CW01187661

Praise for *The TCP/IP Guide*

"It's informative and easy to read, even when discussing rather nasty protocols, and when it covers something, it generally covers it quite completely."
—;LOGIN:

"Keeps things interesting and flowing well enough that working one's way through . . . is actually entertaining instead of torture."
—SLASHDOT

"The most comprehensive guide to TCP/IP protocols we have ever come across. It also is the most readable. This is a book that will be staying on our shelves, and we highly recommend it."
—NETWORK WORLD

"*The TCP/IP Guide* is great for anyone and everyone as it can act both as a reference guide and a textbook."
—LINUX SECURITY

"This is the kind of reference book that might be worth reading cover to cover in spite of its bulk."
—OPEN.ITWORLD.COM

"This book is the Real Deal. . . . If you've read as many bad IT books as I have, you will appreciate the mastery of Kozierok's achievement. His warmth and style don't smack you in the face at first, but keep reading, and you'll discover an IT brother."
—WATCHGUARD WIRE

"The author does a great job of discussing the significance of the information he is presenting. . . . Whereas some books seem to throw illustrations in simply to break up the text, this book adds just the right amount in the right places to make sure you understand."
—LINUX MAGAZINE

"Covers a great breadth and depth of information . . . an excellent reference."
—ABOUT.COM

"In short, this is a really well-done book, and well worth the price if you need up-to-date, easy-to-digest information about TCP/IP. I wish I'd written this puppy."
—IBM'S DEVELOPERWORKS

"Nicely organized, from an introduction to networking through administration and troubleshooting, the book clearly explains each topic."
—LIBRARY JOURNAL

"Kozierok's description of IPv4 addressing is probably the clearest I have ever read. And his chapters about IP subnetting and classless addressing are masterful. . . . I continue to be astounded that this much information, presented in a clear and entertaining fashion, is available for so little."
—KICKSTART NEWS

"This is both an encyclopedic and comprehensible guide to the TCP/IP protocol suite that will appeal to newcomers and the seasoned professional."
—DOMINOPOWER MAGAZINE

"A mind-boggling contribution to understanding and applying TCP/IP protocols to network administration. . . . This is a truly impressive work . . . comprehensive and readable."
—JAVARANCH

"A 'must' for any serious web operator."
—MIDWEST BOOK REVIEW

"Now I can retire all my other TCP/IP books I have gathering dust on my bookshelves. . . . This book, however, may become timeless, because it not only talks about, but shows everything."
—MACCOMPANION

"Smartly illustrated, the book is easily navigated for both brief overviews of the subject matter and more in-depth study of TCP/IP-related topics"
—ABOUT THIS PARTICULAR MAC (ATPM)

"Focuses on the nuts and bolts of how the protocols work while maintaining an emphasis on the present state of the art (including extensive coverage of IPv6)."
—BOOK NEWS

"Anything and everything you ever wanted to or needed to know about the ins and outs of the TCP/IP . . . you could not find a better, more comprehensive book on the subject. I would give it two thumbs up for sure."
—CARIBOO COMPUTER MAGAZINE

"I can't think of a reason why any datacenter or beginning IT technician wouldn't want to own this volume. . . . And it's not one of those books that's going to be outdated in six months' time."
—BLOGCRITICS.ORG

THE TCP/IP GUIDE

A Comprehensive, Illustrated Internet Protocols Reference

by Charles M. Kozierok

San Francisco

Thirteenth printing

23 22 21 20 13 14 15 16

Printed in USA

ISBN-10: 1-59327-047-X
ISBN-13: 978-1-59327-047-6

Publisher: William Pollock
Production Manager: Susan Berge
Cover and Interior Design: Octopod Studios
Developmental Editor: William Pollock
Technical Reviewers: Fernando Gont, Barry Margolin
Copyeditors: Marilyn Smith, Lisa Theobald, Mark Nigara
Compositor: Riley Hoffman
Proofreader: Stephanie Provines

For information on distribution, translations, or bulk sales, please contact No Starch Press, Inc. directly:

No Starch Press, Inc.
245 8th Street, San Francisco, CA 94103
phone: 1.415.863.9900; info@nostarch.com; http://www.nostarch.com

Library of Congress Cataloging-in-Publication Data

Kozierok, Charles.
The TCP/IP guide : a comprehensive, illustrated internet protocols reference / Charles Kozierok.
p. cm.
Includes index.
ISBN 1-59327-047-X
1. TCP/IP (Computer network protocol) I. Title.
TK5105.585.K69 2005
004.6'2--dc22

2004008863

DEDICATION

This book is dedicated to my family: my wife, Robyn, and my three sons, Ryan, Matthew, and Evan.

I suppose that it's a cliché to dedicate a book to your wife. If so, it's for a very good reason. Who plays a more important role in the life of an author than his or her spouse? Robyn is my partner—the person who is always there and the one who shares my life in so many ways. The expression about a great woman being behind every good man is true, yet my wife is deserving of recognition for reasons that go far beyond the usual one of being "supportive."

She agreed to take on a regular working position to make it possible for me to spend time on a very long project with an uncertain payoff. She took on most of the tasks of taking our children to school and dealing with their needs, to give me time to write. She also gracefully agreed to "do without" many things that many other wives would not have been too happy about forgoing.

But most of all, she deserves a world of credit for putting up with *me*. For constantly reassuring me that it was okay that I was spending years on a project that might not be successful. For listening to me talk for countless hours, and for giving her opinions on many portions of my writing, all on a subject that really doesn't interest her. And most important, for encouraging me when I felt this was a waste of time, and even kicking me in the butt when I felt like giving up. Without Robyn, this book simply would not exist. Thanks, R.

My three boys deserve credit for similar reasons, but to a lesser extent. They have had to put up with my constantly sitting at the computer, trying to tune them out so I could concentrate; my too-frequent grouchy moods; and my reluctance to spend time with them when I had work on my plate. I am sure there were many times that they wished I just had a regular "day job."

Ryan, my big boy, has been very patient in waiting for me to finish this project so we can resume several activities that we used to engage in regularly. Matthew, my fun-loving and rambunctious middle son, has also had to deal with me not being able to spend as much time as I would have liked with him. And little Evan has had a father working on a long-term project for his entire life! All three of my boys have been very understanding and provided me with much-needed joy and laughter at times when I needed them most.

BRIEF CONTENTS

Contents in Detail xiii

List of Figures xlv

List of Tables lv

Acknowledgments lxv

About the Author lxvii

Introduction lxix

SECTION I: TCP/IP OVERVIEW AND BACKGROUND INFORMATION

PART I-1: NETWORKING FUNDAMENTALS

Chapter 1: Networking Introduction, Characteristics, and Types 5

Chapter 2: Network Performance Issues and Concepts 31

Chapter 3: Network Standards and Standards Organizations 45

Chapter 4: A Review of Data Representation and the Mathematics of Computing 61

PART I-2: THE OPEN SYSTEMS INTERCONNECTION (OSI) REFERENCE MODEL

Chapter 5: General OSI Reference Model Issues and Concepts 81

Chapter 6: OSI Reference Model Layers 101

Chapter 7: OSI Reference Model Summary 113

PART I-3: TCP/IP PROTOCOL SUITE AND ARCHITECTURE

Chapter 8: TCP/IP Protocol Suite and Architecture 121

SECTION II: TCP/IP LOWER-LAYER CORE PROTOCOLS

PART II-1: TCP/IP NETWORK INTERFACE LAYER PROTOCOLS

Chapter 9: TCP/IP Serial Line Internet Protocol (SLIP) and Point-to-Point Protocol (PPP) Overview and Fundamentals 139

Chapter 10: PPP Core Protocols: Link Control, Network Control, and Authentication 155

Chapter 11: PPP Feature Protocols 167

Chapter 12: PPP Protocol Frame Formats 181

PART II-2: TCP/IP NETWORK INTERFACE/INTERNET LAYER CONNECTION PROTOCOLS

Chapter 13: Address Resolution and the TCP/IP Address Resolution Protocol (ARP) 203

Chapter 14: Reverse Address Resolution and the TCP/IP Reverse Address Resolution Protocol (RARP) 227

PART II-3: INTERNET PROTOCOL VERSION 4 (IP/IPV4)

Chapter 15: Internet Protocol Versions, Concepts, and Overview 235

Chapter 16: IPv4 Addressing Concepts and Issues 241

Chapter 17: Classful (Conventional) Addressing 255

Chapter 18: IP Subnet Addressing (Subnetting) Concepts 273

Chapter 19: IP Subnetting: Practical Subnet Design and Address Determination Example 297

Chapter 20: IP Classless Addressing—Classless Inter-Domain Routing (CIDR)/Supernetting 315

Chapter 21: Internet Protocol Datagram Encapsulation and Formatting 329

Chapter 22: IP Datagram Size, Fragmentation, and Reassembly 339

Chapter 23: IP Routing and Multicasting 351

PART II-4: INTERNET PROTOCOL VERSION 6 (IPV6)

Chapter 24: IPv6 Overview, Changes, and Transition 365

Chapter 25: IPv6 Addressing 373

Chapter 26: IPv6 Datagram Encapsulation and Formatting 401

Chapter 27: IPv6 Datagram Size, Fragmentation, Reassembly, and Routing 415

PART II-5: IP-RELATED FEATURE PROTOCOLS

Chapter 28: IP Network Address Translation (NAT) Protocol 425

Chapter 29: IP Security (IPsec) Protocols 449

Chapter 30: Internet Protocol Mobility Support (Mobile IP) 475

PART II-6: IP SUPPORT PROTOCOLS

Chapter 31: ICMP Concepts and General Operation 507

Chapter 32: ICMPv4 Error Message Types and Formats 521

Chapter 33: ICMPv4 Informational Message Types and Formats 535

Chapter 34: ICMPv6 Error Message Types and Formats 547

Chapter 35: ICMPv6 Informational Message Types and Formats 557

Chapter 36: IPv6 Neighbor Discovery (ND) Protocol 575

PART II-7: TCP/IP ROUTING PROTOCOLS (GATEWAY PROTOCOLS)

Chapter 37: Overview of Key Routing Protocol Concepts 591

Chapter 38: Routing Information Protocol (RIP, RIP-2, and RIPng) 597

Chapter 39: Open Shortest Path First (OSPF) 625

Chapter 40: Border Gateway Protocol (BGP/BGP-4) 647

Chapter 41: Other Routing Protocols 677

PART II-8: TCP/IP TRANSPORT LAYER PROTOCOLS

Chapter 42: Overview and Comparison of TCP and UDP 689

Chapter 43: TCP and UDP Addressing: Ports and Sockets 695

Chapter 44: TCP/IP User Datagram Protocol (UDP) 711

Chapter 45: TCP Overview, Functions, and Characteristics 719

Chapter 46: Transmission Control Protocol (TCP) Fundamentals and General Operation 727

Chapter 47: TCP Basic Operation: Connection Establishment, Management, and Termination 745

Chapter 48: TCP Message Formatting and Data Transfer 769

Chapter 49: TCP Reliability and Flow Control Features 793

SECTION III: TCP/IP APPLICATION LAYER PROTOCOLS

PART III-1: NAME SYSTEMS AND TCP/IP NAME REGISTRATION AND NAME RESOLUTION

Chapter 50: Name System Issues, Concepts, and Techniques 825

Chapter 51: TCP/IP Name Systems Overview and the Host Table Name System 841

Chapter 52: Domain Name System (DNS) Overview, Functions, and Characteristics 847

Chapter 53: DNS Name Space, Architecture, and Terminology 857

Chapter 54: DNS Name Registration, Public Administration, Zones, and Authorities 867

Chapter 55: DNS Name Server Concepts and Operation 887

Chapter 56: DNS Resolution Concepts and Resolver Operations 909

Chapter 57: DNS Messaging and Message, Resource Record, and Master File Formats 927

PART III-2: NETWORK FILE AND RESOURCE SHARING PROTOCOLS

Chapter 58: Network File and Resource Sharing and the TCP/IP Network File System (NFS) 953

PART III-3: HOST CONFIGURATION AND TCP/IP HOST CONFIGURATION PROTOCOLS

Chapter 59: Host Configuration Concepts, Issues, and Motivation 973

Chapter 60: TCP/IP Bootstrap Protocol (BOOTP) 977

Chapter 61: DHCP Overview and Address Allocation Concepts 997

Chapter 62: DHCP Configuration and Operation 1013

Chapter 63: DHCP Messaging, Message Types, and Formats 1035

Chapter 64: DHCP Client/Server Implementation, Features, and IPv6 Support 1053

PART III-4: TCP/IP NETWORK MANAGEMENT FRAMEWORK AND PROTOCOLS

Chapter 65: TCP/IP Internet Standard Management Framework Overview 1069

Chapter 66: TCP/IP Structure of Management Information (SMI) and Management Information Bases (MIBs) 1083

Chapter 67: TCP/IP Simple Network Management Protocol (SNMP) Concepts and Operation 1099

Chapter 68: SNMP Protocol Messaging and Message Formats 1113

Chapter 69: TCP/IP Remote Network Monitoring (RMON)....1133

PART III-5: TCP/IP APPLICATION LAYER ADDRESSING AND APPLICATION CATEGORIES

Chapter 70: TCP/IP Application Layer Addressing: Uniform Resource Identifiers, Locators, and Names (URIs, URLs, and URNs) 1139

Chapter 71: File and Message Transfer Overview and Application Categories....1163

PART III-6: TCP/IP GENERAL FILE TRANSFER PROTOCOLS

Chapter 72: File Transfer Protocol (FTP) 1169

Chapter 73: Trivial File Transfer Protocol (TFTP)....1199

PART III-7: TCP/IP ELECTRONIC MAIL SYSTEM: CONCEPTS AND PROTOCOLS

Chapter 74: TCP/IP Electronic Mail System Overview and Concepts....1217

Chapter 75: TCP/IP Electronic Mail Addresses and Addressing....1225

Chapter 76: TCP/IP Electronic Mail Message Formats and Message Processing: RFC 822 and MIME....1233

Chapter 77: TCP/IP Electronic Mail Delivery Protocol: The Simple Mail Transfer Protocol (SMTP) 1263

Chapter 78: TCP/IP Electronic Mail Access and Retrieval Protocols and Methods....1285

PART III-8: TCP/IP WORLD WIDE WEB AND THE HYPERTEXT TRANSFER PROTOCOL (HTTP)

Chapter 79: World Wide Web and Hypertext Overview and Concepts 1317

Chapter 80: HTTP General Operation and Connections....1329

Chapter 81: HTTP Messages, Methods, and Status Codes....1341

Chapter 82: HTTP Message Headers....1357

Chapter 83: HTTP Entities, Transfers, Coding Methods, and Content Management....1369

Chapter 84: HTTP Features, Capabilities, and Issues 1381

PART III-9: OTHER FILE AND MESSAGE TRANSFER APPLICATIONS

Chapter 85: Usenet (Network News) and the TCP/IP Network News Transfer Protocol (NNTP) 1397

Chapter 86: Gopher Protocol (Gopher) 1431

PART III-10: INTERACTIVE AND ADMINISTRATIVE UTILITIES AND PROTOCOLS

Chapter 87: TCP/IP Interactive and Remote Application Protocols 1437

Chapter 88: TCP/IP Administration and Troubleshooting Utilities and Protocols 1461

INDEX 1491

RFCs BY NUMBER 1537

CONTENTS IN DETAIL

LIST OF FIGURES xlv
LIST OF TABLES lv
ACKNOWLEDGMENTS lxv
ABOUT THE AUTHOR lxvii
INTRODUCTION lxix
Goals of *The TCP/IP Guide* lxix
Scope of *The TCP/IP Guide* lxxi
The TCP/IP Guide Features lxxii
The TCP/IP Guide Online! lxxiii
Your Feedback and Suggestions lxxiii

SECTION I TCP/IP OVERVIEW AND BACKGROUND INFORMATION

PART I-1 NETWORKING FUNDAMENTALS 3

1 Networking Introduction, Characteristics, and Types 5

Introduction to Networking 6
What Is Networking? 6
The Advantages and Benefits of Networking 7
The Disadvantages and Costs of Networking 8
Fundamental Network Characteristics 10
Networking Layers, Models, and Architectures 10
Protocols: What Are They, Anyway? 11
Circuit-Switching and Packet-Switching Networks 13
Connection-Oriented and Connectionless Protocols 15
Messages: Packets, Frames, Datagrams, and Cells 17
Message Formatting: Headers, Payloads, and Footers 19
Message Addressing and Transmission Methods: Unicast, Broadcast, and Multicast 20
Network Structural Models and Client-Server and Peer-to-Peer Networking 23
Types and Sizes of Networks 25
Segments, Networks, Subnetworks, and Internetworks 27
The Internet, Intranets, and Extranets 29

2 Network Performance Issues and Concepts 31

Putting Network Performance in Perspective 32
Balancing Network Performance with Key Nonperformance Characteristics 33
Performance Measurements: Speed, Bandwidth, Throughput, and Latency 34
Speed 34
Bandwidth 35
Throughput 35
Latency 35
Summary of Performance Measurements 36
Understanding Performance Measurement Units 37
Bits and Bytes 37
Baud 38

Theoretical and Real-World Throughput, and Factors Affecting Network Performance 39
Normal Network Overhead 39
External Performance Limiters 40
Network Configuration Problems 40
Asymmetry 41
Simplex, Full-Duplex, and Half-Duplex Operation 41
Simplex Operation 42
Half-Duplex Operation 42
Full-Duplex Operation 42
Quality of Service (QoS) 43

3 Network Standards and Standards Organizations 45

Proprietary, Open, and De Facto Standards 46
Proprietary Standards 46
Open Standards 47
De Facto Standards 48
Networking Standards 48
International Networking Standards Organizations 49
Networking Industry Groups 51
Internet Standards Organizations (ISOC, IAB, IESG, IETF, IRSG, and IRTF) 52
Internet Registration Authorities and Registries (IANA, ICANN, APNIC, ARIN, LACNIC, and RIPE NCC) 55
Internet Centralized Registration Authorities 55
Modern Hierarchy of Registration Authorities 56
Internet Standards and the Request for Comment (RFC) Process 57
RFC Categories 58
The Internet Standardization Process 58

4 A Review of Data Representation and the Mathematics of Computing 61

Binary Information and Representation: Bits, Bytes, Nibbles, Octets, and Characters 62
Binary Information 62
Binary Information Representation and Groups 63
Byte Versus Octet 64
Decimal, Binary, Octal, and Hexadecimal Numbers 65
Binary Numbers and Their Decimal Equivalents 65
Making Binary Numbers Easier to Use by Grouping Bits 66
Octal Numbers 66
Hexadecimal Numbers 67
Decimal, Binary, Octal, and Hexadecimal Number Conversion 68
Binary, Octal, and Hexadecimal Conversions 68
Conversion from Binary, Octal, or Hexadecimal to Decimal 69
Conversion from Decimal to Binary, Octal, or Hexadecimal 70
Binary, Octal, and Hexadecimal Arithmetic 71
Binary Arithmetic 72
Octal and Hexadecimal Arithmetic 72
Boolean Logic and Logical Functions 73
Boolean Logical Functions 73
Combining Boolean Expressions 75
Bit Masking (Setting, Clearing, and Inverting) Using Boolean Logical Functions 75
Setting Groups of Bits with OR 76
Clearing Bits with AND 76
Inverting Bits with XOR 77

PART I-2 THE OPEN SYSTEMS INTERCONNECTION (OSI) REFERENCE MODEL 79

5 General OSI Reference Model Issues and Concepts 81

History of the OSI Reference Model ... 82
General Reference Model Issues ... 83
The Benefits of Networking Models ... 83
Why Understanding the OSI Reference Model Is Important to You ... 84
How to Use the OSI Reference Model ... 85
Other Network Architectures and Protocol Stacks ... 86
Key OSI Reference Model Concepts ... 87
OSI Reference Model Networking Layers, Sublayers, and Layer Groupings ... 87
"N" Notation and Other OSI Model Layer Terminology ... 89
Interfaces: Vertical (Adjacent Layer) Communication ... 91
Protocols: Horizontal (Corresponding Layer) Communication ... 93
Data Encapsulation, Protocol Data Units (PDUs), and Service Data Units (SDUs) ... 95
Indirect Device Connection and Message Routing ... 98

6 OSI Reference Model Layers 101

Physical Layer (Layer 1) ... 102
Data Link Layer (Layer 2) ... 103
Network Layer (Layer 3) ... 105
Transport Layer (Layer 4) ... 106
Session Layer (Layer 5) ... 109
Presentation Layer (Layer 6) ... 110
Application Layer (Layer 7) ... 111

7 OSI Reference Model Summary 113

Understanding the OSI Model: An Analogy ... 113
Remembering the OSI Model Layers: Some Mnemonics ... 116
Summarizing the OSI Model Layers: A Summary Chart ... 117

PART I-3 TCP/IP PROTOCOL SUITE AND ARCHITECTURE 119

8 TCP/IP Protocol Suite and Architecture 121

TCP/IP Overview and History ... 122
TCP/IP History and Development ... 122
Important Factors in the Success of TCP/IP ... 123
TCP/IP Services ... 125
The TCP/IP Client/Server Structural Model ... 125
Hardware and Software Roles ... 127
Transactional Roles ... 127
TCP/IP Architecture and the TCP/IP Model ... 128
Network Interface Layer ... 128
Internet Layer ... 129
Host-to-Host Transport Layer ... 130
Application Layer ... 130
TCP/IP Protocols ... 131

SECTION II
TCP/IP LOWER-LAYER CORE PROTOCOLS

PART II-1 TCP/IP NETWORK INTERFACE LAYER PROTOCOLS 137

9 TCP/IP Serial Line Internet Protocol (SLIP) and Point-to-Point Protocol (PPP) Overview and Fundamentals 139

SLIP versus PPP 140
Serial Line Internet Protocol (SLIP) 141
    SLIP Data Framing Method and General Operation 141
    Problems and Limitations of SLIP 142
Point-to-Point Protocol (PPP) Overview and Fundamentals 144
    Development and Standardization 144
    Function and Architecture 145
    Advantages and Benefits 145
    PPP Main Components 146
    PPP Functional Groups 147
    General Operation 147
    PPP Link Setup and Phases 148
    PPP Standards 151

10 PPP Core Protocols: Link Control, Network Control, and Authentication 155

Link Control Protocol (LCP) 155
    LCP Packets 156
    LCP Link Configuration 157
    LCP Link Maintenance 159
    LCP Link Termination 159
    Other LCP Messages 159
The Network Control Protocols (IPCP, IPXCP, NBFCP, and Others) 159
    Operation of NCPs 160
    The Internet Protocol Control Protocol (IPCP): An Example NCP 162
PPP Authentication Protocols: PAP and CHAP 162
    PAP 162
    CHAP 163

11 PPP Feature Protocols 167

PPP Link Quality Monitoring and Reporting (LQM, LQR) 168
    LQR Setup 168
    Using Link Quality Reports 169
PPP Compression Control Protocol (CCP) and Compression Algorithms 169
    CCP Operation: Compression Setup 170
    CCP Configuration Options and Compression Algorithms 171
    Compression Algorithm Operation: Compressing and Decompressing Data 171
PPP Encryption Control Protocol (ECP) and Encryption Algorithms 172
    ECP Operation: Encryption Setup 173
    ECP Configuration Options and Encryption Algorithms 173
    Encryption Algorithm Operation: Encrypting and Decrypting Data 174
PPP Multilink Protocol (MP, MLP, MLPPP) 175
    PPP Multilink Protocol Architecture 176
    PPP Multilink Protocol Setup and Configuration 177
    PPP Multilink Protocol Operation 177

PPP Bandwidth Allocation Protocol (BAP) and Bandwidth Allocation Control Protocol (BACP) 178
BACP Operation: Configuring the Use of BAP 179
BAP Operation: Adding and Removing Links 179

12 PPP Protocol Frame Formats **181**

PPP General Frame Format 182
Protocol Field Ranges 183
Protocol Field Values 184
PPP Field Compression 185
PPP General Control Protocol Frame Format and Option Format 186
PPP Control Messages and Code Values 187
PPP Control Message Option Format 188
Summary of PPP Control Message Formatting 190
PPP Link Control Protocol (LCP) Frame Formats 190
PAP and CHAP Frame Formats 192
PPP PAP Control Frame Formats 192
PPP CHAP Control Frame Formats 194
PPP Multilink Protocol (MP) Frame Format 195
PPP MP Frame Fragmentation Process 196
PPP MP Fragment Frame Format 196
PPP MP Fragmentation Demonstration 198

PART II-2 TCP/IP NETWORK INTERFACE/INTERNET LAYER CONNECTION PROTOCOLS **201**

13 Address Resolution and the TCP/IP Address Resolution Protocol (ARP) **203**

Address Resolution Concepts and Issues 204
The Need for Address Resolution 204
Address Resolution Through Direct Mapping 206
Dynamic Address Resolution 209
TCP/IP Address Resolution Protocol (ARP) 212
ARP Address Specification and General Operation 213
ARP Message Format 216
ARP Caching 218
Proxy ARP 221
TCP/IP Address Resolution for IP Multicast Addresses 223
TCP/IP Address Resolution for IP Version 6 224

14 Reverse Address Resolution and the TCP/IP Reverse Address Resolution Protocol (RARP) **227**

The Reverse Address Resolution Protocol (RARP) 228
RARP General Operation 229
Limitations of RARP 231

PART II-3 INTERNET PROTOCOL VERSION 4 (IP/IPV4) **233**

15 Internet Protocol Versions, Concepts, and Overview **235**

IP Overview and Key Operational Characteristics 236
IP Functions 238

IP History, Standards, Versions, and Closely Related Protocols 239
IP Versions and Version Numbers 239
IP-Related Protocols 240

16 IPv4 Addressing Concepts and Issues 241

IP Addressing Overview and Fundamentals 242
Number of IP Addresses Per Device 243
Address Uniqueness and Network Specificity 243
Contrasting IP Addresses and Data Link Layer Addresses 244
Private and Public IP Network Addresses 244
IP Address Configuration and Addressing Types 244
IP Address Size, Address Space, and Notation 245
IP Address Size and Binary Notation 245
IP Address Dotted Decimal Notation 245
IP Address Space 246
IP Basic Address Structure and Main Components 247
Network ID and Host ID 247
Location of the Division Between Network ID and Host ID 248
IP Addressing Categories and IP Address Adjuncts 249
Conventional (Classful) Addressing 250
Subnetted Classful Addressing 250
Classless Addressing 250
Subnet Mask and Default Gateway 251
Number of IP Addresses and Multihoming 251
IP Address Management and Assignment Methods and Authorities 252

17 Classful (Conventional) Addressing 255

IP Classful Addressing Overview and Address Classes 256
IP Address Classes 256
Rationale for Classful Addressing 257
IP Classful Addressing Network and Host Identification and Address Ranges 258
Classful Addressing Class Determination Algorithm 258
Determining Address Class from the First Octet Bit Pattern 260
IP Address Class A, B, and C Network and Host Capacities 262
IP Addresses with Special Meanings 263
IP Reserved, Private, and Loopback Addresses 265
Reserved Addresses 265
Private, Unregistered, Nonroutable Addresses 265
Loopback Addresses 266
Reserved, Private, and Loopback Addressing Blocks 267
IP Multicast Addressing 268
Multicast Address Types and Ranges 268
Well-Known Multicast Addresses 269
Problems with Classful IP Addressing 269

18 IP Subnet Addressing (Subnetting) Concepts 273

IP Subnet Addressing Overview, Motivation, and Advantages 274
IP Subnetting: Three-Level Hierarchical IP Subnet Addressing 276
IP Subnet Masks, Notation, and Subnet Calculations 277
Function of the Subnet Mask 277
Subnet Mask Notation 278
Applying the Subnet Mask: An Example 279
Rationale for Subnet Mask Notation 280

IP Default Subnet Masks for Address Classes A, B, and C 281
IP Custom Subnet Masks 283
Deciding How Many Subnet Bits to Use 283
Determining the Custom Subnet Mask 284
Subtracting Two from the Number of Hosts per Subnet and (Possibly) Subnets per Network 285
IP Subnet Identifiers, Subnet Addresses, and Host Addresses 286
Subnet Identifiers 286
Subnet Addresses 287
Host Addresses Within Each Subnet 288
IP Subnetting Summary Tables for Class A, Class B, and Class C Networks 288
IP Variable Length Subnet Masking (VLSM) 292
The Solution: Variable Length Subnet Masking 294
Multiple-Level Subnetting Using VLSM 294

19 IP Subnetting: Practical Subnet Design and Address Determination Example 297

IP Subnetting Step 1: Analyzing Requirements 298
IP Subnetting Step 2: Partitioning Network Address Host Bits 299
Class C Subnetting Design Example 300
Class B Subnetting Design Example 301
IP Subnetting Step 3: Determining the Custom Subnet Mask 302
Calculating the Custom Subnet Mask 303
Determining the Custom Subnet Mask Using Subnetting Tables 305
IP Subnetting Step 4: Determining Subnet Identifiers and Subnet Addresses 305
Class C Subnet ID and Address Determination Example 306
Class B Subnet ID and Address Determination Example 307
Using Subnet Address Formulas to Calculate Subnet Addresses 309
IP Subnetting Step 5: Determining Host Addresses for Each Subnet 310
Class C Host Address Determination Example 310
Class B Host Address Determination Example 313
Shortcuts for Computing Host Addresses 313

20 IP Classless Addressing—Classless Inter-Domain Routing (CIDR)/Supernetting 315

IP Classless Addressing and Supernetting Overview 316
The Main Problem with Classful Addressing 316
The Solution: Eliminate Address Classes 317
The Many Benefits of Classless Addressing and Routing 317
IP Supernetting: CIDR Hierarchical Addressing and Notation 319
CIDR (Slash) Notation 319
Supernetting: Subnetting the Internet 320
Common Aspects of Classful and Classless Addressing 321
IP Classless Addressing Block Sizes and Classful Network Equivalents 322
IP CIDR Addressing Example 324
First Level of Division 324
Second Level of Division 327
Third Level of Division 327

21 Internet Protocol Datagram Encapsulation and Formatting 329

IP Datagram Encapsulation 330
IP Datagram General Format 332
IP Datagram Time to Live (TTL) Field 335
IP Datagram Type of Service (TOS) Field 335
IP Datagram Options and Option Format 336

22 IP Datagram Size, Fragmentation, and Reassembly 339

IP Datagram Size, MTU, and Fragmentation Overview 340
IP Datagram Size and the Underlying Network Frame Size 340
MTU and Datagram Fragmentation 341
Multiple-Stage Fragmentation 342
Internet Minimum MTU: 576 Bytes 343
MTU Path Discovery 343
IP Message Fragmentation Process 344
The IP Fragmentation Process 344
Fragmentation-Related IP Datagram Header Fields 346
IP Message Reassembly 347

23 IP Routing and Multicasting 351

IP Datagram Delivery 352
Direct Datagram Delivery 353
Indirect Datagram Delivery (Routing) 353
The Relationship Between Datagram Routing and Addressing 354
IP Routing Concepts and the Process of Next-Hop Routing 355
IP Routes and Routing Tables 357
IP Routing in a Subnet or Classless Addressing (CIDR) Environment 359
IP Multicasting 360
Multicast Addressing 361
Multicast Group Management 361
Multicast Datagram Processing and Routing 361

PART II-4 INTERNET PROTOCOL VERSION 6 (IPV6) 363

24 IPv6 Overview, Changes, and Transition 365

IPv6 Motivation and Overview 366
IPv6 Standards 366
Design Goals of IPv6 367
Major Changes and Additions in IPv6 368
Transition from IPv4 to IPv6 370
IPv4 to IPv6 Transition: Differences of Opinion 370
IPv4 to IPv6 Transition Methods 371

25 IPv6 Addressing 373

IPv6 Addressing Overview: Addressing Model, Address Types, and Address Size 374
IPv6 Addressing Model Characteristics 374
IPv6 Supported Address Types 375
IPv6 Address Size and Address Space 376
IPv6 Address and Address Notation and Prefix Representation 378
IPv6 Address Hexadecimal Notation 378
Zero Compression in IPv6 Addresses 379
IPv6 Mixed Notation 380
IPv6 Address Prefix Length Representation 381
IPv6 Address Space Allocation 381
IPv6 Global Unicast Address Format 383
Rationale for a Structured Unicast Address Block 383
Generic Division of the Unicast Address Space 384

IPv6 Implementation of the Unicast Address Space 384
Original Division of the Global Routing Prefix: Aggregators 385
A Sample Division of the Global Routing Prefix into Levels 386
IPv6 Interface Identifiers and Physical Address Mapping 388
IPv6 Special Addresses: Reserved, Private, Unspecified, and Loopback 389
Special Address Types 390
IPv6 Private Addresses Type Scopes 391
IPv6/IPv4 Address Embedding 392
IPv6 Multicast and Anycast Addressing 394
IPv6 Multicast Addresses 394
IPv6 Anycast Addresses 398
IPv6 Autoconfiguration and Renumbering 398
IPv6 Stateless Autoconfiguration 399
IPv6 Device Renumbering 400

26 IPv6 Datagram Encapsulation and Formatting 401

IPv6 Datagram Overview and General Structure 402
IPv6 Datagram Main Header Format 404
IPv6 Next Header Field 405
Key Changes to the Main Header Between IPv4 and IPv6 406
IPv6 Datagram Extension Headers 407
IPv6 Header Chaining Using the Next Header Field 407
Summary of IPv6 Extension Headers 409
IPv6 Routing Extension Header 410
IPv6 Fragment Extension Header 411
IPv6 Extension Header Order 411
IPv6 Datagram Options 412

27 IPv6 Datagram Size, Fragmentation, Reassembly, and Routing 415

Overview of IPv6 Datagram Sizing and Fragmentation 416
Implications of IPv6's Source-Only Fragmentation Rule 417
The IPv6 Fragmentation Process 418
IPv6 Datagram Delivery and Routing 420

PART II-5 IP-RELATED FEATURE PROTOCOLS 423

28 IP Network Address Translation (NAT) Protocol 425

IP NAT Overview 426
Advantages of IP NAT 428
Disadvantages of IP NAT 429
IP NAT Address Terminology 430
IP NAT Static and Dynamic Address Mappings 433
Static Mappings 433
Dynamic Mappings 433
Choosing Between Static and Dynamic Mapping 433
IP NAT Unidirectional (Traditional/Outbound) Operation 434
IP NAT Bidirectional (Two-Way/Inbound) Operation 437
IP NAT Port-Based (Overloaded) Operation 439
IP NAT Overlapping/Twice NAT Operation 442
IP NAT Compatibility Issues and Special Handling Requirements 445

29 IP Security (IPsec) Protocols 449

IPsec Overview, History, and Standards 450
Overview of IPsec Services and Functions 451
IPsec Standards 451
IPsec General Operation, Components, and Protocols 452
IPsec Core Protocols 453
IPsec Support Components 453
IPsec Architectures and Implementation Methods 454
Integrated Architecture 455
Bump in the Stack (BITS) Architecture 455
Bump in the Wire (BITW) Architecture 456
IPsec Modes: Transport and Tunnel 457
Transport Mode 457
Tunnel Mode 457
Comparing Transport and Tunnel Modes 457
IPsec Security Constructs 460
Security Policies, Security Associations, and Associated Databases 460
Selectors 461
Security Association Triples and Security Parameter Index (SPI) 461
IPsec Authentication Header (AH) 461
AH Datagram Placement and Linking 462
AH Format 465
IPsec Encapsulating Security Payload (ESP) 466
ESP Fields 466
ESP Operations and Field Use 467
ESP Format 470
IPsec Internet Key Exchange (IKE) 471
IKE Overview 472
IKE Operation 472

30 Internet Protocol Mobility Support (Mobile IP) 475

Mobile IP Overview, History, and Motivation 476
The Problem with Mobile Nodes in TCP/IP 476
The Solution: Mobile IP 478
Limitations of Mobile IP 479
Mobile IP Concepts and General Operation 480
Mobile IP Device Roles 481
Mobile IP Functions 482
Mobile IP Addressing: Home and Care-Of Addresses 483
Foreign Agent Care-Of Address 484
Co-Located Care-Of Address 485
Advantages and Disadvantages of the Care-Of Address Types 485
Mobile IP Agent Discovery 486
Agent Discovery Process 486
Agent Advertisement and Agent Solicitation Messages 487
Mobile IP Home Agent Registration and Registration Messages 491
Mobile Node Registration Events 491
Registration Request and Registration Reply Messages 491
Registration Process 492
Registration Request Message Format 493
Registration Reply Message Format 495
Mobile IP Data Encapsulation and Tunneling 495
Mobile IP Conventional Tunneling 496
Mobile IP Reverse Tunneling 498
Mobile IP and TCP/IP Address Resolution Protocol (ARP) Operation 498

Mobile IP Efficiency Issues ... 500
Mobile IP Security Considerations ... 503

PART II-6 IP SUPPORT PROTOCOLS 505

31 ICMP Concepts and General Operation 507

ICMP Overview, History, Versions, and Standards ... 508
ICMP General Operation ... 510
- The ICMP Message-Passing Service ... 510
- ICMP Error Reporting Limited to the Datagram Source ... 511

ICMP Message Classes, Types, and Codes ... 512
- ICMP Message Classes ... 512
- ICMP Message Types ... 512
- ICMP Message Codes ... 513
- ICMP Message Class and Type Summary ... 513

ICMP Message Creation and Processing Conventions and Rules ... 515
- Limitations on ICMP Message Responses ... 516
- ICMP Message Processing Conventions ... 517

ICMP Common Message Format and Data Encapsulation ... 518
- ICMP Common Message Format ... 518
- Original Datagram Inclusion in ICMP Error Messages ... 519
- ICMP Data Encapsulation ... 520

32 ICMPv4 Error Message Types and Formats 521

ICMPv4 Destination Unreachable Messages ... 522
- ICMPv4 Destination Unreachable Message Format ... 522
- ICMPv4 Destination Unreachable Message Subtypes ... 523
- Interpretation of Destination Unreachable Messages ... 524

ICMPv4 Source Quench Messages ... 525
- ICMPv4 Source Quench Message Format ... 526
- Problems with Source Quench Messages ... 526

ICMPv4 Time Exceeded Messages ... 527
- ICMPv4 Time Exceeded Message Format ... 528
- Applications of Time Exceeded Messages ... 529

ICMPv4 Redirect Messages ... 530
- ICMPv4 Redirect Message Format ... 530
- Redirect Message Interpretation Codes ... 532
- Limitations of Redirect Messages ... 532

ICMPv4 Parameter Problem Messages ... 533
- ICMPv4 Parameter Problem Message Format ... 533
- Parameter Problem Message Interpretation Codes and the Pointer Field ... 534

33 ICMPv4 Informational Message Types and Formats 535

ICMPv4 Echo (Request) and Echo Reply Messages ... 536
- ICMPv4 Echo and Echo Reply Message Format ... 536
- Application of Echo and Echo Reply Messages ... 537

ICMPv4 Timestamp (Request) and Timestamp Reply Messages ... 537
- ICMPv4 Timestamp and Timestamp Reply Message Format ... 538
- Issues Using Timestamp and Timestamp Reply Messages ... 539

ICMPv4 Router Advertisement and Router Solicitation Messages ... 539
- The Router Discovery Process ... 540
- ICMPv4 Router Advertisement Message Format ... 540

ICMPv4 Router Solicitation Message Format 542
Addressing and Use of Router Advertisement and Router Solicitation Messages 542
ICMPv4 Address Mask Request and Reply Messages 543
ICMPv4 Address Mask Request and Address Mask Reply Message Format 543
Use of Address Mask Request and Address Mask Reply Messages 544
ICMPv4 Traceroute Messages 544
ICMPv4 Traceroute Message Format 545
Use of Traceroute Messages 546

34 ICMPv6 Error Message Types and Formats 547

ICMPv6 Destination Unreachable Messages 548
ICMPv6 Destination Unreachable Message Format 548
ICMPv6 Destination Unreachable Message Subtypes 549
Processing of Destination Unreachable Messages 550
ICMPv6 Packet Too Big Messages 550
ICMPv6 Packet Too Big Message Format 550
Applications of Packet Too Big Messages 551
ICMPv6 Time Exceeded Messages 552
ICMPv6 Time Exceeded Message Format 553
Applications of Time Exceeded Messages 554
ICMPv6 Parameter Problem Messages 554
ICMPv6 Parameter Problem Message Format 555
Parameter Problem Message Interpretation Codes and the Pointer Field 555

35 ICMPv6 Informational Message Types and Formats 557

ICMPv6 Echo Request and Echo Reply Messages 558
ICMPv6 Echo and Echo Reply Message Format 558
Application of Echo and Echo Reply Messages 559
ICMPv6 Router Advertisement and Router Solicitation Messages 560
ICMPv6 Router Advertisement Message Format 560
ICMPv6 Router Solicitation Message Format 562
Addressing of Router Advertisement and Router Solicitation Messages 562
ICMPv6 Neighbor Advertisement and Neighbor Solicitation Messages 563
ICMPv6 Neighbor Advertisement Message Format 563
ICMPv6 Neighbor Solicitation Message Format 564
Addressing of Neighbor Advertisement and Neighbor Solicitation Messages 565
ICMPv6 Redirect Messages 566
ICMPv6 Redirect Message Format 566
Application of Redirect Messages 568
ICMPv6 Router Renumbering Messages 568
IPv6 Router Renumbering 568
ICMPv6 Router Renumbering Message Format 569
Addressing of Router Renumbering Messages 571
ICMPv6 Informational Message Options 571
Source Link-Layer Address Option Format 571
Target Link-Layer Address Option Format 572
Prefix Information Option Format 572
Redirected Header Option Format 573
MTU Option Format 574

36 IPv6 Neighbor Discovery (ND) Protocol 575

IPv6 ND Overview 576
Formalizing Local Network Functions: The Neighbor Concept 577
Neighbor Discovery Standards 577

IPv6 ND General Operational Overview 578
Host-Router Discovery Functions 579
Host-Host Communication Functions 579
Redirect Function 579
Relationships Between Functions 580
ICMPv6 Messages Used by ND 580
IPv6 ND Functions Compared to Equivalent IPv4 Functions 580
IPv6 ND Host-Router Discovery Functions 582
Host-Router Discovery Functions Performed by Routers 582
Host-Router Discovery Functions Performed by Hosts 583
IPv6 ND Host-Host Communication Functions 583
Next-Hop Determination 584
Address Resolution 584
Updating Neighbors Using Neighbor Advertisement Messages 585
Neighbor Unreachability Detection and the Neighbor Cache 585
Duplicate Address Detection 586
IPv6 ND Redirect Function 586

PART II-7 TCP/IP ROUTING PROTOCOLS (GATEWAY PROTOCOLS) 589

37 Overview of Key Routing Protocol Concepts 591

Routing Protocol Architectures 591
Core Architecture 592
Autonomous System (AS) Architecture 592
Modern Protocol Types: Interior and Exterior Routing Protocols 593
Routing Protocol Algorithms and Metrics 594
Distance-Vector (Bellman-Ford) Routing Protocol Algorithm 594
Link-State (Shortest-Path First) Routing Protocol Algorithm 595
Hybrid Routing Protocol Algorithms 595
Static and Dynamic Routing Protocols 595

38 Routing Information Protocol (RIP, RIP-2, and RIPng) 597

RIP Overview 598
RIP Standardization 598
RIP Operational Overview, Advantages, and Limitations 599
Development of RIP Version 2 (RIP-2) and RIPng for IPv6 600
RIP Route Determination Algorithm and Metric 600
RIP Routing Information and Route Distance Metric 600
RIP Route Determination Algorithm 601
RIP Route Determination and Information Propagation 601
Default Routes 604
RIP General Operation, Messaging, and Timers 604
RIP Messages and Basic Message Types 604
RIP Update Messaging and the 30-Second Timer 605
Preventing Stale Information: The Timeout Timer 605
Removing Stale Information: The Garbage-Collection Timer 606
Triggered Updates 606
RIP Problems and Some Resolutions 606
Issues with RIP's Algorithm 607
Issues with RIP's Metric 610
RIP Special Features for Resolving RIP Algorithm Problems 610
RIP Version-Specific Message Formats and Features 614
RIP Version 1 (RIP-1) Message Format and Features 614
RIP Version 2 (RIP-2) Message Format and Features 617
RIPng (RIPv6) Message Format and Features 620

39 Open Shortest Path First (OSPF) 625

OSPF Overview ... 626
  Development and Standardization of OSPF ... 626
  Overview of OSPF Operation ... 627
  OSPF Features and Drawbacks ... 627
OSPF Basic Topology and the Link-State Database (LSDB) ... 628
  OSPF Basic Topology ... 628
  LSDB Information Storage and Propagation ... 629
OSPF Hierarchical Topology ... 630
  OSPF Areas ... 630
  Router Roles in OSPF Hierarchical Topology ... 631
OSPF Route Determination Using SPF Trees ... 633
  The SPF Tree ... 633
  OSPF Route Determination ... 634
OSPF General Operation ... 637
  OSPF Message Types ... 638
  OSPF Messaging ... 638
  OSPF Message Authentication ... 639
OSPF Message Formats ... 639
  OSPF Common Header Format ... 639
  OSPF Hello Message Format ... 641
  OSPF Database Description Message Format ... 641
  OSPF Link State Request Message Format ... 643
  OSPF Link State Update Message Format ... 643
  OSPF Link State Acknowledgment Message Format ... 644
  OSPF Link State Advertisements and the LSA Header Format ... 644

40 Border Gateway Protocol (BGP/BGP-4) 647

BGP Overview ... 648
  BGP Versions and Defining Standards ... 649
  Overview of BGP Functions and Features ... 650
BGP Topology ... 651
  BGP Speakers, Router Roles, Neighbors, and Peers ... 652
  BGP AS Types, Traffic Flows, and Routing Policies ... 653
BGP Route Storage and Advertisement ... 656
  BGP Route Information Management Functions ... 656
  BGP Routing Information Bases (RIBs) ... 656
BGP Path Attributes and Algorithm Overview ... 657
  BGP Path Attribute Classes ... 658
  BGP Path Attribute Characteristics ... 659
BGP Route Determination and the BGP Decision Process ... 659
  BGP Decision Process Phases ... 660
  Criteria for Assigning Preferences to Routes ... 660
  Limitations on BGP's Ability to Select Efficient Routes ... 661
  Originating New Routes and Withdrawing Unreachable Routes ... 661
BGP General Operation and Messaging ... 662
  Speaker Designation and Connection Establishment ... 662
  Route Information Exchange ... 662
  Connectivity Maintenance ... 663
  Error Reporting ... 663
BGP Detailed Messaging, Operation, and Message Formats ... 663
  BGP Message Generation and Transport ... 663
  BGP General Message Format ... 664
  BGP Connection Establishment: Open Messages ... 666
  BGP Route Information Exchange: Update Messages ... 667
  BGP Connectivity Maintenance: Keepalive Messages ... 672
  BGP Error Reporting: Notification Messages ... 673

41 Other Routing Protocols 677

TCP/IP Gateway-to-Gateway Protocol (GGP) ... 678
The HELLO Protocol (HELLO) ... 679
Interior Gateway Routing Protocol (IGRP) ... 681
Enhanced Interior Gateway Routing Protocol (EIGRP) ... 682
TCP/IP Exterior Gateway Protocol (EGP) ... 684

PART II-8 TCP/IP TRANSPORT LAYER PROTOCOLS 687

42 Overview and Comparison of TCP and UDP 689

Two Protocols for TCP/IP Transport Layer Requirements ... 690
Applications of TCP and UDP ... 691
    TCP Applications ... 691
    UDP Applications ... 692
Summary Comparison of UDP and TCP ... 692

43 TCP and UDP Addressing: Ports and Sockets 695

TCP/IP Processes, Multiplexing, and Client/Server Application Roles ... 696
    Multiplexing and Demultiplexing ... 696
    TCP/IP Client Processes and Server Processes ... 697
TCP/IP Ports: TCP/UDP Addressing ... 698
    Multiplexing and Demultiplexing Using Ports ... 699
    Source Port and Destination Port Numbers ... 699
    Summary of Port Use for Datagram Transmission and Reception ... 701
TCP/IP Application Assignments and Server Port Number Ranges ... 701
    Reserved Port Numbers ... 702
    TCP/UDP Port Number Ranges ... 702
TCP/IP Client (Ephemeral) Ports and Client/Server Application Port Use ... 703
    Ephemeral Port Number Assignment ... 704
    Ephemeral Port Number Ranges ... 704
    Port Number Use During a Client/Server Exchange ... 705
TCP/IP Sockets and Socket Pairs: Process and Connection Identification ... 706
Common TCP/IP Applications and Well-Known and Registered Port Numbers ... 707

44 TCP/IP User Datagram Protocol (UDP) 711

UDP Overview, History, and Standards ... 712
UDP Operation ... 713
    What UDP Does ... 713
    What UDP Does Not Do ... 713
UDP Message Format ... 714
UDP Common Applications and Server Port Assignments ... 716
    Why Some TCP/IP Applications Use UDP ... 716
    Common UDP Applications and Server Port Use ... 717
    Applications That Use Both UDP and TCP ... 718

45 TCP Overview, Functions, and Characteristics 719

TCP Overview, History, and Standards ... 720
    TCP History ... 720
    Overview of TCP Operation ... 721
    TCP Standards ... 721

TCP Functions 722
Functions That TCP Performs 723
Functions That TCP Doesn't Perform 723
TCP Characteristics 724
The Robustness Principle 726

46 Transmission Control Protocol (TCP) Fundamentals and General Operation 727

TCP Data Handling and Processing 728
Increasing the Flexibility of Application Data Handling: TCP's Stream Orientation 728
TCP Data Packaging: Segments 728
TCP Data Identification: Sequence Numbers 729
The Need for Application Data Delimiting 731
TCP Sliding Window Acknowledgment System 731
The Problem with Unreliable Protocols: Lack of Feedback 732
Providing Basic Reliability Using Positive Acknowledgment with Retransmission (PAR) 732
Improving PAR 734
TCP's Stream-Oriented Sliding Window Acknowledgment System 734
More Information on TCP Sliding Windows 740
TCP Ports, Connections, and Connection Identification 741
TCP Common Applications and Server Port Assignments 742

47 TCP Basic Operation: Connection Establishment, Management, and Termination 745

TCP Operational Overview and the TCP Finite State Machine (FSM) 746
Basic FSM Concepts 746
The Simplified TCP FSM 747
TCP Connection Preparation 750
Storing Connection Data: The Transmission Control Block (TCB) 751
Active and Passive Opens 751
Preparation for Connection 752
TCP Connection Establishment Process: The Three-Way Handshake 752
Connection Establishment Functions 752
Control Messages Used for Connection Establishment: SYN and ACK 753
Normal Connection Establishment: The Three-Way Handshake 753
Simultaneous Open Connection Establishment 755
TCP Connection Establishment Sequence Number Synchronization and Parameter Exchange 757
Initial Sequence Number Selection 757
TCP Sequence Number Synchronization 758
TCP Parameter Exchange 759
TCP Connection Management and Problem Handling 760
The TCP Reset Function 760
Handling Reset Segments 761
Idle Connection Management and Keepalive Messages 761
TCP Connection Termination 762
Requirements and Issues In Connection Termination 762
Normal Connection Termination 763
The TIME-WAIT State 765
Simultaneous Connection Termination 766

48 TCP Message Formatting and Data Transfer 769

TCP Message (Segment) Format 770
TCP Checksum Calculation and the TCP Pseudo Header 774
Detecting Transmission Errors Using Checksums 774
Increasing the Scope of Detected Errors: The TCP Pseudo Header 774
Advantages of the Pseudo Header Method 776

TCP Maximum Segment Size (MSS) 777
MSS Selection 778
TCP Default MSS 778
Nondefault MSS Value Specification 779
TCP Sliding Window Data Transfer and Acknowledgment Mechanics 780
Sliding Window Transmit and Receive Categories 780
Send (SND) and Receive (RCV) Pointers 781
TCP Segment Fields Used to Exchange Pointer Information 783
An Example of TCP Sliding Window Mechanics 784
Real-World Complications of the Sliding Window Mechanism 789
TCP Immediate Data Transfer: Push Function 790
TCP Priority Data Transfer: Urgent Function 791

49 TCP Reliability and Flow Control Features **793**

TCP Segment Retransmission Timers and the Retransmission Queue 794
Managing Retransmissions Using the Retransmission Queue 794
Recognizing When a Segment Is Fully Acknowledged 795
TCP Noncontiguous Acknowledgment Handling and Selective Acknowledgment (SACK) 798
Policies for Dealing with Outstanding Unacknowledged Segments 799
A Better Solution: Selective Acknowledgment (SACK) 801
TCP Adaptive Retransmission and Retransmission Timer Calculations 803
Adaptive Retransmission Based on RTT Calculations 803
Acknowledgment Ambiguity 804
Refinements to RTT Calculation and Karn's Algorithm 804
TCP Window Size Adjustment and Flow Control 805
Reducing Send Window Size to Reduce the Rate Data Is Sent 806
Reducing Send Window Size to Stop the Sending of New Data 808
Closing the Send Window 808
TCP Window Management Issues 809
Problems Associated with Shrinking the TCP Window 809
Reducing Buffer Size Without Shrinking the Window 810
Handling a Closed Window and Sending Probe Segments 811
TCP Silly Window Syndrome 812
How Silly Window Syndrome Occurs 812
Silly Window Syndrome Avoidance Algorithms 815
TCP Congestion Handling and Congestion Avoidance Algorithms 816
Congestion Considerations 816
TCP Congestion-Handling Mechanisms 817

SECTION III
TCP/IP APPLICATION LAYER PROTOCOLS

PART III-1 NAME SYSTEMS AND TCP/IP NAME REGISTRATION AND NAME RESOLUTION **823**

50 Name System Issues, Concepts, and Techniques **825**

Name System Overview 826
Symbolic Names for Addressing 826
A Paradox: Name Systems Are Both Essential and Unnecessary 826
Factors That Determine the Necessity of a Name System 828
Basic Name System Functions: Name Space, Name Registration, and Name Resolution 829

Name Spaces and Name Architectures 831
Name Space Functions 831
Flat Name Architecture (Flat Name Space) 832
Hierarchical Name Architecture (Structured Name Space) 832
Comparing Name Architectures 833
Name Registration Methods, Administration, and Authorities 834
Name Registration Functions 834
Hierarchical Name Registration 835
Name Registration Methods 835
Name Resolution Techniques and Elements 836
Name Resolution Methods 837
Client/Server Name Resolution Functional Elements 838
Efficiency, Reliability, and Other Name Resolution Considerations 838
Efficiency Considerations 839
Reliability Considerations 839
Other Considerations 840

51 TCP/IP Name Systems Overview and the Host Table Name System 841

A Brief History of TCP/IP Host Names and Name Systems 842
Developing the First Name System: ARPAnet Host Name Lists 842
Storing Host Names in a Host Table File 842
Outgrowing the Host Table Name System and Moving to DNS 843
The TCP/IP Host Table Name System 843
Host Table Name Resolution 844
Host Table Name Registration 844
Weaknesses of the Host Table Name System 845
Use of the Host Table Name System in Modern Networking 846

52 Domain Name System (DNS) Overview, Functions, and Characteristics 847

DNS Overview, History, and Standards 848
Early DNS Development and the Move to Hierarchical Domains 848
Standardization of DNS and Initial Defining Standards 849
DNS Evolution and Important Additional Standards 850
DNS Adaptation for Internet Protocol Version 6 850
DNS Design Goals, Objectives, and Assumptions 851
DNS Design Goals and Objectives 851
DNS Design Assumptions 852
DNS Components and General Functions 853
DNS Name Space 854
Name Registration (Including Administration and Authorities) 854
Name Resolution 854

53 DNS Name Space, Architecture, and Terminology 857

DNS Domains and the DNS Hierarchical Name Architecture 858
The Essential Concept in the DNS Name Space: Domains 858
The DNS Hierarchical Tree Structure of Names 858
DNS Structural Elements and Terminology 860
DNS Tree-Related Terminology 860
DNS Domain-Related Terminology 860
DNS Family-Related Terminology 861
DNS Labels, Names, and Syntax Rules 863
DNS Labels and Label Syntax Rules 863
Domain Name Construction 864

Absolute (Fully Qualified) and Relative (Partially Qualified) Domain Name Specifications 865
Fully Qualified Domain Names 865
Partially Qualified Domain Names 866

54 DNS Name Registration, Public Administration, Zones, and Authorities 867

DNS Hierarchical Authority Structure and the Distributed Name Database 868
The DNS Root Domain Central Authority 868
TLD Authorities 869
Lower-Level Authority Delegation 869
Authority Hierarchy's Relationship to the Name Hierarchy 869
The DNS Distributed Name Database 869
DNS Organizational (Generic) TLDs and Authorities 870
Original Generic TLDs 870
New Generic TLDs 871
DNS Geopolitical (Country Code) TLDs and Authorities 874
Country Code Designations 874
Country Code TLD Authorities 875
Leasing/Sale of Country Code Domains 875
Drawbacks of the Geopolitical TLDs 876
Public Registration for Second-Level and Lower Domains 876
Registration Authority 877
Registration Coordination 878
DNS Public Registration Disputes and Dispute Resolution 878
Public Registration Disputes 878
Methods of Registration Dispute Resolution 880
The Uniform Domain Name Dispute Resolution Policy 880
DNS Name Space Administrative Hierarchy Partitioning: DNS Zones of Authority 881
Methods of Dividing a Name Space into Zones of Authority 882
The Impact of Zones on Name Resolution: Authoritative Servers 882
DNS Private Name Registration 884
Using Publicly Accessible Private Names 884
Using Private Names for Internal Use 885
Using Private Names on Networks Not Connected to the Internet 885

55 DNS Name Server Concepts and Operation 887

DNS General Operation 888
DNS Name Server Architecture and the Distributed Name Database 888
DNS Server Support Functions 889
The Logical Nature of the DNS Name Server Hierarchy 890
DNS Name Server Data Storage 890
Binary and Text Representations of Resource Records 890
Use of RRs and Master Files 891
Common RR Types 892
RR Classes 893
DNS Name Server Types and Roles 893
Master (Primary)/Slave (Secondary) Servers 893
Name Server Roles 895
Caching-Only Name Servers 895
DNS Zone Management, Contacts, and Zone Transfers 895
Domain Contacts 896
Zone Transfers 896
DNS Root Name Servers 899
Root Name Server Redundancy 899
Current Root Name Servers 900

DNS Name Server Caching 901
Name Server Caching 902
Caching Data Persistence and the Time to Live Interval 902
Negative Caching 904
DNS Name Server Load Balancing 904
Using Multiple Address Records to Spread Out Requests to a Domain 904
Using Multiple DNS Servers to Spread Out DNS Requests 905
DNS Name Server Enhancements 905
Automating Zone Transfers: DNS Notify 906
Improving Zone Transfer Efficiency: Incremental Transfers 907
Dealing with Dynamic IP Addresses: DNS Update/Dynamic DNS 907

56 DNS Resolution Concepts and Resolver Operations 909

DNS Resolver Functions and General Operation 910
Name Resolution Services 910
Functions Performed by Name Resolvers 910
DNS Name Resolution Techniques: Iterative and Recursive Resolution 911
Iterative Resolution 912
Recursive Resolution 913
Contrasting Iterative and Recursive Resolution 913
DNS Name Resolution Efficiency Improvements: Caching and Local Resolution 915
The Motivation for Caching: Locality of Reference 915
Name Resolver Caching 916
Local Resolution 916
DNS Name Resolution Process 917
A Simple Example of DNS Name Resolution 917
Changes to Resolution to Handle Aliases (CNAME Records) 920
DNS Reverse Name Resolution Using the IN-ADDR.ARPA Domain 920
The Original Method: Inverse Querying 921
The IN-ADDR.ARPA Name Structure for Reverse Resolution 921
RR Setup for Reverse Resolution 922
DNS Electronic Mail Support and Mail Exchange (MX) Resource Records 924
Special Requirements for Email Name Resolution 924
The Mail Exchange (MX) Record and Its Use 925

57 DNS Messaging and Message, Resource Record, and Master File Formats 927

DNS Message Generation and Transport 928
DNS Client/Server Messaging Overview 928
DNS Message Transport Using UDP and TCP 929
DNS Message Processing and General Message Format 930
DNS Message Header Format 932
DNS Question Section Format 935
DNS Message Resource Record Field Formats 935
DNS Common RR Format 936
RData Field Formats for Common RRs 936
DNS Name Notation and Message Compression 940
Standard DNS Name Notation 940
DNS Electronic Mail Address Notation 941
DNS Message Compression 941
DNS Master File Format 943
DNS Common Master File Record Format 944
Use and Interpretation of Partially Qualified Domain Names (PQDNs) 944
Master File Directives 945
Syntax Rules for Master Files 945
Specific RR Syntax and Examples 946
Sample Master File 948

DNS Changes to Support IPv6 948
IPv6 DNS Extensions 949
Proposed Changes to the IPv6 DNS Extensions 949

PART III-2 NETWORK FILE AND RESOURCE SHARING PROTOCOLS 951

58 Network File and Resource Sharing and the TCP/IP Network File System (NFS) 953

File and Resource Sharing Concepts and Components 954
The Power of File and Resource Sharing Protocols 954
Components of a File and Resource Sharing Protocol 954
NFS Design Goals, Versions, and Standards 955
NFS Design Goals 955
NFS Versions and Standards 956
NFS Architecture and Components 957
NFS Main Components 957
Other Important NFS Functions 958
NFS Data Definition with the External Data Representation (XDR) Standard 959
A Method of Universal Data Exchange: XDR 959
XDR Data Types 960
NFS Client/Server Operation Using Remote Procedure Calls (RPCs) 961
RPC Operation and Transport Protocol Usage 962
Client and Server Responsibilities in NFS 963
Client and Server Caching 963
NFS Server Procedures and Operations 964
NFS Version 2 and Version 3 Server Procedures 964
NFS Version 4 Server Procedures and Operations 966
NFS File System Model and the Mount Protocol 968
The NFS File System Model 968
The Mount Protocol 968

PART III-3 HOST CONFIGURATION AND TCP/IP HOST CONFIGURATION PROTOCOLS 971

59 Host Configuration Concepts, Issues, and Motivation 973

The Purpose of Host Configuration 973
The Problems with Manual Host Configuration 974
Automating the Process: Host Configuration Protocols 975
The Role of Host Configuration Protocols in TCP/IP 975

60 TCP/IP Bootstrap Protocol (BOOTP) 977

BOOTP Overview, History, and Standards 978
BOOTP: Correcting the Weaknesses of RARP 978
Vendor-Specific Parameters 979
Changes to BOOTP and the Development of DHCP 980
BOOTP Client/Server Messaging and Addressing 980
BOOTP Messaging and Transport 981
BOOTP Use of Broadcasts and Ports 981
Retransmission of Lost Messages 982
BOOTP Detailed Operation 983
BOOTP Bootstrapping Procedure 983
Interpretation of the Client IP Address (CIAddr) Field 984
BOOTP Message Format 985

BOOTP Vendor-Specific Area and Vendor Information Extensions 988
BOOTP Vendor Information Extensions 989
BOOTP Vendor Information Fields 990
BOOTP Relay Agents (Forwarding Agents) 991
The Function of BOOTP Relay Agents 992
Normal BOOTP Operation Using a Relay Agent 993
Relaying BOOTP Requests Using Broadcasts 994

61 DHCP Overview and Address Allocation Concepts 997

DHCP Overview, History, and Standards 998
DHCP: Building on BOOTP's Strengths 999
Overview of DHCP Features 999
DHCP Address Assignment and Allocation Mechanisms 1000
DHCP Address Allocation 1000
DHCP Manual Allocation 1001
DHCP Dynamic Allocation 1001
DHCP Automatic Allocation 1002
DHCP Leases 1003
DHCP Lease Length Policy 1003
Issues with Infinite Leases 1005
DHCP Lease Life Cycle and Lease Timers 1005
DHCP Lease Life Cycle Phases 1006
Renewal and Rebinding Timers 1008
DHCP Lease Address Pools, Ranges, and Address Management 1008
Address Pool Size Selection 1009
Lease Address Ranges (Scopes) 1009
Other Issues with Address Management 1011

62 DHCP Configuration and Operation 1013

DHCP Overview of Client and Server Responsibilities 1014
DHCP Server Responsibilities 1014
DHCP Client Responsibilities 1015
DHCP Client/Server Roles 1015
DHCP Relay Agents 1016
DHCP Configuration Parameters, Storage, and Communication 1016
Configuration Parameter Management 1016
Parameter Storage 1017
Configuration Parameter Communication 1017
DHCP General Operation and the Client Finite State Machine 1017
DHCP Lease Allocation, Reallocation, and Renewal 1021
Initial Lease Allocation Process 1021
DHCP Lease Reallocation Process 1026
DHCP Lease Renewal and Rebinding Processes 1028
DHCP Early Lease Termination (Release) Process 1031
DHCP Parameter Configuration Process for Clients with Non-DHCP Addresses 1033

63 DHCP Messaging, Message Types, and Formats 1035

DHCP Message Generation, Addressing, Transport, and Retransmission 1036
Message Generation and General Formatting 1036
Message Transport 1036
Retransmission of Lost Messages 1037
DHCP Message Format 1038
DHCP Options 1041
Options and Option Format 1042

Option Categories ... 1043
Option Overloading ... 1044
Summary of DHCP Options/BOOTP Vendor Information Fields ... 1045
RFC 1497 Vendor Extensions ... 1045
IP Layer Parameters per Host ... 1046
IP Layer Parameters per Interface ... 1047
Link Layer Parameters per Interface ... 1048
TCP Parameters ... 1048
Application and Service Parameters ... 1048
DHCP Extensions ... 1050

64 DHCP Client/Server Implementation, Features, and IPv6 Support 1053

DHCP Server and Client Implementation and Management Issues ... 1054
DHCP Server Implementations ... 1054
DHCP Client Implementations ... 1056
DHCP Message Relaying and BOOTP Relay Agents ... 1056
BOOTP Relay Agents for DHCP ... 1057
DHCP Relaying Process ... 1057
DHCP Autoconfiguration/Automatic Private IP Addressing (APIPA) ... 1058
APIPA Operation ... 1059
APIPA Limitations ... 1060
DHCP Server Conflict Detection ... 1061
DHCP and BOOTP Interoperability ... 1062
BOOTP Clients Connecting to a DHCP Server ... 1063
DHCP Clients Connecting to a BOOTP Server ... 1063
DHCP Security Issues ... 1063
DHCP Security Concerns ... 1064
DHCP Authentication ... 1064
DHCP for IP Version 6 (DHCPv6) ... 1065
Two Methods for Autoconfiguration in IPv6 ... 1065
DHCPv6 Operation Overview ... 1065
DHCPv6 Message Exchanges ... 1066

PART III-4 TCP/IP NETWORK MANAGEMENT FRAMEWORK AND PROTOCOLS 1067

65 TCP/IP Internet Standard Management Framework Overview 1069

Overview and History of the TCP/IP Internet Standard Management Framework and Simple Network Management Protocol (SNMP) ... 1070
Early Development of SNMP ... 1070
The Two Meanings of SNMP ... 1071
Design Goals of SNMP ... 1071
Further Development of SNMP and the Problem of SNMP Variations ... 1072
TCP/IP SNMP Operational Model, Components, and Terminology ... 1072
SNMP Device Types ... 1072
SNMP Entities ... 1073
SNMP Operational Model Summary ... 1073
TCP/IP Internet Standard Management Framework Architecture and Protocol Components ... 1075
SNMP Framework Components ... 1075
SNMP Framework Architecture ... 1076
TCP/IP Internet Standard Management Framework and SNMP Versions (SNMPv1, SNMPv2 Variants, and SNMPv3) ... 1076
SNMPv1 ... 1077
SNMPsec ... 1077

SNMPv2 1078
SNMPv2 Variants 1078
SNMPv3 1079
TCP/IP Internet Standard Management Framework and SNMP Standards 1079

66 TCP/IP Structure of Management Information (SMI) and Management Information Bases (MIBs) 1083

TCP/IP SMI and MIBs Overview 1084
SNMP's Information-Oriented Design 1084
MIB and MIB Objects 1085
Defining MIB Objects: SMI 1086
TCP/IP MIB Objects, Object Characteristics, and Object Types 1087
MIB Object Characteristics 1087
SMI Data Types 1089
TCP/IP MIB Object Descriptors and Identifiers and the Object Name Hierarchy 1090
Object Descriptors 1091
Object Identifiers 1091
Structure of the MIB Object Name Hierarchy 1092
Recursive Definition of MIB Object Identifiers 1094
TCP/IP MIB Modules and Object Groups 1094
The Organization of MIB Objects into Object Groups 1094
MIB Modules 1096
MIB Module Format 1097

67 TCP/IP Simple Network Management Protocol (SNMP) Concepts and Operation 1099

SNMP Protocol Overview 1100
Early Development of SNMPv1 1100
SNMPv2 and the Division of SNMP into Protocol Operations and Transport Mappings 1101
SNMP Communication Methods 1102
SNMP Protocol Operations 1102
SNMP PDU Classes 1103
Basic Request/Response Information Poll Using GetRequest and (Get)Response Messages 1104
Table Traversal Using GetNextRequest and GetBulkRequest Messages 1105
Object Modification Using SetRequest Messages 1107
Information Notification Using Trap and InformRequest Messages 1109
SNMP Protocol Security Issues and Methods 1110
Problems with SNMPv1 Security 1111
SNMPv2/v3 Security Methods 1111

68 SNMP Protocol Messaging and Message Formats 1113

SNMP Protocol Message Generation 1114
SNMP Transport Mappings 1114
UDP Message Size Issues 1115
Lost Transmission Issues 1115
SNMP General Message Format 1116
The Difference Between SNMP Messages and PDUs 1117
General PDU Format 1117
SNMP Version 1 (SNMPv1) Message Format 1119
SNMPv1 General Message Format 1119
SNMPv1 PDU Formats 1120
SNMP Version 2 (SNMPv2) Message Formats 1122
SNMP Version 2 (SNMPv2p) Message Format 1123
Community-Based SNMP Version 2 (SNMPv2c) Message Format 1124

User-Based SNMP Version 2 (SNMPv2u) Message Format 1124
SNMPv2 PDU Formats 1126
SNMP Version 3 (SNMPv3) Message Format 1129

69 TCP/IP Remote Network Monitoring (RMON) 1133
RMON Standards 1134
RMON MIB Hierarchy and Object Groups 1134
RMON Alarms, Events, and Statistics 1136

PART III-5 TCP/IP APPLICATION LAYER ADDRESSING AND APPLICATION CATEGORIES 1137

70 TCP/IP Application Layer Addressing: Uniform Resource Identifiers, Locators, and Names (URIs, URLs, and URNs) 1139
URI Overview and Standards 1140
URI Categories: URLs and URNs 1141
URI Standards 1142
URL General Syntax 1142
Common Internet Scheme Syntax 1143
Omission of URL Syntax Elements 1144
URL Fragments 1145
Unsafe Characters and Special Encodings 1145
URL Schemes and Scheme-Specific Syntaxes 1146
World Wide Web/Hypertext Transfer Protocol Syntax (http) 1146
File Transfer Protocol Syntax (ftp) 1147
Electronic Mail Syntax (mailto) 1147
Gopher Protocol Syntax (gopher) 1148
Network News/Usenet Syntax (news) 1148
Network News Transfer Protocol Syntax (nttp) 1148
Telnet Syntax (telnet) 1149
Local File Syntax (file) 1149
Special Syntax Rules 1149
URL Relative Syntax and Base URLs 1150
Interpretation Rules for Relative URLs 1151
Practical Interpretation of Relative URLs 1152
URL Length and Complexity Issues 1154
URL Wrapping and Delimiting 1155
Explicit URL Delimiting and Redirectors 1156
URL Abbreviation 1156
URL Obscuration, Obfuscation, and General Trickery 1156
URNs 1159
The Problem with URLs 1159
Overview of URNs 1160
URN Namespaces and Syntax 1160
URN Resolution and Implementation Difficulties 1161

71 File and Message Transfer Overview and Application Categories 1163
File Concepts 1164
Application Categories 1164
General File Transfer Applications 1164
Message Transfer Applications 1164
The Merging of File and Message Transfer Methods 1165

PART III-6 TCP/IP GENERAL FILE TRANSFER PROTOCOLS 1167

72 File Transfer Protocol (FTP) 1169

FTP Overview, History, and Standards 1170
FTP Development and Standardization 1170
Overview of FTP Operation 1171
FTP Operational Model, Protocol Components, and Key Terminology 1172
The Server-FTP Process and User-FTP Process 1172
FTP Control Connection and Data Connection 1172
FTP Process Components and Terminology 1173
Server-FTP Process Components 1173
User-FTP Process Components 1174
Third-Party File Transfer (Proxy FTP) 1174
FTP Control Connection Establishment, User Authentication, and Anonymous FTP Access 1175
FTP Login Sequence and Authentication 1175
FTP Security Extensions 1176
Anonymous FTP 1177
FTP Data Connection Management 1177
Normal (Active) Data Connections 1178
Passive Data Connections 1178
Efficiency and Security Issues Related to the Connection Methods 1179
FTP General Data Communication and Transmission Modes 1181
Stream Mode 1181
Block Mode 1182
Compressed Mode 1182
FTP Data Representation: Data Types, Format Control, and Data Structures 1182
FTP Data Types 1183
ASCII Data Type Line-Delimiting Issues 1184
FTP Format Control 1184
FTP Data Structures 1185
FTP Internal Command Groups and Protocol Commands 1185
FTP Command Groups and Commands 1185
FTP Replies 1188
Advantages of Using Both Text and Numeric Replies 1188
Reply Code Structure and Digit Interpretation 1188
FTP Multiple-Line Text Replies 1192
FTP User Interface and User Commands 1193
Command-Line and Graphical FTP Interfaces 1193
Typical FTP User Commands 1194
Sample FTP Session 1196

73 Trivial File Transfer Protocol (TFTP) 1199

TFTP Overview, History, and Standards 1200
Why TFTP Was Needed 1200
Comparing FTP and TFTP 1201
Overview of TFTP Operation 1201
TFTP General Operation, Connection Establishment, and Client/Server Communication 1202
Connection Establishment and Identification 1203
Lock-Step Client/Server Messaging 1203
Difficulties with TFTP's Simplified Messaging Mechanism 1204
TFTP Detailed Operation and Messaging 1204
Initial Message Exchange 1204
Data Block Numbering 1205
TFTP Read Process Steps 1205
TFTP Write Process Steps 1206

TFTP Options and Option Negotiation 1208
TFTP Option Negotiation Process 1208
TFTP Options 1211
TFTP Message Formats 1211
Read Request and Write Request Messages 1211
Data Messages 1212
Acknowledgment Messages 1213
Error Messages 1213
Option Acknowledgment Messages 1214

PART III-7 TCP/IP ELECTRONIC MAIL SYSTEM: CONCEPTS AND PROTOCOLS 1215

74 TCP/IP Electronic Mail System Overview and Concepts 1217

TCP/IP Electronic Mail System Overview and History 1218
The Early Days of Email 1218
History of TCP/IP Email 1219
Overview of the TCP/IP Email System 1219
TCP/IP Email Communication Overview 1220
TCP/IP Email Message Communication Model 1222
Protocol Roles in Email Communication 1224

75 TCP/IP Electronic Mail Addresses and Addressing 1225

TCP/IP Email Addressing and Address Resolution 1226
Standard DNS-Based Email Addresses 1226
Special Requirements of Email Addresses 1227
TCP/IP Historical and Special Email Addressing 1228
FidoNet Addressing 1228
UUCP-Style Addressing 1229
Addressing for Gatewaying 1229
TCP/IP Email Aliases and Address Books 1230
Multiple Recipient Addressing 1230
Mailing Lists 1231

76 TCP/IP Electronic Mail Message Formats and Message Processing: RFC 822 and MIME 1233

TCP/IP Email RFC 822 Standard Message Format Overview 1234
Development of the RFC 822 Message Format Standard 1235
Overview of RFC 822 Messages 1235
General RFC 822 Message Structure 1236
TCP/IP Email RFC 822 Standard Message Format Header Fields and Groups 1237
Header Field Structure 1237
Header Field Groups 1237
Common Header Field Groups and Header Fields 1238
TCP/IP Email RFC 822 Standard Message Format Processing and Interpretation 1241
MIME Overview 1242
MIME Capabilities 1243
MIME Standards 1244
MIME Basic Structures and Headers 1245
Basic Structures 1246
MIME Entities 1246
Primary MIME Headers 1246
Additional MIME Headers 1247

MIME Content-Type Header and Discrete Media 1248
Content-Type Header Syntax 1248
Discrete Media Types and Subtypes 1249
MIME Composite Media Types: Multipart and Encapsulated Message Structures 1253
MIME Multipart Message Type 1253
Multipart Message Encoding 1254
MIME Encapsulated Message Type 1257
MIME Content-Transfer-Encoding Header and Encoding Methods 1257
7-Bit and 8-Bit Encoding 1258
Quoted-Printable Encoding 1258
Base64 Encoding 1258
MIME Extension for non-ASCII Mail Message Headers 1261

77 TCP/IP Electronic Mail Delivery Protocol: The Simple Mail Transfer Protocol (SMTP) 1263

SMTP Overview, History, and Standards 1264
SMTP Standards 1264
SMTP Communication and Message Transport Methods 1265
Terminology: Client/Server and Sender/Receiver 1267
SMTP Connection and Session Establishment and Termination 1267
Overview of Connection Establishment and Termination 1268
Connection Establishment and Greeting Exchange 1268
Connection Establishment Using SMTP Extensions 1269
Connection Termination 1270
SMTP Mail Transaction Process 1271
Overview of SMTP Mail Transaction 1271
SMTP Mail Transaction Details 1272
SMTP Special Features, Capabilities, and Extensions 1274
SMTP Special Features and Capabilities 1275
SMTP Extensions 1276
SMTP Security Issues 1277
SMTP Commands 1279
SMTP Replies and Reply Codes 1281
Reply Code Structure and Digit Interpretation 1281
SMTP Multiple-Line Text Replies 1284
Enhanced Status Code Replies 1284

78 TCP/IP Electronic Mail Access and Retrieval Protocols and Methods 1285

TCP/IP Email Mailbox Access Model, Method, and Protocol Overview 1286
Email Access and Retrieval Models 1287
TCP/IP Post Office Protocol (POP/POP3) 1288
POP Overview, History, Versions, and Standards 1288
POP3 General Operation 1290
POP3 Session States 1290
TCP/IP Internet Message Access Protocol (IMAP/IMAP4) 1297
IMAP Overview, History, Versions, and Standards 1298
IMAP General Operation 1300
IMAP Session States 1300
IMAP Commands, Results, and Responses 1302
IMAP Not Authenticated State: User Authentication Process and Commands 1306
IMAP Authenticated State: Mailbox Manipulation/Selection Process and Commands 1307
IMAP Selected State: Message Manipulation Process and Commands 1309
TCP/IP Direct Server Email Access 1311
TCP/IP World Wide Web Email Access 1313

PART III-8 TCP/IP WORLD WIDE WEB AND THE HYPERTEXT TRANSFER PROTOCOL (HTTP) 1315

79 World Wide Web and Hypertext Overview and Concepts 1317

World Wide Web and Hypertext Overview and History 1318
- History of Hypertext 1318
- The World Wide Web Today 1319

World Wide Web System Concepts and Components 1320
- Major Functional Components of the Web 1320
- Web Servers and Web Browsers 1321

World Wide Web Media and the Hypertext Markup Language 1322
- Overview of HTML 1322
- HTML Elements and Tags 1323
- Common HTML Elements 1324
- Common Text Formatting Tags 1326

World Wide Web Addressing: HTTP Uniform Resource Locators 1326
- HTTP URL Syntax 1327
- Resource Paths and Directory Listings 1328

80 HTTP General Operation and Connections 1329

HTTP Versions and Standards 1330
- HTTP/0.9 1330
- HTTP/1.0 1330
- HTTP/1.1 1331
- Future HTTP Versions 1332

HTTP Operational Model and Client/Server Communication 1333
- Basic HTTP Client/Server Communication 1333
- Intermediaries and the HTTP Request/Response Chain 1334
- The Impact of Caching on HTTP Communication 1335

HTTP Transitory and Persistent Connections and Pipelining 1336
- Persistent Connections 1337
- Pipelining 1337
- HTTP Persistent Connection Establishment and Management 1338

81 HTTP Messages, Methods, and Status Codes 1341

HTTP Generic Message Format 1342

HTTP Request Message Format 1343
- Request Line 1344
- Headers 1346

HTTP Response Message Format 1346
- Status Line 1347
- Headers 1348

HTTP Methods 1349
- Common Methods 1349
- Other Methods 1350
- Safe and Idempotent Methods 1351

HTTP Status Codes and Reason Phrases 1352
- Status Code Format 1352
- Reason Phrases 1353
- The 100 (Continue) Preliminary Reply 1356

82 HTTP Message Headers 1357

HTTP General Headers 1358
Cache-Control Headers 1358
Warning 1359
Other HTTP General Headers 1360
HTTP Request Headers 1361
HTTP Response Headers 1364
HTTP Entity Headers 1365

83 HTTP Entities, Transfers, Coding Methods, and Content Management 1369

HTTP Entities and Internet Media Types 1370
Media Types and Subtypes 1370
HTTP's Use of Media Types 1371
Differences in HTTP and MIME Constructs 1371
HTTP Content and Transfer Encodings 1372
HTTP's Two-Level Encoding Scheme 1373
Use of Content and Transfer Encodings 1373
HTTP Data Length Issues, Chunked Transfers, and Message Trailers 1374
Dynamic Data Length 1375
Chunked Transfers and Message Trailers 1375
HTTP Content Negotiation and Quality Values 1378
Content Negotiation Techniques 1378
Quality Values for Preference Weights 1380

84 HTTP Features, Capabilities, and Issues 1381

HTTP Caching Features and Issues 1382
Benefits of HTTP Caching 1382
Cache Locations 1383
Cache Control 1384
Important Caching Issues 1385
HTTP Proxy Servers and Proxying 1386
Benefits of Proxies 1386
Comparing Proxies and Caches 1387
Important Proxying Issues 1387
HTTP Security and Privacy 1388
HTTP Authentication Methods 1389
Security and Privacy Concerns and Issues 1389
Methods for Ensuring Privacy in HTTP 1390
HTTP State Management Using Cookies 1390
Issues with Cookies 1391
Managing Cookie Use 1393

PART III-9 OTHER FILE AND MESSAGE TRANSFER APPLICATIONS 1395

85 Usenet (Network News) and the TCP/IP Network News Transfer Protocol (NNTP) 1397

Usenet Overview, History, and Operation 1398
History of Usenet 1398
Usenet Operation and Characteristics 1399
Usenet Transport Methods 1400
Usenet Communication Model 1401
Usenet's Public Distribution Orientation 1402
Usenet Communication Process 1402

Message Propagation and Server Organization 1404
Usenet Addressing: Newsgroups 1404
Usenet Message Format and Special Headers 1408
Usenet Header Categories and Common Headers 1408
Additional Usenet Headers 1410
Usenet MIME Messages 1411
NNTP Overview and General Operation 1411
NNTP Interserver Communication Process: News Article Propagation 1413
The Usenet Server Structure 1413
Basic NNTP Propagation Methods 1414
NNTP Client-Server Communication Process: News Posting and Access 1416
News Posting, Access, and Reading 1417
News Access Methods 1418
Other Client/Server Functions 1418
Article Threading 1419
NNTP Commands and Command Extensions 1420
Command Syntax 1420
Base Command Set 1420
NNTP Command Extensions 1422
NNTP Status Responses and Response Codes 1426

86 Gopher Protocol (Gopher) 1431

Gopher Overview and General Operation 1431
Information Storage on Gopher Servers 1432
Gopher Client/Server Operation 1432
Important Differences Between Gopher and the Web 1433
Gopher's Role in the Modern Internet 1433

PART III-10 INTERACTIVE AND ADMINISTRATIVE UTILITIES AND PROTOCOLS 1435

87 TCP/IP Interactive and Remote Application Protocols 1437

Telnet Protocol 1438
Telnet Overview, History, and Standards 1438
Telnet Connections and Client/Server Operation 1441
Telnet Communications Model and the Network Virtual Terminal (NVT) 1443
Telnet Protocol Commands 1446
Telnet Interrupt Handling 1449
Telnet Options and Option Negotiation 1450
Berkeley Remote (r) Commands 1454
Berkeley Remote Login (rlogin) 1455
Berkeley Remote Shell (rsh) 1456
Other Berkeley Remote Commands 1457
Internet Relay Chat Protocol (IRC) 1458
IRC Communication Model and Client/Server Operation 1459
Messaging and IRC Channels 1459
IRC and the Modern Internet 1460

88 TCP/IP Administration and Troubleshooting Utilities and Protocols 1461

TCP/IP Host Name Utility (hostname) 1462
TCP/IP Communication Verification Utility (ping) 1463
Operation of the ping Utility 1464
Basic Use of ping 1464

Methods of Diagnosing Connectivity Problems Using ping 1465
ping Options and Parameters 1466
TCP/IP Route Tracing Utility (traceroute) 1467
Operation of the traceroute Utility 1468
Basic Use of the traceroute Utility 1469
traceroute Options and Parameters 1470
TCP/IP Address Resolution Protocol Utility (arp) 1471
TCP/IP DNS Name Resolution and Lookup Utilities (nslookup, host, and dig) 1472
The nslookup Utility 1473
The host Utility 1475
The dig Utility 1476
TCP/IP DNS Registry Database Lookup Utility (whois/nicname) 1477
TCP/IP Network Status Utility (netstat) 1479
The UNIX netstat Utility 1480
The Windows netstat Utility 1482
TCP/IP Configuration Utilities (ifconfig, ipconfig, and winipcfg) 1484
The ifconfig Utility for UNIX 1484
The ipconfig for Windows NT, 2000, and XP 1486
The winipcfg Utility for Windows 95, 98, and Me 1488
Miscellaneous TCP/IP Troubleshooting Protocols 1489

INDEX **1491**

RFCs BY NUMBER **1537**

LIST OF FIGURES

		page
Address resolution problems with large hardware address size	Figure 13-3	208
Address Resolution Protocol (ARP) transaction process	Figure 13-5	215
Address resolution through direct mapping	Figure 13-2	207
Address resolution, why necessary	Figure 13-1	205
ARP message format	Figure 13-6	218
ARP Proxy operation	Figure 13-7	222
ARP proxying by Mobile IP home agent	Figure 30-9	500
BGP general message format	Figure 40-2	665
BGP Keepalive message format	Figure 40-5	673
BGP Notification message format	Figure 40-6	674
BGP Open message format	Figure 40-3	668
BGP topology and designations, sample	Figure 40-1	653
BGP Update message format	Figure 40-4	670
Binary, decimal, and hexadecimal representations of IPv6 addresses	Figure 25-2	378
Binary information representations and terms	Figure 4-1	64
Binary, octal, and hexadecimal number representations	Figure 4-2	67
Bit mask, AND, clearing bits using	Figure 4-3	77
BOOTP, general operation of	Figure 60-1	982
BOOTP message format	Figure 60-3	988
BOOTP operation	Figure 60-2	985
BOOTP operation using a relay agent	Figure 60-5	994
BOOTP Vendor-Specific Area format showing vendor information fields	Figure 60-4	990
CIDR (/15) address block, hierarchical division of, example of	Figure 20-3	325
CIDR (slash) notation and its subnet mask equivalent	Figure 20-2	320
Circuit switching	Figure 1-1	14
Class A, Class B, and Class C networks, default subnet masks for	Figure 18-4	282

		page
Class B network, determining subnet addresses for	Figure 19-7	308
Class B network, determining the custom subnet mask for	Figure 19-5	304
Class C (/24) network split into eight conventional subnets	Figure 18-6	293
Class C (/24) network split using VLSM	Figure 18-7	294
Class C network, determining host addresses for	Figure 19-8	312
Class C network, determining subnet addresses for	Figure 19-6	307
Class C network, determining the custom subnet mask for	Figure 19-4	304
Class C networks, custom subnet masks for	Figure 18-5	285
Class determination algorithm for classful IP addresses	Figure 17-2	259
Classful addressing, main problem with	Figure 17-5	271
Classless addressing (CIDR) solves the granularity problem	Figure 20-1	318
Client-server networking	Figure 1-6	25
DHCP Automatic Private IP Addressing (APIPA)	Figure 64-1	1060
DHCP client finite state machine	Figure 62-1	1020
DHCP lease allocation process	Figure 62-2	1025
DHCP lease reallocation process	Figure 62-3	1028
DHCP lease renewal and rebinding processes	Figure 62-4	1032
DHCP life cycle example	Figure 61-1	1007
DHCP message format	Figure 63-1	1039
DHCP multiple-server non-overlapping scopes	Figure 61-3	1011
DHCP Options field format	Figure 63-2	1042
DHCP parameter configuration process	Figure 62-5	1034
DHCP scope	Figure 61-2	1010
DNS common RR format	Figure 57-4	937
DNS functions	Figure 52-1	853
DNS general message format	Figure 57-1	931
DNS IN-ADDR.ARPA reverse name resolution hierarchy	Figure 56-4	922
DNS labels and domain name construction	Figure 53-4	864
DNS message header format	Figure 57-2	934
DNS message Question section format	Figure 57-3	935
DNS name resolution, iterative	Figure 56-1	913
DNS name resolution process, example of	Figure 56-3	919
DNS name resolution, recursive	Figure 56-2	914
DNS name space "family tree"	Figure 53-3	862
DNS root name servers (Internet), geographic locations of	Figure 55-2	901
DNS RR master file and binary field formats	Figure 55-1	891

		page
DNS standard name notation	Figure 57-6	941
DNS Start Of Authority (SOA) RR data format	Figure 57-5	939
DNS tree-related and domain-related terminology	Figure 53-2	861
DNS zones of authority	Figure 54-2	883
Dynamic address resolution	Figure 13-4	210
Email communication model	Figure 74-1	1223
Flat name architecture (flat name space)	Figure 50-4	832
FTP active data connection	Figure 72-3	1179
FTP connection establishment and user authentication	Figure 72-2	1176
FTP operational model	Figure 72-1	1173
FTP passive data connection	Figure 72-4	1180
FTP reply code format	Figure 72-5	1190
Global hierarchical domain architecture, example of	Figure 53-1	859
Global object name hierarchy and SNMP MIB hierarchies	Figure 66-2	1092
Hierarchical address division using CIDR	Figure 20-4	326
Hierarchical name architecture (structured name space)	Figure 50-5	833
HTTP client/server communication	Figure 80-1	1334
HTTP Request message format	Figure 81-1	1344
HTTP request/response chain, impact of caching on	Figure 84-1	1383
HTTP request/response chain using intermediaries	Figure 80-2	1335
HTTP Response message format	Figure 81-2	1347
ICMP common message format	Figure 31-2	519
ICMP general operation	Figure 31-1	511
ICMP Redirect message, host redirection using	Figure 32-5	531
ICMPv4 Address Mask Request and Address Mask Reply message format	Figure 33-5	544
ICMPv4 Destination Unreachable message format	Figure 32-1	523
ICMPv4 Echo and Echo Reply message format	Figure 33-1	537
ICMPv4 Parameter Problem message format	Figure 32-7	533
ICMPv4 Redirect message format	Figure 32-6	531
ICMPv4 Router Advertisement Message format	Figure 33-3	541
ICMPv4 Router Solicitation Message format	Figure 33-4	542
ICMPv4 Source Quench message format	Figure 32-2	526

		page
ICMPv4 Time Exceeded message format	Figure 32-4	529
ICMPv4 Timestamp and Timestamp Reply message format	Figure 33-2	539
ICMPv4 Traceroute message format	Figure 33-6	546
ICMPv6 Destination Unreachable message format	Figure 34-1	548
ICMPv6 Echo Request and Echo Reply message format	Figure 35-1	559
ICMPv6 MTU option format	Figure 35-12	574
ICMPv6 Neighbor Advertisement message format	Figure 35-4	564
ICMPv6 Neighbor Solicitation message format	Figure 35-5	565
ICMPv6 Packet Too Big message format	Figure 34-2	551
ICMPv6 Parameter Problem message format	Figure 34-5	555
ICMPv6 Prefix Information option format	Figure 35-10	573
ICMPv6 Redirect message format	Figure 35-6	567
ICMPv6 Redirected Header option format	Figure 35-11	574
ICMPv6 Router Advertisement message format	Figure 35-2	560
ICMPv6 Router Renumbering message format	Figure 35-7	569
ICMPv6 Router Solicitation message format	Figure 35-3	562
ICMPv6 Source Link-Layer Address option format	Figure 35-8	571
ICMPv6 Target Link-Layer Address option format	Figure 35-9	572
ICMPv6 Time Exceeded message format	Figure 34-4	554
IEEE 802 MAC addresses, converting to IPv6 modified EUI-64 identifiers	Figure 25-5	390
IMAP FSM	Figure 78-4	1301
Internet DNS organizational (generic) TLDs	Figure 54-1	872
Internet standards organizations	Figure 3-1	54
Internetwork access with a name system	Figure 50-2	828
Internetwork access without a name system	Figure 50-1	827
IP address binary, hexadecimal, and dotted decimal representations	Figure 16-2	246
IP address class bit assignments and network/host ID sizes	Figure 17-3	261
IP address division (basic): network ID and host ID	Figure 16-3	248
IP address division, mid-octet	Figure 16-4	249
IP address subnet ID, determining through subnet masking	Figure 18-3	280
IP addresses (multicast), mapping to IEEE 802 multicast MAC addresses	Figure 13-8	224
IP datagram encapsulation	Figure 21-1	331
IP datagram, expiration of, and Time Exceeded message generation	Figure 32-3	528
IP datagram next-hop routing	Figure 23-2	356
IP datagrams, direct and indirect (routed) delivery of	Figure 23-1	352
IP interfaces for common network devices	Figure 16-1	243
IP maximum transmission unit (MTU) and fragmentation	Figure 22-1	341

		page
IP Multicast address ranges and uses	Figure 17-4	268
IP Network Address Translation (NAT) terminology	Figure 28-1	432
IP routing and routing tables	Figure 23-3	358
IP: internetwork datagram delivery, main function of	Figure 15-1	236
IPsec Authentication Header (AH) format	Figure 29-8	465
IPsec bump in the stack (BITS) architecture	Figure 29-2	455
IPsec bump in the wire (BITW) architecture	Figure 29-3	456
IPsec ESP format	Figure 29-11	471
IPsec protocols and components, overview	Figure 29-1	453
IPsec transport mode operation	Figure 29-4	458
IPsec tunnel mode operation	Figure 29-5	459
IPv4 address space, division into classes	Figure 17-1	257
IPv4 and IPv6 address space sizes, relative, a (poor) representation of	Figure 25-1	377
IPv4 datagram format	Figure 21-2	334
IPv4 datagram format with IPsec AH	Figure 29-7	464
IPv4 datagram format with IPsec ESP	Figure 29-10	469
IPv4 datagram fragmentation	Figure 22-2	342
IPv4 datagram fragmentation process	Figure 22-3	345
IPv4 Options field format	Figure 21-3	337
IPv4-compatible embedded IPv6 address representation	Figure 25-6	393
IPv4-mapped embedded IPv6 address representation	Figure 25-7	393
IPv6 datagram format with IPsec Authentication Header (AH)	Figure 29-6	463
IPv6 datagram format with IPsec ESP	Figure 29-9	468
IPv6 datagram fragmentation	Figure 27-1	419
IPv6 extension header linking using the Next Header field	Figure 26-3	408
IPv6 Fragment extension header format	Figure 26-5	411
IPv6 general datagram structure	Figure 26-1	403
IPv6 global unicast address format	Figure 25-3	385
IPv6 Hop-By-Hop Options and Destination Options header formats	Figure 26-6	413
IPv6 main header format	Figure 26-2	405
IPv6 multicast address format	Figure 25-8	394
IPv6 multicast scope	Figure 25-9	396
IPv6 Routing extension header format	Figure 26-4	410
IPv6 solicited-node address calculation	Figure 25-10	397
IPv6 unicast routing prefix structure, example of	Figure 25-4	387
Message routing in the OSI Reference Model	Figure 5-7	99

		page
MIME base64 encoding	Figure 76-2	1260
MIME multipart message structure	Figure 76-1	1256
Mobile devices on IP internetworks, main problem with	Figure 30-1	477
Mobile IP encapsulation and tunneling	Figure 30-8	497
Mobile IP, general operation of	Figure 30-2	481
Mobile IP inefficiency worst-case scenario	Figure 30-10	502
Mobile IP Mobility Agent Advertisement Extension format	Figure 30-4	489
Mobile IP operation with a foreign agent care-of address	Figure 30-3	484
Mobile IP Prefix-Lengths Extension format	Figure 30-5	490
Mobile IP Registration Reply Message format	Figure 30-7	495
Mobile IP Registration Request message format	Figure 30-6	494
Multihomed devices on an IP internetwork	Figure 16-5	253
Multilink PPP architecture	Figure 11-1	176
Name system functions	Figure 50-3	830
NAT, bidirectional (two-way/inbound), operation of	Figure 28-3	438
NAT (Overlapping NAT/Twice NAT), operation of	Figure 28-5	446
NAT, Port-Based (overloaded), operation of	Figure 28-4	441
NAT, unidirectional (traditional/outbound), operation of	Figure 28-2	436
ND host redirection using an ICMPv6 Redirect message	Figure 36-2	587
Neighbor Discovery (ND) protocol functional groups and functions	Figure 36-1	578
Network message formatting	Figure 1-3	19
NFS architectural components	Figure 58-1	958
NNTP article propagation using the push model	Figure 85-3	1415
NNTP full newsgroup retrieval process	Figure 85-4	1419
OSI Reference Model and TCP/IP model layers	Figure 8-2	129
OSI Reference Model data encapsulation	Figure 5-5	96
OSI Reference Model interfaces for vertical communication	Figure 5-3	92
OSI Reference Model layer relationships and terminology	Figure 5-2	91
OSI Reference Model layers	Figure 5-1	89
OSI Reference Model mnemonics	Figure 7-1	116
OSI Reference Model PDU and SDU encapsulation	Figure 5-6	97
OSI Reference Model protocols: horizontal communication	Figure 5-4	94
OSPF AS, sample	Figure 39-1	629
OSPF AS with Costs, sample	Figure 39-3	634
OSPF calculated SPF tree	Figure 39-5	637

		page
OSPF common header format	Figure 39-6	640
OSPF Database Description message format	Figure 39-8	642
OSPF Hello message format	Figure 39-7	641
OSPF hierarchical topology AS, sample	Figure 39-2	632
OSPF Link State Acknowledgment message format	Figure 39-11	644
OSPF Link State Advertisement header format	Figure 39-12	645
OSPF Link State Request Message format	Figure 39-9	643
OSPF Link State Update message format	Figure 39-10	644
OSPF route determination using the SPF algorithm	Figure 39-4	635
Packet switching	Figure 1-2	14
PAP authentication	Figure 10-4	163
PAR, enhanced	Figure 46-4	735
Peer-to-peer networking	Figure 1-5	24
POP3 finite state machine	Figure 78-1	1291
POP3 mail exchange process	Figure 78-3	1296
POP3 user authentication process	Figure 78-2	1292
PPP Challenge Handshake Authentication Protocol (CHAP) authentication	Figure 10-5	164
PPP CHAP Challenge and Response frame format	Figure 12-8	195
PPP CHAP Success and Failure frame format	Figure 12-9	195
PPP control message carrying options	Figure 12-4	189
PPP control message format	Figure 12-3	187
PPP control message option format	Figure 12-5	189
PPP data frame, sample	Figure 12-2	184
PPP general frame format	Figure 12-1	183
PPP IP Control Protocol (IPCP) message exchanges	Figure 10-3	161
PPP LCP link configuration process	Figure 10-2	157
PPP Link Control Protocol (LCP) message exchanges	Figure 10-1	156
PPP location in the TCP/IP architecture	Figure 9-2	145
PPP MP fragmentation	Figure 12-12	199
PPP MP long fragment frame format	Figure 12-10	197
PPP MP short fragment frame format	Figure 12-11	198
PPP operation, overview	Figure 9-3	148
PPP PAP Authenticate-Ack and Authenticate-Nak frame format	Figure 12-7	193
PPP PAP Authenticate-Request frame format	Figure 12-6	193
PPP phases	Figure 9-4	151
Protocol, unreliable, operation of	Figure 46-2	732

		page
Reliability (basic): positive acknowledgment with retransmission (PAR)	Figure 46-3	733
Reverse Address Resolution Protocol (RARP) operation	Figure 14-2	229
Reverse Address Resolution Protocol (RARP), operation of	Figure 14-1	229
RIP AS, sample	Figure 38-1	601
RIP counting to infinity problem	Figure 38-3	608
RIP problem solving using split horizon with poisoned reverse	Figure 38-4	613
RIP, propagation of network routing information using	Figure 38-2	603
RIP-1 message format	Figure 38-5	616
RIP-2 message format	Figure 38-6	620
RIPng message format	Figure 38-7	622
Router loop (example)	Figure 34-3	553
Serial Line Internet Protocol (SLIP), operation of	Figure 9-1	143
SMTP mail transaction process	Figure 77-2	1273
SMTP transaction session establishment and termination	Figure 77-1	1269
SNMP general message format	Figure 68-1	1118
SNMP information poll process	Figure 67-1	1105
SNMP management information base (MIB)	Figure 66-1	1089
SNMP object modification process	Figure 67-2	1108
SNMP operational model	Figure 65-1	1074
SNMP Remote Network Monitoring (RMON) MIB hierarchy	Figure 69-1	1135
SNMPv1 common PDU format	Figure 68-3	1121
SNMPv1 general message format	Figure 68-2	1119
SNMPv1 Trap-PDU format	Figure 68-4	1122
SNMPv2 common PDU format	Figure 68-8	1128
SNMPv2 GetBulkRequest-PDU format	Figure 68-9	1128
SNMPv2c general message format	Figure 68-6	1124
SNMPv2p general message format	Figure 68-5	1123
SNMPv2u general message format	Figure 68-7	1125
SNMPv3 general message format	Figure 68-10	1130
Subnetted network, determining the subnet mask of	Figure 18-2	279
Subnetting, Class B, example of	Figure 19-3	302
Subnetting Class B network	Figure 18-1	277
Subnetting, Class C, example of	Figure 19-2	301
Subnetting design trade-off for Class C networks	Figure 19-1	300
TCP aggressive retransmission example	Figure 49-2	800

		page
TCP connection termination procedure	Figure 47-5	765
TCP data stream processing and segment packaging	Figure 46-1	730
TCP finite state machine (FSM)	Figure 47-1	750
TCP header checksum calculation	Figure 48-3	776
TCP pseudo header for checksum calculation	Figure 48-2	775
TCP receive categories and pointers	Figure 48-5	783
TCP retransmission with selective acknowledgment (SACK)	Figure 49-3	802
TCP segment format	Figure 48-1	772
TCP send window, sliding the	Figure 46-8	739
TCP sequence number synchronization	Figure 47-4	759
TCP silly window syndrome (SWS)	Figure 49-6	814
TCP simultaneous connection termination procedure	Figure 47-6	766
TCP simultaneous open connection establishment procedure	Figure 47-3	756
TCP stream categories and window after sending usable window bytes	Figure 46-7	738
TCP three-way handshake connection establishment procedure	Figure 47-2	755
TCP transaction example showing client's send pointers	Figure 48-7	788
TCP transaction example showing the server's send pointers	Figure 48-6	787
TCP transaction example with retransmission	Figure 49-1	797
TCP transmission categories, send window, and pointers	Figure 48-4	782
TCP transmission stream categories and send window terminology	Figure 46-6	738
TCP transmission stream, conceptual division into categories	Figure 46-5	736
TCP window, problem with shrinking	Figure 49-5	810
TCP window size adjustments and flow control	Figure 49-4	807
TCP/IP autonomous system (AS) routing architecture	Figure 37-1	594
TCP/IP client/server application port mechanics	Figure 43-3	705
TCP/IP client/server operation	Figure 8-1	126
TCP/IP Internet Standard Management Framework, components	Figure 65-2	1076
TCP/IP, process multiplexing and demultiplexing in	Figure 43-1	698
TCP/IP process multiplexing/demultiplexing using TCP/UDP ports	Figure 43-2	700
TCP/IP protocols	Figure 8-3	134
Telnet communication and the Network Virtual Terminal (NVT)	Figure 87-1	1444
TFTP acknowledgment message format	Figure 73-6	1213
TFTP data message format	Figure 73-5	1213
TFTP error message format	Figure 73-7	1213
TFTP OACK message format	Figure 73-8	1214
TFTP read process	Figure 73-1	1206
TFTP read process with option negotiation	Figure 73-3	1210

		page
TFTP RRQ/WRQ message format	Figure 73-4	1212
TFTP write process	Figure 73-2	1207
traceroute/tracert utility, operation of	Figure 88-1	1469
UDP message format	Figure 44-1	714
UDP pseudo header format	Figure 44-2	715
Unicast, multicast, and broadcast message addressing and transmission	Figure 1-4	21
Uniform Resource Locator (URL), example of	Figure 70-1	1144
Usenet (network news) communication model	Figure 85-1	1403
Usenet newsgroup hierarchies	Figure 85-2	1406
VLSM example	Figure 18-8	295
Windows 95/98/Me winipcfg utility	Figure 88-2	1489
World Wide Web, major functional components of	Figure 79-1	1321

LIST OF TABLES

		page
ARP Hardware Type (HRD) Field Values	Table 13-2	217
ARP Message Format	Table 13-1	217
ARP Opcode (OP) Field Values	Table 13-3	218
BGP General Message Format	Table 40-4	664
BGP Keepalive Message Format	Table 40-11	673
BGP Notification Message Error Codes	Table 40-13	675
BGP Notification Message Error Subcodes	Table 40-14	675
BGP Notification Message Format	Table 40-12	674
BGP Open Message Format	Table 40-5	666
BGP Open Message Optional Parameters	Table 40-6	667
BGP Path Attributes, Summary of	Table 40-3	659
BGP Update Message Attribute Flags	Table 40-9	671
BGP Update Message Attribute Type Codes	Table 40-10	671
BGP Update Message Format	Table 40-7	669
BGP Update Message Path Attributes	Table 40-8	669
BGP Versions and Defining Standards	Table 40-1	649
BGP-4, Additional Defining Standards for	Table 40-2	650
Binary Addition	Table 4-7	72
Binary and Decimal Number Equivalents	Table 4-2	66
Binary Information Group Representations and Terms	Table 4-1	63
Bit Mask, AND, Clearing Bits Using	Table 4-15	77
Bit Mask, OR, Setting Bits Using	Table 4-14	76
Bit Mask, XOR, Inverting Bits Using	Table 4-16	77
BOOTP Message Format	Table 60-1	986
BOOTP Message HType Values	Table 60-2	987
BOOTP Vendor Information Field Format	Table 60-3	990
CHAP Challenge and Response Frame Subfields	Table 12-11	194
CIDR Address Blocks and Classful Address Equivalents	Table 20-1	323

		page
Conversion, Binary, Octal, and Hexadecimal Digits	Table 4-3	68
Conversion, Decimal to Binary Numbers	Table 4-5	70
Conversion, Decimal to Hexadecimal Numbers	Table 4-6	71
Conversion, Hexadecimal to Decimal Numbers	Table 4-4	69
DHCP Client Finite State Machine	Table 62-1	1018
DHCP Message Format	Table 63-1	1039
DHCP Message HType Values	Table 63-2	1041
DHCP Message Type (Option 53) Values	Table 63-13	1051
DHCP Option Categories	Table 63-4	1043
DHCP Option Format	Table 63-3	1043
DHCP Options: DHCP Extensions	Table 63-12	1050
DHCP/BOOTP Options: Application and Service Parameters	Table 63-10	1049
DHCP/BOOTP Options: IP Layer Parameters per Host	Table 63-6	1047
DHCP/BOOTP Options: IP Layer Parameters per Interface	Table 63-7	1047
DHCP/BOOTP Options: Link Layer Parameters per Interface	Table 63-8	1048
DHCP/BOOTP Options: RFC 1497 Vendor Extensions	Table 63-5	1045
DHCP/BOOTP Options: TCP Parameters	Table 63-9	1048
DNS Address RR Data Format	Table 57-8	937
DNS Canonical Name RR Data Format	Table 57-10	938
DNS Common Resource Record Format	Table 57-7	936
DNS General Message Format	Table 57-1	930
DNS Mail Exchange RR Data Format	Table 57-13	939
DNS Message Header Format	Table 57-2	933
DNS Message Question Section Format	Table 57-5	935
DNS Name Server RR Data Format	Table 57-9	937
DNS Pointer RR Data Format	Table 57-12	938
DNS Resource Records (Common), Summary of	Table 55-1	892
DNS Start Of Authority RR Data Format	Table 57-11	938
DNS Text RR Data Format	Table 57-14	940
FTP Access Control Commands	Table 72-1	1186
FTP Protocol Service Commands	Table 72-3	1187
FTP Reply Code Format: First Digit Interpretation	Table 72-4	1189
FTP Reply Code Format: Second Digit Interpretation	Table 72-5	1189
FTP Reply Codes	Table 72-6	1190
FTP Session, Sample	Table 72-8	1196
FTP Transfer Parameter Commands	Table 72-2	1187
FTP User Commands, Common	Table 72-7	1194

		page
Header OpCode Values	Table 57-3	933
Header RCode Values	Table 57-4	934
Hexadecimal Addition	Table 4-8	72
host Utility Options and Parameters, Typical	Table 88-6	1475
HTML Elements, Common	Table 79-1	1324
HTTP Cache-Control Directives	Table 82-1	1359
HTTP Status Code Format: First-Digit Interpretation	Table 81-1	1353
HTTP Status Codes and Reason Phrases	Table 81-2	1354
HTTP Warning Header Codes	Table 82-2	1360
ICMP Common Message Format	Table 31-3	518
ICMP Message Classes, Types, and Codes	Table 31-2	513
ICMP Redirect Message Interpretation Codes	Table 32-6	532
ICMPv4 Address Mask Request and Address Mask Reply Message Format	Table 33-5	544
ICMPv4 Destination Unreachable Message Format	Table 32-1	522
ICMPv4 Destination Unreachable Message Subtypes	Table 32-2	523
ICMPv4 Echo and Echo Reply Message Format	Table 33-1	536
ICMPv4 Parameter Problem Message Format	Table 32-7	534
ICMPv4 Parameter Problem Message Interpretation Codes	Table 32-8	534
ICMPv4 Redirect Message Format	Table 32-5	531
ICMPv4 Router Advertisement Message Format	Table 33-3	541
ICMPv4 Router Solicitation Message Format	Table 33-4	542
ICMPv4 Source Quench Message Format	Table 32-3	526
ICMPv4 Time Exceeded Message Format	Table 32-4	529
ICMPv4 Timestamp and Timestamp Reply Message Format	Table 33-2	538
ICMPv4 Traceroute Message Format	Table 33-6	545
ICMPv6 Destination Unreachable Message Format	Table 34-1	549
ICMPv6 Destination Unreachable Message Subtypes	Table 34-2	549
ICMPv6 Echo Request and Echo Reply Message Format	Table 35-1	559
ICMPv6 MTU Option Format	Table 35-16	574
ICMPv6 Neighbor Advertisement Message Flags	Table 35-6	564
ICMPv6 Neighbor Advertisement Message Format	Table 35-5	563
ICMPv6 Neighbor Solicitation Message Format	Table 35-7	565
ICMPv6 Packet Too Big Message Format	Table 34-3	551
ICMPv6 Parameter Problem Message Format	Table 34-5	555
ICMPv6 Parameter Problem Message Interpretation Codes	Table 34-6	556
ICMPv6 Prefix Information Option Flags	Table 35-14	573
ICMPv6 Prefix Information Option Format	Table 35-13	572
ICMPv6 Redirect Message Format	Table 35-8	566
ICMPv6 Redirected Header Option Format	Table 35-15	574

		page
ICMPv6 Router Advertisement Message Autoconfiguration Flags	Table 35-3	561
ICMPv6 Router Advertisement Message Format	Table 35-2	561
ICMPv6 Router Renumbering Message Flags	Table 35-10	570
ICMPv6 Router Renumbering Message Format	Table 35-9	569
ICMPv6 Router Solicitation Message Format	Table 35-4	562
ICMPv6 Source Link-Layer Address Option Format	Table 35-11	571
ICMPv6 Target Link-Layer Address Option Format	Table 35-12	572
ICMPv6 Time Exceeded Message Format	Table 34-4	553
ifconfig Interface Configuration Parameters (UNIX), Typical	Table 88-13	1486
ifconfig Syntaxes, Options, and Parameters (UNIX), Typical	Table 88-11	1485
ifconfig Universal Options and Parameters (UNIX), Typical	Table 88-12	1485
IMAP "Any State" Commands	Table 78-2	1304
IMAP Authenticated State Commands	Table 78-4	1308
IMAP Not Authenticated State Commands	Table 78-3	1306
IMAP Selected State Commands	Table 78-5	1310
Internet DNS Organizational (Generic) Top-Level Domains	Table 54-1	872
Internet DNS Root Name Servers	Table 55-2	900
Internet Protocol Version 4 (IPv4) Datagram Format	Table 21-1	332
IP Address Class Bit Patterns, First-Octet Ranges, and Address Ranges	Table 17-2	260
IP Address Class Network and Host Capacities	Table 17-3	262
IP Address Classes and Class Characteristics and Uses	Table 17-1	256
IP Address Patterns with Special Meanings	Table 17-4	264
IP Addresses, Reserved, Private, and Loopback	Table 17-5	267
IP Multicast Address Ranges and Uses	Table 17-6	268
IP Multicast Addresses, Well-Known	Table 17-7	269
IP Security (IPsec) Standards, Important	Table 29-1	451
ipconfig Options and Parameters (Windows), Typical	Table 88-14	1487
IPsec Authentication Header (AH) Format	Table 29-2	465
IPsec Encapsulating Security Payload (ESP) Format	Table 29-3	470
IPv4 Flags Subfields	Table 21-2	333
IPv4 Option Format	Table 21-5	337
IPv4 Options, Common	Table 21-7	338
IPv4 Options: Option Type Subfields	Table 21-6	337
IPv4 Protocol Subfields	Table 21-3	334
IPv4 Type of Service (TOS) Field, Original Definition of	Table 21-4	336
IPv6 Address Space Allocations	Table 25-1	382
IPv6 Extension Headers	Table 26-4	409
IPv6 Fragment Extension Header Format	Table 26-6	411
IPv6 General Datagram Structure	Table 26-1	403
IPv6 Global Unicast Address Format	Table 25-2	384

		page
IPv6 Global Unicast Address Format, Generic	Table 25-3	384
IPv6 Main Header Format	Table 26-2	404
IPv6 Multicast Address Format	Table 25-6	395
IPv6 Next Header Values, Common	Table 26-3	406
IPv6 Option Format	Table 26-7	414
IPv6 Option Type Subfields	Table 26-8	414
IPv6 Routing Extension Header Format	Table 26-5	410
IPv6 Unicast Routing Prefix Structure, Example	Table 25-5	386
IPv6 Unicast Routing Prefix Structure, Historical	Table 25-4	386
IPv6 Well-Known Multicast Addresses, Important	Table 25-7	397
MIME application Media Type Subtypes	Table 76-8	1252
MIME audio Media Type Subtypes	Table 76-5	1251
MIME base64 Encoding Groups	Table 76-11	1259
MIME image Media Type Subtypes	Table 76-4	1250
MIME message Media Type Subtypes, Common	Table 76-10	1257
MIME model Media Type Subtypes	Table 76-7	1251
MIME multipart Media Type Subtypes, Common	Table 76-9	1253
MIME Standards	Table 76-2	1245
MIME text Media Type Subtypes	Table 76-3	1250
MIME video Media Type Subtypes	Table 76-6	1251
Mobile IP Mobility Agent Advertisement Extension Flags	Table 30-2	490
Mobile IP Mobility Agent Advertisement Extension Format	Table 30-1	489
Mobile IP Prefix-Lengths Extension Format	Table 30-3	490
Mobile IP Registration Reply Message Format	Table 30-6	495
Mobile IP Registration Request Message Format	Table 30-4	493
NAT, Bidirectional (Two-Way/Inbound), Operation of	Table 28-2	439
NAT (Overlapping NAT/Twice NAT), Operation of	Table 28-4	445
NAT, Port-Based (Overloaded), Operation of	Table 28-3	442
NAT, Unidirectional (Traditional/Outbound), Operation of	Table 28-1	435
NetBIOS Over TCP/IP Node Type (Option 46) Values	Table 63-11	1050
netstat Option Groups, Options, and Parameters (UNIX), Typical	Table 88-7	1480
netstat Option Groups, Options, and Parameters (Windows), Typical	Table 88-9	1482
netstat Universal Options and Parameters (UNIX), Typical	Table 88-8	1481
netstat Universal Options and Parameters (Windows), Typical	Table 88-10	1483
NFS External Data Representation (XDR) Data Types	Table 58-1	960
NFS Mount Protocol Server Procedures	Table 58-5	969
NFS Version 2 and Version 3 Server Procedures	Table 58-2	964
NFS Version 4 Server Operations	Table 58-4	966

		page
NFS Version 4 Server Procedures	Table 58-3	966
NNTP Base Commands	Table 85-5	1421
NNTP LIST Command Extensions	Table 85-7	1423
NNTP Newsreader Extensions	Table 85-8	1424
NNTP Reply Code Format: First Digit Interpretation	Table 85-9	1427
NNTP Reply Code Format: Second Digit Interpretation	Table 85-10	1428
NNTP Reply Codes	Table 85-11	1428
NNTP Transport Extensions	Table 85-6	1423
Non-ICMP Internet Standards That Define ICMP Messages	Table 31-1	509
nslookup Utility Commands, Typical	Table 88-5	1474
OSI Reference Model Layer Summary	Table 7-2	117
OSI Reference Model Real-World Analogy	Table 7-1	114
OSPF Common Header Format	Table 39-4	640
OSPF Database Description Message Flags	Table 39-7	642
OSPF Database Description Message Format	Table 39-6	642
OSPF Hello Message Format	Table 39-5	641
OSPF Link State Acknowledgment Message Format	Table 39-10	644
OSPF Link State Advertisement Header Format	Table 39-11	645
OSPF Link State Advertisement Header LS Types	Table 39-12	645
OSPF Link State Request Message Format	Table 39-8	643
OSPF Link State Update Message Format	Table 39-9	643
OSPF Link-State Database (LSDB), Sample	Table 39-1	629
OSPF LSDB with Costs, Sample	Table 39-2	634
OSPF Routes (Calculated), Example of	Table 39-3	637
ping (UNIX) Utility Options and Parameters, Common	Table 88-1	1466
ping (Windows) Utility Options and Parameters, Common	Table 88-2	1467
POP3 Transaction Commands	Table 78-1	1294
PPP Challenge Handshake Authentication Protocol (CHAP) Formats	Table 12-10	194
PPP Compression Control Protocol (CCP) Compression Algorithms	Table 11-1	171
PPP Control Message Format	Table 12-4	187
PPP Control Message Option Format	Table 12-6	189
PPP Control Messages, Code Values, and PPP Protocol Usage	Table 12-5	188
PPP Encryption Control Protocol (ECP) Compression Algorithms	Table 11-2	174
PPP Frames and Protocol Field Values, Common Protocols Carried in	Table 12-3	185
PPP General Frame Format	Table 12-1	182
PPP Link Control Protocol (LCP) Frame Types and Fields	Table 12-7	191
PPP Multilink Protocol Fragment Frame Format	Table 12-12	197
PPP PAP Authenticate-Request Frame Subfields	Table 12-9	194

		page
PPP Password Authentication Protocol (PAP) Frame Formats	Table 12-8	193
PPP Phases	Table 9-1	152
PPP Protocol Field Ranges	Table 12-2	184
PPP Standards	Table 9-2	153
Question Section QType Values	Table 57-6	935
Registration Request Flags	Table 30-5	494
Relative URL Specifications and Absolute Equivalents	Table 70-2	1152
RFC 822 Email Header Field Groups and Fields	Table 76-1	1239
RIP-1 Message Format	Table 38-1	615
RIP-1 RIP Entries	Table 38-2	615
RIP-2 Message Format	Table 38-3	619
RIP-2 Route Table Entries (RTEs)	Table 38-4	619
RIPng Message Format	Table 38-5	622
RIPng RTEs	Table 38-6	622
SMTP Commands	Table 77-2	1279
SMTP Extensions	Table 77-1	1276
SMTP Reply Code Format: First Digit Interpretation	Table 77-3	1281
SMTP Reply Code Format: Second Digit Interpretation	Table 77-4	1282
SMTP Reply Codes	Table 77-5	1283
SNMP Generic MIB Object Groups	Table 66-2	1095
SNMP MIB Modules, Common	Table 66-3	1096
SNMP PDU (Message) Classes	Table 67-1	1103
SNMP RMON MIB Object Groups	Table 69-1	1135
SNMP Security (SNMPsec) Standards	Table 65-3	1080
SNMP SMI Regular Data Types	Table 66-1	1089
SNMP Variable Binding Format	Table 68-1	1118
SNMPv1 Common PDU Format	Table 68-3	1120
SNMPv1 Error Status Field Values	Table 68-4	1120
SNMPv1 General Message Format	Table 68-2	1119
SNMPv1 Standards	Table 65-2	1080
SNMPv1 Trap-PDU Format	Table 68-5	1121
SNMPv2 Common PDU Format	Table 68-10	1126
SNMPv2 GetBulkRequest-PDU Format	Table 68-12	1129
SNMPv2 PDU Error Status Field Values	Table 68-11	1127
SNMPv2c General Message Format, Community-Based	Table 68-7	1124
SNMPv2c Standards, Community-Based	Table 65-4	1081
SNMPv2p General Message Format	Table 68-6	1123
SNMPv2p Standards, Party-Based	Table 65-1	1080

		page
SNMPv2u General Message Format, User-Based	Table 68-8	1125
SNMPv2u Parameter Field Subfields	Table 68-9	1126
SNMPv2u Standards, User-Based	Table 65-5	1081
SNMPv3 General Message Format	Table 68-13	1130
SNMPv3 Msg Flags Subfields	Table 68-14	1131
SNMPv3 Scoped PDU Subfields	Table 68-15	1131
SNMPv3 Standards	Table 65-6	1082
Subnet ID of an IP Address, Determining Through Subnet Masking	Table 18-1	279
Subnet Masks for Class A, Class B, and Class C Networks, Default	Table 18-2	282
Subnetting Summary Table for Class A Networks	Table 18-3	289
Subnetting Summary Table for Class B Networks	Table 18-4	291
Subnetting Summary Table for Class C Networks	Table 18-5	292
TCP Applications and Server Port Assignments, Common	Table 46-1	743
TCP Connection Termination Procedure	Table 47-4	764
TCP Finite State Machine (FSM) States, Events, and Transitions	Table 47-1	748
TCP Options	Table 48-4	773
TCP Pseudo Header for Checksum Calculations	Table 48-5	775
TCP Segment Control Bits	Table 48-2	772
TCP Segment Format	Table 48-1	771
TCP Segment Option Subfields	Table 48-3	773
TCP Simultaneous Connection Termination Procedure	Table 47-5	767
TCP Simultaneous Open Connection Establishment Procedure	Table 47-3	756
TCP Standards, Supplementary	Table 45-1	722
TCP Three-Way Handshake Connection Establishment Procedure	Table 47-2	754
TCP Transaction Example with Send and Receive Pointers	Table 48-6	785
TCP/IP Protocols	Table 8-1	132
TCP/IP Registered Port Numbers and Applications, Common	Table 43-2	709
TCP/IP Well-Known Port Numbers and Applications, Common	Table 43-1	708
Telnet NVT ASCII Control Codes (Standard), Interpretation of	Table 87-1	1445
Telnet Options, Common	Table 87-3	1451
Telnet Protocol Commands	Table 87-2	1448
TFTP Acknowledgment Message Format	Table 73-4	1213
TFTP Data Message Format	Table 73-3	1212
TFTP Error Message Format	Table 73-5	1214
TFTP OACK Message Format	Table 73-6	1214
TFTP Options	Table 73-1	1211
TFTP RRQ/WRQ Message Format	Table 73-2	1212
traceroute (UNIX) Utility Options and Parameters, Common	Table 88-3	1470
tracert (Windows) Utility Options and Parameters, Common	Table 88-4	1471

		page
Troubleshooting Protocols (TCP/IP), Miscellaneous	Table 88-15	1490
Truth Table, AND Operator	Table 4-11	74
Truth Table, Exclusive OR (XOR) Operator	Table 4-13	75
Truth Table, NOT Operator	Table 4-9	73
Truth Table, NOT Operator (Using Bit Values)	Table 4-10	74
Truth Table, OR Operator	Table 4-12	74
UDP and TCP, Summary Comparison of	Table 42-1	693
UDP Applications and Server Port Assignments, Common	Table 44-2	718
UDP Message Format	Table 44-1	715
URL Special Character Encodings	Table 70-1	1145
Usenet Big Eight Newsgroup Hierarchies	Table 85-1	1405
Usenet Headers, Common Additional	Table 85-4	1410
Usenet Mandatory Headers	Table 85-2	1409
Usenet Optional Headers	Table 85-3	1409

ACKNOWLEDGMENTS

I dedicated this book to my wife and children to reflect the important role they have played in my life in general terms, and in accomplishing this book in particular. However, many others also contributed to the completion of this document, and I'd like to take a moment to acknowledge them.

I want to thank my "original" family: my father, Leon, and sisters, Cari and Cindy, for being supportive and lending a helpful ear about various issues during the time I've been engaged in this project. Thanks also to my "adoptive" family: Eli, Marge, Larry, and Steven. And I definitely want to thank the small group of close friends who have helped with ideas, advice, and much-needed laughs.

I would also like to specifically acknowledge the following individuals and organizations for their assistance:

- Bill Pollock, president and publisher of No Starch Press, for constantly expressing his faith in my abilities as an author, for being a sounding board, and for agreeing to publish this book. My thanks also to Susan Berge, Riley Hoffman, and everyone else at No Starch for putting up with me during this long project and helping make this book a reality.
- Adobe Systems Incorporated, for providing this relatively unknown author with two important pieces of software that I used in creating this book. First, Adobe FrameMaker, one of the best desktop publishing programs around, which was used to format and publish this document. Second, Adobe Photoshop, the industry-standard program for photo and graphics editing, which was used for processing graphics and other tasks.

- Frank Stearns, creator of the IXgen tool for FrameMaker. Without IXgen, it would have taken ten times longer to make the index for this book, and Frank himself was very generous with his time in answering questions from a newbie indexer (me!).
- SmartDraw.com, for the excellent SmartDraw diagramming software that was used to create most of the more than 300 illustrations that appear in this book.
- Fernando Gont and Barry Margolin, for their excellent technical review of *The TCP/IP Guide*, and their corrections and suggestions for improvement to the book.
- Tcat Houser, author and instructor, whose generosity, positive attitude, and enthusiasm for my writing helped boost my confidence as I worked to complete this project.
- All the regulars at The PC Guide Discussion Forums, for creating a fun community, keeping the site active, and agreeing to provide opinions on my writing. In fact, everyone who has supported The PC Guide and my other websites, financially and otherwise, helped make it possible for me to spend time on this project.

I've probably missed a few people who should be on this list; I hope all who are deserving of my appreciation will forgive their omission and accept my thanks.

ABOUT THE AUTHOR

I was born in 1966 in Windsor, Ontario, Canada and raised in nearby Toronto. I married my wife Robyn in 1990; we now live in southern Vermont with our three sons, Ryan (12), Matthew (9), and Evan (4).

I have had an interest in the field of computers ever since my early years, starting at the age of 14 when I received my first computer, an Apple][, a gift from my parents. Since that time, I have worked in various computer-related fields in hardware and software. In 1989, I obtained a Bachelor of Applied Science from the University of Waterloo, in Waterloo, Ontario, Canada. I completed my formal education in 1993 with two master's degrees, in management and in electrical engineering and computer science (EECS), from MIT.

After a brief "conventional" technical career, I created and published The PC Guide, an extensive online reference work on personal computers, and in 1998, I decided to devote myself to my writing projects full time. The TCP/IP Guide was part of a larger networking project that I spent time on earlier this decade. I continue to work in the technical writing and editing field on various projects, for myself and other companies.

You may have noticed something missing here: no impressive listings of credentials. No, I'm not a *New York Times* best-selling author; I haven't been a professor at a prestigious Ivy League university for a quarter century; neither am I a top executive at a Silicon Valley giant. In some ways, I am a student of technology, just as you are. And my experience over the years has shown me that many of the people who know the most about how technology works have rather limited success in explaining what they know in a way that will allow me to understand it. My interests, and I believe my skills, lie not in being an expert, but in serving as an *educator*, presenting complex information in a form that is sensible, digestible, and fun to read.

When I'm not working—all too rare these days—I spend time with my family and enjoy the peaceful quiet and natural beauty of the state of Vermont. I am also an avid amateur photographer, with interests particularly in nature and landscapes.

INTRODUCTION

Goals of *The TCP/IP Guide*

Every author who sets out to write a book or other document has certain objectives that he or she hopes to accomplish when the work is completed. This is why you can go into a library or bookstore, pick up several books that cover the same subject, and discover that they are surprisingly different—not just in their content or scope, but in their entire approach to the material.

I, too, had a number of goals when I set out to write this book. You certainly don't need to know them in order to read and appreciate the material, but understanding what I had in mind while I was writing may help you while you are reading. And if you are reading this information prior to buying *The TCP/IP Guide*, knowing what I strove for in writing the book may help you decide if this is the right resource for you.

My overall goal in writing this book was to create a resource that would allow anyone to obtain a deep understanding of how TCP/IP technologies really work. To accomplish this, I had a number of specific objectives that guided my writing efforts:

Comprehensiveness Like most authors writing a resource that covers a large subject, I wanted *The TCP/IP Guide* to be comprehensive. Of course, no single document can cover everything, so I have needed to limit the scope of the material. However, I feel I cover more about TCP/IP as a whole than any other single book or other resource.

Comprehensibility Creating a resource that is comprehensive is important, but I felt that it was even more important that the book be *comprehensible.* Over the past few years, I've had the opportunity to review many hundreds of books, guides, websites, and papers related to networking. I have found that even though most of them are generally high in quality, too many use unexplained technical jargon or assume extensive prior knowledge of networking concepts and technologies on the part of the reader. I worked very hard to ensure that my descriptions, even of very complex concepts, can be understood by almost every student of networking.

Rationale It's certainly important to know how every TCP/IP protocol functions. However, to gain a true understanding of complex material, one also needs to understand the reasons behind why things are what they are. In writing this material, I have always tried to explain not just the *what,* but also the *why* of TCP/IP. I have anticipated and answered questions that I believe might commonly arise in the mind of someone learning about this technology.

Illustrations A picture is worth a thousand words, as they say. There are many concepts that no amount of verbiage will adequately explain, while a simple illustration will do the trick. For this reason, I spent many months creating more than 300 diagrams (some simple and some not so simple!) to complement the written material in *The TCP/IP Guide.*

User-friendliness I have intentionally broken many of the rules of conventional book authorship, in creating a document that uses a conversational, first-person style, and no small amount of humor where appropriate. My intention was to make you feel at home while you read material that can be quite technically difficult. I want you to think of me as a friend sitting next to you at your computer explaining how TCP/IP works, rather than a professor preaching at you from a podium.

Organization Many networking books consist of dozens of subjects just listed one after the other, leaving the reader to wonder how everything fits together. When I first began this book, I spent weeks just organizing it, with the result being a structure that indicates clearly how subjects are interrelated. I also carefully laid out each individual section to ensure that it covered its topic in a way that made sense.

Multiple levels of detail I realize that some people reading a TCP/IP book might want only a quick summary of the operation of its constituent protocols, while others want to learn all the nuances of how everything works. I have provided the full details that most readers will want, while also including overview topics in each chapter that summarize each technology for quick perusal. This gives you the option of either skimming the surface or "diving deep," as you choose.

Platform independence I have endeavored whenever possible to avoid describing TCP/IP in terms specific to any hardware or software platform. Even though I use a PC for most of my computing and UNIX for some tasks, most of the material is not particular to any type of device or operating system (though I do focus more on networks of smaller computers than larger ones).

How successful was I in achieving these goals? I'd like to think I did a pretty good job, but ultimately, you will be the judge!

Scope of *The TCP/IP Guide*

The first step to dealing with a problem is recognizing that you have one. So, I have to come clean with you, my reader. I have a problem: an addiction to . . . detail. Every time I set out to write about a particular protocol, technology, or concept, I start with a modest goal regarding how much I want to write. I always begin knowing that I really need to control myself, to prevent my project from going on forever. But as I explore each subject, I learn more and more, and I start to say to myself things like, "This is important. I simply *must* include coverage for it," and, "If I'm going to cover subject #1, I also should cover subject #2, because they are related." This is how I turn six-month projects into multiyear ordeals.

However, even though self-control in this area is a weakness for me, even *I* realized I could not possibly cover *everything* related to TCP/IP in this book. Consider that the TCP/IP suite contains dozens of protocols and technologies, each written about in thick books. I was willing to spend years on this project, but not decades! Thus, I had to limit the scope of this book somewhat, both to preserve what remains of my sanity and to spare you from having to wade through a ridiculously large document.

Here are a few different points that will help explain decisions that I made to limit the scope of *The TCP/IP Guide*:

Theory versus practice This is primarily a *reference resource* on the TCP/IP protocol suite. The material here is designed to allow a student to learn the nuts and bolts of how TCP/IP works. I do discuss quite a number of "real-world" practical issues related to how TCP/IP internetworks operate, but this is not my primary focus here. If you want to really understand what TCP/IP is and what makes it work, you've come to the right place. If all you want is simple instructions on how to connect a few PCs together in your home using TCP/IP, this probably isn't the book for you.

Current versus future protocols Most of the emphasis in this book is on the present state of the art in TCP/IP. The suite is always changing, new protocols are constantly being written, and revisions to existing protocols continue to be published. I have not provided extensive coverage of technologies still in development, to try to keep the size of the book manageable and to prevent the book from being out-of-date before it even hits the store shelves. The one exception to this general rule of thumb is version 6 of the Internet Protocol (IPv6), which represents a significant change to the core of how most of TCP/IP operates. While not universally deployed yet, IPv6 is sufficiently far along in its development that I feel any student of TCP/IP needs to know what it is, learn how it works, and understand its significance. Thus, I have included several detailed chapters on IPv6, and also mentioned how it impacts the operation of several other key protocols such as the Internet Control Message Protocol (ICMP), Domain Name System (DNS), and Dynamic Host Configuration Protocol (DHCP).

Application coverage Many thousands of different applications run on TCP/IP internetworks, and I could not possibly hope to describe all of them. The scope of this book is limited to the most important, "classic" TCP/IP applications and application protocols, such as electronic mail, general file transfer, and the World Wide Web.

TCP/IP versus the Internet The TCP/IP protocol suite and the Internet are very closely related in many ways, as you will discover as you read this book. In fact, they are often tied together so much that it is hard to discuss one without the other. However, the Internet as a whole is an enormous subject, and trying to describe it in general terms would have substantially increased the size of this book. Thus, I describe Internet issues only within the context of explanations of TCP/IP technologies. For example, while I cover the World Wide Web in this book, I discuss its generalities only briefly. I focus my technical discussions on how the Hypertext Transfer Protocol (HTTP) that implements it works. I don't talk about how to set up a website, how to choose a web browser, or any of those sorts of details. Those subjects are covered in a dazzling array of different books, papers, and, of course, websites.

Limited TCP/IP security coverage Security is a very important and large topic, especially in modern networking. This book does include a fairly detailed section on the operation of the IP Security protocol (IPSec), and also touches on security issues in describing several other protocols and technologies. However, it is not specifically geared toward detailed discussions of security considerations.

Small computer orientation In general terms, TCP/IP technologies can be used to connect together any types of devices that have the appropriate hardware and software. There are some issues, however, where explanations require me to focus on how specific types of underlying networks and devices work; this is especially true of some of my diagrams. In these cases, my preference has generally been to show how TCP/IP is used to connect together typical small computers such as PCs, Macintoshes, and UNIX workstations, which are what most people use.

The TCP/IP Guide Features

I created *The TCP/IP Guide* to provide you with an unparalleled breadth and depth of information about TCP/IP. This meant including a lot of content in this book—it has 88 chapters, several hundred sections, and more than 1,600 pages. However, I recognized as I was writing this tome that the real goal is not just to provide a lot of detailed information, but also to present it in such a way that it can be easily understood by you, the reader. This requires more than just writing large amounts of text and putting it all into a big file.

For this reason, I have incorporated a number of special features into this book to help make it easier for you to "digest." These include the special structure of the book, special inserts to help you remember topics, and more.

First, *The TCP/IP Guide* uses a three-level structure to organize its content. The book as a whole is divided into three overall *sections*, covering overview/background information, lower-layer protocols, and higher-layer application protocols, respectively. Within each section is a number of *parts*, which group together related chapters. Each chapter is, in turn, structured with sections and subsections to present the material in the most understandable way possible.

The TCP/IP Guide contains more than 300 detailed illustrations, which support the textual descriptions of TCP/IP technologies and protocols, and help make sense of difficult concepts. Most include brief descriptions that allow you to quickly understand what the illustration means without even needing to read the full surrounding text. The book also has more than 300 tables, which present large amounts of information in an organized and readable manner or highlight examples.

Most of the discussions in *The TCP/IP Guide* are presented as free-form text, as you would expect in any document. However, I use *notes* when I need to clarify or explain something that I feel you need to know, but which is either not directly related to the topic under discussion or is sufficiently "tangential" that it needs to be separated from the main text to avoid disrupting its flow. Examples include terminology explanations, "sidebar" historical discussions, anecdotes, and clarifications relating to how I am describing particular concepts.

Last, but definitely not least, are the *key concepts* inserts. I tried very hard in crafting this book to provide a variety of ways to present information, to better suit the learning styles of different readers. To that end, I have created hundreds of these special paragraphs, which summarize and highlight the most important concepts and essential pieces of knowledge in *The TCP/IP Guide.* They can be very useful for quickly distilling the essence of a topic without reading an entire explanation, or for refreshing your memory of a subject. Obviously, however, they contain few details, so you should not assume that you fully understand a topic or concept just by reading this sort of summary.

The TCP/IP Guide Online!

This book had its origins as an online website, called appropriately enough, The TCP/IP Guide. The site is still active and presents the same information as this book contains, albeit in a slightly different format and structure.

You may find the online version of the site useful if you are traveling or need to look up TCP/IP information quickly when you don't have the book handy. As a further bonus, the pages of the site are extensively hyperlinked for ease of use, and the diagrams are in full color. The online version also has a full hyperlinked table of contents and a search engine! Visit the site at:

http://www.TCPIPGuide.com.

Your Feedback and Suggestions

One of the ways that this book differs from the typical technical reference book is that it is a very *personal* work. When you read the material here, I want you to feel as though I am explaining the many technologies and concepts to you personally, because that's how I feel when I am writing. A published book of this sort is by its nature a type of "one-way" communication, from me to you; however, I am also interested in what you have to say to me. For this reason I strongly encourage you to provide me with feedback on this book and suggestions that you may have for it.

First, let me point out that all books have mistakes, and despite undergoing a rigorous technical review and multiple-stage editing process, this book is probably no exception. Before contacting me regarding an error or problem with this book, please check the errata page to see if what you found has already been reported. You can find that page here: http://www.tcpipguide.com/bookerrata.htm. I welcome your constructive criticisms and suggestions. If there is something you don't like about the material, please tell me. Even better, make a suggestion for how to improve it. I am also happy to read your compliments or complaints, and I will gladly answer questions that pertain directly to the use of the book. You can contact me at tcpipbook@tcpipguide.com.

SECTION I

TCP/IP OVERVIEW AND BACKGROUND INFORMATION

They say the best place to start is at the beginning, and that's exactly where you are now. This initial section contains background information that will help you to understand what networking is about and where TCP/IP fits into the grand scheme of things. This introductory information will help ease you into your studies of TCP/IP, and it is particularly valuable to those who are new to the world of networking.

This section contains three parts. The first part covers a number of important fundamental aspects of networks, discussing how they are used, the standards that define them, the terminology that describes them, and much more. The second part describes the important OSI Reference Model, which is an essential tool to comprehending the function and organization of networking technologies. The third part contains a high-level overview of the TCP/IP protocol suite, which will frame the more complete discussions of individual TCP/IP protocols that follow in the latter two sections of this book.

Let's get started!

PART I-1

NETWORKING FUNDAMENTALS

Unlike authors of many other TCP/IP-related resources, I do not assume that readers already know what networking is all about. After all, that's why you are reading this book!

This part provides an overview of some of the basic issues related to networking. It includes discussions of some of the most fundamental networking concepts and ideas. It serves not only to provide you with useful background material, but also as a repository for general information, so that I don't need to repeat it in many different places elsewhere in the book (and if you already know about these basics, you don't need to skip over them in many other locations). The topics covered here are useful for understanding certain TCP/IP concepts. However, some of the material is very broadly oriented toward networking as a whole and is not specific to TCP/IP internetworking.

This part consists of four chapters. The first chapter in this part introduces networking in broad terms, describes its fundamental characteristics, and differentiates between network sizes and types. The second chapter talks about many different matters related to network performance. The third chapter explains the importance of networking standards and standards organizations. Finally, the fourth chapter provides background information about how data is stored and manipulated in computers; if you are new to computing, you may find this information useful when reading some other parts of this book. If you are experienced in networking and related technologies, you may wish to skip this part of the book. Or, you can scan the headings in the chapters; if you understand the terminology mentioned in a heading, you can probably skip the discussion. Cross-references in other areas of the book refer to information in this part as appropriate, so if you need to fill in your knowledge of a particular fundamental on the fly, you can do so rather easily.

1

NETWORKING INTRODUCTION, CHARACTERISTICS, AND TYPES

Someone new to networking will usually have some pretty important questions. What is networking all about? What are the most important attributes that describe networks? And what sort of networks exist? The obvious place to begin discussing networking fundamentals is to answer those questions using a high-level introduction to networking as a whole.

This chapter is divided into three sections. The first provides a quick introduction to networking. I define networking in the most basic terms, then place networking in an overall context by describing some of its advantages and benefits, as well as some of its disadvantages and costs.

The second section discusses key concepts that describe and differentiate between types of networks and networking technologies. This is where I'll define terms and "buzzwords" that you cannot avoid if you are going to learn about networks. The topics here include explanations of protocols, switching methods, types of network messages, message formatting, and ways of addressing messages. I also discuss the differences between client-server and peer-to-peer networking.

In the final section, I describe the major types of networks by drawing distinctions between them based on their size and scope, and I also show you how to use each type and size. I discuss LANs, WLANs, and WANs, and a few variations on these three main categories. I also explore the many terms that are related to the various sizes of networks and how they are used, including segments, subnetworks, internetworks, intranets, and extranets.

Introduction to Networking

In this day and age, networks are everywhere, especially in the form of the Internet. The Internet, the ultimate network, has revolutionized not only the computer world, but the lives of millions. We tend to take for granted that computers should be connected together. In fact, these days, whenever I have two computers in the same room, I have a difficult time *not* connecting them!

Given the ubiquitousness of networking, it's hard to believe that the field is still a relatively young one, especially when it comes to hooking up PCs. In approaching any discussion of networking, it is very useful to take a step back and look at networking from a higher level. What is it, exactly, and why is it now considered so important that it is just assumed that most PCs and other devices will be networked?

What Is Networking?

For such an extensive and involved subject that includes so many different technologies, hardware devices, and protocols, networking is actually quite simple. A *network* is simply a collection of computers or other hardware devices that are connected together, either physically or logically, using special hardware and software that allows the devices to exchange information and cooperate. *Networking* is the term that describes the processes involved in designing, implementing, upgrading, managing, and otherwise working with networks and network technologies.

> **KEY CONCEPT** A network is a set of hardware devices connected together, either physically or logically. This allows them to exchange information.

Networks are used for an incredible array of purposes. Most people learning about networking think about networking as interconnecting PCs and other "true" computers, but you use a variety of types of networks every day. Each time you pick up a phone, use a credit card at a store, get cash from an ATM machine, or even plug in an electrical appliance, you are using some type of network.

In fact, the definition can even be expanded beyond the world of technology. I'm sure you've heard the term *networking* used to describe the process of finding an employer or employee through friends and associates. Similarly, the idea here is that independent units are connected together to share information and cooperate.

The widespread networking of personal computers is a relatively new phenomenon. For the first decade or so of their existence, PCs were very much "islands unto themselves," and were rarely connected together. In the early 1990s, PC networking began to grow in popularity as businesses realized the advantages that networking could provide. By the late 1990s, networking in homes with two or more PCs really started to take off as well.

This interconnection of small devices represents, in a way, a return to the good old days of mainframe computers. Before computers were small and personal, they were large and centralized machines that many users operating remote terminals shared. Although having all of that computer power in one place had many disadvantages, one benefit was that all users were connected because they shared the central computer.

Individualized PCs took away that advantage. Networking attempts to move computing to a middle ground. It provides PC users with the best of both worlds: the independence and flexibility of personal computers, and the connectivity and resource sharing of mainframes. In fact, networking today is considered so vital that it's hard to conceive of an organization with two or more computers that would not want to connect them together!

The Advantages and Benefits of Networking

You have undoubtedly heard the expression "The whole is greater than the sum of its parts." This phrase describes networking very well and explains why it has become so popular. A network isn't just a bunch of computers with wires running between them. Properly implemented, a network is a system that provides its users with unique capabilities, above and beyond what the individual machines and their software applications can provide.

Most of the benefits of networking can be divided into two basic categories: *connectivity* and *sharing*. Networks allow computers, and hence their users, to connect to each other. They also allow for the easy sharing of information and resources, and for the simple cooperation between the devices in other ways. Since modern business depends so much on the intelligent flow and management of information, this ease of use tells you a lot about why networking is so valuable.

Here, in no particular order, are some of the specific advantages generally associated with networking:

Connectivity and Communication Networks connect computers and the users of those computers. Individuals within a building or workgroup can be connected through *local area networks (LANs)*; LANs in distant locations can be interconnected to form larger, *wide area networks (WANs)*. Once computers are connected, it is possible for network users to communicate with each other using technologies such as electronic mail. This makes the transmission of business (or nonbusiness) information easier, more efficient, and less expensive than it would be without the network.

Data Sharing One of the most important uses of networking is to allow the sharing of data. Before networking was common, an accounting employee who wanted to prepare a report for her manager would have to produce it on her PC, put it on a floppy disk, and then walk it over to the manager, who would transfer the data to her PC's hard disk. (This sort of "shoe-based network" was sometimes sarcastically called a *sneakernet*.)

True networking allows thousands of employees to share data much more easily and quickly than this. It also makes possible applications that enable many people to access and share the same data, such as databases, group software development, and much more.

Hardware Sharing Networks facilitate the sharing of hardware devices. For example, instead of giving each employee in a department an expensive color printer (or resorting to the sneakernet again), you can place one printer on the network for everyone to share.

Internet Access The Internet is itself an enormous network, so whenever you access the Internet, you are using a network. The significance of the Internet today is hard to exaggerate!

Internet Access Sharing Small computer networks allow multiple users to share a single Internet connection. Special hardware devices allow the bandwidth of the connection to be easily allocated to various individuals as they need it, and these devices permit an organization to purchase one high-speed connection instead of many slower ones.

Data Security and Management In a business environment, a network allows the administrators to manage the company's critical data better. Instead of spreading data over dozens or even hundreds of small computers in a haphazard fashion as users create it, administrators can centralize data on shared servers. This makes it easy for everyone to find the data and makes it possible for the administrators to ensure that the data is regularly backed up. Administrators can also implement security measures to control who can read or change various pieces of critical information.

Performance Enhancement and Balancing Under some circumstances, you can use a network to enhance the overall performance of some applications by distributing the computation tasks to various computers on the network.

Entertainment Networks facilitate many types of games and entertainment. The Internet itself offers many sources of entertainment. In addition, many multiplayer games operate over a LAN. Many home networks are set up for this reason, and gaming across WANs (including the Internet) has also become quite popular. Of course, if you are running a business and have employees who are easily amused, you might insist that this is really a *disadvantage* of networking rather than an advantage!

KEY CONCEPT At a high level, networks are advantageous because they allow computers and people to be connected together so that they can share resources. Some of the specific benefits of networking include communication, data sharing, Internet access, data security and management, application performance enhancement, and entertainment.

The Disadvantages and Costs of Networking

Now that I have discussed the great value and many useful benefits of networking, I must bring you crashing back to Earth with that old nemesis of the realistic: TANSTAAFL. For those who are not Heinlein fans, this acronym stands for "There ain't no such thing as a free lunch." Even though networking really does represent a whole that is greater than the sum of its parts, it does have some real and significant costs and drawbacks associated with it.

Here are a few disadvantages of networking:

Network Hardware, Software, and Setup Costs Computers don't just magically network themselves, of course. Setting up a network requires an investment in hardware and software, as well as funds for planning, designing, and implementing the network. For a home with a small network of two or three PCs, this is relatively inexpensive. It amounts to more or less a hundred dollars with today's low prices for network hardware, and practically no setup costs considering that the operating systems have already been designed for networks. For a large company, however, costs can easily run into tens of thousands of dollars or more.

Hardware and Software Management and Administration Costs In all but the smallest of implementations, ongoing maintenance and management of the network requires the care and attention of an IT professional. In a smaller organization that already has a system administrator, a network may fall within this person's job responsibilities, but it will take time away from other tasks. In more substantial organizations, a network administrator may need to be hired, and in large companies an entire department may be necessary.

Undesirable Sharing With the good comes the bad; though networking allows the easy sharing of useful information, it also allows the sharing of undesirable data. One significant sharing problem in this regard has to do with viruses, which are easily spread over networks and the Internet. Mitigating these effects costs time, money, and administrative effort.

Illegal or Undesirable Behavior Similar to the previous point, networking facilitates useful connectivity and communication, but also brings difficulties with it. Typical problems include the abuse of company resources, distractions that reduce productivity, the downloading of illegal or illicit materials, and even software piracy. In larger organizations, these issues must be managed through explicit policies and monitoring, which, again, further increases management costs.

Data Security Concerns If a network is implemented properly, it is possible to greatly improve the security of important data. In contrast, a poorly secured network puts critical data at risk, exposing it to the potential problems associated with hackers, unauthorized access, and even sabotage.

Most of these costs and potential problems can be managed by those who set up and run networks. In the end, the choice of whether to use a network is a matter of weighing the advantages against the disadvantages. Today, nearly everyone decides that networking *is* worthwhile.

> **KEY CONCEPT** Networking has a few drawbacks that you can weigh against its many positive aspects. Setting up a network has costs in hardware, software, maintenance, and administration. It is also necessary to manage a network to keep it running smoothly and to address possible misuse or abuse issues. Data security also becomes a much bigger concern when computers are connected together.

Fundamental Network Characteristics

There are many different kinds of networks and network technologies that are used to create them. The proliferation of networking methods has generally occurred for a very good reason: Different needs require different solutions. The drawback of this is that there are so many different types of protocols and technologies for the networking student to understand!

Before you can really compare these approaches, you need to understand some of the basic characteristics that make networks what they are. Although network types may be quite dissimilar, they are often described and even contrasted on the basis of a number of common attributes, which I'll discuss in the following sections.

Networking Layers, Models, and Architectures

One of the reasons why many people find networking difficult to learn is that it can be a very complicated subject. One of the chief reasons for this complexity is that networks consist of so many hardware and software elements. While a network user may perceive that he is using only one computer program (like a web browser) and one piece of hardware (like a PC), these are parts of a much larger puzzle. In order for even the simplest task to be accomplished on a network, dozens of different components must cooperate by passing control information and data to accomplish the overall goal of network communication.

The best way to understand any complex system is to break it down into pieces and then analyze what those pieces do and how they interact. The most logical approach is to divide the overall set of functions into modular components, each of which is responsible for a particular function. At the same time, you also need to define interfaces between these components, which describe how they fit together. This enables you to simplify the complexity of networking by approaching it in digestible chunks.

Networking technologies are most often compartmentalized in this manner by dividing their functions into *layers*, each of which contains hardware and software elements. Each layer is responsible for performing a particular type of task and interacts with the layers above and below it. Layers are conceptually arranged into a vertical *stack*. Lower layers are charged with more concrete tasks such as hardware signaling and low-level communication; they provide services to the higher layers. The higher layers, in turn, use these services to implement more abstract functions such as implementing user applications.

Dividing networks into layers this way is somewhat like the division of labor in a manufacturing facility, and it yields similar benefits. Each hardware device or software program can be specialized to perform the function needed by that layer, like a well-trained specialist on an assembly line. The different modules can be combined in different ways as needed. This way, it's also easier to understand how a network functions overall.

One other important benefit of layering is that makes it possible for technologies defined by different groups to interoperate. For this to be possible, it is necessary for everyone to agree on how layers will be defined and used. The most common tool for this purpose is a *networking model*. The model describes what the different layers are in the network, what each is responsible for doing, and how they interact. A univerally accepted model ensures that everyone is on the same page when creating hardware and software.

The most common general model in use today is the Open Systems Interconnection (OSI) Reference Model, which consists of seven stacked layers. These range from the physical layer (layer 1) at the bottom, which is responsible for low-level signaling, to the application layer (layer 7) at the top, where application software is implemented. Understanding the OSI model is essential to understanding networking as a whole. I explain models and layers in more detail, and provide a complete description of the OSI Reference Model, in Part I-2 of this book.

Closely related to the concept of a model is the concept of an *architecture*. An architecture is essentially a set of rules that describes the function of some portion of the hardware and software that constitutes a stack of layers. Such a ruleset usually takes the form of a specification or standard that describes how equipment and programs using the technology must behave. A networking architecture is designed to implement the functions associated with a particular contiguous set of layers of the OSI Reference Model, either formally or informally.

In this book, I discuss TCP/IP, the protocol suite that runs the Internet. TCP/IP is a complex set of technologies that spans many layers of the OSI model. By examining the various components of TCP/IP and how they implement different OSI model layers, you will really learn how TCP/IP works. For starters, the name of the suite, TCP/IP, comes from the Transmission Control Protocol (TCP), which operates at layer 4 of the OSI model, and the Internet Protocol (IP), which runs at OSI model layer 3. IP provides services to layer 4 and uses services from layer 2 below it. TCP uses IP's functions and provides functions to the layers above it.

I'll start a more complete examination of TCP/IP by looking at its architecture, and by looking at a second, special model that was developed specifically to make sense of TCP/IP. Both are explored in Chapter 8.

Protocols: What Are They, Anyway?

If there's one word you will get used to seeing a lot as you go through this book, it is *protocol*. You will see references to networking protocols, internetworking protocols, high-level protocols, low-level protocols, protocol stacks, protocol suites, subprotocols, and so on. Clearly, protocols are important, yet many reference works and standards use the term over and over again without ever explaining it. One reason for this may be because the term is somewhat vague and can have many meanings.

In some cases, understanding a technical term is easier if you go back to look at how the term is used in plain English. In the real world, a protocol often refers to a code of conduct or a form of etiquette observed by diplomats. These people must follow certain rules of ceremony and formality to ensure that they communicate effectively without causing conflict. They also must understand what is expected of them when they interact with representatives from other nations, making sure that, for example, they do not offend anyone due to an unfamiliarity with local customs. In fact, most people follow various protocols; they are sort of the unwritten rules of society.

This may seem to have little to do with networking, but in fact, this is a pretty good high-level description of what networking protocols are about. They define a language and a set of rules and procedures that enable devices and systems to communicate. Obviously, computers do not have local customs, and they hardly have to worry about committing a faux pas that might cause another computer to take offense. Networking protocols concern themselves with ensuring that all the devices on a network or internetwork are in agreement about how various actions must be performed in the total communication process.

A protocol is thus basically a way of ensuring that devices are able to talk to each other effectively. In most cases, an individual protocol describes how communication is accomplished between one particular software or hardware element in two or more devices.

In the context of the OSI Reference Model, a protocol is formally defined as a set of rules governing communication between entities at the same layer. For example, TCP is responsible for a specific set of functions on TCP/IP networks. Each host on a TCP/IP network has a TCP implementation, and those hosts all communicate with each other logically at layer 4 of the OSI model.

NOTE *The formalized OSI Reference Model meaning of the word* protocol *is covered in the OSI Reference Model topic on horizontal layer communication (discussed in Chapter 5, in the section titled "Protocols: Horizontal (Corresponding Layer) Communication").*

While OSI Reference Model definitions are sometimes overly theoretical in nature, this definition of protocol is rather accurate in assessing protocols in real-world networking. If something doesn't specify a means of communication, it arguably isn't a protocol.

KEY CONCEPT A networking protocol defines a set of rules, algorithms, messages, and other mechanisms that enables software and hardware in networked devices to communicate effectively. A protocol usually describes a means for communication between corresponding entities at the same OSI Reference Model layer in two or more devices.

Despite this, the term *protocol* is often used colloquially to refer to many different concepts in networking. Some of the more common alternative uses of the word are listed here:

Protocol Suites It is very common to hear the word *protocol* used to refer to sets of protocols that are more properly called *protocol suites* (or *stacks*, in reference to a stack of layers). For example, TCP/IP is often called just a protocol when it is really a (large) set of protocols.

Microsoft Windows Protocols One important example of the issue of referring to protocol suites as single protocols is the networking software in Microsoft Windows. It usually calls a full networking stack like TCP/IP or IPX/SPX just a protocol. When you install one of these so-called protocols, however, you actually get a software module that supports a full protocol suite.

Other Technologies Sometimes technologies that are not protocols at all are called protocols, either out of convention or perhaps because people think it sounds good. For example, TCP/IP Remote Network Monitoring (RMON) is often called a protocol when it is really just an enhancement to the Simple Network Management Protocol (SNMP), which *is* a protocol! (See Part III-4 for details on SNMP and RMON.)

So, does it really matter whether a protocol is a "true" protocol or not? Well, the networking hardware devices and software programs sure don't care. But hopefully, having read about the term and what it means, you will be able to better understand the word when you encounter it in your studies—especially in the places where it may not always be used in a way that's entirely consistent with its formal definition.

Circuit-Switching and Packet-Switching Networks

Networks are devices that are connected together using special hardware and software that allows them to exchange information. The most important word in that sentence is the final one: *information.* As you will see in your exploration of this book, there are many methods for exchanging information between networked devices. There are also a number of ways of categorizing and describing these methods and the types of networks that use them.

One fundamental way to differentiate between networking technologies is on the basis of the method used to determine the path between devices over which information will flow. In highly simplified terms, there are two approaches: a path can be set up between the devices in advance, or the data can be sent as individual data elements over a variable path.

Circuit Switching

In the *circuit-switching* networking method, a connection called a *circuit,* which is used for the whole communication, is set up between two devices. Information about the nature of the circuit is maintained by the network. The circuit may be either a fixed one that is always present or one that is created on an as-needed basis. Even if many potential paths through intermediate devices may exist between the two devices that are communicating, only one will be used for any given dialogue, as shown in Figure 1-1.

The classic example of a circuit-switched network is the telephone system. When you call someone and she answers, you establish a circuit connection and can pass data in a steady stream. That circuit functions the same way, regardless of how many intermediate devices are used to carry your voice. You use it for as long as you need it and then terminate the circuit. The next time you call, you get a new circuit, which may (probably will) use different hardware than the first circuit did, depending on what's available at that time in the network.

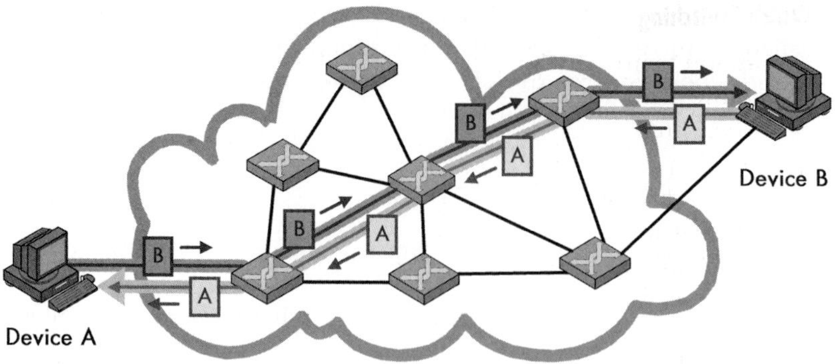

Figure 1-1: Circuit switching In a circuit-switched network, before communication can occur between two devices, a circuit is established between them. This is shown as a darker line for the conduit of data from Device A to Device B, and a matching lighter line from B back to A. Once it's set up, all communication between these devices takes place over this circuit, even though there are other possible ways that data could conceivably be passed over the network of devices between them. Contrast this diagram to Figure 1-2.

Packet Switching

In the *packet-switching* network type, no specific path is used for data transfer. Instead, the data is chopped up into small pieces called *packets* and sent over the network. You can route, combine, or fragment the packets as required to get them to their eventual destination. On the receiving end, the process is reversed—the data is read from the packets and reassembled to form the original data. A packet-switched network is more analogous to the postal system than it is to the telephone system (though the comparison isn't perfect). An example is shown in Figure 1-2.

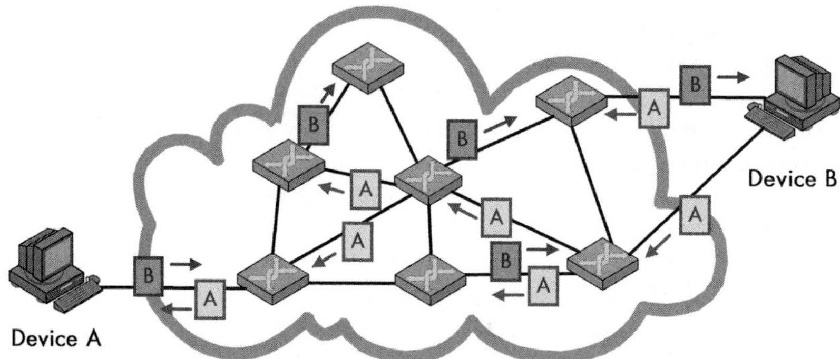

Figure 1-2: Packet switching In a packet-switched network, no circuit is set up prior to sending data between devices. Blocks of data, even from the same file or communication, may take any number of paths as they journey from one device to another. Compare this to Figure 1-1.

> **KEY CONCEPT** One way that networking technologies are categorized is based on the path used to carry data between devices. In circuit switching, a circuit is first established and then used to carry all data between devices. In packet switching, no fixed path is created between devices that communicate; it is broken into packets, each of which may take a separate path from sender to recipient.

Which Switching Method to Choose?

A common temptation when considering alternatives such as these is to ask which is better; the answer is neither. There are places for which one is more suited than the other, but if one were clearly superior, both methods wouldn't be used.

One important issue in selecting a switching method is whether the network medium is *shared* or *dedicated*. Your phone line can be used for establishing a circuit because you are the only one who can use it—assuming you can keep that pesky wife/husband/child/sister/brother/father/mother off it. However, this doesn't work well with LANs, which typically use a single shared medium and baseband signaling. If two devices were to establish a connection, they would lock out all the other devices for a long period of time. It makes more sense to chop the data into small pieces and send them one at a time. Then, if two other devices want to communicate, *their* packets can be interspersed, and everyone can share the network.

The ability to have many devices communicate simultaneously without dedicated data paths is one reason why packet switching is becoming predominant today. However, there are some disadvantages of packet switching compared to circuit switching. One is that since all data does not take the same predictable path between devices, it is possible that some pieces of data may get lost in transit or show up in the incorrect order. In some situations this does not matter, but in others it is very important indeed.

Although the theoretical difference between circuit and packet switching is pretty clear-cut, understanding how to use them is a bit more complicated. One of the major issues is that in modern networks, they are often combined.

For example, suppose you connect to the Internet using a dial-up modem. You will be using IP datagrams (packets) to carry higher-layer data, but it will be over the circuit-switched telephone network. Yet the data may be sent over the telephone system in digital packetized form. So in some ways, both circuit switching and packet switching are being used concurrently.

Another issue is the relationship between circuit and packet switching, and whether a technology is connection-oriented or connectionless. The two concepts are related but not the same, as you will see in a moment.

NOTE *The word* packet *is only one of several terms that are used to refer to messages that are sent over a network. Other terms that you will encounter include frame, datagram, cell, and segment. You will learn more about these terms later in this chapter.*

Connection-Oriented and Connectionless Protocols

I just compared networking technologies based on whether or not they use a dedicated path or *circuit* over which they send data. Another way in which technologies and protocols are differentiated has to do with whether or not they use *connections* between devices. This issue is closely related to the matter of packet versus circuit switching.

Protocols are divided into the following two categories based on their use of connections:

Connection-Oriented Protocols These protocols require you to establish a logical connection between two devices before transferring data. This is generally accomplished by following a specific set of rules that specify how a connection should be initiated, negotiated, managed, and eventually terminated. Usually, one device begins by sending a request to open a connection, and the other responds. The devices pass control information to determine if and how the connection should be set up. If this is successful, data is sent between the devices. When they are finished, the connection is broken.

Connectionless Protocols These protocols do not establish a connection between devices. As soon as a device has data to send to another, it just sends it.

KEY CONCEPT A connection-oriented protocol is one in which a logical connection is first established between devices prior to data being sent. In a connectionless protocol, data is just sent without a connection being created.

You can probably immediately see the relationship between the concepts of circuits and connections. Obviously, in order to establish a circuit between two devices, you must connect them. For this reason, circuit-switched networks are inherently based on connections. This has led to the interchangeable use of the terms *circuit-switched* and *connection-oriented.*

However, this is an oversimplification that results from a common logical fallacy—people make the mistake of thinking that if A implies B, then B implies A, which is like saying that since all apples are fruit, then all fruit are apples! A connection is needed for a circuit, but a circuit is *not* a prerequisite for a connection. There are, therefore, protocols that are connection-oriented, even though they aren't predicated on the use of circuit-based networks at all.

These connection-oriented protocols are important because they enable the implementation of applications that require connections over packet-switched networks that have no inherent sense of a connection. For example, to use the TCP/IP File Transfer Protocol (FTP), you want to be able to connect to a server, enter a login and password, and then execute commands to change directories, send or retrieve files, and so on. This requires the establishment of a connection over which commands, replies, and data can be passed. Similarly, the Telnet Protocol (TP) involves establishing a connection—it lets you remotely use another machine. Yet, both of these work (indirectly) over IP, which is based on the use of packets, through the important principle of layering (see Chapter 5).

KEY CONCEPT Circuit-switched networking technologies are inherently connection-oriented, but not all connection-oriented technologies use circuit switching. Logical connection-oriented protocols can be implemented on top of packet-switching networks to provide higher-layer services to applications that require connections.

To comprehend the relationship between connections and circuits, you must recall the layered nature of modern networking architecture (as I discuss in some detail in Chapter 5). Even though packets may be used at lower layers for the mechanics of sending data, a higher-layer protocol can create logical connections through the use of messages sent in those packets.

TCP/IP has two main protocols that operate at the transport layer of the OSI Reference Model. One is TCP, which is connection-oriented; the other, the User Datagram Protocol (UDP), is connectionless. TCP is used for applications that require the establishment of connections (as well as TCP's other service features), such as FTP; it works using a set of rules, as described earlier, by which a logical connection is negotiated prior to sending data. UDP is used by other applications that don't need connections or other features, but do need the faster performance that UDP can offer by not needing to make such connections before sending data.

Some people consider the layering of a connection-oriented protocol over a connectionless protocol to be like a simulation of circuit switching at higher network layers; this is perhaps a dubious analogy. Even though you can use a TCP connection to send data back and forth between devices, all that data is indeed still being sent as packets; there is no real circuit between the devices. This means that TCP must deal with all the potential pitfalls of packet-switched communication, such as the potential for data loss or receipt of data pieces in the incorrect order. Certainly, the existence of connection-oriented protocols like TCP doesn't obviate the need for circuit-switching technologies, though you will get some arguments about that one too.

The principle of layering also means that there are other ways that connection-oriented and connectionless protocols can be combined at different levels of an internetwork. Just as a connection-oriented protocol can be implemented over an inherently connectionless protocol, the reverse is also true: a connectionless protocol can be implemented over a connection-oriented protocol at a lower level. In a preceding example, I talked about Telnet (which requires a connection) running over IP (which is connectionless). In turn, IP can run over a connection-oriented protocol like Asynchronous Transfer Mode (ATM).

Messages: Packets, Frames, Datagrams, and Cells

Many networking technologies are based on packet switching, which involves the creation of small chunks of data to be sent over a network. Even though *packet* appears in the name of this method, the data items sent between networked devices are most generically called *messages*. *Packet* is one of a variety of similar words that are used in different contexts to refer to messages sent from one device to another.

In some cases, the different terms can be very useful, because the name used to refer to a particular message can tell you something about what the message contains, as you will see shortly. In particular, different message names are usually associated with protocols and technologies operating at specific layers of the OSI Reference Model. Thus, the use of these different names can help clarify discussions that involve multiple protocols operating at different layers.

Unfortunately, these terms can also cause confusion, because they are not always applied in a universal or even consistent manner. Some people are strict about applying particular message designations only to the appropriate technologies where they are normally used, while others use the different terms completely interchangeably. This means that you should be familiar with the different message types and how they are normally used, but you should still be prepared for the unexpected.

The most common terms used for messages are the following:

Packet This term is considered by many to correctly refer to a message sent by protocols operating at the network layer of the OSI Reference Model. So you will commonly see people refer to *IP packets*. However, this term is commonly also used to refer generically to any type of message, as I mentioned earlier.

Datagram This term is basically synonymous with *packet* and is also used to refer to network layer technologies. It is also often used to refer to a message that is sent at a higher level of the OSI Reference Model (more often than *packet* is).

Frame This term is most commonly associated with messages that travel at low levels of the OSI Reference Model. In particular, it is most commonly seen used in reference to data link layer messages. It is occasionally also used to refer to physical layer messages, when message formatting is performed by a layer 1 technology. A frame gets its name from the fact that it is created by taking higher-level packets or datagrams and "framing" them with additional header information needed at the lower level.

Cell Frames and packets, in general, can be of variable length, depending on their contents; in contrast, a *cell* is most often a message that is fixed in size. For example, the fixed-length, 53-byte messages sent in ATM are called cells. Like frames, cells are usually used by technologies operating at the lower layers of the OSI model.

Protocol Data Unit (PDU) and Service Data Unit (SDU) These are the formal terms used in the OSI Reference Model to describe protocol messages. A PDU at layer N is a message sent between protocols at layer N. It consists of layer N header information and an encapsulated message from layer N+1, which is called both the *layer N SDU* and the *layer N+1 PDU*. After you stop scratching your head, see the "Data Encapsulation, Protocol Data Units (PDUs), and Service Data Units (SDUs)" section in Chapter 5 for a discussion of this.

I should also point out that there are certain protocols that use unusual names, which aren't used elsewhere in the world of networking, to refer to their messages. One prominent example is TCP, which calls its messages *segments*.

> **KEY CONCEPT** Communication between devices on packet-switched networks is based on items most generically called messages. These pieces of information also go by other names such as packets, datagrams, frames, and cells, which often correspond to protocols at particular layers of the OSI Reference Model. The formal OSI terms for messages are *protocol data unit (PDU)* and *service data unit (SDU)*.

In this book, I have made a specific effort not to imply anything about the nature of a message solely based on the name it uses, but I do follow the most common name used for a particular technology. For example, messages sent over Ethernet are almost always called Ethernet frames—they are not generally called Ethernet datagrams, for example. However, I do not structure discussions so that the type of name used for a message is the only way to determine what sort of message it is.

Message Formatting: Headers, Payloads, and Footers

Messages are the structures used to send information over networks. They vary greatly from one protocol or technology to the next in how they are used, and as just described, they are also called by many different names. Shakespeare had the right idea about names, however. The most important way that messages differ is not in what they are called but in terms of their *content.*

Every protocol uses a special *formatting method* that determines the structure of the messages it employs. Obviously, a message that is intended to connect a web server and a web browser is going to be quite different from one that connects two Ethernet cards at a low level. This is why I separately describe the formats of dozens of different protocol messages in various areas of this book.

While the format of a particular message type depends entirely on the nature of the technology that uses it, messages on the whole tend to follow a fairly uniform overall structure. In generic terms, each message contains the following three elements (see Figure 1-3):

Header Information that is placed before the actual data. The header normally contains a small number of control-information bytes, which are used to communicate important facts about the data that the message contains and how it is to be interpreted and used. It serves as the communication and control link between protocol elements on different devices.

Data The actual data to be transmitted, often called the *payload* of the message (metaphorically borrowing a term from the space industry!). Most messages contain some data of one form or another, but some messages actually contain none. They are used for only control and communication purposes. For example, these may be used to set up or terminate a logical connection before data is sent.

Footer Information that is placed after the data. There is no real difference between the header and the footer, as both generally contain control fields. The term *trailer* is also sometimes used.

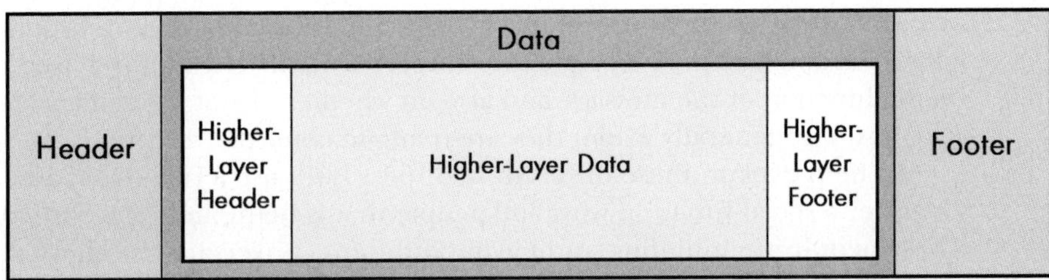

Figure 1-3: Network message formatting *In the most general of terms, a message consists of a data payload that will be communicated, bracketed by a set of header and footer fields. The data of any particular message sent in a networking protocol will itself contain an encapsulated higher-layer message containing a header, data, and a footer. This "nesting" can occur many times as data is passed down a protocol stack. The header is found in most protocol messages; the footer only in some.*

Since the header and footer can contain both control and information fields, you might rightly wonder what the point is of having a separate footer anyway. One reason is that some types of control information are calculated using the values of the data itself. In some cases, it is more efficient to perform this computation as the data payload is being sent, and then transmit the result after the payload in a footer. A good example of a field often found in a footer is redundancy data such as cyclic redundancy check (CRC) code, which can be used for error detection by the receiving device. Footers are most often associated with lower-layer protocols, especially at the data link layer of the OSI Reference Model.

KEY CONCEPT The general format of a networking message consists of a *header*, followed by the *data* or *payload* of the message, followed optionally by a *footer*. Header and footer information is functionally the same except for its position in the message; footer fields are only sometimes used, especially in cases where the data in the field is calculated based on the values of the data being transmitted.

Generally speaking, any particular protocol is concerned with only its *own* header (and footer, if present). It doesn't care much about what is in the data portion of the message, just as a delivery person worries only about driving the truck and not so much about what it contains. At the beginning of that data will normally be the headers of other protocols that were used higher up in the protocol stack; this, too, is shown in Figure 1-3. In the OSI Reference Model, a message handled by a particular protocol is said to be its PDU; the data it carries in its payload is its SDU. The SDU of a lower-layer protocol is usually a PDU of a higher-layer protocol. The discussion of data encapsulation in Chapter 5 contains a full explanation of this important concept.

Message Addressing and Transmission Methods: Unicast, Broadcast, and Multicast

In a networking technology that uses messages to send data, you must undertake a number of tasks in order to successfully transmit the data from one place to another. One is simply *addressing* the message—putting an address on it so that the system knows where it is supposed to go. Another is *transmitting* the message, which is sending it to its intended recipient.

There are several different ways of addressing and transmitting a message over a network. One way in which messages are differentiated is in how they are addressed and how many recipients will receive them. The method used depends on the function of the message and also on whether or not the sender knows specifically or generally whom they are trying to contact.

To help explain these different methods, I will use a real-world analogy. Consider a social function with 300 people that is being held in a large hall. These people are mingling and having different conversations. There are different kinds of messages that you may need to send in this setting, as is the case with networks.

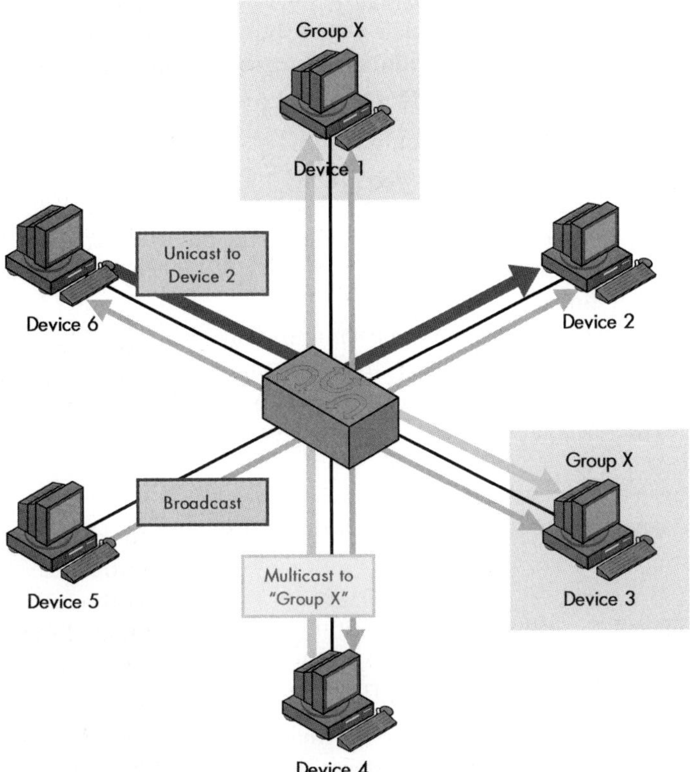

Figure 1-4: Unicast, multicast, and broadcast message addressing and transmission *The three basic types of addressing and message delivery in networking are illustrated in this simplified LAN. Device 6 is sending a* unicast *message to Device 2, shown as the dark, heavy arrow. Device 4 is sending a* multicast *message to multicast group X, shown as the medium-weight arrows. In this case, that group includes Devices 1 and 3, which are highlighted. Finally, Device 5 is sending a* broadcast *message, which goes to all other devices on the LAN, shown as the thin, faint arrows.*

Bearing this analogy in mind, consider these three kinds of message transmissions, which are illustrated in Figure 1-4:

Unicast Messages These are messages that are sent from one device to another device; they are not intended for others. If you have a friend at this social event, this is the equivalent of pulling him aside for a private conversation. Of course, there is still the possibility of someone else at the event overhearing your conversation—or even eavesdropping on it. The same is true in networking as well—addressing a message to a particular computer doesn't guarantee that others won't also read it; it's just that they normally will not do so.

Broadcast Messages As the name suggests, these messages are sent to every device on a network. You use them when you need to communicate a piece of information to everyone on the network, or when the sending station needs to send it to just one recipient, but doesn't know its address. For example, suppose a new arrival at the social gathering saw in the parking lot a blue sedan with its lights left on. She does not know who the car belongs to. The best way to communicate this information is to broadcast it by having the host make an announcement that will be heard by all, including the vehicle's owner. In networks, broadcast messages are used for a variety of purposes, including finding the locations of particular stations or the devices that manage different services.

Multicast Messages These are a compromise between the previous two types. Multicast messages are sent to a group of stations that meet a particular set of criteria. These stations are usually related to each other in some way. For example, they serve a common function or are set up into a particular *multicast group*. (Note that you can also consider broadcast messages to be a special case of multicast in which the group is "everyone.")

Back to our analogy: This would be somewhat like a group of friends who go to this large social hall and then stay together in a small discussion group—or perhaps use radios to talk to each other from a distance. Multicasting requires special techniques that make clear who is in the intended group of recipients.

Since these transmission methods differ based on how many and which devices receive the transmission, they are tied directly to the methods used for addressing, as follows:

Unicast Addressing Unicast delivery requires that a message should be addressed to a specific recipient. This is the most common type of messaging, so this addressing capability is present in almost all protocols.

Broadcast Addressing Broadcasts are normally implemented via a special address that is reserved for that function. Whenever devices see a message sent to that address, they all interpret it as "This message goes to everyone."

Multicast Addressing Multicasts are the most complex type of message because they require a means of identifying a set of specific devices that will receive a message. It is often necessary to create several such groups, which may or may not partially overlap in their membership. Some mechanism is needed to manage which devices are in which groups.

KEY CONCEPT Three basic methods are used to address and transmit data between networked devices. A *unicast* transmission goes from one device to exactly one other; this is the most common method used for most message transactions. A *broadcast* transmission is sent from one device to all connected devices on a network. A *multicast* transmission is addressed and sent to a select group of devices.

Finally, one special case in the field of addressing is worth mentioning. In some networks or links, only two devices are connected together, forming what is often called a *point-to-point network*. In this situation, everything sent by one device is implicitly intended for the other, and vice versa. Thus, no addressing of messages on a point-to-point link is strictly necessary.

NOTE *A new type of message-addressing method was defined as part of IP version 6 (IPv6): the anycast message. This term identifies a message that should be sent to the closest member of a group of devices. Chapter 25 describes this type of addressing and transmission.*

Network Structural Models and Client-Server and Peer-to-Peer Networking

I mentioned in my discussion of the advantages of networking that networks are normally set up for two primary purposes: *connectivity* and *sharing*. If you have a network with a number of different machines on it, each computer can interact with another's hardware and software, which enables you to perform a variety of tasks. How this is actually done depends to a large degree on the overall design of the network.

One very important issue in network design is how to configure the network for the sharing of resources. Specifically, the network designer must decide whether or not to dedicate resource management functions to the devices that constitute it. In some networks, all devices are treated equally in this regard, while in others, each computer is responsible for a particular job in the overall function of providing services. In this latter arrangement, the devices are sometimes said to have *roles*, somewhat like actors in a play.

The following two common terms are used to describe these different approaches to setting up a network:

Peer-to-Peer Networking In a strict peer-to-peer networking setup, every computer is an equal, a *peer* in the network. Each machine can have resources that are shared with any other machine. There is no assigned role for any particular device, and each of the devices usually runs similar software. Any device can and will send requests to any other, as illustrated in Figure 1-5.

Client-Server Networking In this design, a small number of computers are designated as centralized *servers* and are given the task of providing services to a larger number of user machines called *clients*, as shown in Figure 1-6. The servers are usually powerful computers with a lot of memory and storage space, and fast network connections. The clients are typically smaller, regular computers like PCs; they are optimized for human use.

The term *client-server* also frequently refers to protocols and software, which are designed with matching, complementary components. Usually, server software runs on server hardware, and client software is used on client computers that connect to those servers. Most of the interaction on the network is between client and server, not between clients. Server software is designed to efficiently respond to requests, while client software provides the interface to the human users of the network.

KEY CONCEPT Networks are usually configured to share resources using one of two basic *structural models*. In a *peer-to-peer network*, each device is an equal, and none are assigned particular jobs. In a *client-server network*, however, devices are assigned particular roles—a small number of powerful computers are set up as *servers* and respond to requests from the other devices, which are *clients*. Client-server computing also refers to the interaction between complementary protocol elements and software programs. It's rising in popularity due to its prevalence in TCP/IP and Internet applications.

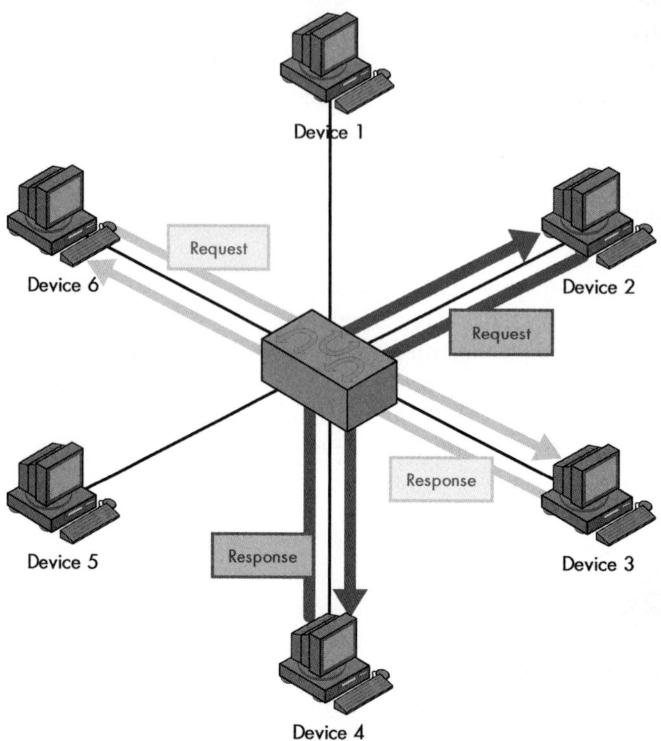

Figure 1-5: Peer-to-peer networking *In this model, each device on the network is treated as a peer, or equal. Each device can send requests and responses, and none are specifically designated as performing a particular role. This model is more often used in very small networks. Contrast this with Figure 1-6.*

The choice of client-server or peer-to-peer is sometimes called choosing a *structural model* for the network. As with most situations in which two different schemes are used, there is no right answer in this regard. Your choice depends entirely on the needs of the particular network.

Peer-to-peer networking has primary advantages of simplicity and low cost, meaning that it has traditionally been used on small networks. Client-server networking provides advantages in the areas of performance, scalability, security, and reliability, but is more complicated and expensive to set up. This makes it better suited to larger networks. Over time, however, there has been a steady evolution toward client-server networking, even on smaller networks. Many years ago, it was common to see even networks with 20 to 50 machines using the peer-to-peer model; today, even networks with only a half-dozen machines are sometimes set up in a client-server mode because of the advantages of centralized resource serving.

The rise in popularity of client-server networking is ironic because, in some ways, it is actually a throwback to the days of large mainframes decades ago. A mainframe with attached terminals can be thought of as a client-server network, with the mainframe itself being the server and the terminals being clients. This analogy is not perfect, of course, because modern client computers do a lot more work than dumb terminals on mainframes.

One of the reasons why the client-server structural model is becoming dominant is that it is the primary model used by the world's largest network: the Internet. Client-server architecture is the basis for most TCP/IP protocols and services. For example, the term *web browser* is really another name for a web client, and a *website* is really a web server.

NOTE *For more information on client-server computing, I recommend that you read the section "TCP/IP Services and Client/Server Operation" in Chapter 8. That topic also contains a very relevant exposition on the different meanings of the terms* client *and* server *in hardware, software, and transactional contexts.*

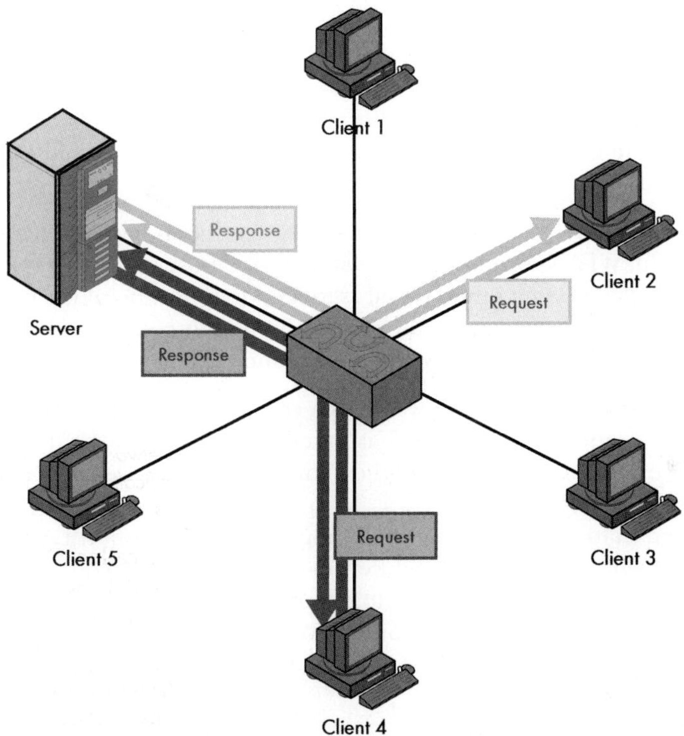

Figure 1-6: Client-server networking *In the client-server model, a small number of devices are designated as servers and equipped with special hardware and software that allows them to interact efficiently and simultaneously with multiple client machines. Though the clients can still interact with each other, most of the time they send requests of various sorts to the server, and the server sends back responses to them. Contrast this with the peer-to-peer networking example in Figure 1-5.*

Types and Sizes of Networks

One of the reasons that understanding networks can be difficult at times is that there are so many different types! When someone talks about a network, she can mean anything from two computers hooked together in an apartment to a globe-spanning entity with millions of nodes. Every network is unique, and each one has an important role to play in filling the communication and data-sharing needs of different individuals and organizations. In fact, the great diversity and flexibility of networking is one of its most important strengths.

Two of the most basic ways that you can distinguish and contrast various networks are the relative distances between the devices that they connect and the general mechanisms used to communicate between them. The reason for making these distinctions is that the technological needs of a network differ greatly depending on the amount of ground you are trying to cover, and also by the overall way that you want to transmit and receive information.

Many people, including me, like to divide the many kinds of networks in existence into three general classes, as follows:

Local Area Networks (LANs) Networks that connect computers that are relatively close to each other—generally, within the same room or building. When most people think about networking PCs and other small computers, this is what they usually have in mind. The vast majority of regular LANs connect using cables, so the term *LAN* by itself usually implies a wired LAN, but not always.

Wireless LANs (WLANs) LANs that connect devices without wires, using radio frequencies or light. WLANs can be entirely wireless, but most are not. They usually connect wireless devices to each other as well as to the wired portion of the network. Due to the limits of most wireless technologies, WLANs usually connect devices that are very close to each other, generally within a few hundred feet at most.

Wide Area Networks (WANs) Networks that connect devices or other networks over a greater distance than that which is practical for LANs. If the distance between devices can be measured in miles, you will generally use WAN and not LAN technology to link them.

More often than not, WANs are used to link physically distant LANs. For example, a company with locations in two different cities would normally set up a LAN in each building and then connect them together in a WAN. I also consider most Internet access technologies to be a form of WAN, though some might not agree with that. There is also the term *wireless WAN (WWAN)*, which just refers to a WAN that uses wireless technology.

As with most other distinctions and categorizations in the world of networking, the lines between these various definitions are not very concrete. As I mentioned already, WLANs are usually not entirely wireless because they contained wired elements. Similarly, trying to say absolutely when a network is "local" and when it is "wide" is difficult.

It's also somewhat pointless to spend too much energy on differentiating these network classes precisely. In some cases it's not the definitions that decide what technology to use, but rather the technology that indicates what kind of network you have! Since some protocols are designed for WANs, if you are using them, many would say you have a WAN, even if all the devices in that technology are near each other. On the other hand, some LAN technologies allow for the use of cables that can run for many miles; most would still consider a mile-long Ethernet fiber link to be a LAN connection, even though it may span WAN distances.

There are many dimensions in which LAN and WAN technologies differ; two of the most important are *cost* and *performance*. It's easy to establish a high-speed conduit for data between two systems that are in the same room, but it's much more difficult if the two are in different states. This means that in the world of WAN, one either pays a lot more or gets a lot less throughput—often it's both.

The gray area between LAN and WAN is becoming more muddled every year. One reason is the emergence of intermediate network types that straddle the line between these more familiar terms. Two of the more common ones are as follows:

Campus Area Networks (CANs) A *CAN* is one created to span multiple buildings in the same location, such as the campus of a university. Campus area networking is a gray area, since neither LANs nor WANs alone are always well suited for this type of application. Often, a mix of LAN and WAN techniques is used for campus networking, depending on the characteristics of the campus and the needs of the organization.

Metropolitan Area Networks (MANs) Another intermediate term that you may see sometimes is the *MAN*. As the name implies, this refers to a network that spans a particular small region or a city. MANs can be considered small WANs that cover a limited geographical area, or large LANs that cover an area greater than what is normally associated with a local network. Wireless MANs are sometimes called *WMANs*; IEEE 802.16 is an example of a WMAN standard.

Finally, there is one other term occasionally used that I should mention: the *personal area network (PAN)*. This type of network generally means a very small LAN with a range of only a few feet. PANs mostly connect devices used by a single person (or very small group). The term is most commonly used in reference to Bluetooth/IEEE 802.15 wireless technology, so you will sometimes see the terms *wireless PAN (WPAN)* and *PAN* used interchangeably.

KEY CONCEPT Networks are often divided by size and general communication method into three classes. *Local area networks (LANs)* generally connect proximate devices, usually using cables. *Wireless LANs (WLANs)* are like cabled LANs but use radio frequency or light technology to connect devices without wires. *Wide area networks (WANs)* connect distant devices or LANs to each other. *Campus area networks (CANs)* and *metropolitan area networks (MANs)* fall between LANs and WANs in terms of overall size. *Personal area networks (PANs)* are like very small LANs and often appear as *wireless PANs (WPANs)*.

Segments, Networks, Subnetworks, and Internetworks

One of the reasons that networks are so powerful is that they can be used to connect not only individual computers, but also groups of computers. Thus, network connections can exist at multiple levels; one network can be attached to another network, and that entire network can be attached to another set of networks, and so on. The ultimate example of this is, of course, the Internet, which is a huge collection of networks that have been interconnected into . . . dare I say, a web?

This means that a larger network can be described as consisting of several smaller networks or even parts of networks that are linked together. Conversely, we can talk about taking individual networks or network portions and assembling them into larger structures. The reason why this concept is important is that certain technologies are best explained when looking at an entire large network at a high level, while others really require that you drill down to the detailed level of how constituent network pieces work.

Over time, a collection of terms has evolved in the networking world to describe the relative sizes of larger and smaller networks. Some of the most common ones are as follows:

Network This is the least specific of the terms mentioned here. Basically, a *network* can be pretty much any size, from two devices to thousands. When networks get very large, however, and are clearly comprised of smaller networks connected together, they are often no longer called networks but *internetworks*, as you will see momentarily. Despite this, it is fairly common to hear someone refer to something like "Microsoft's corporate network," which obviously contains thousands or even tens of thousands of machines.

Subnetwork (Subnet) A *subnetwork* is a portion of a network, or a network that is part of a larger internetwork. This term is also a rather subjective one; subnetworks can be rather large when they are part of a network that is very large.

The abbreviated term *subnet* can refer generically to a subnetwork, but also has a specific meaning in the context of TCP/IP addressing (see Chapter 18).

Segment (Network Segment) A *segment* is a small section of a network. In some contexts, a segment is the same as a subnetwork and the terms are used interchangeably. More often, however, the term *segment* implies something smaller than a subnetwork. Networks are often designed so that, for the sake of efficiency, computers that are related to each other or that are used by the same groups of people are put on the same network segment.

Some LAN technologies—including Ethernet—use the term *segment* to refer specifically to a collection of geographically proximate machines that are connected directly to each other, either by a single cable or single device such as a hub. Such technologies have specific rules about how many devices can be on a segment, how many segments can be connected together, and so on, depending on what sort of network interconnection devices you are using.

Internetwork (or Internet) Most often, this refers to a larger networking structure that is formed by connecting smaller ones. Again, the term can have either a generic or a specific meaning, depending on context. In some technologies, an internetwork is just a very large network that has networks as components. In others, a network is differentiated from an internetwork based on how the devices are connected together.

An important example of the latter definition is TCP/IP, in which a *network* usually refers to a collection of machines that are linked at layer 2 of the OSI Reference Model, using technologies like Ethernet or Token Ring, as well as interconnection devices such as hubs and switches. An internetwork is formed when these networks are linked together at layer 3, using routers that pass IP datagrams between networks. Naturally, this is highly simplified, but in studying TCP/IP, you should keep this in mind when you encounter the terms *network* and *internetwork.*

NOTE *The shorter form of the word internetwork* (internet) *is often avoided by people who wish to avoid confusion with the proper noun form* (Internet). *The latter, of course, refers only to the well-known global internetwork of computers and all the services it provides. I personally try to use the word* internetwork *most of the time in this book instead of* internet, *for this very reason.*

Understanding these different terms is important not only for helping you comprehend what you read about networks, but also because they are important concepts in network design. This is particularly true for LANs in which decisions regarding how to set up segments and how to connect them to each other have an important impact on the overall performance and usability of the network.

KEY CONCEPT Several terms are often used to describe the relative sizes of networks and parts of networks. The most basic term is *network* itself, which can refer to most anything, but often means a set of devices connected using an OSI layer 2 technology. A *subnetwork* is a part of a network (or internetwork), as is a *segment*, though the latter often has a more specific meaning in certain technologies. An *internetwork* refers either generically to a very large network, or specifically, to a set of layer 2 networks connected using routers at layer 3.

The term *segment* is notably problematic because it is routinely used in two different ways, especially in discussions related to Ethernet. Traditionally, a *segment* referred to a specific cable. The earliest forms of Ethernet used coaxial cables, and the coaxial cable segment was shared and became the collision domain for the network. *Collision domain* is a term that refers generally to a collection of hardware devices in which only one can transmit at a time. Devices such as hubs and repeaters were used to extend collision domains by connecting together these segments of cable into wider networks. Over time, the terms *collision domain* and *segment* started to be used interchangeably. Thus today a segment can refer either to a specific piece of cable or to a collection of cables connected electrically that represent a single collision domain.

NOTE *As if that potential ambiguity in the use of the word* segment *isn't bad enough, it also has another, totally unrelated meaning: It is the name of the messages sent in TCP!*

The Internet, Intranets, and Extranets

I mentioned in the preceding discussion of segments, networks, subnetworks, and internetworks that the Internet is really the king of internetworks. After all, you don't get to be called "the" something unless you pretty much define it!

In fact, the Internet is not just a large internetwork, but substantially more. The Internet is defined not just as the computers that are connected to each other around the world, but as the set of services and features that it offers. More than that, the Internet defines a specific way of doing things, of sharing information and resources between people and companies. And though it might be a bit melodramatic to say so, to many people, the Internet is a way of life.

As Internet use exploded in the 1990s, many people realized that the techniques and technologies used on the Internet would be useful if applied to internal company networks as well. The term *intranet* was coined to refer to an internal network that functioned like a private Internet. It comes from the prefix *intra*, which means within. Of course, *inter* is the opposite of intra, so this makes some people think that an intranet is the opposite of an internet. In fact, most intranets *are* internetworks as well!

As if that weren't bad enough from a jargon standpoint, the buzzword buzzards then decided to take matters a step further. If an intranet is extended to allow access to it not only by people or groups strictly from within the organization, but also by people or groups outside the main company, this is sometimes called an *extranet*. *Extra*, of course, is a prefix that means outside, or beyond.

So, an extranet is a type of internal, private Internet that, well, isn't entirely internal. An extranet is an extended intranet, which is really a type of internet that works like the Internet. (You can start to see why I am not a big fan of these fancy terms. But then, I don't get to choose them; I just have to help you understand them!) An extranet isn't public and open to all—it is controlled by a private organization. At the same time, it isn't entirely private either.

KEY CONCEPT The generic noun *internet* is a short form for the word internetwork, while the proper noun *Internet* refers to the global internetwork of TCP/IP networks that we all know and use. The term *intranet* refers to an internal network that uses TCP/IP technologies as the Internet does. An *extranet* is like an intranet that is extended to individuals or organizations outside the company. All these terms can be used ambiguously, so you must take care to determine exactly what they mean in any given context.

As you can see, the lines between the Internet, intranets, and extranets were pretty blurry from the start, and the concepts are rapidly blending into a diffuse gray mass as the whole computing world becomes more tightly integrated. For example, even if you have an entirely private intranet, you will want to connect it to the Internet to communicate with the outside world and to allow access to Internet resources. And an extranet may be implemented, in part, through the public Internet infrastructure, using technologies such as virtual private networking (VPN). I think you get the picture.

The key that binds all of these concepts together is that they all use *Internet technologies*, which is a term that is also somewhat vague. This usually refers to the use of the TCP/IP protocol suite, which is the defining technology of the Internet as well as the set of services that are available on the Internet.

The bottom line is that being told that a company has an intranet or an extranet—as opposed to a plain old boring network—doesn't tell you much at all. It is best not to rely on the slogans and instead look at the underlying characteristics of the network or internetwork itself. Furthermore, when designing such a network, you should focus on using the technologies and protocols that make sense—let the marketing people decide what to call it later.

2

NETWORK PERFORMANCE ISSUES AND CONCEPTS

Networking is largely about connecting together devices so that information can be shared between them. Since the idea is to send data from one place to another, a very important characteristic of any network is its *speed*: How fast can data be transmitted and received? This matter of speed turns out to be only one of several issues that determine the overall *performance* of a network.

In the computing world, performance is, in general, one of the most discussed but least understood characteristics of any system or hardware device. This is true of networking as well. For example, most people know the raw throughput rating of their network hardware, and they may even start to draw conclusions about its capabilities based on those numbers. Many, however, don't realize that they will never actually achieve that rated amount of performance in the real world.

Most of the other subtle issues related to performance are also typically ignored or misunderstood, such as the impact of software drivers on hardware performance, and the fact that certain applications need more than just raw bit speed—they need *reliable* delivery of data. But even beyond all of this, one of the most important issues related to network performance is understanding what your needs are, because then you can make sure you don't spend too much money for performance you don't need—or worse, create a network that can't meet your requirements.

In this chapter, I discuss various performance issues and concepts that are related to networking in one way or another. First and foremost, I try to put performance in context and also contrast it with nonperformance issues. Then I talk about several key performance terms and metrics: speed, bandwidth, throughput, and latency. I also discuss some of the units used to measure network performance. I then explain how the real-world performance of a network differs from its theoretical performance and talk about factors that have an impact on network performance. I conclude by contrasting full-duplex and half-duplex network operation, and talking about quality of service, which is a concept that is especially important in the use of networks for real-time applications such as streaming multimedia.

Putting Network Performance in Perspective

Performance is probably the mother of all buzzwords in the computer industry. There are many people who consider it the ultimate goal of any computer or computer system, and by extension, any network. A lot of people spend many dollars and hours of time trying to maximize it. There's good reason for this: Performance *is* very important. A network that does not offer adequate performance simply will not get the job done for those that rely on it. However, it is very important to keep performance in perspective. Successfully maximizing performance requires that you first take a step back and look at the big picture.

The first question you must ask yourself is also the most essential one: How important is performance to you? Before you answer this question, recall the old auto racing adage: "Speed costs money—how fast do you want to go?" While there are some situations in which you can get much better performance in a network by spending just a little more money, in general, you don't get more performance without paying for it in some way. That may mean a higher cost for the network, or it may mean a trade-off of some nonperformance feature.

If you are designing or specifying a network, it's very important to keep in mind that your goal is to come up with a system that will meet the needs that were determined for it during requirements analysis. This means coming up with a network that has a level of performance that matches the requirements and leaves some room for expansion. Unless you have an unlimited budget—and who does, right?—your objective is not "performance at any cost." It is to create a network that meets *all* of your users' needs, including balancing performance and nonperformance characteristics, as you will see shortly.

NOTE *Buyer beware. Companies are constantly coming out with the "latest and greatest" high-performance networking technologies. They usually try to sell their technologies by attempting to convince you that you just cannot live without this latest advance; that you "need" to upgrade—*

immediately, if not sooner! Well, it's simply not the case. For example, even though you can find Ethernet hardware that runs with a theoretical throughput of 10,000 megabits per second, there are many older networks that continue to work just fine at one 1/100th that speed—or even 1/1,000th!

Finally, remember that designing a network is usually not an irreversible, permanent decision. Networks can be upgraded and expanded. While it is prudent to build some slack into any network to allow for growth, it is not wise to spend too much time and money planning for the future when changes can be made later. This is especially true given that network hardware prices drop over time. Again, this is a matter of drawing an appropriate balance between future performance planning and budget.

Balancing Network Performance with Key Nonperformance Characteristics

We all know that performance is very important to any network. However, anyone putting together a network must also be concerned with many different nonperformance characteristics as well. Depending on the network, these can be just as essential to the users of the network as performance, and possibly even more critical. More than this, nonperformance issues often *trade off* against performance, and in fact, more often than not they have to be reduced to get performance to increase.

Before you can create a very high-performance network, you must understand the key nonperformance network characteristics that you may need to compromise. The following are a few of these issues:

Design and Implementation Cost Unless you have bottomless pockets, you must be concerned with the network's costs. As mentioned earlier, cost is the main trade-off with performance. Going faster usually costs more money.

Quality The quality of the network is a function of the quality of the components used and how they are installed. Quality is important because it impacts all of the other factors, such as reliability and ease of administration, as well as performance. Quality doesn't trade off *directly* with performance—you can design high-quality, high-performance networks—but it does *compete* with performance for resources in the budget. All else being equal, it costs a great deal more to implement a high-quality, high-performance network than a high-quality, low-speed one.

Standardization Network protocols and hardware can be designed to meet either universally accepted standards or nonstandard, proprietary ones. Standard designs are almost always preferable, because they make interoperability, upgrading, support, and training easier. Proprietary standards may include enhancements that improve performance, but may increase cost or make management more difficult.

Reliability This is related to several other issues, especially quality and performance. Faster networks aren't necessarily less reliable, but they are more difficult and expensive to make run reliably than slower ones.

Expandability and Upgradability It's very important to always plan for the future when creating a network. Higher-performance networks can be more difficult to expand, and they are certainly more expensive to expand. Once again, the matter of implementing a network with a capacity for future needs now, as opposed to upgrading later if it becomes necessary, is an important network design decision.

Ease of Administration and Maintenance Higher-performance networks require more work and resources to administer and maintain, and they are more likely to require troubleshooting than slower ones.

Premises and Utility Issues Implementation of high-speed networks may be limited by the physical premises or may have an impact on how they are laid out. Choosing a higher-speed option may require more infrastructure to be put in place, thus increasing cost. The classic example of this is choosing between wired and wireless options for a home or small office network. You can go much faster with wires, but do you really want to run them?

KEY CONCEPT While performance is one of the most important characteristics of any network, there are others that are equally important. In many cases, you must weigh the cost, quality, reliability, expandability, maintainability, and other attributes of a network against overall performance. The faster you want your network to go, the more difficult it is to ensure that these other attributes are kept at sufficiently high levels.

Performance Measurements: Speed, Bandwidth, Throughput, and Latency

A number of terms are commonly used to refer to various aspects of network performance. Some of them are quite similar to each other, and you will often see them used—and in many cases, misused or even *ab*used! I'll examine each of them to see how they are commonly used and what they really mean.

NOTE *More than just the issue of different terms related to performance, however, is the more important reality that there are multiple* facets *to performance. Depending on the application, the manner in which data is sent across the network may be more important than the raw speed at which it is transported. In particular, many multimedia applications require real-time performance; they need data sent in such a manner that it will be delivered steadily. For these purposes, raw speed isn't as important as* consistent *speed. This is an issue that is often not properly recognized.*

Speed

Speed is the most generic performance term used in networking. As such, it can mean just about *anything*. Most commonly, however, it refers to the *rated* or *nominal* speed of a particular networking technology. For example, Fast Ethernet has a nominal speed of 100 Mbps (megabits per second); for that reason, it is often called 100 Mbps Ethernet, or given a designation such as 100BASE-TX.

Rated speed is the biggest performance magic number in networking—you see it used to label hardware devices, and many people bandy the numbers about as if those numbers actually represented the network's real speed. The problem with using nominal speed ratings is that they are only *theoretical*, and as such, tell an incomplete story. No networking technology can run at its full-rated speed, and many run *substantially* below it, due to real-world performance factors.

Speed ratings such as 100 Mbps Ethernet are also often referred to as the *throughput* of a technology, even though the maximum theoretical speed of a technology is more analogous to bandwidth than throughput, and the two are not identical.

Bandwidth

Bandwidth is a widely used term that usually refers to the data-carrying capacity of a network or data-transmission medium. It indicates the maximum amount of data that can pass from one point to another in a unit of time. The term comes from the study of electromagnetic radiation, where it refers to the width of a band of frequencies used to carry data. It is usually given in a theoretical context, though not always.

Bandwidth is still used in these two senses: frequency bandwidth and data capacity. For example, radio frequencies are used for wireless technologies, and the bandwidth of such technologies can refer to how wide the radio frequency band is. More commonly, though, bandwidth refers to how much data can be sent down a network, and it is often used in relative terms. For example, for Internet access, a cable or xDSL connection is considered high-bandwidth access; using a regular analog modem is low-bandwidth access.

Throughput

Throughput is a measure of how much actual data can be sent per unit of time across a network, channel, or interface. While throughput can be a theoretical term like bandwidth, it is more often used in a practical sense—for example, to measure the amount of data actually sent across a network in the real world. Throughput is limited by bandwidth, or by rated speed: If an Ethernet network is rated at 100 Mbps, that's the absolute upper limit on throughput, even though you will normally get quite a bit less. So, you may see someone say that they are using a 100 Mbps Ethernet connection but getting throughput of, say, 71.9 Mbps on their network.

The terms *bandwidth* and *throughput* are often used interchangeably, even though they are really not exactly the same.

Latency

Latency is a very important, often overlooked term, which refers to the *timing* of data transfers on a communications channel or network. One important aspect of latency is how long it takes from the time a request for data is made until it starts to arrive. Another aspect is how much control a device has over the timing of the data that is sent, and whether the network can be arranged to allow for the consistent delivery of data over a period of time. Low latency is considered better than high latency.

Summary of Performance Measurements

As with all networking terms, there are no hard-and-fast rules; many people are rather loose with their use of terms relating to performance measurement. You will even see terms such as *throughput bandwidth, bandwidth throughput,* and other charming inventions from the department of redundancy department. More often, you will just see a lot of mishmashed term usage, and especially, spurious conclusions being drawn about what data streams a network can handle based on its rated speed. Making matters worse is that speed ratings are usually specified in bits per second, but throughput may be given in bits or bytes per second.

> **KEY CONCEPT** The three terms used most often to refer to the overall performance of a network are *speed, bandwidth,* and *throughput.* These are related and often used interchangeably, but are not identical. The term *speed* is the most generic and often refers to the rated or nominal speed of a networking technology. *Bandwidth* can mean either the width of a frequency band used by a technology or more generally, data capacity, where it's used as more of a theoretical measure. *Throughput* is a specific measure of how much data flows over a channel in a given period of time. It is usually a practical measurement.

In general, *speed, bandwidth,* and *throughput* get a lot of attention, while *latency* gets little. Yet latency considerations are very important for many real-time applications such as streaming audio and video and interactive gaming. In fact, they are often more important than raw bandwidth.

For example, suppose you move to a rural home, and your choices for Internet access are a regular 28.8 Kbps modem connection or fancy satellite Internet. The companies selling satellite connectivity call it "broadband" and advertise very high rated speeds—400 Kbps or more. They make a big deal about it being "over ten times as fast as dial-up," and they certainly charge a lot for this very high-tech service. This is a slam dunk, right?

Wrong. The satellite connection has high bandwidth, but very poor (high) latency due to the time it takes for the signals to travel to and from the satellite. It is definitely much better than the modem for downloading that nice little 150 MB patch from Microsoft. However, it is much *worse* than the modem for playing the latest online video game with your buddy over the Internet, because of the latency, or *lag,* in transmissions. Every move you make in your game will be delayed for over half a second as the signal bounces around between the satellite and the earth, making online gaming nearly impossible. Thus, whether satellite Internet is worth the extra money depends entirely on what you plan to use it for.

NOTE *An important issue closely related to latency is* quality of service, *a general term that refers (among other things) to the ability of networks to deliver necessary bandwidth and reliable data transfer for applications that need it. See the section "Quality of Service (QoS)" later in the chapter.*

> **KEY CONCEPT** Where bandwidth and throughput indicate how fast data moves across a network, *latency* describes the nature of how it is conveyed. It is most often used to describe the delay between the time that data is requested and the time when it arrives. A networking technology with very high throughput and bad (high) latency can be worse for some applications than one with relatively low throughput but good (low) latency.

Understanding Performance Measurement Units

People who make networking hardware, or write materials that try to tell you how to operate it, use many terms to describe performance, such as *throughput* and *bandwidth*. (These terms are explained in the previous section.) In addition, they also use several different *units* to measure performance. Unfortunately, these units are often used incorrectly, and they are also very similar to each other in name. Worse, they also have overlapping abbreviations, and lots of people use these abbreviations without making clear what the heck they are talking about. Isn't that great?

Bits and Bytes

The first issue is the infamous letter *B*. Or rather, I should say, the matter of the big *B* and the little *b*. By popular convention, the capitalized *B* is supposed to be used for byte, and the lowercase *b* for bit—this is the way these abbreviations are always used in this book.

NOTE *A byte is normally eight bits; sometimes the term* octet *is used instead. If you aren't familiar with these terms, refer to Chapter 4 for a primer on binary basics, where you will also find a discussion of the small controversy related to bytes and octets.*

Unfortunately, this convention is not followed strictly by everyone. As a result, you may on occasion see *b* being used to refer to bytes, and *B* used for bits. This *b* and *B* business causes a tremendous amount of confusion sometimes, with people mistaking bits for bytes and accidentally thinking that networks are running eight times faster or slower than they really are.

Bear in mind when looking at speed ratings that they are almost always given in terms of bits, not bytes. The 56K in a modem rating means 56,000 bits, not 56,000 bytes of theoretical transfer speed. (This is true even if someone calls it a "56K" modem.) Similarly, Fast Ethernet operates at 100 mega*bits* per second, not megabytes, and a 1.544 Mbps T1 link sends a theoretical maximum of 1,544,000 bits each second. This, at least, is usually pretty consistent.

When it comes to throughput measurements, however, both bits and bytes are used, so you have to be careful. Raw throughput values are normally given in bits per second, but many software applications report transfer rates in bytes per second, including many web browsers and FTP client programs. This often leads to users wondering why they are only getting one-eighth of their expected download or transfer speeds.

KEY CONCEPT In most cases in discussions of networking performance, the lowercase letter *b* refers to bits and the uppercase *B* to bytes. However, these conventions are not always universally followed, so context must be used to interpret a particular measurement.

The standard unit for bit throughput is the bit per second, which is commonly abbreviated bit/s, bps, or b/s. The byte unit is byte per second, abbreviated bytes/s, Bps or B/s—unless some cruel author decides to use a lowercase *b* just to confuse you! This means that the maximum theoretical throughput of 100BASE-TX (100 Mbps) Ethernet is about 12 MB/s. Where the context is unclear, it is better to spell out the unit as 100 Mbits/s or 12 Mbytes/s, which, of course, I try to do in this book.

You will also occasionally, especially when dealing in the realm of communications, see throughput measured in characters per second, or cps. In most computer systems (including PCs), each character takes up one byte, so cps is equivalent to bytes/s, B/s, or Bps.

Of course, most networking technologies don't move just a few bits and bytes around every second; they move, thousands, millions, or even billions. Thus, most speed ratings are not in bits per second, but rather *kilo*bits (Kb), *mega*bits (Mb), or *giga*bits (Gb) per second, and the same thing can be done for bytes. Thus, you find terms such as 100 Mbps Ethernet or 700 kb/s ADSL.

Here, you run into another problem: the existence of both decimal and binary versions of the terms *kilo*, *mega*, and *giga*. For example, the decimal form of the prefix for a million (mega) is 10^6 or 1,000,000, while the binary form is 2^{20} or 1,048,576. This differential of about 5 percent leads to all sorts of confusion. When you see these abbreviations, bear in mind that in networking, they almost always refer to the decimal form. Thus, 100 Mbps Ethernet is rated at 100,000,000 bits per second, not 104,857,600 bits per second.

KEY CONCEPT The unit most often used to express networking throughput is *bits per second* or *bps*. This term is often expressed in thousands, millions, or billions as *Kbps*, *Mbps*, or *Gbps*. It almost always uses the decimal, not binary, versions of the kilo, mega, or giga multipliers.

Baud

Finally, there's another term that you will encounter frequently in discussions of modems and some other technologies: the *baud*. Named for telegraphy pioneer Jean-Maurice-Émile Baudot (1845–1903), this unit measures the number of changes, or transitions, that occur in a signal in each second. So, if the signal changes from a one value to a zero value (or vice versa) one hundred times per second, that is a rate of 100 baud.

In the early days of very slow modems, each bit transition encoded a single bit of data. Thus, 300 baud modems sent a theoretical maximum of 300 bits per second of data. This led to people confusing the terms *baud* and *bits per second*—and the terms are still used interchangeably *far* too often. You will commonly hear people refer to a 28.8 Kbps modem, for example, as running at 28,800 baud.

But the two units are in fact not the same; one measures data (the throughput of a channel), and the other measures transitions (called the *signaling rate*). Modern modems use advanced modulation techniques that encode more than one bit of data into each transition. A 28,800 bps modem typically encodes nine bits into each transition; it runs at 3,200 baud, not 28,800 baud (the latter number being the product of 3,200 and 9). In fact, there's no way to operate a modem on a conventional phone line at 28,800 baud—it exceeds the frequency bandwidth of the phone line. That's the reason why advanced modulation is used to encode more data into each transition.

KEY CONCEPT The *baud* and *bps* units are often treated equivalently, but are not the same. *Baud* measures not the throughput of a network but its signaling rate, meaning the number of times that the signal changes value in each second. Since modern encoding and modulation techniques often encode either greater or less than one bit value into each such transition, the throughput and baud rate of network technologies are usually different.

Theoretical and Real-World Throughput, and Factors Affecting Network Performance

When assessing the performance of networks, keep in mind that there is always a difference between theoretical speed ratings and real-world throughput. If your network is set up well, this difference is relatively small but still significant. Otherwise, the difference can be extremely large. (Notice that the difference between theoretical and practical performance can never be negligible.)

There are many reasons for the difference between what a network or communications method is supposed to be able to do and what it actually can do. The reasons generally fall into three categories: normal network overhead, external performance limiters, and network configuration problems.

NOTE *There are many different ways of measuring and assessing performance. Synthetic benchmark programs are often used to measure throughput, and can produce impressive performance scores, which usually have little to do with how a network will actually operate. Such metrics are best used for comparison purposes by showing that one network or system is faster than another, rather than by paying too much attention to the actual number the metrics produce. Even when doing comparisons, however, caution is wise.*

Normal Network Overhead

Every network has some degree of normal network overhead, which guarantees that you will never be able to use all of the bandwidth of any connection for data. Take as an example 10 Mbps Ethernet. Sure, the line may be able to transmit 10,000,000 bits every second, but not all of those bits are data! Some are used to package and address the data—data can't just be thrown onto the network in raw form. Also, many of those bits are used for general overhead activities, and they deal with collisions on transmissions and other issues. There are natural inefficiencies in any networking technology.

Even beyond this, there are other overhead issues. Any network transaction involves a number of different hardware and software layers, and overhead exists at each of them, from the application and operating system down to the hardware. These overheads mean that you generally lose at least 20 percent of the rated speed of a local area network (LAN) technology off the top, and sometimes even more. For example, 7 Mbps user data throughput on a regular 10 Mbps Ethernet network is actually very good.

External Performance Limiters

There are external factors that limit the performance of a network. Important issues here include the ability of the hardware to process the data and also any bandwidth limitations that exist in the chain of data transmission between two nodes. Hardware issues most often show up with very fast networking technologies.

Consider a gigabit (1,000 Mbps) Ethernet connection between two regular PCs. In theory, this connection should allow the transmission of 1 GB of data every second. Even beyond the matter of overhead mentioned earlier, no regular PC is capable of pumping this much data per second. Only high-end servers have this capacity—and even they would have problems sustaining this unless they were doing nothing else. An older PC's hard disk probably can't even stream data fast enough to keep a 100 Mbps Ethernet connection busy. Thus, upgrading a 100 Mbps Ethernet card in an older machine to gigabit is not likely to help as much as you might expect.

Bandwidth limitations cause network throughput issues because the entire network can run only as fast as its slowest link. These bottlenecks create reduced performance. As a common example, suppose you have a cable modem connection to the Internet that is rated at 1 Mbps for downloads. It may be very fast most of the time, but if the website you are accessing is totally bogged down or it is having connectivity problems itself, you are not going to download from that site at 1 Mbps. In fact, your download probably won't even get close to that speed.

Finally, it's also important to remember that there are many technologies that simply do not always operate at a constant fixed speed, though they may change speeds based on physical network characteristics. A good example is an analog modem, which can vary greatly in performance depending on the quality of the line over which it operates.

Network Configuration Problems

The issues I mentioned earlier are usually ones that you cannot do anything about; they are just the nature of the networking beast. The third category of performance limiters, *misconfiguration*, is different. This refers to network slowdowns that occur because hardware or software has not been set up correctly. Poor cabling, misconfigured interface cards, or bad drivers can *seriously* reduce the performance of a network—by 90 percent or even more.

These problems can usually be corrected, but only if you are looking for them. Driver problems are particularly insidious because the natural tendency is for people to blame hardware when slowdowns occur. However, you cannot get the most of your hardware devices without proper software to run it. These issues are much more significant with bleeding-edge hardware than with established products, incidentally.

Also included in this category of issues are problems that occur due to poor design. For example, putting 30 busy workstations on a shared 10 Mbps Ethernet segment is likely to result in poor performance—using a switch would be much better. Another common mistake is not providing a "fatter pipe" (higher bandwidth connection) to servers in a client/server setup. These issues can be avoided or ameliorated by reconfiguring the network—or even better, by designing it properly in the first place, right?

Asymmetry

Bear in mind that many networking technologies, especially ones used for Internet access, are *asymmetric*, meaning that they offer much higher bandwidth in one direction than the other. Usually, this is arranged so that more bandwidth goes down to the user than from the user to the network, since most Internet users download far more than they upload. However, it's always important to find out if a speed rating is for both directions, or for only one direction, and if so, what the other direction's speed is. Common technologies with asymmetric performance include 56K modems, Asymmetric Digital Subscriber Line (ADSL), cable modems, and satellite Internet access. Beware, because the marketing people who sell these technologies will often try to hide the asymmetry of their services, usually highlighting only the bigger download figure and avoiding mention of the slower uploads.

Asymmetry can also have unexpected effects on network performance, because most communications, even if they seem unidirectional, are not. The most common case is when an Internet access technology has much higher download bandwidth than upload bandwidth. When using TCP/IP to download data, acknowledgments must be sent regularly. If the upstream bandwidth is too low, this may make it impossible to fully exploit the download bandwidth of the link.

KEY CONCEPT The theoretical rated speed of a network is never achieved in practice for a number of reasons. *Overhead* issues mean that not all of the possible capacity of a network can be used for data. *External factors* such as hardware bandwidth limitations restrict data input and output. *Configuration problems* can also greatly reduce real-world performance. Finally, it is important to remember that many technologies are asymmetric, offering higher speed in one direction than the other, and often, the larger number is the one that is advertised.

Simplex, Full-Duplex, and Half-Duplex Operation

Another aspect of performance that is worthy of some attention is the mode of operation of the network or connection. Obviously, whenever we connect together Device A and Device B, there must be some way for Device A to send to Device B and Device B to send to Device A. Many people don't realize, however, that networking technologies can differ in terms of how these two directions of communication are handled. Depending on how the network is set up and the characteristics of the technologies used, you may be able to improve performance through the selection of performance-enhancing modes.

Let's begin with a look at the three basic modes of operation that can exist for any network connection, communications channel, or interface.

Simplex Operation

In *simplex* operation, a network cable or communications channel can send information in only one direction; it's a one-way street. This may seem counter-intuitive: What's the point of communications that travel in only one direction? In fact, there are at least two different places in which simplex operation is encountered in modern networking.

The first is when two distinct channels are used for communication: one transmits from A to B and the other from B to A. This is surprisingly common, even though it isn't always obvious. For example, most, if not all, fiber-optic communication is simplex, meaning that it uses one strand to send data in each direction. But this may not be obvious if the pair of fiber strands are combined into one cable.

Simplex operation is also used in special types of technologies, especially ones that are asymmetric. For example, one type of satellite Internet access sends data over the satellite only for downloads, while a regular dial-up modem is used for upload to the service provider. In this case, both the satellite link and the dial-up connection are operating in a simplex mode.

Half-Duplex Operation

Technologies that employ *half-duplex* operation are capable of sending information in both directions between two nodes, but only one direction or the other can be utilized at a time. This is a fairly common mode of operation when there is only a single network medium (cable, radio frequency, and so forth) between devices.

While this term is often used to describe the behavior of a pair of devices, it can refer more generally to any number of connected devices that take turns transmitting information. For example, in conventional Ethernet networks, any device can transmit, but only one may do so at a time. For this reason, regular (unswitched) Ethernet networks are often said to be half-duplex, even though it may seem strange to describe a LAN that way.

Full-Duplex Operation

In *full-duplex* operation, a connection between two devices is capable of sending data in both directions simultaneously. Full-duplex channels can be constructed either as a pair of simplex links (as described earlier) or by using one channel that's designed to permit bidirectional simultaneous transmissions. A full-duplex link can connect only two devices, so many such links are required if multiple devices are to be connected together.

NOTE *The term* full-duplex *is somewhat redundant;* duplex *would suffice, but everyone still says* full-duplex *(likely, to differentiate this mode from* half-duplex*).*

Of these three options, full-duplex is obviously the one that yields the highest performance. Full-duplex operation doubles the theoretical bandwidth of the connection. If a link normally runs at 1 Mbps but can work in full-duplex mode, it really has 2 Mbps of bandwidth (1 Mbps in each direction). Remember the key word *theoretical*, however—you do not really get double the performance in real life, because communications usually do not involve sending a lot of data in both directions at once. However, you certainly get better throughput than you do in a half-duplex mode.

In some cases, the mode of operation is a function of the technology and cannot be changed. In others, however, full-duplex mode is a matter of the correct hardware settings, and also whether the software supports full-duplex operation. Thus, getting higher performance in this area is sometimes simply a matter of ensuring proper configuration.

Full-duplex operation has been pretty much taken for granted in communications for years. The more interesting development has been the rise in the significance of full-duplex operation for local area networking. Traditionally, LANs have always used half-duplex operation on a shared access medium. As the use of switches has increased, thereby allowing dedicated bandwidth to each computer, full-duplex operation has become very popular. Full-duplex operation in Ethernet not only allows the simultaneous transmission of data in both directions, but also eliminates contention for the formerly shared access medium—thus, no more collisions. The combination of these two effects improves performance, sometimes substantially.

KEY CONCEPT There are three basic operating modes that describe how data is sent between connected devices on a network. In a *simplex* operation, data can flow in only one direction between two devices. *Half-duplex* networks allow any device to transmit, but only one may do so at a time. *Full-duplex* operation means two attached devices can each transmit and receive simultaneously. The latter offers the greatest potential performance, because forcing one device to wait for another before sending data does not decrease throughput.

Quality of Service (QoS)

In my discussion of common network performance measurements earlier in this chapter, I mentioned that there are many different aspects to network performance. I also introduced the concept of *latency*, which measures how long it takes for data to travel across a network. Latency is one important part of a larger issue in networking that is sometimes called *quality of service* or *QoS*.

The inherent nature of most networking technologies is that they are more concerned with pumping data from one place to another as fast as possible than they are with how the data is sent. For example, the Internet is designed on top of the Internet Protocol (IP), a packet-switching technology (described in Chapter 1) that is designed to get packets from point A to point B in the most effective way, without requiring the user to have any knowledge about what route will be taken. In fact, some packets in the same data stream may be sent along different routes. Packets may be stored for a while before being forwarded to their destination, or even dropped and retransmitted.

For most applications, such as simple file or message transfers, this is perfectly fine. However, there are applications for which this sort of service represents low quality. In these cases, the nature of how the data is delivered is more important than merely how fast it is, and there is a need for technologies or protocols that offer QoS. This general term can encompass a number of related features such as the following:

Bandwidth Reservation The ability to reserve a portion of bandwidth in a network or interface for a period of time so that two devices can count on having that bandwidth for a particular operation. This is used for multimedia applications for which data must be streamed in real time, and packet rerouting and retransmission would result in problems. This is also called *resource reservation.*

Latency Management A feature that limits the latency between two devices in any data transfer to a known value.

Traffic Prioritization In conventional networks, all packets are created equal. A useful QoS feature is the ability to handle packets so that more important connections receive priority over less important ones.

Traffic Shaping This refers to the use of buffers and limits, both of which restrict traffic across a connection to a value below a predetermined maximum.

Network Congestion Avoidance This QoS feature refers to monitoring particular connections in a network and rerouting data when a particular part of the network is becoming congested.

So, in essence, QoS in the networking context is analogous to QoS in the real world. It is the difference between getting take-out and sit-down service at a nice French restaurant—both cure the hunger pangs, but they meet very different needs. Some applications, especially multimedia applications such as voice, music, and video, are time dependent and require a constant flow of information more than raw bandwidth.

KEY CONCEPT The generic term *quality of service (QoS)* describes the characteristics of how data is transmitted between devices, rather than how quickly it is sent. QoS features seek to provide more predictable streams of data rather than faster ones. Examples of such features include bandwidth reservation, latency minimums, traffic prioritization and shaping, and congestion limitation. QoS is more important for specialty applications, such as multimedia, than for routine applications, such as those that transfer files or messages.

To support QoS requirements, many newer technologies have been developed or enhanced to add QoS features to them. This includes the ability to support *isochronous transmissions* that can reserve a specific amount of bandwidth over time to support applications that must send data in real time. One technology that has received a lot of attention for its QoS features is Asynchronous Transfer Mode (ATM). ATM is designed to support traffic-management features that are not generally available on networks that haven't been optimized to provide QoS features (such as Ethernet).

QoS has become a big buzzword lately. By itself, this term conveys about as much useful information about what the technology offers as being told that it is high performance. You have to dig past the marketing-speak and find out exactly what QoS features are being offered.

3

NETWORK STANDARDS AND STANDARDS ORGANIZATIONS

You can't study networking and its related technologies without very quickly encountering a whole host of standards that are related to the subject, as well as the organizations that create these standards. Network standards facilitate the interoperability of network technologies and are extremely important. It may be an exaggeration to say that networking would not exist without standards, but it isn't an exaggeration to say that networking *as we know it* would not exist without them. Networks are literally everywhere, and every hardware device or protocol is governed by at least one standard and usually many.

In this chapter, I briefly examine the often overlooked subject of network standards and standards organizations. I begin with a background discussion of why standards are important, highlighting the differences between proprietary, de facto, and open standards. I give an overview of networking standards in general terms and then describe the most important international standards organizations and industry groups related to networking. I then describe the structure of the organizations responsible for

Internet standards, including the registration authorities and registries that manage resources such as addresses, domain names, and protocol values. I conclude with a discussion of the Request for Comment (RFC) process used for creating Internet standards.

Proprietary, Open, and De Facto Standards

Why are standards important? An old saw in the computer world says, "The beauty of standards is that there are so many to choose from." This little joke reflects the frustration that technicians often feel at the thousands of standards that are found in the industry. Aside from differing in terms of content—what technologies and protocols they describe—standards also often differ in terms of their type and how they came about. In fact, part of the reason why there are sometimes so many to choose from in a particular area is *because* of how they come about.

Proprietary Standards

In the early days of computing, many people didn't quite understand just how important universal standards were. Most companies were run by skilled inventors, who came up with great ideas for new technologies, but who weren't particularly interested in sharing them. It wasn't considered a smart business move to share information about new inventions with other companies—the competition! Oh sure, companies believed that standards were important, but they thought it was even more important that *they* be the ones to control those standards.

For example, imagine that it's 1985, and I have just come up with a great networking technology, which I have incorporated into a fancy new local area networking (LAN) product called SooperDooperNet. SooperDooperNet is *my* product. I have patents on the technology, I control its design and manufacture, and I sure as heck don't tell anyone else how it works, because if I did, someone would copy me.

I could sell interface cards, cables, and accessories for SooperDooperNet, and companies that wanted to use it could install the cards in all of their PCs and be assured that those computers would be able to talk to each other. This solves the interoperability problem for this company by creating a "SooperDooperNet standard." This would be an example of a *proprietary* standard—it's owned by one company or person.

The problem with proprietary standards is that other companies are excluded from the standard development process, and therefore have little incentive to cooperate with the standard owner. In fact, just the opposite: They have a strong motivation to develop a competing proprietary standard, even if it doesn't improve on the existing one.

So when my competition sees what I am doing, he is not going to also create network interface cards that can work with SooperDooperNet, which would require paying me a royalty. Instead, he is going to develop a new line of networking hardware called MegaAwesomeNet, which is very similar to SooperDooperNet in operation but uses different connectors, cable, and logic. He, too, will try to sell bunches of cards and cables to my customers.

The problem here is that the market ends up with different companies using different products that don't work together. If you install SooperDooperNet, you *have* to come to me for any upgrades or changes—you have no choice. Worse, what happens if Acme Manufacturing, which has 50 PCs running SooperDooperNet, merges with Emca Manufacturing, which has 40 PCs running MegaAwesomeNet? The IT people have a problem. Sure, there would be ways to solve it, but wouldn't everyone be better off avoiding these difficulties in the first place? And how could you create something like the Internet if everyone's networks use different "standards"?

Open Standards

Eventually, companies learned that they would be better off with standards that everyone agreed on. This is particularly true of networking, where devices need to talk to each other. If many companies get together and agree to cooperate, they can create an *open standard* instead of a bunch of proprietary ones. The name is rather self-explanatory; rather than being the closely guarded secret of one organization, an open standard is available to anyone who is interested in using it.

One key to the success of an open standard is a steering organization to promote it. Usually, a neutral, nonprofit trade association or working group is established to develop the standard, and the various for-profit hardware and software companies join this group and support it financially. These groups also work with standards approval bodies like the International Telecommunication Union (ITU) and International Organization for Standardization (ISO) to gain acceptance for their standards. These and other standards organizations are described in the "International Networking Standards Organizations" section later in this chapter.

Of course, the companies aren't doing this just to be nice to their customers. In creating open standards, they split the market-share pie among them, but they make the pie grow much larger by attracting more customers. Customers like open standards more than proprietary ones, because those standards give them more choices and increase their ability to interact with other companies, troubleshoot problems, hire skilled workers, and expand in the future. As for the companies, they still compete with their specific offerings, so it's not like they all end up making the same products. For all of these reasons, open standards are now far more common than proprietary ones.

However, the process involved in creating these standards is often a difficult one. In some cases, the standards organization will draft the standard from the ground up, but in others, it may select one technology as the basis for the standard from several that are submitted in what is commonly called a "technology bake-off." Thus, many different companies may come to the table with different approaches, each of them vying for selection as the standard for use by the group. Politics can cause groups to get bogged down for years fighting over various options, or even to split into multiple groups. Good examples are what occurred in the conflict between supporters of 100VG-AnyLAN and Fast Ethernet, and the problems with standards politics that have plagued the world of powerline networking.

Furthermore, there are still some companies that believe strongly in proprietary standards, because they really want to control and direct the market. One of the most famous (infamous) in this regard is Sony, a company that makes excellent hardware but frequently refuses to accept established standards. For this reason, some people avoid Sony's products, even though they are good, because they want to stick to industry standards.

De Facto Standards

This brings me to the third type of standard that is often seen in the computer world: the *de facto standard*. "De facto" is Latin for "in fact." A de facto standard is one that is used as a universal standard just because, over time, it has been widely used, and not because the standard was developed and approved by a standards committee.

A good example of a de facto standard is the AT command set used by modems. Virtually all modems use it, but this acceptance didn't result from an industry group agreeing to adopt and deploy it. Rather, it was developed unilaterally by Hayes, the pioneering modem company, and then adopted by virtually every other modem maker until it became a standard.

One reason why proprietary standards are still sometimes seen is that some companies want to produce a standard that will become so universally used that it becomes the de facto standard, thus giving them a leadership position in that market. Again, in my estimation, Sony falls into this category—the developers often want to do things their way and create proprietary standards that they try to promote using their powerful market presence.

Sometimes this succeeds, but often it does not, resulting in a fragmented market of incompatible products. An excellent example is when Sony created a new format for a digital camera's flash memory (the Memory Stick) rather than using the CompactFlash format used by other camera manufacturers. The end result was that not everyone used memory sticks as Sony had hoped, and there were now two incompatible standards that increased confusion and yielded no real benefit to the customer.

KEY CONCEPT Networking standards can be classified as *proprietary*, *open*, or *de facto*. Proprietary standards are owned by one particular organization. If that organization has sufficient market clout and the industry lacks alternatives to its standard, it may be adopted by the whole industry, becoming a de facto standard. Usually, however, differing proprietary standards compete with each other, resulting in a fragmented market. In contrast, open standards are not owned by anyone—they are created by neutral organizations to ensure that compatible products can be designed and developed by many different companies. This makes life easier for the customer and also promotes the market as a whole.

Networking Standards

All networking technologies have standards associated with them. These are usually highly technical documents, and they often presume that the reader has a fair bit of knowledge about networking. If you aren't an expert, you will probably have some difficulty understanding networking standards.

In fact, many technologies have quite a number of standards associated with them. A networking technology may have more than one standard for any or all of the following reasons:

- The original standard has been revised or updated.
- The technology is sufficiently complex that it needs to be described in more than one document.
- The technology borrows from or builds on documents used in related technologies.
- More than one organization has been involved in developing the technology.

Standards documents created in the United States are usually developed in English, but are also routinely translated into other languages. European standards are often published simultaneously in English, French, German, and perhaps other languages as well.

Today, virtually all networking standards are open standards, administered by a standards organization or industry group. As I explained in the previous section, open standards are more popular than proprietary ones in the computer industry, and that's especially true when it comes to networking. In fact, the few technologies for which there is no universally accepted open standard have been losing ground to those with open standards, particularly in the areas of wireless LANs and home networking. This pretty much proves how important an open process really is.

NOTE *You'll find discussions of various standards throughout this book. These can usually be found in an overview chapter introducing each technology type, though the discussions of more complex protocols include a section discussing relevant standards.*

International Networking Standards Organizations

The rise of open standards has been a great boon to customers of computer and networking products, as well as to the manufacturers that sell to them. In order to facilitate the development of open standards, however, we need organizations that will coordinate the creation and publishing of these documents. Generally, these are nonprofit organizations that specifically take a neutral stance regarding technologies and work for the betterment of the industry as a whole.

Here is a selective list of some of the standards organizations that you are likely to encounter when reading about networking and the Internet:

International Organization for Standardization (ISO) Probably the biggest standards organization in the world, the ISO is really a federation of standards organizations from dozens of nations. In the networking world, the ISO is best known for its OSI Reference Model, which is discussed in Part I-2 of this book.

NOTE *The shortened name of the International Organization for Standardization is indeed ISO, not IOS, as you might imagine. In fact, it is not an acronym at all. Since the full name of the body differs from one language the next, any acronym for that name would differ as well. Instead, the organization chose the name ISO from the Greek word* isos, *meaning equal. Many people, especially in the United States, think ISO is short for International Standards Organization, but this is incorrect.*

American National Standards Institute (ANSI) ANSI is the main organization responsible for coordinating and publishing computer and information technology standards in the United States. Although many people think that this organization develops and maintains standards, it does neither. Instead, it oversees and accredits the organizations that actually create the standards, qualifying them as *Standards Developing Organizations* or *SDOs.* ANSI also publishes the standards documents created by the SDOs and serves as the United States' representative to the ISO.

Information Technology Industry Council (ITIC) ITIC is a group of several dozen companies in the information technology (computer) industry. ITIC is the SDO approved by ANSI to develop and process standards related to many computer-related topics. It was formerly known as the *Computer and Business Equipment Manufacturers Association (CBEMA).*

National Committee for Information Technology (NCITS) NCITS is a committee established by the ITIC to develop and maintain standards related to the information-technology world. NCITS was formerly known by the name *Accredited Standards Committee X3, Information Technology*, or more commonly, just *X3.* It maintains several subcommittees that develop and maintain standards for various technical subjects.

Institute of Electrical and Electronics Engineers (IEEE) The IEEE (pronounced "eye-triple-ee") is a well-known professional organization for those in the electrical or electronics fields, including computers and networking. IEEE's main claim to fame in the networking industry is the IEEE 802 Project, which encompasses many popular networking technologies, including Ethernet.

Electronic Industries Alliance (EIA) The EIA is an international industry association that is best known for publishing electrical wiring and transmission standards.

Telecommunications Industry Association (TIA) The TIA is the communications sector of the EIA, and it is responsible for developing communications standards. Since communications, wiring, and transmission are all related, and since the TIA and EIA organizations are also related, standards produced by the EIA or TIA are often labeled with the combined prefixes EIA/TIA or TIA/EIA.

International Telecommunication Union—Telecommunication Standardization Sector (ITU-T) ITU-T is another large international body that develops standards for the telecommunications industry. The ITU-T was formerly named the International Telephone and Telegraph Consultative Committee (CCITT; the abbreviation comes from the French version of the organization's name: *Comité Consultatif International Téléphonique et Télégraphique*).

European Telecommunications Standards Institute (ETSI) An organization with members from dozens of countries both within and outside Europe that is dedicated to developing telecommunications standards for the European market (and elsewhere). ETSI is known for, among other things, regulating the use of radio bandwidth in Europe and developing standards such as HiperLAN.

Many of these organizations do not actually develop the various standards. Generally, these are oversight organizations—high-level management, if you will—that work with many other smaller groups who actually develop the standards. Also, in many cases, a particular standard may be published by more than one standards organization, so it may be labeled with more than one name.

NOTE *The set of related organizations responsible for creating Internet standards is not shown in this list because I have elected to cover them in two dedicated sections later in this chapter, on Internet standards organizations and registration authorities.*

KEY CONCEPT There are a number of well-known international organizations that play important roles in the development of open networking standards. Some of the most important of these are ISO, ANSI, ITIC, IEEE, EIA/TIA, ITU-T, and ETSI. These are oversight organizations, responsible for overall management of the standards development process, rather than for the particulars of creating individual standards.

Networking Industry Groups

While most open standards are coordinated and published by a small number of large, often international, standards organizations, these are not the only groups involved in the development of standards for networking and Internet technologies. Many different networking *industry groups* play an important role in the standard creation process.

Networking industry groups differ in a few ways from standards organizations. They are typically dedicated to the promotion of a specific technology, whereas standards organizations are more generic and oversee hundreds of different ones. Industry groups are also generally smaller than standards organizations, with members drawn primarily from the field of developers and manufacturers that create products for the particular technology the group promotes.

Perhaps most important, industry groups often actually write and maintain the standards, whereas standards organizations generally act as supervisors who ensure that the standards are clear enough to be implemented. Some industry groups, however, are concerned only with marketing and promotion activities.

Obviously, these industry groups work closely together with the standards organizations. In some cases, they may even be part of the same overall organization, and all of the different groups are related in some way. For example, the IEEE 802 Project consists of a number of working groups charged with maintaining and developing specific technology standards, which the larger IEEE organization approves and publishes.

One of these working groups is the 802.11 working group, which develops wireless Ethernet technology. At the same time that this group does its thing, there is an industry group called the *Wireless Ethernet Compatibility Alliance (WECA)*. This group works to ensure the cross-vendor compatibility of 802.11b wireless networking hardware and software.

Other industry groups are formed specifically to develop independent standards that are not approved through a formal standardization process. Examples include groups such as HomePNA, IrDA, and HomeRF.

One of the problems with these groups is that they usually do not make their standards open to the public. This is undoubtedly due to some sort of security concern or desire to keep the inner workings of their technology secret. Unfortunately for these groups, this policy harms the ability of regular people to learn how their technologies work.

NOTE *As an example of what I mean about these closed standards, I can point to my own experience in writing this and other reference works. I was almost always unable to obtain specifications from most of the private industry groups. They either refused to allow me to get the document at all or wanted to charge me a great deal of money for the privilege (well into the thousands of dollars in some cases). In doing this, these groups harm their own cause, thereby making it more difficult for those interested in their technologies to learn about them. This is another key advantage of having open standards managed by public organizations such as ANSI or the IEEE.*

Internet Standards Organizations (ISOC, IAB, IESG, IETF, IRSG, and IRTF)

High-quality, widely accepted open standards become more important as the number of people that use a network grows. The largest network of all is of course the *Internet*, which connects millions of people on thousands of individual networks into a globe-spanning internetwork. The Internet has revolutionized not only networking and computing, but also communication, business, and even society as a whole. One of the critical factors in the success of the Internet has been its development using open standards.

Of course, nobody sat down one day and said, “Hey, let’s create the Internet!” (No, not even Al Gore.) It began as a small research network, and was developed over time concurrently with the technology set that implemented it: TCP/IP. At first, a relatively small organization was sufficient for managing the development of Internet standards and overseeing its activities, but as the Internet continued to grow, this organization became inadequate. Eventually, a more formalized structure of organizations was required in order to manage the Internet development process and other activities. This ensured the continued success and growth of the Internet and the TCP/IP technologies that powered it.

Today, six organizations are responsible for the development of the Internet’s architecture, standards and policies, and related activities. They are closely related, with certain organizations responsible for overseeing others. These organizations perform many tasks and can be somewhat confusing to understand, since many have similar-sounding names and responsibilities. Therefore, I will concentrate mostly on their role in the development of Internet standards, since that is the primary interest in this discussion.

Here are brief descriptions, rather simplified, of the key Internet standards organizations:

Internet Society (ISOC) A professional society responsible for general, high-level activities related to the management, development, and promotion of the Internet. ISOC has thousands of individual and organizational members that engage in activities such as research, education, public policy development, and standardization.

It is responsible for providing financial and administrative support to the other organizations listed in this chapter. From the standpoint of standards development, ISOC's key role is its responsibility for oversight of the IAB.

Internet Architecture Board (IAB) Formerly the *Internet Activities Board*, the IAB is charged with the overall management of the development of Internet standards. It makes "big-picture" policy decisions related to how Internet technologies and structures should work. This ensures that various standardization efforts are coordinated and consistent with overall development of the Internet. It is responsible for publishing Internet standards (RFCs), as described in the "Internet Standards and the Request for Comment (RFC) Process" section at the end of this chapter. It advises the ISOC and oversees the IETF and IRTF; it also acts as an appeals body for complaints about the standardization activities performed by the IETF. The charter of the IAB is described in RFC 2850.

Internet Engineering Task Force (IETF) The IETF focuses on issues related to the development of current Internet and TCP/IP technologies. It is divided into a number of *working groups*, each of which is responsible for developing standards and technologies in a particular area, such as routing or security. Each area is managed by an *area director*, who serves on the IESG. The IETF is overseen directly by the IESG and in turn by the IAB; it is described in RFC 3160.

Internet Engineering Steering Group (IESG) The IESG is directly responsible for managing the IETF and the Internet standards development process. It consists of each of the IETF area directors, who make final decisions about the approval of proposed standards, and works to resolve any issues that may arise in the standardization process. The IESG is technically considered part of the IETF and is also described in RFC 3160.

Internet Research Task Force (IRTF) Where the IETF is focused primarily on short-term development issues, the IRTF is responsible for longer-term research related to the Internet and TCP/IP technologies. It is a much smaller organization than the IETF, consisting of a set of *research groups*, which are analogous to the IETF's working groups. The IRTF is overseen by the IRSG and IAB. It is described in RFC 2014.

Internet Research Steering Group (IRSG) The IRSG manages the IRTF in a similar way to how the IESG manages the IETF. It consists of the chairs of each of the IRTF research groups and works with the chair of the whole IRTF to make appropriate decisions on research activities. It is also discussed in RFC 2014.

Figure 3-1 shows the relationship between the Internet standards associations. The ISOC oversees the IAB, which in turn directs the IETF and IRTF. The IETF develops current Internet and TCP/IP standards and is headed by the IESG, which manages IETF working groups. The IRTF is the IETF's research counterpart, containing *research groups* led by the IRSG.

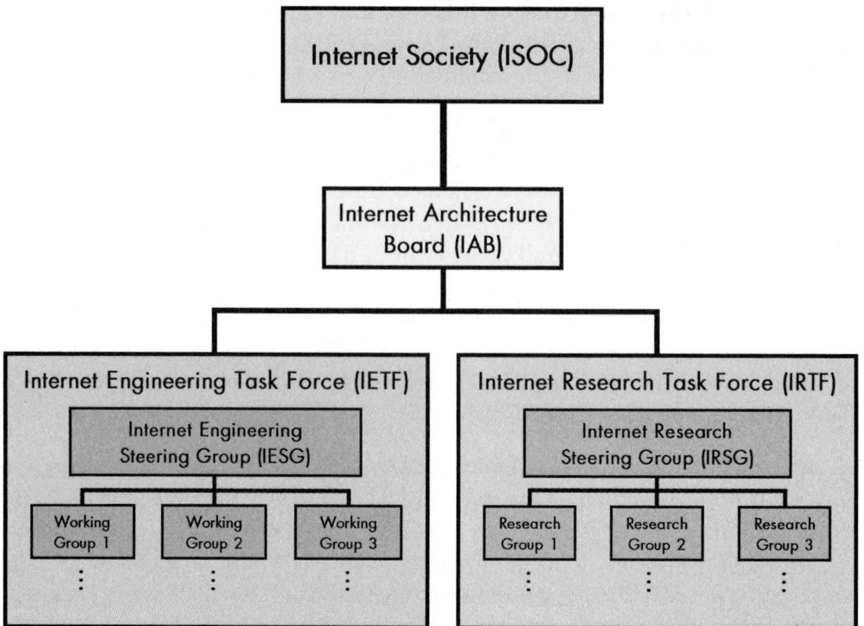

Figure 3-1: Internet standards organizations *The ISOC is responsible for overseeing the IAB, which in turn is responsible for the two task forces, the IETF and IRTF, which are headed by the IESG and IRSG, respectively.*

Of these organizations, the IETF is the one that you will most often hear referenced, because it is directly responsible for the development of the majority of Internet standards. Thus, whenever I mention Internet standards development efforts in this book, I'm referring to the IETF as the organization doing the work. This is, of course, a bit of an oversimplification, since all of these organizations play a role in the standards development process, as described later in this chapter, in the discussion of the RFC process.

Many of these organizations are responsible for a great deal more than just standards development. This is especially true of the ISOC, for which standardization is just one of many activities. The IAB also performs a number of functions not strictly associated with standards development, including managing the assignment of protocol values done by the Internet Assigned Numbers Authority and acting as a liaison between the Internet standards organizations and other standards bodies.

> **KEY CONCEPT** A group of related organizations is responsible for the development of TCP/IP standards and Internet technologies. The *Internet Society (ISOC)* has overall responsibility for many Internet activities, including standards development. It oversees the *Internet Architecture Board (IAB)*, which makes high-level decisions about Internet technology development. Most of the actual work of creating current Internet standards is performed by the *Internet Engineering Task Force (IETF)*, which is managed by the *Internet Engineering Steering Group (IESG)*. Longer-term research is done by the IETF's sibling organization, the *Internet Research Task Force (IRTF)*, which is led by the *Internet Research Steering Group (IRSG)*.

Internet Registration Authorities and Registries (IANA, ICANN, APNIC, ARIN, LACNIC, and RIPE NCC)

The success of the global Internet relies on the development of universally accepted standards for protocols and other technologies. Internet standards organizations such as the IETF are thus critically important. They manage the standards development process, which ensures that everyone agrees on how to create hardware and software that will work together to communicate worldwide.

While the need to standardize protocols seems obvious, there are a couple of other aspects to Internet standardization that are equally important but perhaps not quite as well understood:

Parameter Standardization Most protocols rely on the use of parameters that control how they function. As just two of many, many examples, the IP has a set of numbers that define different IP options, and the Address Resolution Protocol (ARP) has an Operation Code field that can take on many different values. Just as it is essential for devices to agree on what protocols to use, so they must also agree on what parameters to use for those protocols, if communication is to be successful.

Global Resource Allocation and Identifier Uniqueness There are a number of resources that are used on the Internet that must be allocated from a fixed set of values. Uniqueness in assignment is essential for these values. The most obvious example is that each TCP/IP host must have a unique IP address. Another important example is ensuring that only one organization uses a given Domain Name System (DNS) domain name. If two devices have the same IP address or two organizations try to use the same domain name, the results would be unpredictable, but almost certainly bad!

In both of these cases, some sort of centralized organization is required. We need a group to take responsibility for managing parameters. It must ensure that everyone uses the same parameters, and the same protocols. We also need to coordinate the assignment of identifiers such as addresses and names. This ensures that the identifiers are created and allocated in a way that is acceptable to all. In the world of the Internet, these are sometimes called *management authorities* or *registration authorities.*

Internet Centralized Registration Authorities

The organization originally responsible for managing parameters and identifiers was the Internet Assigned Numbers Authority (IANA). Amazingly, while the name makes it sound like the IANA was a huge bureaucracy, it was effectively one man: Jonathan B. (Jon) Postel, one of the most important pioneers of Internet and TCP/IP technologies. Jon Postel ran IANA until his untimely death in 1998.

IANA was originally charged with managing which IP address blocks had been assigned to different companies and groups, and it maintained lists of periodically published Internet parameters such as UDP and TCP port numbers. It also was in charge of the registrations of DNS domain names, which were more directly handled by the Internet Network Information Center (InterNIC), a service managed by the United States government. Network Solutions, Inc. (NSI) was later granted the contract to manage the InterNIC and was eventually purchased by VeriSign.

As the Internet continued to grow, an effort commenced in the mid-1990s to define a new organization that would be responsible for the central registration of Internet addresses and names. This took the form of a new private, nonprofit company called the Internet Corporation for Assigned Names and Numbers (ICANN). ICANN is officially charged with all of the centralized registration tasks I have mentioned so far, including IP address assignment, DNS domain name assignment, and protocol parameters management.

In a simpler world, this development would have meant that ICANN would have replaced IANA, which would no longer exist. Instead, ICANN kept IANA around, leaving that organization in charge of overseeing IP address registration and Internet parameters. ICANN is now in charge of IANA, so both organizations are responsible for IP addresses and parameters. This often leads to confusion, and to make things worse, it is common to see IANA and ICANN mentioned in conjunction as IANA/ICANN or ICANN/IANA.

KEY CONCEPT Internet registration authorities are centralized organizations responsible for coordinating protocol parameters and globally assigned resources such as IP addresses. The first such organization was the *Internet Assigned Numbers Authority (IANA)*, which was initially in charge of IP address assignment, DNS domain name management, and protocol parameters. Today, the *Internet Corporation for Assigned Names and Numbers (ICANN)* has overall responsibility for these activities; the IANA operates under the auspices of ICANN and is still responsible for IP address assignment and parameter coordination.

Modern Hierarchy of Registration Authorities

In the original "classful" IP addressing scheme, addresses were assigned to organizations directly by IANA in address blocks: Class A, Class B, and Class C. Today, a hierarchical, classless addressing system called *Classless Inter-Domain Routing (CIDR)* is used instead. Address assignment in CIDR involves the hierarchical allocation of blocks of addresses, starting with large blocks that are given to big organizations, which split them to assign to smaller groups. (Much more detail on these methods can be found in Chapters 16 through 20, which cover IP addressing.)

IANA, as the organization in charge of all IP addresses, assigns the largest blocks of addresses to *regional Internet registries (RIRs)* that are responsible for further allocation activities. Each RIR manages IP addresses and other Internet number resources (such as autonomous system numbers) for a particular region. The four regional registries are as follows:

Asia Pacific Network Information Centre (APNIC) Covers the Asia/Pacific region.

American Registry for Internet Numbers (ARIN) Manages North America, part of the Caribbean, and subequatorial Africa.

Latin American and Caribbean Internet Addresses Registry (LACNIC) Responsible for Latin America and part of the Caribbean.

Réseaux IP Européens Network Coordination Center (RIPE NCC) Takes care of Europe, the Middle East, Central Asia, and Africa north of the equator.

Each registry may assign address blocks to Internet service providers (ISPs) directly or further delegate them to *national Internet registries* or smaller *local Internet registries.* (See Chapter 16, which covers IP address allocation issues, for more details.)

Name registration has changed over the last several years. It is no longer part of IANA's responsibilities, and ICANN has opened up the name registration business, so it is no longer the province of a single organization such as InterNIC/NSI/VeriSign. Now, many different accredited registrars can be used for name registration in many of the popular top-level domains. This is discussed in Chapter 54, which covers DNS public registration. The complete list of documents containing Internet and TCP/IP parameters can be found on the IANA's website at http://www.iana.org/numbers.html.

Internet Standards and the Request for Comment (RFC) Process

The precursors of the modern Internet were diminutive networks developed and run by a small group of computer scientists and engineers. These technologists knew that developing open, widely adopted standards would be essential to the eventual growth of the Internet and the TCP/IP protocol suite. But there was no formalized standards development mechanism back then.

Standardization was achieved largely through building consensus through discussion about new technologies and protocols. If someone had a proposal for a new protocol or technology, or an idea for a change to an existing one, that person would create a memorandum describing it and circulate it to others. Since the goal was to solicit comments on the proposal, these memos were called *Requests for Comments (RFCs).* Not all RFCs described formalized standards; many were just descriptive documents, clarifications, or contained miscellaneous information.

NOTE *The documents defining early standards were originally called* Internet Engineering Notes (IENs) *before they were called RFCs.*

Today, of course, the Internet is enormous, and there is an official structure of Internet standards organizations that is responsible for creating new Internet and TCP/IP standards. Due to the many thousands of people who play an active role in developing Internet technologies, an informal system where anyone could just write an RFC would lead to chaos. Thus, Internet and TCP/IP standards are still called RFCs, but the process of creating one is much more formal and organized today.

The IETF is the standards body that is most directly responsible for the creation of Internet standards. The IETF's working groups, overseen by the IESG and the IAB, develop new protocols and technologies continuously, and these developments are formalized in RFCs.

The office of the RFC Editor handles the publishing of RFCs. For nearly 30 years, beginning in 1969, the RFC Editor was Internet pioneer Jon Postel. After his death in 1998, the function was assigned to the networking division of the USC Information Sciences Institute (ISI), where Jon Postel was once director. The function of the RFC Editor is to publish and archive RFCs, and to maintain an online repository of these documents so that they can be accessed and used by the Internet community.

The open and free access to RFCs has greatly contributed to the Internet's success. Even today, if you consider that standards bodies charge thousands of dollars for access to a single standard, the ability to log on and immediately retrieve any of the thousands of RFCs is noteworthy.

NOTE *An up-to-date list of RFCs with hyperlinks to each document (except for some of the early ones) can be found at the office of the RFC Editor. Go to http://www.rfc-editor.org/rfc-index.html.*

RFC Categories

As I mentioned, not all RFCs are official Internet standards. This is important to remember. Each RFC has a *category* or *status* associated with it that indicates its disposition:

Proposed Standard/Draft Standard/Standard These documents describe technologies that are on the standards track. That means they are either already formally approved as standards, or they are likely to become standards in the future. In many cases, the document is just listed as "standards track," rather than one of those three precise labels.

Best Current Practice A document providing guideline information or recommendations from the IETF that is not a formal standard.

Informational A document that provides general information or commentary.

Experimental A proposal for an experimental standard that is not on the standards track. In some cases, protocols or proposed changes to existing protocols that are not accepted as formal standards are changed to experimental status.

Historic Former standards that have been made obsolete.

The Internet Standardization Process

Before a proposal will be considered for the Internet standardization process, it must be published as an *Internet Draft (ID)*. The IETF publishes a set of guidelines that specify how IDs must be created and submitted. Members of working groups within the IETF who are involved in specific projects write most IDs. However, because the standards process is open, any member of the public can independently submit a standard for review by creating an ID for consideration by the IETF and IESG. IDs are usually revised many times based on feedback from other working groups within the IETF.

If an ID has been reviewed and is considered valuable, well understood, and stable (meaning that it is not being rapidly updated with new revisions), it may become a candidate for standardization. The IESG can place the ID on the Internet standards track by changing its status to *proposed standard*. Documents of this status are considered mostly complete, but may still be revised based on further review, testing, and experimentation with the technology.

Once the specification is sufficiently mature and widely accepted, it may be elevated from proposed standard to *draft standard.* A key requirement for such advancement is that the technology must be demonstrated to be functional on at least two independent and interoperable implementations. This proves that the standard has been cleared and completed, and that at least two different groups have been able to implement it compatibly.

A document only reaches draft standard when the IETF community believes it is technically mature and the specification is complete. Changes are usually only made to draft standards to correct problems encountered in testing or resolve new issues that arise.

The final station on the Internet standards track is *Internet standard.* This designation is applied to only very mature specifications that are popular and that have been widely implemented. A document that reaches this status often describes a technology that is or will become universally implemented, and is assigned an STD (standard) number.

The RFC development process can take months or even years, depending on how complex the technology is, how many changes are required to the documents, and whether or not the proposal is considered important or interesting. Many RFCs never make it officially to Internet standard status; draft standard status is generally considered stable enough that the technology is often just implemented by companies when that level is reached. Some RFCs never even make it to draft standard status, and the technologies they describe are still used in products.

Once an RFC is published, it cannot be changed. This is a specific policy decision intended to avoid the confusion that would otherwise result from the fact that there were multiple versions of the same RFC. The RFC publication process incorporates a number of steps at which RFC authors can revise their documents and check for editorial omissions and errors.

This need for a new document whenever a change is made is also why proposals are typically published with a category designation of standards track rather than proposed standard, draft standard, and Internet standard. This eliminates the need to publish a new RFC when a proposal advances down the standards track without requiring any real changes aside from a different category designation.

I've just outlined the process for creating and publishing an Internet standard here. The full details of the standards process can be found in RFC 2026 (where else but an RFC?).

KEY CONCEPT Internet standards are described in a series of documents called *Requests for Comments (RFCs).* The RFC process describes how an Internet standard is usually created. An idea for a new technology or enhancement begins with the creation of an *Internet Draft (ID).* After review and feedback, if the proposal has support, it may be placed on the Internet standards track, and its status will be changed to *proposed standard.* As the fledgling standard matures, its status may advance to *draft standard* and eventually, *Internet standard.* However, many RFCs are implemented in products without reaching Internet standard status. There are also other RFCs that define experimental technologies or provide information without describing official Internet standards.

4

A REVIEW OF DATA REPRESENTATION AND THE MATHEMATICS OF COMPUTING

We use decimal (base 10) numbers to represent numeric information, and we use various alphabets and symbol systems to represent other types of information. In contrast, computers understand only one basic type of information: ones and zeros, which themselves are representative of either an on or off electrical state within the hardware of the device. These ones and zeros are combined in various ways to form more common data elements that we are used to finding in computers: regular numbers, characters, and files. However, all of these are really only abstractions; the ones and zeros are always underneath whatever logical structures are used within the computer.

This same basic foundation of ones and zeros applies to networking as well. Even though most of the information in a network is exchanged in a logical fashion between higher-layer protocols, ones and zeros sent over the network medium underlie all networking structures. Understanding how data is represented and manipulated in computer systems is important because it will help you comprehend many of the different technologies.

Computer data representation and mathematics are important for explaining how low-level physical layer modulation and encoding techniques work. Those two elements come into play even for higher-level concepts, such as how IP addresses are set up and used on the Internet.

In this chapter, I provide some general background information on how numerical data is represented, stored, and manipulated within computers and networking hardware. I begin with a description of binary numbers and the different terms used to refer to collections of binary information of various sizes. I describe the different types of numbering systems used in computer systems, such as octal, decimal, and hexadecimal, and how data can be converted between these different types. I explain how arithmetic is performed on binary and hexadecimal numbers. I then discuss boolean logic and how logical functions are used to manipulate binary data.

These explanations then form the basis for a discussion of how logical functions are used for setting, clearing, inverting, and masking bits. These operations are employed extensively in certain networking technologies and protocols. Masking operations especially are often used in IP addressing, so even though this section seems rather low-level, it is quite relevant to the world of TCP/IP.

NOTE *Needless to say, you may know most or all of the information in this chapter, so feel free to skip (or just skim) those topics that you already know. I provide this background detail for the sake of those new to computing or those needing a refresher. However, even those of you who know what a bit and a byte are, and know the difference between binary and decimal numbers, may find the discussion of bit masking worth perusing.*

Binary Information and Representation: Bits, Bytes, Nibbles, Octets, and Characters

The essence of computing is *information*. Computer hardware and software are designed to allow the input, storage, transfer, and expression of various types of information. One primary way by which types of information are differentiated is as either *analog* or *digital*.

Consider, for example, a light switch and a dimmer. A light switch allows a light to be turned on or off; there are no in-between states. These discrete states, on or off, represent digital information. In contrast, a dimmer allows you to fine-tune the light output from fully on to fully off, with an infinite number of intermediate states in between; that's analog information.

Binary Information

Modern digital computers store information digitally. In the same way a light bulb has only an on or off value, so do the components that store and manipulate information within computers. Millions of *transistors* compose computer processors and other circuits, and are, in highly simplified form, digital switches. Thus, all information in computers is manipulated as collections of information pieces that can be only on or off, like a switch.

Since there are only two possible states—on or off—this is called *binary* information (the prefix *bi* means two). There are several advantages to using binary representation for information. It is a simple way to represent many types of information, whether a light switch is on or off or a file has been successfully copied. It is also possible to combine binary values to represent more complex information.

Perhaps most important, binary information is *unambiguous*: On is always on, and off is always off. This property is important because it allows devices to detect clearly the value of a particular piece of information. Computers like black and white; they are not particularly good at dealing with shades of gray. (This becomes especially important in the field of networking, in which transmission of data can cause signals to become polluted by noise.)

The on or off condition of a binary value can be expressed in a number of different ways. In logical expressions, we may consider the value to be true or false. When representing mathematical values, the most common representation is one (on) or zero (off).

Binary Information Representation and Groups

The fundamental building block of computer information is the *bit* (a contraction of *binary digit*). Every bit can be either 0 or 1. Making the value of a bit 1 is commonly called *setting* the bit; changing it to 0 is *resetting* or *clearing* it.

Of course, bits represent only a very small amount of information: a single fact or value. We must make collections of these bits so that we can use them to store large amounts of information and more complex data types. The most common grouping is to take 8 bits and reference them as a single unit. A collection of 8 bits is technically called an *octet*, but is more commonly called a *byte* (more on that in a moment).

Byte is a jocular play on the term *bit*. Over time, various sizes of bit collections have been defined. Some geek comedian decided that if 8 bits made a byte, then 4 bits must be a *nybble* (or "nibble"). Hilarious, no? Larger collections have also been defined and given various names. Table 4-1 summarizes the most common representations of groups of bits and the terms used for them; their relative sizes are also shown graphically in Figure 4-1.

Table 4-1: Binary Information Group Representations and Terms

Number of Bits	Common Representation Terms
1	Bit/Digit/Flag
4	Nybble/Nibble
8	Byte/Octet/Character
16	Double Byte/Word
32	Double Word/Long Word
64	Very Long Word

A few of the new terms that appear in Table 4-1 are worth special mention. A bit is also sometimes called a *flag*; this term is most often heard when a bit is used by itself to represent a particular information state. For example, a computer might use a Changed flag to represent whether a particular file has been modified; this is an analogy to a flag either being raised or lowered to indicate a condition. These flags are often seen in networking message formats.

The term *character* is also used to express a set of 8 bits. This use comes from the fact that computers often store alphanumeric characters, such as letters and numbers, one to a byte. The 16-bit *word* is used fairly often, but not nearly as much as *byte*. The larger collections of bits, such as double word and so on, are not often encountered in everyday parlance; they are used to represent chunks of data in technical fields such as hardware design or programming.

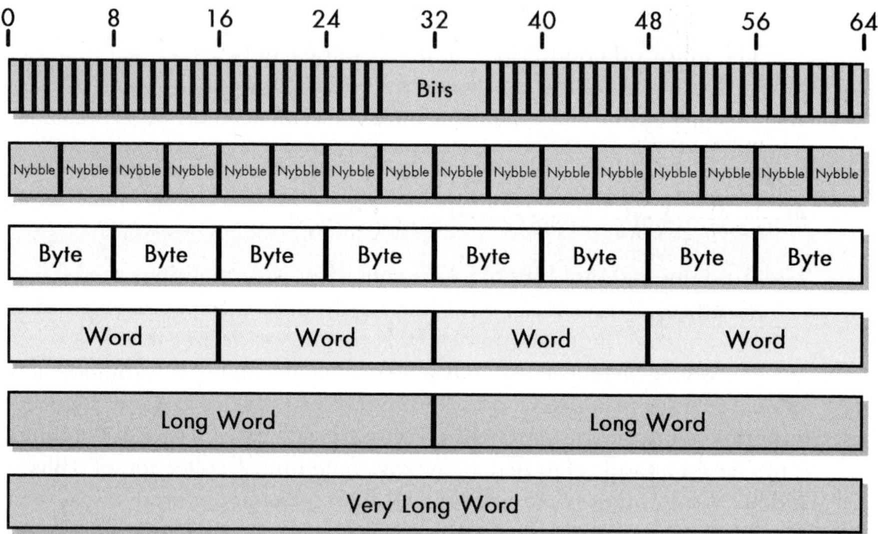

Figure 4-1: Binary information representations and terms *This diagram shows the relative sizes of the most commonly sized collections of binary information.*

Notice that the number of bits used for each of these terms is a power of two. As you will see later in this section, this occurs because when bits come in sets that are a power of two in size, they are easier to represent and manipulate.

> **KEY CONCEPT** Computers store all information in *binary digital form*. This means that all data—whether it's text, photographs, audio, or whatever else—is composed of only collections of ones and zeros. The fundamental building block of digital information is the *binary digit* or *bit*, which represents a single zero or one state. To represent larger amounts of information, bits can be collected into groups of 4, 8, 16, 32, or 64, called *nybbles, bytes, words, long words,* and *very long words*, respectively.

Byte Versus Octet

There has been some disagreement, and even controversy, surrounding the use of the words *byte* and *octet*. The word *byte* has traditionally been the most commonly used term for a set of 8 bits, especially in North America. However, it is *technically* not the correct term.

A byte is, formally, the smallest unit of data that can be read from or written to at one time in a computer system. In almost all cases today, that is indeed 8 bits, but there have been some systems in which a byte was not 8 bits. Some older 36-bit computers used 9-bit bytes, and others had byte sizes of 6 or 7 bits, or even variable-sized bytes. For this reason, many people, especially techie professionals, prefer the term *octet*, which clearly and unambiguously implies 8. This term is much more common outside North America.

NOTE *This matter of* octets *and* bytes *is the kind of tempest in a teapot that computer people love so much. The bottom line in modern computer systems, however, is that an octet is a byte and a byte is an octet, and the terms can generally be used interchangeably without too much danger. You will more often see* octets *used in technical standards. In this book, I use the term* bytes *because it is the term that most people are familiar with.*

KEY CONCEPT Formally, an *octet* is the correct term for exactly 8 bits, while a *byte* is the smallest number of bits that can be accessed in a computer system, which may or may not equal 8. In practice, modern computers use 8-bit bytes, and the terms are used interchangeably (with *byte* being more common in North America, and *octet* often being preferred in Europe).

Decimal, Binary, Octal, and Hexadecimal Numbers

The numbers we are accustomed to using in everyday life are called *decimal numbers*. The word *decimal* refers to the number 10. Every digit can take on one of ten values: 0 to 9. Arithmetic performed on decimal numbers is also called *base 10* mathematics, because of this orientation around the number 10. (Why is the number 10 the foundation of our normal mathematical system? Hold both hands up and count!)

Computer systems, however, don't have fingers or toes; they deal only with binary numbers, which have just two values. Each bit can represent only a 0 or a 1. A single 0 or 1 value is sufficient for encoding a single fact, such as whether something is true or false, or whether the answer is yes or no. But a bit is not enough to hold more complex information, such as your bank account balance, a text document, or a picture of the Yellowstone Canyon.

Binary Numbers and Their Decimal Equivalents

For this reason, larger collections of bits have been created by computer scientists, such as bytes (octets), words, and so forth. When individual bits are collected into sets in this way, they can represent larger integers, called *binary numbers*. Since there are only two possible values for each digit in a binary number (0 or 1), binary numbers are also called *base 2* numbers.

The key to understanding binary numbers is to realize that they are exactly the same as decimal numbers, except that each digit has a value in the range of 0 to 1, instead of 0 to 9. For example, when you count in decimals, you go up to 9 in the ones place, and then you need a second place for tens. If you go above 99, you need a third place for hundreds. Each additional place added on the left is a higher power of ten.

Binary is the same, except the limit for each place is 1 instead of 9. So, in binary, you go up to 1 in the ones place, and then need a second place for twos (instead of tens). If you go above 3, you need a third place for fours (instead of hundreds). Each added digit is a subsequent higher power of two, rather than ten.

Thus, where counting in decimal goes 0, 1, 2, 3, 4, 5, 6, 7, 8, 9, 10, 11, 12, 13, and so on, counting in binary goes 0, 1, 10, 11, 100, 101, 110, 111, 1000, 1001, 1010, 1011, 1100, 1101. For example, the number 13 in decimal is the same as 1101 in binary. How? Well, in decimal, we have a 3 in the ones place, plus a 1 in the tens place, which has a value of 10. This is 3 + 10, or 13. In binary, we start with a 1 in the ones place, add a 1 in the fours place (for a value of 4), plus a 1 in the eights place, for a value of 8. This is 1 + 4 + 8, or 13.

To take a more complex example, 211 in decimal is 11010011 in binary. Table 4-2 shows how the two are equivalent, by adding the values for each binary digit place where there is a 1. Read it from left to right, going top to bottom. Starting in the leftmost column, you can see that the example number has a 1 in the 128s place. So you start with a sum of 128. In the next column there is a 1 in the 64s place, so you add 64 for a running sum of 192. But in the 32s place, the binary digit value is 0, so you don't add 32 to the sum. If you continue down to the ones place, you'll get the decimal equivalent of the binary number.

Table 4-2: Binary and Decimal Number Equivalents

Binary Number	1	1	0	1	0	0	1	1
Power of Two	2^7	2^6	2^5	2^4	2^3	2^2	2^1	2^0
Value of Digit Place	128	64	32	16	8	4	2	1
Value for This Number	128	64	0	16	0	0	2	1
Running Sum (from Left to Right)	128	128+64 = 192	192	192+16 = 208	208	208	208+2 = 210	210+1 = **211**

As you can see, a binary number with N digits can hold up to 2^N values. So a byte with 8 bits can hold 2^8, or 256 different values, which are numbered from 0 to 255. A 16-bit word can hold 2^{16}, or 65,536 values.

Making Binary Numbers Easier to Use by Grouping Bits

One problem with binary numbers is that although computers love them, people have trouble with them because they quickly become long and cumbersome to deal with. For example, 1,000,000 in the decimal system is 11110100001001000000 in the binary system. To make binary numbers easier to work with, two different shorthand notations have been defined. In both of these, instead of working with each bit individually, the numbers are collected into subgroups, each of which is assigned a single digit in an alternative numbering system.

Octal Numbers

Consider the binary number 11110100, which is 244 in decimal. Instead of looking at each bit individually, chop them into groups of three, starting from the right: 11110100 becomes (11)(110)(100). Each of those groups has three bits, so each can have 2^3 values: from 0 to 7. In this case, (11)(110)(100) = (3)(6)(4), or 364 in the *octal* or *base 8* numbering system (see Figure 4-2). As with binary, octal numbers are the same as decimal numbers, except that they use base 8 instead of base 10. So 364 in octal is just $3 \times 64 + 6 \times 8 + 4$, or 244. As you can see, octal is a lot less cumbersome than binary, especially when dealing with larger numbers. In the decimal system, 1,000,000 is 3641100 in octal. Compare that with 11110100001001000000 in binary.

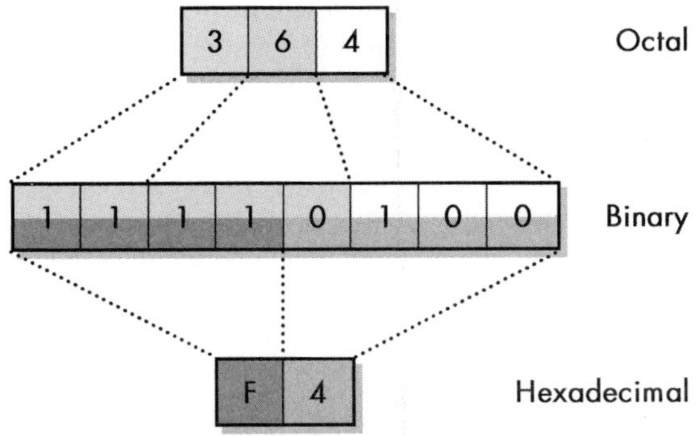

Figure 4-2: Binary, octal, and hexadecimal number representations *A binary number can be represented in octal form by grouping its bits into sets of three, or in hexadecimal by using sets of four bits. These base 8 and base 16 numbers are far shorter than binary numbers, and hence much easier to work with.*

Hexadecimal Numbers

Octal numbers were at one time quite commonly used, but are much less popular today. The problem with octal is that it divides bits into groups of three, but sets of binary numbers typically use a number of bits that is a multiple of *four*.

Hexadecimal or the *base 16* numbering system is an alternative method that works like octal, but uses groups of four. Since there are 4 bits in each group, each can have one of 16 values. Hexadecimal is commonly called *hex* for short.

KEY CONCEPT Regular numbers are called *decimal numbers* because they are built upon the base 10 system of mathematics. Computers use collections of one or zero bits called *binary numbers*, which can be treated just like regular numbers except that each digit can only be 0 or 1 instead of 0 to 9. Bits in a binary number can be expressed as *octal numbers* by grouping three bits into an *octal* digit that ranges from 0 to 7, or taking sets of four bits to create a single *hexadecimal* digit from 0 to 15. To represent the values 10 through 15 in hexadecimal numbers using a single character, you use the letters A through F.

NOTE *The term* hexadecimal *was not the first name used for base 16 numbers in computing. Originally, these were called* sexadecimal *numbers. This is actually the correct term, since Latin prefixes* (sexa-) *are normally used for numbers, not Greek ones* (hexa-). *However, in the early 1950s, IBM decided that the word* sexadecimal *was just a little too provocative for their tastes, so they changed it to* hexadecimal. *IBM being IBM—especially back then—meant everyone else followed suit.*

Now back to the previous example: 11110100 in binary, 244 in decimal. Next you divide this into groups of four to get (1111)(0100). The binary value 1111 is 15, and 0100 is 4, so you have (15)(4). You need to be able to represent 15, but you only have ten numerals. To solve this problem, the values 10, 11, 12, 13, 14, or 15 in hexadecimal are represented by the letters A, B, C, D, E, and F, respectively. So 11110100 in binary is (15)(4), or F4 in hexadecimal (also shown in Figure 4-2).

Hexadecimal numbers are in some ways even less intuitive than binary ones (it takes some practice to get used to thinking of letters as numbers). Still, hexadecimal is particularly useful as a way to compactly represent binary information. Where 1,000,000 in decimal numbers is 11110100001001000000 in binary, it is only F4240 in hexadecimal numbers—even shorter than the decimal number, since 16 is larger than 10. Also, a single byte has 8 bits, so it can be represented using only two hexadecimal digits. This is why hexadecimal numbers are widely used in computing and networking. For example, you will often see hexadecimal numbers used as network addresses or representing different types of information in frame or packet formats.

NOTE *If you see a number that has a letter from A to F in it, you know it is a hex number, but not all hex numbers use these letters. Hex numbers are usually displayed in a special notation, to avoid confusing them with decimal numbers. That notation is either a prefix of* 0x *or a suffix of* h *(sometimes both). Thus, the number 54 is just 54, but 0x54 is 54 in hexadecimal numbers, which is 5 × 16 + 4, or 84 in decimal numbers. Be sure to watch for these representations.*

Decimal, Binary, Octal, and Hexadecimal Number Conversion

Because people and computers speak different number languages, it is often necessary to convert numbers from one system to another. The easiest way to perform the conversion is with a scientific calculator. However, there will be cases for which you need to perform the conversion by hand.

NOTE *If you don't have a scientific calculator, the Windows Calculator program is a reasonable facsimile. Open it, go to the View menu, and change the setting from Standard to Scientific. Click the button next to a numbering system. Then enter a number, and if you click a button next to a different numbering type, the number will be converted for you. There are similar tools for UNIX and Mac OS.*

Binary, Octal, and Hexadecimal Conversions

To convert between binary, octal, and hex, remember that each octal digit is three binary digits, and each hexadecimal digit is four binary digits. To perform the conversion, group the digits, and convert each group into an octal or hex digit. To convert from hex or octal to binary, convert each hex or octal digit into a set of bits. Table 4-3 shows the conversions from each of the octal and hexadecimal single-digit values to binary (with decimal digits thrown in for convenience).

Table 4-3: Binary, Octal, and Hexadecimal Digit Conversion

Binary Digits	Octal Digit	Hexadecimal Digit	Decimal Digit
0000	0	0	0
0001	1	1	1
0010	2	2	2
0011	3	3	3
0100	4	4	4
0101	5	5	5
0110	6	6	6

(continued)

Table 4-3: Binary, Octal, and Hexadecimal Digit Conversion (continued)

Binary Digits	Octal Digit	Hexadecimal Digit	Decimal Digit
0111	7	7	7
1000	-	8	8
1001	-	9	9
1010	-	A	-
1011	-	B	-
1100	-	C	-
1101	-	D	-
1110	-	E	-
1111	-	F	-

Here are some examples:

Binary to Octal Start with the binary number 110101001010. Divide this into groups of three: (110)(101)(001)(010), and then convert each group to a number from 0 to 7 (which is easy to do in your head if you practice a bit). The result is (6)(5)(1)(2), or 6512 octal.

Hexadecimal to Binary Start with the hex number 0x4D1B. Convert each digit as given in Table 4-3. Now you have 0x4D1B = (0100)(1101)(0001)(1011), or 0100110100011011.

Conversion from Binary, Octal, or Hexadecimal to Decimal

Conversions to and from decimal are more complicated, because 2, 8, and 16 are powers of two but ten is not. Of the two directions, conversions *to* decimal are easier: You take the value of each binary, octal, or hexadecimal digit, convert it to decimal, and then multiply it by the power of 2, 8, or 16 represented by the digit's place in the number. Then you add all the numbers together. I did this with the example of the decimal number 211 (see Table 4-2).

Table 4-4 shows the hexadecimal number 0x830C converted to decimal (octal uses a similar process). Read the table from left to right, top to bottom; each digit's value is multiplied by the appropriate power of 16 and added together, yielding the decimal result of 33,548.

Table 4-4: Hexadecimal to Decimal Number Conversion

Hexadecimal Number	8	3	0	C
Decimal Value of Digit	8	3	0	12
Power of 16	16^3	16^2	16^1	16^0
Value of Digit Place	4096	256	16	1
Value for This Number	8×4096 = 32768	3×256 = 768	0×16 = 0	12×1 = 12
Running Sum (from left to right)	32768	32768+768 = 33536	33536	33536+12 = 33548

Conversion from Decimal to Binary, Octal, or Hexadecimal

Conversions *from* decimal requires you to perform the opposite of the previous calculation: You divide and subtract instead of multiply and add.

Conversion from Decimal to Binary

The easiest of the three conversions from decimal is to binary. Because the maximum value of each digit is 1, there is no dividing, just subtraction. To perform the conversion, do the following:

1. Find the largest power of two that is smaller than the number.
2. Put a 1 in the digit place for that power of two and subtract that power of two from the decimal number.
3. Repeat steps 1 and 2 until you are reduced to zero.

This is easier to explain using an example and a table. Let's convert the decimal number 689, as shown in Table 4-5. Again, read the table starting from the upper left, and going down and then across. You start by noticing that 1024 is not less than or equal to 689, so the 1024s place gets a 0. In the next place, 512 is less than 689, so you make the 512s place a 1 and subtract 512 from 689 to leave 177. The calculation continues, before it eventually shows that the 689 decimal is 1010110001 binary.

Table 4-5: Decimal to Binary Number Conversion

Decimal Value Before Considering This Digit Place	689	689	177	177	49	49	17	1	1	1	1
Power of Two	2^{10}	2^9	2^8	2^7	2^6	2^5	2^4	2^3	2^2	2^1	2^0
Value of Digit Place	1024	512	256	128	64	32	16	8	4	2	1
Value of Digit Place Equal to or Less Than Current Decimal Number?	No	Yes	No	Yes	No	Yes	Yes	No	No	No	Yes
Subtraction Step	Skip	689 –512 = 177	Skip	177 –128 = 49	Skip	49 –32 = 17	17 –16 = 1	Skip	Skip	Skip	1 –1 = 0
Binary Digits	0	1	0	1	0	1	1	0	0	0	1

Conversion from Decimal to Octal or Hexadecimal

The process for octal and hexadecimal is almost the same, except that you must divide by powers of two instead of just subtracting, as shown here:

1. Start with the highest power of 16 (hexadecimal) or 8 (octal) that is smaller than the number.
2. Divide the decimal number by that power, keeping only the integer part of the result.

3. Keep the remainder after the division is done.
4. Repeat steps 1 through 3 until you get to the ones place, and then enter whatever is left after the higher digits were done.

Table 4-6 shows the same example as Table 4-5, but goes from decimal to hexadecimal instead of decimal to binary: 689 in decimal is 0x2B1 in hexadecimal.

Table 4-6: Decimal to Hexadecimal Number Conversion

Decimal Value Before Considering This Digit Place	689	689	177	1
Power of 16	16^3	16^2	16^1	16^0
Value of Digit Place	4096	256	16	1
Value of Digit Place Smaller Than Current Decimal Number?	No	Yes	No	n/a
Division Step	Skip	689/256 = 2.691 (use 2 for this digit)	177/16 = 11.0625 (use B for this digit)	n/a
Remainder After Division	Skip	177	1	n/a
Hexadecimal Digits	0	2	B	1

Binary, Octal, and Hexadecimal Arithmetic

We use arithmetic every day to give us the information we need to make decisions. Like us, computers perform arithmetic operations constantly as part of their normal operation, except that computers use binary numbers to perform their calculations incredibly fast.

Binary, octal, and hexadecimal numbers are essentially different representations of numbers, and as such they are not really much different than decimal numbers; they simply have a different number of values per digit. In a similar vein, doing arithmetic with binary, octal, or hexadecimal numbers is not that different from the equivalent operations with decimal numbers. You just have to keep in mind that you are working with powers of 2, 8, or 16, instead of 10, which isn't always easy.

As with number system conversions, calculators are usually the way to go if you need to do math with binary, octal, or hexadecimal numbers. If your calculator does math with only decimal numbers, you can use the trick of converting the numbers to decimal, and then performing the operation and converting the result. However, you can fairly easily do the same addition, subtraction, multiplication, and division on binary, octal, or hexadecimal numbers that you would with decimal numbers by using the Windows Calculator program.

Computers often need to perform multiplication and division operations on binary numbers, but people working with computers don't often perform these operations. Addition and subtraction are much more common operations (especially addition), and they have the added bonus of being much easier to explain. You probably won't need to do this type of arithmetic that often, but it's good to understand it. I'll provide a couple of examples to give you the general idea.

Binary Arithmetic

Let's start with binary. Adding binary numbers is the same as adding decimal ones, except that you end up doing *a lot* of the carrying of ones since there are so few values allowed per digit. Table 4-7 shows an example, with one digit in each column; read it from right to left and top to bottom, just as you would usually do with a manual addition. You start by adding the 1 in the ones place from the first number with the 1 in that place from the second number, thereby yielding a raw digit sum of 2. This means the result for the ones digit is 1, and you carry a 1 to the twos place. You continue with this process until you have added all the digits.

Table 4-7: Binary Addition

Carry		1	1			1	1	—
First Binary Number	1	0	1	1	0	0	1	1
Second Binary Number	0	0	1	1	1	0	0	1
Raw Digit Sum	1	1	3	2	1	1	2	2
Result	1	1	1	0	1	1	0	0
Carry to Next Higher Digit			1	1			1	1

Octal and Hexadecimal Arithmetic

Octal and hexadecimal are pretty much the same, except that you carry the number if the sum in a particular digit exceeds either 8 or 16, respectively. Hexadecimal is more common, and more interesting, so let's examine how to add two hexadecimal numbers. While performing the operation, you will need to convert single-digit hexadecimal numbers to decimal and back again, but this isn't too difficult.

The example shown in Table 4-8 should be read from right to left. You start by adding 8 (decimal 8) to A (decimal 10) in the ones place. This yields a raw sum of 18, from which you carry 16 as a 1 to the 16s place and leave a result of 2. You add this 1 to the D (value 13) and E (14 value) of the 16s place. This is a total of 28, leaving 12 (C in hexadecimal), and you carry a 1 to the 256s place. This continues until you are left with a sum of 6DC2h.

Table 4-8: Hexadecimal Addition

Carry		1	1	
First Hex Number	2	C	D	8
Second Hex Number	4	0	E	A
Raw Digit Sum	2+4 = 6	1+12+0 = 13	1+13+14 = 28	8+10 = 18
Result	6	D	C	2
Carry to Next Higher Digit			1	1

Boolean Logic and Logical Functions

You'll recall that every bit in a computer system can hold a value of either 1 or 0, representing the basic on or off states inherent in a binary digital system, and that you can interpret these on or off values as true or false states, respectively. These values can represent various logical conditions within a system, and you can use various logical operations to manipulate and combine these values to represent more complex logical states.

British mathematician George Boole (1815–1864) was one of the pioneering users of binary values in logical equations, and in recognition of his contribution we call this *boolean logic*.

Boolean Logical Functions

Boolean logic defines a number of *boolean logical functions*, which are sometimes called *operators*. Each of these functions uses a logical algorithm to compute an output value based on the value of one or more inputs. The algorithm determines when the output is true, based on the combination of true and false values the inputs take. Thus, the table that shows the inputs and outputs for a logical function is called a *truth table*. Each of the logical functions is analogous to a real-world logical operation that you can use to define various logical situations (as you will soon see).

NOT

Consider the simplest function: *NOT*. As you might expect, this is a just a negation; the output is the opposite of the input. The NOT function takes only one input, so it is called a *unary* function or operator. The truth table for NOT is shown in Table 4-9. As you can see, the output is true when the input is false, and vice versa.

Table 4-9: NOT Operator Truth Table

Input	Output
False	True
True	False

The NOT function logically represents the opposite of a condition. For example, suppose you have a bit called B1 whose logical meaning is that when the bit is true, a particular pixel on a screen is lit up. Then the *boolean expression* NOT B1 would be the opposite: It would be false when the pixel is lit up, and thus true only when the pixel is *not* lit up.

Since true and false values are represented in computers by 1 or 0 values, boolean logic is often expressed in terms of ones and zeros, instead of true and false. The circuits inside computer processors and other devices manipulate one and zero bits directly using these functions. In some (but not all) cases, they interpret one and zero as true and false, but in either case, the two representations are functionally equivalent.

Table 4-10 shows the same truth table as Table 4-9, but using bit values. Each true is represented as a 1, and each false is represented as a 0.

Table 4-10: NOT Operator Truth Table (Using Bit Values)

Input	Output
0	1
1	0

AND and OR

The two other primary boolean functions that are widely used are *AND* and *OR*. The output of an AND function is true only if its first, and second, and third inputs and so on are true. The output of an OR function is true if the first input is true *or* the second input is true, and so on.

Both AND and OR can have any number of inputs, with a minimum of two. Table 4-11 shows the truth table for the AND function, with two inputs. You can see that the output is a 1 only when both inputs are 1, but it's 0 otherwise.

Table 4-11: AND Operator Truth Table

Input 1	Input 2	Output
0	0	0
0	1	0
1	0	0
1	1	1

Like NOT, AND represents a logical operation similar to how we use the word *and* in our everyday speech. For example, at lunchtime, I might say to a colleague, "Let's go out for lunch *and* stop at the post office."

The truth table for the OR function (again with two inputs) is shown in Table 4-12. Here, the output is 1 whenever a 1 appears in at least one input, not necessarily both as in the previous table.

Table 4-12: OR Operator Truth Table

Input 1	Input 2	Output
0	0	0
0	1	1
1	0	1
1	1	1

Interestingly, unlike AND, the OR function does *not* have the same meaning as what we take the word *or* to mean in everyday English. In boolean, the word OR means that the output is true as long as *any* of the inputs is true.

Exclusive-OR (XOR or EOR)

A modification of OR called *Exclusive-OR* (abbreviated either *XOR* or *EOR*) represents the way we normally use *or* in the real world. Its output is only true if one input or the other is true, but *not both.* The truth table for XOR is as shown in Table 4-13. Notice the difference between this table and Table 4-12: The output is 0 in the case where both inputs are 1.

Table 4-13: Exclusive OR (XOR) Operator Truth Table

Input 1	Input 2	Output
0	0	0
0	1	1
1	0	1
1	1	0

Combining Boolean Expressions

The functions described earlier can also be combined arbitrarily to produce more complex logical conditions. For example, when searching the Web, you might enter "cheese AND (cheddar OR swiss) NOT wisconsin" into a search engine. In response, the search engine might return pages that contain the word *cheese* and the word *cheddar* or *swiss* (or both), but pages that do *not* contain the word *wisconsin.*

Boolean functions are important because they are the building blocks of much of the circuitry within computer hardware. The functions are implemented as tiny *gates* that are designed to allow electrical energy to flow only to the output based on certain combinations of inputs as described by the truth tables for functions like NOT, AND, OR, and others. In networking, boolean logic is important for describing certain conditions and functions in the operation of networks. Boolean functions are also very important because they are used to set, clear, and mask strings of binary digits, which I will explore in the next section.

KEY CONCEPT *Boolean logic* is a system that uses boolean functions to produce output based on varying conditions in input data. The most common boolean functions are as follows: *NOT*, which produces output that is the opposite of its input; *AND*, which is true only if all of its inputs are true; *OR*, which is true if any of its input is true; and *XOR*, which is true only if exactly one of its inputs is true (that is, if the inputs are different). These functions can be used in boolean logic expressions that represent conditional states for making decisions, and they can also be used for bit manipulation.

Bit Masking (Setting, Clearing, and Inverting) Using Boolean Logical Functions

The boolean functions NOT, AND, OR, and XOR describe different ways that logical expressions can be used to manipulate true and false values to represent both simple and complex decisions or conditions. However, these functions can also be used in a more mundane manner to allow the direct manipulation of binary data. This use of boolean logic is very important in a number of different applications in networking.

You should recall that when you give a bit a value you *set* the bit, and when you give it a value of 0, you *reset* or *clear* it. In some situations bits are handled individually and are set or cleared simply by assigning a 0 or 1 value to each bit. However, it is common to have large groups of bits that are used collectively to represent a great deal of information, whenever many bits need to be set or cleared at once. In this situation, the boolean functions come to the rescue.

Setting Groups of Bits with OR

You can set bits en masse with the OR function. Recall that an OR's output is true (equal to 1) if any of its inputs are true (equal to 1). Thus, if you OR a bit with a value known to be 1, the result will always be 1, no matter what the other value is. In contrast, if you OR with a 0, the original value, 1 or 0, is not changed.

By using a string with 0s and 1s in particular spots, you can set certain bits to 1 while leaving others unchanged. This procedure is comparable to how a painter *masks* areas that he does not want to be painted, using plastic or perhaps masking tape. Thus, the process is called *masking*. The string of digits used in the operation is called the *bit mask*, or simply the *mask*.

For example, suppose you have the 12-bit binary input number 101001011010, and you want to set the middle six bits to be all ones. To do this, you OR the number with the 12-bit mask 000111111000. Table 4-14 shows how this works with the changed bits in the result in bold—you simply OR each bit in the input with its corresponding bit in the mask:

Table 4-14: Setting Bits Using an OR Bit Mask

Input	1	0	1	0	0	1	0	1	1	0	1	0
Mask	0	0	0	1	1	1	1	1	1	0	0	0
Result of OR Operation	1	0	1	1	1	1	1	1	1	0	1	0

Clearing Bits with AND

To clear a certain pattern of bits, you perform a similar masking operation, but using the AND function instead. If you AND a bit with 0, it will clear it to 0, regardless of what the bit was before, while ANDing with 1 will leave the bit unchanged. For example, to clear the middle six bits in Table 4-14, you AND with the reverse bit mask, 111000000111.

Table 4-15 and Figure 4-3 show how a bit mask can be used to clear certain bits in a binary number while preserving others. Each 1 represents a "transparent" area that keeps the corresponding input bit value, while each 0 is a bit where the original value is to be cleared. After performing an AND on each bit pair, the first three and last three bits are preserved, while the middle six, since they were each ANDed with 0, are forced to 0 in the output.

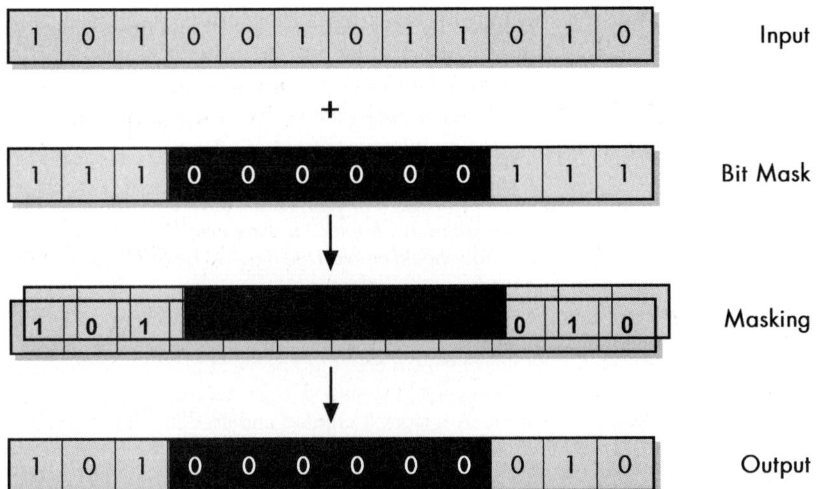

Figure 4-3: Clearing bits using an AND bit mask Applying a bit mask to an input binary number using the AND function clears to 0 all bits where the mask bit was 0 and leaves alone bits where the mask was 1.

Table 4-15: Clearing Bits Using an AND Bit Mask

Input	1	0	1	0	0	1	0	1	1	0	1	0
Mask	1	1	1	0	0	0	0	0	0	1	1	1
Result of AND Operation	1	0	1	0	0	0	0	0	0	0	1	0

You can also look at this clearing function a different way. You are clearing the bits where the mask is a 0, and in so doing selecting the bits where the mask is a 1. Thus, ANDing with a bit mask essentially means that you keep the bits where the mask is a 1 and remove the bits where it is a 0.

Inverting Bits with XOR

There are also situations in which you want to *invert* some bits; that is, change a 1 value to a 0, or a 0 value to a 1. To do this, you use the XOR function. While this is not as intuitive as masking, if you refer to the XOR truth table (Table 4-13) you will see that if you XOR with a 1, the input value is flipped, while XORing with a 0 causes the input to be unchanged. To see how this works, use the same input example and invert the middle six bits, as shown in Table 4-16.

Table 4-16: Inverting Bits Using an XOR Bit Mask

Input	1	0	1	0	0	1	0	1	1	0	1	0
Mask	0	0	0	1	1	1	1	1	1	0	0	0
Result of XOR Operation	1	0	1	1	1	0	1	0	0	0	1	0

In the world of networking, bit masking is most commonly used to manipulate addresses. In particular, masking is perhaps best known for its use in differentiating between the host and subnetwork (subnet) portions of Internet Protocol (IP) addresses, a process called *subnet masking* (see Chapter 18, which discusses IP subnet addressing).

NOTE *Masks are often expressed in either hexadecimal or decimal notation for simplicity, as shown in the IP subnetting summary tables in Chapter 18. However, the masks are always applied in binary, as described previously. You should convert the mask to binary if you want to see exactly how the masking operation will work.*

KEY CONCEPT The properties of the *OR* and *AND* boolean functions make them useful when certain bits of a data item need to be set (changed to 1) or cleared (changed to 0). This process is called *bit masking*. To set bits to 1, a mask is created and used in a bit-by-bit OR function with the input. When the mask has a value of 1, the bit is forced to a 1, while each 0 bit leaves the corresponding original bit unchanged. Similarly, a mask used with the AND function clears certain bits; each 1 bit in the mask leaves the original bit alone, while each 0 forces the output to 0. Finally, *XOR* can be used to invert selected bits using a mask.

PART I-2

THE OPEN SYSTEMS INTERCONNECTION (OSI) REFERENCE MODEL

Models are useful because they help us understand difficult concepts and complicated systems. When it comes to networking, there are several models that are used to explain the roles played by various technologies and how they interact. Of these, the most popular and commonly used is the Open Systems Interconnection (OSI) Reference Model. The OSI Reference Model makes it easier for networks to be analyzed, designed, built, and rearranged, by allowing them to be considered as modular pieces that interact in predictable ways, rather than enormous, complex monoliths.

You'll find that it's nearly impossible to read a lot about networking without encountering discussions that presume at least some knowledge of how the OSI Reference Model works. This is why I strongly advise that if you are new to the OSI Reference Model, you read this part carefully. While it is all arguably background material, this information will give you a foundation for understanding networks, as well as make the rest of the book easier to follow. If you are quite familiar with the OSI Reference Model, you may wish to skip this part or just skim through it.

This part is geared to a discussion of networks and internetworks in general, and not specifically to the TCP/IP protocol suite. Therefore, not all of the material in this section is directly relevant to learning about TCP/IP, although much of it is. You may also wish to refer to Part I-3, which includes a discussion of how the TCP/IP and OSI models compare.

In this part, I describe the OSI Reference Model in detail. I begin with a discussion of some general concepts related to the OSI Reference Model and networking models overall. I then describe each of the seven layers of the OSI Reference Model. I conclude with a summary chapter that includes a useful analogy to help you understand how the reference model works to explain the interaction of networks on multiple levels. That chapter also presents a reference table of the layers and their respective functions.

5

GENERAL OSI REFERENCE MODEL ISSUES AND CONCEPTS

The idea behind the OSI Reference Model is to provide a framework for both designing networking systems and explaining how they work. As you read about networking, you will frequently find references to the various levels, or *layers*, of the OSI Reference Model. However, before I can properly discuss the actual OSI model layers, you need to understand the model as a whole.

In this chapter, I introduce the OSI Reference Model and provide some useful background information to help you understand it. I begin with a brief history of the model, including a look at its development and goals. I then introduce networking models in general terms, describing why they are beneficial and how they can best be used. The bulk of the chapter contains important OSI model concepts, which will help you begin to really understand the way model works, the terminology used to describe it, and how it can be of value in explaining the operation of networking technologies.

History of the OSI Reference Model

A look at the origins of the OSI Reference Model takes us back to several issues related to standards and standards organizations that were discussed in Chapter 3. The idea behind the creation of networking standards is to define widely accepted ways of setting up networks and connecting them together. The OSI Reference Model represented an early attempt to get all of the various hardware and software manufacturers to agree on a framework for developing various networking technologies.

In the late 1970s, two projects began independently with the same goal: to define a unifying standard for the architecture of networking systems. One was administered by the *International Organization for Standardization (ISO)*, while the other was undertaken by the *International Telegraph and Telephone Consultative Committee*, or *CCITT* (the abbreviation is from the French version of the name). These two international standards bodies each developed a document that defined similar networking models.

In 1983, these two documents were merged to form a standard called *The Basic Reference Model for Open Systems Interconnection.* That's a mouthful, so the standard is usually referred to as the *Open Systems Interconnection Reference Model*, the *OSI Reference Model*, or even just the *OSI model.* It was published in 1984 by both the ISO, as standard ISO 7498, and the renamed CCITT (now called the *Telecommunications Standardization Sector of the International Telecommunication Union* or *ITU-T*) as standard X.200. (Incidentally, isn't the new name for the CCITT *much* catchier than the old one? Just rolls off the old tongue, doesn't it?)

One interesting aspect of the history of the OSI Reference Model is that the original objective was *not* to create a model primarily for educational purposes, even though many people today think that this was the case. It was intended to serve as the foundation for the establishment of a widely adopted suite of protocols that would be used by international internetworks—basically, what the Internet became. This was called, unsurprisingly, the OSI protocol suite.

However, things didn't quite work out as planned. The rise in popularity of the Internet and its TCP/IP protocols met the OSI protocol suite head on, and in a nutshell, TCP/IP won. Some of the OSI protocols were implemented, but as a whole, the OSI protocols lost out to TCP/IP when the Internet started to grow.

The OSI model itself, however, found a home as a device for explaining the operation of not just the OSI protocols, but networking in general. It's used widely as an educational tool—much as I use it myself—and it's also used to help describe interactions between the components of other protocol suites and even hardware devices. Although most technologies were not designed specifically to meet the dictates of the OSI model, many are described in terms of how they fit into its layers. This includes networking protocols, software applications, and even different types of hardware devices, such as switches and routers. The model is also useful to those who develop software and hardware products because it clarifies the roles performed by each of the components in a networking system.

KEY CONCEPT The *Open Systems Interconnection Reference Model* (*OSI Reference Model* or *OSI model*) was originally created as the basis for designing a universal set of protocols called the *OSI protocol suite*. This suite never achieved widespread success, but the model became a very useful tool for both education and development. The model defines a set of layers and a number of concepts for their use that make understanding networks easier.

General Reference Model Issues

Let's discuss some of the basic issues related to reference models. In part, I want to explain why I place so much emphasis on the OSI model, even going so far as to build much of this book's organization around this model and its layers. I also want you to understand why the model is important, and how it benefits networking not only on a conceptual level, but in reality.

In the topics that follow, I describe several issues that relate to reference models in general terms, and of course, to the OSI Reference Model specifically. I begin with an overview of why networking models are beneficial and why it is important for you to understand how the OSI model works. I then talk about how best to use the model and contrast it with some "real-world" network architectures and protocol stacks.

The Benefits of Networking Models

Networking is complicated, and special pains must be taken to try to *simplify* it. One of the ways in which networking technology is made easier to understand is by splitting it into pieces, each of which plays a particular role or is responsible for a specific job or function.

However, if this is to be done, you must have a way of ensuring that these various pieces can interoperate; that is, each must know what is expected of it and also what it can expect from the other pieces. This is one of the important roles of networking models. They split the multitude of tasks required to implement modern networks into smaller chunks that can be more easily managed. Just as importantly, they establish "walls" between those pieces and rules for passing information over those walls.

A good analogy of a networking model is that of an assembly line at a manufacturer. No company attempts to have one person build an entire car; even if the company did, it wouldn't expect that individual to be able to learn how to do it all at once. The division of labor offers several advantages to a company that builds a complex product, such as an automobile. Generally speaking, these include the following:

Training and Documentation It is easier to explain how to build a complex system by breaking the process into smaller parts. Training can be done for a specific job without everyone needing to know how everything else works.

Specialization If everyone is responsible for doing every job, no one gets enough experience to become an expert at anything. Through specialization, certain individuals develop expertise at particular jobs.

Easier Design Modification and Enhancement By separating the automobile into systems as well as the particular jobs required to build those systems, you can make changes in the future more easily. Without such divisions, it would be much more difficult to determine what the impact might be of a change, which would serve as a disincentive for innovation.

Modularity This is related to each of the previous items. If the automobile's systems and manufacturing steps are broken down according to a sensible architecture or model, it becomes easier to interchange parts and procedures between vehicles. This saves time and money.

Networking models yield very similar benefits to the networking world. They represent a framework for dividing up the tasks needed to implement a network by splitting the work into different levels, or *layers*. Hardware and software running on each layer are responsible for interacting with corresponding hardware and software that are running on other devices on the same layer. The responsibilities of each hardware or software element are defined in part by specifically dividing lines between the layers.

As a result, you get all of the benefits listed in the previous points: easier training, specialized capabilities at each layer, improved capabilities for modification, and modularity. Modularity is particularly important, because it allows you to interchange technologies that run at different layers. While no one would try to build a vehicle that is partly a compact sedan, partly an SUV, and partly a motorcycle, there are situations in networking for which you may want to do something surprisingly similar to this. Networking models help make this possible.

KEY CONCEPT Networking models such as the *OSI Reference Model* provide a framework for breaking down complex internetworks into components that can more easily be understood and utilized. The model defines networking functions not as a large, complicated whole, but as a set of layered, modular components, each of which is responsible for a particular function. The result is better comprehension of network operations, improved performance and functionality, easier design and development, and the ability to combine different components in a way that's best suited to the needs of the network.

Why Understanding the OSI Reference Model Is Important to You

A lot of networking books and other resources gloss over the OSI Reference Model or relegate it to the back pages of a hard-to-find appendix. The reason usually stated for this is that the OSI model is "too theoretical" and "doesn't apply to modern networking protocols like TCP/IP."

This is a misguided notion. While it is certainly true that the OSI model is primarily theoretical, and that networking protocols aren't always designed to fit strictly within the confines of their layers, it's *not* true that the OSI model has little applicability to the real world. In fact, it is difficult to read about networking technology today without seeing references to the OSI model and its layers, because the model's structure helps to frame discussions of protocols and contrast various technologies.

For example, the OSI Reference Model provides the basis for understanding how technologies like Ethernet and HomePNA are similar; it explains how a PC can communicate using any of several different sets of protocols, even simultaneously; it is an important part of understanding the differences between interconnection devices such as repeaters, hubs, bridges, switches, and routers; and it also explains how many WAN technologies interoperate.

Far from being obsolete, the OSI model layers are now showing up more than ever in discussions of technology. In fact, some protocols are even *named* specifically in terms of their place in the OSI Reference Model! For an example, consider the Layer Two Tunneling Protocol. Also, switches are now commonly categorized as layer 2, layer 3, or even higher-layer switches.

In theoretical discussions, the OSI Reference Model helps you to understand how networks and network protocols function in the real world. It also helps you to figure out which protocols and devices can interact with each other. So I encourage you to read on. It's time well spent.

> **KEY CONCEPT** While many people scoff at the notion of studying the OSI Reference Model, understanding it is very helpful in making sense of networking protocols and technologies. The model is theoretical, but its concepts are employed regularly to describe the operation of real-world networks.

How to Use the OSI Reference Model

Although some people tend to downplay the OSI model too much, others go to the opposite extreme. They use it too much, overanalyzing and trying to use it in a way that was never intended.

The most common mistake is made when attempting to try to "make everything fit" into the layered structure of the OSI model. I must confess to falling into this trap myself on occasion. When I first started laying out the structure of this book, I wanted to organize *everything* based on where it fell in terms of OSI model layers. I quickly discovered that this was like attempting to put pegs of various shapes into a board containing only round holes. I had to change my approach. I ended up organizing it based on the OSI layers where it made sense and using a different structure where it did not.

Learn from my experience. A simple rule of thumb is this: Refer to the OSI Reference Model if it helps you make sense of technologies and understand how they work; *don't* use it if it makes things more complicated. In particular, bear the following in mind:

- It can be very hard to figure out where some technologies fall within the model. Many protocols were designed without the OSI model in mind, and they may not fall neatly into one layer or another. Some overlap two or more layers; other protocol suites may have two protocols that share a layer.
- The boundaries between the upper layers (session, presentation, and application) get particularly fuzzy. Some protocols are clearly designed to fit on one of these layers, while others may overlap all three. This is one reason why I do not categorize higher-level protocols by layer. (The OSI Reference Model was designed to account for the fact that differentiating between these layers might not make sense.)

- The OSI Reference Model was designed primarily with LANs in mind. WAN technologies often fit very poorly into the model, with a lot of overlapping and partial layer coverage. However, it's still useful in most cases to look at these protocols in terms of their approximate fit in the OSI model, since parts of WAN technologies are sometimes interchanged.
- The people who design products don't generally worry about ensuring that their latest inventions implement only specific layers of the model. Thus, sometimes new products come out that break the rules and implement functions across more than one layer, which used to be done by multiple devices at the individual layers. This is usually progress—a good thing!

Finally, an observation: I have noticed that people learning about networking—especially those trying to memorize easy answers to difficult questions so they can pass exams—often ask, "At what layer does this piece of hardware operate?" The problem here is not the answer but rather the question, which is simplistic. With the exception of simple physical devices such as connectors and cables, pretty much *all* networking devices operate at many layers. While a router, for example, is usually associated with layer 3, it has two or more device interfaces that implement layers 2 and 1. A better question is what is the *highest* layer at which a device functions?

The bottom line is that the OSI Reference Model is a tool. If you use it wisely, it can be immensely helpful to you. Just remember not to be too inflexible in how you apply it, and you'll be fine.

KEY CONCEPT It is just as much a mistake to assign too much importance to the OSI Reference Model as too little. While the model defines a framework for understanding networks, not all networking components, protocols, and technologies will necessarily fall into the model's strict layering architecture. There are cases in which trying to use the model to describe certain concepts can lead to less clarity rather than more. You should remember that the OSI model is a *tool* and should be used accordingly.

Other Network Architectures and Protocol Stacks

The OSI Reference Model is not the only model used to describe the structure of networks; several other models and systems are used to describe various sets of networking technologies that work together. These don't generally describe theoretical models, but rather groupings of protocols that are actively used in actual networks. They are, therefore, more often called *networking architectures* and *protocol suites* than models.

As you just saw, many technologies and protocols don't "fit" well into the specific layers used in the OSI model. Similarly, most of the protocol suites used in the real world don't fit the OSI model exactly. This happens, of course, because they were developed independently of the OSI model. Still, most of these architectures and suites still use layers—they are just different from the ones that the OSI model uses.

Since the OSI model is referenced so often, it can be very helpful in making sense of other architectures and even comparing them. Regardless of what the individual layers and technologies are called, networking protocol suites all try to accomplish the same goals in implementing a network. Thus, even though the layers are not the same, they are often comparable.

In the case of TCP/IP, a special model called the DoD (Department of Defense) model or TCP/IP model is usually used in discussions of the suite (see Chapter 8). This model has many similarities to the OSI model, but also some important differences. In other areas in the field of networking, still other models are used, such as the IEEE 802 networking architecture model. These, too, are similar in some ways to the OSI model, but they have their own unique characteristics.

Even within the scope of some individual specific technologies, you can see a layered structure of related protocols. There are technologies that are generally considered to implement a single level of the OSI model, even though they actually have portions that overlap several OSI layers; examples include Ethernet and Asynchronous Transfer Mode (ATM). In fact, some protocols even have *subprotocols* that are layered within the confines of what is considered a single layer under OSI. A good example is the TCP/IP Point-to-Point Protocol (PPP), which, despite the name, is not a single protocol but a protocol suite unto itself (see Part II-1).

Key OSI Reference Model Concepts

The OSI Reference Model is valuable as a tool for explaining how networks function, and for describing the relationships between different networking technologies and protocols. To accomplish this, the model relies on a number of important concepts and terms, which I'll discuss in the following sections.

I'll begin with a discussion of how the model uses layers. This is perhaps the single most important of all model concepts. I then talk about some of the notation and jargon you are likely to see in general discussions of the model. I define in more detail what *interfaces* and *protocols* are in the context of the model. I then explain the important concept of data encapsulation and the terminology used to refer to messages in the OSI Reference Model: protocol data units (PDUs) and service data units (SDUs). Finally, I connect most of the preceding issues by describing how the various layers work to handle the routing of messages on a theoretical basis.

OSI Reference Model Networking Layers, Sublayers, and Layer Groupings

The most important OSI Reference Model concept is that of networking *layers*. It's not an exaggeration to say that layers are really the heart of the OSI model—the entire point of the model is to separate networking into distinct functions that operate at different levels. Each layer is responsible for performing a specific task or set of tasks and dealing with the layers above and below it.

The OSI Reference Model is composed of seven conceptual layers, each of which is assigned a number from 1 to 7. The layer number represents the position of the layer in the model as a whole, and indicates how close the layer is to the actual hardware used to implement a network. The first and lowest layer is the *physical layer*, which is where low-level signaling and hardware are implemented. The seventh and highest layer is the *application layer*, which deals with high-level applications employed by users: both end users and the operating system software.

You can see that as you proceed from the first layer to the seventh, you move up the *layer stack* and, in so doing, increase your level of *abstraction*. This means that the higher a layer is in the stack, the more it deals with logical concepts and software, and the less it deals with the hardware of a network and the nuts and bolts of making it work. The first layer is the most concrete, because it deals with the actual hardware of networks and the specific methods of sending bits from one device to another. It is the domain of hardware engineers and signaling experts. The second layer is a bit more abstract but still deals with signaling and hardware. As you proceed through the third, fourth, and subsequent layers, the technologies at those layers become increasingly abstract. By the time you reach the seventh layer, you are no longer dealing with hardware or even operating system concepts very much; you are in the realm of the user and high-level programs that rely on lower levels to do the "heavy lifting" for them.

The OSI Reference Model does not formally assign any relationship between groups of adjacent layers. However, to help explain how the layers work, it is common to categorize them into two *layer groupings*:

Lower Layers (Layers 1, 2, 3, and 4) As shown in Figure 5-1, the lower layers of the model—*physical*, *data link*, *network*, and *transport*—are primarily concerned with the formatting, encoding, and transmission of data over the network. They don't care that much about what the data is or what it is being used for; instead, they just want to know about moving it around. They are implemented in both hardware and software, with the transition from hardware to software occurring as you proceed up from layer 1 to layer 4.

Upper Layers (Layers 5, 6, and 7) The higher layers of the model—*session*, *presentation*, and *application*—are concerned primarily with interacting with the user and implementing the applications that run over the network. The protocols that run at higher layers are less concerned with the low-level details of how data gets sent from one place to another; they rely on the lower layers to deliver the data. These layers are almost always implemented as software running on a computer or other hardware device.

There are some people who would not necessarily agree with how I have chosen to divide the layers in Figure 5-1. In particular, valid arguments can be made for including the transport layer in the upper layer group, since it is usually implemented as software and is fairly abstract. I place it in the lower layer group because its primary job is still providing services to higher layers for moving data. Really, layer 4 is somewhat of a transition zone and is hard to categorize. Figure 5-1 indicates the special position of layer 4 in the stack.

KEY CONCEPT The most fundamental concept in the OSI Reference Model is the division of networking functions into a set of *layers*, from layer 1 at the bottom to layer 7 at the top. As you go up the layer stack, you move away from concrete, hardware-specific functions to ones that are increasingly abstract, until you reach the realm of user applications at layer 7. The seven layers are sometimes divided into groupings: the lower layers (1 through 3) and the upper layers (4 through 7). There is some disagreement on whether layer 4 is a lower or upper layer.

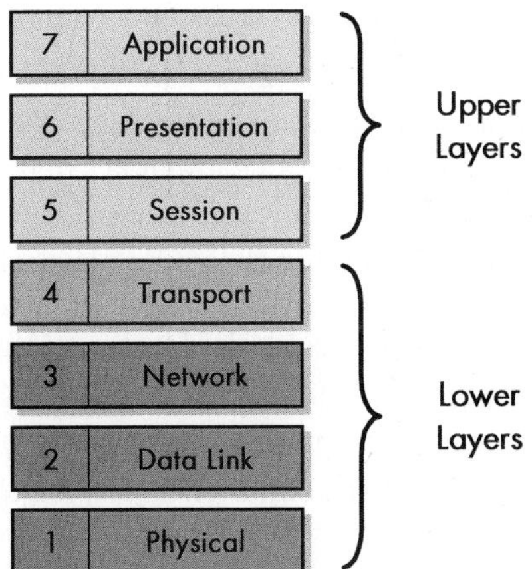

Figure 5-1: OSI Reference Model layers *The OSI Reference Model divides networking functions into a stack of seven layers, numbered 1 through 7 from the bottom up, and sometimes divided into two* layer *groupings—the* lower layers *and the* upper layers*.*

There are also certain OSI layers that have natural relationships to each other. The physical and data link layers, in particular, are closely related. For example, most people talk about Ethernet as a layer 2 technology, but Ethernet specifications really deal with both layer 2 and layer 1. Similarly, layers 3 and 4 are often related; protocol suites are often designed so that layer 3 and 4 protocols work together. Good examples are TCP and IP in the TCP/IP protocol suite, and IPX and SPX in the Novell suite.

In some areas, the layers are so closely related that the lines between them become *blurry*. This is particularly the case when looking at the higher layers; many technologies implement two or even all three of these layers, which is another reason why I feel they best belong in a group together. One important reason why the distinctions between layers 5 through 7 are blurry is that the TCP/IP protocols are based on the TCP/IP model (covered in Chapter 8), which combines the functions of layers 5 through 7 in a single, thick layer.

> **KEY CONCEPT** The four lower layers of the OSI model are most often discussed individually, because the boundaries between them are reasonably clear-cut. In contrast, the lines between the session, presentation, and application layers are somewhat blurry. As a result, sometimes protocols span two or even all three of these layers; this is especially true of TCP/IP application protocols, since the TCP/IP model treats layers 5 through 7 as a single layer.

Finally, note that some OSI Reference Model layers are further divided into *sublayers* to help define more precisely the internal details of protocols and technologies at those layers. This is commonly done at the lower layers, especially at the physical layer and the data link layer.

"N" Notation and Other OSI Model Layer Terminology

As a theoretical model, the OSI Reference Model comes complete with a set of terminology that is used to describe it and its constituent parts. This is sort of both good news and bad news. The good news is that if you understand this terminology, it can help you comprehend how technologies relate to the model as well as most OSI model discussions in general. The bad news is that the terminology can also increase confusion—especially since it isn't always used consistently.

Here are a few terminology concepts you will often see used to refer to the OSI Reference Model:

Layer Names and Numbers The various layers of the OSI Reference Model are referred to in a variety of ways. They may have their names spelled out in full, or they may be abbreviated. They are also often simply referenced by their layer number. So, for example, all of these refer to the same thing: data link layer, Data Link Layer, DLL, L2, layer two, and layer 2. Similarly, you will often see layer names being used as adjectives to describe protocols and technologies. For example, a layer 3 technology is one that operates primarily at the network layer.

N Notation The letter *N* is often used to generically refer to a number within the computer world. With respect to the OSI model, it's common to see this letter used in discussions that relate generically to individual layers without mentioning a specific layer. You will hear terms like *N-functions* and *N-services,* which just refer to the functions and services provided within a particular layer. As another example, you might hear someone say that a particular technology "provides a useful service to the N+1 layer." This just means it provides a function to the layer above the one at which it operates. Conceptually, every layer but the first and seventh have an N-1 layer, an N+1 layer, and so on. If you are looking at the network layer (layer 3), then the N+2 layer is the session layer (layer 5).

Protocols and Interfaces These words have special meaning within the context of the OSI model. A *protocol* represents communication between logical or physical devices at the same layer of the model. An *interface* represents information moving between adjacent layers within the same device. Thus, in N notation, protocols represent communication between layer N on one device and layer N on another device, while interfaces deal with communication between layer N and N+1 or layer N and N-1 on the same device.

Network Stacks What do you get when you take a bunch of layers and pile them up on top of each other? You get a *stack.* This term is used to refer to the entire set of layers in a model or suite of technologies, or a partial set. Since each layer has protocols associated with it, this is also sometimes called the *protocol stack.*

Entities, Functions, Facilities, and Services These often interchanged, somewhat vague terms refer to specific tasks or jobs performed at various layers in the model. An *N-entity* is a term that refers to a specific operation or job done at layer N. A *function* is basically the same thing. *Facilities* and *services* are what a layer provides to the layers above it. This is often expressed in N-notation as well: the N+1 layer often uses a set of N services or N facilities provided by the N layer.

Figure 5-2 serves as a summary of the previous information by showing the relationships between OSI model layers and the terminology used to refer to adjacent layers in the context of any particular layer. Each layer (except layer 7) provides services to the layer above it; each layer (other than layer 1) uses services provided by the layer below it. Another way of saying this is that each layer N provides services to layer N+1 and uses the services of layer N-1. Taking the example of layer 3, the network layer, you see that it provides services to layer 4 and uses services of layer 2. From the standpoint of the network layer, the transport layer is layer N+1 and the data link layer is N-1.

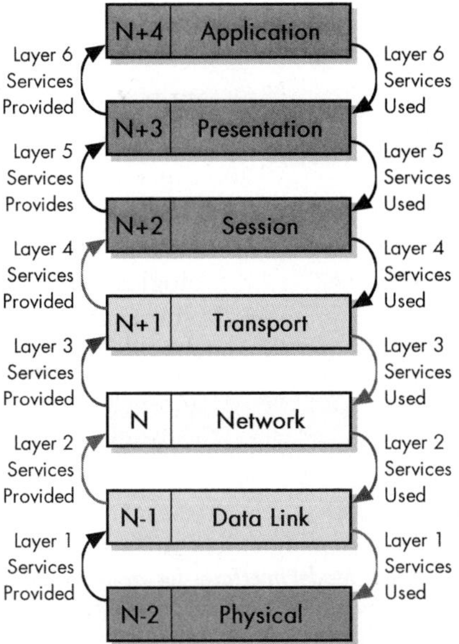

Figure 5-2: OSI Reference Model layer relationships and terminology *Each layer has a relationship with the layer above and below it; here, if the network layer is layer N, it provides services to the transport layer (layer N+1) and uses services of the data link layer (layer N-1).*

You may have just read all of that and said to yourself, "Why do they bother making this so *complicated* anyway?" Good question. Remember, I *did* say there was bad news here! Now that you know what all of this stuff is about, if you run into it, you won't be *too* confused.

Fortunately, the use of the previous buzzwords is somewhat limited. Most references are to specific layer names or numbers, and in particular, the N-1 and N+1 stuff is rarely used in discussions of real-world technologies. However, it can be very useful in explaining the model itself, as you will see in some of these terms when you read the rest of this chapter.

Interfaces: Vertical (Adjacent Layer) Communication

The seven layers of the OSI Reference Model are used to divide the various functions that are required to implement a networking system. On any given device in a network, different software and hardware routines and devices may be functioning on any or all of these layers simultaneously. Because, in general, all of these are supposed to be working together to implement networking functions, there is a need for layers to communicate *vertically* between the layers within a particular host.

In OSI Reference Model parlance, the mechanism for communication between adjacent layers in the model is called an *interface.* Of course, the term *interface* is also used widely in other contexts in the computer and networking worlds, since its generic meaning refers to connecting just about *anything* together. However, when someone talks about an interface between OSI model layers, that person typically refers to the process by which data is passed between layer N of the model and layer N-1 or layer N+1. These relationships are demonstrated in Figure 5-3. For example, the *layer 2/3 interface* is used by a layer 2 and layer 3 protocol to pass data and control information; the *layer 3/4 interface* connects layers 3 and 4 together.

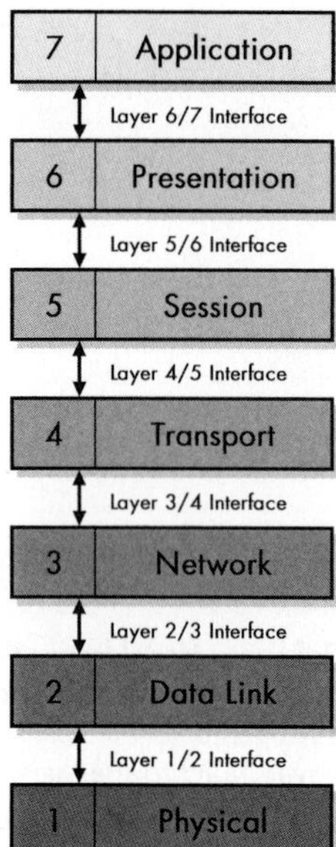

Figure 5-3: OSI Reference Model interfaces for vertical communication
In OSI model terminology, an interface is a conduit for communication between adjacent layers in the layer stack.

NOTE *Remember that not all layers may be implemented in every system or protocol stack in the real world. So it's possible that a process that is technically running at layer 7 might communicate with one running at layer 5. However, I am talking about the theoretical model here.*

Vertical communication is done up and down the protocol stack every time anything is sent across the network, and of course, whenever anything is received. This occurs because the higher levels are implemented as logical functions in software; there is no actual physical connection. The higher layers package data and send it down to the lower layers for it to be sent across the network. At the very lowest level, the data is sent over the network. On the receiving end, the process is reversed, with the data traveling back up to the higher layers on the receiving device. I'll discuss this logical interaction between corresponding layers momentarily.

One of the primary goals of the OSI Reference Model is to allow the interconnection of different implementations of various layers. Thus, the intention is to have somewhat autonomous individual layers that you can mix and match—to a point. The only way to make this work is to have well-defined ways that the layers connect together, and that brings me back to the matter of interfaces. Each layer must present a consistent, well-documented interface to the layers above it so that any upper layer implementation can use the lower layer properly.

I'll provide an example from the world of TCP/IP to illustrate what I mean. The heart of the TCP/IP protocol suite is the Internet Protocol (IP). Whenever you use any application on the Internet—email, websites, FTP, chat rooms, and so on—you are indirectly using IP.

However, you never use IP directly—you generally use one of two transport layer (layer 4) protocols: the Transmission Control Protocol (TCP) or the User Datagram Protocol (UDP) (see Part II-8). A standard interface exists between the network layer and the transport layer in the TCP/IP protocol stack, which defines how IP is to be used by upper layer protocols; this enables TCP and UDP to interface to it. Similarly, both TCP and UDP present a particular interface to the hundreds of higher-layer protocols and applications that use them at higher layers.

Many different types of communication actually take place between layers. Control information is passed to enable the higher layers to utilize the lower ones, and for the lower ones to pass status and results information back to the higher ones. Data is also passed in both directions across the interface. For transmission, it flows down to the lower layer, which normally results in data encapsulation. Upon reception, the process is reversed, with data being sent back up across the interface from a lower to higher layer.

> **KEY CONCEPT** In the OSI Reference Model, an *interface* defines the mechanism for vertical communication between adjacent layers. The existence of well-defined interfaces between layers is what permits a higher layer to use the services of any of a number of lower layers, without requiring knowledge of how those layers are implemented.

Protocols: Horizontal (Corresponding Layer) Communication

Each layer in the OSI Reference Model has a particular role (or roles)—a set of general tasks for which it is responsible. On each system on the network, hardware and software are running at many of the different levels in the model. The routines doing a particular job on Machine A are designed to communicate with similar or complementary ones that are running on Machine B. This *horizontal communication* is the very heart of what networking is about. It is what enables web browsers and web servers to talk, email applications to exchange messages, and so much more.

Of course, all communication types function only if everyone agrees to the same methods of accomplishing it. Each set of rules describing one type of communication is called a *protocol*. You can think of a protocol as a language or a set of instructions. Each function or service of a network has its own language; like human languages, some are similar to each other while others are quite unique.

If you've done any reading at all about networks, you have probably seen the term *protocol* many, many times. Like the word *interface*, the word *protocol* can have many meanings. In fact, it is so fundamental to networking, and used in so many different ways, that I have a discussion devoted to it in Chapter 1.

All that aside, you must remember that the OSI Reference Model is intended to be a formal way of describing networks. As such, the term *protocol* has a formal meaning in the context of the model. It refers specifically to a set of communication rules, instructions, and procedures that describe communication between specific software or hardware elements running *at the same layer* on different machines within a network.

Let's consider how these corresponding layers communicate using protocols. First, you'll recall that every layer in the model, except the bottom (physical) layer, is really a program or algorithm running on a computer. There is no way for, say, a web browser and a web server to actually connect together directly—they are just software programs, after all. Instead, the software running at various layers communicates *logically*. That is to say, through the use of software and procedures, a process running at layer 5 on one machine can accomplish *logical communication* with a similar process running at layer 5 on another machine.

Since machines are only physically connected at layer 1, the data on the sending machine must pass down the data through the layers between layer 5 and layer 1 in order for a protocol at layer 5 to function. The data is then transmitted over the physical connection to layer 1 of the other machine and passed up on the protocol stack of the receiving machine to layer 5. This is how the two machines are logically linked at layer 5, even though they have no physical connection at that layer.

Thus, with the exception of the actual physical connection at layer 1, all horizontal communication also requires vertical communication—down the stack on one machine, and then back up the stack on the other. (The communication doesn't always go all the way back up the stack for each connection, however, as in the case of routing, as discussed in the "Indirect Device Connection and Message Routing" section at the end of this chapter.)

Figure 5-4 illustrates how horizontal communication works. As an example, IP is said to be a layer 3 protocol because each device uses IP software to communicate at layer 3. The actual transmission and reception of data occurs only at the lowest, physical layer; higher-layer protocols communicate *logically* by passing data down interfaces until it reaches layer 1, transmitting at layer 1, and then passing the data back up to the appropriate layer at the recipient.

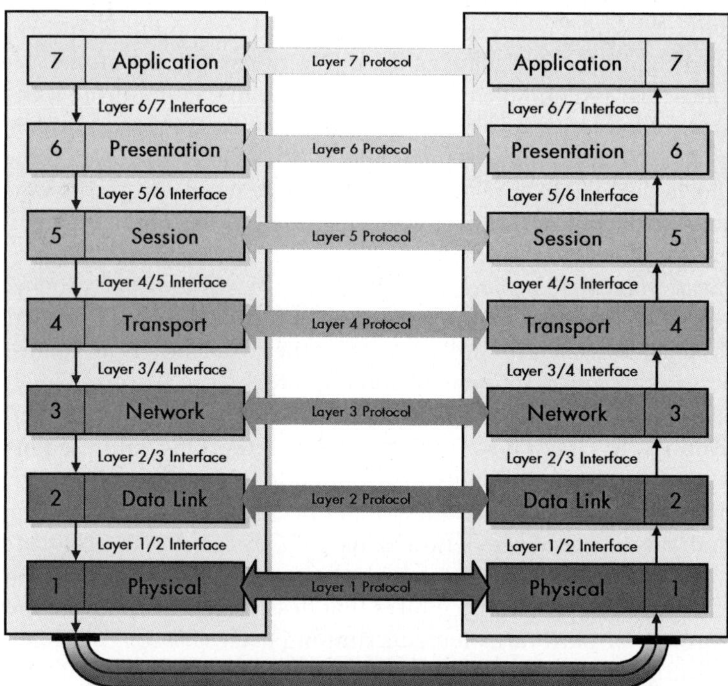

Figure 5-4: OSI Reference Model protocols: horizontal communication *The term* protocol *has many meanings; in the context of the OSI Reference Model, it refers specifically to software or hardware elements that accomplish communication between corresponding layers on two or more devices.*

KEY CONCEPT In the OSI Reference Model, a *protocol* refers specifically to a set of rules or procedures that define communication between software or hardware elements running at the same layer on network devices. Physical layer protocols are responsible for the actual transmission and reception of data at layer 1. Protocols at higher layers pass data down through the layers below them to layer 1 for transmission, then across the network and back up to the corresponding entity at the same layer on the receiving device. The result is that software processes running at say, layer 4 on each of two devices can communicate *logically* as if they were directly connected at layer 4, even though they are not.

Data Encapsulation, Protocol Data Units (PDUs), and Service Data Units (SDUs)

Protocols are what describe the rules that control horizontal communication, that is, conversations between processes that run at corresponding layers within the OSI Reference Model. At every layer (except layer 1), these communications ultimately take the form of some sort of message that is sent between corresponding software elements on two or more devices. Since these messages are the mechanism for communicating information between protocols, they are most generally called *protocol data units (PDUs)*. Each PDU has a specific format that implements the features and requirements of the protocol.

As discussed in the previous section, the communication between layers higher than layer 1 is *logical*; the only hardware connection is at the physical layer. Thus, in order for a protocol to communicate, it must pass down its PDU to the next lower layer for transmission. You've also already seen that, using OSI terminology, lower layers are said to provide *services* to the layers immediately above them. One of the services each layer provides is this function: to handle and manage data received from the layer above.

At any particular layer N, a PDU is a complete message that implements the protocol at that layer. However, when this layer N PDU is passed down to layer N-1, it becomes the *data* that the layer N-1 protocol is supposed to *service*. Thus, the layer N protocol data unit (PDU) is called the layer N-1 *service data unit (SDU)*. The job of layer N-1 is to transport this SDU, which it does by placing the layer N SDU into its own PDU format, preceding the SDU with its own headers and appending footers as necessary. This process is called *data encapsulation*, because the entire contents of the higher-layer message are encapsulated as the data payload of the message at the lower layer.

What does layer N-1 do with its PDU? It passes it down to the next lower layer, where it is treated as a layer N-2 SDU. Layer N-2 creates a layer N-2 PDU containing the layer N-1 PDU and layer N-2's headers and footers. And so the process continues, all the way down to the physical layer. In the theoretical model, what you end up with is a message at layer 1 that consists of application-layer data that is encapsulated with headers and footers from layers 7 through 2.

Figure 5-5 shows a layer 7 PDU consisting of a layer 7 header (labeled L7H) and application data. When this is passed to layer 6, it becomes a layer 6 SDU. The layer 6 protocol prepends to it a layer 6 header (labeled L6H) to create a layer 6 PDU, which is passed to layer 5. The encapsulation process continues all the way down to layer 2, which creates a layer 2 PDU—in this case, shown with both a header and a footer—that is converted to bits and sent at layer 1.

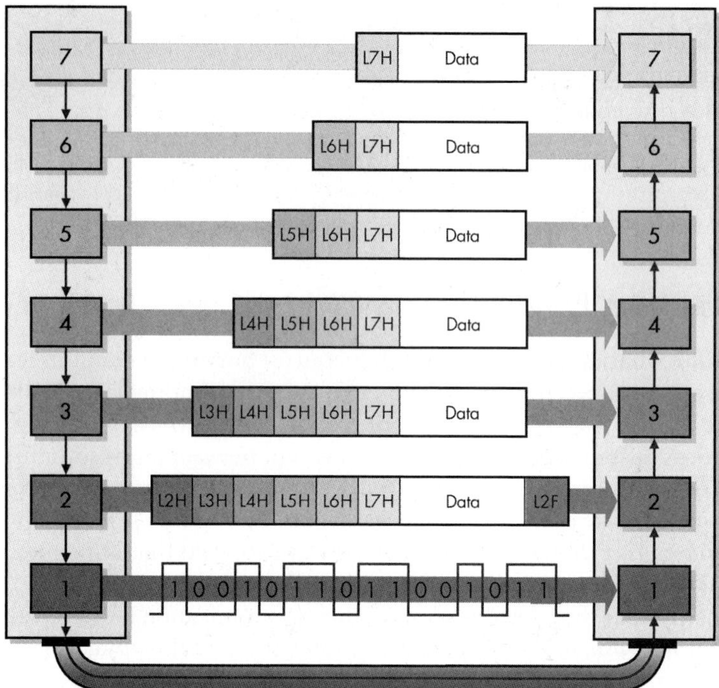

Figure 5-5: OSI Reference Model data encapsulation *Each protocol creates a* protocol data unit (PDU) *for transmission, each of which includes headers required by that protocol and data to be transmitted. This data becomes the* service data unit (SDU) *of the next layer below it.*

> **KEY CONCEPT** The message used to communicate information for a particular protocol is called its *protocol data unit (PDU)* in OSI model terminology. That PDU is passed down to the next lower layer for transmission; since that layer is providing the service of handling that PDU, it is called the lower layer's *service data unit (SDU)*. The SDU is encapsulated into that layer's own PDU and, in turn, sent to the next lower layer in the stack, proceeding until the physical layer is reached. The process is reversed on the recipient device. In summary, a layer N PDU is a layer N-1 SDU, which is *encapsulated* into a layer N-1 PDU.

The "N-1, N-2" stuff makes this seem more difficult than it really is, so let's use a real-world (simplified) example instead. TCP operates at layer 4 of the OSI model. It transmits messages called *segments* that contain data encapsulated from higher-layer protocols. The layer below TCP is IP at layer 3. It receives data from TCP and encapsulates it for transmission.

So, in the formal language of the OSI Reference Model, TCP segments are created as layer 4 PDUs. When passed to IP, they are treated as layer 3 SDUs. The IP software packages these SDUs into messages called *IP packets* or *IP datagrams*, which are layer 3 PDUs. These are passed down to a layer 2 protocol, say Ethernet, which treats IP datagrams as layer 2 SDUs, and packages them into layer 2 PDUs (Ethernet frames), which are sent on to layer 1. (Actually, in some technologies, further encapsulation even occurs at layer 1 prior to transmission.)

On the receiving device, the process of encapsulation is reversed. The Ethernet software inspects the layer 2 PDU (Ethernet frame) and removes from it the layer 2 SDU (IP datagram), which it passes up to IP as a layer 3 PDU. The IP layer removes the layer 3 SDU (TCP segment) and passes it to TCP as a layer 4 PDU. TCP continues the process, going back up the protocol layer stack.

Figure 5-6 shows in more detail how OSI PDUs and SDUs are created and encapsulated. A TCP segment (layer 4 PDU) becomes a layer 3 SDU, which is encapsulated into a layer 3 PDU through the addition of an IP header. This becomes the payload of an Ethernet frame, which is a layer 2 PDU containing an Ethernet header, a layer 2 SDU (the IP datagram), and an Ethernet footer. The receiving device extracts the IP datagram from the Ethernet header and passes it to layer 3; the IP software extracts the TCP segment and passes it up to the TCP software.

This whole matter of encapsulation, passing data up and down the protocol stack, and so on may seem needlessly complex. It also may appear to be rather inefficient; why send a message with so many headers and footers? However, the notion of data encapsulation is critical to creating modular, flexible networks.

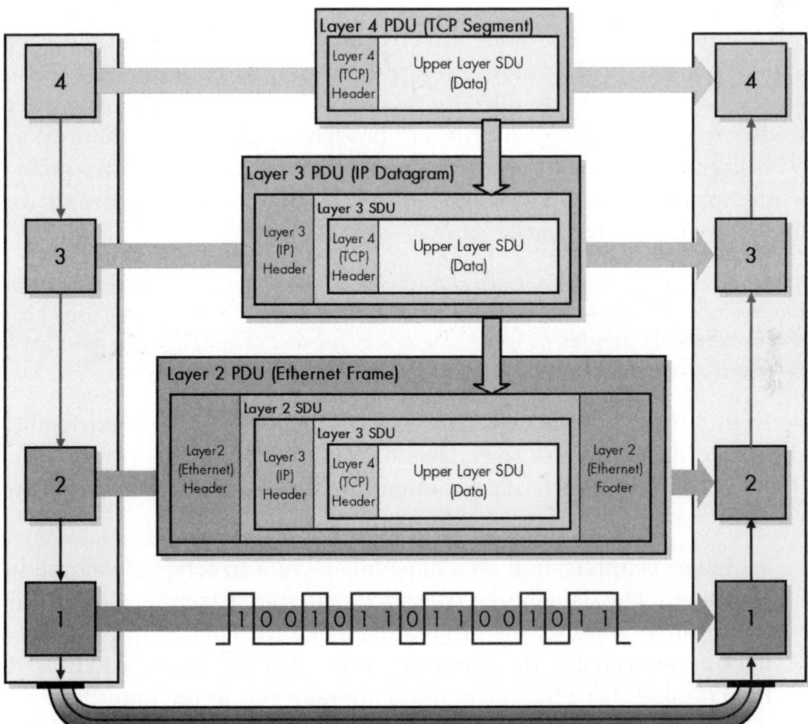

Figure 5-6: OSI Reference Model PDU and SDU encapsulation *Each PDU at one layer of the OSI model becomes an SDU at the next lower layer and is encapsulated into that layer's PDU.*

The term *protocol data unit* or PDU is rather formal. You will see it used in standards and sometimes in discussions, but more often than not, you'll encounter the message terms, such as *frame* and *datagram*, as discussed in Chapter 1. Similarly, data encapsulated by these messages is not normally called a *service data unit* or SDU, but rather simply the *message body* or *payload*, as you saw when you looked at message formatting in Chapter 1. There are cases, however, for which knowing the difference between an SDU and a PDU is important to understanding the technology. One example is the IEEE 802.11 physical layer—the 802.11 standards talk about SDUs and PDUs constantly!

RELATED INFORMATION *See the OSI Reference Model analogy in the "The Benefits of Networking Models" section earlier in this chapter for an example that compares networking encapsulation to something done in a real-world, nonnetworking context.*

Indirect Device Connection and Message Routing

Most of the explanations that I have provided in the other sections of this chapter have discussed the mechanisms by which machines connect to each other over a network *directly*. However, one of the most powerful aspects of networking is that it is possible to create internetworks—networks of networks—that allow devices to be connected *indirectly*. For example, Machine A may send a message to Machine B without really even knowing where it is on the network.

If a message is being sent between devices that are not on the same network, then it must be passed between directly connected networks until it reaches its final destination. The process of transmitting a message from one network to another is called *forwarding*, and the collective process of forwarding from one device to another is *routing*. These concepts are fundamental to all internetworking, including the Internet itself. Every time you access an Internet resource such as a website, you are sending messages that get routed to that site, and the responses you receive get routed back.

NOTE *Even though the technically correct term for moving a message from one network to an adjacent network is* forwarding, *over time, the term* routing *has come to be used both for a single network-to-network transfer, as well as the overall process of transmitting a message from one device to another.*

In the context of the OSI Reference Model, routing is an activity that generally takes place at the network layer, layer 3. You'll recall that data encapsulation causes a higher-layer message to be surrounded by headers and footers at the lower layers. When a message is routed, here's what happens:

- A high-level application on a machine decides to send a datagram to a distant computer. The datagram is packaged, and then passed down vertically through the protocol stack on the originating machine. Each layer encapsulates the data, as described in the previous section. The datagram is addressed to the final destination device. When the message gets to the lower layers, however, it is not packaged for local delivery directly to its ultimate destination, but rather passed to an *intermediate device*. This is the device that is responsible for routing to that destination network. The message is passed down to the data link and physical layers for transmission to that intermediate device.
- The intermediate device (often called a *router*) receives the message at the physical layer. It is passed up to the data link layer, where it is processed, checked for errors and so on, and the data link layer headers are removed. The resulting packet is passed up to the network layer. There, the intermediate device determines if the destination machine is on its local network, or if it needs to

be forwarded to another intermediate device. It then repackages the message and passes it back *down* to the data link layer to be sent on the next leg of its journey.

- After several potential intermediate devices handle the message, it eventually reaches its destination. Here, it travels back up the protocol stack until it reaches the same layer as the one from the application that generated the message on the originating machine.

The key to this description is that in the intermediate devices, the message travels back up the OSI layers *only to the network layer*. It is then repackaged and sent back along its way. The higher layers are involved only on the source and destination devices. The protocol used at layer 3 must be common across the internetwork, but each individual network can be different. This demonstrates some of the power of layering by enabling even rather dissimilar physical networks to be connected together.

Figure 5-7 shows how routing is accomplished conceptually in the OSI model. The intermediate device connects the networks of the message transmitter and recipient. When data is sent, it is passed up to the network layer on the intermediate device, where it is repackaged and sent back down the stack for the next leg of its transmission. Note that the intermediate device actually has two different layer 1 and 2 implementations—one for the interface to each network. Also note that while the layer 3 protocol must be the same across the internetwork, each network can use different technologies at layers 1 and 2.

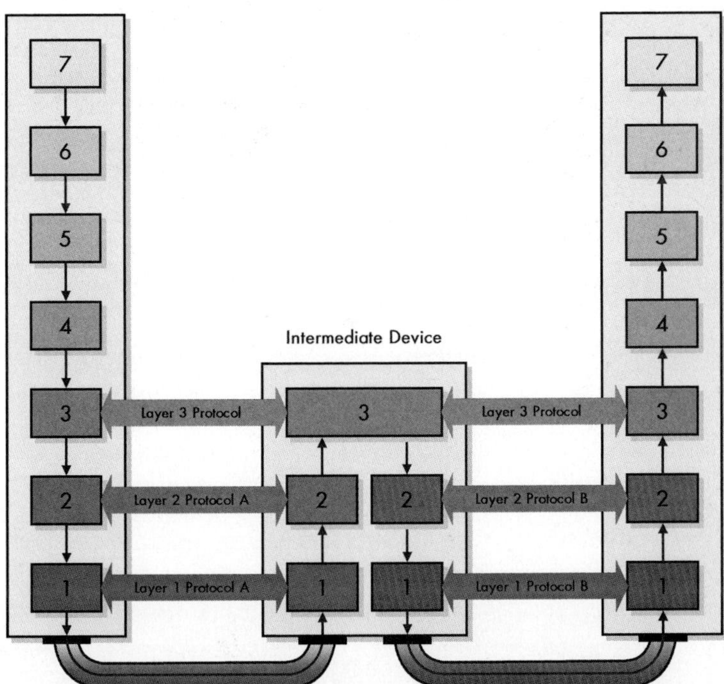

Figure 5-7: Message routing in the OSI Reference Model *Routing in the OSI model is accomplished using an intermediate device that connects networks at layer 3. Data passes up to layer 3 in that device on one network and then passes back down to layer 1 on another.*

KEY CONCEPT In the OSI model, the process of *routing* occurs when data is sent not directly from transmitter to ultimate recipient, but indirectly through the use of an intermediate system. That device, normally called a *router*, connects to two or more physical networks, and thus has multiple interfaces to layer 2. When it receives data, the data passes up only to the network layer, where it is repackaged and then sent on the next leg of its journey over the appropriate layer 2 interface.

6

OSI REFERENCE MODEL LAYERS

In this chapter, we look at the individual layers of the OSI Reference Model. Each layer in the OSI model has certain characteristics that define it, and also various protocols normally associated with it. I'll describe how each layer functions in the OSI layer stack, outline the specific types of activities for which each is normally responsible, and provide some examples of the technologies and protocols that reside at each layer. Understanding the nuances of each layer will help you understand all the technologies that use them.

Keep in mind, however, that the descriptions in this section are *generic*. To really comprehend the details of the various layers and how they are used, read the details of the individual protocols that function at each layer later in this book.

RELATED INFORMATION *Chapter 7 contains summary information that may be helpful to you in understanding the OSI model layers. This includes some common mnemonics for remembering the order of the layers and a summary chart for quickly comparing the layers' key characteristics.*

Physical Layer (Layer 1)

The lowest layer of the OSI Reference Model is layer 1, the *physical layer*; it is commonly abbreviated PHY. This layer is the only one where data is physically moved across the network interface. All other layers perform functions to create messages that implement various protocols, but these messages must all be transmitted down the protocol stack to the physical layer, and they are eventually sent out over the network.

First, a bit of clarification. The name *physical layer* can be a bit problematic because it suggests that this layer relates only to the actual network hardware, which is not the case. While some people say that the physical layer is the network interface cards and cables, this is not actually true. The physical layer defines a number of network functions in addition to interfaces with hardware cables and cards.

People also suggest that all network hardware belongs to the physical layer. Again, this isn't strictly accurate. All hardware must have *some* relation to the physical layer in order to send data over the network, but hardware devices generally implement multiple layers of the OSI model in addition to the physical layer. For example, an Ethernet network interface card performs functions at both the physical layer and the data link layer.

The physical layer technologies deal with the actual ones and zeros that are sent over the network. For example, repeaters, conventional hubs, and transceivers all operate at the physical layer. These devices have no knowledge of the contents of a message; they simply take input bits and send them as output. The physical layer is responsible for the following:

Hardware Specifications Definition The details of operation of cables, connectors, wireless radio transceivers, network interface cards, and other hardware devices are generally a function of the physical layer (although also partially the data link layer, layer 2).

Encoding and Signaling The physical layer is responsible for various encoding and signaling functions that transform the data from bits that reside within a computer or another device into signals that can be sent over the network.

Data Transmission and Reception After encoding the data appropriately, the physical layer actually transmits the data, and of course, receives it. (This applies equally to wired and wireless networks, even if there is no tangible cable in a wireless network.)

Topology and Physical Network Design The physical layer is also considered the domain of many hardware-related network design issues, such as local area network (LAN) and wide area network (WAN) topology.

While the physical layer of a network primarily defines the hardware it uses, it is also closely related to the data link layer. Thus, it is not generally possible to define hardware at the physical layer independently from the technology being used at the data link layer. For example, Ethernet is a technology that describes specific types of cables and network hardware, but the physical layer of Ethernet can be isolated from its data link layer aspects only to a point. Though Ethernet cables are the physical layer, the cables' maximum length is related closely to message format rules that exist at the data link layer.

Furthermore, some technologies perform functions at the physical layer that are normally more closely associated with the data link layer. For example, it is common to have the physical layer perform low-level (bit-level) repackaging of data link layer frames for transmission. Error detection and correction may also be done at layer 1 in some cases, though most people would consider these layer 2 functions.

In many technologies, a number of physical layers can be used with a data link layer. The classic example is Ethernet, for which dozens of different physical layer implementations exist. Each implementation uses the same data link layer (possibly with slight variations).

KEY CONCEPT The lowest layer in the OSI Reference Model is the *physical layer*. It is the realm of networking hardware specifications, and is the place where technologies that perform data encoding, signaling, transmission, and reception functions reside. The physical layer is closely related to the data link layer.

Many technologies further subdivide the physical layer into *sublayers* in order to allow different network media to be supported by the same technology, while sharing other functions at the physical layer that are common between the various media. A good example of this is the physical layer architecture used for Fast Ethernet, Gigabit Ethernet, and 10-Gigabit Ethernet.

NOTE *In some contexts, the physical layer technology that's used to convey bits across a network or communications line is called a* transport method *(not to be confused with the OSI transport layer, layer 4).*

Data Link Layer (Layer 2)

The second-lowest layer (layer 2) in the OSI Reference Model stack is the *data link layer*, often called simply the *link layer*, or abbreviated DLL. The data link layer is where many wired and wireless LAN technologies primarily function. For example, Ethernet, Token Ring, FDDI, and 802.11 (wireless Ethernet or Wi-Fi) are all sometimes called data link layer technologies. The set of devices connected at the data link layer is commonly considered a simple network (as opposed to an internetwork, which is a collection of networks connected at layer 3).

The data link layer is often conceptually divided into two sublayers: *logical link control (LLC)* and *media access control (MAC)*. This split is based on the architecture used in the IEEE 802 Project, which is the IEEE working group responsible for creating the standards that define many networking technologies. By separating LLC and MAC functions, interoperability of different network technologies is made easier, as explained in the discussion of networking models in Chapter 5.

The following are the key tasks performed at the data link layer:

Logical Link Control (LLC) Logical link control refers to the functions required for the establishment and control of logical links between local devices on a network. This is usually considered a sublayer; it provides services to the network layer above it and hides the rest of the details of the data link layer, which allows different technologies to work seamlessly with the higher layers. Most LAN technologies use the IEEE 802.2 LLC protocol to implement this part of the data link layer.

Media Access Control (MAC) This refers to the procedures used by devices to control access to the network medium. Since many networks use a shared medium (such as a single network cable, or a series of cables that are electrically connected into a single virtual medium), it is necessary to have rules for managing the medium to avoid conflicts. For example, Ethernet uses the CSMA/CD method of media access control, while Token Ring uses token passing.

Data Framing The data link layer is responsible for data framing, which is the final encapsulation of higher-level messages into *frames* that are sent over the network at the physical layer.

Addressing The data link layer is the lowest layer in the OSI model that is concerned with addressing. It labels information with a particular destination location. Each device on a network has a unique number that is used by the data link layer protocol to ensure that data intended for a specific machine gets to it properly. This is usually called a *hardware address* (since it is intimately related with low-level hardware) or a *MAC address* (after the MAC function described earlier).

Error Detection and Handling The data link layer handles errors that occur at the lower levels of the network stack. For example, a cyclic redundancy check (CRC) field is often calculated based on the frame's contents and then included in it. This can be employed to allow the station receiving data to detect if it was received correctly.

Physical Layer Standards The physical layer and the data link layer are very closely related. The requirements for the physical layer of a network are often part of the data link layer standard that describes a particular technology. Certain physical-layer hardware and encoding aspects are specified by the data link layer technology being used. The best example of this is the Ethernet standard, IEEE 802.3, which specifies not just how Ethernet works at the data link layer, but also its various physical layers.

> **KEY CONCEPT** The second OSI Reference Model layer is the *data link layer*. This is where most LAN and wireless LAN technologies are defined. Layer 2 is responsible for *logical link control (LLC)*, *media access control (MAC)*, hardware addressing, error detection and handling, and defining physical layer standards. It is often divided into the LLC and MAC sublayers based on the IEEE 802 Project that uses that architecture.

Many types of hardware are associated with the data link layer. Network interface cards typically implement a specific data link layer technology, so they are often called Ethernet cards, Token Ring cards, and so on. There are also a number of network interconnection devices that are said to operate at layer 2 in whole or in part because they make decisions about what to do with data they receive by looking at data link layer frames. These devices include most bridges, switches, and brouters, though the latter two also encompass functions performed by layer 3.

Some of the most popular technologies and protocols generally associated with layer 2 are Ethernet, Token Ring, FDDI (plus CDDI), HomePNA, IEEE 802.11, Asynchronous Transfer Mode (ATM), TCP/IP's Serial Line Interface Protocol (SLIP), and TCP/IP's Point-to-Point Protocol (PPP).

Network Layer (Layer 3)

The third-lowest layer of the OSI Reference Model is the *network layer.* If the data link layer defines the boundaries of what is considered a network, the network layer defines how *internetworks* (interconnected networks) function. The network layer is the lowest one in the OSI model that is concerned with actually getting data from one computer to another even if it is on a remote network; in contrast, the data link layer only deals with devices that are local to each other.

While layers 2 through 6 all act as fences between the layers above and below them, the network layer is particularly important in terms of separating higher and lower-layer functions. It is here that the transition really begins from the more abstract functions of the higher layers—which don't concern themselves as much with data delivery—into the specific tasks required to get data to its destination. (The transport layer continues this abstraction transition as you go up the OSI protocol stack.)

Some of the specific jobs normally performed by the network layer include the following:

Logical Addressing Every device that communicates over a network has a logical address associated with it, which identifies the device regardless of its particular location. This is sometimes called a *layer 3* address. For example, on the Internet, the Internet Protocol (IP) is the network layer protocol and every machine has an IP address. Logical addresses are independent of particular hardware and must be unique across an entire internetwork.

NOTE *Addressing is done at the data link layer as well, but those addresses refer to local physical devices.*

Routing The defining function of the network layer is routing—moving data across a series of interconnected networks. It is the job of the devices and software routines that function at the network layer to handle incoming packets from various sources, determine their final destination, and then figure out where they need to be sent to get them where they are supposed to go. (You'll find a more complete discussion of routing in the OSI model in the section covering indirect device connection in Chapter 5.)

Datagram Encapsulation The network layer normally *encapsulates* messages received from higher layers by placing them into *datagrams* (also called *packets*) with a network layer header (the previous chapter discusses encapsulation).

Fragmentation and Reassembly The network layer must send messages down to the data link layer for transmission. Some data link layer technologies limit the length of any message that can be sent. If the packet that the network layer wants to send is too large, the network layer must split the packet up (fragment it), send each piece to the data link layer, and then have the pieces reassembled once they arrive at the network layer on the destination machine. The IP is the best-known example of a protocol that performs these functions; see Chapter 22 for a discussion of IP datagram fragmentation.

Error Handling and Diagnostics The network layer uses special protocols to allow devices that are logically connected (or that are trying to route traffic) to exchange information about the status of hosts on the network or the devices themselves.

Network layer protocols offer either connection-oriented or connectionless services for delivering packets across the network. Connectionless ones are far more common at the network layer. In many protocol suites, the network layer protocol is connectionless, and connection-oriented services are provided by the transport layer. For example, in TCP/IP, IP is connectionless, while the layer 4 Transmission Control Protocol (TCP) is connection-oriented. Connection-oriented and connectionless protocols are discussed thoroughly in Chapter 1.

The most common network layer protocol is IP, which is why I have already mentioned it a couple of times. IP is the backbone of the Internet and the foundation of the entire TCP/IP protocol suite. There are also several protocols directly related to IP that work with it at the network layer, such as IPsec, IP NAT, and Mobile IP. The Internet Control Message Protocol (ICMP) is the main error-handling and control protocol that is used along with IP. Another notable network layer protocol outside the TCP/IP world is the Novell Internetworking Packet Exchange (IPX) protocol.

> **KEY CONCEPT** The OSI Reference Model's third layer is the *network layer*. This is one of the most important layers in the model; it is responsible for the tasks that link together individual networks into *internetworks*. Network layer functions include internetwork-level addressing, routing, datagram encapsulation, fragmentation and reassembly, and certain types of error handling and diagnostics. The network layer and transport layer are closely related to each other.

The network interconnection devices that operate at the network layer are usually called *routers*. They are responsible for the routing functions I have mentioned, because they receive packets as they are sent along each "hop" of a route and send them on the next leg of their trip. They communicate with each other using routing protocols in order to determine the best routes for sending traffic efficiently. So-called brouters also reside, at least in part, at the network layer, as do the rather obviously named layer 3 switches.

Transport Layer (Layer 4)

The fourth layer of the OSI Reference Model protocol stack is the *transport layer*, also called the *middle layer*. The transport layer is in some ways part of both the lower and upper groups of layers in the OSI model. It is more often associated with the lower layers, because it concerns itself with the *transport* of data, but its functions are also somewhat high level, resulting in its having a fair bit in common with layers 5 through 7 as well.

You'll recall that layers 1 through 3 are concerned with the actual packaging, addressing, routing, and delivery of data. The physical layer handles the bits, the data link layer deals with local networks, and the network layer handles routing between networks. The transport layer, in contrast, is sufficiently conceptual that it no longer concerns itself with these nuts-and-bolts matters. It relies on the lower layers to move data between devices.

The transport layer acts as a liaison of sorts between the abstract world of applications at the higher layers and the concrete functions of layers 1 to 3. Its overall job is to provide the necessary functions to enable communication between software application processes on different computers, which encompasses a number of different but related duties.

Because modern computers are multitasking, many different software applications may be trying to send and receive data to the same machine at any given point. The transport layer is charged with providing a means by which these applications can all send and receive data using the same lower-layer protocol implementation. Thus, it is sometimes said to be responsible for *end-to-end* or *host-to-host* transport (in fact, the equivalent layer in the TCP/IP model is called the host-to-host transport layer).

To accomplish this communication between processes, the transport layer must perform several different but related jobs. For transmission, it must track the data from each application, then combine it into a single flow of data to send to the lower layers. The device receiving information must reverse these operations, fragment the data, and funnel it to the appropriate recipient processes. The transport layer is also responsible for defining the means by which potentially large amounts of application data are fragmented for transmission.

The transport layer is also responsible for providing *connection services* for the protocols and applications that run at the levels above it. These can be categorized as either connection-oriented services or connectionless services, and each has its uses. While connection-oriented services can be handled at the network layer, they are more often seen in the transport layer in the real world. (Some protocol suites, such as TCP/IP, provide both a connection-oriented and a connectionless transport layer protocol that suits the needs of different applications.)

The transport layer is also where functions are normally included for adding features to end-to-end data transport. Whereas network layer protocols are normally concerned with just "best-effort" communications for which delivery is not guaranteed, transport layer protocols are given intelligence in the form of algorithms that ensure the reliable and efficient communication between devices. This intelligence encompasses several related jobs, including lost transmission detection and handling, and managing the rate at which data is sent in order to ensure that the receiving device is not overwhelmed.

Transmission quality—ensuring that transmissions are received as sent—is so important that some networking books define the transport layer on the basis of reliability and flow-control functions. However, not all transport layer protocols provide these services. Just as a protocol suite may have a connection-oriented and a connectionless transport layer protocol, it may also have one transport layer protocol that provides reliability and data management services, and one that doesn't. Again, this is the case with TCP/IP: There is one main transport layer protocol, TCP, that includes reliability and flow-control features, and a second, User Datagram Protocol (UDP), that doesn't.

Let's look at the specific functions often performed at the transport layer in more detail:

Process-Level Addressing Addressing at the transport layer is used to differentiate between software programs. This is part of what enables many different software programs to use a network layer protocol simultaneously. The best example of transport-layer process-level addressing is the TCP and UDP port mechanism that's used in TCP/IP, which allows applications to be individually referenced on any TCP/IP device.

Multiplexing and Demultiplexing Using the process-level addresses, transport layer protocols on a sending device *multiplex* the data received from many application programs for transport, combining them into a single stream of data to be sent. The same protocols receive data and then *demultiplex* it from the incoming stream of datagrams, and direct each one to the appropriate recipient application processes.

Segmentation, Packaging, and Reassembly The transport layer segments the large amounts of data it sends over the network into smaller pieces on the source machine, and then reassembles them on the destination machine. This function is similar to the fragmentation function of the network layer. Just as the network layer fragments messages to fit the limits of the data link layer, the transport layer segments messages to suit the requirements of the underlying network layer.

Connection Establishment, Management, and Termination Transport layer connection-oriented protocols are responsible for the series of communications required to establish a connection, maintain it as data is sent over it, and then terminate the connection when it is no longer required.

Acknowledgments and Retransmissions As mentioned earlier, the transport layer is where many protocols that guarantee reliable delivery of data are implemented. This is done using a variety of techniques, most commonly by combining *acknowledgment* and *retransmission timers*. The sending device starts a timer on each occasion that data is sent; if the data is received, the recipient sends back an acknowledgment to the sender to indicate successful transmission. If no acknowledgment is returned before the timer expires, the data is retransmitted. Other algorithms and techniques are usually required to support this basic process.

Flow Control Transport layer protocols that offer reliable delivery also often implement *flow-control* features. These features allow one device in a communication to specify to another that it must throttle back the rate at which it is sending data. This will prevent the receiver from being bogged down with data. These features allow mismatches in speed between sender and receiver to be detected and handled.

KEY CONCEPT The fourth and middle OSI Reference Model layer is the *transport layer*. This layer represents the transition point between the lower layers that deal with data delivery issues, and the higher ones that work with application software. The transport layer is responsible for enabling *end-to-end communication* between application processes, which it accomplishes in part through the use of process-level addressing and multiplexing or demultiplexing. Transport layer protocols are responsible for segmenting application data into blocks for transmission and may be either connection-oriented or connectionless. Protocols at this layer also often provide data delivery management services such as reliability and flow control.

In theory, the transport and network layers are distinct, but in practice, they are often very closely related to each other. You can see this easily just by looking at the names of common protocol stacks. They are often named after the layer 3 and 4 protocols in the suite, thereby implying their close relationship. For example, the name TCP/IP comes from the suite's most commonly used transport layer protocol (TCP) and network layer protocol (IP). Similarly, the Novell NetWare suite is often called IPX/SPX for its layer 3 (IPX) and layer 4 (Sequenced Packet Exchange, or SPX) protocols.

Typically, specific transport layer protocols use the network layers in the same family. You won't often find a network using the transport layer protocol from one suite and the network layer protocol from another. The most commonly used transport layer protocols are TCP and UDP in the TCP/IP suite, SPX in the NetWare protocol suite, and NetBEUI in the NetBIOS/NetBEUI/NBF suite (though NetBEUI is more difficult to categorize).

Session Layer (Layer 5)

The fifth layer in the OSI Reference Model is the *session layer*. As you proceed up the OSI layer stack from the bottom, the session layer is the first one where essentially all practical matters related to the addressing, packaging, and delivery of data are left behind; they are functions of layers 4 and below. The session layer is the lowest of the three upper layers, which, as a group, are concerned mainly with software application issues and not with the details of network and internetwork implementation.

The name session layer is telling: It is designed to allow devices to establish and manage *sessions*. In general terms, a session is a persistent logical linking of two software application processes that allows them to exchange data over time. In some discussions, these sessions are called *dialogs*, and, in fact, they are roughly analogous to a telephone call made between two people.

Session layer protocols primarily provide the necessary means for setting up, managing, and ending sessions. In fact, in some ways, session-layer software products resemble sets of tools more than specific protocols. These session-layer tools are normally provided to higher-layer protocols through command sets that are often called *application program interfaces* or *APIs*.

Common APIs include NetBIOS, TCP/IP Sockets, and Remote Procedure Calls (RPCs). APIs allow an application to easily accomplish certain high-level communications over the network by using a standardized set of services. Most of these session-layer tools are of primary interest to the developers of application software. The programmers use the APIs to write software that is able to communicate using TCP/IP without developers having to know the implementation details of how TCP/IP works.

For example, the Sockets interface lies conceptually at layer 5 and is used by TCP/IP application programmers to create sessions between software programs over the Internet on the UNIX operating system. Windows Sockets similarly lets programmers create Windows software that is Internet capable and able to interact easily with other software that uses that interface. (Strictly speaking, Sockets is not a protocol, but rather a programming method.)

NOTE *The boundaries between layers start to blur once you get to the session layer. This makes it hard to categorize what exactly belongs at layer 5, and some technologies really span layers 5 through 7. In the world of TCP/IP in particular, it is not common to identify protocols that are specific to the OSI session layer.*

KEY CONCEPT The fifth layer in the OSI Reference Model layer is the *session layer*. As its name suggests, it is the layer intended to provide functions for establishing and managing sessions between software processes. Session layer technologies are often implemented as sets of software tools called *application program interfaces (APIs)*, which provide a consistent set of services that allow programmers to develop networking applications without needing to worry about lower-level details of transport, addressing, and delivery.

NOTE *The term "session" is somewhat vague, which means that there is sometimes disagreement on the specific functions that belong at the session layer, or about whether certain protocols belong at the session layer or not. To add to this potential confusion, there is the matter of differentiating between a* connection *and a* session. *Connections are normally the province of layer 4 and layer 3, yet a TCP connection, for example, can persist for a long time. The longevity of TCP connections makes them hard to distinguish from sessions (and there are some people who feel that the TCP/IP host-to-host transport layer really straddles OSI layers 4 and 5).*

Presentation Layer (Layer 6)

The *presentation layer* is the sixth layer of the OSI Reference Model protocol stack and second from the top. It differs from the other layers in two key respects. First, it has a much more limited and specific function than the other layers. Second, it is used much less often than the other layers and is not required by many types of communications.

This layer deals with the *presentation* of data. More specifically, it is charged with taking care of any issues that might arise when data sent from one system needs to be viewed in a different way by the receiving system. The presentation layer also handles any special processing that must be done to data from the time an application tries to send it until the time it is sent over the network.

Here are some of the specific types of data-handling issues that the presentation layer handles:

Translation Many different types of computers can exist on the same network, such as PCs, Macs, UNIX systems, AS/400 servers, and mainframes. Each has many distinct characteristics and represents data in different ways (with different character sets, for example). The presentation layer hides the differences between machines.

Compression Compression (and decompression) may be done at the presentation layer to improve the throughput of data.

Encryption Some types of encryption (and decryption) are performed at the presentation layer to ensure the security of the data as it travels down the protocol stack. For example, one of the most popular encryption schemes usually associated with the presentation layer is the Secure Sockets Layer (SSL) protocol. (Some encryption is done at lower layers in the protocol stack in technologies such as IPsec.)

The presentation layer is not always used in network communications because these functions mentioned are simply not always needed. Compression and encryption are usually considered optional, and translation features are needed only in certain circumstances. Also, the presentation layer's functions may be performed at the application layer.

NOTE *Since its translation job isn't always needed, the presentation layer is commonly skipped by actual protocol stack implementations; in such implementations protocols at layer 7 may talk directly with those at layer 5. This is part of the reason why all of the functions at layers 5 through 7 may be included in the same software package, as described in the overview of layers and layer groupings in the previous chapter.*

KEY CONCEPT The sixth OSI model layer is the *presentation layer*. Protocols at this layer take care of manipulation tasks that transform data from one representation to another, such as translation, compression, and encryption. In many cases, no such functions are required in a particular networking stack; if so, there may not be any protocol active at layer 6, so layer 7 may deal with layer 5.

Application Layer (Layer 7)

At the very top of the OSI Reference Model stack of layers, you find layer 7, the *application layer*. Continuing the trend that you saw in layers 5 and 6, this one is also named very appropriately. The application layer is the one that is used by network applications. These programs are what actually implement the functions performed by users to accomplish various tasks over the network.

It's important to understand that what the OSI model calls an application is not exactly the same as what you normally think of as an application. In the OSI model, the application layer provides services for user applications to employ.

For example, when you use your web browser, that actual software is an application running on your PC. It doesn't really reside at the application layer. Rather, it makes use of the services offered by a protocol that operates at the application layer, which is called the Hypertext Transfer Protocol (HTTP). The distinction between the browser and HTTP is subtle but important.

Not all user applications use the network's application layer in the same way. Sure, your web browser, email client, and Usenet newsreader do, but if you open a file over the network with a text editor, that editor is not using the application layer—it just sees a file addressed with a name that has been mapped to a network somewhere else. The operating system redirects what the editor does, over the network.

Similarly, not all uses of the application layer are by applications. The operating system itself can (and does) use services directly at the application layer.

That caveat aside, under normal circumstances, whenever you interact with a program on your computer that is designed specifically for use on a network, you are dealing directly with the application layer. For example, sending an email message, firing up a web browser, and using a chat program involve protocols that reside at the application layer.

NOTE *There are dozens of different application layer protocols. Some of the most popular ones include HTTP, FTP, SMTP, DHCP, NFS, Telnet, SNMP, POP3, NNTP, and IRC. I describe all of these and more in Section III.*

As the top-of-the-stack layer, the application layer is the only one that does not provide any services to the layer above it in the stack—there isn't one! Instead, it provides services to programs that want to use the network, and to you, the user. So the responsibilities at this layer are simply to implement the functions that are needed by users of the network and to issue the appropriate commands to make use of the services provided by the lower layers.

KEY CONCEPT The *application layer* is the seventh and highest layer in the OSI Reference Model. Application protocols that implement specific user applications and other high-level functions are defined at this layer. Since they are at the top of the stack, application protocols are the only ones that do not provide services to a higher layer; they use services provided by the layers below.

As you've seen, the distinctions between the top three layers in the OSI Model are not very clear. In the case of TCP/IP, this is exacerbated by the decision not to separate out the session, presentation, and application layer functions. All of the protocols mentioned earlier are from the TCP/IP protocol family, and some may cover all three of the top three OSI layers, two of them, or one; in the TCP/IP model, they are all just considered applications.

7

OSI REFERENCE MODEL SUMMARY

Many students of networking find the OSI Reference Model challenging to deal with. One main reason for this is that the model is somewhat *abstract*, making it hard to understand and even more difficult to apply to real networking situations. For this reason, I have included in this chapter a set of three tools that I hope will help you better understand and remember the OSI Reference Model's and concepts: an analogy, a set of mnemonics, and a summary table of OSI model layers.

Understanding the OSI Model: An Analogy

I have attempted in this discussion of the OSI Reference Model to provide as much a plain English explanation of how it works as possible. However, there are situations in which a good analogy can accomplish what lots of descriptions cannot. So I am going to illustrate the key OSI model concepts by way of a real-life analogy. You can be the judge of whether it is a *good* analogy or not. Just remember that no analogy is perfect!

Our scenario seems relatively simple and common: The CEO of a Fortune 500 company needs to send a letter to the CEO of another company. Simple, right? Just like firing up your web browser and connecting to your favorite website is simple. However, in both cases, a lot goes on behind the scenes to make the communication happen. In the analogy shown in Table 7-1, I compare these real-world and cyber-world communications.

Table 7-1: OSI Reference Model Real-World Analogy

Phase	OSI Layer	CEO Letter	Website Connection (Simplified)
Transmission	7	The CEO of a company in Phoenix decides he needs to send a letter to a peer in Albany. He dictates the letter to his administrative assistant.	You decide you want to connect to the web server at IP address 10.0.12.34, which is within your organization but not on your local network. You type the address into your browser.
	6	The administrative assistant transcribes the dictation into writing.	With a website connection, nothing usually happens here. Format translation may be done in some cases.
	5	The administrative assistant puts the letter in an envelope and gives it to the mail room. The assistant doesn't actually know how the letter will be sent, but knows it is urgent, so he says, "Get this to its destination quickly."	The request is sent via a call to an API, which issues the command necessary to contact the server at that address.
	4	The mail room must decide how to get the letter where it needs to go. Since it is a rush, the people in the mail room decide to give the envelope to a courier company to send.	TCP is used to create a segment that will be sent to IP address 10.0.12.34.
	3	The courier company receives the envelope, but it needs to add its own handling information, so it places the smaller envelope in a courier envelope (encapsulation). The courier then consults its airplane route information and determines that to get this envelope to Albany, it must be flown through its hub in Chicago. It hands this envelope to the workers who load packages on its planes.	Your computer creates an IP datagram encapsulating the TCP datagram created earlier. It then addresses the packet to 10.0.12.34, but discovers that it is not on its local network. Instead, it realizes it needs to send the message to its designated routing device at IP address 10.0.43.21. It hands the packet to the driver for your Ethernet card (the software that interfaces to the Ethernet hardware).
Routing	2	The workers take the courier envelope and put a tag on it with the code for Chicago. They then put it in a handling box and load it on the plane to Chicago.	The Ethernet card driver forms a frame containing the IP datagram and prepares it to be sent over the network. It packages the message and puts the address 10.0.43.21 (for the router) in the frame.
	1	The plane flies to Chicago.	The frame is sent over the twisted-pair cable that connects your local area network. (I'm ignoring overhead, collisions, and so on, here, but then I also ignored the possibility of collisions with the plane.)

(continued)

Table 7-1: OSI Reference Model Real-World Analogy (continued)

Phase	OSI Layer	CEO Letter	Website Connection (Simplified)
Routing	2	In Chicago, the box is unloaded, and the courier envelope is removed from it and given to the people who handle routing in Chicago.	The Ethernet card at the machine with IP address 10.0.43.21 receives the frame, strips off the frame headers, and hands it up to the network layer.
	3	The tag marked "Chicago" is removed from the outside of the courier envelope. The envelope is then given back to the airplane workers to be sent to Albany.	The IP datagram is processed by the router, which realizes the destination (10.0.12.34) can be reached directly. It passes the datagram back down to the Ethernet driver.
	2	The envelope is given a new tag with the code for Albany, placed in another box, and loaded on the plane to Albany.	The Ethernet driver creates a new frame and prepares to send it to the device that uses IP address 10.0.12.34.
	1	The plane flies to Albany.	The frame is sent over the network.
	2	The box is unloaded, and the courier envelope is removed from the box. It is given to the Albany routing office.	The Ethernet card at the device with IP address 10.0.12.34 receives the frame, strips off the headers, and passes it up the stack.
Reception	3	The courier company in Albany sees that the destination is in Albany and delivers the envelope to the destination CEO's company.	The IP headers are removed from the datagram, and the TCP segments are handed up to TCP.
	4	The mail room removes the inner envelope from the courier envelope and delivers it to the destination CEO's assistant.	TCP removes its headers and hands the data up to the drivers on the destination machine.
	5	The assistant takes the letter out of the envelope.	The request is sent to the web-server software for processing.
	6	The assistant reads the letter and decides whether to give the letter to the CEO, transcribe it to email, call the CEO on her cell phone, or whatever.	Again, in this example nothing probably happens at the presentation layer.
	7	The second CEO receives the message that was sent by the first one.	The web server receives and processes the request.

As you can see, the processes have a fair bit in common. The vertical communication and encapsulation are pretty obvious, as is the routing. Also implied is the horizontal communication that occurs logically—the two CEOs seem to be "connected" despite all that happens to enable this to occur. Similarly, in a way, the two assistants are logically connected as well, even though they never actually converse. Of course, this example is highly simplified in just about every way imaginable, so please don't use it as a way of trying to learn about how TCP/IP works—or courier services, for that matter!

Remembering the OSI Model Layers: Some Mnemonics

If you spend any amount of time at all dealing with networking design or implementation issues, or learning about how the various protocols operate, the names and numbers of the various layers will eventually become second nature.

Many people, however, especially those just learning about networks, find it difficult to recall the names of all the layers, and especially, their exact order. For these people, a number of mnemonics have been created as memory aids. You probably remember mnemonics from elementary school. These are cute phrases in which each word starts with the first letter of an OSI model layer, arranged in the correct order. Some of these go in ascending layer number order, and some go in the other direction.

These two go from physical layer to application layer:

- Please Do Not Throw Sausage Pizza Away
- Please Do Not Touch Steve's Pet Alligator

And these go the other direction, from application to physical:

- All People Seem To Need Data Processing (a popular one)
- All People Standing Totally Naked Don't Perspire (hmm, that's interesting!)

For your convenience, I have illustrated all four of these in Figure 7-1.

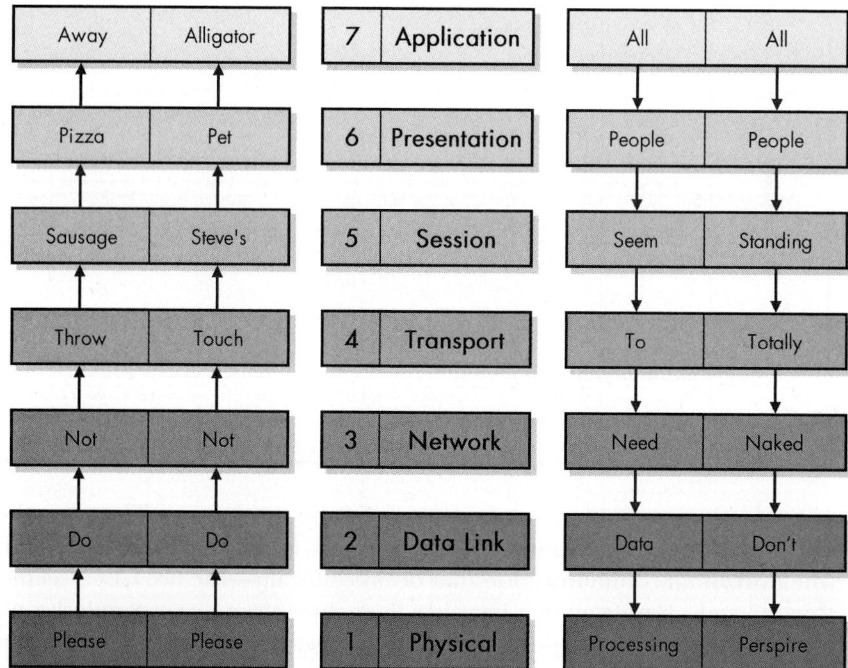

Figure 7-1: OSI Reference Model mnemonics *These mnemonics may help you to remember the order of the OSI Reference Model layers.*

Or try my own creation: All People Should Teach Networking Daily Please.

Summarizing the OSI Model Layers: A Summary Chart

To assist you in quickly comparing the layers of the OSI Reference Model, and understanding where they are different and how they relate to each other, I'm offering you the summary chart shown in Table 7-2. It shows each layer's name and number, describes its key responsibilities, talks about what type of data is generally handled at each layer, and also describes the scope of each layer in approximate terms. I also show some of the more common protocols that are associated with each layer.

The standard disclaimers still apply to this table. Namely, the layers aren't always hard-fast; I haven't listed every single protocol here, so some may really fit into more than one layer, and so on. In particular, note that many of the technologies listed as being in the data link layer are there because that is the layer where their primary functionality resides. In reality, most of these technologies include components in other layers, especially the physical layer.

Table 7-2: OSI Reference Model Layer Summary

Group	#	Layer Name	Key Responsibilities	Data Type Handled	Scope	Common Protocols and Technologies
Lower Layers	1	Physical	Encoding and signaling; physical data transmission; hardware specifications; topology and design	Bits	Electrical or light signals sent between local devices	Physical layers of most of the technologies listed for the data link layer
	2	Data Link	Logical link control; media access control; data framing; addressing; error detection and handling; defining requirements of physical layer	Frames	Low-level data messages between local devices	IEEE 802.2 LLC, Ethernet family; Token Ring; FDDI and CDDI; IEEE 802.11 (WLAN, Wi-Fi); HomePNA; HomeRF; ATM; SLIP and PPP
	3	Network	Logical addressing; routing; datagram encapsulation; fragmentation and reassembly; error handling and diagnostics	Datagrams/ packets	Messages between local or remote devices	IP; IPv6; IP NAT; IPsec; Mobile IP; ICMP; IPX; DLC; PLP; routing protocols such as RIP and BGP
	4	Transport	Process-level addressing; multiplexing/ demultiplexing; connections; segmentation and reassembly; acknowledgments and retransmissions; flow control	Datagrams/ segments	Communication between software processes	TCP and UDP; SPX; NetBEUI/NBF

(continued)

Table 7-2: OSI Reference Model Layer Summary (continued)

Group	#	Layer Name	Key Responsibilities	Data Type Handled	Scope	Common Protocols and Technologies
Upper Layers	5	Session	Session establishment, management, and termination	Sessions	Sessions between local or remote devices	NetBIOS, Sockets, named pipes, RPC
	6	Presentation	Data translation; compression and encryption	Encoded user data	Application data representations	SSL; shells and redirectors; MIME
	7	Application	User application services	User data	Application data	DNS; NFS; BOOTP; DHCP; SNMP; RMON; FTP; TFTP; SMTP; POP3; IMAP; NNTP; HTTP; Telnet

PART I-3

TCP/IP PROTOCOL SUITE AND ARCHITECTURE

In the first two parts of this "TCP/IP Overview and Background Information" section, I have laid the groundwork for understanding how networks function in general terms. Now we can begin to turn our attention to the main subject of this book: TCP/IP.

Just as Ethernet rules the roost when it comes to local area network (LAN) technologies, and IEEE 802.11 is the boss of the wireless LAN (WLAN) world, TCP/IP dominates and even defines the world of modern internetworking, including the Internet.

Since TCP/IP is the subject of this entire book, you might be wondering why this part is so small, containing only a single chapter. The reason is that it provides only a high-level overview of the TCP/IP protocol suite. TCP/IP is a collection of several dozen constituent protocols and technologies. These are described in the following two sections of the book, which cover lower-layer and application protocols, respectively. These protocols are summarized in the TCP/IP introduction chapter that follows, which also provides a brief history of TCP/IP and describes its services and model.

8

TCP/IP PROTOCOL SUITE AND ARCHITECTURE

Named for two of its key protocols, the TCP/IP protocol suite has been in continual use and development for about three decades. In that time, it has evolved from an experimental technology that was used to hook together a handful of research computers to the powerhouse of the largest and most complex computer network in history: the global Internet, connecting together millions of networks and end devices.

In this chapter, we begin a magical tour through the mystical world of TCP/IP with an overview and a brief look at its very interesting history. I discuss the services provided in TCP/IP networks and then explain the architectural model used under TCP/IP. I then provide a brief description of each of the most important TCP/IP protocols that are discussed in the remainder of the book.

TCP/IP Overview and History

The best place to begin an examination of TCP/IP is probably with the name itself. In fact, TCP/IP consists of dozens of different protocols, of which two are usually considered the most important. The *Internet Protocol (IP)* is the primary OSI model network layer (layer 3) protocol that provides addressing, datagram routing, and other functions in an internetwork. The *Transmission Control Protocol (TCP)* is the primary transport layer (layer 4) protocol and is responsible for connection establishment and management, and reliable data transport between software processes on devices. Because these two protocols are so important, their abbreviations have come to represent the entire suite: TCP/IP.

IP and TCP are important because many of TCP/IP's most critical functions are implemented at layers 3 and 4, where these protocols live. However, there is much more to TCP/IP than just TCP and IP. The protocol suite as a whole requires the work of many different protocols and technologies to make a functional network that can properly provide users with the applications they need.

TCP/IP uses its own four-layer architecture (which corresponds roughly to the OSI Reference Model), to provide a framework for the various protocols that compose it. It also includes numerous high-level applications, some of which are well known by Internet users who may not realize they are part of TCP/IP, such as the Hypertext Transfer Protocol (HTTP, which powers the World Wide Web) and File Transfer Protocol (FTP). In the coming discussions on TCP/IP architecture and protocols, we'll look at most of the important TCP/IP protocols and how they fit together.

TCP/IP History and Development

The history of the Internet and the history of TCP/IP are so closely related that it is difficult to discuss one without also talking about the other. They were developed together, with TCP/IP providing the mechanism for implementing the Internet. Over the years, TCP/IP has continued to evolve to meet the needs of the Internet and also smaller, private networks that use the technology. We'll take a brief look at that history here.

The TCP/IP protocols were initially created as part of the research network developed by the United States *Defense Advanced Research Projects Agency* (*DARPA* or *ARPA*). Initially, this fledgling network, called the *ARPAnet*, was designed to use a number of protocols that had been adapted from existing technologies. However, they all had flaws or limitations either in concept or in practical matters, such as capacity when used on the ARPAnet. The developers of the new network recognized that trying to use these existing protocols might eventually lead to problems as the ARPAnet increased in size and was adapted for newer uses and applications.

In 1973, the development of a full-fledged system of internetworking protocols for the ARPAnet began. Interestingly, early versions of this technology included only one core protocol: TCP. And in fact, these letters didn't even stand for what they do today; they stood for the *Transmission Control Program*. The first version of this predecessor of modern TCP was written in 1973, then revised and formally documented in RFC 675, Specification of Internet Transmission Control Program, published in December 1974.

NOTE *Internet standards are defined in documents called Requests for Comments (RFCs). These documents, and the process used to create them, are described in Chapter 3.*

Testing and development of TCP continued for several years. In March 1977, version 2 of TCP was documented. In August 1977, a significant turning point came in TCP/IP's development. Jon Postel, one of the most important pioneers of the Internet and TCP/IP, published a set of comments on the state of TCP. In that document (known as *Internet Engineering Note number 2*, or *IEN 2*), he provided an excellent example of how reference models and layers aren't just for textbooks:

> We are screwing up in our design of internet protocols by violating the principle of layering. Specifically we are trying to use TCP to do two things: serve as a host level end to end protocol, and to serve as an internet packaging and routing protocol. These two things should be provided in a layered and modular way. I suggest that a new distinct internetwork protocol is needed, and that TCP be used strictly as a host level end to end protocol.
>
> —Jon Postel, IEN 2, 1977

Postel was essentially saying that the version of TCP created in the mid-1970s was trying to do too much. Specifically, it was encompassing both OSI layer 3 and layer 4 activities. His vision was prophetic, because we now know that having TCP handle all of these activities would have indeed led to problems down the road.

Postel's observation led to the definition of TCP/IP architecture, and the splitting of TCP into TCP at the transport layer and IP at the network layer. The process of dividing TCP into two portions began in 1978 with version 3 of TCP. The first formal standard for the versions of IP and TCP used in modern networks (version 4) was created in 1980.

TCP/IP quickly became the standard protocol set for running the ARPAnet. In the 1980s, more and more machines and networks were connected to the evolving ARPAnet using TCP/IP protocols, and the TCP/IP Internet was born.

KEY CONCEPT TCP/IP was initially developed in the 1970s as part of an effort to define a set of technologies to operate the fledgling Internet. The name TCP/IP came about when the original *Transmission Control Program (TCP)* was split into the *Transmission Control Protocol (TCP)* and *Internet Protocol (IP)*. The first modern versions of these two key protocols were documented in 1980 as TCP version 4 and IP version 4, respectively.

Important Factors in the Success of TCP/IP

TCP/IP was at one time just one of many different sets of protocols that could be used to provide network-layer and transport-layer functionality. Today there are still other options for internetworking protocols, such as Novell's IPX/SPX, but TCP/IP is the universally accepted worldwide standard.

TCP/IP's growth in popularity has been due to a number of important factors. Some of these are historical, such as the fact that it is tied to the Internet as described earlier, while others are related to the characteristics of the protocol suite itself.

Integrated Addressing System TCP/IP includes within it (as part of IP primarily) a system for identifying and addressing devices on both small and large networks. The addressing system is designed to allow devices to be addressed regardless of the lower-level details of how each constituent network is constructed. Over time, the mechanisms for addressing in TCP/IP have improved to meet the needs of growing networks, especially the Internet. The addressing system also includes a centralized administration capability for the Internet to ensure that each device has a unique address.

Design for Routing TCP/IP is specifically designed to facilitate the routing of information over a network of arbitrary complexity. In fact, TCP/IP is conceptually concerned more with connecting networks than with connecting devices. TCP/IP routers enable data to be delivered between devices on different networks by moving it one step at a time from one network to the next. A number of support protocols in TCP/IP are designed to allow routers to exchange critical information and manage the efficient flow of information from one network to another.

Underlying Network Independence TCP/IP operates primarily at layers 3 and above, and includes provisions to allow it to function on almost any lower-layer technology, including local area networks (LANs), wireless LANs, and wide area networks (WANs) of various sorts. This flexibility means that you can mix and match a variety of different underlying networks and connect them all using TCP/IP.

Scalability One of the most amazing characteristics of TCP/IP is the scalability of its protocols. Over the decades, it has proven its mettle as the Internet has grown from a small network with just a few machines to a huge internetwork with millions of hosts. While some changes have been required periodically to support this growth, these changes have taken place as part of the TCP/IP development process, yet the core of TCP/IP is basically the same as it was 25 years ago.

Open Standards and Development Process The TCP/IP standards, rather than being proprietary, are open ones, freely available to the public. Furthermore, the process used to develop the TCP/IP standards is also completely open. The TCP/IP standards and protocols are developed and modified using the unique, democratic Request for Comments (RFC) process (described in Chapter 3), with all interested parties invited to participate. This ensures that anyone with an interest in the TCP/IP protocols is given a chance to provide input into their development and also ensures the worldwide acceptance of the protocol suite.

Universality Everyone uses TCP/IP because everyone uses it! This last point is, perhaps ironically, arguably the most important. Not only is TCP/IP the underlying language of the Internet, it is also used in most private networks today. Even former competitors to TCP/IP, such as Novell's NetWare, now use TCP/IP to carry traffic.

> **KEY CONCEPT** While TCP/IP is not the only internetworking protocol suite, it is definitely the most important one. Its unparalleled success is due to a wide variety of factors. These include its technical features, such as its routing-friendly design and scalability, its historical role as the protocol suite of the Internet, and its open standards and development process, which reduce barriers to acceptance of TCP/IP protocols.

TCP/IP Services

TCP/IP is most often studied in terms of its layer-based architecture and the protocols that it provides at those different layers. These protocols, however, represent the technical details of *how* TCP/IP works. They are of interest to us as students of technology, but are normally hidden from users who do not need to see the guts of TCP/IP to know that it works. Before proceeding to these details, let's take a bigger picture look at *what* TCP/IP does.

In the discussion of the OSI Reference Model concepts (in Chapter 5), I mentioned that the theoretical operation of the model is based on the idea of one layer providing services to the layers above it. TCP/IP covers many layers of the OSI model, and so it collectively provides services of this sort as well in many ways. Conceptually, we can divide TCP/IP services into two groups:

Services Provided to Other Protocols The first group of services consists of the core functions implemented by the main TCP/IP protocols such as IP, TCP, and User Datagram Protocol (UDP). These services are designed to actually accomplish the internetworking functions of the protocol suite. For example, at the network layer, IP provides functions such as addressing, delivery, datagram packaging, fragmentation, and reassembly. At the transport layer, TCP and UDP are concerned with encapsulating user data and managing connections between devices. Other protocols provide routing and management functionality. Higher-layer protocols use these services, allowing them to concentrate on what they are intended to accomplish.

End-User Services The second group of services provided by TCP/IP is the set of end-user services. These facilitate the operation of the applications that users run to make use of the power of the Internet and other TCP/IP networks. For example, the Web is arguably the most important Internet application. Web services are provided through HTTP, a TCP/IP application layer protocol. HTTP in turn uses services provided by lower-level protocols. All of these details are hidden from end users, entirely on purpose.

The TCP/IP Client/Server Structural Model

TCP/IP services primarily operate in the *client/server* model. It's a system in which a relatively small number of server machines provides services to a much larger number of client hosts (see Chapter 1).

Just as client/server networking applies to hardware, this same concept underlies the design of the TCP/IP protocols and software applications, as shown in Figure 8-1.

TCP/IP protocols are not set up so that two machines that want to communicate use identical software. Instead, a conscious decision was made to make communication function using matched, complementary pairs of client and server software. The client initiates communication by sending a request to a server for data or other information. The server then responds with a reply to the client, giving the client what it requested, or else it replies with an alternative response, such as an error message or information about where else it might find the data. Most (but not all) TCP/IP functions work in this manner.

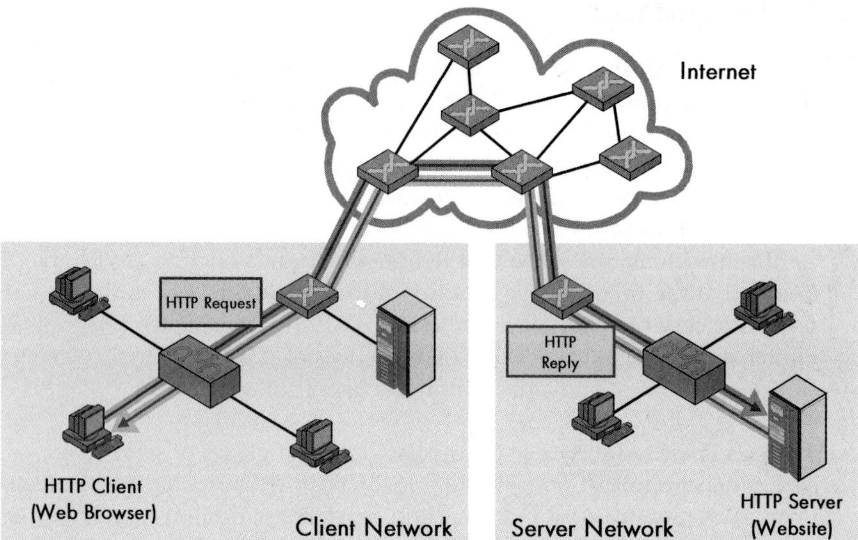

Figure 8-1: TCP/IP client/server operation *Most TCP/IP protocols involve communication between two devices, typically as* client *and* server, *such as this web (HTTP) transaction over the Internet.*

Figure 8-1 is a simplified illustration that shows a common example—a web transaction using HTTP. The web browser is an HTTP client and initiates the communication with a request for a file or other resource sent over the Internet to a website, which is an HTTP server. The server responds to the client with the information requested. (Servers generally respond to many clients simultaneously.)

There are numerous advantages to client/server operation in TCP/IP. Just as client hardware and server hardware can be tailored to their very different jobs, client software and server software can also be optimized to perform their jobs as efficiently as possible. For example, to get information from the Web, web-client software (usually called a *browser*) sends requests to a web server. The web server then responds with the requested content. (There's more to it than that, of course, but that's how it appears to the user.) Among other things, the web browser allows the user to communicate with web servers; the web-server software is designed to receive and respond to requests.

The terms *client* and *server* can be confusing in TCP/IP because they are used in several different ways, sometimes simultaneously.

> **KEY CONCEPT** The TCP/IP protocol suite is oriented around the notion of *client/server* network communication. Rather than all devices and protocol software elements being designed as peers, they are constructed as matched sets. Clients normally initiate communications by sending requests, and servers respond to such requests, providing the client with the desired data or an informative reply.

Hardware and Software Roles

The terms *client* and *server* usually refer to the primary roles played by networked hardware. A *client* computer is usually something like a PC or Macintosh used by an individual; it primarily initiates conversations by sending requests. A *server* is usually a high-powered machine dedicated to responding to client requests, sitting in a computer room somewhere that no one but its administrator ever sees.

As mentioned earlier, TCP/IP uses different software for many protocols to implement client and server roles. For example, a web browser is a piece of client software, while web-server software is completely different. Client software is usually found on client hardware and server software on server hardware, but some devices may run both client and server software.

Transactional Roles

In any exchange of information, the client is normally the device that initiates communication or sends a query, and then the server responds, usually by providing information. Again, the client software on a client device usually initiates the transaction.

In a typical organization there will be many smaller individual computers designated as clients and a few larger ones that are servers. The servers normally run server software, and the clients run client software. But servers can also be set up with client software, and clients can be set up with server software.

For example, suppose you are an administrator working in the computer room on server 1 and need to transfer a file to server 2. You start an FTP session to initiate the file transfer with server 2. In this transaction, server 1 is the client, since it is initiating communication. Theoretically, you could even start an FTP transfer from server 1 to a particular client, if that client had FTP server software to answer the server's request. (This is less common, because server software is often not installed on client machines.)

Transactional roles come into play when communication occurs between servers in certain protocols. For example, when two Simple Mail Transfer Protocol (SMTP) servers communicate to exchange email (even though they are both server programs running on server hardware), during any transaction, one device acts as the client while the other acts as the server. In some cases, devices can even swap client and server roles in the middle of a session.

> **KEY CONCEPT** Understanding client/server computing concepts in TCP/IP is made more complex due to the very different meanings that the terms client and server can have in various contexts. The two terms can refer to *hardware roles*—designations given to hardware devices based on whether they usually function as clients or as servers. The terms can also refer to *software roles*, meaning whether protocol software components function as clients or servers. And they can refer to *transactional roles*, meaning whether a device and program functions as a client or server in any given exchange of data.

NOTE *The client and server roles I have discussed are the traditional ones. The rise of powerful personal computers and widespread Internet access (especially always-on broadband connectivity) has led to a significant blurring of client and server hardware and software. Many client machines now include server software that allows them to, for example, respond to World Wide Web queries from other clients. Also, many file-sharing programs allow clients to communicate using the peer-to-peer structural model. However, most TCP/IP communication is still client/server in nature, so it's important to keep these roles in mind.*

TCP/IP Architecture and the TCP/IP Model

The OSI Reference Model's seven layers divide up the tasks required to implement a network, as described in Part I-2 of this book. However, it is not the only such model. In fact, the TCP/IP protocol suite was developed before the OSI Reference Model; as such, its inventors didn't use the OSI model to explain TCP/IP architecture (even though the OSI model is often used in TCP/IP discussions today). The developers of TCP/IP created their own architectural model, which goes by different names including the *TCP/IP model*, the *DARPA model* (after the agency that was largely responsible for developing TCP/IP) and the *DoD model* (after the United States Department of Defense). Most people call it the TCP/IP model.

Regardless of the model you use to represent the function of a network, the model's functions are pretty much the same. The TCP/IP and the OSI models are really quite similar, even if they don't carve up the network functionality precisely the same way.

Since the OSI model is so widely used, it is common to explain the TCP/IP architecture both in terms of the TCP/IP layers and the corresponding OSI layers. Figure 8-2 shows the relationship between the two models. The TCP/IP model does not address the physical layer, where hardware devices reside. The next three layers—*network interface*, *internet*, and *host-to-host transport*—correspond to layers 2, 3, and 4 of the OSI model. The TCP/IP *application* layer conceptually blurs the top three OSI layers. Note, too, that some people consider certain aspects of the OSI session layer to be part of the TCP/IP host-to-host transport layer.

As shown in Figure 8-2, the TCP/IP model uses four layers that logically span the equivalent of the top six layers of the OSI model. (The physical layer is not covered by the TCP/IP model because the data link layer is considered the point at which the interface occurs between the TCP/IP stack and the underlying networking hardware.) Starting from the bottom, the TCP/IP layers are described in the following sections.

Network Interface Layer

As its name suggests, the network interface layer is where the actual TCP/IP protocols running at higher layers interface to the local network. This layer is somewhat controversial in that some people don't even consider it a legitimate part of TCP/IP, usually because none of the core IP protocols run at this layer. Despite this, the network interface layer is part of the architecture. It is equivalent to the data link layer (layer 2) in the OSI Reference Model (see Chapter 6) and is also sometimes called the *link layer*. You may also see the name *network access layer* used.

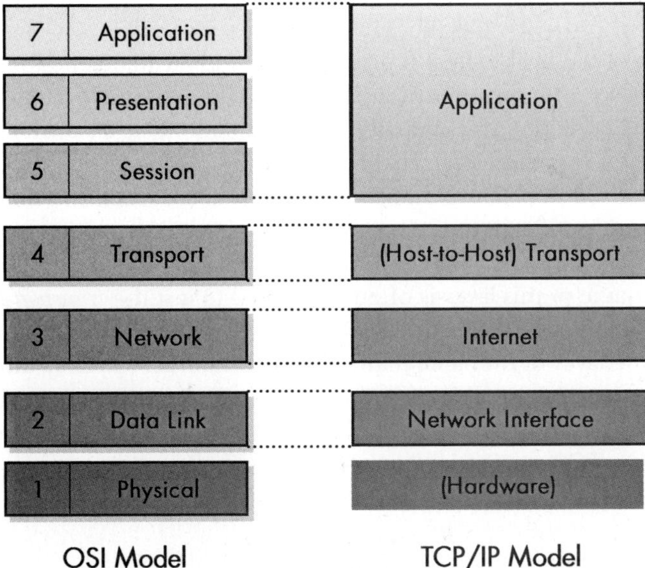

Figure 8-2: OSI Reference Model and TCP/IP model layers *The TCP/IP architectural model has four layers that approximately match six of the seven layers in the OSI Reference Model.*

On many TCP/IP networks, there is no TCP/IP protocol running at all on this layer, because it is simply not needed. For example, if you run TCP/IP over Ethernet, then Ethernet handles layer 2 (and layer 1) functions. However, the TCP/IP standards do define protocols for TCP/IP networks that do not have their own layer 2 implementation. These protocols, the Serial Line Internet Protocol (SLIP) and the Point-to-Point Protocol (PPP), fill the gap between the network layer and the physical layer. They are commonly used to facilitate TCP/IP over direct serial line connections (such as dial-up telephone networking) and other technologies that operate directly at the physical layer.

Internet Layer

The Internet layer corresponds to the network layer in the OSI Reference Model (thus it is sometimes called the *network layer* even in TCP/IP model discussions). It is responsible for typical layer 3 jobs, such as logical device addressing, data packaging, manipulation and delivery, and routing. At this layer, you find IP, which is arguably the heart of TCP/IP, as well as support protocols such as the Internet Control Message Protocol (ICMP) and the routing protocols (RIP, OSFP, BGP, and so on). IP version 6, the next-generation IP, is also at this layer.

Host-to-Host Transport Layer

This primary job of the host-to-host transport layer is to facilitate end-to-end communication over an internetwork. It is in charge of allowing logical connections to be made between devices that allow data to be sent either unreliably (with no guarantee that it gets there) or reliably (where the protocol keeps track of the data sent and received in order to make sure it arrives, and resends it if necessary). It is also here that identification of the specific source and destination application process is accomplished.

The formal name of this layer is often shortened to just the *transport layer*. The key TCP/IP protocols at this layer are TCP and UDP. The TCP/IP transport layer corresponds to the layer of the same name in the OSI model (layer 4) but includes certain elements that are arguably part of the OSI session layer. For example, TCP establishes a connection that can persist for a long period of time, which some people say makes a TCP connection more like a session.

Application Layer

The application layer is the highest layer in the TCP/IP model. It is a rather broad layer, encompassing layers 5 through 7 in the OSI model. While this seems to represent a loss of detail compared to the OSI model, that's probably a good thing. The TCP/IP model better reflects the somewhat fuzzy nature of the divisions between the functions of the higher layers in the OSI model, which in practical terms often seem rather arbitrary. It really is hard to separate some protocols in terms of which portions of layers 5, 6, or 7 they encompass.

Numerous protocols reside at the application layer. These include application protocols such as HTTP, FTP, and SMTP for providing end-user services as well as administrative protocols like Simple Network Management Protocol (SNMP), Dynamic Host Configuration Protocol (DHCP), and Domain Name System (DNS).

NOTE *The Internet and host-to-host transport layers are usually considered the core of TCP/IP architecture, because they contain most of the key protocols that implement TCP/IP internetworks.*

In the following section, I provide a brief look at each of the TCP/IP protocols covered in detail in this book and offer more detail on where they all fit into the TCP/IP architecture. I also discuss a couple of protocols that, interestingly, don't really fit into the TCP/IP layer model very well at all.

KEY CONCEPT The architecture of the TCP/IP protocol suite is often described in terms of a layered reference model called the *TCP/IP model, DARPA model*, or *DoD model*. The TCP/IP model includes four layers: the *network interface layer* (responsible for interfacing the suite to the physical hardware on which it runs), the *Internet layer* (where device addressing, basic datagram communication, and routing take place), the *host-to-host transport layer* (where connections are managed and reliable communication is ensured), and the *application layer* (where end-user applications and services reside). The first three layers correspond to layers 2 through 4 of the OSI Reference Model respectively; the application layer is equivalent to OSI layers 5 to 7.

TCP/IP Protocols

Since TCP/IP is a protocol suite, it is most often discussed in terms of the protocols that compose it. Each protocol resides in a particular layer of the TCP/IP architectural model that I just discussed and is charged with performing a certain subset of the total functionality required to implement a TCP/IP network or application. The protocols work together to allow TCP/IP as a whole to operate.

NOTE *You will sometimes hear TCP/IP called just a protocol instead of a protocol suite. This is a simplification that, while technically incorrect, is widely used. I believe it arises in large part due to Microsoft referring to protocol suites as protocols in its operating systems. I discuss this issue in more detail in Chapter 1.*

As mentioned earlier, a few TCP/IP protocols are usually called the core of the suite, because they are responsible for its basic operation. In this core, most people would include the main protocols at the Internet and transport layers: IP, TCP, and UDP. These core protocols support many other protocols in order to perform a variety of functions at each of the TCP/IP model layers.

NOTE *On the whole, there are many hundreds of TCP/IP protocols and applications, and I could not begin to cover each and every one in this book. I do include chapters in which I discuss several dozen of the protocols that I consider important for one reason or another. Full coverage of each of these protocols (to varying levels of detail) can be found in Section II and Section III of this book.*

Table 8-1 contains a summary of each of the TCP/IP protocols discussed in this book. I have organized them by layer, and I have provided cross-references to the chapters where each is discussed. The organization of protocols in the TCP/IP protocol suite can also be seen at a glance in Figure 8-3. I have also shown in the network interface layer where TCP/IP hardware drivers conceptually reside; these are used at layer 2 when TCP/IP is implemented on a LAN or WAN technology, rather than using SLIP or PPP.

Table 8-1: TCP/IP Protocols

TCP/IP Layer	Protocol Name	Protocol Abbr.	Description
Network Interface (Layer 2)	Serial Line Internet Protocol	SLIP	Provides basic TCP/IP functionality by creating a layer 2 connection between two devices over a serial line. See Chapter 9.
	Point-to-Point Protocol	PPP	Provides layer 2 connectivity like SLIP, but is much more sophisticated and capable. PPP is itself a suite of protocols (subprotocols, if you will) that allow for functions such as authentication, data encapsulation, encryption, and aggregation, thereby facilitating TCP/IP operation over WAN links. See Chapters 9-12.
Network Interface/ Internet (Layer 2/3)	Address Resolution Protocol	ARP	Used to map layer 3 IP addresses to layer 2 physical network addresses. See Chapter 13.
	Reverse Address Resolution Protocol	RARP	Determines the layer 3 address of a machine from its layer 2 address. Now mostly superseded by BOOTP and DHCP. See Chapter 14.
Internet Layer (Layer 3)	Internet Protocol, Internet Protocol Version 6	IP, IPv6	Provides encapsulation and connectionless delivery of transport layer messages over a TCP/IP network. Also responsible for addressing and routing functions. See Part II-3 and Part II-4.
	IP Network Address Translation	IP NAT	Allows addresses on a private network to be automatically translated to different addresses on a public network, thereby providing address sharing and security benefits. (Note that some people don't consider IP NAT to be a protocol in the strict sense of that word.) See Chapter 28.
	IP Security	IPsec	A set of IP-related protocols that improve the security of IP transmissions. See Chapter 29.
	Internet Protocol Mobility Support	Mobile IP	Resolves certain problems with IP associated with mobile devices. See Chapter 30.
	Internet Control Message Protocol	ICMP/ ICMPv4, ICMPv6	A support protocol for IP and IPv6 that provides error reporting and information request-and-reply capabilities to hosts. See Part II-6.
	Neighbor Discovery Protocol	NDP	A new support protocol for IPv6 that includes several functions performed by ARP and ICMP in conventional IP. See Chapter 36.
	Routing Information Protocol, Open Shortest Path First, Gateway-to-Gateway Protocol, HELLO Protocol, Interior Gateway Routing Protocol, Enhanced Interior Gateway Routing Protocol, Border Gateway Protocol, Exterior Gateway Protocol	RIP, OSPF, GGP, HELLO, IGRP, EIGRP, BGP, EGP	Protocols used to support the routing of IP datagrams and the exchange of routing information. See Part II-7.
Host-to-Host Transport Layer (Layer 4)	Transmission Control Protocol	TCP	The main transport layer protocol for TCP/IP. Establishes and manages connections between devices and ensures reliable and flow-controlled delivery of data using IP. See Part II-8.

(continued)

Table 8-1: TCP/IP Protocols (continued)

TCP/IP Layer	Protocol Name	Protocol Abbr.	Description
Host-to-Host Transport Layer (Layer 4) *continued*	User Datagram Protocol	UDP	A transport protocol that can be considered a severely stripped-down version of TCP. It is used to send data in a simple way between application processes, without the many reliability and flow-management features of TCP, but often with greater efficiency. See Chapter 44.
Application Layer (Layer 5/6/7)	Domain Name System	DNS	Provides the ability to refer to IP devices using names instead of just numerical IP addresses. Allows machines to resolve these names into their corresponding IP addresses. See Part III-1.
	Network File System	NFS	Allows files to be shared seamlessly across TCP/IP networks. See Chapter 58.
	Bootstrap Protocol	BOOTP	Developed to address some of the issues with RARP and used in a similar manner: to allow the configuration of a TCP/IP device at startup. Generally superseded by DHCP. See Chapter 60.
	Dynamic Host Configuration Protocol	DHCP	A complete protocol for configuring TCP/IP devices and managing IP addresses. The successor to RARP and BOOTP, it includes numerous features and capabilities. See Part III-3.
	Simple Network Management Protocol	SNMP	A full-featured protocol for remote management of networks and devices. See Part III-4.
	Remote Monitoring	RMON	A diagnostic "protocol" (really a part of SNMP) used for remote monitoring of network devices. See Chapter 69.
	File Transfer Protocol, Trivial File Transfer Protocol	FTP, TFTP	Protocols designed to permit the transfer of all types of files from one device to another. See Part III-6.
	RFC 822, Multipurpose Internet Mail Extensions, Simple Mail Transfer Protocol, Post Office Protocol, Internet Message Access Protocol	RFC 822, MIME, SMTP, POP, IMAP	Protocols that define the formatting, delivery, and storage of email messages on TCP/IP networks. See Part III-7.
	Network News Transfer Protocol	NNTP	Enables the operation of the Usenet online community by transferring Usenet news messages between hosts. See Chapter 85.
	Hypertext Transfer Protocol	HTTP	Transfers hypertext documents between hosts; implements the World Wide Web. See Part III-8.
	Gopher Protocol	Gopher	An older document-retrieval protocol, now largely replaced by the World Wide Web. See Chapter 86.
	Telnet Protocol	Telnet	Allows a user on one machine to establish a remote terminal session on another. See Chapter 87.
	Berkeley "r" Commands	—	Permit commands and operations on one machine to be performed on another. See Chapter 87.
	Internet Relay Chat	IRC	Allows real-time chatting between TCP/IP users. See Chapter 87.
	Administration and Troubleshooting Utilities and Protocols	—	A collection of software tools that allows administrators to manage, configure, and troubleshoot TCP/IP internetworks. See Chapter 88.

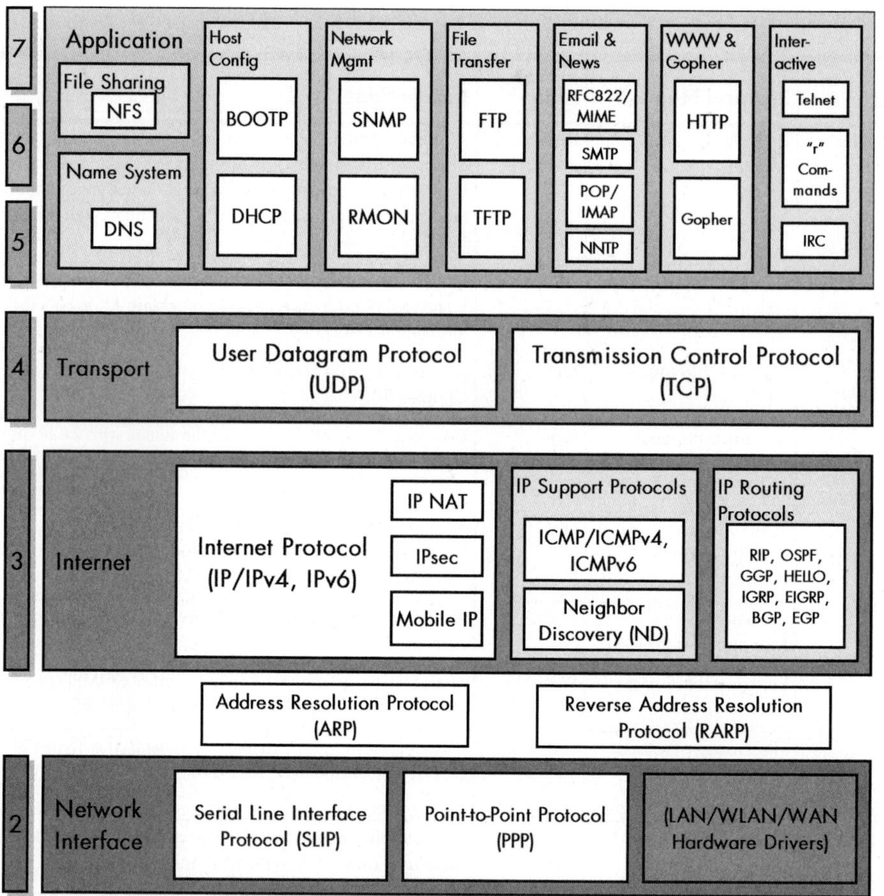

Figure 8-3: TCP/IP protocols *This diagram shows all the TCP/IP protocols covered in this book, arranged by TCP/IP and OSI Reference Model layer (with the exception of the administration utilities).*

You can see in the previous table and figure that ARP and RARP are the oddballs. In some ways they belong in both layer 2 and layer 3, and in other ways they belong in neither. They really serve to link together the network interface layer and the Internet layer. For this reason, I believe they belong *between* these two and call them "layer connection" protocols. See Chapters 13 and 14 for more on this issue.

SECTION II

TCP/IP LOWER-LAYER CORE PROTOCOLS

The TCP/IP protocol suite is largely defined in terms of the protocols that constitute it, and several dozen are covered in this book. Most of the critical protocols of the suite function at the lower layers of the OSI Reference Model (covered in Part I-2): layers 2, 3 and 4, which correspond to the network interface, Internet, and transport layers in the TCP/IP model architecture (described in Part I-3). Included here are the all-important Internet Protocol (IP) at layer 3 and Transmission Control Protocol (TCP) at layer 4, which combine to give TCP/IP its name.

Due to the importance of these and other TCP/IP protocols at the lower layers, this is the largest of the three sections of this book. It contains eight parts. The first describes the two TCP/IP protocols that reside at the network interface layer (layer 2 of the OSI Reference Model): the Point-to-Point Protocol (PPP) and the Serial Line Interface Protocol (SLIP). The second part describes a couple of special protocols that reside architecturally between layers 2 and 3: the Address Resolution Protocol (ARP) and the Reverse Address Resolution Protocol (RARP). The third and fourth parts describe the IP versions 4 and 6 (IPv4 and IPv6). The fifth and sixth parts discuss IP-related feature and support protocols, and the seventh part describes IP routing protocols. Finally, the eighth part covers the two TCP/IP transport layer protocols, the Transmission Control Protocol (TCP) and the User Datagram Protocol (UDP), and related topics such as the use of TCP/IP ports.

PART II-1

TCP/IP NETWORK INTERFACE LAYER PROTOCOLS

The lowest layer of the OSI Reference Model is the physical layer, which is responsible for the nitty-gritty details of transmitting information from one place to another on a network. The layer just above the physical layer is the *data link layer*, called the *network interface layer*, or just the *link layer*, in the TCP/IP architectural model. Its primary jobs are to implement networks at the local level and to interface between the hardware-oriented physical layer and the more abstract, software-oriented functions of the network layer and the layers above it.

In the case of TCP/IP, the Internet Protocol (IP) is the main protocol at layer 3, and it serves as the foundation of the whole TCP/IP protocol suite. IP is designed to be layered on top of any number of layer 2 technologies. However, some types of connections do not include a layer 2 protocol over which IP can run. To enable TCP/IP to operate on these kinds of links, two special TCP/IP protocols operate at the network interface layer, connecting IP to the physical layer below.

In this part, I provide a description of the two protocols that reside at the data link, or network interface layer, in the TCP/IP protocol suite. These are the older, simple Serial Line Interface Protocol (SLIP) and the newer, more capable Point-to-Point Protocol (PPP). I begin with a chapter that provides a brief overview of SLIP and PPP, showing how they fit into the TCP/IP protocol suite as a whole and describing them in general terms.

The rest of this part contains three chapters that describe the more important of the two protocols, PPP, in more detail. The first of these three explains the core protocols that are responsible for setting up PPP links and basic operation. The second covers the protocols used to implement various special features in PPP, such as compression and encryption. The last chapter on PPP provides detailed information about the various frame formats used by PPP protocols.

9

TCP/IP SERIAL LINE INTERNET PROTOCOL (SLIP) AND POINT-TO-POINT PROTOCOL (PPP) OVERVIEW AND FUNDAMENTALS

TCP/IP's core protocols operate at layers 3 and 4 of the OSI model, corresponding to the Internet layer and host-to-host transport layer of the TCP/IP architectural model (introduced in Chapter 8). That model also defines the network interface layer, which corresponds to the data link layer. However, in most network implementations, TCP/IP doesn't define any protocols operating at this layer. Instead, TCP/IP assumes that layer 2 functionality is provided by a wide area network (WAN) or local area network (LAN) technology like Ethernet, Token Ring, or IEEE 802.11. These technologies are responsible for the classic layer 2 functions: physical layer addressing, media access control, and especially, layer 2 framing of datagrams received from layer 3.

There's a problem with the assumption that Internet Protocol (IP) can run on top of an existing layer 2 protocol because sometimes there isn't one. Certain technologies, such as a simple serial connection between two devices, establish only a basic, low-level connection at the physical layer.

And, of course, one type of serial connection is still *very* popular: serial dial-up networking. When you connect with a dial-up modem to your ISP, the modems negotiate a connection that architecturally exists only at the physical layer.

Since IP assumes certain services will be provided at layer 2, there is no way to make it operate directly over a serial line or other physical layer connection. At a minimum, the most important layer 2 function that is required is some mechanism for framing the IP datagram for transmission; that is, a mechanism that provides the necessary data packaging to let datagrams be transmitted over the physical layer network. Without this, IP datagrams cannot be sent over the link.

SLIP versus PPP

To fill the gap between IP at layer 3 and the physical connection at layer 1, two protocols operate at layer 2 and provide the services that IP requires to function. One protocol is *Serial Line Internet Protocol* (SLIP), a very simple layer 2 protocol that provides only basic framing for IP. The other is *Point-to-Point Protocol* (PPP), a more complex, full-featured data link layer protocol that provides framing as well as many additional features that improve security and performance.

SLIP is extremely simple and easy to implement but lacks certain features of PPP (like authentication, compression, and error detection), which is full featured but more complicated. To draw an analogy, SLIP is a mostly sturdy, ten-year-old compact sedan, while PPP is a shiny, new luxury SUV. Both will get you from here to grandma's house, but the SUV is going to be safer, more comfortable, and better able to deal with problems that might crop up on the road. If they cost the same to buy and operate, you'd probably choose the SUV. Both SLIP and PPP cost about the same, and unlike an SUV, PPP causes no air pollution and doesn't guzzle gas. For this reason, PPP is the choice of most serial line connections today and has all but replaced SLIP.

> **KEY CONCEPT** *SLIP* and *PPP* provide layer 2 connectivity for TCP/IP implementations that run directly over a physical layer link without a layer 2 technology. While SLIP is simpler, PPP is favored due to its many features and capabilities.

Both SLIP and PPP are designed for connections between just two devices; thus, the name point-to-point protocol. Since there are only two devices, A and B, communication is straightforward: A sends to B and B sends to A, and since both deal only with simple two-device connections, they do not have to manage complexities like media access control, collisions, and unique addressing schemes in the way that technologies like Ethernet must.

NOTE *Some people don't consider SLIP and PPP to be part of the true TCP/IP protocol suite. They argue that TCP/IP is defined at layers 3 and higher on the OSI model, that IP is the basis of TCP/IP at layer 3, and that SLIP and PPP are just extra protocols that can be used under TCP/IP. To support their argument, they note that PPP can be used for protocols other than IP, which is true.*

Serial Line Internet Protocol (SLIP)

The need for a data link layer protocol to allow IP to operate over serial links was identified very early on in the development of TCP/IP. Engineers working on IP needed a way to send IP datagrams over serial links. To solve the problem, they created the very simple protocol SLIP to frame IP messages for transmission across the serial line.

Unlike most TCP/IP protocols, SLIP has never been defined as a formalized standard. It was created informally in the early 1980s, and it became the de facto standard before it was ever described in a Request for Comment (RFC). When it was published in 1988 (RFC 1055, "A Nonstandard for Transmission of IP Datagrams over Serial Lines: SLIP"), the decision was made to designate it a "nonstandard protocol."

SLIP was designated nonstandard because it was developed as a very rudimentary, stopgap measure to provide layer 2 framing when needed. SLIP is so simple that there really isn't much to standardize. Too, it has so many deficiencies that the Internet Engineering Task Force (IETF) apparently didn't want to formalize it as a standard. RFC 1055 specifically mentions various problems with SLIP (as I'll discuss later in this chapter) and the fact that work was already under way to define PPP as a more capable successor to SLIP.

KEY CONCEPT SLIP provides a *layer 2 framing service* for IP datagrams but no other features or capabilities.

SLIP Data Framing Method and General Operation

SLIP performs only one function: the framing of data for transmission. Here's how SLIP framing works. An IP datagram is passed down to SLIP, which breaks it into bytes and sends those bytes one at a time over the link. After the last byte of the datagram is sent, a special byte value is sent that tells the receiving device that the datagram has ended. This is called the SLIP *END character*, and it has a byte value of 192 in decimal numbers (C0 in hexadecimal and 11000000 binary). That's basically SLIP framing in a nutshell: Take the whole datagram, send it one byte at a time, and then send the byte 192 to delimit the end of the datagram.

One minor enhancement to SLIP's basic operation is to *precede* the datagram with an *END* character as well, thus clearly separating the start of the datagram from anything that precedes it. To see why this might be needed, you can imagine that at a particular time you have only one datagram to send: datagram 1. You send 1, and then send the *END* character to delimit it. Now, suppose there is a pause before the next datagram shows up. During that time, you aren't transmitting, but if there is line noise, the other device might pick up spurious bytes here and there. If you later receive datagram 2 and just start sending it, the receiving device might think the noise bytes were part of datagram 2.

Starting datagram 2 off with an *END* character tells the recipient that anything received between this *END* character and the previous one is a separate datagram. If that's just noise, then this "noise datagram" is just gibberish that will be rejected at the IP layer. Meanwhile, it doesn't corrupt the real datagram you wish to send. If no noise occurred on the line between datagrams, then the recipient will just see the *END* at the start of datagram 2 right after the one at the end of datagram 1 and will ignore the "null datagram" between the two.

But what if the *END* character is 192 in decimal numbers; what happens if the byte value 192 appears in the datagram itself? Transmitting it as is would fool the recipient into thinking that the datagram ended prematurely. To avoid this, an *Escape character* (*ESC*) is defined, which has a decimal value of 219 (DB in hex, 11011011 in binary). This symbol means that "this byte and the next are special." When a value of 192 appears in the datagram, the sending device replaces it with the ESC character followed by the value 220 decimal. Thus, a single 192 becomes 219 220 (or DB DC in hexadecimal). The recipient translates back from 219 220 to 192.

NOTE *The SLIP ESC character is not the same as the ASCII ESC character. They both perform an "escaping" operation but are otherwise unrelated. If the ESC character itself is in the original datagram—that is, if there's a byte value of 219 in the IP datagram to be sent—the device uses 219 221 instead of just 219.*

To summarize, SLIP does the following:

- Breaks an IP datagram into bytes
- Sends the *END* character (value 192) after the last byte of the datagram; in better implementations, it sends the *END* character before the first byte as well
- Replaces any byte to be sent in the datagram that is 192 with 219 220
- Replaces any byte to be sent that is 219 with 219 221

Figure 9-1 shows an example of how this is done with a sample IP datagram. IP datagrams are passed down to the SLIP software at layer 2 (a simplified one with only five bytes is shown here). There, they are framed by surrounding them with *END* characters (hexadecimal value C0h, shown with diagonal hatching). Special characters with hexadecimal values DBh and C0h are replaced by two-byte sequences. Note that the presence of the bracketing *END* characters forces the receiving device to see the noise byte (03h, in black) as a separate IP datagram, rather than part of either of the real ones. It will be rejected when passed up to the IP layer.

Problems and Limitations of SLIP

SLIP's simplicity does not come without costs. SLIP simply doesn't provide many of the features and capabilities you really need on modern serial links. SLIP is most deficient in the following areas:

Standardized Datagram Size Specification SLIP's maximum supported datagram size is not standardized and depends on each implementation. The usual default is 1,006 bytes, which becomes the maximum transmission unit (MTU) for the link (see Chapter 27). If a different size is used, you must program this into the IP layer.

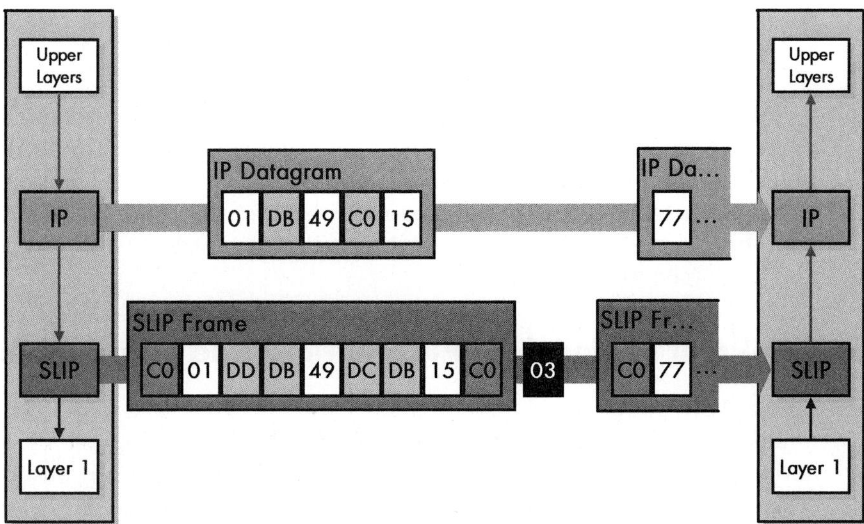

Figure 9-1: Operation of the Serial Line Internet Protocol (SLIP) *SLIP's only function is to frame data from layer 3 (usually IP datagrams) by surrounding them with* END *characters and replacing special characters as needed.*

Error Detection and Correction Mechanism SLIP doesn't provide any way of detecting or correcting errors in transmissions. While such protection is provided at higher layers through IP header checksums and other mechanisms, it is a job traditionally also done at layer 2. The reason is that relying on those higher layers means that errors are detected only after an entire datagram has been sent and passed back up the stack at the recipient. Error correction can come only in the form of resending any datagrams that were corrupted. This is inefficient, especially because serial links are generally much slower than normal LAN links.

Control Messaging SLIP offers no way for the two devices to communicate control information that may be required to manage the link.

Type Identification Since SLIP includes no headers of its own, it is not possible to identify that SLIP is being used. While developed for IP, there is no reason why other layer 3 protocols could not be sent using SLIP (if you were running more than one internetworking protocol at the higher layers). However, without type identification, there is no way to mix datagrams from two or more layer 3 protocols on the same link.

Address Discovery Method Addressing isn't needed at layer 2 because there are only two devices in a point-to-point connection, so each device is obviously only sending to the other one. However, devices do need some way of learning each other's IP addresses for routing at layer 3. SLIP provides no method for this.

Support for Compression Compression would improve performance over serial lines that are otherwise slow compared to other technologies. SLIP provides no compression features. (Note, however, that modems usually do support compression at layer 1 for serial connections that use them.) A variant on SLIP called *Compressed SLIP* or *CSLIP* was created in the late 1980s, but it was not as widely deployed as regular SLIP.

Security Features SLIP lacks even basic security features, with no means for authenticating connections or encrypting data.

SLIP's many shortcomings have led most implementations to move from SLIP to the PPP, which is a much richer data link protocol for direct connections that resolves SLIP's problems. SLIP is now outdated. Still, SLIP continues to be used in many places. Simplicity is attractive, and people are famous for their inertia: If something is implemented and is working well, many will refuse to change unless they are forced to do so.

Point-to-Point Protocol (PPP) Overview and Fundamentals

Even as SLIP was being documented, work was underway on a newer protocol that would provide full-featured IP transmission over direct links between pairs of devices. The result is *PPP*, which defines a complete method for robust data link connectivity between devices using serial lines or other physical layers. It includes numerous capabilities and features, including error detection, compression, authentication, and encryption.

The proliferation of serial links, especially for dial-up Internet access, has led to the widespread use of PPP. PPP is now one of the most popular layer 2 WAN technologies in the networking world, and has replaced SLIP as the standard for serial connections on all but legacy implementations. While most often associated with dial-up modem use, PPP can run across any similar type of physical layer link. For example, it is often used to provide layer 2 functionality on Integrated Services Digital Network (ISDN).

NOTE *Although PPP is called a protocol and is usually considered part of TCP/IP, it is really more a protocol suite, since its operation is based on procedures defined in many individual protocols. Alternatively, its components can be viewed as subprotocols within PPP, even though they are not usually called that in the standards.*

Development and Standardization

Unlike SLIP, PPP was developed to be a complete protocol suite that would enable fully functional layer 2 connectivity to support not just IP, but the transmission of other network layer protocols as well.

PPP's history goes back to the late 1980s, when SLIP was the de facto standard for serial IP implementations. The first formal IETF document related to PPP was RFC 1134 (1989). This RFC was not the standard itself, but a proposal for what would eventually be defined as the first main PPP standard, RFC 1171 (1990). RFC 1171 was revised several times, and several other documents were added to it to define the various protocols that compose the entire PPP suite.

NOTE *Rather than try to develop PPP from scratch, the IETF decided to base it on the ISO High-Level Data Link Control (HDLC) protocol, which was initially developed by IBM. HDLC is a derivative of the Synchronous Data Link Control (SDLC) Protocol. PPP's developers adapted its framing structure and some of its general operation from HDLC.*

Function and Architecture

PPP is a connection-oriented protocol that enables layer 2 links over a variety of different physical layer connections. It is supported on both synchronous and asynchronous lines and can operate in half-duplex or full-duplex mode. It was designed to carry IP traffic, but is general enough to allow any type of network layer datagram to be sent over a PPP connection. As its name implies, PPP is designed for point-to-point connections between two devices, and it assumes that frames are sent and received in the same order.

PPP fits into TCP/IP in the network interface layer (link layer), as shown in Figure 9-2. PPP's operation follows a specific sequence, including a multistep Link Establishment phase that may include optional authentication.

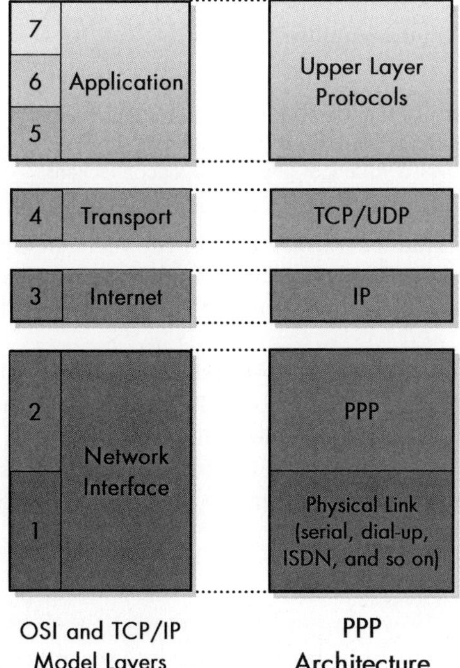

Figure 9-2: PPP location in the TCP/IP architecture *PPP is the interface between the IP and a physical link such as a serial line or dial-up networking connection. This corresponds to layer 2 in the OSI Reference Model.*

Advantages and Benefits

A list of PPP's strengths reads very much like a list of SLIP's weaknesses, as explained earlier in this chapter. Some of PPP's specific benefits include the following:

- A more comprehensive framing mechanism compared to the single *END* character in SLIP
- Specification of the encapsulated protocol to allow multiple layer 3 protocols to be multiplexed on a single link
- Error detection for each transmitted frame through the use of a cyclic redundancy check (CRC) code in each frame header
- A robust mechanism for negotiating link parameters, including the maximum frame size permitted

- A method for testing links before datagram transmission takes place and for monitoring link quality
- Support for authentication of the connection using multiple authentication protocols
- Support for additional optional features, including compression, encryption, and link aggregation (allowing two devices to use multiple physical links as if they were a single, higher-performance link)

The proliferation of serial links, especially for dial-up Internet access, has led to widespread use of PPP. It is now one of the most popular layer 2 WAN technologies in the networking world, and it has replaced SLIP as the standard for serial connections on all but legacy implementations. While most often associated with dial-up modem use, PPP can run across any similar type of physical layer link. For example, it is often used to provide layer 2 functionality on ISDN.

KEY CONCEPT PPP is a complete link layer protocol suite for devices using TCP/IP. It provides framing, encapsulation, authentication, quality monitoring, and other features that enable robust operation of TCP/IP over a variety of physical layer connections.

One key advantage of PPP is that it is *extensible*. Over the years, new protocols have been added to the suite in order to provide additional features or capabilities. For example, PPP is designed not to use just a single authentication protocol, but to allow a choice.

PPP's success has even led to the development of derivative protocols like PPP over Ethernet (PPPoE) and PPP over ATM (PPPoA). These derivatives actually layer PPP over existing data link layer technologies, which demonstrates how valued PPP's features are. Even when a layer 2 technology is already in use, you can apply PPP on top to provide authentication and management benefits for services like Digital Subscriber Line (DSL).

PPP Main Components

At the highest level, PPP's functions can be broken down into several components. Each encompasses a general class of PPP functionality and is represented by either one protocol in the suite or a set of protocols. The PPP standard describes three main components of PPP:

PPP Encapsulation Method The primary job of PPP is to take higher-layer messages, such as IP datagrams, and encapsulate them for transmission over the underlying physical layer link. To this end, PPP defines a special frame format for encapsulating data for transmission, based on the framing used in HDLC. The PPP frame was designed to be small and contain only simple fields in order to maximize bandwidth efficiency and speed in processing.

Link Control Protocol (LCP) LCP is responsible for setting up, maintaining, and terminating the link between devices. It is a flexible, extensible protocol that allows many configuration parameters to be exchanged to ensure that both devices agree on how the link will be used.

Network Control Protocols (NCPs) PPP supports the encapsulation of many different layer 3 datagram types. Some of these require additional setup before the link can be activated. Once the general link setup is completed with LCP, control is passed to the NCP that is specific to the layer 3 protocol being carried on the PPP link. For example, when IP is carried over PPP, the NCP used is the PPP Internet Protocol Control Protocol (IPCP). Other NCPs are defined for supporting the Internetworking Packet Exchange (IPX) protocol, the NetBIOS Frames (NBF) protocol, and so forth.

The PPP encapsulation method and LCP are defined in the main PPP standard and some support standards; the NCPs are described in separate standard documents, one per NCP.

PPP Functional Groups

While PPP's main components constitute much of the total package, I would add two additional functional groups. These represent some of the many extra protocols that have been added to the suite over time to support or enhance its basic operation:

LCP Support Protocols Several protocols in the PPP suite are used during the link negotiation process, either to manage it or to configure options. Examples include the authentication protocols Challenge Handshake Authentication Protocol (CHAP) and Password Authentication Protocol (PAP), which are used by LCP during the optional Authentication phase. These are discussed in Chapter 10.

LCP Optional Feature Protocols A number of protocols have been added to the basic PPP suite over the years to enhance its operation once a link has been set up and datagrams are being passed between devices. For example, the PPP Compression Control Protocol (CCP) allows compression of PPP data; the PPP Encryption Control Protocol (ECP) enables datagrams to be encrypted for security; and the PPP Multilink Protocol (PPP MP) allows a single PPP link to be operated over multiple physical links. These protocols often also require additional setup during link negotiation, so many of them define extensions (such as extra configuration options) that are negotiated as part of LCP.

NOTE *Each optional protocol is defined by a specific standards document, as you will see later in this chapter.*

General Operation

Although the PPP suite includes dozens of protocols, its general operation is really quite straightforward. Essentially, PPP involves the following three basic steps (see Figure 9-3):

1. **Link Setup and Configuration** Before the two devices can exchange information, they must make contact and set up a link between them. During link setup, the devices agree on all the parameters needed to manage the operation of the link. LCP begins this process and invokes the help of support protocols

as needed, for options like authentication. Once the link is set up, in order to complete link setup, the appropriate NCP is called for whatever layer 3 technology is being carried on the link.

2. **Link Operation** The devices use the link to send datagrams. Each device transmits by encapsulating layer 3 datagrams and sending them down to layer 1 to be transmitted. Each device receives by taking PPP frames sent up from its own physical layer, stripping off the PPP header and passing the datagram up to layer 3. Where appropriate, optional protocols are used at this stage to offer features such as compression (CCP).
3. **Link Termination** When either device decides that it no longer wants to communicate, it terminates the link.

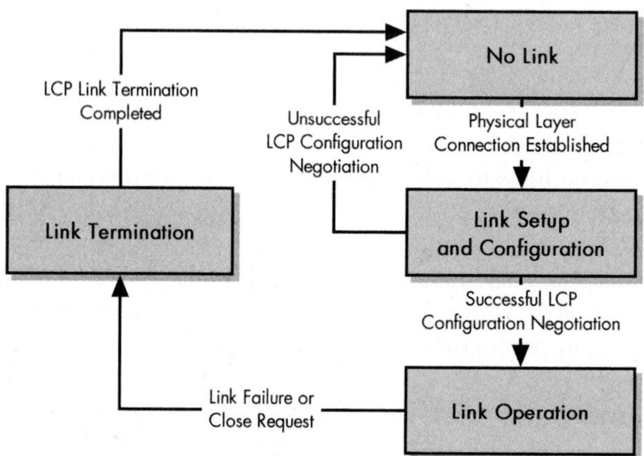

Figure 9-3: Overview of PPP operation *In simplest terms, PPP consists of only three basic steps: link setup, link operation, and link termination.*

Link setup is by far the most complicated of these general steps, because it involves several substeps used to negotiate link parameters and options.

PPP Link Setup and Phases

Before data can be exchanged on a PPP connection, a link must be set up between the two devices. As part of this setup task, a configuration process is undertaken whereby the devices configure the link and agree on the parameters for how data should be passed between them. Only when this is completed can frames actually pass over the link.

LCP is generally in charge of setting up and maintaining PPP links. LCP may invoke an authentication protocol (PAP or CHAP) when PPP is configured to use authentication. Once an LCP link has been opened, PPP invokes one or more NCPs for the layer 3 protocol being carried on the link. These perform any network-layer-specific configuration needed before the link can carry that particular network layer protocol.

The operation of a PPP link can be described as having a life of sorts: A PPP link is established, configured, used, and eventually terminated. The process of setting up, using, and closing a PPP link is described in the PPP standard as a series of *phases* or *states*. This is a type of *finite state machine (FSM)*, which is a tool used to explain the operation of protocols. The general concept behind an FSM is described in the section discussing the finite state machine of the Transmission Control Protocol (TCP), in Chapter 47.

To better understand how PPP works, let's look at these phases and how the transition is made from one to the next during the lifetime of the link. For the sake of clarity, this description is based on an example for which Device A is a PC connecting via dial-up networking to Remote Host B (see Figure 9-4).

NOTE *When we talk about a PPP link overall, we are talking about the status of the LCP connection between the two devices. Once an LCP link has been opened, each of the NCPs used on the link can be opened or closed independently of the overall PPP (LCP) link. You'll see how this works momentarily.*

Link Dead Phase

By design, the PPP link always begins and ends in the *Link Dead* phase. This phase represents the situation in which there is no physical layer link established between the two devices. The link remains here until the physical layer link is set up, at which point it proceeds to the *Link Establishment* phase.

In this example, when Device A is first turned on, there is no physical layer connection (modem connection) between it and Device B. Once the connection is made, the link can proceed to phase 2.

NOTE *In a direct connection, such as a serial cable linking two PCs, the link may stay in the Link Dead phase for only a fraction of a second, until the physical layer connection is detected.*

Link Establishment Phase

The physical layer is now connected and LCP performs the basic setup of the link. Device A sends an LCP configuration request message to Device B over the physical link, specifying the parameters it wishes to use. If Device B agrees, it replies with an acknowledgment. If Device B doesn't agree, it returns a negative acknowledgment or rejection, telling Device A what it won't accept. Device A can then try a different configuration request with new parameters that Device B may accept. (This process is described in more detail in Chapter 10.)

If Device A and Device B eventually come to agreement, the link status is considered *LCP open* and will proceed to the *Authentication* phase. If they cannot agree, the physical link is terminated, and it returns to the Link Dead phase.

Authentication Phase

In many cases, a device may require authentication before it will permit another device to connect. (This is usually the case when PPP is used for dial-up.) Authentication is not mandatory in PPP, however. When it is used, the appropriate authentication protocol (CHAP or PAP) is employed.

After successful authentication, the link proceeds to the *Network Layer Protocol* phase. If authentication is not successful, the link fails and transitions to the *Link Termination* phase.

Network Layer Protocol Phase

Once the basic link has been configured and authentication has completed, the general setup of the LCP link is complete. Now, the specific configuration of the appropriate network layer protocol is performed by invoking the appropriate NCP, such as IPCP, IPXCP, and so forth.

Each particular network layer protocol whose NCP is successfully configured is considered to be open on the LCP link. More than one NCP can be open on a particular PPP link, and each can be closed independently when it is no longer needed. Once all necessary NCPs have been invoked, the link proceeds to the *Link Open* state, even if none of the NCPs were successfully opened.

NOTE *Some PPP features require the negotiation of additional options between the two devices, which may perform their own link establishment process during the* Network Layer Protocol *phase. The PPP Compression Control Protocol (CCP) sets up data compression in this manner.*

Link Open Phase

In the Link Open state, the LCP link and one or more NCP links are open and operational. Data can be passed for each NCP that has been successfully set up.

The link can be terminated at any time by either device for a variety of reasons. These may include a user request (you click Disconnect when you want to log off your dial-up session); link quality problems (the modem hangs up on you due to line noise); or some other cause (you spend too much time in the bathroom and your ISP's idle timer logs you out). When any of these occur, the LCP link is broken, and the link transitions to the *Link Termination* phase.

Link Termination Phase

The device terminating the link sends a special LCP termination frame, and the other device acknowledges it. The link then returns to the Link Dead phase. If the termination was by request and the physical layer connection is still active, the PPP implementation should specifically signal the physical layer to terminate the layer 1 connection.

You should remember that the basic link is established by LCP, and NCP links are set up within the LCP link. Closing an NCP link does not cause the LCP link to be closed. Even if all NCPs are closed, the LCP link remains open. (Of course, no data can be passed until an appropriate NCP link is reestablished; a device is required to discard frames received that contain any layer 3 protocol that does not have an open NCP.) To terminate a PPP connection, only the LCP link needs to be terminated in the *Link Termination* phase; the NCPs do not need to be explicitly closed.

Figure 9-4 shows the PPP phases and the circumstances under which transitions occur between them. The PPP connection between two devices begins in the Link Dead state and proceeds through three intermediate phases until the link is fully opened. It remains in the stable Link Open phase until terminated. The lighter boxes show the corresponding change in the status of the PPP link as transitions are made between phases.

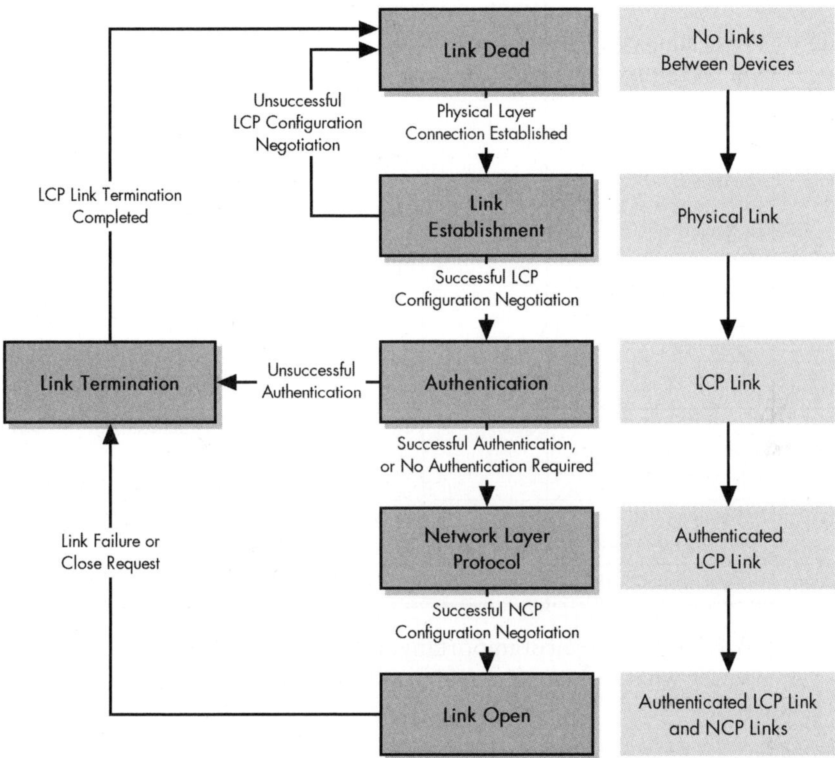

Figure 9-4: PPP phases *A PPP connection follows a mainly linear sequence of transitions from the Link Dead Phase through the Link Open Phase.*

Table 9-1 summarizes the PPP phases; the LCP Link Status and NCP Link Status columns show the status of the link as the phase starts.

PPP Standards

While it makes sense for different parts of PPP to be covered in different standards, this does make it much harder to learn how PPP works. Also, literally *dozens* of RFCs cover PPP's main operation, its various protocols, and other related issues. You can find most of them by consulting a master list of RFCs and searching for the string "PPP," but you will find them in numerical (RFC number) order, which isn't very meaningful in terms of how the protocols are used. You also have to differentiate between the ones that are current and those that are obsolete.

Table 9-1: PPP Phases

Phase/State	Phase Summary	LCP Link Status Upon Entry to Phase	NCP Link Status Upon Entry to Phase	Transition Requirement	Transition to Phase
Link Dead	Default state; physical layer not connected.	Closed	Closed	Successful physical layer connection	Link establishment
Link Establishment	Physical layer connected, basic configuration of link performed by LCP.	Closed	Closed	Successful negotiation	Authentication
				Unsuccessful negotiation	Link dead
Authentication	Basic link is now opened, and optional authentication of device is performed.	Open	Closed	Successful authentication or no authentication required	Network layer protocol
				Unsuccessful authentication	Link termination
Network Layer Protocol	One or more NCPs open an NCP link within the LCP link.	Open	Closed	All NCPs opened	Link open
Link Open	Link is open and operating normally.	Open	Open	Link failure or close request	Link termination
Link Termination	LCP link is shut down.	Open	Open		Link dead

Table 9-2 lists the most important and interesting PPP-related RFCs. To make it easier to see what the RFCs are about, I have organized them into five groups, as follows:

Core These are PPP's main documents. They cover the basic operation of PPP including the PPP LCP and encapsulation of datagrams.

LCP Support These protocols support the basic operation of LCP. I've only included the ones that provide authentication services during link startup.

NCPs These protocols negotiate parameters specific to various layer 3 protocols carried over PPP.

Features These protocols define optional features used with PPP, such as compression and encryption.

Applications and Miscellaneous These are the protocols that describe how PPP can be adapted to run over particular types of links or that don't really fit into any of the previous groups.

Within each group, the RFCs are listed in numerical order, which is also date order. Only the most recent RFC is listed, not earlier ones that were made obsolete (with the exception of RFC 1334, which, despite being made obsolete, is still important).

Table 9-2: PPP Standards

Group	RFC Number	Standard Name	Description
Core	1570	PPP LCP Extensions	Defines two features for LCP that allow devices to identify each other and for each device to tell the other how much time remains in the current session.
	1661	The Point-to-Point Protocol (PPP)	Base standard for PPP. Describes PPP architecture, general operation (including the process of link establishment, maintenance, and termination), and details of LCP.
	1662	PPP in HDLC-like Framing	Defines the specific framing method for PPP frames, based on that used in HDLC. This standard can be considered a companion to the main PPP standard, RFC 1661.
LCP Support	1334	PPP Authentication Protocols	Defines the two PPP authentication protocols: PAP and CHAP. Note that RFC 1994 obsoletes RFC 1334, but does not discuss the PAP. (That tells you that the IETF doesn't think highly of PAP; see Chapter 10 for more on this.)
	1994	PPP Challenge Handshake Authentication Protocol (CHAP)	Updates the information about CHAP provided in RFC 1334.
NCPs	1332	The PPP Internet Protocol Control Protocol (IPCP)	The NCP for IP.
	1377	The PPP OSI Network Layer Control Protocol (OSINLCP)	The NCP for OSI protocol suite network layer protocols, such as CNLP, ES-IS, and IS-IS.
	1378	The PPP AppleTalk Control Protocol (ATCP)	The NCP for the AppleTalk protocol.
	1552	The PPP Internetworking Packet Exchange Control Protocol (IPXCP)	The NCP for the Novell IPX protocol.
	2043	The PPP SNA Control Protocol (SNACP)	The NCP for IBM's Systems Network Architecture (SNA).
	2097	The PPP NetBIOS Frames Control Protocol (NBFCP)	The NCP for NetBIOS Frames (NBF, also commonly called NetBEUI).
	2472	IP Version 6 over PPP	The NCP for IPv6: the IPv6 Control Protocol (IPv6CP).
Features	1962	The PPP Compression Control Protocol (CCP)	Defines a mechanism for compressing data sent over PPP links to improve performance. This standard describes how compression is negotiated between two devices on a PPP link. It is used in conjunction with several compression algorithms that actually do the compression of data.
	1968	The PPP Encryption Control Protocol (ECP)	Defines a mechanism for encrypting data sent over PPP links to improve performance. This standard describes how encryption is negotiated between two devices. It is used with several encryption algorithms.

(continued)

Table 9-2: PPP Standards (continued)

Group	RFC Number	Standard Name	Description
Features, *continued*	1989	PPP Link Quality Monitoring	Defines a protocol that lets PPP devices generate reports to each other about the quality of the link.
	1990	The PPP Multilink Protocol (MP)	Defines a method for running PPP over a set of aggregated links, thereby allowing two devices to use multiple low-bandwidth links as a single, high-bandwidth virtual link.
	2125	The PPP Bandwidth Allocation Protocol (BAP)/The PPP Bandwidth Allocation Control Protocol (BACP)	Defines two support protocols that manage the allocation of bandwidth in links aggregated using PPP MP.
Applications and Miscellaneous	1618	PPP over ISDN	Describes application particulars for running PPP over ISDN links.
	1973	PPP in Frame Relay	Describes how PPP may be modified to run over Frame Relay at layer 2.
	2290	Mobile-IPv4 Configuration Option for PPP IPCP	Defines changes to the PPP Internet Protocol Control Protocol (IPCP) to support Mobile IP.
	2364	PPP over AAL5	Defines a method for sending PPP frames over AAL5 (ATM), commonly called PPPoA.
	2516	A Method for Transmitting PPP over Ethernet (PPPoE)	Defines a technique for encapsulating PPP frames over Ethernet (PPPoE).
	2615	PPP over SONET/SDH	Discusses how to encapsulate PPP frames over SONET/SDH links.

10

PPP CORE PROTOCOLS: LINK CONTROL, NETWORK CONTROL, AND AUTHENTICATION

This chapter describes the protocols responsible for PPP link setup and basic operation, including Link Control Protocol (LCP) and the Network Control Protocols (NCPs) used to configure PPP for different layer 3 protocols. I also discuss the two PPP authentication protocols, Password Authentication Protocol (PAP) and Challenge Handshake Authentication Protocol (CHAP), which are used to provide authentication during link setup.

Link Control Protocol (LCP)

Of all the PPP suite protocols, LCP is the most important. It is responsible for PPP's overall successful operation, and plays a key role in each PPP link stage: configuration, maintenance, and termination (as discussed in Chapter 9). Link configuration is performed during the initial link establishment phase; link maintenance occurs while the link is open, and link termination happens in the link termination phase.

Figure 10-1 provides an overview of many of the message exchanges performed by LCP during different phases of a PPP connection. Link configuration is shown here as a simple exchange of a Configure-Request and Configure-Ack. After subsequent exchanges using other PPP protocols to authenticate and configure one or more NCPs, the link enters the link open phase. In this example, Echo-Request and Echo-Reply messages are first used to test the link, followed by the sending and receiving of data by both devices. One Data message is shown being rejected due to an invalid Code field. Finally, the link is terminated using Terminate-Request and Terminate-Ack messages.

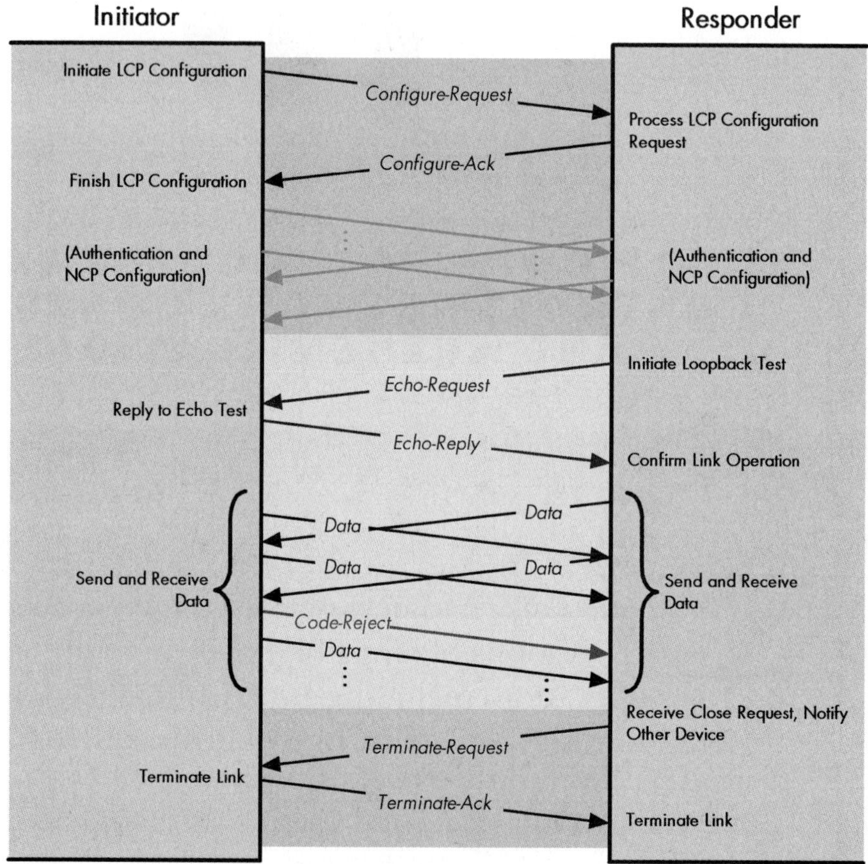

Figure 10-1: PPP Link Control Protocol (LCP) message exchanges *This diagram shows the different message exchanges performed by LCP during link configuration, maintenance, and termination.*

LCP Packets

Devices use LCP to control the PPP link by sending LCP messages across the physical link between them. These messages are called both *LCP packets* and *LCP frames*. Although the standard uses *packet*, the term *frame* is preferred because layer 2 messages are normally called frames. The main PPP document defines 11 different LCP frames, which are divided into three groups that correspond to the three link stages. Four LCP frame types are used for link configuration, five for maintenance, and two for termination.

In the following section I'll discuss each of the three major functions of LCP and how the frames are used in each. (Chapter 12 describes the frame formats for the packets themselves.)

LCP Link Configuration

Link configuration is arguably LCP's most important job in PPP. During the link establishment phase, the two physically connected devices exchange LCP frames that help them negotiate the conditions under which the link will operate. Figure 10-2 shows the entire procedure.

The process begins with the initiating device (Device A) creating a Configure-Request frame that contains a variable number of configuration options that it wants to see set up on the link. This is basically Device A's "wish list" for how it wants the link created.

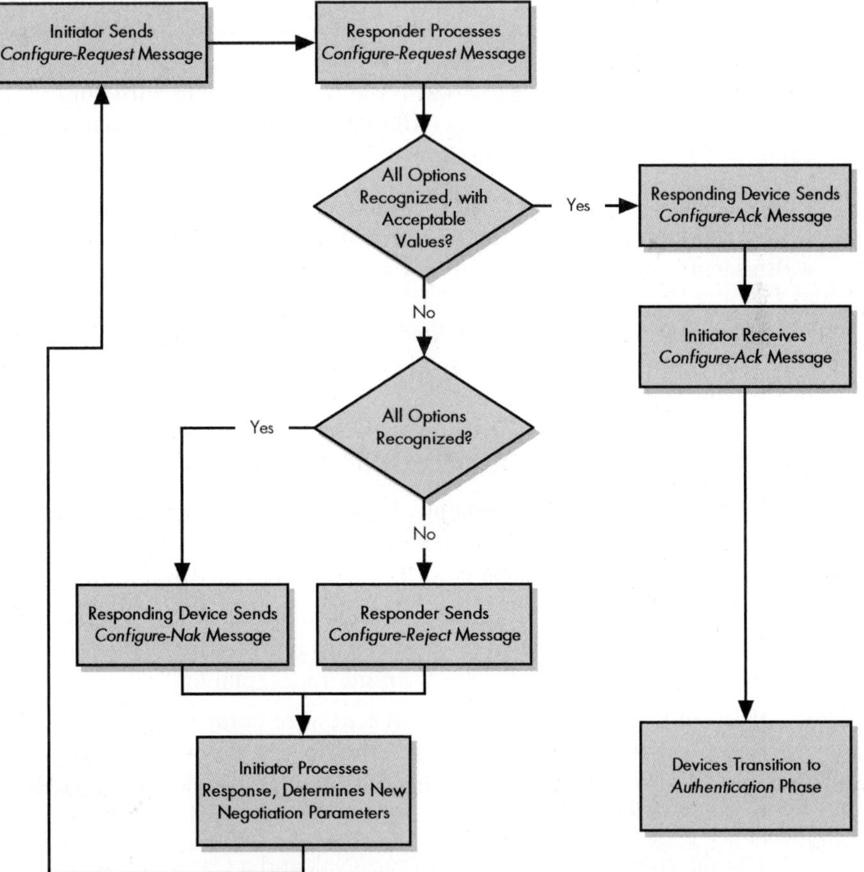

Figure 10-2: PPP LCP link configuration process *The negotiation process undertaken to configure the link by LCP. This process begins when the PPP link enters the link establishment phase. After successful configuration, the connection transitions to the authentication phase.*

RFC 1661, the main PPP document, defines a number of different configuration options that the initiator can specify in this request. Any one of these can be included and if so, filled in with the value corresponding to what Device A wants for that option. If absent, Device A isn't requesting that option. The six options are as follows:

Maximum Receive Unit (MRU) Lets Device *A* specify the maximum size datagram it wants the link to be able to carry.

Authentication Protocol Device *A* can indicate the type of authentication protocol it wishes to use (if any).

Quality Protocol If Device *A* wants to enable quality monitoring on the link, what quality monitoring protocol to use (though there is only one currently defined: LQR).

Magic Number Used to detect looped-back links or other anomalies in the connection.

Protocol Field Compression Allows Device *A* to specify that it wants to use "compressed" (8-bit) Protocol fields in PPP data frames instead of the normal 16-bit Protocol field. This provides a small (one byte) but free savings on each PPP frame. (Note that this has nothing to do with the compression feature offered by Compression Control Protocol, or CCP; see the PPP general frame format discussion in Chapter 12 for more on this feature.)

Address and Control Field Compression (ACFC) The same as Protocol Field Compression, but used to compress the Address and Control fields for small bandwidth savings. (See the PPP general frame format topic in Chapter 12 for more.)

Other options may also be added to this list by optional feature protocols. For example, Multilink PPP (Chapter 11) adds several options that must be negotiated during link setup.

The other device (Device B) receives the Configure-Request and processes it. It then has the following three choices of how to respond:

- If every option in it is acceptable, Device B sends back a Configure-Ack (acknowledge) frame. The negotiation is complete.
- If Device B recognizes all the options that Device A sent as valid and is capable of negotiating, but it doesn't accept the values, Device B returns a Configure-Nak (negative acknowledge) frame. This message includes a copy of each configuration option that Device B found unacceptable.
- If any of the options that Device A sent were either unrecognized by Device B or represent ways of using the link that Device B considers not only unacceptable, but not even subject to negotiation, it returns a Configure-Reject containing each of the objectionable options.

The difference between a Configure-Nak and a Configure-Reject is that the former is like Device B saying, "I don't accept your terms, but I'll discuss," while the latter is Device B basically saying, "No way Jose!" For example, if Device A tries to request PAP as the authentication protocol, but Device B wants to use CHAP, it will send a Configure-Nak. If Device B doesn't support authentication at all, it will send a Configure-Reject.

NOTE *Even after receiving a rejection, Device A can retry the negotiation with a new Configure-Request.*

LCP Link Maintenance

Once the link has been negotiated, LCP passes control to the appropriate authentication and NCP protocols (as discussed below). Eventually the link setup will complete and go into the open state, at which point, LCP messages can then be used by either device to manage or debug the link, as follows:

Code-Reject and Protocol-Reject These frame types are used to provide feedback when one device receives an invalid frame due to either an unrecognized LCP code (LCP frame type) or a bad protocol identifier.

Echo-Request, Echo-Reply, and Discard-Request These frames can be used for testing the link.

LCP Link Termination

When the link is ready to be shut down, LCP terminates it. The device initiating the shutdown (which may not be the one that initiated the link in the first place) sends a Terminate-Request message. The other device replies with a Terminate-Ack message. A termination request indicates that the device sending it needs to close the link. This is a request that cannot be denied.

Other LCP Messages

The standard RFC 1570, "PPP LCP Extensions," also defines two new LCP message types. The Identification message is used to allow a device to identify itself to its peer on the link. The Time-Remaining message lets one device tell the other how much time remains in the current session.

Many of the other protocols used in PPP are modeled after LCP. They use the same basic techniques for establishing protocol connections, and send and receive a subset of LCP message types. They also exchange configuration options in a similar manner.

The Network Control Protocols (IPCP, IPXCP, NBFCP, and Others)

Although PPP was originally created to carry IP datagrams, its designers realized that it could easily carry data from many types of network layer protocols, and that, on some networks, it might even be advantageous to let it carry datagrams from different layer 3 protocols simultaneously.

Allowing PPP to support multiple network layer protocols would require it to have knowledge of each one's idiosyncrasies. If you used only LCP for link configuration, the device would need to know all the unique requirements of each layer 3 protocol. This would also require you to update LCP constantly as new layer 3 protocols were defined and as new parameters were defined for existing ones.

To eliminate this potential issue, PPP takes a modular approach to link establishment. LCP performs the basic link setup, and after (optional) authentication, invokes an *NCP* that is specific to each layer 3 protocol that is to be carried over the link. The NCP negotiates any parameters that are unique to the particular network layer protocol, and more than one NCP can be run for each LCP link (see the discussion of PPP link setup and phases in Chapter 9).

Each of the common network layer technologies has a PPP NCP defined for it in a separate RFC. The most common ones, "The PPP Internet Protocol Control Protocol (IPCP)," "The PPP Internetworking Packet Exchange Control Protocol (IPXCP)," and "The PPP NetBIOS Frames Control Protocol (NBFCP)," are NCPs for IP, IPX, and NBF (also called NetBEUI), respectively. A separate NCP is also defined for IP version 6, the "PPP IP Version 6 Control Protocol (IPv6CP)."

Operation of NCPs

Each NCP operates very much like a light version of LCP, as you can see in Figure 10-3. (To see the similarities, you should compare Figure 10-3 to Figure 10-1, which shows the messaging for LCP.) Like LCP, each NCP performs functions for link setup, maintenance, and termination, except that it deals only with its particular type of NCP link and not the overall LCP link. Each NCP uses a subset of the following seven of the message types defined in LCP in very much the same way that LCP uses each message type of the same name, as shown for each of these three main link activities:

Link Configuration The process of setting up and negotiating the parameters of a particular NCP link (once an LCP link is established) is accomplished using Configure-Request, Configure-Ack, Configure-Nak, and Configure-Reject messages as discussed for LCP (except that these are particular to each NCP). The configuration options are the network layer protocol parameters being negotiated.

Link Maintenance Code-Reject messages can be sent to indicate invalid code values (NCP frame types).

Link Termination An NCP link can be terminated using Terminate-Request and Terminate-Ack messages. But remember that NCP links are set up within an LCP link, and that there can be more than one NCP link open. Closing NCP links doesn't terminate the LCP link. (NCP links do not need to be closed when an LCP link is terminated.)

Figure 10-3 shows how the overall operation of the NCPs, such as IPCP, is very similar to that of LCP. Once LCP configuration (including authentication) is complete, IPCP Configure-Request and Configure-Ack messages are used to establish an IPCP link. IP data can then be sent over the link. If the IPCP connection is no longer needed, it may be terminated, after which the LCP link remains open for other types of data to be transmitted. It is not necessary, however, to explicitly terminate the IPCP link before terminating the LCP connection.

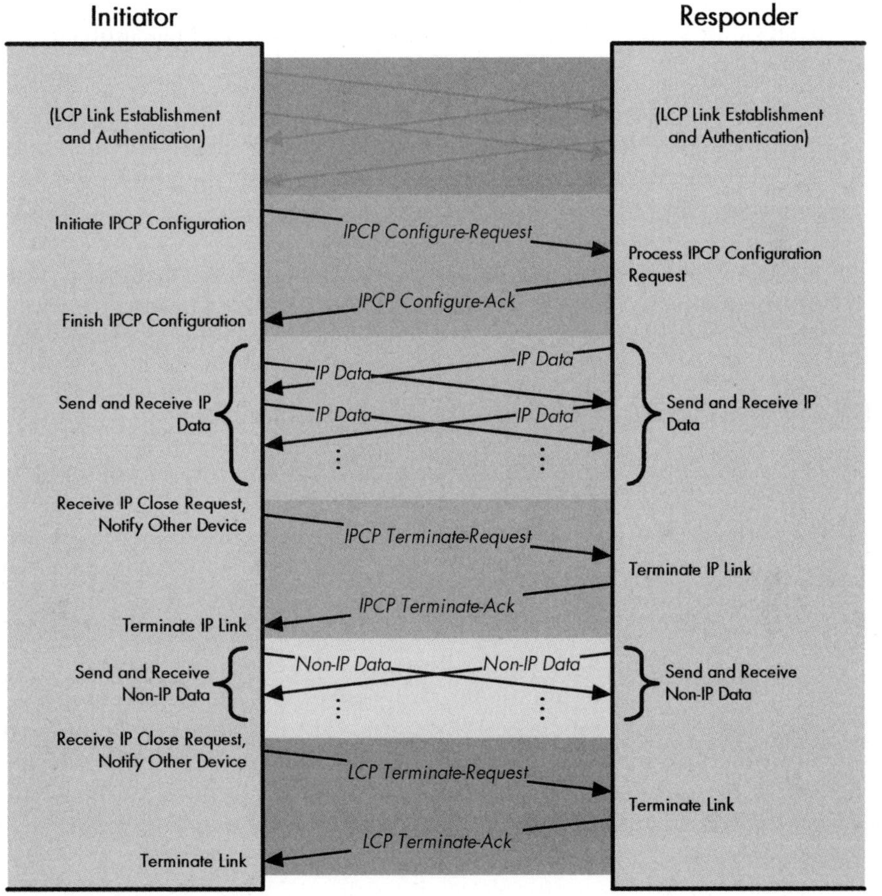

Figure 10-3: PPP IP Control Protocol (IPCP) message exchanges *The message exchanges, performed to configure and terminate IPCP, are quite similar to those used for LCP.*

KEY CONCEPT Once the primary PPP link is established using LCP, each network layer protocol to be carried over the link requires the establishment of the appropriate NCP link. The most important of these is the *PPP Internet Protocol Control Protocol (IPCP)*, which allows IP datagrams to be carried over PPP.

The Internet Protocol Control Protocol (IPCP): An Example NCP

Let's look at the NCP for IP: IPCP. When PPP is set up to carry IP datagrams, IPCP is invoked in the network layer protocol phase to set up an IP NCP link between the two devices. The setup is carried out using the four Configure- messages. For IP, two configuration options can be specified in an IPCP Configure-Request message:

IP Compression Protocol Allows devices to negotiate the use of Van Jacobson TCP/IP header compression, which shrinks the size of TCP and IP headers to save bandwidth. This is similar in concept to the Protocol-Field-Compression and ACFC options in LCP.

IP Address Allows the device sending the Configure-Request message either to specify an IP address it wants to use for routing IP over the PPP link or to request that the other device supply it with one. This is most commonly used for dial-up networking links.

Once configuration is complete, data can be sent for the layer 3 protocol corresponding to the NCP negotiated. This is indicated by using the appropriate value for the Protocol field in PPP data frames containing that layer 3 data.

PPP Authentication Protocols: PAP and CHAP

PPP was designed to provide layer 2 connectivity over a variety of serial links and other physical layer technologies, some of which introduce more security concerns than others. For example, suppose you connect two machines in your office with a serial cable and want to run PPP between them. When one of these initiates a PPP link with the other, you don't really need to worry about who's calling. On the other hand, consider an Internet service provider (ISP) using PPP for remote dial-in users. They generally want to allow only their customers to connect.

The PPP protocol suite allows for the use of an optional authentication protocol when devices negotiate the basic link setup. The PPP suite initially defined two such protocols: PAP and CHAP. Once an LCP link is set up between two devices, a series of authentication messages are sent using these protocols to verify the identity of the device initiating the link. Only if authentication is successful can the link configuration proceed.

PAP

PAP is a very straightforward authentication scheme, consisting of only two basic steps, as shown in Figure 10-4.

Authentication Request The initiating device sends an Authenticate-Request message that contains a name and a password.

Authentication Reply The responding device looks at the name and password and decides whether to accept the initiating device and continue setting up the link. If so, it sends back an Authenticate-Ack message. Otherwise, it sends an Authenticate-Nak message.

PAP is another example of something that is just too simple for its own good. Chief among its flaws is that it transmits the user name and password in clear text across the link. This is a big "no-no" because eavesdroppers can get the password.

PAP also provides no protection against various security attacks. For example, an unauthorized user could try different passwords indefinitely until he discovered the correct one. PAP also puts control of the authentication squarely on the shoulders of the initiating device (usually a client machine), which is not considered desirable, because this is normally a server function that administrators prefer to manage.

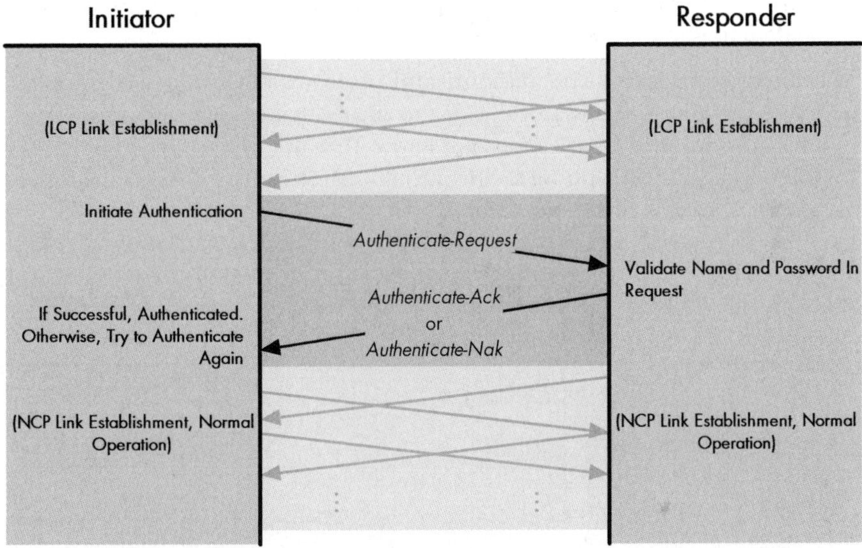

Figure 10-4: PAP authentication *PAP uses a simple exchange of a request containing name and password information and a reply indicating whether or not authentication was successful.*

CHAP

The most important difference between PAP and CHAP is that CHAP doesn't transmit the password across the link. When using PAP, the initiator (calling client) sends the authenticator (generally the server that is deciding whether to grant authentication) a message saying essentially, "Here's the password I know; see if it matches yours." Each device uses the password to perform a cryptographic computation, and then checks to see if it gets the same result. If so, they know they have the same password.

In CHAP, a basic LCP link is first set up between the initiator and authenticator. The authenticator then takes charge of the authentication process, using a technique called a *three-way handshake.*

NOTE *Three-way handshakes are a fairly common general authentication procedure. The same basic technique is used, for example, in shared key authentication on IEEE 802.11 wireless networking.*

The three-way handshake steps are as follows (see Figure 10-5):

Challenge The authenticator generates a frame called a Challenge and sends it to the initiator. This frame contains a simple text message (sometimes called the *challenge text*). The message has no inherent special meaning, so it doesn't matter if anyone intercepts it. The important thing is that after receipt of the Challenge, both devices have the same Challenge message.

Response The initiator uses its password (or some other shared secret that the authenticators also know) to encrypt the challenge text. It then sends the encrypted challenge text as a Response back to the authenticator.

Success or Failure The authenticator performs the same encryption on the challenge text that the initiator did. If the authenticator gets the same result that the initiator sent it in the Response, it knows that the initiator had the right password when it did its encryption, so the authenticator returns a Success message. Otherwise, it sends a Failure message.

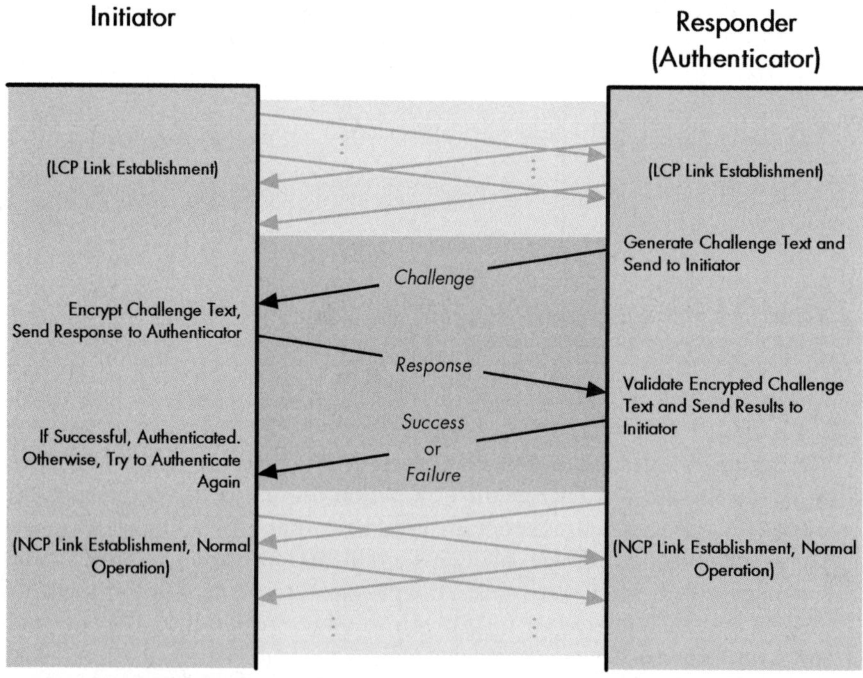

Figure 10-5: PPP Challenge Handshake Authentication Protocol (CHAP) authentication *CHAP uses a three-way handshake beginning with a Challenge from the authenticating device. This message is encrypted and returned to the authenticating device, which checks to see if the device trying to authenticate used the correct password (or other shared secret).*

The beauty of this is that it verifies that the two devices have the same shared secret, but it doesn't require them to send the secret over the link. The Response is calculated based on the password, but the content of the Response is encrypted, and thus it's much harder to derive the password from. CHAP also provides protection against replay attacks, whereby an unauthorized user captures a message and tries to send it again later on. This is done by changing an identifier in each message and varying the challenge text. Also, in CHAP, the server controls the authentication process, not the client that is initiating the link.

KEY CONCEPT PPP supports two authentication protocols: *PAP* and *CHAP*. PAP is a simple request-and-reply authentication protocol that is widely considered to be inadequate because it sends the user name and password in clear text and provides little protection against many security concerns. CHAP uses a three-way handshake procedure and is preferred over PAP in most implementations.

CHAP is not perfect, but it's much better than PAP. In fact, the IETF made a rather strong statement in this regard when it revised the original RFC that described PAP and CHAP to include only CHAP in the new standard. Despite this, PAP is still used in some applications because it is simple. PAP can suffice in situations where security is not a big deal, but CHAP is a much better choice.

NOTE *Incidentally, in addition to PAP and CHAP, it is possible to use proprietary authentication schemes. This requires that the appropriate configuration option values be programmed into LCP for placement in the Authentication Protocol configuration option.*

11

PPP FEATURE PROTOCOLS

Point-to-Point Protocol (PPP) is the standard for data link layer connectivity over serial links because its core protocols provide a solid operational foundation, as you saw in Chapter 10. However, PPP's popularity is based not just on its highly capable link establishment and management features, but it also has a number of very useful features that provide important security and performance benefits to network users.

In this chapter, I describe the protocols that implement several of the most common extra features in PPP. I begin with a discussion of PPP link quality monitoring. I describe the sets of protocols used to configure and implement data compression and data encryption. I then discuss the PPP Multilink Protocol (MP, MLPPP), which allows PPP to bundle multiple low-speed links into a single high-speed link. I also cover the *Bandwidth Allocation Protocol (BAP)* and *Bandwidth Allocation Control Protocol (BACP)*, which are used to manage the operation of MLPPP.

PPP Link Quality Monitoring and Reporting (LQM, LQR)

PPP includes optional authentication in recognition of the varying *security* needs of the many different kinds of links over which PPP may operate. These links also differ greatly in terms of their *quality*. Just as you don't need to worry about authentication much when two machines are linked with a short cable, you also can feel pretty confident that data sent between them is going to arrive intact. Now contrast that with a PPP session established over a long-distance telephone call. For that matter, how about PPP over a dial-up call using an analog cellular phone?

PPP includes in its basic package a provision for detecting errors in sent frames, and higher-layer protocols like TCP also include methods of providing robustness on noisy lines. These techniques allow a link to tolerate problems, but provide little in the way of useful information about what the status of the link is. In some situations, devices may want to be able to keep track of how well the link is working, and perhaps take action on it. For example, a device experiencing too many errors on a dial-up connection might want to cut off and retry a new call. In some cases, a device might want to try an alternate method of attachment if the current physical link is not working well.

Recognizing this need, the PPP suite includes a feature that allows devices to analyze the quality of the link between them. This is called *PPP Link Quality Monitoring* or *LQM*. PPP is set up generically to allow any number of different monitoring functions to be used, but at present, there is only one, called *Link Quality Reporting (LQR)*. LQR allows a device to request that its peer (the other device on the link) keep track of statistics about the link and send periodic reports about them.

LQR Setup

Before LQR can be used, it must be set up, which is done by LCP as part of the negotiation of basic link parameters in the Link Establishment phase (see Chapter 10). The device opening the link requests link monitoring by including the Quality Protocol configuration option in its Configure-Request frame. The configuration option also specifies a *reporting period* that indicates the longest period of time that the requesting device wants to go between receiving reports.

Assuming that the negotiation is successful, LQR will be enabled. A number of counters are set up that keep track of various link statistics, and a timer is used to regulate the sending of quality reports over the link. Each time the timer expires, a link quality report is generated and sent in a PPP frame over the link using the special PPP Protocol field hexadecimal value 0xC025.

Each counter holds information about a different statistic regarding the use of the link. Each counter is reset to zero when LQR is set up and then incremented each time a transmission is made or an event occurs that is relevant to the counter. The statistics tracked include the following:

- The number of frames sent or received
- The number of octets (bytes) in all frames sent or received
- The number of errors that have occurred

- The number of frames that had to be discarded
- The number of link quality reports generated

These counters are reset only at the start of the link, so they contain figures that are kept cumulatively over the life of the connection. The counters can be used in the absolute sense, meaning that the counter value itself is reported. Alternatively, they can be expressed as relative (or *delta*) values, which represent the change since the last report. This is done when a report is received, simply by subtracting the previous report's numbers from the ones in the current report.

Using Link Quality Reports

LQR specifies the quality reporting mechanism, but not specific standards for link quality, since these are so implementation-dependent. Based on the numbers in these reports, a device can decide for itself what conclusions to draw about link quality and what action to take, if any. Here are some possible behaviors:

- Some devices might decide to shut down a link if the absolute number of errors seen in any report reaches a certain threshold.
- Some might look at the trend in successive reporting periods and take action if they detect certain trends, such as an increase in the rate of discarded frames.
- Some devices might just log the information and take no action at all.

NOTE *LQR aggregates its statistics for all higher-layer protocols transmitted over a particular link. It doesn't keep track of statistics for different higher-layer protocols separately, which makes sense, since the quality of the link shouldn't vary from one higher-layer protocol to the next.*

PPP Compression Control Protocol (CCP) and Compression Algorithms

PPP is primarily used to provide data link layer connectivity to physical serial links. One of the biggest problems with serial links compared to many other types of layer 1 connections is that they are relatively slow. Consider that while 10 Mbps regular Ethernet is considered sluggish by modern LAN standards, it is actually much faster than most serial lines used for WAN connectivity, which can be ten, one hundred, or even one thousand times slower.

One way to improve performance over serial links is to compress the data sent over the line. Depending on the data transferred, this can double the performance compared to uncompressed transmissions, and can, in some cases, do even better than that. For this reason, many hardware devices include the ability to compress the data stream at the physical layer. The best example of this is probably the set of compression protocols used on analog modems.

Some physical links don't provide any compression capabilities, but could still benefit from it. To this end, an optional compression feature was created for PPP. It is implemented using the following two distinct protocol components:

PPP Compression Control Protocol (CCP) This protocol is responsible for negotiating and managing the use of compression on a PPP link.

PPP Compression Algorithms A set of compression algorithms that perform the actual compression and decompression of data. Several of these are defined in RFCs. In addition, it is possible for two devices to negotiate the use of a proprietary compression method if they want to use one that isn't defined by a public standard.

> **KEY CONCEPT** PPP includes an optional compression feature that can improve performance over slow physical links. A variety of different compression algorithms are supported. To enable compression, both devices on a PPP link use the *PPP Compression Control Protocol (CCP)* to negotiate a compression algorithm to use. The compression algorithm is then used to compress and decompress PPP data frames.

CCP Operation: Compression Setup

When most people talk about compression in PPP, they mention CCP, which is considered "the" compression protocol for PPP. However, CCP is actually used only to configure and control the use of compression; in fact, the algorithms do the real work of compressing and decompressing. This separation of powers provides flexibility, because it allows each implementation to choose what type of compression it wants to use.

CCP is analogous to the Network Control Protocols (NCPs) that negotiate parameters specific to a network layer protocol sent on the link. An NCP lets two devices decide how they will carry layer 3 traffic, such as how Internet Protocol Control Protocol (IPCP) lets the devices determine how to carry IP. CCP lets two devices decide how they will compress data, in the same basic way.

Similarly, just as each NCP is like a "light" version of LCP, CCP is like a light version of LCP. It is used to set up a compression connection called a *CCP link* within an LCP link between two devices. Once established, compressed frames can be sent between the two devices. CCP also provides messaging capabilities for managing and eventually terminating a CCP link. Again, this is very similar to how each network layer protocol sets up an NCP link within LCP. A CCP link is maintained independently of any NCP links.

CCP uses the same subset of seven LCP message types that the NCPs use, and it adds two additional ones. The use of these messages for each of the life stages of a CCP link is as follows (this should look familiar if you've read about how the NCPs and LCP work in Chapter 10):

Link Configuration Like the NCPs, compression configuration is done once CCP reaches the *network layer protocol* phase. The process of setting up compression and negotiating parameters is accomplished using Configure-Request, Configure-Ack, Configure-Nak, and Configure-Reject messages, just as it is for LCP, except the configuration options are particular to CCP.

Link Maintenance Code-Reject messages can be sent to indicate invalid code values in CCP frames. The two new message types are Reset-Request and Reset-Ack, which are used to reset the compression (the CCP link) in the event of a detected failure in decompression.

Link Termination A CCP link can be terminated using Terminate-Request and Terminate-Ack. Again, remember that, like the NCP links, the CCP link is set up within an LCP link, and closing it doesn't terminate the LCP link, which controls PPP overall.

CCP Configuration Options and Compression Algorithms

CCP configuration options are used only to negotiate the type of compression to be used by the two devices, and to acquire the specifics of how that algorithm is to be employed. The device initiating the negotiation sends a Configure-Request with one option for each of the compression algorithms it supports. The other device compares this list of options to the algorithms it understands. It also checks for any specific details relevant to the option to see if it agrees on how that algorithm should be used. It then sends back the appropriate reply (Ack, Nak, or Reject), and a negotiation ensues until the two devices come up with a common algorithm that both understand. If so, compression is turned on; otherwise, it is not enabled.

The CCP configuration options begin with a Type value that indicates the compression algorithm. When the Type value is 0, this indicates that the option contains information about a special, proprietary compression algorithm that isn't covered by any RFC standards. This information can be used if both devices understand it. Values from 1 to 254 indicate compression algorithms that have been defined for use with CCP. Table 11-1 shows the most common values of the Type field, including the compression algorithm each corresponds to and the number of the RFC that defines it.

Table 11-1: PPP Compression Control Protocol (CCP) Compression Algorithms

CCP Option Type Value	Defining RFC	Compression Algorithm (As Given in RFC Title)
0	—	Proprietary
1 and 2	1978	PPP Predictor Compression Protocol
17	1974	PPP Stac LZS Compression Protocol
18	2118	Microsoft Point-to-Point Compression (MPPC) Protocol
19	1993	PPP Gandalf FZA Compression Protocol
21	1977	PPP BSD Compression Protocol
23	1967	PPP LZS-DCP Compression Protocol (LZS-DCP)
26	1979	PPP Deflate Protocol

Compression Algorithm Operation: Compressing and Decompressing Data

Once an algorithm has been successfully negotiated, the compression algorithm is used to compress data before transmission and to decompress it once received. To compress, the transmitting device takes the data that would normally be put in the Information field of an uncompressed PPP frame and runs it through the compression algorithm. To indicate that a frame has been compressed, the special value

0x00FD (hexadecimal) is placed in the PPP Protocol field. When compression is used with multiple links and the links are compressed independently, a different value is used: 0x00FB.

You'll recall that in a regular uncompressed frame, the Protocol field indicates which layer 3 protocol the data comes from. Since you still need to know this, the original Protocol value is actually prepended to the data before compression. When the data is decompressed, this value is used to restore the original Protocol field, so the receiving device knows to which higher layer the data belongs.

For example, if you use IPCP to encapsulate IP data in PPP, the uncompressed frame would have a value of 0x8021 in the Protocol field. This value (0x8021) would be placed at the start of the data to be compressed. The compressed data would be put in a PPP frame with a Protocol value of 0x00FD. The receiving device would see the value 0x00FD in the Protocol field, recognize the frame as compressed, decompress it, and restore the original frame with 0x8021 as the Protocol value. The discussion of the PPP general frame format in Chapter 12 covers this in more detail.

In theory, a compression algorithm can put more than one PPP data frame into a compressed PPP data frame. Despite this, many, if not most, of the algorithms maintain a one-to-one correspondence, putting each PPP data frame into one compressed frame. Note that LCP frames are not compressed, nor are the control frames used for other protocols. For example, a data frame carrying IP traffic would be compressed, but a control frame for IPCP (the NCP for IP) would not be.

Compression can be combined with encryption. In this case, compression is done before encryption.

NOTE *The compression performed by CCP has nothing to do with the header compression options that can be negotiated as part of LCP. That type of compression doesn't involve compressing a data stream using a compression algorithm, but rather a simple way of saving space in headers when both ends of a link agree to do so.*

PPP Encryption Control Protocol (ECP) and Encryption Algorithms

The PPP authentication protocols Password Authentication Protocol (PAP) and Challenge Handshake Authentication Protocol (CHAP) can be used to ensure that only authorized devices can establish a PPP connection. Once that is done, PPP normally provides no other security to the data being transmitted. In particular, all data is normally sent in the clear (unencrypted), thereby making it easy for someone who intercepts it to read.

For important data that must be kept secure, encryption prior to transmission is a good idea. This can be done at higher layers using something like IPsec, but PPP also provides an optional feature that allows data to be encrypted and decrypted at the data link layer itself using two protocol components:

PPP Encryption Control Protocol (ECP) This protocol is responsible for negotiating and managing the use of encryption on a PPP link.

PPP Encryption Algorithms A family of encryption algorithms that perform the actual encryption and decryption of data. Several of these are defined in RFCs, and two devices can also negotiate a proprietary encryption method if they want to use one that isn't defined by a public standard.

> **KEY CONCEPT** PPP includes an optional encryption feature that provides privacy for data transported over PPP. A number of encryption algorithms are supported. To enable encryption, both devices on a PPP link use the *PPP Encryption Control Protocol (ECP)* to negotiate which algorithm to use. The selected algorithm is then used to encrypt and decrypt PPP data frames.

ECP Operation: Encryption Setup

ECP is usually the only part mentioned when encryption in PPP is discussed, but it is actually used only to configure and control the use of encryption; the algorithms do the real work. This technique allows each implementation to choose which type of encryption it wishes to use.

The original ECP defined only a single encryption method, and a couple of others have since been added. Like CCP, ECP is analogous to the NCPs that negotiate parameters specific to a network layer protocol sent on the link, but it deals with how devices encrypt data, rather than how they transport layer 3 traffic. This also means that like the NCPs, ECP is a light version of LCP and works in the same basic way. Once an ECP link is negotiated, devices can send encrypted frames between each other. When no longer needed, the ECP link can be terminated.

ECP uses the same subset of seven LCP message types that the NCPs use, and it adds two more. The use of these messages for each of the life stages of an ECP link is as follows:

Link Configuration Like the NCPs (and also like CCP, of course), encryption configuration is done once ECP reaches the *network layer protocol* phase. The process of setting up encryption and negotiating parameters is accomplished using Configure-Request, Configure-Ack, Configure-Nak, and Configure-Reject messages, as I explained in the description of LCP in Chapter 10, except the configuration options are particular to ECP.

Link Maintenance Code-Reject messages can be sent to indicate invalid code values in ECP frames. The two new message types are Reset-Request and Reset-Ack, which are used to reset the encryption (the ECP link) in the event of a detected failure in decryption.

Link Termination An ECP link can be terminated using Terminate-Request and Terminate-Ack. Again, remember that like the NCP links, the ECP link is set up within an LCP link, so closing it doesn't terminate the LCP link.

ECP Configuration Options and Encryption Algorithms

ECP configuration options are used solely to negotiate the type of encryption algorithm that will be used by the two devices and the specifics of how that algorithm will be employed. The device initiating the negotiation sends a Configure-Request with one option for each of the encryption algorithms it supports. The other device compares this list of options to the algorithms it understands. It also checks for any details relevant to the option to see if it agrees on how that algorithm should be used. It then sends back the appropriate reply (Ack, Nak, or Reject), and a negotiation ensues until the two devices come up with a common algorithm that they both understand. If so, encryption is enabled; otherwise, it is turned off.

The ECP configuration options begin with a Type value that indicates the encryption algorithm. When the Type value is 0, this indicates that the option contains information about a special, proprietary encryption method that isn't covered by any RFC standards, which can be used if both devices understand it. Values in the range from 1 to 254 indicate encryption algorithms that have been defined for use with ECP; at present, only two are defined. Table 11-2 shows the values of the Type field, including the encryption algorithm each corresponds to and the number of the RFC that defines it.

Table 11-2: PPP Encryption Control Protocol (ECP) Compression Algorithms

ECP Option Type Value	Defining RFC	Encryption Algorithm (As Given in RFC Title)
0	—	Proprietary
2	2420	The PPP Triple-DES Encryption Protocol (3DESE)
3	2419	The PPP DES Encryption Protocol, Version 2 (DESE-bis)

NOTE *Type value 1 was for the original DES algorithm, which was defined in RFC 1969. It was superseded by DES version 2 in RFC 2419.*

Encryption Algorithm Operation: Encrypting and Decrypting Data

Once an encryption algorithm has been successfully negotiated, it is used to encrypt data before transmission and to decrypt data that has been received. To encrypt, the transmitting device takes the data that would normally be put in the Information field of an unencrypted PPP frame and runs it through the encryption algorithm. To indicate that a frame has been encrypted, the special value 0x0053 (hexadecimal) is placed in the PPP Protocol field. When encryption is used with multiple links and the links are encrypted independently, a different value is used: 0x0055.

You'll recall that in a regular unencrypted frame, the Protocol field indicates which layer 3 protocol the data comes from. Since you still need to know this, the original Protocol value is actually prepended to the data before encryption. When the data is decrypted, this value is used to restore the original Protocol field, so the receiving device knows which higher layer the data belongs to.

For example, if you use IPCP to encapsulate IP data in PPP, the unencrypted frame would have a value of 0x8021 (hex) in the Protocol field. This value (0x8021) would be placed at the start of the data to be encrypted. The encrypted data would be put in a PPP frame with a Protocol value of 0x0053. The receiving device would see the value 0x0053 in the Protocol field, recognize the frame as encrypted, decrypt it, and restore the original frame with 0x8021 as the Protocol value. The discussion of the PPP general frame format in Chapter 12 covers this more completely.

Each encrypted PPP data frame carries exactly one PPP data frame. Note that, unlike what you saw in compression, LCP frames and the control frames used for other protocols *can* be encrypted. Compression can be combined with encryption; in this case, compression is done before encryption.

PPP Multilink Protocol (MP, MLP, MLPPP)

Most of the time, there is only a single physical layer link between two devices. However, there are some situations for which there may actually be two layer 1 connections between the same pair of devices. This may seem strange. Why would there be more than one link between any pair of machines?

There are a number of situations in which this can occur. A common one is when two links are intentionally placed between a pair of devices. This is often done to increase performance by widening the pipe between two devices, without going to a newer, more expensive technology. For example, if two machines are connected to each other using a regular analog modem that's too slow, a relatively simple solution is to use two analog modem pairs connecting the machines to double bandwidth.

A slightly different situation occurs when multiplexing creates the equivalent of several physical layer channels between two devices, even if they have only one hardware link between them. Consider ISDN, for example. The most common form of ISDN service (ISDN basic rate interface or BRI) creates two 64,000 bps *B channels* between a pair of devices. These B channels are time division multiplexed and carried along with a D channel on a single pair of copper wire, but to the devices, they appear *as if* there were two physical layer links between devices, each of which carries 64 Kbps of data. And the ISDN primary rate interface (PRI) actually creates 23 or more channels, all between the same pair of hardware devices.

In a situation where you have multiple links, you could just establish PPP over each connection independently. However, this is far from an ideal solution, because you would then have to manually distribute the traffic over the two (or more) channels or links that connect them. If you wanted to connect to the Internet, you would need to make separate connections and then choose which one to use for each action. That isn't exactly a recipe for fun, and what's worse is that you could never use all the bandwidth for a single purpose, such as downloading the latest 100 MB Microsoft security patch.

What you really want is a solution that will let you combine multiple links and use them as if they were one high-performance link. Some hardware devices actually allow this to be done at the hardware level itself. In ISDN, this technology is sometimes called *bonding* when done at layer 1. For those hardware units that don't provide this capability, PPP makes it available in the form of the PPP Multilink Protocol (MP). This protocol was originally described in RFC 1717 and was updated in RFC 1990.

NOTE *The* PPP Multilink Protocol *is properly abbreviated MP, but it is common to see any of a multitude of other abbreviations used for it. Many of these are actually derived from changing the order of the words in the name into Multilink PPP, so you will frequently see this called ML PPP, MLPPP, MPPP, MLP, and so forth. These are technically incorrect, but widely used, especially MLPPP. I use the correct abbreviation in this book.*

PPP Multilink Protocol Architecture

MP is an optional feature of PPP, so it must be designed to integrate seamlessly into regular PPP operation. To accomplish this, MP is implemented as a new architectural sublayer within PPP. In essence, an MP sublayer is inserted between the regular PPP mechanism and any network layer protocols using PPP, as shown in Figure 11-1. This allows MP to take all network layer data to be sent over the PPP link and spread it over multiple physical connections, without causing either the normal PPP mechanisms or the network layer protocol interfaces to PPP to break.

The column on the left in Figure 11-1 shows the TCP/IP model architecture with corresponding OSI Reference Model layer numbers. The center column shows the normal PPP layer architecture. When MP is used, there are separate PPP implementations running over each of two or more physical links. MP sits, architecturally, between these links and any network layer protocols that will be transported over those links. (In this diagram, only IP is shown because it is most common, but MP can work with multiple network layer protocols, each of which are being sent over each physical link.)

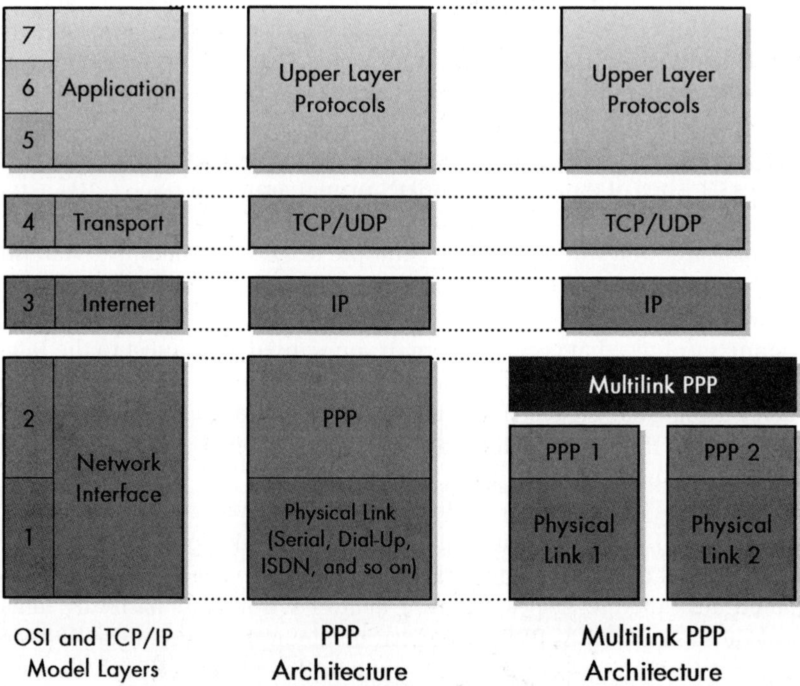

Figure 11-1: Multilink PPP architecture *When Multilink PPP is used to combine two or more physical links, it sits architecturally above the PPP layers that operate on each physical link.*

KEY CONCEPT The *PPP Multilink Protocol (MP)* allows PPP to bundle multiple physical links and use them like a single, high-capacity link. It must be enabled during link configuration. Once operational, it works by fragmenting whole PPP frames and sending the fragments over different physical links.

PPP Multilink Protocol Setup and Configuration

To use MP, both devices must have it implemented as part of their PPP software and must negotiate its use. This is done by LCP as part of the negotiation of basic link parameters in the *link establishment* phase (just like LQR, as described earlier in this chapter). Three new configuration options are defined to be negotiated to enable MP:

Multilink Maximum Received Reconstructed Unit Provides the basic indication that the device starting the negotiation supports MP and wants to use it. The option contains a value specifying the maximum size of the PPP frame it supports. If the device receiving this option does not support MP, it must respond with a Configure-Reject LCP message.

Multilink Short Sequence Number Header Format Allows devices to negotiate the use of a shorter sequence number field for MP frames, for efficiency. (See the section on MP frames in Chapter 12 for a full discussion.)

Endpoint Discriminator Uniquely identifies the system. It is used to allow devices to determine which links go to which other devices.

Before MP can be used, a successful negotiation of at least the Multilink Maximum Received Reconstructed Unit option must be performed on each of the links between the two devices. Once this is done and an LCP link exists for each of the physical links, a virtual *bundle* is made of the LCP links, and MP is enabled.

PPP Multilink Protocol Operation

As mentioned previously, MP basically sits between the network layer and the regular PPP links and acts as a middleman. Here is what it does for each direction of communication:

Transmission MP accepts datagrams received from any of the network layer protocols configured using appropriate NCPs. It first encapsulates them into a modified version of the regular PPP frame, and then takes that frame and decides how to transmit it over the multiple physical links. Typically, this is done by dividing the frame into *fragments* that are evenly spread out over the set of links. These are then encapsulated and sent over the physical links. However, you can also implement an alternative strategy as well, such as alternating full-sized frames between the links. Also, smaller frames typically aren't fragmented, and neither are control frames such as the ones used for link configuration.

Reception MP takes the fragments received from all physical links and reassembles them into the original PPP frame. That frame is then processed like any PPP frame by looking at its Protocol field and passing it to the appropriate network layer protocol.

The fragments used in MP are similar in concept to IP fragments, but of course these are different protocols running at different layers. To PPP or MP, an IP fragment is just an IP datagram like any other.

The fragmenting of data in MP introduces a number of complexities that the protocol must handle. For example, since fragments are being sent roughly concurrently, you need to identify them with a sequence number to facilitate reassembly. You also need some control information to identify the first and last fragments. A special frame format is used for MP fragments to carry this extra information. I describe this in Chapter 12, which also contains more information about how fragmenting is accomplished, as well as an illustration that demonstrates how it works.

PPP Bandwidth Allocation Protocol (BAP) and Bandwidth Allocation Control Protocol (BACP)

The PPP MP allows multiple links between a pair of devices, whether physical or in the form of virtual channels, to be combined into a fat pipe (high-capacity channel). This offers tremendous advantages to many PPP users, because it lets them make optimal use of all their bandwidth, especially for applications such as Internet connectivity. It's no surprise, then, that MP has become one of the most popular features of PPP.

The original standard defining MP basically assumed that multiple links would be combined into a single bundle. For example, if you had two modem links, they would both be connected and then combined, or two B channels in an ISDN link would be combined. After MP was set up, the bundle would be available for either device to use in its entirety.

There's one drawback to this system: The fat pipe is always enabled, and in many cases, it is expensive to have this set up all the time. It often costs more to connect two or more layer 1 links than a single one, and it's not always needed. For example, some ISDN services charge per minute for calls on either of the B channels. In the case of modem dial-up, there are per-minute charges in some parts of the world. Even where regular phone calls are free, there is a cost in the form of tying up a phone line. Consider that in many applications, the amount of bandwidth needed varies over time.

It would be better if you could set up MP so that it could dynamically add links to the bundle when needed (such as when you decided to download some large files), and then automatically drop them when no longer required. This enhancement to the basic MP package was provided in the form of a pair of new protocols described in RFC 2125:

Bandwidth Allocation Protocol (BAP) Describes a mechanism where either device communicating over an MP bundle of layer 1 links may request that a link be added to the bundle or removed from it.

Bandwidth Allocation Control Protocol (BACP) Allows devices to configure how they want to use BAP.

> **KEY CONCEPT** *BAP* and *BACP* are used to provide dynamic control over how PPP MP functions.

BACP Operation: Configuring the Use of BAP

Let's start with BACP, since it is the protocol used for the initial setup of the feature. BACP is very similar conceptually to all those other PPP protocols with "Control" in their names, such as LCP, the NCP family, CCP, and ECP, but is actually even simpler. It is used only during link configuration to set up BAP. This is done using Configure-Request, Configure-Ack, Configure-Nak, and Configure-Reject messages, just as described in the LCP topic.

The only configuration option that is negotiated in BACP is one called Favored-Peer, which is used to ensure that a problem does not occur if the two devices on the link try to send the same request at the same time. If both devices support BAP, then the BACP negotiation will succeed and BAP will be activated.

BAP Operation: Adding and Removing Links

BAP defines a set of messages that can be sent between devices to add or drop links to and from the current PPP bundle. What's particularly interesting about BAP is that it includes the tools necessary to have a device actually initiate different types of physical layer connections (such as dialing a modem for bundled analog links or enabling an extra ISDN channel) when more bandwidth is required. It then shuts them down when they're no longer needed.

Here's a brief description of the BAP message types:

Call-Request and Call-Response When one device on the link wants to add a link to the bundle and initiate the new physical layer link itself, it sends a Call-Request frame to tell the other device, which replies with a Call-Response.

Callback-Request and Callback-Response These are just like the two previous message types, except that they're used when a device wants its peer (the other device on the link) to initiate the call to add a new link. So, if Device A says, "I need more bandwidth but I want you to call me, instead of me calling you," it sends Device B a Callback-Request.

Call-Status-Indication and Call-Status-Response After a device attempts to add a new link to the bundle (after sending a Call-Request or receiving a Callback-Request), it reports the status of the new link using the Call-Status-Indication frame. The other device then replies with a Call-Status-Response.

Link-Drop-Query-Request and Link-Drop-Query-Response One device uses these messages to request that a link be dropped, and the other uses them to respond to that request.

Note that the decision of when to add or remove links is not made by these protocols. It is left up to the particular implementation.

12

PPP PROTOCOL FRAME FORMATS

The Point-to-Point Protocol (PPP) protocol suite includes a number of different protocols used to send both data and control information in different ways. Each of these packages information into messages called *frames*, each of which follows a particular *frame format.* PPP starts with a general frame format that encompasses all frames sent on the link and then includes more specific formats for different purposes. Understanding these formats not only makes diagnosing PPP issues easier, but also helps make more clear how the key PPP protocols function.

In this chapter, I illustrate the most common frame formats used for sending both data and control information over PPP. I begin with an explanation of the overall format used for all PPP frames. I also describe the general format used for the various control protocols and the option format that most of them use. (One of the nice things about PPP is that so many of the protocols use control frames with a common format.)

I then specifically list the frames used for Link Control Protocol (LCP) and the authentication protocols (PAP and CHAP). I also describe the special format used by the PPP Multilink Protocol (MP) to transport fragments of data over bundled links.

NOTE *Due to the sheer number of different protocols in PPP (dozens) and the fact that many have their own unique options, I won't describe all the specific frame formats and option formats for every protocol in detail here. Please refer to the appropriate RFCs (listed in Chapter 9 for more detail).*

PPP General Frame Format

All messages sent using PPP can be considered either *data* or *control information.* The word *data* describes the higher-layer datagrams you are trying to transport here at layer 2. This is what our "customers" are giving us to send. Control information is used to manage the operation of the various protocols within PPP itself. Even though different protocols in the PPP suite use many types of frames, at the highest level, they all fit into a single, *general* frame format.

You'll recall that the basic operation of the PPP suite is based on the ISO High-Level Data Link Control (HDLC) protocol. This becomes very apparent when you look at the structure of PPP frames overall—they use the same basic format as HDLC, even to the point of including certain fields that aren't strictly necessary for PPP itself. The only major change is the addition of a new field to specify the protocol of the encapsulated data. The general structure of PPP frames is defined in RFC 1662, a companion to the main PPP standard RFC 1661.

The general frame format for PPP, showing how the HDLC framing is applied to PPP, is described in Table 12-1 and illustrated in Figure 12-1.

Table 12-1: PPP General Frame Format

Field Name	Size (Bytes)	Description
Flag	1	Indicates the start of a PPP frame. Always has the value 01111110 binary (0x7E hexadecimal, or 126 decimal).
Address	1	In HDLC this is the address of the destination of the frame. But in PPP you are dealing with a direct link between two devices, so this field has no real meaning. It is thus always set to 11111111 (0xFF or 255 decimal), which is equivalent to a broadcast (it means "all stations").
Control	1	This field is used in HDLC for various control purposes, but in PPP it is set to 00000011 (3 decimal).
Protocol	2	Identifies the protocol of the datagram encapsulated in the Information field of the frame. See the "Protocol Field Ranges" section for more information on the Protocol field.
Information	Variable	Zero or more bytes of payload that contain either data or control information, depending on the frame type. For regular PPP data frames, the network layer datagram is encapsulated here. For control frames, the control information fields are placed here instead.
Padding	Variable	In some cases, additional dummy bytes may be added to pad out the size of the PPP frame.
Frame Check Sequence	2 (or 4)	A checksum computed over the frame to provide basic protection against errors in transmission. This is a CRC similar to the one used for other layer 2 protocol error-protection schemes such as the one used in Ethernet. It can be either 16 bits or 32 bits in size (the default is 16 bits). The FCS is calculated over the Address, Control, Protocol, Information, and Padding fields.
Flag	1	Indicates the end of a PPP frame. Always has the value 01111110 binary (0x7E hexadecimal, or 126 decimal).

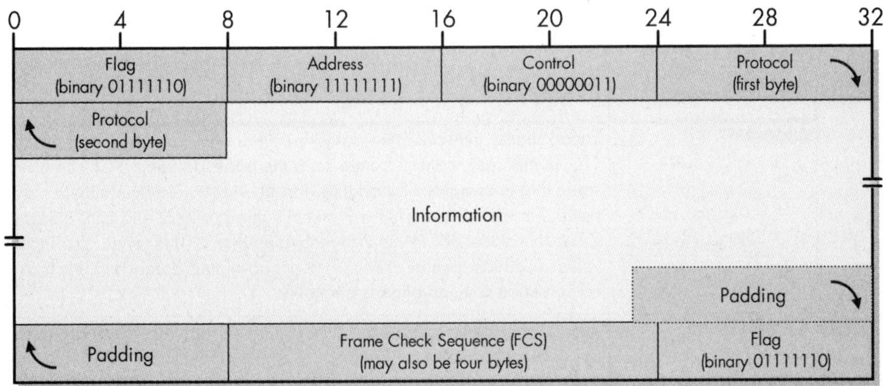

***Figure 12-1:** PPP general frame format*

Protocol Field Ranges

The Protocol field is the main frame type indicator for the device receiving the frame. For data frames, this is normally the network layer protocol that created the datagram; for control frames, it is usually the PPP protocol that created the control message. In the case of protocols that modify data such as when compression (CCP) or encryption (ECP) are used (as explained in the previous chapter), this field identifies the data as being either compressed or encrypted, and the original Protocol value is extracted after the Information field is decompressed/decrypted.

All PPP frames are built on the general format shown in Figure 12-1. The first three bytes are fixed in value, followed by a two-byte Protocol field that indicates the frame type. The variable-length Information field is formatted in a variety of ways, depending on the PPP frame type. Padding may be applied to the frame, which concludes with an FCS field of either two or four bytes (two bytes shown here) and a trailing Flag value of 0x7E. (See Figure 12-2 for an example of how this format is applied.)

There are dozens of network layer protocols and PPP control protocols, and a correspondingly large number of Protocol values. The main PPP standard defines four ranges for organizing these values, as shown in Table 12-2.

The standard also specifies that the Protocol value must be assigned so that the first octet is even and the second octet is odd. So, for example, 0x0021 is a valid value, but 0x0121 and 0x0120 are not. (The reason for this will become apparent shortly.) There are also certain blocks that are reserved and not used.

Figure 12-2 shows one common application of the PPP general frame format: carrying data. The value 0x0021 in the *Protocol* field marks this as an IPv4 datagram. This sample has 1 byte of *Padding* and a 2-byte *FCS* as well. (Obviously real IP datagrams are longer than the 32 bytes shown here! These bytes are arbitrary and don't represent a real datagram.) See Figure 12-12 for an illustration of how this same data frame is formatted and then fragmented for transmission over multiple links using the PPP Multilink Protocol (MP).

Table 12-2: PPP Protocol Field Ranges

Protocol Field Range (Hexadecimal)	Description
0000–3FFF	Encapsulated network layer datagrams that have an associated NCP (see Chapter 10). In this case, control frames from the corresponding NCP use a Protocol field value that is computed by adding 8 to the first octet of the network layer Protocol value. For example, for IP the Protocol value is 0021, and control frames from the IP Control Protocol (IPCP) use Protocol value 8021. This range also includes several values used for specially processed encapsulated datagrams, such as when compression or encryption is employed.
4000–7FFF	Encapsulated datagrams from "low-volume" protocols. These are protocols that do not have an associated NCP.
8000–BFFF	NCP control frames that correspond to the network layer Protocol values in the 0000–3FFF range.
C000–FFFF	Control frames used by LCP and LCP support protocols such as PAP and CHAP. Some miscellaneous protocol values are included here as well.

0 – 8	8 – 16	16 – 24	24 – 32
Flag = 7E	Address = FF	Control = 03	Protocol (byte 1) = 00
Protocol (byte 2) = 21	2A	00	1D
47	9F	BC	19
88	18	E5	01
73	A3	69	AF
1B	90	54	BA
00	7C	D1	AA
Padding = 00	Frame Check Sequence = ????		Flag = 7E

Figure 12-2: Sample PPP data frame *An example of a PPP data frame containing an abbreviated 23-byte IP datagram.*

Protocol Field Values

The full list of PPP Protocol values is maintained by the Internet Assigned Numbers Authority (IANA), along with all the other different reserved numbers for Internet standards. Table 12-3 shows some of the more common values.

Table 12-3: Common Protocols Carried in PPP Frames and Protocol Field Values

Protocol Type	Protocol Field Value (Hex)	Protocol
Encapsulated Network Layer Datagrams	0021	Internet Protocol version 4 (IPv4)
	0023	OSI Network Layer
	0029	AppleTalk
	002B	Novell Internetworking Packet Exchange (IPX)
	003D	PPP Multilink Protocol (MP) fragment
	003F	NetBIOS Frames (NBF/NetBEUI)
	004D	IBM Systems Network Architecture (SNA)
	0053	Encrypted Data (using ECP and a PPP encryption algorithm)
	0055	Individual Link Encrypted Data under PPP Multilink
	0057	Internet Protocol version 6 (IPv6)
	00FB	Individual Link Compressed Data under PPP Multilink
	00FD	Compressed Data (using CCP and a PPP compression algorithm)
Low-Volume Encapsulated Protocols	4003	CDPD Mobile Network Registration Protocol
	4025	Fibre Channel
Network Control Protocol (NCP) Control Frames	8021	PPP Internet Protocol Control Protocol
	8023	PPP OSI Network Layer Control Protocol
	8029	PPP AppleTalk Control Protocol
	802B	PPP IPX Control Protocol
	803F	PPP NetBIOS Frames Control Protocol
	804D	PPP SNA Control Protocol
	8057	PPP IPv6 Control Protocol
LCP and Other Control Frames	C021	PPP Link Control Protocol (LCP)
	C023	PPP Password Authentication Protocol (PAP)
	C025	PPP Link Quality Report (LQR)
	C02B	PPP Bandwidth Allocation Control Protocol (BACP)
	C02D	PPP Bandwidth Allocation Protocol (BAP)
	C223	PPP Challenge Handshake Authentication Protocol (CHAP)

PPP Field Compression

PPP uses the HDLC basic framing structure, which includes two fields that are needed in HDLC but aren't in PPP due to how the latter operates. The fields are the Address and Control fields. Why bother sending two bytes that have the same value for every frame and aren't used for anything? Originally, they were maintained for compatibility, but this reduces efficiency.

To avoid wasting two bytes in every frame, it is possible during initial link setup using the Link Control Protocol (LCP) for the two devices on the link to negotiate a feature called *Address and Control Field Compression (ACFC)* using the LCP option by that same name. When enabled, this feature simply causes these two fields not to be sent for most PPP frames (but not for LCP control frames). In fact, the feature would be better named *Address and Control Field Suppression*, because the fields are just suppressed and compressed down to nothing.

Even when devices agree to use field compression, they must still be capable of receiving both compressed and uncompressed frames. They differentiate one from the other by looking at the first two bytes after the initial Flag field. If they contain the value 0xFF03, they must be the Address and Control fields; otherwise, those fields were suppressed. (The value 0xFF03 is not a valid Protocol field value, so there is no chance of ambiguity.)

Similarly, it is also possible for the two devices on the link to negotiate compression of the Protocol field, so it takes only one byte instead of two. This is done generally by dropping the first byte if it is zero, a process called *Protocol Field Compression (PFC)*. Recall that the first byte must be even and the second odd. Thus, a receiving device examines the evenness of the first byte of the Protocol field in each frame. If it is odd, this means that a leading byte of zeros in the Protocol field has been suppressed, because the first byte of a full two-byte Protocol value must be even.

NOTE *This field compression (really suppression) has nothing to do with data compression using PPP's Compression Control Protocol (CCP) and compression algorithms.*

PPP General Control Protocol Frame Format and Option Format

The general frame format you just saw is used for all of the many frame types defined in the PPP protocol suite. Within that format, the Information field carries either encapsulated layer 3 user data or encapsulated control messages. These control messages contain specific information that is used to configure, manage, and discontinue PPP links, and to implement the various features that comprise PPP.

There are many different PPP control protocols that usually can be distinguished by the word *Control* appearing their names. These include the main PPP Link Control Protocol (LCP); a family of Network Control Protocols (NCPs) such as IPCP, IPXCP, and so forth; and also control protocols for implementing features, such as the Compression Control Protocol (CCP) and the Encryption Control Protocol (ECP). The authentication protocols Password Authentication Protocol (PAP) and Challenge Handshake Authentication Protocol (CHAP) lack Control in the name but also fall into this category.

The control protocols each use control messages in a slightly different way, but there is also a great deal of commonality between the messages. This is because, as I explained in my discussions of the PPP protocols, most of the control protocols—such as the NCP family, CCP, and ECP—are implemented as subsets of the functionality of the LCP. They perform many of the same functions, so the PPP designers wisely adapted the LCP messaging system for these other control protocols.

This all means that control protocol frames have a common format that fits within the overall general frame format in PPP. Even protocols like PAP and CHAP, which aren't based on LCP, use this general control frame format, which is described in Table 12-4.

Table 12-4: PPP Control Message Format

Field Name	Size (Bytes)	Description
Code (Type)	1	A single byte value that indicates what type of control message is in this control frame. It is sometimes instead called Type in certain PPP standards.
Identifier	1	This is a label field that's used to match up requests with replies. When a request is sent, a new Identifier is generated. When a reply is created, the value from the Identifier field in the request that prompted the reply is used for the reply's Identifier field.
Length	2	Specifies the length of the control frame. This is needed because the Data field is variable in length. The Length field is specified in bytes and includes all the fields in the control frame including the Code, Identifier, Length, and Data fields.
Data	Variable	Contains information specific to the message type. The different uses of this field are described later in this chapter.

This entire structure becomes the payload of a PPP frame, meaning that it fits into the Information field of a PPP frame, as shown in Figure 12-3. The four fields of the PPP control message format fit within the Information field of the PPP general frame format. The Data field is subsequently filled in with data specific to the control message type. Thus, the Length field is equal in size to that of the Information field in the PPP frame. The Protocol field of a control frame is set to match the protocol that generated the control frame. For example, it would be 0xC021 for an LCP frame.

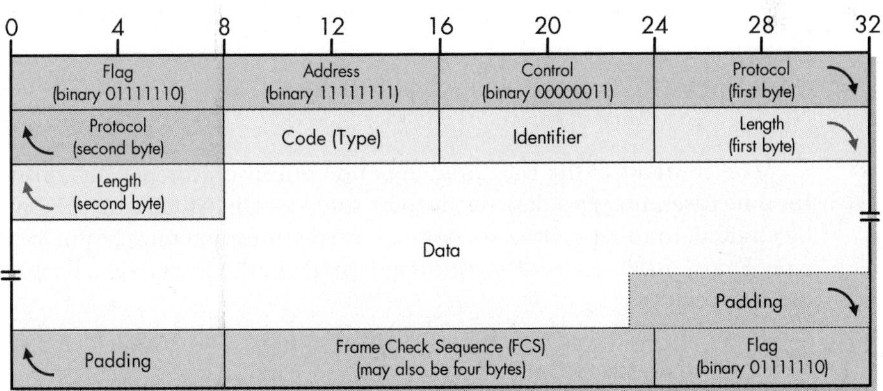

Figure 12-3: PPP control message format

PPP Control Messages and Code Values

The Code field indicates the type of control frame within the particular control protocol. Some protocols have a unique set of codes used only by that particular protocol; examples include the authentication protocols (PAP and CHAP) and the

Bandwidth Allocation Protocol (BAP). Since the NCPs and many of the feature control protocols like CCP and ECP are based on LCP, they use a common set of message codes and types. Table 12-5 shows these common message codes and indicates which control protocols use them.

Table 12-5: PPP Control Messages, Code Values, and PPP Protocol Usage

Code Value	Control Message	LCP	NCPs	CCP and ECP
1	Configure-Request	✓	✓	✓
2	Configure-Ack	✓	✓	✓
3	Configure-Nak	✓	✓	✓
4	Configure-Reject	✓	✓	✓
5	Terminate-Request	✓	✓	✓
6	Terminate-Ack	✓	✓	✓
7	Code-Reject	✓	✓	✓
8	Protocol-Reject	✓		
9	Echo-Request	✓		
10	Echo-Reply	✓		
11	Discard-Request	✓		
12	Identification	✓		
13	Time-Remaining	✓		
14	Reset-Request			✓
15	Reset-Ack			✓

NOTE *I describe the specific ways these frame types are used in the individual topics on LCP, the NCPs, CCP, and ECP in Chapters 10 and 11.*

The contents of the Data field depend entirely on the type of control message. In some cases, no extra data needs to be sent at all, in which case the Data field may be omitted. In other control messages, it carries information relevant to the message type. For example, a *Code-Reject* message carries in the Data field a copy of the frame that was rejected.

PPP Control Message Option Format

The various *Configure-* messages are used to negotiate configuration options in LCP and the other control protocols. In their Data fields, they carry one or more options that are, again, specific to the protocol using them. For example, LCP uses one set of configuration options for the link as a whole, CCP uses options to negotiate a compression algorithm, MP uses it to set up multilink bundles, and so on. Figure 12-4 shows how these options, which can vary in length, are placed in the Data field of a PPP control message (which is nested inside the general PPP frame format).

This diagram shows a sample PPP control message carrying options in its Data field. Any number of options can be included and mixed with other data, depending on the needs of the message.

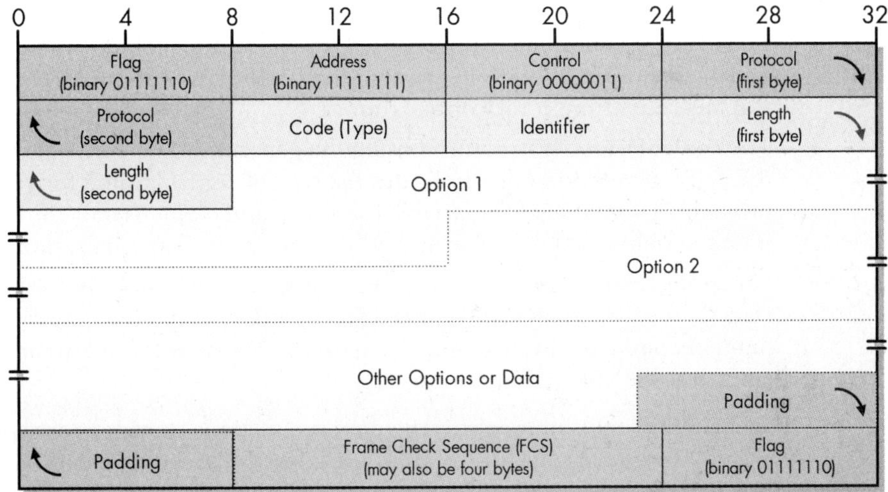

Figure 12-4: PPP control message carrying options

Again, there is commonality here. While every option is different, they all use the same basic format. Each option that appears in any of the many PPP control message types consists of the triplet of Type, Length, and Data, as shown in Table 12-6 and illustrated in Figure 12-5.

Table 12-6: PPP Control Message Option Format

Field Name	Size (Bytes)	Description
Type	1	A type value that indicates the option type. The set of Type values is unique to each protocol. So, for example, LCP has one set of Type values corresponding to its configuration options, each NCP has a different set, CCP has its own set, and so on.
Length	1	Specifies the length of the option in bytes.
Data	Variable	Contains the specific data for the configuration option.

The configuration options are described briefly in the individual protocol topics. I am not showing the specific contents of each option because there are just too many of them. These are in the RFCs.

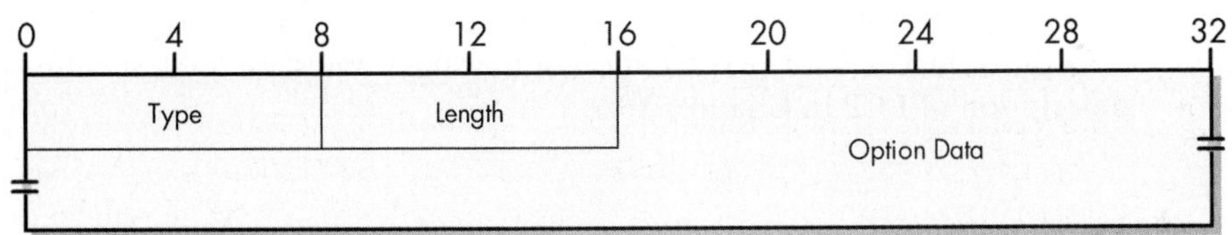

Figure 12-5: PPP control message option format

Summary of PPP Control Message Formatting

My intention here has been to show you the general format used for the different control protocols because they are so similar and I don't have the time or space to describe each protocol's frames individually. Here's a quick summary:

- The PPP general frame format is used for all frames, including all control frames. Its Information field contains the payload, which carries the entire control message within it for control frames.
- The control frame is structured using the general format I gave at the start of this topic. The Code value indicates the type of control frame for each control protocol. The Data field is variable in length, and contains data for that control frame, which in some cases may include one or more configuration options.
- For configuration control frames like *Configure-Request* and *Configure-Ack*, the Data field contains an encapsulated set of options using the general structure in the second table in this topic. Each option has its own Data subfield that contains data specific to that option.

To help make this more clear, the next two sections provide more specific examples of frame formats for LCP and the authentication protocols.

PPP Link Control Protocol (LCP) Frame Formats

You just explored the general format used by the various protocols in PPP that exchange control messages. Of the many control protocols in PPP, LCP is the most important, because it is responsible for basic PPP link setup and operation. It is also the protocol used as a template for many of the other control protocols.

Since it is so central to PPP, and since many of the other protocols use a similar messaging system, let's make the general frame format (shown in Figure 12-5) more concrete by showing the specific frame formats used for each of the LCP control frames. There are 13 different frame formats, however, and since they have many fields in common I've combined them into a single large summary table. Table 12-7 shows the contents and meaning for each of the fields in the 13 LCP frame types.

NOTE *LCP frame types 5, 6, 9, 10, 11, 12, and 13 allow an additional amount of data to be included in the Data field in a manner not strictly described by the protocol. The PPP standard says that there may be zero or more octets that "contain uninterpreted data for use by the sender" and "may consist of any binary value" (RFC 1661). The inclusion of this uninterpreted data is left as an implementation-dependent option.*

All LCP control frames are encapsulated into a PPP frame by placing the frame structure into its Information field, as you saw earlier. The Protocol field is set to 0xC021 for LCP. (For an explanation of how the frames are used, see the operational description of LCP in Chapter 10.)

Table 12-7: PPP Link Control Protocol (LCP) Frame Types and Fields

Frame Type	Code Field	Identifier Field	Length Field	Data Field
Configure-Request	1	New value generated for each frame	4 + length of all included configuration options	Configuration options to be negotiated by the two peers on a link. (The previous section in this chapter describes the general format of configuration options.)
Configure-Ack	2	Copied from the Identifier field of the Configure-Request frame for which this Configure-Ack is a reply	4 + length of all included configuration options	Configuration options being positively acknowledged (accepted during negotiation of the link).
Configure-Nak	3	Copied from the Identifier field of the Configure-Request frame for which this Configure-Nak is a reply	4 + length of all included configuration options	Configuration options being negatively acknowledged (renegotiation requested).
Configure-Reject	4	Copied from the Identifier field of the Configure-Request frame for which this Configure-Reject is a reply	4 + length of all included configuration options	Configuration options being rejected (since the device cannot negotiate them).
Terminate-Request	5	New value generated for each frame	4 (or more if extra data is included)	Not required. See note preceding this table.
Terminate-Ack	6	Copied from the Identifier field of the matching Terminate-Request	4 (or more if extra data is included)	Not required. See note preceding this table.
Code-Reject	7	New value generated for each frame	4 + length of rejected frame	A copy of the LCP frame that was rejected. This is not the complete PPP frame, just the LCP control portion from its Information field.
Protocol-Reject	8	New value generated for each frame	6 + length of rejected frame	The first two bytes contain the Protocol value of the frame rejected. The rest contains a copy of the Information field from the frame rejected.
Echo-Request	9	New value generated for each frame	8 (or more if extra data is included)	Contains a four-byte "magic number" used to detect looped-back links, if the appropriate configuration option has been negotiated; otherwise, set to zero. May also contain additional uninterpreted data; see note preceding this table.
Echo-Reply	10	Copied from the Identifier field of the matching Echo-Request	8 (or more if extra data is included)	Contains a four-byte "magic number" used to detect looped-back links, if the appropriate configuration option has been negotiated; otherwise, set to zero. May also contain additional uninterpreted data; see note preceding this table.

(continued)

Table 12-7: PPP Link Control Protocol (LCP) Frame Types and Fields (continued)

Frame Type	Code Field	Identifier Field	Length Field	Data Field
Discard-Request	11	New value generated for each frame	8 (or more if extra data is included)	Contains a four-byte "magic number" used to detect looped-back links, if the appropriate configuration option has been negotiated; otherwise, set to zero. May also contain additional uninterpreted data; see note preceding this table.
Identification	12	New value generated for each frame	8 (or more if extra data is included)	Contains a four-byte "magic number" used to detect looped-back links, if the appropriate configuration option has been negotiated; otherwise, set to zero. May also contain additional uninterpreted data; see note preceding this table.
Time-Remaining	13	New value generated for each frame	12 (or more if extra data is included)	Contains a four-byte "magic number" used to detect looped-back links, if the appropriate configuration option has been negotiated; otherwise, set to zero. Also contains a four-byte value indicating the number of seconds remaining in the current session. A value of all ones in this field is interpreted as forever, meaning the session will not expire. May also contain additional uninterpreted data; see note preceding this table.

PAP and CHAP Frame Formats

For links where security is important, PPP provides two optional authentication protocols, PAP and CHAP. These are used during initial link setup by the LCP to deny PPP connections to unauthorized devices.

PAP and CHAP are control protocols and thus use the same basic control protocol frame format described earlier in this section. However, since they have a very different purpose than LCP and many of the other control protocols, they use a distinct set of frames with their own unique set of Code values. PAP uses three different control frame types, and CHAP uses four. Let's look at how PAP and CHAP frames are constructed.

PPP PAP Control Frame Formats

PAP's three control frames are constructed as shown in Tables 12-8 and 12-9. The *Authenticate-Request* uses one format, as illustrated in Figure 12-6, while the other two frame types use a different format, as shown in Figure 12-7.

Table 12-8: PPP Password Authentication Protocol (PAP) Frame Formats

Frame Type	Code Field	Identifier Field	Length Field	Data Field
Authenticate-Request	1	New value generated for each frame	6 + length of Peer-ID + length of password	Contains the user name and password for authentication. This is carried in four subfields and arranged as shown in Table 12-9.
Authenticate-Ack	2	Copied from the Identifier field of the Authenticate-Request frame for which this is a reply	5 + length of included Message	Contains a one-byte Msg-Length subfield that specifies the length of the Message subfield that follows it. The Message subfield contains an arbitrary string of data whose use is implementation-dependent. It may be used to provide an indication of authentication success or failure to the user. If not used, the Msg-Length field is still included, but its value is set to zero.
Authenticate-Nak	3			

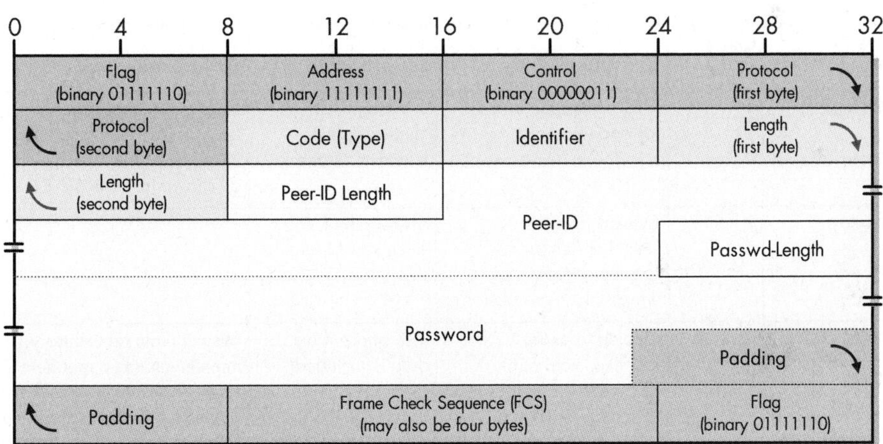

Figure 12-6: *PPP PAP Authenticate-Request frame format*

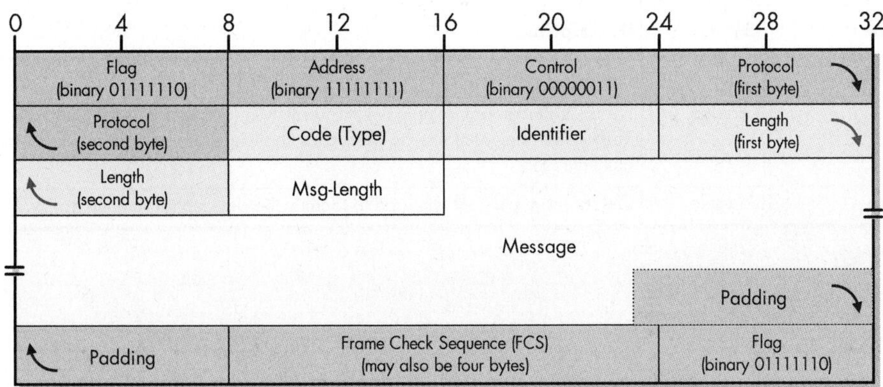

Figure 12-7: *PPP PAP Authenticate-Ack and Authenticate-Nak frame format*

Table 12-9: PPP PAP Authenticate-Request Frame Subfields

Subfield Name	Size (Bytes)	Description
Peer-ID Length	1	Length of the Peer-ID field, in bytes
Peer-ID	Variable	Name of the device to be authenticated; equivalent in concept to a user name
Passwd-Length	1	Length of the Password field, in bytes
Password	Variable	Password corresponding to the name being authenticated

PPP CHAP Control Frame Formats

The four CHAP frame types are formatted as shown in Tables 12-10 and 12-11. The Challenge and Response frames use one message format, as illustrated in Figure 12-8, while the Success and Failure frames use a different one, as shown in Figure 12-9.

Table 12-10: PPP Challenge Handshake Authentication Protocol (CHAP) Formats

Frame Type	Code Field	Identifier Field	Length Field	Data Field
Challenge	1	New value generated for each frame	5 + length of challenge text + length of Name	Carries the challenge text or response text and a system identifier. This information is carried in three subfields, as shown in Table 12-11.
Response	2	Copied from the Identifier field of the Challenge frame for which this is a reply	5 + length of Value + length of Name	
Success	3	Copied from the Identifier field of the Response frame for which this is a reply	4 (or more if extra data is included)	May contain an arbitrary, implementation-dependent Message field to indicate to the user whether authentication was successful or failed.
Failure	4			

Table 12-11: CHAP Challenge and Response Frame Subfields

Subfield Name	Size (Bytes)	Description
Value-Size	1	Length of the Value subfield that follows, in bytes
Value	Variable	For a Challenge frame, contains the challenge text used in the initial challenge; for a Response frame, contains the encrypted challenge text being returned to the authenticator
Name	Variable	One or more bytes of text used to identify the device that sent the frame

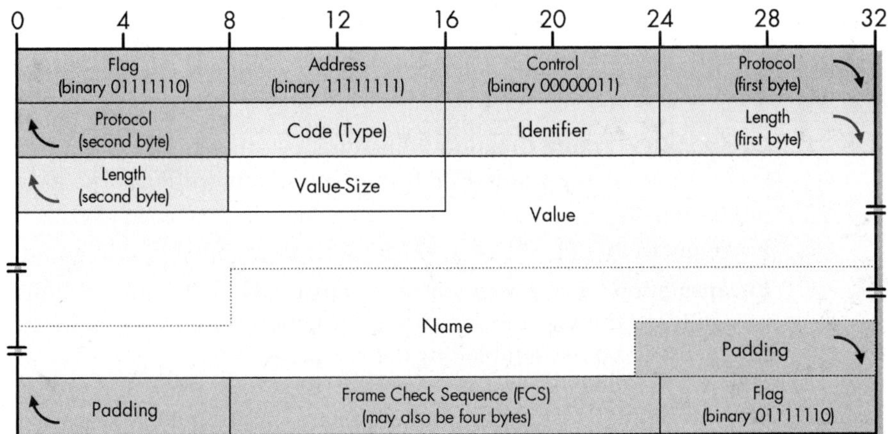

Figure 12-8: *PPP CHAP Challenge and Response frame format*

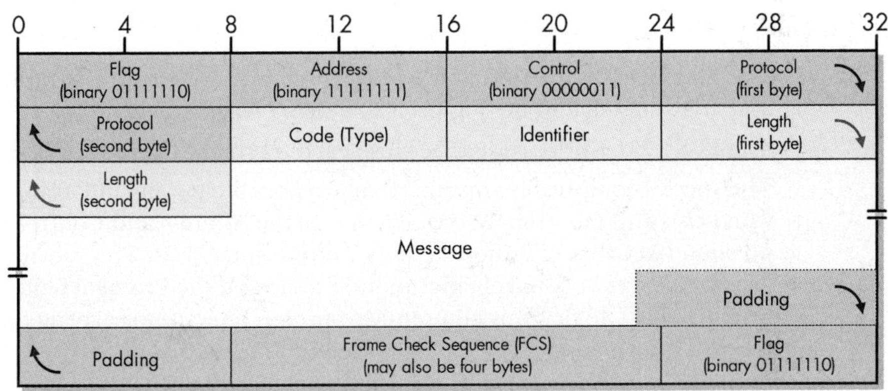

Figure 12-9: *PPP CHAP Success and Failure frame format*

PPP Multilink Protocol (MP) Frame Format

Some devices are connected not by a single physical layer link but by two or more. These may be either multiple physical connections, such as two connected pairs of modems, or multiplexed virtual layer 1 connections like ISDN B channels. In either case, PPP MP can be used to aggregate the bandwidth of these physical links to create a single, high-speed *bundle*. I describe how this is done in Chapter 11.

After MP is configured and starts working, it operates by employing a strategy for dividing up regular PPP frames among the many individual physical links that compose the MP bundle. This is usually accomplished by chopping up the PPP frames into pieces called *fragments* and spreading them across the physical links. This allows the traffic on the physical links to be easily balanced.

PPP MP Frame Fragmentation Process

To accomplish this fragmentation process, the device must follow this three-step process:

1. **Original PPP Frame Creation** The data or other information to be sent is first formatted as a whole PPP frame, but in a modified form, as we will see momentarily.
2. **Fragmentation** The full-sized PPP frame is chopped into fragments by MP.
3. **Encapsulation** Each fragment is encapsulated in the Information field of a new PPP MP fragment frame, along with control information that allows the fragments to be reassembled by the recipient.

Several of the fields that normally appear in a whole PPP frame aren't needed if that frame is going to then be divided and placed into other PPP MP frames, so when fragmentation is to occur, they are omitted when the original PPP frame is constructed for efficiency's sake. These are fields that are not used when MP is employed:

- The Flag fields at the start and end are used only for framing for transmission and aren't needed in the logical frame being fragmented.
- The FCS field is not needed, because each fragment has its own FCS field.
- The special compression options that are possible for any PPP frame are used when creating this original frame—that is, the Address and Control Field Compression (APCP) and Protocol Field Compression (PFC). This means that there are no Address or Control fields in the frame, and the Protocol field is only one byte in size. Note that this inherently restricts fragments to carrying only certain types of information.

KEY CONCEPT The PPP Multilink Protocol (MP) normally divides data among physical links by creating an original PPP frame with unnecessary headers removed, and then dividing it into fragment frames. Each fragment includes special headers that allow for the reassembly of the original frame by the recipient device.

These changes save a full eight bytes on each PPP frame that will be fragmented. As a result, the original PPP frame has a very small header, consisting of only a one-byte Protocol field. The Protocol value of each fragment is set to 0x003D to indicate a MP fragment, while the Protocol field of the original frame becomes the first byte of data in the first fragment.

PPP MP Fragment Frame Format

The Information field of each fragment uses a substructure that contains a four-field *MP header* along with one fragment of the original PPP frame, as shown in Table 12-12.

Table 12-12: PPP Multilink Protocol Fragment Frame Format

Field Name	Size (Bytes)	Description
B	1/8 (1 bit)	Beginning Fragment Flag: When set to 1, flags this fragment as the first of the split-up PPP frame. It is set to 0 for other fragments.
E	1/8 (1 bit)	Ending Fragment Flag: When set to 1, flags this fragment as the last of the split-up PPP frame. It is set to 0 for other fragments.
Reserved	2/8 (2 bits) or 6/8 (6 bits)	Not used; set to 0.
Sequence Number	1 1/2 (12 bits) or 3 (24 bits)	When a frame is split up, the fragments are given consecutive sequence numbers so the receiving device can properly reassemble them.
Fragment Data	Variable	The actual fragment from the original PPP frame.

As you can see, the MP frame format comes in two versions: the long format uses a four-byte header, while the short format requires only four bytes. The default MP header format uses a 24-bit Sequence Number and has 6 reserved bits, as shown in Figure 12-10. When MP is set up, it is possible for devices to negotiate the Multilink Short Sequence Number Header Format configuration option. If this is done successfully, shorter 12-bit Sequence Numbers are used instead. Four of the reserved bits are also truncated, to save two bytes on each frame, as illustrated in Figure 12-11. (Considering that 12 bits still allows for over 4,000 fragments per PPP frame, this is usually more than enough!)

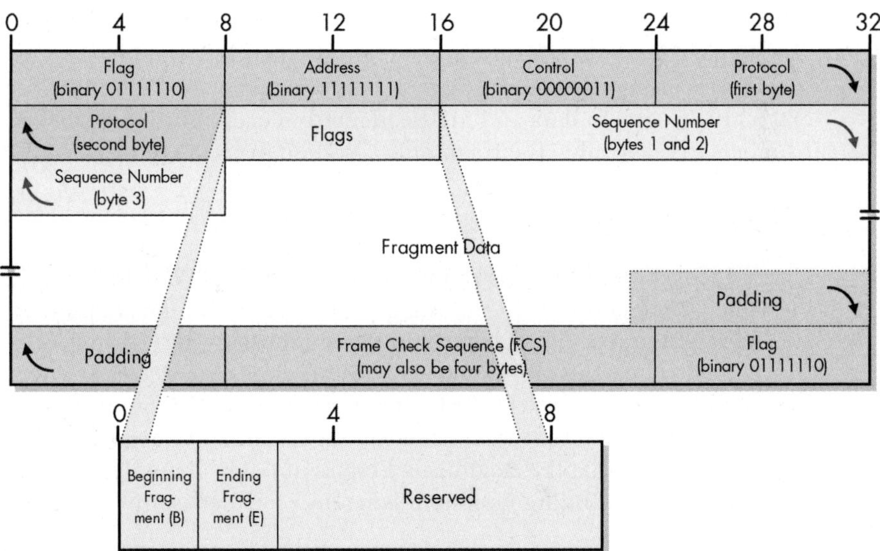

Figure 12-10: PPP MP long fragment frame format *The long PPP MP frame format uses a full byte for flags and a 24-bit Sequence Number.*

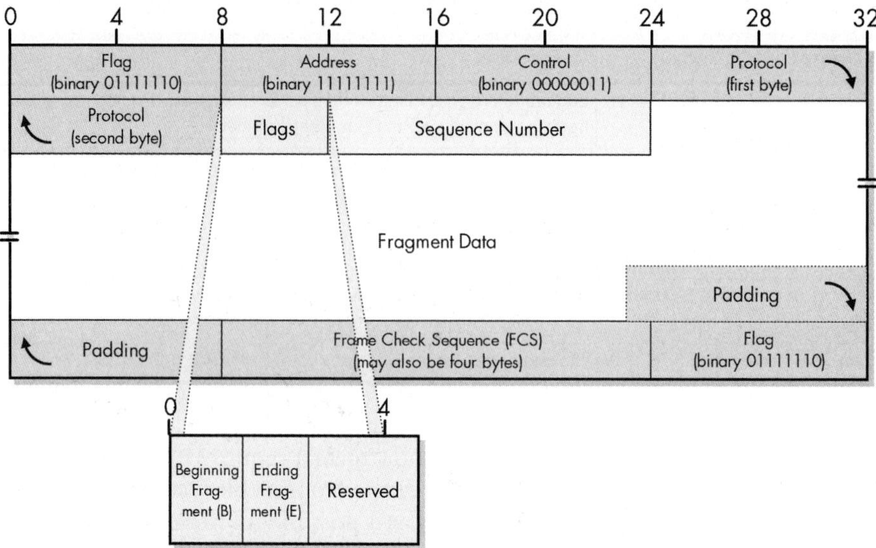

Figure 12-11: PPP MP short fragment frame format *The short version of the PPP MP format uses 4 bits for flags and a 12-bit Sequence Number.*

The Fragment Data field contains the actual fragment to be sent. Since the original PPP header (including the Protocol field) is at the start of the original PPP frame, this will appear at the start of the first fragment. The remaining fragments will have just portions of the Information field of the original PPP frame. The last fragment will end with the last bytes of the original PPP frame.

The receiving device will collect all the fragments for each PPP frame and extract the fragment data and MP headers from each. It will use the Sequence Numbers to reassemble the fragments and then process the resulting PPP frame.

PPP MP Fragmentation Demonstration

Figure 12-12 shows a demonstration of fragmenting a PPP data frame. At the top is the same PPP data frame shown in Figure 12-2 earlier in the chapter.

The eight grayed-out bytes are the ones not used when a frame is to be fragmented. Thus, the PPP frame used for MP is 24 bytes long. This frame is split into eight-byte chunks, each of which is carried in the Fragment Data fields of an MP fragment. Note the consecutive Sequence Number values in the fragment frames. Also note that the Beginning Fragment field is set only for the first fragment, and the Ending Fragment is set only for the last one.

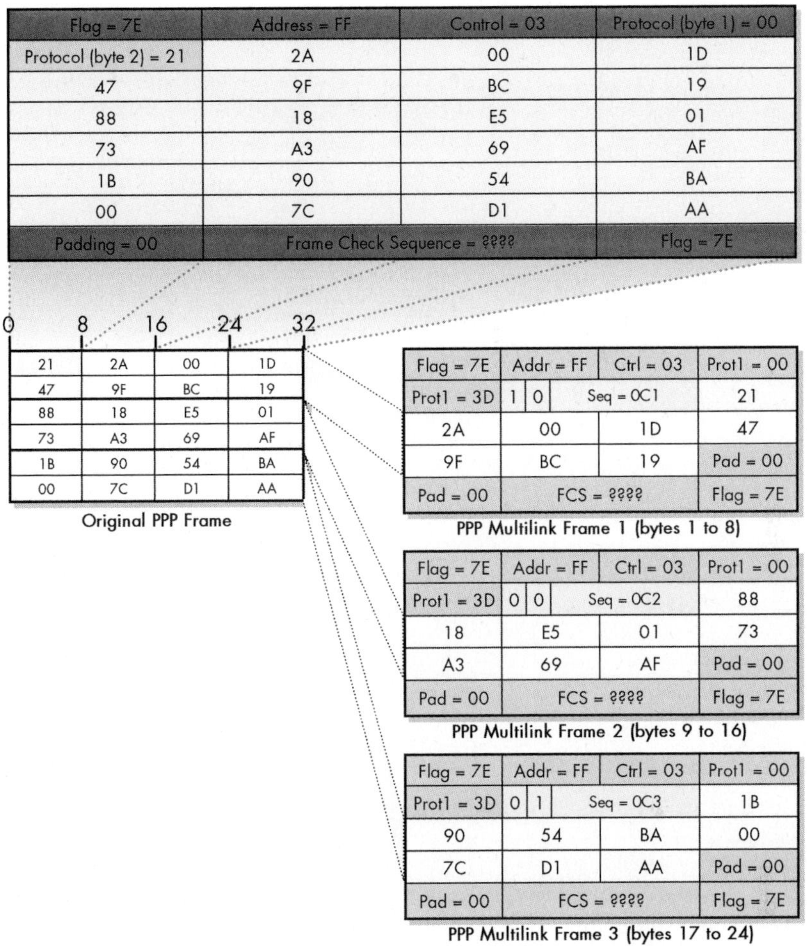

Flag = 7E	Address = FF	Control = 03	Protocol (byte 1) = 00
Protocol (byte 2) = 21	2A	00	1D
47	9F	BC	19
88	18	E5	01
73	A3	69	AF
1B	90	54	BA
00	7C	D1	AA
Padding = 00	Frame Check Sequence = ????		Flag = 7E

0 8 16 24 32

21	2A	00	1D
47	9F	BC	19
88	18	E5	01
73	A3	69	AF
1B	90	54	BA
00	7C	D1	AA

Original PPP Frame

Flag = 7E	Addr = FF	Ctrl = 03	Prot1 = 00
Prot1 = 3D	1 0 Seq = 0C1		21
2A	00	1D	47
9F	BC	19	Pad = 00
Pad = 00	FCS = ????		Flag = 7E

PPP Multilink Frame 1 (bytes 1 to 8)

Flag = 7E	Addr = FF	Ctrl = 03	Prot1 = 00
Prot1 = 3D	0 0 Seq = 0C2		88
18	E5	01	73
A3	69	AF	Pad = 00
Pad = 00	FCS = ????		Flag = 7E

PPP Multilink Frame 2 (bytes 9 to 16)

Flag = 7E	Addr = FF	Ctrl = 03	Prot1 = 00
Prot1 = 3D	0 1 Seq = 0C3		1B
90	54	BA	00
7C	D1	AA	Pad = 00
Pad = 00	FCS = ????		Flag = 7E

PPP Multilink Frame 3 (bytes 17 to 24)

Figure 12-12: PPP MP fragmentation *This diagram shows how a single PPP frame is fragmented into three smaller ones.*

PART II-2

TCP/IP NETWORK INTERFACE/ INTERNET LAYER CONNECTION PROTOCOLS

The second layer of the OSI Reference Model is the *data link layer*; it corresponds to the TCP/IP *network interface layer*. At this layer, most local area network (LAN), wide area network (WAN), and wireless LAN (WLAN) technologies are defined, such as Ethernet and IEEE 802.11.

The third layer of the OSI Reference Model is the *network layer*, also called the *internet layer* in the TCP/IP model. At this layer, internetworking protocols are defined, the most notable being the Internet Protocol (IP).

The second and third layers are intimately related, because messages sent at the network layer must be carried over individual physical networks at the data link layer. They perform different tasks, but as neighbors in the protocol stack, they must cooperate with each other.

A set of protocols serves the important task of linking together these two layers and allowing them to work together. The problem is deciding where exactly these protocols should live. They are sort of the black sheep of the networking world. Nobody denies their importance, but they always think they belong in "the other guy's" layer. For example, since these protocols pass data on layer 2 networks, the folks who deal with layer 2 technologies say the protocols belong at layer 3. But those who work with layer 3 protocols consider these low-level protocols that provide services to layer 3, and hence put them as part of layer 2.

So where do these protocols go? Well, to some extent, it doesn't really matter. I consider them somewhat special, so I gave them their own home. Welcome to networking layer limbo, also known as OSI model layer 2.5. This is where I put a couple of protocols that serve as glue between the data link and network layers. The main job performed here is address resolution, or providing mappings between layer 2 and layer 3 addresses. This resolution can be done in either direction, and is represented by the two TCP/IP protocols described in this part: the Address Resolution Protocol (ARP) and the Reverse Address Resolution Protocol (RARP), which, despite their similarities, are used for rather different purposes.

I suggest familiarity with the basics of layer 2 and layer 3 (described in Parts I-2 and I-3) before proceeding here. In particular, some understanding of IP addressing is helpful, though not strictly necessary.

13

ADDRESS RESOLUTION AND THE TCP/IP ADDRESS RESOLUTION PROTOCOL (ARP)

Communication on an internetwork is accomplished by sending data at layer 3 using a network layer address, but the actual transmission of that data occurs at layer 2 using a data link layer address. This means that every device with a fully specified networking protocol stack will have both a layer 2 and a layer 3 address. It is necessary to define some way of being able to link these addresses together. Usually, this is done by taking a network layer address and determining what data link layer address goes with it. This process is called *address resolution*.

In this chapter, I look at the problem of address resolution at both a conceptual and practical level, with, of course, a focus on how it is done in the TCP/IP protocol suite. I begin with an overview of address resolution in general terms, which describes the issues involved in the process. I then fully describe the TCP/IP Address Resolution Protocol (ARP), probably the best-known and most commonly used address resolution technique. I then provide a brief look at how address resolution is done for multicast addresses in the Internet Protocol (IP), and finally, the method used in the new IP version 6 (IPv6).

Address Resolution Concepts and Issues

Due to the prominence of TCP/IP in the world of networking, most discussions of address resolution jump straight to TCP/IP's ARP. This protocol is indeed important, and we will take a look at it later in this chapter. However, the basic problem of address resolution is not unique to any given implementation that deals with it, such as ARP. To provide better understanding of resolving addresses between the data link layer and the network layer and to support our examination of ARP, we'll begin by looking at the matter in more general terms.

I start by discussing the need for address resolution in general terms. I then describe the two main methods for solving the address resolution problem: direct mapping and dynamic resolution. I also explore some of the efficiency issues involved in practical dynamic address resolution, with a focus on the importance of caching.

The Need for Address Resolution

Some people may balk at the notion of address resolution and the need for protocols that perform this function. In Chapter 5's discussion of the OSI Reference Model, I talked extensively about how the whole point of having conceptual layers was to separate logical functions and allow higher-layer protocols to be hidden from lower-layer details. Given this, why do you need address resolution protocols that tie protocols and layers together?

This is true. However, the OSI Reference Model is exactly that—a *model*. There are often practicalities that arise that require solutions that don't strictly fit the layer model. When the model doesn't fit reality, the model must yield. And so it is in dealing with the problem of address resolution.

Addressing at Layer 2 and Layer 3

When you consider the seven layers of the OSI Reference Model, there are two that deal with addressing: the data link layer and the network layer. The physical layer is not strictly concerned with addressing at all, but rather, only with sending at the bit level. The layers above the network layer all work with network layer addresses.

But why is addressing done at two different layers? The answer is that they are very different types of addresses that are used for different purposes. The layer 2 addresses (such as IEEE 802 MAC addresses) are used for local transmissions between hardware devices that can communicate directly. They are used to implement basic local area network (LAN), wireless LAN (WLAN), and wide area network (WAN) technologies. In contrast, layer 3 addresses (most commonly, IP addresses) are used in internetworking to create the equivalent of a massive virtual network at the network layer.

The most important distinction between these types of addresses is between layers 2 and 3: Layer 2 deals with directly connected devices (on the same network), while layer 3 deals with *indirectly* connected devices (as well as directly connected ones). Say, for example, you want to connect to the web server at http://www.tcpipguide.com. This is a website that runs on a server that has an Ethernet card in it that's used for connecting it to its Internet service provider site. However, even if you know its MAC address, you cannot use it to talk directly to this server using the Ethernet card in your home PC, because the devices are on different networks—in fact, they may be on different continents!

Instead, you communicate at layer 3, using the IP and higher-layer protocols such as the Transmission Control Protocol (TCP) and Hypertext Transfer Protocol (HTTP). Your request is *routed* from your home machine, through a sequence of routers to the server at *The TCP/IP Guide*, and the response is routed back to you. The communication is, logically, at layers 3 and above; you send the request not to the MAC address of the server's network card, but rather to the server's IP address.

However, though you can *virtually* connect devices at layer 3, these connections are really conceptual only. When you send a request using IP, it is sent one *hop* at a time, from one physical network to the next. At each of these hops, an actual transmission occurs at the physical and data link layers. When your request is sent to your local router at layer 3, the actual request is encapsulated in a frame using whatever method you physically connect to the router, and then passed to the router using its data link layer address. The same happens for each subsequent step, until finally, the router nearest the destination sends to the destination using its data link (MAC) address. This is illustrated in Figure 13-1.

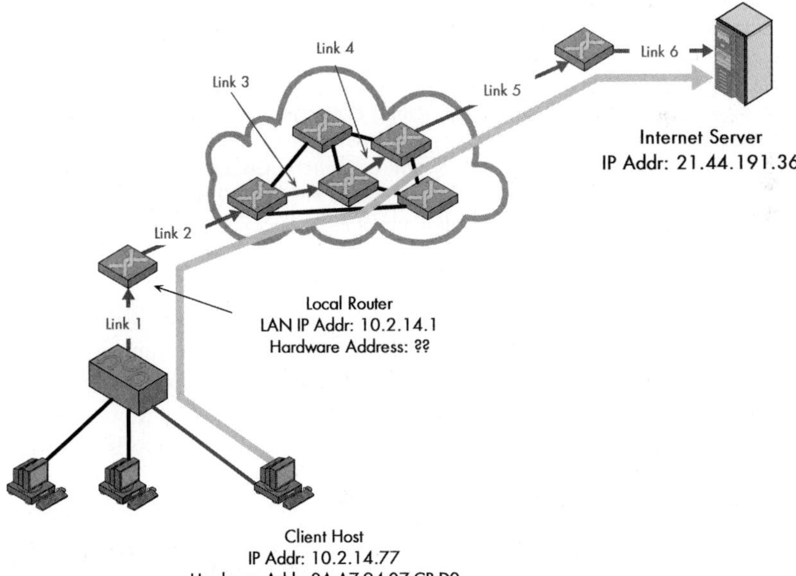

Figure 13-1: Why address resolution is necessary *Even though conceptually the client and server are directly connected at layer 3, in reality, information passing between them goes over multiple layer 2 links. In this example, a client on the local network is accessing a server somewhere on the Internet. Logically, this connection can be made directly between the client and server, but in reality, it is a sequence of physical links at layer 2. In this case, there are six such links, most of them between routers that lie between the client and server. At each step, the decision of where to send the data is made based on a layer 3 address, but the actual transmission must be performed using the layer 2 address of the next intended recipient in the route.*

The basic problem is that IP addresses are at *too high of a level* for the physical hardware on networks to deal with; they don't understand what they are. When your request shows up at the router that connects to *The TCP/IP Guide*, it can see the http://www.tcpipguide.com server's IP address, but that isn't helpful: It needs to send to server's *MAC address*.

The identical issue exists even with communication between devices on a LAN. Even if the web server is sitting on the same desk as the client, the communication is logically at the IP layer, but must also be accomplished at the data link layer. This means you need a way of translating between the addresses at these two layers. This process is called *address resolution*.

> **KEY CONCEPT** Address resolution is required because internetworked devices communicate logically using layer 3 addresses, but the actual transmissions between devices take place using layer 2 (hardware) addresses.

General Address Resolution Methods

In fact, not only do you need to have a way of making this translation, but you need to be concerned with the manner in which it is done. Since the translation occurs for each hop of every datagram sent over an internetwork, the efficiency of the process is extremely important. You don't want to use a resolution method that takes a lot of network resources.

Address resolution can be accomplished in two basic ways: direct mapping and dynamic resolution.

NOTE *By necessity, it is not possible to have a fully general address resolution method that works automatically. Since it deals with linking data link layer addresses to network layer addresses, the implementation must be specific to the technologies used in each of these layers. The only method that could really be considered generic would be the use of static, manually updated tables that say, link this layer 3 address to this layer 2 address." This, of course, is not automatic and brings with it all the limitations of manual configuration.*

Address Resolution Through Direct Mapping

Network layer addresses must be resolved into data link layer addresses numerous times during the travel of each datagram across an internetwork. You therefore want the process to be as simple and efficient as possible. The easiest method of accomplishing this is to do *direct mapping* between the two types of addresses.

How Direct Mapping Works

In the direct mapping technique, a formula is used to map the higher-layer address into the lower-layer address. This is the simpler and more efficient technique, but it has some limitations, especially regarding the size of the data link layer address compared to the network layer address.

The basic idea behind direct mapping is to choose a scheme for layer 2 and layer 3 addresses so that you can determine one from the other using a simple algorithm. This enables you to take the layer 3 address and follow a short procedure to convert it into a layer 2 address. In essence, whenever you have the layer 3 address, you already have the layer 2 address.

The simplest example of direct mapping would be if you used the same structure and semantics for both data link and network layer addresses. This is generally impractical, because the two types of addresses serve different purposes, and are therefore based on incompatible standards. However, you can still perform direct mapping if you have the flexibility of creating layer 3 addresses that are large enough to encode a complete data link layer address within them. Then determining the layer 2 address is a simply matter of selecting a certain portion of the layer 3 address.

As an example, consider a simple LAN technology like ARCNet. It uses a short, 8-bit data link layer address, with valid values of 1 to 255, which can be assigned by an administrator. You could easily set up an IP network on such a LAN by taking a Class C network and using the ARCNet data link layer as the last octet. So, if the network was, for example, 222.101.33.0, you could assign the IP address 222.101.33.1 to the device with ARCNet address #1, the IP address 222.101.33.29 to the device with ARCNet address #29, and so forth, as shown in Figure 13-2.

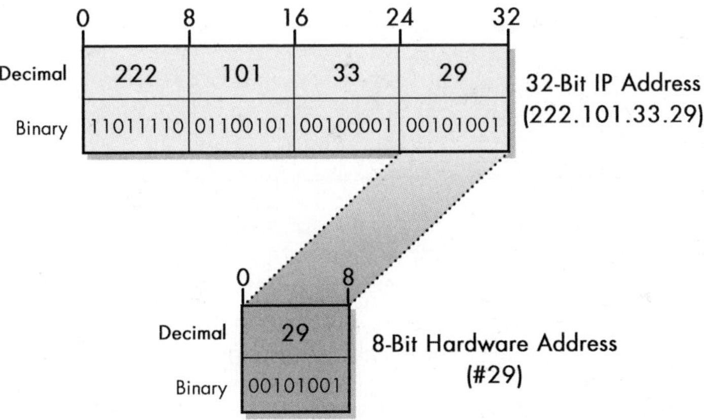

Figure 13-2: Address resolution through direct mapping *With a small hardware address size, you can easily map each hardware address to a layer 3 address. As you can see in this figure, when the hardware address is small, it is easy to define a mapping that directly corresponds to a portion of a layer 3 address. In this example, an 8-bit MAC address, such as the one used for ARCNet, is mapped to the last byte of the device's IP address, thereby making address resolution a trivial matter.*

The appeal of this system is obvious. Conceptually, it is trivial to understand—to get the hardware address for a device, you just use the final eight bits of the IP address. It's also very simple to program devices to perform, and highly efficient, requiring no exchange of data on the network at all.

KEY CONCEPT When the layer 2 address is smaller than the layer 3 address, it is possible to define a direct mapping between them so that the hardware address can be determined directly from the network layer address. This makes address resolution extremely simple, but reduces flexibility in how addresses are assigned.

Problems with Direct Mapping

Unfortunately, direct mapping works only when it is possible to express the data link layer address as a function of the network layer address. Consider instead the same IP address, 222.101.33.29, which is running on an Ethernet network. Here, the data link layer addresses are hardwired into the hardware itself (they can sometimes be overridden, but usually this is not done). More important, the MAC address is 48 bits wide, not 8. This means the layer 2 address is bigger than the layer 3 address, and there is no way to do direct mapping, as Figure 13-3 illustrates. As you can see, when the layer 2 address is larger in size than the layer 3 address, it is not possible to define a mapping between them that can be used for address resolution.

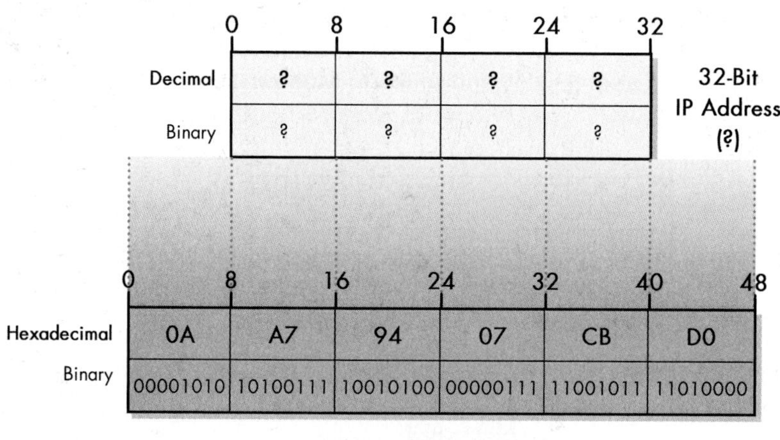

Figure 13-3: Address resolution problems with large hardware address size *Direct mapping is impossible when the layer 2 address is larger in size than the layer 3 address.*

NOTE *When the hardware address size exceeds the network layer address size, you could do a partial mapping. For example, you could use the IP address to get part of the MAC address and hope you don't have any duplication in the bits you didn't use. This method is not well suited to regular transmissions, but is used for resolving multicast addresses in IPv4 to Ethernet addresses. You'll see how this is done near the end of the chapter.*

In general, then, direct mapping is not possible when the layer 3 address is smaller than the layer 2 address. Consider that Ethernet is the most popular technology at layer 2 and uses a 48-bit address, and IP is the most popular technology at layer 3 and uses a 32-bit address. This is one reason why direct mapping is a technique that is not widely used.

What about the next generation of IP? IPv6 supports massive 128-bit addresses (see Chapter 25). Furthermore, regular (unicast) addresses are even defined using a method that creates them from data link layer addresses using a special mapping. This would, in theory, allow IPv6 to use direct mapping for address resolution.

However, the decision was made to have IPv6 use dynamic resolution just as IPv4 does. One reason might be historical, since IPv4 uses dynamic resolution. However, the bigger reason is probably due to a disadvantage of direct mapping: its inflexibility. Dynamic resolution is a more generalized solution, because it allows data link layer and network layer addresses to be independent, and its disadvantages can be mostly neutralized through careful implementation, as you will see.

In fact, evidence for this can be seen in the fact that dynamic resolution of IP is defined on ARCNet, the example I just used. You could do direct mapping there, but it restricts you to a certain pattern of IP addressing that reduces flexibility.

Dynamic Address Resolution

You just saw that direct mapping provides a simple and highly efficient means of resolving network layer addresses into data link layer addresses. Unfortunately, it is a technique that you either cannot or should not use in a majority of cases. You cannot use it when the size of the data link layer address is larger than that of the network layer address. You shouldn't use it when you need flexibility, because direct mapping requires you to make layer 3 and layer 2 addresses correspond.

The alternative to direct mapping is a technique called *dynamic address resolution*. This uses a special protocol that allows a device with only an IP address to determine the corresponding data link layer address, even if the two address types take completely different forms. This is normally done by interrogating one or more other devices on a local network to determine what data link layer address corresponds to a given IP address. This is more complex and less efficient than direct mapping, but it's more flexible.

How Dynamic Addressing Works

To understand how dynamic addressing works, you can consider a simple analogy. I'm sure you've seen a limousine driver who is waiting to pick up a person at the airport. (Well, you've seen it in a movie, haven't you?) This is similar to the problem here: The driver knows the name of the person who will be transported, but not the person's face (a type of "local address" in a manner of speaking!). To find the person, the driver holds up a card bearing that person's name. Everyone other than that person ignores the card, but the named individual should recognize it and approach the driver.

You do the same thing with dynamic address resolution in a network. Let's say that Device A wants to send to Device B but knows only Device B's network layer address (its "name") and not its data link layer address (its "face"). It broadcasts a layer 2 frame containing the layer 3 address of Device B—this is like holding up the card with someone's name on it. The devices other than Device B don't recognize this layer 3 address and ignore it. Device B, however, knows its own network layer address. It recognizes this in the broadcast frame and sends a direct response back to Device A. This tells Device A what Device B's layer 2 address is, and the resolution is complete. Figure 13-4 illustrates the process.

> **KEY CONCEPT** *Dynamic address resolution* is usually implemented using a special protocol. A device that knows only the network layer address of another device can use this protocol to request the other device's hardware address.

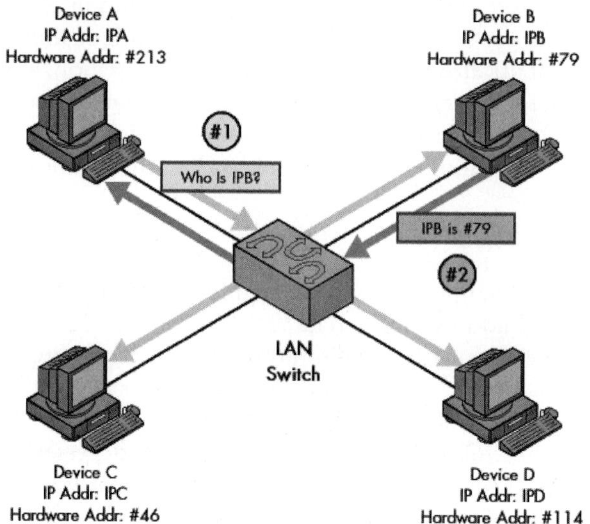

Figure 13-4: Dynamic address resolution *The device that wants to send data broadcasts a request asking for a response with a hardware address from the other device. Device A needs to send data to Device B, but knows only its IP address (IPB) and not its hardware address. Device A broadcasts a request asking to be sent the hardware address of the device using the IP address IPB. Device B responds back to Device A directly with the hardware address.*

Direct mapping is very simple, but as you can see, dynamic resolution isn't exactly rocket science either! It's a simple technique that is easily implemented. Furthermore, it removes the restrictions associated with direct mapping. There is no need for any specific relationship between the network layer address and the data link layer address; they can have a completely different structure and size.

There is one nagging issue though: the efficiency problem. Where direct mapping involves a quick calculation, dynamic resolution requires you to use a protocol to send a message over the network. Fortunately, there are techniques that you can employ to remove some of the sting of this cost through careful implementation.

Dynamic Address Resolution Caching and Efficiency Issues

You've now seen how dynamic address resolution removes the restrictions that you saw in direct mapping, thereby allowing you to easily associate layer 2 and layer 3 addresses of any size or structure. The only problem with it is that each address resolution requires you to send an extra message that would not be required in direct mapping. Worse yet, since you don't know the layer 2 identity of the recipient, you must use a broadcast message (or at least a multicast), which means that many devices on the local network must take resources to examine the data frame and check which IP address is being resolved.

Sure, sending one extra message may not seem like that big of a deal, and the frame doesn't have to be very large since it contains only a network layer address and some control information. However, when you have to do this for *every* hop of *every* datagram transmission, the overhead really adds up. For this reason, while basic dynamic address resolution is simple and functional, it's usually not enough. You must add some *intelligence* to the implementation of address resolution in order to reduce the impact on the performance of continual address resolutions.

Consider that most devices on a local network send to only a small handful of other physical devices and tend to do so over and over again. This is a phenomenon known as *locality of reference*, which is observed in a variety of different areas in the computing field. If you send a request to an Internet website from your office PC, it will need to go first to your company network's local router, so you will need to resolve the router's layer 2 address. If you later click a link on that site, that request will also need to go to the router. In fact, almost everything you do off your local network probably goes first to that same router (commonly called a *default gateway*). Having to do a fresh resolution each time would be, well, stupid. It would be like having to look up the phone number of your best friend every time you want to call to say hello.

To avoid being accused of making address resolution protocols that are, well, stupid, designers always include a *caching* mechanism. After a device's network layer address is resolved to a data link layer address, the link between the two is kept in the memory of the device for a period of time. When it needs the layer 2 address the next time, the device just does a quick lookup in its cache. This means that instead of doing a broadcast on every datagram, you do it only once for a whole sequence of datagrams.

Caching is by far the most important performance-enhancing tool in dynamic resolution. It transforms what would otherwise be a very wasteful process into one that, most of the time, is no less efficient than direct mapping. It does, however, add complexity. The cache table entries must be maintained. There is also the problem that the information in the table may become *stale* over time. What happens if you change the network layer address or the data link layer address of a device? For this reason, cache entries must be set to expire periodically. The discussion of caching in TCP/IP's ARP later in this chapter shows some of the particulars of how these issues are handled.

Other Enhancements to Dynamic Resolution

Other enhancements are also possible to the basic dynamic resolution scheme. Let's consider again our example of sending a request to the Internet. You send a request that needs to go to the local router, so you resolve its address and send it the request. A moment later, the reply comes back to the router to be sent to you, so the router needs *your* address. Thus, it would have to do a dynamic resolution on you, even though you just exchanged frames. Again, this is stupid. Instead, you can improve efficiency through *cross-resolution*; when Device A resolves the address of Device B, Device B also adds the entry for Device A to *its* cache.

Another improvement can be made, too. If you think about it, the devices on a local network are going to talk to each other fairly often, even if they aren't chatting right now. If Device A is resolving Device B's network layer address, it will broadcast a frame that Devices C, D, E, and so on all see. Why not have them also update *their* cache tables with resolution information that they see, for future use?

These and other enhancements all serve to cut down on the efficiency problems with dynamic address resolution. They combine to make dynamic resolution close enough to direct mapping in overall capability that there is no good reason not to use it. Once again, you can see some more particulars of this in the section that describes ARP's caching feature.

Incidentally, one other performance-improving idea sometimes comes up during this discussion: Instead of preceding a datagram transmission with an extra broadcast step for address resolution, why not just broadcast the datagram and be done with it? You actually could do this, and if the datagram were small enough, it would be more efficient. Usually, though, datagrams are large, while resolution frames can be quite compact; it makes sense to do a small broadcast and then a large unicast rather than a large broadcast. Also, suppose you did broadcast this one datagram. What about the next datagram and the one after that? Each of these would then need to be broadcast also. When you do a resolution with caching, you need to broadcast only once in a while, instead of continually.

TCP/IP Address Resolution Protocol (ARP)

ARP is a full-featured, dynamic resolution protocol used to match IP addresses to underlying data link layer addresses. Originally developed for Ethernet, it has now been generalized to allow IP to operate over a wide variety of layer 2 technologies.

NOTE *The Address Resolution Protocol described here is used for resolving unicast addresses in version 4 of the Internet Protocol (IPv4). Multicast addresses under IPv4 use a direct mapping method, and IPv6 uses the new Neighbor Discovery (ND) Protocol instead of ARP. These methods are both discussed near the end of this chapter.*

RELATED INFORMATION *For a discussion of ARP-related issues in networks with mobile IP devices, see Chapter 30.*

RELATED INFORMATION *The software application* `arp`*, which is used to administer the TCP/IP ARP implementation on a host, is covered in Chapter 88.*

Physical networks function at layers 1 and 2 of the OSI Reference Model and use data link layer addresses. In contrast, internetworking protocols function at layer 3, interconnecting these physical networks to create a possibly huge internetwork of devices specified using network layer addresses. Address resolution is the process whereby network layer addresses are resolved into data link layer addresses. This permits data to be sent one hop at a time across an internetwork.

The problem of address resolution was apparent from the very start in the development of the TCP/IP protocol suite. Much of the early development of IP was performed on the then-fledgling Ethernet LAN technology; this was even before Ethernet had been officially standardized as IEEE 802.3. It was necessary to define a way to map IP addresses to Ethernet addresses to allow communication over Ethernet networks.

As we have already seen in this chapter, there are two basic methods to correlate IP and Ethernet addresses: direct mapping or dynamic resolution. However, Ethernet addresses are 48 bits long, while IP addresses are only 32 bits, which immediately rules out direct mapping. Furthermore, the designers of IP wanted the flexibility that results from using the dynamic resolution model. To this end, they developed the TCP/IP *Address Resolution Protocol (ARP)*. This protocol is described in one of the earliest of the Internet RFCs still in common use: RFC 826, "An Ethernet Address Resolution Protocol," which was published in 1982.

The name makes clear that ARP was originally developed for Ethernet. Thus, it represents a nexus between the most popular layer 2 LAN protocol and the most popular layer 3 internetworking protocol. This is true even two decades later. However, it was also obvious from the beginning that even though Ethernet was a very common way of transporting IP, it would not be the only one. Therefore, ARP was made a general protocol that was capable of resolving addresses from IP to Ethernet as well as numerous other data link layer technologies.

The basic operation of ARP involves encoding the IP address of the intended recipient in a broadcast message. It is sent on a local network to allow the intended recipient of an IP datagram to respond to the source with its data link layer address. This is done using a simple request and reply method. A special format is used for ARP messages, which are passed down to the local data link layer for transmission.

> **KEY CONCEPT** *ARP* was developed to facilitate dynamic address resolution between IP and Ethernet and can now be used on other layer 2 technologies as well. It works by allowing an IP device to send a broadcast on the local network, and it requests a response with a hardware address from another device on the same local network.

This basic operation is supplemented by methods to improve performance. Since it was known from the start that having to perform a resolution using broadcast for each datagram was ridiculously inefficient, ARP has always used a cache, where it keeps bindings between IP addresses and data link layer addresses on the local network. Over time, various techniques have been developed to improve the methods used for maintaining cache entries. Refinements and additional features, such as support for cross-resolution by pairs of devices as well as proxy ARP, have also been defined over the years and added to the basic ARP feature set.

ARP Address Specification and General Operation

An ARP transaction begins when a source device on an IP network has an IP datagram to send. It must first decide whether the destination device is on the local network or a distant network. If it's the former, it will send directly to the destination; if it's the latter, it will send the datagram to one of the routers on the physical network for forwarding. Either way, it will determine the IP address of the device that needs to be the immediate destination of its IP datagram on the local network. After packaging the datagram it will pass it to its ARP software for address resolution.

The basic operation of ARP is a *request and response* pair of transmissions on the local network. The source (the one that needs to send the IP datagram) transmits a broadcast containing information about the destination (the intended recipient of the datagram). The destination then responds via unicast back to the source, telling the source the hardware address of the destination.

ARP Message Types and Address Designations

The terms *source* and *destination* apply to the same devices throughout the transaction. However, there are two different messages sent in ARP: one from the source to the destination and one from the destination to the source. For each ARP message, the *sender* is the one that is transmitting the message and the *target* is the one receiving it. Thus, the identity of the sender and target changes for each message. Here's how the sender and target identities work for requests and replies:

Request For the initial request, the sender is the source (the device with the IP datagram to send), and the target is the destination.

Reply For the reply to the ARP request, the sender is the destination. It replies to the source, which becomes the target.

Each of the two parties in any message has two addresses (layer 2 and layer 3) to be concerned with, so the following four different addresses are involved in each message:

Sender Hardware Address The layer 2 address of the sender of the ARP message.

Sender Protocol Address The layer 3 (IP) address of the sender of the ARP message.

Target Hardware Address The layer 2 address of the target of the ARP message.

Target Protocol Address The layer 3 (IP) address of the target.

These addresses each have a position in the ARP message format, which we'll examine shortly.

ARP General Operation

With that background in place, let's look at the steps that occur in an ARP transaction. (These steps are also shown graphically in the illustration in Figure 13-5.) This diagram shows the sequence of steps that occur in a typical ARP transaction, as well as the message exchanges between a source and destination device, and the cache checking and update functions. (Incidentally, those little stacks are hard disks, not cans of soup!)

1. **Source Device Checks Cache** The source device will first check its cache to determine if it already has a resolution of the destination device. If so, it can skip to step 9.
2. **Source Device Generates ARP Request Message** The source device generates an ARP Request message. It puts its own data link layer address as the Sender Hardware Address and its own IP address as the Sender Protocol Address. It fills in the IP address of the destination as the Target Protocol Address. (It must leave the Target Hardware Address blank, since that it is what it is trying to determine!)
3. **Source Device Broadcasts ARP Request Message** The source broadcasts the ARP Request message on the local network.

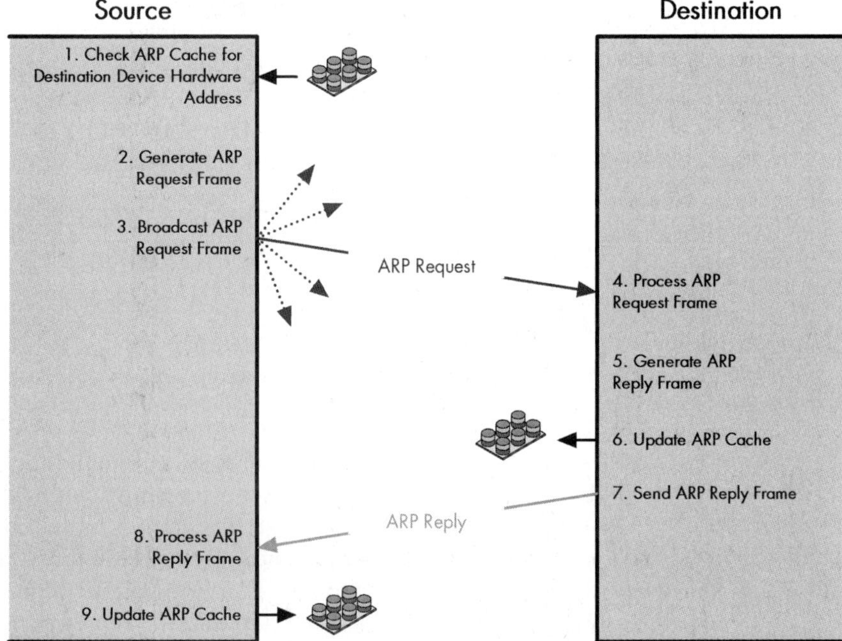

Figure 13-5: Address Resolution Protocol (ARP) transaction process *ARP works by having the source device broadcast a request to find the destination, which responds using a reply message. ARP caches are also consulted and updated as needed.*

4. **Local Devices Process ARP Request Message** The message is received by each device on the local network. It is processed, with each device looking for a match on the Target Protocol Address. Those that do not match will drop the message and take no further action.
5. **Destination Device Generates ARP Reply Message** The one device whose IP address matches the contents of the Target Protocol Address of the message will generate an ARP Reply message. It takes the Sender Hardware Address and Sender Protocol Address fields from the ARP Request message and uses these as the values for the Target Hardware Address and Target Protocol Address of the reply. It then fills in its own layer 2 address as the Sender Hardware Address and its IP address as the Sender Protocol Address. Other fields are filled in, as explained in the description of the ARP message format in the following section.
6. **Destination Device Updates ARP Cache** If the source needs to send an IP datagram to the destination now, it makes sense that the destination will probably need to send a response to the source at some point soon. (After all, most communication on a network is bidirectional.) Next, as an optimization, the destination device will add an entry to its own ARP cache that contains the hardware and IP addresses of the source that sent the ARP Request. This saves the destination from needing to do an unnecessary resolution cycle later on.

7. **Destination Device Sends ARP Reply Message** The destination device sends the ARP Reply message. This reply is, however, sent unicast to the source device, because there is no need to broadcast it.
8. **Source Device Processes ARP Reply Message** The source device processes the reply from the destination. It stores the Sender Hardware Address as the layer 2 address of the destination and uses that address for sending its IP datagram.
9. **Source Device Updates ARP Cache** The source device uses the Sender Protocol Address and Sender Hardware Address to update its ARP cache for use in the future when transmitting to this device.

KEY CONCEPT ARP is a relatively simple request-and-reply protocol. The source device broadcasts an ARP Request that's looking for a particular device based on the device's IP address. That device responds with its hardware address in an ARP Reply message.

Note that this description goes a bit beyond the basic steps in address resolution, because two enhancements are mentioned. One is caching, which you'll explore shortly. The other is cross-resolution (described earlier in this chapter in the overview of caching issues in dynamic resolution), which is step 6 of the process. This is why the source device includes its IP address in the request. It isn't really needed for any other reason, so you can see that this feature was built into ARP from the start.

ARP Message Format

You've just seen how address resolution is accomplished in ARP, through an exchange of messages between the source device seeking to perform the resolution and the destination device that responds to it. As with other protocols, a special *message format* is used for containing the information required for each step of the resolution process.

ARP messages use a relatively simple format. It includes a field describing the type of message (its *operational code* or *opcode*) and information on both layer 2 and layer 3 addresses. In order to support addresses that may be of varying length, the format specifies the type of protocol used at both layer 2 and layer 3, as well as the length of the addresses used at each of these layers. It then includes space for all four of the address combinations described earlier in this chapter: Sender Hardware Address, Sender Protocol Address, Target Hardware Address, and Target Protocol Address.

The format used for ARP messages is described in Table 13-1. Figure 13-6 shows how the ARP message format is designed to accommodate layer 2 and layer 3 addresses of various sizes. This diagram shows the most common implementation, which uses 32 bits for the layer 3 ("Protocol") addresses and 48 bits for the layer 2 hardware addresses. These numbers correspond to the address sizes of the IPv4 and IEEE 802 MAC addresses that are used by Ethernet.

Table 13-1: ARP Message Format

Field Name	Size (Bytes)	Description
HRD	2	Hardware Type: This field specifies the type of hardware used for the local network transmitting the ARP message; thus, it also identifies the type of addressing used. Some of the most common values for this field are shown in Table 13-2.
PRO	2	Protocol Type: This field is the complement of the Hardware Type field, specifying the type of layer 3 addresses used in the message. For IPv4 addresses, this value is 2048 (0800 hex), which corresponds to the EtherType code for IP.
HLN	1	Hardware Address Length: Specifies how long hardware addresses are in this message. For Ethernet or other networks using IEEE 802 MAC addresses, the value is 6.
PLN	1	Protocol Address Length: Again, the complement of the preceding field; specifies how long protocol (layer 3) addresses are in this message. For IPv4 addresses, this value is 4.
OP	2	Opcode: This field specifies the nature of the ARP message being sent. The first two values (1 and 2) are used for regular ARP. Numerous other values are also defined to support other protocols that use the ARP frame format, such as RARP, as shown in Table 13-3. Some protocols are more widely used than others.
SHA	Variable, equals value in HLN field	Sender Hardware Address: The hardware (layer 2) address of the device sending this message, which is the IP datagram source device on a request, and the IP datagram destination on a reply.
SPA	Variable, equals value in PLN field	Sender Protocol Address: The IP address of the device sending this message.
THA	Variable, equals value in HLN field	Target Hardware Address: The hardware (layer 2) address of the device this message is being sent to. This is the IP datagram destination device on a request, and the IP datagram source on a reply.
TPA	Variable, equals value in PLN field	Target Protocol Address: The IP address of the device this message is being sent to.

Table 13-2: ARP Hardware Type (HRD) Field Values

Hardware Type (HRD) Value	Hardware Type
1	Ethernet (10 Mb)
6	IEEE 802 Networks
7	ARCNeT
15	Frame Relay
16	Asynchronous Transfer Mode (ATM)
17	HDLC
18	Fibre Channel
19	Asynchronous Transfer Mode (ATM)
20	Serial Line

Table 13-3: ARP Opcode (OP) Field Values

Opcode	ARP Message Type
1	ARP Request
2	ARP Reply
3	RARP Request
4	RARP Reply
5	DRARP Request
6	DRARP Reply
7	DRARP Error
8	InARP Request
9	InARP Reply

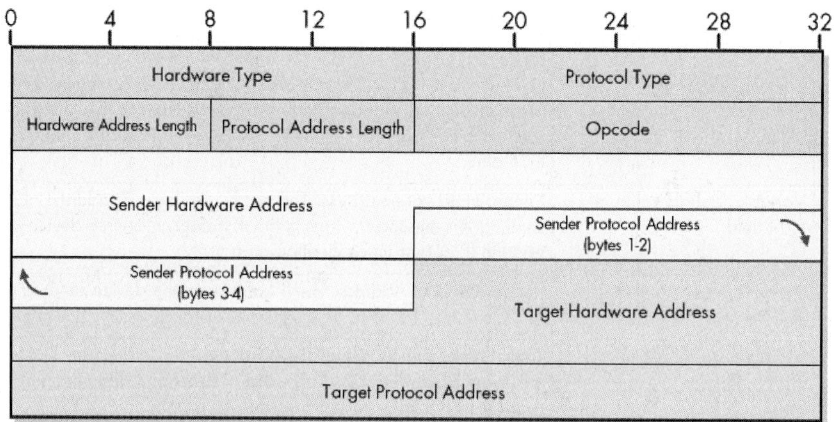

Figure 13-6: *ARP message format*

Once the ARP message has been composed, it is passed down to the data link layer for transmission. The entire contents of the ARP message become the payload for the message actually sent on the network, such as an Ethernet frame on an Ethernet LAN. Note that the total size of the ARP message is variable, since the address fields are of variable length. Normally, though, these messages are quite small. For example, they are only 28 bytes for a network carrying IPv4 datagrams in IEEE 802 MAC addresses.

ARP Caching

ARP is a dynamic resolution protocol, which means that every resolution requires the interchange of messages on the network. Each time a device sends an ARP message, it ties up the local network, consuming network bandwidth that cannot be used for other traffic. ARP messages aren't large, but having to send them for every hop of every IP datagram would represent an unacceptable performance hit on the network. It also wastes time compared to the simpler direct mapping method of resolution. On top of this, the ARP Request message is broadcasted, which means every device on the local network must spend CPU time examining the contents of each one.

The general solution to the efficiency issues with dynamic resolution is to employ *caching*. In addition to reducing network traffic, caching also ensures that the resolution of commonly used addresses is fast, thereby making overall performance comparable to direct mapping. For this reason, caching functionality has been built into ARP from the start.

Static and Dynamic ARP Cache Entries

The ARP cache takes the form of a table containing matched sets of hardware and IP addresses. Each device on the network manages its own ARP cache table. There are two different ways that cache entries can be put into the ARP cache:

Static ARP Cache Entries These are address resolutions that are manually added to the cache table for a device and are kept in the cache on a permanent basis. Static entries are typically managed using a tool such as the arp software utility (see Chapter 88).

Dynamic ARP Cache Entries These are hardware and IP address pairs that are added to the cache by the software itself as a result of past ARP resolutions that were successfully completed. They are kept in the cache for only a period of time and are then removed.

A device's ARP cache can contain both static and dynamic entries, each of which has advantages and disadvantages. However, dynamic entries are used most often because they are automatic and don't require administrator intervention.

Static ARP entries are best used for devices that a given device needs to communicate with on a regular basis. For example, a workstation might have a static ARP entry for its local router and file server. Since the entry is static, it is always found in step 1 of the ARP transaction process, and there is no need to ever send resolution messages for the destination in that entry. The disadvantage is that these entries must be manually added, and they must also be changed if the hardware or IP addresses of any of the hardware in the entries change. Also, each static entry takes space in the ARP cache, so you don't want to overuse static entries. It wouldn't be a good idea to have static entries for every device on the network, for example.

Cache Entry Expiration

Dynamic entries are added automatically to the cache on an as-needed basis, so they represent mappings for hosts and routers that a given device is actively using. They do not need to be manually added or maintained. However, it is also important to realize that dynamic entries cannot be added to the cache and left there forever—dynamic entries left in place for a long time can become stale.

Consider Device A's ARP cache, which contains a dynamic mapping for Device B, which is another host on the network. If dynamic entries stayed in the cache forever, the following situations might arise.

Device Hardware Changes Device B might experience a hardware failure that requires its network interface card to be replaced. The mapping in Device A's cache would become invalid, since the hardware address in the entry is no longer on the network.

Device IP Address Changes Similarly, the mapping in Device A's cache also would become invalid if Device B's IP address changed.

Device Removal Suppose Device B is removed from the local network. Device A would never need to send to it again at the data link layer, but the mapping would remain in Device A's cache, wasting space and possibly taking up search time.

To avoid these problems, dynamic cache entries must be set to automatically expire after a period of time. This is handled automatically by the ARP implementation, with typical timeout values being 10 or 20 minutes. After a particular entry times out, it is removed from the cache. The next time that address mapping is needed, a fresh resolution is performed to update the cache. This is very slightly less efficient than static entries, but sending two 28-byte messages every 10 or 20 minutes isn't a big deal.

As mentioned in the overview of ARP operation, dynamic cache entries are added not only when a device initiates a resolution, but when it is the destination device as well. This is another enhancement that reduces unnecessary address resolution traffic.

Other Caching Features

Other enhancements are also typically put into place, depending on the implementation. Standard ARP requires that if Device A initiates resolution with a broadcast, each device on the network should update its own cache entries for Device A, even if they are not the device that Device A is trying to reach. However, these "third-party" devices are *not* required to create new cache entries for Device A in this situation.

The issue here is a trade-off. Creating a new cache entry would save any of those devices from needing to resolve Device A's address in the near future. However, it also means every device on the network will quickly have an ARP cache table filled up with the addresses of most of the other devices on the network. This may not be desirable in larger networks. Even in smaller ones, this model may not make sense, given that modern computing is client/server in nature and peer devices on a LAN may not often communicate directly. Some devices may choose to create such cache entries, but they may set them to expire after a very short time to avoid filling the cache.

Each ARP implementation is also responsible for any other housekeeping required to maintain the cache. For example, if a device is on a local network with many hosts and its cache table is too small, it might be necessary for older, less frequently used entries to be removed to make room for newer ones. Ideally, the cache should be large enough to hold all the other devices with which a device communicates on a regular basis on the network, along with some room for ones it occasionally talks to.

Proxy ARP

ARP was designed to be used by devices that are directly connected on a local network. Each device on the network should be capable of sending both unicast and broadcast transmissions directly to one another. Normally, if Device A and Device B are separated by a router, they would not be considered local to each other. Device A would not send directly to Device B or vice versa; they would send to the router instead at layer 2 and would be considered two hops apart at layer 3.

In some networking situations, however, there might be two physical network segments that are in the same IP network or subnetwork and are connected by a router. In other words, Device A and Device B might be on different networks at the data link layer level, but on the same IP network or subnet. When this happens, Device A and Device B will each think the other is on the local network when they look to send IP datagrams.

In this situation, suppose that Device A wants to send a datagram to Device B. It doesn't have Device B's hardware address in the cache, so it begins an address resolution. When it broadcasts the ARP Request message to get Device B's hardware address, however, it will quickly run into a problem: Device B is not on Device A's local network. The router between them will not pass Device A's broadcast onto Device B's part of the network, because routers don't pass hardware-layer broadcasts. Device B will never get the request, and thus Device A will not get a reply containing Device B's hardware address.

The solution to this situation is called *ARP proxying* or *Proxy ARP*. In this technique, the router that sits between the local networks is configured to respond to Device A's broadcast on behalf of Device B. It does not send back to Device A the hardware address of Device B. Since they are not on the same network, Device A cannot send directly to Device B anyway. Instead, the router sends Device A its own hardware address. Device A then sends to the router, which forwards the message to Device B on the other network. Of course, the router also does the same thing on Device A's behalf for Device B, and for every other device on both networks, when a broadcast is sent that targets a device that isn't on the same actual physical network as the resolution initiator. This is illustrated in Figure 13-7.

Proxy ARP provides flexibility for networks where hosts are not all actually on the same physical network but are configured as if they were at the network layer. It can be used to provide support in other special situations where a device cannot respond directly to ARP message broadcasts. It may be used when a firewall is configured for security purposes. A type of proxying is also used as part of Mobile IP to solve the problem of address resolution when a mobile device travels away from its home network.

KEY CONCEPT Since ARP relies on broadcasts for address resolution, and broadcasts are not propagated beyond a physical network, ARP cannot function between devices on different physical networks. When such operation is required, a device, such as a router, can be configured as an ARP proxy to respond to ARP requests on the behalf of a device on a different network.

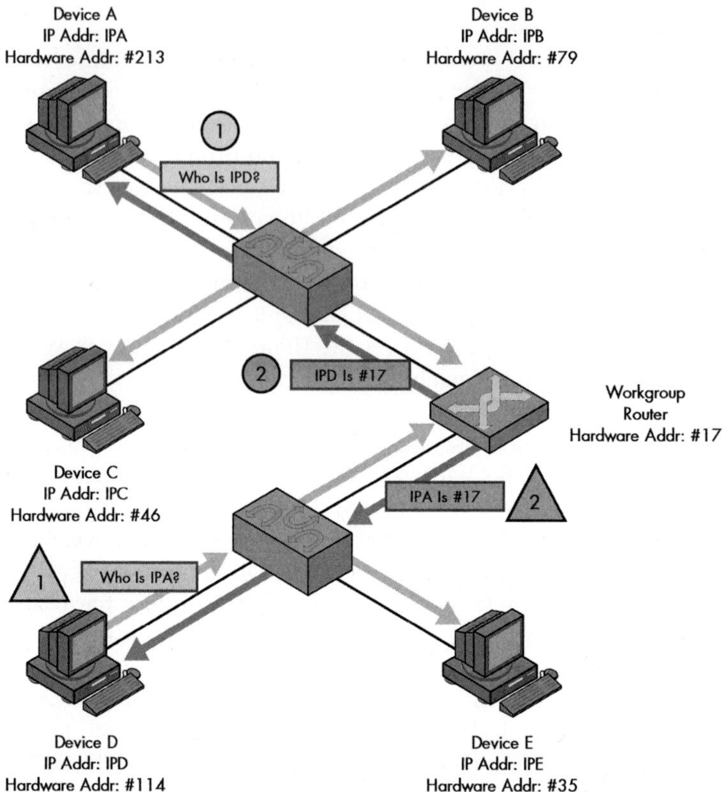

Figure 13-7: ARP Proxy operation *These two examples show how a router acting as an ARP proxy returns its own hardware address in response to requests by one device for an address on the other network. In this small internetwork shown, a single router connects two LANs that are on the same IP network or subnet. The router will not pass ARP broadcasts, but has been configured to act as an ARP proxy. In this example, Device A and Device D are each trying to send an IP datagram to the other, and so each broadcasts an ARP Request. The router responds to the request sent by Device A as if it were Device D, giving to Device A its own hardware address (without propagating Device A's broadcast). It will forward the message sent by Device A to Device D on Device D's network. Similarly, it responds to Device D as if it were Device A, giving its own address, then forwarding what Device D sends to it over to the network where Device A is located.*

The main advantage of proxying is that it is transparent to the hosts on the different physical network segments. The technique has some drawbacks, however. First, it introduces added complexity. Second, if more than one router connects two physical networks using the same network ID, problems may arise. Third, it introduces potential security risks; since it essentially means that a router impersonates devices by acting as a proxy for them, the potential for a device spoofing another is real. For these reasons, it may be better to redesign the network so that routing is done between physical networks separated by a router, if possible.

TCP/IP Address Resolution for IP Multicast Addresses

Like most discussions of address resolution, most of this chapter so far has focused on unicast communication, where a datagram is sent from one source device to one destination device. Whether direct mapping or dynamic resolution is used for resolving a network layer address, it is a relatively simple matter to resolve addresses when there is only one intended recipient of the datagram. As you've seen, TCP/IP uses ARP for its dynamic resolution scheme, which is designed for unicast resolution only.

However, IP also supports *multicasting* of datagrams, as I explain in the sections on IP multicasting and IP multicast addressing in Chapters 23 and 17, respectively. In this situation, the datagram must be sent to multiple recipients, which complicates matters considerably. You need to establish a relationship of some sort between the IP multicast group address and the addresses of the devices at the data link layer. You could do this by converting the IP multicast datagram to individual unicast transmissions at the data link layer with each using ARP for resolution, but this would be horribly inefficient.

When possible, IP makes use of the multicast addressing and delivery capabilities of the underlying network to deliver multicast datagrams on a physical network. Perhaps surprisingly, even though ARP employs dynamic resolution, multicast address resolution is done using a version of the direct mapping technique. By defining a *mapping* between IP multicast groups and data link layer multicast groups, you enable physical devices to know when to pay attention to multicasted datagrams.

The most commonly used multicast-capable data link addressing scheme is the IEEE 802 addressing system best known for its use in Ethernet networks. These data link layer addresses have 48 bits, arranged into two blocks of 24. The upper 24 bits are arranged into a block called the *organizationally unique identifier (OUI)*, with different values assigned to individual organizations; the lower 24 bits are then used for specific devices.

The Internet Assigned Number Authority (IANA) itself has an OUI that it uses for mapping multicast addresses to IEEE 802 addresses. This OUI is 01:00:5E. To form a mapping for Ethernet, 24 bits are used for this OUI, and the 25th (of the 48) is always zero. This leaves 23 bits of the original 48 to encode the multicast address. To do the mapping, the lower-order 23 bits of the multicast address are used as the last 23 bits of the Ethernet address starting with 01:00:5E for sending the multicast message.

Figure 13-8 illustrates how the multicast address mapping process works.

KEY CONCEPT IP multicast addresses are resolved to IEEE 802 (Ethernet) MAC addresses using a direct mapping technique that uses 23 of the 28 bits in the IP multicast group address.

Of course, there are 28 unique bits in IP multicast addresses, so this is a "bit" of a problem! What it means is that there is no unique mapping between IP multicast addresses and Ethernet multicast addresses. Since 5 of the 28 bits of the multicast group cannot be encoded in the Ethernet address, 32 (2^5) different IP multicast addresses map onto each possible Ethernet multicast address. In theory, this would be a problem, but in practice, it isn't. The chances of any two IP multicast addresses on a single network mapping to the same Ethernet multicast address at the same time are pretty small.

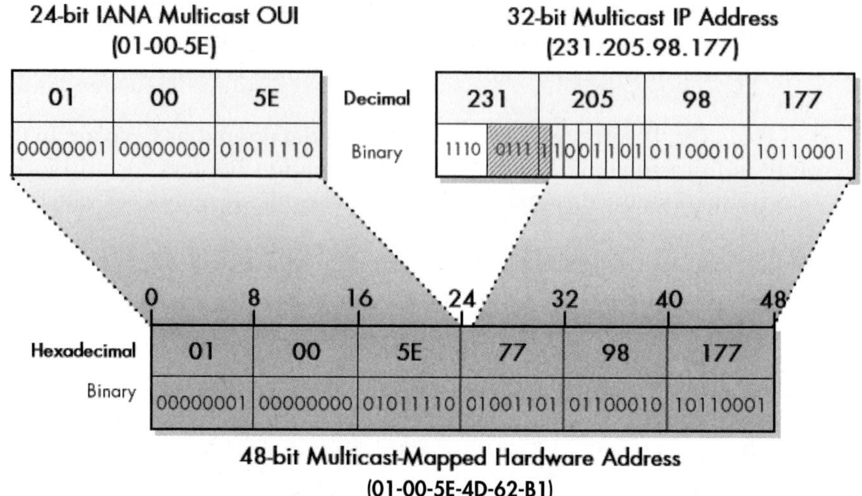

Figure 13-8: Mapping of multicast IP addresses to IEEE 802 multicast MAC addresses *Multicast IP addresses are mapped to IEEE 802 multicast MAC addresses by copying the IANA multicast OUI value (01-00-5E) to the top 24 bits, setting the 25th bit to zero, and copying the bottom 23 bits of the multicast address to the remaining 23 bits. To create a 48-bit multicast IEEE 802 (Ethernet) address, the top 24 bits are filled in with the IANA's multicast OUI, 01-00-5E. The 25th bit is zero, and the bottom 23 bits of the multicast group are put into the bottom 23 bits of the MAC address. This leaves 5 bits (shown hatched) that are not mapped to the MAC address, meaning that 32 different IP addresses may have the same mapped multicast MAC address.*

Still, it is possible that two IP multicast groups might be in use on the same physical network and might map to the same data link layer multicast address. For this reason, devices must not assume that all multicast messages they receive are for their groups; they must pass up the messages to the IP layer to check the full IP multicast address to make sure that they really were supposed to get the multicast datagram they received. If they accidentally get one that was intended for a multicast group they are not a member of, they discard it. This happens infrequently, so the relative lack of efficiency is not a large concern.

TCP/IP Address Resolution for IP Version 6

The TCP/IP ARP is a fairly generic protocol for dynamically resolving network layer addresses into data link layer addresses. Even though it was designed for IPv4, the message format allows for variable-length addresses at both the hardware and network layers. This flexibility means it would have been theoretically possible to use it for the new version of IP, IPv6. Some minor changes might have been required, but the technique could have been about the same.

The designers of IPv6 chose not to do this, however. Changing IP is a big job that has been under way for many years, providing a rare opportunity to change various aspects of TCP/IP. The Internet Engineering Task Force (IETF) decided to take advantage of the changes in IPv6 to overhaul not only IP itself, but also many of the protocols that support or assist it. In IPv6, the address resolution job of ARP has been combined with several functions performed by the Internet Control Message Protocol (ICMP) in the original TCP/IP suite, supplemented with additional capabilities and defined as the new Neighbor Discovery (ND) Protocol.

The term *neighbor* in IPv6 simply refers to devices on a local network, and as the name implies, ND is responsible for tasks related to communicating information between neighbors (among other things). I describe ND briefly in Chapter 36, including a discussion of the various tasks it performs. Here, I focus specifically on how ND performs address resolution.

The basic concepts of address resolution in IPv6 ND aren't all that different from those in IPv4 ARP. Resolution is still dynamic and is based on the use of a cache table that maintains pairings of IPv6 addresses and hardware addresses. Each device on a physical network keeps track of this information for its neighbors. When a source device needs to send an IPv6 datagram to a local network neighbor but doesn't have its hardware address, it initiates the resolution process. For clarity in the text let's say that, as usual, Device A is trying to send to Device B.

Instead of sending an ARP Request message, Device A creates an ND Neighbor Solicitation message. Now, here's where the first big change can be seen from ARP. If the underlying data link protocol supports multicasting, as Ethernet does, the Neighbor Solicitation message is not broadcast. Instead, it is sent to the *solicited-node address* of the device whose IPv6 address you are trying to resolve. So Device A won't broadcast the message, but it will multicast it to Device B's solicited-node multicast address.

The solicited-node multicast address is a special mapping that each device on a multicast-capable network creates from its unicast address; it is described in Chapter 25's discussion of IPv6 multicast addresses. The solicited-node address isn't unique for every IPv6 address, but the odds of any two neighbors on a given network having the same one are small. Each device that receives a multicasted Neighbor Solicitation must still check to make sure it is the device whose address the source is trying to resolve.

Why bother with this, if devices still have to check each message? The multicast will affect at most a small number of devices. With a broadcast, each and every device on the local network would receive the message, while the use of the solicited-node address means at most that a couple of devices will need to process it. Other devices don't even have to bother checking the Neighbor Solicitation message at all.

Device B will receive the Neighbor Solicitation and respond back to Device A with a Neighbor Advertisement. This is analogous to the ARP Reply and tells Device A the physical address of Device B. Device A then adds Device B's information to its neighbor cache. For efficiency, cross-resolution is supported, as in IPv4 address resolution. This is done by having Device A include its own layer 2 address in the Neighbor Solicitation, assuming it knows it. Device B will record this along with Device A's IP address in Device B's neighbor cache.

KEY CONCEPT Address resolution in IPv6 uses the new *Neighbor Discovery (ND) Protocol* instead of the Address Resolution Protocol (ARP). A device trying to send an IPv6 datagram sends a Neighbor Solicitation message to get the address of another device, which responds with a Neighbor Advertisement. When possible, to improve efficiency, the request is sent using a special type of multicast address rather than broadcast.

This is actually a fairly simplified explanation of how resolution works in IPv6, because ND is quite complicated. Neighbor solicitations and advertisements are also used for other functions, such as testing the reachability of nodes and determining if duplicate addresses are in use. There are many special cases and issues that ND addresses to ensure that no problems develop during address resolution. ND also supports proxied address resolution.

NOTE *Even though I put this discussion where it would be near the other discussions of address resolution, ND really isn't a layer connection or lower-level protocol like ARP. It is analogous to ICMP (Chapter 31) in its role and function, and, in fact, makes use of ICMP(v6) messages. One advantage of this architectural change is that there is less dependence on the characteristics of the physical network, so resolution is accomplished in a way that's more similar to other network support activities. Thus, it is possible to make use of facilities that can be applied to all IP datagram transmissions, such as IP security features. Chapter 36 contains much more information on this subject.*

14

REVERSE ADDRESS RESOLUTION AND THE TCP/IP REVERSE ADDRESS RESOLUTION PROTOCOL (RARP)

In Chapter 13, you explored the operation of the TCP/IP Address Resolution Protocol (ARP). ARP is used when a device needs to determine the layer 2 (hardware) address of some other device but has only its layer 3 (network, IP) address. It broadcasts a hardware layer request, and the target device responds with the hardware address that matches the known IP address.

In theory, it is also possible to use ARP in the opposite way. If you know the hardware address of a device but not its IP address, you could broadcast a request containing the hardware address and get back a response that contains the IP address. In this chapter, you will briefly explore this concept of *reverse address resolution.*

The obvious first question is why would you ever need to do this? Since you are dealing with communication on an Internet Protocol (IP) internetwork, you are always going to know the IP address of the destination of the datagram you need to send—it's right there in the datagram itself. You also know your own IP address as well. Or do you?

In a traditional TCP/IP network, every normal host on a network knows its IP address because it is stored somewhere on the machine. When you turn on your PC, the TCP/IP software reads the IP address from a file, which allows your PC to learn and start using its IP address. However, there are some devices, such as diskless workstations, that don't have any means of storing an IP address where it can be easily retrieved. When these units are powered up, they know their physical address only (because it's wired into the hardware) but not their IP address.

The problem you need to solve here is what is commonly called *bootstrapping* in the computer industry. This refers to the concept of starting something from a zero state; it is analogous to "pulling yourself up by your own bootstraps." This is seemingly impossible, just as it seems paradoxical to use TCP/IP to configure the IP address that is needed for TCP/IP communications. However, it is indeed possible to do this, by making use of broadcasts, which allow local communication even when the target's address is not known.

The Reverse Address Resolution Protocol (RARP)

The first method devised to address the bootstrapping problem in TCP/IP was the backward use of ARP, which is described in the previous chapter. This technique was formalized in RFC 903, "A Reverse Address Resolution Protocol (RARP)," published in 1984. ARP allows Device A to say, "I am Device A, and I have Device B's IP address. Device B please tell me your hardware address." RARP is used by Device A to say, "I am Device A, and I am sending this broadcast using my hardware address; can someone please tell me *my* IP address?"

The two-step operation of RARP is illustrated in Figure 14-1. As the name suggests, RARP works like ARP but in reverse, which is why this diagram is similar to Figure 13-4.

The next question then is who knows Device A's IP address if Device A doesn't? The answer is that a special *RARP server* must be configured to listen for RARP requests and then issue replies to them. Each physical network where RARP is in use must have RARP software running on at least one machine.

RARP is not only very similar to ARP, it basically *is* ARP. RFC 903 doesn't define a whole new protocol from scratch; it just describes a new method for using ARP to perform the opposite of its normal function. RARP uses ARP messages in the same format as ARP (described in Chapter 13), but uses different opcodes to accomplish its reverse function. As in ARP, a request and reply are used in an exchange. The meaning of the address fields is the same, too: The sender is the device transmitting a message, while the target is the one receiving it.

> **KEY CONCEPT** The *Reverse Address Resolution Protocol (RARP)* is the earliest and simplest protocol that's designed to allow a device to obtain an IP address for use on a TCP/IP network. It is based directly on ARP and works in basically the same way, but in reverse: A device sends a request containing its hardware address, and a device set up as an RARP server responds back with the device's assigned IP address.

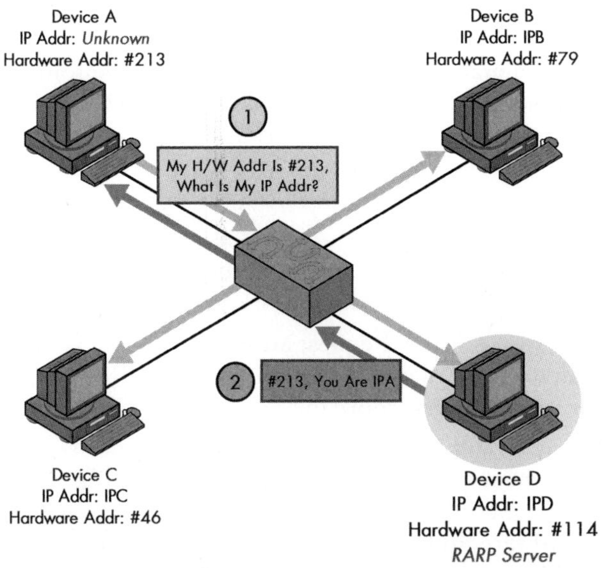

Figure 14-1: Operation of the Reverse Address Resolution Protocol (RARP) *RARP works like ARP but in reverse; a device broadcasts its hardware address and an RARP server responds with its IP address. Here, instead of Device A providing the IP address of another device and asking for its hardware address, it is providing its own hardware address and asking for an IP address it can use. The answer, in this case, is provided by Device D, which is serving as an RARP server for this network.*

RARP General Operation

Figure 14-2 shows the steps followed in a RARP transaction. As you can see, RARP uses a simple request and reply exchange to allow a device to obtain an IP address.

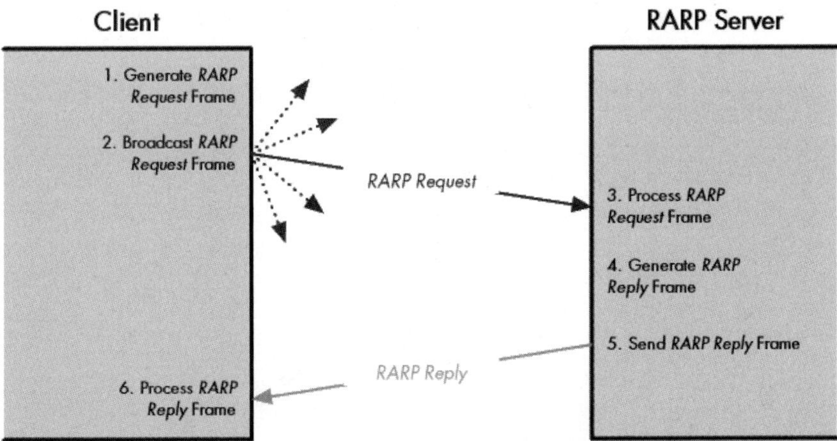

Figure 14-2: Reverse Address Resolution Protocol (RARP) operation *RARP consists of the exchange of one broadcast request message and one unicast reply message.*

Here's what happens at each step:

1. **Source Device Generates RARP Request Message** The source device generates an RARP Request message. Thus, it uses the value 3 for the *opcode* in the message. It puts its own data link layer address as both the Sender Hardware Address and also the Target Hardware Address. It leaves both the Sender Protocol Address and the Target Protocol Address blank, since it doesn't know either.
2. **Source Device Broadcasts RARP Request Message** The source broadcasts the ARP Request message on the local network.
3. **Local Devices Process RARP Request Message** The message is received by each device on the local network and processed. Devices that are not configured to act as RARP servers ignore the message.
4. **RARP Server Generates RARP Reply Message** Any device on the network that is set up to act as an RARP server responds to the broadcast from the source device. It generates an RARP Reply using an opcode value of 4. It sets the Sender Hardware Address and Sender Protocol Address to its own hardware and IP address, since it is the sender of the reply. It then sets the Target Hardware Address to the hardware address of the original source device. It looks up in a table the hardware address of the source, determines that device's IP address assignment, and puts it into the Target Protocol Address field.
5. **RARP Server Sends RARP Reply Message** The RARP server sends the RARP Reply message unicast to the device looking to be configured.
6. **Source Device Processes RARP Reply Message** The source device processes the reply from the RARP server. It then configures itself using the IP address in the Target Protocol Address supplied by the RARP server.

NOTE *More than one RARP server may respond to a request, if two or more are configured on any local network. The source device will typically use the first reply and discard the others.*

Limitations of RARP

RARP is the earliest and most rudimentary of the class of technologies I call *host configuration protocols*, which I describe in general terms in Chapter 59. As the first of these protocols, RARP was a useful addition to TCP/IP in the early 1980s, but has several shortcomings, the most important of which are as follows:

Low-Level Hardware Orientation RARP works using hardware broadcasts. This means that if you have a large internetwork with many physical networks, you need an RARP server on *every* network segment. Worse, if you need reliability to make sure RARP keeps running even if one RARP server goes down, you need *two* on each physical network. This makes centralized management of IP addresses difficult.

Manual Assignment RARP allows hosts to configure themselves automatically, but the RARP server must still be set up with a manual table of bindings between hardware and IP addresses. These must be maintained for each server, which is, again, a lot of work for an administrator.

Limited Information RARP provides a host with only its IP address. It cannot provide other needed information such as, for example, a subnet mask or default gateway.

The importance of host configuration has increased dramatically since the early 1980s. Many organizations assign IP addresses dynamically even for hosts that have disk storage, because of the many advantages this provides in administration and because of the efficient use of address space. For this reason, RARP has been replaced by two more capable technologies that operate at higher layers in the TCP/IP protocol stack: BOOTP and DHCP. They are discussed in the application layer section on host configuration protocols, in Chapters 60 through 64.

Limitations of RARP

PART II-3

INTERNET PROTOCOL VERSION 4 (IP/IPV4)

The idea of singling out any one protocol as being more important than the others in a network is kind of pointless, if you think about it. The protocols and technologies work as a team to accomplish the goal of communication across the network. As with any team, no single member can get the job done alone, no matter how good it is. Still, if we were to try to pick a "most valuable player" in the world of networking, a good case could be made that we have it in the TCP/IP *Internet Protocol (IP)*.

Even though it gets second billing in the name of the TCP/IP protocol suite, IP is the workhorse of TCP/IP. It implements key network layer functions including addressing, datagram handling, and routing, and it is the foundation on which other TCP/IP protocols are built. Even the ones lower in the TCP/IP architecture, such as the Address Resolution Protocol (ARP) and the Point-to-Point Protocol (PPP), are easier to understand when you know how IP works.

This part includes nine chapters that provide considerable coverage of IP. The first chapter gives an overview of IP as a whole, including a discussion of its versions, while the rest of the chapters focus on the details of operation of the most popular current version of the protocol, *IP version 4 (IPv4)*.

The second through sixth chapters discuss in great detail the concepts and practice behind IP addressing. The second chapter provides an overview of IPv4 addressing concepts and issues. The third discusses the original, class-based *(classful)* IP addressing scheme and how the different classes work. The fourth and fifth chapters are devoted to IP subnets and subnet addressing. They discuss subnetting concepts and include an illustration of practical step-by-step subnetting. The sixth chapter describes the new classless addressing system, also sometimes called *supernetting*.

The seventh through ninth chapters discuss important practical issues related to how IPv4 datagrams are created and handled. You'll find a full description of the IPv4 message format and options in the seventh chapter; explanations of IP datagram sizing, fragmentation, and reassembly in the eighth chapter; and coverage of routing and multicasting in the ninth chapter.

As the title of this part implies, the coverage here is limited to IPv4. (For simplicity, in this part, I use the simpler designation *IP* rather than *IPv4*, except where the version number is required for clarity.) IP version 6 (IPv6) is covered in its separate section (Part II-4), as are the IP-related protocols. That said, some of the principles here will also apply to IPv6, as well as IP Network Address Translation (NAT), IPsec, and Mobile IP (Part II-4) in a limited manner.

15

INTERNET PROTOCOL VERSIONS, CONCEPTS, AND OVERVIEW

The Internet Protocol (IP) is a very important protocol in internetworking. It would be no exaggeration to say that you can't really comprehend modern networking without a good understanding of IP. Unfortunately, IP can be somewhat difficult to understand. A large amount of complexity has become associated with it over the years, and this has allowed it to meet the many demands placed on it.

Before diving into the details of how IP works, we'll look at the basic concepts underlying IP. In this chapter, I explain how IP operates in basic terms and the most important aspects of how it does its job. We'll look at its main functions, its history, and how it has spawned the development of several IP-related protocols.

IP Overview and Key Operational Characteristics

IP is the core of the TCP/IP protocol suite and the main protocol at the network layer. The network layer is primarily concerned with the delivery of data between devices that may be on different networks, which are interconnected in an arbitrary manner. In other words, an *internetwork*. IP is the mechanism by which this data is sent on TCP/IP networks (with help from other protocols at the network layer, too, of course).

Let's look at the TCP/IP layer model and consider what IP does from an architectural standpoint. As the layer 3 protocol, it provides a service to layer 4 in the TCP/IP stack, represented mainly by the Transmission Control Protocol (TCP) and User Datagram Protocol (UDP) (see Part II-8). IP takes data that has been packaged by either TCP or UDP, manipulates it as necessary, and sends it out (see Figure 15-1).

This service is sometimes called *internetwork datagram delivery*. There are many details that explain exactly how this service is accomplished, but in a nutshell, IP sends data from point A to point B over an internetwork of connected networks.

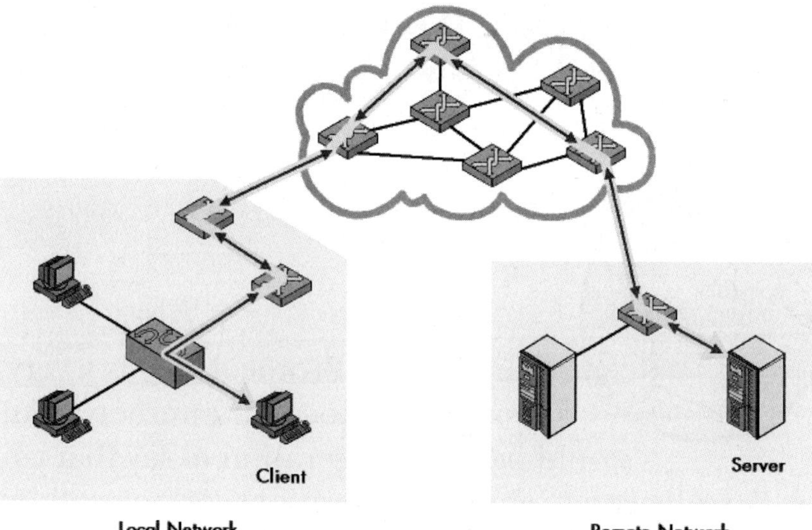

Figure 15-1: The main function of IP: internetwork datagram delivery *IP's overall responsibility is to deliver data between devices on unconnected networks. This figure shows how IP delivers datagrams from one device to another over an internetwork; in this case, a distant client and server communicate with each other by passing IP datagrams over a series of interconnected networks.*

> **KEY CONCEPT** While the *Internet Protocol* has many functions and characteristics, it can be boiled down to one primary purpose: the delivery of datagrams across an internetwork of connected networks.

Of course, there are many ways in which IP could have been implemented in order to accomplish this task. To understand how the designers of TCP/IP made IP work, let's take a look at the key characteristics used to describe IP and the general manner in which it operates:

Universally Addressed In order to send data from point A to point B, it is necessary to ensure that devices know how to identify which device is point B. IP defines the addressing mechanism for the network and uses these addresses for delivery purposes.

Underlying Protocol-Independent IP is designed to allow the transmission of data across any type of underlying network that is designed to work with a TCP/IP stack. It includes provisions that allow it to adapt to the requirements of various lower-level protocols such as Ethernet or IEEE 802.11. IP can also run on the special data link protocols, Serial Line Interface Protocol (SLIP) and Point-to-Point Protocol (PPP), that were created for it (see Part II-1). An important example is IP's ability to fragment large blocks of data into smaller ones in order to match the size limitations of physical networks, and then have the recipient reassemble the pieces again as needed.

Connectionless Delivery IP is a *connectionless protocol.* This means that when point A wants to send data to point B, it doesn't first set up a connection to point B and then send the data—it just makes the datagram and sends it. (See the section in Chapter 1 on connection-oriented and connectionless protocols for more information on this.)

Unreliable Delivery IP is said to be an unreliable protocol. That doesn't mean that one day your IP software will decide to go fishing rather than run your network. It does mean that when datagrams are sent from Device A to Device B, Device A just sends each one and then moves on to the next. IP doesn't keep track of the ones it sent. It does not provide reliability or service-quality capabilities, such as error protection for the data it sends (though it does on the IP header), flow control, or retransmission of lost datagrams. For this reason, IP is sometimes called a *best-effort* protocol. It does what it can to get data to where it needs to go, but makes no guarantees that the data will actually get there.

Unacknowledged Delivery Corresponding with its unreliable nature, IP doesn't use acknowledgements. When Device B gets a datagram from Device A, it doesn't send back a "thank you note" to tell Device A that the datagram was received. It leaves Device A in the dark, so to speak.

These last three characteristics might be enough to make you cringe, thinking that giving your data to IP would be somewhat like trusting a new car to your 16-year-old son. If you are going to build an entire network around this protocol, why design it so that it works without connections, doesn't guarantee that the data will get there, and has no means of acknowledging receipt of data?

The reason is simple: Establishing connections, guaranteeing delivery, error checking, and similar insurance-type functions have a cost in *performance.* It takes time, computer resources, and network bandwidth to perform these tasks, and they aren't always necessary for every application. Now, consider that IP carries pretty much *all* user traffic on a TCP/IP network. To build this complexity into IP would burden all traffic with this overhead, whether or not it was needed.

The solution taken by the designers of TCP/IP was to exploit the power of layering. If service-quality features such as connections, error checking, or guaranteed delivery are required by an application, they are provided at the transport layer (or possibly, the application layer). On the other hand, applications that don't need these features can avoid using them. This is the major distinction between the two TCP/IP transport layer protocols: TCP and UDP. TCP is full featured but a bit slower than UDP; UDP is spartan in its capabilities, but faster than TCP. This system is really the best of both worlds, and it works.

IP Functions

The exact number of IP functions depends on where you draw the line between certain activities. For explanatory purposes, however, I view IP as having four basic functions (or more accurately, function sets):

Addressing Before it can deliver datagrams, IP must know where to deliver them. For this reason, IP includes a mechanism for host addressing. Furthermore, since IP operates over internetworks, its system is designed to allow for the unique addressing of devices across arbitrarily large networks. It also contains a structure to facilitate the routing of datagrams to distant networks, if that is required. Since most of the other TCP/IP protocols use IP, an understanding the IP addressing scheme is of vital importance to comprehending much of what goes on in TCP/IP. It is explored fully in Chapters 16 through 20.

Data Encapsulation and Formatting/Packaging As the TCP/IP network layer protocol, IP accepts data from the transport layer protocols UDP and TCP. It then encapsulates this data into an IP datagram using a special format prior to transmission.

Fragmentation and Reassembly IP datagrams are passed down to the data link layer for transmission on the local network. However, the maximum frame size of each physical and data link network using IP may be different. For this reason, IP includes the ability to *fragment* IP datagrams into pieces, so that they can each be carried on the local network. The receiving device uses the *reassembly* function to re-create the whole IP datagram. Some people view fragmentation and reassembly as distinct functions, though clearly they are complementary, and I view them as being part of the same job.

Routing and Indirect Delivery When an IP datagram must be sent to a destination on the same local network, you can do this easily with the network's underlying local area network (LAN), wireless LAN (WLAN), or wide area network (WAN) protocol, using what is sometimes called *direct delivery*. However, in many (if not most cases) the final destination is on a distant network that isn't directly attached to the source. In this situation, the datagram must be delivered indirectly. This is accomplished by routing the datagram through intermediate devices (*routers*). IP accomplishes this in concert with support from the other protocols including the Internet Control Message Protocol (ICMP) and the TCP/IP gateway/routing protocols such as the Routing Information Protocol (RIP) and the Border Gateway Protocol (BGP).

IP History, Standards, Versions, and Closely Related Protocols

Since IP is really the architectural foundation for the entire TCP/IP protocol suite, you might have expected that it was created first, and that the other protocols were built upon it. That's usually how you build a structure, after all! The history of IP, however, is a bit more complex. The functions it *performs* were defined at the birth of the protocol, but IP itself didn't exist for the first few years that the protocol suite was being defined.

I explore the early days of TCP/IP in Chapter 8, which provides an overview of the suite as a whole. What is notable about the development of IP is that its functions were originally part of TCP. As a formal protocol, IP was born when an early version of TCP developed in the 1970s for predecessors of the modern Internet was split into TCP at layer 4 and IP at layer 3. The key milestone in the development of IP was the publication of RFC 791, "Internet Protocol," in September 1981. This standard, a revision of the similar RFC 760 of the previous year, defined the core functionality and characteristics of the version of IP that has been in widespread use for the last two decades.

IP Versions and Version Numbers

The IP defined in RFC 791 was the first widely used version of IP. Interestingly, however, it is not version 1 of IP but version 4! This would of course imply that there were earlier versions of the protocol at one point. Interestingly, however, there really weren't. IP was created when its functions were split out from an early version of TCP that combined both TCP and IP functions. TCP evolved through three earlier versions and was split into TCP and IP for version 4. That version number was applied to both TCP and IP for consistency.

KEY CONCEPT Version 4 of the *Internet Protocol* (IP) is actually the first version that was widely deployed and is currently the one in widespread use.

So, when you use IP today, you are using IP version 4, which is frequently abbreviated IPv4. Unless otherwise qualified, it's safe to assume that *IP* means IP version 4—at least for the next few years. (This version number is carried in the appropriate field of all IP datagrams, as described in the topic discussing the IP datagram format in Chapter 21.)

Given that it was originally designed for an internetwork a tiny fraction of the size of our current Internet, IPv4 has proven itself remarkably capable. Various additions and changes have been made over time to how IP is used, especially with respect to addressing, but the core protocol is basically what it was in the early

1980s. There's good reason for this. Changing something as fundamental as IP requires a great deal of development effort and also introduces complexities during transition.

IPv4 has served us well, but people understood that, for various reasons, a new version of IP would eventually be required. Due to the difficulties associated with making such an important change, development of this new version of IP has actually been under way since the mid-1990s. This new version of IP is formally called *Internet Protocol version 6 (IPv6)* and also sometimes referred to as *IP Next Generation* or *IPng*. I discuss the reasons why IPv6 was developed and how it differs from IPv4 in considerable detail in Part II-4 of this book.

A natural question at this point is, "What happened to version 5 of IP?" The answer is that it doesn't exist. While this may seem confusing, version 5 was in fact intentionally skipped in order to *avoid* confusion, or at least to rectify it. The problem with version 5 relates to an experimental TCP/IP protocol called the *Internet Stream Protocol, version 2*, originally defined in RFC 1190. This protocol was originally seen by some as being a peer of IP at the Internet layer in the TCP/IP architecture, and in its standard version, these packets were assigned IP version 5 to differentiate them from normal IP packets (version 4). This protocol apparently never went anywhere, but to be absolutely sure that there would be no confusion, version 5 was skipped over in favor of version 6.

IP-Related Protocols

In addition to the old and new versions of IP, there are several protocols that are *IP-related*. These are protocols that add to or expand on the capabilities of IP functions for special circumstances, but they are not part of IP proper. These are as follows:

IP Network Address Translation (IP NAT or NAT) This protocol provides IP address translation capabilities that allow private networks to be interfaced to public networks in a flexible manner. It allows public IP addresses to be shared and improves security by making it more difficult for hosts on the public network to gain unauthorized access to hosts. It is commonly called *NAT*. This protocol is discussed in Chapter 28.

IP Security (IPsec) IPsec defines a set of subprotocols that provide a mechanism for the secure transfer of data using IP. It is rapidly growing in popularity as a security protocol that enables virtual private networks. This protocol is discussed in Chapter 29.

Mobile IP This is a protocol that addresses some of the difficulties associated with using IP on computers that frequently move from one network to another. It provides a mechanism that allows data to be automatically routed to a mobile host (such as a notebook computer), without requiring a constant reconfiguration of the device's IP address. This protocol is discussed in Chapter 30.

16

IPV4 ADDRESSING CONCEPTS AND ISSUES

The primary job of the Internet Protocol (IP) is delivering messages between devices, and like any good delivery service, it can't do its job too well if it doesn't know where the recipients are located. Obviously then, one of the most important functions of IP is *addressing*. IP addressing is used not only to uniquely identify IP addresses, but also to facilitate the routing of IP datagrams over internetworks. IP addresses are used and referred to extensively in TCP/IP networking.

Even though the original IP addressing scheme was relatively simple, it has become complex over time as changes have been made to it to allow it to deal with various addressing requirements. The more advanced styles of IP addressing, such as subnetting and classless addressing, are the ones used most in modern networks. However, they can be a bit confusing to understand. To help make sense of them, we must start at the beginning with a discussion of the fundamentals of IP addressing.

In this chapter, I begin a larger exploration of IP addressing by explaining the key concepts and issues behind it. I begin with an overview of IP addressing and a discussion of what it is all about. I describe the size of IP addresses, the concept of its address space, and the notation usually used for IP addresses. I provide basic information on the structure of an IP address and how it is divided into a network identifier and host identifier. I then describe the different types of IP addresses and the additional information, such as a subnet mask and default gateway, that often accompanies an IP address on larger networks. I provide a brief description of how multiple addresses are sometimes assigned to single devices and why. I conclude with a description of the process by which public IP addresses are registered and managed, and the organizations that do this work for the global Internet.

BACKGROUND INFORMATION *If you are not familiar with at least the basics of how binary numbers work, and also with how to convert between binary and decimal numbers, I recommend reading Chapter 4, which provides some background on data representation and the mathematics of computing, before you proceed here.*

IP Addressing Overview and Fundamentals

IP addressing is important because it facilitates the primary function of the IP: the delivery of datagrams across an internetwork. When you examine this in more detail, it becomes apparent that the IP address actually has two different functions, as follows:

Network Interface Identification Like a street address, the IP address provides unique identification of the interface between a device and the network. This is required to ensure that the datagram is delivered to the correct recipients.

Routing When the source and destination of an IP datagram are not on the same network, the datagram must be delivered indirectly using intermediate systems. This is a process called *routing*. The IP address is an essential part of the system used to route datagrams.

You may have noticed a couple of things about this short list. One is that I said the IP address identifies the *network interface*, not that it identifies the *device* itself. This distinction is important because it underscores the concept that IP is oriented around connections to a large, virtual network at layer 3, which can span multiple physical networks. Some devices, such as routers, will have more than one network connection, necessary to take datagrams from one network and route them onto another. This means they will also have more than one IP address—one per connection.

You might also find it curious that I said that the IP address facilitates routing. How can it do that? The answer is that the addressing system is designed with a structure that can be interpreted to allow routers to determine what to do with a datagram based on the values in the address. Numbers related to the IP address, such as the subnet mask when subnetting is used, support this function.

Let's look at some of the more important issues and characteristics associated with IP addresses in general terms.

Number of IP Addresses Per Device

Any device that has data sent to it at the network layer will have at least one IP address: one per network interface. This means that normal hosts such as computers and network-capable printers usually get one IP address, while routers get more than one IP address. Some special hosts may have more than one IP address if they are multihomed—connected to more than one network.

Lower-level network interconnection devices—such as repeaters, bridges, and switches—don't require an IP address because they pass traffic based on layer 2 (data link layer) addresses. Network segments connected by bridges and switches form a single broadcast domain, and any devices on them can send data to each other directly without routing. To IP, these devices are essentially invisible; they are no more significant than the wires that connect devices together (with a couple of exceptions). Such devices may, however, optionally have an IP address for management purposes. In this regard, they are acting like a regular host on the network.

Figure 16-1 shows the IP interfaces of a few common LAN devices as small circles. Each regular host has one interface, while the router that serves this LAN has three, since it connects to three different networks. Note that the LAN switch has no IP interfaces; it connects the hosts and router at layer 2. (Also see Figure 16-5, which shows the IP interfaces of devices in a more complex configuration.)

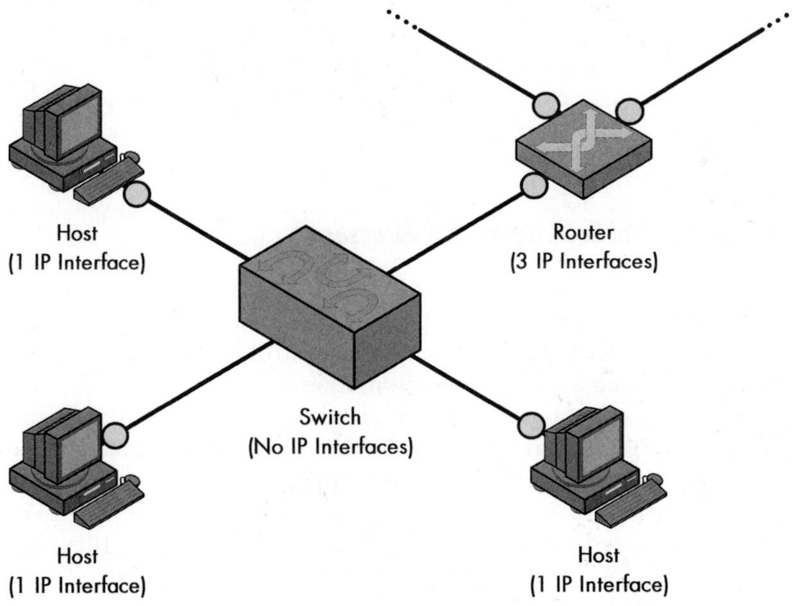

Figure 16-1: IP interfaces for common network devices *Regular hosts have one interface; routers usually have more than one; and switches have none (because they operate at layer 2).*

Address Uniqueness and Network Specificity

Each IP address on a single internetwork must be unique. (This seems rather obvious, although there are exceptions in IPv6, in the form of special anycast addresses, as discussed in Chapter 25.)

Since IP addresses represent network interfaces and are used for routing, the IP address is specific to the network to which it is connected. If the device moves to a new network, the IP address will usually have to change as well. For the full reason why, see the discussion of basic IP address structure later in this chapter. This issue was a primary motivation for the creation of Mobile IP (covered in Chapter 30).

Contrasting IP Addresses and Data Link Layer Addresses

IP addresses are used for network-layer data delivery across an internetwork. This makes IP addresses quite different from the data link layer address of a device, such as its Ethernet MAC address. (In TCP/IP parlance, these are sometimes called *physical addresses* or *hardware addresses.*)

At the network layer, a single datagram may be sent from Device A to Device B. However, the actual delivery of the datagram may require that it passes through a dozen or more physical devices if Device A and Device B are not on the same network.

It is also necessary to provide a function that maps between IP and data link layer addresses. In TCP/IP, this is the job of the Address Resolution Protocol (ARP; see Chapter 13).

In a physical network such as an Ethernet, the MAC address is all the information needed to send data between devices. In contrast, an IP address represents only the final delivery point of the datagram. The route taken depends on the characteristics of the network paths between the source and destination devices. It is even possible that there may not be a route between any two devices, which means two devices cannot exchange data, even if they know each other's addresses!

Private and Public IP Network Addresses

There are two distinct ways that a network can be set up with IP addresses. On a *private network*, a single organization controls the assignment of the addresses for all devices; they have pretty much absolute control to do what they wish in selecting numbers, as long as each address is unique.

In contrast, on a *public network*, a mechanism is required to ensure that organizations don't use overlapping addresses and that they enable efficient routing of data between organizations. The best-known example of this is the Internet, where public IP registration and management facilities have been created to address this issue. There are also advanced techniques now, such as IP Network Address Translation (NAT), which allow a network using private addresses to be interfaced to a public TCP/IP network.

IP Address Configuration and Addressing Types

IP addresses can be set up as either a static or dynamic configuration. In a *static configuration* setup, each device is manually configured with an IP address that doesn't change. This is fine for small networks but quickly becomes an administrative nightmare in larger networks, when changes are required. The alternative, *dynamic configuration*, allows IP addresses to be assigned to devices and changed under software control. The two host configuration protocols, BOOTP and DHCP, were created to fill this latter function (see Part III-3).

Additionally, provision is included in the IP addressing scheme for all three basic types of addressing: unicast, multicast, and broadcast.

> **KEY CONCEPT** IP addresses serve the dual function of device identification and routing. Each network interface requires one IP address, which is network specific. IP addresses can be either statically or dynamically allocated, and come in unicast, multicast, and broadcast forms.

IP Address Size, Address Space, and Notation

Now that you have looked at the general issues and characteristics associated with IP addresses, it's time to get past the introductions and dig into the "meat" of the IP address discussion. Let's start by looking at the physical construction and size of the IP address and how it is referred to and used.

IP Address Size and Binary Notation

At its simplest, the IP address is just a 32-bit binary number: a set of 32 ones or zeros. At their lowest levels, computers always work in binary, and this also applies to networking hardware and software. While different meanings are ascribed to different bits in the address, the address itself is just a 32-digit binary number.

People don't work too well with binary numbers, because they are long and complicated, and the use of only two digits makes them hard to differentiate. (Quick, which of these is larger: 11100011010100101001100110110001 or 11100011010100101001101110110001?) For this reason, when you use IP addresses, you don't work with them in binary except when absolutely necessary.

The first thing that people would naturally do with a long string of bits is to split it into four eight-bit octets (or bytes, even though the two aren't technically the same; see Chapter 4), to make it more manageable. So 11100011010100101001101110110001 would become 11100011 - 01010010 - 10011101 - 10110001. Then you could convert each of those octets into a more manageable two-digit hexadecimal number to yield the following: E3 - 52 - 9D - B1. This is, in fact, the notation used for IEEE 802 MAC addresses, except that they are 48 bits long, so they have six two-digit hex numbers, and they are usually separated by colons, not dashes, as I used here.

(Incidentally, the second binary number is the larger one.)

IP Address Dotted Decimal Notation

Most people still find hexadecimal a bit difficult to work with. So, IP addresses are normally expressed with each octet of eight bits converted to a decimal number and the octets separated by a period (a *dot*). Thus, the previous example would become 227.82.157.177, as shown in Figure 16-2. This is usually called *dotted decimal notation* for rather obvious reasons. Each of the octets in an IP address can take on the values from 0 to 255, so the lowest value is theoretically 0.0.0.0 and the highest is 255.255.255.255.

KEY CONCEPT IP addresses are 32-bit binary numbers, which can be expressed in binary, hexadecimal, or decimal form. Most commonly, they are expressed by dividing the 32 bits into four bytes and converting each to decimal, then separating these numbers with dots to create dotted decimal notation.

	0–8	8–16	16–24	24–32
Binary	11100011	01010010	10011101	10110001
Hexadecimal	E3	52	9D	B1
Dotted Decimal	227	82	157	177

Figure 16-2: IP address binary, hexadecimal, and dotted decimal representations *The binary, hexadecimal, and decimal representations of an IP address are all equivalent.*

Dotted decimal notation provides a convenient way to work with IP addresses when communicating among people. Never forget that to the computers, the IP address is always a 32-bit binary number; you'll understand the importance of this when you look at how the IP address is logically divided into components in the next topic, and when you examine techniques that manipulate IP addresses, such as subnetting.

IP Address Space

Since the IP address is 32 bits wide, this provides a theoretical *address space* of 2^{32}, or 4,294,967,296 addresses. This seems like quite a lot of addresses, and in some ways, it is. However, as you will see, due to how IP addresses are structured and allocated, not every one of those addresses can actually be used.

One of the unfortunate legacies of the fact that IP was originally created on a rather small internetwork is that decisions were made that wasted much of the address space. For example, all IP addresses starting with 127 in the first octet are reserved for the loopback function. Just this one decision makes 1/256th of the total number, or 16,277,216 addresses, no longer available. There are also other ways that the IP address space was not conserved. This caused difficulty as the Internet grew in size. (You'll see more about this in Chapter 17, which covers classful addressing.)

KEY CONCEPT Since IP addresses are 32 bits long, the total address space of IPv4 is 2^{32} or 4,294,967,296 addresses. However, not all of these addresses can be used, for a variety of reasons.

This IP address space dictates the limit on the number of addressable interfaces in *each* IP internetwork. So, if you have a private network, you can, in theory, have four-billion-plus addresses. However, in a public network such as the Internet, all devices must share the available address space. Techniques such as Classless Inter-Domain Routing (CIDR), or supernetting, and NAT were designed in part to utilize the existing Internet IP address space more efficiently. IPv6 expands the IP address size from 32 bits all the way up to 128, which increases the address space to a ridiculously large number and makes the entire matter of address space size moot.

IP Basic Address Structure and Main Components

As I mentioned in the IP addressing overview, one of the ways that IP addresses are used is to facilitate the routing of datagrams in an IP internetwork. This is made possible because of the way that IP addresses are structured and how that structure is interpreted by network routers.

Network ID and Host ID

As you just saw, each IPv4 address is 32 bits long. When you refer to the IP address, you use a dotted decimal notation, while the computer converts this into binary. However, even though these sets of 32 bits are considered a single entity, they have an internal structure containing two components:

Network Identifier (Network ID) A certain number of bits, starting from the left-most bit, is used to identify the network where the host or other network interface is located. This is also sometimes called the *network prefix* or even just the *prefix.*

Host Identifier (Host ID) The remainder of the bits is used to identify the host on the network.

NOTE *By convention, IP devices are often called* hosts *for simplicity, as I do throughout this book. Even though each host* usually *has a single IP address, you should remember that IP addresses are strictly associated with network layer network interfaces, not physical devices, and a device may therefore have more than one IP address (especially a router or multihomed host).*

As you can see in Figure 16-3, this really is a fairly simple concept. The fundamental division of the bits of an IP address is into a network ID and host ID. In this illustration, the network ID is 8 bits long, and the host ID is 24 bits in length. This is similar to the structure used for phone numbers in North America. The telephone number (401) 555-7777 is a ten-digit number that's usually referred to as a single phone number. However, it has a structure. In particular, it has an area code (401) and a local number (555-7777).

The fact that the network ID is contained in the IP address is what partially facilitates the routing of IP datagrams when the address is known. Routers look at the network portion of the IP address to first determine if the destination IP address is on the same network as the host IP address. Then routing decisions are made based on information the routers keep about where various networks are located. Again, this is conceptually similar to how the area code is used by the equivalent of routers in the phone network to switch telephone calls. The host portion of the address is used by devices on the local portion of the network.

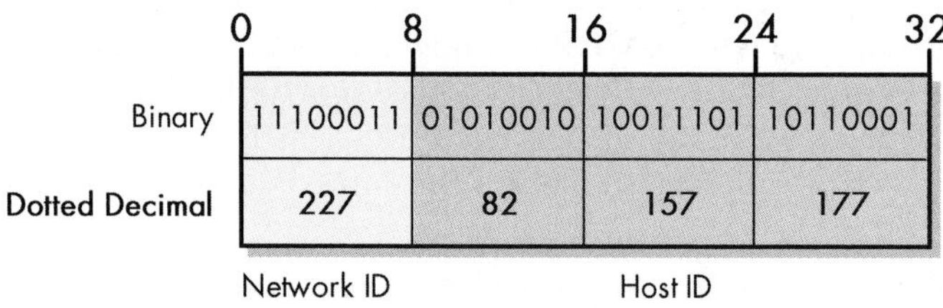

Figure 16-3: Basic IP address division: network ID and host ID *This diagram shows one of the many ways to divide an IP address into a network ID and host ID.*

Location of the Division Between Network ID and Host ID

One difference between IP addresses and phone numbers is that the dividing point between the bits used to identify the network and those that identify the host isn't fixed. It depends on the nature of the address, the type of addressing being used, and other factors.

Take the previous example of 227.82.157.177 (see Figure 16-2). It is possible to divide this into a network ID of 227.82 and a host ID of 157.177. Alternatively, the network ID might be 227 and the host ID might be 82.157.177 within that network.

To express the network and host IDs as 32-bit addresses, you add zeros to replace the missing pieces. With a network ID of 227 and a host ID of 82.157.177, the address of the network becomes 227.0.0.0 and the address of the host 0.82.157.177. (In practice, network addresses of this sort are routinely seen with the added zeros; network IDs are not seen as often in 32-bit form this way.)

Lest you think from these examples that the division must always be between whole octets of the address, you should know that it's also possible to divide it in the middle of an octet. For example, you could split the IP address 227.82.157.177 so that there were 20 bits for the network ID and 12 bits for the host ID. The process is the same, but determining the dotted decimal ID values is more tricky because here, the 157 is split into two binary numbers. The results are 227.82.144.0 for the network ID and 0.0.0.13.177 for the host ID, as shown in Figure 16-4.

Since IP addresses are normally expressed as four dotted-decimal numbers, educational resources often show the division between the network ID and host ID occurring on an octet boundary. However, it's essential to remember that the dividing point often appears in the middle of one of these eight-bit numbers. In Figure 16-4, the network ID is 20 bits long, and the host ID 12 bits long. This results in the third number of the original IP address, 157, being split into 144 and 13.

The place where the line is drawn between the network ID and the host ID must be known in order for devices such as routers to know how to interpret the address. This information is conveyed either implicitly or explicitly, depending on the type of IP addressing in use, as I discuss next.

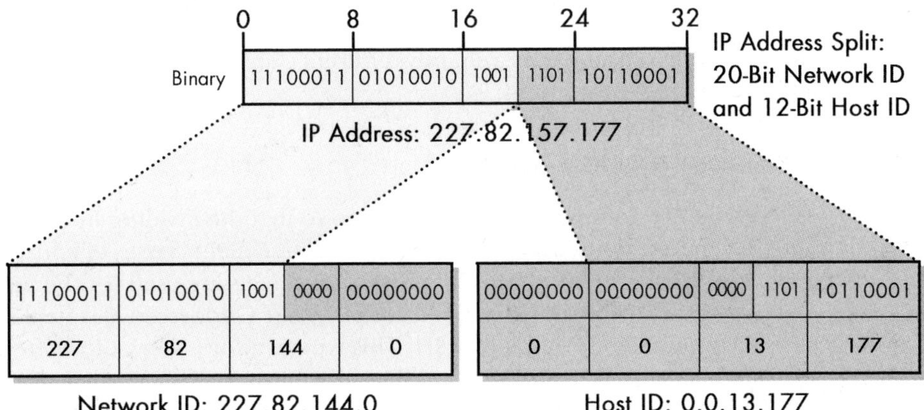

Figure 16-4: Mid-octet IP address division *IP addresses need not be divided between network ID and host ID on octet boundaries. The division here is into a 20-bit network ID and a 12-bit host ID.*

> **KEY CONCEPT** The basic structure of an IP address consists of two components: the network ID and host ID. The dividing point of the 32-bit address is not fixed, but depends on a number of factors and can occur in a variety of places, including in the middle of a dotted-decimal octet.

Since the IP address can be split into network ID and host ID components, it is also possible to use either one or the other by itself, depending on context. These addresses are assigned special meanings. For example, if the network ID is used with all ones as the host ID, this indicates a broadcast to the entire network. Similarly, if the host ID is used by itself with all zeros for the network ID, this implies an IP address sent to the host of that ID on the local network, whatever that might be. This is explained in much more detail in Chapter 17.

It is the inclusion of the network ID in the IP address of each host on the network that causes the IP addresses to be network-specific. If you move a device from one network to a different one, the network ID must change to that of the new network. Therefore, the IP address must change as well. This is an unfortunate drawback that shows up most commonly when dealing with mobile devices; see Chapter 30.

IP Addressing Categories and IP Address Adjuncts

We just explored how the 32 bits in an IP address are fundamentally divided into the network ID and host ID. The network ID is used for routing purposes, and the host ID uniquely identifies each network interface on the network. In order for devices to know how to use IP addresses on the network, they must be able to tell which bits are used for each ID. However, the dividing line is not predefined. It depends on the type of addressing used in the network.

Understanding how these IDs are determined leads us into a larger discussion of the three main categories of IP addressing schemes: classful, subnetted, and classless. Each of these uses a slightly different system of indicating where in the IP address the host ID is found.

Conventional (Classful) Addressing

The original IP addressing scheme is set up so that the dividing line occurs only in one of a few locations: on octet boundaries. Three main classes of addresses—A, B, and C—are differentiated based on how many octets are used for the network ID and how many for the host ID. For example, Class C addresses devote 24 bits to the network ID and 8 bits to the host ID. This type of addressing is now often referred to by the made-up word *classful* to differentiate it from the newer classless scheme.

This most basic addressing type uses the simplest method to divide the network and host IDs: The class, and therefore the dividing point, are encoded into the first few bits of each address. Routers can tell from these bits which octets belong to which identifier.

Subnetted Classful Addressing

In the subnet addressing system, the two-tier network and host division of the IP address is made into a three-tier system by taking some number of bits from a Class A, B, or C host ID and using them for a *subnet identifier (subnet ID).* The network ID is unchanged. The subnet ID is used for routing within the different subnetworks that constitute a complete network, thereby providing extra flexibility for administrators. For example, consider a Class C address that normally uses the first 24 bits for the network ID and remaining 8 bits for the host ID. The host ID can be split into, say, 3 bits for a subnet ID and 5 bits for the host ID.

This system is based on the original classful scheme, so the dividing line between the network ID and full host ID is based on the first few bits of the address as before. The dividing line between the subnet ID and the "subhost" ID is indicated by a 32-bit number called a *subnet mask.* In the previous example, the subnet mask would be 27 ones followed by 5 zeros—the zeros indicate what part of the address is the host. In dotted decimal notation, this would be 255.255.255.224.

Classless Addressing

In the classless system, the classes of the original IP addressing scheme are tossed out the window. The division between the network ID and host ID can occur at an arbitrary point, not just on octet boundaries, as in the classful scheme.

The dividing point is indicated by putting the number of bits used for the network ID, called the *prefix length,* after the address. (Recall that the network ID bits are also sometimes called the *network prefix,* so the network ID size is the prefix length.) For example, if 227.82.157.177 is part of a network where the first 27 bits are used for the network ID, that network would be specified as 227.82.157.160/27. The /27 is conceptually the same as the 255.255.255.224 subnet mask, since it has 27 one bits followed by 5 zeros.

KEY CONCEPT An essential factor in determining how an IP address is interpreted is the addressing scheme in which it is used. The three methods, arranged in increasing order of age, complexity, and flexibility, are classful addressing, subnetted classful addressing, and classless addressing.

This introduction to the concepts of classful, subnetted, and classless addressing was designed to show you how they impact the way the IP address is interpreted. I have greatly summarized important concepts here. All three methods are explained in their own chapters in full detail.

Subnet Mask and Default Gateway

In the original classful scheme, the division between network ID and host ID is implied. However, if either subnetting or classless addressing is used, then the *subnet mask* (or *slash number*, which is equivalent) is required to fully qualify the address. These numbers are considered adjuncts to the IP address and usually mentioned with the address itself, because without them, it is not possible to know where the network ID ends and the host ID begins.

One other number that is often specified along with the IP address for a device is the *default gateway* identifier. In simplest terms, this is the IP address of the router that provides default routing functions for a particular device. When a device on an IP network wants to send a datagram to a device it can't see on its local IP network, it sends it to the default gateway, which takes care of routing functions. Without this, each IP device would also need to have knowledge of routing functions and routes, which would be inefficient. See Chapter 23, which discusses IP routing concepts, and Chapter 37 through 41, which cover TCP/IP routing protocols, for more information.

Number of IP Addresses and Multihoming

Each network interface on an IP internetwork has a separate IP address. In a classic network, each regular computer, usually called a *host*, attaches to the network in exactly only one place, so it will have only one IP address. This is what most of us are familiar with when using an IP network (and is also why most people use the term *host* when they really mean *network interface*).

If a device has more than one interface to the internetwork, it will have more than one IP address. The most obvious case where this occurs is with routers, which connect together different networks and thus must have an IP address for the interface on each one. It is also possible for hosts to have more than one IP address, however. Such a device is sometimes said to be *multihomed.*

There are two ways that a host can be multihomed:

Two or More Interfaces to the Same Network Devices such as servers or high-powered workstations may be equipped with two physical interfaces to the same network for performance and reliability reasons. They will have two IP addresses on the same network with the same network ID.

Interfaces to Two or More Different Networks Devices may have multiple interfaces to different networks. The IP addresses will typically have different network IDs in them.

Figure 16-5 shows examples of both types of multihomed device. Of course, these could be combined, with a host having two connections to one network and a third to another network. There are also some other special cases, such as a host with a single network connection having multiple IP address aliases.

NOTE *When subnetting is used, the same distinction can be made between multihoming to the same subnet or a different subnet.*

Now, let's consider the second case. If a host has interfaces to two or more different networks, could it pass IP datagrams between them? Yes, if it had the right software running on it. And wouldn't that make the host a router, of sorts? In fact, that is exactly the case. A multihomed host with interfaces to two networks can use software to function as a router. This is sometimes called *software routing*.

Using a host as a router has certain advantages and disadvantages compared to a hardware router. A server that is multihomed can perform routing functions and also, well, act as a server. A dedicated hardware router is designed for the job of routing and usually will be more efficient than a software program running on a host.

KEY CONCEPT A host with more than one IP network interface is said to be multihomed. A multihomed device can have multiple connections to the same network, to different networks, or both. A host connected to two networks can be configured to function as a router.

Multihoming was once considered a fairly esoteric application, but has become more common in recent years. This is also true of multihoming on different networks for software routing use. In fact, you may be doing this in your home without realizing it.

Suppose you have two PCs networked together and a single phone line to connect to the Internet. One computer dials up to your Internet service provider (ISP) and runs software such as Microsoft's Internet Connection Sharing (ICS) to let the other computer access the Internet. Millions of people do this every day—they have a multihomed system (the one connecting to the Internet and the other PC) with ICS acting in the role of a software router (though there are some technical differences between ICS and a true router, of course).

IP Address Management and Assignment Methods and Authorities

What would happen if you told someone that you lived at 34 Elm Street, and when he turned onto your road, he found four different houses with the number 34 on them? He probably would find your place eventually but wouldn't be too pleased. Neither would you or your mail carrier! And all of you folks are much smarter than computers. Like street addresses, IP addresses must be unique for them to be useful.

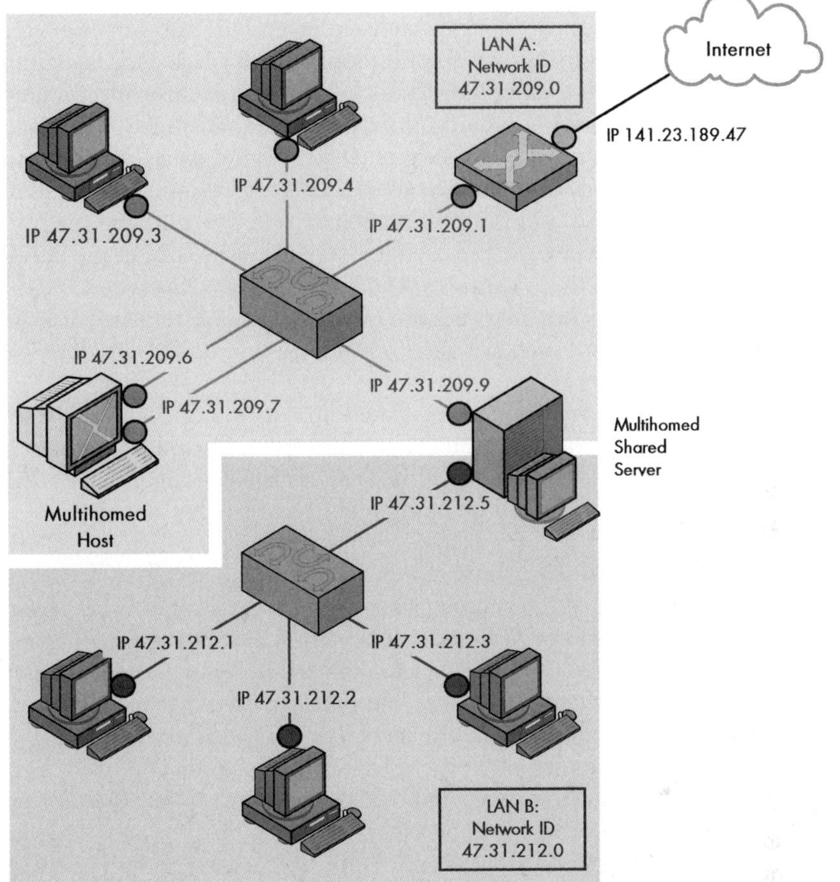

Figure 16-5: Multihomed devices on an IP internetwork *This internetwork consists of two LANs, A (above) and B (below). LAN A has a multihomed workstation, shown with two IP network interface "circles." The two LANs are connected together through a multihomed, shared server that has been configured to route traffic between them. Note that this server also handles all traffic passing between LAN B and the Internet (since the Internet connection is in LAN A only).*

Since IP datagrams are sent only within the confines of the IP internetwork, they must be unique within each internetwork. If you are a company with your own private internetwork, this isn't really a big problem. Whoever is in charge of maintaining the internetwork keeps a list of what numbers have been used where and makes sure that no two devices are given the same address. However, what happens in a public network with many different organizations? Here, it is essential that the IP address space be managed across the organizations to ensure that they use different addresses. It's not feasible to have each organization coordinate its activities with each other one. Therefore, some sort of centralized *management authority* is required.

At the same time that you need someone to ensure that there are no conflicts in address assignment, you don't want users of the network to have to go to this central authority every time they need to make a change to their network. It makes more sense to have the authority assign numbers in blocks or chunks to organizations based on the number of devices they want to connect to the network. The organizations can manage those blocks as they see fit, and the authority's job is made easier because it deals in blocks instead of billions of individual addresses and machines.

The Internet, as the big IP internetwork, requires this coordination task to be performed for millions of organizations worldwide. The job of managing IP address assignment on the Internet was originally carried out by a single organization: the *Internet Assigned Number Authority (IANA)*. IANA was responsible for allocating IP addresses, along with other important centralized coordination functions such as managing universal parameters used for TCP/IP protocols. In the late 1990s, a new organization called the *Internet Corporation for Assigned Names and Numbers (ICANN)* was created. ICANN now oversees the IP address assignment task of IANA, as well as managing other tasks such as Domain Name System (DNS) name registration (see Chapter 54).

IP addresses were originally allocated directly to organizations. The original IP addressing scheme was based on classes, and so IANA would assign addresses in Class A, B, and C blocks. Today, addressing is classless, using CIDR's hierarchical addressing scheme. IANA doesn't assign addresses directly, but rather delegates them to regional Internet registries (RIRs). These are APNIC, ARIN, LACNIC, and RIPE NCC. Each RIR can, in turn, delegate blocks of addresses to lower-level registries such as national Internet registries (NIRs) and local Internet registries (LIRs).

Eventually, blocks of addresses are obtained by ISPs for distribution to end-user organizations. Some of the ISP's customers are end-user organizations, but others are (smaller) ISPs themselves. They can, in turn, use or delegate the addresses in their blocks. This can continue for several stages in a hierarchical fashion. This arrangement helps ensure that IP addresses are assigned and used in the most efficient manner possible. See Chapter 20, which discusses CIDR, for more information on how this works.

IANA, ICANN, and the RIRs are responsible for more than just IP address allocation, though I have concentrated on IP addresses here for obvious reasons. For more general information on IANA, ICANN, APNIC, ARIN, LACNIC, and RIPE NCC, try a can of alphabet soup—or Chapter 3, which provides an overview of the Internet registration authorities.

17

CLASSFUL (CONVENTIONAL) ADDRESSING

The original addressing method for IP addresses divided the IP address space into five chunks of different sizes called *classes,* and assigned blocks of addresses to organizations from these classes based on the size and requirements of the organization. In this classful addressing scheme, each class is reserved for a particular purpose, with the main address classes differentiated based on how many octets are used for the network identifier (network ID) and how many are used for the host identifier (host ID).

In this chapter, I describe classful IP addressing. I begin with an overview of the concept and general description of the different classes. I discuss the network and host IDs and address ranges associated with the different classes. I discuss the capacities of each of the commonly used classes, meaning how many networks belong to each and how many hosts each network can contain. I discuss the special meanings assigned to certain IP address patterns and the special ranges reserved for private IP addressing, loopback functions, and multicasting. I conclude with a discussion of the problems with this type of addressing, which led to it being abandoned in favor of subnetting, and eventually, classless assignment of the IP address space.

NOTE *The classful addressing scheme has been replaced by the classless addressing system described in Chapter 20. However, I think it is still important to understand how this original system operates, as it forms the basis for the more sophisticated addressing mechanisms.*

IP Classful Addressing Overview and Address Classes

The developers of the Internet Protocol (IP) recognized that organizations come in different sizes and would therefore need varying numbers of IP addresses on the Internet. They devised a system to divide the IP address space into *classes*, each of which contained a portion of the total addresses and was dedicated to specific uses. Some classes would be devoted to large networks on the Internet, while others would be reserved for smaller organizations or special purposes.

This original system had no name; it was simply "the" IP addressing system. Today it is called the *classful addressing scheme* to differentiate it from the newer classless scheme.

IP Address Classes

There are five classes in the classful system, which are assigned the letters A through E. Table 17-1 provides some general information about the classes, their intended uses, and their characteristics.

Table 17-1: IP Address Classes and Class Characteristics and Uses

IP Address Class	Fraction of Total IP Address Space	Number of Network ID Bits	Number of Host ID Bits	Intended Use
Class A	1/2	8	24	Unicast addressing for very large organizations with hundreds of thousands or millions of hosts to connect to the Internet
Class B	1/4	16	16	Unicast addressing for medium to large organizations with many hundreds to thousands of hosts to connect to the Internet
Class C	1/8	24	8	Unicast addressing for smaller organizations with no more than about 250 hosts to connect to the Internet
Class D	1/16	n/a	n/a	IP multicasting
Class E	1/16	n/a	n/a	Reserved for experimental use

Looking at this table (and Figure 17-1), you can see that Classes A, B, and C take up most of the total address space (seven-eighths of it). These are the classes used for *unicast* IP addressing and messages sent to a single network interface. (The blocks also include associated broadcast addresses for these networks.) This is what I usually consider normal IP addressing.

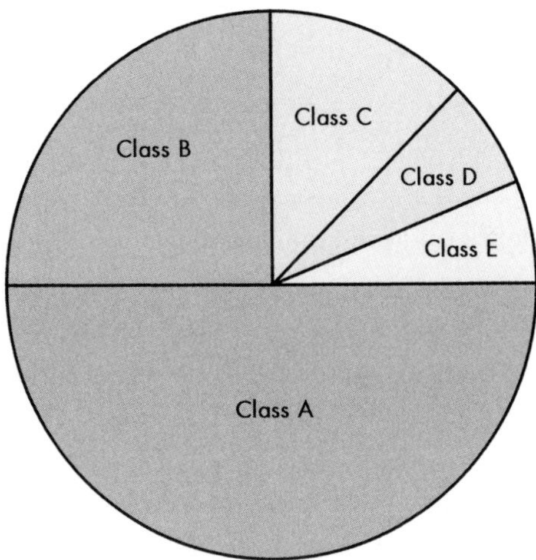

Figure 17-1: Division of IPv4 address space into classes

You can think of Classes A, B, and C as the papa bear, mama bear, and baby bear of traditional IP addressing. They allow the Internet to provide addressing for a small number of very large networks, a moderate number of medium-sized organizations, and a large number of smaller companies. This approximately reflects the distribution of organization sizes in the real world, though the large gulf in the maximum number of hosts allowed for each address class leads to inflexibility, as I will discuss later in the chapter.

As you can see, the classes differ in where they draw the line between the network ID and the host ID portions of the addresses they contain. However, in each case, the division is made on octet boundaries. In classful addressing, the division does not occur within an octet.

Classes D and E are special—to the point where many people don't even realize they exist. Class D is used for IP multicasting, while Class E is reserved for experimental use (by designers of the Internet). I discuss IP multicast addressing later in this chapter.

> **KEY CONCEPT** The classful IP addressing scheme divides the IP address space into five classes, A through E, of differing sizes. Classes A, B, and C are the most important ones, designated for conventional unicast addresses and taking up seven-eighths of the address space. Class D is reserved for IP multicasting, and Class E is reserved for experimental use.

Rationale for Classful Addressing

While the drawbacks of the classful system are often discussed today (as you'll see later in this chapter), it's important to keep in context what the size of the Internet was when this system was developed. The Internet was tiny then, and the 32-bit address space seemed enormous by comparison to even the number of machines its creators envisioned years into the future. It's only fair to also remember the following advantages of the classful system developed over 25 years ago:

Simplicity and Clarity There are only a few classes to choose from, and it's very simple to understand how the addresses are split up. The distinction between classes is clear and obvious. The divisions between network ID and host ID in Classes A, B, and C are on octet boundaries, making it easy to tell what the network ID is of any address.

Reasonable Flexibility Three levels of granularity match the sizes of large, medium-sized, and small organizations reasonably well. The original system provided enough capacity to handle the anticipated growth rate of the Internet at the time.

Routing Ease As you will see shortly, the class of the address is encoded right into the address to make it easy for routers to know what part of any address is the network ID and what part is the host ID. There was no need for adjunct information such as a subnet mask.

Reserved Addresses Certain addresses are reserved for special purposes. This includes not just Classes D and E, but also special reserved address ranges for private addressing.

Of course, it turned out that some of the decisions in the original IP addressing scheme were regrettable—but that's the benefit of hindsight. I'm sure we would all like to have back the 268-odd million addresses that were set aside for Class E. While it may seem wasteful now to have reserved a full one-sixteenth of the address space for experimental use, remember that the current size of the Internet was never anticipated even 10 years ago, never mind 25. Furthermore, it's good practice to reserve some portion of any scarce resource for future use.

IP Classful Addressing Network and Host Identification and Address Ranges

The classful IP addressing scheme divides the total IP address space into five classes, A through E. One of the benefits of the relatively simple classful scheme is that information about the classes is encoded directly into the IP address. This means you can determine in advance which address ranges belong to each class. It also means the opposite is possible: You can identify which class is associated with any address by examining just a few bits of the address. This latter benefit was one of the main motivators for the initial creation of the classful system.

Classful Addressing Class Determination Algorithm

When TCP/IP was first created, computer technology was still in its infancy. Routers needed to be able to quickly make decisions about how to move IP datagrams around. The IP address space was split into classes in such a way that, by looking at only the first few bits of any IP address, the router could easily tell how to choose between the network and host ID, and thus what to do with the datagram.

The number of bits the router needs to look at may be as few as one or as many as four, depending on what it finds when it starts looking. The algorithm used to determine the class corresponds to the system used to divide the address space, as illustrated in Figure 17-2.

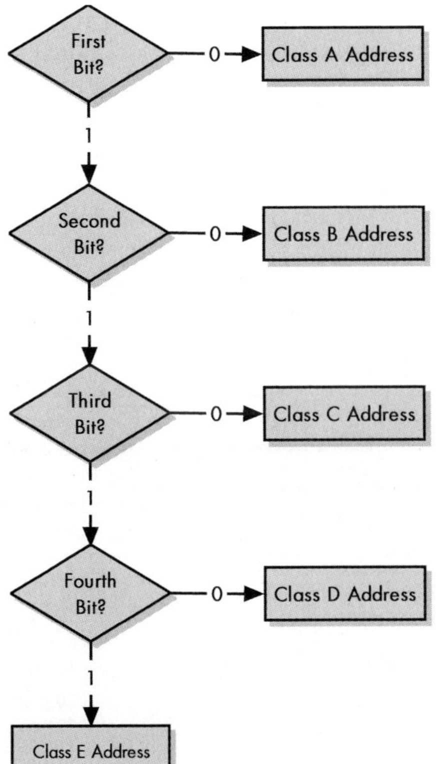

Figure 17-2: Class determination algorithm for classful IP addresses *The simplicity of the classful IP addressing can be seen in the very uncomplicated algorithm used to determine the class of an address.*

Here are the four very basic steps in the algorithm:

1. If the first bit is a 0, it's a Class A address, and you're done. (Half the address space has a 0 for the first bit, so this is why Class A takes up half the address space.) If it's a 1, continue to step 2.
2. If the second bit is a 0, it's a Class B address, and you're done. (Half of the remaining non–Class A addresses, or one quarter of the total.) If it's a 1, continue to step 3.
3. If the third bit is a 0, it's a Class C address, and you're done. (Half again of what's left, or one-eighth of the total.) If it's a 1, continue to step 4.
4. If the fourth bit is a 0, it's a Class D address. (Half the remainder, or one-sixteenth of the address space.) If it's a 1, it's a Class E address. (The other half, one-sixteenth.)

And that's pretty much it.

Determining Address Class from the First Octet Bit Pattern

As humans, of course, we generally work with addresses in dotted decimal notation and not in binary, but it's pretty easy to see the ranges that correspond to the classes. For example, consider Class B. The first two bits of the first octet are 10. The remaining bits can be any combination of ones and zeros. This is normally represented as 10xx xxxx (shown as two groups of four for readability). Thus, the binary for the first octet can range from **10**00 0000 to **10**11 1111 (128 to 191 in decimal). So in the classful scheme, any IP address whose first octet is between 128 and 191 inclusive is a Class B address.

Table 17-2 shows the bit patterns for each of the five classes and the way that the first octet ranges can be calculated. The first column shows the format of the first octet of the IP address; the *x*s can be either a zero or a one. Next are the lowest and highest value columns for each class in binary (the fixed few bits are in bold print so you can see that they do not change while the others do), followed by the corresponding range for the first octet, in decimal.

Table 17-2: IP Address Class Bit Patterns, First-Octet Ranges, and Address Ranges

IP Address Class	First Octet of IP Address	Lowest Value of First Octet (Binary)	Highest Value of First Octet (Binary)	Range of First Octet Values (Decimal)	Octets in Network ID/Host ID	Theoretical IP Address Range
Class A	**0**xxx xxxx	**0**000 0001	**0**111 1110	1 to 126	1 / 3	1.0.0.0 to 126.255.255.255
Class B	**10**xx xxxx	**10**00 0000	**10**11 1111	128 to 191	2 / 2	128.0.0.0 to 191.255.255.255
Class C	**110**x xxxx	**110**0 0000	**110**1 1111	192 to 223	3 / 1	192.0.0.0 to 223.255.255.255
Class D	**1110** xxxx	**1110** 0000	**1110** 1111	224 to 239	—	224.0.0.0 to 239.255.255.255
Class E	**1111** xxxx	**1111** 0000	**1111** 1111	240 to 255	—	240.0.0.0 to 255.255.255.255

This table also shows the *theoretical* lowest and highest IP address ranges for each of the classes. This means that they are the result of taking the full span of binary numbers possible in each class. In reality, some of the values are not available for normal use. For example, even though the range 192.0.0.0 to 192.0.0.255 is technically in Class C, it is reserved and not actually used by hosts on the Internet.

Also, certain IP addresses cannot be used because they have special meaning. For example, 255.255.255.255 is a reserved broadcast address. In a similar vein, note that the range for Class A is from 1 to 126 and not 0 to 127 as you might have expected. This is because Class A networks 0 and 127 are reserved; 127 is the network that contains the IP loopback address. These special and reserved addresses are discussed later in this chapter.

Recall that Classes A, B, and C differ in where the dividing line is between the network ID and the host ID: 1 for network and 3 for host for Class A, 2 for each for Class B, and 3 for network and 1 for host for Class C. Based on this division, in Table 17-2, I have highlighted the network ID portion of the IP address ranges for each of Classes A, B, and C. The plain text corresponds to the range of host IDs for each allowable network ID. Figure 17-3 shows graphically how bits are used in each of the five classes.

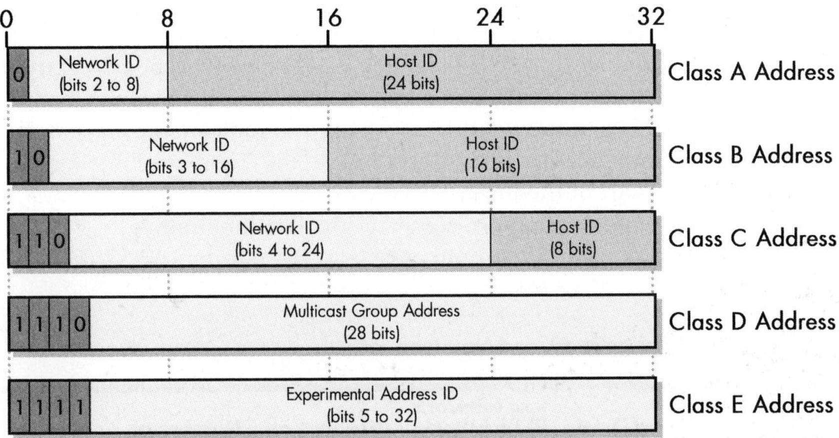

Figure 17-3: IP address class bit assignments and network/host ID sizes *This illustration shows how the 32 bits of IP address are assigned for each of the five IP address classes. Classes A, B, and C are the normal classes used for regular unicast addresses; each has a different dividing point between the network ID and host ID. Classes D and E are special and are not divided in this manner.*

KEY CONCEPT In the classful IP addressing scheme, the class of an IP address is identified by looking at the first one, two, three, or four bits of the address. This can be done both by humans working with these addresses and routers making routing decisions. The use of these bit patterns means that IP addresses in different classes fall into particular address ranges that allow an address's class to be determined by looking at the first byte of its dotted decimal address.

For example, consider Class C. The lowest IP address is **192.0.0**.0, and the highest is **223.255.255**.255. The first three octets are the network ID and can range from **192.0.0** to **223.255.255**. For each network ID in that range, the host ID can range from 0 to 255.

NOTE *It is common to see resources refer to the network ID of a classful address as including only the significant bits; that is, only the ones that are not common to all networks of that class. For example, you may see a Class B network ID shown in a diagram as having 14 bits, with the 10 that starts all such networks shown separately, as if it were not part of the network ID. Remember that the network ID does include those bits as well; it is 8 full bits for Class A, 16 for Class B, and 24 for Class C. In the case of Class D addresses, all 32 bits are part of the address, but only the lower 28 bits are part of the multicast group address; see the topic on multicast addressing later in this chapter for more.*

IP Address Class A, B, and C Network and Host Capacities

So far, I have introduced the concepts of IP address classes and showed how the classes relate to ranges of IP addresses. Of the five classes, D and E are dedicated to special purposes, so I will leave those alone for now. Classes A, B, and C are the ones actually assigned for normal (unicast) addressing purposes on IP internetworks, and therefore they are the primary focus of our continued attention.

As you've seen, the classes differ in the number of bits (and octets) used for the network ID compared to the host ID. The number of different networks possible in each class is a function of the number of bits assigned to the network ID, and likewise, the number of hosts possible in each network depends on the number of bits provided for the host ID. You must also take into account the fact that one, two, or three of the bits in the IP address are used to indicate the class itself, so it is effectively excluded from use in determining the number of networks (though again, it is still part of the network ID).

Based on this information, you can calculate the number of networks in each class, and for each class, the number of host IDs per network. Table 17-3 shows the calculations.

Table 17-3: IP Address Class Network and Host Capacities

IP Address Class	Total # of Bits for Network ID/Host ID	First Octet of IP Address	# of Network ID Bits Used To Identify Class	Usable # of Network ID Bits	Number of Possible Network IDs	# of Host IDs Per Network ID
Class A	8/24	0xxx xxxx	1	8-1 = 7	2^7-2 = 126	2^{24}-2 = 16,777,214
Class B	16/16	10xx xxxx	2	16-2 = 14	2^{14} = 16,384	2^{16}-2 = 65,534
Class C	24/8	110x xxxx	3	24-3 = 21	2^{21} = 2,097,152	2^8-2 = 254

Let's walk through one line of this table so you can see how it works using Class B as an example. The basic division is into 16 bits for network ID and 16 bits for host ID. However, the first 2 bits of all Class B addresses must be 10, so that leaves only 14 bits to uniquely identify the network ID. This gives us a total of 2^{14} or 16,384 Class B network IDs. For each of these, you have 2^{16} host IDs, less two, for a total of 65,534.

Why less two? For each network ID, two host IDs cannot be used: the host ID with all zeros and the ID with all ones. These are addresses with special meanings, as described in the next section. Also notice that two is subtracted from the number of network IDs for Class A. This is because two of the Class A network IDs (0 and 127) are reserved.

Several other address ranges are set aside in all three of the classes shown here. They are listed in the "IP Reserved, Private, and Loopback Addresses" section later in this chapter.

KEY CONCEPT In the classful IP addressing scheme, a Class A network contains addresses for about 16 million network interfaces; a Class B network contains about 65,000; and a Class C network contains 254.

As you can see, there is quite a disparity in the number of hosts available for each network in each of these classes. What happens if an organization needs 1,000 IP addresses? It must use either four Class Cs or one Class B (and in so doing, waste over 90 percent of the possible addresses in the Class B network). Bear in mind that there are only about 16,000 Class B network IDs available worldwide, and you begin to understand one of the big problems with classful addressing.

IP Addresses with Special Meanings

Some IP addresses do not refer directly to specific hardware devices; instead, they are used to refer indirectly to one or more devices. To draw an analogy with language, most IP addresses refer to proper nouns, like "John" or "the red table in the corner." However, some are used more the way you use pronouns such as "this one" or "that group over there." I call these IP addresses with *special meanings.*

These special addresses are constructed by replacing the normal network ID or host ID (or both) in an IP address with one of two special patterns:

All Zeros When the network ID or host ID bits are replaced by a set of all zeros, the special meaning is the equivalent of the pronoun *this,* referring to whatever was replaced. It can also be interpreted as *the default* or *the current.* For example, if you replace the network ID with all zeros but leave the host ID alone, the resulting address means "the device with the host ID given, on *this network,*" or "the device with the host ID specified, on *the default network* or *the current network.*"

All Ones When the network ID or host ID bits are replaced by a set of all ones, this has the special meaning of *all,* meaning that the IP address refers to all hosts on the network. This is generally used as a broadcast address for sending a message to everyone.

KEY CONCEPT When the network ID or host ID of an IP address is replaced by a pattern of all ones or all zeros, the result is an address with a special meaning. Examples of such addresses include "all hosts" broadcast addresses and addresses that refer to a specific host or a whole network.

There are many special addresses. A small number apply to the entire TCP/IP network, while others exist for each network or host ID. Since two special patterns can be applied to the network ID, host ID, or both, there are six potential combinations, each of which has its own meaning. Of these, five are used.

Table 17-4 describes each of these special meanings and includes examples from Class A, B, and C. Note how an IP address in each of the common classes can be modified to have special meaning forms. (The first row shows the examples in their normal form, for reference.)

Table 17-4: IP Address Patterns with Special Meanings

Network ID	Host ID	Class A Example	Class B Example	Class C Example	Special Meaning and Description
Network ID	Host ID	77.91.215.5	154.3.99.6	227.82.157.160	**Normal Meaning:** Refers to a specific device.
Network ID	All Zeros	77.0.0.0	154.3.0.0	227.82.157.0	**The Specified Network:** This notation, with a 0 at the end of the address, refers to an entire network.
All Zeros	Host ID	0.91.215.5	0.0.99.6	0.0.0.160	**Specified Host on This Network:** This addresses a host on the current or default network when the network ID is not known or when it doesn't need to be explicitly stated.
All Zeros	All Zeros	0.0.0.0			**Me:** Used by a device to refer to itself when it doesn't know its own IP address. (Alternatively, "this host," or "the current/default host.") The most common use is when a device attempts to determine its address using a host-configuration protocol like DHCP. May also be used to indicate that any address of a multihomed host may be used.
Network ID	All Ones	77.255.255.255	154.3.255.255	227.82.157.255	**All Hosts on the Specified Network:** Used for broadcasting to all hosts on the local network.
All Ones	All Ones	255.255.255.255			**All Hosts on the Network:** Specifies a global broadcast to all hosts on the directly connected network. Note that there is no address that would imply sending to all hosts everywhere on the global Internet, since this would be very inefficient and costly.

NOTE *The missing combination from Table 17-4 is that of the network ID being all ones and the host ID normal. Semantically, this would refer to "all hosts of a specific ID on all networks," which doesn't really mean anything useful in practice, so it's not used. Note also that, in theory, a special address where the network ID is all zeros and the host ID is all ones would have the same meaning as the all-ones limited broadcast address. The latter is used instead, however, because it is more general, not requiring knowledge of where the division is between the network ID and the host ID.*

Since the all-zeros and all-ones patterns are reserved for these special meanings, they cannot be used for regular IP addresses. This is why, when you looked at the number of hosts per network in each of the classes, you had to subtract two from the theoretical maximum: one for the all-zeros case and one for the all-ones case.

Similarly, the network ID cannot be all zeros either. However, this doesn't require specific exclusion because the entire block of addresses with 0 in the first octet (0.x.x.x) is one of the reserved sets of IP addresses. These reserved addresses, described in the next section, further restrict the use of certain addresses in the IP address space for regular uses.

IP Reserved, Private, and Loopback Addresses

In addition to the unusable numbers with special meanings just discussed, several other sets of IP addresses have special uses, and are therefore not available for normal address assignment. These generally fall into three categories: reserved, private, and loopback addresses.

Reserved Addresses

Several blocks of addresses were designated as reserved with no specific indication given as to what they were reserved for. Perhaps they were set aside for future experimentation or for internal use in managing the Internet. (In general, it's a good idea to set aside some portion of any limited resource for unanticipated needs.)

A couple of these blocks appear in each of the three main classes (A, B, and C), at the beginning and end of each class. (All of Class D and E are also reserved, since they aren't used for regular addressing.)

Private, Unregistered, Nonroutable Addresses

You'll recall that in the IP address overview in Chapter 16, I contrasted private and public IP addresses. Every IP address on an IP network must be unique. In the case of a public IP network, addresses are allocated by a central authority to ensure that there is no overlap. In contrast, on a private network, you can use whatever addresses you want.

Then why not just pick any random block of Class A, B, or C addresses for your private network and use that? You could, and some people did. For example, if you weren't connected to the Internet you could use, say, the Class A network 18.x.x.x that is reserved on the Internet to the Massachusetts Institute of Technology (MIT). Since you aren't connected to MIT, you would think that wouldn't matter.

However, as the Internet grew, those disconnected private networks needed to connect to the public Internet after all, and then they had a conflict. If they used the 18.x.x.x addresses, they would have to renumber all their devices to avoid getting a big bunch of computer geeks really angry. (There were, in fact, cases where companies that had used IP address space belonging to other companies accidentally connected those machines to the Internet, causing a small amount of ruckus in the process.)

RFC 1918 (superseding RFC 1597) provided the solution. It defines a set of unroutable, special address blocks just for private addresses. These addresses simply don't exist on the public Internet. For this reason, they are not registered like other public addresses; they are sometimes called *unregistered*. Anyone can use them, but they cannot connect to the Internet because routers are not programmed to forward traffic with these address ranges outside of local organizations. RFC 1918 was published to encourage the use of these private blocks in order to cut down on the number of devices on the public Internet that didn't really need to be publicly accessible. This was in response to the need to conserve the public address space.

NOTE *In order to connect a network using private addressing to the public Internet, it is necessary to employ additional hardware and software. A gateway machine can be used as an interface between the public and private networks. Technologies such as Network Address Translation (NAT; see Chapter 28) are often used in conjunction with private IP addresses to allow these hosts to communicate on the public IP network.*

KEY CONCEPT Private address blocks were created to allow private IP Internets to be created using addresses that were guaranteed not to conflict with public IP addresses. They are commonly used in internetworks that aren't connected to the global Internet; devices using them can also access the global Internet by using NAT.

Loopback Addresses

Normally, when a TCP/IP application wants to send information, that information travels down the protocol layers to IP, where it is encapsulated in an IP datagram. That datagram then passes down to the data link layer of the device's physical network for transmission to the next hop, on the way to the IP destination.

However, one special range of addresses, 127.0.0.0 to 127.255.255.255, is set aside for *loopback* functionality. IP datagrams sent by a host to a 127.x.x.x loopback address are not passed down to the data link layer for transmission; instead, they loop back to the source device at the IP level. In essence, this short-circuits the normal protocol stack; data is sent by a device's layer 3 IP implementation and then immediately received by it.

This loopback range is used for testing the TCP/IP protocol implementation on a host. Since the lower layers are short-circuited, sending to a loopback address allows you to isolate and test the higher layers (IP and above) without interference from the lower layers. 127.0.0.1 is the address most commonly used for testing purposes.

KEY CONCEPT Portions of the IP address space are set aside for reserved, private, and loopback addresses.

Reserved, Private, and Loopback Addressing Blocks

Table 17-5 shows all of the special blocks set aside from the normal IP address space in numerical order, with a brief explanation of how each is used. It lists both the classful and the classless notation representing each of these blocks because the Internet now uses classless addressing, and because some of the private blocks don't correspond to single Class A, B, or C networks.

Note especially the private address block from 192.168.0.0 to 192.168.255.255. This is the size of a Class B network, but it isn't Class B in the classful scheme, because the first octet of 192 puts it in the Class C part of the address space. It is actually 256 contiguous Class C networks.

You may also notice the special Class B (/16) block 169.254.x.x. This is reserved for *Automatic Private IP Addressing (APIPA)*, discussed in Chapter 64. Systems that are configured to use this feature will automatically assign systems addresses from this block to enable them to communicate even if no server can be found for proper IP address assignment using the Dynamic Host Control Protocol (DHCP).

Table 17-5: Reserved, Private, and Loopback IP Addresses

Range Start Address	Range End Address	Classful Address Equivalent	Classless Address Equivalent	Description
0.0.0.0	**0.255.255.255**	Class A network 0.x.x.x	0/8	Reserved
10.0.0.0	**10.255.255.255**	Class A network 10.x.x.x	10/8	Class A private address block
127.0.0.0	**127.255.255.255**	Class A network 127.x.x.x	127/8	Loopback address block
128.0.0.0	**128.0.255.255**	Class B network 128.0.x.x	128.0/16	Reserved
169.254.0.0	**169.254.255.255**	Class B network 169.254.x.x	169.254/16	Class B private address block reserved for automatic private address allocation (see Chapter 64 for details)
172.16.0.0	**172.31.255.255**	16 contiguous Class B networks from 172.16.x.x through 172.31.x.x	172.16/12	Class B private address blocks
191.255.0.0	**191.255.255.255**	Class B network 191.255.x.x	191.255/16	Reserved
192.0.0.0	**192.0.0.255**	Class C network 192.0.0.x	192.0.0/24	Reserved
192.168.0.0	**192.168.255.255**	256 contiguous Class C networks from 192.168.0.x through 192.168.255.x	192.168/16	Class C private address blocks
223.255.255.0	**223.255.255.255**	Class C network 223.255.255.x	223.255.255/24	Reserved

IP Multicast Addressing

The vast majority of traffic on IP internetworks is *unicast*, which is one source device sending to one destination device. IP also supports *multicasting*, which is a source device sending to a group of devices. Multicasting is not used a great deal on the present-day Internet, mainly due to a lack of widespread hardware support, though it is useful in certain circumstances, especially as a more efficient alternative to broadcasting.

The classful IP addressing scheme sets aside one-sixteenth of the address space for multicast addresses as Class D. Multicast addresses are identified by the pattern 1110 in the first four bits, which corresponds to a first octet of 224 to 239. Thus, the full range of multicast addresses is from 224.0.0.0 to 239.255.255.255.

Since multicast addresses represent a group of IP devices (sometimes called a *host group*), they can be used only as the destination of a datagram, never the source.

Multicast Address Types and Ranges

The other 28 bits in the IP address define the *multicast group address*. The size of the Class D multicast address space is therefore 2^{28}, or 268,435,456 multicast groups. No substructure defines the use of these 28 bits, and there is no specific concept of a network ID and host ID as in Class A, B, and C. However, certain portions of the address space are set aside for specific uses. Table 17-6 and Figure 17-4 show the general allocation of the Class D address space.

Table 17-6: IP Multicast Address Ranges and Uses

Range Start Address	Range End Address	Description
224.0.0.0	224.0.0.255	Reserved for special well-known multicast addresses
224.0.1.0	238.255.255.255	Globally scoped (Internetwide) multicast addresses.
239.0.0.0	239.255.255.255	Administratively scoped (local) multicast addresses

NOTE *As with the other IP address classes, the entire 32 bits of the address is always used. It is only the least significant 28 bits that are interesting, because the upper four bits never change.*

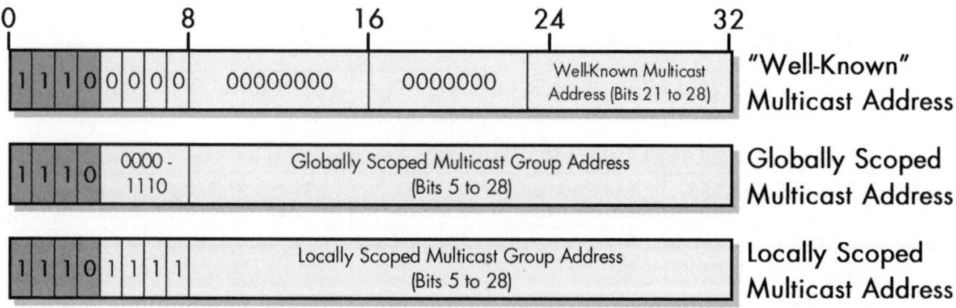

Figure 17-4: IP Multicast address ranges and uses *All multicast addresses begin with 1110. The well-known group has zeros for the first 20 bits of the multicast group address, with 8 bits available to define 255 special multicast addresses. Multicast addresses starting with 1110 1111 are locally scoped; all other addresses are globally scoped (this includes addresses starting with 1110 0000 other than the 255 well-known addresses).*

RELATED INFORMATION *The concept of multicast address scope was more completely defined in IPv6, and I discuss it in more detail in the in the discussion of IPv6 multicast addresses in Chapter 25.*

The bulk of the address space is in the middle multicast range. These are normal multicast addresses, like the Class A, B, and C unicast addresses, and they can be assigned to various groups.

The last address range is for *administratively scoped* multicast groups. This is a fancy term for multicast groups used within a private organization. This block, representing one-sixteenth of the total multicast address space, is comparable to the private addresses you saw earlier in this chapter. It is further subdivided into site-local multicast addresses, organization-local addresses, and so forth.

Well-Known Multicast Addresses

The first block of 256 addresses is used to define special, well-known multicast address blocks (Table 17-7 has a selective listing). These do not represent arbitrary groups of devices and cannot be assigned in that manner. Instead, they have a special meaning that allows a source to send a message to a predefined group.

Table 17-7: Well-Known IP Multicast Addresses

Range Start Address	Description
224.0.0.0	Reserved; not used
224.0.0.1	All devices on the subnet
224.0.0.2	All routers on the subnet
224.0.0.3	Reserved
224.0.0.4	All routers using DVMRP
224.0.0.5	All routers using OSPF
224.0.0.6	Designated routers using OSPF
224.0.0.9	Designated routers using RIP-2
224.0.0.11	Mobile agents (for Mobile IP)
224.0.0.12	DHCP server/relay agent

Delivery of IP multicast traffic is more complex than unicast traffic due to the existence of multiple recipients. Instead of the normal resolution method through the Address Resolution Protocol (ARP) used for unicast datagrams, the IP multicast group and a hardware multicast group are mapped.

Problems with Classful IP Addressing

The classful addressing system was the first major attempt to define a method for universal addressing of a large IP internetwork. There was a reasonable rationale for the system, as I mentioned in the overview of the classful scheme, and given that it was developed decades ago for a network that was limited in size, it did the job remarkably well for a long time.

No one ever expected the Internet to mushroom to anything close to its current size. As the Internet grew, the classful IP addressing mechanism showed some problems.

The three main problems with classful addressing are as follows:

Lack of Internal Address Flexibility Big organizations are assigned large, monolithic blocks of addresses that aren't a good match for the structure of their underlying internal networks.

Inefficient Use of Address Space The existence of only three block sizes (Classes A, B, and C) leads to a waste of limited IP address space.

Proliferation of Router Table Entries As the Internet grows, more and more entries are required for routers to route IP datagrams. This causes performance problems for routers. Attempting to reduce inefficient address space allocation leads to even more router table entries.

The first issue results primarily from the fact that in the classful system, big companies are assigned a rather large (Class B) or truly enormous (Class A) block of addresses. They are considered by the Internet routers to be a single network, with one network ID. Now imagine that you are running a medium-to-large-sized company with 5,000 computers, and you are assigned a Class B address for your network. Do you really have 5,000 computers all hooked into a single network? I sure as heck hope you don't! Yet you would be forced to try to fit all of these into a single IP network in the original classful method. There was no way to create an internal hierarchy of addresses.

The second and third issues both stem from the fact that the granularity in the classful system is simply too low to be practical in a large internetwork; there are simply too few choices in the sizes of available networks. Three sizes seem fine in principle, but the gaps between the sizes are enormous, and the sizes don't match up well with the distribution of organizations in the real world. Consider the difference in size between Class C and Class B networks—a jump from 254 hosts all the way up to over 65,000! There are many, many companies that need more than 254 IP address but a lot fewer than 65,000. And what about Class A? How many companies need 16 *million* IP addresses, even the truly large ones? Probably none, if you think about it, yet that's half the IP address space right there.

What class of network should the company with 5,000 computers use? As Figure 17-5 shows, the classful scheme offers no good match for this company's needs. If it were assigned a Class B, over 90 percent of the IP addresses would be wasted.

The alternative to wasting all these IP addresses would be to give this fictitious company a bunch of Class C addresses instead of one Class B; but they would need 20 of them. While this would use the address space more efficiently, it leads to the third issue: Every router on the Internet then has to replace the single Class B router table entry with 20 Class C router entries. Multiply this by a few thousand medium-sized companies, and you can see that this method would add dramatically to the size of router tables. The larger these tables, the more time it takes for routers to make routing decisions.

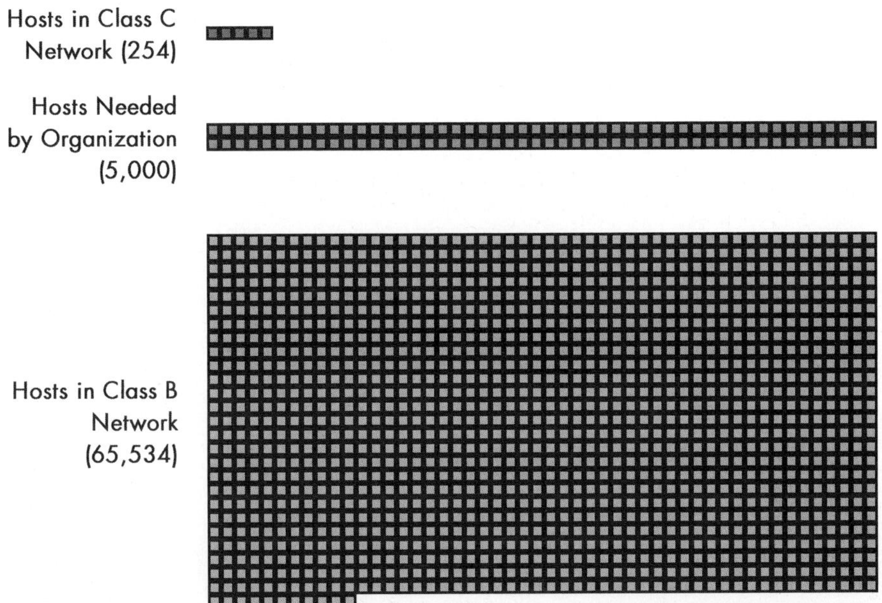

Figure 17-5: The main problem with classful addressing *In this scale diagram, each square represents 50 available addresses. Since a Class C address has only 254 addresses, and a Class B contains 65,534 addresses, an organization with 5,000 hosts is caught in the middle. It can only choose to either waste 90 percent of a Class B address or use 20 different Class C networks.*

The problems with classful addressing have been solved by three enhancements, as you'll see in later chapters. The first, which primarily addresses the first issue, was the development of subnetting. The second was the move to classless addressing and routing, which replaces the classful system with a new method with higher granularity. This tackles the second and third issues by letting addresses be assigned based on real organizational needs, without requiring numerous routing table entries for each organization. The third improvement is the new IP version 6 (IPv6), which finally does away with the cramped 32-bit IP address space in favor of a gargantuan 128-bit one.

Other support technologies, such as NAT, have helped to extend the life of IPv4 by allowing multiple devices to share public addresses. This alone has added years to the life of the IPv4 addressing system.

18

IP SUBNET ADDRESSING (SUBNETTING) CONCEPTS

In the previous chapter, we looked at the original classful IP addressing scheme, which conceptually divides a large internetwork into a simple two-level hierarchy that includes many *networks* of different sizes, each of which contains a number of *hosts*. The system works well for smaller organizations that may connect all their machines in a single network. However, it lacks flexibility for large organizations that often have many subnetworks, or *subnets*. To better meet the administrative and technical requirements of larger organizations, the classful IP addressing system was enhanced through a technique known as *subnet addressing*, or more simply, *subnetting*.

In this chapter, I describe the concepts and general techniques associated with IP subnet addressing. I begin with an overview of subnetting, including a discussion of the motivation for the system and its advantages. I discuss how the traditional two-level method for dividing IP addresses becomes three-level for subnetting. I talk about subnet masks and how they are used in calculations for addressing and routing. I discuss the default subnet masks used to represent the classful Class A, B, and C networks in a subnetting environment and then how custom subnet masks are used for these classes. I then discuss subnet identifiers and general concepts behind determining subnet and host addresses in a subnet environment. I provide summary tables for subnetting Class A, B, and C networks. I conclude with a brief discussion of *Variable Length Subnet Masking (VLSM)*, an enhancement of conventional subnetting that improves its flexibility further.

NOTE *I provide a great deal of coverage of subnetting, because understanding it is an important part of learning about how IP addresses work, and hence, how TCP/IP functions. However, the technique is today considered mostly* historical *because it is based on classful addressing. The concept of a subnet and subnet mask has certainly not disappeared, but the idea of being assigned a Class A, B, or C Internet address block and then explicitly subnetting it is no longer relevant.*

RELATED INFORMATION *This is the first of two chapters dedicated to IP address subnetting. Chapter 19 describes the step-by-step process for subnetting using examples. If you find that after reading this concepts section that you don't quite understand subnetting, try reading the example-based section, and you may find that it helps make it all click. On the other hand, if you are already somewhat familiar with subnetting, you may find that you can skip this concepts section and just go through the step-by-step examples. You will find much more in that chapter in the way of gory details of subnet mask, subnet address, and host address calculations. Putting the practical details there allows this section to concentrate on concepts without getting too bogged down in numbers.*

BACKGROUND INFORMATION *Understanding subnetting requires familiarity with binary numbers and how they are manipulated. This includes the concept of using boolean operators such as* AND *to "mask" binary digits. If reading that last sentence made you go "huh?" I strongly recommend reviewing the background section on computing mathematics (Chapter 4) before you proceed.*

IP Subnet Addressing Overview, Motivation, and Advantages

As I discussed in the previous chapter, IP addressing was originally designed around the assumption of a strict two-level hierarchy for internetworks: the first level was the network, and the second level the host. Each organization was usually represented by a single network identifier (network ID) that indicated a Class A, B, or C block dedicated to them. Within that network, the organization needed to put all of the devices it wanted to connect to the public IP network.

It did not take long after this scheme was developed for serious inadequacies in it to be noticed, especially by larger organizations. In order to address this problem, RFC 950 [1985] defined a new addressing procedure called *subnet addressing* or *subnetting*.

Subnet addressing adds an additional hierarchical level to the way IP addresses are interpreted: Instead of having just hosts, the network has *subnets* and hosts. Each subnet is a subnetwork, and functions much the way a full network does in conventional classful addressing. A three-level hierarchy is thus created: networks, which contain subnets, each of which then has a number of hosts. Thus, an organization can organize hosts into subnets that reflect the way internal networks are structured. In essence, subnet addressing allows each organization to have its own internetwork within the Internet. This change brought numerous advantages over the old system, such as the following:

Better Match to Physical Network Structure Hosts can be grouped into subnets that reflect the way they are actually structured in the organization's physical network.

Flexibility The number of subnets and number of hosts per subnet can be customized for each organization. Each can decide on its own subnet structure and change it as required.

Invisibility to Public Internet Subnetting was implemented so that the internal division of a network into subnets is visible only within the organization. To the rest of the Internet, the organization is still just one big, flat network. This also means that any changes made to the internal structure are not visible outside the organization.

No Need to Request New IP Addresses Organizations don't need to constantly requisition more IP addresses, as they would in the workaround of using multiple small Class C blocks.

No Routing Table Entry Proliferation Since the subnet structure exists only within the organization, routers outside that organization know nothing about it. The organization still maintains a single (or perhaps a few) routing table entries for all of its devices. Only routers inside the organization need to worry about routing between subnets.

The change to subnetting affects both addressing and routing in IP networks. Addressing changes because, instead of having just a network ID and host ID, you now also have a *subnet ID* to be concerned with. The size of the subnet ID can vary for each network, so an additional piece of information is needed to supplement the IP address to indicate what part of the address is the subnet ID and what part is the host ID. This is a 32-bit number commonly called a *subnet mask*. The mask is used both for calculating subnet and host addresses, and by routers for determining how to move IP datagrams around a subnetted network.

Routing changes because of the additional level of hierarchy. In regular classful addressing, when a router receives an IP datagram, it only needs to decide if the destination is on the same network or a different network. Under subnetting, it must also look at the subnet ID of the destination and make one of three choices: same subnet, different subnet on the same network, or different network. Changes are also required to routing protocols, such as the Routing Information Protocol (RIP; see Chapter 38), to deal with subnets and subnet masks.

KEY CONCEPT Subnet addressing adds an additional hierarchical level to how IP addresses are interpreted by dividing an organization's IP network into subnets. This allows each organization to structure its address space to match its internal physical networks, rather than being forced to treat them a flat block. This solves a number of problems with the original classful addressing scheme, but requires changes to how addressing and routing work, as well as modifications to several TCP/IP protocols.

It's funny, but the main drawbacks to subnetting, compared with the older addressing scheme, have more to do with understanding how subnetting works than with the technology itself. More effort is required to deal with addressing and routing in a subnet environment, and administrators must learn how to subdivide their network into subnets and properly assign addresses. This can be a bit confusing to someone who is new to subnetting. However, the technology today is quite well established, so even this is not much of a problem.

IP Subnetting: Three-Level Hierarchical IP Subnet Addressing

As I mentioned earlier, subnetting adds an additional level to the hierarchy of structures used in IP addressing. To support this, IP addresses must be broken into three elements instead of two. This is done by leaving the network ID alone and dividing the host ID into a subnet ID and host ID. These subnet ID bits are used to identify each subnet within the network. Hosts are assigned to the subnets in whatever manner makes the most sense for that network.

Interestingly, the earlier analogy to telephone numbers still holds in the world of subnetting and shows how subnetting changes the way IP addresses are interpreted. For example, a phone number like (401) 555-7777 has an area code (401) and a local number (555-7777). The local number, however, can itself be broken down into two parts: the exchange (555) and the local extension (7777). This means phone numbers really are comprised of three hierarchical components, just as IP addresses are in subnetting.

Of course, the number of bits in an IP address is fixed at 32. This means that in splitting the host ID into subnet ID and host ID, you reduce the size of the host ID portion of the address. In essence, you are stealing bits from the host ID to use for the subnet ID. Class A networks have 24 bits to split between the subnet ID and host ID; Class B networks have 16; and Class C networks have only 8.

> **KEY CONCEPT** A classful network is subnetted by dividing its host ID portion, leaving some of the bits for the host ID while allocating others to a new subnet ID. These bits are then used to identify individual subnets within the network, into which hosts are assigned.

Now remember that when we looked at the sizes of each of the main classes in the previous chapter, we saw that, for each class, the number of networks and the number of hosts per network are a function of how many bits we use for each. The same applies to the splitting of the host ID. Since we are dealing with binary numbers, the number of subnets is two to the power of the size of the subnet ID field. Similarly, the number of hosts per subnet is two to the power of the size of the host ID field (less two for excluded special cases).

Let's take a brief example to see how this works. Imagine that you start with Class B network 154.71.0.0, with 16 bits for the network ID (154.71) and 16 are for the host ID. In regular classful addressing, there are no subnets and 65,534 hosts total. To subnet this network, you can decide to split those 16 bits however you feel best suits the needs of the network: 1 bit for the subnet ID and 15 for the host ID, or 2 and 14, 3 and 13, and so on. Most any combination will work, as long as the total is 16; I've used 5 and 11 in the example shown in Figure 18-1. The more bits you steal from the host ID for the subnet ID, the more subnets you can have, but the fewer hosts you can have for each subnet.

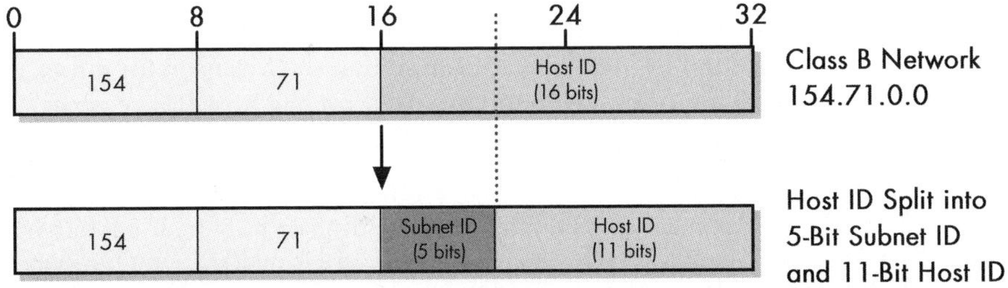

Figure 18-1: Subnetting Class B network *We begin with the Class B network 154.71.0.0, which has 16 bits in its host ID block. We then subnet this network by dividing the host ID into a subnet ID and host ID. In this case, 5 bits have been allocated to the subnet ID, leaving 11 bits for the host ID.*

Choosing how to split the host ID into subnet and host bits is one of the most important design considerations in setting up a subnetted IP network. The number of subnets is generally determined based on the number of physical subnetworks in the overall organizational network, and the number of hosts per subnetwork must not exceed the maximum allowed for the particular subnetting choice you make. Choosing how to divide the original host ID bits into subnet ID bits and host ID bits is sometimes called *custom subnetting* and is described in more detail later in this chapter.

IP Subnet Masks, Notation, and Subnet Calculations

Subnetting divides an organization's network into a two-level structure of subnets and hosts that is entirely internal and hidden from all other organizations on the Internet. One of the many advantages of this is that each organization gets to make its own choice about how to divide the classful host ID into subnet ID and host ID.

In a nonsubnetted classful environment, routers use the first octet of the IP address to determine what the class of the address is, and from this they know which bits are the network ID and which are the host ID. When you use subnetting, these routers also need to know how that host ID is divided into subnet ID and host ID. However, this division can be arbitrary for each network. Furthermore, there is no way to tell how many bits belong to each simply by looking at the IP address.

In a subnetting environment, the additional information about which bits are for the subnet ID and which are for the host ID must be communicated to devices that interpret IP addresses. This information is given in the form of a 32-bit binary number called a *subnet mask.* The term *mask* comes from the binary mathematics concept called *bit masking*. This is a technique where a special pattern of ones and zeros can be used in combination with boolean functions such as AND and OR to select or clear certain bits in a number. (I explain bit masking in the background section on binary numbers and mathematics, in Chapter 4.)

Function of the Subnet Mask

There's something about subnet masks that seems to set people's hair on end, especially if they aren't that familiar with binary numbers. However, the idea behind them is quite straightforward. The mask is a 32-bit number, just as the IP address is a 32-bit number. Each of the 32 bits in the subnet mask corresponds to the bit in the IP address in the same location in the number. The bits of the mask in any given subnetted network are chosen so that the bits used for either the network ID or subnet ID are ones, while the bits used for the host ID are zeros.

KEY CONCEPT The *subnet mask* is a 32-bit binary number that accompanies an IP address. It is created so that it has a one bit for each corresponding bit of the IP address that is part of its network ID or subnet ID, and a zero for each bit of the IP address's host ID. The mask thus tells TCP/IP devices which bits in that IP address belong to the network ID and subnet ID, and which are part of the host ID.

Why bother doing this with a 32-bit binary number? The answer is the magic of boolean logic. You use the subnet mask by applying the boolean AND function between it and the IP address. For each of the 32 "bit pairs" in the IP address and subnet mask, you employ the AND function, the output of which is one only if both bits are one. What this means in practical terms is the following, for each of the 32 bits:

Subnet Bit Is a One In this case, you are ANDing either a zero or one in the IP address with a one. If the IP address bit is a zero, the result of the AND will be zero; if it is a one, the AND will be one. In other words, *where the subnet bit is a one, the IP address is preserved unchanged.*

Subnet Bit Is a Zero Here, you are ANDing with a zero, so the result is always zero, regardless of what the IP address is. Thus, *when the subnet bit is a zero, the IP address bit is always cleared to zero.*

Thus, when you use the subnet mask on an IP address, the bits in the network ID and subnet ID are left intact, while the host ID bits are removed. Like a mask that blocks part of your face but lets other parts show, the subnet mask blocks some of the address bits (the host bits) and leaves others alone (the network and subnet bits). A router that performs this function is left with the address of the subnet. Since it knows from the class of the network what part is the network ID, it also knows what subnet the address is on.

KEY CONCEPT To use a subnet mask, a device performs a boolean AND operation between each bit of the subnet mask and each corresponding bit of an IP address. The resulting 32-bit number contains only the network ID and subnet ID of the address, with the host ID cleared to zero.

Subnet Mask Notation

Like IP addresses, subnet masks are always used as a 32-bit binary number by computers. And like IP addresses, using them as 32-bit binary numbers is difficult for humans. Therefore, they are usually converted to dotted decimal notation for convenience, just as IP addresses are.

For example, suppose you decide to subnet the Class B network 154.71.0.0 using 5 bits for the subnet ID and 11 bits for the host ID (see Figure 18-2). In this case, the subnet mask will have 16 ones for the network portion (since this is Class B) followed by 5 ones for the subnet ID, and 11 zeros for the host ID. That's 11111111 11111111 **11111**000 00000000 in binary, with the bits corresponding to the subnet ID highlighted. In dotted decimal, the subnet mask would be 255.255.248.0.

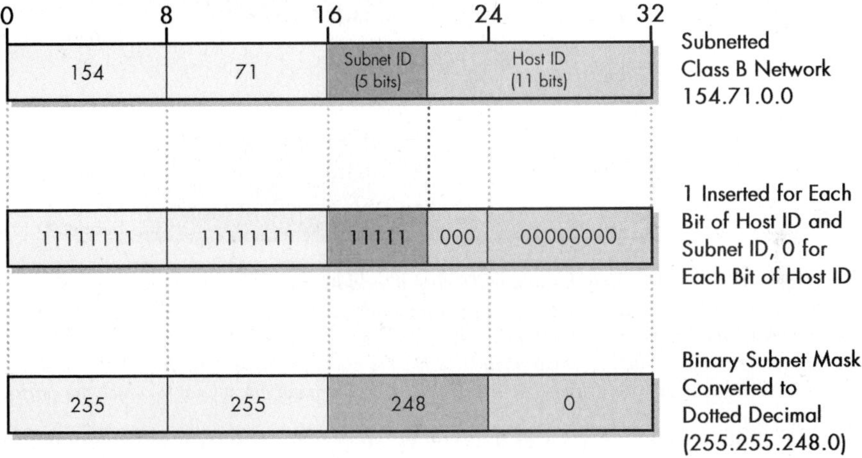

Figure 18-2: Determining the subnet mask of a subnetted network *The Class B network from Figure 18-1 is shown at the top, with 5 bits assigned to the subnet ID and 11 bits left for the host ID. To create the subnet mask, you fill in a 32-bit number with 1 for each network ID and subnet ID bit, and 0 for each host ID bit. You can then convert this to dotted decimal.*

Applying the Subnet Mask: An Example

Now, let's see how the subnet mask might be used. Suppose you have a host on this network with an IP of 154.71.150.42 and a router needs to figure out which subnet this address is on. To do so, it performs the masking operation shown in Table 18-1 and Figure 18-3.

Table 18-1: Determining the Subnet ID of an IP Address Through Subnet Masking

Component	Octet 1	Octet 2	Octet 3	Octet 4
IP Address	10011010 (154)	01000111 (71)	10010110 (150)	00101010 (42)
Subnet Mask	11111111 (255)	11111111 (255)	**11111**000 (248)	00000000 (0)
Result of AND Masking	10011010 (154)	01000111(71)	**10010**000 (144)	00000000 (0)

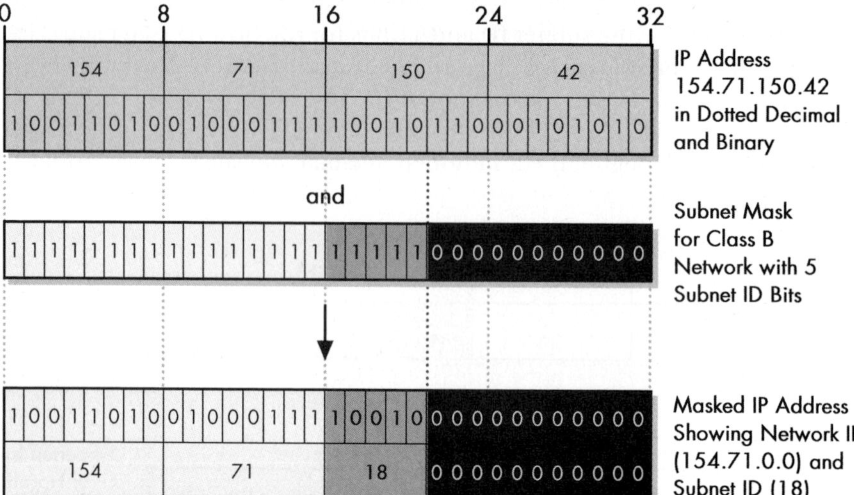

Figure 18-3: Determining the subnet ID of an IP address through subnet masking *Subnet masking involves performing a boolean AND between each corresponding bit in the subnet mask and the IP address. The subnet mask can be likened to a physical mask; each 1 in it lets the corresponding bit of the IP address show through, while each 0 blocks the corresponding IP address bit. In this way the host ID bits of the address are stripped so the device can determine the subnet to which the address belongs.*

This result, 154.71.144.0, is the IP address of the subnet to which 154.71.150.42 belongs. There is no need to explicitly differentiate the network ID bits from the subnet ID bits, because you are still using classful addresses. Any router can see that since the first two bits of the address are 10, this is a Class B address. So the network ID is 16 bits, and this means the subnet ID must be bits 17 to 21, counting from the left. Here, the subnet is the portion highlighted earlier: 10010, or subnet 18. (I'll explain this better in the "IP Custom Subnet Masks" section later in this chapter.)

> **KEY CONCEPT** The subnet mask is often expressed in dotted decimal notation for convenience, but is used by computers as a binary number and usually must be expressed in binary to understand how the mask works and the number of subnet ID bits it represents.

Rationale for Subnet Mask Notation

In practical terms, the subnet mask actually conveys only a single piece of information: the line between the subnet ID and host ID. Then why bother with a big 32-bit binary number in that case, instead of just specifying the bit number where the division occurs? Instead of carrying the subnet mask of 255.255.248.0 around, why not just divide the IP address after bit 21? Even if devices want to perform a masking operation, couldn't they just create the mask as needed?

That's a very good question. There are two historical reasons: efficiency considerations and support for noncontiguous masks. The subnet mask expression is efficient because it allows routers to perform a quick masking operation to determine the subnet address. (This is not really an issue today given the speed of today's machines.)

When splitting the bits in the host ID for subnet ID and host ID, RFC 950 specifies that they may be split in more than one place. In the previous example, you could, instead of splitting the 16 bits into 5 bits for subnet ID and 11 for host ID, have done it as 2 bits for the subnet ID, then 4 bits for the host ID, then 3 more bits for the subnet ID, and finally 7 more bits for host ID. This would be represented by the subnet mask pattern 11000011 10000000 for those 16 bits (following the 16 ones for the network ID). Of course, subnetting this way makes assigning addresses *extremely* confusing. For this reason, while technically legal, noncontiguous subnet masking is not recommended and not done in practice.

Given that noncontiguous masks are not used, and today's computers are faster, the alternative method of expressing masks with just a single number is now often used. Instead of writing "IP address of 154.71.150.42 with subnet mask of 255.255.248.0," you can simply write "154.71.150.42/**21**." This is sometimes called *slash notation* or *Classless Inter-Domain Routing (CIDR) notation.* While this is more commonly used in Variable Length Subnet Masking (VLSM) environments and is the standard for specifying classless addresses under the CIDR addressing scheme (see Chapter 20), it is also sometimes seen in regular subnetting discussions.

NOTE *Since these weird masks were never really used, some resources say that the subnet mask always had to be contiguous, but this is not true—originally, it was legal but advised against. Later, this practice became so out of favor that many hardware devices would not support it. Today, now that classless addressing and CIDR are standard, noncontiguous masks are simply illegal.*

IP Default Subnet Masks for Address Classes A, B, and C

In order to better understand how subnets divide a Class A, B, or C network, let's look at how the Class A, B, and C networks are represented in a subnetted environment. This might seem unnecessary if you aren't planning to create subnets, but the fact is, once subnetting became popular, most operating systems, networking hardware, and software assumed that subnetting would be used. Even if you decide not to subnet, you may need to express your unsubnetted network using a subnet mask.

In essence, a nonsubnetted Class A, B, or C network can be considered the default for the more general, custom-subnetted network. You can think of a nonsubnetted network as being the case where you choose to divide the host ID so that exactly zero bits are used for the subnet ID, and all the bits are used for the host ID. This default case is the basis for the more practical subnetting you will examine shortly.

As is always the case, the subnet mask for a default, unsubnetted Class A, B, or C network has ones for each bit that is used for the network ID or subnet ID and zeros for the host ID bits. Of course, I just said you aren't subnetting, so there *are* no subnet ID bits! Thus, the subnet mask for this default case has ones for the network ID portion and zeros for the host ID portion. This is called the *default subnet mask* for each of the IP address classes.

Since Class A, B, and C divide the network ID from the host ID on octet boundaries, the subnet mask will always have all ones or all zeros in an octet. Therefore, the default subnet masks will always have 255s or 0s when expressed in decimal notation. Table 18-2 summarizes the default subnet masks for each of the classes. They are also shown graphically in Figure 18-4.

Table 18-2: Default Subnet Masks for Class A, Class B, and Class C Networks

IP Address Class	Total # of Bits for Network ID/Host ID	Default Subnet Mask			
		First Octet	Second Octet	Third Octet	Fourth Octet
Class A	8/24	11111111 (255)	00000000 (0)	00000000 (0)	00000000 (0)
Class B	16/16	11111111 (255)	11111111 (255)	00000000 (0)	00000000 (0)
Class C	24/8	11111111 (255)	11111111 (255)	11111111 (255)	00000000 (0)

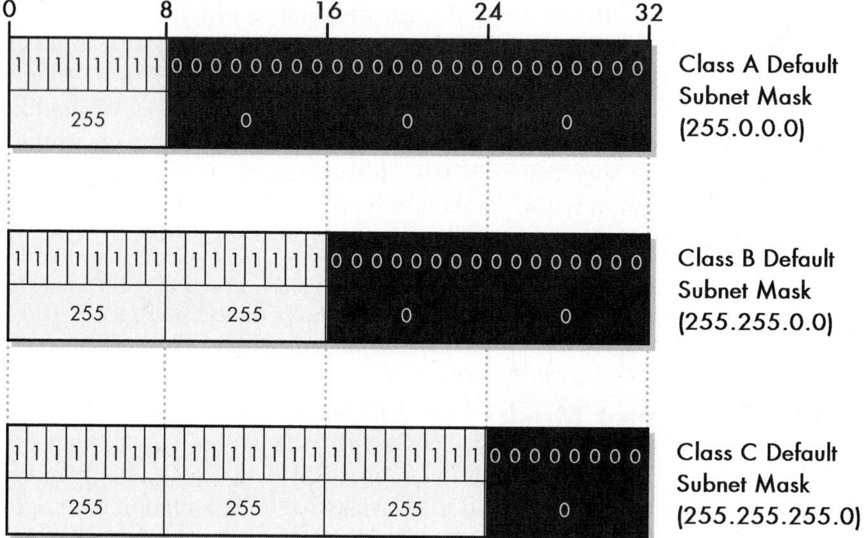

Figure 18-4: Default subnet masks for Class A, Class B, and Class C networks

Thus, the three default subnet masks are 255.0.0.0 for Class A, 255.255.0.0 for Class B, and 255.255.255.0 for Class C.

While all default subnet masks use only 255 and 0, not all subnet masks with 255 and 0 are defaults. There are a small number of custom subnets that divide on octet boundaries as well. These are as follows:

255.255.0.0 This is the default mask for Class B, but can also be the custom subnet mask for dividing a Class A network using 8 bits for the subnet ID (leaving 16 bits for the host ID).

255.255.255.0 This is the default subnet mask for Class C, but can be a custom Class A with 16 bits for the subnet ID *or* a Class B with 8 bits for the subnet ID.

KEY CONCEPT Each of the three IP unicast and broadcast address classes, A, B, and C, has a *default subnet mask* defined that has a one for each bit of the class's network ID, a zero for each bit of its host ID, and no subnet ID bits. The three default subnet masks are 255.0.0.0 for Class A, 255.255.0.0 for Class B, and 255.255.255.0 for Class C.

IP Custom Subnet Masks

A default subnet mask doesn't really represent subnetting because you are assigning zero bits to the subnet ID. To do real subnetting, you must dedicate at least one of the bits of the presubnetted host ID to the subnet ID.

Since you can choose the dividing point between subnet ID and host ID to suit the network, this is sometimes called *customized subnetting*. The subnet mask that you use when creating a customized subnet is, in turn, called a *custom subnet mask*. The custom subnet mask is used by network hardware to determine how you have decided to divide the subnet ID from the host ID in the network.

Deciding How Many Subnet Bits to Use

The key decision in customized subnetting is how many bits to take from the host ID portion of the IP address to put into the subnet ID. You'll recall that the number of subnets possible on the network is two to the power of the number of bits you use to express the subnet ID, and the number of hosts possible per subnet is two to the power of the number of bits left in the host ID (less two, as I explain later in this section).

Thus, the decision of how many bits to use for each of the subnet ID and host ID represents a fundamental trade-off in subnet addressing:

- Each bit taken from the host ID for the subnet ID doubles the number of subnets that are possible in the network.
- Each bit taken from the host ID for the subnet ID (approximately) halves the number of hosts that are possible within each subnet on the network.

For example, say you start with a Class B network with the network address 154.71.0.0. Since this is Class B, 16 bits are for the network ID (154.71) and 16 are for the host ID. In the default case, there are no subnets and 65,534 hosts total. To subnet this network, you can use the following:

- One bit for the subnet ID and 15 bits for the host ID. If you do this, then the total number of subnets is 2^1, or 2. The first subnet is 0, and the second is 1. The number of hosts available for each subnet is $2^{15}-2$, or 32,766.
- Two bits for the subnet ID and 14 for the host ID. In this case, you double the number of subnets. You now have 2^2, or 4 subnets: 00, 01, 10, and 11 (subnets 0, 1, 2, and 3). But the number of hosts is now only $2^{14}-2$, or 16,382.
- Any combination of bits that add up to 16 as long as they allow you at least two hosts per subnet: 4 and 12, 5 and 11, and so on.

The way you decide to divide the classful host ID into subnet ID and host ID bits is the key design decision in subnetting. You make your choice based on the number of subnets in the network, and also on the maximum number of hosts that need to be assigned to each subnet in the network. For example, if you have 10 total subnets for your Class B network, you need 4 bits to represent this, because 2^4 is 16 while 2^3 is only 8. This leaves 12 bits for the host ID, for a maximum of 4,094 hosts per subnet.

However, suppose instead that you have 20 subnets. If so, 4 bits for subnet ID won't suffice; you need 5 bits (2^5=32). This means that you now have only 11 bits for the host ID, for a maximum of 2,046 hosts per subnet. (Step 2 of the practical subnetting example in Chapter 19 discusses these decisions in more detail.)

Now if you have 20 subnets and also need a maximum of 3,000 hosts per subnet, you have a problem. You need 5 bits to express 20 different subnets, but you need 12 bits to express the number 3,000 for the host ID. That's 17 bits—too many. What's the solution? You might be able to shuffle your physical networks so that you only have 16. If not, you need a second Class B network.

KEY CONCEPT The fundamental trade-off in subnetting is that each addition of a bit to the subnet ID (and thus, subtraction of that bit from the host ID) doubles the number of subnets, and approximately halves the number of hosts in each subnet. Each subtraction of a bit from the subnet ID (and addition of that bit to the host ID) does the opposite.

Determining the Custom Subnet Mask

Once you determine how many bits to devote to the subnet and host IDs, you can determine the subnet mask. You begin with the default subnet mask in binary for the appropriate class of the network. You start with the leftmost zero in that mask and change as many bits to one as you have dedicated to the subnet ID, at which point you can express the subnet mask in dotted decimal form. Figure 18-5 shows how the custom subnet mask can be determined for each of the subnetting options of a Class C network in both binary and decimal.

Consider the Class C network 200.13.94.0 in Figure 18-5. There are eight bits in the original host ID, which gives you six different subnetting options (you can't use seven or eight bits for the subnet ID, for reasons I will discuss shortly). Suppose you use three of these for the subnet ID, leaving five for the host ID. To determine the custom subnet mask, you start with the Class C default subnet mask:

11111111 11111111 11111111 00000000

You then change the first three zeros to ones, to get the custom subnet mask:

11111111 11111111 11111111 **111**00000

In dotted decimal format, this is 255.255.255.224.

NOTE *Once you've made the choice of how to subnet, you determine the custom subnet mask by starting with the default subnet mask for the network and changing each subnet ID bit from a zero to a one.*

NOTE *In regular subnetting, the choice of how many bits to use for the subnet ID is fixed for the entire network. You can't have subnets of different sizes—they must all be the same. Thus, the number of hosts in the largest subnet will dictate how many bits you need for the host ID. This means that in the previous case, if you had a strange configuration where 19 subnets had only 100 hosts each but the 20th had 3,000, you would have a problem. If this were the case, you could solve the problem easily by dividing that one oversized subnet into two or more smaller ones. An enhancement to subnetting called Variable Length Subnet Masking (VLSM) was created in large part to remove this restriction. VLSM is described later in the chapter.*

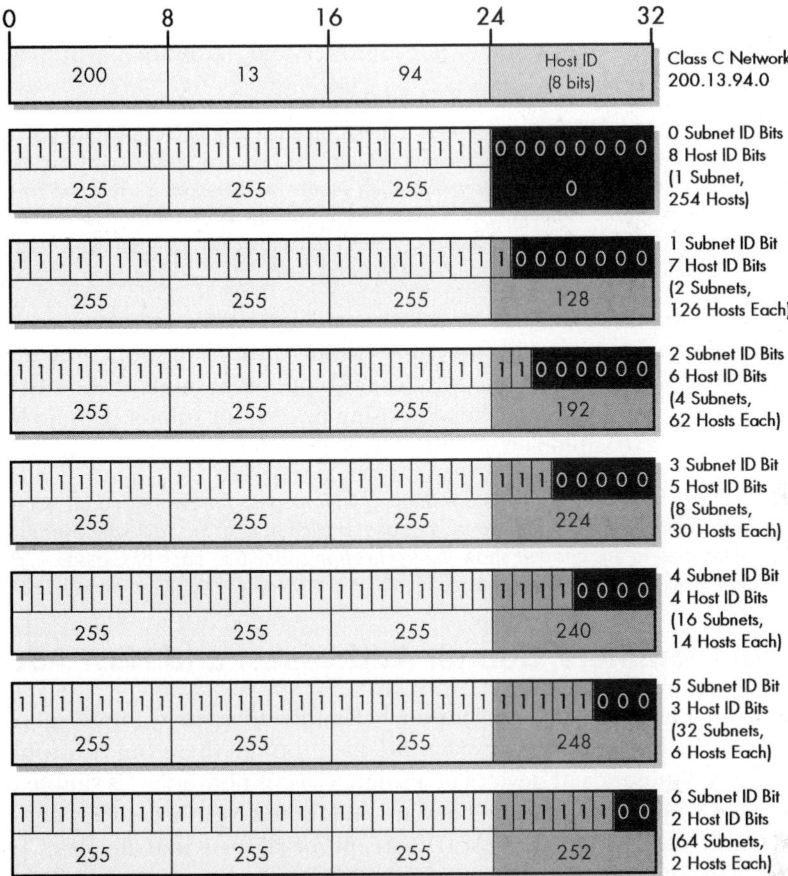

Figure 18-5: Custom subnet masks for Class C networks *Since there are host ID bits in a Class C network address, there are six different ways that the network can be subnetted. Each corresponds to a different custom subnet mask, which is created by changing the allocated subnet ID bits from zero to one.*

Subtracting Two from the Number of Hosts per Subnet and (Possibly) Subnets per Network

You've seen how you must subtract two from the number of hosts allowed in each network in regular classful addressing. This is necessary because two host IDs in each subnet have special meanings: the all-zeros host ID (for "this network") and the all-ones host ID (for broadcasts to all hosts on the network). These restrictions apply to each subnet under subnetting, too, which is why you must continue to subtract two from the number of hosts per subnet. (This is also why dividing the eight host ID bits of a Class C network into seven bits for subnet ID and one bit for host ID is meaningless: It leaves $2^1-2 = 0$ hosts per subnet, which is not particularly useful.)

A similar issue occurs with the subnet ID as well. When subnetting was originally defined in RFC 950, the standard specifically excluded the use of the all-zeros and all-ones subnets. This was due to concern that routers might become confused by these cases. A later standard, RFC 1812, "Requirements for IP Version 4 Routers," removed this restriction in 1995. Thus, modern hardware now has no problem with the all-zeros or all-ones subnets, but some very old hardware may still balk at it.

KEY CONCEPT The number of hosts allowed in each subnet is the binary power of the number of host ID bits remaining after subnetting, less two. The reduction by two occurs because the all-zeros and all-ones host IDs within each subnet are reserved for two special meaning addresses: to refer to the subnetwork itself and to refer to its local broadcast address. In some implementations, the number of subnets is also reduced by two because the all-zeros and all-ones subnet IDs were originally not allowed to be used.

For this reason, you will sometimes see discussions of subnetting that exclude these cases. When that is done, you lose two potential subnets: the all-zeros and all-ones subnets. If you do this, then choosing one bit for subnet ID is no longer valid, as it yields $2^1-2=0$ subnets. You must choose two bits if you need two subnets.

NOTE *In this book, I assume you are dealing with modern hardware and do not exclude the all-zeros and all-ones subnets, but I do try to make explicit note of this fact wherever relevant. Summary tables later in this chapter show the trade-off in subnetting each of Classes A, B, and C, and the subnet mask for each of the choices.*

IP Subnet Identifiers, Subnet Addresses, and Host Addresses

The main advantage that conventional classful addressing without subnets offers over subnets is simplicity. For example, even though there can be problems with managing thousands of devices in a single Class B network, it is simple to assign addresses within the network: They are all lumped together, so any combination of bits can be used within the host ID (except for all-zeros and all-ones).

When you subnet, however, you create a two-level structure within the classful host ID: subnet ID and host ID. This means you must choose IP addresses for devices more carefully. In theory, you are selecting subnets to correspond to the physical networks within the organization, so you want to assign IP addresses in a way that is consistent with the physical network structure.

Subnet Identifiers

Once you decide how many subnets you will have, you need to identify the subnets and determine their addresses. You begin with the *subnet identifier*, the *subnet ID* of any subnets on our network. Subnets are numbered starting with zero and increasing up to one less than the maximum number of subnets, which is a function of how many bits are in the subnet ID. (If the all-zero and all-ones subnet IDs are excluded, as specified in RFC 950, then the first subnet ID is one.)

Of course, you may not need all of the subnets that can be defined. For example, if you have 20 subnets, you need five bits for the subnet identifier, which allows a theoretical maximum of 32 subnets. You would use only subnets 0 to 19; 20 through 31 would be reserved for future use. These subnets could be expressed either in decimal form (0, 1, 2 . . . up to 19) or in binary (00000, 00001, 00010, and so on, up to 10011).

Subnet Addresses

For each subnet, you can also determine the *subnet address*. To do this, you start with the IP address for the overall network, which has all zeros in the classful host ID field (8 bits, 16 bits, or 24 bits). You then insert the subnet ID for a particular subnet into the designated subnet bits.

For example, to subnet the Class B network 154.71.0.0 shown in Figure 18-2, in which you use five subnet ID bits, you start with the following network IP address, with the subnet ID bits highlighted:

10011010 01000111 **00000**000 00000000

To find the address of say, subnet 11, you substitute 01011 for these bits, leaving the host ID bits zero, as follows:

10011010 01000111 **01011**000 00000000

You can then convert this from binary form to dotted decimal, resulting in a subnet address of 154.71.**88**.0.

KEY CONCEPT The *subnet identifier* of a subnet is just its subnet ID. The subnet address of a subnet is determined by substituting its subnet ID into the subnet bits of the overall network address.

When you look at subnet addressing, especially when you substitute subnet IDs in sequence, a pattern becomes immediately visible. The first subnet address is always the address of the overall network, because the subnet ID is all zeros. Then you find the second subnet address in decimal form by adding a specific multiple of two to one of the octets. The third address is then found by adding this same number to the second address, and so on.

In fact, the decimal value of each subnet address can be expressed as a formula, based on the class of the original network and the number of bits being used for the subnet ID. For example, consider a Class B network with the overall address of x.y.0.0 (it doesn't matter what x and y are for these purposes). Now say you are using two bits for the subnet ID. You have four subnet addresses here:

- The address of subnet 0 will be the same as the network address: x.y.0.0.
- The address of subnet 1 will be found by substituting 01 for the first two bits of the third octet. This yields an address of x.y.01000000.0000000, or x.y.64.0 in straight decimal.
- Subnet 2's address is found by substituting 10 for the subnet ID bits, so it is x.y.10000000.0000000, or x.y.128.0 in straight decimal.
- Subnet 3's address will be x.y.192.0.

So, the formula in this case for subnet *N* is x.y.*N**64.0. If you use five bits for a subnet, the formula is x.y.*N**8.0. As you saw earlier, the subnet address for subnet 11 in network 154.71.0.0 is 154.71.**88**.0. I have shown the formulas for all of the combinations of subnet ID and host ID size in the subnetting summary tables (Tables 18-3, 18-4, and 18-5). These formulas can be a real time-saver once you become more familiar with subnetting.

Host Addresses Within Each Subnet

Once you know the subnet address for a particular subnet, you assign IP addresses by plugging in values into the remaining host ID bits. You skip the all-zeros value, so the first host in the subnet has all zeros for the host ID except for a one in the right-most bit position. Then the next host has all zeros except for "10" at the end (2 in decimal). You can do this all the way up to one less than the all-ones value. Again, you then convert each IP address from binary to decimal.

NOTE *You can find exactly these details in Chapter 19's coverage of practical subnetting.*

IP Subnetting Summary Tables for Class A, Class B, and Class C Networks

Since there are only a few options for how to subnet Class A, Class B, and Class C networks, I list the options for each class in summary Tables 18-3 through 18-5. These tables can help you quickly decide how many bits to use for subnet ID and host ID, and then what the subnet mask is for their selection. They also summarize nicely what I've discussed so far in this chapter.

Each row of each table shows one possible subnetting option for that class, including the number of bits for each of the subnet ID and host ID, and the number of subnets and hosts based on the number of bits. I then show the subnet mask in binary and decimal form, as well as in CIDR notation (covered in Chapter 20). Finally, I include the formula for calculating the addresses for each subnet under each of the options.

A few additional explanatory notes are in order regarding these tables:

- The values for the number of subnets per network assume that the all-zeros and all-ones subnets are allowed. If not, you must subtract two from those figures. This also means that the option using only one bit for the subnet ID becomes invalid, and the subnet address formulas no longer work as shown.
- The number of hosts per subnet excludes the all-zeros and all-ones cases, so it is two to the power of the number of host ID bits, less two.
- The first row of each table shows the default case where the number of subnet bits is zero, and thus the subnet mask is the default subnet mask for the class.
- In the subnet mask for all options but the default, I have highlighted the portion of the subnet mask corresponding to the subnet ID, for clarity. This has been done for each individual bit of the binary mask, and for each octet in the dotted decimal representation of the mask where part of the subnet ID is found.
- In looking at these tables, you will see that not all of the divisions make a great deal of sense in the real world, though you might be surprised. For example, at first glance, it seems silly to think that you might want to assign 14 bits of a Class B host ID to the subnet ID and leave 2 bits for the host ID—what sort of real network has 16,384 subnets with two hosts on each? Yet, some larger

Internet service companies may indeed require thousands of tiny subnets when setting up connections between routers or between their core network and their customers.

- The subnet address formulas in the last column of each table show the address for subnet *N* (numbering from zero up to one less than the maximum number of subnets). See the end of step 4 in the step-by-step subnetting discussion (Chapter 19) for a full explanation of how these formulas work.

Table 18-3: Subnetting Summary Table for Class A Networks

# of Subnet ID Bits	# of Host ID Bits	# of Subnets per Network	# of Hosts per Subnet	Subnet Mask (Binary/ Dotted Decimal)	Subnet Mask (Slash/ CIDR Notation)	Subnet Address #N Formula (N=0, 1, # of Subnets -1)
0 (Default)	**24**	1	16,277,214	11111111.00000000 .00000000.00000000 255.0.0.0	/8	—
1	**23**	2	8,388,606	11111111.**1**0000000 .00000000.00000000 255.**128**.0.0	/9	x.N*128.0.0
2	**22**	4	4,194,302	11111111.**11**000000 .00000000.00000000 255.**192**.0.0	/10	x.N*64.0.0
3	**21**	8	2,097,150	11111111.**111**00000 .00000000.00000000 255.**224**.0.0	/11	x.N*32.0.0
4	**20**	16	1,048,574	11111111.**1111**0000 .00000000.00000000 255.**240**.0.0	/12	x.N*16.0.0
5	**19**	32	524,286	11111111.**11111**000 .00000000.00000000 255.**248**.0.0	/13	x.N*8.0.0
6	**18**	64	262,142	11111111.**111111**00 .00000000.00000000 255.**252**.0.0	/14	x.N*4.0.0
7	**17**	128	131,070	11111111.**1111111**0 .00000000.00000000 255.**254**.0.0	/15	x.N*2.0.0
8	**16**	256	65,534	11111111.**11111111** .00000000.00000000 255.**255**.0.0	/16	x.N.0.0
9	**15**	512	32,766	11111111.**11111111** **.1**0000000.00000000 255.**255.128**.0	/17	x.N/2.(N%2)*128.0
10	**14**	1,024	16,382	11111111.**11111111** **.11**000000.00000000 255.**255.192**.0	/18	x.N/4.(N%4)*64.0

(continued)

Table 18-3: Subnetting Summary Table for Class A Networks (continued)

# of Subnet ID Bits	# of Host ID Bits	# of Subnets per Network	# of Hosts per Subnet	Subnet Mask (Binary/ Dotted Decimal)	Subnet Mask (Slash/ CIDR Notation)	Subnet Address #N Formula (N=0, 1, # of Subnets -1)
11	13	2,048	8,190	11111111.**11111111** .**111**00000.00000000 255.**255.224**.0	/19	x.N/8.(N%8)*32.0
12	12	4,096	4,094	11111111.**11111111** .**1111**0000.00000000 255.**255.240**.0	/20	x.N/16.(N%16)*16.0
13	11	8,192	2,046	11111111.**11111111** .**11111**000.00000000 255.**255.248**.0	/21	x.N/32.(N%32)*8.0
14	10	16,384	1,022	11111111.**11111111** .**111111**00.00000000 255.**255.252**.0	/22	x.N/64.(N%64)*4.0
15	9	32,768	510	11111111.**11111111** .**1111111**0.00000000 255.**255.254**.0	/23	x.N/128.(N%128)*2.0
16	8	65,536	254	11111111.**11111111** .**11111111**.00000000 255.**255.255**.0	/24	x.N/256.N%256.0
17	7	131,072	126	11111111.**11111111** .**11111111**.**1**0000000 255.**255.255.128**	/25	x.N/512. (N/2)%256.(N%2)*128
18	6	262,144	62	11111111.**11111111** .**11111111**.**11**000000 255.**255.255.192**	/26	x.N/1024. (N/4)%256.(N%4)*64
19	5	524,288	30	11111111.**11111111** .**11111111**.**111**00000 255.**255.255.224**	/27	x.N/2048. (N/8)%256.(N%8)*32
20	4	1,048,576	14	11111111.**11111111** .**11111111**.**1111**0000 255.**255.255.240**	/28	x.N/4096. (N/16)%256.(N%16)*16
21	3	2,097,152	6	11111111.**11111111** .**11111111**.**11111**000 255.**255.255.248**	/29	x.N/8192. (N/32)%256.(N%32)*8
22	2	4,194,304	2	11111111.**11111111** .**11111111**.**111111**00 255.**255.255.252**	/30	x.N/16384. (N/64)%256.(N%64)*4

Table 18-4: Subnetting Summary Table for Class B Networks

# of Subnet ID Bit	# of Host ID Bits	# of Subnets per Network	# of Hosts per Subnet	Subnet Mask (Binary/ Dotted Decimal)	Subnet Mask (Slash/ CIDR Notation)	Subnet Address #N Formula (N=0, 1, # of Subnets -1)
0 (Default)	16	1	65,534	11111111.11111111 .00000000.00000000 255.255.0.0	/16	-
1	15	2	32,766	11111111.11111111 .**1**0000000.00000000 255.255.**128**.0	/17	x.y.N*128.0
2	14	4	16,382	11111111.11111111. **11**000000.00000000 255.255.**192**.0	/18	x.y.N*64.0
3	13	8	8,190	11111111.11111111 .**111**00000.00000000 255.255.**224**.0	/19	x.y.N*32.0
4	12	16	4,094	11111111.11111111 .**1111**0000.00000000 255.255.**240**.0	/20	x.y.N*16.0
5	11	32	2,046	11111111.11111111 .**11111**000.00000000 255.255.**248**.0	/21	x.y.N*8.0
6	10	64	1,022	11111111.11111111 .**111111**00.00000000 255.255.**252**.0	/22	x.y.N*4.0
7	9	128	510	11111111.11111111 .**1111111**0.00000000 255.255.**254**.0	/23	x.y.N*2.0
8	8	256	254	11111111.11111111 .**11111111**.00000000 255.255.**255**.0	/24	x.y.N.0
9	7	512	126	11111111.11111111 .**11111111**.**1**0000000 255.255.**255**.**128**	/25	x.y.N/2.(N%2)*128
10	6	1,024	62	11111111.11111111 .**11111111**.**11**000000 255.255.**255**.**192**	/26	x.y.N/4.(N%4)*64
11	5	2,048	30	11111111.11111111 .**11111111**.**111**00000 255.255.**255**.**224**	/27	x.x.N/8.(N%8)*32
12	4	4,096	14	11111111.11111111 .**11111111**.**1111**0000 255.255.**255**.**240**	/28	x.y.N/16.(N%16)*16

(continued)

Table 18-4: Subnetting Summary Table for Class B Networks (continued)

# of Subnet ID Bit	# of Host ID Bits	# of Subnets per Network	# of Hosts per Subnet	Subnet Mask (Binary/ Dotted Decimal)	Subnet Mask (Slash/ CIDR Notation)	Subnet Address #N Formula (N=0, 1, # of Subnets -1)
13	3	8,192	6	11111111.11111111 .**11111111.11111**000 255.255.**255.248**	/29	x.y.N/32.(N%32)*8
14	2	16,384	2	11111111.11111111 .**11111111.111111**00 255.255.**255.252**	/30	x.y.N/64.(N%64)*4

Table 18-5: Subnetting Summary Table for Class C Networks

# of Subnet ID Bit	# of Host ID Bits	# of Subnets per Network	# of Hosts per Subnet	Subnet Mask (Binary/ Dotted Decimal)	Subnet Mask (Slash/ CIDR Notation)	Subnet Address #N Formula (N=0, 1, # of Subnets-1)
0 (Default)	8	1	254	11111111.11111111 .11111111.00000000 255.255.255.0	/24	—
1	7	2	126	11111111.11111111 .11111111.**1**0000000 255.255.255.**128**	/25	x.y.z.N*128
2	6	4	62	11111111.11111111 .11111111.**11**000000 255.255.255.**192**	/26	x.y.z.N*64
3	5	8	30	11111111.11111111 .11111111.**111**00000 255.255.255.**224**	/27	x.y.z.N*32
4	4	16	14	11111111.11111111 .11111111.**1111**0000 255.255.255.**240**	/28	x.y.z.N*16
5	3	32	6	11111111.11111111 .11111111.**11111**000 255.255.255.**248**	/29	x.y.z.N*8
6	2	64	2	11111111.11111111 .11111111.**111111**00 255.255.255.**252**	/30	x.y.z.N*4

IP Variable Length Subnet Masking (VLSM)

The main weakness with conventional subnetting is that the subnet ID represents only *one* additional hierarchical level in how IP addresses are interpreted and used for routing.

It may seem greedy to look at subnetting and say, "What, only *one* additional level?" However, in large networks, the need to divide the entire network into only one level of subnetworks doesn't represent the best use of the IP address block.

Furthermore, you have already seen that since the subnet ID is the same length throughout the network, you can have problems if you have subnetworks with very different numbers of hosts on them. The subnet ID must be chosen based on whichever subnet has the greatest number of hosts, even if most of subnets have far fewer. This is inefficient even in small networks, and can result in the need to use extra addressing blocks while wasting many of the addresses in each block.

For example, consider a relatively small company with a Class C network, 201.45.222.0/24. The administrators have six subnetworks in their network. The first four subnets (S1, S2, S3, and S4) are relatively small, containing only 10 hosts each. However, one of them (S5) is for their production floor and has 50 hosts, and the last (S6) is their development and engineering group, which has 100 hosts. The total number of hosts needed is thus 190.

Without subnetting, the company has enough hosts in the Class C network to handle them all. However, when they try to subnet, they have a big problem. In order to have six subnets, they need to use three bits for the subnet ID. This leaves only five bits for the host ID, which means every subnet has the identical capacity of 30 hosts, as shown in Figure 18-6. This is enough for the smaller subnets but not enough for the larger ones. The only solution with conventional subnetting, other than shuffling the physical subnets, is to get another Class C block for the two big subnets and use the original for the four small ones. But this is expensive and means wasting hundreds of IP addresses!

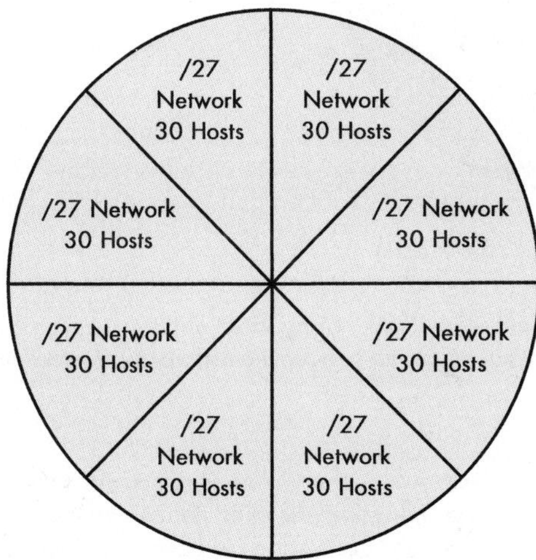

Figure 18-6: Class C (/24) network split into eight conventional subnets *With traditional subnetting, all subnets must be the same size, which creates problems when there are some subnets that are much larger than others. Contrast this with Figure 18-7.*

The Solution: Variable Length Subnet Masking

The solution is an enhancement to the basic subnet addressing scheme called *Variable Length Subnet Masking (VLSM)*. The idea is that you subnet the network and then subnet the subnets just the way you originally subnetted the network. In fact, you can do this multiple times, creating subnets of subnets of subnets, as many times as you need (subject to how many bits you have in the host ID of your address block).

It is possible to choose to apply this multiple-level splitting to only some of the subnets, thereby allowing you to selectively cut the IP address pie so that some of the slices are bigger than others. This means that the company in the previous example could create six subnets to match the needs of its networks, as shown in Figure 18-7.

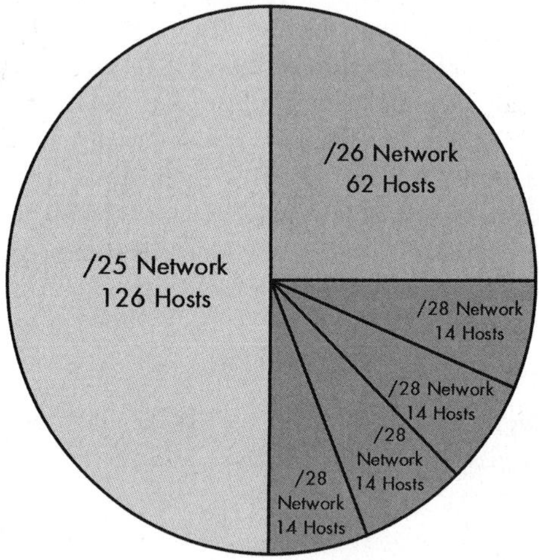

Figure 18-7: Class C (/24) network split using VLSM *Using VLSM, an organization can divide its IP network multiple times to create subnets that match the size requirements of its physical networks much better. Contrast this with Figure 18-6.*

> **KEY CONCEPT** *Variable Length Subnet Masking (VLSM)* is a technique for which subnetting is performed multiple times in iteration to allow a network to be divided into a hierarchy of subnetworks that vary in size. This allows an organization to better match the size of its subnets to the requirements of its networks.

Multiple-Level Subnetting Using VLSM

VLSM subnetting is done the same way as regular subnetting; it just involves extra levels of subnetting hierarchy. To implement it, you first subnet the network into large subnets and then further break down one or more of the subnets as required. You add bits to the subnet mask for each of the sub-subnets and sub-sub-subnets to reflect their smaller size.

In VLSM, the slash notation of classless addressing is commonly used instead of binary subnet masks (it works very much like CIDR), so that's what I will use.

NOTE *If you're feeling a bit uncomfortable with how subnetting works, consider reading the chapter on practical subnetting (Chapter 19) before proceeding with the VLSM example that follows.*

For example, consider the class C network, 201.45.222.0/24. You do three subnettings as follows (see Figure 18-8 for an illustration of the process).

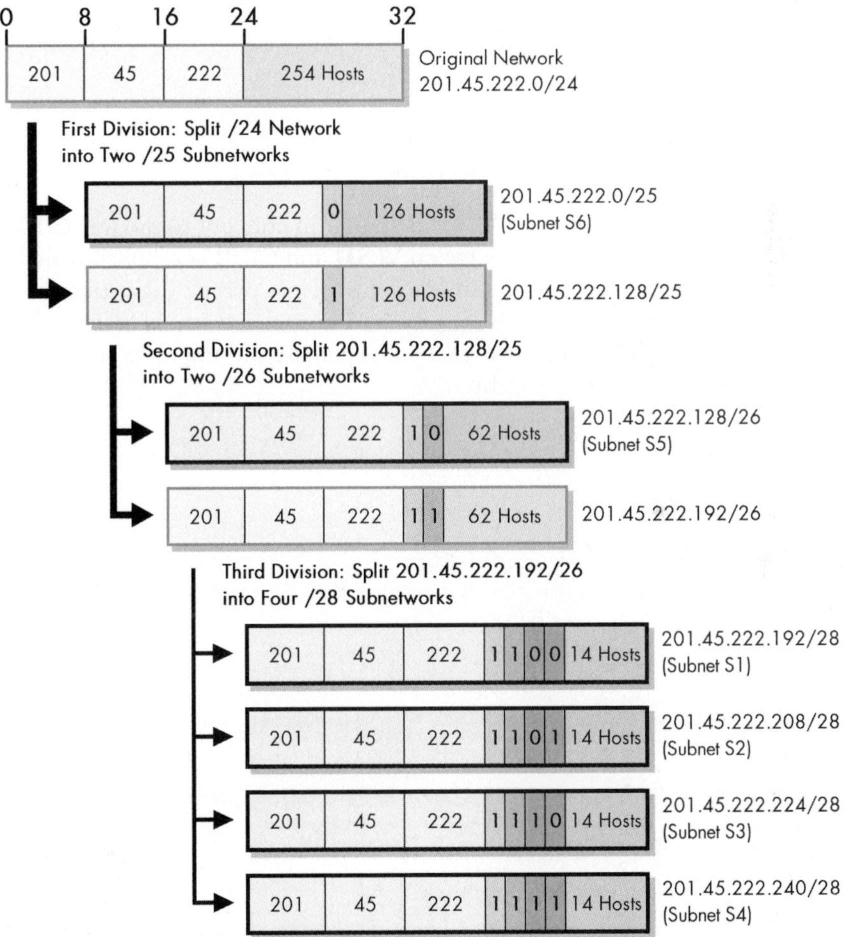

Figure 18-8: VLSM example *This diagram illustrates the example described in the text, of a Class C (/24) network divided using three hierarchical levels. It is first divided into two subnets; one subnet is divided into two sub-subnets; and one sub-subnet is divided into four sub-sub-subnets. The resulting six subnets, shown with thick black borders, have a maximum capacity of 126, 62, 14, 14, 14, and 14 hosts.*

- You first do an initial subnetting by using one bit for the subnet ID, leaving you seven bits for the host ID and two subnets: 201.45.222.0/25 and 201.45.222.128/25. Each of these can have a maximum of 126 hosts. You set aside the first of these for subnet S6 and its 100 hosts.

- You take the second subnet, 201.45.222.128/25, and subnet it further into two sub-subnets by taking one bit from the seven bits left in the host ID. This gives you the sub-subnets 201.45.222.128/26 and 201.45.222.192/26, each of which can have 62 hosts. You set aside the first of these for subnet S5 and its 50 hosts.
- You take the second sub-subnet, 201.45.222.192/26, and subnet it further into four sub-sub-subnets. You take two bits from the six that are left in the host ID, which gives you four sub-sub-subnets that each can have a maximum of 14 hosts. These are used for S1, S2, S3, and S4.

Although I've chosen these numbers so that they work out perfectly, you should get the picture. VLSM greatly improves both the flexibility and the efficiency of subnetting.

NOTE *In order to use VLSM, routers that support VLSM-capable routing protocols must be employed. VLSM also requires more care in how routing tables are constructed to ensure that there is no ambiguity in how to interpret an address in the network.*

As I mentioned earlier, VLSM is similar in concept to the way CIDR is performed. The difference between VLSM and CIDR is primarily one of focus. VLSM deals with subnets of a single network in a private organization. CIDR takes the concept you just saw in VLSM to the Internet as a whole by changing how organizational networks are allocated, replacing the single-level classful hierarchy with a multiple-layer hierarchy.

19

IP SUBNETTING: PRACTICAL SUBNET DESIGN AND ADDRESS DETERMINATION EXAMPLE

When educators ask students what they consider to be the most confusing aspect in learning about networking, many say that it is IP address subnetting. While subnetting isn't all that difficult in concept, it can be a bit mind-boggling, in part due to the manipulations of binary numbers required. Many people understand the ideas behind subnetting but find it hard to follow the actual steps required to subnet a network.

For this reason, even though I explained the concepts behind subnetting in detail in the previous chapter, I felt it would be valuable to have another that provides a step-by-step look at how to perform custom subnetting. This chapter divides subnetting into five relatively straightforward stages that cover determining requirements; deciding how many bits to use for the subnet ID and host ID; and then determining important numbers such as the subnet mask, subnet addresses, and host addresses.

My focus here is on showing the practical "how" of subnetting. The topics work through two examples using a Class B and a Class C sample network to show you how subnetting is done, and I am explicit in showing how everything is calculated. This means the section is a bit number heavy. Also, I try not to duplicate conceptual issues covered in the previous section, though a certain amount of overlap does occur. Overall, if you are not familiar with how subnetting works at all, you will want to read the previous chapter first. I do refer to topics in that chapter where appropriate, especially the summary tables. Incidentally, I only cover conventional subnetting here, not Variable Length Subnet Masking (VLSM).

This section may serve as a useful refresher or summary of subnetting for someone who is already familiar with the basics but just wants to review the steps performed in subnetting. Again, bear in mind that subnetting is based on the older, classful IP addressing scheme, and today's Internet is classless, using Classless Inter-Domain Routing (CIDR; see Chapter 20).

NOTE *If in reading this chapter, you find yourself wanting to do binary-to-decimal conversions or binary math, remember that most versions of Windows (and many other operating systems) have a calculator program that incorporates scientific functions.*

IP Subnetting Step 1: Analyzing Requirements

When you are building or upgrading a network as a whole, the first step isn't buying hardware, or figuring out protocols, or even design. It's *requirements analysis,* the process of determining what it is the network needs to do. Without this foundation, you risk implementing a network that may perfectly match your design, but not meet the needs of your organization. The same rule applies to subnetting as well. Before you look at the gory details of host addresses and subnet masks, you must decide how to subnet the network. To do that, you must understand the requirements of the network.

Analyzing the requirements of the network for subnetting isn't difficult, because there are only a few issues that you need to consider. Since requirements analysis is usually done by asking questions, here's a list of the most important questions in analyzing subnetting requirements:

- What class is the IP address block?
- How many physical subnets are on the network today? (A *physical subnet* generally refers to a broadcast domain on a LAN—a set of hosts on a physical network bounded by routers.)
- Do you anticipate adding any more physical networks in the near future, and if so, how many?
- How many hosts do you have in the largest of the subnets today?
- How many hosts do you anticipate having in the largest subnet in the near future?

KEY CONCEPT To successfully subnet a network, you must begin by learning what the requirements of the network will be. The most important parameters to determine are the number of subnets required and the maximum number of hosts needed per subnet. Numbers should not be based on just present needs, but also take into account requirements anticipated in the near future.

The first question is important because everything in subnetting is based around dividing up a Class A, Class B, or Class C network, so you need to know which one you are dealing with. If you are in the process of designing a network from scratch and don't have a Class A, B, or C block yet, then you will determine which one you need based on the approximate size of the organization.

After that, you need to determine two key numbers: how many physical subnets you have and the maximum number of hosts per subnet. You need to know these not only for the present network, but for the *near future* as well. The current values for these two numbers represent how the network needs to be designed today. However, designing only for the present is not a good idea.

Suppose you have exactly four subnetworks in the network now. In theory, you could use only two bits for the subnet ID, since 2^2 equals 4. However, if the company were growing rapidly, this would be a poor choice. When you needed to add a fifth subnet, you would have a problem!

Similarly, consider the growth in the number of hosts in a subnet. If the current largest subnet has 60 hosts, you don't want six bits for the host ID, because that limits you to 62 hosts. You can divide large subnets into smaller ones, but this may just mean unnecessary additional work.

So what is the "near future?" The term is necessarily vague, because it depends on how far into the future the organization wants to look. On the one hand, planning for several years' growth can make sense, if you have enough IP addresses to do it. On the other, you don't want to plan too far out, since changes in the short term may cause you to completely redesign your network anyway.

IP Subnetting Step 2: Partitioning Network Address Host Bits

After you complete the brief requirements analysis, you should know the two critical parameters that you must have in order to subnet the network: the number of subnets required for the network and the maximum number of hosts per subnetwork. In using these figures to design the subnetted network, you will be faced with the key design decision in subnetting: how to divide the 8, 16, or 24 bits in the classful host ID into the subnet ID and host ID.

Put another way, you need to decide how many bits to steal from the host ID to use for the subnet ID. As I explained in the section on custom subnet masks in the previous chapter, the fundamental trade-off in choosing this number is as follows:

- Each bit taken from the host ID for the subnet ID doubles the number of subnets that are possible in the network.
- Each bit taken from the host ID for the subnet ID (approximately) halves the number of hosts that are possible within each subnet on the network.

There are six possible ways this decision can be made for a Class C network, as illustrated in Figure 19-1.

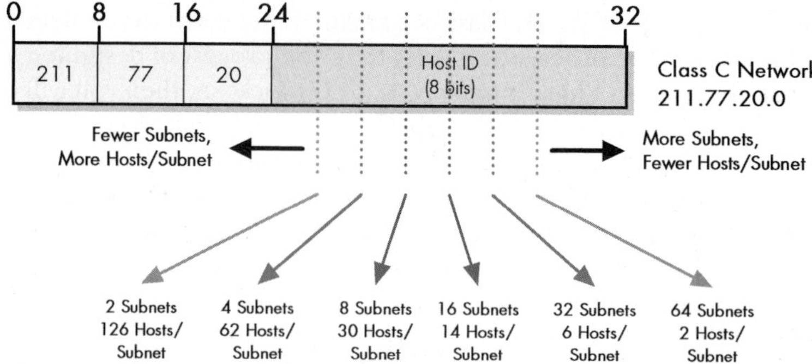

Figure 19-1: Subnetting design trade-off for Class C networks *This drawing shows the options for subnetting a Class C network. As you increase the number of bits for the host ID, you increase the number of subnets, but decrease the size of each.*

The relationship between the bits and the number of subnets and hosts is as follows:

- The number of subnets allowed in the network is two to the power of the number of subnet ID bits.
- The number of hosts allowed per subnet is two to the power of the number of host ID bits, less two.

You subtract two from the number of hosts in each subnet to exclude the special meaning cases where the host ID is all zeros or all ones. As I explained in the previous chapter, this exclusion was originally also applied to the subnet ID, but is no longer in newer systems.

To choose how many bits to use for the subnet, you could use trial and error. By this, I mean you could try to first calculate the number of subnets and hosts when you use one bit for the subnet ID and leave the rest for the host ID. You could then try with two bits for the subnet ID, and then try with three, and so on. This would be silly, however; it's time-consuming and makes it hard for you to choose the best option. There's an easier method: You can use the subnetting summary tables, presented in the previous chapter. They let you look at all the options, and you can usually see immediately the best one for you.

Class C Subnetting Design Example

Let's take an example. Suppose you have a Class C network, base address 211.77.20.0, with a total of seven subnets. The maximum number of hosts per subnet is 25. Looking at the subnetting summary table for Class C (Table 18-5 in Chapter 18), the answer is instantly clear: You need three bits for the subnet ID. Why? This allows you eight subnets and 30 hosts per subnet. If you try to choose two bits, you can't define enough subnets (only four). As Figure 19-2 shows, if you choose four bits for the subnet ID, then you can have only 14 hosts per subnet.

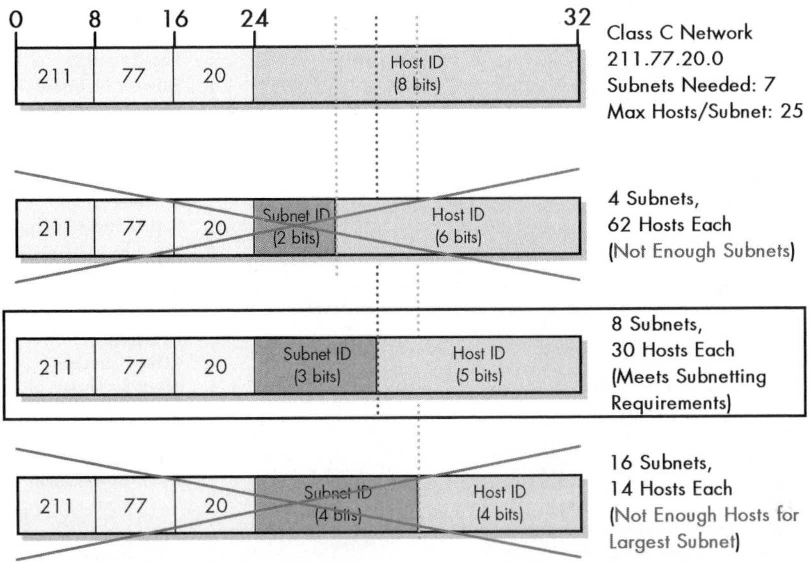

Figure 19-2: Example of Class C subnetting *In this particular example, where seven subnets are needed and 25 hosts are needed for the largest subnet, there is only one choice of subnet ID size that meets the requirements. It's an easy decision!*

Class B Subnetting Design Example

In some cases, especially with larger networks, you may have multiple choices. Consider, as a more interesting example, the larger Class B network 166.113.0.0, where you have a total of 15 subnets and the largest has 450 hosts. Examining the subnet summary table for Class B (Table 18-4 in Chapter 18) suggests four acceptable options, as shown in Figure 19-3.

In all four of these options, the number of subnets is equal to 15 or greater, and the number of hosts per subnet is over 450. So which option should you choose? Usually, you want to pick something in the middle. If you use four bits for the subnet ID, this gives you a maximum of only 16 subnets, which limits growth in the number of subnets, since you already have 15. The same applies to the choice of seven bits for the subnet ID, since you already have 450 hosts in one subnet now, and that limits you to 510. Thus, you probably want either five or six bits here. If you expect more growth in the number of hosts in the largest subnet, you should choose five bits; if you expect more growth in the number of subnets, you should choose six bits. If you're unsure, it's probably best to assume more growth in the number of hosts per subnet, so here you would choose five bits.

The converse problem may also occur: You may be in a position where there don't appear to be any options—no rows in the summary table match. For example, if the Class C example had 35 hosts in the largest subnet instead of 25, you would be out of luck, because there is no combination of subnet ID and host ID size that works. The same is true in the Class B example if you had 4,500 hosts in that big subnet instead of 450. In this situation, you would need to divide the large subnet into a smaller one, use more than one IP address block, or upgrade to a larger block.

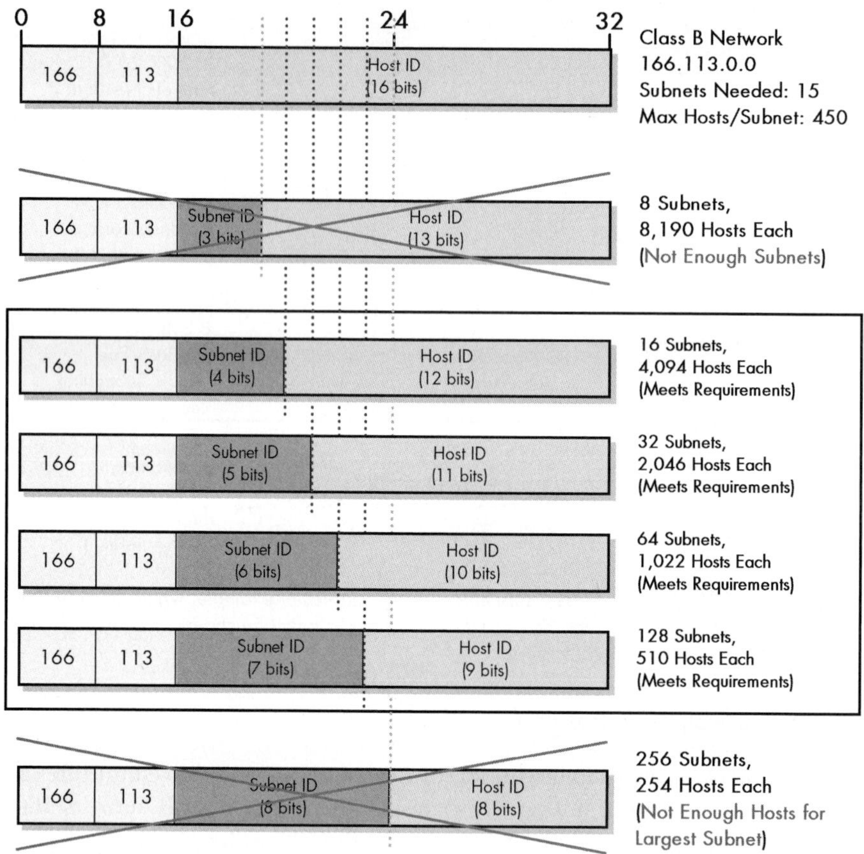

Figure 19-3: Example of Class B subnetting *This Class B network needs at least 15 subnets and must allow up to 450 hosts per subnet. Three subnet ID bits are too few, and eight bits means only 254 hosts per subnet, which is insufficient. This leaves four acceptable options, so you must choose wisely.*

> **KEY CONCEPT** If there is more than one combination of subnet ID and host ID sizes that will meet requirements, try to choose a middle-of-the-road option that best anticipates future growth requirements. If no combination meets the requirements, the requirements have to change!

IP Subnetting Step 3: Determining the Custom Subnet Mask

Once you have decided how many bits to use for the subnet ID and how many to leave for the host ID, you can determine the custom subnet mask for the network. Now, don't go running for cover on me. A lot of people's eyes glaze over at mention of the subnet mask, but it's really quite simple to figure out once you have done the homework in making the design decision you did in step 2. In fact, there are two ways of doing this; one is less work than the other, but they're both quite easy. I was going to call them the hard way and the easy way, but instead, I'll call them easy and easier.

Calculating the Custom Subnet Mask

Let's start with the easy method, in which you calculate the subnet mask in binary form from the information you already have about the network, and then convert the mask to decimal. To refresh your memory and guide the process, remember this: The subnet mask is a 32-bit binary number where a one represents each bit that is part of the network ID or subnet ID, and a zero represents each bit of the host ID.

Class C Custom Subnet Mask Calculation Example

Refer back to the Class C example in the previous section (Figure 19-2). Say you decided to use three bits for the subnet ID, leaving five bits for the host ID. Here are the steps you will follow to determine the custom subnet mask for this network (illustrated in Figure 19-4):

1. **Determine Default Subnet Mask** Each of Classes A, B, and C has a default subnet mask, which is the subnet mask for the network prior to subnetting. It has a one for each network ID bit and a zero for each host ID bit. For Class C, the subnet mask is 255.255.255.0. In binary, this is:

   11111111 11111111 11111111 00000000

2. **Change Leftmost Zeros to Ones for Subnet Bits** You have decided to use three bits for the subnet ID. The subnet mask must have a one for each of the network ID or subnet ID bits. The network ID bits are already one from the default subnet mask, so, you change the three *leftmost* zero bits in the default subnet mask from a 0 to 1, as shown in bold here. This results in the following custom subnet mask for the network:

   11111111 11111111 11111111 **111**00000

3. **Convert Subnet Mask to Dotted Decimal Notation** You take each of the octets in the subnet mask and convert it to decimal. The result is the custom subnet mask in the form you usually see it: 255.255.255.224.

4. **Express Subnet Mask in Slash Notation** Alternatively, you can express the subnet mask in *slash notation*. This is just a slash followed by the number of ones in the subnet mask. 255.255.255.224 is equivalent to /27.

Class B Custom Subnet Mask Calculation Example

Now let's do the same example with the Class B network (166.113.0.0) with five bits for the subnet ID (with a bit less narration this time; see Figure 19-5):

1. **Determine Default Subnet Mask** For Class B, the subnet mask is 255.255.0.0. In binary, this is:

   11111111 11111111 00000000 00000000

2. **Change Leftmost Zeros to Ones for Subnet Bits** If you use five bits for the subnet ID, you change the five leftmost zero bits from a 0 to 1, as shown in bold, to give you the binary custom subnet mask, as follows:

   11111111 11111111 **11111**000 00000000

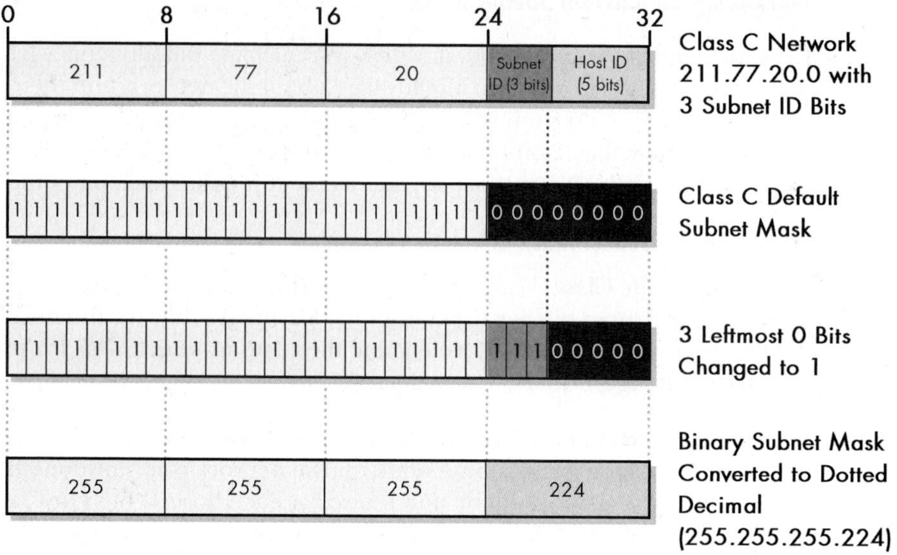

Figure 19-4: *Determining the custom subnet mask for a Class C network*

3. **Convert Subnet Mask to Dotted Decimal Notation** You take each of the octets in the subnet mask and convert it to decimal to give you a custom subnet mask of 255.255.**248**.0.
4. **Express Subnet Mask in Slash Notation** You can express the subnet mask 255.255.248.0 as /21, since it is 21 ones followed by 11 zeros. In other words, its prefix length is 21.

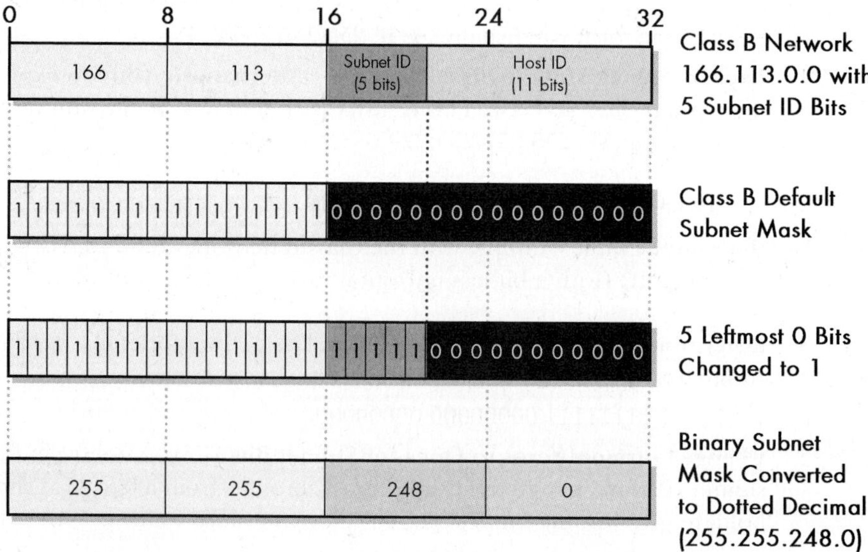

Figure 19-5: *Determining the custom subnet mask for a Class B network*

Determining the Custom Subnet Mask Using Subnetting Tables

Now, what could be easier than that? Well, you could simply refer to the subnetting summary tables, presented in Chapter 18. Find the table for the appropriate class, and then find the row that you selected in the previous step that matches the number of subnet ID bits you want to use. You can see the matching subnet mask right there.

(Hey, it's good to know how to do it yourself! You may not always have tables to refer to!)

IP Subnetting Step 4: Determining Subnet Identifiers and Subnet Addresses

The network ID assigned to the network applies to the entire network. This includes all subnets and all hosts in all subnets. Each subnet, however, needs to be identified with a unique *subnet identifier*, or *subnet ID*, so it can be differentiated from the other subnets in the network. This is the purpose of the subnet ID bits that you took from the host ID bits in subnetting. After you have identified each subnet, you need to determine the address of each subnet, so you can use this in assigning hosts specific IP addresses.

This is another step in subnetting that is not really hard to understand or do. The key to understanding how to determine subnet IDs and subnet addresses is to always work in binary form, and then convert to decimal later. You will also look at a shortcut for determining addresses in decimal directly, which is faster but less conceptually simple.

NOTE *I assume in this description that you will be using the all-zeros and all-ones subnet numbers. In the original RFC 950 subnetting system, those two subnets are not used, which changes most of the following calculations. See Chapter 18 for an explanation.*

You number the subnets starting with 0, and then 1, 2, 3, and so on, up to the highest subnet ID that you need. You determine the subnet IDs and addresses as follows:

Subnet ID This is just the subnet number, and it can be expressed in either binary or decimal form.

Subnet Address This is the address formed by taking the address of the network as a whole and substituting the (binary) subnet ID for the subnet ID bits. You need to do this in binary, but only for the octets where there are subnet ID bits; the ones where there are only network ID bits or only host ID bits are left alone.

Seem complicated? Let's go back to the examples, and you'll see that it really isn't.

Class C Subnet ID and Address Determination Example

You'll recall the Class C example network, 211.77.20.0. The network address in binary is as follows:

11010011 01001101 00010100 00000000

You are subnetting using three bits for the subnet ID, leaving five bits for the host ID. Now let's see the network address with the subnet bits in bold:

11010011 01001101 00010100 **000**00000

These are the bits that you substitute with the subnet ID for each subnet. Notice that since the first three octets contain network ID bits, and the network ID is the same for every subnet, they never change. You don't even really need to look at them in binary form, though for clarity, you will do so here.

Here's how you determine the subnet IDs and addresses, again, starting with 0 (see Figure 19-6):

Subnet 0 This has a subnet ID of 0, or 000 in binary. To find the address, you start with the network address in binary and substitute 000 for the subnet ID bits. Well gee, those bits are already all zero! What this means is that the address for subnet 0 is the same as the address for the network as a whole: 211.77.20.0. This is always the case: subnet 0 always has the same address as the network.

Subnet 1 This has a subnet ID of 1 in decimal or 001 in binary. To find the address, you substitute 001 for the subnet ID bits, which yields the following:

11010011 01001101 00010100 **001**00000

Converting to decimal, you get 211.77.20.32.

Subnet 2 This has a subnet ID of 2, or 010 in binary. To find its address, you substitute 010 for the subnet ID bits, to give you the following:

11010011 01001101 00010100 **010**00000

Which is 211.77.20.64 in binary.

Subnet 3 This has a subnet ID of 011. As you can see, the first three octets of the address are always 211.77.20. The last octet here is **011**00000, which is 96 in decimal, so the whole address is 211.77.20.96.

Starting to see a pattern here? Yes, the address of any subnet can be found by adding 32 to the last octet of the previous subnet. This pattern occurs for all subnetting choices; the increment depends on how many bits you are using for the subnet ID. Here, the increment is 32, which is 2^5; 5 is the number of host ID bits left after you took three subnet ID bits.

Subnet 4 This has a subnet ID of 100. Its address is 211.77.20.128.

Subnet 5 This has a subnet ID of 101. Its address is 211.77.20.160.

Subnet 6 This has a subnet ID of 110. Its address is 211.77.20.192.

Subnet 7 This has a subnet ID of 111. Its address is 211.77.20.224.

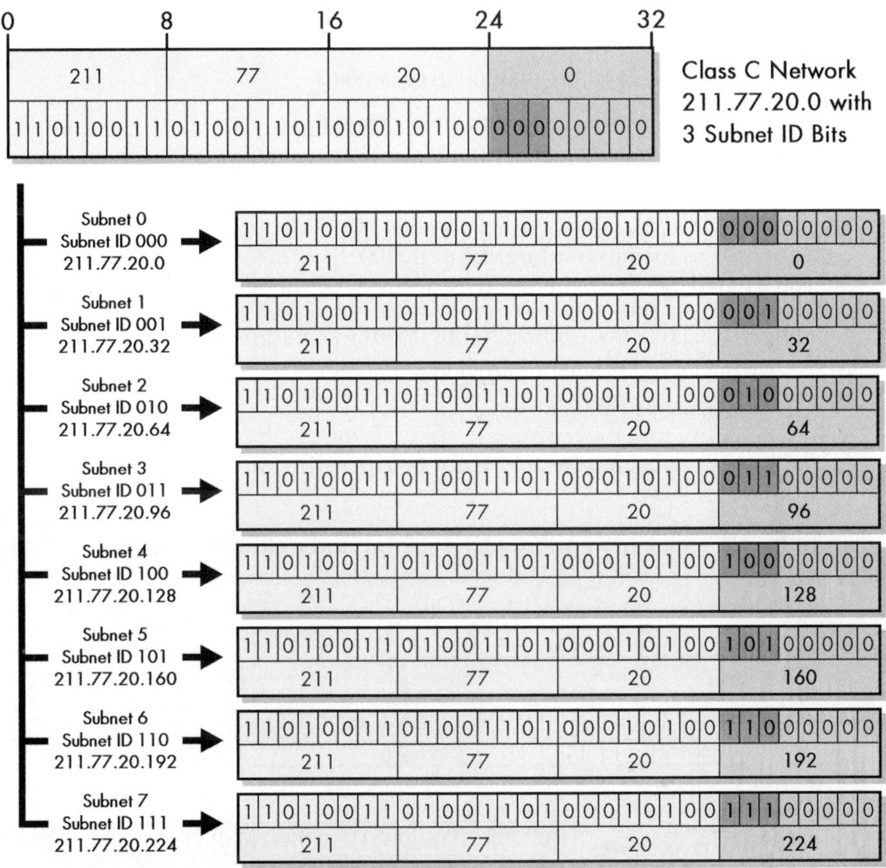

Figure 19-6: Determining subnet addresses for a Class C network *This diagram shows each of the eight possible subnets created when you use three bits for the subnet ID in a Class C network. The binary subnet ID is simply substituted for the subnet bits, and the resulting 32-bit number is converted to dotted decimal form.*

> **KEY CONCEPT** The subnet addresses in a subnetted network are always evenly spaced numerically, with the spacing depending on the number of subnet ID bits.

This example needed only seven subnets, 0 through 6. Subnet 7 would be a spare. Notice that the last subnet has the same last octet as the subnet mask for the network? That's because I substituted 111 for the subnet ID bits, just as in the subnet mask calculation.

Class B Subnet ID and Address Determination Example

Let's look at the other example now, Class B network 166.113.0.0. In binary this is as follows:

10100110 01110001 00000000 00000000

You're using five bits for the subnet ID, leaving 11 host ID bits. The network address with the subnet ID bits highlighted is as follows:

10100110 01110001 **00000**000 00000000

Here, only the third octet will ever change for the different subnets. The first two will always be 166.113, and the last octet will always be 0. There are 32 possible subnets; I'll list the first few so you can see the pattern (refer to Figure 19-7 as well):

Subnet 0 This has a subnet ID of 00000. This means the address will be 166.113.0.0, which is the network address, as you would expect.

Subnet 1 This has a subnet ID of 00001. The address becomes

10100110 01110001 **00001**000 00000000

This is 116.113.8.0 in decimal.

Subnet 2 This has a subnet ID of 00010, giving an address of 116.113.**00010**000.0 or 116.113.16.0.

Subnet 3 This has a subnet ID of 00011 and a subnet address of 116.113.24.0.

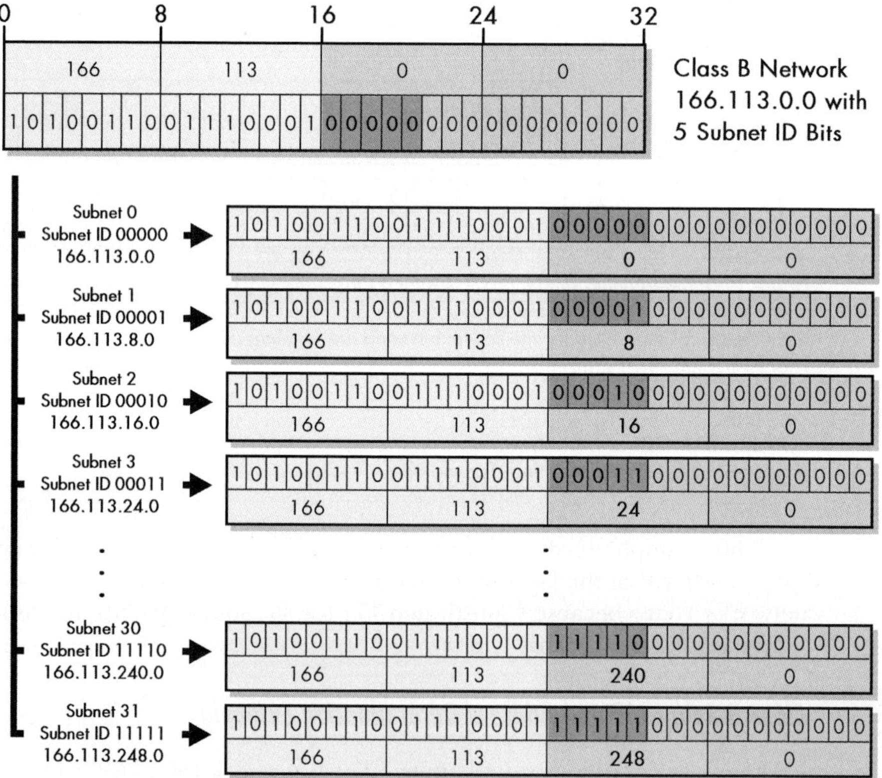

Figure 19-7: Determining subnet addresses for a Class B network *This is the same as Figure 19-6, but for a Class B network with five subnet ID bits (I have not shown all 32 subnets, for obvious reasons).*

Again, the pattern here is obvious: You add eight to the third octet to get successive addresses. The last subnet here is 31, which has a subnet address of 166.113.248.0, which has the same third and fourth octets as the subnet mask of 255.255.248.0.

Using Subnet Address Formulas to Calculate Subnet Addresses

Since the subnet addresses form a pattern, and the pattern depends on the number of subnet ID bits, it is possible to express the subnet addresses using a single formula for each subnetting option. I have shown these formulas for each of the Classes A, B, and C in the subnetting summary tables in Chapter 18. The formulas can be used to directly calculate the address of subnet *N*, where *N* is numbered from 0 up to one less than the total number of subnets, as I have done earlier.

In these formulas, the network ID bits are shown as x., x.y., or x.y.z. for the three classes. This just means that the subnet addresses have as those octets whatever the numbers are in those octets for the network address. In the examples, x.y would be 166.113 for the Class B network, and x.y.z would be 211.77.20 for the Class C network.

When the number of subnet bits is eight or less, the formula is relatively simple, and a calculation is done for only one octet, as a multiplication of *N*, such as *N**4 or *N**32. This is usually the case, since the number of subnets is usually less than 256, and it's the case with both of the examples.

In the Class C network with three subnet ID bits, the formula from the table is x.y.z.*N**32. For this network, all subnets are of the form 211.77.20.*N**32, with *N* going from zero to seven. So, subnet 5 is 211.77.20.(5*32), which is 211.77.20.160, as you saw before. Similarly, in the Class B network with five subnet ID bits, the formula is x.y.*N**8.0. In this case, x.y is 166.113. Subnet 26 would have the address 166.113.(26*8).0, or 166.113.208.0.

This is pretty simple stuff, and it makes the formulas a good shortcut for quickly determining subnet addresses, especially when there are many subnets. They can also be used in a spreadsheet.

The only place where using the formulas requires a bit of care is when the number of subnet bits is nine or more. This means that the subnet identifier crosses an octet boundary, and this causes the formula to become more complex.

When the number of subnet bits is greater than eight, some of the octets are of the form *N* divided by an integer, such as *N*/8. This is an integer division, which means divide *N* by 8, keep the integer part, and drop the fractional part or remainder. Other octets are calculated based on the modulo of *N*, shown as *N*%8. This is the exact opposite: It means divide *N* by 8, drop the integer, and keep the remainder. For example, 33/5 in integer math is 6 (6 with a remainder of 3, drop the remainder, or alternately, 6.6, drop the fraction), and 33%5 is 3 (6 with a remainder of 3, drop the 6, keep the remainder).

Let's take as an example the Class B network and suppose that for some strange reason you decided to use ten bits for the subnet ID instead of five. In this case, the formula is x.y.*N*/4.(N%4)*64. Subnet 23 in this case would have the address 166.113.23/4.(23%4)*64. The 23/4 becomes just 5 (the fractional .75 is dropped). 23 modulo 4 is 3, which is multiplied by 64 to get 192. So the subnet address is 166.113.5.192. Subnet 709 would be 116.113.709/4.(709%4)*64, which is 116.113.177.64.

Okay, now for the real fun! If you subnet a Class A address using more than 16 bits for the subnet ID, you are crossing *two* octet boundaries, and the formulas become very . . . interesting, involving both integer division *and* modulo. Suppose you were in charge of Class A address 21.0.0.0 and decide to subnet it. However, you sat down to do this after having had a few stiff ones at the office holiday party, so your judgment is a bit impaired. You decide that it would be a great idea to choose 21 bits for the subnet ID, since you like the number 21. This gives you a couple million subnets.

The formula for subnet addresses in this case is rather long and complicated: x.*N*/8192.(*N*/32)%256.(*N*%32)*8. Yikes. Well, this is a bit involved—so much so that it might be easier to just take a subnet number and do it in binary, the long way. But let's take an example and see how it works for, say, subnet 987654. The first octet is 21. The second octet is 987654/8192, integer division. This is 120. The third octet is (987654/32)%256. The result of the division is 30864 (you drop the fraction). Then you take 30864%256, which yields a remainder of 144. The fourth octet is (987654%32)*8. This is 6*8 or 48. So subnet address 987654 is 21.120.144.48.

(Don't drink and drive. Don't drink and subnet either.)

IP Subnetting Step 5: Determining Host Addresses for Each Subnet

Once you know the addresses of each of the subnets in the network, you use these addresses as the basis for assigning IP addresses to the individual hosts in each subnet. You start by associating a subnet base address with each physical network (since at least in theory, the subnets correspond to the physical networks). You then sequentially assign hosts particular IP addresses within the subnet (or in a different manner, if you prefer!).

Determining host addresses is really quite simple once you know the subnet address. All you do is substitute the numbers 1, 2, 3, and so on for the host ID bits in the subnet address. You must do this in binary and then convert the address to decimal form. Again, you can take some shortcuts once the rather obvious pattern of how to assign addresses emerges. You'll look at those near the end of the chapter.

Class C Host Address Determination Example

Let's start with the Class C example again, 211.77.20.0, which you divided into eight subnets using three subnet bits. Here's how the address appears with the subnet bits shown in bold, and the host ID bits shown in italics:

11010011 01001101 00010100 **000***00000*

The first subnet is subnet 0, which has all zeros for those subnet bits, and thus the same address as the network as a whole: 211.77.20.0. You substitute the numbers 1, 2, 3, and so on for the italicized bits to get the host IDs. (Remember that you don't start with zero here because for the host ID, the all-zeros and all-ones binary patterns have special meaning.) So it goes like this:

The first host address has the number 1 for the host ID, or 00001 in binary. So it is as follows:

11010011 01001101 00010100 **000*00001***

In decimal, this is 211.77.20.1.

The second host address has the number 2 for the host ID, or 00010 in binary. Its binary value is as follows:

11010011 01001101 00010100 **000*00010***

In decimal, this is 211.77.20.2.

I'm sure you get the picture already; the third host will be 211.77.20.3, the fourth 211.77.20.4, and so on. There is a maximum of 30 hosts in each subnet, as you saw earlier. So the last host in this subnet will be found by substituting 30 (11110 in binary) for the host ID bits, resulting in a decimal address of 211.77.20.30.

You can do the same thing for each of the other subnets; the only thing that changes is the values in the subnet ID bits. Let's take subnet 6, for example. It has 110 for the subnet bits instead of 000. So its subnet base address is 211.77.20.192, or

11010011 01001101 00010100 **110*00000***

You assign hosts to this subnet by substituting 00001, then 00010, then 00011 for the host ID bits as shown earlier. Let's take the hosts one at a time:

The first host address is as follows:

11010011 01001101 00010100 **110*00001***

or 211.77.20.193.

The second host address is

11010011 01001101 00010100 **110*00010***

or 211.77.20.194.

And so on, all the way up to the last host in the subnet, which is 211.77.20.222. Figure 19-8 shows graphically how subnet and host addresses are calculated for this sample network.

One more address you may wish to calculate is the broadcast address for the subnet. This is one of the special cases, as discussed in Chapter 18, found by substituting all ones for the host ID. For subnet 0, this would be 211.77.20.31. For subnet 6, it would be 211.77.20.223. That's pretty much all there is to it.

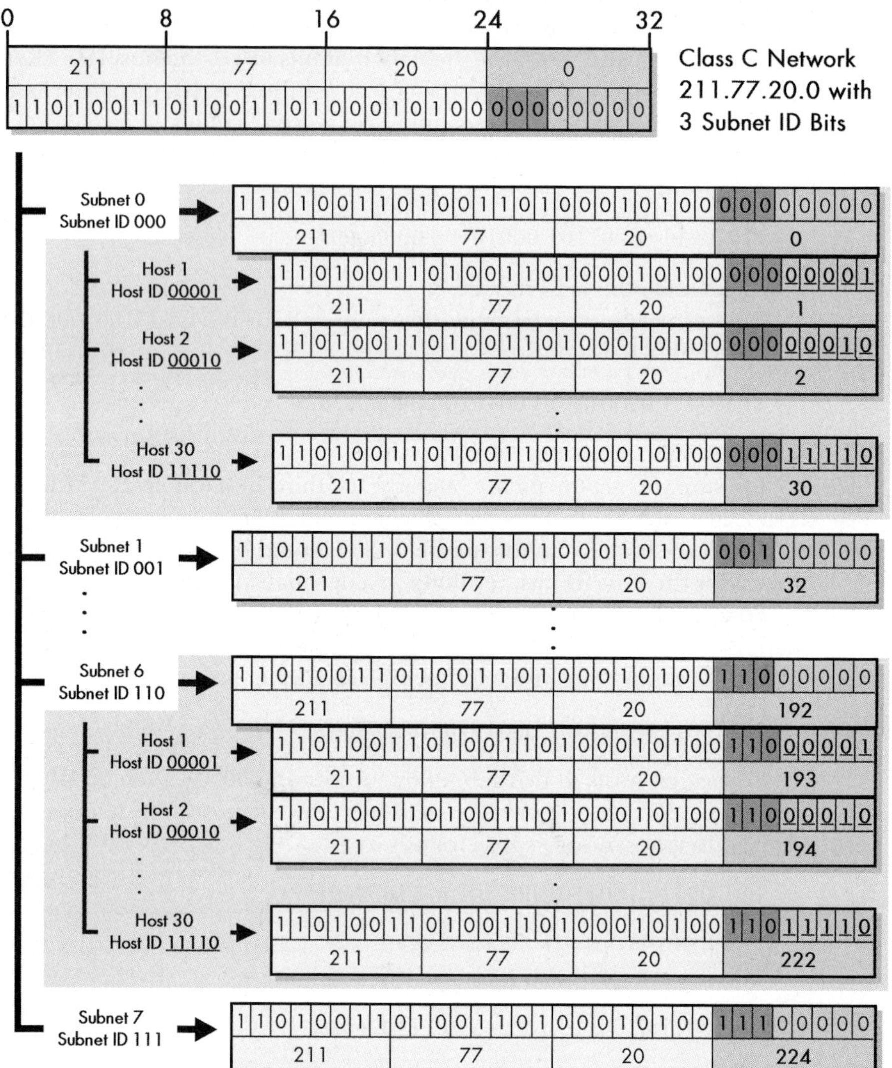

Figure 19-8: Determining host addresses for a Class C network *This diagram shows how both subnet addresses and host addresses are determined in a two-step process. The subnet addresses are found by substituting subnet ID values (shown in bold) for the subnet ID bits of the network. Then, for any given subnet address, you can determine a host address by substituting a host number (shown in bold and italicized) for the host ID bits within that subnet. So, for example, host 2 in subnet 6 has 110 for the subnet ID and 00010 for the host ID, resulting in a final octet value of 11000010, or 194.*

Class B Host Address Determination Example

You can do the same thing for the Class B network, naturally. The address of that network is 166.113.0.0. Now say you want to define the hosts that go in subnet 13. You substitute 13 in binary (01101) for the subnet ID bits to get the following subnet address, which is shown with the subnet ID bits in bold and the host ID bits in italics:

10100110 01110001 **01101***000 00000000*

This is the subnet address 166.113.104.0. Now you have 11 bits of host ID, so you can have a maximum of 2,046 hosts. The first is found by substituting 000 00000001 for the host ID bits, which gives an address of 166.113.104.1. The second host is 166.113.104.2, and so on. The last is found by substituting 111 11111110, which gives an address of 166.113.111.254. Note that since the host ID bits extend over two octets, two octets change as you increment the host ID, unlike the Class C example. The broadcast address is 166.113.111.255.

> **KEY CONCEPT** In a subnetted network, the address of Host H within subnet number *S* is found by plugging in the binary value of *S* for the network's subnet ID bits, and the binary value of *H* for the subnet's host ID bits.

Shortcuts for Computing Host Addresses

As you can see, defining the host IDs is really quite straightforward. If you can substitute bits and convert to decimal, you have all you need to know. You can also see that, as was the case with defining the subnet addresses, there are patterns that you can use in defining host IDs and understanding how they work. These generally define ways for which you can more quickly determine certain host addresses by working directly in decimal instead of bothering with binary substitutions. This is a bit more complex conceptually, so proceed only if you are feeling a bit brave.

The following are some of the shortcuts you can use in determining host IP addresses in a subnet environment:

First Host Address *The first host address is always the subnet address with the last octet incremented by 1.* So in the Class C example, subnet 3's base address is 211.77.20.96. The first host address in subnet 3 is thus 211.77.20.97.

Subsequent Host Addresses After you find the first host address, to get the next one, you just add one to the last octet of the previous address. If this makes the last octet 256 (which can happen only if there are more than eight host ID bits), you "wrap around" this to zero and increment the third octet.

Directly Calculating Host Addresses If the number of host ID bits is eight or less, you can find host *N*'s address by adding *N* to the last octet's decimal value. For example, in the Class C example, subnet 3's base address is 211.77.20.96. Therefore, host 23 in this subnet has an address of 211.77.20.119. If there are more than eight bits in the host ID, this works for only the first 255 hosts, after which you need to wrap around and increase the value of the third octet. Consider again subnet 13 in the Class B example, which has a base address of 166.113.104.0. Host 214 on this subnet has address 166.113.104.0, but host 314 isn't 166.113.104.314. It is 166.113.105.58 (host 255 is 166.113.104.255, then host 256 is 166.113.105.0, and you count up 58 more (314–256) to get to 314, 166.113.105.58).

Range of Host Addresses For a range of hosts for any subnet, the first address is the base address of subnet with last octet incremented by one. The last address is the base address of *next subnet after this one,* less two in the last octet (which may require changing a 0 in the last octet to 254 and reducing the value of the third octet by 1). For example, consider subnet 17 in the Class B example. Its subnet address is 166.113.136.0. The address of subnet 18 is 166.113.144.0. So the range of hosts for subnet 17 is 166.113.136.1 to 166.113.143.254.

Broadcast Address *The broadcast address for a subnet is always one less than the base address of the subsequent subnet.* Or alternatively, one more than the last real host address of the subnet. So for subnet 17 in the Class B example, the broadcast address is 166.113.143.255.

Did I just confuse you? Well, remember that these are shortcuts, and sometimes when you take a shortcut, you get lost. Just kidding; it's really not that hard once you play around with it a bit.

In closing, remember the following quick summary when working with IP addresses in a subnet environment:

- The network ID is the same for all hosts in all subnets and for all subnets in the network.
- The subnet ID is the same for all hosts in each subnet, but it's unique to each subnet in the network.
- The host ID is unique within each subnet. Each subnet has the same set of host IDs.
- Subnetting is fun! (Okay, okay, sorry. . . .)

20

IP CLASSLESS ADDRESSING—CLASSLESS INTER-DOMAIN ROUTING (CIDR)/SUPERNETTING

As the Internet began to grow dramatically, three main problems arose with the original classful addressing scheme described in the previous chapters. These difficulties were addressed partially through subnet addressing, which provides more flexibility for the administrators of individual networks on an Internet. Subnetting, however, doesn't really tackle the problems in general terms. Some of these issues remain due to the use of classes even with subnets.

While development began on version 6 of the Internet Protocol (IPv6; see Part II-4) and its roomy 128-bit addressing system in the mid-1990s, developers recognized that it would take many years before widespread deployment of IPv6 would be possible. In order to extend the life of IPv4 until the newer version could be completed, it was necessary to take a new approach to addressing IPv4 devices. This new system calls for eliminating the notion of address classes entirely, creating a new *classless addressing* scheme sometimes called *Classless Inter-Domain Routing (CIDR)*.

In this chapter, I describe modern classless IP addressing. I begin with an overview of the concepts behind classless addressing and the idea behind *supernetting*, including why it was created and what its advantages and disadvantages are. I then define CIDR and describe how the system works in more detail, including the notation used for address blocks. I list each of the CIDR address block sizes and show how they relate to the older Class A, B, and C networks. I conclude with a CIDR addressing example that's similar to the examples in Chapter 19, but this one focuses on CIDR and is a bit more condensed.

IP Classless Addressing and Supernetting Overview

Subnet addressing was an important development in the evolution of IP addressing, because it solved some important issues with the conventional, two-level class-based addressing scheme. Subnetting's contribution to flexibility in IP addressing was to allow each network to have its own two-level hierarchy, thereby giving the administrator of each network the equivalent of an Internet within the Internet.

When you looked at the advantages of subnetting in Chapter 18, you saw that subnetting was local within each organization and invisible to other organizations. This is an advantage in that it lets each organization tailor its network without other groups having to worry about the details of how this is done. Unfortunately, this invisibility also represents a key *disadvantage* of subnetted classful addressing: It cannot correct the fundamental inefficiencies associated with that type of addressing, because organizations are still assigned address blocks based on classes.

The Main Problem with Classful Addressing

A key weakness of the subnetting system is its low granularity. A Class B address block contains a very large number of addresses (65,534), but a Class C block has only a relatively small number (254). There are many thousands of medium-sized organizations that need more than 254 IP addresses, but a small percentage of these needs 65,534 or anything even close to it. (The lack of a good match to a medium-sized organization with 5,000 hosts is illustrated in Figure 17-5 in Chapter 17.) When setting up their networks, these companies and groups would tend to request Class B address blocks and not Class C blocks, because they needed more than 254 hosts, without considering how many of the 65,000-odd addresses they really would use.

Due to how the classes of the older system were designed, there are over two million Class C address blocks, but only 16,384 Class B networks. While 16,384 seems like a lot at first glance, there are millions of organizations and corporations around the world. Class B allocations were being consumed at a rapid pace, while the smaller Class C networks were relatively unused.

The folks handing out Internet addresses needed a way to better utilize the address space so that it would not run out before the transition to IPv6. Subnetting didn't help a great deal with this problem. Why? Because it only works *within* the classful address blocks. If an organization needing 2,000 IP addresses requested a Class B block, they could use subnetting to more efficiently manage their block. However, subnetting could do nothing about the fact that this organization would never use over 62,000 of the addresses in its block—about 97 percent of their allocated address space.

The only solution to this would be to convince—or at worst case, force—companies to use many smaller Class C blocks instead of wasting the bulk of a Class B assignment. Many organizations resisted this due to the complexity involved, and this caused the other main problem that subnetting didn't correct: the growth of Internet routing tables. Replacing one Class B network with 10 Class C networks means ten times as many entries for routers to maintain.

The Solution: Eliminate Address Classes

It was clear that as long as there were only three sizes of networks, the allocation efficiency problem could never be properly rectified. The solution was to get rid of the classes completely, in favor of a *classless* allocation scheme. This system would solve both of the main problems with classful addressing: inefficient address space use and the exponential growth of routing tables.

This system was developed in the early 1990s and formalized in 1993 in RFCs 1517, 1518, 1519, and 1520. The technology was called *Classless Inter-Domain Routing (CIDR)*. Despite this name, the scheme deals with both addressing and routing matters, since they are inextricably linked.

The idea behind CIDR is to adapt the concept of subnetting a single network to the entire Internet. In essence, classless addressing means that instead of breaking a particular network into subnets, you can aggregate networks into larger "supernets." CIDR is sometimes called *supernetting* for this reason: It applies the principles of subnetting to larger networks. It is this aggregation of networks into supernets that allowed CIDR to resolve the problem of growing Internet routing tables.

Of course, if you are going to apply subnetting concepts to the entire Internet, you need to be able to have subnets of different sizes. After all, that's one of the primary goals in eliminating the classes. So, more accurately, CIDR is an Internet-wide application of not just regular one-level subnetting, but of Variable Length Subnet Masking (VLSM), introduced in Chapter 18. Just as VLSM allows you split a network as many times as you want to create subnets, sub-subnets, and sub-sub-subnets, CIDR lets you do this with the entire Internet, as many times as needed.

> **KEY CONCEPT** *Classless Inter-Domain Routing (CIDR)* is a system of IP addressing and routing that solves the many problems of classful addressing by eliminating fixed address classes in favor of a flexible, multiple-level, hierarchical structure of networks of varying sizes.

The Many Benefits of Classless Addressing and Routing

CIDR provides numerous advantages over the classful addressing scheme, whether or not subnetting is used:

Efficient Address Space Allocation Instead of allocating addresses in fixed-size blocks of low granularity, under CIDR, addresses are allocated in sizes of any binary multiple. So a company that needs 5,000 addresses can be assigned a block of 8,190 instead of 65,534, as shown in Figure 20-1. Or to think of it another way, the equivalent of a single Class B network can be shared among eight companies that each need 8,190 or fewer IP addresses.

Elimination of Class Imbalances There are no more Class A, B, and C networks, so there is no problem with some portions of the address space being widely used while others are neglected.

Efficient Routing Entries CIDR's multiple-level hierarchical structure allows a small number of routing entries to represent a large number of networks. Network descriptions can be aggregated and represented by a single entry. Since CIDR is hierarchical, the detail of lower-level, smaller networks can be hidden from routers that move traffic between large groups of networks. This is discussed more completely in Chapter 23, which covers IP routing issues.

No Separate Subnetting Method CIDR implements the concepts of subnetting within the Internet itself. An organization can use the same method used on the Internet to subdivide its internal network into subnets of arbitrary complexity, without needing a separate subnetting mechanism.

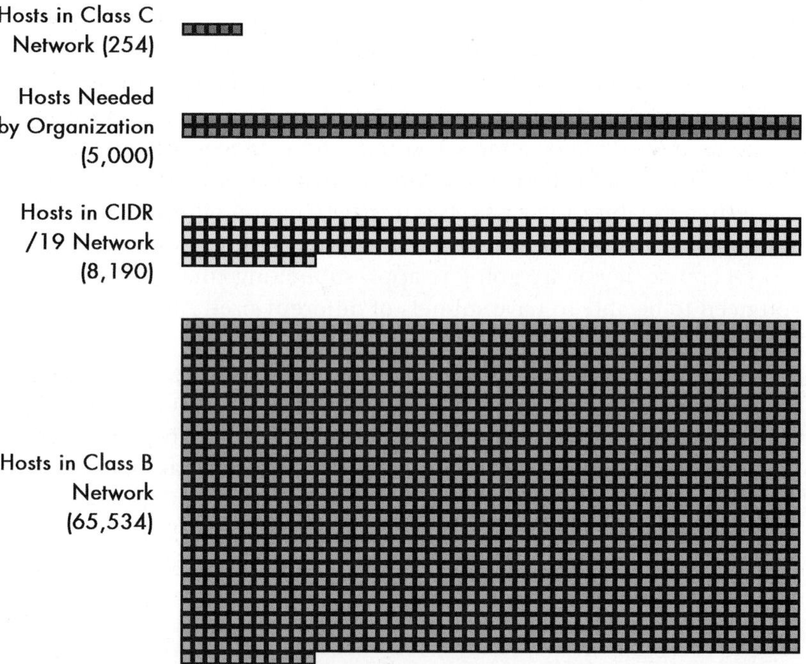

Figure 20-1: Classless addressing (CIDR) solves the granularity problem *Figure 17-5 in Chapter 17 illustrates the primary problem with classful addressing: the great distance between the size of Class B and Class C networks. CIDR solves this issue by allowing any number of bits to be used for the network ID. In the case of an organization with 5,000 hosts, a /19 network with 8,190 hosts can be assigned. This reduces the address space waste for such an organization by about 95.*

Since the main benefit of classful addressing was its simplicity, it's no surprise that the main drawback of CIDR is its greater complexity. One issue is that it is no longer possible to determine, by looking at the first octet, how many bits of an IP address represent the network ID and how many represent the host ID. A bit more care needs to be used in setting up routers as well, to make sure that routing is accomplished correctly.

IP Supernetting: CIDR Hierarchical Addressing and Notation

When you first looked at IP addressing in Chapter 17, you saw that IP addresses were designed to be divided into a network identifier (network ID) and host identifier (host ID). Then, when subnets were introduced, you "stole" bits from the host ID to create a subnet ID, giving the IP address a total of three hierarchical levels. With VLSM, you further subnetted the subnets, taking more bits from the host ID to give you a multiple-level hierarchy with sub-subnets, sub-sub-subnets, and so forth.

In a classless environment, you completely change how you look at IP addresses by applying VLSM concepts not just to one network, but to the entire Internet. In essence, the Internet becomes just one giant network that is subnetted into a number of large blocks. Some of these large blocks are then broken down into smaller blocks, which can in turn be broken down further. This breaking down can occur multiple times, allowing you to split the "pie" of Internet addresses into slices of many different sizes to suit the needs of the organization.

As the name implies, classless addressing completely eliminates the prior notions of classes. There are no more Class A, B, and C blocks that are divided by the first few bits of the address. Instead, under CIDR, all Internet blocks can be of arbitrary size. Instead of having all networks use 8 (Class A), 16 (Class B), or 24 (Class C) bits for the network ID, you can have large networks with, say, 13 bits for the network ID (leaving 19 bits for the host ID), or very small ones that use 28 bits for the network ID (only 4 bits for the host ID). The size of the network is still based on the binary power of the number of host ID bits.

CIDR (Slash) Notation

You'll recall that when you used subnetting, you had a problem: Subnetting could be done by taking any number of available host ID bits, so how would devices know where the line was between the subnet ID and host ID? The same problem occurs under CIDR. There are no classes, so you can't tell anything by looking at the first few bits of an IP address. Since addresses can have the dividing point between host ID and network ID occur anywhere, you need additional information in order to interpret IP addresses properly. Under CIDR, this impacts not only addresses within an organization, but also addresses in the entire Internet, since there are no classes and each network can be a different size.

For this reason, just as subnetting required the use of a subnet mask to show which bits belong to the network ID or subnet ID and which belong to the host ID, CIDR uses a subnet mask to show where the line is drawn between host ID and network ID. However, for simplicity, under CIDR you don't usually work with 32-bit binary subnet masks. Instead, you use *slash notation*, more properly called *CIDR notation*. This notation shows the size of the network, sometimes called the *prefix length*, by following an IP address with an integer that tells you how many bits are used for the network ID (prefix).

KEY CONCEPT Since there are no address classes in CIDR, you cannot tell the size of the network ID of an address from the address alone. In CIDR, the length of the prefix (network ID) is indicated by placing it following a slash after the address. This is called *CIDR notation*, or *slash notation*.

For example, consider the network specification 184.13.152.0/22. The 22 means this network has 22 bits for the network ID and 10 bits for the host ID. This is equivalent to specifying a network with an address of 184.13.152.0 and a subnet mask of 255.255.252.0, as you can see in Figure 20-2. This sample network provides a total of 1,022 hosts (2^{10}–2). The table in the following section shows all the different possible network sizes that can be configured under CIDR.

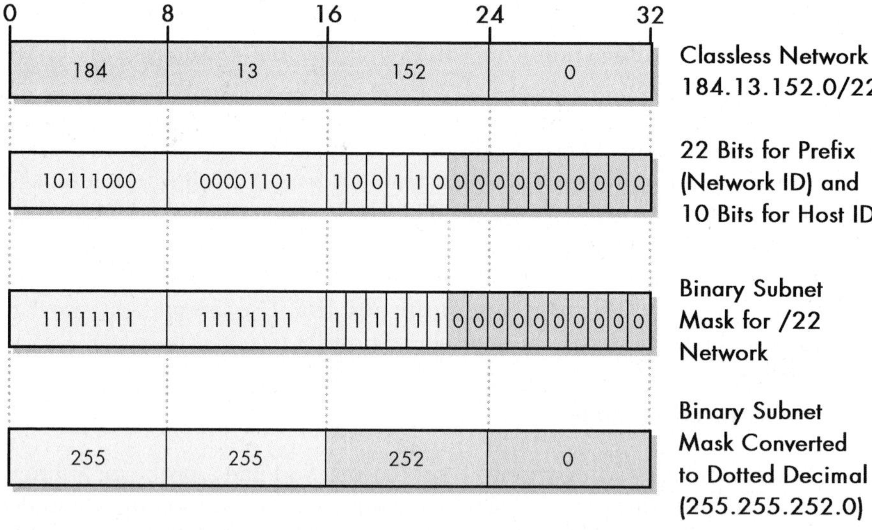

Figure 20-2: CIDR (slash) notation and its subnet mask equivalent *A classless network is normally specified in CIDR, or slash notation, such as this example: 184.13.152.0/22. Here, the /22 means the first 22 bits of the address are the network ID. The equivalent subnet mask can be calculated by creating a 32-bit number with 22 ones followed by 10 zeros.*

NOTE *You may recall that under classful subnetting, the bits used for the subnet ID did not need to be contiguous. Even though this ability was almost never used to avoid confusion, noncontiguous subnet ID bits were possible. Under CIDR, the requirement for contiguous subnet ID bits has been made official—you could not use slash notation otherwise.*

Supernetting: Subnetting the Internet

In theory, then, what CIDR does is provide the central address-assignment authority with the flexibility to hand out address blocks of different sizes to organizations based on their need. However, when CIDR was developed, a shift was made in the method by which public IP addresses were assigned. Having everyone in the world attempt to get addresses from one organization wasn't the best method. It was necessary under the classful scheme because the hierarchy was only two levels deep. The Internet Assigned Numbers Authority (IANA) handed out network IDs to everyone, who then assigned host IDs (or subnetted).

Under CIDR, you have many hierarchical levels: You split big blocks into smaller blocks, and then still-smaller blocks, and so on. It makes sense to manage blocks in a similar hierarchical manner as well. So what happens is that IANA/ICANN divides addresses into large blocks, which it distributes to the four *regional Internet registries (RIRs)*: APNIC, ARIN, LACNIC, and RIPE NCC. These then further divide the address blocks and distribute them to lower-level national Internet registries (NIRs), local Internet registries (LIRs), and/or individual organizations such as Internet service providers (ISPs). This is all explained in the background discussion of Internet authorities and registries in Chapter 3.

ISPs can then divide these blocks into smaller ones and then allocate them to their customers. These customers are sometimes smaller ISPs themselves, which repeat the process. They split their blocks into pieces of different sizes and allocate them to their customers, some of whom are even smaller ISPs and some of whom are end users. The number of times this can occur is limited only by how many addresses are in the original block.

It's also worth noting that while CIDR is based on subnetting concepts, subnetting itself is not used in CIDR—or at least, not in the way it is used under classful addressing. There is no explicit subnetting using a subnet ID within CIDR. All IP addresses are interpreted only as having a network ID and a host ID. An organization does the equivalent of subnetting by dividing its own network into subnetworks using the same general method that ISPs do. This probably seems a bit confusing. Later in this chapter, I provide a detailed example of hierarchical address block assignments and how splitting works under CIDR.

Common Aspects of Classful and Classless Addressing

There are a few aspects of addressing that were defined under the "classful" scheme that don't change under CIDR:

Private Address Blocks Certain blocks of addresses are still reserved for private network addressing. These addresses are not directly routed on the Internet, but can be used in conjunction with Network Address Translation (NAT; see Chapter 28) to allow IP hosts without public addresses to access the Internet.

Addresses with Special Meanings The special meanings assigned to certain network ID and host ID patterns are the same as before. This is also why you still must subtract two from the number of hosts in each network. These represent the all-zeros case that refers to the network as a whole and the all-ones address used for broadcast.

Loopback Addresses The network 127.0.0.0 is still reserved for loopback functionality. (In CIDR it is given the notation 127.0.0.0/8.)

Finally, note that use of classless addressing requires hardware and software designed to handle it. If the hardware and software are still assuming that they are operating in a classful environment, they will not properly interpret addresses. Since CIDR has now been around for more than a decade, this is usually not a problem with modern systems.

IP Classless Addressing Block Sizes and Classful Network Equivalents

Because CIDR allows you to divide IP addresses into network IDs and host IDs along any bit boundary, it allows for the creation of dozens of different sizes of networks. As with subnetting, the size of network is a trade-off between the number of bits used for the network ID and the number used for the host ID. Unlike conventional subnetting, where a single choice is made for all subnets, CIDR allows many levels of hierarchical division of the Internet, so many sizes of networks exist simultaneously. Larger networks are created and subdivided into smaller ones.

Since many people are used to looking at IP address blocks in terms of their classful sizes, it is common to express CIDR address blocks in terms of their classful equivalents. First, at this point it should be simple to see that a CIDR /8 network is equal in size to a Class A network, a /16 is equivalent to a Class B network, and a /24 is equivalent to a Class C network. This is because Class A networks use 8 bits for the network ID, Class B networks use 16, and Class C networks use 24. However, remember that these CIDR equivalents do not need to have any particular ranges for their first octets as in the classful scheme.

Each time you reduce the prefix length, you are defining a network about double the size of the one with the higher number, since you have increased the number of bits in the host ID by one. So, a /15 network is equal in size to two /16 networks.

Table 20-1 shows each of the possible theoretical ways to divide the 32 bits of an IP address into network ID and host ID bits under CIDR. For each, I have shown the number of hosts in each network, and the way a network of each size is represented in both slash notation and as a conventional subnet mask. I have also shown the equivalent number of Class A, Class B, and Class C networks for each.

Keep the following things in mind while looking at this table:

- Some of the entries shown are more theoretical than practical and are included merely for completeness. This is particularly the case with the larger networks. For example, I doubt anyone ever actually works with a /1 or /2 CIDR network; there would be only two of the former and four of the latter encompassing the entire IP address space! Most of the time, you will be working with smaller networks, /16 and below.
- Under normal circumstances, you cannot have a /31 or /32 CIDR network, because it would have zero valid host IDs. (There is a special case: /31 networks can be used for point-to-point links, where it is obvious who the intended recipient is of each transmission, and where broadcasts are not necessary. This is described in RFC 3021.)
- In the columns showing the number of equivalent Class A, B, and C networks I have only shown numbers in the range of 1/256 to 256 for simplicity. Obviously, a /6 network, in addition to being equal in size to four Class A networks, also equals 1,024 Class B networks, and 262,144 Class C networks, but few people would bother referring to a /6 as being 262,144 Class C networks.

Table 20-1: CIDR Address Blocks and Classful Address Equivalents

# of Bits for Network ID	# of Bits for Host ID	# of Hosts per Network	Prefix Length in Slash Notation	Equivalent Subnet Mask	# of Equivalent Classful Addressing Networks		
					Class A	Class B	Class C
1	31	2,147,483,646	/1	128.0.0.0	128	—	—
2	30	1,073,741,822	/2	192.0.0.0	64	—	—
3	29	536,870,910	/3	224.0.0.0	32	—	—
4	28	268,435,454	/4	240.0.0.0	16	—	—
5	27	134,217,726	/5	248.0.0.0	8	—	—
6	26	67,108,862	/6	252.0.0.0	4	—	—
7	25	33,554,430	/7	254.0.0.0	2	—	—
8	24	16,777,214	/8	255.0.0.0	1	256	—
9	23	8,388,606	/9	255.128.0.0	1/2	128	—
10	22	4,194,302	/10	255.192.0.0	1/4	64	—
11	21	2,097,150	/11	255.224.0.0	1/8	32	—
12	20	1,048,574	/12	255.240.0.0	1/16	16	—
13	19	524,286	/13	255.248.0.0	1/32	8	—
14	18	262,142	/14	255.252.0.0	1/64	4	—
15	17	131,070	/15	255.254.0.0	1/128	2	—
16	16	65,534	/16	255.255.0.0	1/256	1	256
17	15	32,766	/17	255.255.128.0	—	1/2	128
18	14	16,382	/18	255.255.192.0	—	1/4	64
19	13	8,190	/19	255.255.224.0	—	1/8	32
20	12	4,094	/20	255.255.240.0	—	1/16	16
21	11	2,046	/21	255.255.248.0	—	1/32	8
22	10	1,022	/22	255.255.252.0	—	1/64	4
23	9	510	/23	255.255.254.0	—	1/128	2
24	8	254	/24	255.255.255.0	—	1/256	1
25	7	126	/25	255.255.255.128	—	—	1/2
26	6	62	/26	255.255.255.192	—	—	1/4
27	5	30	/27	255.255.255.224	—	—	1/8
28	4	14	/28	255.255.255.240	—	—	1/16
29	3	6	/29	255.255.255.248	—	—	1/32
30	2	2	/30	255.255.255.252	—	—	1/64

IP CIDR Addressing Example

The multiple hierarchical levels of CIDR make the technology seem rather complicated. However, understanding how CIDR works really is not that difficult, assuming you already know how subnetting is done. In particular, if you know how VLSM functions, you basically already know how CIDR works, since they are pretty much the same thing. They differ only in the way that the hierarchical division of networks is accomplished, and in the terminology.

To show how CIDR works better, let's take an example that will illustrate the power of classless addressing: its ability to selectively subdivide a large block of addresses into smaller ones that suit the needs of various organizations. Since address allocation in CIDR typically starts with larger blocks owned by larger ISPs, let's start there as well.

Suppose you have an ISP that is just starting up. It's not a major ISP, but a moderate-sized one with only a few customers, so it needs only a relatively small allocation. It begins with the block 71.94.0.0/15. The /15 on the end of the block address tells you that this is a block of addresses where the first 15 bits are the network ID and the last 17 are the host ID. This block was obtained from a larger ISP, carved from a larger block of addresses by that ISP. For example, 71.94.0.0/15 would be equal to half of the address block 71.92.0.0/14, a quarter of the block 71.88.0.0/13, and so on.

The ISP's block is equal in size to two Class B networks and has a total of 131,070 possible host addresses. This ISP can choose to divide this block in a variety of ways, depending on the needs of its clients and its own internal use. However, this ISP is just starting up, so it is not even sure of what its ultimate needs will be. Let's say it expects to resell about half of its address space to other ISPs, but isn't sure what sizes they will need yet. Of the other half, it plans to split it into four different sizes of blocks to match the needs of different-sized organizations.

To imagine how the ISP divides its address space, you can consider the analogy of cutting up a pie. The ISP will first cut the pie in half and reserve one-half for its future ISP customers. It will then cut the other half into some large pieces and some small pieces. This is illustrated in Figure 20-3. (Okay, I know it's a square pie. I wanted to show the individual small blocks to scale.)

The actual process of division might follow the progression described in the following section and illustrated in Figure 20-4.

First Level of Division

The "pie" is initially cut down the middle by using the single leftmost host ID bit as an extra network bit. Here's the network address block, 71.94.0.0/15 in binary, with the leftmost host ID bit shown in bold:

01000111 0101111**0** 00000000 00000000

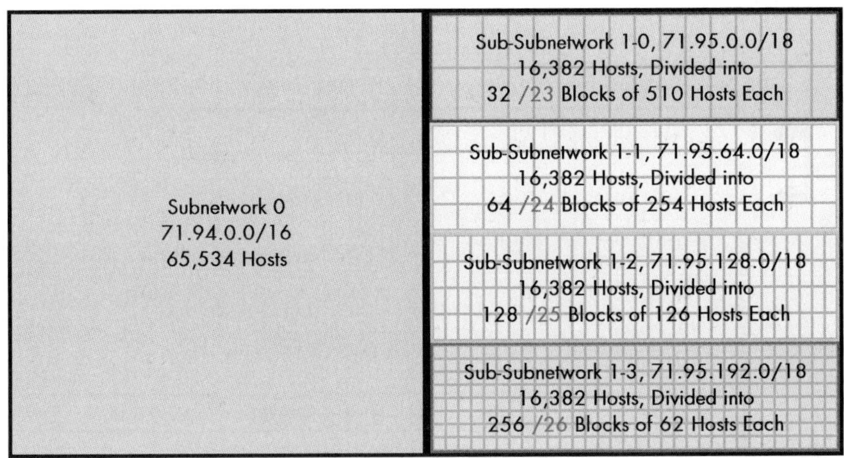

Figure 20-3: Example of a hierarchical division of a /15 CIDR address block *This diagram shows one method by which an ISP with a relatively large /15 address block (131,070 hosts) might choose to hierarchically divide it. In this case it is first divided in half into two /16 blocks. One is reserved, while the other is divided into four /18 blocks. Each of those is divided into blocks of a different size to allow allocation to organizations requiring up to 62, 126, 254, or 510 hosts, respectively.*

To make the split, you make one network equal to this binary network address with the highlighted bit remaining zero, and the other one with it changed to a one. This creates two subnetworks—not subnets as in the classful sense of the word, but portions of the original network—that I have numbered based on the numeric value of what is substituted into the new network ID bits, as follows:

Subnetwork 0: 01000111 0101111**0** 00000000 00000000

Subnetwork 1: 01000111 0101111**1** 00000000 00000000

Because bit 16 is now also part of the network address, these are /16 networks, the size of a classful Class B network. So the subnetworks are as follows:

Subnetwork 0: 71.94.0.0/16

Subnetwork 1: 71.95.0.0/16

You'll notice subnetwork 0 has the same IP address as the larger network it came from; this is always true of the subnetwork 0 in a network.

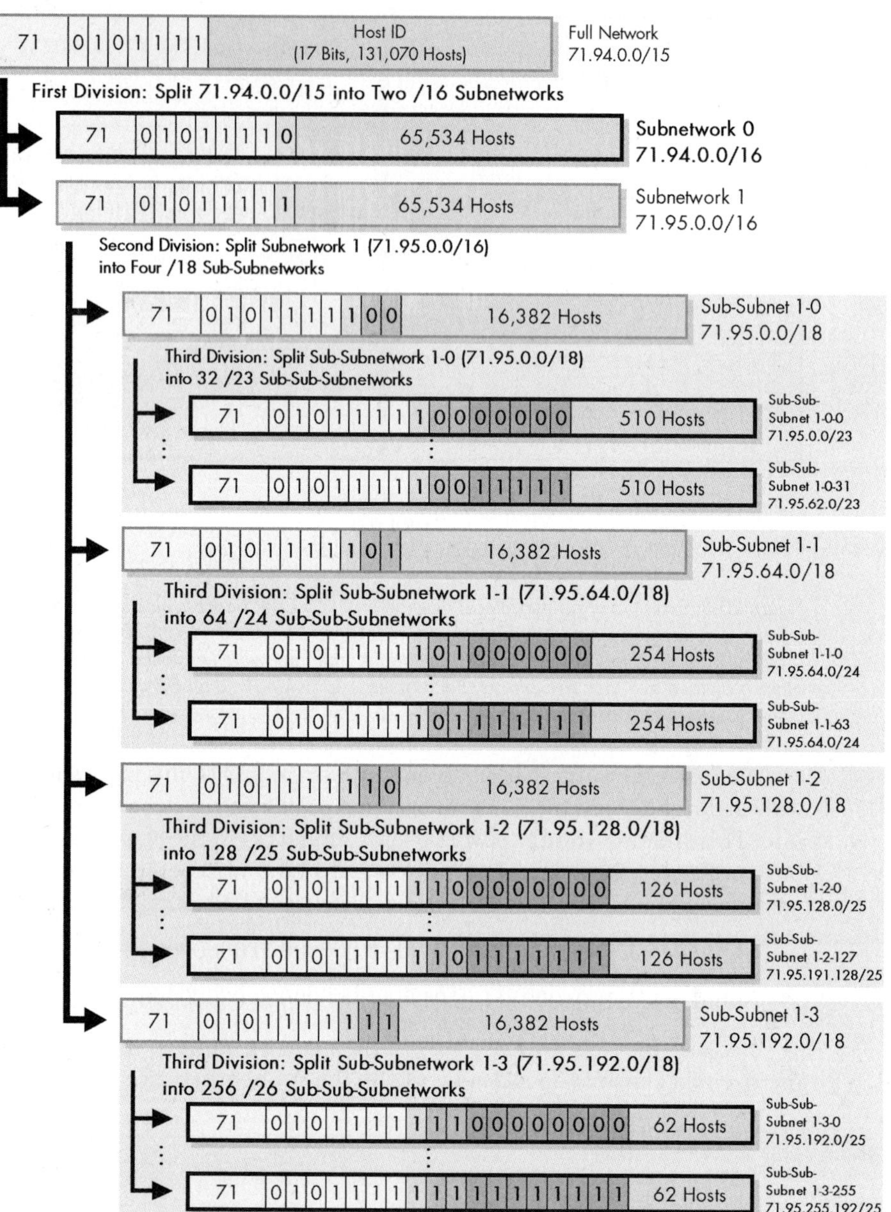

Figure 20-4: *Hierarchical address division using CIDR*

Second Level of Division

Let's say you set aside subnetwork 0 earlier for future ISP allocations. You then choose to divide the second subnetwork into four. These you will then further subdivide into different sizes to meet the customer's needs. To divide into four groups, you need two more bits from the host ID of subnetwork 1, as shown here in bold and underlined next to the original subnet bit:

01000111 0101111**1** **00**000000 00000000

These two bits are replaced by the patterns 00, 01, 10, and 11 to get four sub-subnetworks. They will be /18 networks, since you took two extra bits from the host ID of a /16 as shown here:

Sub-subnetwork 1-0: 01000111 0101111**1** **00**000000 00000000 (71.95.0.0/18)

Sub-subnetwork 1-1: 01000111 0101111**1** **01**000000 00000000 (71.95.64.0/18)

Sub-subnetwork 1-2: 01000111 0101111**1** **10**000000 00000000 (71.95.128.0/18)

Sub-subnetwork 1-3: 01000111 0101111**1** **11**000000 00000000 (71.95.192.0/18)

Each of these has 16,382 addresses.

Third Level of Division

You now take each of the four /18 networks and further subdivide it. You want to make each of these contain a number of blocks of different sizes corresponding to the potential customers. One way to do this would be as follows:

Larger Organizations Customers needing up to 510 addresses require a /23 network. You divide sub-subnetwork 1-0, 71.95.0.0/18 by taking five bits from the host ID field:

01000111 0101111**1** **00*00000***0 00000000

You substitute into these five bits 00000, 00001, 00010 and so on, giving you 32 different /23 networks in this block, each containing nine bits for the host ID, for 510 hosts. The first will be sub-sub-subnetwork 1-0-0, 71.95.0.0/23; the second sub-sub-subnetwork 1-0-1, 71.95.2.0/23; the last will be sub-sub-subnetwork 1-0-31: 71.95.62.0/23.

Medium-Sized Organizations For customers needing up to 254 addresses, you divide sub-subnetwork 1-1, 71.95.64.0/18, by taking six bits from the host ID field:

01000111 0101111**1** **01*000000*** 00000000

This gives you 64 different /24 networks. The first will be sub-sub-subnetwork 1-1-0, 71.95.64.0/24, the second sub-sub-subnetwork 1-1-1, 71.95.65.0/24, and so on.

Smaller Organizations For customers with up to 126 hosts, you divide sub-subnetwork 1-2, 71.95.128.0/18, by taking seven bits from the host ID field, as follows:

01000111 01011111 **10*000000*** *0*0000000

Seven bits allow 128 of these /25 networks within the /18 block. The first will be 71.95.128.0/25, the second 71.95.128.128/25, the third 71.95.129.0/25, and so on.

Very Small Organizations For customers with up to 60 hosts, you divide sub-sub-network 1-3, 71.95.192.0/18, by taking eight bits from the host ID field:

01000111 01011111 **11*000000*** *00*000000

This gives you 256 different /26 networks within the /18 block. The first will be 71.95.192.0/26, the second 71.95.192.64/26, and so on.

This example shows only one of many different ways to slice up this pie. The ISP might decide that creating four different sizes of customer networks in advance was not the right way to go. It might instead just take the tack of dividing the pie in half, dividing it in half again, and so on, as many times as needed to create slices of the right size. Alternatively, if most of their customers needed around 50, 100, 200, or 500 hosts, the previous example might be the easiest to administer.

It would still be possible for the ISP to divide any of the smaller blocks further if they needed to do so. They could split a /26 sub-sub-subnetwork into four /28 sub-sub-sub-subnetworks for very small customers, for example. Also, an individual customer of this ISP could do the same thing, dividing its own block to suit the internal structure of its network.

21

INTERNET PROTOCOL DATAGRAM ENCAPSULATION AND FORMATTING

The primary job of the Internet Protocol (IP) is to deliver data between devices over an internetwork. On its journey between two hosts in an internetwork, this data may travel across many physical networks. To help ensure that the data is sent and received properly, it is *encapsulated* within a message called an *IP datagram.* This datagram includes several fields that help manage the operation of IP and ensure that data gets where it needs to go.

In this chapter, I take a look at how IP takes data passed to it from higher layers and packages it for transmission. I begin with a general discussion of IP datagrams and encapsulation. I then describe the general format of IP datagrams, including the fields used in the IP header and how they are interpreted. I also include a brief discussion of IP datagram options and their use.

BACKGROUND INFORMATION *This chapter assumes at least passing familiarity with IP addressing concepts, as outlined in Chapters 16–20. It also makes reference to the chapter on datagram fragmentation and reassembly (Chapter 22).*

NOTE *IP datagrams are sometimes called* IP packets. *Whether* datagram *or* packet *is the preferred term seems to depend on whom you ask; even the standards don't use one term exclusively. On the other hand, I have seen IP datagrams called* IP frames, *and that's definitely not correct! Chapter 1 describes these terms more completely.*

IP Datagram Encapsulation

In Chapter 5, which described OSI Reference Model concepts, I looked at several ways that protocols at various layers in a networking protocol stack interact with each other. One of the most important concepts in interprotocol operation is that of *encapsulation*. Most data originates within the higher layers of the OSI model. The protocols at these layers pass the data down to lower layers for transmission, usually in the form of discrete messages. Upon receipt, each lower-level protocol takes the entire contents of the message received and encapsulates it into its own message format, adding a header and possibly a footer that contain important control information.

You might think of encapsulation as similar to sending a letter enclosed in an envelope. You write a letter and put it in an envelope with a name and address, but if you give it to a courier for overnight delivery; the courier takes that envelope and puts it in a larger delivery envelope. In a similar way, messages at higher networking layers are encapsulated in lower-layer messages, which can then in turn be further encapsulated.

Due to the prominence of TCP/IP, IP is one of the most important places where data encapsulation occurs on a modern network. Data is passed to IP typically from one of the two main transport layer protocols: the Transmission Control Protocol (TCP) or User Datagram Protocol (UDP). This data is already in the form of a TCP or UDP message with TCP or UDP headers. This is then encapsulated into the body of an IP message, usually called an *IP datagram* or *IP packet*. Encapsulation and formatting of an IP datagram is also sometimes called *packaging*—again, the envelope is an obvious comparison.

Figure 21-1 displays this entire process, which looks very similar to the drawing of the OSI Reference Model as a whole, as shown in Figure 5-5 in Chapter 5. As you can see, an upper-layer message is packaged into a TCP or UDP message. This then becomes the payload of an IP datagram, shown here with only one header (things can get a bit more complex than this). The IP datagram is then passed down to layer 2, where it is encapsulated into some sort of local area network (LAN), wide area network (WAN), or wireless LAN (WLAN) frame, and then converted to bits and transmitted at the physical layer.

If the message to be transmitted is too large to pass through the underlying network, it may first be fragmented. This is analogous to splitting up a large delivery into multiple smaller envelopes or boxes. In this case, each IP datagram carries only part of the higher-layer message. The receiving device must reassemble the message from the IP datagrams.

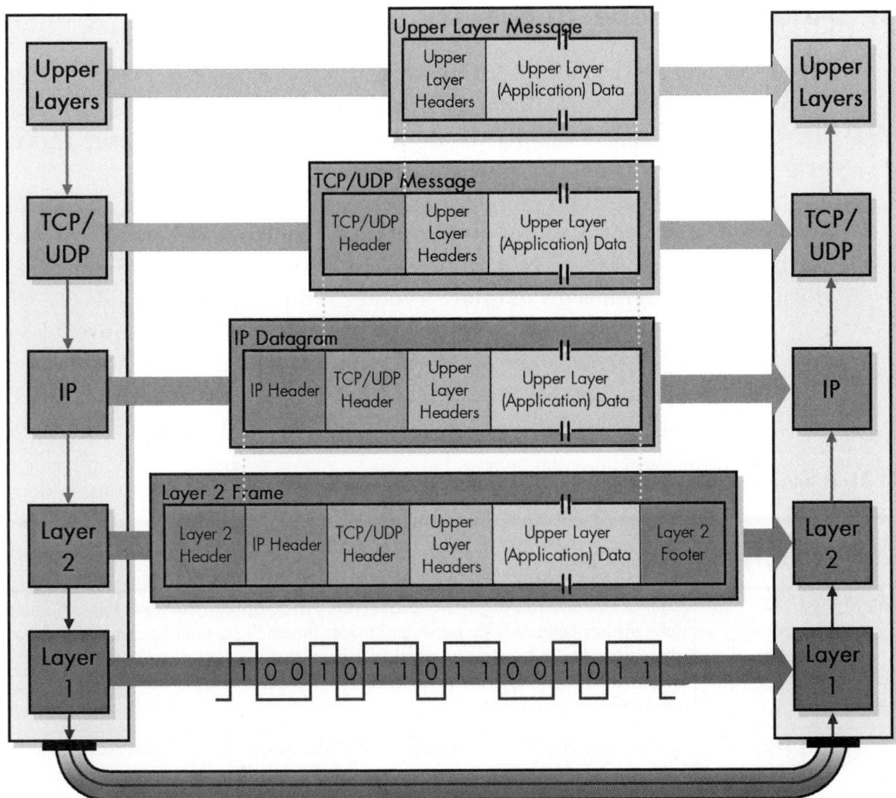

Figure 21-1: IP datagram encapsulation *The upper-layer message is packaged into a TCP or UDP message, which becomes the payload of an IP datagram. The IP datagram is then passed down to layer 2, where it is encapsulated in a LAN, WAN, or WLAN frame. It is then converted to bits and transmitted at the physical layer.*

The IP datagram is somewhat similar in concept to a frame used in Ethernet or another data link layer, except that IP datagrams are designed to facilitate transmission across an internetwork, while data link layer frames are used only for direct delivery within a physical network. The fields included in the IP header are used to manage internetwork datagram delivery. This includes key information for delivery, such as the address of the destination device, identification of the type of frame, and control bits. The header follows a format that you will examine shortly.

Once data is encapsulated into an IP datagram, it is passed down to the data link layer for transmission across the current "hop" of the internetwork. There it is further encapsulated, IP header and all, into a data link layer frame such as an Ethernet frame. An IP datagram may be encapsulated into many such data link layer frames as it is routed across the internetwork; on each hop, the IP datagram is removed from the data link layer frame and then repackaged into a new one for the next hop. The IP datagram, however, is not changed (except for some control fields) until it reaches its final destination.

IP Datagram General Format

Data transmitted over an internetwork using IP is carried in messages called *IP datagrams.* As is the case with all network protocol messages, IP uses a specific format for its datagrams. Here, I will discuss the IP version 4 (IPv4) datagram format, which was defined in RFC 791 along with the rest of IPv4.

The IPv4 datagram is conceptually divided into two pieces: the *header* and the *payload.* The header contains addressing and control fields, while the payload carries the actual data to be sent over the internetwork. Unlike some message formats, IP datagrams do not have a footer following the payload.

Even though IP is a relatively simple, connectionless, and unreliable protocol, the IPv4 header carries a fair bit of information, which makes it rather large. It is at least 20 bytes long, and with options it can be significantly longer. The IP datagram format is described in Tables 21-1, 21-2, and 21-3, and illustrated in Figure 21-2.

Table 21-1: Internet Protocol Version 4 (IPv4) Datagram Format

Field Name	Size (Bytes)	Description
Version	1/2 (4 bits)	Identifies the version of IP used to generate the datagram. For IPv4, this is the number 4. This field ensures compatibility between devices that may be running different versions of IP. In general, a device running an older version of IP will reject datagrams created by newer implementations, under the assumption that the older version may not be able to interpret the newer datagram correctly.
IHL	1/2 (4 bits)	Specifies the length of the IP header, in 32-bit words. This includes the length of any options fields and padding. The normal value of this field when no options are used is 5 (5 32-bit words = 5*4 = 20 bytes). Contrast this with the longer Total Length field in this table.
TOS	1	A field designed to carry information to provide quality-of-service features, such as prioritized delivery for IP datagrams. This has not been as widely used as originally defined, and its meaning has been redefined for use by a technique called *Differentiated Services (DS)*, as discussed in the "IP Datagram Type of Service (TOS) Field" section of this chapter.
TL	2	Specifies the total length of the IP datagram, in bytes. Since this field is 16 bits wide, the maximum length of an IP datagram is 65,535 bytes, though most are much smaller.
Identification	2	This field contains a 16-bit value that is common to each of the fragments belonging to a particular message; for datagrams originally sent unfragmented, it is still filled in so it can be used if the datagram must be fragmented by a router during delivery. The recipient uses this field to reassemble messages without accidentally mixing fragments from different messages. This is needed because fragments may arrive from multiple messages mixed together, since IP datagrams can be received out of order from any device. (See the discussion of IP message fragmentation in Chapter 22.)
Flags	3/8 (3 bits)	Three control flags, two of which are used to manage fragmentation (as described in the topic on fragmentation), and one that is reserved. See Table 21-2.
Fragment Offset	1 5/8 (13 bits)	When fragmentation of a message occurs, this field specifies the offset, or position, in the message where the data in this fragment goes in units of eight bytes (64 bits). The first fragment has an offset of 0. (See the discussion of fragmentation in Chapter 27 for a description of how the field is used.)
TTL	1	This specifies how long the datagram is allowed to live on the network, in router hops. Each router decrements the value of the TTL field (reduces it by one) prior to transmitting it. If the TTL field drops to zero, the datagram is assumed to have taken too long a route and is discarded. (See the "IP Datagram Time to Live (TTL) Field" section later in this chapter for more information.)

(continued)

Table 21-1: Internet Protocol Version 4 (IPv4) Datagram Format (continued)

Field Name	Size (Bytes)	Description
Protocol	1	Identifies the higher-layer protocol (generally either a transport layer protocol or encapsulated network layer protocol) carried in the datagram. Table 21-3 shows the protocol values of this field, which were originally defined by the IETF "Assigned Numbers" standard, RFC 1700, and are now maintained by the Internet Assigned Numbers Authority (IANA).
Header Checksum	2	A checksum is computed over the header to provide basic protection against corruption in transmission. This is not the more complex cyclic redundancy check (CRC) code that's typically used by data link layer technologies such as Ethernet; it's just a 16-bit checksum. It is calculated by dividing the header bytes into words (a word is two bytes) and then adding them together. Only the header is checksummed; not the data. At each hop, the device receiving the datagram does the same checksum calculation, and if there is a mismatch, it discards the datagram as damaged.
Source Address	4	This is the 32-bit IP address of the originator of the datagram. Note that even though intermediate devices such as routers may handle the datagram, they do not normally put their address into this field—the address is always that of the device that originally sent the datagram.
Destination Address	4	This is the 32-bit IP address of the intended recipient of the datagram. Again, even though devices such as routers may be the intermediate targets of the datagram, this field is always used to specify the ultimate destination.
Options	Variable	One or more of several types of options may be included after the standard headers in certain IP datagrams, as discussed later in this chapter, in the "IP Datagram Options and Option Format" section.
Padding	Variable	If one or more options are included, and the number of bits used for them is not a multiple of 32, enough 0 bits are added to pad out the header to a multiple of 32 bits (four bytes).
Data	Variable	This is the data that will be transmitted in the datagram. It is either an entire higher-layer message or a fragment of one.

Table 21-2: IPv4 Flags Subfields

Subfield Name	Size (Bytes)	Description
Reserved	1/8 (1 bit)	Not used.
DF	1/8 (1 bit)	When set to 1, this says that the datagram should not be fragmented. Since the fragmentation process is generally invisible to higher layers, most protocols don't care about this and don't set this flag. It is, however, used for testing the maximum transmission unit (MTU) of a link.
MF	1/8 (1 bit)	When set to 0, this indicates the last fragment in a message; when set to 1, it indicates that more fragments are yet to come in the fragmented message. If no fragmentation is used for a message, there is only one fragment (the whole message), and this flag is 0. If fragmentation is used, all fragments but the last set this flag to 1 so that the recipient knows when all fragments have been sent.

Table 21-3: IPv4 Protocol Subfields

Value (Hexadecimal)	Value (Decimal)	Protocol
00	0	Reserved
01	1	ICMP
02	2	IGMP
03	3	GGP
04	4	IP-in-IP Encapsulation
06	6	TCP
08	8	EGP
11	17	UDP
32	50	Encapsulating Security Payload (ESP) Extension Header
33	51	Authentication Header (AH) Extension Header

NOTE *The last two entries in Table 21-3 are used when IPSec inserts additional headers into the datagram: the AH or ESP headers. See Chapter 29 for more information.*

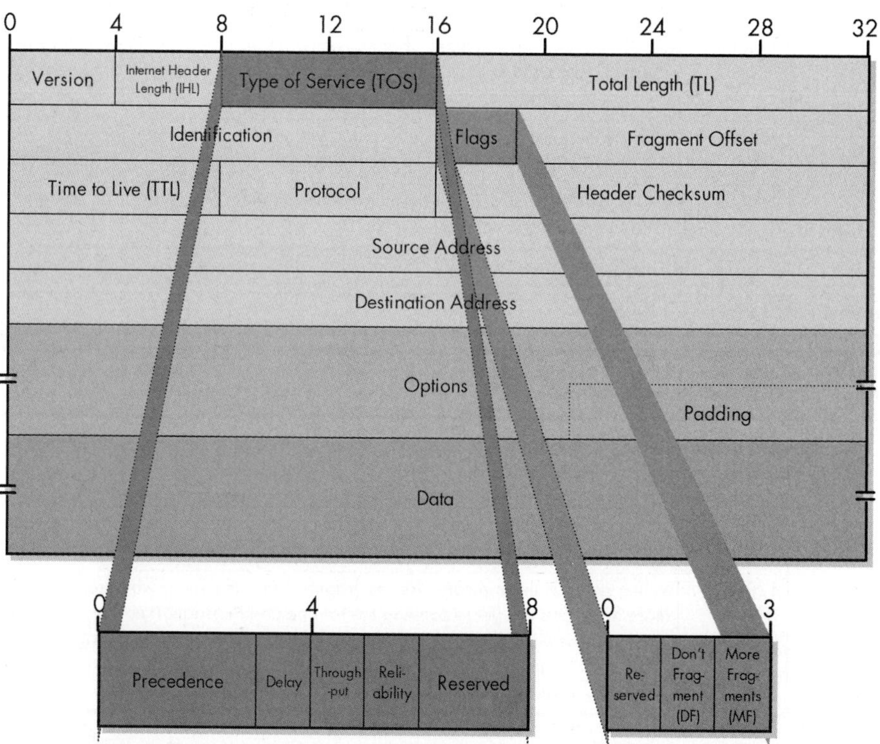

Figure 21-2: IPv4 datagram format *This diagram shows the all-important IPv4 datagram format. The first 20 bytes are the fixed IP header, followed by an optional Options section, and a variable-length Data area. Note that the Type of Service field is shown as originally defined in the IPv4 standard.*

IP Datagram Time to Live (TTL) Field

Let's look at the Time to Live (TTL) field. Since IP datagrams are sent from router to router as they travel across an internetwork, a datagram could be passed from Router A to Router B to Router C, and then back to Router A. This is called a *router loop*, and it's something that we don't want to happen.

To ensure that datagrams don't circle around endlessly, the TTL field was designed to contain a time value (in seconds), which would be filled in when the datagram was originally sent. Routers would decrease the time value periodically, and if it ever hit zero, destroy the datagram. The TTL field was also designed to ensure that time-critical datagrams wouldn't become stale or pass their expiration date.

In practice, this field is not used in exactly this manner. Routers today are fast and usually take far less than a second to forward a datagram, which makes it impractical to measure the time that a datagram lives. Instead, this field is used as a maximum hop count for the datagram. Each time a router processes a datagram, it reduces the value of the TTL field by one. If doing this results in the field being zero, the datagram is said to have expired, at which point it is dropped, and usually an Internet Control Message Protocol (ICMP) Time Exceeded message is sent to inform the originator of the message that it has expired. The TTL field is one of the primary mechanisms by which networks are protected from router loops. (See the description of ICMP Time Exceeded messages in Chapter 32 for more on how TTL helps IP handle router loops.)

IP Datagram Type of Service (TOS) Field

The Type of Service (TOS) field is a one-byte field that was originally intended to provide certain quality-of-service (QoS) features for IP datagram delivery. It allowed IP datagrams to be tagged with information indicating not only their precedence, but also the preferred manner in which they should be delivered. It was divided into a number of subfields, as shown in Table 21-4 and Figure 21-2.

The lack of QoS features has been considered a weakness of IP for a long time. But as you can see in Table 21-4, these features were built into IP from the start. The fact is that even though this field was defined in the standard in the early 1980s, it was not widely used by hardware and software. For years, it was just passed around with all zeros in the bits and mostly ignored.

The Internet Engineering Task Force (IETF), seeing the field unused, attempted to revive its use. In 1998, RFC 2474 redefined the first six bits of the TOS field to support a technique called *Differentiated Services (DS)*. Under DS, the values in the TOS field are called *codepoints* and are associated with different service levels. (See RFC 2474 for all the details.)

RELATED INFORMATION *Be sure to read the remainder of this chapter for more information on how IP options are used in datagrams and Chapter 22 for some more context on the use of fragmentation-related fields such as Identification, Fragment Offset, and More Fragments.*

Table 21-4: Original Definition of IPv4 Type of Service (TOS) Field

Subfield Name	Size (Bytes)	Description
Precedence	3/8 (3 bits)	A field indicating the priority of the datagram. There were eight defined values, from lowest to highest priority: 000: Routine 001: Priority 010: Immediate 011: Flash 100: Flash Override 101: CRITIC/ECP 110: Internetwork Control 111: Network Control
D	1/8 (1 bit)	Set to 0 to request normal delay in delivery; set to 1 if a low delay delivery is requested.
T	1/8 (1 bit)	Set to 0 to request normal delivery throughput; set to 1 if higher throughput delivery is requested.
R	1/8 (1 bit)	Set to 0 to request normal reliability in delivery; set to 1 if higher reliability delivery is requested.
Reserved	2/8 (2 bits)	Not used.

IP Datagram Options and Option Format

All IP datagrams must include the standard 20-byte header that contains key information such as the source and destination address of the datagram, fragmentation control parameters, length information, and more. In addition to these invariable fields, the creators of IPv4 included the ability to add *options* that provide additional flexibility in how IP handles datagrams. Use of these options is, of course, optional. However, all devices that handle IP datagrams must be capable of properly reading and handling them.

The IP datagram may contain zero, one, or more options, so the total length of the Options field in the IP header is variable. Each of the options can be a single byte or multiple bytes in length, depending on how much information the option needs to convey. When more than one option is included, they are concatenated and put into the Options field as a whole. Since the IP header must be a multiple of 32 bits, a Padding field is included if the number of bits in all options together is not a multiple of 32 bits.

Each IP option has its own subfield format, generally structured as shown in Tables 21-5 and 21-6, and illustrated in Figure 21-3. For most options, all three subfields are used: Option Type, Option Length, and Option Data. For a few simple options, however, this complex substructure is not needed. In those cases, the option type itself communicates all the information required, so the Option Type field appears, and the Option Length and Option Data subfields are omitted.

Table 21-5: IPv4 Option Format

Subfield Name	Size (Bytes)	Description
Option Type	1	The Option Type subfield is divided into three subsubfields, as shown in Table 21-6.
Option Length	0 or 1	For variable-length options, indicates the size of the entire option, including all three subfields shown here, in bytes.
Option Data	0 or variable	For variable-length options, contains data to be sent as part of the option.

Table 21-6: IPv4 Options: Option Type Subfields

Sub-Subfield Name	Size (Bytes)	Description
Copied Flag	1/8 (1 bit)	This bit is set to 1 if the option is intended to be copied into all fragments when a datagram is fragmented; it is cleared to 0 if the option should not be copied into fragments.
Option Class	2/8 (2 bits)	Specifies one of four potential values that indicate the general category into which the option belongs. In fact, only two of the values are used: 0 is for Control options, and 2 for Debugging and Measurement.
Option Number	5/8 (5 bits)	Specifies the kind of option. 32 different values can be specified for each of the two option classes. Of these, a few are more commonly employed. See Table 21-7 for more information on the specific options.

Table 21-7 lists the most common IPv4 options, showing the option class, option number, and length for each (a length of 1 indicates that an option consists of only an Option Type field). The table also provides a brief description of how each is used.

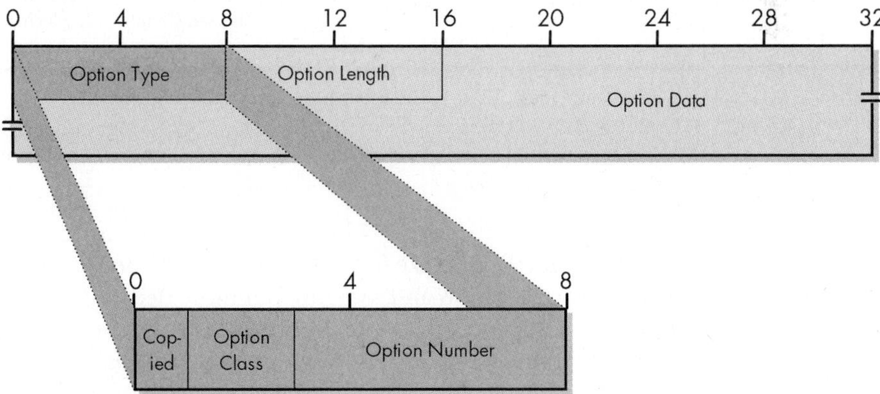

Figure 21-3: IPv4 Options field format *This diagram shows the full field format for an IPv4 option. Note that a few simple options may consist of only the Option Type subfield, with the Option Length and Option Data subfields omitted.*

Table 21-7: Common IPv4 Options

Option Class	Option Number	Length (Bytes)	Option Name	Description
0	0	1	End of Options List	An option containing just a single zero byte, used to mark the end of a list of options.
0	1	1	No Operation	A "dummy option" used as internal padding to align certain options on a 32-bit boundary when required.
0	2	11	Security	An option provided for the military to indicate the security classification of IP datagrams.
0	3	Variable	Loose Source Route	One of two options for source routing of IP datagrams.
0	7	Variable	Record Route	Allows the route used by a datagram to be recorded within the header for the datagram itself. If a source device sends a datagram with this option in it, each router that handles the datagram adds its IP address to this option. The recipient can then extract the list of IP addresses to see the route taken by the datagram. Note that the length of this option is set by the originating device. It cannot be enlarged as the datagram is routed, and if it fills up before it arrives at its destination, only a partial route will be recorded.
0	9	Variable	Strict Source Route	One of two options for source routing of IP datagrams.
2	4	Variable	Timestamp	Works similar to the Record Route option, but each device puts in a timestamp, so the recipient can see how long it took for the datagram to travel between routers. As with the Record Route option, the length of this option is set by the originating device and cannot be enlarged by intermediate devices.
2	18	12	Traceroute	Used in the enhanced implementation of the traceroute utility, as described in RFC 1393. Also see Chapter 33, which discusses ICMP traceroute messages.

KEY CONCEPT Each IPv4 datagram has a 20-byte mandatory header and may also include one or more *options*. Each option has its own field format, and most are variable in size.

Normally, IP datagrams are routed without any specific instructions from devices about the path a datagram should take from the source to the destination. It's the job of routers to use routing protocols and to figure out those details. In some cases, however, it may be advantageous to have the source of a datagram specify the route a datagram takes through the network. This process is called *source routing*.

There are two IP options that support source routing. In each, the option includes a list of IP addresses that specify the routers that must be used to reach the destination. When *strict* source routing is used, the path specified in the option must be used exactly, in sequence, with no other routers permitted to handle the datagram at all. In contrast, *loose* source routing specifies a list of IP addresses that must be followed in sequence, but it allows intervening hops between the devices on the list. (For full details on the exact structure used by each option type, please refer to RFC 791.)

22

IP DATAGRAM SIZE, FRAGMENTATION, AND REASSEMBLY

The main responsibility of the Internet Protocol (IP) is to deliver data between internetworked devices. As you saw in the preceding chapter, this requires that data received from higher layers be encapsulated into IP datagrams for transmission. These datagrams are then passed down to the data link layer, where they are sent over physical network links. In order for this to work properly, each datagram must be small enough to fit within the frame format of the underlying technology. If the message is bigger than the maximum frame size of the underlying network, it may be necessary to fragment the message. The datagrams are then sent individually and reassembled into the original message.

IP is designed to manage datagram size and to make fragmentation and reassembly seamless. This chapter explores issues related to managing the size of IP datagrams. I start with an overview of datagram size issues and the important concept of a network's maximum transmission unit (MTU), discussing why fragmentation is necessary. I then describe the process by which messages are fragmented by the source device, and possibly by routers along the path to the destination, and how they are reassembled by the recipient.

BACKGROUND INFORMATION *Understanding fragmentation and reassembly requires some knowledge of the basic format of IP datagrams and some of the fields they contain. If you haven't yet read the chapter describing the general format of IP datagrams in Chapter 21, you may wish to review it before proceeding here.*

IP Datagram Size, MTU, and Fragmentation Overview

As the core network layer protocol of the TCP/IP protocol suite, IP is designed to implement potentially large internetworks of devices. When we work with IP, we get used to the concept of hosts being able to send information back and forth, even though the hosts may be quite far apart. Although we can usually consider the TCP/IP internetwork to be like a large, abstract virtual network of devices, we must always remember that underneath the network layer, data always travels across one or more physical networks. The implementation of IP must take this reality into account as well.

In order to send messages using IP, we encapsulate the higher-layer data into IP datagrams. These datagrams must then be sent down to the data link layer, where they are further encapsulated into the frames of whatever technology will be used to physically convey them, either directly to their destination or indirectly to the next intermediate step in their journey to their intended recipient. The data link layer implementation puts the entire IP datagram into the data portion (the payload) of its frame format, just as IP puts transport layer messages—transport headers and all—into its IP Data field. This immediately presents us with a potential issue: matching the size of the IP datagram to the size of the underlying data link layer frame size.

IP Datagram Size and the Underlying Network Frame Size

The underlying network that a device uses to connect to other devices could be a local area network (LAN) connection (like Ethernet or Token Ring), wireless LAN (WLAN) link (such as 802.11), dial-up connection, Digital Subscriber Line (DSL) connection, T1 link, or other wide area network (WAN) connection. Each physical network will generally use its own frame format, and each format has a limit on how much data can be sent in a single frame. If the IP datagram is too large for the data link layer frame format's payload section, we have a problem!

For example, consider a Fiber Distributed Data Interface (FDDI) network. The maximum size of the data field in FDDI is around 4,470 bytes. This means FDDI can handle an IP datagram of up to 4,470 bytes. In contrast, a regular Ethernet frame uses a frame format that limits the size of the payload it sends to 1,500 bytes. This means that Ethernet cannot deal with IP datagrams greater than 1,500 bytes.

Now, remember that in sending a datagram across an internetwork, it may pass across more than one physical network. To access a site on the Internet, for example, we typically send a request through our local router, which then connects to other routers that eventually relay the request to the Internet site. Each hop as the datagram is forwarded may use a different physical network, with a different maximum underlying frame size.

The whole idea behind a network layer protocol is to implement this concept of a virtual network where devices can communicate over great distances. This means that higher layers shouldn't need to worry about details like the size limits of underlying data link layer technologies. This task falls to IP.

MTU and Datagram Fragmentation

Each device on an IP internetwork must know the capacity of its immediate data link layer connection to other devices. This capacity is called the *maximum transmission unit (MTU)* of the network, also known as the *maximum transfer unit.*

If an IP layer receives a message to be sent across the internetwork, it looks at the size of the message and then computes how large the IP datagram would be after the addition of the 20 or more bytes needed for the IP header. If the total length is greater than the MTU of the underlying network, the IP layer will fragment the message into multiple IP fragments. Thus, if a host is connected to its local network using an Ethernet LAN, it may use an MTU of 1,500 bytes for IP datagrams, and it will fragment anything larger.

Figure 22-1 shows an example of different MTUs and fragmentation.

> **KEY CONCEPT** The size of the largest IP datagram that can be transmitted over a physical network is called that network's *maximum transmission unit (MTU)*. If a datagram is passed from a network with a high MTU to one with a low MTU, it must be *fragmented* to fit the other network's smaller MTU.

Since some physical networks on the path between devices may have a smaller MTU than others, it may be necessary to fragment the datagram more than once. For example, suppose the source device wants to send an IP message 12,000 bytes long. Its local connection has an MTU of 3,300 bytes. It will need to divide this message into four fragments for transmission: three that are about 3,300 bytes long and a fourth remnant about 2,100 bytes long. (I'm oversimplifying by ignoring the extra headers required; the "The IP Message Fragmentation Process" section later in this chapter includes the full details of the fragmentation process.)

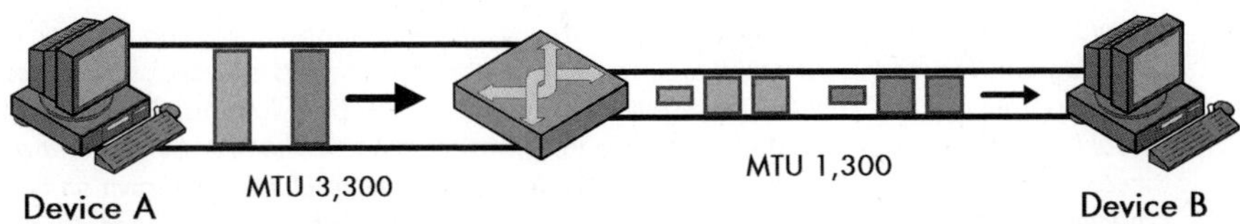

Figure 22-1: IP maximum transmission unit (MTU) and fragmentation *In this simple example, Device A is sending to Device B over a small internetwork consisting of one router and two physical links. The link from Device A to the router has an MTU of 3,300 bytes, but from the router to Device B, it is only 1,300 bytes. Thus, any IP datagrams larger than 1,300 bytes will need to be fragmented.*

Multiple-Stage Fragmentation

While the IP fragments are in transit, they may need to pass over a hop between two routers where the physical network's MTU is only 1,300 bytes. In this case, each of the fragments will again need to be fragmented. The 3,300-byte fragments will end up in three pieces each (two of about 1,300 bytes and one of around 700 bytes), and the final 2,100-byte fragment will become a 1,300-byte and 800-byte fragment. So, instead of having four fragments, we will end up with eleven (3*3+1*2) fragments, as shown in Figure 22-2.

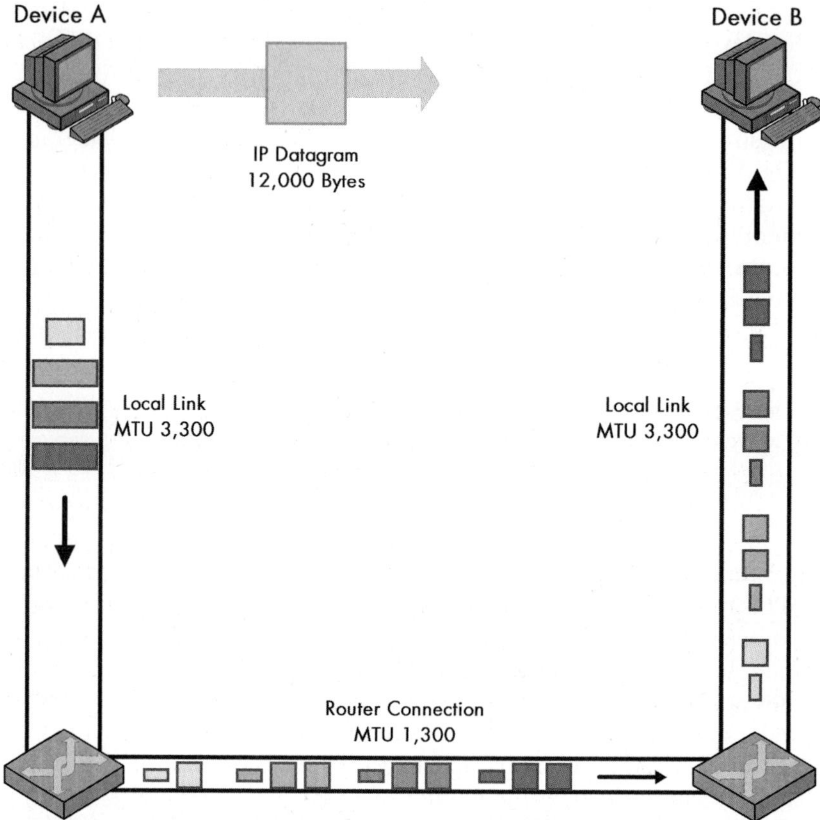

Figure 22-2: IPv4 datagram fragmentation. *This example illustrates a two-step fragmentation of a large IP datagram. The boxes represent datagrams or datagram fragments and are shown to scale. The original datagram is 12,000 bytes, represented by the large, gray box. To transmit this data over the first local link, Device A splits it into four fragments, shown on the left. The first router must fragment each of these into smaller fragments to send them over the 1,300-byte MTU link, as shown on the bottom. Note that the second router does not reassemble the 1,300-byte fragments, even though its link to Device B has an MTU of 3,300 bytes. (The "IP Fragmentation Process" section later in this chapter describes the process by which the fragments in this example are created.)*

Internet Minimum MTU: 576 Bytes

Routers are required to handle an MTU of at least 576 bytes. This value is specified in RFC 791; it was chosen to allow a data block of at least 512 bytes, plus room for the standard IP header and options. Since this is the minimum size specified in the IP standard, 576 bytes has become a common default MTU value used for IP datagrams. Even if a host is connected over a local network with an MTU larger than 576 bytes, it may choose to use an MTU value of 576 to ensure that no further fragmentation will be required by intermediate routers.

NOTE *While intermediate routers may further fragment an already-fragmented IP message, they do not reassemble fragments. Reassembly is done only by the recipient device. This has some advantages and some disadvantages, as we will see when we examine the reassembly process in the "IP Message Reassembly" section later in this chapter.*

MTU Path Discovery

When we're trying to send a great deal of data, efficiency in message transmissions becomes important. The larger the IP datagram we send, the smaller the percentage of bytes wasted for overhead such as header fields. This means that, ideally, we want to use the largest MTU possible without requiring fragmentation for its transmission.

To determine the optimal MTU to use for a route between two devices, we would need to know the MTU of every link on that route—information that the endpoints of the connection simply don't have. However, the connection endpoint can determine the MTU of the overall route by using *MTU path discovery*, which uses an error-reporting mechanism built into TCP/IP Internet Control Message Protocol (ICMP).

One of the message types defined in ICMP version 4 (ICMPv4) is the Destination Unreachable message (see Chapter 32), which is returned under various conditions where an IP datagram cannot be delivered. One of these situations is when a datagram is too large to be forwarded by a router over a physical link, but this datagram has its Don't Fragment (DF) flag set to prevent fragmentation. In this case, the datagram must be discarded and a Destination Unreachable message sent back to the source. A device can exploit this capability by testing the path with datagrams of different sizes, to see how large they must be before they are rejected.

The source node typically sends a datagram that has the MTU of its local physical link, since that represents an upper bound for any path to or from that device. If this datagram goes through without any errors, the device knows it can use that value for future datagrams to that destination. If it gets back any Destination Unreachable - Fragmentation Needed and DF Set messages, it knows that a link between it and the destination has a smaller MTU. It tries again using a smaller datagram size, and it continues until it finds the largest MTU that can be used on the path.

IP Message Fragmentation Process

As explained in the previous section, when an IP datagram is too large for the MTU of the underlying data link layer technology used for the next leg of its journey, it must be fragmented before it can be sent across the network. The higher-layer message to be transmitted is not sent in a single IP datagram, but rather broken down into fragments that are sent separately. In some cases, the fragments themselves may need to be fragmented further.

Fragmentation is key to implementing a network-layer internetwork that is independent of lower-layer details, but it introduces significant complexity to IP. Remember that IP is an unreliable, connectionless protocol. IP datagrams can take any of several routes on their way from the source to the destination, and some may not even make it to the destination at all. When a message is fragmented, this converts a single datagram into many, which introduces several new concerns:

Sequencing and Placement The fragments will typically be sent in sequential order from the beginning of the message to the end, but they won't necessarily show up in the order in which they were sent. The receiving device must be able to determine the sequence of the fragments to reassemble them in the correct order. In fact, some implementations send the last fragment first, so the receiving device will immediately know the full size of the original, complete datagram. This makes keeping track of the order of segments even more essential.

Separation of Fragmented Messages A source device may need to send more than one fragmented message at a time, or it may send multiple datagrams that are fragmented en route. This means that the destination may be receiving multiple sets of fragments that must be put back together. Imagine a box containing pieces from two, three, or more jigsaw puzzles, and you understand this issue.

Completion The destination device must be able to tell when it has received all of the fragments so it knows when to start reassembly (or when to give up if it didn't get all the pieces).

To address these concerns and allow the proper reassembly of the fragmented message, IP includes several fields in the IP format header that convey information from the source to the destination about the fragments. Some of these fields contain a common value for all the fragments of the message; others are different for each fragment.

The IP Fragmentation Process

The device performing the fragmentation follows a specific algorithm to divide the message into fragments for transmission. The exact implementation of the fragmentation process depends on the device. For example, consider an IP message 12,000 bytes wide (including the 20-byte IP header) that needs to be sent over a link with an MTU of 3,300 bytes. Figure 22-3 depicts a typical method by which this fragmentation might be performed.

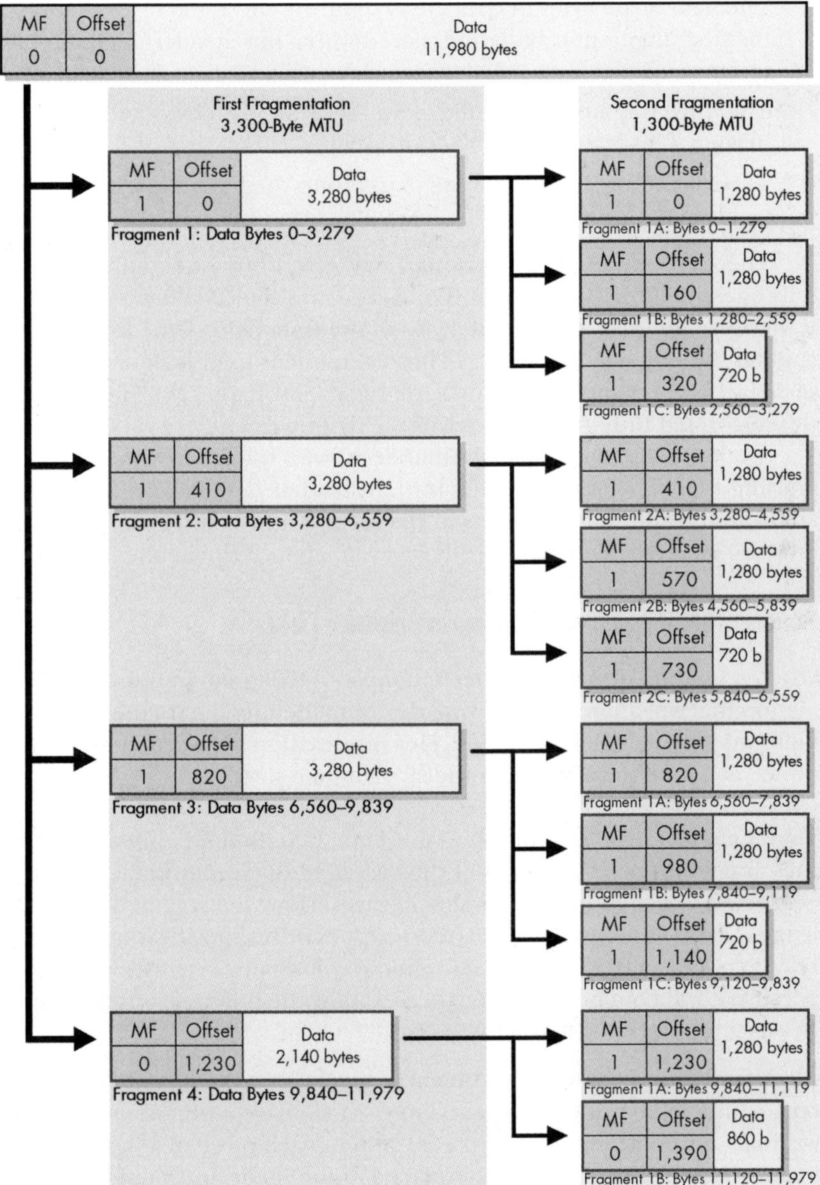

Figure 22-3: IPv4 datagram fragmentation process *In this diagram, the MF and Fragment Offset fields of each fragment are shown for reference. The Data fields are shown to scale (the length of each is proportional to the number of bytes in the fragment).*

The four fragments shown in Figure 22-3 are created as follows:

- The first fragment is created by taking the first 3,300 bytes of the 12,000-byte IP datagram. This includes the original header, which becomes the IP header of the first fragment (with certain fields changed, as described in the next section). So, 3,280 bytes of data are in the first fragment. This leaves 8,700 bytes (11,980–3,280) to encapsulate.

- The next 3,280 bytes of data are taken from the 8,700 bytes that remain after the first fragment is built and paired with a new header to create the second fragment. This leaves 5,420 bytes.
- The third fragment is created from the next 3,280 bytes of data, with a 20-byte header. This leaves 2,140 bytes of data.
- The remaining 2,140 bytes are placed into the fourth fragment, with a 20-byte header.

There are two important points here. First, IP fragmentation does *not* work by fully encapsulating the original IP message into the Data fields of the fragments. If this were the case, the first 20 bytes of the Data field of the first fragment would contain the original IP header. (This technique is used by some other protocols, such as the PPP Multilink Protocol, discussed in Chapter 9.) The original IP header is transformed into the IP header of the first fragment.

Second, note that the total number of bytes transmitted increases: we are sending 12,060 bytes (3,300*3+2,160), instead of 12,000 bytes. The extra 60 bytes are from the additional headers in the second, third, and fourth fragments. (The increase in size could theoretically be even larger if the headers contain options.)

Fragmentation-Related IP Datagram Header Fields

When a sending device or router fragments a datagram, it must provide information that will allow the receiving device to identify the fragments and reassemble them into the original datagram. This information is recorded by the fragmenting device in a number of fields in the IP datagram header:

Total Length After fragmenting, the Total Length field indicates the length of each fragment, not the length of the overall message. Normally, the fragment size is selected to match the MTU value in bytes. However, fragments must have a length that is a multiple of 8, to allow proper offset specification (handled by the Fragment Offset field). The last fragment will usually be shorter than the others because it will contain a leftover piece, unless the message length happens to be an exact multiple of the fragment size.

Identification To solve the problem of pieces from many jigsaw puzzles in the same box, a unique identifier is assigned to each message being fragmented. This is like writing a different number on the bottom of each piece of a jigsaw puzzle before tossing it in the box. This value is placed in the Identification field in the IP header of each fragment sent. The Identification field is 16 bits wide, so a total of 65,536 different identifiers can be used. Obviously, we want to make sure that each message that is being fragmented for delivery has a different identifier. The source can decide how it generates unique identifiers. This may be done through something as simple as a counter that is incremented each time a new set of fragments is created.

More Fragments The More Fragments flag is set to a 1 for all fragments except the last one, which has it set to 0. When the fragment with a value of 0 in the More Fragments flag is seen, the destination knows it has received the last fragment of the message.

Fragment Offset The Fragment Offset field solves the problem of sequencing fragments by indicating to the recipient device where in the overall message each particular fragment should be placed. The field is 13 bits wide, so the offset can be from 0 to 8,191. Fragments are specified in units of 8 bytes, which is why fragment length must be a multiple of 8. Uncoincidentally, 8,191*8 is 65,528, just about the maximum size allowed for an IP datagram. In the example shown in Figure 22-3, the first fragment would have a Fragment Offset of 0, the second would have an offset of 410 (3,280/8), the third would have an offset of 820 (6,560/8), and the fourth would have an offset of 1,230.

An IP datagram has a couple of other fields related to fragmentation. First, if a datagram containing options must be fragmented, some of the options may be copied to each of the fragments. This is controlled by the Copied flag in each option field.

Second, in the IP header, there is a flag called Don't Fragment. This field can be set to 1 by a transmitting device to specify that a datagram should not be fragmented in transit. This may be used in certain circumstances where the entire message must be delivered intact for some reason. It may also be used if the destination device has a limited IP implementation and cannot reassemble fragments, and it is also used for testing the MTU of a link. Normally, however, devices don't care about fragmentation, and this field is left at 0.

If a router encounters a datagram too large to pass over the next physical network but with the Don't Fragment bit set to 1, it cannot fragment the datagram and it cannot pass it along either, so it is stuck. It will generally drop the datagram and return an ICMP Destination Unreachable error message: "Fragmentation Needed and Don't Fragment Bit Set." This is used in MTU path discovery, as described earlier in this chapter.

> **KEY CONCEPT** When an MTU requirement forces a datagram to be fragmented, it is split into several smaller IP datagrams, each containing part of the original. The header of the original datagram is changed into the header of the first fragment, and new headers are created for the other fragments. Each is set to the same Identification value to mark them as part of the same original datagram. The Fragment Offset of each is set to the location where the fragment belongs in the original. The More Fragments field is set to 1 for all fragments but the last, to let the recipient know when it has received all the fragments.

IP Message Reassembly

When a datagram is fragmented, it becomes multiple fragment datagrams. The destination of the overall message must collect these fragments and reassemble them into the original message.

While reassembly is the complement to fragmentation, the two processes are not symmetric. A primary differentiation between the two is that intermediate routers can fragment a single datagram or further fragment a datagram that is already a fragment, but intermediate devices do not perform reassembly; reassembly happens only at the message's ultimate destination. Thus, if a datagram at an intermediate router on one side of a physical network with an MTU of 1,300 bytes causes fragmentation of a 3,300-byte datagram, the router on the other end of this 1,300 MTU link will *not* restore the 3,300-byte datagram to its original state. It will send all the 1,300-byte fragments on down the internetwork, as shown in Figure 22-2, earlier in the chapter.

In IP version 4 (IPv4), fragmentation can be performed by a router between the source and destination of an IP datagram, but reassembly is done only by the destination device.

There are a number of reasons why the decision was made to implement IP reassembly this way. Perhaps the most important reason is that fragments can take different routes to get from the source to destination, so any given router may not see all the fragments in a message. Another reason is that if routers needed to worry about reassembling fragments, their complexity would increase. Finally, reassembly of a message requires that we wait for all fragments before sending on the reassembled message. Having routers do this would slow down routing. Since routers don't reassemble messages, they can immediately forward all fragments on to the ultimate recipient.

However, there are drawbacks to this design as well. One is that it results in more, smaller fragments traveling over longer routes than if intermediate reassembly occurred. This increases the chances of a fragment getting lost and the entire message being discarded. Another is a potential inefficiency in the utilization of data link layer frame capacity. In the example of a 3,300-byte datagram being fragmented for a 1,300-byte MTU link, the 1,300-byte fragments would not be reassembled back into a 3,300-byte datagram at the end of the 1,300-MTU link. If the next link after that one also had an MTU of 3,300 bytes, we would need to send three frames, each encapsulating a 1,300-byte fragment, instead of a single larger frame, which is slightly slower.

As described in the previous section, several IP header fields are filled in when a message is fragmented to give the receiving device the information it requires to properly reassemble the fragments. The receiving device follows a procedure to keep track of the fragments as they are received and build up its copy of the total received message from the source device. Most of its efforts are geared toward dealing with the potential difficulties associated with IP being an unreliable protocol.

The details of implementation of the reassembly process are specific to each device, but reassembly generally includes the following functions:

Fragment Recognition and Fragmented Message Identification The recipient knows it has received a message fragment the first time it sees a datagram with the More Fragments bit set to 1 or the Fragment Offset a value other than 0. It identifies the message based on the source and destination IP addresses, the protocol specified in the header, and the Identification field generated by the sender.

Buffer Initialization The receiving device initializes a buffer where it can store the fragments of the message as they are received. It keeps track of which portions of this buffer have been filled with received fragments, perhaps using a special table. By doing this, it knows when the buffer is partially filled with received fragments and when it is completely full.

Timer Initialization The receiving device sets up a timer for reassembly of the message. Since it is possible that some fragments may never show up, this timer ensures that the device will not wait an infinite time trying to reassemble the message.

Fragment Receipt and Processing Whenever a fragment of this message arrives (as indicated by its having the same source and destination addresses, protocol, and Identification as the first fragment), the fragment is processed. It is inserted into the message buffer in the location indicated by its Fragment Offset field. The device also makes note of the fact that this portion of the message has been received.

Reassembly is complete when the entire buffer has been filled and the fragment with the More Fragments bit set to 0 is received, indicating that it is the last fragment of the datagram. The reassembled datagram is then processed in the same way as a normal, unfragmented datagram. On the other hand, if the timer for the reassembly expires with any of the fragments missing, the message cannot be reconstructed. The fragments are discarded, and an ICMP Time Exceeded message is generated. Since IP is unreliable, it relies on higher-layer protocols such as the Transmission Control Protocol (TCP) to determine that the message was not properly received and then retransmit it.

23

IP ROUTING AND MULTICASTING

The essential functions of Internet Protocol (IP) datagram encapsulation and addressing are sometimes compared to putting a letter in an envelope and then writing the address of the recipient on it. Once our IP datagram "envelope" is filled and labeled, it is ready to go, but it's still sitting on our desk. The last of the main functions of IP is to get the envelope to our intended recipient. This is the process of datagram *delivery*. When the recipient is not on our local network, this delivery requires that the datagram be *routed* from our network to the one where the destination resides.

This chapter concludes our look at IP version 4 (IPv4) with a discussion of some of the particulars of how it routes datagrams over an internetwork. I begin with an overview of the process and contrast direct and indirect delivery of data between devices. I discuss the main method used to route datagrams over the internetwork, and I explain briefly how IP routing tables are built and maintained. I describe how the move from classful to classless addressing using Classless Inter-Domain Routing (CIDR) has impacted routing.

I conclude with a brief look at the issues related to IP multicasting. Multicasting isn't really a part of routing, but many of the issues in multicasting are related to datagram delivery and routing.

RELATED INFORMATION *This chapter focuses on routing issues that are directly related to how IP works. Routing is a complex and important topic in networking, and you'll find much more information about it in Chapters 37 through 41.*

IP Datagram Delivery

The overall job of IP is to transmit messages from higher-layer protocols over an internetwork of devices. These messages must be packaged and addressed, and fragmented if necessary, and then they must be *delivered*. The process of delivery can be either simple or complex, depending on the proximity of the source and destination devices. We can divide all IP datagram deliveries into two general types: direct delivery and indirect delivery. Figure 23-1 shows some examples of IP datagram delivery types.

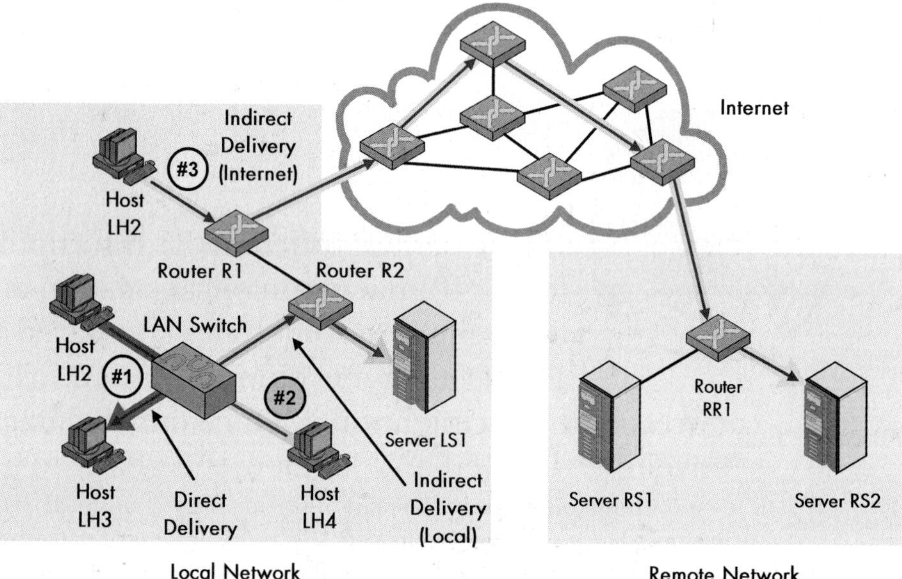

Figure 23-1: Direct and indirect (routed) delivery of IP datagrams This diagram shows three examples of IP datagram delivery. The first transmission (#1, dark arrow) shows a direct delivery between two devices on the local network. The second (#2, light arrow) shows indirect delivery within the local network, between a client and server separated by a router. The third (#3, medium arrow) shows a more distant indirect delivery, between a client on the local network and a server across the Internet.

Direct Datagram Delivery

When datagrams are sent between two devices on the same physical network, the datagrams may be delivered directly from the source to the destination. For example, if you wanted to deliver a letter to a neighbor on your street, you would probably just put her name on the envelope and stick it right in her mailbox.

Direct delivery is obviously a simple delivery method. The source simply sends the IP datagram down to its data link layer implementation. The data link layer encapsulates the datagram in a frame that is sent over the physical network directly to the recipient's data link layer, which passes it up to the IP layer.

Indirect Datagram Delivery (Routing)

When two devices are not on the same physical network, the delivery of datagrams from one to the other is *indirect*. Since the source device cannot see the destination on its local network, it must send the datagram through one or more intermediate devices to deliver it. Indirect delivery is like mailing a letter to a friend in a different city. You don't deliver it yourself; you use the postal system. The letter journeys through the postal system, possibly taking several intermediate steps, and ends up in your friend's neighborhood, where a postal carrier puts it into his mailbox.

Indirect delivery is much more complicated, because we can't send the data straight to the recipient. In fact, we usually will not even know exactly where the recipient is. Sure, we have its address, but we may not know what network it is on, or where that network is relative to our own. (If I told you my address, you would know it's somewhere in Bennington, Vermont, but could you find it?) Just as we must rely on the postal system in the envelope analogy, we must rely on the internetwork itself to indirectly deliver datagrams. And like the postal system, IP doesn't require you to know how to get the message to its recipient; you just put it into the system.

The devices that accomplish this magic of indirect delivery are generally known as *routers*, and indirect delivery is more commonly called *routing*. Like entrusting a letter to your local mail carrier or mailbox, a host that needs to deliver a message to a distant device generally sends datagrams to its local router. The router connects to one or more other routers, and they each maintain information about where to send datagrams so that they reach their final destination.

Indirect delivery is almost always required when communicating with distant devices, such as those on the Internet or across a wide area network (WAN) link. However, it may also be needed even to send a message to a device in the next room of your office, if that device is not connected directly to your device at layer 2.

NOTE *In the past, routers were often called* gateways*. Today, this term more generally can refer to devices that connect networks in a variety of ways. You will still sometimes hear routers called gateways, especially in the context of terms like default gateway, but since it is ambiguous, the term* router *is preferred.*

The Relationship Between Datagram Routing and Addressing

Each time a datagram is to be sent, the sender must determine first whether it can be delivered directly or if routing is required. IP addressing is what allows a device to quickly determine whether or not it is on the same network as its intended recipient. The following are the three main categories of addressing (see Chapter 16):

Conventional Classful Addressing We know the class of each address by looking at the first few bits. This tells us which bits of an address are the network ID. If the network ID of the destination is the same as our own, the recipient is on the same network; otherwise, it is not. Refer to Chapter 17 for more on classful addressing.

Subnetted Classful Addressing We use our subnet mask to determine our network ID and subnet ID and that of the destination address. If the network ID and subnet are the same, the recipient is on the same subnet. If only the network ID is the same, the recipient is on a different subnet of the same network. If the network ID is different, the destination is on a different network entirely. See Chapter 18 for a full discussion of subnetting.

Classless Addressing The same basic technique is used as for subnetted classful addressing, except that there are no subnets. We use the slash number to determine what part of the address is the network ID and compare the source and destination as before; see Chapter 20. (There are complications here, however, as discussed in the "IP Routing in a Subnet or Classless Addressing (CIDR) Environment" section later in this chapter.)

KEY CONCEPT The delivery of IP datagrams is divided into two categories: *direct* and *indirect*. Direct delivery is possible when two devices are on the same physical network. When they are not, indirect delivery, more commonly called *routing*, is required to get the datagrams from the source to the destination. A device can tell which type of delivery is required by looking at the IP address of the destination, in conjunction with supplemental information such as the subnet mask, which tells the device what network or subnet it is on.

The determination of what type of delivery is required is the first step in the source deciding where to send a datagram. If it realizes the destination is on the same local network, it will address the datagram to the recipient directly at the data link layer. Otherwise, it will send the datagram to the data link layer address of one of the routers to which it is connected. The IP address of the datagram will still be that of the ultimate destination. Mapping between IP addresses and data link layer addresses is accomplished using the TCP/IP Address Resolution Protocol (ARP), which is discussed in Chapter 13.

Routing is done in indirect delivery to get the datagram to the local network of the recipient. Once the datagram has been routed to the recipient's physical network, it is sent to the recipient by the recipient's local router. So, you could say that indirect delivery includes direct delivery as its final step.

NOTE *Strictly speaking, any process of delivery between a source and destination device can be considered routing, even if the devices are on the same network. It is common, however, for the process of routing to refer more specifically to indirect delivery.*

IP Routing Concepts and the Process of Next-Hop Routing

IP's ability to route information is what allows us to use it to create the equivalent of a virtual internetwork that spans potentially thousands of physical networks, allowing devices even on opposite ends of the globe communicate. Let's take a brief look at key IP routing concepts.

To continue with our postal system analogy, I can send a letter from my home in the United States to someone in, say, India, and the postal systems of both countries will work (or should work) to deliver the letter to its destination. However, when I drop a letter in the mailbox, it's not like someone shows up, grabs the letter, and hand-delivers it to the right address in India. The letter travels from the mailbox to my local post office. From there, it probably goes to a regional distribution center, and then from there, to a hub for international traffic. It goes to India, perhaps via an intermediate country. When it gets to India, the Indian postal system uses its own network of offices and facilities to route the letter to its destination. The envelope hops from one location to the next, until it reaches its destination.

IP routing works in very much the same manner. Even though IP lets devices connect over the internetwork using indirect delivery, all of the actual communication of datagrams occurs over physical networks using routers. We don't know exactly where the destination device's network is, and we certainly don't have any way to connect directly to each of the thousands of networks out there. Instead, we rely on these intermediate devices—routers—that are each physically connected to each other in a variety of ways to form a mesh containing millions of paths between networks. The datagram is handed off from one router to the next, until it gets to the physical network of the destination device. This process is called *next-hop routing*, as illustrated in Figure 23-2.

This is a critical concept in how IP works: routing is done step by step, one hop at a time. When we decide to send a datagram to a device on a distant network, we don't know the exact path that the datagram will take; we have only enough information to send it to the correct router to which we are attached. That router, in turn, looks at the IP address of the destination and decides where the datagram should hop to next. This process continues until the datagram reaches the destination host's network.

At first, next-hop routing may seem like a strange way of sending datagrams over an internetwork. In fact, it is part of what makes IP so powerful. On each step of the journey to any other host, a router needs to know only where the next step for the datagram is. Without this concept, each device and router would need to know what path to take to every other host on the internetwork, which would be quite impractical.

> **KEY CONCEPT** Indirect delivery of IP datagrams is accomplished using a process called *next-hop routing*, where each message is handed from one router to the next until it reaches the network of the destination. The main advantage of this is that each router needs to know only which neighboring router should be the next recipient of a given datagram, rather than needing to know the exact route to every destination network.

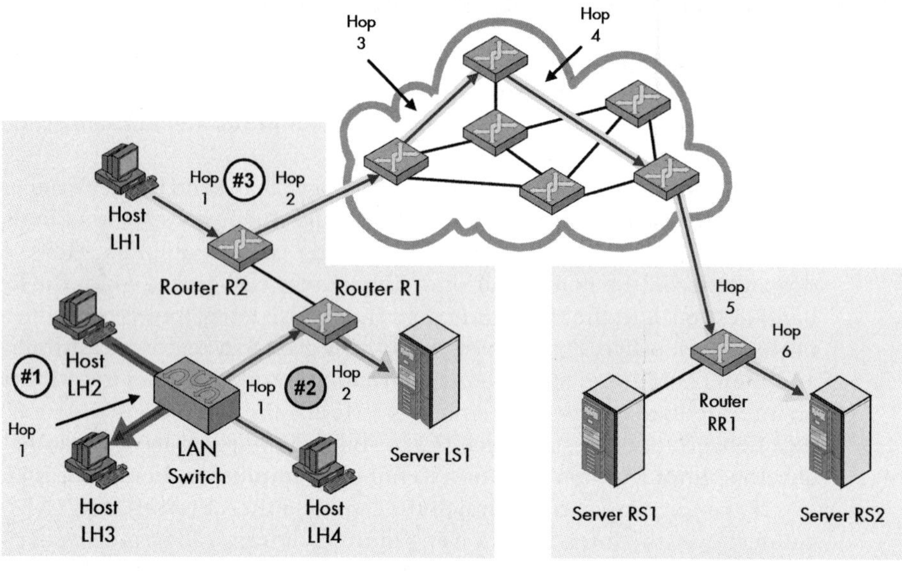

Figure 23-2: IP datagram next-hop routing *This is the same diagram as that shown in Figure 23-1, except it explicitly shows the hops taken by each of the three sample transmissions. The direct delivery of the first transmission has only one hop (remember that the switch doesn't count because it is invisible at layer 3). The local indirect delivery passes through one router, so it has two hops. The Internet delivery has six hops. (Actual Internet routes can be much longer.)*

Another key concept related to the principle of next-hop routing is that routers, not hosts, are designed to accomplish routing. Most hosts are connected to the rest of the internetwork (or Internet) using only one router. It would be a maintenance nightmare to need to give each host the intelligence to know how to route to every other host. Instead, hosts decide only if they are sending to their own local network or to another network. If the destination is another network, a host just sends the datagram to its router and says, "Here, *you* take care of this." If a host has a connection to more than one router, it needs to know only which router to use for certain sets of distant networks.

Again, each hop consists of the traversal of a physical network. Once a source sends a datagram to its local router, the data link layer on the router passes it up to the router's IP layer. There, the datagram's header is examined, and the router decides which device should get the datagram next. It then passes the datagram back down to the data link layer to be sent over one of the router's physical network links, typically to another router. The router will have a record of the physical addresses of the routers to which it is connected, or it will use ARP to determine these addresses.

IP Routes and Routing Tables

As described in the previous section, routers are responsible for forwarding traffic on an IP internetwork. Each router accepts datagrams from a variety of sources, examines the IP address of the destination, and decides the next hop that the datagram needs to take to get it that much closer to its final destination. But how does a router know where to send different datagrams?

Each router maintains a set of information that provides a mapping between different network IDs and the other routers to which it is connected. This information is contained in a data structure normally called a *routing table.* Each entry in the table, called a *routing entry,* provides information about one network (or subnetwork or host). It basically says, "If the destination of this datagram is in the following network, the next hop you should take is to the following device." Each time a datagram is received, the router checks its destination IP address against the routing entries in its table to decide where to send the datagram and then sends it on to its next hop.

> **KEY CONCEPT** A router make decisions about how to route datagrams using its internal *routing table.* The table contains entries specifying to which router datagrams should be sent in order to reach a particular network.

Obviously, the fewer entries in this table, the faster the router can decide what to do with datagrams. (This was a big part of the motivation for classless addressing, which aggregates routes into supernetworks to reduce router table size, as described in the next section.) Some routers have connections to only two other devices, so they don't have much of a decision to make. Typically, the router will simply take datagrams coming from one of its interfaces and, if necessary, send them out on the other one. For example, consider a small company's router acting as the interface between a network of three hosts and the Internet. Any datagrams sent to the router from a host on this network will need to go over the router's connection to the router at the Internet service provider (ISP).

When a router has connections to more than two devices, things become considerably more complex. A certain distant network may be more easily reachable using a particular connection. The routing table not only contains information about the networks directly connected to the router, but also information that the router has learned about more distant networks.

Figure 23-3 shows an example with four routers. Routers R1, R2, and R3 are connected in a triangle, so that each router can send directly to the others, as well as to its own local network. R1's local network is 11.0.0.0/8, R2's is 12.0.0.0/8, and R3's is 13.0.0.0/8. R1 knows that any datagram it sees with 11 as the first octet is on its local network. It will also have a routing entry that says that any IP address starting with 12 should go to R2, and any IP address starting with 13 should go to R3. R1 also connects to router R4, which has 14.0.0.0/8 as its local network. R1 will have an entry for this local network, but R2 and R3 also need to know how to reach 14.0.0.0/8, even though they don't connect to its router directly. Most likely, they will have an entry that says that any datagrams intended for 14.0.0.0/8 should be sent to R1. R1 will then forward them to R4. Similarly, R4 will send any traffic intended for 12.0.0.0/8 or 13.0.0.0/8 through R1.

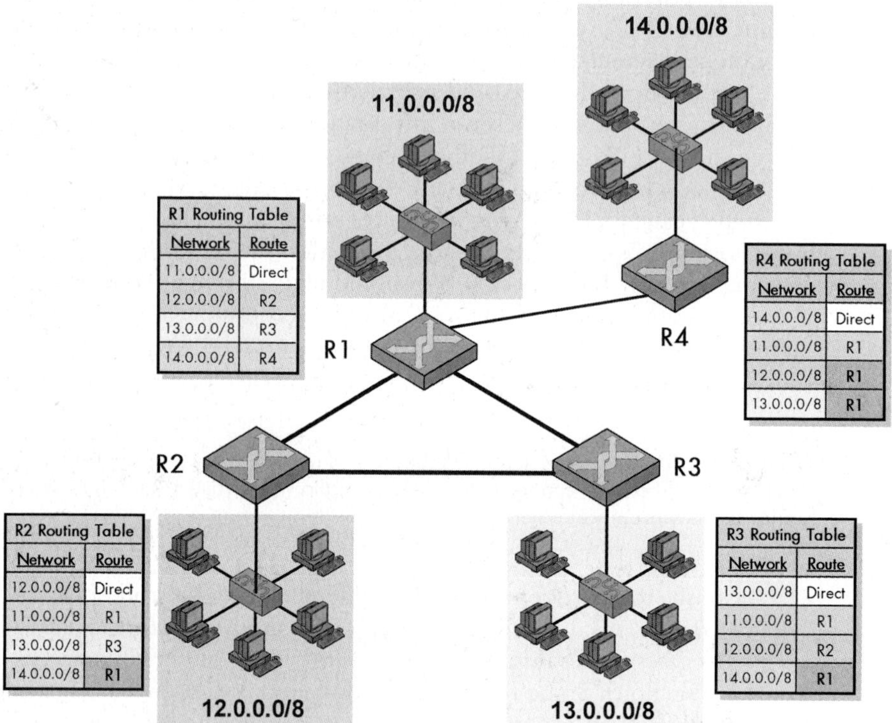

Figure 23-3: IP routing and routing tables *This diagram shows a small, simple internetwork consisting of four LANs each served by a router. The routing table for each lists the router to which datagrams for each destination network should be sent. Notice that due to the triangle, R1, R2, and R3 can send to each other. However, R2 and R3 must send through R1 to deliver to R4, and R4 must use R1 to reach either of the others.*

Now, imagine that this process is expanded to handle thousands of networks and routers. Not only do routers need to know which of their local connections to use for each network, but they want to know, if possible, what is the *best* connection to use for each network. Since routers are interconnected in a mesh, there are usually multiple routes between any two devices, but we want to take the best route whenever we can. This may be the shortest route, the least congested route, or the route considered optimal based on other criteria.

Determining which routes we should use for different networks is an important but very complex job. Routers plan routes and exchange information about routes and networks using IP *routing protocols.* R2 and R3 use these protocols to find out that 14.0.0.0/8 exists and that it is connected to them via R1. (I discuss these support protocols in Chapters 37 through 41.)

NOTE *There is a difference between a* routable protocol *and a* routing protocol. *IP is a* routable *protocol, which means its messages (datagrams) can be routed. Examples of* routing protocols *are the Routing Information Protocol (RIP) and Border Gateway Protocol (BGP), which are used to exchange routing information between routers (see Chapter 38 and Chapter 40).*

IP Routing in a Subnet or Classless Addressing (CIDR) Environment

As discussed in the previous chapters, there are three main categories of IP addressing: classful, subnetted classful, and classless. The method used for determining whether direct or indirect delivery of a datagram is required is different for each type of addressing. The type of addressing used in the network also impacts how routers decide to forward traffic in an internetwork.

One of the main reasons why the traditional class-based addressing scheme was created was that it made both addressing and routing relatively simple. Remember that IPv4 was developed in the late 1970s, when the cheap and powerful computer hardware we take for granted today was still science fiction. For the internetwork to function properly, routers needed to be able to look at an IP address and quickly decide what to do with it.

Classful addressing was intended to make this possible. There was only a two-level hierarchy for the entire internetwork: network ID and host ID. Routers could tell by looking at the first four bits which of the bits in any IP address were the network ID and which were the host ID. Then they needed only consult their routing tables to find the network ID and see which router offered the best route to that network.

The addition of subnetting to conventional addressing didn't really change this for the main routers on the Internet, because subnetting is internal to the organization. The main routers handling large volumes of traffic on the Internet didn't look at subnets at all. The additional level of hierarchy that subnets represent existed only for the routers within each organization that chose to use subnetting. These routers, when deciding what to do with datagrams within the organization's network, needed to extract not only the network ID of IP addresses, but also the subnet ID. This told them which internal physical network should get the datagram.

Classless addressing is formally called *Classless Inter-Domain Routing* (*CIDR*). The fact that the name includes *routing* but not *addressing* is evidence that CIDR was introduced in large part to improve the efficiency of routing. This improvement occurs because classless networks use a multiple-level hierarchy. Each network can be broken down into subnetworks, sub-subnetworks, and so on. This means that when we are deciding how to route in a CIDR environment, we can also describe routes in a hierarchical manner. Many smaller networks can be described using a single, higher-level network description that represents them all to routers in the rest of the internetwork. This technique, sometimes called *route aggregation*, reduces routing table size.

Let's refer back to the detailed example I presented in Chapter 20. An ISP started with the block 71.94.0.0/15 and subdivided it multiple times to create smaller blocks for itself and its customers. To the customers and users of this block, these smaller blocks must be differentiated; the ISP obviously needs to know how to route traffic to the correct customer. To everyone else on the Internet, however, these details are unimportant in deciding how to route datagrams to anyone in that ISP's block.

For example, suppose I am using a host with IP address 211.42.113.5 and I need to send a message to 71.94.1.43. My local router and the main routers on the Internet don't know where in the 71.94.0.0/15 block that address is, and they don't need to know. They just know that anything with the first 15 bits containing the binary equivalent of 71.94 goes to the router that handles 71.94.0.0/15, which is the aggregated address of the entire block. They let the ISP's routers figure out which of its constituent subnetworks contains 71.94.1.43.

Contrast this with a classful environment. Here, each of the customers of this ISP would probably have one or more Class C address blocks, each of which would require a separate routing entry, and these blocks would need to be known by *all* routers on the Internet. Thus, instead of just one 71.94.0.0/15 entry, there would be dozens or even hundreds of entries for each customer network. In the classless scheme, only one entry exists, for the parent ISP.

CIDR provides benefits to routing but also increases its complexity. Under CIDR, we cannot determine which bits are the network ID and which are the host ID just from the IP address. To make matters worse, we can have networks, subnetworks, sub-subnetworks, and so on that all have the same base address!

In our example, 71.94.0.0/15 is the complete network, and subnetwork 0 is 71.94.0.0/16. They have a different prefix length (the number of network ID bits) but the same base address. If a router has more than one match for a network ID in this manner, it must use the match with the longest network identifier first, since it represents a more specific network description.

IP Multicasting

The great bulk of TCP/IP communications uses IP to send messages from one source device to one recipient device, in a process called *unicast* communication. This is the type of messaging we normally use TCP/IP for, so when you use the Internet, you are using unicast for pretty much everything.

IP does, however, also support the ability to have one device send a message to a set of recipients. This is called *multicasting*. IP multicasting has been officially supported since IPv4 was first defined, but has not seen widespread use over the years, due largely to lack of support for multicasting in many hardware devices. Interest in multicasting has increased in recent years, and support for multicasting was made a standard part of the next-generation IP version 6 (IPv6) protocol. Here, we will take a brief look at multicasting, which is a large and complex subject.

The idea behind IP multicasting is to allow a device on an IP internetwork to send datagrams not to just one recipient, but to an arbitrary collection of other devices. IP multicasting is modeled after the similar function used in the data link layer to allow a single hardware device to send to various members of a group. Multicasting is relatively easy at the data link layer, however, because all the devices can communicate directly. In contrast, at the network layer, we are connecting together devices that may be quite far away from each other and must route datagrams between these different networks. This necessarily complicates multicasting when done using IP (except in the special case where we use IP multicasting only between devices on the same data link layer network).

There are three primary functions that must be performed to implement IP multicasting: addressing, group management, and datagram processing/routing.

Multicast Addressing

Special addressing must be used for multicasting. A *multicast address* identifies not a single device, but a *multicast group* of devices that listen for certain datagrams sent to them. In IPv4, one-sixteenth of the entire address space was set aside for multicast addresses: the Class D block of the original classful addressing scheme. Various techniques are used to define the meaning of addresses within this block and to define a mapping between IP multicast and data link layer multicast addresses. (See the discussion of IP multicast addressing in Chapter 17; mapping of IP multicast addresses to hardware layer multicast addresses is discussed in Chapter 13.)

Multicast Group Management

Group management encompasses all of the activities required to set up groups of devices. Devices must be able to dynamically join groups and leave groups, and information about groups must be propagated around the IP internetwork. To support these activities, additional techniques are required. The *Internet Group Management Protocol (IGMP)* is the chief tool used for this purpose. It defines a message format to allow information about groups and group membership to be sent between devices and routers on the Internet.

Multicast Datagram Processing and Routing

Handling and routing datagrams in a multicast environment is probably the most complicated function. There are several issues here:

- Since we are sending from one device to many, we need to actually create multiple copies of the datagram for delivery, in contrast to the single datagram used in the unicast case. Routers must be able to tell when they need to create these copies.
- Routers must use special algorithms to determine how to forward multicast datagrams. Since each one can lead to many copies being sent to various places, efficiency is important to avoid creating unnecessary volumes of traffic.
- Routers must be able to handle datagrams sent to a multicast group, even if the source is not a group member.

Routing in a multicast environment requires significantly more intelligence on the part of router hardware. Several special protocols, such as the Distance Vector Multicast Routing Protocol (DVMRP) and the multicast version of Open Shortest Past First (OSPF), are used to enable routers to forward multicast traffic effectively. These algorithms must balance the need to ensure that every device in a group receives a copy of all datagrams intended for that group with the need to prevent unnecessary traffic from moving across the internetwork.

KEY CONCEPT IP multicasting allows special applications to be developed where one device sends information to multiple devices, across a private internetwork or the global Internet. It is more complex than conventional unicast IP and requires special attention, particularly in the areas of addressing and routing.

This overview has only scratched the surface of IP multicasting. The complexity involved in handling groups and forwarding messages to multicast groups is one reason why support for the feature has been quite uneven and, as a consequence, it is not used widely. Another issue is the demanding nature of multicasting: It uses a great deal of network bandwidth for copies of messages, and it also requires more work of already-busy routers.

PART II-4

INTERNET PROTOCOL VERSION 6 (IPV6)

Since 1981, TCP/IP has been built on version 4 of the Internet Protocol (IPv4), discussed at length in the preceding part. IPv4 was created when the giant, worldwide Internet we take for granted today was just a small, experimental network. Considering how much the Internet has grown and changed over the course of two decades, IPv4 has done its job admirably. At the same time, it has been apparent for many years that certain limitations in this venerable protocol would hold back the future growth of the Internet if they were not addressed.

Due to the key role that IP plays, changing it is no simple feat. It means a substantial modification to the way that nearly everything in TCP/IP operates. However, even though we find change difficult, most of us know that it is necessary. For the past several years, development of a new version of IP has been under way, officially called *Internet Protocol version 6 (IPv6)* and also sometimes referred to as *IP Next Generation* or *IPng*. IPv6 is poised to take over for IPv4, and it will be the basis for the Internet of the future.

In this part, I provide a detailed description of IPv6. Since IPv6 is still IP, just like IPv4, it performs the same functions: addressing, encapsulation, fragmentation and reassembly, and datagram delivery and routing. For this reason, this discussion of IPv6 is patterned after the discussion of IPv4. There are four chapters: The first covers IPv6 concepts and issues; the second discusses IPv6 addressing; the third discusses IPv6 encapsulation and formatting; and the fourth discusses IPv6 datagram fragmentation, reassembly, and routing.

Since IPv6 represents the evolution of IP, many of its concepts of operation are built on those introduced in IPv4. To avoid unnecessary duplication in this part, I've assumed you are familiar with the operation of IPv4, especially addressing and how datagrams are packaged and delivered. If you have not read Part II-3, reviewing it first would be wise, because the description of IPv6 focuses on how it differs from the current IP version.

You may also wish to refer to the Part II-6, which covers the Internet Control Message Protocol (ICMP), part of which is ICMP version 6—ICMP for IPv6, and the IPv6 Neighbor Discovery (ND) protocol, since these are companions to IPv6.

24

IPV6 OVERVIEW, CHANGES, AND TRANSITION

Internet Protocol version 6 (IPv6) is destined to be the future of IP, and due to IP's critical importance, it will form the basis for the future of TCP/IP and the Internet as well. In fact, it's been under development since the middle of the last decade, and a real IPv6 internetwork has been used for testing for a number of years as well. Despite this, many people don't know much about IPv6, other than the fact that it's a newer version of IP. Some have never even heard of it at all! I'm going to rectify that, of course—but before I delve into the important changes made in IPv6 addressing, packaging, fragmentation, and other functions, let's start with a bird's-eye view of IPv6.

In this chapter, I provide a brief higher-level overview of IPv6, including a look at how it differs from IP version 4 (IPv4) in general terms. I begin with a brief overview of IPv6 and why it was created. I list the major changes made in IPv6 and the new additions to the protocol. I also explain some of the difficulties associated with transitioning the enormous global Internet from IPv4 to IPv6.

IPv6 Motivation and Overview

"If it ain't broke, don't fix it." This is one of my favorite pieces of folk wisdom. I generally like to stick with what works, as do most people. And IPv4 works pretty darned well. It's been around for decades now and has survived the growth of the Internet from a small research network into a globe-spanning powerhouse. So, like a trusty older car that you've operated successfully for years, why should you replace it if it still gets the job done?

Like that older car, you could continue to use IPv4 for the foreseeable future. The question is: at what cost? An older car can be kept in good working order if you are willing to devote the time and money it takes to maintain and service it. However, it will still be limited in some of its capabilities. Its reliability may be suspect. It won't have the latest features. With the exception of those who like to work on cars as a hobby, it eventually stops making sense to keep fixing up an older vehicle.

In some ways, this isn't that great of an analogy. Our highways aren't all that much different than they were in the 1970s, and most other issues related to driving a car haven't changed all that much in the past 25 years either. The choice of updating a vehicle or not is based on practical considerations more than necessity.

In contrast, look at what has happened to the computer and networking worlds in the last 25 years! Today's handheld PCs can do more than the most powerful servers could back then. Networking technologies are 100 or even 1,000 times as fast. The number of people connecting to the global Internet has increased by an even larger factor. And the ways that computers communicate have, in many cases, changed dramatically.

IPv4 could be considered in some ways like an older car that has been meticulously maintained and repaired over time. It gets the job done, but its age is starting to show. The main problem with IPv4 is its relatively small address space, a legacy of the decision to use only 32 bits for the IP address. Under the original classful addressing allocation scheme, we would have probably already run out of IPv4 addresses by now. Moving to classless addressing has helped postpone this, as have technologies like IP Network Address Translation (NAT), which allows privately addressed hosts to access the Internet.

In the end, however, these represent patch jobs and imperfect repairs applied to keep the aging IPv4 automobile on the road. The core problem, the 32-bit address space that is too small for the current and future size of the Internet, can be solved only by moving to a larger address space. This was the primary motivating factor in creating the next version of IP, *IPv6*.

NOTE *The reason why the successor to IPv4 is version 6 and not version 5 is because version number 5 was used to refer to an experimental protocol called the* Internet Stream Protocol, *which was never widely deployed. See Chapter 15 for a full discussion of IP history and versions.*

IPv6 Standards

IPv6 represents the first major change to IP since IPv4 was formalized in 1981. For many years, its core operation was defined in a series of RFCs published in 1998: RFCs 2460 through 2467. The most notable of these are the main IPv6 standard, RFC 2460, "Internet Protocol, Version 6 (IPv6) Specification," and documents describing the two helper protocols for IPv6: RFC 2461, which describes the IPv6 Neighbor Discovery Protocol (ND), and RFC 2463, which describes Internet Control Message Protocol version 6 (ICMPv6) for IPv6.

In addition to these, two documents were also written in 1998. They discuss more about IP addressing: RFC 2373, "IP Version 6 Addressing Architecture," and RFC 2374, "An IPv6 Aggregatable Global Unicast Address Format." Due to changes in how IPv6 addressing was to be implemented, these were updated in 2003 by RFC 3513, "Internet Protocol Version 6 (IPv6) Addressing Architecture," and RFC 3587, "IPv6 Global Unicast Address Format."

Many other RFCs define more specifics of how IPv6 works, and many also describe IPv6-compatible versions of other TCP/IP protocols like the Domain Name System (DNS; see Chapter 52) and Dynamic Host Control Protocol (DHCP; see Chapter 61). IPv6 is still very much a work in progress, with new standards being proposed and adopted on a regular basis.

Because IPv6 is the version of IP that's designed for the next generation of the Internet, it is also sometimes called *IP Next Generation* or *IPng*. Personally, I don't care for this name; it reminds me too much of *Star Trek: The Next Generation.* Regardless of its name, IPv6 or IPng was designed to take TCP/IP and the Internet "where none have gone before." (Sorry, I *had* to!)

Design Goals of IPv6

The problem of addressing was the main motivation for creating IPv6. Unfortunately, this has caused many people to think that the address space expansion is the *only* change made in IP, which is definitely not the case. Since making a change to IP is such a big deal, it's something done rarely. It made sense to correct not just the addressing issue, but also to update the protocol in a number of other respects in order to ensure its viability. In fact, even the addressing changes in IPv6 go far beyond just adding more bits to IP address fields.

Some of the most important goals in designing IPv6 include the following:

Larger Address Space IPv6 needed to provide more addresses for the growing Internet.

Better Management of Address Space Developers wanted IPv6 to include not only more addresses, but also a more capable way of dividing the address space and using the bits in each address.

Elimination of Addressing Kludges Technologies like NAT are effectively kludges that make up for the lack of address space in IPv4. IPv6 eliminates the need for NAT and similar work-arounds, allowing every TCP/IP device to have a public address.

Easier TCP/IP Administration The designers of IPv6 hoped to resolve some of the current labor-intensive requirements of IPv4, such as the need to configure IP addresses. Even though tools like DHCP eliminate the need to manually configure many hosts, it only partially solves the problem.

Modern Design for Routing In contrast to IPv4, which was designed before anyone had an idea what the modern Internet would be like, IPv6 was created specifically for efficient routing in the current Internet, and with the flexibility for the future.

Better Support for Multicasting Multicasting was an option in IPv4 from the start, but support for it has been slow in coming.

Better Support for Security IPv4 was designed at a time when security wasn't much of an issue because there were a relatively small number of networks on the Internet, and those networks' administrators often knew each other. Today, security on the public Internet is a big issue, and the future success of the Internet requires that security concerns be resolved.

Better Support for Mobility When IPv4 was created, there really was no concept of mobile IP devices. The problems associated with computers that move between networks led to the need for Mobile IP. IPv6 builds on Mobile IP and provides mobility support within IP itself.

> **KEY CONCEPT** The new version of the IP is *Internet Protocol version 6 (IPv6)*. It was created to correct some of the significant problems of IPv4, especially the looming deficiency of the IPv4 address space, to improve the operation of the protocol as a whole, and to take TCP/IP into the future.

At the same time that IPv6 was intended to address these and many other issues with traditional IP, its changes are nevertheless *evolutionary*, not *revolutionary*. During the many discussions in the Internet Engineering Task Force (IETF) in the 1990s, there were some who said that while we were updating IP, perhaps we should make a complete, radical change to a new type of internetworking protocol completely. The end decision was not to do this, but to define a more capable version of the IP that we've been using all along.

The reason for this is simple: IP, like our trusted older car, *works.* IPv6 represents an update that strives to add to the best characteristics of IPv4, rather than making everyone start over from scratch with something new and unproven. This design ensures that whatever pain may result from the change from IPv4 to IPv6 can be managed, and hopefully, minimized.

Major Changes and Additions in IPv6

In the preceding overview, I explained that the primary motivation for creating a new version of IP was to fix the problems with addressing under IPv4. But as you also saw, numerous other design goals existed for the new protocol as well. Once the decision was made to take the significant step of creating a new version of a protocol as important as IP, it made sense to use the opportunity to make as many improvements as possible.

Of course, there is still the problem of the pain of change to worry about, so each potential change or addition in IPv6 needed to have benefits that would outweigh its costs. The resulting design does a good job of providing useful advantages while maintaining most of the core of the original IP. The following are some of the most important changes between IPv4 and IPv6, and they demonstrate some of the ways that the IPv6 team met the design goals for the new protocol:

Larger Address Space IPv6 addresses are 128 bits long instead of 32 bits. This expands the address space from around 4 billion addresses to, well, an astronomical number (over 300 trillion trillion trillion addresses).

Hierarchical Address Space One reason why the IPv6 address size was expanded so much was to allow it to be hierarchically divided to provide a large number of many classes of addresses.

Hierarchical Assignment of Unicast Addresses A special global unicast address format was created to allow addresses to be easily allocated across the entire Internet. It allows for multiple levels of network and subnetwork hierarchies at both the Internet service provider (ISP) and the organizational level. It also permits the generation of IP addresses based on underlying hardware interface device IDs such as Ethernet MAC addresses.

Better Support for Nonunicast Addressing Support for multicasting is improved, and support for a new type of addressing, *anycast* addressing, has been added. This new kind of addressing basically says, "Deliver this message to the easiest-to-reach member of this group," and potentially enables new types of messaging functionality.

Autoconfiguration and Renumbering A provision is included to allow easier autoconfiguration of hosts and renumbering of the IP addresses in networks and subnetworks as needed. A technique also exists for renumbering router addresses.

New Datagram Format The IP datagram format has been redefined and given new capabilities. The main header of each IP datagram has been streamlined, and support has been added for the ability to easily extend the header for datagrams that require more control information.

Support for Quality of Service (QoS) IPv6 datagrams include QoS features that allow for better support for multimedia and other applications that require QoS.

Security Support Security support is designed into IPv6 using the authentication and encryption extension headers and other features.

Updated Fragmentation and Reassembly Procedures The way that the fragmentation and reassembly of datagrams works has been changed in IPv6. The improved routing efficiency better reflects the realities of today's networks.

Modernized Routing Support IPv6 is designed to support modern routing systems and allow for expansion as the Internet grows.

Transition Capabilities Since it was recognized from the start that going from IPv4 to IPv6 is a big move, support for the IPv4/IPv6 transition has been provided in numerous areas. This includes a plan for interoperating IPv4 and IPv6 networks, for mapping between IPv4 and IPv6 addresses, and other transition support.

Changes to Other Protocols With the introduction of IPv6, several other TCP/IP protocols that deal intimately with IP have also had to be updated. One of these is ICMP, the most important support protocol for IPv4, which has been revised through the creation of ICMPv6 for IPv6. An addition to TCP/IP is the ND protocol, which performs several functions for IPv6 that were done by the Address Resolution Protocol (ARP) and ICMP in version 4.

The following chapters on IPv6 provide much more detail on these changes and additions to IP. You'll notice that the majority of these are related to addressing, because that is where the greatest number of important changes were made in IPv6. Of course, routing and addressing are closely related, and the changes to addressing have had a big impact on routing as well.

Transition from IPv4 to IPv6

IP is the foundation of the TCP/IP protocol suite and the Internet, and thus it's somewhat comparable to the foundation of a house in terms of its structural importance. Given this, changing IP is somewhat analogous to making a substantial modification to the foundation of your house. Since IP is used to connect together many devices, it is like changing not just your house, but every house in the world!

How do you change the foundation of a house? Very carefully. The same caution is required with the implementation of IPv6. While most people think IPv6 is something new, the reality is that the planning and development of IPv6 has been underway for nearly a full decade, and if we were starting from scratch, the protocol would have been ready for action years ago. However, there is a truly enormous installed base of IPv4 hardware and software. This means the folks who develop TCP/IP could not just flip a switch and have everyone move over to using IPv6. Instead, a *transition* from IPv4 to IPv6 had to be planned.

The transition is already under way, though most people don't know about it. As I said, development of IPv6 itself is pretty much complete, though work continues on refining the protocol and also on the development of IPv6-compatible versions of other protocols. The implementation of IPv6 began with the creation of development networks to test IPv6's operation. These were connected together to form an experimental IPv6 internetwork called the *6BONE* (which is a contraction of the phrase *IPv6 backbone*). This internetwork has been in operation for several years.

IPv4 to IPv6 Transition: Differences of Opinion

Experimental networks are well and good, but the big issue is transitioning the Internet to IPv6, and here, opinion diverges rather quickly. In one camp are the corporations, organizations, and individuals. All of these groups are quite eager to transition to IPv6 quickly in order to gain the many benefits it promises in the areas of addressing, routing, and security. Others are taking a much more cautious approach, noting that the dire predictions in the mid-1990s of IPv4's imminent doom have not come to pass, and arguing that we should take our time to make sure IPv6 is going to work on a large scale.

These two groups will continue to play tug-of-war for the next few years, but it seems that the tide is now turning toward those who want to speed up the now-years-long transition. The move toward adoption of IPv6 as a *production* protocol is being spearheaded by a number of groups and organizations. IPv6 has a lot of support in areas outside the United States, many of which are running short of IPv4 addresses due to small allocations relative to their size. One such area is Asia, a region with billions of people, rapidly growing Internet use, and a shortage of IPv4 addresses.

Within the United States, which has the lion's share of IPv4 addresses (because the Internet was developed here), there seems to be a bit less enthusiasm for rapid IPv6 deployment. Even here, however, IPv6 got a major shot in the arm in July 2003 when the United States Department of Defense (DoD) announced that starting in October of that year, it would purchase only networking products that included compatibility with IPv6. The DoD (which was responsible for the development of the Internet in the first place) hopes to be fully transitioned to IPv6 by 2008. This will likely have a big impact on the plans of other governmental and private organizations in the United States.

The creators of IPv6 knew from the start that transition was going to be an important issue with the new protocol. IPv6 is not compatible with IPv4 because the addressing system and datagram format are different. Yet the IPv6 designers knew that since the transition would take many years, it was necessary that they provide a way for IPv4 and IPv6 hosts to interoperate. Consider that in any transition there are always stragglers. Like the old Windows 3.11 PC in the corner that you still need to use once in a while, some devices will remain on IPv4, even when most of the Internet is IPv6, because they were never upgraded.

> **KEY CONCEPT** Due to the many differences between IPv4 and IPv6, and the fundamental importance of IP to TCP/IP, an orderly transition has been planned from IPv4 to IPv6 over a period of many years.

IPv4 to IPv6 Transition Methods

The IETF has been working on specific provisions to allow a smooth transition from IPv4 to IPv6, and hardware and software interoperability solutions to let newer IPv6 devices access IPv4 hosts. A technique was included in IPv6 to allow administrators to embed IPv4 addresses within IPv6 addresses. Special methods are defined to handle interoperability, including the following:

Dual-Stack Devices Routers and some other devices may be programmed with both IPv4 and IPv6 implementations to allow them to communicate with both types of hosts.

IPv4/IPv6 Translation Dual-stack devices may be designed to accept requests from IPv6 hosts, convert them to IPv4 datagrams, send the datagrams to the IPv4 destination, and then process the return datagrams similarly.

IPv4 Tunneling of IPv6 IPv6 devices that don't have a path between them consisting entirely of IPv6-capable routers may be able to communicate by encapsulating IPv6 datagrams within IPv4. In essence, they would be using IPv6 on top of IPv4; that is, two network layers. The encapsulated IPv4 datagrams would travel across conventional IPv4 routers.

Bear in mind that these solutions generally address only backward compatibility to allow IPv6 devices to talk to IPv4 hardware. Forward compatibility between IPv4 and IPv6 is not possible because IPv4 hosts cannot communicate with IPv6 hosts; they lack the knowledge of how IPv6 works. It is possible that certain special adaptations might be created to allow IPv4 hosts to access IPv6 hosts. But eventually, all IPv4 devices of any importance will want to migrate to IPv6.

The IETF has done such a good job in the past with introducing new technologies, and so much effort has been put into the IPv6 transition, that I am quite confident that the transition to IPv6 will come off with few, if any, problems. One good thing about the transition is that IPv4 is, at the present time, still getting the job done, so there is no big hurry to make the move to IPv6. While technologies such as CIDR and NAT are like Band-Aids on IPv4, they have been very successful ones in extending the useful life of the aging protocol.

25

IPV6 ADDRESSING

The primary motivation for creating Internet Protocol version 6 (IPv6) was to rectify the addressing problems in version 4 (IPv4). Along with acquiring more addresses, the IPv6 designers desired a way of interpreting, assigning, and using addresses in a way that was more consonant with modern internetworking. So, it's no surprise that many of the changes in IPv6 are associated with IP addressing. The IPv6 addressing scheme is similar in concept to IPv4 addressing, but has been completely overhauled to create an addressing system that's capable of supporting continued Internet expansion and new applications for the foreseeable future.

This chapter describes the concepts and methods associated with addressing under IPv6. I begin with a look at some addressing generalities in IPv6, including the addressing model, address types' size, and address space. I discuss the unique and sometimes confusing representations and notations used for IPv6 addresses and prefixes. Then I look at how addresses are arranged and allocated into types, beginning with an overall look at address space composition and then at the global unicast address format. I describe the new methods used for mapping IP addresses to underlying physical network addresses. I then describe special IPv6 addressing issues, including reserved and private addresses, IPv4 address embedding, anycast and multicast addresses, and autoconfiguration and renumbering of addresses.

Addressing under IPv6 is outlined in the main IPv6 RFC, RFC 2460, "Internet Protocol, Version 6 (IPv6) Specification." However, most of the details of IPv6 addressing are contained in two other standards: RFC 3513, "Internet Protocol Version 6 (IPv6) Addressing Architecture," and RFC 3587, "IPv6 Global Unicast Address Format." These replaced the 1998 standards RFC 2373, "IP Version 6 Addressing Architecture," and RFC 2374, "An IPv6 Aggregatable Global Unicast Address Format."

BACKGROUND INFORMATION *As with the other IPv6 chapters in this book, my look at addressing is based somewhat on a contrast to how addressing is done in IPv4. I strongly recommend a thorough understanding of IPv4 addressing, including classless addressing using Classless Inter-Domain Routing (CIDR), as presented in Chapters 16 through 23, before proceeding here. As with the IPv4 addressing sections, familiarity with how binary numbers work, and conversion between binary and decimal numbers is also a good idea. Chapter 4, which provides some background on data representation and the mathematics of computing, may be of assistance in that respect.*

IPv6 Addressing Overview: Addressing Model, Address Types, and Address Size

As you saw in the previous chapter, IPv6 represents a significant update to IP, but its modifications and additions are made without changing the core nature of how IP works. Addressing is the place where most of the differences between IPv4 and IPv6 are seen, but the changes are mostly in how addresses are implemented and used. The overall model used for IP addressing in IPv6 is pretty much the same as it was in IPv4; some aspects have not changed at all, while others have changed only slightly.

IPv6 Addressing Model Characteristics

Here are some of the general characteristics of the IPv6 addressing model that are basically the same as in IPv4:

Core Functions of Addressing The two main functions of addressing are still network interface identification and routing. Routing is facilitated through the structure of addresses on the internetwork.

Network Layer Addressing IPv6 addresses are still the ones associated with the network layer in TCP/IP networks and are distinct from data link layer (also sometimes called *physical*) addresses.

Number of IP Addresses per Device Addresses are still assigned to network interfaces, so a regular host like a PC will usually have one (unicast) address, and routers will have more than one for each of the physical networks to which it connects.

Address Interpretation and Prefix Representation IPv6 addresses are like classless IPv4 addresses in that they are interpreted as having a network identifier part and a host identifier part (a network ID and a host ID), but that the delineation is not encoded into the address itself. A prefix-length number, using CIDR-like notation, is used to indicate the length of the network ID (prefix length).

Private and Public Addresses Both types of addresses exist in IPv6, though they are defined and used somewhat differently.

IPv6 Supported Address Types

One important change in the addressing model of IPv6 is the *address types* supported. IPv4 supported three address types: unicast, multicast, and broadcast. Of these, the vast majority of actual traffic was unicast. IP multicast support was not widely deployed until many years after the Internet was established and it continues to be hampered by various issues. Use of broadcast in IP had to be severely restricted for performance reasons (we don't want any device to be able to broadcast across the entire Internet!).

IPv6 also supports three address types, but with the following changes:

Unicast Addresses These are standard unicast addresses as in IPv4, one per host interface.

Multicast Addresses These are addresses that represent various groups of IP devices. A message sent to a multicast address goes to all devices in the group. IPv6 includes much better multicast features and many more multicast addresses than IPv4. Since multicast under IPv4 was hampered in large part due to lack of support of the feature by many hardware devices, support for multicasting is a required, not optional, part of IPv6.

Anycast Addresses Anycast addressing is used when a message must be sent to any member of a group, but does not need to be sent to all of them. Usually the member of the group that is easiest to reach will be sent the message. One common example of how anycast addressing could be used is in load sharing among a group of routers in an organization.

Broadcast addressing as a distinct addressing method is gone in IPv6. Broadcast functionality is implemented using multicast addressing to groups of devices. A multicast group to which all nodes belong can be used for broadcasting in a network, for example.

> **KEY CONCEPT** IPv6 has unicast and multicast addresses like IPv4. There is, however, no distinct concept of a broadcast address in IPv6. A new type of address, the *anycast* address, has been added to allow a message to be sent to any one member of a group of devices.

An important implication of the creation of anycast addressing is removal of the strict uniqueness requirement for IP addresses. Anycast is accomplished by assigning the same IP address to more than one device. The devices must also be specifically told that they are sharing an anycast address, but the addresses themselves are structurally the same as unicast addresses.

The bulk of the remainder of this chapter focuses on unicast addressing, since it is by far the most important type. Multicast and anycast addressing are given special attention in a separate section later in this chapter.

IPv6 Address Size and Address Space

Of all the changes introduced in IPv6, easily the most celebrated is the increase in the size of IP addresses, which resulted in a corresponding massive increase in the size of the address space as well. It's not surprising that these sizes were increased compared to IPv4—everyone has known for years that the IPv4 address space was too small to support the future of the Internet. What's remarkable is the level of increase and the implications for how Internet addresses are used.

In IPv4, IP addresses are 32 bits long; these are usually grouped into 4 octets of 8 bits each. The theoretical IPv4 address space is 2^{32}, or 4,294,967,296 addresses. To increase this address space, we simply increase the size of addresses; each extra bit we give to the address size doubles the address space. Based on this, some folks expected the IPv6 address size to increase from 32 to 48 bits, or perhaps 64 bits. Either of these numbers would have given a rather large number of addresses.

However, IPv6 addressing doesn't use either of these figures. Instead, the IP address size jumps all the way to 128 bits, or 16 8-bit octets/bytes. The size of the IPv6 address space is, quite literally, astronomical. Like the numbers that describe the number of stars in a galaxy or the distance to the furthest pulsars, the number of addresses that can be supported in IPv6 is mind-boggling. See Figure 25-1 for an idea of what I mean by *astronomical.*

Since IPv6 addresses are 128 bits long, the theoretical address space, if all addresses were used, is 2^{128} addresses. This number, when expanded out, is 340,282,366,920,938,463,463,374,607,431,768,211,456, which is normally expressed in scientific notation as about $3.4*10^{38}$ addresses. Whoa! That's about 340 trillion, *trillion, trillion* addresses. As I said, it's pretty hard to grasp just how large this number is. Consider these comparisons:

- It's enough addresses for many trillions of addresses to be assigned to every human being on the planet.
- The Earth is about 4.5 billion years old. If you had been assigning IPv6 addresses at a rate of 1 billion per second since the Earth was formed, you would have by now used up less than one trillionth of the address space.
- The Earth's surface area is about 510 trillion square meters. If a typical computer has a footprint of about one-tenth of a square meter, you would have to stack computers 10 billion high—blanketing the entire surface of the Earth—to use up that same trillionth of the address space.

OK, I think you get the idea. It's clear that one goal of the decision to go to 128-bit addresses is to make sure that we will never run out of address space again, and it seems quite likely that this will be the case.

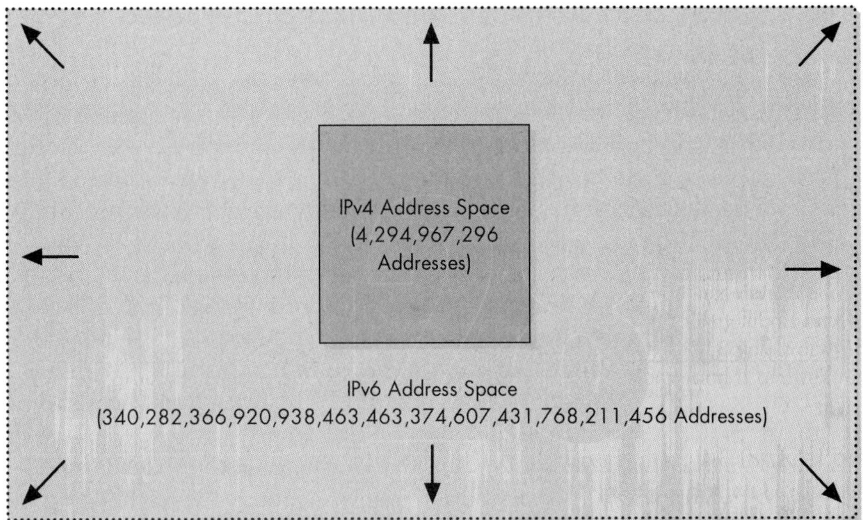

Figure 25-1: A (poor) representation of relative IPv4 and IPv6 address space sizes *I wanted to make a cool graphic to show the relative sizes of the IPv4 and IPv6 address spaces. You know, where I would show the IPv6 address space as a big box and the IPv4 address space as a tiny one. The problem is that the IPv6 address space is so much larger than the IPv4 space that there is no way to show it to scale! To make this diagram to scale, imagine the IPv4 address space is the 1.6-inch square above. In that case, the IPv6 address space would be represented by a square the size of the solar system!*

There are drawbacks to having such a huge address space, too. Consider that even with a 64-bit address, we would have a very large address space; 2^{64} equals 18,446,744,073,709,551,616, or about 18 million trillion. These are still probably more addresses than the Internet will ever need. However, by going to 128 bits instead, this has made dealing with IP addresses unruly (as you'll see in the next section). This has also increased overhead, since every datagram header or other place where IP addresses are referenced must use 16 bytes for each address instead of the 4 bytes that were needed in IPv4, or the 8 bytes that might have been required with a 64-bit address.

KEY CONCEPT The IPv6 address space is really, *really* big!

So why the overkill of going to 128 bits? The main reason is *flexibility*. Even though you can have a couple zillion addresses if we allocate them one at a time, this makes assignment difficult. The developers got rid of class-oriented addressing in IPv4 because it wasted address space. The reality, though, is that being able to waste address space is a useful luxury.

Having 128 bits allows us to divide the address space and assign various purposes to different bit ranges, while still not having to worry about running out of space. Later in this chapter, in the section describing the IPv6 global unicast address format, you'll see one way that those 128 bits are put to good use: They allow you to create a hierarchy of networks while still saving 64 bits for host IDs. This hierarchy has its own advantages.

IPv6 Address and Address Notation and Prefix Representation

Increasing the size of IP addresses from 32 bits to 128 bits expands the address space to a gargantuan size, thereby ensuring that we will never again run out of IP addresses, and thereby allowing flexibility in how they are assigned and used. Unfortunately, there are some drawbacks to this method, and one of them is that 128-bit numbers are very large. The size makes them awkward and difficult to use.

Computers work in binary, and they have no problem dealing with long strings of ones and zeros, but humans find them confusing. Even the 32-bit addresses of IPv4 are cumbersome for us to deal with, which is why we use dotted decimal notation for them unless we need to work in binary (as with subnetting). However, IPv6 addresses are so much larger than IPv4 addresses that it becomes problematic to use dotted decimal notation. To use this notation, we would split the 128 bits into 16 octets and represent each with a decimal number from 0 to 255. However, we would end up not with 4 of these numbers, but *16*. A typical IPv6 address in this notation would appear as follows:

128.91.45.157.220.40.0.0.0.0.252.87.212.200.31.255

The binary and dotted decimal representations of this address are shown near the top of Figure 25-2. In either case, the word *elegant* doesn't exactly spring to mind.

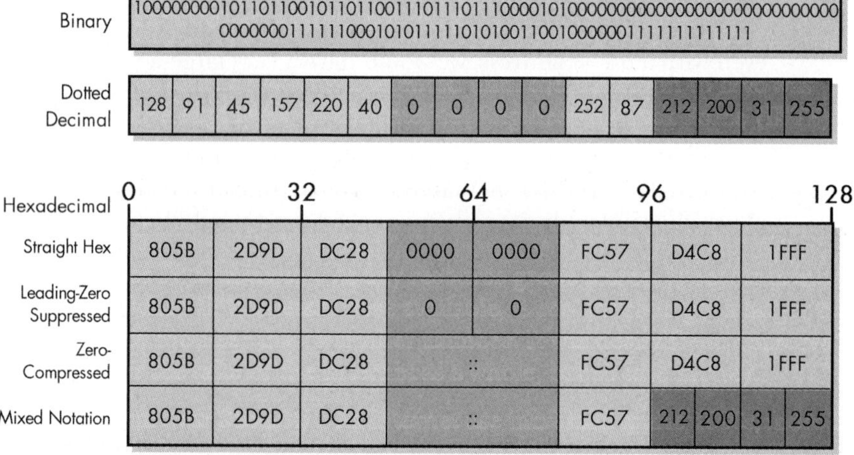

Binary
10000000010110110010110110011101110111000010100000000000000000000000000000
00000001111110001010111110101001100100000001111111111111
Dotted Decimal
128 91 45 157 220 40 0 0 0 0 252 87 212 200 31 255
Hexadecimal
0
32
64
96
128
Straight Hex
805B 2D9D DC28 0000 0000 FC57 D4C8 1FFF
Leading-Zero Suppressed
805B 2D9D DC28 0 0 FC57 D4C8 1FFF
Zero-Compressed
805B 2D9D DC28 :: FC57 D4C8 1FFF
Mixed Notation
805B 2D9D DC28 :: FC57 212 200 31 255

Figure 25-2: Binary, decimal, and hexadecimal representations of IPv6 addresses *The top two rows show binary and dotted decimal representations of an IPv6 address; neither is commonly used (other than by computers themselves!). The top row of the lower table shows the full hexadecimal representation, while the next two rows illustrate zero suppression and compression. The last row shows mixed notation, with the final 32 bits of an IPv6 address shown in dotted decimal notation (212.200.31.255). This is most commonly used for embedded IPv4 addresses.*

IPv6 Address Hexadecimal Notation

To make addresses shorter, the decision was made in IPv6 to change the primary method of expressing addresses to use hexadecimal instead of decimal. The advantage of this is that it requires fewer characters to represent an address, and converting from hexadecimal to binary and back again is much easier than converting from binary to decimal or vice versa. The disadvantage is that many people find hexadecimal difficult to comprehend and work with, especially because the notion of 16 values in each digit is a bit strange.

The hexadecimal notation used for IPv6 addresses is similar to the same method used for IEEE 802 MAC addresses, and for technologies like Ethernet. With these MAC addresses, 48 bits are represented by 6 octets, each octet being a hexadecimal number from 0 to FF, separated by a dash or colon, like this:

0A-A7-94-07-CB-D0

Since IPv6 addresses are larger, they are instead grouped into eight 16-bit *words*, separated by colons, to create what is sometimes called *colon hexadecimal notation*, as shown in Figure 25-2. So, the IPv6 address given in the previous example would be expressed as follows:

805B:2D9D:DC28:0000:0000:FC57:D4C8:1FFF

To keep the address size down, leading zeros can be suppressed in the notation so you can immediately reduce this to the following:

805B:2D9D:DC28:0:0:FC57:D4C8:1FFF

Well, it's definitely shorter than dotted decimal, but still pretty long. When you are dealing with numbers this big, there's only so much you can do. This is part of why the use of Domain Name System (DNS) names for hosts becomes much more important under IPv6 than it is in IPv4: Who could remember a hex address that long?

Zero Compression in IPv6 Addresses

Fortunately, there is a shortcut that can be applied to shorten some addresses even further. This technique is sometimes called *zero compression.* The method allows a single string of contiguous zeros in an IPv6 address to be replaced by double colons. So, for example, the previous address could be expressed as follows:

805B:2D9D:DC28::FC57:D4C8:1FFF

You know how many zeros are replaced by the two colons (::) because you can see how many fully expressed (uncompressed) hexadecimal words are in the address. In this case, there are six, so the :: represents two zero words. To prevent ambiguity, the double colons can appear only once in any IP address, because if it appeared more than once, you could not tell how many zeros were replaced in each instance. So, if the example address were 805B:2D9D:DC28:0:0:FC57:0:0, you could replace either the first pair of zeros or the second, but not both.

Zero compression doesn't make the example much shorter, but due to how IPv6 addresses are structured, long strings of zeros are common. For example, consider this address:

FF00:4501:0:0:0:0:0:32

With compression, this could be shortened as follows:

FF00:4501::32

The technique works even better on special addresses. The full IPv6 loopback address is written as follows:

0:0:0:0:0:0:0:1

With compression, the loopback address looks like this:

::1

For even more fun, consider the especially odd IPv6 unspecified address, as shown here:

0:0:0:0:0:0:0:0

Apply zero compression to an address that is all zeros, and what do you get?

::

No numbers at all! Of course, thinking of :: as an address *does* take some getting used to.

> **KEY CONCEPT** For brevity, IPv6 addresses are represented using eight sets of four hexadecimal digits, a form called *colon hexadecimal notation*. Additional techniques, called *zero suppression* and *zero compression*, are used to reduce the size of displayed addresses further by removing unnecessary zeros from the presentation of the address.

IPv6 Mixed Notation

There is also an alternative notation used in some cases, especially for expressing IPv6 addresses that embed IPv4 addresses (discussed later in this chapter). For these, it is useful to show the IPv4 portion of the address in the older dotted decimal notation, since that's what you use for IPv4. Since embedding uses the last 32 bits for the IPv4 address, the notation has the first 96 bits in colon hexadecimal notation and the last 32 bits in dotted decimal. So, to take the earlier example again, in *mixed notation* it would be shown as follows:

805B:2D9D:DC28::FC57:**212.200.31.255**

This isn't really a great example of mixed notation, because embedding usually involves long strings of zeros followed by the IPv4 address. Thus, zero compression comes in very handy here. Instead of seeing something like this:

0:0:0:0:0:0:212.200.31.255

You will typically see this:

::212.200.31.255

At first glance, this appears to be an IPv4 address. You must keep a close eye on those colons in IPv6!

KEY CONCEPT A special mixed notation is defined for IPv6 addresses whose last 32 bits contain an embedded IPv4 address. In this notation, the first 96 bits are displayed in regular colon hexadecimal notation, and the last 32 bits are displayed in IPv4-style dotted decimal.

IPv6 Address Prefix Length Representation

Like IPv4 classless addresses, IPv6 addresses are fundamentally divided into a number of network ID bits followed by a number of host ID bits. The network identifier is called the *prefix*, and the number of bits used is the *prefix length.* This prefix is represented by adding a slash after the address and then putting the prefix length after the slash. This is the same method used for classless IPv4 addressing with CIDR. For example, if the first 48 bits of the sample address were the network ID (prefix), then we would express this as 805B:2D9D:DC28::FC57:D4C8:1FFF/48.

KEY CONCEPT In IPv6, the size of an address's prefix is indicated by the prefix length that follows the address, separated with a slash, just as it is done in IPv4 classless addressing.

As in IPv4, specifiers for whole networks will typically end in long strings of zeros. These can be replaced by double colons (::) using zero compression. For example, the 48-bit network ID for the previous example is 805B:2D9D:DC28:0:0:0:0:0/48, or 805B:2D9D:DC28::/48. You *must* include the "::" if replacing the trailing zeros.

IPv6 Address Space Allocation

After dealing for so many years with the very small IPv4 address space, the enormous number of addresses in IPv6 must have made the Internet Engineering Task Force (IETF) engineers feel like kids in a candy shop. They were good kids, however, and didn't run wild, grabbing all the candy they could find and gobbling it up. They very carefully considered how to divide the address space for various uses. Of course, when you have this much candy, sharing becomes pretty easy.

As was the case with IPv4, the two primary concerns in deciding how to divide the IPv6 address space were address assignment and routing. The designers of IPv6 wanted to structure the address space to make allocation of addresses to Internet service providers (ISPs), organizations, and individuals as easy as possible.

At first, perhaps ironically, this led the creators of IPv6 back full circle to the use of specific bit sequences to identify different types of addresses, just like the old classful addressing scheme. The address type was indicated by a set of bits at the start of the address, called the format prefix (FP). The format prefix was conceptually identical to the one to four bits used in IPv4 classful addressing to denote address classes, but was variable in length, ranging from three to ten bits. Format prefixes were described in RFC 2373.

In the years following the publication of RFC 2373, the gurus who run the Internet had a change of heart regarding how address blocks should be considered. They still wanted to divide the IPv6 address space into variably sized blocks for different purposes. However, they realized that many people were starting to consider the use of format prefixes to be equivalent to the old class-oriented IPv4 system. Their main concern was that implementers might program into IPv6 hardware logic to make routing decisions based only on the first few bits of the address. This was specifically *not* how IPv6 is supposed to work; for one thing, the allocations are subject to change.

Thus, one of the modifications made in RFC 3513 was to change the language regarding IPv6 address allocations, and specifically, to remove the term *format prefix* from the standard. The allocation of different parts of the address space is still done based on particular patterns of the first three to ten bits of the address to allow certain categories to have more addresses than others. The elimination of the specific term denoting this is intended to convey that these bits should not be given special attention.

Table 25-1 shows the allocations of the IPv6 address space and what fraction of the total address space each represents.

Table 25-1: IPv6 Address Space Allocations

Leading Bits	Fraction of Total IPv6 Address Space	Allocation
0000 0000	1/256	Unassigned (Includes special addresses such as the unspecified and loopback addresses)
0000 0001	1/256	Unassigned
0000 001	1/128	Reserved for NSAP address allocation
0000 01	1/64	Unassigned
0000 1	1/32	Unassigned
0001	1/16	Unassigned
001	1/8	Global unicast addresses
010	1/8	Unassigned
011	1/8	Unassigned
100	1/8	Unassigned
101	1/8	Unassigned
110	1/8	Unassigned
1110	1/16	Unassigned
1111 0	1/32	Unassigned
1111 10	1/64	Unassigned
1111 110	1/128	Unassigned
1111 1110 0	1/512	Unassigned
1111 1110 10	1/1024	Link-local unicast addresses
1111 1110 11	1/1024	Site-local unicast addresses
1111 1111	1/256	Multicast addresses

This is more complicated than the IPv4 classful scheme because there are so many more categories and they range greatly in size, even if most of them are currently unassigned.

An easier way to make sense of this table is to consider the division of the IPv6 address space into *eighths*. Of these eight groups, one (001) has been reserved for unicast addresses; a second (000) has been used to carve out smaller reserved blocks, and a third (111) has been used for sub-blocks for local and multicast addresses. Five are completely unassigned.

You can see that the IPv6 designers have taken great care to allocate only the portion of these "eighths" of the address space that they felt was needed for each type of address. For example, only a small portion of the part of the address space beginning 111 was used, with most of it left aside. In total, only 71/512ths of the address space is assigned right now, or about 14 percent. The other 86 percent is unassigned and kept aside for future use. (Bear in mind that even 1/1024th of the IPv6 address space is gargantuan—it represents trillions of trillions of addresses.)

Later sections in this chapter provide more information on several of these address blocks. Note that the 0000 0000 reserved block is used for several special address types, including the loopback address, the unspecified address, and IPv4 address embedding. The 1111 1111 format prefix identifies multicast addresses; this string is FF in hexadecimal, so any address beginning with FF is a multicast address in IPv6.

IPv6 Global Unicast Address Format

It is anticipated that unicast addressing will be used for the vast majority of Internet traffic under IPv6, as is the case for IPv4. It is for this reason that the largest of the assigned blocks of the IPv6 address space is dedicated to unicast addressing. A full one-eighth slice of the enormous IPv6 address "pie" is assigned to unicast addresses, which are indicated by a 001 in the first three bits of the address. The question is: How do we use the remaining 125 bits in the spacious IP addresses?

Rationale for a Structured Unicast Address Block

When IPv4 was first created, the Internet was rather small, and the model for allocating address blocks was based on a central coordinator: the Internet Assigned Numbers Authority (IANA). Everyone who wanted address blocks would go straight to the central authority. As the Internet grew, this model became impractical. Today, IPv4's classless addressing scheme allows variable-length network IDs and hierarchical assignment of address blocks. Big ISPs get large blocks from the central authority, and then subdivide them and allocate them to their customers, and so on. This is managed by today's ISPs, but there is nothing in the address space that helps manage the allocation process. In turn, each organization has the ability to further subdivide its address allocation to suit its internal requirements.

The designers of IPv6 had the benefit of this experience and realized there would be tremendous advantages to designing the unicast address structure to reflect the overall topology of the Internet. These include the following:

- Easier allocation of address blocks at various levels of the Internet topological hierarchy.
- IP network addresses that automatically reflect the hierarchy by which routers move information across the Internet, thereby allowing routes to be easily aggregated for more efficient routing.

- Flexibility for organizations like ISPs to subdivide their address blocks for customers.
- Flexibility for end-user organizations to subdivide their address blocks to match internal networks, much as subnetting did in IPv4.
- Greater meaning to IP addresses. Instead of just being a string of 128 bits with no structure, it would become possible to look at an address and know certain things about it.

Generic Division of the Unicast Address Space

The most generic way of dividing up the 128 bits of the unicast address space is into three sections, as shown in Table 25-2.

Table 25-2: Generic IPv6 Global Unicast Address Format

Field Name	Size (Bits)	Description
Prefix	n	Global Routing Prefix: The network ID or prefix of the address, used for routing.
Subnet ID	m	Subnet Identifier: A number that identifies a subnet within the site.
Interface ID	$128-n-m$	Interface Identifier: The unique identifier for a particular interface (host or other device). It is unique within the specific prefix and subnet.

The *global routing prefix* and *subnet identifier* represent the two basic levels at which addresses need to be hierarchically constructed: that is, global and site-specific. The routing prefix consists of a number of bits that can be further subdivided according to the needs of Internet registries and ISPs. This subdivision reflects the topography of the Internet as a whole. The subnet ID gives a number of bits to site administrators for creating an internal network structure suiting each administrator's needs.

IPv6 Implementation of the Unicast Address Space

In theory, any size for n and m (see Table 25-2) could be used. The implementation chosen for IPv6, however, assigns 48 bits to the routing prefix and 16 bits to the subnet identifier. This means 64 bits are available for interface identifiers, which are constructed based on the IEEE EUI-64 format, as described in the next section. Thus, the overall IPv6 unicast address format is constructed as shown in Table 25-3 and illustrated in Figure 25-3.

Table 25-3: IPv6 Global Unicast Address Format

Field Name	Size (Bits)	Description
Prefix	48	Global Routing Prefix: The network ID or prefix of the address that's used for routing. The first three bits are 001 to indicate a unicast address.
Subnet ID	16	Subnet Identifier: A number that identifies a subnet within the site.
Interface ID	64	Interface ID: The unique identifier for a particular interface (host or other device). It is unique within the specific prefix and subnet.

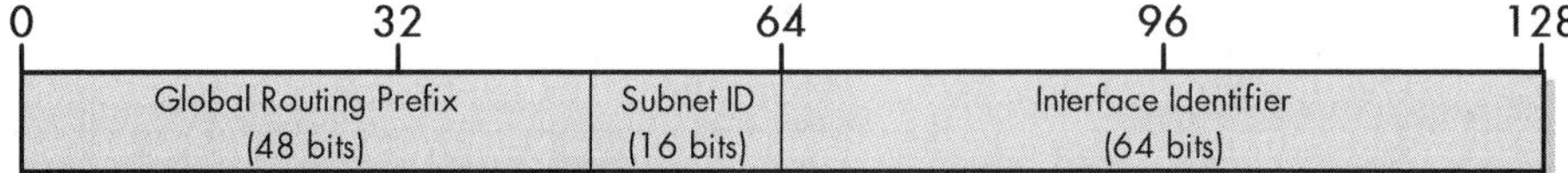

Figure 25-3: *IPv6 global unicast address format*

KEY CONCEPT The part of the IPv6 address space set aside for unicast addresses is structured into an address format that uses the first 48 bits for the *routing prefix* (like a network ID), the next 16 bits for a *subnet ID,* and the final 64 bits for an *interface ID* (like a host ID).

Due to this structure, most end sites (regular companies and organizations, as opposed to ISPs) will be assigned IPv6 networks with a 48-bit prefix. In common parlance, these network identifiers have now come to be called *48s* or */48s.*

The 16 bits of subnet ID allow each site considerable flexibility in creating subnets that reflect the site's network structure. Here are some example uses of the 16 bits:

- A smaller organization can just set all the bits in the subnet ID to zero and have a flat internal structure.
- A medium-sized organization could use all the bits in the subnet ID to perform the equivalent of straight subnetting under IPv4, thereby assigning a different subnet ID to each subnet. There are 16 bits here, and this allows a whopping 65,536 subnets!
- A larger organization can use the bits to create a multiple-level hierarchy of subnets, exactly like IPv4's Variable Length Subnet Masking (VLSM). For example, the company could use two bits to create four subnets. It could then take the next three bits to create eight sub-subnets in some or all of the four subnets. There would still be 11 more bits to create sub-sub-subnets, and so forth.

Original Division of the Global Routing Prefix: Aggregators

The global routing prefix is similarly divided into a hierarchy, but one that has been designed for the use of the entire Internet, like CIDR. There are 45 bits available here (48 bits minus the first three that are fixed at 001). That is a lot. When the unicast address structure was first detailed in RFC 2374, that document described a specific division of the 45 bits based on a two-level hierarchical topology of Internet registries and providers. These organizations were described as follows:

Top-Level Aggregators (TLAs) These refer to the largest Internet organizations, which were to be assigned large blocks of IPv6 addresses from registration authorities.

Next-Level Aggregators (NLAs) These organizations would get blocks of addresses from TLAs and divide them for end-user organizations (sites).

The 45 bits were split between these two uses, with a few bits reserved in the middle to allow expansion of either field if needed. Thus, the RFC 2374 structure for the 45 bits appeared as listed in Table 25-4.

Table 25-4: Historical IPv6 Unicast Routing Prefix Structure

Field Name	Size (Bits)	Description
TLA ID	13	Top-Level Aggregation (TLA) Identifier: A globally unique identifier for the top-level aggregator. There are 13 bits, so there were a maximum of 8,192 TLAs allowed.
RES	8	Reserved: These 8 bits were reserved for future use and set to zero. By leaving these 8 bits between the TLA ID and NLA ID unused, they could later be used to expand either the TLA ID or NLA ID fields as needed.
NLA ID	24	Next-Level Aggregation (NLA) Identifier: Each TLA was given this 24-bit field to generate blocks of addresses for allocation to its customers. The NLA ID is unique for each TLA ID. The use of the 24 bits was left up to the TLA organization.

You'll notice my use of the past tense in the description of the TLA/NLA structure, and that table heading is a pretty big giveaway, too. In August 2003, RFC 3587 was published, which in a nutshell says, "Uh, never mind about all that TLA/NLA stuff." The decision was made that having this structure hardwired into an Internet standard was inflexible, and it made more sense to let the regional Internet registries (APNIC, ARIN, LACNIC, and RIPE) decide for themselves how to use the 45 bits.

NOTE *The obsoleting of the TLA/NLA structure occurred after many years of people getting used to it, so for some time to come, you will still routinely see those terms mentioned in IPv6 descriptions. (This is why I included discussion of them here.)*

A Sample Division of the Global Routing Prefix into Levels

There is no single structure for determining how the 48-bit routing prefix is divided in the global unicast hierarchy. As one example, it might be possible to divide it into three levels, as shown in Table 25-5 and illustrated in Figure 25-4.

Table 25-5: Example IPv6 Unicast Routing Prefix Structure

Field Name	Size (Bits)	Description
(Unicast Indicator)	3	Each unicast address starts with 001; there is no official name for this (it used to be called the *format prefix*).
Level1 ID	10	Level 1 Identifier: The identifier of the highest level in the hierarchy. This would be used for assigning the largest blocks of addresses in the global hierarchy to the biggest Internet organizations. The number of level 1 organizations would be 210, or 1,024.
Level2 ID	12	Level 2 Identifier: Each block assigned to a level 1 organization would use 12 bits to create 4,096 address blocks to divide among the lower-level organizations it serves.
Level3 ID	23	Level 3 Identifier: Each level 2 organization has 23 bits to use to divide its level 2 address block. Thus, it could create over 8 million individual /48 address blocks to assign to end-user sites. Alternatively, the 23 bits could be divided further into still lower levels to reflect the structure of the level 2 organization's customers.

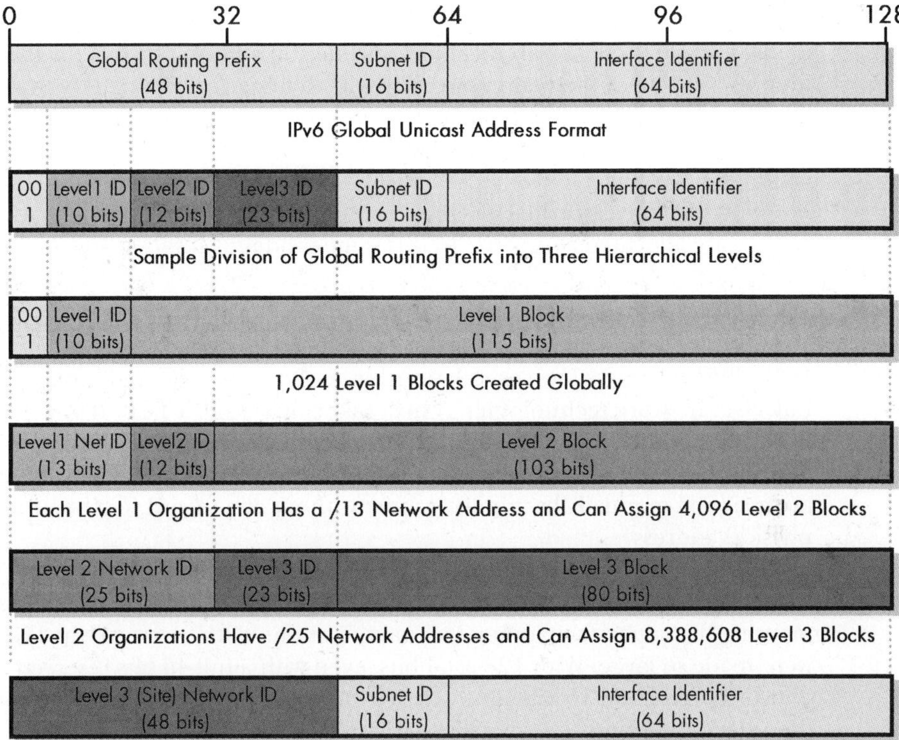

Figure 25-4: Example of IPv6 unicast routing prefix structure *The top row shows the global IPv6 unicast address format. The second shows one way to divide the global routing prefix into three levels using 10, 12, and 23 bits, respectively. The third row shows how the first 10 bits are used to create* 2^{10}*, or 1,024, different level 1 blocks. The next row illustrates that for each of these 13-bit prefixes, you could have* 2^{12}*, or 4,096, level 2 blocks. Then, within each 25-bit level 2 ID, you have 23 bits, or 8,388,608, level 3 blocks. At the bottom, a level 3 or /48 would be assigned to an individual organization.*

This is just one possible theoretical way that the bits in a /48 network address could be assigned. As you can see, with so many bits, there is a lot of flexibility. In the previous scheme, you can have over four million level 2 organizations, each of which can assign eight million /48 addresses. And each of those is equivalent in size to an IPv4 Class B address (over 65,000 hosts)!

The removal of RFC 2374's fixed structure for the global routing prefix is consistent with the IPv6 development team's efforts to emphasize that bit fields and structures are used only for allocating addresses and not for routing purposes. The addresses themselves, once created, are not interpreted by hardware on an internetwork based on this format. To routers, the only structure that matters is the division between the network ID and host ID, given by the prefix length that trails the IP address, and this division can occur at any bit boundary. These hardware devices just see 128 bits of an IP address and use it without any knowledge of hierarchical address divisions or levels.

Incidentally, the key to obtaining the allocation benefits of the aggregatable unicast address format is the abundance of bits available to us under IPv6. The ability to have these hierarchical levels while still allowing 64 bits for the interface identifier is one of the main reasons why IPv6 designers went all the way from 32 bits to 128 bits for address size. By creating this structure, we maintain flexibility, while avoiding the potential chaos of trying to allocate many different network sizes within the 128 bits.

Note that anycast addresses are structured in the same way as unicast addresses, so they are allocated according to this same model. (Multicast addresses are not.)

IPv6 Interface Identifiers and Physical Address Mapping

In IPv4, IP addresses have no relationship to the addresses used for underlying data link layer network technologies. A host that connects to a TCP/IP network using an Ethernet network interface card (NIC) has an Ethernet MAC address and an IP address, but the two numbers are distinct and unrelated in any way. IP addresses are assigned manually by administrators without any regard for the underlying physical address.

With the overhaul of addressing in IPv6, an opportunity presented itself to create a better way of mapping IP unicast addresses and physical network addresses. Implementing this superior mapping technique was one of the reasons why IPv6 addresses were made so large. With 128 total bits, even with a full 45 bits reserved for the network prefix and 16 bits for the site subnet, we are still left with 64 bits to use for the *interface identifier (interface ID)*, which is analogous to the host ID under IPv4.

Having so many bits at our disposal gives us great flexibility. Instead of using arbitrary, made-up identifiers for hosts, we can base the interface ID on the underlying data link layer hardware address, as long as that address is no greater than 64 bits in length. Since virtually all devices use layer 2 addresses of 64 bits or fewer, there is no problem in using those addresses for the interface ID in IP addresses. This provides an immediate benefit: It makes networks easier to administer, since we don't need to record two arbitrary numbers for each host. The IP address can be derived from the MAC address and the network ID. It also means that we can tell the IP address from the MAC address and vice versa.

The actual mapping from data link layer addresses to IP interface IDs depends on the particular technology. It is essential that all devices on the same network use the same mapping technique, of course. By far, the most common type of layer 2 addresses in networking are IEEE 802 MAC addresses, which are used by Ethernet and other IEEE 802 Project networking technologies. These addresses have 48 bits, arranged into two blocks of 24. The upper 24 bits are arranged into a block called the *organizationally unique identifier (OUI)*, with different values assigned to individual organizations. The lower 24 bits are then used for an identifier for each specific device.

The IEEE has also defined a format called the *64-bit extended unique identifier*, which is abbreviated *EUI-64*. It is similar to the 48-bit MAC format, except that while the OUI remains at 24 bits, the device identifier becomes 40 bits instead of 24. This gives each manufacturer 65,536 times as many device addresses within its OUI.

A form of this format, called *modified EUI-64*, has been adopted for IPv6 interface IDs. To get the modified EUI-64 interface ID for a device, you simply take the

EUI-64 address and change the seventh bit from the left (the universal/local, or U/L, bit) from a 0 to a 1.

Of course, most devices still use the older 48-bit MAC address format. These can be converted to EUI-64 and then modified to EUI-64 form for creating an IPv6 interface ID. The process is as follows:

1. Take the 24-bit OUI portion, the leftmost 24 bits of the Ethernet address, and put them into the leftmost 24 bits of the interface ID. Take the 24-bit local portion (the rightmost 24 bits of the Ethernet address) and put it into the rightmost 24 bits of the interface ID.
2. In the remaining 16 bits in the middle of the interface ID, put the value 11111111 11111110, FFFE in hexadecimal.
3. The address is now in EUI-64 form. Change the universal/local bit (bit 7 from the left, shown in bold in Figure 25-5) from a 0 to a 1. This gives the modified EUI-64 interface ID.

KEY CONCEPT The last 64 bits of IPv6 unicast addresses are used for interface IDs, which are created in a special format called *modified EUI-64*. A simple process can be used to determine the interface ID from the 48-bit MAC address of a device like an Ethernet network interface card. This can then be combined with a network prefix (routing prefix and subnet ID) to determine a corresponding IPv6 address for the device.

Let's take as an example the Ethernet address of 39-A7-94-07-CB-D0. Here are the steps for conversion (illustrated in Figure 25-5):

1. Take 39-A7-94, the first 24 bits of the identifier, and put it into the first (leftmost) 24 bits of the address. The local portion of 07-CB-D0 becomes the last 24 bits of the identifier.
2. The middle 16 bits are given the value FF-FE.
3. Change the seventh bit from 0 to 1, which changes the first octet from 39 to 3B.

The identifier thus becomes 3B-A7-94-FF-FE-07-CB-D0, or in IPv6 colon hexadecimal notation, 3BA7:94FF:FE07:CBD0. The first 64 bits of the device's address are supplied using the global unicast address format.

The only drawback of this technique is that if the physical hardware changes, so does the IPv6 address.

IPv6 Special Addresses: Reserved, Private, Unspecified, and Loopback

Just as certain IPv4 address ranges are designated for reserved, private, and other unusual addresses, a small part of the monstrous IPv6 address space has been set aside for special addresses. The purpose of these addresses and address blocks is to provide addresses for special requirements and private use in IPv6 networks. Since even relatively small pieces of IPv6 are still enormous, setting aside 0.1 percent of the address space for a particular use still generally yields more addresses than anyone will ever need.

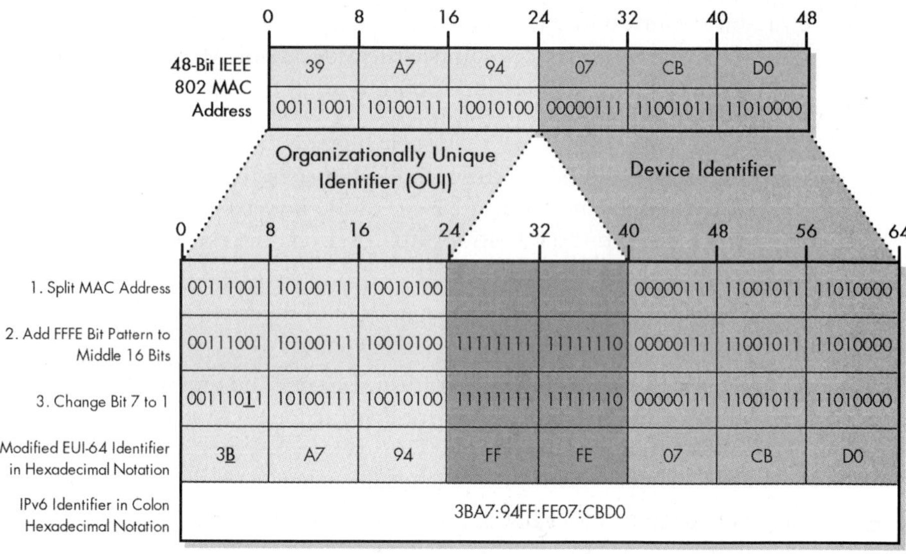

Figure 25-5: *Converting IEEE 802 MAC addresses to IPv6 modified EUI-64 identifiers*

Special Address Types

There are four basic types of special IPv6 addresses:

Reserved Addresses A portion of the address space is set aside as reserved for various uses by the IETF, both present and future. Unlike IPv4, which has many small reserved blocks in various locations in the address space, the reserved block in IPv6 is at the "top" of the address space, beginning with 0000 0000 (or 00 for the first hexadecimal octet). This represents 1/256th of the total address space. Some of the special addresses you'll see shortly come from this block. IPv4 address embedding is also done within this reserved address area.

NOTE *Reserved addresses are not the same as* unassigned *addresses. The latter term just refers to blocks whose use has not yet been determined.*

Private/Unregistered/Nonroutable Addresses A block of addresses is set aside for private addresses, just as in IPv4, except that like everything in IPv6 the private address block in IPv6 is much larger. These private addresses are local only to a particular link or site and, therefore, are never routed outside a particular company's network. Private addresses are indicated by the address having "1111 1110 1" for the first nine bits. Thus, private addresses have a first octet value of FE in hexadecimal, with the next hexadecimal digit being from 8 to F. These addresses are further divided into two types based on their scope: site-local and link-local, as discussed shortly.

Loopback Address Like IPv4, a provision has been made for a special loopback address for testing; datagrams sent to this address "loop back" to the sending device. However, in IPv6, there is just one address for this function, not a whole block (which was never needed in the first place). The loopback address is 0:0:0:0:0:0:0:1, which is normally expressed using zero compression as ::1.

Unspecified Address In IPv4, an IP address of all zeros has a special meaning: It refers to the host itself and is used when a device doesn't know its own address. In IPv6, this concept has been formalized, and the all-zeros address (0:0:0:0:0:0:0:0) is named the *unspecified address*. It is typically used in the source field of a datagram sent by a device seeking to have its IP address configured. Zero compression can be applied to this address; since it is all zeros, the address becomes just ::. (I consider this confusing, myself. I think something like 0::0 is a lot clearer and short enough.)

> **KEY CONCEPT** In IPv6, a special *loopback address*, 0:0:0:0:0:0:0:1 (::1 in compressed form) is set aside for testing purposes. The *unspecified address*, 0:0:0:0:0:0:0:0 (:: in compressed form) is used to indicate an unknown address. A block of *private* or *local* addresses is defined. This block is the set of all addresses beginning with 1111 1110 1 as the first nine bits.

IPv6 Private Addresses Type Scopes

Now let's take a closer look at private addresses. In IPv6, these are called *local-use* addresses, with the name conveying clearly what they are for. They are also sometimes called *link-layer* addresses. You'll recall that IPv4 private addresses were commonly used when public addresses could not be obtained for all devices, sometimes in combination with technologies like Network Address Translation (NAT). In IPv6, trickery like NAT isn't required. Instead, local-use addresses are intended for communication that is inherently designed to be sent to local devices only. For example, neighbor discovery functions using the IPv6 Neighbor Discovery (ND) protocol employ local-use addresses.

The *scope* of local addresses is obviously a local network, not the global scope of public Internet addresses. Local addresses in IPv6 are further divided into two types, reflecting a division of local scope:

Site-Local Addresses These addresses have the scope of an entire site or organization. They allow addressing within an organization without having to use a public prefix. Routers will forward datagrams using site-local addresses within the site, but not addresses outside it to the public Internet. Site-local addresses are differentiated from link-local addresses by having a tenth bit of 1 following the nine starting address bits that are common to all private IPv6 addresses. Thus, they begin with 1111 1110 11. In hexadecimal, site-local addresses begin with FE, and then C to F for the third digit. So, these addresses start with FEC, FED, FEE, or FEF.

Link-Local Addresses These addresses have a smaller scope than site-local addresses; they refer only to a particular physical link (physical network). Routers will not forward datagrams using link-local addresses at all—not even within the organization. These addresses are only for local communication on a particular physical network segment. They can be used for address configuration or for ND functions such as address resolution and ND. Link-local addresses are differentiated from site-local addresses by having a tenth bit of 0 following the nine initial address bits common to all private IPv6 addresses: 1111 1110 1. Thus, site-local addresses begin with FE, and then 8 to B for the third hexadecimal digit. So, these addresses start with FE8, FE9, FEA, or FEB.

> **KEY CONCEPT** IPv6 site-local addresses allow data to be sent only to the devices within a site or organization. They begin with FEC, FED, FEE, or FEF in hexadecimal. IPv6 link-local addresses are used only on a particular local link (physical network), typically for special purposes such as address resolution or Neighbor Discovery (ND). They start with FE8, FE9, FEA, or FEB.

Note that site-local IPv6 addresses are the equivalent of IPv4 private addresses, since they are routed throughout the organization. The concept of link-local scope is new to IPv6.

IPv6/IPv4 Address Embedding

Due to the importance of IP and the significance of the changes made in IPv6, deployment of the newer version of the protocol will not occur all at once. A *transition* from IPv4 to IPv6 will be required. This transition requires careful planning. It is anticipated that the migration from IPv4 to IPv6 will take many years, as I mentioned earlier.

IPv6 is backward-compatible with IPv4 provided that you use special techniques. For example, to enable communication between islands of IPv6 devices connected by IPv4 networks, you may need to employ tunneling. To support IPv4/IPv6 compatibility, a scheme was developed to allow IPv4 addresses to be *embedded* within the IPv6 address structure. This method takes regular IPv4 addresses and puts them in a special IPv6 format, so that they are recognized as being IPv4 addresses by certain IPv6 devices.

Since the IPv6 address space is so much bigger than the one in IPv4, embedding the latter within the former is easy—it's like tucking a compact sedan into the hold of a cargo ship! The embedding address space is part of the reserved address block whose addresses begin with eight 0 bits, but it's only a relatively small part. Two different embedding formats are used to indicate the capabilities of the device that's using the embedded address:

IPv4-Compatible IPv6 Addresses These are special addresses assigned to IPv6-capable devices, such as *dual-stack* devices that use both IPv4 and IPv6. They have all zeros for the middle 16 bits; thus, they start off with a string of 96 zeros, followed by the IPv4 address. An example of such an address would be 0:0:0:0:0:0:101.45.75.219 in mixed notation, or more succinctly, ::101.45.75.219. Figure 25-6 illustrates IPv4-compatible IPv6 representation.

IPv4-Mapped IPv6 Addresses These are regular IPv4 addresses that have been mapped into the IPv6 address space. They are used for devices that are IPv4-capable only. They have a set of 16 ones after the initial string of 80 zeros and then the

IPv4 address. So if an IPv4 device has the address 222.1.41.90, such as the one shown in Figure 25-7, it would be represented as 0:0:0:0:0:FFFF:222.1.41.90, or ::FFFF:222.1.41.90.

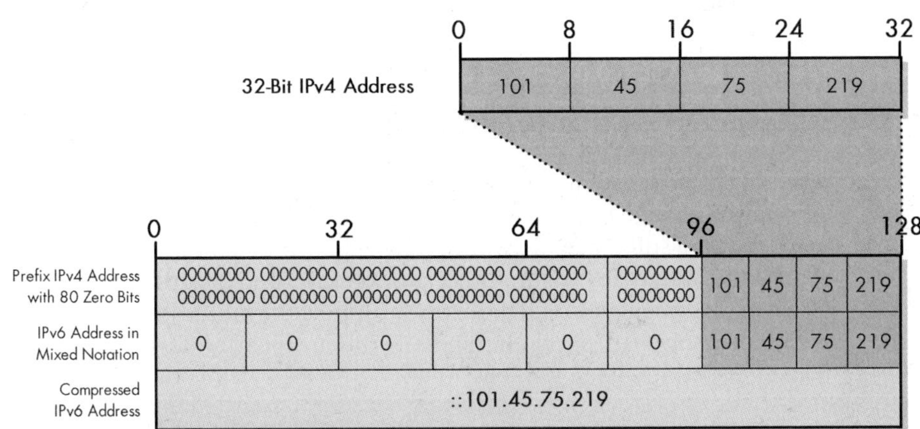

Figure 25-6: *IPv4-compatible embedded IPv6 address representation*

The difference between these two is subtle but important. Both have zeros for the first 80 bits of the address and put the embedded IPv4 address into the last 32 bits of the IPv6 address format. They differ in the value of the 16 remaining bits in between (bits 81 to 96, counting from the left). IPv4-compatible IPv6 addresses are used only for devices that are actually IPv6-aware; the IPv4-compatible address is in addition to its conventional IPv6 address. In contrast, if the FFFF is seen for the 16 bits after the initial 80, this designates a conventional IPv4 devices whose IPv4 address has been mapped into the IPv6 format. It is not an IPv6-capable device.

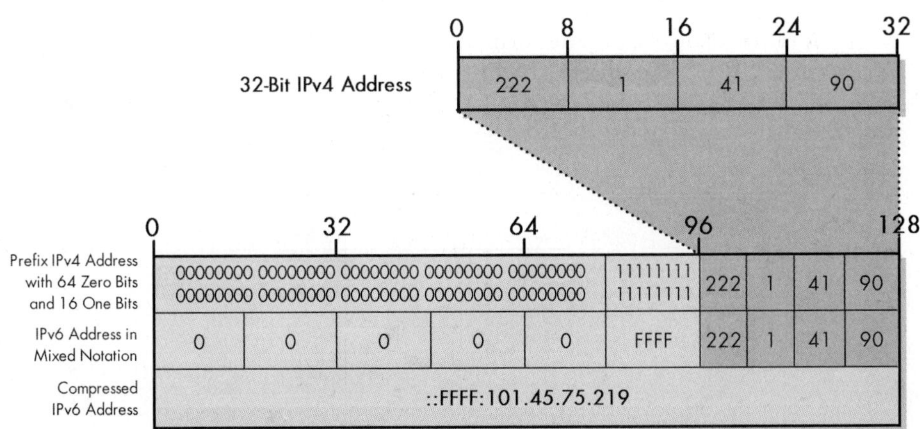

Figure 25-7: *IPv4-mapped embedded IPv6 address representation*

> **KEY CONCEPT** *IPv4 address embedding* is used to create a relationship between an IPv4 address and an IPv6 address to help you transition from IPv4 to IPv6. One type, the *IPv4-compatible IPv6 address,* is used for devices that are compatible with both IPv4 and IPv6; it begins with 96 zero bits. The other, the *IPv4-mapped address,* is used for mapping IPv4 devices that are not compatible with IPv6 into the IPv6 address space; it begins with 80 zeros followed by 16 ones.

IPv6 Multicast and Anycast Addressing

One of the most significant modifications in the general addressing model in IPv6 was a change to the basic types of addresses and how they were used. Unicast addresses are still the choice for the vast majority of communications as in IPv4, but the "bulk" addressing methods are different in IPv6. Broadcast as a specific addressing type has been eliminated. Instead, support for multicast addressing has been expanded and made a required part of the protocol, and a new type of addressing called *anycast* has been implemented.

IPv6 Multicast Addresses

Let's start by looking at multicast under IPv6. Multicasting is used to allow a single device to send a datagram to a group of recipients. IPv4 supported multicast addressing using the Class D address block in the classful addressing scheme (see Chapter 17). Under IPv6, multicast addresses are allocated from the multicast block. This is 1/256th of the address space, and it consists of all addresses that begin with 1111 1111. Thus, any address starting with FF in colon hexadecimal notation is an IPv6 multicast address.

The remaining 120 bits of address space are enough to allow the definition of, well, a gazillion or three multicast addresses. (OK, it's officially about 1.3 trillion trillion trillion addresses.) The allocation of unicast addresses was organized by using a special format to divide these many bits, and the same thing was done for multicast addresses. The format for multicast addresses is explained in Table 25-6 and illustrated in Figure 25-8.

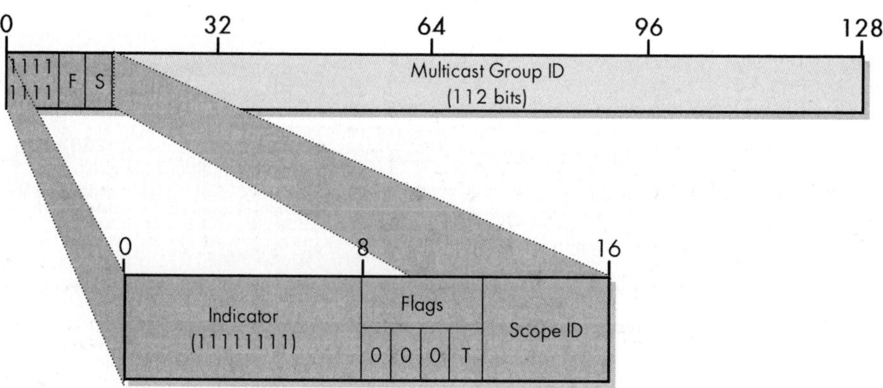

Figure 25-8: *IPv6 multicast address format*

Table 25-6: IPv6 Multicast Address Format

Field Name	Size (Bits)	Description
(Indicator)	8	The first eight bits are always 1111 1111, which indicates a multicast address. This used to be called the *format prefix* before the term was dropped (as explained in the section about IPv6 address space allocation earlier in this chapter). The field now has no name.
Flags	4	Four bits are reserved for flags that can be used to indicate the nature of certain multicast addresses. Currently, the first three of these are unused and set to zero. The fourth is the T (Transient) flag. If left as zero, this marks the multicast address as a permanently assigned, well-known multicast address, as you will see shortly. If set to one, this means this is a *transient* multicast address, meaning that it is not permanently assigned.
Scope ID	4	These four bits are used to define the scope of the multicast address; 16 different values from 0 to 15 are possible. This field allows creation of multicast addresses that are global to the entire Internet, or restricted to smaller spheres of influence such as a specific organization, site, or link. The currently defined values (in decimal) are as follows: 0 = Reserved 1 = Node-Local Scope 2 = Link-Local Scope 5 = Site-Local Scope 8 = Organization-Local Scope 14 = Global Scope 15 = Reserved
Group ID	112	Defines a particular group within each scope level.

Multicast Scopes

The notion of explicitly scoping multicast addresses is important. Globally scoped multicast addresses must be unique across the entire Internet, but locally scoped addresses are unique only within the organization. This provides tremendous flexibility, as every type of multicast address actually comes in several versions: one that multicasts only within a node, one that multicasts on the local link (local network), one that multicasts on the local site, and so on. The scope also allows routers to immediately determine how broadly they should propagate multicast datagrams in order to improve efficiency and eliminate problems with traffic being sent outside the area for which it is intended. Figure 25-9 illustrates the notion of multicast scope graphically.

> **KEY CONCEPT** Multicast addresses are used to send data to a number of devices on an internetwork simultaneously. In IPv6, each multicast address can be specified for a variety of different *scopes*, thereby allowing a transmission to be targeted to either a wide or a narrow audience of recipient devices.

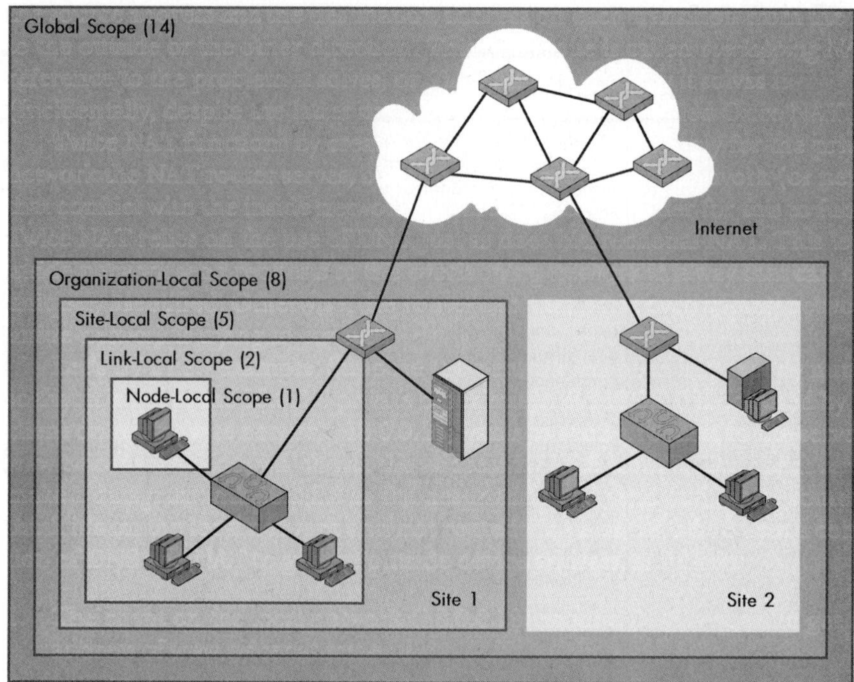

Figure 25-9: IPv6 multicast scope This diagram shows how the notion of scope allows IPv6 multicasts to be limited to specific spheres of influence. The tightest scope is node-local scope, with a scope ID value of 1. As the scope ID value increases, the scope expands to cover the local network, site, organization, and finally, entire Internet.

Well-Known Multicast Addresses

The Transient flag allows for the explicit determination of which multicast addresses are available for normal use compared to which ones are set aside as well known. Several well-known multicast addresses are defined by setting aside certain group IDs that are used for a number of different scope ID values. Table 25-7 shows these values; the *x* in the multicast address pattern is the hexadecimal digit corresponding to the four-bit scope ID field.

The all-nodes and all-routers multicast addresses enable the equivalent function of what broadcast used to perform in IPv4. Again, the concept of scope is important in a multicast of this type, because we don't want to try to send a message to all nodes on the global Internet, for example. So when the all-routers address is used with a scope value of 2, it means "all routers on the local link." If it is used with a value of 5, it means "all routers in this site."

Solicited-Node Multicast Addresses

In addition to the regular multicast addresses, each unicast address has a special multicast address called its *solicited-node address*. This address is created through a special mapping from the device's unicast address. Solicited-node addresses are used by the IPv6 ND protocol (see Chapter 36) to provide more efficient address resolution than the Address Resolution Protocol (ARP; see Chapter 13) technique used in IPv4.

Table 25-7: Important IPv6 Well-Known Multicast Addresses

Multicast Address Pattern	Valid Scope Values (Decimal)	Designation	Description
FF0x:0:0:0:0:0:0:0	0 to 15	Reserved	All multicast addresses where the 112-bit group ID is zero are reserved.
FF0x:0:0:0:0:0:0:1	1, 2	All Nodes	When the group ID is equal to exactly 1, this is a multicast to all nodes. Both node-local (FF01:0:0:0:0:0:0:1) and link-local (FF02:0:0:0:0:0:0:1) all-nodes multicast addresses are possible.
FF0x:0:0:0:0:0:0:2	1, 2, 5	All Routers	When the group ID is equal to exactly 2, this designates all routers within a specific scope as the recipients. Valid scope values are node-local, link-local, and site-local.

All solicited-node addresses have their T flag set to zero and a scope ID of 2, so they start with FF02. The 112-bit group ID is broken down as follows (see Figure 25-10):

- Eighty bits consisting of 79 zeros followed by a single one. This means that the next five hexadecimal values are 0000:0000:0000:0000:0001 in colon hexadecimal notation, or more succinctly, 0:0:0:0:1.
- Eight ones: FF.
- Twenty-four bits taken from the bottom 24 bits of its unicast address.

So, these addresses start with FF02:0:0:0:0:1:FF, followed by the bottom 24 bits of the unicast address. Thus, the node with IP address 805B:2D9D:DC28:0:0:FC57:D4C8:1FFF would have a solicited-node address of FF02:0:0:0:0:1:FFC8:1FFF (or FF02::1:FFC8:1FFF).

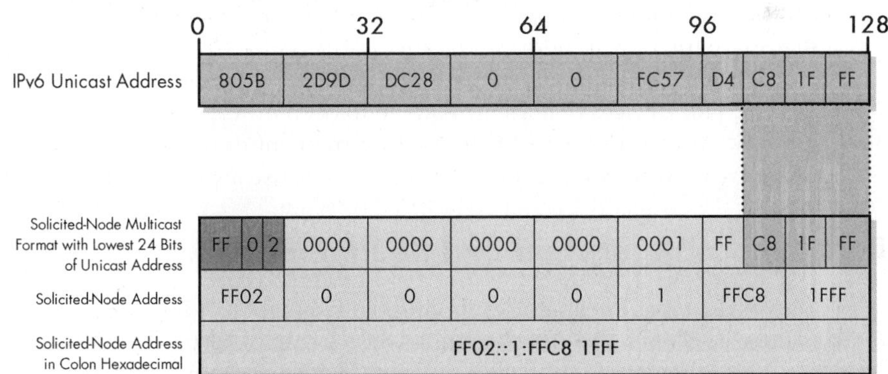

Figure 25-10: IPv6 solicited-node address calculation *The solicited-node multicast address is calculated from a unicast address by taking the last 24 bits of the address and prepending them with the IPv6 partial address FF02:0:0:0:0:1:FF. This shows the example address from Figure 25-2 converted to its solicited-node address, FF02::1:FFC8:1FFF.*

KEY CONCEPT Each unicast address has an equivalent *solicited-node multicast address* that is created from the unicast address and used when other devices need to reach it on the local network.

IPv6 Anycast Addresses

Anycast addresses are a unique type of address that is new to IP in IPv6. The IPv6 implementation is based on the material in RFC 1546, "Host Anycasting Service." Anycast addresses can be considered a conceptual cross between unicast and multicast addressing. Where unicast says, "Send this to one address," and multicast says, "Send this to every member of this group," anycast says, "Send this to any one member of this group." Naturally, in choosing which member to send to, we would, for efficiency, normally send to the closest one—that is, the closest in routing terms. So, we can normally also consider *anycast* to mean, "Send this to the closest member of this group."

The idea behind anycast is to enable functionality that was previously difficult to implement in TCP/IP. Anycast was specifically intended to provide flexibility in situations where we need a service that is provided by a number of different servers or routers but don't really care which one provides it. In routing, anycast allows datagrams to be sent to whichever router in a group of equivalent routers is closest, and to allow load sharing among routers and dynamic flexibility if certain routers go out of service. Datagrams sent to the anycast address will automatically be delivered to the device that is easiest to reach.

Perhaps surprisingly, there is no special anycast-addressing scheme. Anycast addresses are the same as unicast addresses. An anycast address is created automatically when a unicast address is assigned to more than one interface.

> **KEY CONCEPT** Anycast addresses are new in IPv6 and can be used to set up a group of devices, any one of which can respond to a request sent to a single IP address.

Like multicast, anycast creates more work for routers, because it is more complicated than unicast addressing. In particular, the further apart the devices that share the anycast address are, the more complexity. Anycasting across the global Internet would be potentially difficult to implement, and IPv6 anycasting was designed for devices that are proximate to each other, generally within the same network. Also, at present, due to the Internet community's relative inexperience with anycast, only routers, not individual hosts, use anycast addresses.

IPv6 Autoconfiguration and Renumbering

One of the most interesting and potentially valuable addressing features implemented in IPv6 is a facility that allows devices on an IPv6 network to actually configure themselves independently. In IPv4, hosts were originally configured manually. Later, host configuration protocols like the Dynamic Host Configuration Protocol (DHCP; see Chapter 61) enabled servers to allocate IP addresses to hosts that joined the network. IPv6 takes this a step further by defining a method for some devices to automatically configure their IP address and other parameters without the need for a server. It also defines a method whereby the IP addresses on a network can be renumbered (changed en masse). These are the sorts of features that make TCP/IP network administrators drool.

The IPv6 autoconfiguration and renumbering feature is defined in RFC 2462, "IPv6 Stateless Address Autoconfiguration." The word *stateless* contrasts this method to the server-based method using something like DHCPv6, which is called *stateful*. (This word, like *classful*, makes me cringe.) This method is called stateless because it begins with no information (or *state*) at all for the host to work with. It has no need for a DHCP server.

IPv6 Stateless Autoconfiguration

Stateless autoconfiguration exploits several other new features in IPv6, including link-local addresses, multicasting, the ND protocol, and the ability to generate the interface ID of an address from the underlying data link layer address. The general idea is to have a device generate a temporary address until it can determine the characteristics of the network it is on, and then create a permanent address it can use based on that information. In the case of multihomed devices, autoconfiguration is performed for each interface separately.

The following is a summary of the steps a device takes when using stateless autoconfiguration:

1. **Link-Local Address Generation** The device generates a link-local address. You'll recall that this is one of the two types of local-use IPv6 addresses. Link-local addresses have 1111 1110 10 for the first 10 bits. The generated address uses those 10 bits, followed by 54 zeros and then the 64-bit interface ID. Typically, this will be derived from the data link layer (MAC) address as explained in the "IPv6 Interface Identifiers and Physical Address Mapping" section earlier in this chapter, or it may be a "token" generated in some other manner.
2. **Link-Local Address Uniqueness Test** The node tests to ensure that the address it generated isn't already in use on the local network. (This is very unlikely to be an issue if the link-local address came from a MAC address; it is more likely that the address is already in use if it was based on a generated token.) It sends a Neighbor Solicitation message using the ND protocol. In response, it listens for a Neighbor Advertisement, which indicates that another device is already using its link-local address. If so, either a new address must be generated or autoconfiguration fails, and another method must be employed.
3. **Link-Local Address Assignment** Assuming the uniqueness test passes, the device assigns the link-local address to its IP interface. This address can be used for communication on the local network, but not on the wider Internet (since link-local addresses are not routed).
4. **Router Contact** The node next attempts to contact a local router for more information on continuing the configuration. This is done either by listening for Router Advertisement messages sent periodically by routers or by sending a specific Router Solicitation message to ask a router for information on what to do next. This process is described in the section on the IPv6 ND protocol, in Chapter 36.

5. **Router Direction** The router provides direction to the node about how to proceed with the autoconfiguration. It may tell the node that on this network stateful autoconfiguration is in use, and it may give it the address of a DHCP server to use. Alternatively, it will tell the host how to determine its global Internet address.
6. **Global Address Configuration** Assuming that stateless autoconfiguration is in use on the network, the host will configure itself with its globally unique Internet address. This address is generally formed from a network prefix provided to the host by the router. The prefix is combined with the device's identifier, as generated in step 1.

Clearly, this method has numerous advantages over both manual and server-based configuration. It is particularly helpful in supporting the mobility of IP devices, because they can move to new networks and get a valid address without any knowledge of local servers or network prefixes. At the same time, it still allows for the management of IP addresses using the (IPv6-compatible) version of DHCP, if that is desired. Routers on the local network will typically tell hosts which type of autoconfiguration is supported using special flags in Internet Control Message Protocol version 6 (ICMPv6) Router Advertisement messages (see Chapter 35).

> **KEY CONCEPT** IPv6 includes an interesting feature called *stateless address autoconfiguration,* which allows a host to actually determine its own IPv6 address from its layer 2 address by following a special procedure.

IPv6 Device Renumbering

The renumbering of devices is a method related to autoconfiguration. Like host configuration, it can be implemented using protocols like DHCP through the use of IP address leases that expire after a period of time. Under IPv6, networks can be renumbered by having routers specify an expiration interval for network prefixes when autoconfiguration is done. Later, they can send a new prefix to tell devices to regenerate their IP addresses. Devices can actually maintain the old deprecated address for a while, and then move over to the new address.

RFC 2894 defined a similar technique for renumbering router addresses. It uses special ICMPv6 messages and is described in Chapter 35.

26

IPV6 DATAGRAM ENCAPSULATION AND FORMATTING

Delivery of data over Internet Protocol version 6 (IPv6) internetworks is accomplished by encapsulating higher-layer data into IPv6 datagrams. These serve the same general purpose for IPv6 as IPv4 datagrams do in the older version of the protocol. However, they have been redesigned as part of the overall changes represented by IPv6. IPv6 datagrams have a flexible structure, and their format better matches the needs of current IP networks.

In this chapter, I take a look at the format used for IPv6 datagrams. I begin with an overview of the general structure of IPv6 datagrams, describe the major changes, and show how main and extension headers are arranged in the datagram. I then describe the format of the main header, and define and describe the various extension header types. I conclude with a brief explanation of IPv6 options and how they are implemented.

BACKGROUND INFORMATION *This chapter assumes basic understanding of IPv6 addressing concepts (see the previous chapter) and general familiarity with the IPv4 datagram format (described in Chapter 21).*

IPv6 Datagram Overview and General Structure

The method by which IPv6 encapsulates data received from higher-layer protocols for transmission across the internetwork is basically the same as the one used by IPv4. The data received from the transport or higher layers is made the payload of an IPv6 datagram, which has one or more headers that control the delivery of the message. These headers provide information to routers in order to enable them to move the datagram across the network. They also provide information to hosts so they can tell which datagrams they are intended to receive.

While the basic use of datagrams hasn't changed since IPv4, many modifications were made to their structure and format when IPv6 was created. This was done partly out of necessity: IPv6 addresses are different from IPv4 addresses, and IP addresses go in the datagram header. The increase in the size of IP addresses from 32 bits to 128 bits adds a whopping extra 192 bits, or 24 bytes, of information to the header. This led to an effort to remove fields that weren't strictly necessary in order to compensate for the necessary increase in size. However, changes were also made to IPv6 datagrams to add features to them and to make them better suit the needs of modern internetworking.

The following is a list of the most significant overall changes to datagrams in IPv6:

Multiple-Header Structure Rather than a single header that contains all fields for the datagram (possibly including options), the IPv6 datagram supports a main header and then extension headers for additional information when needed.

Streamlined Header Format Several fields have been removed from the main header to reduce its size and increase efficiency. Only the fields that are truly required for pretty much *all* datagrams remain in the main header; others are put into extension headers and used as needed. Some were removed because they were no longer needed, such as the Internet Header Length field. The IPv6 header is of fixed length. I'll examine this more thoroughly in a moment.

Renamed Fields Some fields have been renamed to better reflect their actual use in modern networks.

Greater Flexibility The extension headers allow for a great deal of extra information that will accompany datagrams when needed. Options are also supported in IPv6.

Elimination of Checksum Calculation In IPv6, a checksum is no longer computed on the header. This saves both the calculation time spent by every device that packages IP datagrams (hosts and routers) and the space the checksum field took up in the IPv4 header.

Improved Quality of Service Support A new field, the Flow Label, is defined to help support the prioritization of traffic.

> **KEY CONCEPT** IPv6 datagrams use a general structure that begins with a mandatory main header that's 40 bytes in length, followed by optional extension headers, and then a variable-length Data area. This structure was created to allow the main header to be streamlined, while allowing devices to add extra information to datagrams when needed.

As I mentioned previously, IPv6 datagrams now include a main header format (which has no official name in the standards; it's just "the header") and zero or more extension headers. The overall structure of an IPv6 datagram is shown in Table 26-1 and illustrated in Figure 26-1.

Table 26-1: IPv6 General Datagram Structure

Component	Number of Components per Datagram	Size (Bytes)	Description
Main Header	1	40	Contains the source and destination addresses, and important information that's required for every datagram.
Extension Headers	0 or more	Variable	Each contains one type of extra information that supports various features, including fragmentation, source routing, security, and options.
Data	1	Variable	The payload from the upper layer that will be transmitted in the datagram.

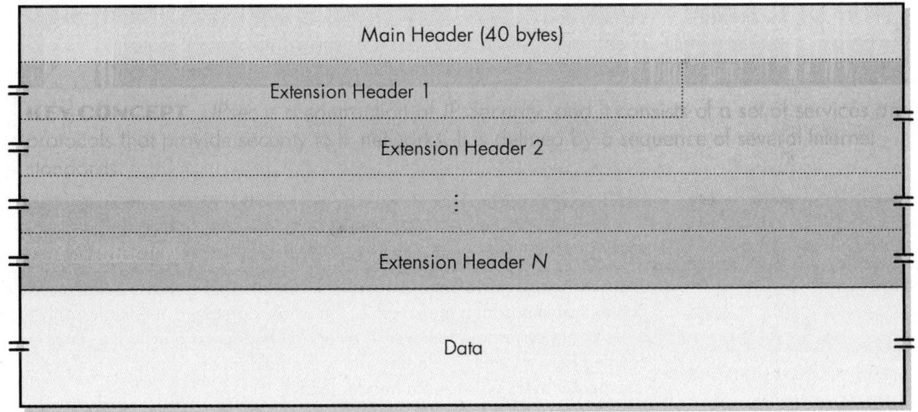

Figure 26-1: *IPv6 general datagram structure*

Note that as with IPv4, large payloads may be fragmented prior to encapsulation in order to ensure that the total size of the datagram doesn't exceed the maximum size permitted on an underlying network. However, the details of fragmentation in IPv6 are different than in IPv4, as explained in Chapter 27.

IPv6 Datagram Main Header Format

IPv6 datagrams use a structure that includes a regular header and, optionally, one or more extension headers. This regular header is like the header of IPv4 datagrams, though it has a different format, as you will see shortly. The standards don't give this header a name; it is just "*the* IPv6 header." To differentiate it from IPv6 extension headers, I call it the *main header*.

The IPv6 main header is required for every datagram. It contains addressing and control information that are used to manage the processing and routing of the datagram. The main header format of IPv6 datagrams is described in Table 26-2 and illustrated in Figure 26-2.

Table 26-2: IPv6 Main Header Format

Field Name	Size (Bytes)	Description
Version	1/2 (4 bits)	This identifies the version of IP that's used to generate the datagram. This field is used the same way as in IPv4, except that it carries the value 6 (0110 binary).
Traffic Class	1	This field replaces the Type of Service (TOS) field in the IPv4 header. It is used not in the original way that the TOS field was defined (with Precedence, D, T, and R bits), but rather, using the new *Differentiated Services (DS)* method defined in RFC 2474. That RFC actually specifies quality-of-service (QoS) techniques for both IPv4 and IPv6; see the IPv4 format description (Chapter 21) for a bit more information.
Flow Label	2 1/2 (20 bits)	This large field was created to provide additional support for real-time datagram delivery and QoS features. The concept of a *flow* is defined in RFC 2460 as a sequence of datagrams sent from a source device to one or more destination devices. A unique flow label is used to identify all the datagrams in a particular flow, so that routers between the source and destination all handle them the same way. This helps to ensure uniformity in how the datagrams in the flow are delivered. For example, if a video stream is being sent across an IP internetwork, the datagrams containing the stream could be identified with a flow label to ensure that they are delivered with minimal latency. Not all devices and routers may support flow label handling, and the use of the field by a source device is entirely optional. Also, the field is still somewhat experimental and may be refined over time.
Payload Length	2	This field replaces the Total Length field from the IPv4 header, but it is used differently. Rather than measuring the length of the whole datagram, it contains only the number of bytes of the payload. However, if extension headers are included, their length is counted here as well. In simpler terms, this field measures the length of the datagram less the 40 bytes of the main header itself.
Next Header	1	This field replaces the Protocol field and has two uses. When a datagram has extension headers, this field specifies the identity of the first extension header, which is the next header in the datagram. When a datagram has just this "main" header and no extension headers, it serves the same purpose as the old IPv4 *Protocol* field and has the same values, though new numbers are used for the IPv6 versions of common protocols. In this case the "next header" is the header of the upper layer message the IPv6 datagram is carrying. I'll discuss this in more detail a bit later in this chapter.
Hop Limit	1	This replaces the Time to Live (TTL) field in the IPv4 header; its name better reflects the way that TTL is used in modern networks (because TTL is really used to count hops, not time).

(continued)

Table 26-2: IPv6 Main Header Format (continued)

Field Name	Size (Bytes)	Description
Source Address	16	The 128-bit IP address of the originator of the datagram. As with IPv4, this is always the device that originally sent the datagram.
Destination Address	16	The 128-bit IP address of the intended recipient of the datagram: unicast, anycast, or multicast. Again, even though devices such as routers may be the intermediate targets of the datagram, this field is always for the ultimate destination.

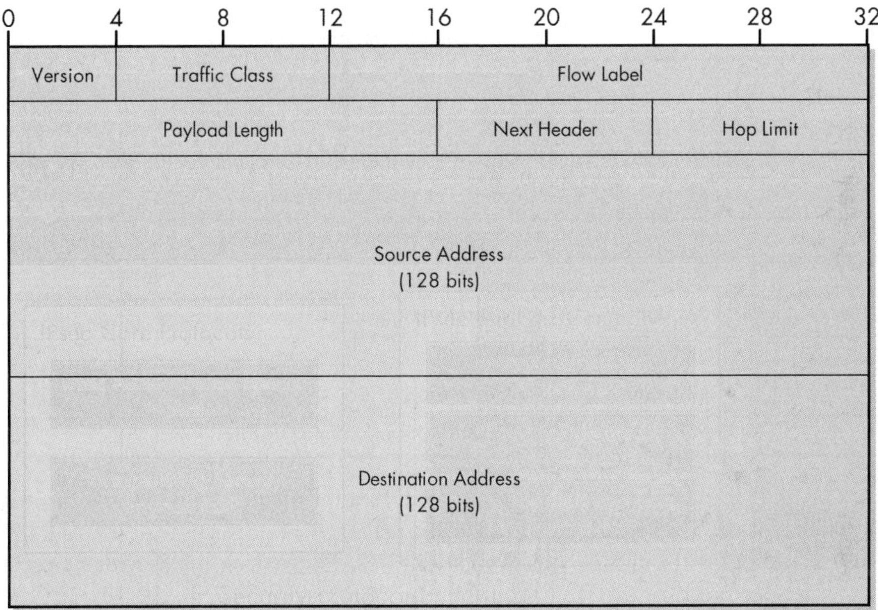

Figure 26-2: *IPv6 main header format*

IPv6 Next Header Field

The Next Header field is one of the most important additions to the IPv6 datagram format. When an IPv6 datagram uses extension headers, this field contains an identifier for the first extension header, which, in turn, uses its own Next Header field to point to the next header, and so on. The last extension header then references the encapsulated higher-layer protocol. Because the higher-layer protocol's header appears at the start of the IPv6 Data field, it is like the "next header" to the device receiving the datagram. For some folks, this is a bit tough to see conceptually; you can find more detail on how the field works (including a useful illustration, Figure 26-3) in the "IPv6 Header Chaining Using the Next Header Field" section later in this chapter.

Some of the most common values for the Next Header field in IPv6 are shown in Table 26-3.

Table 26-3: Common IPv6 Next Header Values

Value (Hexadecimal)	Value (Decimal)	Protocol/Extension Header
00	0	Hop-By-Hop Options Extension Header (Note that this value was "Reserved" in IPv4)
01	1	Internet Control Message Protocol version 4 (ICMPv4)
02	2	Internet Group Management Protocol version 4 (IGMPv4)
04	4	IP-in-IP Encapsulation
06	6	Transmission Control Protocol (TCP)
08	8	Exterior Gateway Protocol (EGP)
11	17	User Datagram Protocol (UDP)
29	41	IPv6
2B	43	Routing Extension Header
2C	44	Fragmentation Extension Header
2E	46	Resource Reservation Protocol (RSVP)
32	50	Encrypted Security Payload (ESP) Extension Header
33	51	Authentication Header (AH) Extension Header
3A	58	ICMPv6
3B	59	No Next Header
3C	60	Destination Options Extension Header

The total length of the main IPv6 header format is 40 bytes. This is double the size of the IPv4 header without options, largely because of the extra 24 bytes needed for the monstrous IPv6 addresses. There are only 8 bytes of nonaddress header fields in the IPv6 main header, compared to 12 in the IPv4 header.

Key Changes to the Main Header Between IPv4 and IPv6

To summarize, the IPv6 main header compares to the IPv4 header as follows:

Unchanged Fields Three fields are used the same way, and they retain the same name (though they have different content and/or size): Version, Source Address, and Destination Address.

Renamed Fields Two fields are used the same way, but they are renamed: Traffic Class and Hop Limit.

Modified Fields Two fields are used in a way similar way to their IPv4 predecessors, but they are slightly different in meaning and also renamed: Payload Length and Next Header.

Added Field There is one new field: Flow Label.

Removed Fields To cut down on header length and unnecessary work, five IPv4 header fields are removed from the IPv6 header:

- The *Internet Header Length* field is no longer needed, because the main IPv6 header is fixed in length at 40 bytes.
- The *Identification*, *Flags*, and *Fragment Offset* fields are used for fragmentation, which is done less in IPv6 than IPv4, so these fields are now found only when needed in the Fragmentation extension header.
- The *Header Checksum* field is no longer needed, because the decision was made to eliminate header checksum calculations in IPv6. It was viewed as redundant with higher-layer error-checking and data link layer CRC calculations. This saves processing time for routers and 2 bytes in the datagram header.

In addition, while options were formerly considered part of the main header in IPv4, they are separate in IPv6.

IPv6 Datagram Extension Headers

After the mandatory main header in an IPv6 datagram, one or more extension headers may appear before the encapsulated payload. These headers were created in an attempt to provide both flexibility and efficiency in the creation of IPv6 datagrams. All the fields that are needed for only special purposes are put into extension headers and placed in the datagram when needed. This allows the size of the main datagram header to be made small and streamlined, containing only those fields that really must be present all the time.

There is often confusion regarding the role of extension headers, especially when compared to datagram options. The IPv4 datagram had only one header, but it included a provision for options, and IPv6 also has options, so why bother with extension headers?

It would have been possible to do everything using options. However, it was deemed a better design to employ extension headers for certain sets of information that are needed for common functions such as fragmenting. Options are indeed still supported in IPv6; they are used to supply even more flexibility by providing variable-length fields that can be used for any purpose. They are themselves defined using extension headers, as you will see shortly.

When extension headers are included in an IPv6 datagram, they appear one after the other following the main header. Each extension header type has its own internal structure of fields.

IPv6 Header Chaining Using the Next Header Field

The only field common to all extension header types is the Next Header field, which actually appears at the end of one header type, the ESP header. The 8-bit Next Header field is used to logically link all the headers in an IPv6 datagram, as follows:

- The Next Header field in the main header contains a reference number for the first extension header type.

- The Next Header field in the first extension header contains the number of the second extension header type, if there is a second one. If there's a third, the second header's Next Header points to it, and so on.
- The Next Header field of the last extension header contains the protocol number of the encapsulated higher-layer protocol. In essence, this field points to the "next header" within the payload itself.

For example, suppose a datagram that encapsulates TCP has a Hop-By-Hop Options extension header and a Fragment extension header. Then, the Next Header fields of these headers would contain the following values:

- The main header would have a Next Header value of 0, indicating the Hop-By-Hop Options header.
- The Hop-By-Hop Options header would have a Next Header value of 44 (decimal), which is the value for the Fragment extension header.
- The Fragment header would have a Next Header value of 6.

This is illustrated in Figure 26-3.

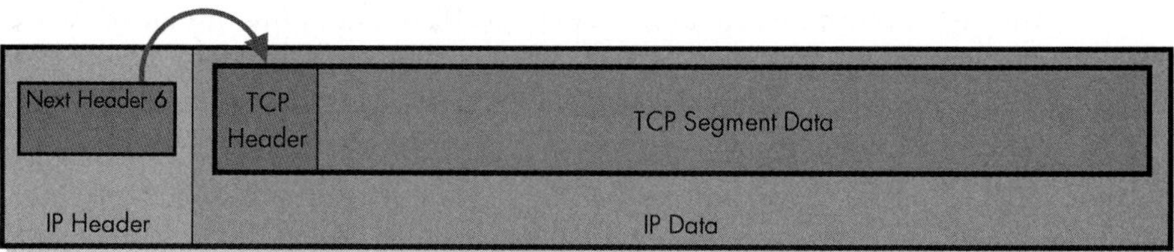

IPv6 Datagram with No Extension Headers Carrying TCP Segment

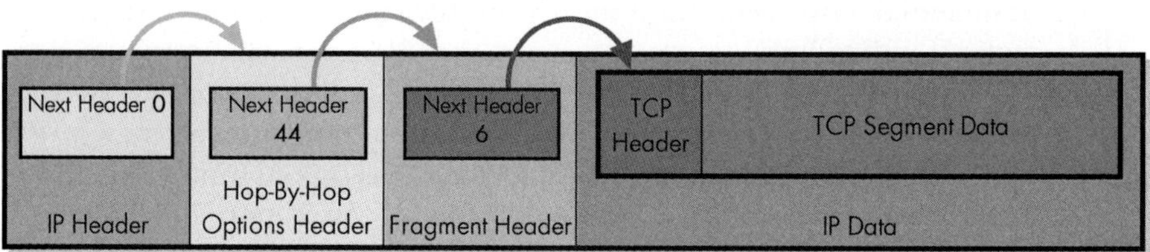

IPv6 Datagram with Two Extension Headers Carrying TCP Segment

Figure 26-3: IPv6 extension header linking using the Next Header field *The Next Header field allows a device to more easily process the headers in a received IPv6 datagram. When a datagram has no extension headers, the "next header" is actually the header at the start of the IP Data field, which, in this case, is a TCP header with a value of 6. This is the same way the Protocol field is used in IPv4. When extension headers do appear, the Next Header value of each header contains a number indicating the type of the following header in the datagram, so they logically chain together the headers.*

KEY CONCEPT The IPv6 Next Header field is used to chain together the headers in an IPv6 datagram. The Next Header field in the main header contains the number of the first extension header; its Next Header contains the number of the second, and so forth. The last header in the datagram contains the number of the encapsulated protocol that begins the Data field.

Summary of IPv6 Extension Headers

Table 26-4 lists the different extension headers, showing each one's Next Header value, length, defining RFC, and a brief description of how it is used.

Table 26-4: IPv6 Extension Headers

Next Header Value (Decimal)	Extension Header Name	Length (Bytes)	Description	Defining RFC
0	Hop-By-Hop Options	Variable	Defines an arbitrary set of options that are intended to be examined by all devices on the path from the source to destination device(s). This is one of two extension headers used to define variable-format options.	2460
43	Routing	Variable	Defines a method for allowing a source device to specify the route for a datagram. This header type actually allows the definition of multiple routing types. The IPv6 standard defines the Type 0 Routing extension header, which is equivalent to the "loose" source routing option in IPv4. It's used in a similar way. See the "IPv6 Routing Extension Header" section in this chapter for the format of this extension header.	2460
44	Fragment	8	When a datagram contains only a fragment of the original message, contains the Fragment Offset, Identification, and More Fragment fields that were removed from the main header. See the "IPv6 Fragment Extension Header" section in this chapter for the format of this extension header, and the topic on fragmentation and reassembly (Chapter 27) for details on how the fields are used.	2460
50	Encapsulating Security Payload (ESP)	Variable	Carries encrypted data for secure communications. This header is described in detail in Chapter 29, which covers IPsec.	2406
51	Authentication Header (AH)	Variable	Contains information used to verify the authenticity of encrypted data. This header is described in detail in Chapter 29.	2402
60	Destination Options	Variable	Defines an arbitrary set of options that are intended to be examined only by the destination(s) of the datagram. This is one of two extension headers used to define variable-format options.	2460

Note that the Next Header value of the IPv6 main header is 41; that of an IPv4 header is 4 (its protocol number). There is also a "dummy" extension header called No Next Header that has a value of 59. This is a placeholder that, when found in the Next Header field, indicates that there is nothing after that extension header.

As mentioned in Table 26-4, the formats for several of the headers are provided in other areas of this book. I will describe two of them here, however: the Routing extension header and the Fragment extension header.

IPv6 Routing Extension Header

The Routing extension header is used to perform source routing in IPv6. It is described in Table 26-5 and illustrated in Figure 26-4.

Table 26-5: IPv6 Routing Extension Header Format

Field Name	Size (Bytes)	Description
Next Header	1	Contains the protocol number of the next header after the Routing header. Used to link headers together, as described earlier in this chapter.
Hdr Ext Len	1	For Header Extension Length, specifies the length of the Routing header in 8-byte units, not including the first 8 bytes of the header. For a Routing Type field of 0, this value is thus two times the number addresses embedded in the header.
Routing Type	1	Allows multiple routing types to be defined; at present, the only value used is 0.
Segments Left	1	Specifies the number of explicitly named nodes remaining in the route until the destination.
Reserved	4	Not used; set to zeros.
Address1 . . . AddressN	Variable (Multiple of 16)	A set of IPv6 addresses that specify the route to be used.

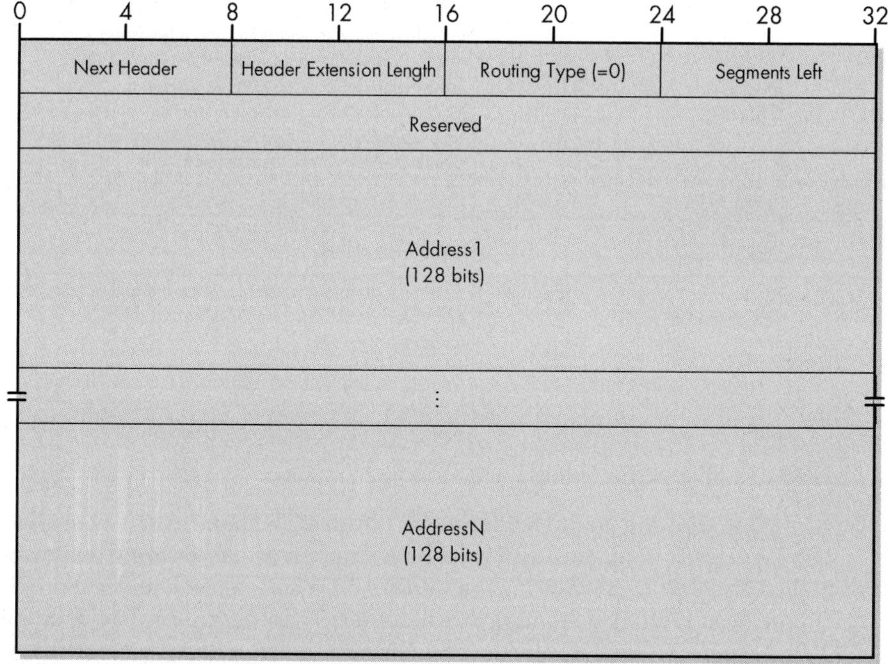

Figure 26-4: *IPv6 Routing extension header format*

IPv6 Fragment Extension Header

The Fragment extension header is included in fragmented datagrams to provide the information that's necessary to allow the fragments to be reassembled. It is described in Table 26-6 and illustrated in Figure 26-5.

Table 26-6: IPv6 Fragment Extension Header Format

Field Name	Size (Bytes)	Description
Next Header	1	Contains the protocol number of the next header after the Fragment header. Used to link headers together, as described earlier in this chapter.
Reserved	1	Not used; set to zeros.
Fragment Offset	13/8 (13 bits)	Specifies the offset, or position, in the overall message where the data in this fragment goes. It is specified in units of 8 bytes (64 bits) and used in a manner very similar to the field of the same name in the IPv4 header.
Res	1/4 (2 bits)	Not used; set to zeros.
M Flag	1/8 (1 bit)	For More Fragments Flag, same as the flag of the same name in the IPv4 header. When set to 0, indicates the last fragment in a message; when set to 1, indicates that more fragments are yet to come in the fragmented message.
Identification	4	Same as the field of the same name in the IPv4 header, but expanded to 32 bits. It contains a specific value that is common to each of the fragments belonging to a particular message. This ensures that pieces from different fragmented messages are not mixed together.

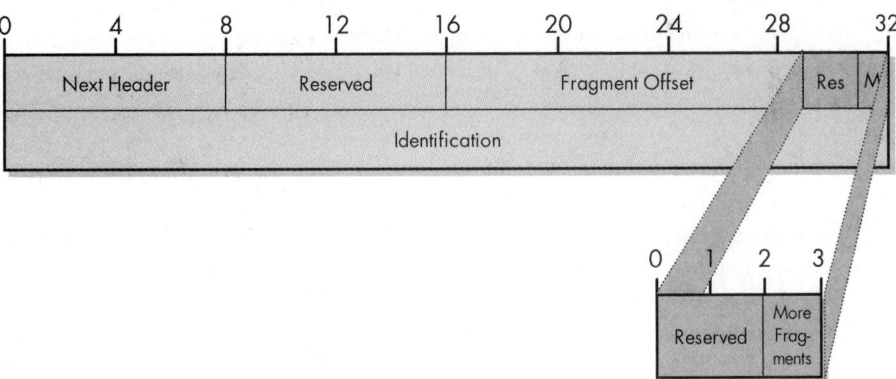

Figure 26-5: IPv6 Fragment extension header format

IPv6 Extension Header Order

Each extension header appears only once in any datagram (with one exception, as you'll see shortly). Also, only the final recipients of the datagram examine extension headers, not intermediate devices (again with one exception, which you will see momentarily).

RFC 2460 specifies that when multiple headers appear, they should be in the following order, after the main header and before the higher-layer encapsulated header in the IPv6 datagram payload:

1. Hop-By-Hop Options
2. Destination Options (for options to be processed by the destination as well as devices specified in a Routing header)
3. Routing
4. Fragmentation
5. Authentication Header
6. Encapsulating Security Payload
7. Destination Options (for options processed only by the final destination)

Now let's look at those exceptions. The only header that can appear twice is Destination Options. Normally, it appears as the last header. However, the datagram may also have a Destination Options header that contains options that must be examined by a list of devices specified in a source route, in addition to the destination. In this case, the Destination Options header for these options is placed before the Routing header. A second such header containing options for only the final destination may also appear.

KEY CONCEPT Each extension header may appear only once in an IPv6 datagram, and each one must appear in a fixed order. The exception is the Destination Options header, which may appear twice: near the start of the datagram for options to be processed by devices en route to the destination and at the end of the extension headers for options intended for only the final destination.

The only header normally examined by all intermediate devices is the Hop-By-Hop Options extension header. It is used specifically to convey management information to all routers in a route. The Hop-By-Hop Options extension header must appear as the first extension header if present. Since it is the only one that every router must read (and this represents a performance drain on routers), it is given top billing to make it easier and faster to find and process.

Finally, note that all extension headers must be a multiple of eight bytes in length for alignment purposes. Also, remember that the Next Header value for a particular extension header appears in the Next Header field of the preceding header, not the header itself.

IPv6 Datagram Options

In IPv4, all extra information required for various purposes is placed into the datagram in the form of options that appear in the IPv4 header. In IPv6, the new concept of extension headers is introduced, as you just saw. These headers take the place of many of the predefined IPv4 options. However, the concept of options is still maintained in IPv6 for a slightly different purpose.

Options allow the IPv6 datagram to be supplemented with arbitrary sets of information that aren't defined in the regular extension headers. They provide maximum flexibility, thereby allowing the basic IPv6 protocol to be extended in ways the designers never anticipated, with the goal of reducing the chance of the protocol becoming obsolete in the future.

I said that IPv6 options supplement extension headers; in fact, they are actually implemented as extension headers. There are two different ones used to encode options. These two headers differ only in terms of how devices will process the options they contain; otherwise, they are formatted the same and used in the same way.

The two extension header types are as follows:

Destination Options Contains options that are intended only for the ultimate destination of the datagram (and perhaps a set of routers in a Routing header, if present).

Hop-By-Hop Options Contains options that carry information for every device (router) between the source and destination.

Each of these header types has a one-byte Next Header field, and a one-byte Header Extension Length field that indicates the header's overall length. The rest of the header has one or more option fields.

Figure 26-6 illustrates the overall format of these two headers. The format of each option is similar to that of IPv4 options, as shown in Tables 26-7 and 26-8.

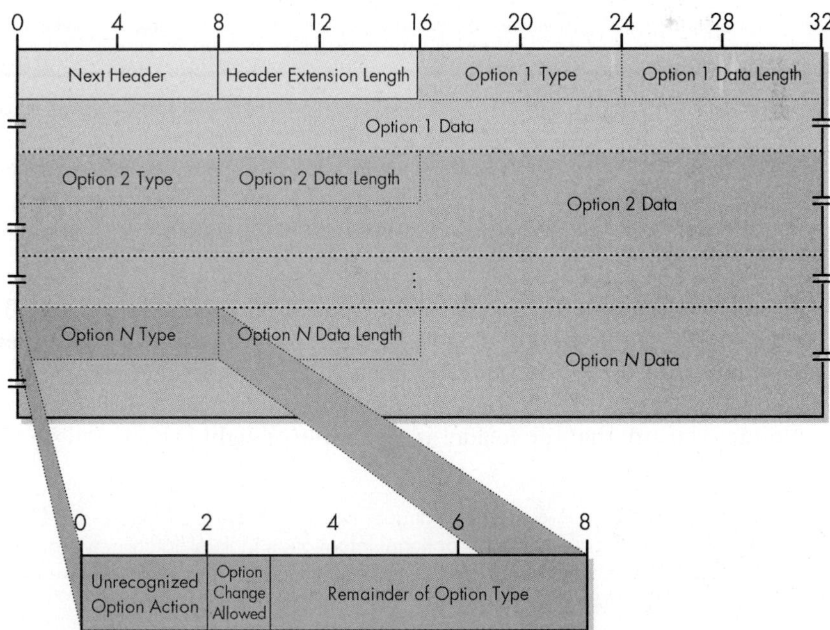

Figure 26-6: IPv6 Hop-By-Hop Options and Destination Options header formats *Each of these extension headers begins with two fixed fields, Next Header and Header Extension Length. The rest of the header consists of a sequence of variable-length options. Each option has a structure that consists of a type/length/value triplet, shown in Table 26-7.*

Table 26-7: IPv6 Option Format

Subfield Name	Size (Bytes)	Description
Option Type	1	This field indicates the type of option. The bits are interpreted according to the sub-subfield" structure, described in Table 26-8.
Opt Data Len	1	Specifies the length of the Option Data subfield. Note that this is a change in semantics from IPv4, where the Length field indicated the size of the entire option; in IPv6 the length of the Option Type and Option Data Length fields are not included.
Option Data	Variable	The data to be sent as part of the option, which is specific to the option type. Also sometimes referred to as the Option Value.

Table 26-8: IPv6 Option Type Subfields

Sub-Subfield Name	Size (Bytes)	Description
Unrecognized Option Action	2/8 (2 bits)	The first two bits specify what action should be taken if the device processing the option doesn't recognize the Option Type. The four values are as follows: 00: Skip option; process rest of header. 0: Discard datagram; do nothing else. 10: Discard datagram and send an ICMP Parameter Problem message with code 2 back to the datagram source. 11: Discard datagram and send the ICMP message as for value 10, only if destination was not a multicast address.
Option Change Allowed Flag	1/8 (1 bit)	Set to 1 if the Option Data can change while the datagram is en route, or left at 0 if it cannot.
Remainder of Option Type	5/8 (5 bits)	Five remaining bits that allow the specification of 32 different combinations for each combination of the three preceding bits.

NOTE *The Option Type subfield is a bit strange in terms of how it is interpreted. Even though it has a substructure with three sub-subfields (as shown in Table 26-8, that structure is informal—the eight bits of this field are taken as a single entity. Despite the special meaning of the three highest-order bits, the entire field is called the Option Type, not just the last five bits, and the whole is used as a single value from 0 to 255. In fact, the sub-subfield names aren't even specified in the standard; I made them up.*

Since each option has a subfield for type, length, and value (data), the options are sometimes said to be TLV-encoded. If there are multiple options, they are placed one after each other in the header. At the end of all the options, in a Hop-By-Hop Options or Destination Options extension header, a device may place padding to ensure that the header is a multiple of eight bytes in length.

KEY CONCEPT Two IPv6 extension header types, Hop-By-Hop Options and Destination Options, are used to carry arbitrary optional information in IPv6 datagrams. Each consists of a set of variable-length options that are defined using three subfields that indicate the option's type, length, and value.

27

IPV6 DATAGRAM SIZE, FRAGMENTATION, REASSEMBLY, AND ROUTING

Internet Protocol version 6 (IPv6) changes many of the operating details of IP, but most of the basics are the same. In particular, devices still need to deliver datagrams over an internetwork that may use different underlying network technologies. This means that we must be concerned here, as we were in IPv4, with the mechanics of datagram sizing, handling fragmentation and reassembly, and dealing with issues related to routing.

In this chapter, I complete the discussion of IPv6 by examining these matters, with an eye toward contrasting how they work in IPv6. This includes a look at IPv6 datagram sizing, changes to the maximum transmission unit (MTU), and fragmentation and reassembly. I also briefly discuss areas where IPv6 routing is performed in the same way as in IPv4, as well as where routing has changed.

Overview of IPv6 Datagram Sizing and Fragmentation

The job of IP is to convey messages across an internetwork of connected networks. When datagrams are sent between hosts on distant networks, they are carried along their journey by routers, one hop at a time, over many physical network links. On each step of this journey, the datagram is encoded in a data link layer frame for transmission.

In order for a datagram to be successfully carried along a route, its size must be small enough to fit within the lower-layer frame at each step of the way. The term *maximum transmission unit (MTU)* describes the size limit for any given physical network. If a datagram is too large for the MTU of a network, it must be broken into pieces—a process called *fragmentation*—and then the pieces are *reassembled* at the destination device. This has been a requirement since IPv4, and I explain the concepts and issues related to datagram size, MTUs, fragmentation, and reassembly in detail in the associated IPv4 discussion, in Chapter 22.

All of these issues apply to sending datagrams in IPv6 as much as they did in IPv4. However, as in other areas of the protocol, some important details of how fragmentation and reassembly are done have changed. These changes were made to improve the efficiency of the routing process and to reflect the realities of current networking technologies: Most can handle average IP datagrams without needing fragmentation.

The most important differences between IPv4 and IPv6 with respect to datagram size, MTU, and fragmentation and reassembly are as follows:

Increased Default MTU In IPv4, the minimum MTU that routers and physical links were required to handle was 576 bytes. In IPv6, all links must handle a datagram size of at least 1280 bytes. This more than doubling in size improves efficiency by increasing the ratio of maximum payload to header length and reduces the frequency with which fragmentation is required.

Elimination of en Route Fragmentation In IPv4, datagrams may be fragmented by either the source device or by routers during delivery. In IPv6, only the source node can fragment; routers do not. The source must fragment to the size of the smallest MTU on the route before transmission. This has both advantages and disadvantages, as you will see. Reassembly is still done only by the destination, as in IPv4.

MTU Size Error Feedback Since routers cannot fragment datagrams, they must drop them if they are forced to try to send a too-large datagram over a physical link. Using the Internet Control Message Protocol version 6 (ICMPv6; see Chapter 31), a feedback process has been defined that allows routers to tell source devices that they are using datagrams that are too large for the route.

Path MTU Discovery Since source devices must decide on the correct size of fragments, it is helpful if they have a mechanism for determining what this should be. This capability is provided through a special technique called *Path MTU Discovery*, which was originally defined for IPv4 but has been refined for IPv6.

Movement of Fragmentation Header Fields To reflect the decreased importance of fragmentation in IPv6, the permanent fields related to the process that were in the IPv4 header have been farmed out to a Fragment extension header and are included only when needed.

Implications of IPv6's Source-Only Fragmentation Rule

I find the changes in the fragmentation and reassembly process interesting. While many other changes in IPv6 represent a shift in responsibility for functions from host devices to routers, this one is the opposite. In IPv4, a source node can send a datagram of any size that its local link can handle, and let the routers take care of fragmenting it as needed. This seems like a sensible model; nodes communicate on a large, virtual network, and the details of splitting messages as needed for physical links are handled invisibly.

The problem with this is that it represents a performance drag on routing. It is much faster for a router to forward a datagram intact than to spend time fragmenting it. In some cases, fragmentation would need to occur multiple times during the transmission of a datagram, and remember that this must happen for every datagram on a route. It is a lot more efficient for the source to just send datagrams that are the right size in the first place.

Of course, there's a problem here: How does the source know what size to use? The source has no understanding of the physical networks used by the route datagrams will take to a destination; in fact, it doesn't even know what the routes are! Thus, it has no idea of what MTU would be best. It has two choices:

Use the Default MTU The first option is simply to use the default MTU of 1280 bytes, which all physical networks must be able to handle. This is a good choice, especially for short communications or for sending small amounts of data.

Use Path MTU Discovery The alternative is to make use of the Path MTU Discovery feature, as described later in the chapter. This feature, defined in RFC 1981, defines a method whereby a node sends messages over a route to determine what the overall minimum MTU for the path is. It's a technique that's very similar to the way it is done in IPv4, as discussed in Chapter 22.

Since routers can't fragment in IPv6, if a datagram is sent by a source that is too large for a router, it must drop the datagram. It will then send back to the source feedback about this occurrence, in the form of an ICMPv6 Packet Too Big message. This tells the source that its datagram was dropped and that it must fragment (or reduce the size of its fragments).

This feedback mechanism is also used in discovering path MTUs. The source node sends a datagram that has the MTU of its local physical link, since that represents an upper bound on the MTU of the path. If this goes through without any errors, it knows it can use that value for future datagrams to that destination. If it gets back any Packet Too Big messages, it tries again using a smaller datagram size. The advantage of this over the 1280 default is that it may allow a large communication to proceed with a higher MTU, which improves performance.

KEY CONCEPT In IPv6, fragmentation is performed only by the device that's sending a datagram, not by routers. If a router encounters a datagram too large to send over a physical network with a small MTU, the router sends an ICMPv6 *Packet Too Big* message back to the source of the datagram. This can be used as part of a process called *Path MTU Discovery* to determine the minimum MTU of an entire route.

One drawback of the decision to only fragment at the source is that it introduces the potential for problems if there is more than one route between devices or if routes change. In IPv4, fragmentation is dynamic and automatic; it happens on its own and adjusts as routes change. Path MTU Discovery is a good feature, but it is static. It requires that hosts keep track of MTUs for different routes and update them regularly. IPv6 does this by redoing Path MTU Discovery if a node receives a Packet Too Big message on a route for which it has previously performed Path MTU Discovery. However, this takes time.

The IPv6 Fragmentation Process

The actual mechanics of fragmentation in IPv6 are similar to those in IPv4, with the added complication that extension headers must be handled carefully. For purposes of fragmentation, IPv6 datagrams are broken into the following two pieces:

Unfragmentable Part This includes the main header of the original datagram, as well as any extension headers that need to be present in each fragment. This means the main header, and any of the following headers, if present: Hop-By-Hop Options, Destination Options (for those options to be processed by devices along a route), and Routing.

Fragmentable Part This includes the data portion of the datagram, along with the other extension headers, if present—Authentication Header, Encapsulating Security Payload, and/or Destination Options (for options to be processed only by the final destination).

The Unfragmentable Part must be present in each fragment, while the Fragmentable Part is split up among the fragments. So to fragment a datagram, a device creates a set of fragment datagrams, each of which contains the following, in order:

1. **Unfragmentable Part** The full Unfragmentable Part of the original datagram, with its Payload Length changed to the length of the fragment datagram.
2. **Fragment Header** A Fragment header with the Fragment Offset, Identification, and M flags set in the same way they are used in IPv4.
3. **Fragment** A fragment of the Fragmentable Part of the original datagram. Note that each fragment must have a length that is a multiple of 8 bytes, because the value in the Fragment Offset field is specified in multiples of 8 bytes.

> **KEY CONCEPT** Fragmentation is done in IPv6 in a manner similar to that of IPv4, except that extension headers must be handled specially. Certain extension headers are considered *unfragmentable* and appear in each fragment; others are fragmented along with the data.

Let's use an example to illustrate how IPv6 fragmentation works. Suppose you have an IPv6 datagram exactly 370 bytes wide, consisting of a 40-byte IP header, four 30-byte extension headers, and 210 bytes of data. Two of the extension headers are unfragmentable, while two are fragmentable. (In practice you would never need to fragment such a small datagram, but I am trying to keep the numbers simple.) Suppose you need to send this over a link with an MTU of only 230 bytes. You would actually require three fragments, not the two you might expect, because of the need to put the two 30-byte unfragmentable extension headers in each fragment, and the requirement that each fragment be a length that is a multiple of 8. Here is how the fragments would be structured (see Figure 27-1):

1. **First Fragment** The first fragment would consist of the 100-byte Unfragmentable Part, followed by an 8-byte Fragment header and the first 120 bytes of the Fragmentable Part of the original datagram. This would contain the two fragmentable extension headers and the first 60 bytes of data. This leaves 150 bytes of data to send.
2. **Second Fragment** This would also contain the 100-byte Unfragmentable Part, followed by a Fragment header, and 120 bytes of data (bytes 60 to 179). This would leave 30 bytes of data remaining.
3. **Third Fragment** The last fragment would contain the 100-byte Unfragmentable Part, a Fragment header, and the final 30 bytes of data.

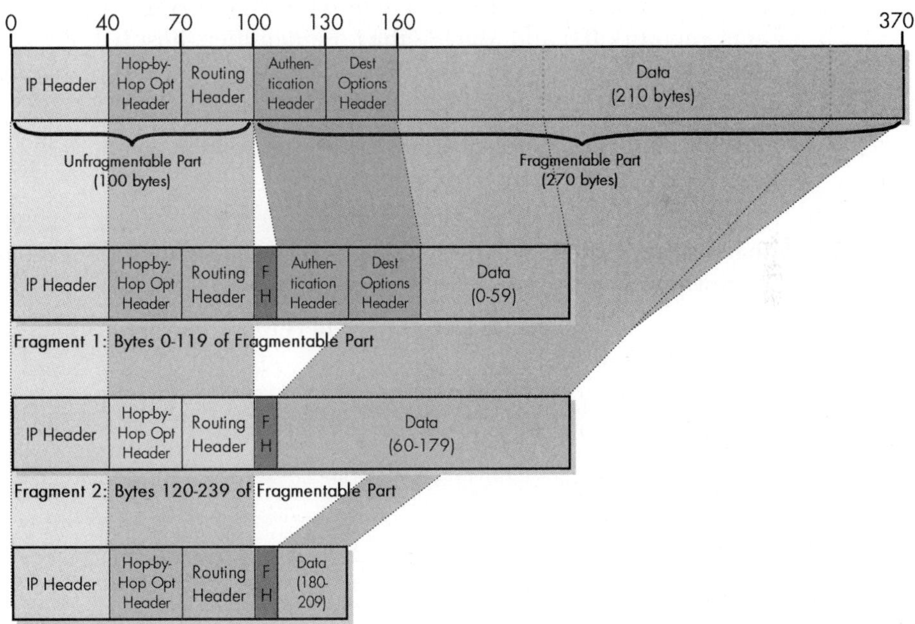

Figure 27-1: IPv6 datagram fragmentation *In this illustration, a 370-byte IPv6 datagram, containing four 30-byte extension headers, is broken into three fragments. The sizes of the fields are shown to scale. The Unfragmentable Part, shown in lighter shading on the left, begins each fragment, followed by the Fragment header (abbreviated as FH in the figure and shown in dark gray). Then, portions of the Fragmentable Part are placed into each fragment in sequence. The Authentication and Destination Options extension headers are part of the Fragmentable Part, so that they appear as part of the first fragment.*

The M (More Fragments) flag would be set to 1 in the first two fragments and 0 in the third, and the Fragment Offset values would be set appropriately. See Chapter 22, which covers IPv4 fragmentation, for more on how these fields are used.

The receiving device reassembles by taking the Unfragmentable Part from the first fragment and then assembling the Fragment data from each fragment in sequence.

IPv6 Datagram Delivery and Routing

IP functions such as addressing, datagram encapsulation, and, if necessary, fragmentation and reassembly, all lead up to the ultimate objective of the protocol: the actual delivery of datagrams from a source device to one or more destination devices. Most of the concepts related to how datagram delivery is accomplished in IPv6 are the same as in IPv4:

- Datagrams are delivered directly when the source and destination nodes are on the same network. When they are on different networks, delivery is indirect, using routing to the destination's network, and then direct to the destination.
- Routers look at IP addresses and determine which portion is the network identifier (network ID) and which is the host identifier (host ID). IPv6 does this in the same basic way as in classless IPv4, despite the fact that IPv6 unicast addresses are assigned using a special hierarchical format.
- Routing is still done on a next-hop basis, with sources generally not knowing how datagrams get from point A to point B.
- Routing is performed by devices called *routers*, which maintain tables of routes that tell them where to forward datagrams to reach different destination networks.
- Routing protocols are used to allow routers to exchange information about routes and networks.

Most of the changes in routing in IPv6 are directly related to changes in other areas of the protocol, as discussed in the previous chapters. Some of the main issues of note related to routing and routers in IPv6 include the following:

Hierarchical Routing and Aggregation One of the goals of the structure used for organizing unicast addresses was to improve routing. The unicast addressing format is designed to provide a better match between addresses and Internet topology and to facilitate route aggregation. Classless addressing using CIDR in IPv4 was an improvement but lacked any formal mechanism for creating a scalable hierarchy.

Scoped Local Addresses Local-use addresses, including site-local and link-local addresses, are defined in IPv6, and routers must be able to recognize them. They must route them or *not* route them when appropriate. Multicast addresses also have various levels of scope.

Multicast and Anycast Routing Multicast is standard in IPv6, not optional as in IPv4, so routers must support it. Anycast addressing is a new type of addressing in IPv6.

More Support Functions Capabilities must be added to routers to support new features in IPv6. For example, routers play a key role in implementing autoconfiguration without the help of a server and Path MTU Discovery in the new IPv6 fragmentation scheme.

New Routing Protocols Routing protocols such as RIP must be updated to support IPv6.

Transition Issues Last, but certainly not least, routers play a major role in supporting the transition from IPv4 to IPv6. They will be responsible for connecting together IPv6 "islands" and performing translation to allow IPv4 and IPv6 devices to communicate with each other during the multiyear migration to the new protocol.

PART II-5

IP-RELATED FEATURE PROTOCOLS

The previous two parts thoroughly explored versions 4 and 6 of the Internet Protocol (IP). IP is a very capable protocol that provides the functionality necessary to address, package, and deliver information on TCP/IP internetworks. However, IP was intentionally designed to be simple, without a lot of bells and whistles. To deal with special needs, a number of other protocols have been created to enhance or expand on IP's capabilities. I call these *IP-related feature protocols*.

This part contains three chapters that provide complete explanations of three of the more important IP-related feature protocols. The first chapter describes *IP Network Address Translation (IP NAT or NAT)*, which allows private networks to be accessed on the Internet and IP addresses to be shared. The second chapter explores *IP Security (IPsec)*, a set of subprotocols that allows IP datagrams to be authenticated and/or encrypted. The third chapter covers the *Mobile IP* protocol, which corrects some of the problems associated with using TCP/IP with mobile hosts.

This part assumes that you have a good understanding of the operation of IP, discussed in Parts II-3 and II-4.

28

IP NETWORK ADDRESS TRANSLATION (NAT) PROTOCOL

To help extend the life of the Internet Protocol version 4 (IPv4) addressing scheme while the newer IPv6 protocol is developed and deployed, other technologies have been developed. One of the most important of these is *IP Network Address Translation (NAT)*. This technology allows a small number of public IP addresses to be shared by a large number of hosts using private addresses. This essential work-around allows the global Internet to actually have far more hosts on it than its address space would normally support. At the same time, it provides some security benefits by making hosts more difficult to address directly by foreign machines on the public Internet.

In this chapter, I provide a description of the concepts behind IP NAT and an explanation of operation of IP NAT types. I begin with an overview of the protocol and discussion of its advantages and disadvantages. I describe the address terminology that you need to know in order to understand how NAT functions and the differences between various translation techniques. I explain the way that address mappings are performed and the difference between static and dynamic address mapping.

I then explain the operation of the four main types of NAT: unidirectional, bidirectional, port-based, and overlapping. I conclude with a bit more information on compatibility issues associated with NAT.

NAT was developed in large part to deal with the address shortage problem in IPv4, so it is associated and used with IPv4. It is possible to implement an IPv6-compatible version of NAT, but address translation isn't nearly as important in IPv6, which was designed to give every TCP/IP device its own unique address. For this reason, in this chapter, I focus in on the use of NAT with IPv4.

NOTE *Incidentally, most people just call this technology* Network Address Translation *without the IP. However, this sounds to me rather generic, and since the version I'm discussing here is specific to IP, I prefer to make it clear that this is an IP feature. That said, for simplicity I often just say "NAT," too, since that's shorter. I should also point out that there are quite a few people who don't consider NAT to be a protocol in the strictest sense of the word.*

IP NAT Overview

The decision to make IP addresses only 32 bits long as part of the original design of IP led to a serious problem when the Internet exploded in popularity beyond anyone's expectations: the exhaustion of the address space. Classless addressing helped make better use of the address space, and IPv6 was created to ensure that we will never run out of addresses again. However, classless addressing has only slowed the consumption of the IPv4 address space, and IPv6 has taken years to develop and will require years more to deploy.

The shortage of IP addresses promised to grow critical by the end of the 1990s unless some sort of solution was implemented until the transition to IPv6 was completed. Creative engineers on the Internet Engineering Task Force (IETF) were up to the challenge. They created a technique that would not only forestall the depletion of the address space, but could also be used to address the following two other growing issues in the mid- to late 1990s:

Increasing Cost of IP Addresses As any resource grows scarce, it becomes more expensive. Even when IP addresses were available, it cost more to get a larger number from a service provider than a smaller number. It was desirable to conserve them not only for the sake of the Internet as a whole, but to save money.

Growing Concerns over Security As Internet use increased in the 1990s, more bad guys started using the network also. The more machines a company had directly connected to the Internet, the greater their potential exposure to security risks.

One solution to these problems was to set up a system whereby a company's network was not connected directly to the Internet, but rather *indirectly*. Setting up a network this way is possible due to the following important characteristics of how most organizations use the Internet:

Most Hosts Are Client Devices The Internet is client/server based, and the majority of hosts are clients. Client devices generally don't need to be made publicly accessible. For example, when using your local PC to access the World Wide Web, you issue requests to servers and they respond back, but servers don't have any reason to try to initiate contact with you. Clients, not servers, begin most correspondence, by definition.

Few Hosts Access the Internet Simultaneously When you have a large number of hosts that are connected to the Internet on the same network, usually only a small number of those hosts are trying to access the Internet at any given time. It isn't necessary to assume they will all need to access servers at once. Even while you actively browse the Web, you pause for a number of seconds to read information from time to time; you are only accessing the web server for the time it takes to perform a transaction.

Internet Communications Are Routed Communications between an organization's network and the Internet go through a router, which acts as a control point for traffic flows.

The best way to explain why these attributes matter is to draw an analogy to how telephones are used an organization, because many of the same attributes apply there. Most of the telephones in a typical organization are used to let employees make calls out. Usually there is no need to have any way to call employees directly; instead, one system or person can handle all incoming calls. Only a few employees are ever making a call to the outside world at any given time. And all calls are routed through a central point that manages the telephone system.

For these reasons, to save money, organizations don't run separate public telephone lines to every employee's desk. Instead, they set up a telephone system whereby each employee gets an *extension*, which is basically a local telephone number valid only within the organization. A small number of outside lines is made available in a pool for employees to share, and the telephone system matches the inside extensions to the outside lines as needed. A voice mail system and human receptionist handle the routing of calls into the organization. (Yes, of course some companies have a direct mapping between extension numbers and real telephone numbers.)

A very similar technique can be used for connecting an organization's computers to the Internet. In TCP/IP networks, this technology was first formalized in RFC 1631, "The IP Network Address Translator (NAT)," which was adopted in May 1994. The word *translator* refers to the device (router) that implements NAT. More commonly, the technology as a whole is called *IP Network Address Translation* (*IP NAT* or *NAT*).

NOTE *The document status of RFC 1631 is informational. This means that, technically, IP NAT is not an official Internet standard.*

A basic implementation of NAT involves setting up an organization's internal network using one of the private addressing ranges set aside for local IP networks. One or more public (Internet) addresses are also assigned to the organization as well, and one or more NAT-capable routers are installed between the local network and the public Internet. The public IP addresses are like outside lines in the telephone system, and the private addresses are like internal extensions.

The NAT router plays the role of telephone system computer and receptionist. It maps internal extensions to outside lines as needed, and also handles "incoming calls" when required. It does this by not just routing IP datagrams, but also by modifying them as needed, thereby translating addresses in datagrams from the private network into public addresses for transmission on the Internet, and back again.

KEY CONCEPT *IP Network Address Translation* (*IP NAT* or *NAT*) is a technique that allows an organization to set up a network using private addresses, while still allowing for communication on the public Internet. A NAT-capable router translates private to public addresses and vice versa as needed. This allows a small number of public IP addresses to be shared among a large number of devices and provides other benefits as well, but it also has some drawbacks.

Over time, newer versions of NAT have also been created. They solve other problems or provide additional capabilities. *Port-Based NAT* allows for the sharing of even more hosts on a limited number of IP addresses by letting two or more devices share one IP address at a time. So-called *twice NAT* helps with the implementation of virtual private networks (VPNs) by translating both source and destination addresses in both incoming and outgoing datagrams.

Advantages of IP NAT

NAT is one of those technologies that has a long list of advantages and disadvantages. This means it can be extremely useful in a variety of scenarios, but also problematic in others. The main advantages are as follows:

Public IP Address Sharing A large number of hosts can share a small number of public IP addresses. This saves money and also conserves IP address space.

Easier Expansion Since local network devices are privately addressed and a public IP address isn't needed for each one, it is easy to add new clients to the local network.

Greater Local Control Administrators get all the benefits of control that come with a private network, but can still connect to the Internet.

Greater Flexibility in Internet Service Provider (ISP) Service Changing the organization's ISP is easier, because only the public addresses change. It isn't necessary to renumber all the client machines on the network.

Increased Security The NAT translation represents a level of indirection. Thus, it automatically creates a type of firewall between the organization's network and the public Internet. It is more difficult for any client devices to be accessed directly by someone malicious because the clients don't have publicly known IP addresses.

(Mostly) Transparent NAT implementation is mostly transparent, because the changes take place in one or perhaps a few routers. The dozens or hundreds of hosts themselves don't need to be changed.

Disadvantages of IP NAT

The previously listed advantages are all good reasons to use NAT, but there are drawbacks to the technique as well:

Complexity NAT represents one more complexity in terms of setting up and managing the network. It also makes troubleshooting more confusing due to address substitutions.

Problems Due to Lack of Public Addresses Certain functions won't work properly due to lack of a real IP address in the client host machines.

Compatibility Problems with Certain Applications I said earlier that NAT was only mostly transparent. There are, in fact, compatibility issues with certain applications that arise because NAT tinkers with the IP header fields in datagrams but not in the application data. This means tools like the File Transfer Protocol (FTP; see Chapter 72), which pass IP addresses and port numbers in commands, must be specially handled, and some applications may not work.

Problems with Security Protocols Protocols like IPsec are designed to detect modifications to headers and commonly balk at the changes that NAT makes, since they cannot differentiate those changes from malicious datagram hacking. It is still possible to combine NAT and IPsec, but this becomes more complicated.

Poor Support for Client Access The lack of a public IP address for each client is a double-edged sword; it protects against hackers trying to access a host, but it also makes it difficult for legitimate access to clients on the local network. Peer-to-peer applications are harder to set up, and something like an organizational website (accessed from the Internet as a whole) usually needs to be set up without NAT.

Performance Reduction Each time a datagram transitions between the private network and the Internet, an address translation is required. In addition, other work must be done as well, such as recalculating header checksums. Each individual translation takes little effort, but when you add it up, you are giving up some performance.

Some of these cancel out some of the benefits of certain items in the previous list. However, many organizations feel that the advantages outweigh the disadvantages, especially if they use the Internet in primarily a client/server fashion, as most do. For this reason, NAT has become quite popular. However, bear in mind that the main problem that led to NAT is lack of address space. IPv6 fixes this problem, while NAT merely finds a clever work-around for it. For this reason, many people consider NAT a kludge. Once IPv6 is deployed, it will no longer be needed, and some folks don't like it even for IPv4. On the other hand, some feel its other benefits make it worthy of consideration even in IPv6.

NOTE *A* kludge *(or* kluge*) is something that is used to address a problem in an inelegant way, like hammering a nail using the side of an adjustable wrench.*

IP NAT Address Terminology

As its name clearly indicates, IP NAT is all about the *translation* of IP addresses. When datagrams pass between the private network of an organization and the public Internet, the NAT router changes one or more of the addresses in these datagrams. This translation means that every transaction in a NAT environment involves not just a source address and a destination address, but also potentially multiple addresses for each of the source and destination.

In order to make clearer the explanation of how NAT operates, several special designations have been developed to refer to the different types of addresses that can be found in an IP datagram when NAT is used. Unfortunately, the terminology used for addressing in NAT can be confusing, because it's hard to visualize what the differences are between the (often similar-sounding) names. However, without knowing what these addresses mean, a proper understanding of NAT operation is impossible.

The first way that addresses are differentiated is based on where the device is in the network that the address is referring to, as follows:

Inside Address Any device on the organization's private network that is using NAT is said to be on the inside network. Thus, any address that refers to a device on the local network in any form is called an *inside address.*

Outside Address The public Internet—that is, everything outside the local network—is considered the outside network. Any address that refers to a public Internet device is an *outside address.*

> **KEY CONCEPT** In NAT, the terms *inside* and *outside* are used to identify the location of devices. *Inside addresses* refer to devices on the organization's private network. *Outside addresses* refer to devices on the public Internet.

An inside device always has an inside address; an outside device always has an outside address. However, there are two different ways of addressing either an inside or an outside device, depending on the part of the network in which the address appears in a datagram:

Local Address This term describes an address that appears in a datagram on the inside network, *whether it refers to an inside or outside address.*

Global Address This term describes an address that appears in a datagram on the outside network, again *whether it refers to an inside or outside address.*

> **KEY CONCEPT** In NAT, the terms *local* and *global* are used to indicate in what network a particular address appears. *Local addresses* are used on the organization's private network (whether to refer to an inside device or an outside device). *Global addresses* are used on the public Internet (again, whether referring to an inside or outside device).

This is a bit confusing, so I will try to explain further. The NAT translating router has the job of interfacing the inside network to the outside network (the Internet). Inside devices need to be able to talk to outside devices and vice versa, but inside devices can use only addressing consistent with the local network-addressing scheme. Similarly, outside devices cannot use local addressing. Thus, both inside and outside devices can be referred to with local or global address versions. This yields four different specific address types:

Inside Local Address An address of a device on the local network, expressed using its normal local device representation. So, for example, if you had a client on a network using the 10.0.0.0 private address block and assigned it address 10.0.0.207, this would be its *inside local* address.

Inside Global Address This is a global, publicly routable IP address that's used to represent an inside device to the outside world. In a NAT configuration, *inside global* addresses are those real IP addresses assigned to an organization for use by the NAT router. Let's say that device 10.0.0.207 wants to send an HTTP request to an Internet server located at address 204.51.16.12. It forms the datagram using 10.0.0.207 as the source address. However, if this datagram is sent out to the Internet as is, the server cannot reply back because 10.0.0.207 is not a publicly routable IP address. So the NAT router will translate 10.0.0.207 in the datagram into one of the organization's registered IP addresses, let's say, 194.54.21.10. This is the *inside global* address that corresponds to 10.0.0.207. It will be used as the destination when the server sends its HTTP response. Note that, in some situations, the inside local address and outside local address may be the same.

Outside Global Address An address of an external (public Internet) device as it is referred to on the global Internet. This is basically a regular, publicly registered address of a device on the Internet. In the previous example, 204.51.16.12 is an *outside global* address of a public server.

Outside Local Address An address of an external device as it is referred to by devices on the local network. In some situations, this may be identical to the *outside global* address of that outside device.

Phew, it's still confusing, isn't it? Let's try another way of looking at this. Of these four addresses, two types are the addresses as they are known natively by either an inside or outside device, while the other two are translated addresses. Here is a summary:

Inside Device Designations For an inside device, the *inside local* address is its normal, or native, address. The *inside global* address is a translated address used to represent the inside device on the outside network, when necessary.

Outside Device Designations For an outside device, the *outside global* address is its normal, or native, address. The *outside local* address is a translated address used to represent the outside device on the inside network, when necessary.

So what NAT does then is translate the identity of either inside or outside devices from local representations to global representations and vice versa. Which addresses are changed and how will depend on the specific type of NAT employed. For example, in traditional NAT, inside devices refer to outside devices using their proper (global) representation, so the outside global and outside local addresses of these outside devices are the same.

KEY CONCEPT A NAT router translates *local* addresses to *global* ones and vice versa. Thus, an *inside local* address is translated to an *inside global* address (and vice versa) and an *outside local* address is translated to an *outside global* address (and vice versa).

And after all that, it's still confusing! One of the big problems is that the words *inside* and *local* are somewhat synonymous, as are *outside* and *global*, yet they mean different things in NAT. And the typical paradox in trying to explain networking concepts rears its ugly head here again: I wanted to define these addresses to make describing NAT operation easier, but find myself wanting to use an example of NAT operation to clarify how the addresses are used.

Even after writing this material I find these terms confusing, so I created Figure 28-1, which shows this same terminology in graphical form and may be of some help. That diagram is also used as a template for the illustrations of each of the different types of NAT in the rest of this chapter. As you read about NAT operation, look back here if you want to double-check the meaning of address types. Don't get discouraged if it takes a couple of times to get the addresses straight.

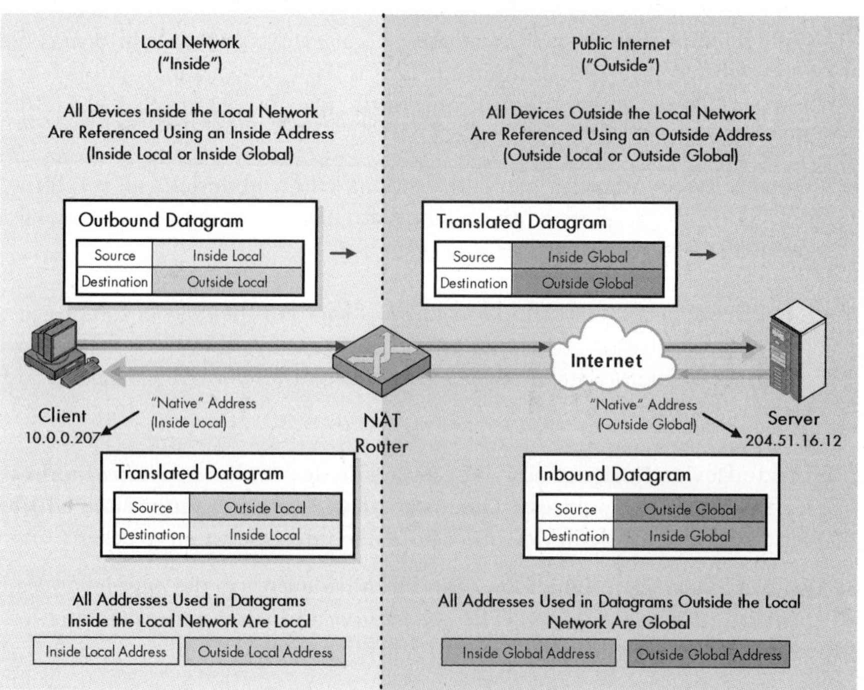

Figure 28-1: IP Network Address Translation (NAT) terminology *Hopefully this diagram will help you to better understand the whole "inside/outside/local/global" thing.*

IP NAT Static and Dynamic Address Mappings

NAT allows you to connect a private (inside) network to a public (outside) network such as the Internet by using an address translation algorithm implemented in a router that connects the two. Each time a NAT router encounters an IP datagram that crosses the boundary between the two networks, it must translate addresses as appropriate. But how does it know what to translate and what to use for the translated address?

The NAT software in the router must maintain a *translation table* to tell it how to operate. The translation table contains information that maps the *inside local* addresses of internal devices (their regular addresses) to *inside global* address representations (the special public addresses used for external communication). It may also contain mappings between *outside global* addresses and *outside local* addresses for inbound transactions, if appropriate.

There are two basic ways that entries can be added to the NAT translation table: statically or dynamically.

Static Mappings

A static mapping represents a permanent, fixed relationship defined between a *global* and a *local* representation of the address of either an *inside* or an *outside* device. For example, you can use a static translation if you want the internal device with an *inside local* address of 10.0.0.207 to *always* use the *inside global* address of 194.54.21.10. Whenever 10.0.0.027 initiates a transaction with the Internet, the NAT router will replace that address with 194.54.21.10.

Dynamic Mappings

With dynamic mapping, *global* and *local* address representations are generated automatically by the NAT router, which is used as needed and then discarded. The most common way that this is employed is in allowing a *pool* of *inside global* addresses to be shared by a large number of *inside* devices.

For example, say you were using dynamic mapping with a pool of *inside global* addresses available from 194.54.21.1 through 194.54.21.20. When 10.0.0.207 sent a request to the Internet, it would not automatically have its source address replaced by 194.54.21.10. One of the 20 addresses in the pool would be chosen by the NAT router. The router would then watch for replies back using that address and translate them back to 10.0.0.207. When the session was completed, it would discard the entry to return the *inside global* address to the pool.

Choosing Between Static and Dynamic Mapping

The trade-offs between static and dynamic NAT mappings are pretty much the same as they always are when the choice is between static and dynamic. For example, the same issues arises in Address Resolution Protocol (ARP) caching; see Chapter 13.

Static mappings are permanent and therefore ideal for devices that need to be always represented with the same public address on the outside network. They may also be used to allow inbound traffic to a particular device; that is, they can be used for transactions initiated on the public network that send to a special server on the inside network. However, they require manual setup and maintenance, and they don't allow IP sharing on the internal network.

Dynamic mapping is normally used for regular clients in order to facilitate public IP address sharing—a prime goal of most NAT implementations. It is more complicated than static mapping, but once you set it up, it's automatic.

It is possible to mix dynamic and static mapping on the same system, of course. You can designate certain devices that are statically mapped and let the rest use dynamic mapping. You just have to make sure that the static mappings don't overlap with the pool used for dynamic assignment.

Incidentally, another way you can perform dynamic mapping of global and local addressing is through domain name resolution using the Domain Name System (DNS; see Chapter 52). This is particularly common when external devices access internal hosts using bidirectional NAT (inbound transactions). Since hosts on the public Internet know nothing about the organization's private network, they issue a request for the DNS name of the device they want to access. This causes the generation of a NAT translation entry that maps the inside local public address of the host to an inside global address for use by those outside the network. See the description of bidirectional NAT later in this chapter for more details on how this works.

IP NAT Unidirectional (Traditional/Outbound) Operation

Now it's time to get down to the nitty gritty of how it works. There are many different flavors of NAT, and four common ones are covered in this chapter. It makes sense to start by looking at the original variety of NAT described in RFC 1631. This is the simplest NAT method, and therefore the easiest one to explain.

NAT was designed to allow hosts on a private network to share public IP addresses in accessing an Internet. Since most hosts are clients that initiate transactions, NAT was designed under the assumption that a client/server request/response communication would begin with a datagram sent from the *inside* network to the *outside*. For this reason, this first type of NAT is sometimes called *unidirectional* or *outbound* NAT. Since it is the oldest flavor, it is also now called *traditional* NAT to differentiate it from newer varieties.

To show how unidirectional NAT works, I will use an example. Let's assume the inside network has 250 hosts that use private (inside local) addresses from the 10.0.0.0/8 address range (which I selected because it has small numbers!). These hosts use dynamic NAT sharing a pool of 20 inside global addresses from 194.54.21.1 through 194.54.21.20.

In this example, device 10.0.0.207 wants to access the World Wide Web server at public address 204.51.16.12. Table 28-1 shows the four basic steps that are involved in this (simplified) transaction. I did this in table form so I could show you explicitly what happens to the addresses in both the request datagram (in steps 1 and 2) and the response datagram (steps 3 and 4). I have also highlighted the translated address values for clarity, and provided Figure 28-2, which shows the process graphically.

Table 28-1: Operation of Unidirectional (Traditional/Outbound) NAT

Step #	Description	Datagram Type	Datagram Source Address	Datagram Destination Address
1	**Inside Client Generates Request and Sends to NAT Router:** Device 10.0.0.207 generates an HTTP request that is eventually passed down to IP and encapsulated in an IP datagram. The source address is itself, 10.0.0.207, and the destination is 204.51.16.12. The datagram is sent to the NAT-capable router that connects the organization's internal network to the Internet.	Request (from inside client to outside server)	10.0.0.207 (inside local)	204.51.16.12 (outside local)
2	**NAT Router Translates Source Address and Sends to Outside Server:** The NAT router realizes that 10.0.0.207 is an *inside local* address and knows it must substitute an *inside global* address in order to let the public Internet destination respond. It consults its pool of addresses and sees the next available one is 194.54.21.11. It changes the source address in the datagram from 10.0.0.207 to 194.54.21.11. The destination address is not translated in traditional NAT. In other words, the *outside local* address and *outside global* address are the same. The NAT router puts the mapping from 10.0.0.207 to 194.54.21.11 into its translation table. It sends out the modified datagram, which is eventually routed to the server at 204.51.16.12.		194.54.21.11 (inside global)	204.51.16.12 (outside global)
3	**Outside Server Generates Response and Sends Back to NAT Router:** The server at 204.51.16.12 generates an HTTP response. It has no idea that NAT was involved; it sees 194.54.21.11 in the request sent to it, so that's where it sends back the response. It is then routed back to the original client's NAT router.	Response (from outside server to inside client)	204.51.16.12 (outside global)	194.54.21.11 (inside global)
4	**NAT Router Translates Destination Address and Delivers Datagram to Inside Client:** The NAT router sees 194.54.21.11 in the response that arrived from the Internet. It consults its translation table and knows this datagram is intended for 10.0.0.207. This time, the destination address is changed but not the source. It then delivers the datagram back to the originating client.		204.51.16.12 (outside local)	10.0.0.207 (inside local)

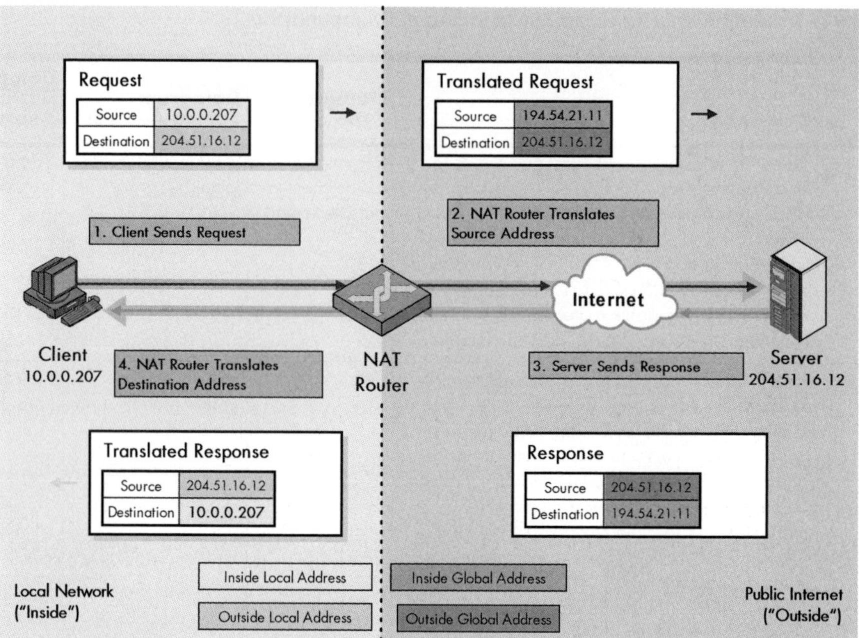

Figure 28-2: Operation of unidirectional (traditional/outbound) NAT *You can see the four steps in this process by following the steps in clockwise order. Translated addresses are shown in bold. Refer to Table 28-1 and Figure 28-1 for an explanation of the four address types.*

As you can see, this really isn't rocket science, and it's fairly easy to understand what is going on as soon as you get used to the terminology and concepts. In unidirectional NAT, the source address is translated on outgoing datagrams and the destination address is translated on incoming ones. Traditional NAT supports only this sort of outbound transaction, which is started by a device on the inside network. It cannot handle a device that sends a request to a private address on the public Internet.

KEY CONCEPT In *unidirectional* (traditional) NAT, the NAT router translates the source address of an outgoing request from inside local to inside global form. It then transforms the destination address of the response from inside global to inside local. The outside local and outside global addresses are the same in both request and reply.

Also note that even though I am focusing on the changes that the NAT router makes to addresses, it also must make other changes to the datagram. Changing any field in the IP header means that the IP Header Checksum field will need to be recalculated. User Datagram Protocol (UDP) and Transmission Control Protocol (TCP) checksums need to be recalculated, and depending on the nature of the data in the datagram, other changes may also be required. I discuss these issues in the section on NAT compatibility issues, at the end of this chapter.

Incidentally, this simplified example assumes the existence of just one router between the private and public networks. It is possible to have more than one router between these networks. If this configuration is used, however, it is essential that they both use the same translation table. Otherwise, if Router R1 processes the request, but Router R2 receives the response, Router R2 won't know how to translate back the destination address on the incoming datagram. This makes dynamic mapping extremely difficult: Routers would have to coordinate their address mappings.

IP NAT Bidirectional (Two-Way/Inbound) Operation

Traditional NAT is designed to handle only outbound transactions; clients on the local network initiate requests and devices on the Internet and send back responses. However, in some circumstances, we may want to go in the opposite direction. That is, we may want to have a device on the outside network initiate a transaction with one on the inside. To permit this, we need a more capable type of NAT than the traditional version. This enhancement goes by various names, most commonly Bidirectional NAT, Two-Way NAT, and Inbound NAT. All of these convey the concept that this kind of NAT allows both the type of transaction you saw in the previous topic and also transactions initiated from the outside network.

Performing NAT on inbound transactions is more difficult than conventional outbound NAT. To understand why, remember that the network configuration when using NAT is inherently *asymmetric*: The inside network generally knows the IP addresses of outside devices, since they are public, but the outside network doesn't know the private addresses of the inside network. Even if they did know them, they could never be specified as the target of an IP datagram initiated from outside since they are not routable—there would be no way to get them to the private network's local router.

Why does this matter? Well, consider the case of outbound NAT from Device A on the inside network to Device B on the outside. The local client, A, always starts the transaction, so Device A's NAT router is able to create a mapping between Device A's inside local and inside global address during the request. Device B is the recipient of the already-translated datagram, so the fact that Device A is using NAT is hidden. Device B responds back, and the NAT router does the reverse translation without Device B ever even knowing NAT was used for Device A.

Now let's look at the inbound case. Here, Device B is trying to send to Device A, which is using NAT. Device B can't send to Device A's private (inside local) address. It needs Device A's inside global address in order to start the ball rolling. However, Device A's NAT router isn't proximate to Device B. In fact, Device B probably doesn't even know the identity of Device A's NAT router!

This leaves only two methods. One is to use static mapping for devices like servers on the inside network that need to be accessed from the outside. When static mapping is employed, the global address of the device that is using the static mapping will be publicly known, which solves the "where do I send my request to" problem.

The other solution is to make use of DNS. As explained in detail in the section on DNS (see Part III-1), this protocol allows requests to be sent as names instead of IP addresses. The DNS server translates these names to their corresponding addresses. It is possible to integrate DNS and NAT so they work together. This process is described in RFC 2694, "DNS Extensions to Network Address Translators (DNS_ALG)."

In this technique, an outside device can make use of dynamic mapping. The basic process (highly simplified) is as follows:

1. The outside device sends a DNS request using the name of the device on the inside network it wishes to reach. For example, it might be www.ilikenat.com.
2. The DNS server for the internal network resolves the www.ilikenat.com name into an *inside local* address for the device that corresponds to this DNS entry.
3. The *inside local* address is passed to NAT and used to create a dynamic mapping between the *inside local* address of the server being accessed from the outside, and an *inside global* address. This mapping is put into the NAT router's translation table.
4. When the DNS server sends back the name resolution, it tells the outside device the *inside global* (public) address mapped in the previous step, not the *inside local* (private) address of the server being sought.

Once the inside global address of the device on the inside network is known by the outside device, the transaction can begin. Let's use the same example as in the previous section, but let's reverse it so that the outside device 204.51.16.12 is initiating a request (and is thus now the *client*) to inside device 10.0.0.207 (which is the *server*). Let's say that either static mapping or DNS has been used so that the outside device knows the inside global address of 10.0.0.207 is actually 194.54.21.6. Table 28-2 describes the transaction in detail, and it is illustrated Figure 28-3.

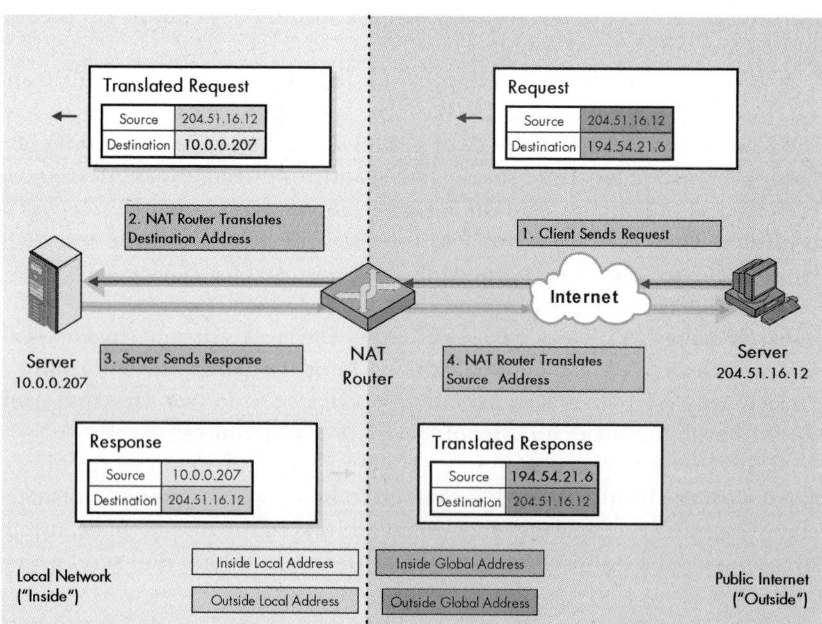

Figure 28-3: Operation of bidirectional (two-way/inbound) NAT *This figure is very similar to Figure 28-2, except that the transaction is in reverse, so start at the upper right and go counterclockwise. Translated addresses are shown in bold. Table 28-2 contains a complete explanation of the four steps. Refer to Figure 28-1 for an explanation of address types.*

Table 28-2: Operation of Bidirectional (Two-Way/Inbound) NAT

Step #	Description	Datagram Type	Datagram Source Address	Datagram Destination Address
1	**Outside Client Generates Request and Sends to NAT Router:** Device 204.51.16.12 generates a request to the inside server. It uses the *inside global* address 194.54.21.6 as the destination. The datagram will be routed to the address's local router, which is the NAT router that services the inside network where the server is located.	Request (from outside client to inside server)	204.51.16.12 (outside global)	194.54.21.6 (inside global)
2	**NAT Router Translates Destination Address and Sends to Inside Server:** The NAT router already has a mapping from the *inside global* address to the *inside local* address of the server. It replaces the 194.54.21.6 destination address with 10.0.0.207, and performs checksum recalculations and other work as necessary. The source address is not translated. The router then delivers the modified datagram to the inside server at 10.0.0.207.		204.51.16.12 (outside local)	10.0.0.207 (inside local)
3	**Inside Server Generates Response and Sends Back to NAT Router:** The server at 10.0.0.207 generates a response, which it addresses to 204.51.16.12 since that was the source of the request to it. This is then routed to the server's NAT router.	Response (from inside server to outside client)	10.0.0.207 (inside local)	204.51.16.12 (outside local)
4	**NAT Router Translates Source Address and Routes Datagram to Outside Client:** The NAT router sees the private address 10.0.0.207 in the response and replaces it with 194.54.21.6. It then routes this back to the original client on the outside network.		194.54.21.6 (inside global)	204.51.16.12 (outside global)

As you can see, once the outside device knows the inside device's *inside global* address, you'll find that inbound NAT is very similar to outbound NAT. It just does the exact opposite translation. Instead of modifying the source address on the outbound request and the destination on the inbound response, the router changes the destination on the inbound request and the source on the outbound reply.

KEY CONCEPT In traditional NAT, a transaction must begin with a request from a client on the local network, but in *bidirectional* (two-way/inbound) NAT, it is possible for a device on the public Internet to access a local network server. This requires the use of either static mapping or DNS to provide to the outside client the address of the server on the inside network. Then the NAT transaction is pretty much the same as in the unidirectional case, except in reverse: The incoming request has its destination address changed from *inside global* to *inside local*; the response has its source changed from *inside local* to *inside global*.

IP NAT Port-Based (Overloaded) Operation

Both traditional NAT and bidirectional NAT work by swapping inside network and outside network addresses as needed in order to allow a private network to access a public one. For each transaction, there is a one-to-one mapping between the *inside local* address of a device on the private network and the *inside global* address that represents it on the public network. We can use dynamic address assignment to allow a large number of private hosts to share a small number of registered public addresses.

However, there is a potential snag here. Consider the earlier NAT example, where 250 hosts share 20 inside global (public) addresses. If 20 hosts already have transactions in progress, what happens when the 21st tries to access the Internet? There aren't any *inside global* addresses available for it to use, so it won't be able to.

Fortunately, there is a mechanism already built into TCP/IP that can help us alleviate this situation. The two TCP/IP transport layer protocols, TCP and UDP, both make use of additional addressing components called *ports*. The port number in a TCP or UDP message helps identify individual connections between two addresses. It is used to allow many different applications on a TCP/IP client and server to talk to each simultaneously, without interference. For example, you use this capability when you open multiple browser windows to access more than one web page on the same site at the same time. This sharing of IP addresses among many connections is called *multiplexing*. Chapter 43, which describes TCP and UDP ports, covers all of this in much more detail.

Now let's come back to NAT. We are already translating IP addresses as we send datagrams between the public and private portions of the internetwork. What if we could also translate port numbers? Well, we can! The combination of an address and port uniquely identifies a connection. As a datagram passes from the private network to the public one, we can change not just the IP address, but also the port number in the TCP or UDP header. The datagram will be sent out with a different source address and port. The response will come back to this same address and port combination (called a *socket*) and can be translated back again.

This method goes by various names. Since it is a technique that can have multiple inside local addresses share a single inside global address, it is called *overloading* of an *inside global* address, or alternatively, just *overloaded NAT*. More elegant names that better indicate how the technique works include *Port-Based NAT*, *Network Address Port Translation (NAPT)*, and *Port Address Translation (PAT)*.

KEY CONCEPT *Port-Based* or overloaded NAT is an enhancement of regular NAT that allows a large number of devices on a private network to simultaneously share a single inside global address by changing the port numbers used in TCP and UDP messages.

Whatever its name, the use of ports in translation has tremendous advantages. It can allow all 250 hosts on the private network to use only 20 IP addresses—and potentially even fewer than that. In theory, you could even have all 250 share a single public IP address at once! You don't want to share so many local hosts that you run out of port numbers, but there are thousands of port numbers to choose from.

Port-Based NAT requires a router that is programmed to make the appropriate address and port mappings for datagrams as it transfers them between networks. The disadvantages of the method include this greater complexity, and also the potential for more compatibility issues (such as with applications like FTP), since you must now watch for port numbers at higher layers and not just IP addresses.

The operation of NAPT/PAT is very similar to the way regular NAT works, except that port numbers are also translated. For a traditional outbound transaction, the source port number is changed on the request at the same time that the source address is modified; the destination port number is modified on the response with the destination address.

Let's consider again the example you looked at in the topic on traditional NAT, but this time in a PAT environment. Device 10.0.0.207 was one of 250 hosts on a private network accessing the World Wide Web server at 204.51.16.12. Let's say that because PAT is being used, in order to save money, all 250 hosts are sharing a single *inside global* address, 194.54.21.7, instead of a pool of 20. The transaction would proceed as described in Table 28-3 and illustrated in Figure 28-4.

> **KEY CONCEPT** In Port-Based NAT, the NAT router translates the source address and port of an outgoing request from inside local to inside global form. It then transforms the destination address and port of the response from inside global to inside local. The outside local and outside global addresses are the same in both request and reply.

One other issue related to NAPT/PAT is worth mentioning: It assumes that all traffic uses either UDP or TCP at the transport layer. Although this is generally the case, it may not always be true. If there is no port number, port translation cannot be done and the method will not work.

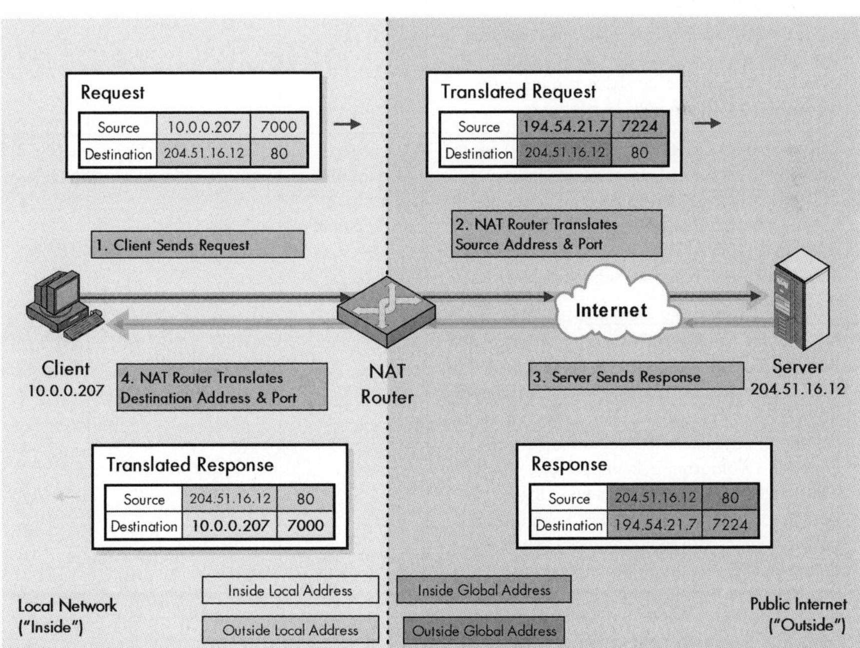

Figure 28-4: Operation of Port-Based (overloaded) NAT *This figure is very similar to Figure 28-4, except that the source and destination port numbers have been shown, since they are used in this type of NAT. Translated addresses and ports are in bold. Table 28-3 contains a complete explanation of the four steps in Port-Based NAT. Refer to Figure 28-1 for an explanation of address types.*

Table 28-3: Operation of Port-Based (Overloaded) NAT

Step #	Description	Datagram Type	Datagram Source Address:Port	Datagram Destination Address:Port
1	**Inside Client Generates Request and Sends to NAT Router:** Device 10.0.0.207 generates an HTTP request to the server at 204.51.16.12. The standard server port for WWW is 80, so the destination port of the request is 80; let's say the source port on the client is 7000. The datagram is sent to the NAT-capable router that connects the organization's internal network to the Internet.	Request (from inside client to outside server)	10.0.0.207:7000 (inside local)	204.51.16.12:80 (outside local)
2	**NAT Router Translates Source Address and Port and Sends to Outside Server:** The NAT router realizes that 10.0.0.207 is an *inside local* address and knows it must substitute an *inside global* address. Here though, there are multiple hosts sharing the single *inside global* address 194.54.21.7. Let's say that port 7000 is already in use for that address by another private host connection. The router substitutes the *inside global* address and also chooses a new source port number, say 7224, for this request. The destination address and port are not changed. The NAT router puts the address and port mapping into its translation table. It sends the modified datagram out, which arrives at the server at 204.51.16.12.		194.54.21.7:7224 (inside global)	204.51.16.12 (outside global)
3	**Outside Server Generates Response and Sends Back to NAT Router:** The server at 204.51.16.12 generates an HTTP response. It has no idea that NAT was involved; it sees an address of 194.54.21.7 and port of 7224 in the request sent to it, so it sends back to that address and port.	Response (from outside server to inside client)	204.51.16.12:80 (outside global)	194.54.21.7:7224 (inside global)
4	**NAT Router Translates Destination Address and Port and Delivers Datagram to Inside Client:** The NAT router sees the address 94.54.21.7 and port 7224 in the response that arrived from the Internet. It consults its translation table and knows this datagram is intended for 10.0.0.207, port 7000. This time, the destination address and port are changed but not the source. The router then delivers the datagram back to the originating client.		204.51.16.12:80 (outside local)	10.0.0.207:7000 (inside local)

IP NAT Overlapping/Twice NAT Operation

All three of the versions of NAT discussed so far—traditional, bidirectional, and Port-Based—are normally used to connect a network using private, nonroutable addresses to the public Internet, which uses unique, registered, routable addresses. With these kinds of NAT, there will normally be no overlap between the address spaces of the inside and outside network, since the former are private and the latter are public. This enables the NAT router to be able to immediately distinguish inside addresses from outside addresses just by looking at them.

In the examples you've seen so far, the inside addresses were all from the RFC 1918 block 10.0.0.0. These can't be public Internet addresses, so the NAT router knew any address referenced by a request from the inside network within this range was a local reference within the inside network. Similarly, any addresses outside this range are easy to identify as belonging to the outside world.

There are circumstances, however, in which there may indeed be an overlap between the addresses used for the inside network, and the addresses used for part of the outside network. Consider the following cases:

Private Network–to–Private Network Connections The example network using 10.0.0.0 block addresses might want to connect to another network using the same method. This situation might occur if two corporations merged and happened to be using the same addressing scheme (and there aren't that many private IP blocks, so this isn't that uncommon).

Invalid Assignment of Public Address Space to Private Network Some networks might have been set up, not by using a designated private address block, but rather by using a block containing valid Internet addresses. For example, suppose an administrator decided that the network he was setting up would never be connected to the Internet (ha!), and numbered the whole thing using 18.0.0.0 addresses, which belong to the Massachusetts Institute of Technology (MIT). Then later, this administrator's shortsightedness would backfire when the network did indeed need to be connected to the Internet.

Stale Public Address Assignment Company A might have been using a particular address block for years that was reassigned or reallocated for whatever reason to Company B. Company A might not want to go through the hassle of renumbering its network, and would then keep its addresses, even while Company B started using them on the Internet.

What these situations all have in common is that the inside addresses used in the private network *overlap* with addresses on the public network. When a datagram is sent from within the local network, the NAT router can't tell if the intended destination is within the inside network or the outside network. For example, if you want to connect host 10.0.0.207 in the private network to host 10.0.0.199 in a different network, and you put 10.0.0.199 in the destination of the datagram and send it, how does the router know if you mean 10.0.0.199 on your own local network or the remote one? For that matter, you might need to send a request to 10.0.0.207 in the other private network, your own address! Take the network that was numbered with MIT's address block. How does the router know when a datagram is actually being sent to MIT as opposed to another device on the private network?

The solution to this dilemma is to use a more sophisticated form of NAT. The other versions you have seen so far always translate either the source address *or* the destination address as a datagram passes from the inside network to the outside network or vice versa. To cope with overlapping addresses, we must translate both the source address *and* the destination address on each transition from the inside to the outside or the other direction. This technique is called *overlapping NAT* in reference to the problem it solves, or *Twice NAT* due to how it solves it. (Incidentally, despite the latter name, regular NAT is *not* called Once NAT.)

Twice NAT functions by creating a set of mappings not only for the private network the NAT router serves, but also for the overlapping network (or networks) that conflict with the inside network's address space. In order for this to function, Twice NAT relies on the use of DNS, just as does bidirectional NAT. This lets the inside network send requests to the overlapping network in a way that can be uniquely identified. Otherwise, the router can't tell what overlapping network our inside network is trying to contact.

Let's try a new example. Suppose the network has been improperly numbered so that it is not in the 10.0.0.0 private block but in the 18.0.0.0 block used by MIT. A client on our private network, 18.0.0.18, wants to send a request to the server www.twicenat.mit.edu, which has the address 18.1.2.3 at MIT. The client can't just make a datagram with 18.1.2.3 as the destination and send out, as the router will think it's on the local network and not route it. Instead, 18.0.0.18 uses a combination of DNS and NAT to get the outside device address, as follows:

1. The client on the local network (18.0.0.18) sends a DNS request to get the address of www.twicenat.mit.edu.
2. The (Twice-NAT compatible) NAT router serving the local network intercepts this DNS request. It then consults its tables to find a special mapping for this outside device. Let's say that it is programmed to translate www.twicenat.mit.edu into the address 172.16.44.55. This is a private, nonroutable RFC 1918 address.
3. The NAT router returns this value, 172.16.44.55, to the source client, which uses it for the destination.

Once the client has the translated address, it initiates a transaction just as before. NAT will now perform translation of the inside devices and the outside devices as well. The outside device address must be translated because the inside device is using 172.16.44.55, which isn't a valid address for the server it is trying to reach. The inside device address must still be translated as in regular NAT because 18.0.0.18 is not a valid public address for you. It may refer to a real machine in MIT and you aren't supposed to be using it on the Internet!

Let's say that you are still using the pool of 20 inside global addresses from 194.54.21.1 through 194.54.21.20 for inside addresses, and let's further suppose that the NAT router chooses 194.54.21.12 for this particular exchange. The transaction sequence would be roughly as described in Table 28-4 and illustrated in Figure 28-5.

Overlapping NAT is used in situations where both the source and destination addresses in a datagram are private addresses or otherwise cannot be used regularly on the public Internet. In this case, unlike with the other types of NAT, the NAT router translates both the source and destination addresses of incoming and outgoing datagrams. On outgoing messages, *inside local* addresses are changed to *inside global* and *outside local* to *outside global*; on incoming messages, *inside global* addresses are changed to *inside local* and *outside global* addresses are changed to *outside local*.

Table 28-4: Operation of Overlapping NAT/Twice NAT

Step #	Description	Datagram Type	Datagram Source Address	Datagram Destination Address
1	**Inside Client Generates Request and Sends to NAT Router:** Device 18.0.0.18 generates a request using the destination 172.16.44.55, which it got from the (NAT-intercepted) DNS query for www.twicenat.mit.edu. The datagram is sent to the NAT router for the local network.	Request (from inside client to outside server)	18.0.0.18 (inside local)	172.16.44.55 (outside local)
2	**NAT Router Translates Source Address and Destination Address and Sends to Outside Server:** The NAT router makes two translations. First, it substitutes the 18.0.0.18 address with a publicly registered address, which is 194.54.21.12 for this example. It then translates the bogus 172.16.44.55 back to the real MIT address for www.twicenat.mit.edu. It routes the datagram to the outside server.		194.54.21.12 (inside global)	18.1.2.3 (outside global)
3	**Outside Server Generates Response and Sends Back to NAT Router:** The MIT server at 18.1.2.3 generates a response and sends it back to 194.54.21.12, which causes it to arrive back at the NAT router.	Response (from outside server to inside client)	18.1.2.3 (outside global)	194.54.21.12 (inside global)
4	**NAT Router Translates Source Address and Destination Address and Delivers Datagram to the Inside Client:** The NAT router translates back the destination address to the actual address that's being used for the inside client, as in regular NAT. It also substitutes back in the 172.16.44.55 value it is using as a substitute for the real address of www.twicenat.mit.edu.		172.16.44.55 (outside local)	18.0.0.18 (inside local)

As you can see, in this example, the *outside local* and *outside global* addresses are different, unlike in the preceding NAT examples. Twice NAT can also handle an inbound transaction by watching for datagrams coming in from the Internet that overlap with the addresses used on the local network and doing double substitutions as required.

IP NAT Compatibility Issues and Special Handling Requirements

In a perfect world NAT could be made transparent to the devices using it. We would like to be able to have a NAT router change IP addresses in request datagrams as they leave the network and change them back in responses that come back, and have none of the hosts be any wiser. Unfortunately, this isn't a perfect world.

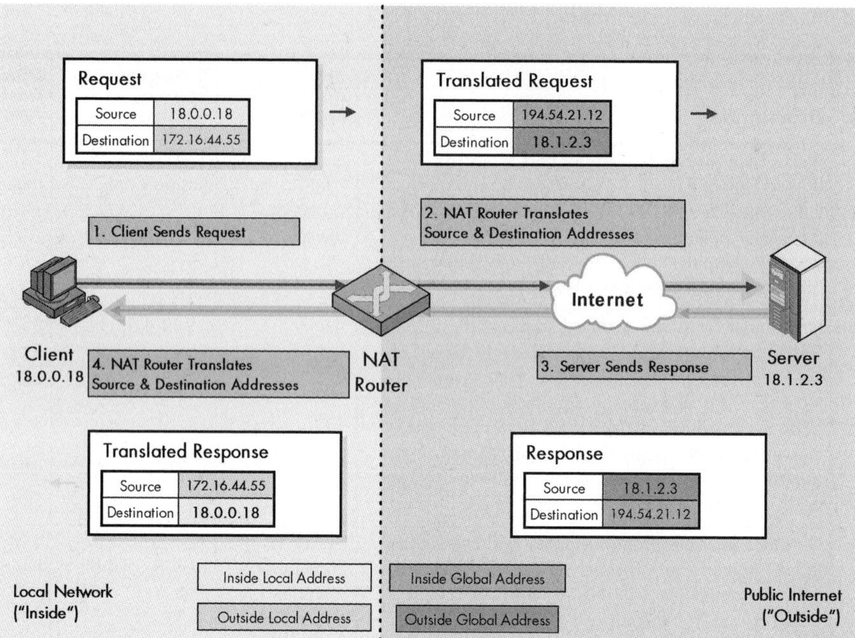

Figure 28-5: Operation of Overlapping NAT/Twice NAT *This figure is very similar to Figure 28-2, except that as you can see, the NAT router translates both source and destination addresses each time (shown in bold). Table 28-4 contains a complete explanation of the four steps in overlapping NAT. Refer to Figure 28-1 for an explanation of address types.*

It is not possible for NAT to be completely transparent to the devices that use it. There are potential compatibility problems that arise if NAT doesn't perform certain functions. These functions go beyond simply swapping IP addresses and possibly port numbers in the IP header. The main problem is that even though IP addresses are supposedly the domain of IP, they are really used by other protocols as well, both at the network layer and in higher layers. When NAT changes the IP address in an IP datagram, it must often also change addresses in other places to make sure that the addresses in various headers and payloads still match.

These compatibility issues require that even though NAT should theoretically work only at the level of IP at the network layer, in practical terms, NAT routers must be aware of many more protocols and perform special operations as required. Some are required for all datagrams that are translated; others only apply to certain datagrams and not others. And even when these techniques are added to NAT routers, some things still may not work properly in a NAT environment.

Let's take a look at some of the main issues and requirements:

TCP and UDP Checksum Recalculations Changing the IP addresses in the IP header means that the IP header checksum must be calculated. Since both UDP and TCP also have checksums, and these checksums are computed over a pseudo header that contains the IP source and destination address as well, they too, must be recalculated each time a translation is made.

ICMP Manipulations Since NAT works so intimately with IP headers, and since IP is closely related to its "assistant" protocol the Internet Control Management Protocol (ICMP; see Chapter 31), NAT must also look for certain ICMP messages and make changes to addresses contained within them. Many ICMP messages, such as Destination Unreachable and Parameter Problem, contain the original IP header of the datagram that lead to the ICMP message as data. Since NAT is translating addresses in IP headers, it must watch for these messages and translate addresses in included headers as required.

Applications That Embed IP Addresses A number of TCP/IP applications embed IP addresses within the actual application data payload. The most notorious example of this is FTP, which actually sends address and port assignments as text information in datagrams between devices during a connection. In order for NAT to support FTP, it must be specifically programmed with algorithms to look for this information and make changes as needed. The level of complication can go even beyond this. Consider what happens when an FTP message containing these text addresses or port numbers is *fragmented*. Part of the address that will be translated may be in two different IP datagrams and may be hard to recognize!

Additional Issues with Port Translation When Port-Based NAT (PAT) is used, the previous issues that apply to addresses now apply to ports as well, making even more work for the router to perform.

Cascading Impact of Changes to Address or Port Numbers Take the example of an FTP datagram encoding an IP address that NAT must change. The address being substituted might require more characters than the original; in the first example, 10.0.0.207 (10 ASCII characters) is replaced by 194.54.21.11 (12 ASCII characters). Making this substitution changes the size of the payload! This means that TCP sequence numbers (see Chapter 46) also must be modified. In these situations, NAT itself is supposed to take care of any additional work that may be required.

Problems with IPsec When IPsec is used in transport mode, both the Authentication Header (AH) and Encapsulating Security Payload (ESP) protocols use an integrity check that is based on the value of the entire payload. When NAT tries to update the TCP or UDP checksum in the IP datagram, this changes the value of data that the receiving device uses in performing the AH or ESP integrity check. The check will fail. Thus, NAT can't be used in IPsec transport mode. It may still work in tunnel mode, but there can be complications here as well.

Most NAT implementations do take at least some of the previous issues into account. Certainly, common applications like FTP are widely supported by NAT routers, or no one would want to use NAT. That said, there might be some applications that will not work over NAT. The fact that NAT really isn't transparent and must do these extra sorts of "hacks" to other protocol headers and even payloads is a big part of the reason why many people refer to NAT as a kludge; elegant solutions don't have so many special cases that need special handling.

29

IP SECURITY (IPSEC) PROTOCOLS

One of the weaknesses of the original Internet Protocol (IP) is that it lacks any sort of general-purpose mechanism for ensuring the authenticity and privacy of data as it is passed over the internetwork. Since IP datagrams must usually be routed between two devices over unknown networks, any information in them is subject to being intercepted and even possibly changed. With the increased use of the Internet for critical applications, security enhancements were needed for IP. To this end, a set of protocols called *IP Security* or *IPsec* was developed.

In this chapter, I provide a brief description of IPsec concepts and protocols. I begin with an overview of IPsec, including a discussion of the history of the technology and a definition of the standards. I describe the main components and protocols of the IPsec suite and its different architectures and methods for implementation. I then move to actually discussing how IPsec works, beginning with a description of the two IPsec modes (transport and tunnel) and how they differ. I describe security associations and related constructs such as the Security Parameter Index (SPI). The last three topics cover the three main IPsec protocols: IPsec Authentication Header (AH), IPsec Encapsulating Security Payload (ESP), and the IPsec Internet Key Exchange (IKE).

NOTE *IPsec was initially developed with IPv6 in mind, but has been engineered to provide security for both IPv4 and IPv6 networks, and operation in both versions is similar. There are some differences in the datagram formats used for AH and ESP. These differences depend on whether you use IPsec in IPv4 or IPv6, because the two versions have different datagram formats and addressing. I highlight these differences where appropriate.*

IPsec Overview, History, and Standards

The big problem with the original IP version (IPv4) is the pending exhaustion of its address space. This situation arose due to the rapid expansion of the Internet beyond anyone's expectations when IPv4 was developed. This same mismatch between how the Internet was when IPv4 was created and how it is now has led to another major problem with IP: the lack of a definitive means of ensuring security on IP internetworks.

The security problem arose because 25 years ago, the Internet was tiny and relatively private. Today it is enormous and truly public. As the Internet has grown, the need for security has grown with it. Consider that TCP/IP and the early Internet precursors were developed as very small networks used by government researchers at the United States Defense Advanced Research Projects Agency (*DARPA* or *ARPA*). People who were well known and would generally have had security clearance controlled all the hardware. In such a network, you don't need to build security in to the protocols—you build it into the building! It's easier to use locks and guards to ensure security than fancy encryption. The easiest way to keep someone from snooping or tampering with data on the network is simply to deny them access to the hosts that connect to the network.

This worked fine at first when there were only a few dozen machines on the Internet. And even when the Internet first started to grow, it was used pretty much only to connect together researchers and other networking professionals. New sites were added to the network slowly at first, and at least someone knew the identity of each new site added to the growing internetwork. However, as the Internet continued to increase in size and was eventually opened to the public, maintaining security of the network as a whole became impossible. Today, the "great unwashed masses" are on the Internet. Many routers—owned by "who knows" and administered by "who knows"—stand between you and most other devices you want to connect with. You cannot assume that the data you send or receive is secure.

A number of methods have evolved over the years to address the need for security. Most of these are focused at the higher layers of the OSI protocol stack in order to compensate for IP's lack of security. These solutions are valuable for certain situations, but they can't be generalized easily because they are particular to various applications. For example, we can use Secure Sockets Layer (SSL) for certain applications like World Wide Web access or File Transfer Protocol (FTP), but there are dozens of applications that this type of security was never intended to work with.

What was really needed was a solution to allow security at the IP level so all higher-layer protocols in TCP/IP could take advantage of it. When the decision was made to develop a new version of IP (IPv6), this was the golden opportunity to resolve not just the addressing problems in the older IPv4, but the lack of security as well. New security technology was developed with IPv6 in mind, but since IPv6 has taken years to develop and roll out, and the need for security is now, the solution was designed to be usable for both IPv4 and IPv6.

The technology that brings secure communications to the IP is called *IP Security*, commonly abbreviated *IPsec*. The capitalization of this abbreviation is variable, so you'll see IPSec and IPSEC.

Overview of IPsec Services and Functions

IPsec is not a single protocol, but rather a set of services and protocols that provide a complete security solution for an IP network. These services and protocols combine to provide various types of protection. Since IPsec works at the IP layer, it can provide these protections for any higher-layer TCP/IP application or protocol without the need for additional security methods, which is a major strength. Some of the kinds of protection services offered by IPsec include the following:

- Encryption of user data for privacy
- Authentication of the integrity of a message to ensure that it is not changed en route
- Protection against certain types of security attacks, such as replay attacks
- The ability for devices to negotiate the security algorithms and keys required to meet their security needs
- Two security modes, tunnel and transport, to meet different network needs

> **KEY CONCEPT** *IPsec* is a contraction of *IP Security*, and it consists of a set of services and protocols that provide security to IP networks. It is defined by a sequence of several Internet standards.

IPsec Standards

Since IPsec is actually a collection of techniques and protocols, it is not defined in a single Internet standard. Instead, a collection of RFCs defines the architecture, services, and specific protocols used in IPsec. Some of the most important of these are shown in Table 29-1, all of which were published in November 1998.

Table 29-1: Important IP Security (IPsec) Standards

RFC Number	Name	Description
2401	Security Architecture for the Internet Protocol	The main IPsec document, describing the architecture and general operation of the technology, and showing how the different components fit together.
2402	IP Authentication Header	Defines the IPsec Authentication Header (AH) protocol, which is used for ensuring data integrity and origin verification.
2403	The Use of HMAC-MD5-96 within ESP and AH	Describes a particular encryption algorithm for use by the AH and Encapsulation Security Payload (ESP) protocols called Message Digest 5 (MD5), HMAC variant.

(continued)

Table 29-1: Important IP Security (IPsec) Standards (continued)

RFC Number	Name	Description
2404	The Use of HMAC-SHA-1-96 within ESP and AH	Describes a particular encryption algorithm for use by AH and ESP called Secure Hash Algorithm 1 (SHA-1), HMAC variant.
2406	IP Encapsulating Security Payload (ESP)	Describes the IPsec ESP protocol, which provides data encryption for confidentiality.
2408	Internet Security Association and Key Management Protocol (ISAKMP)	Defines methods for exchanging keys and negotiating security associations.
2409	The Internet Key Exchange (IKE)	Describes the IKE protocol that's used to negotiate security associations and exchange keys between devices for secure communications. Based on ISAKMP and OAKLEY.
2412	The OAKLEY Key Determination Protocol	Describes a generic protocol for key exchange.

Deployment of IPsec has only really started to take off in the last few years. A major use of the technology is in implementing virtual private networks (VPNs). It appears that the future is bright for IPsec, as more and more individuals and companies decide that they need to take advantage of the power of the Internet, while also protecting the security of the data they transport over it.

IPsec General Operation, Components, and Protocols

IPsec isn't the only difficult topic in this book, but it is definitely a subject that baffles many. Most discussions of it jump straight to describing the mechanisms and protocols, without providing a general description of what it does and how the pieces fit together. Well, I recognized that IPsec is important, and I don't shy away from a challenge. Thus, here's my attempt to provide a framework for understanding IPsec's various bits and pieces.

So what exactly does IPsec do, and how does it do it? In general terms, it provides security services at the IP layer for other TCP/IP protocols and applications to use. What this means is that IPsec provides the tools that devices on a TCP/IP network need in order to communicate securely. When two devices (either end-user hosts or intermediate devices such as routers or firewalls) want to engage in secure communications, they set up a *secure path* between themselves that may traverse across many insecure intermediate systems. To accomplish this, they must perform (at least) the following tasks:

- They must agree on a set of security protocols to use so that each one sends data in a format the other can understand.
- They must decide on a specific encryption algorithm to use in encoding data.
- They must exchange keys that are used to "unlock" data that has been cryptographically encoded.
- Once this background work is completed, each device must use the protocols, methods, and keys previously agreed upon to encode data and send it across the network.

IPsec Core Protocols

To support these activities, a number of different components make up the total package known as IPsec, as shown in Figure 29-1. The two main pieces are a pair of technologies sometimes called the *core protocols* of IPsec, which actually do the work of encoding information to ensure security:

IPsec Authentication Header (AH) This protocol provides authentication services for IPsec. It allows the recipient of a message to verify that the supposed originator of a message was actually fact the one that sent it. It also allows the recipient to verify that intermediate devices en route haven't changed any of the data in the datagram. It also provides protection against so-called *replay attacks*, whereby a message is captured by an unauthorized user and resent.

Encapsulating Security Payload (ESP) AH ensures the integrity of the data in datagram, but not its privacy. When the information in a datagram is "for your eyes only," it can be further protected using ESP, which encrypts the payload of the IP datagram.

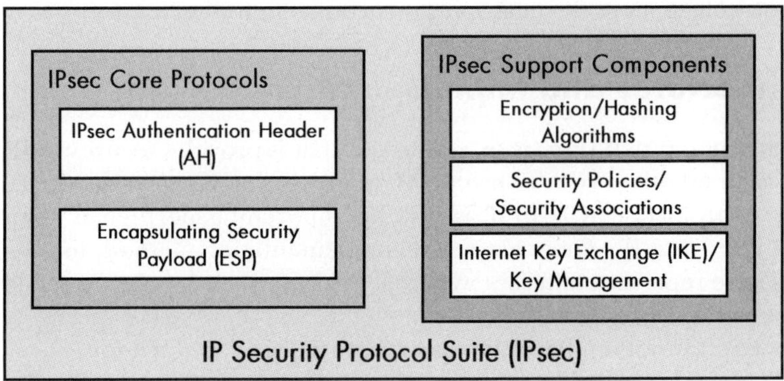

Figure 29-1: Overview of IPsec protocols and components *IPsec consists of two core protocols, AH and ESP, and three supporting components.*

IPsec Support Components

AH and ESP are commonly called *protocols*, though this is another case where the use of this term is debatable. They are not really distinct protocols but are implemented as headers that are inserted into IP datagrams, as you will see. They thus do the "grunt work" of IPsec, and can be used together to provide both authentication and privacy. However, they cannot operate on their own. To function properly, they need the support of several other protocols and services (see Figure 29-1). The most important of these include the following:

Encryption/Hashing Algorithms AH and ESP are generic and do not specify the exact mechanism used for encryption. This gives them the flexibility to work with a variety of such algorithms and to negotiate which one to use as needed. Two common ones used with IPsec are *Message Digest 5 (MD5)* and *Secure Hash Algorithm 1 (SHA-1)*. These are also called *hashing* algorithms because they work by computing a formula called a *hash* based on input data and a key.

Security Policies, Security Associations, and Management Methods Since IPsec provides flexibility in letting different devices decide how they want to implement security, they require some means to keep track of the security relationships between themselves. This is done in IPsec using constructs called *security policies* and *security associations*, and by providing ways to exchange security association information.

Key Exchange Framework and Mechanism For two devices to exchange encrypted information, they need to be able to share keys for unlocking the encryption. They also need a way to exchange security association information. In IPsec, a protocol called the *Internet Key Exchange (IKE)* provides these capabilities.

KEY CONCEPT IPsec consists of a number of different components that work together to provide security services. The two main ones are protocols called the *Authentication Header (AH)* and *Encapsulating Security Payload (ESP)*, which provide authenticity and privacy to IP data in the form of special headers added to IP datagrams.

Well, that's at least a start at providing a framework for understanding what IPsec is all about and how the pieces fit together. You'll examine these components and protocols in more detail as you proceed through this chapter.

IPsec Architectures and Implementation Methods

The main reason that IPsec is so powerful is that it provides security to IP, which is the basis for all other TCP/IP protocols. In protecting IP, you are protecting pretty much everything else in TCP/IP as well. An important issue, then, is how exactly do you get IPsec into IP? There are several implementation methods for deploying IPsec. These represent different ways that IPsec may modify the overall layer architecture of TCP/IP.

Three different implementation architectures are defined for IPsec in RFC 2401. The one you use depends on various factors including the version of IP used (IPv4 or IPv6), the requirements of the application, and other factors. These, in turn, rest on a primary implementation decision: Should IPsec be programmed into all hosts on a network, or just into certain routers or other intermediate devices? This is a design decision that must be based on the requirements of the network:

End-Host Implementation Putting IPsec into all host devices provides the most flexibility and security. It enables end-to-end security between any two devices on the network. However, there are many hosts on a typical network, so this means far more work than just implementing IPsec in routers.

Router Implementation This option is much less work because it means you make changes to only a few routers instead of hundreds or thousands of clients. It provides protection only between pairs of routers that implement IPsec, but this may be sufficient for certain applications such as VPNs. The routers can be used to provide protection for just the portion of the route that datagrams take outside the organization, thereby leaving connections between routers and local hosts unsecured (or possibly, secured by other means).

Three different architectures are defined that describe methods for how to get IPsec into the TCP/IP protocol stack: integrated, bump in the stack, and bump in the wire.

Integrated Architecture

Under ideal circumstances, we would integrate IPsec's protocols and capabilities directly into IP itself. This is the most elegant solution, because it allows all IPsec security modes and capabilities to be provided just as easily as regular IP. No extra hardware or architectural layers are needed.

IPv6 was designed to support IPsec. Thus, it's a viable option for hosts or routers. With IPv4, integration would require making changes to the IP implementation on each device, which is often impractical (to say the least!).

Bump in the Stack (BITS) Architecture

In the bump in the stack (BITS) technique, IPsec is made a separate architectural layer between IP and the data link layer. The cute name refers to the fact that IPsec is an extra element in the networking protocol stack, as you can see in Figure 29-2. IPsec intercepts IP datagrams as they are passed down the protocol stack, provides security, and passes them to the data link layer.

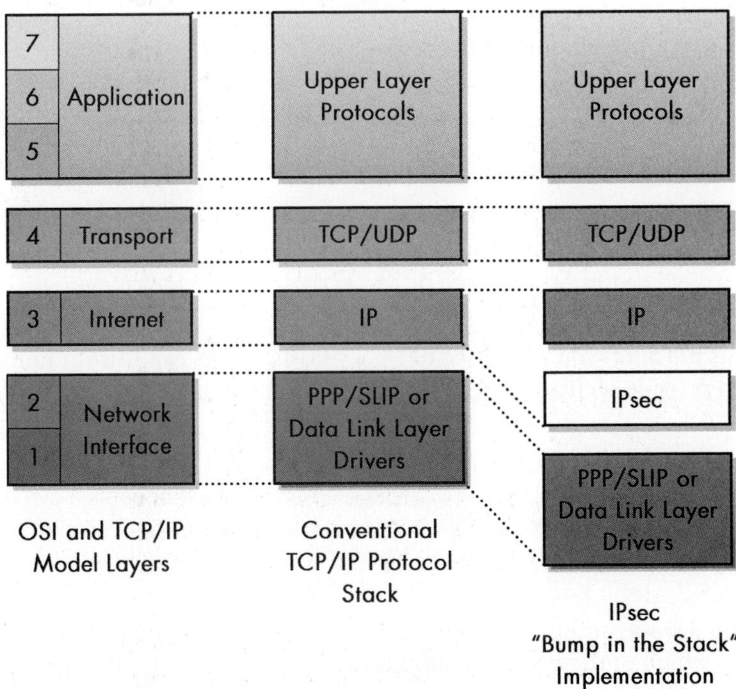

Figure 29-2: IPsec bump in the stack (BITS) architecture *In this type of IPsec implementation, IPsec becomes a separate layer in the TCP/IP stack. It is implemented as software that sits below IP and adds security protection to datagrams created by the IP layer.*

The advantage of this technique is that IPsec can be retrofitted to any IP device, since the IPsec functionality is separate from IP. The disadvantage is that there is a duplication of effort compared to the integrated architecture. BITS is generally used for IPv4 hosts.

Bump in the Wire (BITW) Architecture

In the bump in the wire (BITW) method, we add a hardware device that provides IPsec services. For example, suppose we have a company with two sites. Each has a network that connects to the Internet using a router that is not capable of IPsec functions. We can interpose a special IPsec device between the router and the Internet at both sites, as shown in Figure 29-3. These devices will then intercept outgoing datagrams, add IPsec protection to them, and strip it off incoming datagrams.

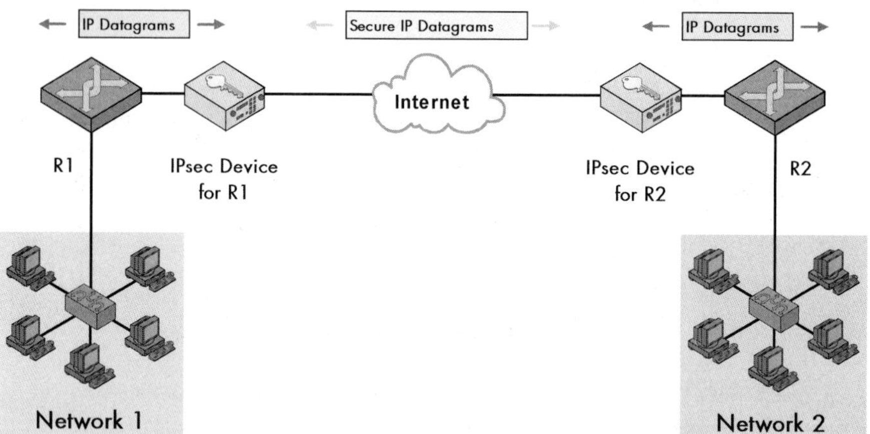

Figure 29-3: IPsec bump in the wire (BITW) architecture *In this IPsec architecture, IPsec is actually implemented in separate devices that sit between the devices that wish to communicate securely. These repackage insecure IP datagrams for transport over the public Internet.*

Just as BITS lets you add IPsec to legacy hosts, BITW can retrofit non-IPsec routers to provide security benefits. The disadvantages are complexity and cost.

> **KEY CONCEPT** Three different architectures or implementation models are defined for IPsec. The best is integrated architecture, in which IPsec is built into the IP layer of devices directly. The other two are *bump in the stack (BITS)* and *bump in the wire (BITW)*, which are ways of layering IPsec underneath regular IP, using software and hardware solutions, respectively.

As you will see in the next section, the choice of architecture has an important impact on which of the two IPsec modes can be used. Incidentally, even though BITS and BITW seem quite different, they are actually do the same thing. In the case of BITS, we have an extra software layer that adds security to existing IP datagrams; in BITW, distinct hardware devices do this same job. In both cases, the result is the same, and the implications on the choice of IPsec mode is likewise the same.

IPsec Modes: Transport and Tunnel

You just saw that three different basic implementation architectures could be used to provide IPsec facilities to TCP/IP networks. The choice of which implementation you use, as well as whether you implement in end hosts or routers, impacts the specific way that IPsec functions. Two specific modes of operation that are related to these architectures are defined for IPsec. They are called *transport mode* and *tunnel mode.*

IPsec modes are closely related to the function of the two core protocols, AH and ESP. Both of these protocols provide protection by adding a header (and possibly other fields) containing security information to a datagram. The choice of mode does not affect the method by which each generates its header, but rather, changes what specific parts of the IP datagram are protected and how the headers are arranged to accomplish this. In essence, the mode really describes, not prescribes, how AH or ESP do their thing. It is used as the basis for defining other constructs, such as security associations (SAs).

Transport Mode

As its name suggests, in transport mode, the protocol protects the message passed down to IP from the transport layer. The message is processed by AH and/or ESP, and the appropriate header(s) are added in front of the transport (UDP or TCP) header. The IP header is then added in front of that by IP.

Another way of looking at this is as follows: Normally, the transport layer packages data for transmission and sends it to IP. From IP's perspective, this transport layer message is the payload of the IP datagram. When IPsec is used in transport mode, the IPsec header is applied only over this IP payload, not the IP header. The AH and ESP headers appear between the original, single IP header and the IP payload. This is illustrated in Figure 29-4.

Tunnel Mode

In tunnel mode, IPsec is used to protect a completely encapsulated IP datagram after the IP header has already been applied to it. The IPsec headers appear in front of the original IP header, and then a new IP header is added in front of the IPsec header. That is to say, the entire original IP datagram is secured and then encapsulated within another IP datagram. This is shown in Figure 29-5.

Comparing Transport and Tunnel Modes

The bottom line in understanding the difference between the two IPsec modes is this: Tunnel mode protects the original IP datagram as a whole, header and all, while transport mode does not. Thus, in general terms, the order of the headers is as follows:

Transport Mode IP header, IPsec headers (AH and/or ESP), IP payload (including transport header)

Tunnel Mode New IP header, IPsec headers (AH and/or ESP), old IP header, IP payload

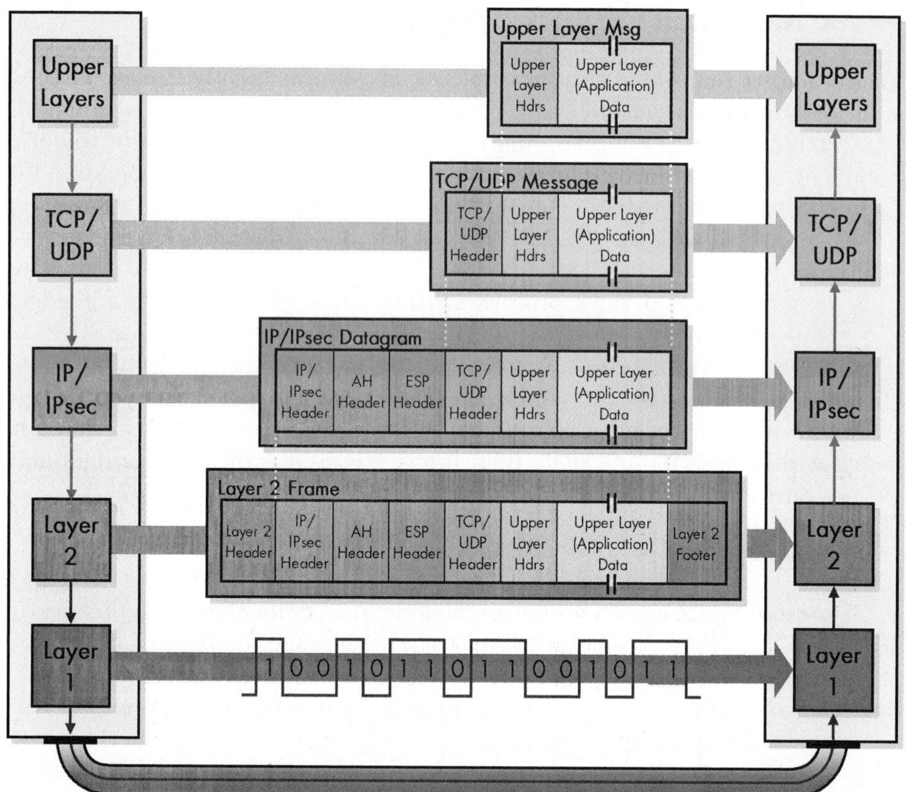

Figure 29-4: IPsec transport mode operation When IPsec operates in transport mode, it is integrated with IP and used to transport the upper layer (TCP/UDP) message directly. After processing, the datagram has just one IP header that contains the AH and ESP IPsec headers. Contrast this to tunnel mode, shown in Figure 29-5.

Again, this is a simplified view of how IPsec datagrams are constructed; the reality is significantly more complex. The exact way that the headers are arranged in an IPsec datagram in both transport and tunnel modes depends on which version of IP is being used. IPv6 uses extension headers that must be arranged in a particular way when IPsec is used. The header placement also depends on which IPsec protocol is being used, AH or ESP. Note that it is also possible to apply both AH and ESP to the same datagram; if so, the AH header always appears before the ESP header.

There are thus three variables and eight basic combinations of mode (tunnel or transport), IP version (IPv4 or IPv6) and protocol (AH or ESP). The coming discussions of AH and ESP describe the four format combinations of transport/tunnel mode and IPv4/IPv6 applicable to each protocol. Note that ESP also includes an ESP trailer that goes after the data protected.

You could probably tell by reading these descriptions how the two modes relate to the choice of IPsec architecture you looked at earlier. Transport mode requires that IPsec be integrated into IP, because AH/ESP must be applied as the original IP packaging is performed on the transport layer message. This is often the choice for implementations requiring end-to-end security with hosts that run IPsec directly.

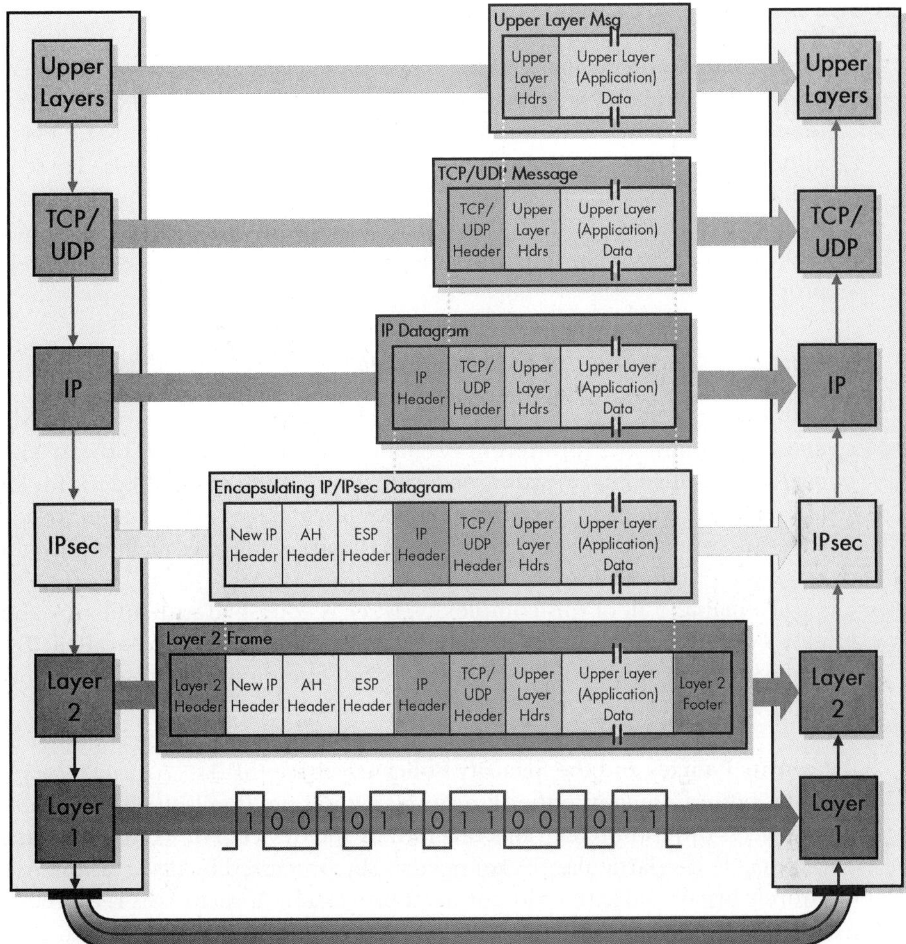

Figure 29-5: IPsec tunnel mode operation IPsec tunnel mode *is so named because it represents an encapsulation of a complete IP datagram, thereby forming a virtual tunnel between IPsec-capable devices. The IP datagram is passed to IPsec, where a new IP header is created with the AH and ESP IPsec headers added. Contrast this to transport mode, shown in Figure 29-4.*

Tunnel mode represents an encapsulation of IP within the combination of IP plus IPsec. Thus, it corresponds with the BITS and BITW implementations, where IPsec is applied after IP has processed higher-layer messages and has already added its header. Tunnel mode is a common choice for VPN implementations, which are based on the tunneling of IP datagrams through an unsecured network such as the Internet.

KEY CONCEPT IPsec has two basic modes of operation. In *transport mode*, IPsec AH and ESP headers are added as the original IP datagram is created. Transport mode is associated with integrated IPsec architectures. In *tunnel mode*, the original IP datagram is created normally, and then the entire datagram is encapsulated into a new IP datagram containing the AH/ESP IPsec headers. Tunnel mode is most commonly used with *bump in the stack (BITS)* and *bump in the wire (BITW)* implementations.

IPsec Security Constructs

Important IPsec security constructs include security associations, the security association database, security policies, the security policy database, selectors, and the security parameter index. These items are all closely related and essential to understand before you begin looking at the core IPsec protocols. These constructs are used to guide the operation of IPsec in a general way and particularly to guide exchanges between devices. The constructs control how IPsec works and ensure that each datagram coming into or leaving an IPsec-capable device is treated properly.

Security Policies, Security Associations, and Associated Databases

Let's begin by considering the problem of how to apply security in a device that may be handling many different exchanges of datagrams with others. There is overhead involved in providing security, so you do not want to do it for every message that comes in or out. Some types of messages may need more security; others may need less. Also, exchanges with certain devices may require different processing than others.

To manage all of this complexity, IPsec is equipped with a flexible, powerful way of specifying how different types of datagrams should be handled. To understand how this works, you must first define the following two important logical concepts:

Security Policies and the Security Policy Database (SPD) A *security policy* is a rule that is programmed into the IPsec implementation. It tells the implementation how to process different datagrams received by the device. For example, security policies decide if a particular packet needs to be processed by IPsec or not. AH and ESP entirely bypass those that do not need processing. If security is required, the security policy provides general guidelines for how it should be provided, and if necessary, links to more specific detail. Security policies for a device are stored in the device's *security policy database (SPD).*

Security Associations (SAs) and the Security Association Database (SAD) A security association (SA) is a set of security information that describes a particular kind of secure connection between one device and another. You can consider it a contract, if you will, that specifies the particular security mechanisms that are used for secure communications between the two. A device's security associations are contained in its *security association database (SAD).*

It's often hard to distinguish between the SPD and the SAD, because they are similar in concept. The main difference between them is that security policies are general, while security associations are more specific. To determine what to do with a particular datagram, a device first checks the SPD. The security policies in the SPD may reference a particular SA in the SAD. If so, the device will look up that SA and use it for processing the datagram.

Selectors

One issue I haven't covered yet is how a device determines what security policies or SAs to use for a specific datagram. Again here, IPsec defines a very flexible system that lets each security association define a set of rules for choosing datagrams that the SA applies to. Each of these rule sets is called a *selector*. For example, you might define a selector that says that a particular range of values in the Source Address of a datagram, combined with another value in the Destination Address, means that a specific SA must be used for the datagram.

Security Association Triples and Security Parameter Index (SPI)

Each secure communication that a device makes to another requires that an SA be established. SAs are unidirectional, so each one only handles either inbound or outbound traffic for a particular device. This allows the level of security for a flow from Device A to Device B to be different than the level for traffic coming from Device B to Device A. In a bidirectional communication of this sort, both Device A and Device B would have two SAs; Device A would have SAs that you could call SAdeviceBin and SAdeviceBout. Device B would have SAs SAdeviceAin and SAdeviceAout.

SAs don't actually have names, however. They are instead defined by a set of three parameters, called a *triple*:

Security Parameter Index (SPI) A 32-bit number that is chosen to uniquely identify a particular SA for any connected device. The SPI is placed in AH or ESP datagrams and thus links each secure datagram to the security association. It is used by the recipient of a transmission so it knows what SA governs the datagram.

IP Destination Address The address of the device for which the SA is established.

Security Protocol Identifier Specifies whether this association is for AH or ESP. If both are in use with this device, they have separate SAs.

As you can see, the two security protocols AH and ESP are dependent on SAs, security policies, and the various databases that control the operation of those SAs and policies. Management of these databases is important, but it's another complex subject entirely. Generally, SAs can either be set up manually (which is of course extra work) or you can deploy an automated system using a protocol like IKE (discussed near the end of this chapter).

Confused? I don't blame you, despite my best efforts, and remember that this is all highly simplified. Welcome to the wonderful world of networking security. If you are ever besieged by insomnia, I highly recommend RFC 2401!

IPsec Authentication Header (AH)

As I mentioned earlier in this chapter, AH is one of the two core security protocols in IPsec. This is another protocol whose name has been well chosen. It provides *authentication* of either all or part of the contents of a datagram through the addition of a *header* that is calculated based on the values in the datagram. The parts of the datagram that are used for the calculation, and the placement of the header, depend on the mode (tunnel or transport) and the version of IP (IPv4 or IPv6).

The operation of AH is surprisingly simple, especially for any protocol that has anything to do with network security. The simplicity is analogous to the algorithms used to calculate checksums or perform cyclic redundancy (CRC) checks for error detection. In those cases, the sender uses a standard algorithm to compute a checksum or CRC code based on the contents of a message. This computed result is transmitted along with the original data to the destination, which repeats the calculation and discards the message if any discrepancy is found between its calculation and the one done by the source.

This is the same idea behind AH, except that instead of using a simple algorithm known to everyone, it uses a special hashing algorithm and a specific key known only to the source and the destination. An SA between two devices specifies these particulars, so that the source and destination know how to perform the computation but nobody else can. On the source device, AH performs the computation and puts the result (called the *integrity check value*, or *ICV*) into a special header with other fields for transmission. The destination device does the same calculation using the key that the two devices share. This enables the device to see immediately if any of the fields in the original datagram were modified (due to either error or malice).

Just as a checksum doesn't change the original data, neither does the ICV calculation change the original data. The presence of the AH header allows us to verify the integrity of the message, but doesn't encrypt it. Thus, AH provides *authentication* but not *privacy* (that's what ESP is for).

AH Datagram Placement and Linking

The calculation of AH is similar for both IPv4 and IPv6. One difference is in the exact mechanism used for placing the header into the datagram and for linking the headers together. I'll describe IPv6 first because it is simpler, and because AH was really designed to fit into its mechanism for this.

IPv6 AH Placement and Linking

In IPv6, the AH is inserted into the IP datagram as an extension header, following the normal IPv6 rules for extension header linking. It is linked by the previous header (extension or main), which puts the assigned value for the AH header (51) into its Next Header field. The AH header then links to the next extension header or the transport layer header using its Next Header field.

In transport mode, the AH is placed into the main IP header and appears before any Destination Options header that contains options intended for the final destination, and before an ESP header if present, but after any other extension headers. In tunnel mode, it appears as an extension header of the new IP datagram that encapsulates the original one being tunneled. This is shown graphically in Figure 29-6.

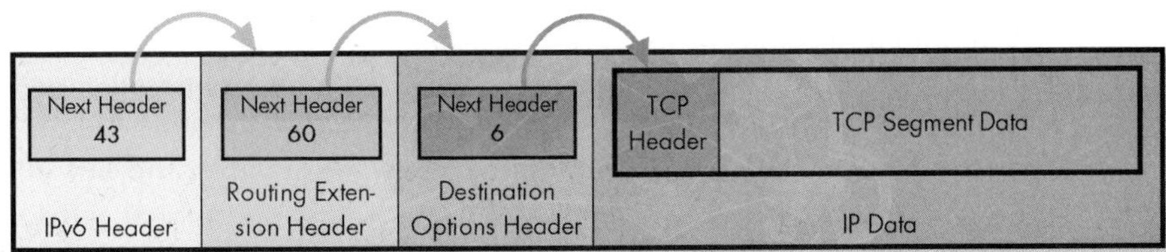

Original IPv6 Datagram Format (Including Routing Extension Header and Destination-Specific Destination Options Extension Header)

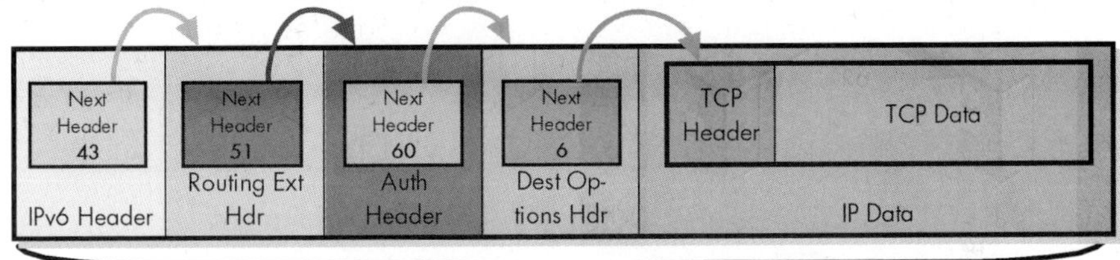

IPv6 AH Datagram Format - IPSec Transport Mode

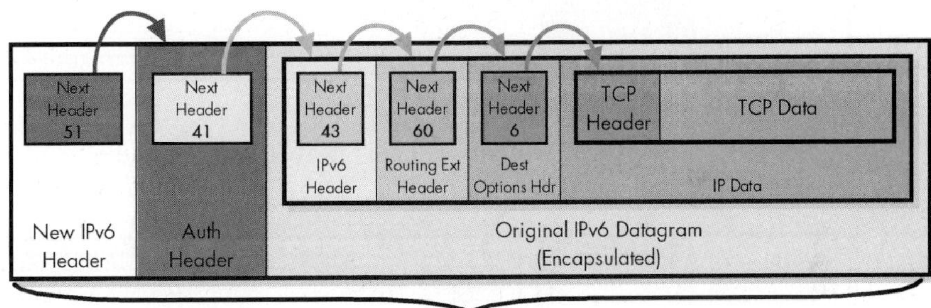

IPv6 AH Datagram Format - IPsec Tunnel Mode

Figure 29-6: IPv6 datagram format with IPsec Authentication Header (AH) *This is an example of an IPv6 datagram with two extension headers that are linked using the standard IPv6 mechanism (see Figure 26-3 in Chapter 26). When AH is applied in transport mode, it is simply added as a new extension header (as shown in dark shading) that goes between the Routing extension header and the Destination Options header. In tunnel mode, the entire original datagram is encapsulated into a new IPv6 datagram that contains the AH header. In both cases, the Next Header fields are used to link each header one to the next. Note the use of Next Header value 41 in tunnel mode, which is the value for the encapsulated IPv6 datagram.*

IPv4 AH Placement and Linking

In IPv4, a method that is similar to the IPv6 header-linking technique is employed. In an IPv4 datagram, the Protocol field indicates the identity of the higher-layer protocol (typically TCP or UDP) that's carried in the datagram. As such, this field points to the next header, which is at the front of the IP payload. AH takes this value and puts it into its Next Header field, and then places the protocol value for AH itself (51 in dotted decimal) into the IP Protocol field. This makes the IP header point to the AH, which then points to whatever the IP datagram pointed to before.

Again, in transport mode, the AH header is added after the main IP header of the original datagram; in tunnel mode it is added after the new IP header that encapsulates the original datagram that's being tunneled. This is shown in Figure 29-7.

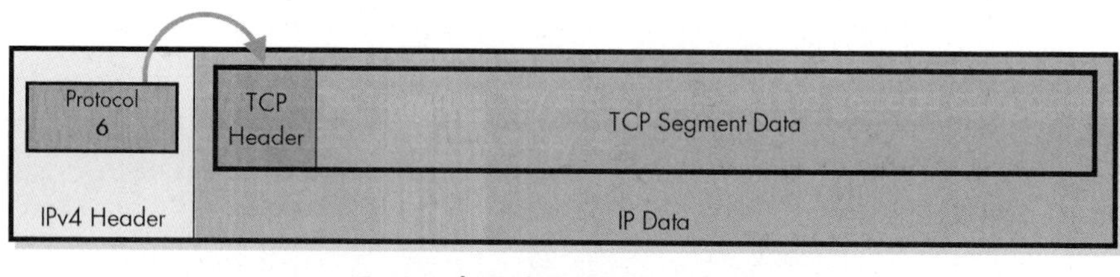

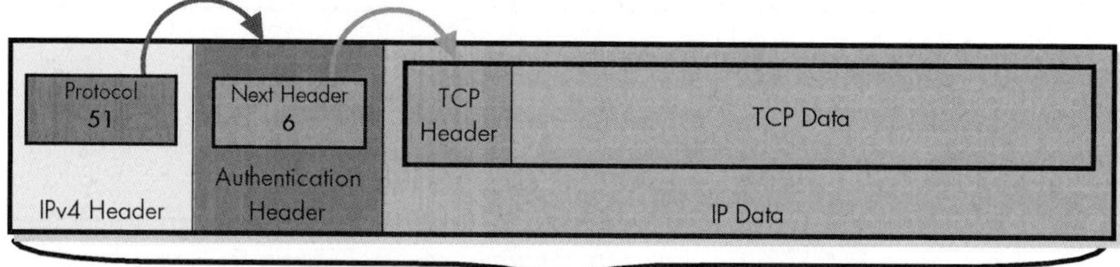

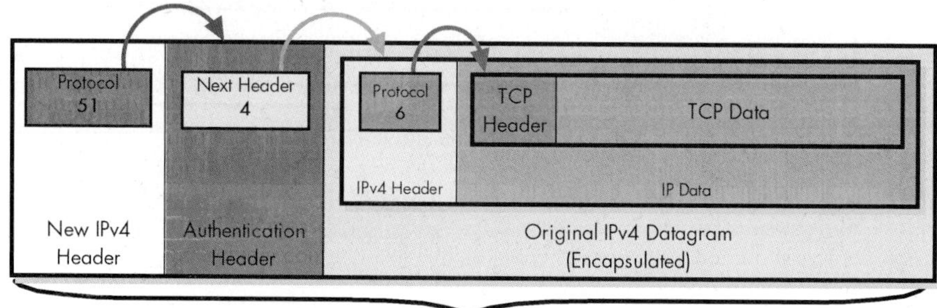

Figure 29-7: IPv4 datagram format with IPsec AH *Here is an example of an IPv4 datagram; it may or may not contain IPv4 options (which are not distinct entities as they are in IPv6). In transport mode, the AH header is added between the IP header and the IP data; the Protocol field of the IP header points to it, while its Next Header field contains the IP header's prior protocol value (in this case 6, for TCP). In tunnel mode, the IPv4 datagram is encapsulated into a new IPv4 datagram that includes the AH header. Note that in tunnel mode, the AH header uses the value 4 (which means IPv4) in its Next Header field.*

KEY CONCEPT The IPsec *Authentication Header (AH)* protocol allows the recipient of a datagram to verify its authenticity. It is implemented as a header that's added to an IP datagram that contains an *integrity check value (ICV)*, which is computed based on the values of the fields in the datagram. The recipient can use this value to ensure that the data has not been changed in transit. AH does not encrypt data and thus does not ensure the privacy of transmissions.

AH Format

The format of AH is described in Table 29-2 and illustrated in Figure 29-8.

Table 29-2: IPsec Authentication Header (AH) Format

Field Name	Size (Bytes)	Description
Next Header	1	Contains the protocol number of the next header after the AH. Used to link headers together.
Payload Len	1	Despite its name, this field measures the length of the authentication header itself, not the payload. (I wonder what the history is behind that!) It is measured in 32-bit units, with 2 subtracted for consistency with how header lengths are normally calculated in IPv6.
Reserved	2	Not used; set to zeros.
SPI	4	A 32-bit value that, when combined with the destination address and security protocol type (which is obviously the one for AH here), identifies the security association (SA) that will be used for this datagram. (SAs are discussed earlier in this chapter.)
Sequence Number	4	A counter field that is initialized to zero when an SA is formed between two devices, and then incremented for each datagram sent using that SA. This uniquely identifies each datagram on an SA and is used to provide protection against replay attacks by preventing the retransmission of captured datagrams.
Authentication Data	Variable	Contains the result of the hashing algorithm, called the integrity check value (ICV), performed by the AH protocol.

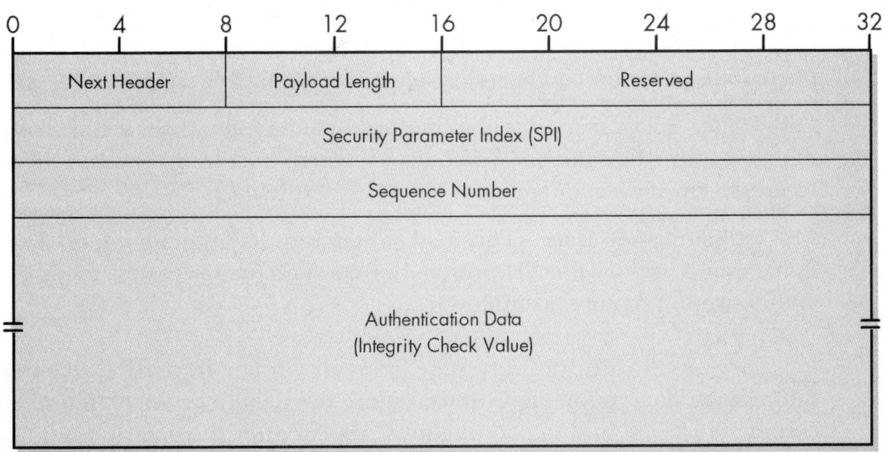

Figure 29-8: *IPsec Authentication Header (AH) format*

The size of the Authentication Data field is variable to support different datagram lengths and hashing algorithms. Its total length must be a multiple of 32 bits. Also, the entire header must be a multiple of either 32 bits (for IPv4) or 64 bits (for IPv6), so additional padding may be added to the Authentication Data field if necessary.

You may also notice that no IP addresses appear in the header, which is a prerequisite for it being the same for both IPv4 and IPv6.

IPsec Encapsulating Security Payload (ESP)

The IPsec AH provides integrity authentication services to IPsec-capable devices so that they can verify that messages are received intact from other devices. For many applications, however, this is only one piece of the puzzle. We want to not only protect against intermediate devices changing the datagrams, but also to protect against them examining their contents as well. For this level of private communication, AH is not enough; we need to use the ESP protocol.

The main job of ESP is to provide the privacy we seek for IP datagrams by encrypting them. An encryption algorithm combines the data in the datagram with a key to transform it into an encrypted form. This is then repackaged using a special format that you will see shortly, and then transmitted to the destination, which decrypts it using the same algorithm. ESP also sports its own authentication scheme like the one used in AH, or it can be used in conjunction with AH.

ESP Fields

ESP has several fields that are the same as those used in AH, but it packages its fields in a very different way. Instead of having just a header, it divides its fields into three components:

ESP Header This contains two fields, SPI and Sequence Number, and comes before the encrypted data. Its placement depends on whether ESP is used in transport mode or tunnel mode, as explained earlier in this chapter.

ESP Trailer This section is placed after the encrypted data. It contains padding that is used to align the encrypted data through a Padding and Pad Length field. Interestingly, it also contains the Next Header field for ESP.

ESP Authentication Data This field contains an ICV that's computed in a manner that's similar to how the AH protocol works. The field is used when ESP's optional authentication feature is employed.

There are two reasons why these fields are broken into pieces like this. The first is that some encryption algorithms require the data to be encrypted to have a certain block size, and so padding must appear after the data and not before it. That's why padding appears in the ESP Trailer field. The second is that the ESP Authentication Data appears separately because it is used to authenticate the rest of the encrypted datagram after encryption. This means that it cannot appear in the ESP Header or ESP Trailer.

ESP Operations and Field Use

This is still a bit boggling so I'm going to try to explain this procedurally by considering three basic steps performed by ESP: calculating the header, then the trailer, and then the Authentication field.

Header Calculation and Placement

The first thing to consider is how the ESP header is placed. This is similar to how AH works and depends on the IP version, as follows:

IPv6 The ESP Header field is inserted into the IP datagram as an extension header, following the normal IPv6 rules for extension-header linking. In transport mode, it appears before a Destination Options header that contains options intended for the final destination, but after any other extension headers, if present. In tunnel mode, it appears as an extension header of the new IP datagram that encapsulates the original one being tunneled. This is shown in Figure 29-9.

IPv4 As with AH, the ESP Header field is placed after the normal IPv4 header. In transport mode, it appears after the IP header of the original datagram; in tunnel mode, it appears after the IP header of the new IP datagram that's encapsulating the original one. You can see this in Figure 29-10.

Trailer Calculation and Placement

The ESP Trailer field is appended to the data that will be encrypted. ESP then performs the encryption. The payload (TCP/UDP message or encapsulated IP datagram) and the ESP trailer are both encrypted, but the ESP header is not. Note again that any other IP headers that appear between the ESP header and the payload are also encrypted. In IPv6, this can include a Destination Options extension header.

Normally, the Next Header field would appear in the ESP Header and would be used to link the ESP Header to the header that comes after it. However, the Next Header field in ESP appears in the trailer and not the header, which makes the linking seem a bit strange in ESP. The method is basically the same as what's used in AH and in IPv6 in general, with the Next Header and Protocol fields being used to tie everything together. However, in ESP the Next Header field appears *after* the encrypted data, and so it points back to one of the following: a Destination Options extension header (if present), a TCP/UDP header (in transport mode), or an IPv4/IPv6 header (in tunnel mode). This is also shown in Figures 29-9 and 29-10.

ESP Authentication Field Calculation and Placement

If the optional ESP authentication feature is being used, it is computed over the entire ESP datagram (except the Authentication Data field itself, of course). This includes the ESP header, payload, and trailer.

> **KEY CONCEPT** The IPsec ESP protocol allows the contents of a datagram to be encrypted, which ensures that only the intended recipient is able to see the data. ESP is implemented using three components: an *ESP Header* that's added to the front of a protected datagram, an *ESP Trailer* that follows the protected data, and an optional *ESP Authentication Data* field that provides authentication services similar to those provided by AH.

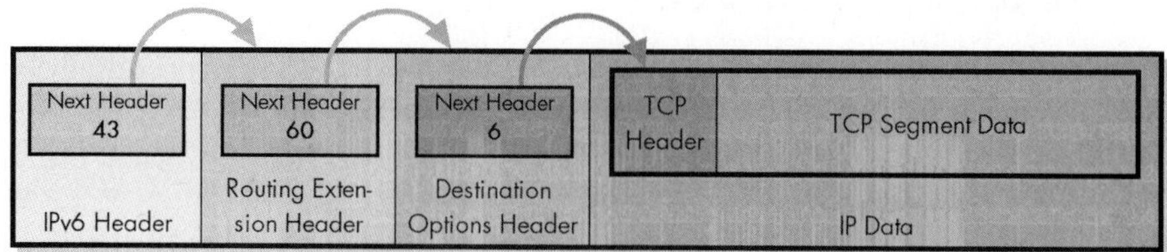

Original IPv6 Datagram Format (Including Routing Extension Header and Destination-Specific Destination Options Extension Header)

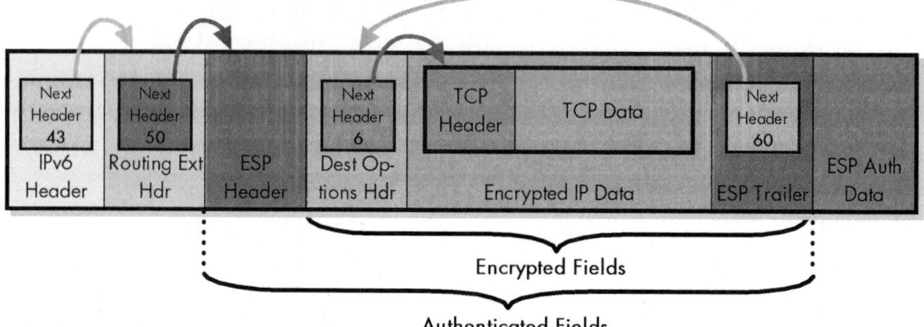

IPv6 ESP Datagram Format - IPsec Transport Mode

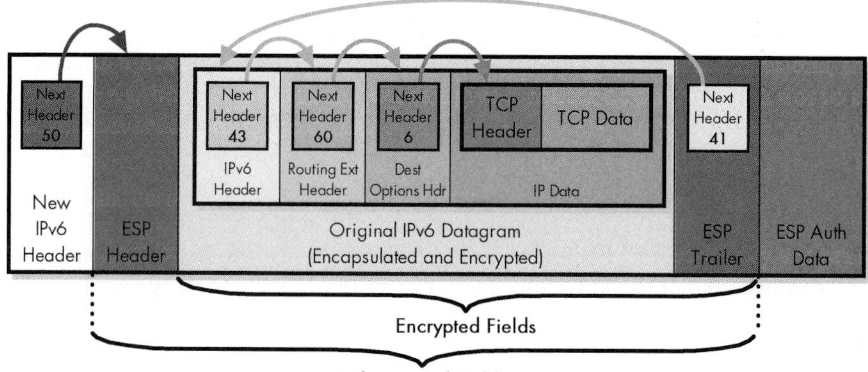

IPv6 ESP Datagram Format - IPsec Tunnel Mode

Figure 29-9: IPv6 datagram format with IPsec ESP *Here is the same example of an IPv6 datagram with two extension headers that you saw in Figure 29-6. When ESP is applied in transport mode, the ESP Header field is added to the existing datagram as in AH, and the ESP Trailer and ESP Authentication Data fields are placed at the end. In tunnel mode, the ESP Header and Trailer fields bracket the entire encapsulated IPv6 datagram. Note the encryption and authentication coverage in each case, and also how the Next Header field points back into the datagram since it appears in the ESP Trailer.*

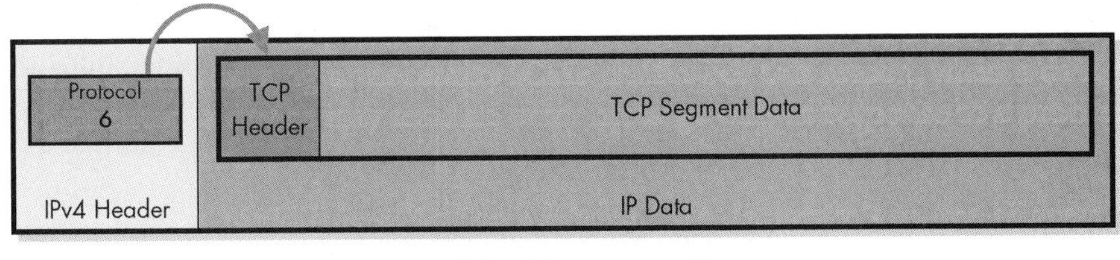

Original IPv4 Datagram Format

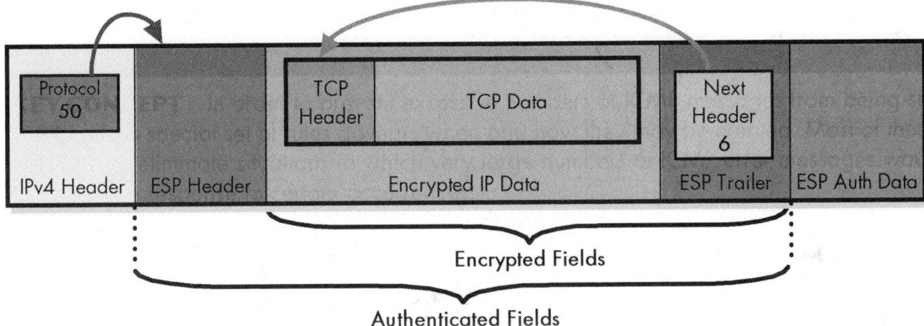

IPv4 ESP Datagram Format - IPsec Transport Mode

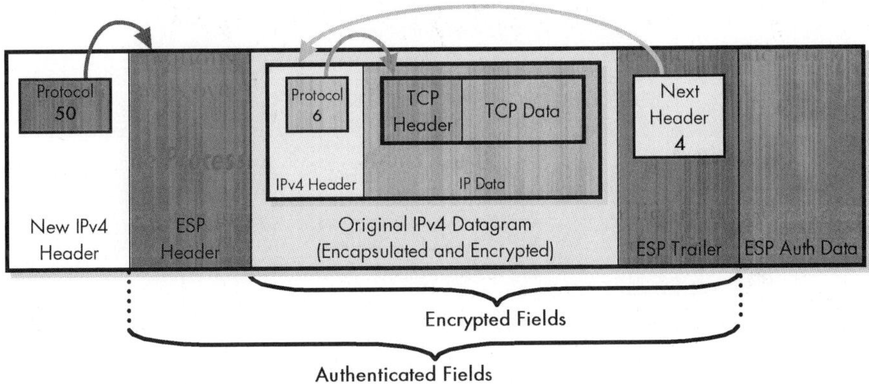

IPv4 ESP Datagram Format - IPsec Tunnel Mode

Figure 29-10: IPv4 datagram format with IPsec ESP *Here is the same sample IPv4 datagram that you saw in Figure 29-7. When ESP processes this datagram in transport mode, the ESP Header field is placed between the IPv4 header and data, with the ESP Trailer and ESP Authentication Data fields following. In tunnel mode, the entire original IPv4 datagram is surrounded by these ESP components, rather than just the IPv4 data. Again, as in Figure 29-9, note the encryption and authentication coverage, and how the Next Header field points back to specify the identity of the encrypted data or datagram.*

ESP Format

The format of the ESP sections and fields is described in Table 29-3 and illustrated in Figure 29-11. In both the figure and the table, I have shown the encryption and authentication coverage of the fields explicitly, to clarify how it all works.

Table 29-3: IPsec Encapsulating Security Payload (ESP) Format

Section	Field Name	Size (Bytes)	Description	Encryption Coverage	Authentication Coverage
ESP Header	SPI	4	A 32-bit value that is combined with the destination address and security protocol type to identify the SA that will be used for this datagram. (SAs are discussed earlier in this chapter.)		
	Sequence Number	4	A counter field initialized to zero when an SA is formed between two devices, and then incremented for each datagram that's sent using that SA. This is used to provide protection against replay attacks.		
Payload	Payload Data	Variable	The encrypted payload data, which consists of a higher-layer message or encapsulated IP datagram. It may also include support information such as an initialization vector that's required by certain encryption methods.		
ESP Trailer	Padding	Variable (0 to 255)	Additional padding bytes are included as needed for encryption or for alignment.		
	Pad Length	1	The number of bytes in the preceding Padding field.		
	Next Header	1	Contains the protocol number of the next header in the datagram. Used to chain together headers.		
ESP Authentication Data		Variable	Contains the ICV resulting from the application of the optional ESP authentication algorithm.		

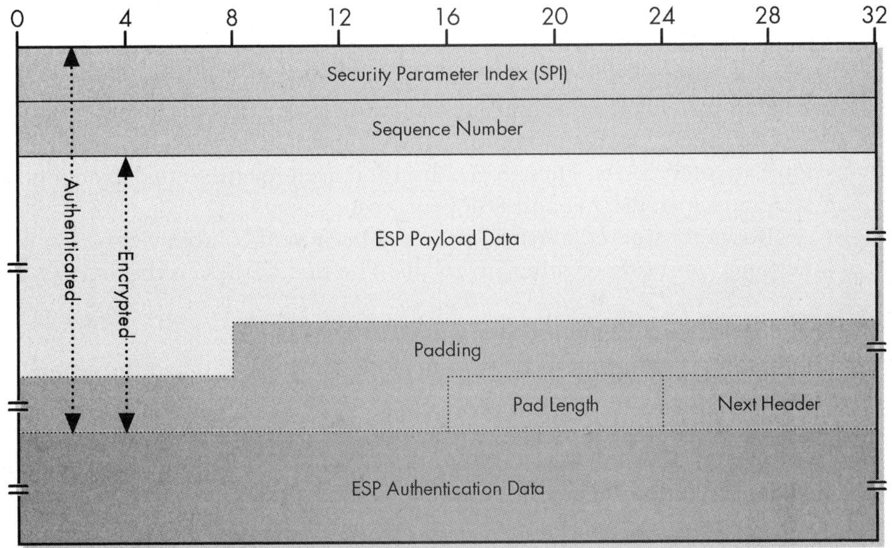

Figure 29-11: IPsec ESP format *Note that most of the fields and sections in this format are variable length. The exceptions are the SPI and Sequence Number fields, which are four bytes long, and the Pad Length and Next Header fields, which are one byte each.*

The Padding field is used when encryption algorithms require it. Padding is also used to make sure that the ESP Trailer field ends on a 32-bit boundary. That is, the size of the ESP Header field plus the Payload field, plus the ESP Trailer field must be a multiple of 32 bits. The ESP Authentication Data field must also be a multiple of 32 bits.

IPsec Internet Key Exchange (IKE)

IPsec, like many secure networking protocol sets, is based on the concept of a shared secret. Two devices that want to send information securely encode and decode it using a piece of information that only the devices know. Anyone who isn't in on the secret is able to intercept the information but is prevented either from reading it (if ESP is used to encrypt the payload) or from tampering with it undetected (if AH is used). Before either AH or ESP can be used, however, it is necessary for the two devices to exchange the secret that the security protocols themselves will use. The primary support protocol used for this purpose in IPsec is called *Internet Key Exchange (IKE)*.

IKE is defined in RFC 2409, and it is one of the more complicated of the IPsec protocols to comprehend. In fact, it is simply impossible to truly understand more than a real simplification of its operation without significant background in cryptography. I don't have a background in cryptography, and I must assume that you, my reader, do not either. So rather than fill this topic with baffling acronyms and unexplained concepts, I will just provide a brief outline of IKE and how it is used.

IKE Overview

The purpose of IKE is to allow devices to exchange information that's required for secure communication. As the title suggests, this includes cryptographic keys that are used for encoding authentication information and performing payload encryption. IKE works by allowing IPsec-capable devices to exchange SAs, which populate their SADs. These SADs are then used for the actual exchange of secured datagrams with the AH and ESP protocols.

IKE is considered a hybrid protocol because it combines (and supplements) the functions of three other protocols. The first of these is the *Internet Security Association and Key Management Protocol (ISAKMP)*. This protocol provides a framework for exchanging encryption keys and security association information. It operates by allowing security associations to be negotiated through a series of phases.

ISAKMP is a generic protocol that supports many different key exchange methods. In IKE, the ISAKMP framework is used as the basis for a specific key exchange method that combines features from two key exchange protocols:

OAKLEY Describes a specific mechanism for exchanging keys through the definition of various key exchange modes. Most of the IKE key exchange process is based on OAKLEY.

SKEME Describes a different key exchange mechanism than OAKLEY. IKE uses some features from SKEME, including its method of public key encryption and its fast rekeying feature.

IKE Operation

IKE doesn't strictly implement either OAKLEY or SKEME but takes bits of each to form its own method of using ISAKMP. Clear as mud, I know. Because IKE functions within the framework of ISAKMP, its operation is based on the ISAKMP phased-negotiation process. There are two phases, as follows:

ISAKMP Phase 1 The first phase is a setup stage where two devices agree on how to exchange further information securely. This negotiation between the two units creates an SA for ISAKMP itself: an *ISAKMP SA*. This security association is then used for securely exchanging more detailed information in Phase 2.

ISAKMP Phase 2 In this phase, the ISAKMP SA established in Phase 1 is used to create SAs for other security protocols. Normally, this is where the parameters for the "real" SAs for the AH and ESP protocols would be negotiated.

An obvious question is why IKE bothers with this two-phased approach. Why not just negotiate the SA for AH or ESP in the first place? Well, even though the extra phase adds overhead, multiple Phase 2 negotiations can be conducted after one Phase 1, which amortizes the extra cost of the two-phase approach. It is also possible to use a simpler exchange method for Phase 2 once the ISAKMP SA has been established in Phase 1.

The ISAKMP SA negotiated during Phase 1 includes the negotiation of the following attributes used for subsequent negotiations:

- An encryption algorithm, such as the *Data Encryption Standard (DES)*
- A hash algorithm (MD5 or SHA, as used by AH or ESP)
- An authentication method, such as authentication using previously shared keys
- A *Diffie-Hellman* group

NOTE *Diffie and Hellman were two pioneers in the industry who invented public-key cryptography. In this method, instead of encrypting and decrypting with the same key, data is encrypted using a public key that anyone can know, and decrypted using a private key that is kept secret. A Diffie-Hellman group defines the attributes of how to perform this type of cryptography. Four predefined groups derived from OAKLEY are specified in IKE, and provision is allowed for defining new groups as well.*

Note that even though SAs in general are unidirectional, the ISAKMP SA is established bidirectionally. Once Phase 1 is complete, either device can set up a subsequent SA for AH or ESP using the ISAKMP SA.

30

INTERNET PROTOCOL MOBILITY SUPPORT (MOBILE IP)

The Internet Protocol (IP) is the most successful network layer protocol in computing due to its many strengths, but it also has some weaknesses, most of which have become more important as networks has evolved over time. Technologies like classless addressing and Network Address Translation (NAT) combat the exhaustion of the IP version 4 (IPv4) address space, while IPsec provides it with the secure communications it lacks. Another weakness of IP is that it was not designed with mobile computers in mind.

While mobile devices can certainly use IP, the way that devices are addressed and datagrams routed causes a problem when they are moved from one network to another. At the time IP was developed, computers were large and rarely moved. Today, we have millions of notebook computers and smaller devices, some of which even use wireless networking to connect to the wired network. The importance of providing full IP capabilities for these mobile devices has grown dramatically. To support IP in a mobile environment, a new protocol called *IP Mobility Support*, or more simply, *Mobile IP*, was developed.

In this chapter, I describe the special protocol that was developed to overcome the problems with mobile computers attaching to IP internetworks. I begin with an overview of Mobile IP and a more detailed description of why it was created. I discuss important concepts that define Mobile IP and its general mode of operation. I then move on to some of the specifics of how Mobile IP works. This includes a description of the special Mobile IP addressing scheme, an explanation of how agents are discovered by mobile devices, a discussion of the process of registration with the device's home agent, and finally, an explanation of how data is encapsulated and routed. I discuss the impact that Mobile IP has on the operation of the TCP/IP Address Resolution Protocol (ARP). I end the chapter by examining some of the efficiency and security issues that come into play when Mobile IP is used.

NOTE *This section specifically describes how IP mobility support is provided for IPv4 networks. It does not deal with the more specific details for how mobility is implemented in IPv6.*

BACKGROUND INFORMATION *If you are not familiar with the basics of IP addressing and routing, I strongly suggest reading at least Chapters 16 and 23 before reading about Mobile IP.*

Mobile IP Overview, History, and Motivation

Mobile computing has greatly increased in popularity over the past several years, largely due to advances in miniaturization. Today, we can get the power that once required a hulking behemoth of a machine in a notebook PC or even a handheld computer. We also have wireless LAN (WLAN) technologies that easily let a device move from place to place and retain networking connectivity at the data link layer. Unfortunately, IP was developed back in the era of the behemoths, and it isn't designed to deal gracefully with computers that move around. To understand why IP doesn't work well in a mobile environment, you must take a look back at how IP addressing and routing work.

The Problem with Mobile Nodes in TCP/IP

If you've read any of the materials in this book on IP addressing—and I certainly hope that you have—you know that IP addresses are fundamentally divided into two portions: a network identifier (network ID) and a host identifier (host ID). The network ID specifies which network a host is on, and the host ID uniquely specifies hosts within a network. This structure is fundamental to datagram routing, because devices use the network ID portion of the destination address of a datagram to determine if the recipient is on a local network or a remote one, and routers use it to determine how to route the datagram.

This is a great system, but it has one critical flaw: The IP address is tied tightly to the network where the device is located. Most devices never (or at least rarely) change their attachment point to the network, so this is not a problem for them, but it is certainly an issue for a mobile device. When the mobile device travels away from its home location, the system of routing based on IP address breaks. This is illustrated in Figure 30-1.

The tight binding of network ID and host IP address means that there are only two real options under conventional IP when a mobile device moves from one network to another:

Change IP Address We can change the IP address of the host to a new address that includes the network ID of the network to which it is moving.

Decouple IP Routing from Address We can change the way routing is done for the device, so that instead of routers sending datagrams to a device based on its network ID, they route based on its entire address.

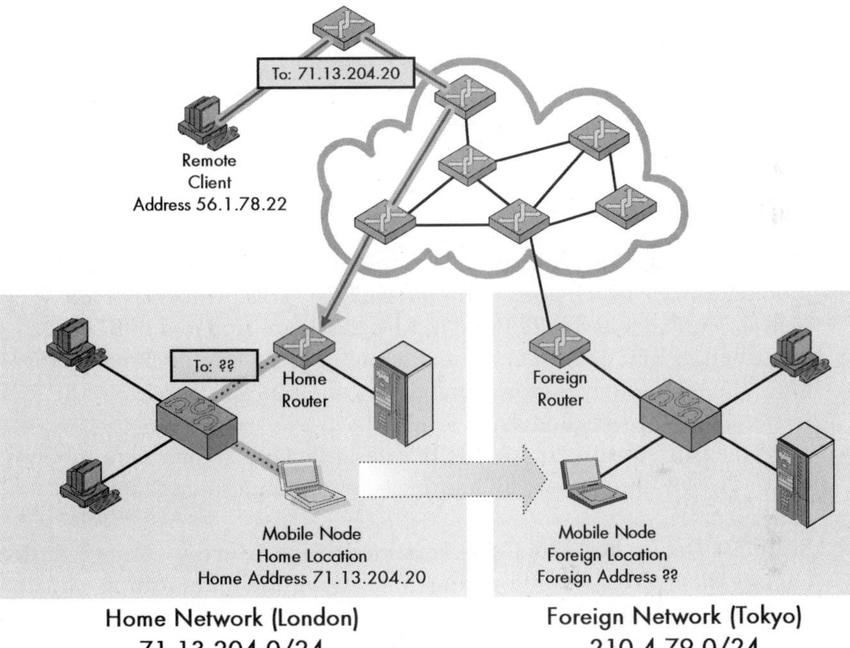

Figure 30-1: The main problem with mobile devices on IP internetworks *In this example, a mobile device (the notebook PC) has been moved from its home network in London to another network in Tokyo. A remote client (upper left) decides to send a datagram to the mobile device. However, it has no idea the device has moved. Since it sends by using the mobile node's home address, 71.13.204.20, its request is routed to the router responsible for that network, which is in London. The mobile device isn't there, so the router can't deliver it. Mobile IP solves this problem by giving mobile devices and routers the capability to forward datagrams from one location to another.*

These both seem like viable options at first glance, and if only a few devices tried them, they might work. Unfortunately, they are both inefficient, often impractical, and neither is scalable (practical when thousands or millions of devices try them) for these reasons:

- Changing the IP address each time a device moves is time-consuming and normally requires manual intervention. In addition, the entire TCP/IP stack would need to be restarted, thereby breaking any existing connections.

- If we change the mobile device's IP address, how do we communicate the change of address to other devices on the Internet? These devices will only have the mobile node's original home address, which means they won't be able to find it, even if we give it a new address matching its new location.
- Routing based on the entire address of a host would mean the entire Internet would be flooded with routing information for each and every mobile computer. Considering how much trouble has gone into developing technologies like classless addressing to reduce routing table entries, it's obvious this is a Pandora's box no one wants to touch.

KEY CONCEPT The basic problem with supporting mobile devices in IP internetworks is that routing is performed using the IP address. This means the IP address of a device is tied to the network where that the device is located. If a device changes networks, data sent to its old address cannot be delivered by conventional means. Traditional work-arounds, such as routing by the full IP address or changing IP addresses manually, often create more problems.

The Solution: Mobile IP

The solution to these difficulties was to define a new protocol especially to support mobile devices, which adds to the original IP. This protocol, called *IP Mobility Support for IPv4*, was first defined in RFC 2002, was updated in RFC 3220, and is now described in RFC 3344. The formal name given in that document title is rather long; the technology is more commonly called *Mobile IP*, both in the RFC itself and by networking professionals.

To ensure its success, Mobile IP's designers had to meet a number of important goals. The resulting protocol has these key attributes and features:

Seamless Device Mobility Using Existing Device Address Mobile devices can change their physical network attachment method and location while continuing to use their existing IP address.

No New Addressing or Routing Requirements The overall scheme for addressing and routing as in regular IP is maintained. IP addresses are still assigned in the conventional way by the owner of each device. No new routing requirements are placed on the internetwork, such as host-specific routes.

Interoperability Mobile IP devices can still send to and receive from existing IP devices that do not know how Mobile IP works, and vice versa.

Layer Transparency The changes made by Mobile IP are confined to the network layer. Transport layer and higher-layer protocols and applications are able to function as in regular IPv4, and existing connections can even be maintained across a move.

Limited Hardware Changes Changes are required to the mobile device's software as well as to routers used directly by the mobile device. Other devices, however, do not need changes, including routers between the ones on the home and visited networks.

Scalability Mobile IP allows a device to change from any network to any other, and supports this for an arbitrary number of devices. The scope of the connection change can be global; you could detach a notebook from an office in London and move it to Australia or Brazil, for example, and it will work the same as if you took it to the office next door.

Security Mobile IP works by redirecting messages, and includes authentication procedures to prevent an unauthorized device from causing problems.

Mobile IP accomplishes these goals by implementing a *forwarding system* for mobile devices. When a mobile unit is on its home network, it functions normally. When it moves to a different network, datagrams are sent from its home network to its new location. This allows normal hosts and routers that don't know about Mobile IP to continue to operate as if the mobile device had not moved. Special support services are required to implement Mobile IP; these services allow activities such as letting a mobile device determine where it is, telling the home network where to forward messages, and more.

KEY CONCEPT *Mobile IP* solves the problems associated with devices that change network locations by setting up a system whereby datagrams sent to the mobile node's home location are forwarded to it wherever it may be located. It is particularly useful for wireless devices, but can be used for any device that moves between networks periodically.

Mobile IP is often associated with wireless networks, since devices using WLAN technology can move so easily from one network to another. However, it wasn't designed specifically for wireless. It can be equally useful for moving from an Ethernet network in one building to a network in another building, city, or country. Mobile IP can be of great benefit in numerous applications for traveling salespeople, consultants who visit client sites, administrators who walk around a campus troubleshooting problems, and many more.

Limitations of Mobile IP

It's important to realize that Mobile IP has certain limitations in its usefulness in a wireless environment. It was designed to handle the mobility of devices, but only relatively infrequent mobility. This is due to the work involved with each change. This overhead isn't a big deal when you move a computer once a week, once a day, or even once an hour. It can be an issue for "real-time" mobility, such as roaming in a wireless network, where handoff functions operating at the data link layer may be more suitable. Mobile IP was designed under the specific assumption that the attachment point would not change more than once per second.

Mobile IP is intended to be used with devices that maintain a static IP configuration. Since the device needs to be able to always know the identity of its home network and normal IP address, it is much more difficult to use it with a device that obtains an IP address dynamically, using something like the Dynamic Host Configuration Protocol (DHCP).

Mobile IP Concepts and General Operation

I like analogies because they provide a way of explaining often dry technical concepts in terms that you can relate to. The problem of mobile devices in an IP internetwork can easily be compared to a real-life mobility and information transmission problem: mail delivery for those who travel.

Suppose you are a consultant working for a large corporation with many offices. Your home office is in London, England, and you spend about half your time there. The rest of the time is split between other offices in, say, Rome, Tokyo, New York City, and Toronto. You also occasionally visit client sites that can be just about anywhere in the world. You may be at these remote locations for weeks at a time.

The problem is how do you arrange things so that you can receive your mail regardless of your location? You have the same problem that regular IP has with a mobile device, and without taking special steps, you have the same two unsatisfactory options for resolving it: address changing or decoupling routing from your address. You can't change your address each time you move because you would be modifying it constantly; by the time you told everyone about your new address, it would change again. And you certainly can't "decouple" the routing of mail from your address, unless you want to set up your own postal system!

The solution to this dilemma is *mail forwarding*. Let's say that you leave London for Tokyo for a couple of months. You tell the London post office (PO) that you will be in Tokyo. They intercept mail headed for your normal London address, relabel it, and forward it to Tokyo. Depending on where you are staying, this mail might be redirected either straight to a new address in Tokyo or to a Tokyo PO where you can pick it up. If you leave Tokyo to go to another city, you just call the London PO and tell them your new location. When you come home, you cancel the forwarding and get your mail as always. (Yes, I'm assuming London and Tokyo each have only one PO.)

The advantages of this system are many. It is relatively simple to understand and implement. It is also transparent to everyone who sends you mail; they still send to you in London and it gets wherever it needs to go. And handling of the forwarding mechanism is done only by the London PO and possibly the PO where you are presently located; the rest of the postal system doesn't even know anything out of the ordinary is going on.

There are some disadvantages, too. The London PO may allow occasional forwarding for free, but would probably charge you if you did this on a regular basis. You might also need a special arrangement in the city you travel to. You need to keep communicating with your home PO each time you move. And every piece of mail must be sent through the system twice—first to London and then to wherever you are located—which is inefficient.

Mobile IP works in a manner very similar to the mail-forwarding system I just described. The traveling consultant is the device that goes from network to network. Each network can be considered like a different city, and the internetwork of routers is like the postal system. The router that connects any network to the Internet is like that network's post office, from an IP perspective.

The mobile node is normally resident on its home network, which is the one that is indicated by the network ID in its IP address. Devices on the internetwork always route using this address, so the pieces of "mail" (datagrams) always arrive at a router at the device's "home." When the device travels to another network, the home router ("post office") intercepts these datagrams and forwards them to the device's current address. It may send them straight to the device using a new, temporary address, or it may send them to a router on the device's current network (the "other post office" or Tokyo in our analogy) for final delivery. You can see an overview of Mobile IP operation in Figure 30-2.

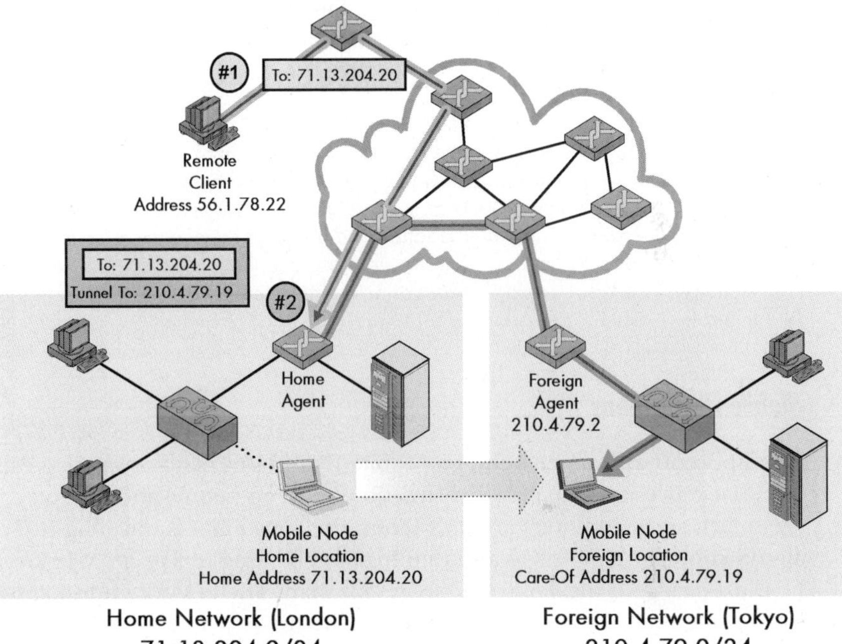

Figure 30-2: General operation of Mobile IP *This diagram is similar to Figure 30-1, except that it shows Mobile IP implemented. The mobile node's home router serves as home agent, and the router in Tokyo serves as the foreign agent. The mobile has been assigned a temporary "care-of" address to use while in Tokyo (which in this case is a co-located care-of address, meaning that it is assigned directly to the mobile node. Figure 30-3 shows the same example using the other type of care-of address). In step 1, the remote client sends a datagram to the mobile using its home address, as in normal TCP/IP. It arrives in London as usual. In step 2, the home agent encapsulates that datagram in a new one and sends it to the mobile node in Tokyo.*

Mobile IP Device Roles

As you can see, just as mail forwarding requires support from one or more POs, Mobile IP requires the help of two routers. The following special names are given to the three main players that implement the protocol (also shown in Figure 30-2):

Mobile Node This is the mobile device, the one moving around the internetwork.

Home Agent This is a router on the home network that is responsible for catching datagrams intended for the mobile node and forwarding them to it when it is traveling. It also implements other support functions that are necessary to run the protocol.

Foreign Agent This is a router on the network to which the mobile node is currently attached. It serves as a "home away from home" for the mobile node, and normally acts as its default router and implements Mobile IP functions. Depending on the mode of operation, it may receive forwarded datagrams from the home agent and forward them to the mobile node. It also supports the sharing of mobility information to make Mobile IP operate. The foreign agent may not be required in some Mobile IP implementations but is usually considered part of how the protocol operates.

> **KEY CONCEPT** Mobile IP operates by setting up the TCP/IP equivalent of a mail-forwarding system. A router on a *mobile node*'s home network serves as the mobile device's *home agent*, and one on its current network acts as the *foreign agent*. The home agent receives datagrams destined for the mobile's normal IP address and forwards them to the mobile node's current location, either directly or by sending the datagrams to the foreign agent. The home agent and foreign agent are also responsible for various communication and setup activities that are required for Mobile IP to work.

Mobile IP Functions

An important difference between Mobile IP and this mail-forwarding example is one that represents the classic distinction between people and computers: People are smart, and computers are not. When the consultant is traveling in Tokyo, he always knows he's in Tokyo and that his mail is being forwarded. He knows that he must deal with the Tokyo PO to get his mail. The PO in London knows what forwarding is all about and how to do it. The traveler and the POs can communicate easily using the telephone.

In contrast, in the computer world, when a device travels using Mobile IP, things are more complicated. Let's suppose the consultant flies to Tokyo, turns on his notebook, and plugs it in to the network. When the notebook is first turned on, it has no clue what is going on. The notebook has to figure out that it is in Tokyo. It needs to find a foreign agent in Tokyo. It needs to know what address to use while in Tokyo. It needs to communicate with its home agent back in London to tell it that it is in Tokyo and that the agent should start forwarding datagrams. Furthermore, it must accomplish its communication without any telephone.

To this end, Mobile IP includes a host of special functions that are used to set up and manage datagram forwarding. To see how these support functions work, let's look at the general operation of Mobile IP as a simplified series of steps:

1. **Agent Communication** The mobile node finds an agent on its local network by engaging in the *Agent Discovery* process. It listens for Agent Advertisement messages that are sent out by agents, and from this it can determine where it is located. If it doesn't hear these messages it can ask for one using an Agent Solicitation message.

2. **Network Location Determination** The mobile node determines whether it is on its home network or on a foreign one by looking at the information in the Agent Advertisement message.

If it is on its home network, it functions using regular IP. To show how the rest of the process works, let's say the device sees that it just moved to a foreign network. The remaining steps are as follows:

1. **Care-Of Address Acquisition** The device obtains a temporary address called a *care-of address.* This either comes from the Agent Advertisement message from the foreign agent or through some other means. This address is used only as the destination point for forwarding datagrams, and for no other purpose.
2. **Agent Registration** The mobile node informs the home agent on its home network of its presence on the foreign network and enables datagram forwarding by *registering* with the home agent. This may be done either directly between the node and the home agent or indirectly using the foreign agent as a conduit.
3. **Datagram Forwarding** The home agent captures datagrams intended for the mobile node and forwards them. It may send them either directly to the node or indirectly to the foreign agent for delivery, depending on the type of care-of address in use.

Datagram forwarding continues until the current agent registration expires. The device can then renew it. If it moves again, it repeats the process to get a new care-of address and then registers its new location with the home agent. When the mobile node returns to its home network, it *deregisters* to cancel datagram forwarding and resumes normal IP operation.

The following sections look in more detail at the functions summarized in each of the previous steps.

Mobile IP Addressing: Home and Care-Of Addresses

Just as most of us have only a single address used for mail, most IP devices have only a single address. Our traveling consultant, however, needs to have two addresses; a normal one and one that is used while he is away. Continuing the earlier analogy, the Mobile IP–equipped notebook the consultant carries needs to have two addresses:

Home Address The normal, permanent IP address assigned to the mobile node. This is the address used by the device on its home network, and the one to which datagrams intended for the mobile node are always sent.

Care-Of Address A secondary, temporary address used by a mobile node while it is traveling away from its home network. It is a normal 32-bit IP address in most respects, but is used only by Mobile IP for forwarding IP datagrams and for administrative functions. Higher layers never use it, nor do regular IP devices when creating datagrams.

The care-of address is a slightly tricky concept. There are two different types, which correspond to two distinctly different methods of forwarding datagrams from the home agent router.

Foreign Agent Care-Of Address

The care-of address is provided by a foreign agent in its *Agent Advertisement* message. It is, in fact, the IP address of the foreign agent itself. When this type of care-of address is used, all datagrams captured by the home agent are not relayed directly to the mobile node, but indirectly to the foreign agent, which is responsible for final delivery. In this arrangement, the mobile node has no distinct IP address valid on the foreign network, so this is typically done using a layer 2 technology. This arrangement is illustrated in Figure 30-3.

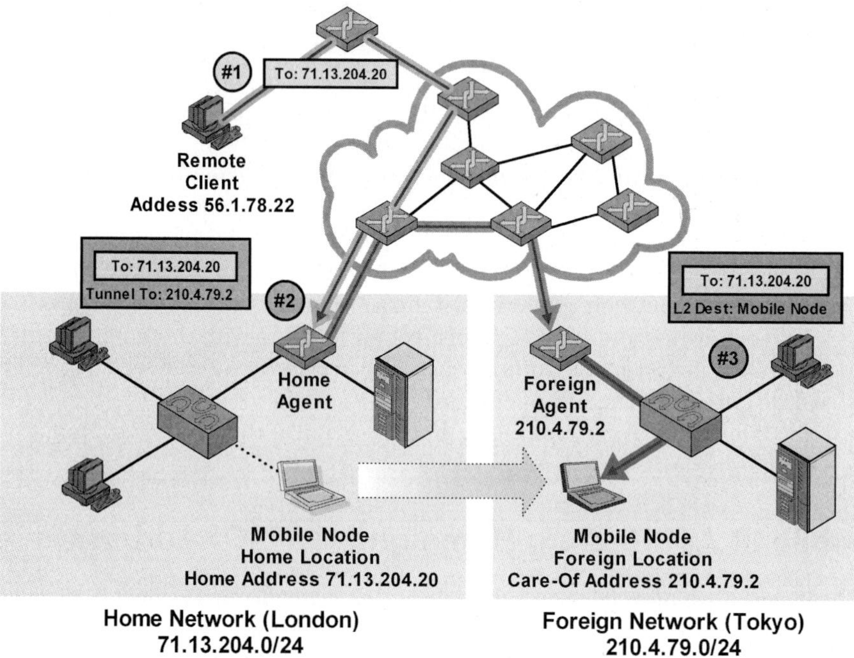

Figure 30-3: Mobile IP operation with a foreign agent care-of address *This diagram is similar to Figure 30-2, except that instead of the mobile node having a co-located (distinct) IP address, here the mobile node is using a foreign agent care-of address. This means that the node's care-of address is actually that of the foreign agent itself. Step 1 is the same as in Figure 30-2, but in step 2, the home agent forwards not to the mobile node directly, but to the foreign agent (since that router is the one whose IP address the mobile is using). In step 3, the foreign agent strips off the home agent's packaging and delivers the original datagram to the mobile node. This is typically done using whatever layer 2 (LAN or WLAN) technology connects the mobile node and foreign agent.*

In the consultant analogy, this type of care-of address is like forwarding from the London PO to the Tokyo PO. The London personnel would take a letter for John Smith sent to his London address, and repackage it for delivery to John Smith, care of the Tokyo post office. The Tokyo PO (or John Smith himself) would need to worry about the last leg of the delivery.

Co-Located Care-Of Address

The co-located care-of address is assigned directly to the mobile node using some means that is external to Mobile IP. For example, it may be assigned on the foreign network manually, or it may be assigned automatically using DHCP. In this situation, the care-of address is used to forward traffic from the home agent directly to the mobile node. This was the type of address shown earlier in Figure 30-2.

In the consultant analogy, this is like John Smith obtaining a temporary address for his use while in Tokyo. The London PO would forward directly to his Tokyo address. They would not specifically send it to the Tokyo PO (although that PO would handle the mail at some point).

> **KEY CONCEPT** In Mobile IP, each mobile device uses a temporary care-of address while on a foreign network. A co-located care-of address is one that is assigned directly to the mobile node and enables direct delivery of datagrams to the node. The alternative is to use a foreign agent care-of address. In this situation, the mobile node actually uses the IP address of the foreign agent. Datagrams are sent to the foreign agent, which delivers them to the mobile node.

Advantages and Disadvantages of the Care-Of Address Types

The foreign agent care-of address is considered the type used in classic Mobile IP, where there is both a home agent and a foreign agent. While it seems less efficient than the co-located address method, it offers some important advantages, a key one being that the same foreign agent care-of address can be used for all mobile nodes visiting that network. Datagrams for all mobile nodes on that network are sent to the foreign agent, which completes the delivery to the individual nodes. Since the mobile nodes use the foreign agent's address, no extra addresses or extra work is required for each mobile node.

The co-located care-of address has the advantage that traffic can be forwarded directly from the home agent to the mobile node. In this type of arrangement, it is possible for a Mobile IP device to travel to a foreign network where there is no Mobile IP–aware router to act as a foreign agent. This does mean, however, that the Mobile IP implementation must include all the functions of communicating with the home agent that the foreign agent normally performs.

When co-located care-of addresses are used, an issue is how the temporary address is obtained. In many foreign networks, automatic assignment of an IP address using something like DHCP may be possible, but if not, a temporary IP address would need to be assigned. Either way, some of the foreign network's limited IP address space would need to be set aside for mobile nodes, each of which would use an address while present on the network. In some cases, this could lead to an address depletion issue.

Foreign agent care-of addressing is usually preferred due to its more automatic nature, when a foreign agent is present on the visited network. Considering that all datagrams will need to go through some router on the foreign network to reach the mobile node anyway, we might as well save the extra IP addresses. Co-located care-of addresses would be used when there is no foreign agent, or might be practical for long-term connections even when a foreign agent is present.

KEY CONCEPT In Mobile IP, *co-located care-of addresses* have the advantage of flexibility, but require each device to have a unique IP address on the remote network. Foreign agent care-of addresses have the chief advantage of allowing many mobile devices on a foreign network without each requiring a distinct IP address.

Remember that the care-of address represents only the destination to which mobile node datagrams are forwarded. Foreign agents provide services other than forwarding, so it is possible for a mobile node to use a co-located care-of address even when a foreign agent is present, while continuing to take advantage of the other foreign agent services.

For more information on how datagrams are forwarded between the home agent and the mobile node's care-of address, see the section on Mobile IP encapsulation and tunneling, later in this chapter.

Mobile IP Agent Discovery

When a mobile node is first turned on, it cannot assume that it is still at home, the way normal IP devices do. It must first determine where it is, and if it is not at home, begin the process of setting up datagram forwarding from its home network. This process is accomplished by communicating with a local router that's serving as an agent through the process called *Agent Discovery*.

Agent Discovery Process

Agent discovery encompasses the first three steps in the simplified five-step Mobile IP operational summary I gave earlier in discussing general Mobile IP operation. The main goals of Agent Discovery include the following:

Agent/Node Communication Agent Discovery is the method by which a mobile node first establishes contact with an agent on the local network to which it is attached. Messages containing important information about the agent are sent from the agent to the node. A message can also be sent from the node to the agent asking for this information to be sent.

Orientation The node uses the Agent Discovery process to determine where it is. Specifically, it learns whether it is on its home network or a foreign network by identifying the agent that sends it messages.

Care-Of Address Assignment The Agent Discovery process is the method used to tell a mobile node the care-of address it should use, when foreign agent care-of addressing is used.

Mobile IP agents are routers that have been given additional programming to make them Mobile IP-aware. The communication between a mobile node and the agent on its local network is basically the same as the normal communication required between a device on an IP network and its local router, except more information needs to be sent when the router is an agent.

Agent Advertisement and Agent Solicitation Messages

Provision already exists for exchanges of data between a router and a node in the form of Internet Control Message Protocol (ICMP) messages that are used for the regular IP *Router Discovery* process. Two messages are used for this purpose: Router Advertisement messages that let routers tell local nodes that they exist and describe their capabilities, and Router Solicitation messages that let a node prompt a router to send an advertisement. These are described in Chapter 33.

Given the similarity to normal Router Discovery, it made sense to implement Agent Discovery as a modification to the existing process rather than set up a whole new system. The messages used in the Agent Discovery process are as follows:

Agent Advertisement This is a message transmitted regularly by a router acting as a Mobile IP agent. It consists of a regular Router Advertisement message that has one or more *extensions* added that contain Mobile IP–specific information for mobile nodes.

Agent Solicitation This message can be sent by a Mobile IP device to nudge a local agent to send an Agent Advertisement message.

The use of these messages is described in the Mobile IP standard in detail, and unsurprisingly, is very similar to how regular Router Advertisement and Router Solicitation messages are employed. Agents are normally configured to send out Agent Advertisements on a regular basis, with the rate set to ensure reasonably fast contact with mobile nodes without consuming excessive network bandwidth. They are required to respond to any Agent Solicitation messages they receive by sending an Advertisement. It is possible that some agents may be configured to send Advertisements only upon receipt of a Solicitation.

Mobile nodes are required to accept and process Agent Advertisements. They distinguish these from regular Router Advertisements by looking at the size of the message. They then parse the extension(s) to learn the capabilities of the local agent. They determine whether they are on their home network or a foreign network, and in the case of a foreign agent, how the agent should be used. Mobile nodes are required to use Agent Advertisements to detect when they have moved, using one of two algorithms defined in the standard. Mobile nodes are also required to detect when they have returned to their home network after they have been traveling. Finally, they are also required to be able to send Agent Solicitation messages if they don't receive an Agent Advertisement after a certain period of time. They are restricted to sending these only infrequently, however, in order to keep traffic manageable.

Now let's look at the formats of the two message types.

Agent Solicitation Message Format

The Agent Solicitation message is simple. In fact, there is no new message format defined for this at all; it is identical to the format of a Router Solicitation message (see Chapter 33).

The reason no new message type is required here is that a solicitation is an extremely simple message: "Hey, if there are any routers out there, please tell me who you are and what you can do." No extra Mobile IP information needs to be sent. When a regular IP router receives a Router Solicitation, it will send a Router Advertisement, but a Mobile IP router automatically sends the longer Agent Advertisement instead when prompted by any solicitation, whether it comes from a Mobile IP node or a regular IP device.

Agent Advertisement Message Format

The Agent Advertisement begins with the normal fields of an ICMP Router Advertisement message (see Chapter 33). The destination of the message is either the "all devices" multicast address (224.0.0.1) if multicast is supported on the local network, or the broadcast address (255.255.255.255) otherwise. The *Router Address* fields are filled in with the address(es) of the agent.

NOTE *It is possible that a device may wish to advertise its ability to handle Mobile IP messages, but not act as a regular router. In this case it changes the normal Code field in the header of the Router Advertisement message from 0 to 16.*

Following the regular fields, one or more extensions are added:

Mobility Agent Advertisement Extension This is the main extension used to convey Mobile IP capabilities of the agent to mobile nodes on the local network. This field is described in Tables 30-1 and 30-2 and illustrated in Figure 30-4.

Prefix-Lengths Extension This is an optional extension that tells a mobile node the prefix length(s) of the router address(es) contained in the regular portion of the Agent Advertisement message; that is, the Router Address field in the regular Router Advertisement part of the message. The prefix length is another term for the number of bits of a network ID in an address, so this specifies the network ID in the router addresses. This field is described in Table 30-3 and illustrated in Figure 30-5.

One-Byte Padding Extension Some implementations require ICMP messages to be an even number of bytes, so a byte of padding is needed. This field is just a single byte of all zeros.

KEY CONCEPT Mobile IP *Agent Discovery* is the process by which a mobile node determines where it is located and establishes contact with a home or foreign agent. To indicate their capabilities, routers that can function as agents regularly send *Agent Advertisement* messages, which are modified versions of regular *Router Advertisements*. To request the sending of an *Advertisement*, a mobile node can also send an *Agent Solicitation*, which is the same as a regular *Router Solicitation*.

I should point out that Mobile IP does not include any provisions for the authentication of *Agent Advertisement* and *Agent Solicitation* messages. They may be authenticated using IPsec, if that has been implemented.

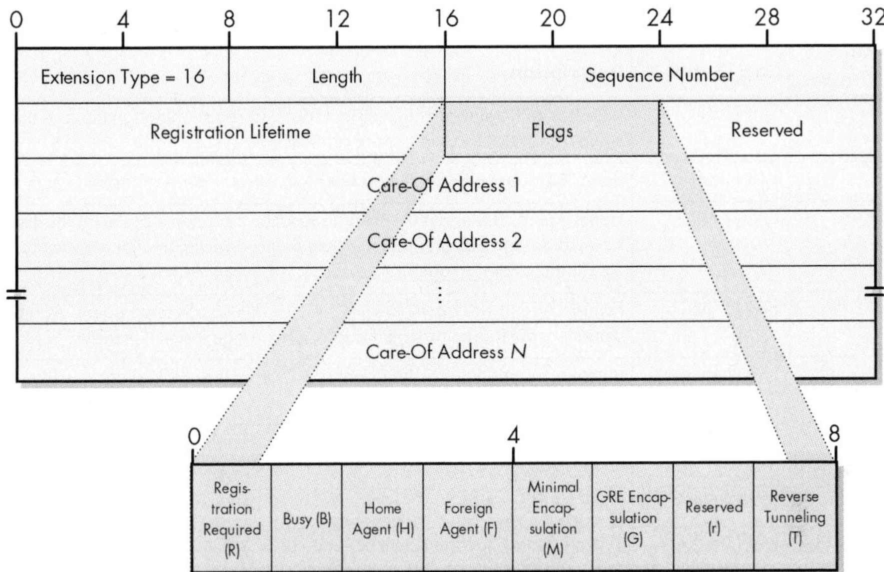

Figure 30-4: Mobile IP Mobility Agent Advertisement Extension format *This extension appears after the normal fields of a* Router Advertisement *message, as shown in Chapter 33.*

Table 30-1: Mobile IP Mobility Agent Advertisement Extension Format

Field Name	Size (Bytes)	Description
Type	1	Identifies the Agent Advertisement extension type. For the Mobility Agent Advertisement Extension, it is set to 16.
Length	1	Length of the extension in bytes, excluding the Type and Length fields. Thus, it is equal to 6 plus 4 for each care-of address in the message.
Sequence Number	2	A sequential counter is set to zero when the router initializes and then incremented for each advertisement sent out.
Registration Lifetime	2	The maximum length of time, in seconds, that the agent is willing to accept for registration requests. A value of 65,535 (all ones) means infinite. Note that this field is for registration only and has no relation to the regular Lifetime field in the regular Router Advertisement part of the message.
Flags	1	A one-byte field containing several informational flags that convey specific information about the agent's capabilities and status. There are seven one-bit flags, which, when set, convey the meanings shown in Table 30-2.
Reserved	1	Sent as zero and ignored by recipient.
Care-Of Addresses	Variable (4 per address)	Zero or more addresses provided by a foreign agent for a mobile node to use as a foreign agent care-of address. A foreign agent must always provide at least one address in its advertisement. A router that cannot act as a foreign agent will typically omit this field.

Table 30-2: Mobile IP Mobility Agent Advertisement Extension Flags

Subfield Name	Size (Bytes)	Description
R	1/8 (1 bit)	Registration Required: The mobile node must register through the foreign agent, even when using a co-located care-of address.
B	1/8 (1 bit)	Busy: The agent is currently too busy to accept further registrations from mobile nodes.
H	1/8 (1 bit)	Home Agent: The agent is willing to function as a home agent on this link (it will forward datagrams, and so on). Note that a device can offer services as both a home agent and a foreign agent.
F	1/8 (1 bit)	Foreign Agent: The agent is willing to function as a foreign agent. Again, a device can act as both a home agent and a foreign agent simultaneously.
M	1/8 (1 bit)	Minimal Encapsulation: The agent can receive tunneled datagrams using minimal encapsulation.
G	1/8 (1bit)	GRE Encapsulation: The agent can receive tunneled datagrams using GRE encapsulation.
r	1/8 (1 bit)	Reserved: Not used; sent as zero.
T	1/8 (1 bit)	Reverse Tunneling: The agent supports reverse tunneling.

Table 30-3: Mobile IP Prefix-Lengths Extension Format

Field Name	Size (Bytes)	Description
Type	1	Identifies the Agent Advertisement extension type. For the Prefix-Lengths Extension, it is set to 19.
Length	1	Length of the extension in bytes, excluding the Type and Length fields. Thus, it is equal to the number of prefix lengths (since each takes 1 byte).
Prefix Lengths	Variable (1 per length)	One prefix length number for each router address in the regular, Router Advertisement portion of the Agent Advertisement.

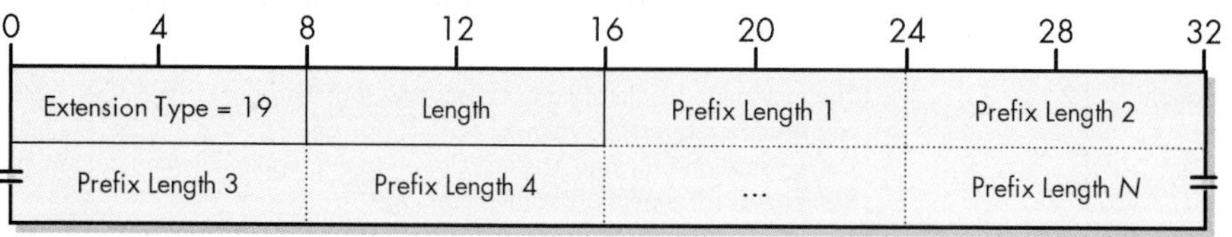

Figure 30-5: Mobile IP Prefix-Lengths Extension format *This extension appears after the normal fields of a Router Advertisement message, as shown in Chapter 33.*

See the section on Mobile IP encapsulation later in this chapter for details on minimal and Generic Routing Encapsulation (GRE) encapsulation and reverse tunneling.

Mobile IP Home Agent Registration and Registration Messages

Once a mobile node has completed Agent Discovery, it knows whether it is on its home network or a foreign network. If it's on its home network, it communicates as a regular IP device, but if it's on a foreign network, it must activate Mobile IP. This requires that it communicate with its home agent so that information and instructions can be exchanged between the two. This process is called *home agent registration*, or more simply, just *registration*.

The main purpose of registration is to actually start Mobile IP working. The mobile node must contact the home agent and tell it that it is on a foreign network and request that datagram forwarding be turned on. It also must let the home agent know its care-of address so the home agent knows where to send the forwarded datagrams. The home agent needs to communicate various types of information back to the mobile node when registration is performed. Note that the foreign agent is not really involved in registration, except perhaps to relay messages.

Mobile Node Registration Events

Successful registration establishes what is called in the standard a *mobility binding* between a home agent and a mobile node. For the duration of the registration, the mobile node's regular home address is tied to its current care-of address, and the home agent will encapsulate and forward datagrams addressed to the home address over to the care-of address. The mobile node is supposed to manage its registration and handle various events using the following actions:

Registration The mobile node initiates a *registration* when it first detects it has moved from its home network to a foreign network.

Deregistration When the mobile node returns home, it should tell the home agent to cancel forwarding—a process called *deregistration*.

Reregistration If the mobile node moves from one foreign network to another, or if its care-of address changes, it must update its registration with the home agent. It also must do so if its current registration is about to expire, even if it remains stationary on one foreign network.

Each registration is established only for a specific length of time, which is why regular reregistration is required whether or not the device moves. Registrations are time-limited to ensure that they do not become stale. If, for example, a node forgets to deregister when it returns home, the datagram forwarding will eventually stop when the registration expires.

Registration Request and Registration Reply Messages

To perform registration, two new message types have been defined in Mobile IP: the *Registration Request* and the *Registration Reply*. Each of these does what you would expect from its name. Interestingly, these are not ICMP messages like the ones used in Agent Discovery; they are User Datagram Protocol (UDP) messages. Thus, technically speaking, registration is performed at a higher layer than the rest of Mobile IP communication. Agents listen for Registration Requests on well-known UDP port 434, and respond back to mobile nodes using whatever ephemeral port the node used to send the message.

Registration Process

There are two different procedures defined for registration, depending on the type of care-of address used by the mobile node, and other specifics that I will get into shortly. The first is the direct registration method, which has only two steps:

1. The mobile node sends a Registration Request to the home agent.
2. The home agent sends a Registration Reply back to the mobile node.

In some cases, however, a slightly more complex process is required, whereby the foreign agent conveys messages between the home agent and the mobile node. In this situation, the process has four steps:

1. The mobile node sends a Registration Request to the foreign agent.
2. The foreign agent processes a Registration Request and forwards it to the home agent.
3. The home agent sends a Registration Reply to a foreign agent.
4. The foreign agent processes a Registration Reply and sends back to the mobile node.

The first, simpler method is normally used when a mobile node is using a co-located care-of address. In that situation, the node can easily communicate directly with the home agent, and the mobile node is also set up to directly receive information and datagrams from the home agent. When there is no foreign agent, this is obviously the only method available. It is also obviously the only method when a mobile node is deregistering with its home agent after it arrives back on the home network.

The second method is required when a mobile node is using a foreign care-of address. You'll recall that in this situation, the mobile node doesn't have its own unique IP address at all; it is using a shared address that was given to it by the foreign agent, which precludes direct communication between the node and the home agent. Also, if a mobile node receives an Agent Advertisement with the R flag set, it also should go through the foreign agent, even if it has a co-located care-of address.

Note that the foreign agent really is just a middleman; the exchange is still really between the home agent and the mobile node. However, the foreign agent can deny registration if the request violates whatever rules are in place for using the foreign network. It is for this reason that some foreign agents may require that they be the conduits for registrations even if the mobile node has a co-located care-of address. Of course, if the foreign agent can't contact the home agent the registration will not be able to proceed.

KEY CONCEPT Mobile IP *home agent registration* is the process by which a *mobility binding* is created between a home agent and a traveling mobile node to enable datagram forwarding to be performed. The mobile node that sends a Registration Request message performs registration, and the home agent returns a Registration Reply. The foreign agent may be required to act as a middleman in order to facilitate the transaction, but is otherwise not involved.

The previous description is really a highly simplified explanation of the basics of registration. The Mobile IP standard specifies many more details on exactly how agents and nodes perform registration, including particulars on when requests and replies are sent, how to handle various special conditions such as invalid requests, rules for how home agents maintain a table of mobility bindings, and much more. The standard covers the definition of extensions to the regular registration messages that support authentication, which is required for secure communications (see the section on security issues later in this chapter for more details). It also includes the ability to have a mobile node that maintains more than one concurrent binding, when needed.

Registration Request Message Format

Registration Request messages have the format shown in Tables 30-4 and Table 30-5 and illustrated in Figure 30-6. See the section on Mobile IP encapsulation later in this chapter for details on minimal and GRE encapsulation and reverse tunneling.

Table 30-4: Mobile IP Registration Request Message Format

Field Name	Size (Bytes)	Description
Type	1	Identifies the registration message type. For a request, this field is 1.
Flags	1	A one-byte field containing several informational flags that convey specific requests that are being made by the mobile node to the home agent. When set, the flags conveys the meanings shown in Table 30-5.
Lifetime	2	Length of time, in seconds, that the mobile node requests from the home agent for this registration.
Home Address	4	The home (normal) IP address of the mobile node when on its home network. Uniquely identifies the device regardless of how the request is conveyed to the home agent.
Home Agent	4	The IP address of the device acting as the mobile node's home agent.
Care-Of Address	4	The IP address being used by the mobile node as its care-of address.
Identification	8	A 64-bit number that uniquely identifies the *Registration Request* and is used to match requests to replies. It also provides protection against replay attacks; see the section on Mobile IP security issues later in this chapter for more information.
Extensions	Variable	Extension fields are included here for authentication of the request. Other extensions may also be included.

Table 30-5: Registration Request Flags

Subfield Name	Size (Bytes)	Description
S	1/8 (1 bit)	Simultaneous Bindings: Mobile node requests that prior mobility bindings be retained in addition to the one in the current request.
B	1/8 (1 bit)	Broadcast Datagrams: Mobile node requests that broadcasts on the home network be forwarded to it.
D	1/8 (1 bit)	Decapsulation by Mobile Node: Mobile node is telling the home agent that it will itself decapsulate encapsulated datagrams, as opposed to a foreign agent. In other words, when this is one, the mobile node is using a co-located care-of address; when zero, it is using a foreign agent care-of address.
M	1/8 (1 bit)	Minimal Encapsulation: Mobile node requests that home agent use minimal encapsulation for forwarded datagrams.
G	1/8 (1 bit)	GRE Encapsulation: Mobile node requests that home agent use GRE encapsulation for forwarded datagrams.
r	1/8 (1bit)	Reserved: Not used; sent as zero.
T	1/8 (1 bit)	Reverse Tunneling: Mobile node requests that reverse tunneling be used by the home agent.
x	1/8 (1 bit)	Reserved: Not used; sent as zero.

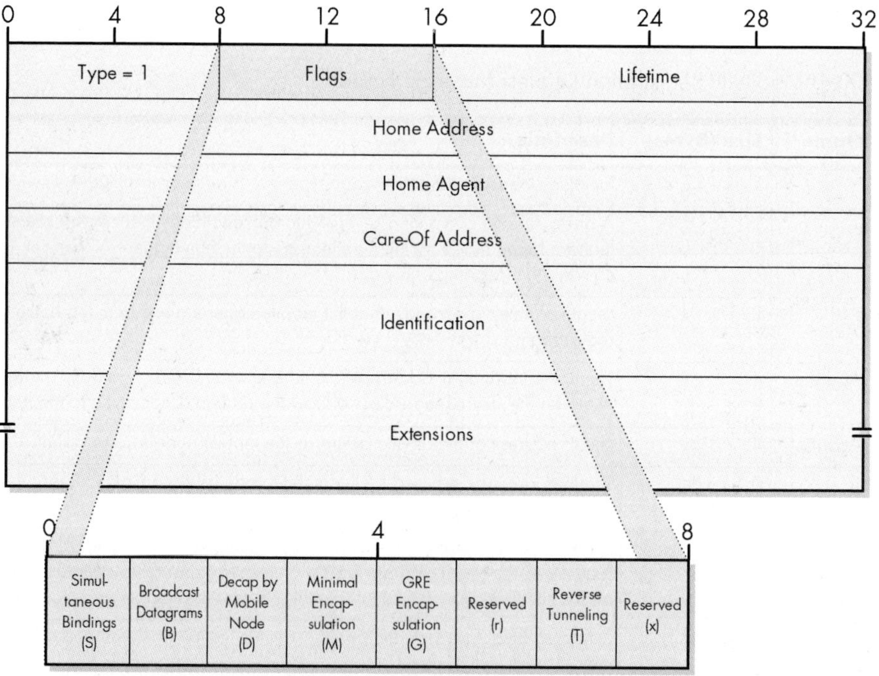

Figure 30-6: Mobile IP Registration Request message format *This message is carried in the payload of a User Datagram Protocol (UDP) message, the headers of which are not shown.*

Registration Reply Message Format

Registration Reply messages are formatted as shown in Table 30-6 and illustrated in Figure 30-7.

Table 30-6: Mobile IP Registration Reply Message Format

Field Name	Size (Bytes)	Description
Type	1	Identifies the registration message type. For a reply, this field is 3.
Code	1	Indicates the result of the registration request. This field is set to 0 if the registration was accepted, 1 if it was accepted but simultaneous bindings were requested and are not supported. If the registration was denied, a different reason code is provided that indicates the reason for the rejection, as well as whether it was the home agent or foreign agent that denied it.
Lifetime	2	If the registration was accepted, this represents the length of time in seconds until the registration expires. This may be a different value than the mobile node requested.
Home Address	4	The home (normal) IP address of the mobile node when it's on its home network. Uniquely identifies the device regardless of how the request is conveyed to the home agent so that the message can be delivered to it if the same foreign agent serves multiple mobile nodes.
Home Agent	4	The IP address of the device acting as the mobile node's home agent.
Identification	8	A 64-bit number that uniquely identifies the *Registration Reply* and is matched to the Identification field of the request that precipitated it.
Extensions	Variable	Extension fields are included here for the authentication of the reply. Other extensions may also be included.

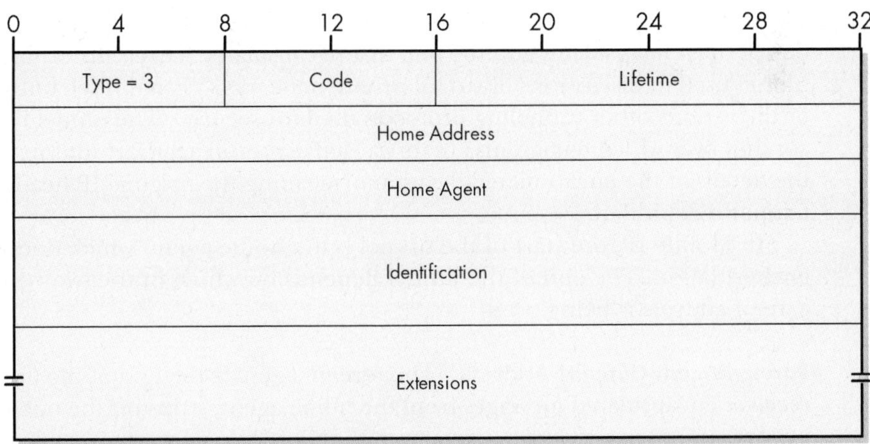

Figure 30-7: Mobile IP Registration Reply Message format *This message is carried in the payload of a UDP message, the headers of which are not shown.*

Mobile IP Data Encapsulation and Tunneling

Once a mobile node on a foreign network has completed a successful registration with its home agent, the Mobile IP datagram forwarding process described earlier in this chapter will be fully "activated." The home agent will intercept datagrams intended for the mobile node as they are routed to its home network, and forward them to the mobile node. Encapsulating the datagrams, and then sending them to the node's care-of address, does this.

Encapsulation is required because each datagram that you intercept and forward needs to be resent over the network to the device's care-of address. In theory, the designers might conceivably have done this by just having the home agent change the destination address and stick it back out on the network, but there are various complications that make this unwise. It makes more sense to take the entire datagram and wrap it in a new set of headers before retransmitting. In my mail-forwarding analogy, this is comparable to taking a letter received for the traveling consultant and putting it into a fresh envelope for forwarding, as opposed to just crossing off the original address and putting a new one on.

The default encapsulation process used in Mobile IP is called *IP Encapsulation within IP*, which is as it's defined in RFC 2003. It's commonly abbreviated *IP-in-IP*. It is a relatively simple method that describes how to take an IP datagram and make it the payload of another IP datagram. In Mobile IP, the new headers specify how to send the encapsulated datagram to the mobile node's care-of address.

In addition to IP-in-IP, the following two encapsulation methods may be optionally used: *Minimal Encapsulation within IP*, which is defined in RFC 2004, and *Generic Routing Encapsulation (GRE)*, which is defined in RFC 1701. To use either of these, the mobile node must request the appropriate method in its Registration Request, and the home agent must agree to use it. If foreign agent care-of addressing is used, the foreign agent also must support the method desired.

Mobile IP Conventional Tunneling

The encapsulation process creates a logical construct called a *tunnel* between the device that encapsulates and the one that decapsulates. This is the same idea of a tunnel used in discussions of virtual private networks (VPNs), IPsec tunnel mode, or the various other tunneling protocols used for security. The tunnel represents a conduit over which datagrams are forwarded across an arbitrary internetwork, with the details of the encapsulated datagram (meaning the original IP headers) temporarily hidden.

In Mobile IP, the start of the tunnel is the home agent, which does the encapsulation. The end of the tunnel depends on which of the two types of care-of address is being used:

Foreign Agent Care-Of Address The foreign agent is the end of the tunnel. It receives encapsulated messages from the home agent, strips off the outer IP header, and then delivers the datagram to the mobile node. This is generally done using layer 2, because the mobile node and foreign agent are on the same local network, and the mobile node does not have its own IP address on that network, because it is using the foreign agent's address.

Co-Located Care-Of Address The mobile node itself is the end of the tunnel and strips off the outer header.

Normally, the tunnel described previously is used only for datagrams that have been sent to the mobile node and captured by the home agent. When the mobile node wants to send a datagram, it doesn't tunnel it back to the home agent; this would be needlessly inefficient. Instead, it just sends out the datagram directly using whatever router it can find on its current network, which may or may not be a foreign agent. When it does this, it uses its own home address as the source address for any requests it sends. As a result, any response to those requests will go back to the home network. This sets up a triangle of three transmissions for these kinds of transactions (illustrated in Figure 30-8):

1. The mobile node sends a request from the foreign network to some third-party device somewhere on the internetwork.
2. The third-party device responds back to the mobile node. However, this sends the reply back to the model node's home address on its home network.
3. The home agent intercepts the response on the home network and tunnels it back to the mobile node.

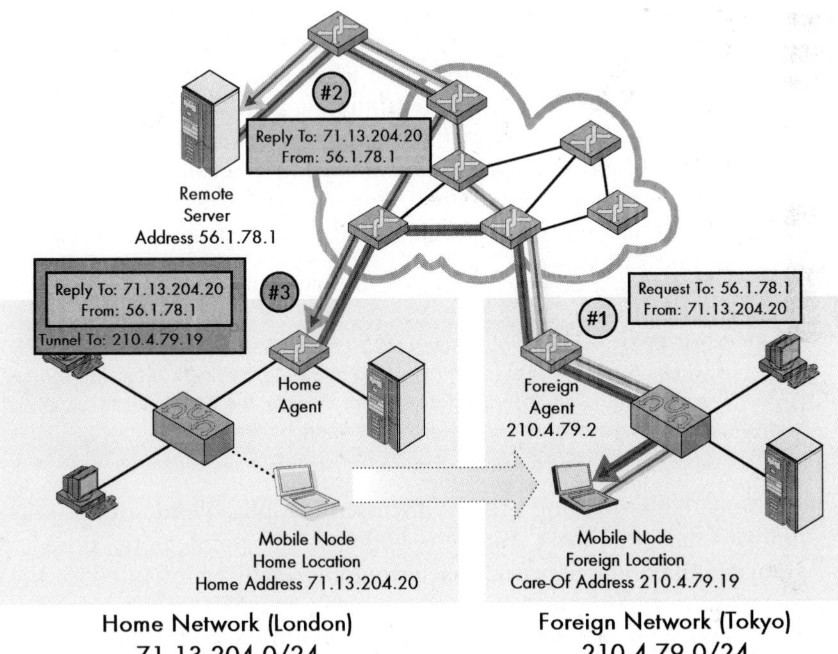

Figure 30-8: Mobile IP encapsulation and tunneling *This example illustrates how a typical request/reply message exchange in Mobile IP results in a triangle of communication. In step 1, the mobile node sends a request to a remote server somewhere on the Internet. It uses its own home address as the source for this request, so in step 2, the reply goes back to the home agent. Step 3 consists of the home agent tunneling the reply back to the mobile node.*

The reverse transaction would be pretty much the same, except in the reverse order. In that case, the third-party (Internet) device would send a request to mobile node, which would be received and forwarded by the home agent. The mobile node would reply back directly to the Internet host.

KEY CONCEPT Once Mobile IP is set up and operational, it works by having the home agent *encapsulate* and *tunnel* received datagrams to the mobile node. The mobile device normally sends datagrams directly to Internet hosts, which respond back to the mobile's home agent, which forwards those datagrams to the mobile node. This means a request/reply communication takes three transmissions.

Mobile IP Reverse Tunneling

There may be situations where it is not feasible or desired to have the mobile node send datagrams directly to the internetwork using a router on the foreign network, as you just saw. In this case, an optional feature called *reverse tunneling* may be deployed if it is supported by the mobile node, the home agent, and, if relevant, the foreign agent. When this is done, a reverse tunnel that complements the normal one is set up between the mobile node and the home agent, or between the foreign agent and the home agent, depending on the care-of address type. All transmissions from the mobile node are tunneled back to the home network where the home agent transmits them over the internetwork, thereby resulting in a more symmetric operation as opposed to the triangle just described. This is basically what I described earlier as being needlessly inefficient, because it means each communication requires four steps. Thus, it is used only when necessary.

One situation for which reverse tunneling may be required is if the network where the mobile node is located has implemented certain security measures that prohibit the node from sending datagrams using its normal IP address. In particular, a network may be set up to disallow outgoing datagrams with a source address that doesn't match its network prefix. This is often done to prevent *spoofing* (impersonating another's IP address).

KEY CONCEPT An optional feature called *reverse tunneling* may be used in certain cases, such as when a network does not allow outgoing datagrams with a foreign source IP address. When enabled, rather than sending datagrams directly, the mobile node tunnels all transmissions back to the home agent, which sends them on the Internet.

Note that everything I've just discussed is applicable to normal—meaning unicast—datagrams that are sent to and from the mobile node. Broadcast datagrams on the home network, which would normally be intended for the mobile node if it were at home, are not forwarded unless the node specifically asks for this service during registration. Multicast operation on the foreign network is also supported, but extra work is required by the mobile node to set it up.

Mobile IP and TCP/IP Address Resolution Protocol (ARP) Operation

Mobile IP is a protocol that does a good job of implementing a difficult function: It transparently allows an IP device to travel to a different network. Unfortunately, a problem with any protocol that tries to change how IP works is dealing with special cases. Having a home agent intercept datagrams and tunnel them to the mobile node works well in general terms, but there are some instances in which extra work is required. One of these is the use of ARP, which breaks under Mobile IP unless we take special steps.

BACKGROUND INFORMATION *Some understanding of how ARP works in general terms is assumed in this topic. This includes ARP proxying, which is described in Chapter 13.*

To understand what the problem is with ARP, consider a mobile node that is on a foreign network and has successfully registered with its home agent. The home agent will intercept all datagrams that come onto the home network, particularly the ones intended for the mobile node, and then encapsulate and forward them. For this to happen, though, the home agent (home router) must see the datagram. This normally occurs only when a datagram comes onto the home network from the outside and is processed by the router.

What happens when a local device on the home network itself wants to transmit to a mobile node that has traveled elsewhere? Remember that this device may not be mobile itself and probably knows nothing about Mobile IP. It will follow the standard process for deciding what to do with a datagram that it needs to send, as explained in Chapter 23. It will compare its network ID to that of the mobile node and realize that it doesn't need to route its datagram; it can send it directly to the mobile node.

The local host will attempt to use ARP to find the data link layer address of the mobile node so that it can send the datagram to it directly. The host will start by looking in its ARP cache, and if it finds the node's data link layer address there, it will use it to send at layer 2. The mobile node is no longer on the local network segment, so the message will never be received. If there is no ARP cache entry, the host on the home network will attempt to send an ARP Request to the mobile node to determine its layer 2 address. Again, the mobile node has traveled away, so this request will go unanswered.

Solving this problem requires the intervention of, you guessed it, the home agent. It must perform two tasks to enable local hosts to send to the mobile node:

ARP Proxying The home agent must listen for any ARP Requests that are sent by nodes on the same network as any of the mobile nodes that are currently registered to it. When it hears one, it replies in the mobile node's stead, and specifies its own data link layer address as the binding for the mobile node's IP address. This will cause hosts on the home network to send any datagrams that are intended for the mobile node to the home agent where they can be forwarded. This process is illustrated in Figure 30-9.

Gratuitous ARP Proxying helps with ARP Requests, but what about devices that already have cache entries for the mobile node? As soon as the mobile node leaves the network, these become automatically stale. To correct them, the home agent sends what is called a *gratuitous* ARP message, which tells devices on the local network to associate the mobile node's IP address with the home agent's data link layer address. The term *gratuitous* refers to the fact that the device isn't sending the message in order to perform an actual address resolution, but merely to cause caches to be updated. It may be sent more than once to ensure that every device gets the message.

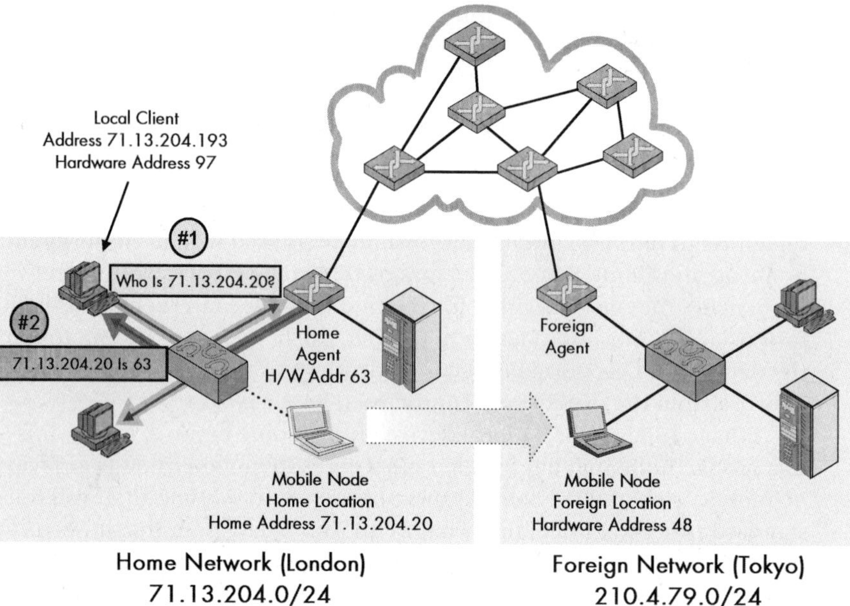

Figure 30-9: ARP proxying by Mobile IP home agent *The home agent must take special steps to deal with transmissions from devices on the local network to the mobile node. In this example (using short hardware addresses for simplicity), the hardware address of the mobile node is 48 and the home agent is 63. A local client on the home network with hardware address 97 sends an ARP Request to find out the hardware address of the mobile node. The home agent responds on the mobile's behalf, specifying not hardware address 48 but rather its own address: 63. The client will thus send to the home agent, which can then forward the data to the mobile node on the foreign network.*

KEY CONCEPT In theory, problems can occur with hosts on the mobile node's home network that are trying to send datagrams to the host at layer 2. To address these issues, the home agent is required to use proxy ARP to direct such devices to send to the home agent so they can be forwarded. It must also use *gratuitous* ARP to update any existing ARP caches to that effect.

Once these steps are taken, ARP should function normally on the home link. When the mobile device returns back to the home network, the process must be reversed. Upon deregistration with the home agent, the mobile device will stop proxying for the mobile node. Both the mobile node and the home agent will also send gratuitous ARP broadcasts that update local device caches. These will again associate the mobile node's IP address with its own layer 2 address, instead of the layer 2 address of the home agent.

Mobile IP Efficiency Issues

Having the home agent forward all datagrams to the mobile node wherever it may be is a convenient solution to mobility, but it's also a rather inefficient one. Since the device must send every datagram first to the home network and then forward it to the mobile node, the datagrams are going to travel over some part of the internetwork twice. The degree of inefficiency represented by forwarding can be significant and may lead to problems with certain applications.

To see what the problem is, let's consider a traveling mobile Node M and a regular device that wants to send to it, Device A. The degree of the inefficiency of Mobile IP is a function of the internetwork distance between Device A and Node M's home network, compared to the internetwork distance between Device A and Node M's current network. By *distance,* I mean the term as it is used in determining routes on an internetwork. Two devices are closer when it takes less time and fewer hops to communicate between them, and they are farther when more hops are required. (I use geography in the following examples to represent this notion of distance, but remember that geographical distance is only one factor in internetwork distance.)

Let's consider the case in which mobile Node M is on a foreign network that's quite far from home, and Device A wants to send a datagram using Node M's home IP address. Suppose the home network is in London and the device is again in Tokyo. Let's look at the inefficiency factor of Mobile IP, compared to the alternative of having the mobile node just get a new temporary IP address on the foreign network and not use Mobile IP. The following examples are arranged in order of increasing inefficiency:

Sending Device on Home Network In this situation, Device A will send a datagram that is immediately intercepted by the home agent on the home network and forwarded to the mobile node. There is really no inefficiency here at all (except for overhead for encapsulation and such), because even if Device A did send the datagram directly to the mobile node with a new foreign address, the datagram would probably be routed through the home agent router anyway.

Sending Device on Network Close to Home Network Let's say a device in Paris wants to send to the mobile node. The datagram goes from Paris to London and then to Tokyo. That's not too bad.

Sending Device on Network Close to Foreign Network Now suppose the sending device is in Taipei, Taiwan. In this situation, Mobile IP becomes quite inefficient. The datagram must be sent from Taipei all the way to London, and then all the way back to Tokyo.

Sending Device on Foreign Network The greatest inefficiency occurs when the sending device is actually on the foreign network that the mobile node is visiting. If Device A is on the mobile node's current network in Tokyo, it must send all the way to London, and then have the result forwarded all the way back again to Tokyo. Without Mobile IP, all you would need to do is use ARP and then deliver directly at layer 2 without needing routing at all! This scenario is illustrated in Figure 30-10.

Unfortunately, the worst-case scenario of the sending device on a foreign network is one that occurs quite often. It's common for a mobile device to connect with a foreign network in order for it to communicate specifically with the hosts on that network.

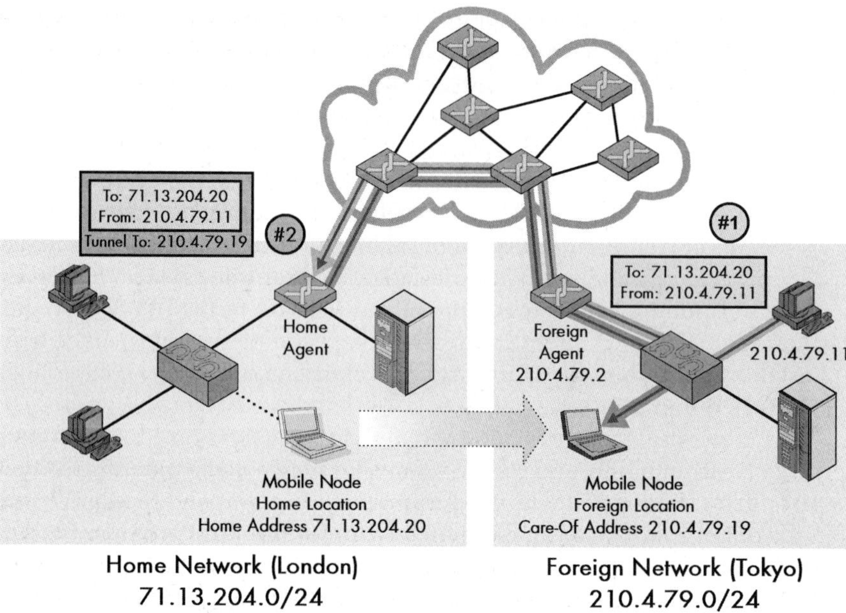

Figure 30-10: A Mobile IP inefficiency worst-case scenario *This diagram shows the worst possible case of Mobile IP inefficiency. When a device on the foreign network where the mobile is located tries to send data to the mobile device. The sender here, 210.4.79.11, uses the mobile node's home address so that the transmission must be routed all the way back to London, and then forwarded back to Tokyo, even though the two devices might be sitting on the same desk!*

To make matters worse, consider what happens if reverse tunneling is used! Here, tunneling is done not just for datagrams sent to the mobile node, but for datagrams sent from the device as well. In the worst-case example, a request/reply pair from the mobile node to another device on the foreign network requires *two* complete round-trips from Tokyo to London and back. Clearly, this is far from ideal.

> **KEY CONCEPT** Since datagrams are sent to a Mobile IP at its home address, each datagram sent to the mobile device must first go back to its home network and then be forwarded to its current location. The level of inefficiency that results depends on how far the sender is from the mobile's home network. The worst case actually occurs if the sender and mobile are on the same foreign network, in which case each transmission must make a round-trip to the mobile's home network and then back again.

There really isn't any solution to this problem within Mobile IP itself; it's just a natural consequence of how the protocol works. The only way to really improve things is to "hack in" a solution that ultimately boils down to one of the two options we always have in IP without mobility support: Either give the mobile device a temporary real IP address on the foreign network, or use a host-specific route for the mobile device while it's on the foreign network.

You've already seen that these both have problems, which is why Mobile IP was created in the first place. There may be situations, however, in which efficiency is more important than the transparent portability that Mobile IP provides. For a long-term deployment on a foreign network far from the home network, or for applications where efficiency is paramount, it may make sense to employ one of these techniques. For example, a corporation that has a small number of offices in different cities that are connected using the Internet might set up special routing. This would let mobile devices visiting from other cities talk directly to nodes that are local to the foreign part of the network without being routed across the Internet.

Mobile IP Security Considerations

Security is always a concern in any internetworking environment these days, but is especially important with Mobile IP. There are a number of reasons for this. The reasons are related to both how the protocol is used and the specific mechanisms by which it is implemented.

In terms of use, security was kept in mind during Mobile IP's development because mobile devices often use wireless networking technologies. Wireless communication is inherently less secure than wired communication, because transmissions are sent out in the open, where they can be intercepted. It's also easier for malicious users to disrupt the operation of wireless devices.

In terms of operation, Mobile IP has a number of risks due to the fact that it uses a registration system and then forwards datagrams across an unsecured internetwork. A malicious device could interfere with registration process, thereby causing the datagrams intended for a mobile device to be diverted. A bad guy might also interfere with the data forwarding process itself by encapsulating a bogus datagram to trick a mobile node into thinking it was sent something that it never was.

For these reasons, the Mobile IP standard includes a limited number of explicit provisions to safeguard against various security risks. One security measure was considered sufficiently important that it was built into the Mobile IP standard directly: the authentication of Registration Request and Registration Reply messages. This authentication process is accomplished in a manner that's somewhat similar to how the IPsec Authentication Header (AH) operates, as described in Chapter 29. Its goal is to prevent unauthorized devices from intercepting traffic by tricking an agent into setting up, renewing, or canceling a registration improperly.

All Mobile IP devices are required to support authentication. Nodes must use it for requests, and agents must use it for replies. Keys must be assigned manually because there is no automated system for secure key distribution. The default authentication method uses *HMAC-MD5* (specified in RFC 2403), which is one of two hashing algorithms used by IPsec.

Another concern is a security problem called a *replay attack*. In this type of attack, a third party intercepts a datagram, holds on to it, and then resends it later on. This seems fairly harmless, but consider the importance of timing. Imagine a mobile node that registers with its home agent, and then later returns home and deregisters. If a malicious device captures a copy of the original Registration Request and resends it, the home agent might be fooled into thinking the node has traveled away from home when it has not. It could then intercept the forwarded datagrams.

The Identification field used in Registration Request and Registration Reply messages is designed to prevent replay attacks. Since each request has a different Identification number, nodes and agents can match up requests with replies and reject any datagrams they receive that are repeats of ones they have seen already. The Mobile IP standard also specifies alternative methods for protecting against replays.

While Mobile IP includes authentication measures for registration messages, it does not for other types of messages. It also doesn't specify authentication of encapsulated datagrams being forwarded from the home agent to the mobile node. Encryption is also not provided to safeguard the privacy of either control messages or forwarded datagrams. The obvious solution when stronger assurances of privacy or authenticity are required is to make use of the IPsec AH and/or Encapsulating Security Payload (ESP) protocols (described in Chapter 29).

PART II-6

IP SUPPORT PROTOCOLS

The Internet Protocol (IP) is the key network layer protocol that implements the TCP/IP protocol suite. Since IP is the protocol that provides the mechanism for delivering datagrams between devices, it is designed to be relatively basic. For example, it lacks provisions for some way to allow errors to be reported back to a transmitting device, and for tests and special tasks to be accomplished. These auxiliary capabilities are necessary for the operation of an internetwork, however, so TCP/IP includes *support protocols* that help IP perform these tasks. This part examines the two main IP support protocols: the *Internet Control Message Protocol (ICMP)* and the *Neighbor Discovery (ND)* protocol.

The bulk of this part thoroughly describes ICMP, which was initially developed to be a companion to the original IP version 4 (IPv4). With the creation of IP version 6 (IPv6), a new version of ICMP, called ICMP version 6 (ICMPv6), was created as well. The original ICMP is now sometimes called *ICMPv4* to differentiate it, just as the original IP is now often called IPv4.

The two versions of ICMP have some differences in their specifics, but they are very similar in overall operation. For this reason, I have integrated the general operation description of both versions of ICMP in the first chapter of this part. The area where ICMPv4 and ICMPv6 most differ is in specific message types and formats, so these have been described separately in the second through fifth chapters. These chapters describe the error messages and informational messages in each version.

The final chapter describes ND, which was created specifically to assist in the operation of IPv6 and is closely related to ICMPv6.

Due to the close relationship between ICMP and IP, this part assumes that you are familiar with basic IP concepts, including IP addressing, the general format of IP datagrams, and how they are routed (covered in Part II-3). To better understand ICMPv6 details, you may also want to reference the IPv6 addressing and datagram encapsulation information (covered in Part II-4).

31

ICMP CONCEPTS AND GENERAL OPERATION

The Internet Control Message Protocol (ICMP) is one of the underappreciated "worker bees" of the networking world. Everyone knows how important key protocols such as the Internet Protocol (IP) are to TCP/IP, but few realize that the suite as a whole relies on many functions that ICMP provides. Originally created to allow the reporting of a small set of error conditions, ICMP messages are now used to implement a wide range of error-reporting, feedback, and testing capabilities. While each message type is unique, they are all implemented using a common message format, sent, and then received based on relatively simple protocol rules. This makes ICMP one of the easiest TCP/IP protocols to understand. (Yes, I actually said something in this book was easy!)

In this chapter, I provide a general description of ICMP. I begin with an overview of ICMP, discussing its purpose, history, and the versions and standards that define it. I describe the general method by which ICMP operates and discuss the rules that govern how and when ICMP messages are created and processed. I then outline the common format used for ICMP messages in versions 4 and 6 of the protocol (ICMPv4 and ICMPv6), and how data is encapsulated in them in general terms. I conclude with a discussion of ICMP message classifications and a summary of different message types and codes for both ICMPv4 and ICMPv6.

ICMP Overview, History, Versions, and Standards

IP is the foundation of the TCP/IP protocol suite, because it is the mechanism responsible for delivering datagrams. Three of the main characteristics that describe IP's datagram delivery method are *connectionless*, *unreliable*, and *unacknowledged*. This means that datagrams are just sent over the internetwork with no prior connection established, no assurance they will show up, and no acknowledgment sent back to the sender that they arrived. On the surface, this seems like it would result in a protocol that is difficult to use and impossible to rely on, and thus would be a poor choice for designing a protocol suite. However, even though IP makes no guarantees, it works very well because most of the time, IP internetworks are sufficiently robust that messages get where they need to go.

Even the best-designed system still encounters problems, of course. Incorrect packets are occasionally sent, hardware devices have problems, routes are found to be invalid, and so forth. IP devices also often need to share specific information in order to guide them in their operation, and they need to perform tests and diagnostics. However, IP itself includes no provision that allows devices to exchange low-level control messages. Instead, these features are provided in the form of a companion protocol to IP called the *Internet Control Message Protocol (ICMP)*.

A good analogy for the relationship between IP and ICMP is to consider the one between a high-powered executive and her experienced administrative assistant. The executive is busy and her time is very expensive. She is paid to do a specific job and to do it well, and not to spend time on administrative tasks. However, without someone doing those tasks, the executive could not do her job properly. The administrative assistant does the important support jobs that make it possible for the executive to focus on her work. The working relationship between them is very important; a good pair will work together like a cohesive team, even anticipating each other's needs.

In TCP/IP, IP is the executive, and ICMP is its administrative assistant. IP focuses on its core activities, such as addressing, datagram packaging, and routing. ICMP provides critical support to IP in the form of *ICMP messages* that allow different types of communication to occur between IP devices. These messages use a common general format and are encapsulated in IP datagrams for transmission. They are divided into different categories, and each type has a specific use and internal field format.

Just as an administrative assistant often has a special location in an organization chart, and usually connects with a dotted line directly to the executive she assists, ICMP occupies a unique place in the TCP/IP protocol architecture (see Chapter 8). Technically, you might consider ICMP to belong to layer 4, because it creates messages that are encapsulated in IP datagrams and sent using IP at layer 3. However, in the standard that first defined it, ICMP is specifically declared to be not only part of the network layer, but also, as stated in RFC 792, is "actually an integral part of IP, [that] must be implemented by every IP module." This was the initial defining standard for ICMP, titled simply "Internet Control Message Protocol." It was published at the same time as the standard for IP, which was RFC 791. This is further indication that IP and ICMP really are a team of sorts.

Due to the close relationship between the two, when the new version 6 of the Internet Protocol (IPv6) was developed in the mid-1990s, it was necessary to define a new version of ICMP as well. This was of course called the "Internet Control Message Protocol (ICMPv6) for the Internet Protocol Version 6 (IPv6) Specification." It was first published as RFC 1885 in 1995, and revised in RFC 2463 in 1998. Just as the original IP is now often called IPv4 to differentiate it from IPv6, the original ICMP is now also called *ICMPv4*.

> **KEY CONCEPT** In TCP/IP, diagnostic, test, and error-reporting functions at the internetwork layer are performed by the *Internet Control Message Protocol (ICMP)*, which is like IP's "administrative assistant." The original version, now called ICMPv4, is used with IPv4, and the newer ICMPv6 is used with IPv6.

These two RFCs, 792 and 2463, define the basic operation of ICMPv4 and ICMPv6, respectively, and also describe some of the ICMP message types supported by each version of the protocol. ICMPv4 and ICMPv6 are very similar in most respects, although they have some differences, most of which are a direct result of the changes made to IP itself. Another document, RFC 1122, "Requirements for Internet Hosts—Communication Layers," contains rules for how ICMPv4 is used, as you will see soon in the section on ICMP message creation and processing conventions later in this chapter. RFC 1812, "Requirements for IP Version 4 Routers," is also relevant.

Both versions of the protocol define a general messaging system that was designed to be expandable. This means that in addition to the messages defined in the ICMP standards themselves, other protocols may also define message types used in ICMP. Some of the more important of these are shown in Table 31-1.

Table 31-1: Non-ICMP Internet Standards That Define ICMP Messages

ICMP Version of Message Types Defined	RFC Number	Name	ICMP Message Types Defined
ICMPv4	950	Internet Standard Subnetting Procedure	Address Mask Request, Address Mask Reply
	1256	ICMP Router Discovery Messages	Router Advertisement, Router Solicitation
	1393	Traceroute Using an IP Option	Traceroute
	1812	Requirements for IP Version 4 Routers	Defines three new codes (subtypes) for the Destination Unreachable message.
ICMPv6	2461	Neighbor Discovery for IP Version 6 (IPv6)	Router Advertisement, Router Solicitation, Neighbor Advertisement, Neighbor Solicitation, Redirect
	2894	Router Renumbering for IPv6	Router Renumbering

This chapter includes a full list of the ICMPv4 and ICMPv6 message types covered in this book and the standards that define each one.

ICMP General Operation

ICMP is one of the simplest protocols in the TCP/IP protocol suite. Most protocols implement a particular type of functionality to either facilitate basic operation of a part of the network stack or an application. To this end, they include many specific algorithms and tasks that define the protocol, which is where most of the complexity lies. ICMP, in contrast, is exactly what its name suggests: a protocol that defines control messages. As such, pretty much all of what ICMP is about is providing a mechanism for any IP device to send control messages to another device.

The ICMP Message-Passing Service

Various message types are defined in ICMP that allow different types of information to be exchanged. These are usually either generated for the purpose of reporting errors or for exchanging important information of different sorts that is needed to keep IP operating smoothly. ICMP itself doesn't define how all the different ICMP messages are used; this is done by the protocols that use the messages. In this manner, ICMP describes a simple message-passing service to other protocols.

> **KEY CONCEPT** ICMP is not like most other TCP/IP protocols in that it does not perform a specific task. It defines a mechanism by which various control messages can be transmitted and received to implement a variety of functions.

As mentioned in the preceding section, ICMP is considered an integral part of IP, even though it uses IP to send its messages. Typically, the operation of ICMP involves some portion of the TCP/IP protocol software on a machine detecting a condition that causes it to generate an ICMP message. This is often the IP layer itself, though it may be some other part of the software. The message is then encapsulated and transmitted like any other TCP/IP message, and is given no special treatment compared to other IP datagrams. The message is sent over the internetwork to the IP layer at the receiving device, as shown in Figure 31-1.

Again, since many of the ICMP messages are actually intended to convey information to a device's IP software, the IP layer itself may be the ultimate destination of an ICMP message once a recipient gets it. In other cases, the ultimate destination may be some other part of the TCP/IP protocol software, which is determined by the type of message received. ICMP does not use ports like the User Datagram Protocol (UDP) or Transmission Control Protocol (TCP) to direct its messages to different applications on a host. The software recognizes the message type and directs it accordingly within the software.

ICMP was originally designed with the idea that most messages would be sent by routers, but they can be sent by both routers and by regular hosts as well, depending on the message type. Some are obviously sent only by routers, such as Redirect messages; others may be sent by either routers or hosts. Many of the ICMP messages are used in matched pairs, especially in various kinds of Request and Reply messages, and Advertisement and Solicitation messages.

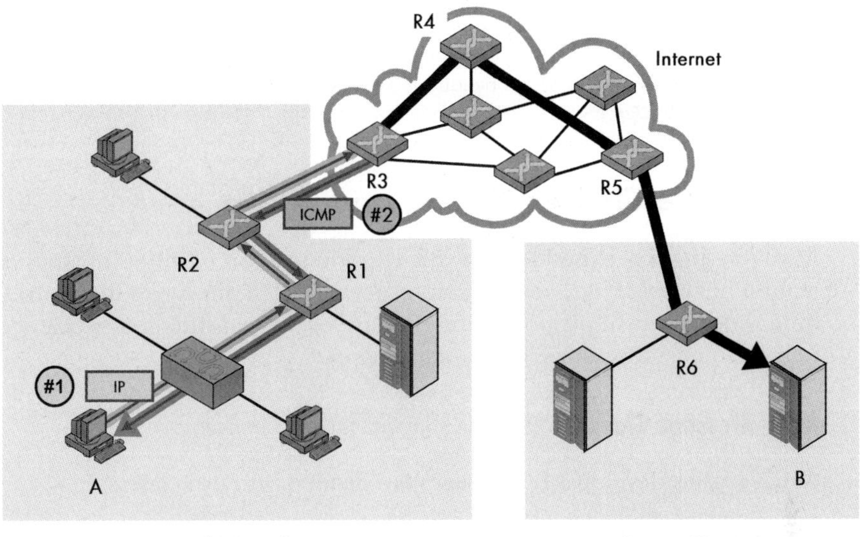

Figure 31-1: ICMP general operation *A typical use of ICMP is to provide a feedback mechanism when an IP message is sent. In this example, Device A is trying to send an IP datagram to Device B. However, when it gets to Router R3, a problem of some sort is detected that causes the datagram to be dropped. Router R3 sends an ICMP message back to Device A to tell it that something happened, hopefully with enough information to let Device A correct the problem, if possible. Router R3 can only send the ICMP message back to Device A, not to Router R2 or R1.*

ICMP Error Reporting Limited to the Datagram Source

One interesting general characteristic of ICMP's operation is that when errors are detected, they can be reported using ICMP, but only back to the original source of a datagram. This is actually a big drawback in how ICMP works. Refer back to Figure 31-1 and consider again client Host A sending a message to server Host B, with a problem detected in the datagram by Router R3. Even if Router R3 suspects that the problem was caused by one of the preceding routers that handled the message, such as Router R2, it *cannot* send a problem report to Router R2. It can send an ICMP message only back to Host A.

This limitation is an artifact of how IP works. You may recall from looking at the IP datagram format that the only address fields are for the original source and ultimate destination of the datagram. (The only exception is if the IP Record Route option is used, but devices cannot count on this.) When Router R3 receives a datagram from Router R2 that Router R2 in turn received from Router R1 (and prior to that, from Device A), it is only Device A's address in the datagram. Thus, Router R3 *must* send a problem report back to Device A, and Device A must decide what to do with it. Device A may decide to change the route it uses or to generate an error report that an administrator can use to troubleshoot Router R2.

In addition to this basic limitation, several special rules and conventions have been put in place to govern the circumstances under which ICMP messages are generated, sent, and processed. I'll discuss these later in the chapter.

> **KEY CONCEPT** ICMP error-reporting messages sent in response to a problem seen in an IP datagram can be sent back only to the originating device. Intermediate devices cannot be the recipients of an ICMP message because their addresses are normally not carried in the IP datagram's header.

ICMP Message Classes, Types, and Codes

ICMP messages are used to allow the communication of different types of information between IP devices on an internetwork. The messages themselves are used for a wide variety of purposes, and they are organized into general categories as well as numerous specific types and subtypes.

ICMP Message Classes

At the highest level, ICMP messages are divided into two classes:

Error Messages These messages are used to provide feedback to a source device about an error that has occurred. They are typically generated specifically in response to some sort of action, usually the transmission of a datagram, as shown in the example in Figure 31-1. Errors are usually related to the structure or content of a datagram or to problem situations on the internetwork encountered during datagram routing.

Informational (or Query) Messages These are messages that are used to let devices exchange information, implement certain IP-related features, and perform testing. They do not indicate errors and are typically not sent in response to a regular datagram transmission. They are generated either when directed by an application or on a regular basis to provide information to other devices. An informational ICMP message may also be sent in reply to another informational ICMP message, since they often occur in request/reply or solicitation/advertisement functional pairs.

> **KEY CONCEPT** ICMP messages are divided into two general categories: *error messages* that are used to report problem conditions, and *informational messages* that are used for diagnostics, testing, and other purposes.

ICMP Message Types

Each individual kind of message in ICMP is given its own unique Type value, which is put into the field of that name in the ICMP common message format. This field is 8 bits wide, so a theoretical maximum of 256 message types can be defined. A separate set of Type values is maintained for each of ICMPv4 and ICMPv6.

In ICMPv4, Type values were assigned sequentially to both error and informational messages on a first-come, first-served basis (sort of), so we cannot tell just by the Type value what type of message each is. One minor improvement made in ICMPv6 was that the message types were separated. In IPv6, error messages have Type values from 0 to 127, and informational messages have values from 128 to 255. Only some of the Type values are currently defined.

> **KEY CONCEPT** A total of 256 different possible message types can be defined for each of ICMPv4 and ICMPv6. The Type field that appears in the header of each message specifies the kind of ICMP message. In ICMPv4, there is no relationship between Type value and message type. In ICMPv6, error messages have a Type value of 0 to 127, and informational messages have a Type value of 128 to 255.

ICMP Message Codes

The message type indicates the general purpose of each kind of ICMP message. ICMP also provides an additional level of detail within each message type in the form of a Code field, which is also 8 bits. You can consider this field as a message subtype. Thus, each message type can have up to 256 subtypes that are more detailed subdivisions of the message's overall functionality. A good example is the Destination Unreachable message, which is generated when a datagram cannot be delivered. In this message type, the Code value provides more information on exactly why the delivery was not possible.

ICMP Message Class and Type Summary

The next four chapters of the book describe all of the major ICMP message types for both ICMPv4 and ICMPv6. For convenience, I have summarized all these message types in Table 31-2, which shows each of the Type values for the messages covered in this book, the name of each message, a very brief summary of its purpose, and the RFC that defines it. (To keep the table from being egregiously large, I have not shown each of the Code values for each Type value; these can be found in the individual message type descriptions.) The table is organized into sections that correspond to the four chapters that describe ICMP message types, except this table is sorted by ascending Type value within each category for easier reference.

Table 31-2: ICMP Message Classes, Types, and Codes

Message Class	Type Value	Message Name	Summary Description of Message Type	Defining RFC Number
ICMPv4 Error Messages	3	Destination Unreachable	Indicates that a datagram could not be delivered to its destination. The Code value provides more information on the nature of the error.	792
	4	Source Quench	Lets a congested IP device tell a device that is sending it datagrams to slow down the rate at which it is sending them.	792
	5	Redirect	Allows a router to inform a host of a better route to use for sending datagrams.	792
	11	Time Exceeded	Sent when a datagram has been discarded prior to delivery due to expiration of its Time to Live field.	792
	12	Parameter Problem	Indicates a miscellaneous problem (specified by the Code value) in delivering a datagram.	792

(continued)

Table 31-2: ICMP Message Classes, Types, and Codes (continued)

Message Class	Type Value	Message Name	Summary Description of Message Type	Defining RFC Number
ICMPv4 Informational Messages (part 1 of 2)	0	Echo Reply	Sent in reply to an Echo (Request) message; used for testing connectivity.	792
	8	Echo (Request)	Sent by a device to test connectivity to another device on the internetwork. The word *Request* sometimes appears in the message name.	792
	9	Router Advertisement	Used by routers to tell hosts of their existence and capabilities.	1256
	10	Router Solicitation	Used by hosts to prompt any listening routers to send a Router Advertisement.	1256
	13	Timestamp (Request)	Sent by a device to request that another send it a timestamp value for propagation time calculation and clock synchronization. The word *Request* sometimes appears in the message name.	792
	14	Timestamp Reply	Sent in response to a Timestamp (Request) to provide time calculation and clock synchronization information.	792
	15	Information Request	Originally used to request configuration information from another device. Now obsolete.	792
ICMPv4 Informational Messages (part 2 of 2)	16	Information Reply	Originally used to provide configuration information in response to an Information Request message. Now obsolete.	792
	17	Address Mask Request	Used to request that a device send a subnet mask.	950
	18	Address Mask Reply	Contains a subnet mask sent in reply to an Address Mask Request.	950
	30	Traceroute	Used to implement the experimental enhanced traceroute utility.	1393
ICMPv6 Error Messages	1	Destination Unreachable	Indicates that a datagram could not be delivered to its destination. *Code* value provides more information on the nature of the error.	2463
	2	Packet Too Big	Sent when a datagram cannot be forwarded because it is too big for the maximum transmission unit (MTU) of the next hop in the route. This message is needed in IPv6 and not IPv4 because in IPv4, routers can fragment oversized messages, but in IPv6 they cannot.	2463
	3	Time Exceeded	Sent when a datagram has been discarded prior to delivery due to the Hop Limit field being reduced to zero.	2463
	4	Parameter Problem	Indicates a miscellaneous problem (specified by the *Code* value) in delivering a datagram.	2463

(continued)

Table 31-2: ICMP Message Classes, Types, and Codes (continued)

Message Class	Type Value	Message Name	Summary Description of Message Type	Defining RFC Number
ICMPv6 Informational Messages	128	Echo Request	Sent by a device to test connectivity to another device on the internetwork.	2463
	129	Echo Reply	Sent in reply to an Echo (Request) message; used for testing connectivity.	2463
	133	Router Solicitation	Prompts a router to send a Router Advertisement.	2461
	134	Router Advertisement	Sent by routers to tell hosts on the local network that the router exists. It also describes its capabilities.	2461
	135	Neighbor Solicitation	Sent by a device to request the layer 2 address of another device while providing its own as well.	2461
	136	Neighbor Advertisement	Provides information about a host to other devices on the network.	2461
	137	Redirect	Redirects transmissions from a host to either an immediate neighbor on the network or a router.	2461
	138	Router Renumbering	Conveys renumbering information for router renumbering.	2894

You can see that several of the message types are quite similar in ICMPv4 and ICMPv6, but there are some slight differences. An obvious one is that Redirect is considered an error message in ICMPv4, but it's an informational message in ICMPv6. Messages are often used differently as well. In IPv6, the use of many of the ICMP informational messages is described in the Neighbor Discovery (ND) protocol, which is new to IPv6 (see Chapter 36).

Note that the Information Request and Information Reply messages were originally created to allow devices to determine an IP address and possibly other configuration information. This function was later implemented using host configuration protocols such as the Reverse Address Resolution Protocol (RARP; see Chapter 14), Boot Protocol (BOOTP; see Chapter 60), and Dynamic Host Configuration Protocol (DHCP, discussed in Chapters 61 through 64). These message types are now obsolete.

ICMP Message Creation and Processing Conventions and Rules

In the overview of ICMP earlier in this chapter, I compared the relationship between IP and ICMP to that between an executive and an administrative assistant. One of the characteristics that many executives value in a good assistant is that the assistant does his work independently, without causing unnecessary disruption. A good assistant should save the executive time, not cost her time.

As the assistant to IP, ICMP must similarly help IP function without taking up too much of its resources. Here, the resource being conserved is not so much time as bandwidth. ICMP messages are important, but must be considered part of the overhead of running a network. They carry no user data, so each one represents a small loss of overall end-user bandwidth on the network. For this reason, we want to send them only when necessary, and to carefully control the circumstances under which they are generated.

Administrative assistants have some serious advantages over networking protocols: common sense and experience. They usually know where the line is drawn between help and hindrance; computers don't. To partially compensate, ICMP's operation is guided by a set of *conventions* or *rules* for how messages are created and processed. For ICMPv4, these conventions are described in part in the defining RFC 792, but much more in RFC 1122, "Requirements for Internet Hosts—Communication Layers," which provides specific information on implementing TCP/IP in host devices. In ICMPv6, the information related to ICMP implementation that appears in RFC 1122 has been largely incorporated into the main document that defines ICMPv6, RFC 2463.

Most of the issues related to message generation have to do with error messages, not informational messages. The latter class of messages usually doesn't cause problems because they are generated based on specific rules already established in the protocols that use them. For example, routers send Router Advertisement messages on a regular basis, and the routers make sure this is infrequent. They are also sent in response to Router Solicitation messages sent on occasion by hosts, and as long as a host doesn't go haywire and start sending tons of Solicitations, there won't be a problem. Even then, you can give a router enough smarts not to send Router Advertisements too often.

Limitations on ICMP Message Responses

The problem comes up with error messages specifically because they are sent *in response* to so many situations. Potentially, they may even be sent in response to each other. Without special care, loops or cascading message generation might occur. For example, consider a situation in which Device A encounters an error and sends an error report to Device B. Device B finds an error in Device A's message and sends an error report back to Device A. This could result in billions of messages being sent back and forth, thereby clogging the network, until a human figures out what is wrong and fixes it.

To prevent such problems, an ICMP error message *must not* be generated in response to any of the following:

An ICMP Error Message This prevents loops of the type just mentioned. Note, however, that an ICMP error message *can* be generated in response to an ICMP informational message.

A Broadcast or Multicast Datagram What would happen if a datagram were broadcast to 5,000 hosts, and each of them found an error in it and tried to send a report back to the source? Something unpleasant!

IP Datagram Fragments Except the First In many cases, the same situation that might cause a device to generate an error for one fragment would also apply to each successive one, causing unnecessary ICMP traffic. For this reason, when a datagram is fragmented, a device may send an error message only in response to a problem in the first fragment.

Datagrams with Non-Unicast Source Address If a datagram's source address doesn't define a unique, unicast device address, an error message cannot be sent back to that source. This prevents ICMP messages from being broadcast, unicast, or sent to nonroutable special addresses such as the loopback address.

> **KEY CONCEPT** In order to prevent excessive numbers of ICMP messages from being sent on a network, a special set of rules governs when and how they may be created. Most of these are designed to eliminate situations in which very large numbers of ICMP error messages would be generated in response to certain occurrences.

These rules apply to both ICMPv4 and ICMPv6, but in ICMPv6 there are a couple of special cases. In certain circumstances, an ICMPv6 Packet Too Big message may be sent to a multicast address, as this is required for Path MTU Discovery (described in Chapter 27) to work. Certain Parameter Problem messages may also be sent to multicast or broadcast addresses. Finally, in addition to the rules just mentioned, IPv6 implementations are specifically directed to limit the rate at which they send ICMPv6 messages overall.

ICMP Message Processing Conventions

Message processing generally takes place as described earlier in the section on ICMP general operation, with the ICMP message delivered either to the IP software or other protocol software implementation as required. What is done with the message usually depends on its type. Some messages are destined for only the IP software itself, but many are intended for the higher-layer protocol that generated the datagram that led to the error. In the next section, you will see that ICMP error messages include information that allows the upper-layer protocol to be extracted for the purpose of passing the message to the appropriate software layer.

In IPv6, the class of message (error or informational) can be determined from the Type value. This knowledge can then be used to guide processing of ICMP messages with unknown Type values. The rule is that ICMP error messages with unknown Type values must be passed to the appropriate upper-layer protocol. Informational messages with unknown Type values are discarded without taking action.

In addition to these general rules, there are specific rules put into place to guide the processing of some of the message types. I describe some of these conventions in the chapters that discuss individual ICMP messages.

An important final point is that ICMP messages, especially error messages, are not considered binding on the device that processes them. To stick with the office analogy, they have the equivalent status in an office of only of an FYI memo, not an assignment. It is often the case that a device *should* take action upon processing an

ICMP message, but the device is not required to. The exception, again, is when informational messages are used for specific purposes. For example, most of the messages that come in pairs are designed so that a Request results in the matching Reply and a Solicitation yields an Advertisement.

KEY CONCEPT A device receiving an ICMP message is not required to take action unless a protocol using a message type dictates a specific response to a particular message type. In particular, devices are not mandated to perform any specific task when receiving an ICMP error message.

ICMP Common Message Format and Data Encapsulation

As you have seen so far in this chapter, ICMP is not so much a protocol that performs a specific function as a framework for the exchange of error reports and information. Since each of the message types is used for a different purpose, they differ in the types of information they contain. This means each ICMP message has a slightly different format. At the same time, however, ICMP message types also have a degree of commonality—a portion of each message is common between message types.

ICMP Common Message Format

You can think of the structure of an ICMP message as having a *common part* and a *unique part*. The common part consists of three fields that have the same size and same meaning in all ICMP messages (although the values in the fields aren't the same for each ICMP message type). The unique part contains fields that are specific to each type of message.

Interestingly, the common message format is basically the same for ICMPv4 and ICMPv6. It is described in Table 31-3 and illustrated in Figure 31-2.

Table 31-3: ICMP Common Message Format

Field Name	Size (Bytes)	Description
Type	1	Identifies the ICMP message type. For ICMPv6, values from 0 to 127 are error messages, and values 128 to 255 are informational messages. Common values for this field are given in Table 31-2.
Code	1	Identifies the subtype of message within each ICMP message Type value. Thus, up to 256 subtypes can be defined for each message type. Values for this field are shown in the following chapters on individual ICMP message types.
Checksum	2	A 16-bit checksum field that is calculated in a manner similar to the IP header checksum in IPv4. It provides error-detection coverage for the entire ICMP message. Note that in ICMPv6, a pseudo header of IPv6 header fields is prepended for checksum calculation; this is similar to the way this is done in TCP.
Message Body/Data	Variable	Contains the specific fields used to implement each message type. This is the unique part of the message.

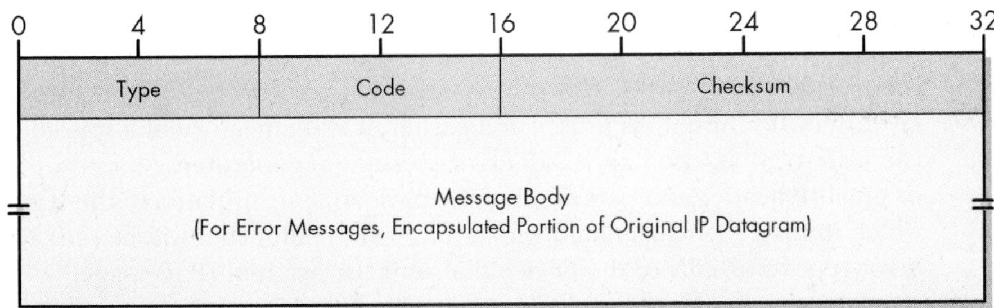

Figure 31-2: ICMP common message format *This overall, generic message format is used for both ICMPv4 and ICMPv6 message types.*

Original Datagram Inclusion in ICMP Error Messages

The message body typically contains one or several fields that carry information of relevance to each specific type of ICMP message. All ICMP error messages include a portion of the original IP datagram that led to the ICMP error message. This aids in diagnosing the problem that caused the ICMP message to be generated, by allowing the error to be communicated to higher layers.

The inclusion of original IP datagram information is done differently for the two ICMP versions:

ICMPv4 Error Messages Each error message includes the full IP header and the first 8 bytes of the payload. Since the beginning of the payload will contain the encapsulated higher-layer header, the ICMP message also carries either the full UDP header or the first 8 bytes of the TCP header. In both cases, the source and destination port numbers are part of what is included. If the original header was a standard IP header with no options, the Message Body will therefore have a length of 28 bytes; if options are present, it will be larger.

ICMPv6 Error Messages Each error message includes as much of the IPv6 datagram as will fit without causing the size of the ICMPv6 error message (including its IP header encapsulation) to exceed the minimum IPv6 maximum transmission unit size, which is 1280 bytes. This provides additional information for diagnostic purposes when compared to ICMPv4, while ensuring that no ICMPv6 error messages will be too large for any physical network segment. The larger size of the included data allows the IPv6 extension headers to be included in the error message, since the error could be in one of those extension headers.

NOTE *Remember that in IPv6, routers cannot fragment IP datagrams; any datagram that is oversized for an underlying physical network is dropped. ICMPv6 is thus designed to ensure that this does not happen by not creating ICMPv6 datagrams over the universal IPv6 MTU size of 1280.*

KEY CONCEPT Each kind of ICMP message contains data unique to that message type, but all messages are structured according to a common ICMP message format. ICMP error messages always include in their message body field some portion of the original IP datagram that resulted in the error being generated.

ICMP Data Encapsulation

After an ICMP message is formatted, it is encapsulated in an IP datagram like any other IP message. This is why some people believe ICMP is architecturally a higher layer than IP, though as I discussed earlier, it is really more of a special case. You can also see that when an ICMP error message is generated, we end up with the original IP header and part or all of the payload, encapsulated in the ICMP message, which in turn is encapsulated within a new IP header that will be sent back as an error report, usually to the device that sent the original IP message.

32

ICMPV4 ERROR MESSAGE TYPES AND FORMATS

Routers and hosts use Internet Control Message Protocol (ICMP) error messages to tell a device that sent a datagram about problems that were encountered during delivery. The original ICMP version 4 (ICMPv4) defined five different error messages, which are all described in the original ICMP standard, RFC 792. These are some of the most important ICMP messages. They provide critical feedback about error conditions and may help a transmitting device take corrective action to ensure reliable and efficient datagram delivery.

In this first of four chapters on specific ICMP types, I look at the ICMPv4 error messages. I begin with Destination Unreachable messages, which are sent due to datagram delivery failures, and Source Quench messages, which are used to tell a device to slow down the rate at which it sends datagrams. Next, I describe Time Exceeded messages, which are sent when a datagram has been traveling the network too long or takes too long to be reassembled from fragments, and Redirect messages, which let a router provide feedback about better routes to a host. Finally, I discuss Parameter Problem messages, which are generic messages used for problems not covered by other ICMP error messages.

ICMPv4 Destination Unreachable Messages

Since the Internet Protocol (IP) is an unreliable protocol, there are no guarantees that a datagram sent by one device to another will ever actually get there. The internetwork of hosts and routers will make a best effort to deliver the datagram, but it may not get where it needs to for any number of reasons. Devices on an IP network understand that and are designed accordingly. IP software never assumes its datagrams will always be received, and higher-layer protocols like the Transmission Control Protocol (TCP) take care of providing reliability and acknowledgments of received data for applications that need these features.

This setup, with higher layers handling failed deliveries, is sufficient in some cases. For example, suppose Device A tries to send to Device B, but a router near Device B is overloaded, so it drops the datagram. In this case, the problem is likely intermittent, so Device A can retransmit and eventually reach Device B. But what about a situation where a device is trying to send to an IP address that doesn't exist, or a problem with routing that isn't easily corrected? Having the source just continually retry in this case would be inefficient, to say the least.

IP is designed to allow IP datagram deliveries to fail, and we should take any such failures seriously. What we really need is a feedback mechanism that can tell a source device that something improper is happening and why. In IP version 4 (IPv4), this service is provided through the transmission of *Destination Unreachable* ICMP messages. When a source node receives one of these messages, it knows there was a problem sending a datagram, and can then decide what action, if any, it wants to take. Like all ICMP error messages, Destination Unreachable messages include a portion of the datagram that could not be delivered, which helps the recipient of the error figure out what the problem is.

ICMPv4 Destination Unreachable Message Format

Table 32-1 and Figure 32-1 show the specific format for ICMPv4 Destination Unreachable messages.

Table 32-1: ICMPv4 Destination Unreachable Message Format

Field Name	Size (Bytes)	Description
Type	1	Identifies the ICMP message type; for Destination Unreachable messages, this is set to 3.
Code	1	Identifies the subtype of unreachable error being communicated. See Table 32-2 for a full list of codes and what they mean.
Checksum	2	A 16-bit checksum field for the ICMP header (see Chapter 31).
Unused	4	The 4 bytes that are left blank and not used.
Original Datagram Portion	Variable	The full IP header and the first 8 bytes of the payload of the datagram that prompted this error message to be sent.

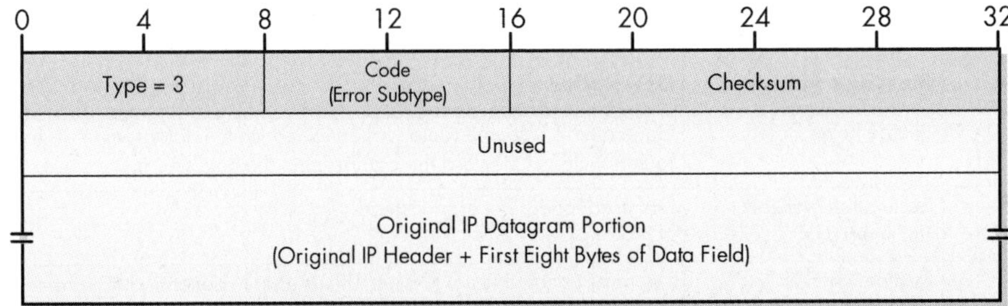

Figure 32-1: *ICMPv4 Destination Unreachable message format*

ICMPv4 Destination Unreachable Message Subtypes

There are many different reasons why it may not be possible for a datagram to reach its destination. Some of these may be due to erroneous parameters (like the invalid IP address example mentioned earlier). A router might have a problem reaching a particular network for whatever reason. There can also be other more esoteric reasons related to why a datagram cannot be delivered.

For this reason, the ICMPv4 Destination Unreachable message type can be considered as a class of related error messages. The receipt of a Destination Unreachable message tells a device that the datagram it sent couldn't be delivered, and the Code field in the ICMP header indicates the reason for the nondelivery. Table 32-2 shows the different Code values, corresponding message subtypes, and a brief explanation of each.

Table 32-2: ICMPv4 Destination Unreachable Message Subtypes

Code Value	Message Subtype	Description
0	Network Unreachable	The datagram could not be delivered to the network specified in the network ID portion of the IP address. This usually means a problem with routing but could also be caused by a bad address.
1	Host Unreachable	The datagram was delivered to the network specified in the network ID portion of the IP address but could not be sent to the specific host indicated in the address. Again, this usually implies a routing issue.
2	Protocol Unreachable	The protocol specified in the Protocol field was invalid for the host to which the datagram was delivered.
3	Port Unreachable	The destination port specified in the UDP or TCP header was invalid.
4	Fragmentation Needed and DF Set	This is one of those esoteric codes. Normally, an IPv4 router will automatically fragment a datagram that it receives if it is too large for the maximum transmission unit (MTU) of the next physical network link the datagram needs to traverse. However, if the DF (Don't Fragment) flag is set in the IP header, this means the sender of the datagram does not *want* the datagram ever to be fragmented. This puts the router between the proverbial rock and a hard place, and it will be forced to drop the datagram and send an error message with this code. This message type is most often used in a clever way by intentionally sending messages of increasing size to discover the MTU size that a link can handle. This process is called Path MTU Discovery (described in Chapter 27).

(continued)

Table 32-2: ICMPv4 Destination Unreachable Message Subtypes (continued)

Code Value	Message Subtype	Description
5	Source Route Failed	Generated if a source route was specified for the datagram in an option but a router could not forward the datagram to the next step in the route.
6	Destination Network Unknown	Not used; code 0 is used instead.
7	Destination Host Unknown	The host specified is not known. This is usually generated by a router local to the destination host and usually means a bad address.
8	Source Host Isolated	Obsolete, no longer used.
9	Communication with Destination Network Is Administratively Prohibited	The source device is not allowed to send to the network where the destination device is located.
10	Communication with Destination Host Is Administratively Prohibited	The source device is allowed to send to the network where the destination device is located, but not that particular device.
11	Destination Network Unreachable for Type of Service	The network specified in the IP address cannot be reached due to the inability to provide service specified in the Type of Service field of the datagram header (see Chapter 31).
12	Destination Host Unreachable for Type of Service	The destination host specified in the IP address cannot be reached due to the inability to provide service specified in the datagram's Type of Service field.
13	Communication Administratively Prohibited	The datagram could not be forwarded due to filtering that blocks the message based on its contents.
14	Host Precedence Violation	Sent by a first-hop router (the first router to handle a sent datagram) when the Precedence value in the Type of Service field is not permitted.
15	Precedence Cutoff in Effect	Sent by a router when receiving a datagram whose Precedence value (priority) is lower than the minimum allowed for the network at that time.

As you can see in Table 32-2, not all of these codes are actively used at this time. For example, code 8 is obsolete and code 0 is used instead of 6. Also, some of the higher numbers related to the Type of Service field aren't actively used because Type of Service isn't actively used.

> **KEY CONCEPT** ICMPv4 *Destination Unreachable* messages are used to inform a sending device of a failure to deliver an IP datagram. The message's Code field provides information about the nature of the delivery problem.

Interpretation of Destination Unreachable Messages

It's important to remember that just as IP is a best effort, the reporting of unreachable destinations using ICMP is also a best effort. Realize that these ICMP messages are themselves carried in IP datagrams. More than that, however, remember that there may be problems that prevent a router from detecting failure of delivery of an

ICMP message, such as a low-level hardware problem. A router could, theoretically, also be precluded from sending an ICMP message even when failure of delivery *is* detected for whatever reason.

For this reason, the sending of Destination Unreachable messages should be considered supplemental. There is no guarantee that every problem sending a datagram will result in a corresponding ICMP message. No device should count on receiving an ICMP Destination Unreachable for a failed delivery any more than it counts on the delivery in the first place. This is why the higher-layer mechanisms mentioned at the start of this discussion are still important.

ICMPv4 Source Quench Messages

When a source device sends out a datagram, it will travel across the internetwork and eventually arrive at its intended destination (at least, that's what we hope will happen). At that point, it is up to the destination device to process the datagram by examining it and determining which higher-layer software process to hand the datagram.

If a destination device is receiving datagrams at a relatively slow rate, it may be able to process each datagram on the fly as it is received. However, datagram receipt in a typical internetwork can tend to be uneven or bursty, with alternating higher and lower rates of traffic. To allow for times when datagrams are arriving faster than they can be processed, each device has a *buffer* where it can temporarily hold datagrams it has received until it has a chance to deal with them.

However, this buffer is itself limited in size. Assuming the device has been properly designed, the buffer may be sufficient to smooth out high-traffic and low-traffic periods most of the time. Certain situations can still arise in which traffic is received so rapidly that the buffer fills up entirely. Some examples of scenarios in which this might happen include the following:

- A single destination is overwhelmed by datagrams from many sources, such as a popular website being swamped by HTTP requests.
- Device A and Device B are exchanging information, but Device A is a much faster computer than Device B, and can generate outgoing and process incoming datagrams much faster than Device B can.
- A router receives a large number of datagrams over a high-speed link that it needs to forward over a low-speed link; they start to pile up while waiting to be sent over the slow link.
- A hardware failure or other situation causes datagrams to sit at a device unprocessed.

A device that continues to receive datagrams when it has no more buffer space is forced to discard them and is said to be *congested*. A source that has its datagram discarded due to congestion won't have any way of knowing this, since IP itself is unreliable and unacknowledged. Therefore, while it is possible to simply allow higher-layer protocols to detect the dropped datagrams and generate replacements, it makes a lot more sense to have the congested device provide feedback to the sources by telling them that it is overloaded.

In IPv4, a device that is forced to drop datagrams due to congestion provides feedback to the sources that overwhelmed it by sending them ICMPv4 *Source Quench* messages. Just as you use water to quench a fire, a Source Quench message is a signal that attempts to quench a source device that is sending too fast. In other words, it's a polite way for one IP device to tell another, "Slow down!" When a device receives one of these messages, it knows it needs to reduce the speed at which it is sending datagrams to the device that sent it.

ICMPv4 Source Quench Message Format

Table 32-3 and Figure 32-2 show the specific format for ICMPv4 Source Quench messages.

Table 32-3: ICMPv4 Source Quench Message Format

Field Name	Size (Bytes)	Description
Type	1	Identifies the ICMP message type; for Source Quench messages, this is set to 4.
Code	1	Identifies the subtype of error being communicated. For Source Quench messages, this is not used, and the field is set to 0.
Checksum	2	A 16-bit checksum field for the ICMP header (see Chapter 31).
Unused	4	The 4 bytes that are left blank and not used.
Original Datagram Portion	Variable	The full IP header and the first 8 bytes of the payload of the datagram that was dropped due to congestion.

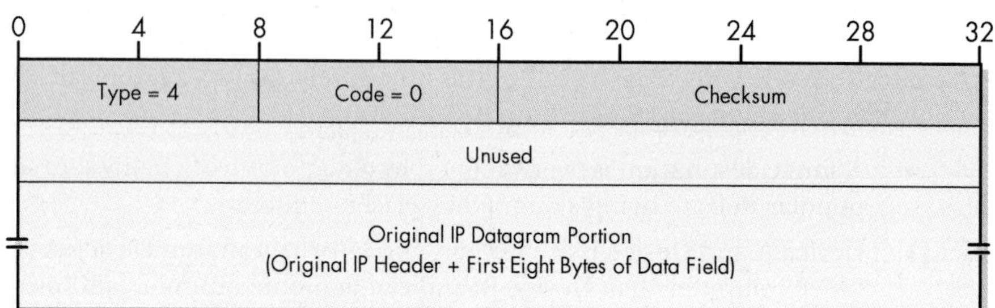

***Figure 32-2:** ICMPv4 Source Quench message format*

Problems with Source Quench Messages

What's interesting about the Source Quench format is that it is basically a null message. It tells the source that the destination is congested but provides no specific information about that situation, nor does it specify what exactly the destination wants the source to do other than cut back on its transmission rate in some way. There is also no method for the destination to signal a source that it is no longer congested, and that the source should resume its prior sending rate. This means the response to a Source Quench message is left up to the device that receives it. Usually, a device will cut back its transmission rate until it no longer receives the messages, and then it may try to slowly increase the rate again.

In a similar manner, there are no rules about when and how a device generates Source Quench messages in the first place. A common convention is that one message is generated for each dropped datagram. However, more intelligent algorithms may be employed, especially on higher-end routers, to predict when the device's buffer will be filled and preemptively quench certain sources that are sending too quickly. Devices may also decide whether to quench all sources when they become busy, or only certain ones. As with other ICMP error messages, a device cannot count on a Source Quench message being sent when a busy device discards one of its datagrams.

The lack of information communicated in Source Quench messages makes them a rather crude tool for managing congestion. In general terms, the process of regulating the sending of messages between two devices is called *flow control*, and this is usually a function of the transport layer. TCP actually has a flow control mechanism (discussed in Chapter 49) that is far superior to the use of ICMP Source Quench messages.

Another issue with Source Quench messages is that they can be abused. Transmission of these messages by a malicious user can cause a host to be slowed down when there is no valid reason. This security issue, combined with the superiority of the TCP method for flow control, has caused the use of Source Quench messages to largely fall out of favor.

> **KEY CONCEPT** ICMPv4 *Source Quench* messages are sent by a device to request that another reduce the rate at which it is sending datagrams. The messages are a rather crude method of flow control compared to more capable mechanisms such as those provided by TCP.

ICMPv4 Time Exceeded Messages

Large IP internetworks can have thousands of interconnected routers that pass datagrams between devices on various networks. In large internetworks, the topology of connections between routes can become complex, which makes routing more difficult. Routing protocols will normally allow routers to find the best routes between networks, but in some situations, an inefficient route might be selected for a datagram. In the worst case, a *router loop* may occur. An example of this situation is where Router A thinks datagrams intended for Network X should next go to Router B, which thinks they should go to Router C, which thinks they need to go to Router A. (See the ICMPv6 Time Exceeded Message description in Chapter 34 for an illustration of a router loop.)

If a loop like this occurred, datagrams for Network X that were entering this part of the internetwork would circle forever, chewing up bandwidth and eventually leading to the network being unusable. As insurance against this occurrence, each IP datagram includes in its header a Time to Live (TTL) field. This field was originally intended to limit the maximum time (in seconds) that a datagram could be on the internetwork, but now limits the life of a datagram by limiting the number of times the datagram can be passed from one device to the next. The TTL is set to a value by the source that represents the maximum number of hops it wants for the datagram. Each router decrements the value; if it ever reaches zero, the datagram is said to have *expired* and is discarded.

When a datagram is dropped due to expiration of the TTL field, the device that dropped the datagram will inform the source of this occurrence by sending it an ICMPv4 *Time Exceeded* message, as shown in Figure 32-3. Receipt of this message indicates to the original sending device that there is a routing problem when sending to that particular destination, or that it set the TTL field value too low in the first place. As with all ICMP messages, the device receiving it must decide whether and how to respond to receipt of the message. For example, it may first try to resend the datagram with a higher TTL value.

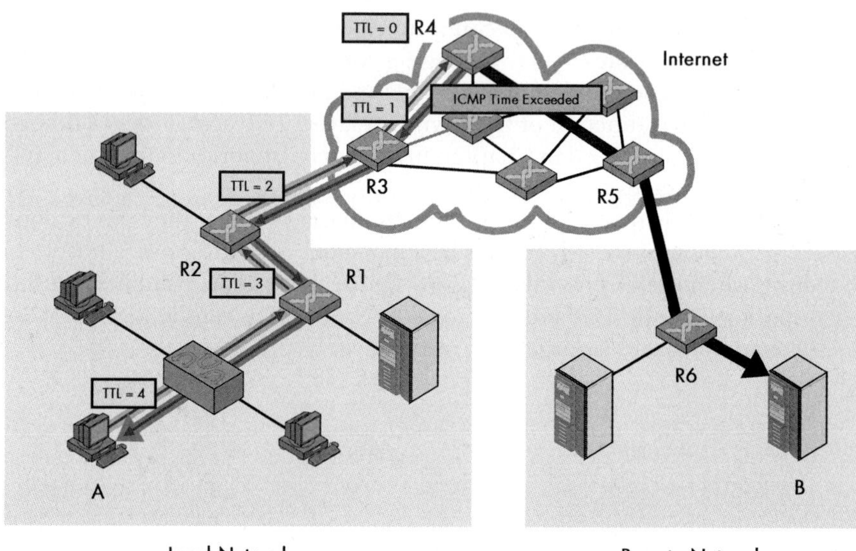

Figure 32-3: Expiration of an IP datagram and Time Exceeded message generation *In this example, Device A sends an IP datagram to Device B, which has a Time to Live (TTL) field value of only 4 (perhaps not realizing that Device B is seven hops away). On the fourth, hop the datagram reaches Router R4, which decrements its TTL field to 0 and then drops it as it expires. Router R4 then sends an ICMP Time Exceeded message back to Device A.*

There is another time expiration situation where ICMP Time Exceeded messages are used. When an IP message is broken into fragments, the destination device is charged with reassembling them into the original message. One or more fragments may not make it to the destination, so to prevent the device from waiting forever, it sets a timer when the first fragment arrives. If this timer expires before the others are received, the device gives up on this message. The fragments are discarded, and a Time Exceeded message is generated.

ICMPv4 Time Exceeded Message Format

Table 32-4 and Figure 32-4 show the specific format for ICMPv4 Time Exceeded messages.

Table 32-4: ICMPv4 Time Exceeded Message Format

Field Name	Size (Bytes)	Description
Type	1	Identifies the ICMP message type; for Time Exceeded messages, this is set to 11.
Code	1	Identifies the subtype of error being communicated. A value of 0 indicates expiration of the IP TTL field; a value of 1 indicates that the fragment reassembly time has been exceeded.
Checksum	2	A 16-bit checksum field for the ICMP header (see Chapter 31).
Unused	4	The 4 bytes that are left blank and not used.
Original Datagram Portion	Variable	The full IP header and the first 8 bytes of the payload of the datagram that was dropped due to expiration of the TTL field or reassembly timer.

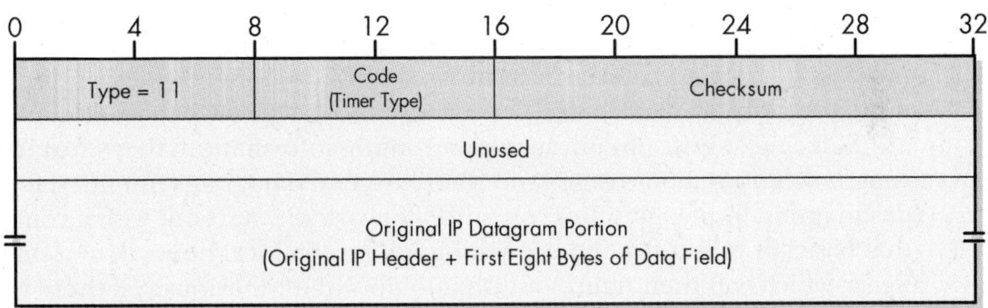

Figure 32-4: *ICMPv4 Time Exceeded message format*

Applications of Time Exceeded Messages

ICMP Time Exceeded messages are usually sent in response to the two conditions described in Table 32-4: TTL or reassembly timer expiration. Generally, routers generate TTL expiration messages as they try to route a datagram, while end hosts indicate reassembly violations. However, there is actually a very clever application of these messages that has nothing to do with reporting errors at all.

The TCP/IP *traceroute* (or *tracert*) utility is used to show the sequence of devices over which a datagram is passed on a particular route between a source and destination. The traceroute utility also shows the amount of time it takes for a datagram to reach each hop in that route. This utility was originally implemented using Time Exceeded messages by sending datagrams with successively higher TTL values.

First, a dummy datagram is sent with a TTL value of 1, causing the first hop in the route to discard the datagram and send back an ICMP Time Exceeded message; the time elapsed for this could then be measured. Then, a second datagram is sent with a TTL value of 2. This causes the second device in the route to report back a Time Exceeded message, and so on. By continuing to increase the TTL value you can get reports back from each hop in the route. See Chapter 88 for more details on traceroute's operation.

> **KEY CONCEPT** ICMPv4 *Time Exceeded* messages are sent in two different time-related circumstances. The first is if a datagram's Time to Live (TTL) field is reduced to zero, causing it to expire and the datagram to be dropped. The second is when all the pieces of a fragmented message are not received before the expiration of the recipient's reassembly timer.

ICMPv4 Redirect Messages

Every device on an internetwork needs to be able to send to every other device. If hosts were responsible for determining the routes to each possible destination, each host would need to maintain an extensive set of routing information. Since there are so many hosts on an internetwork, this would be a very time-consuming and maintenance-intensive situation.

Instead, IP internetworks are designed around a fundamental design decision: Routers are responsible for determining routes and maintaining routing information. Hosts determine only when they need a datagram routed, and then hand the datagram off to a local router to be sent where it needs to go. I discuss this in more detail in my overview of IP routing concepts (see Chapter 23).

Since most hosts do not maintain routing information, they must rely on routers to know about routes and where to send datagrams intended for different destinations. Typically, a host on an IP network will start out with a routing table that basically tells it to send everything not on the local network to a single *default router*, which will then figure out what to do with it. Obviously, if there is only one router on the network, the host will use that as the default router for all nonlocal traffic. However, if there are two or more routers, sending all datagrams to just one router may not make sense. It is possible that a host could be manually configured to know which router to use for which destinations, but another mechanism in IP can allow a host to learn this automatically.

Consider a Network N1 that contains a number of hosts (H1, H2, and so on) and two routers, R1 and R2. Host H1 has been configured to send all datagrams to Router R1, as its default router. Suppose it wants to send a datagram to a device on Network N2. However, Network N2 is most directly connected to Network N1 using Router R2, not R1. The datagram will first be sent to Router R1, which will look in its routing table and see that datagrams for Network N2 need to be sent through Router R2. "But wait," R1 says. "R2 is on the local network, and H1 is on the local network—so why am I needed as a middleman? H1 should just send datagrams for N2 directly to R2 and leave me out of it."

In this situation, Router R1 will send an ICMPv4 *Redirect* message back to Host H1, telling it that in the future, it should send this type of datagram directly to Router R2. This situation is shown in Figure 32-5. Router R1 will also forward the datagram to Router R2 for delivery, since there is no reason to drop the datagram. Thus, despite usually being grouped along with true ICMP error messages, Redirect messages are really arguably not error messages at all. They represent a situation in which only inefficiency exists, not outright error. (In fact, in ICMPv6, they have been reclassified.)

ICMPv4 Redirect Message Format

Table 32-5 and Figure 32-6 show the specific format for ICMPv4 Redirect messages.

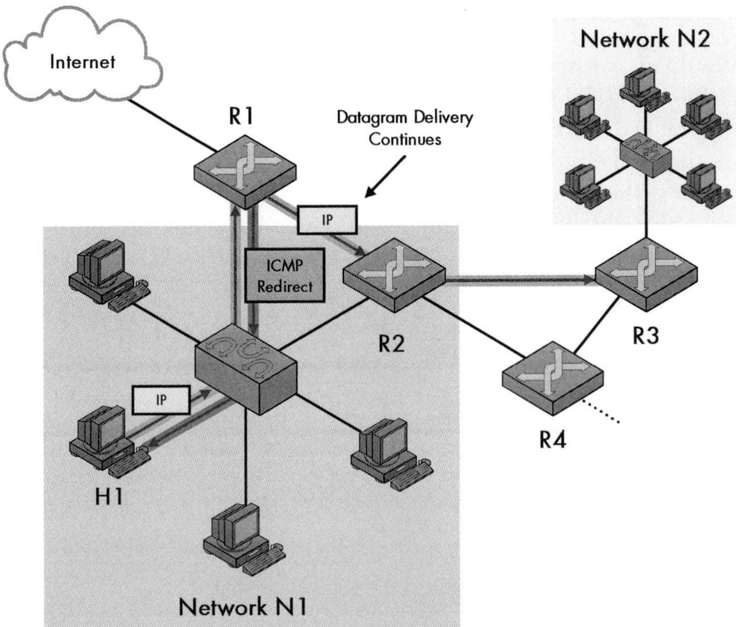

Figure 32-5: Host redirection using an ICMP Redirect message In this example, Host H1 sends to Router R1 a datagram destined for Network N2. However, Router R1 notices that Router R2 is on the same network and is a more direct route to Network N2. It forwards the datagram on to Router R2, but also sends an ICMP Redirect message back to Host H1 to tell it to use Router R2 next time.

Table 32-5: ICMPv4 Redirect Message Format

Field Name	Size (Bytes)	Description
Type	1	Identifies the ICMP message type; for Redirect messages, this value is 5.
Code	1	Identifies the meaning or scope of the Redirect message. See Table 32-6 for an explanation of how this field is used in Redirect messages.
Checksum	2	A 16-bit checksum field for the ICMP header (see Chapter 31).
Internet Address	4	The address of the router to which future datagrams sent to the original destination should be sent.
Original Datagram Portion	Variable	The full IP header and the first 8 bytes of the payload of the datagram that led to the creation of the Redirect.

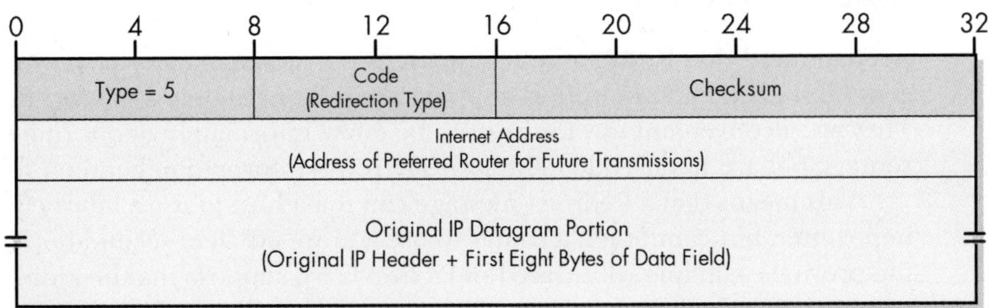

Figure 32-6: ICMPv4 Redirect message format

Redirect Message Interpretation Codes

When a Redirect message is received back by a device, it inspects the included portion of the original datagram. Since this contains the original destination address of the redirected target device, this tells the original sender which addresses should be redirected in the future. The Internet Address field tells it which router it should use for subsequent datagrams. The Code field tells the sender how broadly to interpret the redirection. There are four different Code values, as shown in Table 32-6.

Table 32-6: ICMP Redirect Message Interpretation Codes

Code Value	Message Subtype	Meaning
0	Redirect Datagrams for the Network (or Subnet)	Redirect all future datagrams sent not only to the device whose address caused this Redirect, but also to all other devices on the network (or subnet) where that device is located. (This code is now obsolete; see the note that follows this table.)
1	Redirect Datagrams for the Host	Redirect all future datagrams only for the address of the specific device to which the original datagram was sent.
2	Redirect Datagrams for the Type of Service (TOS) and Network (or Subnet)	Same as for Code value 0, but only for future datagrams that have the same TOS value as the original datagram. (This code is now obsolete; see the note that follows this table.)
3	Redirect Datagrams for the TOS and Host	As for Code value 1, but only for future datagrams that have the same TOS value as the original datagram.

NOTE *One problem with* Redirects *for whole networks is that the network specification may be ambiguous in an environment where subnetting or classless addressing is used. For this reason, the use of Code values 0 and 2 was prohibited by RFC 1812; the values are considered obsolete on the modern Internet.*

Obviously, routers usually generate Redirect messages and send them to hosts; hosts do not normally create them. The specific rules for when Redirect messages are created can be fairly complex, as a number of conditions may exist that preclude these messages from being sent. In particular, special rules exist for when a router may redirect an entire network (or subnet) instead of just a single host. Also, remember that the TOS field is optional and often not used, so Redirects with Code values of 2 or 3 are less common than those with values of 0 and 1.

Limitations of Redirect Messages

Keep in mind that ICMP Redirect messages are *not* a mechanism by which the general routing process in IP is implemented; they are only a support function. They are a convenient way for hosts to be given information about routes by local routers, but are not used to communicate route information between routers.

This means that a Redirect message can tell a host to use a more efficient first-hop router, but cannot tell a router to use a more efficient second-hop router. In the previous example (illustrated in Figure 32-5), suppose that in addition to the connections mentioned, Router R2 is connected to Router R3 and Router R4. Router R2 sends the datagram in question to Router R3, which realizes it needs to send to Router R4, a router already directly connected to Router R2. Router R3 *cannot* send a Redirect message to Router R2 telling it to use Router R4 next time. The messages are simply not designed for this purpose—remember that ICMP messages always go back to the source of the original datagram, which would not be Router R2 in this case. Such inefficiencies must be resolved using routing protocols.

> **KEY CONCEPT** A router uses ICMPv4 *Redirect* messages to inform a host of a preferred router that will be used for future datagrams that are sent to a particular host or network. They are not used to alter routes between routers.

ICMPv4 Parameter Problem Messages

The previous sections in this chapter describe four specific ICMPv4 message types that allow a device to report various error conditions to the original sender of a datagram. However, other error situations may arise that don't correspond to any of these four specific message types. Typically, the problem results when a device attempts to process the header fields of an IP datagram and finds something in it that doesn't make sense.

If a device finds a problem with any of the parameters in an IP datagram header that is serious enough that it cannot complete processing the header, it must discard the datagram. As in other cases where a datagram must be tossed out, this is serious enough to warrant communication of the problem back to the device that sent the original datagram. This is accomplished in ICMPv4 using the *Parameter Problem* message type.

This is a catchall type of message that can be used to indicate an error in any header field of an IP datagram. The message type does not contain any specific fields or coding to indicate what the problem is. This was done intentionally to keep the Parameter Problem message generic and ensure that it could indicate any sort of error. Instead of special error codes, most Parameter Problem messages tell the original source which parameter caused the problem by including a special pointer that indicates which field in the original datagram header caused the problem. Both hosts and routers can generate Parameter Problem messages.

ICMPv4 Parameter Problem Message Format

Table 32-7 and Figure 32-7 show the specific format for ICMPv4 Parameter Problem messages.

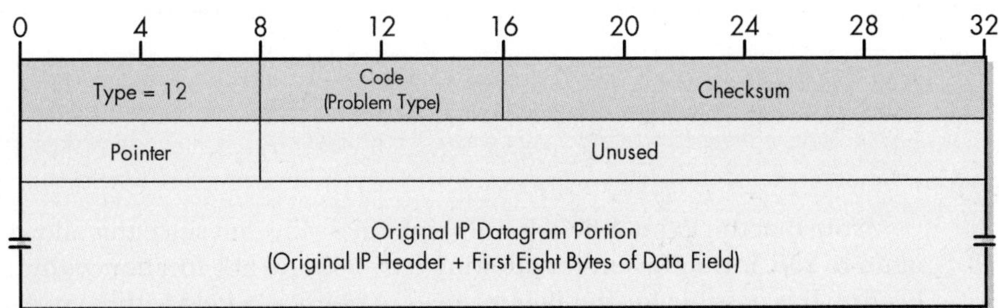

***Figure 32-7:** ICMPv4 Parameter Problem message format*

Table 32-7: ICMPv4 Parameter Problem Message Format

Field Name	Size (Bytes)	Description
Type	1	Identifies the ICMP message type; for Parameter Problem messages, this value is 12.
Code	1	Identifies the subtype of the problem being communicated. See Table 32-8 for more information about this field as it relates to Parameter Problem messages.
Checksum	2	A 16-bit checksum field for the ICMP header (see Chapter 31).
Pointer	1	An offset that points to the byte location in the datagram that caused the Parameter Problem message to be generated. The device receiving the ICMP message can use this value to get an idea of which field in the original message had the problem. This field is used only when the Code value is 0.
Unused	3	3 bytes that are left blank and not used.
Original Datagram Portion	Variable	The full IP header and the first 8 bytes of the payload of the datagram that prompted this error message to be sent.

Parameter Problem Message Interpretation Codes and the Pointer Field

When a Parameter Problem message is generated due to a specific bad field in the original message, the Pointer field is used to show the location of the problem. This meaning of the Parameter Problem message is the one that was defined in the original ICMP standard, RFC 792, and is associated with Code value 0. There are some cases of a parameter problem in which a pointer to a specific field in the original message really wouldn't make sense, so other standards have defined two new Code field values for Parameter Problem messages. Table 32-8 shows the three Code values and provides a brief explanation of each one.

Table 32-8: ICMPv4 Parameter Problem Message Interpretation Codes

Code Value	Message Subtype	Description
0	Pointer Indicates the Error	This is the normal use of the Parameter Problem message. When this Code value is used, the Pointer field indicates the location of the problem.
1	Missing a Required Option	The IP datagram needed to have an option in it that was missing. Since the option was missing, there is no way to point to it.
2	Bad Length	The length of the datagram overall was incorrect, indicating a general problem with the message as a whole. Again, the Pointer field makes no sense here.

KEY CONCEPT The ICMPv4 *Parameter Problem* message is a generic catchall that can be used to convey an error of any type in an IP datagram. A special Pointer field is normally used to indicate to the message's recipient where the problem was in the original datagram.

Note that the Pointer field is only eight bits wide, but since this allows for values of up to 256, it is sufficient for allowing it to point to any location within the IP header. It is possible for the Pointer field to point to a field within an IP option.

33

ICMPV4 INFORMATIONAL MESSAGE TYPES AND FORMATS

The five Internet Control Message Protocol (ICMP) error message types we examined in the previous chapter communicate important information about error or problem conditions encountered during the operation of an Internet Protocol (IP) internetwork. In contrast, the other class of ICMP messages contains those messages that are *informational*. They are not sent in response to some issue with a regular IP datagram, but are used on their own to implement various support functions for IP. Informational messages are used for testing and diagnostic purposes, as well as for allowing devices to share critical information that they need to function correctly.

In this chapter, I describe nine different ICMP version 4 (ICMPv4) informational messages. Because many of these messages are used in functional sets, pairs of related messages are described together. I begin with a discussion of the Echo (Request) and Echo Reply messages used for network testing, and Timestamp (Request) and Timestamp Reply messages used for clock synchronization. I explain the use and format of Router Advertisement and Router Solicitation messages, which allow hosts to discover the identity of local routers and learn important information about them. I also describe the Address Mask Request and Address Mask Reply messages that communicate subnet mask information. I conclude with a look at the Traceroute message, which implements a more sophisticated version of the traceroute utility.

NOTE *The original ICMP standard also defined two more informational message types: Information Request and Information Reply. These were intended to allow devices to determine an IP address and possibly other configuration information. This function was later implemented using host configuration protocols such as the Reverse Address Resolution Protocol (RARP), Boot Protocol (BOOTP), and Dynamic Host Configuration Protocol (DHCP). These message types are now obsolete; therefore, they are not discussed in this chapter.*

ICMPv4 Echo (Request) and Echo Reply Messages

One of the main purposes of ICMP informational messages is to enable testing and diagnostics in order to help identify and correct problems on an internetwork. The most basic test that can be conducted between two devices is simply checking if they are capable of sending datagrams to each other. The usual way that this is done is to have one device send a test message to a second device, which receives the message and replies back to tell the first device it received the message.

ICMPv4 includes a pair of messages specifically for connection testing. Suppose Device A wants to see if it can reach Device B. Device A begins the test process by sending an ICMPv4 *Echo* message to Device B. Device B, when it receives the Echo, responds back to Device A with an *Echo* Reply message. When Device A receives this message, it knows that it is able to communicate (both send and receive) successfully with Device B.

NOTE *The name of the first message in this pair is often given as Echo Request. While this does convey the paired nature of the Echo and Echo Reply messages, the formal name used in the standards is simply an Echo message.*

ICMPv4 Echo and Echo Reply Message Format

Table 33-1 and Figure 33-1 show the format for both ICMPv4 Echo and Echo Reply messages.

Table 33-1: ICMPv4 Echo and Echo Reply Message Format

Field Name	Size (Bytes)	Description
Type	1	Identifies the ICMP message type. For Echo messages, the value is 8; for Echo Reply messages, the value is 0.
Code	1	Not used for Echo and Echo Reply messages; set to 0.
Checksum	2	A 16-bit checksum field for the ICMP header (see Chapter 31).
Identifier	2	An identification field that can be used to help in matching Echo and Echo Reply messages.
Sequence Number	2	A sequence number to help in matching Echo and Echo Reply messages.
Optional Data	Variable	Additional data to be sent along with the message (not specified).

It is possible that a source device may want to send more than one Echo message to either a single destination or multiple destinations. Conversely, a single destination might receive Echo messages from more than one source. It is essential that a device receiving an Echo Reply message knows which Echo message prompted it to be sent.

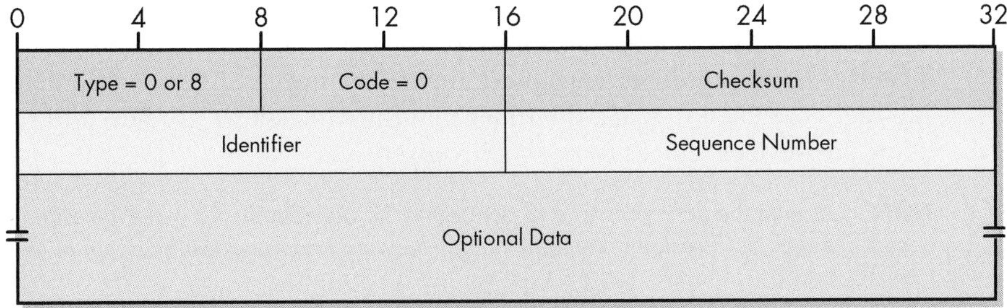

Figure 33-1: ICMPv4 Echo and Echo Reply message format *Two special fields are used within the format of these messages. They allow devices to match Echo and Echo Reply messages together, and exchange a sequence of messages. The Identifier field was envisioned as being used as a higher-level label, like a session identifier, while the Sequence Number was seen as something to identify individual test messages within a series. However, the use of these fields is up to the particular implementation. In some cases, the Identifier field is filled in with the process number of the application that is using the Echo or Echo Reply message to allow several users to use utilities like ping without interference.*

Application of Echo and Echo Reply Messages

The most common way that you may use the Echo and Echo Reply messages is through the popular utility *ping*, which is used to test host reachability. While the basic test simply consists of sending an Echo message and waiting for an Echo Reply message, modern versions of ping are quite sophisticated. They allow the user to specify many parameters, including the number of Echo messages sent, how often they are sent, the size of message transmitted, and more. They also provide a great deal of information about the connection, including the number of Echo Reply messages received, the time elapsed for the pair of messages to be exchanged, and a lot more. See the description of ping in Chapter 88 for a full explanation of the utility.

> **KEY CONCEPT** ICMPv4 *Echo (Request)* and *Echo Reply* messages are used to facilitate network reachability testing. A device can test its ability to perform basic communication with another one by sending an Echo message and waiting for an Echo Reply message to be returned by the other device. The ping utility, a widely used diagnostic tool in TCP/IP internetworks, makes use of these messages.

ICMPv4 Timestamp (Request) and Timestamp Reply Messages

All of the hosts and routers on an internetwork operate independently of each other. One aspect of this autonomy is that each device maintains a separate system clock. There's a problem, however: Even highly accurate clocks have slight differences in both how accurately they keep time and the time with which they were initialized at startup. This means that under normal circumstances, no two devices on an internetwork are guaranteed to have exactly the same time.

The creators of TCP/IP recognized that certain applications might not work properly if there were too much differential between the system clocks of a pair of devices. To support this requirement, they created a pair of ICMP messages that allow devices to exchange system time information. The initiating device creates a Timestamp message and sends it to the device with which it wishes to synchronize. That device responds with a Timestamp Reply message. Timestamp fields in these messages are used to mark the times that these messages are sent and received to allow the devices' clocks to be synchronized.

NOTE *As with the Echo message (described in the previous section), the Timestamp message is sometimes seen as Timestamp Request, though the word* Request *doesn't appear in its formal name.*

ICMPv4 Timestamp and Timestamp Reply Message Format

The ICMPv4 *Timestamp* and *Timestamp Reply* messages have the same format. The originating device fills in some of the fields, and the replying device fills in others. The format is as shown in Table 33-2 and Figure 33-2.

Table 33-2: ICMPv4 Timestamp and Timestamp Reply Message Format

Field Name	Size (Bytes)	Description
Type	1	Identifies the ICMP message type. For Timestamp messages, the value is 13; for Timestamp Reply messages, the value is 14.
Code	1	Not used for Timestamp and Timestamp Reply messages; set to 0.
Checksum	2	A 16-bit checksum field for the ICMP header (see Chapter 31).
Identifier	2	An identification field that can be used to help in matching Timestamp and Timestamp Reply messages.
Sequence Number	2	A sequence number to help in matching Timestamp and Timestamp Reply messages.
Originate Timestamp	4	A time value filled in by the originating device just before sending the Timestamp message.
Receive Timestamp	4	A time value filled in by the responding device just as it receives the Timestamp message.
Transmit Timestamp	4	A time value filled in by the responding device just before sending back the Timestamp Reply message.

The Identifier and Sequence Number fields are used to match Timestamp and Timestamp Reply messages, exactly as they are used for Echo and Echo Reply messages. The Identifier field is intended as a higher-level label, like a session identifier, while the Sequence Number is often used to identify individual messages within a series. However, the use of these fields is up to the particular implementation.

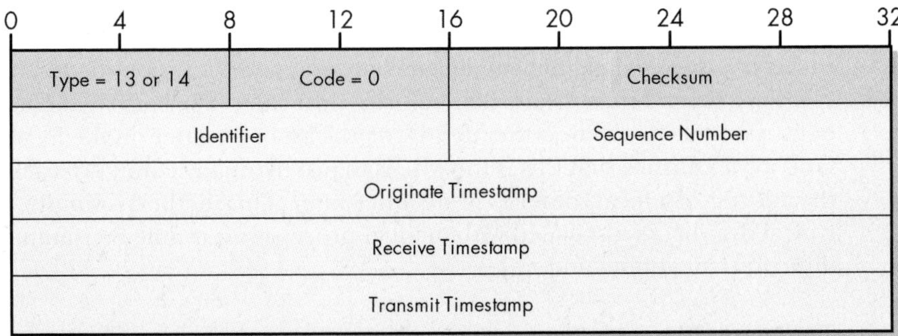

Figure 33-2: *ICMPv4 Timestamp and Timestamp Reply message format*

All three timestamps are represented as the number of milliseconds since midnight, *Universal Time* (*UT*, also called *Greenwich mean time* or *GMT*). The reason there are three timestamps instead of the two you might ordinarily expect is that the responding device records a separate timestamp when it receives the Timestamp message and when it generates the Timestamp Reply. When the Reply message is received back by the originating device, it then has the times that both the Timestamp and the Timestamp Reply messages were sent. This allows the originating device to differentiate between the time required for transmitting datagrams over the network and the time for the other device to process the Timestamp message and turn it into a Timestamp Reply message.

Issues Using Timestamp and Timestamp Reply Messages

In practice, even with these three timestamp fields, it is difficult to coordinate system clocks over an internetwork, especially a large one like the Internet. The main problem is that the amount of time it takes to send a datagram between any pair of devices varies from one datagram to the next. And again, since IP is unreliable, it's possible that the time for a datagram to be received could be infinite. In fact, it might be lost or dropped by a router.

This means that a simple exchange of Timestamp and Timestamp Reply messages is simply not a method that's reliable enough to ensure that two devices are synchronized on a typical IP internetwork. For this reason, modern devices often use a more sophisticated method for time synchronization, such as the Network Time Protocol (NTP).

Note that unlike many of the other ICMP message types, support for Timestamp and Timestamp Reply messages is optional, for both hosts and routers.

ICMPv4 Router Advertisement and Router Solicitation Messages

In Chapter 23, which described IP routing fundamentals, I discussed a critical aspect of IP internetwork design: the difference between the roles of a router and the roles of a host with regard to routing. Routers are charged with the job of routing datagrams, and therefore, of knowing routes and exchanging route information. Hosts generally do not know a great deal about routes; they rely on routers to convey datagrams intended for destinations outside the local network.

This dependence means that before a host can really participate on an internetwork, it needs to know the identity of at least one router on the local network. One way to ensure that this is the case is to just manually configure each host with the address of a local router as its default router. This method is simple, but has the typical drawbacks associated with manual processes: It is time-consuming to set up, difficult to maintain, and inflexible.

The Router Discovery Process

It would be better if there were some method whereby a host could automatically discover the identity of local routers and learn important information about them. In IP, this process is called *Router Discovery* and was first defined in RFC 1256, "ICMP Router Discovery Messages." The messages referenced in the RFC title are the ICMP Router Advertisement message and the Router Solicitation message. They were added to the ICMP message types that were defined in earlier standards such as RFC 792.

Routers are responsible for sending *Router Advertisement* messages. These messages tell listening devices that the router exists, and they provide important information about the router such as its address (or addresses, if it has more than one) and how long the host should retain information about the router. Routine Router Advertisement messages are sent on a regular basis, and an administrator can configure the time between messages (usually between seven and ten minutes). Hosts listen for these messages; when an advertisement is received, the host processes it and adds the information about the router to its routing table.

A host that does not have any manually configured routing information will have no knowledge of routers when it first powers on. Having it sit for many minutes while it looks for a routine Router Advertisement message is inefficient. Instead of waiting, the host may send a *Router Solicitation* message on its local network(s). This will prompt any router that hears it to immediately send out an extra Router Advertisement message directly to that host.

ICMPv4 Router Advertisement Message Format

The ICMPv4 Router Advertisement message format is shown in Table 33-3 and Figure 33-3.

Table 33-3: ICMPv4 Router Advertisement Message Format

Field Name	Size (Bytes)	Description
Type	1	Identifies the ICMP message type. For Router Advertisement messages, the value is 9.
Code	1	Normally set to 0. When a Mobile IP agent is sending a Router Advertisement with an Agent Advertisement extension, it may set the value to 16 only if the device is a mobile agent and doesn't intend to handle normal traffic. See the discussion of Mobile IP agent discovery for details (Chapter 30).
Checksum	2	A 16-bit checksum field for the ICMP header (see Chapter 31).
Num Addrs	1	The number of addresses associated with this router that are included in this advertisement.
Addr Entry Size	1	The address entry size—number of 32-bit words of information included with each address. Since in this message format each router address has a 32-bit address and a 32-bit preference level, this value is fixed at 2.
Lifetime	2	The number of seconds that a host should consider the information in this message valid.
Router Address Entries	Value of Num Addrs field * 8	A number of router address entries equal to the value of the Num Addrs field. Each is 8 bytes and has two subfields, each 4 bytes in size. The Router Address subfield is a valid address for an interface to the router sending this message. The Preference Level subfield is the preference level of this address. When more than one address is included in an advertisement, this field indicates which address the router would prefer hosts to use. Higher values mean greater preference.

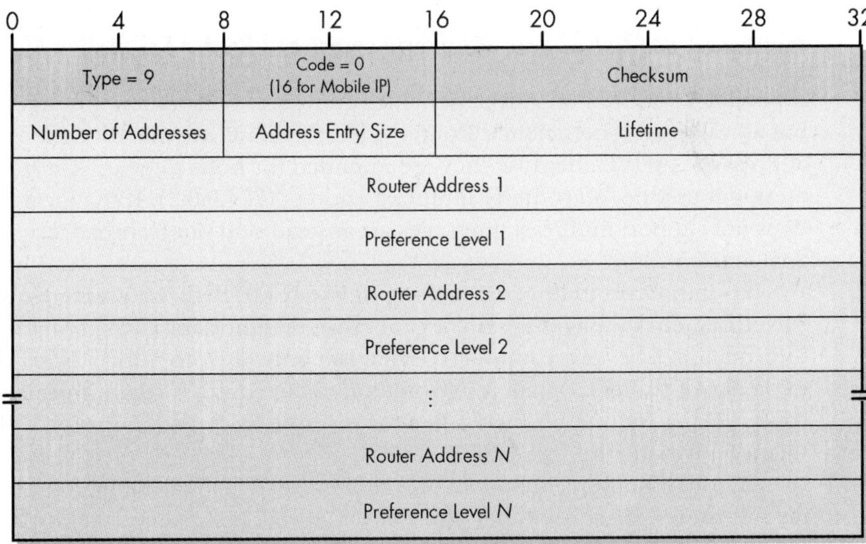

***Figure 33-3:** ICMPv4 Router Advertisement Message format*

ICMPv4 Router Solicitation Message Format

ICMPv4 Router Solicitation messages are much simpler, because they need to convey only the following single piece of information: "If you are a router and can hear this, please send a Router Advertisement to me." The format is therefore just the trivial set of fields shown in Table 33-4 and illustrated in Figure 33-4.

Table 33-4: ICMPv4 Router Solicitation Message Format

Field Name	Size (Bytes)	Description
Type	1	Identifies the ICMP message type. For Router Solicitation messages, the value is 10.
Code	1	Not used; value set to 0.
Checksum	2	A 16-bit checksum field for the ICMP header (see Chapter 31).
Reserved	4	The 4 reserved bytes sent as 0.

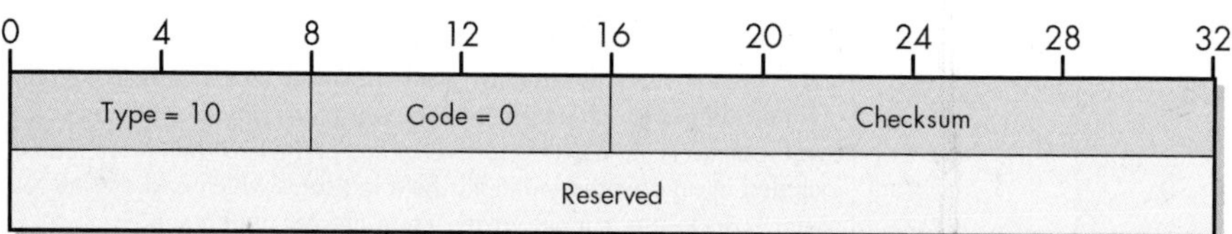

Figure 33-4: *ICMPv4 Router Solicitation Message format*

Addressing and Use of Router Advertisement and Router Solicitation Messages

If possible, both Router Advertisement and Router Solicitation messages are sent out as multicast for efficiency. Router Advertisements use the "all devices" multicast address (224.0.0.1), because they are intended for hosts to hear. *Router Solicitation* messages use the "all routers" multicast address (224.0.0.2). If the local network does not support multicast, messages are instead sent out by broadcast (to address 255.255.255.255).

It is important to remember that just like ICMP Redirect messages, Router Advertisement messages are not a generalized method for exchanging routing information. They are a support mechanism only, used to inform hosts about the existence of routers. Detailed information about routes is communicated between routers using routing protocols, like the Routing Information Protocol (RIP) and Open Shortest Path First (OSPF).

Although Router Discovery is one alternative to manual configuration of a host's default router, there are other alternatives as well. For example, a host configuration protocol like the Dynamic Host Configuration Protocol (DHCP) can allow a host to learn the address of a default router on the local network.

Finally, note that when Mobile IP is implemented, Router Advertisement messages are used as the basis for Mobile IP–aware routers to send Agent Advertisements. One or more special extensions are added to the regular Router Advertisement format to create an Agent Advertisement. This is discussed extensively in the section on Mobile IP Agent Discovery in Chapter 31.

KEY CONCEPT ICMP *Router Advertisement* messages are sent regularly by IP routers to inform hosts of their presence and characteristics. This way, hosts know to use them for delivery of datagrams to distant hosts. A host that is new to a network and wants to find out immediately what routers are present may send a *Router Solicitation* message, which will prompt listening routers to send out Router Advertisement messages.

ICMPv4 Address Mask Request and Reply Messages

When IP was first developed, IP addresses were based on a simple two-level structure, with a network identifier (network ID) and host identifier (host ID). To provide more flexibility, a technique called *subnetting* was soon developed. Subnetting expands the addressing scheme into a three-level structure, with each address containing a network ID, subnet identifier, and host ID. The *subnet mask* is a 32-bit number that tells devices (and users) which bits are part of the subnet identifier, as compared to the host ID. All of this is described in considerable detail in the part on IP addressing (Part II-3).

To function properly in a subnetting environment, each host must know the subnet mask that corresponds to each address it is assigned. Without the mask, it cannot properly interpret IP addresses. Just as in determining the identity of a local router, a host can be informed of the local network's subnet mask either manually or automatically. The manual method is to simply manually assign the subnet mask to each host. The automatic method makes use of a pair of ICMP messages designed for subnet mask determination, which were defined in RFC 950, the same standard that defined subnetting itself.

To use this method, a host sends an *Address Mask Request* message on the local network, usually to get a response from a router. If it knows the address of a local router, it may send the request directly (unicast); otherwise, the host will broadcast the request to any listening router. A local router (or other device) will receive this message and respond back with an *Address Mask Reply* message that contains the subnet mask for the local network. This process is somewhat similar to the mechanism used by a host to solicit a router to respond with a Router Advertisement message, except that routers do not routinely send subnet mask information—that information must be requested.

ICMPv4 Address Mask Request and Address Mask Reply Message Format

The Address Mask Request and Address Mask Reply, like some other request and reply pairs, have the same basic format. The host creates the request with all fields filled in except for the subnet mask value itself, and the router supplies the mask and sends the reply back to the host. The format is described in Table 33-5 and illustrated in Figure 33-5.

Table 33-5: ICMPv4 Address Mask Request and Address Mask Reply Message Format

Field Name	Size (Bytes)	Description
Type	1	Identifies the ICMP message type. For Address Mask Request messages, the value is 17; for Address Mask Reply messages, it is 18.
Code	1	Not used for either message type; set to 0.
Checksum	2	A 16-bit checksum field for the ICMP header (see Chapter 31).
Identifier	2	An identification field that can be used to help in matching Address Mask Request and Address Mask Reply messages.
Sequence Number	2	A sequence number to help in matching Address Mask Request and Address Mask Reply messages.
Address Mask	4	The subnet mask for the local network, filled in by the router in the Address Mask Reply message.

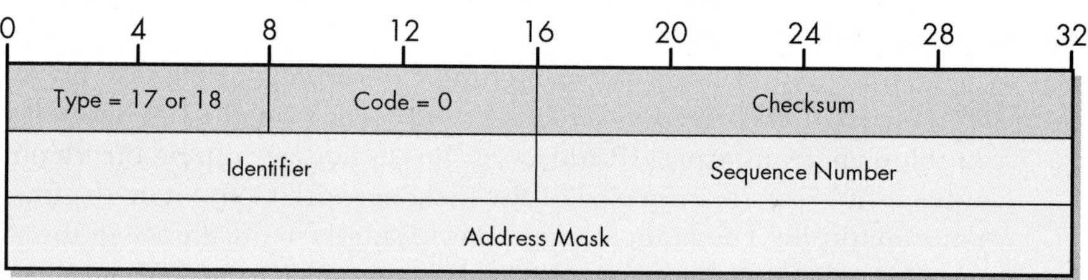

Figure 33-5: *ICMPv4 Address Mask Request and Address Mask Reply message format*

The Identifier and Sequence Number fields can be used to match up requests and replies, as they are for Echo and Echo Reply messages. However, a host won't normally send multiple requests for subnet masks the way it might send Echo messages for testing. For this reason, the Identifier and Sequence Number fields may be ignored by some implementations.

Use of Address Mask Request and Address Mask Reply Messages

Note that the use of Address Mask Request and Address Mask Reply messages is optional, just as the Router Discovery described in the previous section is. Other methods besides these messages or manual configuration may be used to tell a host what subnet mask to use. Again, a common alternative to ICMP for this is to use a host configuration protocol like DHCP. Routers do need to be able to respond to Address Mask Requests for hosts that choose to send them.

ICMPv4 Traceroute Messages

The Echo and Echo Reply messages you saw earlier in this chapter are used for the most basic type of test that can be conducted between two devices: checking if they can communicate. A more sophisticated test can also be performed in order to see not only if the devices are able to talk, but also to discover the exact sequence of routers used to move datagrams between them. In TCP/IP, this diagnostic is performed using the traceroute (or tracert) utility.

The first implementation of *traceroute* used a clever application of Time Exceeded error messages, as described in the previous chapter. By sending a test message to a destination first with a Time to Live (TTL) value of 1, then 2, then 3, and so on, each router in the path between the source and destination would successively discard the test messages and send back a Time Exceeded message. Each router would then display the sequence of routers between the two hosts. This bit of trickery works well enough in general terms, but is suboptimal in a couple of respects. For example, it requires the source device to send one test message for each router in the path, instead of just a single test message. It also doesn't take into account the possibility that the path between two devices may change during the test.

Recognizing these limitations, a new experimental standard was developed in 1993 that defined a more efficient way to conduct a traceroute: RFC 1393, "Traceroute Using an IP Option." As the title suggests, this method of doing a traceroute works by having the source device send a single datagram to the destination that contains a special Traceroute IP option. Each router that sees that option while the test message is conducted along the route responds back to the original source with an ICMP Traceroute message, which is also defined in RFC 1393.

ICMPv4 Traceroute Message Format

Since the *Traceroute* message was specifically designed for the traceroute utility, it was possible to incorporate extra information in it that a host tracing a route could use. The message format is as shown in Table 33-6 and Figure 33-6.

Table 33-6: ICMPv4 Traceroute Message Format

Field Name	Size (Bytes)	Description
Type	1	Identifies the ICMP message type; in this case, 30.
Code	1	Set to the value 0 if the datagram the source device sent was successfully sent to the next router, or 1 to indicate that the datagram was dropped (meaning the traceroute failed).
Checksum	2	A 16-bit checksum field for the ICMP header (see Chapter 31).
ID Number	2	An identification field used to match up this Traceroute message to the original message sent by the source (the one containing the Traceroute IP option).
Unused	2	Not used, set to 0.
Outbound Hop Count	2	The number of routers the original message has already passed through.
Return Hop Count	2	The number of routers the return message has passed through.
Output Link Speed	4	The speed of the link over which the Traceroute message is being sent, in bytes per second.
Output Link MTU	4	The maximum transmission unit (MTU) of the link over which the Traceroute message is being sent, in bytes.

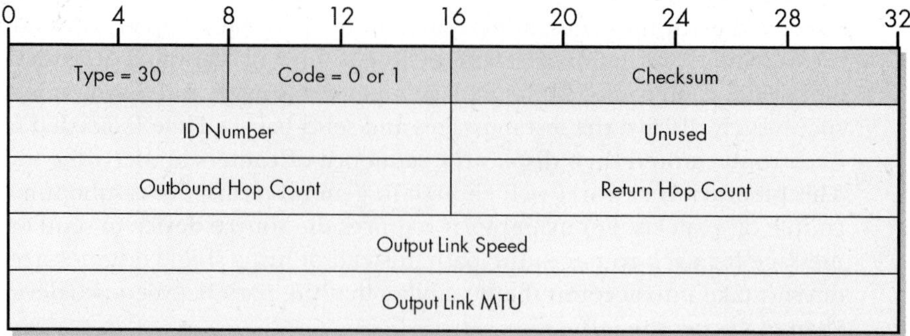

Figure 33-6: *ICMPv4 Traceroute message format*

Use of Traceroute Messages

Although this method of implementing traceroute has advantages over the older Time Exceeded messages method, it has one critical flaw as well: It requires changes to both hosts and routers to support the new IP option and the Traceroute ICMP message. People aren't big on change, especially when it comes to the basic operation of IP. For this reason, RFC 1393 never moved beyond experimental status, and most IP devices still use the older method of implementing traceroute. It is possible that you may encounter ICMP Traceroute messages, however, so it's good that you know they exist.

KEY CONCEPT ICMP *Traceroute* messages were designed to provide a more capable way of implementing the traceroute (tracert) utility. However, most TCP/IP implementations still use ICMP Time Exceeded messages for this task.

34

ICMPV6 ERROR MESSAGE TYPES AND FORMATS

The original Internet Control Message Protocol (ICMP) defined for version 4 of the Internet Protocol (IPv4) has a number of error messages that allow for the communication of problems on an internetwork. When IP version 6 (IPv6) was developed, the differences between IPv4 and IPv6 were significant enough that a new version of ICMP was also required: version 6 *(ICMPv6)*, which is currently specified in RFC 2463. Like ICMPv4, ICMPv6 defines several error messages for informing a source that something has gone wrong.

In this chapter, I describe the four ICMPv6 error messages defined in RFC 2463. I first discuss ICMPv6 Destination Unreachable messages, which are used to tell a device that the datagram it sent could not be delivered for a variety of reasons. I describe Packet Too Big error messages, which are sent when a datagram can't be sent due to being too large for an underlying network it needs to traverse. I explain the use of Time Exceeded messages, which indicate that too much time was taken to accomplish a transmission.

I conclude with a look at Parameter Problem messages, which provide a generalized way of reporting errors that are not described by any of the preceding ICMPv6 error message types.

NOTE *Three of the four ICMPv6 error messages (all except Packet Too Big) are equivalent to the ICMPv4 error messages that have the same names. However, to allow this chapter to stand on its own, I describe each one fully, in addition to pointing out any significant differences between the ICMPv4 and ICMPv6 version of the message.*

ICMPv6 Destination Unreachable Messages

IPv6 includes some important enhancements over the older version 4, but the basic operation of the two protocols is still fundamentally the same. Like IPv4, IPv6 is an unreliable network protocol that makes a best effort to deliver datagrams, but offers no guarantees that they will always get there. Just as they did in IPv4, devices on an IPv6 network must not assume that datagrams sent to a destination will always be received.

When a datagram cannot be delivered, recovery from this condition normally falls to higher-layer protocols like the Transmission Control Protocol (TCP), which will detect the miscommunication and resend the lost datagrams. In some situations, such as a datagram that was dropped due to the congestion of a router, this is sufficient, but in other cases, a datagram may not be delivered due to an inherent problem with how it is being sent. For example, the source may have specified an invalid destination address, which means that even if it were resent many times, the datagram would never get to its intended recipient.

In general, having the source just resend undelivered datagrams while having no idea why they were lost is inefficient. It is better to have a feedback mechanism that can tell a source device about undeliverable datagrams and provide some information about why the datagram delivery failed. As in ICMPv4, in ICMPv6 this is done with *Destination Unreachable* messages. Each message includes a code that indicates the basic nature of the problem that caused the datagram not to be delivered, as well as all or part of the datagram that was undelivered in order to help the source device diagnose the problem.

ICMPv6 Destination Unreachable Message Format

Table 34-1 and Figure 34-1 show the specific format for ICMPv6 Destination Unreachable messages.

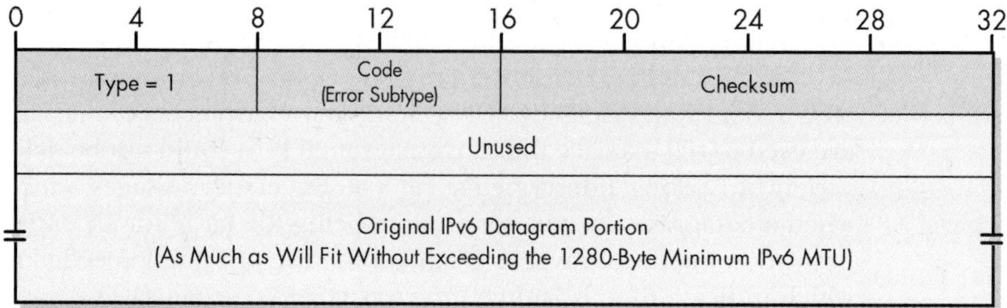

Figure 34-1: ICMPv6 Destination Unreachable message format

Table 34-1: ICMPv6 Destination Unreachable Message Format

Field Name	Size (Bytes)	Description
Type	1	Identifies the ICMPv6 message type; for Destination Unreachable messages, this is set to 1.
Code	1	Identifies the subtype of unreachable errors that are being communicated. See Table 34-2 for a full list of codes and what they mean.
Checksum	2	A 16-bit checksum field for the ICMP header (see Chapter 31).
Unused	4	The 4 bytes that are left blank and not used.
Original Datagram Portion	Variable	As much of the IPv6 datagram as will fit without causing the size of the ICMPv6 error message (including its own IP header) to exceed the minimum IPv6 maximum transmission unit (MTU) of 1280 bytes.

ICMPv6 Destination Unreachable Message Subtypes

There are a number of different reasons why a destination may be unreachable. To provide additional information about the nature of the problem to the device that originally tried to send the datagram, a value is placed in the message's Code field. One interesting difference between ICMPv4 and ICMPv6 Destination Unreachable messages is that there are many fewer Code values for ICMPv6. The ICMPv6 Code values were streamlined, mainly because several of the ICMPv4 codes were related to relatively obscure features that aren't applicable to ICMPv6.

Table 34-2 shows the different Code values, corresponding message subtypes, and a brief explanation of each.

Table 34-2: ICMPv6 Destination Unreachable Message Subtypes

Code Value	Message Subtype	Description
0	No Route to Destination	The datagram was not delivered because it could not be routed to the destination. Since this means that the datagram could not be sent to the destination device's local network, this is basically equivalent to the Network Unreachable message subtype in ICMPv4.
1	Communication with Destination Administratively Prohibited	The datagram could not be forwarded due to filtering that blocks the message based on its contents. Equivalent to the message subtype with the same name (and *Code* value 13) in ICMPv4.
3	Address Unreachable	There was a problem attempting to deliver the datagram to the host specified in the destination address. This code is equivalent to the ICMPv4 Host Unreachable code and usually means that the destination address was bad or that there was a problem with resolving it into a layer 2 address.
4	Port Unreachable	The destination port specified in the UDP or TCP header was invalid or does not exist on the destination host.

Note that Code value 2 is not used. Also, Destination Unreachable messages are sent only when there is a fundamental problem with delivering a particular datagram; they are not sent when a datagram is dropped simply due to congestion of a router.

Processing of Destination Unreachable Messages

It is up to the recipient of an ICMPv6 Destination Unreachable message to decide what to do with it. However, just as the original datagram may not reach its destination, the Destination Unreachable message may do the same. Therefore, a device cannot rely on the receipt of one of these error messages to inform it of every delivery problem. This is especially true given that it is possible that some unreachable destination problems may not be detectable.

KEY CONCEPT ICMPv6 *Destination Unreachable* messages are used in the same manner as the ICMPv4 Destination Unreachable messages: to inform a sending device of a failure to deliver an IP datagram. The message's Code field provides information about the nature of the delivery problem (though the Code values are different from those in ICMPv4).

ICMPv6 Packet Too Big Messages

One of the most interesting changes made to the operation of IP in version 6 is related to the process of datagram fragmentation and reassembly. In IPv4, a host can send a datagram of any size that's allowed by the IP specification out onto the internetwork. If a router needs to send the datagram over a physical link that has a maximum transmission unit (MTU) size that is too small for the size of the datagram, it will automatically fragment the datagram and send the fragments individually so they will fit. The destination device will receive the fragments and reassemble them. I explain the basics behind this in Chapter 22.

Even though it is convenient for hosts to be able to rely on routers to automatically fragment messages as needed, it is inefficient for routers to spend time doing this. For this reason, in IPv6 developers made the decision to not allow routers to fragment datagrams. This puts the responsibility on each host to ensure that the datagrams they send out are small enough to fit over every physical network between itself and any destination. This is done either by using the IPv6 default minimum MTU of 1280, which every physical link must support, or a special Path MTU Discovery process for determining the minimum MTU between a pair of devices. Again, the full details are in Chapter 22.

If an IPv6 router is not allowed to fragment an IPv6 datagram that is too large to fit on the next physical link over which it must be forwarded, what should the router do with it? The datagram can't be forwarded, so the router has no choice but to discard it. When this happens, the router is required to report this occurrence back to the device that initially sent the datagram, using an ICMPv6 *Packet Too Big* message. The source device will know that it needs to fragment the datagram in order to have it successfully reach its destination.

NOTE *Recall that* packet *is a synonym for* datagram, *so you can think of this as the "Datagram Too Big" message.*

ICMPv6 Packet Too Big Message Format

Table 34-3 and Figure 34-2 show the format for ICMPv6 Packet Too Big messages.

Table 34-3: ICMPv6 Packet Too Big Message Format

Field Name	Size (Bytes)	Description
Type	1	Identifies the ICMPv6 message type; for Packet Too Big messages, this is set to 2.
Code	1	Not used for this message type; set to 0.
Checksum	2	A 16-bit checksum field for the ICMP header (see Chapter 31).
MTU	4	The MTU size, in bytes, of the physical link over which the router wanted to send the datagram, but was not able to do so due to the datagram's size. Including this value in the Packet Too Big message tells the source device the size it needs to use for its next transmission to this destination in order to avoid this problem in the future (at least for this particular link).
Original Datagram Portion	Variable	As much of the IPv6 datagram as will fit without causing the size of the ICMPv6 message (including its own IP header) to exceed the minimum IPv6 MTU of 1280 bytes.

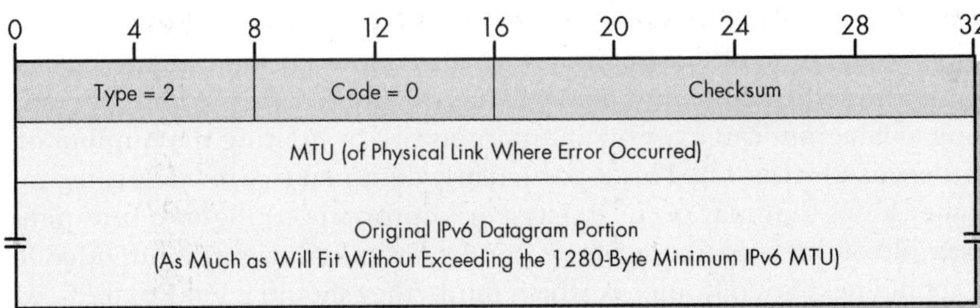

Figure 34-2: *ICMPv6 Packet Too Big message format*

KEY CONCEPT In IPv6, routers are not allowed to fragment datagrams that are too large to send over a physical link to which they are connected. An oversized datagram is dropped, and an ICMPv6 *Packet Too Big* message is sent back to the datagram's originator to inform it of this occurrence.

Applications of Packet Too Big Messages

While Packet Too Big is obviously an error message, it also has another use: the implementation of Path MTU Discovery. This process, described in RFC 1981, defines a way for a device to determine the minimum MTU for a path to a destination. To perform Path MTU Discovery, the source device sends a series of test messages, decreasing the size of the datagram until it no longer receives Packet Too Big messages back in response to its tests. See Chapter 27 for a bit more detail on this.

NOTE *The Packet Too Big message is new to ICMPv6. However, its use is somewhat similar to the use of the Fragmentation Needed and DF Set version of the ICMP4 Destination Unreachable message type, which is used as part of IPv4's Path MTU Discovery feature.*

Incidentally, Packet Too Big is an exception to the rule that ICMP messages are sent only in response to unicast datagrams; it may be sent in reply to an oversized multicast datagram. If this occurs, it is important to realize that some of the intended targets of the multicast may still have received it, if the path the multicast took to them did not go through the link with the small MTU that caused the error.

ICMPv6 Time Exceeded Messages

The engineers who first designed IP recognized that due to the nature of how routing works on an internetwork, there was always a danger that a datagram might get lost in the system and spend too much time being passed from one router to another. They included in IPv4 datagrams a field called *Time to Live (TTL)*, which was intended to be set to a time value by the device sending the datagram and used as a timer to cause the datagram to be discarded if it took too long to get to its destination.

Eventually, the meaning of this field was changed, so it represented not a time in seconds but the number of hops the datagram was allowed to traverse. In IPv6, the new meaning of this field was formalized when it was renamed *Hop Limit*. Regardless of its name, the field still has the same basic purpose: It restricts how long a datagram can exist on an internetwork by limiting the number of times routers can forward it. This is particularly designed to provide protection against router loops that may occur in large or improperly configured internetworks. An example of this situation is where Router A thinks datagrams intended for Network X should next go to Router B, which thinks they should go to Router C, which thinks they need to go to Router A. Without a Hop Limit, such datagrams would circle forever, clogging networks and never accomplishing anything useful. Figure 34-3 illustrates the router loop problem.

Each time a router passes an IPv6 datagram, it decreases the Hop Limit field. If the value ever reaches zero, the datagram expires and is discarded. When this happens, the router that dropped the datagram sends an ICMPv6 Time Exceeded message back to the datagram's originator to inform it that the datagram was dropped. This is basically the same as the ICMPv4 *Time Exceeded* message. As in the ICMPv4 case, the device receiving the message must decide whether and how to respond to receipt of the message. For example, since a device using a Hop Limit that was too low can cause the error, the device may try to resend the datagram with a higher value before concluding that there is a routing problem and giving up. (Chapter 32 for an illustration of how TTL expiration works.)

Just as with the ICMPv4 equivalent, there is also another time expiration situation in which ICMPv6 Time Exceeded messages are used. When an IP message is broken into fragments that are sent independently, the destination device is charged with reassembling the fragments into the original message. One or more fragments may not make it to the destination, however. To prevent the device from waiting forever, it sets a timer when the first fragment arrives. If this timer expires before all of the other fragments are also received, the device gives up on this message. The fragments are tossed out, and a Time Exceeded message is generated.

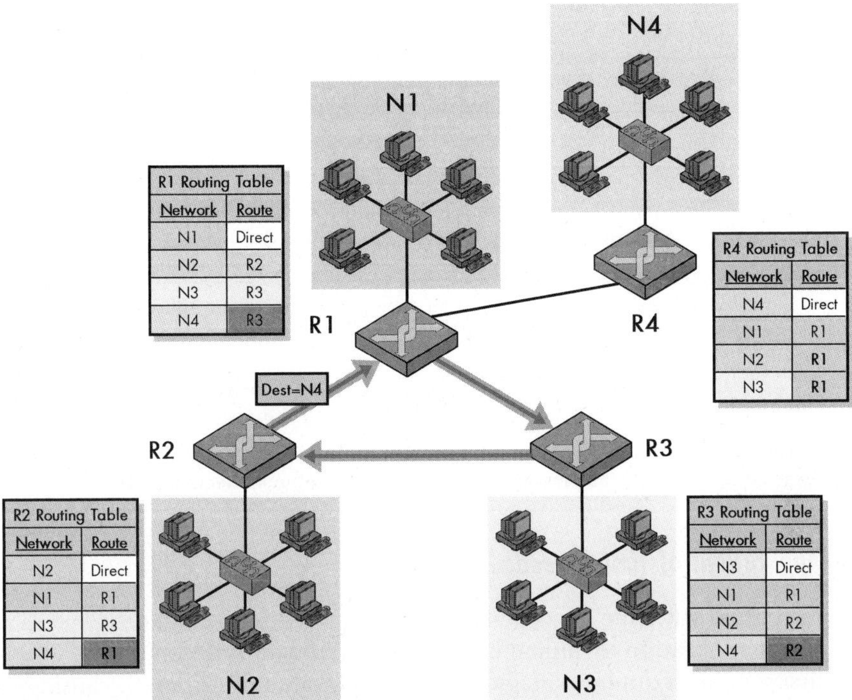

Figure 34-3: An example of a router loop *This diagram shows a simple internetwork consisting of four networks, each of which is served by a router. It is an adaptation of Figure 23-3 from Chapter 23, but in this case, the routing tables have been set up incorrectly. Router R1 thinks that it needs to route any traffic intended for Network N4 to Router R3, which thinks it goes to Router R2, which thinks it goes back to Router R1. This means that when any device tries to send to Network N4, the datagram will circle this triangle until its* Hop Limit *is reached, at which point an ICMPv6 Time Exceeded message will be generated.*

ICMPv6 Time Exceeded Message Format

Table 34-4 and Figure 34-4 show the format for ICMPv6 Time Exceeded messages.

Table 34-4: ICMPv6 Time Exceeded Message Format

Field Name	Size (Bytes)	Description
Type	1	Identifies the ICMPv6 message type; for Time Exceeded messages, this is set to 3.
Code	1	Identifies the subtype of time error that's being communicated. A value of 0 indicates expiration of the Hop Limit field; a value of 1 indicates that the fragment reassembly time has been exceeded.
Checksum	2	A 16-bit checksum field for the ICMP header (see Chapter 31).
Unused	4	The 4 bytes left blank and not used.
Original Datagram Portion	Variable	As much of the IPv6 datagram as will fit without causing the size of the ICMPv6 error message (including its own IP header) to exceed the minimum IPv6 MTU of 1280 bytes.

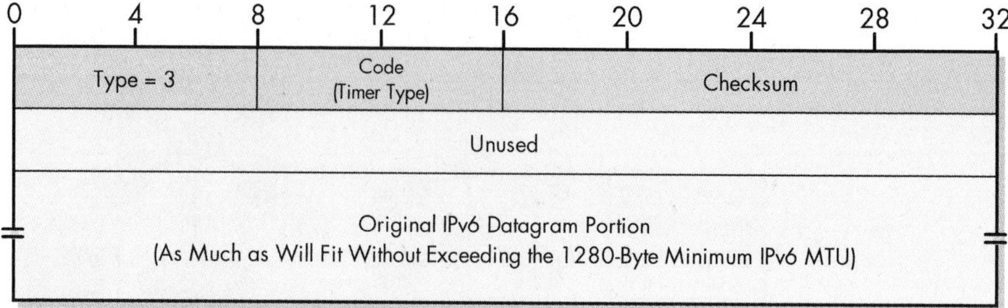

Figure 34-4: *ICMPv6 Time Exceeded message format*

> **KEY CONCEPT** Like their ICMPv4 namesakes, ICMPv6 *Time Exceeded* messages are sent in two different time-related circumstances. The first is if a datagram's *Hop Limit* field is reduced to zero, thereby causing it to expire and the datagram to be dropped. The second is when all the pieces of a fragmented message are not received before the recipient's reassembly timer expires.

Applications of Time Exceeded Messages

In IPv4, ICMP Time Exceeded messages are used both as an error message and in a clever application to implement the TCP/IP traceroute command. This is done by first sending a dummy datagram with a TTL value of 1, thereby causing the first hop in the route to discard the datagram and send back an ICMP Time Exceeded message. Then a second datagram is sent to the same destination with a TTL value of 2, thus causing the second device in the route to report back a Time Exceeded message, and so on.

There is an IPv6 version of traceroute that is sometimes called *traceroute6*. Due to the fact that IPv6 and its protocols and applications are still in development, I have not been able to confirm definitively that traceroute6 is implemented using ICMPv6 Time Exceeded messages in the manner described earlier, but I believe this is the case (and it certainly would make sense). See Chapter 88 for more information about traceroute.

ICMPv6 Parameter Problem Messages

The ICMPv6 Destination Unreachable, Packet Too Big, and Time Exceeded messages described in the previous sections are used to indicate specific error conditions to the original sender of a datagram. Recognizing that a router or host may encounter some other problem in processing a datagram that is not covered by any of these message types, ICMPv6 includes a generic error message type, just as ICMPv4 did. This is called the ICMPv6 *Parameter Problem* message.

As the name suggests, a Parameter Problem message indicates that a device found a problem with a parameter (another name for a datagram field) while attempting to work its way through the header (or headers) in an IPv6 datagram. This message is generated only when the error encountered is serious enough that the device could not make sense of the datagram and had to discard it. So, if an error is found that a device is able to recover from (does not need to drop the datagram), no Parameter Problem message is created.

As was the case for the ICMPv4 version of this message, the ICMPv6 message was designed to be generic, so it can indicate an error in basically any field in the original datagram. A special Pointer field is used that points to the place in that datagram where the error was encountered. By looking at the structure of the original message (which, as you may recall, is included up to a certain size in the ICMP message format), the original device can tell which field contained the problem. The Code value is also used to communicate additional general information about the nature of the problem.

ICMPv6 Parameter Problem Message Format

Table 34-5 and Figure 34-5 show the format for ICMPv6 Parameter Problem messages.

Table 34-5: ICMPv6 Parameter Problem Message Format

Field Name	Size (Bytes)	Description
Type	1	Identifies the ICMPv6 message type; for Parameter Problem messages, this is set to 4.
Code	1	Identifies the general class of the parameter problem. See Table 34-6 for more information.
Checksum	2	A 16-bit checksum field for the ICMP header (see Chapter 31).
Pointer	4	An offset that points to the byte location in the original datagram that caused the Parameter Problem message to be generated. The device receiving the ICMP message can use this value to get an idea of which field in the original message had the problem.
Original Datagram Portion	Variable	As much of the IPv6 datagram as will fit without causing the size of the ICMPv6 error message (including its own IP header) to exceed the minimum IPv6 MTU of 1280 bytes.

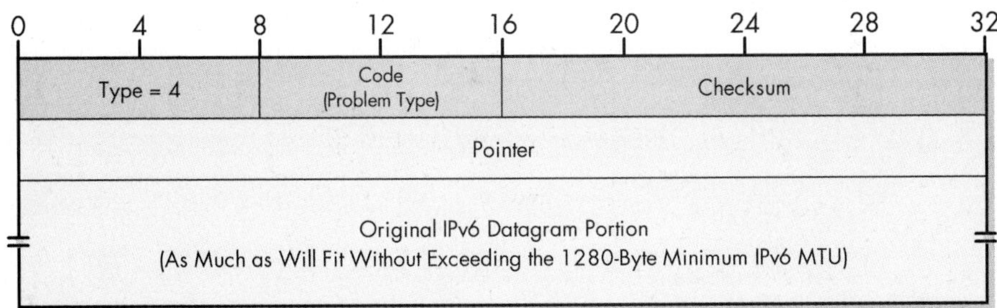

Figure 34-5: ICMPv6 Parameter Problem message format

Parameter Problem Message Interpretation Codes and the Pointer Field

The Pointer field, which was only 8 bits wide in ICMPv4, has been widened to 32 bits in ICMPv6 in order to provide more flexibility in isolating the error. The Code value is also used somewhat differently in ICMPv6 than it was in the ICMPv4 version of this message type. In ICMPv4, the Pointer was used only when the Code field was 0, and other code values indicated other problem categories for which the Pointer field did not make sense. In ICMPv6, the Pointer field is used with all Code types to indicate the general nature of what the problem is. This means the Pointer field tells the recipient of the Parameter Problem message where the problem happened in the message, and the Code field tells it what the nature of the problem is. Table 34-6 shows the three Code values and provides a brief explanation of each.

Table 34-6: ICMPv6 Parameter Problem Message Interpretation Codes

Code Value	Message Subtype	Description
0	Erroneous Header Field Encountered	The Pointer field points to a header that contains an error or otherwise could not be processed.
1	Unrecognized Next Header Type Encountered	As explained in Chapter 26, in IPv6, a datagram can have multiple headers, each of which contains a Next Header field that points to the next header in the datagram. This code indicates that the Pointer field points to a Next Header field containing an unrecognized value.
2	Unrecognized IPv6 Option Encountered	The Pointer field points to an IPv6 option that was not recognized by the processing device.

KEY CONCEPT The ICMPv6 *Parameter Problem* message is a generic error message that can be used to convey an error of any type in an IP datagram. The Pointer field is used to indicate where the problem was in the original datagram to the recipient of the message.

35

ICMPV6 INFORMATIONAL MESSAGE TYPES AND FORMATS

In the previous chapter, we explored a number of Internet Control Message Protocol version 6 (ICMPv6) error messages. These are sent back to the originator of an Internet Protocol version 6 (IPv6) datagram when the originator detects an error it, thereby making it impossible for the error to be delivered. Like the original version of ICMP (ICMPv4), ICMPv6 also defines another message class: *informational* messages. These ICMPv6 messages are used not to report errors, but to allow the sharing of information required to implement various test, diagnostic, and support functions critical to the operation of IPv6.

In this chapter, I describe eight different ICMPv6 informational messages in five topics (six of these messages are used in matching pairs, and the pairs are described together). I begin by describing ICMPv6 Echo Request and Echo Reply messages, which are used for network connectivity testing. I explain the format of Router Advertisement and Router Solicitation messages, which are used to let hosts discover local routers and learn necessary parameters from them. I then describe ICMPv6 Neighbor Advertisement and

Neighbor Solicitation messages, which are used for various communications between hosts on a local network, including IPv6 address resolution. I discuss IPv6 Redirect messages, which let routers inform hosts of better first-hop routers, and IPv6 Router Renumbering messages.

Several of the ICMPv6 informational messages include additional information that is either optional, recommended, or mandatory, depending on the circumstances under which the message is generated. Some of these are shared between message types, so they are described in a separate topic at the end of the chapter.

In IPv4, the use of many of the ICMP informational messages was described in a variety of different standards. In IPv6, many of the functions using informational messages have been gathered together and formalized in the IPv6 *Neighbor Discovery (ND) protocol.* The solicitation and advertisement of local routers and neighboring hosts, as well as the communication of redirection information are both examples of activities for which ND is responsible. In fact, five of the ICMP messages described in this chapter are actually defined in the ND standard, RFC 2461.

RELATED INFORMATION *Neighbor Discovery (ND) and ICMPv6 are obviously closely related, given that ND describes the use of several of the ICMP messages: Router Advertisement, Router Solicitation, Neighbor Advertisement, Neighbor Solicitation, and Redirect. Thus, just as ICMPv4 is an important assistant to IPv4, both ICMPv6 and ND are important helpers for IPv6. In this book, I provide most of the description of how these messages are used in the next chapter, which discusses ND. In this chapter, I provide only a brief summary of their use, while focusing primarily on message format and the meaning of each of the fields in that format.*

ICMPv6 Echo Request and Echo Reply Messages

IP is a relatively simple protocol that does not include any method for performing tests between devices to help in diagnosing internetwork problems. This means that this job, like other support tasks, falls to ICMP. The simplest test performed when there is a problem using TCP/IP is usually a check that a pair of devices is able to send datagrams to each other. This is most often done by an initiating device that sends a test message to a second device, which receives it and replies back to tell the first device it received the message.

Like ICMPv4, ICMPv6 includes a pair of messages specifically for connection testing. To use them, Device A begins the test process by sending an ICMPv4 *Echo Request* message to Device B, which responds back to Device A with an *Echo Reply* message. When Device A receives this message, it knows that it is able to communicate (both send and receive) successfully with Device B.

NOTE *In ICMPv4 the first message type was named just* Echo *but was often called* Echo Request. *In ICMPv6,* Request *is part of the formal message name—a modest but useful improvement from a clarity standpoint.*

ICMPv6 Echo and Echo Reply Message Format

The format for ICMPv6 Echo Request and Echo Reply messages is very similar to that of the ICMPv4 version, as shown in Table 35-1 and Figure 35-1.

Table 35-1: ICMPv6 Echo Request and Echo Reply Message Format

Field Name	Size (Bytes)	Description
Type	1	Identifies the ICMPv6 message type; for Echo Request messages, the value is 128, and for Echo Reply messages, it's 129. (In ICMPv6, informational messages always have a Type value of 128 or higher.)
Code	1	Not used; set to 0.
Checksum	2	A 16-bit checksum field for the ICMP header (see Chapter 31).
Identifier	2	An optional identification field that can be used to help in matching Echo Request and Echo Reply messages.
Sequence Number	2	A sequence number to help in matching Echo Request and Echo Reply messages.
Optional Data	Variable	Additional optional data to be sent along with the message. If this is sent in the Echo Request, it is copied into the Echo Reply to be sent back to the source.

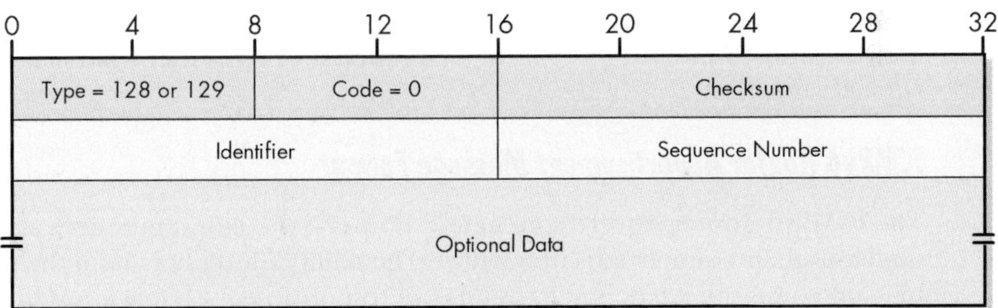

Figure 35-1: *ICMPv6 Echo Request and Echo Reply message format*

It is often necessary to match an Echo Reply message with the Echo Request message that led to it being generated. Two special fields are used within the format of these messages to allow Echo Request and Echo Reply messages to be matched together, and to allow a sequence of messages to be exchanged. The Identifier field is provided so that a particular test session can be identified, and the Sequence Number field allows a series of tests in a session to be numbered. The use of both fields is optional.

Application of Echo and Echo Reply Messages

ICMPv6 Echo Request and Echo Reply messages are used via the IPv6 version of the IP ping utility, which is commonly called *ping6*. Like its IPv4 predecessor, this utility allows an administrator to configure a number of test options to perform either a simple or rigorous test of the connection between a pair of devices. See Chapter 88 for a full explanation.

KEY CONCEPT ICMPv6 *Echo Request* and *Echo Reply* messages are used to facilitate network reachability testing. A device tests its ability to communicate with another by sending it an Echo Request message and waiting for an Echo Reply in response. The *ping* utility, a widely used diagnostic tool in TCP/IP internetworks, makes use of these messages.

ICMPv6 Router Advertisement and Router Solicitation Messages

At the highest level, we can separate IP devices into two groups: hosts and routers. Both participate in the use of the internetwork, but they have different roles. An important IP principle related to this division is that routers take care of routing—moving data between networks—while hosts generally don't need to worry about this job. Hosts rely on the routers on their local networks to facilitate communication to all other hosts except those on the local network.

The implications of this are clear: A host cannot really use an internetwork until it knows the identity of at least one local router and the method by which that router is to be used. In IPv4, a technique known as *Router Discovery* was invented, which provides a means by which a host can locate a router and learn important parameters related to the operation of the local network. Router Discovery in IPv6 works in a very similar manner by having routers send *Router Advertisement* messages both on a regular basis and in response to hosts prompting for them using *Router Solicitation* messages. The Router Discovery function has been incorporated into the ND protocol, where it is part of a larger class of tools that I call *host–Router Discovery* functions.

ICMPv6 Router Advertisement Message Format

The ICMPv6 Router Advertisement and Router Solicitation messages are fairly similar to their counterparts in ICMPv4. The main differences are in the parameters that are communicated. Since routers are responsible for a few more functions in IPv6 than they are in IPv4, the Router Advertisement message in ICMPv6 has a few more fields than the older version.

The format of an ICMPv6 Router Advertisement message is described in Table 35-2 and shown in Figure 35-2.

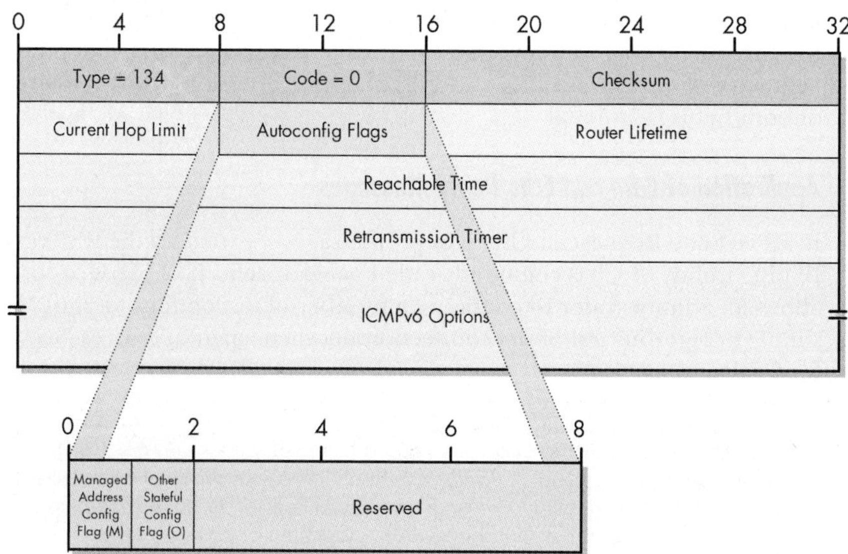

Figure 35-2: ICMPv6 Router Advertisement message format

Table 35-2: ICMPv6 Router Advertisement Message Format

Field Name	Size (Bytes)	Description
Type	1	Identifies the ICMPv6 message type; for Router Advertisement messages, the value is 134.
Code	1	Not used; set to 0.
Checksum	2	A 16-bit checksum field for the ICMP header (see Chapter 31).
Cur Hop Limit	1	Current Hop Limit: This is a default number that the router recommends that hosts on the local network use as a value in the Hop Limit field of datagrams they send. If 0, the router is not recommending a Hop Limit value in this Router Advertisement.
Autoconfig Flags	1	Two flags that let the router tell the host how autoconfiguration is performed on the local network, as described in Table 35-3. (See Chapter 25 for details on IPv6 autoconfiguration.)
Router Lifetime	2	Tells the host receiving this message how long, in seconds, this router should be used as a default router. If 0, it tells the host this router should not be used as a default router. Note that this is an expiration interval only for the status of the router as a default, not for other information in the Router Advertisement message.
Reachable Time	4	Tells hosts how long, in milliseconds, they should consider a neighbor to be reachable after they have received reachability confirmation. (See Chapter 36 for more information.)
Retrans Timer	4	Retransmission Timer: The amount of time, in milliseconds, that a host should wait before retransmitting Neighbor Solicitation messages.
Options	Variable	Router Advertisement messages may contain three possible options (see the "ICMPv6 Informational Message Options" section later in this chapter for more on ICMPv6 options): • Source Link-Layer Address: Included when the router sending the Advertisement knows its link-layer (layer 2) address. • MTU: Used to tell local hosts the MTU of the local network when hosts on the network may not know this information. • Prefix Information: Tells local hosts what prefix or prefixes to use for the local network. (You'll recall that the "prefix" indicates which bits of an IPv6 address are the network identifier when compared to the host identifier; it is thus analogous to an IPv4 subnet mask.)

Table 35-3: ICMPv6 Router Advertisement Message Autoconfiguration Flags

Subfield Name	Size (Bytes)	Description
M	1/8 (1 bit)	Managed Address Configuration Flag: When set, this flag tells hosts to use an administered or stateful method for address autoconfiguration, such as the Dynamic Host Configuration Protocol (DHCP).
O	1/8 (1 bit)	Other Stateful Configuration Flag: When set, this tells hosts to use an administered or stateful autoconfiguration method for information other than addresses.
Reserved	6/8 (6 bits)	Reserved for future use; sent as zeros.

ICMPv6 Router Solicitation Message Format

The format of an ICMPv6 Router Solicitation message is shown in Table 35-4 and Figure 35-3.

Table 35-4: ICMPv6 Router Solicitation Message Format

Field Name	Size (Bytes)	Description
Type	1	Identifies the ICMPv6 message type; for Router Solicitation messages, the value is 133.
Code	1	Not used; set to 0.
Checksum	2	A 16-bit checksum field for the ICMP header (see Chapter 31).
Reserved	4	The 4 reserved bytes set to 0.
Options	Variable	If the device sending the Router Solicitation knows its layer 2 address, it should be included in a Source Link-Layer Address option. Option formats are described in the "ICMPv6 Informational Message Options" section later in this chapter.

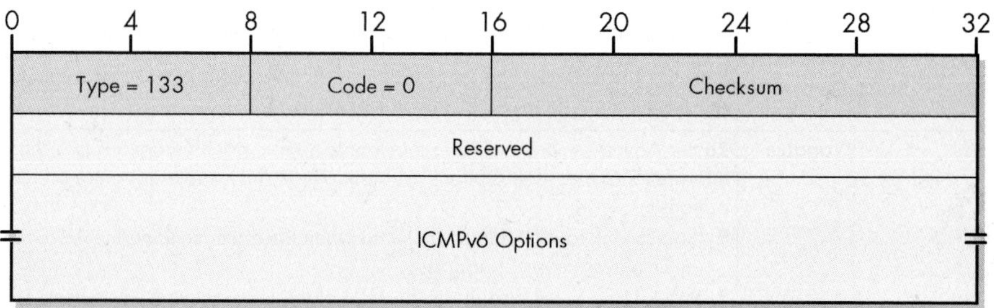

Figure 35-3: *ICMPv6 Router Solicitation message format*

Addressing of Router Advertisement and Router Solicitation Messages

Router Solicitation messages are normally sent to the IPv6 "all routers" multicast address; this is the most efficient method, because routers are required to subscribe to this multicast address while hosts will ignore it. A routine (unsolicited) Router Advertisement message is sent to all devices using the "all nodes" multicast address for the local network. A Router Advertisement message that is sent in response to a Router Solicitation message goes in unicast back to the device that sent the solicitation.

KEY CONCEPT ICMPv6 *Router Advertisement* messages are sent regularly by IPv6 routers to inform hosts of their presence and characteristics, and to provide hosts with parameters that they need to function properly on the local network. A host that wants to find out immediately which routers are present may send a *Router Solicitation* message, which will prompt listening routers to send out Router Advertisements.

ICMPv6 Neighbor Advertisement and Neighbor Solicitation Messages

The previous section described the Router Advertisement and Router Solicitation messages, which are used to facilitate host–Router Discovery functions as part of the IPv6 ND protocol. The other main group of tasks for which ND is responsible relates to the exchange of information between neighboring hosts on the same network. I call these *host-host communication* or *host-host discovery* functions.

Arguably, the most important additions to the ND protocol are the functions that formalize the exchange of parameters and the methods that determine the existence of neighboring hosts. These tasks include the new method of address resolution in IPv6 as well as the processes of next-hop determination and neighbor unreachability detection. They require the use of two ICMPv6 messages: the *Neighbor Solicitation message* and the *Neighbor Advertisement message.*

The Neighbor Solicitation message allows a device to check that a neighbor exists and is reachable, and lets a device initiate address resolution. The Neighbor Advertisement message confirms the existence of a host or router, and also provides layer 2 address information when needed. As you can see, these two messages are comparable to the Router Advertisement and Router Solicitation messages, but they are used differently and include different parameters.

ICMPv6 Neighbor Advertisement Message Format

The format for the Neighbor Advertisement message is shown in Table 35-5 and Figure 35-4.

Table 35-5: ICMPv6 Neighbor Advertisement Message Format

Field Name	Size (Bytes)	Description
Type	1	Identifies the ICMPv6 message type; for Neighbor Advertisement messages, the value is 136.
Code	1	Not used; set to 0.
Checksum	2	A 16-bit checksum field for the ICMP header (see Chapter 31).
Flags	4	Three flags that convey information about the message (and a lot of empty space for future use), as described in Table 35-6.
Target Address	16	If the Neighbor Advertisement is being sent in response to a Neighbor Solicitation, this is the same value as in the Target Address field of the Solicitation. This field will commonly contain the IPv6 address of the device, thereby sending the Neighbor Advertisement, but not in all cases. For example, if a device responds as a proxy for the target of the Neighbor Solicitation, the Target Address field contains the address of the target, not the device sending the response. (See Chapter 13 for details on address resolution proxying.) If the Neighbor Advertisement is being sent unsolicited, then this is the IPv6 address of the device sending it.
Options	Variable	When sent in response to a multicast Neighbor Solicitation, a Neighbor Advertisement message must contain a Target Link-Layer Address option, which carries the link-layer address of the device sending the message. This is a good example of an option that's not really "optional." When the Neighbor Advertisement is sent in response to a unicast Neighbor Solicitation, this option is technically not required (since the sender of the Solicitation must already have the target's link-layer address to have sent it unicast). Despite this, it is still normally included to ensure that the link-layer address of the target is refreshed in the cache of the device that sent the Neighbor Solicitation.

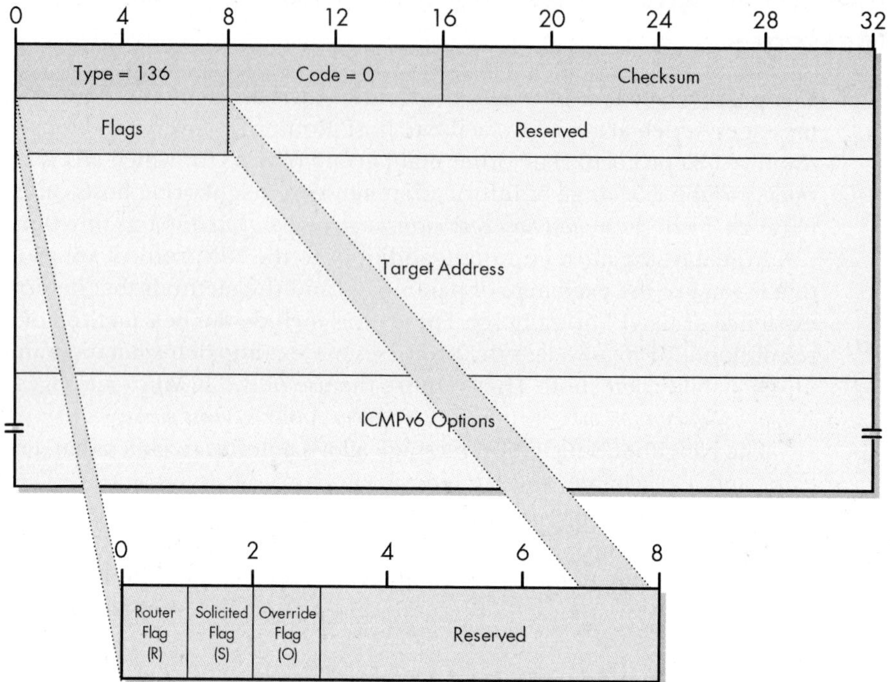

Figure 35-4: ICMPv6 Neighbor Advertisement message format

Table 35-6: ICMPv6 Neighbor Advertisement Message Flags

Subfield Name	Size (Bytes)	Description
R	1/8 (1 bit)	Router Flag: Set when a router sends a Neighbor Advertisement, and cleared when a host sends one. This identifies the type of device that sent the datagram, and is also used as part of neighbor unreachability detection to detect when a device changes from acting as a router to functioning as a regular host.
S	1/8 (1 bit)	Solicited Flag: When set, indicates that this message was sent in response to a Neighbor Solicitation message. Cleared for unsolicited Neighbor Advertisements.
O	1/8 (1 bit)	Override Flag: When set, tells the recipient that the information in this message should override any existing cached entry for the link-layer address of this device. This bit is normally set in unsolicited Neighbor Advertisements, since these are sent when a host needs to force a change of information in the caches of its neighbors.
Reserved	3 5/8 (29 bits)	A big set of reserved bits.

ICMPv6 Neighbor Solicitation Message Format

The Neighbor Solicitation message format is much simpler, as shown in Table 35-7 and Figure 35-5.

Table 35-7: ICMPv6 Neighbor Solicitation Message Format

Field Name	Size (Bytes)	Description
Type	1	Identifies the ICMPv6 message type; for Neighbor Solicitation messages, the value is 135.
Code	1	Not used; set to 0.
Checksum	2	A 16-bit checksum field for the ICMP header (see Chapter 31).
Reserved	4	The 4 reserved bytes set to 0.
Target Address	16	The IPv6 address of the target of the solicitation. For IPv6 address resolution, this is the actual unicast IP address of the device whose layer 2 (link-layer) address we are trying to resolve.
Options	Variable	If the device sending the Neighbor Solicitation knows both its own IP address and layer 2 address, it should include the layer 2 address in a Source Link-Layer Address option. The inclusion of this option will allow the destination of the Neighbor Solicitation to enter the layer 2 and layer 3 addresses of the source of this message into its own address cache. (See the discussion of IPv6 address resolution in Chapter 25.)

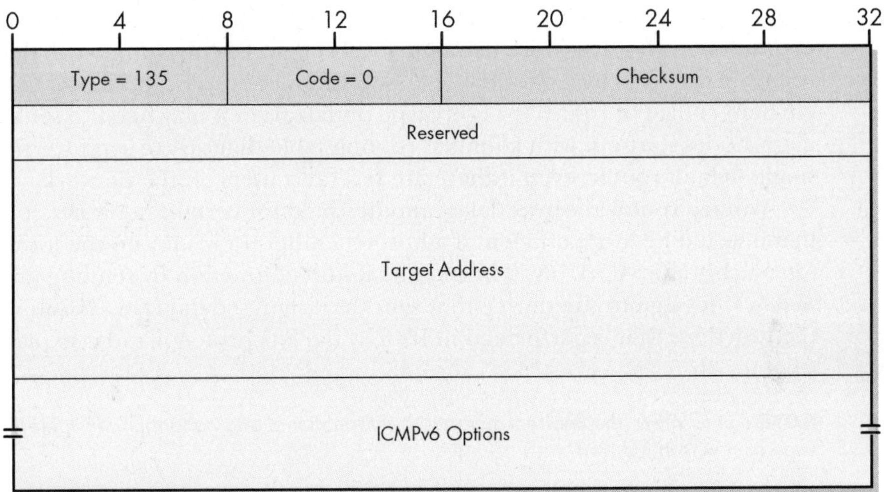

Figure 35-5: ICMPv6 Neighbor Solicitation message format

Addressing of Neighbor Advertisement and Neighbor Solicitation Messages

Neighbor Solicitation messages are sent either unicast to the address of the target device or to the solicited-node multicast address of the target. This latter address is a special type that's used to allow a device to send a multicast that will be heard by the target whose address it is trying to resolve, but won't be heard by most other devices; it is explained in Chapter 25, which describes IPv6 address resolution.

When a Neighbor Advertisement message is generated in response to a Neighbor Solicitation message, it is sent unicast back to the device that sent the Solicitation message, unless that message was sent from the unspecified address, in which case it is multicast to the "all nodes" multicast address. If the Neighbor

Advertisement message is sent unsolicited (for example, by a device that wishes to inform others of a change in link-layer address), it is sent to the "all nodes" multicast address.

KEY CONCEPT ICMPv6 *Neighbor Advertisement* and *Neighbor Solicitation* messages are similar in many ways to the Router Advertisement and Router Solicitation messages. However, rather than being used to communicate parameters from routers to hosts, they are used for various types of communication between hosts on a physical network, such as address resolution, next-hop determination, and neighbor unreachability detection.

ICMPv6 Redirect Messages

Because of the different roles of routers and hosts in an IPv6 internetwork, hosts don't need to know very much about routes. They send datagrams intended for destinations on the local network directly, while they send those for other networks to their local routers and let them "do the driving," so to speak.

If a local network has only a single router, it will send all such nonlocal traffic to that router. If it has more than one local router, the host then must decide which router to use for which traffic. In general terms, a host will not know the most efficient choice of router for every type of datagram it may need to send. In fact, many nodes start out with a limited routing table that says to send *everything* to a single default router, even if there are several routers on the network.

When a router receives datagrams destined for certain networks, it may realize that it would be more efficient if a host to a different router on the local network sent such traffic. If so, it will invoke the Redirect function by sending an ICMPv6 *Redirect* message to the device that sent the original datagram. This is the last of the functions that is performed in IPv6 by the ND protocol and is explained in Chapter 36.

NOTE *In ICMPv6, the Redirect message is informational and no longer considered an error message as it was in ICMPv4.*

ICMPv6 Redirect Message Format

The format of ICMPv6 Redirect messages is shown in Table 35-8 and Figure 35-6.

Table 35-8: ICMPv6 Redirect Message Format

Field Name	Size (Bytes)	Description
Type	1	Identifies the ICMPv6 message type; for Redirect messages, the value is 137.
Code	1	Not used; set to 0.
Checksum	2	A 16-bit checksum field for the ICMP header (see Chapter 31).
Reserved	4	The 4 bytes sent as zeros.

(continued)

Table 35-8: ICMPv6 Redirect Message Format (continued)

Field Name	Size (Bytes)	Description
Target Address	16	The address of the router that the router creating the Redirect is telling the recipient of the Redirect to use as a first hop for future transmissions to the destination. For example, if Router R2 generated a Redirect telling Host A that, in the future, transmissions to Host B should be sent first to Router R1, then Router R1's IPv6 address would be in this field.
Destination Address	16	The address of the device whose future transmissions are being redirected; this is the destination of the datagram that originally led to the Redirect being generated. Repeating the previous example: If Router R2 generated a Redirect telling Host A that, in the future, transmissions to Host B should be sent first to Router R1, then Host B's IPv6 address would be in this field.
Options	Variable	Redirect messages normally include two ICMPv6 option fields (see the "ICMPv6 Informational Message Options" section later in this chapter): • Target Link-Layer Address: The layer 2 address of the Target Address, if known. This saves the recipient of the Redirect message from needing to perform an address resolution on the target. • Redirected Header: As much of the IPv6 datagram that spawned this Redirect as will fit without causing the size of the ICMPv6 error message (including its own IP header) to exceed the minimum IPv6 MTU of 1280 bytes.

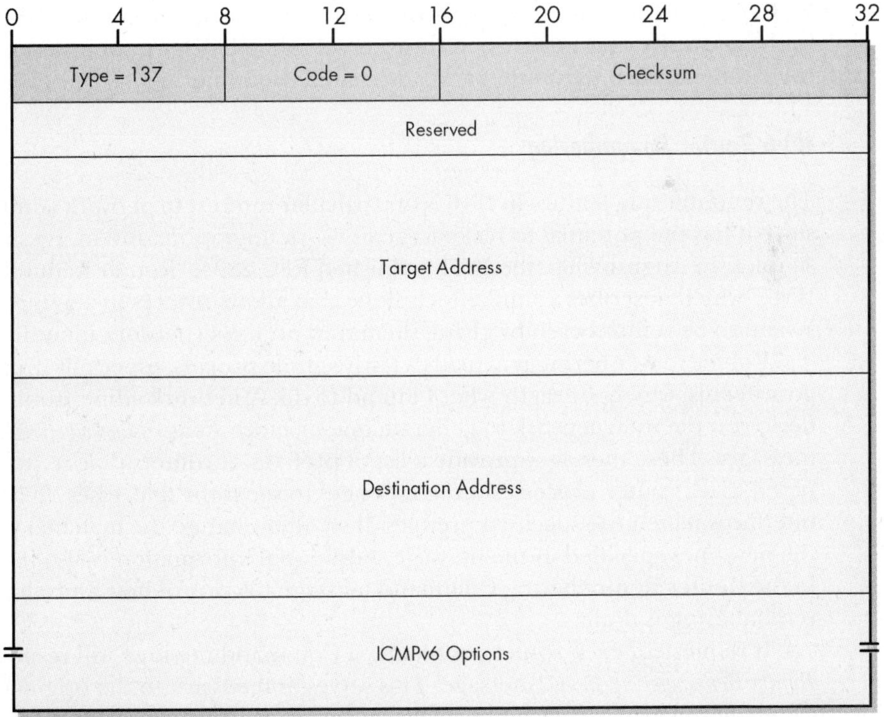

Figure 35-6: *ICMPv6 Redirect message format*

Redirect messages are always sent in unicast to the address of the device that originally sent the datagram that originally created the Redirect message.

Application of Redirect Messages

The Redirect message has always been somewhat of an oddball. In ICMPv4, it is considered an error message, but this makes it different from other error messages. For one thing, it's not really an error, since it doesn't represent a failure to deliver, only an inefficiency in doing so. For this reason, in ICMPv6 it was moved into the set of informational message types. Here, too, it doesn't really fit in with the others, since it is sent in reaction to a regular IP message, and it also includes a copy of (part of) the datagram that spawned it, as error messages do.

KEY CONCEPT ICMPv6 *Redirect* messages are used by a router to inform a host of a better router to use for future datagrams that were sent to a particular host or network. They are not used to alter routes between routers, however.

ICMPv6 Router Renumbering Messages

One of the more interesting decisions made in IPv6 was the selection of a very large 128-bit address size. This provides an address space far larger than what humans are ever likely to need, and probably larger than needed for IPv6, strictly speaking. What this wealth of bits provides is the flexibility to assign meaning to different bits in the address structure. This, in turn, serves as the basis for important features such as the autoconfiguration and automated renumbering of IPv6 addresses.

IPv6 Router Renumbering

The renumbering feature in IPv6 is of particular interest to network administrators, since it has the potential to make large network migrations and merges much simpler. In August 2000, the IETF published RFC 2894, "Router Renumbering for IPv6," which describes a similar technique that allows routers in an autonomous system to be renumbered by giving them new prefixes (network identifiers).

Router renumbering is actually a fairly simple process, especially if we avoid the gory details, which is exactly what I intend to do. A network administrator uses a device on the internetwork to generate one or more *Router Renumbering Command* messages. These messages provide a list of prefixes of routers that are to be renumbered. Each router processes these messages to see if the addresses on any of their interfaces match the specified prefixes. If so, they change the matched prefixes to the new ones specified in the message. Additional information is also included in the Router Renumbering Command message to control how and when the renumbering is done.

If requested, each router processing a Command message will respond with a *Router Renumbering Result* message. This serves as feedback to the originator of the Command message, indicating whether the renumbering was successful, and what changes, if any, were made.

The router renumbering standard also defines a few important management features. Many of these reflect the great power of something that can mass-renumber routers, and hence, they represent the potential for such power to be abused. Command messages may be sent in a test mode, in which they are processed but the renumbering is not actually done. Messages include a sequence number to guard against replay attacks, and a special *Sequence Number Reset* message can be used to reset the sequence number information that was previously sent. For added security, the standard specifies that messages be authenticated and have their identity checked.

ICMPv6 Router Renumbering Message Format

The format of Router Renumbering messages is shown in Table 35-9 and Figure 35-7.

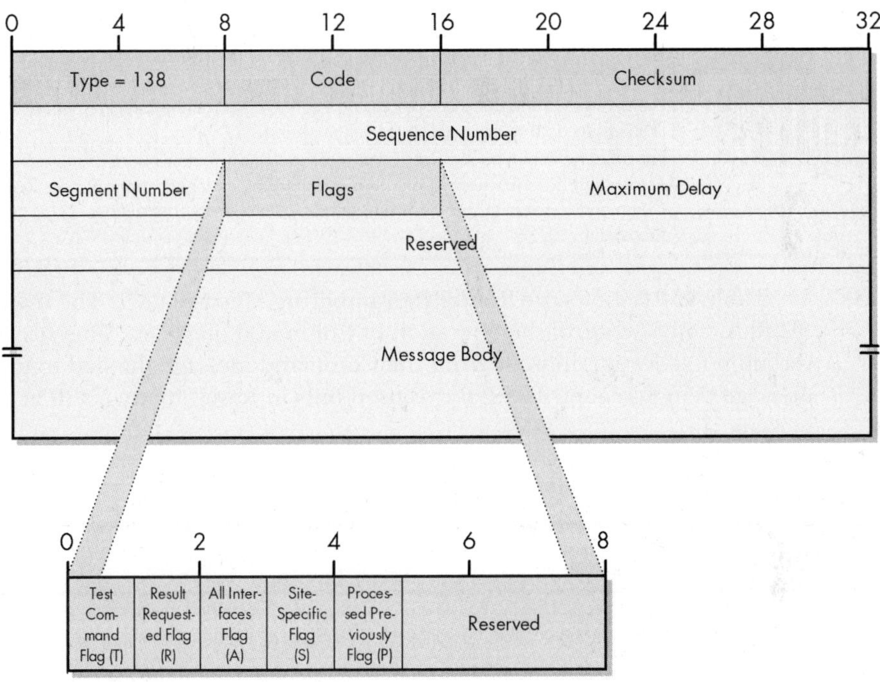

Figure 35-7: *ICMPv6 Router Renumbering message format*

Table 35-9: ICMPv6 Router Renumbering Message Format

Field Name	Size (Bytes)	Description
Type	1	Identifies the ICMPv6 message type; for Router Renumbering messages, the value is 138.
Code	1	Indicates the subtype of Router Renumbering message: 0 = Router Renumbering Command 1 = Router Renumbering Result 255 = Sequence Number Reset
Checksum	2	A 16-bit checksum field for the ICMP header (see Chapter 31).
Sequence Number	4	A 32-bit number that guards against replay attacks by letting a recipient detect stale, duplicate, or out-of-order commands.

(continued)

Table 35-9: ICMPv6 Router Renumbering Message Format (continued)

Field Name	Size (Bytes)	Description
Segment Number	1	Differentiates between valid Router Renumbering messages within the same Sequence Number.
Flags	1	Five flags used to control the renumbering process, as described in Table 35-10.
Max Delay	2	Tells a router receiving a message the maximum amount of time (in milliseconds) it is allowed to delay before sending a reply.
Reserved	4	The 4 reserved bytes.
Message Body	Variable	For a Router Renumbering Command, the message body contains two sets of information. The first is a Match-Prefix Part for the prefix being renumbered. The second is one or more Use-Prefix Parts that describe the new prefix for each match. A router receiving a Command checks its own interface addresses, and if they match the Match-Prefix-Part, they use Use-Prefix Parts data to accomplish the renumbering. For a Router Renumbering Result, the message body contains zero or more Match Results entries that describe each prefix that a router has matched from a Router Renumbering Command. Each entry provides information about whether renumbering for a prefix was successful.

Table 35-10 shows the Router Renumbering Message flags. The first four flags (T, R, A, and S) control the operation of Command messages. They are just copied verbatim in a Result message from the Command message that led to the Result message being created. The P flag is used only in Result messages (0 in Command messages).

Table 35-10: ICMPv6 Router Renumbering Message Flags

Subfield Name	Size (Bytes)	Description
T	1/8 (1 bit)	Test Command Flag: When set to 1, this flags this Command messageas being a test message. This tells the recipient to only simulate processing of the renumbering, not to actually do it.
R	1/8 (1 bit)	Result Requested Flag: When set to 1, requests that a Result message be sent after processing the Command message. When set to 0, says not to send one.
A	1/8 (1 bit)	All Interfaces Flag: When this flag is clear (0), the Command message is not applied to any router interfaces that have been administratively shut down. When 1, it is applied to all interfaces.
S	1/8 (1 bit)	Site-Specific Flag: This flag has meaning only when a router treats its interfaces as belonging to different sites. If so, a value of 1 tells it to apply the Command message only to interfaces on the same site as the interface for which the Command message was received. A value of 0 applies it to all interfaces regardless of site.
P	1/8 (1 bit)	Processed Previously Flag: This flag is normally 0, meaning the Command message was not previously seen and the Result message contains the report of processing it. When 1, this indicates that the recipient of the Command message believes it has seen it before and is not processing it. (Test commands are not included in the assessment of whether a Command message has been seen before.)
Reserved	3/8 (3 bits)	Three bits reserved for future flags.

Addressing of Router Renumbering Messages

Since Router Renumbering messages are intended for all routers on a site, they are normally sent to the "all routers" multicast address, using either link-local or site-local scope. They may also be sent to local unicast addresses.

ICMPv6 Informational Message Options

Each of the five ICMPv6 informational message types defined and used by the protocol has an Options field into which one or more options may be inserted. This probably isn't the best name for these sets of data, since they are only optional in certain cases. In fact, in some cases the option is actually the entire point of the message. For example, a Neighbor Advertisement message containing a link-layer address for address resolution carries it in an Options field, but the message wouldn't be of much use without it!

Each option has its own structure of subfields based on the classic type, length, and value triplet used in many message formats. The Type subfield indicates the option type, and the Length field indicates its length, so that the device processing the option can determine where it ends. The value may be contained in one or more fields, which hold the actual information for which the option is being used.

Some options are used for only one kind of ICMPv6 message; others are used for more than one variety. So, they are best thought of as modular components used in different types of messages as needed. I describe the format of each of these five options in the following sections.

Source Link-Layer Address Option Format

The Source Link-Layer Address Option carries the link-layer address of a device sending an ICMPv6 message, as shown in Table 35-11 and Figure 35-8. It's used in Router Advertisement, Router Solicitation, and Neighbor Solicitation messages.

Table 35-11: ICMPv6 Source Link-Layer Address Option Format

Field Name	Size (Bytes)	Description
Type	1	Identifies the ICMPv6 option type. For the Source Link-Layer Address option, the value is 1.
Length	1	The length of the entire option (including the Type and Length fields), expressed in units of 8 octets (64 bits).
Source Link-Layer Address	Variable	The link-layer (layer 2) address of the device sending the ICMPv6 message.

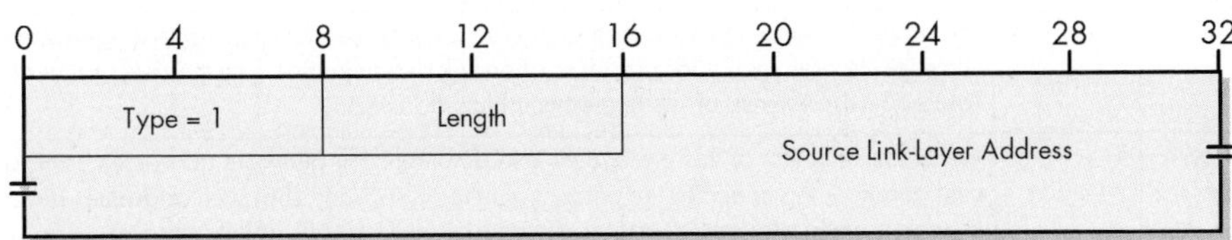

Figure 35-8: ICMPv6 Source Link-Layer Address option format

Target Link-Layer Address Option Format

The Target Link-Layer Address option carries the link-layer address corresponding to the Target Address field in Neighbor Advertisement and Redirect messages. Its format is shown in Table 35-12 and Figure 35-9.

Table 35-12: ICMPv6 Target Link-Layer Address Option Format

Field Name	Size (Bytes)	Description
Type	1	Identifies the ICMPv6 option type. For the Target Link-Layer Address option, the value is 2.
Length	1	The length of the entire option (including the Type and Length fields), expressed in units of 8 octets (64 bits).
Target Link-Layer Address	Variable	The link-layer (layer 2) address of the target device.

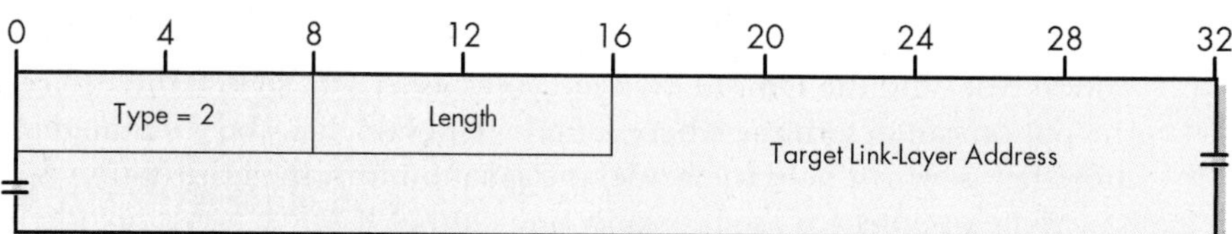

Figure 35-9: ICMPv6 Target Link-Layer Address option format

Prefix Information Option Format

The *Prefix Information* option provides a prefix and related information in Router Advertisement messages. This is the longest and most complex of the options, as you can see in Table 35-13 and Figure 35-10.

Table 35-13: ICMPv6 Prefix Information Option Format

Field Name	Size (Bytes)	Description
Type	1	Identifies the ICMPv6 option type. For the Prefix Information option, the value is 3.
Length	1	The length of the entire option (including the Type and Length fields), expressed in units of 8 octets (64 bits). The Prefix Information option is fixed in size at 32 bytes, so the value of the Length field is 4.
Prefix Length	1	The number of bits in the Prefix field that are considered part of the network identifier (the remainder are used for the host identifier and ignored). See Chapter 25 for details on prefix lengths.
Flags	1	A pair of flags that convey information about the prefix, as described in Table 35-14.
Valid Life-time	4	The amount of time, in seconds, that the recipient of the message containing this option should consider the prefix valid for purposes of on-link determination (see the description of the L flag in Table 35-14). A value of all 1s means infinity (forever).
Preferred Lifetime	4	When the recipient of this prefix uses it to automatically generate addresses using address auto-configuration, this specifies the amount of time, in seconds, that such addresses remain preferred (meaning, valid and freely usable). A value of all 1s means infinity (forever).
Reserved	4	The 4 unused bytes sent as zeros.

(continued)

Table 35-13: ICMPv6 Prefix Information Option Format (continued)

Field Name	Size (Bytes)	Description
Prefix	16	The prefix being communicated from the router to the host in the Router Advertisement message. The Prefix Length field indicates how many of the 128 bits in this field are significant (part of the network ID). Only these bits are placed in the Prefix field; the remaining bits are cleared to zero.

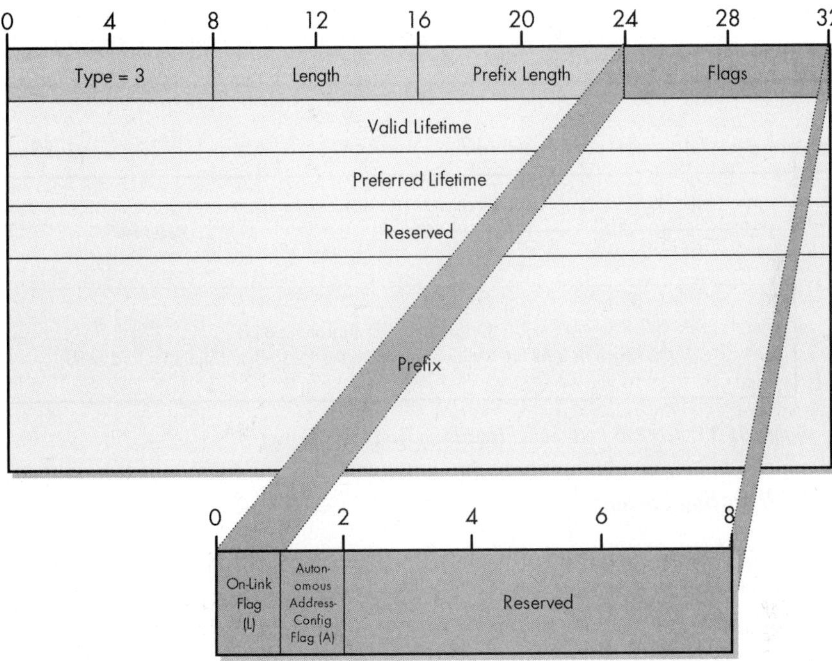

Figure 35-10: ICMPv6 Prefix Information option format

Table 35-14: ICMPv6 Prefix Information Option Flags

Subfield Name	Size (Bytes)	Description
L	1/8 (1 bit)	On-Link Flag: When set to 1, tells the recipient of the option that this prefix can be used for on-link determination. This means the prefix can be used for deciding whether or not an address is *on-link* (on the recipient's local network). When 0, the sender is making no statement regarding whether the prefix can be used for this or not.
A	1/8 (1 bit)	Autonomous Address-Configuration Flag: When set to 1, specifies that this prefix can be used for IPv6 address autoconfiguration. (See Chapter 25 for details on IPv6 autoconfiguration.)
Reserved	6/8 (6 bits)	6 leftover bits reserved and sent as zeros.

Redirected Header Option Format

In a Redirect message, the *Redirected Header* option provides a copy of the original message (or a portion of it) that led to the Redirect message being generated. This option's format is shown in Table 35-15 and Figure 35-11.

Table 35-15: ICMPv6 Redirected Header Option Format

Field Name	Size (Bytes)	Description
Type	1	Identifies the ICMPv6 option type. For the Redirected Header option, the value is 4.
Length	1	The length of the entire option (including the Type and Length fields), expressed in units of 8 octets (64 bits).
Reserved	6	The 6 reserved bytes sent as zeros.
IP Header + Data	Variable	As much of the original IPv6 datagram as will fit without causing the size of the ICMPv6 error message (including its own IP header) to exceed the minimum IPv6 MTU of 1280 bytes.

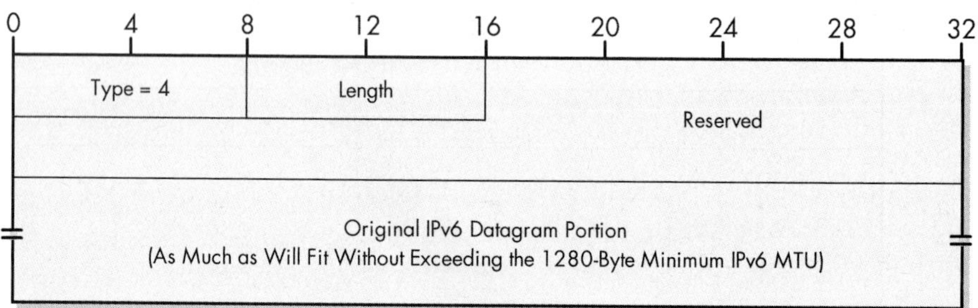

Figure 35-11: *ICMPv6 Redirected Header option format*

MTU Option Format

The *MTU* option lets a router convey a recommended MTU value in Router Advertisement messages. Its format is shown in Table 35-16 and Figure 35-12.

Table 35-16: ICMPv6 MTU Option Format

Field Name	Size (Bytes)	Description
Type	1	Identifies the ICMPv6 option type. For the MTU option, the value is 5.
Length	1	The length of the entire option (including the Type and Length fields), expressed in units of 8 octets (64 bits). The MTU option is fixed in length at 8 bytes, so the value of this field is 1.
Reserved	2	The 2 reserved bytes sent as zeros.
MTU	4	The MTU value, in bytes, that the router is recommending for use on the local link.

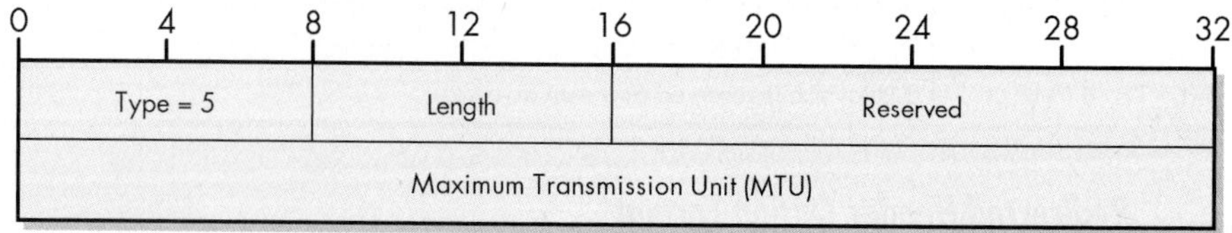

Figure 35-12: *ICMPv6 MTU option format*

36

IPV6 NEIGHBOR DISCOVERY (ND) PROTOCOL

The new Internet Protocol version 6 (IPv6) represents an evolution of the venerable IP. It maintains the same basic operational principles of IPv4, but makes some important modifications, particularly in the area of addressing. In fact, some of the more significant changes in IPv6 are actually not in IP itself, but in the protocols that support IP. One of the most interesting of these was the creation of an entirely new support protocol for IPv6. It combines several tasks previously performed by other protocols in IPv4, adds some new functions, and makes numerous improvements to the whole package. This new standard is called the IPv6 *Neighbor Discovery (ND)* protocol.

In this chapter, I describe the new ND protocol used in IPv6. I begin with an overview of the protocol, discussing its history, the motivation for its creation, and the standards that define it. I then describe its operation in general terms, listing the fundamental functions that ND performs, the three groups these functions fit into, and the Internet Control Message Protocol version 6 (ICMPv6) message types used to carry them out. I describe the key differences between ND and the way that its functions were carried out in IPv4. I then provide more information on the three functional groups in ND: those that involve discovery of important internetwork information from routers, those that are related to address resolution and neighbor communication between hosts, and finally, those involved with router redirection.

BACKGROUND INFORMATION *This chapter assumes basic comprehension of IPv6, which, in turn, requires understanding IPv4. ND uses ICMPv6 messages, so I reference Chapters 31 to 35, which discuss them. Finally, since ICMP performs some of the functions done by the Address Resolution Protocol (ARP) in IPv4, you may need to refer to Chapter 13 if you're unfamiliar with ARP's operation.*

IPv6 ND Overview

The purpose of network layer protocols like IP is to provide a means of connecting together individual local networks to create a much larger internetwork. To higher-layer protocols and to users, this internetwork behaves in most respects as if it were a single large network, because the lower layers hide the details that hold together the individual networks. Any device can send information to any other regardless of where it is located, and like magic, it will work—at least most of the time.

The existence of an internetwork means that devices can treat all other devices as peers, at least from the perspective of higher-layer protocols and applications. From the standpoint of lower layers, however, there is a very important difference between devices that are on a host's local network and those that are elsewhere. In a general sense, most devices have a more important relationship with the devices that are on their local network than those that are far away. Some of the most obvious tasks that a device must perform specifically with other devices on its local network include the following:

Direct Datagram Delivery Devices deliver data directly to other devices on their local network, while data going to distant devices must be indirectly delivered (routed).

Layer 2 Addressing To facilitate direct delivery, devices need to know the layer 2 addresses of the other devices on the local network; they don't need to know them for nonlocal devices.

Router Identification To deliver indirectly, a device needs to find a router on its local network that it can talk to.

Router Communication The local router must communicate information to each of the local hosts using it, so the hosts know how best to use it.

Configuration Hosts will usually look to information provided by local devices to let them perform configuration tasks such as determining their own IP address.

To support these and other requirements, several special protocols and functions were developed along with the original IP (version 4). The IP addressing scheme lets devices differentiate local addresses from distant ones. The Address Resolution Protocol (ARP) lets devices determine layer 2 addresses from layer 3 addresses. ICMP provides a messaging system to support various communication requirements between local devices, including the ability of a host to find a local router and the router to provide information to local hosts.

These features all work properly in IPv4, but they were developed in sort of an ad hoc manner. They are defined not in a single place, but rather in a variety of different Internet standards. There were also some limitations with the way these local device functions were implemented.

Formalizing Local Network Functions: The Neighbor Concept

IPv6 represents the biggest change in decades to not just the IP itself, but the entire TCP/IP suite. It thus provided an ideal opportunity to formalize and integrate the many disparate functions and tasks related to communication between local devices. The result was the creation of a new protocol: *Neighbor Discovery for IP version 6*, also commonly called the *IPv6 Neighbor Discovery* protocol. Since this protocol is new in IPv6, there is no IPv4 version of it, so the name is usually just seen as the *ND* protocol with no further qualifications; its use with IPv6 is implied.

The term *neighbor* is one that has been used for years in various networking standards and technologies to refer to devices that are local to each other. In the context of the current discussion, two devices are *neighbors* if they are on the same local network, meaning that they can send information to each other directly. The term can refer to either a regular host or a router. I think this is a good analogy to the way humans refer to those who live or work nearby. Just as most of us have a special relationship with people who are our neighbors and communicate more with them than with those who are far away, so do IP devices.

Since a neighbor is a local device, the name of the ND protocol would seem to indicate that ND is all about how neighbors discover each other's existence. In the context of this protocol, however, the term *discovery* has a much more generic meaning: It refers to discovering not just who are neighbors are, but also discovering important information about them. In addition to letting devices identify their neighbors, ND facilitates all the tasks listed earlier, including such functions as address resolution, parameter communication, autoconfiguration, and much more, as you will see in this chapter.

> **KEY CONCEPT** The new *IPv6 Neighbor Discovery (ND)* protocol formalizes for IPv6 a number of functions related to communication between devices on a local network that are performed in IPv4 by protocols such as ARP and ICMP. ND is considered another helper protocol for IPv6 and is closely related to ICMPv6.

Neighbor Discovery Standards

The ND protocol was originally defined in RFC 1970, published in August 1996, and revised in the current defining standard, RFC 2461, published December 1998. Most of the functions of the ND protocol are implemented using a set of five special ICMPv6 control messages, which were discussed in the previous chapter. Thus, to some extent, the operation of ND is partially described by the ICMPv6 standard, RFC 2463. Where ICMPv4 can be considered IPv4's "administrative assistant," IPv6 really has two such assistants working closely together: ICMPv6 and ND. I discuss more of the differences between the ways IPv4 and IPv6 implement ND's functions later in this chapter.

IPv6 ND General Operational Overview

As I just mentioned, the name of the ND protocol really does not do it justice. The protocol facilitates not merely the discovery of neighboring devices, but also a substantial number of functions related to local network connectivity, datagram routing, and configuration. Both regular hosts and routers in an IPv6 environment count on the ND protocol to facilitate important exchanges of information that are necessary for proper internetwork operation.

The ND protocol has a number of similarities to ICMP. An important one is that like ICMP, ND is a *messaging* protocol. It doesn't implement a single specific function, but rather a group of activities that are performed through the exchange of messages. This means I can't explain the operation of ND through a specific description of what ND does, but rather must define its operation by means of a list of messages that ND provides, and the specific ways that those messages are used.

Any local network on an internetwork will have both regular hosts and routers, and the term *neighbor* can refer to either. Of course, hosts and routers play different roles on a network, and as a result, ND is very different for each. The ND standard describes nine specific functions performed by the protocol. To better understand these functions and how they are related, we can divide them into three functional groups based on communication type and the kinds of devices involved, as illustrated in Figure 36-1.

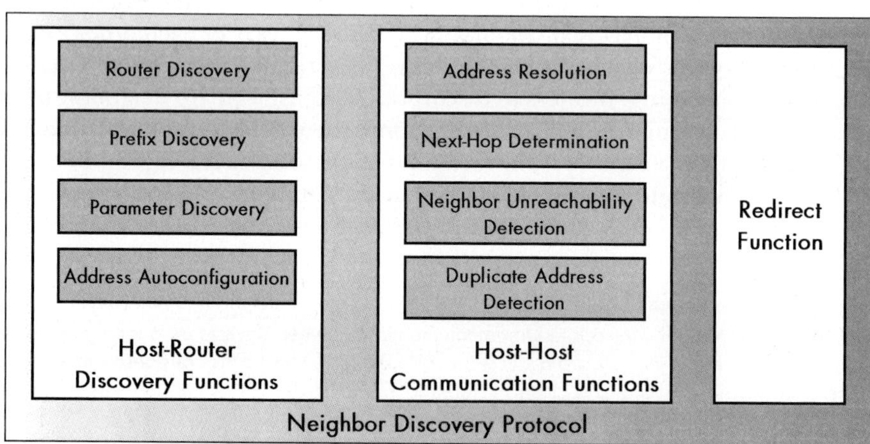

Figure 36-1: *Neighbor Discovery (ND) protocol functional groups and functions*

Two main groups of functions in ND are those for handling router discovery and those for handling communications between hosts. A third functional group consists of just the Redirect function.

Host-Router Discovery Functions

ND host-router discovery functions are those that facilitate the discovery of local routers and the exchange of information between routers and hosts. This includes four specific functions:

Router Discovery (RD) RD is the core function of this group. It's the method by which hosts locate routers on their local network.

Prefix Discovery Closely related to the process of RD is Prefix Discovery. Recall that the term *prefix* refers to the network identifier portion of an IP address. Hosts use this function to determine the network they are on, which, in turn, tells them how to differentiate between local and distant destinations and whether to attempt direct or indirect delivery of datagrams.

Parameter Discovery Also closely related to RD, this is the method by which a host learns important parameters about the local network and/or routers, such as the maximum transmission unit (MTU) of the local link.

Address Autoconfiguration Hosts in IPv6 are designed to be able to automatically configure themselves, but this requires information that is normally provided by a router.

Host-Host Communication Functions

The other main group of functions is associated with information determination and communication directly between nodes, usually hosts. Some of these functions can be performed between hosts and routers, but this group is not specifically related to RD. Host-host communcation functions include the following:

Address Resolution The process by which a device determines the layer 2 address of another device on the local network from that device's layer 3 (IP) address. This is the job performed by ARP in IPv4.

Next-Hop Determination The method for looking at an IP datagram's destination address and determining where it should next be sent.

Neighbor Unreachability Detection The process of determining whether or not a neighbor device can be directly contacted.

Duplicate Address Detection Determining if an address that a device wishes to use already exists on the network.

Redirect Function

The last functional group contains just one function: *Redirect.* This is the technique whereby a router informs a host of a better next-hop node to use for a particular destination.

> **KEY CONCEPT** ND encompasses nine individual functions, many of which are related to each other. They are organized into three functional groups: *host-router discovery functions*, *host-host communications functions*, and the *Redirect function*.

Relationships Between Functions

The division of ND's overall functionality into nine tasks in three groups is somewhat arbitrary, but provides a good frame of reference for understanding what the protocol does. Some of the functions in different groups are related; next-hop determination uses information obtained as part of Parameter Discovery. The Redirect function is also a form of router-host communication but is distinct from RD.

ICMPv6 Messages Used by ND

Just as ND is similar to ICMP in its operation, the two protocols are related in another way: the way that they perform messaging. ND actually implements its functions using ICMPv6 messages. A set of five message types is described in the ND standard:

Router Advertisement Messages Sent regularly by routers to tell hosts that they exist and provide important prefix and parameter information to them.

Router Solicitation Messages Sent by hosts to request that any local routers send a Router Advertisement message so they don't have to wait for the next regular advertisement message.

Neighbor Advertisement Messages Sent by hosts to indicate the existence of the host and provide information about it.

Neighbor Solicitation Messages Sent to verify the existence of another host and to ask it to transmit a Neighbor Advertisement message.

Redirect Messages Sent by a router to tell a host of a better method to route data to a particular destination.

We'll look at how these message types are used later in this chapter. See Chapter 35 for the structures of each of these five ICMPv6 message types used by ND.

IPv6 ND Functions Compared to Equivalent IPv4 Functions

The IPv6 ND protocol has the distinction of being the only truly new protocol created as part of the core of IPv6; there is no previous version of ND. Of course, most of the services that ND provides to IPv6 were also required in IPv4. They were just provided in a rather diverse set of protocols and standards that the ND protocol has formalized, integrated, and improved.

What this means is that while ND is new, the jobs it does are equivalent to the tasks performed by several other protocols in IPv4. Specifically, the bulk of ND functions correspond to the following set of standards, features, and message types in IPv4:

ICMPv4 Router Discovery Most of the functions associated with identifying and obtaining information from routers in ND are based on the use of ICMPv4 Router Advertisement and Router Solicitation messages, as defined in RFC 1256.

Address Resolution Protocol ND provides enhanced address resolution capabilities that are similar to the functions provided in IPv4 by ARP.

ICMPv4 Redirect ND's Redirect function and Redirect messages are based on similar functionality defined in IPv4 and ICMPv4.

There are other aspects of ND that only somewhat correlate to how things work in IPv4. There are also improvements or new functionality compared to how these IPv4 functions work. Some of these are due to differences in how IPv6 itself operates compared to IPv4. For example, Prefix Discovery in ND is sort of related to the Address Mask Request and Address Mask Reply messaging in ICMPv4.

Overall, ND represents a substantial improvement compared to the way its job was done in IPv4. Like IPv6 itself, ND is generally better suited to the needs of modern networks than the older protocols. Some of the more important specific improvements made in ND compared to how its job was done in IPv4 include the following:

Formalizing of Router Discovery In IPv4, the process of RD and solicitation was arguably an afterthought. ND formalizes this process and makes it part of the core of the TCP/IP protocol suite.

Formalizing of Address Resolution In a similar manner, address resolution is handled in a superior way in ND, which functions at layer 3 and is tightly tied to IP, just as ICMP is. There is no more need for an ambiguously layered protocol like ARP, whose implementation depends greatly on the underlying physical and data link layers.

Ability to Perform Functions Securely ND operates at the network layer, so it can make use of the authentication and encryption capabilities of IPsec for tasks such as address resolution and RD.

Autoconfiguration In combination with features built into IPv6, ND allows many devices to automatically configure themselves, without the need for something like a Dynamic Host Configuration Protocol (DHCP) server (though DHCPv6 does also exist).

Dynamic Router Selection Devices use ND to detect if neighbors are reachable. If a device is using a router that stops being reachable, it will detect this and automatically switch to another one.

Multicast-Based Address Resolution Address resolution is performed using special multicast addresses instead of broadcasts, thereby reducing unnecessary disruption of "innocent bystanders" when resolution messages must be sent.

Better Redirection Improvements have been made to the method for generating and using Redirect messages.

IPv6 ND Host-Router Discovery Functions

Connecting individual networks together creates internetworks. The devices that are responsible for this connection of networks are routers, which send data from one network to the next. A host must rely on a router to forward transmissions to all devices other than those on the local network. For this reason, before a host can properly use an internetwork, it needs to find a local router and learn important information about both the router and the network itself. Enabling this information exchange is one of the most important jobs of the IPv6 ND protocol.

The general term used to describe most of the ND communication between hosts and routers on a local network is *discovery*. As I mentioned earlier in this chapter, the term encompasses not merely discovery of the router, but also communication of important parameters. Most of this communication flows from the routers to the hosts, since routers control the way that each network is used. They provide information to hosts so the hosts know how best to operate.

The various discovery features related to host-router communication are all facilitated by the same exchange of two different ICMPv6 message types. Router Advertisement messages are sent only by routers, and they contain information about the router and the network on which it is located. Router Solicitation messages are optional, and they are sent by hosts when they want to find a local router. The format of each of these messages is described in Chapter 35.

Note that both Router Advertisement and Router Solicitation messages may include an optional layer 2 address of the device sending the message. This is used to update address resolution caches to save time when address resolution is needed later.

The mechanisms for using these messages are not really that complicated. The best way to see how the discovery process works overall is to look at the specific tasks performed both by routers and hosts in ND. Let's start by looking at the functions that routers perform.

Host-Router Discovery Functions Performed by Routers

Routers are responsible for the following functions:

Routine Advertisement The main job that routers do in ND is to regularly transmit Router Advertisement messages. Each router maintains a timer that controls how often an advertisement is sent out. Advertisements are also sent when any sort of special situation arises. For example, a message will be sent if key information about the router changes, such as its address on the local network. Router Advertisement messages include key information about both the router and the network. See Chapter 35 for a full description of the Router Advertisement message format.

Parameter Maintenance Routers are responsible for maintaining key parameters about the local network, so they can be sent in advertisements. These include the default Hop Limit field value that should be used by hosts on the network, a default MTU value for the network, and information such as network prefixes, which are used for both first-hop routing by hosts and autoconfiguration. Again, some more details on these can be found in Chapter 35.

Solicitation Processing Routers listen for Router Solicitation messages. When one is received, they will immediately send a Router Advertisement to the requesting host.

Host-Router Discovery Functions Performed by Hosts

For their part, hosts are responsible for three main functions:

Advertisement Processing Hosts listen for advertisements on their local network and process them. They then set appropriate parameters based on the information in these messages. This includes maintaining various data structures such as lists of prefixes and routers, which are updated regularly as new advertisement information comes in.

Solicitation Generation Under certain conditions, a host will generate a Router Solicitation and send it out on the local network. This very simple message just requests that any local routers that hear it immediately send a Router Advertisement message back to the device that made the request. This is most often done when a host is first turned on, so it doesn't have to sit waiting for the next routine advertisement.

Autoconfiguration When required, and if the network supports the function, the host will use information from the local router to allow it to automatically configure itself with an IP address and other parameters.

> **KEY CONCEPT** One of the two main functional groups of ND is the set of *host-router discovery* functions. They allow hosts on a local network to discover the identity of a local router and learn important parameters about how the network is to be used. Host-router discovery operations are performed using ICMPv6 Router Advertisement and Router Solicitation messages.

IPv6 ND Host-Host Communication Functions

The delivery of datagrams in IP can be divided into two methods: direct and indirect. Indirect datagram delivery requires that routers provide help to hosts, which leads to the host-router discovery functions described in the previous section. Direct delivery of datagrams is performed from one host to another on the same network. This doesn't require the use of routers, but necessitates other IPv6 ND protocol functions that involve communication directly between local hosts. These include next-hop determination, address resolution, neighbor unreachability detection, and duplicate address detection.

Next-Hop Determination

The first task that any host must perform when it wants to send a datagram is *next-hop determination.* This is the process by which a device looks at the destination address in a datagram and decides whether direct or indirect delivery is required. In early IPv4, this was done by looking at the class of the address, and later on, by using the subnet mask. In IPv6, the prefix information obtained from local routers is compared to the destination of the datagram to determine if the destination device is local or distant. If it is local, the next hop is the same as the destination address; if it is not local, the next hop is chosen from the device's list of local routers (which are determined either by manual configuration or using the host-router discovery features of ND).

For efficiency purposes, hosts do not perform this next-hop determination for each and every datagram. They maintain a destination cache that contains information about what the next hop should be for recent devices to which datagrams have been sent. Each time a next-hop determination is performed for a particular destination, information from that determination is entered into the cache so that it can be used the next time datagrams are sent to that device.

Address Resolution

If a host determines that the destination of a datagram is local, it will then need to send the datagram to that device. The actual transmission will occur using whatever physical layer and data link layer technology has been used to implement the local network. This requires the host to know the layer 2 address of the destination, even though it generally has only the layer 3 address from the datagram. Getting from the layer 3 address to the layer 2 address is known as the address resolution problem.

In IPv6, the ND protocol is responsible for address resolution. When a host wants to get the layer 2 address of a datagram destination it sends an ICMPv6 Neighbor Solicitation message containing the IP address of the device whose layer 2 address it wishes to determine. That device responds back with a Neighbor Advertisement message that contains its layer 2 address. Instead of using a broadcast that would disrupt each device on the local network, the solicitation is sent using a special multicast to the destination device's solicited-node address. See Chapters 13 and 25 for more information about address resolution in IPv6.

Note also that even though this discussion does concentrate on communication between hosts, address resolution may also be done when a host needs to send a datagram to a local router and has no entry for it in its destination cache. In the context of address resolution, a destination device is just a neighbor. Whether it is a host or a router matters only in terms of what happens after the datagram has been sent and received. In other words, these host-to-host functions are so named only because they are not specific to the communication between hosts and routers like the tasks in the preceding section.

Updating Neighbors Using Neighbor Advertisement Messages

Devices do not routinely send Neighbor Advertisement messages the way that routers send Router Advertisement messages. There really isn't any need for this: Neighbors don't change much over time, and resolution will occur naturally over time as devices send datagrams to each other. In addition, having advertisements sent regularly by so many devices on a network would be wasteful.

A host may, however, send an unsolicited Neighbor Advertisement message under certain conditions where it feels it is necessary to immediately provide updated information to other neighbors on the local network. A good example of this is a hardware failure—in particular, the failure of a network interface card. When the card is replaced, the device's layer 2 (MAC) address will change. Assuming the device's IP layer can detect this, it can send out an unsolicited Neighbor Advertisement message to tell other devices to update their resolution caches with the new MAC address.

Neighbor Unreachability Detection and the Neighbor Cache

Neighbor Solicitation and Neighbor Advertisement messages are most often associated with address resolution, but they also have other purposes. One of these is neighbor unreachability detection. Each device maintains information about each of its neighbors and updates it dynamically as network conditions change. The information is kept for both host and router devices that are neighbors on the local network. Knowing that a device has become unreachable is important because a host can adapt its behavior accordingly. In the case of an unreachable host, a device may wait a certain period of time before trying to send datagrams to an unreachable host, instead of flooding the network with repeated attempts to send to the host. An unreachable router, on the other hand, is a signal that the device needs to find a new router to use, if an alternate is available.

Each host maintains a neighbor cache that contains information about neighboring devices. Each time a host receives a datagram from a neighbor, it knows the neighbor is reachable at that particular moment, so the device makes an entry in the cache for the neighbor to indicate this. Of course, receiving a datagram from a neighbor means only that the neighbor is reachable now; the more time that elapses since the last datagram was received, the greater the chance that something has happened to make the neighbor no longer reachable.

For this reason, neighbor reachability information must be considered temporary. Each time a neighbor is entered into the cache as reachable, a timer is started. When the timer expires, the reachability information for that neighbor is considered stale, and reachability is no longer assumed for that neighbor. When a new datagram is received from the neighbor in question, the timer is reset and the cache is again set to indicate that the device is reachable. The amount of time a host should consider a neighbor reachable before expiring it is communicated by a local router using a field in a Router Advertisement message.

A host can also dynamically seek out a neighbor if it needs to know its reachability status. It sends a Neighbor Solicitation message to the device and waits for a Neighbor Advertisement message in response. It then updates the cache accordingly.

Duplicate Address Detection

The last use of the two messages we have been discussing here is for duplicate address detection. When a host uses the IPv6 autoconfiguration facility, one of the steps in the process is to ensure that the address it is trying to use doesn't already exist on the network. This is done by sending a Neighbor Solicitation message to the address the device wishes to use. If a Neighbor Advertisement message is received in reply, the address is already in use.

> **KEY CONCEPT** The second of the two main functional groups of ND is the set of *host-host communication* functions. Two ICMPv6 messages, Neighbor Advertisement and Neighbor Solicitation, are defined. They enable a variety of types of essential communication between adjacent hosts on a local network. These include address resolution, determining the next hop to which a datagram should be sent, and also the assessment of a neighboring device's reachability.

IPv6 ND Redirect Function

The last of the major responsibilities of the IPv6 ND protocol is the *Redirect* function. This is used by a router to inform a host of a better route to use for datagrams that have been sent to a particular destination. An argument could be made that the Redirect function should be part of the host-router group since it represents a form of communication between routers and regular hosts. However, it is somewhat different from the other discovery functions, and so the standard treats it separately.

Routers are responsible for detecting situations where a host on the local network has made an inefficient first-hop routing decision, and then attempting to correct it. For example, consider a network that has two routers on it, R1 and R2. A Host H1 wants to send a datagram to Device X2 on another network that is connected to Host H1's network through Router R2. If Host H1 sends the datagram to Router R1, that router will know it must go through Router R2, and will send it there. Seeing that Router R2 was also on the local network, Router R1 therefore knows that Host H1 made a poor initial routing decision: The datagram should have been sent to Router R2 directly, not Router R1. If this sounds very similar to ICMPv4's redirect feature, that's because it is!

In response, Router R1 will create a special ICMPv6 Redirect message. This message will tell Host H1 that for any subsequent datagrams that will be sent to Device X2 should be first sent to Router R2, instead of to Router R1. It is also possible that a router may determine other situations where the first hop from a particular host should be different and will advise the host using a Redirect message. This is illustrated in Figure 36-2.

Only routers send Redirect messages, not hosts. Hosts are responsible for looking for these Redirect messages and processing them. A host receiving such a message will look in it to see which destination's datagram led to the redirection notice, and which new first hop the router is saying the host should use in the future for that destination. In this example, Host H1 will see that Router R1 is saying that any further datagrams to Device X2 should be sent to Router R2 instead of Router R1. Host H1 will update its destination cache for Device X2 accordingly.

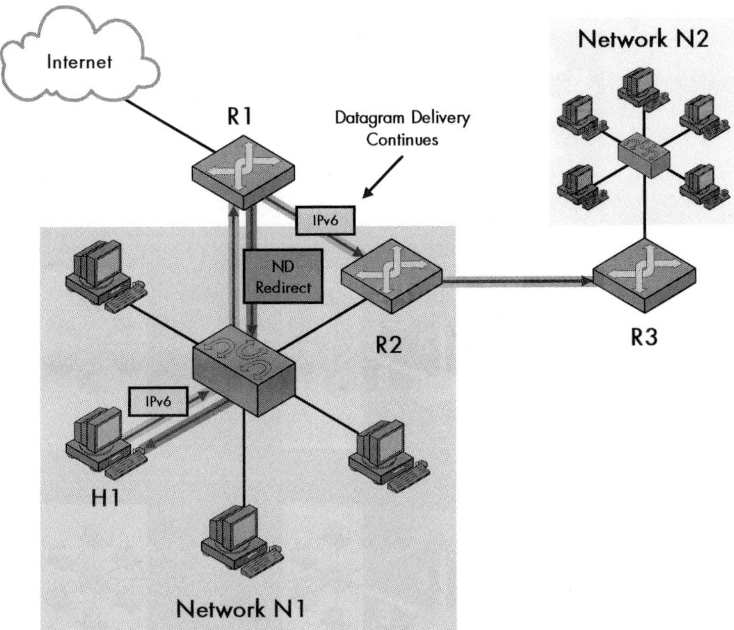

Figure 36-2: ND host redirection using an ICMPv6 Redirect message Host H1 sends to Router R1 an IPv6 datagram destined for a device on Network N2. However, Router R1 notices that Router R2 is on the same network as the source device and is a more direct route to Network N2. It forwards the datagram on to Router R2 but also sends an ICMPv6 Redirect message back to Host H1 to tell it to use Router R2 next time.

KEY CONCEPT The ND *Redirect* function allows a router to tell a host to use a different router for future transmissions to a particular destination. It is similar to the IPv4 redirect feature and is implemented using ICMPv6 Redirect messages.

When a router sends a Redirect message, it may also include in the message the data link layer address of the destination to which it is redirecting. This address is used by the host to update its address resolution cache, if necessary. This may save bandwidth in the future by eliminating an address resolution cycle, when the redirected host tries to send to the new, redirected location. In the example, Router R1 may include Router R2's own layer 2 address in the Redirect message. This can be used by Host H1 the next time it has a datagram for Device X2.

IPv6 also supports the authentication of Redirect messages to prevent unauthorized devices from causing havoc by sending inappropriate Redirect messages. A host may be configured to discard Redirect messages that are not properly authenticated.

PART II-7

TCP/IP ROUTING PROTOCOLS (GATEWAY PROTOCOLS)

Routing is not just one of the most important activities that take place at the network layer; it is also the function that really *defines* layer 3 of the OSI Reference Model. Routing is what enables small local networks to be linked together to form potentially huge internetworks that can span cities, countries, or even the entire globe. The job of routing is done by special devices called *routers*, which forward datagrams from network to network, allowing any device to send to any other device, even if the source has no idea where the destination is.

Strictly speaking, an argument could be made that some routing protocols don't belong in layer 3. For example, many of these protocols send messages using the Transmission Control Protocol (TCP) or User Datagram Protocol (UDP) at layer 4. Despite this, routing is inherently a layer 3 activity, and for this reason, it is traditional to consider routing protocols part of layer 3.

Routing is a complicated subject. The short summary of the process is that routers decide how to forward a datagram based on its destination address, which is compared to information the router keeps in special routing tables. These tables contain entries for each of the networks the router knows about, telling the router which adjacent router the datagram should be sent to in order for it to reach its eventual destination.

As you can imagine, routing tables are critically important to the routing process. It is possible for these tables to be manually maintained by network administrators, but this is tedious and time-consuming and doesn't allow routers to deal with changes or problems in the internetwork. Instead, most modern routers are designed with functionality that lets them share route information with other routers, so they can keep their routing tables up-to-date automatically. This information exchange is accomplished through the use of *routing protocols*.

This part contains five chapters that provide a description of the most common routing (or *gateway*) protocols used in TCP/IP. The first chapter provides an overview of various concepts that are important to know in order to understand how routing protocols work, including an explanation of the difference between interior and exterior routing protocols. This sets the stage for the chapters that follow.

In the second and third chapters, I thoroughly explain the two most commonly used interior routing protocols in TCP/IP: the Routing Information Protocol (RIP) and the Open Shortest Path First (OSPF) protocol. In the fourth chapter, I describe the Border Gateway Protocol (BGP), which is the exterior routing protocol used today on the Internet. The fifth chapter briefly discussing five historical, proprietary, or less commonly used routing protocols.

You may notice that the title of this part refers to both *routing protocols* and *gateway protocols*. These terms are interchangeable, and the word *gateway* appears in the name of several of the protocols. This is an artifact of the historical use of the term *gateway* in early TCP/IP standards to refer to the devices we now call routers. Today, the term *gateway* normally refers not to a router, but to a different type of network interconnection device, so this can be particularly confusing. The term *routing protocol* is now preferred, and it is the one I use.

Like all topics related to routing, routing protocols are generally quite complex. I cover the major ones here in more detail than most general networking references, but even so, I am only scratching the surface, especially of the more complicated ones like OSPF. You can check out the referenced Internet standards (RFCs) for more details if you desire. Also note that there are some routing protocols in use on IP networks that I do not cover here, such as IS-IS (which is actually an OSI protocol and not formally part of TCP/IP).

37

OVERVIEW OF KEY ROUTING PROTOCOL CONCEPTS

Routing protocols play an important part in the overall process of routing in an internetwork. It is therefore easiest to understand them in the scope of an overall discussion of routing. It's difficult to describe the individual TCP/IP routing protocols without some background information on how routing protocols work. For this reason, I feel it is worth taking a brief look at key routing protocol concepts so that you will have more luck making sense of the routing protocols described in the next few chapters.

In this chapter, I will provide an overview of the routing protocol architectures, protocol types, algorithms, and metrics.

Routing Protocol Architectures

Let's start with a look at routing protocol architectures. In this context, the word *architecture* refers to the way that an internetwork is structured. Once you have some networks and routers that you wish to connect together, there are any number of ways that you can do this. The architecture you choose is based on the way that routers are linked, and this has an impact on the way that routing is done and how routing protocols operate.

Core Architecture

TCP/IP and the Internet were developed simultaneously, so TCP/IP routing protocols evolved as the Internet itself did. Early architecture of the Internet consisted of a small number of *core* routers that contained comprehensive information about the internetwork. When the Internet was very small, adding more routers to this core expanded it. However, each time the core was expanded, the amount of routing information that needed to be maintained grew.

Eventually, the core became too large, so a two-level hierarchy was formed to allow further expansion. *Noncore* routers were located on the periphery of the core and contained only partial routing information; they relied on the core routers for transmissions that went across the internetwork. A special routing protocol called the *Gateway-to-Gateway Protocol (GGP)* was used within the core of the internetwork, while another protocol called the *Exterior Gateway Protocol (EGP)* was used between noncore and core routers. The noncore routers were sometimes single, stand-alone routers that connected a single network to the core, or they could be sets of routers for an organization.

This architecture served for a while, but it did not scale very well as the Internet grew. The problem was mainly due to the fact that there was only a single level to the architecture: Every router in the core had to communicate with every other router. Even with peripheral routers being kept outside the core, the amount of traffic in the core kept growing.

Autonomous System (AS) Architecture

To resolve the scaling problem, a new architecture was created that moved away from the centralized concept of a core toward an architecture that was better suited to a larger and growing internetwork. This decentralized architecture treats the internetwork as a set of independent groups, with each group called an *autonomous system (AS)*. An AS consists of a set of routers and networks controlled by a particular organization or administrative entity, which uses a single consistent policy for internal routing.

The power of this system is that routing on the internetwork as a whole occurs between ASes and not individual routers. Information is shared between one and maybe a couple of routers in each AS, not every router in each AS. The details of routing within an AS are also hidden from the rest of the internetwork. This provides both flexibility for each AS to do routing as it sees fit (thus the name *autonomous*) and efficiency for the overall internetwork. Each AS has its own number, and the numbers are globally managed to make sure that they are unique across an internetwork (such as the Internet).

> **KEY CONCEPT** Large, modern TCP/IP internetworks can contain thousands of routers. To better manage routing in such an environment, routers are grouped into constructs called *autonomous systems (ASes)*, each of which consists of a group of routers managed independently by a particular organization or entity.

Modern Protocol Types: Interior and Exterior Routing Protocols

The different nature of routing within an AS and between ASes can be seen in the fact that the following distinct sets of TCP/IP routing protocols are used for each type:

Interior Routing Protocols These protocols are used to exchange routing information between routers within an AS. Interior routing protocols are not used between ASes.

Exterior Routing Protocols These protocols are used to exchange routing information between ASes. They may in some cases be used between routers within an AS, but they primarily deal with exchanging information between ASes.

> **KEY CONCEPT** Interior routing protocols are used to share routing information within an autonomous system; each AS may use a different interior routing protocol because the system is, as the name says, autonomous. Exterior routing protocols convey routing data between ASes; each AS must use the same exterior protocol to ensure that it can communicate.

Since ASes are just sets of routers, you connect ASes by linking a router in one AS to a router in another AS. Architecturally, an AS consists of a set of routers with two different types of connectivity:

Internal Routers Some routers in an AS connect only to other routers in the same AS. These run interior routing protocols.

Border Routers Some routers in an AS connect both to routers within the AS and to routers in one or more other ASes. These devices are responsible for passing traffic between the AS and the rest of the internetwork. They run both interior and exterior routing protocols.

Due to its advantages, the AS architecture, an example of which can be seen in Figure 37-1, has become the standard for TCP/IP networks, most notably the Internet. The division of routing protocols into the interior and exterior classifications has thus also become standard, and all modern TCP/IP routing protocols are first subdivided by type in this manner.

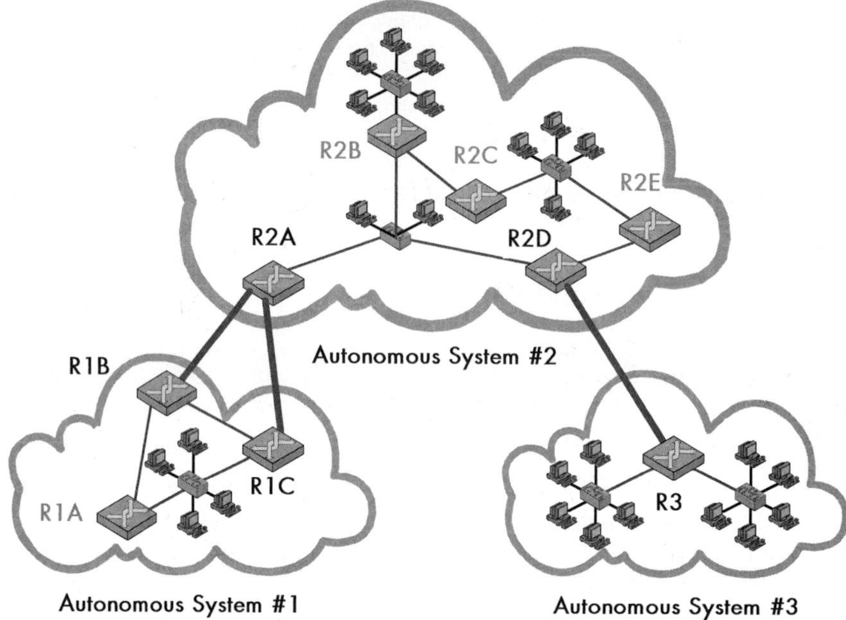

Figure 37-1: TCP/IP autonomous system (AS) routing architecture *This diagram shows a simplified Internet organized into three ASes, each of which is managed independently from the others. Communication within each AS is done using an interior routing protocol chosen by that AS's administrators (thin links). Communication between ASes must be done using a common exterior routing protocol (thick links). Internal routers are shown in lighter text, and border routers are shown in black text.*

Routing Protocol Algorithms and Metrics

Another key differentiation of routing protocols is on the basis of the *algorithms* and *metrics* they use. An algorithm refers to a method that the protocol uses for determining the best route between any pair of networks, and for sharing routing information between routers. A metric is a measure of "cost" that is used to assess the efficiency of a particular route. Since internetworks can be quite complex, the algorithms and metrics of a protocol are very important, and they can be the determining factor in deciding that one protocol is superior to another.

There are two routing protocol algorithms that are most commonly encountered: distance vector and link state. There are also protocols that use a combination of these methods or other methods.

Distance-Vector (Bellman-Ford) Routing Protocol Algorithm

A *distance-vector* routing algorithm, also called a *Bellman-Ford* algorithm after two of its inventors, is one where routes are selected based on the distance between networks. The distance metric is something simple—usually the number of *hops*, or routers, between them.

Routers using this type of protocol maintain information about the distance to all known networks in a table. They regularly send that table to each router they immediately connect with (their *neighbors* or *peers*). These routers then update their tables and send those tables to their neighbors. This causes distance information to propagate across the internetwork, so that eventually, each router obtains distance information about all networks on the internetwork.

Distance-vector routing protocols are somewhat limited in their ability to choose the best route. They also are subject to certain problems in their operation that must be worked around through the addition of special heuristics and features. Their chief advantages are simplicity and history (they have been used for a long time).

Link-State (Shortest-Path First) Routing Protocol Algorithm

A *link-state* algorithm selects routes based on a dynamic assessment of the shortest path between any two networks. For that reason, it's also called a *shortest-path first* method.

Using this method, each router maintains a map describing the current topology of the internetwork. This map is updated regularly by testing reachability of different parts of the Internet, and by exchanging link-state information with other routers. The determination of the best route (or shortest path) can be made based on a variety of metrics that indicate the true cost of sending a datagram over a particular route.

Link-state algorithms are much more powerful than distance-vector algorithms. They adapt dynamically to changing internetwork conditions, and they also allow routes to be selected based on more realistic metrics of cost than simply the number of hops between networks. However, they are more complicated to set up and use more computer processing resources than distance-vector algorithms, and they aren't as well established.

Hybrid Routing Protocol Algorithms

There are also hybrid protocols that combine features from both types of algorithms, and other protocols that use completely different algorithms. For example, the *Border Gateway Protocol (BGP)* is a path-vector algorithm, which is somewhat similar to the distance-vector algorithm, but communicates much more detailed route information. It includes some of the attributes of distance-vector and link-state protocols, but is more than just a combination of the two.

Static and Dynamic Routing Protocols

Finally, you may also occasionally see routing protocols categorized by type as *static* and *dynamic*. This terminology is somewhat misleading.

The term *static routing* simply refers to a situation where the routing tables are manually set up so that they remain static. In contrast, *dynamic routing* is the use of routing protocols to dynamically update routing tables. Thus, all routing protocols are dynamic. There is no such thing as a static routing protocol (unless you consider a network administrator who is editing a routing table a protocol).

38

ROUTING INFORMATION PROTOCOL (RIP, RIP-2, AND RIPNG)

The most popular of the TCP/IP interior routing protocols is the *Routing Information Protocol (RIP)*. The simplicity of the name matches the simplicity of the protocol. Of all the routing protocols, RIP is one of the easiest to configure and least demanding of resources. Its popularity is due both to this simplicity and its long history. In fact, support for RIP has been built into operating systems for as long as TCP/IP itself has existed.

There are three versions of RIP: RIP versions 1 and 2 for IP version 4 (IPv4) and RIPng for IP version 6 (IPv6). The basic operation of the protocol is mostly the same for all three versions, but there are also some notable differences between them, especially in terms of the format of messages sent.

RIP was one of the first interior routing protocols used in TCP/IP. More than 20 years later, it continues to be widely used. Even though RIP has important limitations, it continues to have an important place in TCP/IP routing to this day. Evidence that RIP has a future can be seen in the creation of an IPv6 version of the protocol: RIPng.

I will open the examination of RIP with an overall description of its characteristics and how it works in general terms. I start with an overview and history of the protocol, including a brief discussion of its different versions and the standards that define them. I describe the method that RIP uses to determine routes and the metric used to assess route cost. I describe the general operation of the protocol including message types and when they are sent. I then describe the most important limitations and issues with RIP, and the special features that have been added to the protocol to resolve several problems with the basic RIP algorithm. Finally, I take a closer look at each version, showing the message format used for each and discussing version-specific features as well.

RIP Overview

RIP has been the most popular interior routing protocol in the TCP/IP protocol suite for many years. The history of the protocol and how it came to achieve prominence is a rather interesting one. Unlike many of the other important protocols in the TCP/IP suite, RIP was not first developed formally using the RFC standardization process (see Chapter 3). Rather, it evolved as a de facto industry standard and became an Internet standard later.

The history of RIP has something in common with another networking heavyweight: Ethernet. Like that formidable local area network (LAN) technology, RIP's roots go back to that computing pioneer, Xerox's Palo Alto Research Center (PARC). At the same time that Ethernet was being developed for tying together LANs, PARC created a higher-layer protocol to run on Ethernet called the Xerox PARC Universal Protocol (PUP). PUP required a routing protocol, so Xerox created a protocol called the Gateway Information Protocol (GWINFO). This was later renamed the Routing Information Protocol and used as part of the Xerox Network System (XNS) protocol suite.

RIP entered the mainstream when developers at the University of California at Berkeley adapted it for use in the Berkeley Standard Distribution (BSD) of the UNIX operating system. RIP first appeared in BSD version 4.2 in 1982, where it was implemented as the UNIX program *routed* (pronounced "route-dee," not "rout-ed"—the "d" stands for "daemon," a common UNIX term for a server process).

BSD was (and still is) a very popular operating system, especially for machines connected to the early Internet. As a result, RIP was widely deployed and became the industry standard for internal routing protocols. It was used both for TCP/IP and other protocol suites. In fact, a number of other routing protocols, such as the RTP protocol in the AppleTalk suite, were based on this early version of RIP.

RIP Standardization

For a while, the BSD implementation of routed was actually considered the standard for the protocol itself. However, this was not a formally defined standard, and this meant that there was no formal definition of exactly how it functioned. This led to slight differences in various implementations of the protocol over time. To resolve potential interoperability issues between implementations, the Internet Engineering Task Force (IETF) formally specified RIP in the Internet standard RFC 1058, "Routing Information Protocol," which was published in June 1988. This

RFC was based directly on the BSD routed program. This original version of RIP is now also sometimes called RIP version 1 or RIP-1 to differentiate it from later versions.

RIP's popularity was due in large part to its inclusion in BSD, and it was included in BSD because of the relative simplicity of the protocol.

RIP Operational Overview, Advantages, and Limitations

RIP uses the distance-vector algorithm to determine routes, as described in Chapter 37. Each router maintains a routing table containing entries for various networks or hosts in the internetwork. Each entry contains two primary pieces of information: the address of the network or host and the distance to it, measured in hops, which is simply the number of routers that a datagram must pass through to get to its destination.

On a regular basis, each router in the internetwork sends out its routing table in a special message on each of the networks to which it is connected, using the User Datagram Protocol (UDP). Other routers receive these tables and use them to update their own tables. This is done by taking each of the routes they receive and adding an extra hop. For example, if Router A receives an indication from Router B that Network N1 is four hops away, since Router A and Router B are adjacent, the distance from Router A to Network N1 is five. After a router updates its tables, it sends out this information to other routers on its local networks. Over time, routing distance information for all networks propagates over the entire internetwork.

RIP is straightforward in operation, easy to implement, and undemanding of router processing power, which makes it especially attractive in smaller autonomous systems (ASes). There are, however, some important limitations that arise due to the simplicity of the protocol. For starters, hops are often not the best metric to use in selecting routes. There are also a number of problems that arise with the algorithm itself. These include slow convergence (delays in having all routers agree on the same routing information) and problems dealing with network link failures. RIP includes several special features to resolve some of these issues, but others are inherent limitations of the protocol. For example, RIP supports a maximum of only 15 hops between destinations, making it unsuitable for very large ASes, and this cannot be changed.

More than two decades after it was first created, RIP continues to be a popular interior routing protocol. Its limitations have led to many internetworking experts hoping that the protocol would eventually be replaced by newer protocols such as Open Shortest Path First (OSPF) that are superior on a strictly technical basis. Some have gone so far as to sarcastically suggest that maybe it would be best if RIP would R. I. P. Once a protocol becomes popular, however, it's hard to resist momentum, and RIP is likely to continue to be used for many years to come.

> **KEY CONCEPT** The *Routing Information Protocol (RIP)* is one of the oldest and most popular interior routing protocols. With each router, it uses a distance-vector algorithm that maintains a table, which indicates how to reach various networks in the AS and the distance to it in hops. RIP is popular because it is well established and simple, but it has a number of important limitations.

Development of RIP Version 2 (RIP-2) and RIPng for IPv6

Some other issues with RIP came about as a result of the protocol having been developed in the early 1980s, when TCP/IP was still in its infancy. Over time, as the use of TCP/IP protocols changed, RIP became outdated. In response, *RIP version 2*, or *RIP-2* was created in the early 1990s.

RIP-2 defines a new message format for RIP and includes a number of new features, including support for classless addressing, authentication, and the use of multicasting instead of broadcasting, which improves network performance. It was first defined in RFC 1388, "RIP Version 2 Carrying Additional Information," published in January 1993. This RFC was revised in RFC 1723 and finalized in RFC 2453, "RIP Version 2," published in November 1998.

In order to ensure that RIP can work with TCP/IP in the future, it was necessary to define a version that would work with the IPv6. In 1997, RFC 2080 was published, titled "RIPng for IPv6." The *ng* stands for *next generation*; you'll recall that IPv6 is also sometimes called *IPng*.

RIPng is not just a new version of RIP, like RIP-2, but is defined as a new standalone protocol. It is, however, based closely on the original RIP and RIP-2 standards. A distinct protocol (as opposed to a revision of the original) was needed due to the changes made between IPv4 and IPv6, though RIP and RIPng work in the same basic way. RIPng is sometimes also called *RIPv6*.

KEY CONCEPT The original version of RIP has the fewest features and is now called *RIP-1*. *RIP-2* was created to add support for classless addressing and other capabilities. *RIPng* is the version created for compatibility with IPv6.

RIP Route Determination Algorithm and Metric

As I mentioned in the previous chapter, one of the defining characteristics of any routing protocol is the algorithm it uses for determining routes. RIP falls into the class of protocols that use a distance-vector, or Bellman-Ford, routing algorithm. To help you understand exactly how RIP determines routes, this section presents the specific implementation of the algorithm for RIP and provides an example.

Note that the description presented here is the basic algorithm used by RIP. This is modified in certain ways to address some of the problems that can occur in special circumstances due to how the algorithm works. Later in this chapter, we will explore these problems and the special features RIP includes to address them.

RIP Routing Information and Route Distance Metric

The job of RIP, like any routing protocol, is to provide a mechanism for exchanging information about routes so routers can keep their routing tables up-to-date. Each router in an RIP internetwork keeps track in its routing table of all networks (and possibly individual hosts) in the internetwork. For each network or host, the device includes a variety of information, of which the following is the most important:

- The address of the network or host
- The distance from that router to the network or host

- The first hop for the route: the device to which datagrams must first be sent to eventually get to the network or host

In theory, the distance metric can be any assessment of cost, but in RIP, distance is measured in hops. As you probably already know, in TCP/IP vernacular, a datagram makes a *hop* when it passes through a router. Thus, the RIP distance between a router and a network measures the number of routers that the datagram must pass through to get to the network. If a router connects to a network directly, then the distance is 1 hop. If it goes through a single router, the distance is 2 hops, and so on. In RIP, a maximum of 15 hops are allowed for any network or host. The value 16 is defined as infinity, so an entry with 16 in it means "this network or host is not reachable."

RIP Route Determination Algorithm

On a regular basis, each router running RIP will send out its routing table entries to provide information to other routers about the networks and hosts it knows how to reach. Any routers on the same network as the one sending out this information will be able to update their own tables based on the information they receive.

Any router that receives a message from another router on the same network saying it can reach Network X at a cost of *N* knows it can reach Network X at a cost of *N*+1 by sending to the router it received the message from.

RIP Route Determination and Information Propagation

Let's take a specific example to help you understand how routes are determined and how route information is propagated using RIP. Consider a relatively simple internetwork with four individual networks, connected as follows:

- Router RA connects Network N1 to Network N2.
- Router RB and Router RC connect Network N2 to Network N3.
- Router RD connects Network N3 to Network N4.

This sample AS is illustrated in Figure 38-1.

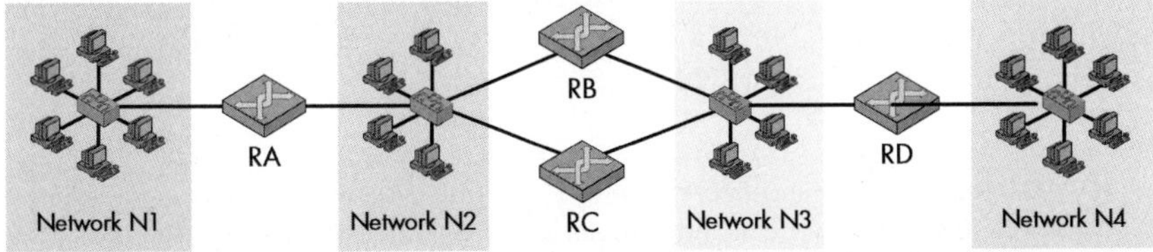

Figure 38-1: Sample RIP AS *This is an example of a simple AS that contains four physical networks and four routers.*

Now let's suppose that we just turned on Router RA. It sees that it is directly connected to Network N1 and Network N2, so it will have an entry in its routing table indicating that it can reach Network N1 at a cost of 1, which we can represent as {N1,1}. Information about Network N1 will propagate from Router RA across the internetwork in the following sequence of steps (which are illustrated in Figure 38-2):

1. Router RA sends out an RIP message containing the entry {N1,1} on each of the networks to which it is connected. There are no other routers on Network N1, so nothing happens there. But Routers RB and RC are on Network N2, so they receive the information.
2. Routers RB and RC will look in their routing tables to see if they already have entries for Network N1. Assuming neither does, they will each create a routing table entry {N1,2} for Router RA. This means, "I can reach Network N1 at a cost of 2 hops by sending to Router RA."
3. Routers RB and RC will each send their own routing tables out over the networks to which they are connected: Networks N2 and N3. This will contain the entry {N1,2}. Router RA will receive that message on Network N2 but will ignore it, since it knows it can reach Network N1 directly (cost of 1, which is less than 2). But Router RD will receive the message on Network N3.
4. Router RD will examine its routing table, and seeing no entry for Network N1, it will add the entry {N1,3} for Routers RB or RC. Either one will work, so whichever is chosen depends entirely on whether Router RD received information about Network N1 first from Router RB or Router RC.
5. Router RD will send the entry {N1,3} on Network N4, but there are no other routers there to hear it.

Note that RIP is designed so that a routing entry is replaced only if information is received about a *shorter* route; ties go to the incumbent, if you will. This means that once Router RD creates an entry for Network N1 with a cost of 3 going through Router RB, if it receives information that it can reach Network N1 at the same cost of 3 through Router RC, it will ignore it. Similarly, if it gets Router RC's information first, it will ignore the information from Router RB.

Naturally, this same propagation scheme will occur for all the other networks as well. I have shown only how information about Network N1 moves from router to router. For example, Router RA will eventually install an entry for Network N4 saying that it is reachable at a cost of 3 going through either Router RB or RC; this will be either {N4,RB,3} or {N4,RC,3}.

KEY CONCEPT Routing information is propagated between routers in RIP using a simple algorithm. On a regular basis, each router sends out RIP messages that specify which networks it can reach and how many hops it takes to reach them. Other routers directly connected to that one know that they can then reach those networks through that router at a cost of one additional hop. So if Router A sends a message saying it can reach Network X for a cost of *N* hops, every other router that connects directly to Router A can reach Network X for a cost of *N*+1 hops. It will put that information into its routing table, unless it knows of an alternate route through another router that has a lower cost.

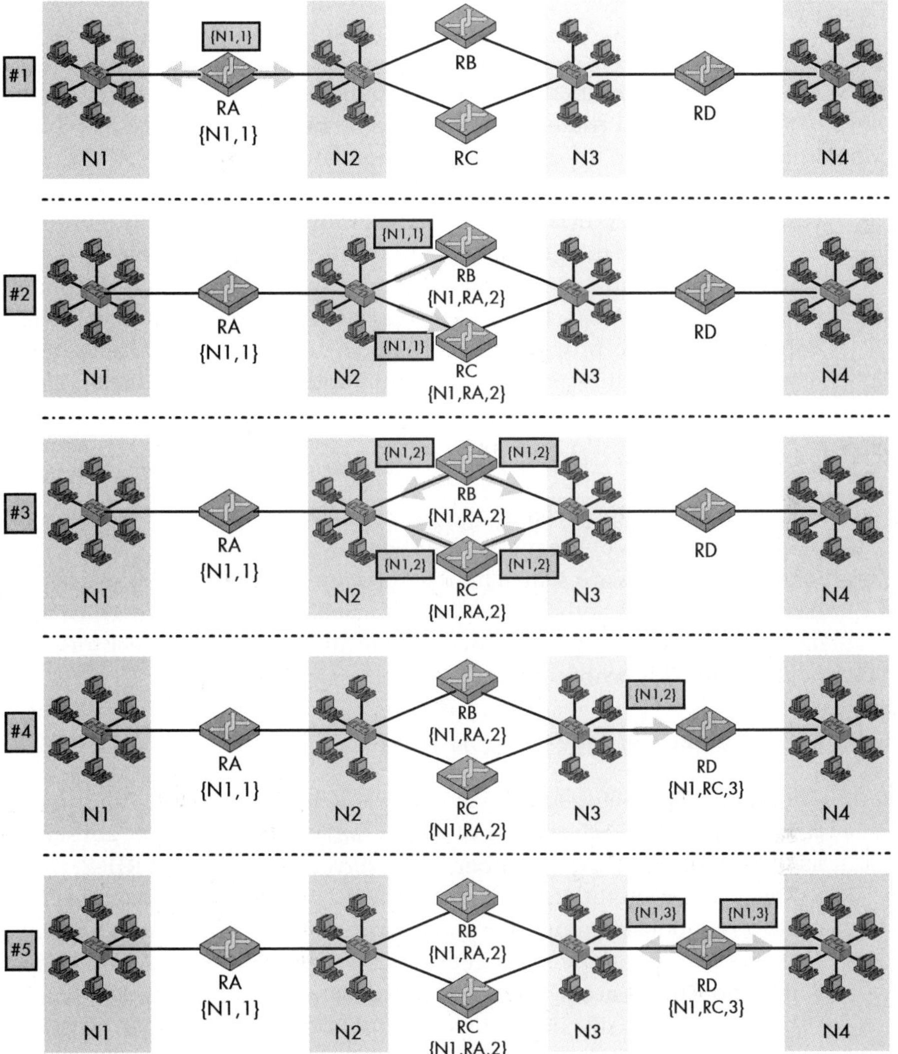

Figure 38-2: Propagation of network routing information using RIP *This composite diagram illustrates the five steps in propagating route information about Network N1 from Router RA to the rest of the AS. In step 1, the information is sent from Router RA to both of its connected networks. In step 2, it reaches Routers RB and RC, which then know they can reach Network N1 through Router RA at a cost of one additional hop. In step 3, these two routers send this information on their networks, and in step 4, it reaches Router RD. In step 5, Router RD sends out the information, but no other routers are around to receive it.*

This propagation of network routing information occurs on a regular basis, and also when the structure of the network changes (due to intentional changes in topography or failure of links or routers). When this happens, the change information will move through the internetwork so that all routers are eventually updated. For example, suppose a connection were added from Router RC to Network N1. If Router RD previously had the entry {N1,RB,3}, it would eventually change this to {N1,RC,2}, since it could now reach Network N1 more quickly by going through Router RC.

Default Routes

In some cases, it is not convenient for every network or host in a large internetwork to be fully specified with its own routing entry. Then it may be advantageous to specify a default route for the network to use in reaching hosts or networks for which they have no information. The most common example of this is when an AS connects to the public Internet through a single router. Except for that router, the rest of the local network doesn't need to know how to access the Internet.

In RIP, information about a default route is communicated by having routers that are intended to handle such traffic send information about a "dummy" network with the address 0.0.0.0. This is treated as if it were a regular network when information about routes is propagated on the internetwork using RIP messages, but other devices recognize this special address and understand that it means a default route.

RIP General Operation, Messaging, and Timers

RIP is a protocol for exchanging routing information, so its operation can best be described in terms of the messages used to exchange this information and the rules for when messages are sent. The RIP software in each router sends messages and takes other actions both in reaction to certain events and in response to triggers set off by timers. Timers are also used to determine when routing information should be discarded if it is not updated.

RIP Messages and Basic Message Types

Communication between RIP software elements in routers on an internetwork is accomplished through the use of *RIP messages.* These messages are sent using the UDP, with the UDP port number 520 reserved for RIP-1 and RIP-2, and 521 for RIPng. Thus, even though RIP is considered part of layer 3 like other routing protocols, it behaves more like an application in terms of how it sends messages. The exact format of the message is version-dependent, and all three formats (RIP, RIP-2, and RIPng) are described in detail later in this chapter. RIP messages can be either sent to a specific device or sent out for multiple devices to receive. If directed to one device, they are sent unicast; otherwise, they are either broadcast (in RIP) or multicast (RIP-2 and RIPng).

There are only two basic message types for all three versions of RIP:

RIP Request A message sent by a router to another router asking it to send back all or part of its routing table.

RIP Response A message sent by a router containing all or part of its routing table. Note that despite the name, this message is *not* sent just in response to an RIP Request message, as you will see.

NOTE *The original RIP also defined a few other message types: Traceon, Traceoff, and a special message type reserved for use by Sun Microsystems. These are obsolete and no longer used. They were removed from the RIP-2 and RIPng standards.*

RIP Update Messaging and the 30-Second Timer

RIP Request messages are sent under special circumstances when a router requires that it be provided with immediate routing information. The most common example of this is when a router is first powered on. After initializing, the router will typically send an RIP Request message on its attached networks to ask for the latest information about routes from any neighboring routers. It is also possible for RIP Request messages to be used for diagnostic purposes.

A router receiving an RIP Request message will process it and send an RIP Response message containing either all of its routing table or just the entries the Request message asked for, as appropriate. Under normal circumstances, however, routers do not usually send RIP Request messages asking specifically for routing information. Instead, each RIP router has a special timer that goes off every 30 seconds. (This timer is not given a specific name in the RIP standards; it is just the 30-second timer.)

Each time the timer expires, an unsolicited (unrequested) broadcast or multicast is made of an RIP Response message containing the router's entire routing table. The timer is then reset, and 30 seconds later, it goes off again, causing another routine RIP Response message to be sent. This process ensures that route information is regularly sent around the Internet, so routers are always kept up-to-date about routes.

> **KEY CONCEPT** RIP uses two basic message types: the RIP Request and RIP Response. Both are sent using the User Datagram Protocol (UDP). RIP Response messages, despite their name, are used both for routine periodic routing table updates as well as to reply to RIP Request messages. Requests are sent only in special circumstances, such as when a router first joins a network.

Preventing Stale Information: The Timeout Timer

When a router receives routing information and enters it into its routing table, that information cannot be considerd valid indefinitely. In the example presented earlier in the "RIP Route Determination and Information Propagation" section, suppose that after Router RB installs a route to Network N1 through Router RA, the link between Router RA and Network N2 fails. Once this happens, Network N1 is no longer reachable from Router RB, but Router RB has a route indicating that it can reach Network N1.

To prevent this problem, routes are kept in the routing table for only a limited amount of time. A special Timeout timer is started whenever a route is installed in the routing table. Whenever the router receives another RIP Response message with information about that route, the route is considered refreshed, and its Timeout timer is reset. As long as the route continues to be refreshed, the timer will never expire.

If, however, RIP Response messages containing that route stop arriving, the timer will eventually expire. When this happens, the route is marked for deletion by setting the distance for the route to 16 (which you may recall is RIP infinity and indicates an unreachable network). The default value for the Timeout timer is usually 180 seconds. This allows several periodic updates of a route to be missed before a router will conclude that the route is no longer reachable.

Removing Stale Information: The Garbage-Collection Timer

When a route is marked for deletion, a new Garbage-Collection timer is also started. *Garbage collection* is a computer-industry phrase for a task that looks for deleted or invalid information and cleans it up. Thus, this is a timer that counts a number of seconds before the newly invalid route will be actually removed from the table. The default value for this timer is 120 seconds.

The reason for using this two-stage removal method is to give the router that declared the route that's no longer reachable a chance to propagate this information to other routers. Until the Garbage-Collection timer expires, the router will include that route, with the unreachable metric of 16 hops, in its own RIP Response messages, so that the problem with that route is conveyed to the other routers. When the timer expires, the route is deleted. If during the garbage collection period a new RIP Response message for the route is received, then the deletion process is aborted. In this case, the Garbage-Collection timer is cleared, the route is marked as valid again, and a new Timeout timer starts.

Triggered Updates

In addition to the two situations already described where an RIP Response is sent—in reply to an RIP Request message and on expiration of the 30-second timer—an RIP Response message is also sent out when a route changes.

This action, an enhancement to a basic RIP operation, called a *triggered update*, is intended to ensure that information about route changes is propagated as fast as possible across the internetwork. This will help reduce the slow convergence problem in RIP. For example, in the case of a route timing out and the Garbage-Collection timer starting, a triggered update would be sent out about the now-invalid route immediately. This is described in more detail later in the chapter, in the "RIP Special Features for Resolving RIP Algorithm Problems" section.

RIP Problems and Some Resolutions

The simplicity of RIP is often given as the main reason for its popularity. Simplicity is great most of the time, but an unfortunate price of simplicity in too many cases is that problems crop up, usually in unusual cases or special situations, and so it is with RIP. The straightforward distance-vector algorithm and operation mechanism work well most of the time, but they have some important weaknesses. We need to examine these problems to understand both the limitations of RIP and some of the complexities that have been added to the protocol to resolve them.

Issues with RIP's Algorithm

The most important area where we find serious issues with RIP is with the basic function of the distance-vector algorithm described earlier in this section and the way that messages are used to implement it, as described in the following sections.

Slow Convergence

The distance-vector algorithm is designed so that all routers share all their routing information regularly. Over time, all routers eventually end up with the same information about the location of networks and which are the best routes to use to reach them. This is called *convergence.* Unfortunately, the basic RIP algorithm is rather slow to achieve convergence. It takes a long time for all routers to get the same information, and in particular, it takes a long time for information about topology changes to propagate.

Consider the worst-case situation of two networks separated by 15 routers. Since routers normally send RIP Response messages only every 30 seconds, a change to one of this pair of networks might not be seen by the router nearest to the other one until many minutes have elapsed—an eternity in networking terms.

The slow convergence problem is even more pronounced when it comes to the propagation of route failures. Failure of a route is detected only through the expiration of the 180-second Timeout timer, so that adds up to three minutes more delay before convergence can even begin.

Routing Loops

A routing loop occurs when Router A has an entry telling it to send datagrams for Network 1 to Router B, and Router B has an entry saying that datagrams for Network 1 should be sent to Router A. Larger loops can also exist: Router A says to send to B, which says to send to Router C, which says to send to Router A. Under normal circumstances, these loops should not occur, but they can happen in special situations.

RIP does not include any specific mechanism to detect or prevent routing loops. The best it can do is try to avoid them.

Counting to Infinity

A special case of slow convergence can lead to a routing loop situation where one router passes bad information to another router, which sends more bad information to another router, and so on. This causes a situation where the protocol is sometimes described as unstable. The problem is called *counting to infinity*, for reasons you will soon see.

To understand how this happens, let's modify the example presented earlier in the "RIP Route Determination and Information Propagation" section, as shown in Figure 38-3. Suppose that the internetwork is operating properly for a while. Router RB has an entry indicating it can reach Network N1 through Router RA at a cost of 2. But let's say the link from Network N1 to Router RA fails. After the Timeout timer for Network N1 expires on Router RA, that router will change the metric for Network N1 to 16 to indicate that it is unreachable. In the absence of any mechanism to force Router RA to immediately inform other routers of this failure, those routers will not know about the change. Router RB will continue to think it can reach Network N1 through Router RA.

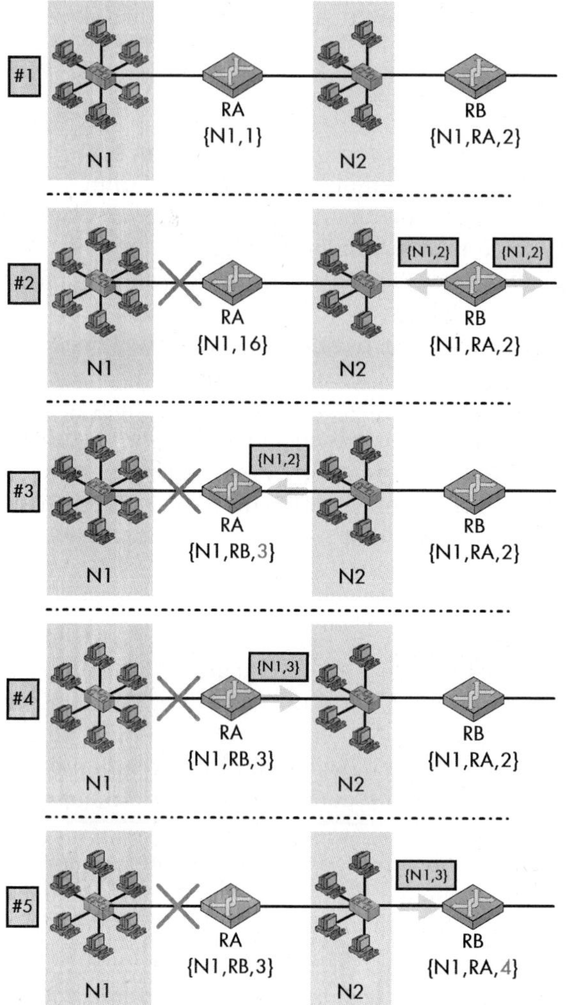

Figure 38-3: The RIP counting to infinity problem *This composite diagram shows part of the AS illustrated previously in Figure 38-1. The top panel (1) shows the normal state of the network, with Router RB able to reach Network N1 through Router RA at a cost of 2. In panel 2, the link between Router RA and Network N1 is broken. Router RA changes its cost to reach Network N1 to 16 (RIP infinity). In panel 3, before Router RA can send out this update to Router RB, it receives a routine RIP message from Router RB indicating that Network N1 can be reached for a cost of 2. Router RA is then fooled into thinking that it can use Router RB as an alternate route to Network N1, even though Router RB's information originally came from Router RA in the first place. In panel 4, Router RA then sends this bogus information out, which is received by Router RB in panel 5. Router RB then increases its cost to 4, and on its next cycle will send this to Router RA, which will increase its cost to 5, and so on. This cycle will continue, with both routers "counting to infinity" (cost of 16).*

Now suppose Router RB's regular 30-second timer goes off before Router RA's next broadcast. Router RB will send its normal routing table, *which contains a route to Network N1 at a cost of 2*. Router RA will see this and say, "Hey look, Router RB has a route to Network N1 with a cost of 2! That means I can get there with a cost of 3, which sure beats my current cost of 16. Let's use that!" So Router RA installs this route and cancels its Timeout timer. Of course, this is bogus information—Router RA doesn't realize that Router RB's claim of being able to reach Network N1 was based on old information from Router RA itself!

It only gets worse from there. When it is time for Router RA's regular routing table update, it will broadcast a route to Network N1 with a cost of 3. Now Router RB will see this and say, "Well, my route to Network N1 is through Router RA. Router RA was saying before that its cost was 1; but now it says the cost is 3. That means I have to change my cost to 4."

Router RB will later send back to Router RA, and back and forth they will go, each incrementing the cost two at a time. This won't stop until the value of infinity cost of 16 is hit—thus the name counting to infinity. At this point, both routers will finally agree that Network N1 is unreachable, but as you can see, it takes a long time for it to happen.

Small Infinity

The use of a relatively small value for the infinity cost limits the slow convergence problem. Even in a situation where we count to infinity, the total amount of time elapsed is at least manageable. (Imagine if infinity were defined as say, 1,000!) Unfortunately, the drawback of this is that it limits the size of the internetwork that can be used for RIP.

Many people balk at the limit of a span of 15 routers in RIP, but to be honest I think it is much ado about, well, if not nothing, then nothing much. The 15 value is not a limit on the total number of routers you can use, but rather a limit on the number of routers between any two networks. Consider that most internetworks are set up hierarchically. Even if you have a rather complex four-level hierarchy, you wouldn't be close to the 15-router limit. In fact, you could create a huge AS with thousands of routers, without having more than 15 routers between any two devices. So this is a limitation for only the very largest of ASes.

On the other hand, RIP's need to send out its entire routing table many times each hour makes it a potentially poor choice for a large internetwork regardless of the infinity=16 issue. In an internetwork with many routers, the amount of traffic RIP generates can become excessive.

> **KEY CONCEPT** One of the most important problems with the operation of RIP is slow convergence, which describes the fact that it can take a long time for information about changes to a network to propagate between routers. One specific instance of this problem is the counting to infinity problem, in which out-of-date information causes many bogus RIP messages to be exchanged between routers about an unreachable network.

To be fair, these problems are mostly general to distance-vector routing algorithms and not RIP in particular. Some of them are corrected through the implementation of specific changes to the algorithm or the rules under which RIP messages are sent, as described in the next section. According to RFC 2453, there was actually a proposal to increase RIP's infinity cost to a number larger than 16, but this would have caused compatibility problems with older devices (which would view any route with a metric of 16 or higher as unreachable), so it was rejected.

Issues with RIP's Metric

In addition to these concerns with the algorithm itself, RIP is also often criticized because of its choice of metric. The first issue here is RIP's use of hop count as a distance metric. Simply put, hop count is a poor metric of the cost of sending a datagram between two networks. I believe the use of hop count as the metric in RIP is partially due to the desire for simplicity (it's easy to make the protocol work when hop count is all the routers need to consider). But the use of hop count is also partially an artifact of RIP being around for more than 20 years.

Decades ago, computers were slow, so each time a datagram passed through a router there was probably a significant delay. Hop count was not a perfect metric even then, but I think it had more correspondence with how long it took to move a datagram across an internetwork than it does today.

Modern routers are lightning fast, making hop count a flawed way of measuring network distance. The number of hops taken often has no correlation with the actual amount of time it takes to move data across a route. To take an extreme case, consider two networks that are connected by a direct dial-up telephone networking link using 56K modems. Let's say they are also connected by a sequence of three routers using high-speed DS-3 lines. RIP would consider the 56K link a better route because it has fewer hops, even though it clearly is much slower.

Another issue is RIP's lack of support for dynamic (real-time) metrics. Even if RIP were to use a more meaningful metric than hop count, the algorithm requires that the metric should be fixed for each link. There is no way to have RIP calculate the best route based on real-time data about various links the way protocols like OSPF do (see Chapter 39).

Most of these problems are built into RIP and cannot be resolved. Interestingly, some RIP implementations apparently do let administrators "fudge" certain routes to compensate for the limitations of the hop count metric. For example, the routers on either end of the 56K link mentioned earlier could be configured so that they considered the 56K link to have a hop count of ten instead of one. This would cause any routes using the link to be more expensive than the DS-3 path. This is clever, but hardly an elegant or general solution.

Note that in addition to the rather long list of problems that I've mentioned, there were also some specific issues with the first version of RIP. Some of the more important of these include lack of support for Classless Inter-Domain Routing (CIDR), lack of authentication, and a performance reduction caused by the use of broadcasts for messaging. These were mostly addressed through extensions in RIP-2.

RIP Special Features for Resolving RIP Algorithm Problems

The simplicity of RIP is its most attractive quality, but as you just saw, this leads to certain problems with how it operates. Most of these limitations are related to the basic algorithm used for determining routes, and the method of message passing that's being used to implement the algorithm. In order for RIP to be a useful protocol, some of these issues needed to be addressed, in the form of changes to the basic RIP algorithm and operational scheme we explored earlier in this section.

The solution to problems that arise due to RIP being too simple is to add complexity in the form of features that add more intelligence to the way that RIP operates. In the following sections, we'll take a look at four of these: *split horizon*, *split horizon with poisoned reverse*, *triggered updates*, and *hold down*.

Note that while I describe these as "features," at least some of them are really necessary to ensure the proper RIP functionality. Therefore, they are generally considered standard parts of RIP, and most were described even in the earliest RIP documents. However, sometimes performance or stability issues may arise when these techniques are used, especially in combination. For this reason different RIP implementations may omit some features. For example, hold down slows down route recovery and may not be needed when other features such as split horizon are used. As always, care must be taken to ensure that all routers are using the same features, or even greater problems may arise.

Also, see the upcoming section on RIP-2's specific features, later in this chapter, for a description of the Next Hop feature, which helps reduce convergence and routing problems when RIP is used.

Split Horizon

The counting to infinity problem is one of the most serious issues with the basic RIP algorithm. In the example in the previous section, the cause of the problem is immediately obvious: After Network N1 fails and Router RA notices it go down, Router RB "tricks" Router RA into thinking it has an alternate path to Network N1 by sending Router RA a route advertisement to Network N1.

If you think about it, it doesn't really make sense under *any* circumstances to have Router RB send an advertisement to Router RA about a network that Router RB can access only through Router RA in the first place. In the case where the route fails, it causes this problem, which is obviously a good reason not do it. But even when the route is operational, what is the point of Router RB telling Router RA about it? Router RA already has a shorter connection to the network and will therefore never send traffic intended for Network N1 to Router RB anyway.

Clearly, the best solution is simply to have Router RB not include any mention of the route to Network N1 in any RIP Response messages it sends to Router RA. We can generalize this by adding a new rule to RIP operation: When a router sends out an RIP Response message on any of the networks to which it is connected, it omits any route information that it originally learned from that network. This feature is called *split horizon*, because the router effectively splits its view of the internetwork, sending different information on certain links than on others.

With this new rule, let's consider the behavior of Router RB. It has an interface on Network N2, which it shares with Router RA. It will therefore not include any information on routes it originally obtained from Router RA when sending on Network N2. This will prevent the counting to infinity loop you saw in the previous section. Similarly, because Router RD is on Network N3, Router RB will not send any information about routes it got from Router RD when sending on Network N3.

Note, however, that split horizon may not always solve the counting to infinity problem, especially in the case where multiple routers are connected indirectly. The classic example would be three routers configured in a triangle. In this situation, problems may still result due to data that is propagated in two directions between any two routers. In this case, the hold down feature, described shortly, may be of assistance.

Split Horizon with Poisoned Reverse

Adding "poisoned reverse" provides an enhancement of the basic split horizon feature. Instead of omitting routes learned from a particular interface when sending RIP Response messages on that interface, we include those routes but set their metric to RIP infinity, or 16. So in the previous example, Router RB *would* include the route to Network N1 in its transmissions on Network N2, but it would say the cost to reach Network N1 was 16 instead of its real cost (which is 2).

The *poisoned reverse* refers to the fact that we are poisoning the routes that we want to make sure routers on that interface don't use. Router RA will see Router RB advertise Network N1 but with a cost of 16, which serves as an explicit message to Router RA: "There is absolutely no way for you to get to Network N1 through Router RB." This provides more insurance than the regular split horizon feature, because if the link from Router RA to Network N1 is broken, Router RA will know for certain that it can't try to get a new route through Router RB. Figure 38-4 shows how split horizon with poisoned reverse works.

This technique also works in normal circumstances (meaning when there is no issue such as a broken link to a network). In that case, Router RA will receive updates from Router RB with a cost of 16 on a periodic basis, but Router RA will never try to reach Network N1 through Router RB anyway, since it is directly connected to Network N1 (cost of 1).

Triggered Updates

The routing loop problem we looked at earlier in this chapter occurred because Router RB advertised Router RA's route back to Router RA. There's another aspect of the problem that is also significant: After Router RA discovered that the link to Network N1 failed, it had to wait up to 30 seconds until its next scheduled transmission time to tell other routers about the failure.

For RIP to work well, when something significant happens, we want to tell other routers on the internetwork immediately. For this reason, a new rule should be added to the basic RIP router operation: Whenever a router changes the metric for a route it is required to (almost) immediately send out an RIP Response message to tell its immediate neighbor routers about the change. If these routers, seeing this change, update their routing information, they are in turn required to send out updates. Thus, the change of any network route information causes cascading updates to be sent throughout the internetwork, significantly reducing the slow convergence problem. Note that this includes the removal of a route due to expiration of its Timeout timer, since the first step in route removal is setting the route's metric to 16, which triggers an update.

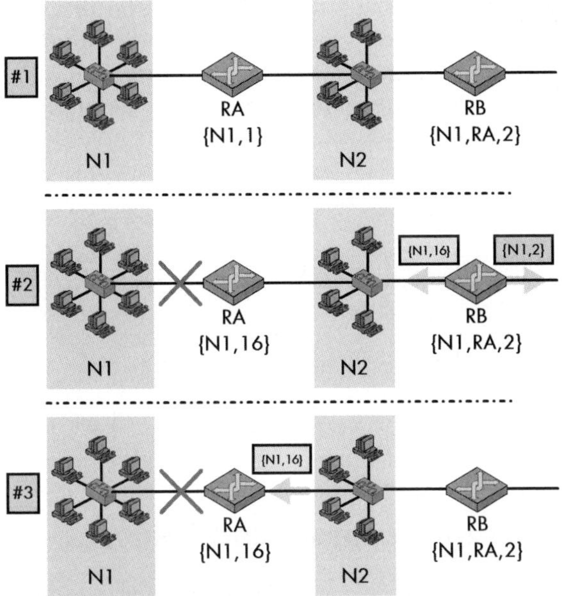

Figure 38-4: RIP problem solving using split horizon with poisoned reverse *The top panel in this diagram (1) shows the same example as in Figure 38-3. In panel 2, as before, the link between Router RA and Network N1 is broken, just as Router RB is ready to send out its routine update. However, the* split horizon with poisoned reverse *feature means it sends different messages on its two links. On the network that connects it to Router RA, it sends a route advertisement with a cost of 16. In panel 3, Router RA receives this, which it will discard, ensuring no counting to infinity problem occurs. On Router RA's next cycle, it will update Router RB to tell it that Network N1 is no longer reachable.*

You probably noticed that I said that triggered updates were sent "almost" immediately. In fact, before sending a triggered update a route waits a random amount of time, from 1 to 5 seconds. This is done to reduce the load on the internetwork that would result from many routers sending update messages nearly simultaneously.

Hold Down

Split horizon tries to solve the counting to infinity problem by suppressing the transmission of invalid information about routes that fail. For extra insurance, we can implement a feature that changes how devices receiving route information process it in the case of a failed route. The *hold down* feature works by having each router start a timer when it first receives information about a network that is unreachable. Until the timer expires, the router will discard any subsequent route messages that indicate that the route is in fact reachable. A typical Hold Down timer runs for 60 or 120 seconds.

The main advantage of this technique is that a router won't be confused by receiving spurious information about a route being accessible when it was just recently told that the route was no longer valid. It provides a period of time for out-of-date information to be flushed from the system, which is valuable especially on complex internetworks. Adding hold down to split horizon can also help in situations where split horizon alone is insufficient for preventing counting to infinity, such as when a trio of routers are linked in a triangle, as discussed earlier.

The main disadvantage of hold down is that it forces a delay in a router responding to a route once it is fixed. Suppose that a route went down for just five seconds for some reason. After the network is up again, routers will want to again know about this. However, the Hold Down timer must expire before the router will try to use that network again. This makes internetworks using hold down relatively slow to respond to corrected routes, and it could lead to delays in accessing networks that fail intermittently.

KEY CONCEPT Four special features represent changes to RIP operation that ameliorate or eliminate the problems with the operation of the basic protocol. *Split horizon* and *split horizon with poisoned reverse* prevent a router from sending invalid route information back to the router from which it originally learned the route. *Triggered updates* reduce the slow convergence problem by causing the immediate propagation of changed route information. Finally, the *hold down* feature may be used to provide robustness when information about a failed route is received.

RIP Version-Specific Message Formats and Features

As I've noted, RIP has been in widespread use for more than two decades. During that time, internetworks and internetworking technologies have changed. To keep up with the times, RIP has also evolved and today has three different versions. The basic operation of all three is fairly similar, and it was described in the previous sections of this chapter. As you might expect, there are also some differences between the versions. One of the more important of these is the format used for RIP messages in each version, and the meaning and use of the fields within that format.

It's now time to take a look at the message format used by each of the three versions of RIP as well as certain specific features not common to all versions. I begin with the original RIP, now also known as *RIP version 1*. I then describe the updated version of RIP called *RIP version 2* or *RIP-2*. Finally, I discuss *RIPng*, also sometimes called *RIPv6*; it's the version of RIP used for IPv6. (Note that this is not technically a new version of the original RIP but a new protocol closely based on the earlier RIP versions.)

RIP Version 1 (RIP-1) Message Format and Features

RIP evolved as an industry standard and was popularized by its inclusion in the Berkeley Standard Distribution of UNIX (BSD UNIX). This first version of RIP (now sometimes called RIP-1 to differentiate it from later versions) was eventually standardized in RFC 1058. As part of this standard, the original RIP-1 message format was defined, which of course serves *RIP-1* itself, and is also the basis for the format used in later versions.

RIP-1 Messaging

As explained in the general discussion on RIP operation in the previous sections, route information is exchanged in RIP through the sending of two different types of RIP messages: RIP Request and the RIP Response. These are transmitted as regular TCP/IP messages using UDP, which uses the UDP reserved port number 520. This port number is used as follows:

- RIP Request messages are sent to UDP destination port 520. They may have a source port of 520 or may use an ephemeral port number (see Chapter 43 for an explanation of ephemeral ports).
- RIP Response messages sent in reply to an RIP Request are sent with a source port of 520 and a destination port equal to whatever source port the RIP Request used.
- Unsolicited RIP Response messages (sent on a routine basis and not in response to a request) are sent with both the source and destination ports, which are set to 520.

RIP-1 Message Format

The basic message format for RIP-1 is described in Table 38-1 and illustrated Figure 38-5.

Table 38-1: RIP-1 Message Format

Field Name	Size (Bytes)	Description
Command	1	Command Type: Identifies the type of RIP message being sent. A value of 1 indicates an RIP Request, while 2 means an RIP Response. Originally, three other values and commands were also defined: 3 and 4 for the Traceon and Traceoff commands, and 5, which was reserved for use by Sun Microsystems. These are obsolete and no longer used.
Version	1	Version Number: Set to 1 for RIP version 1.
Must Be Zero	2	Field reserved; value must be set to all zeros.
RIP Entries	20 to 500, in increments of 20	The body of an RIP message consists of 1 to 25 sets of RIP entries. These entries contain the actual route information that the message is conveying. Each entry is 20 bytes long and has the subfields shown in Table 38-2.

Table 38-2: RIP-1 RIP Entries

Subfield Name	Size (Bytes)	Description
Address Family Identifier	2	A fancy name for a field that identifies the type of address in the entry. The routers are using IP addresses, for which this field value is 2.
Must Be Zero	2	Field reserved; value must be set to all zeros.
IP Address	4	The address of the route the routers are sending information about. No distinction is made between addresses of different types of devices in RIP, so the address can be for a network, a subnet, or a single host. It is also possible to send an address of all zeros, which is interpreted as the default route for other devices on the network to use for reaching routes with no specified routing entries. This is commonly used to allow a network to access the Internet.

(continued)

Table 38-2: RIP-1 RIP Entries (continued)

Subfield Name	Size (Bytes)	Description
Must Be Zero	4	Field reserved; value must be set to all zeros.
Must Be Zero	4	Field reserved; value must be set to all zeros. (Yes, two of them in a row.)
Metric	4	The distance for the network indicated by the IP address in the IP Address field. Values of 1 to 15 indicate the number of hops to reach the network, while a value of 16 represents infinity (an unreachable destination). See the general discussion of the RIP algorithm earlier in this chapter for more information about the use of metrics.

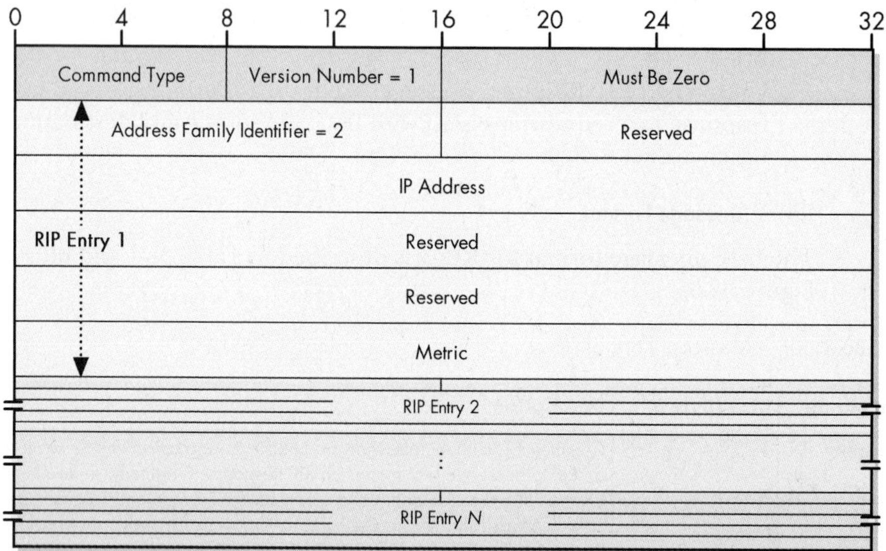

Figure 38-5: RIP-1 message format *The RIP-1 message format can contain up to 25 RIP entries. Here, RIP entry 1 is shown with each of its constituent subfields.*

If you're like me, the first thing that comes to mind after looking at this message format is this: What's with all the extra space? I mean, we have four different fields that are reserved (must be zero), and even most of the other fields are larger than they need to be (a metric of 1 to 16 needs only 4 bits, not 32). The command type and version number could also easily have been made only 4 bits each, if not less. And why bother having a 2-byte field to identify the address type when we are only going to deal with IP addresses anyway?

This seeming wastefulness is actually an artifact of the generality of the original RIP design. The protocol was intended to be able to support routing for a variety of different internetworking protocols, not just Internet Protocol (IP). Remember that it wasn't even originally developed with IP in mind. So, the Address Family Identifier was included to specify address type, and RIP entries were made large enough to handle large addresses. IP requires only 4 bytes per address, so some of the space is not used.

RIP-1 Version-Specific Features

Since RIP-1 was the first version of the protocol, its features formed the basis for future RIP versions; it doesn't really have any version-specific features. What RIP-1 has is a number of limitations, such as a lack of support for specifying classless addresses and no means for authentication. RIP-2 was created to address some of RIP-1 shortcomings. As you will see in the next section, RIP-2's features put to good use those "Must Be Zero" bytes in the RIP-1 format!

KEY CONCEPT RIP-1 was the first version of RIP and is the simplest in terms of operation and features. The bulk of an RIP-1 message consists of sets of RIP entries that specify route addresses and the distance to the route in hops.

RIP Version 2 (RIP-2) Message Format and Features

The original RIP (RIP-1) has a number of problems and limitations. As the TCP/IP protocol suite evolved and changed, RIP-1's problems were compounded by it becoming somewhat out of date. It was unable to handle newer IP features. There were some who felt that the existence of newer and better interior routing protocols meant that it would be best to just give up on RIP entirely and move over to something like OSPF.

However, RIP's appeal was never its technical superiority, but its simplicity and ubiquity in the industry. By the early 1990s, RIP was already in use in many thousands of networks. For those who liked RIP, it made more sense to migrate to a newer version that addressed some of RIP-1's shortcomings than to go to an entirely different protocol. To this end, a new version of the protocol, RIP-2 was developed. It was initially published in RFC 1388 in 1993. It is now defined in RFC 2453, "RIP Version 2," which was published in November 1998.

RIP-2 Version-Specific Features

RIP-2 represents a very modest change to the basic RIP. RIP-2 works in the same basic way as RIP-1. In fact, the new features introduced in RIP-2 are described as *extensions* to the basic protocol, thereby conveying the fact that they are layered upon regular RIP-1 functionality. The five key RIP-2 extensions are as follows:

Classless Addressing Support and Subnet Mask Specification When RIP-1 was developed, the use of subnets in IP (as described in RFC 950) had not yet been formally defined. It was still possible to use RIP-1 with subnets through the use of a heuristic to determine if the destination is a network, subnet, or host. However, there was no way to clearly specify the subnet mask for an address using RIP-1 messages. RIP-2 adds explicit support for subnets by allowing a subnet mask within the route entry for each network address. It also provides support for Variable Length Subnet Masking (VLSM; see Chapter 18) and CIDR.

Next Hop Specification In RIP-2, each RIP entry includes a space where an explicit IP address can be entered as the next-hop router for datagrams that are intended for the network in that entry. This feature can help improve efficiency of routing by eliminating unnecessary extra hops for datagrams sent to certain destinations. One common use of this field is when the most efficient route to a network is through a router that is not running RIP. Such a router will not exchange RIP messages and would therefore not normally be selected by RIP routers as a next hop for any network. The explicit Next Hop field allows the router to be selected as the next hop, regardless of this situation.

Authentication RIP-1 included no authentication mechanism, which is a problem because it could potentially allow a malicious host to attack an internetwork by sending bogus RIP messages. RIP-2 provides a basic authentication scheme that allows routers to ascertain the identity of a router before it will accept RIP messages from it.

Route Tag Each RIP-2 entry includes a Route Tag field where additional information about a route can be stored. This information is propagated along with other data about the route as RIP entries are sent around the internetwork. A common use of this field is when a route is learned from a different AS in order to identify the AS from which the route was obtained.

Use of Multicasting To help reduce network load, RIP-2 allows routers to be configured to use multicasts instead of broadcasts for sending out unsolicited RIP Response messages. These datagrams are sent out using the special reserved multicast address 224.0.0.9. All routers on an internetwork must use multicast if this is to work properly.

As you can see, many of these extensions require more information to be included with each advertised route. This is where all that extra space in the message format of RIP-1 routing entries comes in handy, as you will see shortly.

> **KEY CONCEPT** RIP-2 is the most recent version of RIP used in IPv4. It includes a number of enhancements over the original RIP-1, including support for subnet masks and classless addressing, explicit next-hop specification, route tagging, authentication, and multicast. For compatibility, it uses the same basic message format as RIP-1, putting the extra information required for its new features into some of the unused fields of the RIP-1 message format.

RIP-2 Messaging

RIP-2 messages are exchanged using the same basic mechanism as RIP-1 messages. Two different message types exist: RIP Request and RIP Response. They are sent using UDP, which uses the reserved port number 520. The semantics for the use of this port are the same as for RIP-1. For convenience, I'll repeat the description here:

- RIP Request messages are sent to UDP destination port 520. They may have a source port of 520 or may use an ephemeral port number.
- RIP Response messages sent in reply to an RIP Request message are sent with a source port of 520 and a destination port equal to whatever source port the RIP Request message used.
- Unsolicited RIP Response messages (sent on a routine basis and not in response to a request) are sent with both the source and destination ports set to 520.

RIP-2 Message Format

The basic message format for RIP-2 is also pretty much the same as it was for RIP-1, with the Version field set to 2 in order to clearly identify the message as being RIP-2. Table 38-3 and Figure 38-6 illustrate the RIP-2 message format. The real differences are in the individual RIP entries, as you can see in Table 38-4.

Table 38-3: RIP-2 Message Format

Field Name	Size (Bytes)	Description
Command	1	Command Type: Identifies the type of RIP message being sent. A value of 1 indicates an RIP Request, while 2 means an RIP Response.
Version	1	Version Number: Set to 2 for RIP version 2.
Must Be Zero	2	Field reserved; value must be set to all zeros.
Route Table Entries (RTEs)	20 to 500, in increments of 20	As with RIP-1, the body of an RIP-2 message consists of 1 to 25 sets of route information. In RIP-2 these are labeled Route Table Entries, or RTEs. Each RTE is 20 bytes long and has the subfields shown in Table 38-4.

Table 38-4: RIP-2 Route Table Entries (RTEs)

Subfield Name	Size (Bytes)	Description
Address Family Identifier	2	Same meaning as for RIP-1; value is 2 to identify IP addresses.
Route Tag	2	Additional information to be carried with this route.
IP Address	4	Same as in RIP-1: the address of the route the router is sending information about. No distinction is made between the address of different types of devices in RIP, so the address can be for a network, a subnet, or a single host. It is also possible to send an address of all zeros, which is interpreted as the default route, as in RIP-1.
Subnet Mask	4	The subnet mask associated with this address.
Next Hop	4	Address of the device to use as the next hop for the network advertised in this entry.
Metric	4	The distance for the network indicated by the IP address, as in RIP-1. Values of 1 to 15 indicate the number of hops to reach the network (as described in the discussion of the RIP algorithm earlier in this chapter), while a value of 16 represents infinity (an unreachable destination).

As you can see, the unused fields allow the new RIP-2 features to be implemented without changing the basic structure of the RIP entry format. This allows RIP-1 and RIP-2 messages and devices to coexist in the same network. An RIP-2 device can handle both RIP-1 and RIP-2 messages, and will look at the version number to see which version the message is. An RIP-1 device should handle both RIP-2 and RIP-1 messages the same way, simply ignoring the extra RIP-2 fields it doesn't understand.

NOTE *If authentication is used, one of the RTEs contains authentication information, thus limiting the message to 24 "real" RTEs.*

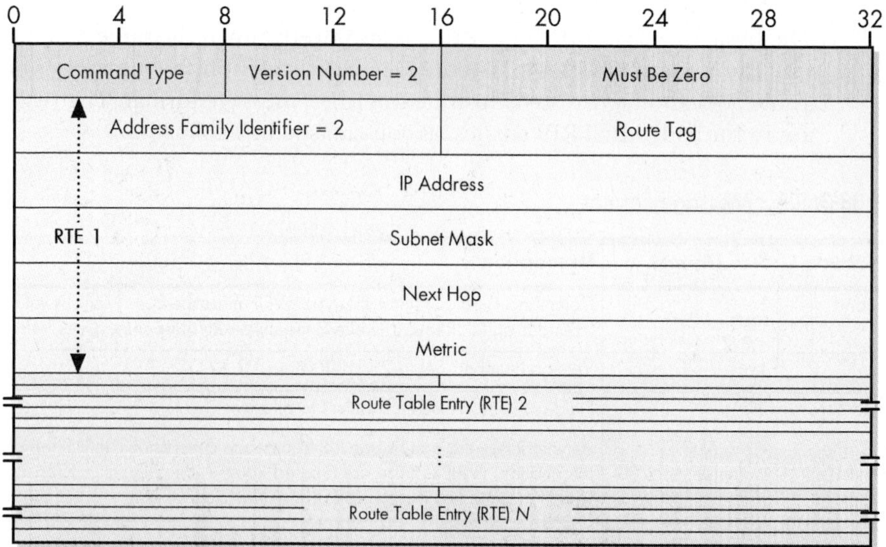

Figure 38-6: RIP-2 message format The RIP entries of RIP-1 are called Route Table Entries (RTEs) in RIP-2; the message format can contain up to 25. The format of RTE 1 is shown here with each of its subfields (the others are summarized to save space).

RIPng (RIPv6) Message Format and Features

The future of TCP/IP is IPv6, which makes some very important changes to IP, especially with regard to addressing. Since IPv6 addresses are different than IPv4 addresses, everything that works with IP addresses must change to function under IPv6. This includes routing protocols, which exchange addressing information.

To ensure a future for the RIP, a new IPv6-compatible version had to be developed. This new version was published in 1997 in RFC 2080, *RIPng for IPv6*, where the *ng* stands for next generation (IPv6 is also sometimes called *IP next generation*).

RIPng, which is also occasionally seen as RIPv6 for obvious reasons, was designed to be as similar as possible to the current version of RIP for IPv4, which is RIP-2. In fact, RFC 2080 describes RIPng as the minimum change possible to RIP to allow it to work on IPv6. Despite this effort, it was not possible to define RIPng as just a new version of the older RIP, as RIP-2 was defined. RIPng is a new protocol, which was necessary because of the significance of the changes between IPv4 and IPv6—especially the change from 32-bit to 128-bit addresses in IPv6, which necessitated a new message format.

RIPng Version-Specific Features

Even though RIPng is a new protocol, a specific effort was made to make RIPng like its predecessors. Its basic operation is almost entirely the same, and it uses the same overall algorithm and operation, as you saw earlier in this chapter. RIPng also does not introduce any specific new features compared to RIP-2, except those needed to implement RIP on IPv6.

RIPng maintains most of the enhancements introduced in RIP-2; some are implemented as they were in RIP-2, while others appear in a modified form. Here's specifically how the five extensions in RIP-2 are implemented in RIPng:

Classless Addressing Support and Subnet Mask Specification In IPv6 all, addresses are classless and specified using an address and a prefix length, instead of a subnet mask. Thus, a field for the prefix length is provided for each entry instead of a subnet mask field.

Next Hop Specification This feature is maintained in RIPng, but implemented differently. Due to the large size of IPv6 addresses, if you include a Next Hop field in the format of RIPng, the RTEs would almost double the size of every entry. Since Next Hop is an optional feature, this would be wasteful. Instead, when a Next Hop is needed, it is specified in a separate routing entry.

Authentication RIPng does not include its own authentication mechanism. It is assumed that if authentication and/or encryption are needed, they will be provided using the standard IPsec features, which are defined for IPv6 at the IP layer. This is more efficient than having individual protocols like RIPng perform authentication.

Route Tag This field is implemented in the same way as it is in RIP-2.

Use of Multicasting RIPng uses multicasts for transmissions, specifically the reserved IPv6 multicast address FF02::9.

RIPng Messaging

There are two basic RIPng message types, RIP Request and RIP Response, which are exchanged using the UDP as with RIP-1 and RIP-2. Since RIPng is a new protocol, it cannot use the same UDP reserved port number 520, which is used for RIP-1/RIP-2. Instead, RIPng uses well-known port number 521. The semantics for the use of this port are the same as those used for port 520 in RIP-1 and RIP-2. For convenience, here are the rules again:

- RIP Request messages are sent to UDP destination port 521. They may have a source port of 521 or may use an ephemeral port number.
- RIP Response messages sent in reply to an RIP Request message are sent with a source port of 521 and a destination port equal to whatever source port the RIP Request message used.
- Unsolicited RIP Response messages (sent on a routine basis and not in response to a request) are sent with both the source and destination ports set to 521.

RIPng Message Format

The message format for RIPng is similar to that of RIP-1 and RIP-2, except for the format of the RTEs. It is shown in Table 38-5 and illustrated in Figure 38-7.

Table 38-5: RIPng Message Format

Field Name	Size (Bytes)	Description
Command	1	Command Type: Identifies the type of RIPng message being sent. A value of 1 indicates an RIPng Request, while 2 means an RIPng Response.
Version	1	Version Number: Set to 1 (not 6, since this is the first version of the new protocol RIPng).
Must Be Zero	2	Field reserved; value must be set to all zeros.
Route Table Entries (RTEs)	Variable	The body of an RIPng message consists of a variable number of Route Table Entries (RTEs) that contain information about routes. Each entry is 20 bytes long and has the subfields shown in Table 38-6.

Table 38-6: RIPng RTEs

Subfield Name	Size (Bytes)	Description
IPv6 Prefix	16	The 128-bit IPv6 address of the network whose information is contained in this RTE.
Route Tag	2	Additional information to be carried with this route, as defined in RIP-2.
Prefix Len	1	The number of bits of the IPv6 address that is the network portion (the remainder being the host portion). This is the number that normally would appear after the slash when specifying an IPv6 network address. It is analogous to an IPv4 subnet mask. See the description of IPv6 prefix notation in Chapter 25 for more details.
Metric	1	The distance for the network indicated by the IP address, as in RIP-1. Values of 1 to 15 indicate the number of hops to reach the network (as described in the general discussion of the RIP algorithm earlier in this chapter) while a value of 16 represents infinity (an unreachable destination).

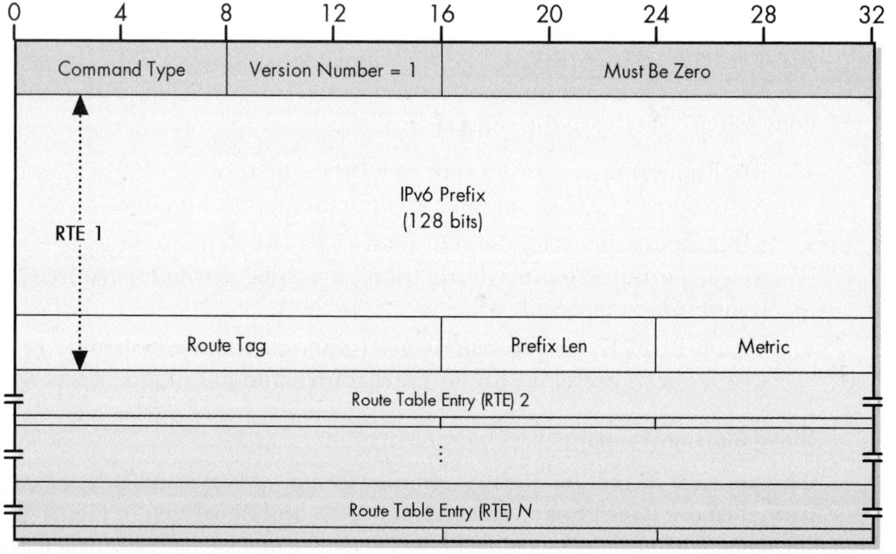

Figure 38-7: RIPng message format *RIPng retains the use of RTEs from RIP-2, but their format has been changed to accommodate the much larger IPv6 address size. The limit of 25 entries per message has also been eliminated.*

The maximum number of RTEs in RIPng is not restricted to 25 as it is in RIP-1 and RIP-2. It is limited only by the maximum transmission unit (MTU) of the network over which the message is being sent.

KEY CONCEPT RIPng is the version of RIP that was developed for use on IPv6 internetworks. It is technically a distinct protocol from RIP-1 and RIP-2, but is very similar to both. It retains the enhancements to RIP made in RIP-2, making changes to these features and to the RIP message format wherever needed for compatibility with IPv6.

When a Next Hop field needs to be specified, a special RTE is included, as I mentioned earlier. This RTE is included before all the RTEs to which it applies. It has the same basic structure as shown for regular RTEs in Table 38-6, with the IPv6 Prefix subfield containing the next hop address, the Route Tag and Prefix Len fields set to 0, and the Metric field set to 255 (0xFF).

39

OPEN SHORTEST PATH FIRST (OSPF)

Interior routing protocols using a distance-vector routing algorithm, such as the Routing Information Protocol (RIP) we explored last chapter, have a long history and work well in a small group of routers. However, they also have some serious limitations in both scalability and performance that make them poorly suited to larger autonomous systems (ASes) or those with specific performance issues. Many organizations that start out using RIP quickly find that its restrictions and issues make it less than ideal.

To solve this problem, a new routing protocol was developed in the late 1980s. This protocol, called *Open Shortest Path First (OSPF)*, uses the more capable (and more complex) link-state or *shortest-path first* routing algorithm. It fixes many of the issues with RIP and allows routes to be selected dynamically based on the current state of the network, not just a static picture of how routers are connected. It also has numerous advanced features, including support for a hierarchical topology and automatic load sharing among routes. On the downside, it is a complicated protocol, which means it is often not used unless it is really needed. This makes it the complement of RIP and is the reason they both have a place in the spectrum of TCP/IP routing protocols.

In this chapter, I provide a condensed explanation of the concepts and operation behind OSPF. As usual, I begin with an overview of the protocol, discussing how it was developed, its versions, and the standards that define them. I describe the concepts behind OSPF, including basic topology and the link-state database. I then discuss the more complex optional hierarchical topology of routers and the roles routers play when this topology is used. I briefly explain the method used for determining routes in OSPF, and the general operation and messaging used in the protocol, including a description of the five OSPF message types. I conclude with descriptions of the formats used for OSPF messages.

NOTE *The difficult thing about networking is that so many protocols and technologies are so involved that each deserves its own book. This is certainly the case with OSPF itself, which is sufficiently complex that the RFC defining OSPF version 2 is more than 240 pages long! Thus, this chapter, despite being fairly comprehensive, is only a high-level description of OSPF.*

OSPF Overview

In the early days of TCP/IP, RIP became the standard protocol for routing within an autonomous system (AS), almost by default. RIP had two big things going for it: It was simple and easy to use, and it was included in the popular Berkeley Standard Distribution (BSD) of UNIX starting in 1982. Most organizations using TCP/IP started out with relatively small networks and were able to use RIP with some degree of success.

However, as I discussed in Chapter 38, that protocol has some serious technical issues, and they are exacerbated when RIP is used on a larger AS. Many of RIP's problems are due to it being a distance-vector protocol, because the algorithm itself simply limits the ability of RIP to choose the best route and adapt to changing network conditions. Other problems with RIP were based on its implementation, such as the selection of a cost value of 16 for infinity, which makes it impossible to use RIP in a situation where more than 15 hops might occur between devices. Problems such as the lack of classless addressing support were addressed in version 2 of RIP, but the basic difficulties with the protocol as a whole persist.

Development and Standardization of OSPF

The Internet Engineering Task Force (IETF) recognized that RIP by itself simply would not meet the needs of all ASes on the Internet. It formed a working group in 1988 to develop a new routing protocol based on the more capable link-state algorithm, also called shortest path first (SPF). Research into this type of protocol had already begun as early as the 1970s, with some of it conducted on the ARPAnet, the predecessor of the Internet, upon which much of TCP/IP was developed.

This new protocol's name conveys two of its most important characteristics. The first word refers to the fact that the protocol, like all TCP/IP standards, was developed using the open and public RFC process, so it is not proprietary, and no license is required to use it. The SPF portion of the name refers to the type of algorithm it uses, which is designed to allow routers to dynamically determine the shortest path between any two networks.

The first version of OSPF was described in RFC 1131, which was published in October 1989. This was quickly replaced by OSPF version 2 in July 1991, which is described in RFC 1247. Since then, there have been several revisions to the OSPF version 2 standard, in RFCs 1583, 2178, and 2328, with the last of these now the current standard. OSPF version 2 is the only version in use today, so it is usually what is meant when people (including myself) refer to OSPF.

Overview of OSPF Operation

The fundamental concept behind OSPF is a data structure called the *link-state database (LSDB)*. Each router in an AS maintains a copy of this database, which contains information in the form of a directed graph that describes the current state of the AS. Each link to a network or another router is represented by an entry in the database, and each has an associated cost (or metric). The metric can be made to include many different aspects of route performance, not just a simple hop count, as is used in RIP.

Information about the AS moves around the AS in the form of *link-state advertisements (LSAs)*, which are messages that let each router tell the others what it currently knows about the state of the AS. Over time, the information that each router has about the AS converges with that of the others, and they all have the same data. When changes occur to the internetwork, routers send updates to ensure that all the routers are kept up-to-date.

To determine actual routes, each router uses its LSDB to construct a shortest-path tree. This tree shows the links from the router to each other router and network and allows the lowest-cost route to any location to be determined. As new information about the state of the internetwork arrives, this tree can be recalculated, so the best route is dynamically adjusted based on network conditions. When more than one route with an equal cost exists, traffic can be shared among the routes.

OSPF Features and Drawbacks

In addition to the obvious benefits of the link-state algorithm, OSPF includes several other features of value, especially to larger organizations. It supports authentication for security and all three major types of IP addressing (classful, subnetted classful, and classless). For very large ASes, OSPF also allows routers to be grouped and arranged into a hierarchical topology. This allows for better organization and improved performance through reduced LSA traffic.

Naturally, the superior functionality and many features of OSPF do not come without a cost. In this case, the primary cost is that of complexity. Where RIP is a simple and easy-to-use protocol, OSPF requires more work and more expertise to properly configure and maintain. This means that even though OSPF is widely considered better than RIP, technically, it's not for everyone. The obvious role for OSPF is as a routing protocol for larger or higher-performance ASes, leaving RIP to cover the smaller and simpler internetworks.

KEY CONCEPT *Open Shortest Path First (OSPF)* was developed in the late 1980s to provide a more capable interior routing protocol for larger or more complex ASes that were not being served well by RIP. It uses the dynamic shortest path first, or link-state, routing algorithm, with each router maintaining a database containing information about the state and topology of the internetwork. As changes to the internetwork occur, routers send out updated state information, which allows each router to dynamically calculate the best route to any network at any point in time. OSPF is a complement to RIP in that RIP is simple but limited, whereas OSPF is more capable but more complicated.

OSPF Basic Topology and the Link-State Database (LSDB)

OSPF is designed to facilitate routing in both smaller and larger ASes. To this end, the protocol supports two topologies. When there is only a small number of routers, the entire AS is managed as a single entity. This doesn't have a specific name, but I call it *OSPF basic topology* to convey the simple nature of the topology and to contrast it with the hierarchical topology you will explore in the next section.

When OSPF basic topology is used, all the routers in the AS function as peers. Each router communicates routing information with each other one, and each maintains a copy of the key OSPF data structure: the LSDB, which is essentially a computerized representation of the topology of the AS. It is the method by which routers see the state of the links in the AS—thus the name *link-state database* (and for that matter, the name of the entire class of link-state algorithms of which OSPF is a part).

The LSDB is a bit hard to visualize, but is best viewed as a set of data that is equivalent to a graphical picture that shows the topology of an AS. In such a diagram, we typically show routers and networks as nodes, and connections between routers and networks as lines that connect them. The OSPF LSDB takes that information and puts it into a table to allow a router to maintain a virtual picture of all the connections between routers and networks in the AS.

The LSDB therefore indicates which routers can directly reach which other routers and which networks each router can reach. Furthermore, it stores for each of these links a *cost* to reach the network. This cost is an arbitrary metric that can be set up based on any criteria important to the administrator. OSPF is not restricted to the overly simple hop-count metric used in RIP.

OSPF Basic Topology

For example, let's consider the same AS that you looked at in the examination of the RIP route determination algorithm in Chapter 38. This internetwork has four individual networks, connected as follows:

- Router RA connects Network N1 to Network N2.
- Routers RB and RC connect Network N2 to Network N3.
- Router RD connects Network N3 to Network N4.

To make this example more interesting, I added a direct link between Routers RB and RC.

The resulting AS is shown in Figure 39-1. Table 39-1 shows what the LSDB for this AS might look like.

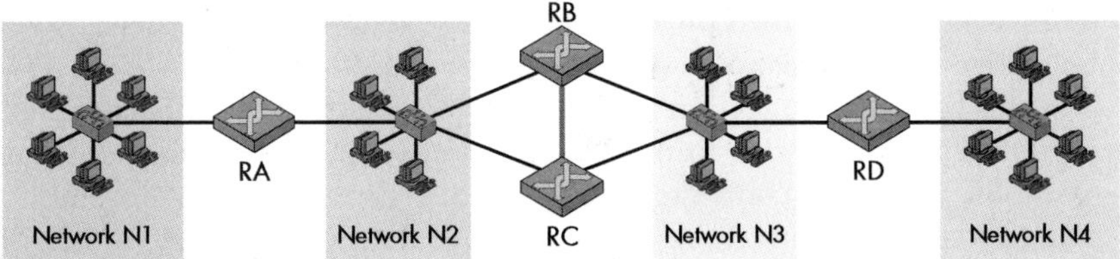

Figure 39-1: Sample OSPF AS This is the same AS that you looked at in RIP (as shown in Figure 38-1 in Chapter 38), but with the addition of a link between the two Routers RB and RC.

Table 39-1: Sample OSPF Link-State Database (LSDB)

To Router/ Network	From Router				From Network			
	RA	RB	RC	RD	N1	N2	N3	N4
RA					0	0		
RB			•			0	0	
RC		•				0	0	
RD							0	0
N1	•							
N2	•	•	•					
N3		•	•	•				
N4				•				

In practice, each of the bullets (•) in Table 39-1 would be replaced by a metric value indicating the cost to send a datagram from the particular router to another router or network. Note that the chart is symmetric, because if Router RB can reach Router RC, Router RC can reach Router RB. However, the *costs* do not have to be symmetric. It is possible for Router RB to have a metric that is higher for it to send to Router RC than for Router RC to send to Router RB.

Note too that there is no cost to reach a router *from* a network. This ensures that only one cost is applied for a router to send to another router over a network. The cost is to reach the network from the router. This makes sense, since each router is a member of the network on which it is connected.

LSDB Information Storage and Propagation

An important thing to remember about the LSDB is that even though each router maintains it, the database isn't constructed from the perspective of the individual router. A router's LSDB represents the topology of the entire AS, including links between routers that may be rather distant from it. So, for example, Router RA would keep the entire database in its storage area, including information about Router RC and Router RD, to which it does not connect directly.

Since in the basic topology, all the routers are peers and maintain information for the entire AS, in theory, they should have the exact same LSDB contents. When a router is first turned on, it may have different LSDB information than its neighbors, but this will be corrected through the exchange of update messages containing LSAs. Eventually, all routers should converge to the same information. You will see how this works in the section about OSPF messaging later in this chapter.

OSPF, as an interior routing protocol, is used only within the AS. In most cases, the AS will be connected to other ASes through one or more of its routers. The routers that connect the AS to other ASes are often called *boundary routers.* These devices will use OSPF to communicate within the AS, and an exterior routing protocol (typically BGP) to talk to routers outside the AS. The word *boundary* in its name refers to the fact that these devices are usually located on the periphery of the AS.

KEY CONCEPT In basic OSPF topology, each of the routers running OSPF is considered a peer of the others. Each maintains a *link-state database (LSDB)* that contains information about the topology of the entire AS. Each link between a router and network or between two routers is represented by an entry in the LSDB that indicates the cost to send data over the link. The LSDB is updated regularly through the exchange of OSPF *link-state advertisements (LSAs).*

OSPF Hierarchical Topology

When the number of routers in an AS is relatively small, using the previously described basic topology works well. Each router maintains a common picture of the network topology in the form of an identical LSDB. The routers communicate as peers using LSAs. While changes in the AS may cause a router to temporarily have different information than its peers, routine exchanges of data will keep all the LSDBs synchronized and up-to-date, and not that much information needs to be sent around because the AS is small.

This simpler topology does scale reasonably well, and it can support many smaller and even moderate-sized ASes. However, as the number of routers increases, the amount of communication required to update LSDBs increases as well. In a very large internetwork with dozens or even hundreds of routers, having all the routers be OSPF peers using the basic topology can result in performance degradation. This problem occurs due to the amount of routing information that needs to be passed around and to the need for each router to maintain a large LSDB containing every router and network in the entire AS.

OSPF Areas

To provide better support for these larger internetworks, OSPF supports the use of a more advanced, hierarchical topology. In this technique, the AS is no longer considered a single, flat structure of interconnected routers all of which are peers. Instead, a two-level hierarchical topology is constructed. The AS is divided into constructs called *areas,* each of which contains a number of contiguous routers and networks. These areas are numbered and managed independently by the routers within them, so each area is almost as if it were an AS unto itself. The areas are interconnected so that routing information can be shared among areas across the entire AS.

The easiest way to understand this hierarchical topology is to consider each area like a sub-AS within the AS as a whole. The routers within any area maintain an LSDB that contains information about the routers and networks within that area. Routers within more than one area maintain LSDBs about each area that they are a part of, and they also link the areas together to share routing information between them.

KEY CONCEPT To allow for better control and management over larger internetworks, OSPF allows a large AS to be structured into a hierarchical form. Contiguous routers and networks are grouped into areas that connect together using a logical backbone. These areas act as the equivalent of smaller ASes within the larger AS, yielding the same benefits of localized control and traffic management that ASes provide for a large internetwork between organizations.

Router Roles in OSPF Hierarchical Topology

The topology just described is hierarchical because the routers in the AS are no longer all peers in a single group. The two-level hierarchy consists of the lower level, which contains individual areas, and the higher level that connects them together, which is called the *backbone* and is designated as Area 0. The routers play different roles, depending on where they are located and how they are connected. There are three different labels applied to routers in this configuration:

Internal Routers These are routers that are connected only to other routers or networks within a single area. They maintain an LSDB for only that area and have no knowledge of the topology of other areas.

Area Border Routers These are routers that connect to routers or networks in more than one area. They maintain an LSDB for each area of which they are a part. They also participate in the backbone.

Backbone Routers These are routers that are a part of the OSPF backbone. By definition, these include all area border routers, since those routers pass routing information between areas. However, a backbone router may also be a router that connects only to other backbone (or area border) routers and is therefore not part of any area (other than Area 0).

To summarize, an *area border router* is also always a *backbone router*, but a backbone router is not necessarily an area border router.

NOTE *The classifications that I just mentioned are independent of the designation of a router as being a* boundary router, *as described in the previous section. A boundary router is one that talks to routers or networks outside the AS. A boundary router will also often be an area border router or a backbone router, but this is not necessarily the case. A boundary router could be an internal router in one area.*

The point of all this is the same as the point of using AS architecture in the first place. The topology of each area matters only to the devices in that area. This means that changes in that topology need to be propagated only within the area. It also means that internal routers within Area 1 don't need to know about anything that goes on within Area 2 and don't need to maintain information about any area other than their own. Only the backbone routers (which include at least one area border router within each area) need to know the details of the entire AS. These backbone routers condense information about the areas so that only a summary of each area's topology needs to be advertised on the backbone.

Routing in a hierarchical topology AS is performed in one of two ways, depending on the location of the devices:

- If the source and destination are in the same area, routing occurs only over networks and routers in that area.
- If the source and destination are in different areas, the datagram is routed from the source to an area border router in the source's area, over the backbone to an area border router in the destination's area, and then finally delivered to the destination.

Again, this is analogous to how routing works between ASes in the big-picture internetwork.

Let's take an example to help make things more concrete. We can use the AS in the preceding example. This AS is really small enough that it's unlikely we would use hierarchical topology, but it will suffice for sake of illustration. Let's divide this AS into two areas, as follows (see Figure 39-2):

- Area 1 contains Network N1, Router RA, Network N2, Router RB, and Router RC.
- Area 2 contains Router RB, Router RC, Network N3, Router RD, and Network N4.

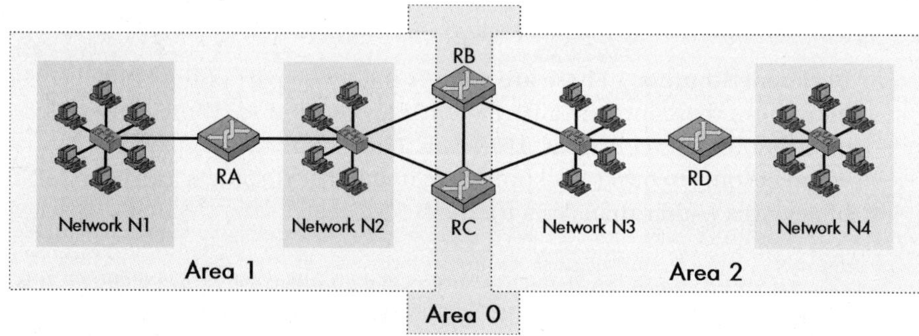

Figure 39-2: Sample OSPF hierarchical topology AS *This is the same AS you saw in Figure 39-1, but it's arranged into OSPF hierarchical topology. The AS has been split evenly into Area 1 and Area 2. Area 0 contains Routers RB and RC, which are area border routers for both Area 1 and Area 2 in this very simple example.*

In this example, Router RA and Router RD are internal routers. Router RB and Router RC are area border routers that make up the backbone (Area 0) of the internetwork. Routers RA, RB, and RC will maintain an LSDB describing Area 1, while Routers RB, RC, and RD will maintain an LSDB describing Area 2. Routers

RB and RC maintain a separate LSDB for the backbone. There is no backbone router other than the area border routers RB and RC. However, suppose we had a Router RE that had only direct connections to Routers RB and RC. This would be a backbone router only.

This example has illustrated the chief drawback to hierarchical topology mentioned earlier in this chapter: complexity. For large ASes, however, it has significant advantages over making every router a peer. At the same time, the conceptual complexity is made worse by the need for very careful design, especially of the backbone. If the hierarchy is not set up properly, a single failure of a link between routers could disrupt the backbone and isolate one or more of the areas (including all the devices on all networks within the area!).

OSPF Route Determination Using SPF Trees

The key data structure maintained by each router in an OSPF AS is the LSDB, which contains a representation of the topology of either the entire AS (in the basic topology) or a single area (in the hierarchical topology). As you have seen, each router in the AS or area has the same LSDB, so it represents a neutral view of the connections between routers and networks.

The SPF Tree

Each router needs to participate in keeping the LSDB up-to-date, but it also has its own concerns. It needs to be able to determine what routes it should use for datagrams it receives from its connected networks—this is, after all, the entire point of a routing protocol. To find the best route, it must determine the shortest path between itself and each router or network in the AS or area. For this, it needs not a neutral view of the internetwork but a view of it from its own perspective.

The router creates this perspective by taking the information in the LSDB and transforming it into an *SPF tree*. The term *tree* refers to a data structure with a root that has branches coming out that go to other nodes, which also have branches. The structure as a whole looks like an upside-down tree. In this case, the SPF tree shows the topology information of the AS or area with the router that constructs the tree at the top. Each directly connected router or network is one step down in the tree; each router or network connected to these first-level routers or networks is then connected, and so on, until the entire AS or area has been represented.

Again, the router doesn't really *make* the tree; it is just an algorithmic calculation performed by the computer within the router. Once this is done, however, this logical construct can be used to calculate the cost for that router to reach any router or network in the AS (or area). In some cases, there may be more than one way to reach a router or network, so the tree is constructed to show only the shortest (lowest-cost) path to the network.

Each router is responsible only for sending a datagram on the next leg of its journey, and not for what happens to the journey as a whole. After the SPF tree is created, the router will create a routing table with an entry for each network, showing the cost to reach it, and also the next-hop router to use to reach it.

The SPF tree is created dynamically based on the current state of the LSDB. If the LSDB ever changes, the SPF tree and the routing information are recalculated.

> **KEY CONCEPT** To determine what routes it should use to reach networks in its AS, a router generates a *shortest-path first tree (SPF tree)* from its LSDB. This tree contains the same basic information as the LSDB, but presents it from the point of view of the router doing the calculation, so that router can see the costs of various paths to different networks.

OSPF Route Determination

I can almost see your eyes glazing over, so let's go back to the example we have been using in this chapter. Let's assume that we are looking at the AS as a whole in basic topology, for simplicity. Table 39-2 repeats the LSDB for this AS shown earlier in Table 39-1, but I have taken the liberty of replacing the bullets with cost metrics; these are shown in Figure 39-3 as well. Again, remember that there is no cost to reach a router from a network, so those links have a nonzero cost only going from the router to the network.

Table 39-2: Sample OSPF LSDB with Costs

To Router/ Network	From Router				From Network			
	RA	**RB**	**RC**	**RD**	**N1**	**N2**	**N3**	**N4**
RA					0	0		
RB			5			0	0	
RC		5				0	0	
RD							0	0
N1	2							
N2	3	4	3					
N3		5	6	1				
N4				4				

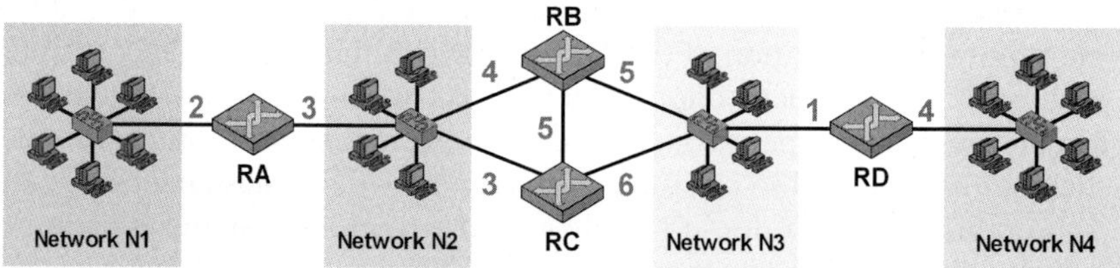

Figure 39-3: Sample OSPF AS with Costs *This is the same sample AS that is shown in Figure 39-1, but with costs assigned to each of the links between routers and networks. Costs between routers and networks are applied only in the direction from the router to the network.*

Now let's construct the SPF tree for RC. We can do this in iterations, as follows (see Figure 39-4).

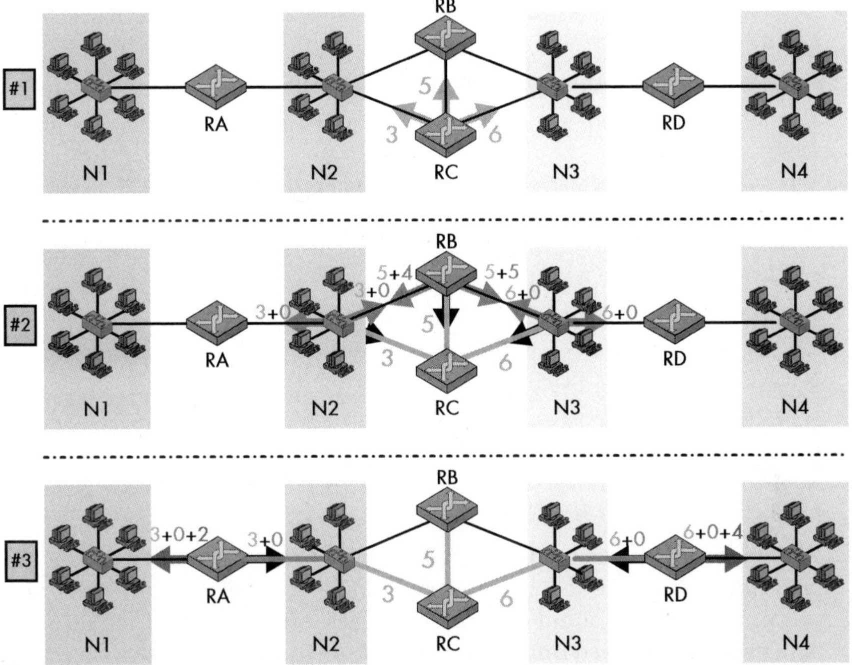

Figure 39-4: OSPF route determination using the SPF algorithm *This diagram shows graphically how a router, in this case Router RC, determines the best path to various networks. The arrows here represent not the transfer of data, but rather the examination of various links from a router to other routers or networks. In panel 1, Router RC examines its LSDB and determines the cost for each of its directly linked devices. In panel 2, the second level of the SPF tree is constructed by adding to those numbers the costs of all routers/networks that connect to the routers/networks found in panel 1. (The black arrows represent looking back in the direction we came from in the prior step, which we don't pursue.) In panel 3 the process continues, resulting in the determination of a cost of 5 for Router RC to reach Network N1 and 10 to reach Network N4.*

First Level

To construct the first level of the tree, we look for all devices that Router RC can reach directly. We find the following:

- Router RB, with a cost of 5
- Network N2, with a cost of 3
- Network N3, with a cost of 6

Second Level

To construct the second level, we look for all devices that the devices on the first level can reach directly. We then add the cost to reach each device on the first level to the cost of each device at the second level.

RB: Router RB has a cost of 5 and can reach the following:

- Router RC, with a cost of 5, total cost of 10
- Network N2, with a cost of 4, total cost of 9
- Network N3, with a cost of 5, total cost of 10

N2: Network N2 has a cost of 3 and can reach the following:

- Router RA, with a cost of 0, total cost of 3
- Router RB, with a cost of 0, total cost of 3
- Router RC, with a cost of 0, total cost of 3

N3: Network N3 has a cost of 6 and can reach the following:

- Router RB, with a cost of 0, total cost of 6
- Router RC, with a cost of 0, total cost of 6
- Router RD, with a cost of 0, total cost of 6

You probably can see immediately that we ended up with a number of different paths to the same devices or networks, some of which make no sense. For example, we don't really care about any path that goes to Router RC, since we *are* Router RC! Similarly, we can weed out certain paths immediately because we already have a shorter path to them. Taking a path through Router RB to Network N3 with a cost of 10 makes no sense when we can go directly at the first level for a cost of 6. So, after separating out the chaff, we end up with the following wheat at the second level:

- Network N2 to Router RA, with a cost of 3
- Network N3 to Router RD, with a cost of 6

Third Level

We continue the process by looking for devices that connect to the weeded-out devices that we found on the second level (this time I am only showing the meaningful ones):

RA: Router RA connects to Network N1, with a cost of 2, total cost of 5.

RD: Router RD connects to Network N4, with a cost of 4, total cost of 10.

In this simple example, we only need three levels to construct the tree for Router RC. (We would need more for Router RA or RD.) The final results would be the tree shown in Figure 39-5 and the routing information for RC to the four networks that is shown in Table 39-3.

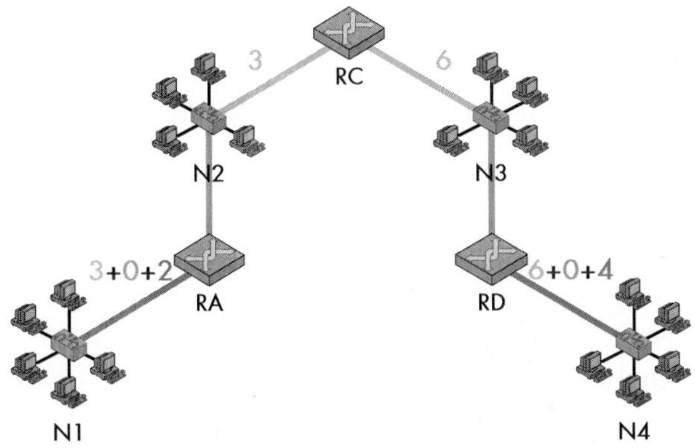

Figure 39-5: OSPF calculated SPF tree *This is a graphical representation of the SPF tree calculated in Figure 39-4, showing only the final results of the calculation process.*

Table 39-3: Example of Calculated OSPF Routes

Destination Network	Cost	Next Hop
N1	5	RA
N2	3	(local)
N3	6	(local)
N4	10	RD

This is what you would expect in this very simple example. Note that there are no specific entries for other routers, since they are the means to the end of reaching networks. However, if one of the other routers were a boundary router that connected the AS to the outside world, there would be entries for the networks to which the boundary router connected, so Router RC knew to send traffic for those networks to that boundary router.

OSPF General Operation

As a routing protocol, the main job of OSPF is to facilitate the exchange of routing information between routers. Each router in an OSPF AS that runs OSPF software is responsible for various tasks, such as setting timers to control certain activities that must occur on a regular basis, and the maintenance of important data structures, such as the LSDB. Most important, each OSPF router must both generate and respond to OSPF messages. It is this messaging system that allows important routing information to be shared within an AS or area, which makes it crucial to understanding how OSPF works. So it's worth starting a discussion of OSPF operation by taking a look at the message types and how they are used.

OSPF Message Types

Unlike RIP, OSPF does not send its information using the User Datagram Protocol (UDP). Instead, OSPF forms IP datagrams directly, packaging them using protocol number 89 for the Internet Protocol (IP) Protocol field. OSPF defines five different message types, for various types of communication:

Hello As the name suggests, these messages are used as a form of greeting to allow a router to discover other adjacent routers on its local links and networks. The messages establish relationships between neighboring devices (called *adjacencies*) and communicate key parameters about how OSPF is to be used in the AS or area.

Database Description These messages contain descriptions of the topology of the AS or area; that is, they convey the contents of the LSDB for the AS or area from one router to another. Communicating a large LSDB may require several messages to be sent; this is done by designating the sending device as a master device and sending messages in sequence, with the slave (recipient of the LSDB information) responding with acknowledgments.

Link State Request These messages are used by one router to request updated information about a portion of the LSDB from another router. The message specifies the link(s) about which the requesting device wants more current information.

Link State Update These messages contain updated information about the state of certain links on the LSDB. They are sent in response to a Link State Request message, and they are also broadcast or multicast by routers on a regular basis. Their contents are used to update the information in the LSDBs of routers that receive them.

Link State Acknowledgment These messages provide reliability to the link-state exchange process by explicitly acknowledging receipt of a Link State Update message.

OSPF Messaging

The use of these messages is approximately as follows. When a router first starts up it will send out a Hello message to see if any neighboring routers are around running OSPF, and it will also send them out periodically to discover any new neighbors that may show up. When an adjacency is set up with a new router, Database Description messages will then be sent to initialize the router's LSDB.

Routers that have been initialized enter a steady state mode. They will each routinely flood their local networks with Link State Update messages, advertising the state of their links. They will also send out updates when they detect a change in topology that needs to be communicated. They will receive Link State Update messages sent by other devices, and respond with Link State Acknowledgments accordingly. Routers may also request updates using Link State Request messages.

When the hierarchical topology is used, internal routers maintain a single LSDB and perform messaging only within an area. Area border routers have multiple LSDBs and perform messaging in more than one area. They, along with any other OSPF backbone routers, also exchange messaging information on the backbone, including summarized link-state information for the areas they border.

Again, all of this is highly simplified; the OSPF standard contains pages and pages of detailed rules and procedures governing the exact timing for sending and receiving messages.

KEY CONCEPT The operation of OSPF involves five message types. Hello messages establish contact between routers. Database Description messages initialize a router's LSDB. Routine LSDB updates are sent using Link State Update messages, which are acknowledged using Link State Acknowledgments. A device may also request a specific update using a Link State Request message.

OSPF Message Authentication

The OSPF standard specifies that all OSPF messages are authenticated for security. This is a bit misleading, however, since one of the authentication methods supported is null authentication, meaning no authentication is used. More security is provided by using the optional simple password authentication method, and the most security is available through the use of cryptographic authentication. These methods are described in Appendix D of RFC 2328.

NOTE *The Hello messages used in OSPF are also sometimes called the* Hello Protocol. *This is especially poor terminology, because there is an actual routing protocol called the* HELLO Protocol. *The two protocols are not related. However, I suspect that the OSPF Hello messages may have been so named because they serve a similar purpose to the messages used in the independent HELLO Protocol.*

OSPF Message Formats

As explained in the previous section, OSPF uses five different types of messages to communicate both link-state and general information between routers within an AS or area. To help illustrate how the OSPF messages are used, it's worth taking a look at the format of each of these messages.

OSPF Common Header Format

Naturally, each type of OSPF message includes a slightly different set of information; otherwise, there wouldn't be different message types. However, all message types share a similar message structure, beginning with a shared 24-byte header. This common header allows certain standard information to be conveyed in a consistent manner, such as the number of the version of OSPF that generated the message. It also allows a device receiving an OSPF message to quickly determine which type of message it has received, so it knows whether or not it needs to bother examining the rest of the message. Table 39-4 and Figure 39-6 show the common OSPF header format.

Table 39-4: OSPF Common Header Format

Field Name	Size (Bytes)	Description
Version #	1	Set to 2 for OSPF version 2.
Type	1	Indicates the type of OSPF message: 1 = Hello 2 = Database Description 3 = Link State Request 4 = Link State Update 5 = Link State Acknowledgment
Packet Length	2	The length of the message, in bytes, including the 24 bytes of this header.
Router ID	4	The ID of the router that generated this message (generally its IP address on the interface over which the message was sent).
Area ID	4	An identification of the OSPF area to which this message belongs, when areas are used.
Checksum	2	A 16-bit checksum computed in a manner similar to a standard IP checksum. The entire message is included in the calculation except for the Authentication field.
AuType	2	Indicates the type of authentication used for this message: 0 = No Authentication 1 = Simple Password Authentication 2 = Cryptographic Authentication
Authentication	8	A 64-bit field used for authentication of the message, as needed.

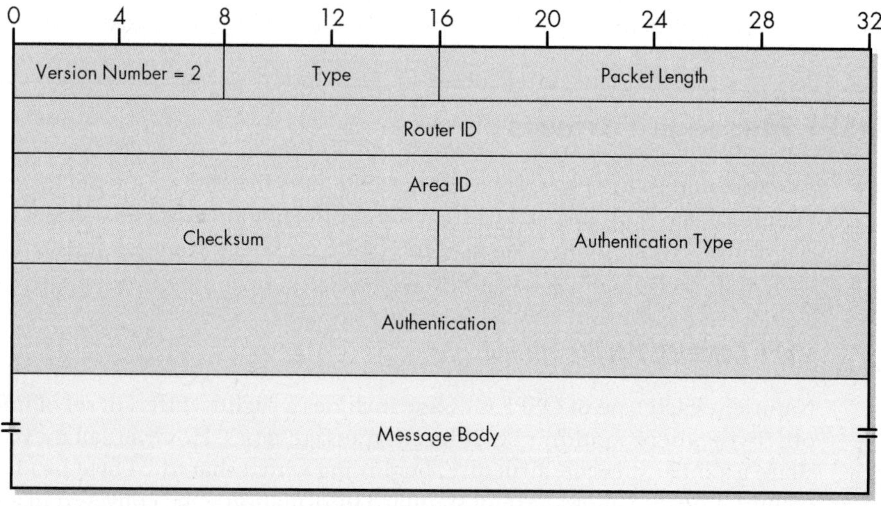

Figure 39-6: OSPF common header format *Following this header, the body of the message includes a variable number of fields that depend on the message type. Each of the message formats is described in detail in RFC 2328. Since some are quite long, I will describe their fields only briefly here.*

OSPF Hello Message Format

Hello messages have a Type value of 1 in the header, and the field structure shown in Table 39-5 and Figure 39-7 in the body of the message.

Table 39-5: OSPF Hello Message Format

Field Name	Size (Bytes)	Description
Network Mask	4	The subnet mask of the network the router is sending to.
Hello Interval	2	The number of seconds this router waits between sending Hello messages.
Options	1	Indicates which optional OSPF capabilities the router supports.
Rtr Pri	1	Indicates the router's priority, when electing a backup designated router.
Router Dead Interval	4	The number of seconds a router can be silent before it is considered to have failed.
Designated Router	4	The address of a router designated for certain special functions on some networks. Set to zeros if there is no designated router.
Backup Designated Router	4	The address of a backup designated router. Set to all zeros if there is no backup designated router.
Neighbors	Multiple of 4	The addresses of each router from which this router has received Hello messages recently.

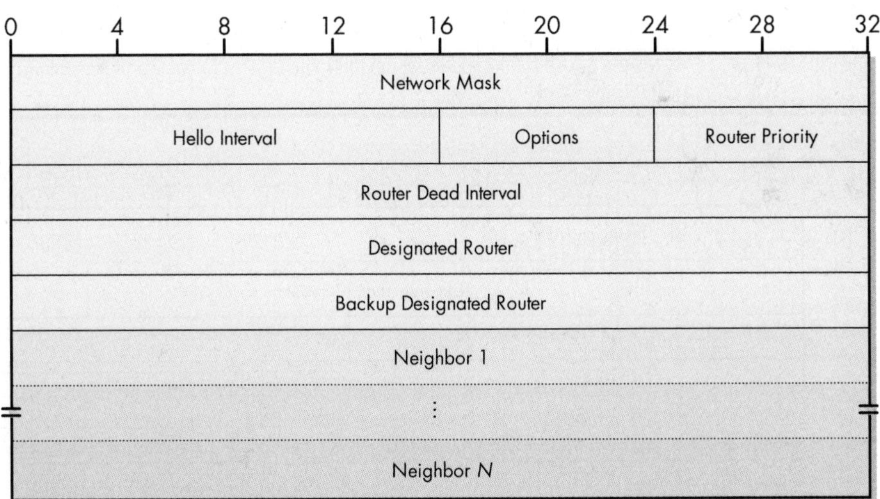

***Figure 39-7:** OSPF Hello message format*

OSPF Database Description Message Format

Database Description messages have a Type value of 2 in the header and the body structure depicted in Table 39-6 and Figure 39-8.

Table 39-6: OSPF Database Description Message Format

Field Name	Size (Bytes)	Description
Interface MTU	2	The size of the largest IP message that can be sent on this router's interface without fragmentation.
Options	1	Indicates which of several optional OSPF capabilities the router supports.
Flags	1	Special flags used to indicate information about the exchange of Database Description messages, as shown in Table 39-7.
DD Sequence Number	4	Used to number a sequence of Database Description messages so that they are kept in order.
LSA Headers	Variable	Contains LSA headers, which carry information about the LSDB. See the "OSPF Link State Advertisements and the LSA Header Format" section later in this chapter for more information about LSAs. Please add correct cross-ref info.

Table 39-7: OSPF Database Description Message Flags

Subfield Name	Size (Bytes)	Description
Reserved	5/8 (5 bits)	Reserved: Sent and received as zero.
I	1/8 (1 bit)	I-Bit: Set to 1 to indicate that this is the first (initial) in a sequence of Database Description messages.
M	1/8 (1 bit)	M-Bit: Set to 1 to indicate that more Database Description messages follow this one.
MS	1/8 (1 bit)	MS-Bit: Set to 1 if the router sending this message is the master in the communication, or 0 if it is the slave.

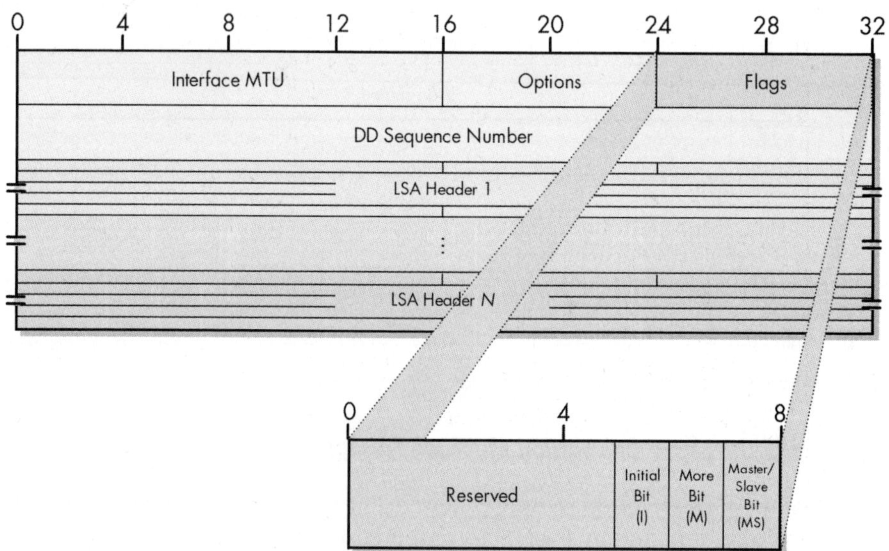

***Figure 39-8:** OSPF Database Description message format*

OSPF Link State Request Message Format

Link State Request messages have a Type value of 3 in the header. Following the header comes one or more sets of three fields, each of which identify an LSA for which the router is requesting an update, as shown in Figure 39-9. Each LSA identification has the format described in Table 39-8.

Table 39-8: OSPF Link State Request Message Format

Field Name	Size (Bytes)	Description
LS Type	4	The type of LSA being sought.
Link State ID	4	The identifier of the LSA, usually the IP address of either the router or network linked.
Advertising Router	4	The ID of the router that created the LSA whose update is being sought.

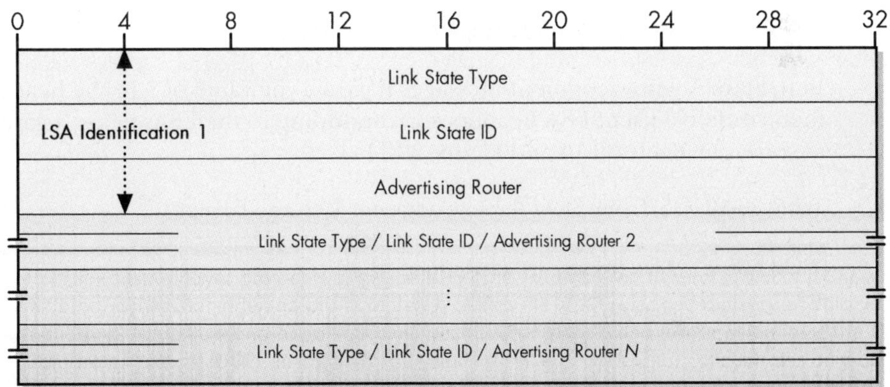

***Figure 39-9:** OSPF Link State Request Message format*

OSPF Link State Update Message Format

Link State Update messages have a Type value of 4 in the header and the fields illustrated in Table 39-9 and Figure 39-10.

Table 39-9: OSPF Link State Update Message Format

Field Name	Size (Bytes)	Description
# LSAs	4	The number of LSAs included in this message.
LSAs	Variable	One or more LSAs. See the "OSPF Link State Advertisements and the LSA Header Format" section later in this chapter for more details.

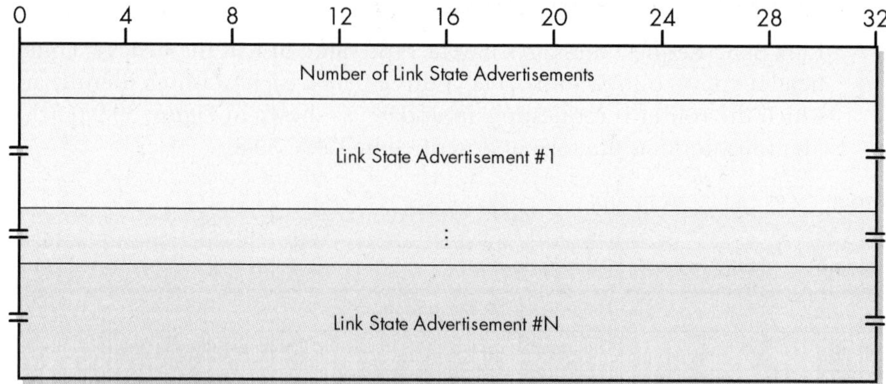

Figure 39-10: *OSPF Link State Update message format*

OSPF Link State Acknowledgment Message Format

Link State Acknowledgment messages have a Type value of 5 in the header. They then contain a list of LSA headers corresponding to the LSAs being acknowledged, as shown in Table 39-10 and Figure 39-11.

Table 39-10: OSPF Link State Acknowledgment Message Format

Field Name	Size (Bytes)	Description
LSA Headers	Variable	Contains LSA headers that identify the LSAs acknowledged.

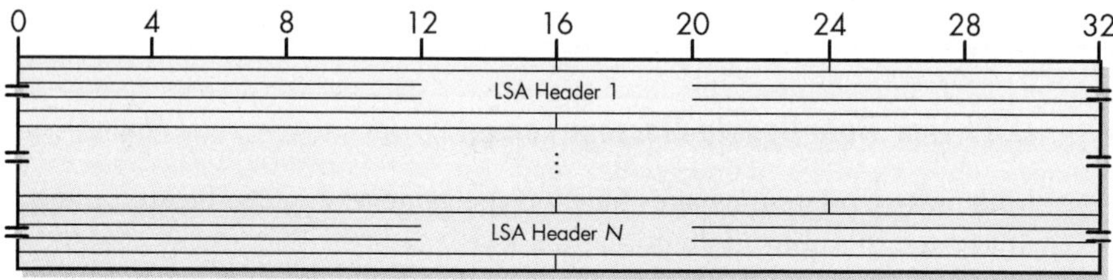

Figure 39-11: *OSPF Link State Acknowledgment message format*

OSPF Link State Advertisements and the LSA Header Format

Several of the previous message types include LSAs, which are the fields that actually carry topological information about the LSDB. There are several types of LSAs, which are used to convey information about different types of links. Like the OSPF messages themselves, each LSA has a common header with 20 bytes and then a number of additional fields that describe the link.

The LSA header contains sufficient information to identify the link. It uses the subfield structure shown in Table 39-11 and Figure 39-12.

Table 39-11: OSPF Link State Advertisement Header Format

Subfield Name	Size (Bytes)	Description
LS Age	2	The number of seconds elapsed since the LSA was created.
Options	1	Indicates which of several optional OSPF capabilities the router supports.
LS Type	1	Indicates the type of link this LSA describes, as shown in Table 39-12.
Link State ID	4	Identifies the link. This usually is the IP address of either the router or the network the link represents.
Advertising Router	4	The ID of the router originating the LSA.
LS Sequence Number	4	A sequence number used to detect old or duplicate LSAs.
LS Checksum	2	A checksum of the LSA for data corruption protection.
Length	2	The length of the LSA, including the 20 bytes of the header.

Table 39-12: OSPF Link State Advertisement Header LS Types

Value	Link Type	Description
1	Router-LSA	Link to a router.
2	Network-LSA	Link to a network.
3	Summary-LSA (IP Network)	When areas are used, summary information is generated about a network.
4	Summary-LSA (ASBR)	When areas are used, summary information is generated about a link to an AS boundary router.
5	AS-External-LSA	An external link outside the AS.

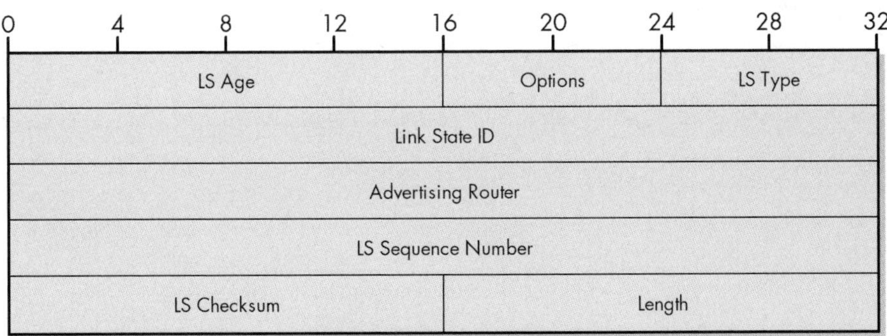

Figure 39-12: OSPF Link State Advertisement header format

Following the LSA header comes the body of the LSA. The specific fields in the body depend on the value of the LS Type field (see Table 39-12). Here is a summary:

- For normal links to a router, the LSA includes an identification of the router and the metric to reach it, as well as details about the router such as whether it is a boundary or area border router.

- LSAs for networks include a subnet mask and information about other routers on the network.
- Summary LSAs include a metric and a summarized address as well as a subnet mask.
- External LSAs include a number of additional fields that allow the external router to be communicated.

Refer to Appendix A of RFC 2328 if you want all the details about the fields in the LSA body.

40

BORDER GATEWAY PROTOCOL (BGP/BGP-4)

Modern TCP/IP internetworks are composed of autonomous systems (ASes) that are run independently. Each may use an interior routing protocol such as Routing Information Protocol (RIP), Open Shortest Path First (OSPF), Interior Gateway Routing Protocol (IGRP), or Enhanced Interior Gateway Routing Protocol (EIGRP) to select routes between networks within the AS. To form larger internetworks, and especially the "mother of all internetworks," the Internet, these ASes must be connected together. This requires use of a consistent exterior routing protocol that all ASes can agree upon, and in today's TCP/IP, that protocol is the *Border Gateway Protocol (BGP)*.

If you were to ask the average Internet user, or even the typical network administrator, to make a list of the ten most important TCP/IP protocols, BGP probably wouldn't show up frequently. Routing protocols are worker bees of the TCP/IP protocol suite, and they just are not very exciting. The reality, however, is that BGP is a critically important protocol to the operation of larger internetworks and the Internet itself. It is the glue that binds smaller internetworks (ASes) together, and it ensures that every organization is able to share routing information. It is this function that lets us take disparate networks and internetworks and find efficient routes from any host to any other host, regardless of location.

In this chapter, I describe the characteristics, general operation, and detailed operation of BGP. I start, as usual, with an overview of the protocol and discuss its history, standards, and versions, including a discussion of its key features and characteristics. I then cover basic operational concepts, including topology, the notion of BGP speakers, and neighbor relationships. I discuss BGP traffic types and how policies can be used to control traffic flows on the internetwork. I explain how BGP routers store and advertise routes and how Routing Information Bases function. I describe the basic algorithm used by BGP and how path attributes describe routes. I provide a summary of how the BGP route selection process operates. I then give a general description of BGP's operation and its high-level use of various messages. Finally, I present a more detailed analysis of the different message types, how they are used, and their format.

BGP is another in the rather large group of protocols and technologies that is so complex it would take dozens of chapters to do justice. Therefore, I include here my somewhat standard disclaimer that you will find in this chapter only a relatively high-level look at BGP. You will need to refer to the BGP standards (described in the section on BGP standards and versions) if you need more details.

NOTE *The current version of BGP is version 4, also called* BGP-4*. This is the only version widely used today, so unless otherwise indicated, assume that I'm talking about BGP-4 wherever you see* BGP*.*

BGP Overview

As I described briefly in the overview of routing protocol concepts in Chapter 37, the way that routers were connected in the early Internet was quite different than it is today. The early Internet had a set of centralized routers functioning as a core AS. These routers used the Gateway-to-Gateway Protocol (GGP) for communication between them within the AS and the aptly named Exterior Gateway Protocol (EGP) to talk to routers outside the core. GGP and EGP are discussed in Chapter 41.

When the Internet grew and moved to AS architecture, EGP was still able to function as the exterior routing protocol for the Internet. However, as the number of ASes in an internetwork grew, the importance of communication between them grew as well. EGP was functional but had several weaknesses that became more problematic as the Internet expanded. It was necessary to define a new exterior routing protocol that would provide enhanced capabilities for use on the growing Internet.

In June 1989, the first version of this new routing protocol was formalized, with the publishing of RFC 1105, "A Border Gateway Protocol (BGP)." This initial version of the BGP standard defined most of the concepts behind the protocol, as well as key fundamentals such as messaging, message formats, and how devices operate in general terms. It established BGP as the Internet's exterior routing protocol of the future.

BGP Versions and Defining Standards

Due to the importance of a protocol that spans the Internet, work continued on BGP for many years after the initial standard was published. The developers of BGP needed to correct problems with the initial protocol, refine BGP's operation, improve efficiency, and add features. It was also necessary to make adjustments to allow BGP to keep pace with other changes in the TCP/IP protocol suite, such as the invention of classless addressing and routing.

The result of this ongoing work is that BGP has evolved through several versions and standards. These are sometimes called BGP-*N*, where *N* is the version number. Table 40-1 shows the history of BGP standards, providing the RFC numbers and names, and a brief summary of the changes made in each version.

Table 40-1: Border Gateway Protocol (BGP) Versions and Defining Standards

RFC Number	Date	Name	BGP Version	Description
1105	June 1989	A Border Gateway Protocol (BGP)	BGP-1	Initial definition of the BGP.
1163	June 1990	A Border Gateway Protocol (BGP)	BGP-2	This version cleaned up several issues with BGP-1 and refined the meaning and use of several of the message types. It also added the important concept of path attributes, which communicate information about routes. BGP-1 was designed around the notion of a directional topology, with certain routers being up, down, or horizontal relative to each other; BGP-2 removed this concept, making BGP better suited to an arbitrary AS topology. (Note that the RFC title is not a typo; they didn't put "version 2" in the title.)
1267	October 1991	Border Gateway Protocol 3 (BGP-3)	BGP-3	This version optimized and simplified route information exchange, adding an identification capability to the messages used to establish BGP communications, and incorporating several other improvements and corrections. (They left the "A" off the title of this one for some reason.)
1654	July 1994	A Border Gateway Protocol 4 (BGP-4)	BGP-4	Initial standard for BGP-4, revised in RFC 1771.
1771	March 1995	A Border Gateway Protocol 4 (BGP-4)	BGP-4	Current standard for BGP-4. The primary change in BGP-4 is support for Classless Inter-Domain Routing (CIDR). The protocol was changed to allow prefixes to be specified that represent a set of aggregated networks. Other minor improvements were also made to the protocol.

As you might imagine, changing the version of a protocol like BGP is not an easy undertaking. Any modification of the protocol would require the coordination of many different organizations. The larger the Internet grows, the more difficult this would be. As a result, despite frequent version changes in the early 1990s, BGP-4 remains today the current version of the standard and is the one that is widely used. Unless otherwise specified, any mention of BGP in this book refers to BGP-4.

Supplementing RFC 1771 are three other consecutively numbered RFCs published simultaneously with it, which provide supporting information about BGP's functions and use, as shown in Table 40-2.

Table 40-2: Additional Defining Standards for BGP-4

RFC Number	Name	Description
1772	Application of the Border Gateway Protocol in the Internet	Provides additional conceptual information on the operation of BGP and how it is applied to and used on the Internet. This document is sometimes considered a companion of RFC 1771 with the pair defining BGP-4.
1773	Experience with the BGP-4 Protocol	Describes the experiences of those testing and using BGP-4 and provides information that justified its acceptance as a standard.
1774	BGP-4 Protocol Analysis	Provides more detailed technical information about the operation of BGP-4.

KEY CONCEPT The exterior routing protocol used in modern TCP/IP internetworks is the *Border Gateway Protocol (BGP)*. Initially developed in the late 1980s as a successor to the Exterior Gateway Protocol (EGP), BGP has been revised many times; the current version is 4, so BGP is also commonly called BGP-4. BGP's primary function is the exchange of network reachability information between ASes to allow each AS on an internetwork to send messages efficiently to every other one.

Overview of BGP Functions and Features

If I were to summarize the job of BGP in one phrase, it would be to exchange network reachability information between ASes and from this information determine routes to networks. In a typical internetwork (and in the Internet), each AS designates one or more routers that run BGP software. BGP routers in each AS are linked to those in one or more other ASes. Each BGP stores information about networks and the routes to them in a set of Routing Information Bases (RIBs). This route information is exchanged between BGP routers and propagated throughout the entire internetwork, allowing each AS to find paths to each other AS, and thereby enabling routing across the entire internetwork.

BGP supports an arbitrary topology of ASes, meaning that they can be connected in any manner. An AS must have a minimum of one router running BGP, but can have more than one. It is also possible to use BGP to communicate between BGP routers within the same AS.

BGP uses a fairly complex system for route determination. The protocol goes beyond the limited notion of considering only the next hop to a network the way distance-vector algorithms like RIP function. Instead, the BGP router stores more complete information about the path (sequence of ASes) from itself to a network. Special path attributes describe the characteristics of paths and are used in the process of route selection. Because of its storage of path information, BGP is sometimes called a *path-vector* protocol.

BGP chooses routes using a deterministic algorithm that assesses path attributes and chooses an efficient route, while avoiding router loops and other problem conditions. The selection of routes by a BGP router can also be controlled through a set of BGP policies that specify, for example, whether an AS is willing to carry traffic from other ASes. However, BGP cannot guarantee the most efficient route to any destination, because it cannot know what happens within each AS and therefore what the cost is to traverse each AS.

BGP's operation is based on the exchange of messages that perform different functions. BGP routers use Open messages to contact neighboring routers and establish BGP sessions. They exchange Update messages to communicate information about reachable networks, sending only partial information as needed. They also use Keepalive and Notification messages to maintain sessions and inform peers of error conditions. The use of these messages is explained thoroughly later in this chapter.

> **KEY CONCEPT** BGP supports an arbitrary topology of ASes. Each AS using BGP assigns one or more routers to implement the protocol. These devices then exchange messages to establish contact with each other and share information about rates through the internetwork using the Transmission Control Protocol (TCP). BGP employs a sophisticated path vector route calculation algorithm that determines routes from path attributes that describe how different networks can be reached.

BGP uses the Transmission Control Protocol (TCP) as a reliable transport protocol so that it can take advantage of the many connection setup and maintenance features of that protocol. This also means that BGP doesn't need to worry about issues such as message sequencing, acknowledgments, or lost transmissions. Since unauthorized BGP messages could wreak havoc with the operation of the Internet, BGP includes an authentication scheme for security.

NOTE *BGP maintains backward compatibility with the older exterior routing protocol, EGP.*

BGP Topology

In the preceding section, I boiled down the function of BGP into this summary: the exchange of network reachability information between ASes of routers and networks, and the determination of routes from this information. The actual method that BGP uses to accomplish this, however, is fairly complex.

One of the most important characteristics of BGP is its flexibility. The protocol can connect together any internetwork of ASes using an arbitrary topology. The only requirement is that each AS have at least one router that is able to run BGP and that this router connect to at least one other AS's BGP router. Beyond that, "the sky is the limit," as they say. BGP can handle a set of ASes connected in a full mesh topology (each AS to each other AS), a partial mesh, a chain of ASes linked one to the next, or any other configuration. It also handles changes to topology that may occur over time.

Another important assumption that BGP makes is that it doesn't know anything about what happens within the AS. This is an important prerequisite to the notion of an AS being autonomous—it has its own internal topology and uses its own choice of routing protocols to determine routes. BGP just takes the information conveyed to it from the AS and shares it with other ASes.

BGP Speakers, Router Roles, Neighbors, and Peers

Creating a BGP internetwork begins with the designation of certain routers in each AS as ones that will run the protocol. In BGP parlance, these are called *BGP speakers,* since they speak the BGP language. A protocol can reasonably be called a language, but I have not encountered this notion of a speaker in any other protocol, so it's somewhat interesting terminology.

An AS can contain many routers that are connected in an arbitrary topology. We can draw a distinction between routers in an AS that are connected only to other routers within the AS versus those that connect to other ASes. Routers in the former group are usually called *internal routers,* while those in the latter group are called *border routers* in BGP (as well as similar names in other protocols; for example, in OSPF they are called *boundary routers*).

The notion of a border is the basis for the name of the BGP itself. To actually create the BGP internetwork, the BGP speakers bordering each AS are physically connected to one or more BGP speakers in other ASes, in whatever topology the internetwork designer decrees. When a BGP speaker in one AS is linked to a BGP speaker in another AS, they are deemed *neighbors.* The direct connection between them allows them to exchange information about the ASes of which they are a part.

Most BGP speakers will be connected to more than one other speaker. This provides both greater efficiency in the form of more direct paths to different networks and redundancy to allow the internetwork to cope with either device or connection failures. It is possible (and in many cases, likely) for a BGP speaker to have neighbor relationships with other BGP speakers both within its own AS and outside its AS. A neighbor within the AS is called an *internal peer,* while a neighbor outside the AS is an *external peer.* BGP between internal peers is sometimes called *Internal BGP (IBGP);* use of the protocol between external peers is *External BGP (EBGP).* The two are similar, but differ in certain areas, especially path attributes and route selection. You can see an example of BGP topology and the designation of internal and external peers in Figure 40-1.

This diagram is a variation on Figure 37-1 in Chapter 37. It shows the names used by BGP to refer to different types of routers and ASes. Internal routers are shown in faint type, while border routers are in bold type. BGP speakers that communicate within an AS are internal peers, while those that communicate between ASes are external peers. This highly simplified internetwork shows two stub ASes, both of which only connect to the multihomed AS 2. A peer connection between BGP speakers can be either a direct link using some form of layer 2 technology or an indirect link using TCP. This allows the BGP speakers to establish BGP sessions and then exchange routing information, using the messaging system you will see later in this chapter. It also is the means by which actual end-user traffic moves between ASes. External peers are normally connected directly, while internal peers are often linked indirectly.

You will see in a moment that the method in which ASes are connected has an important impact on the overall function of the internetwork and how traffic is carried on it.

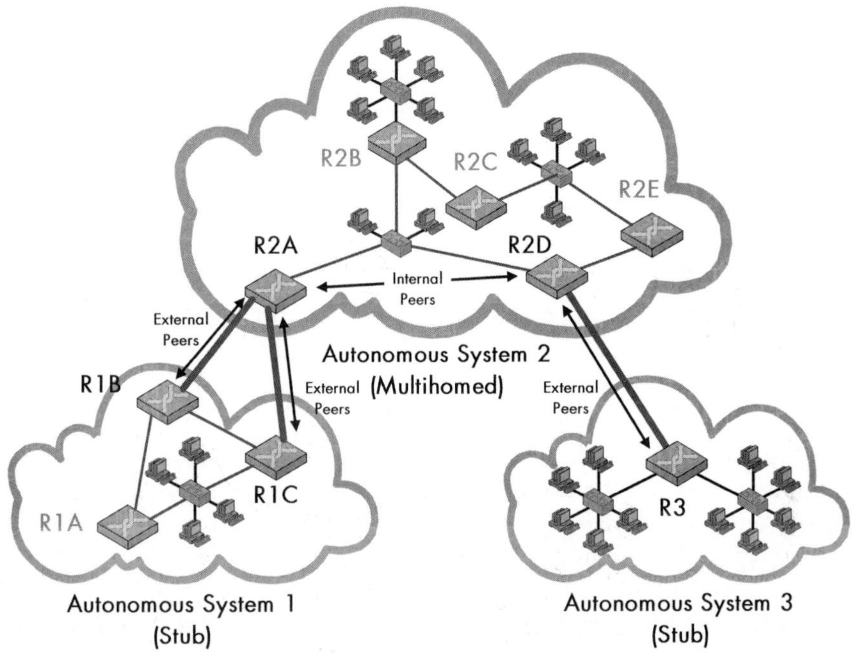

Figure 40-1: *Sample BGP topology and designations*

> **KEY CONCEPT** Each router configured to use BGP is called a BGP *speaker*; these devices exchange route information using the BGP *messaging system*. Routers that connect only to other routers in the same AS are called *internal routers*, while those that connect to other ASes are *border routers*. Neighboring BGP speakers in the same AS are called *internal peers*, while those in different ASes are *external peers*.

BGP AS Types, Traffic Flows, and Routing Policies

When we connect ASes together to form an internetwork, the paths between AS border routers form the conduit by which messages move from one AS to another. It is very important that the flow of messages between ASes be carefully controlled. Depending on circumstances, we may wish to limit or even prohibit certain types of messages from going to or from a certain AS. These decisions in turn have a direct impact on BGP route determination.

BGP Traffic Flow and Traffic Types

The flow of messages in an internetwork is sometimes collectively called *traffic*. This term presents a good analogy, because we can consider the matter of traffic flow control in a BGP internetwork in much the same way that we do the streets of a city. You have probably seen signs on residential streets that say "No Through Traffic" or "Local Traffic Only." These are attempts to control the flow of traffic over those streets. A more extreme example of this would be a street in the neighborhood where I used to live, where a barricade was intentionally erected in the middle to turn a busy through street into a pair of dead ends. Again, the goal was traffic control.

These measures highlight a key distinction between local traffic and through traffic in a neighborhood. The very same categorization is important in BGP, as shown here:

Local Traffic Traffic carried within an AS that either originated in that same AS *or* is intended to be delivered within that AS. This is like local traffic on a street.

Transit Traffic Traffic that was generated outside that AS and is intended to be delivered outside the AS. This is like through traffic on streets.

BGP AS Types

In the previous section, I discussed the distinction between internal routers and border (or boundary) routers in an AS. We can make a similar distinction between different types of ASes, based on how they are interconnected in the overall BGP topology. There are two main types of ASes:

Stub AS This is an AS that is connected to only one other AS. It is comparable to a cul-de-sac (dead-end street) in a road analogy; usually, only vehicles coming from or going to houses on the street will be found on that street.

Multihomed AS This is an AS that is connected to two or more other ASes. It is comparable to a through street in the road analogy, because it is possible that vehicles may enter the street and pass through it, without stopping at any of the street's houses.

In the example BGP internetwork in Figure 40-1, I have linked border routers in AS 2 to both AS 1 and AS 3. While traffic from AS 2 can flow both to and from AS 1 and AS 3, it is possible that traffic from AS 1 may also flow to AS 3 and vice versa. AS 2 acts as the "through street" for these datagrams.

BGP AS Routing Policies

The reason why BGP makes a distinction between traffic types and AS types is the same reason why it is done on the streets: Many folks have a dim view of through traffic. In a neighborhood, everyone wants to be able to get from their homes to anywhere they need to go in the city, but they don't want a lot of other people using their streets. Similarly, every AS must use at least one other AS to communicate with distant ASes, but many are less than enthusiastic about being a conduit for a lot of external traffic.

This reluctance really does make sense in many cases, either in the case of a neighborhood or in the case of BGP. Having many cars and trucks on a residential street can be a problem in a number of ways: safety issues, wear and tear on the road, pollution, and so forth. Similarly, if a multihomed AS was forced to carry all transit traffic that other ASes want to send to it, it might become overloaded.

To provide control over the carrying of transit traffic, BGP allows an AS to set up and use routing policies. These are sets of rules that govern how an AS will handle transit traffic. A great deal of flexibility exists in how an AS decides to handle transit traffic. Some of the many options include the following:

No Transit Policy An AS can have a policy that it will not handle transit traffic at all.

Restricted AS Transit Policy An AS may allow for the handling of traffic from certain ASes but not others. In this case, it tells the ASes it will handle that they may send it traffic, but does not say this to the others.

Criteria-Based Transit Policy An AS may use a number of different criteria to decide whether to allow transit traffic. For example, it might allow transit traffic only during certain times or only when it has enough spare capacity.

NOTE *An AS that is willing to carry transit traffic is sometimes called a* transit AS.

In a similar manner, policies can be set that control how an AS will have its own traffic handled by other ASes. A stub AS will always connect to the internetwork as a whole using the single AS to which it connects. A multihomed AS, however, may have policies that influence route selection by specifying the conditions under which one AS should be used over another. These policies may be based on considerations of security (if one connecting AS is deemed more secure than another), performance (if one AS is faster than another), reliability, or other factors.

KEY CONCEPT One important issue in BGP is how to handle the flow of traffic between ASes. Each AS in a BGP internetwork is either a *stub AS* if it connects to only one other AS, or a *multihomed AS* if it connects to two or more others. BGP allows the administrators of a multihomed AS to establish routing policies that specify under what conditions the AS is willing to handle transit traffic (messages sent over the AS whose source and destination are both external to that AS).

Issues with Routing Policies and Internetwork Design

What would happen to a city if every street only allowed local traffic? It would be pretty hard to get around. Of course this problem never occurs in well-designed cities, because traffic planners understand the dual need for connectivity and through-traffic avoidance in residential areas. Cities are laid out in a somewhat hierarchical fashion, so local traffic funnels to thoroughfares intended specifically to carry nonlocal traffic.

The same basic situation exists in an internetwork. It wouldn't work very well if every AS declared that it was not interested in carrying transit traffic! Usually, internetworks are designed so that certain ASes are intended to carry large amounts of transit traffic. This is typically the function of high-speed, high-capacity backbone connections that serve other ASes as customers. An AS will usually carry another AS's traffic only if arrangements have been made to allow this.

BGP Route Storage and Advertisement

The job of the BGP is to facilitate the exchange of route information between BGP devices so that each router can determine efficient routes to each of the networks on an IP internetwork. This means that descriptions of routes are the key data that BGP devices work with. Every BGP speaker is responsible for managing route descriptions according to specific guidelines established in the BGP standards.

BGP Route Information Management Functions

Conceptually, the overall activity of route information management can be considered to encompass four main tasks:

Route Storage Each BGP stores information about how to reach networks in a set of special databases. It also uses databases to hold routing information received from other devices.

Route Update When a BGP device receives an Update message from one of its peers, it must decide how to use this information. Special techniques are applied to determine when and how to use the information received from peers to properly update the device's knowledge of routes.

Route Selection Each BGP uses the information in its route databases to select good routes to each network on the internetwork.

Route Advertisement Each BGP speaker regularly tells its peers what it knows about various networks and methods to reach them. This is called *route advertisement* and is accomplished using BGP Update messages. You'll learn more about these messages later in the chapter.

BGP Routing Information Bases (RIBs)

The heart of BGP's system of routing information management and handling is the database where routes are stored. This database is collectively called the *Routing Information Base (RIB)*, but it is not actually a monolithic entity. It is composed of three separate sections that are used by a BGP speaker to handle the input and output of routing information. Two of these sections consist of several individual parts, or copies.

The three RIB sections (using the cryptic names given them by the BGP standards) are as follows:

Adj-RIBs-In A set of input database parts that holds information about routes received from peer BGP speakers.

Loc-RIB The local RIB. This is the core database that stores routes that have been selected by this BGP device and are considered valid to it.

Adj-RIBs-Out A set of output database parts that holds information about routes that this BGP device has selected to be disseminated to its peers.

Thus, the RIB can be considered either a single database or a set of related databases, depending on how you look at it. (The previous divisions are conceptual in nature; the entire RIB can be implemented as a single database with an internal structure representing the different components, or implemented as separate databases.)

The RIB is a fairly complex data structure, not just because of this multisection structure, but also because BGP devices store considerably more information about routes than simpler routing protocols. Routes are also called *paths* in BGP, and the detailed descriptions of them are stored in the form of special BGP path attributes, which we will examine shortly.

The three sections of the RIB are the mechanism by which information flow is managed in a BGP speaker. Data received from Update messages transmitted by peer BGP speakers is held in the Adj-RIBs-In, with each Adj-RIB-In holding input from one peer. This data is then analyzed and appropriate portions of it are selected to update the Loc-RIB, which is the main database of routes this BGP speaker is using. On a regular basis, information from the Loc-RIB is placed into the Adj-RIBs-Out to be sent to other peers using Update messages. This information flow is accomplished as part of the system of route update, selection, and advertisement known as the BGP decision process, which I'll discuss in the "BGP Route Determination and the BGP Decision Process" section later in this chapter.

KEY CONCEPT The routine operation of BGP requires BGP speakers to store, update, select, and advertise routing information. The central data structure used for this purpose is the *BGP Routing Information Base (RIB)*. The RIB actually consists of three sections: a set of input databases *(Adj-RIBs-In)* that hold routing information received from peers; a local database *(Loc-RIB)* that contains the router's current routes; and a set of output databases *(Adj-RIBs-Out)* used by the router to send its routing information to other routers.

BGP Path Attributes and Algorithm Overview

Routing protocols that use a distance-vector algorithm, such as RIP, are relatively simple in large part because the information each device stores about each route is itself simple. Each router only knows that it can reach a network at a specific cost through a particular next-hop router. It doesn't have knowledge of the route that datagrams will take to reach any of these networks. This level of knowledge is simply insufficient for the needs of a protocol like BGP.

In order to handle the calculation of efficient, nonlooping routes in an arbitrary topology of ASes, we need to know not just that we must get Network N7 to send to Router R4, but also the characteristics of the entire path between ourselves and Network N7. By storing this additional information, it is possible to make decisions about how to compute and change routes, using knowledge of the entire path between a router and a network. Thus, instead of advertising networks in terms of a destination and the distance to that destination, BGP devices advertise networks as destination addresses and path descriptions to reach those destinations. This means BGP uses, instead of a distance-vector algorithm, a *path-vector algorithm.*

Each communication of a reachable network provides considerable information about the entire sequence of routers to a destination. Due to this inclusion of topology information, path-vector protocols are sometimes described as a combination of distance-vector and link-state algorithms. This doesn't really do them justice, however, since they do not function in the same way as either of those algorithm types. (If you are interested in additional general information about path-vector algorithms, you can find some in RFC 1322, "A Unified Approach to Inter-Domain Routing." (Warning: do not read before operating heavy machinery.)

The information about the path to each route is stored in the RIB of each BGP speaker in the form of BGP path attributes. These attributes are used to advertise routes to networks when BGP devices send out Update messages. The storing, processing, sending, and receiving of path attributes is the method by which routers decide how to create routes, so understanding them is obviously quite important.

There are several different path attributes, each of which describes a particular characteristic of a route. Attributes are divided into different categories based on their level of importance and specific rules designed to manage their propagation. The most important path attributes are called *well-known attributes*; every BGP speaker must recognize and process these, but only some are required to be sent with every route. Other attributes are optional and may or not be implemented. These are further differentiated based on how they are handled when received by a device that does not recognize them.

BGP Path Attribute Classes

The four formal classifications of path attributes are as follows:

Well-Known Mandatory These are the most important path attributes. They must be included in every route description in Update messages, and must be processed by each BGP device receiving them.

Well-Known Discretionary A BGP device, if received, must recognize these path attributes, but they may or may not be included in an Update message. Thus, they are optional for a sender of information, but mandatory for a receiver to process.

Optional Transitive These path attributes may be recognized by a BGP router and may be included in an Update message. They must be passed on to other BGP speakers when the route is advertised, even if received by a device that does not recognize the attribute.

Optional Nontransitive Optional attributes that may be recognized by a BGP device and may be included in an Update message. If received by a device that does not recognize the attribute, it is dropped and not passed on to the next router.

> **KEY CONCEPT** Unlike simpler routing protocols that store only limited information about how to reach a network, BGP stores detailed information about complete routes to various networks. This information takes the form of *path attributes* that describe various characteristics of a path (route) through the ASes that connect a router to a destination network.

NOTE *As you might imagine, all well-known attributes are by definition transitive—they must be passed on from one BGP speaker to the next.*

BGP Path Attribute Characteristics

Table 40-3 provides a summary of the characteristics of each of the most common BGP path attributes used to describe the route to a destination. It also provides a summary of the Attribute Type code assigned to each characteristic in BGP Update messages.

Table 40-3: Summary of BGP Path Attributes

BGP Path Attribute	Classification	Attribute Type Value	Description
Origin	Well-Known Mandatory	1	Specifies the origin of the path information. This attribute indicates whether the path came originally from an interior routing protocol, the older exterior routing protocol, or some other source.
AS_Path	Well-Known Mandatory	2	A list of AS numbers that describes the sequence of ASes through which this route description has passed. This is a critically important attribute, since it contains the actual path of ASes to the network. It is used to calculate routes and to detect routing loops.
Next_Hop	Well-Known Mandatory	3	The next-hop router to be used to reach this destination.
Multi_Exit_Disc (MED)	Optional Non-Transitive	4	When a path includes multiple exit or entry points to an AS, this value may be used as a metric to discriminate between them (that is, choose one exit or entry point over the others).
Local_Pref	Well-Known Discretionary	5	Used in communication between BGP speakers in the same AS to indicate the level of preference for a particular route.
Atomic_Aggregate	Well-Known Discretionary	6	In certain circumstances, a BGP speaker may receive a set of overlapping routes whereby one is more specific than the other. For example, consider a route to the network 34.15.67.0/24 and to the network 34.15.67.0/26. The latter network is a subset of the former, which makes it more specific. If the BGP speaker uses the less-specific route (in this case, 34.15.67.0/24), it sets this path attribute to a value of 1 to indicate that this was done.
Aggregator	Optional Transitive	7	Contains the AS number and BGP ID of the router that performed route aggregation; used for troubleshooting.

Some of these path attributes are straightforward; others are fairly cryptic and probably confusing. Delving into any more detail on the path attributes leads us into a full-blown description of detailed inter-AS route calculations. We'll look at that to some degree in the next section.

BGP Route Determination and the BGP Decision Process

You have now looked at the fundamentals of how BGP devices store and manage information about routes to networks. This included an overview of the four route information management activities performed by BGP speakers: route storage, update, selection, and advertisement. Route storage is the function of the RIB in each BGP speaker. Path attributes are the mechanism by which BGP stores details about routes and also describes those details to BGP peers.

BGP Decision Process Phases

As you have seen, the RIB also contains sections for holding input information received from BGP peers and for holding output information that each BGP device wants to send to those peers. The functions of route update, selection, and advertisement are concerned with analyzing this input information. They also decide what to include in the local database, update that database, and then choose what routes to send from it to peer devices. In BGP, a mechanism called the *decision process* is responsible for these tasks. It consists of three overall phases:

Phase 1 Each route received from a BGP speaker in a neighboring AS is analyzed and assigned a preference level. The routes are then ranked according to preference and the best one for each network advertised to other BGP speakers within the AS.

Phase 2 The best route for each destination is selected from the incoming data based on preference levels, and it's used to update the local routing information base (the Loc-RIB).

Phase 3 Routes in the Loc-RIB are selected to be sent to neighboring BGP speakers in other ASes.

Criteria for Assigning Preferences to Routes

Obviously, if a BGP speaker only knows of a single route to a network, it will install and use that route (assuming there are no problems with it). The assigning of preferences among routes becomes important only when more than one route has been received by a BGP speaker for a particular network. Preferences can be determined based on a number of different criteria. The following are a few typical ones:

- The number of ASes between the router and the network (fewer generally being better).
- The existence of certain policies that may make certain routes unusable; for example, a route may pass through an AS that as the BGP speaker is not willing to trust with its data.
- The origin of the path—that is, where it came from.

In the case where a set of routes to the same network are all calculated to have the same preference, a tie-breaking scheme is used to select from among them. Additional logic is used to handle special circumstances, such as the case of overlapping networks (see the description of the Atomic_Aggregate path attribute in Table 40-3 for an example of this).

The selection of routes for dissemination to other routers in phase 3 is based on a rather complex algorithm that I cannot explain adequately here. Route advertisement is guided by the routing policies I discussed earlier in this chapter.

Different rules are used to select routes for advertising to internal peers compared to external peers.

KEY CONCEPT The method used by a BGP speaker to determine what new routes to accept from its peers and what routes to advertise back them is called the *BGP decision process*. It is a complex algorithm in three phases that involves the computation of the best route based on both preexisting and incoming path information.

Limitations on BGP's Ability to Select Efficient Routes

When considering route selection, it's very important to remember that BGP is a routing protocol that operates at the inter-AS level. Thus, routes are chosen between ASes, not at the level of individual routers within an AS. So, for example, when BGP stores information about the path to a network, it stores it as a sequence of ASes, not a sequence of specific routers.

BGP cannot deal with individual routers in an AS because, by definition, the details of what happens within an AS are supposed to be hidden from the outside world. It doesn't know the structure of ASes outside its own. This has an important implication for how BGP selects routes: BGP cannot guarantee that it will pick the fastest, lowest-cost route to every network. It can select a route that minimizes the number of ASes that lie between itself and a particular network, but, of course, ASes are not all the same. Some ASes are large and consist of many slow links; others are small and fast. Choosing a route through two of the latter types of AS will be better than choosing a route through one of the former, but BGP can't know that. Policies can be used to influence AS selection to some extent, but in general, since BGP doesn't know what happens in an AS, it cannot guarantee the efficiency of a route overall. (Incidentally, this is the reason why there is no general cost or distance path attribute in BGP.)

KEY CONCEPT As an exterior routing protocol, BGP operates at the AS level. Its routes are calculated based on paths between ASes, not individual routers. Since BGP, by definition, does not know the internal structure of routers within an AS, it cannot know for certain the cost to send a datagram across a given AS. This means that BGP cannot always guarantee that it will select the absolute lowest-cost route between any two networks.

Originating New Routes and Withdrawing Unreachable Routes

Naturally, a facility exists to allow BGP speakers to originate new routes to networks. A BGP speaker may obtain knowledge about a new route from an interior routing protocol on an AS to which it is directly attached, and then it may choose to share this information with other ASes. It will create a new entry in its RIB for this network and then send information about it out to other BGP peers.

BGP also includes a mechanism for advertising routes it cannot reach. These are called unfeasible or withdrawn routes and are mentioned in Update messages to indicate that a router can no longer reach the specific network.

BGP General Operation and Messaging

In the previous sections, you have seen how BGP stores information about routes and uses it to determine paths to various networks. Let's now take a high-level look at how BGP operates in general terms. Like many other protocols covered in this book, BGP's operation can be described primarily in the form of messaging. The use of messages is the means by which route information is communicated between BGP peers. This eventually allows the knowledge of how to reach networks to spread throughout the entire internetwork.

Speaker Designation and Connection Establishment

Before messaging can begin, BGP speakers must be designated and then linked together. The BGP standard does not specify how neighboring speakers are determined; this must be done outside the protocol. Once accomplished, ASes are connected into a BGP-enabled internetwork. Topological linking provides the physical connection and the means for datagrams to flow between ASes. At this point, the dance floor is prepared, but nobody is dancing; BGP can function but isn't yet in operation.

BGP operation begins with BGP peers forming a transport protocol connection. BGP uses TCP for its reliable transport layer, so the two BGP speakers establish a TCP session that remains in place during the course of the subsequent message exchange. When this is done, each BGP speaker sends a BGP Open message. This message is like an invitation to dance, and it begins the process of setting up the BGP link between the devices. In this message, each router identifies itself and its AS, and also tells its peer what parameters it would like to use for the link. This includes an exchange of authentication parameters. Assuming that each device finds the contents of its peer's Open message acceptable, it acknowledges it with a Keepalive message, and the BGP session begins.

Under normal circumstances, most BGP speakers will maintain simultaneous sessions with more than one other BGP speaker, both within the speaker's own AS and outside its AS. Links between ASes are what enable BGP routers to learn how to route through the internetwork. Links within the AS are important to ensure that each BGP speaker in the AS maintains consistent information.

Route Information Exchange

Assuming the link is initialized, the two peers begin an ongoing process of telling each other what they know about networks and how to reach them. Each BGP speaker encodes information from its RIBs into BGP Update messages. These messages contain lists of known network addresses, as well as information about paths to various networks, as described in the form of path attributes, as you have already seen. This information is then used for the route determination, as described in the preceding section.

When a link is first set up between two peers, those peers ensure that each router holds complete information by exchanging their complete routing tables. Subsequently, Update messages are sent. They contain only incremental updates about routes that have changed. Exchanging only updated information as needed reduces unnecessary bandwidth on the network, thereby making BGP more efficient than it would be if it sent full routing table information on a regular basis.

Connectivity Maintenance

The TCP session between BGP speakers can be kept open for a very long time. Update messages need to be sent only when changes occur to routes, which are usually infrequent. This means many seconds may elapse between the transmission of Update messages.

To ensure that the peers maintain contact with each other, they both send Keepalive messages on a regular basis when they don't have other information to send. These are null messages that contain no data and just tell the peer device "I'm still here." These messages are sent infrequently—no more often than one per second—but regularly enough that the peers won't think the session was interrupted.

Error Reporting

The last type of BGP message is the BGP Notification message. This is an error message; it tells a peer that a problem occurred and describes the nature of the error condition. After sending a BGP Notification message, the device that sent it will terminate the BGP connection between the peers. A new connection will then need to be negotiated, possibly after the problem that led to the Notification message has been corrected.

> **KEY CONCEPT** BGP is implemented through the exchange of four different message types between BGP speakers. A BGP session begins with a TCP connection being established between two routers and each sending an Open message to the other. BGP Update messages are the primary mechanism by which routing information is exchanged between devices. Small BGP Keepalive messages are used to maintain communication between devices between periods when they need to exchange information. Finally, Notification messages are used for problem reporting.

BGP Detailed Messaging, Operation, and Message Formats

So far, I have discussed the concepts and general operation of the BGP. To get a better understanding of exactly how BGP works, it is helpful to take a detailed look at its four different message types—Open, Update, Keepalive, and Notification—and how they are used. As we do this, we can examine the fields in each message type, so that you can comprehend not just the way that messaging is accomplished, but the way that routing data is actually communicated. Let's begin with a description of common attributes of BGP message generation and transport, and the general format used for all BGP messages.

BGP Message Generation and Transport

Each router running BGP generates messages to implement the various functions of the protocol. Some of these messages are created on a regular basis by the BGP software during the course of its normal operation. These are generally controlled by timers that are set and counted down to cause them to be sent. Other messages are sent in response to messages received from BGP peers, possibly after a processing step.

BGP is different from most other routing protocols in that it was designed from the start to operate using a reliable method of message delivery. TCP is present in the software of every Internet Protocol (IP) router, thereby making it the obvious choice for reliable data communication in a TCP/IP Internet, and that's what BGP uses. Routing protocols are usually considered part of layer 3, but this one runs over a layer 4 protocol, thereby making BGP a good example of why architectural models are best used only as a guideline.

TCP provides numerous advantages to BGP by taking care of most of the details of session setup and management, thereby allowing BGP to focus on the data it needs to send. TCP takes care of session setup and negotiation, flow control, congestion handling, and any necessary retransmissions of lost messages, thereby ensuring that messages are received and acknowledged. BGP uses well-known TCP port 179 for connections.

BGP General Message Format

The use of TCP also has an interesting impact on the way BGP messages are structured. One thing that stands out when you look at the BGP message format (as you will see shortly) is that a BGP message can have an odd number of bytes. Most routing protocols are sized in units of 4 or 8 bytes, but since TCP sends data as a stream of octets, there is no need for BGP messages to break on a 32-bit or 64-bit boundary. The other impact is the need of a special Marker field to help ensure that BGP messages can be differentiated from each other in the TCP stream (more about this in a moment).

Like most messaging protocols, BGP uses a common message format for each of its four message types. Each BGP message is conceptually divided into a header and a body (called the *data portion* in the BGP standard). The header has three fields and is fixed in length at 19 bytes. The body is variable in length and is omitted entirely in Keepalive messages, since it is not needed for them.

The general format for all BGP message types is shown in Table 40-4 and illustrated in Figure 40-2.

Table 40-4: BGP General Message Format

Field Name	Size (Bytes)	Description
Marker	16	This large field at the start of each BGP message is used for synchronization and authentication.
Length	2	The total length of the message in bytes, including the fields of the header. The minimum value of this field is 19 for a Keepalive message; it may be as high as 4096.
Type	1	Indicates the BGP message type: 1 = Open 2 = Update 3 = Notification 4 = Keepalive
Message Body/ Data Portion	Variable	Contains the specific fields used to implement each message type for Open, Update, and Notification messages.

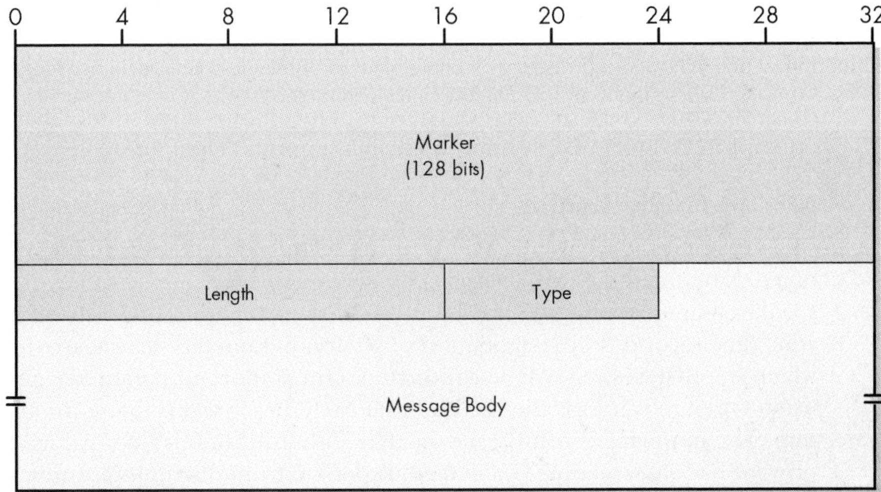

Figure 40-2: *BGP general message format*

The Marker field is the most interesting one in the BGP message format. It is used for both synchronization and authentication. BGP uses a single TCP session to send many messages in a row. TCP is a stream-oriented transport protocol that sends bytes across the link without any knowledge of what the bytes represent. This means that the protocol using TCP is responsible for deciding where the line is drawn between data units—in this case, BGP messages.

Normally, the Length field tells each BGP device where to draw the line between the end of one message and the start of the next. However, it is possible that, due to various conditions, a device might lose track of where the message boundary is. The Marker field is filled with a recognizable pattern that clearly marks the start of each message; BGP peers keep synchronized by looking for that pattern.

Before a BGP connection is established, the Marker field is filled with all ones. Thus, this is the pattern used for Open messages. Once a BGP session is negotiated, if agreement is reached on an authentication method between the two devices, the Marker field takes on the additional role of authentication. Instead of looking for a Marker field containing all ones, BGP devices look for a pattern generated using the agreed-upon authentication method. Detection of this pattern simultaneously synchronizes the devices and ensures that messages are authentic.

In extreme cases, BGP peers may be unable to maintain synchronization, and if so, a Notification message is generated and the session is closed. This will also happen if the Marker field contains the wrong data when authentication is enabled.

> **KEY CONCEPT** All four BGP message types use a general message format that contains three fixed header fields—Marker, Length, and Type—and room for a message body that differs for each message type. The large Marker field is used to denote the start of a new BGP message, and it is also used to facilitate the BGP authentication method.

BGP Connection Establishment: Open Messages

Before a BGP session can be used to exchange routing information, a connection must first be established between BGP peers. This process begins with the creation of a TCP connection between the devices. Once this is done, the BGP devices will attempt to create a BGP session by exchanging BGP Open messages.

BGP Open Message Functions

The Open message has two main purposes. The first is identification and initiation of a link between the two devices; it allows one peer to tell the other, "I am a BGP speaker named X on AS Y, and I want to start exchanging BGP information with you." The second is the negotiation of session parameters. These are the terms by which the BGP session will be conducted. One important parameter negotiated using Open messages is the method that each device wants to use for authentication. The importance of BGP means that authentication is essential in order to prevent bad information or a malicious person from disrupting routes.

Each BGP receiving an Open message processes it. If the message's contents are acceptable, including the parameters the other device wants to use, it responds with a Keepalive message as an acknowledgment. Each peer must send an Open message and receive a Keepalive acknowledgment for the BGP link to be initialized. If either is not willing to accept the terms of the Open message, the link is not established. In that case, a Notification message may be sent to convey the nature of the problem.

BGP Open Message Format

The specific format for BGP Open messages is shown in Table 40-5 and Figure 40-3.

Table 40-5: BGP Open Message Format

Field Name	Size (Bytes)	Description
Marker	16	This large field at the start of each BGP message is used for synchronization and authentication.
Length	2	The total length of the message in bytes, including the fields of the header. Open messages are variable in length.
Type	1	BGP message type; value is 1 for Open messages.
Version	1	Indicates the BGP version the sender of the Open message is using. This field allows devices to reject connections with devices using versions that they may not be capable of understanding. The current value is 4, for BGP-4, and is used by most, if not all, current BGP implementations.
My Autonomous System	2	Identifies the AS number of the sender of the Open message. AS numbers are centrally managed across the Internet in a manner similar to how IP addresses are administered.
Hold Time	2	The number of seconds that this device proposes to use for the BGP hold timer, which specifies how long a BGP peer will allow the connection to be left silent between receipt of BGP messages. A BGP device may refuse a connection if it doesn't like the value that its peer is suggesting; usually, however, the two devices agree to use the smaller of the values suggested by each device. The value must be at least 3 seconds, or 0. If 0, this specifies that the hold timer is not used. See the Keepalive message discussion later in this chapter for more on how the hold timer is used.

(continued)

Table 40-5: BGP Open Message Format (continued)

Field Name	Size (Bytes)	Description
BGP Identifier	4	Identifies the specific BGP speaker. You'll recall that IP addresses are associated with interfaces, not devices, so each router will have at least two IP addresses. Normally, the BGP identifier is chosen as one of these addresses. Once chosen, this identifier is used for all BGP communications with BGP peers. This includes BGP peers on the interface from which the identifier was chosen, and also BGP peers on other interfaces as well. So, if a BGP speaker with two interfaces has addresses IP1 and IP2, it will choose one as its identifier and use it on both of its interfaces.
Opt Parm Len	1	The number of bytes used for Optional Parameters (see the following entry). If 0, no optional parameters are in this message.
Optional Parameters	Variable	Allows the Open message to communicate any number of extra parameters during BGP session setup. Each parameter is encoded using a rather standard type/length/value triple, as shown in Table 40-6.

Table 40-6: BGP Open Message Optional Parameters

Subfield Name	Size (Bytes)	Description
Parm Type	1	Parameter Type: The type of the optional parameter. At present, only one value is defined, 1, for Authentication Information.
Parm Length	1	Parameter Length: Specifies the length of the Parameter Value subfield (thus, this value is the length of the entire parameter, less 2).
Parm Value	Variable	Parameter Value: The value of the parameter being communicated.

BGP Open messages currently use only one optional parameter: Authentication Information. Its Parameter Value subfield contains a one-byte Authentication Code sub-subfield, which specifies the type of authentication a device wishes to use. Following this is a variable-length Authentication Data sub-subfield. The Authentication Code specifies how authentication is to be performed, including the meaning of the Authentication Data field, and the manner in which Marker fields are to be calculated.

KEY CONCEPT BGP sessions begin with each peer in a connection sending the other a BGP Open message. The purpose of this message is to establish contact between devices, identify the sender of the message and its AS, and negotiate important parameters that dictate how the session will be conducted.

BGP Route Information Exchange: Update Messages

Once BGP speakers have made contact and a link has been established using Open messages, the devices begin the actual process of exchanging routing information. Each BGP router uses the BGP decision process described earlier in this chapter to select certain routes to be advertised to its peer. This information is then placed into BGP Update messages, which are sent to every BGP device for which a session has been established. These messages are the way that network reachability knowledge is propagated around the internetwork.

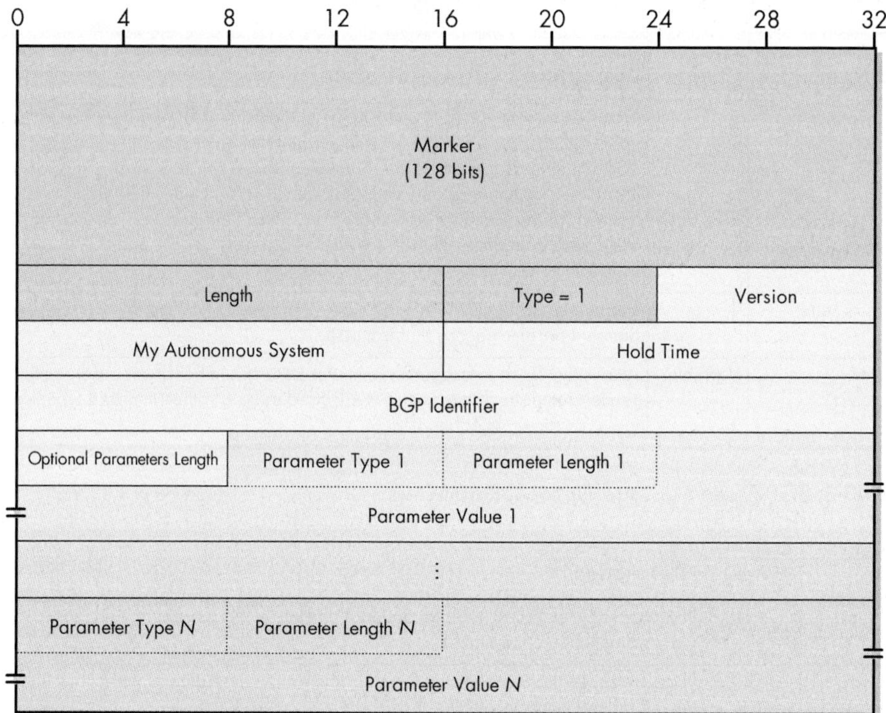

Figure 40-3: *BGP Open message format*

BGP Update Message Contents

Each Update message contains either one or both of the following:

Route Advertisement The characteristics of a single route.

Route Withdrawal A list of networks that are no longer reachable.

Only one route can be advertised in an Update message, but several can be withdrawn. This is because withdrawing a route is simple; it requires just the address of the network for which the route is being removed. In contrast, a route advertisement requires a fairly complex set of path attributes to be described, which takes up a significant amount of space. (Note that it is possible for an Update message to specify only withdrawn routes and not advertise a route at all.)

BGP Update Message Format

Because of the amount of information it contains and the complexity of that information, BGP Update messages use one of the most complicated structures in TCP/IP. The basic structure of the message is described in Table 40-7 and illustrated in Figure 40-4. As you can see in that table, several of the fields have their own substructure. The Path Attributes field has a complex substructure, which I have shown separately in other tables.

Table 40-7: BGP Update Message Format

Field Name	Size (Bytes)	Description
Marker	16	This large field at the start of each BGP message is used for synchronization and authentication.
Length	2	The total length of the message in bytes, including the fields of the header. Update messages are variable in length.
Type	1	BGP message type; value is 2 for Update messages.
Unfeasible Routes Length	2	The length of the Withdrawn Routes field, in bytes. If 0, no routes are being withdrawn and the Withdrawn Routes field is omitted.
Withdrawn Routes	Variable	Specifies the addresses of networks for which routes are being withdrawn from use. Each address is specified using the two subfields. The 1-byte Length field is the number of bits in the IP address Prefix subfield that are significant. The variable-length Prefix subfield is the IP address prefix of the network whose route is being withdrawn. If the number of bits in the prefix is not a multiple of 8, this field is padded with zeros so that it falls on a byte boundary. The length of this field is 1 byte if the preceding Length field is 8 or less; 2 bytes if it is 9 to 16; 3 bytes if it is 17 to 24; and 4 bytes if it is 25 or greater.
Total Path Attribute Length	2	The length of the Path Attributes field, in bytes. If 0, indicates no route is being advertised in this message, so Path Attributes and Network Layer Reachability Information are omitted.
Path Attributes	Variable	Describes the path attributes of the route advertised. Since some attributes require more information than others, attributes are described using a flexible structure that minimizes message size compared to using fixed fields that would often be empty. Unfortunately, it also makes the field structure confusing. Each attribute has the subfields shown in Table 40-8.
Network Layer Reachability Information (NLRI)	Variable	Contains a list of IP address prefixes for the route being advertised. Each address is specified using the same general structure as the one used for Withdrawn Routes. The 1-byte Length subfield is the number of bits in the Prefix subfield that are significant. The variable-length Prefix subfield is the IP address prefix of the network whose route is being advertised. If the number of bits in the prefix is not a multiple of 8, this field is padded with zeros so that it falls on a byte boundary. The length of this field is 1 byte if the preceding Length field is 8 or less; 2 bytes if it is 9 to 16; 3 bytes if it is 17 to 24; and 4 bytes if it is25 or greater. Unlike most of the other fields in the Update message, the length of the NLRI field is not explicitly stated. It is computed from the overall message Length field, minus the lengths of the other fields that are explicitly specified.

Table 40-8: BGP Update Message Path Attributes

Subfield Name	Size (Bytes)	Description
Attribute Type	2	Defines the type of attribute and describes it. This subfield itself has a two-level substructure, with Attribute Type flags and Attribute Type codes, so it won't even fit it here! See Tables 40-9 and 40-10 for details.
Attribute Length	1 or 2	The length of the attribute in bytes. This field is normally 1 byte, thereby allowing for fields with a length up to 255 bytes. For longer attributes, the Extended Length flag is set (see Table 40-9), indicating that this Attribute Length field is 2 bytes, for attributes up to 65,535 bytes.
Attribute Value	Variable	The value of the attribute. The size and meaning of this field depends on the type of path attribute. For example, for an Origin attribute, it is a single integer value indicating the origin of the route; for an AS_Path attribute, this field contains a variable-length list of the ASes in the path to the network.

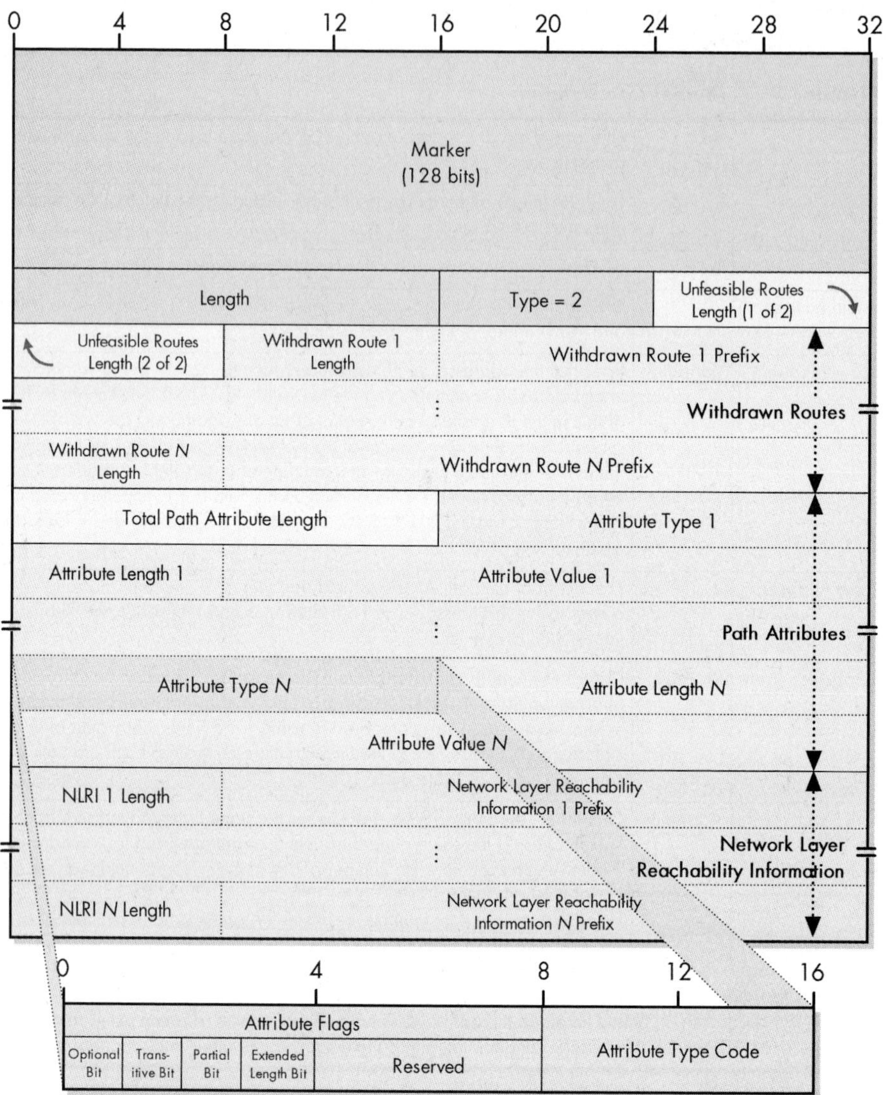

Figure 40-4: BGP Update message format *This diagram shows the complete BGP Update message format, including a set of withdrawn routes, path attributes, and NLRI entries. The exploded view shows the substructure of the Attribute Type subfield of the Path Attributes, as described in Tables 40-9 and 40-10.*

Table 40-9 shows the structure of the Attribute Flags sub-subfield of the Attribute Type subfield of the Path Attributes field. This subfield contains a set of flags that describe the nature of the attribute and how to process it. You may need to refer to the path attributes description in the "BGP Path Attributes and Algorithm Overview" section earlier in this chapter to make sense of these flags.

Table 40-9: BGP Update Message Attribute Flags

Sub-Sub-Subfield Name	Size (Bytes)	Description
Optional	1/8 (1 bit)	Set to 1 for optional attributes; 0 for well-known attributes.
Transitive	1/8 (1 bit)	Set to 1 for optional transitive attributes; 0 for optional nontransitive attributes. Always set to 1 for well-known attributes.
Partial	1/8 (1 bit)	When 1, indicates that information about an optional transitive attribute is partial. This means that since it was optional and transitive, one or more of the routers that passed the path along did not implement that attribute but was forced to pass it along, so information about it may be missing (not supplied by the routers that didn't recognize it but just passed along). If 0, it means information is complete. This bit has meaning only for optional transitive attributes; for well-known or nontransitive attributes, it is 0.
Extended Length	1/8 (1 bit)	Set to 1 for long attributes to indicate that the Attribute Length field is 2 bytes in size. Normally 0, meaning the Attribute Length field is a single byte.
Reserved	4/8 (4 bits)	Set to 0 and ignored.

The Attribute Type Code sub-subfield of the Attribute Type subfield of the Path Attributes field contains a number that identifies the attribute type. Table 40-10 shows the current values.

Table 40-10: BGP Update Message Attribute Type Codes

Value	Attribute Type
1	Origin
2	AS_Path
3	Next_Hop
4	Multi_Exit_Disc (MED)
5	Local_Pref
6	Atomic_Aggregate
7	Aggregator

It may seem confusing that there can be more than one prefix in the Network Layer Reachability Information (NLRI) field, even though I said earlier that an Update message advertises only one route. There is, in fact, no inconsistency here. A single route may be associated with more than one networks; to put it another way, multiple networks may have the same path and path attributes. In that case, specifying multiple network prefixes in the same Update message is more efficient than generating a new one for each network.

KEY CONCEPT The most important message type in BGP is the Update message, which is used to send detailed information about routes between BGP devices. It uses a complex structure that allows a BGP speaker to efficiently specify new routes, update existing ones, and withdraw routes that are no longer valid. Each message may include the full description of one existing route and may also withdraw from use a list of multiple routes.

BGP Connectivity Maintenance: Keepalive Messages

Once a BGP connection is established using Open messages, BGP peers will initially use Update messages to send each other a large amount of routing information. They will then settle into a routine in which the BGP session is maintained, but Update messages are sent only when needed. Since these updates correspond to route changes, and route changes are normally infrequent, this means many seconds may elapse between the receipt of consecutive Update messages.

The BGP Hold Timer and Keepalive Message Interval

While a BGP peer is waiting to hear the next Update message, it remains sort of like a person who has been put on hold on the telephone. Now seconds may not seem like much to us, but to a computer, they are a very long time. Like you, a BGP speaker that is put on hold for too long might become impatient and might start to wonder if maybe the other guy hung up. Computers don't get offended at being put on hold, but they might wonder if perhaps a problem arose that led to the connection being interrupted.

To keep track of how long it has been on hold, each BGP device maintains a special *hold timer*. This hold timer is set to an initial value each time its peer sends a BGP message. The timer then counts down until the next message is received, and then it is reset. If the hold timer ever expires, the connection is assumed to have been interrupted and the BGP session is terminated.

The length of the hold timer is negotiated as part of session setup using Open messages. It must be at least three seconds long, or may be negotiated as a value of zero. If zero, the hold timer is not used; this means the devices are infinitely patient and don't care how much time elapses between messages.

To ensure that the timer doesn't expire even when no Update messages need to be sent for a long while, each peer periodically sends a BGP Keepalive message. The name says it all: The message just keeps the BGP connection alive. The rate at which Keepalive messages is sent depends on the implementation, but the standard recommends that they be sent with an interval of one-third the value of the hold timer. So if the hold timer has a value of three seconds, each peer sends a Keepalive message every second (unless it needs to send some other message type in that second). To prevent excess bandwidth use, Keepalive messages must be sent no more often than once per second, so that is the minimum interval, even if the hold timer is shorter than three seconds.

BGP Keepalive Message Format

The point of a Keepalive message is the message itself; there's no data to be communicated. In fact, we want to keep the message short and sweet. Thus, it is really a dummy message that contains only a BGP header—a nice change after that incredibly long Update message format! The format of the Keepalive message is shown in Table 40-11 and Figure 40-5.

Table 40-11: BGP Keepalive Message Format

Field Name	Size (Bytes)	Description
Marker	16	This large field at the start of each BGP message is used for synchronization and authentication.
Length	2	The total length of the message in bytes, including the fields of the header. Keepalive messages are fixed in length at 19 bytes.
Type	1	BGP message type; value is 4 for Keepalive messages.

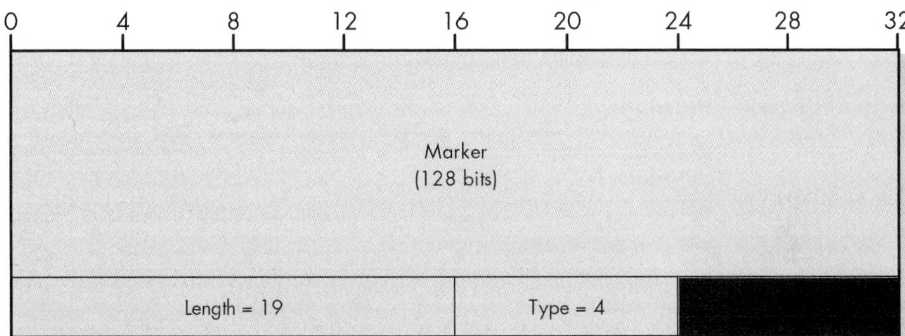

Figure 40-5: BGP Keepalive message format

There is also a special use for Keepalive messages: They acknowledge the receipt of a valid Open message during the initial BGP session setup.

> **KEY CONCEPT** BGP Keepalive messages are sent periodically during idle periods when no real information needs to be sent between connected BGP speakers. They serve only to keep the session alive, and thus contain only a BGP header and no data.

BGP Error Reporting: Notification Messages

Once established, a BGP session will remain open for a considerable period of time, allowing routing information to be exchanged between devices on a regular basis. During the course of operation, certain error conditions may crop up that may interfere with normal communication between BGP peers.

BGP Notification Message Functions

Some of the error conditions that arise are serious enough that the BGP session must be terminated. When this occurs, the device detecting the error will inform its peer of the nature of the problem by sending it a BGP Notification message, and then it will close the connection.

Of course, having someone tell you, "I found an error, so I quit" is not of much value. Therefore, the BGP Notification message contains a number of fields that provide information about the nature of the error that caused the message to be sent. This includes a set of primary error codes as well as subcodes within some of these error codes. Depending on the nature of the error, an additional data field may also be included to aid in diagnosing the problem.

In addition to the use of Notification messages to convey the occurrence of an error, this message type is also used for other purposes. For example, one may be sent if two devices cannot agree on how to negotiate a session, which isn't, strictly speaking, an error. A Notification message is also used to allow a device to tear down a BGP session for reasons that have nothing to do with an error.

BGP Notification Message Format

The format for the BGP Notification messages is detailed in Table 40-12 and illustrated in Figure 40-6.

Table 40-12: BGP Notification Message Format

Field Name	Size (Bytes)	Description
Marker	16	This large field at the start of each BGP message is used for synchronization and authentication.
Length	2	The total length of the message in bytes, including the fields of the header. Notification messages are variable in length.
Type	1	BGP message type; value is 3 for Notification messages.
Error Code	1	Specifies the general class of the error. Table 40-13 shows the possible error types with a brief description of each.
Error Subcode	1	Provides a more specific indication of the cause of the error for three of the Error Code values. The possible values of this field for each Error Code value are shown in Table 40-14.
Data	Variable	Contains additional information to help diagnose the error. Its meaning depends on the type of error specified in the Error Code and Error Subcode fields. In most cases, this field is filled in with whatever bad value caused the error to occur. For example, for "Message Header Error / Bad Message Type," the value of the bad Type field is placed here.

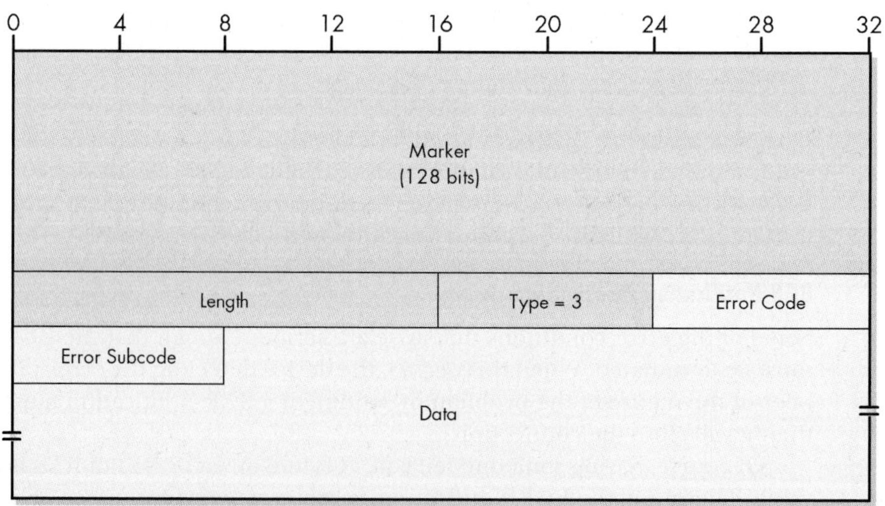

Figure 40-6: BGP Notification message format

Tables 40-13 and 40-14 show the values permitted for the Error Code and Error Subcode fields, respectively, and thus provide a good summary of the types of errors that Notification messages can report. They also demonstrate the other nonerror uses of the message type.

Table 40-13: BGP Notification Message Error Codes

Error Code Value	Code Name	Description
1	Message Header Error	A problem was detected either with the contents or length of the BGP header. The Error Subcode field provides more details on the nature of the problem.
2	Open Message Error	A problem was found in the body of an Open message. The Error Subcode field describes the problem in more detail. Note that authentication failures or the inability to agree on a parameter such as hold time are included here.
3	Update Message Error	A problem was found in the body of an Update message. Again, the Error Subcode field provides more information. Many of the problems that fall under this code are related to issues detected in the routing data or path attributes sent in the Update message, so these messages provide feedback about such problems to the device sending the erroneous data.
4	Hold Timer Expired	A message was not received before the hold time expired. See the description of the Keepalive message earlier in this chapter for details on this timer.
5	Finite State Machine Error	The BGP finite state machine refers to the mechanism by which the BGP software on a peer moves from one operating state to another based on events (see the TCP finite state machine description in Chapter 47 for some background on this concept). If an event occurs that is unexpected for the state the peer is currently in, it will generate this error.
6	Cease	Used when a BGP device wants to break the connection to a peer for a reason not related to any of the error conditions described by the other codes.

Table 40-14: BGP Notification Message Error Subcodes

Error Type	Error Subcode Value	Subcode Name	Description
Message Header Error (Error Code 1)	1	Connection Not Synchronized	The expected value in the Marker field was not found, indicating that the connection has become unsynchronized. See the description of the Marker field in Table 40-12.
	2	Bad Message Length	The message was less than 19 bytes, greater than 4096 bytes, or not consistent with what was expected for the message type.
	3	Bad Message Type	The Type field of the message contains an invalid value.

(continued)

Table 40-14: BGP Notification Message Error Subcodes (continued)

Error Type	Error Subcode Value	Subcode Name	Description
Open Message Error (Error Code 2)	1	Unsupported Version Number	The device does not "speak" the version number its peer is trying to use.
	2	Bad Peer AS	The router doesn't recognize the peer's AS number or is not willing to communicate with it.
	3	Bad BGP Identifier	The BGP Identifier field is invalid.
	4	Unsupported Optional Parameter	The Open message contains an optional parameter that the recipient of the message doesn't understand.
	5	Authentication Failure	The data in the Authentication Information optional parameter could not be authenticated.
	6	Unacceptable Hold Time	The router refuses to open a session because the proposed hold time its peer specified in its Open message is unacceptable.
Update Message Error (Error Code 3)	1	Malformed Attribute List	The overall structure of the message's path attributes is incorrect, or an attribute has appeared twice.
	2	Unrecognized Well-Known Attribute	One of the mandatory well-known attributes was not recognized.
	3	Missing Well-Known Attribute	One of the mandatory well-known attributes was not specified.
	4	Attribute Flags Error	An attribute has a flag set to a value that conflicts with the attribute's type code.
	5	Attribute Length Error	The length of an attribute is incorrect.
	6	Invalid Origin Attribute	The Origin attribute has an undefined value.
	7	AS Routing Loop	A routing loop was detected.
	8	Invalid Next_Hop Attribute	The Next_Hop attribute is invalid.
	9	Optional Attribute Error	An error was detected in an optional attribute.
	10	Invalid Network Field	The Network Layer Reachability Information field is incorrect.
	11	Malformed AS_Path	The AS_Path attribute is incorrect.

Note that, perhaps ironically, no mechanism exists to report an error in a Notification message itself. This is likely because the connection is normally terminated after such a message is sent.

KEY CONCEPT BGP Notification messages are used for error reporting between BGP peers. Each message contains an Error Code field that indicates what type of problem occurred. For certain Error Code fields, an Error Subcode field provides additional details about the specific nature of the problem. Despite these field names, Notification messages are also used for other types of special nonerror communication, such as terminating a BGP connection.

41

OTHER ROUTING PROTOCOLS

The Routing Information Protocol (RIP), Open Shortest Path First (OSPF), and Border Gateway Protocol (BGP)—detailed in the preceding chapters—are the three most well-known routing protocols used in the TCP/IP protocol suite. But there are several other TCP/IP routing protocols, and they fall into one of two categories. Some protocols are no longer in use today but are nevertheless interesting from a historical perspective. Others are proprietary RIP and OSPF alternatives that you may occasionally encounter in today's networking world.

In this chapter, I provide a brief description of five additional TCP/IP routing protocols. I begin with a look at two obsolete interior routing protocols that played an important role in the early Internet: the Gateway-to-Gateway Protocol (GGP) and the HELLO Protocol. I then describe two interior routing protocols (developed by Cisco Systems) that are sometimes seen in the industry today as alternatives to RIP and OSPF: the Interior Gateway Routing Protocol (IGRP) and the Enhanced Interior Gateway Routing Protocol (EIGRP). I conclude with a discussion of the Exterior Gateway Protocol (EGP), the exterior routing protocol that preceded BGP.

TCP/IP Gateway-to-Gateway Protocol (GGP)

In Chapter 37, I described the evolution of TCP/IP routing architectures. The modern Internet is based on the concept of independent autonomous systems (ASes), which run interior routing protocols within them and exterior routing protocols between them. The early Internet, however, was somewhat simpler. It consisted of a relatively small number of core routers that carried detailed information about the Internet as a whole, as well as noncore routers that knew only partial information about the whole internetwork and were located around the core.

These core routers used a special routing protocol to communicate called the *Gateway-to-Gateway Protocol (GGP)*. Bolt, Beranek, and Newman, one of the pioneers of the Internet and TCP/IP, originally developed GGP in the early 1980s. It was documented in RFC 823, "The DARPA Internet Gateway," published September 1982. This protocol is now obsolete, but it played an important role in the early Internet by introducing certain concepts that developers used in later routing protocols.

GGP is similar in general operation to RIP (described in Chapter 38) in that it uses a distance-vector algorithm to determine the best routes between devices. Like RIP, the metric is a simple hop count, so GGP will select a route with the shortest number of hops. Although you have seen that hop count is not always the best metric of cost for a router in RIP, it was actually a pretty good method of route determination back then. This is because the early Internet used both computers and links that would be considered glacially slow by today's standards, thereby making each hop fairly expensive (in terms of the time required to send data) compared to modern routing.

A router using GGP initially starts out in a null state. It then tests the status of its local networks by seeing if it can send and receive messages on the network. Every 15 seconds, the router sends a GGP Echo message to each of its neighbors. If the neighbor receives the message, it responds with a GGP Echo Reply message. The router sending the Echo messages considers the neighbor up if it receives replies to a certain percentage of messages (the default is 50 percent).

NOTE *These messages serve a similar function to the Internet Control Message Protocol version 4 (ICMPv4) Echo and Echo Reply messages (described in Chapter 33), but are not the same.*

Actual routing information is communicated by sending GGP Routing Update messages. These are similar in nature to RIP Response messages used in RIP. Each Routing Update message contains the information in the sending router's routing table, which specifies the networks the router can reach and what the cost (in hops) will be for each.

A router that receives a Routing Update message knows that it can reach the router that sent the update. Because of that, it can reach all of the other routers' reachable networks at the cost of an additional hop. The router uses the information to update its own internal tables of destinations and metrics, and then it sends out its own Routing Update on its own attached networks. This way, it can propagate the information it acquired from other routers on its own networks. This process continues until eventually, routes to all GGP routers spreads across the internetwork, just as this process occurs in RIP.

One interesting difference between GGP and RIP is that in GGP networks and costs aren't sent in pairs. Instead, a GGP router sends its routing table in groups. If it has three networks it can communicate with directly at a cost of 1, it sends those in a group with a distance value of 1. Next, if the GGP router has a few networks it can reach at a cost of 2, it sends those in a group with a distance value of 2, and so on.

Another difference is that GGP Routing Update messages are acknowledged. Each Routing Update message is sent with a sequence number, which ensures that out-of-date information is not propagated. If the Routing Update is received and it has a new sequence number (indicating that it contains recent information), the router processing returns a GGP Acknowledgment message to the originator. If the sequence number indicates the message is stale, a Negative Acknowledgment is sent instead and the message is discarded.

As a distance-vector algorithm using hop count as a metric, GGP shared most of the same pros and cons as RIP. It had simplicity on its side, but it had numerous problems such as slow convergence and the counting to infinity issue. GGP was a much more rudimentary protocol than RIP, however, and did not include many of the features included in RIP to handle such issues, such as split horizon. GGP was also limited to unsubnetted classful networks, due to its age.

When Internet architecture moved to the use of ASes, GGP was obsoleted. While it was an important part of TCP/IP history, it is today not formally considered a part of the TCP/IP protocol suite.

KEY CONCEPT The *Gateway-to-Gateway Protocol (GGP)* was used to communicate route information between core routers on the early Internet. It is a distance-vector protocol that operates in a manner that's very similar to RIP. Each router periodically sends out its routing table to neighboring routers so that each router can learn the cost, in hops, to reach every network in the AS. GGP is now considered a historical protocol and is no longer part of TCP/IP.

The HELLO Protocol (HELLO)

The TCP/IP Internet as we know it today evolved over the course of decades. It began as an experimental research project started by the United States Defense Advanced Research Projects Agency (DARPA or ARPA). Called the ARPAnet, the project grew through the addition of other networks, such as the important NSFnet developed by the National Science Foundation (NSF). The NSFnet backbone grew over the course of many years and was instrumental to the eventual creation of the modern Internet.

The original NSFnet backbone consisted of six Digital Equipment Corporation (absorbed by Compaq years ago) LSI-11 computers located across the United States. These computers ran special software that was colloquially called "fuzzball." This software enabled the computers to function as routers. These fuzzball routers connected various networks to the NSFnet and the ARPAnet.

The six NSFnet routers worked as an AS, and like any AS, used an interior routing protocol to exchange routing information. The routing protocol used in these early routers was called the *HELLO Protocol*. Developed in the early 1980s, it was documented in RFC 891, "DCN Local-Network Protocols," which was published in December 1983. The name *HELLO* is capitalized, but it is not an acronym; it simply refers to the word *hello*, because the protocol uses messages that are sort of analogous to the routers greeting each other.

NOTE *The OSPF routing protocol has a message type called* Hello. *The use of these messages is sometimes referred to as the* Hello protocol. *OSPF is not directly related to the HELLO Protocol described in this section, other than the fact that an AS could use both protocols for routing. OSPF may have borrowed the name Hello from the HELLO Protocol.*

The HELLO Protocol uses a distance-vector algorithm, like RIP and GGP. What's interesting about it, however, is that unlike RIP and GGP, HELLO does not use hop count as a metric. Instead, it attempts to select the best route by assessing network delays and choosing the path with the shortest delay.

One of the key jobs of routers that use HELLO is to compute the time delay required to send and receive datagrams to and from its neighbors. On a regular basis, routers exchange HELLO messages that contain clock and timestamp information. By using a special algorithm to compare the clock value and timestamp in the message to its own clock, a receiving device can compute an estimate for the amount of time it takes to send a datagram over the link.

Like RIP and GGP messages, HELLO messages also contain routing information in the form of pairs of destinations and metrics. These represent places that the sending router is able to reach and a cost to communicate with each one. However, in HELLO, the metric is an estimate of the round-trip delay cost for each destination. This information is added to the computed round-trip delay time for the link over which the message was received, and it is used to update the receiving router's own routing table.

This seems a bit confusing, but is really similar to the way a hop-count distance-vector protocol like RIP works. Router A, which is using RIP to receive an RIP Response message from Router B, knows it can reach every destination Router B can, but at a cost of one extra hop (the hop from Router A to Router B). Similarly, Router A, which receives a HELLO message from Router B, knows it can reach every destination that Router B can, but at an additional cost of the computed delay for the link between Router A and Router B.

In theory, using delay calculations should result in more efficient route selection than simply using a hop-count algorithm, but this comes at the cost of more complexity. This makes HELLO very interesting indeed, especially for a protocol that is more than 20 years old. However, since the latency of a link is often unrelated to its bandwidth, using time delay as a link metric may lead to spurious results.

Furthermore, it is normal for the delay on any link to vary over time; for example, if two routes are similar in cost, fluctuations in the delay for each route could result in rapid changes between routes (a phenomenon sometimes called *route flapping*). Adjustments are needed to the basic overview of the operation of the HELLO Protocol in order to avoid these sorts of problems.

Like other early routing protocols, HELLO does not include anything fancy like authentication. Such features were not needed in the early days of the Internet, when the internetworks were small and could easily be controlled. As the Internet grew, newer routing protocols such as RIP eventually replaced HELLO. It is now considered a historical protocol (in other words, obsolete) and is no longer used.

KEY CONCEPT The *HELLO Protocol* was used on very early routers on the precursors of the Internet to exchange routing information. It is a distance-vector protocol like RIP and GGP, but differs because it uses calculated delay instead of hop count as a metric. Like GGP, it is now considered a historical protocol and is no longer part of TCP/IP.

Interior Gateway Routing Protocol (IGRP)

I greatly prefer universal, open standards to proprietary standards. I explain the reasons why in Chapter 3, which discusses networking standards. I am not alone in this view, and it's no exaggeration to say that much of the success of TCP/IP and the Internet is tied to the fact that they were both developed, and still are being developed, with the open RFC process.

That said, in certain situations, a proprietary protocol can be a benefit and can even achieve considerable success if a minimum of two factors is true:

- There is a lack of a suitable open protocol or a gap in the feature coverage of existing open protocols, creating an opportunity for a proprietary protocol to succeed.
- The proprietary protocol must be either initiated or strongly supported by a big player in the industry. This helps to ensure that other companies will take notice and give the protocol a chance to become a standard.

This situation arose in the 1980s in the world of routing protocols. At that time, the most popular interior routing protocol was RIP, which does a basically good job, but has a number of limitations and problems that are inherent to the protocol and are not easily resolved. In the mid-1980s, open alternatives like OSPF did not yet exist; even if they had, OSPF is much more complex than RIP and therefore sometimes not a good alternative to it.

Cisco Systems—definitely one of the big names in networking, internetworking, and routing—decided to develop a new routing protocol that would be similar to RIP but would provide greater functionality and solve some of RIP's inherent problems. Called the *Interior Gateway Routing Protocol (IGRP)*, it conveniently uses the words *gateway* and *routing* in its name, illustrating that these two words are used interchangeably in internetworking standards. Cisco designed it as a replacement for RIP. It is similar in many ways and keeps RIP's simplicity, one of its key strengths. At the same time, IGRP overcomes two key limitations of RIP: the use of hop count solely as a routing metric and the hop count limit of 15.

Like RIP, IGRP is a distance-vector routing protocol designed for use with an AS, and thus uses the same basic mechanism for route determination. Each router routinely sends out a message on each attached local network that contains a copy of its routing table. This message contains pairs of reachable networks and costs (metrics) to reach each network. A router receiving this message knows it can reach all the networks in the message as long as it can reach the router that sent the message. It computes the cost to reach those networks by adding what it costs to reach the router that sent the message to the networks' costs. The routers update their tables accordingly and send this information out in their next routine update. Eventually, each router in the AS will have information about the cost to reach each network in it.

There's an important difference between RIP and IGRP, however. RIP allows the cost to reach a network to be expressed only in terms of hop count; IGRP provides a much more sophisticated metric. In IGRP, the overall cost to reach a network is computed based on several individual metrics, including internetwork delay, bandwidth, reliability, and load. An administrator can customize the calculation of cost by setting relative weightings to the component metrics that reflect the priorities of that AS. So, if a particular administrator feels that emphasizing reliability over bandwidth would best minimize route cost, he can do this. Such a system provides tremendous flexibility over the rigid hop-count system of RIP. Unlike RIP, IGRP also does not have an inherent limit of 15 hops between networks.

To this basic algorithm, IGRP adds a feature called *multipath routing*. This allows multiple paths between routes to be used automatically, with traffic shared between them. The traffic can either be shared evenly or apportioned unevenly based on the relative cost metric of each path. This provides improved performance and flexibility.

Since IGRP is a distance-vector protocol like RIP, it shares many of RIP's algorithmic issues. Unsurprisingly, then, IGRP must incorporate many of the same stability features as RIP, including the use of split horizon, split horizon with poisoned reverse (in certain circumstances), and the employment of hold-down timers. Like RIP, IGRP also uses timers to control how often updates are sent, how long routers are held down, and how long routes are held in the routing table before they expire.

Cisco originally developed IGRP for Internet Protocol (IP) networks, and since IP is predominant in the industry, these networks are where it is most often seen. IGRP is not specific to IP, however, and can be used with other internetworking protocols if implemented for them. As you will see, Cisco also used IGRP as the basis for an improved routing protocol called EIGRP, which it developed several years after the original.

> **KEY CONCEPT** In the 1980s, Cisco Systems created the *Interior Gateway Routing Protocol (IGRP)* as an improvement over the industry standard protocol, RIP. Like RIP, IGRP is a distance-vector protocol, but it includes several enhancements. Most important, it eliminates the 15-hop limit between routers and provides the ability to use metrics other than hop count to determine optimal routes.

Enhanced Interior Gateway Routing Protocol (EIGRP)

As discussed in the previous section, IGRP represented a substantial improvement over RIP, but like any successful company, Cisco was not content to rest on its laurels. Cisco developers knew that IGRP had significant room for improvement, so they set to work on creating a better version of IGRP in the early 1990s. The result was the *Enhanced Interior Gateway Routing Protocol (EIGRP)*.

Compared to the original protocol, EIGRP is more of an evolution than a revolution. EIGRP is still a distance-vector protocol, but it is more sophisticated than other distance-vector protocols like IGRP or RIP, and it includes certain features that are more often associated with link-state routing protocols like OSPF than distance-vector algorithms. Also, since the Cisco developers realized that many of the organizations that had decided to use EIGRP would be migrating to it from IGRP, they took special steps to ensure compatibility between the two.

The chief differences between IGRP and EIGRP are not in what they do, but how they do it. In an effort to improve the efficiency and speed of route convergence (that is, to improve the agreement between different routers in the internetwork), EIGRP changes the way that routes are calculated. EIGRP is based on a new route calculation algorithm called the *Diffusing Update Algorithm (DUAL)*, developed at SRI International by Dr. J. J. Garcia-Luna-Aceves.

DUAL differs from a typical distance-vector algorithm primarily in that it maintains more topology information about the internetwork than RIP or IGRP do. It uses this information to automatically select least-cost, loop-free routes between networks. EIGRP uses a metric that combines an assessment of the bandwidth of a link with the total delay to send over the link. (Other metrics are configurable as well, though not recommended.) When a neighboring router sends changed metric information, routes are recalculated and updates sent as needed. DUAL will query neighboring routers for reachability information if needed (for example, if an existing route fails).

This "as needed" aspect of operation highlights an important way that EIGRP improves performance over IGRP. EIGRP does not send routine route updates, but instead sends only partial updates as required, thereby reducing the amount of traffic generated between routers. Furthermore, these updates are designed so that only the routers that need the updated information receive them.

In order to build the tables of information that it needs to calculate routes, EIGRP requires routers to make and maintain contact with other routers on their local networks. To facilitate this, EIGRP incorporates a neighbor discovery and recovery process. This system involves the exchange of small Hello messages that let routers discover the other routers on the local network and periodically check to see whether they're reachable. This is very similar to the way the identically named Hello messages are used in OSPF (as described in Chapter 39) and has a low impact on bandwidth use because the messages are small and infrequently sent.

Some of the features in IGRP carry through to its successor, such as the use of split horizon with poisoned reverse for improved stability. In addition to the basic improvements of efficiency and route convergence that accrue from the algorithm itself, EIGRP includes some other features. These include support for Variable Length Subnet Masks (VLSM) as well as support for multiple network-layer protocols. This means that EIGRP could be configured to function on a network that is running IP as well as another layer 3 protocol.

> **KEY CONCEPT** Developed in the 1990s, the *Enhanced Interior Gateway Routing Protocol (EIGRP)* is an improved version of Cisco's IGRP. It is similar to IGRP in many respects, but it uses a more sophisticated route calculation method called the *Diffusing Update Algorithm (DUAL)*. EIGRP also includes several features that make it more intelligent with regard to how it computes routes; it borrows concepts from link-state routing protocols and uses more efficient partial updates, rather than sending out entire routing tables.

TCP/IP Exterior Gateway Protocol (EGP)

In the days of the early Internet, a small number of centralized core routers that maintained complete information about network reachability did the routing. These core routers exchanged information using the historical interior routing protocol, GGP, which we examined earlier in this chapter. Other noncore routers located around the periphery of this core, both stand-alone and in groups, exchanged network reachability information with the core routers using the first TCP/IP exterior routing protocol: the *Exterior Gateway Protocol (EGP).*

Internet pioneers Bolt, Beranek, and Newman developed EGP in the early 1980s. It was first formally described in an Internet standard in RFC 827, "Exterior Gateway Protocol (EGP)," published in October 1982, which was later superseded by RFC 904, "Exterior Gateway Protocol Formal Specification," in April 1984. Like GGP, EGP is now considered obsolete, having been replaced by BGP. However, like GGP, it is an important part of the history of TCP/IP routing, so it is worth examining briefly.

NOTE *As I explained in Chapter 37, routers were in the past often called* gateways. *As such, exterior routing protocols were* exterior gateway protocols. *The EGP protocol discussed here is a specific instance of an exterior gateway protocol (also known as* EGP*). Thus, you may occasionally see BGP also called an* exterior gateway protocol *or an* EGP, *which is the generic use of the term.*

EGP is responsible for the communication of network reachability information between neighboring routers that may or may not be in different ASes. The operation of EGP is somewhat similar to that of BGP (discussed in Chapter 40). Each EGP router maintains a database of information about which networks it can reach and how to reach them. It sends this information out on a regular basis to each router to which it is directly connected. Routers receive these messages and update their routing tables, and then use this new information to update other routers. Information about how to reach each network propagates across the entire internetwork.

The actual process of exchanging routing information involves several steps that discover neighbors and then set up and maintain communications. The steps are as follows:

1. **Neighbor Acquisition** Each router attempts to establish a connection to each of its neighboring routers by sending Neighbor Acquisition Request messages. A neighbor hearing a request can respond with a Neighbor Acquisition Confirm message, which says that it recognized the request and wishes to connect. It may reject the acquisition by replying with a Neighbor Acquisition Refuse message. For an EGP connection to be established between a pair of neighbors, each message must first successfully acquire the other with a Confirm message.

2. **Neighbor Reachability** After acquiring a neighbor, a router checks to make sure the neighbor is reachable and functioning properly on a regular basis. This is done by sending an EGP Hello message to each neighbor for which a connection has been established. The neighbor replies with an I Heard You (IHU) message. These messages are somewhat analogous to the BGP Keepalive message, but they are used in matched pairs.
3. **Network Reachability Update** A router sends Poll messages on a regular basis to each of its neighbors. The neighbor responds with an Update message, which contains details about the networks that it is able to reach. This information is used to update the routing tables of the device that sent the Poll message.

A neighbor can decide to terminate a connection (called *neighbor deacquisition*) by sending a Cease message; the neighbor responds with a Cease-ack (acknowledge) message.

An Error message, similar to the BGP Notification message in role and structure (see Chapter 40), is also defined. A neighbor may send this message in response to the receipt of an EGP message either when the message itself has a problem (such as a bad message length or unrecognized data in a field) or to indicate a problem with how the message is being used (such as receipt of Hello or Poll messages at a rate deemed excessive). Unlike with the BGP Notification message, an EGP router does not necessarily close the connection when sending an Error message.

> **KEY CONCEPT** The *Exterior Gateway Protocol (EGP)* was the first TCP/IP exterior routing protocol and was used with GGP on the early Internet. It functions in a manner similar to BGP. For example, an EGP router makes contact with neighboring routers and exchanges routing information with them. A mechanism is also provided to maintain a session and report errors. EGP is more limited than BGP in capability and is now considered a historical protocol.

The early Internet was designed to connect peripheral routers or groups of routers to the Internet core. It was therefore designed under the assumption that the internetwork was connected as a hierarchical tree, with the core as the root. EGP was designed based on this assumption of a tree structure and, for that reason, cannot handle an arbitrary topology of ASes like BGP. It likewise cannot guarantee the absence of routing loops if such loops exist in the interconnection of neighboring routers. This is part of why BGP needed to be developed as the Internet moved to a more arbitrary structure of AS connections, where loops would be possible if steps weren't taken to avoid them.

PART II-8

TCP/IP TRANSPORT LAYER PROTOCOLS

The first three layers of the OSI Reference Model—the physical layer, data link layer, and network layer—are very important layers for understanding how networks function. The physical layer moves bits over wires; the data link layer moves frames on a network; and the network layer moves datagrams on an internetwork. Taken as a whole, they are the parts of a protocol stack that are responsible for the actual nuts and bolts of getting data from one place to another.

Immediately above these three layers is the fourth layer of the OSI Reference Model: the *transport layer*, called the host-to-host transport layer in the TCP/IP model. This layer is interesting in that it resides in the very architectural center of the model. Accordingly, it represents an important transition point between the hardware-associated layers below it that do the grunt work and the layers above that are more software-oriented and abstract.

Protocols running at the transport layer are charged with providing several important services to enable software applications in higher layers to work over an internetwork. They are typically responsible for allowing connections to be established and maintained between software services on possibly distant machines. Many higher-layer applications need to send data in a reliable way, without needing to worry about error correction, lost data, or flow management. However, network layer protocols are typically unreliable and unacknowledged. Transport layer protocols are often very tightly tied to the network layer protocols directly below them and designed specifically to take care of functions that are not dealt with by those protocols.

This part describes transport layer protocols and related technologies used in the TCP/IP protocol suite. There are two main protocols at this layer: the Transmission Control Protocol (TCP) and the User Datagram Protocol (UDP). UDP is the simpler of the two and doesn't take a great deal of time to explain. In contrast, TCP is a rather complex protocol that is also a very important part of the TCP/IP protocol suite, and thus it requires considerably more explanation.

The first chapter in this part provides a quick overview of the roles of these two protocols in the TCP/IP protocol suite, a discussion of why they are both important, and a summary that compares their key attributes. The second chapter describes the method that both protocols employ for addressing, using transport layer ports and sockets. The third chapter contains a discussion of UDP.

The remaining five chapters encompass a comprehensive description of the concepts, characteristics, and functions of TCP. The fourth chapter in this part provides an overview of TCP, describing its history, what it does, and how it works. The fifth chapter covers some important background information that is necessary to understanding how TCP operates, explaining key concepts such as streams and segments, sliding windows, and TCP ports and connections. The sixth chapter describes the process used by TCP to establish, maintain, and terminate sessions. The seventh chapter describes TCP messages and how they are formatted and transferred. Finally, the last chapter in this part shows how TCP provides reliability and other important transport layer functions, such as flow control, retransmission of lost data, and congestion avoidance.

Since TCP is built on top of the Internet Protocol (IP), in describing TCP, I assume that you have at least a basic familiarity with IP (covered in Part II-3; specifically, see Chapters 15 and 16 for descriptions of basic IP concepts).

42

OVERVIEW AND COMPARISON OF TCP AND UDP

TCP/IP is the most important internetworking protocol suite in the world. It is the basis for the Internet and the "language" spoken by the vast majority of the world's networked computers. TCP/IP includes a large set of protocols that operate at the network layer and the layers above it. The suite as a whole is anchored at layer 3 by the Internet Protocol (IP), which many people consider the single most important protocol in the world of networking.

Of course, there's a bit of *architectural distance* between the network layer and the applications that run at the layers well above that layer. IP is the protocol that performs the bulk of the functions needed to make an internetwork work, but it does not include some capabilities that many applications need. In TCP/IP, a pair of protocols that operate at the transport layer performs these tasks. The protocols are the *Transmission Control Protocol (TCP)* and the *User Datagram Protocol (UDP).*

Of these two, TCP gets the most attention. It is the transport layer protocol that is most often associated with TCP/IP. It is also the transport protocol that many of the Internet's most popular applications use.

UDP, on the other hand, gets second billing. However, UDP and TCP are really peers that play the same role in TCP/IP. They function very differently and provide different benefits for and drawbacks to the applications that use them. Yet they are both important to the protocol suite as a whole. This chapter introduces what TCP and UDP do and highlights the similarities and differences between them.

Two Protocols for TCP/IP Transport Layer Requirements

The transport layer in a protocol suite is responsible for a specific set of functions. For this reason, you might expect that the TCP/IP suite would have a single main transport protocol that performs those functions, just as it has IP as its core protocol at the network layer. But there are *two* different widely used TCP/IP transport layer protocols, an arrangement that is probably one of the best examples of the power of protocol layering (showing that it was worth all the time you spent learning to understand that pesky OSI Reference Model back in Chapters 5 through 7).

Let's start with a look back at layer 3. In my overview of the key operating characteristics of IP in Chapter 15, I described several limitations of IP. The most important limitations are that IP is *connectionless, unreliable*, and *unacknowledged.* Using a best-effort paradigm, data is sent over an IP internetwork without first establishing a connection. Messages *usually* get where they need to go, but there are no guarantees, and the sender usually doesn't even know if the data arrived at its destination.

These characteristics present serious problems for software. Many, if not most, applications need to be able to count on the fact that the data they send will get to its destination without loss or error. Applications also want the connection between two devices to be automatically managed, with problems such as congestion and flow control taken care of as needed. Unless some mechanism is provided for this at lower layers, every application would need to perform these jobs, and that would be a massive duplication of effort.

In fact, you might argue that establishing connections, providing reliability, and handling retransmissions, buffering, and data flow are sufficiently important that it might have been best to simply build these abilities directly into IP. Interestingly, that was exactly the case in the early days of TCP/IP. In the beginning there was just a single protocol called TCP. It combined the tasks of IP with the reliability and session management features that I just mentioned. There's a big problem with this, however: Establishing connections, providing a mechanism for reliability, managing flow control, managing acknowledgments, and managing retransmissions all come at a cost of time and bandwidth. Building all of these capabilities into a single protocol that spanned layers 3 and 4 would mean that all applications would receive the benefits of reliability, but would also take on the costs. While this approach would be fine for many applications, there are others that either don't need the reliability or can't afford the overhead required to provide it.

The solution was simple: Let the network layer (IP) take care of basic data movement on the internetwork, and define two protocols at the transport layer. One protocol would provide a rich set of services for applications that need that functionality, and the understanding would be that some overhead would be required when using this protocol. The other protocol would be simpler, providing little in the way of classic layer 4 functions, but it would be fast and easy to use. Thus, the result was two TCP/IP transport layer protocols:

Transmission Control Protocol (TCP) TCP is a full-featured, connection-oriented, reliable transport protocol for TCP/IP applications. It provides transport layer addressing that allows multiple software applications to simultaneously use a single IP address, and it allows a pair of devices to establish a virtual connection and then pass data bidirectionally. Transmissions are managed using a special *sliding window* system, with unacknowledged transmissions detected and automatically retransmitted. Additional functionality allows the flow of data between devices to be managed, and special circumstances to be addressed.

User Datagram Protocol (UDP) In contrast, UDP is a very simple transport protocol that provides transport layer addressing like TCP, but little else. UDP is barely more than a wrapper protocol that provides a way for applications to access IP. No connection is established, transmissions are unreliable, and data can be lost.

KEY CONCEPT Many TCP/IP applications require different transport requirements, thus two TCP/IP transport layer protocols are necessary. The *Transmission Control Protocol (TCP)* is a full-featured, connection-oriented protocol that provides the acknowledged delivery of data while managing traffic flow and handling issues such as congestion and transmission loss. The *User Datagram Protocol (UDP)*, in contrast, is a much simpler protocol that concentrates only on delivering data in order to maximize the speed of communication when the features of TCP are not required.

Applications of TCP and UDP

To use an analogy, TCP is a fully loaded luxury performance sedan with a chauffeur and a satellite tracking/navigation system. It provides a lot of frills, comfort, and performance. It virtually guarantees that you will get where you need to go without any problems, and any concerns that do arise can be corrected. In contrast, UDP is a stripped-down race car. Its goal is simplicity and speed; everything else is secondary. You will probably get where you need to go, but you can have trouble keeping race cars up and running.

Having two transport layer protocols with such complementary strengths and weaknesses provides considerable flexibility to the creators of networking software.

TCP Applications

Most typical applications need the reliability and other services provided by TCP, and most applications don't care about the loss of a small amount of performance due to TCP's overhead requirements. For example, most applications that transfer files or important data between machines use TCP, because the loss of any portion of the file renders the data useless. Examples include such well-known applications as the Hypertext Transfer Protocol (HTTP), which is used by the World Wide Web (WWW), the File Transfer Protocol (FTP), and the Simple Mail Transfer Protocol (SMTP). I describe TCP applications in more detail in Section III.

UDP Applications

What sort of application doesn't care if its data gets there, and why would anyone want to use such an unreliable application? You might be surprised. A lot of TCP/IP protocols use UDP. It is a good match when the application doesn't really care if some of the data gets lost, such as if you are streaming video or multimedia. The application won't notice one lost byte of data. UDP is also a good match when the application itself chooses to provide some other mechanism to make up for the lack of functionality in UDP.

Applications that send very small amounts of data often use UDP and assume that the client will just send a new request later on if a request is sent and a reply is not received. This provides enough reliability without the overhead of a TCP connection. I discuss some common UDP applications in Chapter 44.

> **KEY CONCEPT** Most typical applications, especially ones that send files or messages, require that data be delivered reliably, and therefore use TCP for transport. The loss of a small amount of data usually is not a concern to applications that use UDP or that use their own application-specific procedures for dealing with potential delivery problems.

Note that even though TCP is often described as being *slower* than UDP, this is a *relative* measurement. TCP is a very well-written protocol that is capable of highly efficient data transfers. It is slow only compared to UDP because of the overhead of establishing and managing connections. The difference can be significant, but it is not enormous.

Incidentally, if you want a good real-world illustration of why it's valuable to have both UDP and TCP, consider message transport under the Domain Name System (DNS). As described in Chapter 57, DNS actually uses UDP for certain types of communication and TCP for others.

Summary Comparison of UDP and TCP

In the next few chapters, we will explore both UDP and TCP in further detail. I will help you to understand much better the strengths and drawbacks of both protocols. While informative, these chapters are time-consuming to read. Thus, for your convenience, I have included Table 42-1, which describes the most important attributes of both protocols and how they contrast with each other.

Table 42-1: Summary Comparison of UDP and TCP

Characteristic/ Description	UDP	TCP
General Description	Simple, high-speed, low-functionality wrapper that interfaces applications to the network layer and does little else	Full-featured protocol that allows applications to send data reliably without worrying about network layer issues
Protocol Connection Setup	Connectionless; data is sent without setup	Connection-oriented; connection must be established prior to transmission
Data Interface to Application	Message-based; the application sends data in discrete packages	Stream-based; the application sends data with no particular structure
Reliability and Acknowledgments	Unreliable, best-effort delivery without acknowledgments	Reliable delivery of messages; all data is acknowledged
Retransmissions	Not performed; application must detect lost data and retransmit if needed	Delivery of all data is managed, and lost data is retransmitted automatically
Features Provided to Manage Flow of Data	None	Flow control using sliding windows; window size adjustment heuristics; congestion-avoidance algorithms
Overhead	Very low	Low, but higher than UDP
Transmission Speed	Very high	High, but not as high as UDP
Data Quantity Suitability	Small to moderate amounts of data (up to a few hundred bytes)	Small to very large amounts of data (up to a few gigabytes)
Types of Applications That Use the Protocol	Applications where data delivery speed matters more than completeness, where small amounts of data are sent, or where multicast/broadcast are used	Most protocols and applications sending data that must be received reliably, including most file and message transfer protocols
Well-Known Applications and Protocols	Multimedia applications, DNS, BOOTP, DHCP, TFTP, SNMP, RIP, NFS (early versions)	FTP, Telnet, SMTP, DNS, HTTP, POP, NNTP, IMAP, BGP, IRC, NFS (later versions)

43

TCP AND UDP ADDRESSING: PORTS AND SOCKETS

Internet Protocol (IP) addresses are the main form of addressing used on a TCP/IP network. These network layer addresses uniquely identify each network interface, and as such, they serve as the mechanism by which data is routed to the correct network on the internetwork and then to the correct device on that network.

But there is an additional level of addressing that occurs at the transport layer in TCP/IP, above that of the IP address. Both of the TCP/IP transport protocols—the Transmission Control Protocol (TCP) and the User Datagram Protocol (UDP)—use the concepts of *ports* and *sockets* for virtual software addressing. Ports and sockets enable many applications to function simultaneously on an IP device.

In this chapter, I describe the special mechanism used for addressing in both TCP and UDP. I begin with a discussion of TCP/IP application processes, including the client/server nature of communication, which provides a background for explaining how ports and sockets are used. I then give an overview of the concept of ports and how they enable the multiplexing of data over an

IP address. I describe the way that port numbers are categorized in ranges and assigned to server processes for common applications. I explain the concept of ephemeral port numbers used for clients. I then discuss sockets and their use for connection identification, including the means by which multiple devices can talk to a single port on another device. I then provide a summary table of the most common registered port numbers.

TCP/IP Processes, Multiplexing, and Client/Server Application Roles

The most sensible place to start learning about how the TCP/IP protocol suite works is by examining IP itself, as well as the support protocols that function in tandem with it at the network layer. IP is the foundation upon which most of the rest of TCP/IP is built. It is the mechanism by which data is packaged and routed throughout a TCP/IP internetwork.

It makes sense, then, that when we examine the operation of TCP/IP from the perspective of IP, we talk very generically about sending and receiving datagrams. To the IP layer software that sends and receives IP datagrams, the higher-level application that datagrams come from and go to is really unimportant. To IP, a datagram is a datagram. All datagrams are packaged and routed in the same way, and IP is mainly concerned with lower-level aspects of moving them between devices in an efficient manner. It's important to remember, however, that this is really an abstraction for the convenience of describing a layer 3 operation. It doesn't consider how datagrams are really generated and used above layer 3.

Layer 4 represents a transition point between the OSI model hardware-related layers (1, 2, and 3) and the software-related layers (5 to 7). This means that the TCP/IP transport layer protocols, TCP and UDP, need to pay attention to the way that software uses TCP/IP, even if IP really does not.

Ultimately, the entire point of having networks, internetworks, and protocol suites like TCP/IP is to enable networking *applications*. Most Internet users employ these applications on a daily basis. In fact, most of us run many different applications simultaneously. For example, you might use a web browser to check the news, a File Transfer Program (FTP) client to upload some pictures to share with family, and an Internet Relay Chat (IRC) program to discuss something with a friend or colleague. In fact, it is common to have multiple instances of a single application. The most common example is having multiple web browser windows open (I sometimes find myself with as many as 30 going at one time!).

Multiplexing and Demultiplexing

Most communication in TCP/IP takes the form of exchanges of information between a program running on one device and a matching program running on another device. Each instance of an application represents a copy of that application's software that needs to send and receive information. These application instances are commonly called *processes*. A TCP/IP application process is any piece of networking software that sends and receives information using the TCP/IP protocol suite. This includes classic end-user applications such as the ones described earlier, and support protocols that behave like applications when they send messages. Examples of the latter would include a network management protocol like the Simple Network Management Protocol (SNMP; see Chapters 65 through 69), or even the routing protocol Border Gateway Protocol (BGP; see Chapter 40), which sends messages using TCP the way an application does.

So, a typical TCP/IP host has multiple processes, and each one needs to send and receive datagrams. All of these datagrams, however, must be sent using the same interface to the internetwork, using the IP layer. This means that the data from all applications (with some possible exceptions) is initially funneled down to the transport layer, where TCP or UDP handles it. From there, messages pass to the device's IP layer, where they are packaged in IP datagrams and sent out over the internetwork to different destinations. The technical term for this is *multiplexing*. This term simply means combining, and its use here is a software analog to the way multiplexing is done with signals (such as how individual telephone calls are packaged).

A complementary mechanism is responsible for the receipt of datagrams. At the same time that the IP layer multiplexes datagrams to send from many application processes, it receives many datagrams that are intended for different processes. The IP layer must take this stream of unrelated datagrams and pass them to the correct process (through the transport layer protocol above it). This is *demultiplexing*, the opposite of multiplexing.

You can see an illustration of the concept behind TCP/IP process multiplexing and demultiplexing in Figure 43-1.

> **KEY CONCEPT** TCP/IP is designed to allow many different applications to send and receive data simultaneously using the same IP software on a given device. To accomplish this, it is necessary to *multiplex* transmitted data from many sources as it is passed down to the IP layer. As a stream of IP datagrams is received, it is *demultiplexed* and the appropriate data passed to each application software instance on the receiving host.

TCP/IP Client Processes and Server Processes

TCP/IP software is generally *asymmetric*. This means that when a TCP/IP application process on one computer tries to talk to an application process on another computer, the two processes are usually not exactly the same. They are instead *complements* of each other, designed to function together as a team.

As I explained in the overview description of TCP/IP in Chapter 8, most networking applications use a *client/server* model of operation. This term can be used to refer to the roles of computers, where a *server* is a relatively powerful machine that provides services to a large number of user-operated *clients*. It also applies to software. In a software context, a *client process* usually runs on a client machine and initiates contact to perform some sort of function. A *server process* usually runs on a hardware server, listens for requests from clients, and responds to them.

The classic example of this client/server operation is the World Wide Web (WWW). The Web uses the Hypertext Transfer Protocol (HTTP; see Chapter 80), which is a good example of an application protocol. A web browser is an HTTP client that normally runs on an end-user client machine. It initiates an exchange of HTTP (web) data by sending a request to a web (HTTP) server. A server process on that web server hears the request and replies either with the requested item(s)—a web page or other data—or an error message. The server is usually specifically designed to handle many incoming client requests, and in many cases, has no other use.

Why am I telling you all of this in a section that is supposed to explain TCP and UDP ports? I started here because many application processes run simultaneously and have their data multiplexed for transmission. The simultaneity of application processes and the multiplexing of data are the impetus for why higher-level addressing is a necessity in TCP/IP. The client/server arrangement used by TCP/IP has an important impact on the way that ports are used and the mechanisms for how they are assigned. The next two sections explore these concepts more completely.

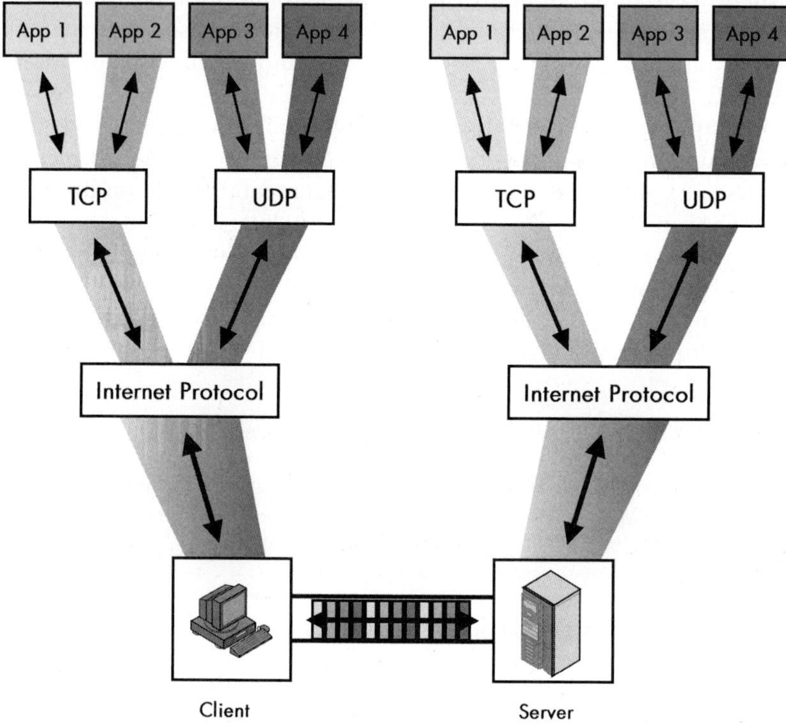

Figure 43-1: Process multiplexing and demultiplexing in TCP/IP *In a typical machine that is running TCP/IP, there are many different protocols and applications running simultaneously. This example shows four different applications communicating between a client and server machine. All four are multiplexed for transmission using the same IP software and physical connection; received data is demultiplexed and passed to the appropriate application. IP, TCP, and UDP provide a way of keeping the data from each application distinct.*

TCP/IP Ports: TCP/UDP Addressing

A typical host on a TCP/IP internetwork has many different software application processes running concurrently. Each process generates data that it sends to either TCP or UDP, which then passes it to IP for transmission. The IP layer sends out this multiplexed stream of datagrams to various destinations. Simultaneously, each device's IP layer is receiving datagrams that originated in numerous application processes on other hosts. These datagrams need to be demultiplexed so that they end up at the correct process on the device that receives them.

Multiplexing and Demultiplexing Using Ports

The question is how do we demultiplex a sequence of IP datagrams that need to go to many different application processes? Let's consider a particular host with a single network interface bearing the IP address 24.156.79.20. Normally, every datagram received by the IP layer will have this value in the IP Destination Address field. The consecutive datagrams that IP receives may contain a piece of a file you are downloading with your web browser, an email your brother sent to you, and a line of text a buddy wrote in an IRC chat channel. How does the IP layer know which datagrams go where if they all have the same IP address?

The first part of the answer lies in the Protocol field included in the header of each IP datagram. This field carries a code that identifies the protocol that sent the data in the datagram to IP. Since most end-user applications use TCP or UDP at the transport layer, the Protocol field in a received datagram tells IP to pass data to either TCP or UDP as appropriate. Of course, this just defers the problem to the transport layer.

Many applications use both TCP and UDP at once. This means that TCP or UDP must figure out which process to send the data to. To make this possible, an additional addressing element is necessary. This address allows a more specific location—a software process—to be identified within a particular IP address. In TCP/IP, this transport layer address is called a *port.*

Source Port and Destination Port Numbers

In UDP and TCP messages two addressing fields appear: a *source port* and a *destination port.* These are analogous to the source address and destination address fields at the IP level, but at a higher level of detail. They identify the originating process on the source machine and the destination process on the destination machine. The TCP or UDP software fills them in before transmission, and they direct the data to the correct process on the destination device.

NOTE *The term* port *has many meanings aside from this one in TCP/IP. For example, a physical outlet in a network device is often called a* port. *Usually, you can discern whether the port in question refers to a hardware port or a software port from the context.*

TCP and UDP port numbers are 16 bits in length. Valid port numbers can theoretically take on values from 0 to 65,535. As you will see in the next section, these values are divided into ranges for different purposes, with certain ports reserved for particular uses.

One fact that is sometimes a bit confusing is that both UDP and TCP use the same range of port numbers, but they are independent. In theory, it is possible for UDP port number 77 to refer to one application process and TCP port number 77 to refer to an entirely different one. There is no ambiguity, at least to the computers, because as mentioned earlier, each IP datagram contains a Protocol field that specifies whether it is carrying a TCP message or a UDP message. IP passes the datagram to either TCP or UDP, which sends the message on to the right process using the port number in the TCP or UDP header. This mechanism is illustrated in Figure 43-2.

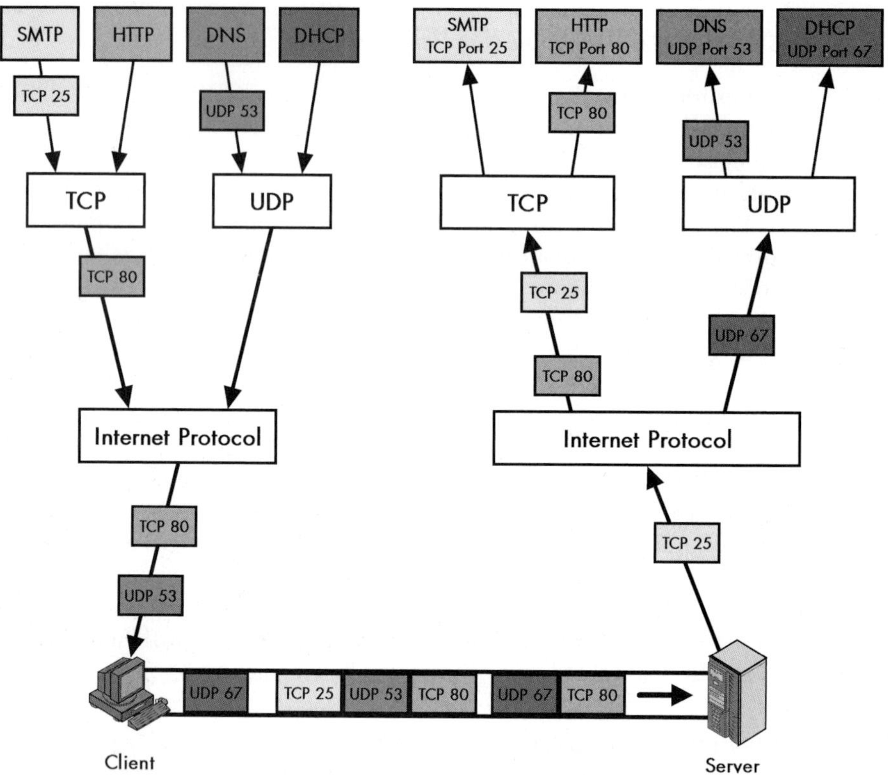

Figure 43-2: TCP/IP process multiplexing/demultiplexing using TCP/UDP ports *A more concrete version of Figure 43-1, this figure shows how TCP and UDP ports accomplish software multiplexing and demultiplexing. Again there are four different TCP/IP applications communicating, but this time I am showing only the traffic going from the client to the server. Two of the applications use TCP, and two use UDP. Each application on the client sends messages using a specific TCP or UDP port number. The server's UDP or TCP software uses these port numbers to pass the datagrams to the appropriate application process.*

In practice, having TCP and UDP use different port numbers is confusing, especially for the reserved port numbers that common applications use. To avoid confusion, by convention, most reserved port numbers are reserved for both TCP and UDP. For example, port 80 is reserved for HTTP for both TCP and UDP, even though HTTP only uses TCP. We'll examine this in greater detail in the following section.

> **KEY CONCEPT** TCP/IP transport layer addressing is accomplished by using TCP and UDP *ports*. Each port number within a particular IP device identifies a particular software process.

Summary of Port Use for Datagram Transmission and Reception

Here's how transport layer addressing (port addressing) works in TCP and UDP:

Sending Datagrams An application specifies the source and destination port it wishes to use for the communication. The port numbers are encoded into the TCP or UDP header, depending on which transport layer protocol the application is using. When TCP or UDP passes data to IP, IP indicates the protocol type that's appropriate for TCP or UDP in the Protocol field of the IP datagram. The source and destination port numbers are encapsulated as part of the TCP or UDP message, within the IP datagram's data area.

Receiving Datagrams The IP software receives the datagram, inspects the Protocol field, and decides which protocol the datagram belongs to (in this case, TCP or UDP). TCP or UDP receives the datagram and passes its contents to the appropriate process based on the destination port number.

> **KEY CONCEPT** Application process multiplexing and demultiplexing in TCP/IP is implemented using the IP Protocol field and the UDP/TCP Source Port and Destination Port fields. Upon transmission, the Protocol field is given a number to indicate whether TCP or UDP was used, and the port numbers are filled in to indicate the sending and receiving software process. The device receiving the datagram uses the Protocol field to determine whether TCP or UDP was used and then passes the data to the software process that the destination port number indicates.

TCP/IP Application Assignments and Server Port Number Ranges

The port numbers I just discussed provide a method of transport layer addressing that allows many applications to use TCP and UDP simultaneously. By specifying the appropriate destination port number, an application sending data can be sure that the right process on the destination device will receive the message. Unfortunately, there's still a problem to be solved.

Let's go back to using the World Wide Web. You fire up a web browser, which is client software that sends requests using HTTP. You need to know the IP address of the website you want to access, or you may have the Domain Name System (DNS) supply the IP address to you automatically. Once you have the address, the web browser can generate an HTTP message and send it to the website's IP address.

This HTTP message is intended for the web server process on the site you are trying to reach. The problem is how does the web browser (client process) know which port number has been assigned to the server process on the website? Port numbers can range from 0 to 65535, which means a lot of choices. And, in theory, every website could assign a different port number to its web server process.

There are a couple of different ways to resolve this problem. TCP/IP takes what is probably the simplest possible approach: It *reserves* certain port numbers for particular applications.

Reserved Port Numbers

Server processes, which listen for requests for that application and then respond to them, assign each common application a specific port number. To avoid chaos, the software that implements a particular server process normally uses the same reserved port number on every IP device so that clients can find it easily.

In the example of accessing a website with a web browser, the reserved port number for HTTP is 80. Every web browser knows that web designers design websites to listen for requests sent to port 80. The web browser will thus use this value in requests to ensure that the IP and TCP software on the web browser directs these HTTP messages to the web server software. It is possible for a particular web server to use a different port number, but in this case, the web server must inform the user of this number somehow, and must explicitly tell the web browser to use it instead of the default port number (80).

> **KEY CONCEPT** To allow client devices to establish connections to TCP/IP servers more easily, server processes for common applications use universal server port numbers. Clients are preprogrammed to know to use the port numbers by default.

In order for this system to work well, universal agreement on port assignments is essential. Thus, this becomes another situation where a central authority is needed to manage a list of port assignments that everyone uses. For TCP/IP, it is the same authority responsible for the assignment and coordination of other centrally managed numbers, including IP addresses, IP protocol numbers, and so forth: the Internet Assigned Numbers Authority (IANA; see Chapter 3).

TCP/UDP Port Number Ranges

As you have seen, there are 65,536 port numbers that can be used for processes. But there are also a fairly large number of TCP/IP applications, and the list grows every year. IANA needs to carefully manage the port number address space in order to ensure that port numbers are not wasted on protocols that won't be widely used. IANA also needs to provide flexibility for organizations that must make use of obscure applications. To this end, the full spectrum of TCP and UDP port numbers is divided into three ranges:

Well-Known (Privileged) Port Numbers (0 to 1023) IANA manages these port numbers and reserves them for only the most universal TCP/IP applications. The IANA assigns these port numbers only to protocols that have been standardized using the TCP/IP RFC process, protocols that are in the process of being standardized, or protocols that are likely to be standardized in the future. On most computers, only server processes run by system administrators or privileged users use these port numbers. These processes generally correspond to processes that implement key IP applications, such as web servers, FTP servers, and the like. For this reason, these processes are sometimes called *system port numbers*.

Registered (User) Port Numbers (1024 to 49151) There are many applications that need to use TCP/IP, but are not specified in RFCs or are not as universally used as other applications, so they do not warrant a worldwide well-known port number. To ensure that these various applications do not conflict with each other, IANA uses the bulk of the overall port number range for registered port numbers. Anyone who creates a viable TCP/IP server application can request to reserve one of these port numbers, and if the request is approved, the IANA will register that port number and assign it to the application. Any user on a system can generally access registered port numbers; thus they are sometimes called *user port numbers.*

Private/Dynamic Port Numbers (49152 to 65535) IANA neither reserves nor maintains these ports. Anyone can use them for any purpose without registration, so they are appropriate for a private protocol that only a particular organization uses.

KEY CONCEPT IANA manages port-number assignments to ensure universal compatibility around the global Internet. The numbers are divided into three ranges: well-known port numbers used for the most common applications, registered port numbers for other applications, and private/dynamic port numbers that can be used without IANA registration.

Use of these ranges ensures that there will be universal agreement on how to access a server process for the most common TCP/IP protocols. They also allow flexibility for special applications. Most of the TCP/IP applications and application protocols use numbers in the well-known port number range for their servers. These port numbers are not generally used for client processes, but there are some exceptions. For example, port 68 is reserved for a client using the Bootstrap Protocol (BOOTP) or Dynamic Host Configuration Protocol (DHCP).

TCP/IP Client (Ephemeral) Ports and Client/Server Application Port Use

The significance of the asymmetry between clients and servers in TCP/IP becomes evident when you examine in detail how port numbers are used. Since clients initiate application data transfers using TCP and UDP, they need to know the port number of the server process. Consequently, servers are required to use universally known port numbers. Thus, well-known and registered port numbers identify server processes. Clients that send requests use the well-known or registered port number as the destination port number.

In contrast, servers respond to clients; they do not initiate contact with them. Thus, the client doesn't need to use a reserved port number. In fact, this is really an understatement. A server shouldn't use a well-known or registered port number to send responses back to clients because it is possible for a particular device to have client and server software from the same protocol running on the same machine. If a server received an HTTP request on port 80 of its machine and sent the reply back to port 80 on the client machine, the server would be sending the reply to the client machine's HTTP server process (if present), rather than the client process that sent the initial request.

To know where to send the reply, the server must know the port number the client is using. The client supplies the port number as the *source port* in the request, and then the server uses the source port as the destination port to send the reply. Client processes don't use well-known or registered ports. Instead, each client process is assigned a temporary port number for its use. This is commonly called an *ephemeral port number.*

NOTE *Your $10 word for the day:* ephemeral*: "short-lived; existing or continuing for a short time only." — Webster's Revised Unabridged Dictionary.*

Ephemeral Port Number Assignment

The TCP/IP software assigns ephemeral port numbers as needed to processes. Obviously, each client process that's running concurrently needs to use a unique ephemeral port number, so the TCP and UDP layers must keep track of which ones are in use. The TCP/IP software generally assigns these port numbers in a *pseudo-random* manner from a reserved pool of numbers. I say pseudo-random because there is no specific meaning to an ephemeral port number that is assigned to a process, so the TCP/IP software could select a random one for each client process. However, since it is necessary to reuse the port numbers in this pool over time, many implementations use a set of rules to minimize the chance of confusion due to reuse.

Consider a client process that used only ephemeral port number 4121 to send a request. The client process received a reply and then terminated. Suppose you immediately reallocate 4121 to some other process. However, the prior user of port 4121 accesses the server, which for some reason sends an extra reply. The reply would go to the new process, thereby creating confusion. To avoid this, it is wise to wait as long as possible before reusing port number 4121 for another client process. Some implementations will therefore cycle through the port numbers in order to ensure that the maximum amount of time elapses between consecutive uses of the same ephemeral port number.

KEY CONCEPT Well-known and registered port numbers are needed for server processes since a client must know the server's port number to initiate contact. On the other hand, client processes can use any port number. Each time a client process initiates a UDP or TCP communication, the TCP/IP software assigns it a temporary, or *ephemeral*, port number to use for that conversation. The TCP/IP software assigns these port numbers in a pseudo-random way because the exact number that the software uses is not important as long as each process has a different number.

Ephemeral Port Number Ranges

The range of port numbers that TCP/IP software uses for ephemeral ports on a device also depends on the implementation. The TCP/IP implementation in Berkeley Standard Distribution (BSD) UNIX established the classic ephemeral port range. BSD UNIX defined it as 1024 to 4999, thereby providing 3,976 ephemeral ports. This seems like a very large number, and it is indeed usually more than enough for a typical client. However, the size of this number can be deceiving.

Many applications use more than one process, and it is theoretically possible to run out of ephemeral port numbers on a very busy IP device. For this reason, most of the time, the ephemeral port number range can be changed. The default range may be different for other operating systems.

Just as well-known and registered port numbers are used for server processes, ephemeral port numbers are for client processes only. This means that the use of a range of addresses from 1024 to 4999 does not conflict with the use of that same range for registered port numbers. I discussed this in the previous section, "Ephemeral Port Number Assignment."

Port Number Use During a Client/Server Exchange

Now let's return to the matter of client/server application message exchange. Once a client is assigned an ephemeral port number, that port number is used as the source port in the client's request TCP/UDP message. The server receives the request and then generates a reply. In forming this response message, the server *swaps* the source and destination port numbers, just as it does the source and destination IP addresses. So the server's reply is sent from the well-known or registered port number on the server process back to the ephemeral port number on the client machine.

Now back to the web browser example. The web browser, with IP address 177.41.72.6, wants to send an HTTP request to a particular website at IP address 41.199.222.3. The TCP/IP software sends the HTTP request with a *destination port* number of 80 (the one reserved for HTTP servers). The TCP/IP software allocates the *source port* number from a pool of ephemeral ports; let's say it's port 3022. When the HTTP request arrives at the web server, it is conveyed to port 80 where the HTTP server receives it. That process generates a reply and sends it back to 177.41.72.6, using *destination port* 3022 and *source port* 80. The two processes can exchange information back and forth each time the TCP/IP software swaps the source port number and destination port number along with the source and destination IP addresses. This example is illustrated in Figure 43-3.

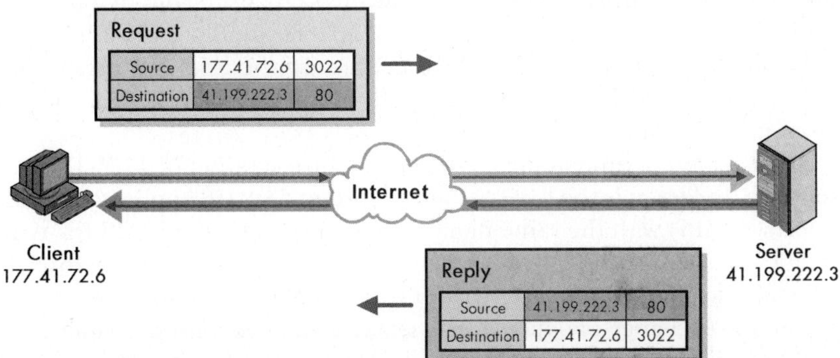

Figure 43-3: TCP/IP client/server application port mechanics *This highly simplified example shows how clients and servers use port numbers for a request.reply exchange. The client is making an HTTP request and sends it to the server at HTTP's well-known port number, 80. Its port number for this exchange is the pseudo-randomly selected port 3022. The server sends its reply back to that port number, which it reads from the request.*

KEY CONCEPT In most TCP/IP client/server communications, the client uses a random ephemeral port number and sends a request to the appropriate reserved port number at the server's IP address. The server sends its reply back to whatever port number it finds in the Source Port field of the request.

TCP/IP Sockets and Socket Pairs: Process and Connection Identification

In this chapter, I have discussed the key difference between addressing at the level of IP and addressing with regard to application processes. To summarize, at layer 3 an IP address is all that is really important for properly transmitting data between IP devices. In contrast, application protocols must be concerned with the port assigned to each instance of the application so that the protocols can properly use TCP or UDP.

So, the overall identification of an application process actually uses the combination of the IP address of the host it runs on—or the network interface over which it is talking, to be more precise—and the port number that has been assigned to it. This combined address is called a *socket.* Sockets are specified using the notation *<IP Address>:<Port Number>*. For example, if you have a website running on IP address 41.199.222.3, the socket corresponding to the HTTP server for that site would be *41.199.222.3:80*.

KEY CONCEPT The overall identifier of a TCP/IP application process on a device is the combination of its IP address and port number, which is called a *socket*.

You will also sometimes see a socket specified using a host name instead of an IP address, like this: *<Host Name>:<Port Number>*. To use this descriptor, the web browser must first resolve the name to an IP address using DNS. For example, you might find a website URL such as http://www.thisisagreatsite.com:8080. This tells the web browser to *resolve* the name www.thisisagreatsite.com first to an IP address using DNS. Then it tells the browser to send a request to that address using the nonstandard server port 8080, which the browser occasionally uses instead of port 80. (See Chapter 70's discussion of application layer addressing using URLs for more information.)

The *socket* is a fundamental concept to the operation of TCP/IP application software. In fact, it is the basis for an important TCP/IP application program interface (API) with the same name: *sockets.* A version of this API for Windows is called *Windows Sockets* or *Winsock*, which you may have heard of before. These APIs allow application programs to easily use TCP/IP to communicate.

So the exchange of data between a pair of devices consists of a series of messages sent from a socket on one device to a socket on the other. Each device will normally have multiple simultaneous conversations going on. In the case of TCP, a connection is established for each pair of devices for the duration of the communication session. These connections must be managed, and this requires that they be uniquely identified. This is done using the socket identifiers for each of the two devices that are connected.

KEY CONCEPT Each device may have multiple TCP connections active at any given time. Each connection is uniquely identified using the combination of the client socket and server socket, which in turn contains four elements: the client IP address and port, and the server IP address and port.

Let's return to the example in Figure 43-3. You are sending an HTTP request from your client at 177.41.72.6 to the website at 41.199.222.3. The server for that website will use well-known port number 80, so its socket is 41.199.222.3:80, as you saw before. You have been ephemeral port number 3022 for the web browser, so the client socket is 177.41.72.6:3022. The overall connection between these devices can be described using this socket pair: (41.199.222.3:80, 177.41.72.6:3022).

For much more on how TCP identifies connections, see the topic on TCP ports and connection identification in Chapter 46.

Unlike TCP, UDP is a connectionless protocol, so it obviously doesn't use connections. The pair of sockets on the sending and receiving devices can still be used to identify the two processes that are exchanging data, but because there are no connections, the socket pair doesn't have the significance that it does in TCP.

Common TCP/IP Applications and Well-Known and Registered Port Numbers

The great popularity of the TCP/IP protocol suite has led to the development of literally thousands of different applications and protocols. Most of these use the client/server model of operation that I discussed earlier in this chapter. Server processes for a particular application are designed to use a particular reserved port number, and clients use an ephemeral (temporary) port number to initiate a connection to the server. To ensure that everyone agrees on which port numbers each server application should use for each application, port numbers are centrally managed by the IANA.

Originally, IANA kept the list of well-known and registered port numbers in a lengthy text document along with all the many other parameters for which IANA was centrally responsible (such as IP Protocol field numbers, Type and Code field values for ICMP, and so on). These port numbers were published on a periodic basis in Internet (RFC) standards documents titled "Assigned Numbers." This system worked fine in the early days of the Internet, but by the mid-1990s, these values were changing so rapidly that using the RFC process was not feasible. It was too much work to keep publishing them, and the RFC was practically out of date the day after it was published.

The last "Assigned Numbers" standard was RFC 1700, which was published in October 1994. After that time, IANA moved to a set of World Wide Web documents that contained the parameters they manage. This allowed IANA to keep the lists constantly up-to-date, and enabled TCP/IP users to get more current information. RFC 1700 was officially obsoleted in 2002.

You can find complete information on all the parameters that IANA maintains at http://www.iana.org/numbers.html. The URL of the file that contains TCP/UDP port assignments is http://www.iana.org/assignments/port-numbers.

This document is the definitive list of all well-known and registered TCP and UDP port assignments. Each port number is assigned a short *keyword* with a brief description of the protocol that uses it. There are two problems with this document. First, it is incredibly long; it contains over 10,000 lines of text. Most of the protocols mentioned in those thousands of lines are for obscure applications that you have probably never heard of before (I certainly have never heard of most of them!). This makes it hard to easily see the port assignments for the protocols that are most commonly used.

The other problem with this document is that it shows the same port number as reserved for both TCP and UDP for an application. As I mentioned earlier, TCP and UDP port numbers are actually independent, so, in theory, one port number could assign TCP port 80 to one server application type and UDP port 80 to another. It was believed that this would lead to confusion, so with very few exceptions, the same port number is shown in the list for the same application for both TCP and UDP. Nevertheless, showing this in the list has a drawback: You can't tell which protocol the application actually uses, and which has just been reserved for consistency.

Given all that, I have decided to include a couple of summary tables that show the well-known and registered port numbers for the most common TCP/IP applications. I have indicated whether or not the protocol uses TCP, UDP, or both. Table 43-1 lists the well-known port numbers for the most common TCP/IP application protocols.

Table 43-1: Common TCP/IP Well-Known Port Numbers and Applications

Port #	TCP/UDP	Keyword	Protocol Abbreviation	Application or Protocol Name/Comments
7	TCP + UDP	echo	—	Echo Protocol
9	TCP + UDP	discard	—	Discard Protocol
11	TCP + UDP	systat	—	Active Users Protocol
13	TCP + UDP	daytime	—	Daytime Protocol
17	TCP + UDP	qotd	QOTD	Quote of the Day Protocol
19	TCP + UDP	chargen	—	Character Generator Protocol
20	TCP	ftp-data	FTP (data)	File Transfer Protocol (default data port)
21	TCP	ftp	FTP (control)	File Transfer Protocol (control/commands)
23	TCP	telnet	—	Telnet Protocol
25	TCP	smtp	SMTP	Simple Mail Transfer Protocol
37	TCP + UDP	time	—	Time Protocol
43	TCP	nicname	—	Whois Protocol (also called Nicname)
53	TCP + UDP	domain	DNS	Domain Name Server (Domain Name System)
67	UDP	bootps	BOOTP/DHCP	Bootstrap Protocol/Dynamic Host Configuration Protocol (server)
68	UDP	bootpc	BOOTP/DHCP	Bootstrap Protocol/Dynamic Host Configuration Protocol (client)

(continued)

Table 43-1: Common TCP/IP Well-Known Port Numbers and Applications (continued)

Port #	TCP/UDP	Keyword	Protocol Abbreviation	Application or Protocol Name/Comments
69	UDP	tftp	TFTP	Trivial File Transfer Protocol
70	TCP	gopher	—	Gopher Protocol
79	TCP	finger	—	Finger User Information Protocol
80	TCP	http	HTTP	Hypertext Transfer Protocol (World Wide Web)
110	TCP	pop3	POP	Post Office Protocol (version 3)
119	TCP	nntp	NNTP	Network News Transfer Protocol
123	UDP	ntp	NTP	Network Time Protocol
137	TCP + UDP	netbios-ns	—	NetBIOS (Name Service)
138	UDP	netbios-dgm	—	NetBIOS (Datagram Service)
139	TCP	netbios-ssn	—	NetBIOS (Session Service)
143	TCP	imap	IMAP	Internet Message Access Protocol
161	UDP	snmp	SNMP	Simple Network Management Protocol
162	UDP	snmptrap	SNMP	Simple Network Management Protocol (Trap)
179	TCP	bgp	BGP	Border Gateway Protocol
194	TCP	irc	IRC	Internet Relay Chat
443	TCP	https	HTTP over SSL	Hypertext Transfer Protocol over Secure Sockets Layer
500	UDP	isakmp	IKE	IPsec Internet Key Exchange
520	UDP	router	RIP	Routing Information Protocol (RIP-1 and RIP-2)
521	UDP	ripng	RIPng	Routing Information Protocol - Next Generation

The registered port numbers are by definition for protocols that are not standardized using the RFC process, so they are mostly esoteric applications, and I don't think it's necessary to list all of them. Table 43-2 shows a few that I feel are of particular interest.

Table 43-2: Common TCP/IP Registered Port Numbers and Applications

Port #	TCP/UDP	Keyword	Protocol Abbreviation	Application or Protocol Name/Comments
1512	TCP + UDP	wins	WINS	Microsoft Windows Internet Naming Service
1701	UDP	l2tp	L2TP	Layer 2 Tunneling Protocol
1723	TCP	pptp	PPTP	Point-to-Point Tunneling Protocol
2049	TCP + UDP	nfs	NFS	Network File System
6000–6063	TCP	x11	X11	X Window System

44

TCP/IP USER DATAGRAM PROTOCOL (UDP)

The very fact that the TCP/IP protocol suite bears the name of the Internet Protocol (IP) and the Transmission Control Protocol (TCP) suggests that these are the two key protocols in the suite. IP resides at the network layer, and TCP is at the transport layer. It's no wonder that many people don't even realize that there is a second transport layer protocol in TCP/IP.

Like a shy younger brother, the *User Datagram Protocol (UDP)* sits in the shadows while TCP gets the glory. The fancier sibling deserves much of this limelight, since TCP is arguably the more important of the two. However, UDP fills a critical niche in the TCP/IP protocol suite, because it allows many applications to work at their best when using TCP would be less than ideal.

In this chapter, I discuss UDP, the simpler and less-known TCP/IP transport protocol. I begin with an overview of the protocol and describe its history and standards. I outline how UDP operates, and explain the format used for UDP messages. I conclude with a discussion of what kinds of applications use UDP and the well-known or registered ports that are assigned to them.

UDP Overview, History, and Standards

I suppose the sibling rivalry analogy I mentioned in the introduction to this section may be a bit silly. I highly doubt that protocols lie awake at night worrying about how much we use them. However, it's interesting to discover just how important UDP really is, given how little attention it gets compared to TCP. In fact, in true older-sibling, spotlight-stealing fashion, you can't even really understand the history of UDP without first discussing TCP.

In Chapter 8, where I described the history of TCP/IP, I explained that very early on in the development of the protocol suite, there was only one protocol that handled the functions IP and TCP perform. This protocol, called TCP, provided network layer connectivity like IP, and also established connections, offered reliability, and took care of the typical transport layer quality requirements that you associate with modern TCP, such as flow control and retransmission handling.

It didn't take long before the developers of the fledgling combined TCP protocol quickly realized that mixing these functions together was a mistake. While most conventional applications needed the classic transport layer reliability functions, some did not. These features introduced overhead, which was added whether or not applications actually needed the reliability features. Worse, there were some applications for which the features not only were of no value, but also were a detriment, since even a small amount of lost performance due to the overhead would be a problem.

The solution was to separate the original protocol into IP and TCP. IP would do basic internetworking, and TCP would do the reliability features. This paved the way for the creation of an alternative transport layer protocol—UDP—for applications that didn't want or need the features that TCP provided.

There are two main attributes that are always associated with UDP: simple and fast. UDP is a simple protocol that uses a very straightforward messaging structure that is similar to the message format that many other TCP/IP protocols use (in contrast to the more complex data structures—streams and segments—that TCP uses). In fact, when you boil it down, UDP's only real goal is to serve as an interface between networking application processes that are running at the higher layers, and the internetworking capabilities of IP.

Like TCP, UDP layers a method of transport layer addressing (and hence, process identification) on top of IP through the use of UDP port numbers. UDP includes an optional checksum capability for error detection, but adds virtually no other functionality.

The best way to see the simplicity of UDP is to look at the standards that define it. Or rather, I should say *standard* in the singular, because there is only one. UDP was defined in RFC 768, "User Datagram Protocol," in 1980. This document is three pages in length, and no one has ever needed to revise it.

UDP is a fast protocol specifically because it doesn't have all the bells and whistles of TCP. This makes it unsuitable for use by many, if not most, typical networking applications. But for some applications, this speed is exactly what the applications want from a transport layer protocol, namely something that takes the applications' data and quickly shuffles it down to the IP layer with minimal fuss. In choosing to use UDP, the application writer takes it upon himself to take care of issues such as reliability and retransmissions, if necessary. This can be a recipe for success or failure, depending on the application and how carefully the writer uses UDP.

KEY CONCEPT *The User Datagram Protocol (UDP)* was developed for use by application protocols that do not require reliability, acknowledgment, or flow control features at the transport layer. It is designed to be simple and fast. It provides only transport layer addressing (in the form of UDP ports), an optional checksum capability, and little else.

UDP Operation

UDP is so simple that I can't say a great deal about how it works. It is designed to do as little as possible.

What UDP Does

UDP's only real task is to take data from higher-layer protocols and place it in UDP messages, which are then passed down to IP for transmission. The basic steps for transmission using UDP are as follows:

1. **Higher-Layer Data Transfer** An application sends a message to the UDP software.
2. **UDP Message Encapsulation** The higher-layer message is encapsulated into the Data field of a UDP message. The headers of the UDP message are filled in, including the Source Port field of the application that sent the data to UDP and the Destination Port field of the intended recipient. The checksum value may also be calculated.
3. **Transfer Message to IP** The UDP message is passed to IP for transmission.

And that's about it. Of course, when the destination device receives the message, this short procedure is reversed.

What UDP Does Not Do

UDP is so simple that its operation is often described in terms of what it does not do, instead of what it does. As a transport protocol, UDP does not do the following:

- Establish connections before sending data. It just packages the data and sends it off.
- Provide acknowledgments to show that data was received.
- Provide any guarantees that its messages will arrive.
- Detect lost messages and retransmit them.
- Ensure that data is received in the same order that it was sent.
- Provide any mechanism to handle congestion or manage the flow of data between devices.

KEY CONCEPT UDP is probably the simplest protocol in all of TCP/IP. It takes application layer data that has been passed to it, packages it in a simplified message format, and sends it to IP for transmission.

If these limitations sound similar the ones for IP, then you're paying attention. UDP is basically IP with transport layer port addressing. (For this reason, UDP is sometimes called a *wrapper protocol,* since all it does is wrap application data in its simple message format and send it to IP.)

However, despite the previous list, there are a couple of limited feedback and error-checking mechanisms that do exist within UDP. One is the optional checksum capability, which can allow for the detection of an error in transmission or the situation in which a UDP message is delivered to the wrong place (see the next section, "UDP Message Format" for details). The other is Internet Control Message Protocol (ICMP) error reporting (see Chapter 31). For example, if a UDP message is sent that contains a destination port number that the destination device does not recognize, the destination host will send an ICMP Destination Unreachable message back to the original source. Of course, ICMP exists for all IP errors of this sort, so I'm stretching a bit here.

UDP Message Format

What's the magic word when it comes to UDP? It's *simple.* This is true of the operation of the protocol, and it is also true of the format used for UDP messages. Interestingly, however, there is one aspect of UDP that is not simple.

In keeping with the goal of efficiency, the UDP header is only 8 bytes in length. You can contrast this with the TCP header size of 20 bytes or more. Table 44-1 and Figure 44-1 show the format of UDP messages.

The UDP Checksum field is the one area where the protocol is a bit confusing. The concept of a checksum itself is nothing new; checksums are used widely in networking protocols to provide protection against errors. What's a bit odd is this notion of computing the checksum over the regular datagram as well as a pseudo header. So instead of calculating the checksum over only the fields in the UDP datagram, the UDP software first constructs a fake additional header that contains the following fields:

- IP Source Address field
- IP Destination Address field
- IP Protocol field
- UDP Length field

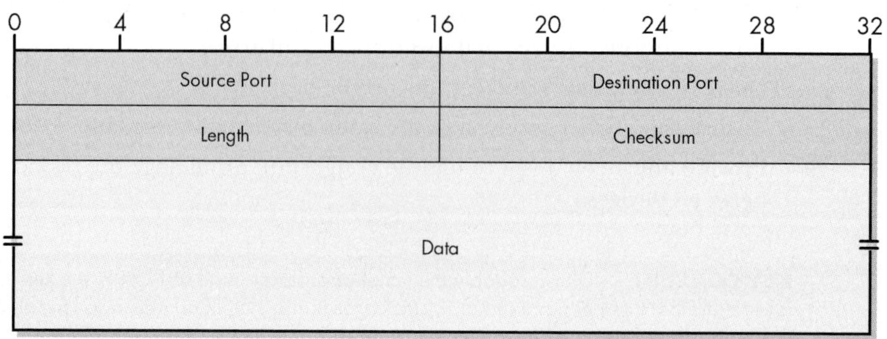

Figure 44-1: *UDP message format*

Table 44-1: UDP Message Format

Field Name	Size (Bytes)	Description
Source Port	2	The 16-bit port number of the process that originated the UDP message on the source device. This will normally be an ephemeral (client) port number for a request that a client sends to a server or a well-known/registered (server) port number for a reply that a server sends to a client. (See Chapter 43 for details.)
Destination Port	2	The 16-bit port number of the process that is the ultimate intended recipient of the message on the destination device. This will usually be a well-known/registered (server) port number for a client request or an ephemeral (client) port number for a server reply. (See Chapter 43 for details.)
Length	2	The length of the entire UDP datagram, including both header and Data fields.
Checksum	2	An optional 16-bit checksum computed over the entire UDP datagram plus a special pseudo header of fields. See below for more information.
Data	Variable	The encapsulated higher-layer message that will be sent.

The UDP pseudo header format is illustrated in Figure 44-2.

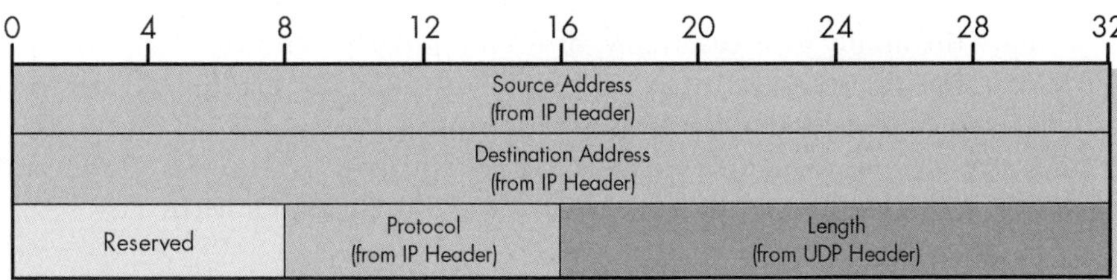

Figure 44-2: UDP pseudo header format

The total length of this pseudo header is 11 bytes. It is padded to 12 bytes with a byte of zeros and then prepended to the real UDP message. The checksum is then computed over the combination of the pseudo header and the real UDP message, and the value is placed into the Checksum field. The pseudo header is used only for this calculation and is then discarded; it is not actually transmitted. The UDP software in the destination device creates the same pseudo header when calculating its checksum in order to compare it to the one transmitted in the UDP header.

Computing the checksum over the regular UDP fields protects the UDP message against bit errors. Adding the pseudo header allows the checksum to also protect the UDP message against other types of problems as well, most notably the accidental delivery of a message to the wrong destination. The checksum calculation in UDP, including the use of the pseudo header, is exactly the same as the method used in TCP (except that the Length field is different in TCP). See Chapter 48 for a full description of why the pseudo header is important, as well as some of the interesting implications of using IP fields in transport layer datagram calculations.

> **KEY CONCEPT** UDP packages application layer data into a very simple message format that includes only four header fields. One of these is an optional Checksum field. When the Checksum field is used, the checksum is computed over both the real header and a pseudo header of fields from the UDP and IP headers, in a manner that's very similar to the way the TCP checksum is calculated.

Note that the use of the Checksum field is optional in UDP. If UDP doesn't use the Checksum field, UDP sets it to a value of all zeros. This could potentially create confusion, however, since when UDP uses the checksum, the calculation can sometimes result in a value of zero. To avoid having the destination think that UDP didn't use the checksum in this case, UDP instead represents this zero value as a value of all ones (65,535 decimal).

UDP Common Applications and Server Port Assignments

As you have seen, UDP contains very little functionality. With the exception of the important addressing capability that UDP ports represent, using UDP is very much like using IP. This means that UDP has most of the same disadvantages that IP has. It doesn't establish a lasting connection between devices; it doesn't acknowledge received data or retransmit lost messages; and it certainly isn't concerned with obscurities such as flow control and congestion management.

The absence of those features makes UDP simply unsuitable for the majority of classic networking applications. These applications usually need to establish a connection so that the two devices can exchange data. Many applications also must have the ability to occasionally, or even regularly, send very large amounts of data that must be received intact for it to be of value. For example, consider a message transfer protocol like the Hypertext Transfer Protocol (HTTP). If only part of a web page gets from a server back to a web browser, it's useless. HTTP and other file and message transfer protocols like it need the capabilities of TCP.

Why Some TCP/IP Applications Use UDP

So what applications use UDP then? UDP's classic limitation is that because it doesn't provide reliability features, an application that uses UDP is responsible for those functions. In reality, if an application needs the features that TCP provides but not the ones that UDP provides, it's inefficient to allow the application to implement those features, except in special cases. If the application needs what TCP provides, it should just use TCP! However, applications that only need some of what TCP implements are sometimes better off using UDP and implementing that limited set of functionality at the application level.

So, the applications that run over UDP are normally the ones that do not require all or even most of the features that TCP has. These applications can benefit from the increased efficiency that comes about from avoiding the setup and overhead associated with TCP. Applications usually (but not always) meet this description because the data they send falls into one of two categories:

Data Where Performance Is More Important Than Completeness The classic example of this category is a multimedia application. For streaming a video clip over the Internet, the most important feature is that the stream starts flowing quickly and keeps flowing. Human beings notice only significant disruptions in the flow of this type of information, so a few bytes of data missing due to a lost datagram is not a big problem. Furthermore, even if someone used TCP for something like this and noticed and retransmitted a lost datagram, it would be useless, because the lost datagram would belong to a part of the clip that is long past—and the time spent in that retransmission might make the current part of the clip arrive late. Clearly, UDP is best for this situation.

Data Exchanges That Are "Short and Sweet" There are many TCP/IP applications in which the underlying protocol consists of only a very simple request/reply exchange. A client sends a short request message to a server, and a short reply message goes back from the server to the client. In this situation, there is no real need to set up a connection the way that TCP does. Also, if a client sends only one short message, a single IP datagram can carry the message. This means that there is no need to worry about data arriving out of order, flow control between the devices, and so forth. How about the loss of the request or the reply? These can be handled simply at the application level using timers. If a client sends a request and the server doesn't get it, the server won't reply, and the client will eventually send a replacement request. The same logic applies if the server sends a response that never arrives.

These are the most common cases where UDP is used, but there are other reasons. For example, if an application needs to multicast or broadcast data, it must use UDP, because TCP is supported only for unicast communication between two devices.

> **KEY CONCEPT** A protocol uses UDP instead of TCP in two situations. The first is when an application values timely delivery over reliable delivery, and when TCP's retransmission of lost data would be of limited or even no value. The second is when a simple protocol can handle the potential loss of an IP datagram itself at the application layer using a timer/retransmit strategy, and when the other features of TCP are not required. Applications that require multicast or broadcast transmissions also use UDP, because TCP does not support those transmissions.

Incidentally, I have read about problems that have occurred in the past in applications using UDP. Sometimes, programmers don't realize how little UDP does, how it leaves the application responsible for handling all the potential vagaries of an internetworking environment. Someone writing a UDP-based application must always keep in mind that no one can make assumptions about how or even whether a destination will receive any message. Insufficient testing can lead to disaster in worst-case scenarios on a larger internetwork, especially the Internet.

Common UDP Applications and Server Port Use

Table 44-2 shows some of the more interesting protocols that use UDP and the well-known and registered port numbers used for each one's server processes. It also provides a very brief description of why these protocols use UDP instead of TCP.

Applications That Use Both UDP and TCP

There are some protocols that use both of the TCP/IP transport layer protocols. This is often the case either for utility protocols that are designed to accept connections using both transport layer protocols, or for applications that need the benefits of TCP in some cases but not others.

The classic example of the latter is the TCP/IP Domain Name System (DNS), which normally uses UDP port 53 for simple requests and replies, which are usually short. Larger messages requiring reliable delivery, such as zone transfers, use TCP port 53 instead. Note that in Table 44-2, I have omitted some of the less-significant protocols such as the ones used for diagnostic purposes (Echo, Discard, CharGen, and so on). For a full list of all common applications, see Chapter 43.

Table 44-2: Common UDP Applications and Server Port Assignments

Port #	Keyword	Protocol	Comments
53	domain	Domain Name Server (DNS)	Uses a simple request/reply messaging system for most exchanges (but also uses TCP for longer ones).
67 and 68	bootps/ bootpc	Bootstrap Protocol (BOOTP) and Dynamic Host Configuration Protocol (DHCP)	Host configuration protocols that consist of short request and reply exchanges.
69	tftp	Trivial File Transfer Protocol (TFTP)	TFTP is a great example of a protocol that was specifically designed for UDP, especially when you compare it to regular FTP. The latter protocol uses TCP to establish a session between two devices and then makes use of its own large command set and TCP's features in order to ensure the reliable transfer of possibly very large files. In contrast, TFTP is designed for the quick and easy transfer of small files. To avoid file corruption, TFTP includes simple versions of some of TCP's features, such as acknowledgments.
161 and 162	snmp	Simple Network Management Protocol	An administrative protocol that uses relatively short messages.
520 and 521	router/ ripng	Routing Information Protocol (RIP-1, RIP-2, RIPng)	Unlike more complex routing protocols like BGP, RIP uses a simple request/reply messaging system, doesn't require connections, and does require multicasts/broadcasts. This makes it a natural choice for UDP. If a routing update is sent due to a request and is lost, it can be replaced by sending a new request. Routine (unsolicited) updates that are lost are replaced in the next cycle.
2049	nfs	Network File System	NFS is an interesting case. Since it is a file-sharing protocol, you would think that it would use TCP instead of UDP, but it was originally designed to use UDP for performance reasons. There were many people who felt that this was not the best design decision, and later versions moved to the use of TCP. The latest version of NFS uses only TCP.

45

TCP OVERVIEW, FUNCTIONS, AND CHARACTERISTICS

As I mentioned in Chapter 42, the Transmission Control Protocol (TCP) is a critically important part of the TCP/IP protocol suite. It's also a fairly complicated protocol, with a lot of important concepts and mechanisms that you need to understand. The old joke says the "best way to eat an elephant is one bite at a time." Similarly here, you can best comprehend the operation of this complicated protocol by going slowly, starting with a high-level look at it, where it came from, and what it does.

In this chapter, I begin by introducing you to TCP. I first provide an overview and history of TCP and then describe the standards that define it. Then I illustrate what TCP actually does by listing its functions and explaining how TCP works by describing its most important characteristics. This will give you a feel for what TCP is all about, and it will set the stage for the more complex technical discussions in subsequent chapters.

TCP Overview, History, and Standards

Between them, layers 3 and 4 of the OSI Reference Model represent the interface between networking software (the applications that need to move data across networks) and networking hardware (the devices that carry the data over networks). Any protocol suite must have a protocol or set of protocols that handles these layer 3 and layer 4 functions.

The TCP/IP protocol suite is named for the two main protocols that provide these capabilities. Both TCP and the Internet Protocol (IP) allow software to run on an internetwork. IP deals with internetwork datagram delivery and routing, while TCP handles connections and provides reliability. What's interesting, however, is that in the early days of the protocol suite, there was, in fact, no TCP/IP at all.

TCP History

Due to its prominent role in the history of networking, TCP is impossible to describe without going back to the early days of the protocol suite. In the early 1970s, what we know today as the global Internet was a small research internetwork called the *ARPAnet*, an acronym that came from the United States Defense Advanced Research Projects Agency (DARPA or ARPA). This network used a technology called the *Network Control Protocol (NCP)*, which allowed hosts to connect to each other. NCP did approximately the same job that TCP and IP do together today.

Due to limitations in NCP, development began on a new protocol that would be better suited to a growing internetwork. This new protocol, first formalized in RFC 675, was called the Internet *Transmission Control Program (TCP)*. Like its predecessor NCP, TCP was responsible for basically everything that was needed to allow applications to run on an internetwork. Thus, TCP was at first both TCP and IP.

As I explain in detail in the description of the history of TCP/IP as a whole in Chapter 8, several years were spent adjusting and revising TCP, with version 2 of the protocol documented in 1977. While the functionality of TCP was steadily improved, there was a problem with the basic concept behind the protocol. Having TCP handle datagram transmissions, routing (layer 3 functions), and connections, reliability, and data-flow management (layer 4 functions) meant that TCP violated key concepts of protocol layering and modularity. TCP forced all applications to use the layer 4 functions in order to use the layer 3 functions. This made TCP inflexible and poorly suited to the needs of applications that required only the lower-level functions and not the higher-level ones.

As a result, the decision was made to split TCP into two: the layer 4 functions were retained, with TCP renamed the *Transmission Control Protocol* (as opposed to Transmission Control Program). The layer 3 functions became the Internet Protocol. This split was finalized in version 4 of TCP, and so the first IP was given "version 4" as well, for consistency. RFC 793, "Transmission Control Protocol," published in September 1981, defined TCP version 4, and it is still the current version of the standard.

Even though it is more than 20 years old and is the first version most people have ever used, version 4 was the result of several years' work and many earlier TCP versions tested on the early Internet. It is therefore a very mature protocol for its age. A precocious protocol, you might say. (To be fair, other standards have described many additional features and modifications to TCP, rather than upgrading the main document.)

Overview of TCP Operation

TCP is a full-featured transport layer protocol that provides all the functions that a typical application needs for the reliable transportation of data across an arbitrary internetwork. It provides transport layer addressing for application processes in the form of TCP ports and allows machines to use these ports in order to establishing connections between them. Once the devices have connected to each other, they can pass data bidirectionally between them. Applications can send data to TCP as a simple stream of bytes, and TCP takes care of packaging and sending the data as segments that TCP packages into IP datagrams. The receiving device's TCP implementation reverses the process, passing up to the application the stream of data that the device originally sent.

TCP includes an extensive set of mechanisms. These mechanisms ensure that data gets from source to destination reliably, consistently, and in a timely fashion. The key to its operation in this regard is the *sliding window acknowledgment system*, which allows each device to keep track of the bytes of data it has sent and to confirm the receipt of data received from the other device in the connection. Unacknowledged data is eventually retransmitted automatically, and the parameters of the system can be adjusted to the needs of the devices and the connection. This same system also provides buffering and flow control capabilities between devices. These capabilities handle uneven data delivery rates and other problems.

KEY CONCEPT The primary transport layer protocol in the TCP/IP protocol suite is the *Transmission Control Protocol (TCP)*. TCP is a connection-oriented, acknowledged, reliable, full-featured protocol designed to provide applications with a reliable way to send data using the unreliable Internet Protocol (IP). It allows applications to send bytes of data as a stream of bytes and automatically packages them into appropriately sized segments for transmission. It uses a special *sliding window acknowledgment system* to ensure that its recipient receives all data, handles necessary retransmissions, and provides flow control so that each device in a connection can manage the rate at which other devices send data to it.

Because of TCP's many capabilities, it's likely that the protocol will satisfy just about any application that requires reliable, connection-oriented data delivery. A primary goal of TCP, reliable data delivery means that higher-layer applications don't need to provide TCP's common functions. Because the majority of conventional message-passing applications employ it, the TCP/IP transport protocol is the most widely used transport protocol.

TCP Standards

RFC 793 is the defining standard for TCP, but it doesn't include all the details about how modern TCP operates. Several other standards include additional information about how the protocol works and describe enhancements to the basic

TCP mechanisms that were developed over the years. Some of these are fairly esoteric, but they are useful for gaining a more complete understanding of TCP. I have listed some of them in Table 45-1.

Table 45-1: Supplementary TCP Standards

RFC #	Name	Description
813	Window and Acknowledgment Strategy in TCP	Discusses the TCP sliding window acknowledgment system, describes certain problems that can occur with it, and offers methods to correct them.
879	The TCP Maximum Segment Size and Related Topics	Discusses the important maximum segment size (MSS) parameter that controls the size of TCP messages, and then relates this parameter to IP datagram size.
896	Congestion Control in IP/TCP Internetworks	Talks about congestion problems and how you can use TCP to handle them. Note the interesting inversion of the normal protocol suite name: IP/TCP.
1122	Requirements for Internet Hosts — Communication Layers	Describes important details of how TCP should be implemented on hosts.
1146	TCP Alternate Checksum Options	Specifies a mechanism for having TCP devices use an alternative method of checksum generation.
1323	TCP Extensions for High Performance	Defines extensions to TCP for high-speed links and new TCP options.
2018	TCP Selective Acknowledgment Options	An enhancement to basic TCP functionality that allows TCP devices to selectively specify specific segments for retransmission.
2581	TCP Congestion Control	Describes four algorithms used for congestion control in TCP networks: slow start, congestion avoidance, fast retransmit, and fast recovery.
2988	Computing TCP's Retransmission Timer	Discusses issues related to setting the TCP retransmission timer, which controls how long a device waits for acknowledgment of sent data before retransmitting it.

There are hundreds of higher-layer application protocols that use TCP and whose defining standards therefore make at least glancing reference to it.

TCP is designed to use IP, since they were developed together and as you have seen, were even once part of the same specification. They were later split up in order to respect the principles of architectural layering. For this reason, TCP tries to make as few assumptions as possible regarding the underlying protocol over which it runs. It is not as strictly tied to the use of IP as you might imagine, and you can even adapt it for use over other network layer protocols. For our purposes, however, this should be considered mainly an interesting aside.

TCP Functions

You have now seen where TCP comes from and the standards that describe it. As I said in the introduction to this chapter, TCP is a complicated protocol, so it will take some time to explain how it works. Here, I'll describe what TCP does and what it doesn't do.

Functions That TCP Performs

Despite the TCP's complexity, I can simplify its basic operation by describing its primary functions. The following are what I believe to be the six main tasks that TCP performs:

Addressing/Multiplexing Many different applications use TCP for a transport protocol. Therefore, like its simpler sibling, the User Datagram Protocol (UDP), multiplexing the data that TCP receives from these different processes so that the data can be sent out using the underlying network layer protocol is an important job for TCP. At the same time, these higher-layer application processes are identified using TCP ports. Chapter 43 contains a great deal of detail about how this addressing works.

Establishing, Managing, and Terminating Connections TCP provides a set of procedures that devices can follow in order to negotiate and establish a TCP connection over which data can travel. Once a connection is opened, TCP includes logic for managing the connection and handling problems that may result with the connection. When a device is finished with a TCP connection, a special process is followed to terminate it.

Handling and Packaging Data TCP defines a mechanism by which applications are able to send data to TCP from higher layers. This data is then packaged into messages that will be sent to the destination TCP software. The destination software unpackages the data and gives it to the application on the destination machine.

Transferring Data Conceptually, the TCP implementation on a transmitting device is responsible for the transfer of packaged data to the TCP process on the other device. Following the principle of layering, this transfer is done by having the TCP software on the sending machine pass the data packets to the underlying network layer protocol, which again normally means IP.

Providing Reliability and Transmission Quality Services TCP includes a set of services and features that allows an application to consider the protocol a reliable means of sending of data. This means that normally a TCP application doesn't need to worry about data being sent and never showing up or arriving in the wrong order. It also means that other common problems that might arise if IP were used directly are avoided.

Providing Flow Control and Congestion Avoidance Features TCP allows the flow of data between two devices to be controlled and managed. It also includes features that deal with congestion that devices may experience during communication between each other.

Functions That TCP Doesn't Perform

Clearly, TCP is responsible for a fairly significant number of key functions. The items listed in the preceding section may not seem that impressive, but this is just a high-level look at the protocol. When you look at these functions in detail, you will see that each one actually involves a rather significant amount of work for TCP to do.

Conversely, sometimes TCP is described as doing everything an application needs in order to use an internetwork. However, the protocol doesn't do everything. It has limitations and certain areas that its designers specifically did not address. The following are some of the notable functions that TCP does not perform:

Specifying Application Use TCP defines the transport protocol. It does not specifically describe how applications should use TCP. That is up to the application protocol.

Providing Security TCP does not provide any mechanism for ensuring the authenticity or privacy of data that it transmits. If authenticity and privacy are important to applications, they must accomplish them using some other means, such as IPsec, for example.

Maintaining Message Boundaries TCP sends data as a continuous stream rather than discrete messages. It is up to the application to specify where one message ends and the next begins.

Guaranteeing Communication Wait a minute; isn't TCP supposed to guarantee that data will get to its destination? Well, yes and no. TCP will detect unacknowledged transmissions and resend them if needed. However, if some sort of problem prevents reliable communication, all TCP can do is keep trying. It can't make any guarantees, because there are too many things out of its control. Similarly, it can attempt to manage the flow of data, but it cannot resolve every problem.

This last point might seem a bit pedantic, but it is important to keep in mind, especially since many people tend to think of TCP as bulletproof. The overall success of communication depends entirely on the underlying internetwork and the networks that constitute it. A chain is as strong as its weakest link, and if there is a problem at the lower layers, nothing TCP can do will guarantee successful data transfer.

> **KEY CONCEPT** TCP provides reliable communication only by detecting failed transmissions and resending them. It cannot guarantee any particular transmission, because it relies on IP, which is unreliable. All it can do is keep trying if an initial delivery attempt fails.

TCP Characteristics

In many ways, it is more interesting to look at how TCP does its job than the functions of the job. By examining the most important attributes of TCP and its operation, you can get a better handle on the way TCP works. You can also see the many ways that it contrasts with its simpler transport layer sibling, UDP.

TCP has the following characteristics, which allow it to perform its functions:

Connection-Oriented TCP requires that devices first establish a connection with each other before they send data. The connection creates the equivalent of a circuit between the units; it is analogous to a telephone call. A process of negotiation occurs, and that process establishes the connection, thereby ensuring that both devices agree on how they will exchange data.

Bidirectional Once a connection is established, TCP devices send data bidirectionally. Both devices on the connection can send and receive, regardless of which one initiated the connection.

Multiply Connected and Endpoint Identified The pair of sockets used by the two devices in the connection identifies the endpoints of the TCP connection. This identification method allows each device to have multiple connections opened, either to the same IP device or different IP devices, and to handle each connection independently without conflicts.

Reliable Communication using TCP is said to be reliable because TCP keeps track of data that has been sent and received to ensure that all the data gets to its destination. As you saw in the previous section earlier, TCP can't really guarantee that data will always be received. However, it can guarantee that all data sent will be checked for reception, checked for data integrity, and then retransmitted when needed.

Acknowledged A key to providing reliability is that TCP acknowledges all transmissions at the TCP layer. Furthermore, TCP cannot guarantee that the remote application will receive all such transmissions. The recipient must tell the sender, "Yes, I got that" for each piece of data transferred. This is in stark contrast to typical messaging protocols in which the sender never knows what happened to its transmission. As you will see, this acknowledgment is fundamental to the operation of TCP as a whole.

Stream-Oriented Most lower-layer protocols are designed so that higher-layer protocols must send them data in blocks in order to use them. IP is the best example of this; you send it a message to be formatted and IP puts that message into a datagram. UDP works the same way. In contrast, TCP allows applications to send it a continuous stream of data for transmission. Applications don't need to worry about dividing this stream into chunks for transmission; TCP does it.

Unstructured Data An important consequence of TCP's stream orientation is that there are no natural divisions between data elements in the application's data stream. When multiple messages are sent over TCP, applications must provide a way of differentiating one message (data element, record, and so on) from the next.

Managed Data Flow TCP does more than just package data and send it as fast as possible. A TCP connection is managed to ensure that data flows evenly and smoothly and that connection includes the ability to deal with problems that arise along the way.

You'll notice that I have not listed "slow" as one of TCP's characteristics. It is true that applications use UDP for performance reasons when they don't want to deal with the overhead that TCP incorporates for connections and reliability. That, however, should not lead you to conclude that TCP is glacially slow. It is in fact quite efficient—were it not, it's unlikely that it would have ever achieved such widespread use.

KEY CONCEPT To summarize TCP's key characteristics, we can say that it is connection-oriented, bidirectional, multiply connected, reliable, acknowledged, stream-oriented, and flow-managed.

The Robustness Principle

The TCP standard says that TCP follows the *robustness principle*, which is described in this way: "Be conservative in what you do; be liberal in what you accept from others." This rule means that every TCP implementation tries to avoid doing anything that would cause a problem for another device's TCP layer. At the same time, every TCP implementation is also trying to anticipate problems that another TCP may cause and attempting to deal with those problems gracefully.

This principle represents a "belt and suspenders" approach that helps provide extra protection against unusual conditions in TCP operation. In fact, this general principle is applied to many other protocols in the TCP/IP protocol suite, which is part of the reason why it has proven to be so capable over the years. The principle allows TCP and other protocols to deal with unanticipated problems that might show up in the difficult environment of a large internetwork such as the Internet.

46

TRANSMISSION CONTROL PROTOCOL (TCP) FUNDAMENTALS AND GENERAL OPERATION

Many people have a difficult time understanding how the Transmission Control Protocol (TCP) works. After spending dozens of hours writing almost 100 pages on the protocol, I am quite sympathetic! I think a main reason for the difficulty is that many descriptions of the protocol leap too quickly from a brief introduction straight into the mind-boggling details of TCP's operation. The problem is that TCP works in a very particular way. Its operation is built around a few very important fundamentals that you absolutely must understand before the details of TCP operation will make much sense.

In this chapter, I describe some of the key operating fundamentals of TCP. I begin with a discussion of how TCP handles data and introduce the concepts of streams, segments, and sequences. I then describe the very important TCP sliding window system, which is used for acknowledgment, reliability, and data flow control. I discuss how TCP uses ports and how it identifies connections. I also describe the most important applications that use TCP and what ports they use for server applications.

TCP Data Handling and Processing

One of the givens in the operation of most of the protocols you'll find at upper layers in the OSI Reference Model is that the protocols are oriented around the use of messages. These messages are analogous to a written letter in an envelope that contains a specific piece of information. They are passed from higher layers down to lower ones, where they are encapsulated in the lower layers' headers (like putting them in another envelope), and then passed down further until they are actually sent out at the physical layer.

You can see a good example of this by looking at the User Datagram Protocol (UDP), TCP's transport layer peer. To use UDP, an application passes it a distinct block of data that is usually fairly short. The block is packaged into a UDP message, then sent to the Internet Protocol (IP). IP packs the message into an IP datagram and eventually passes it to a layer 2 protocol such as Ethernet. There, IP places it into a frame and sends it to layer 1 for transmission.

Increasing the Flexibility of Application Data Handling: TCP's Stream Orientation

The use of discrete messaging is pretty simple, and it obviously works well enough since most protocols make use of it. However, it is inherently limiting because it forces applications to create discrete blocks of data in order to communicate. There are many applications that need to send information continuously in a manner that doesn't lend itself well to creating "chunks" of data. Others need to send data in chunks that are so large that applications could never send them as a single message at the lower layers.

To use a protocol like UDP, many applications would be forced to artificially divide their data into messages of a size that has no inherent meaning to them. This would immediately introduce new problems that would require more work for the application. The application would have to keep track of what data is in what message, and replace any data that was lost. It would need to ensure that the messages could be reassembled in the correct order, since IP might deliver them out of order.

Of course, you could program applications to do this, but it would make little sense, because these functions are already ones that TCP is charged with handling. Instead, the TCP designers took the very smart approach of generalizing TCP so that it could accept application data of any size and structure without requiring the data to be in discrete pieces. More specifically, TCP treats data coming from an application as a *stream*—thus, the description of TCP as *stream-oriented.* Each application sends the data it wishes to transmit as a steady stream of octets (bytes). The application doesn't need to carve the data into blocks or worry about how lengthy streams will get across the internetwork. It just "pumps bytes" to TCP.

TCP Data Packaging: Segments

TCP must take the bytes it gets from an application and send them using a network layer protocol, which is IP in this case. IP is a message-oriented protocol; it is not stream-oriented. Thus, we have simply "passed the buck" to TCP, which must take the stream from the application and divide it into discrete messages for IP. These messages are called *TCP segments.*

NOTE *Segment is one of the most confusing data structure names in the world of networking. From a dictionary definition standpoint, referring to a piece of a stream as a* segment *is sensible, but most people working with networks don't think of a message as being a segment. In the industry, the term also refers to a length of cable or a part of a local area network (LAN), among other things, so watch out for that.*

IP treats TCP segments like all other discrete messages for transmission. IP places them into IP datagrams and transmits them to the destination device. The recipient unpackages the segments and passes them to TCP, which converts them back to a byte stream in order to send them to the application. This process is illustrated in Figure 46-1.

KEY CONCEPT TCP is designed to have applications send data to it as a stream of bytes, rather than requiring fixed-size messages to be used. This provides maximum flexibility for a wide variety of uses, because applications don't need to worry about data packaging and can send files or messages of any size. TCP takes care of packaging these bytes into messages called *segments*.

The TCP layer on a device accumulates data that it receives from the application process stream. On regular intervals, the TCP layer forms segments that it will transmit using IP. Two primary factors control the size of the segment. First, there is an overall limit to the size of a segment, chosen to prevent unnecessary fragmentation at the IP layer. A parameter called the *maximum segment size (MSS)* governs this size limit. The MSS is determined during connection establishment. Second, TCP is designed so that once a connection is set up, each of the devices tells the other how much data it is ready to accept at any given time. If the data is lower than the MSS value, the device must send a smaller segment. This is part of the sliding window system described a little later in this chapter.

TCP Data Identification: Sequence Numbers

The fact that TCP treats data coming from an application as a stream of octets has a couple of very significant implications for the operation of the protocol. The first is related to data identification. Since TCP is reliable, it needs to keep track of all the data it receives from an application so it can make sure that the destination receives all the data. Furthermore, TCP must make sure that the destination receives the data in the order that the application sent it, and the destination must retransmit any lost data.

If a device conveyed data to TCP in block-like messages, it would be fairly simple to keep track of the data by adding an identifier to each message. Because TCP is stream-oriented, however, that identification must be done for each byte of data! This may seem surprising, but it is actually what TCP does through the use of sequence numbers. Each byte of data is assigned a sequence number that is used to keep track of it through the process of transmission, reception, and acknowledgment (though in practice, blocks of many bytes are managed using the sequence numbers of bytes at the start and end of the block). These sequence numbers are used to ensure that the sending application transmits and reassembles the segmented data into the original stream of data. The sequence numbers are required to implement the sliding window system, which enables TCP to provide reliability and data flow control.

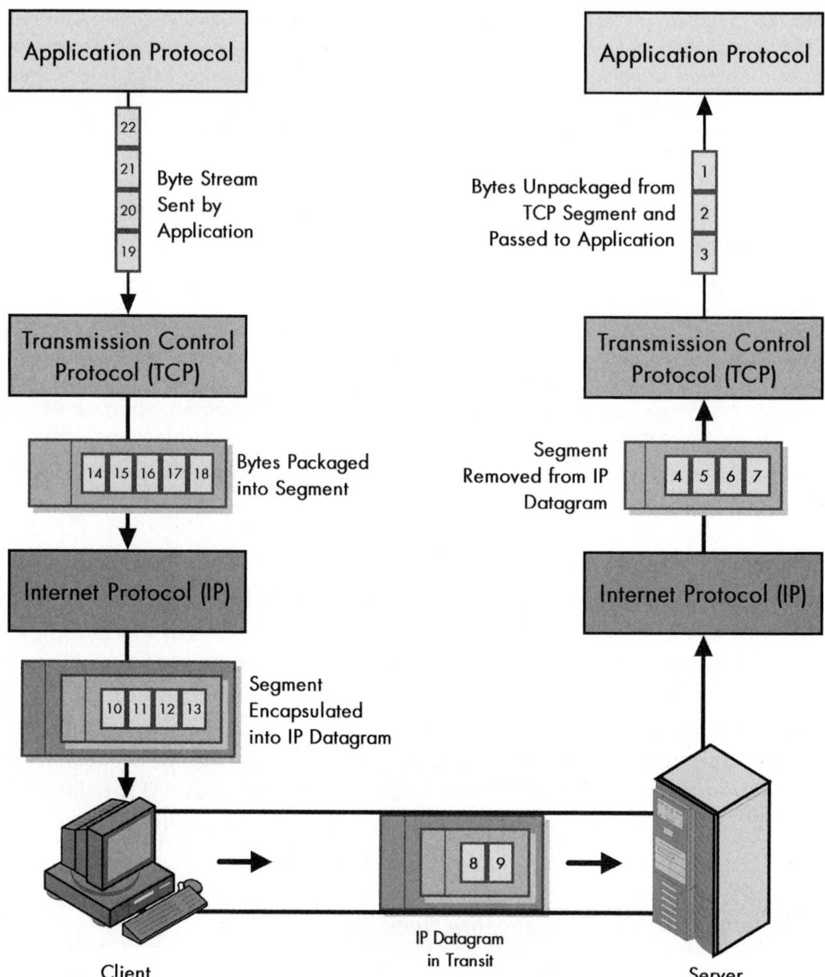

Figure 46-1: TCP data stream processing and segment packaging *TCP is different from most protocols because it does not require applications that use it to send data to it in messages. Once a TCP connection is set up, an application protocol can send TCP a steady stream of bytes that does not need to conform to any particular structure. TCP packages these bytes into segments that are sized based on a number of different parameters. These segments are passed to IP, where they are encapsulated into IP datagrams and transmitted. The receiving device reverses the process: Segments are removed from IP datagrams, and then the bytes are taken from the segments and passed up to the appropriate recipient application protocol as a byte stream.*

KEY CONCEPT Since TCP works with individual bytes of data rather than discrete messages, it must use an identification scheme that works at the byte level to implement its data transmission and tracking system. This is accomplished by assigning a sequence number to each byte that TCP processes.

The Need for Application Data Delimiting

When TCP treats incoming data as a stream, the data the application using TCP receives is called *unstructured.* For transmission, a stream of data goes into TCP on the sending device, and on reception, a stream of data goes back to the application on the receiving device. Even though TCP breaks the stream into segments for transmission, these segments are TCP-level details that remain hidden from the application. When a device wants to send multiple pieces of data, TCP provides no mechanism for indicating where the dividing line is between the pieces, since TCP doesn't examine the meaning of the data. The application must provide a means for doing this.

Consider, for example, an application that is sending database records. It needs to transmit record 579 from the Employees database table, followed by record 581 and record 611. It sends these records to TCP, which treats them all collectively as a stream of bytes. TCP will package these bytes into segments, but in a way that the application cannot predict. It is possible that each byte will end up in a different segment, but more likely that they will all be in one segment, or that part of each will end up in different segments, depending on their length. The records must have some sort of explicit markers so that the receiving device can tell where one record ends and the next starts.

KEY CONCEPT Since applications send data to TCP as a stream of bytes as opposed to prepackaged messages, each application must use its own scheme to determine where one application data element ends and the next begins.

TCP Sliding Window Acknowledgment System

What differentiates TCP from simpler transport protocols like UDP is the quality of the manner in which it sends data between devices. Rather than just sticking data in a message and saying, "off you go," TCP carefully keeps track of the data it sends. This management of data is required to facilitate the following two key requirements of the protocol:

Reliability Ensuring that data that is sent actually arrives at its destination, and if it doesn't arrive, detecting this and resending it.

Data Flow Control Managing the rate at which data is sent so that it does not overwhelm the device that is receiving it.

To accomplish these tasks, the entire operation of the protocol is oriented around something called the *sliding window acknowledgment system.* It is no exaggeration to say that comprehending how sliding windows work is critical to understanding just about everything else in TCP. It is also, unfortunately, a bit hard to follow if you try to grasp it all at once. I wanted to make sure that I explained the mechanism thoroughly without assuming that you already understood it. For this reason, I am going to start by explaining the concepts behind sliding windows, particularly how the technique works and why it is so powerful.

The Problem with Unreliable Protocols: Lack of Feedback

A simple "send and forget" protocol like IP is unreliable and includes no flow control for one main reason: It is an open-loop system in which the transmitter receives no feedback from the recipient. (I am ignoring error reports using ICMP and the like for the purpose of this discussion.) A datagram is sent, and it may or may not get there, but the transmitter will never have any way of knowing because there is no mechanism for feedback. This concept is illustrated in Figure 46-2.

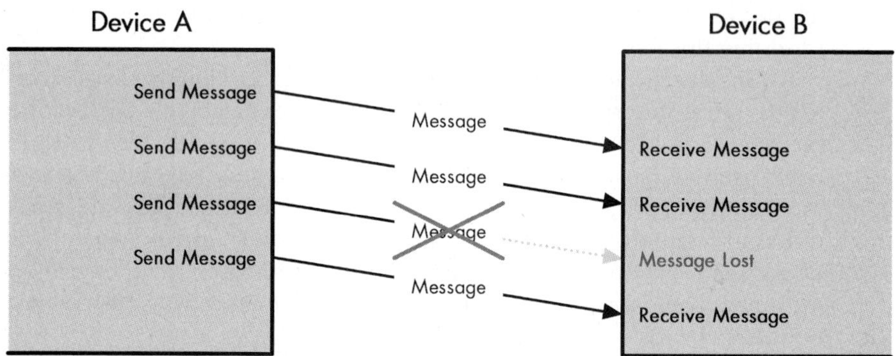

Figure 46-2: Operation of an unreliable protocol *In a system such as the one that IP uses, if a message gets to its destination, that's great; otherwise, nobody will have a clue. Some external mechanism is needed to take care of the lost message, unless the protocol doesn't really care whether a few bits and pieces are missing from its message stream.*

Providing Basic Reliability Using Positive Acknowledgment with Retransmission (PAR)

Basic reliability in a protocol running over an unreliable protocol like IP can be implemented by closing the loop so the recipient provides feedback to the sender. This is most easily done with a simple acknowledgment system. Device A sends a piece of data to Device B, which receives the data and sends back an acknowledgment saying, "Device A, I received your message." Device A then knows its transmission was successful.

But since IP is unreliable, that message may in fact never get to where it is going. Device A will sit and wait for the acknowledgment and never receive it. Conversely, it is also possible that Device B gets the message from Device A, but the acknowledgment itself vanishes somehow. In either case, we don't want Device A to sit forever waiting for an acknowledgment that is never going to arrive.

To prevent this from happening, Device A starts a timer when it first sends the message to Device B, which allows sufficient time for the message to get to Device B and for the acknowledgment to travel back, plus some reasonable time to allow for possible delays. If the timer expires before the acknowledgment is received, Device A assumes that there was a problem and retransmits its original message. Since this method involves positive acknowledgments ("Yes, I got your message") and a facility for retransmission when needed, it is commonly called *positive acknowledgment with retransmission (PAR)*, as shown in Figure 46-3.

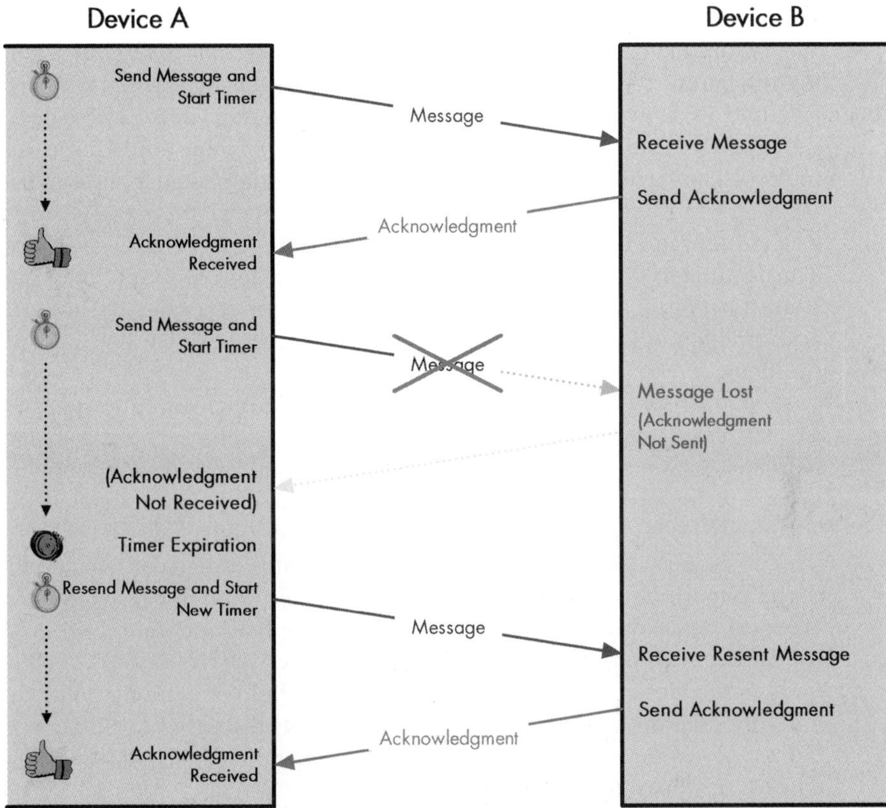

Figure 46-3: Basic reliability: positive acknowledgment with retransmission (PAR) *This diagram shows one of the most common and simple techniques for ensuring reliability. Each time Device A sends a message, it starts a timer. Device B sends an acknowledgment back to Device A when it receives a message, so that Device A knows that it successfully transmitted the message. If a message is lost, the timer goes off, and Device A retransmits the data. Note that only one message can be outstanding at any time, making this system rather slow.*

> **KEY CONCEPT** A basic technique for ensuring reliability in communications uses a rule that requires a device to send back an acknowledgment each time it successfully receives a transmission. If a device doesn't acknowledge the transmission after a period of time, its sender retransmits the acknowledgment. This system is called *positive acknowledgment with retransmission (PAR)*. One drawback with this basic scheme is that the transmitter cannot send a second message until after the first device has acknowledged the first.

PAR is a technique that is used widely in networking and communications for protocols that exchange relatively small amounts of data, or protocols that exchange data infrequently. The basic method is functional, but it is not well suited to a protocol like TCP. One main reason is that it is *inefficient.* Device A sends a message, and then waits for the acknowledgment. Device A cannot send another message to Device B until it hears that Device B received its original message, which is very wasteful and would make the protocol extremely slow.

Improving PAR

The first improvement we can make to the PAR system is to provide some means of identification to the messages that were sent, as well as the acknowledgments. For example, we could put a message ID field in the message header. The device sending the message would uniquely identify it, and the recipient would use this identifier in the acknowledgment. For example, Device A might send a piece of data in a message with the message ID 1. Device B would receive the message and then send its own message back to Device A, saying "Device A, I received your message 1." The advantage of this system is that Device A can send multiple messages at once. It must keep track of each one that it sends, and whether or not Device B sent an acknowledgment. Each device also requires a separate timer, but that's not a big problem.

Of course, we also need to consider this exchange from the standpoint of Device B. Before, Device B had to deal with only one message at a time from Device A. Now it may have several show up all at once. What if it is already busy with transmissions from another device (or ten)? We need some mechanism that lets Device B say, "I am only willing to handle the following number of messages from you at a time." We could do that by having the acknowledgment message contain a field, such as send limit, which specifies the maximum number of unacknowledged messages Device A was allowed to have in transit to Device B at one time.

Device A would use this send limit field to restrict the rate at which it sent messages to Device B. Device B could adjust this field depending on its current load and other factors to maximize performance in its discussions with Device A. This enhanced system would thus provide reliability, efficiency, and basic data flow control, as illustrated in Figure 46-4.

> **KEY CONCEPT** The basic PAR reliability scheme can be enhanced by identifying each message to be sent, so multiple messages can be in transit at once. The use of a send limit allows the mechanism to also provide flow control capabilities, by allowing each device to control the rate at which other devices send data to it.

TCP's Stream-Oriented Sliding Window Acknowledgment System

So does TCP use this variation on PAR? Of course not! That would be too simple. Conceptually, the TCP sliding window system is very similar to this method, which is why it is important that you understand it. However, it requires some adjustment. The main reason has to do with the way TCP handles data: the matter of stream orientation compared to message orientation discussed earlier in this chapter. The technique I have outlined involves explicit acknowledgments and (if necessary) retransmissions for messages. Thus, it would work well for a protocol that exchanged reasonably large messages on a fairly infrequent basis.

TCP, on the other hand, deals with individual bytes of data as a stream. Transmitting each byte one at a time and acknowledging each one at a time would quite obviously be absurd. It would require too much work, and even with overlapped transmissions (that is, not waiting for an acknowledgment before sending the next piece of data), the result would be horribly slow.

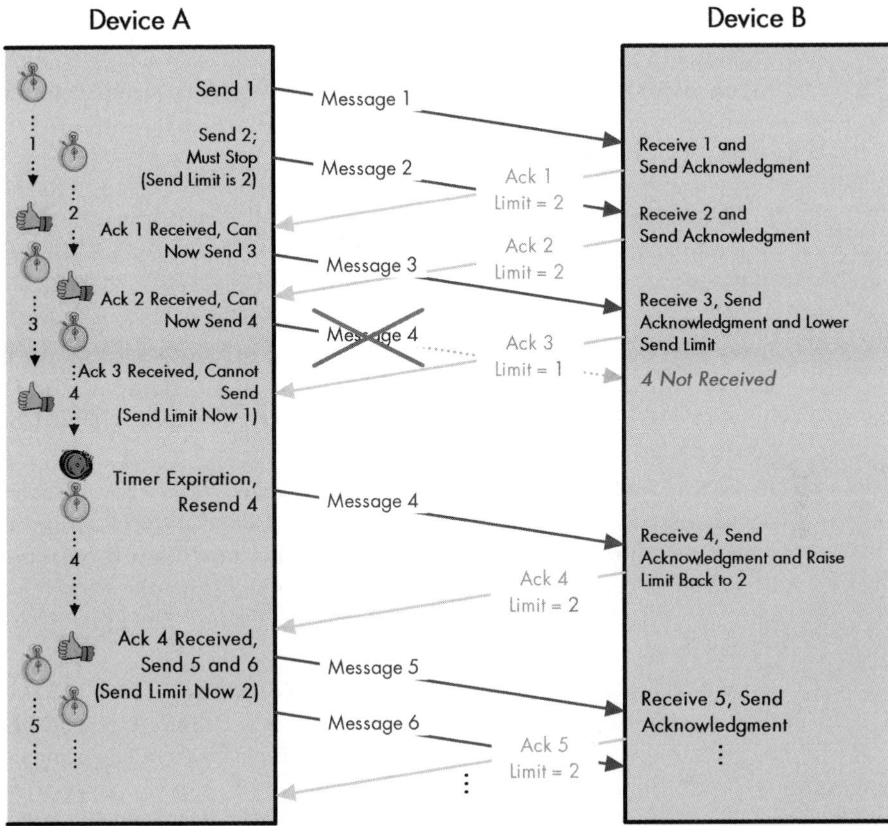

Figure 46-4: Enhanced PAR *This diagram shows two enhancements to the basic PAR scheme from Figure 46-3. First, each message now has an identification number; each can be acknowledged individually, so more than one message can be in transit at a given time. Second, Device B regularly communicates to Device A a send limit parameter, which restricts the number of messages Device A can have outstanding at once. Device B can adjust this parameter to control the flow of data from Device A.*

This slowness is why TCP does not send bytes individually but divides them into segments. All of the bytes in a segment are sent together and received together, and thus acknowledged together. TCP uses a variation on the method I described earlier, in which the sequence numbers I discussed earlier identify the data sent and acknowledged. Instead of acknowledging the use of something like a message ID field, we acknowledge data using the sequence number of the last byte of data in the segment. Thus, we are dealing with a range of bytes in each case, and the range represents the sequence numbers of all the bytes in the segment.

Conceptual Division of TCP Transmission Stream into Categories

Imagine a newly established TCP connection between Device A and Device B. Device A has a long stream of bytes that it will transmit, but Device B can't accept them all at once, so it limits Device A to sending a particular number of bytes at once in segments, until the bytes in the segments already sent have been acknowledged. Then Device A is allowed to send more bytes. Each device keeps track of which bytes have been sent and which have not, and which have been acknowledged.

At any point in time, we can take a "snapshot" of the process. If we do, we can conceptually divide the bytes that the sending TCP has in its buffer into the following four categories, and view them as a timeline (see Figure 46-5):

1. **Bytes Sent and Acknowledged** The earliest bytes in the stream will have been sent and acknowledged. These bytes are basically viewed from the standpoint of the device sending data. In the example in Figure 46-5, 31 bytes of data have already been sent and acknowledged. These would fall into category 1.
2. **Bytes Sent but Not Yet Acknowledged** These are the bytes that the device has sent but for which it has not yet received an acknowledgment. The sender cannot consider these handled until they are acknowledged. In Figure 46-5, there are 14 bytes here, in category 2.
3. **Bytes Not Yet Sent for Which Recipient Is Ready** These are bytes that the device has not sent, but which the recipient has room for based on its most recent communication to the sender regarding how many bytes it is willing to handle at once. The sender will try to send these immediately (subject to certain algorithmic restrictions that you'll explore later). In Figure 46-5, there are 6 bytes in category 3.
4. **Bytes Not Yet Sent for Which Recipient Is Not Ready** These are the bytes further down the stream, which the sender is not yet allowed to send because the receiver is not ready. In Figure 46-5, there are 44 bytes in category 4.

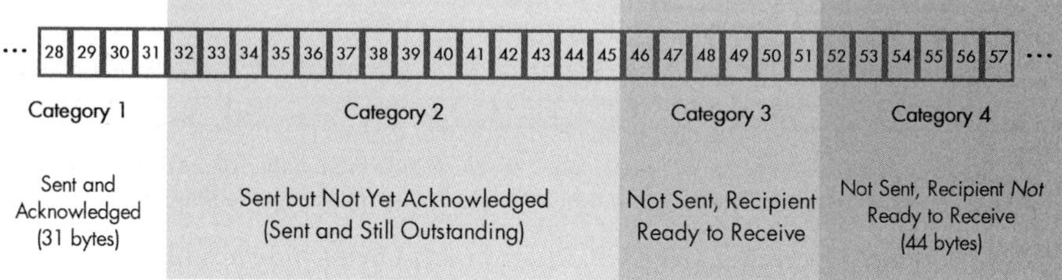

Figure 46-5: Conceptual division of TCP transmission stream into categories

NOTE *I am using very small numbers here to keep the example simple and to make the diagrams a bit easier to construct! TCP does not normally send tiny numbers of bytes around for efficiency reasons.*

The receiving device uses a similar system in order to differentiate between data received and acknowledged, data not yet received but ready to receive, and data not yet received and not yet ready to be received. In fact, both devices maintain a separate set of variables to keep track of the categories into which bytes fall in the stream they are sending, as well as the stream they are receiving. This is explored further in Chapter 48's section named "TCP Sliding Window Data Transfer and Acknowledgment Mechanics," which describes the detailed sliding window data transfer procedure.

KEY CONCEPT The TCP *sliding window system* is a variation on the enhanced PAR system, with changes made to support TCP's stream orientation. Each device keeps track of the status of the byte stream that it needs to transmit. The device keeps track by dividing the byte streams into four conceptual categories: bytes sent and acknowledged, bytes sent but not yet acknowledged, bytes not yet sent but that can be sent immediately, and bytes not yet sent that cannot be sent until the recipient signals that it is ready for them.

Sequence Number Assignment and Synchronization

The sender and receiver must agree on the sequence numbers that they will assign to the bytes in the stream. This is called *synchronization* and is done when the TCP connection is established. For simplicity, let's assume that the first byte was sent with sequence number 1 (this is not normally the case). Thus, in the example shown in Figure 46-5, the byte ranges for the four categories are as follows:

1. The bytes sent and acknowledged are bytes 1 to 31.
2. The bytes sent but not yet acknowledged are bytes 32 to 45.
3. The bytes not yet sent for which the recipient is ready are bytes 46 to 51.
4. The bytes not yet sent for which the recipient is not ready are bytes 52 to 95.

The Send Window and Usable Window

The key to the operation of the entire process is the number of bytes that the recipient is allowing the transmitter to have unacknowledged at one time. This is called the *send window*, or often, just the *window*. The window is what determines how many bytes the sender is allowed to transmit, and is equal to the sum of the number of bytes in category 2 and category 3. Thus, the dividing line between the last two categories (bytes not sent that the recipient is ready for and bytes the recipient is not ready for) is determined by adding the window to the byte number of the first unacknowledged byte in the stream. In the example shown in Figure 46-5, the first unacknowledged byte is 32. The total window size is 20.

The term *usable window* is defined as the amount of data the transmitter is still allowed to send given the amount of data that is outstanding. It is thus exactly equal to the size of category 3. You may also commonly hear the *edges* of the window mentioned. The left edge marks the first byte in the window (byte 32). The right edge marks the last byte in the window (byte 51). See Figure 46-6 for an illustration of these concepts.

KEY CONCEPT The *send window* is the key to the entire TCP sliding window system. It represents the maximum number of unacknowledged bytes that a device is allowed to have outstanding at one time. The *usable window* is the amount of the send window that the sender is still allowed to send at any point in time; it is equal to the size of the send window less the number of unacknowledged bytes already transmitted.

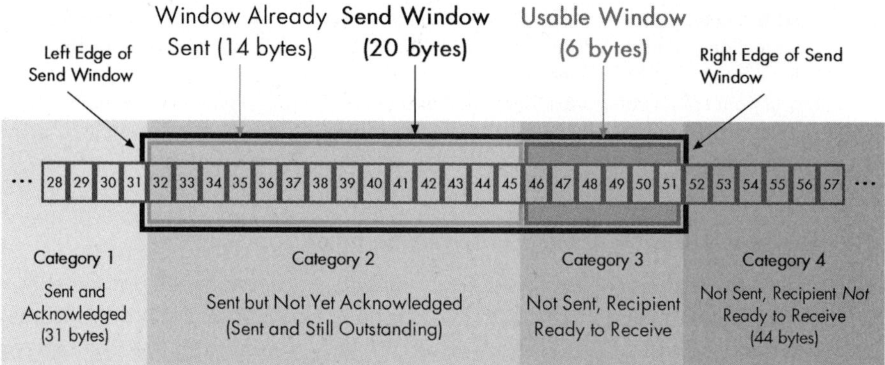

Figure 46-6: TCP transmission stream categories and send window terminology *This diagram shows the same categories as the ones in Figure 46-5, except that it shows the send window as well. The black box is the overall send window (categories 2 and 3 combined); the light gray box represents the bytes already sent (category 2), and the dark gray box is the usable window (category 3).*

Changes to TCP Categories and Window Sizes After Sending Bytes in the Usable Window

Now let's suppose that in the example shown in Figure 46-6 there is nothing stopping the sender from immediately transmitting the 6 bytes in category 3 (the usable window). When the sender transmits them, the 6 bytes will shift from category 3 to category 2. The byte ranges will now be as follows (see Figure 46-7):

1. The bytes sent and acknowledged are bytes 1 to 31.
2. The bytes sent but not yet acknowledged are bytes 32 to 51.
3. The bytes not yet sent for which the recipient is ready are none.
4. The bytes not yet sent for which the recipient is not ready are bytes 52 to 95.

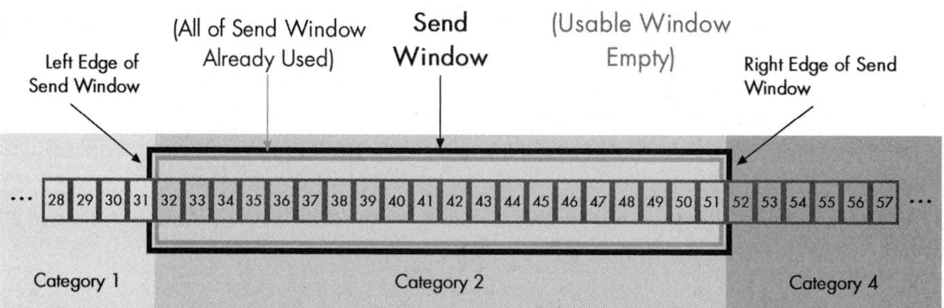

Figure 46-7: TCP stream categories and window after sending usable window bytes *This diagram shows the result of the device sending all the bytes that it is allowed to transmit in its usable window. It is the same as Figure 46-6, except that all the bytes in category 3 have moved to category 2. The usable window is now zero and will remain so until it receives an acknowledgment for bytes in category 2.*

Processing Acknowledgments and Sliding the Send Window

Some time later, the destination device sends back a message to the sender and provides an acknowledgment. The destination device will not specifically list out the bytes that it has acknowledged, because as I said earlier, listing the bytes would be inefficient. Instead, the destination device will acknowledge a range of bytes that represents the longest contiguous sequence of bytes it has received since the ones it had previously acknowledged.

For example, let's suppose that the bytes already sent but not yet acknowledged at the start of the example (bytes 32 to 45) were transmitted in four different segments. These segments carried bytes 32 to 34, 35 to 36, 37 to 41, and 42 to 45, respectively. The first, second, and fourth segments arrived, but the third did not. The receiver will send back an acknowledgment only for bytes 32 to 36 (32 to 34 and 35 to 36). The receiver will hold bytes 42 to 45 but won't acknowledge them, because this would imply that the receiver has received bytes 37 to 41, which have not shown up yet. This is necessary because TCP is a cumulative acknowledgment system that can use only a single number to acknowledge data. That number is the number of the last contiguous byte in the stream that was successfully received. Let's also say that the destination keeps the window size the same at 20 bytes.

NOTE *An optional feature called* selective acknowledgments *does allow noncontiguous blocks of data to be acknowledged. This is explained in Chapter 49's section named "TCP Noncontiguous Acknowledgment Handling and Selective Acknowledgment (SACK)"; we'll ignore this complication for now.*

When the sending device receives this acknowledgment, it will be able to transfer some of the bytes from category 2 to category 1, because they have now been acknowledged. When it does so, something interesting will happen. Since 5 bytes have been acknowledged, and the window size didn't change, the sender is allowed to send 5 more bytes. In effect, the window shifts or slides over to the right in the timeline. At the same time 5 bytes move from category 2 to category 1, 5 bytes move from category 4 to category 3, creating a new usable window for subsequent transmission. So, after the groups receive the acknowledgment, they will look like what you see in Figure 46-8. The byte ranges will be as follows:

1. The bytes sent and acknowledged are bytes 1 to 36.
2. The bytes sent but not yet acknowledged are bytes 37 to 51.
3. The bytes not yet sent for which the recipient is ready are bytes 52 to 56.
4. The bytes not yet sent for which the recipient is not ready are bytes 57 to 95.

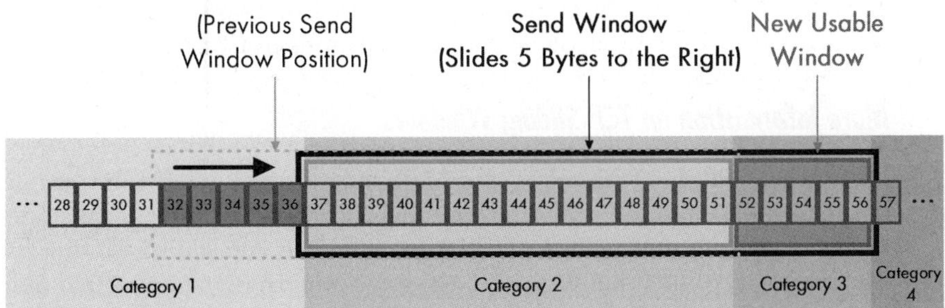

Figure 46-8: Sliding the TCP send window *After receiving acknowledgment for bytes 32 to 36, the bytes move from category 2 to 1 (shown in dark shading). The send window shown in Figure 46-7 slides right by 5 bytes; shifting 5 bytes from category 4 to 3, and opening a new usable window.*

This process will occur each time an acknowledgment is received, thereby causing the window to slide across the entire stream in order to be transmitted. And thus, ladies and gentlemen, you have the TCP sliding window acknowledgment system!

It is a very powerful technique that allows TCP to easily acknowledge an arbitrary number of bytes using a single acknowledgment number. It provides reliability to the byte-oriented protocol without spending time on an excessive number of acknowledgments. For simplicity, the example I've used here leaves the window size constant, but in reality, it can be adjusted to allow a recipient to control the rate at which data is sent, thereby enabling flow control and congestion handling.

> **KEY CONCEPT** When a device gets an acknowledgment for a range of bytes, it knows the destination has successfully received them. It moves them from the "sent but unacknowledged" to the "sent and acknowledged" category. This causes the send window to slide to the right, allowing the device to send more data.

Dealing with Missing Acknowledgments

But what about bytes 42 through 45 in the example shown in Figure 46-8? Until segment 3 (containing bytes 37 to 41) shows up, the receiving device will not send an acknowledgment for those bytes, and it won't send any others that show up after it. The sending device will be able to send the new bytes that were added to category 3, namely, bytes 52 to 56. The sending device will then stop, and the window will be stuck on bytes 37 to 41.

> **KEY CONCEPT** TCP acknowledgments are cumulative and tell a transmitter that the receiving device successfully received all the bytes up to the sequence number indicated in the acknowledgment. Thus, if the receiving device receives bytes out of order, the device cannot acknowledge them until all the preceding bytes are received.

Like the PAR system, TCP includes a system for timing transmissions and retransmitting. Eventually, the TCP device will resend the lost segment. Unfortunately, one drawback of TCP is that since it does not separately acknowledge segments, it may have to retransmit other segments that the recipient actually received (such as the segment with bytes 42 to 45). This starts to get very complex, as I discussed in the topic on TCP retransmissions in Chapter 49.

More Information on TCP Sliding Windows

Despite the length of this explanation, the preceding is just a summary description of the overall operation of sliding windows. This chapter does not include all of the modifications used in modern TCP! As you can see, the sliding window mechanism is at the heart of the operation of TCP as a whole. In the chapter that describes segments and discusses data transfer, you will see in more detail how TCP transmitters decide how and when to create segments for transmission. Chapter 49 provides much more information about how sliding windows enable a device to manage the flow of data to it on a TCP connection. It also discusses special problems that can arise if window size is not carefully managed and how you can avoid problems such as congestion in TCP implementations through key changes to the basic sliding window mechanism described in this section.

TCP Ports, Connections, and Connection Identification

The two TCP/IP transport layer protocols, TCP and UDP, play the same architectural role in the protocol suite, but do it in very different ways. In fact, one of the few functions that the two have in common is that they both provide a method of transport layer addressing and multiplexing. Through the use of *ports*, both protocols allow the data from many different application processes to be aggregated and sent through the IP layer, and then returned up the stack to the proper application process on the destination device. I explain TCP ports in detail in Chapter 43.

Despite this commonality, TCP and UDP diverge somewhat even in how they deal with processes. UDP is a connectionless protocol, which means that devices do not set up a formal connection before sending data. UDP does not have to use sliding windows or keep track of how long it has been since UDP sent a transmission and so forth. When the UDP layer on a device receives data, it just sends it to the process that the destination port indicates, and that's that. UDP can seamlessly handle any number of processes that are sending it messages because UDP handles them all identically.

In contrast, since TCP is connection-oriented, it has many more responsibilities. Each TCP software layer needs to be able to support connections to several other TCPs simultaneously. The operation of each connection is separate from of each other connection, and the TCP software must manage each operation independently. TCP must be sure that it not only routes data to the right process, but that it also manages transmitted data on each connection without any overlap or confusion.

The first consequence of this is that TCP must uniquely identify each connection. It does this by using the pair of socket identifiers that correspond to the two endpoints of the connection, where a socket is simply the combination of the IP address and the port number of each process. This means a socket pair contains four pieces of information: source address, source port, destination address, and destination port. Thus, TCP connections are sometimes said to be described by this addressing quadruple.

I introduced this concept in Chapter 43, where I gave the example of a Hypertext Transfer Protocol (HTTP) request that a client sends at 177.41.72.6 to a website at 41.199.222.3. The server for that website will use well-known port number 80, so the server's socket is 41.199.222.3:80. If the server assigns a client ephemeral port number 3022 for the web browser, the client socket is 177.41.72.6:3022. The overall connection between these devices can be described using this socket pair: (41.199.222.3:80, 177.41.72.6:3022).

This identification of connections using both client and server sockets is what provides the flexibility in allowing multiple connections between devices that we probably take for granted on the Internet. For example, busy application server processes (such as web servers) must be able to handle connections from more than one client; otherwise, the Web would be pretty much unusable. Since the client and server's socket identify the connection, this is no problem. At the same time that the web server maintains the connection, it can easily have another connection to say, port 2199 at IP address 219.31.0.44. The connection identifier that represents this as follows: (41.199.222.3:80, 219.31.0.44:2199).

In fact, you can have multiple connections from the same client to the same server. Each client process will be assigned a different ephemeral port number, so even if they all try to access the same server process (such as the web server process at 41.199.222.3:80), they will all have a different client socket and represent unique connections. This difference is what lets you make several simultaneous requests to the same website from your computer.

Again, TCP keeps track of each of these connections independently, so each connection is unaware of the others. TCP can handle hundreds or even thousands of simultaneous connections. The only limit is the capacity of the computer running TCP, and the bandwidth of the physical connections to it—the more connections running at once, the more each one has to share limited resources.

KEY CONCEPT Each device can handle simultaneous TCP connections to many different processes on one or more devices. The socket numbers of the devices in the connection, called the connection's *endpoints*, identify each connection. Each endpoint consists of the device's IP address and port number, so the four-way communication between client IP address and port number, and server IP address and port number identifies each connection.

TCP Common Applications and Server Port Assignments

In the overview of TCP in Chapter 45, you saw that the protocol originally included the functions of both modern TCP and IP. TCP was split into TCP and IP in order to allow applications that didn't need TCP's complexity to bypass it, using the much simpler UDP as a transport layer protocol instead. This bypass was an important step in the development of the TCP/IP protocol suite, since there are several important protocols for which UDP is ideally suited, and even some for which TCP is more of a nuisance than a benefit.

Most commonly, however, UDP is used only in special cases. I describe the two types of applications that may be better suited to UDP than TCP in Chapter 44: applications where speed is more important than reliability, and applications that send only short messages infrequently. The majority of TCP/IP applications do not fall into these categories. Thus, even though the layering of TCP and IP means that most protocols aren't required to use TCP, most of them do anyway. The majority of the protocols that use TCP employ all, or at least most, of the features that it provides. The establishment of a persistent connection is necessary for many interactive protocols, such as Telnet, as well as for ones that send commands and status replies, like HTTP. Reliability and flow control are essential for protocols like the File Transfer Protocol (FTP) or the email protocols, which send large files.

Table 46-1 shows some of the more significant application protocols that run on TCP. For each protocol, I have shown the well-known or registered port number that's reserved for that protocol's server process (clients use ephemeral ports, not the port numbers in the table). I have also shown the special keyword shortcut for each port assignment and provided brief comments on why the protocol is well matched to TCP.

Table 46-1: Common TCP Applications and Server Port Assignments

Port #	Keyword	Protocol	Comments
20 and 21	ftp-data/ftp	File Transfer Protocol (FTP, data and control)	Used to send large files, so it is ideally suited for TCP.
23	telnet	Telnet Protocol	Interactive session-based protocol. Requires the connection-based nature of TCP.
25	smtp	Simple Mail Transfer Protocol (SMTP)	Uses an exchange of commands, and sends possibly large files between devices.
53	domain	Domain Name Server (DNS)	An example of a protocol that uses both UDP and TCP. For simple requests and replies, DNS uses UDP. For larger messages, especially zone transfers, DNS uses TCP.
70	gopher	Gopher Protocol	A messaging protocol that has been largely replaced by the WWW.
80	http	Hypertext Transfer Protocol (HTTP/World Wide Web)	The classic example of a TCP-based messaging protocol.
110	pop3	Post Office Protocol (POP version 3)	Email message retrieval protocols that use TCP to exchange commands and data.
119	nntp	Network News Transfer Protocol (NNTP)	Used for transferring NetNews (Usenet) messages, which can be lengthy.
139	netbios-ssn	NetBIOS Session Service	A session protocol, clearly better suited to TCP than UDP.
143	imap	Internet Message Access Protocol (IMAP)	Another email message retrieval protocol.
179	bgp	Border Gateway Protocol (BGP)	While interior routing protocols like RIP and OSPF use either UDP or IP directly, BGP runs over TCP. This allows BGP to assume reliable communication even as it sends data over potentially long distances.
194	irc	Internet Relay Chat (IRC)	IRC is like Telnet in that it is an interactive protocol that is strongly based on the notion of a persistent connection between a client and server.
2049	nfs	Network File System (NFS)	NFS was originally implemented using UDP for performance reasons. Given that it is responsible for large transfers of files and given UDP's unreliability, NFS was probably not the best idea, so developers created TCP versions. The latest version of NFS uses TCP exclusively.
6000–6063	TCP	x11	Used for the X Window graphical system. Multiple ports are dedicated to allow many sessions.

A couple of the protocols in Table 46-1 use both TCP and UDP in order to get the best of both worlds. UDP can send short, simple messages, while TCP moves larger files. Many of the protocols that use both TCP and UDP are actually utility/diagnostic protocols (such as Echo, Discard, and the Time Protocol). These are special cases, because they developers designed them to use both UDP and TCP specifically to allow their use for diagnostics on both protocols.

I have not included an exhaustive list of TCP applications in Table 46-1. See Chapter 42 for common TCP/IP applications and port numbers, and also a reference to the full (massive) list of well-known and registered TCP server ports.

47

TCP BASIC OPERATION: CONNECTION ESTABLISHMENT, MANAGEMENT, AND TERMINATION

While I have described the Transmission Control Protocol (TCP) as *connection-oriented*, this term isn't just any old characteristic of TCP. The overall operation of the entire protocol can be described in terms of how TCP software prepares, negotiates, establishes, manages, and terminates connections. TCP implementations certainly do more than handle connections, but the other major tasks they perform, such as data handling and providing reliability and flow control, can occur only over a stable connection. This stability makes connections the logical place to begin exploring the details of how TCP works.

In this chapter, I describe TCP connections from start to finish. I begin with an overview of TCP's operation by providing a summary of the *finite state machine* that formally defines the stages of a connection. State machines can be a bit mind-boggling when you read about them in standards, but a simplified, explained version provides an excellent high-level view of the life of a connection, so it is a good place to start.

From there, I move on to provide details about TCP's handling of connections. I describe how you prepare and set up connections and *transmission control blocks (TCBs)*, and explain the difference between a passive and an active socket Open. I explain the three-way handshake that you can use to create a connection and the method by which parameters are exchanged and sequence numbers synchronized. I talk about how an established connection is managed, including the method by which TCP handles problem conditions and resets the connection when necessary. Finally, I describe how a connection can be terminated when it is no longer needed.

BACKGROUND INFORMATION *The following detailed sections assume that you're familiar with the concepts in the previous chapter, especially the notion of sequence numbers.*

TCP Operational Overview and the TCP Finite State Machine (FSM)

It is essential that all devices that implement a networking protocol do so in a consistent manner. Otherwise, one device might behave in a manner that the other would not expect. Naturally, this inconsistency is why there are standards that describe the operation of each protocol. The problem with a protocol like TCP is that it performs so many tasks that it is difficult to specify the exact operation of all aspects of the protocol succinctly.

One way that computer scientists describe how a complex protocol works is through a theoretical tool called a *finite state machine (FSM)*. An FSM attempts to describe a protocol or algorithm by considering it like a virtual machine that progresses through a series of stages of operation in response to various occurrences.

Basic FSM Concepts

You need to understand the following four essential concepts to comprehend the workings of an FSM:

State The particular circumstance or status that describes the protocol software on a machine at a given time.

Transition The act of moving from one state to another.

Event Something that causes a transition to occur between states.

Action Something a device does in response to an event before it transitions to another state.

An FSM describes the protocol by explaining all the different states the protocol can be in, the events that can occur in each state, what actions are taken in response to the events, and what transitions happen as a result. The protocol usually starts in a particular *beginning state* when it is first run. It then follows a sequence of steps that get it into a regular operating state, and moves to other states in response to particular types of input or other circumstances. The state machine is called *finite* because there are a limited number of states.

The Simplified TCP FSM

In the case of TCP, the FSM describes the life stages of a connection. Each connection between one TCP device and another begins in a null state where there is no connection and then proceeds through a series of states until a connection is established. The connection remains in that state until something occurs to cause the connection to be closed again, at which point it proceeds through another sequence of transitional states and returns to the closed state.

> **KEY CONCEPT** Many computer scientists use the *finite state machine (FSM)* to describe the operation of a protocol or algorithm. The FSM describes the different actions that a piece of software takes over time by defining a finite number of operating *states*, *events* that can cause *transitions* between states, and *actions* taken in response to events.

The full description of the states, events, and transitions in a TCP connection is lengthy and complicated. This is not surprising, because those three elements would cover much of the entire TCP standard. That level of detail would be a good cure for insomnia, but not much else. However, a simplified look at the TCP FSM will help give you a nice overall feel for how TCP establishes connections and then functions when a connection has been created.

Table 47-1 briefly explains each of the TCP states in a TCP connection, the main events that occur in each state, and what actions and transitions occur as a result. For brevity, three abbreviations are used for the three types of messages that control transitions between states, which correspond to the TCP header flags that are set to indicate that a message is serving that function. These are as follows:

SYN A *Synchronize* message; initiates and establishes a connection. It is so named since one of its functions is to synchronize sequence numbers between devices.

FIN A *Finish* message, which is a TCP segment with the FIN bit set; it indicates that a device wants to terminate the connection.

ACK An *Acknowledgment message*; indicates receipt of a message such as a SYN or a FIN.

Again, I have not shown every possible transition, just the ones normally followed in the life of a connection. Error conditions also cause transitions, but including these would move us well beyond a simplified state machine. The FSM, including how state transitions occur, is illustrated in Figure 47-1.

It's important to remember that this state machine is followed for each connection. This means that, at any given time, TCP may be in one state for one connection to socket *X*, and in another for its connection to socket *Y*. Also, the typical movement between states for the two processes in a particular connection is not symmetric, because the roles of the devices are not symmetric. For example, one device initiates a connection, and the other responds; one device starts termination, and the other replies. There is also an alternate path taken for connection establishment and termination if both devices initiate simultaneously (which is unusual, but can happen). This is shown by the shading in Figure 47-1.

Table 47-1: TCP Finite State Machine (FSM) States, Events, and Transitions

State	State Description	Event and Transition
CLOSED	The default state that each connection starts in before the process of establishing it begins. The state is called "fictional" in the standard because this state represents the situation in which there is no connection between devices. It either hasn't been created yet or has just been destroyed (if that makes sense).	Passive Open: A server begins the process of connection setup by doing a passive open on a TCP port. At the same time, it sets up the data structure (transmission control block, or TCB) that it needs in order to manage the connection. It then transitions to the LISTEN state.
		Active Open, Send SYN: A client begins the connection setup by sending a SYN message, and it sets up a TCB for this connection. It then transitions to the SYN-SENT state.
LISTEN	A device (normally a server) is waiting to receive a SYN message from a client. It has not yet sent its own SYN message.	Receive Client SYN, Send SYN+ACK: The server device receives a SYN from a client. It sends back a message that contains its own SYN and acknowledges the one it received. The server moves to the SYN-RECEIVED state.
SYN-SENT	The device (normally a client) has sent a SYN message and is waiting for a matching SYN from the other device (usually a server).	Receive SYN, Send ACK: If the device that has sent its SYN message receives a SYN from the other device but not an ACK for its own SYN, it acknowledges the SYN it receives and then transitions to SYN-RECEIVED in order to wait for the acknowledgment to its own SYN.
		Receive SYN+ACK, Send ACK: If the device that sent the SYN receives both an acknowledgment to its SYN and a SYN from the other device, it acknowledges the SYN received and then moves straight to the ESTABLISHED state.
SYN-RECEIVED	The device has received a SYN (connection request) from its partner and sent its own SYN. It is now waiting for an ACK to its SYN in order to finish the connection setup.	Receive ACK: When the device receives the ACK to the SYN that it sent, it transitions to the ESTABLISHED state.
ESTABLISHED	The steady state of an open TCP connection. Both devices can exchange data freely once both devices in the connection enter this state. This will continue until they close the connection.	Close, Send FIN: A device can close the connection by sending a message with the FIN bit sent, and then it can transition to the FIN-WAIT-1 state.
		Receive FIN: A device may receive a FIN message from its connection partner asking that the connection be closed. It will acknowledge this message and transition to the CLOSE-WAIT state.
CLOSE-WAIT	The device has received a close request (FIN) from the other device. It must now wait for the application on the local device to acknowledge this request and generate a matching request.	Close, Send FIN: The application using TCP, having been informed that the other process wants to shut down, sends a close request to the TCP layer on the machine on which it is running. TCP then sends a FIN to the remote device that already asked to terminate the connection. This device now transitions to LAST-ACK.
LAST-ACK	A device that has already received a close request and acknowledged has sent its own FIN and is waiting for an ACK to this request.	Receive ACK for FIN: The device receives an acknowledgment for its close request. We have now sent our FIN and had it acknowledged, and received the other device's FIN and acknowledged it, so we go straight to the CLOSED state.
FIN-WAIT-1	A device in this state is waiting for an ACK for a FIN it has sent, or is waiting for a connection termination request from the other device.	Receive ACK for FIN: The device receives an acknowledgment for its close request. It transitions to the FIN-WAIT-2 state.
		Receive FIN, Send ACK: The device does not receive an ACK for its own FIN, but receives a FIN from the other device. It acknowledges it and then moves to the CLOSING state.

(continued)

Table 47-1: TCP Finite State Machine (FSM) States, Events, and Transitions (continued)

State	State Description	Event and Transition
FIN-WAIT-2	A device in this state has received an ACK for its request to terminate the connection and is now waiting for a matching FIN from the other device.	Receive FIN, Send ACK: The device receives a FIN from the other device. It acknowledges it and then moves to the TIME-WAIT state.
CLOSING	The device has received a FIN from the other device and has sent an ACK for it, but has not yet received an ACK for its own FIN message.	Receive ACK for FIN: The device receives an acknowledgment for its close request. It transitions to the TIME-WAIT state.
TIME-WAIT	The device has now received a FIN from the other device and acknowledged it, and sent its own FIN and received an ACK for it. We are finished, except for waiting to ensure the ACK is received and preventing potential overlap with new connections. (See the "TCP Connection Termination" section later in this chapter for more details on this state.)	Timer Expiration: After a designated wait period, the device transitions to the CLOSED state.

Thus, for example, at the start of connection establishment, the two devices will take different routes to get to the ESTABLISHED state. One device (the server usually) will pass through the LISTEN state, while the other (the client) will go through SYN-SENT state. Similarly, one device will initiate connection termination and take the path through the FIN-WAIT-1 state in order to get back to the CLOSED state; the other will go through the CLOSE-WAIT and LAST-ACK states. However, if both try to open at once, they each proceed through SYN-SENT and SYN-RECEIVED states, and if both try to close at once, they go through FIN-WAIT-1, CLOSING, and TIME-WAIT states roughly simultaneously.

Although FSM may seem a bit intimidating at first, if you spend a few minutes with it, you can get a good handle on how TCP works. The FSM will be of great use in making sense of the connection establishment and termination processes discussed later in this chapter, and reading those sections will help you make sense of the FSM.

KEY CONCEPT The TCP finite state machine (FSM) describes the sequence of steps that both devices take in a TCP session as they establish, manage, and close the connection. Each device may take a different path through the states, because under normal circumstances, the operation of the protocol is not symmetric—one device initiates connection establishment or termination, and the other responds.

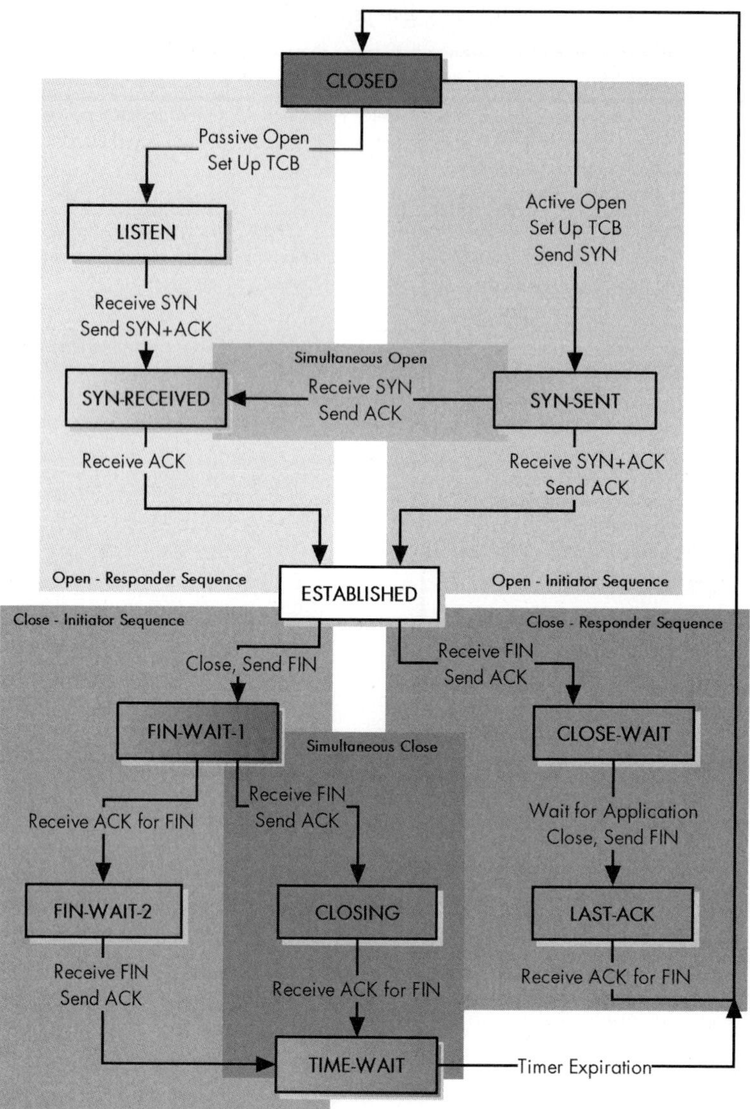

Figure 47-1: The TCP finite state machine (FSM) *This diagram illustrates the simplified TCP FSM. The shadings are not an official part of the definition of the FSM; I have added them to show more clearly the sequences the two devices took to open and close a link. For establishment and termination, there is a regular sequence, in which the initiating and responding devices go through different states, and a simultaneous sequence, in which each uses the same sequence.*

TCP Connection Preparation

In Chapter 43, I raised an important point about TCP operation, particularly that it must be capable of handling many connections simultaneously. For this reason, we must uniquely identify each connection using the *quadruple* of the socket identifiers

(IP address and port number) for each of the two devices on the connection. The process of setting up, managing, and terminating a connection is performed independently for each connection.

Storing Connection Data: The Transmission Control Block (TCB)

Since each connection is distinct, we must maintain data about each connection separately. TCP uses a special data structure for this purpose, called a *transmission control block (TCB)*. The TCB contains all the important information about the connection, such as the two socket numbers that identify it and pointers to buffers that hold incoming and outgoing data. The TCB also implements the sliding window mechanism. It holds variables that keep track of the number of bytes received and acknowledged, bytes received and not yet acknowledged, current window size, and so forth. Each device maintains its own TCB for the connection.

Before the process of setting up a TCP connection can begin, the devices on each end must perform some "prep work." One of the tasks required in order to prepare for the connection is to set up the TCB that will be used to hold information about it. This is done right at the very start of the connection establishment process, when each device transitions out of the CLOSED state.

Active and Passive Opens

TCP/IP is based on the client/server model of operation, and TCP connection setup is based on the existence of these roles as well. The client and server each prepare for the connection by performing an *Open* operation. However, there are two different kinds of Open operations:

Active Open A client process using TCP takes the active role and initiates the connection by sending a TCP message to start the connection (a SYN message).

Passive Open A server process designed to use TCP takes a more "laid-back" approach. It performs a *passive Open* by contacting TCP and saying, "I'm here, and I'm waiting for clients that may wish to talk to me to send me a message on the following port number." The Open is called *passive* because, aside from indicating that the process is listening, the server process does nothing. A passive Open can specify that the server is waiting for an active Open from a specific client, though not all TCP/IP APIs support this capability. More commonly, a server process is willing to accept connections from all comers. Such a passive Open is said to be *unspecified.*

> **KEY CONCEPT** A client process initiates a TCP connection by performing an *active Open*, sending a SYN message to a server. A server process using TCP prepares for an incoming connection request by performing a *passive Open*. For each TCP session, both devices create a data structure, called a *transmission control block (TCB)*, that is used to hold important data related to the connection.

Preparation for Connection

Both the client and the server create the TCB for the connection at the time that they perform the Open. The client already knows the IP addresses and port numbers for both the client process and the server process it is trying to reach, so it can use these to uniquely identify the connection and the TCB that goes with it.

For the server, the concept of a TCB at this stage of the game is a bit more complex. If the server is waiting for a particular client, it can identify the connection using its own socket and the socket of the client for which it is waiting. Normally, however, the server doesn't know which client is trying to reach it. In fact, more than one client could contact it at nearly the same time.

In this case, the server creates a TCB with an unspecified (zero) client socket number and waits to receive an active Open. It then *binds* the socket number of the client to the TCB for the passive Open as part of the connection process. To allow the server to handle multiple incoming connections, the server process may perform several unspecified passive Opens simultaneously.

The TCB for a connection is maintained throughout the connection and destroyed when the connection is completely terminated, and the device returns to the CLOSED state. TCP does include a procedure that handles the situation in which both devices perform an active Open simultaneously, as I discuss the next section.

TCP Connection Establishment Process: The Three-Way Handshake

Before TCP can be employed for any actually useful purpose—that is, sending data—a connection must be set up between the two devices that wish to communicate. This process, usually called *connection establishment*, involves an exchange of messages that transitions both devices from their initial connection state (CLOSED) to the normal operating state (ESTABLISHED).

Connection Establishment Functions

The connection establishment process actually accomplishes the following tasks as it creates a connection suitable for data exchange:

Contact and Communication The client and server make contact with each other and establish communication by sending each other messages. The server usually doesn't even know which client it will be talking to before this point, so it discovers this during connection establishment.

Sequence Number Synchronization Each device lets the other know what initial sequence number it wants to use for its first transmission.

Parameter Exchange The two devices exchange certain parameters that control the operation of the TCP connection.

I'll discuss the sequence number synchronization and parameter exchange tasks in the "TCP Connection Establishment Sequence Number Synchronization and Parameter Exchange" section later in this chapter.

Control Messages Used for Connection Establishment: SYN and ACK

TCP uses control messages to manage the process of contact and communication. There aren't, however, any special TCP control message types; all TCP messages use the same segment format. A set of control flags in the TCP header indicates whether a segment is being used for control purposes or just to carry data. As I introduced in the discussion of the TCP FSM earlier in the chapter, two control message types are used in connection setup, which are specified by setting the following two flags:

SYN Indicates that the segment is being used to initialize a connection. SYN stands for *synchronize*, in reference to the sequence number synchronization task in the connection establishment process.

ACK Indicates that the device sending the segment is conveying an *acknowledgment* for a message it has received (such as a SYN).

There are also other control bits (*FIN*, *RST*, *PSH*, and *URG*) that aren't important to connection establishment, so I will discuss them in other topics. In common TCP parlance, a message with a control bit set is often named for that bit. For example, if the SYN control bit is set, the segment is often called a SYN message. Similarly, a segment with the ACK bit set is an ACK message, or even just an ACK.

Normal Connection Establishment: The Three-Way Handshake

To establish a connection, each device must send a SYN message and receive an ACK message for it from the other device. Thus, conceptually, we need to have four control messages pass between the devices. However, it's inefficient to send a SYN and an ACK in separate messages when one could communicate both simultaneously. Thus, in the normal sequence of events in connection establishment, one of the SYNs and one of the ACKs are sent together by setting both of the relevant bits (a message sometimes called a *SYN+ACK*). This makes a total of three messages, and for this reason the connection procedure is called a *three-way handshake*.

> **KEY CONCEPT** The normal process of establishing a connection between a TCP client and server involves the following three steps: The client sends a *SYN* message. The server sends a message that combines an *ACK* for the client's *SYN* and contains the server's SYN. And the client sends an ACK for the server's SYN. This is called the *TCP three-way handshake*.

Table 47-2 describes in detail how the three-way handshake works (including a summary of the preparation discussed in the previous section). It is adapted from the table describing the TCP FSM (Table 47-1), but shows what happens for both the server and the client over time. Each row shows the state the device begins in, what action it takes in that state, and the state to which it transitions. The transmit and receive parts of each of the three steps of the handshake process are shown as well. The same process is also illustrated in 47-2.

Table 47-2: TCP Three-Way Handshake Connection Establishment Procedure

Client			Server		
Start State	**Action**	**Move to State**	**Start State**	**Action**	**Move to State**
CLOSED	The client cannot do anything until the server has performed a passive Open and is ready to accept a connection.	—	CLOSED	The server performs a passive Open, creating a TCB for the connection and readying itself for the receipt of a connection request (SYN) from a client.	LISTEN
CLOSED	Step 1 Transmit: The client performs an active Open, creating a TCB) for the connection and sending a SYN message to the server.	SYN-SENT	LISTEN	The server waits for contact from a client.	—
SYN-SENT	The client waits to receive an ACK to the SYN that it has sent, as well as the server's SYN.	—	LISTEN	Step 1 Receive, Step 2 Transmit: The server receives the SYN from the client. It sends a single SYN+ACK message back to the client that contains an ACK for the client's SYN, as well as the server's own SYN.	SYN-RECEIVED
SYN-SENT	Step 2 Receive, Step 3 Transmit: The client receives from the server the SYN+ACK containing the ACK to the client's SYN, and the SYN from the server. It sends the server an ACK for the server's SYN. The client is now finished with the connection establishment.	ESTABLISHED	SYN-RECEIVED	The server waits for an ACK to the SYN it sent previously.	—
ESTABLISHED	The client is waiting for the server to finish connection establishment so they can operate normally.		SYN-RECEIVED	Step 3 Receive: The server receives the ACK to its SYN and is now finished with connection establishment.	ESTABLISHED
ESTABLISHED	The client is ready for normal data transfer operations.		ESTABLISHED	The server is ready for normal data transfer operations.	

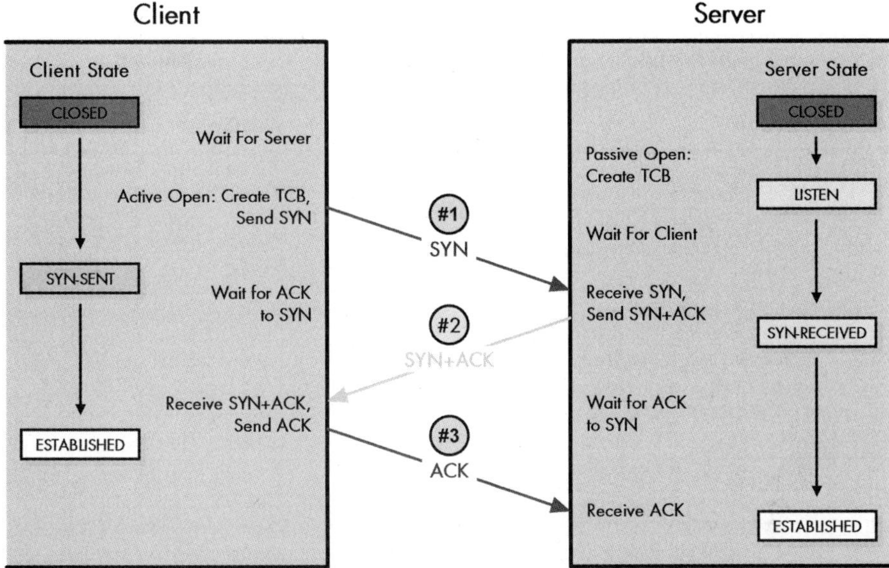

Figure 47-2: TCP three-way handshake connection establishment procedure *This diagram illustrates how a client and server establish a conventional connection. It shows how the three messages sent during the process and how each device transitions from the CLOSED state through intermediate states until the session is in the ESTABLISHED state.*

Simultaneous Open Connection Establishment

TCP is also set up to handle the situation in which both devices perform an active Open instead of one doing a passive Open. This may occur if two clients are trying to reach each other instead of a client and a server. It is uncommon, however, and only happens under certain circumstances. Simultaneous connection establishment can also happen only if one of the devices uses a well-known port as its source port.

In the case of simultaneous open connection establishment, the steps are different for both devices. Each client will perform an active Open and will then proceed through both the SYN-SENT and SYN-RECEIVED states until the clients acknowledge each other's SYNs. This means that there is no three-way handshake; instead, there is something like two simultaneous two-way handshakes. Each client sends a SYN, receives the other's SYN, acknowledges the SYN with an ACK it, and then waits for its own ACK.

I have described the transaction for establishing open connections simultaneously, in a simplified way, in Table 47-3 and illustrated it in Figure 47-3. To limit the table size, I have shown the activities performed by the two devices occurring simultaneously (in the same row). In reality, the actions don't need to occur at exactly the same time and probably won't. All that must happen for the simultaneous procedure to be followed is that each device receives a SYN before getting an ACK for its own SYN, as Figure 47-3 shows.

Table 47-3: TCP Simultaneous Open Connection Establishment Procedure

Client A			Client B		
Start State	**Action**	**Move to State**	**Start State**	**Action**	**Move to State**
CLOSED	Client A Step 1 Transmit: Client A performs an active Open, creating a TCB and sending a SYN to the server.	SYN-SENT	CLOSED	Client B Step 1 Transmit: Client B performs an active Open, creating a TCB and sending a SYN to the server.	SYN-SENT
SYN-SENT	Client B Step 1 Receive and Step 2 Transmit: Client A receives Client B's SYN and sends it an ACK. It is still waiting for an ACK to its own SYN.	SYN-RECEIVED	SYN-SENT	Client A Step 1 Receive and Step 2 Transmit: Client B receives Client A's SYN and sends it an ACK. It is still waiting for an ACK to its own SYN.	SYN-RECEIVED
SYN-RECEIVED	Client A Step 2 Receive: Client A receives the ACK from Client B for its SYN and finishes connection establishment.	ESTABLISHED	SYN-RECEIVED	Client B Step 2 Receive: Client B receives the ACK from Client A for its SYN and finishes connection establishment.	ESTABLISHED

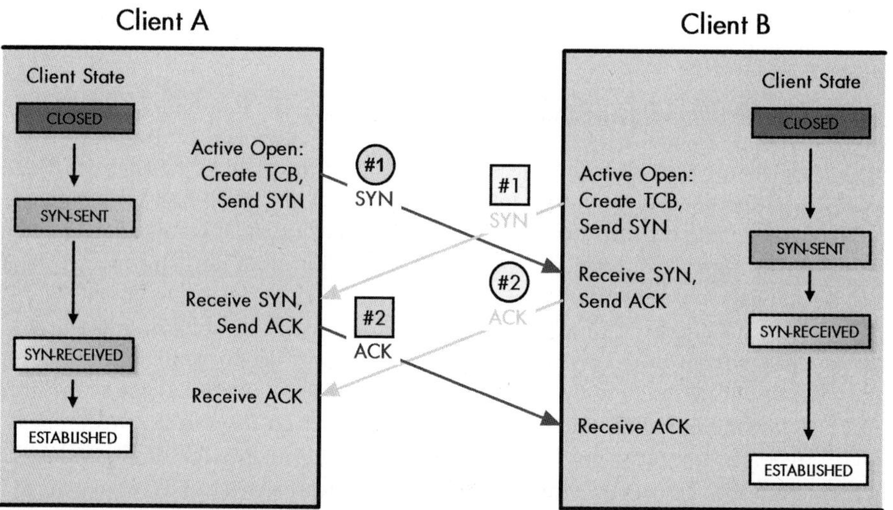

Figure 47-3: TCP simultaneous open connection establishment procedure *This diagram shows what happens when two devices try to open a connection to each other at the same time. In this case, instead of a three-way handshake, each sends a SYN and receives an ACK. They each follow the same sequence of states, which differs from both sequences in the normal three-way handshake.*

KEY CONCEPT If one device setting up a TCP connection sends a SYN and then receives a SYN from the another device before it acknowledges its SYN, the two devices perform a *simultaneous OPEN*, which consists of the exchange of two independent SYN and ACK message sets. The end result is the same as the conventional three-way handshake, but the process of getting to the ESTABLISHED state is different.

TCP Connection Establishment Sequence Number Synchronization and Parameter Exchange

The TCP three-way handshake describes the mechanism of message exchange that allows a pair of TCP devices to move from a closed state to one that is a ready-to-use, established connection. Connection establishment is about more than just passing messages between devices in order to establish communication. The TCP layers on the devices must also exchange information about the sequence numbers each device wants to use for its first data transmission. The layers must also exchange information about the parameters that will control how the connection operates. The sequence numbers exchange is usually called *sequence number synchronization*, and it is such an important part of connection establishment that the messages that each device sends to start the connection are called *SYN (synchronization)* messages.

You may recall from the TCP fundamentals discussion in Chapter 46 that TCP refers to each byte of data individually and uses sequence numbers to keep track of which bytes have been sent and received. Since each byte has a sequence number, we can acknowledge each byte, or more efficiently, use a single number to acknowledge a range of bytes received.

In the example I gave in Chapter 46, I assumed that each device would start a connection by giving the first byte of data sent between them sequence number 1. A valid question is why wouldn't we *always* just start off each TCP connection by sending the first byte of data with a sequence number of 1? The sequence numbers are arbitrary, after all, and this is the simplest method. In an ideal world, this would probably work, but we don't live in an ideal world.

The problem with starting off each connection with a sequence number of 1 is that it introduces the possibility of segments from different connections getting mixed up. Suppose we established a TCP connection and sent a segment containing bytes 1 through 30. However, a problem with the internetwork caused a delay with this segment, and eventually, the TCP connection itself was terminated. We then started up a new connection and again used a starting sequence number of 1. As soon as this new connection was started, however, the old segment with bytes labeled 1 to 30 showed up. The other device would erroneously think those bytes were part of the *new* connection.

This is but one of several similar problems that could occur. To avoid them, each TCP device, at the time a connection is initiated, chooses a 32-bit *initial sequence number (ISN)* for the connection. Each device has its own ISN, and those ISNs normally won't be the same.

Initial Sequence Number Selection

Traditionally, each device chose the ISN by making use of a timed counter, like a clock of sorts, that was incremented every 4 microseconds. TCP initialized the counter when it started up, and then the counter's value increased by one every 4 microseconds until it reached the largest 32-bit value possible (4,294,967,295), at which point it wrapped around to 0 and resumed incrementing. Any time a new connection was set up, the ISN was taken from the current value of this timer. Since it takes over 4 hours to count from 0 to 4,294,967,295 at 4 microseconds per increment, this virtually ensured that each connection would not conflict with any previous ones.

One issue with this method is that it made ISNs predictable. A malicious person could write code to analyze ISNs and then predict the ISN of a subsequent TCP connection based on the ISNs used in earlier ones. Malicious hackers have exploited this security risk in the past (such as in the case of the famous Mitnick attack). To defeat the malicious hackers, implementations now use a random number in their ISN selection process.

TCP Sequence Number Synchronization

Once each device chooses its ISN, it sends the ISN value to the other device in the Sequence Number field in the device's initial SYN message. The device receiving the SYN responds with an ACK message that acknowledges the SYN (which may also contain its own SYN, as in step 2 of the three-way handshake). In the ACK message, the Acknowledgment Number field is set to the value of the ISN that is received from the other device *plus one*. This represents the next sequence number the device expects to receive from its peer; the ISN actually represents the sequence number of the last byte received (fictitious in this case, since the connection is new and nothing yet has been received).

> **KEY CONCEPT** As part of the process of connection establishment, each of the two devices in a TCP connection informs the other of the sequence number it plans to use for its first data transmission. Each device informs the other by putting the preceding sequence number in the Sequence Number field of its SYN message. The other device confirms this by incrementing that value and putting it into the Acknowledgment Number field of its ACK message, telling the other device that it is the sequence number it is expecting for the first data transmission. This process is called *sequence number synchronization*.

Here's a simplified example of the three-way handshake steps (see Figure 47-4). I chose small ISNs for readability, but remember that ISNs can be any 32-bit number.

1. **Connection Request by Client** The client chooses an ISN for its transmissions of 4,567. It sends a SYN with the Sequence Number field set to 4,567.
2. **Acknowledgment and Connection Request by Server** The server chooses an ISN for its transmissions of 12,998. It receives the client's SYN. It sends a SYN+ACK with an Acknowledgment Number field value of 4,568 (one more than the client's ISN). This message has a Sequence Number field value of 12,998.
3. **Acknowledgment by Client** The client sends an ACK with the Acknowledgment Number field set to 12,999.

With the connection now established, the client will send data whose first byte will be given sequence number 4,568. The server's first byte of data will be numbered 12,999.

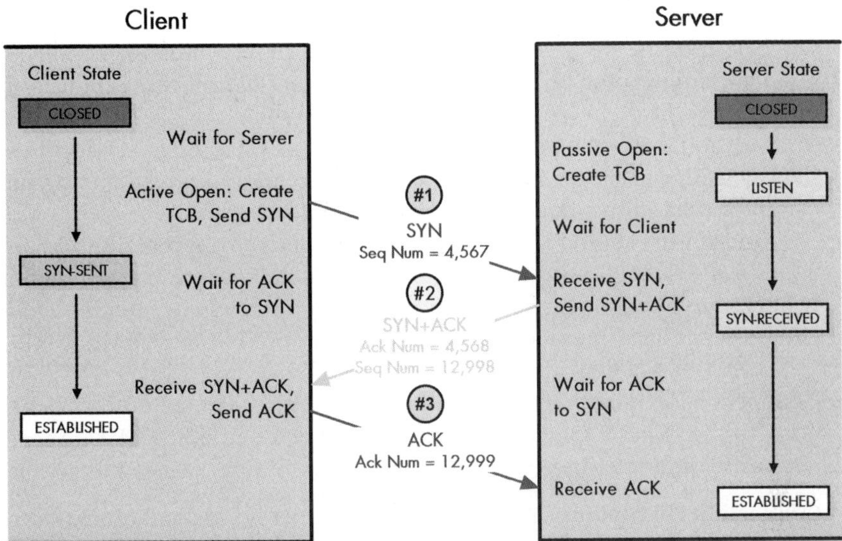

Figure 47-4: TCP sequence number synchronization *This diagram illustrates the same three-way handshake connection establishment procedure that I introduced in Figure 47-2, except this time I have shown the Sequence Number and Acknowledgment Number fields in each message, so that you can see how each of the two devices use them to establish initial sequence numbers for data exchange.*

TCP Parameter Exchange

In addition to the initial sequence numbers, SYN messages also are designed to convey important parameters about how the connection should operate. TCP includes a flexible scheme for carrying these parameters, in the form of a variable-length *Options* field in the TCP segment format, which can be expanded to carry multiple parameters. In RFC 793, only a single parameter is defined to be exchanged during connection setup: *maximum segment size (MSS)*. I explain the significance of this parameter in the TCP data transfer discussion in Chapter 48.

Each device sends the other the MSS that it wants to use for the connection; that is, if the device wishes to use a nondefault value. When receiving the SYN, the server records the MSS value that the client sent, and it will never send a segment larger than that value to the client. The client does the same for the server. The client and server MSS values are independent, so they can establish a connection where the client can receive larger segments than the server or vice versa.

Later RFCs have defined additional parameters that may be exchanged during connection setup. Some of these include the following:

Window Scale Factor Allows a pair of devices to specify larger window sizes than would normally be possible given the 16-bit size of the TCP *Window* field.

Selective Acknowledgment Permitted Allows a pair of devices to use the optional selective acknowledgment feature to allow only certain lost segments to be retransmitted.

Alternate Checksum Method Lets devices specify an alternative method of performing checksums than the standard TCP checksum mechanism.

TCP Connection Management and Problem Handling

Once both of the devices in a TCP connection have completed connection setup and have entered the ESTABLISHED state, the TCP software is in its normal operating mode. The TCP software will package bytes of data into segments for transmission using the mechanisms described in Chapter 48. TCP will use the sliding windows scheme to control segment size and to provide flow control, congestion handling, and retransmissions as needed.

Once in the sliding windows mode, both devices can remain there indefinitely. Some TCP connections can be very long-lived—in fact, some users maintain certain connections like Telnet sessions for hours or even days at a time. The following two circumstances can cause a connection to move out of the ESTABLISHED state:

Connection Termination Either of the devices decides to terminate the connection. This involves a specific procedure that I cover in the "TCP Connection Termination" section later in this chapter.

Connection Disruption A problem of some sort occurs and interrupts the connection.

The TCP Reset Function

In order for it to live up to its job of being a reliable and robust protocol, TCP includes intelligence that allows it to detect and respond to various problems that can occur during an established connection. One of the most common is the *half-open connection.* This situation occurs when, due to some sort of problem, one device closes or aborts the connection without the other one knowing about it. This means one device is in the ESTABLISHED state, while the other may be in the CLOSED state (no connection) or some other transient state. This could happen if, for example, one device had a software crash and someone restarted it in the middle of a connection, or if some sort of glitch caused the states of the two devices to become unsynchronized.

To handle half-open connections and other problem situations, TCP includes a special *reset function.* A *reset* is a TCP segment that TCP sends with the *RST* flag set to 1 in its header. Generally speaking, the TCP software generates a reset whenever something unexpected happens. The following are some of the most common cases in which the TCP software generates a reset:

- Receipt of any TCP segment from any device with which the device receiving the segment does not currently have a connection (other than a SYN requesting a new connection)
- Receipt of a message with an invalid or incorrect Sequence Number or Acknowledgment Number field, indicating that the message may belong to a prior connection or is spurious in some other way
- Receipt of a SYN message on a port where there is no process listening for connections

Handling Reset Segments

When a device receives a segment with the RST bit, it tells the other device to reset the connection so that the device can reestablish the connection. Like all segments, the reset itself must be checked to ensure that it is valid (by looking at the value of its Sequence Number field). This check prevents a spurious reset from shutting down a connection. Assuming the reset is valid, the handling of the message depends on the state of the device that receives it, as follows:

- If the device is in the LISTEN state, it ignores the reset and remains in that state.
- If the device is in the SYN-RECEIVED state but was previously in the LISTEN state (which is the normal course of events for a server setting up a new connection), it returns to the LISTEN state.
- In any other situation, the reset causes the device to abort the connection and the device returns to the CLOSED state for that connection. The device will advise the higher-layer process that is using TCP that it has closed the connection.

KEY CONCEPT TCP includes a special *connection reset feature* that allows devices to deal with problem situations, such as *half-open connections* or the receipt of unexpected message types. To use the feature, the device detecting the problem sends a TCP segment with the RST (reset) flag set to 1. The receiving device either returns to the LISTEN state, if it was in the process of connection establishment, or closes the connection and returns to the CLOSED state pending a new session negotiation.

Idle Connection Management and Keepalive Messages

One final connection management issue in TCP is how to handle an idle connection; that is, a TCP session that is active but that has no data being transmitted by either device for a prolonged period of time. The TCP standard specifies that the appropriate action to take in this situation is nothing. The reason is that, strictly speaking, there is no need to do anything to maintain an idle connection in TCP. The protocol is perfectly happy to allow both devices to stop transmitting for a very long period of time. Then it simply allows both devices to resume transmissions of data and acknowledgment segments when each one has data to send.

However, in the same way that people become antsy when they are on a telephone call and don't hear anything for a long time, some TCP implementors were concerned that an idle TCP connection might mean that something had broken the connection.

Thus, TCP software often includes an unofficial feature that allows a device with a TCP link to periodically send a null segment, which contains no data, to its peer on the connection. If the connection is still valid, the other device responds with a segment that contains an acknowledgment; if it is not, the other device will reply with a connection reset segment as I described earlier. These segments are sometimes called TCP *keepalive messages*, or just *keepalives*. They are analogous to Border Gateway Protocol (BGP) Keepalive messages (described in Chapter 40).

The use of these messages is quite controversial, and therefore, not universal. Those who oppose using them argue that they are not really necessary, and that sending them represents a waste of internetwork bandwidth and a possible additional cost on metered links (those that charge for each datagram sent). Their key point is that if the connection is not presently being used, it doesn't matter if it is still valid or not; as soon as the connection is used again, if it has broken, in the meantime, TCP can handle that using the reset function mentioned earlier.

Sending a keepalive message can, in theory, break a good TCP session unnecessarily. This may happen if the keepalive is sent during a time when there is an intermittent failure between the client and server. The failure might otherwise have corrected itself by the time the next piece of real data must be sent. In addition, some TCP implementations may not properly deal with the receipt of these segments.

Those in favor of using keepalives point out that each TCP connection consumes a certain amount of resources, and this can be an issue, especially for busy servers. If many clients connect to such a server and don't terminate the TCP connection properly, the server may sit for a long time with an idle connection, using system memory and other resources that it could apply elsewhere.

Since there is no wide acceptance on the use of this feature, devices implementing it include a way to disable it if necessary. Devices are also programmed so that they will not terminate a connection simply because they did not receive a response to a single keepalive message. They may terminate the connection if they do not receive a reply after several such messages have been sent over a period of time.

TCP Connection Termination

As the saying goes, all good things must come to an end, and so it is with TCP connections. The link between a pair of devices can remain open for a considerable period of time, assuming that a problem doesn't force the device to abort the connection. Eventually, however, one or both of the processes in the connection will run out of data to send and will shut down the TCP session, or the user will instruct the device to shut down.

Requirements and Issues In Connection Termination

Just as TCP follows an ordered sequence of operations in order to establish a connection, it also includes a specific procedure for terminating a connection. As with connection establishment, each of the devices moves from one state to the next in order to terminate the connection. This process is more complicated than you might imagine. In fact, an examination of the TCP FSM shows that there are more distinct states involved in shutting down a connection than in setting one up.

The reason that connection termination is complex is that during normal operation, both devices are sending and receiving data simultaneously. Usually, connection termination begins with one device indicating to TCP that it wants to close the connection. The matching process on the other device may not be aware that its peer wants to end the connection at all. Several steps are required to ensure that both devices shut down the connection gracefully and that no data is lost in the process.

Ultimately, shutting down a TCP connection requires the application processes on both ends of the connection to recognize that "the end is nigh" for the connection and that they should stop sending data. For this reason, connection termination is implemented so that each device terminates its end of the connection separately. The act of closing the connection by one device means that device will no longer send data, but can continue to receive it until the other device has decided to stop sending. This allows all data that is pending to be sent by both sides of the communication to be flushed before the connection is ended.

Normal Connection Termination

In the normal case, each side terminates its end of the connection by sending a special message with the FIN (finish) bit set. The FIN message serves as a connection termination request to the other device, while also possibly carrying data like a regular segment. The device receiving the FIN responds with an acknowledgment to the FIN that indicates that it received the acknowledgment. Neither side considers the connection terminated until they both have sent a FIN and received an ACK, thereby finishing the shutdown procedure.

Thus, termination isn't a three-way handshake as with establishment. It is a pair of two-way handshakes. The states that the two devices in the connection move through during a normal connection shutdown are different because the device initiating the shutdown must behave differently than the one that receives the termination request. In particular, the TCP on the device receiving the initial termination request must inform its application process and wait for a signal that the process is ready to proceed. The initiating device doesn't need to do this, since the application started the ball rolling in the first place.

> **KEY CONCEPT** A TCP connection is terminating using a special procedure by which each side independently closes its end of the link. The connection normally begins with one of the application processes signaling to its TCP layer that the session is no longer needed. That device sends a FIN message to tell the other device that it wants to end the connection, which the other device acknowledges. When the responding device is ready, it too sends a FIN that the other device acknowledges; after waiting a period of time for the device to receive the ACK, the device closes the session.

Table 47-4 describes in detail how the connection termination process works. You can also see the progression of states and messages exchanged in Figure 47-5. The table is adapted from Table 47-1, which describes the TCP FSM, but shows what happens for both the server and the client over time during connection shutdown. Either device can initiate connection termination; in this example, I am assuming the client does it. Each row shows the state each device begins in, what action it takes in that state, and what state it transitions to. I have also shown the send and receive stages of both of the steps for each of the client and server's close operations.

Table 47-4: TCP Connection Termination Procedure

Client			Server		
Start State	**Action**	**Transitions to State**	**Start State**	**Action**	**Transitions to State**
ESTABLISHED	Client Close Step 1 Transmit: The application using TCP signals that the connection is no longer needed. The client TCP sends a segment with the FIN bit set to request that the connection be closed.	FIN-WAIT-1	ESTABLISHED	At this stage the server is still in normal operating mode.	—
FIN-WAIT-1	The client, having sent a FIN, is waiting for a device to acknowledge it and for the server to send its own FIN. In this state, the client can still receive data from the server but will no longer accept data from its local application to be sent to the server.	—	ESTABLISHED	Client Close Step 1 Receive and Step 2 Transmit: The server receives the client's FIN. It sends an ACK to acknowledge the FIN. The server must wait for the application using it to be told that the other end is closing, so the application here can finish what it is doing.	CLOSE-WAIT
FIN-WAIT-1	Client Close Step 2 Receive: The client receives the ACK for its FIN. It must now wait for the server to close.	FIN-WAIT-2	CLOSE-WAIT	The server waits for the application process on its end to signal that it is ready to close.	—
FIN-WAIT-2	The client is waiting for the server's FIN.	—	CLOSE-WAIT	Server Close Step 1 Transmit: The server's TCP receives a notice from the local application that it is done. The server sends its FIN to the client.	LAST-ACK
FIN-WAIT-2	Server Close Step 1 Receive and Step 2 Transmit: The client receives the server's FIN and sends back an ACK.	TIME-WAIT	LAST-ACK	The server is waiting for an ACK for the FIN that it sent.	—
TIME-WAIT	The client waits for a period of time equal to double the maximum segment life (MSL) time; this wait ensures that the ACK it sent was received.	—	LAST-ACK	Server Close Step 2 Receive: The server receives the ACK to its FIN and closes the connection.	CLOSED
TIME-WAIT	The timer expires after double the MSL time.	CLOSED	CLOSED	The connection is closed on the server's end.	
CLOSED	The connection is closed.		CLOSED	The connection is closed.	

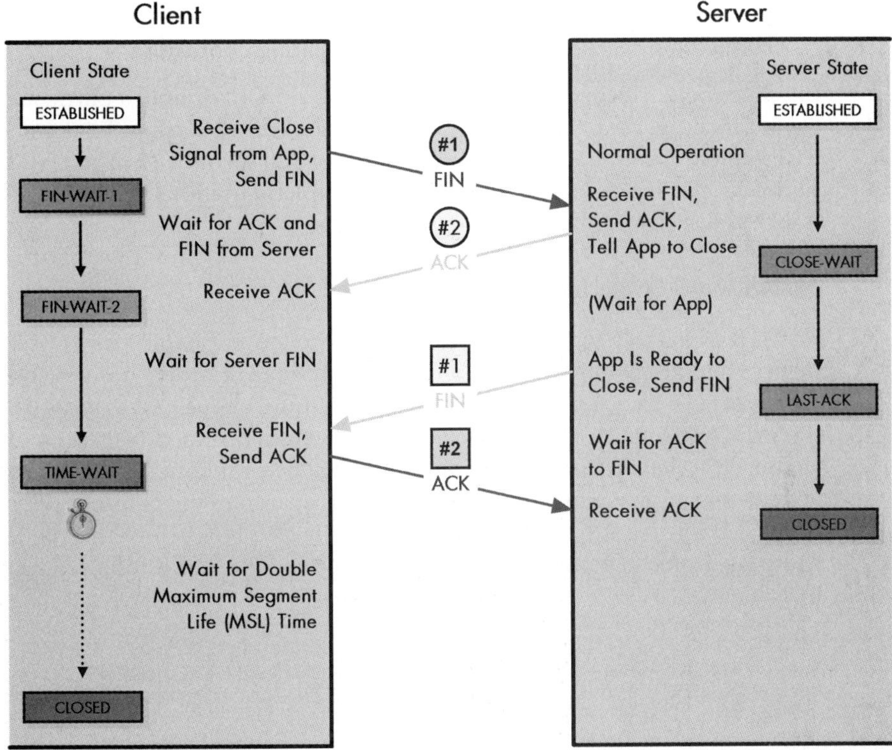

Figure 47-5: TCP connection termination procedure *This diagram shows the conventional termination procedure for a TCP session, with one device initiating termination and the other responding. In this case, the client initiates; it sends a FIN, which the server acknowledges. The server waits for the server process to be ready to close and then sends its FIN, which the client acknowledges. The client waits for a period of time in order to ensure that the device receives its ACK, before proceeding to the CLOSED state.*

The device receiving the initial FIN may have to wait a fairly long time (in networking terms) in the CLOSE-WAIT state for the application it is serving to indicate that it is ready to shut down. TCP cannot make any assumptions about how long this will take. During this period of time, the server in the previous example may continue sending data, and the client will receive it. However, the client will not send data to the server.

Eventually, the second device (the server in the example) will send a FIN to close its end of the connection. The device that originally initiated the close (the client) will send an ACK for this FIN. However, the client cannot immediately go to the CLOSED state right after sending that ACK because it must allow time for the ACK to travel to the server. Normally, this will be quick, but delays might slow it down somewhat.

The TIME-WAIT State

The TIME-WAIT state is required for two main reasons:

- To provide enough time to ensure that the other device receives the ACK, and to retransmit it if it is lost

- To provide a buffering period between the end of this connection and any subsequent ones. If not for this period, it is possible that packets from different connections could be mixed, thereby creating confusion.

The standard specifies that the client should wait double a particular length of time, called the *maximum segment lifetime (MSL)*, before closing the connection. The TCP standard defines MSL as being a value of 120 seconds (2 minutes). In modern networks, this is an eternity, so TCP allows implementations to choose a lower value if it believes that will lead to better operation.

Simultaneous Connection Termination

Just as it is possible to change the normal connection establishment process if two devices decide to actively open a connection to each other, it is also possible for two devices to try to terminate a connection simultaneously. This term *simultaneously* does not mean that they both decide to shut down at exactly the same time—variances in network delays mean nothing can be simultaneous on an internetwork anyway. It simply means that, in the previous example, the client decides to shut down and sends a FIN, but the server sends its own FIN before the client's FIN shows up at the server. In that case, a different procedure is followed, as described in Table 47-5 and illustrated in Figure 47-6.

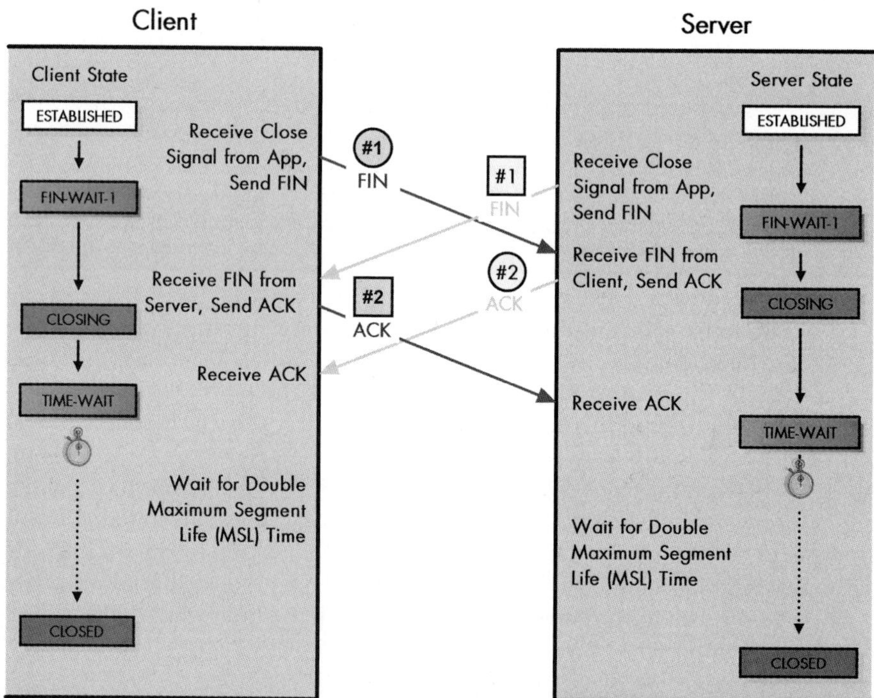

Figure 47-6: TCP simultaneous connection termination procedure *Under certain circumstances, both devices may decide to terminate a connection simultaneously, or nearly simultaneously. In this case, each sends a FIN and, before getting an ACK for it, receives the other device's FIN. Each acknowledges the other's FIN and waits for a period of time before closing the connection. Note the transition through the CLOSING state, which is used only as part of simultaneous termination.*

Table 47-5: TCP Simultaneous Connection Termination Procedure

Client			Server		
Start State	**Action**	**Transitions to State**	**Start State**	**Action**	**Transitions to State**
ESTABLISHED	Client Close Step 1 Transmit: The application using TCP signals that the connection is no longer needed. The TCP on the client sends the next segment with the FIN bit set, indicating a request to close the connection.	FIN-WAIT-1	ESTABLISHED	Server Close Step 1 Transmit: Before the server can receive the FIN that the client sent, the application on the server also signals a close. The server also sends a FIN.	FIN-WAIT-1
FIN-WAIT-1	Server Close Step 1 Receive and Step 2 Transmit: The client has sent a FIN and is waiting for it to be acknowledged. Instead, it receives the FIN that the server sends. It acknowledges the server's close request with an ACK and continues to wait for its own ACK.	CLOSING	FIN-WAIT-1	Client Close Step 1 Receive and Step 2 Transmit: The server has sent a FIN and is waiting for it to be acknowledged. Instead, it receives the FIN that the client sends. It acknowledges the client's close request with an ACK and continues to wait for its own ACK.	CLOSING
CLOSING	Client Close Step 2 Receive: The client receives the ACK for its FIN.	TIME-WAIT	CLOSING	Server Close Step 2 Receive: The server receives the ACK for its FIN.	TIME-WAIT
TIME-WAIT	The client waits for a period of time equal to double the MSL time. This gives enough time to ensure that the ACK it sent to the server was received.	—	TIME-WAIT	The server waits for a period of time equal to double the MSL time. This gives enough time to ensure the ACK it sent to the client was received.	—
TIME-WAIT	The timer expires after double the MSL time.	CLOSED	TIME-WAIT	The timer expires after double the MSL time.	CLOSED
CLOSED	The connection is closed.	—	CLOSED	The connection is closed.	—

As you can see, the process is much more symmetric in this case, with both devices transitioning through the same states. In either case the end result is the same, with the connection in the CLOSED state—meaning no connection. Each TCP will make sure all outstanding data is sent to the application, sometimes referred to as an implied *push* (see the description of the push function in Chapter 48 for an explanation of this term). The TCBs established for the connection in both devices are destroyed when the connection is closed down.

KEY CONCEPT Just as two devices can simultaneously open a TCP session, they can terminate it simultaneously as well. In this case, a different state sequence is followed, with each device responding to the other's FIN with an ACK, then waiting for receipt of its own ACK, and pausing for a period of time to ensure that the other device received its ACK before ending the connection.

48

TCP MESSAGE FORMATTING AND DATA TRANSFER

The previous chapter described how two devices using the Transmission Control Protocol (TCP) establish a TCP connection, as well as how that connection is managed and eventually terminated. While connections are a key part of how TCP works, they are really just a means to the ultimate end of the protocol: sending data. By employing the TCP sliding window mechanism, a special segment format, and several features, TCP devices are able to package and send data over the connection, enabling applications to communicate.

This chapter describes the actual mechanism by which TCP messages are formatted and data is transferred between devices. I begin with a look at the important *TCP segment format*, which describes the fields in each TCP message and how they are used. Next, I provide a description of the method used to calculate the checksum in TCP (as well as UDP) messages, and explain the reason why a special pseudo header is used. Then I discuss the maximum segment size (MSS) parameter and its significance. Following that, I talk about exactly how the sliding window mechanism is used to transfer and acknowledge data. I conclude with a description of two special data transfer features: the push feature, for immediate data transfer, and the urgent feature for priority data transfer.

BACKGROUND INFORMATION *This chapter assumes that you are already familiar with TCP concepts such as sequence numbers, segments, and the basics of the TCP sliding window mechanism. If you are not, read Chapter 46 before proceeding with this one.*

TCP Message (Segment) Format

In the TCP overview in Chapter 45, I described one of the most interesting jobs that TCP performs: It allows an application to send data as an unstructured sequence of bytes, transparently packaging that data in distinct messages as required by the underlying protocol that TCP uses (normally IP, of course). TCP messages are called *segments*, the name referring to the fact that each is a portion of the overall data stream passing between the devices.

TCP segments are very much jack-of-all-trade messages—they are flexible and serve a variety of purposes. A single field format is used for all segments, with a number of header fields that implement the many functions and features for which TCP is responsible. One of the most notable characteristics of TCP segments is that they are designed to carry both control information and data simultaneously. This reduces the number of segments sent, since a segment can perform more than one function.

For example, there is no need to send separate acknowledgments in TCP, because each TCP message includes a field for an acknowledgment byte number. Similarly, one can request that a connection be closed while sending data in the same message. The nature of each TCP segment is indicated through the use of several special control bits. More than one bit can be sent to allow a segment to perform multiple functions, such as when a bit is used to specify an initial sequence number (ISN) and acknowledge receipt of another such segment at the same time.

The price we pay for this flexibility is that the TCP header is large: 20 bytes for regular segments and more for those carrying options. This is one of the reasons why some protocols prefer to use the User Datagram Protocol (UDP) if they don't need TCP's features. The TCP header fields are used for the following general purposes:

Process Addressing The processes on the source and destination devices are identified using port numbers.

Implementing the Sliding Window System Sequence Number, Acknowledgment Number, and Window Size fields implement the TCP sliding window system (discussed in the "TCP Sliding Window Data Transfer and Acknowledgment Mechanics" section later in this chapter).

Setting Control Bits and Fields These are special bits that implement various control functions and fields that carry pointers and other data needed for them.

Carrying Data The Data field carries the actual bytes of data being sent between devices.

Performing Miscellaneous Functions These include a checksum for data protection and options for connection setup.

The format for TCP messages (segments) is described fully in Tables 48-1 through 48-3 and illustrated in Figure 48-1.

Table 48-1: TCP Segment Format

Field Name	Size (Bytes)	Description
Source Port	2	This is the 16-bit port number of the process that originated the TCP segment on the source device. This will normally be an ephemeral (client) port number for a request sent by a client to a server, or a well-known/registered (server) port number for a reply from a server to a client.
Destination Port	2	This is the 16-bit port number of the process that is the ultimate intended recipient of the message on the destination device. This will usually be a well-known/registered (server) port number for a client request, or an ephemeral (client) port number for a server reply.
Sequence Number	4	For normal transmissions, this is the sequence number of the first byte of data in this segment. In a connection request (SYN) message, this carries the ISN of the source TCP. The first byte of data will be given the next sequence number after the contents of this field, as described in Chapter 47.
Acknowledgment Number	4	When the ACK bit is set, this segment is serving as an acknowledgment (in addition to other possible duties), and this field contains the sequence number the source is next expecting the destination to send. See the "TCP Sliding Window Data Transfer and Acknowledgment Mechanics" section later in this chapter for details.
Data Offset	1/2 (4 bits)	This specifies the number of 32-bit words of data in the TCP header. In other words, this value times four equals the number of bytes in the header, which must always be a multiple of four. It is called a *data offset* since it indicates by how many 32-bit words the start of the data is offset from the beginning of the TCP segment.
Reserved	3/4 (6 bits)	This field is 6 bits reserved for future use; sent as zero.
Control Bits	3/4 (6 bits)	TCP does not use a separate format for control messages. Instead, certain bits are set to indicate the communication of control information. The 6 bits are described in Table 48-2.
Window	2	This indicates the number of octets of data the sender of this segment is willing to accept from the receiver at one time. This normally corresponds to the current size of the buffer allocated to accept data for this connection. In other words, this field is the current receive window size for the device sending this segment, which is also the send window for the recipient of the segment. See the "TCP Sliding Window Data Transfer and Acknowledgment Mechanics" section later in this chapter for details.
Checksum	2	This is a 16-bit checksum for data integrity protection, computed over the entire TCP datagram, plus a special pseudo header of fields. It is used to protect the entire TCP segment against errors in transmission as well as errors in delivery. Optional alternate checksum methods are also supported.
Urgent Pointer	2	This is used in conjunction with the URG control bit for priority data transfer (see Table 48-2). This field contains the sequence number of the last byte of urgent data. See the "TCP Priority Data Transfer: Urgent Function" section later in this chapter for details.
Options	Variable	TCP includes a generic mechanism for including one or more sets of optional data in a TCP segment. Each of the options can be either one byte in length or variable in length. The first byte is the Option-Kind subfield, and its value specifies the type of option, which in turn indicates whether the option is just a single byte or multiple bytes. Options that are many bytes consist of three fields, which are described in Table 48-3.
Padding	Variable	If the Options field is not a multiple of 32 bits in length, enough zeros are added to pad the header so it is a multiple of 32 bits.
Data	Variable	This is the bytes of data being sent in the segment.

Table 48-2: TCP Segment Control Bits

Subfield Name	Size (Bytes)	Description
URG	1/8 (1 bit)	Urgent bit: When set to 1, indicates that the priority data transfer feature has been invoked for this segment, and that the Urgent Pointer field is valid.
ACK	1/8 (1 bit)	Acknowledgment bit: When set to 1, indicates that this segment is carrying an acknowledgment, and the value of the Acknowledgment Number field is valid and carrying the next sequence expected from the destination of this segment.
PSH	1/8 (1 bit)	Push bit: The sender of this segment is using the TCP push feature, requesting that the data in this segment be immediately pushed to the application on the receiving device.
RST	1/8 (1 bit)	Reset bit: The sender has encountered a problem and wants to reset the connection.
SYN	1/8 (1 bit)	Synchronize bit: This segment is a request to synchronize sequence numbers and establish a connection; the Sequence Number field (see Table 48-1) contains the ISN of the sender of the segment.
FIN	1/8 (1 bit)	Finish bit: The sender of the segment is requesting that the connection be closed.

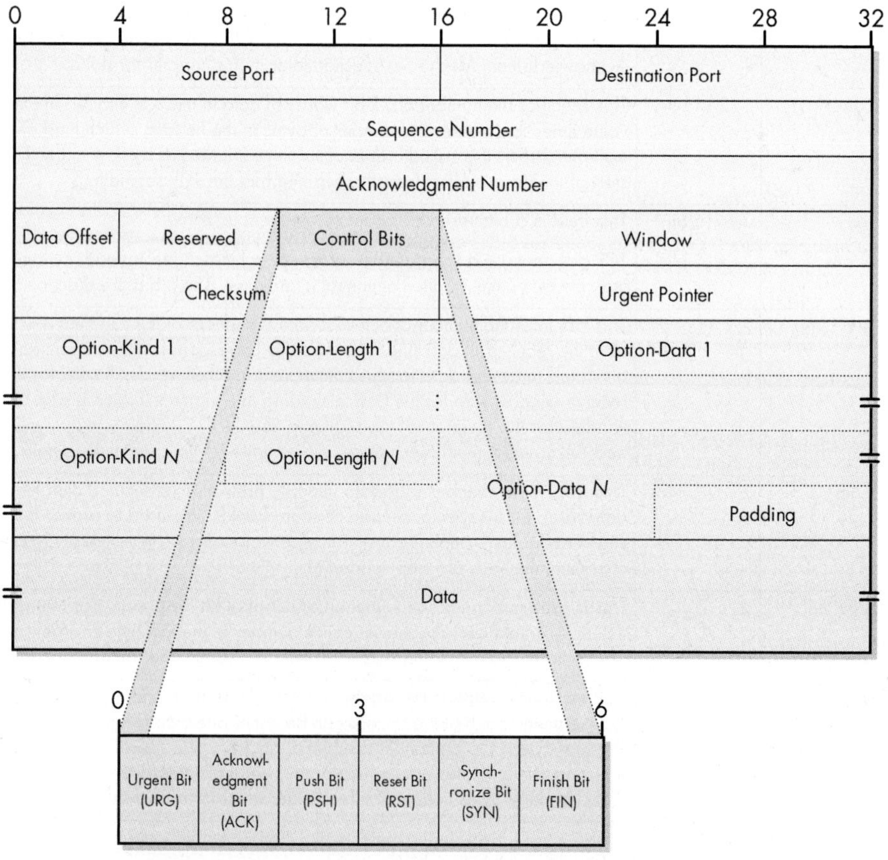

***Figure 48-1:** TCP segment format*

Table 48-3: TCP Segment Option Subfields

Subfield Name	Size (Bytes)	Description
Option-Kind	1	This specifies the option type.
Option-Length	1	This is the length of the entire option in bytes, including the Option-Kind and Option-Length fields.
Option-Data	Variable	This field contains the option data itself. In at least one oddball case, this field is omitted (making Option-Length equal to 2).

Table 48-4 shows the main options currently defined for TCP

Table 48-4: Some TCP Options

Option-Kind	Option-Length	Option-Data	Description
0	—	—	End of Option List: A single-byte option that marks the end of all options included in this segment. This needs to be included only when the end of the options doesn't coincide with the end of the TCP header.
1	—	—	No-Operation: A "spacer" that can be included between options to align a subsequent option on a 32-bit boundary if needed.
2	4	Maximum Segment Size Value	Maximum Segment Size: Conveys the size of the largest segment the sender of the segment wishes to receive. Used only in connection request (SYN) messages.
3	3	Window Size Shift Bits	Window Scale: Implements the optional window scale feature, which allows devices to specify much larger window sizes than would be possible with the normal Window field. The value in Option-Data specifies the power of 2 that the Window field should be multiplied by to get the true window size the sender of the option is using. For example, if the value of Option-Data is 3, this means values in the Window field should be multiplied by 8, assuming both devices agree to use this feature. This allows very large windows to be advertised when needed on high-performance links. See the "TCP Sliding Window Data Transfer and Acknowledgment Mechanics" section later in this chapter for details.
4	2	—	Selective Acknowledgment Permitted: Specifies that this device supports the selective acknowledgment (SACK) feature. This was implemented as a 2-byte option with no Option-Data field, instead of a single-byte option like End of Option List or No-Operation. This was necessary because it was defined after the original TCP specification, so an explicit option length needed to be indicated for backward compatibility.
5	Variable	Blocks of Data Selectively Acknowledged	Selective Acknowledgment: Allows devices supporting the optional selective acknowledgment feature to specify noncontiguous blocks of data that have been received so they are not retransmitted if intervening segments do not show up and need to be retransmitted.
14	3	Alternate Checksum Algorithm	Alternate Checksum Request: Lets a device request that a checksum-generation algorithm other than the standard TCP algorithm be used for this connection. Both devices must agree to the algorithm for it to be used.
15	Variable	Alternate Checksum	Alternate Checksum: If the checksum value needed to implement an alternate checksum is too large to fit in the standard 16-bit Checksum field, it is placed in this option.

The table does not include every TCP option; it just shows the basic ones defined in RFC 793 and a few others that are interesting and correspond to features described elsewhere in this book. Note that most options are sent only in connection request (SYN) segments. This includes the Maximum Segment Size, Window Scale, Selective Acknowledgment Permitted, and Alternate Checksum Request options. In contrast, the Selective Acknowledgment and Alternate Checksum options appear in regular data segments when they are used.

TCP Checksum Calculation and the TCP Pseudo Header

TCP is designed to provide reliable data transfer between a pair of devices on an IP internetwork. Much of the effort required to ensure reliable delivery of data segments is focused on the problem of ensuring that data is not lost in transit. But there's another important critical impediment to the safe transmission of data: the risk of *errors* being introduced into a TCP segment during its travel across the internetwork.

Detecting Transmission Errors Using Checksums

If the data gets where it needs to go but is corrupted, and we do not detect the corruption, this is in some ways worse than it never showing up at all. To provide basic protection against errors in transmission, TCP includes a 16-bit Checksum field in its header. The idea behind a checksum is very straightforward: Take a string of data bytes and add them all together, then send this sum with the data stream and have the receiver check the sum. In TCP, the device sending the segment uses a special algorithm to calculate this checksum. The recipient then employs the same algorithm to check the data it received and ensure that there were no errors.

The checksum calculation used by TCP is a bit different than a regular checksum algorithm. A conventional checksum is performed over all the bytes that the checksum is intended to protect, and it can detect most bit errors in any of those fields. The designers of TCP wanted this bit-error protection, but they also wanted protection against other types of problems. To this end, a change was made in how the TCP checksum is computed. This special TCP checksum algorithm was eventually also adopted for use by UDP; see Chapter 44.

Increasing the Scope of Detected Errors: The TCP Pseudo Header

Instead of computing the checksum over only the actual data fields of the TCP segment, a 12-byte TCP *pseudo header* is created prior to checksum calculation. This header contains important information taken from fields in both the TCP header and the Internet Protocol (IP) datagram into which the TCP segment will be encapsulated (see Chapter 21 for a description of the IP datagram format). The TCP pseudo header has the format described in Table 48-5 and illustrated in Figure 48-2.

Table 48-5: TCP Pseudo Header for Checksum Calculations

Field Name	Size (Bytes)	Description
Source Address	4	This is the 32-bit IP address of the originator of the datagram, taken from the IP header.
Destination Address	4	This is the 32-bit IP address of the intended recipient of the datagram, also from the IP header.
Reserved	1	This consists of 8 bits of zeros.
Protocol	1	This is the Protocol field from the IP header. This indicates the higher-layer protocol that is carried in the IP datagram. Of course, we already know that this protocol is TCP. So, this field will normally have the value 6.
TCP Length	2	This is the length of the TCP segment, including both header and data. Note that this is not a specific field in the TCP header; it is computed.

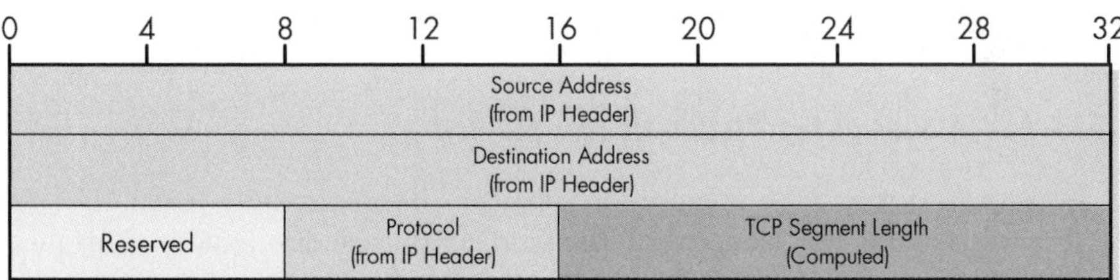

Figure 48-2: TCP pseudo header for checksum calculation

Once this 96-bit header has been formed, it is placed in a buffer, followed by the TCP segment itself. Then the checksum is computed over the entire set of data (pseudo header plus TCP segment). The value of the checksum is placed in the Checksum field of the TCP header, and the pseudo header is discarded; it is *not* an actual part of the TCP segment and is not transmitted. This process is illustrated in Figure 48-3.

NOTE *The Checksum field is itself part of the TCP header and thus one of the fields over which the checksum is calculated, creating a "chicken-and-egg" situation of sorts. This field is assumed to be all zeros during calculation of the checksum.*

When the TCP segment arrives at its destination, the receiving TCP software performs the same calculation. It forms the pseudo header, prepends it to the actual TCP segment, and then performs the checksum (setting the Checksum field to zero for the calculation as before). If there is a mismatch between its calculation and the value the source device put in the Checksum field, this indicates that an error of some sort occurred, and the segment is normally discarded.

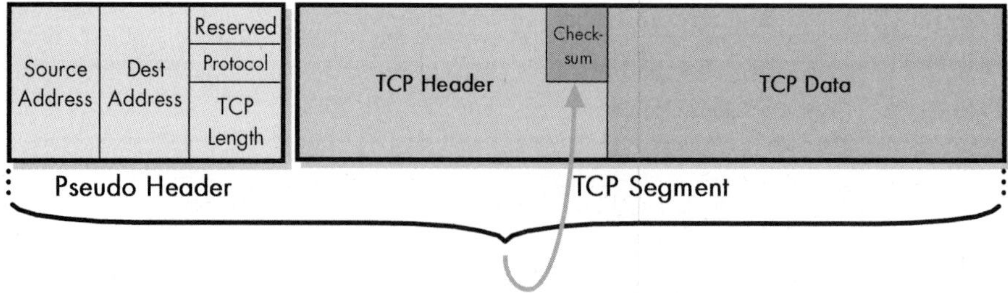

Figure 48-3: TCP header checksum calculation *To calculate the TCP segment header's Checksum field, the TCP pseudo header is first constructed and placed, logically, before the TCP segment. The checksum is then calculated over both the pseudo header and the TCP segment. The pseudo header is then discarded.*

Advantages of the Pseudo Header Method

So, why bother with this pseudo header? The source and destination devices both compute the checksum using the fields in this pseudo header. This means that if, for any reason, the two devices don't use the same values for the pseudo header, the checksum will fail. When we consider what's in the header, we find that this means the checksum now protects against not just errors in the TCP segment fields, but also against the following problems:

Incorrect Segment Delivery If there is a mismatch in the Destination Address between what the source specified and what the destination that received the segment used, the checksum will fail. The same will happen if the Source Address does not match.

Incorrect Protocol If a datagram is routed to TCP that actually belongs to a different protocol for whatever reason, this can be immediately detected.

Incorrect Segment Length If part of the TCP segment has been omitted by accident, the lengths the source and destination used won't match, and the checksum will fail.

What's clever about the pseudo header is that by using it for the checksum calculation, we can provide this protection without actually needing to send the fields in the pseudo header itself. This eliminates duplicating the IP fields used in the pseudo header within the TCP header, which would be redundant and wasteful of bandwidth. The drawback of the pseudo header method is that it makes checksum calculation take more time and effort (though this is not much of an issue today).

KEY CONCEPT TCP checksums are computed over not just the TCP segment, but also over a TCP *pseudo header* that contains the length of the TCP segment as well as the IP Source Address, Destination Address, and Protocol fields. Since these fields are part of the checksum, if the segment is received by the wrong device or has the incorrect Protocol field or segment length, it will be rejected. The technique is clever because the checksum can provide this protection, even though the pseudo header itself is not actually transmitted.

In the context of today's modern, high-speed, highly reliable networks, the use of the pseudo header sometimes seems archaic. How likely is it that a datagram will be delivered to the wrong address? Not very. At the time TCP was created, however, there was significant concern that there might not be proper end-to-end checking of the delivery of datagrams at the IP level. Including IP information in the TCP checksum was seen as a useful additional level of protection.

NOTE *There is one interesting implication of the TCP pseudo header: It violates the architectural layering principles that the designers of TCP sought to respect in splitting up TCP and IP. For the checksum, TCP must know IP information that technically it shouldn't know. TCP checksum calculation requires, for example, that the protocol number from the IP header be given to the TCP layer on the receiving device from the IP datagram that carried the segment. The TCP pseudo header is a good example of a case where strict layering was eschewed in favor of practicality.*

TCP also supports an optional method of having two devices agree on an alternative checksum algorithm. This must be negotiated during connection establishment.

TCP Maximum Segment Size (MSS)

TCP *segments* are the messages that carry data between TCP devices. The Data field is where the actual data being transmitted is carried, and since the length of the Data field in TCP is variable, this raises an interesting question: How much data should we put into each segment? TCP accepts data as a constant stream from the applications that use it, which means that it must decide how many bytes to put into each message that it sends.

A primary determinant of how much data to send in a segment is the current status of the sliding window mechanism on the part of the receiver. When Device A receives a TCP segment from Device B, it examines the value of the Window field to know the limit on how much data Device B is allowing Device A to send in its next segment. (This process is described in the "TCP Sliding Window Data Transfer and Acknowledgment Mechanics" section later in this chapter.) There are also important issues in the selection and adjustment of window size that impact the operation of the TCP system as a whole, which are discussed in Chapter 46.

In addition to the dictates of the current window size, each TCP device also has associated with it a *ceiling* on TCP size—a segment size that will never be exceeded, regardless of how large the current window is. This is called the *maximum segment size (MSS)*. When deciding how much data to put into a segment, each device in the TCP connection will choose the amount based on the current window size, in conjunction with the various algorithms described in Chapter 46, but it will never be so large that the amount of data exceeds the MSS of the device to which it is sending.

NOTE *The name* maximum segment size *is misleading. The value actually refers to the maximum amount of data that a segment can hold. It does not include the TCP headers. So if the MSS is 100, the actual maximum segment size could be 120 (for a regular TCP header) or larger (if the segment includes TCP options).*

MSS Selection

The selection of the MSS is based on the need to balance various competing performance and implementation issues in the transmission of data on TCP/IP networks. The main TCP standard, RFC 793, doesn't say much about MSS, so there was potential for confusion about how the parameter should be used. RFC 879 was published a couple of years after the TCP standard to clarify this parameter and the issues surrounding it.

Some issues with the MSS are fairly mundane; for example, certain devices are limited in the amount of space they have for buffers to hold TCP segments, and therefore may wish to limit segment size to a relatively small value. In general, though, the MSS must be chosen by balancing two competing performance issues:

Overhead Management The TCP header takes up 20 bytes of data (or more if options are used); the IP header also uses 20 or more bytes. This means that between them, a minimum of 40 bytes is needed for headers, and all of that is nondata overhead. If we set the MSS too low, this results in very inefficient use of bandwidth. For example, if we set it to 40 bytes, a *maximum* of 50 percent of each segment could actually be data; the rest would just be headers. Many segment datagrams would be even worse in terms of efficiency.

IP Fragmentation TCP segments will be packaged into IP datagrams. As you saw in Chapter 22, datagrams have their own size limit issues: the matter of the maximum transmission unit (MTU) of an underlying network. If a TCP segment is too large, it will lead to an IP datagram that is too large to be sent without fragmentation. Fragmentation reduces efficiency and increases the chances of part of a TCP segment being lost, resulting in the entire segment needing to be retransmitted.

TCP Default MSS

The solution to the two competing issues of overhead management and IP fragmentation was to establish a default MSS for TCP that was as large as possible, while avoiding fragmentation for most transmitted segments. This was computed by starting with the minimum MTU for IP networks of 576 bytes. All networks are required to be able to handle an IP datagram of this size without fragmenting. From this number, we subtract 20 bytes for the TCP header and 20 bytes for the IP header, leaving 536 bytes. This is the standard MSS for TCP.

KEY CONCEPT TCP is designed to restrict the size of the segments it sends to a certain maximum limit, to reduce the likelihood that segments will need to be fragmented for transmission at the IP level. The TCP *maximum segment size (MSS)* specifies the maximum number of bytes in the TCP segment's Data field, regardless of any other factors that influence segment size. The default MSS for TCP is 536 bytes, which is calculated by starting with the minimum IP MTU of 576 bytes and subtracting 20 bytes each for the IP and TCP headers.

The selection of this MSS value was a compromise of sorts. It means that most TCP segments will be sent unfragmented across an IP internetwork. However, if any TCP or IP options are used, the minimum MTU of 576 bytes will be exceeded, and fragmentation will occur. Still, it makes more sense to allow some segments to be fragmented, rather than use a much smaller MSS to ensure that none are ever fragmented. If we chose, say, an MSS of 400 bytes, we would probably never have fragmentation, but we would lower the data/header ratio from 536:40 (93 percent data) to 400:40 (91 percent data) for all segments.

Nondefault MSS Value Specification

Naturally, there will be cases where the default MSS is not ideal. TCP provides a means for a device to specify that the MSS it wants to use is either smaller or larger than the default value of 536 bytes. A device can inform the other device of the MSS it wants to use through parameter exchange during the connection establishment process. A device that chooses to do so includes in its SYN message the TCP option called, appropriately, Maximum Segment Size. The other device receives this option and records the MSS for the connection. Each device can specify the MSS it wants for the segments it receives independently.

NOTE *The exchange of MSS values during setup is sometimes called* MSS negotiation. *This is actually a misleading term, because it implies that the two devices must agree on a common MSS value, which is not the case. The MSS value used by each may be different, and there is no negotiation at all.*

Devices may wish to use a larger MSS if they know that the MTUs of the networks the segments will pass over are larger than the IP minimum of 576 bytes. This is most commonly the case when large amounts of data are sent on a local network. The process of MTU path discovery, as described in Chapter 22, is used to determine the appropriate MSS. Devices might use a smaller MSS if they know that TCP segments use a particular optional feature that would consistently increase the size of the IP header, such as when the segments employ IPsec for security (see Chapter 29).

KEY CONCEPT Devices can indicate that they wish to use a different MSS value from the default by including a Maximum Segment Size option in the SYN message they use to establish a connection. Each device in the connection may use a different MSS value.

TCP Sliding Window Data Transfer and Acknowledgment Mechanics

The TCP connection establishment process is employed by a pair of devices to create a TCP connection between them. Once all the setup is done—transmission control blocks (TCBs) have been set up, parameters have been exchanged, and so forth—the devices are ready to get down to the business of transferring data.

The sending of data between TCP devices on a connection is accomplished using the sliding window system we explored in Chapter 46. Here, we will take a more detailed look at exactly how sliding windows are implemented to allow data to be sent and received. For ease of explanation, we'll assume that our connection is between a client and a server—this is easier than the whole "Device A/Device B" business.

Sliding Window Transmit and Receive Categories

Each of the two devices on a connection must keep track of the data it is sending, as well as the data it is receiving from the other device. This is done by conceptually dividing the bytes into *categories*. For data being transmitted, there are four transmit categories:

Transmit Category 1 Bytes sent and acknowledged

Transmit Category 2 Bytes sent but not yet acknowledged

Transmit Category 3 Bytes not yet sent for which recipient is ready

Transmit Category 4 Bytes not yet sent for which recipient is not ready

For data being received, there is no need to separate into "received and acknowledged" and "received and unacknowledged," the way the transmitter separates its first two categories into "sent and acknowledged" and "sent but not yet acknowledged." The reason is that the transmitter must wait for acknowledgment of each transmission, but the receiver doesn't need acknowledgment that it received something. Thus, one receive category corresponds to Transmit Categories 1 and 2, while the other two correspond to Transmit Category 3 and Transmit Category 4, respectively, for a total of three receive categories. To help make more clear how the categories relate, I number them as follows:

Receive Category 1+2 Bytes received and acknowledged. This is the receiver's complement to Transmit Categories 1 and 2.

Receive Category 3 Bytes not yet received for which recipient is ready. This is the receiver's complement to Transmit Category 3.

Receive Category 4 Bytes not yet received for which recipient is not ready. This is the receiver's complement to Transmit Category 4.

Send (SND) and Receive (RCV) Pointers

Both the client and server must keep track of both streams being sent over the connection. This is done using a set of special variables called *pointers*, which carve the byte stream into the categories described in the previous section.

The four transmit categories are divided using three send (SND) pointers. Two of the pointers are absolute (refer to a specific sequence number), and one is an offset that is added to one of the absolute pointers, as follows:

Send Unacknowledged (SND.UNA) The sequence number of the first byte of data that has been sent but not yet acknowledged. This marks the first byte of Transmit Category 2; all previous sequence numbers refer to bytes in Transmit Category 1.

Send Next (SND.NXT) The sequence number of the next byte of data to be sent to the other device (the server, in this case). This marks the first byte of Transmit Category 3.

Send Window (SND.WND) The size of the send window. Recall that the window specifies the total number of bytes that any device may have outstanding *(unacknowledged)* at any one time. Thus, adding the sequence number of the first unacknowledged byte (SND.UNA) and the send window (SND.WND) marks the first byte of Transmit Category 4.

Another way of looking at these pointers is how they indicate the number of bytes a transmitting device can send at any point in time—that is, the number of bytes in Transmit Category 3. The start of Transmit Category 3 is marked by SND.NXT. The end is marked by the first byte of Transmit Category 4, given by SND.UNA+SND.WND. Thus, the number of bytes in Transmit Category 3 is given by the following formula:

SND.UNA + SND.WND – SND.NXT

This is called the *usable window*, since it indicates how many bytes the transmitter can use at any point in time. When data is acknowledged, this causes bytes to move from Transmit Category 2 to Transmit Category 1, by increasing the value of SND.UNA. Assuming that the send window size doesn't change, this causes the window to *slide* to the right, permitting more data to be sent. Figure 48-4 illustrates the SND pointers.

KEY CONCEPT The TCP sliding windows scheme uses three pointers that keep track of which bytes are in each of the four transmit categories. SND.UNA points to the first unacknowledged byte and indicates the start of Transmit Category 2; SND.NXT points to the next byte of data to be sent and marks the start of Transmit Category 3. SND.WND contains the size of the send window; it is added to SND.NXT to mark the start of Transmit Category 4. Adding SND.WND to SND.UNA and then subtracting SND.NXT yields the current size of the usable transmit window.

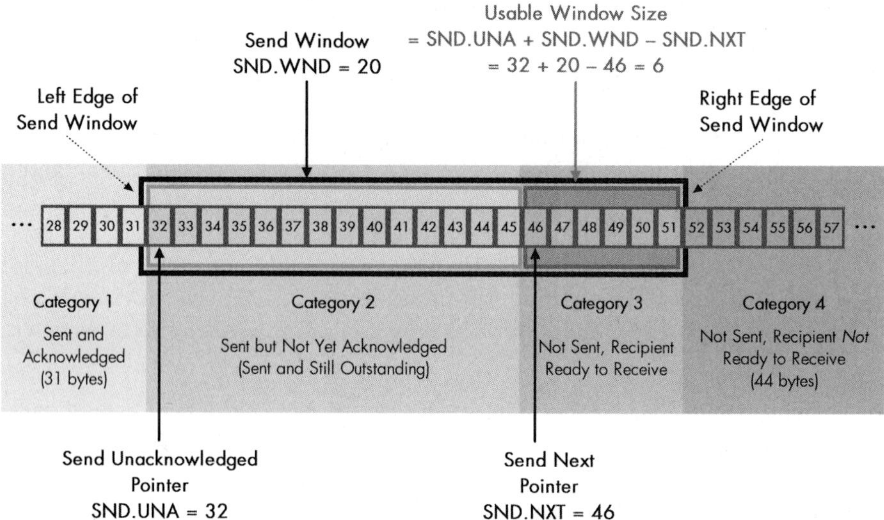

Figure 48-4: TCP transmission categories, send window, and pointers *This diagram is the same as Figure 46-6 (in Chapter 46), but shows the TCP send pointers. SND.UNA points to the start of Transmit Category 2, SND.NXT points to the start of Transmit Category 3, and SND.WND is the size of the send window. The size of the usable window (the hatched rectangle) can be calculated as shown from those three pointers.*

The three receive categories are divided using two pointers:

Receive Next (RCV.NXT) The sequence number of the next byte of data that is expected from the other device. This marks the first byte in Receive Category 3. All previous sequence numbers refer to bytes already received and acknowledged, in Receive Categories 1 and 2.

Receive Window (RCV.WND) The size of the receive window advertised to the other device. This refers to the number of bytes the device is willing to accept at one time from its peer, which is usually the size of the buffer allocated for receiving data for this connection. When added to the RCV.NXT pointer, this pointer marks the first byte of Receive Category 4.

The receive categories and pointers are illustrated in Figure 48-5.

The SND and RCV pointers are complementary, just as the categories are, with each device managing both the sending of its data and receiving of data from its peer. Assuming we have a client and a server, the relationship between these pointers is as follows:

Client The SND pointers keep track of the client's outgoing data stream; the RCV pointers refer to the data coming in from the server. The client's SND categories correspond to the server's RCV categories.

Server The SND pointers keep track of the server's outgoing data stream; the RCV pointers refer to the data being received from the client. The server's SND categories correspond to the client's RCV categories.

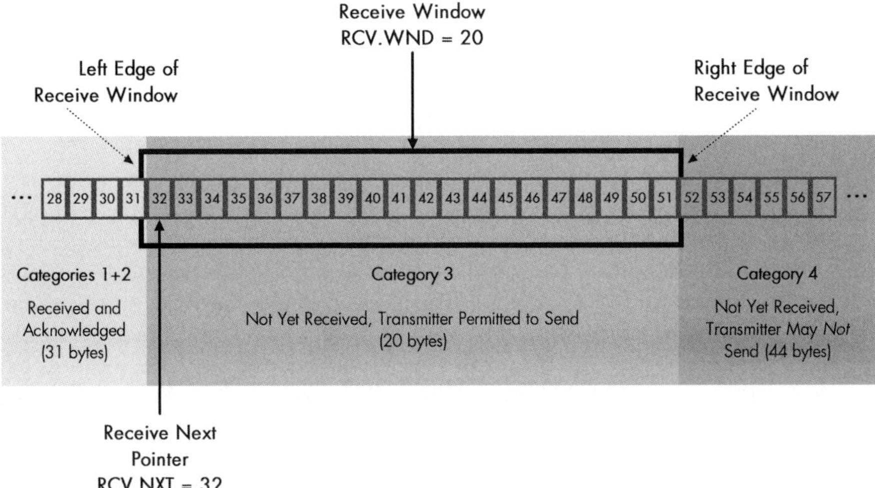

Figure 48-5: TCP receive categories and pointers *This diagram is the complement of Figure 48-4, showing how the categories are set up for the receiving device. Categories 1 and 2 have been combined since there is no differentiation between "received and unacknowledged" and "received and acknowledged." This example shows the state of the receiving device prior to receipt of the 14 bytes that in Figure 48-4 have already been sent.*

> **KEY CONCEPT** A set of *receive (RCV) pointers* is maintained by each device. These receive pointers are the complement of the *send (SND) pointers.* A device's send pointers keep track of its outgoing data, and its receive pointers keep track of the incoming data. The two receive pointers are RCV.NXT, which indicates the number of the next byte of data expected from the other device, and RCV.WND, which is the size of the receive window for that device. The RCV.WND of one device equals the SND.WND of the other device on the connection.

Since the SND and RCV values are complementary, the send window of one device is the receive window of the other, and vice versa. Note, however, that the values of the pointers do not always match exactly on the two devices, because at any given time, some bytes may be in transit between the two. Figure 48-5, for example, shows the receive pointers of the recipient *prior* to receiving bytes 32 to 45, which are shown in transit in Figure 48-4.

TCP Segment Fields Used to Exchange Pointer Information

Both SND and RCV pointers are maintained in the TCB for the connection held by each device. As data is exchanged, the pointers are updated, and information about the state of the send and receive streams is exchanged using control fields in the TCP segment format. The following are the three most important TCP segment fields used to exchange pointer information:

Sequence Number Identifies the sequence number of the first byte of data in the segment being transmitted. This will normally be equal to the value of the SND.UNA pointer at the time that data is sent.

Acknowledgment Number Acknowledges the receipt of data by specifying the sequence number that the sender of the segment expects in the segment recipient's next transmission. This field will normally be equal to the RCV.NXT pointer of the device that sends it.

Window The size of the receive window of the device sending the segment (and thus, the send window of the device receiving the segment).

The Acknowledgment Number field is critical because a device uses this field to tell its peer which segments it has received. The system is *cumulative*. The Acknowledgment Number field says, "I have received all data bytes with sequence numbers less than this value." This means if a client receives many segments of data from a server in rapid succession, it can acknowledge all of them using a single number, as long as they are contiguous. If they are not contiguous, then things get more complicated; see "TCP Noncontiguous Acknowledgment Handling and Selective Acknowledgment (SACK)" in Chapter 49.

KEY CONCEPT Three essential fields in the TCP segment format are used to implement the sliding windows system. The Sequence Number field indicates the number of the first byte of data being transmitted. The Acknowledgment Number is used to acknowledge data received by the device sending this segment. The Window field tells the recipient of the segment the size to which it should set its send window.

An Example of TCP Sliding Window Mechanics

To see how all of this works, let's consider an example of a client and server using a mythical file-retrieval protocol. This protocol specifies that the client sends a request and receives an immediate response from the server. The server then sends the file requested when it is ready.

The two devices will first establish a connection and synchronize sequence numbers. For simplicity, let's say the client uses an ISN of 0, and the server uses an ISN of 240. The server will send the client an ACK with an Acknowledgment Number of 1, indicating it is the sequence number it expects to receive next. Let's say the server's receive window size is set to 360, so this is the client's send window size. The client will send its ACK with an Acknowledgment Number of 241. Let's say its receive window size is 200 (and the server's client window size is thus 200). Let's assume that both devices maintain the same window size throughout the transaction. This won't normally happen, especially if the devices are busy, but the example is complicated enough. Let's also say the MSS is 536 bytes in both directions. This means that the MSS won't affect the size of actual segments in this example (since the MSS is larger than the send window sizes for both devices).

We'll follow a sample transaction to show how the send and receive pointers are created and changed as messages are exchanged between client and server. Table 48-6 describes the process in detail, showing for each step what the send and receive pointers are for both devices. It is rather large, so beware. The transaction is also graphically illustrated in Figures 48-6 and 48-7. Both illustrate the same exchange of messages, using the step numbers of Table 48-6, but from the perspective of one of the devices. Figure 48-6 shows the server's send pointers and client's receive pointers. Figure 48-7 shows the client's send pointers and server's receive pointers. (I would have put them all in one diagram, but they wouldn't fit!)

Table 48-6: TCP Transaction Example with Send and Receive Pointers

Client						**Server**					
Process Step	**SND. UNA**	**SND. NXT**	**SND. WND**	**RCV. NXT**	**RCV. WND**	**Process Step**	**SND. UNA**	**SND. NXT**	**SND. WND**	**RCV. NXT**	**RCV. WND**
Description						**Description**					
(setup)	1	1	360	241	200	**(setup)**	241	241	200	1	360
During connection establishment, the client sets up its pointers based on the parameters exchanged during setup. Notice that the SND.UNA and SND.NXT values are the same. No data has been sent yet, so nothing is unacknowledged. RCV.NXT is the value of the first byte of data expected from the server.						The server sets up its pointers just as the client does. Notice how its values are the complement of the client's.					
1. Send Request	1	141	360	241	200	**(wait)**	241	241	200	1	360
The client transmits a request to the server. Let's say the request is 140 bytes in length. It will form a segment with a data field of this length and transmit it with the Sequence Number set to 1, the sequence number of the first byte. Once this data has been sent, the client's SND.NXT pointer will be incremented to the value 141 to indicate this is the next data to be sent to the server.						The server does nothing, waiting for a request.					
(wait)	1	141	360	241	200	**2. Receive Request, Send Ack & Reply**	241	321	200	141	360
At this point, the client hasn't received an acknowledgment for its request. At present, SND.UNA+SND.WND is 361, while SND.NXT is 141. This means the current usable window is 220 bytes. The client could send up to 220 more bytes of data before getting back an acknowledgment. For now, let's say it has nothing more to transmit.						The server receives the 140-byte request from the client. The server sends back an 80-byte response that also acknowledges the client's TCP segment. The Sequence Number field will be 241, the first sequence number of the server's 80 bytes of data. The Acknowledgment Number will be 141, telling the client that is the next sequence number the server expects to hear, and thereby implicitly acknowledging receipt of bytes 1 through 140. The server increases its RCV.NXT pointer to 141 to reflect the 140 bytes of data received. It increases its SND.NXT pointer by 80.					
3. Receive Ack & Reply, Send Ack	141	141	360	321	200	**4. Send Part 1 of File**	241	441	200	141	360
The client receives the server's response. It sees the Acknowledgment Number of 141 and knows bytes 1 to 140 were successfully received. It increases its SND.UNA to 141, effectively "sliding the send window" by 140. The client also accepts the 80 bytes of data the server sent, increasing its RCV.NXT pointer by 80. Assuming it has no more data to send, it sends back a TCP segment that is a pure acknowledgment of the server's response. This segment has no data and an Acknowledgment Number value of 321.						While the client was receiving its response, the server's TCP was supplied with a 280-byte file to be sent to the client. It cannot send all this in one segment, however. The current value of SND.UNA+SND.WND is 441, while SND.NXT is 321. Thus, the server's usable window contains 120 bytes of data. It creates a TCP segment with this much data and a Sequence Number of 321. It increases the SND.NXT pointer to 441. The server has now filled the send window. Note that the server does not need to wait for an acknowledgment to the reply it sent in step 2. This is a key factor in TCP's ability to ensure high throughput.					

(continued)

Table 48-6: TCP Transaction Example with Send and Receive Pointers (continued)

Client						Server					
Process Step	**SND. UNA**	**SND. NXT**	**SND. WND**	**RCV. NXT**	**RCV. WND**	**Process Step**	**SND. UNA**	**SND. NXT**	**SND. WND**	**RCV. NXT**	**RCV. WND**
Description						**Description**					
5. Receive Part 1 of File, Send Ack	141	141	360	441	200	**6. Receive Ack for Reply**	321	441	200	141	360
The client receives the first 120-byte part of the file the server was sending. It increases the RCV.NXT pointer to 441 and sends an acknowledgment back with an Acknowledgment Number of 441. Again, if it had another request to make of the server, it could include it here, but we'll assume it does not.						The server receives the client's acknowledgment of its earlier 80-byte response (sent in step 2). It increases its SND.UNA to 321. Since it just received acknowledgment of 80 bytes (and the client's window didn't change), the server's usable window is now 80 bytes. However, as we will see in Chapter 49, sending small segments like this can lead to performance issues. Let's say the server has been programmed to not send segments under 100 bytes when it has a lot of data to transmit. It decides to wait.					
(wait)	141	141	360	441	200	**7. Receive Ack for Part 1 of File**	441	441	200	141	360
The client waits for the rest of the file.						The server receives the acknowledgment for the first part of the file. It increases SND.UNA to 441. This now restores the full 200-byte window.					
(still waiting?)	141	141	360	441	200	**8. Send Part 2 of File**	441	601	200	141	360
The client continues to wait for the rest of the file.						The server sends the remaining 160 bytes of data in the file in one segment. It increases SND.NXT by 160, and sends the data with a Sequence Number value of 441.					
9. Receive Part 2 of File, Send Ack	141	141	360	601	200	**(wait)**	441	601	200	141	360
The client receives the rest of the file and acknowledges it. It increases RCV.NXT to 601 and sends back a segment with an Acknowledgment Number of 601.						The server is done for now. It waits for the acknowledgment of the second part of the file.					
(done)	141	141	360	601	200	**10. Receive Ack for Part 2 of File**	601	601	200	141	360
The client is done with this exchange.						The server receives the second acknowledgment and slides its send window forward by 160 bytes. The transaction is now completed.					

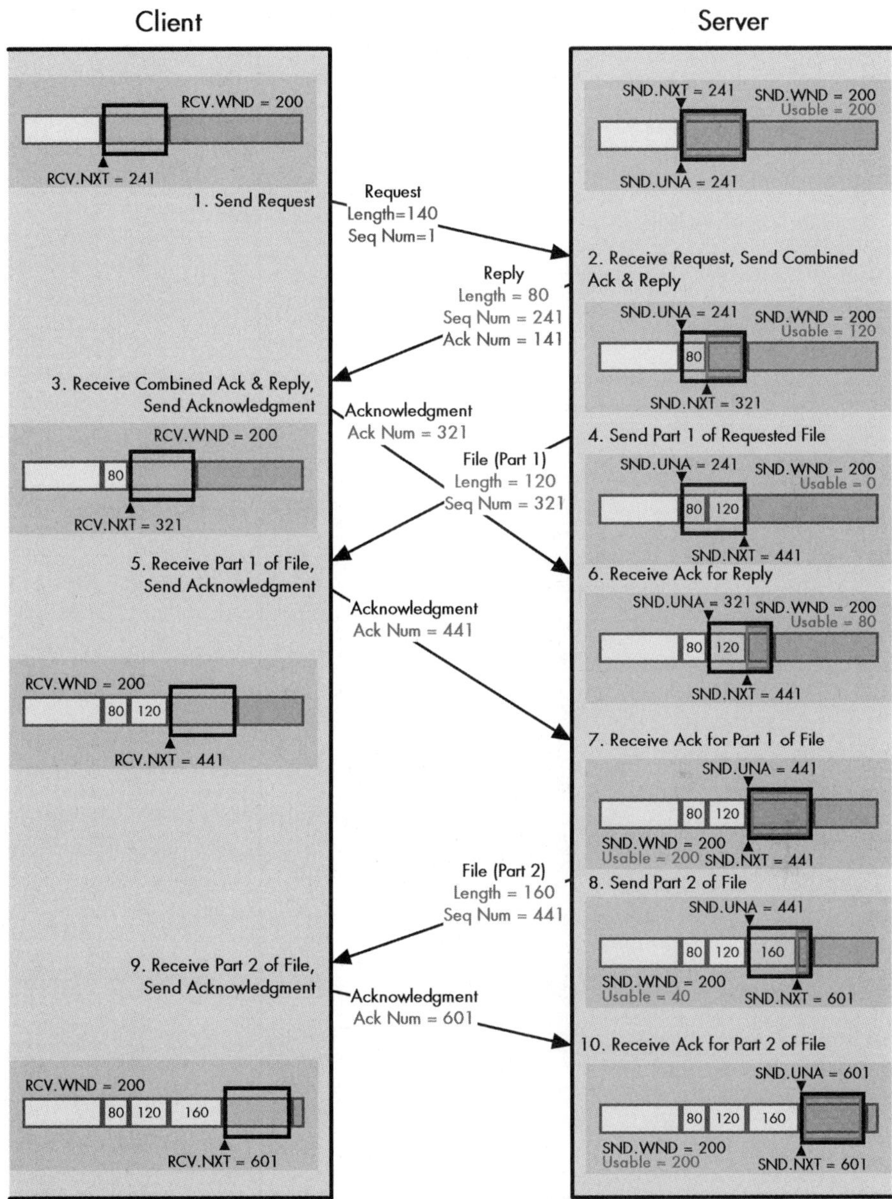

Figure 48-6: TCP transaction example showing the server's send pointers *The transaction of Table 48-6 from the perspective of the server. See Figure 48-7 for the client's pointers.*

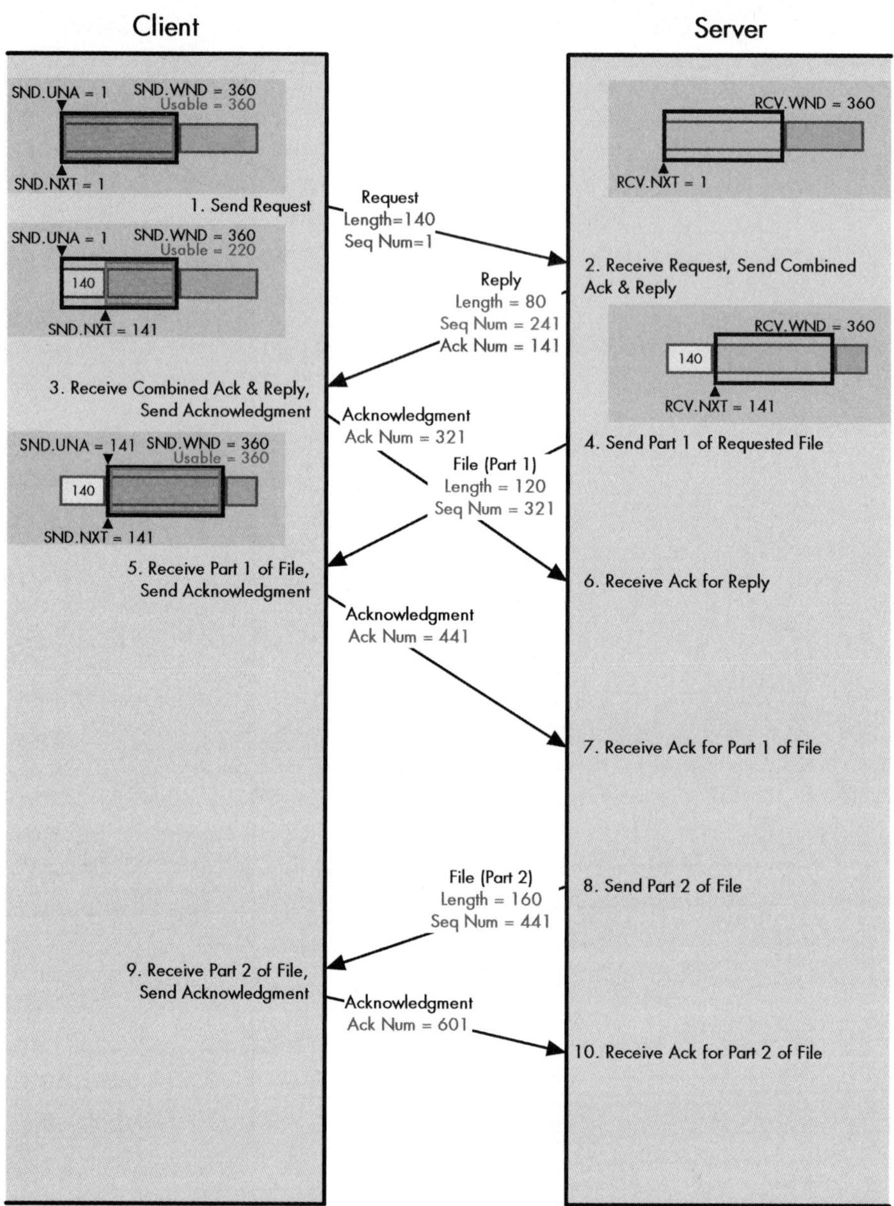

Figure 48-7: TCP transaction example showing client's send pointers *The transaction of Table 48-6 from the perspective of the client. See Figure 48-6 for the server's pointers.*

Real-World Complications of the Sliding Window Mechanism

I'm sure the process outlined in the previous section seems rather complicated, but in fact, the example is highly *simplified*, to show you how the basic data transfer mechanism works without too much going on. Scary, isn't it? A real-world connection would include several complications:

Overlapping Transmissions I intentionally showed only one request from the client and the response from the server. In reality, the client and server could be pumping many requests and responses at each other in rapid-fire succession. The client would be acknowledging segments received from the server with segments that themselves contained new requests, and so on.

Acknowledgment of Multiple Segments I also didn't show a case where two segments are received by a device and acknowledged with a single acknowledgment, although this can certainly happen. Suppose that, in the example, the two parts of the 280-byte file were sent at once and received by the client at the same time. The client would acknowledge both by sending a single segment with an Acknowledgment Number of 601. Remember that this field is a *cumulative* acknowledgment of all segments containing data through the number preceding it, so this would acknowledge all data up to byte 600.

Fluctuating Window Sizes for Flow Control The window sizes in the example remained constant, but in a real connection, this will not always be the case. A very busy server may not be able to process and remove data from its buffer as fast as it acknowledges it. It may need to shrink its receive window to reduce the amount of data the client sends it, and then increase the window when more space becomes available. This is how TCP implements flow control, as you will see in the next chapter.

Lost Transmissions In a real connection, some transmitted segments will be lost and need to be retransmitted. This is handled by TCP's retransmission scheme (described in Chapter 49).

Avoiding Small Window Problems I hinted in the description of the example that we don't necessarily always want to send data as fast as we can, to avoid sending a very small segment. The reason is that this can lead to performance degradation, including a phenomenon called *silly window syndrome.* This will also be explored in the next chapter, where we will see how handling it requires that we change the simple sliding windows scheme we examined so far.

Congestion Handling and Avoidance The basic sliding window mechanism has been changed over the years to avoid having TCP connections cause internetwork congestion and to have them handle congestion when it is detected. Congestion issues are discussed, as you may have guessed, in the next chapter.

TCP Immediate Data Transfer: Push Function

The fact that TCP takes incoming data from a process as an unstructured stream of bytes gives it great flexibility in meeting the needs of most applications. There is no need for an application to create blocks or messages; it just sends the data to TCP when it is ready for transmission. For its part, TCP has no knowledge or interest in the meaning of the bytes of data in this stream. They are just bytes, and TCP sends them without any real concern for their structure or purpose.

This has a couple of interesting effects on how applications work. One is that TCP does not provide any natural indication of the dividing point between pieces of data, such as database records or files. The application must take care of this. Another result of TCP's byte orientation is that TCP cannot decide when to form a segment and send bytes between devices based on the contents of the data. TCP will generally accumulate data sent to it by an application process in a buffer. It chooses when and how to send data based solely on the sliding window system discussed in the previous section, in combination with logic that helps to ensure efficient operation of the protocol.

This means that while an application can control the rate and timing with which it sends data to TCP, it cannot inherently control the timing with which TCP itself sends the data over the internetwork. Now, if we are sending a large file, for example, this isn't a big problem. As long as we keep sending data, TCP will keep forwarding it over the internetwork. It's generally fine in such a case to let TCP fill its internal transmit buffer with data and form a segment to be sent when TCP feels it is appropriate.

However, there are situations where letting TCP accumulate data before transmitting it can cause serious application problems. The classic example of this is an interactive application such as the Telnet protocol (see Chapter 87). When you are using such a program, you want each keystroke to be sent immediately to the other application; you don't want TCP to accumulate hundreds of keystrokes and then send them all at once. The latter may be more efficient, but it makes the application unusable, which is really putting the cart before the horse.

Even with a more mundane protocol that transfers files, there are many situations in which we need to say, "Send the data *now.*" For example, many protocols begin with a client sending a request to a server—like the hypothetical one in the preceding example or a request for a web page sent by a web browser. In that case, we want the client's request sent immediately; we don't want to wait until enough requests have been accumulated by TCP to fill an optimal-sized segment.

Naturally, the designers of TCP realized that we needed a way to handle these situations. When an application has data that it needs to have sent across the internetwork immediately, it sends the data to TCP, and then uses the TCP *push* function. This tells the sending TCP to immediately "push" all the data it has to the recipient's TCP as soon as it is able to do so, without waiting for more data.

When this function is invoked, TCP will create a segment (or segments) that contains all the data it has outstanding and then transmit it with the PSH control bit set to 1. The destination device's TCP software, seeing this bit sent, will know that it should not just take the data in the segment it received and buffer it, but rather push it through directly to the application.

KEY CONCEPT TCP includes a special *push* function to handle cases where data given to TCP needs to be sent immediately. An application can send data to its TCP software and indicate that it should be pushed. The segment will be sent right away rather than being buffered. The pushed segment's PSH control bit will be set to 1 to tell the receiving TCP that it should immediately pass the data up to the receiving application.

It's important to realize that the push function only forces immediate delivery of data. It does not change the fact that TCP provides no boundaries between data elements. It may seem that an application could send one record of data and then push it to the recipient, then send the second record and push that, and so on. However, the application cannot assume that because it sets the PSH bit for each piece of data it gives to TCP, each piece of data will be in a single segment. It is possible that the first push may contain data given to TCP earlier that wasn't yet transmitted, and it's also possible that two records pushed in this manner may end up in the same segment anyway.

TCP Priority Data Transfer: Urgent Function

As noted earlier, the fact that TCP treats data to be transmitted as just an unstructured stream of bytes has some important implications on how it used. One aspect of this characteristic is that since TCP doesn't understand the content of the data it sends, it normally treats all the data bytes in a stream as *equals*. The data is sent to TCP in a particular sequence, and it is transmitted in that same order. This makes TCP, in this regard, like those annoying voice mail systems that tell you not to hang up because they will answer calls in the order received.

Of course, while waiting on hold is irritating, this *first-in, first-out* behavior is usually how we want TCP to operate. If we are transmitting a message or a file, we want to be able to give TCP the bytes that compose that file and have TCP transmit that data in the order we gave it. However, just as special circumstances can require the use of the push function described in the previous section, there are cases where we may not want to always send all data in the exact sequence it was given to TCP.

The most common example of this is when it is necessary to interrupt an application's data transfer. Suppose we have an application that sends large files in both directions between two devices. The user of the application realizes that the wrong file is being transferred. When she tells the application to stop the file being sent, she wants this to be communicated to the other end of the TCP connection immediately. She doesn't want the abort command to just be placed at the end of the line after the file she is trying to send!

TCP provides a means for a process to prioritize the sending of data in the form of its *urgent* function. To use it, the process that needs to send urgent data enables the function and sends the urgent data to its TCP layer. TCP then creates a special TCP segment that has the URG control bit set to 1. It also sets the Urgent Pointer field to an offset value that points to the last byte of urgent data in the segment. So, for example, if the segment contained 400 bytes of urgent data followed by 200 bytes of regular data, the URG bit would be set, and the Urgent Pointer field would have a value of 400.

Upon receipt of a segment with the URG flag set to 1, the receiving device looks at the Urgent Pointer and from its value determines which data in the segment is urgent. It then forwards the urgent data to the process with an indication that the data is marked as urgent by the sender. The rest of the data in the segment is processed normally.

KEY CONCEPT To deal with situations where a certain part of a data stream needs to be sent with a higher priority than the rest, TCP incorporates an *urgent* function. When critical data needs to be sent, the application signals this to its TCP layer, which transmits it with the URG bit set in the TCP segment, bypassing any lower-priority data that may have already been queued for transmission.

Since we typically want to send urgent data, well, urgently, it makes sense that when such data is given to TCP, the push function is usually also invoked. This ensures that the urgent data is sent as soon as possible by the transmitting TCP and also forwarded up the protocol stack right away by the receiving TCP. Again, we need to remember that this does not guarantee the contents of the urgent segment. Using the push function may mean the segment contains only urgent data with no regular data following, but again, an application cannot assume that this will always be the case.

49

TCP RELIABILITY AND FLOW CONTROL FEATURES

The main task of the Transmission Control Protocol (TCP) is simple: packaging and sending data. Of course, almost every protocol packages and sends data! What distinguishes TCP from these protocols is the sliding window mechanism we explored in the previous chapter, which controls the flow of data between devices. This system not only manages the basic data transfer process, but it also ensures that data is sent reliably and manages the flow of data between devices to transfer data efficiently, without either device sending data faster than the other can receive it.

To enable TCP to provide the features and quality of data transfer that applications require, the protocol needed to be enhanced beyond the simplified data transfer mechanism we saw in preceding chapters. The developers needed to give extra "smarts" to the protocol to handle potential problems and make changes to the basic way that devices send data, to avoid inefficiencies that might otherwise have resulted.

In this chapter, I describe how TCP ensures that devices on a TCP connection communicate in a reliable and efficient manner. I begin with an explanation of the basic method by which TCP detects lost segments and retransmits them. I discuss some of the issues associated with TCP's acknowledgment scheme and an optional feature for improving its efficiency. I then describe the system by which TCP adjusts how long it will wait before deciding that a segment is lost. I discuss how the window size can be adjusted to implement flow control and some of the issues involved in window size management. This includes a look at the infamous "silly window syndrome" problem and special heuristics for addressing issues related to small window size that modify the basic sliding windows scheme. I conclude with a discussion of TCP's mechanisms for handling and avoiding congestion.

BACKGROUND INFORMATION *This section assumes that you are already familiar with TCP sequence numbers and segments, and the basics of the TCP sliding window mechanism. It also assumes you have already read the section on TCP message formatting and data transfer. If not, you may want to review at least the section about TCP data transfer mechanics in Chapter 48. Several of the sections in this chapter extend that simplified discussion of TCP data transfer to show what happens in nonideal conditions.*

TCP Segment Retransmission Timers and the Retransmission Queue

TCP's basic data transfer and acknowledgment mechanism uses a set of variables maintained by each device to implement the sliding window system. These pointers keep track of the bytes of data sent and received by each device, as well as differentiating between acknowledged and unacknowledged transmissions. In the preceding chapter, I described this mechanism and gave a simplified example showing how a client and server use it for basic data transfer.

One of the reasons why that example is simplified is that every segment that was transmitted by the server was received by the client and vice versa. It would be nice if we could always count on this happening, but as we know, in an Internet environment, this is not realistic. Due to any number of conditions—such as hardware failure, corruption of an Internet Protocol (IP) datagram, or router congestion—a TCP segment may be sent but never received. To qualify as a reliable transport protocol, TCP must be able detect lost segments and *retransmit* them.

Managing Retransmissions Using the Retransmission Queue

The method for detecting lost segments and retransmitting them is conceptually simple. Each time we send a segment, we start a *retransmission timer.* This timer starts at a predetermined value and counts down over time. If the timer expires before an acknowledgment is received for the segment, we retransmit the segment.

TCP uses this basic technique, but implements it in a slightly different way. The reason for this is the need to efficiently deal with many segments that may be unacknowledged at once, to ensure that they are each retransmitted at the appropriate time if needed. The TCP system works according to the following specific sequence.

Placement on Retransmission Queue, Timer Start As soon as a segment containing data is transmitted, a copy of the segment is placed in a data structure called the *retransmission queue.* A retransmission timer is started for the segment when it is placed on the queue. Thus, at some point, *every* segment is placed in this queue. The queue is kept sorted by the time remaining in the retransmission timer, so the TCP software can keep track of which timers have the least time remaining before they expire.

Acknowledgment Processing If an acknowledgment is received for a segment before its timer expires, the segment is removed from the retransmission queue.

Retransmission Timeout If an acknowledgment is *not* received before the timer for a segment expires, a *retransmission timeout* occurs, and the segment is automatically retransmitted.

Of course, we have no more guarantee that a retransmitted segment will be received than we had for the original segment. For this reason, after retransmitting a segment, it remains in the retransmission queue. The retransmission timer is reset, and the countdown begins again. If an acknowledgment is not received for the retransmission, the segment will be retransmitted again and the process repeated.

Certain conditions may cause even repeated retransmissions of a segment to fail. We don't want TCP to just keep retransmitting forever, so TCP will retransmit a lost segment only a certain number of times before concluding that there is a problem and terminating the connection.

KEY CONCEPT To provide basic reliability for sent data, each device's TCP implementation uses a *retransmission queue.* Each sent segment is placed in the queue and a *retransmission timer* started for it. When an acknowledgment is received for the data in the segment, it is removed from the retransmission queue. If the timer goes off before an acknowledgment is received, the segment is retransmitted and the timer restarted.

Recognizing When a Segment Is Fully Acknowledged

But how do we know when a segment has been fully acknowledged? Retransmissions are handled on a segment basis, but TCP acknowledgments, as we have seen, are done on a cumulative basis using sequence numbers. Each time a segment is sent by Device A to Device B, Device B looks at the value of the Acknowledgment Number field in the segment. All bytes with sequence numbers lower than the value of this field have been received by Device A. Thus, a segment sent by Device B to Device A is considered acknowledged when all of the bytes that were sent in the segment have a lower sequence number than the latest Acknowledgment Number sent by Device B to Device A. This is determined by calculating the last sequence number of the segment using its first byte number (in the Sequence Number field) and length of the segment's Data field.

> **KEY CONCEPT** TCP uses a *cumulative acknowledgment system.* The Acknowledgment Number field in a segment received by a device indicates that all bytes of data with sequence numbers less than that value have been successfully received by the other device. A segment is considered acknowledged when all of its bytes have been acknowledged; in other words, when an Acknowledgment Number containing a value larger than the sequence number of its last byte is received.

Let's use the example illustrated in Figure 49-1 to clarify how acknowledgments and retransmissions work in TCP. Suppose the server in a connection sends out four contiguous segments (numbered starting with 1 for clarity):

Segment 1 Sequence Number field is 1 and segment length is 80. So the last sequence number in Segment 1 is 80.

Segment 2 Sequence Number field is 81 and segment length is 120. The last sequence number in Segment 2 is 200.

Segment 3 Sequence Number field is 201 and segment length is 160. The last sequence number in Segment 3 is 360.

Segment 4 Sequence Number field is 361 and segment length is 140. The last sequence number in Segment 4 is 500.

Again, these segments can be sent one after the other, without needing to wait for each preceding transmission to be acknowledged. This is a major benefit of TCP's sliding window mechanism.

Now let's say the client receives the first two transmissions. It will send back an acknowledgment with an Acknowledgment Number field value of 201. This tells the server that the first two segments have been successfully received by the client; they will be removed from the retransmission queue (and the server's send window will slide 200 bytes to the right). Segment 3 will remain on the retransmission queue until a segment with an Acknowledgment Number field value of 361 or higher is received; Segment 4 requires an acknowledgment value of 501 or greater.

Now, let's further suppose in this example that Segment 3 gets lost in transit, but Segment 4 is received. The client will store Segment 4 in its receive buffer, but will not be able to acknowledge it, because of TCP's cumulative acknowledgment system—acknowledging Segment 4 would imply receipt of Segment 3 as well, which never showed up. So, the client will need to wait for Segment 3. Eventually, the retransmission timer that the server started for Segment 3 will expire. The server will then retransmit Segment 3. It will be received by the client, which will then be able to acknowledge both Segments 3 and 4 to the server.

There's another important issue here, however: How exactly should the server handle Segment 4? While the client is waiting for the missing Segment 3, the server is receiving no feedback, so it doesn't know that Segment 3 is lost, and it also doesn't know what happened to Segment 4 (or any subsequent transmissions). It is possible that the client has already received Segment 4 but just couldn't acknowledge it. Then again, maybe Segment 4 got lost as well. Some implementations may choose to resend only Segment 3, while some may choose to resend both Segments 3 and 4. This is an important issue that we will discuss next.

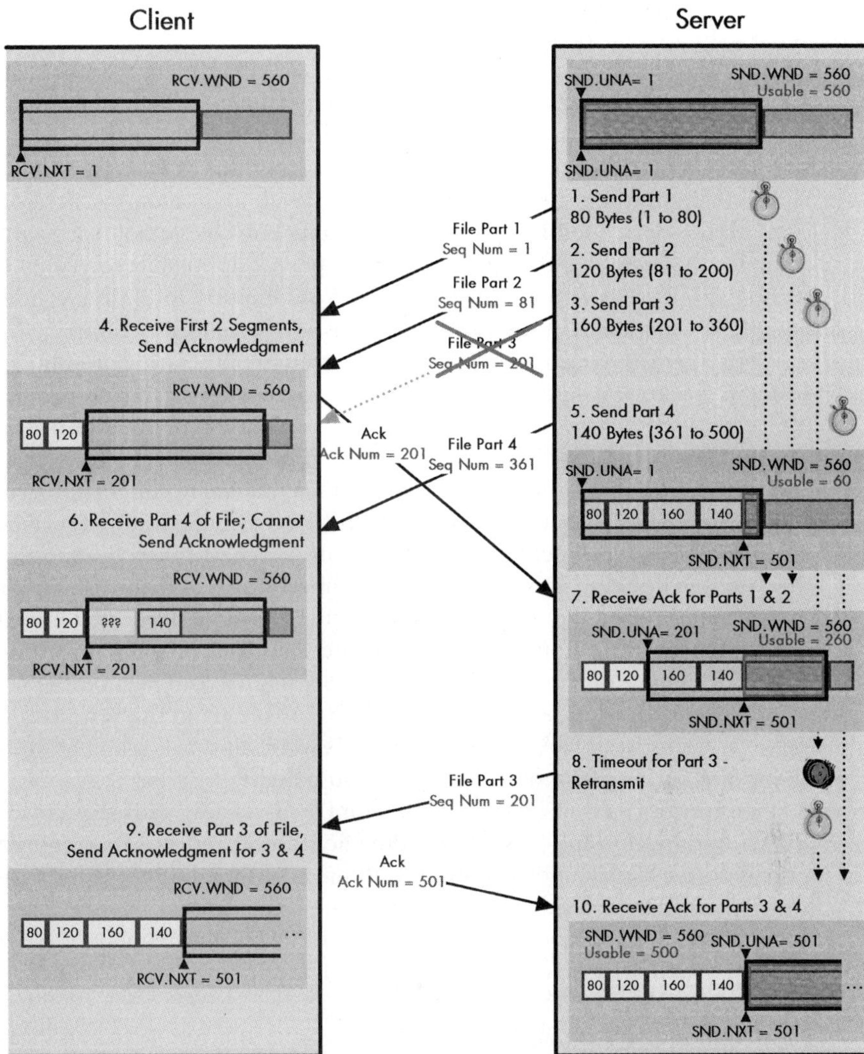

Figure 49-1: TCP transaction example with retransmission *This diagram illustrates a simple transaction and shows the server's send pointers and client's receive pointers. The server sends three segments to the client in rapid succession, setting a retransmission timer for each. Parts 1 and 2 are received, and the client sends an acknowledgment for them. Upon receipt of this ACK, Parts 1 and 2 are taken off the retransmission queue. However, Part 3 is lost in transit. When Part 4 is received, the client cannot acknowledge it; this would imply receipt of the missing Part 3. Eventually, the retransmission timer for Part 3 expires and it is retransmitted, at which time both Part 3 and Part 4 are acknowledged.*

A final issue is what value we should use for the retransmission timer when we put a segment on the retransmission queue. If it is set too low, excessive retransmissions occur; if set too high, performance is reduced due to extraneous delays in resending lost segments. In fact, TCP cannot use a single number for this value. It must determine the value dynamically using a process called adaptive retransmission, which we will examine later in the chapter.

TCP Noncontiguous Acknowledgment Handling and Selective Acknowledgment (SACK)

Computer science people sometimes use the term *elegant* to describe a simple but effective solution to a problem or need. I think the term applies fairly well to the cumulative acknowledgment method that is part of the TCP sliding window system. With a single number, returned in the Acknowledgment Number field of a TCP segment, the device sending the segment can acknowledge not just a single segment it has received from its connection peer, but possibly several of them. We saw how this works in the discussion of the fundamentals of sliding windows in Chapter 46, and again in the previous discussion of retransmissions.

Even the most elegant technique has certain weaknesses, however. In the case of the TCP acknowledgment system, it is the inability to effectively deal with the receipt of *noncontiguous* TCP segments. The Acknowledgment Number specifies that *all* sequence numbers lower than its value have been received by the device sending that number. If we receive bytes with sequence numbers in two noncontiguous ranges, there is no way to specify this with a single number.

This can lead to potentially serious performance problems, especially on internetworks that operate at high speed or over inherently unreliable physical networks. To see what the problem is, let's go back to the example illustrated in Figure 49-1. There, the server sent four segments and received back an acknowledgment with an Acknowledgment Number value of 201. Segment 1 and Segment 2 were thus considered acknowledged. They would be removed from the retransmission queue, and this would also allow the server's send window to slide 80+120 bytes to the right, allowing 200 more bytes of data to be sent.

However, let's again imagine that Segment 3, starting with sequence number 201, is somehow lost in transit. Since the client never receives this segment, it can never send back an acknowledgment with an Acknowledgment Number higher than 201. This causes the sliding window system to get stuck. The server can continue to send additional segments until it fills up the client's receive window, but until the client sends another acknowledgment, the server's send window will not slide.

The other problem we saw is that if Segment 3 gets lost, the client has no way to tell the server that it has received any *subsequent* segments. It's entirely possible that the client has received the server's Segment 4 and later segments, until the window filled up. But the client can't send an acknowledgment with a value of 501 to indicate receipt of Segment 4, *because this implies receipt of Segment 3 as well.*

NOTE *In some cases, the client may still send an acknowledgment upon receipt of Segment 4, but containing only a repeated acknowledgment of the bytes up to the end of Segment 2. See the coverage of congestion avoidance later in this chapter for an explanation.*

And here we see the drawback of the single-number, cumulative acknowledgment system of TCP. We could imagine a worst-case scenario, in which the server is told it has a window of 10,000 bytes, and sends 20 segments of 500 bytes each. The first segment is lost, and the other 19 are received. But since it is the first segment that never showed up, none of the other 19 segments can be acknowledged!

KEY CONCEPT TCP's acknowledgment system is *cumulative*. This means that if a segment is lost in transit, no subsequent segments can be acknowledged until the missing one is retransmitted and successfully received.

Policies for Dealing with Outstanding Unacknowledged Segments

How do we handle retransmissions when there are subsequent segments outstanding beyond the lost segment? In our example, when the server experiences a retransmission timeout on Segment 3, it must decide what to do about Segment 4, when it simply doesn't know whether or not the client received it. In our worst-case scenario, we have 19 segments that may or may not have shown up at the client after the first one that was lost.

We have two possible ways to handle this situation:

Retransmit Only Timed-Out Segments This is the more conservative, or if you prefer, optimistic approach. We retransmit only the segment that timed out, hoping that the other segments beyond it were successfully received. This method is best if the segments after the timed-out segment actually showed up. It doesn't work so well if they did not. In the latter case, each segment would need to time out individually and be retransmitted. Imagine that in our worst-case scenario, all twenty 500-byte segments were lost. We would need to wait for Segment 1 to time out and be retransmitted. This retransmission would be acknowledged (we hope), but then we would get stuck waiting for Segment 2 to time out and be resent. We would need to do this many times.

Retransmit All Outstanding Segments This is the more aggressive, or pessimistic, method. Whenever a segment times out, we resend not only that segment, but all other segments that are still unacknowledged. This method ensures that any time there is a holdup with acknowledgments, we refresh all outstanding segments to give the other device an extra chance at receiving them, in case they, too, were lost. In the case where all 20 segments were lost, this saves substantial amounts of time over the alternative, optimistic approach. The problem here is that these retransmissions may not be necessary. If the first of 20 segments was lost and the other 19 were actually received, we would be resending 9500 bytes of data (plus headers) for no reason.

Since TCP doesn't know whether these other segments showed up, it cannot know which method is better. It must simply make an executive decision to use one approach or the other and hope for the best. In the example shown in Figure 49-1, I demonstrated the conservative, optimistic approach: Only the lost segment of the file was retransmitted. Figure 49-2 illustrates the alternative aggressive, pessimistic approach to retransmission.

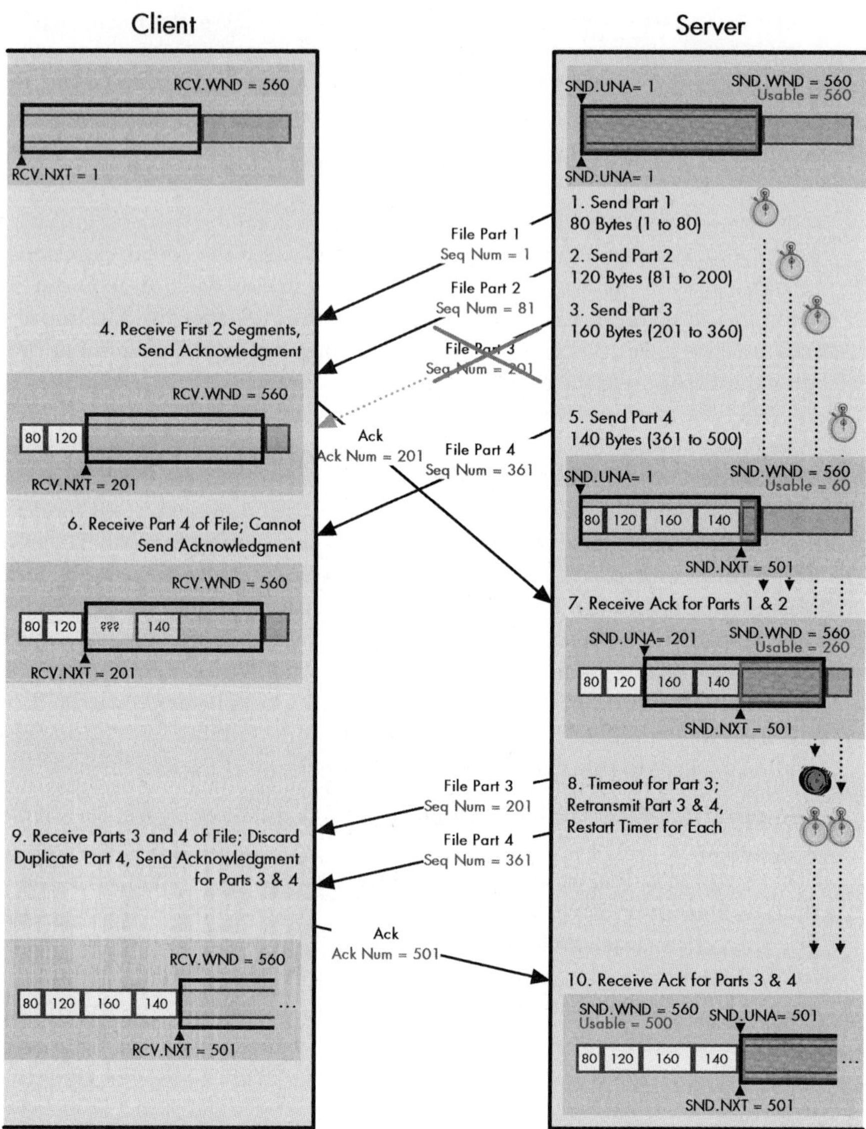

Figure 49-2: TCP aggressive retransmission example *This example is the same as that shown in Figure 49-1, except that here the server is taking an "aggressive" approach to retransmitting lost segments. When Segment 3 times out, both Segments 3 and 4 are retransmitted, and their retransmission timers restarted. (In this case, Segment 4 already arrived, so this extra transmission was not useful.)*

> **KEY CONCEPT** There are two approaches to handling retransmission in TCP. In the more conservative approach, only the segments whose timers expire are retransmitted. This saves bandwidth, but it may cause performance degradation if many segments in a row are lost. The alternative is that when a segment's retransmission timer expires, both it and all subsequent unacknowledged segments are retransmitted. This provides better performance if many segments are lost, but it may waste bandwidth on unnecessary retransmissions.

This lack of knowledge about noncontiguous segments is the core of the problem. The solution is to extend the basic TCP sliding window algorithm with an optional feature that allows a device to acknowledge noncontiguous segments individually. This feature, introduced in RFC 1072 and refined in RFC 2018, is called TCP *selective acknowledgment*, abbreviated *SACK*.

A Better Solution: Selective Acknowledgment (SACK)

To use SACK, the two devices on the connection must both support the feature, and must enable it by negotiating the Selective Acknowledge Permitted (SACK-Permitted) option in the SYN segment they use to establish the connection. Assuming this is done, either device is then permitted to include in a regular TCP segment a Selective Acknowledgment (SACK) option. This option contains a list of sequence number ranges of segments of data that have been received but have not been acknowledged, since they are noncontiguous.

Each device modifies its retransmission queue so that each segment includes a flag that is set to 1 if the segment has been selectively acknowledged—the SACK bit. The device then uses a modified version of the aggressive method illustrated in Figure 49-2, where upon retransmission of a segment, all later segments are also retransmitted *unless* their SACK bits are set to 1.

> **KEY CONCEPT** The optional TCP *selective acknowledgment* feature provides a more elegant way of handling subsequent segments when a retransmission timer expires. When a device receives a noncontiguous segment, it includes a special *Selective Acknowledgment (SACK)* option in its regular acknowledgment that identifies noncontiguous segments that have already been received, even if they are not yet acknowledged. This saves the original sender from needing to retransmit them.

For example, in our four-segment case, if the client receives Segment 4 but not Segment 3, when it sends back a segment with an Acknowledgment Number field value of 201 (for Segments 1 and 2), it can include a SACK option that specifies, "I have received bytes 361 through 500, but they are not yet acknowledged." This can also be done in a second acknowledgment segment if Segment 4 arrives well after Segments 1 and 2. The server recognizes this as the range of bytes for Segment 4, and turns on the SACK bit for Segment 4. When Segment 3 is retransmitted, the server sees that the SACK bit for Segment 4 is on and does not retransmit it. This is illustrated in Figure 49-3.

After Segment 3 is retransmitted, the SACK bit for Segment 4 is cleared. This is done for robustness, to handle cases where, for whatever reason, the client changes its mind about having received Segment 4. The client *should* send an acknowledgment with an Acknowledgment Number of 501 or higher, officially indicating receipt of Segments 3 and 4. If this does not happen, the server must receive another selective acknowledgment for Segment 4 to turn its SACK bit back on. Otherwise, it will be automatically resent when its timer expires or when Segment 3 is retransmitted.

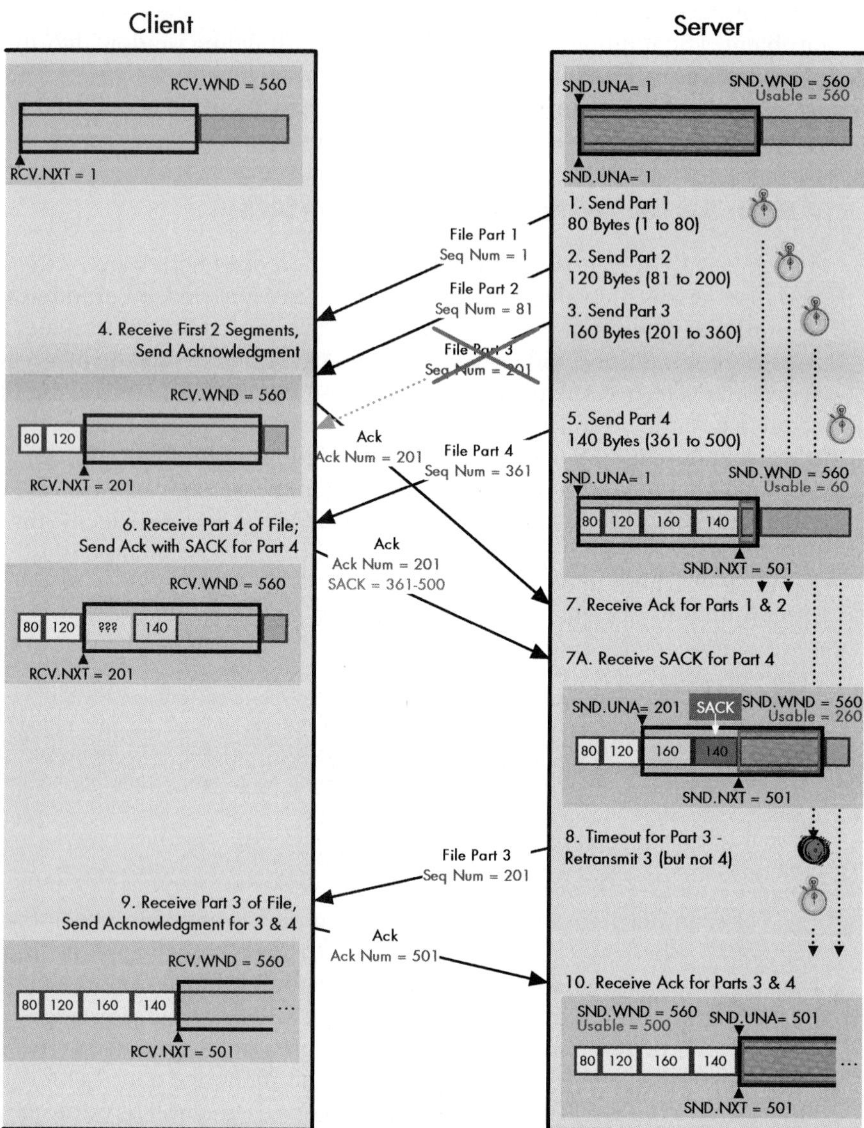

Figure 49-3: TCP retransmission with selective acknowledgment (SACK) *This is the example from Figures 49-1 and 49-2, changed to use the optional selective acknowledge feature. After receiving Parts 1, 2, and 4 of the file, the client sends an acknowledgment for 1 and 2 that includes a SACK for Part 4. This tells the server not to resend Part 4 when Part 3's timer expires.*

TCP Adaptive Retransmission and Retransmission Timer Calculations

Whenever a TCP segment is transmitted, a copy of it is also placed on the retransmission queue. When the segment is placed on the queue, a retransmission timer is started for the segment, which starts from a particular value and counts down to zero. This timer controls how long a segment can remain unacknowledged before the sender gives up, concludes that the segment is lost, and sends it again.

The length of time we use for retransmission timer is thus very important. If it is set too low, we might start retransmitting a segment that was actually received, because we didn't wait long enough for the acknowledgment of that segment to arrive. Conversely, if we set the timer too long, we waste time waiting for an acknowledgment that will never arrive, reducing overall performance.

Ideally, we would like to set the retransmission timer to a value just slightly larger than the *round-trip time (RTT)* between the two TCP devices; that is, the typical time it takes to send a segment from a client to a server and the server to send an acknowledgment back to the client (or the other way around, of course). The problem is that there *is* no such typical RTT. There are two main reasons for this:

Differences in Connection Distance Suppose you are at work in the United States, and during your lunch hour, you transfer a large file between your workstation and a local server connection using 100 Mbps Fast Ethernet. At the same time, you are downloading a picture of your nephew from your sister's personal website, which is connected to the Internet using an analog modem to an ISP in a small town near Lima, Peru. Would you want both of these TCP connections to use the same retransmission timer value? I certainly hope not!

Transient Delays and Variability The amount of time it takes to send data between any two devices will vary over time due to various happenings on the internetwork: fluctuations in traffic, router loads, and so on. To see an example of this for yourself, try typing `ping www.tcpipguide.com` from the command line of an Internet-connected PC, and you'll see how the reported times can vary.

It is for these reasons that TCP does not attempt to use a static, single number for its retransmission timers. Instead, TCP uses a dynamic, or *adaptive* retransmission scheme.

Adaptive Retransmission Based on RTT Calculations

TCP attempts to determine the approximate RTT between the devices and adjusts it over time to compensate for increases or decreases in the average delay. The practical issues of how this is done are important, but they are not covered in much detail in the main TCP standard. However, RFC 2988, "Computing TCP's Retransmission Timer," discusses the issue extensively.

RTTs can bounce up and down, so we want to aim for an *average* RTT value for the connection. This average should respond to consistent movement up or down in the RTT, without overreacting to a few very slow or fast acknowledgments. To allow this to happen, the RTT calculation uses a *smoothing* formula:

New RTT = (α * Old RTT) + ((1-α) * Newest RTT Measurement)

where α (alpha) is a *smoothing factor* between 0 and 1. Higher values of α (closer to 1) provide better smoothing and avoiding sudden changes as a result of one very fast or very slow RTT measurement. Conversely, this also slows down how quickly TCP reacts to more sustained changes in RTT. Lower values of alpha (closer to 0) make the RTT change more quickly in reaction to changes in measured RTT, but can cause overreaction when RTTs fluctuate wildly.

Acknowledgment Ambiguity

Measuring the RTT between two devices is simple in concept: Note the time that a segment is sent, note the time that an acknowledgment is received, and subtract the two. The measurement is more tricky in actual implementation, however.

One of the main potential "gotchas" occurs when a segment is assumed lost and is retransmitted. The retransmitted segment carries nothing that distinguishes it from the original. When an acknowledgment is received for this segment, it's unclear whether this corresponds to the retransmission or the original segment. Even though we decided the segment was lost and retransmitted it, it's possible the segment eventually got there, after taking a long time, or that the segment got their quickly but the *acknowledgment* took a long time!

This is called *acknowledgment ambiguity*, and it is not trivial to resolve. We can't just decide to assume that an acknowledgment always goes with the oldest copy of the segment sent, because this makes the RTT appear too high. We also don't want to just assume an acknowledgment always goes with the latest sending of the segment, as that may artificially lower the average RTT.

Refinements to RTT Calculation and Karn's Algorithm

TCP's solution is based on the use of a technique called *Karn's algorithm*, after its inventor, Phil Karn. The main change this algorithm makes is the separation of the calculation of average RTT from the calculation of the value to use for timers on retransmitted segments.

The first change made under Karn's algorithm is to not use measured RTT for any segments that are retransmitted in the calculation of the overall average RTT for the connection. This completely eliminates the problem of acknowledgment ambiguity.

However, this by itself, would not allow increased delays due to retransmissions to affect the average RTT. For this, we need the second change: incorporation of a *timer backoff* scheme for retransmitted segments. We start by setting the retransmission timer for each newly transmitted segment based on the current average RTT. When a segment is retransmitted, the timer is not reset to the same value it was set for the initial transmission. It is "backed off," or increased, using a multiplier (typically 2) to give the retransmission more time to be received. The timer continues to be increased until a retransmission is successful, up to a certain maximum value. This prevents retransmissions from being sent too quickly and further adding to network congestion.

Once the retransmission succeeds, the RTT is kept at the longer (backed-off) value until a valid RTT can be measured on a segment that is sent and acknowledged without retransmission. This permits a device to respond with longer timers to occasional circumstances that cause delays to persist for a period of time on a connection, while eventually having the RTT settle back to a long-term average when normal conditions resume.

> **KEY CONCEPT** TCP uses an *adaptive* retransmission scheme that automatically adjusts the amount of time to which retransmission timers are set, based on the average amount of time it takes to send segments between devices. This helps avoid retransmitting potentially lost segments too quickly or too slowly.

TCP Window Size Adjustment and Flow Control

We have seen the importance of the concept of *window size* to TCP's sliding window mechanism. In a connection between a client and a server, the client tells the server the number of bytes it is willing to receive at one time from the server; this is the client's *receive window*, which becomes the server's *send window*. Likewise, the server tells the client how many bytes of data it is willing to take from the client at one time; this is the server's *receive window* and the client's *send window*.

The use of these windows is demonstrated in Chapter 48, where we discussed TCP's basic data transfer and acknowledgment mechanism. However, just as the example in that chapter was simplified because I didn't show what happens with lost segments, there's another way that it doesn't reflect the real-world conditions of an actual Internet: the send and receive window sizes never changed during the course of communication.

To understand why the window size may fluctuate, we need to understand what it represents. The simplest way of considering the window size is that it indicates the size of the device's receive buffer for the particular connection. That is, window size represents how much data a device can handle from its peer at one time before it is passed to the application process. Let's consider the example in Chapter 48. I said that the server's window size was 360. This means the server is willing to take no more than 360 bytes at a time from the client.

When the server receives data from the client, it places it into this buffer. The server must then do two distinct things with this data:

Acknowledgment The server must send an acknowledgment back to the client to indicate that the data was received.

Transfer The server must process the data, transferring it to the destination application process.

It is critically important that we differentiate between these two activities. Unfortunately, the TCP standards don't do a great job in this regard, which makes them very difficult to understand. The key point is that in the basic sliding window system, data is acknowledged when received, but *not necessarily* immediately transferred out of the buffer. This means that is possible for the buffer to fill up with received data faster than the receiving TCP can empty it. When this occurs, the receiving device may need to adjust the window size to prevent the buffer from being overloaded.

Since the window size can be used in this manner to manage the rate at which data flows between the devices at the ends of the connection, it is the method by which TCP implements *flow control*, one of the classic jobs of the transport layer. Flow control is vitally important to TCP, as it is the method by which devices communicate their status to each other. By reducing or increasing window size, the server and client each ensure that the other device sends data just as fast as the recipient can deal with it.

Reducing Send Window Size to Reduce the Rate Data Is Sent

To understand window size adjustment, let's go back to our earlier example in Chapter 48, but with a few changes. First, to keep things simple, let's just look at the transmissions made from the client to the server, not the server's replies (other than acknowledgments)—this is illustrated in Figure 48-7. As before, the client sends 140 bytes to the server. After sending the 140 bytes, the client has 220 bytes remaining in its usable window: 360 bytes in the send window less the 140 bytes it just sent.

Sometime later, the server receives the 140 bytes and puts them in the buffer. Now, in an ideal world, the 140 bytes go into the buffer, and they are acknowledged and immediately removed from the buffer. Another way of thinking of this is that the buffer is of infinite size and can hold as much as the client can send. The buffer's free space remains 360 bytes in size, so the same window size can be advertised back to the client. This was the simplification in the previous example.

As long as the server can process the data as fast as it comes in, it will keep the window size at 360 bytes. The client, upon receipt of the acknowledgment of 140 bytes and the same window size it had before, slides the full 360-byte window 140 bytes to the right. Since there are now 0 unacknowledged bytes, the client can now once again send 360 bytes of data. These correspond to the 220 bytes that were formerly in the usable window, plus 140 new bytes for the ones that were just acknowledged.

In the real world, however, that server might be dealing with dozens, hundreds, or even thousands of TCP connections. TCP might not be able to process the data immediately. Alternatively, it is possible the application itself might not be ready for the 140 bytes for whatever reason. In either case, the server's TCP may not be able to immediately remove all 140 bytes from the buffer. If so, upon sending an acknowledgment back to the client, the server will want to change the window size that it advertises to the client, to reflect the fact that the buffer is partially filled.

Suppose that we receive 140 bytes, but are able to send only 40 bytes to the application, leaving 100 bytes in the buffer. When we send back the acknowledgment for the 140 bytes, the server can reduce its send window by 100 bytes, to 260 bytes. When the client receives this segment from the server, it will see the acknowledgment of the 140 bytes sent and slide its window 140 bytes to the right. However, as it slides this window, it reduces its size to only 260 bytes. We can consider this as sliding the *left edge* of the window 140 bytes, but the *right edge* only 40 bytes. The new, smaller window ensures that the server receives a maximum of 260 bytes from the client, which will fit in the 260 bytes remaining in its receive buffer. This is illustrated in the first exchange of messages (steps 1 through 3) at the top of Figure 49-4.

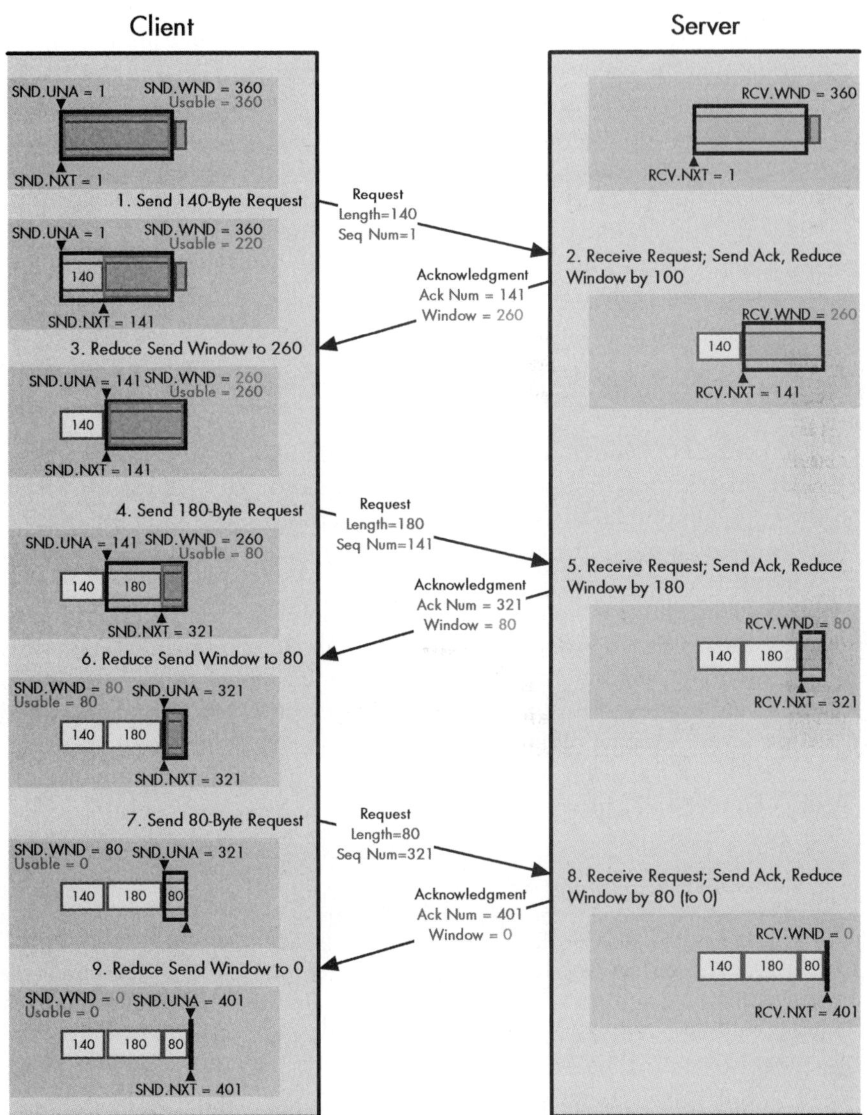

Figure 49-4: TCP window size adjustments and flow control *This diagram shows three message cycles, each of which results in the server reducing its receive window. In the first cycle, the server reduces it from 360 to 260 bytes, so the client's usable window can increase by only 40 bytes when it gets the server's acknowledgment. In the second and third cycles, the server reduces the window size by the amount of data it receives, which temporarily freezes the client's send window size, halting it from sending new data.*

Reducing Send Window Size to Stop the Sending of New Data

What if the server is so bogged down that it cannot process *any* of the bytes received? Let's suppose that the next transmission from the client is 180 bytes in size, but the server is so busy it cannot remove any of them.

In this case, the server could buffer the 180 bytes and, in the acknowledgment it sends for those bytes, reduce the window size by the same amount: from 260 to 80 bytes. When the client received the acknowledgment for 180 bytes, it would see the window size had reduced by 180 bytes as well. It would slide its window by the same amount as the window size was reduced! This is effectively like the server saying, "I acknowledge receipt of 180 bytes, but I am not allowing you to send any new bytes to replace them." Another way of looking at this is that the left edge of the window slides 180 bytes, while the right edge remains fixed. And as long as the right edge of the window doesn't move, the client cannot send any more data than it could before receipt of the acknowledgment. This is the middle exchange (steps 4 to 6) in Figure 49-4.

Closing the Send Window

This process of window adjustment can continue, and, of course, can be done by both devices, even though we are considering only the client-sends-to-server side of the equation here. If the server continues to receive data from the client faster than it can pump it out to the application, it will continue to reduce the size of its receive window.

To continue our example, suppose that after the send window is reduced to 80 bytes, the client sends a third request, this one 80 bytes in length, but the server is still busy. The server then reduces its window all the way down to 0, which is called *closing* the window. This tells the client the server is very overloaded, and it should stop routine sending of data entirely, as shown in the bottom third of Figure 49-4. Later on, when the server is less loaded down, it can increase the window size for this connection again, permitting more data to be transferred.

KEY CONCEPT The TCP sliding window system is used not just for ensuring reliability through acknowledgments and retransmissions, but it is also the basis for TCP's *flow control* mechanism. By increasing or reducing the size of its receive window, a device can raise or lower the rate at which its connection partner sends it data. In the case where a device becomes extremely busy, it can even reduce the receive window to zero. This will close the window and halt any further transmissions of data until the window is reopened.

While conceptually simple, flow control using window size adjustment can be very tricky. If we aren't careful about how we make changes to window size, we can introduce serious problems in the operation of TCP. There are also special situations that can occur, especially in cases where the window size is made small in response to a device becoming busy. The next two sections explore window management issues and changes that need to be made to the basic sliding window system to address them.

TCP Window Management Issues

Each of the two devices on a TCP connection can adjust the window size it advertises to the other, to control the flow of data over the connection. Reducing the size of the window forces the other device to send less data; increasing the window size lets more data flow. In theory, we should be able to just let the TCP software on each of the devices change the window size as needed to match the speed at which data both enters the buffer and is removed from it to be sent to the receiving application.

Unfortunately, certain changes in window size can lead to undesirable consequences. These can occur both when the size of the window is reduced and when it is increased. For this reason, there are a few issues related to *window size management* that we need to consider. As in previous sections, we'll use for illustration a modification of the same client/server example introduced in Chapter 48.

Problems Associated with Shrinking the TCP Window

One window size management matter is related to just how quickly a device reduces the size of its receive window when it gets busy. Let's say the server starts with a 360-byte receive window, as in the aforementioned example, and receives 140 bytes of data that it acknowledges but cannot remove from the buffer immediately. The server can respond by reducing the size of the window it advertises back to the client. In the case where no bytes can be removed from the buffer at all, the window size is reduced by the same 140 bytes that were added to the buffer. This freezes the right edge of the client's send window, so it cannot send any additional data when it gets an acknowledgment.

What if the server were so overloaded that we actually needed to reduce the size of the *buffer* itself? Say memory was short and the operating system said, "I know you have 360 bytes allocated for the receive buffer for this connection, but I need to free up memory, so now you only have 240." The server still cannot immediately process the 140 bytes it received, so it would need to drop the window size it sent back to the client all the way from 360 bytes down to 100 bytes (240 in the total buffer less the 140 already received).

In effect, doing this actually moves the right edge of the client's send window *back to the left*. It says, "Not only can't you send more data when you receive this acknowledgment, but you now can send *less* when you do send data." In TCP parlance, this is called *shrinking the window.*

There's a very serious problem with doing this, however: While the original 140 bytes were in transit from the client to the server, the client still thought it had 360 bytes of total window, of which 220 bytes were *usable* (360 less 140). The client may well have already sent some of those 220 bytes of data to the server before it got the notification that the server had shrunk the window! If so, and the server reduced its buffer to 240 bytes with 140 used, when those 220 bytes showed up at the server, only 100 would fit, and any additional ones would need to be discarded. This would force the client to need to retransmit that data, which is inefficient. Figure 49-5 illustrates graphically how this situation would play out.

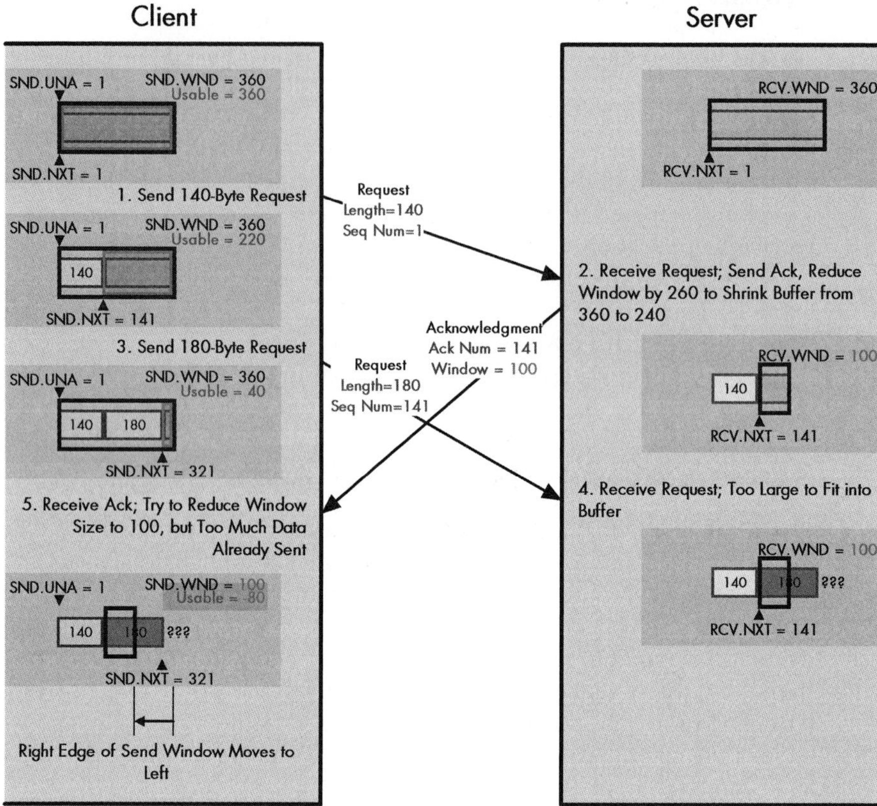

Figure 49-5: The problem with shrinking the TCP window *In this modification of the example of Figure 49-4, the client begins with a usable window size of 360 bytes. It sends a 140-byte segment and then a short time thereafter sends one of 180 bytes. The server is busy, however, and when it receives the first transmission, it decides to reduce its buffer to 240 bytes. It holds the 140 bytes just received and reduces its receive window all the way down to 100 bytes. When the client's 180-byte segment arrives, there is room for only 100 of the 180 bytes in the server's buffer. When the client gets the new window size advertisement of 100, it will have a problem, because it already has 180 bytes sent but not acknowledged.*

Reducing Buffer Size Without Shrinking the Window

To prevent the problems associated with shrinking windows from occurring, TCP adds a simple rule to the basic sliding window mechanism: A device is not allowed to shrink the window.

Note that there is a potential terminology ambiguity here. The words *shrinking* and *reducing* are sometimes used synonymously in colloquial discussions. As we've seen, there's nothing wrong with *reducing* the size of the window. The problem of *shrinking* the window refers only to the case where we reduce the window size so much that we contradict a prior window advertisement by *taking back* permission to send a certain number of bytes.

Another way of looking at this is that *shrinking* occurs whenever the server sends back a window size advertisement smaller than what the client considers its usable window size to be at that time. In this case, the server shrunk the window, because at the time it was acknowledging the 140 bytes, it sent back a window size of 100, which is less than the 220-byte usable window the client had then.

Of course, there may be cases where we *do* need to reduce a buffer, so how should this be handled? Instead of shrinking the window, the server must be more patient. In the example in the previous section, where the buffer needs to be reduced to 240 bytes, the server must send back a window size of 220, freezing the right edge of the client's send window. The client can still fill the 360-byte buffer, but it cannot send more than that. As soon as 120 bytes are removed from the server's receive buffer, the buffer can then be reduced in size to 240 bytes with no data loss. Then the server can resume normal operation, increasing the window size as bytes are taken from the receive buffer.

> **KEY CONCEPT** A phenomenon called *shrinking the window* occurs when a device reduces its receive window so much that its partner device's usable transmit window shrinks in size (meaning that the right edge of its send window moves to the left). Since this can result in data already in transit needing to be discarded, devices must instead reduce their receive window size more gradually.

Handling a Closed Window and Sending Probe Segments

Another special window management problem is how to deal with the case where a device must reduce the send window size all the way down to zero. As noted earlier, this is called *closing the receive window*. Since the server's receive window is the client's send window, reducing its size to zero means the client cannot send any more data. This situation continues until the client receives from the server a new acknowledgment with a nonzero Window field, which reopens the window. Then the client is able to send again.

The problem with this situation is that the client must depend on receipt of the "window opening" segment from the server. Like all TCP segments, this segment is carried over IP, which is unreliable. Remember that TCP is reliable only because it acknowledges sent data and retransmits lost data if necessary, but it can never *guarantee* that any particular segment gets to its destination. This means that when the server tries to reopen the window with an acknowledgment segment containing a larger Window field, it's possible that the client will never get the message. The client might conclude that a problem had occurred and terminate the connection.

To prevent this from happening, the client can regularly send special *probe* segments to the server. The purpose of these probes is to prompt the server to send back a segment containing the current window size. The probe segment can contain either zero or one byte of data, even when the window is closed. The probes will continue to be sent periodically until the window reopens, with the particular implementation determining the rate at which the probes are generated.

KEY CONCEPT A device that reduces its receive window to zero is said to have *closed* the window. The other device's send window is thus closed; it may not send regular data segments. It may, however, send *probe* segments to check the status of the window, thus making sure it does not miss notification when the window reopens.

When the server decides to reopen the closed window, there is another potential pitfall: opening the window to too small a value. In general, when the receive window is too small, this leads to the generation of many small segments, greatly reducing the overall efficiency of TCP. The next section explores this well-known problem and how it is resolved through changes to the basic sliding window mechanism.

TCP Silly Window Syndrome

In the description of TCP's maximum segment size (MSS) parameter in Chapter 48, I explained the trade-off in determining the optimal size of TCP segments. If segments are too large, we risk having them become fragmented at the IP level. If they're too small, we get greatly reduced performance, because we are sending a small amount of data in a segment with at least 40 bytes of header overhead. We also use up valuable processing time that is required to handle each of these small segments.

The MSS parameter ensures that we don't send segments that are too large; TCP is not allowed to create a segment larger than the MSS. Unfortunately, the basic sliding windows mechanism doesn't provide any *minimum* size of segment that can be transmitted. In fact, not only is it *possible* for a device to send very small, inefficient segments, the simplest implementation of flow control using unrestricted window size adjustments *ensures* that under conditions of heavy load, window size will become small, leading to significant performance reduction!

How Silly Window Syndrome Occurs

To see how the *silly window syndrome (SWS)* can happen, let's consider an example that is a variation on the one we've been using so far in this section. We'll assume the MSS is 360 bytes and a client/server pair where the server's initial receive window is set to this same value, 360. This means the client can send a full-sized segment to the server. As long as the server can keep removing the data from the buffer as fast as the client sends it, we should have no problem. (In reality, the buffer size would normally be larger than the MSS.)

Now, imagine that instead, the server is bogged down for whatever reason while the client needs to send it a great deal of data. For simplicity, let's say that the server is able to remove only 1 byte of data from the buffer for every 3 bytes it receives. Let's say it also removes 40 additional bytes from the buffer during the time it takes for the next client's segment to arrive. Here's what will happen:

1. The client's send window is 360 bytes, and it has a lot of data to send. It immediately sends a 360-byte segment to the server. This uses up its entire send window.

2. When the server gets this segment, it acknowledges it. However, it can remove only 120 bytes, so the server reduces the window size from 360 to 120 bytes. It sends this in the Window field of the acknowledgment.
3. The client receives an acknowledgment of 360 bytes and sees that the window size has been reduced to 120. It wants to send its data as soon as possible, so it sends off a 120-byte segment.
4. The server has removed 40 more bytes from the buffer by the time the 120-byte segment arrives. The buffer thus contains 200 bytes (240 from the first segment, less the 40 removed). The server is able to immediately process one-third of those 120 bytes, or 40 bytes. This means 80 bytes are added to the 200 that already remain in the buffer, so 280 bytes are used up. The server must reduce the window size to 80 bytes.
5. The client will see this reduced window size and send an 80-byte segment.
6. The server started with 280 bytes and removed 40, so 240 bytes remain. It receives 80 bytes from the client and removes one-third, so 53 are added to the buffer, which becomes 293 bytes. It reduces the window size to 67 bytes (360 minus 293).

This process, which is illustrated in Figure 49-6, will continue for many rounds, with the window size getting smaller and smaller, especially if the server gets even more overloaded. Its rate of clearing the buffer may decrease even more, and the window may close entirely.

Let's suppose this happens. Now, eventually, the server will remove some of the data from this buffer. Let's say it removes 40 bytes by the time the first closed-window probe from the client arrives. The server then reopens the window to a size of 40 bytes. The client is still desperate to send data as fast as possible, so it generates a 40-byte segment. And so it goes, with likely all the remaining data passing from the client to the server in tiny segments, until either the client runs out of data or the server clears the buffer more quickly.

Now imagine the worst-case scenario. This time, it is the application process on the server that is overloaded. It is drawing data from the buffer one byte at a time. Every time it removes a byte from the server's buffer, the server's TCP opens the window with a window size of exactly 1 and puts this in the Window field in an acknowledgment to the client. The client then sends a segment with exactly one byte, refilling the buffer until the application draws off the next byte.

None of this represents a *failure* per se of the sliding window mechanism. It is working properly to keep the server's receive buffer filled and to manage the flow of data. The problem is that the sliding window mechanism is concerned only with managing the buffer. It doesn't take into account the inefficiency of the small segments that result when the window size is micromanaged in this way. In essence, by sending small window size advertisements, we are winning the battle but losing the war.

Early TCP/IP researchers who discovered this phenomenon called it *silly window syndrome (SWS)*, a play on the phrase *sliding window system*, which expresses their opinion on how it behaves when it gets into this state.

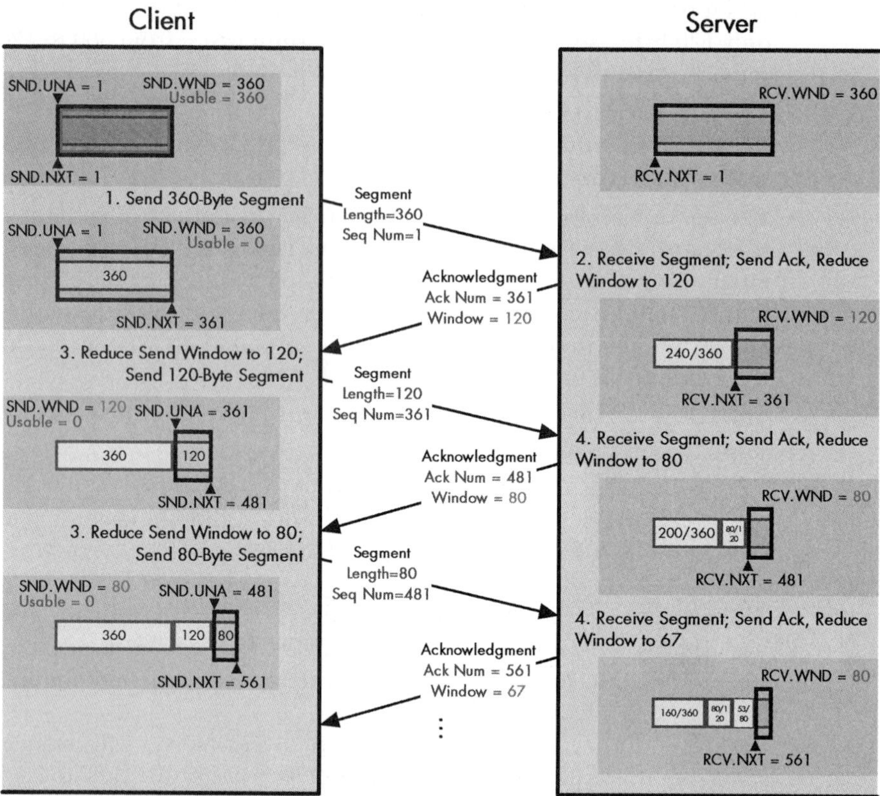

Figure 49-6: TCP silly window syndrome (SWS) *This diagram shows one example of how the phenomenon known as* TCP silly window syndrome *can arise. The client is trying to send data as fast as possible to the server, which is very busy and cannot clear its buffers promptly. Each time the client sends data, the server reduces its receive window. The size of the messages the client sends shrinks until it is sending only very small, inefficient segments. Note that in this diagram, I have shown the server's buffer fixed in position, rather than sliding to the right, as in the other diagrams in this chapter. This way, you can see the receive window decreasing in size more easily.*

The examples discussed show how SWS can be caused by the advertisement of small window sizes by a receiving device. It is also possible for SWS to happen if the sending device isn't careful about how it generates segments for transmission, regardless of the state of the receiver's buffers. For example, suppose the client TCP in the example shown in Figure 49-6 was receiving data from the sending application in blocks of 10 bytes at a time. However, the sending TCP was so impatient to get the data to the client that it took each 10-byte block and immediately packaged it into a segment, even though the next 10-byte block was coming shortly thereafter. This would result in a needless swarm of inefficient 10-byte segments.

> **KEY CONCEPT** The basic TCP sliding window system sets no minimum size on transmitted segments. Under certain circumstances, this can result in a situation where many small, inefficient segments are sent, rather than a smaller number of large ones. Affectionately termed *silly window syndrome (SWS)*, this phenomenon can occur either as a result of a recipient advertising window sizes that are too small or a transmitter being too aggressive in immediately sending out very small amounts of data.

Silly Window Syndrome Avoidance Algorithms

Since SWS is caused by the basic sliding window system not paying attention to the result of decisions that create small segments, dealing with SWS is conceptually simple: Change the system so that we avoid small window size advertisements, and at the same time, also avoid sending small segments. Since both the sender and recipient of data contribute to SWS, changes are made to the behavior of both to avoid SWS. These changes are collectively termed *SWS avoidance algorithms.*

Receiver SWS Avoidance

Let's start with SWS avoidance by the receiver. As we saw in the previous example, the receiver contributed to SWS by reducing the size of its receive window to smaller and smaller values. This caused the right edge of the sender's send window to move by ever-smaller increments, leading to smaller and smaller segments. To avoid SWS, we simply make the rule that the receiver may not update its advertised receive window in such a way that this leaves too little usable window space on the part of the sender. In other words, we restrict the receiver from moving the right edge of the window by too small an amount. The usual minimum that the edge may be moved is either the value of the MSS parameter or one-half the buffer size, whichever is less.

Let's see how we might use this in the example shown in Figure 49-6. When the server receives the initial 360-byte segment from the client and can process only 120 bytes, it does not reduce the window size to 120. It reduces it all the way to zero, closing the window. It sends this back to the client, which will then stop and not send a small segment. Once the server has removed 60 more bytes from the buffer, it will now have 180 bytes free, half the size of the buffer. It now opens the window up to 180 bytes in size and sends the new window size to the client.

It will continue to advertise only either 0 bytes or 180 or more bytes, not smaller values in between. This seems to slow down the operation of TCP, but it really doesn't. Because the server is overloaded, the limiting factor in overall performance of the connection is the rate at which the server can clear the buffer. We are just exchanging many small segments for a few larger ones.

Sender SWS Avoidance and Nagle's Algorithm

SWS avoidance by the sender is accomplished generally by imposing "restraint" on the part of the transmitting TCP. Instead of trying to immediately send data as soon as we can, we wait to send it until we have a segment of a reasonable size. The specific method for doing this is called *Nagle's algorithm*, named for its inventor, John Smith. (Just kidding, it was John Nagle.) Simplified, this algorithm works as follows:

- As long as there is no unacknowledged data outstanding on the connection, as soon as the application wants, data can be immediately sent. For example, in the case of an interactive application like Telnet, a single keystroke can be pushed in a segment.
- While there *is* unacknowledged data, all subsequent data to be sent is held in the transmit buffer and not transmitted until either all the unacknowledged data is acknowledged or we have accumulated enough data to send a full-sized (MSS-sized) segment. This applies even if a push is requested by the user.

This might seem strange, especially the part about buffering data despite a push request! You might think this would cause applications like Telnet to break. In fact, Nagle's algorithm is a very clever method that suits the needs of both low-data-rate interactive applications like Telnet and high-bandwidth file-transfer applications.

If you are using something like Telnet where the data is arriving very slowly (humans are very slow compared to computers), the initial data (first keystroke) can be pushed right away. The next keystroke must wait for an acknowledgment, but this will probably come reasonably soon relative to how long it takes to hit the next key. In contrast, more conventional applications that generate data in large amounts will automatically have the data accumulated into larger segments for efficiency.

Nagle's algorithm is actually far more complex than this description, but this section is already getting too long. RFC 896 discusses it in (much) more detail.

> **KEY CONCEPT** Modern TCP implementations incorporate a set of *SWS avoidance algorithms*. When receiving, devices are programmed not to advertise very small windows, waiting instead until there is enough room in the buffer for one of a reasonable size. Transmitters use *Nagle's algorithm* to ensure that small segments are not generated when there are unacknowledged bytes outstanding.

TCP Congestion Handling and Congestion Avoidance Algorithms

By changing the window size that a device advertises to a peer on a TCP connection, the device can increase or decrease the rate at which its peer sends it data. This is how the TCP sliding window system implements flow control between the two connected devices. We've seen how this works in this chapter, including the changes required to the basic mechanism to ensure performance remains high by reducing the number of small segments sent.

Flow control is a very important part of regulating the transmission of data between devices, but it is limited in the following respect: It considers only what is going on within each of the devices on the connection, and *not* what is happening in devices between them. In fact, this "self-centeredness" is symptomatic of architectural layering. Since we are dealing with how TCP works between a typical server and client at layer 4, we don't worry about how data gets between them; that's the job of IP at layer 3.

Congestion Considerations

In practice, what is going on at layer 3 can be quite important. Considered from an abstract point of view, our server and client may be connected directly using TCP, but all the segments we transmit are carried across an internetwork of networks and routers between them. These networks and routers are also carrying data from many other connections and higher-layer protocols. If the internetwork becomes very busy, the speed at which segments are carried between the endpoints of our connection will be reduced, and they could even be dropped. This is called *congestion.*

Again, at the TCP level, there is no way to directly comprehend what is causing congestion or why. It is perceived simply as inefficiencies in moving data from one device to another, through the need for some segments to be retransmitted. However, even though TCP is mostly oblivious to what is happening on the internetwork, it *must* be smart enough to understand how to deal with congestion and not exacerbate it.

Recall that each segment that is transmitted is placed in the retransmission queue with a retransmission timer. Now, suppose congestion dramatically increased on the internetwork, and there were no mechanisms in place to handle congestion. Segments would be delayed or dropped, which would cause them to time out and be retransmitted. This would increase the amount of traffic on the internetwork between our client and server. Furthermore, there might be thousands of other TCP connections behaving similarly. Each would keep retransmitting more and more segments, increasing congestion further, leading to a vicious circle. Performance of the entire internetwork would decrease dramatically, resulting in a condition called *congestion collapse.*

The message is clear: TCP cannot just ignore what is happening on the internetwork between its connection endpoints. To this end, TCP includes several specific algorithms that are designed to respond to congestion or avoid it in the first place. Many of these techniques can be considered, in a way, to be methods by which a TCP connection is made less selfish; that is, it tries to take into account the existence of other users of the internetwork over which it operates. While no single connection by itself can solve congestion of an entire internetwork, having all devices implement these measures collectively reduces congestion due to TCP.

The first issue is that we need to know when congestion is taking place. By definition, congestion means intermediate devices—routers—are overloaded. Routers respond to overloading by dropping datagrams. When these datagrams contain TCP segments, the segments don't reach their destination, and they are therefore left unacknowledged and will eventually expire and be retransmitted. This means that when a device sends TCP segments and does not receive acknowledgments for them, it can be assumed that, in most cases, they have been dropped by intermediate devices due to congestion. By detecting the rate at which segments are sent and not acknowledged, a TCP device can infer the level of congestion on the network between itself and its TCP connection peer.

TCP Congestion-Handling Mechanisms

After getting information about congestion, we must then decide what to do with that information. The main TCP standard, RFC 793, includes very little information about TCP congestion-handling issues. That is because early versions of TCP based solely on this standard didn't include congestion-handling measures. Problems with these early implementations led to the discovery that congestion was an important issue. The measures used in modern devices were developed over the years, and eventually documented in RFC 2001, "TCP Slow Start, Congestion Avoidance, Fast Retransmit, and Fast Recovery Algorithms."

KEY CONCEPT TCP flow control is an essential part of regulating the traffic flow between TCP devices, but takes into account only how busy the two TCP endpoints are. It is also important to take into account the possibility of *congestion* of the networks over which any TCP session is established, which can lead to inefficiency through dropped segments. To deal with congestion and avoid contributing to it unnecessarily, modern TCP implementations include a set of Congestion Avoidance algorithms that alter the normal operation of the sliding window system to ensure more efficient overall operation.

RFC 2001 refers to four algorithms: Slow Start, Congestion Avoidance, Fast Retransmit, and Fast Recovery. In practice, these features are all related to each other. Slow Start and Congestion Avoidance are distinct algorithms but are implemented using a single mechanism, involving the definition of a *congestion window* that limits the size of transmissions and whose size is increased or decreased depending on congestion levels. Fast Retransmit and Fast Recovery are implemented as changes to the mechanism that implements Slow Start and Congestion Avoidance.

The following sections provide simplified summaries of how these algorithms work. My goal is simply to help you get a feel for how congestion is handled in TCP in general terms.

NOTE *Congestion handling is a rather complex process. If you want to learn more, RFC 2001 contains the technical details, showing how each of the algorithms is implemented in each device.*

Slow Start

In the original implementation of TCP, as soon as a connection was established between two devices, they could each go "hog wild," sending segments as fast as they liked as long as there was room in the other device's receive window. In a busy internetwork, the sudden appearance of a large amount of new traffic could exacerbate any existing congestion. To alleviate this, modern TCP devices are restrained in the rate at which they initially send segments.

Each sender is at first restricted to sending only an amount of data equal to one full-sized segment—that is, equal to the MSS value for the connection. Each time an acknowledgment is received, the amount of data the device can send is increased by the size of another full-sized segment. Thus, the device starts slow in terms of how much data it can send, with the amount it sends increasing until either the full window size is reached or congestion is detected on the link. In the latter case, the Congestion Avoidance feature, described next, is used.

Congestion Avoidance

When potential congestion is detected on a TCP link, a device responds by throttling back the rate at which it sends segments. A special algorithm is used that allows the device to drop the rate at which segments are sent quickly when congestion occurs. The device then uses the Slow Start algorithm to gradually increase the transmission rate back up again to try to maximize throughput without congestion occurring again.

Fast Retransmit

We've already seen in our look at TCP segment retransmission that when segments are received by a device out of order (noncontiguously), the recipient will acknowledge only the ones received contiguously. The Acknowledgment Number field will specify the sequence number of the byte it expects to receive next. So, in the example given in that section, Segments 1 and 2 were acknowledged, while Segment 4 was not because Segment 3 was not received.

It is possible for a TCP device to respond with an acknowledgment when it receives an out-of-order segment, simply reiterating that it is stuck waiting for a particular byte number. So, when the client in that example receives Segment 4 and not Segment 3, it could send back an acknowledgment saying, "I am expecting the first byte of Segment 3 next."

Now, suppose this happens over and over. The server, not realizing that Segment 3 was lost, sends Segments 5, 6, and so on. Each time a segment is received, the client sends back an acknowledgment specifying the first byte number of Segment 3. Eventually, the server can reasonably conclude that Segment 3 is lost, even if its retransmission timer has not expired.

The Fast Retransmit feature dictates that if three or more of these acknowledgments are received, all saying, "I want the segment starting with byte *N*," then it's probable that the segment starting with byte *N* has been lost, usually because it was dropped due to congestion. In this case, the device will immediately retransmit the missing segment, without going through the normal retransmission queue process. This improves performance by eliminating delays that would suspend effective data flow on the link.

Fast Recovery

When Fast Retransmit is used to resend a lost segment, the device using it performs Congestion Avoidance, but does not use Slow Start to increase the transmission rate back up again. The rationale for this is that since multiple ACKs were received by the sender, all indicating receipt of out-of-order segments, this indicates that several segments have already been removed from the flow of segments between the two devices. For efficiency reasons, then, the transmission rate can be increased more quickly than when congestion occurs in other ways. This improves performance compared to using the regular Congestion Avoidance algorithm after Fast Retransmit.

SECTION III

TCP/IP APPLICATION LAYER PROTOCOLS

The OSI Reference Model is used to describe the architecture of networking protocols and technologies and to show how they relate to one another. In the chapter describing OSI Reference Model concepts (Chapter 5), I mentioned that its seven layers could be organized into two layer groupings: the lower layers (1 through 4) and the upper layers (5 through 7). While there are certainly other ways to divide the layers, this split best reflects the different roles that the layers play in a network.

The lower layers are concerned primarily with the mechanics of formatting, encoding, and sending data over a network. These layers involve software elements, but they are often closely associated with networking hardware devices. In contrast, the upper layers are concerned mainly with user interaction and the implementation of software applications, protocols, and services that let us actually use the network. These elements generally don't need to worry about details, relying on the lower layers to ensure that data gets to where it needs to go reliably.

In this section, I describe the details of the many protocols and applications that occupy the upper layers in TCP/IP. The organization of this section is quite different from the previous section's organization. Since the TCP/IP protocol suite uses an architecture that lumps all the higher layers together, even attempting to differentiate between these layers is not worthwhile. For these reasons, this section is divided by functions, rather than by layers. It contains ten parts: four that discuss application layer protocols that support the operation of TCP/IP, and six that discuss actual application protocols.

The first part discusses naming systems, especially the TCP/IP Domain Name System (DNS). The second part overviews file and resource sharing protocols, with a focus on the Network File System (NFS). The third part covers TCP/IP host configuration and the host configuration protocols: the Boot Protocol (BOOTP) and the Dynamic Host Configuration Protocol (DHCP). The fourth part describes the TCP/IP network management framework, including the Simple Network Management Protocol (SNMP) and Remote Network Monitoring (RMON).

The fifth part introduces TCP/IP applications with a look at application layer addressing and an overview of file and message transfer applications. The sixth part covers the general file transfer protocols: the File Transfer Protocol (FTP) and the Trivial File Transfer Protocol (TFTP). The seventh part explains the many related protocols that together form TCP/IP's electronic mail application. The eighth part covers the Web and the important Hypertext Transfer Protocol (HTTP). The ninth part describes Usenet (network news) and Gopher. Finally, the tenth part discusses interactive and administrative protocols.

PART III-1

NAME SYSTEMS AND TCP/IP NAME REGISTRATION AND NAME RESOLUTION

Humans and computers first started dealing with each other several decades ago. The relationship between man (and woman!) and machine has been a pretty good one overall, and this is reflected in the fact that while computers were once just the province of techies, they are now *mainstream*. However, there are areas where humans and computers simply don't see eye to eye. One of these is in the way that we deal with information.

Computers work best with numbers, while most people prefer not to work with numbers. This fundamental difference represented a problem for the designers of networking technology. It made sense from a technical standpoint to design addressing schemes for networks and internetworks using simple numeric identifiers, for simplicity and efficiency. Unfortunately, identifying computers using numeric addresses is cumbersome for people and becomes more so as the number of devices on a network increases. To solve this problem, the techies went to work and came up with *name systems* for networks. These mechanisms allow computers to continue to use simple, efficient numeric addresses, while letting humans specify names to identify network devices.

This part includes eight chapters that explain both the theory and practice behind networking name systems. The first chapter describes the motivation for name systems and the important concepts and techniques behind how they work. The second chapter provides an introduction to name systems on TCP/IP and a brief description of the simple host table name system.

The remaining chapters describe the very important Domain Name System (DNS). The third chapter provides an overview of DNS, including a description of its characteristics and components. The fourth chapter discusses the DNS name space and architecture, and the fifth chapter covers the DNS name registration process, including hierarchical authorities and administration. The sixth chapter describes DNS name servers and how they represent, manage, and provide data when resolution is invoked. The seventh chapter describes DNS clients, called *resolvers,* how they initiate resolution, and the steps involved in the resolution process. Finally, the eighth chapter ties together the information about name servers and resolvers by providing a look at message exchange between these units, and describing the formats of messages, resource records, and DNS master files. This chapter includes a brief look at the changes made to DNS to support the new version 6 of the Internet Protocol (IPv6) and its much longer addresses.

Note that even though the abbreviation *DNS* usually stands for *Domain Name System,* you will also sometimes see the *S* stand for other words, especially *Service* or *Server.* Also, some documents refer to this name system as *the DNS.* Most people just say *DNS,* without the definite article, and that's the convention I follow here as well.

A set of related TCP/IP utilities called *nslookup, host,* and *dig* can be used by an administrator to query DNS name servers for information. They are useful for a variety of purposes, including manually determining the IP address of a host, checking for specific resource records maintained for a DNS name, and verifying the name resolution function. You can find more information about these utilities in Part III-10.

50

NAME SYSTEM ISSUES, CONCEPTS, AND TECHNIQUES

Name systems can be considered as the diplomats of the networking protocol stack. Just as a political diplomat is skilled at speaking multiple languages and ensuring good communications between those who may view the world in different ways, name systems bridge the gulf between the numeric addresses that computers like to use and the simpler names that humans prefer.

Before looking at specific name systems, it makes sense to discuss them generally. This will help you to understand the reasons why these systems are important and the concepts that underlie all name systems, regardless of their specific implementation.

I begin this chapter with an overview of name systems and a discussion of why they were created. I then discuss the three main functions of a name system: the name space, name registration, and name resolution. I then expand on this functional overview, illustrating how name spaces and architectures work, the issues behind name registration and administration, and finally, name resolution techniques and the practical issues in the resolution process.

This chapter provides an introduction to name systems and doesn't discuss specific name systems. I like to use examples to explain concepts and, for this purpose, do make reference to the TCP/IP Domain Name System (DNS) at times. However, you do not need to be familiar with DNS to follow this chapter.

Name System Overview

One of several important differences between humans and computers is how we prefer to deal with information. Computers work with numbers, while very few humans like to do so. This distinction becomes particularly important when we look at how identifiers, or addresses, are assigned to network devices.

Symbolic Names for Addressing

To a computer, there is no problem with simply giving a number to each device on the network and using those numbers to move information around. Your computer would be perfectly happy if you assigned a number like 341,481,178,295 to it and all the other machines on your network, and then issued commands such as, "Send this file to machine 56,712,489,901." However, most humans don't want to use a network in this manner. These long, cryptic numbers don't mean anything to them. They want to tell their machine, "Send this file to Joe's computer," or "Print this on the color laser in the Sales department," or "Check the latest headlines on CNN's website."

This difference led to the development of *name systems*. These technologies allow computers on a network to be given both a conventional numeric address and a more user-friendly, human-readable name, composed of letters, numbers, and other special symbols. Sometimes called a *symbolic name*, this can be used as an alternative form of addressing for devices. The name system takes care of the functions necessary to manage this system, including ensuring that names are unique, translating from names to numbers, and managing the list of names and numbers.

A Paradox: Name Systems Are Both Essential and Unnecessary

What's interesting about name systems is that they are extremely important to networks, but at the same time, they often aren't strictly necessary for a network to operate. This seeming paradox is due again to the difference between humans and computers. Computers need only the numeric addressing scheme, not the names assigned to them. So, without name systems, the computers and the network can still work, but it will be much harder for people to use them!

An example of this can most readily be seen when a problem disables the operation of a part of DNS used to provide naming services on the Internet. Technically, DNS isn't needed to use most parts of the Internet, because all communications use IP addresses. This means that even though you might normally access CNN's website at www.cnn.com, you could instead just use the IP address 64.236.16.20.

The problem is that prior to reading this, you probably had no idea what the IP address of CNN's website is, and that's true of almost everyone else who uses the site as well. Also, you might want to check not just CNN's website, but perhaps 1, 2, or 20 other news sites. It would be difficult to remember the numbers for even a small percentage of the thousands of different websites on the Internet, so each time you wanted to access a resource, you would need to manually look up its address, as shown in Figure 50-1.

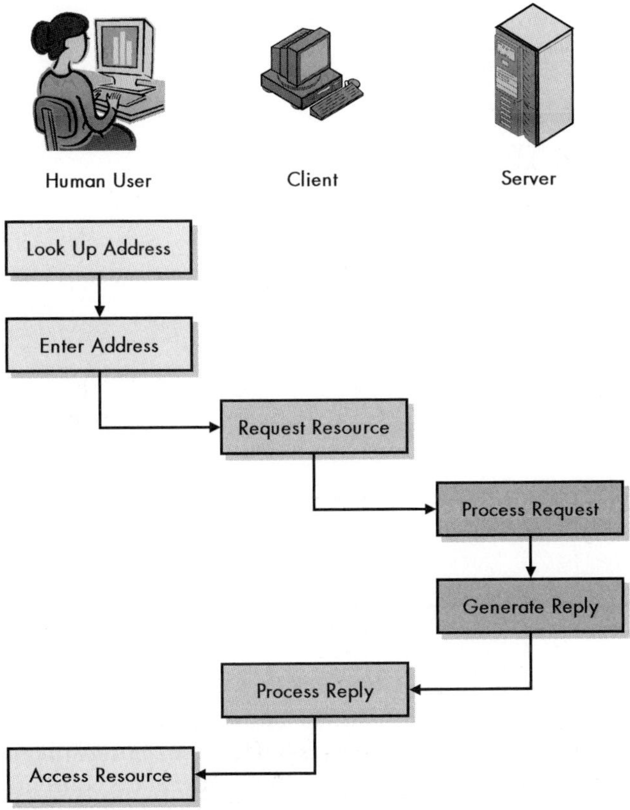

Figure 50-1: Internetwork access without a name system *When there is no name system, a user must know the address of any device he or she wishes to access on the internetwork. Since most of us have limited memories for numbers, this means each access must be preceded by an inefficient, tedious, manual address lookup.*

In contrast, it's much easier to remember the names of resources. With a name system, you just enter the name of a device, and the name system converts it to an address, as shown in Figure 50-2. This is why name systems are so important, even if they aren't needed by the networking technologies themselves. In fact, the reliance on name systems like DNS is so significant that many people don't even realize they can enter IP addresses into their web browsers!

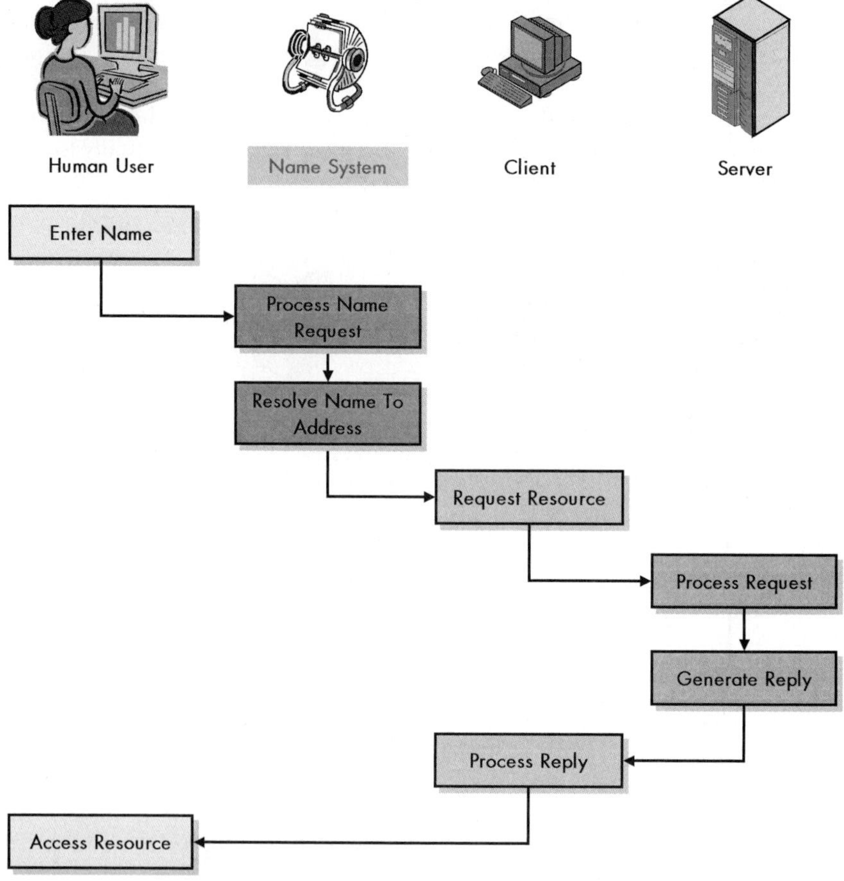

Figure 50-2: *Internetwork access with a name system*

When an internetwork is equipped with a name system, the user no longer needs to know the address of a device to access it. He or she enters the name, and the name system converts it into an address automatically, like a computerized Rolodex, as shown here. The name system then passes the address to the client software, which uses that address to access the requested resource as if the user had entered it directly.

Factors That Determine the Necessity of a Name System

More generally, the importance of a name system depends greatly on the characteristics of the network where it is used. The following are the three main issues in determining the need for a name system:

Network Size With a really small network and only a handful of computers, having human users remember the numeric addresses for these machines is at least feasible, if not ideal. For example, a small home network with two or three machines doesn't really *need* a name system, in theory. If you have thousands or millions of devices, however, the name system becomes essential.

Address Size and Complexity The more complex the numeric addressing scheme, or the larger the numbers used, the more difficult it is for humans to remember the numbers. This makes having a name system all the more essential for the users of those addresses.

User Base Size and Skill In the early days of networks, a small number of highly skilled and well-trained engineers used them, and these people sometimes just memorized the numbers of the machines they worked with every day. In modern networks with thousands or millions of regular users, expecting the average person to remember device numbers is not reasonable.

> **KEY CONCEPT** Networking name systems are important because they allow devices to be assigned efficient numeric addresses, while still enabling humans to access them using names that are easier to remember. Name systems become more important as you increase the size of the network, the address, or the user base. They are also more essential when the user base is limited in skill or experience.

Looking at these issues, we can see that the trends in today's networks are all in the direction of increasing the importance of name systems. Our networks, both private and public, are growing larger, and we have more people using them, including more people without a technical background. We are also increasingly moving from small addresses to larger ones. The best example of this is the upcoming change to IP. While DNS is important for the 32-bit addresses used in IPv4, it's even *more* important for dealing with the enormous 128-bit addresses of IPv6 (see Part II-4).

Basic Name System Functions: Name Space, Name Registration, and Name Resolution

While the difference between numeric addresses and symbolic names is very significant to the users of network devices, it's important to remember that both numbers and names really serve the same basic purpose: *device identification.* Even when we use a name system to make devices easier to access, the computers themselves will still normally need to use the underlying numeric identifier. In essence, every device will end up with (at least) two identifiers: a number *and* a name.

The fact that devices end up with multiple identifiers is what allows both people and their machines to use the method of identification they prefer. However, it means that there must be ways of managing the assignment of names to devices and converting between them. A name system involves more than just slapping names on computers. It must be a complete *system* that allows names to be used by the humans while numbers continue to be used by the devices.

At the highest level, a name system must handle three basic functions:

Name Space Definition The name system defines a *name space* for the networking system on which it runs. The name space, also sometimes called a *name architecture,* describes the rules for how names are structured and used. It also defines how the name of one device is related to the names of other devices in the system and how to ensure that there are no invalid names that would cause problems with the system as a whole.

Name Registration To implement the name system, a name must be assigned to each device on the network. Like any addressing system, a name system cannot work properly unless every name on the system is unique. We need some way of managing how the names are assigned so the result is sensible. The process of linking specific names to particular devices is usually called *name registration.*

Name Resolution Even though humans like symbolic names, computers usually have little use for them. It is necessary to define a mechanism by which a device's symbolic name can be translated into its numeric address. This process is usually called *name resolution.*

The name space is more of a descriptive function, which defines how names work in the system. Name registration and resolution are more active functions, with each name system including one or more specific procedures for how these jobs are carried out. Name registration and resolution are in some ways complements of each other, so certain registration techniques are most often associated with particular resolution methods. In turn, the types of registration and resolution methods that are possible depend on the name space, and in particular, its architecture. These relationships are shown in simplified form in Figure 50-3.

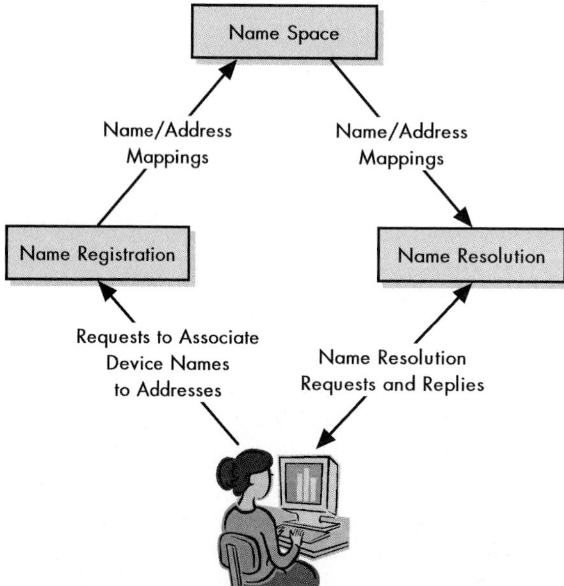

Figure 50-3: *Name system functions*

This diagram shows the relationships between the three main functions of a name system. The *name space* defines the structure of the name system and the rules for creating names. The name space is used as the basis for the *name registration* method, which defines the mappings between names and addresses. When a user wants to access a device by name, a *name resolution* method is used to consult the name space, determine what address is associated with a name, and then convert the name to an address. The processes of registration and resolution can be either quite plain or fairly complicated, depending on the type of name system used. Simple name systems are largely manual in operation, easy to understand, and best used in smaller networks. Larger, more complex networks and internetworks require more sophisticated methods of registration and resolution, which involve less administrator intervention and *scale* better as new machines are added to the network.

Although name registration and name resolution work as functions at the highest level, they are probably better thought of as *sets* of functions. Name registration is necessarily tied to issues such as name system administration and management, and understanding resolution requires that we look at a number of important implementation issues in the areas of efficiency and reliability. The rest of this chapter expands on this overview by considering each of these three functions in more detail.

> **KEY CONCEPT** A name system consists of three theoretical high-level functions: the *name space*, which describes how names are created and organized; the *name registration* technique, which is used to set up relationships between names and addresses; and the *name resolution* method, which is responsible for translating names to addresses.

Name Spaces and Name Architectures

The main idea of a name system is to provide a way to identify devices using symbolic names. Like any identification mechanism, before it can be used, we must define the way that identification will be performed. Numeric addressing schemes (like IP addresses) have rules for how addresses are created and assign addresses to each device from their *address space*. In a similar way, devices in a name system are given names from the system's *name space*.

Name Space Functions

Of the three main components of a name system, the name space is the most abstract. It is also the most fundamental part of the system, since it actually describes how the names are created. There are several aspects to what the name space defines in a name system:

Name Size and Maximum Number of Names The name space specifies the number of characters (symbols) that compose names. It also defines the maximum number of names that can appear in the system.

Name Rules and Syntax The name space specifies which characters and symbols are allowed in a name. This is used to allow legal names to be chosen for all devices, while avoiding illegal names.

Name Architecture and Semantics Each name space uses a specific *architecture* or *structure*, which describes how names are constructed and interpreted.

The concepts of name size and name syntax are relatively straightforward. The *name architecture* is probably the most important differentiating characteristic of name systems. For this reason, name spaces are sometimes even *called* name architectures. The architecture of the name space determines whether names are assigned and used as a simple unstructured set of symbols or have a more complex internal structure. In the latter case, the name space also must define how elements of a particular name are related to each other.

Theoretically, many different name architectures are possible. In practice, most fall into one of two categories: flat and hierarchical.

Flat Name Architecture (Flat Name Space)

In a *flat name architecture*, names are assigned as a sequence of symbols that are interpreted as a single, whole label without any internal structure. There is no clear relationship between any name and any other name.

An example of this sort of architecture would be a name system where computers are given unstructured names like Engineering Workstation 1 or Joanne's PC, as shown in the example in Figure 50-4.

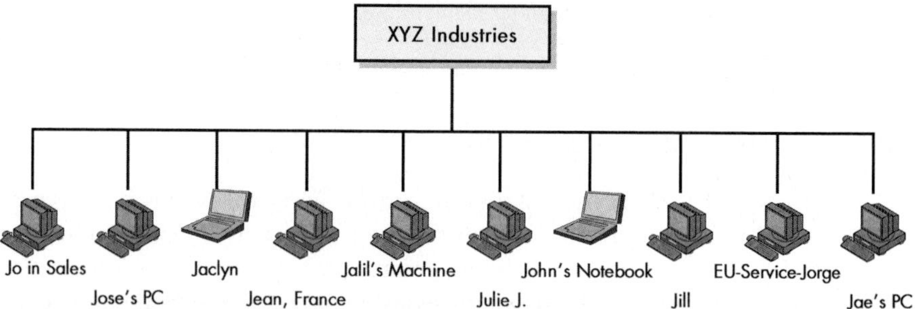

Figure 50-4: Flat name architecture (flat name space) *This diagram shows an example of a flat name architecture. There is no structure that organizes the names or dictates how they must be constructed. Logically, each device is a peer of each of the others.*

Hierarchical Name Architecture (Structured Name Space)

In a *hierarchical name architecture*, or structured name space, the names are a sequence of symbols, but these symbols are assigned using a specific and clear structure. Each name consists of discrete elements that are related to each other, usually by using hierarchical parent/child semantics. There are many naming architectures in various contexts that use this type of hierarchical structure. For example, consider how a large company might set up an organization chart and name the executives and officers in the organization. One hypothetical example of a hierarchical name architecture is illustrated in Figure 50-5.

The best-known real-world example of a hierarchical name space is the name space of DNS (see Chapter 53), which uses text labels separated by periods (or *dots*) to form an internal structure. All the names in the system are organized into a structure, and a particular device's place in the structure can be determined by looking at its name. For example, www.tcpipguide.com refers to the World Wide Web server for *The TCP/IP Guide*, which is named under the umbrella of commercial (.com) companies.

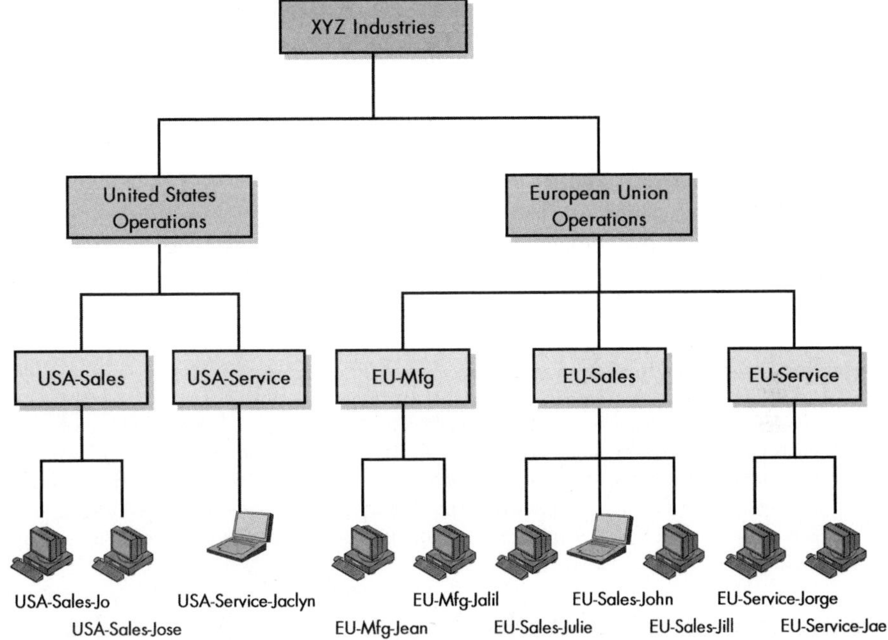

Figure 50-5: *Hierarchical name architecture (structured name space)*

This diagram contains the same devices as Figure 50-4, but they have been arranged using a hierarchical, structured name architecture. In this case, the organization has chosen to structure its device names first by facility location, and then by department. Each name starts with something like USA-Service- or EU-Mfg-. This has immediate benefits by providing local control over device naming without risk of conflicts. If someone named John were hired into the USA sales force, his machine could be named USA-Sales-John, without conflicting with the machine owned by John of the European sales force (EU-Sales-John). The structure also makes it easier to know immediately where a device can be found within the organization.

Comparing Name Architectures

As you will see in the next two sections in this chapter, the architecture of the name space is intimately related to how names are registered and managed, and ultimately, how they are resolved. A flat name space requires a central authority of some sort to assign names to all devices in the system to ensure uniqueness. A hierarchical name architecture is ideally suited to a more distributed registration scheme that allows many authorities to share in the registration and administrative process.

All of this means that the advantages and disadvantages of each of these architectures are not a great mystery. Flat name spaces have the advantage of simplicity and the ability to create short and easily remembered names, as shown in Figure 50-4. However, they do not scale well to name systems containing hundreds or thousands of machines, due to the difficulties in ensuring each name is unique. For example, what happens if there are four people named John who all try to name their computers John's PC? Another issue is the overhead needed to centrally manage these names.

In contrast, hierarchical name spaces are more sophisticated and flexible, because they allow names to be assigned using a logical structure. We can name our machines using a hierarchy that reflects our organization's structure, for example, and give authority to different parts of the organization to manage parts of the name space. As long as each department is named uniquely and that unique department name is part of each machine name, we don't need to worry about each assigned name being unique across the entire organization; it just needs to be unique within the department. Thus, we can have four different machines named with their department name and John, as Figure 50-5 demonstrates. The price of this flexibility is the need for longer names and more complexity in name registration and resolution.

> **KEY CONCEPT** The two most common types of name architecture are the flat name space and the hierarchical name space. Names in a flat name space are all peers with no relationship. In a hierarchical architecture, a multiple-level structure is used to organize names in a specific way. The flat system is simpler and satisfactory for small networks. The hierarchical name space is more flexible and powerful, and better suited to larger networks and internetworks.

Name Registration Methods, Administration, and Authorities

It seems obvious that for our name system to be implemented, we need some method of assigning names to each of the devices that will use the system. Just as a name system has a name space that is comparable to an addressing system's address space, it also must implement a set of rules and procedures for assigning names, comparable to how an addressing system assigns addresses. This is called *name registration.*

Name Registration Functions

In general, name registration encompasses the following four concepts and tasks:

Name Assignment and Guarantee of Uniqueness The core task of the name registration process is assigning names to devices. Like all identification schemes, a key requirement of name registration is ensuring that each name is unique. Duplicated names cause ambiguity and make consistent name resolution impossible.

Central Registration Authority Designation Ensuring uniqueness of names requires that there be someone in charge of the name assignment process. This *central registration authority* may be a single individual that maintains a file containing names, or it may be an organization that is responsible for the overall name registration process. The authority is also charged with resolving problems and conflicts that may arise in registrations.

Registration Authority Delegation In smaller name systems, the central registration authority may be responsible for the actual registration process for all devices. In larger, hierarchical name systems, having this process centralized is impractical. Instead, the central registration authority will divide the name space and *delegate* authority for registering names in different parts of it to subordinate organizations. This requires a delegation policy to be developed and implemented.

Hierarchical Structure Definition When a hierarchical name space is used, the central authority is responsible for defining how the structure will look. This, in turn, dictates how names can be registered in different parts of the hierarchy, and of course, also impacts how authority is delegated.

The complexity of the name registration process depends to a great extent on the size and complexity of the name system as a whole, and, in particular, on the architecture of the name space. In a simple name system using a flat name space, registration is usually accomplished using a single authority. There is no structure and usually no delegation of authority, so there isn't much to registration. For hierarchical name systems, name registration is tied tightly to the hierarchy used for names.

Hierarchical Name Registration

The central authority defines the structure of the hierarchy and decides how the hierarchy is to be *partitioned* into subsets that can be independently administered by other authorities. Those authorities may, in turn, delegate subsets of their name spaces as well, creating a flexible and extensible system.

This ability to delegate authority for name registration is one of the most powerful benefits of a hierarchical name space. For example, in DNS, a central authority is responsible for name registration as a whole. This central authority is in charge of deciding which top-level domains—such as .com, .edu, .info, and .uk—are allowed to exist. Authority for managing each of these subsets of the worldwide hierarchy is then delegated to other organizations. These organizations continue the process of dividing the hierarchy as they see fit. Eventually, each organization is able to decide how it will name its own internal systems independently; for example, IBM can register names in any way it sees fit within the ibm.com name.

Name Registration Methods

There are several common methods by which the actual process of registration is carried out. These include table name registration, broadcast name registration, and database registration. Each of these has its strengths and weaknesses, and again, some are better suited to flat name spaces and some to hierarchical ones.

Table Name Registration

Using table name registration, name assignments are maintained in a table by an administrator. When names need to be added, deleted, or changed, the table is edited.

This technique is usually associated with small, flat name space name systems. It has the same benefits and drawbacks as flat architecture in general: It is simple and easy to implement, but doesn't scale well to larger systems. With a dozen machines, having someone edit name registration tables is practical; with thousands of machines, it is not. It is also not conducive to a hierarchical system where there are multiple authorities, because the table needs to be kept in one place.

In larger internetworks, tables may be used as an adjunct to one of the other, more sophisticated, registration techniques.

Broadcast Name Registration

Broadcast name registration is a trial-and-error technique. A device that wants to use a particular name sends out a message to all other devices on the network, asking if anyone else is already using it. If so, it chooses a different name. If not, the name is considered registered and can then be used.

This technique is more sophisticated than using tables, but it is still limited to use in relatively small systems. It is not practical to attempt to broadcast to thousands of systems, and this method could not be used over the Internet, since there is no way to broadcast to every device on an internetwork.

Database Registration

With database registration, a database of name assignments is maintained. To register a name, a request must be made to have the name assignment added to the database. If the authority for the name system is entirely centralized, the database will be centralized and maintained by that authority. If authority for parts of the hierarchy is delegated, then a *distributed database* is used for registration, with each authority maintaining the part of the database describing its section of the hierarchy.

This is the most sophisticated technique and one normally associated with hierarchical name systems like DNS. It has several benefits, including flexibility, reliability, and distribution of maintenance effort. Its main drawback is complexity.

> **KEY CONCEPT** *Name registration* is the process by which names are linked to addresses in a name system. It encompasses activities such as central registry authority designation and delegation, and name space structure management. The most common methods of name registration, in order of both increasing capability and complexity, are manual table maintenance, broadcast registration, and database registration.

Name Resolution Techniques and Elements

As we discussed earlier in this chapter, using a name system creates two parallel identification systems for computers: the numbers used by machines and the names used by people. The job of the name system is to integrate these two schemes. Name registration allows humans to specify which machines use which names. This is only half the process, however; we also need a way for machines to take a name given to them by a human and translate it into the numeric address it can actually use for communication. This is called *name resolution.*

Name resolution, also sometimes called *name translation, mapping,* or *binding,* is the most well-known aspect of name systems, because it is where most of the "heavy lifting" of a name system occurs. The name space is generally set up once, and name registration occurs infrequently—only when names must be created or changed. In contrast, every user of a name system instructs the machines he or she uses to perform name resolution, hundreds or even thousands of times a day.

Name Resolution Methods

Several different techniques can be used for name resolution. How this function is implemented depends a great deal on the other two name system functions: name space and name registration. As you might imagine, a simple name system with a simple name registration method will most often use a simple resolution method as well. Complex hierarchical systems with distributed databases require more sophistication in how names are resolved. There are three common name resolution methods: table name resolution, broadcast name resolution, and client/server name resolution.

Table-Based Name Resolution

The table used for table-based name registration is consulted by a device when resolution needs to be performed. The table tells the device how to transform the name of the machine it needs to contact into an address.

This technique obviously corresponds to table name registration. It is the simplest and least capable of the three methods. Table name resolution is suitable for stand-alone use only in very small name systems, but it can be a supplement to other methods as well.

Broadcast Name Resolution

When a device needs to resolve a name, it broadcasts a query that says something to this effect: "I need to send to the device named *X.* Who is that?" The device whose name is *X* responds, "I'm *X,* and my numeric address is *N.*"

This is the complement of broadcast name registration. It, too, can be used only in simple systems where every device can hear a broadcast. The use of broadcasts also makes it wasteful of network bandwidth.

Client/Server Name Resolution

With client/server name resolution, servers are programmed with software that allows them to respond to name resolution requests sent by clients. These servers take the name in the request, look up the associated numeric identifier in a database, and send it back in a response.

This technique is generally used in conjunction with database name registration. It is the most complex name resolution method, but it is also the most efficient and the only one that can really work properly on a large, distributed hierarchical name system.

Client/Server Name Resolution Functional Elements

Client/server name resolution is the method used for most large, modern name systems. The client/server method of request/reply resolution is similar to how many other protocols function. One thing that is unique about name resolution, however, is that name resolution isn't often invoked directly by the client. It's rare, for example, for a human user to say, "Please resolve the following name." We also certainly wouldn't want users to need to manually resolve a name to an address each time they wished to contact a device, as this would be cumbersome.

Instead, the system is automated by having software accept machine names input by users. The software resolves the name by passing it to a *name resolver* software component. The resolver acts as the client in the name resolution process. It contacts a *name server*, which responds to the request. The name resolver and name server constitute the two main functional elements in name resolution.

> **KEY CONCEPT** *Name resolution* is arguably the most important of the main functional elements of a name system, because it is the part of the system that actually converts names into addresses. The two main components of name resolution are *name resolvers*, which act as clients in the resolution process, and *name servers*. The three main name resolution methods—table-based, broadcast, and client/server—correspond closely to the table, broadcast, and database methods of name registration.

In a distributed database for a hierarchical name system, multiple requests may be required, since name servers will contain only information for certain machines and not others. Resolvers follow a special procedure to travel the hierarchy until they find the server that has the information they want. Again, DNS's name resolution is the best example of this method.

Efficiency, Reliability, and Other Name Resolution Considerations

As described in the previous section, the primary function of name resolution is allowing humans to identify devices using names, then converting these names into numbers so that computers can use the numbers instead. This basic task is conceptually quite simple, but it can become quite complex in implementation. The reason for this is the key characteristic that makes name resolution so different from the other tasks performed by a name system: the frequency with which it is done.

Name registration is seldom done, but name resolution is done very often. If you consider a large internetwork with thousands of users running various applications, millions of names must be resolved every day. Now, consider something like the Internet, which must process billions of client/server requests and replies daily! Ensuring that such systems work requires that we do more than just implement a resolution process; we must add facilities to ensure that resolution is done as effectively as possible.

Efficiency Considerations

The first major concern with name resolution is *efficiency*. Name resolution uses up system resources, especially with resolution techniques that require requests and replies to be sent. This means we want to minimize the number of times resolution is performed, if at all possible. Now, consider that many people will frequently access the same machines over and over again. For example, if you go to a website called www.thisisasite.com for the first time, your system will need to resolve that name. After the home page for that site loads, if you click a link to another page on that site, the page will also be found at that same name: www.thisisasite.com. So, it would be wasteful to need to resolve that name a second time.

To avoid this, name systems almost always include some sort of *caching* capability, which allows devices to remember recent name resolutions and retain the mapping from name to address for a period of time. Whenever a name needs to be resolved, the cache is first checked before going through the formal process of resolution. The use of caching eliminates the vast majority of actual name resolution requests that would otherwise be required.

The drawbacks of caching are that it requires some system resources of its own and that it adds complexity to the system. One issue is deciding how long to retain data in the cache. If we keep it too short a time, we generate extra unnecessary resolution requests. If we keep it too long, we risk having the mapping become stale if the name assignment for the machine changes. These are issues that a sophisticated name system must handle. A typical solution is to allow each name registration to specify how long information about that name-to-address link may be cached.

Reliability Considerations

The next main concern after efficiency is name resolution *reliability*. As I said earlier in this chapter, having a name system isn't strictly necessary for the computers, but it's very important for the users, especially on a large network like the Internet.

While having a single central place that maintains all information about a name system may make administration simpler, it creates a dangerous single point of failure. If anything happens to the device storing the information, the entire name system fails. Modern name systems employ redundancies to prevent having the entire system rely on any particular device for resolution. A typical approach in a client/server system is to have multiple servers in different locations (or attached to different networks) that can respond to name resolution requests.

> **KEY CONCEPT** Since name resolution is the part of a name system that is used most often, it is here that we must pay careful attention to implementation issues. The two most important ones are efficiency and reliability. Efficiency is essential due to the many thousands or millions of resolutions performed every day on a large system. Reliability is a consideration because users of the name system quickly come to rely on it, so we must make sure it is robust.

Other Considerations

An optional feature in some name resolution systems is *load balancing*. When properly implemented, load balancing allows a single name to map to more than one underlying address. This allows requests sent to a particular virtual device to actually be directed to a number of different actual physical devices, spreading the load over multiple machines. A common use of this feature is for very popular websites that are visited often.

Finally, while name resolution is obviously designed to allow names to be mapped to addresses, there are cases where we may wish to go in the other direction: given a numeric address, find the name that goes with it. This process, called *reverse resolution*, is analogous to having a phone number and trying to find the name of the person or company to which it belongs. Just as we can't easily find the name matching a phone number using a conventional phone book (we would need to scan every page looking for the number), reverse resolution requires special support on the part of the name system. This is especially true if the name system data is distributed over many servers.

51

TCP/IP NAME SYSTEMS OVERVIEW AND THE HOST TABLE NAME SYSTEM

TCP/IP has become sufficiently popular that many people—even those who aren't geeks—are fairly comfortable working with its numeric identifiers (IP addresses). Even so, it's a lot easier to work with names than numbers, and it's certainly easier to remember names. We can consider also that name systems become more important when used on larger networks, and TCP/IP is used to implement the Internet, the world's largest internetwork. Having a good name system is vital to the operation of the Internet, and thus, has become an important element of TCP/IP as a whole.

In this chapter, I begin the discussion of TCP/IP's name systems with a look at the history of the use of host names in TCP/IP and the early development of its name systems. I then provide a description of the simple host table name system, the first one used in the protocol suite. I discuss why host tables were replaced by the Domain Name System (DNS) and how, even today, they can be used to complement DNS functions.

BACKGROUND INFORMATION *This chapter assumes that you are already familiar with the general concepts and issues of name systems explained in the preceding chapter.*

A Brief History of TCP/IP Host Names and Name Systems

In the previous chapter, I described an interesting paradox: Even though name systems aren't strictly necessary for the functioning of a networking system, they make using a network so much easier for people that they are considered an essential part of most networks. No better evidence of this can be found than in the history of name system development in TCP/IP.

Developing the First Name System: ARPAnet Host Name Lists

The history of name systems in the TCP/IP protocol suite actually goes back well before the Transmission Control Protocol (TCP) and Internet Protocol (IP) were themselves even created. In the late 1960s and early 1970s, when the predecessor of the Internet, called the *ARPAnet*, was being developed, it used older networking protocols that served the same function that TCP and IP do today.

The ARPAnet was very small by today's standards, containing at first only a few machines, referred to as *hosts*, just as TCP/IP machines often are called today. The addressing scheme was also very simple, consisting of just the combination of a computer number and a port number for each host. With only a handful of machine names, it was easy to memorize addresses, but as the ARPAnet grew to several dozen machines, this scheme became untenable.

As early as 1971, it was apparent to the engineers designing the ARPAnet that symbolic names were much easier for everyone to work with than numeric addresses. They began to assign simple host names to each of the devices on the network. Each site managed its own *host table*, which listed the mappings of names to addresses.

Naturally, the ARPAnet engineers immediately recognized the dangers of having each site maintain a list of possibly inconsistent host names. Since the internetwork was just a small "club" at this point, they used the Request for Comment (RFC) process itself to document standard host-name-to-address mappings. RFC 226, "Standardization of Host Mnemonics," is the first RFC I could find showing how host names were assigned. It was published on September 20, 1971.

This initial name system was about as manual as a system could be. As additions and changes were made to the network, the list of host names was updated in a new RFC, leading to a series of RFCs being published in the 1970s. Each host administrator still maintained his or her own host table, which was updated when a new RFC was published. During this time, the structure of host names was still under discussion, and changes were made to just about every aspect of the name system as new ideas were explored and refined.

Storing Host Names in a Host Table File

This early name system worked fine while the ARPAnet was very small, but it presented many problems as the internetwork grew. One problem was that it was extremely slow in responding to network modifications, because additions and changes would be entered into device tables only after a new list was published. Also, even with the centralized list, there were still potential consistency issues, because a site manager might forget to update a file or make a typographical error.

The first improvement was to make the list of host name assignments a standard "master" text file, which was centrally managed and could be downloaded using network protocols like the File Transfer Protocol (FTP). The file was maintained at the Network Information Center (NIC) at Stanford University. The process for defining and using this file was described in RFCs 606 and 608, both entitled "Host Names On-Line," published in December 1973 and January 1974, respectively. These documents also formally specified the syntax for the TCP/IP host table name system, described later in this chapter.

The use of a centrally managed host table continued through the 1970s. When TCP/IP was developed, the system was maintained, and the mappings were made between host names and 32-bit IP addresses. RFC 810, "DoD Internet Host Table Specification," shows how host tables were defined for use with IP addresses. It was published in March 1982.

Outgrowing the Host Table Name System and Moving to DNS

The continuing growth of the ARPAnet/Internet made it apparent that the simple host table name system would eventually become unmanageable. With at first dozens, and then hundreds and thousands of new hosts connecting to the internetwork, a single text file maintained in a central location just wasn't up to the task.

The idea of moving to a hierarchical name system based on the concept of *domains* was first introduced in September 1981 in RFC 799, "Internet Name Domains." Considerable discussion and development of this concept occurred in the early 1980s. By 1983, a plan was put in place to migrate from the flat host table name system to the new Domain Name System (DNS). The detailed history of the development of this name system is continued in the overview of DNS in Chapter 52.

The TCP/IP Host Table Name System

The pioneers of the modern Internet made the first name system for the TCP/IP suite when they created simple files containing the names and addresses of the machines in the early ARPAnet, as explained in the preceding section. This system was so simple that it originally wasn't even formally specified as a name system per se. Since the files contained names for network hosts, the process for relating names to addresses was simply called the *host name* mechanism. Later, these files were called *host tables*, and for this reason, this technology is commonly called the TCP/IP *host table name system.*

As a system, it is extremely simple, since it consists of nothing more than a text file maintained on each machine on the network. This file is normally called /etc/hosts on a UNIX system and HOSTS on a Windows system (usually residing in the main Windows directory). The file usually begins with some comment lines and then lists pairs of IP addresses and host names. A very simplified example (using the modern table structure, which is slightly different from the original host table format) is shown in Listing 51-1.

```
# Host Database
# This file should contain the addresses and aliases
# for local hosts that share this file.
#
# Each line should take the form:
# <address>            <host name>
#
127.0.0.1              localhost
209.68.14.80           www.pcguide.com
216.92.177.143         www.desktopscenes.com
198.175.98.64          ftp.intel.com
```

Listing 51-1: *Example TCP/IP host table*

The name space and architecture for the host table name system is theoretically flat, with each name being able to take any form, without any real structure. Despite this, for consistency, certain rules were eventually put in place regarding how names should be created, as discussed in Chapter 53. As you will learn later in this chapter, it's also possible to use host tables to support the implementation of a hierarchical name space, which would mean that the names would need to be created using that name space's structural rules.

Host Table Name Resolution

Name resolution in the host table name system is very simple. Each device reads the host table into memory when it starts up. Users of the system can refer to the names in that host table by using names, instead of a numeric IP addresses, in their invocation of various applications. When the software detects a name has been used in this manner, it refers the name to the internal resolver routine in the device, which looks up the name in the host table in memory and returns its address. There is no need for any transmissions or servers to be contacted; resolution is entirely local.

Host Table Name Registration

Now, here is the part where I am supposed to say that name registration in the host table name system is simple as well, right? Well, yes and no. From a purely technical standpoint, it certainly is simple. A name is registered on a particular device when the name and corresponding IP address are entered into the device's host table, and that's it.

However, name registration is much more complicated from an administrative standpoint, and this is where we find the major weakness of using host tables. Each network device maintains its own host table independent of the others, usually stored as a file on its local hard disk. This is in contrast to database registration systems (see Chapter 50), where the data is centrally stored and managed. This approach to name registration leads to two very important concerns:

Consistency Since every device has its own host table, how do we ensure that information is consistent throughout all the tables on the different devices?

Modifications How do we ensure that information about new device mappings and changes to existing ones are propagated to all devices?

As explained earlier in this chapter, the original mechanism for name registration was simply hand-editing, with administrators consulting updated published lists of device names. This was a very inefficient method that was prone to error and slow to acknowledge changes to the network. The revised system used a centrally managed master file that was downloaded by all sites on a regular basis. Name registration in this method required that the name/address mapping be submitted to the authority managing the central file, the NIC.

Weaknesses of the Host Table Name System

The use of a centralized master file for name registration certainly worked better than using the equivalent of interoffice memos to publish host name lists, but it was practical only in the early days of TCP/IP. As the internetwork grew, more weaknesses of the host table system became apparent:

Central Administration Overload The changes to the central file became more frequent, increasing the administrative load on the individual managing the master file, to the point where changes were being made many times per day. As the Internet continued to grow, it would eventually have become impossible for human beings to enter the changes as fast as they were being submitted.

Growth in the Master File Size Every host needed a line in the master file. When the Internet grew to be thousands and eventually millions of devices, the file size would have become excessive.

Excessive Bandwidth Use Since the master file was changing so often, this also meant that all the devices on the network needed to keep downloading this master file repeatedly to stay current. At the same time, the file was also growing in size. Frequent downloads of a big file meant large amounts of network bandwidth were being consumed on something that was, in essence, an overhead activity.

Flat Name Space Problems The lack of a hierarchical name space led to conflicts when users chose identical names for their devices, and this further increased the workload on the central administrator. These issues were ameliorated in part by using naming conventions, such as using a prefix with a location before each individual machine name (like the example we saw in Chapter 50), but this was not an ideal solution.

All of these are reasons why the designers of the Internet eventually moved away from using host tables for the entire Internet to the more capable DNS.

> **KEY CONCEPT** The *host table name system* was the original mechanism used for implementing names on the early Internet. It consists simply of a set of tables containing mappings between names and addresses maintained on each machine in the internetwork. When a name needs to be resolved, the table is consulted to determine the appropriate address. This system is extremely simple, but not very capable and not well suited to a large global Internet, which is why it was eventually abandoned in favor of DNS.

Use of the Host Table Name System in Modern Networking

Although the host table name system has critical weaknesses, it has not gone away entirely. There are two circumstances in which this technique is still of value, as explained in this section.

Small "Island" Networks

If you are setting up a small local area network (LAN) using TCP/IP, and you don't need the names of your devices to be accessible by those outside your network, then guess what: You have the equivalent, of sorts, of the early Internet. In that case, the host table system is as applicable to you as it was to the Internet in the 1970s. You can simply set up host tables on each device and manage them manually.

As long as the LAN is small enough that editing these files periodically is not a hassle, this is actually a fast and effective name system, because no exchange of messages is needed for resolution. You can even maintain a master file on one machine and copy it to the others when changes are required using a script, to save time.

Local Name Mappings to Supplement DNS

Even though modern systems use DNS for most name resolution, they also usually still support the use of host table files. You can manually enter common name mappings into this file, even for devices that are on the global Internet. Your system can then be set up to consult this list before making use of its assigned DNS server.

The use of the HOSTS file in conjunction with DNS allows you to manually specify mappings for commonly accessed sites, which may provide a slight performance improvement since there is no need to access a server. Since the HOSTS file doesn't enforce any particular structure to names, it is naturally quite possible to put DNS-style hierarchical names into the file, as I showed in Listing 51-1. The file is loaded into memory and used to *override* the normal DNS process for names listed in it.

Of course, you then subject yourself to all the potential maintenance headaches of manually edited files. You must update these files as host names or addresses are changed in the DNS system. For this reason, this second use of the HOSTS file for Internet sites served by DNS is less popular than the use of the file for local machines.

KEY CONCEPT Even though the host table name system is not the primary mechanism used for TCP/IP naming, it is still used in two circumstances. The first is to implement a basic name system in a small local TCP/IP internetwork. The second is as an adjunct to DNS, where it allows manual mappings to be created that override the DNS process when needed.

52

DOMAIN NAME SYSTEM (DNS) OVERVIEW, FUNCTIONS, AND CHARACTERISTICS

The creation of host tables to map computer names to addresses greatly improved the usability of the early Internet and the TCP/IP protocol suite that implemented it. Unfortunately, while the host table name system worked well when the internetwork was small, it did not scale particularly well as the Internet started to grow in size and complexity. The name system had to stay, but the use of host tables had to be dispensed with in favor of a newer, more capable system.

Over the period of several years, many engineers worked to create a system that would meet not just the needs of TCP/IP internetworks of the time, but also those of the future. The new name system was based on a hierarchical division of the network into groups and subgroups, with names reflecting this structure. It was designed to store data in a distributed fashion to facilitate decentralized control and efficient operation, and included flexible and extensible mechanisms for name registration and resolution. This new name system for TCP/IP was called the *Domain Name System (DNS)*.

We'll begin our look at DNS in this introductory chapter. I start by providing an overview of DNS's development, history, and standards, continuing the history begun in the overall look at TCP/IP name systems. I discuss the design goals and objectives of the creators of DNS, to help you understand better what its designers were trying to do. I then talk about the main components of DNS and the functions it performs, relating these to the basic functions explained in the overview section on name systems.

DNS Overview, History, and Standards

The aversion that most people have to trying to remember numeric identifiers led to the very quick adoption of a name system for devices on the predecessors of what we now call the Internet. In the 1960s and early 1970s, names were given to machines, and these names were maintained in host tables. The TCP/IP host table name system (described in Chapter 51) worked well for a number of years, with a centrally maintained master list used by device administrators to ensure a consistent view of the network.

Unfortunately, such a system works well only when the number of devices is small. As the budding Internet grew, numerous weaknesses became apparent in the host table method, as I detailed in Chapter 51. Furthermore, the problems with the system weren't something that could be easily patched with small changes; the problems were structural, part of the basic idea of host tables as a whole. A completely new approach was needed for how names would be used on the Internet.

Early DNS Development and the Move to Hierarchical Domains

The most important paradigm shift made by the TCP/IP engineers was the decision to change the name system from one that used a single, centralized list of names to a more decentralized system. The idea was to create a structured topology where names were organized into *domains.* This idea was first introduced in RFC 799, "Internet Name Domains," published in September 1981.

RFC 799 actually describes more the mechanics of delivering electronic mail messages between domains than the domains themselves. Interestingly, the standard assumes a flat structure of domains in its discussion, while mentioning the possibility of creating a hierarchical structure instead. It was the decision to go to such a hierarchical name space for domains that led to the creation of DNS in the form in which we know it today.

Many RFC documents describing the development of different aspects of DNS were published in the early 1980s. The first real milestone in DNS's history was probably the publishing, in November 1983, of three initial documents discussing DNS concepts:

- RFC 881, "Domain Names Plan and Schedule," discusses the issues involved in implementing the new DNS and how to migrate from the older host table system.

- RFC 882, "Domain Names: Concepts and Facilities," describes the concepts and functional elements of DNS in fairly extensive detail. It includes a discussion of the name space, resource records, and how name servers and resolvers work.
- RFC 883, "Domain Names: Implementation Specification," provides the nitty-gritty details on DNS messaging and operation.

Standardization of DNS and Initial Defining Standards

The three "Domain Names" RFC documents published in November 1983 were discussed frequently over the months that followed, and the basic DNS mechanism was revised many times. Several subsequent RFCs were published, updating the DNS transition plan and schedule. Finally, in November 1987, agreement on the operation of the system was finalized, and four new RFCs were published that formalized the DNS system for the first time:

- RFC 1032, "Domain Administrators Guide," specifies administrative procedures and policies for those running a domain.
- RFC 1033, "Domain Administrators Operations Guide," provides technical details on how to operate a DNS server, including how to maintain portions of the DNS distributed database of names.
- RFC 1034, "Domain Names - Concepts and Facilities," replaces RFC 882, providing an introduction and conceptual description of DNS.
- RFC 1035, "Domain Names - Implementation and Specification," is an update to RFC 883, specifying how DNS works in detail, including resource record definitions, message types, master file format, and resolver and name server implementation details.

These last two documents, RFCs 1034 and 1035, are considered the definitive original specification for the operation of DNS. While they are now many years old, they still provide the essential description of how DNS works.

As the Internet has grown to include thousands and then millions of sites, the importance of DNS has grown as well. Today, most people use DNS almost every time they use TCP/IP to access the Internet. It has gone from an alternative form of addressing for applications to one that is preferred by most users. It is also an important building block of the more complete application layer addressing scheme developed for TCP/IP: Uniform Resource Identifiers (URIs) (described in Chapter 70).

The hierarchical nature of the DNS name space has allowed the Internet to grow by making the assignment and mapping of names manageable. The authority structure (which defines who is in charge of parts of the name space) is also hierarchical, giving local administrators control over the names of devices they manage, while ensuring name consistency across the hierarchy as a whole. The distribution of data using many name servers and a standardized resolution technique following a standard message protocol provides efficiency and reliability. These concepts will become clearer as we explore DNS more completely in later sections of this chapter.

DNS Evolution and Important Additional Standards

TCP/IP and the Internet have both changed a lot since 1987, of course, and DNS has also had to change. Many RFCs have been written since the base documents were published in the late 1980s, most of which further clarify the operation of DNS, expand on its capabilities, or define new features for it. You can find all of these by searching for "domain" or "DNS" in a list of RFCs. There are dozens of these. The following are a few of the more interesting ones:

- RFC 1183, "New DNS RR Definitions," defines several new experimental resource record types. Other subsequent RFCs have also defined new resource records.
- RFC 1794, "DNS Support for Load Balancing," discusses load balancing for greater performance in DNS servers.
- RFC 1995, "Incremental Zone Transfer in DNS," specifies a new feature that allows only part of a zone to be transferred to a secondary name server for efficiency.
- RFC 1996, "A Mechanism for Prompt Notification of Zone Changes (DNS NOTIFY)," adds a new message type to DNS to allow primary (authoritative) DNS servers to tell secondary servers that information has changed in the main database.
- RFC 2136, "Dynamic Updates in the Domain Name System (DNS UPDATE)," describes a technique for dynamically making resource record changes in the DNS database (also called *Dynamic DNS*).
- RFC 2181, "Clarifications to the DNS Specification," discusses several issues with the main DNS standards as defined in RFCs 1034 and 1035 and how to address them.
- RFC 2308, "Negative Caching of DNS Queries (DNS NCACHE)," specifies the operation of negative caching, a feature that allows a server to maintain information about names that do not exist more efficiently.

DNS Adaptation for Internet Protocol Version 6

Version 6 of the Internet Protocol (IPv6, covered in Part II-4) was developed starting in the mid-1990s and brought with it the need to make changes and enhancements to the operation of DNS. (Even though DNS operates at the higher layers, it deals intimately with addresses, and addresses have changed in IPv6, as discussed in Chapter 25.) The modifications required to allow DNS to support IPv6 were first defined in RFC 1886, "IPv6 DNS Extensions," which was part of a group of RFCs that laid out the fundamentals of IPv6. Several subsequent standards have been published since that time; these are discussed in the section on IPv6 DNS near the end of Chapter 57.

The rest of this chapter provides a more complete overview of DNS and its development, by discussing the design goals of its creators and the protocol's key characteristics.

DNS Design Goals, Objectives, and Assumptions

As we just saw, the elapsed time from the first RFC discussing TCP/IP domain names to the publishing of the official standards describing the operation of DNS was more than six years. This is a very long time for the development of a system, but it isn't surprising. A lot of thought had to go into the creation of DNS, to be certain that it would meet all of the many demands that would be placed on it.

The first problem was that the creators of DNS needed to worry about both how to define the new system and how to migrate from the old one. Considerable time was spent figuring out how all the existing hosts would be moved over to the new DNS name space and how the new protocols for exchanging DNS information would be implemented on them.

The creators of DNS knew they were making the new system because the old one didn't scale very well. They also knew that if migration was a difficult problem with the small number of hosts in existence at that time, it would be much more difficult if they needed to go to another new system in the future. This made the key challenge in DNS to create a system that would meet the needs of the Internet not just the day it was introduced, or the following year, but even ten years or more down the road.

DNS Design Goals and Objectives

Back in the 1980s, no one had any idea how the Internet would grow as it has in the last decade. That DNS still works as well as it does is a testament to the skill of its designers. Much of this success is due to the early groundwork put into the design of the system. DNS engineers documented some of what they considered to be the main design goals in creating it, which can help us understand not just what DNS does, but also why. These design goals and objectives are as follows:

Creation of a Global, Scalable, Consistent Name Space The name space needed to be capable of spanning a large, global internetwork containing millions of machines. It was necessary that it provide a consistent and predictable method for naming devices and resources, so they could be easily found. It was also, obviously, essential that name duplication be avoided, even when conflicts could potentially be between devices on different continents.

Local Control over Local Resources Administrators of networks and small internetworks on the Internet as a whole needed to be able to have control over the naming of their own devices. It would not be acceptable to need to go through a central authority for naming every single object, nor would it be acceptable for every administrator to need to know the names of everyone else's networks and machines.

Distributed Design to Avoid Bottlenecks The designers of DNS knew that they would need to abandon the idea of a centralized database in favor of a distributed approach to data storage, to avoid the bottlenecks that would result in using DNS with many devices.

Application Universality The system needed to be general enough that it would support a wide variety of applications. For example, it needed to support host identification, mail delivery, and other functions.

Multiple Underlying Protocol Support DNS needed to be inherently able to support different underlying protocols. Many people don't realize, for example, that DNS can support not just IP addresses, but other types of addresses, simply because IP is so dominant in networking today.

Hardware Universality Both large and small computers needed to be able to use the system.

Keep these objectives in mind as you learn more about DNS, and they will help you understand better why certain design attributes were chosen. For example, if we consider the first two objectives listed, they seem almost contradictory: How can we have a global name space with unique names if individual administrators were able to assign local names? As you will see, this is where the power of the DNS hierarchical name space shines through.

DNS Design Assumptions

The design goals tell us what DNS's creators wanted to make sure the new system addressed. In addition, the engineers that worked on the protocol's implementation details needed to make decisions based on certain assumptions of how it would be used:

Rapidly Growing Database Size By the mid-1980s, it was obvious that the DNS database of names would start out rather small but would grow quickly. The system needed to be capable of handling this rapid growth.

Variable Data Modification Rate Most of the data in the name database would change only infrequently, but some data would change more often than that. This meant flexibility would be required in how data changes were handled and how information about those changes was communicated.

Delegatable Organizational Responsibility Responsibility for portions of the name database would be delegated primarily on the basis of organizational boundaries. Many organizations would also run their own hardware and software to implement portions of the overall system.

Relative Importance of Name Information Access It was assumed that the most important thing about DNS was providing reliable name resolution, so the system was created so that it was always possible for a user to access a name and determine its address. A key decision in creating the system was deciding that even if the information were slightly out of date, it was better than no information at all. If a name server were unable to provide the latest data to fill a request, it would return the best information it had available.

Handling of Requests for Missing Information Since the name data was to be distributed, a particular name server might not have the information requested by a user. In this case, the name server should not just say, "I don't know." It should provide a referral to a more likely source of the information or take care of finding the data by issuing its own requests. This led to the creation of the several DNS name resolution techniques: local, iterative, and recursive.

Use of Caching for Performance From the start, it was assumed that DNS would make extensive use of caching to avoid unnecessary queries to servers containing parts of the distributed name database.

Arguably, a lot more assumptions were made in creating this system, as is the case in the development of every system. For example, DNS needed to make assumptions about how exactly data would be stored, the transport mechanism for sending messages, the role of administrators, and so on. You'll learn more about these as we go through our look at the system.

DNS Components and General Functions

To meet the many objectives set for it by its designers, DNS requires a great deal of functionality. It is a true name system with the emphasis on *system*, and as such, is considerably more complex than the host table name system used earlier in TCP/IP. In Chapter 50, I divided the many tasks of a full-featured name system into three categories. DNS includes functions in all of these categories, and so using these categories is a good way to take a high-level look at the way DNS works (see Figure 52-1).

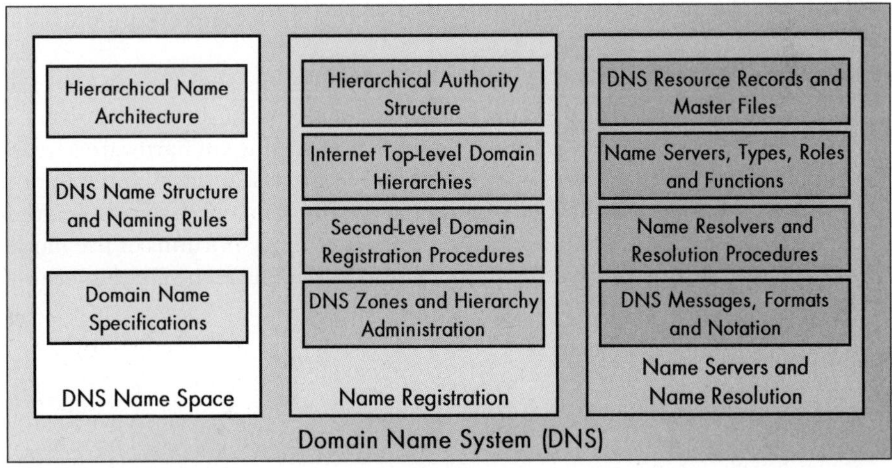

Figure 52-1: DNS functions *DNS consists of three main functional categories: name space, name registration, and name servers/resolution. Each of these consists of a number of specific tasks and responsibilites.*

DNS Name Space

DNS uses a hierarchical name space consisting of a single, complex, multiple-level structure into which all names in the system fit. The name space is organized starting from a single root into which containers (called *domains*) are placed. Each can contain either individual device names or more specific subcontainers. The overall structure is somewhat analogous to how a directory system on a computer organizes files from general to specific, using an arbitrary structure that can be optimized to various needs. A specific syntax is used to define valid names, and special terminology is used to describe parts of the structure and identify domain names, from the root down to the device level.

Name Registration (Including Administration and Authorities)

DNS name registration is used to enter individual names into the DNS distributed database. DNS uses a hierarchical arrangement of authorities that complements the hierarchical name space. A centralized authority determines the overall shape and structure of the name space and handles registration of names at the highest level. Authority is then *delegated* to different organizations to manage various parts of the name space. A set of universal policies controls the registration process and deals with problems and conflicts.

Name Resolution

DNS uses a powerful, distributed, client/server name resolution mechanism. This is probably the area where the most attention needed to be put into the design of DNS, to ensure that it could scale to handle millions and eventually billions of name resolution requests each day.

The name resolution process is implemented using two basic software elements that play the role of server and client: name servers and name resolvers.

DNS name servers are special programs running on hardware servers that are the heart of DNS. Servers are maintained by organizations that have administrative control over part of the DNS name space. They contain *resource records* that describe names, addresses, and other characteristics of those portions of the name space. As such, the servers themselves are arranged into a hierarchy analogous to that of the name space, although not identical in structure.

The main job of name servers is to receive requests for name resolution and respond with either the data requested from the database or with the name of another name server that will lead to the requested information. Name servers are also responsible for data caching and other administrative tasks to ensure efficient operation of the system as a whole.

Name resolvers are the usual clients in the name resolution process. When a user makes reference to a name in a networking application, the name is passed to the resolver, which issues a request to a name server. Depending on the configuration, more than one request may be needed, and several different resolution processes may be combined to find the needed information. Resolvers also may employ caching or implement other features.

NOTE *The division between resolvers and servers is based on roles. As you'll see when we look at name resolution, name servers may also function as clients in certain exchanges of data. See Chapter 56 for an explanation of this apparent paradox.*

If this seems a lot like the classic description of a name system that I gave in Chapter 50, that's not a coincidence. DNS is considered *the* name system against which most others are usually compared. If you understand these high-level descriptions, then you already know the basics of how DNS works. The next three chapters delve into each of these three functional areas in more detail and will help you really learn how DNS does its thing.

KEY CONCEPT As a complete name system, DNS provides numerous capabilities that implement each of the three basic name system functions. The DNS *name space* is hierarchical and is organized using a multilevel structure with particular naming rules. The DNS *name registration system* is based on the idea of a hierarchy of domains and registration authorities responsible for them. DNS *name resolution* is similarly hierarchical, and it is designed around interaction between *name resolver* and *name server* software components that consult databases of DNS *resource records* and communicate using a special messaging protocol to answer client queries.

53

DNS NAME SPACE, ARCHITECTURE, AND TERMINOLOGY

The name space is the most fundamental part of any name system, since it is what defines the ways that the names themselves are created. The name space tells us what form names may take and provides the rules for how they are created. Most important, it specifies the *architecture* of the names—the internal structure of names themselves. This, in turn, has a critical influence on how name registration and resolution work, making an examination of name space and architecture issues the obvious place to start in learning the details of the Domain Name System (DNS).

In this chapter, I describe the concepts behind the DNS name space and its structure. I begin with an overview of the DNS name space and description of the hierarchical architecture it uses. I then explain the terminology often used to refer to parts of the name space. Next, I provide a formal description of DNS labels and the official and unofficial rules for creating domain names. I conclude with a description of domain name specifications, and I explain the concept of qualification and how fully qualified and partially qualified names differ.

DNS Domains and the DNS Hierarchical Name Architecture

The most important element of a name system's name space is its *name architecture*, which describes how names are constructed and interpreted. The architecture of DNS is, unsurprisingly, based on the concept of an abstraction called a *domain*. This is obviously a good place to start in explaining how DNS works.

The Essential Concept in the DNS Name Space: Domains

Dictionary definitions of the word *domain* generally convey the notion of a sphere of influence or an area of control or rulership. An essential concept is that in various contexts, control or authority can be exerted at many different levels. One sphere of influence may contain smaller ones, which can, in turn, contain still smaller ones. This means that such domains are naturally arranged in a hierarchy.

As an example, consider geopolitical domains. We have no centralized "world government" on earth, but we do have the United Nations, which deals with worldwide issues. At the next level down, we have individual countries. Some of these countries have divisions such as states and provinces. Still lower levels have counties, municipalities, neighborhoods, and individual residences or businesses. The "domains" are inherently hierarchical in organization.

DNS uses the word *domain* in a manner very similar to this, and it employs a hierarchical structure that works in much the same way as the geopolitical example. In DNS, a *domain* is defined as either a single object or a set of objects that have been collected together based on some type of commonality. Usually, in DNS, that commonality is that they are all administered by the same organization or authority, which makes the name hierarchy tightly linked to the notion of the DNS hierarchical authority structure (see Chapter 54).

NOTE *The term* domain *is also used in other contexts in the world of networking. The most notable example of this is in Microsoft networking, where* domain *is also used to represent the notion of a collection of objects under common authority. However, the two types of domains are completely different and not related beyond this conceptual level.*

The DNS Hierarchical Tree Structure of Names

We could construct a tree diagram with the United Nations on top, with lines pointing to each of the countries in the world. Then, within the United States, we could draw lines to each of the states. Within each state, we could draw lines to each county, and so on. The result would be something that looks like an upside-down tree, as illustrated in Figure 53-1. This is called a *tree structure.*

Tree structures are common in computing and networking. For example, trees are a type of topology used to connect networks into a local area network.

For understanding DNS, the best example of a tree structure is the directory tree used to store files on a computer's hard disk. The root directory is at the top of the structure and may contain named files and/or named directories. Each directory can itself contain individual files or subdirectories, which can, in turn, contain their own subdirectories, and so on. The domain name structure in DNS is conceptually arranged in the same way, but instead of dealing with files, DNS deals with named objects, usually devices like Internet Protocol (IP) hosts.

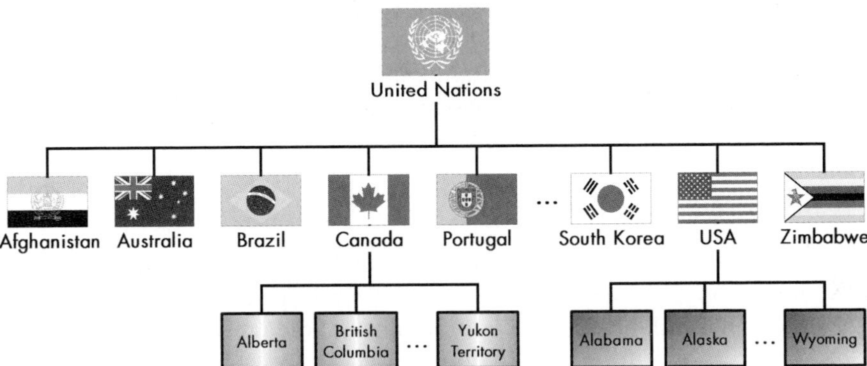

Figure 53-1: Example of a global hierarchical domain architecture *This diagram shows an example of hierarchical architecture, based on political divisions. The United Nations is an umbrella organization representing (to one extent or another) all of the world's nations. It is the* root *of the tree; underneath it we find individual nations. Each nation then is further subdivided in a manner it chooses. For example, Canada has provinces and territories, and the United States has individual states. These can be further subdivided in any number of ways.*

The highest level is still the *root* of the tree. It contains a number of domains, each of which can contain individual objects (names) and/or lower-level domains. Lower-level domains can, in turn, have still lower-level domains, allowing the tree as a whole to take on an arbitrary structure.

Like a directory structure, the DNS hierarchical name architecture allows names to be organized from most general to most specific. It also has complete flexibility, allowing us to arrange the structure in any way that we want. For example, we could make a name system that is structured exactly paralleling the geopolitical organization chart shown in Figure 53-1. We could have the root of the name structure represent the United Nations and create a domain for each country. Then, for those countries that have states, we could create state domains within those country domains. Smaller countries not needing those domains could have city domains directly under the country domain. The hierarchy is flexible, because at each level, it can be given a suitable substructure.

KEY CONCEPT The DNS name space is arranged into a *hierarchy of domains* shaped like an inverted tree. It is structurally similar to the directory structure of a file system, with a root that contains domains, each of which can contain subdomains and so forth.

It's important to remember that every stand-alone internetwork can have its own name space and unique hierarchical structure. Many times, people conflate the idea of *a* DNS name space with *the* DNS name space. The latter refers to the DNS hierarchy used for the global Internet, and it's obvious that this deserves a great deal of attention. But it is just one possible arrangement, although an important one, of an infinite number of possible structures.

NOTE *Chapter 54 provides more specific information about the Internet's DNS hierarchy. As you'll see, geopolitical structures are, in fact, used to assign names to some of the Internet's computers, but other parts of the hierarchy are different.*

DNS Structural Elements and Terminology

Now that we've reviewed the fundamentals of the DNS name space, let's look at its structure in more detail. At the same time, I'll define the many different terms used to refer to parts of the DNS domain name hierarchy.

DNS Tree-Related Terminology

As I explained in the previous section, the DNS name structure is shaped somewhat like a tree. The comparison between structured elements and trees is a common one in networking. The main difference between technology and biology is that DNS trees grow from the top down, instead of reaching for the sky. The analogy to a tree naturally leads to the use of several tree-related terms in describing the DNS name structure, some of which are illustrated in Figure 53-2:

Root This is the conceptual top of the DNS name structure. The *root* domain in DNS contains the entire structure. By definition, it has no name; it is *null*.

Branch A *branch* is any contiguous portion of DNS hierarchy. It consists of a domain and all the domains and objects within it. All branches connect together to the root, just as in a real tree. (Yes, it would be better if the root were called the *trunk*, but computer science majors apparently don't take botany electives.)

Leaf This is an end object in the structure; that is, a domain that doesn't have anything underneath it. The analogy to a leaf being at the end of a sequence of branches is apt.

There is no specific term to refer to a domain that is not a leaf. These are sometimes called *interior nodes*, meaning that they are in the middle of the structure. A *node* is the generic computing term for an object in a topology or structure. So, in DNS, every node is a domain, and it may be an interior node that contains additional domains and/or objects or a leaf that is a specific, named device. The term *domain* is thus somewhat ambiguous, as it can refer to either a collection of objects that represents a branch of the tree or to a specific leaf.

DNS Domain-Related Terminology

There are also several domain-like terms that are often used to refer to domains at different levels of the hierarchy. These terms are also shown in Figure 53-2:

Root Domain This is the root of the tree.

Top-Level Domains (TLDs) These are the highest-level domains directly under the root of the tree. They are also sometimes called *first-level domains*.

Second-Level Domains Shockingly enough, these are the domains located directly below the top-level domains.

Subdomains In some contexts, this term refers only to domains that are located directly below the second-level domains.

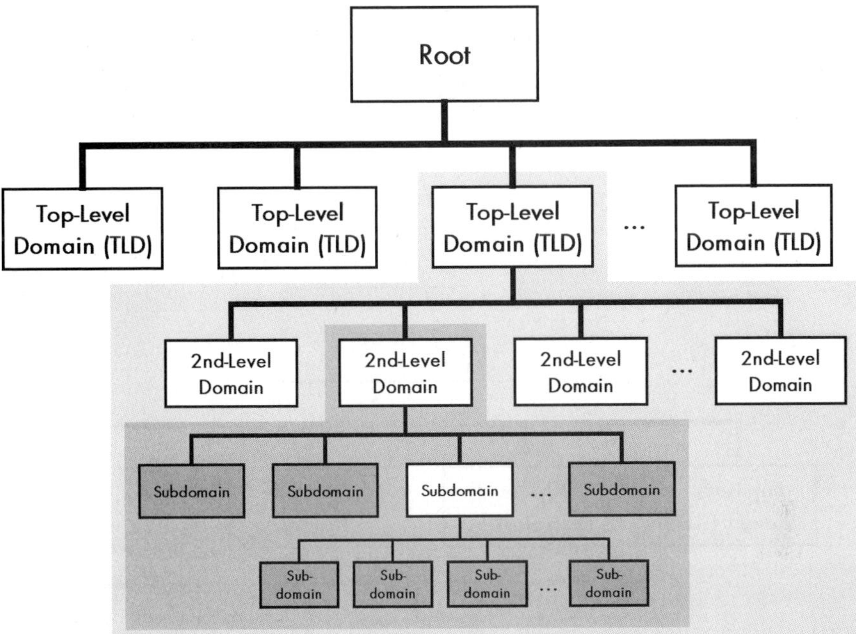

Figure 53-2: DNS tree-related and domain-related terminology *The top of the DNS name space is the root of the tree, and it has no name. Under the root comes any number of top-level domains (TLDs). Within each of these can be placed second-level domains, then within those subdomains, and so forth. Some of the tree terminology used in DNS is also shown here. The portion of the tree with the light shading is one branch; the darker area highlights a smaller subbranch within that branch. The darkest nodes within that area are the leaves of that smaller branch of the tree.*

KEY CONCEPT The top of the DNS name space is the *root*. Under the root come *top-level domains*, and within these are *second-level domains* and then *subdomains*. In theory, any number of levels of subdomains can be created. A *branch* is any contiguous portion of the DNS tree. A *leaf* is a domain with nothing underneath it in the structure, and it usually represents a single device.

The term *subdomain* can also be used generically, like the word *domain* itself. In that case, it refers simply to the relationship between two domains, with a subdomain being under another domain in the structure. This means, for example, that top-level domains can be said to be subdomains of the root; every second-level domain is a subdomain of a top-level domain, and so on. But again, sometimes *subdomain* means specifically a third-level or lower domain.

DNS Family-Related Terminology

Another set of terminology related to DNS compares the tree structure not to a living tree, but to another analogy: a family tree. These terms are most often used to describe how a particular domain relates to the other domains or subdomains around it, so they are relative terms. The following family-related terms are common (see Figure 53-3).

Parent Domain This is the domain that is above this one in the hierarchy. For example, the root domain is the parent of all top-level domains.

Child This is a domain at the next level down from this one in the hierarchy. Thus, the top-level domains are *children* of the root.

Sibling This is a peer at the same level as this one in the hierarchy, with the same parent. Thus, all top-level domains are *siblings* with the root as a parent; all second-level domains within a particular top-level domain are siblings, and so on.

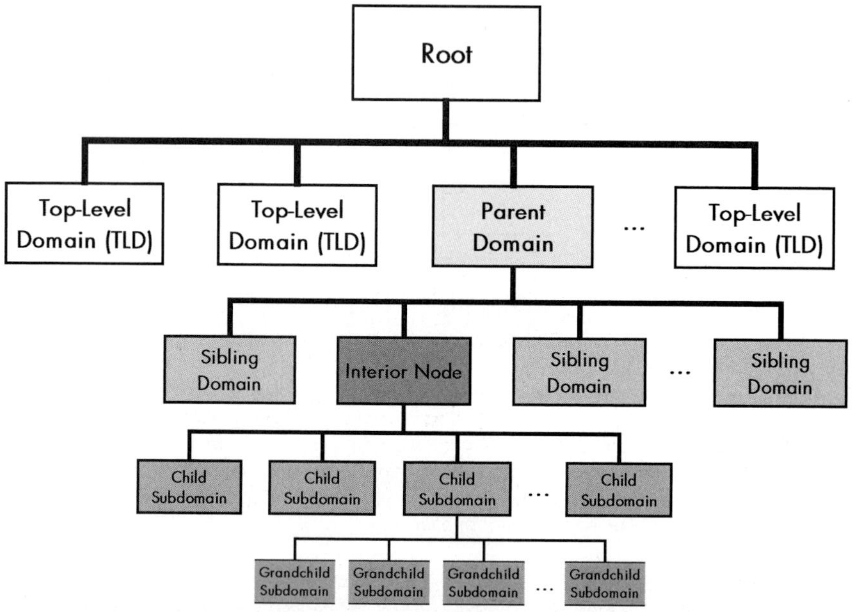

Figure 53-3: DNS name space "family tree" *This diagram is similar to Figure 53-2, but the nodes are labeled to show the family-oriented terminology sometimes used in DNS. In this case, the names are relative to the interior node shown in the darker shade. The domain immediately above it is its parent node. Other nodes on the same level are siblings, and subdomains within it are children of that node.*

> **KEY CONCEPT** The domain above a given domain in the DNS name space is called its *parent domain*. Domains at the same level within the same parent are *siblings*. Subdomains are called *children* of that domain.

Like a real tree, the DNS name structure must be a true tree in its structure. Every domain can have only one parent (except the root), just as every branch of a tree connects to only one limb (except the root/trunk). Also, no loops can appear in the structure; you cannot have a domain whose child is also its parent, for example.

> **KEY CONCEPT** A DNS name space must be arranged as a true topological tree. This means each domain can have only one parent, and no loops are permitted in the structure.

Keep in mind that even though the name hierarchy represents an arrangement of named devices, it is only a logical structure. There is no necessary correspondence to the physical location of devices. A domain with 10 children may represent 11 devices in 11 different countries. We'll explore this more when we look at DNS authority structures in the next chapter.

DNS Labels, Names, and Syntax Rules

We've seen how the DNS name space hierarchy allows us to arrange domains into a virtual tree that reflects the characteristics of how the devices themselves are organized. While using a hierarchical name space is inherently more complex than a flat name space, it yields a powerful result: the ability to specify names that can be locally managed while remaining globally unique. At the same time, the complexity of the tree yields the benefit of relatively simple name construction using domain identifiers.

DNS Labels and Label Syntax Rules

Naming in DNS begins with giving each domain, or node, in the DNS name space a text *label*. The label identifies the domain within the structure and must follow several syntax rules:

Length Each label can theoretically be from 0 to 63 characters in length. In practice, a length of 1 to about 20 characters is most common, with a special exception for the label assigned to the root of the tree (which is 0 characters in length, as explained in the next section).

Symbols Letters and numbers are allowed, as well as the dash character (-). No other punctuation is permitted. For example, an underscore (_) cannot be used in a label.

Case Labels are not case-sensitive. For example, *Jabberwocky* and *jabberwocky* are equivalent domain name labels.

Every label must be unique within its parent domain. So, for example, if we have a top-level domain called Rocks, we can have only one subdomain within Rocks called Crystal. Due to the case-insensitivity of labels, we cannot have both CRYSTAL and Crystal within Rocks, because they are considered the same.

It is this concept of *local uniqueness* within a parent domain that ensures the uniqueness of names as a whole, while allowing local control over naming. Whoever is in charge of the Rocks domain can assign names to as many individual objects or subdomains as he likes, as long as those names are unique within the domain. Someone else, say, the maintainer of the Glass domain, can also create a subdomain called Crystal within Glass. There will not be a conflict, because the Glass and Rocks domains are separate. Of course, since all top-level domains have the same parent (the root), all top-level domains must be unique.

KEY CONCEPT Each node in the DNS name space is identified by a *label*. Each label must be unique within a parent domain, but it does not need to be unique across domains. This enables each domain to have local control over the names of subdomains, without causing any conflicts in the full domain names created on a global level.

Domain Name Construction

Each individual domain within the domain name structure can be uniquely identified using the sequence of labels that starts from the root of the tree and progresses down to that domain. The labels at each level in the hierarchy are listed in sequence, starting with the highest level, from right to left, separated by dots. The result is the formal definition of a *domain name.*

The root of the name space is given a zero-length, null name by default; that is, the label for the root exists, but it's empty. This is done because the root technically is part of every domain name, so it must be included in every domain name. If it were something long like Root, we would need to include that at the end of every domain name. This would simply make every name longer, while not really adding any useful information—we already know every domain name is under the root.

Consider the example of a top-level domain called Rocks, within which is a second-level domain Crystal. The domain name of Rocks is "Rocks.", with the dot separating Rocks and the empty label (the null root). In practice, the trailing dot is often omitted, so the domain name of the top-level domain Rocks can be considered as just "Rocks". The subdomain Crystal within Rocks has the domain name "Crystal.Rocks". If we had a device named Salt within the Crystal.Rocks domain, it would be called "Salt.Crystal.Rocks". This is fairly straightforward, as you can see in Figure 53-4.

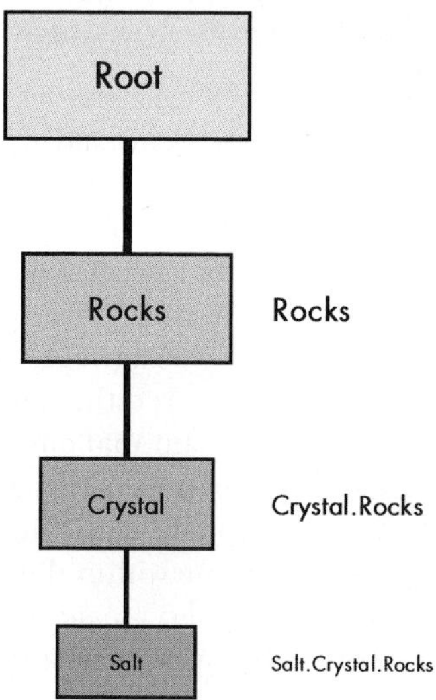

Figure 53-4: DNS labels and domain name construction *Each node in the DNS name space has a label (except the root, whose label is null). The domain name for a node is constructed simply by placing in order the sequence of labels from the top of the tree down to the individual domain, going from right to left, separating each label with a dot (period).*

We can use these names to easily identify subdomains of a particular domain. For example, if we start with Salt.Crystal.Rocks, it's obvious that Crystal.Rocks is its parent domain. It's also clear that both Crystal.Rocks and Salt.Crystal.Rocks are subdomains of Rocks; one is a single level down from Rocks, and the other is two levels down.

Note that there is a maximum limit of 255 characters for a complete domain name, for implementation purposes. In practice, most domain names are much shorter than this limit, as it would violate the whole purpose of domain names if we let them get so long that no one could remember them.

> **KEY CONCEPT** A *domain name* is a string of text that uniquely identifies a particular node in the name space. The domain name for a node is constructed by concatenating in right-to-left order all the labels in the branch of the DNS tree, starting from the top of the tree down to the particular node, separating each by a dot (period).

Finally, note that in many protocols, it is possible to specify a particular resource within a domain name by providing a directory structure after a name. This is done using the standard TCP/IP URL syntax, where a path is indicated using slashes to separate subdirectories. For example, a specific file at Salt.Crystal.Rocks might be located at Salt.Crystal.Rocks/chem/composition. While DNS names are case-insensitive, the labels in a path are case-sensitive. So, this example would be different from Salt.Crystal.Rocks/chem/Composition. See the discussion of URL syntax in Chapter 70 for more details.

Absolute (Fully Qualified) and Relative (Partially Qualified) Domain Name Specifications

As explained in the previous section, we can specify the domain name of any node in the DNS name hierarchy by simply starting at the root node and following the sequence of subdomains down to the node in question, listing each level's labels separated by a dot. When we do this, we get a single name that uniquely identifies a particular device. In practice, domain names can be specified by their fully qualified names or their partially qualified names.

Fully Qualified Domain Names

Technically, if a top-level domain A contains a subdomain B that contains subdomain C, the full domain name for C is "C.B.A.". This is called the *fully qualified domain name (FQDN)* for the node. Here, the word *qualified* is synonymous with *specified.* The domain name C.B.A. is fully qualified because it gives the full location of the specific domain that bears its name within the whole DNS name space.

FQDNs are also sometimes called *absolute* domain names. This term reflects the fact that you can refer unambiguously to the name of any device using its FQDN from any other portion of the name space. Using the FQDN always instructs the person or software interpreting the name to start at the root, and then follow the sequence of domain labels from right to left, going top to bottom within the tree.

Partially Qualified Domain Names

There are also some situations in which you may refer to a device using an incomplete name specification. This is called a *partially qualified domain name (PQDN)*, which means that the name only partially specifies the location of the device. By definition, a PQDN is ambiguous, because it doesn't give the full path to the domain. Thus, you can use a PQDN only within the context of a particular parent domain, whose absolute domain name is known.

We can find the FQDN of a partially specified domain name by appending the partial name to the absolute name of the parent domain. For example, if we have the PQDN Z within the context of the FQDN "Y.X.", we know the FQDN for Z is "Z.Y.X.".

Why bother with this? The answer is convenience. An administrator for a domain can use PQDNs as a shorthand to refer to devices or subdomains without needing to repeat the entire full name. For example, suppose you are in charge of the computer science department at the University of Widgetopia. The domain name for the department as a whole is "cs.widgetopia.edu.", and the individual hosts you manage are named after fruit. In the DNS files you maintain, you could refer to each device by its FQDN every time; for example, "apple.cs.widgetopia.edu.", "banana.cs .widgetopia.edu.", and so on. But it's easier to tell the software, "If you see a name that is not fully qualified, assume it is in the cs.widgetopia.edu domain." Then you can just call the machines apple, banana, and so on. Whenever the DNS software sees a PQDN such as kiwi, it will treat it as "kiwi.cs.widgetopia.edu.".

KEY CONCEPT A *fully qualified domain name (FQDN)* is a complete domain name that uniquely identifies a node in the DNS name space by giving the full path of labels from the root of the tree down to that node. It defines the absolute location of a domain. In contrast, a *partially qualified domain name (PQDN)* specifies only a portion of a domain name. It is a relative name that has meaning only within a particular context. The partial name must be interpreted within that context to fully identify the node.

I mentioned earlier in this chapter that the trailing dot for the null root domain is usually omitted. This is true in common parlance and when users specify a domain name in an application. You don't use the trailing dot in your web browser, for instance. However, the dot is used to clearly distinguish a FQDN from a PQDN within DNS master files. This allows us to use both FQDNs and PQDNs together. In our example, apple would refer to "apple.cs.widgetopia.edu.", but "apple.com." would refer to the FQDN for Apple Computer, Inc. You must be careful about watching the dots here, because apple.com (without a trailing period) would be a PQDN and would refer to "apple.com.cs.widgetopia.edu.", not the domain of Apple Computer.

54

DNS NAME REGISTRATION, PUBLIC ADMINISTRATION, ZONES, AND AUTHORITIES

The previous chapter explained how the Domain Name System (DNS) name space consists of a hierarchy of domains and subdomains. From the root, we have a number of top-level domains, then second-level domains below them, and still lower-level domains below that. The obvious questions then become: How do we determine the shape and structure of the name space, and who will manage it? More specifically, who will control the root of the tree and decide what the top-level domains will be called? How will we then subdivide control over the rest of the name space? How do we ensure there are no conflicts in choosing the names of sibling subdomains within a domain?

DNS can be used on private networks controlled by a single organization, and if so, that organization is obviously in charge of the name space. We'll discuss private naming, but in reality, it's just not that interesting. The vast majority of DNS use occurs on the public Internet. Here, we have a much greater challenge, because we need to construct a name space that spans the globe and covers millions of machines managed by different organizations. For this, we need a very capable *name registration* process and administration methods to support it.

In this chapter, I will describe the process of name registration and how authorities are managed within DNS, focusing on the public Internet. I begin with a description of the DNS hierarchical authority structure and how it relates to the hierarchical name space, and a discussion of the concepts behind the DNS distributed name database. I describe the Internet's organizational and geopolitical top-level domains, and how they are administered by various authorities. I then discuss how authority is delegated to the second-level and lower-level domains, and how public registration of domain names works, including how public registration issues and problems are resolved. I explain how the DNS name space is partitioned into administrative zones of authority, and then I conclude with a brief discussion of private DNS name registration.

RELATED INFORMATION *Most TCP/IP implementations include a special utility called* whois *that can be used to interrogate the DNS distributed name database to obtain registration information about domains. This application can be very useful for troubleshooting. For details, see the section discussing whois in Chapter 88.*

DNS Hierarchical Authority Structure and the Distributed Name Database

In the previous chapter, I explained that the central concept of naming in DNS is based on *domains*. Each domain can be considered akin to a sphere of influence or control. A domain "spreads its wings" over all the objects and subdomains that it contains. Due to this concept of influence, when we consider any DNS name space, we see that it is hierarchical because it reflects a hierarchy of organizations that control domains and the nodes within them. This means that there is a *hierarchical authority structure* that complements the hierarchical name structure in DNS.

The primary reason why the name space hierarchy leads to an authority hierarchy is the requirement that sibling subdomains be unique within a domain. As soon as we have a need for uniqueness, we must have some sort of authority or process that ensures that each subdomain or object picks a different name within that domain. This is what name registration is all about.

This concept of a hierarchical authority structure is a bit abstract, but it's easier to understand if we examine a sample DNS name space and discuss the issues involved in assigning names within it. Naturally, we want to start at the top of the name hierarchy, with the root domain, null.

The DNS Root Domain Central Authority

To start off the name space, we must create top-level domains (TLDs) within the root. Now, each of these must be unique, so one authority must manage the creation of all TLDs. This means that the authority that controls the root domain controls the entire name space.

In the case of the Internet, this central authority is ultimately responsible for every name in DNS. The central DNS authority for the Internet, which controls the creation of TLDs, was initially called the *Network Information Center*. It was later the *Internet Assigned Numbers Authority (IANA)*, which is also responsible for protocol numbers, IP addresses, and more. These functions are now shared by IANA and the *Internet Corporation for Assigned Names and Numbers (ICANN)*. We'll discuss the specific TLDs of the Internet in the next few chapters; IANA, ICANN, and related organizations are discussed in the section on Internet registration authorities in Chapter 3.

TLD Authorities

At the next level down in the authority hierarchy, we create second-level domains within each of the TLDs. Each TLD must itself be managed using a coordinating authority, however, this is not necessarily the organization that runs the root (IANA). IANA *delegates* authority for some of the TLDs to other organizations.

IANA may delegate control for each TLD to a different authority at this level of the hierarchy. In fact, there can be completely different rules for managing the creation of second-level domains in one TLD than there are in another. And in some TLDs, there are multiple authorities that work together on name registration.

Lower-Level Authority Delegation

This process of authority delegation continues as we move down the name space hierarchy. At each level, the name space becomes more specific.

If we use an organizational hierarchy, like the .COM TLD, we generally delegate authority for each second-level domain to the organization whose name it represents. So, for example, IBM.COM is managed by IBM. Since IBM is huge, it may itself subdivide the authority structure further, but smaller organizations probably won't.

Authority Hierarchy's Relationship to the Name Hierarchy

The authority hierarchy is complementary to the name hierarchy; they are not exactly the same. It is not necessary that there be a different authority for every level of the hierarchy. In many cases, a single authority may manage a section of the name space that spans more than one level of the structure. For example, IANA manages the Internet root domain (null) and also the .INT TLD, but other TLDs are managed by other organizations. The name hierarchy is divided into *zones of authority* that reflect the hierarchy of authorities that manage parts of the name space.

Also, authority over a domain doesn't necessarily imply physical control. A domain can contain subdomains that are managed by organizations on different continents, and a single subdomain can contain named devices that are on different continents as well.

The DNS Distributed Name Database

Of course, with authority comes responsibility, and the main responsibility an authority has for a domain is registering names within the domain. When a name is registered, a set of data is created for it, which can then be used by internetwork devices to resolve the name into an address or perform other functions.

The set of all the data describing all DNS domains constitutes the DNS *name database.* Just as registration authority is distributed and hierarchical, this database is distributed and hierarchical. In other words, there is no single place where all DNS name information is stored. Instead, DNS servers carry resource records (see Chapter 57) that describe the domains for which they have authority. As you'll see, the fact that this database is distributed has major implications on how name resolution is carried out.

> **KEY CONCEPT** The name space of the public Internet is managed by a *hierarchy of authorities* that is similar in structure to the hierarchical DNS name space, though not identical. The top of the hierarchy is centrally managed by IANA/ICANN, which delegates authority to other organizations for registering names in various other parts of the hierarchy. The information about name registrations is maintained in resource records stored in various locations, which form a distributed name database on the Internet.

DNS Organizational (Generic) TLDs and Authorities

The top of the DNS name hierarchy is managed by a central authority, which controls the entire name space by virtue of deciding which TLDs are allowed to exist. Obviously, it is very important that a great deal of thought go into how the TLDs are chosen. A poor design at this top level would make the entire hierarchy poorly reflect the actual structure of organizations using the name space.

The creators of DNS could have chosen any number of ways to structure the Internet's name hierarchy. One obvious possibility is to structure the Internet based on geopolitical boundaries: countries, states, and so forth. Another sensible idea is to structure the name space based on types of organizations.

The beauty of the hierarchical name space is that we don't need to choose between different methods of structuring the name space. We can use more than one technique at the same time, and this is exactly what was done when DNS was first implemented. Both the organization type and geography structures were used for TLDs. This gives multiple options for name registration for most groups and individuals.

I'll begin here by discussing organizational TLDs, and then we'll look at geopolitical ones. As you'll see, although there are only a handful of organizational TLDs, there is no doubt that they have been much more popular than the geopolitical ones.

Original Generic TLDs

The initial deployment of DNS featured a set of seven top-level domains that are called *generic* TLDs. The idea was that each company or organization could choose a name within one of these TLDs; they were generic enough that every organization would find a place that suited them. I prefer to call them *organizational*, because they divide the generic portion of the name space by organization type.

The initial TLDs and their original intended organization types were as follows:

.ARPA A temporary domain used many years ago for transition to DNS; today, this domain is used for reverse name resolution (see Chapter 56).

.COM Corporations and businesses

.EDU Universities and other educational organizations

.GOV Government agencies

.MIL Military organizations

.NET Organizations that implement, deal with, or manage networking technologies and/or the Internet

.ORG Other organizations that don't fit into any of the previous classifications

At first glance, this seems like a reasonable way to cover the organizations of the world. However, since the .ARPA domain (whose name refers to the ARPAnet, the precursor of the modern Internet, as described in Chapter 8) was temporary, this left only six categories for all other organizations. Also, the TLDs weren't all used as was originally foreseen. For example, the .GOV and .MIL domains were not used for all types of government and military organizations, but primarily for the United States federal government and military. The .EDU domain ended up being used only for universities, again in the United States.

This left only three common TLDs—.COM, .NET, and .ORG—for almost all other groups and companies that wanted to use the organizational hierarchy. Since there were only three such TLDs, they quickly became very crowded, especially the .COM domain. A new fourth domain, .INT for international organizations, was added fairly soon to the original seven. However, it was intended only for a small number of organizations, such as international standards bodies.

Of course, there was no inherent reason why the generic domains should be limited to only the few that were originally created.

New Generic TLDs

Over the years, many suggestions were made for new generic TLDs that would expand the number of possible second-level domain names and also provide better categorization for different organization types—that is, to make the generic TLDs less generic. There was some resistance at first to adopting these new names, especially because there were so many different ideas about what new TLDs should be created.

IANA took input from a lot of people and followed a complex procedure to determine what new TLDs should be made. In 2001 and 2002, approval was given for the creation of several new TLDs, and decisions were made about authorities for administering them.

Of the new TLDs approved in the past few years, the number that has achieved widespread popularity is, to my knowledge, zero. Humans are creatures of inertia, and most people are still used to names ending in .COM, .NET, or .ORG. In time this may change, but it will probably take a few years.

NOTE *Some people actually felt that adding new generic TLDs was a bad idea, since it makes organizations potentially more difficult to locate (due to the possibility of a name ending in a variety of different TLDs). This is debatable, however, especially since the exhaustion of address space in the existing TLDs means many companies have needed to choose unintuitive domain names anyway.*

Table 54-1 shows all the current generic TLDs and describes how they are used, and it lists the current central authority that manages each. The original TLDs are highlighted in italics (I am including .INT as an original TLD, since it was created long before the "new" ones). Figure 54-1 shows the 15 generic TLDs in graphical form.

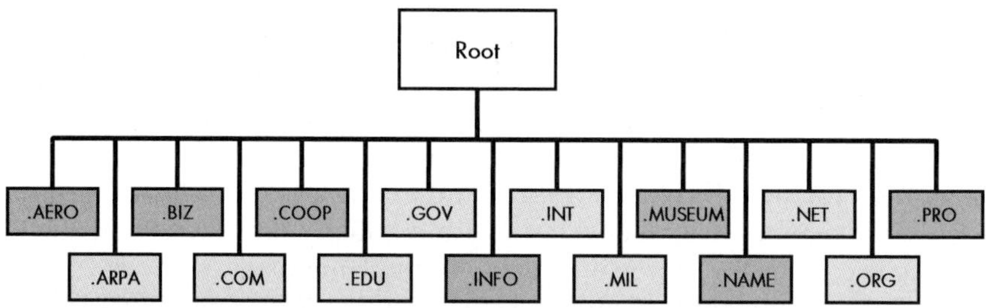

Figure 54-1: Internet DNS organizational (generic) TLDs *There are 15 generic TLDs currently defined for the Internet. They are shown here in alphabetical order, with the original TLDs shown in light shading and the new ones added in 2001/2002 in darker shading.*

Table 54-1: Internet DNS Organizational (Generic) Top-Level Domains

Generic TLD	Abbreviation For	Authority	Description
.AERO	Aerospace	Société Internationale de Télécommunications Aéronautiques (SITA)	Used for members of the aerospace industry, such as airlines and airports. (Yes, that is French!)
.ARPA	Address and Routing Parameter Area	IANA/ ICANN	First defined as a temporary domain for migration from the older host table system, the *ARPA* of course originally stood for the Advanced Research Projects Agency, creators of the predecessors of the Internet. Today, the .ARPA domain is used for internal Internet management purposes; the expanded name shown in this table was, I believe, chosen to fit the acronym. The best-known use of this domain is for reverse DNS lookups.
.BIZ	Business	NeuLevel, Inc.	Used for businesses. Intended as a competitor to .COM.
.COM	Commercial Organizations	VeriSign, Inc.	Originally intended for corporations and other commercial interests, .COM is also widely used for other purposes, including small businesses and even individuals who like the popularity of the .COM domain.

(continued)

Table 54-1: Internet DNS Organizational (Generic) Top-Level Domains (continued)

Generic TLD	Abbreviation For	Authority	Description
.COOP	Cooperative Associations	Dot Cooperation, LLC	Used for cooperative associations.
.EDU	Education	Educause	Originally intended for all types of educational organizations, .EDU is now used only for degree-granting higher-education institutions accredited in the US. Other educational institutions such as public schools usually use the country code TLDs.
.GOV	Government	U.S. General Services Administration	Reserved for the U.S. federal government.
.INFO	Information	Afilias, Ltd.	A very generic TLD designed for information resources of various sorts. It is unrestricted, in that anyone can register any sort of organization in .INFO. It's also positioned as an alternative to .COM.
.INT	International	IANA .int Domain Registry	Used only for large organizations established by international treaty.
.MIL	Military	U.S. DoD Network Information Center	Reserved for the U.S. military.
.MUSEUM	Museum	Museum Domain Management Association	Take a guess. See http://index.museum for a complete list of museums using this TLD.
.NAME	Names	Global Name Registry	In the original generic hierarchy, there was no place set aside for individuals to register names for themselves, so people would create domains like jonesfamily.org. This was not ideal, so .NAME was created as a place for individuals and families to register a domain for their names. .NAME also competes with the country code TLDs.
.NET	Network	VeriSign, Inc.	This was supposed to be used only for Internet service providers (ISPs) and other organizations working intimately with the Internet or networking. Due to the exhaustion of name spaces in .COM and .ORG, many .NET domains are registered to other organizations, however.
.ORG	Organizations	Public Interest Registry	Originally intended for organizations not fitting into the other generic TLDs, .ORG quickly became associated with professional and nonprofit organizations. It is possible, however, to have a for-profit company use an .ORG name.
.PRO	Professional	RegistryPro	Reserved for credentialed professionals such as lawyers and doctors.

KEY CONCEPT One of the two ways in which the Internet's DNS name space is divided is using a set of generic TLDs. These TLDs are intended to provide a place for all companies and organizations to be named based on their organization type. There were originally six such domains, but this has been expanded so that there are now 15.

DNS Geopolitical (Country Code) TLDs and Authorities

In theory, the generic TLDs would be sufficient to meet the needs of all the individuals, companies, and groups in the world. This is especially true since .ORG, by definition, is a catchall that can include anyone or anything. Thus, in an ideal world, everyone in the world would have been able to find a place in those simple domains.

However, back at the beginning of DNS, its creators recognized that the generic TLDs might not meet the needs of everyone around the world, especially in certain cases. There are several reasons for this:

Americentricism of the Generic Domains I don't mean this as a criticism (I'm an American citizen and love my country!). It is indisputable, however, that United States organizations and companies dominate the generic TLDs. This is not surprising, given that the Internet was first developed in the United States, but it still presents a problem for certain groups. For example, if the United States military controls the .MIL domain, where does, say, Great Britain's military fit into the name space?

Language Most of the generic domains are populated by organizations that primarily do business in English. There are hundreds of languages in the world, however, and it's easier for the speakers of those tongues if they can more readily locate resources they can understand.

Local Control Countries around the world rarely agree on much, and they certainly differ on how organizations within their nations should have their Internet presence arranged. There was a desire on the parts of many to allow nations to have the ability to set up subsets of the name space for their own use.

For these and other reasons, the Internet's name space was set up with a set of *country code* TLDs paralleling the generic ones, sometimes called *ccTLDs*. I call these *geopolitical* TLDs, since they are based on geopolitical divisions of the world (similar to the example I used in the overview of the DNS name space in Chapter 53). In this hierarchy, every country of the world is assigned a particular two-letter code as a TLD, with a specific authority put in charge of administering the domain. For example, the ccTLD for Great Britain is .UK, the one for Canada is .CA, and the one for Japan is .JP. The codes often are more meaningful in the local language than in English. For example, Germany's is .DE, and Switzerland's is .CH.

Country Code Designations

When I said that countries rarely agree on anything, I wasn't kidding. In fact, they can't even agree on what's a country! Real shooting wars have been fought over whether or not a particular territory was independent or part of another nation, and the creators of DNS wanted no part of this sort of controversy. As the IANA website says, "The IANA is not in the business of deciding what is and what is not a country, nor what code letters are appropriate for a particular country."

To remain neutral, IANA's ccTLD codes are taken directly from the standard country abbreviations maintained by the International Organization for Standardization (ISO) in ISO Standard 3166-1. When a country is recognized by the ISO and a code assigned to it on this list, IANA creates it as a TLD. There are presently more than 200 different geopolitical TLDs. You can find the current list of IANA country code TLDs at http://www.iana.org/cctld/cctld-whois.htm.

KEY CONCEPT Due to the limitations of the generic TLDs, a set of *country code* top-level domains was created. This *geopolitical hierarchy* allows each nation on earth to set up its own name system based on its own requirements and to administer it in the manner it sees fit. The IANA determines what is a country based on official decisions made by ISO.

Country Code TLD Authorities

Each country has the authority to set up its TLD with whatever internal substructure it chooses; again, this is the power of a hierarchical structure.

Some countries enforce a further geographical substructure at the lower levels. For example, the .US domain for the United States was originally set up so that all second-level domains were two-letter state abbreviations (this was later changed).

Other countries may actually use organizational subdomains within their country code. For example, Great Britain has .CO.UK for companies in the country (like .COM but for the UK only; they left off the *M*), and .COM.AU is for corporations in Australia.

Other countries may not have any particular substructure at all, especially if they are small.

Leasing/Sale of Country Code Domains

Interestingly, some very small countries with recognizable country codes, especially to English speakers, have used their codes for very creative purposes, including selling or renting the name space to enterprising companies.

A good example is the .TV domain, which technically belongs to the island nation of *Tuvalu.* Of course, to most people, "TV" means something quite different. Some folks thought that domain names ending in .TV might be popular in the English-speaking world, so they formed a company called The .TV Corporation and negotiated with the government of Tuvalu to use the .TV domain. Today, the authority for this TLD is this corporation, headquartered in California! Similar arrangements can be found with the .CC, .NU, .TO, and other TLDs.

This serves as a good reminder that the name space is logical and not physical. Obviously, the many computers with .TV names are not actually located on a remote island in the South Pacific. Similarly, if a website ends with .CA, for example, it probably represents a Canadian organization, but that doesn't necessarily mean the website itself is actually hosted in Canada.

Drawbacks of the Geopolitical TLDs

The geopolitical domains have been very popular for certain uses. National governments and other official institutions like to use them, for obvious reasons. Typing www.gov.*xx* or www.government.*xx*, where *xx* is a country code is likely to bring you to the national government website of most countries. Some companies and organizations use the ccTLDs because they allow them to choose a name already taken in the generic hierarchies or simply to express national pride.

For many other companies and organizations, however, the generic TLDs have been much more popular than the country codes. I think the most important reason for this is that organizations are easier to locate using the generic domains.

Here's a good example of what I mean. In the town near where I live, a new grocery store called Aldi recently opened. I like the store and wanted to learn more about it, so I fired up my web browser and sought out its website. Yes, I could have typed it into a search engine, but like most people, I'm lazy. It was much easier to just enter www.aldi.com into my browser, and lo and behold, up popped the website of Aldi International.

Now, Aldi is actually headquartered in Germany, and the company does have a website at www.aldi.de as well. But I didn't know that. I found them easily by going to www.aldi.com, because I didn't need to know their physical location, and because I know that most large companies have a .COM domain. Of course, being findable is very important, especially for commercial organizations trying to do business.

Another good example is the United States, which has its own country code, .US, in addition to dominating the generic TLDs. The authority in charge of this domain initially chose to make it follow a strict geographical hierarchy, so every domain had to be of the form *organization.city.state-code*.us. So, to use this part of the name space, a company in Boston must be within the .boston.ma.us domain. That's very neat and logical, but it makes names both longer and harder to guess than the generic equivalents.

Suppose you wanted to get information on metals giant Alcoa. If you're in the industry, you might know Alcoa is located in Pittsburgh, but if not, which is easier to find: www.alcoa.pittsburgh.pa.us or www.alcoa.com? Anyone here know how to spell Albuquerque?

It is for this reason that the .US domain achieved success in certain segments of society but not in others, especially commercial entities (corporations). The strict hierarchy does have some real advantages, such as avoiding name space conflicts, but its disadvantages were such that the rules were recently relaxed in the .US domain.

Public Registration for Second-Level and Lower Domains

The IANA is in charge of deciding which TLDs exist in the Internet name space, and as such, they are ultimately responsible for all names in the Internet. The entire point of the authority hierarchy, however, is that IANA should not be responsible for the whole name space. So, while IANA maintains control over certain TLDs, such as .INT and .ARPA, control for managing the others is delegated to secondary authorities for each TLD.

Just as IANA had the choice of how to delegate authority to the subdomains of the root domain, the organization in charge of each TLD gets to make the same decision about how second-level domains are to be created under the TLD.

In many TLDs, especially the generic ones, second-level domains are assigned directly to individuals or organizations. For example, a company named XYZ Industries might want to get the domain xyzindustries.com.

In other TLDs, second-level domains are set up in a particular structure, like the state codes used in the .US domain. There, you need to go down more levels, but eventually you get to the point where companies and people register their own domains. For example, in the .US domain, XYZ Industries might want to register xyz.phoenix.az.us if it were headquartered in Phoenix.

This transition point between the authorities granted responsibility for parts of the name space and the regular people and groups who want to get names is important. A process of *public registration* had to be established to allow such name assignment to occur in a consistent and manageable way. This was not that difficult to accomplish back when the original generic TLDs and country code TLDs were first created. The Internet was quite small, and it made sense to just have the authority in charge of each TLD perform registrations within that TLD. This ensured that there was no duplication of names within a TLD with a minimum of fuss.

Registration Authority

For very important generic TLDs such as .COM, .NET, and .ORG, the authority in charge of registration was the Internet Network Information Center (the InterNIC). The InterNIC was set up as a service administered by the United States government, who later granted the contract to manage it to Network Solutions Inc. (NSI). NSI was eventually purchased by VeriSign, who later spun it off as a separate venture. (Things change quickly in the networking world!)

NSI single-handedly performed all registrations within the .COM, .NET, and .ORG TLDs for many years. The popularity of the original generic TLDs, however, led to an explosion in demand for name registration in these domains in the 1990s. Having a single company in charge of registration led to this becoming another bottleneck in the Internet's Domain Name System. There were also many folks who didn't like the lack of accountability and competition that came with having a single monopoly in charge of registration. The InterNIC could set its own price and originally charged $35 per year per domain name, then later $50 per year.

In the late 1990s, responsibility for name registration was given to ICANN. The registration process was *deregulated*, to borrow a term referring to removal of monopolies from industries like power generation. As of December 1999, there was still a single authority with overall responsibility for each TLD, including .COM, .NET, and .ORG.

Today, NSI is still the authority running .COM and .NET. However, it isn't the only organization that registers names within these TLDs. It further delegates registration authority to a multitude of other companies, called *accredited registrars*. Any registrar can register names within the TLD(s) for which they are accredited.

Registration Coordination

Naturally, coordination becomes much more of a concern when you have multiple companies registering names in a TLD. A special set of technical and administrative procedures is followed to ensure that there are no problems, such as two registrars trying to grab a name at the same time.

The system has worked well, and those who wish to use TLDs where competition exists now can choose from a variety of registering companies. The most noticeable result of this was also the most predictable one: the cost of registering a domain name in the deregulated generic TLDs is usually much lower than the fees originally charged by the InterNIC.

Once a company, individual, or organization has a registered lower-level domain, he/she/it becomes the authority for that domain. Use of the domain then becomes private, but depending on how the domain is used, further public name registration may be required. See the discussion of private registration, near the end of this chapter, for more information.

DNS Public Registration Disputes and Dispute Resolution

The Internet started off as a medium for research into networking, evolved into a system for interconnecting scientists, and ended up as a global communications tool used by just about everyone. As part of this evolution, the Internet also became a very important part of how business is done in the world. Money started to come into the Internet picture in the early 1990s, and just a few short years later, its impact on the Internet was so significant that the growth of the stock market to dizzying heights in the late 1990s is now often called "the Internet bubble."

Public Registration Disputes

Unfortunately, the increasing importance of the Internet to commercial interests crashed headlong into the noncommercial original design of Internet technology, and nowhere was this more evident than in DNS. Since there were only a few generic TLDs, each name within a TLD had to be unique, and humans are often confrontational creatures, it didn't take long before arguments broke out over who should be able to use what name and why. And, of course, from there, it didn't take long before lawsuits and other unpleasantries were common.

There are a surprising number of significant problems associated with public registration of domain names:

Corporate Name Conflicts The .COM domain is for corporations, but many corporations have the same name. The ACME Furniture Company, the ACME Restaurant Supply Corporation, and ACME Footwear, Inc., probably all would like to have the acme.com domain. But there can be only one such domain within .COM. (These are fictional examples; acme.com is actually owned by an organization called *Acme Labs.*)

Corporate/Individual/Small Business Name Conflicts There are many corporations that have names similar to or even identical to the names of individuals, leading to potential conflicts. For example, suppose your first name is Wendy and you own a small fabric store called Wendy's Fabrics. But you are Internet savvy and decide you want to register wendys.com as soon as you hear about the Internet in 1993. Then this big hamburger chain comes along and has a problem with that.

NOTE *To my knowledge, no such issue arose with respect to Wendy's, but there actually was a widely publicized case that shows just how recently most corporations were out of the loop with respect to domain naming. In 1994, a writer for* Wired *magazine was astonished to find that the mcdonalds.com domain name was unregistered! To show just how unregulated the registration process was, he registered it himself, and caused a bit of a stir as a result. The Golden Arches folks eventually acquired the domain from him in an amicable arrangement, where he relinquished the name and they made a donation to charity.*

Corporate Warfare A particularly ugly type of conflict is when companies intentionally try to take business from each other by registering names that have nothing to do with their own companies. An example would be if Burger King had tried to register mcdonalds.com and use it to advertise Burger King products. (Which they didn't do, I might add, so please nobody sue me!) Another example is when companies try to use alternate TLDs, such as registering burgerking.org to confuse people trying to find burgerking.com. In fact, many companies have taken the step of registering their names in many different TLDs to prevent this sort of thing from happening.

Cybersquatting Some ambitious (to choose a nice term) individuals, recognizing early on the potential value of certain names, registered large volumes of names with the hopes of reselling them. Many people condemned this as exploitative, and the term *cybersquatting* was created to refer to this type of activity. Unfortunately, a lot of money was made this way, and there are many domain names that, to this day, cannot be used because they have been reserved indefinitely by people or individuals who will never use them.

Deceptive Naming Practices Another type of somewhat diabolic creativity has been displayed by people who seek to take advantage of the inability of some of us to spell. For example, if you were a competitor of a large company called Superb Transceivers Inc., which registered superbtransceivers.com, you might register superbtransceivers.com and redirect traffic from there to your own domain. Another example takes advantage of the common mix-up between the letter *O* and 0 (zero). For example, a software company once registered micros0ft.com, much to the chagrin of the Redmond, Washington software giant.

Incidentally, it was all this nonsense that led, in part, to the clamor for new generic TLDs. Even though the more complicated schemes used by TLDs like .US are not very popular, they have a huge advantage over the generic domains. Since all these registrations are geographic, there are far fewer conflicts. For example, the ACME Furniture Company might use acme.seattle.wa.us, the ACME Restaurant Supply Corporation might have acme.mendocino.ca.us, and ACME Footwear, Inc., could go with acme.anchorage.ak.us. A dispute would arise only when organizations have the same name and also are in the same state and town. You could still have three Joe's Pizza Parlors in Chicago duke it out, but it's not likely to be a problem for big companies.

Methods of Registration Dispute Resolution

So, how do we resolve these situations? As the saying goes, it can be done either the easy way or the hard way. Here are some methods that have been used for dispute resolution:

Domain Name Sharing Sometimes, the antagonists agree on a productive solution. One particularly constructive idea is to agree to *share* the domain name. For example, the three different ACME companies could each create their own more specifically named domains, such as acmefurniture.com, acmerestaurantsupply.com, and acmefootwear.com. Then they might agree to have the www.acme.com registered to nobody, by having one company register it and not use it for anything. Even better, they could set it up with a simple web page that says the domain is shared, with a link to the three sites. Unfortunately, it seems grade school children understand the concept of sharing better than most corporate executives do, so this type of resolution is rare.

Domain Name Purchase Another option is purchase. If a big company wants a domain name already registered by an individual or a small business, it will often just purchase the name, as this is the easiest thing to do. During the height of the Internet mania, there were domain names that sold for *millions* of dollars—just for the right to use the name! Many cybersquatters and other speculators got rich selling names.

Litigation Often, the combatants don't play nice, and the usual occurs: threats, intimidation, lawsuits, and so forth. Sometimes, a letter from a lawyer is enough to resolve the issue, especially when some poor individual owning a website gets threatened with legal action by a large company—this has happened many times. However, often the disagreeing parties stick to their guns, especially if two companies lock horns and their lawyers refused to back down. Usually, the matter then ends up in the courts, where it is eventually resolved one way or the other. Usually, claims of trademark infringement would be used by a company challenging a prior domain name registration.

The Uniform Domain Name Dispute Resolution Policy

Lawsuits are expensive and time-consuming, so there was a desire that some other mechanism exist for resolving these conflicts as well. Since the authority for each TLD controls what happens within it, it also has the right to create its own policies for how to deal with these sorts of issues. For the generic TLDs, the original registering authority, the InterNIC, had a dispute resolution policy that allowed people with a complaint to challenge a domain name registration if they had a trademark interest in that name. The policy was controversial for a number of reasons, not the least of which because it led to some domain names being successfully challenged, even if there was no proof of trademark infringement.

The current authority for the generic TLDs, IANA/ICANN, created a new Uniform Domain Name Dispute Resolution Policy (UDRP) in 1999, to better handle domain name conflicts. This policy specifies a procedure whereby a company that has a valid trademark can challenge a domain name if it infringes on the trademark, is confusingly similar to it, or was registered by someone else in bad faith. At the same time, it also lists ways that the original registrant can prove that the registration is valid and should be maintained. This new system eliminates many of the problems associated with public registration of domain names—such as deceptive naming, corporate warfare, and cybersquatting—while not automatically allowing a second-comer to shut down a legitimate domain.

DNS Name Space Administrative Hierarchy Partitioning: DNS Zones of Authority

I explained earlier in this chapter that the DNS name space is arranged in a hierarchy and that there is also a hierarchy of authorities that is related to that hierarchical name structure. However, the two hierarchies are not exactly the same. If they were the same, we would need a separate authority for every domain at every level of the tree, and that's something we are very unlikely to want to have everywhere in the structure.

At the very top levels of the DNS tree, it seems reasonable that we might want to designate a separate authority at each level of the structure. Consider the geopolitical name hierarchy; IANA/ICANN manages the root domain, but each of the ccTLDs is managed by a distinct national authority.

However, when we get to the lower levels of the structure, it is often inconvenient or downright impossible to have each level correspond to a separate authority. As an example, let's suppose you are in charge of the Googleplex University IT department, which runs its own DNS servers for the googleplex.edu domain. Suppose there were only two schools at this university, teaching fine arts and computer science. Suppose also that the name space for the computers were divided into three subdomains: finearts.googleplex.edu, compsci.googleplex.edu, and admin.googleplex.edu (for central administrative functions, including the IT department itself).

Most likely, you don't want or need the Fine Arts department running its own DNS servers. The same is likely true of the administration machines. However, it's possible that the Computer Science department does want to run its own DNS servers, because this department probably has many more computers than the other departments, and the staff might use running a DNS server as part of the curriculum.

In this case, you might want yourself, the administrator for googleplex.edu, to maintain authority for the finearts.googleplex.edu and admin.googleplex.edu subdomains and everything within them, while delegating authority for compsci.googleplex.edu to whomever in the Computer Science department is designated for the task. DNS is specifically designed to allow these divisions between the name hierarchy and the authority structure to be created.

Methods of Dividing a Name Space into Zones of Authority

The complete DNS name structure is divided by making *cuts* (as RFC 1034 calls them) between adjacent nodes to create groups of contiguous nodes in the structure. Each group is called a *zone of authority*, or more commonly, just a *zone*. Each zone is usually identified by the domain name of the highest-level node in the zone; that is, the one closest to the root. The zones in DNS are by definition *non-overlapping*—every domain or subdomain is in exactly one zone. The division of the name space into zones can be made in an arbitrary way. At one extreme, we could place a cut between every node, and thereby divide the entire name space so each domain (and subdomain, and so on) was a separate zone. If we did this, the name hierarchy and authority hierarchy would indeed be the same for the entire DNS tree. At the other end of the scale, we could use no cuts at all, defining a single zone encompassing the entire DNS structure. This would mean the root was the authority for the entire tree.

Of course in practice, neither of these methods is particularly useful, as neither reflects how the real-world administration of DNS works. Instead, we generally divide the name structure in a variety of places, depending on the needs of different parts of the name space. There are many cases where we might want to create a subdomain that is responsible for its own DNS server operation; there are others where we might not want to do that. The significance of a cut in the name hierarchy is that making such a cut represents, in essence, a *declaration of DNS independence* by the node below the cut from the one above the cut.

Returning to our example, if googleplex.edu is in charge of its own DNS servers, then there would be a cut in the name space between googleplex.edu and .EDU at the next-higher level. This means that the DNS server for .EDU is no longer in charge of DNS for the googleplex.edu domain; instead, either the unversity itself or someone hired as a third party must provide DNS for it. In this case, we are assuming the folks at Googleplex U. themselves run their own DNS. Without making any other cuts, the googleplex.edu domain would be a single zone containing everything below that name, including both finearts.googleplex.edu and compsci.googleplex.edu.

In our example, however, we would make another cut, between googleplex.edu and compsci.googleplex.edu. This, in effect, *liberates* compsci.googleplex.edu, allowing its administrators to be in charge of their own DNS server. In doing this, we end up with two distinct zones: one encompassing googleplex.edu, finearts.googleplex.edu, and admin.googleplex.edu (and everything underneath them) and another for compsci.googleplex.edu (and everything below it). This is illustrated in Figure 54-2.

The Impact of Zones on Name Resolution: Authoritative Servers

The concept of zones is critical to understanding how DNS name servers work, and therefore, how name resolution is performed. All of the information about the subdomains and individual devices in the zone is represented using a set of resource records stored on a DNS name server. Usually, this name server is associated with the highest-level domain name in the zone. A name server that contains the definitive information for the zone is said to be *authoritative* for the zone.

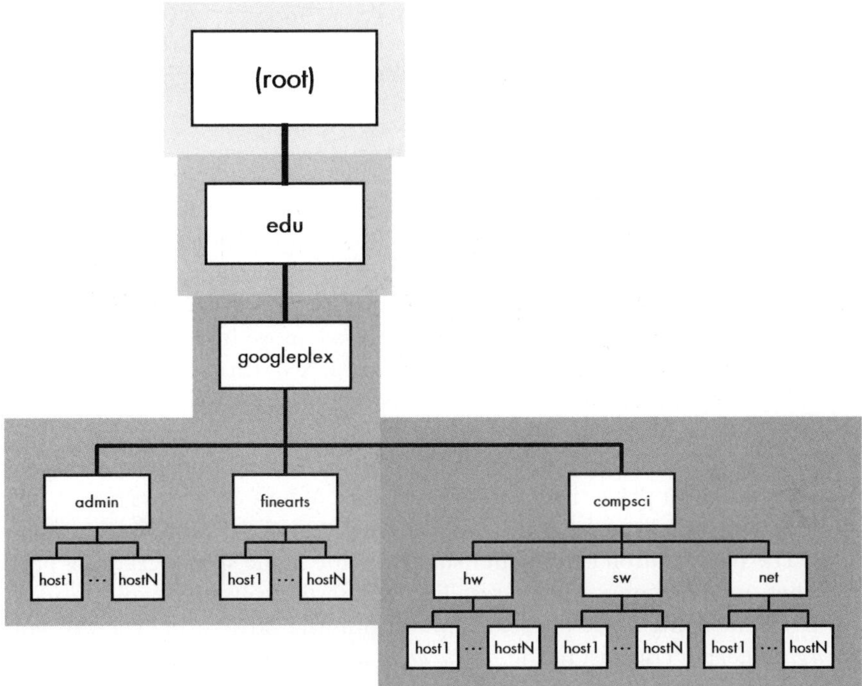

Figure 54-2: DNS zones of authority *Cuts can be made between nodes in the DNS name tree to create an arbitrary hierarchy of name authorities. This example shows the DNS tree branch for googleplex.edu, with each zone indicated using a different shading. IANA/ICANN is responsible for the root domain, and a separate authority named* Educause *takes care of .EDU. The third zone covers much of googleplex.edu, except that a cut has been made between googleplex and compsci to create an independent zone of authority for compsci.googleplex.edu.*

An authoritative server for a zone is one that maintains the official information about the zone, and the one that is ultimately responsible for providing name resolution information about it. We'll discuss this in the section on DNS servers and name resolution in Chapter 56.

> **KEY CONCEPT** The DNS name registration hierarchy is divided into regions called *zones of authority*. Each zone represents an area that is administered independently and consists of a contiguous segment of the DNS name tree.

Every DNS zone has a set of authoritative servers, which are usually a pair called the *primary* (or *master*) and *secondary* (or *slave*) servers. However, it is also possible for a single DNS name server to be authoritative for more than one zone.

As mentioned earlier, it is not always necessary for the actual owner of a domain to provide DNS services for it. Very often, especially for the domains owned by small businesses or individuals, DNS services are provided by a third party, often an ISP. For example, I have had pcguide.com registered as a domain since 1997, but my long-time web-hosting provider, pair Networks, has provided DNS services for me since the beginning. This means that pair's DNS servers in the pair.com hierarchy are responsible for pcguide.com. They are also responsible for many other domains for the company's customers.

DNS Private Name Registration

We have now reviewed the hierarchical nature of the DNS name space and the authority structure that administers it. Name registration begins with the generic and country code TLDs within the root of the name hierarchy, then proceeds to second-level domains within the TLDs and then lower-level subdomains below those. As we progress down the name tree, we move from the most general, public authority (IANA/ICANN, which runs all of DNS), through the high-level TLD authorities, and eventually down to the level of individual organizations, corporations, and individuals.

This dividing line between public authorities and private authorities occurs in many different places in the name structure. Wherever it does occur, below that line, responsibility for the domain becomes that of the organization that registered it. The organization can further subdivide the name space, granting parts of it to other organizations, or even reselling it. Alternatively, an organization may decide to use the name space to create a purely internal structure. I call this *private name registration*, in contrast to the *public name registration* described earlier in this chapter.

For example, if a company called XYZ Industries registers xyzindustries.com, that company becomes the owner of not just that domain name, but any subdomain structure or named items within it that the company may choose to create. This is the beauty and power of authority delegation and the hierarchical structure. The company has an important decision to make, however: whether they want to create names that are part of the global DNS name structure or use names within the structure purely privately.

Using Publicly Accessible Private Names

If an organization's administrators want names within their domain to be part of the global DNS name structure, they must perform the work required to properly set up and manage these names so they fit into DNS. The most common example is creating a public World Wide Web server. Most companies name such servers beginning with www, so XYZ Industries would probably wish to have the name www.xyzindustries.com for its web server address.

Obviously, the XYZ Industries owners want and need anyone on the Internet to be able to locate this server. Thus, even though they have private control of the xyzindustries.com domain, and own the name www.xyzindustries.com, they must follow proper procedures for ensuring that DNS resource records are set up for their www subdomain so everyone on the Internet can find it. They may do this themselves, if they run their own DNS servers, or may have an ISP or other third party do it for them, as described earlier.

Using Private Names for Internal Use

The alternative is to create purely private names for use only within the organization. For example, it is likely that even if XYZ wants a public web server, the administrators may wish to name many other machines that are to be accessed only within the company itself. In this case, they don't need to set up these machines so they are publicly recognizable. They can create private machine names and manage them internally within their own network.

> **KEY CONCEPT** Once an organization registers a particular domain name, it becomes the owner of that name and can decide whether and how to create a substructure within that domain. If an organization wants objects in the domain to be accessible on the public Internet, it must structure its domain to be consistent with Internet DNS standards. Alternately, it can create a purely private domain using any structure and rules it prefers.

One common way to do this is to make use of the older host table name system. This system is now archaic for large internetworks, but is often still used in smaller companies due to its simplicity. A name is *registered* by being added to the host tables on each of the computers within the organization, and *resolved* when the operating system on a host checks this file prior to using standard DNS resolution methods. The host table supplements DNS in this case (it is not really a part of DNS). The two systems are complementary and can work together, as explained in Chapter 51.

Using Private Names on Networks Not Connected to the Internet

Note that if you are running a purely private network not connected to the Internet at all, you can actually set up your own entirely private name hierarchy and run DNS yourself. In this case, you are in charge of the DNS root and can use any naming system you like.

This approach is sometimes considered attractive, because you can then use very simple machine names on small networks, without needing to perform any public registration or use names that correspond to the global hierarchy. Instead of the accounting computer in XYZ Industries being named accounting.xyzindustries.com, internally it could be named accounting. You can mix these with real DNS names, too, when accessing resources. For example, Joe's machine could be called just joe, while the website of UPS would, of course, still be www.ups.com.

The most common example of this mixing of private and public names is the definition of the private local name for the loopback address of a computer. Most Windows and UNIX machines define the name *localhost* to be the address 127.0.0.1, which means "this computer" on any TCP/IP machine.

55

DNS NAME SERVER CONCEPTS AND OPERATION

Of all the components and functional elements that combine to form the Domain Name System (DNS), name servers are arguably the most important. These servers, which may be either dedicated devices or software processes running on machines that also perform other tasks, are the workhorses of DNS. They store and manage information about domains, and respond to resolution requests for clients—in some cases, millions of times each day. Understanding how they perform this most basic task and the many support jobs for which they are also responsible is crucial to understanding DNS as a whole.

In this chapter, I describe the concepts related to DNS name servers and explain how they operate. I begin with an overview of DNS name server functions and general operation. I describe the way that DNS name server data is stored in resource records and the role of classes. I discuss the different roles of name servers in DNS and explain the all-important root name servers. I discuss how DNS zones are managed, the notions of domain contacts and zone transfers, and how caching and load balancing are used to improve efficiency in DNS. I conclude with a brief outline of several enhancements to basic DNS server operation, including the new Notify and Update message types and incremental zone transfers.

RELATED INFORMATION *The information in this section should be considered complementary to that in the following chapter on DNS resolvers.*

DNS General Operation

The three major functions of a name system are creating a name space, performing name registration, and providing name resolution services. The previous chapters describe how DNS uses a hierarchical tree structure for its name space (Chapter 53), and a hierarchical tree for name authorities and registration (Chapter 54). I'm sure that, given this, you will have to struggle to contain your surprise when I tell you that name resolution is also oriented around the notion of a hierarchical structure.

The devices that are primarily charged with performing the functions required to enable name resolution are *name servers*. They are arranged in a hierarchy that is closely related to the authority structure of the name system. Just as the authority structure complements the name structure but is not exactly the same as it, the name server architecture complements both the authority structure and the name structure, but may be different from them in its actual composition.

DNS Name Server Architecture and the Distributed Name Database

In a large DNS implementation, information about domains is not centralized in a single database run by one authority. Instead, it is *distributed* across many different authorities that manage particular top-level domains (TLDs), second-level domains, or lower-level subdomains. In the case of the global Internet, literally millions of different authorities, many of them responsible only for their own local domain space, participate cooperatively in running the DNS system.

With authority for registration distributed in this manner, the information about domains is similarly spread among many entities, resulting in a *distributed database*. A key concept in DNS name resolution is that each entity that maintains responsibility for a part of the name space must also arrange to have that information stored on a DNS server. This is required so that the server can provide the information about that part of the name space when resolution is performed. As you can see, the existence of a structured hierarchy of authorities directly implies the need for a hierarchy of servers that store that hierarchical name information.

Each DNS zone of authority is required to have one or more DNS servers that are in charge of managing information about that zone. These servers are said to be *authoritative* for the zone. Storing information about the domains, subdomains, and objects in the zone is done by recording the data in special resource records that are read from DNS master lists maintained by administrators. Servers then respond to requests for this information.

KEY CONCEPT DNS public name information is stored in a *distributed database* of DNS name servers that are structured in a hierarchy comparable to the hierarchy of authorities. Each zone has one or more DNS name servers in charge of the zone's information, called *authoritative name servers*.

Since information in DNS is stored in a distributed form, there is no single server that has information about every domain in the system. As you'll see in the next chapter, the process of resolution instead relies on the hierarchy of name servers. At the top of the DNS hierarchy is the *root* domain, and in that domain are root name servers. These are the most important servers, because they maintain information about the TLDs within the root. They also have knowledge of the servers that can be used to resolve domains one level below them. Those servers, in turn, are responsible for the TLDs and can reference servers that are responsible for second-level domains. Thus, a DNS resolution may require that requests be sent to more than one server.

DNS Server Support Functions

The storing and serving of name data (through responses to requests from DNS resolvers) is the main function of a DNS server. However, other support jobs are also typically required of a DNS server:

Interacting with Other Servers Because the DNS resolution process often requires that multiple servers be involved, servers must maintain not just name information, but information about the existence of other servers. Depending on the type of DNS request, servers may themselves become clients and generate requests to other servers.

Zone Management and Transfers The server must provide a way for DNS information within the zone to be managed. A facility also exists to allow a *zone transfer* to be performed between the master (primary) server for a zone and slave (secondary) servers.

Performance Enhancement Functions Due to the large number of requests servers handle, they employ numerous techniques to reduce the time required to respond to queries. The most important of these is caching of name information. A variation of regular caching called *negative caching* may also be used to improve performance, and load balancing is a feature that can be used to improve efficiency of busy devices registered within the DNS system.

Administration Various other administrative details are required of name servers, such as storing information about the different types of contacts (humans) who are responsible for certain tasks related to management of a domain or zone.

As you'll see later in this chapter, not all name servers perform all of these tasks described; some perform only a subset.

The Logical Nature of the DNS Name Server Hierarchy

Like the other hierarchies, the name server hierarchy is logical in nature. I already mentioned that it often is not exactly the same as the authority hierarchy. For one thing, it is common for a single DNS name server to be the authoritative server for a number of domains. Even if a particular group has authority for a subdomain of a particular domain, it's possible they will share the DNS servers with the authority of their parent domain for efficiency reasons. For example, a university might delegate control over parts of its domain space to different groups (as in the example of DNS zones in Chapter 54) but still manage all subdomains on the same server. In practice, the lower the level of the subdomain in the DNS name hierarchy, the less likely that subdomain has its own DNS server.

Another important aspect of the logical nature of the name server hierarchy is that there is no necessary relationship between the structure of the name servers and their location. In fact, in many cases, name servers are specifically put in different places for reliability reasons. The best example of this is the set of root name servers. These are all at the top of the DNS server architecture, but they are spread around the globe to prevent a single problem from taking all of them out. Also remember not to be fooled by the structure of a name in the geopolitical DNS name hierarchy (as discussed in Chapter 53). A name server called ns1.blahblah.ca might be in Canada, but it very well might not be located there.

KEY CONCEPT The DNS name server hierarchy is logical in nature and not exactly the same as the DNS name server tree. One server may be responsible for many domains and subdomains. Also, the structure of the DNS name server hierarchy doesn't necessarily indicate the physical locations of name servers.

DNS Name Server Data Storage

One of the most important jobs performed by name servers is the storage of name data. Since the authority for registering names is distributed across the internetwork using DNS, the database of name information is likewise distributed. An *authoritative* server is responsible for storing and managing all the information for the zones of authority it is assigned.

Each DNS server is, in essence, a type of database server. The database contains many kinds of information about the subdomains and individual devices within the domain or zone for which the server is responsible. In DNS, the database entries that contain this name information are called *resource records (RRs)*. A specific set of RRs is associated with each node within the zone.

Binary and Text Representations of Resource Records

The entire point of DNS is to allow humans to work with names and computers to work with numbers. This principle is further reflected in the two very different representations that exist for the DNS RRs themselves (see Figure 55-1):

RR Field Format (Binary) Representation Name servers are required to respond to queries for name information by sending RRs within DNS messages. Obviously, we want to do this in as efficient a way as possible, so each RR is internally stored using a special field format that is similar to the many field formats used for messages in other protocols. All RRs use a general field format for some of their fields and then have a unique portion that is specific to the RR type.

Master File (Text) Representation Computers are happy to exchange binary-encoded field formats and have no problem remembering that, for example, RR type 15 corresponds to a mail exchange (MX) record. However, human administrators want to be able to quickly and easily maintain DNS information without needing to remember cryptic codes or work with binary values. For this reason, DNS uses a *master file* format for its user-machine interface, which allows RRs to be specified in text form for easier maintenance.

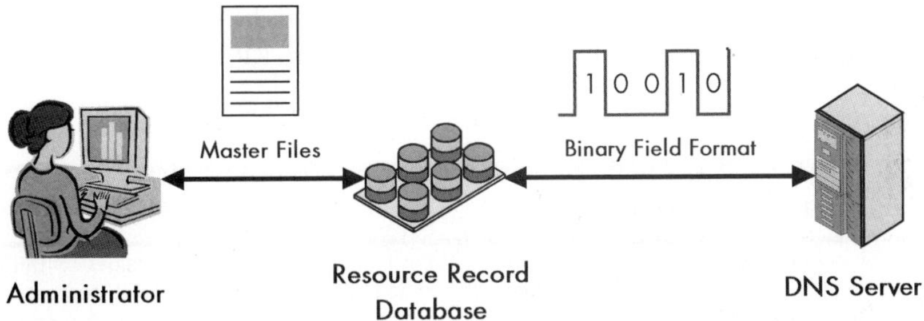

Figure 55-1: *DNS RR master file and binary field formats*

To meet the needs of humans and computers, DNS uses two representations for the data stored in RRs. Administrators enter and maintain information in textual DNS master files. These are read by DNS server software and internally stored in binary format for answering DNS requests.

Use of RRs and Master Files

Each node may have a variable number of records, depending on the node type and what information is being kept for it. The RRs are added, changed, or deleted when DNS information changes, by administrators who make modifications to the text master files on the server computer. These files are then read into memory by the DNS server software, parsed (interpreted), and converted into binary form. Then they are ready for use in resolving DNS name requests and other queries. I describe both the binary RR field formats and master file format in Chapter 57.

KEY CONCEPT DNS name servers store DNS information in the form of *resource records (RRs)*. Each RR contains a particular type of information about a node in the DNS tree. There are two representations for RRs: Conventional binary field formats are used for communication between DNS name servers and resolvers, and text *master files* are edited by administrators to manage DNS zones.

Common RR Types

The main DNS standards, RFC 1034 and 1035, defined a number of RR types. Over time, the list has changed, with new RR types being created in subsequent standards and the use of others changed. Like other Internet parameters, the list of DNS RR types is maintained in a file by the Internet Assigned Numbers Authority (IANA). Also like other Internet parameters, there are actually several dozen defined RRs in DNS, but only a few are commonly used; others are now obsolete, used for special purposes, or experimental in nature. The current list of DNS resource records is maintained in a file that can be found at http://www.iana.org/assignments/dns-parameters.

Table 55-1 summarizes the most important RR types. For each, I have shown the numeric Type value for the record, which is used to identify the RR type in message exchanges, and the text code used for the RR in master files.

Table 55-1: Summary of Common DNS Resource Records

RR Type Value	RR Text Code	RR Type	Description
1	A	Address	Contains a 32-bit IP address. This is the "meat and potatoes" of DNS, since it is where the address of a node is stored for name resolution purposes.
2	NS	Name Server	Specifies the name of a DNS name server that is authoritative for the zone. Each zone must have at least one NS record that points to its primary name server, and that name must also have a valid Address (A) record.
5	CNAME	Canonical Name	Used to allow aliases to be defined that point to the real name of a node. The CNAME record provides a mapping between this alias and the canonical (real) name of the node. It is commonly used to hide changes in the internal DNS structure from outside users, by letting them use an unchanging alias, while the internal names are modified based on the needs of the organization. See the discussion of name resolution in Chapter 56 for an example.
6	SOA	Start Of Authority	Used to mark the start of a DNS zone and provide important information about it. Every zone must have exactly one SOA record, which contains the name of the zone, its primary (master) authoritative server name, and technical details such as the email address of its administrator and parameters for how often slave (secondary) name servers are updated.
12	PTR	Pointer	Provides a pointer to another location in the name space. These records are best known for their use in reverse resolution through the IN-ADDR.ARPA domain (described in Chapter 54).
15	MX	Mail Exchange	Specifies the location (device name) that is responsible for handling email sent to the domain.
16	TXT	Text String	Allows arbitrary additional text associated with the domain to be stored.

All of these RRs are used in different ways to define zones and devices within them and then permit name resolution and other functions to take place. You'll see how they are used in more detail in Chapter 56, which covers name resolution. You can also find a more lengthy description of some of them in the section in Chapter 57 devoted to RR field formats.

RELATED INFORMATION *See the topic on IPv6 DNS support near the end of Chapter 57 for IPv6-specific RR types.*

RR Classes

Finally, I would like to mention a historical note about RRs. When DNS was first created, its inventors wanted it to be as generic as possible. To that end, they designed it so that a DNS server could, theoretically, provide name service for more than one type of underlying protocol; that is, DNS could support TCP/IP as well as other protocols simultaneously.

Of course, protocols have different addressing schemes and also varying needs for name resolution. Therefore, DNS was defined so that each protocol could have a distinct set of RR types. Each set of RR types was called a *class*. Technically, an RR must be identified using both a class identifier and an RR type. Like the RR types, classes have a numeric code number and a text abbreviation. The class for TCP/IP uses the number 1, with the text code IN (for Internet).

In practice, this notion of multiple classes of RRs never took off. Today, DNS is, to my knowledge, used only for TCP/IP. (There may be some obscure exceptions.) Several other classes have been defined by RFC 1035 and are in the IANA DNS parameters list, but they are for relatively obscure, experimental, or obsolete network types, with names such as CSNET, CHAOS, and Hesiod. You'll still see this concept of class in the specification of DNS message and RR formats, but there really is only class today: IN for TCP/IP. For this reason, in most cases, the class name can be omitted in DNS-related commands and data entries, and IN will be assumed by default.

> **KEY CONCEPT** The DNS standards were originally created to allow them to work with multiple protocols, by specifying the class of each RR. Today, the only class commonly used is that for TCP/IP, which is called IN (for Internet).

DNS Name Server Types and Roles

So far, we have looked at the functions of DNS servers, focusing on the important job of storing name server information. There are many thousands of DNS servers on the Internet, and not all are used in the same way. Each DNS server has a particular role in the overall operation of the name system. The different kinds of servers also interact with each other in a variety of ways.

Master (Primary)/Slave (Secondary) Servers

Every zone needs to have at least one DNS name server that is responsible for it. These DNS name servers are called *authoritative* servers for the zone, because they contain the full set of RRs that describe the zone. When any device on the Internet wants to know something about a zone, it consults one of its authoritative servers.

From a strictly theoretical perspective, having one name server for each zone or domain is sufficient to provide name resolution services for the entire DNS name structure. From an implementation standpoint, however, having only one name server for each part of the name space is not a wise idea. Instead, each zone usually has associated with it at least two name servers: one *primary* or *master* name server, and one *secondary* or *slave* name server. Some zones may have more than one secondary name server.

NOTE *The terms* primary *and* secondary *are used often in the DNS standards to refer to the roles of the two authoritative servers for a zone. However,* master *and* slave *are now the preferred terms, because* primary *and* secondary *are somewhat ambiguous and used in other contexts. You should be prepared to see both terms used.*

The master name server is obviously the most essential server. It is on this name server that the master files for the zone's RRs are maintained, so the master name server is the final word on information on the zone. However, there are several reasons why slave servers are also important:

Redundancy If there were only one name server and it failed, no one would be able to resolve names such as www.xyzindustries.com into IP addresses, and that would be a Bad Thing. Slave name servers act as a backup for the masters they support. Redundancy is the most important consideration in setting up master and slave name servers. Sticking two machines side by side in a server room, plugged into the same electrical service, both connected to the Internet with the same Internet service provider (ISP), and making one your master DNS server and the other your slave is not a smart move. Ideally, the primary and secondary servers should be as independent as possible; they should be physically distant and have separate connections to the Internet.

Maintenance With more than one server, we can easily take the primary server down for maintenance when needed without name resolution service being disrupted.

Load Handling Busy zones can use multiple servers to spread the load of name resolution requests to improve performance.

Efficiency There are many cases where there is an advantage to positioning a name server in a particular geographical location for the sake of efficiency. For example, a company may have an office in a distant location connected using a low-speed wide area network link. To reduce name resolution traffic across that link, it makes sense to have that zone's information available in a name server on both sides of the connection, which would require two physical servers.

Just as the names *master* and *slave* suggest, the secondary name servers are not the original source of information about a zone. They normally obtain their RRs not from human-edited master files, but from updates from the master server. This is accomplished using a process called a *zone transfer*. These transfers are performed on a regular basis to ensure that the slave servers are kept up-to-date. The slaves can then respond to name resolution requests with current information. Both the master and the slave are considered authoritative for the zone.

Name Server Roles

The master and slave roles for a zone are logical and do not always correspond to individual physical hardware devices. A single physical name server can play multiple roles in the following cases:

- It can be the master name server for more than one zone. Each zone in this case has a distinct set of RRs maintained in separate master files.
- It can be a slave name server for more than one zone.
- It can be a slave name server for certain zones as well as a primary for others.

Note, however, that a single physical name server cannot be a master and a slave server for the same zone.

> **KEY CONCEPT** The master DNS server for a zone is its primary server, which maintains the master copy of DNS information. Most DNS zones also have at least one slave or secondary DNS server. These are important because they serve as backups for the primary server, and they can also help share the load of responding to requests in busy zones. Secondary name servers get their information from primary servers on a routine basis. Both master and slave servers are considered authoritative for the zones whose data they maintain.

Caching-Only Name Servers

For efficiency, all DNS servers—both masters and slaves—perform caching of DNS information so it can be used again if requested in the near future. (Caching is described in the "Name Server Caching" section later in this chapter.) The importance of caching is so significant that some servers are set up only to cache information from other DNS servers. Unsurprisingly, these are called *caching-only* name servers.

These name servers are not authoritative for any zone or domain, and they don't maintain any RRs of their own. They can answer name resolution requests only by contacting other name servers that *are* authoritative and then relaying the information. They then store the information for future requests. Why bother? The reason is performance. Through strategic placement, a caching-only server can increase DNS resolution performance substantially in some networks by cutting down on requests to authoritative servers.

> **KEY CONCEPT** There are DNS servers that do not maintain DNS RRs of their own but solely hold recently used information from other zones. These are called *caching-only* name servers and are not authoritative for any zone.

DNS Zone Management, Contacts, and Zone Transfers

The authority for a particular DNS zone is responsible for performing a variety of tasks to manage it. *Zone management* encompasses the entire gamut of jobs related to a zone: deciding on the name hierarchy within the zone, specifying procedures for name registration, technical work related to keeping DNS servers running, and other administrative overhead of all sorts. This job can be either very small or incredibly large, depending on the type of organization. A small domain owned by an individual doesn't require much work to manage, while one for a huge company might require a dedicated staff to maintain.

Domain Contacts

It is important that it be possible for anyone on an internetwork to be able to determine who the owner of a domain is, so that person can be reached for whatever reason. On the Internet, each DNS domain has associated with it a set of three *contacts* that are responsible for different facets of managing a domain:

Administrative Contact The main contact, responsible for the domain as a whole. This individual or organization is considered the overall owner of the domain.

Billing Contact A contact responsible for handling payment for domain services and other accounting matters.

Technical Contact A contact who handles the technical details of setting up DNS for the domain and making sure it works.

For smaller domains, there usually is no separate billing contact; it is the same as the administrative contact. In contrast, the technical contact is often different from the administrative contact in both large and small domains. Large organizations will make the technical contact someone in their information technology department. Small organizations often let their ISP provide DNS services, and in that case, the technical contact will be someone at that ISP.

KEY CONCEPT Each DNS domain has associated with it a set of three contact names that indicate who is responsible for managing it. The *administrative contact* is the person with overall responsibility for the domain. The *billing contact* is responsible for payment issues; this may be the same as the administrative contact. The *technical contact* is in charge of technical matters for the domain and is often a different person than the administrative contact, especially when DNS services are outsourced.

Zone Transfers

The ultimate purpose of zone management is to ensure that information about the zone is kept current on the zone's master and slave name servers, so it can be efficiently provided to name resolvers. Thus, the management of a zone begins with decision-making and administrative actions that result in changes to the RRs for the zone. These are reflected in changes made to the DNS master files on the master (primary) DNS server for the zone.

In contrast, each zone's secondary DNS server(s) act as slaves to the master primary server. They carry information about the zone, but do not load it from local master files that are locally edited. Instead, they obtain their information from the master name server on a regular basis. The procedure responsible for this is called a *zone transfer*.

The records on the master name server can be updated at any time. As soon as the master name server's records have been changed, the information at the slave name servers becomes partially out-of-date. This is not generally a big deal, because most of the data will still be accurate, and the secondary server will continue to respond to resolution requests using the most current information it has. However, it is obviously important that we update the slave servers on a regular basis; if this is not done, eventually their data will become stale and unreliable. To this end, it is necessary that zone transfers be performed on a regular basis.

Control of When Zone Transfers Occur

Controlling when zone transfers happen requires implementation of a communication process between the servers that consists of two basic parts. First, we need a mechanism to allow slave servers to regularly check for changes to the data on the master. Second, we must have a mechanism for copying the RRs for the zone from the primary name server to the secondary server when needed.

Both mechanisms make use of standard DNS query/response facilities and special fields in the RRs for the zone. Of particular importance is the Start Of Authority (SOA) record for the zone, which contains several parameters that control zone status checking and zone transfers. While the formal description of these parameters can be found in the description of RR formats in Chapter 57, I'll discuss how they are used here.

When a slave name server starts up, it may have no information about the zone at all, or it may have a copy of the zone's RRs stored on its local storage, from the last time it was running. In the former case, it must immediately perform a full zone transfer, since it has no information. In the latter case, it will read its last-known copy of the zone from local storage; it may immediately perform a *poll* on the master server to see if the data has changed, depending on configuration. A poll is done by requesting the SOA RR for the zone.

The Serial field in the SOA record contains a serial number (which may be arbitrary or may be encoded so it has a particular meaning) that acts as the version number of the master server's zone database. Each time the master file for the zone is modified (either manually by editing or automatically through another means), this serial number is increased. Therefore, a slave server can detect when changes have been made on the master by seeing if the Serial field in the most recent SOA record is greater than the one the slave stored the last time it polled the master. If the serial number has changed, the slave begins a zone transfer.

Three other fields in the SOA record control the timing that slave name servers use for polling and updating their information:

Refresh This field specifies how many seconds a slave server waits between attempts to check for an update on the master. Assuming the slave can make contact, this is the longest period of time that data on a slave will become stale when the master changes.

Retry This field controls how long the slave must wait before trying again to check in with the master if its last attempt failed. This is used to prevent rapid-fire attempts to contact a master that may clog the network.

Expire If, for whatever reason, the slave name server is not able to make contact with the master for a number of seconds given by this field's value, it must assume that the information it has is stale and stop using it. This means that it will stop acting as an authoritative name server for the zone until it receives an update.

The fact that these parameters are part of the SOA record for the zone gives the administrator of the zone complete control over how often master name servers are updated. In a small zone where changes are rare, the interval between checks made by the slave servers can be increased; for larger zones or ones that are changed often, the Refresh interval can be decreased.

Zone Transfer Mechanism

When a zone transfer is required, it is accomplished using a DNS query sent to the master server using the regular DNS query/response messaging method used for name resolution (discussed in the next section). A special DNS question type, called AXFR (address transfer) is used to initiate the zone transfer. The server will then transfer the RRs for the zone using a series of DNS response messages (assuming that the server that requested the transfer is authorized to do so). Since it's important that zone transfers be received reliably, and since the amount of data to be sent is large and needs to be managed, a Transmission Control Protocol (TCP) session must first be established and used for zone transfers. This is in contrast to the simpler User Datagram Protocol (UDP) transport used for regular DNS messages (as described in the section discussing the use of UDP and TCP for DNS at the start of Chapter 57).

Once the zone transfer is complete, the slave name server will update its database and return to regular operation. It will continue to perform regular polls of the master server every Refresh seconds. If it has a problem with a regular poll, it will try again after Retry seconds. Finally, if an amount of time equal to Expires seconds elapses, the slave name server will stop serving data from the zone until it reestablishes contact with the primary name server.

> **KEY CONCEPT** Slave name servers do not have their DNS information managed directly by an administrator. Instead, they obtain information from their master name server on a periodic basis through a process called a *zone transfer*. Several fields in the Start Of Authority (SOA) DNS RR control the zone transfer process, including specifying how often transfers are done and how slave name servers handle problem conditions such as an inability to contact the master server.

Note that the DNS *Notify* feature is an enhancement to the basic zone status check/zone transfer model. It allows the master server to notify a slave server when the master's database has changed. Another new feature allows only part of a zone to be transferred instead of the entire zone. See the discussion of DNS name server enhancements later in this chapter for more information.

DNS Root Name Servers

DNS is strongly oriented around the notion of hierarchical structure. The name space, registration authorities, and name servers are all arranged in a tree structure. Like these structures, the name resolution process is also hierarchical. As explained in Chapter 53, a fully qualified domain name (FQDN) is resolved by starting with the least specific domain name element (label) and working toward the most specific one.

Naturally, the least specific portion of every name is the root node under which the entire DNS structure exists. This means that, absent caching and other performance enhancements, all name resolution begins with the root of the name tree. We find here a set of name servers that are responsible for name server functions for the DNS root: the DNS *root name servers.*

Like all name servers, DNS root name servers store information about and provide name resolution services for all the nodes within the root zone. This includes certain specific TLDs and subdomains. Most TLDs, however, are in their own zones. The root name servers are used as the "go-to" spot to obtain the names and addresses of the authoritative servers for each of these TLDs. For example, if we want to resolve the name www.xyzindustries.co.uk, the root name servers are where a resolver would find the identity of the name server that is responsible for .UK.

Root Name Server Redundancy

Clearly, these root name servers are extremely important to the functioning of the DNS system as a whole. If anything were to ever happen to cause the root name servers to stop operating, the entire DNS system would essentially shut down. For this reason, there obviously isn't just one root server, nor are there two or three; there are (at present) thirteen different root name servers.

In fact, there are actually far more than 13 physical servers. Most of the 13 name servers are implemented as clusters of several independent physical hardware servers. Some are distributed collections of servers that are in different physical locations. The best example is the F root server, which has been implemented as a set of more than a dozen *mirrors* in various places around the world, to provide better service.

The principles of redundancy that are a good idea for choosing a secondary name server for a regular domain obviously apply that much more to the root. This is why the various physical devices that compose the 13 root servers are all located in different places all around the globe. Many of them are in the United States, but even these are in many locations throughout the country (albeit concentrated in a couple of hot spots in California and near Washington, DC) and are set up to use different networks to connect to the Internet.

The root name servers are, of course, rather powerful. Despite there being several dozen pieces of hardware to spread the load, they must each handle large amounts of data, 24 hours a day. They are run by networking professionals who ensure that they function efficiently. An Internet standard, RFC 2870, "Root Name Server Operational Requirements," spells out the basic rules and practices for the operation of these name servers. It specifies extensive procedures for ensuring the security of the servers and for avoiding performance problems due to their pivotal role.

> **KEY CONCEPT** Information about the DNS root and its TLDs is managed by a set of *root name servers.* These servers are essential to the operation of DNS. They are arranged into 13 groups and physically distributed around the world.

Despite all the efforts taken to ensure that the root servers are widely distributed and secure, they still collectively represent a point of weakness in the global Internet. Millions and millions of people depend on these servers. There have been incidents in the past where rogue elements on the Internet have attempted to disrupt DNS by attacking the root name servers. One widely publicized incident was a denial-of-service (DoS) attack against the root servers on October 21, 2002. The attack failed, but it significantly raised awareness of the importance of these servers and how essential DNS security is.

Current Root Name Servers

Originally, the root name servers were given domain names reflecting the organizations that ran them. In these historical names, we can see a veritable who's who of the big players in the development of the Internet: the Information Sciences Institute (ISI), National Aeronautics and Space Administration (NASA), United States military, and others. Several of the servers are still run by government agencies or the United States military, where added security can be put into place to protect them. For convenience, however, all the root name servers are now given alphabetical letter names in the special domain root-servers.net.

Table 55-2 shows the most current information about the DNS root name servers as of the date of publishing of this book. For your interest and amusement, I have also mapped the locations of these servers in Figure 55-2 .

Table 55-2: Internet DNS Root Name Servers

Root Server Name	IP Address	Historical Name	Location(s)
a.root-servers.net	198.41.0.4	ns.internic.net	Dulles, VA, U.S.
b.root-servers.net	128.9.0.107	ns1.isi.edu	Marina Del Rey, CA, U.S.
c.root-servers.net	192.33.4.12	c.psi.net	Herndon, VA and Los Angeles, CA, U.S.
d.root-servers.net	128.8.10.90	terp.umd.edu	College Park, MD, U.S.
e.root-servers.net	192.203.230.10	ns.nasa.gov	Mountain View, CA, U.S.
f.root-servers.net	192.5.5.241	ns.isc.org	Auckland, New Zealand; Sao Paulo, Brazil; Hong Kong, China; Johannesburg, South Africa; Los Angeles, CA, U.S.; New York, NY, U.S.; Madrid, Spain; Palo Alto, CA, U.S.; Rome, Italy; Seoul, Korea; San Francisco, CA, U.S.; San Jose, CA, U.S.; Ottawa, ON, Canada

(continued)

Table 55-2: Internet DNS Root Name Servers (continued)

Root Server Name	IP Address	Historical Name	Location(s)
g.root-servers.net	192.112.36.4	ns.nic.ddn.mil	Vienna, VA, U.S.
h.root-servers.net	128.63.2.53	aos.arl.army.mil	Aberdeen, MD, U.S.
i.root-servers.net	192.36.148.17	nic.nordu.net	Stockholm, Sweden; Helsinki, Finland
j.root-servers.net	192.58.128.30	—	Dulles, VA, U.S.; Mountain View, CA, U.S.; Sterling, VA, U.S.; Seattle, WA, U.S.; Atlanta, GA, U.S.; Los Angeles, CA, U.S.; Amsterdam, The Netherlands
k.root-servers.net	193.0.14.129	—	London, UK; Amsterdam, The Netherlands
l.root-servers.net	198.32.64.12	—	Los Angeles, CA, U.S.
m.root-servers.net	202.12.27.33	—	Tokyo, Japan

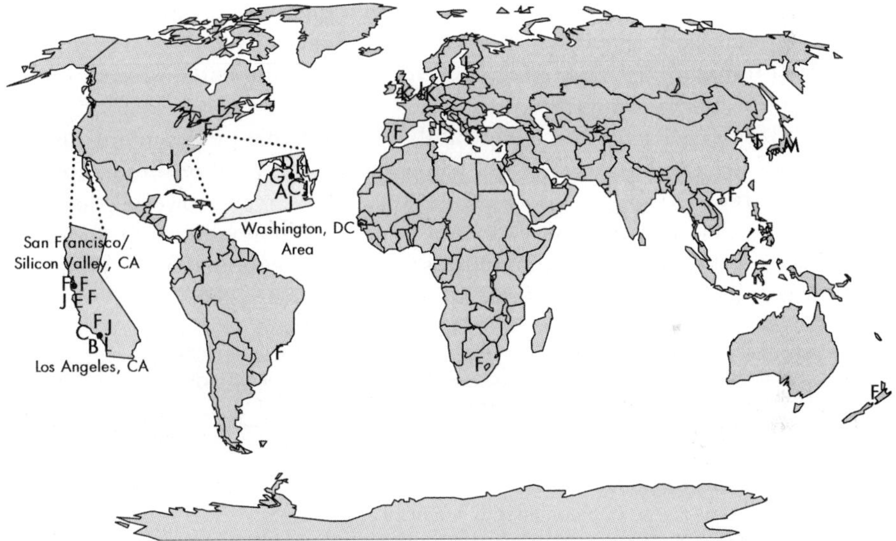

Figure 55-2: Geographic locations of Internet DNS root name servers

The current list of root name servers can be found in the file ftp://ftp.rs.internic.net/domain/named.root. You can also find the information in a more user-friendly format at http://www.root-servers.org.

DNS Name Server Caching

Most of the grunt work done by name servers is responding to name resolution requests. Busy servers—like the root name servers, the ones that carry zone information for the TLDs, and ones that serve very busy zones—must handle hundreds or even thousands of name resolution requests each *second*. Each of these requests takes time and resources to resolve and takes internetwork bandwidth away from the business of transferring data. It is essential, therefore, that DNS server implementations employ mechanisms to improve their efficiency and cut down on unnecessary name resolution requests. One of the most important of these is *caching*.

Name Server Caching

The word *cache* refers to a store, or a place where something is kept. In the computer world, the term usually refers to an area of memory set aside for storing information that has been recently obtained so it can be used again. In the case of DNS, caching is used by DNS name servers to store the results of recent name resolution and other requests, so that if the request occurs again, it can be satisfied from the cache without requiring another complete run of the name resolution process. Due to how most people use computers, a particular request is often followed by another request for the same name, so caching can significantly reduce the number of requests that result in complete name resolution procedures.

An example is the best way to illustrate this. Suppose you are using a host on your company's local network. This host is probably configured to use your company's DNS name server to handle resolution requests. You type www.xyzindustries.com into your web browser, which causes a resolution attempt to be made for that address. Most likely, your local DNS server doesn't know that name, so it will follow the complete name resolution process (described in Chapter 56) to get its address. After doing this, your local DNS server will *cache* the name www.xyzindustries.com and the address associated with it.

If you click a link for a page at that website, that new page will also probably be somewhere at the www.xyzindustries.com site. This will result in another DNS resolution request being sent off to your local DNS server. However, this time, the local server will not need to perform a resolution. It remembers that this name is in its cache and returns the saved address for the name immediately. Voilà! You get your answer faster, and unnecessary Internet traffic is avoided.

> **KEY CONCEPT** *Caching* is an essential efficiency feature that reduces DNS message traffic by eliminating unnecessary requests for recently resolved names. Whenever a name is resolved, the resulting DNS information is cached so it can be used for subsequent requests that occur shortly thereafter.

Of course, things aren't entirely this simple. One very important issue that comes up with every caching system, including the one used in DNS, is the matter of the *freshness* of the cache.

Caching Data Persistence and the Time to Live Interval

Suppose your local DNS server resolves the name www.xyzindustries.com, and then caches its address. In this example, where you click a link a few seconds after the XYZ Industries home page loads, you aren't likely to be too concerned about how fresh the DNS data is. But how about if you shut down your computer to go on vacation for two weeks, and then come back to work and type the name into your browser again. If your local server still has the name in its cache, how do you know the IP address of www.xyzindustries.com hasn't changed during that two-week period?

Two different mechanisms are used to address this issue. The first is that when data is cached, the caching server also makes a note of the authoritative server from which it came. When a resolver (client) asks for a name resolution and the address is drawn from the cache, the server marks the answer as *non-authoritative* to clearly tell the client that the name came from the cache. The server also supplies the name of the authoritative server that originally supplied the data.

The client then has a choice: It can either use the non-authoritative answer or issue a request for a fresh name resolution from the authoritative server. This is a trade-off between performance (using the cached data) and currency (asking for a fresh resolution each time). Usually, the cached data can be used safely, because DNS information doesn't change very often.

The second technique for ensuring that caching data doesn't get too old is a procedure for limiting the *persistence* of DNS cached data. Each RR has associated with it a time interval, called the *Time to Live (TTL)*. Whenever an RR is read from a server, the TTL for the record is also read. Any server caching the record is supposed to discard the record after that time interval expires.

Each zone also has associated with it a default value for the TTL field to be applied to all records in the zone. This allows an administrator to select a TTL value for all records in a zone without needing to enter TTL numbers for each record individually. At the same time, the administrator can assign an override TTL value to any records that need a number that is different from the default. This default TTL was originally kept in the special SOA RR for each zone, but is now handled using a special directive in the zone's master file.

NOTE *This Time to Live (TTL) field is not related to the one used in Internet Protocol (IP) datagrams (see Chapter 21). Obviously, IP and DNS are totally different protocols, but more than that, the TTL fields in IP and DNS don't have the same meaning at all.*

It's worth emphasizing that DNS gives control over caching to the owner of the record, not whoever is running the DNS server doing the caching. While it is possible for a particular caching server to override the TTL and specify how long data will be held in its own cache, DNS is not supposed to work that way. The ability to specify a TTL on a record-by-record basis allows the persistence of cache data to be tailored to the needs of the individual data elements. Data that changes often can be given a small TTL value; infrequently modified records can be given a higher TTL. Selecting the TTL value must be done carefully. This is another trade-off between performance (which is optimized with higher TTL values, reducing the number of queries made for cached data) and freshness of the data (which increases as the TTL values are lowered).

KEY CONCEPT Cached information can become stale over time and result in incorrect responses sent to queries. Each RR can have associated with it a time interval, called the *Time to Live (TTL)*, that specifies how long the record may be held in a cache. The value of this field is controlled by the owner of the RR, who can tailor it to the specific needs of each RR type.

Negative Caching

Classic DNS caching stores only the results of successful name resolutions. It is also possible for DNS servers to cache the results of *unsuccessful* name resolution attempts; this is called *negative caching*. To extend the example we've been using in this section, suppose you mistakenly thought the name of the company's website was www.xyz-industries.com and typed that into your browser. Your local DNS server would be unable to resolve the name and would mark that name as unresolvable in its cache—a negative cache entry.

Suppose you typed the name in incorrectly because someone mistyped it on an internal memo. If a colleague later tried the same name, the DNS server would say, "I already know this is a bogus name," and not try to resolve it again. Since there is no RR for an invalid name, the server itself must decide how long to cache this negative information. Negative caching improves performance because resolving a name that doesn't exist takes resources, just as resolving an existing one does. Note that regular caching is sometimes called *positive caching* to contrast it with negative caching.

The value to be used for negative caching in a zone is now specified by the Minimum field in the SOA RR for each zone. As mentioned in the previous section, this was formerly used to specify the default TTL for a zone.

DNS Name Server Load Balancing

The Address (A) RR is the most fundamental one in DNS, since it records an actual mapping between a domain name and an IP address. Let's consider for a moment one of the words in that sentence in more detail. No, I don't mean *address* or *RR* or *mapping*. I mean the word *an*!

The Address record mentions only a single address for each domain name. This means that each domain name maps to only a single physical hardware device. When the number of requests that a particular server or other device needs to handle is relatively small, this is not a problem; the function can usually be implemented using a single physical hardware device. If the server gets busier, the usual solution is to throw more hardware at the problem—get a bigger machine.

However, some hosts on a large internetwork, especially the Internet, feature servers that must handle tremendous amounts of traffic from many clients. There simply is no single hardware device that can readily handle the traffic of a site like www.cnn.com or www.microsoft.com, for example, without becoming unwieldy. Sites like these must use a technique called *load balancing* to spread requests across multiple hardware servers.

Using Multiple Address Records to Spread Out Requests to a Domain

One simple way to do load balancing would be to have multiple machine names. For example, CNN could create several different websites called www1.cnn.com, www2.cnn.com, and so on, each pointing to a different hardware device. DNS certainly supports this type of solution. The problem with this solution is that it is cumbersome; it requires users to remember multiple server names.

It would be better if we could balance the load automatically. DNS supports this by providing a simple way to implement load balancing. Instead of specifying a single Address RR for a name, we can create several such records, thereby associating more than one IP address with a particular DNS name. When we do this, each time the authoritative name server for the zone in which that name exists resolves that name, it sends all the addresses on the list back to the requester. The server changes the order of the addresses supplied in the response, choosing the order randomly or in a sequential, round-robin fashion. The client will usually use the first address in the list returned by the server, so by changing the list, the server ensures that requests for that device's name are resolved to multiple hardware units.

> **KEY CONCEPT** Rather than creating a single Address (A) RR for a DNS domain name, it is possible to create multiple ones. This associates several IP addresses with one name, which can be used to spread a large number of requests for one domain name over many physical IP devices. This allows DNS to implement load balancing for busy Internet servers.

As Internet traffic increases, load balancing is becoming more popular. In early 2003, I saw a survey that indicated approximately 10 percent of Internet names at that time used load balancing—a fairly significant number. Most employed either two or three addresses, but some used as many as sixty addresses! Incidentally, at last check, www.cnn.com was associated with eight different IP addresses. (You can check the number of addresses associated with a name using the `host` command, as described in Chapter 88.)

Using Multiple DNS Servers to Spread Out DNS Requests

The term *DNS load balancing* also has a completely different meaning from what I described in the previous section. In the discussion of DNS server roles, I talked about how each zone should have at least one slave (secondary) DNS server in addition to the master (primary) server. The usually stated main reason for this is redundancy, in case something happens to cause the master server to fail. However, having a slave server can also allow the load of DNS resolution requests to be balanced between the servers. In fact, some busy domains have more than two servers specifically for this reason.

Thus, *DNS load balancing* can refer to either using DNS to spread the load of requests (such as web page requests) to a device that is named using DNS or to spreading the load of DNS requests themselves.

DNS Name Server Enhancements

The fundamentals of operation of DNS servers, as explained in the preceding sections in this chapter, are specified in the main DNS standards, RFC 1034 and 1035. These documents are pretty old by computer industry standards; they were published in 1987. To the credit of the designers of DNS, most of what they originally put into the DNS protocol is still valid and in use today. The creators of DNS knew that it had to be able to scale to a large size, and the system has successfully handled the expansion of the Internet to a degree far beyond what anyone could have imagined 15 or so years ago.

As originally defined, DNS requires that DNS information be updated manually by editing master files on the master server for a zone. The zone is then copied in its entirety to slave servers using the polling/zone-transfer mechanism described earlier in this chapter. This method is satisfactory when the internetwork is relatively small and changes to a zone are made infrequently. However, in the modern Internet, large zones may require nearly constant changes to their RRs. Hand-editing and constantly copying master files can be impractical, especially when they grow large, and having slave servers get out of date between zone transfers may lead to reliability and performance concerns. For these reasons, several enhancements to the operation of DNS servers have been proposed over the years. We'll take a closer look at three of them here: DNS Notify, incremental zone transfers, and Dynamic DNS.

Automating Zone Transfers: DNS Notify

The first problem that many DNS administrators wanted to tackle was the reliance on polling for updating slave name servers. Imagine that you placed an order for a new music CD at your favorite online music store, but it was out of stock—backordered. Which makes more sense: having you call them every six hours to ask if your CD has arrived yet, or having the store simply call you when it shows up?

The answer is so obvious that the question seems ridiculous. Yet DNS uses the first model: slave name servers must constantly call up their zone masters and ask them, "Has anything changed yet?" This both generates unnecessary traffic and results in the slave name server being out of date from the time the master *does* change until the next poll is performed. Tweaking the Refresh time for the zone allows only the choice between more polls or more staleness when changes happen; neither is really good.

To improve this situation, a new technique was developed and formalized in RFC 1996, published in 1996 (weird coincidence!). This standard, "A Mechanism for Prompt Notification of Zone Changes (DNS NOTIFY)," defines a new DNS message type called *Notify* and describes a protocol for its use. The Notify message is a variation on the standard DNS message type, with some of the fields redefined to support this new feature.

If both the master and slave name servers support this feature, when a modification is made to an RR, the master server will automatically send a Notify message to its slave server(s), saying, "Your CD has arrived!" er... "The database has changed." The slave then acts as if its Refresh timer had just expired. Enabling this feature allows the Refresh interval to be dramatically increased, since slave servers don't need to constantly poll the master for changes.

> **KEY CONCEPT** The optional DNS *Notify* feature allows a master name server to inform slave name servers when changes are made to a zone. This has two advantages: It cuts down on unnecessary polling by the slave servers to find out if changes have occurred to DNS information, and it also reduces the amount of time that slave name servers have out-of-date records.

Improving Zone Transfer Efficiency: Incremental Transfers

The second issue with regular DNS is the need to transfer the entire zone whenever a change to any part of it is made. There are many zones on the Internet that have truly enormous master files that change constantly. Consider the master files for the .COM zone, for example. Having to copy the entire database to slave name servers every time there is a change to even one record is beyond inefficient—it's downright insane!

RFC 1995, "Incremental Zone Transfer in DNS," specifies a new type of zone transfer called an *incremental zone transfer*. When this feature is implemented on master and slave name servers in a zone, the master server keeps track of the most recent changes made to the database. Each time a slave server determines that a change has occurred and the slave's database needs to be updated, it sends an IXFR (incremental transfer) query to the master, which contains the serial number of the slave's current copy of the database. The master then looks to see what RRs have changed since that serial number was the current one and sends only the updated RRs to the slave server.

To conserve storage, the master server obviously doesn't keep all the changes made to its database forever. It will generally track the last few modifications to the database, with the serial number associated with each. If the slave sends an IXFR request that contains a serial number for which recent change information is still on the master server, only the changes are sent in reply. If the request has a serial number so old that the master server no longer has information about some of the changes since that version of the database, a complete zone transfer is performed instead of an incremental one.

> **KEY CONCEPT** The DNS *incremental zone transfer* enhancement uses a special message type that allows a slave name server to determine what changes have occurred since it last synchronized with the master server. By transferring only the changes, the amount of time and bandwidth used for zone transfers can be significantly reduced.

Dealing with Dynamic IP Addresses: DNS Update/Dynamic DNS

The third problem with classic DNS is that it assumes changes are made infrequently to zones, so they can be handled by hand-editing master files. Some zones are so large that hand-editing of the master files would be nearly continuous. However, the problem goes beyond just inconvenience. Regular DNS assumes that the IP address for a host is relatively static. Modern networks, however, make use of host technologies such as the Dynamic Host Configuration Protocol (DHCP) (described in Part III-3), to assign IP addresses dynamically to devices. When DHCP is used, the IP address of each host in a zone could change on a weekly, daily, or even hourly basis! Clearly, there would be no hope of keeping up with this rate of change using a human being and a text editor.

In April 1997, RFC 2136, "Dynamic Updates in the Domain Name System (DNS UPDATE)," was published. This standard describes an enhancement to basic DNS operation that allows DNS information to be dynamically updated. When this feature is implemented, the resulting system is sometimes called *Dynamic DNS (DDNS)*.

RFC 2136 defines a new DNS message type: the Update message. Like the Notify message, the Update message is designed around the structure of regular DNS messages, but with changes to the meanings of several of the fields. As the name implies, Update messages allow RRs to be selectively changed within the master name server for a zone. Using a special message syntax, it is possible to add, delete, or modify RRs.

Obviously, care must be taken in how this feature is used, since we don't want just anyone to be making changes willy-nilly to our master records. The standard specifies a detailed process for verifying Update messages, as well as security procedures that must be put into place so the server accepts such messages from only certain individuals or systems.

Dynamic DNS allows administrators to make changes much more easily, but its true power becomes evident only when it is used to integrate DNS with other address-related protocols and services. Dynamic DNS solves a major weakness with traditional DNS: the inability to easily associate a host name with an address assigned using a protocol like DHCP.

With DNS servers supporting this feature, DNS and DHCP can be integrated, allowing automatic address and name assignment, and automatic update of DNS records when a host's IP address changes. One common application of Dynamic DNS is to allow the use of DNS names by those who access the Internet using a service provider that dynamically assigns IP addresses. Dynamic DNS is similarly used by certain directory services, notably Microsoft's Active Directory, to associate addresses with device names.

KEY CONCEPT An enhancement to DNS, commonly called *Dynamic DNS (DDNS)*, allows DNS information in a server's database to be updated automatically, rather than always requiring hand-editing of master files. This can not only save time and energy on the part of administrators, but it also allows DNS to better handle dynamic address assignment, such as the type performed by host configuration protocols like DHCP.

56

DNS RESOLUTION CONCEPTS AND RESOLVER OPERATIONS

In the preceding three chapters, I have described the Domain Name System (DNS) name space, authorities, registration mechanism, and name servers. These elements can all be considered part of the infrastructure of DNS; they are the parts of the system that must be established first to enable it to be used. Once we have these components in place, we can actually get down to the business at hand: name resolution. This is accomplished using a specific set of procedures carried out by DNS clients called *resolvers.*

In this chapter, I describe DNS name resolvers and the process of name resolution itself. I begin with an overview of the functions performed by DNS resolvers and how they work in general terms. I then describe the two fundamental methods of name resolution used in DNS: iterative and recursive resolution. I discuss the way that resolvers improve efficiency through local resolution and caching. I describe the steps in the actual name resolution algorithm. I then cover two special cases of name resolution: reverse name resolution using the special IN-ADDR.ARPA domain, and the way that DNS provides mail support using Mail Exchange resource records.

RELATED INFORMATION *The information in this section complements that in the previous chapter on DNS name servers. I assume in the topics here that you have at least basic familiarity with DNS servers.*

DNS Resolver Functions and General Operation

Name servers are arguably the most important part of the DNS system as a whole. After all, they store all the data on the system and actually provide the addresses we need when names are given to them. Without these servers, there would be no DNS at all. Of course, what use is a server if nobody is asking for service? The clients in the system, called *resolvers*, are also important, because they initiate the process of name resolution. Resolvers are where the rubber meets the road, so to speak.

The operation of DNS resolvers is explained in the two main DNS standards. RFC 1034 describes the functions performed by resolvers and how they work in general terms. This includes a discussion of the algorithm used to conduct name resolution. RFC 1035 deals more with the implementation details of resolvers and the fine points of how they do their jobs. Several subsequent standards have modified these base standards, changing some of the ways that resolvers work in different ways.

Name Resolution Services

Just as the main job of a DNS server is to store DNS name data and serve it when it receives requests, the main job of a DNS resolver is to, well, resolve. While most people think of name resolution as only the process of transforming a DNS name into an IP address, this is just one of several types of resolution services performed by DNS. The following are a few of the most typical types of DNS resolution:

Standard Name Resolution Taking a DNS name as input and determining its corresponding IP address.

Reverse Name Resolution Taking an IP address and determining what name is associated with it.

Electronic Mail Resolution Determining where to send electronic mail (email) messages based on the email address used in a message.

Functions Performed by Name Resolvers

There are other types of resolution activities as well, though again, most name resolution requests are of the standard variety, making it the primary focus in our discussion. To accomplish this task, name resolvers perform a number of related functions:

Providing the User Interface Normal name resolution usually doesn't involve explicitly running a piece of resolver software. In your web browser, you don't have to say, "Please find the IP address for www.xyzindustries.com," and then say, "Please connect to this IP address for XYZ Industries." You just type www.xyzindustries.com, and the name resolution happens. There is no magic involved. The resolver is just called *implicitly* instead of explicitly. The web browser recognizes that a name has been entered instead of an IP address and feeds it to the resolver, saying, "I need you to resolve this name, please." (Hey, it never hurts to be polite.) The resolver takes care of resolution and provides the IP address to the web browser, which connects to the site. Thus, the resolver is the interface between the user (both the human user and the software user, the browser) and the DNS system.

Forming and Sending Queries Given a name to resolve, the DNS resolver must create an appropriate query using the DNS messaging system, determine what type of resolution to perform, and send the query to the appropriate name server.

Processing Responses The resolver must accept back responses from the DNS server to which it sent its query and decide what to do with the information within the reply. As you'll see, it may be necessary for more than one server to be contacted for a particular name resolution.

> **KEY CONCEPT** The primary clients in DNS are software modules called DNS *name resolvers.* They are responsible for accepting names from client software, generating resolution requests to DNS servers, and processing and returning responses.

These tasks seem fairly simple, and they are in some ways, but implementation can become rather complicated. The resolver may need to juggle several outstanding name resolutions simultaneously. It must keep track of the different requests, queries, and responses and make sure everything is kept straight.

Name resolvers don't need to perform nearly as many administrative jobs as name servers do; clients are usually simpler than servers in this regard. One important support function that many name resolvers do perform, however, is caching. Like name servers, name resolvers can cache the results of the name resolutions they perform to save time if the same resolution is required again. (Not all resolvers perform caching, however.)

Even though resolvers are the DNS components that are most associated with name resolution, name servers can also act as clients in certain types of name resolution. In fact, it is possible to set up a network so that the resolvers on each of the client machines do nothing more than hand resolution requests to a local DNS server and let the server take care of it. In this case, the client resolver becomes little more than a shell, sometimes called a *stub resolver.* This has the advantage of centralizing name resolution for the network, but a potential disadvantage of performance reduction.

DNS Name Resolution Techniques: Iterative and Recursive Resolution

Conventional name resolution transforms a DNS name into an IP address. At the highest level, this process can be considered to have two phases. In the first phase, we locate a DNS name server that has the information we need: the address that goes with a particular name. In the second phase, we send that server a request containing the name we want to resolve, and it sends back the address required.

Somewhat ironically, the second phase (the actual mapping of the name into an address) is fairly simple. It is the first phase—finding the right server—that is potentially difficult and represents most of the work in DNS name resolution.

While perhaps surprising, this is a predictable result of how DNS is structured. Name information in DNS is not centralized, but rather distributed throughout a hierarchy of servers, each of which is responsible for one zone in the DNS name space. This means we must follow a special sequence of steps to find the server that has the information we need.

The formal process of name resolution parallels the treelike hierarchy of the DNS name space, authorities, and servers. Resolution of a particular DNS name starts with the most general part of the name and proceeds to the most specific part. Naturally, the most general part of every name is the *root* of the DNS tree, represented in a name as a trailing dot (.), sometimes omitted. The next most specific part is the top-level domain (TLD), then the second-level domain, and so forth. The DNS name servers are linked in that the DNS server at one level knows the name of the servers that are responsible for subdomains in zones below it at the next level.

Suppose we start with C.B.A. as the fully qualified domain name (FQDN). Formally, every name resolution begins with the root of the tree—this is why the root name servers are so important. It's possible that the root name servers are authoritative for this name, but this is probably not the case; that's not what the root name servers are usually used for. What the root name server does know is the name of the server responsible for the TLD: A.. The name server for A. may have the information to resolve C.B.A., but it's still fairly high level, so C.B.A. is probably not directly within its zone. In that case, it will not know the address we seek, but it will know the name of the server responsible for B.A.. In turn, that name server may be authoritative for C.B.A., or it may just know the address of the server for C.B.A., which will have the information we need. As you can see, it is very possible that several different servers may be needed in a name resolution.

KEY CONCEPT Since DNS name information is stored as a distributed database spread across many servers, name resolution cannot usually be performed using a single request/response communication. It is first necessary to find the server that has the information that the resolver requires. This usually requires a sequence of message exchanges, starting from a root name server and proceeding down to the specific server containing the resource records (RRs) that the client requires.

The DNS standards actually define two distinct ways of following this hierarchy of servers to discover the correct one. They both eventually lead to the right device, but they differ in how they assign responsibility for resolution when it requires multiple steps. The two techniques are *iterative resolution* and *recursive resolution.*

Iterative Resolution

When a client sends an iterative request to a name server, the server responds with either the answer to the request (for a regular resolution, the IP address we want) *or* the name of another server that has the information or is closer to it. The original client must then *iterate* by sending a new request to this referred server, which again may either answer it or provide another server name. The process continues until the correct server is found. The iterative resolution method is illustrated in Figure 56-1.

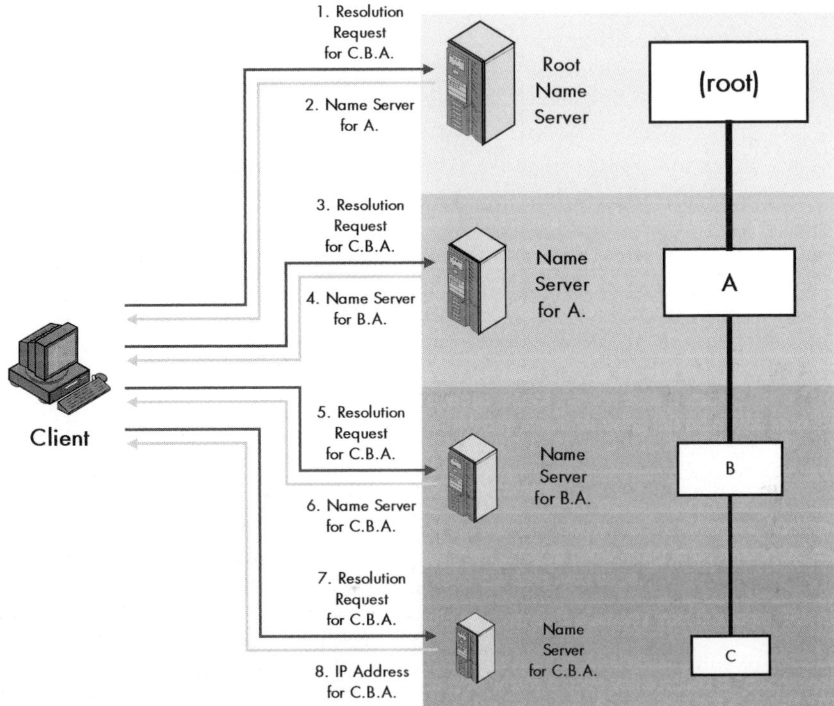

Figure 56-1: Iterative DNS name resolution *In this example, the client is performing a name resolution for C.B.A. using strictly iterative resolution. It is thus responsible for forming all DNS requests and processing all replies. It starts by sending a request to the root name server for this mythical hierarchy. That server doesn't have the address of C.B.A., so it instead returns the address of the name server for A. The client then sends its query to that name server, which points the client to the server for B.A. That name server refers the client to the name server that actually has the address for C.B.A., which returns it to the client. Contrast this to Figure 56-2.*

Recursive Resolution

When a client sends a recursive request to a name server, the server responds with the answer if it has the information sought. If it doesn't, the server takes responsibility for finding the answer by becoming a client on behalf of the original client and sending new requests to other servers. The original client sends only one request and eventually gets the information it wants (or an error message if it is not available). This technique is shown in Figure 56-2.

Contrasting Iterative and Recursive Resolution

To help explain the difference between iterative and recursive resolution, let's take a side trip to a real-world case. Suppose you are trying to find the phone number of your old friend Carol, with whom you haven't spoken in years. You call your friend Joe. He doesn't have Carol's number, but he gives you John's number, suggesting you call him. So you call John. He doesn't have the information, but he knows the number of Carol's best friend, Debbie, and gives that to you. You call Debbie, and she gives you Carol's information. This is an example of an iterative process.

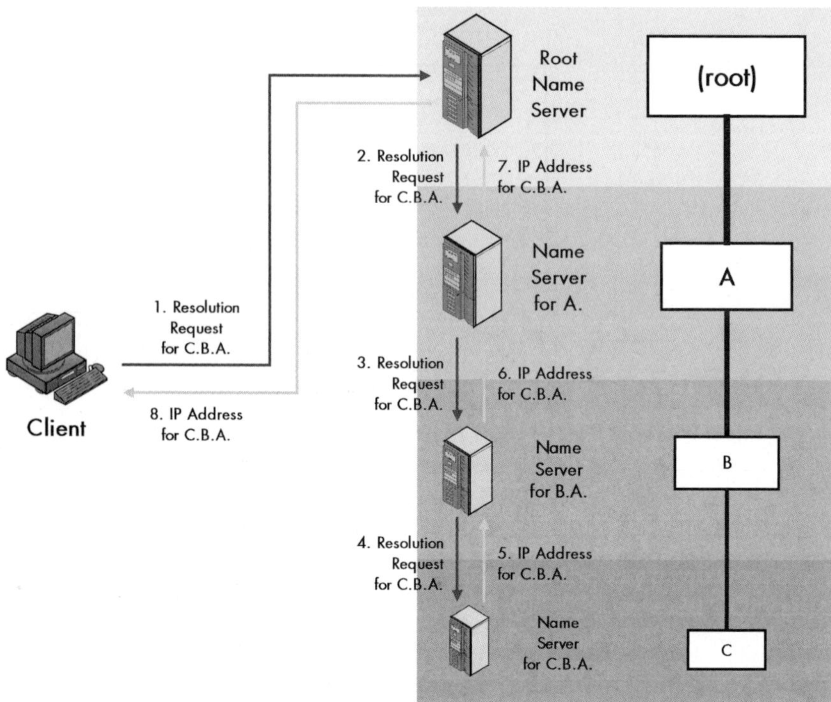

Figure 56-2: Recursive DNS name resolution *This is the same theoretical DNS resolution shown in Figure 56-1, but this time, the client asks for the name servers to perform recursive resolution, and they agree to do so. As in the iterative case, the client sends its initial request to the root name server. That server doesn't have the address of C.B.A., but instead of merely returning to the client the address of the name server for A., it sends a request to that server itself. That name server sends a request to the server for B.A., which sends a request to the server for C.B.A.. The address of C.B.A. is then carried back up the chain of requests, from the server of C.B.A. to that of B.A., then A., then the root, and then finally, back to the client.*

In contrast, suppose you call Joe and Joe says, "I don't know, but I think I know how to find out." He calls John, and then Debbie, and then calls you back with the phone number. That would be like recursive resolution.

So, in essence, iteration is like doing the job yourself, while recursion is like passing the buck. You might think that everyone would always want to use recursion since it makes the other guy do the work. This is true, but passing the buck is not considered good form if it is not done with permission. Not all name servers support recursion, especially servers near the top of the hierarchy. Obviously, we don't want to bog down certain name servers—such as the root name servers, the ones that handle .COM, and other critical TLDs—with doing recursion. It is for this reason that clients must request that name servers perform recursion for them. One place where recursion is often used is with the local name server on a network. Rather than making client machine resolvers perform iterative resolution, it is common for the resolver to generate a recursive request to the local DNS server, which then generates iterative requests to other servers as needed. As you can see, recursive and iterative requests can be combined in a single resolution, providing significant flexibility to the process as a whole. This is demonstrated in a more realistic example in the "DNS Name Resolution Process" section later in this chapter.

Again, remember that for the purpose of understanding resolution, a DNS server can act as a client. As soon as a DNS server accepts a recursive request for resolution on a name it cannot resolve itself, it becomes a client in the process. Also, it is common for resolvers to know the names of not one, but two local DNS servers, so if a problem occurs reaching the first, they can try the second.

> **KEY CONCEPT** The two methods of name resolution in DNS are *iterative resolution* and *recursive resolution*. In iterative resolution, if a client sends a request to a name server that does not have the information the client needs, the server returns a pointer to a different name server, and the client sends a new request to that server. In recursive resolution, if a client sends a request to a server that doesn't have the requested information, that server takes on the responsibility for sending requests to other servers to find the necessary records, and then returns them to the client. A server doing this takes on the role of client for its requests to other servers.

DNS Name Resolution Efficiency Improvements: Caching and Local Resolution

The basic resolution techniques—iterative and recursive—can be considered complete from an algorithmic standpoint. By starting at the top (root) and working our way down, we are "guaranteed" to always eventually arrive at the server that has the information we need. I put *guaranteed* in quotation marks because, as always, there are no real guarantees in networking—we might have asked for a nonexistent name, or a server might have bad data, for example. But in the absence of such atypical problems, the process leads to the information eventually.

The problem is that last word: *eventually*. Both iterative and recursive resolution will get us to the right server, but they take a long time to do it, especially if the name we are trying to resolve is in a deep part of the DNS hierarchy (for example, F.E.D.C.B.A.). Since resolution is done so often, it is helpful to define changes to the basic resolution process that improve efficiency as much as possible.

The Motivation for Caching: Locality of Reference

A computer science principle called *locality of reference* describes two common phenomena related to how computers (and networks) are used. The first, sometimes called *spatial locality of reference*, observes that a resource is more likely to be referenced if it is near another resource that was recently referenced. The second, *temporal locality of reference*, says a resource is more likely to be accessed if it was recently accessed.

We can observe both of these phenomena by using the example of browsing the Web. To observe spatial locality of reference, notice what happens when you visit a site such as http://www.tcpipguide.com. The initial request asks the server for the main index document of *The TCP/IP Guide*. However, that document contains links to several images and other items, all of which are also located at the domain tcpipguide.com. When your browser asks for the main document, it will shortly thereafter also ask for a number of graphics. As you navigate the site, you will click links to go to other web pages. Again, most of these will be at the same domain, tcpipguide.com.

What this means is that if we resolve a particular domain name, it is likely that we will need to resolve it again very soon in the future. It would be silly to need to interrogate the same domain server dozens of times, asking it to resolve the same name each time.

The second phenomenon, *temporal locality of reference*, is one you have probably noticed yourself. You are far more likely to access a resource you have used recently than one you have not looked at in a year. This means that maintaining information about recently used resources can be inherently advantageous.

These two phenomena are the rationale for caching in the computer world in general, and as you have seen in Chapter 55, in DNS servers in particular. The same advantages apply to resolvers, and many of them perform caching also, in a way rather similar to how it is done in servers.

Name Resolver Caching

On a particular client computer, once a particular name is resolved, it is cached and remains ready for the next time it is needed. Again, this eliminates traffic and load on DNS servers. (Note, however, that not all resolvers perform caching.)

You might be wondering why we bother having caching on both resolvers and servers. This is not redundant, as it may appear. Or rather, it's redundant, but in a good way. To understand why, we must recognize that a fundamental trade-off in caching is that a cache provides better performance the closer it is the requester of the data, but better coverage the farther it is from the user.

If resolvers didn't cache results but our local server did, we could get the information from the server's cache, but it would require waiting for the exchange of a query and response. The resolver's cache is closer to the user and so more efficient. At the same time, this doesn't obviate the need for caching at our network's local DNS server. The server is farther away from the user than the resolver, but its cache is shared by many machines. They can all benefit from its cache. For example, if you look up a particular name, and then someone else does a few minutes later, she can use your cached resolution, even though she is typing it for the first time.

KEY CONCEPT In addition to the caching performed by DNS name servers, many (but not all) DNS resolvers also cache the results of recent resolution requests. This cache is checked prior to beginning a name resolution, to save time when multiple requests are made for the same name.

Caching by name resolvers follows the same general principles and rules as caching by name servers, outlined in Chapter 55. The amount of time a resource record (RR) is held in the cache is specified by its Time to Live (TTL) value. Also, resolvers will not cache the results of certain queries, such as reverse lookups, and may also not cache a resolution if they suspect (for whatever reason) that the data returned is unreliable or corrupted.

Local Resolution

One other area where resolution efficiency can be improved is the special case where we are trying to resolve the names of computers in our own organizations.

Suppose that you, an employee at XYZ Industries, want to get some sales information using the File Transfer Protocol (FTP) from sales.xyzindustries.com. Your FTP client will invoke your local resolver to resolve that name, by sending it to your local DNS server. Now, would it be smart for that server, which is here inside the company, to start the resolution process up at the root name server? Not really.

The local DNS server that accepts local resolution requests from resolvers on the network may be the authoritative name server for sales.xyzindustries.com. In other cases, it may know how to answer certain resolution requests directly. Obviously, it makes sense for the server to check to see if it can answer a resolver's query before heading up to the root server, since this provides a faster answer to the client and saves internetwork traffic. This is called *local resolution.*

Most DNS servers will perform this check to see if they have the information needed for a request before commencing the formal top-down resolution process. The exception is DNS servers that do not maintain information about any zones: *caching-only servers.* In some cases, DNS resolvers on client machines may also have access to certain local zone information, in which case, they can use it instead of sending a resolution query at all.

NOTE *Most operating systems support the use of the old host table mechanism (described in Chapter 51), which can be useful for local machines on a network. If a host has a host table, the resolver will check the host table to see if it can find a mapping for a name before it will bother with the more time-consuming DNS resolution process. This is not technically part of DNS, but is often used in conjunction with it.*

DNS Name Resolution Process

In the first half of this chapter, I have described what name resolvers do, explained the basic top-down resolution process using iterative and recursive resolution, and discussed how local resolution and caching are used to improve resolution performance. Now it's time to tie all this background material together and see how the name resolution process works as a whole.

As usual, the best way to do this is by example. Here, I will actually combine two examples I have used earlier: the fictitious company XYZ Industries and the nonexistent college, Googleplex University.

A Simple Example of DNS Name Resolution

Let's say that XYZ Industries runs its own DNS servers for the xyzindustries.com zone. The master name server is called ns1.xyzindustries.com, and the slave is ns2.xyzindustries.com. These are also used as local DNS servers for resolvers on client machines. We'll assume for this example that, as is often the case, our DNS servers will accept recursive requests from machines within our company, but we will not assume that other machines will accept such requests. Let's also assume that both the server and resolver perform caching, and that the caches are empty.

Let's say that Googleplex University runs its own DNS servers for the googleplex .edu domain, as in the example in Chapter 54. There are three subdomains: finearts.googleplex.edu, compsci.googleplex.edu, and admin.googleplex.edu. Of these, compsci.googleplex.edu is in a separate zone with dedicated servers, while the other subdomains are in the googleplex.edu zone (see Figure 54-2).

Now, suppose you are an employee within XYZ Industries and one of your clients is in charge of the networking department at Googleplex U. You type into your web browser the address of that department's web server, www.net.compsci.googleplex.edu. In simplified terms, the procedure would involve the following steps (Figure 56-3 shows the process graphically):

1. Your web browser recognizes the request for a name and invokes your local resolver, passing to it the name www.net.compsci.googleplex.edu.
2. The resolver checks its cache to see if it already has the address for this name. If it does, it returns it immediately to the web browser, but in this case, we are assuming that it does not. The resolver also checks to see if it has a local host table file. If so, it scans the file to see if this name has a static mapping. If so, it resolves the name using this information immediately. Again, let's assume it does not, since that would be boring.
3. The resolver generates a recursive query and sends it to ns1.xyzindustries.com (using that server's IP address, of course, which the resolver knows).
4. The local DNS server receives the request and checks its cache. Again, let's assume it doesn't have the information needed. If it did, it would return the information, marked non-authoritative, to the resolver. The server also checks to see if it has in its zone resource records that can resolve www.net.compsci.googleplex.edu. Of course, it does not in this case, since they are in totally different domains.
5. ns1.xyzindustries.com generates an iterative request for the name and sends it to a root name server.
6. The root name server does not resolve the name. It returns the name and address of the name server for the .edu domain.
7. ns1.xyzindustries.com generates an iterative request and sends it to the name server for .edu.
8. The name server for .edu returns the name and address of the name server for the googleplex.edu domain.
9. ns1.xyzindustries.com generates an iterative request and sends it to the name server for googleplex.edu.
10. The name server for googleplex.edu consults its records. It sees, however, that this name is in the compsci.googleplex.edu subdomain, which is in a separate zone. It returns the name server for that zone.
11. ns1.xyzindustries.com generates an iterative request and sends it to the name server for compsci.googleplex.edu.
12. The name server for compsci.googleplex.edu is authoritative for www.net.compsci.googleplex.edu. It returns the IP address for that host to ns1.xyzindustries.com.
13. ns1.xyzindustries.com caches this resolution.
14. The local name server returns the resolution to the resolver on your local machine.
15. Your local resolver also caches the information.

16. The local resolver gives the address to your browser.
17. Your browser commences an HTTP request to the Googleplex machine's IP address.

This seems rather complicated and slow. Of course, computers work faster than you can read (or I can type, for that matter). Even given that, the benefits of caching are obvious—if the name were in the cache of the resolver or the local DNS server, most of these steps would be avoided.

Note that this example is highly simplified and also shows only one possible way that servers might be set up. For one thing, it is possible that even though compsci .googleplex.edu is in a separate zone from googleplex.edu, they might use the same server. In that case, one iteration in the process would be skipped. The example also doesn't show what happens if an error occurs in the process. Also, if the name entered were an alias, indicated by a CNAME record, this would change the processing as well.

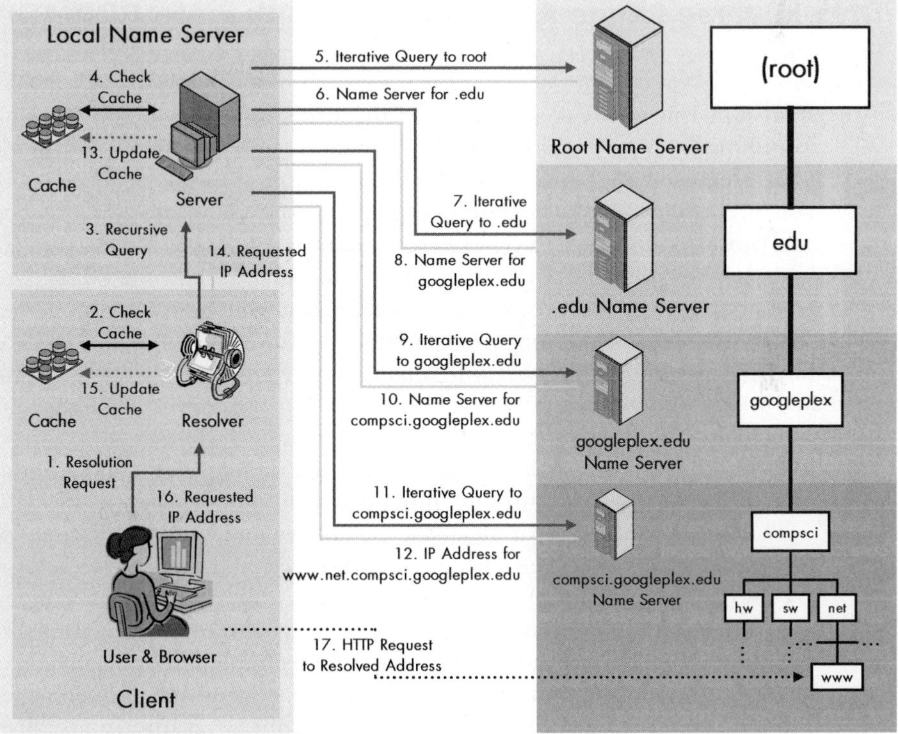

Figure 56-3: Example of the DNS name resolution process *This fairly complex example illustrates a typical DNS name resolution using both iterative and recursive resolution. The user types a DNS name (www.net.compsci.googleplex.edu) into a web browser, which causes a DNS resolution request to be made from her client machine's resolver to a local DNS name server. That name server agrees to resolve the name recursively on behalf of the resolver, but uses iterative requests to accomplish it. These requests are sent to a DNS root name server, followed in turn by the name servers for .edu, googleplex.edu, and compsci.googleplex.edu. The IP address is then passed to the local name server and then back to the user's resolver, and finally, to her web browser software.*

Changes to Resolution to Handle Aliases (CNAME Records)

CNAME records are used to allow a constant name for a device to be presented to the outside world, while allowing the actual device that corresponds to the name to vary inside the organization. When a CNAME is used, it changes the name resolution process by adding an extra step: First we resolve the alias to the canonical name, and then we resolve the canonical name.

For example, web servers are almost always named starting with www., so at XYZ Industries, we want people to be able to find our website at www.xyzindustries.com. However, the web server may be shared with other services on bigserver.xyzindustries.com. We can set up a CNAME record to point www.xyzindustries.com to bigserver.xyzindustries.com. Resolution of www will result in a CNAME pointing to bigserver, which is then itself resolved. If in the future, our business grows and we decide to upgrade our web service to run on biggerserver.xyzindustries.com, we just change the CNAME record, and users are unaffected.

DNS Reverse Name Resolution Using the IN-ADDR.ARPA Domain

If most people were asked to identify the core job of DNS to one function, they would probably say it was converting the names of objects into the numeric IP addresses associated with them. (Well, they would if they knew much about DNS.) For this reason, DNS is sometimes compared to a telephone book, or to telephone 411 (information) service. There are certain problems with this analogy, but at the highest level, it is valid. In both cases, we take a name, consult a database (of one type or another), and produce from it a number that matches that name.

In the real world, there are sometimes situations where you don't want to find the phone number that goes with a name, but rather, you have a phone number and want to know what person it belongs to. For example, this might happen if your telephone records the number of incoming calls but you don't have caller ID to display the name associated with a number. You might also find a phone number on a piece of paper and not remember whose number it is.

Similarly, in the networking world, there are many situations where we have an IP address and want to know what name goes with it. For example, a World Wide Web server records the IP address of each device that connects to it in its server logs, but these numbers are generally meaningless to humans, who prefer to see the names that go with them. A more serious example might be a hacker trying to break into your computer; by converting the IP address into a name, you might be able to find out what part of the world he is from, what Internet service provider (ISP) he is using, and so forth. There are also many reasons why a network administrator might want to find out the name that goes with an address, for setup or troubleshooting purposes.

DNS originally included a feature called *inverse querying* that would allow this type of "opposite" resolution.

The Original Method: Inverse Querying

For inverse querying, a resolver could send a query which, instead of having a name filled in and a space for the server to fill in the IP address, had the IP address and a space for the name. The server would check its RRs and return the name to the resolver.

This works fine in theory, and even in practice, if the internetwork is very small. However, remember that due to the distributed nature of DNS information, the biggest part of the job of resolution is finding the right server. Now, in the case of regular resolution, we can easily find the right server by traversing the hierarchy of servers. This is possible because the servers are connected together following a hierarchy of names.

DNS servers are not, however, arranged based on IP address. This means that to use inverse queries, we need to use the right name server for the IP address we want to resolve into a name, with no easy way to find out what it is. Sure, we could try sending the inverse query to the authoritative DNS server for every zone in the hierarchy. If you tried, it would probably take you longer than it took to write this book, so let's not go there. The end result of all of this is that inverse queries were never popular, except for local server troubleshooting. They were formally removed from DNS in November 2002 through the publishing of RFC 3425.

So, what to do? Well, the problem is that the servers are arranged by name and not by IP address. The solution, therefore, is as simple as it sounds: Arrange the servers by IP address. This doesn't mean we remove the name hierarchy, or duplicate all the servers, or anything silly like that. Instead, we create an additional, numerical hierarchy that coexists with the name hierarchy. We then use this to find names from numbers, using a process commonly called *reverse name resolution*.

The IN-ADDR.ARPA Name Structure for Reverse Resolution

The name hierarchy for the Internet is implemented using a special domain called *IN-ADDR.ARPA*, located within the reserved .ARPA TLD (*IN-ADDR* stands for *INternet ADDRess*). Recall from the discussion in Chapter 54 that .ARPA was originally used to transition old Internet hosts to DNS and is now used by the folks that run the Internet for various purposes.

A special numerical hierarchy is created within IN-ADDR.ARPA that covers the entire IP address space (see Figure 56-4):

- At the first level within IN-ADDR.ARPA there are 256 subdomains called 0, 1, 2, and so on, up to 255; for example, 191.IN-ADDR.ARPA. (Actually, there may not be all 256 of these, since some IP addresses are reserved, but let's ignore that for now.)
- Within each of the first-level subdomains, there are 256 further subdomains at the second level, numbered the same way. So, for example, one of these would be 27.191.IN-ADDR.ARPA.
- Again, there are 256 subdomains at the third level within each of the second-level subdomains, such as 203.27.191.IN-ADDR.ARPA.
- Finally, there are 256 subdomains at the fourth level within each of the third-level subdomains, such as 8.203.27.191.IN-ADDR.ARPA.

As you can see, within IN-ADDR.ARPA, we have created a name space that parallels the address space of the Internet Protocol (IP). Yes, this means there are several billion nodes and branches in this part of the Internet DNS name space!

RR Setup for Reverse Resolution

With this structure in place, we can now associate one entry in this name space with each entry in the real DNS name space. We do this using the Pointer (PTR) RR type. For example, if www.xyzindustries.com has the IP address 191.27.203.8, then the DNS server for its zone will have an Address (A) RR indicating this. In master file text format, it will say something like this:

```
www.xyzindustries.com.   A   191.27.203.8
```

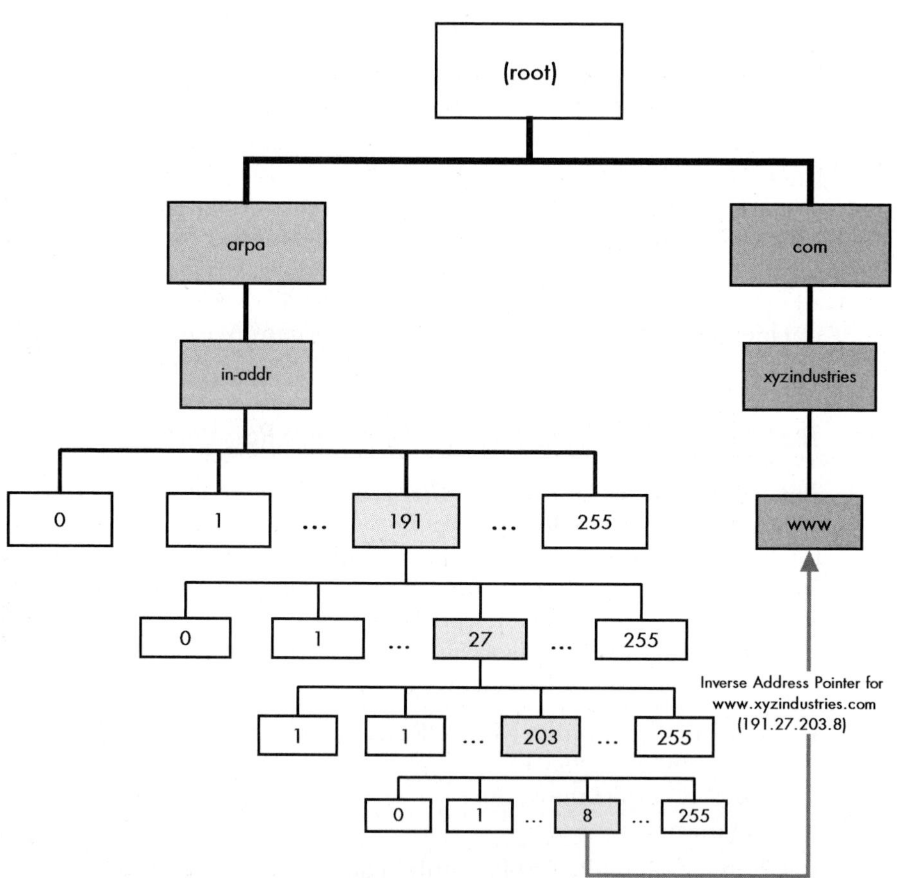

Figure 56-4: The DNS IN-ADDR.ARPA reverse name resolution hierarchy *The special IN-ADDR.ARPA hierarchy was created to allow easy reverse lookups of DNS names. IN-ADDR.ARPA contains 256 subdomains numbered 0 to 255, each of which has 256 subdomains numbered 0 to 255, and so forth, down to four levels. Thus, each IP address is represented in the hierarchy. This example shows the DNS domain name www.xyzindustries.com. It would have a conventional RR pointing to its IP address, 191.27.203.8, as well as a reverse resolution record at 8.203.27.191.IN-ADDR.ARPA, pointing to the domain name www.xyzindustries.com.*

However, there will also be the following entry for it within the IN-ADDR.ARPA domain:

```
8.203.27.191.IN-ADDR.ARPA    PTR    www.xyzindustries.com
```

NOTE *Remember that DNS names are case-insensitive, so* IN-ADDR.ARPA *could also be given as* in-addr.arpa.

Once this is done, reverse name resolution can be easily performed by doing a name resolution on 8.203.27.191.in-addr.arpa. If we do this, a server for the IN-ADDR.ARPA domain will return to us the name www.xyzindustries.com. This is shown in Figure 56-4.

KEY CONCEPT Most name resolutions require that we transform a DNS domain name into an IP address. However, there are cases where we want to perform a *reverse name resolution*, by starting with an IP address and finding out what domain name matches it. This is difficult to do using the conventional DNS distributed name hierarchy, because there is no easy way to find the DNS server containing the entries for a particular IP address. To this end, a special hierarchy called *IN-ADDR.ARPA* was set up for reverse name lookups. This hierarchy contains four levels of numerical subdomains structured so that each IP address has its own node. The node for an IP address contains an entry that points to the DNS domain name associated with that address.

I'm sure you've noticed that the numbers are backward in the IN-ADDR.ARPA domain. We've already seen the reason for this: Name resolution proceeds from the least specific to the most specific element, going from right to left. In contrast, IP addresses have the least specific octet on the left and the most specific on the right. Thus, we reverse them to maintain consistency with the DNS name space.

This immediately yields one extra benefit. Just as we can delegate authority for portions of the regular name space, for example, letting XYZ Industries be in charge of everything in xyzindustries.com, we can also delegate authority for parts of the IN-ADDR.ARPA name space. For example, since the Massachusetts Institute of Technology (MIT) owns all IP addresses with a first octet of 18 (at least, I think it still does), it is possible that if MIT wanted to, it could control the 18.IN-ADDR.ARPA domain as well for reverse queries. This would not be possible without reversing the octets.

Note that for this system to work reliably, it is essential that the data in the regular name space and the reverse name space remain consistent. Whenever a new DNS name is registered, an appropriate entry must be made within IN-ADDR.ARPA as well. Special procedures have been put into place to allow these pointer entries to be created automatically.

RELATED INFORMATION *A similar scheme using a different reverse domain is used for DNS under version 6 of the Internet Protocol (IPv6). See the end of Chapter 57 for more information.*

DNS Electronic Mail Support and Mail Exchange (MX) Resource Records

Most savvy users of the Internet know that DNS exists, and they usually associate it with the most common Internet applications. Of these applications, the "Big Kahuna" is the World Wide Web. It's probably the case that the majority of DNS name resolution requests are spawned as a result of web server domain names being typed into browsers billions of times a day, as well as requests for named pages generated by both user mouse clicks and web-based applications.

Of course, DNS is not tied specifically to any one application. We can specify names in any place where an IP address would go. For example, you can use a DNS name instead of an address for an FTP client, or even for a troubleshooting utility like traceroute or ping (see Chapter 88). The resolver will, in each case, take care of translating the name for you.

There's one application that has always used DNS, but it's one that doesn't usually spring to mind when you think about DNS: electronic mail (discussed in Part III-7). Electronic mail (email) is, in fact, more reliant on DNS than just about any other TCP/IP application. Consider that while you may sometimes type an IP address for a command like traceroute, or even type it into a browser, you probably have never sent anyone mail by entering joe@14.194.29.60 into your email client. You type something like joe@xyzindustries.com, and DNS takes care of figuring out where email for XYZ Industries is to go.

Special Requirements for Email Name Resolution

Name resolution for email addresses is different from other applications in DNS, for three reasons (which I describe in more detail in the discussion of TCP/IP email addressing and address resolution in Chapter 75):

- We may not want email to go to the exact machine specified by the address.
- We need to be able to change server names without changing everyone's email address.
- We need to be able to support multiple servers for handling mail.

For example, XYZ Industries might want to use a dedicated mail server called mail.xyzindustries.com to handle incoming mail, but actually construct all of its email addresses to use @xyzindustries.com. This makes addresses shorter and allows the server's name to be changed without affecting user addresses. If the company wishes, it might decide to use two servers, mail1.xyzindustries.com and mail2.xyzindustries.com, for redundancy, and again have just @xyzindustries.com for addresses.

To allow the flexibility needed for these situations, a special DNS RR type, called a *Mail Exchange (MX)* record, is defined.

The Mail Exchange (MX) Record and Its Use

Each MX record specifies a particular mail server that is to be used to handle incoming email for a particular domain. Once this record is established, resolution of email messages is pretty much similar to regular resolution. Suppose you want to send a message to joe@xyzindustries.com. The basic process is as follows:

1. Your email client invokes the resolver on your local machine to perform an email resolution on xyzindustries.com.
2. Your local resolver and local DNS server follow the process described earlier in this chapter to find the authoritative server for xyzindustries.com, which is ns1.xyzindustries.com.
3. ns1.xyzindustries.com finds the MX record for xyzindustries.com and replies back indicating that mail.xyzindustries.com should be used for email.

The email client can't actually send anything to mail.xyzindustries.com; it needs its IP address. So, it would then need to resolve that name. This resolution request will likely end up right back at the same DNS name server that just handled the MX request. To eliminate the inefficiency of two separate resolutions, the DNS name server can combine the information. In our example, ns1.xyzindustries.com will include the A (Address) RR for mail.xyzindustries.com in the Additional section of the DNS message that it sends in step 3.

NOTE *RFC 1035 originally defined several other RR types related to email as well: Mailbox (MB), Mail Group (MG), and Mail Rename (MR). These are called "experimental" in the standard. I think the experiment failed, whatever it was, because I don't believe these are used today. There are also two even older mail-related RRs, Mail Destination (MD) and Mail Forwarder (MF), which must have been used at one time but were already obsolete at the time RFC 1035 itself was written.*

It is also possible to specify multiple MX records for a particular domain, each pointing to a different mail server's name. This provides redundancy, so if there is a problem with one mail server, another can pick up the slack. DNS allows each mail server to be specified with a *preference* value, so you can clearly indicate which is the main mail server, which is the first backup, the second backup, and so on. The DNS server will choose the mail server with the lowest preference value first, then the next highest one, and so on.

KEY CONCEPT Since email is sent using host names and not IP addresses, DNS contains special provisions to support the transfer of email between sites. Special *Mail Exchange (MX)* DNS RRs are set up that contain the names of mail servers that a domain wants to use for handling incoming email. Before sending email to a site, a device performs a name resolution to get that site's MX record, so it knows where to send the message.

57

DNS MESSAGING AND MESSAGE, RESOURCE RECORD, AND MASTER FILE FORMATS

Networking is all about the communication of information between connected devices. In the case of the Domain Name System (DNS), information about names and objects on the internetwork is exchanged during each of the many types of operations DNS performs. This involves sending *messages* between devices. Like most protocols, DNS uses its own set of messages with distinct field formats, and it follows a particular set of rules for generating them and transporting them over the internetwork.

In this chapter, I explain how messages are generated and sent in DNS, and I describe the formats used for messages and resource records (RRs). I begin with an overview discussion of DNS messages and how they are generated and transported. I provide an overview of the general DNS message format and the five sections it contains. I describe the notation used for names and the special compression method that helps keep DNS messages down in size. I then show the fields in the DNS message Header and Question section. I illustrate the common field format used for all RRs and the specific fields in the most important record types. I also provide a description of the format used for DNS text master files.

I conclude with a brief discussion of the changes made to DNS to support Internet Protocol version 6 (IPv6). Most of these changes (but not all of them) are associated with message formats and RRs, the subject of this chapter.

BACKGROUND INFORMATION *This chapter assumes that you are already familiar with DNS concepts and operation as described in Chapters 52 through 56.*

DNS Message Generation and Transport

In the preceding chapters in this part of the book, we have explored the many different tasks that servers and resolvers perform: regular name resolution, reverse name resolution, email resolution, zone transfers, and more. Each of these operations requires that information be exchanged between a pair of DNS devices. Like so many other TCP/IP protocols, DNS is designed to accomplish this information transfer using a *client/server* model. All DNS exchanges begin with a client sending a request and a server responding with an answer.

DNS Client/Server Messaging Overview

In Chapter 8's overview of TCP/IP's client/server nature, I explained a potential source of confusion regarding these terms: the fact that they refer to hardware roles, software roles, and transactional roles. This issue definitely applies when it comes to DNS. You've already seen that DNS implementation consists of two sets of software elements: resolvers that act as clients and name servers that are the servers. Resolver software usually runs on client machines like PCs, while name server software often runs on dedicated server hardware. However, these designations are based on the overall role of the hardware and software.

From a messaging viewpoint, the client is the initiator of the communication, regardless of what type of machine does this initiating, and the server is the device that responds to the client. A resolver usually acts as a client and a name server as a server. However, in a particular exchange, a DNS name server can act as a client, in at least two cases. First, in recursive name resolution, a server generates requests to others servers and therefore acts as a client. Second, in administrative functions like zone transfers, one server acts as a client and sends a request to another server. (There are no cases in DNS that I know of where a resolver acts as a server, incidentally.)

Most transactions in DNS consist of the exchange of a single query message and a single response message. The device acting as client for the transaction creates the query and sends it to the server; the server then sends back a reply. In certain cases where a great deal of data needs to be sent, such as zone transfers, the server may send back multiple messages. Multiple such transactions may be required to perform a complete name resolution, as the example of the DNS resolution process in the previous chapter demonstrated.

DNS Message Transport Using UDP and TCP

TCP/IP has two different transport layer protocols: the User Datagram Protocol (UDP) and Transmission Control Protocol (TCP) (see Part II-8). UDP and TCP share layer 4 in the TCP/IP model, because they are so different in terms of capabilities and operation. Some application layer protocols need the services of TCP and can use it to take advantage of them, while others are better off with the simpler UDP. DNS is itself a perfect example of the valid reasons for having both UDP and TCP in the protocol suite (see Chapter 42), because it uses both.

UDP is a simple connectionless protocol that provides no real features but is very fast. It is ideally suited for small, quick exchanges of information and can be faster than TCP because there is no need to establish a connection. This makes it a good choice for most of the conventional queries used in DNS, because they are normally very short, and fast data exchange is important. For this reason, the DNS standards recommend use of UDP for queries and replies as part of regular and reverse name resolution. UDP DNS messages are limited to 512 bytes; longer messages are truncated, and a special bit in the header is set to indicate that this has occurred. If a message being truncated causes a problem for its recipient, the query must be repeated using TCP.

NOTE *The 512-byte limit on DNS UDP messages can be surpassed if the optional Extension Mechanisms for DNS (EDNS0) are implemented. These are described in RFC 2671.*

Since UDP does not provide reliable delivery of messages, DNS clients must keep track of requests they have sent. If no response is received after a particular amount of time, the request must be retransmitted. The need to take care of these details is considered an acceptable trade-off for the lower setup costs involved with UDP, such as not requiring a connection. The rate at which retransmissions are sent is usually set at a minimum of two to five seconds to prevent excessive DNS traffic on the internetwork.

For certain special DNS transactions, UDP is simply inappropriate. The most common example of such a transaction is a zone transfer. While the query for a zone transfer is small in size, the amount of data sent in response can be quite large. The limit of 512 bytes for UDP is not even close to enough. Furthermore, we really do need to make sure that a zone transfer is accomplished reliably and with flow control and other data transfer management features, or we risk having corrupted zone information in our secondary DNS server databases.

The solution is to use TCP for these types of exchanges. TCP allows messages to be of arbitrary length, and as a connection-oriented, acknowledged, reliable protocol, automatically provides the mechanisms we need to ensure that zone transfers and other lengthy operations complete successfully. The cost is the small amount of overhead needed to establish the connection, but since zone transfers are infrequent (compared to the sheer volume of regular name resolutions), this is not a problem.

You can see how DNS nicely illustrates the roles of both TCP and UDP in TCP/IP. Since both transport protocols can be used, name servers listen for UDP and TCP requests on the same well-known port number, 53. The device acting as the client uses an ephemeral port number for the transaction. All DNS messages are sent unicast from one device directly to another.

KEY CONCEPT DNS uses both UDP and TCP to send messages. Conventional message exchanges are short, and thus well suited to the use of the very fast UDP; DNS itself handles the detection and retransmission of lost requests. For larger or more important exchanges of information, especially zone transfers, TCP is used—both for its reliability and its ability to handle messages of any size.

DNS Message Processing and General Message Format

As we've just discussed, DNS message exchanges are all based on the principle of client/server computing. In a particular exchange, one device acts as a client, initiating the communication by sending a query; the other acts as the server by responding to the query with an answer. This query/response behavior is an integral part of DNS, and it is reflected in the format used for DNS messages.

A common message format is used for DNS queries and responses. This message format contains five sections that provide a place for the query asked by the client, the answer(s) provided by the server, and header information that controls the entire process. Table 57-1 describes the DNS general message format, providing a brief summary of each of its sections and how they are used. You can also see a simplified illustration of the message format in Figure 57-1.

Table 57-1: DNS General Message Format

Section Name	Description
Header	Contains fields that describe the type of message and provide important information about it. Also contains fields that indicate the number of entries in the other sections of the message.
Question	Carries one or more questions—that is, queries for information being sent to a DNS name server.
Answer	Carries one or more RRs that answer the question(s) indicated in the Question section.
Authority	Contains one or more RRs that point to authoritative name servers that can be used to continue the resolution process.
Additional	Conveys one or more RRs that contain additional information related to the query that is not strictly necessary to answer the queries (questions) in the message.

The Header section is always present in all messages and is fixed in length. In addition to containing important DNS control information, it has a flag (QR) that indicates whether a message is a query or a response. It also has four "count" fields that tell the recipient the number of entries in the other four sections.

When a client initiates a query, it creates a message with the fields in the Header section filled in, and one or more queries (requests for information) in the Question section. It sets the QR flag to 0 to indicate that this is a query, and it places a number in the QDCount field of the header that indicates the number of questions in the Question section. The number of entries in the other sections are usually 0, so their count fields (ANCount, NSCount, and ARCount) are set to 0 in the header. (Although more than one question can be put into a query, usually only one is included.)

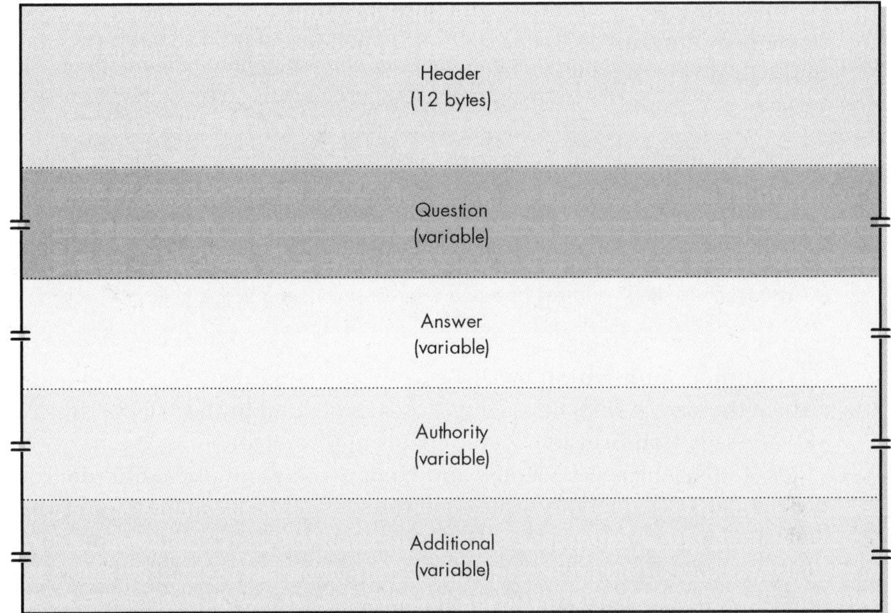

Figure 57-1: *DNS general message format*

When the server receives the query, it processes it and performs the information retrieval operation requested (if it can). It then uses the query as the basis for its response message. The Header and Question sections are copied to the response message, and the QR flag is set to 1 to indicate that the message is a reply. Certain fields are also changed in the Header section to provide information back to the client. For example, the server sets the RCode (Response Code) field to indicate whether the query was successful or if an error occurred, and if one did occur, to indicate what the problem was. The next section of this chapter illustrates all the Header fields and indicates how each is used by both client and server.

The server is also responsible for filling in the other three sections of the message: Answer, Authority, and Additional. These sections share the same basic format, each carrying one or more RRs that use a common record format. The number of records in each section is indicated using the count fields in the message header. The sections differ only in terms of the types of records they carry. Answer records are directly related to the question asked, while Authority records carry RRs that identify other name servers. Authority records are thus the means by which name servers are hierarchically linked when the server doesn't have the information the client requested.

The Additional section exists for the specific purpose of improving DNS efficiency. There are cases where a server supplies an answer to a query that it has reason to believe will lead to a subsequent question that the server can also answer. For example, suppose a server provides the name of another name server in the Authority section (an NS RR). The client may not have the address for that server, which would mean it must perform an extra name resolution to contact the referenced server. If the server providing the NS record already knows the IP address for this name server, it can include it in the Additional section. The same goes for a server providing an MX record as I explained in the discussion of DNS mail support in the previous chapter.

> **KEY CONCEPT** DNS uses a general message format for all messages. It consists of a fixed 12-byte header, a Question section that contains a query, and then three additional sections that can carry RRs of different types. The Answer section usually contains records that directly answer the question of the message; the Authority section holds the names of name servers being sent back to the client; and the Additional section holds extra information that may be of value to the client, such as the IP address of a name server mentioned in the Authority section.

Another optimization by DNS is a special compression technique used to reduce the size of DNS messages. This is explained in the "DNS Name Notation and Message Compression" section later in this chapter.

Note that the special Notify and Update messages use a different format than the regular DNS query/response messages. These special messages (whose use is described in the section about DNS server enhancements in Chapter 55) are based on the regular format but with the meanings of certain fields changed. You can find these field formats in RFC 1996 and RFC 2136, respectively.

The client/server information exchange in DNS is facilitated using query/response messaging. Both queries and responses have the same general format, containing up to five individual sections carrying information. Of these, two are usually found in both queries and responses: the Header section and the Question section. We will look at these two sections first, and then examine the RR formats used by servers for the other three message sections.

DNS Message Header Format

The header is the most important part of any message, since it is where critical control fields are carried. In DNS messages, the Header section carries several key control flags, and it also indicates which of the other sections are used in the message. Examining the Header section can help you understand several of the nuances of how messaging works in DNS.

The format of the Header section used in all DNS messages is illustrated in Figure 57-2 and described in detail in Tables 57-2, 57-3, and 57-4. Where fields are used differently by the client and server in an exchange, I have mentioned in Table 57-2 how the use is differentiated between the two.

Note that the current lists of valid question types, query operation codes, and response codes are maintained by the Internet Assigned Numbers Authority (IANA) as one of its many lists of Internet parameters. Response codes 0 to 5 are part of regular DNS and are defined in RFC 1035; codes 6 to 10 implement Dynamic DNS and are defined in RFC 2136.

Table 57-2: DNS Message Header Format

Field Name	Size (Bytes)	Description
ID	2	Identifier: A 16-bit identification field generated by the device that creates the DNS query. It is copied by the server into the response, so it can be used by that device to match that query to the corresponding reply received from a DNS server. This is used in a manner similar to how the Identifier field is used in many of the Internet Control Message Protocol (ICMP) message types.
QR	1/8 (1 bit)	Query/Response Flag: Differentiates between queries and responses. Set to 0 when the query is generated; changed to 1 when that query is changed to a response by a replying server.
OpCode	1/2 (4 bits)	Operation Code: Specifies the type of query the message is carrying. This field is set by the creator of the query and copied unchanged into the response. See Table 57-3 for the OpCode values.
AA	1/8 (1 bit)	Authoritative Answer Flag: This bit is set to 1 in a response to indicate that the server that created the response is authoritative for the zone in which the domain name specified in the Question section is located. If it is 0, the response is non-authoritative.
TC	1/8 (1 bit)	Truncation Flag: When set to 1, indicates that the message was truncated due to its length being longer than the maximum permitted for the type of transport mechanism used. TCP doesn't have a length limit for messages; UDP messages are limited to 512 bytes, so this bit being sent usually is an indication that the message was sent using UDP and was too long to fit. The client may need to establish a TCP session to get the full message. On the other hand, if the portion truncated was part of the Additional section, it may choose not to bother.
RD	1/8 (1 bit)	Recursion Desired: When set in a query, requests that the server receiving the query attempt to answer the query recursively, if the server supports recursive resolution. The value of this bit is not changed in the response.
RA	1/8 (1 bit)	Recursion Available: Set to 1 or cleared to 0 in a response to indicate whether the server creating the response supports recursive queries. This can then be noted by the device that sent the query for future use.
Z	3/8 (3 bits)	Zero: Three reserved bits set to 0.
RCode	1/2 (4 bits)	Response Code: Set to 0 in queries, then changed by the replying server in a response to convey the results of processing the query. This field is used to indicate if the query was answered successfully or if some sort of error occurred. See Table 57-4 for the RCode values.
QDCount	2	Question Count: Specifies the number of questions in the Question section of the message.
ANCount	2	Answer Record Count: Specifies the number of RRs in the Answer section of the message.
ARCount	2	Additional Record Count: Specifies the number of RRs in the Additional section of the message.

Table 57-3: Header OpCode Values

OpCode Value	Query Name	Description
0	Query	A standard query.
1	IQuery	An inverse query; now obsolete. RFC 1035 defines the inverse query as an optional method for performing inverse DNS lookups; that is, finding a name from an IP address. Due to implementation difficulties, the method was never widely deployed, however, in favor of reverse mapping using the IN-ADDR.ARPA domain. Use of this OpCode value was formally obsoleted in RFC 3425, November 2002.
2	Status	A server status request.
3	Reserved	Reserved, not used.

(continued)

Table 57-3: Header OpCode Values (continued)

OpCode Value	Query Name	Description
4	Notify	A special message type added by RFC 1996. It is used by a primary (master, authoritative) server to tell secondary servers that data for a zone has changed and prompt them to request a zone transfer. See the discussion of DNS server enhancements in Chapter 55 for more details.
5	Update	A special message type added by RFC 2136 to implement Dynamic DNS. It allows RRs to be added, deleted, or updated selectively. See the discussion of DNS server enhancements in Chapter 55 for more details.

Table 57-4: Header RCode Values

RCode Value	Response Code	Description
0	No Error	No error occurred.
1	Format Error	The server was unable to respond to the query due to a problem with how it was constructed.
2	Server Failure	The server was unable to respond to the query due to a problem with the server itself.
3	Name Error	The name specified in the query does not exist in the domain. This code can be used by an authoritative server for a zone (since it knows all the objects and subdomains in a domain) or by a caching server that implements negative caching.
4	Not Implemented	The type of query received is not supported by the server.
5	Refused	The server refused to process the query, generally for policy reasons and not technical ones. For example, certain types of operations, such as zone transfers, are restricted. The server will honor a zone transfer request only from certain devices.
6	YX Domain	A name exists when it should not.
7	YX RR Set	An RR set exists that should not.
8	NX RR Set	An RR set that should exist does not.
9	Not Auth	The server receiving the query is not authoritative for the zone specified.
10	Not Zone	A name specified in the message is not within the zone specified in the message.

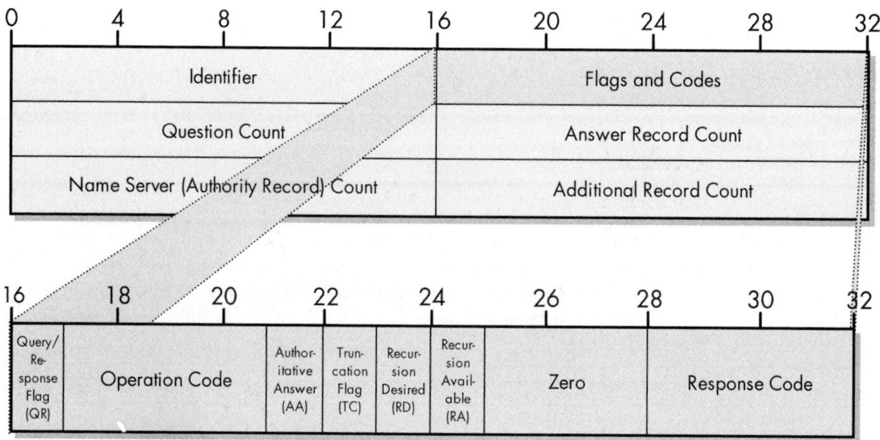

***Figure 57-2:** DNS message header format*

DNS Question Section Format

DNS queries always contain at least one entry in the Question section that specifies what the client in the exchange is trying to find out. These entries are copied to the response message unchanged, for reference on the part of the client if needed. The format used for each entry in the Question section of a DNS message described in detail in Tables 57-5 and 57-6, and illustrated in Figure 57-3.

Table 57-5: DNS Message Question Section Format

Field Name	Size (Bytes)	Description
QName	Variable	Question Name: Contains the object, domain, or zone name that is the subject of the query, encoded using standard DNS name notation, which is explained later in this chapter.
QType	2	Question Type: Specifies the type of question being asked by the device acting as a client. This field may contain a code number corresponding to a particular type of RR being requested. (Table 55-1 in Chapter 55 contains the numbers for the most common RRs.) If so, this means the client is asking for that type of record to be sent for the domain name listed in QName. The QType field may also contain one of the codes listed in Table 57-6, corresponding to a special type of requests.
QClass	2	Question Class: Specifies the class of the RR being requested, normally the value 1 for Internet (IN). See the discussion of classes and RR types in Chapter 56 for an explanation. In addition, the QClass value 255 is defined to have the special meaning "any class."

Table 57-6: Question Section QType Values

QType Value	Question Type	Description
251	IXFR	A request for an incremental (partial) zone transfer, per RFC 1995
252	AXFR	A request for a zone transfer
253	MAILB	A request for mailbox-related records (RR types MB, MG, or MR; now obsolete)
254	MAILA	A request for mail agent RR (now obsolete; MX records are used instead)
255	* (asterisk)	A request for all records

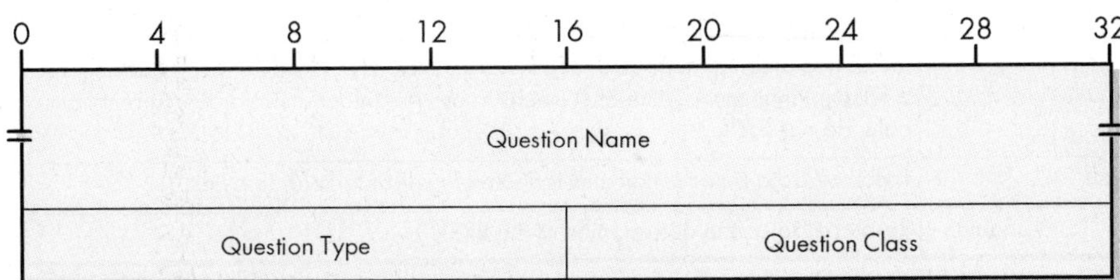

Figure 57-3: DNS message Question section format

DNS Message Resource Record Field Formats

As you've learned in this and the previous chapter, the exchange of information in DNS consists of a series of client/server transactions. Clients send requests, or *queries*, to servers, and the servers send back *responses*. DNS servers are database servers, and they store DNS name database information in the form of RRs. The questions asked by clients are requests for information from a DNS server's database, and they are answered by the DNS server looking up the requested RRs and putting them into the DNS response message.

The Answer, Authority, and Additional sections of the overall DNS message format are the places where servers put DNS RRs to be sent back to a client. Each section consists of zero or more records, and in theory, any record can be placed in any section. The sections differ only in the semantics (meaning) that the client draws from a record being in one section rather than in another section.

RRs have two representations: binary and text. The text format is used for master files edited by humans and is discussed in the "DNS Master File Format" section later in this chapter. The binary representation consists of regular numeric and text fields, just like the other fields in the DNS message format.

DNS Common RR Format

There are certain types of information that are common to all RRs and other types that are unique to each type of record. To handle this, all RRs are represented using a common field format, which contains a single RData field that varies by record type. The common RR format is described in Table 57-7 and illustrated in Figure 57-4.

Table 57-7: DNS Common Resource Record Format

Field Name	Size (Bytes)	Description
Name	Variable	Name: Contains the object, domain, or zone name that is the subject of the RR, encoded using standard DNS name notation, which is explained later in this chapter. All of the information in the RR is associated with this object, which I call the *named object* for the record.
Type	2	Type: A code value specifying the type of resource record. The type values for the most common kinds of RRs are shown in Table 55-1, in Chapter 55 and also in the following sections of this chapter.
Class	2	Class: Specifies the class of the RR being requested, normally the value 1 for Internet (IN). See Chapter 55 for an explanation.
TTL	4	Time to Live: Specifies the number of seconds that the record should be retained in the cache of the device reading the record. See the discussion of DNS name server caching in Chapter 55 for a full explanation. A value of 0 means to use this information for the current name resolution only; do not cache it.
RDLength	2	Resource Data Length: Indicates the size of the RData field, in bytes.
RData	Variable	Resource Data: The data portion of the RR.

RData Field Formats for Common RRs

The RData field consists of one or more subfields that carry the actual payload for the RR. The following sections present the most common RR types. For each, I have indicated the RR text code, name, and type value; provided a brief summary of the RR's use; and shown the structure of the RData field in a table.

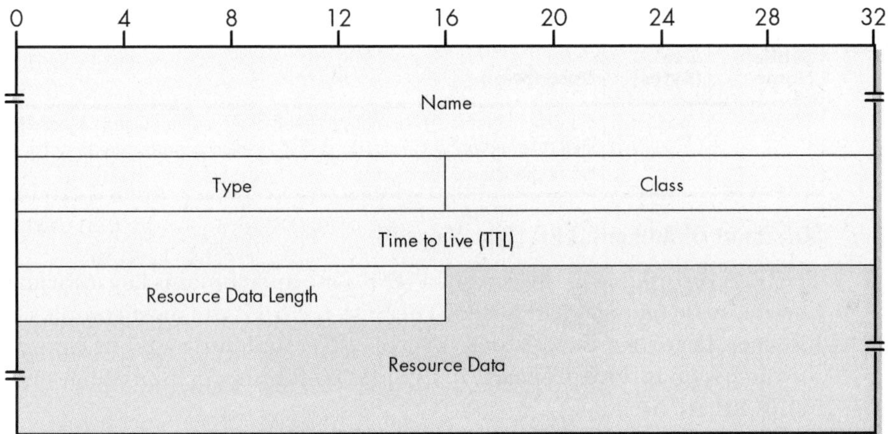

Figure 57-4: *DNS common RR format*

A (Address) RR (Type Value 1)

A (Address) is the primary RR type in DNS. It contains a 32-bit IP address associated with a domain name, as shown in Table 57-8.

Table 57-8: DNS Address RR Data Format

Subfield Name	Size (Bytes)	Description
Address	4	Address: The 32-bit IP address corresponding to this record's named object.

NS (Name Server) RR (Type Value 2)

The NSDName data field carries the domain name of a name server, as shown in Table 57-9.

Table 57-9: DNS Name Server RR Data Format

Subfield Name	Size (Bytes)	Description
NSDName	Variable	Name Server Domain Name: A variable-length name of a name server that should be authoritative for this record's named object. Like all names, this name is encoded using standard DNS name notation. A request for this RR type normally results in an A record for the name server specified also being returned in the Additional section of the response, if available.

CName (Canonical Name) RR (Type Value 5)

The CName data field contains the real name of a named object that has been referenced using an alias, as shown in Table 57-10.

Table 57-10: DNS Canonical Name RR Data Format

Subfield Name	Size (Bytes)	Description
CName	Variable	Canonical Name: The canonical (real) name of the named object. This name is then resolved using the standard DNS resolution procedure to get the address for the originally specified name.

SOA (Start Of Authority) RR (Type Value 6)

The SOA record marks the start of a DNS zone and contains key information about how it is to be managed and used. The SOA record is the most complex of the DNS RR types. Its format is explained in Table 57-11 and illustrated in Figure 57-5. See the discussion of zone transfers in Chapter 55 for information about how the fields in this RR are used.

Table 57-11: DNS Start Of Authority RR Data Format

Subfield Name	Size (Bytes)	Description
MName	Variable	Master Name: The domain name of the name server that is the source of the data for the zone. This is normally the primary authoritative server for the zone. It is encoded using the standard DNS name format.
RName	Variable	Responsible Name: The email address of the person responsible for this zone. Email addresses in DNS are encoded using a special variation of the regular DNS name notation, discussed later in this chapter.
Serial	4	Serial Number: The serial number, or version number, of the RR database for this zone. Used to determine when changes have been made to the database to trigger zone transfers.
Refresh	4	Refresh Interval: The number of seconds that secondary name servers for this zone will wait between attempts to check for changes made to the zone database on the primary name server.
Retry	4	Retry Interval: The number of seconds a secondary name server waits before trying again to check with a primary for changes if its previous attempt failed.
Expire	4	Expire Interval: The number of seconds that can elapse between successful contacts with the primary name server before a secondary name server must consider the information it holds stale.
Minimum	4	Negative Caching TTL: Originally carried the default TTL value for records where no explicit TTL value was specified. Now represents the zone's negative cache TTL. See the discussion of DNS name server caching in Chapter 55.

PTR (Pointer) RR (Type Value 12)

The PTR record carries a pointer to an RR. It's used for reverse address lookups. It contains one data field, shown in Table 57-12.

Table 57-12: DNS Pointer RR Data Format

Subfield Name	Size (Bytes)	Description
PTRDName	Variable	Pointer Domain Name: A variable-length domain name. This is a name pointed to by the RR. See the description of reverse resolution in Chapter 56 for the most common way that this record type is used.

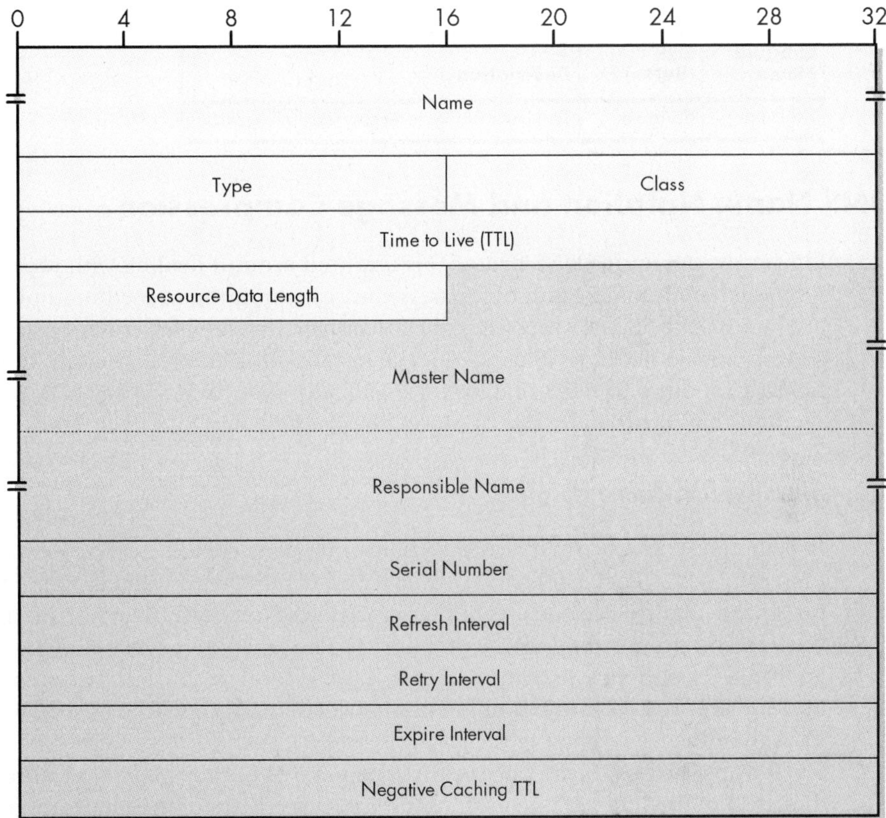

Figure 57-5: *DNS Start Of Authority (SOA) RR data format*

MX (Mail Exchange) RR (Type Value 15)

The special MX record contains information about the mail server(s) to be used for sending email to the domain (see Chapter 56). Each record contains two fields, as shown in Table 57-13.

Table 57-13: DNS Mail Exchange RR Data Format

Subfield Name	Size (Bytes)	Description
Preference	2	Preference Value: The preference level for this mail exchange. Lower values signify higher preference.
Exchange	Variable	Exchange Domain Name: The domain name, encoded using standard DNS name notation, of a host willing to provide mail exchange services for this named object.

TXT (Text) RR (Type Value 16)

The TXT record contains additional descriptive information about the named object, as shown in Table 57-14.

Table 57-14: DNS Text RR Data Format

Subfield Name	Size (Bytes)	Description
TXT-Data	Variable	Text Data: Variable-length descriptive text.

DNS Name Notation and Message Compression

Obviously, the entire DNS protocol is oriented around dealing with names for domains, subdomains, and objects. As you've seen in the preceding topics, there are many fields in DNS messages and RRs that carry the names of objects, name servers, and so forth. DNS uses a special notation for encoding names in RRs and fields, a variation of this notation for email addresses, and a special compression method that reduces the size of messages for efficiency.

Standard DNS Name Notation

In Chapter 53, you learned how DNS names are constructed. Each node in the name hierarchy has a label associated with it. The fully qualified domain name (FQDN) for a particular device consists of the sequence of labels that starts from the root of the tree and progresses down to that device. The labels at each level in the hierarchy are listed in sequence, starting with the highest level, from right to left, separated by dots. This results in the domain names we are used to working with, such as www.xyzindustries.com.

It would be possible to encode these names into RRs or other DNS message fields directly: Put the letter *w* into each of the first three bytes of the name, then put a dot (.) into the fourth byte, an *x* into the fifth byte, and so on. The disadvantage of this is that as a computer was reading the name, it wouldn't be able to tell when each name was finished. We would need to include a length field for each name.

Instead, DNS uses a special notation for DNS names. Each label is encoded, one after the next, in the name field. Before each label, a single byte is used that holds a binary number indicating the number of characters in the label. Then the label's characters are encoded, one per byte. The end of the name is indicated by a null label, representing the root; this has a length of zero, so each name ends with just a 0 character, indicating this zero-length root label.

Note that the dots between the labels aren't necessary, since the length numbers delineate the labels. The computer reading the name also knows how many bytes are in each label as it reads the name, so it can easily allocate space for the label as it reads it from the name.

For example, www.xyzindustries.com would be encoded as follows:

```
[3] w w w [13] x y z i n d u s t r i e s [3] c o m [0]
```

I have shown the label lengths in square brackets to distinguish them. Remember that these label lengths are binary encoded numbers, so a single byte can hold a value from 0 to 255; that [13] is one byte, not two, as you can see in Figure 57-6. Labels are actually limited to a maximum of 63 characters, and you'll see shortly why this is significant.

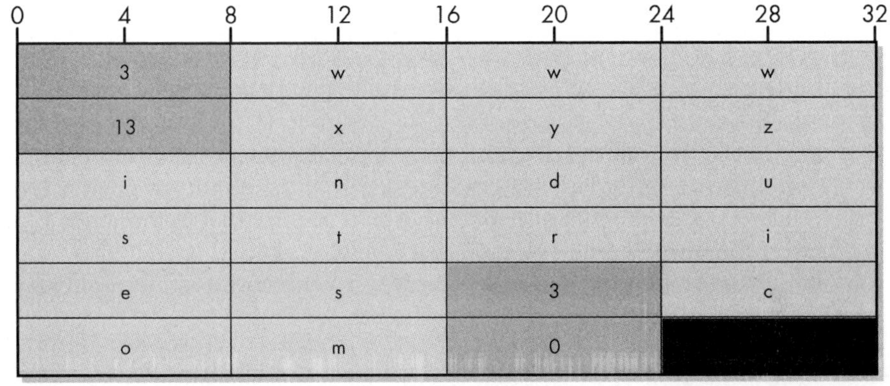

0–8	8–16	16–24	24–32
3	w	w	w
13	x	y	z
i	n	d	u
s	t	r	i
e	s	3	c
o	m	0	

Figure 57-6: DNS standard name notation *In DNS, every named object or other name is represented by a sequence of label lengths and then labels, with each label length taking one byte and each label taking one byte per character. This example shows the encoding of the name www.xyzindustries.com.*

DNS Electronic Mail Address Notation

Email addresses are used in certain DNS resource records, such as the RName field in the SOA RR. Email addresses take the form *<name>@<domain-name>*. DNS encodes these in exactly the same way as regular DNS domains, simply treating the @ like another dot. So, johnny@somewhere.org would be treated as johnny.somewhere .org and encoded as follows:

```
[6] j o h n n y [9] s o m e w h e r e [3] o r g [0]
```

Note that there is no specific indication that this is an email address. The name is interpreted as an email address instead of a device name based on context.

DNS Message Compression

A single DNS message may contain many domain names. Now, consider that when a particular name server sends a response containing multiple domain names, they are all usually in the same zone or are related to the zone. Most of these names will have common elements to their names.

Consider our previous mail example of a client asking for an MX record for xyzindustries.com. The response to this client will contain, among other things, these two records:

MX Record An MX record that has xyzindustries.com in the Name field of the record and mail.xyzindustries.com in the RData field.

A Record Assuming the name server knows the IP address of mail.xyzindustries .com, the Additional section will contain an A record that has mail.xyzindustries.com in the Name field and its address in the RData field.

This is just one small example of name duplication. It can be much more extreme with other types of DNS messages, with certain string patterns being repeated many times. Normally, this would require that each name be spelled out fully using the encoding method described here. But this would be wasteful, since a large portion of these names is common. To cut down on this duplication, a special technique called *message compression* is used.

Using Message Compression to Avoid Duplication of a Full Name

Using message compression, instead of a DNS name encoded using the combination of labels and label lengths, a two-byte subfield represents a *pointer* to another location in the message where the name can be found. The first two bits of this subfield are set to 1 (the value 11 in binary), and the remaining 14 bits contain an *offset* that specifies where in the message the name can be found, counting the first byte of the message (the first byte of the ID field) as 0.

Let's go back to our example. Suppose that in the DNS message, the RData field of the MX record, containing mail.xyzindustries.com, begins at byte 47. In this first instance, we would find the name encoded in full as follows:

```
[4] m a i l [13] x y z i n d u s t r i e s [3] c o m [0]
```

However, in the second instance, where mail.xyzindustries.com shows up in the Name field of the A record, we would instead put two 1 bits, followed by the number 47 encoded in binary. So, this would be the 16-bit binary pattern 11000000 00101111, or two numeric byte values 192 and 47. This second instance now takes 2 bytes instead of duplicating the 24 bytes needed for the first instance of the name.

How does a device reading a Name field differentiate a pointer from a real name? This is the reason that 11 is used at the start of the field. Doing this guarantees that the first byte of the pointer will always have a value of 192 or larger. Since labels are restricted to a length of 63 or less, when the host reads the first byte of a name, if it sees a value of 63 or less in a byte, it knows this is a real name; a value of 192 or more means it is a pointer.

Using Message Compression to Avoid Duplication of Part of a Name

The previous example shows how pointers can be used to eliminate duplication of a whole name: The name mail.xyzindustries.com was used in two places, and a pointer was used instead of the second. Pointers are even more powerful than this, however. They can also be used to point to only part of a real name or can be combined with additional labels to provide a compressed representation of a name related to another name in a RR. This provides even greater space savings.

In the previous example, this means that even the first instance of mail.xyzindustries.com can be compressed. Recall that the MX record will have xyzindustries.com in the Name field and mail.xyzindustries.com in the RData field. If the Name field of that record starts at byte 19, then we can encode the RData field as follows:

```
[4] m a i l [pointer-to-byte-19]
```

The device reading the record will get "mail" for the first label and then read "xyzindustries.com" from the Name field to get the complete name, mail.xyzindustries.com.

Similarly, suppose we had a record in this same message that contained a reference to the parent domain for xyzindustries.com, which is "com." This could simply be encoded as follows:

```
[pointer-to-byte-33]
```

The reason is that byte 33 is where we find the `[3] c o m [0]` part of the Name field containing `[13] x y z i n d u s t r i e s [3] c o m [0]`.

DNS Master File Format

DNS servers answer queries from clients by sending reply messages containing RRs. You have already seen in this chapter the binary message formats used to encode these RRs. These message formats are great for transmitted messages, because they are compact and efficient. Computers have no problem reading fields very quickly and knowing how to interpret a particular string of ones and zeros.

Humans, on the other hand, don't deal well with cryptic codes in binary. Before an RR can be provided by a server, it is necessary for a human administrator to tell the server what those records are and what information they contain. To make this job easier, DNS includes a special text representation for zones and RRs. Administrators edit special *master files* that describe the zone and the records it contains. These files are then read into memory by the server's DNS software and converted into binary form for responding to client requests. This is described in more detail in Chapter 56.

Each master file consists of a simple, flat text file that can be created with any sort of text editor. Each file contains a number of lines expressed using a simple set of syntax rules that describe a zone and the records within it. The basic syntactic rules for DNS master files are specified in RFC 1035, Section 5.1. Certain DNS implementations use their own variations on the syntax in the standard, though they are all pretty similar.

DNS Common Master File Record Format

Just as all RRs are stored internally using a common field format, they also use a common master file format. Each record normally appears on a separate line of the file. This format is as follows, with optional fields shown in square brackets:

```
<domain-name> [<ttl>] <class> <type> <rdata>
```

The fields are as follows:

<domain-name> A DNS domain name, which may be either an FQDN or a partially qualified name (PQDN).

<ttl> A TTL value, in seconds, for the record. If omitted, the default TTL value for the zone is used. In fact, most RRs do not have a specified TTL and just use the default provided by the SOA record.

<class> The RR class. For modern DNS, this field is optional, and it defaults to IN, for Internet.

<type> The RR type, specified using a text code such as A or NS, not the numeric code.

<rdata> RR data, which is a set of space-separated entries that depends on the record type.

The *<rdata>* can be either a single piece of information or a set of entries, depending on the record type. In the case of longer record types, especially the SOA record, multiple entry *<rdata>* fields are spread over several lines and enclosed in parentheses; the parentheses make all the entries act as if they were on a single line. Note that if the *<ttl>* field is present, the order of it and the *<class>* field may be switched without any problems, because one is a number and the other text (IN).

Use and Interpretation of Partially Qualified Domain Names (PQDNs)

Domain names may be mixed between FQDNs and PQDNs (described in Chapter 53). PQDNs are used to make master files faster to create and more readable, by cutting down on the common parts of names. They are sort of the human equivalent of DNS message compression. An FQDN is shown as a full domain name ending in a dot (.) to represent the DNS name tree root. A PQDN is given as just a partial name with no root, and is interpreted as an FQDN by the software reading the master file. (See the description of the `$ORIGIN` directive in the next section for more information.)

It is important to remember the trailing dot to mark FQDNs. If the origin is xyzindustries.com and in its zone file the name bigisp.net appears, the server will read this as bigisp.net.xyzindustries.com—probably not what you want. Also, email addresses, such as the *<r-name>* field in the SOA record, have the @ of the email address converted to a dot, following the standard DNS convention.

Master File Directives

In addition to RRs, most master file implementations also support the use of *directives.* These are commands that specify certain important pieces of information to guide how the master file is to be interpreted. The following are three of the most common directives:

$ORIGIN Specifies the domain name that is appended to unqualified specifications. This is the base used to convert PQDNs to FQDNs. For example, if the origin is xyzindustries.com., then a PQDN such as "sales" will be interpreted as sales.xyzindustries.com. Once defined, the origin can be referenced by just using @ in place of a name, as you will see in the example of a sample master file shown at the end of this section.

$TTL Specifies the default TTL value to be used for any RRs that do not specify a TTL value in the record itself. (This value was formerly specified by the Minimum field in the SOA record.)

$INCLUDE Allows one master file to include the contents of another. This is sometimes used to save the duplication of certain entries that are common between zones.

Syntax Rules for Master Files

There are a few other syntax rules for DNS master files, some of which are intended to save time or energy on the part of administrators:

Multiple-Record Shorthand If multiple consecutive records pertain to the same domain, the *<domain-name>* is specified for the first one and can be then be left blank for the subsequent ones. The server will assume that any RRs without a *<domain-name>* indicated apply to the last *<domain-name>* it saw.

Comments A semicolon (;) marks a comment. Any text from the semicolon until the end of the line is ignored.

Escape Character A backslash (\) is used to "escape" the special meaning of a character. For example, a double-quotation (quote) mark (") is used to delimit text strings; a literal double-quote character is indicated by a backslash–double-quote combination (\").

White Space Tabs and spaces are used as delimiters and blank lines are ignored. For readability, most smart administrators indent using tabs to clarify which records belong with which names, and group records using blank lines and comments.

Case Like DNS domain names, master file entries are case-insensitive.

Specific RR Syntax and Examples

The following sections show the specific formats and examples for each of the common RR types. The fields are basically the same as the ones explained in the DNS binary record formats. The examples include explanatory comments using the DNS comment format. Assume that these examples are for the zone googleplex.edu.

A (Address) RR

The format for an A record is as follows:

```
<domain-name> [<ttl>] IN A <ip-address>
```

Here is an example:

```
admin1.googleplex.edu IN A 204.13.100.3     ; An FQDN
admin2 IN A 204.13.100.44                   ; A PQDN equivalent to
                                            ; admin2.googleplex.edu
```

NS (Name Server) RR

The format for an NS record is as follows:

```
<domain-name>  [<ttl>]  IN  NS  <name-server-name>
```

Here is an example:

```
< googleplex.edu. IN NS custns.bigisp.net  ; Secondary NS
```

CName (Canonical Name) RR

The format for a CName record is as follows:

```
<domain-name>  [<ttl>]  IN  CNAME  <canonical-name>
```

Here is an example:

```
www IN CNAME bigserver   ; www.googleplex.edu is really
                         ; bigserver.googleplex.edu.
```

SOA (Start Of Authority) RR

The format for an SOA record is as follows:

```
<domain-name> [<ttl>] IN SOA <m-name> <r-name> (
      <serial-number>
      <refresh-interval>
```

```
    <retry-interval>
    <expire-interval>
    <default-ttl>)
```

Here is an example:

```
< googleplex.edu. IN SOA ns1.googleplex.edu it.googleplex.edu (
      42      ; Version 42 of the zone.
      21600   ; Refresh every 6 hours.
      3600    ; Retry every hour.
      604800  ; Expire after one week.
      86400)  ; Negative Cache TTL is one day.
```

PTR (Pointer) RR

The format for a PTR record is as follows:

```
<reverse-domain-name> [<ttl>] IN PTR <domain-name>
```

Here is an example:

```
3.100.13.204.IN-ADDR.ARPA. IN PTR admin1.googleplex.edu.
```

Note that the PTR record would actually be in the IN-ADDR.ARPA domain.

MX (Mail Exchange) RR

The format of an MX record is as follows:

```
<domain-name> [<ttl>] IN MX <preference-value> <exchange-name>
```

Here is an example:

```
googleplex.edu.      IN MX 10 mainmail.googleplex.edu.
                     IN MX 20 backupmail.googleplex.edu
```

TXT (Text) RR

The format of a TXT record is as follows:

```
<domain-name> [<ttl>] IN TXT <text-information>
```

Here is an example:

```
googleplex.edu. IN TXT "Contact Joe at X321 for more info."
```

Sample Master File

The following is a real-world example of a DNS master file, taken from my own pcguide.com server (slightly modified), hosted by (and DNS information provided by) the fine folks at pair.com. Note the use of @ as a shortcut to mean "this domain" (pcguide.com).

```
$ORIGIN pcguide.com.
@ IN SOA ns23.pair.com. root.pair.com. (
      2001072300  ; Serial
      3600        ; Refresh
      300         ; Retry
      604800      ; Expire
      3600 )      ; Minimum

@ IN NS ns23.pair.com.
@ IN NS ns0.ns0.com.

localhost  IN A  127.0.0.1
@          IN A  209.68.14.80
           IN MX 50  qs939.pair.com.

www    IN CNAME   @
ftp    IN CNAME   @
mail   IN CNAME   @
relay  IN CNAME   relay.pair.com.
```

DNS Changes to Support IPv6

Version 4 of the Internet Protocol (IPv4) is the basis of today's Internet and the foundation upon which the TCP/IP protocol suite is built. While IPv4 has served us well for over two decades, it has certain important drawbacks that would limit internetworks of the future if it were to continue to be used. For this reason, the next generation of IP, IP version 6 (IPv6), has been in development for many years. IPv6 will eventually replace IPv4 and take TCP/IP into the future.

The change from IPv4 to IPv6 will have effects that ripple to other TCP/IP protocols, including DNS. DNS is a higher-level protocol, so you might think that based on the principle of layering, a change to IP should not affect it. However, this is another example of how strict layering doesn't always apply. DNS works directly with IP addresses, and one of the most significant modifications that IPv6 makes to IP is in the area of addressing, so this means that using DNS on IPv6 requires some changes to how the protocol works.

IPv6 DNS Extensions

In fact, because DNS is so architecturally distant from IP down there at layer 3, the changes required are not extensive. RFC 1886, "IPv6 DNS Extensions," published in December 1995, was the Internet Engineering Task Force's (IETF's) first formalized attempt to describe the changes needed in DNS to support IPv6. It defines three specific modifications to DNS for IPv6:

New RR Type—AAAA (IPv6 Address) The regular DNS Address (A) RR is defined for a 32-bit IPv4 address, so a new one was created to allow a domain name to be associated with a 128-bit IPv6 address. The four *A*s (AAAA) are a mnemonic to indicate that the IPv6 address is four times the size of the IPv4 address. The AAAA record is structured in very much the same way as the A record in both binary and master file formats; it is just much larger. The DNS RR Type value for AAAA is 28.

New Reverse Resolution Hierarchy A new hierarchical structure similar to IN-ADDR.ARPA is defined for IPv6 reverse lookups, but the IETF put it in a different top-level domain (TLD). The new domain is *IP6.INT* and is used in a way similar to how IN-ADDR.ARPA works. However, since IPv6 addresses are expressed in hexadecimal instead of dotted-decimal, IP6.INT has 16 subdomains 0 through F, and each of those has 16 subdomains 0 through F, and so on, 16 layers deep. Yes, this leads to a potentially frightfully large reverse resolution database!

Changes to Query Types and Resolution Procedure All query types that work with A records or result in A records being included in the Additional section of a reply must be changed to also handle AAAA records. Also, queries that would normally result in A records being returned in the Additional section must return the corresponding AAAA records only in the Answer section, not in the Additional section.

> **KEY CONCEPT** Even though DNS resides far above IP in the TCP/IP protocol suite architecture, it works intimately with IP addresses. For this reason, changes are required to allow it to support the new IPv6. These changes include the definition of a new IPv6 address RR (AAAA), a new reverse resolution domain hierarchy, and certain changes to how messaging is performed.

Proposed Changes to the IPv6 DNS Extensions

In 2000, the IETF published RFC 2874, "DNS Extensions to Support IPv6 Address Aggregation and Renumbering." This standard proposed a replacement for the IPv6 support introduced in RFC 1886, using a new record type, A6, instead of RFC 1886's AAAA. The main difference between AAAA and A6 records is that the former are just whole addresses like A records, while A6 records can contain either a whole or partial address.

The idea behind RFC 2874 was that A6 records could be set up in a manner that complements the IPv6 format for unicast addresses (see Chapter 25). Then name resolution would involve a technique called *chaining* to determine a full address for a name from a set of partially specified address components. In essence, this would make the addresses behave much the way hierarchical names themselves work, providing some potential flexibility benefits.

For a couple of years, both RFC 1886 and RFC 2874 were proposed standards, and this led to considerable confusion. In August 2002, RFCs 3363 and 3364 were published, which clarified the situation with these two proposals. RFC 3363 represents the "Supreme Court decision," which was that RFC 2874 and the A6 record be changed to experimental status and the AAAA record of RFC 1886 be kept as the DNS IPv6 standard.

The full explanation for the decision can be found in RFC 3364. In a nutshell, it boiled down to the IETF believing that there were significant potential risks in the successful implementation of RFC 2874. While the capabilities of the A6 record were interesting, it was not clear that they were needed, and given those risks, the IETF felt that sticking with RFC 1886 was the better move.

PART III-2

NETWORK FILE AND RESOURCE SHARING PROTOCOLS

To the typical end user, networks were created for one main reason: to permit the sharing of information. Most information on computers exists in the form of files that reside on storage devices such as hard disks; thus, one primary purpose of networks is to let users share files. File transfer and message transfer protocols allow users to manually move files from one place to the next, but a more automated method is preferable in many cases. Internetworking protocols provide such capabilities in the form of *network file and resource sharing protocols.*

In this brief part, I describe network file and resource sharing protocols from the standpoint of TCP/IP networks. The one chapter here provides an overview of the concepts and operation of this class of protocols, discussing some of the elements common to the different types. It then describes the most common one defined specifically for TCP/IP: the Network File System (NFS).

Obviously, network file and resource sharing protocols and services are closely related to the file and message transfer protocols I mentioned earlier. For example, NFS can be used to accomplish tasks similar to those performed by TCP/IP file and message transfer applications such as the File Transfer Protocol (FTP) and the Hypertext Transfer Protocol (HTTP). I consider those protocols more like specific end-user applications unto themselves, and therefore describe them in later parts on application protocols (FTP in Part III-6 and HTTP in Part III-8). I realize that this distinction between manual and automatic file transfer is somewhat arbitrary, but then, so are a lot of other things in the great world of networking.

58

NETWORK FILE AND RESOURCE SHARING AND THE TCP/IP NETWORK FILE SYSTEM (NFS)

File and resource sharing protocols are important because they let users seamlessly share files over a network. Due to the dominance of Microsoft operating systems in the industry, many people are familiar with the way Microsoft networking can be used in this way. However, Microsoft is somewhat of a "Johnny come lately" to file sharing protocols. Long before Microsoft Windows even existed, the *Network File System (NFS)* was letting users share files over a network using the UNIX operating system.

In this chapter, I provide a brief look at network file and resource sharing in TCP/IP, with a focus on the operation of NFS. I begin with a general look at file and resource sharing protocol concepts. Then I provide an overview and history of NFS, and discuss its common versions and standards. I describe the architecture of NFS and the three components that compose it. I then describe the NFS file system model and how data is encoded using the *External Data Representation (XDR)* standard. I explain the client/server operation of NFS using *Remote Procedure Calls (RPCs)*. I then list the procedures and operations used in NFS, and conclude with a description of the separate NFS Mount protocol, used to attach network resources to a device.

File and Resource Sharing Concepts and Components

A primary reason why networks and internetworks are created is to allow files and other resources to be shared among computers. Thus, in any internetworking protocol stack, we need some mechanism by which users can easily move files across a network in a simple way. Application layer file and message transfer protocols like the File Transfer Protocol (FTP) and Hypertext Transfer Protocol (HTTP) were created for just this purpose: to let users access resources across a network while hiding the details of how the network operates at the layers below them.

However, even though these protocols hide the lower layers, they are somewhat *manual* in nature. They require a user to invoke an application protocol and use specific commands that accomplish network-based resource access. In fact, the problem with such protocols isn't so much that they require manual intervention, but that they make sharing more difficult because they don't allow a file to be used directly on another resource.

Consider a protocol like FTP. It does lets you share files between machines, but it draws a clear distinction between a file that is yours and a file that is someone else's. If you want to use a file on Joe's machine, you must transfer it to your machine, use it, and then transfer it back. Also, if you don't transfer the file back, Joe might never even see the updated version.

The Power of File and Resource Sharing Protocols

The ultimate in file and resource sharing is achieved when we can hide even the details of where the files are located and the commands required to move them around. Such a system would use an *automatic* sharing protocol that lets files and resources be used over a network seamlessly. Once set up, a network resource in such a scheme can be used in much the same way that one on a local computer is. Such protocols are sometimes called *network file and resource sharing protocols*.

It is this blurring of the line between a local file and a remote one that makes file and resource sharing protocols so powerful. Once the system is set up, users can access resources on another host as readily as on their own host. This is an extremely useful capability, especially in the modern era of client/server computing. For example, it allows a company to store information that is used by many individuals in a common place, such as in a directory on a server, where each of those individuals can access it. In essence, there is a virtual file system that spans network devices, instead of being simply on one storage device on a single computer.

Components of a File and Resource Sharing Protocol

File and transfer protocols allow users to share files effortlessly, but that doesn't mean no work is involved. The work is still there, but it's shouldered by those who write the protocol and those who administer its operation. Generally speaking, these protocols require at least the following general components:

File System Model and Architecture A mechanism for defining resources and files to be shared, and for describing how the virtual file system works.

Resource Access Method Procedures that describe how users can attach or detach a distant resource from their local host.

Operation Set A set of operations for accomplishing various tasks that the users need to perform on files on other hosts.

Messaging Protocol Message formats that carry operations to be performed, status information, and more, and a protocol for exchanging these messages between devices.

Administrative Tools Miscellaneous functionality needed to support the operation of the protocol and tie the other elements together.

NFS Design Goals, Versions, and Standards

The histories of TCP/IP and the Internet are inextricably linked, as I discussed in Chapter 8. However, there is a third partner that is less often mentioned but very much part of the development history of these technologies. That is the operating system that ran on the machines in the early Internet and is still used on a large percentage of Internet servers today: the *UNIX* operating system.

Sun Microsystems was one of the early pioneers in the development of UNIX and in TCP/IP networking. Early in the evolution of TCP/IP, certain tools were created to allow a user to access another machine over the network—after all, this is arguably the entire point of networking. Remote-access protocols such as Telnet allowed a user to log in to another host computer and use resources there. FTP allowed people to copy a file from a distant machine to their own and edit it. However, neither of these solutions really fit the bill of allowing a user to access a file on a remote machine in a way similar to how a local file is used. To fill this need, Sun created the *Network File System (NFS).*

NFS Design Goals

NFS was specifically designed with the goal of eliminating the distinction between a local and a remote file. To a user, after the appropriate setup is performed, a file on a remote computer can be used as if it were on a hard disk on the user's local machine. Sun also crafted NFS specifically to be vendor-independent, to ensure that both hardware made by Sun and that made by other companies could interoperate.

One of the most important design goals of NFS was performance. Obviously, even if you set up a file on a distant machine as if it were local, the actual read and write operations must travel across a network. Usually, this takes more time than simply sending data within a computer, so the protocol itself needed to be as lean and mean as possible. This decision led to some interesting choices, such as the use of the unreliable User Datagram Protocol (UDP) for transport in TCP/IP, instead of the reliable Transmission Control Protocol (TCP), as with most file transfer protocols. This, in turn, has interesting implications on how the protocol works as a whole.

Another key design goal for NFS was simplicity (which of course is related to performance). NFS servers are said to be *stateless*, which means that the protocol is designed so that servers do not need to keep track of which files have been opened by which clients. This allows requests to be made independently of each other, and allows a server to gracefully deal with events such as crashes without the need for complex recovery procedures.

The protocol is also designed so that if requests are lost or duplicated, file corruption will not occur.

> **KEY CONCEPT** The *Network File System (NFS)* was created to allow client hosts to access files on remote servers as if they were local. It was designed primarily with the goals of performance, simplicity, and cross-vendor compatibility.

NFS Versions and Standards

Since it was initially designed and marketed by Sun, NFS began as a de facto standard. The first widespread version of NFS was version 2 (NFSv2), and this is still the most common version of the protocol. NFSv2 was eventually codified as an official TCP/IP standard when RFC 1094, "NFS: Network File System Protocol Specification," was published in 1989.

NFS version 3 (NFSv3) was subsequently developed, and it was published in 1995 as RFC 1813, "NFS Version 3 Protocol Specification." It is similar to NFSv2, but makes a few changes and adds some new capabilities. These include support for larger files and file transfers, better support for setting file attributes, and several new file access and manipulation procedures.

NFS version 4 (NFSv4) was published in 2000 as RFC 3010, "NFS Version 4 Protocol." Where NFSv3 contained only relatively small changes to the previous version, NFSv4 is virtually a rewrite of NFS. It includes numerous changes, most notably the following:

- Reflecting the needs of modern internetworking, NFSv4 puts greater emphasis on security.
- NFSv4 introduces the concept of a *compound* procedure, which allows several simpler procedures to be sent from a client to a server as a group.
- NFSv4 almost doubles the number of individual procedures that a client can use in accessing a file on an NFS server.
- NFSv4 makes a significant change in messaging, with the specification of TCP as the transport protocol for NFS.
- NFSv4 integrates the functions of the Mount protocol into the basic NFS protocol, eliminating it as a separate protocol as it is in previous versions.

The NFSv4 standard also has a lot more details about implementation and optional features than the earlier standards—it's 275 pages long. So much for simplicity! RFC 3010 was later updated by RFC 3530, "Network File System (NFS) Version 4 Protocol," in April 2003. This standard makes several further revisions and clarifications to the operation of NFSv4.

NFS Architecture and Components

NFS follows the classic TCP/IP client/server model of operation. A hard disk or a directory on a storage device of a particular computer can be set up by an administrator as a shared resource. This resource can then be accessed by client computers, which *mount* the shared drive or directory, causing it to appear as if it were a local directory on the client machine. Some computers may act as only servers or only clients; others may be both, sharing some of their own resources and accessing resources provided by others.

Considered from the perspective of the TCP/IP protocol suite as a whole, NFS is a single protocol that resides at the application layer of the TCP/IP (DOD) model (described in Chapter 8). This TCP/IP layer encompasses the session, presentation, and application layers of the OSI Reference Model (described in Chapter 6). As I have said before in this book, I don't see much value in trying to differentiate between layers 5 through 7 most of the time. In some situations, however, these layers can be helpful in understanding the architecture of a protocol, and that's the case with NFS.

NFS Main Components

The operation of NFS is defined in the form of three main components that can be viewed as logically residing at each of the three OSI model layers corresponding to the TCP/IP application layer, as illustrated in Figure 58-1:

Remote Procedure Call (RPC) RPC is a generic session layer service used to implement client/server internetworking functionality. It extends the notion of a program calling a local procedure on a particular host computer to the calling of a procedure on a remote device across a network.

External Data Representation (XDR) XDR is a descriptive language that allows data types to be defined in a consistent manner. XDR conceptually resides at the presentation layer. Its universal representations allow data to be exchanged using NFS between computers that may use very different internal methods of storing data.

NFS Procedures and Operations The actual functionality of NFS is implemented in the form of procedures and operations that conceptually function at layer 7 of the OSI model. These procedures specify particular tasks to be carried out on files over the network, using XDR to represent data and RPC to carry the commands across an internetwork.

These three key "subprotocols," if you will, compose the bulk of the NFS protocol. Each is described in more detail in a separate section in this chapter.

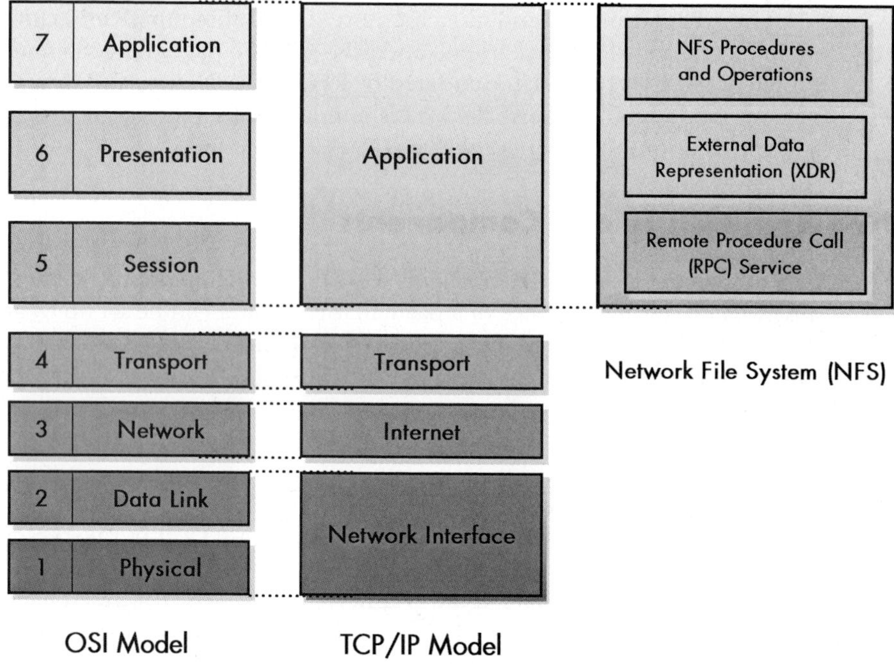

Figure 58-1: *NFS architectural components*

> **KEY CONCEPT** NFS resides architecturally at the TCP/IP application layer. Even though in the TCP/IP model no clear distinction is made generally between the functions of layers 5 through 7 of the OSI Reference Model, NFS's three subprotocols correspond well to those three layers as shown.NFS resides architecturally at the application layer of the TCP/IP model. Its functions are implemented primarily through three distinct functional components that implement the functions of layers 5 through 7 of the OSI Reference Model: the *Remote Procedure Call (RPC)*, which provide session-layer services; the *External Data Representation (XDR)* standard, which manages data representation and conversion; and *NFS procedures and operations*, which allow application layer tasks to be performed using the other two components.

Other Important NFS Functions

Aside from it three main components, the NFS protocol as a whole involves a number of other functions, most notably the following:

Mount Protocol A specific decision was made by the creators of NFS to not have NFS deal with the particulars of file opening and closing. Instead, a separate protocol called the *Mount* protocol is used for this purpose. Accessing a file or other resource over the network involves first *mounting* it using this protocol. The Mount protocol is architecturally distinct, but obviously closely related to NFS, and is even defined in an appendix of the NFS standard. I describe it in the last section in this chapter. (Note that in NFSv4, the functions of the Mount protocol have been incorporated into NFS proper.)

NFS File System Model NFS uses a particular model to implement the directory and file structure of the systems that use it. This model is closely based on the file system model of UNIX, but is not specific to only that operating system. It is discussed in conjunction with the explanation of the Mount protocol at the end of this chapter.

Security Versions 2 and 3 of NFS include only limited security provisions. They use UNIX-style authentication to check permissions for various operations. NFSv4 greatly increases the security options available for NFS implementations. These include provisions for multiple authentication and encryption algorithms, and many changes to the protocol as a whole to make it more secure.

NFS Data Definition with the External Data Representation (XDR) Standard

The overall idea behind NFS is to allow you to read from or write to a file on another computer as readily as you do on your local machine. Of course, the files on your local machine are all stored in the same file system, using the same file structure and the same means of representing different types of data. You can't be sure that this will be the case when accessing a remote device, and this creates a bit of a Tower of Babel problem.

One approach would be to simply restrict access only to remote files on machines that use the same operating system. However, this would remove much of the effectiveness of NFS. It would also be highly impractical to require every computer to understand the internal representation of every other one. A more general method is needed to allow even very dissimilar machines to share data. To this end, the creators of NFS defined NFS so that it deals with data using a universal data description language. This language is called the *External Data Representation* (*XDR*) standard and was originally described in RFC 1014. It was updated in RFC 1832, "XDR: External Data Representation Standard," in 1995.

A Method of Universal Data Exchange: XDR

The idea behind XDR is simple, and it can be easily understood in the form of an analogy. If you had delegates speaking 50 different languages at a convention, they would have a hard time communicating. You could hire translators to facilitate, but you would never find translators to handle all the different possible combinations of languages. A more practical solution is to declare one language, such as English, to be a common language. You then need only 49 translators: one to translate from English to each of the non-English languages and back again. To translate from Swedish to Portuguese, you translate from Swedish to English and then from English to Portuguese. The common language could be French, Spanish, or something else, as long as a translator could be found from all the other languages.

XDR works in the same manner. When information about how to access a file is to be transferred from Device A to Device B, Device A first converts it from Device A's internal representation to the XDR representation of those data types. The information is transmitted across the network using XDR encoding. Then Device B translates from XDR back to its own internal representation, so it can be presented to the user as if it were on the local file system. Each device needs to know only how to convert from its own language to XDR and back again; Device A doesn't need to know Device B's internal details and vice versa. This sort of translation is a classic job of the presentation layer, which is where XDR resides in the OSI Reference Model. XDR is itself based on an International Organization for Standardization (ISO) standard called "Abstract Syntax Notation."

NOTE *The idea behind XDR is also used in other protocols to allow the exchange of data independent of the nature of the underlying systems. For example, a similar idea is behind the way management information is exchanged using the Simple Network Management Protocol (SNMP), which is described in Chapter 66. The same basic idea underlies the important Network Virtual Terminal (NVT) paradigm used in the Telnet protocol, which is described in Chapter 87.*

KEY CONCEPT The purpose of the *External Data Representation (XDR)* standard is to define a common method for representing common data types. Using this universal representation, data can be exchanged between devices, regardless of what internal file system each uses. This enables NFS to exchange file data between clients and servers that may be implemented using very different hardware and software platforms.

XDR Data Types

For XDR to be universal, it must allow the description of all the common types of data that are used in computers. For example, it must allow integers, floating-point numbers, strings, and other data constructs to be exchanged. The XDR standard describes the structure of many data types using a notation somewhat similar to the C programming language. As you may know, this is one of the most popular languages in computing history, and it is closely associated with UNIX (and thus, certain TCP/IP technologies as well).

Table 58-1 shows the data types defined by XDR, which can be used by NFS in exchanging data between the client and server. For each, I have included the data type code, its size in bytes, and a brief description.

Table 58-1: NFS External Data Representation (XDR) Data Types

Data Type Code	Size (Bytes)	Description
int	4	Signed integer: A 32-bit signed integer in two's complement notation, capable of holding a value from -2,147,483,648 to +2,147,483,647.
unsigned int	4	Unsigned integer: A 32-bit unsigned integer, from 0 to 4,294,967,295.
enum	4	Enumeration: An alternate way of expressing a signed integer where some of the integer values are used to stand for particular constant values. For example, you could represent the colors of the rainbow, by defining the value 1 to stand for PURPLE, 2 to stand for BLUE, and so on.
bool	4	Boolean: A logical representation of an integer, analogous to a two-level enumeration where a value of 0 is defined as FALSE and 1 is TRUE.
hyper	8	Signed hyper integer: Same as a regular signed integer, but 8 bytes wide to allow much larger numbers.
unsigned hyper	8	Unsigned hyper integer: Same as a regular unsigned integer but 8 bytes wide to allow much larger numbers.

(continued)

Table 58-1: NFS External Data Representation (XDR) Data Types (continued)

Data Type Code	Size (Bytes)	Description
float	4	Floating-point number: A 32-bit signed floating-point number. 1 bit holds the sign (positive or negative), 8 bits hold the exponent (power), in base 2, and 23 bits hold the mantissa (fractional part of the number).
double	8	Double-precision floating-point number: The same as float but with more bits to allow greater precision. 1 bit is for the sign, 11 bits for the exponent, and 52 bits for the mantissa.
quadruple	16	Quadruple-precision floating-point number: The same as float and double but with still more bits to allow greater precision. 1 bit is for the sign, 15 bits for the exponent, and 112 bits for the mantissa.
opaque	Variable	Opaque data: Data that is to be passed between devices without being given a specific representation using XDR. The term *opaque* means that the data is treated like a "black box" whose insides cannot be seen. Obviously, any machines using this data type must themselves know how to deal with it, since NFS does not.
string	Variable	String: A variable-length string of ASCII characters.
(array)	Variable	Arrays: A group of any single type of the elements above, such as integers, floating-point numbers, and so on, may be specified in an array to allow many to be referenced as a single unit. They are not indicated using a separate data type code.
struct	Variable	Structure: An arbitrary structure containing other data elements from this table. This allows the definition of complex data types.
union	Variable	Discriminated union: A complex data type where a code value called a "discriminant" is used to determine the nature of the rest of the structure. See section 3.14 of RFC 1014 for details.
void	0	Void: A null data type that contains nothing.
const	0	Constant: A constant value used in other representations.

As you can see, XDR provides considerable data description capabilities. If you know the C language, much of what is in Table 58-1 is probably familiar to you. Unfortunately, I can't really describe many of the more complex data types without turning this into a guide to C programming.

XDR also provides a means of defining new data types and a method for specifying optional data. This offers even more flexibility beyond the large number of specific types already specifically described. Each version of NFS has a slightly different list of data types it supports.

NFS Client/Server Operation Using Remote Procedure Calls (RPCs)

Almost all applications deal with files and other resources. When a software program on a particular computer wants to read a file, write a file, or perform related tasks, it needs to use the correct software instructions for this purpose. It would be inefficient to require each software program to contain a copy of these instructions, so instead, they are encoded as standardized software modules, sometimes called *procedures*. To perform an action, a piece of software *calls* the procedure. The procedure temporarily takes over for the main program and performs a task such as reading or writing data. The procedure then returns control of the program back to the software that called it, and optionally, returns data as well.

Since the key concept of NFS was to make remote file access look like local file access, it was designed around the use of a network-based version of this procedure calling method. A software application that wants to do something with a file still makes a procedure call, but it makes the call to a procedure on a different computer instead of the local one. A special set of routines is used to handle the transmission of the call across the network, in a way largely invisible to software performing the call.

This functionality could have been implemented directly in NFS, but instead Sun created a separate session-layer protocol component called the *Remote Procedure Call (RPC)* specification, which defines how this works. RPC was originally created as a subcomponent of NFS, but it is generic enough and useful enough that it has been used for other client/server applications in TCP/IP. For this reason, it is really considered in many respects a distinct protocol.

Because RPC is the actual process of communicating in NFS, NFS itself is different from many other TCP/IP protocols. Its operation can't be described in terms of specific message exchanges and state diagrams the way a protocol like HTTP or the Dynamic Host Configuration Protocol (DHCP), or even TCP can, because RPC does all of that. NFS is defined in terms of a set of RPC server procedures and operations that an NFS server makes available to NFS clients. These procedures and operations each allow a particular type of action to be taken on a file, such as reading from it, writing to it, or deleting it.

RPC Operation and Transport Protocol Usage

When a client wants to perform some type of action on a file on a particular machine, it uses RPC to make a call to the NFS server on that machine. The server accepts the request and performs the action required, then returns a result code and possibly data back to the client, depending on the request. The result code indicates if the action was successful. If it was, the client can assume that whatever it asked to be done was completed. For example, in the case of writing data, the client can assume the data has been successfully written to long-term storage.

> **KEY CONCEPT** NFS does not use a dedicated message format, like most other protocols do. Instead, clients and servers use the *Remote Procedure Call (RPC)* protocol to exchange file operation requests and data.

NFS can operate over any transport mechanism that has a valid RPC implementation at the session layer. NFS has seen an evolution of sorts in its use of transport protocol. The NFSv2 standard says that it operates normally using UDP, and this is still a common way that NFS information is carried. NFSv3 says that either UDP or TCP may be used, but NFSv4 specifies TCP to carry data. The nominal registered port number for use by NFS is 2049, but other port numbers are sometimes used for NFS, through the use of RPC's *port mapper* capability.

Client and Server Responsibilities in NFS

Since UDP is unreliable, the use of that protocol to transport important information may seem strange. For example, we obviously don't want data that we are trying to write to a file to be lost in transit. Remember, however, that UDP doesn't preclude the use of measures to ensure reliable communications; it simply doesn't provide those capabilities itself. UDP can be used by NFS because the protocol itself is designed to tolerate loss of transmitted data and to recover from it.

Consistent with this concept, the general design of NFS puts most of the responsibility for implementing the protocol on the client, not the server. As the NFSv3 standard says, "NFS servers are dumb, and NFS clients are smart." What this means is that the servers focus only on responding to requests, while clients must take care of most of the nitty-gritty details of the protocol, including recovery from failed communications. This is a common requirement when UDP is used, because if a client request is lost in transit, the server has no way of knowing that it was ever sent.

As mentioned in the NFS overview earlier in this chapter, NFS servers are designed to be stateless. In simplified terms, this means that the NFS server does not keep track of the state of the clients using it from one request to another. Each request is independent of the previous one, and the server in essence has no memory of what it did before when it gets a new command from a client. This again requires more intelligence to be put into the clients, but has the important advantage of simplifying recovery in the case that the server crashes. Since there is nothing that the server was keeping track of for the client, there's nothing that can be lost. This is an important part of ensuring that files are not damaged as a result of network problems or congestion.

Client and Server Caching

Both NFS clients and servers can make use of caching to improve performance. Servers may use caching to store recently requested information in case it is needed again. They may also use *predictive* caching, sometimes called *prefetching*. In this technique, a server that receives a request to read a block of data from a file may load into memory the next block after it, on the theory that it will likely be requested next.

Client-side caching is used to satisfy repeat NFS requests from applications while avoiding additional RPC calls. Like almost everything else about NFS, caching is implemented much more thoroughly in NFSv4 than in the previous versions.

> **KEY CONCEPT** NFS is designed to be a *stateless* protocol, with intelligent clients and relatively dumb servers that respond to requests and do not maintain status information about what files are in use. NFS was originally designed to use UDP for transport, for efficiency purposes. This requires that NFS clients take care of detecting lost requests and retransmitting them. NFSv4 uses TCP to take advantage of TCP's reliability and other features.

NFS Server Procedures and Operations

The actual exchange of information between an NFS client and server is performed by the underlying RPC protocol. NFS functionality is therefore described not in terms of specific protocol operations, but by delineating the different actions that a client may take on files residing on a server. In the original version of NFS, NFSv2, these are called NFS *server procedures*.

Each procedure represents a particular action that a client may perform, such as reading from a file, writing to a file, or creating or removing a directory. The operations performed on the file require that the file be referenced using a data structure called a *file handle*. As the name suggests, the file handle, like the handle of a real object, lets the client and server "grasp" the file. The Mount protocol, described later in this chapter, is used to mount a file system, to enable a file handle to be accessed for use by NFS procedures.

NFSv3 uses the same basic model for server procedures, but makes certain changes. Two of the NFSv2 procedures were removed, and several new ones added to support new functionality. The numbers assigned to identify each procedure were also changed.

NFS Version 2 and Version 3 Server Procedures

Table 58-2 shows the server procedures defined in versions 2 and 3 of NFS. The table shows the procedure numbers for both NFSv2 and NFSv3, as well as the name of each procedure and a description of what it does. I have kept the descriptions short so the table can serve as a useful summary of what NFS can do. They are listed in order of the procedure number used in NFSv2.

Table 58-2: NFS Version 2 and Version 3 Server Procedures

Procedure No. (v2)	Procedure No. (v3)	Procedure Name	Procedure Summary	Description
0	0	null	Do nothing	Dummy procedure provided for testing purposes.
1	1	getattr	Get file attributes	Retrieves the attributes of a file on a remote server.
2	2	setattr	Set file attributes	Sets (changes) the attributes of a file on a remote server.
3	—	root	Get file system root (obsolete)	This procedure was originally defined to allow a client to find the root of a remote file system, but is now obsolete. This function is instead now implemented as part of the Mount protocol. It was removed in NFSv3.
4	3	lookup	Look up filename	Returns the file handle of a file for the client to use.
5	5	readlink	Read from symbolic link	Reads the name of a file specified using a symbolic link.
6	6	read	Read from rile	Reads data from a file.
7	—	writecache	Write to cache	Proposed for future use in NFSv2 but abandoned and removed from NFSv3.

(continued)

Table 58-2: NFS Version 2 and Version 3 Server Procedures (continued)

Procedure No. (v2)	Procedure No. (v3)	Procedure Name	Procedure Summary	Description
8	7	write	Write to file	Writes data to a file.
9	8	create	Create file	Creates a file on the server.
10	12	remove	Remove file	Deletes a file from the server.
11	14	rename	Rename file	Changes the name of a file.
12	15	link	Create link to file	Creates a hard (nonsymbolic) link to a file.
13	10	symlink	Create symbolic link	Creates a symbolic link to a file.
14	9	mkdir	Create directory	Creates a directory on the server.
15	13	rmdir	Remove directory	Deletes a directory.
16	16	readdir	Read from directory	Reads the contents of a directory.
17	—	statfs	Get file system attributes	Provides to the client general information about the remote file system, including the size of the file system and the amount of free space remaining. In NFSv3, this was replaced by fsstat and fsinfo.
—	4	access	Check access permission	Determines the access rights that a user has for a particular file system object. This is new in NFSv3.
—	11	mknod	Create a special device	Creates a special file such as a named pipe or device file. This is new in NFSv3.
—	17	readdirplus	Extended read from directory	Retrieves additional information from a directory. This is new in NFSv3.
—	18	fsstat	Get dynamic file system information	Returns volatile (dynamic) file system status information such as the current amount of file system free space and the number of free file slots. This is new in NFSv3.
—	19	fsinfo	Get static file system information	Returns static information about the file system, such as general data about how the file system is used and parameters for how requests to the server should be structured. This is new in NFSv3.
—	20	pathconf	Retrieve POSIX information	Retrieves additional information for a file or directory. This is new in NFSv3.
—	21	commit	Commit cached data on a server to stable storage	Flushes any data that the server is holding in a write cache to storage. This is used to ensure that any data that the client has sent to the server but that the server has held pending write to storage is written out. This is new in NFSv3.

It is common that a client may want to perform multiple actions on a file, such as several consecutive reads. One of the problems with the server procedure system in NFSv2 and NFSv3 is that each client action required a separate procedure call. This was somewhat inefficient, especially when NFS was used over a high-latency link.

NFS Version 4 Server Procedures and Operations

To improve the efficiency of server procedures, NFSv4 makes a significant change to the way that server procedures are implemented. Instead of each client action being a separate procedure, a single procedure, called a *compound procedure*, is defined. Within this compound procedure, a large number of *server operations* are encapsulated. These are all sent as a single unit, and the server interprets and follows the instructions in each operation in sequence.

This change means there are actually only two RPC procedures in NFSv4, as shown in Table 58-3.

Table 58-3: NFS Version 4 Server Procedures

Procedure Number	Procedure Name	Procedure Summary	Description
0	null	Do nothing	Dummy procedure provided for testing purposes.
1	compound	Compound operations	Combines a number of NFS operations into a single request.

All the real client actions are defined as operations within the compound procedure, as shown in Table 58-4. You'll notice that the number of NFSv4 operations is much larger than the number of procedures in NFSv2 and NFSv3. This is due both to the added features in NSFv4 and the fact that it incorporates functions formerly performed by the separate Mount protocol.

Table 58-4: NFS Version 4 Server Operations

Operation Number	Operation Name	Operation Summary	Description
3	access	Check access rights	Determines the access rights a user has for an object.
4	close	Close file	Closes a file.
5	commit	Commit cached data	Flushes any data that the server is holding in a write cache to storage, to ensure that any pending data is permanently recorded.
6	create	Create a nonregular file object	This is similar to the mknod procedure in NFSv3; it creates a "nonregular" (special) object file. (Regular files are created using the open operation.)
7	delepurge	Purge delegations awaiting recovery	NFSv4 has a feature where a server may delegate to a client responsibility for certain files. This operation removes delegations awaiting recovery from a client.
8	delegreturn	Return delegation	Returns a delegation from a client to the server that granted it.
9	getattr	Get attributes	Obtains the attributes for a file.
10	getfh	Get current file handle	Returns a file handle, which is a logical object used to allow access to a file.
11	link	Create link to a file	Creates a hard (nonsymbolic) link to a file.
12	lock	Create lock	Creates a lock on a file. Locks are used to manage access to a file—for example, to prevent two clients from trying to write to a file simultaneously and thus corrupting it.

(continued)

Table 58-4: NFS Version 4 Server Operations (continued)

Operation Number	Operation Name	Operation Summary	Description
13	lockt	Test for lock	Tests for the existence of a lock on an object and returns information about it.
14	locku	Unlock lile	Removes a lock previously created on a file.
15	lookup	Look up filename	Looks up or finds a file.
16	lookupp	Look up parent directory	Returns the file handle of an object's parent directory.
17	nverify	Verify difference in attributes	Checks to see if attributes have changed on a file.
18	open	Open a regular file	Opens a file.
19	openattr	Open named attribute directory	Opens an attribute directory associated with a file.
20	open_confirm	Confirm open	Confirms information related to an opened file.
21	open_ downgrade	Reduce open file access	Adjusts the access rights for a file that is already open.
22	putfh	Set current file handle	Replaces one file handle with another.
23	putpubfh	Set public file handle	Sets the current file handle to be the public file handle of the server. This may or may not be the same as the root file handle.
24	putrootfh	Set root file handle	Sets the current file handle to be the root of the server's file system.
25	read	Read from file	Reads data from a file.
26	readdir	Read directory	Reads the contents of a directory.
27	readlink	Read symbolic link	Reads the name of a file specified using a symbolic link.
28	remove	Remove file system object	Removes (deletes) an object.
29	rename	Rename directory entry	Changes the name of an object.
30	renew	Renew a lease	Renews an NFS delegation made by a server. (Note that these leases have nothing to do with DHCP leases, which are discussed in Chapter 61.)
31	restorefh	Restore saved file handle	Allows a file handle previously saved to be made the current file handle.
32	savefh	Save current file handle	Allows a file handle to be saved so it can later be restored when needed.
33	secinfo	Obtain available security	Retrieves NFS security information.
34	setattr	Set attributes	Changes one or more attributes of a file.
35	setclientid	Negotiate client ID	Allows a client to communicate information to the server regarding how the client wants to use NFS.
36	setclientid_ confirm	Confirm client ID	Used to confirm the results of a previous negotiation using setclientid.

(continued)

Table 58-4: NFS Version 4 Server Operations (continued)

Operation Number	Operation Name	Operation Summary	Description
37	verify	Verify same attributes	Allows a client to verify certain attributes before proceeding with a particular action.
38	write	Write to file	Writes data to a file.
39	release_ lockowner	Release lock owner state	Used by a client to tell a server to release certain information related to file locks.
10044	illegal	Illegal operation	A placeholder (dummy) operation used to support error reporting when an invalid operation is used in a request from a client.

KEY CONCEPT File operations in NFS are carried out using NFS *server procedures*. In versions 2 and 3 of NFS, each procedure performs one action, such as reading data from a file. In NFSv4, a special *compound* action is defined that allows many individual *operations* to be sent in a single request to a server.

NFS File System Model and the Mount Protocol

Since NFS is used by a client to simulate access to remote directories of files as if they were local, the protocol must present the files from the remote system to the local user. Just as files on a local storage device are arranged using a particular file system, NFS uses a *file system model* to represent how files are shown to a user.

The NFS File System Model

The file system model used by NFS is the same one that most of us are familiar with: a hierarchical arrangement of directories that contain files and subdirectories. The top of the hierarchy is the *root*, which contains any number of files and first-level directories. Each directory may contain more files or other directories, allowing an arbitrary tree structure to be created.

A file can be uniquely specified by using its *filename* and a *path name* that shows the sequence of directories one must traverse from the root to find the file. Since NFS is associated with UNIX, files in NFS discussions are usually shown in UNIX notation; for example, */etc/hosts*. The same basic tree idea can also be expressed using the method followed by Windows operating systems: *C:\WINDOWS\HOSTS*.

The Mount Protocol

Before NFS can be used to allow a client to access a file on a remote server, the client must be given a way of accessing the file. This means that a portion of the remote file system must be made available to the client, and the file opened for access. A specific decision was made when NFS was created to not put file access, opening, and closing functions into NFS proper. Instead, a separate protocol was created to work with NFS, so that if the method of providing file access needed to be changed later, it wouldn't require changes to NFS itself. This separate mechanism is called the *Mount protocol* and is described in Appendix A of RFC 1094 (NFSv2). Note that while its functionally distinct, Mount is considered part of the overall NFS package.

When NFS was revised to version 3, the Mount protocol was similarly modified. The NFSv3 version of the Mount protocol is defined in Appendix I of RFC 1813 (NFSv3). It contains some changes to how the protocol works, but the overall operation of the two versions of Mount is pretty much the same.

The term *mount* is actually an analog to a hardware term that refers to making a physical storage volume available. In the past, storage devices were usually removable disk packs, and to use one, you mounted it onto a drive unit. In a similar manner, NFS resources are logically mounted using the Mount protocol, which makes the shared file system available to the client. A file can then be opened and a file handle returned to the NFS client, so it can reference the file for operations such as reading and writing.

KEY CONCEPT Versions 2 and 3 of NFS do not include procedures for opening or closing resources on a remote server. Before NFS tasks can be accomplished on these versions, the special *Mount* protocol must be employed to mount a file system and create a file handle to access a file on it. The protocol is also used to unmount the file system when no longer required. The Mount protocol is implemented in a manner similar to NFS itself, defining a sequence of procedures that use RPC and XDR. In NFSv4, the Mount protocol is no longer needed, because the tasks it performs have been implemented as NFSv4 operations.

The actual implementation of the Mount protocol is very similar to that of NFS itself. Like NFS, the Mount protocol uses XDR to define data types to be exchanged between the client and server and RPC to define a set of server procedures that clients may use to perform different operations. The main difference between Mount and NFS is simply that Mount defines procedures related to opening and closing file systems, rather than file access operations. Table 58-5 shows the server procedures used in the Mount protocol.

Table 58-5: NFS Mount Protocol Server Procedures

Procedure Number	Procedure Name	Procedure Summary	Description
0	null	Do nothing	Dummy procedure provided for testing purposes.
1	mnt	Add mount entry	Performs a mount operation by mapping a path on a server to a file handle for the client to use.
2	dump	Return mount entries	Returns a list of remotely mounted file systems.
3	umnt	Remove mount entry	Performs an unmount operation by removing a mount entry. (Yes, it should be *dismount*; techies usually aren't English majors.)
4	umntall	Remove all mount entries	Removes all mount entries, thus eliminating all mounted file systems between server and client.
5	export	Return export list	Returns a list of exported file systems and indicates which clients are allowed to mount them. This is used to let the client see which served file systems are available for use.

Again, NFSv4 does away with the notion of a separate Mount protocol, incorporating file mounting operations into NFS directly.

PART III-3

HOST CONFIGURATION AND TCP/IP HOST CONFIGURATION PROTOCOLS

Each host that is placed on a network or internetwork must be set up and configured before it can be used. Configuration ensures that the host functions properly and that it is told the parameters needed for it to successfully communicate with other hosts and devices. In the good old days, administrators would manually set up each host as it was added to the network, and they would also manually make changes to the configuration as required.

Modern networks, however, are very large, and manual configuration of hosts is a time-consuming chore. Furthermore, we often need features that only automated configuration can provide, particularly for special hosts that have no internal storage. It is for these reasons that *host configuration* protocols were developed.

This part includes six chapters that describe the concepts behind host configuration protocols and then illustrate the operation of two of the most important ones in use today. The first chapter is an overview of host configuration concepts and issues, which will help you understand why these protocols are so important. In the second chapter, I describe the TCP/IP Bootstrap Protocol (BOOTP), the first truly capable automated configuration tool for Internet Protocol (IP) hosts.

The remaining chapters in this part cover BOOTP's successor, the feature-filled Dynamic Host Configuration Protocol (DHCP). The third chapter introduces DHCP and talks about the different ways DHCP can assign addresses, with a focus on dynamic addressing. The fourth chapter discusses how DHCP operates, including a look at configuration parameter management and the procedures for allocating addresses and managing those allocations. The fifth chapter describes DHCP messaging and illustrates the DHCP message format. The final chapter details DHCP clients and servers, looks at special features and issues with DHCP, and describes DHCP changes to support the new IP version 6 (IPv6).

Technically, the very first host configuration protocol for TCP/IP was the Reverse Address Resolution Protocol (RARP). RARP is a simple, crude protocol that allows very basic host configuration to be performed, but little else. RARP is very different from BOOTP and DHCP, not only because of its more limited capabilities, but because it operates between layers 2 and 3, like the Address Resolution Protocol (ARP) on which it is based. It is therefore covered in Part II-2, which also describes ARP.

59

HOST CONFIGURATION CONCEPTS, ISSUES, AND MOTIVATION

Putting a host on an internetwork requires that certain setup and configuration procedures be followed. Hardware must be selected and set up, and software must be chosen and installed on the hardware. Once the software is set up, we aren't finished, however. We must also perform other configuration tasks that tell the software how we want it to operate and give it certain parameters, so it knows its role on the network and how to function.

In this brief chapter, I discuss the purpose of host configuration, the problems associated with it, and host configuration protocols.

The Purpose of Host Configuration

Probably the most important configuration task that must be performed for each host on an internetwork is to give it an *identity*, in the form of an address that is unique to it alone. In TCP/IP networks, each device must be given an

IP address. Hosts also often require other parameters to ensure that they operate properly. For a TCP/IP network, we might want to tell each host some of the following:

- The address of a default router on the local network
- The network mask the host should use
- The addresses of servers providing particular services to the host, such as a mail server or a Domain Name System (DNS) name server
- The maximum transmission unit (MTU) of the local network (see Chapter 22)
- What Time to Live (TTL) value to use for IP datagrams (see Chapter 21)

There may be a lot more information that must be relayed to the host. Dozens of different parameters must be set up for certain networks. Many of these may be common to all the machines on a network, but IP addresses must be unique. The administrator must therefore ensure that each IP address is assigned to only one computer, even as machines are added to and removed from the network.

The Problems with Manual Host Configuration

If you're an administrator in charge of a small local area network (LAN) with ten hosts, performing setup and configuration is simple. For each host, you set up the hardware, install the software, and then configure the software. Even making changes and keeping track of IP addresses wouldn't be a big deal; a single sheet of paper would suffice. However, what happens when your network has a hundred computers, or a thousand computers, or even ten thousand?

As the size of the network grows, the work needed for manual configuration grows with it. And while initial hardware setup may be time-consuming, at least it is done mainly when the host is first set up, and rarely changed thereafter. This is not the case with configuration parameters. If the address of the local router changes on a network with a thousand hosts, do you really want to go to each host to edit a configuration file?

The drudge work associated with manual configuration is significant, but the problems go well beyond the inefficiency issue. There are situations where manual configuration is not just inconvenient, but is actually impossible:

Remote Configuration An administrator cannot be everywhere; modern networks can span cities or nations. Unless we want to train every user on how to configure network hosts, we must use an automated protocol.

Mobile Device Configuration IP was designed when computers were large and attached to each other using heavy cables; today, we have computers that fit in a shirt pocket and communicate using radio waves. IP addresses must be assigned based on the network to which they are attached, and this makes reconfiguration required when a device is moved. This is not conducive to manual configuration at all.

Dumb Host Configuration Most of the hosts we use today are full-fledged computers, with their own internal storage. We can assign such a device an address by entering it into a file that the device reads when it starts up. There are certain devices, however, that do not include any form of storage. Since they are mass-produced, they are all identical and cannot have individualized parameters stored within them. Such a device relies on a configuration protocol to learn what it needs to function on a network—especially including its individual identity.

Address Sharing The proliferation of devices attached to the global Internet has led to a situation where IP addresses must be carefully managed to ensure that they are not wasted on devices that aren't using them. Some organizations even find themselves with more potential hosts than they have addresses. A host configuration protocol can allow an address to be automatically assigned to a host when needed, and then have that address returned to a common pool for reuse when the host leaves the network. This permits addresses to be shared and reduces the need for more address space.

Automating the Process: Host Configuration Protocols

Even though most of us don't have robots that can automate the hardware portions of the setup and configuration job, we can employ tools that will make the rest of the job easier. This includes the use of special *host configuration* protocols. These protocols allow hosts to be automatically configured when they are set up and to have additional parameters assigned when needed.

Host configuration protocols generally function by having a host send a request for an address and other parameters, which is satisfied by a response from a server. The information in the response is used by the client to set its address, identify a local router, and perform other necessary setup so it can communicate.

The use of an automated protocol solves all of the problems associated with manual configuration. We can configure devices remotely, rather than needing to walk to each one. We can instantly assign a valid address to mobile devices. We can have dumb hosts boot up and obtain the information they need to operate. Finally, we can maintain a pool of addresses that is shared by a group of hosts.

> **KEY CONCEPT** *Host configuration protocols* enable administrators to set up hosts so that they can automatically determine their address and other key parameters. They are useful not only because of the effort they save over manual configuration, but because they enable the automatic setup of remote, storageless, or mobile devices.

The Role of Host Configuration Protocols in TCP/IP

You might find it strange that host configuration protocols would exist in the lofty heights of the application layer. It certainly sounds like host configuration is a function related more to the network layer, where internetwork addresses such as IP addresses function. In fact, some host configuration protocols, like the rudimentary Reverse Address Resolution Protocol (RARP, discussed in Chapter 14), do exist down at that level.

However, there are advantages to having host configuration protocols reside at higher levels. A major one is that the operation of the protocol does not depend on the hardware on which it runs, making it more universal. Another is being able to convey host configuration messages between networks, which is not possible with a low-level protocol operating on the local network.

60

TCP/IP BOOTSTRAP PROTOCOL (BOOTP)

Before a device on a TCP/IP network can effectively communicate, it needs to know its IP address. While a conventional network host can read this information from its internal disk, some devices have no storage, so they do not have this luxury. They need help from another device on the network to provide them with an IP address and the other information and/or software they need to become active Internet Protocol (IP) hosts. This problem of getting a new machine up and running is commonly called *bootstrapping*, and to provide this capability to IP hosts, the TCP/IP *Bootstrap Protocol (BOOTP)* was created.

In this chapter, I provide a detailed look at BOOTP. I begin with an overview and history of the protocol and a look at the standards that define it. I then discuss the general client/server nature of BOOTP and how addressing is done in communication between the client and the server. I describe the operation of BOOTP step by step and illustrate the format of BOOTP messages. I conclude with a description of BOOTP vendor extensions, which are used to allow the information sent in BOOTP messages to be customized, and a discussion of BOOTP relay agents, which allow the protocol to operate even when the BOOTP server and client are on different networks.

RELATED INFORMATION *BOOTP was the predecessor of the Dynamic Host Configuration Protocol (DHCP). DHCP was built to be substantially compatible with BOOTP, and so the two protocols have a fair degree of commonality. To avoid duplication, certain information has been included only in the following chapters about DHCP (with references to this chapter where appropriate). On the other hand, some of the historical background information behind features like vendor information extensions and relay agents, which were first developed for BOOTP and adopted by DHCP, is in this chapter and referenced from the DHCP chapters. If you plan to read about DHCP as well as BOOTP, I recommend reading this section first. If you don't plan to read up on DHCP, you may wish to check the discussion of DHCP/BOOTP interoperability in Chapter 64.*

BOOTP Overview, History, and Standards

The TCP/IP protocol suite has been with us for over two decades, and the problem of how to automate the configuration of parameters on IP hosts has been around almost as long. Back in the early 1980s, networks were small and relatively simple, so manual configuration wasn't that difficult. Automated host configuration was primarily needed because it was the only way to configure devices like diskless workstations.

As I discussed in Chapter 59, without a form of internal storage, a device must rely on someone or something to tell it "who it is" (its address) and how to function each time it is powered up. When a device like this is turned on, it is in a difficult position: It needs to use IP to communicate with another device that will tell it how to communicate using IP! This process, called *bootstrapping* or *booting*, comes from an analogy to a person "pulling himself up using his own bootstraps." You've likely encountered this term before, if at no other time then when some tech support person has told you to "reboot" your computer.

BOOTP: Correcting the Weaknesses of RARP

The Reverse Address Resolution Protocol (RARP) was the first attempt to resolve this bootstrap problem. Created in 1984, RARP is a direct adaptation of the low-level Address Resolution Protocol (ARP) that binds IP addresses to link-layer hardware addresses (see Chapter 13). RARP is capable of providing a diskless device with its IP address, using a simple client/server exchange of a request and reply between a host and an RARP server.

The difficulty with RARP is that it has so many limitations. It operates at a fairly low level using hardware broadcasts, so it requires adjustments for different hardware types. An RARP server is also required on every physical network to respond to layer 2 broadcasts. Each RARP server must have address assignments manually provided by an administrator. And perhaps worst of all, RARP provides only an IP address to a host and none of the other information a host may need. (I describe these issues in detail in Chapter 14.)

RARP clearly wasn't sufficient for the host configuration needs of TCP/IP. To support both diskless hosts and other situations where the benefits of autoconfiguration were required, BOOTP was created. BOOTP was standardized in RFC 951, published in September 1985. This relatively straightforward protocol was designed specifically to address the shortcomings of RARP:

- BOOTP is still based on a client/server exchange, but is implemented as a higher-layer software protocol, using the User Datagram Protocol (UDP) for message transport (see Chapter 44). It is not dependent on the particular hardware of the network as RARP is.
- It supports sending additional configuration information to a client beyond just an IP address. This extra information can usually be sent in one message for efficiency.
- It can handle having the client and server on different networks of an internetwork. This allows the administration of the server providing IP addresses to be more centralized, saving money as well as administrative time and hassle.

It should be noted that, even though the name of BOOTP implies that it defines everything needed for a storageless device to boot, this isn't really the case. As the BOOTP standard itself describes, bootstrapping generally requires two phases. In the first, the client is provided with an address and other parameters. In the second, the client downloads software, such as an operating system and drivers, that let it function on the network and perform other tasks. BOOTP really deals with only the first of these phases: address assignment and configuration. The second is assumed to take place using a simple file transfer protocol like the Trivial File Transfer Protocol (TFTP, discussed in Chapter 73).

> **KEY CONCEPT** The first widely used host configuration protocol for TCP/IP was the *Boot Protocol (BOOTP)*. It was created specifically to enable host configuration while addressing many of the weaknesses of RARP. BOOTP is intended to be used as the first phase of a two-phase boot procedure for storageless devices. After obtaining an IP address and other configuration parameters using BOOTP, the device employs a protocol such as TFTP to download software necessary to function on the network.

Vendor-Specific Parameters

One smart decision made when BOOTP was created was the inclusion of a *vendor-specific area.* This was intended to provide a place where hardware vendors could define parameters relevant to their own products. As the complexity of TCP/IP increased, it was realized that this field could be used to define a method of communicating certain parameters that were commonly needed by IP hosts, and were in fact vendor-independent. This was first proposed in RFC 1048, "BOOTP Vendor Information Extensions," published in February 1988.

The fact that BOOTP can be used to provide information to a client beyond just an IP address makes it useful even in cases where a device already knows its address. BOOTP can be used to send parameters that the administrator wants all hosts to have, to ensure that they use the network in a consistent manner. Also, in the case of devices that do have local storage (and therefore do not need BOOTP to get an IP address), BOOTP can still be used to let these devices get the name of a boot file for phase two of bootstrapping, in which the client downloads software.

Changes to BOOTP and the Development of DHCP

BOOTP was the TCP/IP host configuration protocol of choice from the mid-1980s through the end of the 1990s. The vendor extensions introduced in RFC 1048 were popular, and over the years, additional vendor extensions were defined. RFC 1048 was replaced by RFCs 1084, 1395, and 1497 in succession.

Some confusion also resulted over the years in how some sections of RFC 951 should be interpreted and how certain features of BOOTP work. RFC 1542, "Clarifications and Extensions for the Bootstrap Protocol," was published in October 1993 to address this and also to make some slight changes to the protocol's operation. (RFC 1542 is actually a correction of the nearly identical RFC 1532, which had some small errors.)

While BOOTP was obviously quite successful, it also had certain weaknesses. One of the most important of these was the lack of support for *dynamic* address assignment. The need for dynamic assignment became much more pronounced when the Internet really started to take off in the late 1990s. This led directly to the development of the Dynamic Host Configuration Protocol (DHCP).

While DHCP replaced BOOTP as the TCP/IP host configuration protocol of choice, it would be inaccurate to say that BOOTP is gone. It is still used to this day in some networks. Furthermore, DHCP was based directly on BOOTP, and they share many attributes, including a common message format. BOOTP vendor extensions were used as the basis for DHCP *options*, which work in the same way but include extra capabilities. In fact, the successor to RFC 1497 is RFC 1533, which officially merges BOOTP vendor extensions and DHCP options into the same standard.

BOOTP Client/Server Messaging and Addressing

While BOOTP can be used for a variety of devices, one of the primary motives behind its creation was to provide a way to automatically configure "dumb" devices that have no storage. Most of these devices are relatively limited in their capabilities, so requiring them to support a fancy boot protocol would not make sense. BOOTP is thus an uncomplicated protocol, which accomplishes host configuration without a lot of complicated concepts or implementation requirements.

Like so many other TCP/IP protocols, BOOTP is client/server in nature. The operation of the protocol consists of a single exchange of messages between a *BOOTP client* and a *BOOTP server*. A BOOTP client can be any type of device that needs to be configured. A BOOTP server is a network device that has been specially set up to respond to BOOTP client requests, and has been programmed with addressing and other information it can provide to clients when required.

The BOOTP server maintains a special set of information about the clients it serves. One key part of this is a table that maps the hardware (layer 2, the data link layer) addresses of each client to an assigned IP address for that device. The client specifies its hardware address in its request, and the server uses that address to look up the client's IP address and return it to the client. (Other techniques can also be used, but a mapping table is most common.)

BOOTP Messaging and Transport

BOOTP messaging uses UDP as its layer 4 transport protocol, for a couple of reasons:

- UDP is a lot less complex than the other layer 4 transport protocol, the Transmission Control Protocol (TCP), and is ideal for simple request/reply protocols like BOOTP.
- Since the client obviously doesn't know the address of a BOOTP server, the request is broadcast on its local network. UDP supports broadcasts; TCP does not.

UDP uses a special well-known (reserved) port number for BOOTP servers: UDP port 67. BOOTP servers listen on port 67 for these broadcast BOOTP requests sent by clients. After processing the request, the server sends a reply back to the client. How this is handled depends on whether or not the client knows its own address.

BOOTP is often used to provide an IP address to a client that doesn't know its address. This is sometimes called a chicken-and-egg problem, because it represents a loop of sorts like the old conundrum of which came first, the chicken or the egg? To resolve this dilemma, the BOOTP server has two choices. If the operating system supports it, the server can use the client's hardware address to create an ARP entry for the device, and then use a layer 2 unicast to deliver the reply. Otherwise, it must send the reply as a broadcast as well on the local network.

However, in the case where the BOOTP client already knows its own address, that address can be used by the BOOTP server to send back its reply directly.

BOOTP Use of Broadcasts and Ports

The fact that BOOTP servers may need to broadcast back to the client necessitates a bit of a change from the way most TCP/IP protocols use client ports. Recall that normally, the client in a client/server transaction using UDP or TCP generates a temporary, or ephemeral, port number that it uses as the source port in its request. The server sends the reply back to the client's IP address using that ephemeral port number.

Ephemeral port numbers must be unique for a particular IP address, but may not necessarily be unique across all the devices on a network. For example, Device A may be using ephemeral port number 1248 for an HTTP request to a web server, while Device B may be using port number 1248 on its TCP/IP stack to send a Domain Name System (DNS) request. Since the server in BOOTP is broadcasting, it is not targeting a particular device with a unicast transmission. This means it cannot safely send to an ephemeral port number. This is because some other device on the network may have selected the same ephemeral port number for some other transaction and may mistake the BOOTP server's response as being intended for itself. To avoid this problem, another well-known port number is used just for BOOTP clients: UDP port 68. Clients listen on this port for broadcast or unicast transmissions; devices that have not sent a BOOTP request will ignore it. This dual-broadcast BOOTP communication process is illustrated in Figure 60-1.

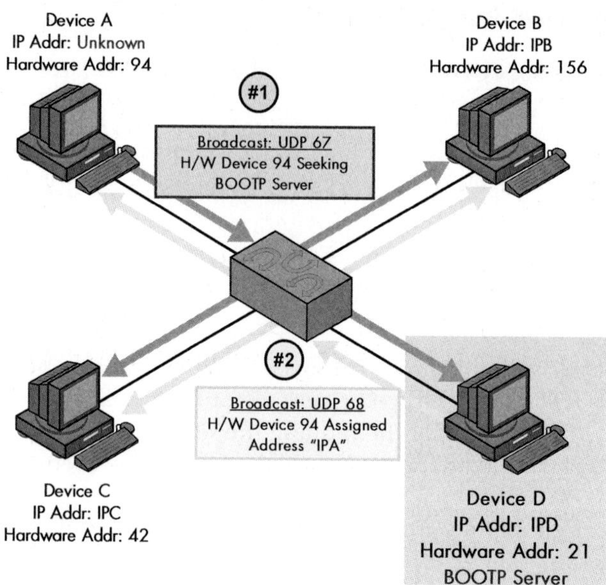

Figure 60-1: *General operation of BOOTP*

KEY CONCEPT BOOTP is a relatively simple client/server protocol that relies on broadcasts to permit communication with devices that do not have an assigned IP address. In this example, Device A is trying to determine its IP address and other parameters. It broadcasts a BOOTP request on the local network using UDP port 67 and then listens for a reply on port 68. Device D is configured as a BOOTP server and listens on this port. When it receives the request, it sends a broadcast on port 68 telling Device A what its IP address is. A BOOTP client uses broadcasts to send its requests to any listening BOOTP server. In most cases, the BOOTP client device does not know its own IP address when it uses the protocol. For this reason, a BOOTP server will also typically use broadcast in sending its reply, to be sure it reaches the client.

Retransmission of Lost Messages

The drawback of the simplicity of using UDP for BOOTP messaging is that UDP is unreliable, which means a BOOTP request might be lost before it gets to the server, or the server's response may not get back to the client. Like many other protocols using UDP, BOOTP clients take care of this by using a retransmission timer. If after a certain period of time the client has not received a response, it resends its request.

However, BOOTP clients must take care in how they implement their retransmission strategy. Consider a scenario where a network with 200 BOOTP clients loses power. These machines are all pretty much the same, so when the power comes back on, they all restart and try to send BOOTP requests at about the same time. Most likely, problems will occur due to all these requests: Some will be lost, or the server may drop some due to overload. If all the clients use the same amount of time for retransmission, then after that time elapses, a whole bunch of machines will again send requests and re-create the original problem.

To avoid retransmission problems, the BOOTP standard recommends using an exponential backoff scheme for retransmissions, starting with a retransmission interval of 4 seconds and doubling it for successive tries. A randomness element is also added to prevent many devices from overlapping their retransmissions. The idea is very similar to the backoff method used by Ethernet (in fact, the standard even refers to the Ethernet specification). For example, the first retransmission would occur after a random period of time between 0 and 4 seconds (plus or minus a random amount); a second retransmission, if needed, after a random time interval between 0 and 8 seconds, plus or minus, and so forth. This helps reduce the chances of retransmissions being lost and also helps ensure BOOTP traffic doesn't bog down the network.

> **KEY CONCEPT** BOOTP uses UDP for transport, which provides no reliability features. For this reason, the BOOTP client must detect when its requests are lost and, if necessary, retransmit them.

BOOTP Detailed Operation

Now that you have seen how BOOTP messaging works in general terms, let's take a closer look at the detailed operation of the protocol. This will clarify how clients and servers create and process messages, and also help make sense of some of the important fields in the BOOTP message field format. Understanding the basic operation of BOOTP will also be of use when we examine BOOTP relay agents later in this chapter, and even when we discuss DHCP in the following chapters.

BOOTP Bootstrapping Procedure

The following are the basic steps performed by the client and server in a regular BOOTP bootstrapping procedure (see Figure 60-2).

Client Creates Request The client machine begins the procedure by creating a BOOTP request message. In creating this message, it fills in the following information:

- It sets the message type (Op) to the value 1, for a BOOTREQUEST message.
- If it knows its own IP address that it plans to keep using, it specifies it in the CIAddr (Client IP Address) field. Otherwise, it fills this field with zeros. (The CIAddr field is discussed in more detail in the next section.)
- It puts its own layer 2 hardware address in the CHAddr field. This is used by the server to determine the right address and other parameters for the client.
- It generates a random transaction identifier and puts this in the XID field.
- The client may specify a particular server that it wants to send it a reply and put that in the SName field. It may also specify the name of a particular type of boot file that it wants the server to provide in the File field.
- The client may specify vendor-specific information, if programmed to do so.

Client Sends Request The client broadcasts the BOOTREQUEST message by transmitting it to address 255.255.255.255. Alternatively, if it already knows the address of a BOOTP server, it may send the request unicast.

Server Receives Request and Processes It A BOOTP server, listening on UDP port 67, receives the broadcasted request and processes it. If a name of a particular server was specified and this name is different from the name of this server, the server may discard the request. This is especially true if the server knows that the server the client asked for is also on the local network. If no particular server is specified, or this particular server was the one the client wanted, the server will reply.

Server Creates Reply The server creates a reply message by copying the request message and changing several fields:

- It changes the message type (Op) to the value 2, for a BOOTREPLY message.
- It takes the client's specified hardware address from the CHAddr field and uses it in a table lookup to find the matching IP address for this host. It then places this value into the YIAddr (Your IP Address) of the reply.
- It processes the File field and provides the filename type the client requested, or if the field was blank, the default filename.
- It puts its own IP address and name in the SIAddr and SName fields.
- It sets any vendor-specific values in the Vend field.

Server Sends Reply The server sends the reply. The method it uses depends on the contents of the request:

- If the B (Broadcast) flag is set, this indicates that the client can't have the reply sent unicast, so the server will broadcast it.
- If the CIAddr field is nonzero, the server will send the reply unicast back to that CIAddr.
- If the B flag is zero and the CIAddr field is also zero, the server may either use an ARP entry or broadcast, as described earlier.

Client Processes Reply The client receives the server's reply and processes it, storing the information and parameters provided. (See the next section for one important issue related to this processing.)

Client Completes Boot Process Once configured, the client proceeds to phase two of the bootstrapping process, by using a protocol such as TFTP to download its boot file containing operating system software, using the filename the server provided.

Interpretation of the Client IP Address (CIAddr) Field

A complication can arise when a client chooses to specify an IP address in the CIAddr field in its request. The problem is how exactly to interpret this field. Does it mean that the client is already using this IP address? Or is it just the one it used last time it was booted? Then there is the related problem of what to do if the server supplies an address in the YIAddr that is different from the one the client is using. Should the server's provided address override the client's address? Or should the client ignore it? Who makes the decision, the server or the client?

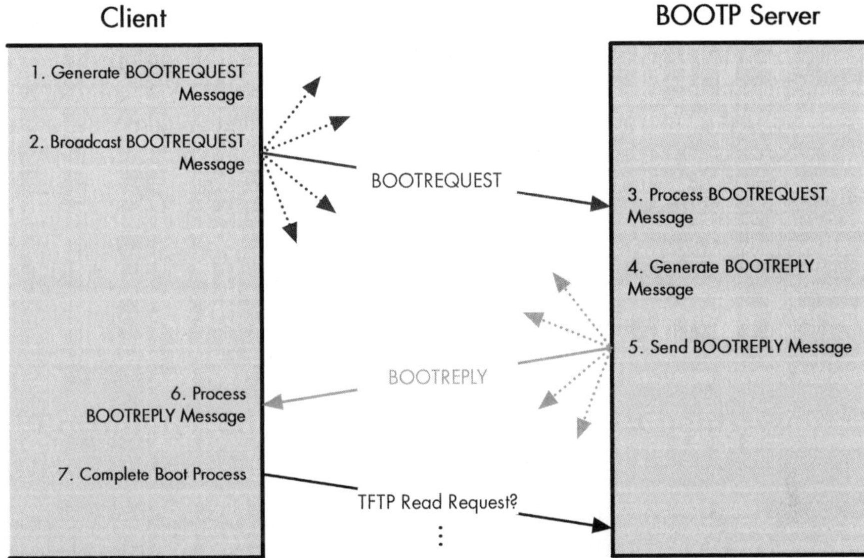

Figure 60-2: BOOTP operation *BOOTP uses a simple two-step message exchange consisting of a broadcast request and broadcast reply. After the client receives configuration information from the BOOTP server, it completes the bootstrapping process using a protocol such as TFTP.*

Much confusion occurred due to the vagueness of the original standard in this regard, and this led to nonuniformity in how different implementations chose to handle this issue. There were even some implementations that used the CIAddr to mean "the client requests this IP address," which was never part of BOOTP functionality. This is an especially bad idea since it could lead to BOOTP replies never reaching the client.

RFC 1542 was written in part to try to clean up this mess. It suggests that the following is the best way to handle the meaning of these fields:

- If a client is willing to accept whatever IP address the server provides, it sets CIAddr to all zeros, even if it knows a previous address.
- If the client fills in a value for the field, it is saying it will use this address, and it must be prepared to receive unicast messages sent to that address.
- If the client specifies an address in CIAddr and receives a different address in the YIAddr field, the server-provided address is ignored.

Note that not all hardware devices may necessarily agree with this interpretation as provided by RFC 1542, so there are still potential interoperability concerns here with older equipment. Then again, RFC 1542 was written in 1993, so this is probably no longer much of an issue!

BOOTP Message Format

The exchange of information in BOOTP takes the form of a request sent by a client and a reply sent back by the server. BOOTP, like a number of other request/reply protocols, uses a common message format for requests and replies. The client starts by setting aside memory space for the message and clearing it to all zeros. It then fills in the fields of the message and sends the request, as you saw in the previous section. The server creates its reply not from scratch, but by copying the request and changing certain fields.

BOOTP messages contain a considerable number of fields, so the message format is rather large. It is described in Tables 60-1 and 60-2, and illustrated in Figure 60-3.

Table 60-1: BOOTP Message Format

Field Name	Size (Bytes)	Description
Op	1	Operation Code: Specifies the type of message. A value of 1 indicates a request (BOOTREQUEST message). A value of 2 is a reply (BOOTREPLY message).
HType	1	Hardware Type: This field specifies the type of hardware used for the local network and is used in exactly the same way as the equivalent field (HRD) in the ARP message format (see Chapter 13). Some of the most common values for this field are shown in Table 60-2.
HLen	1	Hardware Address Length: Specifies how long hardware addresses are in this message. For Ethernet or other networks using IEEE 802 MAC addresses, the value is 6. This is the same as the field with a similar name (HLN) in the ARP field format.
Hops	1	Hops: Set to 0 by a client before transmitting a request and used by BOOTP relay agents to control the forwarding of BOOTP messages.
XID	4	Transaction Identifier: A 32-bit identification field generated by the client, to allow it to match up the request with replies received from BOOTP servers.
Secs	2	Seconds: According to RFC 951, the client enters into this field the number of seconds "elapsed since [the] client started trying to boot." This is supposed to provide information to BOOTP servers to help them decide which requests to respond to first. Unfortunately, it isn't clear if this meant the amount of time since the machine was powered on or since the first BOOTREQUEST message was sent. In addition, some devices incorrectly implemented this field. As a result, it is not always used.
Flags	2	Flags: In the original BOOTP standard (RFC 951), this was an empty 2-byte field. RFC 1542 changed this to a Flags field, which at present contains only one flag. It has a B (Broadcast) flag subfield, 1 bit in size, which is set to 1 if the client doesn't know its own IP address at the time it sends its BOOTP request. This serves as an immediate indicator to the BOOTP server or relay agent that receives the request that it definitely should send its reply by broadcast. The other subfield is Reserved, which is 15 bits, set to 0, and not used.
CIAddr	4	Client IP Address: If the client has a current IP address that it plans to keep using, it puts it in this field. By filling in this field, the client is committing to responding to unicast IP datagrams sent to this address. Otherwise, it sets this field to all 0s to tell the server it wants an address assigned. (See the previous section in this chapter for important information about this field.)
YIAddr	4	Your IP Address: The IP address that the server is assigning to the client. This may be different than the IP address currently used by the client.
SIAddr	4	Server IP Address: The IP address of the BOOTP server sending a BOOTREPLY message.
GIAddr	4	Gateway IP Address: Used to route BOOTP messages when BOOTP relay agents facilitate the communication of BOOTP requests and replies between a client and a server on different subnets or networks. To understand the name, remember that the old TCP/IP term for *router* is *gateway;* BOOTP relay agents are typically routers. Note that this field is set to 0 by the client and should be ignored by the client when processing a BOOTREPLY. It specifically does not represent the server giving the client the address of a default router address to be used for general IP routing purposes.

(continued)

Table 60-1: BOOTP Message Format (continued)

Field Name	Size (Bytes)	Description
CHAddr	16	Client Hardware Address: The hardware (layer 2) address of the client sending a BOOTREQUEST. It is used to look up a device's assigned IP address and also possibly in delivery of a reply message.
SName	64	Server Name: The server sending a BOOTREPLY may optionally put its name in this field. This can be a simple text nickname or a fully qualified DNS domain name (such as myserver .organization.org). Note that a client may specify a name in this field when it creates its request. If it does so, it is saying that it wants to get a reply only from the BOOTP server with this name. This may be done to ensure that the client is able to access a particular boot file stored on only one server.
File	128	Boot Filename: Contains the full directory path and filename of a boot file that can be downloaded by the client to complete its bootstrapping process. The client may request a particular type of file by entering a text description here, or it may leave the field blank and the server will supply the filename of the default file.
Vend	64	Vendor-Specific Area: Originally created to allow vendors to customize BOOTP to the needs of different types of hardware, this field is now also used to hold additional vendor-independent configuration information. The next section, on BOOTP vendor information extensions, contains much more detail on this field. It may be used by the client and/or the server.

Table 60-2: BOOTP Message HType Values

HType Value	Hardware Type
1	Ethernet (10 Mb)
6	IEEE 802 Networks
7	ARCNet
15	Frame Relay
16	Asynchronous Transfer Mode (ATM)
17	High-Level Data Link Control (HDLC)
18	Fibre Channel
19	ATM
20	Serial Line

As I mentioned earlier in this chapter, both requests and replies are encapsulated into UDP messages for transmission. The BOOTP standard specifies that the use of UDP checksums is optional. Using the checksum provides protection against data-integrity errors and is thus recommended. This may cause unacceptable processing demands on the part of very simple clients, so the checksum can legally be skipped.

Similarly, for simplicity, BOOTP assumes that its messages will not be fragmented. This is to allow BOOTP clients to avoid the complexity of reassembling fragmented messages. Since BOOTP messages are only 300 bytes in length, under the maximum transmission unit (MTU) required for all TCP/IP links, this is not normally an issue.

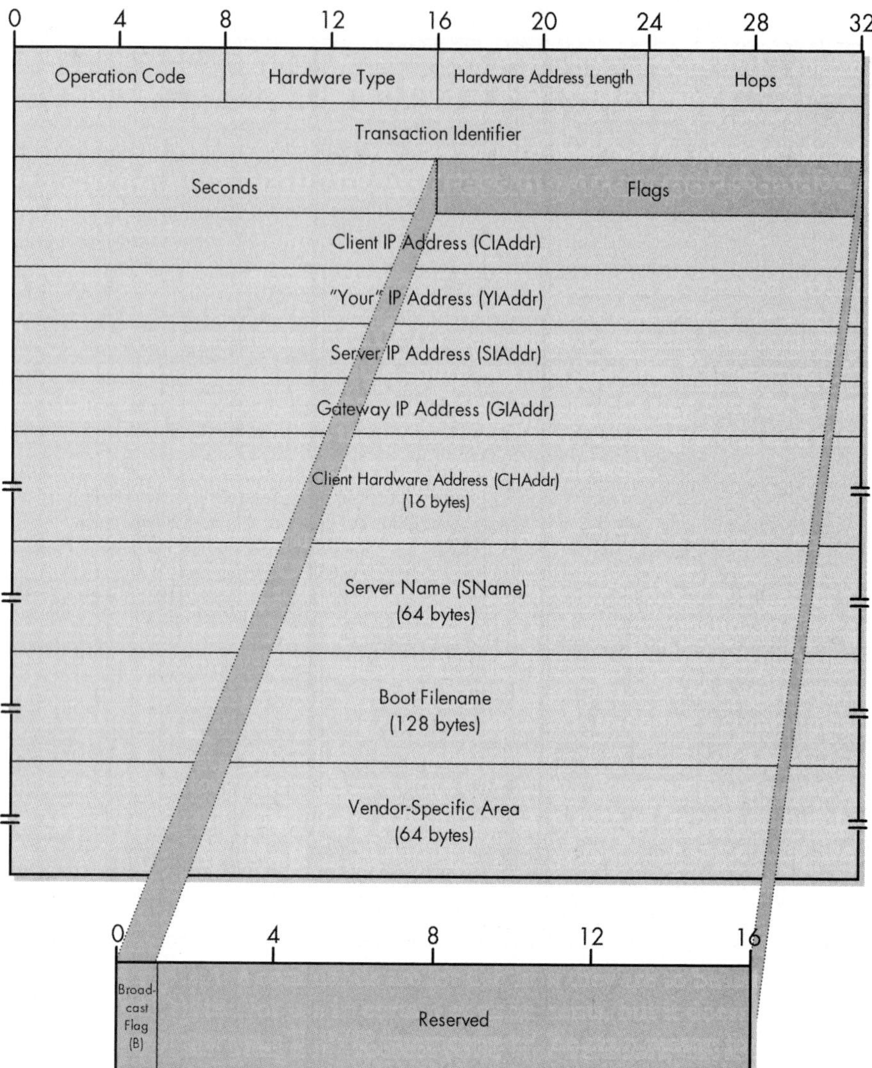

Figure 60-3: *BOOTP message format*

BOOTP Vendor-Specific Area and Vendor Information Extensions

The creators of BOOTP realized that certain types of hardware might require additional information to be passed from the server to the client in order for the client to boot. For this reason, they put into the BOOTP field format the 64-byte Vend field, also called the Vendor-Specific Area. Including this field makes BOOTP flexible, since it allows vendors to decide for themselves how they want to use the protocol and to tailor it to their needs.

A client can use the Vend field by asking for certain types of information in the field when composing its request. The server can then respond to these requests, and it may also include parameters it wants the client to have, even if they were not requested. The original BOOTP protocol does not define any structure for the Vendor-Specific Area, leaving this up to each manufacturer to decide.

Obviously, there is nothing preventing a client made by one manufacturer from trying to send a request to a server made by another one. If each one is expecting the Vend field to contain something different, the results will be less than satisfactory. Thus, for the Vend field to be used properly, both devices must be speaking the same language when it comes to the meaning of this field. This is done by setting the first four bytes of the field to a special value. Each manufacturer chooses its own *magic number*, sometimes called a *magic cookie*, for this four-byte subfield.

NOTE *Why is it called a magic cookie? I'm not sure, to be honest. I have heard that its origin may be the cookie that Alice ate to grow or shrink in the story* Alice in Wonderland.

BOOTP Vendor Information Extensions

Including the Vend field in BOOTP gives the protocol extensibility for vendor-specific information. Unfortunately, the original field format didn't include any way of extending the information sent from a server to a client for *generic*, nonvendor-specific TCP/IP information. This was a significant oversight in the creation of the protocol, because there are many types of information that a TCP/IP host needs when it starts up that really have nothing to do with its vendor. For example, when a host boots, we probably want it to be told the address of a default router, the subnet mask for its local subnet, the address of a local DNS server, the MTU of the local network, and much more. None of these things are vendor-specific, but there is no place to put them in the BOOTP reply message.

Since there was no nonvendor-specific area field in BOOTP, the decision was made to define a way of using the Vendor-Specific Area (Vend field) for communicating this additional generic information. This was first standardized in RFC 1048 and then refined in later RFCs, as I explained in the BOOTP overview earlier in this chapter. This scheme basically represents one particular way of using the Vend field that most TCP/IP BOOTP implementations have chosen to adopt, regardless of their vendor. This enhancement is formally referred to as *BOOTP vendor information extensions.*

KEY CONCEPT The BOOTP message format includes a Vend field that was originally intended for vendor-specific customized fields. It was later changed to a place where additional generic information could be sent from a BOOTP server to a BOOTP client. Each such parameter is carried in a BOOTP *vendor information field.*

To clearly mark that this particular meaning of the Vend field is being used, a special, universal magic cookie value of 99.130.83.99 is inserted into the first four bytes of the field. Then the remaining 60 bytes can contain a sequence of one or more *vendor information fields.* The overall structure of the Vendor-Specific Area when vendor information extensions are used is shown in Figure 60-4.

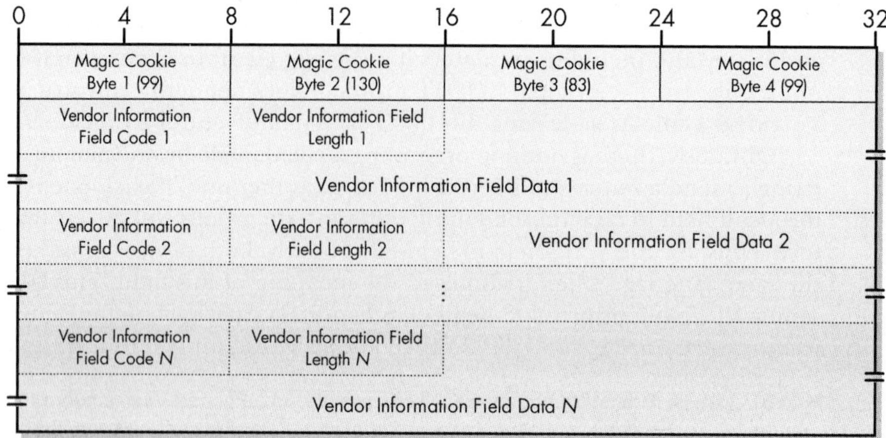

***Figure 60-4:** BOOTP Vendor-Specific Area format showing vendor information fields*

NOTE *The BOOTP Vendor-Specific Area begins with the four-byte magic cookie and then contains a number of variable-length vendor information fields, each of which has the format shown above and in Table 60-3. Despite the use of IP dotted-decimal notation to represent the value 99.130.83.99, this is not an IP address. It's just a marker—a magic number that is universally recognized.*

BOOTP Vendor Information Fields

Each vendor information field specifies a particular type of information to be communicated, and it is encoded using a special subfield structure that specifies the field's type, length, and value. This is a common method of specifying options, called *TLV-encoding* (for *type, length, value*). The same basic method is used for encoding Internet Protocol versions 4 and 6 (IPv4 and IPv6) options. Table 60-3 shows the structure and the common names for the subfields of each vendor information field.

Table 60-3: BOOTP Vendor Information Field Format

Subfield Name	Size (Bytes)	Description
Code	1	Vendor Information Field Code: A single octet that specifies the vendor information field type.
Len	1	Vendor Information Field Length: The number of bytes in this particular vendor information field. This does not include the two bytes for the Code and Len fields.
Data	Variable	Vendor Information Field Data: The data being sent, which has a length indicated by the Len subfield, and which is interpreted based on the Code subfield.

There are two special cases that violate the field format shown in Table 60-3. A Code value of 0 is used as padding when subfields need to be aligned on word boundaries; it contains no information. The value 255 is used to mark the end of the vendor information fields. Both of these codes contain no actual data. To save space, when either is used, just the single Code value is included, and the Len and

Data fields are omitted. A device seeing a Code value of 0 just skips it as filler; a device seeing a Code value of 255 knows it has reached the end of the vendor information fields in this Vend field.

The vendor information extensions of BOOTP have become so popular that the use of this field for sending extra generic information is pretty much standard. In fact, I am not sure if anyone today still uses the Vend field solely for vendor-specific information.

When the vendor information extensions were introduced, one was created that points to a file where vendor-specific information can be found. This lets devices have the best of both worlds—they can use the standard vendor-independent fields and can incorporate vendor-specific fields (through the referenced file) where needed. Later, another field type was created that lets vendor-specific fields be mixed with vendor-independent ones directly in a BOOTP message.

When DHCP was created, the same vendor extension mechanism was maintained and enhanced further, but instead of the field being called vendor information extensions, it was renamed to *Options*. (A much better name!) The BOOTP vendor information fields were retained in DHCP, and new DHCP-specific options were defined. To avoid duplication, I have listed all the BOOTP vendor information fields and DHCP options in a set of tables in Chapter 63, which covers DHCP messaging. This includes a discussion of how vendor-specific and vendor-independent information can be mixed. You may also want to read the section in Chapter 63 that describes DHCP options, which discusses how they were created from BOOTP vendor information extensions.

BOOTP Relay Agents (Forwarding Agents)

One reason why RARP was quickly replaced by BOOTP is that RARP required the client being configured and the server providing it with an IP address to be on the same physical network. This is fine when you run a small organization with ten machines, which are probably all on the same physical network. Larger networks must be divided into multiple physical networks for efficiency, however. RARP would require a separate RARP server for each network, meaning needing to duplicate all the functions of a single server onto multiple machines. Worse yet, all the configuration information would also be duplicated, and any changes would need to be made to all the different servers each time.

BOOTP is designed to allow the BOOTP server and the clients it serves to be on different networks. This centralizes the BOOTP server and greatly reduces the amount of work required of network administrators. However, implementing this feature means increasing the complexity of the protocol. In particular, we need to involve a third-party device in the configuration process.

You might rightly wonder why this would be the case. RARP is a low-level protocol that works at the link layer, so that explains why it would have problems putting the client and server on different physical networks. But wasn't the whole point of making BOOTP a high-level protocol that it was able to use IP? And if BOOTP uses IP, can't we send from one network to another arbitrarily, just like any IP-based messaging protocol?

The answer is that even though we are indeed using IP and UDP, BOOTP still has one of the same issues that RARP had: a reliance on *broadcasts*. The client usually doesn't know the address of a server, so it must send out its request as a broadcast, saying in essence, "Can anyone hear this and give me the information I need?" For efficiency reasons, routers do not route such broadcasts, as they would clog the network. This means that if the server and client are not on the same network, the server can't hear the client's broadcast. Similarly, if the server ever did get the request and broadcast its reply back to the client, the client would never get it anyway. To make this all work, we need something to act as an intermediary between the client and the server: a *BOOTP relay agent*.

The Function of BOOTP Relay Agents

The job of a BOOTP relay agent is to sit on a physical network where BOOTP clients may be located and act as a proxy for the BOOTP server. The agent gets its name because it relays messages between the client and server, and thus enables them to be on different networks.

NOTE *BOOTP relay agents were originally called* forwarding agents. *RFC 1542 changed the name to make explicit the fact that BOOTP relaying was not the same as conventional IP datagram forwarding by regular routers.*

In practice, a BOOTP relay agent is not usually a separate piece of hardware. Rather, it's a software module that runs on an existing piece of hardware that performs other functions. It is common for BOOTP relay agent functionality to be implemented on an IP router. In that case, the router is acting both as a regular router and also playing the role of a BOOTP agent. The forwarding functions required of a BOOTP relay agent are distinct from the normal IP datagram forwarding tasks of a router.

KEY CONCEPT Since BOOTP uses broadcasts, the BOOTP client and BOOTP server must be on the same physical network to be able to hear each other's broadcasted transmissions. For a client and server on different networks to communicate, a third party is required to facilitate the transaction: a *BOOTP relay agent*. This device, which is often a router, listens for transmissions from BOOTP clients and relays them to the BOOTP server. The server responds back to the agent, which then sends the server's response back to the client.

Naturally, the placement of the client and server on different networks and the presence of a relay agent change the normal request/reply process of BOOTP significantly. A couple of specific fields in the BOOTP message format are used to control the process. RFC 951 was rather vague in describing how this process works, so RFC 1542 described it in much more detail.

Normal BOOTP Operation Using a Relay Agent

The following shows, in simplified form, a revised set of BOOTP operation steps when a relay agent is involved. To keep the size of this discussion manageable, I have omitted the details of the basic request/reply process to focus on the relaying functionality, which you can also see graphically in Figure 60-5.

Client Creates Request The client machine creates its request normally. The existence of a relay agent is totally transparent to the client.

Client Sends Request The client broadcasts the BOOTREQUEST message by transmitting it to address 255.255.255.255. (Note that in the case where a client already knows both its own address and the address of a BOOTP server, we don't need the relay agent at all—both the request and reply can be sent unicast over an arbitrary internetwork.)

Relay Agent Receives Request and Processes It The BOOTP relay agent on the physical network where the client is located is listening on UDP port 67 on the server's behalf. It processes the request as follows:

- It checks the value of the Hops field. If the value is less than or equal to 16, it increments it. If the value is greater than 16, it discards the request and does nothing further.
- It examines the contents of the GIAddr field. If this field is all zeros, it knows it is the first relay agent to handle the request and puts its own IP address into this field. (If the agent is a router, it has more than one IP address, so it chooses the one of the interface on which it received the request.)

Relay Agent Relays Request The relay agent sends the BOOTP request to the BOOTP server. If the relay agent knows the server's IP address, it will send it unicast directly to the server. Otherwise, if the agent is a router, it may choose to broadcast the request on a different interface from the one on which it received the request. In the latter case, it is possible that multiple relay agents may be required to convey the request to the server. See the next section for more on this.

Server Receives Request and Processes It The BOOTP server receives the relayed request from the BOOTP relay agent. It processes it as normal.

Server Creates Reply The server creates a reply message as normal.

Server Sends Reply Seeing that the GIAddr field in the request was nonzero, the server knows the request was relayed. Instead of trying to send its reply back to the client that sent the request, it transmits the reply unicast back to the relay agent specified in GIAddr.

Relay Agent Relays Reply The BOOTP relay agent transmits the BOOTREPLY message back to the client. It does this either unicast or broadcast, depending on the value of the CIAddr field and the B (Broadcast) flag, just as a server does in the nonrelay case.

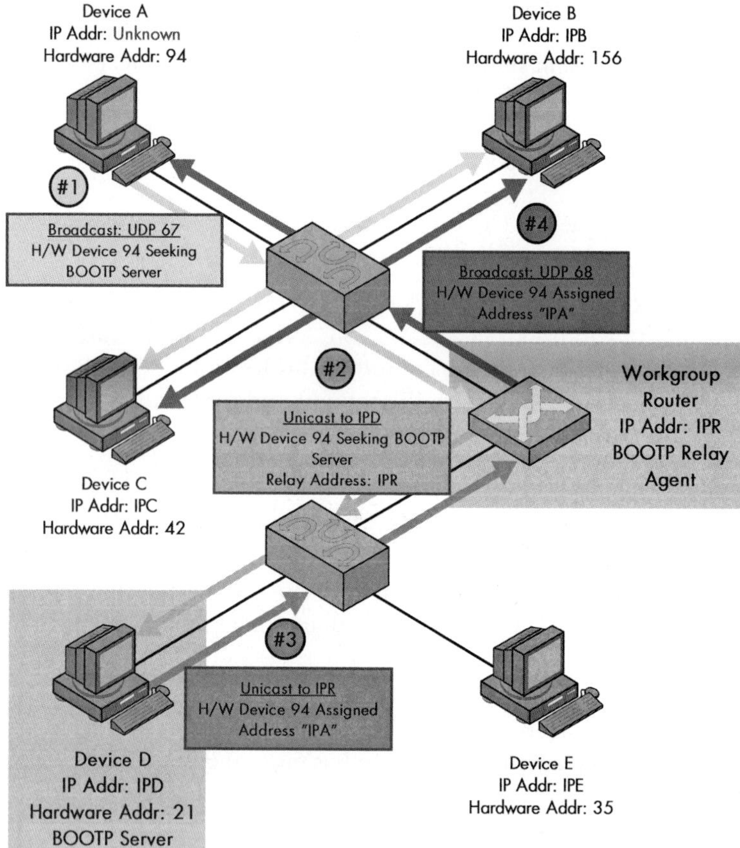

Figure 60-5: BOOTP operation using a relay agent *In this example, Device A is trying to access a BOOTP server, but the only one is on a different network; the two are connected by a workgroup router that is configured to act as a BOOTP relay agent. Device A broadcasts its request, which the router receives. It relays the request to the BOOTP server, Device D, and puts its own IP address (IPR) into the BOOTP GIAddr field. The BOOTP server sends the reply back to the router using address IPR. The router then broadcasts it on Device A's local network so that Device A can receive it.*

Relaying BOOTP Requests Using Broadcasts

The simplest case of relaying is when each network has a relay agent that knows the IP address of the BOOTP server. The relay agent captures the request in step 3 of the procedure described in the preceding section, and sends it directly to the BOOTP server, wherever it may be on the network. The request is relayed as a regular unicast UDP message and routed to the BOOTP server. The BOOTP server's reply is routed back to the BOOTP relay agent, just like any UDP message in an IP datagram, and the relay agent forwards the reply.

It is also possible to set up BOOTP relay agents to relay requests even if they don't know the BOOTP server's address. These agents take requests received on one network and relay them to the next, where they expect another agent to continue the relaying process until a BOOTP server is reached. For example, suppose we have a set of three networks. Network N1 is connected to Network N2 using Router RA, and Network N2 connects to Network N3 using Router RB. Both of these routers function as relay agents but don't know the IP address of the BOOTP server. Here's what would happen if a client on Network N1 sent a request and the server was on Network N3:

1. The client would send its request.
2. Router RA would capture the request and put its address into GIAddr. It would increment the Hops field to a value of 1 and then broadcast the request out on Network N2.
3. Router RB would capture this request. It would see there is already an address in GIAddr, so it would leave that alone. It would increment the Hops field to 2 and broadcast the request on Network N3.
4. The BOOTP server would receive the request, process it, and return the reply directly back to Router RA.
5. Router RA would relay the reply back to the client.

As you can see, the purpose of the Hops field is to ensure that errant requests don't circle around the network endlessly. Each relay agent increments it, and if the value of 16 is ever exceeded, the request is dropped. You can also see that any relay agents other than the first are involved only for handling the request; the reply is sent unicast back to the agent closest to the client.

Incidentally, if this multiple-step relaying process sounds like IP routing (only using broadcasts), and the Hops field sounds like the Time to Live (TTL) field in an IP datagram, then you've been paying attention. It is essentially the same idea (as explained in Chapter 21).

61

DHCP OVERVIEW AND ADDRESS ALLOCATION CONCEPTS

In some ways, technological advancement can be considered more a journey than a destination. When a particular technology is refined or replaced with a superior one, it's usually only a matter of time before it, too, is replaced with something better. And so it was with the TCP/IP Boot Protocol (BOOTP), described in the previous chapter. While BOOTP was far more capable than the protocol it replaced, Reverse Address Resolution Protocol (RARP), after a number of years BOOTP, itself was replaced with a new TCP/IP configuration protocol: the *Dynamic Host Configuration Protocol (DHCP)*.

Where BOOTP represented a revolutionary change from RARP, DHCP is more of an evolution of BOOTP. It was built using BOOTP as a foundation, with the same basic message format. The most significant addition in DHCP is the ability to *dynamically* assign addresses to clients and to centrally manage them. It is this capability that makes DHCP so powerful. Today, DHCP is the standard TCP/IP host configuration protocol and is used in everything from single-client home networks to enterprise-class internetworks.

In this first chapter on DHCP, I provide an overview of the protocol and a description of the concepts behind DHCP address assignment and leasing. I take a high-level look at how DHCP address assignment works and give a description of the three DHCP address allocation mechanisms. I then delve into DHCP leases and the policies and techniques used to decide how to implement DHCP leasing. I provide an overview of the lease life cycle from start to finish and describe the two DHCP lease timers that help control the process. Finally, I describe DHCP lease address pools and ranges, and the general concepts behind address management.

RELATED INFORMATION *Since DHCP builds on BOOTP, they have a number of things in common. For example, DHCP makes use of BOOTP relay agent functionality, and DHCP options are basically the same as BOOTP vendor information fields. Since DHCP is the more common of the two protocols, I have tried to be complete in describing the operation of these features here, highlighting especially any differences between how they work for DHCP and in BOOTP. However, I have avoided duplicating the history and reasoning for the existence of many of these features. Since BOOTP came first, I have placed more of the historical information in the previous chapter. In general, if you plan to read about DHCP as well as BOOTP, I recommend reading the chapter on BOOTP first. If you don't plan to read up on BOOTP, you may wish to check the topic on DHCP/BOOTP interoperability in Chapter 64 instead.*

DHCP Overview, History, and Standards

As you learned in the previous chapter, BOOTP represents a significant improvement over RARP because it solves so many of RARP's problems. BOOTP is a higher-layer protocol, not hardware-dependent like RARP. It can support sending extra information beyond an IP address to a client to enable customized configuration. Also, through the use of BOOTP relay agents, it allows a large organization to use just one or two BOOTP servers to handle clients spread out over many physical networks. In so doing, BOOTP effectively solves one of the major classes of problems that administrators have with manual configuration: the "I have to go configure each host myself" issue. It allows "dumb" (storageless) hosts to configure themselves automatically and saves administrators the hassles of needing to trek to each host individually to specify important configuration parameters.

BOOTP normally uses a static method of determining what IP address to assign to a device. When a client sends a request, it includes its hardware address, which the server looks up in a table to determine the IP address for that client. (It is possible for BOOTP to use other methods of determining the relationship between an IP and hardware address, but static mapping is usually used.) This means BOOTP works well in relatively static environments, where changes to the IP addresses assigned to different devices are infrequent. Such networks were basically the norm in the 1980s and early 1990s.

Over time, many networks quickly started to move away from this model, for a number of reasons. As computers became smaller and lighter, it was more common for them to move from one network to another, where they would require a different address using the new network's network ID. Laptop and even palmtop computers could literally move from one network to another many times per day. Another major issue was the looming exhaustion of the IP address space (see Chapter 17). For many organizations, permanently assigning a static IP address to each and every computer that might connect to their network was a luxury they could not afford.

In many organizations, trying to keep track of constant IP address changes became a daunting task in and of itself. BOOTP, with its static table of mappings between hardware addresses and IP addresses, simply wasn't up to the task. It also offered no way to reuse addresses; once an address had been assigned, a device could keep it forever, even if it were no longer needed.

DHCP: Building on BOOTP's Strengths

A new host configuration protocol was needed to serve modern networks, which would move away from static, permanent IP address assignment. The Internet Engineering Task Force (IETF) supplied this in the form of DHCP, first formalized in RFC 1541, published in October 1993. (Actually, it was really originally specified in RFC 1531 in that same month, but due to minor errors in 1531, the standard was quickly revised and 1541 published.)

Because BOOTP worked well within its limitations and was also already widely deployed, it would not have made sense to start over from scratch with DHCP. This was especially so given that such a decision would have meant dealing with the inevitable painful transition, as well as compatibility problems associated with having both BOOTP and DHCP around for many years.

So, instead of tossing out BOOTP, DHCP was built on it as a foundation. In it simplest form, DHCP consists of two major components: an address allocation mechanism and a protocol that allows clients to request configuration information and servers to provide it. DHCP performs both functions in a manner similar to BOOTP, but with improvements.

Overview of DHCP Features

The most significant differences between BOOTP and DHCP are in the area of address allocation, which is enhanced through the support for *dynamic* address assignment. Rather than using a static table that absolutely maps hardware addresses to IP addresses, a *pool* of IP addresses is used to dynamically allocate addresses. Dynamic addressing allows IP addresses to be efficiently allocated, and even shared among devices. At the same time, DHCP still supports static mapping of addresses for devices where this is needed.

The overall operation and communication between clients and servers are similar to that used by BOOTP, but with changes. The same basic request/reply protocol using UDP was retained for communicating configuration information, but additional message types were created to support DHCP's enhanced capabilities. BOOTP relay agents can be used by DHCP in a manner very similar to how they are used by BOOTP clients and server. The vendor information extensions from BOOTP were retained as well, but were formalized, renamed *DHCP options*, and extended to allow the transmission of much more information.

The result of all of this development effort is a widely accepted, universal host configuration protocol for TCP/IP that retains compatibility with BOOTP while significantly extending its capabilities. Today, DHCP is found on millions of networks worldwide. It is used for everything from assigning IP addresses to corporate networks with thousands of hosts, to allowing a home Internet access router to automatically providing the correct Internet configuration information to a single user's computer.

KEY CONCEPT The *Dynamic Host Configuration Protocol (DHCP)* is the host configuration protocol currently used on modern TCP/IP internetworks. It was based on BOOTP and is similar to its predecessor in many respects, including the use of request/reply message exchanges and a nearly identical message format. However, DHCP includes added functionality, the most notable of which is *dynamic address assignment,* which allows clients to be assigned IP addresses from a shared pool managed by a DHCP server.

The original DHCP specification was revised in March 1997 with the publishing of RFC 2131, also titled "Dynamic Host Configuration Protocol." This standard defined another new DHCP message (DHCPINFORM) type to allow active IP hosts to request additional configuration information. It also made several other small changes to the protocol. Since that time, numerous other DHCP-related RFCs have been published, most of which either define new DHCP option types (other kinds of information DHCP servers can send to DHCP clients) or slightly refine the way that DHCP is used in particular applications.

DHCP Address Assignment and Allocation Mechanisms

The two main functions of DHCP are to provide a mechanism for assigning addresses to hosts and to provide a method by which clients can request addresses and other configuration data from servers. Both functions are based on the ones implemented in DHCP's predecessor, BOOTP, but the changes are much more significant in the area of address assignment than they are in communication. It makes sense to start our look at DHCP here, since this will naturally lead us into a detailed discussion of defining characteristic of DHCP: *dynamic addressing.*

DHCP Address Allocation

Providing an IP address to a client is the most fundamental configuration task performed by a host configuration protocol. To provide flexibility for configuring addresses on different types of clients, the DHCP standard includes three different address allocation mechanisms: manual, automatic, and dynamic.

I don't really care for the names *automatic* and *dynamic* allocation, because they don't do a good job of clearly conveying the differences between these methods. Both methods can be considered automatic, because in each, the DHCP server assigns an address without requiring any administrator intervention. The real difference between them is only in how long the IP address is retained, and therefore, whether a host's address varies over time. I think better names would be *static* or *permanent* automatic allocation and *dynamic* or *temporary* automatic allocation.

Regardless of what you call them, all three of these methods exist for configuring IP hosts using DHCP. It is not necessary for administrators to choose one over the others. Instead, they will normally combine the methods, using each where it makes the most sense.

DHCP Manual Allocation

With manual allocation, a particular IP address is preallocated to a single device by an administrator. DHCP communicates only the IP address to the device.

Manual allocation is the simplest method, and it is equivalent to the method BOOTP uses for address assignment, described in the previous chapter. Each device has an address that an administrator gives it ahead of time, and all DHCP does is look up the address in a table and send it to the client for which it is intended. This technique makes the most sense for devices that are mainstays of the network, such as servers and routers. It is also appropriate for other devices that must have a stable, permanent IP address.

Okay, now here's a fair question you might have. DHCP acts basically like BOOTP in the case of manual allocation. But BOOTP was created for devices that needed help with configuration. Servers and routers are complex devices with their own internal storage, and they obviously don't need a DHCP server to tell them their IP address as a diskless workstation does, so why bother using DHCP for them at all?

Well, in fact, you could just manually assign the address to the device directly and tell DHCP to ignore those addresses. However, using DHCP for manual assignments yields a different benefit: an administrative one. It keeps all the IP address information centralized in the DHCP address database, instead of requiring an administrator to go from machine to machine checking addresses and ensuring there are no duplicates. Updates can be made in a single place as well.

DHCP Dynamic Allocation

While manual allocation is possible in DHCP, dynamic allocation is its real *raison d'etre.* With dynamic allocation, DHCP assigns an IP address from a pool of addresses for a limited period of time chosen by the server, or until the client tells the DHCP server that it no longer needs the address. An administrator sets up the *pool* (usually a range or set of ranges) of IP addresses that are available for use. Each client that is configured to use DHCP contacts the server when it needs an IP address. The server keeps track of which IP addresses are already assigned, and it *leases* one of the free addresses from the pool to the client. The server decides the amount of time that the lease will last. When the time expires, the client must either request permission to keep using the address (*renew* the lease) or must get a new one.

Dynamic allocation is the method used for most client machines in modern DHCP-enabled IP internetworks. It offers numerous benefits, such as the following:

Automation Each client can be automatically assigned an IP address when it is needed, without any administrator intervention. Administrators do not need to manually decide which address goes with which client.

Centralized Management All the IP addresses are managed by the DHCP server. An administrator can easily look to see which devices are using which addresses and perform other network-wide maintenance tasks.

Address Reuse and Sharing By limiting the amount of time that each device holds an IP address, the DHCP server can ensure that the pool of IP addresses is used only by devices actively using the network. After a period of time, addresses no longer being used are returned to the pool, allowing other devices to use them. This allows an internetwork to support a total number of devices larger than the number of IP addresses available, as long as not all the devices connect to the internetwork at the same time.

Portability and Universality BOOTP (and DHCP manual allocation) both require that the DHCP server know the identity of each client that connects to it, so the server can find the client's assigned address. With dynamic allocation, there are no predefined allocations, so any client can request an IP address. This inherently makes dynamic allocation the ideal choice for supporting mobile devices that travel between networks.

Conflict Avoidance Since IP addresses are all assigned from a pool that is managed by the DHCP server, IP address conflicts are avoided. This, of course, assumes that all the clients use DHCP. The administrator must ensure that the address pool is not used by non-DHCP devices.

DHCP Automatic Allocation

With the automatic allocation method, DHCP automatically assigns an IP address permanently to a device, selecting it from a pool of available addresses. This method can be used in cases where there are enough IP addresses for each device that may connect to the network, but where devices don't really care which IP address they use. Once an address is assigned to a client, that device will keep using it. Automatic allocation can be considered a special case of dynamic allocation: It is essentially dynamic allocation where the time limit on the use of the IP address by a client (the lease length) is forever.

In practice, automatic allocation is not used nearly as much as dynamic allocation, for a simple reason: Automatically assigning an IP address to a device permanently is a risky move. Most administrators feel it is better to use manual allocation for the limited number of machines that really need a permanent IP address assignment and to use dynamic addressing for others.

> **KEY CONCEPT** DHCP defines three basic mechanisms for address assignment. *Dynamic allocation* is the method most often used, and it works by having each client *lease* an address from a DHCP server for a period of time. The server chooses the address dynamically from a shared address pool. *Automatic allocation* is like dynamic allocation, but the address is assigned permanently instead of being leased. *Manual allocation* preassigns an address to a specific device, just as BOOTP does, and is normally used only for servers and other permanent, important hosts.

DHCP Leases

Of the three address allocation methods supported by DHCP, dynamic address allocation is by far the most popular and important. The significance of the change that dynamic addressing represents to how IP addresses are used in TCP/IP can be seen in the semantics of how addresses are treated in DHCP. Where conventionally a host was said to *own* an IP address, when dynamic address allocation is used, hosts are said instead to *lease* an address.

The notion of a lease conveys very accurately the difference between dynamic allocation and the other types. A host no longer is strictly entitled to a particular address, with a server merely telling it what the address is. In DHCP, the server remains the real owner of all the IP addresses in the address pool, and it merely gives permission for a client to use the address for a period of time. The server guarantees that it will not try to use the address for another client only during this time. The client is responsible for taking certain actions if it wants to continue using the address. If it does not successfully reacquire permission for using the address after a period of time, it must stop using it or risk creating an IP address conflict on the network.

KEY CONCEPT DHCP's most significant new feature is dynamic allocation, which changes the way that IP addresses are managed. Where in traditional IP each device owns a particular IP address, in DHCP the server owns all the addresses in the address pool, and each client *leases* an address from the server, usually for only a limited period of time.

DHCP Lease Length Policy

When dynamic address allocation is used, the administrator of the network must provide parameters to the DHCP server to control how leases are assigned and managed. One of the most important decisions to be made is the *lease length policy* of the internetwork: how long the administrator wants client leases to last. This choice will depend on the network, the server, and the clients. The choice of lease time, like so many other networking parameters, comes down to a trade-off between *stability* and *allocation efficiency*.

The primary benefit of using long lease times is that the addresses of devices are relatively stable. A device doesn't need to worry about its IP address changing all the time, and neither does its user. This is a significant advantage in many cases, especially when it is necessary for the client to perform certain server functions, accept incoming connections, or use a DNS domain name (ignoring for the moment dynamic DNS capabilities). In those situations, having the IP address of a device moving all over the place can cause serious complications.

The main drawback of using long leases is that they substantially increase the amount of time that an IP address, once it is no longer needed, is tied up before it can be reused. In the worst-case scenario, the amount of wasted time for an allocation can be almost as long as the lease itself. If we give a device a particular address for six months and after two weeks the device is shut down and no longer used, the IP address that it was using is still unavailable for another five and a half more months.

For this reason, many administrators prefer to use short leases. This forces a client to continually renew the lease as long as it needs it. When it stops asking for permission, the address is quickly put back into the pool. This makes shorter leases a better idea in environments where the number of addresses is limited and must be conserved. The drawback is the opposite of the benefit of long leases: constantly changing IP addresses.

Administrators do not need to pick from short and long lease durations. They can compromise by choosing a number that best suits the network. The following are some examples of lease times and the reasoning behind them:

One Hour or Less Ensures maximum IP address allocation efficiency in a very dynamic environment where there are many devices connecting and disconnecting from the network, and the number of IP addresses is limited.

One Day Suitable for situations where guest machines typically stay for a day, to increase IP efficiency when many employees work part time, or otherwise to ensure that every day each client must ask again for permission to use an address.

Three Days The default used by Microsoft, which alone makes it a popular choice.

One Week A reasonable compromise between the shorter and longer times.

One Month Another compromise, closer to the longer end of the lease time range.

Three Months Provides reasonable IP address stability so that addresses don't change very often in reasonably static environments. Also a good idea if there are many IP addresses available and machines are often turned off for many days or weeks at a time. For example, this duration may be used in a university setting to ensure that IP addresses of returning students are maintained over the summer recess.

One Year An approximation of an infinite lease.

Not only is the administrator not restricted to a limited number of possible lease durations, it is not necessary for the administrator to choose a constant lease length policy for all clients. Depending on the capabilities of the DHCP server, an administrator may select different lease lengths for certain clients. For example, the administrator may decide to use long leases for desktop computers that are permanently assigned to a particular subnet and not moved, and a pool of short-leased addresses for notebook computers and visitors. In some DHCP implementations, this can be done by assigning clients to particular classes. Of course, this requires more work (and may even require multiple servers).

In selecting a lease time policy, the administrator must also bear in mind that, by default, after half the length of a lease, the client will begin attempting to renew the lease. This may make it more advisable to use a longer lease time, to increase the amount of time between when a client tries to renew the lease and when the lease expires. For example, in a network with a single DHCP server, an administrator may want to use leases no shorter than eight hours. This provides a four-hour window for maintenance on the server without leases expiring.

When a lease is very short, such as minutes or hours, it will typically expire when a client machine is turned off for a period of time, such as overnight. Longer leases will persist across reboots. The client in this case will still contact the DHCP server each time it is restarted to *reallocate* the address—confirm that it may continue using the address it was assigned.

KEY CONCEPT A key decision that a network administrator using DHCP must make is what the network's *lease length policy* will be. Longer leases allow devices to avoid changing addresses too often; shorter leases are more efficient in terms of reallocating addresses that are no longer required. An administrator can choose from a variety of different lease times and may choose longer leases for some devices than for others.

Issues with Infinite Leases

In addition to choosing a particular lease length number, it is possible to specify an infinite lease length duration for certain clients. This effectively turns dynamic allocation into automatic allocation for a particular client. As I said earlier, however, this is generally not done. The reason is that an infinite lease never expires, and as the old saw goes, "Never is a long time."

Permanently assigning an IP address from a pool is a somewhat risky move, because once assigned, if anything occurs that causes that address to be no longer used, it can never be recovered. A worst-case scenario would be a visitor to a company site who plugs a notebook computer in to the network to check email or transfer a file. If that machine is assigned an IP address using automatic allocation, the visitor will take it with him when he leaves. Obviously, this is not a great idea.

For this reason, most administrators prefer to use dynamic allocation instead, with addresses set to a very long time frame, such as a year or two years. This is considered near enough to infinity that it approximates a permanent assignment, but allows an IP address to eventually be recovered if a device stops using it. In such a policy, anything that really, truly needs a permanent assignment is given an address using *manual* assignment, which requires a conscious decision to dedicate the address to a particular device.

RELATED INFORMATION *For a little more information related to lease length selection, see the section on DHCP server implementation problems and issues in Chapter 64.*

DHCP Lease Life Cycle and Lease Timers

The use of dynamic address allocation in DHCP means a whole new way of thinking about addresses. A client no longer owns an address, but rather leases it. This means that when a client machine is set to use DHCP dynamic addressing, it can never assume that it has an address on a permanent basis. Each time it powers up, it must engage in communications with a DHCP server to begin or confirm the lease of an address. It also must perform other activities over time to manage this lease and possibly terminate it.

Calling dynamic address assignments leases is a good analogy, because a DHCP IP address lease is similar to a real-world lease in a number of respects. For example, when you rent an apartment, you sign the lease. Then you use the apartment for a period of time. Typically, assuming you are happy with the place, you will *renew* the lease before it expires, so you can keep using it. If by the time you get near the end of the lease the owner of the apartment has not allowed you to renew it, you will probably lease a different apartment to ensure you have somewhere to live. And if you decide, say, to move out of the country, you may terminate the lease and not get another.

DHCP Lease Life Cycle Phases

DHCP leases follow a lease life cycle that generally consists of the following six phases:

Allocation A client begins with no active lease, and hence, no DHCP-assigned address. It acquires a lease through a process of *allocation.*

Reallocation If a client already has an address from an existing lease, then when it reboots or starts up after being shut down, it will contact the DHCP server that granted it the lease to confirm the lease and acquire operating parameters. This is sometimes called *reallocation*; it is similar to the full allocation process but shorter.

Normal Operation Once a lease is active, the client functions normally, using its assigned IP address and other parameters during the main part of the lease. The client is said to be *bound* to the lease and the address.

Renewal After a certain portion of the lease time has expired, the client will attempt to contact the server that initially granted the lease to *renew* the lease, so it can keep using its IP address.

Rebinding If renewal with the original leasing server fails (because, for example, the server has been taken offline), the client will try to *rebind* to any active DHCP server, in an attempt to extend its current lease with any server that will allow it to do so.

Release The client may decide at any time that it no longer wishes to use the IP address it was assigned, and may terminate the lease, *releasing* the IP address. Like the apartment renter moving out of the country, this may be done if a device is moving to a different network, for example. (Of course, unlike DHCP servers, landlords usually don't let you cancel a lease at your leisure, but hey, no analogy is perfect.)

Figure 61-1 illustrates the DHCP life cycle using an example that spans three individual leases.

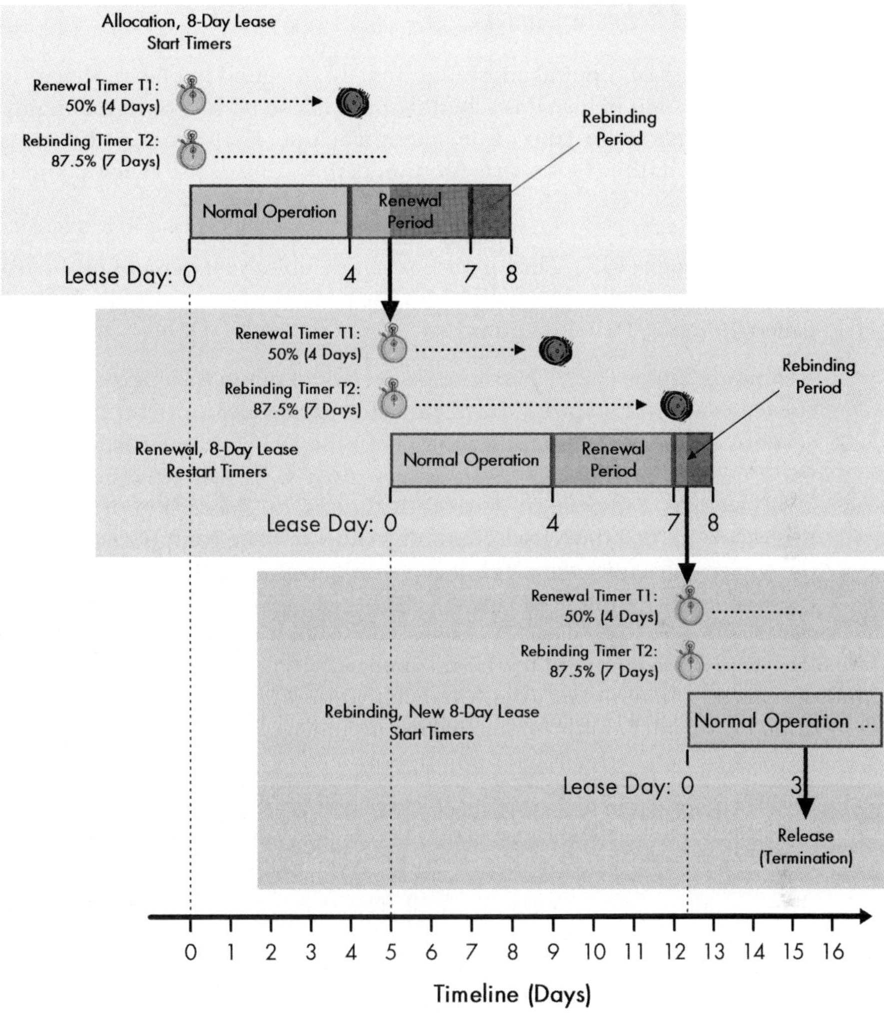

Figure 61-1: DHCP life cycle example *In this example, the initial lease has a duration of 8 days and begins at day 0. The T1 and T2 timers are set for 4 days and 7 days, respectively. When the T1 timer expires, the client enters the renewal period and successfully renews at day 5 with a new 8-day lease. When this second lease's T1 timer expires, the client is unable to renew with the original server. It enters the rebinding period when its T2 timer goes off, and it is granted a renewed 8-day lease with a different server. Three days into this lease, it is moved to a different network and no longer needs its leased address, so it voluntarily releases it.*

Renewal and Rebinding Timers

The processes of renewal and rebinding are designed to ensure that a client's lease can be extended before it is scheduled to end, so no loss of functionality or interruption occurs to the user of the client machine. Each time an address is allocated or reallocated, the client starts two timers that control the renewal and rebinding process:

Renewal Timer (T1) This timer is set by default to 50 percent of the lease period. When it expires, the client will begin the process of renewing the lease. It is simply called *T1* in the DHCP standards.

Rebinding Timer (T2) This timer is set by default to 87.5 percent of the length of the lease. When it expires, the client will try to rebind, as described in the previous section. It is given the snappy name *T2* in the DHCP standards.

Naturally, if the client successfully renews the lease when the T1 timer expires, this will result in a fresh lease, and both timers will be reset. T2 comes into play only if the renewal is not successful. It is possible to change the amount of time to which these timers are set, but obviously T1 must expire before T2, which must expire before the lease itself ends. These usually are not changed from the default, but may be modified in certain circumstances.

> **KEY CONCEPT** DHCP leases follow a conceptual *life cycle*. The lease is first assigned to the client through a process of *allocation*; if the device later reboots, it will *reallocate* the lease. After a period of time controlled by the *renewal timer (T1)*, the device will attempt to *renew* its lease with the server that allocated it. If this fails, the *rebinding timer (T2)* will go off, and the device will attempt to *rebind* the lease with any available server. The client may also *release* its IP address if it no longer needs it.

The lease life cycle is described in the DHCP standards in the form of states that the client moves through as it acquires a lease, uses it, and then either renews or ends it. The next chapter describes these states and the specific exchanges of messages between a client and server to accomplish different lease activities.

DHCP Lease Address Pools, Ranges, and Address Management

Simpler host configuration methods such as BOOTP (or DHCP manual allocation for that matter) associate a single IP address with each client machine. DHCP dynamic addressing removes this one-to-one correspondence, in favor of flexible address mapping to clients on an as-needed basis. The clients no longer own the addresses, but lease them from the true owner, the server. Thus, a primary job of both a DHCP server and the administrator of that server is to maintain and manage these client addresses.

Address Pool Size Selection

The set of all addresses that a DHCP server has available for assignment is most often called the *address pool.* The first issue related to address management is ensuring that the address pool is large enough to serve all the clients that will be using the server. The number of addresses required depends on several factors:

Number of Clients This is an obvious factor.

Stability and Frequency of Use of Clients If most clients are left on and connected to the network all the time, you will probably need to plan on an address for each one. In contrast, if you are serving part-time employees or consultants who frequently travel, you can get away with sharing a smaller number of addresses.

Consequences of Overallocation If having certain clients be unable to get a free address is a problem, you need to more carefully manage the address pool to ensure that you don't run out of IP addresses. If having a client not get an address is *never* acceptable, make sure you have as many or more addresses as clients.

I'm sure you've probably noticed that these issues are similar to those that I raised in discussing lease lengths earlier in this chapter. In fact, the two matters are intimately related. Generally speaking, having more addresses gives the administrator the luxury of using longer leases. If you are short on addresses, you probably need to use shorter leases to reduce the chances of any unused addresses continuing to be allocated to devices not needing them.

Lease Address Ranges (Scopes)

In its simplest form, the address pool takes the form of a list of all addresses that the DHCP server has reserved for dynamic client allocation. Along with each address, the server stores certain parameters, such as a default lease length for the address and other configuration information to be sent to the client when it is assigned that address (for example, a subnet mask and the address of a default router). All of this data is stored in a special database on the server.

Of course, many clients will request addresses from this pool. Most of these clients are equals as far as the DHCP server is concerned, and it doesn't matter which address each individual client gets. This means most of the information stored with each of the addresses in a pool may be the same, except for the address number itself. Due to this similarity, it would be inefficient to need to specify each address and its parameters individually. Instead, a *range* of addresses is normally handled as a single group defined for a particular network or subnet. These are not given any particular name in the DHCP standards, but are commonly called *scopes.* This term has been popularized by Microsoft in its DHCP server implementations. Other operating systems sometimes just call these blocks of addresses *ranges,* but I prefer scope.

> **KEY CONCEPT** Each DHCP server maintains a set of IP addresses that it uses to allocate leases to clients. These are usually contiguous blocks of addresses assigned to the server by an administrator, called DHCP *address ranges* or *scopes.*

The exact method for setting up scopes depends on the particular operating system and DHCP server software. However, each scope definition typically begins by specifying a range of addresses using a starting and an ending IP address. For example, if a company was assigned the IP address block 111.14.56.0/24, the administrator might set up a scope encompassing addresses 111.14.56.20 through 111.14.56.254, as shown in Figure 61-2. Then for that scope, the administrator can set up various parameters to be specified to each client assigned an address from the scope.

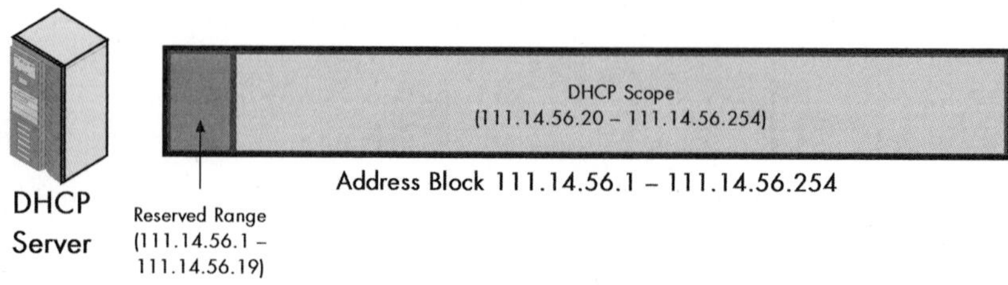

Figure 61-2: DHCP scope *A single DHCP server scope, encompassing addresses 111.14.56.1 through 111.14.56.254.*

Why not start at 111.14.56.1? Usually, we will want to set aside certain IP addresses for manual configuration of servers, routers, and other devices requiring a fixed address. One easy way to do that is to simply reserve a block of addresses that aren't used by DHCP. Alternatively, most DHCP server software will allow you to specify a range but *exclude* an address or set of addresses from the range. So, we could specify 111.14.56.1 through 111.14.56.254 and individually mark as not available addresses we manually assign. Or we could specify that 111.14.56.1 through 111.14.56.19 are reserved.

Instead of putting all of its addresses (except excluded ones) in a single scope, a server may use *multiple* scopes. One common reason for the latter approach is to support more than one subnet on a server. Multiple scopes are also commonly used when multiple DHCP servers are used to serve the same clients. There are two ways to do this: by having either *overlapping* or *non-overlapping* scopes.

Overlapping scopes allows each server to assign any address from the same pool. However, the DHCP standard doesn't specify any way for servers to communicate with each other when they assign an address, so if both servers were told they could assign addresses from the same address pool, this could result in both servers trying to assign a particular address to two different devices. As a result, if you are using two DHCP servers (as is often recommended for redundancy reasons), the administrator generally gives them different, non-overlapping scope assignments. Alternatively, the same scope is given to each server, with each server told to exclude from use the addresses the other server is assigning.

For example, suppose we have two DHCP servers: Server A (the main server) and Server B (the backup). We want to assign most of the addresses to Server A and a few as backup to Server B. We could give both Server A and Server B the scope 111.14.56.1 through 111.14.56.254. We would exclude 111.14.56.1 through 111.14.56.19 from both. Then we would exclude from Server A the range 111.14.56.200 through 111.14.56.254 and exclude from Server B the range 111.14.20 through 111.14.56.199. Figure 61-3 shows how this would work. The main advantage of this method is that if one server goes down, the administrator can quickly remove the exclusion and let the remaining server access all addresses. Also, if one server runs out of addresses while the other has plenty, the allocations can be shifted easily.

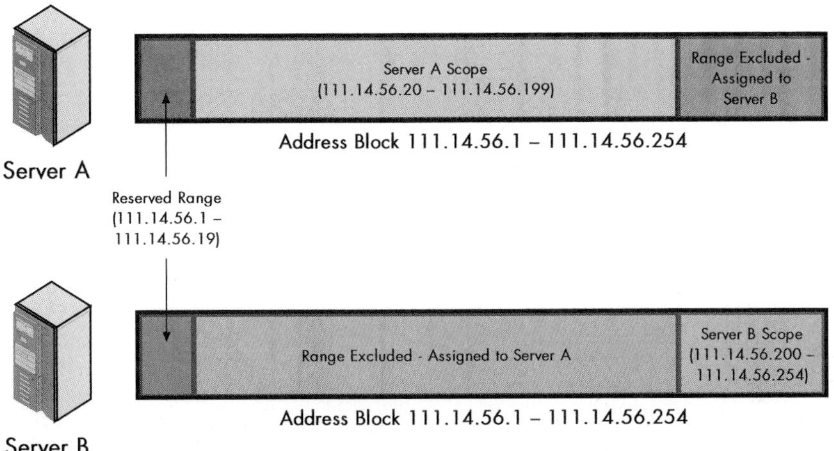

Figure 61-3: DHCP multiple-server non-overlapping scopes *DHCP Servers A and B have been assigned non-overlapping scopes to ensure that they do not conflict. This has been done by starting with the same scope definition for both. The common reserved range is excluded from each. Then Server A has Server B's address range excluded (hatched area at right in the top bar), and Server B has Server A's range excluded (hatched area in the middle at bottom).*

Other Issues with Address Management

There are many other issues related to address management, which start to get into the guts of DHCP server implementation. For example, as was the case with BOOTP, we may need to use relay agents when the DHCP server is responsible for addresses on a subnet different from its own. There are also special DHCP features that affect how addresses are managed. For example, the DHCP conflict detection feature can actually allow two servers to have overlapping scopes, despite what I said in the previous section. Chapter 64, which covers DHCP implementation and features, describes these issues in more detail.

KEY CONCEPT If a site has multiple DHCP servers, they can be set up with either *overlapping* or *non-overlapping* scopes. Overlapping scopes allow each server to assign from the same pool, providing flexibility, but raising the possibility of two clients being assigned the same address unless a feature such as *server conflict detection* is employed. non-overlapping scopes are safer because each server has a dedicated set of addresses for its use, but this means one server could run out of addresses while the other still has plenty, and if a server goes down, its addresses will be temporarily unallocatable.

62

DHCP CONFIGURATION AND OPERATION

The big news in DHCP is dynamic address allocation, along with the concept of address leasing. It is this new functionality that makes DHCP significantly more complex than its predecessor, the Boot Protocol (BOOTP). BOOTP is a simple request/reply protocol—a server only needs to look up a client's hardware address and send back the client's assigned IP address and other parameters. In contrast, DHCP clients and servers must do much more to carry out both parameter exchange and the many tasks needed to manage IP address leasing.

In this chapter, I delve into the nuts and bolts of how DHCP operates. I begin with two background topics. The first provides an overview of the responsibilities of clients and servers in DHCP, and shows in general terms how they relate to each other. The second discusses DHCP configuration parameters and how they are stored and communicated.

In the rest of the chapter, I illustrate the operation of DHCP in detail. I explain the DHCP client *finite state machine*, which will give you a high-level look at the entire client lease life cycle, including address allocation, reallocation, renewal, rebinding, and optionally, lease termination. This theoretical description is then used as the basis for several topics that explain the actual processes by which DHCP client lease activities occur. These show the specific actions taken by both client and server and when and how DHCP messages are created and sent. The last part of the chapter describes the special mechanism by which a device not using DHCP for address allocation can request configuration parameters.

DHCP Overview of Client and Server Responsibilities

DHCP is the newest and most current TCP/IP host configuration protocol. However, as you saw in the previous chapter, it wasn't built from scratch—it was designed as an extension of BOOTP. In many ways, DHCP is like BOOTP with more features, and this can be seen in the basic setup of the protocol and how it works.

Both BOOTP and DHCP are designed based on the common TCP/IP model of client/server operation (see Chapter 8). In any interaction, one device plays the role of client and the other server. Each has specific responsibilities and must send and receive messages following the protocol described in the DHCP standard. The difference is that where BOOTP involves relatively little work for servers and clients and uses a simple single-message exchange for communication, DHCP requires that both servers and clients do more, and it uses several types of message exchanges.

DHCP Server Responsibilities

A *DHCP server* is a network device that has been programmed to provide DHCP services to clients. The server plays a central role in DHCP because DHCP's main function is host configuration, and the server configures hosts (clients) that communicate with it. Smaller networks may have only a single server to support many clients, while larger networks may use multiple servers. Regardless of the number of servers, each will usually service many clients.

The following are the key responsibilities of servers in making DHCP work:

Address Storage and Management DHCP servers are the owners of the addresses used by all DHCP clients. The server stores the addresses and manages their use, keeping track of which addresses have been allocated and which are still available.

Configuration Parameter Storage and Management DHCP servers also store and maintain other parameters that are intended to be sent to clients when requested. Many of these are important configuration values that specify in detail how a client is to operate.

Lease Management DHCP servers use leases to dynamically allocate addresses to clients for a limited time. The DHCP server maintains information about each of the leases it has granted to clients, as well as policy information such as lease lengths.

Response to Client Requests DHCP servers respond to different types of requests from clients to implement the DHCP communication protocol. This includes assigning addresses; conveying configuration parameters; and granting, renewing, and terminating leases.

Administration Services To support all of its other responsibilities, the DHCP server includes functionality to allow a human administrator to enter, view, change, and analyze addresses, leases, parameters, and all other information needed to run DHCP.

DHCP Client Responsibilities

A *DHCP client* is any device that sends DHCP requests to a server to obtain an IP address or other configuration information. Due to the advantages of DHCP, most host computers on TCP/IP internetworks today include DHCP client software, making them potential DHCP clients if their administrator chooses to enable the function. There are several main responsibilities of a DHCP client:

Configuration Initiation The client takes the *active* role by initiating the communication exchange that results in it being given an IP address and other parameters. The server, in contrast, is *passive* and will not really do anything for the client until the client makes contact.

Configuration Parameter Management The client maintains parameters that pertain to its configuration, some or all of which may be obtained from a DHCP server.

Lease Management Assuming its address is dynamically allocated, the client keeps track of the status of its own lease. It is responsible for renewing the lease at the appropriate time, rebinding if renewal is not possible, and terminating the lease early if the address is no longer needed.

Message Retransmission Since DHCP uses the unreliable User Datagram Protocol (UDP, see Chapter 44) for messaging, clients are responsible for detecting message loss and retransmitting requests if necessary.

DHCP Client/Server Roles

The DHCP server and client obviously play complementary roles. The server maintains configuration parameters for all clients. Each client maintains its own parameters, as discussed in the next section.

IP address assignment and lease creation, renewal, rebinding, and termination are accomplished through specific exchanges using a set of eight DHCP message types, as discussed in the "DHCP General Operation and Client Finite State Machine" and "DHCP Lease Allocation, Reallocation, and Renewal" sections later in this chapter. To accomplish this messaging, special rules are followed to generate, address, and transport messages, as explained in Chapter 63.

DHCP Relay Agents

Like BOOTP, DHCP also supports a third type of device: the *relay agent.* Relay agents are neither clients nor servers, but rather intermediaries that facilitate cross-network communication between servers and clients. They are described in more detail in Chapter 64 (where you can also find more of the implementation details of servers and clients).

> **KEY CONCEPT** *DHCP servers* are devices programmed to provide DHCP services to clients. They manage address information and other parameters and respond to client configuration requests. *DHCP clients* are TCP/IP devices that have been set to use DHCP to determine their configuration. They send requests and read responses, and are responsible for managing their own leases, including renewing or rebinding a lease when necessary.

DHCP Configuration Parameters, Storage, and Communication

One of the more important oversights in DHCP's predecessor, BOOTP, was that it allowed a server to tell a client only three pieces of information: its IP address, the name of the server it could use to download a boot file, and the name of the boot file to use. This was a result of BOOTP's legacy as a protocol created primarily to let diskless workstations be bootstrapped.

Obviously, the IP address is a very important parameter, but in modern networks it isn't the only one that a client needs to be given for it to function properly. A typical host needs to be given other essential information to allow it to know how it should operate on its local network and interact with other devices. For example, it needs to know the address of a default local router, the subnet mask for the subnet it is on, parameters for creating outgoing IP datagrams, and much more.

Configuration Parameter Management

The inability to specify additional configuration parameters in BOOTP was resolved by using the special BOOTP Vendor-Specific Area for vendor-independent *vendor information fields,* as first defined in RFC 1048. In DHCP, this idea has been extended further, and more important, formalized, as part of the effort to make DHCP a more general-purpose configuration tool. Configuration parameter storage, maintenance, and communication are no longer optional features; they are an essential part of the host configuration process.

Just as DHCP servers are the bosses that own and manage IP addresses, they also act as the repository for other configuration parameters that belong to DHCP clients. This centralization of parameter storage provides many of the same benefits that centralizing IP addresses in DHCP does: Administrators can check and adjust parameters in a single place, rather than needing to go to each client machine.

Each DHCP server is programmed with parameters that are to be communicated to clients in addition to an IP address when an address is assigned. Alternatively, a client that has already been assigned an address using some other mechanism may still query the DHCP server to get parameter information, using the DHCPINFORM message type. (This was actually added to the protocol in RFC 2131; it was not in the original DHCP standard.)

Parameter Storage

The exact method of storage of client parameters is to some extent implementation-dependent. Typically, there will be some parameters that apply to all clients. For example, on a small network with only one router, that router will probably be the default router for every DHCP client, regardless of address.

The DHCP server will also have certain parameters that are client-specific. The IP address itself is an obvious example, but there are other parameters that may apply to only certain clients on a network. These parameters are stored in some sort of a database and indexed using a particular *client identifier*. The default identifier consists of the client's IP subnet number and its hardware address. Thus, when a server gets a request from a particular subnet, it can use the client's hardware address in the request to look up client-specific parameters and return them. The client identifier can be changed if a different identification scheme is desired.

Clients are also responsible for storing their own parameters. Many of these will be obtained from the DHCP server, although some may be supplied in other ways. The specific implementation of the client determines which parameters it considers important and how they are discovered.

Configuration Parameter Communication

Communication of configuration parameters between DHCP clients and servers is accomplished using *DHCP options*, which replace BOOTP vendor information fields. A number of options were defined when DHCP was first created, and additional new ones have been created over the years.

Today, there are several dozen DHCP options. Obviously, the ability to have so many different parameters automatically delivered to a client provides a great deal of host configuration flexibility to administrators. DHCP options are described further in Chapter 63.

DHCP General Operation and the Client Finite State Machine

Dynamic address allocation is probably the most important new capability introduced by DHCP. In the previous chapter, I discussed the significance of the change from IP address *ownership* to IP address *leasing*. I also provided a high-level look of the activities involved in leasing, by providing an overview of the DHCP lease life cycle.

An overview of this sort is useful to get a general handle on how leases work, but to really understand the mechanics of DHCP address assignment and client/server communication, you need more details on how the devices behave and the messages they send. One tool often employed by networking engineers to describe a protocol is a theoretical model called a *finite state machine (FSM)*. Using this technique, the protocol's specific behavior is illustrated by showing the different *states* a device can be in, what possible *transitions* exist from one state to another, what *events* cause transitions to occur, and what *actions* are performed in response to an event. The TCP operational overview contains more general background information on FSMs (see Chapter 47).

The DHCP standard uses an FSM to describe the lease life cycle from the perspective of a DHCP client. The client begins in an initial INIT state where it has no lease and then transitions through various states as it acquires, renews, rebinds, and/or releases its IP address. The FSM also indicates which message exchanges occurs between the server and client at various stages.

NOTE *The DHCP standard does not describe the DHCP server's behavior in the form of a FSM; only the client's is described this way.*

Some people think FSMs are a little dense and hard to understand, and I can see why. You can skip this topic, of course, but I think the FSM provides a useful way of illustrating in a comprehensive way most of the behavior of a DHCP client.

Table 62-1 describes each of the DHCP client states, and summarizes the messages sent and received by the client in each, as well as showing the state transitions that occur in response. The FSM's states, events, and transitions are easier to envision in Figure 62-1, which also incorporates a shading scheme so you can see which states are associated with each of the main DHCP processes.

Table 62-1: DHCP Client Finite State Machine

State	**State Description**	**Event and Transition**
INIT	This is the initialization state, where a client begins the process of acquiring a lease. It also returns here when a lease ends or when a lease negotiation fails.	Client sends DHCPDISCOVER. The client creates a DHCPDISCOVER message and broadcasts it to try to find a DHCP server. It transitions to the SELECTING state.
SELECTING	The client is waiting to receive DHCPOFFER messages from one or more DHCP servers, so it can choose one.	Client receives offers, selects preferred offer, and sends DHCPREQUEST. The client chooses one of the offers it has been sent, and broadcasts a DHCPREQUEST message to tell DHCP servers what its choice was. It transitions to the REQUESTING state.
REQUESTING	The client is waiting to hear back from the server to which it sent its request.	Client receives DHCPACK, successfully checks that IP address is free. The client receives a DHCPACK message from its chosen server, confirming that it can have the lease that was offered. It checks to ensure that address is not already used, and assuming it is not, records the parameters the server sent it, sets the lease timers T1 and T2, and transitions to the BOUND state.
		Client receives DHCPACK, but IP address is in use. The client receives a DHCPACK message from its chosen server, confirming that it can have the lease that was offered. However, it checks and finds the address already in use. It sends a DHCPDECLINE message back to the server and returns to the INIT state.
		Client receives DHCPNAK. The client receives a DHCPNAK message from its chosen server, which means the server has withdrawn its offer. The client returns to the INIT state.

(continued)

Table 62-1: DHCP Client Finite State Machine (continued)

State	**State Description**	**Event and Transition**
INIT-REBOOT	When a client that already has a valid lease starts up after a power down or reboot, it starts here instead of the INIT state.	Client sends DHCPREQUEST. The client sends a DHCPREQUEST message to attempt to verify its lease and reobtain its configuration parameters. It then transitions to the REBOOTING state to wait for a response.
REBOOTING	A client that has rebooted with an assigned address is waiting for a confirming reply from a server.	Client receives DHCPACK, successfully checks that IP address is free. The client receives a DHCPACK message from the server that has its lease information, confirming that the lease is still valid. To be safe, the client checks anyway to ensure that the address is not already in use by some other device. Assuming it is not, the client records the parameters the server sent it and transitions to the BOUND state.
		Client receives DHCPACK, but IP address is in use. The client receives a DHCPACK message from the server that had its lease, confirming that the lease is still valid. However, the client checks and finds that while the client was offline, some other device has grabbed its leased IP address. The client sends a DHCPDECLINE message back to the server and returns to the INIT state to obtain a new lease.
		Client receives DHCPNAK. The client receives a DHCPNAK message from a server. This tells it that its current lease is no longer valid; for example, the client may have moved to a new network where it can no longer use the address in its present lease. The client returns to the INIT state.
BOUND	A client has a valid lease and is in its normal operating state.	Renewal timer (T1) expires. The client transitions to the RENEWING state.
		Client terminates lease and sends DHCPRELEASE. The client decides to terminate the lease (due to user command, for example). It sends a DHCPRELEASE message and returns to the INIT state.
RENEWING	A client is trying to renew its lease. It regularly sends DHCPREQUEST messages with the server that gave it its current lease specified, and waits for a reply.	Client receives DHCPACK. The client receives a DHCPACK reply to its DHCPREQUEST. Its lease is renewed, it restarts the T1 and T2 timers, and it returns to the BOUND state.
		Client receives DHCPNAK. The server has refused to renew the client's lease. The client goes to the INIT state to get a new lease.
		Rebinding timer (T2) expires. While the client is attempting to renew its lease, the T2 timer expires, indicating that the renewal period has ended. The client transitions to the REBINDING state.
REBINDING	The client has failed to renew its lease with the server that originally granted it and now seeks a lease extension with any server that can hear it. It periodically sends DHCPREQUEST messages with no server specified, until it gets a reply or the lease ends.	Client receives DHCPACK. Some server on the network has renewed the client's lease. The client binds to the new server granting the lease, restarts the T1 and T2 timers, and returns to the BOUND state.
		Client receives DHCPNAK. A server on the network is specifically telling the client it needs to restart the leasing process. This may be the case if a new server is willing to grant the client a lease, but only with terms different from the client's current lease. The client goes to the INIT state.
		Lease expires. The client receives no reply prior to the expiration of the lease. It goes back to the INIT state.

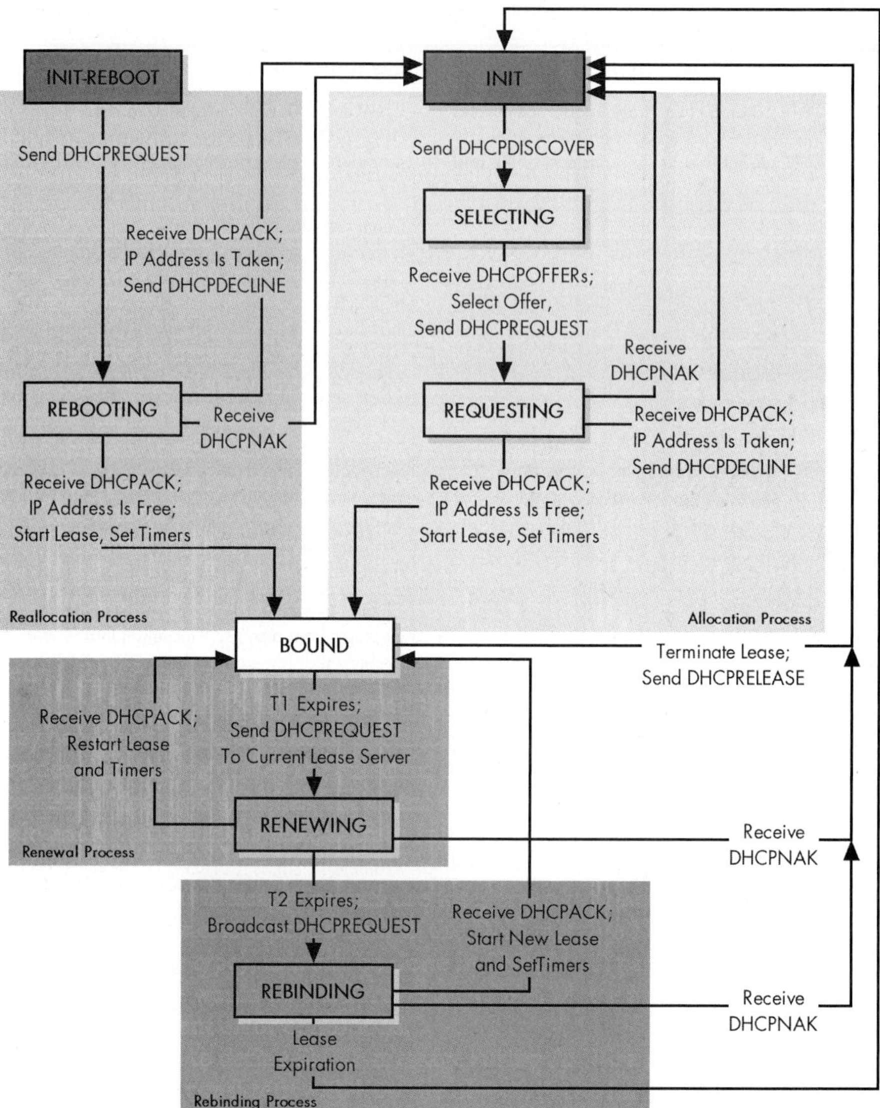

Figure 62-1: DHCP client finite state machine *This diagram shows the finite state machine (FSM) used by DHCP clients. The shaded background areas show the transitions taken by a DHCP client as it moves through the four primary DHCP processes: allocation, reallocation, renewal, and rebinding.*

This is just a summary of the FSM, and it does not show every possible event and transition, since it is complex enough already. For example, if a client that received two offers in the SELECTING state receives a DHCPNAK from its chosen server in the REQUESTING state, it may choose to send a new DHCPREQUEST to its second choice, instead of starting over from scratch. Also, the client must have logic that lets it time out if it receives no reply to sent messages in various states, such as not receiving any offers in the SELECTING state. The next sections discuss these matters in more detail.

Also note that this FSM applies to dynamically allocated clients—that is, ones with conventional leases. A device configured using automatic allocation will go through the same basic allocation process, but does not need to renew its lease. The process for manual allocation is somewhat different.

DHCP Lease Allocation, Reallocation, and Renewal

To implement DHCP, an administrator must first set up a DHCP server and provide it with configuration parameters and policy information: IP address ranges, lease length specifications, and configuration data that DHCP hosts will need to be delivered to them. Host devices can then have their DHCP client software enabled, but nothing will happen until the client initiates communication with the server. When a DHCP client starts up for the first time, or when it has no current DHCP lease, it will be in an initial state where it doesn't have an address and needs to acquire one. It will do so by initiating the process of *lease allocation*.

Before we examine the steps in the lease allocation, reallocation, and renewal processes, I need to clarify some issues related to DHCP lease communications. First, DHCP assumes that clients will normally broadcast messages, since they don't know the address of servers when they initiate contact, but that servers will send replies back unicast to the client. This can be done even before the client has an IP address, by sending the message at the link layer. Some clients don't support this and require that messages to them be broadcast instead.

DHCP uses many of the same basic fields as BOOTP, but much of the extra information the protocol requires is carried in DHCP *options*. Some of these options aren't really optional, despite the name—they are needed for the basic function of DHCP. An obvious example is the DHCP Message Type option, which is what specifies the message type itself.

The details of how messages are created and addressed, along with a full description of all DHCP fields and options, are presented in Chapter 63.

NOTE *I have assumed that no relay agents are in use here. See the discussion of DHCP/BOOTP relay agents in Chapter 60 for more on how they change the allocation process (and other processes).*

Initial Lease Allocation Process

The following are the basic steps taken by a DHCP client and server in the initial allocation of an IP address lease, focusing on the most important tasks each device performs (see Figure 62-2).

1. **Client Creates DHCPDISCOVER Message**

   The client begins in the INIT (initialization) state. It has no IP address and doesn't even know whether or where a DHCP server may be on the network. To find one, it creates a DHCPDISCOVER message, including the following information:

   - Its own hardware address in the CHAddr field of the message, to identify itself

- A random transaction identifier, put into the XID field (used to identify later messages as being part of the same transaction)

Optionally, the client may request a particular IP address using a Requested IP Address DHCP option, a particular lease length using an IP Address Lease Time option, and/or specific configuration parameters by including a Parameter Request List option in the message

2. **Client Sends DHCPDISCOVER Message**

   The client broadcasts the DHCPDISCOVER message on the local network. The client transitions to the SELECTING state, where it waits for replies to its message.

3. **Servers Receive and Process DHCPDISCOVER Message**

   Each DHCP server on the local network receives the client's DHCPDISCOVER message and examines it. The server looks up the client's hardware address in its database and determines if it is able to offer the client a lease and what the terms of the lease will be. If the client has made requests for a particular IP address, lease length, or other parameters, the server will attempt to satisfy these requests, but it is not required to do so. A server may decide not to offer a lease to a particular client if it has not been programmed to provide service for it, it has no remaining IP addresses, or for other reasons.

4. **Servers Create DHCPOFFER Messages**

   Each server that chooses to respond to the client creates a DHCPOFFER message including the following information:

   - The IP address to be assigned to the client, in the YIAddr field (if the server previously had a lease for this client, it will attempt to reuse the IP address it used last time; failing that, it will try to use the client's requested address, if present; otherwise, it will select any available address)
   - The length of the lease being offered
   - Any client-specific configuration parameters either requested by the client or programmed into the server to be returned to the client
   - Any general configuration parameters to be returned to all clients or clients in this client's class
   - The server's identifier in the DHCP Server Identifier option
   - The same transaction ID (XID) used in the DHCPDISCOVER message

5. **Servers Probe and/or Reserve Offered Address (Optional)**

   The DHCP standard specifies that before sending a DHCPOFFER to a client, the server should check to see that the IP address isn't already in use by sending an ICMP Echo message to that address. It is considered a key part of the DHCP server conflict detection feature (discussed in Chapter 64). This may be disabled by an administrator. Whether or not it probes the address offered, the server may also *reserve* the address so that if the client decides to use it, it will be available. This isn't mandatory, because the protocol handles the case where an offered lease is retracted. It is more efficient if servers do reserve addresses, but if IP addresses are in very short supply, such reservations may not be practical.

6. **Servers Send DHCPOFFER Messages**

   Each server sends its DHCPOFFER message. They may not all be sent at exactly the same time. The messages are sent either unicast or broadcast, as mentioned earlier.

7. **Client Collects and Processes DHCPOFFER Messages**

   The client waits for DHCPOFFER messages to arrive in response to its DHCPDISCOVER message. The exact behavior of the client here is implementation-dependent. The client may decide to simply take the first offer it receives, for expediency. Alternatively, it may choose to shop around by waiting for a period of time. It can then process each offer and take the one with the most favorable terms—for example, the one with the longest lease. If no DHCPOFFER messages are received, the client will enter a retransmission mode and try sending the DHCPDISCOVER again for a period of time.

8. **Client Creates DHCPREQUEST Message**

   The client creates a DHCPREQUEST message for the server offer it has selected. This message serves two purposes: It tells the server whose offer the client has accepted, "Yes, I accept your offer, assuming it is still available," and also tells the other servers, "Sorry, your offer was rejected." (Well, except for the "sorry" part; servers are pretty thick-skinned about rejection.) In this message, the client includes the following information:

   - The identifier of the chosen server in the DHCP Server Identifier option, so everyone knows who won
   - The IP address that the DHCP server assigned the client in the DHCPOFFER message, which the client puts in the Requested IP Address DHCP option as a confirmation
   - Any additional configuration parameters it wants in a Parameter Request List option in the message

9. **Client Sends DHCPREQUEST Message**

   The client sends the DHCPREQUEST message. Since it is intended for not just the selected DHCP server, but all servers, it is broadcast. After doing this, the client transitions to the REQUESTING state, where it waits for a reply from the chosen server.

10. **Servers Receive and Process DHCPREQUEST Message**

    Each of the servers receives and processes the client's request message. The servers not chosen will take the message as a rejection. However, a client may select one offer, attempt to request the lease, and have the transaction not complete successfully. The client may then come back and try its second-choice offer by sending a DHCPREQUEST containing a different Server Identifier. This means that if Server A receives a single DHCPREQUEST with a Server Identifier of Server B, that doesn't necessarily mean that Server A is finished with the transaction. For this reason, rejected servers will wait for a while before offering a previously offered lease to another client.

11. **Server Sends DHCPACK or DHCPNAK Message**

    The chosen server will see that its lease has been selected. If it did not previously reserve the IP address that was offered to the client, it must check to make sure it is still available. If it is not, the server sends back a DHCPNAK (*negative acknowledgment*) message, which essentially means, "Never mind, that lease is no longer available." Usually, however, the server will still have that lease. It will create a *binding* for that client, and send back a DHCPACK (*acknowledgment*) message that confirms the lease and contains all the pertinent configuration parameters for the client.

12. **Client Receives and Processes DHCPACK or DHCPNAK Message**

    The client receives either a positive or negative acknowledgment for its request. If the message is a DHCPNAK, the client transitions back to the INIT state and starts over—back to square one (step 1). If it is a DHCPACK, the client reads the IP address from the YIAddr field, and records the lease length and other parameters from the various message fields and DHCP options. If the client receives neither message, it may retransmit the DHCPREQUEST message one or more times. If it continues to hear nothing, it must conclude that the server flaked out and go back to step 1.

13. **Client Checks That Address Is Not in Use**

    The client device should perform a final check to ensure that the new address isn't already in use before it concludes the leasing process. This is typically done by generating an Address Resolution Protocol (ARP) request on the local network, to see if any other device thinks it already has the IP address this client was just leased. If another device responds, the client sends a DHCPDECLINE message back to the server, which basically means, "Hey server, you messed up. Someone is already using that address." The client then goes back to step 1 and starts over.

14. **Client Finalizes Lease Allocation**

    Assuming that the address is not already in use, the client finalizes the lease and transitions to the BOUND state. It also sets its two lease timers, T1 and T2. It is now ready for normal operation.

As you can see in this description, there are a number of situations that may occur that require a client to retransmit messages. This is because DHCP uses UDP, which is unreliable and can cause messages to be lost. If retransmissions don't fix a problem such as not receiving a DHCPOFFER or a DHCPACK from a server, the client may need to start the allocation process over from scratch. The client must include enough intelligence to prevent it from simply trying forever to get a lease when there may not be a point. For example, if there are no DHCP servers on the network, no number of retransmissions will help.

Thus, after a number of retries, the client will give up and the allocation process will fail. If the client is configured to use the Automatic Private IP Addressing (APIPA) feature (see Chapter 64), this is where it would be used to give the client a default address. Otherwise, the client will be, well, dead in the water.

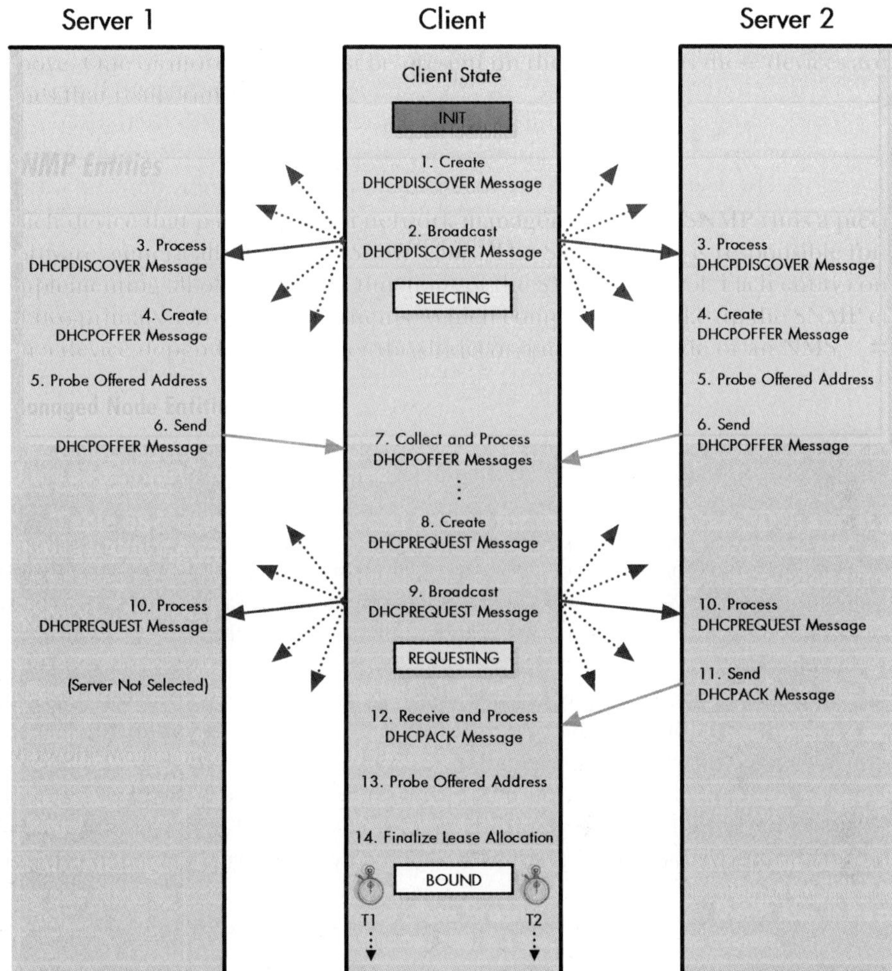

Figure 62-2: DHCP lease allocation process *This diagram shows the steps involved in DHCP client lease allocation. This diagram is a bit different from most of the other client/server exchange diagrams in this book, in that I have shown two servers instead of one. This shows how a client handles responses from multiple DHCP servers and how each server reacts differently, depending on whether its lease offer was chosen by the client.*

KEY CONCEPT The most important configuration process in DHCP is the *lease allocation process*, used by clients to acquire a lease. The client broadcasts a request to determine if any DHCP servers can hear it. Each DHCP server that is willing to grant the client a lease sends it an offer. The client selects the lease it prefers and sends a response to all servers telling them its choice. The selected server then sends the client its lease information.

DHCP Lease Reallocation Process

When a DHCP client starts up for the first time and has no lease, it begins in the INIT (initialize) state and goes through the allocation process described in the preceding section to acquire a lease. The same process is used when a lease ends, if a lease renewal fails, or if something happens to cause a client to need a new lease.

There are, however, certain situations in which a client starts up while it still has a lease already in place. In this situation, the client does not need to go through the entire process of getting an IP address allocation and a new lease setup. Instead, it simply tries to reestablish its existing lease, through a *reallocation process.*

A client performs reallocation rather than allocation when it restarts with an existing lease. The length of time that a client lease lasts can range from minutes to years; it is entirely a matter of the lease length policy set for the network and client by the administrator. Many, if not most, client machines are not connected to the network 24 hours a day. They are turned on during the day and then shut down at night, and also shut down on weekends. A client with a very short lease that is shut down and then later started again will probably find that its lease has expired, and it will need to get a new one. However, if a lease is longer than a few days, it will still probably be in effect when the client starts up again. Clients are also sometimes rebooted, to install new software or correct a problem. In this case, even when the lease length is very short, the restarting client will still have a valid lease when it starts up.

The reallocation process is essentially an abbreviated version of the allocation process described in the previous section. There is no need for the client to go through the whole "Yoohoo, any servers out there want to give me a lease?" routine. Instead, the client attempts to find the server that gave it the lease in the first place, seeking a confirmation that the lease is still valid and that it may resume using its previously allocated IP address. It also receives confirmation of the parameters it should use.

The following steps summarize the reallocation process (see Figure 62-3).

1. **Client Creates DHCPREQUEST Message**

   The client begins in the INIT-REBOOT state instead of the INIT state. It creates a DHCPREQUEST message to attempt to find a server with information about its current lease. This may or may not be the server that originally granted the lease. The server responsible for a lease could, theoretically, have changed in the time since the client obtained the lease. Thus, unlike the DHCPREQUEST message in step 8 in the allocation process, the client does not include a DHCP Server Identifier option. It does includes the following information:

   - Its own hardware address in the CHAddr field of the message, to identify itself
   - The IP address of its existing lease, in the Requested IP Address DHCP option (this address is not put into the CIAddr field)
   - A random transaction identifier, put into the XID field (used to identify later messages as being part of the same transaction)
   - Any additional configuration parameters it wants, in a Parameter Request List option in the message

2. **Client Sends DHCPREQUEST Message**

   The client broadcasts the DHCPREQUEST message. It then transitions to the REBOOTING state, where it waits for a reply from a server.

3. **Servers Receive and Process DHCPREQUEST Message and Generate Replies**

   Each server on the network receives and processes the client's request. The server looks up the client in its database, attempting to find information about the lease. Each server then decides how to reply to the client:

   - If the server has valid client lease information, it sends a DHCPACK message to confirm the lease. It will also reiterate any parameters the client should be using.
   - If the server determines the client lease is invalid, it sends a DHCPNAK message to negate the lease request. Common reasons for this happening are the client trying to confirm a lease after it has moved to a different network or after the lease has already expired.
   - If the server has no definitive information about the client lease, it does not respond. A server is also required not to respond unless its information is guaranteed to be accurate. So, for example, if a server has knowledge of an old expired lease, it cannot assume that the lease is no longer valid and send a DHCPNAK, unless it also has certain knowledge that no other server has a newer, valid lease for that client.

4. **Servers Send Replies**

   Servers that are going to respond to the client's DHCPREQUEST send their DHCPACK or DHCPNAK messages.

5. **Client Receives and Processes DHCPACK or DHCPNAK Message**

   The client waits for a period of time to get a reply to its request. Again, there are three possibilities that match the three in step 3:

   - The client receives a DHCPACK message, which confirms the validity of the lease. The client will prepare to begin using the lease again, and continue with step 6.
   - The client receives a DHCPNAK message, which tells the client that its lease is no longer valid. The client transitions back to the INIT state to get a new lease—step 1 in the allocation process.
   - If the client receives no reply at all, it may retransmit the DHCPREQUEST message. If no reply is received after a period of time, it will conclude that no server has information about its lease and will return to the INIT state to try to get a new lease.

6. **Client Checks That Address Is Not in Use**

   Before resuming use of its lease, the client device should perform a final check to ensure that the new address isn't already in use. Even though this should not be the case when a lease already exists, it's done anyway, as a safety measure. The check is the same as described in step 13 of the allocation process: an ARP request is issued on the local network, to see if any other device thinks it already has the IP address this client was just leased. If another device responds, the client sends a DHCPDECLINE message back to the server, which tells it that the lease is no good because some other device is using the address. The client then goes back to the INIT state to get a new lease.

7. **Client Finalizes Lease Allocation**

   Assuming that the address is not already in use, the client finalizes the lease and transitions to the BOUND state. It is now ready for normal operation.

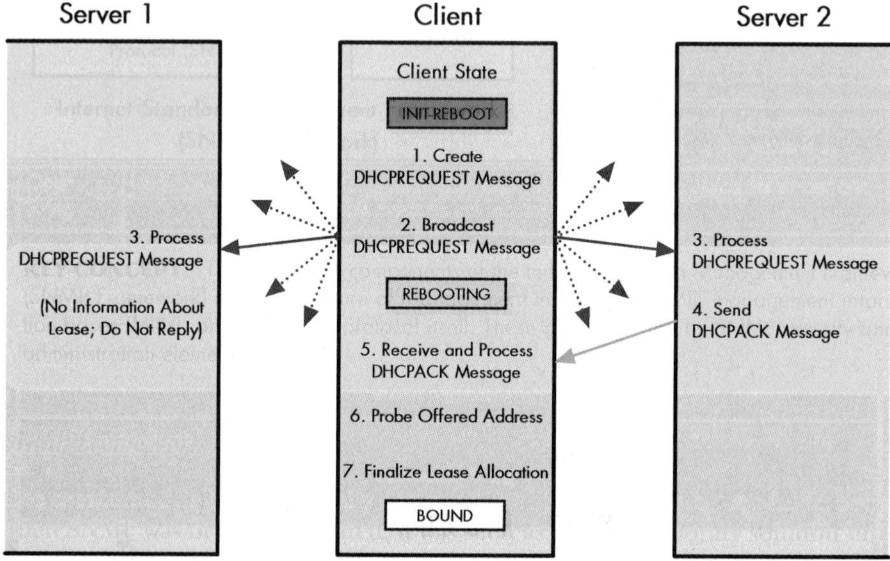

Figure 62-3: DHCP lease reallocation process *The lease reallocation process consists of seven steps that correspond approximately to steps 8 through 14 of the full lease allocation process shown in Figure 62-2. In this example, the server that originally granted the lease to the client is Server 2, so it is normally the only one that responds.*

> **KEY CONCEPT** If a client starts up and already has a lease, it does not need to go through the full lease allocation process; instead, it can use the shorter *reallocation process*. The client broadcasts a request to find the server that has the current information on its lease. That server responds back to confirm that the client's lease is still valid.

DHCP Lease Renewal and Rebinding Processes

Once a DHCP client completes the allocation or reallocation process, it enters the BOUND state. The client is now in its regular operating mode, with a valid IP address and other configuration parameters it received from the DHCP server, and it can be used like any regular TCP/IP host.

While the client is in the BOUND state, DHCP essentially lies dormant. As long as the client stays on and functioning normally, no real DHCP activity will occur while in this state. The most common occurrence that causes DHCP to wake up and become active again is arrival of the time when the lease is to be *renewed.* Renewal ensures that a lease is perpetuated so it can be used for a prolonged period of time, and involves its own message-exchange procedure. (The other way that a client can leave the BOUND state is when it terminates the lease early, as described in the next section.)

If DHCP's automatic allocation is used, or if dynamic allocation is used with an infinite lease period, the client's lease will never expire, so it never needs to be renewed. Short of early termination, the device will remain in the BOUND state forever, or at least until it is rebooted. However, most leases are finite in nature. A client must take action to ensure that its lease is extended and normal operation continues.

To manage the lease extension process, two timers are set at the time that a lease is allocated. The *renewal timer (T1)* goes off to tell the client it is time to try to renew the lease with the server that initially granted it. The *rebinding timer (T2)* goes off if the client is not successful in renewing with that server, and tells it to try any server to have the lease extended. If the lease is renewed or rebound, the client goes back to normal operation. If it cannot be rebound, it will expire, and the client will need to seek a new lease.

The following steps summarize the renewal/rebinding process (see Figure 62-4). Obviously, the exact sequence of operations taken by a client depends on what happens in its attempts to contact a server. For example, if it is successful with renewal, it will never need to attempt rebinding.

1. **Renewal Timer (T1) Expires**

   The renewal timer, T1, is set by default to 50 percent of the length of the lease. When the timer goes off, the client transitions from the BOUND state to the RENEWING state. Note that a client may initiate lease renewal prior to T1 timer expiration, if it desires.

2. **Client Sends DHCPREQUEST Renewal Message**

   The client creates a DHCPREQUEST message that identifies itself and its lease. It then transmits the message directly to the server that initially granted the lease, unicast. Note that this is different from the DHCPREQUEST messages used in the allocation/reallocation processes, where the DHCPREQUEST is broadcast. The client may request a particular new lease length, just as it may request a lease length in its requests during allocation, but as always, the server makes the final call on lease length.

3. **Server Receives and Processes DHCPREQUEST Message and Creates Reply**

   Assuming the server is reachable, it will receive and process the client's renewal request. There are two possible responses:

   - The server decides that the client's lease can be renewed. It prepares to send to the client a DHCPACK message to confirm the lease's renewal, indicating the new lease length and any parameters that may have changed since the lease was created or last renewed.
   - The server decides, for whatever reason, not to renew the client's lease. It will create a DHCPNAK message.

4. **Server Sends Reply**

   The server sends the DHCPACK or DHCPNAK message back to the client.

5. **Client Receives and Processes Server Reply**

   The client takes the appropriate action in response to the server's reply:

   - If the client receives a DHCPACK message, renewing the lease, it notes the new lease expiration time and any changed parameters sent by the server, resets the T1 and T2 timers, and transitions back to the BOUND state. The client does not need to do an ARP IP address check when it is renewing.
   - If the client receives a DHCPNAK message, which tells it its lease renewal request has been denied, it will immediately transition to the INIT state to get a new lease (step 1 in the allocation process).

6. **Rebinding Timer (T2) Expires**

   If the client receives no reply from the server, it will remain in the RENEWING state and will regularly retransmit the unicast DHCPREQUEST to the server. During this period, the client is still operating normally, from the perspective of its user. If no response from the server is received, eventually the rebinding timer (T2) expires. This will cause the client to transition to the REBINDING state. Recall that by default, the T2 timer is set to 87.5 percent (seven-eighths) of the length of the lease.

7. **Client Sends DHCPREQUEST Rebinding Message**

   Having received no response from the server that initially granted the lease, the client gives up on that server and tries to contact any server that may be able to extend its existing lease. It creates a DHCPREQUEST message and puts its IP address in the CIAddr field, indicating clearly that it presently owns that address. It then broadcasts the request on the local network.

8. **Servers Receive and Process DHCPREQUEST Message and Send Reply**

   Each server receives the request and responds according to the information it has for the client (a server that has no information about the lease or may have outdated information does not respond):

   - A server may agree to rebind the client's lease. This happens when the server has information about the client's lease and can extend it. It prepares for the client a DHCPACK message to confirm the lease's renewal, indicating any parameters that may have changed since the lease was created or last renewed.
   - A server may decide that the client cannot extend its current lease. This occurs when the server determines that, for whatever reason, this client's lease should not be extended. It gets ready to send back to the client a DHCPNAK message.

9. **Server Sends Reply**

   Each server that is responding to the client sends its DHCPACK or DHCPNAK message.

10. **Client Receives Server Reply**

    The client takes the appropriate action in response to the two possibilities in the preceding step:

    - The client receives a DHCPACK message, rebinding the lease. The client makes note of the server that is now in charge of this lease, the new lease expiration time, and any changed parameters sent by the server. It resets the T1 and T2 timers, and transitions back to the BOUND state. (It may also probe the new address as it does during regular lease allocation.)
    - The client receives a DHCPNAK message, which tells it that some server has determined that the lease should not be extended. The client immediately transitions to the INIT state to get a new lease (step 1 in the allocation process).

11. **Lease Expires**

    If the client receives no response to its broadcast rebinding request, it will, as in the RENEWING state, retransmit the request regularly. If no response is received by the time the lease expires, it transitions to the INIT state to get a new lease.

So, why bother with a two-step process: rebinding and renewal? The reason is that this provides the best blend of efficiency and flexibility. We first try to contact the server that granted the lease using a unicast request, to avoid taking up the time of other DHCP servers and disrupting the network as a whole with broadcast traffic. Usually this will work, because DHCP servers don't change that often and are usually left on continuously. If that fails, we then fall back on the broadcast, giving other servers a chance to take over the client's existing lease.

> **KEY CONCEPT** Each client's lease has associated with it a *renewal timer (T1)*, normally set to 50 percent of the length of the lease, and a *rebinding timer (T2)*, usually set to 87.5 percent of the lease length. When the T1 timer goes off, the client will try to renew its lease by contacting the server that originally granted it. If the client cannot renew the lease by the time the T2 timer expires, it will broadcast a rebinding request to any available server. If the lease is not renewed or rebound by the time the lease expires, the client must start the lease allocation process over again.

DHCP Early Lease Termination (Release) Process

A TCP/IP host can't really do much without an IP address; it's a fundamental component of the Internet Protocol (IP), on which all TCP/IP protocols and applications run. When a host has either a manual IP address assignment or an infinite lease, it obviously never needs to worry about losing its IP address. When a host has a finite DHCP lease, it will use the renewal/rebinding process to try to hang on to its existing IP address as long as possible.

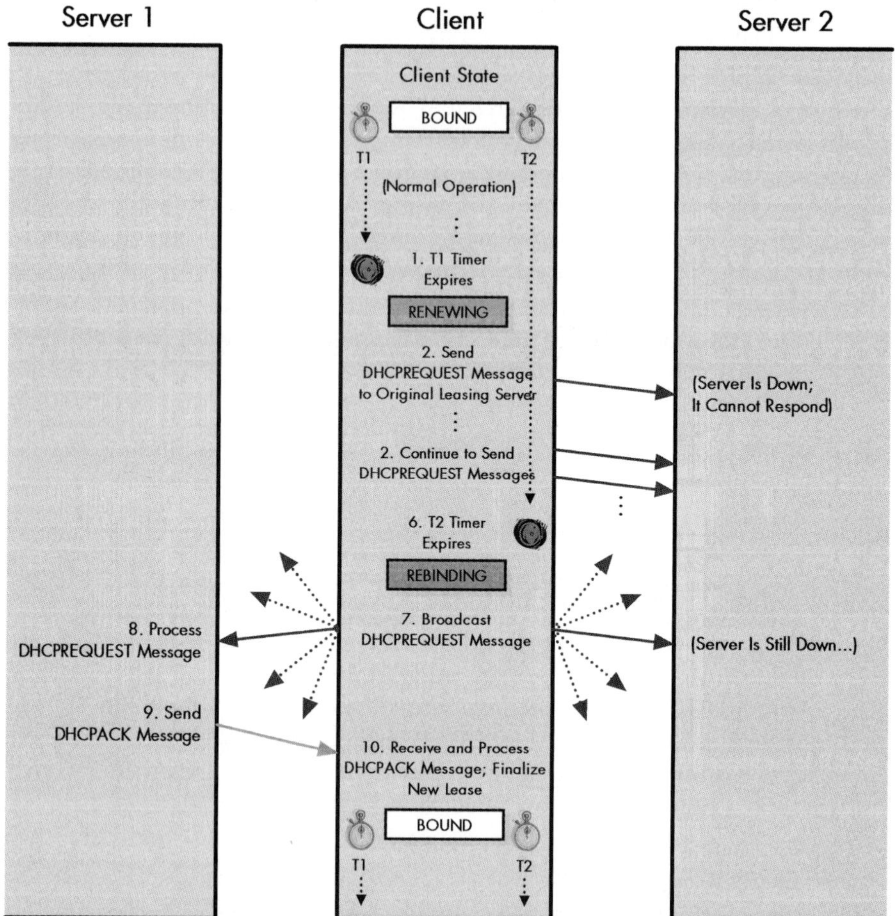

Figure 62-4: DHCP lease renewal and rebinding processes *This diagram shows the example of a client presently holding a lease with Server 2 attempting to contact it to renew the lease. However, in this case, Server 2 is down for maintenance. The server is unable to respond, and the client remains stuck at step 2 in the renewal/rebinding process. It keeps sending DHCPREQUEST messages to Server 2 until its T2 timer expires. It then enters the rebinding state and broadcasts a DHCPREQUEST message, which is heard by Server 1, which agrees to extend its current lease.*

So, under normal circumstances, a client will continue trying to extend its existing lease indefinitely. In certain cases, however, a host may decide to terminate its lease. This usually will not be something the client just decides to do spontaneously. It will occur in response to a specific request from the user to end the lease. A user may terminate a lease for a number of reasons, including the following:

- The client is being moved to a different network.
- The network is having its IP addresses renumbered.
- The user wants the host to negotiate a new lease with a different server.
- The user wants to reset the lease to fix some sort of a problem.

In any of these cases, the user can end the lease through a process called *early lease termination* or *lease release*. This is a very simple, unidirectional communication. The client sends a special DHCPRELEASE message unicast to the server that holds its current lease, to tell it that the lease is no longer required. The server then records the lease as having been ended. It does not need to reply back to the client.

The reason that the client can just assume that the lease termination has been successful is that this is not a mandatory part of the DHCP protocol. Having clients send DHCPRELEASE to end a lease is considered a courtesy, rather than a requirement. It is more efficient to have clients inform servers when they no longer need a lease, and this also allows the IP address in the terminated lease to be reused more quickly. However, DHCP servers are designed to handle the case where a client seemingly disappears without formally ending an existing lease.

DHCP Parameter Configuration Process for Clients with Non-DHCP Addresses

The majority of DHCP clients make use of the protocol to obtain both an IP address and other configuration parameters. This is the reason why so much of DHCP is oriented around address assignment and leasing. A conventional DHCP client obtains all its configuration parameters at the same time it gets an IP address, using the message exchanges and processes described in the preceding sections of this chapter.

There are cases where a device with an IP address assigned using a method other than DHCP still wants to use DHCP servers to obtain other configuration parameters. The main advantage of this is administrative convenience; it allows a device with a static IP address to still be able to automatically get other parameters the same way that regular DHCP clients do.

Ironically, one common case where this capability can be used is in configuring DHCP servers themselves! Administrators normally do not use DHCP to provide an IP address to a DHCP server, but they may want to use it to tell the server other parameters. In this case, the server requesting the parameters actually acts as a client for the purpose of the exchange with another server.

The original DHCP standard did not provide any mechanism for this sort of non-IP configuration to take place. RFC 2131 revised the protocol, adding a new message type (DHCPINFORM) that allows a device to request configuration parameters without going through the full leasing process. This message is used as part of a simple bidirectional communication that is separate from the leasing communications we have looked at so far. Since it doesn't involve IP address assignment, it is not part of the lease life cycle, nor is it part of the DHCP client FSM.

The following steps show how a device with an externally configured address uses DHCP to get other parameters (see Figure 62-5):

1. **Client Creates DHCPINFORM Message**

   The client (which may be a DHCP server acting as a client) creates a DHCP-INFORM message. It fills in its own IP address in the CIAddr field, since that IP address is current and valid. It may request specific parameters using the Parameter Request List option or simply accept the defaults provided by the server.

2. **Client Sends DHCPINFORM Message**

   The client sends the DHCPINFORM message unicast, if it knows the identity and address of a DHCP server; otherwise, it broadcasts it.

3. **Server Receives and Processes DHCPINFORM Message**

   The message is received and processed by the DHCP server or servers (if there are multiple servers and the request was broadcast). Each server checks to see if it has the parameters needed by the client in its database.

4. **Server Creates DHCPACK Message**

   Each server that has the information the client needs creates a DHCPACK message, which includes the needed parameters in the appropriate DHCP option fields. (Often, this will be only a single server.)

5. **Server Sends DHCPACK Message**

   The server sends the message unicast back to the client.

6. **Client Receives and Processes DHCPACK Message**

   The client receives the DHCPACK message sent by the server, processes it, and sets its parameters accordingly.

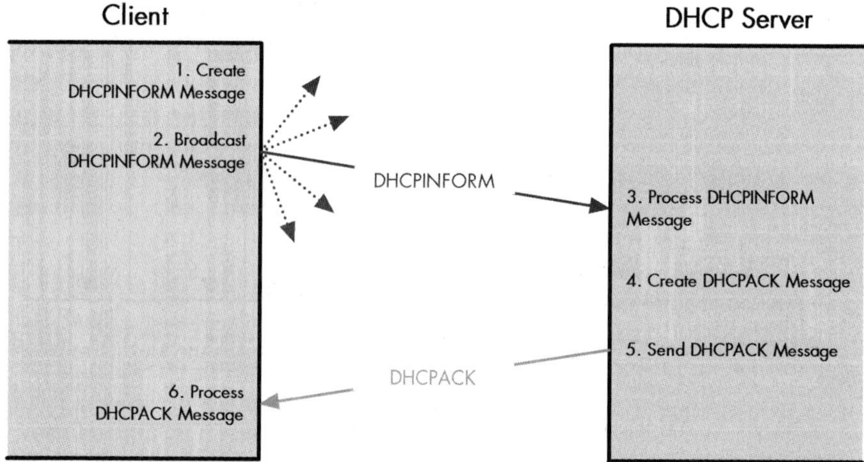

Figure 62-5: DHCP parameter configuration process *A device that already has an IP address can use the simple request/reply exchange shown in this figure to get other configuration parameters from a DHCP server. In this case, the client is broadcasting its request.*

If a client receives no reply to its DHCPINFORM message, it will retransmit it periodically. After a retry period, it will give up and use default configuration values. It will also typically generate an error report to inform an administrator or user of the problem.

> **KEY CONCEPT** Devices that are not using DHCP to acquire IP addresses can still use its other configuration capabilities. A client can broadcast a *DHCPINFORM* message to request that any available server send it parameters for how the network is to be used. DHCP servers respond with the requested parameters and/or default parameters, carried in DHCP options of a *DHCPACK* message.

63

DHCP MESSAGING, MESSAGE TYPES, AND FORMATS

The preceding chapter on DHCP configuration and operation demonstrated how DHCP works by showing the various leasing and information-exchange processes. All of these procedures rely heavily on the exchange of information between the client and server, which is accomplished through DHCP *messages*. Like all protocols, DHCP uses a special message format and a set of rules that govern how messages are created, addressed, and transported.

In this chapter, I provide the details of how DHCP creates and sends messages, and show the formats used for DHCP messages and options. I begin with a description of how DHCP creates, addresses, and transports messages, and how it deals with message retransmission. I then outline the DHCP general message format, showing how it is similar to the BOOTP message format on which it is based and also where it differs. I describe DHCP options, the format used for them, and the special option overloading feature used for efficiency. I conclude the section with a complete list of DHCP options.

RELATED INFORMATION *DHCP is most closely related to BOOTP in the area of messaging. DHCP options are based closely on BOOTP vendor extensions (see Chapter 60), and many of the specific DHCP option types are the same as BOOTP vendor information fields. To avoid duplication, the summary table in this chapter lists the options/extensions for both protocols, indicating which ones are used by both BOOTP and DHCP, and which are used only by DHCP.*

DHCP Message Generation, Addressing, Transport, and Retransmission

As you've learned, nearly every aspect of DHCP's operation is oriented around the notion of a client device exchanging information with a server. You can also see this reflected in all of the major characteristics of DHCP messaging. This includes the format of DHCP messages, as well as the specifics of how DHCP messages are created, addressed, and transmitted, and when necessary, retransmitted.

Message Generation and General Formatting

DHCP messaging is similar in many ways to that of BOOTP, the protocol on which DHCP was based. BOOTP defined only two message types: a request and a reply. DHCP is much more complex. It uses eight different types of messages, but these are still categorized as either request or reply messages, depending on who sends them and why. DHCP uses a special DHCP Message Type option to indicate the exact DHCP message type, but still treats a message from a client seeking information as a request, and a response from a server containing information as a reply.

A client generates a message using the general DHCP message format, which is very similar to the BOOTP message format. When a server replies to a client message, it does not generate the reply as a completely new message, but rather copies the client request, changes fields as appropriate, and sends the reply back to the client. A special transaction identifier (XID) is placed in the request and maintained in the reply, which allows a client to know which reply goes with a particular request.

Message Transport

DHCP uses the User Datagram Protocol (UDP) for transport, just as BOOTP does, and for the same reasons: simplicity and support for broadcasts. It also has many of the same addressing concerns as BOOTP, as discussed in Chapter 60. Clients usually will send requests by broadcast on the local network, to allow them to contact any available DHCP server. The exception to this is when a client is trying to renew a lease with a server that it already knows. For compatibility with BOOTP, DHCP uses the same well-known (reserved) UDP port number, 67, for client requests to servers.

Some DHCP message exchanges require a server to respond back to a client that has a valid and active IP address. An example is a DHCPACK message sent in reply to a DHCPINFORM request. In this situation, the server can always send a reply unicast back to the client. Other message exchanges, however, present the same chicken-and-egg conundrum that we saw with BOOTP: If a client is using DHCP to obtain an IP address, we can't assume that IP address is available for us to use to send a reply.

In BOOTP, there were two possible solutions to this situation: The server could send back its reply using broadcast addressing as well, or the server could send back a reply directly to the host at layer 2. Due to the performance problems associated with broadcasts, DHCP tries to make the latter method the default for server replies. It assumes that a client's TCP/IP software will be capable of accepting and processing an IP datagram delivered at layer 2, even before the IP stack is initialized.

As the standard itself puts it, "DHCP requires creative use of the client's TCP/IP software and liberal interpretation of RFC 1122." RFC 1122 is a key standard describing the detailed implementation requirements of TCP/IP hosts. The DHCP standard, however, acknowledges the fact that not all devices may support this behavior. It allows a client to force servers to send back replies using broadcasts instead. This is done by the client setting the special Broadcast (B) flag to 1 in its request.

Since DHCP, like BOOTP, must use either layer 2 delivery or layer 3 broadcasts for server replies, it requires a separate well-known port number for servers to send to. Again, for compatibility with BOOTP, the same port number is used, 68. This port number is used whether a server reply is sent unicast or broadcast.

KEY CONCEPT Requests from BOOTP clients are normally sent broadcast, to reach any available DHCP server. However, there are certain exceptions, such as in lease renewal, when a request is sent directly to a known server. DHCP servers can send their replies either broadcast to the special port number reserved for DHCP clients or unicast using layer 2. The DHCP standards specify that layer 2 delivery should be used when possible to avoid unnecessary broadcast traffic.

Retransmission of Lost Messages

Using UDP provides benefits such as simplicity and efficiency to DHCP, but since UDP is unreliable, there is no guarantee that messages will get to their destination. This can lead to potential confusion on the part of a client. Consider, for example, a client sending a DHCPDISCOVER message and waiting for DHCPOFFER messages in reply. If it gets no response, does this mean that there is no DHCP server willing to offer it service or simply that its DHCPDISCOVER got lost somewhere on the network? The same applies to most other request/reply sequences, such as a client waiting for a DHCPACK or DHCPNAK message in reply to a DHCPREQUEST or DHCPINFORM message.

The fact that messages can be lost means that DHCP itself must keep track of messages sent, and if there is no response, retransmit them. Since there are so many message exchanges in DHCP, there is much that can go wrong. As in BOOTP, DHCP puts responsibility for this squarely on the shoulders of the client. This makes sense, since the client initiates contact and can most easily keep track of messages sent and retransmit them when needed. A server can't know when a client's request is lost, but a client can react when it doesn't receive a reply from the server.

In any request/reply message exchange, the client uses a retransmission timer that is set to a period of time that represents how long it is reasonable for it to wait for a response. If no reply is received by the time the timer expires, the client assumes that either its request or the response coming back was lost. The client then retransmits the request. If this request again elicits no reply, the client will continue retransmitting for a period of time.

To prevent large numbers of DHCP clients from retransmitting requests simultaneously (which would potentially clog the network), the client must use a randomized exponential backoff algorithm to determine when exactly a retransmission is made. As in BOOTP, this is similar to the technique used to recover from collisions in Ethernet. The DHCP standard specifies that the delay should be based on the speed of the underlying network between the client and the server. More specifically, it says that in a standard Ethernet network, the first retransmission should be delayed 4 seconds plus or minus a random value from 0 to 1 second; in other words, some value is chosen between 3 and 5 seconds. The delay is then doubled with each subsequent transmission (7 to 9 seconds, then 15 to 17 seconds, and so forth) up to a maximum of 64 +/– 1 second.

To prevent it from retrying endlessly, the client normally has logic that limits the number of retries. The amount of time that retransmissions go on depends on the type of request being sent; that is, what process is being undertaken. If a client is forced to give up due to too many retries, it will generally either take some sort of default action or generate an error message.

> **KEY CONCEPT** Like BOOTP, DHCP uses UDP for transport, which does not provide any reliability features. DHCP clients must detect when requests are sent and no response is received, and retransmit requests periodically. Special logic is used to prevent clients from sending excessive numbers of requests during difficult network conditions.

DHCP Message Format

When DHCP was created, its developers had a bit of an issue related to how exactly they should structure DHCP messages. BOOTP was already widely used, and maintaining compatibility between DHCP and BOOTP was an important goal. This meant that DHCP's designers needed to continue using the existing BOOTP message format. However, DHCP has more functionality than BOOTP, and this means that it can hold more information than can easily fit in the limited BOOTP message format.

This apparent contradiction was resolved in two ways:

- The existing BOOTP message format was maintained for basic functionality, but DHCP clients and servers were programmed to use the BOOTP message fields in slightly different ways.
- The BOOTP vendor extensions were formalized and became DHCP *options*. Despite the name *options*, some of these additional fields are for basic DHCP functionality, and they are quite mandatory!

With this dual approach, DHCP devices have access to the extra information they need. Meanwhile, the basic field format is unchanged, allowing DHCP servers to communicate with older BOOTP clients, which ignore the extra DHCP information that doesn't relate to them. See the discussion of BOOTP/DHCP interoperability (in Chapter 64) for more information.

The DHCP message format is illustrated in Figure 63-1 and described fully in Tables 63-1 and 63-2. In the table, I have specifically indicated which fields are used in DHCP in a manner similar to how they are used in BOOTP, and which are significantly different.

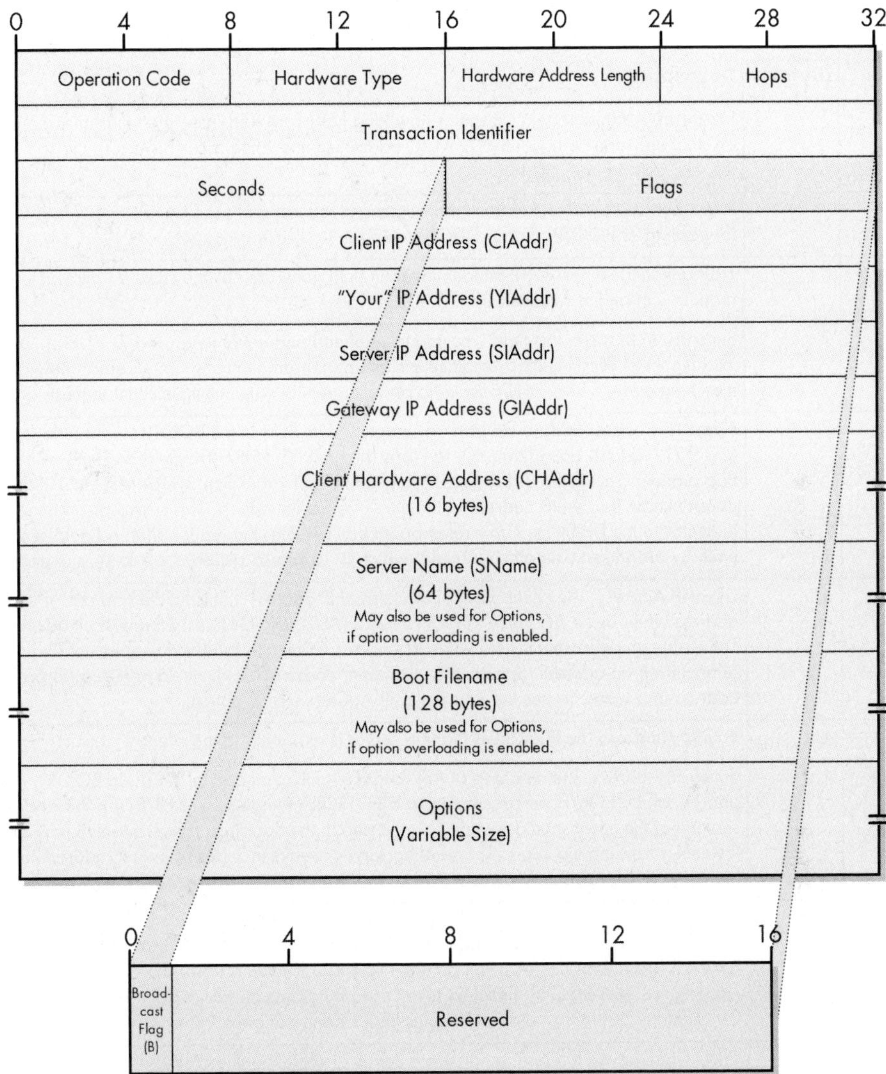

Figure 63-1: *DHCP message format*

Table 63-1: DHCP Message Format

Field Name	Size (Bytes)	Description
Op	1	Operation Code: This code represents the general category of the DHCP message. A client sending a request to a server uses an opcode of 1; a server replying uses a code of 2. So, for example, a DHCPREQUEST would be a request, and a DHCPACK or DHCPNAK is a reply. The actual specific type of DHCP message is encoded using the DHCP Message Type option.
HType	1	Hardware Type: This field specifies the type of hardware used for the local network, and it is used in exactly the same way as the equivalent field (HRD) in the Address Resolution Protocol (ARP) message format. Some of the most common values for this field are shown in Table 63-2.

(continued)

Table 63-1: DHCP Message Format (continued)

Field Name	Size (Bytes)	Description
Hlen	1	Hardware Address Length: Specifies how long hardware addresses are in this message. For Ethernet or other networks using IEEE 802 MAC addresses, the value is 6. This is also the same as a field in the ARP field format, HLN.
Hops	1	Hops: Set to 0 by a client before transmitting a request and used by relay agents to control the forwarding of BOOTP and/or DHCP messages.
XID	4	Transaction Identifier: A 32-bit identification field generated by the client, to allow it to match up the request with replies received from DHCP servers.
Secs	2	Seconds: In BOOTP, this field was vaguely defined and not always used. For DHCP, it is defined as the number of seconds elapsed since a client began an attempt to acquire or renew a lease. This may be used by a busy DHCP server to prioritize replies when multiple client requests are outstanding.
Flags	2	Flags: This corresponds to the formerly empty 2-byte field in the BOOTP message format defined by RFC 951, which was redefined as a Flags field in RFC 1542. The field presently contains just one flag subfield. This is the B (Broadcast) flag subfield, 1 bit in size, which is set to 1 if the client doesn't know its own IP address at the time it sends its request. This serves as an immediate indicator to the DHCP server or relay agent that receives the request that it should send its reply back by broadcast. The other subfield, which is 15 bits, is reserved, set to 0, and not used.
CIAddr	4	Client IP Address: The client puts its own current IP address in this field if and only if it has a valid IP address while in the *BOUND, RENEWING,* or *REBINDING* states; otherwise, it sets the field to 0. The client can only use this field when its address is actually valid and usable, not during the process of acquiring an address. Specifically, the client does not use this field to request a particular IP address in a lease; it uses the Requested IP Address DHCP option.
YIAddr	4	Your IP Address: The IP address that the server is assigning to the client.
SIAddr	4	Server IP Address: The meaning of this field is slightly changed in DHCP. In BOOTP, it is the IP address of the BOOTP server sending a BOOTREPLY message. In DHCP, it is the address of the server that the client should use for the next step in the bootstrap process, which may or may not be the server sending this reply. The sending server always includes its own IP address in the Server Identifier DHCP option.
GIAddr	4	Gateway IP Address: This field is used just as it is in BOOTP, to route BOOTP messages when BOOTP relay agents are involved to facilitate the communication of BOOTP requests and replies between a client and a server on different subnets or networks. See the description of DHCP relaying. As with BOOTP, this field is not used by clients and does not represent the server giving the client the address of a default router (that's done using the Router DHCP option).
CHAddr	16	Client Hardware Address: The hardware (layer 2) address of the client, which is used for identification and communication.
SName	64	Server Name: The server sending a DHCPOFFER or DHCPACK message may optionally put its name in this field. This can be a simple text nickname or a fully qualified DNS domain name (such as myserver.organization.org). This field may also be used to carry DHCP options, using the option overload feature, indicated by the value of the DHCP Option Overload option.
File	128	Boot Filename: Optionally used by a client to request a particular type of boot file in a DHCPDISCOVER message. Used by a server in a DHCPOFFER to fully specify a boot file directory path and filename. This field may also be used to carry DHCP options, using the option overload feature, indicated by the value of the DHCP Option Overload option.
Options	Variable	Options: Holds DHCP options, including several parameters required for basic DHCP operation. Note that this field was fixed at 64 bytes in length in BOOTP but is variable in length in DHCP. See the next section for more information. This field may be used by both the client and server.

Table 63-2: DHCP Message HType Values

HType Value	Hardware Type
1	Ethernet (10 Mb)
6	IEEE 802 Networks
7	ARCNet
11	LocalTalk
12	LocalNet (IBM PCNet or SYTEK LocalNET)
14	Switched Multimegabit Data Service (SMDS)
15	Frame Relay
16	Asynchronous Transfer Mode (ATM)
17	High-Level Data Link Control (HDLC)
18	Fibre Channel
19	ATM
20	Serial Line

The DHCP standard does not specify the details of how DHCP messages are encapsulated within UDP. I would assume that due to the other similarities to BOOTP, DHCP maintains BOOTP's optional use of message checksums. It also most likely assumes that messages will not be fragmented (sent with the Do Not Fragment bit set to 1 in the IP datagram). This is to allow BOOTP clients to avoid the complexity of reassembling fragmented messages.

Unlike with BOOTP, which has a fixed message size, DHCP messages are variable in length. This is the result of changing BOOTP's 64-byte Vend field into the variable-length Options field. DHCP relies on options much more than BOOTP does, and a device must be capable of accepting a message with an Options field at least 312 bytes in length. The SName and File fields may also be used to carry options, as described in the next section.

DHCP Options

When BOOTP was first developed, its message format included a 64-byte Vend field, called the Vendor-Specific Area. The idea behind this field was to provide flexibility to the protocol. The BOOTP standard did not define any specific way of using this field. Instead, the field was left open for the creators of different types of hardware to use it to customize BOOTP to meet the needs of their clients and/or servers.

Including this sort of undefined field is a good idea because it makes a protocol easily *extensible*—allowing the protocol to be easily enhanced in the future through the definition of new fields while not disturbing any existing fields. The problem with the BOOTP Vendor-Specific Area, however, is that the extensibility was vendor-specific. It was useful only for special fields that were particular to a single vendor.

What was really needed was a way to define new fields for general-purpose, vendor-independent parameter communication, but there was no field in the BOOTP message format that would let this happen. The solution came in the form of RFC 1048, which defined a technique called BOOTP *vendor information extensions.*

This method redefines the Vendor-Specific Area to allow it to carry general parameters between a client and server. This idea was so successful that it largely replaced the older vendor-specific use of the Vend field.

DHCP maintains, formalizes, and further extends the idea of using the Vend field to carry general-purpose parameters. Instead of being called vendor information extensions or vendor information fields, these fields are now called simply DHCP *options*. Similarly, the Vend field has been renamed the Options field, reflecting its new role as a way of conveying vendor-independent options between a client and server.

Options and Option Format

Keeping with the desire to maintain compatibility between BOOTP and DHCP, the DHCP Options field is, in most ways, the same as the vendor-independent interpretation of the BOOTP Vend field introduced by RFC 1048. The first four bytes of the field still carry the magic cookie value 99.130.83.99 to identify the information as vendor-independent option fields. The rest of the Option field consists of one or more subfields, each of which has a *type, length, value (TLV-encoded)* substructure, as in BOOTP.

The main differences between BOOTP vendor information fields and DHCP options are the field names and the fact that the DHCP Options field is variable in length (the BOOTP Vend field is fixed at 64 bytes). The structure of the DHCP Options field as a whole is shown in Figure 63-2, and the subfield names of each option are described in Table 63-3.

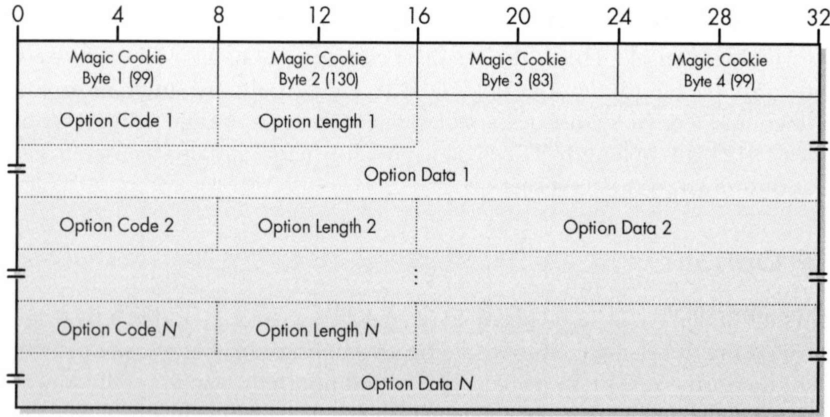

Figure 63-2: DHCP Options field format *The format of the DHCP Options field is, unsurprisingly, very similar to that of the BOOTP Vendor-Specific Area, as shown in Figure 60-4 in Chapter 60. The Options field begins with the same four-byte magic cookie and then contains a number of variable-length option fields. Each option has the format described in Table 63-3.*

All of the DHCP options follow the format shown in Table 63-3, except for two special cases, again the same as with BOOTP. A Code value of 0 is used as a *pad*, when subfields need to be aligned on word boundaries; it contains no information. The value 255 is used to mark the end of the vendor information fields. Both of these codes contain no actual data, so to save space, when either is used, just the single Code value is included and the Len and Data fields are omitted. A device seeing a Code value of 0 just skips it as filler. A device seeing a Code value of 255 knows it has reached the end of the fields in this Options field.

Table 63-3: DHCP Option Format

Subfield Name	Size (Bytes)	Description
Code	1	Option Code: A single octet that specifies the option type.
Len	1	Option Length: The number of bytes in this particular option. This does not include the two bytes for the Code and Len subfields.
Data	Variable	Option Data: The data being sent, which has a length indicated by the Len subfield, and which is interpreted based on the Code subfield.

Option Categories

Before DHCP was invented, a series of BOOTP standards was published defining the current list of BOOTP vendor information extensions. When DHCP was developed, a single standard was created that merged both BOOTP vendor information extensions and DHCP options, since again, they are basically the same. The most recent of these is RFC 2132, entitled (ta-da!) "DHCP Options and BOOTP Vendor Extensions."

RFC 2132 lists several dozen fields that can be used either as DHCP options or BOOTP vendor information fields, grouped into several categories. In addition, there is also a set of fields that are used only in DHCP, not in BOOTP. Despite being called *options*, only some really are optional; others are necessary for the basic operation of DHCP. They are carried as option fields for only one reason: to allow DHCP to keep using the same basic message format as BOOTP for compatibility. Table 63-4 summarizes the categories used for DHCP options.

Table 63-4: DHCP Option Categories

Option Category	Description
RFC 1497 Vendor Extensions	The BOOTP vendor extensions defined in RFC 1497, the last RFC describing vendor extension fields that was BOOTP-specific (before DHCP was created). For easier reference, these were kept in a single group when DHCP options were created, even though some of the functions they represent might fit better in other categories. (See Table 63-5.)
IP Layer Parameters per Host	Parameters that control the operation of the Internet Protocol (IP) on a host, which affect the host as a whole and are not interface-specific. (See Table 63-6.)
IP Layer Parameters per Interface	Parameters that affect the operation of IP for a particular interface of a host. (Some devices have only one interface; others have more.) (See Table 63-7.)
Link Layer Parameters per Interface	Parameters that affect the data link layer operation of a host, on a per-interface basis. (See Table 63-8.)
TCP Parameters	Parameters that impact the operation of the TCP layer; specified on a per-interface basis. (See Table 63-9.)
Application and Service Parameters	Parameters used to configure or control the operation of various miscellaneous applications or services. (See Table 63-10.)
DHCP Extensions	Parameters that are DHCP-specific and used to control the operation of the DHCP protocol itself. (See Table 63-12.)

The tables at the end of this chapter provide a complete list of the DHCP options defined in RFC 2132.

Due to the popularity of DHCP, several other options have been defined since that standard was published. Each time a new option is created, documenting it would have required a new successor to RFC 2132, which would be confusing and time-consuming. Instead, the maintenance of these options and extensions has been moved from the RFC process to a set of files maintained by the Internet Assigned Numbers Authority (IANA), just like so many other parameters. There is also a process by which a developer can request additional standard extensions to be added to DHCP. This is described in section 10 of RFC 2132.

KEY CONCEPT DHCP takes BOOTP's vendor information extensions and formalizes them into an official feature called DHCP *options*. The BOOTP Vendor Specific Area field becomes the DHCP Options field, and it can contain an arbitrary number of parameters to be sent from the server to the client. Some of these include pieces of data that are actually mandatory for the successful operation of DHCP. There are several dozen DHCP options, which are divided into functional categories.

Option Overloading

Since DHCP relies so much more on the use of options than BOOTP did, the size of the Options field could theoretically grow quite large. However, since DHCP is using UDP for transport, the overall size of a message is limited. This theoretically could have led to a situation where a message might run out of room and be unable to carry all its options. Meanwhile, there are two more spacious fields in the message format: SName and File, which are 64 bytes and 128 bytes, respectively. These fields might not even be needed in some cases, because many devices use DHCP for getting a lease and parameters, not to download a boot image. Even if they are needed, they might be carrying much less information than their large fixed size allows.

To make better use of the total space in the message format, DHCP includes a special feature called *option overloading*, which allows the SName and File fields to be used to carry more option fields instead of their conventional information. Use of this option is itself indicated through the use of a DHCP option, Option Overload, which tells a device receiving a message how to interpret the two fields. If option overloading is used, the SName and/or File fields are read and interpreted in the same way as the Options field, after all of the options in the Options field are parsed. If the message actually does need to carry a server name or boot file, these are included as separate options (number 66 and number 67, respectively), which are variable in length and can therefore be made exactly the length needed.

Incidentally, the creators of DHCP did recognize that even though vendor-independent options are important, a vendor might want to be able to send vendor-specific information just as the original BOOTP defined. To this end, they created a DHCP option called Vendor Specific Information. This option allows a vendor to encapsulate a set of vendor-specific option fields within the normal DHCP option structure. In essence, you can think of this as a way of nesting a conventional BOOTP Vend field (of variable length) within a single DHCP option. Other DHCP options can be carried simultaneously, subject to overall message-length limits. Note that this supplements an already existing BOOTP option that allows reference to be made to a file containing vendor-specific information.

KEY CONCEPT Since DHCP messages can contain so many options, a special feature called *option overloading* was created. When enabled, overloading allows options to make use of the large SName and File fields in the DHCP message format for options.

Summary of DHCP Options/BOOTP Vendor Information Fields

BOOTP *vendor information fields* are used to carry additional vendor-independent configuration parameters. These were used as the basis for DHCP *options*, which extend the concept to include parameters used to manage the operation of DHCP as a whole, as described in the previous section. Since BOOTP vendor information fields and DHCP options are essentially the same (except for the DHCP-specific fields), they are described in the same TCP/IP standard, and hence, in this single part of the book.

The following tables list each of the DHCP options/BOOTP vendor information fields. The tables show each option's Code value, the length of the Data subfield for the option, the formal name of the option, and a brief description of how it is used. For simplicity in the tables, where I say *option*, please read it as *option/vendor information field*, since they are the same (except, for the DHCP-specific options).

NOTE *There are a lot of options in these tables, and some of them define parameters that are used by somewhat obscure protocols that I do not cover in this book. The brief descriptions may not be enough for you to completely understand how each and every option is used. Note in particular that many of the original BOOTP vendor information fields that are used to communicate the addresses of certain types of servers are now archaic and may no longer be used.*

RFC 1497 Vendor Extensions

Table 63-5 shows the DHCP/BOOTP options that were originally defined in RFC 1497.

Table 63-5: DHCP/BOOTP Options: RFC 1497 Vendor Extensions

Code Value	Data Length (Bytes)	Name and Description
0	0	Pad: A single byte used as filler to align a subsequent field on a word (2-byte) boundary. It contains no information. One of two options that is a single byte in length, having no Data subfield (the other is the End option).
1	4	Subnet Mask: A 32-bit subnet mask being supplied for the client to use on the current network. It must appear in the option list before the Router option if both are present.
2	4	Time Offset: Specifies the time offset of the client's subnet in seconds from *Coordinated Universal Time (UTC, formerly Greenwich Mean Time or GMT)*. Positive values represent areas east of the prime meridian (in the United Kingdom); negative values represent areas west of the prime meridian. Essentially, this is used to indicate the time zone of the subnet.
3	Variable (multiple of 4)	Router: Specifies a list of 32-bit router addresses for the client to use on the local network. Routers are listed in the order of preference for the client to use.

(continued)

Table 63-5: DHCP/BOOTP Options: RFC 1497 Vendor Extensions (continued)

Code Value	Data Length (Bytes)	Name and Description
4	Variable (multiple of 4)	Time Server: Specifies a list of time server addresses (per RFC 868, see Chapter 88) for the client to use on the local network. Servers are listed in the order of preference for the client to use.
5	Variable (multiple of 4)	IEN-116 Name Server: Specifies a list of IEN-116 name server addresses for the client to use on the local network. Servers are listed in the order of preference for the client to use. Note that this option is not used for DNS name servers.
6	Variable (multiple of 4)	DNS Name Server: Specifies a list of DNS (see Chapter 52) name server addresses for the client to use on the local network. Servers are listed in the order of preference for the client to use.
7	Variable (multiple of 4)	Log Server: Specifies a list of MIT-LCS UDP log server addresses for the client to use on the local network. Servers are listed in the order of preference for the client to use.
8	Variable (multiple of 4)	Cookie Server: Specifies a list of RFC 865 cookie server addresses for the client to use on the local network. Servers are listed in the order of preference for the client to use.
9	Variable (multiple of 4)	LPR Server: Specifies a list of RFC 1179 line printer server addresses for the client to use on the local network. Servers are listed in the order of preference for the client to use.
10	Variable (multiple of 4)	Impress Server: Specifies a list of Imagen Impress server addresses for the client to use on the local network. Servers are listed in the order of preference for the client to use.
11	Variable (multiple of 4)	Resource Location Server: Specifies a list of RFC 887 resource location server addresses for the client to use on the local network. Servers are listed in the order of preference for the client to use.
12	Variable	Host Name: Specifies a host name for the client. This may or may not be a DNS host name; see option15.
13	2	Boot File Size: Specifies the size of the default boot image file for the client, expressed in units of 512 bytes.
14	Variable	Merit Dump File: Specifies the path and filename of the file to which the client should dump its core image in the event that it crashes.
15	Variable	Domain Name: Specifies the DNS domain name for the client. Compare this with option 12.
16	4	Swap Server: Specifies the address of the client's swap server.
17	Variable	Root Path: Specifies the path name of the client's root disk. This allows the client to access files it may need, using a protocol such as the Network File System (NFS; see Chapter 58).
18	Variable	Extensions Path: Specifies the name of a file that contains vendor-specific fields that the client can interpret in the same way as the Options or Vend field in a DHCP/BOOTP message. This was defined to allow a client and server to still exchange vendor-specific information even though the Option/Vend field is now used for the general-purpose fields described in this chapter. Also see option 43.
255	0	End: Placed after all other options to mark the end of the option list. One of two options that is a single byte in length, having no Data subfield (the other is the Pad option).

IP Layer Parameters per Host

Table 63-6 shows the parameters that control the operation of IP on a host as a whole. They are not interface-specific.

Table 63-6: DHCP/BOOTP Options: IP Layer Parameters per Host

Code Value	Data Length (Bytes)	Name and Description
19	1	IP Forwarding Enable/Disable: A value of 1 turns on IP forwarding (that is, routing) on a client that is capable of that function; a value of 0 turns it off.
20	1	Non-Local Source Routing Enable/Disable Option: A value of 1 tells a client capable of routing to allow forwarding of IP datagrams with nonlocal source routes. A value of 0 tells the client not to allow this. See the source routing IP datagram option (see Chapter 21) for a bit more information on this and option 21.
21	Variable (multiple of 8)	Policy Filter: A set of address/mask pairs used to filter nonlocal source-routed datagrams.
22	2	Maximum Datagram Reassembly Size: Tells the client the size of the largest datagram that the client should be prepared to reassemble. The minimum value is 576 bytes.
23	1	Default IP Time to Live: Specifies the default value that the client should use for the Time to Live field in creating IP datagrams.
24	4	Path MTU Aging Timeout: Specifies the number of seconds the client should use in aging path maximum transmission unit (MTU) values determined using path MTU discovery.
25	Variable (multiple of 2)	Path MTU Plateau Table: Specifies a table of values to be used in performing path MTU discovery.

IP Layer Parameters per Interface

Table 63-7 shows the parameters that are specific to a particular host interface at the IP level.

Table 63-7: DHCP/BOOTP Options: IP Layer Parameters per Interface

Code Value	Data Length (Bytes)	Name and Description
26	2	Interface MTU: Specifies the MTU to be used for IP datagrams on this interface. The minimum value is 68.
27	1	All Subnets Are Local: When set to 1, tells the client that it may assume that all subnets of the IP network it is on have the same MTU as its own subnet. When 0, the client must assume that some subnets may have smaller MTUs than the client's subnet.
28	4	Broadcast Address: Tells the client what address it should use for broadcasts on this interface.
29	1	Perform Mask Discovery: A value of 1 tells the client that it should use Internet Control Message Protocol (ICMP; see Chapter 31) to discover a subnet mask on the local subnet. A value of 0 tells the client not to perform this discovery.
30	1	Mask Supplier: Set to 1 to tell the client that it should respond to ICMP subnet mask requests on this interface.
31	1	Perform Router Discovery: A value of 1 tells the client to use the ICMP router discovery process to solicit a local router. A value of 0 tells the client to not do so. Note that DHCP itself can be used to specify one or more local routers using option 3.

(continued)

Table 63-7: DHCP/BOOTP Options: IP Layer Parameters per Interface (continued)

Code Value	Data Length (Bytes)	Name and Description
32	4	Router Solicitation Address: Tells the client the address to use as the destination for router solicitations.
33	Variable (multiple of 8)	Static Route: Provides the client with a list of static routes it can put into its routing cache. The list consists of a set of IP address pairs; each pair defines a destination and a router to be used to reach the destination.

Link Layer Parameters per Interface

Table 63-8 lists the DHCP/BOOTP options that are specific to a particular link layer (layer 2) interface.

Table 63-8: DHCP/BOOTP Options: Link Layer Parameters per Interface

Code Value	Data Length (Bytes)	Name and Description
34	1	Trailer Encapsulation: When set to 1, tells the client to negotiate the use of trailers, as defined in RFC 893. A value of 0 tells the client not to use this feature.
35	4	ARP Cache Timeout: Specifies how long, in seconds, the client should hold entries in its ARP cache (see Chapter 13).
36	1	Ethernet Encapsulation: Tells the client what type of encapsulation to use when transmitting over Ethernet at layer 2. If the option value is 0, it specifies that Ethernet II encapsulation should be used, per RFC 894; when the value is 1, it tells the client to use IEEE 802.3 encapsulation, per RFC 1042.

TCP Parameters

The options impacting the operation of TCP are shown in Table 63-9.

Table 63-9: DHCP/BOOTP Options: TCP Parameters

Code Value	Data Length (Bytes)	Name and Description
37	1	Default TTL: Specifies the default TTL the client should use when sending TCP segments.
38	4	TCP Keepalive Interval: Specifies how long (in seconds) the client should wait on an idle TCP connection before sending a keepalive message. A value of 0 instructs the client not to send such messages unless specifically instructed to do so by an application.
39	1	TCP Keepalive Garbage: When set to 1, tells a client it should send TCP keepalive messages that include an octet of "garbage" for compatibility with implementations that require this.

Application and Service Parameters

Table 63-10 shows the miscellaneous options that control the operation of various applications and services.

Table 63-10: DHCP/BOOTP Options: Application and Service Parameters

Code Value	Data Length (Bytes)	Name and Description
40	Variable	Network Information Service Domain: Specifies the client's Network Information Service (NIS) domain. Contrast this with option 64.
41	Variable (multiple of 4)	Network Information Servers: Specifies a list of IP addresses of NIS servers the client may use. Servers are listed in the order of preference for the client to use. Contrast this with option 65.
42	Variable (multiple of 4)	Network Time Protocol Servers: Specifies a list of IP addresses of Network Time Protocol (NTP) servers the client may use. Servers are listed in the order of preference for the client to use.
43	Variable	Vendor Specific Information: Allows an arbitrary set of vendor-specific information items to be included as a single option within a DHCP or BOOTP message. This information is structured using the same format as the Options or Vend field itself, except that it does not start with a magic cookie. See the "DHCP Options" section earlier in this chapter for more details.
44	Variable (multiple of 4)	NetBIOS over TCP/IP Name Servers: Specifies a list of IP addresses of NetBIOS name servers (per RFC 1001/1002) that the client may use. Servers are listed in the order of preference for the client to use.
45	Variable (multiple of 4)	NetBIOS over TCP/IP Datagram Distribution Servers: Specifies a list of IP addresses of NetBIOS datagram distribution servers (per RFC 1001/1002) that the client may use. Servers are listed in the order of preference for the client to use.
46	1	NetBIOS over TCP/IP Node Type: Tells the client what sort of NetBIOS node type it should use. Four different bit values are used to define the possible node type combinations, as listed in Table 63-11.
47	Variable	NetBIOS over TCP/IP Scope: Specifies the NetBIOS over TCP/IP scope parameter for the client.
48	Variable (multiple of 4)	X Window System Font Servers: Specifies a list of IP addresses of X Window System Font servers that the client may use. Servers are listed in the order of preference for the client to use.
49	Variable (multiple of 4)	X Window System Display Manager: Specifies a list of IP addresses of systems running the X Window System Display Manager that the client may use. Addresses are listed in the order of preference for the client to use.
64	Variable	Network Information Service+ Domain: Specifies the client's NIS+ domain. Contrast this with option 40.
65	Variable (multiple of 4)	Network Information Service+ Servers: Specifies a list of IP addresses of NIS+ servers the client may use. Servers are listed in the order of preference for the client to use. Contrast this with option 41.
68	Variable (multiple of 4)	Mobile IP Home Agent: Specifies a list of IP addresses of home agents that the client can use in Mobile IP (see Chapter 30). Agents are listed in the order of preference for the client to use; normally a single agent is specified.
69	Variable (multiple of 4)	Simple Mail Transport Protocol (SMTP) Servers: Specifies a list of IP addresses of SMTP servers the client may use. Servers are listed in the order of preference for the client to use. See Chapter 77 for more on SMTP.
70	Variable (multiple of 4)	Post Office Protocol (POP3) Servers: Specifies a list of IP addresses of POP3 servers the client may use. Servers are listed in the order of preference for the client to use. See Chapter 78.
71	Variable (multiple of 4)	Network News Transfer Protocol (NNTP) Servers: Specifies a list of IP addresses of NNTP servers the client may use. Servers are listed in the order of preference for the client to use. See Chapter 85.
72	Variable (multiple of 4)	Default World Wide Web (WWW) Servers: Specifies a list of IP addresses of World Wide Web (HTTP) servers the client may use. Servers are listed in the order of preference for the client to use. See Chapter 79.

(continued)

Table 63-10: DHCP/BOOTP Options: Application and Service Parameters (continued)

Code Value	Data Length (Bytes)	Name and Description
73	Variable (multiple of 4)	Default Finger Servers: Specifies a list of IP addresses of Finger servers the client may use. Servers are listed in the order of preference for the client to use.
74	Variable (multiple of 4)	Default Internet Relay Chat (IRC) Servers: Specifies a list of IP addresses of Internet Relay Chat (IRC) servers the client may use. Servers are listed in the order of preference for the client to use.
75	Variable (multiple of 4)	StreetTalk Servers: Specifies a list of IP addresses of StreetTalk servers the client may use. Servers are listed in the order of preference for the client to use.
76	Variable (multiple of 4)	StreetTalk Directory Assistance (STDA) Servers: Specifies a list of IP addresses of STDA servers the client may use. Servers are listed in the order of preference for the client to use.

Table 63-11: NetBIOS Over TCP/IP Node Type (Option 46) Values

Option 46 Subfield Name	Size (Bits)	Description
Reserved	4	Reserved: Not used.
H-Node	1	H-Node: Set to 1 to tell the client to act as a NetBIOS H-node.
M-Node	1	M-Node: Set to 1 to tell the client to act as a NetBIOS M-node.
P-Node	1	P-Node: Set to 1 to tell the client to act as a NetBIOS P-node.
B-Node	1	B-Node: Set to 1 to tell the client to act as a NetBIOS B-node.

DHCP Extensions

Last, but certainly not least, Table 63-12 describes the DHCP-only options that control the operation of the DHCP protocol.

Table 63-12: DHCP Options: DHCP Extensions

Code Value	Data Length (Bytes)	Name and Description
50	4	Requested IP Address: Used in a client's DHCPDISCOVER message to request a particular IP address assignment.
51	4	IP Address Lease Time: Used in a client request to ask a server for a particular DHCP lease duration, or in a server reply to tell the client the offered lease time. It is specified in units of seconds.
52	1	Option Overload: Used to tell the recipient of a DHCP message that the message's SName and/or File fields are being used to carry options, instead having their normal meanings. This option implements the option overload feature. There are three possible values for this single-byte option: 1 means the File field is carrying the option data, 2 means the SName field has the option data, and 3 means both fields have the option data.
53	1	DHCP Message Type: Indicates the specific type of DHCP message, as listed in Table 6-13.

(continued)

Table 63-12: DHCP Options: DHCP Extensions (continued)

Code Value	Data Length (Bytes)	Name and Description
54	4	Server Identifier: The IP address of a particular DHCP server. This option is included in messages sent by DHCP servers to identify themselves as the source of the message. It is also used by a client in a DHCPREQUEST message to specify which server's lease it is accepting.
55	Variable	Parameter Request List: Used by a DHCP client to request a list of particular configuration parameter values from a DHCP server.
56	Variable	Message: Used by a server or client to indicate an error or other message.
57	2	Maximum DHCP Message Size: Used by a DHCP client or server to specify the maximum size of DHCP message it is willing to accept. The minimum legal value is 576 bytes.
58	4	Renewal (T1) Time Value: Tells the client the value to use for its renewal timer.
59	4	Rebinding (T2) Time Value: Tells the client the value to use for its rebinding timer.
60	Variable	Vendor Class Identifier: Included in a message sent by a DHCP client to specify its vendor and configuration. This may be used to prompt a server to send the correct vendor-specific information using option 43.
61	Variable	Client Identifier: Used optionally by a client to specify a unique client identification for itself that differs from the DHCP default. This identifier is expected by servers to be unique among all DHCP clients and is used to index the DHCP server's configuration parameter database.
66	Variable	TFTP Server Name: When the DHCP message's SName field has been used for options using the option overload feature, this option may be included to specify the Trivial File Transfer Protocol (TFTP) server name that would normally appear in the SName field.
67	Variable	Bootfile Name: When the DHCP message's File field has been used for options using the option overload feature, this option may be included to specify the boot filename that would normally appear in the File field.

Table 63-13: DHCP Message Type (Option 53) Values

Option 53 Value	DHCP Message Type
1	DHCPDISCOVER
2	DHCPOFFER
3	DHCPREQUEST
4	DHCPDECLINE
5	DHCPACK
6	DHCPNAK
7	DHCPRELEASE
8	DHCPINFORM

64

DHCP CLIENT/SERVER IMPLEMENTATION, FEATURES, AND IPV6 SUPPORT

The preceding chapters in this part describe the fundamentals of the operation of DHCP: the address leasing system, configuration processes, and messaging. With this foundation in place, we can now proceed to look into some of the more interesting details of how DHCP is implemented. We can also delve into some of the extra capabilities and special features that change the basic DHCP mechanisms we have already studied.

In this chapter, I discuss DHCP client/server implementation issues, special features that enhance the protocol, and some of the problems and issues related to making DHCP work. I begin with a discussion of DHCP server and client implementation and management issues. I discuss DHCP message relaying and how it is related to the relaying feature used for the Boot Protocol (BOOTP). I describe the DHCP feature for providing automatic default addressing when a client cannot contact a server, and the conflict detection feature for multiple servers. I then cover some of the issues related to interoperability of DHCP and BOOTP, and provide an outline of some of the more important problems and issues related to DHCP security. I conclude with an overview of DHCP for IP version 6 (DHCPv6).

DHCP Server and Client Implementation and Management Issues

DHCP is a client/server protocol, relying on both the server and client to fulfill certain responsibilities. Of the two device roles, the DHCP server is arguably the more important, because it is in the server that most of the functionality of DHCP is actually implemented.

DHCP Server Implementations

The server maintains the configuration database, keeps track of address ranges, and manages leases. For this reason, DHCP servers are typically much more complex than DHCP clients. In essence, without a DHCP server, there really is no DHCP. Thus, deciding how to implement DHCP servers is a large part of implementing the protocol.

A classic DHCP server consists of DHCP server software running on a server hardware platform of one sort or another. A DHCP server usually will not be a dedicated computer, except on very large networks. It is more common for a hardware server to provide DHCP services along with performing other functions, such as acting as an application server, serving as a general database server, providing DNS services, and so forth. So, a DHCP server does not need to be a special computer; any device that can run a DHCP server implementation can act as a server.

In fact, the DHCP server may not even need to be a host computer at all. Today, many routers include DHCP functionality. Programming a router to act as a DHCP server allows clients that connect to the router to be automatically assigned IP addresses. This provides numerous potential advantages in an environment where a limited number of public IP addresses is shared among multiple clients, or where IP Network Address Translation (NAT; see Chapter 28) is used to dynamically share a small number of addresses. Since DHCP requires a database, a router that acts as a DHCP server requires some form of permanent storage. This is often implemented using flash memory on routers; "true" servers use hard disk storage.

Virtually all modern operating systems include support for DHCP, including most variants of UNIX, Linux, newer versions of Microsoft Windows, Novell NetWare, and others. In some cases, you may need to run the server version of the operating system to have a host act as a DHCP server. For example, while Microsoft Windows XP supports DHCP, I don't believe that a DHCP server comes in the Windows XP Home Edition, though you could install one yourself.

DHCP Server Software Features

In most networks, you will choose the operating system based on a large number of factors. The choice of operating system will then dictate what options you have for selecting DHCP server software. Most common operating systems have a number of options available for software. While all will implement the core DHCP protocol, they will differ in terms of the usual software attributes: cost, performance, ease of use, and so on. They may also differ in terms of their features, such as the following:

- How they allow address ranges (scopes) to be defined
- How clients can be grouped and managed
- The level of control an administrator has over parameters returned to a client
- The level of control an administrator has over general operation of the protocol, such as specification of the T1 and T2 timers and other variables, and how leases are allocated and renewals handled
- Security features
- Ability to interact with DNS to support dynamic device naming
- Optional features such as BOOTP support, conflict detection, and Automatic Private IP Addressing (all discussed later in this chapter)

Choosing the Number of Servers

In setting up DHCP for a network, there are a number of important factors to consider and decisions to be made. One of the most critical is the number of servers you want to have. In theory, each network requires only one DHCP server; in practice, this is often not a great idea. Servers sometimes experience hardware or software failures, or they must be taken down for maintenance. If there is only one server and clients can't reach it, no DHCP clients will be able to get addresses. For this reason, two or more servers are often used.

If you do use more than one server, you need to carefully plan how you will configure each one. One of the first decisions you will need to make is which servers will be responsible for which addresses and clients. You need to determine whether you want the servers to have distinct or overlapping address pools, as discussed in the explanation of DHCP address ranges in Chapter 61. Distinct pools ensure that addresses remain unique, but result in unallocatable addresses if a server fails. Overlapping addresses are more flexible, but risk address conflicts unless a feature like conflict detection (described later in this chapter) is used.

Server Placement, Setup, and Maintenance

Once you know how many servers you want, you need to determine on which part of the network you want to place them. If you have many physical networks, you may also need to use DHCP relaying to allow all clients to reach a server. Since the structure of the network may affect the number of servers you use, many of these decisions are interrelated.

You must make policy decisions related to all the DHCP operating parameters discussed in the previous chapters. The two big decisions are the size and structure of the address pool, and making lease policy decisions such as the lease length and the settings for the T1 and T2 timers. You also must decide which clients will be dynamically allocated addresses and how manually configured clients will be handled.

Finally, it's essential for the administrator to remember that an organization's DHCP server is a database server and must be treated accordingly. Like any database server, it must be maintained and managed carefully. Administrative policies must be put into place to ensure the security and efficient operation of the server. Also, unlike certain other types of database systems, the DHCP database is not automatically replicated; the server database should therefore be routinely backed up, and using RAID storage is also a good idea.

DHCP Client Implementations

Just as a DHCP server consists of server software running on a server platform or hardware acting as a server, a DHCP client is simply DHCP client software running on a client device. Most often, a client device is a host computer connected to a TCP/IP internetwork. DHCP is so widely accepted today that virtually all hosts include DHCP client software. The DHCP client is usually integrated into graphical operating systems like Windows, or is implemented using a specific client daemon like *dhclient* or *dhcpd* on UNIX/Linux.

Since the entire idea behind DHCP is to put the server in charge of parameter storage, configuration, and address management, DHCP clients are relatively simple. The client implements the messaging protocol and communicates parameters received from the DHCP server to the rest of the TCP/IP software components as needed. It doesn't do a whole lot else.

In fact, there's not really much for an administrator to do to set up a client to use DHCP. In some operating systems, it's as simple as "throwing a switch," by enabling DHCP support within the client itself. This prompts the client to then stop using any manually configured parameters and start searching for a DHCP server instead. The server then becomes responsible for the client's configuration and address assignment.

Since the client doesn't do a great deal in DHCP other than communicate with the server, not much is required in the way of user software for a DHCP client. In most cases, control over the DHCP client software is accomplished using a TCP/IP configuration utility, as described in Chapter 88. Windows clients use the programs *ipconfig* or *winipcfg* to display the status of their current DHCP leases. These programs also allow the client to manually release the current lease or renew it.

Releasing the lease means early lease termination using the DHCPRELEASE message. This is usually the only way that a lease is terminated. Renewing the lease is a manual version of the automated renewal process. Releasing and renewing the lease may be done in sequence to reset a client that is in a confused state or is having some other type of DHCP or connectivity problem.

DHCP Message Relaying and BOOTP Relay Agents

DHCP is the third-generation host configuration protocol for TCP/IP. We've already discussed extensively how it was based directly on BOOTP, which was, in turn, an enhancement of the earlier Reverse Address Resolution Protocol (RARP). Even though each new protocol has made significant improvements over its predecessor, each iteration has retained certain limitations that are actually common to all host configuration protocols.

One of the most important limitations with host configuration protocols is the reliance on broadcasts for communication. Whenever we are dealing with a situation where a client needs to communicate but doesn't know its IP address and doesn't know the address of a server that will provide it, the client needs to use broadcast addressing. However, for performance reasons, broadcasts are normally propagated only on the local network. This means that the client and server would always need to be on the same physical network for host configuration to occur. Of course, we don't want this to be the case. It would require that a large internetwork have a different server on every network, greatly reducing the benefits of centralized configuration information and creating numerous administrative hassles.

RARP didn't have any solution to this problem, which is one reason why it was so limited in usefulness. BOOTP's solution is to allow a client and server to be on different networks through the use of BOOTP *relay agents.*

BOOTP Relay Agents for DHCP

A *relay agent* is a device that is not a BOOTP server, but which runs a special software module that allows it to act in the place of a server. A relay agent can be placed on networks where there are BOOTP clients but no BOOTP servers. The relay agent intercepts requests from clients and relays them to the server. The server then responds back to the agent, which forwards the response to the client. A full rationale and description of operation of BOOTP relay agents can be found in Chapter 60.

The designers of DHCP were satisfied with the basic concepts and operation behind BOOTP relay agents, which had already been in use for many years. For this reason, they made the specific decision to continue using BOOTP relay agent functionality in DHCP. In fact, this is one of the reasons why the decision was made to retain the BOOTP message format in DHCP, and also the basic two-message request/reply communication protocol. This allows BOOTP relay agents to handle DHCP messages as if they were BOOTP messages. This is also why the mention of BOOTP in the title of this topic is not a typo—DHCP uses BOOTP relay agents. Even the DHCP standard says that a "BOOTP relay agent is an Internet host or router that passes DHCP messages between DHCP clients and DHCP servers."

In practice, the agents are indeed sometimes called *DHCP relay agents.* You may also see the terms *BOOTP/DHCP relay agent* and *DHCP/BOOTP relay agent.*

DHCP Relaying Process

Since DHCP was designed specifically to support BOOTP relay agents, the agents behave in DHCP much as they do in BOOTP. Although DHCP has much more complex message exchanges, they are all still designed around the notion of a client request and server response. There are just more requests and responses.

The BOOTP agent looks for broadcasts sent by the client and then forwards them to the server (as described in the BOOTP relay agent behavior discussion in Chapter 60), and then returns replies from the server. The additional information in the DHCP protocol is implemented using additions to the BOOTP message format in the form of DHCP options, which the relay agent doesn't look at. It just treats them as it does BOOTP requests and replies.

KEY CONCEPT To permit DHCP clients and DHCP servers to reside on different physical networks, an intermediary device is required to facilitate message exchange between networks. DHCP uses the same mechanism for this as BOOTP: the deployment of *BOOTP relay agents*. The relay agent captures client requests, forwards them to the server, and then returns the server's responses back to the client.

In summary, when a relay agent is used, here's what the various client requests and server replies in the DHCP operation section become:

Client Request When a client broadcasts a request, the relay agent intercepts it on UDP port 67. It checks the Hops field and discards the request if the value is greater than 16; otherwise, it increments the field. The agent puts its own address into the GIAddr field unless another relay agent has already put its address in the field. It then forwards the client request to a DHCP server, either unicast or broadcast on another network.

Server Reply The server sees a nonzero value in the GIAddr field and sends the reply to the relay agent whose IP address is in that field. The relay agent then sends the reply back to the client, using either unicast or broadcast (as explained in the discussion of DHCP addressing in Chapter 61).

One difference between BOOTP and DHCP is that certain communications from the client to the server are unicast. The most noticeable instance of this is when a client tries to renew its lease with a specific DHCP server. Since it sends this request unicast, it can go to a DHCP server on a different network using conventional IP routing, and the relay agent does not need to be involved.

DHCP Autoconfiguration/Automatic Private IP Addressing (APIPA)

The IP address of a TCP/IP host is, in many ways, its identity. Every TCP/IP network requires that all hosts have unique addresses to facilitate communication. When a network is manually configured with a distinct IP address for each host, the hosts permanently know who they are. When hosts are made DHCP clients, they no longer have a permanent identity; they rely on a DHCP server to tell them who they are.

This dependency is not a problem as long as DHCP is functioning normally and a host can get a lease, and, in fact, has many benefits that we have explored. Unfortunately, a number of circumstances can arise that result in a client failing to get a lease. The client may not be able to obtain a lease, reacquire one after reboot, or renew an existing lease. There are several possible reasons why this might happen:

- The DHCP server may have experienced a failure or may be taken down for maintenance.
- The relay agent on the client's local network may have failed.

- Another hardware malfunction or power failure may make communication impossible.
- The network may have run out of allocatable addresses.

Without a lease, the host has no IP address, and without an address, the host is effectively dead in the water. The base DHCP specification doesn't really specify any recourse for the host in the event that it cannot successfully obtain a lease. It is left up to the implementor to decide what to do, and when DHCP was first created, many host implementations would simply display an error message and leave the host unusable until an administrator or user took action.

Clearly, this is far from an ideal situation. It would be better if we could just have a DHCP client that is unable to reach a server automatically configure itself. In fact, the Internet Engineering Task Force (IETF) reserved a special IP address block for this purpose (see Chapter 17). This block, 169.254.0.1 through 169.254.255.254 (or 169.254.0.0/16 in classless notation) is reserved for autoconfiguration, as mentioned in RFC 3330, "Hosts obtain these addresses by auto-configuration, such as when a DHCP server may not be found."

Strangely, however, no TCP/IP standard was defined to specify how such autoconfiguration works. To fill the void, Microsoft created an implementation that it calls *Automatic Private IP Addressing (APIPA)*. Due to Microsoft's market power, APIPA has been deployed on millions of machines, and has thus become a de facto standard in the industry. Many years later, the IETF did define a formal standard for this functionality, in RFC 3927, "Dynamic Configuration of IPv4 Link-Local Addresses."

APIPA Operation

APIPA is really so simple that it's surprising it took so long for someone to come up with the idea. It takes over at the point where any DHCP lease process fails. Instead of just halting with an error message, APIPA randomly chooses an address within the aforementioned private addressing block. It then performs a test very similar to the one in step 13 in the DHCP allocation process (see Chapter 62): It uses ARP to generate a request on the local network to see if any other client responds using the address it has chosen. If there is a reply, APIPA tries another random address and repeats the test. When the APIPA software finds an address that is not in use, it is given to the client as a default address. The client will then use default values for other configuration parameters that it would normally receive from the DHCP server. This process is illustrated in Figure 64-1.

A client using an autoconfigured address will continue to try to contact a DHCP server periodically. By default, this check is performed every five minutes. If and when it finds one, it will obtain a lease and replace the autoconfigured address with the proper leased address.

APIPA is ideally suited to small networks, where all devices are on a single physical link. Conceivably, with 20 APIPA-enabled DHCP clients on a network with a single DHCP server, you could take the server down for maintenance and still have all the clients work properly, using 169.254.*x.x* addresses.

Bear in mind, however, that APIPA is not a proper replacement for full DHCP.

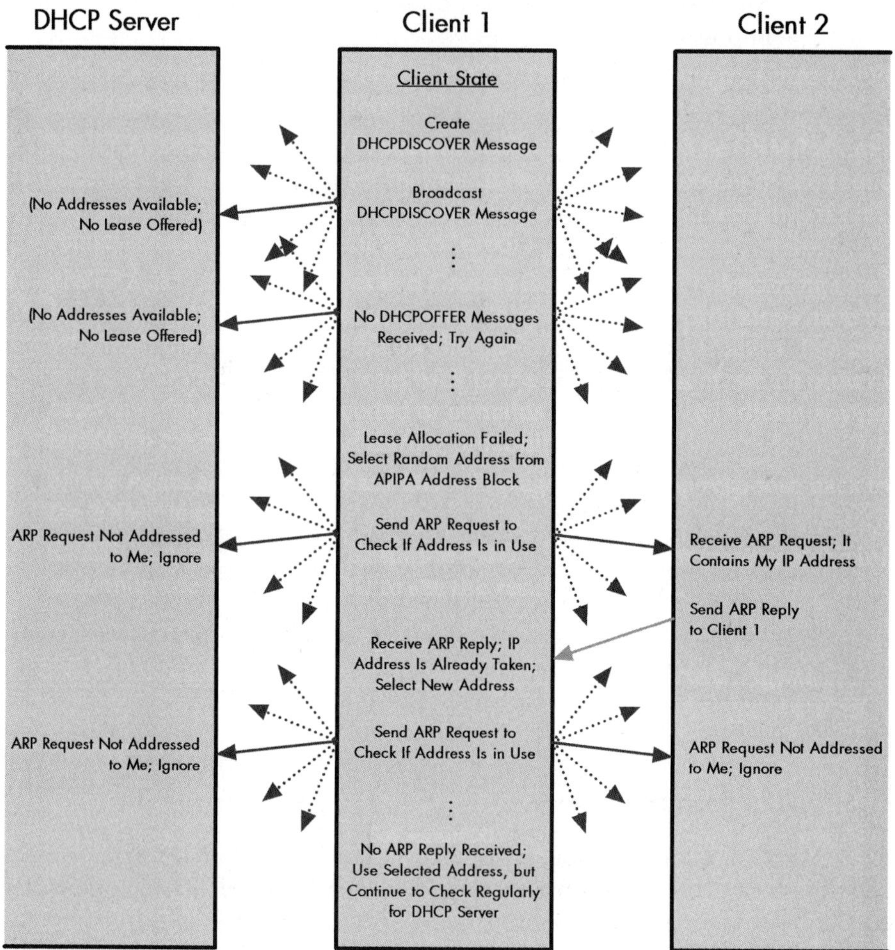

Figure 64-1: DHCP Automatic Private IP Addressing (APIPA) *In this example, Client 1 is trying to get an IP address from its DHCP server, but the server is out of addresses, so it does not respond to the client's requests. The client is configured to use APIPA, so it randomly selects an address from the APIPA address block. It sends an ARP request on the local network to see if any other device is using that address. Usually, there will be no conflict, but here Client 2 is using the address, so it responds. Client 1 chooses a different address, and this time gets no reply. It begins using that address, while continuing to check regularly for a DHCP server to come online.*

APIPA Limitations

The 169.254.0.0/16 block is a private IP range and comes with all the limitations of private IP addresses, including inability to use these addresses on the Internet. Also, APIPA cannot provide the other configuration parameters that a client may need to get from a DHCP server. Finally, APIPA will not work properly in conjunction with proxy ARP, because the proxy will respond for any of the private addresses, so they will all appear to be used.

Since it uses ARP to check for address conflicts, APIPA is not well suited for large internetworks. To use it on an internetwork with multiple subnets would require software that allows each subnet to use a different portion of the full 169.254.0.0/16 blocks, to avoid conflicts.

In practice, APIPA is a solution for small networks. Large internetworks deal with the problem of not being able to contact a DHCP server by taking steps to ensure that a client can always contact a DHCP server.

> **KEY CONCEPT** An optional DHCP feature called *Automatic Private IP Addressing (APIPA)* was developed to allow clients to still be able to communicate in the event that they are unable to obtain an IP address from a DHCP server. When enabled, the client chooses a random address from a special reserved block of private IP addresses and checks to make sure the address is not already in use by another device. It continues to check for a DHCP server periodically until it is able to find one.

DHCP Server Conflict Detection

One of the primary decisions any TCP/IP administrator using DHCP must make is how many DHCP servers to deploy. A single server has the advantage of simplicity, but provides no redundancy in the event of failure. It also means that whenever the DHCP server is down, clients can't get addresses. For these reasons, most larger networks use two or more servers.

When you have two servers or more—let's say two for sake of this discussion—you then have another decision to make: How do you divide the address pool between the servers? As I explored in detail in the discussion of DHCP address pools in Chapter 61, there are two options: give the servers overlapping addresses or making them non-overlapping. Unfortunately, in classic DHCP, neither is really a great solution. Overlapping ranges mean both servers might try to assign the same address, since DHCP includes no provision for communication between servers. Non-overlapping ranges avoid this problem, but make only some of the addresses available to each server.

It's strange that the DHCP standard didn't provide better support for cross-server coordination, even though there clearly was a need for it. However, certain DHCP implementations include an optional feature to allow two servers to have overlapping scopes without address clashes occurring. This is a feature commonly found on Microsoft DHCP servers and may also be present in other implementations. It is called *DHCP server conflict detection.*

The idea behind conflict detection is very simple. Suppose a DHCP server receives a DHCPDISCOVER message from a client and decides to offer it a lease. Before sending the DHCPOFFER message, the server conducts a *probe* by sending ICMP Echo (ping) messages (see Chapter 33) out to the address it plans to offer. It then waits a short period of time to hear if it receives any ICMP Echo Reply messages back. If it does, it knows the IP address is in use and chooses a different one.

If all DHCP servers are configured to do this before offering an address, then it is possible to give all of them the same, overlapping addresses for assignment. They won't have any way of coordinating with each other, but as long as they ask first by doing an ICMP check, there won't be any problems. This provides an administrator with the advantages of overlapping address ranges—simplicity and access to all addresses by all servers—without risk of address conflicts. The only small drawback is a little extra network traffic to perform the check, and possibly a few milliseconds of server CPU time if a new address needs to be chosen.

If you were paying attention when you read about the DHCP allocation process in Chapter 62, you may have noticed that what I am describing here sounds familiar. In fact, it's true that this feature isn't anything new. The use of ICMP to check an address before offering it is actually mentioned in RFC 2131 as part of the standard DHCP allocation process, and you can find it mentioned as step 5 in the allocation process description.

So why was conflict detection required to be an extra feature? The reason is that the use of ICMP wasn't mandatory because the standard says servers *should* do it, not that they *must* do it. This choice was made to provide flexibility in implementing DHCP, but that flexibility comes at a cost. So, if you want to use this feature, you need to look for support for it in your server software.

> **KEY CONCEPT** Some DHCP implementations include a feature called *server conflict detection.* When this feature is activated, it causes each server to always check to make sure an address is not in use before granting it to a client. When conflict detection is used by all DHCP servers on a network, the servers can be given overlapping scopes, so each can assign any of the organization's IP addresses, while at the same time not needing to be concerned about two clients being assigned the same address by different servers.

DHCP and BOOTP Interoperability

I've talked extensively about how DHCP was designed based on BOOTP and how they use the same basic communication method and message format. This was done for several reasons, one of the most important of which was ensuring interoperability of the two protocols. Given this, you might expect that we could simply say that BOOTP and DHCP are compatible with each other, and that's that.

It is true that DHCP was intended to be compatible with BOOTP. RFC 2131 lists the following as one of DHCP's design goals: "DHCP must provide service to existing BOOTP clients." This seems pretty clear. The reuse of the BOOTP message format is one of the keys to DHCP and BOOTP compatibility. DHCP functionality is implemented not through new fields, but rather through DHCP-specific options, such as the DHCP Message Type option that specifies the all-important type of DHCP messages. DHCP devices can look for this extra information, while BOOTP devices can ignore it.

However, while DHCP and BOOTP are similar, they are not the same, and so there are some interoperability concerns that crop up when they are used together. The DHCP message format is structurally the same as the BOOTP format, but the interpretation of certain fields is slightly different. BOOTP clients don't understand DHCP, so when BOOTP and DHCP are used together, the DHCP client or server must sometimes behave slightly differently to compensate. Further complicating matters are the facts that not all implementations of DHCP and BOOTP are necessarily exactly the same and that certain specifications in the DHCP standard are not mandatory.

For these reasons, we cannot just assume that DHCP and BOOTP will work together. To address some of these issues, the IETF published RFC 1534, "Interoperation Between DHCP and BOOTP," at the same time that DHCP was originally created. This document looks at how the protocols work together, focusing on the two distinct client/server interoperating combinations: a BOOTP client connecting to a DHCP server, and a DHCP client connecting to a BOOTP server. Let's consider each case.

BOOTP Clients Connecting to a DHCP Server

As indicated by the preceding quote from RFC 2131, DHCP was specifically intended to allow a DHCP server to handle requests from BOOTP clients. The protocol itself is set up to enable this, but it does require that the DHCP server be given certain intelligence to know how to deal with BOOTP clients.

One of the most important issues is that BOOTP clients will follow the BOOTP configuration process and not the DHCP leasing processes. The DHCP server must use BOOTP messages with the BOOTP meanings for fields when dealing with BOOTP clients. A server determines that a client is using BOOTP instead of DHCP by looking for the presence of the DHCP Message Type option, which must be present in all DHCP messages but is not used for BOOTP.

If a DHCP server detects that it is dealing with a BOOTP client, it can respond with configuration information for the client. The server can use either manual or automatic allocation for the client. Automatic allocation means the server chooses an address from its pool of unused addresses, but assigns it permanently. BOOTP clients are not capable of dynamic allocation, since BOOTP is static in nature.

A DHCP server may include BOOTP vendor information fields in its response to a BOOTP client, including ones defined since BOOTP was created. However, it obviously must not send any DHCP-specific options.

DHCP Clients Connecting to a BOOTP Server

A DHCP client can obtain configuration information from a BOOTP server, because the server will respond to the client's initial DHCPDISCOVER message as if it were a BOOTP BOOTREQUEST message. The DHCP client can tell that a BOOTP reply has been received because there will be no DHCP Message Type option.

A response from a BOOTP server should be treated as an infinite lease, since again, that's all that BOOTP supports. Note that if a DHCP client receives a response from both a BOOTP server and a DHCP server, it should use the DHCP response and not the BOOTP response (even if this means it gets a shorter lease).

DHCP Security Issues

DHCP was designed in the early 1990s, when the number of organizations on the Internet was relatively small. Furthermore, it was based on BOOTP, which was created in the 1980s, when the Internet as we know it today barely even existed. In those days, Internet security wasn't a big issue, because it was mostly a small group of research and educational organizations using TCP/IP on the Internet. As a result, DHCP, like many protocols of that era, doesn't do much to address security concerns.

Actually, this is a bit understated. Not only does DHCP run over the Internet Protocol (IP) and the User Datagram Protocol (UDP), which are inherently insecure, but the DHCP protocol itself has no security provisions whatsoever. This is a fairly serious issue in modern networks, because of the sheer power of DHCP, which deals with critical configuration information.

DHCP Security Concerns

There are two different classes of potential security problems related to DHCP:

Unauthorized DHCP Servers If a malicious person plants a rogue DHCP server, it is possible that this device could respond to client requests and supply them with spurious configuration information. This could be used to make clients unusable on the network, or worse, set them up for further abuse later on. For example, a hacker could exploit a bogus DHCP server to direct a DHCP client to use a router under the hacker's control, rather than the one the client is supposed to use.

Unauthorized DHCP Clients A client could be set up that masquerades as a legitimate DHCP client and thereby obtain configuration information intended for that client. This information could then be used to compromise the network later on. Alternatively, a malicious person could use software to generate a lot of bogus DHCP client requests to use up all the IP addresses in a DHCP server's pool. More simply, this could be used by a thief to steal an IP address from an organization for his own use.

These are obviously serious concerns. The normal recommended solutions to these risks generally involve providing security at lower layers. For example, one of the most important techniques for preventing unauthorized servers and clients is careful control over physical access to the network: layer 1 security. Security techniques implemented at layer 2 may also be of use—for example, in the case of wireless LANs. Since DHCP runs over UDP and IP, one could use IPSec at layer 3 to provide authentication.

DHCP Authentication

To try to address some of the more specific security concerns within DHCP itself, in June 2001, the IETF published RFC 3118, "Authentication for DHCP Messages." This standard describes an enhancement that replaces the normal DHCP messages with authenticated ones. Clients and servers check the authentication information and reject messages that come from invalid sources. The technology involves the use of a new DHCP option type, the Authentication option, and operating changes to several of the leasing processes to use this option.

Unfortunately, 2001 was pretty late in the DHCP game, and there are millions of DHCP clients and servers around that don't support this new standard. Both the client and server must be programmed to use authentication for this method to have value. A DHCP server that supports authentication could use it for clients that support the feature and skip it for those that do not. However, the fact that this option is not universal means that it is not widely deployed, and most networks must rely on more conventional security measures.

DHCP for IP Version 6 (DHCPv6)

DHCP is currently the standard host configuration protocol for the TCP/IP protocol suite. TCP/IP is built on version 4 of IP (IPv4). However, development work has been under way since the early 1990s on a successor to IPv4: version 6 of the Internet Protocol (IPv6; see Part II-4 for more information). This new IP standard will be the future of TCP/IP.

While most of the changes that IPv6 brings impact technologies at the lower layers of the TCP/IP architectural model, the significance of the modifications means that many other TCP/IP protocols are also affected. This is particularly true of protocols that work with addresses or configuration information, including DHCP. For this reason, a new version of DHCP is required for IPv6. Development has been under way for quite some time on *DHCP for IPv6*, also sometimes called *DHCPv6*. At the time of writing, DHCPv6 has not yet been formally published—it is still an Internet draft under discussion.

NOTE *In discussions purely oriented around IPv6, DHCPv6 is sometimes just called* DHCP, *and the original DHCP is called* DHCPv4.

Two Methods for Autoconfiguration in IPv6

One of the many enhancements introduced in IPv6 is an overall strategy for easier administration of IP devices, including host configuration. There are two basic methods defined for autoconfiguration of IPv6 hosts:

Stateless Autoconfiguration A method defined to allow a host to configure itself without help from any other device.

Stateful Autoconfiguration A technique where configuration information is provided to a host by a server.

Which of these methods is used depends on the characteristics of the network. Stateless autoconfiguration is described in RFC 2462 and discussed in Chapter 24. Stateful autoconfiguration for IPv6 is provided by DHCPv6. As with regular DHCP, DHCPv6 may be used to obtain an IP address and other configuration parameters, or just to get configuration parameters when the client already has an IP address.

DHCPv6 Operation Overview

The operation of DHCPv6 is similar to that of DHCPv4, but the protocol itself has been completely rewritten. It is not based on the older DHCP or on BOOTP, except in conceptual terms. It still uses UDP, but it uses new port numbers, a new message format, and restructured options. All of this means that the new protocol is not strictly compatible with DHCPv4 or BOOTP, though I believe work is under way on a method to allow DHCPv6 servers to work with IPv4 devices.

> **KEY CONCEPT** Since DHCP works with IP addresses and other configuration parameters, the change from IPv4 to IPv6 requires a new version of DHCP commonly called *DHCPv6*. This new DHCP represents a significant change from the original DHCP and is still under development. DHCPv6 is used for IPv6 *stateful autoconfiguration*. The alternative is *stateless autoconfiguration*, a feature of IPv6 that allows a client to determine its IP address without need for a server.

DHCPv6 is also oriented around IPv6 methods of addressing, especially the use of link-local scoped multicast addresses (see Chapter 25). This allows efficient communication even before a client has been assigned an IP address. Once a client has an address and knows the identity of a server, it may communicate with the server directly using unicast addressing.

DHCPv6 Message Exchanges

There are two basic client/server message exchanges that are used in DHCPv6: the *four-message exchange* and the *two-message exchange*. The former is used when a client needs to obtain an IPv6 address and other parameters. This process is similar to the regular DHCP address allocation process. Highly simplified, it involves these steps:

1. The client sends a multicast Solicit message to find a DHCPv6 server and ask for a lease.
2. Any server that can fulfill the client's request responds to it with an Advertise message.
3. The client chooses one of the servers and sends a Request message to it, asking to confirm the offered address and other parameters.
4. The server responds with a Reply message to finalize the process.

There is also a shorter variation of the four-message process above, where a client sends a Solicit message and indicates that a server should respond back immediately with a Reply message.

If the client already has an IP address, either assigned manually or obtained in some other way, a simpler process can be undertaken, similar to how in regular DHCP the DHCPINFORM message is used:

1. The client multicasts an Information-Request message.
2. A server with configuration information for the client sends back a Reply message.
3. As in regular DHCP, a DHCPv6 client renews its lease after a period of time by sending a Renew message. DHCPv6 also supports relay agent functionality, as in DHCPv4.

PART III-4

TCP/IP NETWORK MANAGEMENT FRAMEWORK AND PROTOCOLS

Modern networks and internetworks are larger, faster, and more capable than their predecessors of years gone by. As we expand, speed up, and enhance our networks, they become more complex, and as a result, more difficult to manage. Years ago, an administrator could get by with very simple tools to keep a network running, but today, more sophisticated network management technologies are required to match the sophistication of our networks.

Some of the most important tools in the network manager's toolbox are now in the form of software, not hardware. To manage a sprawling, heterogeneous, and complex internetwork, we can employ software applications to gather information and control devices using the internetwork itself. TCP/IP, being the most popular internetworking suite, has such software tools. One of the most important is a pair of protocols that have been implemented as part of an overall method of network management called the *TCP/IP Internet Standard Management Framework*.

This part describes the TCP/IP Internet Standard Management Framework, looking at each of its architectural and protocol components and how they interoperate. The first chapter provides an overview of the network management framework itself and serves as an introduction to the chapters that follow. The second chapter discusses the way that network management information is structured and arranged into information stores called *management information bases (MIBs)*. The third chapter describes the concepts behind and operation of the key protocol in TCP/IP network management: the Simple Network Management Protocol (SNMP). The fourth chapter provides details on SNMP's messaging and message formats. Finally, the fifth chapter takes a brief look at Remote Network Monitoring (RMON), an enhancement of SNMP—sometimes called a protocol, even though it really isn't—that provides administrators with greater management and monitoring abilities on a TCP/IP internetwork.

Note that while you may be tempted to jump straight to the chapter on SNMP, what is written there will make a lot more sense if you read the chapters of this part in order.

65

TCP/IP INTERNET STANDARD MANAGEMENT FRAMEWORK OVERVIEW

TCP/IP network management functions are most commonly associated with the key protocol responsible for implementing those functions: the *Simple Network Management Protocol (SNMP)*. Many people have heard of SNMP, and it is common for SNMP to be considered "the" way that network management is performed in TCP/IP. This is true to an extent, but is really an oversimplification. The actual SNMP protocol is only one part of a higher-level network management strategy called the *Internet Standard Management Framework*. In order to really understand how SNMP works, you need to first have some background on the way this network management is structured as a whole.

In this chapter, I provide an introduction to TCP/IP network management by describing the concepts and components of the TCP/IP Internet Standard Management Framework. I begin with an overview and history of the framework, and discuss how it is related to SNMP. I describe the TCP/IP network management model and the key components that compose a network management system. I provide a summary of the architecture of the

Internet Standard Management Framework. I then describe the three main versions of the Framework and SNMP and how they compare. I conclude with a discussion of the many standards used to describe this technology.

Overview and History of the TCP/IP Internet Standard Management Framework and Simple Network Management Protocol (SNMP)

An adage from the world of professional sports says that a baseball umpire is doing a good job when you forget that he is there. In many ways, the same could be said of a network administrator. The administrator is doing a good job when the network is running so smoothly and efficiently that users forget that the administrator exists. Because, as the administrator knows all too well, the second there is a problem, the users will all remember very quickly that he or she is there.

A primary job of a network administrator is to keep tabs on the network and ensure that it is operating normally. Information about the hardware and software on the network is a key to performing this task properly.

When networks were small, an administrator could stay informed about the status of hardware and software using simple means, such as physically walking over to a computer and using it, or using a low-level link layer management protocol. This is simply not possible with modern internetworks, which are large, geographically diverse, and often consist of many different lower-layer technologies. Usually, the only thing all the devices on the network have in common is an implementation of a particular internetworking protocol suite, such as TCP/IP. This makes the internetwork itself a logical way to facilitate the communication of network management information between devices and a network administrator.

Early Development of SNMP

Many people recognized during the early days of the Internet that some sort of network management technology would be needed for TCP/IP. Unfortunately, at first there was no single standard. In the 1980s, several different technologies were developed by different working groups. There were three main contestants: the *High-level Entity Management System (HEMS)/High-level Entity Management Protocol (HEMP)* as defined by RFCs 1021 through 1024; the *Simple Gateway Monitoring Protocol (SGMP)*, defined by RFC 1028; and the *Common Management Information Protocol (CMIP)*, which is actually part of the OSI protocol suite.

The Internet Engineering Task Force (IETF) recognized the importance of having a unifying management standard for TCP/IP, and in 1988, published RFC 1052, "IAB Recommendations for the Development of Internet Network Management Standards." This memo is not a standard, but more a statement of intention and documentation of a meeting held on this subject. The conclusion of RFC 1052 was that SGMP be used as the basis of a new Internet standard to be called the *Simple Network Management Protocol (SNMP)*. This development was to be carried out by the SNMP Working Group.

The Two Meanings of SNMP

The rationale of the middle two words in the name Simple Network Management Protocol is obvious, but the other two words are slightly more problematic. The word *Protocol* implies that SNMP is just a TCP/IP communication protocol, like other protocols, such as the Dynamic Host Configuration Protocol (DHCP) and the File Transfer Protocol (FTP). Unfortunately, this is both true and untrue: the name is ambiguous.

At a lower level, SNMP does indeed refer specifically to the actual protocol that carries network management information between devices. This is what most people think of when they talk about SNMP. However, as defined by the SNMP working group, the TCP/IP network management solution as a whole consists of a number of different elements arranged in an architecture. This architecture originally had no specific name, but is now called the *Internet Standard Management Framework*. Oddly, this higher-level framework is not abbreviated ISMF, but is *also* called SNMP, which means that context is important in understanding that term.

NOTE *To avoid confusion, I will often use the phrases SNMP Framework and SNMP protocol to differentiate these two uses of the term SNMP.*

Design Goals of SNMP

The word *Simple* in the protocol's name is another problem. Even in its first iteration, it was only somewhat simple. The most current version of SNMP is fairly complicated indeed, with many different standards defining the SNMP Framework, the SNMP protocol itself, and a number of supporting elements.

So why is it called *Simple?* Well, as they say, everything is relative. SNMP is simple when compared to other protocols that are even more complex. Some of this can be seen by looking at the basic goals of the Internet Standard Management Framework and the SNMP protocol as a whole:

- SNMP defines a universal way that management information can be easily defined for any object, and then exchanged between that object and a device designed to facilitate network management.
- SNMP separates the functions of defining and communicating management information from the applications that are used for network management.
- The actual SNMP protocol is fairly simple, consisting of only a few easy-to-understand protocol operations.
- The implementation of SNMP is relatively simple for the designers and manufacturers of products.

KEY CONCEPT The *Simple Network Management Protocol (SNMP)* defines a set of technologies that allow network administrators to remotely monitor and manage TCP/IP network devices. The term SNMP refers both to a specific communication protocol (sometimes called the *SNMP protocol*) and an overall framework for Internet management (the *SNMP Framework*).

Since SNMP is a TCP/IP application layer protocol, it can theoretically run over a variety of transport mechanisms. It is most commonly implemented over the Internet Protocol (IP), but the most recent versions also define *transport mappings* that can allow SNMP information to be carried over other internetworking technologies.

Further Development of SNMP and the Problem of SNMP Variations

The first Internet Standard Management Framework developed (in 1988) is now called *SNMP version 1 (SNMPv1)*. This initial version of SNMP achieved widespread acceptance, and it is still probably the most common version of SNMP.

Much of the history of SNMP since that time has been a rather confusing standards nightmare. SNMPv1 had a number of weaknesses, particularly in the area of security. For this reason, shortly after SNMPv1 was done, work began on a new version of SNMP. Unfortunately, this effort became a quagmire, with many competing variations of SNMPv2 being created. After many years of confusion, none of the SNMPv2 variants achieved significant success.

Recently, a third version of the SNMP Framework and protocol has been published, which adds new features and reunites SNMP under a single, universal protocol again. The discussions of SNMP versions and SNMP standards later in this chapter further explore the history of SNMP since 1988. They can be considered a continuation of this historical overview, as they help clarify the very confusing story behind SNMP versions over the last decade and a half.

RELATED INFORMATION *More background on the SNMP protocol proper can be found in the overview of the actual protocol itself, in Chapter 67.*

TCP/IP SNMP Operational Model, Components, and Terminology

So, it seems the *Simple* Network Management Protocol isn't quite so simple after all. There are many versions and standards and uses of SNMP, and so a lot to learn. I think a good place to start in understanding what SNMP does is to look at its *model of operation.* Then we can examine the components that compose a TCP/IP network management system and define the terminology used to describe them.

SNMP Device Types

The overall idea behind SNMP is to allow the information needed for network management to be exchanged using TCP/IP. More specifically, the protocol allows a network administrator to make use of a special network device that interacts with other network devices to collect information from them and modify how they operate. In the simplest sense, two different basic types of hardware devices are defined:

Managed Nodes Regular nodes on a network that have been equipped with software to allow them to be managed using SNMP. These are, generally speaking, conventional TCP/IP devices. They are also sometimes called *managed devices.*

Network Management Station (NMS) A designated network device that runs special software to allow it to manage the regular managed nodes mentioned just above. One or more NMSs must be present on the network, as these devices are the ones that really run SNMP.

SNMP Entities

Each device that participates in network management using SNMP runs a piece of software, generically called an *SNMP entity*. The SNMP entity is responsible for implementing all of the various functions of the SNMP protocol. Each entity consists of two primary software components. Which components make up the SNMP entity on a device depends on whether the device is a managed node or an NMS.

Managed Node Entities

The SNMP entity on a managed node consists of the following software elements and constructs:

SNMP Agent A software program that implements the SNMP protocol and allows a managed node to provide information to an NMS and accept instructions from it.

SNMP Management Information Base (MIB) An MIB defines the types of information stored about the node that can be collected and used to control the managed node. Information exchanged using SNMP takes the form of objects from the MIB.

Network Management Station Entities

The SNMP entity on an NMS consists of the following:

SNMP Manager A software program that implements the SNMP protocol, allowing the NMS to collect information from managed nodes and to send instructions to them.

SNMP Applications One or more software applications that allow a human network administrator to use SNMP to manage a network.

SNMP Operational Model Summary

So, to integrate and reiterate all of this, let's summarize. SNMP consists of a small number of *network management stations (NMSs)* that interact with regular TCP/IP devices that are called *managed nodes*. The *SNMP manager* on the NMS and the *SNMP agents* on the managed nodes implement the SNMP protocol and allow network management information to be exchanged. *SNMP applications* run on the NMS and provide the interface to the human administrator, and allow information to be collected from the *management information bases (MIBs)* at each SNMP agent. Figure 65-1 illustrates the SNMP operational model.

An SNMP managed node can be pretty much any network device that can communicate using TCP/IP, as long as it is programmed with the proper SNMP entity software. SNMP is designed to allow regular hosts to be managed, as well as intelligent network interconnection devices, such as routers, bridges, hubs, and switches. Other devices—printers, scanners, consumer electronic devices, specialized medical devices, and so on—can also be managed, as long as they connect to a TCP/IP internetwork.

On a larger network, an NMS may be a separate, high-powered TCP/IP computer dedicated to network management. However, it is really software that makes a device into an NMS, so the NMS may not be a separate hardware device. It may act as an NMS and also perform other functions on the network.

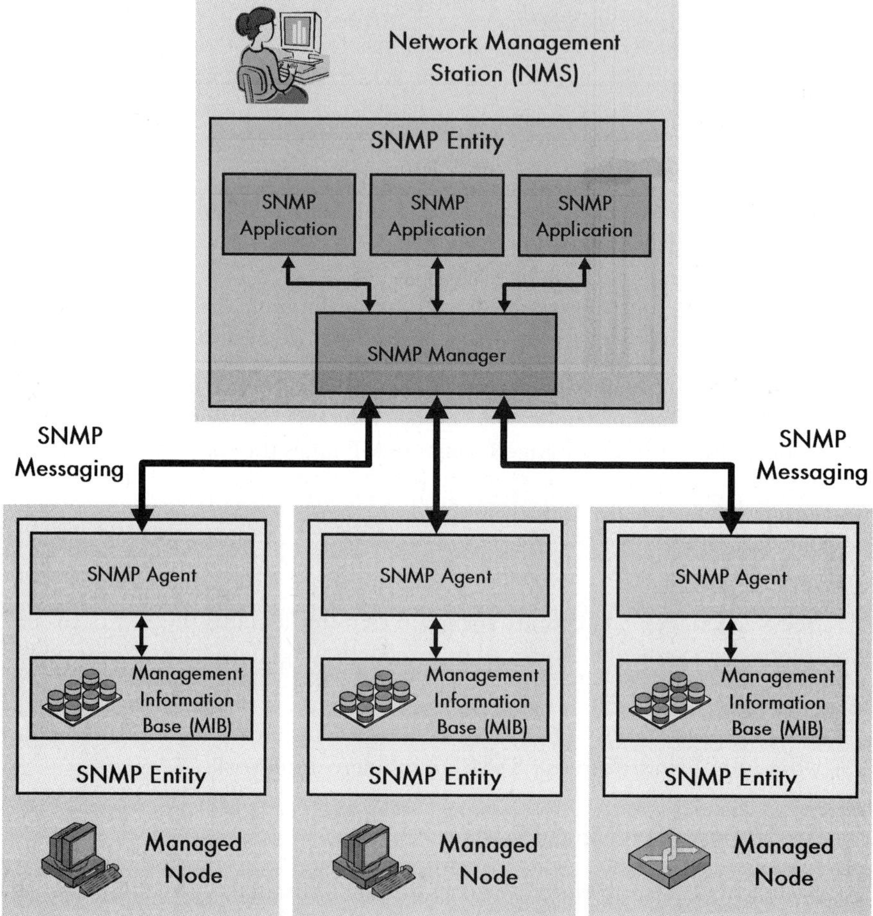

Figure 65-1: SNMP operational model *This diagram shows a simplified implementation of SNMP, with one network management station (NMS) used to maintain three managed nodes. Each device has an* SNMP entity, *and they communicate using SNMP messages. The SNMP entity of the NMS consists of the* SNMP manager *and one or more* SNMP applications. *The managed nodes each run an* SNMP agent *and maintain a* management information base (MIB).

KEY CONCEPT SNMP allows a network administrator using a *network management station (NMS)* to control a set of managed nodes. Each device incorporates an *SNMP entity* that implements the technology. In an NMS, the entity consists of an *SNMP manager* module and a set of SNMP applications. In a managed node, the entity consists of an SNMP agent and *management information base (MIB)*.

TCP/IP Internet Standard Management Framework Architecture and Protocol Components

The Internet Standard Management Framework encompasses all of the technologies that compose the TCP/IP network management solution. The SNMP Framework consists of a number of architectural components that define how management information is structured, how it is stored, and how it is exchanged using the SNMP protocol. The Framework also describes how the different components fit together, how SNMP is to be implemented in network devices, and how the devices interact.

SNMP Framework Components

As we will explore in more detail in the next chapter, the Internet Standard Management Framework is entirely *information-oriented.* It includes four primary components (see Figure 65-2):

Structure of Management Information (SMI) To ensure interoperability of various devices, we want to have a consistent way of describing the characteristics of devices to be managed using SNMP. In computer science, a *data description language (DDL)* is the tool for this job. The *SMI* is a standard that defines the structure, syntax, and characteristics of management information in SNMP.

Management Information Bases (MIBs) Each managed device contains a set of variables that is used to manage it. These variables represent information about the operation of the device that is sent to an NMS, and/or parameters sent to the managed device to control it. The *MIB* is the full set of these variables that describe the management characteristics of a particular type of device. Each variable in a MIB is called a *MIB object,* and it is defined using the SMI data description language. A device may have many objects, corresponding to the different hardware and software elements it contains.

NOTE *Initially, a single document defined the MIB for SNMP, but this model was inflexible. To allow new MIB objects to be more easily defined, groups of related MIB objects are now defined in separate RFC standards called* MIB modules. *More than 100 such MIB modules have been defined so far.*

Simple Network Management Protocol (SNMP) This is the actual SNMP protocol itself. It defines how information is exchanged between SNMP agents and NMSs. The SNMP *protocol operations* define the various SNMP messages and how they are created and used. SNMP *transport mappings* describe how SNMP can be used over various underlying internetworks, such as TCP/IP, IPX, and others.

Security and Administration To the previous three main architectural components, the SNMP Framework adds a number of supporting elements. These provide enhancements to the operation of the SNMP protocol for security and address issues related to SNMP implementation, version transition, and other administrative issues.

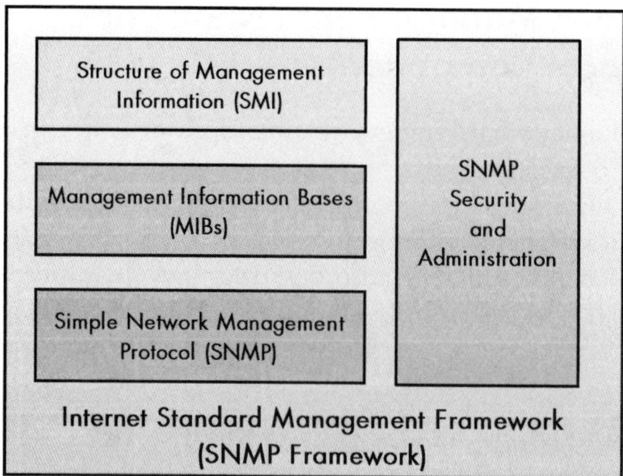

Figure 65-2: *Components of the TCP/IP Internet Standard Management Framework*

KEY CONCEPT The three main components of the Internet Standard Management Framework (SNMP Framework) are the Structure of Management Information (SMI), management information bases (MIBs), and the SNMP protocol itself. These are supported by SNMP security and administration elements.

SNMP Framework Architecture

The creators of SNMP specifically designed the Framework to be modular, because when SNMP was originally created, it was seen as only a temporary solution until a transition could be made to another network management protocol from the OSI protocol suite. The modular architecture separated definitional, data, and functional (protocol) elements, to allow the SNMP protocol itself to be replaced without changing how network management information was defined and described.

This transition to the OSI protocol never occurred, but the architecture has still proven valuable in defining the entire scope of SNMP and in making its implementation much simpler. Each of the major components discussed in the previous section—the SMI, MIBs, and SNMP itself—are described in different standards. The modularity of the SNMP Framework has also allowed changes to be made to these components relatively independently of each other, making the transition between SNMP versions easier than it would have been if one huge document defined everything.

TCP/IP Internet Standard Management Framework and SNMP Versions (SNMPv1, SNMPv2 Variants, and SNMPv3)

In Chapter 3, I explained the differences between proprietary, de facto, and open standards, and described the many benefits of open standards. History is replete with examples of technologies that have succeeded because they used an open standard when a competing standard was proprietary.

TCP/IP and the Internet are often held up as a model for proper open-standards development. Thousands of TCP/IP standards have been developed and published using the well-known Request for Comments (RFC) standardization process. The result has been the most successful set of internetworking protocols in computing history, accepted and used worldwide.

Nobody is perfect, however, and no process is perfect either. Some problems occurred in the introduction of SNMP version 2, leading to a virtual breakdown in the normally smooth protocol standardization method, and a proliferation of incompatible variants that we aren't used to seeing in TCP/IP. The story behind this is a continuation of the general SNMP overview and history from earlier in this chapter, and it explains the many SNMP standard names and numbers, so you can make sense of them. At the same time, the discussion serves as a vivid reminder of how important proper standard development is, and what the consequences are when there isn't universal agreement on how a standard should evolve.

SNMPv1

The first version of SNMP was developed in early 1988 and published in the form of three RFC standards in August 1988. This first version is now known as *SNMP version 1* or *SNMPv1*. The three SNMPv1 standards provided the initial description of the three main Internet Standard Management Framework components: the SMI, MIB, and SNMP protocol itself. However, the term *Internet Standard Management Framework* was not actually used at that time.

SNMPv1 was generally accepted and widely deployed in many networks. SNMPv1 got the job done and became the standard for TCP/IP network management. It is still widely used today. It is the Old Faithful of SNMP versions. Slight revisions were made to the initial standards, and more and more MIB modules were defined over time, but the technology remained the same for a number of years.

As with any technology, users of SNMPv1 identified weaknesses in it and opportunities for improvement. One of the areas in which SNMPv1 was most criticized was the area of security. SNMPv1 used only a "trivial" (as RFC 3410 puts it) authentication scheme, employing a password-like construct called a *community string*.

The issue of security turned out to be the bone of contention that eventually led to serious problems in the development of SNMP. Some people felt that community strings were sufficient security, but many others felt it was important that better security be put into SNMP. There were many different ways proposed to add security to SNMP, but no universal agreement on how to do it. The points raised about the security weaknesses in the original SNMPv1 had some validity, as I explore in the discussion of SNMP protocol operations in Chapter 67.

SNMPsec

The first attempt to add security came in the form of three standards published in July 1992 that defined a new security mechanism using logical identifiers called *parties*. This is sometimes called *SNMP Security* or *SNMPsec*. This method was more secure than the original SNMPv1, but SNMPsec was never widely accepted, and it is now considered historical.

SNMPv2

The idea of party-based security never went away, however. It was used as the basis of the definition of the first full revision of SNMP, when *SNMP version 2 (SNMPv2)* was published in RFCs 1441 through 1452 in April 1993. This new version incorporated the new security model, as well as making changes to the actual SNMP protocol operations, changes to the SMI standard (defining version 2 of SMI, SMIv2), and formalizing the concept of the Internet Standard Management Framework.

Unfortunately, this new standard also was never universally accepted. Some people thought the whole new version was a great advance, but others took issue with the party-based security, claiming it was too complex. A great deal of debate and discussion took place over the next couple of years, as an attempt was made to get everyone on board with the new version.

SNMPv2 Variants

Acceptance of SNMPv2 never happened. Instead, different splinter groups broke off and began work on *variants* of SNMPv2. To prevent confusion, the original SNMPv2 became known as either *SNMPv2 classic* (reminiscent of the name a particular soft drink) or *SNMPv2p*, with the *p* referring to party-based security. Things got very interesting (and confusing) when the following were proposed and/or developed:

SNMPv1.5 You can tell immediately that an idea is probably going to be a problem when it proposes a version number lower than a number already standardized. SNMPv1.5 was an attempt to retain the uncontroversial elements in SNMPv2p—the enhancements to the SNMP protocol and SMI—while going back to community-based security as in SNMPv1. It never became a standard itself, but became the basis of the next variant.

Community-Based SNMPv2 (SNMPv2c) This is SNMPv2p modified to use community strings instead of party-based security; in essence, the same idea as SNMPv1.5, but with a more official-sounding name and a few changes. Interestingly, the standard that defines this, RFC 1901, still has an experimental status, despite the fact that SNMPv2c actually achieved some degree of commercial success, where the standard SNMPv2p did not. SNMPv2c was defined by standards RFC 1902 through 1908, which incorporate other changes, including a new version of SMI (SMIv2).

User-Based SNMPv2 (SNMPv2u) This is an alternative security method for SNMPv2c, which is based on users rather than community strings. It is considered simpler than party-based but more secure than community-string security. It is defined by RFC 1909 and RFC 1910. It, too, is formally considered experimental.

SNMPv2* As if all of the other variants were not enough, a well-known vendor decided to define another variant called *SNMPv2** that combined elements of SNMPv2p and SNMPv2u. This was never formally standardized. (Yes, that's an asterisk in the name. No, there's no footnote at the bottom of the page, so don't bother looking for one. Yes, putting an asterisk in a name is extremely confusing. No, I don't know how it is that marketing people get paid good money to come up with names like this.)

Now, imagine that you were a network administrator in the mid-1990s and were faced with SNMPv2p, SNMPv2c, SNMPv2u, and SNMPv2*. Which one would you choose? Well, if you are like most people, you would choose none of the above, saying, "I think I'll stick with SNMPv1 until these version 2 folks get their act together!" And that's basically what happened. Some proponents of these variations promoted them, but there was never any agreement, and the result was that the success of all of the various and sundry SNMPv2s was limited. As I said, this is a classic illustration of how important universal standardization is.

SNMPv3

I would imagine that, at some point, everyone realized that the situation was a mess and decided enough is enough. In 1996, work began on a new approach to resolve the outstanding issues and return universality to SNMP. In 1998, *SNMP version 3 (SNMPv3)* was developed, which includes additional enhancements to SNMP and finally gets all the players back on the same team.

SNMPv3 is the most current version of SNMP and is still being actively revised. One of the important changes in SNMPv3 is a more formalized way of handing different security approaches to SNMP—obviously, a lesson learned from the SNMPv2 experience.

SNMPv3 uses SNMPv2 protocol operations and its protocol data unit (PDU) message format, and the SMIv2 standard from SNMPv2 as well. SNMPv3 allows a number of different security methods to be incorporated into its architecture, and includes standards describing user-based security as defined in SNMPv2u and SNMPv2*, as well as a new view-based access control model. It also includes additional tools to aid in the administration of SNMP.

TCP/IP Internet Standard Management Framework and SNMP Standards

You've now seen that there are three different versions of the Internet Standard Management Framework. Some of these versions have different variants. Each version or variant of the Framework includes multiple modular components. Each component has one or more documents that define it. Some of these have multiple revisions. Add to that dozens of individual MIBs defined for SNMP and other support documents, and what do you have? A boatload of TCP/IP standards, that's what. There are probably more RFCs defining parts of SNMP than any other single TCP/IP protocol or technology.

It is specifically because there are so many versions and components and documents associated with SNMP that I feel it is important to keep all the standards straight. To that end, Tables 65-1 through 65-6 show the major SNMP standards for each of the versions and variants of the SNMP Framework: SNMPv1, SNMPsec, SNMPv2p, SNMPv2c, SNMPv2u, and SNMPv3. (SNMPv2* was not standardized using the regular RFC process.) Each individual RFC defines one component of one version of the Framework.

The usual way that RFCs work is that when new versions of a standard are released that are direct replacements for older ones, the older ones are obsoleted by the new ones. With SNMP, due to the many versions and the controversy over the variants, this is a bit unclear. For example, the standards defining SNMPv2p are not considered by the IETF to obsolete the standards for SNMPv1, but the IETF says the standards for SNMPv2c and SNMPv2u do obsolete those of SNMPv2p.

To keep all of this distinct, I decided to show the standards for each version or variant separately. I put the RFC numbers for obsolete RFCs only where those RFCs are for the same SNMP version or variant. For example, RFC 3410 obsoletes 2570 because they both deal with SNMPv3 and 3410 is a direct replacement for 2570. Also, there are a few cases where the name of a standard changed slightly between RFC numbers; I have shown the current name. A full, hyperlinked list of RFCs can be found at http://www.rfc-editor.org/rfc-index.html.

Table 65-1: SNMP Version 1 (SNMPv1) Standards

Obsolete RFCs	Most Recent RFC	Date of Most Recent RFC	Standard Name
1065	1155	May 1990	Structure and Identification of Management Information for TCP/IP-Based Internets
1066	1156	May 1990	Management Information Base for Network Management of TCP/IP-Based Internets
1067, 1098	1157	May 1990	Simple Network Management Protocol (SNMP)
1158	1213	March 1991	Management Information Base for Network Management of TCP/IP-Based Internets: MIB-II

Table 65-2: SNMP Security (SNMPsec) Standards

Obsolete RFCs	Most Recent RFC	Date of Most Recent RFC	Standard Name
—	1351	July 1992	SNMP Administrative Model
—	1352	July 1992	SNMP Security Protocols
—	1353	July 1992	Definitions of Managed Objects for Administration of SNMP Parties

Table 65-3: Party-Based SNMP Version 2 (SNMPv2p) Standards

Obsolete RFCs	Most Recent RFC	Date of Most Recent RFC	Standard Name
—	1441	April 1993	Introduction to Version 2 of the Internet-Standard Network Management Framework
—	1442	April 1993	Structure of Management Information for Version 2 of the Simple Network Management Protocol (SNMPv2)
—	1443	April 1993	Textual Conventions for Version 2 of the Simple Network Management Protocol (SNMPv2)
—	1444	April 1993	Conformance Statements for Version 2 of the Simple Network Management Protocol (SNMPv2)

(continued)

Table 65-3: Party-Based SNMP Version 2 (SNMPv2p) Standards (continued)

Obsolete RFCs	Most Recent RFC	Date of Most Recent RFC	Standard Name
—	1445	April 1993	Administrative Model for Version 2 of the Simple Network Management Protocol (SNMPv2)
—	1446	April 1993	Security Protocols for Version 2 of the Simple Network Management Protocol (SNMPv2)
—	1447	April 1993	Party MIB for Version 2 of the Simple Network Management Protocol (SNMPv2)
—	1448	April 1993	Protocol Operations for Version 2 of the Simple Network Management Protocol (SNMPv2)
—	1449	April 1993	Transport Mappings for Version 2 of the Simple Network Management Protocol (SNMPv2)
—	1450	April 1993	Management Information Base for Version 2 of the Simple Network Management Protocol (SNMPv2)
—	1451	April 1993	Manager-to-Manager Management Information Base
—	1452	April 1993	Coexistence Between Version 1 and Version 2 of the Internet-Standard Network Management Framework

Table 65-4: Community-Based SNMP Version 2 (SNMPv2c) Standards

Obsolete RFCs	Most Recent RFC	Date of Most Recent RFC	Standard Name
—	1901	January 1996	Introduction to Community-Based SNMPv2
—	1902	January 1996	Structure of Management Information for Version 2 of the Simple Network Management Protocol (SNMPv2)
—	1903	January 1996	Textual Conventions for Version 2 of the Simple Network Management Protocol (SNMPv2)
—	1904	January 1996	Conformance Statements for Version 2 of the Simple Network Management Protocol (SNMPv2)
—	1905	January 1996	Protocol Operations for Version 2 of the Simple Network Management Protocol (SNMPv2)
—	1906	January 1996	Transport Mappings for Version 2 of the Simple Network Management Protocol (SNMPv2)
—	1907	January 1996	Management Information Base for Version 2 of the Simple Network Management Protocol (SNMPv2)
—	1908	January 1996	Coexistence between Version 1 and Version 2 of the Internet-Standard Network Management Framework

Table 65-5: User-Based SNMP Version 2 (SNMPv2u) Standards

Obsolete RFCs	Most Recent RFC	Date of Most Recent RFC	Standard Name
—	1909	February 1996	An Administrative Infrastructure for SNMPv2
—	1910	February 1996	User-Based Security Model for SNMPv2

Table 65-6: SNMP Version 3 (SNMPv3) Standards

Obsolete RFCs	Most Recent RFC	Date of Most Recent RFC	Standard Name
—	2576	March 2000	Coexistence between Version 1, Version 2, and Version 3 of the Internet-Standard Network Management Framework
—	2578	April 1999	Structure of Management Information Version 2 (SMIv2)
—	2579	April 1999	Textual Conventions for SMIv2
—	2580	April 1999	Conformance Statements for SMIv2
2570	3410	December 2002	Introduction and Applicability Statements for Internet-Standard Management Framework
2261, 2271, 2571	3411	December 2002	An Architecture for Describing Simple Network Management Protocol (SNMP) Management Frameworks
2262, 2272, 2572	3412	December 2002	Message Processing and Dispatching for the Simple Network Management Protocol (SNMP)
2263, 2273, 2573	3413	December 2002	Simple Network Management Protocol (SNMP) Applications
2264, 2274, 2574	3414	December 2002	User-Based Security Model (USM) for Version 3 of the Simple Network Management Protocol (SNMPv3)
2265, 2275, 2575	3415	December 2002	View-Based Access Control Model (VACM) for the Simple Network Management Protocol (SNMP)
—	3416	December 2002	Version 2 of the Protocol Operations for the Simple Network Management Protocol (SNMP)
—	3417	December 2002	Transport Mappings for the Simple Network Management Protocol (SNMP)
—	3418	December 2002	Management Information Base (MIB) for the Simple Network Management Protocol (SNMP)

In addition to all of the standards listed in these tables, there are dozens of supplemental RFCs that describe MIB modules and also clarify various fine points of operation related to SNMP. You can find all the MIBs in an online list of RFCs by searching for "MIB" or "SNMP."

66

TCP/IP STRUCTURE OF MANAGEMENT INFORMATION (SMI) AND MANAGEMENT INFORMATION BASES (MIBS)

The Internet Standard Management Framework defines three major components that describe how devices can be managed on a TCP/IP internetwork. One of these, the actual Simple Network Management Protocol (SNMP) is relatively well known, but is only part of the overall picture. SNMP describes how information is exchanged between SNMP entities, but two other components are equally important, because they describe the information itself.

In this chapter, I describe these two important supporting elements of the TCP/IP Internet Standard Management Framework: the Management Information Base (MIB) standard that describes types of information that SNMP works with, and the Structure of Management Information (SMI) standard that specifies how MIB information is defined. Understanding these two parts of the SNMP Framework is an important initial step before we examine the actual SNMP protocol itself.

I begin with an overview description of the SMI data description language and how MIBs work. I discuss the MIB object name hierarchy and the notation used to refer to names. I also describe how MIB objects work, discussing the different object types and MIB object groups. I describe MIB concepts common to all of the versions of SNMP, and discuss both of the specific versions of SMI (SMIv1 and SMIv2) used in those SNMP versions.

BACKGROUND INFORMATION *If you have not yet already read the preceding chapter describing the SNMP Internet Standard Management Framework, you should do so before proceeding here.*

TCP/IP SMI and MIBs Overview

The key to really understanding TCP/IP network management is to comprehend the *information-oriented* nature of the entire Internet Standard Management Framework (SNMP Framework). To see what I mean by this, let's step back for a moment and consider in general terms the problem of network management, and more specifically, the problem of managing devices on a network.

SNMP's Information-Oriented Design

A network administrator needs to perform two basic types of actions: gather data about devices to learn how they are functioning and give commands to devices to change how they are functioning. In the simplest terms, the first category can be considered as a read operation, and the second is comparable to a write operation.

A classic way of implementing this functionality is to define a communication protocol. Most such protocols are *command-oriented*—they consist of a specific set of commands to perform the read and write operations. For example, a network management protocol might have a read command such as "report on number of hours device has been in use," and a write command might be something like "put this device into test mode." The network manager would control the device by giving the appropriate commands.

A command-oriented management protocol has the advantage of simplicity, since it's clear what the commands are for and how they are to be used. It can be reasonably well suited for use in certain environments, but it doesn't work well on a large, heterogeneous TCP/IP internetwork. The main reason for this is that command-orientation inextricably ties the protocol to the devices being managed. Consider the following problems:

- Every type of device might require a distinct set of commands. For example, the commands given to a router might need to be different than those given to a host. This would lead either to a proliferation of commands in the protocol or to inflexibility in allowing proper management of different device types.
- Every time a company created a new type of device, or made a unique version of a type of device, the network management protocol would need to be changed.
- Whenever the operation of a kind of device changed, due perhaps to a change in another protocol, the management protocol would need to be updated.
- The protocol itself could not be easily changed without affecting a lot of hardware.

The solution to the problems of command-oriented management protocols is to use an *information-oriented* model. Instead of defining specific commands that interrogate or control devices, the devices are defined in terms of units of information that are to be exchanged between the devices and a management station.

Instead of read commands and write commands, we have *variables* that can be read or written. Take the two examples mentioned earlier. Instead of a command like "report on a number of hours device has been in use," the device keeps a variable called "number of hours in use," and the network management station can read this as one of many variables, with no need for a specific protocol command. Instead of a write command called "put this device into test mode," the device has a variable called "current mode." The network manager can change the mode of the device to test mode by changing the value of the variable.

This difference may seem subtle, but it underlies every aspect of how SNMP works. I believe part of why the SNMP Framework is hard to understand is because insufficient emphasis is placed on looking at things in the "SNMP way," which means thinking about information objects and not commands.

> **KEY CONCEPT** Unlike most protocols, which are *command-oriented,* SNMP is *information-oriented.* SNMP operations are implemented using objects called *variables* that are maintained in managed devices. Rather than issuing commands, a network management station checks the status of a device by reading variables, and controls the operation of the device by changing (writing) variables.

MIB and MIB Objects

Given this backdrop, we can look at the SNMP Framework in a new light. The actual SNMP protocol itself, which we'll examine in the next couple of chapters, has only a few, generic commands to accomplish read and write tasks. It deals with only the methods by which network management information is exchanged between SNMP agents and SNMP network management stations (NMSs), which were described in the previous chapter. The network management information is really the heart of TCP/IP network management.

So, instead of SNMP being defined in terms of commands used to control particular devices, it is defined in terms of management information variables, generally called *objects.* Each object describes a particular characteristic of a device. Some objects are fairly generic and are meaningful for any device on a TCP/IP network; for example, an object describing something related to the Internet Protocol (IP) itself, such as the device's IP address. Other objects might be particular to a specific type of device; for example, a router will have objects that a regular host's Ethernet network interface card would not.

A collection of objects used in SNMP is called a *management information base,* or *MIB.* (In fact, SNMP objects are often called *MIB objects.*) The first version of SNMP, SNMPv1, had a single standard that defined the entire MIB for SNMP. Newer versions provide more flexibility by using different *MIB modules* that define sets of variables particular to the hardware or software used by a device.

KEY CONCEPT The management data variables in a managed device are maintained in a logical collection called a *management information base (MIB)*. The objects in the MIB are often called *MIB objects*, and they are typically collected into sets called *MIB modules*.

Defining objects using modules allows for significant flexibility in defining the variables that allow management of different types of devices. A device can incorporate all the MIB modules appropriate to the hardware and software it uses. For example, if you had a device using Ethernet, it would incorporate variables from the Ethernet MIB. A device using Token Ring would use the Token Ring MIB. Both devices would also use the common SNMP MIB that is used by all TCP/IP devices. Other modules might also be included as needed.

NOTE *Due to its name, the MIB is often called a database. This is, strictly speaking, inaccurate. The MIB is a description of objects. The actual MIB in a device may be implemented as a software database, but that is not required.*

Defining MIB Objects: SMI

The use of MIB objects solves the problem of the network management protocol being tied to the network management information. However, we must be very particular about how we define these objects. Again, the reason is the wide variety of devices that TCP/IP allows to be connected together. Each device may represent information in a different way. For all of them to communicate with each other, we need to ensure that management information is represented in a consistent manner.

The part of the SNMP Framework that ensures the universality of MIB objects is the *Structure of Management Information (SMI)* standard. SMI defines the rules for how MIB objects and MIB modules are constructed. In SMI, MIB objects are described using a precise set of definitions based on a data description language called the ISO *Abstract Syntax Notation 1 (ASN.1)* standard.

In essence, we really have three levels of abstraction in SNMP. The actual SNMP protocol moves values that represent the state of management devices. The MIB defines what these variables are. And the SMI defines how the variables in the MIB are themselves defined.

There are two main SMI standards. The original, *SMIv1*, was part of the first SNMP Framework, SNMPv1, defined in RFC 1155. It sets out the basic rules for MIBs and MIB variables. The second, *SMIv2*, was defined as part of SNMPv2p in RFC 1442 and further updated in RFC 2578, part of SNMPv3. It is similar to the earlier version, but defines more object types, as well as the structure of MIB modules.

These SMI standards are responsible for defining the following important information elements in SNMP:

- The general characteristics associated with all MIB objects—the standard way by which all MIB objects are described
- The different types of MIB objects that can be created, such as integers, strings, and more complex data types

- A hierarchical structure for naming MIB objects, so they can be addressed in a consistent manner without names overlapping
- The information associated with each MIB module

> **KEY CONCEPT** The *Structure of Management Information (SMI)* standard is responsible for defining the rules for how MIB objects are structured, described, and organized. SMI allows dissimilar devices to communicate by ensuring that they use a universal data representation for all management information.

TCP/IP MIB Objects, Object Characteristics, and Object Types

As explained in the previous sections, the SNMP Framework is designed to facilitate the exchange of management information. The MIB defines a device's management information and contains a number of variables called *MIB objects*, also called *managed objects*. These objects are defined according to the rules set out in the SMI standard.

The best place to begin looking at MIB objects is by examining the SMI rules that define them. As I mentioned earlier in this chapter, two different versions of SMI have been created: SMIv1 as part of the original SNMP, and SMIv2 as part of SNMPv2 and SNMPv3. The two are similar in terms of how MIB objects are described, but SMIv2 allows more information to be associated with each object.

MIB Object Characteristics

Just as a typical protocol uses a field format for specifying the content of messages sent between devices using the protocol, SMI uses a format that specifies the fundamental characteristics of each MIB object. The most basic of these are five mandatory characteristics defined in SMIv1. These are also used in SMIv2, but a couple of names were changed, and the possible values for some of the fields were modified as well. An MIB object may have the following characteristics (see Figure 66-1):

Object Name Each object has a name that serves to uniquely identify it. Actually, that's not entirely true. Each object has *two* names: a textual name called an *object descriptor* and a numeric *object identifier*, which indicates the object's place in the MIB object name hierarchy. We'll explore these names and how they are used shortly.

Syntax Defines the object's data type and the structure that describes it. This attribute is very important because it defines the data type of information that the object contains. There are two basic categories of data types allowed:

- Regular data types are single pieces of information, of the type we are used to dealing with on a regular basis, such as integers and strings. These are called *base types* in SMIv2. SMIv1 differentiates between *primitive types* like integers defined in ASN.1, and *defined types* that are special forms of primitive types that are still single pieces of information but with certain special meaning attached to how they are used. SMIv2 doesn't use those two terms.

- Tabular data types are collections of multiple data elements. They may take the form of a list of base types or a table of base types. For example, a table of integers could be constructed to represent a set of values. In SMIv1, these are called *constructor types*; in SMIv2 they are *conceptual tables*. They can be accessed using special SNMP mechanisms designed for reading tables. See the topic on SNMP table traversal for more on tables.

Access (Max-Access in SMIv2) This field defines the ways that an SNMP application will normally use the object. In SMIv1, there are four different possible values: *read-only*, *read-write*, *write-only*, and *not-accessible*. In SMIv2 there are five values, which are described as a hierarchy of sorts. SMIv2 calls this characteristic *Max-Access* (*maximum access*) to make it explicit that higher access levels include the lower levels as well. For example, an object with read-create access can also be used in any of the modes below it, such as read-write, but not vice versa. The following are the five SMIv2 access values, in decreasing order of access (note that write-only has been removed in SMIv2):

- *read-create* (object can be read, written, or created)
- *read-write* (object can be read or written)
- *read-only* (object can only be read)
- *accessible-for-notify* (object can be used only using SNMP notification or SNMP traps)
- *not-accessible* (used for special purposes)

Status Indicates the currency of the object definition. In SMIv1 there are three values: *mandatory*, *optional*, and *obsolete*. In SMIv2, the first two are combined into simply *current*, meaning a current definition. The value *obsolete* is retained, and *deprecated* is added, meaning the definition is obsolete but maintained for compatibility.

Definition (Description in SMIv2) A textual description of the object.

Optional Characteristics SMIv2 adds the following optional characteristics that may appear in the definition of an object:

- *Units* is a textual description of the units associated with the object.
- *Reference* is a text cross-reference to a related document or other information relevant to the object.
- *Index* is a value used to define objects that are actually more complex rows of other objects.
- *Augments* is an alternative to the Index field.
- *DefVal* defines an acceptable default value for the object.

KEY CONCEPT Each management information variable, called an *MIB object*, has associated with it five key attributes: its name, syntax, maximum access, status, and definition. It may also have a number of optional characteristics.

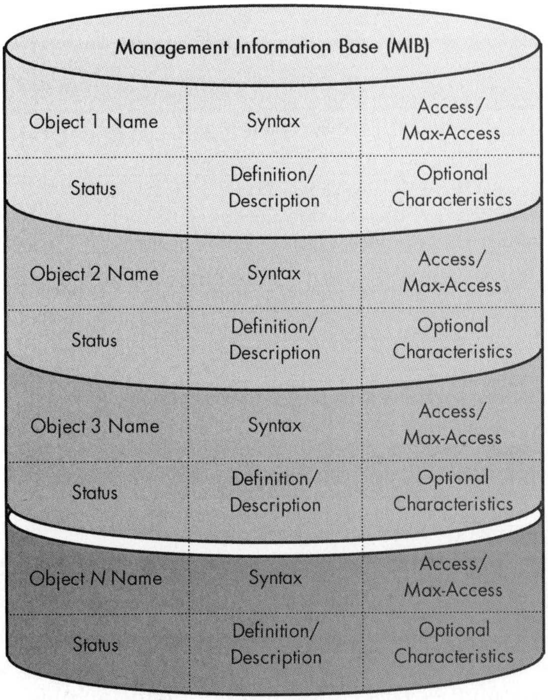

Management Information Base (MIB)

Object 1 Name	Syntax	Access/ Max-Access
Status	Definition/ Description	Optional Characteristics
Object 2 Name	Syntax	Access/ Max-Access
Status	Definition/ Description	Optional Characteristics
Object 3 Name	Syntax	Access/ Max-Access
Status	Definition/ Description	Optional Characteristics
Object *N* Name	Syntax	Access/ Max-Access
Status	Definition/ Description	Optional Characteristics

Figure 66-1: SNMP management information base (MIB) *This diagram shows an SNMP MIB containing N MIB objects. Each object has five mandatory characteristics and a variable number of optional characteristics.*

SMI Data Types

Table 66-1 shows the regular data types supported for objects in both SMIv1 and SMIv2. (The names with 32 in them are the ones used in SMIv2; they were changed to make the type's bit size explicit.) The first five entries in the table are primitive types; the rest are defined types, using the SMIv1 terminology.

Table 66-1: SNMP SMI Regular Data Types

Data Type Code	Description	In SMIv1?	In SMIv2?
Integer/Integer32	A 32-bit signed integer in two's complement notation, capable of holding a value from -2,147,483,648 to +2,147,483,647. Can also be used to represent an enumerated type; for example, where 1 represents a particular constant, 2 represents a different one, and so on.	Yes	Yes
Octet String	A variable-length string of binary or text data.	Yes	Yes
Null	Nothing.	Yes	No
Bits	An enumeration of named bits. Used to allow a set of bit flags to be treated as a single data type.	No	Yes
Unsigned	A 32-bit unsigned integer, from 0 to 4,294,967,295.	No	Yes
Network Address/ IpAddress	An IP address, encoded as a 4-byte octet string.	Yes	Yes

(continued)

Table 66-1: SNMP SMI Regular Data Types (continued)

Data Type Code	Description	In SMIv1?	In SMIv2?
Counter/Counter32	A 32-bit unsigned integer that begins at 0 and increases up to 4,294,967,295, then wraps back to 0.	Yes	Yes
Gauge/Gauge32	A 32-bit unsigned integer that may have a value from 0 to 4,294,967,295 and may increase or decrease, like a gauge. A minimum and maximum value are associated with the gauge, indicating its normal range.	Yes	Yes
TimeTicks	A 32-bit unsigned integer that indicates the number of hundredths of seconds since some arbitrary start date. Used for timestamping and to compute elapsed time.	Yes	Yes
Opaque	Data using arbitrary ASN.1 syntax that is to be passed between devices without being interpreted. As in the Network File System's (NFS) XDR (see Chapter 58), the term *opaque* means that the data is treated like a black box, whose internal details cannot be seen.	Yes	Yes
Counter64	A counter like Counter32 but 64 bits wide, allowing a value from 0 to 18,446,744,073,709,551,615.	No	Yes

In addition to the types shown in Table 66-1, other defined types are also created to indicate more specific semantics for a particular data type. These are called *textual conventions* and are described in RFC 2579 for SMIv2. For example, a type called *TimeStamp* is the same as *TimeTicks*. However, seeing an object using the former rather than the latter makes it more clear that the variable is representing a particular timestamp value. Another is called *TimeInterval*, which is also just an integer underneath its name, but conveys a different interpreted meaning.

If all of this seems very confusing to you, note that this description is actually a significant simplification of SMI's object definitions. Check out Listing 66-1, which shows an object definition from RFC 3418, using SMIv2.

```
sysLocation OBJECT-TYPE
     SYNTAX DisplayString (SIZE (0..255))
     MAX-ACCESS read-write
     STATUS current
     DESCRIPTION "The physical location of this node
      (e.g., 'telephone closet, 3rd floor'). If the location
      is unknown, the value is the zero-length string."
              ::= { system 6 }
```

Listing 66-1: *Example SNMP SMIv2 object definition*

Note that `DisplayString` is a textual convention for a displayed text string. The last part, `{ system 6 }`, will be explained in the next section.

TCP/IP MIB Object Descriptors and Identifiers and the Object Name Hierarchy

Of the many MIB object characteristics, only one is sufficiently interesting that it really deserves its own exposition. Or perhaps I should say that only one is sufficiently complicated to require further explanation. This is the object name, part of the larger naming system used for MIB objects.

Each MIB object actually has two names: an *object descriptor* and an *object identifier*.

Object Descriptors

The object descriptor is a conventional text name that provides a user-friendly handle to refer to the object. The name is assigned based on the particular MIB object group in which the object is located. In the previous example, `sysLocation` is the object descriptor for that MIB object. I describe these names in greater detail later in this chapter, when I discuss MIB modules and object groups.

Object Identifiers

Text names are convenient, but they are generally unstructured. There are at present more than 10,000 different MIB objects, and even if each has a distinct text name, a huge collection of such names doesn't help us to manage these objects and see how they are related. For this, we need a more structured approach to categorizing and naming objects.

This problem is similar to another problem that you may recall reading about: the problem of how to assign names on the Internet. Originally, names for hosts were simple, flat names, but this quickly grew unwieldy. The DNS hierarchical name space (see Chapter 53) allows every device to be arranged into a single hierarchical tree structure. The name of the device can be formed by traversing the tree from the top down to the location of the device, listing the labels traversed separated by dots. For example, the web server of The PC Guide is at http://www.pcguide.com.

This same concept is used to organize MIB objects in SNMP. A single, universal hierarchy that contains all MIB objects is used. It is hierarchical in nature, and it is split into levels from the most general to the most specific. Each object has a particular place in the hierarchy.

There is an important difference between the MIB name hierarchy and the DNS one: the MIB name hierarchy is even more universal than the one for DNS. The entire subtree of all MIB objects is just one branch of the full, international object hierarchy maintained by the International Organization for Standardization (ISO) and the International Telecommunication Union (ITU). This object identification hierarchy is so general that it can contain a name for every object or variable in use by any technology in the entire world (and possibly other planets or solar systems).

The reason for my jocularity will become apparent in a moment. Suffice it to say that this object tree is enormous. Each node in this tree is identified with both a label and an integer. The labels are for descriptive purposes. Object (or subtree) identifiers are formed by listing the numbers in sequence from the top of the tree down to the node, separated by dots. SNMP doesn't reverse the order of the labels the way DNS does, however. They are listed top-down from left to right. (The text labels can be used for names, too, but they are not because they would get very long due to how deep the tree structure is.)

KEY CONCEPT SNMP MIB objects have two names. The first is a text *object descriptor*, which provides a means of addressing the object in a way that is familiar and easy for humans. The second is the *object identifier*, which consists of a sequence of integers that specifies the location of the object in the global object hierarchy maintained by the international standards bodies ISO and ITU.

Structure of the MIB Object Name Hierarchy

Let's explore how the MIB object tree is structured, and more important, how SNMP MIB objects fit into it. Figure 66-2 illustrates the global object name hierarchy and SNMP MIB hierarchies.

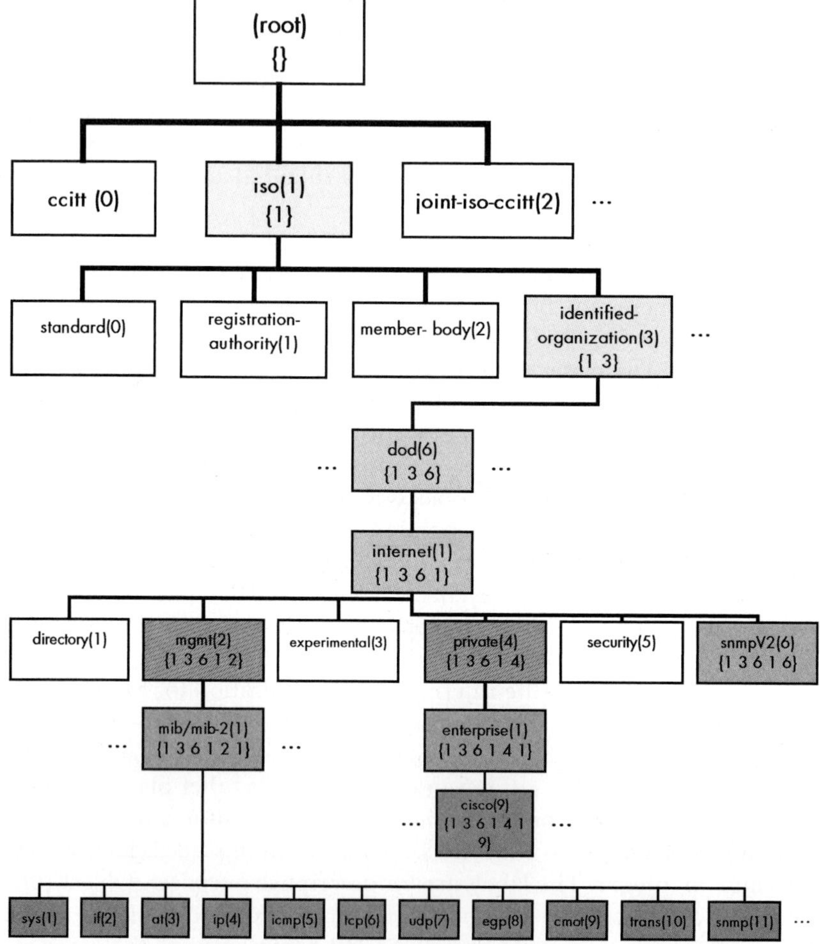

Figure 66-2: Global object name hierarchy and SNMP MIB hierarchies *This diagram shows the object name hierarchy defined by ISO and CCITT (ITU) to allow all types of objects to be universally represented. The path within this larger tree to the tree branches relevant to SNMP can be found by following the shaded boxes. The two subtrees used for SNMP are shown as the hatched boxes under internet(1). Each contains its own substructure (some of which is illustrated here) defining thousands of different MIB objects. The branch on the left side is used for generic MIB objects and the one on the right for private ones. A separate hierarchy is also defined for SNMPv2.*

The tree's root has no label, and has three children:

- ccitt(0) for ITU (formerly the CCITT) standards (also seen as itu(0)).
- iso(1) for ISO standards.
- joint-iso-ccitt(2) for joint standards (also seen as joint-iso-itu(2)).

Following the iso(1) node, we see the following at the next several levels:

- Within iso(1), the ISO has created a subtree for use by other organizations, called org(3).
- Within org(3), there is a subtree for the United States Department of Defense (which, as you may recall, was the originator of the Internet): dod(6).
- Within dod(6), there is a subtree called internet(1).

Everything we work with in SNMP is under this one very specific subtree: 1.3.6.1, which if we used the text labels would be iso.org.dod.internet. Within this part of the name space, there are six subtrees below:

- directory(1) is reserved for future use by ISO.
- mgmt(2) is the primary subtree where MIB objects are located. This is 1.3.6.1.2. It contains a subtree called mib(1), which is 1.3.6.1.2.1. When MIB-II was created, a subtree called mib-2(1) was created using the same number, 1.3.6.1.2.1.
- experimental(3) contains objects used for standards under development. This is 1.3.6.1.3.
- private(4) is used for objects defined by private companies. This node, 1.3.6.1.4, has a subtree called enterprise(1), which is 1.3.6.1.4.1.
- security(5) is reserved for security use.
- snmpV2(6) defines objects used specifically for SNMP version 2.

So, what's the bottom line of all this? Well, basically all MIB module objects are named within one of these two branches of the overall object tree:

Regular MIB Objects These are in the mib(1) subtree under mgmt(2): 1.3.6.1.2.1.

Private MIB Objects These are in the enterprise(1) subtree under private(4), which is 1.3.6.1.4.1. For example, within enterprise(1), there is an entry cisco(9) for Cisco Systems. So all Cisco-specific MIB objects start with 1.3.6.1.4.1.9.

Clear as mud, right? Why didn't they just make a separate hierarchy where "mib" was at the top instead of six levels deep? How dare you even suggest such a thing? Don't you understand the importance of global standards?

All facetiousness aside, this name hierarchy is a bit cumbersome to deal with (okay, more than a bit), but it does allow us to keep MIB objects organized in a sensible way. Within the 1.3.6.1.2.1 subtree, we find most of the regular MIB objects used in SNMP. Each subtree within 1.3.6.1.2.1 corresponds to one of the regular SNMP object groups or a particular MIB module.

KEY CONCEPT All MIB objects have object identifiers that fit within two branches of the global object hierarchy. Regular MIB objects (which are not vendor-specific) fit in the mib(1) subtree under mgmt(2): 1.3.6.1.2.1. Private objects, which can be created by a hardware vendor to assist in managing that vendor's products, are in the enterprise(1) subtree under private(4), which is 1.3.6.1.4.1.

Recursive Definition of MIB Object Identifiers

An object is given a text object descriptor by putting its name at the start of the object, as shown in Listing 66-1, but the definition of numeric object identifiers is, again, more complex. It is done by defining only the number of the object within its particular subtree. This means the object identifiers are defined recursively (one based on another) and are not explicitly stated for each object. This is syntactically precise, but makes it hard to see at a glance what the number is for any particular object.

Consider again the example in Listing 66-1. For this object, `sysLocation` is the object descriptor and `{ system 6 }` is the object identifier. This means it is object number 6 within the node system, which is in turn defined as `{ mib-2 1 }`—it is the first node within the mib-2 subtree. Since mib-2 is 1.3.6.1.2.1, as noted in the previous section, this means `system` is 1.3.6.1.2.1.1 and `sysLocation` is 1.3.6.1.2.1.1.6.

TCP/IP MIB Modules and Object Groups

The MIB contains the collection of MIB objects that describe the characteristics of a device using the SNMP Framework. When SNMP was first created, there were not that many objects in the MIB. Furthermore, they were mostly generic objects that applied fairly universally to TCP/IP devices as a whole. In fact, most of the MIB objects were variables related to the operation of TCP/IP protocols such as IP, the Transmission Control Protocol (TCP), and the Internet Control Message Protocol (ICMP).

For this reason, at first, a single document defined "the" MIB for SNMP. The first of these documents was RFC 1066, part of the initial SNMPv1 specification. It was then revised in RFC 1156. In RFC 1158, a second version of the MIB, *MIB II*, was defined, which was essentially the same but made a few changes.

The Organization of MIB Objects into Object Groups

The number of MIB objects defined in the early MIB standards was relatively small. However, there were still several dozen of them, and it was recognized from the start that more would be created in time. To help organize the objects in a logical way, they were arranged into *object groups*. These groups serve the purpose of separating the objects and defining how they should be given object identifiers in the overall object name hierarchy.

Each group has associated with it three important pieces of information:

Group Name This is a name that is used as a text label in the object identification tree described earlier in this chapter (see Figure 66-2). These objects are all located within the iso.org.dod.internet.mgmt.mib subtree. So, for example, the group system would be iso.org.dod.internet.mgmt.mib.system.

Group Number This number corresponds to the group name used for making numeric identifiers from the object name tree. For example, the group system has the number 1, and so the group's object identifier is 1.3.6.1.2.1.1. All objects in that group will be under that tree; for example, `sysUpTime` is 1.3.6.1.2.1.1.3.

Group Code This is a text label that may be the same as the group name or may be an abbreviation. It is used as a prefix in making object descriptors (the text names of objects). For example, for the group system, the code is sys, and so an object in this group is `sysUpTime`.

Table 66-2 shows the eight generic SNMP groups defined in RFC 1158, along with their codes, names, and numbers.

Table 66-2: SNMP Generic MIB Object Groups

Group Name	Group Code	Group Number	Full Group Identifier	Description
system	sys	1	1.3.6.1.2.1.1	General objects of relevance to all or most devices. For example, a general description of the device is an object in this group, as is the identifier of the object. Later MIB versions greatly expanded the number of variables in this group.
interfaces	`if`	2	1.3.6.1.2.1.2	Objects related to the IP interfaces between this device and the internetwork. (Recall that a regular host normally has one interface, while a router has two or more.)
at (address translation)	`at`	3	1.3.6.1.2.1.3	Objects used for IP address translation. (No longer used.)
ip	`ip`	4	1.3.6.1.2.1.4	Objects related to the IP layer of the device as a whole (as opposed to interface-specific information in the `if` group).
icmp	`icmp`	5	1.3.6.1.2.1.5	Objects related to the operation of ICMP.
tcp	`tcp`	6	1.3.6.1.2.1.6	Objects related to the operation of the TCP.
udp	`udp`	7	1.3.6.1.2.1.7	Objects related to the operation of the User Datagram Protocol (UDP).
egp	`egp`	8	1.3.6.1.2.1.8	Objects related to the operation of the Exterior Gateway Protocol (EGP).
cmot	`cmot`	9	1.3.6.1.2.1.9	Objects related to running the CMIP protocol over TCP (historical, not used).
transmission	`trans`	10	1.3.6.1.2.1.10	Objects related to the specific method of information transmission used by each interface on the system.
snmp	`snmp`	11	1.3.6.1.2.1.11	Objects used to manage SNMP itself.

All of the groups in this table are fairly generic, and with the exception of the one about EGP, apply to pretty much every TCP/IP system using SNMP. (The mention of EGP, a routing protocol now considered obsolete, shows the age of this list.) The first five groups and the last one are mandatory for all systems. The others are used only by devices that use the indicated protocols or functions.

MIB Modules

What's most conspicuous about the object groups listed in Table 66-2 is the groups that are not included. There are no groups for most of the other TCP/IP protocols, nor any for variables that might be needed for specific hardware types. For example, most hosts will have a network card in them using a layer 2 protocol like Ethernet or Token Ring. How does a manager check or control the operation of this hardware? What about newer routing protocols like Open Shortest Path First (OSPF) or Border Gateway Protocol (BGP)? How about objects related to running the Domain Name System (DNS)?

Updating the MIB document constantly would have been impractical. Instead, in SNMPv2, the MIB was changed from a single document to a group of documents. The basic organization into groups of objects was retained, but instead of all groups being in the same standard, they are divided into multiple standards. A method was also defined for how to create *MIB modules* that describe new groups of objects specific to a particular technology. A list of these modules is maintained by the *Internet Assigned Numbers Authority* (IANA), the organization that maintains all of these sorts of numbers. The current list of SNMP MIB modules can be found at http://www.iana.org/assignments/smi-numbers.

The use of MIB modules makes putting SNMP support into a device somewhat like going shopping. The basic groups common to all devices are incorporated into each device, and then other modules/groups are used as needed. Table 66-3 provides a brief selection of MIB modules to give you an idea of what is out there, also showing the module's group number (within the 1.3.6.1.2.1 name subtree). There are many, many more modules than listed in this table.

Table 66-3: Some Common SNMP MIB Modules

MIB Module Name	Group Number	Description
`ospf`	14	Objects related to OSPF
`bgp`	15	Objects related to BGP
`rmon`	16	Objects used as part of Remote Network Monitoring (RMON)
`snmpDot3 RptrMgt`	22	Objects related to IEEE 802.3 (Ethernet) repeaters
`rip-2`	23	Objects used as part of version 2 of the Routing Information Protocol (RIP)
`snmpDot3 MauMgt`	26	Objects related to IEEE 802.3 (Ethernet) medium attachment units
`etherMIB`	35	Ethernet-like generic objects

(continued)

Table 66-3: Some Common SNMP MIB Modules (continued)

MIB Module Name	Group Number	Description
mipMIB	44	Mobile IP objects
ipMIB	48	IP objects for SNMPv2
tcpMIB	49	TCP objects for SNMPv2
udpMIB	50	UDP objects for SNMPv2

The last three entries in Table 66-3 might seem a bit confusing, since there were already groups for IP, TCP, and UDP, as shown in Table 66-2. The reason for these is that when the new modular architecture for MIB objects was created in SNMPv2, the definition of objects for the individual protocols that was part of the one document in SNMPv1 was separated out into individual MIB documents for consistency and to allow them to be updated independently. In fact, the base SNMPv2 and SNMPv3 MIB documents now define only objects in the `system` and `snmp` groups.

> **KEY CONCEPT** MIB objects created early in SNMP's history were organized into *MIB object groups* that reside within the mib(1) subtree, starting with identifier code 1.3.6.1.2.1. As the popularity of TCP/IP grew, it became impractical to centrally define all MIB objects, so sets of objects particular to different hardware devices are now specified in *MIB modules.*

MIB Module Format

The format for MIB modules is described in the SMI standard, version 2 (SMIv2). This document specifies how modules are to be defined in a way similar to how objects themselves are defined: by listing a set of characteristics that must be included in each module description. The module fields are as follows:

Module Name The name of the module. Remember that modules are really objects, syntactically, so like regular objects, they have a textual object descriptor (like `tcpMIB`) and an object identifier (in the case of `tcpMIB`, the number 50).

Last Updated The date and time that the module was last revised.

Organization The name of the organization that is managing the development of the module.

Contact Information The name, address, telephone number, and email address of the point person for this module.

Description A description of the module.

Revision and Revision Description One Revision entry is placed for each revision of the module to show its history. Each entry has a description associated with it.

After the definition of the module itself, the objects in the module are described. For an example, see RFC 2012, which defines the SNMPv2 TCP MIB.

67

TCP/IP SIMPLE NETWORK MANAGEMENT PROTOCOL (SNMP) CONCEPTS AND OPERATION

The overall network management solution for TCP/IP networks is the Internet Standard Management Framework. In the previous two chapters, we have taken a look at the Framework as a whole, and also discussed the two components that define the management information transmitted between TCP/IP devices to accomplish network management. The third major part of the SNMP Framework is the actual *Simple Network Management Protocol (SNMP)*, which is responsible for moving management information between devices.

The core of the protocol consists of a set of *protocol operations* that allow management information to be exchanged between SNMP agents and managers. Having previously examined the generalities of SNMP and what management information base (MIB) objects are, we can now get down to the nitty gritty of how management information is actually communicated using SNMP.

In this chapter, I provide a detailed description of the operations performed by the SNMP protocol. I begin with a brief overview and history of the protocol. I then provide a general description of how SNMP operates and the two basic methods that devices use to communicate. I also describe SNMP's message classes and the basic operations performed in SNMP: basic request/response, table traversal, object modification, and notification. I conclude with a discussion of SNMP security issues and a summary of the security methods in each of the SNMP versions.

NOTE *The number and types of protocol operations in SNMP changed between SNMPv1 and SNMPv2. The operations defined in SNMPv2 have been carried forward into the newest version, SNMPv3. Most of the discussion focuses on SNMPv3 as the newest implementation, noting the differences between it and the original and still widely used SNMPv1.*

SNMP Protocol Overview

As explained in the previous chapters, the SNMP Framework is often described as being *information-oriented.* A specific decision was made in the design of the SNMP Framework to decouple the management information conveyed between SNMP agents and SNMP managers from the protocol used to carry that information. This provides numerous benefits to the technology as a whole, chief among them flexibility and modularity.

In this model, the operation of the management protocol is *not* defined in terms of specific commands made to check the status of a device or change how it operates. Instead, the protocol is defined in terms of management information variables called *objects,* and a communication protocol that allows these objects to be either examined or changed by a network administrator. I describe this concept thoroughly in the previous chapter.

The MIB and Structure of Management Information (SMI) spell out the rules for how MIB objects are created and described. These MIB objects describe the types of information that can be read from the device or written to the device. The last piece of the puzzle is the actual protocol that is responsible for these read- and write-type operations. This is SNMP itself, which I give the somewhat redundant name *SNMP protocol* to differentiate it from the SNMP Framework.

The result of the separation of the protocol from the management information it carries is that the protocol itself becomes significantly reduced in complexity. Instead of the SNMP protocol needing to define dozens or even hundreds of operations that specify particular network management functions, it needs to deal with only the transmission of MIB object information between SNMP agents and managers. The SNMP protocol itself does not pay attention to what is in these objects; it is merely concerned with moving them around. In some ways, the SNMP protocol is the only really simple part of SNMP!

Early Development of SNMPv1

The history of the SNMP protocol goes back to the predecessor of the SNMP Framework, the *Simple Gateway Monitoring Protocol (SGMP),* which was defined in RFC 1028 in 1987. SGMP was designed as an interim solution for network management while larger issues were being explored, as I explained in Chapter 65. However, this standard is where many of the basic design concepts underlying the modern SNMP protocol can be found.

The SGMP standard specified the basic design model used in SNMP by describing SGMP in terms of only retrievals of, or alterations to, variables stored on an Internet gateway (router). The standard also outlines the small number of protocol operations that are still the basis for SNMP's operation today.

The first version of the SNMP Framework, SNMPv1, included the first formal definition of the SNMP protocol in RFC 1067 (later revised by RFCs 1098 and 1157). This standard refines the protocol operations given in the SGMP document. It makes the operation of the SNMP protocol fit into the overall SNMP Framework, working with formally defined MIB objects.

SNMPv2 and the Division of SNMP into Protocol Operations and Transport Mappings

When SNMPv2 was created, the single document describing the SNMP protocol was split into two standards, to make the protocol more modular and better reflective of the layers used in internetworks:

Protocol Operations The first document of the pair describes the actual mechanics by which MIB objects are moved between SNMP devices using particular SNMP message types. In SNMPv3, it is RFC 3416, "Version 2 of the Protocol Operations for the Simple Network Management Protocol (SNMP)." When people talk about just "the SNMP standard," this is the document they usually mean.

Transport Mappings The second document details how the SNMP protocol operations described in the first standard can be transported over a variety of different protocol suites. By using the correct mapping, SNMP operations can be carried out using lower-layer technologies other than the Internet Protocol (IP). This standard is represented in SNMPv3 by RFC 3417, "Transport Mappings for the Simple Network Management Protocol (SNMP)."

KEY CONCEPT The actual mechanism used to communicate management information between network management stations (NMSs) and managed devices is called the *Simple Network Management Protocol*, which may be called the *SNMP protocol* to differentiate it from the SNMP Framework. It consists of a number of *protocol operations* that describe the actual message exchanges that take place between devices, and a set of *transport mappings* that define how these messages are carried over various types of internetworks. The Internet Protocol (IP) is the most common transport mapping used for SNMP.

I discuss transport mappings in a little more detail in the description of SNMP messaging later in this chapter, but since the IP/User Datagram Protocol (UDP) method is by far the most common transport mechanism, there isn't a great deal to say about that aspect of the SNMP protocol.

SNMP Communication Methods

For SNMP to be useful in enabling the management of a network, it must allow a network administrator using a network management station (NMS) to easily check the status of SNMP agents in managed devices. In data communications, there are two general techniques that are used in a situation where one entity needs to be kept informed about activity or occurrences on another:

Poll-Driven Communication This term refers to the general technique of having the one who wants the information ask for it—just like someone might conduct a political poll. In SNMP, the NMS would poll SNMP agents for information. A common real-life example of polling is the model used by the regular mail service; every day you go to check your mailbox to see if you have any mail.

Interrupt-Driven Communication This term refers to having a device with information that another needs to know decide to send the information of its own volition. In SNMP, this would refer to an SNMP agent sending information to an NMS without being asked. This is the model used by that most famous of interrupters—the telephone.

Which communication method is better? The usual answer applies here: Neither is better or worse universally, which is why both options exist. Due to the obvious strengths and weaknesses of these models, the SNMP protocol is designed to use both. Polling is used for the periodic gathering of routine information, such as checking the usage statistics and general status of a device. Interrupts are used in the form of *traps* that a network administrator can set on a managed device. These traps cause an SNMP agent to interrupt an NMS when an event of importance occurs.

> **KEY CONCEPT** SNMP uses two basic methods for exchanging management information. Routine communication uses a *poll-driven* technique, where the network management station (NMS) requests information from managed nodes. An *interrupt-driven* model is also supported. In situations where a managed device needs to tell an NMS about an occurrence immediately, it can send a *trap* message without waiting for a request from the NMS.

The focus of most of our look at SNMP in this chapter will concentrate on SNMP protocol operations: what messages are used, how they are structured, and how they are exchanged. In examining these messages, we will see the two main ways that information exchanges occur in SNMP—by polling and by interrupt—and also discover how the SNMP protocol works with MIB objects.

SNMP Protocol Operations

The actual communication of information in the SNMP protocol is performed in a manner similar to most other protocols, through the exchange of SNMP messages. These messages are sometimes called *protocol data units* or *PDUs*. This is a term you may have heard used in other protocols, and it is part of the formal definition of data encapsulation in the OSI Reference Model, as explained in Chapter 5. A message is, of course, a data unit used by the protocol. SNMP messages all have *-PDU* at the ends of their names to identify them.

Some consider *protocol data unit* to be analogous to the military using oblong, metallic-headed, manually operated, fastener-acceleration device to refer to a hammer. To be fair though, strictly speaking, in SNMP, a PDU and a message are not exactly the same. The PDU is the higher-layer data that SNMP encapsulates, as described by the OSI model. The SNMP message format is a *wrapper* that encapsulates a PDU along with header fields, as I describe in the next chapter on SNMP messaging. However, the point of a message is to send a PDU, so the two are close enough, and the terms are sometimes used interchangeably.

SNMP PDU Classes

SNMPv1 originally defined six PDUs. The number of PDUs was expanded, and some changes were made to their names and uses in SNMPv2 and SNMPv3. The current SNMP Framework categorizes the PDUs into different *classes*. These classes describe both the function of each message type and the kind of communication they use to perform their task (polling versus interrupting).

> **KEY CONCEPT** SNMP messages consist of a set of fields wrapped around a data element called a *protocol data unit* or *PDU*. In some cases, the terms message and PDU are used interchangeably, although they are technically not the same. SNMP PDUs are arranged into *classes* based on their function.

Table 67-1 lists the main SNMPv2/SNMPv3 PDU classes, describes them, and shows which PDUs are in each class in SNMPv2/SNMPv3. These classes were not used in SNMPv1, but for clarity, I also show which messages from SNMPv1 fall into the classes conceptually.

Table 67-1: SNMP PDU (Message) Classes

SNMPv3 PDU Class	Description	SNMPv1 PDUs	SNMPv2/SNMPv3 PDUs
Read	Messages that read management information from a managed device using a polling mechanism.	GetRequest-PDU, GetNextRequest-PDU	GetRequest-PDU, GetNextRequest-PDU, GetBulkRequest-PDU
Write	Messages that change management information on a managed device to affect the device's operation.	SetRequest-PDU	SetRequest-PDU
Response	Messages sent in response to a previous request.	GetResponse-PDU	Response-PDU
Notification	Messages used by a device to send an interrupt-like notification to an SNMP manager.	Trap-PDU	Trapv2-PDU, InformRequest-PDU

The GetBulkRequest-PDU and InformRequest-PDU messages are new in SNMPv2/v3. The GetResponse-PDU message was renamed Response-PDU (since it is a response and not a message that gets anything), and the new Trapv2-PDU replaces Trap-PDU.

There are three other special classes defined by the current SNMP Framework that are of less interest to us because they don't define actively used messages, but which I should mention for completeness. The Internal class contains a special message called Report-PDU defined for internal SNMP communication. The SNMP standards also provide two classes called Confirmed and Unconfirmed, which are used to categorize the messages listed in Table 67-1 based on whether or not they are acknowledged. The Report-PDU, Trapv2-PDU, and Response-PDU messages are considered Unconfirmed, and the rest are Confirmed.

Now we will look at how the major message types in the four main classes are used. Note that in general terms, all protocol exchanges in SNMP are described in terms of one SNMP entity sending messages to another. Most commonly, the entity sending requests is an SNMP manager, and the one responding is an SNMP agent, except for traps, which are sent by agents. For greater clarity, I try to use these more specific terms (*manager* or *agent*) when possible, rather than just *entity*.

Basic Request/Response Information Poll Using GetRequest and (Get)Response Messages

The obvious place to begin our detailed look at SNMP protocol operations is with the simplest type of information exchange. This would be a simple *poll* operation to read one or more management information variables, used by one SNMP entity (typically an SNMP manager) to request or read information from another entity (normally an SNMP agent on a managed device). SNMP implements this as a simple, two-message request/response protocol exchange, similar to the request/reply processes found in so many TCP/IP protocols.

This information request process typically begins with the user of an application wanting to check the status of a device or look at information about it. As we've seen, all this information is stored on the device in the form of MIB objects. The communication, therefore, takes the form of a request for particular MIB objects and a reply from the device containing those objects' values. In simplified form, the steps in the process are as follows (see Figure 67-1):

1. **SNMP Manager Creates GetRequest-PDU** Based on the information required by the application and user, the SNMP software on the NMS creates a GetRequest-PDU message. It contains the names of the MIB objects whose values the application wants to retrieve.
2. **SNMP Manager Sends GetRequest-PDU** The SNMP manager sends the PDU to the device that is being polled.
3. **SNMP Agent Receives and Processes GetRequest-PDU** The SNMP agent receives and processes the request. It looks at the list of MIB object names contained in the message and checks to see if they are valid (ones the agent actually implements). It looks up the value of each variable that was correctly specified.
4. **SNMP Agent Creates Response-PDU** The agent creates a Response-PDU to send back to the SNMP manager. This message contains the values of the MIB objects requested and/or error codes to indicate any problems with the request, such as an invalid object name.

5. **SNMP Agent Sends Response-PDU** The agent sends the response back to the SNMP manager.
6. **SNMP Manager Processes Response-PDU** The manager processes the information in the Response-PDU received from the agent.

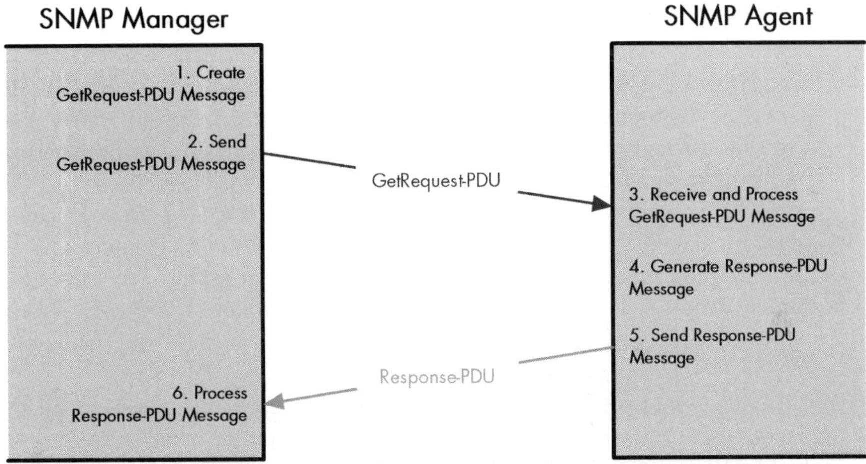

Figure 67-1: SNMP information poll process *The basic SNMP information polling process involves a simple exchange of a GetRequest-PDU sent by an SNMP manager and a Response-PDU returned by an SNMP agent.*

> **KEY CONCEPT** The most basic type of communication in SNMP is an *information poll*, which allows an NMS to read one or more MIB objects from a managed node using a simple request/reply message exchange.

The Response-PDU message is called GetResponse-PDU in SNMPv1. Presumably, this name was chosen based on the fact that it was a response to a get operation, to make the names GetRequest-PDU and GetResponse-PDU somewhat symmetric. The problem is that this name is confusing, for two reasons. First, it sounds to some people like the purpose of the PDU is to "get a response." Second, the GetResponse-PDU was also defined as the response message for operations other than get operations, including the reply message for SetRequest-PDU. Having a GetResponse message be sent in reply to a SetRequest message is disconcerting. The new name is more generic and avoids these problems.

Table Traversal Using GetNextRequest and GetBulkRequest Messages

The GetRequest-PDU message is used by applications to request values for regular, single variables in an SNMP managed object's MIB. As I mentioned in Chapter 66, however, the SMI also allows an MIB to contain *tabular data*.

MIB tables are a useful way for a device to store and organize a set of related data items. It would be far from ideal to try to structure these items just as collections of regular objects. For example, a device may have multiple IP addresses. It would be inefficient to define one MIB object called ipAddr1, another called ipAddr2, and so on to store IP address information. Instead, an object called ipAddrTable is defined in the original SNMPv1 MIB, which specifies a table containing one or more entries called ipAddrEntry. Each entry contains the IP address and subnet mask for one of the interfaces of the device.

SNMPv1 Table Traversal Using GetNextRequest

There needs to be a way to let an SNMP manager read the contents of these tables from a device. This can be done using the regular GetRequest-PDU message, by specifying each entry in the table, one after the other. However, this is somewhat crude, and it leaves a problem: the SNMP manager may not know how many entries are in the table, and therefore, how many entries it should request.

The problem of *table traversal* was addressed in SNMPv1 through the creation of a new message type called GetNextRequest-PDU. You can think of this as a relative of the regular GetRequest-PDU. The GetNextRequest-PDU contains the name of a tabular variable, as well as a particular entry in the table. The device receiving the GetNextRequest-PDU uses this to look up the next value in the table and return it in a GetResponse-PDU message.

The actual protocol exchange is about the same as that described in the previous section: a request is sent by the SNMP manager, and a reply is returned by the SNMP agent. The difference is that instead of the SNMP agent returning the value for the variable specified, it returns the value of the *next* variable in the table. This is then used as the value for the next request, and so on, until the last entry in the table is reached. Once this happens and a GetNextRequest-PDU is sent that contains this last entry, the responding device indicates this by returning the MIB object that conceptually follows the table in the implementation of the MIB. This signals to the SNMP manager that the table has been fully traversed.

> **KEY CONCEPT** The SNMP GetNextRequest-PDU message allows an NMS to request a series of consecutive variables in an MIB. This is most commonly used to allow tabular data to be more easily retrieved, without requiring that each variable in the table be individually specified.

SNMPv2/v3 Table Traversal Using GetBulkRequest

The GetNextRequest-PDU message is functional, but while it is more elegant than using regular GetRequest-PDU messages, it is not any more efficient—each entry in the table must still be requested one at a time. This means that retrieving the information in a table takes a long time and also results in a great deal of traffic being generated, due to the number of requests and replies that must be sent.

To make table traversal easier and more conservative in its use of network resources, SNMPv2 introduced a new message type called GetBulkRequest-PDU. You can probably surmise the idea here from the name. Instead of specifying a particular MIB object to get or to get next, a GetBulkRequest-PDU allows an SNMP manager to send a single request that results in a number of entries in a table being returned in a Response-PDU message.

The GetBulkRequest-PDU is designed to allow both regular variables and tables to be retrieved in a single request. The PDU includes a list of objects, just as in a GetRequest-PDU or GetNextRequest-PDU. The list is organized so that regular objects appear first and table objects come afterwards. Two special parameters are included in the request:

Non Repeaters Specifies the number of nonrepeating, regular objects to be retrieved. This is the number of regular objects at the start of the object list.

Max Repetitions Specifies the number of iterations, or entries, to read for the remaining tabular objects.

For example, suppose an SNMP manager wanted to request four regular variables and three entries from a table. The GetNextRequest-PDU would contain five MIB object specifications, with the table last. The Non Repeaters field would be set to 4, and the Max Repetitions field set to 3.

> **KEY CONCEPT** To improve the efficiency of table traversal, SNMPv2 introduced the GetBulkRequest-PDU message, which allows an NMS to request a sequence of MIB objects from a table using a single request to a managed node.

The original method of traversing tables using GetRequest-PDU and GetNextRequest-PDU from SNMPv1 was retained in SNMPv2 and SNMPv3 when they were developed. However, the introduction of the more efficient GetBulkRequest-PDU means that GetNextRequest-PDU is not as important as it was in SNMPv1. Bear in mind, however, that using GetBulkRequest-PDU does require that the requesting entity know how many entries to ask for. So, some trial and error, or multiple requests, may be required to get a whole table if the number of entries is not known.

Object Modification Using SetRequest Messages

The GetRequest-PDU, GetNextRequest-PDU, and GetBulkRequest-PDU messages are the three members of the SNMP Read class of PDUs—they are used to let an SNMP manager read MIB objects from an SNMP agent. The opposite function is represented by the SNMP Write class, which contains a single member: the SNMP SetRequest-PDU message.

The use of this PDU is fairly obvious; where one of the three Get PDUs specifies a variable whose value is to be retrieved, the SetRequest-PDU message contains a specification for variables whose values are to be modified by the network administrator. Remember that SNMP does not include specific commands to let a network administrator control a managed device. This is the *control* method, which works by setting variables that affect the operation of the managed device.

The set process is the complement of the get process, using the same basic idea, but a reversal in how the object values travel and what is done with them. The process follows these steps (see Figure 67-2):

1. **SNMP Manager Creates SetRequest-PDU** Based on the information changes specified by the user through the SNMP application, the SNMP software on the

NMS creates a SetRequest-PDU message. It contains a set of MIB object names and the values to which they are to be set.

2. **SNMP Manager Sends SetRequest-PDU** The SNMP manager sends the PDU to the device being controlled.
3. **SNMP Agent Receives and Processes SetRequest-PDU** The SNMP agent receives and processes the set request. It examines each object in the request, along with the value to which the object is to be set, and determines if the request should or should not be honored.
4. **SNMP Agent Makes Changes and Creates Response-PDU** Assuming that the information in the request was correct (and any security provisions have been satisfied), the SNMP agent makes changes to its internal variables. The agent creates a Response-PDU to send back to the SNMP manager, which either indicates that the request succeeded or contains error codes to indicate any problems with the request found during processing.
5. **SNMP Agent Sends Response-PDU** The agent sends the response back to the SNMP manager.
6. **SNMP Manager Processes Response-PDU** The manager processes the information in the Response-PDU to see the results of the set.

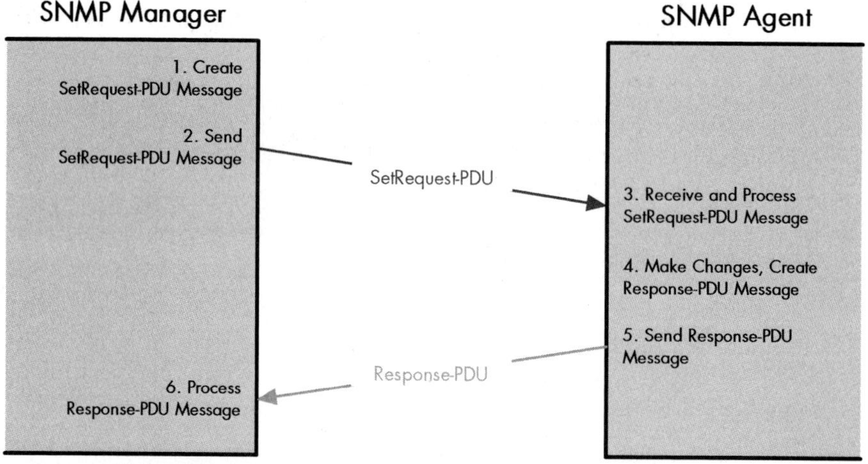

Figure 67-2: SNMP object modification process *The communication process for setting a MIB object value is very similar to that used for reading one. The main difference is that the object values are sent from the SNMP manager to the SNMP agent, carried in the SetRequest-PDU message.*

Obviously, telling a device to change a variable's value is a more significant request than just asking the device to read the value. For this reason, the managed device must very carefully analyze and verify the information in the request to ensure that the request is valid. The checks performed include the following:

- Verifying the names of the objects to be changed
- Verifying that the objects are allowed to be modified (based on their Access or Max-Access object characteristic, as described in Chapter 66)

- Checking the value included in the request to ensure that its type and size are valid for the object to be changed

This is also a place where general protocol security issues become more important, as I'll discuss near the end of this chapter.

> **KEY CONCEPT** SNMP NMSs control the operation of managed devices by changing MIB objects on those devices. This is done using the SetRequest-PDU message, which specifies the objects to be modified and their values.

Information Notification Using Trap and InformRequest Messages

Earlier in this chapter, I introduced the two basic methods of communicating information between SNMP devices: using polls or interrupts. All of the message types and exchanges we have examined thus far in this section have been poll-driven. They consist of an SNMP manager making a specific request that results in action being taken, and a response being generated by an SNMP agent.

Polling is ideal for the exchange of routine information that needs to be gathered on a regular basis. For example, the regular get requests could be used to verify the settings on a device, examine error counts over a period of time, or check its uptime or use statistics. And, obviously, polling is the only real method for performing a set operation, where data is changed.

But polling is not well suited for important information that needs to be communicated quickly. The reason is that poll-driven communication is always initiated by the recipient of the information: the SNMP manager. If something significant occurs on a managed device that the manager wasn't expecting, the manager won't find out about it unless it specifically asks to see the variable that has changed. This means that important variables would need to be checked all the time by the SNMP manager, which is highly efficient.

In the real world, using polling to implement situations where critical information needs to be sent would be like having the emergency response service in your town call everyone every hour to find out if they needed an ambulance or fire truck. Similarly, in SNMP, a mechanism was needed to let an SNMP agent initiate the communication of information. This capability was originally made part of the SNMPv1 protocol through the inclusion of the Trap-PDU message type.

In computer science, a *trap* is simply a set of conditions that a device monitors continuously. If the appropriate conditions occur, the trap is *triggered* and causes some sort of action to be taken. In SNMP, traps are programmed into SNMP agents, and when they are triggered, an SNMP Trap-PDU message is sent to an SNMP manager to inform it of the occurrence. Examples of traps in the SNMPv1 specification include ones that trigger in the event of a communication link failure, restart of the device, or an authentication problem.

Use of SNMP Trap and Trapv2 Messages

The communication in the case of a trap is trivial. The SNMP agent sends the trap, and the SNMP manager is thereby considered informed of what happened. That's pretty much it. These are Unconfirmed messages, and no reply is made back to the SNMP agent. The triggering of the trap may lead the network administrator to take follow-up action at the device that sent the trap.

The designer of a particular MIB must determine which traps to create for a particular group of objects. The implementation must specify the conditions under which the traps will trigger and also the destination to which the Trap-PDU message will be sent when this occurs. In SNMPv2, the trap notification message was retained in the form of the Trapv2-PDU message.

Use of the SNMPv2 InformRequest Message

SNMPv2 also incorporates a second notification message type: the InformRequest-PDU message. This type of message is not the same as a trap, but it is related to traps for two reasons: Both message types are used to communicate information without the recipient initiating the process, and the two messages are sometimes used in conjunction.

The purpose of the InformRequest-PDU is actually to facilitate the communication of information between NMSs. The SNMP manager on one NMS can choose to inform another of some piece of information by sending an InformRequest-PDU to that other SNMP manager. The receiving manager then replies back with a Response-PDU to the one that sent the InformRequest-PDU, confirming receipt of the inform message.

A common way that this message is used is to spread the news when a trap occurs. Suppose a device experiences a power failure, which results in a Trapv2-PDU being sent to NMS 1. The network administrator may want to set up NMS 1 so that receipt of particular traps causes the information in the trap to be forwarded to another NMS. The InformRequest-PDU would be used to carry that information from NMS 1 to, say, NMS 2.

KEY CONCEPT SNMP managed devices can inform an NMS of an important occurrence by sending it a Trap-PDU or Trapv2-PDU message. Network administrators determine the circumstances under which one of these messages should be transmitted. SNMPv2 adds to this capability the InformRequest-PDU message, which can be used to propagate information about an event between management stations.

SNMP Protocol Security Issues and Methods

In my description of the various SNMP versions in Chapter 65, it's possible that I may have been a bit harsh on those who worked on SNMP during the 1990s. The proliferation of many SNMP version 2 variants really was unfortunate, and not something we often see in the world of TCP/IP. However, now that we've seen the sort of work that SNMP does, the desire for security in the protocol would seem to be clear. Given that, and given the very low level of security in the initial SNMPv1 protocol, it's understandable to some extent why a conflict over security issues arose.

The need for security in SNMP is obvious because the MIB objects being communicated contain critical information about network devices. We don't want just anyone snooping into our network to find out our IP addresses, how long our machines have been running, whether our links are down, or pretty much anything else. When it comes to object write operations using a SetRequest-PDU, the concerns are magnified even more, because we definitely don't want strangers being able to control or interfere with our managed devices by issuing bogus commands to change MIB objects that control device operation!

Problems with SNMPv1 Security

Unfortunately, the security incorporated into SNMPv1 was extremely limited. It really took the form of only one policy and one simple technology.

SNMP was created with the mindset that the MIB objects used in the protocol would be relatively *weak*. This means that the objects are designed so that any problems in working with them result in minimal damage. The policy of the designers of SNMP was that MIB objects that are normally read should not contain critical information, and objects that are written should not control critical functions.

So, a read-only MIB object containing a description of a machine is fine, but one containing the administrative password is not. Similarly, a read-write MIB object that controls when the computer next reboots is acceptable, but one that tells the object to reformat its hard disk is definitely not!

All the devices in an SNMP network managed by a particular set of NMSs are considered to be in a *community*. Each SNMPv1 message sent between members of the community is identified by a *community string* that appears in a field in the message header. This string is like a simple password. Any messages received with the wrong string will be rejected by the recipient.

These security features are better than nothing, but not much. The use of weak objects is comparable to a policy that says not to leave your car in front of the convenience store with the doors unlocked and the key in the ignition—it is basically saying, "Don't ask for trouble." This is wise, but it's not a complete security solution.

The community strings protect against obvious tampering in the form of unauthorized messages. However, the strings are sent in plain text, and they can easily be discovered and then used to compromise the community. So, this is like locking your doors when parking your car—it protects against the casual thief but not a pro.

Of course, for some people, not leaving their car running and locking the doors when they park provide enough security, and SNMPv1's security was also sufficient for some users of SNMP. But in newer, larger internetworks, especially ones spanning large distances or using public carriers, SNMPv1 wasn't up to the task. This is why all that fun stuff occurred with SNMPv2.

SNMPv2/v3 Security Methods

During the evolution of SNMPv2 variants, and eventually the creation of SNMPv3, several new security models were created to improve SNMPv1's security:

Party-Based Security Model Party-based security was the model for the original SNMPv2 standard, now called *SNMPv2p*. A logical entity called a *party* is defined for communication that specifies a particular authentication protocol and a privacy (encryption) protocol. The information is used to verify that a particular request is authentic, and to ensure that the sender and receiver agree on how to encrypt and decrypt data.

User-Based Security Model (USM) USM was developed in the SNMPv2u variant and used in SNMPv2* (SNMPv2 asterisk). It eventually was adopted in SNMPv3. The idea here is to move away from tying security to the machines and instead use more traditional security based on access rights of a user of a machine. A variety of authentication and encryption protocols can be used to ensure access rights are respected and to protect message privacy. The method relies on timestamps, clock synchronization, and other techniques to protect against certain types of attacks.

View-Based Access Control Model (VACM) VACM is part of SNMPv3, and it defines a method where more fine control can be placed on access to objects on a device. A *view* specifies a particular set of MIB objects that can be accessed by a particular group in a particular context. By controlling these views, an administrator can manage what information is accessed by whom.

Party-based security pretty much died with SNMPv2p. USM and VACM are part of SNMPv3 and provide enhanced security for those who need it. Again, it's interesting to note how many networks continue to use SNMPv1, security warts and all.

SNMPv3 took another important security-related step in redefining the SNMP architecture to seamlessly support multiple security models. This enables different implementations to choose the security model that is best for them. USM is the default model in SNMPv3.

68

SNMP PROTOCOL MESSAGING AND MESSAGE FORMATS

As we saw extensively in the previous chapter, the communication of management information is accomplished through the exchange of Simple Network Management Protocol (SNMP) messages that contain *protocol data units (PDUs)*. Like the messages of most TCP/IP protocols, these PDUs are designed to use a particular field format, and are created, addressed, and transported according to specific protocol rules. SNMP messages include fields that control the operation of the protocol, and they carry a payload of management information in the form of management information base (MIB) objects.

In this chapter, I describe the details of how messaging is accomplished in the SNMP protocol. I begin with a general discussion of issues related to message generation, addressing, and transport, and a description of how retransmission of messages is handled when necessary. I discuss the way fields are defined in SNMP messages and describe their general format, explaining the difference between the overall message and the PDU it contains. I then examine the message format used in all of the important SNMP versions, showing the structure of each message type and the fields used.

SNMP Protocol Message Generation

Message generation in SNMP is a bit different than the typical TCP/IP client/server model used for most other protocols. There aren't really any formal clients and servers in SNMP, since management information can be obtained from any device; it is distributed. Most of the message exchanges use a matched pair of request and reply messages. The network management station (NMS) usually *acts* as the client in these exchanges, sending a particular get or set request to an SNMP agent, which plays the role of server for the information it contains. However, SNMP agents aren't usually considered servers in the conventional sense.

SNMP traps deviate from the normal request/reply model of message generation entirely. When a trap is triggered, an SNMP agent sends a trap message to an NMS on its own, not in reaction to receiving a request. Since trap messages are unconfirmed, there is no reply. Note, however, that the SNMP versions 2 and 3 (SNMPv2 and SNMPv3) InformRequest-PDU message (discussed later in this chapter) is confirmed, and a response message is thus sent back to the NMS that generates it.

SNMP Transport Mappings

Once a message has been generated, it is sent using the protocols at the levels below the application layer where SNMP resides. As you saw in the overview of the SNMP protocol in the previous chapter, the current SNMP standard set separates the description of protocol operations and PDUs from the methods used to actually send them.

Starting with version 2, SNMP has defined several *transport mappings* that describe how SNMP PDUs can be sent over a variety of internetworking protocol suites, including TCP/IP, OSI, IPX/SPX (Novell), and AppleTalk. Many of the specific details of SNMP messaging depend on the transport mapping that is used in a particular implementation. SNMP is primarily used on TCP/IP internetworks, and TCP/IP is where our interest lies here, so the rest of this discussion will deal with transport issues when SNMP is used over the Internet Protocol (IP).

The standard IP transport mapping for SNMP calls for it to be carried using the User Datagram Protocol (UDP). This decision goes back to the initial implementation of SNMPv1 (before there were distinct transport mappings). UDP was likely chosen because it is more efficient for the simple request/reply messaging scheme SNMP uses. The many Transmission Control Protocol (TCP) features were not considered necessary and add overhead that SNMP's designers wanted to avoid. It is possible that TCP could be used to carry SNMP, defined as a different transport mapping, but I don't believe this is actually done.

Two well-known UDP port numbers are reserved for SNMP. The first is port 161, which is the general-purpose SNMP number. All devices that are set up to listen for SNMP requests—both agents and managers—listen on port 161. Each device receives any messages sent and replies back to the client, the SNMP entity that issued the request, which uses an ephemeral port number to identify the requesting process. The second UDP port number is 162, which is reserved for

SNMP traps. Having two numbers allows regular messages and traps to be kept separate. Normally, only NMSs would listen on port 162, since agents are not recipients of traps.

The use of UDP allows SNMP information communication to be streamlined, since there is no need to establish a TCP connection, and since message headers are shorter and processing time slightly reduced. But the use of UDP introduces a couple of issues that SNMP implementations must be concerned with, including message size and lost messages.

UDP Message Size Issues

The first issue is that of message length. SNMP PDUs can carry many MIB objects, which means they could potentially be rather large. However, UDP is limited in the size of message it can carry (where TCP is not). The standards specify that SNMP entities must accept messages up to at least 484 bytes in size. They also recommend that SNMP implementations be able to accept even larger messages, up to 1,472 bytes, which would correspond to the largest size message that can be encapsulated in an Ethernet frame (1,500 bytes, allowing 20 bytes for the IP header and 8 for the UDP header).

The use of the GetBulkRequest-PDU message type in SNMPv2 and SNMPv3 requires particular care, since it allows a single request to result in many MIB objects being sent back in a response. The Max Repetitions parameter must be chosen conservatively so the SNMP agent doesn't try to send an enormous message that won't fit.

Lost Transmission Issues

The second issue with UDP is the price we pay for its efficiency and simplicity: a lack of transport features. UDP doesn't guarantee data delivery or handle retransmissions, which means a request or reply could, in theory, be lost in transit. Only the device that initially sends a request can know if there was a problem with transport. It sends the request, and if it receives no reply, it knows either the request or response got lost. This puts the responsibility for retransmission on the device that sends the request message.

NMSs sending requests to SNMP agents generally use a timer to keep track of how much time has elapsed since a request was sent. If the response doesn't arrive within a certain time interval, the request is sent again. Because of how SNMP works, having a request be received more than once accidentally will normally not cause any problems (a property known as *idempotence*). The NMS does need to employ an algorithm to ensure that it does not generate too many retransmissions and clog the network (especially since congestion might be causing the loss of its messages in the first place).

Since traps are unconfirmed, there is no way for the intended recipient of a trap PDU to know if did not arrive, nor is there any way for the sender of the trap PDU to know. This is just a weakness in the protocol; the overall reliability of TCP/IP (and the underlying networks) ensures that these messages are not lost very often.

KEY CONCEPT SNMP is designed with a separately defined set of *protocol operations* and *transport mappings*, so it can be carried over many different internetworking technologies. The most common of these transport mechanisms is TCP/IP, where SNMP makes use of UDP running over IP, for its efficient and simple communication. The lack of reliability features in UDP means that requests must be tracked by the device sending them and retransmitted if no reply is received. The limited size of UDP messages restricts the amount of information that can be sent in any SNMP PDU.

SNMP General Message Format

To structure its messages for transport, SNMP uses a special field format, like most protocols. What's interesting about SNMP, however, is that its standards do not describe the SNMP message format using a simple list of fields the way most TCP/IP standards do. Instead, SNMP messages are defined using the same data description language (*Abstract Syntax Notation 1* or *ASN.1*) that is used to describe MIB objects.

The reason for this is that SNMP messages implement the various SNMP protocol operations with the ultimate goal of allowing MIB objects to be conveyed between SNMP entities. These MIB objects become fields within the messages to be sent. The MIB objects carried in SNMP messages are defined using ASN.1 as described in the Structure of Management Information (SMI) standard. So, it makes sense to define SNMP messages and all their fields using the same syntax.

Since all SNMP fields are defined like MIB objects, they are like objects in that they have certain characteristics. Specifically, each field has a name, and its contents are described using one of the standard SMI data types. So, unlike normal message formats where each field has just a name and a length, an SNMP message format field has a name and a *syntax*, such as Integer, Octet String, or IpAddress. The syntax of the field defines its length and how it is formatted and used.

Just as regular message formats use integers to represent specific values (for example, the numeric Opcode field in the DNS message header, which indicates the DNS message type), this can be done in SNMP using an enumerated integer type. An example would be the Error Status field, where a range of integer values represents different error conditions.

The decision to define SNMP messages using ASN.1 allows the message format description to be consistent with how the objects in the format are described, which is nice. Unfortunately, it means that the field formats are very hard to determine from the standards, because they are not described in one place. Instead, the overall message format is defined as a set of components, and those components contain subcomponents that may be defined elsewhere, and so on. In fact, the full message format isn't even defined in one standard; parts are spread across several standards. So, you can't look in one place and see the whole message format. Well, I should say that you can't if you use the standards, but you can if you look here.

To make things easier for you, I have converted these distributed syntax descriptions into the same tabular field formats I use throughout the rest of this book. I will begin here by describing the general format used for SNMP messages, and in the remainder of the chapter, explore the specific formats used in each version of SNMP.

The Difference Between SNMP Messages and PDUs

To understand SNMP messages, it is important that you first grasp the difference between SNMP messages and SNMP PDUs. We've seen in looking at SNMP protocol operations that the two terms are often used interchangeably. This is because each message carries one PDU, and the PDU is the most important part of the message.

However, strictly speaking, an SNMP PDU and an SNMP message are not exactly the same. The PDU is the actual piece of information that is being communicated between SNMP entities. It is carried within the SNMP message along with a number of header fields, which are used to carry identification and security information. Thus, conceptually, the SNMP message format can be considered to have two overall sections:

Message Header Contains fields used to control how the message is processed, including fields for implementing SNMP security.

Message Body (PDU) Contains the main portion of the message. In this case, the message body is the PDU being transmitted.

The overall SNMP message is sometimes called a *wrapper* for the PDU, since it encapsulates the PDU and precedes it with additional fields. The distinction between the PDU and the message format as a whole began as a formality in SNMPv1, but it became quite important in later versions. The reason is that it allows the fields used for basic protocol operations (which are in the PDU) to be kept separate from fields used to implement security features. In SNMPv2, the implementation of security became a very big deal indeed, so this flexibility was quite important.

General PDU Format

The fields in each PDU depend on the PDU type, but can be divided into the following general substructure:

PDU Control Fields A set of fields that describe the PDU and communicate information from one SNMP entity to another.

PDU Variable Bindings A set of descriptions of the MIB objects in the PDU. Each object is described as a *binding* of a name to a value.

Each PDU will follow this general structure, which is shown in Figure 68-1, differing only in the number of control fields and variable bindings and how they are used. In theory, each PDU could have a different message format using a distinct set of control fields, but in practice, most PDUs for a given SNMP version use the same control fields (with some exceptions).

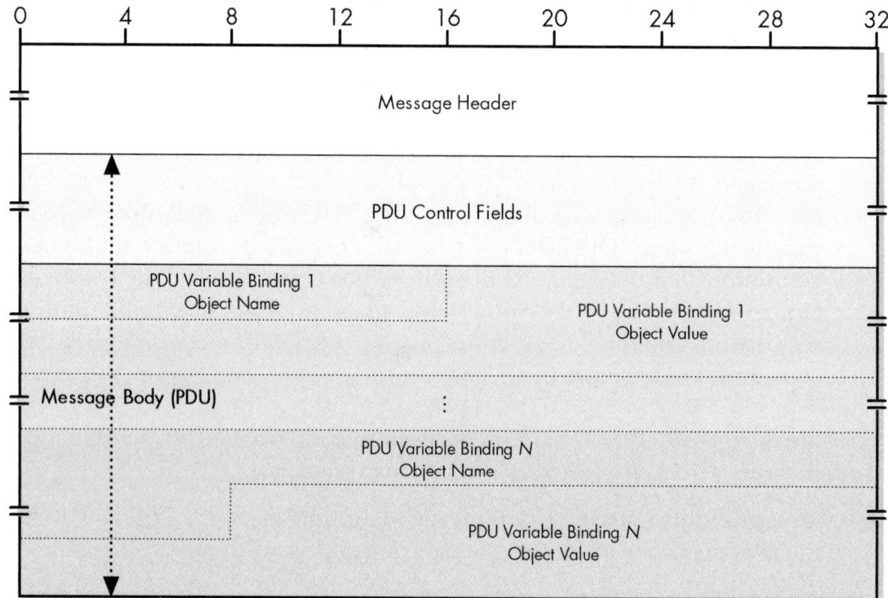

Figure 68-1: *SNMP general message format*

Each variable binding describes one MIB object. The binding consists of a pair of subfields, one specifying the name of the object in standard SNMP object identifier notation and one its value, formatted to match the object's SMI syntax. For example, if the object were of type Integer, the value field would be four bytes wide and contain a numeric integer value. Table 68-1 describes the subfield format for each PDU variable binding.

Table 68-1: SNMP Variable Binding Format

Subfield Name	Syntax	Size (Bytes)	Description
Object Name	Sequence of Integer	Variable	The numeric object identifier of the MIB object, specified as a sequence of integers. For example, the object `sysLocation` has the object identifier 1.3.6.1.2.1.1.6, so it would be specified as 1 3 6 1 2 1 1 6 using ASN.1.
Object Value	Variable	Variable	In any type of get request, this subfield is a placeholder; it is structured using the appropriate syntax for the object but has no value (since the get request is asking for that value!). In a set request (SetRequest-PDU) or in a reply message carrying requested data (GetResponse-PDU or Response-PDU), the value of the object is placed here.

KEY CONCEPT The general format of SNMP messages consists of a *message header* and a *message body*. The body of the message is also called the *protocol data unit*, or *PDU*, and contains a set of PDU *control fields* and a number of *variable bindings*. Each variable binding describes one MIB object and consists of the object's name and value.

SNMP Version 1 (SNMPv1) Message Format

The SNMP general message format was first used to define the format of messages in the original SNMP protocol, SNMPv1. This first version of SNMP is probably best known for its relative simplicity compared to the versions that followed it. This is reflected in its message format, which is quite straightforward.

SNMPv1 General Message Format

The general message format in SNMPv1 is a wrapper consisting of a small header and an encapsulated PDU. Not very many header fields were needed in SNMPv1 because the community-based security method in SNMPv1 is very rudimentary. The overall format for SNMPv1 messages is described in Table 68-2 and illustrated in Figure 68-2.

Table 68-2: SNMP Version 1 (SNMPv1) General Message Format

Field Name	Syntax	Size (Bytes)	Description
Version	Integer	4	Version Number: Describes the SNMP version number of this message; used for ensuring compatibility between versions. For SNMPv1, this value is actually 0, not 1.
Community	Octet String	Variable	Community String: Identifies the SNMP community in which the sender and recipient of this message are located. This is used to implement the simple SNMP community-based security mechanism, described in the previous chapter.
PDU	—	Variable	Protocol Data Unit: The PDU being communicated as the body of the message.

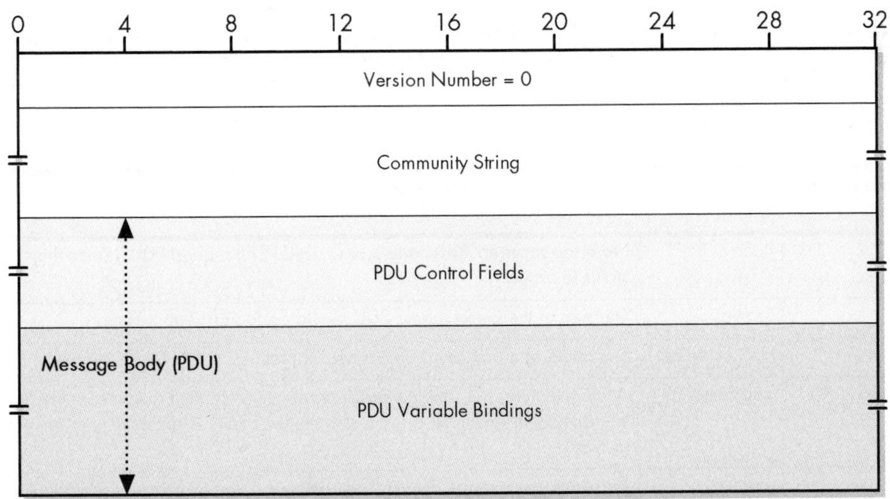

Figure 68-2: SNMPv1 general message format

SNMPv1 PDU Formats

All of the PDUs in SNMPv1 have the same format, with one exception: Trap-PDU. The exact semantics of each field in the PDU depend on the particular message. For example, the ErrorStatus field only has meaning in a reply and not a request, and object values are used differently in requests and replies as well.

Table 68-3 shows the common format for most of the SNMPv1 PDUs: GetRequest-PDU, GetNextRequest-PDU, SetRequest-PDU, and GetResponse-PDU.

Table 68-3: SNMPv1 Common PDU Format

Field Name	Syntax	Size (Bytes)	Description
PDU Type	Integer (Enumerated)	4	PDU Type: An integer value that indicates the PDU type: 0 = GetRequest-PDU 1 = GetNextRequest-PDU 2 = GetNextRequest-PDU 3 = SetRequest-PDU
Request ID	Integer	4	Request Identifier: A number used to match requests with replies. It is generated by the device that sends a request and copied into this field in a GetResponse-PDU by the responding SNMP entity.
Error Status	Integer (Enumerated)	4	Error Status: An integer value that is used in a GetResponse-PDU to tell the requesting SNMP entity the result of its request. A value of zero indicates that no error occurred; the other values indicate what sort of error happened, as listed in Table 68-4.
Error Index	Integer	4	Error Index: When Error Status is nonzero, this field contains a pointer that specifies which object generated the error. Always zero in a request.
Variable Bindings	Variable	Variable	Variable Bindings: A set of name/value pairs identifying the MIB objects in the PDU, and in the case of a SetRequest-PDU or GetResponse-PDU, containing their values. See the discussion of the general SNMP general PDU format earlier in this chapter for more on these bindings.

Table 68-4: SNMPv1 Error Status Field Values

Error Status Value	Error Code	Description
0	noError	No error occurred. This code is also used in all request PDUs, since they have no error status to report.
1	tooBig	The size of the GetResponse-PDU would be too large to transport.
2	noSuchName	The name of a requested object was not found.
3	badValue	A value in the request didn't match the structure that the recipient of the request had for the object. For example, an object in the request was specified with an incorrect length or type.
4	readOnly	An attempt was made to set a variable that has an Access value indicating that it is read-only.
5	genErr	An error other than one of the preceding four specific types occurred.

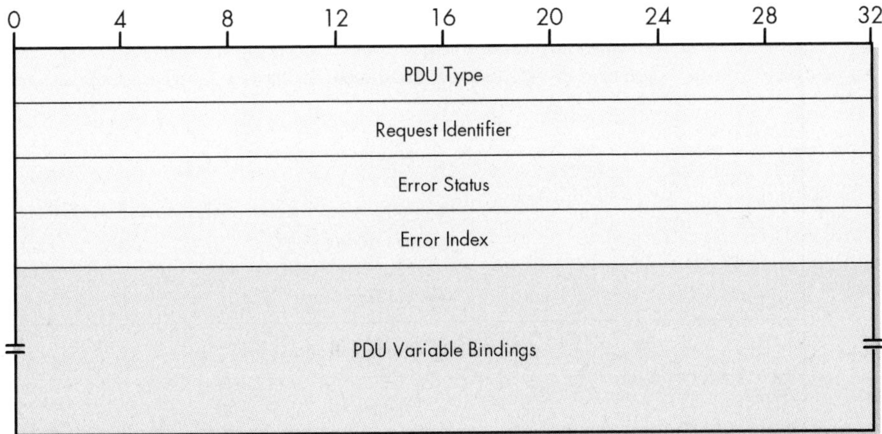

Figure 68-3: *SNMPv1 common PDU format*

Table 68-5 describes the special format for the SNMPv1 Trap-PDU, and it is illustrated in Figure 68-4.

Table 68-5: SNMPv1 Trap-PDU Format

Field Name	Syntax	Size (Bytes)	Description
PDU Type	Integer (Enumerated)	4	PDU Type: An integer value that indicates the PDU type, which is 4 for a Trap-PDU message.
Enterprise	Sequence of Integer	Variable	Enterprise: An object identifier for a group, which indicates the type of object that generated the trap.
Agent Addr	NetworkAddress	4	Agent Address: The IP address of the SNMP agent that generated the trap. This is also in the IP header at lower levels but inclusion in the SNMP message format allows for easier trap logging within SNMP. Also, in the case of a multihomed host, this specifies the preferred address.
Generic Trap	Integer (Enumerated)	4	Generic Trap Code: A code value specifying one of a number of predefined generic trap types.
Specific Trap	Integer	4	Specific Trap Code: A code value indicating an implementation-specific trap type.
Time Stamp	TimeTicks	4	Time Stamp: The amount of time since the SNMP entity sending this message last initialized or reinitialized. Used to time stamp traps for logging purposes.
Variable Bindings	Variable	Variable	Variable Bindings: A set of name/value pairs identifying the MIB objects in the PDU. See the discussion of the general SNMP general PDU format earlier in this chapter for more on these bindings.

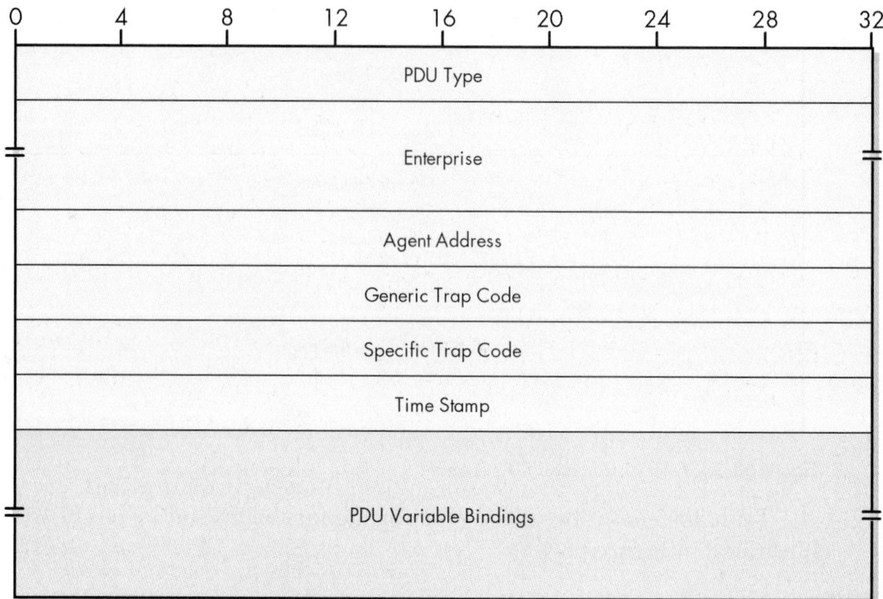

Figure 68-4: *SNMPv1 Trap-PDU format*

SNMP Version 2 (SNMPv2) Message Formats

After SMNPv1 had been in use for several years, certain issues with it were noticed and areas for improvement identified. This led to the development of the original SNMPv2, which was intended to enhance SNMPv1 in many areas, including MIB object definitions, protocol operations, and security. This last area, security, led to the proliferation of SNMPv2 version variants that I described in Chapter 65.

Since there are several different SNMPv2s, there are also several message formats for SNMPv2. This is confusing, but it would be even worse without the modular nature of SNMP messages coming to the rescue. The protocol operations in SNMPv2 were changed from SNMPv1, which necessitated some modifications to the format of SNMPv2 PDUs. However, the protocol operations are the same for all the SNMPv2 variations. The differences between SNMPv2 variants are in the areas of security implementation. Thus, the result of this is that the PDU format is the same for all the SNMPv2 types, while the overall message format differs for each variant. (This is why the distinction between a PDU and a message is not just an academic one!)

During the SNMPv2 divergence, four variations were defined: the original SNMPv2 (SNMPv2p), community-based SNMPv2 (SNMPv2c), user-based SNMPv2 (SNMPv2u), and SNMPv2 asterisk (SNMPv2*). Of these, the first three were documented in sets of SNMP RFC standards, as discussed in Chapter 65; the fourth was not. The structure of the overall message format for each variant is discussed in an administrative or security standard for the variation in question, which makes reference to the shared SNMPv2 standard for the PDU format (RFC 1905).

SNMP Version 2 (SNMPv2p) Message Format

The party-based security model is quite complex, but the basic messaging in this version is described through the definition of a *management communication*, which describes the source and destination party and makes reference to a *context* for the communication. The overall message format is described in detail in RFC 1445. This information is summarized in Table 68-6 and shown graphically in Figure 68-5.

Table 68-6: SNMP Version 2 (SNMPv2p) General Message Format

Field Name	Syntax	Size (Bytes)	Description
Version	Integer	4	Version Number: Describes the SNMP version number of this message; used for ensuring compatibility between versions. For SNMPv2p, this value is 2.
Dst Party	Sequence of Integer	Variable	Destination Party: An object identifier that specifies the party that is the intended recipient of the message.
Src Party	Sequence of Integer	Variable	Source Party: An object identifier that specifies the party that is the sender of the message.
Context	Sequence of Integer	Variable	Context: Defines a set of MIB object resources that is accessible by a particular entity.
PDU	—	Variable	PDU: The protocol data unit of the message.

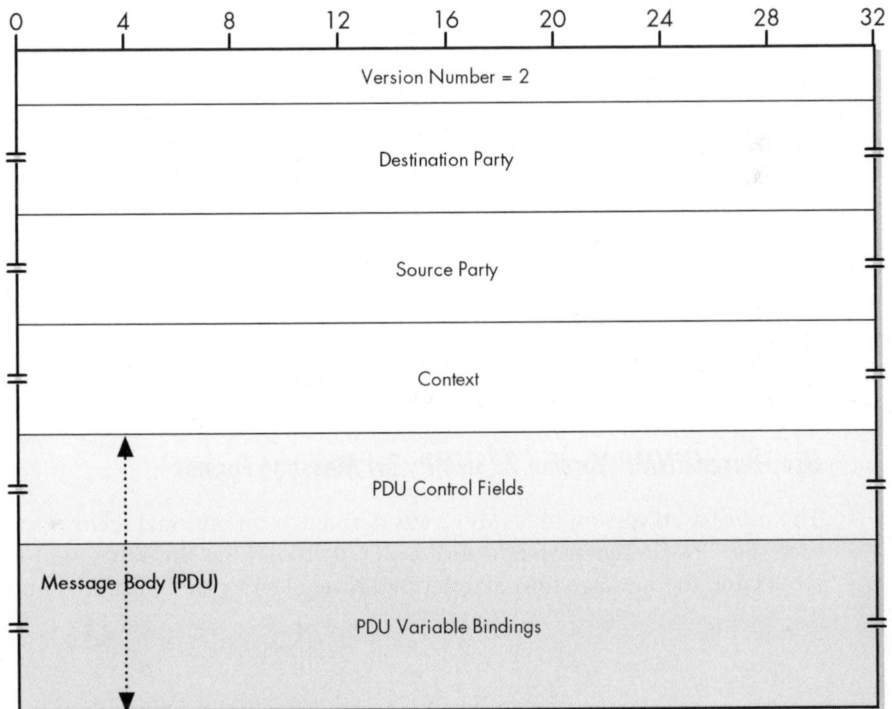

Figure 68-5: SNMPv2p general message format

Community-Based SNMP Version 2 (SNMPv2c) Message Format

The community-based version of SNMPv2 was intended to keep the new protocol enhancements introduced by SNMPv2p but go back to the simple SNMPv1 security model. As such, the defining document for SNMPv2c, RFC 1901, specifies that its overall message format is the same as that of SNMPv1, except that the version number is changed. This is shown in Table 68-7 and illustrated in Figure 68-6.

Table 68-7: Community-Based SNMP Version 2 (SNMPv2c) General Message Format

Field Name	Syntax	Size (Bytes)	Description
Version	Integer	4	Version Number: Describes the SNMP version number of this message; used for ensuring compatibility between versions. For SNMPv2c, this value is 1.
Community	Octet String	Variable	Community String: Identifies the SNMP community in which the sender and recipient of this message are located.
PDU	—	Variable	Protocol Data Unit: The PDU being communicated as the body of the message.

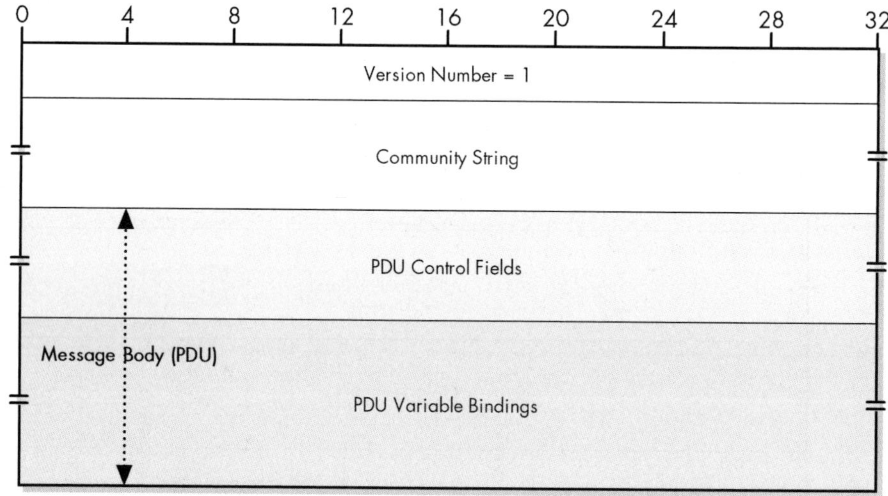

Figure 68-6: *SNMPv2c general message format*

User-Based SNMP Version 2 (SNMPv2u) Message Format

The user-based version of SNMPv2 was defined as an optional security model at the time that SNMPv2c was standardized. RFC 1910 defines the user-based security model and the message format described in Table 68-8 and illustrated in Figure 68-7.

Table 68-8: User-Based SNMP Version 2 (SNMPv2u) General Message Format

Field Name	Syntax	Size (Bytes)	Description
Version	Integer	4	Version Number: Describes the SNMP version number of this message; used for ensuring compatibility between versions. For SNMPv2u, this value is 2. Note that this is the same value as used for SNMPv2p.
Parameters	Octet String	Variable	Parameters: A string of parameters used to implement the user-based security model, which are briefly described in Table 68-9.
PDU	—	Variable	Protocol Data Unit: The PDU being communicated as the body of the message. This may be in either encrypted or unencrypted form.

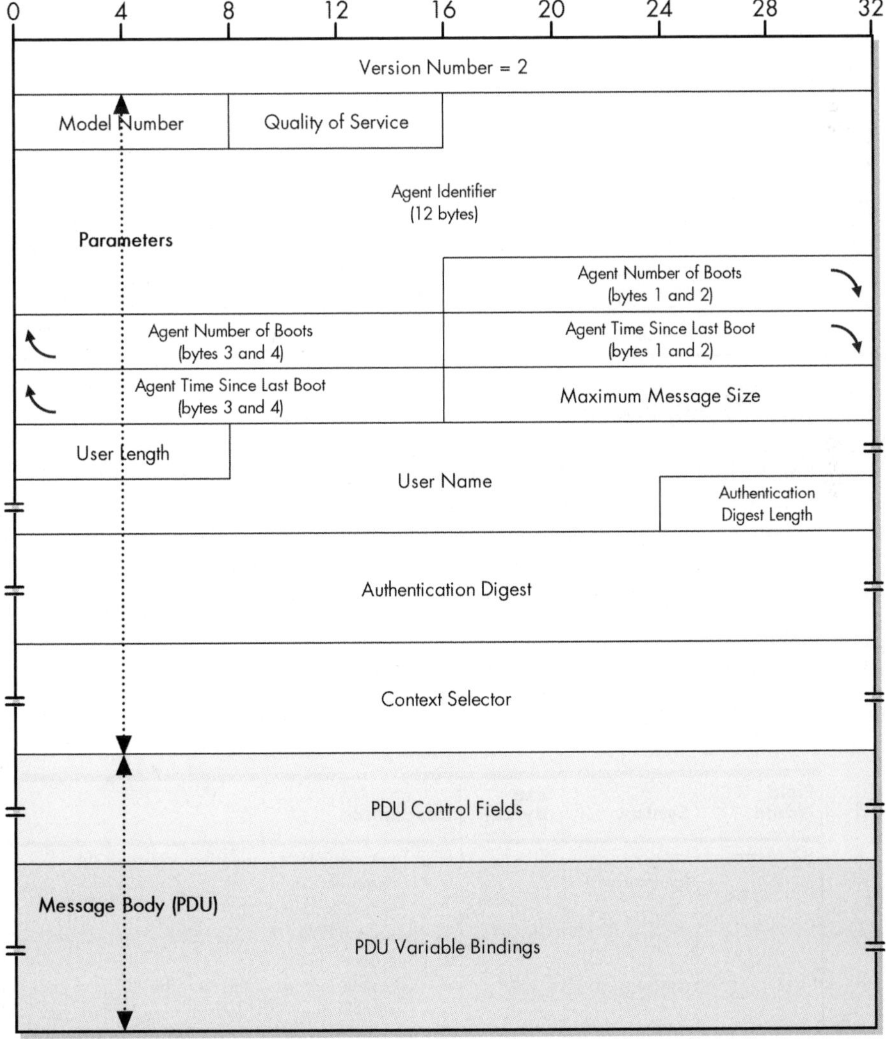

Figure 68-7: SNMPv2u general message format

Table 68-9: SNMPv2u Parameter Field Subfields

Subfield Name	Size (Bytes)	Description
Model	1	Model Number: Set to 1 to identify the user-based model.
QoS	1	Quality of Service: Indicates whether authentication and/or privacy (encryption) have been used and whether generation of a Report-PDU is allowed.
Agent ID	12	Agent Identifier: The identifier of the agent sending the message. Used to defeat replay attacks and certain other types of security attacks.
Agent Boots	4	Agent Number of Boots: The number of times the agent has been booted or rebooted since its Agent ID was set; used to defeat certain security attacks.
Agent Time	4	Agent Time Since Last Boot: The number of seconds since the last boot of this agent. Again, used to defeat replay and other security attacks.
Max Size	2	Maximum Message Size: The maximum size of message that the sender of this message can receive.
User Len	1	User Length: The length of the User Name field below.
User Name	Variable (1 to 16)	User Name: The name of the user on whose behalf the message is being sent.
Auth Len	1	Authentication Digest Length: The length of the Auth Digest field.
Auth Digest	Variable (0 to 255)	Authentication Digest: An authentication value used to verify the identity and genuineness of this message, when authentication is used.
Context Selector	Variable (0 to 40)	Context Selector: A string that is combined with the Agent ID to specify a particular context that contains the management information referenced by this message.

SNMPv2 PDU Formats

The format of protocol data units in SNMPv2 is described in RFC 1905, and it is similar to that of SNMPv1. The format for all PDUs in SNMPv2 is the same, except for the GetBulkRequest-PDU message. (Oddly, this includes the Trapv2-PDU message, even though the Trap-PDU message in SNMPv1 used a distinct format.)

Table 68-10 shows the common SNMPv2 PDU format. Table 68-11 contains a listing of the different values for the Error Status field and how they are interpreted. Figure 68-8 illustrates the SNMPv2 common PDU format.

Table 68-10: SNMPv2 Common PDU Format

Field Name	Syntax	Size (Bytes)	Description
PDU Type	Integer (Enumerated)	4	PDU Type: An integer value that indicates the PDU type: 0 = GetRequest-PDU 1 = GetNextRequest-PDU 2 = Response-PDU 3 = SetRequest-PDU 4 = Obsolete, not used (this was the old Trap-PDU in SNMPv1) 5 = GetBulkRequest-PDU (has its own format; see Table 68-12) 6 = InformRequest-PDU 7 = Trapv2-PDU 8 = Report-PDU

(continued)

Table 68-10: SNMPv2 Common PDU Format (continued)

Field Name	Syntax	Size (Bytes)	Description
Request ID	Integer	4	Request Identifier: A number used to match requests with replies. It is generated by the device that sends a request and copied into this field in a Response-PDU by the responding SNMP entity.
Error Status	Integer (Enumerated)	4	Error Status: An integer value that is used in a Response-PDU to tell the requesting SNMP entity the result of its request. A value of zero indicates that no error occurred; the other values indicate what sort of error happened (see Table 68-11).
Error Index	Integer	4	Error Index: When Error Status is nonzero, this field contains a pointer that specifies which object generated the error. Always zero in a request.
Variable Bindings	Variable	Variable	Variable Bindings: A set of name/value pairs identifying the MIB objects in the PDU, and in the case of messages other than requests, containing their values. See the discussion of the general SNMP general PDU format earlier in this chapter for more on these bindings.

NOTE *The first six Error Status field values (0 to 5) are maintained as used in SNMPv1 for compatibility, but SNMPv2 adds many new error codes that provide more specific indication of the exact nature of an error in a request. The genErr code is still used only when none of the specific error types (either the old codes or the new ones) apply.*

Table 68-11: SNMPv2 PDU Error Status Field Values

Error Status Value	Error Code	Description
0	noError	No error occurred. This code is also used in all request PDUs, since they have no error status to report.
1	tooBig	The size of the Response-PDU would be too large to transport.
2	noSuchName	The name of a requested object was not found.
3	badValue	A value in the request didn't match the structure that the recipient of the request had for the object. For example, an object in the request was specified with an incorrect length or type.
4	readOnly	An attempt was made to set a variable that has an Access value indicating that it is read-only.
5	genErr	An error occurred other than one indicated by a more specific error code in this table.
6	noAccess	Access was denied to the object for security reasons.
7	wrongType	The object type in a variable binding is incorrect for the object.
8	wrongLength	A variable binding specifies a length incorrect for the object.
9	wrongEncoding	A variable binding specifies an encoding incorrect for the object.
10	wrongValue	The value given in a variable binding is not possible for the object.
11	noCreation	A specified variable does not exist and cannot be created.
12	inconsistentValue	A variable binding specifies a value that could be held by the variable but cannot be assigned to it at this time.

(continued)

Table 68-11: SNMPv2 PDU Error Status Field Values (continued)

Error Status Value	Error Code	Description
13	resourceUnavailable	An attempt to set a variable required a resource that is not available.
14	commitFailed	An attempt to set a particular variable failed.
15	undoFailed	An attempt to set a particular variable as part of a group of variables failed, and the attempt to then undo the setting of other variables was not successful.
16	authorizationError	A problem occurred in authorization.
17	notWritable	The variable cannot be written or created.
18	inconsistentName	The name in a variable binding specifies a variable that does not exist.

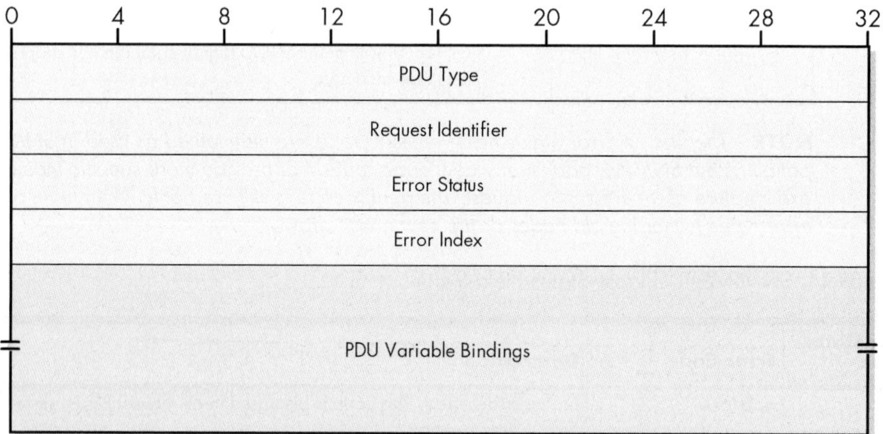

Figure 68-8: *SNMPv2 common PDU format*

The special format of the SNMPv2 GetBulkRequest-PDU message is shown in Table 68-12 and illustrated in Figure 68-9.

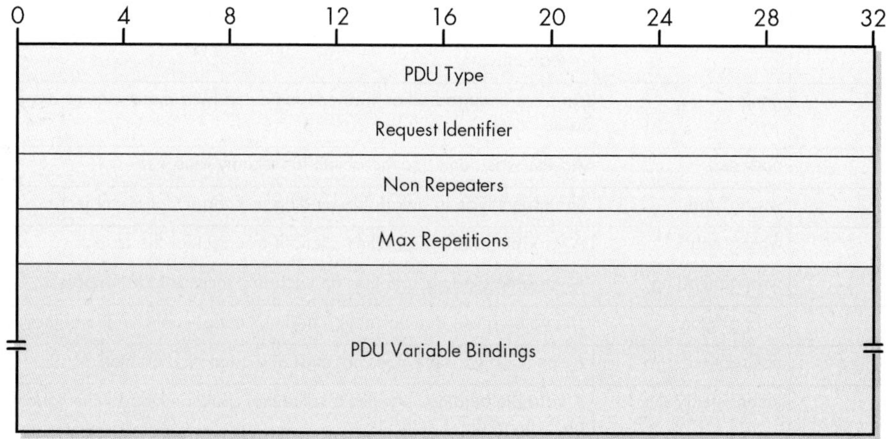

Figure 68-9: *SNMPv2 GetBulkRequest-PDU format*

Table 68-12: SNMPv2 GetBulkRequest-PDU Format

Field Name	Syntax	Size (Bytes)	Description
PDU Type	Integer (Enumerated)	4	PDU Type: An integer value that indicates the PDU type, which is 5 for a GetBulkRequest-PDU message.
Request ID	Integer	4	Request Identifier: A number used to match requests with replies. It is generated by the device that sends a request and copied into this field in a Response-PDU by the responding SNMP entity.
Non Repeaters	Integer	4	Non Repeaters: Specifies the number of nonrepeating, regular objects at the start of the variable list in the request.
Max Repetitions	Integer	4	Maximum Repetitions: The number of iterations in the table to be read for the repeating objects that follow the nonrepeating objects.
Variable Bindings	Variable	Variable	Variable Bindings: A set of name/value pairs identifying the MIB objects in the PDU. See the discussion of the general SNMP general PDU format earlier in this chapter for more on these bindings.

Chapter 67 contains full details on how the Non Repeaters and Max Repetitions fields are used.

SNMP Version 3 (SNMPv3) Message Format

In the late 1990s, SNMPv3 was created to resolve the problems that occurred with the many different variations of SNMPv2. The SNMPv3 Framework adopts many components that were created in SNMPv2, including the SNMPv2 protocol operations, PDU types, and PDU format. The significant changes made in SNMPv3 include a more flexible way of defining security methods and parameters to allow the coexistence of multiple security techniques.

The general message format for SNMPv3 still follows the same idea of an overall message wrapper that contains a header and an encapsulated PDU, but it is further refined. The fields in the header have themselves been divided into those dealing with security and those that do not deal with security matters. The fields not related to security are common to all SNMPv3 implementations. The use of the security fields can be tailored by each SNMPv3 security model, and processed by the module in an SNMP entity that deals with security. This solution provides considerable flexibility while avoiding the problems that plagued SNMPv2.

The overall SNMPv3 message format is described in RFC 3412, which specifies its message processing and dispatching. Table 68-13 describes the SNMPv3 message format, and it is illustrated in Figure 68-10.

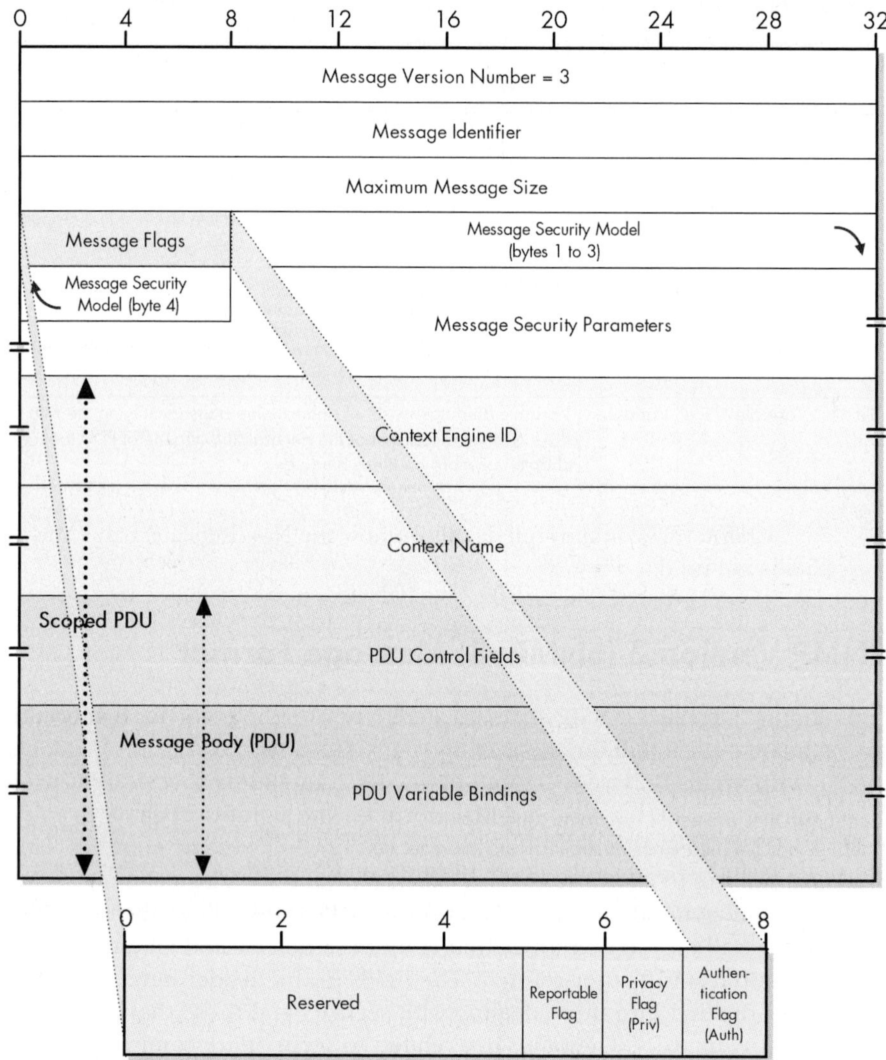

Figure 68-10: *SNMPv3 general message format*

Table 68-13: SNMP Version 3 (SNMPv3) General Message Format

Field Name	Syntax	Size (Bytes)	Description
Msg Version	Integer	4	Message Version Number: Describes the SNMP version number of this message; used for ensuring compatibility between versions. For SNMPv3, this value is 3.
Msg ID	Integer	4	Message Identifier: A number used to identify an SNMPv3 message and to match response messages to request messages. The use of this field is similar to that of the Request ID field in the SNMPv2 PDU format (see Table 68-10), but they are not identical. This field was created to allow matching at the message-processing level, regardless of the contents of the PDU, to protect against certain security attacks. Thus, Msg ID and Request ID are used independently.

(continued)

Table 68-13: SNMP Version 3 (SNMPv3) General Message Format (continued)

Field Name	Syntax	Size (Bytes)	Description
Msg Max Size	Integer	4	Maximum Message Size: The maximum size of message that the sender of this message can receive. Minimum value of this field is 484.
Msg Flags	Octet String	1	Message Flags: A set of flags that controls processing of the message. The current substructure of this field is shown in Table 68-14.
Msg Security Model	Integer	4	Message Security Model: An integer value indicating which security model was used for this message. For the user-based security model (the default in SNMPv3), this value is 3.
Msg Security Parameters	—	Variable	Message Security Parameters: A set of fields that contain parameters required to implement the particular security model used for this message. The contents of this field are specified in each document describing an SNMPv3 security model. For example, the parameters for the user-based model are in RFC 3414.
Scoped PDU	—	Variable	Scoped PDU: Contains the PDU to be transmitted, along with parameters that identify an SNMP context, which describes a set of management information accessible by a particular entity. The PDU is said to be *scoped* because it is applied within the scope of this context. (Yes, security stuff is confusing, sorry; it would take pages and pages to properly explain contexts; see RFC 3411.) The field may be encrypted or unencrypted depending on the value of *Priv Flag*. Its structure is shown in Table 68-15.

Table 68-14: SNMPv3 Msg Flags Subfields

Subfield Name	Size (Bits)	Description
Reserved	5	Reserved: Reserved for future use.
Reportable Flag	1	Reportable Flag: When set to 1, a device receiving this message must send back a Report-PDU whenever conditions arise where such a PDU should be generated.
Priv Flag	1	Privacy Flag: When set to 1, indicates that encryption was used to protect the privacy of the message. May not be set to 1 unless Auth Flag is also set to 1.
Auth Flag	1	Authentication Flag: When set to 1, indicates that authentication was used to protect the authenticity of this message.

Table 68-15: SNMPv3 Scoped PDU Subfields

Subfield Name	Syntax	Size	Description
Context Engine ID	Octet String	Variable	Used to identify to which application the PDU will be sent for processing.
Context Name	Octet String	Variable	An object identifier specifying the particular context associated with this PDU.
PDU	—	Variable	The protocol data unit being transmitted.

Fortunately, SNMPv3 uses the protocol operations from SNMPv2, as described in RFC 3416, which is just an update of RFC 1904. Thus, the PDU formats for SNMPv3 are the same as those of SNMPv2 (see Tables 68-10 through 68-12 and Figures 68-8 and 68-9).

69

TCP/IP REMOTE NETWORK MONITORING (RMON)

We've seen in the preceding chapters of this part that the Simple Network Management Protocol (SNMP) defines both a framework and a specific protocol for exchanging network information on a TCP/IP internetwork. The general model used by SNMP is that of a network management station (NMS) that sends requests to SNMP agents running on managed devices. The SNMP agents may also initiate certain types of communication by sending *trap* messages to tell the NMS when particular events occur.

This model works well, which is why SNMP has become so popular. However, one fundamental limitation of the protocol and the model it uses is that it is oriented around the communication of network information from SNMP agents that are normally part of regular TCP/IP devices, such as hosts and routers. The amount of information gathered by these devices is usually somewhat limited, because obviously hosts and routers have real work to do—that is, doing the jobs of being hosts and routers. They can't devote themselves to network management tasks.

Thus, in situations where more information is needed about a network than is gathered by traditional devices, administrators often use special hardware units called *network analyzers, monitors,* or *probes.* These are dedicated pieces of equipment that are connected to a network and used strictly for the purpose of gathering statistics and watching for events of interest or concern to the administrator. It would obviously be very useful if these devices could use SNMP to allow the information they gather to be retrieved, and to let them generate traps when they notice something important. To enable this, the *Remote Network Monitoring (RMON)* specification was created.

RMON Standards

RMON is often called a protocol, and you will sometimes see SNMP and RMON referred to as the TCP/IP network management protocols. However, RMON really isn't a separate protocol at all—it defines no protocol operations. RMON is actually part of SNMP, and the RMON specification is simply a management information base (MIB) module that defines a particular set of MIB objects for use by network monitoring probes. Architecturally, it is just one of the many MIB modules that compose the SNMP Framework.

> **KEY CONCEPT** SNMP *Remote Network Monitoring (RMON)* was created to enable the efficient management of networks using dedicated management devices such as network analyzers, monitors, or probes. RMON is often called a protocol, but it does not define any new protocol operations. It is actually an MIB module for SNMP that describes objects that permit advanced network management capabilities.

The first standard documenting RMON was RFC 1271, "Remote Network Monitoring Management Information Base," published in 1991. RFC 1271 was replaced by RFC 1757 in 1995, which made a couple of changes to the specification. RFC 2819, published in May 2000, updates RMON to use the new Structure of Management Information version 2 (SMIv2) specification that is part of SNMPv2 but is functionally the same as RFC 1757.

RMON MIB Hierarchy and Object Groups

Since RMON is a MIB module, it consists almost entirely of descriptions for MIB objects, each with the standard characteristics belonging to all such objects. All the objects within RMON are arranged into the SNMP object name hierarchy within the *rmon* group, which is group number 16 within the SNMP mib (mib-2) object tree, 1.3.6.1.2.1. So, all RMON objects have identifiers starting with 1.3.6.1.2.1.16. This single RMON group is broken down into several lower-level groups that provide more structure for the RMON objects defined by the specification. Figure 69-1 shows this structure.

Table 69-1 describes each of the RMON groups, showing its name, group code (which is used as the prefix for object descriptors in the group), and RMON group number and SNMP object hierarchy identifier.

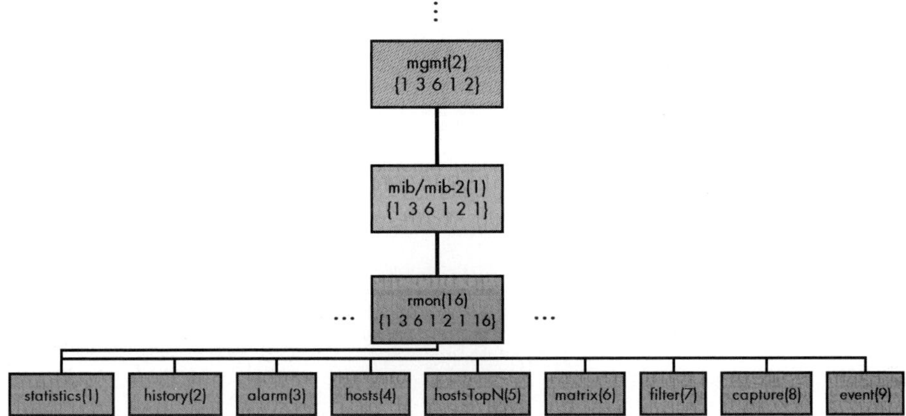

Figure 69-1: SNMP Remote Network Monitoring (RMON) MIB hierarchy *RMON uses a special MIB module, rmon(16), which fits into the overall SNMP object hierarchy tree under mib/mib-2(1) within mgmt(2)—just like other MIB object groups such as sys(1) and if(2); see Figure 66-2 in Chapter 66. Within this group, which has the group identifier 1.3.6.1.2.1.16, are nine subgroups of RMON objects.*

Table 69-1: SNMP RMON MIB Object Groups

RMON Group Name	RMON Group Code	RMON Group Number	Full Group Identifier	Description
statistics	etherStats	1	1.3.6.1.2.1.16.1	This group contains objects that keep track of network statistics measured by the device. Statistics may include network traffic load, average packet size, number of broadcasts observed, counts of errors that have occurred, the number of packets in various size ranges, and so forth.
history	history, etherHistory	2	1.3.6.1.2.1.16.2	The history group contains a single table object that controls how often statistical data is sampled by the probe. The additional etherHistory group is optional and contains extra Ethernet-specific information; it is contained logically within the history group.
alarm	alarm	3	1.3.6.1.2.1.16.3	This group defines the parameters under which an alarm may be generated to inform an administrator of an occurrence of import. The alarm group contains a table that describes the thresholds that will cause an event to be triggered (see the event group description in this table).
hosts	host	4	1.3.6.1.2.1.16.4	This group contains objects that keep track of information for each host on a network.
hostsTopN	hostTopN	5	1.3.6.1.2.1.16.5	This group contains objects that facilitate reporting of hosts sorted in a particular way. The administrator determines how these ordered statistics are tracked. For example, an administrator could generate a report listing hosts sorted by the number of packets transmitted, showing the most active devices.

(continued)

Table 69-1: SNMP RMON MIB Object Groups (continued)

RMON Group Name	RMON Group Code	RMON Group Number	Full Group Identifier	Description
matrix	matrix	6	1.3.6.1.2.1.16.6	This group keeps track of statistics for data exchanges between particular pairs of hosts. The amount of data sent between any two devices on the network could be tracked here. Since a large network could have thousands of such device pairs, to conserve resources on the probe, often only the most recent conversations between device pairs are kept in the MIB.
filter	filter	7	1.3.6.1.2.1.16.7	This group allows an administrator to set up filters that control what sorts of network packets the probe will capture.
capture	buffer, capture	8	1.3.6.1.2.1.16.8	This group is used to allow a probe to capture packets based on particular parameters set up in the filter group.
event	event	9	1.3.6.1.2.1.16.9	When a particular alarm is triggered based on the parameters in the objects in the alarm group, an event is generated. This group controls how these events are processed, including creating and sending an SNMP trap message to an NMS.

The original RMON standard was heavily oriented around Ethernet local area networks (LANs), and you can see some of that in Table 69-1. Probes can also gather and report information related to other networking technologies by using other RMON groups created for that purpose. The best example of this was the definition of a set of groups specifically for Token Ring, which was defined in RFC 1513 in 1993.

RMON Alarms, Events, and Statistics

Alarms and events are particularly useful constructs in RMON, as they allow the immediate communication of important information to an NMS. The administrator has full control over what conditions will cause an alarm to be sounded and how an event is generated. This includes specifying which variables or statistics to monitor, how often to check them, and what values will trigger an alarm. A log entry may also be recorded when an event occurs. If an event results in transmission of a trap message, the administrator will thus be notified and can decide how to respond, depending on the severity of the event.

Like all MIB modules and groups, a particular manufacturer may decide which RMON groups to implement. However, certain groups—such as alarm and event—are related, and some groups—such as statistics—are usually implemented in all RMON probes. Obviously, when RMON is used, the NMS must be aware of RMON groups and must allow a network management application to be run that will exploit the capabilities of the RMON MIB objects.

PART III-5

TCP/IP APPLICATION LAYER ADDRESSING AND APPLICATION CATEGORIES

The TCP/IP protocol suite is the foundation of modern internetworking, and for this reason, has been used as the primary platform for the development and implementation of networking applications. Over the past few decades, as the global TCP/IP Internet has grown, hundreds of new applications have been created. These programs support a myriad of different tasks and functions, ranging from implementing essential business tasks to providing pure entertainment. Users may be in the same room or on different continents.

Of the many TCP/IP applications, a small number are widely considered to be key applications of TCP/IP. Most have been around for a very long time—in some cases, longer than even the modern Internet Protocol (IP) itself. Many of these protocols deal specifically with the sending of information that has been arranged into discrete units called *files* or *messages*. For this reason, one of the most important groups of TCP/IP applications is the one that describes the basic mechanisms for moving these files between internetworked devices: *file and message transfer applications*.

The rest of this book deals with the most common definitive TCP/IP applications and application layer protocols. Before describing the applications themselves, however, I need to lay some groundwork related to application protocols as a whole. To that end, this part contains two chapters. In the first, I explain the universal system set up for TCP/IP applications to use for addressing Internet resources: Uniform Resource Identifiers (URIs), which include Uniform Resource Locators (URLs) and Uniform Resource Names (URNs). In the second chapter, I provide an overview of file and message transfer applications, including a description of the differences between them.

70

TCP/IP APPLICATION LAYER ADDRESSING: UNIFORM RESOURCE IDENTIFIERS, LOCATORS, AND NAMES (URIS, URLS, AND URNS)

The Internet consists of millions of interconnected servers, each of which is capable of providing useful information to Internet users who request it. The more information a network has, the richer it is, but the more difficult it becomes to locate. In order to use information, we need to be able to find it, and that requires, at a minimum, that we employ some means for labeling each file or object.

For this purpose, TCP/IP has defined a system of Uniform Resource Identifiers (URIs) that can be used both on the Internet and on private TCP/IP networks. Each URI uniquely specifies how a client can locate a particular resource and access it so it can be used. URIs are subdivided into Uniform Resource Locators (URLs) and Uniform Resource Names (URNs), which serve a similar purpose but work in different ways.

In this chapter, I describe the system of addressing used on the Internet to identify files, objects, and resources. I begin with an overview, which introduces the concept of URIs and explains the differences between URIs, URLs, and URNs. I then provide a detailed explanation of URLs and how they are used. This includes an overview of the general syntax used for URLs, a description of the URL schemes used for the most common applications, a discussion of relative URLs and how they work, and a comprehensive look at real-world issues associated with URLs, including the intentional obfuscation games being played by some unscrupulous people. Finally, I discuss URNs, including how they solve a major problem with URLs and the impediments to their use.

URI Overview and Standards

If you've been working your way up the OSI Reference Model layers in reading this book, you might have expected that you would be done with addressing by this point. After all, we have already discussed MAC addresses at layer 2, IP addresses at layer 3, and mechanisms for converting between them (see Chapters 13 and 14). We even have ports and sockets that provide transport layer addressing capabilities to let each device run multiple software applications (see Chapter 43). Given all this, the idea of application layer addressing may seem a bit strange, and I am aware that using the term to refer to the subject of this chapter may be a bit unorthodox.

The concept isn't really as odd as it might seem at first, however. It's true that with an IP address and a port number, we can theoretically access any resource on a TCP/IP internetwork; the problem is finding it.

Application layer addressing is not something that is required by the computer software. It is something that makes it easier for humans to identify and locate resources. This is very much the same rationale that is used to justify the creation of name systems, such as the Domain Name System (DNS; see Part III-1). DNS is a form of high-level addressing that allows names to be used instead of IP addresses. It is helpful to people, who find it easier to understand www.intel.com than 198.175.96.33.

The idea behind a comprehensive application layer addressing scheme is to extend to the next level what DNS has already accomplished. DNS names provide essential high-level abstract addressing, but only of whole devices (whether real or virtual). These names can be used as the basis for a more complete labeling scheme that points not just to a site or device, but to a specific file, object, or other resource. In TCP/IP, these labels are called Uniform Resource Identifiers (URIs).

URIs were one of the key technologies developed as part of the World Wide Web (WWW), and they are still most often associated with the Web and the protocol that implements it, the Hypertext Transfer Protocol (HTTP; see Part III-8). You have likely used URIs thousands of times in the past; whenever you enter something like `http://www.myfavoritewebsite.com` into a web browser, you are using a URI.

The reason why URIs are so important to the Web is that they combine into one string all of the information necessary to refer to a resource. This compactness of expression is essential to the entire concept of hypertext resource linking. If we want to be able to have an object in one document point to another, we need to have a simple way of describing that object without requiring a whole set of instructions. URIs allow us to do exactly that.

In fact, URIs are so associated with the Web that they are usually described as being part of Web technology specifically. They are not, however, unique to the Web, which is why this chapter is separate from the discussion of WWW and HTTP.

URI Categories: URLs and URNs

URIs are a general-purpose method for referring to many kinds of TCP/IP resources. They are currently divided into two primary categories based on how they describe a resource:

Uniform Resource Locators (URLs) A URL is a URI that refers to a resource through the combination of a protocol or access mechanism and a specific resource location. A URL begins with the name of the protocol to be used for accessing the resource, and then contains sufficient information to point to how it can be obtained.

Uniform Resource Names (URNs) A URN is a URI that provides a way of uniquely naming a resource without specifying an access protocol or mechanism, and without specifying a particular location.

The difference between a URL and a URN is that the former is much more specific and oriented around how to access a resource, while the latter is more abstract and designed more to identify what the resource is than describe how to get it.

Giving someone a URL is like giving them directions to find a book, as follows: "Take the train to Albuquerque, then Bus #11 to 41 Albert Street, a red brick house owned by Joanne Johnson. The book you want is the third from the right on the bottom of the bookshelf on the second floor."

A URN is more like referring to a book using its International Standard Book Number (ISBN); it uniquely identifies the book, regardless of where the book may be located, and doesn't tell you how to access it. (In fact, ISBNs are one of the identification systems used with URNs, as you will see in the section about URNs at the end of this chapter.)

While URLs and URNs are theoretical peers, in practice, URLs are used far more often than URNs. In fact, URLs are so dominant that most people have never even heard of URIs or URNs. The reason is that even though the example of how to find a book suggests that URNs are more natural than URLs, URLs are easier to use in practice. URLs provide the information needed to access a resource, and without being able to access a resource, simply knowing how to identify it is of limited value.

URNs are an attractive concept because they identify a resource without tying it to a specific access mechanism or location. However, the implementation of URNs requires some means of tying the permanent identifier of a resource to where it is at any given moment, which is not a simple task. For this reason, URNs and the methods for using them have been in development for a number of years, while URLs have been in active use all that time.

KEY CONCEPT Some sort of mechanism is needed on any internetwork to allow resources such as files, directories, and programs to be identified and accessed. In TCP/IP, Uniform Resource Identifiers (URIs) are used for this sort of "application layer addressing." The two types of URIs are Uniform Resource Locators (URLs), which specify how to access an object using a combination of an access method and location, and Uniform Resource Names (URNs), which identify an object by name but do not indicate how to access it.

While URLs began with the Web and most URLs are still used with HTTP, they can and do refer to resources that are accessed using many other protocols, such as the File Transfer Protocol (FTP) and Telnet. The compactness of URIs makes them very powerful for such uses. With a URL, we can use one string to tell a program to retrieve a file using FTP. This replaces the complete FTP process of starting an FTP client, establishing a session, logging in, and issuing commands.

URI Standards

A number of Internet standards published in the 1990s describe the syntax and basic use of URIs, URLs, and URNs. The first was RFC 1630, "Universal Resource Identifiers in WWW," which was published in 1994 and is still a good overview of the topic. In December 1994, a pair of documents, RFCs 1737 and 1738, provided more specific information about URNs and URLs, respectively. RFC 1808 describes how to define and use relative URLs. RFC 2141 provides more information about the URN syntax.

RFC 2396, "Uniform Resource Identifiers (URI): Generic Syntax," was published in August 1998 to revise and replace some of the information in many of the previous RFCs just mentioned. It is probably the definitive standard on URIs at the present time, although RFCs continue to be published discussing issues related to URIs. This is especially true of URNs, which as I noted earlier, are still in active development.

The base documents such as RFC 2396 describe how URLs can be specified for a number of common protocols (called *schemes* in URL-speak, as we will see when we look at URLs more closely). To provide flexibility, a mechanism was also defined to allow new URL schemes to be registered. This is described in RFC 2717, "Registration Procedures for URL Scheme Names," and RFC 2718, "Guidelines for new URL Schemes." There are also a few RFCs that describe specific URL schemes for different protocols, including RFCs 2192 (IMAP), 2224 (NFS), 2368 (email), and 2384 (POP).

URL General Syntax

URLs are text strings that allow a resource such as a file or other object to be labeled based on its location on an internetwork and the primary method or protocol by which it may be accessed. URLs have become the most common type of URI used for application layer addressing in TCP/IP because of their simplicity.

URLs consist of two components that identify how to access a resource on a TCP/IP internetwork: the location of the resource and the method to be used to access it. These two pieces of information, taken together, allow a user with the appropriate software to obtain, read, or otherwise work with many different kinds of resources, such as files, objects, programs, and much more.

The most general form of syntax for a URL contains only two elements, which correspond to the two pieces of information just described: `<scheme>:<scheme-specific-part>`. The term *scheme* refers to a type of access method, which describes the way that the resource is to be used. It usually refers to either an application protocol, such as `http` or `ftp`, or a resource type, such as `file`. A scheme name must contain only letters, plus signs (+), periods (.), and hyphens (-). In practice, scheme names usually contain only letters. Schemes are case-insensitive but usually expressed in lowercase.

The rest of the URL after the scheme (and the required colon separator) is scheme-specific. This is necessary because various protocols and access methods require different types and quantities of information to identify a particular resource. When a URL is read, the scheme name tells the program parsing it how to interpret the syntax of the rest of the URL.

Common Internet Scheme Syntax

In theory, each scheme may use a completely different syntax for the `<scheme-specific-part>` of a URL. However, many of these schemes share a common syntax for this part, by virtue of the similarities in how they refer to internetwork devices and resources on those devices. For example, both HTTP and FTP are used to point to specific TCP/IP devices using a DNS name or IP address, and then access resources stored in a hierarchical directory structure. It makes sense that their URLs would be at least somewhat similar.

> **KEY CONCEPT** URLs are the most widely used type of URI. In its most basic form, a URL consists of two elements: a scheme that defines the protocol or other mechanism for accessing the resource, and a scheme-specific part that contains information that identifies the specific resource and indicates how it should be used. Some schemes use a common syntax for their scheme-specific parts; others use a syntax unique to the scheme.

The most general form of this common Internet scheme syntax is as follows:

```
<scheme>://<user>:<password>@<host>:<port>/<url-path>;<params>?<query>#<fragment>
```

The syntax elements are as follows:

`<scheme>` The URL scheme, which refers to a type of access method.

`<user>` and `<password>` Authentication information for schemes requiring a login, in the form of a user name and password.

`<host>` An Internet host, usually specified either as a fully qualified DNS domain name or an IP address in dotted decimal notation.

`<port>` A Transmission Control Protocol (TCP) or User Datagram Protocol (UDP) port number to use when invoking the protocol appropriate to the scheme.

`<url-path>` A resource location path. This is usually a full directory path expressing the sequence of directories to be traversed from the root directory to the place where the resource is located, and then the resource's name. For example, if on a device there is a directory called project1 and within it a subdirectory called memos containing a text file called June11th-minutes.txt, the URL path `project1/memos/June11th-minutes.txt` would refer to that resource. Note that the slash before the `<url-path>` is required, and while it is technically not considered part of the path, it serves the purpose of acting like the slash denoting the root directory in many file systems. Also, the `<url-path>` may end in a slash, which means that the path refers specifically to a directory. However, this is often not required, as the server will treat the URL as a directory reference by context when needed. A path may also refer to a virtual file, program, or another type of resource.

`<params>` Scheme-specific parameters included to control how the scheme is used to access the resource. Each parameter is generally of the form `<parameter>=<value>`, with each parameter specification separated from the next using a semicolon.

`<query>` An optional query or other information to be passed to the server when the resource is accessed.

`<fragment>` Identifies a particular place within a resource that the user of the URL is interested in.

Figure 70-1 illustrates this common syntax and its elements using an example of an HTTP URL.

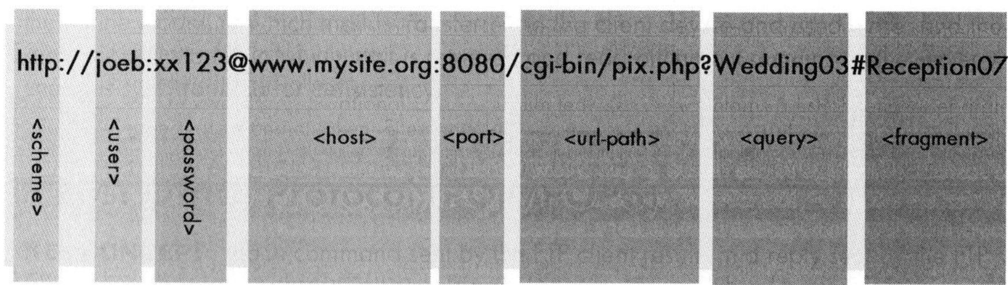

Figure 70-1: Example of a Uniform Resource Locator (URL) *This diagram shows a sample URL that includes almost all of the possible elements in the general scheme syntax, each of them highlighted using shaded boxes. This URL identifies a Web (HTTP) resource that must be accessed using a particular password at the site www.mysite.org using port 8080. The resource in this case is a PHP program in the site's cgi-bin directory that causes a particular page of photographs to be displayed. The `<fragment>` specifier will cause the picture Reception07 on the retrieved page of wedding photos to be displayed to the user.*

Omission of URL Syntax Elements

The full URL syntax may seem very complicated, but bear in mind that this is a formal definition and shows all of the possible elements in a URL at once. Most schemes do not use every one of these elements, and furthermore, many of them are optional, even when they are valid in a particular scheme. For example, the `<login>` and `<password>` elements are officially supported for HTTP URLs, but they are very rarely used. Similarly, port numbers are often omitted, telling the client software to just use the default port number for the scheme. The "URL Schemes and Scheme-Specific Syntaxes" section of this chapter describes some of the most common URL schemes and the specific syntaxes used for them, including how and when these elements are employed.

Even though the richness of the URL syntax isn't often needed, it can be useful for supplying a wide variety of information in special cases. URLs are also very flexible in terms of how they may be expressed. For example, while a `<host>` element is usually a DNS name, it can also be an IP address expressed in many forms, including dotted decimal, regular decimal, hexadecimal, octal, and even a combination of these. Unfortunately, the lack of familiarity that most people have with some of these refinements has led to URLs being abused through deliberate obscuration, to get people to visit "resources" they would normally want to avoid. We'll explore this later in this chapter, in the "URL Obscuration, Obfuscation, and General Trickery" section.

URL Fragments

It's worth noting that, technically, a `<fragment>` element is not considered a formal part of the URL by the standards that describe resource naming. The reason is that it identifies only a portion of a resource, and it is not part of the information required to identify the resource itself. It is not sent to the server but retained by the client software, to guide it in how to display or use the resource. Some would make a valid argument, however, that this distinction is somewhat arbitrary. Consider, for example, that the scheme itself is also used only by the client, as is the host itself.

The most common example of a URL fragment is specifying a particular bookmark to scroll to in displaying a web page. In practice, a fragment identifier is often treated as if it were part of a URL, since it is part of the string that specifies a URL.

Unsafe Characters and Special Encodings

URLs are normally expressed in the standard US ASCII character set, which is the default used by most TCP/IP application protocols. Certain characters in the set are called unsafe, because they have special meaning in different contexts, and including them in a URL would lead to ambiguity or problems in of how they should be interpreted. The space character is the classic unsafe character, because spaces are normally used to separate URLs, so including one in a URL would break the URL into pieces. Other characters are unsafe because they have special significance in a URL, such as the colon (:).

The safe characters in a URL are alphanumerics (*A* to *Z*, *a* to *z*, and 0 to 9) and the following special characters: the dollar sign ($), hyphen (-), underscore (_), period (.), plus sign (+), exclamation point (!), asterisk (*), apostrophe ('), left parenthesis ((), and right parenthesis ()). All other unsafe characters can be represented in a URL using an encoding scheme consisting of a percent sign (%) followed by the hexadecimal ASCII value of the character. The most common examples are given in Table 70-1.

Table 70-1: URL Special Character Encodings

Character	Encoding	Character	Encoding	Character	Encoding
<space>	%20	<	%3C	>	%3E
#	%23	%	%25	{	%7B
}	%7D	|	%7C	\	%5C
^	%5E	~	%7E	[	%5B
]	%5D		`%60	;	%3B

(continued)

Table 70-1: URL Special Character Encodings (continued)

Character	Encoding	Character	Encoding	Character	Encoding
/	%2F	?	%3F	:	%3A
@	%40	=	%3D	&	%26

When these sequences are encountered, they are interpreted as the literal character they represent, without any significance. So, the URL `http://www.myfavesite.com/are%20you%20there%3F` points to a file called "are you there?" on www.myfavesite.com. The `%20` codes prevent the spaces from breaking up the URL, and the `3F` prevents the question mark in the filename from being interpreted as a special URL character.

NOTE *Since the percent sign is used for this encoding mechanism, it itself is special. When it is encountered, the next values are interpreted as character encodings. So, to embed a literal percent sign, it must be encoded as* `%25`.

Again, these encodings are sometimes abused for nefarious purposes, unfortunately, such as using them for regular ASCII characters to obscure URLs.

URL Schemes and Scheme-Specific Syntaxes

As explained in the previous sections, URLs use a general syntax that describes the location and method for accessing a TCP/IP resource:

```
<scheme>://<user>:<password>@<host>:<port>/<urlpath>;<params>?<query>#<fragment>
```

Each access method, called a *scheme*, has its own specific URL syntax, including the various pieces of information required by the method to identify a resource. RFC 1738 includes a description of the specific syntaxes used by several popular URL schemes. Others have been defined in subsequent RFCs using the procedure established for URL scheme registration.

Several of the URL schemes use the common Internet pattern shown in Figure 70-1 earlier in the chapter. Other schemes use entirely different (usually simpler) structures based on their needs.

The following sections describe the most common URL schemes and the scheme-specific syntaxes they use.

World Wide Web/Hypertext Transfer Protocol Syntax (http)

The Web potentially uses most of the elements of the common Internet scheme syntax, as follows:

```
http://<user>:<password>@<host>:<port>/<url-path>?<query>#<bookmark>
```

As discussed in the overview of resource identifiers, the Web is the primary application using URLs today. A URL can theoretically contain most of the common URL syntax elements, but in practice, most are omitted. Most URLs contain only a host and a path to a resource. The port number is usually omitted, implying that the default value of 80 should be used. The <query> construct is often used to pass arguments or information from the client to the web server.

I have provided full details on how Web URLs are used in Chapter 79.

File Transfer Protocol Syntax (ftp)

The syntax for FTP URLs is:

```
ftp://<user>:<password>@<host>:<port>/<url-path>;type=<typecode>
```

FTP (see Chapter 72) is an interactive command-based protocol, so it may seem odd to use a URL for FTP. However, one of the most common uses of FTP is to access and read a single file, and this is what an FTP URL allows a client to do, quickly and easily. The <user> and <password> elements are used for login and may be omitted for anonymous FTP access. The port number is usually omitted and defaults to the standard FTP control channel port, 21.

The <url-path> is interpreted as a directory structure and filename. The appropriate CWD (change working directory) commands are issued to go to the specified directory, and then a RETR (retrieve) command is issued for the named file. The optional `type` parameter can be used to indicate the file type: `a` to specify an ASCII file retrieval or `i` for an image (binary) file. The `type` parameter is often omitted from the URL, with the correct mode being set automatically by the client based on the name of the file.

For example, consider this URL:

```
ftp://ftp.hardwarecompanyx.com/drivers/widgetdriver.zip
```

This is equivalent to starting an FTP client, making an anonymous FTP connection to ftp.hardwarecompanyx.com, then changing to the drivers directory and retrieving the file widgetdriver.zip. The client will retrieve the file in binary mode because it is a compressed ZIP file.

It is also possible to use an FTP URL to get a listing of the files within a particular directory. This allows users to navigate an FTP server's directory structure using URL links to find the file they want, and then retrieve it. This is done by specifying a directory name for the <url-path> and using the `type` parameter with a <typecode> of `d` to request a directory listing. Again, the `type` parameter is usually omitted, and the software figures out to send a LIST command to the server when a directory name is given in a URL.

Electronic Mail Syntax (mailto)

A special syntax is defined to allow a URL to represent the command to send mail to a user:

```
mailto:<email-address>
```

The email address (see Chapter 75) is in standard Internet form: *<username>@<domainname>*. This is really an unusual type of URL because it does not really represent an object at all, though a person can be considered a type of resource. Note that optional parameters, such as the subject of the email, can also be included in a `mailto` URL. This facility is not often used, however.

Gopher Protocol Syntax (gopher)

The syntax for the Gopher protocol is similar to that of HTTP and FTP:

```
gopher://<host>:<port>/<gopher-path>
```

See Chapter 86 for more information about the Gopher protocol.

Network News/Usenet Syntax (news)

Two syntaxes are defined for Usenet newsgroup access:

```
news://<newsgroup-name>
news://<message-id>
```

Both of these URLs are used to access a Usenet newsgroup (see Chapter 85) or a specific message, referenced by message ID. Like the `mailto` scheme, this is a special type of URL because it defines an access method but does not provide the detailed information to describe how to locate a newsgroup or message.

By definition, the first form of this URL is interpreted as being local. So, for example, `news://alt.food.sushi` means, "Access the newsgroup alt.food.sushi on the local news server, using the default news protocol." The default news protocol is normally the Network News Transfer Protocol (NNTP). The second URL form is global, because message IDs are unique on Usenet (or at least, they are supposed to be!).

Network News Transfer Protocol Syntax (nttp)

The `nntp` form is a different URL type for news access:

```
nntp://<host>:<port>/<newsgroup-name>/<article-number>
```

Unlike `news`, this URL form specifically requests the use of NNTP (see Chapter 85) and identifies a particular NNTP server. Then it tells the server which newsgroup to access and which article number within that newsgroup. Note that articles are numbered using a different sequence by each server, so this is still a local form of news addressing. The port number defaults to 119.

Even though the nntp form seems to provide a more complete resource specification, the news URL is more often used, because it is simpler. It's easier just to set up the appropriate NNTP server in the client software once than to specify it each time, since clients usually use only one NNTP server.

Telnet Syntax (telnet)

This syntax is used to open a Telnet connection to a server (see Chapter 87):

```
telnet://<user>:<password>@<host>:<port>
```

In practice, the user name and password are often omitted, which causes the Telnet server to prompt for this information. Alternatively, the <user> can be supplied and the password left out (to prevent it being seen), and the server will prompt for just the password. The port number defaults to the standard port for Telnet, 23, and is also often omitted.

This type of URL is interesting in that it identifies a resource that is not an object but rather a service.

Local File Syntax (file)

A special URL type is used for referring to files on a particular host computer. The standard syntax is:

```
file://<host>:<url-path>
```

This type of URL is also somewhat interesting, in that it describes the location of an object but not an access method. It is not sufficiently general to allow access to a file anywhere on an internetwork, but is often used for referencing files on computers on a local area network (LAN) where names have been assigned to different devices.

A special syntax is also defined to refer specifically to files on the local computer:

```
file:///<url-path>
```

Here, the entire //<host>: element has been replaced by a set of three slashes, meaning to look on the local host.

Special Syntax Rules

Additional syntax rules are often used by browsers to support the quirks of Microsoft operating systems, especially for the file scheme. First, the backslashes used by Microsoft Windows are expressed as forward slashes as required by TCP/IP. Second, since colons are used in drive letters specifications in Microsoft operating systems, these are replaced by the vertical pipe character (|).

So, to refer to the file C:\WINDOWS\SYSTEM32\DRIVERS\ETC\HOSTS, the following URL could be used:

```
file:///C|/WINDOWS/SYSTEM32/DRIVERS/ETC/HOSTS
```

Note, however, that some browsers actually do allow the colon in the drive specification.

URL Relative Syntax and Base URLs

The URL syntax described so far is sometimes said to specify an *absolute URL*. This is because the information in the URL is sufficient to completely identify the resource. Absolute URLs thus have the property of being context-independent, meaning that users can access and retrieve the resource using the URL without any additional information required.

Since the entire point of a URL is to provide the information needed to locate and access a resource, it makes sense that we would want them to be absolute in definition most of the time. The problem with absolute URLs is that they can be long and cumbersome. There are cases where many different resources need to be identified that have a relationship to each other; the URLs for these resources often have many common elements. Using absolute URLs in such situations leads to a lot of excess and redundant verbiage.

In the overview of URIs at the beginning of this chapter, I gave a real-world analogy to a URL in the form of a description of an access method and location for a person retrieving a book: "Take the train to Albuquerque, then Bus #11 to 41 Albert Street, a red brick house owned by Joanne Johnson. The book you want is the third from the right on the bottom of the bookshelf on the second floor."

What if I also wanted the same person to get a second book located in the same house on the ground floor after getting the first one? Should I start by saying again, "Take the train to Albuquerque, then Bus #11 to 41 Albert Street, a red brick house owned by Joanne Johnson?" Why bother, when they are already there at that house? No, I would give a second instruction in relative terms: "Go downstairs, and also get the blue book on the wood table." This instruction only makes sense in the context of the original one.

The same need arises in URLs. Consider a web page located at `http://www.longdomainnamesareirritating.com/index.htm` that has 37 embedded graphic images in it. The poor guy stuck with maintaining this site doesn't want to have to put `http://www.longdomainnamesareirritating.com/` in front of the URL of every image.

Similarly, if we have just taken a directory listing at `ftp://ftp.somesitesomewhere.org/very/deep/directory/structures/also/stink/`, and we want to explore the parent directory, we would like to just say "go up one level," without having to say `ftp://ftp.somesitesomewhere.org/very/deep/directory/structures/also/`.

It is for these reasons that URL syntax was extended to include a relative form. In simplest terms, a relative URL is the same as an absolute URL, but with pieces of information omitted that are implied by context. Like our "Go downstairs" instruction, a relative URL does not by itself contain enough information to specify a resource. A relative URL must be interpreted within a context that provides the missing information.

Interpretation Rules for Relative URLs

The context needed to find a resource from a relative URL is provided in the form of a base URL that provides the missing information. A base URL must be either a specific absolute URL or itself a relative URL that refers to some other absolute base. The base URL may be either explicitly stated or may be inferred from use. The RFCs dealing with URLs define the following three methods for determining the base URL, in the precedence in which they are listed here:

Base URL Within Document Some documents allow the base URL to be explicitly stated. If present, this specification is used for any relative URLs in the document.

Base URL from Encapsulating Entity In cases where no explicit base URL is specified in a document, but the document is part of a higher-level entity enclosing it, the base URL is the URL of the parent document. For example, a document within a body part of a MIME multipart message (see Chapter 76) can use the URL of the message as a whole as the base URL for relative references.

Base URL from Retrieval URL If neither of those two methods are feasible, the base URL is inferred from the URL used to retrieve the document containing the relative URL.

Of these three methods, the first and third are the most common. HTML, the language used for the Web, allows a base URL to be explicitly stated, which removes any doubt about how relative URLs are to be interpreted. Failing this, the third method is commonly used for images and other links in HTML documents that are specified in relative terms.

> **KEY CONCEPT** Regular URLs are absolute, meaning that they include all of the information needed to fully specify how to access a resource. In situations where many resources need to be accessed that are approximately in the same place or are related in some way, completely specifying a URL can be inefficient. Instead, relative URLs can be used, which specify how to access a resource relative to the location of another one. A relative URL can be interpreted only within the context of a base URL that provides any information missing from the relative reference.

For example, let's go back to the poor slob maintaining `http://www.longdomainnamesareirritating.com/index.htm`. By default, any images referenced from that index.htm HTML document can use relative URLs—the base URL will be assumed from the name of the document itself. So he can just say `companylogo.gif` instead of `http://www.longdomainnamesareirritating.com/companylogo.gif`, as long as that file is in the same directory on the same server as index.htm.

If all three of these methods fail for whatever reason, then no base URL can be determined. Relative URLs in such a document will be interpreted as absolute URLs, and since they do not contain complete information, they will not work properly.

Practical Interpretation of Relative URLs

This probably seems confusing, but relative URLs are actually fairly easy to understand, because they are interpreted in a rather common-sense way. You simply take the base URL and the relative URL, and you substitute whatever information is in the relative URL for the appropriate information in the base URL to get the resulting equivalent absolute reference. In so doing, you must drop any elements that are more specific than the ones being replaced.

What do I mean by "more specific?" Well, most URLs can be considered to move from most general to most specific in terms of the location they specify. As you go from left to right, you go through the host name, then high-level directories, subdirectories, the filename, and optionally, the parameters, query, and fragment applied to the filename. If a relative URL specifies a new file name, it replaces the file name in the base URL, and any parameters, query, and fragment elements are dropped, as they no longer have meaning given that the file name has changed. If the relative URL changes the host name, the entire directory structure, filename, and everything else to the right of the host name goes away, replaced with any that might have been included in the new host name specification.

This is hard to explain in words but easy to understand with a few examples. Let's assume we start with the following explicit base URL:

```
http://site.net/dir1/subdir1/file1?query1#bookmark1
```

Table 70-2 shows some examples of relative URLs and how they would be interpreted.

Table 70-2: Relative URL Specifications and Absolute Equivalents

Relative URL	Equivalent Absolute URL	Explanation
#bookmark2	http://site.net/dir1/subdir1/file1?query1#bookmark2	The URL is the same as the base URL, except that the bookmark is different. This can be used to reference different places in the same document in HTML. Technically, the URL has not changed here, since the fragment (bookmark) is not part of the actual URL. A web browser given a new bookmark name will usually not try to reaccess the resource.
?query2	http://site.net/dir1/subdir1/file1?query2	The same file as given by the base URL, but with a different query string. Note that the bookmark reference from the base URL is stripped off.
file2	http://site.net/dir1/subdir1/file2	This refers to a file using the name file2, which replaces file1 in the base URL. Here, both the query and bookmark are removed.

(continued)

Table 70-2: Relative URL Specifications and Absolute Equivalents (continued)

Relative URL	Equivalent Absolute URL	Explanation
/file2	http://site.net/file2	Since a single slash was included, this means file2 is in the root directory. This relative URL replaces the entire `<url-path>` of the base URL.
..	http://site.net/dir1/	The pair of dots refers to the parent directory of the one in the base URL. Since the directory in the base URL is dir1/subdir1. This refers to dir1/.
../file2	http://site.net/dir1/file2	This specifies that we should go up to the parent directory to find the file file2 in dir1.
../subdir2/file2	http://site.net/dir1/subdir2/file2	This says go up one directory with .., then enter the subdirectory subdir2 to find file2.
../../dir2/subdir2/file2	http://site.net/dir2/subdir2/file2	This is the same as the previous example, but going up two directory levels, then down through dir2 and subdir2 to find file2.
//file2	http://file2	Two slashes means that file2 replaces the host name, causing everything to the right of the host name to be stripped. This is probably not what was intended, and it shows how important it is to watch those slashes.
//www.newsite.net/otherfile.htm	http://www.newsite.net/otherfile.htm	In this example, everything but the scheme has been replaced. In practice, this form of relative URL is not that common—the scheme is usually included if the site name is specified, for completeness.
file2?query2#bookmark2	http://site.net/dir1/subdir1/file2?query2#bookmark2	This replaces the filename, query name, and bookmark name.
ftp://differentsite.net/whatever	ftp://differentsite.net/whatever	Using a new scheme forces the URL to be interpreted as absolute.

Relative URLs have meaning only for certain URL schemes. For others, they make no sense and cannot be used. In particular, relative URLs are never used for the `telnet`, `mailto`, and `news` schemes. They are very commonly used for HTTP documents, and may also be used for FTP and file URLs.

Incidentally, there is one other very important benefit of using relative URLs: Avoiding absolute URLs in a document allows it to be more portable by eliminating hard-coded references to names that might change. Going back to our previous example, if the guy maintaining the site `http://www.longdomainnamesareirritating.com` uses only relative links to refer to graphics and other embedded objects, then if the site is migrated to www.muchshortername.com, he will not need to edit all of his links to the new name. The significance of this in Web URLs is explored further in the detailed discussion of HTTP URLs in Chapter 79.

> **KEY CONCEPT** In addition to being more efficient than absolute URLs, relative URLs have the advantage that they allow a resource designer to avoid the specific mention of names. This increases the portability of documents between locations within a site or between sites.

URL Length and Complexity Issues

URLs are the most ubiquitous form of resource addressing for some very good reasons: They represent a simple, convenient, and easy-to-understand way of finding documents. Popularized by their use on the Web, URLs can now be seen in everything from electronic document lists to television commercials—a testament to their universality and ease of use.

At least, this is true most of the time.

When URLs work, they work very well. Unfortunately, there are also some concerns that arise with respect to how URLs are used. Both accidental and intentional misuse of URLs occurs on a regular basis. Part of why I have devoted so much effort to describing URLs is that most people don't really understand how they work, and this is part of why problems occur.

Many of the issues with URLs are directly due to the related matters of length and complexity. URLs work best when they are short and simple, so it is clear what they are about and so they are easy to manipulate. For example, `http://www.ibm.com` is recognizable to almost everyone as the website of the International Business Machines Corporation (IBM). Similarly, you can probably figure out what this URL does without any explanation: `ftp://www.somecomputercompany.com/drivers/video-drivers.zip`.

However, as you have seen earlier in this chapter, URLs can be much more complex. In particular, the common Internet syntax used by protocols such as HTTP and FTP is extremely flexible, containing a large number of optional elements that can be used when required to provide the information necessary for a particular resource access.

The point that many elements in URL syntax are optional is important. The majority of the time, most of these optional parts are omitted, which makes URLs much simpler in practical use than they are in their descriptions. For example, even though an HTTP URL theoretically contains a user name, password, host, port, path, query, and bookmark, most URLs use only a host name and a path. This is what helps keep URLs short and easy to use.

Despite this, you will still find some rather long URLs used on the Internet, for a variety of reasons:

Long DNS Domain and Host Names Some people don't realize that long host names are hard to remember. If you run the Super Auto Body Shop & Pizza Parlor, having a website called www.superauto.com will make it easier for your customers to find you than trying to register www.superautobodyshopandpizza.com. Yet DNS names of 15, 20, or even more characters are surprisingly common.

Long Document or Directory Names Similarly, short filenames are better than long ones, and again, many people don't think about this before putting files on the Internet, which makes things more difficult for those who must access them.

Use of Unsafe Characters As discussed saw earlier in this chapter, URLs have a mechanism for dealing with unsafe characters, but it makes them longer and harder to decipher. If you have a file called "{ABC Corp} budget; draft #3; third quarter 2004.htm," the URL for it will have to be `%7BABC%20Corp%7D%20budget%3B%20draft%20%233%3B%20third%20quarter%202004.htm`.

The original long filename was readable, but the URL is a mess. Naming the file "ABC budget draft 3, 3Q2004.htm" would be a better choice, and still includes enough information to be understandable. Even better, you could replace the spaces with underscores, to avoid the need for the `%20` encoding entirely: "ABC_budget_draft 3,_3Q2004.htm."

Parameter Strings In HTTP URLs, the syntax for specifying a query (following a question mark character) is often used to allow a web browser to send various types of information to a web server, especially parameters for interactive queries. These parameter strings can get quite lengthy. For example, I typed in a query to the great web search engine Google to find recipes for potato salad. This is what the URL for one of the recipe files looks like:

```
http://groups.google.com/groups?q=%22potato+salad%22&hl=en&lr=&ie=
UTF-8&safe=off&selm=B826FB57.89C0%25sbrooks%40ev1.net&rnum=2
```

Almost all of that consists of parameters that tell the Google server exactly what document I want based on my query. It is necessary, but still cumbersome.

URL Wrapping and Delimiting

For humans, long and complex URLs are hard to remember and use. In addition to the sheer difficulty of remembering all those characters, there is the issue of URL wrapping, which occurs when they are presented in certain forms. Most programs can display only 78 or 80 characters in a single line. If a URL is longer than this, the characters of the URL will wrap onto multiple lines; when you read that Google example of parameter strings, you probably noticed that.

URL wrapping can lead to mistakes when copying a URL from one form to another, such as if you copied it from this document into your web browser. If a URL is 81 characters long, and 80 are on the first line and the last character is on the second line, many users may not realize that the URL has wrapped. I have seen URLs that are hundreds of characters long, requiring several manual copy-and-paste operations to get the URL to work.

Perhaps surprisingly, some software may not handle this wrapping properly either. While this is not a problem when a hyperlink is used in something like an HTML document, it can be troublesome when links are included in an email message or Usenet article.

Another issue is delimiting where a URL starts and ends when it appears. A URL begins with a scheme name that could, in theory, be used in other contexts that are not URLs. Without a clear way of labeling a URL as being a URL, a software program might not recognize it. Consider discussion of a URL in a document like this one. If I say, "Please visit http://www.thissite.com; you will see the information you need there," we all know the semicolon is part of the sentence and not part of the URL, but a computer program might not be so sure. And again, this problem is worse when a URL is long and complex, and wraps on to multiple lines of text. How does the program recognize the end of the URL?

Explicit URL Delimiting and Redirectors

To resolve both the wrapping and delimiting problems, a special URL super-syntax is sometimes employed, especially when URLs are used in other text. This is done by surrounding the URL in angle brackets, possibly including the label `URL:`. before the scheme name. For example, all of the following are equivalent:

```
http://www.networkingistoodarnedcomplicated.com
<http://www.networkingistoodarnedcomplicated.com>
<URL:http://www.networkingistoodarnedcomplicated.com>
```

The angle brackets indicate clearly where the URL begins and ends, making it easier for both programs and humans to deal with long URLs.

Another solution sometimes used for long URLs are redirection services, provided by many websites. For example, http://www.tinyurl.com is a free service that allows someone to create a short URL that automatically loads a resource at a much longer URL.

URL Abbreviation

One final issue I want to discuss isn't related directly to long or complex URLs, but is related indirectly to the matter of length: URL abbreviation. Many people use URLs so often that they become lazy when it comes to specifying URLs. They tend to leave off portions of the full URL syntax to save time and energy. I don't mean by this that they specify relative URLs, but rather, they specify absolute URLs with missing pieces.

For example, rather than type `http://www.sitename.com`, they might type `http:www.sitename.com`, leaving off the two slashes. More commonly, people omit the scheme name entirely, just entering `www.sitename.com`. Technically, this is not a URL—it is just a domain name. However, most web browsers can handle this, assuming by default that the scheme is `http://` if none is provided.

URL Obscuration, Obfuscation, and General Trickery

Most of the time, the owner of a resource wants the URL that refers to the resource to be short, simple and easily understood. Thus, long and complex URLs are usually the result of necessity, accident, or ignorance. Some resources need to have long names for a specific reason, such as the use of the long query string in the Google example earlier; other times, URLs are made long because the owner of the resource doesn't realize that using a long DNS host name or file name will make for a long and unwieldy URL.

Whatever the reasons for these situations, they are not deliberate. Recent years, however, have seen a dramatic rise in the use of intentionally long, complex, confusing and deliberately deceptive URLs. These URLs are either structured so that it is impossible to tell what they are, or worse, they are made to appear as if they point to one resource when they really go to another.

Why would people do this? Because they do not want to be open and honest about their "resources." And who would these people be? Why, they would be the spammers and con artists who overload our Internet email boxes with offers of every sort imaginable, from making you rich beyond your wildest dreams to inflating the dimensions of certain body parts to unnatural sizes.

They are afraid that if the URL indicated clearly what the "resource" was, you might not click the link, or that if you identify them as spammers you might filter out their email. They also figure that if they can make the URL appear to be something interesting, you'll load it. Even if it turns out to be something you didn't expect, maybe you'll pay attention anyway.

You may be thinking that you are too smart to be tricked into buying a product through a deceptive URL. And you would never support a spammer anyway. What a coincidence—same with me! Yet the spam keeps coming. It must work, or they wouldn't keep doing it . . . would they?

It is a cruel irony that the complex syntax that was built into URLs to allow them to be so flexible has been subject to exploitation. Tricksters know that most people are used to seeing simple URLs like `http://www.myfavoritesite.com` and do not realize that the full URL syntax allows the same resource to be specified in literally millions of different ways. So, desperate for hits to their websites at any cost, they keep coming up with new tricks for manipulating URLs. These are focused on HTTP scheme URLs, though in theory, the tricks can be applied to several other types as well (though they won't work with some schemes).

Here are some of the more common gimmicks that have been used (note that if you are trying these out as you read, some examples may not work on certain browsers):

Excessive Length In some cases, a URL is just made really long by the addition of a lot of gibberish as a query string, so that the user's eyes glaze over just looking at it. This is a relatively unsophisticated technique, however, since you can easily tell what the real host name is by looking at the start of the URL. Most of the better scammers have moved beyond such simple tricks today.

Regular IP Address Hosts Internet users are so accustomed to using DNS names that they don't realize that you can access a URL using an IP address. So most people don't realize that The PC Guide can be accessed as easily using `<http://209.68.14.80>` as `<http://www.PCGuide.com>`. (Note that this is not true of all Internet hosts; those that use virtual names cannot be accessed using just an IP address.) This is not really trickery per se. It is quite legitimate, and in some ways, even necessary; for example, for accessing a site that is having DNS problems. The problem here is that usually you cannot tell what a site is from the IP address alone, and many people will just click an IP address link without bothering to find out what it is.

Numeric Domain Names It is possible to register a DNS domain name consisting of just a single number. For example, one could register 114.com. And then you could create subdomains within it such as 42.12.205.114.com. At first glance, this appears to be an IP address specification, so someone might think it would resolve to the address 42.12.205.114, but it's actually some other address. I believe that DNS name registrars have been cracking down on this sort of trickery, so it may not be as prevalent now as it once was.

Bogus Authentication Information HTTP URLs theoretically support the inclusion of authentication information, by including `<user>:<password>@` before the host in the URL. Yet the vast majority of websites are open, and neither require nor use this type of information. If you specify an authentication string and it is not needed, it is ignored. One way to abuse this is by including "authentication information" that looks like a benign host, to make the user think the URL is for that host. For example, if I wanted to trick you into visiting The PC Guide, I might use this URL to make it look like clicking it would go to CNN: <http://www.cnn.com@www.PCGuide.com>. This is still too obvious, however, so this method is often combined with some of the following techniques.

Deceptive Character Encoding The use of the percent sign to encode special characters such as spaces and punctuation can also be abused to obscure the name of a domain. For example, the following is another way of expressing the DNS name for The PC Guide: <http://%57%57%57.%50%43%47%55%49%44%45.%43%4F%4D>. Try it!

IP Address Math Trickery Okay, this is where things get really bizarre. Most of the time, we express an IP address as a dotted decimal number. Remember, however, that to computers, the IP address is just a 32-bit binary number. Most browsers support a rather shocking number of methods for expressing these numbers. This is unfortunate, because this flexibility is really not needed and almost never used for legitimate purposes. It can lead to some really bizarre URLs that are unrecognizable or that look like regular IP addresses but are not. Here are some examples, all of which are the same as the IP address form of The PC Guide (<http://209.68.14.80>):

- An IP address in dotted octal uses a leading zero to signify where each byte is in octal, as in <http://0321.0104.016.0120>.
- An IP address in dotted hexadecimal uses a leading zero followed by an *x* to signify where each byte is in hexadecimal, as in <http://0xD1.0x44.0x0E.0x50>.
- We can even take the entire 32-bit number and express it as a single number, and that will work too. In decimal, this would look like <http://3510898256/>; in octal, <http://032121007120/>; and in hexadecimal, <http://0xd1440e50/>.

As if these tricks weren't bad enough taken individually, we can have some real fun by combining them! For example, start with the regular PC Guide URL:

```
<http://www.PCGuide.com>
```

And convert it to IP:

```
<http://209.68.14.80>
```

Then add some bogus authentication gibberish:

```
<http://www.cnn.com@209.68.14.80>
```

And convert the real URL into a single number, so it looks like a document on the CNN website:

```
<http://www.cnn.com@3510898256>
```

Alternatively, we can use the octal form, and even include a lot of extra leading zeros just for fun:

```
<http://www.cnn.com@0000000000000321.0000000104.0000000000016.00000120>
```

Believe it or not, this is just the tip of the iceberg. In some browsers, even the IP address numbers can be expressed using percent sign ASCII encoding!

While quite irritating, I must give these people points for creativity at least—some of the tricks are quite ingenious. At the same time, their inventiveness is potentially hazardous. While these false URLs are usually more a waste of time than anything harmful, there are sometimes good reasons a person would go to great lengths to hide the identity of a resource. Deceptive URLs are just one more danger that network administrators must deal with today.

> **KEY CONCEPT** The syntax of Internet URLs includes many elements that provide great flexibility in how URLs can be constructed. Unfortunately, these capabilities of expression are now often abused by people who create intentionally obfuscated URLs to trick users into accessing their websites and other resources. Some of these can be potentially hazardous, which means that care is required before clicking unknown links or accessing strange URLs.

URNs

"HTTP 404 - NOT FOUND"

Have you ever tried to access a website or other Internet resource, only to see those dreaded words appear? You probably have, and in seeing them, you have experienced firsthand one of the most common problems with URLs.

URLs specify a resource using two key pieces of information: the resource's location and a method by which the resource may be accessed or retrieved. This focus on the means of access for the resource makes URLs very practical, in that the URL usually contains all the data we need to use the resource. This is why URLs are so widely used today. However, this access orientation also means that URLs have a number of serious limitations.

The Problem with URLs

The main difficulty with URLs is that since they describe a resource based on its location, they tie the resource and its location together inextricably. While this may not seem to be a big deal, it is actually a fairly serious matter in a number of ways, because a resource and its location are not the same thing. It is only because most Internet resources rarely change location that we don't notice this issue more often with URLs.

Suppose that your name is Joe Xavier Zachariah and you live at 44 Glendale Crescent in Sydney, Australia. If someone asked you who you were, would you say, "Joe Xavier Zachariah," or "the man living at 44 Glendale Crescent in Sydney, Australia"? Almost certainly, you would supply the former answer. But a URL would be like describing yourself as a "resource" using the latter description.

Since we realize that Mr. Zachariah is obviously not always going to be at 44 Glendale Crescent, we know that describing him using just a location is not sufficient. The same thing occurs with Internet resources when they are identified using only location.

However, the problem with Internet resources and URLs goes beyond just the matter of movement. Consider a situation where a particular resource is very popular and we want to duplicate the same resource in multiple locations. Using URLs, we would need a different identifier for each copy of the resource, even though each copy is the same. Again, the problem is that we are not identifying the resource itself, but rather the place where it can be found.

In recognition of this issue with URLs, an alternative identification mechanism for Internet resources was developed, called *Uniform Resource Names (URNs)*.

Overview of URNs

The basic standard describing URNs is RFC 1737, "Functional Requirements for Uniform Resource Names," which was published in 1994. In 1997, RFC 2141 was published, which specifies the syntax of URNs.

As you can probably tell from that term, a URN is intended to label a resource based on its actual identity, rather than where it can be found. So, where a URL is like Joe Zachariah's address, a URN would be his name. Or, as I gave as an example in the overview of URIs at the beginning of this chapter, a URN would be identifying a book based on its ISBN number rather than specifying which bookshelf it is on in a building.

To be useful in identifying a particular resource, it is necessary that a URN be globally unique, and that's not always as simple as it may at first appear. Consider human names, for example. Even though there is probably only one Charles Marlin Kozierok in the entire world, if your name is John Paul Smith or José Garcia, you likely share that name with thousands of others. This means using common names may not be sufficient for identifying human "resources," and some other method might need to be devised.

URN Namespaces and Syntax

There are many types of resources that URNs are intended to identify on the Internet, each of which may require a different form of naming. To allow URNs to represent many kinds of resources, numerous *URN namespaces* are defined.

A namespace is referenced using a unique string that tells the person or computer interpreting the URN what type of resource the URN identifies. The namespace also ensures the uniqueness of URNs, when a particular identifier might exist in more than one context. For example, both North American telephone numbers and ISBN numbers consist of ten digits, so a particular number such as 4167819249 could represent both a telephone number and a book number. The namespace identifier tells us what the number means when it is encountered in a URN.

The general syntax of a URN is as follows:

```
URN:<namespace-ID>:<resource-identifier>
```

For example, a book with the ISBN number 0-679-73669-7 could be represented as `URN:isbn:0-679-73669-7`. This string identifies that particular book uniquely, wherever it might happen to be in the world. Many other namespaces have also been defined to specify the URNs for other types of resources, such as documents on the Internet.

> **KEY CONCEPT** Where URLs specify a resource based on an access method and location, Uniform Resource Names (URNs) identify a resource by name. A URN consists of a namespace identifier that indicates what type of name it contains, and a resource identifier that specifies the individual resource within the context of that namespace.

URN Resolution and Implementation Difficulties

URNs are a more natural way of identifying resources, which gives them intuitive appeal. Despite this, URNs are still not widely used, even though they have been in development for more than a decade. The main reason for this is somewhat ironic: It is because URNs are independent of location! The very characteristic that provides URNs with identification advantages over URLs also makes URNs much harder to use practically, which has led to long delays in workable URN systems.

To understand the problem, consider the example `URN:isbn:0-679-73669-7`. This uniquely identifies a particular book, and will always refer to it no matter where the book may be, unlike a URL. The problem is that while the URL equivalent tells us how to actually find this book, the URN does not. The same thing goes for our previous human example: Identifying Joe Xavier Zachariah by his name is more sensible than identifying him as the man living at 44 Glendale Crescent in Sydney, Australia, but at least with the latter, we know where Joe is!

In order for URNs to be useful on an internetwork, they require an additional mechanism for translating a simple URN identification string into a particular location and/or access method. In other words, we need to be able to change a URN into the equivalent of a URL, so that the resource can be found. This requirement is analogous to the problem of resolving Internet DNS domain names into IP addresses, and the same term is used to describe it: *URN resolution*.

Ideally, we want to be able to use some sort of technique where we specify the name Joe Xavier Zachariah, and we are told where Joe is so we can find him. Or, we provide the string `URN:isbn:0-679-73669-7`, and we are provided with a list of libraries or other places where the book can be found. The power of URNs can also be taken advantage of in such a system, by having the resolution system specify the location of a copy of the resource that is closest (in terms of network distance, cost, or other measurements) to the entity making the request.

However, setting up URN resolution mechanisms is a nontrivial task. The matter of URN resolution has been the subject of much of the work on URNs over the past decade. RFC 2483, "URI Resolution Services Necessary for URN Resolution," was published in 1999 and discusses some of the important issues in URN resolution. In October 2002, a series of RFCs, 3401 to 3405, defined a new system called the *Dynamic Delegation Discovery System (DDDS)* that was designed not just to resolve URNs, but to handle the entire class of resolution problems where an identifier is given and the output is information about where to get more information about that identifier. RFC 3406 was published at the same time, providing more information about URN namespaces.

> **KEY CONCEPT** Since URNs identify resources by name rather than location, they are a more natural way of identifying resources than using URLs. Unfortunately, this advantage is also a disadvantage, since URNs don't, by themselves, provide a user with the necessary information to find the resource so it can be used. A process of URN resolution must be performed to transform the URN into a set of information that allows the resource to be accessed.

Although progress on URNs has been slow, it has been steady. While it may yet be a few years before URNs are widely used, I believe it is likely that they will play an increasingly prominent role in identifying resources on the Internet in the future.

71

FILE AND MESSAGE TRANSFER OVERVIEW AND APPLICATION CATEGORIES

The purpose of networking applications is to allow different types of information to be sent between networked devices. In the world of computers, information is most often arranged into discrete units called *files*. When those files are created specifically for the purpose of communication, they are often called *messages*.

Transferring files and messages between networked computers is the most basic type of network communication. For this reason, it would not be an exaggeration to say that *file and message transfer applications* may be the most important class of internetworking applications. Some of the members of this group are so common that many people use them every day without even thinking about it.

In this brief introductory chapter, I take a general look at the concepts behind file and message transfer, and how different applications treat them. I begin with a discussion of the general concept behind files, then discuss the categories of applications that use them, contrasting message transfer with file transfer.

File Concepts

To understand the file and message transfer applications, let's first take a quick step back to look at the fundamental concept of a *file*. Simply put, a file is just a collection of information that is treated as a single unit by a computer system.

Files are stored in directories or folders in a *file system*. In modern computers, files are normally expressed as a sequence of bytes or characters, and each file is read, written, copied, or otherwise manipulated as an independent object. In addition to the data it contains, each file has associated with it file *attributes* that describe it.

For our purposes, the critical characteristic of a file is that it is a self-contained object carrying arbitrary information. Since files are the building blocks of information in computer systems, it's no surprise that the transfer of information in networking was originally defined in terms of the movement of files. Some of the protocols describing how to transfer files predate all of the modern protocols in the lower levels of TCP/IP, including Internet Protocol version 4 (IPv4), the Transmission Control Protocol (TCP), and the User Datagram Protocol (UDP). It's not the case that file transfer was an early application of internetworking, but that internetworking was invented in large part to permit file transfer!

Application Categories

Files in modern computing systems are inherently designed to be generic; they can contain any type of information. The significance of the contents of a file depends entirely on the user or software program that examines it. The TCP/IP file and message transfer protocols have in common the notion of moving files from one computer to another. Where they differ is in how the files are handled and processed. There are two basic approaches: file transfer and message transfer.

General File Transfer Applications

General transfer applications normally treat files as a "black box," moving them from place to place and paying little or no attention to what the files contain. The TCP/IP File Transfer Protocol (FTP) and Trivial File Transfer Protocol (TFTP) fall into this category. FTP has been around in one form or another for more than 30 years now and is still widely used.

Message Transfer Applications

Other TCP/IP applications work with particular types of files, processing and interpreting them in various ways. These files are usually designed for the specific purpose of communication, and are thus called *messages*; these applications allow users to construct, send, and receive messages that fit a particular message format. There are several prominent TCP/IP messaging applications we'll examine in this book.

Electronic Mail (Email)

Email is a system that allows users to exchange "letters" (in fact, any type of document) in a manner equivalent to the conventional postal system, but with the advantages of great speed and simplicity. Email has not replaced regular mail entirely, but many people now use it for the vast majority of their correspondence.

Network News (Usenet)

Usenet is an application that is like email in that it allows users to send messages. However, while email is normally used to allow a message to be sent to one user or a small number of recipients, network news is a way for thousands of users to share messages on various topics.

Any user can contribute a message that can be seen by others, any of whom can respond. Unlike the case with email, recipients do not need to be explicitly identified, which makes network news far more suitable to communication among large groups of people who may not even know each other. This was one of the first TCP/IP applications to create something like an electronic bulletin board: an online community.

Hypertext (World Wide Web)

You probably don't even need me to explain what the World Wide Web is, such is its great significance in modern internetworking. Hypertext moves the idea of messaging beyond the simple exchange of text messages or plain files to the notion of rich messages that can contain a variety of types of information. This includes text, graphics, multimedia, and embedded files.

Most important, hypertext allows one document to be linked to another, forming the web of related documents that led to the name World Wide Web. The Web is almost certainly the single most important TCP/IP application, used daily by millions of people.

The Merging of File and Message Transfer Methods

In recent years, a number of developments have caused the lines between applications that transfer files and applications that transfer messages to become greatly blurred. Email is no longer limited to simple text messages; it can now be used to carry general files by encoding them into text form using special methods, and even to carry hypertext documents. World Wide Web clients (browsers) continue to be enhanced to let them access other types of servers and files, and can also be used for general file transfer.

These developments mean even more functionality and flexibility for the TCP/IP user—and a bit more care required on the part of you, the TCP/IP learner.

> **KEY CONCEPT** One of the most important groups of TCP/IP applications is the one that enables files to be moved between devices on an internetwork: file and message transfer applications. This group contains many of the common applications that TCP/IP users employ every day to communicate. It can be broken into two main categories: general file transfer applications that are used to move any type of file between devices, and message transfer applications, which allow different types of communication using special file types, such as electronic-mail messages or hypertext files.

PART III-6

TCP/IP GENERAL FILE TRANSFER PROTOCOLS

File and message transfer protocols represent the most basic type of network communication: the simple movement of blocks of data. Of the many file and message transfer methods, the most fundamental application is what I call *general file transfer*. General file transfer protocols perform one main function: allowing files to be copied from one computer to another.

Since file transfer protocols move files from place to place without much consideration of their contents, they are relatively unsophisticated compared with certain message-processing applications. However, the idea of being able to move files around is so important that general file transfer protocols were one of the very first applications in internetworking. While many people now use electronic mail or web browsers to perform the functions formerly performed exclusively using general file transfer, these older protocols are still very important and widely used, and important to understand.

This part covers the two TCP/IP general file transfer protocols: the File Transfer Protocol (FTP) and the Trivial File Transfer Protocol (TFTP). Each is described in its own chapter.

The relationship between FTP and TFTP is similar to that of the two transport protocols, the Transmission Control Protocol (TCP) and the User Datagram Protocol (UDP) at layer 4 (discussed in Part II-8). FTP is full-featured, session-oriented, and somewhat complex. It is the more often used of the two protocols, providing a full command interface and taking advantage of the reliability and stream-transfer functions of TCP, over which it runs. TFTP, like the UDP it uses at the transport layer, is a stripped-down version of FTP. It has far fewer commands and capabilities than FTP, but it is ideal for cases where simplicity and small software program size are important, such as in the case of embedded software in devices.

72

FILE TRANSFER PROTOCOL (FTP)

The primary general file transfer protocol in the TCP/IP suite shows its generality directly through its unqualified name: the *File Transfer Protocol (FTP)*. FTP is one of the most widely used application protocols in the world. It was designed to allow the efficient transfer of files between any two devices on a TCP/IP internetwork. It automatically takes care of the details of how files are moved, provides a rich command syntax to allow various supporting file operations to be performed (such as navigating the directory structure and deleting files), and operates using the Transmission Control Protocol (TCP) transport service for reliability.

In this chapter, I describe in detail the operation of FTP. I begin with an overview of FTP, a discussion of its long history, and the standards that define it. I then explain the key concepts related to FTP and how it functions. This includes a description of the FTP operational model and a look at how FTP control connections are established, how and when normal and passive data connections are used, and FTP's transmission modes and data representation methods. I then move on to the details of FTP commands and how they work, including a discussion of FTP command groups, reply codes, and user commands. Finally, I provide a sample illustration of a user FTP session showing the internal commands used for each action.

FTP Overview, History, and Standards

The TCP/IP protocol suite as we know it today was developed in the late 1970s and early 1980s, with the watershed event probably the publishing of the version 4 standards of IP and TCP in 1980. Modern TCP/IP was the result of experimentation and development work that had been underway since the 1960s. This work included both the design and implementation of the protocols that would implement internetworks and also the creation of the first networking applications to allow users to perform different tasks.

FTP Development and Standardization

The developers of early applications conceptually divided methods of network use into two categories: *direct* and *indirect*. Direct network applications let a user access a remote host and use it as if it were local, creating the illusion that the remote network doesn't even exist (or at least, minimizing the importance of distance). Indirect network use meant getting resources from a remote host and using them on the local system, and then transferring them back. These two methods of use became the models for the first two formalized TCP/IP networking applications: Telnet for direct access (see Chapter 87) and the FTP for indirect network use.

The first FTP standard was RFC 114, published in April 1971, before TCP and IP even existed. This standard defined the basic commands of the protocol and the formal means by which devices communicate using it. At this time, the predecessor of TCP (called the *Network Control Protocol* or *NCP*) was used for conveying network traffic. There was no Internet back then. Its precursor, the ARPAnet, was tiny, consisting of only a small group of development computers.

A number of subsequent RFCs refined the operation of this early version of FTP, with revisions published as RFC 172 in June 1971 and RFC 265 in November 1971. The first major revision was RFC 354, published in July 1972, which for the first time contained a description of the overall communication model used by modern TCP and details on many of the current features of the protocol. In subsequent months, many additional RFCs were published that defined features for FTP or raised issues with it. In RFC 542, published in August 1973, the FTP specification looks remarkably similar to the one we use today, more than three decades later, except that it was still defined to run over NCP.

After a number of subsequent RFCs that defined and discussed changes, the formal standard for modern FTP was published in RFC 765, "File Transfer Protocol Specification," in June 1980. This was the first standard to define FTP operation over modern TCP/IP and was created at around the same time as the other primary defining standards for TCP/IP.

RFC 959, "File Transfer Protocol (FTP)," was published in October 1985 and made some revisions to RFC 765, including the addition of several new commands, and it is now the base specification for FTP. Since that time, a number of other standards have been published that define extensions to FTP, better security measures, and other features.

Overview of FTP Operation

FTP was created with the overall goal of allowing indirect use of computers on a network by making it easy for users to move files from one place to another. Like most TCP/IP protocols, FTP is based on a client/server model, with an FTP client on a user machine creating a connection to an FTP server to send and retrieve files to and from the server. The main objectives of FTP were to make file transfer simple and to shield the user from implementation details of how the files are actually moved from one place to another. To this end, FTP is designed to deal automatically with many of the issues that can potentially arise due to format differences in files stored on differing systems.

To ensure that files are sent and received without loss of data that could corrupt them, FTP uses the reliable TCP at the transport layer. An authentication system is used to ensure that only authorized clients are allowed to access a server. At the same time, a feature sometimes called *anonymous FTP* allows an organization that wishes it to set up a general information server to provide files to anyone who might want to retrieve them.

After a TCP connection is established, an FTP control connection is created. Internal FTP commands are passed over this logical connection based on formatting rules established by the Telnet Protocol. Each command sent by the client receives a reply from the server to indicate whether it succeeded or failed. A data connection is established for each individual data transfer to be performed. FTP supports normal and passive data connections, allowing either the server or client to initiate the data connection. Multiple data types and file types are supported to allow flexibility for various types of transfers.

The interface between an FTP user and the protocol is provided in the form of a set of interactive user commands. After establishing a connection and completing authentication, two basic commands can be used to send or receive files. Additional support commands are provided to manage the FTP connection as well as to perform support functions such as listing the contents of a directory or deleting or renaming files. In recent years, graphical implementations of FTP have been created to allow users to transfer files using mouse clicks instead of having to memorize commands. Also, other applications can use FTP directly to move files from one place to another.

> **KEY CONCEPT** The most important general file transfer protocol in TCP/IP is the simply named *File Transfer Protocol (FTP)*. The need to be able to move files of any type between machines is so fundamental that FTP's history goes back more than 30 years. FTP runs over TCP to ensure that files are transferred reliably with no data loss. The protocol uses a set of *FTP commands* sent from an FTP client to an FTP server to perform file-transfer operations; the FTP server sends to the client *FTP replies* that indicate the success or failure of commands.

FTP Operational Model, Protocol Components, and Key Terminology

The standards that define FTP describe its overall operation using a simple conceptual tool called the *FTP model*. This model defines the roles of the devices that participate in a file transfer and the two communication channels that are established between them. It also describes the components of FTP that manage these channels and defines the terminology used for the components. This makes it an ideal place for us to see how FTP works in broad terms.

The Server-FTP Process and User-FTP Process

FTP is a classic client/server protocol, as mentioned earlier. However, the client is not called by that name, but rather is called the *user*. The name comes from the fact that the human user that issues FTP commands works on the client machine. The full set of FTP software operating on a device is called a *process*. The FTP software on the server is called the *server-FTP process*, while the software on the client is the *user-FTP process*.

> **KEY CONCEPT** The FTP client is sometimes called the *user device*, since the human user interacts with the client directly. The FTP client software is called the *user-FTP process*; the FTP server software is the *server-FTP process*.

FTP Control Connection and Data Connection

A critical concept in understanding FTP is that, although it uses TCP like many other applications, it does not use just one TCP connection for all communication the way most protocols do. Instead, the FTP model is designed around two logical channels of communication between the server and user FTP processes:

Control Connection This is the main logical TCP connection that is created when an FTP session is established. It is maintained throughout the FTP session and is used only for passing control information, such as FTP commands and replies. It is not used to send files.

Data Connection Each time data is sent from the server to the client or vice versa, a distinct TCP data connection is established between them. Data is transferred over this connection. When the file transfer is complete, the connection is terminated.

Using separate channels provides flexibility in how the protocol is used, but it also adds complexity to FTP.

> **KEY CONCEPT** Unlike most protocols, FTP does not use a single TCP connection. When a session is set up, a permanent *control connection* is established using TCP for passing commands and replies. When files or other data are to be sent, they are passed over separate TCP *data connections* that are created and then dismantled as needed.

FTP Process Components and Terminology

Since the control and data functions are communicated using distinct channels, the FTP model divides the software on each device into two logical protocol components that are responsible for each channel. The *protocol interpreter (PI)* is a piece of software that is charged with managing the control connection, issuing and receiving commands and replies. The *data transfer process (DTP)* is responsible for actually sending and receiving data between the client and server. In addition to these two elements, the user FTP process includes a third component, a *user interface*, that interacts with the human FTP user; it is not present on the server side.

Thus, two server process components and three client (user) process components are included in FTP. These components are referred to in the FTP model by specific names, which are used in the standard to describe the detailed operation of the protocol. I plan to do the same in this chapter, so I will now describe more fully the components in each device of this model, which are illustrated in Figure 72-1.

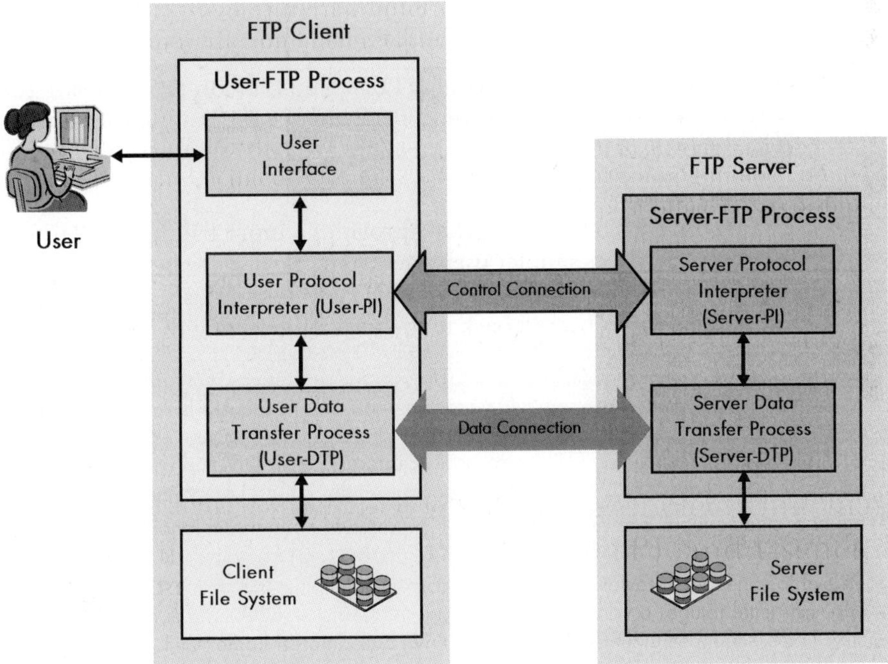

Figure 72-1: FTP operational model *FTP is a client/server protocol, with communication taking place between the user-FTP process on the client and the server-FTP process on the server. Commands, replies, and status information are passed between the user-PI and server-PI over the control connection, which is established once and maintained for the session. Data is moved between devices over data connections that are set up for each transfer.*

Server-FTP Process Components

The server-FTP process contains two protocol elements:

Server Protocol Interpreter (Server-PI) The protocol interpreter is responsible for managing the control connection on the server. It listens on the main reserved

FTP port for incoming connection requests from users (clients). Once a connection is established, it receives commands from the user-PI, sends back replies, and manages the server data transfer process.

Server Data Transfer Process (Server-DTP) The DTP on the server side is used to send or receive data to or from the user-DTP. The server-DTP may either establish a data connection or listen for a data connection coming from the user. It interacts with the server's local file system to read and write files.

User-FTP Process Components

The User-FTP Process contains three protocol elements:

User Protocol Interpreter (User-PI) This protocol interpreter is responsible for managing the control connection on the client. It initiates the FTP session by issuing a request to the server-PI. Once a connection is established, it processes commands received from the user interface, sends them to the server-PI, and receives replies. It also manages the user data transfer process.

User Data Transfer Process (User-DTP) The DTP on the user side sends or receives data to or from the server-DTP. The user-DTP may either establish a data connection or listen for a data connection coming from the server. It interacts with the client device's local file system.

User Interface The user interface provides a more friendly FTP interface to a human user. It allows simpler user-oriented commands to be used for FTP functions rather than the somewhat cryptic internal FTP commands, and it allows results and information to be conveyed back to the person operating the FTP session.

> **KEY CONCEPT** The server-FTP process and user-FTP process both contain a *protocol interpreter (PI)* element and a *data transfer process (DTP)* element. The *server-PI* and *user-PI* are logically linked by the FTP control connection; the *server-DTP* and *user-DTP* are logically linked by data connections. The user-FTP process includes a third component, the *user interface,* which provides the means for the human user to issue commands and see responses from the FTP software.

Third-Party File Transfer (Proxy FTP)

The FTP standard actually defines a separate model for an alternative way of using the protocol. In this technique, a user on one host performs a file transfer from one server to another. This is done by opening two control connections: one each from the user-PI on the user's machine to the two server-PIs on the two servers. Then, a server-DTP is invoked on each server to send data; the user-DTP is not used.

This method, sometimes called *third-party file transfer* or *proxy FTP,* is not widely used today. A major reason for its lack of use is that it raises security concerns and has been exploited in the past. Thus, while it is worth mentioning, I will not be discussing it further in my coverage of FTP.

FTP Control Connection Establishment, User Authentication, and Anonymous FTP Access

You just saw how FTP uses distinct logical data and control channels that are established between an FTP client (user) and an FTP server. Before the data connection can be used to send actual files, the control connection must be established. A specific process is followed to set up this connection and thereby create the permanent FTP session between devices that can be used for transferring files.

As with other client/server protocols, the FTP server assumes a passive role in the control connection process. The server protocol interpreter (server-PI) listens on the special well-known TCP port reserved for FTP control connections: port 21. The user-PI initiates the connection by opening a TCP connection from the user device to the server on this port. It uses an ephemeral port number as its source port in the TCP connection.

Once TCP has been set up, the control connection between the devices is established, allowing commands to be sent from the user-PI to the server-PI and reply codes to be sent back in response. The first order of business after the channel is operating is *user authentication*, which the FTP standard calls the *login sequence*. This process has two purposes:

Access Control The authentication process allows access to the server to be restricted to only authorized users. It also lets the server control what types of access each user has.

Resource Selection By identifying the user making the connection, the FTP server can make decisions about what resources to make available to the user.

FTP Login Sequence and Authentication

The FTP's regular authentication scheme is quite rudimentary: it is a simple *user name/password* login scheme, shown in Figure 72-2. Most of us are familiar with this type of authentication for various types of access on the Internet and elsewhere. First, the user is identified by sending a user name from the user-PI to the server-PI using the USER command. Then, the user's password is sent using the PASS command.

The server checks the user name and password against its user database to verify that the connecting user has valid authority to access the server. If the information is valid, the server sends back a greeting to the client to indicate that the session is opened. If the user improperly authenticates (by specifying an incorrect user name or password), the server will request that the user attempt authorization again. After a number of invalid authorization tries, the server may time out and terminate the connection.

Assuming that the authentication succeeds, the server then sets up the connection to allow the type of access to which the user is authorized. Some users may have access to only certain files or certain types of files. Some servers may allow particular users to read and write files on the server, while other users may only retrieve files. The administrator can thus tailor FTP access as needed.

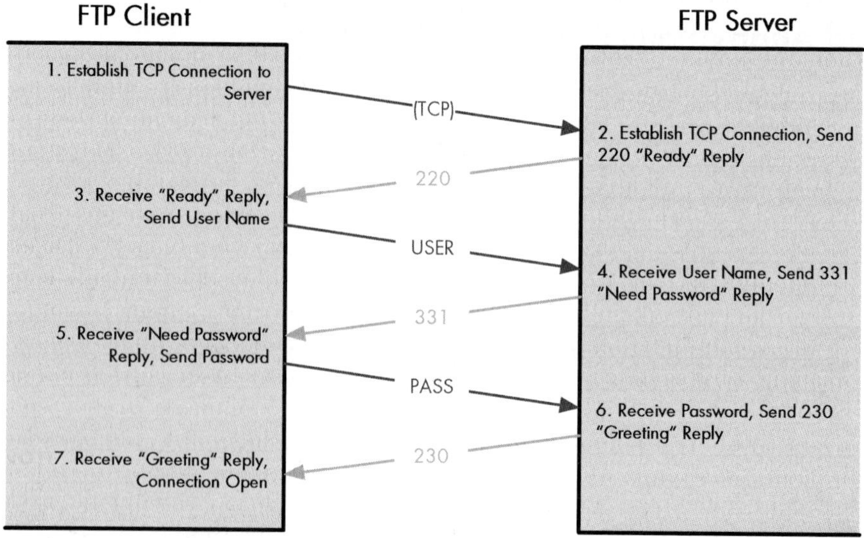

Figure 72-2: FTP connection establishment and user authentication *An FTP session begins with the establishment of a TCP connection between the client and server. The client then sends the user name and password to authenticate with the server. Assuming that the information is accepted by the server, it sends a greeting reply to the client and the session is open.*

Once the connection is established, the server can also make resource selection decisions based on the user's identity. For example, on a system with multiple users, the administrator can set up FTP so that when any user connects, she automatically is taken to her own home directory. The optional ACCT (account) command also allows a user to select a particular account if she has more than one.

FTP Security Extensions

Like most older protocols, the simple login scheme used by FTP is a legacy of the relatively closed nature of the early Internet. It is not considered secure by today's global Internet standards, because the user name and password are sent across the control connection in clear text. This makes it relatively easy for login information to be intercepted by intermediate systems and accounts to be compromised. RFC 2228, "FTP Security Extensions," defines more sophisticated authentication and encryption options for those who need added security in their FTP software.

> **KEY CONCEPT** An FTP session begins with the establishment of a control connection between an FTP client and server. After the TCP connection is made, the user must authenticate with the server using a simple user name/password exchange between client and server. This provides only rudimentary security, so if more security is required, it must be implemented using FTP security extensions or through other means.

Anonymous FTP

Perhaps surprisingly, many organizations did not see the need for an enhanced level of security. These organizations, in fact, went in the opposite direction: They used FTP without any authentication at all. But why would any business want to allow just anybody access to its FTP server? The answer is pretty simple: Anyone who wants to use the server can do so to provide information to the general public.

Today, most organizations use the World Wide Web to distribute documents, software, and other files to customers and others who want to obtain them. But in the 1980s, before the Web became popular, FTP was often used to distribute such information. For example, today, if you had a 3Com network interface card and wanted to obtain a driver for it, you would go to the web server *www.3com.com*, but several years ago, you might have accessed the 3Com FTP server *(ftp.3com.com)* to download a driver.

Clearly, requiring every customer to have a user name and password on such a server would be ridiculously difficult. For this reason, RFC 1635, published in 1994, defined a use for the protocol called *anonymous FTP*. In this technique, a client connects to a server and provides a default user name to log in as a guest. Usually the names *anonymous* or *ftp* are supported. Seeing this name, the server responds back with a special message, saying something like "Guest login OK, send your complete email address as password." The password in this case isn't really a password; it is used simply to allow the server to log who is accessing it.

The guest is then able to access the site, though the server will usually severely restrict the access rights of guests on the system. Many FTP servers support both identified and anonymous access, with authorized users having more permissions (such as being able to traverse the full directory path and having the right to delete or rename files) and anonymous users restricted to only reading files from a particular directory set up for public access.

> **KEY CONCEPT** Many FTP servers support *anonymous FTP*, which allows a guest who has no account on the server to have limited access to server resources. This is often used by organizations that wish to make files available to the public for purposes such as technical support, customer support, or distribution.

FTP Data Connection Management

The control channel created between the server-PI and the user-PI using the FTP connection establishment and authentication process is maintained throughout the FTP session. Over the control channel, the protocol interpreters exchange commands and replies, but not data.

Each time files or other data need to be sent between the server and user FTP processes, a data connection must be created. The data connection links the user-DTP with the server-DTP. This connection is required both for explicit file transfer actions (getting or receiving a file) and for implicit data transfers, such as requesting a list of files from a directory on the server.

The FTP standard specifies two different ways of creating a data connection, though it doesn't really explain them in a way that is very easy to understand. The two methods differ primarily in which device—the client or the server—initiates the connection. This may at first seem like a trivial matter, but as you'll see shortly, it is actually quite important.

Normal (Active) Data Connections

The first method is sometimes called creating a *normal* data connection (because it is the default method) and sometimes an *active* data connection (in contrast with the passive method we will discuss in a moment). In this type of connection, the server-DTP initiates the data channel by opening a TCP connection to the user-DTP. The server uses the special reserved port number 20 (one less than the well-known control FTP port number 21) for the data connection. On the client machine, the default port number used is the same as the ephemeral port number used for the control connection, but as you'll see shortly, the client will often choose a different port for each transfer.

Let's use an example to see how this works. Suppose the user-PI established a control connection from its ephemeral port number 1678 to the server's FTP control port of 21. Then, to create a data connection for data transfer, the server-PI would instruct the server-DTP to initiate a TCP connection from the server's port 20 to the client's port 1678. The client would acknowledge this, and then data could be transferred (in either direction—remember that TCP is bidirectional).

In practice, having the client's control and data connection on the same port is not a good idea; it complicates the operation of FTP and can lead to some tricky problems. For this reason, it is strongly recommended that the client specify a different port number using the PORT command prior to the data transfer. For example, suppose the client specifies port 1742 using PORT. The server-DTP would then create a connection from its port 20 to the client's port 1742 instead of 1678. This process is shown in Figure 72-3.

Passive Data Connections

The second method is called a *passive* data connection. The client tells the server to be passive—that is, to accept an incoming data connection initiated by the client. The server replies, giving the client the server IP address and port number that it should use. The server-DTP then listens on this port for an incoming TCP connection from the user-DTP. By default, the user machine uses the same port number it used for the control connection, as in the active case. However, here again, the client can choose to use a different port number for the data connection if necessary (typically an ephemeral port number).

Let's consider our example again, with the control connection from port 1678 on the client to port 21 on the server, but this time consider data transfer using a passive connection, as illustrated in Figure 72-4. The client would issue the PASV command to tell the server it wanted to use passive data control. The server-PI would reply with a port number for the client to use—say port 2223. The server-PI would then instruct the server-DTP to listen on this port 2223. The user-PI would instruct the user-DTP to create a connection from client port 1742 to server port 2223. The server would acknowledge this, and then data could be sent and received, again in either direction.

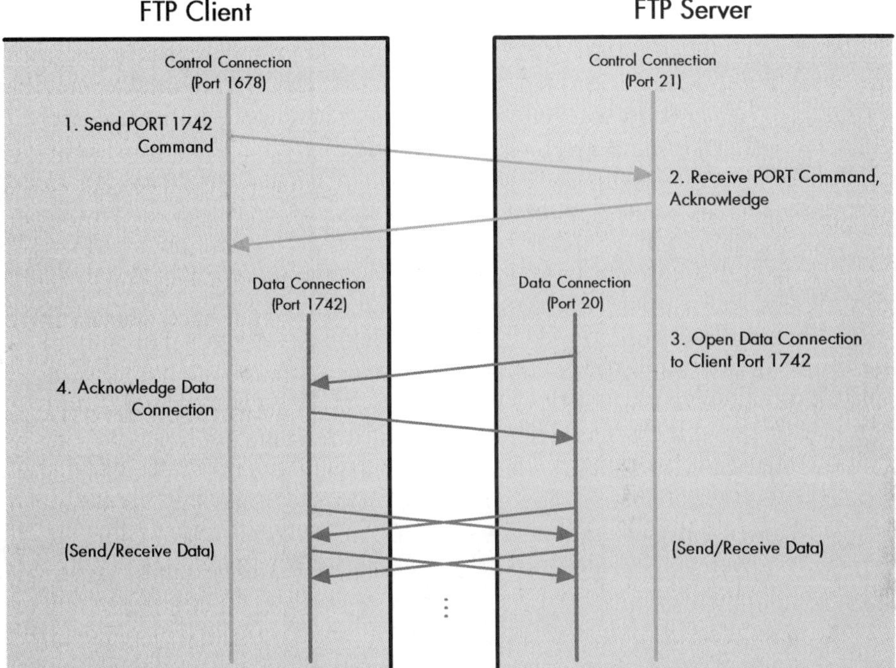

Figure 72-3: FTP active data connection *In a conventional, or active, FTP data connection, the server initiates the transfer of data by opening the data connection to the client. In this case, the client first sends a PORT command to tell the server to use port 1742. The server then opens the data connection from its default port number of 20 to client port 1742. Data is then exchanged between the devices using these ports.*

Efficiency and Security Issues Related to the Connection Methods

At this point, you may be wondering what the practical difference is between the active and passive connection types. I already said that in either case, the data transfer can go in both directions. So what does it matter who initiates the data connection? Isn't this like arguing over who makes a local telephone call?

The answer is related to the dreaded "S word:" *security*. The fact that FTP uses more than one TCP connection can cause problems for the hardware and software that people use to ensure the security of their systems.

Consider what is happening in the case of an active data connection, as described in Figure 72-3. From the perspective of the client, an established control connection exists from the client's port 1678 to the server's port 21. But the data connection is initiated by the server. So the client sees an incoming connection request to port 1678 (or some other port). Many clients are suspicious about receiving such incoming connections, since under normal circumstances, clients *establish* connections—they don't respond to them. Since incoming TCP connections can potentially be a security risk, many clients are configured to block them using firewall hardware or software.

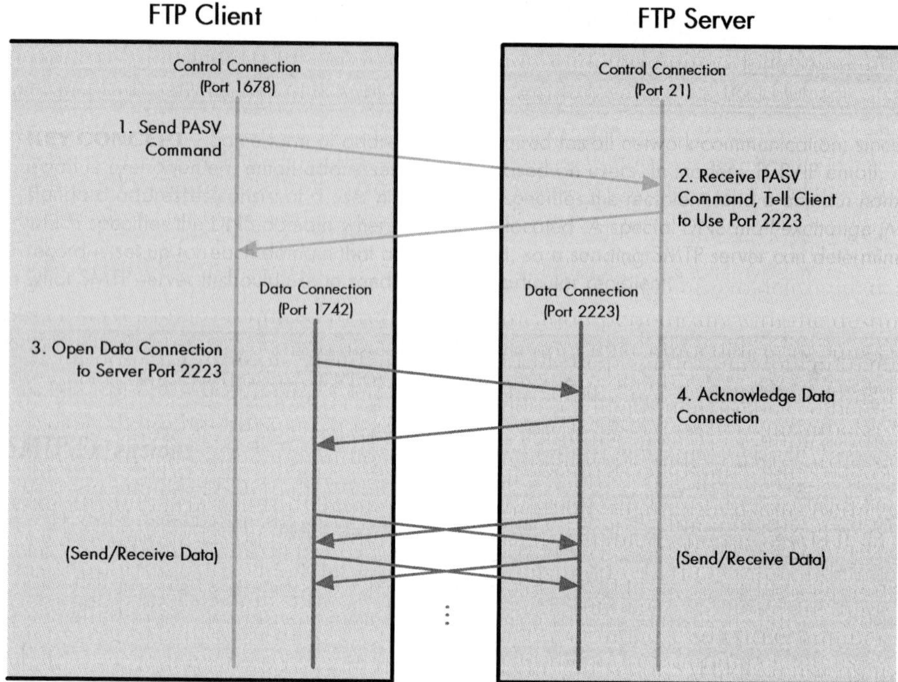

Figure 72-4: FTP passive data connection *In a passive FTP data connection, the client uses the PASV command to tell the server to wait for the client to establish the data connection. The server responds, telling the client what port it should use on the server for the data transmission—in this case, port 2223. The client then opens the data connection using that port number on the server and a client port number of its own choosing—in this case, 1742.*

Why not just make it so that the client always accepts connections to the port number one above the ephemeral number used for the control connection? The problem here is that clients often use different port numbers for each transfer by using the PORT command. This is done because of the rules of TCP. As I describe in Chapter 47, after a connection is closed, a period of time must elapse before the port can be used again to prevent mixing up consecutive sessions. This would cause delays when sending multiple files one after the other, so to avoid this, clients usually use different port numbers for each transfer. This is more efficient, but it means a firewall protecting the client would be asked to accept incoming connections that appear to be going to many unpredictable port numbers.

The use of passive connections largely eliminates this problem. Most firewalls have a lot more difficulty dealing with incoming connections to odd ports than outgoing connections. RFC 1579, "Firewall-Friendly FTP," discusses this issue in detail. It recommends that clients use passive data connections by default instead of using normal connections with the PORT command to avoid the port-blocking problem.

Of course, passive data connections don't really eliminate the problem; they just push it off onto servers. These servers now must face the issue of incoming connections to various ports. Still, it is, generally speaking, easier to deal with security issues on a relatively smaller number of servers than on a large number of clients.

FTP servers must be able to accept passive mode transfers from clients anyway, so the usual approach is to set aside a block of ports for this purpose, which the server's security provisions allow to accept incoming connections, while blocking incoming connection requests on other ports.

> **KEY CONCEPT** FTP supports two different models for establishing data connections between the client and server. In normal, or *active*, data connections, the server initiates the connection when the client requests a transfer, and the client responds; in a *passive* data connection, the client tells the server it will initiate the connection, and the server responds. Since TCP is bidirectional, data can flow either way in both cases; the chief difference between the two modes has to do with security. In particular, passive mode is often used because many modern client devices are not able to accept incoming connections from servers.

Another point worth mentioning is that it is a significant violation of the layering principle of networks to pass IP addresses and port numbers in FTP commands such as PORT and PASV and the replies to them. This isn't just a philosophical issue. Applications aren't supposed to deal with port numbers, and this creates issues when certain lower-layer technologies are used. For example, consider the use of Network Address Translation (NAT; see Chapter 28), which modifies IP addresses and possibly port numbers. To prevent NAT from "breaking" when FTP is used, special provisions must be made to handle the protocol.

FTP General Data Communication and Transmission Modes

Once a data connection has been established between the server-DTP and the user-DTP, data is sent directly from the client to the server, or the server to the client, depending on the specific command issued. Since control information is sent using the distinct control channel, the entire data channel can be used for data communication. (These two logical channels are multiplexed at lower layers along with all other TCP and User Datagram Protocol (UDP) connections on both devices, so this doesn't actually represent a performance improvement over a single channel.)

FTP defines three different *transmission modes* (also called *transfer modes*) that specify exactly how data is sent from one device to another over an open data channel: *stream mode*, *block mode*, and *compressed mode*.

Stream Mode

In stream mode, data is sent simply as a continuous stream of unstructured bytes. The sending device simply starts pushing data across the TCP data connection to the recipient. No message format with distinct header fields is used, making this method quite different from the way many other protocols send information in discrete chunks. It relies strongly on the data streaming and reliable transport services of TCP. Since there is no header structure, the end of the file is indicated simply by the sending device closing the data connection when it is done.

Of the three modes, stream is by far the most widely used in real FTP implementations, for three main reasons:

- It is the default and also the simplest method, so it is the easiest to implement and is required for compatibility.
- It is the most general, because it treats all files as simple streams of bytes without paying attention to their content.
- It is the most efficient method because no bytes are wasted on overhead such as headers.

Block Mode

Block mode is a more conventional data transmission mode, in which data is broken into data blocks and encapsulated into individual FTP blocks, or records. Each record has a three-byte header that indicates its length and contains information about the data blocks being sent. A special algorithm is used to keep track of the transmitted data and to detect and restart an interrupted transfer.

Compressed Mode

Compressed mode is a transmission mode in which a relatively simple compression technique called *run-length encoding* is used to detect repeated patterns in the data being sent, which then represents data in such a way that the overall message takes fewer bytes. The compressed information is sent in a way similar to block mode, using a header-plus-payload record format.

Compressed mode seems on the surface to be useful. In practice, however, compression is often implemented in other places in a typical networking software stack, making it unnecessary in FTP. For example, if you are transferring a file over the Internet using an analog modem, your modem normally performs compression down at layer 1. Large files on FTP servers are also often already compressed using something like the ZIP format, meaning further compression would serve no purpose.

> **KEY CONCEPT** FTP includes three different *transmission modes*: *stream*, *block*, and *compressed*. In stream mode, the most commonly used mode, data is sent as a continuous sequence of bytes. In block mode, data is formatted into blocks with headers. In compressed mode, bytes are compacted using run-length encoding.

FTP Data Representation: Data Types, Format Control, and Data Structures

The most general way of designing FTP would have been to make it treat all files as "black boxes." A file would be represented as just as a set of bytes. FTP would pay no attention to what the file contained and would simply move the file, one byte at a time, from one place to another. In this scenario, FTP would seem to be very similar to the Copy command that is implemented on most file systems, which likewise creates a copy without looking into the file to see what it contains.

So what would be the problem with that, you may wonder? Well, for some types of files, this is exactly what we want, but for others, it introduces a problem. Certain types of files use different representations on different systems. If you copy a file from one place to another on the same computer using a Copy command, there is no problem, because the same representation for files is used everywhere within that computer. But when you copy it to a computer that uses a different representation, you may encounter difficulties.

The most common example of this is a type of file that may surprise you: simple text files. All ASCII text files use the ASCII character set, but they differ in the control characters used to mark the end of a line of text. On UNIX, a line feed (LF) character is used; on Apple computers, a carriage return (CR) is used; and Windows machines use both (CR+LF).

If you move a text file from one type of system to another using regular FTP, the data will all get moved exactly as it is. Moving a text file from a UNIX system to a PC as just a set of bytes would mean programs would not properly recognize end-of-line markers. To avoid this predicament, FTP moves past the idea that all files are just bytes and incorporates some intelligence to handle different types of files. The FTP standard recognizes this by allowing the specification of certain details about a file's internal representation prior to transfer.

FTP Data Types

The first piece of information that can be provided about a file is its *data type*, which dictates the overall representation of the file. Four different data types are specified in the FTP standard:

ASCII This data type defines an ASCII text file, with lines marked by some sort of end-of-line marker.

EBCDIC Conceptually, EBCDIC is the same as the ASCII type, but it is used for files using IBM's EBCDIC character set.

Image With the image data type, the file has no formal internal structure and is sent one byte at a time without any processing; this is the black box mode mentioned earlier.

Local This data type is used to handle files that may store data in logical bytes containing a number of bits other than eight. Specifying this type along with the way the data is structured allows the data to be stored on the destination system in a manner consistent with its local representation.

NOTE *The term* byte *conventionally refers to eight bits, but strictly speaking, the term used to describe eight bits is octet. A byte may in fact contain a number of bits other than eight on certain systems. For details, see "Binary Information and Representation: Bits, Bytes, Nibbles, Octets, and Characters" in Chapter 4.*

In practice, the two data types most often used are ASCII and image. The ASCII type is used for text files, and allows them to be moved between systems with line-end codes converted automatically. The Image type is used for generic binary files, such as graphical images, ZIP files, and other data that is represented in a universal manner. It is also often called the *binary* type for that reason.

ASCII Data Type Line-Delimiting Issues

When the ASCII data type is used, differences in internal representations between systems are handled by using a universal external representation that acts as a common language. Lines of the file being transmitted are converted by the sending FTP process from the sender's internal representation to the neutral ASCII representation used by the Telnet Protocol (NETASCII), with each line ending in CR+LF. The receiving device then converts from this neutral representation to the internal format used by the recipient file system.

For example, when using FTP to move a text file from a Macintosh to a UNIX system, each line would have the CR changed to a CR+LF for transmission over the FTP data channel. The receiving UNIX system would change each CR+LF to just LF so UNIX programs could read it properly.

Note that because of these changes, the resulting file can be bigger or smaller than the original if it is transferred between systems using ASCII mode. Also, since FTP works by converting to a neutral representation for universality, sending an ASCII file from a UNIX system to a UNIX system means each LF is changed to CR+LF for transmission, and then it's changed back to LF by the recipient. It's slightly inefficient, but not that big a deal.

It's very important that the correct data type be specified with the appropriate user command. Sending a text file between dissimilar systems without setting the ASCII mode will result in either a file that cannot be properly read on the destination or one that contains stray characters. Conversely, binary files must be sent in binary mode. If you send something like a ZIP file or a JPG graphic in ASCII mode, the FTP software will think it is a text file. It will treat the file as if it were text, and each time it encounters bytes in the file that look like CR, LF, or CR+LF, it will convert them, which you do not want. (Having the wrong data type set is a leading cause of corrupted files when using FTP to move files between PCs and UNIX systems. I know from experience!)

> **KEY CONCEPT** FTP defines four data types: *ASCII, EBCDIC, image,* and *local. ASCII* and *EBCDIC* are used for text files in the ASCII and EBCDIC character sets, respectively. The *image* type is used for files with no specific structure. The local type is used for local representation. The ASCII type is important because it allows text files to be transferred successfully between file systems that may use different methods of indicating the end of a line of text. The image type, also called binary, is used for files that must be sent and received byte-for-byte with no transformation, such as executable files, graphics, and files with arbitrary formats.

FTP Format Control

For the ASCII and EBCDIC types, FTP defines an optional parameter called *format control,* which allows a user to specify a particular representation for how vertical formatting is used to describe a file. The format control option was created to handle files transferred from host devices to printers. It is not used today, to my knowledge (or if it is used, it is used only in special applications).

Three options can be used in this control:

Non Print This is the default, indicating no vertical formatting.

Telnet Format The file uses vertical format control characters, as specified in the Telnet Protocol.

Carriage Control/FORTRAN The file uses format control characters given as the first character of each line, as specified for the FORTRAN programming language.

FTP Data Structures

In addition to specifying a file's data type, it is also possible to specify the file's *data structure* in three ways:

File Structure The file is a contiguous stream of bytes with no internal structure. This is the default and is used for most types of files.

Record Structure The file consists of a set of sequential records, each of which is delimited by an end-of-record marker. The record structure can be used for ASCII text files, but these are more commonly sent with the regular file structure using the ASCII data type.

Page Structure The file contains a set of special indexed data pages. This structure is not commonly used; it was initially created for a now archaic type of computer used in the early ARPAnet.

FTP Internal Command Groups and Protocol Commands

Once a connection is established between an FTP server and user, all communication to manage the operation of the protocol takes place over the control channel. The user-PI sends *protocol commands* to the server-PI, which processes them and takes appropriate action. The server-PI responds with *reply codes* to tell the user-PI the result of the commands it issued and convey other important information.

Interestingly, the actual transmission of FTP commands over the control channel is done using specifications based on the Telnet Protocol. You may recall from the "FTP Overview, History, and Standards" section earlier in this chapter that Telnet and FTP are two of the very oldest TCP/IP applications, the former being for direct network use and the latter for indirect resource access. They were developed at around the same time, and setting up the FTP control channel to act as a type of Telnet connection is a good example of how Internet standards try not to reinvent the wheel.

FTP Command Groups and Commands

Each command is identified by a short, three- or four-letter *command code* for convenience, and the command performs a specific task in the overall functionality of FTP. Several dozen of these protocol commands are available, and to help organize them, the FTP standard categorizes them into three groups, based on overall function type:

Access Control Commands Commands that are part of the user login and authentication process, are used for resource access, or are part of general session control. See Table 72-1.

Transfer Parameter Commands Commands that specify parameters for how data transfers should occur. For example, commands in this group specify the data type of a file to be sent, indicate whether passive or active data connections will be used, and so forth. See Table 72-2.

FTP Service Commands Commands that actually perform file operations, such as sending and receiving files, and to implement support functions, such as deleting or renaming files. This is the largest group. See Table 72-3.

> **KEY CONCEPT** FTP operation is controlled through the issuing of *protocol commands* from the FTP client to the FTP server. Each command has a three- or four-letter command code that indicates its function. The commands are organized into three groups: *access control commands* used for login and general session control, *transfer parameter commands* that control how transfers are performed, and *FTP service commands* that are used to perform actual file operations.

Since the commands are based on the Telnet specifications, they are sent as plain text, as specified by Telnet's Network Virtual Terminal (NVT) conventions. Tables 72-1, 72-2, and 72-3 list and describe the FTP internal protocol commands in the access control, transfer parameters, and service command groups. They are shown in the order that they appear in the FTP standard (RFC 959).

Table 72-1: FTP Access Control Commands

Command Code	Command	Description
USER	User name	Identifies the user attempting to establish an FTP session.
PASS	Password	Specifies the password for the user given previously by the USER command during login authentication.
ACCT	Account	Specifies an account for an authenticated user during the FTP session. Used only on systems that require this to be separately identified; most select an account automatically based on the name entered in the USER command.
CWD	Change working directory	Allows the user to specify a different directory for file transfer during an FTP session.
CDUP	Change to parent directory ("change directory up")	A special case of the CWD command that goes to the directory one level up in the server's directory structure. It is implemented separately to abstract out differences in directory structures between file systems; the user can use CDUP instead of knowing the specific syntax for navigating up the directory tree on the server.
SMNT	Structure mount	Allows the user to mount a particular file system for access to different resources.
REIN	Reinitialize	Reinitializes the FTP session, flushing all set parameters and user information. This returns the session to the state when the control connection is just established. It is, in essence, the opposite of the USER command. The next command issued is often USER, to log in a different user.
QUIT	Logout	Terminates the FTP session and closes the control connection. Note that the naming of this command was unfortunate. The REIN command is really most similar to a conventional logout command, as it terminates a logged-in user and allows another user to log in. In contrast, the QUIT command shuts down the entire session.

Table 72-2: FTP Transfer Parameter Commands

Command Code	Command	Description
PORT	Data port	Used to tell the FTP server that the client wants to accept an active data connection on a specific port number.
PASV	Passive	Requests that the FTP server allow the user-DTP to initiate passive data connections.
TYPE	Representation type	Specifies for the file to be transferred the data type (ASCII, EBCDIC, image, or local), and optionally the format control (Non Print, Telnet, or Carriage Control).
STRU	File structure	Specifies the data structure for the file (file, record, or page).
MODE	Transfer mode	Specifies the transmission mode to be used (stream, block, or compressed).

Table 72-3: FTP Protocol Service Commands

Command Code	Command	Description
RETR	Retrieve	Tells the server to send the user a file.
STOR	Store	Sends a file to the server.
STOU	Store unique	Like STOR, but instructs the server to make sure the file has a unique name in the current directory. This is used to prevent overwriting a file that may already exist with the same name. The server replies back with the name used for the file.
APPE	Append (with create)	Like STOR, but if a file with the name specified already exists, the data being sent is appended to it instead of replacing it.
ALLO	Allocate	An optional command used to reserve storage on the server before a file is sent.
REST	Restart	Restarts a file transfer at a particular server marker. Used only for block or compressed transfer modes.
RNFR	Rename from	Specifies the old name of a file to be renamed. See the RNTO command.
RNTO	Rename to	Specifies the new name of a file to be renamed. Used with the RNFR command.
ABOR	Abort	Tells the server to abort the last FTP command and/or the current data transfer.
DELE	Delete	Deletes a specified file on the server.
RMD	Remove directory	Deletes a directory on the server.
MKD	Make directory	Creates a directory.
PWD	Print working directory	Displays the current server working directory for the FTP session; shows the users where they are in the server's file system.
LIST	List	Requests a list of the contents of the current directory from the server, including both names and other information. Similar in concept to the `DIR` command in DOS/Windows or the `ls` command in UNIX.
NLST	Name list	Like LIST, but returns only the names in a directory.
SITE	Site parameters	Used to implement site-specific functions.
SYST	System	Requests that the server send to the client information about the server's operating system.
STAT	Status	Prompts the server to send an indication of the status of a file or the transfer currently in progress.

(continued)

Table 72-3: FTP Protocol Service Commands (continued)

Command Code	Command	Description
HELP	Help	Asks the server for any help information that might be useful in allowing the user to determine how the server should be used.
NOOP	No operation	Does nothing, other than prompting the server to send an "OK" response to verify that the control channel is alive.

NOTE *FTP commands are not case-sensitive, but they have been shown in uppercase for clarity in Tables 72-1, 72-2, and 72-3.*

FTP commands are all sent between FTP elements; they are not usually issued directly by users. Instead, a special set of user commands is employed for this purpose. The FTP user interface implements the link between the user and the user-FTP process, including the translation of user commands into FTP commands. We'll explore these commands later in this chapter.

FTP Replies

Each time the user-PI sends a command to the server-PI over the control connection, the server sends back a reply. FTP replies serve three main purposes:

- They serve as confirmation that the server received a command.
- They tell the user device whether or not the command was accepted, and if an error occurred, what it was.
- They communicate various types of information to the user of the session, such as the status of a transfer.

Advantages of Using Both Text and Numeric Replies

For a human user, a string of reply text would be sufficient to satisfy the requirements just mentioned, and FTP replies do include descriptive text. But having only a text string would make it difficult or impossible for FTP software on the client side to interpret results coming from the server. FTP was designed to allow software applications to interact with each other over the FTP command link. For this reason, the protocol's reply system uses *reply codes.*

FTP reply codes are three-digit numeric responses that can be easily interpreted by a computer program. They are also useful for human users who are familiar with FTP, because they communicate at a glance the results of various operations. While each FTP server implementation may differ in the text sent for each type of reply, the reply codes are used in a consistent manner based on the specifications of the FTP standard. It is, therefore, the codes that are examined to determine the results of a command; the text is just descriptive.

Reply Code Structure and Digit Interpretation

To make reply codes even more useful, they are not just assigned in a linear or random order. Rather, a special encoding scheme is used, in which each code has three digits that each communicate a particular type of information and categorize replies. A code can be considered to be of the form *xyz*, where *x* is the first digit, *y* is the second, and *z* is the third.

The first digit indicates the success or failure of the command in general terms, whether a successful command is complete or incomplete, and whether or not an unsuccessful command should be retried. Table 72-4 shows the possible values.

Table 72-4: FTP Reply Code Format: First Digit Interpretation

Reply Code Format	Meaning	Description
1yz	Positive preliminary reply	An initial response indicating that the command has been accepted and processing is still in progress. The user should expect another reply before a new command may be sent.
2yz	Positive completion reply	The command has been successfully processed and completed.
3yz	Positive intermediate reply	The command was accepted, but processing has been delayed, pending receipt of additional information. This type of reply is used in the middle of command sequences. For example, it is used as part of the authentication sequence after receiving a USER command but before the matching PASS command is sent.
4yz	Transient negative completion reply	The command was not accepted and no action was taken, but the error is temporary and the command may be tried again. This is used for errors that may be a result of temporary glitches or conditions that may change—for example, a file being busy due to another resource accessing it at the time a request was made for it.
5yz	Permanent negative completion reply	The command was not accepted and no action was taken. Trying the same command again is likely to result in another error. For example, a request for a file that is not found on the server, or sending an invalid command like BUGU, would fall into this category.

The second digit of the reply code is used to categorize messages into functional groups. These groups are shown in Table 72-5.

Table 72-5: FTP Reply Code Format: Second Digit Interpretation

Reply Code Format	Meaning	Description
x0z	Syntax	Syntax errors or miscellaneous messages
x1z	Information	Replies to requests for information, such as status requests
x2z	Connections	Replies related to the control connection or data connection
x3z	Authentication and accounting	Replies related to login procedures and accounting
x4z	Unspecified	Not defined
x5z	File system	Replies related to the server's file system

The third digit indicates a specific type of message within each of the functional groups described by the second digit. The third digit allows each functional group to have ten different reply codes for each reply type given by the first code digit (preliminary success, transient failure, and so on).

These *x*, *y*, and *z* digit meanings are combined to make specific reply codes. For example, consider reply code 530, diagrammed in Figure 72-5. The first digit tells you that this is a permanent negative reply, and the second indicates that it is related to login or accounting. (It is, in fact, an error message received when a login fails.) The third digit tells you the specific type of error that has occurred.

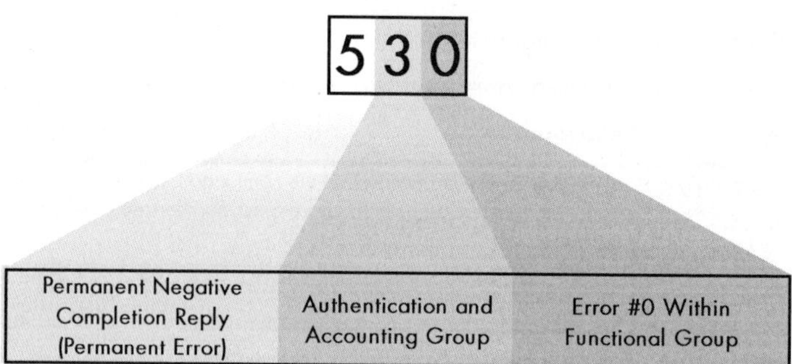

Figure 72-5: FTP reply code format *This diagram shows how the three-digit FTP reply code format is interpreted. In reply code 530, the 5 indicates a permanent error, the 3 specifies that the error is related to authentication or accounting, and the 0 is the specific error type. A similar method is used for reply codes in many other TCP/IP application protocols, including the Simple Mail Transfer Protocol (SMTP) and Hypertext Transfer Protocol (HTTP).*

Using encoded reply codes allows the code itself to communicate information immediately and provides a way of keeping different types of responses organized. This idea was adapted for use by several other application protocols, including the Simple Mail Transfer Protocol (SMTP) for email, the Network News Transfer Protocol (NNTP) for network news, and the Hypertext Transfer Protocol (HTTP) for the World Wide Web.

Table 72-6 contains a list of some of the more common FTP reply codes taken from RFC 959. They are shown in numerical order, along with the reply text presented as typical in that document and additional descriptive information as needed.

Table 72-6: FTP Reply Codes

Reply Code	Typical Reply Text	Description
110	Restart marker reply.	Used as part of the marker restart feature when transferring in block mode.
120	Service ready in *nnn* minutes.	*nnn* indicates the number of minutes until the service will be available.
125	Data connection already open; transfer starting.	
150	File status okay; about to open data connection.	
200	Command okay.	Sometimes the text indicates the name of the command that was successful.

(continued)

Table 72-6: FTP Reply Codes (continued)

Reply Code	Typical Reply Text	Description
202	Command not implemented, or superfluous at this site.	
211	System status, or system help reply.	Will contain system-specific status or help information.
212	Directory status.	
213	File status.	
214	Help message.	Includes help information of use to a human user of this server.
215	*NAME* system type.	*NAME* is the name of a type of operating system. Often sent as a reply to the SYST command.
220	Service ready for new user.	Sent when the command channel is established before the USER command is sent.
221	Service closing control connection.	A "goodbye" message is sent when the session is closed.
225	Data connection open; no transfer in progress.	
226	Closing data connection.	Sent after a successful file transfer or a file abort.
227	Entering Passive Mode (h1,h2,h3,h4,p1,p2).	Sent in reply to the PASV command, indicates the IP address and port to use for the data connection.
230	User logged in, proceed.	Sent after successful USER and PASS authentication. Systems often include additional greeting or other information with this code after a login.
250	Requested file action okay, completed.	The text description will provide more details about what was successfully done, such as confirming a change of directory or deleted file.
257	*PATHNAME* created.	*PATHNAME* is replaced by the path created.
331	User name okay, need password.	Intermediate result after sending USER but before sending PASS.
332	Need account for login.	
350	Requested file action pending further information.	
421	Service not available, closing control connection.	Sometimes sent if the FTP server is in the process of shutting down.
425	Can't open data connection.	
426	Connection closed; transfer aborted.	
450	Requested file action not taken. File unavailable.	The file is not available; for example, it may be locked by another user. Contrast to reply code 550.
451	Requested action aborted: local error in processing.	
452	Requested action not taken. Insufficient storage space in system.	The file system is full.
500	Syntax error, command unrecognized.	Bad or excessively long command line was sent.

(continued)

Table 72-6: FTP Reply Codes (continued)

Reply Code	Typical Reply Text	Description
501	Syntax error in parameters or arguments.	
502	Command not implemented.	
503	Bad sequence of commands.	
504	Command not implemented for that parameter.	
530	Not logged in.	Sent if authentication fails due to a bad user name or incorrect password.
550	Requested action not taken. File unavailable.	File was not found or user does not have access to it. This error code may be sent in reply to any file transfer command if the user has not successfully logged in yet. Contrast to reply code 450.
551	Requested action aborted: page type unknown.	
552	Requested file action aborted. Exceeded storage allocation.	
553	Requested action not taken. File name not allowed.	

KEY CONCEPT Each command sent by the FTP client results in a reply sent by the FTP server. FTP replies consist of a three-digit numeric *reply code,* along with a line of descriptive text. The reply code serves to standardize FTP replies, both so they can be interpreted by client software and so experienced users can see at a glance the results of a command. The reply code is structured so that the first two digits indicate the type of reply and to what category it belongs.

FTP Multiple-Line Text Replies

It is possible for a reply to contain more than one line of text. In this case, each line starts with the reply code, and all lines but the last have a hyphen between the reply code and the reply text, to indicate that the reply continues. The last line includes a space between the reply code and reply text, just like a single-line reply. This facility is often used to provide additional response information after a user logs in, via the 230 reply code. Listing 72-1 contains an example.

```
230-Welcome user to FTP server jabberwockynocky.
230-
230-You are user #17 of 100 simultaneous users allowed.
230-
230-
230-Please see the file "faq.txt" for help using this server.
230-
230 Logged in.
```

Listing 72-1: *FTP multiple-line text reply example*

As I mentioned, the actual text string for each reply code is implementation-specific. You can sometimes find some rather humorous text strings associated with some of these error messages. For example, I tried some commands using the FreeBSD FTP client on one of my Internet accounts. I tried to send or receive a file before I was logged in, and it didn't return an error like "Requested action not taken. File unavailable." Instead, it told me this: "Login first, then I might let you do that."

FTP User Interface and User Commands

The FTP command set provides a rich, complete set of instructions for implementing FTP. A human user could employ these commands to perform file-transfer functions directly with an FTP server. But to do this, the user must have an intimate knowledge of how FTP works. The user must know exactly which commands to send at which time, and in what order.

Gaining knowledge of internal FTP commands might be a reasonable assignment for an internetworking expert, but not for a typical TCP/IP application user. For this reason, the FTP protocol defines an additional protocol component as part of the user-FTP process: the FTP *user interface*. It provides three main benefits to the FTP user:

User Friendliness The FTP user interface presents FTP to the human user in a way that is easier and simpler to use than issuing protocol commands. Instead of requiring the knowledge of all those four-letter codes, the user interface can allow functions to be performed with more intuitive human-language commands. For example, we can say `get` a file instead of having to use the command RETR.

Customization The command used to perform a particular function can be customized based on common parlance in the networking industry, without requiring changes to be made to FTP itself. For example, the image transfer mode is now also commonly called binary mode, so a user command called `binary` has been created to set this mode.

Detail Abstraction and Command Sequence Simplification A single user command can be made to issue multiple FTP protocol commands, hiding internal FTP details and making the protocol easier to use. In particular, commands that are related to the maintenance of the connection and other overhead issues that users don't want to deal with can be automated. For example, an FTP client normally issues a PASV or PORT command prior to each data transfer. The user interface can take care of issuing this command automatically prior to a RETR or STOR command when a user tells FTP to get or send a file.

Command-Line and Graphical FTP Interfaces

Traditionally, FTP clients have used a *command-line interface*. In this familiar arrangement, an FTP client is invoked and the user is automatically asked for a user name and password to establish an FTP session. Then the user is presented with a command prompt, where the user can type various FTP commands to perform different functions. Text responses from the server are displayed to the user to indicate the results of various commands. Normally, the internal protocol commands (such as PASV and STOR) sent by the client are suppressed to avoid screen clutter, but their display can be enabled in a debug mode.

Command-line utilities are efficient, but some folks don't care for them. They are rather "old school" in the context of modern graphical operating systems and applications. Thus, many modern FTP clients are graphical in nature. They allow actions to be performed by the user clicking buttons instead of typing commands. Some FTP clients allow files to be transferred by dragging and dropping from a local file system display to one on a remote server. These make FTP even easier to use.

> **KEY CONCEPT** The FTP *user interface* is the component on the FTP client that acts as an intermediary between the human user and the FTP software. The existence of the user interface allows FTP to be used in a friendly manner without requiring knowledge of FTP's internal protocol commands. Most FTP software uses either a *command-line interface* that understands English-like user commands or a *graphical interface,* where mouse clicks and other graphical operations are translated into FTP commands.

Typical FTP User Commands

To discover the specific commands supported by an FTP client, consult its documentation. In a command-line client, you can enter the command ? to see a list of supported commands. Table 72-7 shows some of the common commands encountered in typical FTP command-line clients, along with the typical parameters they require.

Note how many of these commands are actually synonyms, such as `bye`, `exit`, and `quit`. Similarly, you can use the command `type ascii` to set the ASCII data type or use the `ascii` command. This is all done for the user's convenience and is one of the benefits of having a flexible user interface that is distinct from the FTP command set.

Finally, an alternative way of using FTP is through the specification of an FTP Uniform Resource Locator (URL). While FTP is at its heart an interactive system, FTP URLs allow simple functions, such as retrieving a single file, to be done quickly and easily. They also allow FTP file references to be integrated with hypertext (World Wide Web) documents. See "URL Schemes and Scheme-Specific Syntaxes" in Chapter 70 for more on how FTP uses URLs.

Table 72-7: Common FTP User Commands

User Command	Description
`account <account-name>`	Sends the ACCT command to access a particular account on the server.
`append <file-name>`	Appends data to a file using APPE.
`ascii`	Sets the ASCII data type for subsequent transfers.
`binary`	Sets the image data type for subsequent transfers. Same as the `image` command.
`bye`	Terminates FTP session and exits the FTP client (same as `exit` and `quit`).
`cd <directory-path>`	Changes the remote server working directory (using CWD protocol command).
`cdup`	Goes to parent of current working directory.

(continued)

Table 72-7: Common FTP User Commands (continued)

User Command	Description
`chmod <file-name>`	On UNIX systems, changes file permissions of a file.
`close`	Closes a particular FTP session but user stays at FTP command line.
`debug`	Sets debug mode.
`delete <file-name>`	Deletes a file on the FTP server.
`dir [<optional-file-specification>]`	Lists contents of current working directory (or files matching the specification).
`exit`	Another synonym for bye and `quit`.
`form <format>`	Sets the transfer format.
`ftp <ftp-server>`	Opens session to the FTP server.
`get <file-name> [<dest-file-name>]`	Gets a file. If the *<dest-file-name>* parameter is specified, it is used for the name of the file retrieved; otherwise, the source filename is used.
`help [<optional-command-name>]`	Displays FTP client help information. Same as ?.
`image`	Sets the image data type, like the `binary` command.
`ls [<optional-file-specification>]`	Lists contents of current working directory (or files matching the specification). Same as `dir`.
`mget <file-specification>`	Gets multiple files from the server.
`mkdir <directory-name>`	Creates a directory on the remote server.
`mode` **`<transfer-mode>`**	Sets the file transfer mode.
`mput <file-specification>`	Sends (puts) multiple files to the server.
`msend <file-specification>`	Same as `mput`.
`open <ftp-server>`	Opens a session to the FTP server (same as `ftp`).
`passive`	Turns passive transfer mode on and off.
`put <file-name> [<dest-file-name>]`	Sends a file to the server. If the *<dest-file-name>* parameter is specified, it is used as the name for the file on the destination host; otherwise, the source filename is used.
`pwd`	Prints current working directory.
`quit`	Terminates FTP session and exits FTP client (same as bye and `exit`).
`recv <file-name> [<dest-file-name>]`	Receives file (same as get). If the *<dest-file-name>* parameter is specified, it is used for the name of the file retrieved; otherwise, the source filename is used.
`rename <old-file-name> <new-file-name>`	Renames a file.
`rhelp`	Displays remote help information, obtained using FTP `HELP` command.
`rmdir <directory-name>`	Removes a directory.
`send <file-name> [<dest-file-name>]`	Sends a file (same as put). If the *<dest-file-name>* parameter is specified, it is used as the name for the file on the destination host; otherwise, the source file name is used.
`site`	Sends a site-specific command to the server.
`size <file-name>`	Shows the size of a remote file.
`status`	Displays current session status.

(continued)

Table 72-7: Common FTP User Commands (continued)

User Command	Description
`struct <structure-type>`	Sets the file structure.
`system`	Shows the server's operating system type.
`type <data-type>`	Sets the data type for transfers.
`user <user-name>`	Logs in to server as a new user. Server will prompt for a password.
`? [<optional-command-name>]`	Displays FTP client help information. Same as help.

Sample FTP Session

Having now seen all the details of how FTP works, let's tie everything together by looking at a sample FTP session between an FTP client and server, to see FTP commands and replies in action. In this example, I will invoke FTP from a client to retrieve a text file from an FTP server, and then I'll delete the file from the server and the directory that contained it. In the process, I will issue some additional commands to illustrate more of how FTP works. I will enable debug mode in the FTP client so that for each user command, you can see the actual FTP commands generated.

Table 72-8 shows the sample FTP session, slightly simplified. The first column contains commands entered by the user (that's me, of course) on the FTP client. The second shows the actual protocol command(s) sent to the FTP server in highlighted text and the reply returned from the server to the client in plain text. The third column contains descriptive comments.

Table 72-8: Sample FTP Session

User Command	FTP Protocol Command/FTP Server Reply	Comments

`ftp -d pcguide.com`	`Connected to pcguide.com.`
	`220 ftp199.pair.com NcFTPd Server (licensed copy) ready.`
	`Name (pcguide.com:ixl):`
		This is the command to start up FTP. The -d enables debug mode. In this initial step, the TCP control connection is made and the server replies with a 220 reply code indicating that it's ready for user identification. The FTP client automatically prompts for the user name.

`ixl`	**`USER ixl`** `331 User ixl okay, need password.`	I use `ixl` for user names commonly. Here, the FTP client sends the user name and the server responds, asking for the password.

`****`	**`PASS XXXX`**
	`230-You are user #1 of 300 simultaneous users allowed.`
	`230-`
	`230-`
	`230-Welcome to (<system name>)`
	`230-`
	`230 Logged in.`
	`SYST`
	`215 UNIX Type: L8`
	`Remote system type is UNIX.`
	`Using binary mode to transfer files.`
		I enter my password, which is sent to the FTP server, and the server authenticates me and sends back a 230 message. This tells me the login was successful. It also provides additional information.
		The FTP client then automatically sends a SYST command to tell me what type of system the server is using, which is UNIX in this case. The client tells me that binary mode has been selected by default; this is often the default when doing FTP from UNIX to UNIX (as I am doing here), since there is no need for ASCII mode when moving text files between similar systems.

(continued)

Table 72-8: Sample FTP Session (continued)

User Command	FTP Protocol Command/FTP Server Reply	Comments
pwd	**PWD** 257 "/usr/home/ixl" is cwd.	I check the current working directory (cwd), which the server tells me is my own home directory on this system.
cd ftptest	**CWD ftptest** 550 No such directory.	I try to go to a directory called ftptest, but that was the wrong name, so I get a 550 error for my trouble. (I wasn't trying to do this; I forgot the directory name but figured I might as well show it to you anyway!)
cd ftpdemo	**CWD ftpdemo** 250 "/usr/home/ixl/ftpdemo" is new cwd.	I got the name right this time, and the server confirms the new working directory.
dir	**PASV** 227 Entering Passive Mode (ip1,ip2,ip3,ip4,193,224) **LIST** 150 Data connection accepted from ip5.ip6.ip7.ip8:4279; transfer starting. -rw-r-r- 1 ixl users 16 May 22 17:47 testfile.txt 226 Listing completed.	I request a list of files from the server. The FTP client automatically issues a PASV command, and the server responds with a port number and IP address for it to use. (I have not shown the IP here for security reasons.) The directory listing is then transferred from the server to the client.
asc	**TYPE A** 200 Type okay.	I set ASCII mode, although I didn't really need to do that. Note that this client allowed me to abbreviate the ascii command as asc.
get testfile.txt	**PASV** 227 Entering Passive Mode (ip1,ip2,ip3,ip4,193,226) **RETR testfile.txt** 150 Data connection accepted from ip5.ip6.ip7.ip8:4283; transfer starting for testfile.txt (16 bytes). 226 Transfer completed. 17 bytes received in 0.10 seconds (0.17 KB/s)	I get the file in this demo directory using a get command. The server accepts the PASV command and sends the file. It initially sends a 150 reply as the transfer starts (initial positive reply), and then sends 226 when it is done. Note that the port numbers used here are different (for both server and client) than they were for the directory listing I did earlier.
del testfile.txt	**DELE testfile.txt** 250 Deleted.	I delete the original file on the server.
cdup	**CDUP** 250 "/usr/home/ixl" is new cwd.	I go up to the parent directory.
rmdir ftpdemo	**RMD ftpdemo** 250 Directory removed.	I remove the directory that the file was in.
quit	**QUIT** 221 Goodbye.	I end the FTP session. The quit command also automatically closes the FTP client and returns me to the UNIX shell.

73

TRIVIAL FILE TRANSFER PROTOCOL (TFTP)

In Chapter 72, you saw how the File Transfer Protocol (FTP) implements a full set of commands and reply functionalities that enables a user to perform a wide range of file movement and manipulation tasks. Although FTP is ideal as a general-purpose protocol for file transfer between computers, on certain types of hardware, it is too complex to implement easily and provides more capabilities than are really needed. In cases where only the most basic file transfer functions are required while simplicity and small program size is of paramount importance, a companion to FTP called the *Trivial File Transfer Protocol (TFTP)* can be used.

This chapter provides a description of the operation of TFTP, beginning with an overview description of the protocol, its history and motivation, and the relevant standards that describe it. I discuss its operation in general terms, cover how TFTP clients and servers communicate, and explain TFTP messaging in detail. I then discuss TFTP options and the TFTP option negotiation mechanism. The chapter concludes by showing the various TFTP message formats.

BACKGROUND INFORMATION *While TFTP is a distinct protocol from FTP, explaining the former is easier when the reader is familiar with the latter. I assume that the reader has some understanding of FTP, since it is the more commonly used protocol. If you have come to this chapter prior to reading Chapter 72, I recommend at least reading the section "FTP Overview, History, and Standards" in that chapter before proceeding here.*

TFTP Overview, History, and Standards

FTP is the main protocol used for the majority of general file transfers in TCP/IP internetworks. One of the objectives of the designers of FTP was to keep the protocol relatively simple, but that was possible only to a limited extent. To enable the protocol to be useful in a variety of cases and between many kinds of devices, FTP needed a fairly large set of features and capabilities. As a result, while FTP is not as complex as certain other protocols, it is still fairly complicated in a number of respects.

Why TFTP Was Needed

The complexity of FTP is partly due to the protocol itself, with its dozens of commands and reply codes, and partly due to the need of using TCP for connections and data transport. The reliance on TCP means that any device wanting to use FTP needs not only the FTP program but a full TCP implementation as well. It must handle FTP's need for simultaneous data and control channel connections and other requirements.

For a conventional computer, such as a regular PC, Macintosh, or UNIX workstation, none of this is really an issue, especially with today's large hard disks and fast, cheap memory. But remember that FTP was developed more than three decades ago, when hardware was slow and memory was expensive. Furthermore, even today, regular computers are not the only devices used on networks. Some networked devices do not have the capabilities of true computers, but they still need to be able to perform file transfers. For these devices, a full FTP and TCP implementation is a nontrivial matter.

One of the most notable examples of such devices are *diskless workstations*—computers that have no permanent storage, so when they start up, they cannot read a whole TCP/IP implementation from a hard disk like most computers easily do. They start with only a small amount of built-in software and must obtain configuration information from a server and then download the rest of their software from another network device. The same issue arises for certain other hardware devices with no hard disks.

The process of starting up these devices is commonly called *bootstrapping* and occurs in two phases. First, the workstation is provided with an IP address and other parameters through the use of a host configuration protocol such as the Bootstrap Protocol (BOOTP; see Chapter 60) or the Dynamic Host Control Protocol (DHCP; see Chapters 61 to 64). Second, the client downloads software, such as an operating system and drivers, that let it function on the network like any other device. This requires that the device have the ability to transfer files quickly and easily. The instructions to perform this bootstrapping must fit onto a read-only memory (ROM) chip, and this makes the size of the software an important issue—again, especially many years ago.

The solution to this need was to create a "light" version of FTP that would emphasize small program size and simplicity over functionality. This new protocol, TFTP, was initially developed in the late 1970s and first standardized in 1980. The modern version, *TFTP version 2*, was documented in RFC 783 in 1981, which was revised and published as RFC 1350, "The TFTP Protocol (Revision 2)," in 1992. This is the current version of the standard.

Comparing FTP and TFTP

Probably the best way to understand the relationship between TFTP and FTP is to compare it to the relationship between the Transmission Control Protocol (TCP) and User Datagram Protocol (UDP) at the transport layer. UDP is a simplified, stripped-down alternative to TCP that is used when simplicity is more important than rich functionality. Similarly, TFTP is a greatly simplified version of FTP that allows only basic operations and lacks some of FTP's fancy capabilities in order to keep its implementation easy (even trivial) and its program size small.

Due to its limitations, TFTP is a complement to FTP, not a replacement for it. TFTP is used only when its simplicity is important and its lack of features is not. Its most common application is bootstrapping, as described above, though it can be used for other purposes. One specific application that the TFTP standard describes for the protocol is the transport of electronic mail (email). While the protocol supports this explicitly, TFTP is not generally used for this purpose today.

FTP and TFTP have significant differences in at least four significant areas:

Transport The comparison to TCP and UDP is apt not only based on the features/simplicity trade-off, but because FTP uses TCP for transport while TFTP uses UDP. Like TFTP, UDP is simple, and this makes the two ideal for embedding together as a hardware program set in a network device.

Limited Command Set FTP includes a rich set of commands to allow files to be sent, received, renamed, deleted, and so forth. TFTP allows files only to be sent and received.

Limited Data Representations TFTP does not include some of FTP's fancy data representation options; it allows only simple ASCII or binary file transfers.

Lack of Authentication UDP uses no login mechanism or other means of authentication. This is again a simplification, though it means the operators of TFTP servers must severely restrict the files they make available for access. (It is also part of why TFTP specifically does not allow the client to perform dangerous file operations such as deletion.)

Overview of TFTP Operation

Communication and messaging in TFTP is very different from FTP because of the different transport layer protocols used by each. FTP makes use of TCP's rich functionality, including its stream data orientation, to allow it to send bytes of data directly over the FTP data connection. TCP also takes care of reliable delivery of data for FTP, ensuring that files are received correctly. In contrast, since TFTP uses UDP, it must package data into individual messages for both protocol control and data communication. TFTP must also take care of timing transmissions to detect lost datagrams and then retransmitting as needed.

TFTP servers allow connections from TFTP clients to perform file send and receive operations. Many hosts that run FTP servers will also run a separate TFTP server module. TFTP users initiate connections by starting a TFTP client program, which generally uses a command-line interface similar to that of many FTP clients; the main difference is the much smaller number of commands in TFTP.

> **KEY CONCEPT** For situations in which the full FTP is either unnecessary or impractical, the simpler *Trivial File Transfer Protocol (TFTP)* was developed. TFTP is like FTP in that it is used for general file transfer between a client and server device, but it is stripped down in its capabilities. Rather than including a full command set and using TCP for communication, like FTP, TFTP can be used only for reading or writing a single file, and it uses the fast but unreliable UDP for transport. It is often preferred in situations where small files must be transferred quickly and simply, such as for bootstrapping diskless workstations.

The basic operation of TFTP has not changed since RFC 1350 was published, but a new feature was added to the protocol in 1995. RFC 1782, "TFTP Option Extension," defines a mechanism by which a TFTP client and TFTP server can negotiate certain parameters that will control a file transfer prior to the transfer commencing. This allows more flexibility in how TFTP is used, adding a slight amount of complexity to TFTP, but not a great deal.

The option extension is backward-compatible with regular TFTP and is used only if both server and client support it. Two subsequent RFCs define the actual options that can be negotiated: RFC 1783, "TFTP Blocksize Option," and RFC 1784, "TFTP Timeout Interval and Transfer Size Options." This set of three RFCs (1782, 1783, and 1784) was replaced in 1998 by updated versions in RFCs 2347, 2348, and 2349.

TFTP General Operation, Connection Establishment, and Client/Server Communication

Since the *T* in *TFTP* stands for *Trivial*, and the protocol was specifically designed to be simple, you would think that describing how it works would, in fact, be simple, wouldn't you? And, actually, that's pretty much true. TFTP communication is client/server based, as discussed in the overview. The process of transferring a file consists of three main phases:

Initial Connection The TFTP client establishes the connection by sending an initial request to the server. The server responds back to the client, and the connection is effectively opened.

Data Transfer Once the connection is established, the client and server exchange TFTP messages. One device sends data, and the other sends acknowledgments.

Connection Termination When the last TFTP message containing data has been sent and acknowledged, the connection is terminated.

Connection Establishment and Identification

The matter of a connection is somewhat different in TFTP than it is with a protocol like FTP that uses TCP. FTP must establish a connection at the TCP level before anything can be done by FTP itself. TFTP, however, uses the connectionless UDP for transport, so there is no connection in the sense that one exists in TCP. In TFTP, the connection is more in a *logical* sense, meaning that the client and server are participating in the protocol and exchanging TFTP messages.

The TFTP server listens continuously for requests on well-known UDP port number 69, which is reserved for TFTP. The client chooses for its initial communication an ephemeral port number, as is usually the case in TCP/IP. This port number actually identifies the data transfer and is called a *transfer identifier (TID).*

What's different about TFTP, however, is that the server also selects a pseudo-random TID that it uses for sending responses back to the client; it doesn't send them from port number 69. This is done because by using a unique client port number and source port number, multiple TFTP exchanges can be conducted simultaneously by a server. Each transfer is identified automatically by the source and destination port number, so there is no need to identify in data messages the transfer to which each block data belongs. This keeps the TFTP header size down, allowing more of each UDP message to contain actual data.

For example, suppose the TFTP client selects a TID of 3145 for its initial message. It would send a UDP transmission from its port 3145 to the server's port 69. Say the server selects a TID of 1114. It would send its reply from its port 1114 to the client's port 3145. From then on, the client would send messages back to server port 1114 until the TFTP session was completed.

Lock-Step Client/Server Messaging

After the initial exchange, the client and server exchange data and acknowledgment messages in *lock-step* fashion. Each device sends a message for each message it receives: one device sends data messages and waits for acknowledgments; the other sends acknowledgments and waits for data messages. This form of rigid communication is less efficient than allowing the transmitter to fire away with one data message after another, but it is important because it keeps TFTP simple when it comes to an important issue: retransmissions.

Like all protocols using the unreliable UDP, TFTP has no assurances that any messages sent will actually arrive at their destination, so it must use timers to detect lost transmissions and resend them. What is different about TFTP is that both clients and servers perform retransmission. The device that is sending data messages will resend the data message if it doesn't receive an acknowledgment in a reasonable period of time; the device sending the acknowledgments will resend the acknowledgment if it doesn't receive the next data message promptly. The lock-step communication greatly simplifies this process, since each device needs to keep track of only one outstanding message at a time. It also eliminates the need to deal with complications such as reorganizing blocks received out of order (which protocols like FTP rely on TCP to manage).

> **KEY CONCEPT** Since TFTP uses UDP rather than TCP, no explicit concept of a connection exists as in FTP. A TFTP session instead uses the concept of a logical connection, which is opened when a client sends a request to a server to read or write a file. Communication between the client and server is performed in lock-step fashion: one device sends data messages and receives acknowledgments so it knows the data messages were received; the other sends acknowledgments and receives data messages so it knows the acknowledgments were received.

Difficulties with TFTP's Simplified Messaging Mechanism

One of the most important drawbacks with this technique is that while it simplifies communication, it does so at the cost of performance. Since only one message can be in transit at a time, this limits throughput to a maximum of 512 bytes for exchange of messages between the client and server. In contrast, when using FTP, large amounts of data can be pipelined; there is no need to wait for an acknowledgment for the first piece of data before sending the second.

Another complication is that if a data or an acknowledgment message is resent and the original was not lost but rather just delayed, two copies will show up. The original TFTP rules stated that upon receipt of a duplicate datagram, the device receiving it may resend the current datagram. So, receipt of a duplicate block 2 by a client doing a read would result in the client sending a duplicate acknowledgment for block 2. This would result in two acknowledgments being received by the server, which would in turn send block 3 twice. Then there would be two acknowledgments for block 3, and so on.

The end result of this is that once the initial duplication occurs, every message thereafter is sent twice. This has been affectionately dubbed the *Sorcerer's Apprentice bug*, after the story used as the basis of the famous scene in the movie *Fantasia,* where Mickey Mouse cuts animated brooms in half only to find that each half comes to life. This problem was fixed by changing the rules so that only the device receiving a duplicate data message may send a duplicate acknowledgment. Receipt of a duplicate acknowledgment does not result in sending a duplicate data message. Since only one of the two devices can send duplicates, this fixes the problem.

It's also worth emphasizing that TFTP includes absolutely no security, so no login or authentication process is in place. As mentioned earlier, administrators must use caution in deciding what files to make available via TFTP and in allowing write access to TFTP servers.

TFTP Detailed Operation and Messaging

You saw earlier that TFTP operation consists of three general steps: initial connection, data transfer, and connection termination. All operations are performed through the exchange of specific TFTP messages. Let's take a more detailed look now at these three phases of operation and the specifics of TFTP messaging.

Initial Message Exchange

The first message sent by the client to initiate TFTP is either a read request (RRQ) message or a write request (WRQ) message. This message serves implicitly to establish the logical TFTP connection and to indicate whether the file is to be sent from the server to the client (read request) or the client to the server (write request). The message also specifies the type of file transfer to be performed. TFTP supports two transfer modes: *netascii* mode (ASCII text files as used by the Telnet Protocol) and *octet* mode (binary files).

NOTE *Originally, a third file type option existed, called mail mode, but TFTP was never really designed for transmitting mail and this option is now obsolete.*

Assuming no problem occurred with the request (such as a server problem, inability to find the file, and so on), the server will respond with a positive reply. In the case of a read request, the server will immediately send the first data message back to the client. In the case of a write request, the server will send an acknowledgment message to the client, telling it that it may proceed to send the first data message.

After the initial exchange, the client and server exchange data and acknowledgment messages in lock-step fashion as described earlier. For a read, the server sends one data message and waits for an acknowledgment from the client before sending the next one. For a write, the client sends one data message and the server sends an acknowledgment for it, before the client sends the next data message.

Data Block Numbering

Each data message contains a block of between 0 and 512 bytes of data. The blocks are numbered sequentially, starting with 1. The number of each block is placed in the header of the data message carrying that block and then used in the acknowledgment for that block so the original sender knows it was received. The device sending the data will always send 512 bytes of data at a time for as long as it has enough data to fill the message. When it gets to the end of the file and has fewer than 512 bytes to send, it will send only as many bytes as remain. (Interestingly, this means that if the size of the file is an exact multiple of 512, the last message sent will have zero bytes of data!)

The receipt of a data message with between 0 and 511 bytes of data signals that this is the last data message. Once this is acknowledged, it automatically signals the end of the data transfer. There is no need to terminate the connection explicitly, just as it was not necessary to establish it explicitly.

TFTP Read Process Steps

Let's look at an example that shows how TFTP messaging works. Suppose the client wants to read a particular file that is 1200 bytes long. Here are the steps in simplified form (also displayed in Figure 73-1):

1. The client sends a read request to the server, specifying the name of the file.
2. The server sends back a data message containing block 1, carrying 512 bytes of data.
3. The client receives the data and sends back an acknowledgment for block 1.
4. The server sends block 2, with 512 bytes of data.
5. The client receives block 2 and sends back an acknowledgment for it.

6. The server sends block 3, containing 176 bytes of data. It waits for an acknowledgment before terminating the logical connection.
7. The client receives the data and sends an acknowledgment for block 3. Since this data message had fewer than 512 bytes, it knows the file is complete.
8. The server receives the acknowledgment and knows the file was received successfully.

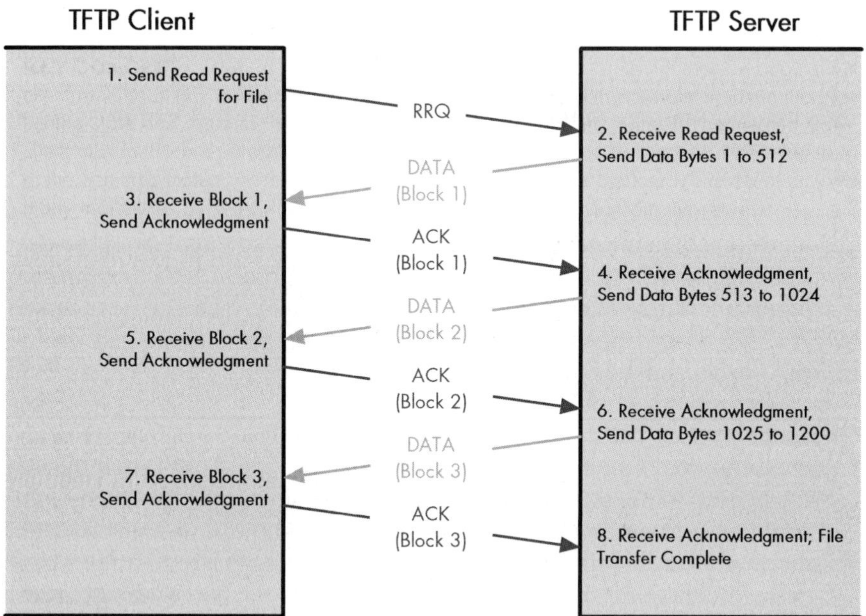

TFTP Client
TFTP Server
1. Send Read Request for File
RRQ
2. Receive Read Request, Send Data Bytes 1 to 512
DATA (Block 1)
3. Receive Block 1, Send Acknowledgment
ACK (Block 1)
4. Receive Acknowledgment, Send Data Bytes 513 to 1024
DATA (Block 2)
5. Receive Block 2, Send Acknowledgment
ACK (Block 2)
6. Receive Acknowledgment, Send Data Bytes 1025 to 1200
DATA (Block 3)
7. Receive Block 3, Send Acknowledgment
ACK (Block 3)
8. Receive Acknowledgment; File Transfer Complete

Figure 73-1: TFTP read process *In this example, the client starts the process of reading a file by sending a request for it to the server. The server acknowledges this request by immediately sending a DATA message carrying block 1, containing the first 512 bytes of the file. The client acknowledges this with an ACK message for block 1. The server then sends block 2, containing bytes 513 to 1024, which the client acknowledges. When the client receives block 3, it realizes it has only 176 bytes, which marks it as the last block of the file.*

TFTP Write Process Steps

Here are the steps in the same process, but where the client is writing the file (see Figure 73-2):

1. The client sends a write request to the server, specifying the name of the file.
2. The server sends back an acknowledgment. Since this acknowledgment is prior to the receipt of any data, it uses block 0 in the acknowledgment.
3. The client sends a data message containing block 1, with 512 bytes of data.
4. The server receives the data and sends back an acknowledgment for block 1.
5. The client sends block 2, containing 512 bytes of data.
6. The server receives the data and sends back an acknowledgment for block 2.

7. The client sends block 3, containing 176 bytes of data. It waits for an acknowledgment before terminating the logical connection.
8. The server receives block 3 and sends an acknowledgment for it. Since this data message had fewer than 512 bytes, the transfer is done.
9. The client receives the acknowledgment for block 3 and knows the file write was completed successfully.

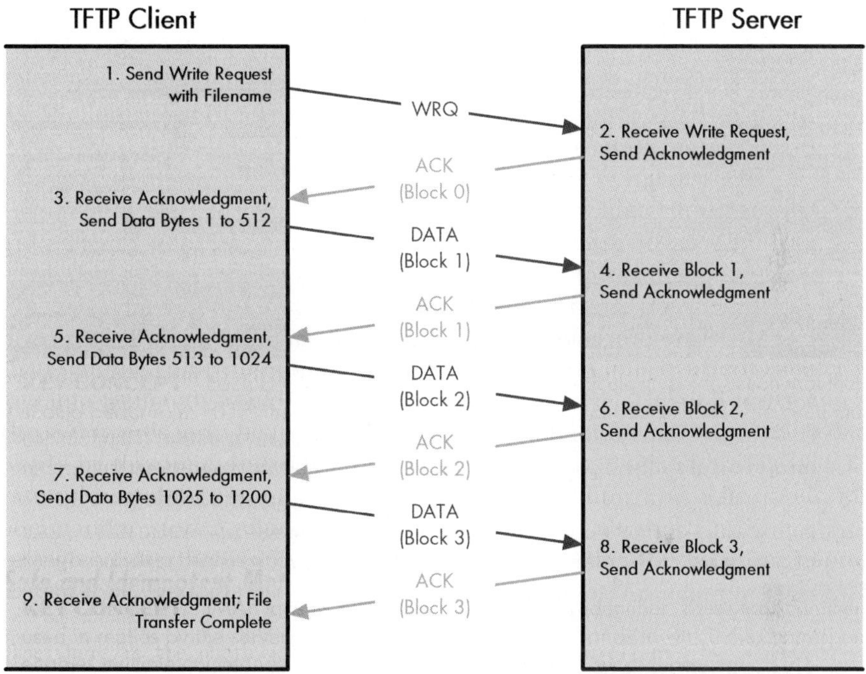

TFTP Client
TFTP Server
1. Send Write Request with Filename
WRQ
2. Receive Write Request, Send Acknowledgment
ACK (Block 0)
3. Receive Acknowledgment, Send Data Bytes 1 to 512
DATA (Block 1)
4. Receive Block 1, Send Acknowledgment
ACK (Block 1)
5. Receive Acknowledgment, Send Data Bytes 513 to 1024
DATA (Block 2)
6. Receive Block 2, Send Acknowledgment
ACK (Block 2)
7. Receive Acknowledgment, Send Data Bytes 1025 to 1200
DATA (Block 3)
8. Receive Block 3, Send Acknowledgment
ACK (Block 3)
9. Receive Acknowledgment; File Transfer Complete

Figure 73-2: TFTP write process *This example shows the client sending the same 1200-byte file to the server that it read in Figure 73-1. The client sends a write request to the server, which acknowledges it; it uses block 0 to represent acknowledgment of the request prior to receipt of any data. The client then sends blocks of data one at a time, each of which is acknowledged by the server. When the server receives block 3 containing fewer than 512 bytes of data, it knows it has received the whole file.*

> **KEY CONCEPT** A TFTP *read operation* begins with the client sending a read request message to the TFTP server; the server then sends the file in 512-byte data messages, waiting after each one for the client to acknowledge receipt before sending the next. A TFTP *write operation* starts with a write request sent by the client to the server, which the server acknowledges. The client then sends the file in 512-byte data blocks, waiting after each for the server to acknowledge receipt. In both cases, there is no explicit means by which the end of a transfer is marked; the device receiving the file simply knows the transfer is complete when it receives a data message containing fewer than 512 bytes.

If a problem is encountered at any stage of the connection establishment or transfer process, a device may reply with an error message instead of a data or acknowledgment message, as appropriate. An error message normally results in the failure of the data transfer; this is one of the prices paid for the simplicity of TFTP.

Each TFTP file transfer proceeds using the process described, which transfers a single file. If another file needs to be sent or received, a new logical communication is established, in a manner analogous to how FTP creates data connections. The main difference is that TFTP has no persistent control connection, as FTP does.

TFTP Options and Option Negotiation

One of the difficulties that designers of simple protocols and applications seem to have is keeping them simple. Many protocols start out small, but over time well-intentioned users suggest improvements that are added slowly but surely. Eventually, the program that was once lean and mean has become, shall we say, "well-marbled." In the software industry, this is called *feature creep* and has happened to many protocols and applications.

The temptation to add features is especially strong when the program or protocol has few to begin with. Given this, the maintainers of TFTP have done a good job over the years of avoiding this pitfall. However, they did allow one new feature to be added to the protocol in 1995: the "TFTP Option Extension," which describes how a TFTP client and server can negotiate *options* before transferring a file.

The reason for adding this capability is that the original TFTP provided no way at all for the client and server to exchange important control information prior to sending a file. This limited the flexibility of the protocol to deal with special cases, such as the transfer of data over unusual network types. The TFTP option negotiation feature allows additional parameters to be exchanged between the client and server that govern how data is transferred. It does this without significantly complicating the protocol and is backward-compatible with normal TFTP. It is used only if both client and server support it, and one device trying to use the feature will not cause problems if the other doesn't support it.

TFTP Option Negotiation Process

The client begins the negotiation by sending a modified TFTP read request or write request message. In addition to the normal information that appears in this message (described in the "TFTP Message Formats" section later in this chapter), a list of options may also be included. Each is specified with an option code and an option value. The names and values are expressed as ASCII strings, terminated by a null character (0 byte). Multiple options may be specified in the request message.

The server receives the request containing the options, and if it supports the option extension, it processes them. It then returns a *special option acknowledgment* (*OACK*) message to the client, where it lists all the options that the client specified that the server recognizes and accepts. Any options that the client requested but the server rejects are not included in the OACK. The client may use only the options that the server accepts. If the client rejects the server's response, it may send back an error message (with error code 8) upon receipt of the unacceptable OACK message.

The server may specify an alternative value in its response for certain options, if it recognizes the option but doesn't like the client's suggested value. Obviously, if the server doesn't support options at all, it will ignore the client's option requests and respond with a data message (for a read) or a regular acknowledgment (for a write) as in normal TFTP.

If the server did send an OACK, the client proceeds to send messages using the regular messaging exchange described in the previous section. In the case of a write, the OACK replaces the regular acknowledgment in the message dialog. In the case of a read, the OACK is the server's first message instead of the first data block that it would normally send. TFTP doesn't allow the same device to send two datagrams in a row, so a reply from the client must be received before that first block can be sent. The client does this by sending a regular acknowledgment with a block number of 0 in it—the same form of acknowledgment a server normally sends for a write.

> **KEY CONCEPT** TFTP is supposed to be a small and simple protocol, so it includes few extra features. One that it does support is *option negotiation*, where a TFTP client and server attempt to come to agreement on additional parameters that they will use in transferring a file. The TFTP client includes one or more options in its read request or write request message; the TFTP server then sends an option acknowledgment (OACK) message listing each option the server agrees to use. The use of options when reading a file means that an extra acknowledgment must be sent by the client—to acknowledge the OACK—before the server sends the first block of the file.

For review, let's take a look at each of the four possible cases: read and write, with and without options.

The initial message exchange for a normal read (without option negotiation), as shown in Figure 73-1, is as follows:

1. Client sends read request.
2. Server sends data block 1.
3. Client acknowledges data block 1.

   And so on . . .

With option negotiation, a read is as follows (see Figure 73-3):

1. Client sends read request with options.
2. Server sends OACK.
3. Client sends regular acknowledgment for block 0; that is, it acknowledges the OACK.
4. Server sends data block 1.
5. Client acknowledges data block 1.

   And so on . . .

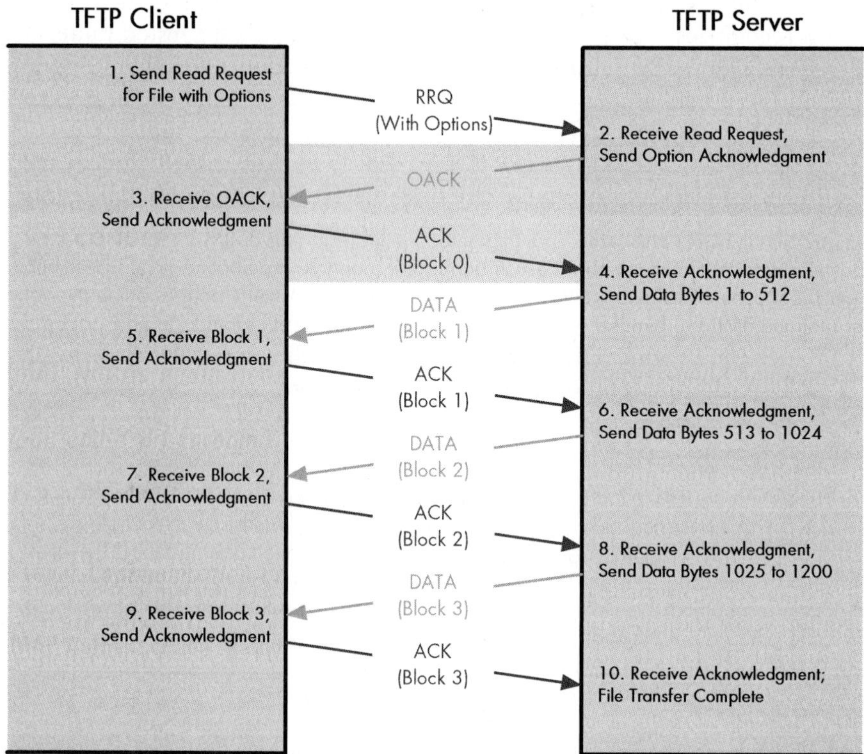
TFTP Client
TFTP Server
1. Send Read Request for File with Options
RRQ (With Options)
2. Receive Read Request, Send Option Acknowledgment
OACK
3. Receive OACK, Send Acknowledgment
ACK (Block 0)
4. Receive Acknowledgment, Send Data Bytes 1 to 512
DATA (Block 1)
5. Receive Block 1, Send Acknowledgment
ACK (Block 1)
6. Receive Acknowledgment, Send Data Bytes 513 to 1024
DATA (Block 2)
7. Receive Block 2, Send Acknowledgment
ACK (Block 2)
8. Receive Acknowledgment, Send Data Bytes 1025 to 1200
DATA (Block 3)
9. Receive Block 3, Send Acknowledgment
ACK (Block 3)
10. Receive Acknowledgment; File Transfer Complete

Figure 73-3: TFTP read process with option negotiation *This diagram shows the same example illustrated in Figure 73-1, but with one added message exchange used for option negotiation. The client's initial read request here includes options that it wants to use for this transfer. The server responds not immediately with the first data block, but with an OACK. The client indicates receipt of the OACK by sending an acknowledgment using block 0. The server sends data block 1, and the rest of the exchange proceeds as normal.*

The initial message exchange for a normal write (without option negotiation) is as follows:

1. Client sends write request.
2. Server sends acknowledgment.
3. Client sends data block 1.
4. Server acknowledges data block 1.

   And so on . . .

And here's a write with option negotiation:

1. Client sends write request with options.
2. Server sends option acknowledgment (instead of regular acknowledgment).
3. Client sends data block 1.
4. Server acknowledges data block 1.

   And so on . . .

TFTP Options

Table 73-1 contains a summary of the three TFTP options currently defined.

Table 73-1: TFTP Options

TFTP Option Name	TFTP Option Code (Used in Request Messages)	Defining RFC	Description
Block Size	blksize	2348	Allows the client and server to send data blocks of a size other than 512 bytes to improve efficiency or address limitations of a particular type of network.
Timeout Interval	interval	2349	Permits the client and server to agree on a specified number of seconds to use for their retransmission timers. Again, may be of value on certain networks with high latency or other special requirements.
Transfer Size	tsize	2349	Lets the device sending the file (client on a write, server on a read) tell the other device the size of the file before the transfer commences. This allows the receiving device to allocate space for it in advance.

TFTP Message Formats

Unlike FTP, all communication in TFTP is accomplished in the form of discrete messages that follow a particular message format. The reason why TFTP and FTP are so different in this regard is because of the different transport protocols they use. FTP uses TCP, which allows data to be streamed a byte at a time; FTP also makes use of a dedicated channel for commands. TFTP runs on UDP, which uses a conventional header/data formatting scheme.

The original TFTP standard defines five different types of messages: read request (RRQ), write request (WRQ), data (DATA), acknowledgment (ACK), and error (ERROR). The TFTP option extension feature defines a sixth message: option acknowledgment (OACK). Of these six messages, the first two share the same message format. The only common field in every TFTP message is the operation code (Opcode), which tells the recipient of the message what type it is.

TFTP's message formats are different than those used for certain other protocols, because many of the fields in TFTP are variable in length. Usually, variable-length fields in messages are expressed using a preceding length field that specifies the length of the variable-sized field. Instead, TFTP sends such fields as strings of ASCII characters using netascii, the Telnet version of ASCII. The end of the string is marked by a zero byte. The exception to this is the data field in data messages, the content of which depends on the transfer mode.

The remainder of the chapter contains the details on each of the TFTP messages.

Read Request and Write Request Messages

These messages use a common message format, described in Table 73-2 and shown graphically in Figure 73-4.

Table 73-2: TFTP RRQ/WRQ Message Format

Field Name	Size (Bytes)	Description
Opcode	2	Operation Code: Specifies the TFTP message type. A value of 1 indicates a RRQ message, while a value of 2 is a WRQ message.
Filename	Variable	The name of the file to be read or written.
Mode	Variable	Transfer Mode: The string netascii or octet, zero-terminated.
Options	Variable	When the client supports TFTP options, it will encode them in sequence following the Mode field. Each option consists of two variable-length subfields. The optN subfield is the option code for option N, containing a string specifying the name of the option; currently, blksize, interval, and tsize are supported. The valueN subfield is the option value for option N, containing the value the client is requesting for this option. (Note that this is a zero-terminated string just like other TFTP variable-length fields, even for a numeric value.)

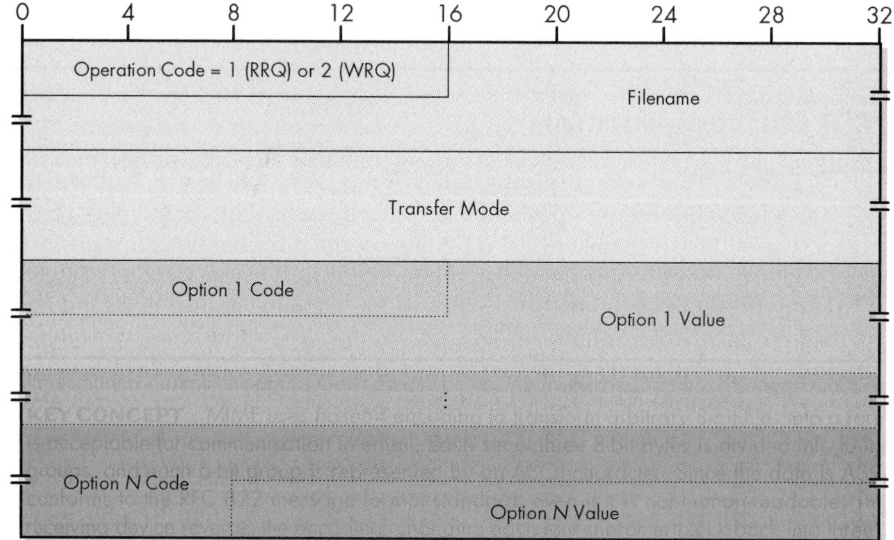

Figure 73-4: TFTP RRQ/WRQ message format

Data Messages

Data blocks are sent using the simplified format shown in Table 73-3 and Figure 73-5.

Table 73-3: TFTP Data Message Format

Field Name	Size (Bytes)	Description
Opcode	2	Operation Code: Specifies the TFTP message type. A value of 3 indicates a data message.
Block #	2	Block Number: The number of the data block being sent.
Data	Variable	Data: 0 to 512 bytes of data.

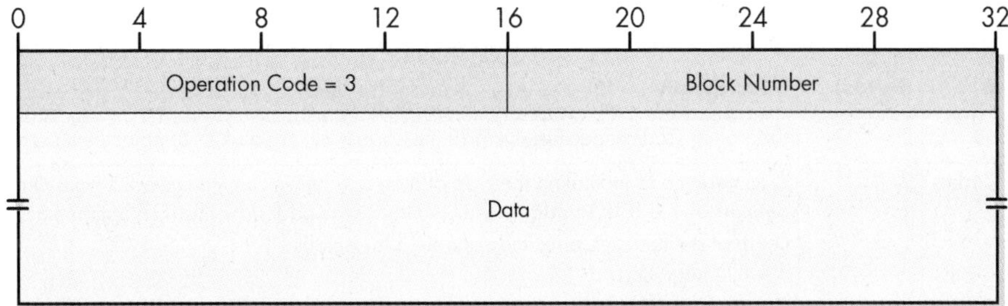

Figure 73-5: TFTP data message format

Acknowledgment Messages

Acknowledgments have the simplest format of any TFTP message, as you can see in Table 73-4 and Figure 73-6.

Table 73-4: TFTP Acknowledgment Message Format

Field Name	Size (Bytes)	Description
Opcode	2	Operation Code: Specifies the TFTP message type. A value of 4 indicates an ACK message.
Block #	2	Block Number: The number of the data block being acknowledged; a value of 0 is used to acknowledge receipt of a write request without options or to acknowledge receipt of an OACK.

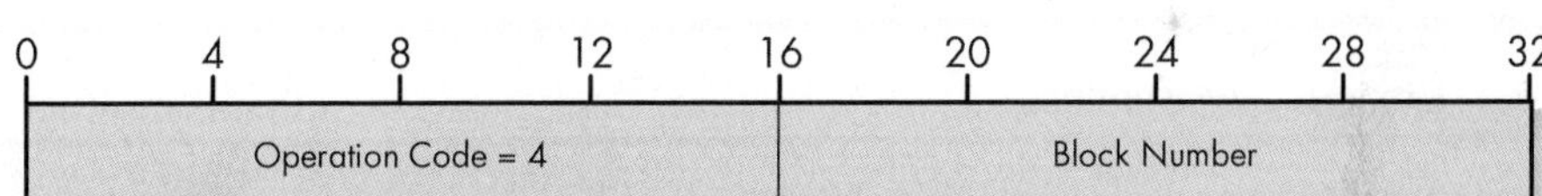

Figure 73-6: TFTP acknowledgment message format

Error Messages

Error messages can be sent by either the client or server in cases where a problem is detected in the communication. They have the format indicated in Table 73-5 and Figure 73-7.

Figure 73-7: TFTP error message format

Table 73-5: TFTP Error Message Format

Field Name	Size (Bytes)	Description
Opcode	2	Operation Code: Specifies the TFTP message type. A value of 5 indicates an error message.
Error Code	2	A numeric code indicating the type of message being communicated. Values 0 to 7 are defined by the TFTP standard, while value 8 was added by the TFTP option extension: 0 = Not defined; see error message field for details 1 = File not found 2 = Access violation 3 = Disk full or allocation exceeded 4 = Illegal TFTP operation 5 = Unknown transfer ID 6 = File already exists 7 = No such user 8 = Client transfer termination due to unacceptable option negotiation
Error Msg	Variable	Error Message: A descriptive text error message string, intended for "human consumption," as the standard puts it.

Option Acknowledgment Messages

OACK messages are used to acknowledge receipt of TFTP options. They are structured as shown in Table 73-6 and Figure 73-8.

Table 73-6: TFTP OACK Message Format

Field Name	Size (bytes)	Description
Opcode	2	Operation Code: Specifies the TFTP message type. A value of 6 indicates an OACK message.
Options	Variable	A list of options being acknowledged by the server. Each option consists of two variable-length subfields. The optN subfield is the option code for option N, containing a string specifying the name of the option, copied from the RRQ or WRQ message. The valueN subfield is the option value for option N, containing the acknowledged value for the option, which may be the value that the client specified or an alternative value, depending on the type of option.

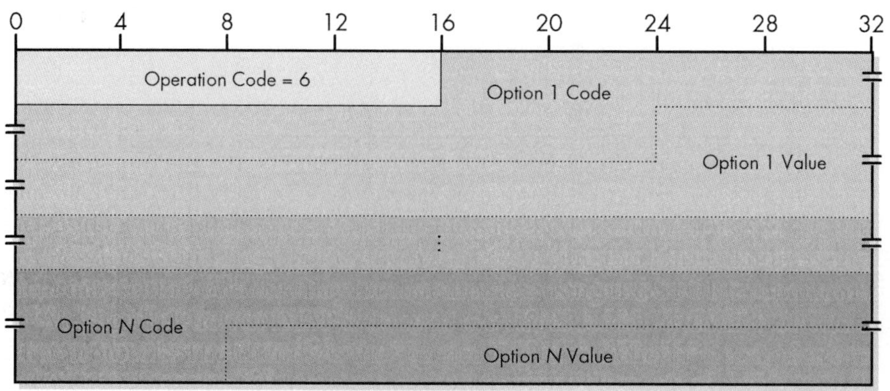

Figure 73-8: TFTP OACK message format

PART III-7

TCP/IP ELECTRONIC MAIL SYSTEM: CONCEPTS AND PROTOCOLS

It is common for human beings to create systems that are reminiscent of ones with which they are already familiar. We are all accustomed to using the regular mail system to send letters and other documents from our location to recipients anywhere that the postal system serves. Naturally, one of the first applications of internetworks was to create an electronic version of this conventional mail system that would allow messages to be sent in a similar manner, but more quickly and easily. Over the course of many years, an *electronic mail system* for TCP/IP was created and refined. It is now the most widely used means of electronic messaging in the world.

In this part, I describe TCP/IP electronic mail (email) in detail, in five chapters that discuss electronic mail concepts and the various components and protocols that comprise the overall TCP/IP email system. The first chapter provides an overview of TCP/IP email and discusses the way that it is used and the different protocols and methods that make up the system. The second chapter discusses how email messages are addressed, and the third chapter covers standard and special formats for email messages. The fourth and fifth chapters describe the TCP/IP protocols that implement email functionality. These include the Simple Mail Transfer Protocol (SMTP), which is responsible for the delivery of email, and several protocols and methods used for mailbox access and mail retrieval, including the Post Office Protocol version 3 (POP3) and the Internet Message Access Protocol (IMAP).

This discussion focuses primarily on the mechanisms used for email composition, delivery, and access in modern internetworks. In the email overview in Chapter 74, I mention some techniques used in the past for TCP/IP email, but only briefly for historical completeness and to contrast these methods to the ones presently used.

74

TCP/IP ELECTRONIC MAIL SYSTEM OVERVIEW AND CONCEPTS

Electronic mail (email) in the TCP/IP protocol suite is not implemented as just a single protocol or technology. Rather, it is a complete system that contains a number of related components that work together. These include standards defining methods for addressing and message formatting and a number of protocols that play different functions in implementing email messaging. Before proceeding to examine each of these pieces, it makes sense to start with an overview of the system as a whole.

In this chapter, I provide an introductory look at TCP/IP email to help you understand the system, how it works, and how different components fit into it. I begin with an overview and history of email and its implementation in TCP/IP. I provide a general overview of the steps involved in the email communication process, concluding with a more specific discussion of the communication model used in TCP/IP and the roles played by various TCP/IP devices and protocols in the sending and receiving of email.

TCP/IP Electronic Mail System Overview and History

The need to communicate is as old as humanity itself. Thousands of years ago, communication was of necessity almost exclusively local. Messages were primarily oral, and even when in writing, they were rarely delivered a great distance. Most people never traveled far from their homes and rarely communicated with those distant from themselves. But even in ancient times, leaders used messengers to send short pieces of critical information from place to place. It was slow and unreliable, but some messages were important enough that an effort to communicate often had to be made despite the difficulties.

Advances in transportation led to advances in communication capability, eventually resulting in the creation of physical mail systems. Today, these systems have evolved to the point at which anyone in the developed world can send a letter or package to just about anyone else. Reliability has vastly improved, despite all the jokes people make about the postal service. Speed is also much better than it used to be, with messages now taking days to reach their destination instead of weeks or months.

Waiting even days for a message to get from one place to another is pretty slow by the standards of our modern world. For this reason, one of the most natural applications of networks was to use them as a replacement for the physical transportation of messages from one place to another. Transforming mail from a physical process to an electronic one yields enormous benefits, including greatly increased communication speed, the ability to send one message to multiple recipients instantly, and the ability to get nearly instantaneous feedback upon receipt of a message.

The Early Days of Email

The idea behind email is not only as old as computer networks, but it actually predates internetworking. The first email systems were implemented on traditional mainframe computers. These were single large computers accessed by many users simultaneously through connected terminals. An email system on a mainframe consisted of a set of software running on the mainframe that implemented the entire email system. Each user simply had a mailbox that resided on this machine, and mail was delivered by moving messages from one mailbox to the next. Users sent and received mail through a user-interface program.

Such an early email system was useful for local communication but not for sending messages to a person in another organization. Mainframe email is somewhat analogous to local mail being sent by one resident of a town to another. There is no way to send mail to a person in a distant town without the infrastructure in place for delivery.

The power of internetworking is what really enables email to become a universal method of communication. Internetworks link together systems the way the postal service's fleet of airplanes and vehicles link together post offices. Mail is sent from user to user over the underlying technology of the internetwork. Since TCP/IP is the most commonly used internetworking protocol suite, and the modern Internet uses TCP/IP to tie together systems across the globe, it is the vehicle used for sending email.

History of TCP/IP Email

As with some other file and message transfer protocols, email on TCP/IP actually goes back to before TCP/IP and the Internet formally existed. The first protocols for email were developed during the days of the ARPAnet. Prior to the creation of email, several Internet RFCs, such as RFC 95 (yes 95, two digits—we are going back a long way here) and RFC 155, describe physical mailing lists that were used for distributing documents in the early 1970s. It was this need to send documents that likely made TCP/IP pioneers realize the usefulness of an electronic messaging system, using the technology they were themselves creating.

The first Internet document describing email was probably RFC 196, published in 1971. It describes the *Mail Box Protocol*, a very rudimentary message transfer method using the predecessors of TCP/IP. This protocol was designed for the specific purpose of sending documents for remote printing. In those days, it was not as common for people to use computers at interactive terminals as it is today, but the idea of electronically mailing documents was the same. The Mail Box Protocol was revised several times in 1971.

In the mid-1970s, developers began working on a more comprehensive method of implementing email on the fledgling Internet. The technique was originally described using a number of existing application layer transfer protocols, including the File Transfer Protocol (FTP). In 1980 the "Mail Transfer Protocol (MTP)" was published in RFC 772. This was the first precursor of today's TCP/IP email and was defined using principles from the Telnet Protocol as well as FTP.

During the time that email protocols were being developed in the 1970s, mail was being exchanged between host systems using a variety of techniques. One of the most common used was the *Unix-to-Unix Copy Protocol (UUCP)*, which was designed to allow files to be transferred between UNIX systems, moving them from one connected system to the next. UUCP was also used for communicating Usenet newsgroup articles and other files.

In 1981, the modern TCP/IP email era came into being with the definition of the *Simple Mail Transfer Protocol (SMTP)*. SMTP described in detail how mail could be moved directly or indirectly from one TCP/IP host to another without the need to use FTP or another file transfer method. (SMTP has its own detailed history and discussion in Chapter 77.) Other complementary specifications were created at around the same time, which formalized or defined other components and elements of the system. We'll explore these pieces of the puzzle throughout the rest of this chapter.

Overview of the TCP/IP Email System

One of the most important general concepts in the modern email system is that a distinction is made between protocols that deliver email between SMTP hosts on the internetwork and those that let users access received mail on their local hosts. To continue the postal mail analogy, different protocols are used for sending mail between post offices and for home delivery. As you'll see, this was done intentionally to make it possible to send mail to users, even if they are not connected to the

Internet when the mail is sent. This decoupling is critical, as it enables delayed communication, where mail can be sent when the sender wants to transmit it and received when the recipient wants to read it.

> **KEY CONCEPT** One of the most important TCP/IP applications is the internetworking equivalent of the real-world postal delivery system, commonly called *electronic mail* or *email*. The history of email goes back to the very earliest days of TCP/IP's development. Today, it is used by millions of people every day to send both simple and complex messages around the world. TCP/IP email is not a single application, but rather a complete system that includes several protocols, software elements, and components.

Over the years, the basic components defined in the early 1980s have not changed substantially, but how they are used has evolved and improved. Early email delivery involved the use of route specifications by one SMTP host to dictate how mail was to be delivered through intermediate systems; today, the Domain Name System (DNS) makes much of that obsolete, facilitating nearly immediate direct mail delivery in most cases. Early email supported only simple text, but we can now send graphical images, programs, and other file attachments in email. Modern high-speed Internet connections and updated access protocols allow email to be the realization of the ultimate goal of nearly instantaneous communication, even across continents.

TCP/IP Email Communication Overview

You've just seen that TCP/IP email is implemented as a complete system, with a number of elements that perform different portions of the complete job of email communication. These included a standard message format, a specific syntax for recipient addressing, and protocols to both deliver mail and allow access to mailboxes from intermittently connected TCP/IP clients.

To help set the groundwork for examining these components, here, I provide an overview of the complete end-to-end process of email communication, so you can see how everything works. I will show the basic steps in simplified form and continue the analogy to the regular mail system for comparison.

The modern TCP/IP email communication process consists of five basic steps:

1. **Mail Composition** A user begins the email journey by creating an email message. The message contains two sections: the *body* and the *header*. The body of the message is the actual information to be communicated. The header contains data that describes the message and controls how it is delivered and processed. The message must be created so that it matches the standard message format for the email system so that it can be processed (see Chapter 76). It must also specify the email addresses of the intended recipients for the message (see Chapter 75). By way of analogy to "snail mail," the body of the message is like a letter, and the header is like the addressed and stamped envelope into which the letter is placed.

2. **Mail Submission** Email is different from many other internetworking applications in that the sender and receiver of a message do not necessarily need to be connected to the network simultaneously, nor even continuously, to use it. The system is designed so that after composing the message, the user decides when to submit it to the email system so it can be delivered. This is done using SMTP (see Chapter 77). This is analogous to dropping off an envelope at the post office or to a postal worker picking up an envelope from a mailbox and carrying it to the local post office to insert into the mail delivery stream.
3. **Mail Delivery** The email message is accepted by the sender's local SMTP system for delivery through the mail system to the destination user. Today, this is accomplished by performing a DNS lookup of the intended recipient's host system and establishing an SMTP connection to that system. SMTP also supports the ability to specify a sequence of SMTP servers through which a message must be passed to reach a destination. Eventually, the message arrives at the recipient's local SMTP system. This is like the transportation of the envelope through the postal system's internal "internetwork" of trucks, airplanes, and other equipment to the intended recipient's local post office.
4. **Mail Receipt and Processing** The local SMTP server accepts the email message and processes it. It places the mail into the intended recipient's mailbox, where it waits for the user to retrieve it. In our physical analogy, this is the step at which the recipient's local post office sorts mail coming in from the postal delivery system and puts the mail into individual post office boxes or bins for delivery.
5. **Mail Access and Retrieval** The intended recipient periodically checks with its local SMTP server to determine whether any mail has arrived. If so, the recipient retrieves the mail, opens it, and reads its content. This is done using a special mail access protocol or method (see Chapter 78). To save time, the access protocol and client email software may allow the user to scan the headers of received mail (such as the subject and sender's identity) to decide which mail messages to download. This is analogous to the step where mail is physically picked up at the post office or delivered to the home.

KEY CONCEPT TCP/IP email communication normally involves a sequence of five steps, each of which is analogous to a portion of the journey taken by a regular letter through the postal system. First, email is *composed* (written); second, it is *submitted* to the email system; third, it is *delivered* to recipient's server; fourth, it is *received and processed*; and fifth, it is *accessed and retrieved* by its recipient.

In some cases, not all of these steps are performed. If a user is sending email from a device that is already an SMTP server, then step 2 can be omitted. If the recipient is logged in to a device that is also an SMTP server, step 5 will be skipped, as the user can read mail directly on the server. Thus, in the simplest case, all that occurs is composition, delivery, and receipt; this occurs when one user of a dial-up UNIX host sends mail to another. In most cases today, however, all five steps occur.

TCP/IP Email Message Communication Model

The purpose of the email system as a whole is to accomplish the transmission of messages from a user of a TCP/IP internetwork to one or more recipients. To accomplish this, a special method of communication is required that makes the email system quite different from that used by most other protocols. To understand what I mean by this, just consider the difference in communication between sending a letter and making a phone call.

Most TCP/IP protocols are analogous to making a phone call in this respect: The sender and the receiver must both be on the network at the same time. You can't call someone and talk to him if he isn't around to answer the phone. (I'm ignoring answering machines and voice mail of course!) Most TCP/IP protocols are like this. To send a file using FTP, for example, you must make a direct connection from the sender's machine to the recipient's machine. If the recipient's machine is not on the network at the exact time that the sender's machine is, no communication is possible. For email, immediate communication of this sort is simply unacceptable.

As with real-world snail mail, Joe wants to be able to put a message into the system at a time that is convenient for him, and Ellen wants to be able to receive Joe's mail at a time that works for her. For this to work, email must use a "send and forget" model, just like real mail, where Joe drops the "envelope" into the email system and it eventually arrives at its destination.

This *decoupling* of the sender and receiver is critical to the design of the email system. This is especially true because many of the users of Internet email are not on the Internet all the time. Just as you wouldn't want real mail to be rejected if it arrived when you are not home, you wouldn't want email to not be delivered if you are not on the Internet when it arrives. Similarly, you may not want to be connected to the Internet for the entire time it takes to write a message, especially if you have access to the Internet for only a limited amount of time each day.

Also critical to the entire email system is that idea that communication is between specific *users*, not between particular machines. This makes email inherently different from many other types of communication on TCP/IP internetworks. You'll see more of why this is important when we look at email addressing in Chapter 75.

To allow the type of communication needed for email, the entire system is designed to facilitate the *delayed delivery* of email messages from one user to another. To see how this works, let's look again at the example communication we discussed earlier—but this time, consider the roles of the different devices in the exchange (as shown in Figure 74-1):

Sender's Client Host The sender composes an email message, generally using a mail client program on her local machine. The mail, once composed, is not immediately sent out over the Internet; it is held in a buffer area called a *spool*. This allows the user to be "unattached" for the entire time that a number of outgoing messages are created. When the user is done, all of the messages can be sent at once.

Sender's Local SMTP Server When the user's mail is ready to be sent, she connects to the internetwork. The messages are then communicated to the user's designated local SMTP server, normally run by the user's Internet service provider

(ISP). The mail is sent from the client machine to the local SMTP server using SMTP. (It is possible for the sender to be working directly on a device with a local SMTP server, in which case sending is simplified.)

Recipient's Local SMTP Server The sender's SMTP server sends the email using SMTP to the recipient's local SMTP server over the internetwork. There, the email is placed into the recipient's incoming mailbox (or inbox). This is comparable to the outgoing spool that existed on the sender's client machine. It allows the recipient to accumulate mail from many sources over a period of time and retrieve them when it is convenient.

Recipient's Client Host In certain cases, the recipient may access her mailbox directly on the local SMTP server. More often, however, a mail access and retrieval protocol, such as Post Office Protocol (POP3) or Internet Message Access Protocol (IMAP), is used to read the mail from the SMTP server and display it on the recipient's local machine. There, it is displayed using an email client program, similar to the one the sender used to compose the message in the first place.

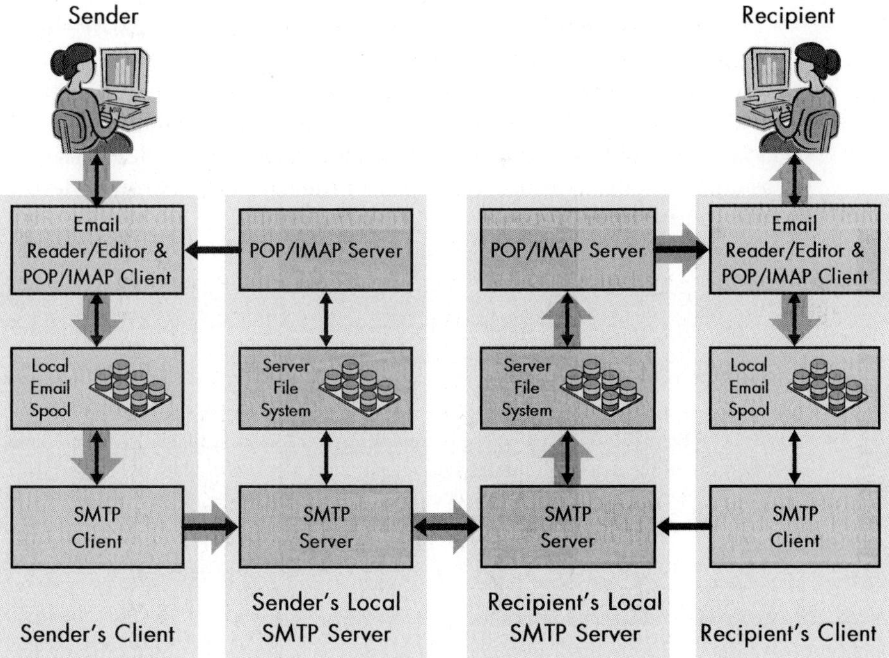

Figure 74-1: Email communication model *This diagram shows the four devices that are involved in a typical email communication between two users. Each device consists of a number of different elements, which communicate as indicated by the black arrows. Note the inherent asymmetry, because the method used to send an email from a user is not the same as that used to retrieve it from the server. The large, shaded arrows show a typical transaction: the sender composes mail and it goes to her local email spool. It is sent to the sender's local SMTP server using SMTP, and then to the recipient's SMTP server, where it goes into that user's inbox. It is then retrieved, usually using a protocol such as POP or IMAP.*

Protocol Roles in Email Communication

You may have noticed that SMTP is used for most of this communication process. In fact, if the recipient uses a machine that runs SMTP software, which is common for those using dial-up UNIX shell Internet access, the process of sending email uses SMTP exclusively. SMTP servers must, however, always be available on the Internet and ready to accept mail. Most people access the Internet using devices that aren't always online or that don't run SMTP software. That is why the last step, email access and retrieval, is usually required.

It might have been possible to define the email system so that this last step of communication was carried out using SMTP as well, which would mean the entire system used the same protocol. However, SMTP was tailored for the specific purpose of transporting and delivering email, not for remote mailbox access. It made more sense to leave the function of mailbox access to dedicated, separate protocols. This not only allows these protocols to be tailored to the needs of email recipients, but it also provides flexibility by giving users more than one option for how email is retrieved. I discuss email access protocols and methods in Chapter 78, highlighting the two most common protocols: POP and IMAP.

The three protocols discussed here—SMTP, POP3, and IMAP—get lead billing on the TCP/IP email stage, but they rely on two other elements to play supporting roles. The first is a method of addressing email messages to ensure that they arrive at their destinations. The second is the set of message formats used to encode messages and control how they are delivered and used. These elements don't usually get as much attention as they deserve, but they do here, as I have devoted the next two chapters to them.

> **KEY CONCEPT** One of the critical requirements of an email system is that the sender and receiver of a message are not required to be on the system at the time mail is sent. TCP/IP therefore uses a communication model with several devices that allow the sender and recipient to be *decoupled.* The sender's client device spools mail and moves it to the sender's local SMTP server when it is ready for transmission; the email is then transmitted to the receiver's SMTP server using SMTP. The email can remain on the recipient's server for an indefinite period of time. When the recipient is ready to read it, he retrieves it using one or more of a set of mail access protocols and methods, the two most popular of which are POP and IMAP.

75

TCP/IP ELECTRONIC MAIL ADDRESSES AND ADDRESSING

The entire concept of electronic mail (email) is based on an analogy: sending electronic messages is like sending paper messages. The analogy works well, because email was indeed intended to be like regular mail, only with the advantages of the technological era: speed and flexibility.

One of the many similarities between email and regular mail is the need for *addressing*. For a message to be delivered, it is necessary for the sender to specify the recipient and provide a reasonable amount of information to indicate how and where the recipient can be reached. In TCP/IP email, a standard *electronic mail address* format is used for this, and support is also provided for alternative addressing schemes that may be used in special cases.

In this chapter, I describe how email messages are addressed. I begin with a discussion of standard email addressing in TCP/IP and how those addresses are used to determine where email should be sent. I then provide a brief discussion of historical and special email addresses that you may encounter from time to time. I also discuss the use of email address books (aliases) and how multiple recipients may be addressed, and I provide an overview of electronic mailing lists, one of the earliest ways in which electronic group communication was implemented.

TCP/IP Email Addressing and Address Resolution

All communication on an internetwork requires some way of specifying the identity of the intended recipient of the communication. Most application protocols, such as the File Transfer Protocol (FTP) and Hypertext Transfer Protocol (HTTP), use conventional TCP/IP constructs—IP addresses and port numbers—to specify the destination of information to be sent. The IP address normally identifies a particular host computer, and the port number indicates a software process or application running on that computer.

Email, however, uses a model for communication that differs from most applications. As you saw in the discussion of the email model in the previous chapter, one element that sets email apart from many other systems is that communication is *user-oriented*. Email is not sent from one machine to another, as a file is transferred using FTP. Instead, it is sent from one user to another. This is critical to the operation of the entire system. For one thing, it allows someone to retrieve email that has been sent from any number of different client computers. This allows the recipient to receive email even when traveling, for example.

Since email messaging is user-based, the addressing scheme must also be user-based. We cannot use conventional IP addresses and ports, so we need a distinct system that specifies two primary pieces of information: who the user is and where the user is located. These are, of course, analogous to a name and address on a regular mail envelope.

The idea of a user name is relatively straightforward, but identifying the location of the user is not. In regular mail, an address refers to a physical place. It would have been possible to define email addresses in the same way; that is, to have an email address refer to the user's client machine. However, recall the other important characteristic of email delivery: it is indirect and based on the concept of a user's local Simple Mail Transfer Protocol (SMTP) server holding received messages until they can be retrieved. The machine that the user employs to access his email may not even routinely be connected to the Internet, and it may thus not be easy to identify. And we also want a user to be able to access email from multiple machines.

For all of these reasons, we want addresses to identify not the user's specific location at any particular time, but the place where the user's permanent mailbox lives—on the user's SMTP server, which is permanently connected to the Internet.

Standard DNS-Based Email Addresses

In TCP/IP, the system used for identifying servers (and other machines) is the *Domain Name System (DNS)*. DNS is a big system and is described in Part III-1 of this book, which you should read if you want to learn more. For now, it is important that you realize that in DNS, all devices on the Internet are arranged into a device-naming hierarchy, and any device can be identified using a *domain name* consisting of a series of text labels separated by dots.

The complete TCP/IP address consists of two components: a user name specification and a domain name specification. The two are connected together using the at symbol (@) to form the TCP/IP email address syntax that most of us are familiar with today: *<username>@<domainname>*.

The format of *<domainname>* follows the syntax rules of DNS (see Chapter 53), which specify that it can contain only numbers and digits for each label, and periods to separate the labels. The format of *<username>* is slightly less restrictive, allowing special characters such as the underscore (_). Other special characters and spaces are also allowed in the *<username>* if they are surrounded by quotation marks (or otherwise marked as being part the name, such as through the use of an escape character). Domain names are case-insensitive; user names may be case-sensitive, depending on the system.

An example of a valid email address is cmk@athena.mit.edu (an address I used when I was in school many years ago). Here, *cmk* is my user name (my initials); *athena.mit.edu* is the name of the host where I was receiving mail; and *athena* is a particular system at Massachusetts Institute of Technology *(mit)*, an educational institution that uses the *.edu* top-level domain.

It is also possible to specify an email address using an Internet-standard Uniform Resource Locator (URL). This allows a link to be embedded in a hypertext (Web) document; when clicked, it invokes an email client to send mail to a user. Email URLs are created by preceding the address by the special URL scheme string *mailto:*, like this: mailto:cmk@athena.mit.edu.

Special Requirements of Email Addresses

Having an email address refer to a user's local SMTP server provides a great deal of flexibility compared to having the address mention a specific client computer. But this doesn't provide enough flexibility to handle the following situations:

- An organization may want to use generic addresses that do not specify the name of the SMTP server to handle email, to make it easier for senders or clients to remember an email address. For example, if someone knew my real name and that I was at MIT, it would be easier for him to remember my email address as cmk@mit.edu than to remember cmk@athena.mit.edu.
- An administrator may change which machines handle mail over a period of time. This would mean all the users' email addresses would have to be changed, too—and most of us know what a pain that is. For example, if I moved from the athena machine to the jabberwocky machine, my old address would need to be changed to cmk@jabberwocky.mit.edu. But if the address were just cmk@mit.edu, a server change would not affect the address.
- In larger organizations, it might be desirable to have multiple servers share the load of handling incoming email.

To address all of these requirements, the DNS system includes a feature that was specifically designed to support email addressing. A special *mail exchange (MX)* record can be set up that specifies which SMTP server should be used for mail arriving at a particular domain name. If properly configured, this allows considerable flexibility to handle the cases described above, and more. For more details, please see the description of the MX record and DNS electronic mail support in Chapter 56.

> **KEY CONCEPT** Some form of addressing is required for all network communication; since email is *user-oriented*, email addresses are also based on users. In modern TCP/IP email, standard addresses consist of a *user name*, which specifies the recipient, and a *domain name*, which specifies the DNS domain where the user is located. A special DNS *mail exchange (MX)* record is set up for each domain that accepts email, so a sending SMTP server can determine what SMTP server it should use to send mail to a particular recipient.

Suppose, for example, that I am the owner of the pcguide.com domain name. Email can be sent to me at pcguide.com, but the mail is not actually stored on any server by that name. Instead, it is redirected to the real server where my inbox is located. This allows me to handle all incoming mail to pcguide.com, regardless of where my mailbox is actually located.

DNS is also significant in that its MX resource records eliminate the need to relay email from one SMTP server to the next to deliver it. In modern TCP/IP, it is possible to send email directly from the sender's SMTP server to the recipient's server, making communication faster and more efficient. This is also discussed in Chapter 56.

TCP/IP Historical and Special Email Addressing

TCP/IP email has been so successful that it is arguably the most important worldwide standard for electronic messaging. The widespread acceptance of email is tied inextricably to that of TCP/IP and the Internet as a whole. Since most organizations want to be part of the Internet, they connect to it and use its technologies, including DNS, which is the basis for TCP/IP email addresses. In turn, the use of simple DNS-style email addresses (*user@domain*) encourages further use of email because people find it conceptually easy to decide how to send messages.

TCP/IP is not, however, the only email system around. Over the years, several other networks have developed email systems. Due to the fact that the Internet is the largest internetwork in the world, TCP/IP email has often been used as a clearinghouse of sorts to link together some of these different email mechanisms. This is called *gatewaying*, and it allows someone using a non-SMTP email system to interact with someone using TCP/IP, and vice versa. Gatewaying is complex, in part because email systems use different ways of addressing mail. Let's take a look at a couple of these systems and how they interact with TCP/IP.

FidoNet Addressing

One of the earliest independent email systems was the *FidoNet*, which has been around for a long time and is still in use today. FidoNet is a worldwide network connected using modems and proprietary protocols; it is, in essence, a "competitor" to the global TCP/IP Internet. I put *competitor* in quotes because FidoNet and the

TCP/IP Internet are not really comparable in terms of number of users and the kinds of applications they support, but they are similar in overall objectives: worldwide electronic communication.

FidoNet users are identified using four numbers that specify the FidoNet *zone, net, node,* and *point (connection point).* These addressing elements are used for sending mail on this system, which again is completely distinct from TCP/IP. However, to allow communication between TCP/IP and FidoNet, the FidoNet administrators have set up a gateway system that allows mail to be sent to FidoNet using TCP/IP-style domain names. This style of mapping was also used by other systems with proprietary mail address formats to allow them to interface with the Internet.

For example, if a user was on machine 4, node 205, net 141, zone 1 (North America), the FidoNet address would be 1:141/205:4. The equivalent domain name would be p4.f205.n141.z1.fidonet.org and could be used for TCP/IP-style *user@domain* addressing.

UUCP-Style Addressing

An older address style commonly associated with email was the UUCP-style address. The *Unix-to-Unix Copy Protocol (UUCP)* was commonly used years ago to route mail before SMTP became widely deployed (again, it is still used, just not as much as before). The addresses in this system are specified as a path of hosts separated by exclamation marks (!). The path dictates the route that mail takes to get to a particular user, passing through a series of intermediate machines running UUCP. For example, if mail to joe at the host joesplace had to go through three hosts—host1, host2, and host3, the address would be host1!host2!host3!joesplace!joe. Since the slang term for an exclamation mark is *bang,* this came to be called *bang path* notation.

The use of UUCP-style notation was sometimes mixed with TCP/IP-style domain name address notation when DNS came into use. So you might have seen something like host1!user@domain. There was some confusion in how exactly to interpret such an address: Does it mean to send mail first to host1 and then to user@domain? Or does it mean to first send it to the domain, which then goes to user at host1? There was no universal answer to this. The problem was mostly resolved both by the decrease in use of UUCP and the move on the part of UUCP systems to TCP/IP-style domain name addressing.

Addressing for Gatewaying

You may encounter email addresses that appear as if multiple TCP/IP addresses have been nested using unusual punctuation. For example, you may see something like this: user%domain1.com@subdomain.domain2.edu. This is a way of addressing sometimes seen when email gateways are used; it will cause the mail to be sent to user%domain1.com at subdomain.domain2.edu. The address then is interpreted as user@domain1.com. However, again, not all systems are guaranteed to interpret this the same way.

Email gatewaying is not a simple matter in general, and as you can see, one reason is the use of different email address styles and the problems of consistency in how complex hybrid addresses are interpreted. However, as the Internet expands and TCP/IP becomes more widespread, it is becoming less and less common to see these older special address formats in use. They are becoming more and more a historical curiosity (unless you happen to use one of them).

TCP/IP Email Aliases and Address Books

Email is analogous to regular mail but superior to it due to two main advantages of digital and electronic communication. One advantage is *speed*, which is why modern Internet users have come up with the slang term *snail mail* to refer to the regular postal service. But the other advantage, *flexibility*, is also essential. Email allows you to send messages easily in ways that would be cumbersome with regular mail. And one of the ways this flexibility can be seen is in addressing.

The first way that email addressing is flexible is that most email clients support advanced features that allow users to specify the identity of recipients in convenient ways. While TCP/IP addressing is fairly straightforward, remembering the addresses of everyone you know is difficult. In the real world, we use address books to help us remember addresses. With email, we can do the same by allowing email software to associate a name with an email address.

This is usually done in one of two ways. In old-fashioned, text-based email such as that used on many UNIX systems, name and address association is performed using *aliases*. These are short forms for email addresses that save typing. For example, I often send email to my wife, Robyn, but I'm too lazy to type in her complete address all the time. So I have defined an alias for her in my email program called simply *r*. I enter the mail command and specify the alias *r* as the intended recipient, and it expands her email address for me.

In modern graphical email systems, aliases aren't used. Instead, an *electronic address book* is usually implemented, which is the equivalent of the paper address book. The difference is that there is no manual copying; you just choose the name from the list using your mouse.

Multiple Recipient Addressing

Another advantage of email addressing is that it allows the easy specification of multiple recipients. With paper mail, sending a message to ten people means you need ten copies of the message, ten envelopes, and ten stamps. With email, you just list the recipient addresses separated by a comma in the recipient list: <user1@domain1>,<user2@domain2>,<user3@domain3>. A separate copy is mailed to each recipient. Of course, aliases and/or address books can be used to specify each recipient here as well, making this even simpler.

Since email makes it so easy for one person to send information to a set of others, so-called *one-to-many* messaging, it was also one of the first ways in which electronic group communication was implemented. Prior to email, sharing information in a group setting required either a face-to-face meeting or a telephone conference call. In both cases, all parties must be present simultaneously, and a cost is involved, especially when the parties are geographically distant.

With email, a group of individuals can share information without needing to meet or even be available at the same time. Suppose a group comprises four individuals: Ellen, Joe, Jane, and Tom. Ellen has a proposal that she wants to discuss. She sends it to Joe, Jane, and Tom. Each recipient will read it at a time convenient for him or her. Each person can then reply back to the group. For example, Tom might have a comment on the proposal, so he just sends it to Ellen, Joe, and Jane. Most email clients include a *group reply* feature for this purpose.

Mailing Lists

In larger groups, communication by typing the addresses of each recipient becomes cumbersome. Instead, a *mailing list* is used. The list is created by an individual termed the *list owner* and contains the email addresses of all the members of the group. A special *list address* is created, which functions just like a regular email address. However, when anyone sends mail to this special address, it is not simply deposited into a mailbox. It is instead intercepted by special software that processes the message and sends it out automatically to all recipients on the list. Any recipient can reply to the list address, and all members will receive the reply.

Many other ways can be used by groups to share information today, such as using World Wide Web bulletin boards, Usenet newsgroups, Internet Relay Chat (IRC), and so forth. Some of these have a lot of features that make mailing lists seem unsophisticated by comparison. Despite this, electronic mailing lists are still very popular, largely because email is the most universal Internet communication method and one of the easiest methods to use.

Many thousands of mailing lists are in use on the Internet, covering every subject imaginable. Each list differs in a number of regards, including the following five aspects:

Implementation Usually, some sort of special software is used to allow the list owner to manage it, add and remove users, and set parameters that control how the list operates. These programs are commonly called *robots* or *listservs (list servers)*. One of the more common listservs is named *Majordomo*. Some mailing lists are actually implemented and managed using the Web. (The line between Internet applications continues to get more and more blurry.)

Subscription Rules and Technique Some mailing lists are open to anyone who wishes to join; others are by invitation only. Most allow a new subscriber to join automatically using software; others require the list owner to add new members.

Management Method and Style The list owner decides what is acceptable for discussion on the list. Some lists are *moderated*, meaning that all submissions to the list must be approved by the list owner before they are sent to list members. Some lists allow mail to the list from nonmembers, and some do not.

Culture Like all groups, groups of people on mailing lists have their own culture, interesting personalities, and other unique traits. New members of a list are often encouraged to read the list and not send to it for a while until they become accustomed to it and how it works. This is similar to the acclimation process for Usenet newbies (Usenet is covered in Chapter 85).

Special Features Some lists support special features, such as the ability to subscribe in *digest mode* (where messages are collected into large digests to reduce the number of individual messages sent) or to access messages on the Web.

> **KEY CONCEPT** One of the many benefits of email is that it is easy to send a message to many people at once, simply by specifying several recipient addresses. This permits easy and simple *group communication*, because each recipient can then send a group reply to respond to each of the people who were sent the original message. Electronic *mailing lists* provide a more formalized way for groups to exchange ideas and information; many thousands of such lists are in use on the Internet.

76

TCP/IP ELECTRONIC MAIL MESSAGE FORMATS AND MESSAGE PROCESSING: RFC 822 AND MIME

The advantages of using computers for communication are obvious, but some limitations are also imposed by the use of computer technology. When I compare electronic mail (email) to regular mail, I always point out that email is much faster and more flexible in how it can be delivered, and this is true. An email message can reach its destination in seconds, while a conventional letter can take days.

However, one significant drawback of using computers to communicate is that they are not very flexible in figuring out how to understand messages. Consider that anyone can put any type of letter, memorandum, or other communication in an envelope and send it to you, and assuming you know the language in which it is written, you can open the envelope and probably understand it. You can figure out how to deal with a date that appears in an unusual place in the letter, or your name appearing at the top compared to the bottom, or the body of the message being structured in different ways. You can read notes that are typed or handwritten in pen, pencil, or crayon—as long as the letters are decipherable, you can understand what is being said.

Computers are not good at deciphering such subtleties. It is for that reason that email systems must rely on standard message formats to ensure that all messages have the same form and structure. This then makes it possible for all devices in the email system to read and understand one another's messages, to enable TCP/IP email to work on many different types of computers.

In this chapter, I describe the two formats used for TCP/IP email messages: the main TCP/IP email standard, which is called the RFC 822 format after the standard that defines it, and the Multipurpose Internet Mail Extensions (MIME) standard, which greatly expands the ability of email to support the communication of different types of information by defining methods of encoding various media and non-English-language text into the standard RFC 822 format.

TCP/IP Email RFC 822 Standard Message Format Overview

One of the most astute observations I have read about internetworking applications asserts that their usefulness is proportional to the number of people who use them. TCP/IP email is a great example. It is a powerful communication method in large part because almost everyone with a computer today participates in the system. The more people who sign on to use email, the more powerful it becomes.

The creators of TCP/IP email realized that people who use the system would employ many different types of hardware and software. To ensure that everyone was able to understand all email messages, regardless of who sent them, they specified a common message format for email messages. This format doesn't have an official fancy name; it is simply known by the name of the standard that defines it: the RFC 822 message format.

RELATED INFORMATION *This discussion will make certain references to the discussion of the Simple Mail Transfer Protocol (SMTP; see Chapter 77) but was designed so that you could read it prior to learning about SMTP without getting confused.*

The primary protocol for delivering email is Simple Mail Transfer Protocol (SMTP). For this reason, the message format used for TCP/IP email could be considered SMTP's protocol message format, not unlike the special message formats discussed for other protocols, such as the Internet Protocol (IP) and the Transmission Control Protocol (TCP). However, the TCP/IP email message format is used not only by SMTP, but by all protocols and applications that deal with email. This includes the mail-access protocols Post Office Protocol (POP3) and Internet Message Access Protocol (IMAP), as well as others. It was also intended to be potentially usable by other non-TCP/IP mail delivery protocols. Perhaps for this reason, the TCP/IP email format was not specified as part of the SMTP itself, RFC 821, but was specified in a companion document, RFC 822. Both were published in 1982.

Development of the RFC 822 Message Format Standard

The history of the message format used in TCP/IP starts long before 1982. It was originally defined as the format for passing text messages on the Internet's precursor, the ARPAnet, in the early 1970s. The format was refined several times, leading to the publication in 1977 of the important email standard RFC 733, "Standard for the Format of ARPA Network Text Messages." RFC 822 later streamlined the contents of RFC 733, removing some of the features described in the earlier standard that failed to gain acceptance and simplifying the specification.

In 2001, both SMTP and the RFC 822 message format were revised; SMTP is now described in RFC 2821 and the message format in RFC 2822. This newer standard makes relatively small changes to the RFC 822 message format to reflect modern use of TCP/IP email. Even though RFC 2822 is the current standard, the original name is still the one most commonly used. I will respect that convention in this discussion, describing the message format based on RFC 2822 while still calling it the RFC 822 message format.

The RFC 822 format describes the form, structure, and content of TCP/IP email messages. It is, as I said, analogous to the message formats used for other protocols in TCP/IP. Like those other formats, the RFC 822 format can be logically divided into two main sections: the *message header*, which contains important control and descriptive information, and the *message body* or *payload*, which carries the data.

Overview of RFC 822 Messages

Where RFC 822 differs from the field formats of other protocols is in expression. Most TCP/IP protocols encode header information into a compact set of bytes that are read and understood based on their location in the message and the semantic meaning assigned to them. Consider IP, for example. The ninth byte of every IP datagram is the Time to Live (TTL) field, which is encoded as a value from 0 to 255. A device reading an IP datagram simply knows that byte number 9 contains the TTL value. If it sees the binary value 00010011 there, it knows the TTL value for this datagram is the decimal value 19.

In contrast, RFC 822 messages do not use a binary format. They are composed entirely of lines of regular ASCII text (as used in the United States, called *US-ASCII* by the standard), even the headers. Each line ends with an ASCII *carriage return (CR)* character, followed by a *line feed (LF)* character; the combination is collectively termed *CRLF*. Each line of text should be 78 or fewer characters (not including the terminating CRLF) and must not be more than 998 characters (again, excluding the CRLF). Also, the CR and LF characters must not appear by themselves within the text.

The RFC 822 message begins with a set of lines of text that collectively make up the message header. Each *header field* is expressed in the following form, in text: *<header name>: <header value>*. So, for example, if a *TTL* field were in an RFC 822 message (which it isn't, as that concept is not particular to email) and a value of 19 needed to be expressed, the header field would appear like this: *Time to Live: 19.*

This expressing of all fields as simple text means each header takes up more space in each message; the string *Time To Live: 19* takes up 18 bytes including the terminating CRLF, whereas the binary-encoded TTL field in the IP header takes only a single byte. What we gain from this are two important benefits:

- Any user can easily check the headers and immediately understand what headers are present and what their values are, which makes RFC 822 messages very readable.
- Since each header is explicitly labeled, RFC 822 messages can vary in terms of the number of headers they contain and even in what order they appear, making them flexible.

General RFC 822 Message Structure

The RFC 822 message always starts with a set of header fields (as described in the next section). After all the headers, an empty line must occur. This consists simply of the characters CRLF alone, immediately following the CRLF at the end of the final header field line. Seeing two CRLF character pairs in sequence tells the device reading the message that the end of the headers has been reached. All the remaining lines are considered the body of the message. Like the header lines, body lines are composed of ASCII text and must be no more than 998 characters, with 78 characters or fewer recommended (for easier reading on standard 80-character terminal displays).

KEY CONCEPT To ensure that every device on a TCP/IP internetwork can read email sent by every other device, all messages are required to adhere to a specific structure. The standard that first specified the form of modern TCP/IP email messages was RFC 822, and as a result, this is now called the *RFC 822 message format.* An RFC 822 message consists of a set of *message headers* and a *message body*, which are separated by a blank line. RFC 822 messages must contain only plain ASCII text characters. Each line must be no more than 1,000 characters in length, and the last two characters must be the ASCII CR and LF characters to mark the end of the line.

Since both the header and body of email messages are simply ASCII text, the entire message is just a text file, so these messages are very readable and also easy to create. You can use a simple text editor to create a complete email message, including headers, and it can be read with a simple text display utility. This contributes to email's universal appeal.

The drawback is that the decision to make messages entirely ASCII means that no native support is available in RFC 822 messages for anything that requires more complex structuring or that cannot be expressed using the limited number of ASCII characters. So, you cannot express pictures, binary files, spreadsheets, sound clips, and similar types of files directly using ASCII. Also, the use of ASCII makes RFC 822 well suited to expressing messages in English but not in many other languages that use characters that ASCII cannot represent. All of these limitations eventually prompted the creation of the enhanced MIME message format, which we will explore in detail later in this chapter.

TCP/IP Email RFC 822 Standard Message Format Header Fields and Groups

The RFC 822 message format describes the structure and content of TCP/IP email messages. The structure is intentionally designed to be simple and easy to create and understand. Each message begins with a set of headers that describe the message and its contents. An empty line marks the end of the headers, and then the message body follows.

The message body contains the actual text that the sender is communicating to the recipient(s), while the message header contains information that serves various purposes. The header helps control how the message is processed by specifying who the recipients are, describing the contents of the message, and providing information to a recipient of a message about processing that occurred on the message as it was delivered.

Header Field Structure

As mentioned earlier, the *<header name>* field is the name of the header, and the *<header value>* is the value associated with that header, which depends on the header type. Like all RFC 822 lines, headers must be no more than 998 characters long and are recommended to be no more than 78 characters in length, for easier readability. The RFC 822 and 2822 standards support a special syntax for allowing headers to be folded onto multiple lines if they are very lengthy. This is done by continuing a header value onto a new line, which must begin with at least one white-space character, such as white space or a tab character, like this:

<header name>: *<header value part 1>*

<white space> <header value part 2>

<white space> <header value part 3>

The tab character is most often used for this purpose. So, for example, if we wanted to specify a large number of recipients for a message, we could do it as follows:

To:*<tab>person1@domain1.org, person2@domain2.com,*

<tab>person3@domain3.net, person4@domain4.edu

Header Field Groups

The RFC 822 message format specifies many types of headers that can be included in email messages. A small number of headers are mandatory, meaning they must be included in all messages. Some are not mandatory but are usually present, because they are fundamental to describing the message. Other optional headers are included only when needed.

To help organize the many headers, the RFC 2822 standard categorizes them into header field groups (as did RFC 822, though the groups are a little different in the older standard):

Origination Date Field Specifies the date and time that the message was made ready for delivery; see the next section for details. (This field is in its own group for reasons that are unclear to me; perhaps just because it is so important.)

Originator Fields Contain information about the sender of the message.

Destination Address Fields Specify the recipient(s) of the message, which may be in one of three different recipient classes: the primary recipients ("To"), copied recipients ("Cc"), and blind-copied recipients ("Bcc").

Identification Fields Contain information to help identify the message.

Informational Fields Contain optional information to help make clear to the recipient what the message is about.

Resent Fields Preserve the original originator, destination, and other fields when a message is resent.

Trace Fields Show the path taken by mail as it was transported.

In addition, the format allows other user-defined fields to be specified, as long as they correspond to the standard *<header name>: <header value>* syntax. This can be used to provide additional information of various sorts. For example, sometimes the email client software will include a header line indicating the name and version of the software used to compose and send the message. As you'll see later in this chapter, MIME uses new header lines to encode information about MIME messages.

> **KEY CONCEPT** Each RFC 822 message begins with a set of *headers* that carry essential information about the message. These headers are used to manage how the message is processed and interpreted, and they also describe the contents of the message body. Each header consists of a *header name* and a *header value*. More than a dozen different standard RFC 822 headers are available for use and organized into groups. It is also possible to define custom user headers.

Common Header Field Groups and Header Fields

Table 76-1 describes the header fields in TCP/IP email messages and how they are used.

Table 76-1: RFC 822 Email Header Field Groups and Fields

Field Group	Field Name	Appearance	Number of Occurrences Per Message	Description
Origination Date	Date:	Mandatory	1	Indicates date and time that the message was made available for delivery by the mail transport system. This is commonly the date/time that the user tells her email client to send the message.
Originator Fields	From:	Mandatory	1	Email address of the user sending the message, who should be the person who is the source of the message.
	Sender:	Optional	1	Email address of the person sending the email, if different from the message originator. For example, if person B is sending an email containing a message from person A on A's behalf, person A's address goes in the From: header and person B's in the Sender: header. If the originator and the sender are the same (commonly the case), this field is not present.
	Reply-To:	Optional	1	Tells the recipient of the message the address the originator would like the recipient to use for replies. If absent, replies are normally sent back to the From: address.
Destination Address Field	To:	Normally present	1	A list of primary recipients of the message.
	Cc:	Optional	1	A list of recipients to receive a copy of the message (*cc* stands for carbon copy, as used in old typewriters). There is no technical difference between how a message is sent to someone listed in the Cc: header and someone in the To: header. The difference is only in how the recipient interprets the message. The person in the To: list is usually the main recipient of the message, while the person in the Cc: list is being copied on the message for informational purposes.
	Bcc:	Optional	1	Contains a list of recipients to receive a "blind" copy of the message without other recipients knowing they have received it. For example, if person X is specified in the *To*: line, person Y is in the *Cc*: line, and person Z is in the *Bcc*: line, all three would get a copy of the message, but X and Y would not know Z had received a copy. This is done by either removing the *Bcc*: line before message delivery or altering its contents.

(continued)

Table 76-1: RFC 822 Email Header Field Groups and Fields (continued)

Field Group	Field Name	Appearance	Number of Occurrences Per Message	Description
Identification Fields	Message-ID:	Should be present	1	Provides a unique code for identifying a message; normally generated when a message is sent.
	In-Reply-To:	Optional, normally present for replies	1	When a message is sent in reply to another, the Message-ID: field of the original message is specified in this field, to tell the recipient of the reply to what original message the reply pertains.
	References:	Optional	1	Identifies other documents related to this message, such as other email messages.
Informational Fields	Subject:	Normally present	1	Describes the subject or topic of the message.
	Comments:	Optional	Unlimited	Contains summarized comments about the message.
	Keywords:	Optional	Unlimited	Contains a list of comma-separated keywords that may be useful to the recipient. May be used optionally when searching for messages on a particular subject matter.
Resent Fields	Resent-Date: Resent-From: Resent-Sender: Resent-To: Resent-Cc: Resent-Bcc: Resent-Message-ID:	Each time a message is resent, a resent block is required	For each resent block, Resent-Date: and Resent-Sender: are required; others are optional	Special fields used only when a message is resent by the original recipient to someone else, called forwarding. For example, person X may send a message to Y, who forwards it to Z. In that case, the original Date:, From:, and other headers are as they were when person X sent the message. The Resent-Date:, Resent-From:, and other resent headers are used to indicate the date, originator, recipient, and other characteristics of the resent message.
Trace Fields	Received: Return-Path:	Inserted by email system	Unlimited	Inserted by computers as they process a message and transport it from the originator to the recipient. Can be used to trace the path a message took through the email system.

TCP/IP Email RFC 822 Standard Message Format Processing and Interpretation

The standards that define SMTP describe the protocol as being responsible for transporting *mail objects*. A mail object is described as consisting of two components: a *message* and an *envelope*. The message is everything in the email message, including both message header and body; the envelope contains all the information necessary to accomplish transport of the message.

The distinction between these objects is important technically. Just as the postal service looks only at the envelope and not its contents in determining what to do with a letter, SMTP likewise looks only at the envelope in deciding how to send a message. It does not rely on the information in the actual message itself for basic transport purposes.

So the envelope is not the same as the message headers. However, as you can tell by looking at the list of email headers, each message includes the recipients and other information needed for mail transport. For this reason, it is typical for an email message to be specified with enough header information to accomplish its own delivery. Email software can process and interpret the message to construct the necessary envelope for SMTP to transport the message to its destination mailbox. The distinction between an email message and its envelope is discussed in more detail in the section describing SMTP mail transfers, in Chapter 77.

The processing of RFC 822 messages is relatively straightforward, due again to the simple RFC 822 message format. The creation of the complete email message begins with the creation of a message body and certain headers by the user creating the message. Whenever a message is "handled" by a software program, the headers are examined so the program can determine what to do with it. Additional headers are also added and changed as needed.

The following is the sequence of events that occur during the lifetime of a message's headers.

Composition The human composer of the message writes the message body and tells the email client program the values to use for certain important header fields. These include the intended recipients, the message subject, other informational fields, and certain optional headers such as the Reply-To field.

Sender Client Processing The email client processes the message, puts the information the human provided into the appropriate header form, and creates the initial email message. At this time, it inserts certain headers into the message, such as the origination date. The client also parses the intended recipient list to create the envelope for transmission of the message using SMTP.

SMTP Server Processing SMTP servers do not pay attention to most of the fields in a message as they forward it. They will, however, add certain headers, especially trace headers such as Received and Return-Path, as they transport the message. These are generally prepended to the beginning of the message to ensure that existing headers are not rearranged or modified. Note, however, that when gatewaying occurs between email systems (as described in Chapter 75), certain headers must actually be changed to ensure that the message is compatible with non-TCP/IP email software.

Recipient Client Processing When the message arrives at its destination, the recipient's SMTP server may add headers to indicate the date and time the message was received.

Recipient Access When the recipient of a message uses client software, optionally via an email access protocol such as POP3 or IMAP, the software analyzes each message in the mailbox. This enables the software to display the messages in a way that's meaningful to the human user and may also permit the selection of particular messages to be retrieved. For example, most of us like to see a summary list of newly received mail, showing the originator, message subject, and the date and time the message was received, so we can decide what mail we want to read first, what mail to defer to a later time, and what to delete without reading (such as spam).

MIME Overview

The RFC 822 email message format is the standard for the exchange of email in TCP/IP internetworks. Its use of simple ASCII text makes it easy to create, process, and read email messages, which has contributed to the success of email as a worldwide communication method.

Unfortunately, while ASCII text is great for writing simple memorandums and other short messages, it provides no flexibility to support other types of communication. To allow email to carry multimedia information, arbitrary files, and messages in languages using character sets other than ASCII, the MIME standard was created.

NOTE *While MIME was developed specifically for email, its encoding and data representation methods have proven so useful that it has been adopted by other application protocols as well. One of the best known of these is the Hypertext Transfer Protocol (HTTP), which uses MIME headers for indicating the characteristics of data being transferred. Some elements of MIME were in fact developed not for email but for use by HTTP or other protocols, and I indicate this where appropriate. Be aware that HTTP only uses some elements of MIME; HTTP messages are not MIME-compliant.*

Most protocols become successful specifically because they are based on open standards that are widely accepted. The RFC 822 email message format standard is an excellent example; it is used by millions of people every day to send and receive TCP/IP email.

However, success of standards comes at a price: *reliance* on those standards. Once a standard is in wide use, it is very difficult to modify it, even when times change and the standard is no longer sufficient for the requirements of modern computing. Again, unfortunately, the RFC 822 email message format is an excellent example.

The Motivation for MIME

TCP/IP email was developed in the 1960s and 1970s. Compared to the way the world of computers and networking is today, almost everything back then was *small.* The networks were small; the number of users was small; the computing capabilities of networked hosts was small; the capacity of network connections was small; the number of network applications was small. (The only thing that wasn't small back then was the size of the computers themselves!)

As a result of this, the requirements for electronic mail messaging were also rather . . . small. Most computer input and output back then was text-based, and it was therefore natural that the creators of SMTP and the RFC 822 standard would have envisioned email as being strictly a text medium. Accordingly, they specified RFC 822 to carry text messages.

The fledgling Internet was also developed within the United States, and at first, the entire internetwork was within American borders. Most people in the United States speak English, a language that as you may know uses a relatively small number of characters that is well-represented using the ASCII character set. Defining the email message format to support United States ASCII (US-ASCII) also made sense at the time.

However, as computers developed, they moved away from a strict text model toward graphical operating systems. And predictably, users became interested in sending more than just text. They wanted to be able to transmit diagrams, non-ASCII text documents (such as Microsoft Word files), binary program files, and eventually multimedia information: digital photographs, MP3 audio clips, slide presentations, movie files and much more. Also, as the Internet grew and became global, other countries came "online," some of which used languages that simply could not be expressed with the US-ASCII character set.

Unfortunately, by this point, the die was cast. RFC 822 was in wide use and changing it would have also meant changes to how protocols such as SMTP, POP and IMAP worked, protocols that ran on millions of machines. Yet by the late 1980s, it was quite clear that the limitations of plain ASCII email were a big problem that had to be resolved. A solution was needed, and it came in the form of the Multipurpose Internet Mail Extensions (MIME).

NOTE *MIME is usually referred to in the singular, as I will do from here forward, even though it is an abbreviation of a plural term.*

MIME Capabilities

The idea behind MIME is both clever and elegant: RFC 822 restricts email messages to ASCII text, but that doesn't mean that we can't define a more specific structure for how that ASCII text is created. Instead of just letting the user type an ASCII text message, we can use ASCII text characters to encode nontext data parcels (commonly called *attachments*). Using this technique, MIME allows regular RFC 822 email messages to carry the following:

Nontext Information Includes graphics files, multimedia clips, and all the other nontext data examples listed earlier.

Arbitrary Binary Files Includes executable programs and files stored in proprietary formats (for example, AutoCAD files, Adobe Acrobat PDF files, and so forth).

Text Messages That Use Character Sets Other Than ASCII Includes the ability to use non-ASCII characters in the headers of RFC 822 email messages.

MIME even goes one step beyond this, by actually defining a structure that allows multiple files to be encoded into a single email message, including files of different types. For example, someone working on a budget analysis could send one email message that includes a text message, a PowerPoint presentation, and a spreadsheet containing the budget figures. This capability has greatly expanded email's usefulness in TCP/IP.

All of this is accomplished through special encoding rules that transform non-ASCII files and information into an ASCII form. Headers are added to the message to indicate how the information is encoded. The encoded message can then be sent through the system like any other message. SMTP and the other protocols that handle mail pay no attention to the message body, so they don't even know MIME has been used.

The only change required to the email software is adding support for MIME to email client programs. Both the sender and receiver must support MIME to encode and decode the messages. Support for MIME was not widespread when MIME was first developed, but the value of the technique is so significant that it is present in nearly all email client software today. Furthermore, most clients today can also use the information in MIME headers to not only decode nontext information but pass it to the appropriate application for presentation to the user.

> **KEY CONCEPT** The use of the RFC 822 message format ensures that all devices are able to read one another's email messages, but it has a critical limitation: It supports only plain ASCII text. This is insufficient for the needs of modern internetworks, yet reliance on the RFC 822 standard would have made replacing it difficult. *MIME* specifies several methods that allow email messages to contain multimedia content, binary files, and text files using non-ASCII character sets, all while still adhering to the RFC 822 message format. MIME also further expands email's flexibility by allowing multiple files or pieces of content to be sent in a single message.

MIME Standards

MIME was first described in a set of two standards, RFC 1341 and RFC 1342, published in June 1992. These were updated by RFCs 1521 and 1522 in September 1993. In March 1994, a supplemental standard was published, RFC 1590, which specified the procedure for defining new MIME media types.

Work continued on MIME through the mid-1990s, and in November 1996, the standards were revised again. This time, the documents were completely restructured to improve the readability of the information and published as a set of five individual standards. These standards are shown in Table 76-2.

Since the time that these five primary MIME standards were released, numerous additional RFCs have been published that have defined various extensions to MIME itself, including additional MIME header types and new media types. Notable examples are RFCs 2183 and 2557, which define the MIME Content-Disposition and Content-Location headers, respectively. Some other MIME capabilities are actually defined as part of other technologies that use MIME; for example, the first HTTP standard, RFC 1945 defines the Content-Length header. Other RFCs define new media types and subtypes (too many to list here).

Table 76-2: MIME Standards

RFC Number	RFC Name	Description
2045	Multipurpose Internet Mail Extensions (MIME) Part One: Format of Internet Message Bodies	Describes the fundamental concepts behind MIME and the structure of MIME messages.
2046	Multipurpose Internet Mail Extensions (MIME) Part Two: Media Types	Explains the concept of MIME media types and subtypes and describes some of the kinds of media whose encoding is defined in the MIME standards.
2047	MIME (Multipurpose Internet Mail Extensions) Part Three: Message Header Extensions for Non-ASCII Text	Describes how RFC 822 headers can be modified to carry non-ASCII text.
2048	Multipurpose Internet Mail Extensions (MIME) Part Four: Registration Procedures	Discusses how organizations can register additional media types for use with MIME.
2049	Multipurpose Internet Mail Extensions (MIME) Part Five: Conformance Criteria and Examples	Provides additional implementation information and examples of how MIME can be used.

MIME Basic Structures and Headers

The creators of the MIME standard had a difficult challenge on their hands: how to bring flexibility in the types of data contained in email messages, when RFC 822 said that messages could contain only ASCII text. To accomplish this, MIME creators had to exploit the areas of flexibility that had already been put into the existing RFC 822.

Two such opportunities were available: The first was the fact that RFC 822 message bodies are allowed to contain any type of ASCII text, as long as lines don't exceed 998 text characters and each line ends with a CRLF control code combination. Even though the creators of RFC 822 naturally assumed this ASCII text would be human-readable, there was nothing stopping it from being machine-readable code. The second opportunity was the facility built into RFC 822 (and the protocols that use it, such as SMTP) that allowed custom user-defined header fields to be added to any email message.

The nonspecific nature of RFC 822 message bodies forms the basis for how MIME itself works. An email client that supports the MIME standard uses special encoding algorithms that transform non-ASCII information into ASCII form. It then places this set of encoded ASCII characters into the body of the message, as if it had been typed by a user, using one of two special structures.

The ability to add new headers to RFC 822 is used to communicate information about the use of MIME from the sender to the recipient. The devices transporting a MIME message don't care that MIME was used, because they don't pay attention to the contents of the message body. However, when the message reaches its destination, the recipient's email client program must have some way of knowing that MIME was used and must also be told how the information in the message was encoded. Otherwise, it might just present the encoded non-ASCII data to the user as ASCII text (which would look like random gibberish).

Basic Structures

The exact method by which data is encoded in the message body and MIME headers are included depends on the overall structure of the MIME message. Two basic structure types are described, based on the kind of media the message carries:

Simple Structure (Discrete Media) MIME messages carrying a single discrete media type, such as a text message or a graphical image, use a simple structure. Only one encoding of information is present in the body of the message.

Complex Structure (Composite Media) Some MIME messages carry a composite media type, which allows multiple different media to be contained in a single message, such as a text message and a graphical image, or which allows the email to encapsulate another email message in its entirety. Many of these messages use a more complex structure, where the body of the message contains several MIME body parts.

MIME Entities

Collectively, both whole MIME messages and individual body parts are called *MIME entities*. Each set of MIME headers provides information about either type of MIME entity: a MIME message as a whole or a body part in a composite message. When a MIME message is received, the recipient first examines the headers in the message as a whole (the RFC 822 headers) to determine the overall message type. This then indicates whether the message uses a simple or complex structure. If the latter is used, the body of the message is parsed and each individual body part is individually interpreted, including its individualized headers. The section "MIME Composite Media Types," later in this chapter, provides more details on how these body parts are formatted.

Primary MIME Headers

The first of the five main MIME standards, RFC 2045, describes a set of five primary MIME headers that communicate basic information about the content of each MIME entity (message or body part).

MIME-Version Each MIME message is required to have a MIME-Version header, which serves two purposes. First, it identifies the email message as being MIME-encoded. Second, even though only one version of MIME has been defined so far, having a version number header provides future proofing in case a new version is created later that may have some incompatibilities with the present one. Currently, all MIME messages use version 1.0. This is the only MIME header that applies to an entire message; it is not used to label individual MIME body parts. This is easy to remember, as it is the only header whose name does not begin with Content-.

Content-Type Describes the nature of the data that is encoded in the MIME entity. This header specifies a content type and a content subtype, which are separated by a slash character. It may optionally also contain certain parameters that convey additional information about the type and subtype. In a message body, this header tells the recipient of the email message what sort of media it contains and whether the body uses a simple or complex structure. In a body part, it describes the media type the body part contains. For example, a message containing an HTML document might have a Content-Type header of `text/html`, where a message containing a JPEG graphical file might be specified as image/jpeg. For a composite MIME type, the Content-Type header of the whole message will contain something like `multipart/mixed` or `multipart/alternative`, and each body part will contain individual Content-Type headers such as `text/html` or `image/jpeg`. These are all discussed in detail in the next two sections. This header is optional. When not present, the default of a regular US-ASCII text message is assumed (the media type of regular RFC 822 messages).

Content-Transfer-Encoding For a message using simple structure, specifies the method used to encode the data in the message body; for a composite message, identifies the encoding method for each MIME body part. For data that is already in ASCII form, no special encoding is needed, but other types of data must be converted to ASCII for transmission. This header tells the recipient how to decode the data back into its normal representation. (MIME encoding methods are described later in this chapter.) This header is optional; the default value, if it is not present, is 7-bit encoding, which again is the encoding of regular ASCII.

Content-ID Allows the MIME content to be assigned a specific identification code. This header is analogous to the RFC 822 Message-ID header field but is specific to the MIME content itself. It is optional and is most often used for body parts in multipart MIME messages.

Content-Description This optional header allows an arbitrary additional text description to be associated with the MIME entity. In a multipart message, each body part might be given a description header to make clear to the recipient what the parts represent.

> **KEY CONCEPT** MIME provides flexibility in the information that can be carried in email messages, by encoding non-ASCII data in ASCII form, and by adding special headers that describe this data and how it is to be interpreted. The most important MIME headers are *Content-Type*, which describes what sort of data is in the message, and *Content-Transfer-Encoding*, which specifies how the data is encoded. MIME supports two basic overall formats: *simple structure*, in which a single type of *discrete media* is encoded in a message, and *complex structure*, which encodes a *composite media* type that can carry multiple kinds of information.

Additional MIME Headers

In addition to the five basic headers, the MIME standard allows additional headers to be defined. The only restriction is that they all must start with the word *Content-*, which clearly labels them as describing content of a MIME entity (message or body part). Both the sender and recipient must support a custom header for it to be useful.

Several new MIME headers have in fact been created and documented in various Internet RFCs. Some are actually designed not specifically for use by email messages, but for use by other protocols that make use of MIME technology, such as HTTP. Three are notable:

Content-Disposition In multipart MIME messages, this header may be given to MIME body parts to control how information is presented to the user. The two most common values are *inline*, which says the content is intended to be displayed automatically along with other body parts, and *attachment*, which indicates that the content is separate from the main document. This header is defined in RFC 2183.

Content-Location Allows the location of a MIME body part to be identified using a Uniform Resource Locator (URL). This is sometimes used when encoding HTML and other multimedia-enabled document formats into email using MIME multipart messages. It is defined in RFC 2557.

Content-Length Specifies the length of a MIME entity in bytes. This header is not commonly used in email applications of MIME but is an important header in HTTP. It is described in the HTTP standards, first appearing in RFC 1945.

MIME Content-Type Header and Discrete Media

MIME uses special techniques to encode various kinds of information into ASCII text form, such as graphical images, sound files, video clips, application programs, compressed data files, and many others. We commonly refer to these as different types of *media*, and MIME uses the same term to describe them.

Since MIME supports so many kinds of media, it is necessary that each message contain information that describes what it contains to permit accurate decoding of message contents. This is the function of the important MIME Content-Type header.

Content-Type Header Syntax

The syntax of the Content-Type header is as follows:

Content-Type: <type>/<subtype> [; parameter1 ; parameter2 .. ; parameterN]

The purpose of these different elements is to describe the media in the MIME entity in a way that proceeds from the general to the specific. The first element, *<type>*, is called the *top-level media type* and describes the overall form of the data. For example, it indicates whether the MIME entity contains text, an image, audio, and so forth. The second element, *<subtype>*, provides specific information about the form or format of the data. For example, a JPEG image and a GIF image are both images, but they are in a different format. Both *<type>* and *<subtype>* are mandatory in the Content-Type header.

Following these elements may appear one or more *parameters*, which are usually optional but may be required for some media types. These provide still more details about the nature of the data, when it is required. Each parameter is preceded by a semicolon and is expressed as an attribute/value pair, separated by an equal (=) sign, like this: *; attribute=value.*

One example of how parameters may be used is in specifying the character set in a text message. The representation of regular RFC 822 ASCII text is as follows:

```
Content-type: text/plain; charset="us-ascii"
```

The top-level media type is `text`, and the subtype is `plain`, so this indicates a plain-text message. The parameter `charset` specifies that the message uses the US-ASCII character set. Another common use for parameters is to specify the name of an attached file, like this:

```
Content-type: image/jpeg; name="ryanpicture.jpg"
```

Discrete Media Types and Subtypes

As I mentioned earlier, MIME supports two basic structures: simple and complex. A simple message carries only one media type, such as a piece of text, a picture, or an executable file. These are called *discrete media types* in MIME. A complex message carries a *composite media type*, which may incorporate multiple body parts. Each body part in turn carries data corresponding to one of the discrete media types. The top-level media type indicates whether the whole message carries a discrete media type or a composite type.

> **KEY CONCEPT** The MIME *Content-Type* header specifies what sort of data is encoded in a MIME message. The header indicates the general form of the message's content through a *top-level media type*, and the more specific nature of the data through the specification of a *subtype*. It may also contain optional *parameters* that provide still more information about the content.

The RFC 2046 standard (part two of the set of five standards that describes MIME) defines five discrete top-level media types: `text`, `image`, `audio`, `video`, and `application`. They each represent one of the major classes of data commonly transmitted over TCP/IP. Each of these has one or more subtypes, and some also have parameters that are used to provide more information about them.

The creators of MIME recognized that the standard could not describe every media type and that new ones would be created in the future. RFC 2048 (part four of the MIME set) describes the process by which new media types, subtypes, and parameters can be described and registered with the Internet Assigned Numbers Authority (IANA).

Thus far, only one new top-level media type has been created; this is the `model` top-level type, defined for CAD modeling files and similar uses, as described in RFC 2077. However, many dozens of new subtypes have been created over the years, some specified in RFCs and others just registered directly with IANA. This includes many vendor-specific subtypes, which are usually identified by either the prefix *x-* or *vnd.* in the subtype name.

Literally hundreds of type/subtype combinations now exist, and I will not list them all. You can find a complete list of MIME media organized by top-level media type on IANA's website: *http://www.iana.org/assignments/media-types/index.html.*

Here, I will briefly describe the six MIME discrete top-level media types. For each, I've provided a table showing some of the more commonly encountered MIME subtypes to give you an idea of what is out there.

Text Media Type (text)

The `text` media type is used for sending data that is primarily in textual form. Table 76-3 describes shows the subtypes.

Table 76-3: MIME text Media Type Subtypes

Type/Subtype	Description	Defining Source
`text/plain`	Plain text, used for regular messages such as those corresponding to the initial RFC 822 standard	RFC 2046
`text/enriched`	Text that includes formatting information or other enrichment that makes it no longer plain	RFC 1896
`text/html`	A document expressed in HTML, commonly used for the World Wide Web	RFC 2854
`text/css`	Cascading style sheet information for the World Wide Web	RFC 2318

Image Media Type (image)

The `image` media type indicates graphical image files, such as pictures. The subtype normally indicates the specific format to allow the recipient to decode and present the file properly. Some of the more common subtypes are shown in Table 76-4.

Table 76-4: MIME image Media Type Subtypes

Type/Subtype	Description	Defining Source
`image/jpeg`	An image in JPEG format	RFC 2046
`image/gif`	A Graphical Interchange Format (GIF) image	IANA says RFC 2046, but it's not there.
`image/tiff`	Tagged Image File Format (TIFF) image	RFC 2302
`image/vnd.dwg`, `image/vnd.dxf`, `image/vnd.svf`	Vector images used in AutoCAD	Registration with IANA

Audio Media Type (audio)

The `audio` media type is used for sending audio information. The subtype normally indicates the specific format. Table 76-5 shows a couple of common values.

Table 76-5: MIME audio Media Type Subtypes

Type/ Subtype	Description	Defining Source
audio/basic	A basic audio type defined in the main MIME standards that describes single-channel audio encoded using 8-bit ISDN mu-law pulse code modulation at 8,000 Hz	RFC 2046
audio/mpeg	MPEG standard audio (including the popular MP3 file format)	RFC 3003

Video Media Type (video)

The video media type is used for sending video information. Again, the subtype normally indicates the specific format, as shown in Table 76-6.

Table 76-6: MIME video Media Type Subtypes

Type/Subtype	Description	Defining Source
video/mpeg	Video encoded to the MPEG digital video standard	RFC 2046
video/dv	Digital video corresponding to several popular standards including SD-VCR, HD-VCR, and DVB, as used by various types of video equipment	RFC 3189
video/quicktime	Apple's QuickTime movie format	Registration with IANA

Model Media Type (model)

The model media type describes a model representation, such as a two-dimensional or three-dimension physical model. Its subtypes are described in Table 76-7.

Table 76-7: MIME model Media Type Subtypes

Type/ Subtype	Description	Defining Source
model/mesh	A mesh, as used in modeling	RFC 2077
model/vrml	A Virtual Reality Modeling Language (VRML) model	RFC 2077
model/iges	A model file corresponding to the Initial Graphics Exchange Specification (IGES)	Registration with IANA

Application Media Type (application)

The application media type is a catchall for any kind of data that doesn't fit into one of the preceding categories or that is inherently application-specific. The subtype describes the data by indicating the kind of application that uses it. This can be used to guide the recipient's email program in choosing an appropriate application program to display it, just as a file extension in Windows tells the operating system how to open different kinds of files.

For example, if you have Microsoft Excel installed on your PC, clicking a filename ending with .XLS will launch Excel automatically. Similarly, an Excel spreadsheet will normally be sent using MIME with a media type of application/vnd.ms-excel. This tells the recipient's email program to launch Excel to read this file.

Since so many applications are out there, more than 100 different subtypes exist within this top-level type. Table 76-8 contains a few representative samples.

Table 76-8: MIME application Media Type Subtypes

Type/Subtype	Description	Defining Source
`application/octet-stream`	An arbitrary set of binary data octets (see the discussion following this table for more details)	RFC 2046
`application/postscript`	A PostScript file, used for printing and for generating Adobe Acrobat (PDF) files	RFC 2046
`application/applefile`	Resource file information for representing Apple Macintosh files	Registration with IANA
`application/msword`	Microsoft Word document (note that this does not have the vnd prefix like most other Microsoft file types)	Registration with IANA
`application/pdf`	A Portable Document Format (PDF) file, as created by Adobe Acrobat	Registration with IANA
`application/vnd.framemaker`	An Adobe FrameMaker file	Registration with IANA
`application/vnd.lotus-1-2-3`	A Lotus 1-2-3 file	Registration with IANA
`application/vnd.lotus-notes`	A Lotus Notes file	Registration with IANA
`application/vnd.ms-excel`	A Microsoft Excel spreadsheet file	Registration with IANA
`application/vnd.ms-powerpoint`	A Microsoft PowerPoint presentation file	Registration with IANA
`application/vnd.ms-project`	A Microsoft Project file	Registration with IANA
`application/zip`	A compressed archive file containing one or more other files, using the ZIP/PKZIP compression format	Registration with IANA

Of these application subtypes, a special one is worth further mention: the `application/octet-stream` subtype. This is the catchall within the catchall of the application type, which just means the file is a sequence of arbitrary binary data. It is usually used when the sender is unsure of what form the data takes or cannot identify it as belonging to a particular application. When this type is used, the recipient will usually be prompted to save the data to a file. He must then figure out what application to use to read it.

The `application/octet-stream` MIME type/subtype may even be used for images, audio, or video in unknown formats. If you try to send a multimedia document that your sending program does not understand, it will generally encode it as `application/octet-stream` for transmission. This is your email program's way of saying to the recipient, "I am sending you this file as-is; you figure out what to do with it."

This `application/octet-stream` type is also often used for transmitting executable files (programs) especially on Windows systems. Unfortunately, while convenient, this can be a serious security hazard. In recent years, the Internet has been subject to a steady stream of viruses and worms that spread by sending themselves to other users through executable file attachments in email. This makes opening and running any unknown `application/octet-stream` attachment potentially dangerous.

MIME Composite Media Types: Multipart and Encapsulated Message Structures

MIME discrete media types allow MIME to represent hundreds of different kinds of data in email messages. This alone would make MIME an incredibly useful technology, but the MIME standard goes one step further by defining *composite* media types. These allow MIME to perform even more spectacular feats, such as sending many types of data at once or encapsulating other messages or information into email.

The use of a MIME composite media type is indicated via the Content-Type header of an RFC 822 message. Instead of one of the six discrete media types (`text`, `image`, `audio`, `video`, `model`, or `application`), one of these two composite media types is used: `multipart`, which allows one or more sets of data to be sent in a single MIME message, and `message`, which allows a message to encapsulate another message.

> **KEY CONCEPT** Two MIME composite media types exist: `message`, which allows one message to encapsulate another, and `multipart`, which allows multiple individual media types to be encoded into a single email message.

MIME Multipart Message Type

The `multipart` media type is the more common of the two types, and for good reason: It is an *incredibly* powerful mechanism. It allows one message to contain many different kinds of information that can be used in different ways. Each piece of data is encoded separately as a MIME body part, and the parts are combined into a single email message. How these parts are used depends on the semantics of the message, indicated by the MIME subtype. RFC 2046 describes several of these, and a few new ones have also been defined by the IANA registration scheme described earlier.

MIME Multipart Message Subtypes

Table 78-9 shows the most common multipart media subtypes and how they are used. The first four are defined in RFC 2046.

Table 76-9: Common MIME multipart Media Type Subtypes

Type/Subtype	Description	Defining Source
`multipart/mixed`	Indicates that the body parts are not really related, but they have been bundled for transport in a single message for convenience. For example, this might be used by someone to send an office memo along with a vacation snapshot just for fun. This subtype is also sometimes used when the parts are related but the relationship is communicated to the recipient in some other way (such as via a description in a distinct body part).	RFC 2046

(continued)

Table 76-9: Common MIME multipart Media Type Subtypes (continued)

Type/Subtype	Description	Defining Source
multipart/ alternative	Specifies that the body parts are alternative representations of the same information. The recipient decodes the parts and chooses the one that is best suited to her needs. A common use of this is in sending Hypertext Markup Language (HTML)-encoded email. Some email clients can't display HTML, so it is courteous to send a *multipart/alternative* message containing the message in both HTML and plain text forms. The alternatives should be placed in the message in increasing order of preference, meaning that the preferred format goes last. In the case of a document that includes plain text and rich text alternatives—such as the preceding example with plain text and HTML versions of a document—the plainest format should go first and the fanciest last.	RFC 2046
multipart/parallel	Tells the recipient that the body parts should all be displayed at the same time (in parallel). For example, someone sends an audio clip along with explanatory text to be displayed alongside it as it plays.	RFC 2046
multipart/digest	Allows a message to carry a digest, such as a collection of other email messages.	RFC 2046
multipart/related	Indicates specifically that the body parts are related to each other. Special parameters are used to provide more information on how they are to be interpreted.	RFC 2387
multipart/encrypted	Used for encrypted data. The first body part contains information on how the data is to be decrypted, and the second contains the data itself.	RFC 1847

Multipart Message Encoding

You can see just from the different subtypes shown in Table 78-9 how much flexibility the multipart type provides to MIME, and there are other subtypes. In all cases, the same syntax is used to encode the constituent body parts into a single message. The basic process is as follows:

1. Each individual piece of data is processed as if it were to be transmitted as the body of a discrete media type MIME message. This includes the specification of appropriate headers, such as Content-Type, Content-ID, and Content-Transfer-Encoding, as needed.
2. A special *boundary delimiter* is chosen to separate the body parts. It must be selected so that it will not appear in any of the body parts; a random string is sometimes used. It is prepended with two dashes (--) when placed in the message to reduce the chance of it being mistaken for data.
3. The multipart message is assembled. It consists of a *preamble* text area, then a boundary line, followed by the first body part. Each subsequent body part is separated from the previous one with another boundary line. After the last body part, another boundary line appears, followed by an *epilogue* text area.
4. The special parameter *boundary* is included in the Content-Type header of the message as a whole, to tell the recipient what pattern separates the body parts.

KEY CONCEPT MIME multipart messages are formed by first processing each individual data component to create a MIME *body part*. Each can have a distinct encoding method and set of headers, as if it were a separate MIME message. These body parts are then combined into a single multipart message and separated with a *boundary delimiter*. The identity of the delimiter is inserted into the *boundary* parameter of the *Content-Type* header, so the recipient can easily separate the individual body parts upon receipt of the message.

These rules may seem rather complicated, but once you've seen a couple of multipart messages, the structure will make sense. To help clarify multipart message encoding, Figure 76-1 shows graphically the overall structure of a multipart MIME message.

Listing 76-1 contains a specific example of a multipart message (with portions abbreviated to keep the length down), so you can see what one looks like in text form. (If you want to see more, you probably have several in your own email inbox right now!)

```
From: Joe Sender <joe@someplace.org>
To: Jane Receiver <jane@somewhereelse.com>
Date: Sun, 1 Jun 2003 13:28:19 -0800
Subject: Photo and discussion
MIME-Version: 1.0
Content-Type: multipart/mixed; boundary="exampledelimtext123"

This is a multipart message in MIME format

—exampledelimtext123
Content-Type: text/plain

Jane, here is the photo you wanted from me for the new client.
Here are some notes on how it was processed.
(Blah blah blah...)
Talk to you soon,
Joe.

—exampledelimtext123

Content-Type: image/jpeg; name="clientphoto.jpg"
Content-Transfer-Encoding: base64

SDc9Pjv/2wBDAQoLCw4NDhwQEBw7KCIoOzs7Ozs7Ozs
...
zv/wAARCADIARoDASIAAhEBAxEB/8QAHAAAAQUBA

—exampledelimtext123

(Epilogue)
```

Listing 76-1: *Example of a MIME multipart message*

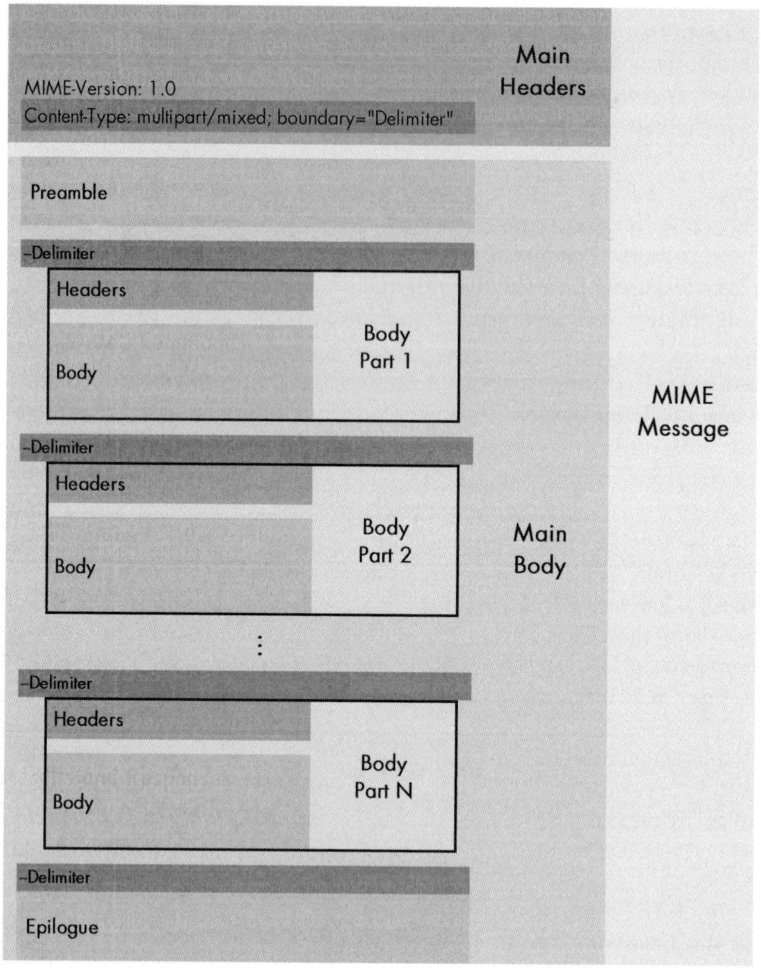

Figure 76-1: MIME multipart message structure *A MIME multipart message consists of a set of main headers and a main body portion, like all messages. Within the main body are one or more body parts, each of which has its own body-part-specific headers followed by the body part itself; each body part is shown in a black box. The Content-Type header of the message as a whole indicates that the message type is multipart, and the* boundary *parameter specifies the name of the delimiter, in this case just called "Delimiter." This delimiter is used to separate the body parts from each other and from the preamble and epilogue that begin and end the message body, respectively.*

In this example, Joe is sending Jane a multipart message containing a JPEG photograph and some explanatory text. The main header of the message specifies the `multipart/mixed` type and a boundary string of `exampledelimtext123`. The message begins with the preamble, which is ignored by the recipient email client but can be seen by the human reader. It is common to put a string here such as the one given in this example. That way, if a person using a client that does not support MIME receives the message, the recipient will know what it is.

The first delimiter string is then placed in the message, followed by the first body part, the text Joe is sending Jane. This is preceded by whatever headers are needed by the body part, in this case `Content-Type: text/plain`. (Note, however, that this is the default in MIME, so it could be omitted here.) After the text message is another delimiter, and then the encoded JPEG photo in the second body part, with its own headers. Finally, there is one more delimiter, and then a space for the epilogue. This is ignored if present and is often not used at all.

It is possible to send a multipart message that has only a single body part. This is sometimes done to take advantage of the preamble area to provide information about how to decode a nontext media type. Of course, this can also be done by including such text decoding instructions as a body part.

MIME Encapsulated Message Type

The other composite media type is the `message` type, which is devoted to the special purpose of encapsulating existing email messages within the body of a new message, or encapsulating other types of messages. This may be another email message previously sent or a message of some other kind. This media type also provides flexibility for sending partial messages and other special types of communication. Table 76-10 shows the three subtypes defined in RFC 2046.

Table 76-10: Common MIME message Media Type Subtypes

Type/Subtype	Description	Defining Source
`message/rfc822`	Indicates that the body contains an encapsulated email, itself formatted according to the RFC 822 standard. Note that this doesn't necessarily mean it is a plain text email message; it could be a MIME message (though encapsulating MIME within MIME must be done carefully).	RFC 2046
`message/partial`	Allows the fragmentation of larger messages into pieces that can later be reassembled.	RFC 2046
`message/external-body`	Indicates that the body of the message is not actually contained in the message itself; instead, a reference is provided to where the body is located. Sufficient information to locate the real message body must be provided.	RFC 2046

MIME Content-Transfer-Encoding Header and Encoding Methods

One of the main reasons why MIME was created was the significant restrictions that the RFC 822 standard places on how data in email messages must be formatted. To follow the rules, messages must be encoded in US-ASCII, a 7-bit data representation. This means that even though each byte can theoretically have any of 256 values, in ASCII only 128 values are valid. Furthermore, lines can be no longer than 1,000 characters including the carriage return and line feed (CRLF) characters at the end, and those two characters cannot appear elsewhere.

For some types of data, such as text files, this is no big deal; but for others it is a serious problem. This is especially the case with binary data. If you look at the data in a video clip, MP3 file, or executable program, it will appear to be random gibberish. In fact, such data is not random; it is represented using specific rules, but the data is expressed in raw binary form, where any 8-bit byte can contain any value from 0 to 255, which is why it looks like junk to humans. More important, this means that this data does not follow the rules for RFC 822 files and cannot be sent directly in this form.

To send non-ASCII data in MIME, it must be encoded. The Content-Transfer-Encoding header is used to specify how a MIME message or body part has been encoded, so that it can be decoded by its recipient. Four types of encoding are defined: `7bit`, `8bit/binary`, `quoted-printable`, and `base64`. The quoted-printable and base64 encodings are the most interesting ones, because they are what allow non-RFC-822 data to be sent using RFC 822.

> **KEY CONCEPT** MIME supports four encoding methods: `7bit`, `8bit (binary)`, `quoted-printable`, and `base64`. `7bit` encoding is standard ASCII and is used for text. `quoted-printable` encoding is for output that is mostly text but has some special characters that must be encoded. `base64` is used for arbitrary binary files. The 8-bit encoding method is defined in MIME but not used for RFC 822 messages.

7-Bit and 8-Bit Encoding

`7bit` encoding indicates that the message is already in ASCII form compatible with RFC 822. It is the default and is what is assumed if no Content-Transfer-Encoding header is present.

The `8bit` and `binary` values are synonymous. They mean the message has been encoded directly in 8-bit binary form. Yes, I did just say that this would violate the rules of RFC 822. These options appear to have been included to support future mechanisms for transporting binary data directly. RFC 1652 describes an SMTP extension that discusses this in part: "SMTP Service Extension for 8bit-MIMEtransport" (there is no space between *MIME* and *transport*). However, the standard clearly states that this still does not allow the transfer of raw binary data using SMTP and RFC 822.

Quoted-Printable Encoding

Quotable-printable encoding is a special type that is used when most of the data is ASCII text, but it contains certain violations of the rules of RFC 822. These illegal sections are converted using special encoding rules so the data as a whole is consistent with RFC 822; only the problem bytes are encoded. The result is that RFC 822 compatibility is achieved while maintaining most of the data as regular text so it can still be easily understood by a human.

An example would be letters with tildes or accents, such as those used in French or Spanish. Another would be a text message formed using an editor that inserts carriage return characters in the middle of a line. Most of the message is still text. The `quoted-printable` encoding can be used here, with the carriage return characters represented as =0D (the hexadecimal value of the character prepended by an equal sign). RFC 2046 contains more details on how this is done.

Base64 Encoding

In contrast, `base64` encoding is more often used for raw binary data that is not in human-readable form anyway, such as graphical image, audio, video, and application files. This encoding is used to allow arbitrary binary data to be represented in ASCII form. The data is then sent as ASCII and decoded back into binary form by the recipient. The idea behind this type of encoding is simple: The data that needs to be sent can have any value for each 8-bit byte, which is not allowed. So why not rearrange the bits so the data fits into the 7-bit ASCII limits of RFC 822?

This is done by processing the data to be sent three bytes at a time. There are 24 bits in each three-byte block, which are carved into four sets of 6 bits each. Each 6-bit group has a value from 0 to 63 and is represented by a single ASCII character, as presented in Table 76-11.

Table 76-11: MIME base64 Encoding Groups

6-Bit Value	Encoding	6-Bit Value	Encoding	6-Bit Value	Encoding	6-Bit Value	Encoding
0	A	16	Q	32	g	48	w
1	B	17	R	33	h	49	x
2	C	18	S	34	i	50	y
3	D	19	T	35	j	51	z
4	E	20	U	36	k	52	0
5	F	21	V	37	l	53	1
6	G	22	W	38	m	54	2
7	H	23	X	39	n	55	3
8	I	24	Y	40	o	56	4
9	J	25	Z	41	p	57	5
10	K	26	a	42	q	58	6
11	L	27	b	43	r	59	7
12	M	28	c	44	s	60	8
13	N	29	d	45	t	61	9
14	O	30	e	46	u	62	+
15	P	31	f	47	v	63	/

For example, suppose the first three bytes of the data to be sent were the decimal values 212, 39, and 247. These cannot all be expressed in 7-bit ASCII. In binary form, they are expressed like so:

11010100 00100111 11110111

We can divide these into four 6-bit groups:

110101 - 00 0010 - 0111 11 - 110111

Which yields the four values 53, 2, 31, and 55. Thus, the values 214, 39, and 247 would be encoded as the three ASCII characters 1Cf3. The conceptual steps of this process are shown in Figure 76-2.

NOTE *The sequence of steps for the encoding are intended to help you understand the process. Computers inherently deal directly with bits and would not bother with converting to decimal before encoding the 6-bit groups into ASCII characters.*

Data Bytes in Decimal Form	212		39		247
Data Bytes in Binary Form	11010100		00100111		11110111
Data Rearranged into 6-Bit Groups	110101	000010		011111	110111
6-Bit Groups in Decimal Form	53	2		31	55
Groups Converted to ASCII Characters	1	C		f	3

Figure 76-2: MIME base64 encoding *In this simplified example, three binary data bytes are encoded as four ASCII characters using MIME base64 encoding. Instead of transmitting those three bytes, two of which would not be valid in RFC 822, the four ASCII characters 1Cf3 are sent.*

This 3-to-4 encoding is done for all the data. The converted ASCII characters are then placed into the body of the entity instead of the raw binary data, 76 characters to a line. I showed how this is done in the second body part in the example in Listing 76-1 (except I didn't use 76 characters per line, to keep the line lengths short). One final character is involved in this scheme, the equal sign (=), which is used as a padding character when needed.

Since base64 characters are regular ASCII, they appear to SMTP like a regular text message. Of course, the data looks like gibberish to us, but that's not a problem since it will be converted back to its regular form and displayed to the recipient as an image, movie, audio, or whatever.

KEY CONCEPT MIME uses *base64* encoding to transform arbitrary 8-bit files into a form that is acceptable for communication in email. Each set of three 8-bit bytes is divided into four 6-bit groups, and each 6-bit group is represented by an ASCII character. Since the data is ASCII, it conforms to the RFC 822 message format standard, even if it is not human-readable. The receiving device reverses the encoding, changing each four-character block back into three 8-bit bytes.

The main drawback of the base64 method is that it is about 33 percent less efficient than sending binary data directly, using a protocol like the File Transfer Protocol (FTP). The reason is that three 8-bit bytes of binary data are sent as four ASCII characters, but of course, each ASCII character is represented using 8 bits itself. So there is one-third more overhead when using base64. In most cases, this is not a big deal, but it can be significant if downloading very large email files over a slow Internet connection.

Note that RFC 2046 also defines two other encodings: `ietf-token` and `x-token`. These are included to allow new encoding types to be defined in the future.

MIME Extension for non-ASCII Mail Message Headers

All of the MIME mechanisms discussed up to this point deal with ways of encoding different kinds of ASCII and non-ASCII data into the *body* of an RFC 822 message. In addition to these capabilities, MIME also includes a way in which non-ASCII data can be encoded into *headers* of an RFC 822 message.

At this point, you might be wondering why anyone would want to do this. Sure, it makes sense to be able to use MIME to encode binary data such as an image into an email, but why do it in a header? Well, if you can't see the need for this, chances are that you are a native English speaker. ASCII does a great job of representing English, but isn't so good with many other languages. With RFC 822, speakers of languages that use non-ASCII characters were unable to use descriptive headers fully, such as the Subject and Comments headers. Some could not even properly express their own names!

The solution to this problem is the subject of RFC 2047, the third of the five main MIME standards. It describes how to encode non-ASCII text into ASCII RFC 822 message headers. The idea is straightforward: As with message bodies, the non-ASCII text is replaced with ASCII, and information is provided to describe how this was done.

With this technique, the value of a regular header is replaced by a MIME *encoded-word* that has the following syntax:

=?<*charset*>?<*encoding*>?<*encoded-text*>?=

The strings `=?` and `?=` are used to *bracket* the non-ASCII header, which flags it as a MIME encoded header to the recipient's email client. The other elements, separated by `?`, indicate how the non-ASCII text is encoded, as follows:

<charset> The character set used, such as `iso-8859-1`.

<encoding> Two different encoding types are defined, each represented by a single letter for brevity: `B` indicates base64 encoding, and `Q` indicates quoted-printable encoding (these encoding types are discussed in the previous section.

<encoded-text> The non-ASCII text that has been encoded as ASCII using the encoding type indicated.

As you can see, this method is analogous to how a non-ASCII message body or body part would be encoded, but the information about the encoding has been condensed so everything can fit in a single header line. The <*charset*> parameter is somewhat analogous to the Content-Type header for a message body, but since headers can contain only text, it specifies what kind of text it is. The <*encoding*> parameter is clearly equivalent to the Content-Transfer-Encoding header.

KEY CONCEPT In addition to its many functions for encoding a variety of data in email message bodies, MIME provides a feature that allows non-ASCII information to be placed into email headers. This is done by encoding the data using either *quoted-printable or base64* encoding, and then using a special format for the header value that specifies its encoding and character set. This technique is especially useful for email sent in languages that cannot be represented easily in standard ASCII, such as many Asian languages.

Here's an example of a non-ASCII header, using the GB2312 character set (for Chinese characters) and base64 encoding:

```
Subject: =?GB2312?B?u7bTrbLOvNPDwLn61bm74Q==?=
```

I hope that doesn't say anything inappropriate; I took it from a piece of spam email I received once!

77

TCP/IP ELECTRONIC MAIL DELIVERY PROTOCOL: THE SIMPLE MAIL TRANSFER PROTOCOL (SMTP)

I emphasized in my overall description of TCP/IP email that communication using email requires the interaction of various protocols and elements. One mistake that some people make is to equate the method used for delivering email with the entire system. This is, however, an understandable mistake—just as the postal service is only a part of the whole system of mailing a letter, it is nonetheless a very big part. Likewise, the delivery of email from sender to recipient is arguably the most important part of email as a whole. In modern TCP/IP, this task is the responsibility of the *Simple Mail Transfer Protocol (SMTP)*.

In this chapter, I describe in detail the operation of SMTP. I begin with an overview and history of the protocol and a discussion of the standards that define it. I then examine the way that SMTP client/server communication and message transport work. I explain the way that SMTP servers establish connections and transaction sessions, and then the process by which mail is transferred from one server to another. I describe some of the special features implemented in SMTP and discuss SMTP security issues. I conclude with a reference summary of SMTP commands and replies.

BACKGROUND INFORMATION *My discussion of SMTP assumes that you already have a basic understanding of the general concepts of TCP/IP email, as well as familiarity with TCP/IP email addressing and message formatting. These topics are discussed in Chapters 74, 75, and 76, respectively.*

SMTP Overview, History, and Standards

The overview and history of the TCP/IP email system in Chapter 74 describes how TCP/IP evolved from its early beginnings to its current form. Since the mechanism used to deliver email is such a big part of the system as a whole, any overview of the system must of necessity discuss how delivery mechanisms have changed as well. In the case of TCP/IP, the delivery of mail evolved through many forms during the 1970s, as developers sought to find effective ways of communicating email messages between systems. Most of these efforts involved attempts to transmit mail using existing protocols; this makes sense, since it is easier to adapt a technology than design one from scratch.

SMTP Standards

One important achievement in the development of a mail system was the publishing of the *Mail Transfer Protocol (MTP)*, which was first defined in RFC 772 in September 1980, and then updated in RFC 780 in May 1981. MTP describes a set of commands and procedures by which two devices can connect using TCP to exchange email messages. Its operation is described largely using elements borrowed from two early TCP/IP application protocols that were already in use at that time: Telnet and the File Transfer Protocol (FTP). The commands of MTP are actually based directly on those of FTP.

Although there was nothing inherently wrong with basing email delivery on FTP, defining it this way made MTP somewhat of a hack. It was also restricted to the capabilities defined by FTP, a general file transfer protocol, so it was not possible to include features in MTP that were specific to sending and receiving mail. Due to the importance of email, a specific protocol designed for the purpose of delivering email was warranted. SMTP was first defined in RFC 788 and published in November 1981.

The name suggests that SMTP is simpler than the protocol that it replaced. Whether or not this is true is somewhat a matter of opinion; I do note that RFC 788 is 61 pages long, while the earlier RFC 780 was only 43 pages. What SMTP definitely has over MTP is *elegance*; the protocol is designed specifically for the transport of email. While it retains certain similarities to FTP, it is an independent protocol running over the Transmission Control Protocol (TCP). So, from a conceptual standpoint, it can be considered simpler than MTP. In terms of mechanics, the process SMTP uses to transfer an email message is indeed rather simple, especially compared to some other protocols.

RFC 788 described the operation of SMTP carrying email messages corresponding to the ARPAnet text message standard as described in RFC 733. Development of both email messages and SMTP continued, and in August 1982, a milestone in TCP/IP email was achieved when RFCs 821 and 822 were published. RFC 821 revised SMTP and became the defining standard for the protocol for the next two decades. RFC 822, its companion standard, became the standard for TCP/IP email messages carried by SMTP.

> **KEY CONCEPT** The most important component of the TCP/IP email system is the *Simple Mail Transfer Protocol (SMTP)*. SMTP was derived from the earlier Mail Transfer Protocol (MTP) and is the mechanism used for the delivery of mail between TCP/IP systems and users. The only part of the email system for which SMTP is not used is the final retrieval step by an email recipient.

As the 1980s progressed, and TCP/IP and the Internet both grew in popularity, SMTP gradually overtook other methods to become the dominant method of email message delivery. For a number of years, the protocol was used mostly as is, with no new RFCs published to define new versions or formally change its behavior. This changed in February 1993, when RFC 1425, "SMTP Service Extensions," was published. As the name suggests, this standard describes a process for adding new capabilities to extend how SMTP works, while maintaining backward compatibility with existing systems. SMTP with these extensions is sometimes called *Extended SMTP* or *ESMTP* (though use of this term seems not to be entirely universal).

As development of SMTP continued, RFC 1425 was revised in RFC 1651 in July 1994, and then in RFC 1869 in November 1995. Along with these revisions, a number of other RFCs defining particular SMTP extensions, such as pipelining and message size declaration, were defined.

In April 2001, another major milestone in TCP/IP email was reached when revisions of RFC 821 and RFC 822 were published, as RFCs 2821 and 2822, respectively. Both documents are consolidations of updates and changes that had been made to RFCs 821 and 822 between 1982 and 2001. And, no, I don't think it is a coincidence that the old and new RFC numbers are exactly 2,000 apart. RFCs 2820 and 2823 were both published in May 2000, so it looks like 2821 and 2822 were reserved for the email standards. I think this naming was a great idea, as it makes it clear that the new RFCs are revisions of the old ones.

RFC 2821 is the current base standard for SMTP. It incorporates the base protocol description from RFC 821 and the latest SMTP extensions as defined in RFC 1869. It updates the description of the email communication model to reflect the realities of modern TCP/IP networks, especially the email features built into the Domain Name System (DNS). We'll examine this in more detail in the next section.

SMTP Communication and Message Transport Methods

The TCP/IP email communication model describes the way email messages are conveyed from the sender to the recipient. In most cases, this involves the sender's client machine sending the email to its local SMTP server, which sends it to the recipient's local SMTP server, which then sends it to the recipient's local host. SMTP handles the transport between SMTP servers. In fact, the overall email communication model is largely described by the RFC 821 and 2821 SMTP standards.

The initial communication takes place between the sender's client machine and a local SMTP server that the sender is allowed to access. After submission of the email message, that SMTP server becomes responsible for delivering the message to the SMTP server responsible for the recipient's mailbox.

Early Email Communication Using Relaying

In the early days of email, when RFC 821 and its predecessors were first defined, the Internet was very different from what it is today. There was no DNS, and this made email delivery complex, because there was no way to map a mailbox address to the IP address of the SMTP server that managed that mailbox. Also, many proprietary networks were connected to the Internet, which meant that it was not always possible for any particular system to communicate with any other.

Given this, how could email be delivered? The most common way in the early days of SMTP was through a process called *relaying*. SMTP routing information was included along with the email address, to specify a sequence of SMTP servers that the mail should be relayed through to get to its destination. For example, if a sender using SMTP Server A wanted to send email to someone whose mailbox was on SMTP Server Z, the sender might have needed to specify that the mail be sent through intermediate SMTP Servers D, P, and U to get there. An SMTP connection would be established from Server A to Server D to send the message on one leg of its journey; then it would go from Server D to P, Server P to U, and then Server U to Z. The process is analogous to how Internet Protocol (IP) routing works, but at the application layer (actually using IP routing at a lower level).

You can probably see the problems with this quite easily: It's cumbersome, requires many devices to handle the mail, results in delays in communication, and requires the communication of source routes between SMTP servers. It was certainly functional, but it was far from ideal.

Modern Email Communication Using DNS and Direct Delivery

The creation of DNS radically changed how email delivery worked. DNS includes support for a special *mail exchange (MX)* record that allows easy mapping from the domain name in an email address to the IP address of the SMTP server that handles mail for that domain. I explain this in the description of the regular email address format in Chapter 76, as well as the section about DNS email support in Chapter 56.

In the new system, SMTP communication is much simpler and more direct. The sending SMTP server uses DNS to find the MX record of the domain to which the email is addressed. This gives the sender the DNS name of the recipient's SMTP server. This is resolved to an IP address, and a connection can be made directly from the sender's SMTP server to the recipient's server to deliver the email. While SMTP still supports relaying, direct email delivery using MX records is faster and more efficient, and RFC 2821 makes clear that this is now the preferred method.

In this new system, SMTP is generally used only for two transfers: first, from the sender's client machine to the sender's local SMTP server, and then from that server to the recipient's local SMTP server, as shown in Figure 74-1 in Chapter 74. (A distinct mail access protocol or method is used by the recipient for the last leg of the journey.) Each transfer of an email message between SMTP servers involves the establishment of a TCP connection, and then the transfer of the email headers and body using the SMTP mail transfer process. The following sections describe in detail how this occurs.

KEY CONCEPT In the early days of SMTP, mail was delivered using the relatively inefficient process of relaying from server to server across the internetwork. Today, when an SMTP server has mail to deliver to a user, it determines the server that handles the user's mail using the Domain Name System (DNS) and sends the mail directly to that server.

Terminology: Client/Server and Sender/Receiver

The original RFC 821 standard referred to the device that initiates an SMTP email transfer as the *sender* and the device that responds to it as the *receiver*. These terms were changed to *client* and *server* in RFC 2821 to "reflect current industry terminology." Strictly speaking, this is correct, but in some ways, the more current terminology is significantly *less* clear.

As I explained in the general discussion of TCP/IP client/server operation in Chapter 8, the terms *client* and *server* are used in many different senses in networking, which often leads to confusion. In common parlance, the computers that handle email on the Internet are usually all called *SMTP servers*. This is because they run SMTP server software to provide SMTP services to client machines, such as end-user PCs. In addition, these devices are usually dedicated hardware servers running in network centers, typically managed by Internet service providers (ISPs).

However, the terms *client* and *server* are now used to refer to the roles in a particular SMTP communication as well. Since all SMTP servers both send and receive email, they all act as both clients and servers at different times. An SMTP server that is relaying an email will act as both server and client for that message, receiving it as a server, and then sending it to the next server as a client. Adding to this potential confusion is the fact that the initial stage in sending an email is from the sender's client machine to the sender's local SMTP server. Thus, the client role in an SMTP transaction may not be an actual SMTP server, but the server role will always be a server.

For all of these reasons, the old terms *sender* and *receiver* are still used in places in RFC 2821, where needed for clarity. I consider them much more straightforward and use them in the rest of this chapter.

KEY CONCEPT SMTP servers both send and receive email. The device sending mail acts as a client for that transaction, and the one receiving it acts as a server. To avoid confusion, it is easier to refer to the device sending email as the *SMTP sender* and the one receiving as the *SMTP receiver*; these terms were used when SMTP was originally created.

SMTP Connection and Session Establishment and Termination

The delivery of email using SMTP involves the regular exchange of email messages among SMTP servers. SMTP servers are responsible for sending email that users of the server submit for delivery. They also receive email intended for local recipients, or for forwarding or relaying to other servers.

Overview of Connection Establishment and Termination

All SMTP communication is done using TCP. This allows SMTP servers to make use of TCP's many features that ensure efficient and reliable communication. SMTP servers generally must be kept running and connected to the Internet 24 hours a day, seven days a week, to ensure that mail can be delivered at any time. (This is a big reason why most end users employ access protocols such as the Post Office Protocol to access their received email rather than running their own SMTP servers.) The server listens continuously on the SMTP server port, well-known port number 25, for any TCP connection requests from other SMTP servers.

An SMTP server that wishes to send email normally begins with a DNS lookup of the MX record corresponding to the domain name of the intended recipient's email address to get the name of the appropriate SMTP server. This name is then resolved to an IP address; for efficiency, this IP address is often included as an *additional* record in the response to the MX request to save the sending server from needing to perform two explicit DNS resolutions.

The SMTP sender then establishes an SMTP session with the SMTP receiver. Once the session is established, mail transactions can be performed to allow mail to be sent between the devices. When the SMTP sender is finished sending mail, it terminates the connection. All of these processes involve specific exchanges of commands and replies, which are illustrated in Figure 77-1.

Let's take a look at these processes in more detail, starting with SMTP session establishment.

Connection Establishment and Greeting Exchange

The SMTP sender begins by initiating a TCP connection to the SMTP receiver. The sending SMTP server uses an ephemeral port number, since it is playing the role of the client in the transaction. Assuming that the server is willing to accept a connection, it will indicate that it is ready to receive instructions from the client by sending reply code 220. This is called the *greeting* or *service ready* response. It commonly includes the full domain name of the server machine, the version of the SMTP server software it is running, and possibly other information.

Now, it would be rude for the server acting as a client to start sending commands to the responding server without saying hello first, wouldn't it? So that's exactly what comes next: the client says, "Hello." In the original SMTP protocol, this is done by issuing a HELO command, which includes the domain name of the sending (client) SMTP server as a courtesy. The receiving device then responds back with a return hello message using an SMTP reply code 250.

For example, if the SMTP server smtp.sendersite.org was making a connection to the SMTP server mail.receiversplace.com, it would say:

```
HELO smtp.sendersite.org.
```

After receiving this greeting, mail.receiversplace.com would respond back with a `hello` message of its own, something like this:

```
250 mail.receiversplace.com Hello smtp.sendersite.org, nice to meet you.
```

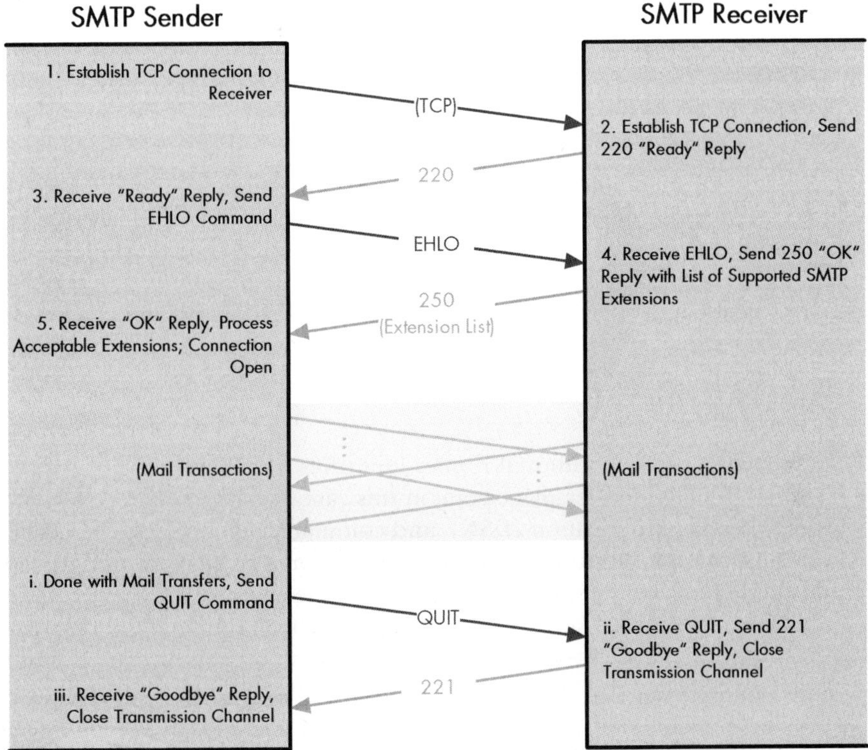

Figure 77-1: SMTP transaction session establishment and termination *An SMTP session begins with the SMTP sender establishing a TCP connection to the SMTP receiver. The receiver sends a ready message; the sender sends a HELO or EHLO command, to which the receiver responds. Assuming no difficulties are encountered, the session is established and mail transactions take place. When the sender is finished, it sends a QUIT command; the receiver responds with a 221 reply and closes the session.*

(The chatty text is of course purely optional; most of the time, SMTP communication is between software programs, so the pleasantries are usually written by programmers who have a sense of humor.)

Connection Establishment Using SMTP Extensions

The SMTP extensions first defined in RFC 1425, and then in subsequent standards up to RFC 2821, define an alternative hello message for the client to use: EHLO (extended hello). An SMTP sender supporting SMTP extensions (and most do) uses EHLO instead of HELO in response to the 220 greeting. This serves both to say hello to the SMTP receiver and to tell it that the sender supports SMTP extensions.

If the SMTP receiver supports the extensions, it replies with the usual 250 reply, as well as a series of extra 250 responses. Each of these lists an EHLO *keyword* that indicates a particular SMTP extension the receiver supports. If the receiving server doesn't support the extensions, it will reject the EHLO command with a 500 reply code ("syntax error, command not recognized"). This tells the SMTP sender that it cannot use extensions. It will then issue a conventional HELO command, or it will QUIT the connection if it requires the SMTP extension to be present. (In practice, it is rare for a server to *require* the use of SMTP extensions.)

Here's the same example used earlier, but using EHLO. The sender says:

```
EHLO smtp.sendersite.org.
```

Assuming mail.receiversplace.com supports the SMTP extensions, a typical reply might look like this:

```
250-mail.receiversplace.com Hello smtp.sendersite.org, nice to meet you.
250-SIZE
250-DSN
250 PIPELINING
```

Each of these additional replies identifies a particular SMTP extension supported by mail.receiversplace.com; in this case, message size declaration (SIZE), delivery status notification (DSN), and command pipelining. (The dashes after the 250 indicate a multiple-line response to a command; this is discussed in the "SMTP Multiple-Line Text Replies" section later in the chapter.)

Once the HELO or EHLO command has been sent and the receiving device has responded, the session is initiated. Further commands can be sent by the sending SMTP server to the responding server. These usually take the form of email message transfer transactions using the process described in the upcoming "SMTP Mail Transaction Process" section, and other command/reply exchanges as needed.

Connection Termination

When the sending device is finished sending all the email it has to transfer to the receiving device, and it has completed all its other activities, it terminates the session by issuing the QUIT command. This normally results in a 221 "goodbye" message from the SMTP receiver, which says something like "closing transmission channel." The TCP connection is then terminated.

> **KEY CONCEPT** An SMTP session consists of three basic phases. The session is first *established* through the creation of a TCP connection and the exchange of identity information between the SMTP sender and receiver using the HELO command. Once established, *mail transactions* can be performed. When the SMTP sender is finished with the session, it *terminates* it using the QUIT command. If *SMTP extensions* are supported, the SMTP sender uses the *EHLO (extended hello)* command instead of *HELO*, and the SMTP receiver replies with a list of extensions it will allow the SMTP sender to use.

A server may also terminate prematurely in special cases. If it is given a local command to shut down (for example, due to imminent rebooting of the hardware server on which it is running), it may respond to any routine command with a 421 response ("Service not available, closing transmission channel"). A server is not supposed to terminate a session simply due to receipt of an invalid command, however; this should happen only in special cases where session termination cannot be avoided.

SMTP Mail Transaction Process

As described in the previous section, the delivery of an email message begins with the establishment of an SMTP session between the devices sending and receiving the message. The SMTP sender initiates a TCP connection to the SMTP receiver and then sends a HELO or an EHLO command, to which the receiver responds. Assuming no problems ensue, the session is then established and ready for actual email message transactions.

Overview of SMTP Mail Transaction

The SMTP mail transaction process itself consists of three steps:

1. **Transaction Initiation and Sender Identification** The SMTP sender tells the SMTP receiver that it wants to start sending a message and gives the receiver the email address of the message's originator.
2. **Recipient Identification** The sender tells the receiver the email address(es) of the intended recipients of the message.
3. **Mail Transfer** The sender transfers the email message to the receiver. This is a complete email message meeting the RFC 822 specification (which may be in MIME format as well).

That's it! So you can see that the word *Simple* in *Simple Mail Transfer Protocol* definitely has at least *some* merit. In fact, one question that sometimes comes up when examining SMTP is "Why couldn't this process be even simpler?" The first two steps identify the sender of the email and the intended recipient(s). But all of this information is already contained in headers in the message itself. Why doesn't SMTP just read that information from the message, which would make the mail transaction a *one-step* process?

The explanation isn't specifically addressed in the SMTP standards, but I believe there are several reasons for this:

- Specifying the sender and recipients separately is more efficient, as it gives the SMTP receiver the information it needs up front before the message itself is transmitted. In fact, the SMTP receiver can decide whether or not to accept the message based on the source and destination email addresses.
- Having this information specified separately gives greater control on how email is distributed. For example, an email message may be addressed to two recipients, but they may be on totally different systems; the SMTP sender might wish to deliver the mail using two separate SMTP sessions to two different SMTP receivers.

- In a similar vein, there is the matter of delivering blind carbon copies. Someone who is BCC'ed a message must receive it without being mentioned in the message itself.
- Having this information separate makes implementing security on SMTP much easier.

For these reasons, SMTP draws a distinction between the message itself, which it calls the *content*, and the sender and recipient identification, which it calls the *envelope*. This is consistent with our running analogy between regular mail and email. Just as the postal service delivers a piece of mail using only the information written on the envelope, SMTP delivers email using the envelope information, not the content of the message. It's not quite the case that the SMTP server doesn't look at the message itself, just that this is not the information it uses to manage delivery.

NOTE *It is possible for the sender of a message to generate envelope information based on the contents of the message, but this is somewhat external to SMTP itself. It is described in the standard, but caution is urged in exactly how this is implemented.*

SMTP Mail Transaction Details

Let's take a more detailed look at the SMTP mail transaction process, using as aids the process diagram in Figure 77-2 and the sample transaction of Listing 77-1 (which has commands highlighted in bold and replies in italics).

```
MAIL FROM:<joe@someplace.org>
250 <joe@someplace.org> . . . Sender ok
RCPT TO:<jane@somewhereelse.com>
250 <jane@somewhereelse.com> . . . Recipient ok
DATA
354 Enter mail, end with "." on a line by itself
From: Joe Sender <joe@someplace.org>
To: Jane Receiver <jane@somewhereelse.com>
Date: Sun, 1 Jun 2003 14:17:31 -0800
Subject: Lunch tomorrow

Hey Jane,

It's my turn for lunch tomorrow. I was thinking we could
[rest of message]
Hope you are free. Send me a reply back when you get a chance.
Joe.
.
250 OK
```

Listing 77-1: *Example of an SMTP mail transaction*

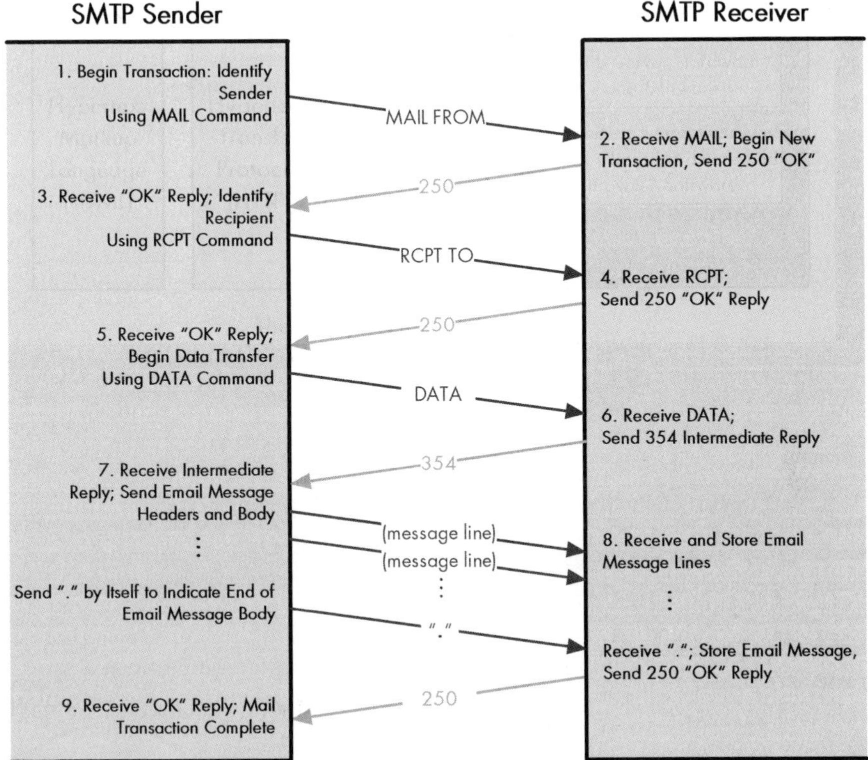
SMTP Sender
SMTP Receiver
1. Begin Transaction: Identify Sender Using MAIL Command
MAIL FROM
2. Receive MAIL; Begin New Transaction, Send 250 "OK"
250
3. Receive "OK" Reply; Identify Recipient Using RCPT Command
RCPT TO
4. Receive RCPT; Send 250 "OK" Reply
250
5. Receive "OK" Reply; Begin Data Transfer Using DATA Command
DATA
6. Receive DATA; Send 354 Intermediate Reply
354
7. Receive Intermediate Reply; Send Email Message Headers and Body
(message line)
(message line)
8. Receive and Store Email Message Lines
Send "." by Itself to Indicate End of Email Message Body
"."
Receive "."; Store Email Message, Send 250 "OK" Reply
250
9. Receive "OK" Reply; Mail Transaction Complete

Figure 77-2: SMTP mail transaction process *Once an SMTP session is established between a sender and receiver, each mail transaction consists of a set of three command/reply sequences. The sender is first identified using the MAIL command and the recipients are specified using one or more RCPT commands. The actual mail message is then transferred using the DATA command, which involves a preliminary reply before the actual message is sent and a completion reply when it has been fully received.*

The first two steps in the mail transaction are responsible for providing the receiving SMTP server with the envelope information just discussed. The transaction begins by the SMTP sender issuing a MAIL command. This serves to inform the receiver that a new transaction is commencing and also to tell it the *from* information on the envelope. Here's an example:

```
MAIL FROM:<joe@someplace.org>
```

The email address of the originator is always enclosed in angle brackets (< and >). The SMTP receiver acknowledges the command with a 250 ("OK") reply message, sometimes sending back the address as a confirmation. Here's an example:

```
250 <joe@someplace.org> . . . Sender ok
```

Next, the SMTP sender uses RCPT commands to specify the intended recipients of the email that is being sent. Each RCPT line can contain only one recipient, so if multiple recipients are indicated, two or more RCPT commands must be issued.

Each one normally specifies an email address, but if relaying is being used, the command may contain routing information as well. (As described earlier in the "SMTP Communication and Message Transport Methods" section, this is not as commonly done as it was in the past.) Here's an example:

```
RCPT TO:<jane@somewhereelse.com>
```

Assuming the server accepts the email, it will give a 250 "OK" reply again, like so:

```
250 <jane@somewhereelse.com> . . . Recipient ok
```

The SMTP sender then issues the DATA command, which tells the SMTP receiver that the message is coming:

```
DATA
```

The SMTP receiver responds with a 354 "intermediate" reply message, such as this:

```
354 Enter mail, end with "." on a line by itself
```

The SMTP sender then sends the email message, one line at a time, with a single dot (.) on a line to terminate it. The server confirms the receipt of the message with another 250 "OK" reply, and the transaction is finished.

> **KEY CONCEPT** After an SMTP session is established, email messages are sent using the SMTP *mail transaction process*. The SMTP sender starts the transaction by identifying the sender of the email and then specifying one or more recipients. The email message itself is then transmitted to the SMTP receiver. Each email to be sent is a separate transaction.

While this indeed is quite simple, notice that I have shown an email transfer from a sender to one recipient, one in which there were no problems or complications in the transaction. Due either to command syntax or server issues, it is possible for various types of errors to occur at different stages of the process, which may result in the transaction failing. As you'll see shortly, security concerns may come also into play, leading to restrictions in what transactions a server may allow.

SMTP Special Features, Capabilities, and Extensions

The primary job of the SMTP is to implement the TCP/IP email delivery system. Whenever the user of an SMTP server gives it an email message addressed to a remote mailbox, the server will attempt to transfer it to the appropriate destination server, using the SMTP mail transaction process. Many billions of such transfers are performed every day on the Internet, allowing email to reach its destination quickly anywhere around the world.

SMTP Special Features and Capabilities

In addition to this basic transfer mechanism, SMTP includes a number of other features and capabilities. These allow SMTP to support special requirements and auxiliary needs of the mail system, as described in detail in RFC 2821. It would take many pages to describe them all in detail, so I will provide a quick summary of the more important ones here so you know a bit about them.

The following are some of SMTP's special features:

Mail Relaying As discussed in the "SMTP Communication and Message Transport Methods" section earlier in this chapter, the protocol was once widely used in a relaying mode, where email was routed from one SMTP server to another to reach its destination. Today, the more efficient, normal method of email transfer on the Internet is directly from the sender's SMTP server to the recipient's server, using DNS MX records to determine the recipient SMTP server address. SMTP still includes the ability to relay mail from one server to another, provided certain conditions are met. Note that many servers won't relay mail because this feature has been abused for spamming and malicious hacking.

Mail Forwarding Under certain conditions, an SMTP server may agree to accept email for a remote mailbox and forward it to the appropriate destination. This sounds similar to relaying but is used in a different way. A common example is when users change their email address. For example, if you have worked at XYZ Industries for years and then retire, the company may no longer wish to let you receive email at the company's SMTP server. As a courtesy, however, they may forward email sent to you there, so that you receive it at your new company.

Mail Gatewaying Certain SMTP servers may be configured as email gateways. These devices translate TCP/IP email into a form suitable for another email system, and vice versa. Gatewaying is a complex topic because email systems can be so different. One of the more important problems is the inconsistency of addressing methods of different email systems.

Address Debugging SMTP includes a VRFY (verify) command that can be used to check the validity of an email address without actually sending mail to it.

Mailing List Expansion The SMTP command EXPN (expand) can be used to determine the individual email addresses associated with a mailing list. (Note, however, that this has nothing directly to do with mailing list software like *Majordomo.*)

Turning The original SMTP included a command that allows the SMTP sender and SMTP receiver to change roles. This could be used to allow SMTP Server A to send email to Server B, and then have Server B send email it has queued for Server A in the same session. In practice, this capability was not widely used for a variety of reasons, including security considerations. It is now officially not recommended but may still be implemented in some SMTP software.

These are just a few of the features that are mentioned in the SMTP standards. In addition, developers of a particular type of SMTP server software may give it other features as well. The HELP command is one way of determining what commands are supported by a particular SMTP server.

SMTP servers also must perform a great deal of background processing that doesn't get a great deal of attention. This includes managing connections, checking for errors in commands and email messages, and reacting accordingly. They must also be on the lookout for problem conditions, such as looping that may result in an email message being passed back and forth between two SMTP servers, each thinking the other is the intended recipient. In the event of an initial failure to deliver mail, an SMTP server is also required to retry communication periodically with the destination device and return a failure message to the sender if it cannot deliver the message after a certain period of time. RFC 2821 contains more details.

SMTP Extensions

As discussed earlier in this chapter, during the 1990s, many extensions to the basic operation of SMTP were defined. These are enabled when two SMTP servers supporting the extension set up a session using the EHLO command and appropriate extension response codes. Table 77-1 summarizes some of the more interesting SMTP extensions that have been defined and gives the RFC number where each is described. You can find the full current set of SMTP extensions at http://www.iana.org/assignments/mail-parameters.

Table 77-1: SMTP Extensions

Extension Keyword	Extension	Defining Document	Description
8BITMIME	8-bit MIME support	RFC 1652	Theoretically defines support for the 8-bit content transfer encoding type in MIME, but complications associated with this. See the discussion of content encoding in Chapter 76 for details.
AUTH	Authorization	RFC 2554	Used to implement an authorization mechanism for servers requiring enhanced security.
DSN	Delivery status notification	RFC 1891	Allows an SMTP sender to request that the SMTP receiver notify it if a problem occurs in delivering a message.
ENHANCEDSTATUSCODES	Enhanced status codes	RFC 2034, RFC 1893	Extends the traditional three-digit SMTP reply code format with extra codes that provide more information. See the "SMTP Replies and Reply Codes" section later in this chapter for more information.
PIPELINING	Command pipelining	RFC 2920	Allows multiple commands to be transmitted in batches from the SMTP sender to the receiver, rather than sending one command at a time and waiting for a response code.
SIZE	Message size declaration	RFC 1870	Allows information about the size of a message to be declared by an SMTP sender prior to transmitting it, so the SMTP receiver can decide if it wants the message or not.

NOTE *Certain commands in the basic SMTP description that are considered optional are also sometimes considered extensions, such as the EXPN and HELP commands; I have not listed these here, since they are not true SMTP extensions.*

SMTP Security Issues

When it comes to security and SMTP, the theme is a common one in TCP/IP: A lack of security in how the protocol is implemented, because it was developed when the Internet was just a small group of machines controlled by individuals who mostly knew and trusted each other or who were able to use physical security. Developers never imagined TCP/IP being used by millions of anonymous average Joes around the world, which necessitates far more attention to security than a small research internetwork like the ARPAnet.

With SMTP, security matters are, if anything, *worse* than they are with some of the other protocols. Not only does SMTP not have any real security mechanism, the original relaying model of SMTP communication is entirely designed around the idea of cooperation and trust among servers. Since most SMTP servers would be asked to handle a certain number of intermediate transfers, each server was required to accept mail from any originator to be delivered to any destination.

The basic assumption in this model is that users of SMTP servers would all be well behaved and not abuse the system by flooding intermediate servers with a lot of mail to be delivered or sending bogus messages to cause problems. This all changed as the Internet exploded in popularity in the 1990s. Con artists, malicious hackers, and disreputable salespeople discovered that email could be used for free delivery of messages simply by submitting them to an SMTP server for delivery. The result was overloaded servers, primarily due to the sending of large quantities of unwanted email, which Internet users commonly call *spam*.

NOTE *The term* spam, *in this context, has nothing directly to do with the Hormel processed meat product. Its use in reference to massive amounts of email comes from a Monty Python comedy sketch in which that word is repeated in phrases over and over again.*

It is actually very easy to impersonate an SMTP server. You can use the Telnet Protocol to connect directly to an SMTP server on port 25. SMTP commands are all sent as text, and so are SMTP replies, so you can have a conversation with a server, and even manually perform a mail transaction. This is useful for debugging, but it also makes abuse of a wide-open SMTP server trivially easy. Since spammers often don't want to be identified, they employ spoofing techniques to make it more difficult to identify them, so resolving these problems is even more difficult.

Despite this obvious dilemma, efforts to implement a general security mechanism in SMTP have been resisted for two main reasons. First, there is no foolproof way to retrofit a new security mechanism onto something as widely used as SMTP without creating incompatibilities between newer and older systems. Second, many administrators were reluctant to do away completely with the general notion of cooperation among sites that has helped make the Internet so successful.

Still, something had to be done. The compromise was for system administrators to tighten up their SMTP servers through the imposition of both technical and policy changes. Naturally, these vary from one organization to another. Some of the more common SMTP security provisions include the following:

- Checking the IP address of a device attempting connection and refusing even to start an SMTP session unless it is in a list of authorized client devices.
- Restricting certain commands or features, such as email relaying, to authorized users or client servers. This is sometimes done by requiring authentication via the SMTP extension AUTH before the command will be accepted.
- Limiting the use of commands such as EXPN to prevent unauthorized users from determining the email addresses of users on mailing lists.
- Checking the validity of envelope information before accepting a message for delivery. Some servers will first verify that the originator's email address is valid before agreeing to accept the MAIL command. Many will check the recipient's address and refuse the message if delivery is not to a local mailbox. Others use even more advanced techniques.
- Limiting the size of email messages that may be sent or the number that may be sent in a given period of time.
- Logging all access to the server to keep records of server use and check for abuse.

Because of all the abuse in recent years, you will find that most SMTP servers implement these or other features, even though most of those features are not formally defined by the SMTP standards. Rather, they are enhancements built into individual SMTP server software packages.

SMTP was designed during an era in which Internet security was not much of an issue; as a result, the base protocol includes no security mechanism at all. Since email is so often abused today, most modern SMTP servers incorporate one or more security features to avoid problems.

Some of these measures can actually be quite sophisticated. For example, the SMTP server run by pair Networks, the great web-hosting company I have used for years, uses *POP-before-SMTP authentication.* This means that before the server will accept outgoing mail from the user via SMTP, the user must first log in to check incoming mail using the Post Office Protocol (POP). Since POP includes authentication, a successful POP login tells the server the user is authorized. This "flips a switch" in the server that allows the user to access the SMTP service after that login for a limited period of time. If this seems convoluted, then you're starting to get an idea of the hassle that spammers and malicious hackers have created for ISPs today.

It's also worth noting that SMTP does not include any mechanism for encryption to ensure the privacy of email transmissions. Users requiring security to control who sees their messages must use a separate encryption scheme to encode the body of the message prior to submission.

SMTP Commands

Early TCP/IP email mechanisms were developed by borrowing techniques and elements from existing application protocols, especially Telnet and FTP. SMTP is an independent protocol, but its heritage can still be seen clearly in a few areas. One of the more obvious of these is in the method by which commands are issued by an SMTP sender and replies returned by an SMTP receiver.

Like FTP, all SMTP commands are sent as plain ASCII text over the TCP connection established between the client and server in an SMTP connection. These commands must end with the two-character CRLF sequence that normally terminates ASCII text as required for the Telnet Network Virtual Terminal (NVT; see Chapter 87). In fact, you can check the function of an SMTP server and even issue commands to it yourself simply by using Telnet to connect to it on port 25.

All SMTP commands are specified using a four-letter command code. Some commands also either allow or require parameters to be specified. The basic syntax of a command is

```
<command-code> <parameters>
```

When parameters are used, they follow the command code and are separated from it by one or more space characters. For example, the HELO and EHLO commands are specified with the command code, a space character, and then the domain name of the SMTP sender, as you saw earlier in the discussion of SMTP connection establishment.

Table 77-2 lists the commands currently used in modern SMTP in the order they are described in RFC 2821, with a brief description of each.

Table 77-2: SMTP Commands

Command Code	Command	Parameters	Description
HELO	Hello	The domain name of the sender	The conventional instruction sent by an SMTP sender to an SMTP receiver to initiate the SMTP session.
EHLO	Extended Hello	The domain name of the sender	Sent by an SMTP sender that supports SMTP extensions to greet an SMTP receiver and ask it to return a list of SMTP extensions the receiver supports. The domain name of the sender is supplied as a parameter.
MAIL	Initiate Mail Transaction	Must include a FROM: parameter specifying the originator of the message, and may contain other parameters as well	Begins a mail transaction from the sender to the receiver.
RCPT	Recipient	Must include a TO: parameter specifying the recipient mailbox, and may also incorporate other optional parameters	Specifies one recipient of the email message being conveyed in the current transaction.

(continued)

Table 77-2: SMTP Commands (continued)

Command Code	Command	Parameters	Description
DATA	Mail Message Data	None	Tells the SMTP receiver that the SMTP sender is ready to transmit the email message. The receiver normally replies with an intermediate "go ahead" message, and the sender then transmits the message one line at a time, indicating the end of the message by a single period on a line by itself.
RSET	Reset	None	Aborts a mail transaction in progress. This may be used if an error is received upon issuing a MAIL or RCPT command, if the SMTP sender cannot continue the transfer as a result.
VRFY	Verify	Email address of mailbox to be verified	Asks the SMTP receiver to verify the validity of a mailbox.
EXPN	Expand	Email address of mailing list	Requests that the SMTP server confirm that the address specifies a mailing list, and return a list of the addresses on the list.
HELP	Help	Optional command name	Requests general help information if no parameter is supplied; otherwise, information specific to the command code supplied.
NOOP	No Operation	None	Does nothing except for verifying communication with the SMTP receiver.
QUIT	Quit	None	Terminates the SMTP session.

Like FTP commands, SMTP commands are not case-sensitive.

KEY CONCEPT The SMTP sender performs operations using a set of *SMTP commands*. Each command is identifies using a four-letter code. Since SMTP supports only a limited number of functions, it has a small command set.

The commands in Table 77-2 are those most commonly used in SMTP today. Certain other commands were also originally defined in RFC 821 but have since become obsolete. These include the following:

SEND, SAML (Send and Mail), and SOML (Send or Mail) RFC 821 defined a distinct mechanism for delivering mail directly to a user's terminal as opposed to a mailbox, optionally in combination with conventional email delivery. These were rarely implemented and obsoleted in RFC 2821.

TURN Reverses the role of the SMTP sender and receiver as described earlier in the SMTP special features discussion. This had a number of implementation and security issues and was removed from the standard in RFC 2821.

Finally, note that certain SMTP extensions make changes to the basic SMTP command set. For example, the *AUTH* extension specifies a new command (also called AUTH) that specifies an authentication method the SMTP client wants to use. Other extensions define new parameters for existing commands. For example, the SIZE extension defines a *SIZE* parameter that can be added to a *MAIL* command to tell the SMTP receiver the size of the message to be transferred.

SMTP Replies and Reply Codes

All SMTP protocol operations consist of the plain ASCII text SMTP commands you saw in Table 77-2, issued by the sender to the receiver. The receiver analyzes each command, carries out the instruction requested by the sender if possible, and then sends a reply to the sender. The reply serves several functions: confirming command receipt, indicating whether or not the command was accepted, and communicating the result of processing the command.

Just as SMTP commands are sent in a manner reminiscent of how FTP internal commands work, SMTP replies are formatted and interpreted in a way almost identical to that of FTP replies. As with FTP, the reply consists of not just a string of reply text, but a combination of reply text and a numerical *reply code*. And as with FTP, these reply codes use three digits to encode various information about the reply, with each digit having a particular significance. The reply code is really the key part of the reply, with the reply text being merely descriptive.

NOTE *The discussion of FTP reply codes in Chapter 72 contains a thorough explanation of the benefits of using these structured numeric reply codes.*

Reply Code Structure and Digit Interpretation

SMTP reply codes can be considered to be of the form *xyz*, where *x* is the first digit, *y* is the second, and *z* is the third.

The first reply code digit (*x*) indicates the success or failure of the command in general terms, whether a successful command is complete or incomplete, and whether an unsuccessful command should be tried again or not. This particular digit is interpreted in exactly the same way as it is in FTP, as shown in Table 77-3.

Table 77-3: SMTP Reply Code Format: First Digit Interpretation

Reply Code Format	Meaning	Description
1yz	Positive Preliminary Reply	An initial response indicating that the command has been accepted and processing of it is still in progress. The SMTP sender should expect another reply before a new command may be sent. Note that while this first digit type is formally defined in the SMTP specification for completeness, it is not currently used by any of the SMTP commands; that is, no reply codes between 100 and 199 exist in SMTP.
2yz	Positive Completion Reply	The command has been successfully processed and completed.

(continued)

Table 77-3: SMTP Reply Code Format: First Digit Interpretation (continued)

Reply Code Format	Meaning	Description
3yz	Positive Intermediate Reply	The command was accepted but processing it has been delayed, pending receipt of additional information. For example, this type of reply is often made after receipt of a DATA command to prompt the SMTP sender to send the actual email message to be transferred.
4yz	Transient Negative Completion Reply	The command was not accepted and no action was taken, but the error is temporary and the command may be tried again. This is used for errors that may be a result of temporary glitches or conditions that may change, such as a resource on the SMTP server being temporarily busy.
5yz	Permanent Negative Completion Reply	The command was not accepted and no action was taken. Trying the same command again is likely to result in another error. An example would be sending an invalid command.

The second reply code digit (*y*) is used to categorize messages into functional groups. This digit is used in the same general way as in FTP, but some of the functional groups are different in SMTP, as you can see in Table 77-4.

Table 77-4: SMTP Reply Code Format: Second Digit Interpretation

Reply Code Format	Meaning	Description
x0z	Syntax	Syntax errors or miscellaneous messages.
x1z	Information	Replies to requests for information, such as status requests.
x2z	Connections	Replies related to the connection between the SMTP sender and SMTP receiver.
x3z	Unspecified	Not defined.
x4z	Unspecified	Not defined.
x5z	Mail System	Replies related to the SMTP mail service itself.

The third reply code digit (*z*) indicates a specific type of message within each of the functional groups described by the second digit. The third digit allows each functional group to have ten different reply codes for each reply type given by the first code digit (preliminary success, transient failure, and so on).

Again, as in FTP, these *x*, *y*, and *z* digit meanings are combined to make specific reply codes. For example, the reply code 250 is a positive reply indicating command completion, related to the mail system. It is usually used to indicate that a requested mail command was completed successfully.

Table 77-5 contains a list of some of the more common SMTP reply codes taken from RFC 2821, in numerical order. For each, I have shown the typical reply text specified in the standard and provided additional descriptive information when needed.

As mentioned earlier, the actual text string for each reply code is implementation-specific. While the standard specifies dry response text such as "Requested action completed" for a 250 message, some servers will customize this code or even give different replies to different 250 messages, depending on the context.

Table 77-5: SMTP Reply Codes

Reply Code	Reply Text	Description
211	System status or system help reply.	
214	*<Help message...>*	Used for text sent in reply to the HELP command.
220	*<servername>* Service ready.	Greeting message sent when TCP connection is first established to an SMTP server.
221	*<servername>* closing transmission channel.	Goodbye message sent in response to a QUIT message.
250	Requested mail action ok, completed	Indicates successful execution of a variety of commands.
251	User not local; will forward to *<forward-path>*	Used when the SMTP receiver agrees to forward a message to a remote user.
252	Cannot VRFY user, but will accept message and attempt delivery	Indicates that a server tried to verify an email address, but was not able to do so completely. Usually means the address appears to be valid but it was not possible to ascertain this to be positively true.
354	Start mail input; end with <CRLF>.<CRLF>	Intermediate reply to a DATA command.
421	*<servername>* Service not available, closing transmission channel	Sent in response to any command when the SMTP receiver prematurely terminates the connection. A common reason for this is receipt of a local shutdown command, due to a hardware reboot, for example.
450	Requested mail action not taken: mailbox unavailable	Sent when a mailbox is busy due to another process accessing it.
451	Requested action aborted: local error in processing	Local processing problem on the server.
452	Requested action not taken: insufficient system storage.	Time to clean out the server's hard disk!
500	Syntax error, command unrecognized	Response to a bad command or one that was too long.
501	Syntax error in parameters or arguments	
502	Command not implemented	Command is valid for SMTP in general but not supported by this particular server.
503	Bad sequence of commands	Commands were not sent in the correct order, such as sending the DATA command before the MAIL command.
504	Command parameter not implemented.	
550	Requested action not taken: mailbox unavailable	Generic response given due to a problem with a specified mailbox. This includes trying to send mail to an invalid address, refusal to relay to a remote mailbox, and so forth.
551	User not local; please try *<forward-path>*	Tells the SMTP sender to try a different path; may be used to support mailbox forwarding.
552	Requested mail action aborted: exceeded storage allocation	User's mailbox is full.
553	Requested action not taken: mailbox name not allowed	Specification of an invalid mailbox address.
554	Transaction failed.	General failure of a transaction.

SMTP Multiple-Line Text Replies

As in FTP, it is possible for an SMTP reply to contain more than one line of text. In this case, each line starts with the reply code, and all lines but the last have a hyphen between the reply code and the reply text to indicate that the reply continues. The last line has a space between the reply code and reply text, just like a single-line reply. See the "Connection Establishment Using SMTP Extensions" section earlier in this chapter for an example of a multiple-line response to an EHLO command.

Enhanced Status Code Replies

When the ENHANCEDSTATUSCODES SMTP extension is enabled, this causes supplemental reply codes to be issued by the SMTP receiver in response to each command. These codes are similar in some respects to the standard reply codes; they also use three digits, but the digits are separated by periods. These enhanced codes provide more information about the results of operations, especially errors.

For example, if you try to issue a RCPT command specifying a remote mailbox on a server that does not support this feature, it will send back a 550 reply, which is a generic error meaning "requested action not taken: mailbox unavailable." When enhanced status codes are active, the response will be 550 5.7.1, which is the more specific message "delivery not authorized, request refused." A full description of these enhanced codes can be found in RFC 1893.

> **KEY CONCEPT** Each time the SMTP sender issues a command, it receives a *reply* from the SMTP receiver. SMTP replies are similar to FTP replies, using both a three-digit reply code and a descriptive text line. A special *enhanced status codes* SMTP extension is also defined; when enabled, this causes the SMTP receiver to return more detailed result information after processing a command.

78

TCP/IP ELECTRONIC MAIL ACCESS AND RETRIEVAL PROTOCOLS AND METHODS

The Simple Mail Transfer Protocol (SMTP) is responsible for most of the process of sending an electronic mail (email) message from the originator to the recipient. SMTP's job ends when the message has been successfully deposited into the recipient's mailbox on his local SMTP server.

In some cases, this mailbox is the end of the message's travels through cyberspace. More often, however, it is only a "rest stop"—the last step of the journey is for the message to be accessed and read by the user to whom it was sent. This may require that it be retrieved from the mailbox and transferred to another client machine. For a variety of reasons, SMTP is not used for the process of accessing a mailbox; instead, a special set of protocols and methods is designed specifically for email access and retrieval.

In this chapter, I describe some of the more common techniques used for TCP/IP email access and retrieval. I begin with an overview of the subject that describes in general the different paradigms used for email access and gives an overview of the protocols.

I then describe the operation of the very popular Post Office Protocol (POP), focusing on version 3 (POP3). I look at the protocol in general terms, discussing its history, the various versions of the protocol, and the standards that define them. I describe POP3's general operation and the communication between a client and server, concentrating on the three main states through which the session transitions. I then describe each of these states in sequence: the *Authorization* state, *Transaction* state, and *Update* state.

Following this, I discuss the other common mail access protocol: the Internet Message Access Protocol (IMAP). This includes a description of its benefits compared to the simpler POP3, a discussion of its operation, and a look at how client and server devices communicate, showing how the IMAP session moves through a series of four states.

Finally, I conclude with a discussion of two alternative methods of email access and retrieval. The first I call *direct server access,* which describes several ways that mailboxes are accessed without the use of special remote-access protocols such as POP and IMAP. The second is email access using a web browser. This is the newest email access method and is growing in popularity every year.

TCP/IP Email Mailbox Access Model, Method, and Protocol Overview

In an ideal world, every device on the Internet would run SMTP server software, and that one protocol would be sufficient to implement the entire TCP/IP email system. You would compose email on your machine, your SMTP software would send it to a recipient's machine, and she would read it.

Here in the real world, however, this is not possible in general terms. An SMTP server must be connected to the Internet and available around the clock to receive email sent at any time by any of the millions of other computers in the world. Most of us either cannot or do not want to run machines continuously connected to the Internet, nor do we want to configure and maintain potentially complex SMTP software. For these reasons, a complete email exchange normally involves not two devices but four: A message is composed on the sender's client machine, and then transferred to the sender's SMTP server, then to the recipient's SMTP server, and finally to the recipient's machine.

The communication between SMTP servers is done with SMTP; so is the initial step of sending the email from the sender's machine to the sender's SMTP server. However, SMTP is not used for the last part of the process, which is accessing the recipient's mailbox. Instead, specific mailbox access and retrieval protocols and methods were devised.

Why not simply have mail wait on the recipient's SMTP server, and then have the mail sent to the recipient client device when it comes online, using SMTP? This isn't possible for two main reasons. First, SMTP was designed for the specific purpose of transporting only email. Having it responsible for client mailbox access would require adding more functionality, making it difficult to keep SMTP *simple.* In the same vein, SMTP works on a *push* model, with transactions being initiated by the sender. It would need changes to allow it to respond to requests from a client device that is only online intermittently.

The second reason is probably more important, because the current protocol configuration allows *flexibility* in how email is accessed. If we used SMTP, all we would be able to do is transfer email to the recipient's client machine. This would be functional, but it would greatly limit the capabilities of how email is used, especially, for example, for users who wish to access mail directly on the server and manipulate it there. Also consider the problem of people with special requirements, such as those who travel and may need to access email from a number of different client devices. There is thus an advantage to providing more than one way to access a mailbox.

Email Access and Retrieval Models

RFC 1733, "Distributed Electronic Mail Models in IMAP4," describes three different paradigms, or models, for mail access and retrieval:

Online Access Model We would all be using this mode of access in my ideal world scenario, where every machine was always connected to the Internet running an SMTP server. We would have constant, direct online access to our mailboxes. In the real world, this model is still used by some Internet users, especially those who have UNIX accounts or run their own SMTP servers. I call this *direct server access.*

Offline Access Model In this paradigm, a user establishes a connection to a server where his mailbox is located. The user downloads received messages to the client device and then deletes them from the server mailbox. All reading and other activity performed on the mail can be done offline once the mail has been retrieved.

Disconnected Access Model This is a hybrid of online and offline access. The user downloads messages from the server, so she can read or otherwise manipulate them without requiring a continuous connection to the server. However, the mail is not deleted from the server, as in the offline model. At some time in the future, the user connects back with the server and synchronizes any changes made on the local device with the mailbox on the server. What sort of changes can be made? Examples include marking whether or not a message has been read to keep track of read and unread mail, and marking messages to which the user has already replied. These are important tools to help those with busy mailboxes keep track of what they need to do.

None of the three models is entirely better than the others. Each has advantages and disadvantages, which is why it is good that we have these options rather than the single SMTP protocol for mail access.

Direct server access has the main benefits of instant speed and universal access from any location. As for disadvantages, you must be online to read mail, and it usually requires that you use UNIX email clients, which with most people are not familiar. However, IMAP can also be used for online access.

Offline access has the main advantages of simplicity and short connection time requirements; you can easily connect to the mailbox, download messages, and then read them locally. But that makes this method somewhat inflexible and poorly suited to access from different machines. Still, it is currently the most popular access method because simplicity is important; it is best typified by POP.

Disconnected access attempts to combine the advantages of offline and online access without combining their disadvantages, and it does a pretty good job. The advantages are significant: the ability to access mail quickly and use it offline, while retaining and updating the mailbox on the server to allow access from different client machines. IMAP is popularly used for disconnected access. In the IMAP overview later in this chapter, I explore its advantages over offline access as well as its main disadvantages, which are complexity and far less universal support than POP (though acceptance of IMAP is slowly increasing).

Finally, in recent years, a somewhat new mailbox access method has become popular: email access using the World Wide Web. This technique allows a user to access his mailbox from any computer with an Internet connection and a web browser. It is a good example of line blurring, not only between the access models discussed here, but between TCP/IP applications—in this case, the Web and email.

> **KEY CONCEPT** For flexibility, TCP/IP uses a variety of mailbox access and retrieval protocols and methods to allow users to read email. Three different models describe how these different methods work: the *online model*, in which email is accessed and read on the server; the *offline model*, in which mail is transferred to the client device and used there; and the *disconnected model*, in which mail is retrieved and read offline but remains on the server with changes synchronized for consistency.

TCP/IP Post Office Protocol (POP/POP3)

The overall communication model used for TCP/IP email provides many options to an email user for accessing her electronic mailbox. The most popular access method today is the simple offline access model, in which a client device accesses a server, retrieves mail, and deletes it from the server. POP was designed for quick, simple, and efficient mail access; it is used by millions of people to access billions of email messages every day.

POP Overview, History, Versions, and Standards

Of the three mailbox access paradigms—online, offline, and disconnected—the offline model is probably the least capable in terms of features. And it is also the most popular. This may seem counterintuitive, but it is in fact a pattern that repeats itself over and over in the worlds of computing and networking. The reason is that *simplicity* and *ease of implementation* are keys to the success of any technology, and the offline mail access model beats the other two in these areas.

The history of offline email access goes back farther than one might expect—to the early 1980s. Two decades ago, not everyone and his brother were accessing the Internet to check email the way we do today. In fact, only a relatively small number of machines were connected using TCP/IP, and most users of these machines could access their email on a server, using the online access model.

However, even back then, developers recognized the advantages of being able to retrieve email from a server directly to a client computer, rather than accessing the mailbox on the server using Telnet or Network File System (NFS). In 1984, RFC

918 was published, defining POP. This protocol provided a simple way for a client computer to retrieve email from a mailbox on an SMTP server so it could be used locally.

The emphasis was on *simple*. The RFC for this first version of POP is only five pages long, and the standard it defined is extremely rudimentary. It describes a simple sequence of operations in which a user provides a name and password for authentication and then downloads the entire contents of a mailbox. Simple is good, but simple has limits.

RFC 937, "Post Office Protocol - Version 2" was published in February 1985. POP2 expanded the capabilities of POP by defining a much richer set of commands and replies. This included the ability to read only certain messages, rather than dumping a whole mailbox. Of course, this came at the cost of a slight increase in protocol complexity, but POP2 was still quite simple as protocols go.

These two early versions of POP were used in the mid-1980s, but not very widely. Again, this is simply because the need for an offline email access protocol was limited at that time; most people were not using the Internet before the 1990s.

In 1988, RFC 1081 was published, describing POP3. By this time, the personal computer (PC) was transitioning from a curiosity to a place of importance in the worlds of computing and networking. POP3 was based closely on POP2, but the new version was refined and enhanced with the idea of providing a simple and efficient way for PCs and other clients not normally connected to the Internet to access and retrieve email.

Development on POP3 continued through the 1990s, with several new RFCs published every couple of years. RFC 1081 was made obsolete by, in turn, RFCs 1225, 1460, 1725, and 1939. Despite the large number of revisions, the protocol itself has not changed a great deal since 1988; these RFCs contain only relatively minor tweaks to the original description of the protocol. RFC 1939 was published in 1996, and POP3 has not been revised since that time, though a few subsequent RFCs define optional extensions and additions to the basic protocol, such as alternative authentication mechanisms.

While POP3 has been enhanced and refined, its developers have remained true to the basic idea of a very simple protocol for quick and efficient email transfer. POP3 is a straightforward state-based protocol, with a client and server proceeding through three stages during a session. A very small number of commands is defined to perform simple tasks, and even after all its changes and revisions, the protocol has a minimum of fluff.

For reasons that are unclear to me, almost everyone refers to POP with its version number—that is, they say *POP3* instead of *POP*. This is true despite most people not using version numbers with many other protocols, and almost no one using any other version of POP. But it is the convention, and I will follow it in the rest of this discussion.

> **KEY CONCEPT** POP is currently the most popular TCP/IP email access and retrieval protocol. It implements the offline access model, allowing users to retrieve mail from their SMTP server and use it on their local client computers. It is specifically designed to be a simple protocol and has only a small number of commands. The current revision of POP is version 3, and the protocol is usually abbreviated *POP3*.

NOTE *Some implementations of POP attempt to implement the disconnected access model, with limited success. More often, however, IMAP is used for this purpose, since it is better suited to that access model. See the overview of IMAP later in this chapter for more details.*

POP3 General Operation

POP3 is a regular TCP/IP client/server protocol. In order to provide access to mailboxes, POP3 server software must be installed and continuously running on the server on which the mailboxes are located. This does not necessarily have to be the same physical hardware device that runs the SMTP server software that receives mail for those boxes—a mechanism such as NFS may be used to allow both the POP3 and SMTP servers to "see" mailboxes locally. POP3 clients are regular end-user email programs that make connections to POP3 servers to get mail; examples include Microsoft Outlook and Eudora Email.

POP3 uses TCP for communication, to ensure the reliable transfer of commands, responses, and message data. POP3 servers listen on well-known port number 110 for incoming connection requests from POP3 clients. After a TCP connection is established, the POP3 session is activated. The client sends commands to the server, which replies with responses and/or email message contents.

POP3 commands are three or four letters long and are case-insensitive. They are all sent in plain ASCII text and terminated with a CRLF sequence, just as with FTP and SMTP commands. POP3 replies are also textual, but the protocol does not use the complex three-digit reply code mechanism of FTP (and SMTP). In fact, it defines only two basic responses:

+OK A positive response, sent when a command or action is successful

-ERR A negative response, sent to indicate that an error has occurred

These messages may be accompanied by explanatory text, especially in the case of an ERR response, to provide more information about the nature of the error.

POP3 Session States

POP3 is described in terms of a *finite state machine (FSM)*, with a session transitioning through three states during the course of its lifetime, as shown in Figure 78-1. (I describe the concepts behind using FSM as a descriptive tool in Chapter 47.) Fortunately, unlike the FSMs of protocols like TCP, this one really is simple, because it is *linear*. The session goes through each state once and only once, in the following sequence:

1. **Authorization State** The server provides a greeting to the client to indicate that it is ready for commands. The client then provides authentication information to allow access to the user's mailbox.
2. **Transaction State** The client is allowed to perform various operations on the mailbox. These include listing and retrieving messages and marking retrieved messages for deletion.

3. **Update State** When the client is finished with all of its tasks and issues the QUIT command, the session enters this state automatically, where the server actually deletes the messages marked for deletion in the Transaction state. The session is then concluded, and the TCP connection between the two is terminated.

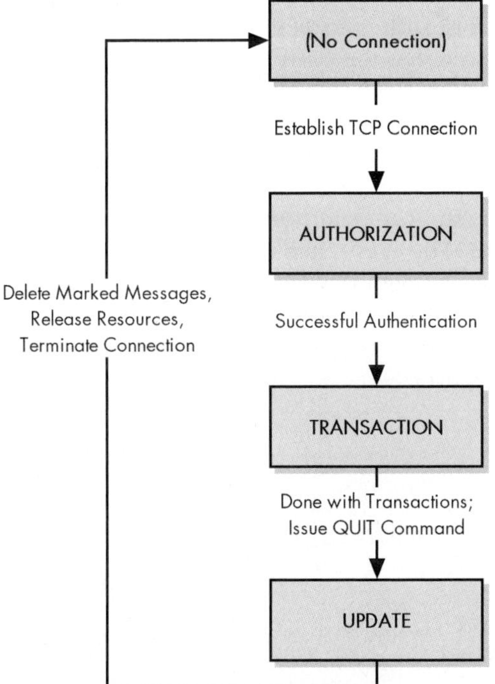

Figure 78-1: POP3 finite state machine
POP uses a finite state machine (FSM) to describe its operation, but it is very simple because it is linear. Once a TCP connection is established between a POP3 client and POP3 server, the session proceeds through three states in sequence, after which the connection is terminated.

POP3 is designed so that only certain commands may be sent in each of these states. Here, I will describe the activities that take place in these three states, including the commands that are issued by the client in each.

KEY CONCEPT POP3 is a client/server protocol that is described using a simple linear sequence of states. A POP3 session begins with a POP3 client making a TCP connection to a POP3 server, at which point the session is in the *Authorization* state. After successful authentication, the session moves to the *Transaction* state, where the client can perform mail access transactions. When it is finished, the client ends the session and the *Update* state is entered automatically, where cleanup functions are performed and the POP3 session ended.

POP3 Authorization State: User Authentication Process and Commands

A session between a POP3 client and a POP3 server begins when the client sends a TCP connection request to the server. The connection is established using the standard TCP three-way handshake, and the POP3 session commences. The first of the three states of a POP3 session, the Authorization state, is responsible for authenticating the POP3 client with the server.

When the session first enters this state, the server sends a greeting message to the client. This tells the client that the connection is alive and ready for the client to send the first command. An example of such a greeting follows:

```
+OK POP3 server ready
```

The client is now required to authenticate the user who is trying to access a mailbox. This proves that the user has the right to access the server and identifies the user so the server knows which mailbox is being requested.

The normal method of authorization in POP3 is a standard user name/password login. This is pretty much identical to how a login is performed in FTP; even the commands are the same. First the client issues a USER command along with the user's mailbox name (his user name or email address). The server responds with an intermediate acknowledgment. The client then uses the PASS command to send the user's password. Assuming the login is valid, the server responds to the client with an acknowledgment that indicates successful authentication. The response will also typically specify the number of messages waiting for the user in the mailbox. This process is illustrated in Figure 78-2.

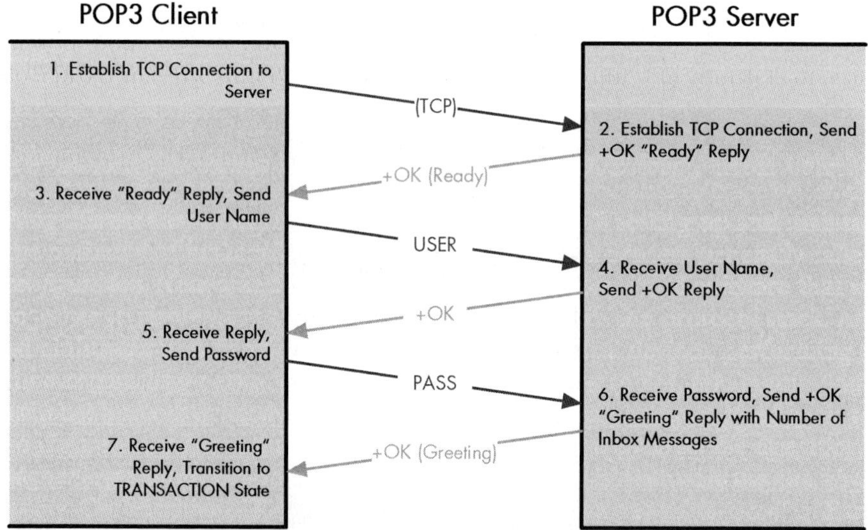

Figure 78-2: POP3 user authentication process *Once the TCP connection is established from the client to the server, the server responds with a greeting message, and the simple POP3 authentication process begins. The client sends a user name and password to the server using the USER and PASS commands, and the server evaluates the information to determine whether or not it will allow the client access.*

Listing 78-1 shows an example POP3 authorization, with the client's commands in boldface and the server's responses in italics.

NOTE *Some servers may require only the name of the user* (jane)*, while others require the full email address, as shown in Listing 78-1.*

```
+OK POP3 server ready
USER jane@somewhereelse.com
+OK
PASS *******
+OK jane@somewhereelse.com has 3 messages
```

Listing 78-1: *Example of POP3 authorization*

If authorization is successful, the POP3 session transitions to the Transaction state, where mail-access commands can be performed. If the user name or password is incorrect, an error response is given, and the session cannot proceed. The authorization may also fail due to technical problems, such as an inability by the server to lock the mailbox (perhaps due to new mail arriving via SMTP).

Since user name/password authorization is considered by many people to be insufficient for the security needs of modern internetworks, the POP3 standard also defines an alternative authentication method using the APOP command. This is a more sophisticated technique based on the Message Digest 5 (MD5) encryption algorithm. If the server supports this technique, in its opening greeting it provides a string indicating a *timestamp* that is unique for each POP3 session. The client then performs an MD5 calculation using this timestamp value and a shared secret known by the server and client. The result of this calculation is included in the client's APOP command. If it matches the server's calculation, authentication is successful; otherwise, the session remains in the Authorization state.

POP was also designed to be extendable through the addition of other authentication mechanisms. This process is based on the use of the optional AUTH command, as described in RFC 1734.

KEY CONCEPT A POP3 session begins in the Authorization state, where the client device is expected to authenticate with the server. By default, POP3 uses only a simple user name/password authentication method. Optional authentication methods are also defined for applications requiring more security.

POP3 Transaction State: Mail and Information Exchange Process and Commands

Once the POP3 client has successfully authenticated the user who is performing mailbox access, the session transitions from the Authorization state to the Transaction state. There's no real mystery as to what this phase of the connection is all about: The POP3 client issues the commands that perform mailbox access and message retrieval transactions.

Most of the commands defined in POP3 are valid only in the Transaction state. Table 78-1 lists each of them, in the order in which they appear in RFC 1939.

Table 78-1: POP3 Transaction Commands

Command Code	Command	Parameters	Description
STAT	Status	None	Requests status information for the mailbox. The server will normally respond, telling the client the number of messages in the mailbox and the number of bytes of data it contains. Optionally, more information may also be returned.
LIST	List Messages	Optional message number	Lists information for the messages in a mailbox; generally this means showing the message number and its size. If a message number is given, only that message's information is provided; otherwise, the full contents of the mailbox are described, one line at a time, with a line containing just a single period at the end.
RETR	Retrieve	Message number	Retrieves a particular message from the mailbox. The server responds with a standard +OK message and then immediately sends the message in RFC 822 format, one line at a time. A line with a single period is sent after the last line.
DELE	Delete	Message number	Marks a message as deleted. Once deleted, any further attempt to access a message (using LIST or RETR, for example) results in an error.
NOOP	No Operation	None	Does nothing; the server just returns an +OK reply.
RSET	Reset	None	Resets the session to the state it was in upon entry to the Transaction state. This includes undeleting any messages already marked for deletion.
TOP	Retrieve Message Top	Message number and number of lines	Allows a client to retrieve only the beginning of a message. The server returns the headers of the message and only the first *N* lines, where *N* is the number of lines specified. This command is optional and may not be supported by all servers.
UIDL	Unique ID Listing	Optional message number	If a message number was specified, returns a unique identification code for that message; otherwise, returns an identification code for each message in the mailbox. This command is optional and may not be supported by all servers.

The Transaction state is relatively unstructured in that commands do not need to be issued in any particular order to meet the requirements of the standard. However, there is a natural progression to how a mailbox is retrieved, and that means the commands are usually used in the following order:

1. The client issues a STAT command to see the number of messages in the mailbox.
2. The client issues a LIST command, and the server tells it the number of each message to be retrieved.
3. The client issues a RETR command to get the first message and, if successful, marks it for deletion with DELE. The client uses RETR/DELE for each successive message.

Listing 78-2 and Figure 78-3 show a sample access sequence for a mailbox containing two messages that total 574 bytes; the client's commands are in boldface and the server's responses are in italics.

```
STAT
+OK 2 574
LIST
+OK
1 414
2 160
.
RETR 1
+OK
(Message 1 is sent)
.
DELE 1
+OK message 1 deleted
RETR 2
+OK
(Message 2 is sent)
.
DELE 2
+OK message 2 deleted
QUIT
```

Listing 78-2: *Example of the POP3 mail exchange process*

The exact message sent in reply to each command is server-dependent; some say +OK, while others provide more descriptive text, as I have done here for the responses to the DELE command.

> **KEY CONCEPT** After successful authorization, the POP3 session transitions to the Transaction state, where the client actually accesses email messages on the server. The client normally begins by first retrieving statistics about the mailbox from the server and obtaining a list of the messages in the mailbox. The client then retrieves each message one at a time, marking each retrieved message for deletion on the server.

In some cases, a POP3 client may be configured to *not* delete messages after retrieving them. This is useful, for example, when Web-based access is being combined with a conventional email client program.

POP3 Update State: Mailbox Update and Session Termination Process and Commands

Once the POP3 client has completed all the email message access and retrieval transactions that it needs to perform, it isn't quite finished yet. The POP3 standard defines a final session state, the Update state, to perform various housekeeping functions, after which both the POP3 session and the underlying TCP connection are terminated.

The transition from the Transaction state to the Update state occurs when the POP3 client issues the QUIT command. This command has no parameters and serves to tell the POP3 server that the client is finished and wishes to end the session. The POP3 standard lists this command as part of its description of the Update state, though it is actually issued from the Transaction state.

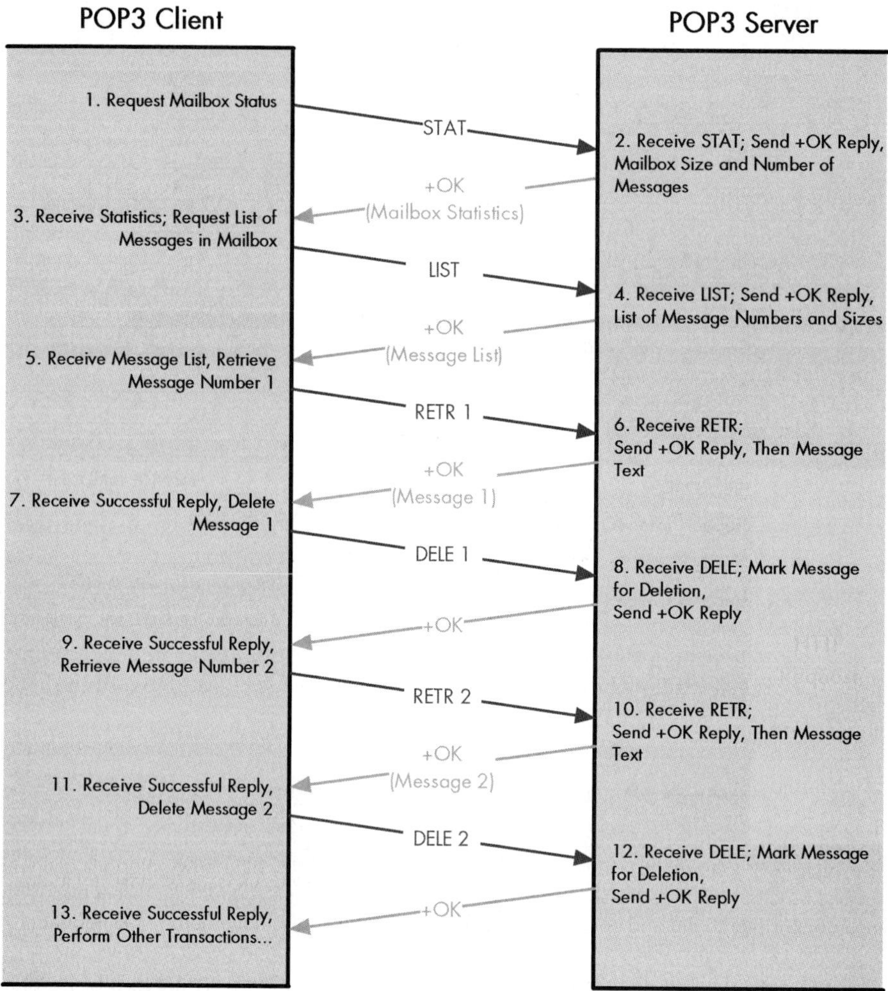

Figure 78-3: POP3 mail exchange process *This diagram shows the typical exchange of commands and replies employed by a POP3 client to retrieve email from a POP3 server. The STAT command is used to get mailbox statistics, followed by the LIST command to obtain a list of message numbers. Each message in turn is then retrieved using RETR and marked for deletion by DELE. (Messages are not actually deleted until the Update state is entered.)*

After the POP3 server receives the QUIT command, it deletes any messages that were previously marked for deletion by the DELE command in the Transaction state. It's interesting to note that POP chose to implement this two-stage deletion process. The standard doesn't describe specifically why this was done, but it seems likely that it is a precaution to insure against accidental deletion and loss of mail.

By delaying actual deletion until the Update state, the server can verify that it has received and processed all commands prior to the move to the Update state. This also allows the deletion of messages to be undone if necessary, using the RSET command, if the user changes her mind about the deletion prior to exiting the Transaction state. Finally, if any problem occurs with communication between the client and server that causes the TCP connection to be interrupted prematurely before the QUIT command is issued, no messages will be removed from the mailbox, giving the client a second chance to retrieve them in case they were not received properly.

Once the deleted messages have been removed, the server returns an acknowledgment to the client: +OK if the update was successful, or -ERR if there was a problem removing one or more of the deleted messages. Assuming no problems occurred, the +OK response will also contain a goodbye message of some sort, indicating that the session is about to be closed. The TCP connection between the client and server is then torn down and the session is done.

> **KEY CONCEPT** When the POP3 client is done with its email transactions, it issues the QUIT command. This causes the Update state to be entered automatically, where the server performs necessary cleanup operations, including deleting any messages marked for deletion in the Transaction state.

A POP3 mail-retrieval session normally lasts a few seconds or minutes, but it can take many minutes if the mailbox is large and the connection between the client and server is slow. There is no limit on how long the client and server can be connected, as long as commands continue to be sent by the client. A POP3 server will normally implement an inactivity timer, however, which is customizable but must have a duration of no less than ten minutes. If the connection is idle for the full duration of the inactivity timer, the server assumes that the client has experienced some sort of a problem and shuts down the connection. If this occurs, the server does not delete any messages marked for deletion—again, this is to give the client another chance to retrieve those messages if a problem occurred getting them the first time.

TCP/IP Internet Message Access Protocol (IMAP/IMAP4)

The offline mailbox access model provides the basic mail access functions that most users need. Using the popular POP3, a user can access her mailbox and retrieve messages so she can read them on her local machine. This model has the advantage of simplicity, but it does not provide many features that are increasingly in demand today, such as keeping track of the status of messages and allowing access from many client devices simultaneously. To provide better control over how mail is accessed and managed, we must use either the online or disconnected access models. IMAP was created to allow these access models to be used; it provides rich functionality and flexibility for the TCP/IP email user.

RELATED INFORMATION *The main price that IMAP pays for having a much richer set of functionality than POP is much more complexity. In this section, I have described IMAP in approximately the same level of detail that I did earlier for POP. Please see the appropriate RFC documents for the full description of the protocol and more discussion of some of its nuances, particularly the syntax of the many commands and parameters, which would take dozens of pages to cover fully here.*

IMAP Overview, History, Versions, and Standards

POP3 has become the most popular protocol for accessing TCP/IP mailboxes, not because of its rich functionality, but in spite of its lack of functionality. POP implements the offline mail access model, where mail is retrieved and then deleted from the server where the mailbox resides, so it can be used on a local machine. Millions of people use POP3 every day to access incoming mail. Unfortunately, due to the way the offline access model works, POP3 cannot be used for much else.

The online model is the one we would use in an ideal world, in which we all would be always connected to the Internet all the time. Offline access is a necessity, however, because most user client machines are connected to the Internet only periodically. The transfer of mail from the server to a client machine removes the requirement that we be online to perform mail functions, but it costs us the benefits of central mail storage on the server.

This may seem counterintuitive: how can it be better to have mail stored on some remote server rather than on our local computer? The main reason for this is flexibility of access. One of the biggest problems with offline access using POP3 is that mail is transferred permanently from a central server to one client machine. This is fine as long as an individual uses only that one machine, but what if the person has separate work and home computers or travels a great deal? And what about a mailbox shared by many users? These concerns have become more and more important in recent years.

Another issue is data security and safety. Mail servers run by Internet service providers (ISPs) are usually located in professionally managed data centers. They are carefully controlled and monitored, and backups occur on a routine basis. Most people do not take this sort of care with their own PCs and Macs, nor do they back up their data routinely. So, it's less likely that people will lose mail that on the server.

Of course, we still have the problem of not wanting to force users to be online all the time to access their mail. The solution is the disconnected mailbox access model, which marries the benefits of online and offline access. Mail is retrieved for local use as in the offline model, so the user does not need to be connected to the server continuously. However, changes made to the mailbox are synchronized between the client and the server. The mail remains on the server, where it can be accessed from a different client in the future, and the server acts as a permanent home base for the user's mail.

Recognizing these benefits, developers made some attempts to implement POP using the disconnected access model. Typically, this was done by using POP commands to retrieve mail but still leave it on the server, which is an option in many client programs. This works, but only to a limited extent; for example, keeping track of which messages are new or old becomes an issue when they are both retrieved and left on the server. POP simply lacks the features required for proper disconnected access because it was not designed for it.

In the mid-1980s, development began at Stanford University on a new protocol that would provide a more capable way of accessing user mailboxes. The result was the Interactive Mail Access Protocol, later renamed the Internet Message Access Protocol (IMAP).

IMAP Features

IMAP was designed for the specific purpose of providing flexibility in how users access email messages. It, in fact, can operate in all three of the access modes: online, offline, and disconnected access. Of these, the online and disconnected access modes are of interest to most users of the protocol; offline access is similar to how POP works.

IMAP allows a user to do all of the following:

- Access and retrieve mail from a remote server so it can be used locally while retaining it on the server.
- Set message flags so that the user can keep track of which messages he has already seen, already answered, and so on.
- Manage multiple mailboxes and transfer messages from one mailbox to another. You can organize mail into categories, which is useful for those working on multiple projects or those who are on various mailing lists.
- Determine information about a message prior to downloading it, to decide whether or not to retrieve it.
- Download only portions of a message, such as one body part from a MIME multipart message. This can be quite helpful in cases where large multimedia files are combined with short text elements in a single message.
- Manage documents other than email. For example, IMAP can be used to access Usenet messages.

Of course, there are some disadvantages to IMAP, but not many. One disadvantage is that it is more complex, but it's really not that complex, and the protocol has been around for enough years that this is not a big issue. The most important sticking point with IMAP is simply that it is used less commonly than POP, so providers that support it are not as easy to find as those that support POP. This is changing, however, as more people discover IMAP's benefits.

> **KEY CONCEPT** POP is popular because of its simplicity and long history, but it has few features and normally supports only the rather limited offline mail access method. To provide more flexibility for users in how they access, retrieve, and work with email messages, IMAP was developed. IMAP is used primarily in the online and disconnected access models. It allows users to access mail from many different devices, manage multiple mailboxes, select only certain messages for downloading, and much more. Due to its many capabilities, it is growing in popularity.

IMAP History and Standards

IMAP has had a rather interesting history—interesting in the sense that the normal orderly development process that is used for most TCP/IP protocols broke down. The result wasn't quite as bad as the chaos that occurred in the development of SNMP version 2 (see Chapter 65), but it was still unusual.

The first version of IMAP formally documented as an Internet standard was IMAP version 2 (IMAP2) in RFC 1064, published in July 1988. This was updated in RFC 1176, August 1990, retaining the same version number. However, it seems that some of the people involved with IMAP were not pleased with RFC 1176, so they created a new document defining version 3 of IMAP (IMAP3): RFC 1203, published in February 1991. This is described by its authors as a "counter proposal."

For whatever reason, however, IMAP3 was never accepted by the marketplace. Instead, people kept using IMAP2 for a while. An extension to the protocol was later created, called IMAP2bis, which added support for Multipurpose Internet Mail Extensions (MIME) to IMAP. This was an important development due to the usefulness of MIME, and many implementations of IMAP2bis were created. Despite this, for some reason IMAP2bis was never published as an RFC. This may have been due to the problems associated with the publishing of IMAP3.

NOTE bis *is a Latin word meaning again. It is sometimes used to differentiate changed technical documents from their previous versions when no official new version number is allocated.*

In December 1994, IMAP version 4 (IMAP4) was published in two RFCs: RFC 1730 describing the main protocol, and RFC 1731 describing authentication mechanisms for IMAP4. IMAP4 is the current version of IMAP that is widely used today. It continues to be refined; the latest specific version is actually called version 4rev1 (IMAP4rev1), defined in RFC 2060, and then most recently by RFC 3501. Most people still just call this *IMAP4*, and that's what I will do in the rest of this section.

IMAP General Operation

IMAP4 is a standard client/server protocol like POP3 and most other TCP/IP application protocols. For the protocol to function, an IMAP4 server must be operating on the server where user mailboxes are located. Again, as with POP3, this does not necessarily need to be the same physical server that provides SMTP service. The mailbox must in some way be made accessible to both SMTP for incoming mail, and to IMAP4 for message retrieval and modification. A mechanism for ensuring exclusive access to avoid interference between the various protocols is also needed.

IMAP4 uses the Transmission Control Protocol (TCP) for communication. This ensures that all commands and data are sent reliably and received in the correct order. IMAP4 servers listen on well-known port number 143 for incoming connection requests from IMAP4 clients. After a TCP connection is established, the IMAP4 session begins.

IMAP Session States

The session between an IMAP4 client and server is described in the IMAP standards using an FSM. Again, this is similar to how POP3 operates, except that IMAP4 is a bit more complex. Its FSM defines four states instead of three, and where a POP3 session is linear (going through each state only once) in IMAP4 the session is not. However, the state flow is still fairly straightforward, mostly following a logical sequence from one state to the next. The IMAP FSM is illustrated in Figure 78-4.

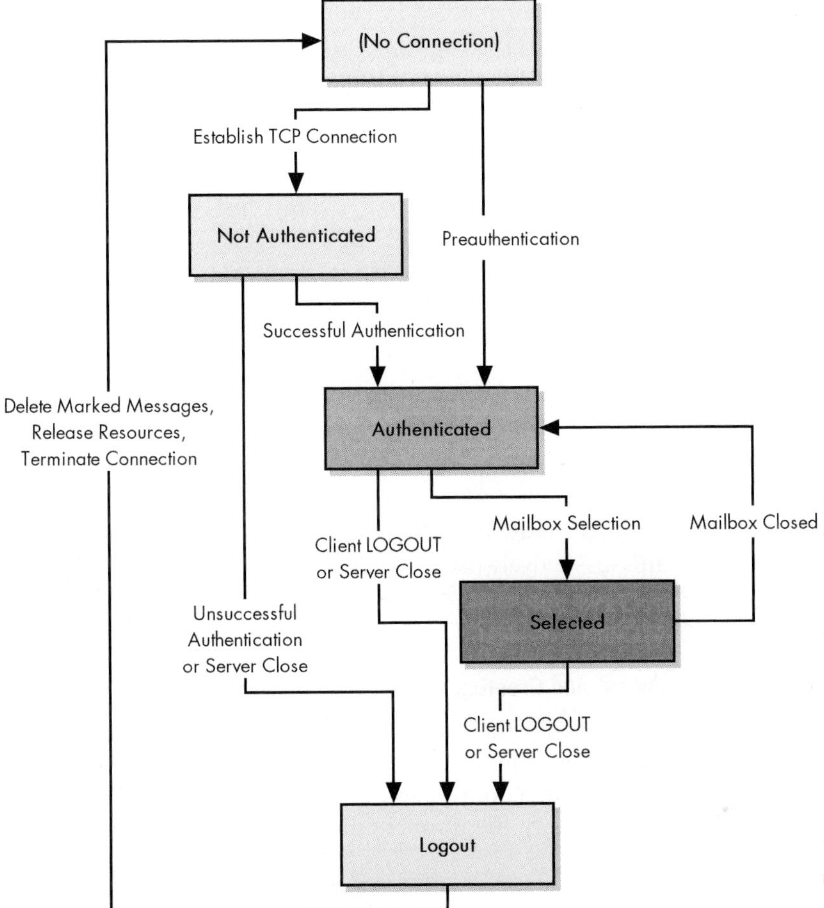

Figure 78-4: IMAP FSM *The IMAP FSM is slightly more complex than that of POP (shown in Figure 78-1) but it's still rather straightforward. Once the TCP connection is made between client and server, the Not Authenticated state is entered; after successful authorization, the session moves to the Authenticated state. The session may move between Authenticated and Selected several times, as different mailboxes are selected for use and then closed when no longer needed. From any state the session may be terminated, entering the Logout state.*

The following are the IMAP states, in the usual sequence in which they occur for a session:

1. **Not Authenticated State** The session normally begins in this state after a TCP connection is established, unless the special IMAP *preauthentication* feature has been used (we'll get to this feature shortly). At this point, the client cannot really do much aside from providing authentication information so it can move to the next state.
2. **Authenticated State** The client has completed authentication, either through an authentication process in the prior state or through preauthentication. The client is now allowed to perform operations on whole mailboxes. The client must select a mailbox before individual message operations are permitted.

3. **Selected State** After a mailbox has been chosen, the client is allowed to access and manipulate individual messages within the mailbox. When the client is finished with the current mailbox, it can close it and return to the Authenticated state to select a new one to work with, or it can log out to end the session.
4. **Logout State** The client may issue a Logout command from any of the other states to request that the IMAP session be ended. The session may also enter this state if the session inactivity timer expires. The server sends a response, and the connection is terminated.

> **KEY CONCEPT** IMAP is a client/server application, and an IMAP session begins with the client making a TCP connection to the server. The session then normally starts in the Not Authenticated state and remains there until successful authentication. In the Authenticated state, the client may perform operations on whole mailboxes, but a mailbox must be *selected* to transition to the Selected state, where individual messages can be manipulated. The client can work with many mailboxes by selecting each one in turn; it then logs out from the server.

Of the four IMAP states, only the first three are *interactive*, meaning states in which commands are actively issued by the client and responses provided by the server. Some IMAP commands can be used while the session is in any state; others are state-specific.

Session Establishment and Greeting

The server determines in which state the IMAP session begins and sends a *greeting* message to tell the client the session is established and indicate which state it is in. Normally, the server will begin the session in the Not Authenticated state. This is conveyed to the client with the normal OK greeting message, such as this:

```
* OK <server-name> server ready
```

Preauthentication

In certain circumstances, a server may already know the identity of the client, perhaps as a result of some external authentication mechanism not part of the IMAP protocol. In this case, a special greeting is used:

```
* PREAUTH <server-name> server ready, logged in as <user-name>
```

This tells the client that it is already in the Authenticated state.

If the server decides for whatever reason not to accept a new session from the client, it can respond with a BYE response, instead of OK or PREAUTH, and close the TCP connection.

IMAP Commands, Results, and Responses

Once an IMAP session is established, all communication between the client and server takes place in the form of *commands* sent by the client and *responses* returned by the server. Like POP3, commands and responses are sent as strings of ASCII text and terminated with a CRLF sequence, making them compatible with the way data is sent using the Telnet Protocol. However, IMAP has a few differences from POP and many other TCP/IP application protocols.

The first interesting thing about IMAP commands is that most are not abbreviated into codes of three or four letters—they are spelled out in full. So where POP3 has a STAT command, the command in IMAP is called STATUS. Commands are normally shown in uppercase, as I do in this book, but they are case-insensitive.

IMAP also uses an interesting system of *command tagging* to match client commands explicitly with certain server responses. Each time a client sends a command, it prefixes it with a tag that is unique for the particular session. The tags are usually short strings with a monotonically increasing number in them; the examples in the IMAP standards have the first command tagged a0001, the second a0002, and so on. That said, as long as each command is uniquely labeled, it doesn't matter what tagging scheme is used. When the server needs to send a response that is specific to a command, it tags the reply with the appropriate command tag. Not all replies are tagged, however.

The standard doesn't state explicitly why this tagging scheme is needed, but I believe it is probably related to IMAP's multiple command feature. IMAP clients are allowed to send a sequence of commands to the server to be processed, rather than sending commands only one at a time. This can improve performance when certain commands would take a long time to complete. The only restriction is that the commands must be independent enough that the result of executing them all would be the same, regardless of the order in which they were processed. For example, sending a command to read a particular entity in combination with a command to store a value into the same entity is not allowed.

KEY CONCEPT IMAP tags its commands with a unique identifier. These tags can then be used in replies by the server to match replies with the commands to which they correspond. This enables multiple commands to be sent to an IMAP server in succession.

Command Groups

IMAP commands are organized into groups based on which session states the IMAP session may be in when they are used:

"Any State" Commands A small number of commands that can be used at any time during an IMAP session.

Not Authenticated State Commands Commands that can be used only in the Not Authenticated state. They are usually used for authentication, of course.

Authenticated State Commands Commands used to perform various actions on mailboxes. (Note that despite the name, these commands can also be used in the Selected state.)

Selected State A set of commands for accessing and manipulating individual messages that can be used only in the Selected state.

The reason for having the distinct Authenticated and Selected states and command groups is that IMAP is designed specifically to enable the manipulation of multiple mailboxes. After the session starts and the client is authenticated, the client is allowed to issue commands that work with entire mailboxes. However, it may not issue commands that manipulate individual messages until it tells the server which mailbox it wants to work with, which puts it in the Selected state. The client can also issue mailbox commands from the Selected state.

NOTE *In addition to these four state groups, the standard also defines an* extension mechanism *that allows new commands to be defined. These must begin with the letter* X.

"Any State" Commands

Table 78-2 describes the IMAP "any state" commands, which can be used whenever needed.

Table 78-2: IMAP "Any State" Commands

Command	Parameters	Description
CAPABILITY	None	Asks the server to tell the client what capabilities and features it supports.
NOOP (No Operation)	None	Does nothing. May be used to reset the inactivity timer or to prompt the server periodically to send notification if new messages arrive.
LOGOUT	None	Tells the server that the client is done and ready to end the session, which transitions to the Logout state for termination.

Results and Responses

Each command sent by the IMAP client elicits some sort of reaction from the IMAP server. The server takes action based on what the client requested and then returns one or more text strings to indicate what occurred. The server can send two types of replies after a command is received:

Result A reply usually indicating the status or disposition of a command. It may be tagged with the command tag of the command whose result it is communicating, or it may be a general message that is not tagged.

Response Any type of information that is being sent by the server to the client. It is usually not tagged with a command tag and is not specifically intended to indicate server status.

NOTE *The IMAP standards sometimes use the terms* result, response, *and* reply *in a manner that I find to be inconsistent. Watch out for this if you examine the IMAP RFCs.*

KEY CONCEPT IMAP servers issue two basic types of replies to client commands: *results* are replies that indicate the success, failure, or status of a command; *responses* are general replies containing many different types of information that the server needs to send to the client.

Result Codes

Three main result codes are sent in reply to a command, and two special ones are used in certain circumstances:

OK A positive result to a command, usually sent with the tag of the command that was successful. May be sent untagged in the server's initial greeting when a session starts.

NO A negative result to a command. When tagged, indicates the command failed; when untagged, serves as a general warning message about some situation on the server.

BAD Indicates an error message. It is tagged when the error is directly related to a command that has been sent and otherwise is untagged.

PREAUTH An untagged message sent at the start of a session to indicate that no authentication is required; the session goes directly to the Authenticated state.

BYE Sent when the server is about to close the connection. It is always untagged and is sent in reply to a Logout command or when the connection is to be closed for any other reason.

Response Codes

In contrast to results, responses are used to communicate a wide variety of information to the client device. Responses normally include descriptive text that provides details about what is being communicated. They may be sent either directly in reply to a command or incidentally to one. An example of the latter case would be if a new message arrives in a mailbox during a session. In this case, the server will convey this information unilaterally at its first opportunity, regardless of what command was recently sent.

The following are the response codes defined by the IMAP standard:

ALERT An alert message to be sent to the human user of the IMAP client to inform him of something important.

BADCHARSET Sent when a search fails due to use of an unsupported character set.

CAPABILITY A list of server capabilities may be sent as part of the initial server greeting so the CAPABILITY command does not need to be used.

PARSE Sent when an error occurs parsing the headers or MIME content of an email message.

PERMANENTFLAGS Communicates a list of message status flags that the client is allowed to manipulate.

READ-ONLY Tells the client that the mailbox is accessible only in a read-only mode.

READ-WRITE Tells the client that the mailbox is accessible in read-write mode.

TRYCREATE Sent when an APPEND or COPY command fails due to the target mailbox not existing, to suggest to the client that it try creating the mailbox first.

UIDNEXT Sent with a decimal number that specifies the next unique identifier value to use in an operation. These identifiers allow each message to be uniquely identified.

UIDVALIDITY Sent with a decimal number that specifies the unique identifier validity value, used to confirm unique message identification.

UNSEEN Sent with a decimal number that tells the client the message that is flagged as not yet seen (a new message).

IMAP Not Authenticated State: User Authentication Process and Commands

An IMAP4 session begins with an IMAP4 client establishing a TCP connection with an IMAP4 server. Under normal circumstances, the IMAP4 server has no idea who the client is, and therefore starts the session in the Not Authenticated state. For security reasons, the client is not allowed to do anything until it is authenticated. Thus, the only purpose of this state is to allow the client to present valid credentials so the session can move on to the Authenticated state.

IMAP Authentication Methods

The IMAP4 standard defines three different mechanisms by which a client may authenticate itself. These are implemented using one or more of the three different commands allowed only in the Not Authenticated state, which are shown in Table 78-3.

Table 78-3: IMAP Not Authenticated State Commands

Command	Parameters	Description
LOGIN	User name and password	Specifies a user name and password to use for authentication.
AUTHENTICATE	Authentication mechanism name	Tells the server that the client wants to use a particular authentication mechanism and prompts the client and server to exchange authentication information appropriate for that mechanism.
STARTTLS	None	Tells the IMAP4 server to use the Transport Layer Security (TLS) protocol for authentication, and prompts TLS negotiation to begin.

In response to a LOGIN or AUTHENTICATE command, the server will send an OK message if the authentication was successful, and then transition to the Authenticated state. It will send a NO response if authentication failed due to incorrect information. The client can then try another method of authenticating or terminate the session with the LOGOUT command.

The three authentication methods are as follows:

Plain Login This is the typical user name/password technique, using the LOGIN command by itself. This is similar to the simple scheme used in POP3, except that in IMAP4 one command is used to send both the user name and password. Since the command and parameters are sent in plain text, this is by far the least secure method of authentication and is not recommended by the standard unless some other means is used in conjunction.

TLS Login This is a secure login where the Transport Layer Security (TLS) protocol is first enabled with the STARTTLS command, and then the LOGIN command can be used securely. Note that STARTTLS only causes the TLS negotiation to begin and does not itself cause the IMAP client to be authenticated. Either LOGIN or AUTHENTICATE must still be used.

Negotiated Authentication Method The AUTHENTICATE command allows the client and server to use any authentication scheme that they both support. The server may indicate which schemes it supports in response to a CAPABILITY command. After specifying the authentication mechanism to be used, the server and client exchange authentication information as required by the mechanism specified. This may require one or more additional lines of data to be sent.

> **KEY CONCEPT** IMAP supports three basic types of authentication: a plain user name/password login, authentication using the Transport Layer Security (TLS) protocol, or the negotiation of some other authentication method between the client and server. In some cases, the IMAP server may choose to preauthenticate clients that it is able to identify reliably; in which case, the Not Authenticated state is skipped entirely.

IMAP Authenticated State: Mailbox Manipulation/Selection Process and Commands

In the normal progression of an IMAP session, the Authenticated state is the first state in which the IMAP client is able to perform useful work on behalf of its user. This state will normally be reached from the Not Authenticated state after successful authentication using the LOGIN or AUTHENTICATE command. Alternately, a server may preauthenticate a client and begin the session in this state directly.

Once in the Authenticated state, the client is considered authorized to issue commands to the server. However, it may issue only commands that deal with *whole mailboxes.* As mentioned in the general operation overview, IMAP was created to allow access to, and manipulation of, multiple mailboxes. For this reason, the client must specify dynamically which mailbox it wants to use before commands dealing with individual messages may be given. This is done in this state using the SELECT or EXAMINE command, which both cause a transition to the Selected state.

It is also possible that the Authenticated state can be reentered during the course of a session. If the CLOSE command is used from the Selected state to close a particular mailbox, the server will consider that mailbox deselected, and the session will transition back to the Authenticated state until a new selection is made. The same can occur if a new SELECT or EXAMINE command is given from the Selected state but fails.

Authenticated State Commands

Table 78-4 provides a brief description of the mailbox-manipulation commands that can be used in the Authenticated state.

Table 78-4: IMAP Authenticated State Commands

Command	Parameters	Description
SELECT	Mailbox name	Selects a particular mailbox so that messages within it can be accessed. If the command is successful, the session transitions to the Selected state. The server will also normally respond with information for the client about the selected mailbox, as described after this table.
EXAMINE	Mailbox name	The same as the SELECT command, except that the mailbox is opened read-only; no changes are allowed.
CREATE	Mailbox name	Creates a mailbox with the given name.
DELETE	Mailbox name	Deletes the specified mailbox.
RENAME	Current and new mailbox names	Renames a mailbox.
SUBSCRIBE	Mailbox name	Adds the mailbox to the server's set of active mailboxes. This is sometimes used when IMAP4 is employed for Usenet message access.
UNSUBSCRIBE	Mailbox name	Removes the mailbox from the active list.
LIST	Mailbox name or reference string	Requests a partial list of available mailbox names, based on the parameter provided.
LSUB	Mailbox name or reference string	The same as LIST but returns only names from the active list.
STATUS	Mailbox name	Requests the status of the specified mailbox. The server responds providing information such as the number of messages in the box and the number of recently arrived and unseen messages.
APPEND	Mailbox name, message, optional flags, and date/time	Adds a message to a mailbox.

NOTE *All of the commands in Table 78-4 may also be used in the Selected state; they should really be called Authenticated+Selected state commands.*

When either the SELECT or EXAMINE command is successfully issued, the server will return to the client a set of useful information about the mailbox, which can be used to guide commands issued from the Selected state. This information includes the following three mandatory responses:

<*n*> EXISTS Tells the client the number of messages in the mailbox.

<*n*> RECENT Tells the client the number of recently arrived (new) messages.

FLAGS (<*flag-list*>) Tells the client which flags are supported in the mailbox. These include the following: `\Seen`, `\Answered`, `\Flagged` (marked for special attention), `\Deleted`, `\Draft`, and `\Recent`. (The backslashes are part of the flag names.)

The reply from the server may also contain these optional replies:

UNSEEN <*n*> The message number of the first unseen message.

PERMANENTFLAGS (<*flag-list*>) A list of flags (as for the FLAGS response above) that the client is allowed to change.

UIDNEXT <*n*> The next unique identifier value. This is used to check for changes made to the mailbox since the client last accessed it.

UIDVALIDITY <*n*> The unique identifier validity value, used to confirm valid UID values.

KEY CONCEPT In the Authenticated state, the IMAP client can perform operations on whole mailboxes, such as creating, renaming, or deleting mailboxes, or listing mailbox contents. The SELECT and EXAMINE commands are used to tell the IMAP server which mailbox the client wants to open for message-specific access. Successful execution of either command causes the server to provide the client with several pieces of important information about the mailbox, after which the session transitions to the Selected state.

IMAP Selected State: Message Manipulation Process and Commands

Once the IMAP client has been authorized to access the server, it enters the Authenticated state, where it is allowed to execute tasks on whole mailboxes. Since IMAP allows multiple mailboxes to be manipulated, message-specific commands cannot be used until the client tells the server which mailbox in wants to work with. Only one mailbox can be accessed at a time in a given session.

After the SELECT or EXAMINE command is successfully issued, the session enters the Selected state. In this state, the full palette of message and mailbox commands is available to the client. This includes the message-specific commands in Table 78-5 as the mailbox commands defined for the Authenticated state. Most of IMAP's message-specific commands do not include a mailbox name as a parameters, since the server knows automatically that the commands apply to whatever mailbox was selected in the Authenticated state.

The session remains in the Selected state for as long as the client continues to have work to do with the particular selected (or examined) mailbox. Three different actions can cause a transition out of the Selected state:

- If the client has nothing more to do when it is done with the current mailbox, it can use the LOGOUT command to end the session.
- The client can use the CLOSE command to tell the server it is finished with the current mailbox but keep the session active. The server will close the mailbox, and the session will go back to the Authenticated state.
- The client can issue a new SELECT or EXAMINE command, which will implicitly close the current mailbox and then open the new one. The transition in this case is from the Selected state back to the Selected state, but with a new current mailbox.

Selected State Commands

Table 78-5 lists the message-specific commands that can be used only in the Selected state.

Table 78-5: IMAP Selected State Commands

Command	Parameters	Description
CHECK	None	Sets a checkpoint for the current mailbox. This is used to mark when a certain sequence of operations has been completed.
CLOSE	None	Explicitly closes the current mailbox and returns the session to the Authenticated state. When this command is issued, the server will also implicitly perform an EXPUNGE operation on the mailbox.
EXPUNGE	None	Permanently removes any messages that were flagged for deletion by the client. This is done automatically when a mailbox is closed.
SEARCH	Search criteria and an optional character set specification	Searches the current mailbox for messages matching the specified search criteria. The server response lists the message numbers meeting the criteria.
FETCH	Sequence of message numbers and a list of message data items (or a macro)	Retrieves information about a message or set of messages from the current mailbox.
STORE	Sequence of message numbers, message data item name, and value	Stores a value for a particular message data item for a set of messages.
COPY	Sequence of message numbers and a mailbox name	Copies the set of messages specified to the end of the specified mailbox.
UID	Command name and arguments	Used to allow one of the other commands above to be performed using unique identifier numbers for specifying the messages to be operated on, rather than the usual message sequence numbers.

The list in Table 78-5 might seem surprisingly short. You might wonder, for example, where the specific commands are to read a message header or body, delete a message, mark a message as read, and so forth. The answer is that these (and much more) are all implemented as part of the powerful and flexible FETCH and STORE commands.

The FETCH command can be used to read a number of specific elements from either one message or a sequence of messages. The list of message data items specifies what information is to be read. The data items that can be read include the headers of the message, the message body, flags that are set for the message, the date of the message, and much more. The FETCH command can even be used to retrieve part of a message, such as one body part of a MIME multipart message, making it very useful indeed. Special macros are also defined for convenience. For example, the client can specify the message data item FULL to get all the data associated with a message.

The complement to FETCH, the STORE command, is used to make changes to a message. However, this command does not modify the basic message information such as the content of headers and the message body. Rather, it exists for changing the message's status flags. For example, after replying to a particular message, the client may set the `\Answered` flag for that message using the STORE command.

Message deletion in IMAP is done in two stages for safety, as in POP and many other protocols. The client sets the `\Deleted` flag for whichever messages are to be removed, using the STORE command. The messages are deleted only when the mailbox is expunged, typically when it is closed.

The search facility in IMAP4 is also surprisingly quite sophisticated, allowing the client to look for messages based on multiple criteria simultaneously. For example, with the appropriate syntax, you could search for "all posts that are flagged as having been answered that were sent by Jane Jones before April 1, 2004." Users of IMAP clients can thus easily locate specific messages even in very large mailboxes without needing to download and hunt through hundreds of messages.

KEY CONCEPT After the client opens a specific mailbox, the IMAP session enters the Selected state, where operations such as reading and copying individual email messages may be performed. The two most important commands used in this state are FETCH, which can be used to retrieve a whole message, part of a message, or only certain message headers or flags; and STORE, which sets a message's status information. IMAP also includes a powerful search facility, providing users with great flexibility in finding messages in a mailbox. When the client is finished working with a particular mailbox, it may choose a different one and reenter the Selected state, close the mailbox and return to the Authenticated state, or log out, automatically entering the Logout state.

TCP/IP Direct Server Email Access

This final portion of the journey of a TCP/IP email message is usually the job of an email access and retrieval protocol like POP3 or IMAP4. These are *customized* protocols, by which I mean that they were created specifically for the last step of the email communication process. However, there are also several *generic* methods by which an email client can gain access to a mailbox, without the use of a special protocol.

These methods are all variations of the online email access model. They generally work by establishing *direct access* to the server where the mailbox is located. The mailbox itself is just a file on a server somewhere, so if that file can be made available, it can be viewed and manipulated like any other file using an email client program that reads and writes the mailbox file. The following are some of the ways in which this can be done:

Using the SMTP Server Directly The simplest method for gaining access to the mailbox is to log on to the server itself. This is not an option for most people, and even in years gone by, it was not often done, for security and other reasons. However, some people do run their own SMTP servers, giving them considerable control over access to their email.

File Sharing Access Using a protocol such as NFS, it is possible to have a mailbox mounted on a user's client machine where it can be accessed as if it were a local file. The mail is still on the server and not the client machine, but the communication between the client and the server occurs transparently to both the user and the email client software.

Dial-Up Remote Server Access A user on a client machine dials up a server where her mailbox is located and logs in to it. The user then can issue commands to access mail on that server as if she were logged in to it directly.

Telnet Remote Server Access Instead of dialing in to the server, a user can connect to it for remote access using the Telnet Protocol.

These techniques are much more commonly associated with timesharing systems, which commonly use the UNIX family of operating systems more than others. They are also often combined; for example, remote access is often provided for UNIX users, but most companies don't want users logging in directly to the SMTP server. Instead, an ISP might run an SMTP server on one machine called *mail.companyname.com* and also operate a different server that is designed for client access called *users.companyname.com*. A user could access email by dialing into the users machine, which would employ NFS to access user mailboxes on the mail machine.

Direct server access is a method that has been around for decades. At one time, this was how the majority of people accessed email, for two main reasons. First, if you go back far enough, protocols like POP or IMAP had not yet been developed; the TCP/IP email system as a whole predates them by many years, and direct access was the only option back then. Second, the general way that email and networks were used years ago was different from what it is today. Most individuals did not have PCs at home, and no Internet as we know it existed. Remotely accessing a UNIX server using a modem or Telnet for email and other services was just the way it was done.

I got started using direct server access for email more than ten years ago, and I still use it today. I Telnet in to a client machine and use a UNIX email program called `elm` to access and manipulate my mailbox. To me, this provides numerous advantages:

- Most important, I can access my email using Telnet from any machine on the Internet, anywhere around the world.
- Since I am logged in directly, I get immediate notification when new mail arrives, without needing to check routinely for new mail.
- My mailbox is always accessible, and all my mail is always on a secure server in a professionally managed data center.
- I have complete control over my mailbox and can edit it, split it into folders, write custom spam filters, or do anything else I need to do.

This probably sounds good, but most people today do not use direct server access because of the disadvantages of this method. One big issue is that you must be logged in to the Internet to access your email. Another one, perhaps even larger, is the need to be familiar with UNIX and a UNIX email program. UNIX is simply not as user-friendly as a graphical operating systems such as Windows or the Mac. For example, my UNIX email program doesn't support color and cannot show me attached graphic images. I must extract images and other files from MIME messages and transfer them to my own PC for viewing.

Most ordinary computer users today don't know UNIX and don't want to know it. They are much happier using a fancy graphical email program based on POP3 or IMAP4. However, a number of us old UNIX dinosaurs are still around and believe the benefits of direct access outweigh the drawbacks. (Oh, one other benefit that I forgot to mention is that it's very hard to get a computer virus in email when you use UNIX!)

KEY CONCEPT Instead of using a dedicated protocol like POP3 or IMAP4 to retrieve mail, on some systems it is possible for a user to have direct server access to email. This is most commonly done on UNIX systems, where protocols like Telnet or NFS can give a user shared access to mailboxes on a server. This is the oldest method of email access. It provides the user with the most control over his mailbox and is well suited to those who must access mail from many locations. The main drawback is that it means the user must be on the Internet to read email, and it also usually requires familiarity with the UNIX operating system, which few people use today.

TCP/IP World Wide Web Email Access

Most email users like the advantages of online access, especially the ability to read mail from a variety of different machines. What they don't care for is direct server access using protocols like Telnet, UNIX, and nonintuitive, character-based email programs. They want online access, but they want it to be simple and easy to use.

In the 1990s, the World Wide Web was developed and grew in popularity very rapidly, due in large part to its ease of use. Millions of people became accustomed to firing up a web browser to perform a variety of tasks, to the point at which using the Web has become almost second nature. It didn't take very long before someone figured out that using the Web would be a natural way of providing easy access to email on a server.

This technique is straightforward. It exploits the flexibility of the Hypertext Transfer Protocol (HTTP) to tunnel email from a mailbox server to the client. A web browser (client) is opened and given a URL for a special web server document that accesses the user's mailbox. The web server reads information from the mailbox and sends it to the web browser, where it is displayed to the user.

This method uses the online access model like direct server access, because requests must be sent to the web server, and this requires the user to be online. The mail also remains on the server, as when NFS or Telnet are used. The big difference between Web-based mail and the UNIX methods is that the former is much easier for nonexperts to use.

Since the idea was first developed, many companies have jumped on the Webmail bandwagon, and the number of people using this technique has exploded into the millions in just a few years. Many free services even popped up in the late 1990s as part of the dot-com bubble, allowing any Internet user to send and receive email using the Web at no charge (except perhaps for tolerating advertising). Many ISPs now offer Web access as an option in additional to conventional POP/IMAP access, which is useful for those who travel.

There are drawbacks to the technique, however, which as you might imagine are directly related to its advantages. Web-based mail is easy to use, but inflexible; the user does not have direct access to her mailbox and can use only whatever features the provider's website implements. For example, suppose the user wants to search for a particular string in her mailbox; this requires that the Web interface provide this function. If it doesn't, the user is out of luck.

Web-based mail also has a disadvantage that is an issue for some people: performance. Using conventional UNIX direct access, it is quick and easy to read through a mailbox; the same is true of access using POP3, once the mail is downloaded.

In contrast, Web-based mail services mean each request requires another HTTP request/response cycle. The fact that many Web-based services are free often means server overload that exacerbates the speed issue.

Note that when Web-based mail is combined with other methods such as POP3, care must be taken to avoid strange results. If the Web interface doesn't provide all the features of the conventional email client, certain changes made by the client may not show up when Web-based access is used. Also, mail retrieval using POP3 by default removes the mail from the server. If you use POP3 to read your mailbox and then later try to use the Web to access those messages from elsewhere, you will find that the mail is gone—it's on the client machine where you used the POP3 client. Many email client programs now allow you to specify that you want the mail left on the server after retrieving it using POP3.

KEY CONCEPT In the past few years, a new method has been developed to allow email access using the World Wide Web. This technique is rapidly growing in popularity, because it provides many of the benefits of direct server access, such as the ability to receive email anywhere around the world, while being much simpler and easier than the older methods of direct access such as making a Telnet connection to a server. In some cases, Web-based email can be used in combination with other methods or protocols, such as POP3, giving users great flexibility in how they read their mail.

PART III-8

TCP/IP WORLD WIDE WEB AND THE HYPERTEXT TRANSFER PROTOCOL (HTTP)

In my overview of file and message transfer protocols in Chapter 71, I said that the World Wide Web was "almost certainly" the most important TCP/IP application. If anything, I was probably understating the case. The Web is not only quite clearly the most important TCP/IP application today, it is arguably the single most important application in the history of networking, and perhaps even computing as a whole.

This may sound a little melodramatic, but consider what the Web has done in the decade or so that it has been around. It has transformed not only how internetworks are used, but in many ways, it has also changed society itself. The Web put the Internet on the map, so to speak, moving it from the realm of technicians and academics to the mainstream world.

This part contains six chapters that describe the World Wide Web and the all-important *Hypertext Transfer Protocol (HTTP)*, the TCP/IP application layer protocol that makes the Web work. The first chapter discusses the Web and the concepts behind hypertext and hypertext documents in general terms. The second chapter provides an overview of HTTP and describes its operation in general terms, focusing on how connections are established and maintained. The third chapter outlines HTTP messages and how they are formatted, and describes HTTP methods (commands) and status codes. The fourth chapter details the many HTTP headers, which are critically important because they are the primary way that information is communicated between HTTP servers and clients. The fifth chapter provides information about how resources, called *entities*, are encoded and transferred in HTTP. The sixth and final chapter explores special features and capabilities of the modern HTTP protocol.

Like so many TCP/IP protocols, when HTTP was designed, its creators borrowed elements from other application protocols. In this case, HTTP uses certain elements from email, especially the Multipurpose Internet Mail Extensions (MIME). I would recommend familiarity with both the RFC 822 email message format and MIME, especially MIME headers and media types, before reading this part (both topics are covered in Chapter 76). The relationship between HTTP and MIME is covered more fully in Chapter 83, which discusses HTTP entities and media types.

79

WORLD WIDE WEB AND HYPERTEXT OVERVIEW AND CONCEPTS

The World Wide Web (the Web) expands the concepts of messaging beyond the limits of simple text file transfer of electronic mail (email), File Transfer Protocol (FTP), and Usenet. Its power is in its combination of *hypertext,* a system that allows related documents to be linked together, its rich document format that supports not just text but graphics and multimedia, and the special protocol that allows efficient movement of those media. The result is a powerful system that, once introduced, caught on almost immediately among everyone from large company users to individuals. In a few short years, the Web came to dominate all other applications on the Internet.

In this chapter, I take a high-level, summarized look at the concepts behind the Web. I begin with a short overview and history of the Web and hypertext and a discussion of the components that make up the Web system. I briefly describe the documents and media used on the Web and explain the importance of the Hypertext Markup Language (HTML). I conclude with an overview of how documents are addressed on the Web using Uniform Resource Locators (URLs).

World Wide Web and Hypertext Overview and History

The World Wide Web is one of the members of the class of Internet messaging applications. But for some reason, it just doesn't seem like a message transfer protocol to me. This led me to wonder, what is so special about the Web that caused it to become popular in a way that no prior messaging applications ever had?

There is no truly accurate one-word answer to this question. However, if I had to give one anyway, it would be this: *hypertext*. Sure, applications like email and Usenet allow users to send and receive information, and FTP lets a user access a set of files on a server. But what these methods lack is any way of easily representing the *relationship* between documents or providing a way of moving from one to another. Highly simplified, hypertext does exactly that: It allows the creator of a document to include links to related information, either elsewhere in that document or in other documents. With the appropriate software, a user can easily move from one location to another. So why is this a big deal? In fact, this is more important than it may initially seem.

Without some way of linking documents together, they remain in unconnected islands. In some ways, hypertext-linked documents are to unlinked documents what networked computers are to those that are not networked.

History of Hypertext

The ideas behind hypertext actually go back far beyond the Web and even electronic computers. Vannevar Bush (1890–1974) is generally credited with introducing the idea in his 1945 description of a theoretical device called the *Memex*, which was intended to be used to store and retrieve documents. He described the concept of a *trail* that would link together related information to make it easier to organize and access the information in the device.

Bush's ideas were used as the basis of the work of several researchers who followed. One of these was Ted Nelson, who coined the term *hypertext* and, in 1960, first described a system called *Xanadu*, which is considered one of the original hypertext software models.

The history of the Web itself goes back to 1989 at *CERN*, the European Organization for Nuclear Research, in Geneva. (The acronym stands for *Conseil Européen pour la Recherche Nucléaire*, the French name of the organization.) Many of the projects undertaken at CERN were large and complex, and they took many years to complete. They also involved many scientists who had to work with and share related documents.

A researcher at CERN, Tim Berners-Lee, proposed the idea of creating a "web" of electronically linked documents. The rapidly growing Internet was the obvious conduit for this project. He designed the first (very crude and simple) version of HTTP for TCP/IP in 1990. He was also responsible for developing or co-developing several of the other key concepts and components behind the Web, such as Uniform Resource Identifiers (URIs) and HTML.

The ability to link documents and files had tremendous appeal, and it took little time before creative individuals found many different uses for this new technology. The early 1990s saw a flurry of development activity. Web server and client software was developed and refined, and the first graphical web browser, *Mosaic*, was created by the National Center for Supercomputer Applications (NCSA) in 1993. (The developer of this program, Marc Andreessen, eventually formed Netscape Communications.)

Once the Web started to form, it grew very quickly indeed. In fact, to call the growth of the Web anything but *explosive* would not do it justice. In early 1993, only 50 active HTTP web servers existed. By late 1993, more than 1,000 were in service. By late 1995, thousands of new websites were coming online every day, and HTTP requests and responses had overtaken all other TCP/IP application traffic. By the end of the decade, *millions* of websites and more than a billion documents were available on the Web.

The World Wide Web Today

While the rapid growth in the size of the Web is amazing, what is even more fascinating is its growth in *scope*. Since you are reading a book about networking, you are most likely a Web user who is familiar with the incredible array of different types of information you can find on the Web today. Early hypertext systems were based on the use of only text documents; today the Web is a world of many media including pictures, sounds, and movies. The term *hypertext* has in many contexts been replaced with the more generic *hypermedia*—functionally, if not officially.

The Web has also moved beyond providing simple document retrieval to providing a myriad of services. A website can serve up much more than just documents, allowing users to run thousands of kinds of programs to do everything from shop to play music or games online. Websites are also blurring the lines between different types of applications, offering Web-based email, Web-based Usenet access, bulletin boards, and other interactive forums for discussion.

The Web has had an impact on both networking and society as a whole that even its most enthusiastic early fans could never have anticipated. In fact, the Web was the ultimate "killer application" for the Internet as a whole. In the early 1990s, big corporations viewed the Web as an amusing curiosity; by the end of the decade, it was for many a business necessity. Millions of individuals and families discovered the wealth of information at their fingertips, and Internet access became for many another necessary utility, like telephone service. In fact, the huge increase in Web traffic volume spawned the spending of billions of dollars on Internet infrastructure.

The dot-com collapse of the early twenty-first century took some of the wind out of the Web's sails. The incredible growth of the Web could not continue at its original pace and has slowed somewhat. But the Web as a whole continues to expand and mature, and it will likely be the most important information and service resource on the Internet for some time to come.

> **KEY CONCEPT** The World Wide Web (the Web or WWW) began in 1989 as a project designed to facilitate the representation of relationships between documents and the sharing of information between researchers. The main feature of the Web that makes it so powerful is hypertext, which allows links to be made from one document to another. The many benefits of the Web caused it to grow in only a few short years from a small application to the largest and arguably most important application in the world of networking. It is largely responsible for bringing the Internet into the mainstream of society.

World Wide Web System Concepts and Components

Hypertext is the main concept that makes the Web more than just another message transfer system. However, the idea behind hypertext had been around for decades before the Web was born, as had certain software products based on that idea. Obviously, more than just a concept is needed for an idea to be developed into a successful system.

The Web became a phenomenon because it combined the basic idea of hypertext with several other concepts and technologies to create a rich, comprehensive mechanism for interactive communication. This system today encompasses so many different concepts and software elements, and is so integrated with other technologies, that it's difficult to find any two people who agree on what exactly the Web comprises, and which parts are most critical.

For example, one of the keys to the success of the Web is undeniably the combination of the TCP/IP internetworking protocol suite and the Internet infrastructure that connects together the computers of the world. Is the Internet then an essential component of the Web? In many ways, it is; and, in fact, due to how popular the Web is today, it is common to hear people refer to the Web as *the Internet.* We know that this is not a precise use of terms, of course, but it shows how important the Web has become and how closely it is tied to the Internet.

Major Functional Components of the Web

While the Internet and TCP/IP are obviously important parts of the Web's success, they are generic in nature. When it comes to defining the Web system itself more specifically, three particular components are usually considered most essential (see Figure 79-1):

Hypertext Markup Language HTML is a text language used to define hypertext documents. The idea behind HTML was to add simple constructs, called *tags*, to regular text documents, to enable the linking of one document to another, as well as to allow special data formatting and the combining of different types of media. HTML has become the standard language for implementing information in hypertext and has spawned the creation of numerous related languages.

Hypertext Transfer Protocol HTTP is the TCP/IP application layer protocol that implements the Web, by enabling the transfer of hypertext documents and other files between a client and server. HTTP began as a very crude protocol for transferring HTML documents between computers, and it has evolved to a full-featured and sophisticated messaging protocol. It supports transfers of many different kinds of documents, streaming of multiple files on a connection, and various advanced features including caching, proxying, and authentication.

Uniform Resource Identifiers URIs are used to define labels that identify resources on an internetwork so that they can be easily found and referenced. URIs were originally developed to provide a means by which the users of the Web could locate hypertext documents so they could be retrieved. URIs are actually not specific to the Web, though they are most often associated with the Web and HTTP.

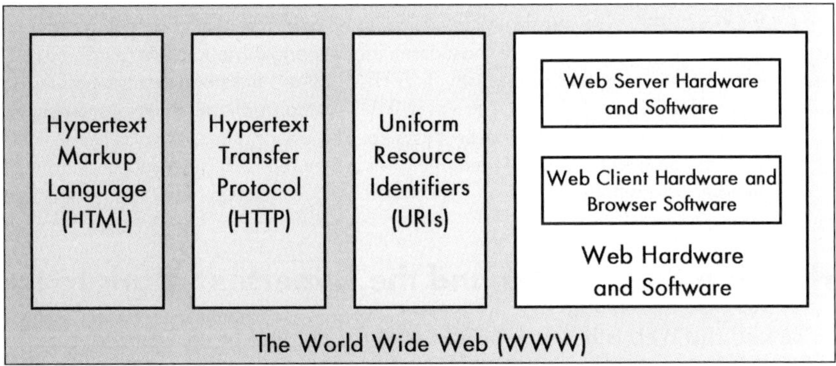

Figure 79-1: *Major functional components of the World Wide Web*

NOTE *Uniform Resource Locators (URLs) are actually a subset of Uniform Resource Identifiers (URIs). The terms are often used interchangeably in World Wide Web discussions.*

All three of these components were created and developed at around the same time, and taken together they represent the key technologies that define the Web. In this chapter, I'll describe HTML and the use of URIs in the context of the Web. HTTP is really the heart of the Web and is covered in the remaining five chapters of this part of the book.

Web Servers and Web Browsers

These three main Web components are supplemented by a number of other elements that play supporting roles in rounding out the system as a whole. Chief among these are the hardware and software used to implement client/server communication that makes the Web work, also illustrated in Figure 79-1: *web servers* and *web browsers.*

Web servers are computers that run special server software that allows them to provide hypertext documents and other files to clients who request them. Millions of such machines around the world now serve as a virtual distributed repository of the enormous wealth of information that the Web represents.

Web browsers are HTTP client software programs that run on TCP/IP client computers to access web documents on web servers. These browser programs retrieve hypertext documents and display them, and they also implement many of the Web's advanced features, such as caching. Today's browsers support a wide variety of media, allowing the Web to implement many different functions aside from hypertext document transfer. Examples include displaying images, playing sounds, and implementing interactive programs.

Last, but certainly not least, the *users* of the Web are perhaps its most important component. User involvement has had more of a role in shaping the development of Web technology than any other networking application. The Web began as a simple means of exchanging documents; today, it has grown to encompass thousands of different applications and services, largely as a result of the creativity of its users. Content providers have pushed the boundaries of what the Web can do by creating new ideas for information and services to satisfy the insatiable demands of the end-user community.

KEY CONCEPT The World Wide Web is a complete system comprising a number of related components, of which three are most essential. Hypertext Markup Language (HTML) describes how hypertext documents are constructed. HTML allows links between documents to be represented. The Hypertext Transfer Protocol (HTTP) is the application layer protocol that moves hypertext and other documents over the Web. The Uniform Resource Identifier (URI) mechanism provides a consistent means of identifying resources, both on the Web and more generally on the Internet as a whole.

World Wide Web Media and the Hypertext Markup Language

I've said the Web is based around the central concept of *hypertext*. The prefix *hyper* usually means above or beyond, and thus *hypertext* is like text but goes beyond it in terms of functionality. Documents written in hypertext are similar to regular text files but include information that implements hypertext functions. These are usually called *hypertext documents* or *hypertext files*.

The extra information in a hypertext document is used to tell the computer program that displays the file how to format it. This information takes the form of special instructions that are interspersed with the actual text of the document itself, which are written according to the syntax of a defining language. This addition of extra elements to the content of a document is commonly called *marking up* the document.

Overview of HTML

HTML is one of the three primary system components of the Web and was invented in 1990 by the creator of the Web, Tim Berners-Lee. It was not created in a vacuum; rather, it is a specific application of the general concept of a markup language that is described in ISO standard 8879:1986—the *Standard Generalized Markup Language (SGML)*.

A markup language defines special items that provide information to the software displaying the document about how it should be presented. For the purposes of hypertext, the most basic type of information in a document is a special instruction that specifies how one document can be linked to another—after all, this linking process is the defining attribute of hypertext.

However, HTML goes far beyond just this; it defines a full set of text codes used for describing nearly every aspect of how a document is shown to a user. This includes instructions for formatting text (such as defining its color, size, and alignment), interactive forms, methods for displaying tabular data, specifications for how to present images and other media along with the document, and much more. In theory, the language is only supposed to define the document and leave how it should be displayed up to the browser, but in practice, modern HTML documents also usually contain rather specific instructions for how their information should be presented.

To do justice to HTML, I would need to devote several dozen pages to the subject. I have decided not to do this, because even though HTML is an important part of the Web, it is actually not that important in understanding how the Web works. Knowing HTML is essential if you are writing Web content, and it is also critical if you want to understand how to write Web software. Perhaps ironically, though, to the actual mechanisms that make the Web work, such as HTTP, a document is a document. HTTP is not designed under the assumption that it will transfer HTML, and in most cases, servers do not even look at the contents of an HTML file—they just transfer it.

That said, a basic understanding of HTML is important, and it just wouldn't seem right not to provide at least an overview of the language, so I will do that here. I encourage you to seek out one of the many good HTML resources if you want to learn more—you'll find dozens of them on the Web (where else?).

HTML Elements and Tags

In simplest terms, an HTML document is a plain ASCII text file, like an email message or other text document. The biggest difference between HTML and regular text is that HTML documents are *structured*; that is, the document is logically organized into a series of *elements* that are arranged according to the rules of the language. Each element defines one part of the document as a whole. The title of a document, a paragraph, a table, and a hyperlink to another document are all examples of elements.

Each element is described using special text *tags* that follow a particular syntax. Each tag begins with the < symbol, which is then followed by the (case-insensitive) element name, and optionally, additional parameters that describe the element. The tag ends with the > symbol. Here's how a tag looks generally:

```
<element parameter1="value1" parameter2="value2". . .>
```

Some elements are entirely described by the presence of a tag, and in such cases, that tag is the entire element. More often, tags occur in pairs surrounding the actual content of the element; the *start tag* begins with the name of the element, and the *end tag* begins with a slash symbol followed by the name of the element. For example, the title of a document is an element that can be defined as follows:

```
<title>This Is A Great Story</title>
```

The content of each element can contain other elements, which causes tags to be nested within each other. For example, if we wanted to highlight the word *Great* in our title by displaying it in bold letters, we can add the `<b>` tag as follows:

```
<title>This Is A <b>Great</b> Story</title>
```

Each whole HTML document is defined as a single element called `html`; the whole document is enclosed in `<html>` and `</html>` tags. Within this element, the document is divided into two standard subelements that must be present in each document: the `head` and the `body`. The `head` of the document contains information that describes the document and how it is to be processed; it most commonly contains the title of the document. The body contains the actual content of the document. These three elements define the basic HTML document structure, as follows:

```
<html>
<head>
(head elements go here...)
</head>
<body>
(body elements go here...)
</body>
</html>
```

The bulk of the document consists of the body elements that are placed between the <body> and </body> tags. HTML documents can range from very simple bodies containing only elements such as text paragraphs and perhaps a few links, to very sophisticated documents that are computer-generated and contain hundreds or even thousands of nested tags of various sorts.

Common HTML Elements

Table 79-1 provides a brief description of some of the more common elements used in the body of an HTML message and the tags that define them, to give you a feel for how the language works.

Table 79-1: Common HTML Elements

Element	Example Element and Tags	Description
Paragraph	`<p>Jack and Jill went up the hill to fetch a pail of water...</p>`	Delineates a paragraph of text. Note that everything between the start and end tags will be considered one paragraph, even if split onto multiple lines as I have done here. Line breaks are not significant in HTML formatting; only tags are recognized.
Line Break	`George W. Bush ` `The White House ` `1600 Pennsylvania Ave., NW ` `Washington, DC 20500`	Forces a line break. Used instead of the paragraph tag to present lines close together, such as addresses.
Heading	`<h1>First Topic</h1>` `<h2>Subtopic</h2>`	Defines section headings to allow information in a long document to be displayed in hierarchical form. Six sets of tags are defined, from <h1> and </h1> to <h6> and </h6>. Browsers will automatically display the higher-level headings in more prominent ways, by using larger fonts, underlining the text, or similar treatment.

List	`<p>Shopping list:`
	`<ul>`
	`<li>Milk`
	`<li>Eggs`
	`<li>Sushi`
	`</ul>`
	`</p>`
		Allows information to be presented as a list. The tag <ul> means unnumbered list and causes the list items to be shown usually as bullet points. Alternatively, <ol> (ordered list) can be used to show the items preceded by 1, 2, 3, and so on.

(continued)

Table 79-1: Common HTML Elements (continued)

Element	Example Element and Tags	Description

Horizontal Rule	`...end of this part of the story.</p>`
	`<hr size= "3">`
	`<p>Start of next part of story...`
		Draws a horizontal line across the page; the size parameter controls its thickness. Used to separate logical sections in a document.

Image	`<img src="companylogo.gif" alt="XYZ Industries Logo" align="center">`	Displays an inline image in the appropriate section of the text. The `src` parameter is a relative or absolute URL for the image, and numerous other parameters can be included to define the image's alignment, size, alternate text to display if the browser is nongraphical (as shown here with the `alt` parameter), and much more.
Link	`<a href="http://www.PCGuide.com">Click here to visit The PC Guide</a>`	Hyperlinks to another document. The *a* in the tag stands for anchor, which is the formal name for a hyperlink. The `href` parameter specifies the URL of the link. Most browsers will underline or otherwise highlight text between the start and end tags to make it clear that the text represents a hyperlink. It is also possible to give a hyperlink to an image by combining the `<img>` and `<a>` tags.
Bookmark	`<a name="Step4">Step 4: Remove paint using scrubbing tool.</a>`	Creates a bookmark that can be used to hyperlink to a particular section in a document. For example, if the bookmark in this example was in a document at URL http://www.homefixitup.com/repainting.htm, the URL http://www.homefixitup.com/repainting.htm#Step4 refers to this particular place in the document. See the discussion of URLs later in this chapter for more details.

Table	`<table>`
	`<tr>`
	`<td>1st row, 1st column.</td>`
	`<td>1st row, 2nd column.</td>`
	`</tr>`
	`<tr>`
	`<td>2nd row, 1st column.</td>`
	`<td>2nd row, 2nd column.</td>`
	`</tr>`
	`</table>`
		Displays information in tabular form. Each `<tr>` and `</tr>` tag set defines one row of the table; within each row, each `<td>` and `</td>` pair defines one table data element. Many different parameters can be provided for each of these tags to control table size and appearance.

Form	`<form method="POST" action="https://www.myfavesite.com/order.php">`
	`<input type="hidden" name="PRODUCT" value="widget">`
	`<input type="text" name="QUANTITY" size="3">`
	`<input type="submit" value="Click Here to Proceed to the Secure Processing Site">`
	`</form>`
		Defines an HTML form, allowing various sorts of information to be submitted by a client to a program on a website designed to process forms. The form consists of the initial `<form>` tag that describes what action to be taken when the submission button is pressed, and other form items such as predefined variables, text-entry fields, and buttons. One example of each of these items is shown here.

Script	`<script language=javascript>`
	`(JavaScript code)`
	`</script>`
		Allows instructions in a scripting language to be included in an HTML document. It is most often used for JavaScript.

Common Text Formatting Tags

Numerous tags are used to format the appearance of text within a document; here are some of the more common ones:

`<b>text</b>` Present the enclosed text in boldface.

`<i>text</i>` Present the enclosed text in italics.

`<u>text</u>` Present the enclosed text underlined.

`<font (parameters)>text</font>` Present the enclosed text using the indicated font type, size, or color.

This is just the tip of the iceberg when it comes to HTML. If you are not familiar with HTML, however, knowing these basic tags should help you interpret basic HTML documents and learn how HTTP works.

KEY CONCEPT The language used by World Wide Web hypertext documents is called HTML. HTML documents are like ASCII text files, but they are arranged using a special structure of HTML elements that define the different parts of the document and how they should be displayed to the user. Each element is described using special text tags that define it and its characteristics.

World Wide Web Addressing: HTTP Uniform Resource Locators

The main reason that hypertext is so powerful and useful is that it allows related documents to be linked together. In the case of the Web, this is done using a special set of HTML tags that specifies in one document the name of another document that is related in some important way. A user can move from one document to the next using a simple mouse click. The Web has succeeded largely on the basis of this simple and elegant method of referral.

The notion of hyperlinking has some important implications on how Web documents and other resources are addressed. Even though the Web is at its heart a message transfer protocol similar to FTP, the need to be able to define hyperlinks meant that the traditional FTP model of using a set of commands to specify how to retrieve a resource had to be abandoned. Instead, a system was needed whereby a resource could be uniquely specified using a simple, compact string.

The result of this need was the definition of one of the three primary elements of the Web: the *URI*. URIs are divided into two categories: *Uniform Resource Locators (URLs)* and *Uniform Resource Names (URNs)*. While URIs, URLs, and URNs grew out of the development of the Web, they have now been generalized to provide an addressing mechanism for a wide assortment of TCP/IP application layer protocols. They are described in detail in Chapter 70. Here, we will look at how they are used specifically for the Web.

Currently, the Web uses URLs almost exclusively; URNs are still in development. Web URLs specify the use of HTTP for resource retrieval and are thus normally called *HTTP URLs*. These URLs allow a resource such as a document, graphical image, or multimedia file to be uniquely addressed by specifying the host name, directory path, and filename where it is located.

> **KEY CONCEPT** Uniform Resource Identifiers (URIs) were developed to allow World Wide Web resources to be easily and consistently identified; they are also now used for other protocols and applications. The type of URI currently used on the Web is the Uniform Resource Locator (URL), which identifies the use of HTTP to retrieve a resource, and provides information on where and how it can be found and retrieved.

HTTP URL Syntax

HTTP URLs may be absolute or relative (see "URL Relative Syntax and Base URLs" in Chapter 70 for details on the difference between them). Absolute URLs are usually used for hyperlinks from one website to another or by users requesting a new document without any prior context. Absolute HTTP URLs are based on the following common Internet URL syntax:

```
<scheme>://<user>:<password>@<host>:<port>/<urlpath>;<params>?<query>#<fragment>
```

For the Web, the scheme is `http:`, and the semantics of the different URL elements are defined to have meanings that are relevant to the Web. The general structure of an HTTP URL looks like this:

```
http://<user>:<password>@<host>:<port>/<url-path>?<query>#<bookmark>
```

These syntactic elements are specifically defined for HTTP absolute URLs as follows:

`<user>` and `<password>` Optional authentication information, for resources located on password-protected servers. This construct is rarely used in practice, so most people don't realize it is an option. It has thus become a target of abuse by con artists who use it to obscure undesirable URLs.

`<host>` The host name of the web server where the resource is located. This is usually a fully qualified Domain Name System (DNS) domain name, but it may also be an IP address.

`<port>` The TCP port number to use for connecting to the web server. This defaults to port 80 for HTTP and is usually omitted. In rare cases, you may see some other port number used, sometimes to allow two copies of web server software devoted to different uses on the same IP address. Port 8080 is especially common as an alternative.

`<url-path>` The path pointing to the specific resource to be retrieved using HTTP. This is usually a full directory path expressing the sequence of directories to be traversed from the root directory to the place where the resource is located, and then the resource's name. It's important to remember that the path is case-sensitive, even though DNS domain names are not.

`<query>` An optional query or other information to be passed to the web server. This feature is commonly used to implement interactive functions, because the query value can be specified by the user and then be passed from the web browser to the web server. The alternative method is by using the HTTP POST method.

`<bookmark>` Identifies a particular location within an HTML document. This is commonly used in very large HTML documents to allow a user to click a hyperlink and scroll to a particular place in the document. See the example near the end of Table 79-1.

Although the URL syntax for the Web is quite rich and potentially complex, most Web URLs are actually quite short. The vast majority of these components are omitted, especially the user, password, port, and bookmark elements. Queries are used only for special purposes. This leaves the more simplified form you will usually encounter for URLs:

```
http://<host>/<url-path>
```

Resource Paths and Directory Listings

The `<url-path>` used to reference a particular document can also be omitted. This provides a convenient way for a user to see what content is offered on a website without needing to know what particular document to request. For example, a user who wants to see the current headlines on CNN would go to http://www.cnn.com. In this case, the request is sent to the web server for the null document (represented by /, which is implied if it is not specified; technically, you are supposed to specify http://www.cnn.com/).

How a / request is handled depends on the server. Technically, such a request is actually asking the server, "Please show me the contents of the root directory of the server." However, this is both ugly (a listing of filenames is not the best way to make a first impression) and a potential security issue (as anyone can see the name of every file on the server). Instead, most HTTP servers are set up to recognize such requests automatically and return a default document, often named something like index.html or default.html. Many servers will similarly return a default document of some sort if any other directory is specified in a URL; for example, typing http://www.pcguide.com/ref in the URL address bar of a web browser actually returns http://www.pcguide.com/ref/index.htm.

NOTE *While it is technically incorrect to leave the* http:// *off an HTTP URL, most web browsers will add it automatically if it's omitted. As a result, many Web users are in the habit of entering URLs that are simply a host name, such as www.tcpipguide.com.*

The forms shown here apply to absolute HTTP URLs. URLs may also be relative, which is the norm for links between closely related documents, such as graphics that go with a document, or between documents in a set or project. In this case, usually only a fractional portion of a URL path is specified. This is described fully in Chapter 70.

80

HTTP GENERAL OPERATION AND CONNECTIONS

The Hypertext Transfer Protocol (HTTP) began as an extremely basic protocol, designed to do just one thing: allow a client to send a simple request for a hypertext file and receive it back from the server. Modern HTTP remains at its heart a straightforward request/reply protocol, but now includes many new features and capabilities to support the growing size of the World Wide Web (the Web) and the ever-increasing variety of ways that people have found to use the Web. Therefore, the best place to start explaining HTTP is by looking at its operation as a whole and how communication takes place between a web server and a web client.

In this chapter, I introduce HTTP by describing its operation in general terms. I start with an overview of HTTP, discussing its versions and the standards that define them. I then discuss its operational model, which is important to understanding how HTTP works. I explain the two types of connections that are supported between HTTP clients and servers, and the method by which requests can be pipelined in the current version of HTTP, HTTP/1.1. I then provide more information about how persistent connections are established, managed, and terminated in HTTP/1.1.

HTTP Versions and Standards

The World Wide Web had humble beginnings as a research project at the Swiss research institute, CERN, the European Organization for Nuclear Research. The primary goal of the project was to allow hypertext documents to be electronically linked, so selecting a reference in one document to a second document would cause the reference document to be retrieved. To implement this system, the researchers needed some sort of mechanism to allow a client computer to tell a server to send it a document. To fill this function, the early developers of the Web created a new TCP/IP application layer protocol: the *Hypertext Transfer Protocol (HTTP)*.

This first version is now known as HTTP/0.9. Subsequent versions are HTTP/1.0 and HTTP/1.1.

HTTP/0.9

The original version of HTTP was intended only for the transfer of hypertext documents, and it was designed to be very simple to make implementation of the fledgling Web easier. This early HTTP specifies that an HTTP client establishes a connection to an HTTP server using the Transmission Control Protocol (TCP). The client then issues a single GET request specifying a resource to be retrieved. The server responds by sending the file as a stream of text bytes, and the connection is terminated. The entire document defining this version of HTTP is only a couple of pages long!

This first version of HTTP was functional but extremely limited in its capabilities. It didn't support the transfer of any types of data other than hypertext, and it didn't provide any mechanism for any sort of intelligent communication between the client and server. This early HTTP prototype was not up to the task of providing the basis for data transfer for the future of the Web. It was never made an official RFC standard, and, in fact, never even had a formal version number; it is known today as HTTP version 0.9, or HTTP/0.9, using the HTTP version format. I believe this number has no particular significance, other than being a bit smaller than the number of the first official version of the protocol.

HTTP/1.0

HTTP/0.9's skeleton of functionality formed the basis for a rapid evolution of HTTP in the early 1990s. As the Web grew in size and acceptance, many new ideas and features were incorporated into HTTP. The result of a great deal of development effort was the formalization of the first HTTP standard: version 1.0. The standard for this much enhanced HTTP was published in May 1996 as RFC 1945, "Hypertext Transfer Protocol—HTTP/1.0." It had been in use for several years prior to that formal publication date, however.

HTTP/1.0 transformed HTTP from a trivial request/response application to a true messaging protocol. It described a complete message format for HTTP, and explained how it should be used for client requests and server responses. One of the most important changes in HTTP/1.0 was the generalization of the protocol to handle many types of different media, as opposed to strictly hypertext documents. To broaden HTTP's scope, its developers borrowed concepts and header constructs from the Multipurpose Internet Mail Extensions (MIME) standard defined for email (discussed in Chapter 76). At the same time that it defined much more capable web servers and web clients, HTTP/1.0 retained backward-compatibility with servers and clients still using HTTP/0.9.

HTTP/1.0 was the version of HTTP that was widely implemented in the mid-1990s as the Web exploded in popularity. After only a couple of years, HTTP accounted for the majority of the traffic on the burgeoning Internet. The popularity of HTTP was so great that it single-handedly prompted the installation of a lot of new hardware to handle the load of browser requests and web server replies.

Unfortunately, much of this huge load of traffic was due to some limitations in HTTP itself. These only became apparent due to the tremendous growth in the use of the protocol, which, combined with the normal growing pains of the Internet, led to many frustrated Web users. The inefficiencies of HTTP/1.0 were a result of design limitations, such as the following:

- The need for each site to be hosted on a different server.
- The fact that each HTTP session handled only one client request.
- A general lack of support for necessary performance-enhancing features such as caching, proxying, and partial resource retrieval.

HTTP/1.1

While impatient pundits coined sarcastic terms such as the "World Wide Wait," the Internet Engineering Task Force (IETF) continued to work to improve HTTP. In January 1997, the first draft version of HTTP/1.1 appeared, in RFC 2068. This document was later revised and published as RFC 2616, "Hypertext Transfer Protocol—HTTP/1.1," in June 1999. HTTP/1.1 retains backward-compatibility with both HTTP/1.0 and HTTP/0.9. It is accompanied by RFC 2617, "HTTP Authentication: Basic and Digest Access Authentication," which deals with security and authentication issues.

HTTP/1.1 introduces several significant improvements over version 1.0 of the protocol, most of which specifically address the performance problems I just described. Some of the more important improvements in HTTP1/1 include the following:

Multiple Host Name Support In HTTP/1.0, there was no way to specify the host name of the server to which the client needed to connect. As a result, the web server at a particular IP address could support only one domain name. This was not only inefficient, but it also was exacerbating the depletion of IP addresses in the 1990s, because each new web server to come online required a new IP address. HTTP/1.1 allows one web server to handle requests for dozens or even hundreds of different virtual hosts.

Persistent Connections HTTP/1.1 allows a client to send multiple requests for related documents to a server in a single TCP session. This greatly improves performance over HTTP/1.0, where each request required a new connection to the server.

Partial Resource Selection In HTTP/1.1, a client can ask for only part of a resource, rather than needing the get the entire document, which reduces the load on the server and saves transfer bandwidth.

Better Caching and Proxying Support HTTP/1.1 includes many provisions to make caching and proxying more efficient and effective than they were in HTTP/1.0. These techniques can improve performance by providing clients with faster replies to their requests while reducing the load on servers, as well as enhancing security and implementing other functionality.

Content Negotiation HTTP/1.1 has an additional negotiation feature that allows the client and server to exchange information to help select the best resource or version of a resource when multiple variants are available.

Better Security HTTP/1.1 defines authentication methods and is generally more security-aware than HTTP/1.0 was.

In addition to these notable improvements, many other minor enhancements were made in HTTP/1.1. Several of these take the form of new headers that can be included in client requests to better control under what circumstances resources are retrieved from the server, and headers in server responses to provide additional information to the client.

Future HTTP Versions

HTTP/1.1 continues to be the current version of HTTP, even though it is now several years old. This may seem somewhat surprising, given how widely used HTTP is. Then again, it may because so many millions of servers and clients implement HTTP/1.1 that no new version has been created. For a while, there was speculation that version 1.2 of HTTP would be developed, but this has not happened yet.

In the late 1990s, work began on a method of expanding HTTP through extensions to the existing version 1.1. Development of the *HTTP Extension Framework* proceeded for a number of years, and in 1998, a proposed draft for a new Internet standard was created. However, HTTP/1.1 is so widely deployed and so important that it was very difficult to achieve consensus on any proposal to modify it. As a result, when the HTTP Extension Framework was finally published in February 2000 as RFC 2774, the universal acceptance required for a new standard did not exist. The framework was given experimental status and never became a formal standard.

KEY CONCEPT The engine of the World Wide Web (the Web) is the application protocol that defines how web servers and clients exchange information: the *Hypertext Transfer Protocol (HTTP)*. The first version of HTTP, HTTP/0.9, was part of the early Web and was a very simple request/response protocol with limited capabilities that could transfer only text files. The first widely used version was HTTP/1.0, which is a more complete protocol that allows the transport of many types of files and resources. The current version is HTTP/1.1, which expands HTTP/1.0's capabilities with several features that improve the efficiency of transfers and address many of the needs of the rapidly growing modern Web.

HTTP Operational Model and Client/Server Communication

While the Web itself has many different facets, HTTP is concerned with only one basic function: the transfer of hypertext documents and other files from web servers to web clients. In terms of actual communication, clients are chiefly concerned with making requests to servers, which respond to those requests.

Thus, even though HTTP includes a lot of functionality to meet the needs of clients and servers, when you boil it down, you get a very simple, client/server, request/response protocol. In this respect, HTTP more closely resembles a rudimentary protocol like the Boot Protocol (BOOTP) or the Address Resolution Protocol (ARP) than it does other application layer protocols like the File Transfer Protocol (FTP) and the Simple Mail Transfer Protocol (SMTP), which involve multiple communication steps and command/reply sequences.

Basic HTTP Client/Server Communication

In its simplest form, the operation of HTTP involves only an HTTP client, usually a *web browser* on a client machine, and an HTTP server, more commonly known as a *web server*. After a TCP connection is created, the two steps in communication are as follows (see Figure 80-1):

Client Request The HTTP client sends a request message formatted according to the rules of the HTTP standard—an *HTTP Request*. This message specifies the resource that the client wishes to retrieve or includes information to be provided to the server.

Server Response The server reads and interprets the request. It takes action relevant to the request and creates an *HTTP Response* message, which it sends back to the client. The response message indicates whether the request was successful, and it may also contain the content of the resource that the client requested, if appropriate.

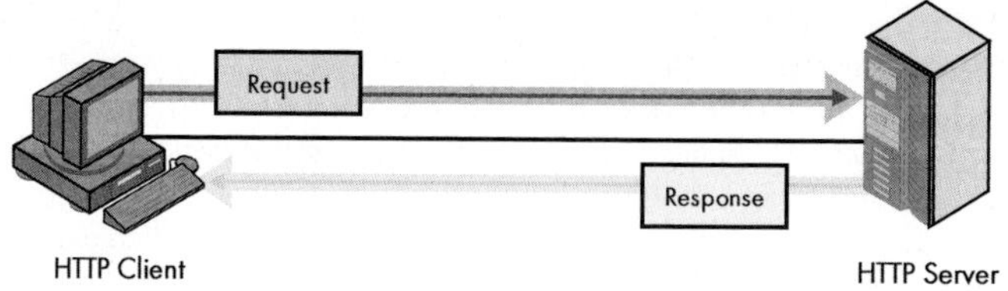

Figure 80-1: HTTP client/server communication *In its simplest form, HTTP communication consists of an HTTP Request message sent by a client to a server, which replies with an HTTP Response message.*

In HTTP/1.0, each TCP connection involves only one such exchange, as shown in Figure 80-1. In HTTP/1.1, multiple exchanges are possible, as you'll see soon. Note also that, in some cases, the server may respond with one or preliminary responses prior to sending the full response. This may occur if the server sends a preliminary response using the 100 Continue status code prior to the actual reply. See the description of HTTP status codes in Chapter 81 for more information.

> **KEY CONCEPT** HTTP is a client/server-oriented, request/reply protocol. Basic communication consists of an *HTTP Request* message sent by an HTTP client to an HTTP server, which returns an *HTTP Response* message back to the client.

Intermediaries and the HTTP Request/Response Chain

The simple request/response pair between a client and server becomes more complex when *intermediaries* are placed in the virtual communication path between the client and server. These are devices such as *proxies*, *gateways*, or *tunnels* that are used to improve performance, provide security, or perform other necessary functions for particular clients or servers. Proxies are particularly commonly used on the Web, because they can greatly improve response time for groups of related client computers.

When an intermediary is involved in HTTP communication, it acts as a middleman. Rather than the client speaking directly to the server and vice versa, each talks to the intermediary. This allows the intermediary to perform functions such as caching, translation, aggregation, and encapsulation. For example, consider an exchange through a single intermediary device. The two-step communication process described in the preceding section would become four steps:

1. **Client Request** The HTTP client sends a request message to the intermediary device.
2. **Intermediary Request** The intermediary processes the request, making changes to it if necessary. It then forwards the request to the server.
3. **Server Response** The server reads and interprets the request, takes appropriate action, and then sends a response. Since it received its request from the intermediary, its reply goes back to the intermediary.
4. **Intermediary Response** The intermediary processes the request, again possibly making changes, and then forwards it back to the client.

As you can see, the intermediary acts as if it were a server from the client's perspective and as a client from the server's viewpoint. Many intermediaries are designed to be able to intercept a variety of TCP/IP protocols, by posing as the server to a client and the client to a server. Most protocols are unaware of the existence of intermediaries. HTTP, however, includes special support for certain intermediaries such as proxy servers, providing headers that control how intermediaries handle HTTP requests and replies. (Proxy servers are discussed in Chapter 84.)

It is possible for two or more intermediaries to be linked together between the client and server. For example, the client might send a request to intermediary 1, which then forwards to intermediary 2, which then talks to the server, as illustrated in Figure 80-2. The process is reversed for the reply. The HTTP standard uses the phrase *request/response chain* to refer collectively to the entire set of devices involved in an HTTP message exchange.

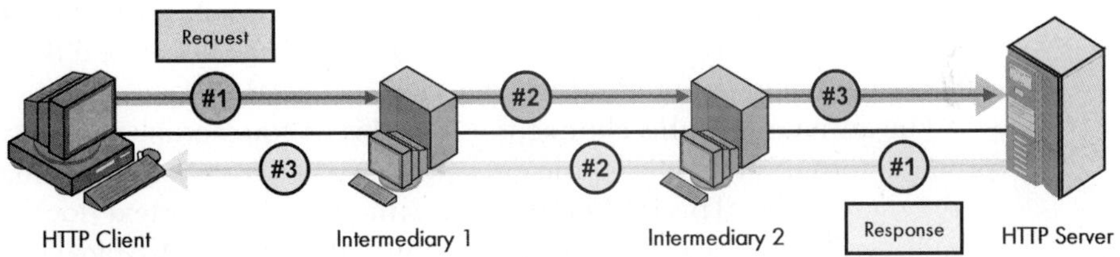

Figure 80-2: HTTP request/response chain using intermediaries *Instead of being connected directly, an HTTP client and server may be linked using one or more intermediary devices such as proxies. In this example, two intermediaries are present. The HTTP Request message sent by the client will actually be transferred three times: from the client to the first intermediary, then to the second, and finally to the server. The HTTP Response message will be created once but transmitted three distinct times. The full set of devices participating in the message exchange is called the request/response chain.*

> **KEY CONCEPT** The simple client/server operational model of HTTP becomes more complicated when *intermediary devices* such as proxies, tunnels, or gateways are inserted in the communication path between the HTTP client and server. HTTP/1.1 is specifically designed with features to support the efficient conveyance of requests and responses through a series of steps from the client through the intermediaries to the server, and back again. The entire set of devices involved in such a communication is called the *request/response chain.*

The Impact of Caching on HTTP Communication

The normal HTTP communication model is changed through the application of *caching* to client requests. Various devices on the Web employ caching to store recently retrieved resources so they can be quickly supplied in reply to a request. The client itself will cache recently accessed web documents, so that if the user asks for them again, they can be displayed without even making a request to a server. If a request is required, any intermediary device can satisfy a request for a file if the file is in its cache.

When a cache is used, the device that has the cached resource requested returns it directly, circumventing the normal HTTP communication process. In the example shown in Figure 80-2, if intermediary 1 has the file the client needs, it will supply it to the client directly, and intermediary 2 and the web server that the client was trying to reach originally will not even be aware that a request was ever made. Chapter 84 provides details on HTTP caching.

NOTE *Most requests for web resources are made using HTTP URLs based on a Domain Name System (DNS) host name. The first step in satisfying such requests is to resolve the DNS domain name into an IP address, but this process is separate from the HTTP communication itself.*

HTTP Transitory and Persistent Connections and Pipelining

You just learned that the basic HTTP communication process is a simple two-step procedure: A client sends a request to a server, and the server replies back to the client. Since this was all that HTTP was intended to do, the first version of the protocol was designed so that after a TCP connection was established between the client and server, a single request/response exchange was performed. After the request was satisfied, the TCP connection was terminated. These *transitory* connections were the only type supported by the original HTTP/0.9, and the same model was maintained in the more widely deployed HTTP/1.0.

The advantage of this connection model is its conceptual simplicity. The problem with it is that it is inefficient when the client needs to make many requests to the same server. This is often the case with modern hypertext documents, which usually carry inline references to images and other media. A typical client request for the home page of a website begins with a single request for a Hypertext Markup Language (HTML) file, but then leads to subsequent requests for each of the other related files that go with that document.

With transitory connections, each of these requests made by the client requires a new, distinct TCP connection to be set up between the client and server. Every connection takes server resources and network bandwidth, so needing to establish a new one for each file is woefully inefficient. Suppose that you were having a conversation with someone whom you needed to ask a series of questions. Now imagine that after answering each question, the other person hung up the phone, and you had to call her again! You get the picture.

There are some people who consider the temporary nature of HTTP/0.9 and HTTP/1.0 connections to be a design flaw of these early versions of HTTP, but I don't think that this is fair. In the early days, this model of operation was really not a big issue; it became problematic only when the use of the Web and hypertext evolved. For the first few years of its existence, hypertext was primarily that: *text.* Having an HTTP session last just long enough for one request/response was generally sufficient, since the whole resource was in one file. It was only in the 1990s that hypertext became *hypermedia,* with a heavy emphasis on embedded graphics and other files. When web pages changed from simple text to multimedia marvels sporting dozens or even hundreds of embedded images, the limitations of HTTP/1.0 became obvious.

The solution to the problem came in HTTP/1.1, which allows an HTTP client and server to set up a *persistent connection.*

Persistent Connections

With persistent connections, the basic operation of HTTP is not changed. The main difference is that, by default, the TCP connection is kept open after each request/response set, so that the next request and response can be exchanged immediately. The session is closed only when the client is finished requesting all the documents it needs.

Keeping the TCP connection between an HTTP client and server alive between requests is probably the single most important way that HTTP/1.1 improves performance over HTTP/1.0. Clients are able to get their files more quickly because they don't need to wait for a TCP connection before each resource is retrieved. Server load is reduced, and memory use in busy servers is conserved. Network congestion is reduced through the elimination of unnecessary TCP handshaking segments.

Pipelining

Persistent connections offer another important performance-enhancing option to HTTP clients: the ability to *pipeline* requests. Suppose the client needs to send a request for Files A, B, and C to a server. Since the requests for all of these files will be sent in the same TCP session, there is no need for the client to wait for a response to its request for File A before sending the request for File B. The client can send requests in a rapid-fire fashion, one after the other. This also improves the efficiency of the server, which will be able to fill the requests in the order in which they are received, as soon as it is able, without needing to pause to wait for each new request to be sent.

> **KEY CONCEPT** HTTP/0.9 and HTTP/1.0 supported only *transitory connections* between an HTTP client and server, where just a single request and response could be exchanged on a TCP connection. This is very inefficient for the modern Web, where clients frequently need to make dozens of requests to a server. By default, HTTP/1.1 operates using *persistent connections*. This means that once a TCP connection is established, the client can send many requests to the server and receive replies to each in turn. This allows files to be retrieved more quickly, and conserves server resources and Internet bandwidth. The client can even *pipeline* its requests, sending the second request immediately, without needing to wait for a reply to the first request. HTTP/1.1 still supports transitory connections for backward-compatibility, when needed.

The obvious advantages of persistent connections make them the default for modern HTTP communication, but they do have one drawback: They complicate the process of sending data from the server to the client. With transitory connections, the client knows that all of the data it receives back from the server is in reply to the one request it sent. Once it has all the bytes the server sent and the TCP session ends, the client knows the file is complete.

With persistent connections, and especially when pipelining is used, the server will typically be sending one file after the other to the client, which must differentiate them. Remember that TCP sends data as just a series of unstructured bytes; the application must take care of specifying where the dividing points are between files. This means that persistent connections and pipelining lead to data length issues that must be specially addressed in HTTP.

To provide compatibility with older versions of the software, HTTP/1.1 servers still support transitory connections, and they will automatically close the TCP connection after one response if they receive an HTTP/0.9 or HTTP/1.0 request. HTTP/1.1 clients may also specify in their initial request that they do not want to use persistent connections.

HTTP Persistent Connection Establishment and Management

As with most TCP/IP client/server protocols, in establishing a persistent connection, the HTTP server plays the passive role by listening for requests on a particular port number. The default port number for HTTP is well-known TCP port number 80, and is used by web browsers for most HTTP requests, unless a different port number is specified in the Uniform Resource Locator (URL). The client initiates an HTTP connection by opening a TCP connection from itself to the server it wishes to contact.

NOTE *A DNS name resolution step may precede the entire HTTP connection, since most URLs contain a host name, while HTTP requires that the client know the server's IP address. This can lead to confusion, because DNS uses the User Datagram Protocol (UDP), but HTTP uses TCP. This causes some people to think that HTTP uses UDP.*

Once the TCP connection is active, the client sends its first request message. The request specifies which version of HTTP the client is using. If this is HTTP/0.9 or HTTP/1.0, the server will automatically work in the transitory connection model, and it will send only one reply and then close the link. If it is HTTP/1.1, the assumption is that a persistent connection is desired. An HTTP/1.1 client can override this by including the special Connection: Close header in its initial request, which tells the server it does not want to keep the session active after the request it is sending has been fulfilled.

Assuming that a persistent connection is being used, the client may begin pipelining subsequent requests after sending its first request, while waiting for a response from the server to the initial query. As the server starts to respond to requests, the client processes them and takes action, such as displaying the data retrieved to the user. The data received from the server may also prompt the client to request more files on the same connection, as in the case of an HTML document that contains references to images.

The server will generally buffer a certain number of pipelined requests from the client. In the case where the client sends too many requests too quickly, the server may throttle back the client using the flow-control mechanism built into TCP. In theory, the server could also just decided to terminate the connection with the client, but it is better for it to use TCP's existing features. Closing the connection will cause the client to initiate a new connection, potentially exacerbating any overloading problem.

The flow of requests and responses continues for as long as the client has requests. The connection can be gracefully terminated by the client by including the Connection: Close header in the last request it needs to send to the server. All requests are filled in order, so the server will satisfy all outstanding requests, and then close the session.

Since HTTP/1.1 supports pipelining of requests, there is usually no need for a client to establish more than one simultaneous connection to the same server. Clients occasionally do this anyway to allow them to get information from a server more quickly. This is considered by many to be "antisocial," because it can lead to a busy server's resources being monopolized by one client to the exclusion of others that want to access it.

Under special circumstances, either the client or the server may unexpectedly close an active persistent connection. For example, if the client detects that too much time has elapsed since the server last replied, it may conclude that the server has crashed and terminate the connection. Similarly, the server might receive a shutdown command from its administrator or for other reasons end a session with a client abruptly. Servers normally avoid closing down a link during the middle of sending a response.

Both clients and servers must be able to handle abrupt session termination. For servers, there is not much to do; if the client terminates the connection, the server simply cleans up any resources associated with the connection, and then goes on to service the next client.

Clients have more to do when a server prematurely terminates a session, and this is especially the case when requests are pipelined. The client must keep track of all requests sent to the server to ensure that each is filled. If the server closes the session unexpectedly, the client will usually attempt to establish a new connection to retransmit the unfilled requests. Since an abrupt session termination is often a sign of a busy server, the HTTP standard specifies that clients use a binary exponential back-off algorithm to wait a variable but increasing amount of time before resubmitting requests for files (similar in concept to the method used to deal with collisions in Ethernet). This helps prevent clients from piling on requests to a device that is already overwhelmed.

81

HTTP MESSAGES, METHODS, AND STATUS CODES

As you saw in the previous chapter, the Hypertext Transfer Protocol (HTTP) is entirely oriented around the sending of client requests and server responses. These take the form of *HTTP messages* sent between clients and servers. As with all protocols, HTTP uses a special format that dictates the structure of both client Request messages and server Response messages. Understanding how these messages work is a big part of comprehending HTTP as a whole.

In this chapter, I describe the messages used by HTTP and the specific commands and responses issued by clients and servers. I begin with a look at the generic HTTP message format and the major components of every HTTP message. I then discuss the specific formats used for both Request and Response messages. I explain the different types of HTTP methods (commands) used in client requests and the HTTP status codes used in server replies.

NOTE *Much of the functionality of HTTP is implemented using* header fields *that appear at the start of each HTTP Request and Response message. Headers are covered in detail in the next chapter.*

HTTP Generic Message Format

As you learned in the previous chapter, all of the communication between devices using HTTP takes place via HTTP messages, of which there are only two types: *Request* and *Response messages.* Clients usually send requests and receive responses, while servers receive requests and send responses. Intermediate devices such as gateways or proxies may send and receive both types of messages.

All HTTP messages are created to fit a message structure that the standard calls the *generic message format.* Like most of the other TCP/IP messaging protocols, HTTP does not use a binary message format; rather, the messages are text-based. HTTP messages are based loosely on the electronic mail (email) RFC 822 and 2822 message standards, as well as the Multipurpose Internet Mail Extensions (MIME) standard (described in Chapter 76). I say "loosely" because HTTP messages are similar in construction to email messages but do not strictly follow all of the email or MIME format requirements. One difference is that not all of the RFC 822 and MIME headers are used; there are other differences as well, which we will soon examine.

The HTTP generic message format is as follows:

<*start-line*>

<*message-headers*>

<*empty-line*>

[<*message-body*>]

[<*message-trailers*>]

You can see that this is pretty much the same as the format used for email messages: headers, an empty line, and then a message body. All text lines are terminated with the standard carriage return-line feed (CRLF) control character sequence. The empty line contains just those two characters and nothing else. The headers are always sent as regular text. The body, however, may be either text or 8-bit binary information, depending on the nature of the data to be sent. (This is another way that HTTP does not adhere strictly to the RFC 822 standard; see the discussion of entities and media types in Chapter 83 for a full discussion.)

The generic message format has the following components:

Start Line The *start line* is a special text line that conveys the nature of the message. In a request, this line indicates the nature of the request, in the form of a *method,* as well as specifying a Uniform Resource Identifier (URI) to indicate the resource that is the object of the request. Responses use the start line to indicate status information in reply to a request. You can find more details on the use of the start line in the following sections in this chapter that detail HTTP Request messages and Response messages.

Message Headers Many dozens of message headers are defined in HTTP. These headers are organized into groups by function, as described in the following sections in this chapter. Almost all of these headers are optional; the one exception is the Host header, which must be present in each request in HTTP/1.1. Headers may be sent in any order, and they all follow the same header format used in email messages: *<header-name>*: *<header-value>*.

Message Body The message body is optional, because it is needed only for certain types of messages. The body may carry a set of information to be communicated between the client and server, such as a detailed error message in a response. More commonly, it carries a file or other resource, which is formally called an *entity* in the HTTP standard. Entities are most often found in the body of a Response message, since most client requests ask for a server to send a file or other resource. However, they can also be found in certain Request messages. HTTP supports many kinds of entities, as described in detail in Chapter 83.

Message Trailers As described in the previous chapter, HTTP/1.1 uses persistent connections by default, so messages are sent in a steady stream from client to server and server to client. This requires some means to mark where one message ends and the next begins, which is usually accomplished in one of two ways. The first is using a special header that indicates the length of the message, so the receiving device knows when the entire message has been received. The second is a method called *chunking*, where a message is broken into pieces for transmission, and the length of each piece is indicated in the message body. When chunking is done, a set of message *trailers* may follow the body of the message. Trailers are actually the same as headers, except for their position in the file, but they may only be used for entity headers. See Chapter 83 for more details on trailers and chunked data.

> **KEY CONCEPT** All HTTP messages conform to a structure called the *generic message format*. This format is based on the RFC 822 and MIME electronic mail message standards, although HTTP does not follow those formats precisely. Each HTTP message begins with a start line, then contains a number of message headers, followed by an empty line and optionally a message body. The body of the message may contain a resource such as a file to be communicated between client and server, called an *entity*.

HTTP Request Message Format

The client initiates an HTTP session by opening a TCP connection to the HTTP server with which it wishes to communicate. It then sends *HTTP Request messages* to the server, each of which specifies a particular type of action that the user of the HTTP client would like the server to take. Requests can be generated either by specific user action (such as clicking a hyperlink in a web browser) or indirectly as a result of a prior action (such as a reference to an inline image in an HTML document leading to a request for that image).

HTTP Request messages use a format that is based on the generic message format described in the previous section, but specific to the needs of requests. The structure of this format is as follows (see Figure 81-1):

<request-line>

<general-headers>

<request-headers>

<entity-headers>

<empty-line>

[*<message-body>*]

[*<message-trailers>*]

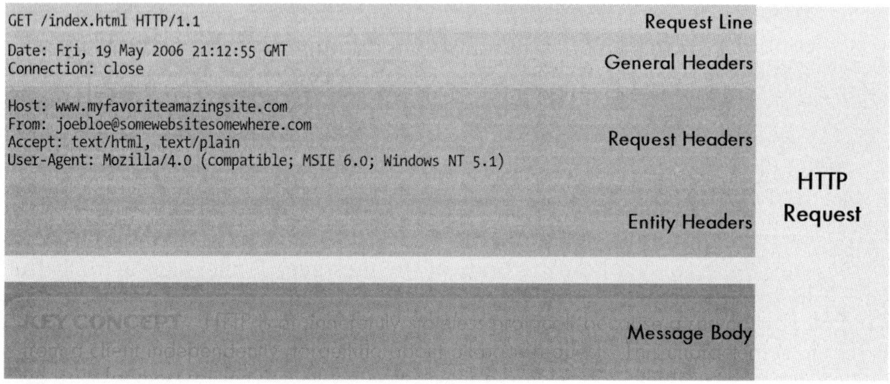
GET /index.html HTTP/1.1
Request Line
Date: Fri, 19 May 2006 21:12:55 GMT
Connection: close
General Headers
Host: www.myfavoriteamazingsite.com
From: joebloe@somewebsitesomewhere.com
Accept: text/html, text/plain
User-Agent: Mozilla/4.0 (compatible; MSIE 6.0; Windows NT 5.1)
Request Headers
Entity Headers
HTTP Request
Message Body

Figure 81-1: HTTP Request message format *This diagram shows the structural elements of an HTTP Request message and an example of the sorts of headers a Request message might contain. Like most HTTP requests, this one carries no entity, so there are no entity headers and the message body is empty. See Figure 81-2 for the HTTP Response message format.*

Request Line

The generic *start line* that begins all HTTP messages is called a *request line* in Request messages. Its has three main purposes:

- To indicate the command or action that the client wants performed
- To specify a resource on which the action should be taken
- To indicate to the server what version of HTTP the client is using

The formal syntax for the request line is as follows:

<METHOD> <request-uri> <HTTP-VERSION>

Each of the request line components is discussed in the following sections.

Method

The *method* is simply the type of action that the client wants the server to take; it is always specified in uppercase letters. There are eight standard methods defined in HTTP/1.1, of which three are widely used: *GET*, *HEAD*, and *POST*. They are called *methods*, rather than *commands*, because the HTTP standard uses terminology from object-oriented programming. I explain this and also describe the methods themselves in the "HTTP Methods" section later in this chapter.

Request URI

The *request URI* is the URI of the resource to which the request applies. While URIs can theoretically refer to either Uniform Resource Locators (URLs) or Uniform Resource Names (URNs), currently, a URI is almost always an HTTP URL that follows the standard syntax rules of Web URLs, as described in Chapter 70.

Interestingly, the exact form of the URL used in the HTTP request line usually differs from that used in HTML documents or entered by users. This is because some of the information in a full URL is used to control HTTP itself. It is needed as part of the communication between the user and the HTTP client, but not in the request from the client to the server. The standard method of specifying a resource in a request is to include the path and filename in the request line (as well as any optional query information), while specifying the host in the special Host header that must be used in HTTP/1.1 Request messages.

For example, suppose the user enters a URL such as `http://www.myfavoritewebsite.com:8080/chatware/chatroom.php`. We obviously don't need to send the `http:` to the server. The client would take the remaining information and split it so the URI was specified as `/chatware/chatroom.php` and the Host line would contain `www.myfavoritewebsite.com:8080`. Thus, the start of the request would look like this:

```
GET /chatware/chatroom.php HTTP/1.1
Host: www.myfavoritewebsite.com:8080
```

The exception to this rule is when a request is being made to a proxy server. In that case, the request is made using the full URL in its original form, so that it can be processed by the proxy just as the original client processed it. The request would look like this:

```
GET http://www.myfavoritewebsite.com:8080/chatware/chatroom.php HTTP/1.1
```

Finally, there is one special case where a single asterisk can be used instead of a real URL. This is for the OPTIONS method, which does not require the specification of a resource. (Nominally, the asterisk means the method refers to the server itself.)

HTTP Version

The *HTTP version* element tells the server which version the client is using, so the server knows how to interpret the request, and what to send and not to send the client in its response. For example, a server receiving a request from a client using HTTP/0.9 or HTTP/1.0 will assume that a transitory connection is being used rather than a persistent one (as explained in the previous section), and the server will avoid using HTTP/1.1 headers in its reply. The version token is sent in uppercase letters, as HTTP/0.9, HTTP/1.0, or HTTP/1.1—just the way I've been doing throughout my discussion of the protocol.

Headers

After the request line come any of the headers that the client wants to include in the message. In these headers, details are provided to the server about the request. The headers all use the same structure, but are organized into the following categories based on the functions they serve and whether they are specific to one kind of message:

General Headers General headers refer mainly to the message itself, as opposed to its contents, and they are used to control its processing or provide the recipient with extra information. They are not particular to either Request or Response messages, so they can appear in either. Also, they are not specifically relevant to any entity the message may be carrying.

Request Headers These headers convey to the server more details about the nature of the client's request, and they give the client more control over how the request is handled. For example, special request headers can be used by the client to specify a conditional request—one that is filled only if certain criteria are met. Others can tell the server which formats or encodings the client is able to process in a Response message.

Entity Headers These are headers that describe the entity contained in the body of the request, if any.

> **KEY CONCEPT** *HTTP Request messages* are the means by which HTTP clients ask servers to take a particular type of action, such as sending a file or processing user input. Each Request message begins with a *request line*, which contains three critical pieces of information: the *method* (type of action) the client is requesting, the *URI* of the resource on which the client wishes the action to be performed, and the version of HTTP that the client is using. After the request line comes a set of message headers related to the request, followed by a blank line, and then optionally, the message body of the request.

Request headers are obviously used only in Request messages, but both general headers and entity headers can appear in either a Request or a Response message. Since there are so many headers and most are not particular to one message type, I describe them in detail in the next chapter.

HTTP Response Message Format

Each Request message sent by an HTTP client to a server prompts the server to send back a *Response message*. Actually, in certain cases, the server may send two responses: a preliminary response, followed by the real one. Usually though, one request yields one response, which indicates the results of the server's processing of the request, and a response often also carries an entity (file or resource) in the message body.

Like Request messages, Response messages use their own specific format that is based on the HTTP generic message format described earlier in this chapter. The format Response message format header is as follows (see Figure 81-2):

<*status-line*>

<*general-headers*>

<*response-headers*>

<*entity-headers*>

<*empty-line*>

[<*message-body*>]

[<*message-trailers*>]

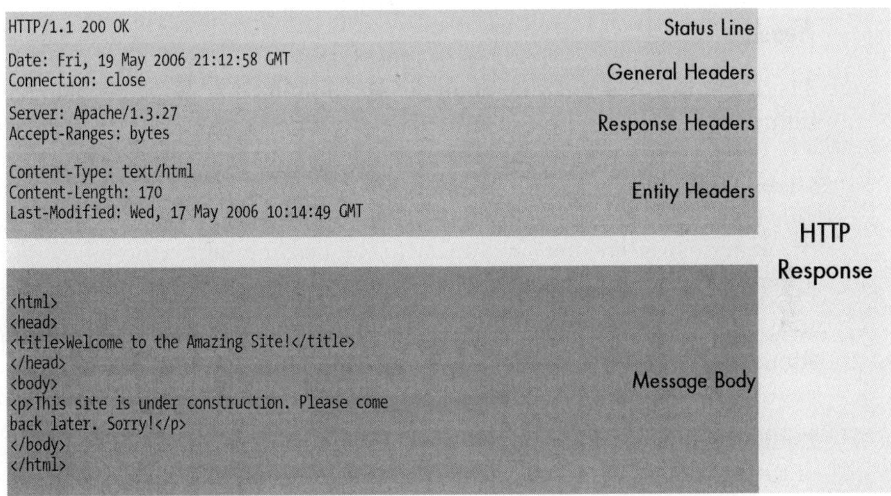

HTTP/1.1 200 OK
Status Line
Date: Fri, 19 May 2006 21:12:58 GMT
Connection: close
General Headers
Server: Apache/1.3.27
Accept-Ranges: bytes
Response Headers
Content-Type: text/html
Content-Length: 170
Last-Modified: Wed, 17 May 2006 10:14:49 GMT
Entity Headers
HTTP Response
<html>
<head>
<title>Welcome to the Amazing Site!</title>
</head>
<body>
<p>This site is under construction. Please come
back later. Sorry!</p>
</body>
</html>
Message Body

Figure 81-2: HTTP Response message format *This figure illustrates the construction of an HTTP Response message and includes an example of both message headers and body. The status code 200 indicates that this is a successful response to a request; it contains a brief text HTML entity in the message body. See Figure 81-1 for the HTTP Request message format.*

Status Line

The *status line* (note that this is not called the *response line*) is the start line used for Response messages. It has two functions: to tell the client what version of the protocol the server is using and to communicate a summary of the results of processing the client's request. The formal syntax for the status line is as follows:

<*HTTP-VERSION*> <*status-code*> <*reason-phrase*>

Each of the status line components is discussed in the following sections.

HTTP Version

The *HTTP-VERSION* label in the status line serves the same purpose as it does in the request line of a Request message (described in the previous section). Here, it tells the client the version number that the server is using for its response. It uses the same format as in the request line, with the version in uppercase as HTTP/0.9, HTTP/1.0, or HTTP/1.1. The server is required to return an HTTP version number that is no greater than the number the client sent in its request.

Status Code and Reason Phrase

The *status code* and *reason phrase* provide information about the results of processing the client's request in two different forms. The status code is a three-digit number that indicates the formal result that the server is communicating to the client. It is intended for the client HTTP implementation to process so the software can take appropriate action. The reason phrase is an additional, descriptive text string, which can be displayed to the human users of the HTTP client so they can see how the server responded. I describe status codes and reason phrases later in this chapter, and also list all of the standard codes.

Headers

The Response message will always include a number of headers that provide extra information about it. Response message headers fall into three categories:

General Headers General headers that refer to the message itself and are not specific to Response messages or the entity in the message body. These are the same as the generic headers that can appear in Request messages (though certain headers appear more often in responses, and others are more common in requests).

Response Headers These headers provide additional data that expands on the summary result information in the status line. The server may also return extra result information in the body of the message, especially when an error occurs.

Entity Headers These are headers that describe the entity contained in the body of the response, if any. These are the same entity headers that can appear in a Request message, but they are seen more often in response messages.

Most Response messages contain an entity in the message body. In the case of a successful request to retrieve a resource, this is the resource itself. Responses indicating unsuccessful requests usually contain detailed error information, often in the form of an HTML-formatted error message.

NOTE *Entity headers may appear in a Response message to describe the resource that is the subject of the request, even if the entity itself is not sent in the message. This occurs when the HEAD method is used to request only the headers associated with an entity.*

Response headers are used only in Response messages, while the others are general with respect to message type. See Chapter 82 for more details about HTTP headers.

KEY CONCEPT Each HTTP Request message sent by a client leads to a server returning one or more *HTTP Response messages*. Each Response message starts with *a status line* that contains the server's HTTP version number, and a numeric *status code* and text *reason phrase* that indicate the result of processing the client's request. The message then contains headers related to the response, followed by a blank line, and then the optional message body. Since most HTTP Request messages ask for a server to return a file or other resource, many HTTP Response messages carry an entity in the message body.

HTTP Methods

An HTTP Request message sent by a client to a server obviously requests that the server do something. All client/server protocols provide a way for the client to prompt the server to take action, generally by having the client give the server a series of commands. HTTP, in contrast, has *methods*, rather than commands. Each client Request message begins with the specification of the method that is the subject of the request.

What is the difference between a method and a command? In practical terms, nothing; they are the same. So why does HTTP use the term *method* instead of *command*? That's a good question. The answer can be found in the abstract of the standard defining HTTP/1.0, RFC 1945. It states, in part, that HTTP is "a generic, stateless, object-oriented protocol which can be used for many tasks. . . ." In highly simplified terms, object-oriented programming is a technique in which software modules are described not as sets of procedures, but as *objects* that possess attributes. These modules send messages to each other to communicate and to cause actions to be performed, where the action taken depends on the nature of the object. In object-oriented programming, the procedures each object can perform are called *methods*.

HTTP is considered to be object-oriented because, in many cases, the action taken by a server depends on the object that is the subject of the request. For example, if you ask a server to retrieve a text document, it will send that document; but if you ask for a directory, the server may instead return a default document for that directory. In contrast, a request that specifies the name of a program will result in the program being executed and its output returned (as opposed to the program's source code being returned).

Common Methods

Each method allows the client to specify a particular type of action to be taken by the server. Method names are always in uppercase letters. There are three methods that are commonly used in HTTP: GET, HEAD, and POST.

GET

The GET method requests that server retrieve the resource specified by the URL on the HTTP request line and send it in a response back to the client. This is the most basic type of request and the one that accounts for the majority of HTTP traffic. When you enter a conventional URL or click a link to a document or other file, you are usually prompting your web browser to send a GET request.

The handling of a GET request depends on a number of factors. If the URL is correct and the server can find the resource, it will send back the appropriate response to the client. The exact resource returned depends on the nature of the object requested. If the request cannot be processed properly, an error message may result. Caching (discussed in Chapter 84) also comes into play, as a proxy server or even the client itself might satisfy the request before it gets to the server.

It's important to remember that the meaning of a GET request may change if certain headers, such as If-Modified-Since or If-Match, are used. These tell the server to send the resource only if certain conditions are met. A request of this sort is sometimes called a *conditional GET*. Similarly, the client may use the Range header to request that the server send it only part of a resource; this is usually used for large files. When this header is included, the request may be called a *partial GET*.

HEAD

The HEAD method is identical to the GET method, but it tells the server not to send the actual body of the message. Thus, the response will contain all of the headers that would have accompanied a reply to the equivalent GET message, including entity headers describing the entity that the server would have sent had the method been GET. The client often uses this method to check the existence, status, or size of a file before deciding whether it wants the server to send the whole file.

HEAD requests are processed in the same way as GET requests, except that only the headers are returned, not the actual resource.

POST

The POST method allows the client to send an entity containing arbitrary data to the server for processing. It is commonly used to enable a client to submit information such as an interactive HTML form to a program on the server, which then takes action based on that input and sends a response. This capability is now used for all sorts of online programs. The URL in the request specifies the name of the program on the server that is to accept the data. Contrast this with the PUT method described in the next section.

Other Methods

The other methods defined by the HTTP standard are not used as often, but I will describe them briefly, as you may still encounter them. Other HTTP methods include the following:

OPTIONS This method allows the client to request that the server send it information about available communication options. A URI of a resource may be specified to request information relevant to accessing that resource, or an asterisk (*) may be used to indicate that the query is about the server itself. The response includes headers that give the client more details about how the server may be accessed.

PUT This method requests that the server store the entity enclosed in the body of the request at the URL specified in the request line. In a PUT, the URI identifies the entity in the request; thus a PUT allows a file to be copied to a server, in the exact complement to how a GET requests that a file be copied to the client. In contrast, with a POST, the URI identifies a program intended to *process* the entity in the request, so it's used for interactive programs. Now, would you like people to be able to store files on your server in the same way that they request them? Neither would I. This is one primary reason why PUT is not often used. It has valid uses, such as uploading content to a website, and it must be used with authentication in this case. However, storing files on a site is more often accomplished using other means, like the File Transfer Protocol (FTP).

DELETE This method requests that the specified resource be deleted. This has the same issues as PUT and is not often used for similar reasons.

TRACE This method allows a client to receive back a copy of the request that it sent to the server, for diagnostic purposes.

In addition to these, the standard reserves the method name CONNECT for future use. An earlier version of HTTP/1.1, RFC 2068, defined the methods PATCH, LINK, and UNLINK. These were removed in the final version, but you may still see references to them.

KEY CONCEPT Each HTTP client request specifies a particular type of action that the server should perform; in HTTP, these are called *methods*, rather than commands. The three most common HTTP methods are *GET*, which prompts a server to return a resource; *HEAD*, which returns just the headers associated with a resource; and *POST*, which allows a client to submit data to a server for processing.

Safe and Idempotent Methods

As you've seen, methods vary greatly in the type of behavior they cause the server to take. The HTTP standard defines two characteristics that can be used to differentiate methods based on the impact they have on a server:

Safe Methods These are methods that an administrator of a server can feel reasonably comfortable permitting a client to send because they are very unlikely to have any negative side effects. The methods usually put into this category are GET, HEAD, OPTIONS, and TRACE. The methods that cause data to be accepted by the server for processing, or lead to changes on the server, are deemed unsafe: POST, PUT, and DELETE. (The fact that they are considered unsafe doesn't mean a server never allows them—just that they require more care and detail in handling than the others.)

Idempotent Methods A method is said to be *idempotent* if repeating the same method request numerous times causes the exact same results, as if the method were issued only once. For example, if you load a web page in your browser, and then type the same URL in again, you get the same result, at least most of the time. In general, all of the methods in HTTP have this property inherently except one: POST.

The POST method is not idempotent because each instance of a POST request causes the receiving server to process the data in the Request message's body. Submitting a POST request two or more times can often lead to undesirable results. The classic example is clicking the Submit button on a form more than once, which can lead to annoyances such as a duplicate message on an Internet forum or a double order at an online store.

There are also situations where a method that is normally idempotent may not be. A GET request for a simple document is idempotent, but a GET for a script can change files on the server and therefore is not idempotent. Similarly, a sequence of idempotent methods may not be idempotent. For example, consider a situation where a PUT request is followed by a GET for the same resource. This sequence is not idempotent because the second request depends on the results of the first.

The significance of nonidempotence is that clients must handle such requests or sequences specially. The client must keep track of them, making sure that they are filled in order and only once. The HTTP standard also specifies that nonidempotent methods should not be pipelined, to avoid problems if an HTTP session is unexpectedly terminated. For example, if two POST requests were pipelined and the server got hung up handling them, the client would need to reissue them but might not know how many of the original requests had been successfully processed.

HTTP Status Codes and Reason Phrases

Every request sent by an HTTP client causes one or more responses to be returned by the server that receives it. As you saw earlier in the discussion of the Response message format, the first line of the response is a status line that contains a summary of the results of processing the request. The purpose of this line is to communicate quickly whether or not the request was successful and why.

HTTP status lines contain both a numeric status code and a text reason phrase. The reason for having both a number and a text string is that computers can more easily understand the results of a request by looking at a number and then can quickly respond accordingly. Humans, on the other hand, find text descriptions easier to comprehend. The idea of using both forms was taken directly from earlier application layer protocols such as FTP, the Simple Mail Transfer Protocol (SMTP), and the Network News Transfer Protocol (NNTP). The explanation of FTP reply codes in Chapter 72 discusses more completely the reasons why numeric reply codes are used in addition to descriptive text.

Status Code Format

HTTP status codes are three digits in length and follow a particular format, where the first digit has particular significance. Unlike the reply codes used by FTP and other protocols, the second digit does not stand for a functional grouping; the second and third digits together just make 100 different options for each of the categories indicated by the first digit. Thus, the general form of an HTTP status code is *xyy*, where the first digit, *x*, is specified as shown in Table 81-1.

Table 81-1: HTTP Status Code Format: First-Digit Interpretation

Status Code Format	Meaning	Description
1yy	Informational message	Provides general information; does not indicate success or failure of a request.
2yy	Success	The method was received, understood, and accepted by the server.
3yy	Redirection	The request did not fail outright, but additional action is needed before it can be successfully completed.
4yy	Client error	The request was invalid, contained bad syntax, or could not be completed for some other reason that the server believes was the client's fault.
5yy	Server error	The request was valid, but the server was unable to complete it due to a problem of its own.

In each of these five groups, the code where *yy* is 00 is defined as a generic status code for that group, while other two-digit combinations are more specific responses. For example, 404 is the well-known specific error message that means the requested resource was not found by the server, and 400 is the less specific Bad Request error. This system was set up to allow the definition of new status codes that certain clients might not comprehend. If a client receives a strange code, it just treats it as the equivalent of the generic response in the appropriate category. So, if a server response starts with the code 491, and the client has no idea what this is, it treats it as a 400 Bad Request reply.

Reason Phrases

The reason phrase is a text string that provides a more meaningful description of the error for people who are bad at remembering what cryptic codes stand for (which would be most of us!). The HTTP standard includes sample reason phrases for each status code, but server administrators can customize these phrases if desired. When a server returns a more detailed HTML error message in the body of its Response message, the reason phrase is often used for the title tag in that message body.

KEY CONCEPT Each HTTP Response message includes both a numeric *status code* and a text *reason phrase*, both of which indicate the disposition of the corresponding client request. The numeric code allows software programs to easily interpret the results of a request, while the text phrase provides more useful information to human users. HTTP status codes are three digits in length, with the first digit indicating the general class of the reply.

Table 81-2 lists in numerical order the status codes defined by the HTTP/1.1 standard, along with the standard reason phrase and a brief description of each.

Table 81-2: HTTP Status Codes and Reason Phrases

Status Code	Reason Phrase	Description
100	Continue	The client should continue sending its request. This is a special status code; see the next section in this chapter for details.
101	Switching Protocols	The client has used the Upgrade header to request the use of an alternative protocol and the server has agreed.
200	OK	This is the generic successful Request message response, which is the code sent most often when a request is filled normally.
201	Created	The request was successful and resulted in a resource being created. This is a typical response to a PUT method.
202	Accepted	The request was accepted by the server, but it has not yet been processed. This is an intentionally noncommittal response that does not tell the client whether or not the request will be carried out. The client determines the eventual disposition of the request in some unspecified way. It is used only in special circumstances.
203	Non-Authoritative Information	The request was successful, but some of the information returned by the server came from a third party, rather than from the original server associated with the resource.
204	No Content	The request was successful, but the server has determined that it does not need to return to the client an entity body.
205	Reset Content	The request was successful; the server is telling the client that it should reset the document from which the request was generated so that a duplicate request is not sent. This code is intended for use with forms.
206	Partial Content	The server has successfully fulfilled a partial GET request. See the section on methods earlier in this chapter for more details on this, as well as the description of the Range header in the next chapter.
300	Multiple Choices	The resource is represented in more than one way on the server. The server is returning information describing these representations, so the client can pick the most appropriate one, a process called agent-driven negotiation (discussed in Chapter 83).
301	Moved Permanently	The resource requested has been moved to a new URL permanently. Any future requests for this resource should use the new URL. This is the proper method of handling situations where a file on a server is renamed or moved to a new directory. Most people don't bother setting this up, which is why URLs break so often, resulting in 404 errors.
302	Found	The resource requested is temporarily using a different URL. The client should continue to use the original URL. See code 307.
303	See Other	The response for the request can be found at a different URL, which the server specifies. The client must do a fresh GET on that URL to see the results of the prior request.
304	Not Modified	The client sent a conditional GET request, but the resource has not been modified since the specified date/time, so the server has not sent it.
305	Use Proxy	To access the requested resource, the client must use a proxy, whose URL is given by the server in its response.
306	(unused)	Defined in an earlier version of HTTP and no longer used.
307	Temporary Redirect	The resource is temporarily located at a different URL than the one the client specified. Note that 302 and 307 are basically the same status code. Code 307 was created to clear up some confusion related to 302 that occurred in earlier versions of HTTP.
400	Bad Request	This is a generic response when the request cannot be understood or carried out due to a problem on the client's end.

(continued)

Table 81-2: HTTP Status Codes and Reason Phrases (continued)

Status Code	Reason Phrase	Description
401	Unauthorized	The client is not authorized to access the resource. This is often returned if an attempt is made to access a resource protected by a password or some other means without the appropriate credentials.
402	Payment Required	This is reserved for future use. Its mere presence in the HTTP standard has caused a lot of people to scratch their chins and go "hmm. . . ."
403	Forbidden	The request has been disallowed by the server. This is a generic "no way" response that is not related to authorization. For example, if the maintainer of website blocks access to it from a particular client, any requests from that client will result in a 403 reply.
404	Not Found	The most common HTTP error message, this is returned when the server cannot locate the requested resource. It usually occurs due to the server having moved (or removed) the resource or the client giving an invalid URL (usually due to misspellings).
405	Method Not Allowed	The requested method is not allowed for the specified resource. The response includes an Allow header that indicates which methods the server will permit.
406	Not Acceptable	The client sent a request that specifies limitations that the server cannot meet for the specified resource. This error may occur if an overly restrictive list of conditions is placed into a request such that the server cannot return any part of the resource.
407	Proxy Authentication Required	This is similar to 401, but the client must first authenticate itself with the proxy.
408	Request Timeout	The server was expecting the client to send a request within a particular time frame and the client didn't send it.
409	Conflict	The request could not be filled because of a conflict of some sort related to the resource. This most often occurs in response to a PUT method, such as if one user tries to PUT a resource that another user has open for editing.
410	Gone	The resource is no longer available at the server, which does not know its new URL. This is a more specific version of the 404 code that is used only if the server knows that the resource was intentionally removed. It is seen rarely (if ever).
411	Length Required	The request requires a Content-Length header field and one was not included.
412	Precondition Failed	This indicates that the client specified a precondition in its request, such as the use of an If-Match header, which evaluated to a false value. This indicates that the condition was not satisfied, so the request is not being filled. This is used by clients in special cases to ensure that they do not accidentally receive the wrong resource.
413	Request Entity Too Large	The server has refused to fulfill the request because the entity that the client is requesting is too large.
414	Request-URI Too Long	The server has refused to fulfill the request because the URL specified is longer than the server can process. This rarely occurs with properly formed URLs, but may be seen if clients try to send gibberish to the server.
415	Unsupported Media Type	The request cannot be processed because it contains an entity using a media type the server does not support.
416	Requested Range Not Satisfiable	The client included a Range header specifying a range of values that is not valid for the resource. An example might be requesting bytes 3000 through 4000 of a 2400-byte file.
417	Expectation Failed	The request included an Expect header that could not be satisfied by the server.
500	Internal Server Error	This is a generic error message indicating that the request could not be fulfilled due to a server problem.

(continued)

Table 81-2: HTTP Status Codes and Reason Phrases (continued)

Status Code	Reason Phrase	Description
501	Not Implemented	The server does not know how to carry out the request, so it cannot satisfy it.
502	Bad Gateway	The server, while acting as a gateway or proxy, received an invalid response from another server it tried to access on the client's behalf.
503	Service Unavailable	The server is temporarily unable to fulfill the request for internal reasons. This is often returned when a server is overloaded or down for maintenance.
504	Gateway Timeout	The server, while acting as a gateway or proxy, timed out while waiting for a response from another server it tried to access on the client's behalf.
505	HTTP Version Not Supported	The request used a version of HTTP that the server does not understand.

The 100 (Continue) Preliminary Reply

Now, let's go back to the top of the list in Table 81-2 and look at the special status code 100. Normally, a client sends a complete request to the server and waits for a response to it (while optionally pipelining additional requests, as described in the previous chapter). In certain circumstances, however, the client might wish to check in advance if the server is willing to accept the request before it bothers sending the whole message. This is not a common occurrence, because most requests are quite small, so checking first isn't worth the bother. However, in cases where a user wants to submit a very large amount of data to an online program or use PUT to store a large file, for example, checking with the server first can be a useful optimization.

In this situation, the client sends a request containing the special header Expect: 100-Continue. Assuming that the server supports the feature, it will process the request's headers and immediately send back the 100 Continue preliminary reply. This tells the client to continue sending the rest of the request. The server then processes it and responds normally. If the server doesn't send the 100 response after a certain amount of time, the client will typically just send the rest of the request anyway. Note that in some cases, servers send these preliminary replies even when they are not supposed to, so clients must be prepared to deal with them (they are simply discarded, since they contain no information).

82

HTTP MESSAGE HEADERS

As you have seen in the preceding two chapters, Hypertext Transfer Protocol (HTTP) communication takes place through the relatively simple exchange of request and response messages. There are only a small number of methods (commands) supported by the protocol, which might give you the impression that the protocol is quite limited. Looks can be deceiving, however. Much of the functionality in HTTP is actually implemented in the form of *message headers*, which convey important details between clients and servers.

Some headers can appear in only HTTP requests, some in only HTTP responses, and some in either type of message. Understanding these headers is important to learning how HTTP works. There are literally dozens of them, and many apply to both Request and Response messages.

In this chapter, I provide a description of each of the many headers used in HTTP Request and Response messages. The chapter is organized by the four basic types of HTTP headers: general headers, request headers, response headers, and entity headers.

BACKGROUND INFORMATION *I assume here that you have already read the preceding chapter describing HTTP message formats.*

NOTE *For the purpose of determining how web caches treat HTTP messages, HTTP headers are categorized as either* end-to-end *or* hop-by-hop *headers. The former are meaningful only to the ultimate recipient of a message, while the latter are relevant to each device in the chain of devices (such as proxies) connecting a client and server. To avoid unnecessary complication, I have not categorized the headers using these categories; see the full discussion of caching in Chapter 84 for more information. In the descriptions of the individual headers, I indicate which headers are hop-by-hop; all others are end-to-end.*

HTTP General Headers

HTTP *general headers* are so named because, unlike headers in the other three categories, they are not specific to any particular kind of message or message component (request, response, or message entity). General headers are used primarily to communicate information about the message itself, as opposed to what content it carries. They provide general information and control how a message is processed and handled.

Despite not being specific to either requests or replies, some general headers are used either mostly or entirely in one or the other type of message. There are also some general headers that can appear in either a Request or a Reply message, but have a somewhat different meaning in each.

Here, I describe the Cache-Control and Warning headers and then the other more straightforward headers.

Cache-Control Headers

A Cache-Control header specifies directives that manage how caching is performed either for an HTTP request or response. These directives affect the handling of a request or response by all devices in the request/response chain from the HTTP client, through any present intermediaries, to the HTTP server (or the other way, from the server, through intermediaries, to the client). They override any default caching behavior performed by a device. See the discussion of caching in Chapter 84 for a full exposition of the subject.

There are a dozen individual directives that can appear in this header, the full details of which can be found in RFC 2616. Even though this is a general header, some directives can appear only in a request or a response. Some also include an additional parameter, such as a number of seconds, that control their interpretation. Table 82-1 provides a brief summary of the different Cache-Control options and how they are used.

Note that only one directive may appear in a Cache-Control header, but more than one such header can appear in a message.

Table 82-1: HTTP Cache-Control Directives

Cache-Control Directive	HTTP Message Type	Description
no-cache	Request or Response	When present, forces a caching device to forward any subsequent requests for the same content to the server for revalidation; that is, the cache must check with the server to ensure that the cached data is still valid. Also see the Pragma header description, for an alternative way of accomplishing the same thing.
public	Response	Indicates that the response may be cached by any cache, including a shared one (a cache used by many clients). See Chapter 84 for more details on shared caches.
private	Response	Specifies that the response is intended for only a particular user and should not be placed into a shared cache.
no-store	Request or Response	Specifies that the entire request or response should not be stored in a cache. This is used sometimes to prevent the storing of sensitive documents in caches where unauthorized people might be able to access them. However, as the HTTP standard points out, this is really a very rudimentary security measure and should not be trusted a great deal (since a malicious cache operator could simply ignore the directive).
max-age	Request or Response	In a request, indicates that the client is willing to accept a response whose age is no greater than the value specified. In a response, indicates the maximum age of the response before it is considered stale. This is an alternative to the use of the Expires header and takes precedence over it.
s-maxage	Response	If present, specifies the maximum age for shared caches receiving the response. Private caches (ones that serve only a single client) use the max-age value (see the preceding description).
min-fresh	Request	Specifies that the client wants a response that is not only not stale at the time the request is received, but that will remain fresh for the specified number of seconds.
max-stale	Request	If sent without a parameter, indicates that the client is willing to accept a stale reply (one that has expired). If a numeric parameter is included, it indicates how stale, in seconds, the response may be.
only-if-cached	Request	Used only in special circumstances, forces the reply to come from a cache only; the content may not come from the actual specified HTTP server.
must-revalidate	Response	Instructs a cache to revalidate its cache entry for the given response with the original server after it becomes stale. This is used to prevent problems with certain types of transactions that can occur if stale cache entries are sent to a client (perhaps as a result of the client using the max-stale directive).
proxy-revalidate	Response	Similar to must-revalidate, but applies only to proxies that service many users. Private caches, such as those on individual client computers, are not affected.
no-transform	Request or Response	Some caches will, by default, change the form in which certain cached entries are stored, to save space or improve performance. In cases where this might cause problems, the client or server can use this directive to request that this transformation not be performed.

Warning

A Warning header is used when it's needed to provide additional information about the status of a message. Many of the defined warning header types are related to caching. More than one Warning header may appear in a message, and each typically includes a three-digit numeric code as well as a plain text message, following the same basic format used in HTTP response status codes (described in Chapter 81). Table 82-2 briefly lists the warnings defined in RFC 2616.

Table 82-2: HTTP Warning Header Codes

Warning Code	Warning Text	Description
110	Response is stale	Must be included when a response provided by a cache is stale (that is, has passed the expiration time set for it).
111	Revalidation failed	A cache attempted to revalidate a cached entry but was unsuccessful, so it returned its (stale) cached entry.
112	Disconnected operation	The cache is disconnected from the rest of the network.
113	Heuristic expiration	Included if the cache chose a freshness lifetime of more than 24 hours, and the age of the response is also greater than 24 hours.
199	Miscellaneous warning	Catchall code for other, nonspecific warnings.
214	Transformation applied	Warns the recipient that an intermediate cache or proxy applied a transformation of some type to change the content coding or media type of the message or message body.
299	Miscellaneous persistent warning	Similar to code 199, but indicates a persistent warning.

Other HTTP General Headers

The following are the other types of HTTP general headers:

Connection Contains instructions that pertain only to this particular connection, and must not be retained by proxies and used for further connections. The most common use of this header is with the `close` parameter, as follows: `Connection: close`. This overrides the default persistent connection behavior of HTTP/1.1 (described in Chapter 80), forcing the connection to terminate after the server's response. Connection is a hop-by-hop header.

Date Indicates the date and time when the message originated. This is the same as the Date header in the RFC 822 email format (described in Chapter 76). A typical example is `Date: Wed, 17 May 2006 16:43:50 GMT`.

Pragma Used to enable implementation-specific directives to be applied to all devices in the request/response chain. One common use of this header is to suppress caching by including `Pragma: no-cache` in a message. This has the same meaning as a `Cache-Control: no-cache` header, and is included in HTTP/1.1 for backward-compatibility with HTTP/1.0 (which supports Pragma but not Cache-Control).

Trailer When chunked transfers are used (as described in Chapter 83), certain headers may be placed as trailers, after the data being sent. In this case, the Trailer header is included before the data, and it lists the names of the headers that are actually trailers in that message. This warns the recipient to look for them after the data. Trailer is a hop-by-hop header.

Transfer-Encoding Indicates what encoding has been used for the body of the message, to ensure that it is able to be transferred properly between devices. This header is most often used with the chunked transfer method. Note that this header describes encoding applied to an entire message, and is thus not the same as the Content-Encoding entity header, which specifically describes the entity carried in a message. See Chapter 83 for a full discussion. This header applies only to a single transfer, so it is a hop-by-hop header.

Upgrade Allows a client device to specify which additional protocols it supports. If the server also supports one of the protocols the client listed, the server may agree to upgrade the connection to the alternative protocol. It indicates the protocol to which it is upgrading by including an Upgrade header in a 101 (Switching Protocols) response to the client. This is a hop-by-hop header.

Via Included by intermediary devices to indicate to the recipient which gateways, proxies, and/or tunnels were used in conveying a request or response. This header allows easy tracing of the path a message took over a potentially complex chain of devices between a client and server.

> **KEY CONCEPT** HTTP *general headers* can appear in either an HTTP Request or HTTP Response message. They are used to communicate information about the message itself, as opposed to its contents. General headers are used for functions such as specifying the date and time of a message, controlling how the message is cached, and indicating its transfer encoding method.

HTTP Request Headers

HTTP *request headers*, as you might imagine, are used only in HTTP Request messages, where they serve a number of functions. First, they allow the client to provide information about itself to the server. Second, they give additional details about the nature of the request that the client is making. Third, they allow the client to have greater control over how its request is processed and how (or even if) a response is returned by the server or intermediary.

This is the largest of the four categories of HTTP headers, containing more than a dozen different types, as follows:

Accept Allows the client to tell the server which Internet media types it is willing to accept in a response. The header may list several different Multipurpose Internet Mail Extensions (MIME) media types and subtypes that the client knows how to deal with. Each may be prepended with a quality value (q parameter) to indicate the client's preference. If this header is not specified, the default is for the server to assume any media type may be sent to the client. See the discussion of entity media types and content negotiation in Chapter 83 for more information about how this header is used.

Accept-Charset Similar to Accept, but specifies which character sets (charsets) the client is willing to accept in a response, rather than which media types. Again, the listed charsets may use a `q` value, and again, the default if the header is omitted is for the client to accept any charset.

Accept-Encoding Similar to Accept and Accept-Charset, but specifies which content encodings the client is willing to accept. This is often used to control whether the server may send content in compressed form. (As you'll learn in Chapter 83, content codings are not the same as transfer encodings.)

Accept-Language Similar to the preceding Accept-type headers, but provides a list of *language tags* that indicates which languages the client supports or expects the server to use in its response.

Authorization Used by the client to present authentication information (called *credentials*) to the server to allow the client to be authenticated. This is required only when the server requests authentication, often by sending a 401 (Unauthorized) response to the client's initial request. This response will contain a WWW-Authenticate header providing the client with details on how to authenticate with the server. See the discussion of security and privacy in Chapter 84 for more information.

Expect Indicates certain types of actions that the client is expecting the server to perform. Usually, the server will accept the indicated parameters; if not, it will send back a 417 (Expectation Failed) response. The most common use of this field is to control when the server sends a 100 (Continue) response. The client indicates that it wants the server to send this preliminary reply by including the Expect: 100-Continue header in its request. (See the discussion of status codes at the end of Chapter 81 for details.)

From Contains the email address of the human user making the request. This is optional, and since it is easily spoofed, should be used only for informational purposes, and not for any type of access rights determination or authentication.

Host Specifies the Internet host as a Domain Name System (DNS) domain name and may also contain a port number specification as well (typically, only if a port other than the HTTP default of 80 is to be used). This header is used to allow multiple domains to be served by the same web server on a particular Internet Protocol (IP) host. It has the distinction of being the only mandatory header—it must be present in all HTTP/1.1 requests.

If-Match Makes a method conditional by specifying the *entity tag* (or tags) corresponding to the specific entity that the client wishes to access. This is usually used in a GET method, and the server responds with the entity only if it matches the one specified in this header. Otherwise, the server sends a 412 (Precondition Failed) reply.

If-Modified-Since Makes a method conditional by telling the server to return the requested entity only if it has been modified since the time specified in this header. Otherwise, the server sends a 304 (Not Modified) response. This is used to check if a resource has changed since it was last accessed, to avoid unnecessary transfers.

If-None-Match The opposite of If-Match; it creates a conditional request that is only filled if the specified tag(s) do not match the requested entity.

If-Range Used in combination with the Range header to effectively allow a client to both check for whether an entity has changed and request that a portion of it be sent in a single request. (The alternative is to first issue a conditional request, and if it fails, issue a second request.) When present, If-Range tells the server to send to the client the part of the entity indicated in the Range header if the entity has not changed. If the entity has changed, the server sends the entire entity in response.

If-Unmodified-Since The logical opposite of the If-Modified-Since header; the request is filled only if the resource has *not* been modified since the specified time. Otherwise, the server sends a 412 reply.

Max-Forwards Specifies a limit on the number of times a request can be forwarded to the next device in the request chain. This header is used with the TRACE or OPTIONS methods only, to permit diagnosis of forwarding failures or looping. When present in one of these methods, each time a device forwards the request, the number in this header is decremented. If a device receives a request with a Max-Forwards value of 0, it must not forward it, but rather it should respond back to the client. (In a way, this is somewhat analogous to how the Time to Live field is used in the IP datagram format, as described in Chapter 21.)

Proxy-Authorization Like the Authorization header, but used to present credentials to a proxy server for authentication, rather than to the end server. It is created using information sent by a proxy in a response containing a Proxy-Authenticate header. This is a hop-by-hop header, sent only to the first proxy that receives the request. If authentication is required with more than one proxy, multiple Proxy-Authorization headers may be put in a message, with each proxy consuming one of the headers.

Range Allows the client to request that the server send it only a portion of an entity, by specifying a range of bytes in the entity to be retrieved. If the requested range is valid, the server sends only the indicated part of the file, using a 206 (Partial Content) status code; if the range requested cannot be filled, the reply is 416 (Requested Range Not Satisfiable).

Referer Tells the server the Uniform Resource Locator (URL) of the resource from which the URL of the current request was obtained. Typically, when a user clicks a link on one web page to load another, the address of the original web page is put into the Referer line when the request for the clicked link is sent. This allows tracking and logging of how the server is accessed. If a human user manually enters a Uniform Resource Identifier (URI) into a web browser, this header is not included in the request. Since this header provides information related to how web pages are used, it has certain privacy implications.

NOTE *The proper spelling of this word is* referrer. *It was misspelled years ago in an earlier version of the HTTP standard, and before this was noticed and corrected, this spelling became incorporated into so much software that the Internet Engineering Task Force (IETF) chose not to correct the spelling in HTTP/1.1.*

TE Provides information to the server about how the client wishes to deal with transfer encodings for entities sent by the server. If extensions to the standard HTTP transfer encodings are defined, the client can indicate its willingness to accept them in this header. The client can also use the header `TE: trailers` to indicate its ability to handle having headers sent as trailers following data when chunking of data is done. This is a hop-by-hop header and applies only to the immediate connection.

User-Agent Provides information about the client software. This is normally the name and version number of the web browser or other program sending the request. It is used for server access statistic logging and also may be used to tailor how the server responds to the needs of different clients. Note that proxies do not modify this field when forwarding a request; rather, they use the Via header.

> **KEY CONCEPT** HTTP *request headers* are used only in HTTP Request messages. They allow a client to provide information about itself to a server, provide more details about a request, and allow control over how the request is carried out.

HTTP Response Headers

The counterpart to request headers, *response headers*, appear only in HTTP responses sent by servers or intermediaries. They provide additional data that expands on the summary information that is present in the status line at the beginning of each server reply. Many of the response headers are sent only in response to the receipt of specific types of requests or even to particular headers within certain requests.

There are nine response headers defined for HTTP/1.1:

Accept-Ranges Tells the client whether the server accepts partial content requests using the Range request header, and if so, what type. For example, include `Accept-Range: bytes` indicates the server accepts byte ranges, and `Accept-Range: none` indicates range requests are not supported. Note that this is header is different from the other Accept- headers, which are used in HTTP requests to perform content negotiation.

Age Tells the client the approximate age of the resource, as calculated by the device sending the response.

ETag Specifies the entity tag for the entity included in the response. This value can be used by the client in future requests to uniquely identify an entity, using the If-Match (or similar) request header.

Location Indicates a new URL that the server is instructing the client to use in place of the one the client initially requested. This header is normally used when the server redirects a client request to a new location, using a 301, 302, or 307 reply. It is also used to indicate the location of a created resource in a 201 (Created) response to a PUT request. Note that this is not the same as the Content-Location entity header, which is used to indicate the location of the originally requested resource.

Proxy-Authenticate The proxy version of the WWW-Authenticate header (described next). It is included in a 407 (Proxy Authentication Required) response, to indicate how the proxy is requiring the client to perform authentication. The header specifies an authentication method, as well as any other parameters needed for authentication. The client will use this to generate a new request containing a Proxy-Authorization header. This is a hop-by-hop header.

Retry-After Sometimes included in unsuccessful requests—such as those resulting in a 503 (Service Unavailable) response—to tell the client when it should try its request again. It may also be used with a redirection response such as 301, 302, or 307 to indicate how long the client should wait before sending a request for the redirected URL. The Retry-After header may specify either a time interval to wait (in seconds) or a full date/time when the server suggests the client try again.

Server The server's version of the User-Agent request header. It identifies the type and version of the server software generating the response. Note that proxies do not modify this field when forwarding a response; they put their identification information into a Via header instead.

Vary Specifies which request header fields fully determine whether a cache is allowed to use this response to reply to subsequent requests for the same resource without revalidation. A caching device inspects the Vary header to ascertain which other headers it needs to examine when the client makes its next request for the resource in this reply, to determine whether it can respond with a cached entry. (See Chapter 84 for more information about caching, which should make the use of this header easier to understand.)

WWW-Authenticate Included in a 401 (Unauthorized) response to indicate how the server wants the client to authenticate. The header specifies an authentication method as well as any other parameters needed for authentication. The client will use this to generate a new request containing an Authorization header.

> **KEY CONCEPT** HTTP *response headers* appear in HTTP Response messages, where they provide additional information about HTTP server capabilities and requirements, and the results of processing a client request.

HTTP Entity Headers

Last, but not least, we come to the fourth group of HTTP headers: *entity headers.* These headers provide information about the resource carried in the body of an HTTP message, called an *entity* in the HTTP standards. They serve the overall purpose of conveying to the recipient of a message the information it needs to properly process and display the entity, such as its type and encoding method.

The most common type of entity is a file or another set of information that has been requested by a client, and for this reason, entity headers most often appear in HTTP Response messages. However, they can also appear in HTTP Request messages, especially those using the PUT and POST methods, which are the ones that transfer data from a client to a server.

At least one entity header should appear in any HTTP message that carries an entity. However, they may also be present in certain responses that do not have an actual entity in them. Most notably, a response to a HEAD request will contain all the entity headers associated with the resource specified in the request; these are the same headers that would have been included with the entity had the GET method been used instead of the HEAD method on the same resource. Entity headers may also be present in certain error responses to provide information to help the client make a successful follow-up request.

NOTE *Many of the entity headers have the same names as certain MIME headers, but they are often used in different ways. See the topic on HTTP Internet media types in Chapter 83 for a full discussion of the relationship between HTTP and MIME.*

There are ten entity headers defined for HTTP/1.1:

Allow Lists all the methods that are supported for a particular resource. This header may be provided in a server response as a guide to the client regarding what methods it may use on the resource in the future. The header must be included when a server returns a 405 (Method Not Allowed) response to a request containing an unsupported method.

Content-Encoding Describes any optional method that may have been used to encode the entity. This header is most often used when transferring entities that have been compressed. It tells the recipient which algorithm has been used so the entity can be uncompressed. Note that this header describes only transformations performed on the entity in a message; the Transfer-Encoding header describes encodings done on the message as a whole. See the discussion of content codings and transfer codings in Chapter 83 for more details.

Content-Language Specifies the natural (human) language intended for using the entity. This is an optional header, and it may not be appropriate for all resource types. Multiple languages may be specified, if needed. This header is intended to provide guidance so the entity can be presented to the correct audience; thus, the language should be selected based on who would best use the material, which may not necessarily include all of the languages used in the entity. For example, a German analysis of Italian operas would probably be best tagged only with the language *de.*

Content-Length Indicates the size of the entity in octets. This header is important, as it is used by the recipient to determine the end of a message. However, it may be included only in cases where the length of a message can be fully determined prior to transmitting the entity. This is not always possible in the case of dynamically generated content, which complicates message-length calculation; the discussion of data length and chunked transfer encoding in Chapter 83 contains a full exploration of this issue.

Content-Location Specifies the resource location of the entity, in the form of an absolute or relative URL. This is an optional header, and it is normally included only in cases where the entity has been supplied from a location different from the one specified in the request. This may occur if a particular resource is stored in multiple places.

Content-MD5 Contains a Message Digest 5 (MD5) digest for the entity, used for checking message integrity.

Content-Range Sent when a message contains an entity that is only part of a complete resource—for example, a fragment of a file sent in response to an HTTP GET request containing the Range header. The Content-Range header indicates which portion of the overall file this message contains, as well as the total size of the resource. This information is given as a byte range, with the first byte numbered 0. For example, if the entity contains the first 1200 bytes of a 2000-byte file, this header would have a value of 0-1199/2000.

Content-Type Specifies the media type and subtype of the entity, in a manner very similar to how this header is used in MIME. See Chapter 83 for a full discussion.

Expires Specifies a date and time after which the entity in the message should be considered stale. This may be used to identify certain entities that should be held in HTTP caches for longer or shorter periods of time than usual. This header is ignored if a Cache-Control header containing the max-age directive is present in the message.

Last-Modified Indicates the date and time when the server believes the entity was last changed. This header is often used to determine if a resource has been modified since it was last retrieved. For example, suppose a client machine already contains a copy of a very large file that was obtained two months ago, and its user wants to check if an update to the file is available. The client can send a HEAD request for the file, and compare the value of the returned Last-Modified header to the date of the copy of the file it already has. Then it needs to request the entire file only if it has changed.

Note the use of the word "believes" in the preceding description of the Last-Modified header. The reason for this wording is that the server cannot always be certain of the time that a resource was modified. With files this is fairly simple—it is usually the last-modified time stored for the file by the operating system. For other more complex resources such as database records or virtual objects, however, it may be more difficult to ascertain when the last change occurred to a particular piece of information. In the case of dynamically generated content, the Last-Modified date/time may be the same as that of the message as a whole, as specified in the Date field.

> **KEY CONCEPT** HTTP *entity headers* appear in either Request or Response messages that carry an entity in the message body. They describe the nature of the entity, including its type, language, and encoding, to facilitate the proper processing and presentation of the entity by the device receiving it.

83

HTTP ENTITIES, TRANSFERS, CODING METHODS, AND CONTENT MANAGEMENT

Hypertext Transfer Protocol (HTTP) message headers are very important, because they are the mechanism that HTTP uses to allow devices to specify the details of client requests and server responses. These headers, however, are only the means to an end, which is the transfer of resources (such as files, form input, and program output) from one device to another. When a resource is carried in the body of an HTTP message, it is called an *entity*. HTTP defines special rules for how these entities are identified, encoded, and transferred.

In this chapter, I explain how HTTP handles entities. I begin with a discussion of entities in general terms and a look at how their contents are identified. This includes an examination of the relationship between HTTP and Multipurpose Internet Mail Extensions (MIME). I discuss the issues behind the transfer of entities between clients and servers, and the difference between content encodings and transfer encodings. I describe the special issues associated with identifying the length of entities in HTTP messages, and detail the special chunked transfer coding and message trailers. Finally, I describe the methods by which devices can perform content negotiation and how quality values allow clients to intelligently select different variations of a resource.

HTTP Entities and Internet Media Types

The presence of the word *text* in the name Hypertext Transfer Protocol is a reminder of the legacy of HTTP. As I explained in Chapter 80, HTTP was originally created to allow text documents to be linked together. This made sense, because at the time that the Web was being created, most computing was being done with text. Accordingly, the first version of HTTP (HTTP/0.9) supported only one type of message body: a plain ASCII text document.

In the early 1990s, the rapid increase in computing power and networking performance transformed the world of information technology from text to multimedia. These were also the Web's formative years, and it did not take long before many users wanted to exploit the power of the Web to share not only text files, but also pictures, drawings, sound clips, movies, and much more. Thus, HTTP had to evolve as well. Starting with HTTP/1.0, the protocol's developers made significant changes to allow HTTP to transport and process much more than just text. Today, HTTP really would be better described as dealing with *hypermedia* than *hypertext.*

One drawback of supporting many types of files in HTTP is added complexity. Previously, every message recipient knew the body contained ASCII text; now any message can contain any of many kinds of data. When HTTP was expanded to support flexible media, it needed a system that would address two specific issues: encoding entities of various types into an HTTP message body and clearly identifying the entity's characteristics for the recipient of the message.

At the same time that HTTP was being changed to support nontext entities, another important TCP/IP application was also moving away from its decades-long role as a text-messaging medium to one that could transport multimedia: electronic mail (email). This was accomplished using a technology called MIME (introduced in Chapter 76), which define a mechanism for encoding and identifying nontext data—exactly what HTTP needed to do. Since TCP/IP developers wisely reuse technologies that work, the creators of HTTP borrowed many concepts from MIME, including many of the MIME email headers that are used to identify the contents of a MIME message.

Media Types and Subtypes

The most important concept that HTTP adopted from MIME was the use of standardized Internet media types, which describe the contents of an HTTP entity. The formal syntax of an HTTP media type is the same as that used in MIME:

<type>/<subtype> [; *parameter1* ; *parameter2* ... ; *parameterN*]

Each media type consists of a top-level media type that defines its general nature and a more specific subtype that indicates its form or structure. For example, text documents use the top-level media type `text`, with subtypes such as `plain` for regular unformatted text and `html` for HTML documents. So, an HTML document of the type commonly transported using HTTP will be identified with a media type of `text/html`. Similarly, `image` is a top-level media type, with subtypes such as `jpeg`, `gif`, and `tiff`. Photographs usually are identified as `image/jpeg`, while line drawings are often seen as `image/gif`. Additional parameters may also be supplied to provide more information to help a recipient interpret the entity.

HTTP's Use of Media Types

In HTTP, media types are most often seen in a special Content-Type entity header, which is present in any HTTP message that carries an entity. This header uses the same format as the header of the same name in MIME:

Content-Type: <*type*>/<*subtype*> [; *parameter1* ; *parameter2* ... ; *parameterN*]

RELATED INFORMATION *I provide a more complete description of both the Content-Type header and Internet media types, including a description of many types and subtypes, in Chapter 76. HTTP can also support composite media types, such as the multipart media type.*

The other place where media types are used in HTTP is in the Accept request header, which may appear in an HTTP request sent by a client. If present, the purpose of this header is to tell the server what sorts of media types the client can handle, so the server will not send a response that cannot be processed. For example, if a client can process only text documents, it might send a request specifying this in an Accept header. This is part of the overall content negotiation process supported by HTTP, which I describe in the "HTTP Content Negotiation and Quality Values" section later in this chapter.

When a media type is specified in an Accept header, either the subtype or both the type and subtype can be replaced by the asterisk (*) wildcard to represent any acceptable type. For example, in an Accept header, the specification `text/html` refers to an HTML document, while `text/*` means any text type. The string `*/*` means any type of media; this is usually used in combination with a `q` value, as explained in the discussion of the HTTP content negotiation process later in this chapter.

KEY CONCEPT While HTTP is most often associated with hypertext, its messages can transport a large variety of different types of files, including images, audio, video, and much more. To indicate the type of entity contained in an HTTP message, its sender must identify its media *type* and *subtype*. This is done using the HTTP Content-Type header, which was borrowed from the Multipurpose Internet Mail Extensions (MIME) specification.

Differences in HTTP and MIME Constructs

In addition to media types, HTTP also borrows from MIME in several other ways, such as MIME's notion of content codings and the use of a header to indicate the length of an entity. It's important to recognize, however, that even though HTTP's handling of Internet media is very similar to that of MIME, it is not identical. In fact, there was an early proposal that HTTP use MIME exactly as defined, but HTTP's developers specifically decided not to do this. We will explore a possible reason why HTTP is not strictly MIME-compliant in the next section.

The bottom line is that HTTP's developers chose to adopt concepts from MIME that made sense and to leave other parts out. As a result, HTTP messages are not MIME-compliant, even though you may see several headers in HTTP messages starting with MIME's Content- prefix. For example, even though HTTP has a Content-Encoding header, its use is quite different from that of MIME's. The fact that HTTP does not use the MIME-Version header that is required in MIME messages confirms the difference between HTTP and MIME.

> **KEY CONCEPT** Even though HTTP borrows several concepts and header types from MIME, the protocol is not MIME-compliant.

HTTP Content and Transfer Encodings

Two specific issues that HTTP must address in order to carry a wide variety of media types in its messages are encoding the data and identifying its type and characteristics. HTTP borrows from MIME the notion of media types and the Content-Type header to handle type identification, as explained in the previous section. It similarly borrows concepts and headers from MIME to deal with the encoding issue. Here, however, we run into some of the important differences between HTTP and MIME.

Encoding was a significant issue for MIME, because it was created for the specific purpose of sending nontext data using the old RFC 822 email message standard (discussed in Chapter 76). RFC 822 imposes several significant restrictions on the messages it carries, the most important of which is that data must be encoded using 7-bit ASCII. RFC 822 messages are also limited to lines of no more than 1,000 characters that end in a carriage return/line feed (CRLF) sequence.

These limitations mean that arbitrary binary files, which have no concept of lines and consist of bytes that can each contain a value from 0 to 255, cannot be sent using RFC 822 in their native format. In order for MIME to transfer binary files, they must be encoded using a method such as base64 (described in Chapter 76), which converts three 8-bit characters to a set of four 6-bit characters that can be represented in ASCII. When this sort of transformation is done, the MIME Content-Transfer-Encoding header is included in the message, so the recipient can reverse the encoding to return the data to its normal form. Although this technique works, it is less efficient than sending the data directly in binary, because base64 encoding increases the size of the message by 33 percent (three bytes are encoded using four ASCII characters, each of which takes one byte to transmit).

HTTP messages are transmitted directly between the client and server over a Transmission Control Protocol (TCP) connection, and they do not use the RFC 822 standard. Thus, binary data can be sent between HTTP clients and servers without the need for base64 encoding or other transformation techniques. Since it is more efficient to send the data unencoded, this may be one reason why HTTP's developers decided not to make the protocol strictly MIME-compliant.

HTTP's Two-Level Encoding Scheme

So, encoding would seem to be an area where HTTP is simpler than MIME. There is no need to encode the entity, and thus no need for the Content-Transfer-Encoding header, so we have one less thing to worry about. It is true that HTTP could have been designed so that all entities were just sent one byte at a time with no need to specify encodings, but the developers of the protocol recognized that this would have made the protocol inflexible. There are situations where it might be useful to transform or encode an entity or message for transmission, and then reverse the operation on receipt.

This effort to make HTTP flexible resulted in a system of representing encodings that is actually more complicated than MIME's! The key to understanding it is to recognize that HTTP/1.1 actually splits MIME's notion of content transfer encoding into two different encoding levels:

Content Encoding This encoding is applied specifically to the entity carried in an HTTP message, to prepare or package it prior to transmission. Content encodings are said to be *end-to-end,* because the encoding of the entity is done once before it sent by the client or server, and decoded only on receipt by the ultimate recipient: server or client. When this type of encoding is done, the method is identified in the special Content-Encoding entity header. A client may also specify which content encodings it can handle, using the Accept-Encoding header, as you will see in the section on content negotiation later in this chapter.

Transfer Encoding This encoding is done specifically for the purpose of ensuring that data can be safely transferred between devices. It is applied across an entire HTTP message and not specifically to the entity. This type of encoding is *hop-by-hop,* because a different transfer encoding may be used for each hop of a message that is transmitted through many intermediaries in the request/response chain. The transfer encoding method, if any, is indicated in the Transfer-Encoding general header.

Use of Content and Transfer Encodings

Since the content and transfer encodings are applied at different levels, it is possible for both to be used at the same time. A content encoding may be applied to an entity and then placed into a message. On some or all of the hops that are used to move the message containing that entity, a transfer encoding may be applied to the entire message (including the entity). The transfer encoding is removed first, and then the content encoding is removed.

So, what are these types of encodings used for in practice? The answer is not a great deal. The HTTP standard defines a small number of content and transfer encodings, and specifies that additional methods may be registered with the Internet Assigned Numbers Authority (IANA). Currently, only the ones defined in the HTTP/1.1 standard are in use.

Content encodings are used only to implement compression. This is a good example of an encoding that, while not strictly necessary, can be useful since it improves performance dramatically for some types of data. RFC 2616 defines three different encoding algorithms:

- `gzip`, which is the compression used by the UNIX `gzip` program, described in RFC 1952
- `compress`, which also represents the compression method used by the UNIX program of that name
- `deflate`, which is a method defined in RFCs 1950 and 1951

NOTE *It is also possible to apply compression to an entire HTTP message as a transfer encoding. Obviously, if the entity is already compressed using content encoding, this will result in some duplication of effort. Since the size of HTTP headers is not that large compared to some entities that HTTP messages carry, it is usually simpler just to compress the entity using content encoding.*

Since transfer encodings are intended to be used to make data safe for transfer, and we've already discussed the fact that HTTP can handle arbitrary binary data, this suggests that transfer encodings are not really necessary. However, there is one situation where safe transport does become an issue: the matter of identifying the end of a message. This issue is the subject of the next section.

KEY CONCEPT HTTP supports two levels of codings for data transfer. The first is *content encoding*, which is used in certain circumstances to transform the entity carried in an HTTP message. The second is *transfer encoding*, which is used to encode an entire HTTP message to ensure its safe transport. Content encodings are often employed when entities are compressed to improve communication efficiency. Transfer encoding is used primarily to deal with the problem of identifying the end of a message.

HTTP Data Length Issues, Chunked Transfers, and Message Trailers

As you've learned, two different levels of encodings are used in HTTP: *content encodings*, which are applied to HTTP entities, and *transfer encodings*, which are used over entire HTTP messages. Content encodings are used for convenience to package entities for transmission. Transfer encodings are hop-specific, and they are intended for use in situations where data needs to be made safe for transfer.

However, we've already seen that HTTP can transport arbitrary binary data, so unlike the situation where MIME needed to make binary data safe (as defined in RFC 822), this is not an issue with HTTP. Therefore, why are transport encodings needed at all? In theory, they are not, and HTTP/1.0 did not even have a Transfer-Encoding header (though it did use content encodings). The concept of transfer encoding became important in HTTP/1.1 due to another key feature of that version of HTTP: persistent connections (described in Chapter 80).

Dynamic Data Length

Recall that HTTP uses TCP for connections. One of the key characteristics of TCP is that it transmits all data as a stream of unstructured bytes (see Chapter 46). TCP itself does not provide any way of differentiating between the end of one piece of data and the start of the next; this is left up to each application. In HTTP/1.0 (and HTTP/0.9), this was not a problem, because those versions used only transitory connections. Each HTTP session consisted of only one request and one response. Since the client and server each sent only one piece of data, there was no need to worry about differentiating HTTP messages on a connection.

HTTP/1.1's persistent connections improve performance by letting devices send requests and responses one after the other over a single TCP connection. However, the fact that messages are sent in sequence makes differentiating them a concern. There are two usual approaches to dealing with this sort of data length issue: using an explicit delimiter to mark the end of the message, or including a length header or field to tell the recipient how long each message is. The first approach could not really have been done easily while maintaining compatibility with older versions of the protocol. This left the second approach. Since HTTP already had a Content-Length entity header, the solution was to use this to indicate the length of each message at transmission time.

Using the Content-Length header works fine in cases where the size of the entity to be transferred is known in advance, such as when transmitting a text document, an image, or an executable program needs. However, there are many types of resources that are generated dynamically. In those cases, the total size of such a resource is not known until it has been completely processed.

While not typical in HTTP's early days, dynamic resources account for a large percentage of Web traffic today. Many web pages are often not static Hypertext Markup Language (HTML) files, but instead are created as output from scripts or programs based on user input; discussion forums are a good example. Even modern HTML files are often not static. They usually contain program elements such as *server-side includes (SSIs)* that cause code to be generated on the fly, so their exact size cannot be determined in advance.

The problem of unknown message length could be resolved by buffering the entire resource before transmission. However, this would be wasteful of server memory and would delay the transmission of the entity unnecessarily, since no part could be sent until the entire entity was ready. Instead, a special transfer encoding method was developed to handle the particular problem of not knowing the length of a file. The method is called *chunking*.

Chunked Transfers and Message Trailers

When the chunking technique is used, instead of sending an entity as a raw sequence of bytes, it is broken into, well, chunks. This allows HTTP to send a dynamically generated resource, such as output from a script, a piece at a time as the data becomes available from the software processing it. To indicate that this method has been used, the special header `Transfer-Encoding: chunked` is placed in the message. A special format is also used for the body of the HTTP message to delineate the chunks:

<*chunk-1-length*>

<*chunk-1-data*>

<*chunk-2-length*>

<*chunk-2-data*>

...

0

<*message-trailers*>

Basically, instead of putting the whole entity in the body and indicating its length in a Content-Length header, each chunk is placed in the body sequentially, each preceded by the length of the chunk. The length is specified in hexadecimal and represented using ASCII characters. All chunk lengths and chunk data are terminated with a CRLF sequence. The recipient knows it has received the last chunk when it sees a chunk length of zero.

NOTE *An HTTP/1.1 client can specify that it does not want to use persistent connections by including the* `Connection: close` *header in its request. In this case, the server does not have to use chunking in its response. Since the server will close the connection after the first response message, the client knows that everything it receives from the server is part of that response. However, some servers may use chunked transfers anyway, even in this situation.*

When chunked transfer encoding is used, the sender of the message may also choose to specify one or more *message trailers.* These are the same as entity headers, describing the contents of the message body, but appear *after* the entity, rather than *before* it. Message trailers provide flexibility in the same way that chunking itself does: They allow a device to include an HTTP header that may contain information that was not available when the HTTP message transmission began. A good example would be an integrity check field calculated based on the byte values of the entire entity.

Trailers are optional, and they will not always be needed. When they are used, they are processed just like regular entity headers. To give the recipient of a message a "heads up" that trailers have been used, the special Trailer header is included at the start of the message, which lists the names of each header that appears as a trailer.

Yes, I really did say that headers can actually be trailers, in which case, a header called Trailer lists each header that is actually a trailer. An example will help clarify matters somewhat. Suppose we have a server that contains a program that, when supplied with a filename, returns a simple HTML response that contains the size and last modification date of the file. This is obviously dynamic content, so the length of the response cannot be determined in advance. If the server were to buffer the entire output of this program (since it is small), it could construct a conventional HTTP response using the Content-Length header, as shown in the sample output of Listing 83-1.

```
HTTP/1.1 200 OK
Date: Tue, 22 Mar 2005 11:15:03 GMT
Content-Type: text/html
Content-Length: 129
Expires: Sun, 27 Mar 2005 21:12:00 GMT

<html><body><p>The file you requested is 3,400 bytes long and was last modified:
Sun, 20 Mar 2005 21:12:00 GMT.</p></body></html>
```

Listing 83-1: *Example of an HTTP Response using a Content-Length header*

Using chunking instead allows the server to send out parts of the response as soon as they become available from the program. The equivalent output of the example shown in Listing 83-1 using chunked transfers is shown in Listing 83-2.

```
HTTP/1.1 200 OK
Date: Tue, 22 Mar 2005 11:15:03 GMT
Content-Type: text/html
Transfer-Encoding: chunked
Trailer: Expires

29
<html><body><p>The file you requested is
5
3,400
23
 bytes long and was last modified:
1d
Sun, 20 Mar 2005 21:12:00 GMT
13
.</p></body></html>
0
Expires: Sun, 27 Mar 2005 21:12:00 GMT
```

Listing 83-2: *Example of an HTTP Response using chunked transfer encoding*

In Listing 83-2, notice that the Expires header is now a trailer, so it can be calculated based on the output of the program, and this is indicated by the Trailer: Expires header. Remember that the Content-Length header specifies the length as a decimal number while chunking specifies chunk lengths in hexadecimal; the chunks in this example are 41, 5, 35, 29, and 19 decimal bytes, respectively.

KEY CONCEPT Since HTTP/1.1 uses persistent connections that allow multiple requests and responses to be sent over a TCP connection, clients and servers need some way to identify where one message ends and the next begins. The easier solution is to use the Content-Length header to indicate the size of a message, but this works only when the length of a message can be determined in advance. For dynamic content or other cases where message length cannot be easily computed before sending the data, the special *chunked* transfer encoding can be used, where the message body is sent as a sequence of chunks, each preceded by the length of the chunk. When chunked transfer encoding is used, the sender of the message may move certain headers from the start of the message to the end, where they are known as *trailers*. Trailers are interpreted in the same way as normal headers by the recipient. The special Trailer header is used in such messages to tell the recipient to look for trailers after the body of the message.

HTTP Content Negotiation and Quality Values

Many Internet resources have only one representation, meaning a single way in which they are stored or made available. In this situation, a client request to a server is an all-or-nothing proposition. The client may specify conditions under which it would like the server to send the resource, using the If- series of request headers described in the previous chapter. If the condition is met, the resource will be sent in the server's response in the one form in which it exists; if the condition is not met, no entity will be returned.

Other resources, however, may have multiple representations. The most common example is a document that is available in multiple languages, or one that is stored using more than one character set. Similarly, a graphical image might exist in two different formats: a Tagged Image File Format (TIFF) file, for those who want maximum image quality despite the large size of TIFF images, and a more compact JPEG file, for those who need to see the image quickly and don't care as much about its quality level.

To provide flexibility in allowing clients to obtain the best version of resources that exist in multiple forms, HTTP/1.1 defines a set of features that are collectively called *content negotiation*.

Content Negotiation Techniques

The HTTP/1.1 standard defines two basic methods by which this negotiation may be performed.

Server-Driven Negotiation In this technique, the client includes headers in its request that provide guidance to the server about its desired representation for the resource. The server uses an algorithm that processes this information and provides the version of the resource that it feels best matches the client's preferences.

Agent-Driven Negotiation This method puts the client in charge of the negotiation process. It first sends a preliminary request for the resource to the server. If the resource is available in multiple forms, the server typically sends back a 300 (Multiple Choices) response, which contains a list of the various representations in which the resource is available. The client then sends a second request for the one that it prefers.

To draw an analogy, suppose a co-worker offers to go out at lunchtime to pick up lunch for the two of you. He is going to a new restaurant, where neither of you have eaten before. You could provide him with some parameters regarding what you like to eat—"I like roast beef sandwiches, fish and chips, and pizza, but not chicken"—and then trust him to pick something you will like. Alternatively, he could go to the restaurant, call you on his cell phone, read the menu to you, and let you make a selection. This former approach is like server-driven negotiation; the latter is like agent-driven negotiation.

This analogy not only points out the differences between the two methods, but it also highlights the key advantages and disadvantages of each. Trusting your co-worker with your lunch selection is simple and efficient, but not foolproof. It's possible that the restaurant may not have any of the items you specified, or that your friend may get you something containing another ingredient that you don't like but forgot to mention. Similarly, server-based negotiation is a best-guess process that does not guarantee that the client will receive the resource in the format it wants. This is exacerbated by the fact that there are only so many ways for the client to specify its preferences using a handful of request headers.

Agent-based negotiation, on the other hand, allows the client to select exactly what it wants from the available choices, just as you can choose your favorite dish from the menu of the restaurant. The problem here is that it is inefficient, because two requests and responses are required for each resource access. (Would you really want to read a restaurant's menu over the phone to someone so he could choose his ideal dish?)

In practice, server-based negotiation is the type that is most commonly used today. The client specifies its preferences using a set of four request headers that indicate what it would prefer in the representation of the resource. The headers each represents one characteristic of a resource: Accept (media type), Accept-Charset (character set), Accept-Encoding (content encoding), and Accept-Language (resource language). Any or all of these may be included in the request. Each Accept- header contains a list of acceptable values that is appropriate to the characteristic that it specifies, separated by a comma. For example, the Accept header lists media types the client considers acceptable, and Accept-Language contains language tags.

For example, suppose you have a friend who is trilingual in English, French, and Spanish. She can read a particular document in any of these languages, so she might instruct her browser to include the following header in her requests:

```
Accept-Language: en, fr, sp
```

KEY CONCEPT HTTP includes a feature called *content negotiation* that allows the selection of a particular variation of a resource that has more than one representation. There are two negotiation techniques: *server-driven*, where the client includes headers in its request that indicate what it wants and the server does its best to select the most appropriate variant, and *agent-driven*, where the server sends the client a list of the available resource alternatives and the client chooses one.

Quality Values for Preference Weights

To improve the results of server-driven negotiation, HTTP allows the client to *weight* each of the items in such a list, to indicate which is preferred of the alternatives. The client specifies weights by adding a decimal *quality value* after each parameter using the syntax `q=<value>`, which represents the relative priority of that parameter relative to others. The highest priority is 1, and the lowest priority is 0. The default if no value is indicated is 1. A value of 0 means that the client will not accept documents with that characteristic.

For example, suppose your trilingual friend knows English, French, and Spanish, but her French is a bit rusty. Furthermore, she may need to share the document she is requesting with a friend of hers who knows only a little Spanish, so it would be best if she got the document in English. Finally, she knows there is a German version of the resource that she definitely does not want. This could be represented as follows:

```
Accept-Language: en, fr;q=0.3, sp;q=0.7, de;q=0
```

Translated to English, this means, "I would prefer if you sent me the document in English. If not, Spanish is okay, or French if that is all you have, but definitely don't send it to me in German."

Incidentally, the name *quality value* is the one used in the HTTP standard, but it is really a poor choice of terminology (a point which, to be fair, is also mentioned in the standard). These values do not have anything to do with quality; for all we know, the German version of this document may be the original and the others could be lousy translations. The `q` values specify only the relative preference of the client making the request.

Finally, the asterisk (*) wildcard can be used in the Accept family of headers to represent any value or everything else. This is often used to tell the server, "If you can't find what I specifically asked for, then here are my preferences for the alternatives." Let's take an example using the Accept header:

```
Accept: text/html, text/*;q=0.6, */*;q=0.1
```

This header represents the client saying, "My preference (`q=1`, the default since no `q` value is indicated) is an HTML text document. If not available, I would prefer some other type of text document. Failing that, you may send me any other type of document relevant to the requested resource."

> **KEY CONCEPT** Server-driven content negotiation is the type most often used in HTTP. A client sending a request can include up to four different headers that provide information about how the server should fill its request. These may include optional *quality values* that specify the client's relative preference among a set of alternative resource characteristics such as media type, language, character set, and encoding.

84

HTTP FEATURES, CAPABILITIES, AND ISSUES

The previous chapters covered the fundamental concepts and basic operation of the Hypertext Transfer Protocol (HTTP). Modern HTTP, however, goes beyond the simple mechanics by which HTTP requests and responses are exchanged. It includes a number of features and capabilities that extend the basic protocol to improve performance and meet the various needs of organizations using modern TCP/IP internetworks.

In this chapter, I complete my description of HTTP by discussing several important matters that are essential to the operation of the modern World Wide Web. I begin with an overview of HTTP caching, which is the single most important feature that promotes efficiency in web transactions. I discuss the different uses of proxies in HTTP and some of the issues associated with them. I briefly examine the issues related to security and privacy in HTTP and conclude with a discussion of the matter of state management and how it is implemented despite HTTP being an inherently stateless protocol.

HTTP Caching Features and Issues

The explosive growth of the Web was a marvel for its users but a nightmare for networking engineers. The biggest problem that the burgeoning Web created was an overloading of the internetworks over which it ran. Many of the features that were added to HTTP/1.1 were designed specifically to improve the efficiency of the protocol and reduce unnecessary bandwidth consumed by HTTP requests and responses. Arguably, the most important of these is a set of features designed to support *caching*.

The subject of caching comes up again and again in discussions of computers and networking, because of a phenomenon that is widely observed in these technologies: Whenever a user, hardware device, or software process requests a particular piece of data, there is a good chance it will ask for that same data again in the near future. Thus, by storing recently retrieved items in a cache, we can eliminate duplicated effort. This is the reason that caching plays an important role in the efficiency of protocols such as the Address Resolution Protocol (ARP) and the Domain Name System (DNS).

Benefits of HTTP Caching

Caching is important to HTTP because Web users tend to request the same documents over and over again. For example, in writing this section on HTTP, I made reference to RFC 2616 many, many times. Each time, I loaded it from a particular web server. Since the document never changes, it would have been more efficient to just load it from a local cache rather than needing to retrieve it from the distant web server each time.

However, caching is even more essential to HTTP than to most other protocols or technologies where it used. The reason is that web documents tend to be structured so that a request for one resource leads to a request for many others. Even if you load a number of *different* documents, they may each refer to common elements that do not change between your requests. Thus, caching can be of benefit in HTTP even if a user never asks for the same document twice, or if a single document changes over time so that caching the document itself would be of little value.

For example, suppose that each morning, you load CNN's website to see what is going on in the world. Obviously, the headlines will be different every day, so caching of the main CCN.com home page won't be of much value. However, many of the graphical elements on the page (CNN's logo, dividing bars, perhaps a "breaking news" graphic, and so on) will be the same every day, and these can be cached. Another example would be a set of discussion forums on a website. As you load different topics to read, each one is different, but they have common elements (such as icons and other images) that would be wasteful to need to retrieve over and over again.

Caching in HTTP yields two main benefits:

- Reduced bandwidth use, by eliminating unneeded transfers of requests and responses
- Faster response time for the user loading a resource

Consider that on many web pages today, the image files are much larger than the HTML page that references them. Caching these graphics will allow the entire page to load far more quickly. Figure 84-1 illustrates how caching reduces bandwidth and speeds up resource retrieval by short-circuiting the request/response chain.

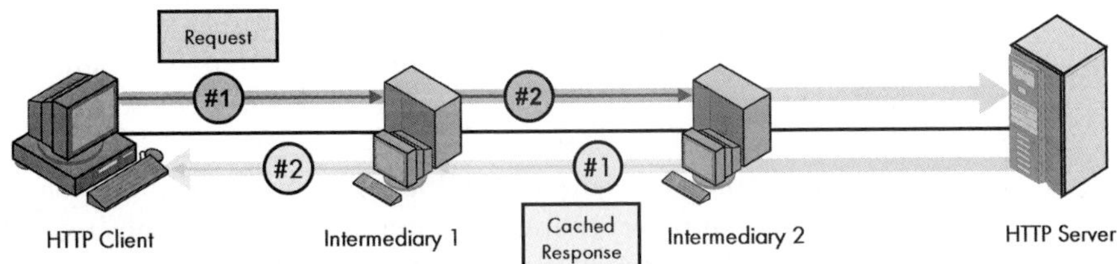

Figure 84-1: Impact of caching on the HTTP request/response chain *This diagram illustrates the impact of caching on the request/response chain of (see Figure 80-2 in Chapter 80). In this example, intermediary 2 is able to satisfy the client's request from its cache. This short-circuits the communication chain after two transfers, which means the client gets its resource more quickly, and the HTTP server is spared the need to process the client's request.*

The obvious advantages of caching have made it a part of the Web since pretty much the beginning. However, it was not until HTTP/1.1 that the importance of caching was really recognized in the protocol itself, and many features were added to support it. Where the HTTP/1.0 standard makes passing mention of caching and some of the issues related to it, HTTP/1.1 devotes 26 full pages to caching (more than 20 percent of the main body of the document!).

Cache Locations

HTTP caching can be implemented in a variety of places in the request/response chain. The choice of location involves the fundamental trade-off that always occurs in caching: proximity versus universality. Simply put, the closer the cache is to the requester of the information, the more savings that result when data is pulled from the cache, rather than being fetched from the source. However, the further the cache is from the requester (and thus closer to the source), the greater the number of devices that can benefit from the cache. Let's see how this manifests itself in the three classes of devices where caches may be found: the web client, intermediary, and web server.

Caching on the Web Client

The cache with which most Internet users are familiar is that found on the local client. It is usually built into the web browser software, and for this reason, it's called a *web browser cache*. This cache stores recent documents and files accessed by a particular user, so that they can be made quickly available if that user requests them again.

Since the cache is in the user's own machine, a request for an item that the cache contains is filled instantly, resulting in no network transaction and instant gratification for the user. However, that user is the only one who can benefit from the cache, so it's sometimes called a *private cache*.

Caching on the Intermediary

Devices such as proxy servers that reside between web clients and servers are also often equipped with a cache. If users want documents that are not in their local client cache, the intermediary may be able to provide it, as shown in Figure 84-1. This is not as efficient as retrieving from the local cache, but far better than going back to the web server.

An advantage is that all devices using the intermediary can benefit from its cache, which may be termed a *public* or *shared cache*. This can be useful, because members of an organization often access similar documents. For example, in an organization developing a hardware product to be used on Apple computers, many different people might be accessing documents on Apple's website. With a shared cache, a request from User A would often result in items being cached that could be used by User B as well.

Caching on the Web Server

Web servers themselves may also implement a cache. While it may seem a bit strange to have a server maintain a cache of its own documents, this can be of benefit in some circumstances. A resource might require a significant amount of server resources to create. For example, consider a web page that is generated using a complex database query. If this page is retrieved frequently by many clients, there can be a large benefit to creating it periodically and caching it, rather than generating it on the fly for each request.

Since the web server cache is the farthest from the users, this results in the least savings for a cache hit, as the client request and server response must still travel the full path over the network between the client and server. However, this distance from the client also means that all users of the server can benefit from the cache.

> **KEY CONCEPT** The most important feature that improves the efficiency of operation of HTTP is *caching*—the storing of recently requested resources in a temporary area. If the same resource is then needed again a short time later, it can be retrieved from the cache rather than requiring a fresh request to the server, resulting in a savings of both time and bandwidth. Caching can be performed by web clients, web servers, and intermediaries. The closer the cache is to the user, the greater the efficiency benefits; the farther from the user, the greater the number of users who can benefit from the cache.

Cache Control

Caching in clients and servers is controlled in the same manner as most other types of control are implemented in HTTP: through the use of special headers. The most important of these is the Cache-Control general header, which has a number of directives that allow the operation of caches to be managed. There are other important caching-related headers, including Expires and Vary. For a great deal of more specific information related to HTTP caching, see RFC 2616, section 13.

Important Caching Issues

While the performance advantages of caching are obvious, caching has one significant drawback: it complicates the operation of HTTP in a number of ways. The following are some of the more important issues that HTTP/1.1 clients, servers, and intermediaries need to address. This list is not exhaustive, but it gives you an idea of what is involved with caching in HTTP.

Cache Aging and Staleness When users retrieve a document directly from its original source on the server, they are assured of getting the current version of that resource. When caching is used, that is no longer the case. While many resources change infrequently, almost all will change at some point. For example, at CNN's website, it is probable that the CNN logo won't change very often, but it's possible that the site may be redesigned periodically and the logo modified in some way, such as its size or color. For this reason, a device cannot keep items in an HTTP cache indefinitely. The longer an item is held in a cache—a process called *aging*—the more likely it is that the resource on the server has changed and the cache has become stale. To make matters even more complex, some resources become stale more quickly than others. As a result, much of the caching-related functionality of HTTP involves dealing with this matter of cache aging.

Cache Expiration and Validation One of the ways that HTTP deals with the cache aging issue is through headers and logic that allow caches, clients, and servers to specify how long items should be cached before they expire and must be refreshed. A validation process allows a cache to check with a server at appropriate times to see if an item it has stored has been modified.

Communication of Cache Status to the User In most cases, the fact that an item has been retrieved from a cache rather than its source is transparent to users (though they may notice that the resource loads faster than expected). In certain cases, however, the user may need to be informed that a resource came from a cache and not its original source. This is especially true when a cached item may be stale; in which case, the client should warn the user that the information might be out-of-date.

Header Caching Caching in HTTP is complicated by the fact that it can occur in multiple places, and some HTTP headers are treated differently than others. HTTP headers are divided into two general categories: *end-to-end headers* that are intended to accompany a resource all the way to its ultimate recipient, and *hop-by-hop headers* that are used only for a particular communication between two devices (by the client, server, or intermediary device). End-to-end headers must be stored with a cached resource. Hop-by-hop headers have meaning only for a particular transfer and are not cached.

Impact of Resource Updates Some HTTP methods (discussed in Chapter 81) will automatically cause cache entries to become invalidated, because they inherently cause a change to the underlying resource. For example, if a user performs a PUT on a resource that was previously retrieved using GET, any cached copies of that resource should be automatically invalidated to prevent the old version from being supplied from the cache.

Privacy Concerns In the case of shared caches (such as might exist in a proxy), there are potential privacy issues. In most cases, having User A's cached resource be made available to User B is advantageous, but we must be careful not to cache any items that might be specific to User A, which User B should not see.

HTTP Proxy Servers and Proxying

In my overview of the HTTP operational model in Chapter 80, I described how HTTP was designed to support not just communication between a client and server, but also the inclusion of intermediaries that may sit in the communication path between them. One of the most important types of intermediary is a device called a *proxy server*, or more simply, just a *proxy*.

A proxy is a middleman that acts as both a client and a server. It accepts requests from a client as if it were a server, then forwards those requests (possibly modifying them) to the real server, which sees the proxy as a client. The server responds back to the proxy, which forwards the reply back to the client. Proxies can be either *transparent*, meaning that they do not modify requests and responses, or *nontransparent*, if they do modify messages in order to provide a particular service.

NOTE *The term* transparent proxy *can also be used to refer to a proxy that is interposed automatically between a client and server—such as an organization-wide firewall—as opposed to one that a user manually configures.*

Benefits of Proxies

Since proxies have the ability to fully process all client requests and server responses, they can be extremely useful in a number of circumstances. They can be used to implement or enhance many important capabilities, such as the following:

Security Proxies can be set up to examine both outgoing requests and incoming responses, to address various security concerns. For example, filtering can be set up to prevent users from requesting objectionable content or to screen out harmful replies, such as files containing hidden viruses.

Caching As you saw earlier, it can be advantageous to set up a shared cache that is implemented on an intermediary, so resources requested by one client can be made available to another. This can be done within a proxy server.

Performance In some circumstances, using a proxy server can significantly improve performance, particularly by reducing latency.

An excellent example of how a proxy server can improve performance is how proxying is used by my own satellite Internet connection. Due to the distance from the Earth to the satellite, it takes more than 500 milliseconds for a round-trip request/response cycle between my PC and my Internet server provider (ISP). If I loaded a web page containing images, I would need to wait 500+ milliseconds to get the HTML page, and then my browser would need to generate new requests for each graphical element, meaning another 500+ millisecond delay for each. Instead, my ISP has a proxy server to which I send my requests for web pages. The proxy server looks through the HTML of these pages and automatically requests any elements such as graphics for me. It then sends them straight back to my machine, thus drastically reducing the time required to display a full web page.

KEY CONCEPT One of the most important types of intermediary devices in HTTP is a *proxy server*, which acts as a middleman between the client and server, handling both requests and responses. A proxy server may transport messages unchanged or may modify them to implement certain features and capabilities. Proxies are often used to increase the security and/or performance of Web access.

Comparing Proxies and Caches

Proxying and caching are concepts that have a number of similarities, especially in terms of the impact that they have on basic HTTP operation. Like caching, proxying has become more important in recent years, and it also complicates HTTP in a number of ways. The HTTP/1.1 standard includes a number of specific features to support proxies, and it also addresses a number of concerns related to proxying.

The fact that both proxying and caching represent ways in which basic HTTP client/server communication is changed, combined with the ability of proxies to perform caching, sometimes leads people to think caches and proxies are the same, which is not true. A proxy is a separate element that resides in the HTTP request/response chain. Caches can be implemented within any device in that chain, including a proxy.

Another key way that caches and proxies differ is that caches are used automatically when they are enabled, but proxies are not. To use a proxy, client software must be told to use the proxy and supplied with its IP address or domain name. The client then sends all requests to the proxy, rather than to the actual server that the user specifies.

NOTE *Most of my explanations here have focused on hardware proxy servers, but proxies are also commonly implemented as software in a client device. A software proxy performs the same tasks of processing requests and responses. A software proxy is much cheaper to implement than a hardware proxy, but it cannot be shared by many devices.*

Important Proxying Issues

As with caching, issues arise when proxies are used in HTTP. The following are some of the more important ones. (For much more information about proxying, refer to RFC 2616).

Capability Inconsistencies Issues arise when a client and server don't use the same version of HTTP or don't support the same features. For example, some servers may not support all of the methods that a client may try to use. This becomes more complex when a proxy enters the picture. Of particular concern is the situation where a client and server may agree on a particular feature that the proxy does not. The proxy must make sure that it passes along headers or other elements that it may not comprehend.

Authentication Requirements The use of proxy servers often introduces new authentication or security requirements. In addition to authenticating with an end server, the proxy may specify that the client needs to present separate authentication credentials to it as well. This is done using the HTTP Proxy-Authorization and Proxy-Authenticate headers, as discussed in the next section in this chapter.

Caching Interaction Not only do both caching and proxying both complicate HTTP, they can complicate each other. Many of the issues in handling caching—such as header caching, expiration, and validation—become more complex when proxies are involved. Some of the Cache-Control general header directives are specific to proxying. Another issue is that the use of proxying and caching together can lead to distortions in the apparent number of times that a web resource is accessed. This is important in situations where web pages are supported by advertising, based on the number of times the page is accessed. In some cases, special codes called *cache busters* are placed in URLs to force pages not to be stored in shared caches.

Encodings Content encodings (discussed in Chapter 83) are applied end-to-end and so should not be affected by proxies. Transfer encoding is done hop-by-hop, so a proxy may use different encodings in handling different transfers of a single request or response.

Tracing Proxy Handling It is useful in some circumstances, especially when multiple proxies may be in the request/response chain, to be able to trace which proxies have processed a particular message. To this end, HTTP/1.1 requires that each proxy that handles a message identify itself in the Via header.

HTTP Security and Privacy

Many TCP/IP protocols lack security measures, largely because they were developed when security wasn't a big concern. As the Internet has developed, security has become extremely important, however. In the case of the Web, the issue is even more important due to the significance of the changes that have occurred in the content of HTTP messages since the protocol was first developed.

HTTP has become the vehicle for transporting any and every kind of information, including a large amount of personal data. HTTP was initially designed to carry academic documents such as memos about research projects. Today, an HTTP message is more likely to carry someone's mortgage application, credit card number, or medical details. Thus, not only does HTTP have the usual security issues such as preventing unauthorized access, but it also needs to deal with privacy concerns.

HTTP Authentication Methods

The main HTTP/1.1 standard, RFC 2616, does not deal extensively with security matters. These are addressed in detail instead in the companion document, RFC 2617, which explains the two methods of HTTP authentication:

Basic Authentication This is a conventional user name/password type of authentication. When a client sends a request to a server that requires authentication to access a resource, the server sends a response to the client's initial request that contains a WWW-Authenticate header. The client then sends a new request containing the Authorization header, which carries a base64-encoded user name and password combination. Basic authentication is not considered strong security because it sends credentials unencrypted, which means that they can be intercepted.

Digest Authentication Digest authentication uses the same headers as basic authentication, but employs more sophisticated techniques, including encryption, that protect against a malicious person snooping credentials information. Digest authentication is not considered as strong as public key encryption, but it is a lot better than basic authentication. It's also a lot more complicated. The full details of how it works are in RFC 2617.

Security and Privacy Concerns and Issues

Both RFC 2616 and 2617 address some of the specific security concerns and threats that can potentially affect HTTP clients and servers. These include actions such as spoofing, counterfeit servers, replay attacks, and much more. One concern addressed is the potential for man-in-the-middle attacks, where an attacker interposes between the client and server. Since proxies are inherently middlemen, they represent a security concern in this area. The same authentication methods used for servers can also be applied to authentication with proxies. In this case, the Proxy-Authenticate and Proxy-Authorization headers are used instead of WWW-Authenticate and Authorization headers.

The HTTP standards also discuss a number of privacy issues. The following are particularly worthy of examining.

Sensitive Information Handling The HTTP protocol can carry any type of information, and it does not inherently protect the privacy of data in HTTP message entities. To ensure the privacy of sensitive information, other techniques must be used (as described in the next section).

Information in URLs One issue that sometimes arises in HTTP is that poorly designed websites may inadvertently encode private information into URLs. These URLs may be recorded in web logs, where they could fall into the hands of people who could abuse them. An example of this is a website that submits a user name and password to a server by encoding them as parameters of a GET request such as this: `GET http://www.somesite.com/login?name=xxx&password=yyy`. The POST method should be used instead for this sort of functionality, because it transmits its data in the body of the message instead of putting it into the URL.

Information in Accept Headers While this may seem strange at first, it is possible that private information about the user could be transmitted through the use of certain Accept headers used for content negotiation. For example, some users might not want others to know what languages they speak, so they may be concerned about who looks at the Accept-Language header.

Information in Referer Headers The Referer (yes, that's how it's spelled; see my note in Chapter 82) request header is a double-edged sword. It can be very useful to those who operate websites because it lets them see the sources of links to their resources. At the same time, it can be abused by those who might employ it to study users' Web-access patterns. There are also potential privacy issues that the HTTP standard raises. For example, a user might not want the name of a private document that references a public web page to be transmitted in a Referer header.

Methods for Ensuring Privacy in HTTP

As mentioned earlier, HTTP does not include any mechanism to protect the privacy of transmitted documents or messages. There are two different methods by which this is normally accomplished:

Encryption The simplest way is to encrypt the resource on the server and supply valid decryption keys only to authorized users. Even if the entire message is intercepted, the entity itself will still be secured. The level of protection here depends on the quality of the encryption.

Secure Sockets Layer (SSL) Another more common method is to use a protocol designed specifically to ensure the privacy of HTTP transactions. The one often used today is called *Secure Sockets Layer (SSL)*. Servers employ SSL to protect sensitive resources, such as those associated with financial transactions. They are accessed by using the URL scheme *https* rather than *http* in a web browser that supports the protocol. SSL was originally developed by Netscape and is now widely used across the Web.

HTTP State Management Using Cookies

Even though modern HTTP has a lot of capabilities and features, it is still, at its heart, a simple request/reply protocol. One of the unfortunate problems that results from this is that HTTP is entirely *stateless*. This means that each time a server receives a request from a client, it processes the request, sends a response, and then forgets about the request. The next request from the client is treated as independent of any previous ones.

NOTE *The persistent connection feature of HTTP/1.1 (described in Chapter 80) does not change the stateless nature of the protocol. Even though multiple requests and responses can be sent on a single Transmission Control Protocol (TCP) connection, they are still not treated as being related in any way.*

So why is HTTP being stateless a problem? Isn't this what we would expect of a protocol designed to allow a client to quickly and efficiently retrieve resources from a server? Well, this is, yet again, another place where HTTP's behavior was well suited to its original intended uses but not to how the Web is used today. Sure, if all we want to do is to say, "Hey server, please give me that file over there," then the server doesn't need to care about whether or not it may have previously provided that client with any other files in the past. This is how HTTP was originally intended to be used.

Today, the Web is much more than a simple resource-retrieval protocol. If you go to an online store, you want to be able to select a number of items to put into a "shopping cart" and have the store's server remember them. You might also want to participate in a discussion forum, which requires you to provide a user name and password in order to post a message. Ideally, the server should let you log in once, and then remember who you are so you can post many messages, without needing to enter your login information each and every time. (I have used forums where the latter is required—it gets old very quickly, believe me.)

For these and other interactive applications, the stateless nature of HTTP is a serious problem. The solution was the addition of a new technology called *state management*, which allows the state of a client session with a server to be maintained across a series of HTTP transactions. Initially developed by Netscape, this technique was later made a formal Internet standard in RFC 2109, later revised in RFC 2965, "HTTP State Management Mechanism." This feature is actually not part of HTTP; it is an optional element, but one that has been implemented in most web browsers due to its usefulness.

The idea behind state management is very simple. When a server implements a function that requires state to be maintained across a set of transactions, it sends a small amount of data called a *cookie* to the web client. The cookie contains important information relevant to the particular web application, such as a customer name, items in a shopping cart, or a user name and password. The client stores the information in the cookie, and then uses it in subsequent requests to the server that set the cookie. The server can then update the cookie based on the information in the new request and send it back to the client. In this manner, state information can be maintained indefinitely, allowing the client and server to have a memory that persists over a period of time.

NOTE Cookie *may seem like an odd term, but it is used in a few contexts to refer to a small piece of significant data. Another example is found in the Boot Protocol (BOOTP) and Dynamic Host Configuration Protocol (DHCP) message format. Today, most knowledgeable web users would blink at you if you mentioned the "HTTP state management mechanism," but they usually know what cookies are.*

Issues with Cookies

Cookies sound like a great idea, right? Cookies are absolutely essential for many of the applications that make the Web the powerhouse it is today. Online shopping and discussion forums are just two of the many interactive applications that benefit from cookies. Most of the time, cookies are used for these sorts of useful and benign purposes. Unfortunately, some people have turned cookies to the "dark side" by finding ways to abuse them. There can even be potential problems with cookies when there is no nefarious intent. For this reason, cookies are rather controversial.

Here are some of the issues with cookies:

Transmission of Sensitive Information Suppose you use an online banking system. You log in to the server, which then stores your user name and password (which controls access to your account) in a cookie. If the application is not implemented carefully, the message containing that cookie could be intercepted, giving someone access to your account. Even if it is not intercepted, someone knowledgeable who gained access to your computer could retrieve the information from the file where cookies are stored.

Undesirable Use of Cookies In theory, cookies should be a help to the user, not a hindrance. However, any server can set a cookie for any reason. In some cases, a server could set a cookie for the purpose of tracking the websites that a user visits, which some people consider a violation of their privacy. Since some web browsers do not inform the user when a cookie is being set, the user may not even be aware that this is happening.

Third-Party or Unintentional Cookies While most people think of cookies as being set in the context of a resource they specifically request, a cookie may be set by any server to which a request is sent, whether the user realizes it or not. Suppose you send a request to http://www.myfavoritesite.com/index.htm, and that page contains a reference to a tiny image that is on the server http://www.bigbrotherishere.com. The second site can set a cookie on your machine even though you never intended to visit it. This is called a *third-party cookie.*

> **KEY CONCEPT** HTTP is an inherently *stateless* protocol, because a server treats each request from a client independently, forgetting about all prior requests. This characteristic of HTTP is not an issue for most routine uses of the Web, but is a problem for interactive applications such as online shopping where the server needs to keep track of a user's information over time. To support these applications, most HTTP implementations include an optional feature called *state management.* When enabled, a server sends to a client a small amount of information called a *cookie,* which is stored on the client machine. The data in the cookie is returned to the server with each subsequent request, allowing the server to update it and send it back to the client again. Cookies thus enable servers to remember user data between requests. However, they are controversial, because of certain potential privacy and security concerns related to their use.

Managing Cookie Use

The RFCs describing the cookie state management technique deal extensively with these and other issues, but there is no clear-cut resolution to these concerns. Like most security and privacy matters, the most important determinant of how significant potential cookie abuse may be is your own personal comfort level. Millions of people browse the Web every day letting any and all sites set whatever cookies they want and never have a problem. Others consider cookies an offensive idea and disable all cookies, which eliminates the privacy concerns but can cause problems with useful applications like interactive websites. As usual, the best approach is usually something in the middle, where you choose when and how you will allow cookies to be set.

The degree to which cookie control is possible depends greatly on the quality and feature set of your web client software. Many browsers do not provide a great deal of control in how and when cookies are set; others are much better in this regard. Some browsers allow cookies to be disabled, but come with them turned on by default. Since many people are not even aware of the issues associated with cookies, they do not realize when cookies are being sent. Most notable in this regard is the popular Microsoft Internet Explorer, which normally comes set by default to accept all cookies without complaint or even comment.

Internet Explorer does allow you to disable cookies, but you must do it yourself. It also allows you to differentiate between first-party and third-party cookies, but again, you must turn on this feature. Other browsers have more sophisticated settings, which will let you dictate conditions under which cookies may be set and others when they may not. Some browser will even let you allow certain websites to send cookies while prohibiting them from others. Better browsers will also let you visually inspect cookies, and selectively clear the ones you do not want on your machine.

Third-party cookies can be used by online advertising companies and others to track the sites that a Web user visits. For this reason, they are considered by many people to fall into the general category of undesirable software called *spyware*. There are numerous tools that will allow you to identify and remove tracking cookies from your computer; many are available free on the Web.

PART III-9

OTHER FILE AND MESSAGE TRANSFER APPLICATIONS

The previous three parts of this book have examined several of the most widely used TCP/IP file and message transfer protocols: the File Transfer Protocol (FTP), the Trivial File Transfer Protocol (TFTP), electronic mail (email), and the World Wide Web. Of course, hundreds of other applications are in use on the Internet today, and we couldn't possibly examine them all here. However, there are a couple of other protocols that are considered part of the group of classic applications of TCP/IP like FTP, email, and the Web that I feel are worth discussing.

This part contains two chapters that cover these other file and message transfer applications. The first chapter describes Usenet (network news), which is one of the original methods of group communication on the Internet. The second chapter describes the Gopher protocol, which while no longer widely used today is worth a brief discussion, especially due to its role as a historical precursor of the Web.

85

USENET (NETWORK NEWS) AND THE TCP/IP NETWORK NEWS TRANSFER PROTOCOL (NNTP)

Electronic mail (email) is one of the stalwarts of message transfer on the modern Internet, but it is really designed only for communication within a relatively small group of specific users. There are many situations in which email is not ideally suited, such as when information needs to be shared among a large number of participants, not all of whom may necessarily even know each other. One classic example of this is sharing *news*. In this case, the person providing news often wants to make it generally available to anyone who is interested, rather than specifying a particular set of recipients.

For distributing news and other types of general information over internetworks, a messaging system called both *Usenet* and *network news* was created. Like email, this application allows messages to be written and read by large numbers of users. However, it is designed using a very different model than email—one that is focused on public sharing and feedback. In Usenet, anyone can write a message that can be read by any number of recipients, and anyone can respond to messages written by others. Usenet was one of the first widely deployed internetwork-based group communication applications, and it has grown into one of the largest online communities in the world, used by millions of people for sharing information, asking questions, and discussing thousands of different topics.

In this chapter, I describe Usenet and network news in detail, discussing how they are used and how they work. I provide an overview and history of Usenet, a high-level look at its model of communication and how messages are created and manipulated, an explanation of Usenet newsgroups, and a description of the Usenet message format and headers. Then I provide a detailed description of the operation of the Network News Transfer Protocol (NNTP), the means used for transferring messages on modern Usenet. Starting as usual with an overview of the protocol, I then explain the two fundamentals ways that NNTP is used: for the propagation of news articles between servers and for client article posting and access. From there, I move on to the technical details of NNTP commands, command extensions, responses, and response codes.

BACKGROUND INFORMATION *Several aspects of how Usenet works are closely related to the standards and techniques used for email. If you have not read Part III-7, which covers email, I suggest that you at least review the overview of the email system in Chapter 74 and the discussion of the email message format in Chapter 76, since Usenet messages are based on the RFC 822 email message standard.*

Usenet Overview, History, and Operation

Where email is the modern equivalent of the handwritten letter or the interoffice memo, *Usenet* is the updated version of the company newsletter, the cafeteria bulletin board, the coffee break chat, and the watercooler gossip session, all rolled into one. Spread worldwide over the Internet, Usenet newsgroup messages provide a means for people with common interests to form online communities to discuss happenings, solve problems, and provide support to each other, as well as to engage in plain old socializing and entertainment.

We are by nature both highly social and creative animals, and as a result, we are always finding new ways to communicate. It did not take long after computers were first connected together for it to be recognized that those interconnections provided the means to link together people as well. The desire to use computers to create an *online community* led to the creation of Usenet more than two decades ago.

History of Usenet

Like almost everything associated with networking, Usenet had very humble beginnings. In 1979, Tom Truscott was a student at Duke University in North Carolina, and he spent the summer as an intern at Bell Laboratories, the place where the UNIX operating system was born. He enjoyed the experience so much that when he returned to school that autumn, he missed the intensive UNIX environment at Bell Labs. He used the *Unix-to-Unix Copy Protocol (UUCP)* to send information from his local machine to other machines and vice versa, including establishing electronic connectivity back to Bell Labs.

Building on this idea, Truscott and a fellow Duke student, Jim Ellis, teamed up with other UNIX enthusiasts at Duke and the nearby University of North Carolina (UNC) at Chapel Hill, to develop the idea of an online community. The goal was to create a system where students could use UNIX to write and read messages, to allow them to obtain both technical help and maintain social contacts. They designed the system based on an analogy to an online newsletter that was open to all users of a connected system. To share information, messages were posted to *newsgroups*, where any user could access the messages to read them and respond to them.

The early work at Duke and UNC resulted in the development of both the initial message format and the software for the earliest versions of this system, which became known both as *network news (net news)* and *Usenet* (a contraction of *User's network*). At first, the system had just two computers, sharing messages posted in a pair of different newsgroups. The value of the system was immediately recognized, however, and soon many new sites were added to the system. These sites were arranged in a structure to allow messages to be efficiently passed using direct UUCP connections. The software used for passing news articles also continued to evolve and become more capable, as did the software for reading and writing articles.

The newsgroups themselves also changed over time. Many new newsgroups were created, and a hierarchical structure was defined to help keep the newsgroups organized in a meaningful way. As more sites and users joined Usenet, more areas of interest were identified. Today, there are a staggering number of Usenet newsgroups: more than 100,000. While many of these groups are not used, many thousands of active ones discuss nearly every topic imaginable—from space exploration, to cooking, to biochemistry, to PC troubleshooting, to raising horses. There are also regional newsgroups devoted to particular areas; for example, there is a set of newsgroups for discussing events in Canada and another for discussing happenings in the New York area, and so on.

Usenet Operation and Characteristics

Usenet begins with a user writing a message to be distributed. After the message is *posted* to say, the group on TCP/IP networking, it is stored on that user's local news server, and special software sends copies of it to other connected news servers. The message eventually propagates around the world, where anyone who chooses to read the TCP/IP networking newsgroup can see the message.

The real power of Usenet is that after reading a message, any user can respond to it on the same newsgroup. Like the original message, the reply will propagate to each connected system, including the one used by the author of the original message. This makes Usenet very useful for sharing information about recent happenings, for social discussions, and especially for receiving assistance with problems, such as resolving technical glitches or getting help with a diet program.

What is particularly interesting about Usenet is that it is not a formalized system in any way, and it is not based on any formally defined standards. It is a classic example of the development of a system in an entirely ad hoc manner: The software was created, people started using it, the software was refined, and things just took off from there. Certain standards have been written to codify how Usenet works—such as RFC 1036, which describes the Usenet message format—but these serve more as historical documents than as prescriptive standards.

There is likewise no central authority that is responsible for Usenet's operation, even though new users often think there is one. Unlike a dial-up bulletin board system or Web-based forum, Usenet works simply by virtue of cooperation between sites; there is no manager in charge. For this reason, Usenet is sometimes called an anarchy, but this is not accurate. It isn't the case that there are no rules. It is up to the managers of participating systems to make policy decisions such as which newsgroups to support. There are also certain dictatorial aspects of the system, in that only certain people (usually system administrators) can decide whether to create some kinds of new newsgroups. The system also has socialistic elements in that machine owners are expected to share messages with each other. So, the simplified political labels really don't apply to Usenet.

Every community has a *culture*, and the same is true of online communities, including Usenet. There is an overall culture that prescribes acceptable behavior on Usenet, and also thousands of newsgroup-specific cultures in Usenet, each of which has evolved through the writings of thousands of participants over the years. There are even newsgroups devoted to explaining how Usenet itself operates, where you can learn about *newbies* (new users), *netiquette* (rules of etiquette for posting messages), and related subjects.

Usenet Transport Methods

As I said earlier, Usenet messages were originally transported using UUCP, which was created to let UNIX systems communicate directly, usually using telephone lines. For many years, all Usenet messages were simply sent from machine to machine using computerized telephone calls (just as email once was). Each computer joining the network would connect to one already on Usenet and receive a *feed* of messages from it periodically. The owner of that computer had to agree to provide messages to other computers.

Once TCP/IP was developed in the 1980s and the Internet grew to a substantial size and scope, it made sense to start using it to carry Usenet messages rather than UUCP. The *Network News Transfer Protocol (NNTP)* was developed specifically to describe the mechanism for communicating Usenet messages over the Transmission Control Protocol (TCP). It was formally defined in RFC 977, published in 1986, with NNTP extensions described in RFC 2980, published in October 2000.

For many years, Usenet was carried using both NNTP and UUCP, but NNTP is now the mechanism used for the vast majority of Usenet traffic, and for this reason is the primary focus of my Usenet discussion. NNTP is employed not only to distribute Usenet articles to various servers, but also for other client actions, such as posting and reading messages. It is thus used for most of the steps in Usenet message communication.

NOTE *Many people often equate the Usenet system as a whole with the NNTP protocol that is used to carry Usenet messages on the Internet. They are not the same however; Usenet predates NNTP, which is simply a protocol for conveying Usenet messages.*

It is because of the critical role of NNTP and the Internet in carrying messages in today's Usenet that the concepts are often confused. It's essential to remember, however, that Usenet does not refer to any type of physical network or internetworking technology; rather, it is a logical network of users. That logical network has evolved from UUCP data transfers to NNTP and TCP/IP, but Usenet itself is the same.

Today, Usenet faces competition from many other group messaging applications and protocols, including Web-based bulletin board systems and chat rooms. After a quarter of a century, however, Usenet has established itself and is used by millions of people every day. While to some, the primarily text-based medium seems archaic, it is a mainstay of global group communication and likely to continue to be so for many years to come.

KEY CONCEPT One of the very first online electronic communities was set up in 1979 by university students who wanted to keep in touch and share news and other information. Today, *Usenet* (for *User's network*), also called *network news*, has grown into a logical network that spans the globe. By posting messages to a Usenet newsgroup, people can share information on a variety of subjects of interest. Usenet was originally implemented in the form of direct connections established between participating hosts. Today, the Internet is the vehicle for message transport.

Usenet Communication Model

When the students at Duke University decided to create their online community, email was already in wide use, and there were many mailing lists in operation as well. Email was usually transported using UUCP—the same method that Usenet was designed to employ—during these pre-Internet days. Then why not simply use email to communicate between sites?

The main reason is that email is not designed to facilitate the creation of an online community where information can be easily shared in a group. The main issue with email in this respect is that only the individuals who are specified as recipients of a message can read it. There is no facility whereby someone can write a message and put it in an open place where anyone who wants to can read it, analogous to posting a newsletter in a public place.

Another problem with email in large groups is related to efficiency. Consider that if you put 1,000 people on a mailing list, each message sent to that list must be duplicated and delivered 1,000 times. Early networks were limited in bandwidth and resources, so using email for wide-scale group communication was possible, but far from ideal.

KEY CONCEPT While email can be used for group communications, it has two important limitations. First, a message must be specifically addressed to each recipient, making public messaging impossible. Second, each recipient requires delivery of a separate copy of the message, so sending a message to many recipients requires the use of a large number of resources.

Usenet's Public Distribution Orientation

To avoid the problems of using email for group messaging, Usenet was designed using a rather different communication and message-handling model than email. The defining difference between the Usenet communication model and that used for email is that Usenet message handling is oriented around the concept of *public distribution*, rather than private delivery to an individual user. This affects every aspect of how Usenet communication works, as follows:

Addressing Messages are not addressed from a sender to any particular recipient or set of recipients, but rather to a *group*, which is identified with a newsgroup name.

Storage Messages are not stored in individual mailboxes, but rather in a central location on a server, where any user of the server can access them.

Delivery Messages are not conveyed from the sender's system to the recipient's system, but rather are spread over the Internet to all connected systems so anyone can read them.

Usenet Communication Process

To help illustrate in more detail how Usenet communication works, let's take a look at the steps involved in writing, transmitting, and reading a typical Usenet message (also called an *article*—the terms are used interchangeably). Let's suppose the process begins with a user, Ellen, posting a request for help with a sick horse to the newsgroup misc.rural. Since she is posting the message, she would be known as the message *poster*. Simplified, the steps in the process (illustrated in Figure 85-1) are as follows:

1. **Article Composition** Ellen begins by creating a Usenet article, which is structured according to the special message format required by Usenet. This message is similar to an email message in that it has a *header* and a *body*. The body contains the actual message to be sent, while the header contains header lines that describe the message and control how it is delivered. For example, one important header line specifies for which newsgroup(s) the article is intended.
2. **Article Posting and Local Storage** After completing her article, Ellen submits the article to Usenet, a process called *posting*. A client software program on Ellen's computer transmits Ellen's message to her local Usenet server. The message is stored in an appropriate file storage area on that server. It is now immediately available to all other users of that server who decide to read misc.rural.
3. **Article Propagation** At this point, Ellen's local server is the only one that has a copy of her message. The article must be sent to other sites, a process called *distribution*, or more commonly, *propagation*. Ellen's message travels from her local Usenet server to other servers to which her server directly connects. It then propagates from those servers to others *they* connect to, and so on, until all Usenet servers that want it have a copy of the message.

4. **Article Access and Retrieval** Since Usenet articles are stored on central servers, in order to read them, they must be accessed on the server. This is done using a Usenet *newsreader* program. For example, some other reader of misc.rural named Jane might access that group and find Ellen's message. If Jane were able to help Ellen, she could reply to Ellen by posting an article of her own. This would then propagate back to Ellen's server, where she could read it and reply. All other readers of *misc.rural* could jump into the conversation at any time as well, which is what makes Usenet so useful for group communication.

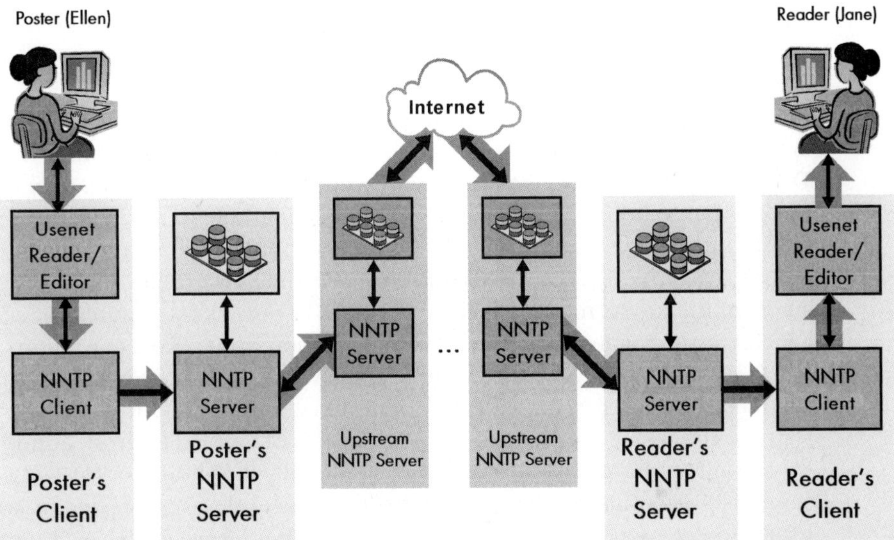

Figure 85-1: Usenet (network news) communication model *This figure illustrates the method by which messages are created, propagated, and read using NNTP on modern Usenet; it is similar in some respects to the email model diagram (Figure 74-1 in Chapter 74). In this example, a message is created by the poster, Ellen, and read by a reader, Jane. The process begins with Ellen creating a message in an editor and posting it. Her NNTP client sends it to her local NNTP server. It is then propagated from that local server to adjacent servers, usually including its upstream server, which is used to send the message around the Internet. Other NNTP servers receive the message, including the one upstream from Jane's local server. It passes the message to Jane's local server, and Jane accesses and reads the message using an NNTP client. Jane could respond to the message; in which case, the same process would repeat, but going in the opposite direction, back to Ellen (and also back to thousands of other readers, not shown here).*

> **KEY CONCEPT** Usenet communication consists of four basic steps. A message is first composed and then posted to the originator's local server. The third step is propagation, where the message is transmitted from its original server to others on the Usenet system. The last step in the process is article retrieval, where other members of the newsgroup access and read the article. The Network News Transfer Protocol (NNTP) is the technology used for moving Usenet articles from one host to the next.

Message Propagation and Server Organization

Propagation is definitely the most complex part of the Usenet communication process. In the past, UUCP was used for propagation. Each Usenet server would be programmed to regularly dial up another server and give it all new articles it had received since the last connection. Articles would *flood* across Usenet from one server to another. This was time-consuming and inefficient, and it worked only because the volume of articles was relatively small.

As I noted in the previous section, in modern Usenet, NNTP is used for all stages of transporting messages between devices. Articles are posted using an NNTP connection between a client machine and a local server, which then uses the same protocol to propagate the articles to other adjacent NNTP servers. The client newsreader software also uses NNTP to retrieve messages from a server.

NNTP servers are usually arranged in a hierarchy of sorts, with the largest and fastest servers providing service to smaller servers downstream from them. Depending on how the connections are arranged, an NNTP server may establish a connection to immediately send a newly posted article to an upstream server for distribution to the rest of Usenet, or the server may passively wait for a connection from the upstream server to ask if there are any new articles to be sent. With the speed of the modern Internet, it typically takes only a few minutes (or seconds) for articles to propagate from one server to another, even across continents.

It is also possible to restrict the propagation of a Usenet message, a technique often used for discussions that are of relevance only in certain regions or on certain systems. Discussing rural issues such as horses is of general interest, and Ellen might find help anywhere around the world, so global propagation of her message makes sense. However, if Ellen lived in the Boston area and was interested in knowing the location of a good local restaurant, posting a query to *ne.food* (New England food discussions) with only local distribution would make more sense. There are also companies that use Usenet to provide "in-house" newsgroups that are not propagated off the local server at all. However, because so many news providers are now national or international, limiting the distribution of messages has largely fallen out of practice.

Usenet Addressing: Newsgroups

A key concept in Usenet communication is the *newsgroup*. Newsgroups are the addressing mechanism for Usenet, and sending a Usenet article to a newsgroup is equivalent to sending email to an email address. Newsgroups are analogous to other group communication venues such as mailing lists, chat rooms, Internet Relay Chat (IRC) channels, or bulletin board system (BBS) forums (though calling a newsgroup a *list*, *room*, *channel*, or *BBS* is likely to elicit a negative reaction from Usenet old-timers!).

Like any addressing mechanism, newsgroups must be uniquely identifiable. Each newsgroup has a *newsgroup name* that describes the topic of the newsgroup and differentiates it from other newsgroups. Since there are many thousands of different newsgroups, they are arranged into sets called *hierarchies*. Each hierarchy contains a tree structure of related newsgroups.

The Usenet Newsgroup Hierarchies

The total collection of newsgroup hierarchies is in many ways similar to the domain name tree structure used in the Domain Name System (DNS). Each Usenet hierarchy is like a collection of all the domain names within a DNS top-level domain. Just as a domain name like www.pcguide.com is formed by appending the label of the top-level domain *.com* to the second-level domain name *pcguide* and the subdomain *www*, newsgroup names are created in the same way. They are created from a top-level newsgroup hierarchy name, to which are attached a set of descriptive labels that describes the newsgroup's place in the hierarchy.

One difference between DNS and Usenet hierarchies is that while DNS names are created from right to left as you go down the tree, Usenet newsgroup names are formed in the more natural (for English speakers) left-to-right order. For example, one of the main Usenet hierarchies is the *comp* hierarchy, devoted to computer topics. Within comp is a subhierarchy on data communications called *dcom*, and within that is a group that discusses data cabling. This group is called comp.dcom.cabling. Almost all newsgroups are structured in this manner.

The "Big Eight" Newsgroup Hierarchies

One problem with the decentralized nature of Usenet is ensuring coordination in certain areas where we want everyone to be on the same page, and one of these is newsgroup naming. If we let just anyone create a newsgroup, we might end up with many groups that all discuss the same topic. Imagine that someone had a question on data cabling and didn't realize that comp.dcom.cabling existed, so he created a new group called comp.datacomm.cabling. The two groups could coexist, but this would lead to both confusion and fragmenting of the pool of people interested in this topic.

To avoid problems with newsgroup creation, administrators of large Usenet systems collaborated on a system for organizing many of the more commonly used Usenet groups into eight hierarchies, and devised a specific procedure for creating new newsgroups within them. Today, these are called the *Big Eight* Usenet hierarchies, which are summarized in Table 85-1.

Table 85-1: Usenet Big Eight Newsgroup Hierarchies

Hierarchy	Description
comp.*	Newsgroups discussing computer-related topics, including hardware, software, operating systems, and techniques
humanities.*	Newsgroups discussing the humanities, such as literature and art
misc.*	Newsgroups discussing miscellaneous topics that don't fit into other Big Eight hierarchies
news.*	Newsgroups discussing Usenet itself and its administration
rec.*	Newsgroups discussing recreation topics, such as games, sports, and activities
sci.*	Science newsgroups, covering specific areas such as physics and chemistry, research topics, and so forth
soc.*	Society and social discussions, including groups on specific cultures
talk.*	Newsgroups primarily oriented around discussion and debate of current events and happenings

These eight hierarchies contain many of the most widely used groups on Usenet today. For example, professional baseball is discussed in rec.sport.baseball, Intel computers in comp.sys.intel, and Middle East politics in talk.politics.mideast.

The Big Eight hierarchies are rather tightly controlled in terms of their structure and the newsgroups they contain. The process to create a new Big Eight newsgroup is democratic and open. Anyone can propose a new group, and if there is enough support, it will be created by the cooperating system administrators who agree to follow the Big Eight system. However, this creation process is rather complex and time-consuming. Some people find this unacceptable and even object to the entire concept of this restricted process. Others consider the system advantageous, as it keeps the Big Eight hierarchies relatively orderly by slowing the rate of change to existing newsgroups and the number of new groups added.

Alt and Other Newsgroup Hierarchies

For those who prefer a more freewheeling environment and do not want to submit to the Big Eight procedures, there is an alternative Usenet hierarchy, which begins with the hierarchy name *alt*. This hierarchy includes many thousands of groups. Some are quite popular, but many are not used at all; this is a side effect of the relative ease with which an alt group can be created.

In addition to these nine hierarchies, there are dozens of additional, smaller hierarchies. Many of these are regional or even company-specific. For example, the *ne.* hierarchy contains a set of newsgroups discussing issues of relevance to New England; *fr.** covers France, and *de.** pertains to Germany. Microsoft has its own set of public newsgroups in the *microsoft.** hierarchy. Figure 85-2 shows the Big Eight hierarchies and some of the other hierarchies that exist.

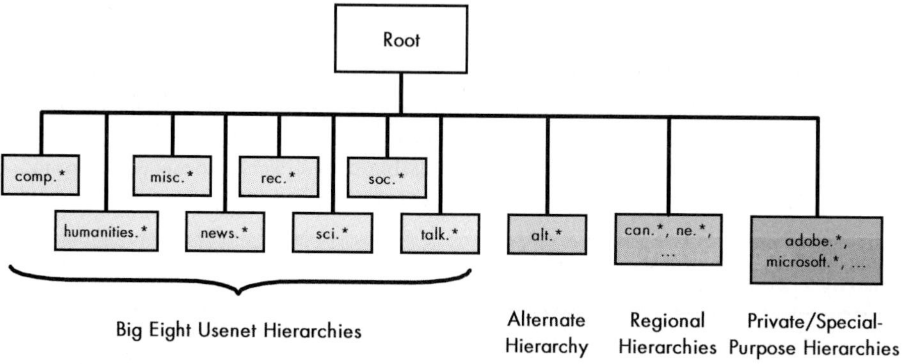

Figure 85-2: Usenet newsgroup hierarchies *Usenet newsgroups are arranged into tree-like structures called* hierarchies. *Eight of these are centralized, widely used, general-purpose hierarchies, which are today called the Big Eight. The alternate (alt) hierarchy is a very loosely structured set of thousands of groups covering every topic imaginable. In addition to these, there are many hundreds of regional, private, and special-purpose hierarchies.*

KEY CONCEPT Usenet messages are not addressed to individual users; rather, they are posted to newsgroups. Each newsgroup represents a topic. Those with an interest in the subject of a group can read messages in it and reply to them as well. Usenet newsgroups are arranged into tree-like hierarchies that are similar in structure to DNS domains. Many of the most widely used newsgroups are found in a collection of general-interest hierarchies called the Big Eight. An alternate (alt) hierarchy offers an alternative to the Big Eight. There are also many regional and special-purpose hierarchies.

Unmoderated and Moderated Newsgroups

Most newsgroups are open to all to use and are called *unmoderated* because a message sent to them goes directly out to the whole Usenet server internetwork. In contrast, a small percentage of newsgroups is *moderated*, which means that all messages sent to the group are screened and only the ones that are approved by a moderator (or moderator team) are really posted.

The purpose of moderated groups is to ensure that discussions in a particular group remain on-topic. They are often created to handle topics that are controversial, to ensure that debates remain constructive and disruption is avoided. For example, rec.guns is moderated to ensure that discussions focus on the use of guns and not on endless political arguments related to gun control and the like (which has a place, in talk.politics.guns). Moderated groups are also sometimes used for specialty groups intended only for announcements, or for groups where the content is restricted. For example, rec.food.recipes is moderated so that it contains only recipes and recipe requests, which helps people find recipes easily without needing to wade through a lot of discussion. Finally, moderated versions of unmoderated groups are sometimes created when a few disruptive elements choose to post large volumes in the unmoderated groups, making normal discussion difficult.

Cross-Posting to Multiple Newsgroups

It is possible for a single article to be posted to multiple newsgroups. This process, called *cross-posting*, is used when a message pertains to two topics, or to allow a sender to reach a wider audience. For example, if you live in the Seattle area and have a problem with your house, you might legitimately cross-post to *seattle.general* and *misc.consumers.house*.

Cross-posting is more efficient than posting the same message to each group independently for two reasons:

- Only one copy of the message will be stored on each Usenet server rather than two.
- Usenet participants who happen to read both groups won't see the message twice.

However, cross-posting to very large numbers of newsgroups is usually considered disruptive and a breach of Usenet etiquette.

Usenet Message Format and Special Headers

Usenet is designed to permit users to exchange information in the form of messages that are sent from one computer to another. As is necessary with any message-based networking application, all Usenet client software and server software agree to use a common *message format*. This ensures that all devices and programs are able to interpret all Usenet articles in a consistent manner.

While Usenet was created as an alternative to email, and there are obviously differences in how each treats messages, there are also many similarities. Both are text-oriented messaging systems with similar needs for communicating content and control information. The creators of Usenet realized that there would be many advantages to basing the Usenet message format on the one used for email, rather than creating a new format from scratch. The email message format was already widely used, and adopting it for Usenet would save implementation time and effort. It would also enhance compatibility between email and Usenet messages, allowing software designed to process or display email to also work with Usenet articles. For this reason, the Usenet message format was defined based on the RFC 822 standard for email messages (introduced in Chapter 76).

RFC 822 messages begin with a set of *headers* that contain control and descriptive information about the message, followed by a blank line and then the message *body*, which contains the actual content.

One important attribute of the RFC 822 standard is the ability to define custom headers that add to the regular set of headers defined in the standard itself. Usenet articles require some types of information not needed by email, and these can be included in specially defined headers while still adhering to the basic RFC 822 format. At the same time, headers specific to email that are not needed for Usenet can be omitted. Thus, there is no structural difference at all between a Usenet article and an email message. They differ only in the kinds of headers they contain and the values for those headers. For example, a Usenet message will always contain a header specifying the newsgroup(s) to which the article is being posted, but will not carry a "To:" line as an email message would.

KEY CONCEPT Usenet articles use the same RFC 822 message format as email messages. The only difference between a Usenet article and an email message is in the header types and values used in each.

Usenet Header Categories and Common Headers

All Usenet headers are defined according to the standard header format specified in RFC 822: <*header name*>: <*header value*>. As with email messages, headers may extend onto multiple lines, following the indenting procedure described in the RFC 822 standard.

The current standard for Usenet messages, RFC 1036, describes the header types for Usenet messages. The headers are divided into two categories: *mandatory* headers (see Table 85-2) and *optional* headers (see Table 85-3). Some are the same as headers of the equivalent name used for email, some are similar to email headers but used in a slightly different way, and others are unique to Usenet.

Table 85-2: Usenet Mandatory Headers

Header Name	Description
From:	The email address of the user sending the message, as for email.
Date:	The date and time that the message was originally posted to Usenet. This is usually the date/time that the user submitted the article to his or her local NNTP server.
Newsgroups:	Indicates the newsgroup or set of newsgroups to which the message is being posted. Multiple newsgroups are specified by separating them with a comma; for example: Newsgroups: news.onegroup,rec.secondgroup.
Subject:	Describes the subject or topic of the message. Note that this header is mandatory on Usenet despite being optional for email; it is important because it is used by readers to decide what messages to open.
Message-ID:	Provides a unique code for identifying a message; normally generated when a message is sent. The message ID is very important in Usenet, arguably more so than in email. The reason is that delivery of email is performed based on recipient email addresses, while the propagation of Usenet messages is controlled using the message ID header.
Path:	An informational field that shows the path of servers that a particular copy of a message followed to get to the server where it is being read. Each time a server forwards a Usenet article, it adds its own name to the list in the Path header. The entries are usually separated by exclamation points. For example, if a user on Usenet Server A posts a message, and it is transported from Server A to Server G, then Server X, then Server F, and finally to Server Q, where a second user reads it, the person on Server Q would see something like this in the Path header: "Q!F!X!G!A."

Table 85-3: Usenet Optional Headers

Header Name	Description
Reply-To:	It is possible to reply back to a Usenet article author using email, which by default, goes to the address in the From: line. If this header is present, the address it contains is used instead of the default From: address.
Sender:	Indicates the email address of the user who is sending the message, if different from the message originator. This is functionally the same as the Sender: header in email messages, but is used in a slightly different way. Normally, when a Usenet message is posted, the sender's email address is automatically filled in to the From: line. If the user manually specifies a different From: line, the address from which the message was actually sent is usually included in the Sender: line. This is used to track the true originating point of articles.
Followup-To:	A reply to a Usenet message is usually made back to Usenet itself and is called a *follow-up*. By default, a follow-up goes to the newsgroup(s) specified in the original message's Newsgroups: header. However, if the Followup-To: header is included, follow-ups to that message go to the newsgroups specified in the Followup-To: header instead. This header is sometimes used to route replies to a message to a particular group. Note, however, that when a user replies to a message, this field controls only what appears in the new message's Newsgroups: line by default. The user can override the Newsgroups: header manually.
Expires:	All Usenet messages are maintained on each server for only a certain period of time, due to storage limitations. The expiration interval for each newsgroup is controlled by the administrator of each site. If present, this line requests a different expiration for a particular message; it is usually used only for special articles. For example, if a weekly announcement is posted every Monday morning, each article might be set to expire the following Monday morning, to make sure that people see the most current version.
References:	Lists the message IDs of prior messages in a conversation. For example, if someone posts a question to a newsgroup with message ID AA207, and a reply to that message is made, the software will automatically insert the line "References: AA207" into the reply. This is used by software to group together articles into conversations (called *threads*) to make it easier to follow discussions on busy newsgroups.

(continued)

Table 85-3: Usenet Optional Headers (continued)

Header Name	Description
Control:	Indicates that the article is a control message and specifies a control action to be performed, such as creating a new newsgroup.
Distribution:	By default, most messages are propagated on Usenet worldwide. If specified, this line restricts the distribution of a message to a smaller area, either geographical or organizational.
Organization:	Describes the organization to which the article sender belongs. Often filled in automatically with the name of the user's Internet service provider (ISP).
Keywords:	Contains a list of comma-separated keywords that may be of use to the readers of the message. Keywords can be useful when searching for messages on a particular subject matter. This header is not often used.
Summary:	A short summary of the message. This is rarely used in practice.
Approved:	Added by the moderator of a moderated newsgroup to tell the Usenet software that the message has been approved for posting.
Lines:	A count of the number of lines in the message.
Xref:	While Usenet articles are identified by message ID, they are also given a number by each Usenet server as they are received. These article numbers, which differ from one system to the next, are usually listed in this cross-reference header. This information is used when a message is cross-posted to multiple groups. In that case, as soon as a user reads the message in one group, it is marked as having been read in all the others where it was posted. This way, if the user later reads one of those other groups, that user will not see the message again.

Additional Usenet Headers

Usenet messages may also contain additional headers, just as is the case with email messages. Some of these are custom headers included by individual users to provide extra information about an article. Others are used in many current Usenet articles and have become almost de facto standard headers through common use. Many of these custom headers are preceded by *X-*, indicating that they are experimental or extra headers.

Some of the more frequently encountered additional Usenet headers are shown in Table 85-4.

Table 85-4: Common Additional Usenet Headers

Header Name	Description
NNTP-Posting-Host:	Specifies the IP address or the DNS domain name of the host used to originally post the message. This is usually either the address of the client that the author used for posting the message or the sender's local NNTP server.
User-Agent: (or) X-Newsreader:	The name and version number of the software used to post the message.
X-Trace:	Provides additional information that can be used to trace the message.
X-Complaints-To:	An email address to use to report abusive messages. This header is now included automatically by many ISPs.

Usenet MIME Messages

Since Usenet follows the RFC 822 standard, Multipurpose Internet Mail Extensions (MIME) can be used to format Usenet messages. When this is done, you will see the usual MIME headers (such as MIME-Version, Content-Type, and so forth) in the message.

Note that the use of MIME in Usenet messages is somewhat controversial. Some newsreaders are not MIME-compliant and make a mess when trying to display some of these messages, and many Usenet veterans object to the use of anything but plain text in Usenet messages. Despite this, MIME messages are becoming more common, for better or worse.

NNTP Overview and General Operation

As I explained earlier in this chapter, Usenet started out as an informal network of UNIX computers using dial-up UUCP connections to transmit messages between servers. This arrangement arose out of necessity, and it worked fairly well, though it had a number of problems. Once the Internet became widely used in the 1980s, it provided the ideal opportunity for a more efficient means of distributing Usenet articles. NNTP was developed as a special TCP/IP protocol for sending these messages. Now NNTP carries billions of copies of Usenet messages from computer to computer every day.

BACKGROUND INFORMATION *NNTP is similar to the Simple Mail Transfer Protocol (SMTP) in many ways, including its basic operation and command set and reply format. You may find the information about NNTP easier to understand if you are familiar with SMTP, covered in Chapter 77.*

Usenet began as a *logical* internetwork of cooperating hosts that contacted each other directly. In the early Usenet, a user would post a message to her local server, where it would stay until that server either contacted or was contacted by another server. The message would then be transferred to the new server, where it would stay until the second server contacted a third one, and so on. This transport mechanism was functional, but seriously flawed in a number of ways.

Servers were not continually connected to each other; they could communicate only by making a telephone call using an analog modem. Thus, messages would often sit for hours before they could be propagated. Modems in those days were also very slow by today's standards—2400 bits per second or even less—so it took a long time to copy a message from one server to another. Worst of all, unless two sites were in the same city, these phone calls were long distance, making them quite expensive.

Why was this system used despite all of these problems? The answer is simply because there was no alternative. In the late 1970s and early 1980s, there was no Internet as we know it, and no other physical infrastructure existed to link Usenet sites together. It was either use UUCP over telephone lines or nothing.

That all changed as the fledgling ARPAnet grew into the modern Internet. As the Internet expanded, more and more sites connected to it, including many sites that were participating in Usenet. Once both sites in an exchange were on the Internet, it was an easy decision to use the Internet to send Usenet articles, rather than relying on slow, expensive phone calls. Over time, more and more Usenet sites joined the Internet, and it became clear that just as email had moved from UUCP to the TCP/IP Internet, the future of Usenet was on the Internet as well.

The shifting of Usenet from UUCP connections to TCP/IP internetworking meant that some rethinking was required as to how Usenet articles were moved from server to server. On the Internet, Usenet was just one of many applications, and the transfer of messages had to be structured using TCP or the User Datagram Protocol (UDP). Thus, like other applications, Usenet required an application-level protocol to describe how to carry Usenet traffic over TCP/IP. Just as Usenet had borrowed its message format from email's RFC 822, it made sense to model its message delivery protocol on the one used by email: SMTP. The result was the creation of NNTP, published as RFC 977 in February 1986.

The general operation of NNTP is indeed very similar to that of SMTP. NNTP uses TCP, with servers listening on well-known TCP port 119 for incoming connections, either from client hosts or other NNTP servers. As in SMTP, when two servers communicate using NNTP, the one that initiates the connection plays the role of client for that exchange.

After a connection is established, communication takes the form of commands sent by the client to the server and replies returned from the server to the client device. NNTP commands are sent as plain ASCII text, just like those used by SMTP, the File Transfer Protocol (FTP), the Hypertext Transfer Protocol (HTTP), and other protocols. NNTP responses take the form of three-digit reply codes as well as descriptive text, again just like SMTP (which, in turn, borrowed this concept from FTP).

NNTP was designed to be a comprehensive vehicle for transporting Usenet messages. It is most often considered as a delivery protocol for moving Usenet articles from one server to another, but it is also used for connections from client hosts to Usenet servers for posting and reading messages. Thus, the NNTP command set is quite extensive and includes commands to handle communications between servers and between clients and servers. For message propagation, a set of commands allows a server to request new articles from another server or to send new articles to another server. For message posting and access, commands allow a client to request lists of new newsgroups and messages, and to retrieve messages for display to a user.

The commands defined in RFC 977 were the only official ones for over a decade. However, even as early as the late 1980s, implementers of NNTP server and client software were adding new commands and features to make NNTP both more efficient and useful to users. These *NNTP extensions* were eventually documented in RFC 2980, published in 2000. I describe them in more detail later in this chapter, in the "NNTP Commands and Command Extensions" section.

> **KEY CONCEPT** The Network News Transfer Protocol (NNTP) is the protocol used to implement message communication in modern Usenet. It is used for two primary purposes: to propagate messages between NNTP servers and to permit NNTP clients to post and read articles. It is a stand-alone protocol, but shares many characteristics with email's Simple Mail Transfer Protocol (SMTP).

NNTP is used for all of the transfer steps in the modern Usenet communication process. However, NNTP is most often associated with the process of Usenet article *propagation*. This is arguably the most important function of NNTP: providing an efficient means of moving large volumes of Usenet articles from one server to another. It is thus a sensible place to start looking at the protocol.

NNTP Interserver Communication Process: News Article Propagation

To understand how NNTP propagation works, we must begin with a look at the way that the modern Usenet network itself is organized. Usenet sites are now all on the Internet, and theoretically, any NNTP server can contact any other to send and receive Usenet articles. However, it would be ridiculous to have a new article submitted to a particular server need to be sent via separate NNTP connections to each and every other NNTP server. For this reason, the Usenet logical network continues to be very important, even in the Internet era.

The Usenet Server Structure

In theory, all that is required of the Usenet structure is that each site be connected to at least one other site in some form. The logical network could be amorphous and without any formal structure at all, as long as every site could form a path through some sequence of intermediate servers to each other one. However, the modern Usenet is very large, with thousands of servers and gigabytes of articles being posted every day. This calls for a more organized structure for distributing news.

For this reason, the modern Usenet logical network is structured loosely in a hierarchy. A few large Internet service providers (ISPs) and big companies with high-speed Internet connections and large servers are considered to be at the top of the hierarchy, in what is sometimes called the Usenet *backbone.* Smaller organizations connect to the servers run by these large organizations; these organizations are considered to be *downstream* from the backbone groups. In turn, still smaller organizations may connect further downstream from the ones connected to the large organizations.

This hierarchical structure means that most Usenet servers maintain a direct connection only to their upstream neighbor and to any downstream sites to which they provide service. A server is said to receive a *news feed* from its upstream connection, since that is the place from which it will receive most of its news articles. It then provides a news feed to all the servers downstream from it. I illustrated this structure earlier in Figure 85-1.

As an example, suppose Company A runs a large Usenet server called Largenews that is connected to the backbone. Downstream from this server is the NNTP server Mediumnews. That server provides service to the server named Smallnews. If a user posts an article to Mediumnews, it will be placed on that server immediately. That server will send the article downstream, to Smallnews, so that it can be read by that server's users. Mediumnews will also, at some point, send the article to Largenews. From Largenews, the message will be distributed to other backbone sites, which will pass the message down to their own downstream sites. In this way, all sites eventually get a copy of the message, even though Mediumnews needs to connect directly to only two other servers.

The term used to describe how news is propagated with NNTP is *flooding*. This is because of the way that a message begins in one server and floods outward from it, eventually reaching the backbone sites, and then going down all the downstream "rivers" to reach every site on Usenet.

Even though I described the logical Usenet network as a hierarchy, it is not a strict hierarchy. For redundancy, many NNTP servers maintain connections to multiple other servers to ensure that news propagates quickly. The transmission of articles can be controlled by looking at message IDs to avoid duplication of messages that may be received simultaneously by one server from more than one neighbor.

Basic NNTP Propagation Methods

Now let's look at how messages are actually propagated between servers using NNTP. There are two techniques by which this can be done:

- In the *push model*, as soon as a server receives a new message, it immediately tells its upstream and downstream neighbors about the message and asks them if they want a copy of it.
- In the *pull model*, servers do not offer new articles to their neighbors. The neighboring servers must ask for a list of new messages if they want to see what has arrived since the last connection was established, and then request that the new messages be sent to them.

Both techniques have advantages and disadvantages, but pushing is the model most commonly used today.

KEY CONCEPT One important role that NNTP plays is its propagation of articles between Usenet servers, which is what makes the entire system possible. Two models are used for article propagation: the push model, in which a server that receives a new message offers it to connected servers immediately, and the pull model, where servers that receive new messages hold them until they are requested by other servers. The push model is usually preferred since it allows for quicker communication of messages around the system.

Article Propagation Using the Push Model

Using the push model, when the administrators of an NNTP server establish a service relationship with an upstream Usenet service provider, they furnish the provider with a list of newsgroups that the downstream server wants to carry. Whenever a new article arrives at the upstream server within that list of groups, it is automatically sent to the downstream site. This saves the downstream server from constantly having to ask whether anything has arrived.

In the classic NNTP protocol as defined in RFC 977, the exchange of articles is based on the push model and performed using the IHAVE command. Returning to the example in the previous section, suppose three new messages arrive at the Largenews server. It would establish an NNTP connection to the Mediumnews server and use IHAVE to provide the message IDs of each of the three new messages, one at a time. (NNTP commands are described later in this chapter.) The Mediumnews server would respond to each one, indicating whether or not it already had that message. If not, Largenews would send it the message. An example of an article transaction using the push model of propagation is illustrated in Figure 85-3.

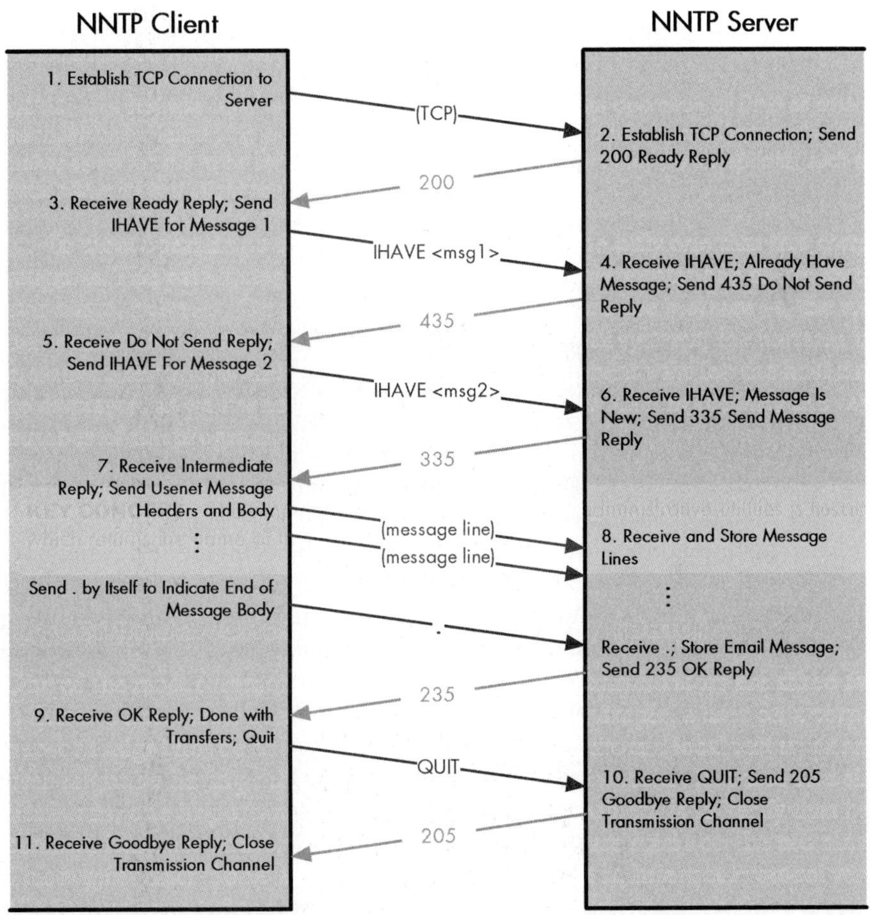

Figure 85-3: NNTP article propagation using the push model *This example shows how Usenet articles are moved between servers using the conventional push model of propagation. Here, the device acting as an NNTP client (which may, in fact, be an NNTP server) has two messages available to offer to the server. It sends the IHAVE command specifying the message ID of the first message, but the server already has that message, so it sends a 435 (Do Not Send) reply. The client then issues an IHAVE with the second message ID. The server wants this one, so it sends a 335 reply. The client sends the Usenet message, ending with a single period on a line by itself. The server indicates that it received the message, and the client, finished with its transactions, quits the session.*

The main advantage of this technique is that it ensures that a server is not sent a duplicate copy of a message that it already has. The problem with it in modern Usenet is that it is slow, because the server must respond to the IHAVE command before the message or the next command can be sent by the client.

Improving Propagation Efficiency with Streaming Mode

One of the more important NNTP extensions is *streaming mode*, which changes how news pushing is done. (NNTP command extensions are described later in this chapter.) When this mode is enabled, the client machine uses the CHECK command instead of IHAVE to ask the server if it wants a particular message. The server responds to indicate if it wants the message; if it does, the client sends the message with the TAKETHIS command.

The benefit of CHECK/TAKETHIS is that the client does not need to wait for a reply to CHECK before sending the next command. While the client is waiting for a reply to the first CHECK command, it can do something else, like sending the next CHECK command, allowing commands to be streamed for greater efficiency. So, the client could send a CHECK command for the first new message, then a CHECK for the second, while waiting for a reply from the server to the first one. Many CHECK commands could be sent in a stream, and then TAKETHIS commands sent for each reply received to CHECK commands sent earlier indicating that the message was wanted by the server.

Article Propagation Using the Pull Model

The pull model is implemented using the NEWNEWS and ARTICLE commands. The client connects to the server and sends the NEWNEWS command with a date specifying the date and time that it last checked for new messages. The server responds with a set of message IDs for new articles that have arrived since that date. The client then requests each new message using the ARTICLE command.

Note that the push and pull models can be combined in a single session. A client can connect to a server, use NEWNEWS to check for new messages on that server, and then IHAVE or CHECK inform the server about new messages the client wants to send. In practice, it is more common for only one or the other of the models to be used between a pair of servers for any given exchange.

In addition to propagating new messages, NNTP is also used to allow servers to communicate information about new newsgroups that have been created. This is done using the NEWGROUPS command, which is specified with a date and time like NEWNEWS. In response, the server sends to the client a list of new newsgroups that have been created since the specified date and time.

NNTP Client-Server Communication Process: News Posting and Access

One critical area where NNTP differs from its progenitor, SMTP, is that NNTP is not just used for interserver communication. It is also used for the initial posting of Usenet messages, as well as reading the messages. In fact, the majority of NNTP commands deals with the interaction between user client machines and NNTP servers, not communication between servers.

An NNTP client is any software program that knows the NNTP protocol and is designed to provide user access to Usenet. NNTP clients are usually called *newsreaders*, and they provide two main capabilities to a user: *posting* and *reading*

Usenet messages. Usenet newsreaders exist for virtually all hardware and software platforms, and they range greatly in terms of capabilities, user interface, and other characteristics. Most people today use a Usenet newsreader on a client computer that must make NNTP connections to a separate NNTP server to read and post news. These programs are analogous to email clients, and, in fact, many email clients also function as NNTP clients.

News Posting, Access, and Reading

Posting a Usenet message is the first step in the overall Usenet communication process (although many Usenet articles are actually replies to other articles, so it's a bit of a chicken-and-egg situation). Article posting is quite straightforward with NNTP. The client establishes a connection to the server and issues the POST command. If the server is willing to accept new articles, it replies with a prompt for the client to send it the article. The article is then transmitted by the client to the server. Some newsreaders may batch new articles, so they can be sent in a single NNTP session, rather than submitting them one at a time.

Newsreaders also establish an NNTP connection to a server to read Usenet articles. NNTP provides a large number of commands to support a variety of different article access and retrieval actions that may be taken by a user. The first step in reading is sometimes to examine the list of available newsgroups. Using the LIST command, the client requests from the server a list of the newsgroups available for reading and posting. RFC 977 defines the basic LIST command, which returns a list of all groups to the client. RFC 2980 defines numerous extensions to the command to allow a client to retrieve only certain types of information about groups on the server. Since the number of Usenet newsgroups is so large today, this listing of newsgroups is usually skipped unless the user specifically requests it.

The next step in Usenet message access is typically to select a newsgroup to read from the list of groups available. Again, since there are so many groups today, most newsreaders allow a user to search for a group name using a pattern or partial name string. The GROUP command is then sent to the server with the name of the selected group. The server returns the first and last current article numbers for the group to the client.

Messages are identified in two ways: one absolute and the other site-specific. The article's message ID is a fixed identifier that can be used to uniquely represent it across Usenet; this is what is used in interserver communication to determine whether each site has a copy of a given message. In contrast, *article numbers* are server-specific; they represent the numbers assigned to those articles as they arrived at that server and are used as a shorthand to more easily refer to articles in a newsgroup. Thus, the same message will have a different article number on each NNTP server. Article numbers are used for convenience, since they are much shorter than message IDs. During a session, the NNTP server also maintains a current article pointer, which can be used for stepping sequentially through a newsgroup.

News Access Methods

There are several different ways that the newsreader can access messages in a group, depending on how it is programmed and what the user of the software wants. The news access methods include the following:

Full Newsgroup Retrieval The brute-force technique is for the client to simply request that the server send it all the messages in the group. The client issues the ARTICLE command to select the first current message in the group, using the first article number returned by the GROUP command. This sets the server's internal pointer for the session to point to the first article, so it can be retrieved. The NEXT command is then used to advance the pointer to the next message, and the ARTICLE command is used to retrieve it. This continues until the entire group has been read. Figure 85-4 illustrates the process. The retrieved messages are stored by the newsreader and available for instant access by the user. This method is most suitable for relatively small newsgroups and/or users with fast Internet connections.

Newsgroup Header Retrieval Since downloading an entire newsgroup is time-consuming, many newsreaders compromise by downloading the headers of all messages instead of the full message. The process is the same as for full newsgroup retrieval, but the HEAD command is used to retrieve just an article's headers. This takes less time than retrieving each message in its entirety using the ARTICLE command. The XHDR command extension can also be used, if the server supports it, to more efficiently retrieve only a subset of the headers for the messages, such as the subject line and author.

Individual Article Retrieval It is also possible to retrieve a single message from a group, using the ARTICLE command and specifying the article's message identifier.

> **KEY CONCEPT** While NNTP is best known for its role in interserver propagation, it is also used by Usenet clients to write and read articles. Different commands provide flexibility in how articles can be read by a client device. A client can retrieve an entire newsgroup, only a set of newsgroup headers, or individual articles. Other commands also support various administrative functions.

Other Client/Server Functions

In addition to reading and posting, NNTP includes commands to support other miscellaneous tasks that a Usenet user may wish to perform. The client can ask the server for help information by using the HELP command or get a list of new newsgroups by using the NEWGROUPS command.

Most modern newsreaders include capabilities that go far beyond the basic posting and reading functions previously described. Most maintain their own sets of configuration files that allow a user to maintain a set of favorite subscribed newsgroups, rather than needing to choose a group to read from the master list each time Usenet is accessed. Newsreaders also keep track of which articles have been read by a user in each subscribed newsgroup, so users do not need to wade through a whole newsgroup to see new messages that have been posted.

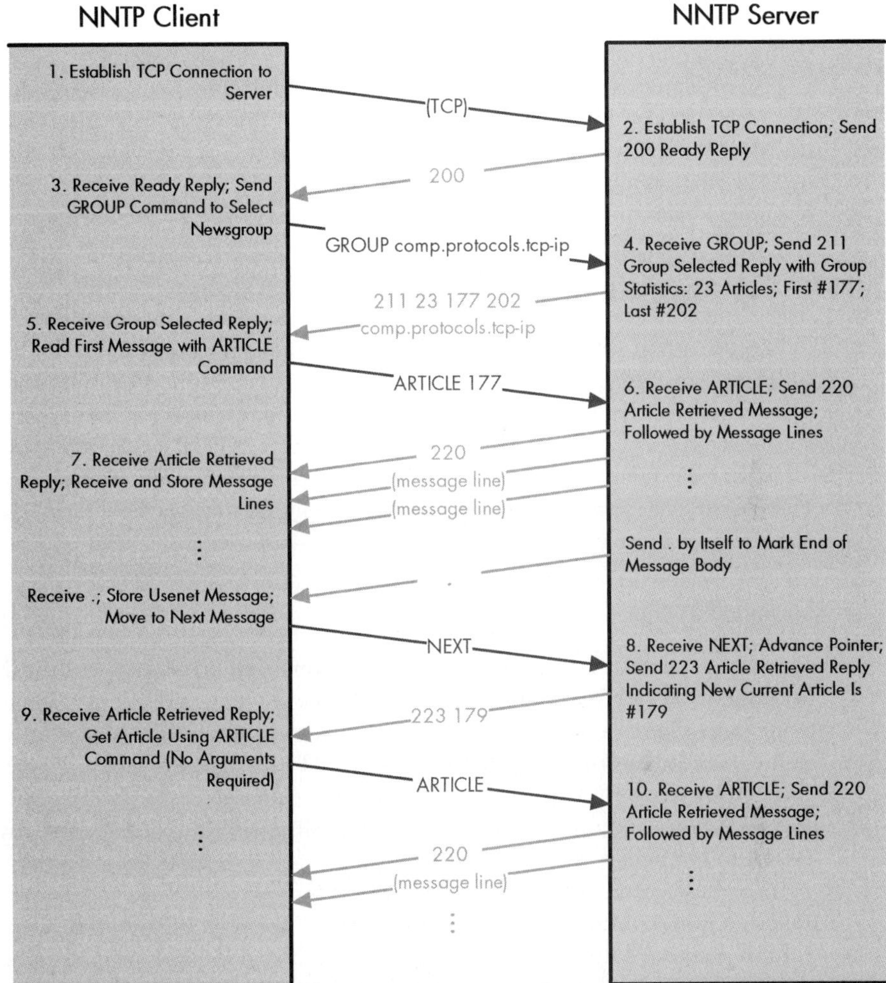

NNTP Client
NNTP Server
1. Establish TCP Connection to Server
(TCP)
2. Establish TCP Connection; Send 200 Ready Reply
200
3. Receive Ready Reply; Send GROUP Command to Select Newsgroup
GROUP comp.protocols.tcp-ip
4. Receive GROUP; Send 211 Group Selected Reply with Group Statistics: 23 Articles; First #177; Last #202
211 23 177 202 comp.protocols.tcp-ip
5. Receive Group Selected Reply; Read First Message with ARTICLE Command
ARTICLE 177
6. Receive ARTICLE; Send 220 Article Retrieved Message; Followed by Message Lines
220
(message line)
(message line)
7. Receive Article Retrieved Reply; Receive and Store Message Lines
Send . by Itself to Mark End of Message Body
.
Receive .; Store Usenet Message; Move to Next Message
NEXT
8. Receive NEXT; Advance Pointer; Send 223 Article Retrieved Reply Indicating New Current Article Is #179
223 179
9. Receive Article Retrieved Reply; Get Article Using ARTICLE Command (No Arguments Required)
ARTICLE
10. Receive ARTICLE; Send 220 Article Retrieved Message; Followed by Message Lines
220
(message line)

Figure 85-4: NNTP full newsgroup retrieval process *There are many ways that an NNTP client can access and read Usenet messages on a server. One common method is to retrieve the entire contents of a newsgroup. In this example, the client uses the GROUP command to select the newsgroup comp.protocols.tcp-ip for reading; the server responds with a 211 (Group Selected) reply, which includes important statistics about the group. The client uses the ARTICLE command with the number of the first article in the group, 177, to read it from the server. The server then sends the message line by line, ending it with a single period on a line. The client uses the NEXT command to tell the server to advance its internal article pointer to the next message, which often will not be the next consecutive number after the one just read; here it is 179. The client can then read that message by sending the ARTICLE command by itself. Since no parameters are given, the server returns the current message (179).*

Article Threading

One particularly useful enhancement to basic Usenet article reading is *threading*. This feature allows a newsreader to display articles not strictly in either alphabetical or chronological order, but rather grouped into conversations using the information in the articles' References headers. Threading is especially useful in busy newsgroups, as it allows users to see all the articles in a particular discussion at once, rather than trying to juggle messages from many conversations simultaneously.

A problem with threading is that it takes a long time for a newsreader to sift through all those References lines and construct the article threads. To speed up this process, many servers now cache extra threading or overview information for newsgroups, which can be retrieved by the client to save time when a newsgroup is opened. This is done using the XTHREAD or XOVER NNTP command extensions.

NNTP Commands and Command Extensions

One of the great strengths of the open, cooperative process used to develop Internet standards is that new protocols are usually designed by building on older ones. This saves development time and effort, and promotes compatibility between technologies. As I explained earlier in the chapter, NNTP was based in many ways on principles from SMTP; SMTP, in turn, borrowed ideas from earlier protocols: Telnet and FTP. This legacy can be seen in the similarities between NNTP commands and those of these earlier protocols.

Command Syntax

As in SMTP, all NNTP commands are ASCII text that are sent over the NNTP TCP connection to an NNTP server, from the device acting as the client (which may be a newsreader client or an NNTP server itself). These are standard text strings adhering to the Telnet Network Virtual Terminal (NVT) format, terminated by the two-character carriage return/line feed (CRLF) sequence. As is the case with SMTP and FTP, you can conduct an interactive session with an NNTP server by using Telnet to connect to it on port 119.

The basic syntax of an NNTP command is *<command-code> <parameters>*. Unlike SMTP, NNTP commands are not restricted to a length of four characters. The parameters that follow the command are separated by one or more space characters, and are used to provide necessary information to allow the server to execute the command. NNTP commands are not case-sensitive.

Base Command Set

The main NNTP specification, RFC 977, describes the base set of commands supported by NNTP clients and servers. They are not broken into categories, but rather listed alphabetically, as I have done in Table 85-5. (The details on how many of these commands are used for news article propagation and news posting/access were provided earlier in this chapter.)

Table 85-5: NNTP Base Commands

Command Code	Command	Parameters	Description
ARTICLE	Retrieve Article	Message ID or server article number	Tells the server to send the client a particular Usenet article. The article to be retrieved may be specified using either its absolute, universal message ID or its locally assigned article number. When the command is issued with an article number, this causes the server's internal message pointer to be set to the specified article. If the message pointer is already set to a particular article, the ARTICLE command can be issued without an article number, and the current message will be retrieved.
HEAD	Retrieve Article Headers	Message ID or server article number	Same as the ARTICLE command, but retrieves only the article's headers.
BODY	Retrieve Article Body	Message ID or server article number	Same as the ARTICLE command, but returns only the body of the article.
STAT	Retrieve Article Statistics	Server article number	Conceptually the same as the ARTICLE command, but does not return any message text, only the message ID of the article. This command is usually used for setting the server's internal message pointer, so STAT is normally invoked only with an article number (and not a message ID).
GROUP	Select Newsgroup	Newsgroup name	Tells the server the name of the newsgroup that the client wants to access. Assuming the group specified exists, the server returns to the client the numbers of the first and last articles currently in the group, along with an estimate of the number of messages in the group. The server's internal article pointer is also set to the first message in the group.
HELP	Get Help Information	None	Prompts the server to send the client help information, which usually takes the form of a list of valid commands that the server supports.
IHAVE	Offer Article to Server	Message ID	Used by the client in an NNTP session to tell the server that it has a new article that the server may want. The server will check the message ID provided and respond to the client, indicating whether or not it wants the client to send the article.
LAST	Go to Last Message	None	Tells the server to set its current article pointer to the last message in the newsgroup.
LIST	List Newsgroups	None	Asks the server to send a list of the newsgroups that it supports, along with the first and last article number in each group. The command as described in RFC 977 is simple, supporting no parameters and causing the full list of newsgroups to be sent to the client. NNTP command extensions significantly expand the syntax of this command, as described in the following section of this chapter.
NEWGROUPS	List New Newsgroups	Date and time, and optional distribution specification	Prompts the server to send a list of new newsgroups created since the date and time specified. The client may also restrict the command to return only new newsgroups within a particular regional distribution.
NEWNEWS	List New News Articles	Date and time, and optional distribution specification	Requests a list from the server of all new articles that have arrived since a particular date and time. Like the NEWGROUPS command, this may be restricted in distribution. The server responds with a list of message IDs of new articles.

(continued)

Table 85-5: NNTP Base Commands (continued)

Command Code	Command	Parameters	Description
NEXT	Go to Next Message	None	Advances the server's current article pointer to the next message in the newsgroup.
POST	Post Article	None	Tells the server that the client would like to post a new article. The server responds with either a positive or negative acknowledgment. Assuming that posting is allowed, the client then sends the full text of the message to the server, which stores it and begins the process of propagating it to other servers.
QUIT	End Session	None	Terminates the NNTP session. To be "polite," the client should issue this command prior to closing the TCP connection.
SLAVE	Set Slave Status	None	Intended for use in special configurations where one NNTP server acts as a subsidiary to others. It is not often used in practice.

KEY CONCEPT The main NNTP standard defines a number of base NNTP commands that are used by the device initiating an NNTP connection to accomplish article propagation, posting, and reading functions. NNTP commands consist of a command code and, optionally, parameters that specify how the command is to be carried out.

NNTP Command Extensions

The base command set described in RFC 977 was sufficient to enable client-server and interserver functionality, but in many ways, it was quite basic and limited in efficiency and usefulness. As Usenet grew larger and more popular in the late 1980s, NNTP needed changes to improve its usability. In 1991, work began on a formal revision to the NNTP standard, but was never completed. Despite this, many of the concepts from that effort were adopted informally in NNTP implementations in subsequent years. In addition, some Usenet software authors created their own nonstandard features to improve the protocol, and some of these features also became de facto standards through widespread adoption.

As a result, by the late 1990s, most Usenet software actually implemented variations of NNTP with capabilities far exceeding what was documented in the standard. Naturally, not all NNTP software supported the same extra features, leading to potential compatibility difficulties between servers and clients. RFC 2980, "Common NNTP Extensions," was published in October 2000 to formalize many of these extensions to the base NNTP standard as defined in RFC 977.

The NNTP extensions primarily consist of new NNTP commands that are added to the basic NNTP command set, as well as some minor changes to how other commands and functions of NNTP work. The extensions generally fall into three categories:

- Extensions that improve the efficiency of NNTP message transport between servers
- Extensions that make NNTP more effective for client message access
- Miscellaneous extensions, which don't fall into either of the preceding groups

NNTP Transport Extensions

The first group is called the NNTP *transport extensions* and consists of a small group of related commands that are designed to improve interserver message propagation. Most of these implement NNTP's *stream mode*, which provides a more effective way of moving large numbers of articles from one server to another, as described in the discussion of interserver communication earlier in this chapter. Table 85-6 describes the new transport commands.

Table 85-6: NNTP Transport Extensions

Command Code	Command	Parameters	Description
MODE STREAM	Set Stream Mode	None	Used to tell the server that the client wants to operate in stream mode, using the CHECK and TAKETHIS commands.
CHECK	Check If Article Exists	Message ID	Used in stream mode by a server acting as a client to ask another server if it has a copy of a particular article. The server responds back indicating whether or not it wishes to be sent a copy of the article. This command is similar to IHAVE, except that the client does not need to wait for a reply before sending the next command.
TAKETHIS	Send Article to Server	Message ID	When a server responds to a CHECK command indicating that it wants a copy of a particular message, the client sends it using this command.
XREPLIC	Replicate Articles	List of newsgroups and article numbers	Created for the special purpose of copying large numbers of articles from one server to another. It is not widely used.

NNTP Newsreader Extensions

The second group of extensions defined by RFC 2980 consists of *newsreader extensions*, which focus primarily on commands used by newsreader clients in interactions with NNTP servers. These extensions consist of several new commands, as well as significant enhancements to one important command that was very limited in its functionality in RFC 977: LIST.

The original LIST command has no parameters and only allows a client to retrieve the entire list of newsgroups a server carries. This may have been sufficient when there were only a few hundred Usenet newsgroups, but there are now tens of thousands. RFC 2980 defines a number of new variations of the LIST command to allow the client much more flexibility in the types of information the server returns. Table 85-7 shows the new LIST command variations.

Table 85-7: NNTP LIST Command Extensions

Command Code	Command	Parameters	Description
LIST ACTIVE	List Active Newsgroups	Newsgroup name or pattern	Provides a list of active newsgroups on the server. This is semantically the same as the original LIST command, but the client may provide a newsgroup name or a pattern to restrict the number of newsgroups returned. For example, the client can ask for a list of only the newsgroups that contain "football" in them.

(continued)

Table 85-7: NNTP LIST Command Extensions (continued)

Command Code	Command	Parameters	Description
LIST ACTIVE.TIMES	List Active Newsgroup Creation Times	None	Prompts the server to send the client its *active.times* file, which contains information about when the newsgroups carried by the server were created.
LIST DISTRIBUTIONS	List Distributions	None	Causes the server to sent the client the contents of the *distributions* file, which shows what regional distribution strings the server recognizes (for use in the Distribution header of a message).
LIST DISTRIB.PATS	List Distribution Patterns	None	Asks the server for its *distribution.pats* file, which is like the distributions file but uses patterns to summarize distribution information for different newsgroups.
LIST NEWSGROUPS	List Newsgroups	Newsgroup name or pattern	Provides a list of newsgroup names and descriptions. This differs from LIST ACTIVE in that only the newsgroup name and description are returned, not the article numbers for each newsgroup. It is functionally the same as XGTITLE (see Table 85-8) and is usually employed by a user to locate a newsgroup to be added to his or her subscribed list.
LIST OVERVIEW.FMT	Display Overview Format	None	Prompts the server to display information about the format of its *overview* file. See the XOVER command description in Table 85-8 for more information.
LIST SUBSCRIPTIONS	Retrieve Default Subscription List	None	Asks the server to send the client a default list of subscribed newsgroups. This is used to set up a new user with a suggested list of newsgroups. For example, if an organization has an internal support newsgroup, it could put this group on the default subscription list so all new users learn about it immediately when they first start up their newsreader.

In addition to these changes to the LIST command, many new newsreader-related command extensions are defined, which are described in Table 85-8.

Table 85-8: NNTP Newsreader Extensions

Command Code	Command	Parameters	Description
LISTGROUP	List Article Numbers In Newsgroup	Newsgroup name	Causes the server to return a list of local article numbers for the current messages in the newsgroup. The server's current article pointer is also set to the first message in the group.
MODE READER	Set Newsreader Mode	None	Tells the server that the device acting as a client is a client newsreader and not another NNTP server. While technically not required—all commands can be sent by any device acting as client—some servers may be optimized to respond to newsreader-oriented commands if given this command.

(continued)

Table 85-8: NNTP Newsreader Extensions (continued)

Command Code	Command	Parameters	Description
XGTITLE	Retrieve Newsgroup Descriptions	Newsgroup name or pattern	Used to list the descriptions for a newsgroup or a set of newsgroups matching a particular text pattern. This command is functionally the same as the LIST NEWSGROUP command extension (see Table 85-7). It is therefore recommended that XGTITLE no longer be used.
XHDR	Retrieve Article Headers	Header name and optionally, either a message ID or a range of article numbers	Allows a client to ask for only a particular header from a set of messages. If only the header name is provided, the header is returned for all messages in the current group. Otherwise, the header is provided for the selected messages. This extension provides a newsreader client with a more efficient way of retrieving and displaying important headers in a newsgroup to a user.
XINDEX	Retrieve Index Information	Newsgroup name	Retrieves an *index* file, used by the newsreader called *TIN* to improve the efficiency of newsgroup perusal. TIN now supports the more common overview format, so the XOVER command is preferred to this one.
XOVER	Retrieve Overview Information	Article number or range of article numbers in a newsgroup	Retrieves the *overview* for an article or set of articles. Servers supporting this feature maintain a special database for their newsgroups that contains information about current articles in a format that can be used by a variety of newsreaders. Retrieving the overview information allows features like message threading to be performed more quickly than if the client had to retrieve the headers of each message and analyze them manually.
XPAT	Retrieve Article Headers Matching a Pattern	Header name, pattern, and either a message ID or a range of article numbers	Similar to XHDR in that it allows a particular header to be retrieved for a set of messages. The difference is that the client can specify a pattern that must be matched for the header to be retrieved. This allows the client to have the server search for and return certain messages, such as those with a subject line indicating a particular type of discussion, rather than requiring the client to download all the headers and search through them.
XPATH	Retrieve File Name Information	Message ID	Allows a client to ask for the name of the actual file in which a particular message is stored on the server.
XROVER	Retrieve Overview Reference Information	Article number or range of article numbers in a newsgroup	Like the XOVER command, but specifically retrieves information in the References header for the indicated articles. This is the header containing the data needed to create threaded conversations.
XTHREAD	Retrieve Threading Information	Optional DBINIT parameter	Similar to XINDEX, but retrieves a special threading information file in the format used by the newsreader named *TRN*. Like TIN, TRN now supports the common overview format, so XOVER is preferred to this command. The DBINIT parameter can be used to check for the existence of a thread database.

Other NNTP Extensions

The last extension group contains the miscellaneous extensions not strictly related to either interserver or client-server NNTP interaction. There are two commands in this group: AUTHINFO and DATE. The latter is a simple command that causes the server to tell the client its current date and time. AUTHINFO is more interesting. It is used by a client to provide authentication data to a server.

You may have noticed that there are no commands related to security described in the RFC 977 protocol. That's because the original NNTP had no security features whatsoever. Like many protocols written before the modern Internet era, security was not considered a big issue back in the early 1980s. Most news servers were used only by people within the organization owning the server, and simple security measures were used, such as restricting access to servers by IP address or through the use of access lists.

One of the more important changes made by many NNTP software implementations as soon as Usenet grew in size was to require authentication. Modern clients will usually issue AUTHINFO as one of their first commands on establishing a connection to a server, because the server will refuse to accept most other commands before this is done. A special reply code is also added to NNTP for a server to use if it rejects a command due to improper authentication.

The AUTHINFO command can be invoked in several different ways. The original version of the command required the client to issue an AUTHINFO USER command with a user name, followed by AUTHINFO PASS with a password. This is simple user/password login authentication. A variation of this is the AUTHINFO SIMPLE command, where the client needs to send just a password.

A client and server can also agree to use more sophisticated authentication methods by employing the AUTHINFO GENERIC command. The client provides to the server the name of the authentication method it wants to use, along with any arguments required for authentication. The client and server then exchange messages and authentication information as required by the particular authenticator they are using.

> **KEY CONCEPT** A number of limitations in its base command set led to a proliferation of nonstandard enhancements to NNTP during the 1980s and 1990s. These were eventually documented in a set of NNTP command extensions that formally supplement the original RFC 977 commands. The extensions are conceptually divided into three groups: transport extensions that refine how NNTP propagates messages, newsreader extensions that improve client article access, and miscellaneous extensions. The most important miscellaneous extension is AUTHINFO, which adds security to NNTP.

NNTP Status Responses and Response Codes

Each time the device acting as a client in an NNTP connection sends a command, the server sends back a *response*. The response serves to acknowledge receipt of the command, to inform the client of the results of processing the command, and possibly to prompt for additional information. Since NNTP commands are structured and formatted in a way very similar to that of SMTP commands, I'm sure it will come as no great surprise that NNTP responses are very similar to those of SMTP (described in Chapter 77). In turn, SMTP responses are based on the system designed for replies in FTP.

The first line of an NNTP response consists of a three-digit numerical *response code*, as well as a line of descriptive text that summarizes the response. These response codes are structured so that each digit has a particular significance, which allows the client to quickly determine the status of the command to which the reply was sent. After the initial response line, depending on the reply, a number of additional response lines may follow. For example, a successful LIST command results in a 215 response code, followed by a list of newsgroups.

BACKGROUND INFORMATION *The discussion of FTP reply codes in Chapter 72 explains the reasons why numeric reply codes are used in addition to descriptive text.*

As with SMTP and FTP, NNTP reply codes can be considered to be of the form *xyz*, where *x* is the first digit, *y* the second, and *z* the third. The first reply code digit (*x*) indicates the success, failure, or progress of the command in general terms; whether a successful command is complete or incomplete; and the general reason why an unsuccessful command did not work. The values of this digit are defined slightly differently than they are in SMTP and FTP. In some cases, the terminology is just simplified; for example, the second category is Command OK, instead of the more cryptic Positive Completion Reply. Table 85-9 shows the specific meaning of the possible values of this digit.

Table 85-9: NNTP Reply Code Format: First Digit Interpretation

Reply Code Format	Meaning	Description
1yz	Informative Message	General information; used for help information and debugging.
2yz	Command OK	The command was completed successfully.
3yz	Command OK So Far; Send the Rest	An intermediate reply, sent to prompt the client to send more information. Typically used for replies to commands such as IHAVE or POST, where the server acknowledges the command, and then requests that an article be transmitted by the client.
4yz	Command Was Correct, but Couldn't Be Performed	The command was valid but could not be performed. This type of error usually occurs due to bad parameters, a transient problem with the server, a bad command sequence, or similar situations.
5yz	Command Unimplemented or Incorrect, or Serious Program Error	The command was invalid or a significant program error prevented it from being performed.

The second reply code digit (*y*) is used to categorize messages into functional groups. This digit is used in the same general way as in SMTP and FTP, but the functional groups are different, as described in Table 85-10.

Table 85-10: NNTP Reply Code Format: Second Digit Interpretation

Reply Code Format	Meaning	Description
x0z	Connection, Setup, and Miscellaneous	Generic and miscellaneous replies.
x1z	Newsgroup Selection	Messages related to commands used to select a newsgroup.
x2z	Article Selection	Messages related to commands used to select an article.
x3z	Distribution Functions	Messages related to the transfer of messages.
x4z	Posting	Messages related to posting messages.
x5z	Authentication	Messages related to authentication and the AUTHINFO command extension. (This category is not officially listed in the standard, but these responses have a middle digit of 5.)
x8z	Nonstandard Extensions	Reserved for private, nonstandard implementation use.
x9z	Debugging	Debugging output messages.

The third reply code digit (*z*) indicates a specific type of message within each of the functional groups described by the second digit. The third digit allows each functional group to have ten different reply codes for each reply type given by the first code digit.

As in FTP and SMTP, these *x*, *y*, and *z* digit meanings are combined to make specific reply codes. For example, the reply code 435 is sent by the server if a client issues the IHAVE command but the server doesn't want the article being offered. The command was correct but the reply is negative, thus it starts with 4, and the message is related to message distribution, so the middle digit is 3.

Table 85-11 contains a list of some of the more common NNTP reply codes in numerical order, along with typical reply text from the standard and additional descriptive information.

Table 85-11: NNTP Reply Codes

Reply Code	Reply Text	Description
100	help text follows	Precedes response to HELP command.
111	(date and time)	Response to DATE command extension.
199	(debugging output)	Debugging information.
200	server ready - posting allowed	Sent by the server on initiation of the session, if the client is allowed to post messages.
201	server ready - no posting allowed	Sent by the server on initiation of the session, if the client is not allowed to post messages.
202	slave status noted	Response to the SLAVE command.
203	streaming is ok	Successful response to MODE STREAM command.
205	closing connection - goodbye!	Goodbye message sent in response to a QUIT message.
211	n f l s group selected	Successful response to the GROUP command, indicating the estimated number of messages in the group (*n*), first and last article numbers (*f* and *l*) and group name (*s*).

(continued)

Table 85-11: NNTP Reply Codes (continued)

Reply Code	Reply Text	Description
215	list of newsgroups follows (OR) information follows	Successful response to LIST command. The second form is for variations of LIST defined as NNTP command extensions.
218	tin-style index follows	Successful response to XINDEX command extension.
220	n <a> article retrieved - head and body follow	Successful response to the ARTICLE command, indicating the article number and message ID of the article.
221	n <a> article retrieved - head follows	Successful response to the HEAD command, indicating the article number and message ID of the article.
222	n <a> article retrieved - body follows	Successful response to the BODY command, indicating the article number and message ID of the article.
223	n <a> article retrieved - request text separately	Successful response to the STAT command, indicating the article number and message ID of the article.
224	overview information follows	Successful response to the XOVER command extension.
230	list of new articles by message-id follows	Successful response to the NEWNEWS command.
235	article transferred ok	Successful response to the IHAVE command, after the article has been sent.
239	article transferred ok	Successful response to the TAKETHIS command.
240	article posted ok	Successful response to the POST command, after the article has been posted.
250 or 281	authentication accepted	Successful authentication using the AUTHINFO command extension.
282	list of groups and descriptions follows	Positive response to the XGTITLE command extension.
288	binary data to follow	Successful response to the XTHREAD command extension.
335	send article to be transferred	Preliminary response to the IHAVE command.
340	send article to be posted	Preliminary response to the POST command.
381	more authentication information required	Preliminary response to the AUTHINFO command extension.
400	service discontinued	Session is being terminated, perhaps due to user request.
411	no such newsgroup	Invalid newsgroup name specified.
412	no newsgroup has been selected	Attempt to issue a command that refers to the current newsgroup before one has been selected using GROUP.
420	no current article has been selected	Attempt to issue a command that refers to the current article using the server's current article pointer, before the pointer has been set through article selection.
421	no next article in this group	Response to NEXT command when at the last article of a newsgroup.
422	no previous article in this group	Possible response to LAST (I have no idea why the word "previous" is in there).
423	no such article number in this group	Command with invalid article number.
430	no such article found	Article not found; it may have been deleted.

(continued)

Table 85-11: NNTP Reply Codes (continued)

Reply Code	Reply Text	Description
435	article not wanted - do not send it	Negative response to IHAVE if server doesn't need the article.
436	transfer failed - try again later	Temporary failure of article transfer; retry.
437	article rejected - do not try again	Article refused for whatever reason.
438	already have it, please don't send it to me	Same as reply code 435, but for the CHECK command extension.
440	posting not allowed	POST command issued when posting is not allowed.
441	posting failed	POST command failed.
450	authorization required for this command	Response sent when server requires authentication but client has not yet authenticated.
452	authorization rejected	Failed authentication.
480	transfer permission denied	Response to CHECK if transfer is not allowed.
500	command not recognized	Bad command.
501	command syntax error	Bad syntax in command.
502	access restriction or permission denied	Permission denied; sent if the client has not properly authentication but the server requires it.
503	program fault - command not performed	General fatal error message.

KEY CONCEPT Each command sent by the device acting as the client in an NNTP connection results in the server returning a reply. NNTP replies consist of a three-digit reply code and a string of descriptive text. These codes are modeled after those of SMTP, and in turn, FTP.

86

GOPHER PROTOCOL (GOPHER)

Let's suppose that I told you I was going to describe a TCP/IP application layer protocol designed for the specific purpose of distributed document search and retrieval. This protocol uses a client/server model of operation, where servers provide links to related resources such as files or programs that users access with client software that displays options for the user to select. You might think that I was talking about the World Wide Web, and for good reason. However, in this case, I am actually talking about one of the Web's predecessors: the *Gopher Protocol*.

In this chapter, I briefly describe Gopher's history, operation, differences from the World Wide Web, and role in the modern Internet.

Gopher Overview and General Operation

A good place to start our discussion of this protocol is with its name, which is well chosen for a number of reasons. The Gopher Protocol was developed at the University of Minnesota, whose sports teams are called the Golden Gophers (Minnesota is known as the Gopher State). This is the direct origin of the name, but it is also appropriate because the rodent that shares it is known for burrowing, just as the protocol is designed to "burrow" through the Internet. And of course, the term *gopher* also applies to a person who performs errands, such as retrieving documents (they "go fer" this and "go fer" that).

The Gopher Protocol was developed in the late 1980s to provide a mechanism for organizing documents for easy access by students and faculty at the university. The core principle that guided the development of the system was *simplicity*. Gopher is designed on the basis of a small number of core principles, and it uses a very straightforward mechanism for passing information between client and server devices. It is described in RFC 1436, published in March 1993.

Information Storage on Gopher Servers

Information accessible by Gopher is stored as files on *Gopher servers*. It is organized in a hierarchical manner similar to the file system tree of a computer such as a Windows PC or UNIX workstation.

Just as a file system consists of a top-level directory (or folder) that contains files and subdirectories (subfolders), Gopher servers present information as a top-level directory that contains resources such as files, and/or subdirectories containing additional resources. Resources on different servers can be linked together by having them mentioned in each others' resource hierarchies. It is also possible for virtual resources to be created that act as if they were files, such as programs that allow Gopher servers to be searched.

Gopher Client/Server Operation

Typical use of Gopher begins with a user on a client machine creating a TCP connection to a Gopher server using well-known TCP port number 70. After the connection is established, the server waits for the client to request a particular resource by sending the server a piece of text called a *selector string*. Often, when a user first accesses a server, he does not know what resource to request, so a null (empty) selector string is sent. This causes the server to send back to the client a list of the resources available at the top (root) directory of the server's file system tree.

A directory list sent by the server consists of a set of lines, each of which describes one available resource in that directory. Each line contains the following elements, each separated by a tab character:

Type Character and Resource Name The first character of the line tells the client software what sort of resource the line represents. The most common type characters are 0 (zero) for a file, 1 for a subdirectory, and 7 for a search service. The rest of the characters up to the first tab character contain the name of the resource to be presented to the user.

Selector String The string of text to be sent to the server to retrieve this resource.

Server Name The name of the server where the resource is located.

Server Port Number The port number to be used for accessing this resource's server; normally 70.

Each line ends with a carriage return/line feed (CRLF) character sequence consistent with the Telnet Network Virtual Terminal (NVT) specification. Upon sending the directory listing (or any other response) the connection between the client and server is closed.

After receiving this sort of directory list, the Gopher client software will display a menu to the user containing all the resource names the server provided. The user then selects his desired item from the menu, and the client retrieves it by making a connection to the appropriate server and port number, and sending the selector string of that resource. If this itself represents a subdirectory, the server will send a new directory listing for that subdirectory; if it represents some other type of resource, it will be accessed according to the requirements of the resource type.

For example, suppose this line were sent from the server to the client:

```
0Gopher Introduction<Tab>intro<Tab>gopher.someserver.org<Tab>70
```

This would be presented to the user as the file called Gopher Introduction in a menu containing other options. If the user chose it, the client would initiate a connection to the Gopher server gopher.someserver.org at port 70, and then send the selector string `intro` to that server to retrieve the document.

Important Differences Between Gopher and the Web

As I hinted at the start of this discussion, both Gopher and the Web are intended for the same basic purpose: providing access to repositories of information, with links between related documents and resources. However, they take a very different approach to how that information is accessed, especially in two key areas: user interface and resource linking.

Gopher's presentation to the user is entirely oriented around its hierarchical file system. As a result, Gopher is inherently menu-based, and the user interface is usually based on a simple text presentation of those menus. In contrast, information on web servers can be organized in any manner and presented to the user in whatever form or fashion the owner of the server desires. The Web is much more free-form, and there is no need to use a directory structure unless that is advantageous in some way.

Linking in the Web is done directly between documents, most often using Hypertext Markup Language (HTML) tags. When someone writing Document A mentions something relevant to Document B, she puts a link to Document B directly in Document A. Gopher, on the other hand, is not designed to use links in this way. Instead, linking is intended to be done using the directory tree I described earlier.

Gopher's Role in the Modern Internet

There are some people who believe that Gopher is technically superior to the Web in a number of respects. They consider it cleaner to have servers do the linking, rather than having links embedded in documents. An argument can also be made that the text orientation of Gopher is efficient, better able to ensure compatibility between platforms, and also more suited to special needs situations such as low-bandwidth links and access by those with visual impairments. Some Gopher enthusiasts thus consider it to be a purer hypertext system than the Web.

However, history shows us that despite Gopher predating the Web, the Web overtook it in popularity in only a few short years. Today, the Web is the 900-pound gorilla of the Internet, while most people have never even heard of Gopher. What happened?

I believe the main reason why Gopher lost out to the Web is that the Web is far more flexible. Gopher's use of text hyperlinks and server directory structures may be efficient, but it is limiting. In contrast, the Web allows information to be presented in a wide variety of ways. The open, unstructured nature of the Web makes it an ideal vehicle for the creativity of information providers and application developers. In the mid-1990s, the Web was also perfectly poised to support the transition of computing from text to graphics, and Gopher was not.

Simply put, you can do more with the Web than you can with Gopher, and most people care more about functionality and breadth of options than straight efficiency. Once the Web started to gain momentum, it very quickly snowballed. It took only a couple of years before Web use was well entrenched, and Gopher was unable to compete.

For its part, the University of Minnesota likely hastened Gopher's demise with its controversial decision to charge licensing fees to companies that wanted to use Gopher for commercial purposes. I do not believe there was anything nefarious about this. The university was on a limited budget and wanted companies that could afford it to pay a small fee to support development of Gopher software. However, computing history has shown time and time again that there is no faster way to kill a protocol or standard than to try to charge licensing or royalty fees for it, no matter what the reason.

By the late 1990s, Gopher was well on its way to obsolescence. As use of the protocol dwindled, many organizations could no longer justify the cost of continuing to run Gopher servers. Even the University of Minnesota itself eventually shut down its own Gopher servers due to low utilization. The final nail in the coffin for Gopher occurred in 2002, when a security vulnerability related to Gopher was discovered in Internet Explorer, and Microsoft chose to simply remove Gopher support from the product rather than fix the problem. Today, Gopher is still around, but it is a niche protocol used only by a relatively small group of enthusiasts and a handful of organizations that have a past history of using it.

KEY CONCEPT The Gopher Protocol is a distributed document search and retrieval protocol that was developed at the University of Minnesota in the late 1980s. Resources are stored on Gopher servers, which organize information using a hierarchical directory structure. Gopher clients access servers to retrieve directory listings of available resources, which are presented to the user as a menu from which an item may be selected for retrieval. Gopher's chief advantage is simplicity and ease of use, but it lacks flexibility in presentation and the ability to effectively present graphics and multimedia. For this reason, despite Gopher predating the World Wide Web, the Web has almost entirely replaced it, and Gopher is now a niche protocol.

PART III-10

INTERACTIVE AND ADMINISTRATIVE UTILITIES AND PROTOCOLS

File and message transfer applications include the File Transfer Protocol (FTP), electronic mail (email), and the World Wide Web, which makes file and message transfer the most important category of classic TCP/IP applications. However, those applications do not represent the only ways that TCP/IP internetworks are used. While not as glamorous as some of the application protocols we have examined so far in this section, interactive and administrative protocols are also important and worth understanding.

This final part of the book covers a couple other categories of TCP/IP applications. The first chapter describes interactive and remote application protocols, which are used traditionally to allow a user of one computer to access another, or to permit the real-time exchange of information. The second chapter discusses TCP/IP administration and troubleshooting utilities, which can be employed by both administrators and end users to manage TCP/IP networks and diagnose problems with them.

87

TCP/IP INTERACTIVE AND REMOTE APPLICATION PROTOCOLS

When it comes to TCP/IP applications, file and message transfer applications get the most attention, because they are the ones used most often on modern internetworks. Another category of TCP/IP application protocols that is less well known is the group that allows users to interactively access and use other computers directly over an internetwork, such as the public Internet. These applications are not often employed by end users today, but they are still important—both from a historical perspective and because of their usefulness in certain circumstances, especially to network administrators.

In this chapter, I provide a brief description of the classic interactive and remote application protocols used in TCP/IP. I first describe the Telnet Protocol, one of the earliest and most conceptually important application protocols in TCP/IP. This discussion includes a description of Telnet client/server communication, the Telnet Network Virtual Terminal (NVT), and Telnet's protocol commands and options. I then describe the Berkeley remote access family, often called the *r commands* or protocols because their command names begin with that letter. Finally, I provide a brief overview of the Internet Relay Chat (IRC) protocol, the original interactive chat application of the Internet and one still used widely today.

Telnet Protocol

In the very earliest days of internetworking, one of the most important problems that computer scientists needed to solve was how to allow someone operating one computer to access and use another as if that remote user were connected to it locally. The protocol created to meet this need was called *Telnet*, and the effort to develop it was tied closely to that of the Internet and TCP/IP as a whole. Even though most Internet users today never invoke the Telnet Protocol directly, they use some of its underlying principles indirectly all the time. Every time you send a piece of email, use the File Transfer Protocol (FTP) to transfer a file, or load a web page, you are using technology based on Telnet. For this reason, the Telnet Protocol can make a valid claim to the title of the most historically important application protocol in TCP/IP.

BACKGROUND INFORMATION *A basic comprehension of the Transmission Control Protocol (TCP), especially its sliding window mechanism and flow control features, will be helpful in understanding Telnet. Those topics are covered in Chapters 48 and 49.*

Telnet Overview, History, and Standards

The history of Telnet actually goes back over a decade before the modern TCP/IP protocol suite that we know today. As I mentioned in my overview of FTP, the early developers of TCP/IP internetworking technologies identified two overall application needs for networks to fill: enabling *direct access* to resources and also allowing *indirect access* to resources. FTP was created for indirect access, by allowing users to retrieve a resource from a remote host, use it locally, and if desired, copy it back to its source. Telnet was designed for direct access, by allowing users to access a remote machine and use it as if they were connected to it locally.

Telnet History

Telnet was initially developed in the late 1960s. This was well before the era of the small personal computers that so many of us use exclusively today. All computers of that period were large and usually shared by many users. To work on a computer, you had to access a physical terminal connected to that machine, which was usually specially tailored to the needs and requirements of the host. Two specific issues resulted from this situation:

- If an organization had several different computers, each user needed a separate terminal to access each computer that he or she used. This was expensive and inefficient. I can recall reading a quote from a book that compared this situation to having a room containing a number of television sets, each of which could only display a single channel.

- Perhaps a more significant issue was the difficulty in allowing a user at one site to access and use a machine at another site. The only method at the time for accomplishing this was to install a dedicated data circuit from the site of the computer to the site of the user, to connect the user's terminal to the remote machine. Again, each circuit would enable access to only one machine. Every combination of user and computer required a separate, expensive circuit to be installed and maintained.

The solution to both of these issues was to create a more general way of allowing any terminal to access any computer. The underlying internetwork provided the mechanism for communicating information between computers. This became the physical network connecting sites and the TCP/IP protocol suite connecting networks. On top of this ran an application protocol that allowed a user to establish a session to any networked computer and use it. That application protocol is Telnet.

Telnet was the first application protocol demonstrated on the fledgling ARPAnet, in 1969. The first RFC specifically defining Telnet was RFC 97, "First Cut at a Proposed Telnet Protocol," published in February 1971. Development of Telnet continued throughout the 1970s, with quite a number of different RFCs devoted to revisions of the protocol and discussions of issues related to it. It took many years to refine Telnet and resolve all the difficulties that were associated with its development. The final version of the protocol, "Telnet Protocol Specification," was published as RFC 854 in May 1983. Over the years, other RFCs have been published to clarify the use of the protocol and address various issues such as authentication. There are also a number of other RFCs that define Telnet options, as discussed in the "Telnet Options and Option Negotiation" section later in this chapter.

Fundamental Telnet Concepts

At first glance, it may be surprising that Telnet took so long to develop, because in theory, it should be a very simple protocol to define. All it needs to do is send keystrokes and program output over the network like any other protocol. Its definition would be simple if every terminal and computer used the same communication method, but they do not. Telnet becomes complicated because it needs to allow a terminal from one manufacturer to be able to talk to a computer that may use a very different data representation.

Telnet solves this problem by defining a method that ensures compatibility between terminal types and computers, while allowing special features to be used by computers and terminals that agree to support them. The protocol is built on a foundation of three main concepts.

Network Virtual Terminal (NVT) Telnet defines a standardized, fictional terminal called the *Network Virtual Terminal (NVT)* that is used for universal communication by all devices. A Telnet client takes input from a user and translates it from its native form to the NVT format to send to a Telnet server running on a remote computer. The server translates from NVT to whatever representation the computer being accessed requires. The process is reversed when data is sent from the remote computer back to the user. This system allows clients and servers to communicate even if they use entirely different hardware and internal data representations. Special Telnet commands are interspersed with the data to allow the client and server devices to perform various functions needed to manage the operation of the protocol.

Options and Option Negotiation Having Telnet clients and servers act as NVTs avoids incompatibilities between devices, but does so by stripping all terminal-specific functionality to provide a common base representation that is understood by everyone. Since there are many cases where more intelligent terminals and computers may wish to use more advanced communication features and services, Telnet defines a rich set of options and a mechanism by which a Telnet client and server can negotiate their use. If the client and server agree on the use of an option, it can be enabled; if not, they can always fall back on the NVT to ensure basic communication.

Symmetric Operation While Telnet is a client/server protocol, it is specifically designed to not make assumptions about the nature of the client and server software. Once a Telnet session is established, the computers can each send and receive data as equals. They can also each initiate the negotiation of options. This makes the protocol extremely flexible and has led to its use in a variety of places, as discussed in the next section.

Telnet Applications

Telnet is most often associated with remote login, which is its common traditional use. A user typically uses a Telnet client program to open a Telnet connection to a remote server, which then treats the Telnet client like a local terminal, allowing the user to log in and access the server's resources as if he were using a directly attached terminal. Telnet is still used this way quite extensively by UNIX users, who often need to log in to remote hosts from their local machines (I use Telnet in this manner every day to access a machine hundreds of miles away). However, this use of Telnet is not nearly as common among the majority of Internet users who work on Windows or Apple computers, where network resources are accessed not through direct login, but by other means.

Although remote login is a big part of what Telnet is about, the protocol was not inherently designed for that specific function. When Telnet is used to access a remote device, the protocol itself is used only to set up the connection between the client and server machines, encode data to be transmitted according to the rules of the Telnet NVT, and facilitate the negotiation and use of options. The client and server devices decide whether Telnet is used for remote access or for some other purpose.

This flexibility, combined with Telnet's age in the TCP/IP suite, has led to its being adopted for a variety of other protocols. Since Telnet doesn't make assumptions about what a client is and what a server is, any program or application can use it. Many of the file and message transfer applications—such as FTP, Simple Mail Transfer Protocol (SMTP), Network News Transfer Protocol (NNTP), and Hypertext Transfer Protocol (HTTP)—communicate by sending text commands and messages, and use Telnet's NVT specification to ensure the compatibility of communication between devices. They don't actually establish Telnet sessions or use features like option negotiation; they just send data in a manner consistent with how Telnet works. Thus, even though modern Internet users may never intentionally invoke Telnet specifically, they use it indirectly every time they send or receive email or browse the Web. Administrators can even use Telnet client software to access devices such as FTP and HTTP servers, and send those devices commands manually.

> **KEY CONCEPT** *Telnet* is one of the oldest protocols in the TCP/IP suite, first developed in the 1960s to allow a user on one computer system to directly access and use another. It is most often used for remote login, with Telnet client software on a user's machine establishing a session with a Telnet server on a remote host to let the user work with the host as if connected directly. To ensure compatibility between terminals and hosts that use different hardware and software, communication between Telnet client and server software is based on a simplified, fictional data representation, called the *Network Virtual Terminal (NVT)*, which can be enhanced through the negotiation of options.

Telnet Connections and Client/Server Operation

Telnet's overall function is to define a means by which a user or process on one machine can access and use another machine as if it were locally connected. This makes Telnet inherently client/server in operation, like so many other application protocols in TCP/IP. Usually, the Telnet client is a piece of software that acts as an interface to the user, processing keystrokes and user commands and presenting output from the remote machine. The Telnet server is a program running on a remote computer that has been set up to allow remote sessions.

TCP Sessions and Client/Server Communication

Telnet is used for the interactive communication of data and commands between a client and server over a prolonged period of time, and is thus strongly based on the concept of a *session.* For this reason, Telnet runs over the connection-oriented Transmission Control Protocol (TCP). Telnet servers listen for connections on well-known TCP port number 23. When a client wants to access a particular server, it initiates a TCP connection to the appropriate server, which responds to set up a TCP connection using the standard TCP three-way handshake (described in Chapter 47).

The TCP connection is maintained for the duration of the Telnet session, which can remain alive for hours, days, or even weeks at a time. The quality of service features of TCP guarantee that data is received reliably and in order, and ensure that data is not sent at too high a rate for either client or server. A machine offering Telnet service can support multiple simultaneous sessions with different users, keeping each distinct by identifying it using the IP address and port number of the client.

Since TCP is a full-duplex protocol, both the client and server can send information at will over the Telnet session. By default, both devices begin by using the standard NVT method for encoding data and control commands (which we will explore fully a little later in this chapter). They can also negotiate the use of Telnet options to provide greater functionality for the session. While option negotiation can occur at any time, it is normal for there to be a burst of such option exchanges when a Telnet session is first established and only occasional option command exchanges thereafter.

With the TCP connection in place and the Telnet session active, the client and server software begin their normal jobs of interfacing the user to the remote host. To the user, the Telnet session appears fundamentally the same as sitting down at a terminal directly connected to the remote host. In most cases, the server will begin the user's session by sending a login prompt to ask for a user name and password. The Telnet client will accept this information from the user and send it to the server. Assuming the information is valid, the user will be logged in and can use the host in whatever manner her account authorizes.

As mentioned in the Telnet overview, even though the protocol is commonly used for remote login, it does not need to be used in this manner. The administrator of the computer that is running the Telnet server determines how it is to be used on that machine. As just one example, a Telnet server can be interfaced directly to a process or program providing a service. I can recall years ago using an Internet server that provided weather information to the public using Telnet. After using the protocol to connect to that machine, users were presented not with a login prompt, but with a menu of weather display options. Today, the Web has replaced most of such facilities, as it is far better suited to this type of information retrieval.

KEY CONCEPT Telnet is a client/server protocol that uses TCP to establish a session between a user terminal and a remote host. The Telnet client software takes input from the user and sends it to the server, which feeds it to the host machine's operating system. The Telnet server takes output from the host and sends it to the client to display to the user. While Telnet is most often used to implement remote login capability, it is not specifically designed for logins. The protocol is general enough to allow it to be used for a variety of functions.

Use of Telnet to Access Other Servers

The Telnet NVT representation is used by a variety of other protocols such as SMTP and HTTP. This means that the same Telnet client that allows you to access a Telnet server can be used to directly access other application servers. All you need to do is specify the port number corresponding to the service. For example, the following command will allow you to directly interface to a web server:

```
telnet www.someserversomewhere.org 80
```

You will not receive a login prompt, but instead the server will wait for you to send an HTTP Request message, as if you were a web browser. If you enter a valid request, the server will send you an HTTP Response message. Used in this way, Telnet can be very valuable as a diagnostic tool.

KEY CONCEPT The Telnet Network Virtual Terminal (NVT) data representation has been adopted by a host of other TCP/IP protocols as the basis for their messaging systems. Telnet client software can thus be used not only to connect to Telnet servers, but also to connect to servers of protocols such as SMTP and HTTP, which is useful for diagnostic purposes.

Telnet Communications Model and the Network Virtual Terminal (NVT)

At its heart, Telnet is a rather simple protocol. Once a TCP connection is made and the Telnet session begins, the only real task for the client and server software is to capture input and output, and redirect it over the network. So, when the user presses a key on his local terminal, the Telnet client software captures it and sends it over the network to the remote machine. There, the Telnet server software sends the keypress to the operating system, which treats it as if it had been typed locally. When the operating system produces output, the process is reversed: Telnet server software captures the output and sends it over the network to the user's client program, which displays it on the printer or monitor.

To invoke two well-known clichés, I could say that this looks good on paper, but that the devil is in the details. This simplified implementation would work only if every computer and terminal used the exact same hardware, software, and data representation. Of course, this is far from the case today, and was even worse when Telnet was being developed. Computers back in the "good old days" were highly proprietary and not designed to interoperate. They differed in numerous ways—from the type of keyboard a terminal used and the keystrokes it could send, to the number of characters per line and lines per screen on a terminal, to the character set used to encode data and control functions. In short, Computer A was designed to accept input in a particular form from its own terminals, and not those of Computer B.

This is actually a fairly common issue in the world of networking, and one to which I can draw a real-world analogy to help explain the problem and how it may be solved. Suppose that an important international conference was attended by 30 ambassadors from different nations, each of which had one assistant. Every ambassador and assistant pair spoke only their own language and thus could only speak to each other—just like a computer and terminal designed to interface only to each other. To allow the assistant from one country to speak to the ambassador from the others, one solution would be to train the assistants to speak the languages of all the other attending nations. Back in the computing world, this would be like defining the Telnet Protocol so that every Telnet client software implementation understood how to speak to every computer in existence. This would work, but it would be quite impractical and difficult to do.

An alternative approach is to define a single common language and have all the ambassadors and assistants learn it. While this would require some work, it would be a lot less than requiring people to learn dozens of languages. Each ambassador and assistant would speak both a native language and this chosen common language. Each could communicate with all of the others using this common language, without needing to know all of the languages that might be used by anyone at the conference. Even more important, if an ambassador and assistant showed up at the conference speaking a new, 31st language, all the other delegates wouldn't need to learn it.

Telnet uses a very similar approach for dealing with its problem of hardware and software compatibility. Rather than having terminals and hosts communicate using their various native languages, all Telnet clients and servers agree to send data and commands that adhere to a fictional, virtual terminal type call the NVT.

The NVT

The NVT defines a set of rules for how information is formatted and sent, such as character set, line termination, and how information about the Telnet session itself is sent.

Each Telnet client running on a terminal understands both its native language and the NVT language. When users enter information on their local terminal, it is converted to NVT form for transmission over the network. When the Telnet server receives this information, it translates it from NVT form to the format that the remote host expects to receive it. The identical process is performed for transmissions from the server to the client, in reverse. This is illustrated in Figure 87-1.

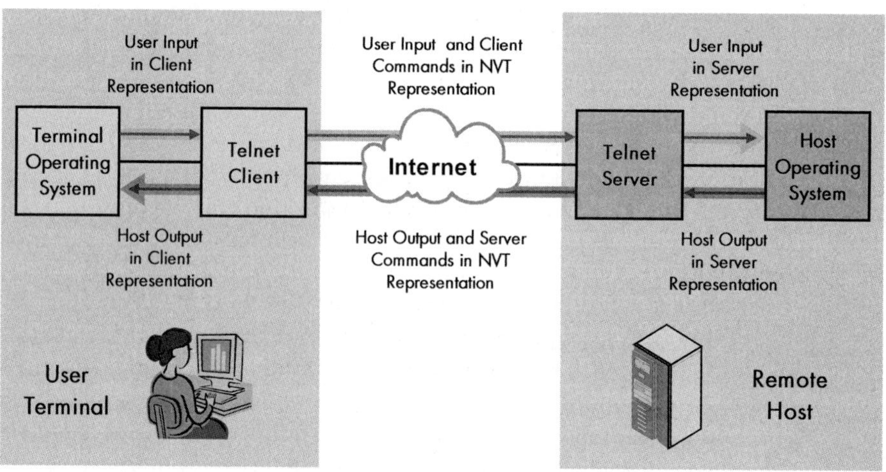

Figure 87-1: Telnet communication and the Network Virtual Terminal (NVT) *Telnet uses the Network Virtual Terminal (NVT) representation to allow a user terminal and remote host that use different internal formats to communicate.*

> **KEY CONCEPT** The Telnet *Network Virtual Terminal (NVT)* is a uniform data representation that ensures the compatibility of communication between terminals and hosts that may use very different hardware, software, and data formats. The Telnet client translates user input from the terminal's native form to NVT form for transport to the Telnet server, where it is converted to the host's internal format. The process is reversed for output from the host to the user.

The NVT is defined to consist of a logical keyboard for input and a logical printer for output (the age of the protocol is reflected in these terms; decades ago there were no monitors, all output was on paper). NVT uses the 7-bit *United States ASCII (US-ASCII)* character set. Each character is encoded using one 8-bit byte.

However, a client and server can use Telnet options to negotiate other data representations, including the transmission of either extended ASCII or even full 8-bit binary data.

NVT ASCII Control Codes

Regular ASCII consists of 95 regular, printable characters (codes 32 through 126) and 33 control codes (0 through 31 and 127). The Telnet standard specifies that the output device must be able to handle all the printable characters, and it mandates how several of the other common ASCII control codes should be interpreted. Of these codes, three (0, 10, and 13) are required to be accepted by all Telnet software; five others are optional, but if supported, must be interpreted in a manner consistent with the Telnet specification. Table 87-1 describes the standard Telnet NVT ASCII control codes.

Table 87-1: Interpretation of Standard Telnet NVT ASCII Control Codes

ASCII Value (Decimal)	ASCII Character Code	ASCII Character	Description	Support Optional/ Mandatory
0	NUL	Null	No operation (no effect on output).	Mandatory
7	BEL	Bell	Produces an audible or visible signal on the output without moving the print head. This notification may be used to get the user's attention, as in the case of an error.	Optional
8	BS	Backspace	Moves the print position one character to the left.	Optional
9	HT	Horizontal Tab	Moves the printer to the next horizontal tab stop. The standard does not specify how devices agree on tab stop positions; this can be negotiated using Telnet options.	Optional
10	LF	Line Feed	Moves the printer to the next line, keeping the print position the same.	Mandatory
11	VT	Vertical Tab	Moves the print line to the next vertical tab stop. As with the HT character, devices must use an option to come to an agreement on vertical tab stop positions.	Optional
12	FF	Form Feed	Moves the printer to the top of the next page (or on a display, clears the screen and positions the cursor at the top).	Optional
13	CR	Carriage Return	Moves the printer to the left margin of the current print line.	Mandatory

The Telnet NVT scheme defines the combination of the carriage return (CR) and line feed (LF) characters to represent the end of a line of ASCII text. The literal meaning of these two characters is return to the left margin (the CR) and go to the next line (the LF). However, NVT treats the CRLF sequence as more than just two independent characters; they are taken collectively to define a *logical end-of-line character.* This is necessary because not all terminal types define an end of line using both CR and LF. Translation of end-of-line characters between the native and NVT formats is one of the functions that Telnet client and server software must perform to ensure compatibility between terminals and hosts.

KEY CONCEPT The Telnet NVT format is based on 7-bit US-ASCII, with each byte carrying one character. The standard specifies that devices must handle all standard printable ASCII characters, as well as three mandatory control characters. Two of these are the carriage return (CR) and line feed (LF) characters; when combined, these define the logical end of a line of text. The Telnet standard also describes the interpretation of five other optional ASCII control characters.

Half-Duplex and Full-Duplex Modes

Another artifact of the age of Telnet is that for maximum compatibility, the NVT specification is designed under the assumption of half-duplex operation: only one device can transmit at a time. A device that is sending data is supposed to end its transmission with the special Telnet Go Ahead command, telling the other device that it may now transmit (the next section describes Telnet protocol commands). This is similar to how people using walkie-talkies end each transmission with "Over," to tell their partners that they may now respond.

Of course, modern networks operate in a full-duplex mode, and using half-duplex communication would be needlessly inefficient. In most cases, the Telnet client and server agree to use an option (Suppress Go Ahead) that eliminates the need to send this command. However, having this as the default is a good example of how NVT acts as a least common denominator in Telnet, in case the simpler operating mode is needed by either device.

Telnet Protocol Commands

Most of the input that users enter at a terminal takes the form of data and commands that are sent to the application program they are using. However, computer systems also provide a means by which users can instruct the terminal to send certain commands that control how the terminal itself operates, and how it interacts with the computer to which it is connected. The best example of this is the command to interrupt a process, which is usually sent by pressing a special key or key combination on the user terminal.

Telnet needs to have a way to allow such commands to be entered by the user. However, here we run into the same problem that arises in the communication of data between terminals and computers: a lack of uniformity in representation. While all terminals and computers support the ability to interrupt a running program, for example, they may each use a different keystroke to invoke it. For example, on most UNIX systems, the key combination CTRL-C interrupts a program, but typing this on a Windows system will not (it usually represents the copy data function!).

Since the problem is the same as the one we ran into in representing data flow, it's not too surprising that the solution is the same: the use of a universal representation for a set of standard commands to be passed between the terminal and host computer. All keystrokes that represent these commands are translated to the standard Telnet codes for transmission, and then translated to the specific needs of the host computer. So, if a user presses CTRL-C on a UNIX terminal where this is defined as the interrupt function, instead of sending that exact keystroke, the Telnet client sends the special Telnet Interrupt Process command, which is translated by the Telnet server to the command code appropriate for the connected host.

The Telnet standard includes a number of these special codes to allow a user to control the operation of the remote computer. It also defines a set of commands that are specific to the Telnet Protocol itself; these let the Telnet client and Telnet server software communicate. Collectively, these are called Telnet *protocol commands*.

All Telnet commands are sent in the same communication stream as regular data. They are represented using special byte values in the range from 240 to 254. To differentiate between data bytes of these values and Telnet commands, every command is preceded by a special *escape character*, given the name *Interpret As Command (IAC)*. IAC has a value of 255; when the recipient sees this character, it knows the next byte is a command, not data. So, since the Telnet Interrupt Process command has the value 244, to send this command, the Telnet client would transmit the byte 255 and then 244. If the actual data byte value 255 needs to be sent, it is transmitted as two 255 bytes. Some Telnet commands also include additional bytes of data, which are sent after the command code itself. A good example is the use of parameters in Telnet option negotiation, as you will see in the "Telnet Options and Option Negotiation" section later in this chapter.

KEY CONCEPT The Telnet Protocol defines a set of *protocol commands* that are used for two purposes: first, to represent standard control functions that need to be sent between a terminal and host, such as the command to interrupt a process, and second, to enable protocol communication between the Telnet client and server software. Protocol commands are sent in the normal data communication stream over the Telnet session's TCP connection. Each is represented by a byte value from 240 to 254, and is preceded by the Interpret As Command (IAC) command, byte value 255, which tells the recipient that the next byte in the stream is a command.

You may be wondering at this point why the IAC character is needed at all. After all, Telnet uses US-ASCII, which is 7-bit data in the byte range of 0 to 127, and the Telnet commands have values higher than 127. One general rationale for using the IAC escape character is to be explicit that a command is being sent. A more specific reason is to accommodate the optional sending of 8-bit binary data over Telnet, which the client and server can negotiate. If this mode were enabled and commands were not preceded by the IAC character, this would require all data bytes with values from 240 to 255 to be marked somehow so they would be interpreted as data and not commands. It is more efficient to include an extra byte for commands than data, since commands are sent less frequently. By escaping commands, only data byte value 255 requires two bytes to be sent.

Table 87-2 lists the Telnet protocol commands in numerical byte value order, showing for each its command code and name, and describing its meaning and use.

Table 87-2: Telnet Protocol Commands

Command Byte Value (Decimal)	Command Code	Command	Description
240	SE	Subnegotiation End	Marks the end of a Telnet option subnegotiation, used with the SB code to specify more specific option parameters. See the "Telnet Options and Option Negotiation" section later in this chapter for details.
241	NOP	No Operation	Null command; does nothing.
242	DM	Data Mark	Used to mark the end of a sequence of data that the recipient should scan for urgent Telnet commands. See the discussion of Telnet interrupt handling in the following section for details.
243	BRK	Break	Represents the pressing of the "break" or "attention" key on the terminal.
244	IP	Interrupt Process	Tells the recipient to interrupt, abort, suspend, or terminate the process currently in use.
245	AO	Abort Output	Instructs the remote host to continue running the current process but discard all remaining output from it. This may be needed if a program starts to send unexpectedly large amounts of data to the user.
246	AYT	Are You There	May be used to check that the remote host is still "alive." When this character is sent, the remote host returns some type of output to indicate that it is still functioning.
247	EC	Erase Character	Instructs the recipient to delete the last undeleted character from the data stream. Used to undo the sending of a character.
248	EL	Erase Line	Tells the recipient to delete all characters from the data stream back to (but not including) the last end-of-line (CRLF) sequence.
249	GA	Go Ahead	Used in Telnet half-duplex mode to signal the other device that it may transmit.
250	SB	Subnegotiation	Marks the beginning of a Telnet option subnegotiation, used when an option requires the client and server to exchange parameters. See the "Telnet Options and Option Negotiation" section later in this chapter for a full description.
251	WILL	Will Perform	In Telnet option negotiation, indicates that the device sending this code is willing to perform or continue performing a particular option.
252	WONT	Won't Perform	In Telnet option negotiation, indicates that the device sending this code is either not willing to perform a particular option or is now refusing to continue to perform it.
253	DO	Do Perform	In Telnet option negotiation, requests that the other device perform a particular option or confirms the expectation that the other device will perform that option.
254	DONT	Don't Perform	In Telnet option negotiation, specifies that the other party not perform an option or confirms a device's expectation that the other party not perform an option.
255	IAC	Interpret As Command	Precedes command values 240 through 254 as described in the preceding descriptions. A pair of IAC bytes in a row represents the data value 255.

Perhaps ironically, the Telnet commands are not used as much today as they were when Telnet was in its early days, because many of the compatibility issues that we discussed earlier no longer exist. ASCII has become the standard character set of the computing world, so many of the functions such as aborting output or interrupting a process no longer require the use of Telnet commands. They are still widely used, however, for internal Telnet operations such as option negotiation.

Telnet Interrupt Handling

All the bytes of data sent from a Telnet client to a server are received in the order that they were sent, and vice versa. This is the way that we expect an application to operate. In fact, ensuring that data is not received out of order is one of the jobs that we assume of the reliable transport protocol TCP, over which Telnet runs. However, this can cause a problem for Telnet because of the way Telnet sends both data and commands over the same connection.

The most important case where this issue arises is when a user needs to interrupt a process. Suppose that you are using Telnet to run an interactive program that takes user input, processes it, and then produces output. You are merrily typing away when you notice that you haven't seen any output from the program for a while. It has apparently hung up due to a programming error or other glitch.

If you were using the program on a directly connected terminal, you would simply use the key or keystroke command appropriate to that terminal to interrupt or abort the process and restart it. Instead, you are using Telnet, so you enter the appropriate keystroke, which gets converted to the special Telnet Interrupt Process command code (byte value 244, preceded by the Telnet Interpret As Command code, 255).

Since Telnet uses only a single stream for commands and data, that code is placed into the TCP data stream to be sent over to the Telnet server. Since you were entering data for a while, that Telnet Interrupt Process code will be sitting behind a bunch of regular data bytes. Now the remote process has stopped reading this data, which means the TCP receive buffer on the server will start to fill up. The Interrupt Process command will thus remain stuck in the buffer, waiting to be read. In fact, if the number of data bytes in front of the command is high enough, the TCP buffer on the server may fill entirely, causing the server to close the client's TCP send window. This means the Interrupt Process command will wait in the client's outgoing TCP queue and *never* be sent to the remote host!

What we need here is some way to be able to flag the Interrupt Process command, so that it can be sent to the remote host regardless of the number of data bytes outstanding in front of it. If you've already perused the chapters devoted to TCP, you may be thinking that you have already read about a feature of that protocol that seems ideally suited for this exact problem, and you would be correct! The TCP urgent function (described in Chapter 48) allows an important piece of data to be marked so that it is given priority over regular data, a process sometimes called *out-of-band signaling* (because the signal is outside the normal data stream). Telnet uses this feature of TCP to define what it calls the *synch function.*

When needed, the synch function is invoked by the client sending the special Telnet Data Mark (DM) protocol command, while instructing its TCP layer to mark that data as urgent. The URG bit in the TCP segment carrying this command causes it to bypass TCP's normal flow control mechanism so it is sent over to the remote host. The Telnet server software, seeing the synch in the data stream, searches through all of the data in its buffer looking only for Telnet control commands such as Interrupt Process, Abort Output, and Are You There. These commands are then executed immediately. The server continues to search for important commands up to the point where the Data Mark command is seen. All intervening data is discarded; it will need to be retransmitted. After the Data Mark is processed, the server returns to normal operation.

It is also possible for the server to use the synch function in communication with the user on the client device. For example, if the user sends the Abort Output command to the server, she is telling the server to discard all remaining output from the current process. The server will stop sending that output, and can also use the synch function to clear all outstanding data that is waiting in buffers to be sent to the client machine (since it causes data to be discarded).

KEY CONCEPT Telnet protocol commands are sent in the same stream with user data, which means a problem with the remote host that stops the flow of data might cause user commands to become backed up and never received by the host. Since this may include commands issued by the user to try to fix the problem on the host, this can be a serious problem. To alleviate this situation, Telnet includes the *synch function*, which uses TCP's urgent data transmission feature to force the receipt of essential commands, even when regular data is not being processed.

Telnet Options and Option Negotiation

The basic Telnet NVT specification solves the problem of compatibility between different terminal and computer types by defining a common representation for data and commands that every Telnet client and server uses. The price for this universal representation, however, is very high: All of the advanced or special capabilities of terminals and hosts are stripped off. The result is a language that everyone can speak but that is not capable of much more than basic conversation.

The creators of Telnet recognized that, while it was important to define NVT as a common base to ensure cross-device compatibility, it was also essential that some means be provided by which clients and servers could agree to use more advanced means of communication. They defined a set of *Telnet options* and a mechanism by which a Telnet client and server can *negotiate* which options they want to use.

Most Telnet options are used for improving the efficiency of how data is transferred between devices. For example, by default, the NVT assumes half-duplex operation with each device, requiring it to use the Go Ahead command after each transmission. However, virtually all hardware now supports full-duplex communication, so devices will usually agree to use the Suppress Go Ahead option to eliminate the need to send this character. Similarly, it is possible for devices to negotiate the sending of 8-bit binary data instead of the standard 7-bit ASCII of the Telnet NVT.

The process of Telnet option negotiation is described in the main Telnet standard document, RFC 854, as well as a companion document, RFC 855, "Telnet Option Specifications." The options themselves are described in a separate set of Internet standards. Several of these were published at the same time as RFCs 854 and 855; others were defined earlier as part of previous versions of Telnet; and still others have been added over the years. There are now several dozen different Telnet options in existence. A master list is maintained by Internet Assigned Numbers Authority (IANA), just as it maintains other TCP/IP parameters. An up-to-date listing of all Telnet options can be found on the IANA website at http://www.iana.org/assignments/telnet-options.

Common Telnet Options

Each Telnet option is identified using a decimal byte code with a possible value of 0 to 254. The value 255 is reserved to extend the option list should more than 255 options ever be needed. Each option also has a text code string associated with it, which is often used as a symbol in place of the code number in both protocol discussions and diagnostic output. Table 87-3 lists some of the more interesting Telnet options and provides a brief description of each.

Table 87-3: Common Telnet Options

Option Number	Option Code	Option Name	Description	Defining RFC
0	TRANSMIT-BINARY	Binary Transmission	Allows devices to send data in 8-bit binary form instead of 7-bit ASCII.	856
1	ECHO	Echo	Allows devices to negotiate any of a variety of different echo modes. (When you press a key on a terminal, you also expect to see the character you entered appear on the terminal screen as output; this is called *echoing* the input.)	857
3	SUPPRESS-GO-AHEAD	Suppress Go Ahead	Allows devices not operating in half-duplex mode to no longer need to end transmissions using the Telnet Go Ahead command.	858
5	STATUS	Status	Lets a device request the status of a Telnet option.	859
6	TIMING-MARK	Timing Mark	Allows devices to negotiate the insertion of a special timing mark into the data stream, which is used for synchronization.	860
10	NAOCRD	Output Carriage Return Disposition	Lets the devices negotiate how carriage returns will be handled.	652
11	NAOHTS	Output Horizontal Tab Stops	Allows the devices to determine what horizontal tab stop positions will be used for output display.	653
12	NAOHTD	Output Horizontal Tab Stop Disposition	Allows the devices to negotiate how horizontal tabs will be handled and by which end of the connection.	654
13	NAOFFD	Output Form Feed Disposition	Allows the devices to negotiate how form feed characters will be handled.	655
14	NAOVTS	Output Vertical Tab Stops	Used to determine what vertical tab stop positions will be used for output display.	656
15	NAOVTD	Output Vertical Tab Disposition	Lets devices negotiate the disposition of vertical tab stops.	657
16	NAOLFD	Output Line Feed Disposition	Allows devices to decide how line feed characters should be handled.	658

(continued)

Table 87-3: Common Telnet Options (continued)

Option Number	Option Code	Option Name	Description	Defining RFC
17	EXTEND-ASCII	Extended ASCII	Lets devices agree to use extended ASCII for transmissions and negotiate how it will be used.	698
24	TERMINAL-TYPE	Terminal Type	Allows the client and server to negotiate the use of a specific terminal type. If they agree, this allows the output from the server to be ideally customized to the needs of the particular terminal the user is using.	1091
31	NAWS	Negotiate About Window Size	Permits communication of the size of the terminal window.	1073
32	TERMINAL-SPEED	Terminal Speed	Allows devices to report on the current terminal speed.	1079
33	TOGGLE-FLOW-CONTROL	Remote Flow Control	Allows flow control between the client and the server to be enabled and disabled.	1372
34	LINEMODE	Line Mode	Allows the client to send data one line at a time instead of one character at a time. This improves performance by replacing a large number of tiny TCP transmissions with a smaller number of larger ones.	1184
37	AUTHENTICATION	Authentication	Lets the client and server negotiate a method of authentication to secure connections.	1416

KEY CONCEPT The Telnet NVT specification ensures that all devices using Telnet can talk to each other, but accomplishes this communication at the lowest level. To allow the use of more sophisticated formats and services, Telnet defines a number of *options*. If a client and server both implement a particular option, they can enable its use through a process of *negotiation*.

Telnet Option Negotiation

The first stage in Telnet option negotiation is for the client and server to decide whether they want to enable a particular option. One of the aspects of Telnet's symmetry of operation is that either device may choose to initiate the use of an option. The initiating device may either specify that it wants to start using an option or that it wants the other device to start using it. The responding device may agree or disagree. An option can be enabled only if both devices agree to its use.

This negotiation is performed using four Telnet protocol commands: WILL, WONT, DO, and DONT.

To specify that it wants to start using an option, the initiator sends the WILL command to the other device. There are two possible replies by the responding device:

DO Sent to indicate agreement that the initiator should use the option; it is then considered enabled.

DONT Sent to specify that the initiator must not use the option.

If the initiator wants the other device to start using an option, it sends the DO command. That device may respond in two ways:

WILL Sent to specify that the responding device will agree to use the option; the option is enabled.

WONT Sent to tell the initiator that the responder will not use the option requested.

The symmetry of Telnet and the fact that both DO and WILL can be used either to initiate a negotiation or respond to one make Telnet's option negotiation potentially complicated. Since either device can initiate negotiation of an option at any time, this could result in acknowledgment loops if both devices were to try to enable an option simultaneously or each kept responding to the other's replies. For this reason, the Telnet standard specifies restrictions on when the WILL and DO commands are used. One is that a device may send a negotiation command only to request a change in the status of an option; it cannot send DO or WILL just to confirm or reinforce the current state of the option. Another is that a device receiving a request to start using an option it is already using should not acknowledge it using DO or WILL.

Since an option may be activated only if both devices agree to use it, either may disable the use of an option at any time by sending one of these commands:

WONT Sent by a device to indicate that it is going to stop using an option. The other device must respond with DONT as a confirmation.

DONT Sent by a device to indicate that it wants the other device to stop using an option. The other device must respond with WONT.

KEY CONCEPT Either device may choose to negotiate the use of a Telnet option. The initiator uses the WILL command to specify that it wants to start using a particular option; if the other device agrees, it responds with DO; otherwise, it sends DONT. Alternatively, the initiator can use the DO command to indicate that it wants the other device to start using an option; that device responds with WILL if it agrees to do so or WONT if it does not. Either device may disable the use of an option at any time by sending the other a WONT or DONT command.

Option Subnegotiation

All of the DO/DONT/WILL/WONT negotiation just described serves only to enable or disable an option. Some options, such as the binary transmission option (TRANSMIT-BINARY), are either only off or on; in which case, this option negotiation is sufficient. Other options require that after they are enabled, the client and server exchange parameters to control how the option works. For example, the TERMINAL-TYPE option requires some way for the client to send the server the name of the terminal. Telnet allows the client and server to send an arbitrary amount of data related to the option using a process called *option subnegotiation.*

A device begins the subnegotiation process by sending a special sequence of Telnet protocol commands and data. First, the device sends the SB (subnegotiation) command, followed by the option number and parameters as defined by the particular option, and then ending the subnegotiation data by sending the SE (subnegotiation end) command. Both SB and SE must be preceded by the Interpret As Command (IAC) command byte.

Let's take the terminal type negotiation as an example. Suppose the server supports this option and would like the client to use it. The server starts option negotiation by sending the DO command:

```
IAC DO TERMINAL-TYPE
```

Assuming the client agrees, it will respond with the WILL command:

```
IAC WILL TERMINAL-TYPE
```

Now the terminal type option is in effect, but the server still doesn't know which terminal the client is using. It can prompt the client to provide that information by sending this command:

```
IAC SB TERMINAL-TYPE SEND IAC SE
```

The client receiving this option subnegotiation command will respond with the following:

```
IAC SB TERMINAL-TYPE IS <some_terminal_type> IAC SE
```

KEY CONCEPT The WILL and DO commands only turn on a Telnet option that a client and server agree to use. In some cases, an option requires additional information to be sent between the client and server device for it to function properly. This is accomplished through a process of *option subnegotiation*. Either device sends the other a set of data relevant to the option, bracketed by the SB (subnegotiation) and SE (subnegotiation end) Telnet protocol commands.

Berkeley Remote (r) Commands

TCP/IP has achieved success in large part due to its universality—it has been implemented on virtually every major computing platform. While the suite is thus not specific to any operating system, there is no denying that its history is closely tied to a particular one—UNIX. Most of the computers on the early Internet used UNIX, and the development of TCP/IP has paralleled that of UNIX in a number of respects.

One of the most important organizations involved in the development of UNIX, and thus TCP/IP indirectly, was the University of California at Berkeley (UCB). The well-known UCB-developed *Berkeley Software Distribution (BSD)* UNIX has been in widespread use for over 20 years. They also developed a set of commands for BSD UNIX to facilitate various remote operation functions over a TCP/IP internetwork. Each of these programs begins with the letter *r* (for remote), so they have come to be known as both the *Berkeley remote commands* (or utilities) and also simply the *r commands*. Since their initial creation, they have been adopted for most variations of UNIX and some other operating systems as well.

BACKGROUND INFORMATION *This section will probably make much more sense to those who have some understanding of the UNIX operating system than those who do not.*

Berkeley Remote Login (rlogin)

The head of the Berkeley remote protocol family is the remote login command, `rlogin`. As the name clearly implies, the purpose of this program is to allow a user on a UNIX host to log in to another host over a TCP/IP internetwork. Since Telnet is also often used for remote login, `rlogin` and Telnet are sometimes considered alternatives to each other for TCP/IP remote login. While they can be used in a similar way, they are quite different in a few respects.

From a conceptual standpoint, Telnet is designed as a protocol to enable terminal/host communication. As I mentioned in the Telnet overview earlier in this chapter, that protocol was not designed specifically for the purpose of remote login. In contrast, `rlogin` was intended for that specific purpose, and this is reflected in its operation.

The protocol requires `rlogin` server software to be running on the host that is going to allow remote access; it is usually called `rlogind` (for `rlogin` *daemon*, the latter word being the standard UNIX term for a background server process). The server listens for incoming connection requests on TCP port 513. Users who want to remotely log in to the server run the `rlogin` command on their local host and specify the name of the server. The client makes a TCP connection to the server and then sends to the server a string containing the following information:

- The login name of the user on the client machine
- The login name that the user wants to use on the server (which is often the same as the user's login name on the client, but not always)
- Control information such as the type and speed of the terminal

The server processes this information and begins the login process. It will normally prompt the user for a password to log in to the remote host. Assuming the password is correct, the user will be logged in to the remote host and can use it as if the user were locally connected.

From a practical standpoint, the `rlogin` command is much simpler than Telnet; it does not support Telnet's full command structure, nor capabilities such as option negotiation. It does include a small set of commands, however. The client is able to send to the server one key piece of information: the current size of the terminal window in use. The server is able to tell the client to turn on or off flow control, request that the client send it the current window size, or ask the client to flush pending output that the server has sent, up to a certain point in the data stream.

Some organizations have many different UNIX hosts that are used every day, and needing to constantly type passwords when using `rlogin` can be somewhat of a chore. On these systems, it is possible for administrators to set up control files that specify combinations of host names, user names, and passwords. If set up correctly, this enables an authorized user to use `rlogin` to remotely access a host automatically, without needing to enter either a login name or password.

As originally designed, rlogin is a classic example of a protocol from the early days of TCP/IP, since it emphasizes simplicity and usability over security. This is especially true of the automated login process just described. The original schemes used by rlogin for authentication are considered inadequate for modern TCP/IP internetworks, especially those connected to the Internet. Later versions of rlogin have been enhanced with more secure authorization methods. There is also a newer program called slogin (for *secure login*) that uses stronger authentication and encryption, which is intended to replace rlogin on newer systems.

> **KEY CONCEPT** The Berkeley remote, or *r*, commands facilitate remote operations between UNIX hosts on a TCP/IP internetwork. The base command of the family is the *remote login* command, rlogin, which allows a device on one host to access and use another as if it were locally connected to it. rlogin is often used as an alternative to Telnet. It is simpler than Telnet, both conceptually and practically.

Berkeley Remote Shell (rsh)

A user would normally use rlogin when he needs to log in to a server to perform a number of tasks. There are some situations, however, where a user needs to only enter one command on a remote host. With rlogin, the user would need to log in to the host, execute the command, and then log back out again. This isn't exactly an earth-shattering amount of inconvenience, especially when the correct configuration files are set up to allow automatic login. Over the course of time, however, all the extra logging in and out can become tedious. As a convenience, a variation of rlogin, called rsh (for *remote shell*), allows a user to access a remote host and execute a single command on it without requiring the login and logout steps.

NOTE Shell *is the standard term used in UNIX to refer to the user interface that accepts commands from the user and displays output on the screen.*

The rsh command is based on rlogin and works in much the same way, except that it is oriented around executing a command rather than establishing a persistent login session. The server process on the remote host is usually called rshd (for *remote shell daemon*) and listens for incoming rsh requests. When one is received, the user is logged in through the same mechanism as rlogin. The command runs on the remote host, and then the user is automatically logged out.

rsh is most useful when automatic login is employed, so that the program can be run without the need for the user to enter a login name or password. In that case, it is possible to have programs use rsh to automatically run commands on remote hosts without the need for human intervention, which opens up a number of possibilities for UNIX users. The normal UNIX user interface concepts of *standard input (stdin)*, *standard output (stdout)*, and *standard error (stderr)* also apply to rsh, so you can use it to execute a remote command and redirect the output to a local file. For example, the following command would let a user get a listing of his home directory on the host server and store it in the local file named remotelist:

```
rsh <somehost> ls -l >remotelist
```

> **KEY CONCEPT** The `rsh` (remote shell) command is similar to the Berkeley `rlogin` command, but instead of opening a login session on a remote host, it executes a single, user-provided command. `rsh` can be helpful for users who need to perform a quick operation on a remote host, and it can also be employed by other programs to automate network tasks.

Since `rsh` is based on `rlogin`, all of the concerns that apply to `rlogin` are also relevant here, especially with regard to security. (We really don't want unauthorized users running commands on our servers!) As with `rlogin`, newer versions of `rsh` support more advanced authentication options than the original software. Also, just as `slogin` is a newer, more secure version of `rlogin`, there is a program called `ssh` (for *secure shell*) that replaces `rsh` on many systems.

NOTE *On some systems, if* `rsh` *is entered without a command specified to execute, an interactive remote session is established, exactly as if the* `rlogin` *command had been entered instead of* `rsh`.

Other Berkeley Remote Commands

The `rlogin` and `rsh` commands are the generic members of the Berkeley *r* family of programs that allow remote access to a host. To complement these, the developers also defined a small number of specific remote commands. These are essentially remote versions of some of the more common UNIX functions. Instead of the command being applied to only one system, however, it is used between two systems or across all systems on a TCP/IP network.

All of these commands are based on `rlogin` in the same way as `rsh` is. They work in the same way, but instead of opening a session or passing a user-specified command to the remote host, they execute a particular function. The following are the most common of these remote commands:

Remote Copy (`rcp`) This is the remote version of the UNIX copy (`cp`) command. It allows a file to be copied between the local host and the remote host or between two remote hosts. The usual syntax is basically the same as the regular `cp` command, but the source and/or destination is specified as being on a remote host. The `rcp` command can be used in a manner similar to FTP, but is much simpler and less capable. Or, to put it another way, `rcp` is to FTP what `rlogin` is to Telnet. (That's not a perfect analogy, but it's pretty close.)

Remote Uptime (`ruptime`) The UNIX command `uptime` displays how long a computer has been running since it was last booted, along with information related to its current load. `ruptime` is the remote version of this command; it displays the current status of each machine on the network (up or down), how long each up machine has been up since its last boot, and its load statistics.

Remote Who (`rwho`) This is the remote version of the `who` command. Where `who` shows all the users logged on to the host where it is run, `rwho` shows all users logged on to all machines on the network.

The `ruptime` and `rwho` commands both rely on the presence of the `rwhod` (for *remote who daemon*) running in the background on networked machines. These processes routinely share information with each other about host uptime and who is logged on to each system, so it can be quickly displayed when either `ruptime` or `rwho` is run.

On some operating systems, other remote commands may also be implemented. As with `rlogin` and `rsh`, security issues may apply to these commands, and there may be efficiency concerns with others (such as `rwho`). For these reasons, on many networks, these commands are no longer used.

Internet Relay Chat Protocol (IRC)

The primary advantage that electronic mail (email) offers over conventional mail is *speed*. Instead of needing to wait for days or weeks for a message to be delivered, it usually arrives in minutes or even seconds. This makes email far more useful than the regular postal service for most types of information transfer. There are some cases, however, where speed of delivery is not sufficient to make email an ideal mechanism for communication. One such case is where a *dialogue* is required between two parties.

Consider that even though email may be delivered very quickly, it uses a decoupled model of communication. Say that Ellen sends an email to Jane. The message may show up in Jane's inbox in a matter of seconds, but Jane may not be around to read it at the time it arrives. Jane might not see the message until hours later. Then Jane would send a response to Ellen, who might not see it for a while. If the subject they are discussing requires several dozen iterations of this sort, it could take a very long time before the exchange is completed.

In the real world, of course, most of us would never use email for such a conversation, preferring instead that high-tech communication device that we call the telephone. Many people using computers realized that it would be useful to have a way for two or more people to interactively discuss issues in a manner similar to a telephone conversation. In the online world, this is commonly called *chatting*, and one of the first and most important application protocols designed to implement it in TCP/IP was the *Internet Relay Chat (IRC) Protocol.*

Prior to the widespread use of the Internet, people with computers would often communicate by dialing in to a *bulletin board system (BBS)* or other proprietary service. IRC was originally created by a gentleman from Finland named Jarkko Oikarinen, based on his experience with chat applications on BBSes. He wrote the first client and server software in 1988. The protocol was later formally defined in RFC 1459, "Internet Relay Chat Protocol," published May 1993. In April 2000, the IRC standard was revised and enhanced with several new extended capabilities, and published as a set of four smaller documents: RFCs 2810 through 2813. Each of these focuses on one particular area of IRC functionality.

NOTE *RFC 1459 has the experimental RFC status, and the RFC 2810 to 2813 group is designated Informational. This makes IRC optional; it does not need to be implemented on TCP/IP devices.*

IRC Communication Model and Client/Server Operation

IRC is an interesting protocol in that it is not based strictly on the standard client/server model of TCP/IP protocol operation. *IRC servers* are TCP/IP machines that run IRC server software. They are configured with information that allows them to establish TCP connections to each other. IRC uses TCP because the connections are maintained over a long period of time, and reliable transport of data is required. Server connections are used to exchange control information and user data, forming a logical *IRC network* at the application level, which allows any server to send to any other server, using intermediate servers as conduits. Servers are managed by *IRC operators (IRCops)* who have special privileges that allow them to ensure that everything runs smoothly on the network.

The IRC network forms the backbone of the IRC communication service. A user can access the network by running *IRC client* software on any TCP/IP-enabled device. The user enters the name of one of the servers on the network and establishes a TCP connection to that server. This causes the user to be connected directly to one server, and thus, indirectly to all of the others on the network. This allows that user to send and receive messages to and from all other users connected either to the user's server or other servers.

Messaging and IRC Channels

The most common type of communication in IRC is *group messaging*, which is accomplished using *IRC channels.* A channel is a virtual meeting place of sorts and is also sometimes called a *chat room* (though IRC purists scoff at the use of that term). Every IRC network has hundreds or even thousands of different channels, each of which is dedicated to a particular type of discussion, ranging from the serious to the silly. For example, a group of people interested in talking about meteorology could establish a channel called #weather, where they would meet regularly to discuss various aspects of climatology and interesting weather events.

IRC is an inherently text-based protocol (though it is also possible to use IRC clients to transfer arbitrary files between users, including images and executable programs). To communicate in a channel, all a user needs to do is enter text in the appropriate spot in the IRC client program, and then the program automatically sends this text to every other member of the channel. The IRC network handles the relaying of these messages in real time from the sender's connected server to other servers in the network, and then to all user machines on those servers. When other users see the first user's message, they can reply with messages of their own, which will, in turn, be propagated across the network. Each IRC user chooses a nickname (often abbreviated *nick*) that is like a *handle* used for communication while connected to the network.

IRC also supports one-to-one communication, which can be used for private conversation. To use this method, a user just needs the nickname of another user to whom she wants to talk. She uses a special command to send messages directly to that user, who can respond in kind. This is not a secure form of communication, since the messages are not encrypted, and they pass through servers where they could be monitored. However, there is so much traffic on a typical IRC network that any given message is unlikely to be monitored.

The IRC Protocol defines a rich command set that allows users to perform essential functions, such as joining or leaving a channel, changing nicknames, changing servers, setting operating modes for channels, and so forth. The exact command set and features available depend both on the specific software used for the user's IRC client and the features available on the IRC network itself. Not all IRC networks run the same version of the protocol.

IRC and the Modern Internet

IRC became very popular in the early 1990s because of the powerful way that it allows users from anywhere on the Internet to meet and share information dynamically. It acts like a text-based telephone, but users across the globe don't have the expense of long-distance calls.

One of the most important characteristics of IRC is its open-ended nature; it gives every person the freedom to communicate in whatever way he or she considers best. For example, every IRC channel has an owner, who has certain rights related to how the channel is used, including the ability to decide who should be allowed in the channel. This may seem autocratic, but IRC lets anyone start a new channel instantly and become that channel's owner, without the need for prior registration or authorization. This means that if you don't like how a particular channel is run, you can start your own with a minimum of fuss. You are not forced to adhere to anyone's rules, other than the rules set forth for the server (which are usually just intended to prevent abuse).

This same principle extends to the IRC networks themselves. There isn't just one single IRC network; there are dozens of different ones. Some are large, well-established networks that may have more than 100 servers and thousands of users; others are smaller and devoted to specific areas of interest or geographical regions. Anyone can set up their own IRC network if they have the hardware and software, and some organizations have set up private, dedicated IRC servers for their own use.

IRC is considered by many to be the most important ancestor of the related interactive applications collectively known as *instant messaging*. These services are offered by several organizations, including America Online (AOL), Yahoo, and Microsoft's MSN. The idea behind them is very similar to that of IRC. Each allows a message sent by one user to be displayed immediately to another, though most are focused primarily on user-to-user messages rather than group messaging. Instant messaging has surpassed IRC in overall use, perhaps due to the large subscriber base of services like AOL. However, IRC is still widely used by thousands of enthusiasts on a daily basis for both entertainment and business purposes.

88

TCP/IP ADMINISTRATION AND TROUBLESHOOTING UTILITIES AND PROTOCOLS

This final chapter on application protocols is a bit different from the previous ones. It doesn't describe applications designed for end users. Rather, it discusses a set of TCP/IP troubleshooting utilities and protocols, which are normally the province of internetwork administrators. Even though millions of people use TCP/IP every day without even knowing that these applications exist—much less how they work—they are critically important to those who maintain TCP/IP internetworks. Since many of you are studying TCP/IP so that you can implement and administer this technology, understanding how these applications work is well worth your time.

In this chapter, I provide an overview of a number of software utilities that are commonly employed to help set up, configure, and maintain TCP/IP internetworks. These programs allow a network administrator to perform functions such as checking the identity of a host, verifying connectivity between two hosts, checking the path of routers between devices, examining the configuration of a computer, and looking up a Domain Name System (DNS) domain name.

The goal of this chapter is to provide explanations of the general purpose and function of troubleshooting utilities, so you will know how they can help you manage TCP/IP networks. As part of these descriptions, I demonstrate the typical syntax used to invoke each utility in both UNIX and Windows. Due to variations in software implementations, you will need to consult your operating system documentation for the details on exactly how each program should be used on your network. On Windows systems, try `<program> /?` to see the syntax of the program; on UNIX/Linux, try `man <program>`.

BACKGROUND INFORMATION *Many of the software tools described in this section are designed to manage the operation of other TCP/IP protocols, such as the Internet Protocol (IP), the Domain Name System (DNS), and the Dynamic Host Configuration Protocol (DHCP). To fully appreciate how these utilities work, you need to understand the basics of these and other key TCP/IP protocols. In particular, a number of the utilities discussed here communicate use Internet Control Message Protocol (ICMP) messages, so I would recommend familiarity with ICMP (discussed in Part II-6) before proceeding.*

TCP/IP Host Name Utility (hostname)

One of the most fundamental of tasks in diagnosing problems with a networked computer is identifying it. Just as the first thing we usually do when we meet someone is exchange names, one of the first actions an administrator takes when accessing a device is to determine its name, if it is not known. This is accomplished using the `hostname` utility.

You may recall from our discussion of TCP/IP name systems in Part III-1 that there are two different ways that hosts can be named. The first way is to manually assign flat names to devices using host tables or equivalent means; this is most often used for devices that not going to be accessed on the public Internet. The second is to give a device a domain name within DNS. The `hostname` utility can be used for both types of named hosts, but it functions in a slightly different way for each.

On most systems, including Windows and many UNIX implementations, the `hostname` utility is very simple. When you enter the command by itself on a line with no arguments, it displays the full name of the host. If it is entered with the `-s` (short) parameter and the host name is a fully qualified DNS domain name, only the local label of the node is shown and not the full domain name; if the host has a flat (non-DNS) name, the `-s` parameter has no effect. Here is a simple example:

```
% hostname
fearn.pair.com
% hostname -s
fearn
```

The `hostname` utility is also intended to allow an administrator to set the name of a host. The syntax for this is also simple; you just supply the name of the host as a parameter, as follows:

```
hostname <new-hostname>
```

However, in most implementations, the use of the hostname command for setting a device's name is either disabled or restricted. In Windows systems, a special applet in the Control Panel is used to set the device's name; attempting to set it using hostname will result in an error message. In UNIX, the superuser of the system can use hostname to set the device's name, but it is more common for this to be done by other means, such as editing the configuration file /etc/hosts. If a simple flat name is being assigned to this host, the administrator has full control over it. However, if DNS is used, then the proper procedures for registering the name must be followed.

NOTE *The* hostname *utility is not, strictly speaking, tied into the operation of DNS or other formal mechanisms for identifying a host. It simply displays what the administrator has set it to show. It makes sense for this to be set to the host's DNS name, but there may be exceptions, such as in small networks that might not use DNS.*

In most operating systems, the -s parameter is the only one that this command supports. The parameter is not supported on all implementations of the hostname command, however. On some implementations, if you use hostname -s, the system may report its host name as being *-s*. On certain Linux systems, the hostname utility includes a few additional parameters that allow different ways for the host name to be displayed, as well as some miscellaneous functions such as showing the version number of the program.

KEY CONCEPT The simplest and most basic of TCP/IP administrative utilities is hostname, which returns the name of the host on which it is run.

TCP/IP Communication Verification Utility (ping)

One of the most common problems that network administrators are asked to solve is that two hosts are not able to communicate. For example, a user on a corporate network might not be able to retrieve one of his files from a local server, or another user might be having difficulty loading her favorite website. In these and similar situations, one important step in diagnosing the problem is to verify that basic communication is possible between the TCP/IP software stacks on the two machines. This is most often done using the ping utility, or ping6 in Internet Protocol version 6 (IPv6) implementations. The IPv6 version of ping works in much the same way as IPv4 ping, but ping6's options and parameters reflect the changes made in addressing and routing in IPv6.

NOTE *Some people say that* ping *is an acronym for Packet Internet Groper, while others insist that it is actually based on the use of the term to refer to a sonar pulse sent by a submarine to check for nearby objects. I really don't know which of these is true, but I prefer the second explanation. Consider that the utility works in a way similar to a sonar ping, and that it was originally written by a gentleman named Mike Muuss, who worked at the United States Army Ballistics Research Laboratory.*

ping is one of the most commonly used diagnostic utilities, and it is present in just about every TCP/IP implementation. It is usually implemented and accessed as a command-line utility, though there are also now graphical and menu-based versions of the program on some operating systems.

Operation of the ping Utility

The ping utility is implemented using Internet Control Message Protocol (ICMP) Echo (Request) and Echo Reply messages, which are designed specifically for this type of diagnostic use. When Device A sends an ICMP Echo message to Device B, Device B responds by sending an ICMP Echo Reply message back to Device A. The same functionality exists in ICMPv6, the IPv6 version of ICMP; the ICMPv6 Echo and Echo Reply messages differ from the IPv4 ones only slightly in their field structure.

This would seem to indicate that ping would be an extremely simple utility that would send one Echo message and wait to see if an Echo Reply was received back. If so, this would mean that the two devices were able to communicate; if not, this would indicate a problem somewhere on the internetwork between the two. However, almost all ping implementations are much more complex than this. They use multiple sets of Echo and Echo Reply messages, along with considerable internal logic, to allow an administrator to determine all of the following, and more:

- Whether or not the two devices can communicate
- Whether congestion or other problems exist that might allow communication to succeed sometimes but cause it to fail in others, seen as packet loss; if so, how bad the loss is
- How much time it takes to send a simple ICMP message between devices, which gives an indication of the overall latency between the hosts and also indicates if there are certain types of problems

Basic Use of ping

The most basic use of the ping command is to enter it by itself with the IP address of a host. Virtually all implementations also allow you to use a host name, which will be resolved to an IP address automatically. When you invoke the utility with no additional options, it uses default values for parameters such as what size message to send, how many messages to be sent, how long to wait for a reply, and so on. The utility will transmit a series of Echo messages to the host and report back whether or not a reply was received for each. If a reply is seen, it will also indicate how long it took for the response to be received. When the program is finished, it will provide a statistical summary showing what percentage of the Echo messages received a reply and the average amount of time it took for them to be received.

NOTE *While the inability to get a response from a device to a* ping *has traditionally been interpreted as a problem in communication, this is not always necessarily the case. In the current era of increased security consciousness, some networks are set up to not respond to Echo messages, to protect against attacks that use floods of such messages. In this case, a* ping *will fail, even though the host may be quite reachable.*

Listing 88-1 shows an example of using the ping command on a Windows XP computer (mine!), which, by default, sends four 32-byte Echo messages and allows four seconds before considering an Echo message lost. I use a satellite Internet connection that has fairly high latency and also occasionally drops packets. This isn't great for me, but it is useful for illustrating how ping works.

```
D:\aa>ping www.pcguide.com
Pinging pcguide.com [209.68.14.80] with 32 bytes of data:

Reply from 209.68.14.80: bytes=32 time=582ms TTL=56
Reply from 209.68.14.80: bytes=32 time=601ms TTL=56
Request timed out.
Reply from 209.68.14.80: bytes=32 time=583ms TTL=56

Ping statistics for 209.68.14.80:
    Packets: Sent = 4, Received = 3, Lost = 1 (25% loss),
Approximate round trip times in milli-seconds:
    Minimum = 582ms, Maximum = 601ms, Average = 588ms
```

Listing 88-1: *Verifying communication using the ping utility*

Methods of Diagnosing Connectivity Problems Using ping

Most people find that using ping with default settings is enough for their needs. In fact, the utility can be used in this simplest form to perform a surprising number of diagnostic checks. In many cases, you can use the ping command to diagnose connectivity problems by issuing it multiple times in sequence, often starting with checks at or close to the transmitting device and then proceeding outward toward the other device with which the communication problem has been observed. Here are some examples of how ping can be used in this way:

Internal Device TCP/IP Stack Operation By performing a ping on the device's own address, you can verify that its internal TCP/IP stack is working. This can also be done using the standard IP loopback address, 127.0.0.1.

Local Network Connectivity If the internal test succeeds, it's a good idea to do a ping on another device on the local network, to verify that local communication is possible.

Local Router Operation If there is no problem on the local network, it makes sense to ping whatever local router the device is using to make sure it is operating and reachable.

Domain Name Resolution Functionality If a ping performed on a DNS domain name fails, you should try it with the device's IP address instead. If that works, this implies either a problem with domain name configuration or resolution.

Remote Host Operation If all the preceding checks succeed, you can try performing a ping to a remote host to see if it responds. If it does not, you can try a different remote host. If that one works, it is possible that the problem is actually with the first remote device itself and not with your local device.

KEY CONCEPT The TCP/IP ping utility is used to verify the ability of two devices on a TCP/IP internetwork to communicate. It operates by having one device send ICMP Echo (Request) messages to another, which responds with Echo Reply messages. The program can be helpful in diagnosing a number of connectivity issues, especially if it is used to test the ability to communicate with other devices in different locations. It also allows the average round-trip delay to exchange messages with another device to be estimated.

ping Options and Parameters

In addition to the basic uses described in the previous sections, all ping implementations include a number of options and parameters that allow an administrator to fine-tune how it works. They allow ping to be used for more extensive or specific types of testing. For example, ping can be set in a mode where it sends Echo messages continually, to check for an intermittent problem over a long period of time. You can also increase the size of the messages sent or the frequency with which they are transmitted, to test the ability of the local network to handle large amounts of traffic.

As with the other utilities described in this chapter, the exact features of the ping program are implementation-dependent. Even though UNIX and Windows systems often include many of the same options, they usually use completely different option codes. Table 88-1 shows some of the more important options that are often defined for the utility on many UNIX systems, and where appropriate, the parameters supplied with the option. Table 88-2 shows ping options for a typical Windows system.

Table 88-1: Common UNIX ping Utility Options and Parameters

Option/ Parameters	Description
-c *<count>*	Specifies the number of Echo messages that should be sent.
-f	Flood mode; sends Echo packets at high speed to stress test a network. This can cause serious problems if not used carefully!
-i *<wait-interval>*	Tells the utility how long to wait between transmissions.
-m *<ttl-value>*	Overrides the default Time to Live (TTL) value for outgoing Echo messages.
-n	Numeric output only; suppresses lookups of DNS host names to save time.
-p *<pattern>*	Allows a byte pattern to be specified for inclusion in the transmitted Echo messages. This can be useful for diagnosing certain odd problems that may occur only with certain types of transmissions.
-q	Quiet output; only summary lines are displayed at the start and end of the program's execution, while the lines for each individual message are suppressed.
-R	Tells the utility to include the Record Route IP option, so the route taken by the ICMP Echo message can be displayed. This option is not supported by all implementations. Using the traceroute utility (described in the next section) is usually a better idea.
-s *<packet-size>*	Specifies the size of outgoing message to use.
-S *<src-addr>*	On devices that have multiple IP interfaces (addresses), allows a ping sent from one interface to use an address from one of the others.
-t *<timeout>*	Specifies a timeout period, in seconds, after which the ping utility will terminate, regardless of how many requests or replies have been sent or received.

Table 88-2: Common Windows ping Utility Options and Parameters

Option/ Parameters	Description
-a	If the target device is specified as an IP address, forces the address to be resolved to a DNS host name and displayed.
-f	Sets the Don't Fragment bit in the outgoing datagram.
-i <*ttl-value*>	Specifies the Time to Live (TTL) value to be used for outgoing Echo messages.
-j <*host-list*>	Sends the outgoing messages using the specified loose source route.
-k <*host-list*>	Sends the outgoing messages using the indicated strict source route.
-l <*buffer-size*>	Specifies the size of the data field in the transmitted Echo messages.
-n <*count*>	Tells the utility how many Echo messages to send.
-r <*count*>	Specifies the use of the Record Route IP option and the number of hops to be recorded. It's usually preferable to use the traceroute utility (described in the next section).
-s <*count*>	Specifies the use of the IP Timestamp option to record the arrival time of the Echo and Echo Reply messages.
-t	Sends Echo messages continuously until the program is interrupted.
-w <*timeout*>	Specifies how long the program should wait for each Echo Reply before giving up, in milliseconds (default is 4,000, for 4 seconds).

TCP/IP Route Tracing Utility (traceroute)

The ping utility is extremely helpful for checking whether two devices are able to communicate with each other. However, it provides very little information regarding what is going on between those two devices. In the event that ping shows either a total inability to communicate or intermittent connectivity with high loss of transmitted data, administrators need to know more about what is happening to IP datagrams as they are carried across the internetwork. This is especially important when the two devices are far from each other, especially if you are trying to reach a server on the public Internet.

I described in my overview of IP datagram delivery that when two devices are not on the same network, data sent between them must be delivered from one network to the next until it reaches its destination. This means that any time data is sent from Device A on one network to Device B on another, it follows a route, which may not be the same for each transmission. When communication problems arise, it is very useful to be able to check the specific route taken by data between two devices. A special route tracing utility is provided for this function, called traceroute (abbreviated tracert in Windows systems, a legacy of the old eight-character limit for DOS program names).

The IPv6 equivalent of this program is called traceroute6, which functions in a very similar manner to its IPv4 predecessor. It obviously uses IPv6 datagrams instead of IPv4 ones, and responses from traced devices are in the form of ICMPv6 Time Exceeded and Destination Unreachable messages rather than their ICMPv4 counterparts.

Operation of the traceroute Utility

Like the ping utility, traceroute is implemented using ICMP messages. However, unlike ping, traceroute was not originally designed to use a special ICMP message type intended exclusively for route tracing. Instead, it makes clever use of the IP and ICMP features that are designed to prevent routing problems.

Recall that the IP datagram format includes a Time to Live (TTL) field. This field is set to the maximum number of times that a datagram may be forwarded before it must be discarded; it exists to prevent datagrams from circling an internetwork endlessly. If a datagram must be discarded due to expiration of the TTL field, the device that discards it is supposed to send an ICMP Time Exceeded message back to the device that sent the discarded datagram. (This is explained in detail in Chapter 32.) Under normal circumstances, this occurs only when there is a problem, such as a router loop or another misconfiguration issue. What traceroute does is to force each router in a route to report back to it by intentionally setting the TTL value in test datagrams to a value too low to allow them to reach their destination.

Suppose you have Device A and Device B, which are separated by Routers R1 and R2—three hops total (A to R1, R1 to R2 and R2 to B). If you do a traceroute from Device A to Device B, here's what happens (see Figure 88-1):

1. The traceroute utility sends a dummy User Datagram Protocol (UDP) message (sometimes called a *probe*) to a port number that is intentionally selected to be invalid. The TTL field of the IP datagram is set to 1. When Router R1 receives the message, it decrements the field, which will make its value 0. That router discards the probe and sends an ICMP Time Exceeded message back to Device A.
2. Device A sends a second UDP message with the TTL field set to 2. This time, Router R1 reduces the TTL value to 1 and sends it to Router R2, which reduces the TTL field to 0 and sends a Time Exceeded message back to Device A.
3. Device A sends a third UDP message, with the TTL field set to 3. This time, the message will pass through both routers and be received by Device B. However, since the port number was invalid, the message is rejected by Device B, which sends back a Destination Unreachable message to Device A.

So Device A sends out three messages to Device B, and it gets back three error messages and is happy about it! The route to Device B is thus indicated by the identities of the devices sending back the error messages, in sequence. By keeping track of the time between when it sent each UDP message and received back the corresponding error message, the traceroute utility can also display how long it took to communicate with each device. In practice, usually three dummy messages are sent with each TTL value, so their transit times can be averaged by the user if desired.

NOTE *Not all* traceroute *utility implementations use the technique described here. Microsoft's* tracert *works by sending ICMP Echo messages with increasing TTL values, rather than UDP packets. It knows it has reached the final host when it gets back an Echo Reply message. A special ICMP Traceroute message was also developed in 1993, which was intended to improve the efficiency of* traceroute *by eliminating the need to send many UDP messages for each route tracing. Despite its technical advantages, since this message was introduced long after TCP/IP was widely deployed, it never became a formal Internet standard and its use is not seen as often as the traditional method.*

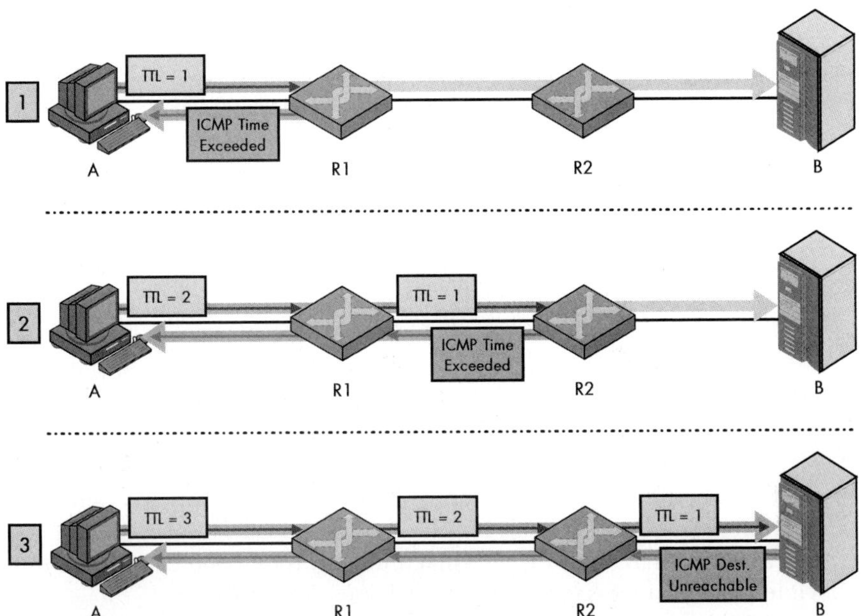

Figure 88-1: Operation of the traceroute/tracert utility *The* `traceroute` *utility identifies the devices in a route by forcing them to report back failures to route datagrams with parameters intentionally set to invalid values. The first message sent by Device A here has a Time to Live (TTL) value of 1, which will cause Router R1 it to drop it and send an ICMP Time Exceeded message back to Device A. The second message has a TTL value of 2, so it will be dropped and reported by Router R2. The third message will pass both routers and get to the destination host, Device B, but since the message is deliberately chosen with a bogus port number, this will cause an ICMP Destination Unreachable message to be returned. These error messages identify the sequence of devices in the route between Devices A and B.*

KEY CONCEPT The `traceroute` utility takes the idea behind `ping` one step further, allowing administrators to not only check communication between two devices, but also letting them see a list of all the intermediate devices between the pair. It works by having the initiating host send a series of test datagrams with TTL values that cause each to expire sequentially at each device on the route. The `traceroute` program also shows how much time it takes to communicate with each device between the sending host and a destination device.

Basic Use of the traceroute Utility

Listing 88-2 shows an example of a `traceroute` sent between two of the UNIX computers I use on a regular basis. I added the `-q2` parameter to change the default of three dummy messages per hop to two, so the output would fit better on the page.

```
traceroute -q2 www.pcguide.com
traceroute to www.pcguide.com (209.68.14.80), 40 hops max, 40 byte packets
 1  cisco0fe0-0-1.bf.sover.net (209.198.87.10)  1.223 ms  1.143 ms
 2  cisco1fe0.bf.sover.net (209.198.87.12)  1.265 ms  1.117 ms
 3  cisco0a5-0-102.wnskvtao.sover.net (216.114.153.170)  8.004 ms  7.270 ms
 4  207.136.212.234 (207.136.212.234)  7.163 ms  7.601 ms
 5  sl-gw18-nyc-2-0.sprintlink.net (144.232.228.145)  15.948 ms  20.931 ms
```

```
 6  sl-bb21-nyc-12-1.sprintlink.net (144.232.13.162)  21.578 ms  16.324 ms
 7  sl-bb27-pen-12-0.sprintlink.net (144.232.20.97)  18.296 ms  *
 8  sl-bb24-pen-15-0.sprintlink.net (144.232.16.81)  18.041 ms  18.338 ms
 9  sl-bb26-rly-0-0.sprintlink.net (144.232.20.111)  20.259 ms  21.648 ms
10  sl-bb20-rly-12-0.sprintlink.net (144.232.7.249)  132.302 ms  37.825 ms
11  sl-gw9-rly-8-0.sprintlink.net (144.232.14.22)  23.085 ms  20.082 ms
12  sl-exped4-1-0.sprintlink.net (144.232.248.126)  43.374 ms  42.274 ms
13  * *
14  pcguide.com (209.68.14.80)  41.310 ms  49.455 ms
```

Listing 88-2: *Route tracing using the traceroute utility*

In this case, the servers are separated by 14 hops. Notice how the elapsed time generally increases as the distance from the transmitting device increases, but it is not consistent because of random elements in the delay between any two devices (see the incongruously large value in hop 10, for example). Also notice the asterisk (*) in the seventh hop, which means that no response was received before the timeout period for the second transmission with a TTL value of 7. Finally, there is no report at all for hop 13. This machine may have been configured not to send Time Exceeded messages.

Additional unusual results may be displayed under certain circumstances. For example, the `traceroute` program may display a code such a `!H`, `!N`, or `!P` to indicate receipt of an unexpected Destination Unreachable message for a host, network, or protocol, respectively. Other error messages may also exist, depending on the implementation.

traceroute Options and Parameters

As is the case with `ping`, `traceroute` can be used with an IP address or host name. If no parameters are supplied, default values will be used for key parameters. On the system I use, the defaults are three probes for each TTL value, a maximum of 64 hops tested, and packets 40 bytes in size. However, my implementation also supports a number of options and parameters to give me more control over how the utility functions (such as the `-q` parameter I used in Listing 88-2). Some of the typical options available in UNIX systems are described in Table 88-3. A smaller set of options exists in Windows, as shown in Table 88-4.

Table 88-3: Common UNIX traceroute Utility Options and Parameters

Option/Parameters	Description
`-g` *<host-list>*	Specifies a source route to be used for the trace.
`-M` *<initial-ttl-value>*	Overrides the default value of 1 for the initial TTL value of the first outgoing probe message.
`-m` *<max-ttl-value>*	Sets the maximum TTL value to be used. This limits how long a route the utility will attempt to trace.
`-n`	Displays the route using numeric addresses only, rather than showing both IP addresses and host names. This speeds up the display by saving the utility from needing to perform reverse DNS lookups on all the devices in the route (ICMP messages use IP addresses, not domain names).

(continued)

Table 88-3: Common UNIX traceroute Utility Options and Parameters (continued)

Option/Parameters	Description
-p <*port-number*>	Specifies the port number to be used as the destination of the probe messages.
-q <*queries*>	Tells the utility how many probes to send to each device in the route (the default is 3).
-r	Tells the program to bypass the normal routing tables and send directly to a host on an attached network.
-s <*src-addr*>	On devices that have multiple IP interfaces (addresses), allows the device to use an address from one interface on a `traceroute` using another interface.
-S	Instructs the program to display a summary of how many probes did not receive a reply.
-v	Sets verbose output mode, which informs the user of all ICMP messages received during the trace.
-w <*wait-time*>	Specifies how long the utility should wait for a reply to each probe, in seconds (the typical default is 3 to 5).

Table 88-4: Common Windows tracert Utility Options and Parameters

Option/Parameters	Description
-d	Displays the route using numeric addresses only, rather than showing both IP addresses and host names, for faster display. This is the same as the -n option on UNIX systems.
-h <*maximum-hops*>	Specifies the maximum number of hops to use for tracing (the default is 30).
-j <*host-list*>	Sends the outgoing probes using the specified loose source route.
-w <*wait-time*>	Specifies how long to wait for a reply to each probe, in milliseconds (the default is 4,000, for 4 seconds).

TCP/IP Address Resolution Protocol Utility (arp)

All devices on an internetwork are considered to be virtually connected at layer 3, since the process of routing lets any device communicate with any other device. However, there is no way for devices on distant networks to communicate directly. The internetwork communication at layer 3 actually consists of a number of steps, called *hops*, that carry the data from its source to destination. Each hop in a route requires that data be sent between a pair of hardware devices, and each transmission must use layer 2 hardware addresses. Since TCP/IP uses layer 3 addresses, this means each hop requires that we translate the IP address of the target of the hop to a hardware address. This is called *address resolution*; the reasons why it is needed and the methods used for it are explained in detail in Chapter 13.

In TCP/IP, address resolution functions are performed by the aptly named Address Resolution Protocol (ARP). When a device needs to transmit to a device with a particular IP address, it can use ARP's request/reply messaging protocol to find out which hardware device corresponds to that IP address. However, each such message exchange takes time and network bandwidth, so for efficiency, every device maintains an ARP cache, which is a table containing mappings between IP and hardware addresses. The ARP cache table can contain a combination of static cache entries that are manually inserted for frequently accessed devices, and dynamic entries, which are entered automatically when a request/reply resolution is done. The next time it is necessary to send a device mapped in the ARP cache table, the lookup process can be avoided.

To allow administrators to manage this ARP cache table, TCP/IP devices include an arp utility. It has the following three basic functions, which are invoked using three different versions of the command (which, for once, are the same in UNIX and Windows):

ARP Cache Table Display When the -a option is used with the utility, it displays the current contents of the ARP cache table. The syntax is arp -d *<host-name>*. Each entry in the table shows the IP address and hardware address pair for one device (interface, actually). Usually, it also indicates whether each entry is static or dynamic. The exact format of the display varies from one implementation to the next; some programs show IP addresses, others show host names, and still others may show both. Some systems default to displaying host names but allow the -n option to also be used to force only IP addresses (not names) to be displayed.

ARP Cache Table Entry Addition This version allows an administrator to make a new manual ARP cache table entry that maps the given host name to the specified hardware address. The syntax is arp -s *<host-name>* *<hw-addr>*.

ARP Cache Table Entry Deletion Using arp with the -d option removes the specified cache entry from the table. Some implementations allow the addition of another parameter to specify that all entries should be removed from the cache. The basic syntax is arp -d *<host-name>*.

> **KEY CONCEPT** The TCP/IP arp utility is used by an administrator to inspect or modify a host's ARP cache table, which contains mappings between TCP/IP host names and IP addresses.

Certain versions of the software may also supplement these basic commands with additional features. One common additional option on UNIX systems is the ability to specify a file from which cache table entries may be read, using the syntax arp -f *<file-name>*. This saves a considerable amount of time and effort compared to typing each entry manually using arp -s.

Note also that the operating system may allow only authorized users to access options that cause the ARP cache table to be changed. This is especially true of the delete function.

TCP/IP DNS Name Resolution and Lookup Utilities (nslookup, host, and dig)

DNS is a critically important part of TCP/IP internetworks, especially the modern Internet, because it allows hosts to be accessed using easily remembered names rather than confusing numerical addresses. Two different primary types of devices are involved in the operation of DNS: DNS name servers that store information about domains and DNS resolvers that query DNS servers to transform names into addresses, as well as perform other necessary functions.

DNS resolvers are employed by Internet users on a continual basis to translate DNS names into address, but under normal circumstances, they are always invoked indirectly. Each time a user types a DNS name into a program such as a web browser or File Transfer Protocol (FTP) client—or even uses it in one of the other utilities described in this chapter, such as `ping` or `traceroute`—the resolver automatically performs the name resolution without the user having to ask. For this reason, there is no need for users to manually resolve DNS names into addresses.

However, administrators often do need to perform a DNS resolution manually. For example, when troubleshooting a problem, the administrator may know a host's name but not its address. In the case of a security problem, the address may show up in a log file but the host name may not be known. In addition, even though users do not need to know the specifics of the resource records that define a DNS domain, administrators often need to be able to check these details, to make sure a domain is set up properly. Administrators also need some way to be able to diagnose problems with DNS servers themselves. To support all of these needs, modern TCP/IP implementations come equipped with one or more DNS name resolution and information lookup utilities. Here, we will look at three such utilities: `nslookup`, `host`, and `dig`.

The nslookup Utility

One of the most common DNS diagnostic utilities is `nslookup` (for name server lookup), which has been around for many years. The details of how the program is implemented depend on the operating system, though most of them offer versions that are quite similar in operation and settings. The utility can normally be used in two modes: interactive or noninteractive.

The noninteractive version of `nslookup` is the simplest, and it is most often used when an administrator wants to just quickly translate a name into an address or vice versa. To run this version, issue the `nslookup` command using the following simple syntax:

```
nslookup <host> [<server>]
```

Here, *<host>* can be a DNS domain name, for performing a normal resolution, or it may be an IP address, for a reverse resolution to return the associated DNS domain name. The *<server>* parameter is optional; if it's omitted, the program uses the default name server of the host where the command was issued. Listing 88-3 shows a simple example of noninteractive use of `nslookup`.

```
D:\aa>nslookup www.pcguide.com
Server:  ns1-mar.starband.com
Address:  148.78.249.200

Non-authoritative answer:
Name:    pcguide.com
Address:  209.68.14.80
Aliases:  www.pcguide.com
```

Listing 88-3: *DNS name resolution using the nslookup utility*

This example was done on my home PC that uses the Starband satellite Internet service, which is configured to use Starband's name server (`ns1-mar.starband.com`). The answer provided here is labeled *non-authoritative*, because it came from the Starband name server's DNS cache, rather than one of the DNS name servers that is a DNS authority for www.pcguide.com.

NOTE *It is also possible to specify one or more options to modify the behavior of the lookup in noninteractive mode. These options are the same as the parameters controlled by the* `nslookup set` *command described in Table 88-5. They are specified by preceding them with a dash. For example,* `nslookup -timeout=10 www.pcguide.com` *would perform the same lookup as in Listing 88-3, but with the timeout interval set to 10 seconds.*

The interactive mode of `nslookup` is selected by simply issuing the name of the command with no parameters. This will cause the program to display the current default name server's DNS name and address, and then provide a prompt at which the administrator may enter commands. Interactive mode allows someone to perform multiple lookups easily without having to type `nslookup` each time. More important, it provides more convenient control over the types of information that can be requested and how the lookups are performed.

You can usually determine the exact command set available in an `nslookup` implementation by issuing the command `help` or `?` at the `nslookup` prompt. Table 88-5 shows some of the commands that are usually found in most `nslookup` implementations.

Table 88-5: Typical nslookup Utility Commands

Command and Parameters	Description
<host> [*<server>*]	Look up the specified host, optionally using the specified DNS name server. Note that there is no actual command here; you just enter the name directly at the command prompt.
server *<server>*	Change the default server to *<server>*, using information obtained from the current default server.
lserver *<server>*	Change the default server to *<server>*, using information obtained from the initial name server; that is, the system's default server that was in place when the nslookup command was started (prior to any preceding changes of the current name server in this session).
root	Changes the default name server to one of the DNS root name servers.
ls [-t *<type>*] *<name>*	Requests a list of information available for the specified domain name, by conducting a zone transfer. By default, the host names and addresses associated with the domain are listed; the -t option may be used to restrict the output to a particular record type. Other options may also be defined. (Most servers restrict the use of zone transfers to designated slave servers, so this command may not work for ordinary clients.)
help	Displays help information (usually a list of valid commands and options).
?	Same as help (works on only some systems).
set all	Displays the current value of all nslookup options.
set *<option>*[=*<value>*]	Sets an option to control the behavior of the utility. Most implementations include quite a number of options, some of which are controlled by just specifying a keyword, while others require a value for the option. For example, set recurse tells the program to use recursive resolution, while set norecurse turns it off. set retry=3 sets the number of retries to 3.
exit	Quits the program.

The nslookup utility is widely deployed on both UNIX and Windows systems, but the program is not without its critics. The complaints about it mainly center around its use of nonstandard methods of obtaining information, rather than standard resolution routines. I have also read reports that it can produce spurious results in some cases. One example of a significant problem with the command is that it will abort if it is unable to perform a reverse lookup of its own IP address. This can cause confusion, because users mistake that error for an error trying to find the name they were looking up. For this and other reasons, a number of people in UNIX circles consider nslookup to be a hack of sorts. In some newer UNIX systems, nslookup has been deprecated (still included in the operating system for compatibility, but not recommended and may be removed in the future). Instead, a pair of newer utilities is provided: host and dig.

The host Utility

The host utility is most often used for simple queries such as those normally performed using nslookup's noninteractive mode. It is invoked in the same way as noninteractive nslookup:

```
host <host> [<server>]
```

The output is also similar to that of noninteractive nslookup, but less verbose. Here is an example:

```
%host www.pcguide.com
www.pcguide.com is an alias for pcguide.com.
pcguide.com has address 209.68.14.80
```

Even though host does not operate interactively, it includes a number of options that can allow an administrator to get the same information that would have been obtained using nslookup's interactive mode. Some of the more common options are shown in Table 88-6.

Table 88-6: Typical host Utility Options and Parameters

Option/ Parameters	Description
-d	Turns on debug mode.
-l	Provides a complete list of information for a domain; this is similar to the ls command in interactive nslookup. This may be used with the -t option to select only a particular type of resource record for the domain.
-r	Disables recursion in the request. When this is specified, only the server directly queried will return any information; it will not query other servers.
-t <*query-type*>	Specifies a query for a particular resource record type, allowing any type of DNS information to be retrieved.
-v	Uses verbose mode for output (additional details are provided).
-w	Waits as long as necessary for a response (no timeout).

The dig Utility

The second alternative to `nslookup` is `dig`, which stands for Domain Information Groper (likely a play on the supposed origin of the name `ping`). It differs from the `host` command in that it provides considerably more information about a domain, even when invoked in the simplest of ways. It is also quite a bit more complicated, with a large number of options and features, such as a batch mode for obtaining information about many domains.

The basic syntax for the `dig` command is different from that of `nslookup` and `host`. If you specify a nondefault name server, it is prepended with an at sign (@) and comes before the host to be looked up. You can also specify a specific type of resource record, like this:

```
dig [@<server>] <host>  [<type>]
```

Listing 88-4 shows the output from running `dig` on the same domain (www.pcguide.com) that I used as an example for nslookup (Listing 88-3) and `host`. You can see that it provides much more information about the domain.

```
%dig www.pcguide.com
; <<>> DiG 9.2.1 <<>> www.pcguide.com
;; global options:  printcmd
;; Got answer:
;; ->>HEADER<<- opcode: QUERY, status: NOERROR, id: 15912
;; flags: qr rd ra; QUERY: 1, ANSWER: 2, AUTHORITY: 2, ADDITIONAL: 0
;; QUESTION SECTION:
;www.pcguide.com.               IN      A

;; ANSWER SECTION:
www.pcguide.com.        3600    IN      CNAME   pcguide.com.
pcguide.com.            3600    IN      A       209.68.14.80

;; AUTHORITY SECTION:
pcguide.com.            3600    IN      NS      ns0.ns0.com.
pcguide.com.            3600    IN      NS      ns23.pair.com.

;; Query time: 1840 msec
;; SERVER: 209.68.1.87#53(209.68.1.87)
;; WHEN: Tue Nov 18 16:05:08 2003
;; MSG SIZE  rcvd: 109Server:  ns1-mar.starband.com
```

Listing 88-4: *DNS name resolution using the nslookup utility*

NOTE *The* `dig` *utility is very useful, but has still not been implemented on some systems. Fortunately, there is an online* `dig` *utility you can access using your browser on the Internet. Find it at http://www.gont.com.ar/tools/dig.*

The dig command includes dozens of options and settings. Since this chapter is already getting very long and dig is by far the most advanced of the three utilities, I will stop here. Consult your system's documentation for the full instructions on how dig works and a list of its parameters.

> **KEY CONCEPT** Most TCP/IP implementations provide one or more utilities that can be employed by an administrator to manually resolve DNS domain names to IP addresses or perform related searches for DNS information. One of the most common is nslookup, which allows a host name to be translated to an address or vice versa; it has both interactive and noninteractive modes. On some operating systems, nslookup has been replaced by the host utility for simple DNS lookups and by the dig program for more detailed inspections of DNS resource information.

TCP/IP DNS Registry Database Lookup Utility (whois/nicname)

Utilities such as nslookup and host allow administrators to resolve a DNS domain name to an address and also view detailed information about a domain's resource records. There are cases, however, where administrators need to know its DNS registration information, rather technical information about a domain. This includes details such as which organization owns the domain, when its registration expires, and who are the designated contacts who manage it.

In the early days of DNS, all domain names were centrally registered by a single authority, called the Internet Network Information Center (InterNIC or just NIC). To allow Internet users to look up information about domains and contacts, InterNIC set up a special server. To allow users to retrieve information from this server, developers created a protocol called both nicname and whois. It was initially described in RFC 812 (in 1982) and then later in RFC 943 (in 1985). Over time, the name whois has become the preferred of the two, and it is the one used today for the utility program that allows an administrator to look up DNS registration data. (It can also be used to look up information about IP addresses, but is used for that purpose much less commonly.)

As the Internet grew and expanded, it moved away from having a single centralized authority. The modern Internet has a hierarchical structure of authorities that are responsible for registering domain names in different portions of the DNS name space. In recent years, this has been further complicated by the deregulation process that allows multiple registries for the generic top-level domains such as .COM, .NET, and .ORG. All of this means that more work is needed to look up domain registration information, since it is distributed across many databases on different servers.

To make it easier for administrators to find information about domains in this large distributed database, modern TCP/IP implementations generally come with an intelligent version of the whois utility. It is able to accept as input the name of a domain and automatically locate the appropriate registry in which that domain's information is located. The utility is usually used as follows:

```
whois [-h <whois-host>] <domain>
```

In this syntax, *<domain>* represents the name about which registration information is requested. The administrator can use the `-h` parameter to force the program to query a particular whois server, but again, this is usually not required. Some implementations also include other options that can be used to direct queries to particular registries.

Listing 88-5 shows the sample output of the `whois` command on a FreeBSD UNIX machine (I have stripped out some of the preliminary general information and legal disclaimers to shorten the listing).

```
%whois pcguide.com
Registrant:
  The PC Guide
  2080 Harwood Hill Road
  Bennington, VT 05201
  US

  ixl@fearn.pair.com
   +1.8025555555

Domain Name: PCGUIDE.COM

Administrative & Technical Contact:
  Charles Kozierok
  The PC Guide
  2080 Harwood Hill Road
  Bennington, VT 05201
  US

  ixl@fearn.pair.com
   +1.8025555555

Domain Name Servers:
  NS23.PAIR.COM
  NS0.NS0.COM

 Created:     August 25, 1997
Modified:     July  7, 2003
 Expires:     August 24, 2008

** Register Now at http://www.pairNIC.com/ **
```

Listing 88-5: *DNS domain registry lookup using the whois program*

In this case, the registrar of the domain pcguide.com is pairNIC, the DNS registry division of pair Networks, the company I have used for web hosting for many years (since 1997, as you can see). This output is public information and lets anyone who has an interest in pcguide.com determine that I own the domain and learn how to contact me. (No, 555-5555 is not my real phone number.) It also tells them that pair Networks runs the name servers that contain domain information for my domain.

Many operating systems, including Windows, do not come with a `whois` command implementation, but there are third-party programs that will support the function. In recent years, many different organizations have also set up websites that implement the `whois` function, which is much more convenient and user-friendly to those more accustomed to graphical user interface operating systems like Windows. Many of these sites are provided as free services by DNS registrars, so customers can check if a name they are interested in is already taken, and if so, by whom.

One drawback of some of these systems is that they usually do not have the intelligence to check all the different registries where domain name records are stored. In most cases, a `whois` service provided by a registrar will search for names only in the particular top-level domains in which the registrar operates. So, if the registrar deals with .COM, .ORG, and .NET, it may support `whois` queries only for those top-level domains. To check the registration information for domains in more obscure domains, such as some of the less common geopolitical (country code) domains, a considerable amount of searching may be required.

> **KEY CONCEPT** The TCP/IP `whois` utility allows registration information to be displayed for a DNS domain, such as its owner, contact information, and the date that its registration expires. The program is most commonly found on UNIX operating systems, where it is given intelligence that allows it to automatically query the correct servers to find the information for most domains. Newer Web-based `whois` utilities also exist, but they are usually limited to displaying information about domains in only a specific subset of top-level domains.

TCP/IP Network Status Utility (netstat)

Given how complex TCP/IP is, it's actually quite amazing that most of the time, all of the different protocols, services, and programs perform their jobs both efficiently and silently. Most of us don't even realize just how much is going on in the background, and that's as it should be. On the other hand, when a problem does occur on a TCP/IP network, the administrator charged with fixing it needs to obtain as much information as possible about what all those bits and pieces of the suite are doing behind the scenes. The network status utility, `netstat`, serves this purpose.

The `netstat` program is very simple in concept, being designed for only one purpose: to show information about the operation of TCP/IP on a device. The complexity of TCP/IP, however, leads to `netstat` being rather elaborate itself. The program can provide a large variety of information. As usual, the options and output of `netstat` depend on the particular operating system type and version. It is somewhat different on UNIX and Windows machines, so I will describe each platform's version separately.

The UNIX netstat Utility

On most UNIX systems, the netstat utility is very full-featured, with a typical implementation including dozens of options that can be used to control what information is displayed. These options may not all be used simultaneously; rather, they are arranged into option groups, each of which presents one class of information. Within each group, one option is mandatory, and that is the one that identifies the group, and hence the general kind of information that will be displayed. Other options are also possible in each group, which are optional and modify the command to provide better control of exactly what is output. In essence, netstat is like many related utilities rolled into one.

Table 88-7 provides a simplified summary of the option groups for a typical UNIX netstat implementation, in this case FreeBSD.

Table 88-7: Typical UNIX netstat Option Groups, Options, and Parameters

Option Group, Options, and Parameters	Description
netstat [-AaLSW] [-f <*family*>] [-p <*protocol*>] [-n]	Default invocation of netstat, with no mandatory options. It prompts the utility to display a list of active sockets on the host machine. The other options shown can be used to control what precisely is output; for example, -a also shows server processes.
netstat -i [-abdt] [-f <*family*>] [-n] netstat -I <*interface*> [-abdt] [-f <*family*>] [-n]	Tells netstat to provide information about all network interfaces (-i) or a particular network interface (-I <*interface*>). The -a option shows multicast addresses as well, -b displays bytes of data in and out on the interface, -d shows the number of dropped packets, and -t displays the value of watchdog timers.
netstat -w <*interval*> -d [-I <*interface*>]	Displays packet traffic information on all interfaces every <*interval*> seconds, or just on the specified interface if -I <*interface*> is included. If -d is included, it also indicates the number of dropped packets.
netstat -s [-s] [-z] [-f <*family*>] [-p <*protocol*>]	Shows systemwide statistics for each of the protocols on the system (which may be modified to show information for only a particular address family or protocol). If the -s option is repeated, counters that have a value of zero are suppressed. The -z option resets the statistics after they are displayed.
netstat -i -s [-f <*family*>] [-p <*protocol*>] netstat -I <*interface*> -s [-f <*family*>] [-p <*protocol*>]	Displays statistics as for netstat -s, but on a per-interface basis rather than aggregated for the whole system.
netstat -m	Outputs memory management routine statistics.
netstat -r [-Aa] [-f <*family*>] [-n] [-W]	Displays the contents of the host's routing tables. The options -A and -a provide additional information about the routes.
netstat -rs [-s]	Displays routing statistics. The -s option suppresses counters with a zero value.
netstat -g [-W] [-f <*family*>]	Shows multicast routing information.
netstat -gs [-s] [-f <*family*>]	Shows multicast routing statistics. The -s option suppresses counters with a zero value.

Most of the options shown in the option groups in Table 88-7 are particular to those groups; for example, you cannot use -s when issuing the command netstat -i. However, there are also a number of universal options that can be used with more than one of these groups to modify the behavior of netstat variations in a consistent way. These options are described in Table 88-8.

Table 88-8: Typical UNIX netstat Universal Options and Parameters

Option/ Parameters	Description
-f <*family*>	Limits the output of the command to information on a particular protocol address family, for hosts running multiple protocol suites. For example, the address family for regular TCP/IP is inet; for IPv6, it is inet6. Others may also be supported.
-p <*protocol*>	Restricts output to data related only to a particular protocol, such as IP, TCP, UDP, or ICMP.
-n	Shows network addresses in numeric form, instead of showing them as symbolic names. Also shows ports as numbers instead of converting well-known UDP and TCP port numbers to the protocol names that use them (for example, 23 rather than telnet).
-W	Suppresses the automatic truncation of addresses (which is sometimes done for display formatting).

The netstat command can produce a startling amount of output, especially if you do not restrict it with some of the options in Table 88-8. This is particularly true for netstat by itself and with the -s option. Listing 88-6 shows sample output from running "plain" netstat, but I have truncated the list of connections so it would not be too long (I also reformatted the listing so it would fit on the page better). Notice the last column, which shows the current state of the TCP connection (see the TCP finite state machine description in Chapter 47).

```
%netstat
Active Internet connections
Prot  Rcv  Snd  Local Address     Foreign Address        (state)
tcp4  0    0    pcguide.com.http  c-24-118-141-124.3384  ESTABLISHED
tcp4  0    827  pcguide.com.http  webcacheB03a.cac.46075 ESTABLISHED
tcp4  0    0    qs36.smtp         MV1-24.171.17.64.1339  ESTABLISHED
tcp4  0    0    pcguide.com.http  1Cust234.tnt1.le.1338  ESTABLISHED
tcp4  0    0    pcguide.com.http  1Cust234.tnt1.le.1337  FIN_WAIT_1
tcp4  0    84   pcguide.com.http  dial81-131-97-70.2902  FIN_WAIT_1
tcp4  0    0    pcguide.com.http  216.76.14.221.9954     FIN_WAIT_2
tcp4  0    0    pcguide.com.http  216.76.14.221.9945     FIN_WAIT_2
tcp4  0    0    pcguide.com.http  1Cust234.tnt1.le.1326  TIME_WAIT
```

Listing 88-6: *Sample connections list from the UNIX netstat utility*

Listing 88-7 shows an example of the output of netstat -s. Here, I have limited the output by using -p ip to tell the program to show me only the statistics for IP.

```
%netstat -s -p ip
ip:
        57156204 total packets received
        0 bad header checksums
        4 with size smaller than minimum
        0 with data size < data length
        0 with ip length > max ip packet size
        0 with header length < data size
        0 with data length < header length
        0 with bad options
```

```
0 with incorrect version number
138 fragments received
6 fragments dropped (dup or out of space)
128 fragments dropped after timeout
2 packets reassembled ok
57085912 packets for this host
24736 packets for unknown/unsupported protocol
0 packets forwarded (0 packets fast forwarded)
44957 packets not forwardable
4 packets received for unknown multicast group
0 redirects sent
66183465 packets sent from this host
177 packets sent with fabricated ip header
0 output packets dropped due to no bufs, etc.
0 output packets discarded due to no route
0 output datagrams fragmented
0 fragments created
0 datagrams that can't be fragmented
0 tunneling packets that can't find gif
22 datagrams with bad address in header
```

Listing 88-7: *Sample IP statistics from the UNIX netstat utility*

The Windows netstat Utility

The Windows netstat utility is quite a bit simpler than the UNIX one, because it has a lot fewer options. This is good news for those learning about the program, but not so wonderful for those who want maximum power and flexibility in using it.

Like the UNIX netstat version, the Windows utility has a set of options groups that dictate the general type of information shown, and a few universal options that can be used with multiple groups. The option groups and generic options are shown in Tables 88-9 and 88-10, respectively.

Table 88-9: Typical Windows netstat Option Groups, Options, and Parameters

Option Group, Options, and Parameters	Description
`netstat [-n] [-o] [<interval>]` `netstat -a [-n] [-o]`	When called with no mandatory options, `netstat` displays information about active TCP connections.
`[-p <protocol> [<interval>]`	Displays all active TCP connections, as well as both TCP and UDP ports to which the host is listening.
`netstat -e [<interval>]`	Shows statistics for Ethernet interfaces.
`netstat -r [<interval>]`	Displays the current routing table for the device.
`netstat -s [-p <protocol>] [<interval>]`	Displays TCP/IP statistics for the system by protocol.

Table 88-10: Typical Windows netstat Universal Options and Parameters

Option/ Parameters	Description
`-n`	Displays network addresses in numeric form instead of symbolic name form. Also shows ports in numeric form instead of displaying standard process names associated with well-known UDP or TCP port numbers.
`-o`	Displays the process ID associated with each connection.
`-p` *<protocol>*	Limits the display to only the information associated with the specified protocol.
<interval>	Causes the `netstat` command to be repeated every *<interval>* seconds, rather than just displaying its information once. This can be used with any of the `netstat` option groups. For example, `netstat -s 5` displays TCP/IP statistics every 5 seconds.

The output from the Windows `netstat` program is fairly similar to that of the UNIX utility when the same or similar options are given, but the UNIX version usually provides more details. Listing 88-8 shows an example illustrating TCP/IP statistics on my home Windows XP machine, using `-p icmp` to restrict the output to ICMP statistics only.

```
D:\aa>netstat -s -p icmp
ICMPv4 Statistics

                            Received    Sent
  Messages                  243         248
  Errors                    0           0
  Destination Unreachable   9           4
  Time Exceeded             7           0
  Parameter Problems        0           0
  Source Quenches           0           0
  Redirects                 0           0
  Echos                     224         20
  Echo Replies              3           224
  Timestamps                0           0
  Timestamp Replies         0           0
  Address Masks             0           0
  Address Mask Replies      0           0
```

Listing 88-8: *Sample ICMP statistics from the Windows netstat utility*

Listing 88-9 shows the routing table display from `netstat` (which I modified slightly to fit the page). You would get similar output using the UNIX `netstat -s -p icmp` or `netstat -r` command, but with additional information.

```
D:\aa>netstat -r
Route Table
===================================================================
Interface List
0x1 ........................... MS TCP Loopback interface
0x2 ...00 04 76 4e 75 3f ...... 3Com 10/100 Mini PCI Ethernet
```

```
===========================================================================
===========================================================================
Active Routes:
  Network Dest      Netmask           Gateway        Interface      Met
  0.0.0.0           0.0.0.0           148.64.128.1   148.64.133.73   30
  127.0.0.0         255.0.0.0         127.0.0.1      127.0.0.1       1
  148.64.128.0      255.255.192.0     148.64.133.73  148.64.133.73   30
  148.64.133.73     255.255.255.255   127.0.0.1      127.0.0.1       30
  148.64.255.255    255.255.255.255   148.64.133.73  148.64.133.73   30
  224.0.0.0         240.0.0.0         148.64.133.73  148.64.133.73   30
  255.255.255.255   255.255.255.255   148.64.133.73  148.64.133.73   1
Default Gateway:       148.64.128.1
===========================================================================
Persistent Routes:
  None
```

Listing 88-9: *Sample routing table display from the Windows netstat utility*

> **KEY CONCEPT** TCP/IP implementations include the `netstat` utility to allow information about network status to be displayed. On UNIX systems, `netstat` is a full-featured program with many options arranged into option groups, each of which shows a particular type of information about the operation of TCP/IP protocols. On Windows systems, `netstat` is somewhat more limited in function, but it still can display a considerable amount of information.

TCP/IP Configuration Utilities (ifconfig, ipconfig, and winipcfg)

A significant part of any network administrator's job is setting up and maintaining the devices that make a TCP/IP network function, a process generally called *configuration*. Networked hosts consist of both hardware and software that work together to implement all the layers and functions of the protocol stack. An administrator uses hardware tools to configure physical devices, performing tasks such as installing network interface cards, connecting cables, and manipulating switches and other hardware settings. Similarly, administrators need tools to configure the software that runs TCP/IP interfaces and controls the operation of higher-layer protocols on networked hosts. UNIX administrators use the `ifconfig` utility. On Windows NT, 2000, and XP, the configuration tool is `ipconfig`. Earlier versions of Windows have the `winipcfg` utility.

The ifconfig Utility for UNIX

On UNIX systems, administrators use the interface configuration utility, `ifconfig`, to view and modify the software settings that control how TCP/IP functions on a host. It is a very powerful program that allows an administrator to set up and manage a very wide array of network settings. The implementation of `ifconfig` varies greatly between flavors of UNIX; while most are similar in general terms, they may have different options and syntaxes.

You can use the ifconfig program for a variety of purposes: to create or remove a network interface, change its settings, or simply examine the existing configuration. Thus, like the netstat utility, ifconfig is like several related programs combined into one, and how it works depends on the syntax you used to invoke it. And also like netstat, ifconfig has a number of universal options that can be applied to many of its different uses.

Table 88-11 provides a simplified summary of the different functions that ifconfig can perform and the syntaxes that are used to specify each in a typical UNIX implementation (NetBSD in this case). You can use ifconfig to modify an interface's configuration by setting any of several dozen configuration parameters, using the syntax shown in the last row of that table. Table 88-12 describes the common options and parameters that can be used for many of these different modes. I have provided a brief description of some sample parameters in Table 88-13 (see your ifconfig documentation for a complete list).

Table 88-11: Typical UNIX ifconfig Syntaxes, Options, and Parameters

Syntax, Options and Parameters	Description
ifconfig [-L] [-m] *<interface>*	When ifconfig is called with just an interface specification and no other options (other than possibly -L and -m), it displays the configuration information for that network interface. Note that entering ifconfig by itself with no interface displays just help information for the parameter. To see all interfaces, use the -a parameter.
ifconfig -a [-L] [-m] [-b] [-d] [-u] [-s] [*<family>*]	Displays information about all the interfaces on the host. The output may be restricted using the universal parameters shown or by specifying an address family (see Table 88-12).
ifconfig -l [-b] [-d] [-u] [-s]	Lists all available interfaces on the system.
ifconfig *<interface>* create	Creates the specified logical network interface on the host, which is then configured using the syntax shown in the last row of this table. Note that some variations of UNIX allow certain parameters to be set at the time of creation.
ifconfig *<interface>* destroy	Destroys the specified logical interface.
ifconfig *<interface>* [*<family>*] [*<address>* [*<dest-address>*]] [*<parameters>*]	Configures parameters for a particular interface on the host. If the address is being set, it is the first parameter specified, after the optional address family, if present. The <dest-address> is used to specify a destination address for a point-to-point link. After this, any of several dozen parameters may be specified for the interface, some of which are shown in Table 88-13.

Table 88-12: Typical UNIX ifconfig Universal Options and Parameters

Option/Parameter	Description
-L	Displays the address lifetime for IPv6 addresses.
-m	Displays all supported media for the interface.
-b	Limits the display of interface information to broadcast interfaces.
-d	Shows only interfaces that are presently down (disabled).
-u	Shows only interfaces that are presently up (operational).

(continued)

Table 88-12: Typical UNIX ifconfig Universal Options and Parameters (continued)

Option/Parameter	Description
`-s`	Shows only interfaces that may be connected.
`<family>`	Specifies a particular address family, either to limit output or indicate what address type is being configured. The value `inet` is used for IPv4 and `inet6` for IPv6.

Table 88-13: Typical UNIX ifconfig Interface Configuration Parameters

Parameters	Description
`alias / -alias`	Establishes or removes a network address alias.
`arp / -arp`	Enables or disables the use of ARP on this interface.
`delete`	Removes the specified network address.
`down`	Marks an interface as being down, disabling it.
`media <type>`	Sets the media type of the interface to a particular value.
`mtu <n>`	Sets the maximum transmission unit (MTU) of the interface.
`netmask <mask>`	Sets the network or subnet mask for the interface's address.
`prefixlen <n>`	Same as `netmask` but allows the mask to be specified using a CIDR-style prefix length.
`up`	Sets an interface up, enabling it.

NOTE *Since creating, destroying, or modifying interfaces can cause a host to stop working properly, administrative (superuser) rights are generally required on most systems in order to do anything with* `ifconfig` *other than examining the existing configuration.*

Listing 88-10 shows sample output of the `ifconfig -a` command on one of the UNIX machines I use regularly, showing the settings for its interfaces.

```
%ifconfig -a
fxp0: flags=8843<UP,BROADCAST,RUNNING,SIMPLEX,MULTICAST> mtu 1500
  address: 00:a0:c9:8c:f4:a1
  media: Ethernet autoselect (100baseTX full-duplex)
  status: active
  inet 166.84.1.3 netmask 0xffffffe0 broadcast 166.84.1.31
  inet alias 166.84.1.13 netmask 0xffffffff broadcast 166.84.1.13
lo0: flags=8009<UP,LOOPBACK,MULTICAST> mtu 33228
  inet 127.0.0.1 netmask 0xff000000
```

Listing 88-10: *Sample output of the UNIX ifconfig -a command*

The ipconfig for Windows NT, 2000, and XP

Windows takes a somewhat different approach to network configuration than UNIX. As described in the previous section, you can use the UNIX `ifconfig` program both to view and modify a wide range of configuration parameters. In Windows, however, most setup and parameter modification is done using the Windows Control Panel. Windows does include a utility that is somewhat similar to UNIX's `ifconfig`, but it has far less functionality and is used mainly to inspect the existing configuration, not change it. It also allows an administrator to easily perform a few simple functions on a host.

On Windows NT, 2000, and XP, the equivalent of ifconfig is a command-line utility called ipconfig. Like ifconfig, the Windows utility is controlled using options that are supplied to the program. However, because it is so much simpler than ifconfig, there are only a few options, as summarized in Table 88-14.

Table 88-14: Typical Windows ipconfig Options and Parameters

Option/Parameters	Description
(none)	When called with no options or parameters, ipconfig displays the IP address, subnet mask, and default gateway for each interface on the host.
/all	Similar to calling ipconfig with no options, but displays more detailed configuration information about the host's interfaces.
/release [<*adapter*>]	Releases (terminates) the DHCP lease on either the specified adapter (interface) or all interfaces, if none is provided.
/renew [<*adapter*>]	Manually renews the DHCP lease for either the specified adapter (interface) or all adapters, if none is mentioned.
/displaydns	Displays the contents of the host's DNS resolver cache.
/flushdns	Clears the host's DNS resolver cache.
/registerdns	Refreshes (renews) all DHCP leases and also reregisters any DNS names associated with the host.
/showclassid <*adapter*>	Displays DHCP class IDs associated with this adapter (these are used to arrange clients into groups that are given different treatment by DHCP servers). The adapter must be specified, even if there is only one.
/setclassid <*adapter*> [<*classid*>]	Modifies the DHCP class ID for the specified adapter.

As mentioned earlier, ipconfig is most often used to just examine the existing configuration. You can see from the list of options in Table 88-14 that most of the other uses of ipconfig are related to controlling the operation of protocols such as DNS and the Dynamic Host Configuration Protocol (DHCP), rather than configuring a host. One common use of ipconfig is to force a host to seek out a new DHCP lease, which can be done using ipconfig /release followed by ipconfig /renew.

Listing 88-11 shows an example of the output from using the ipconfig command without any options. For detailed information on interfaces, you can use the /all option, as shown in the example in Listing 88-12 (which I've modified slightly so it is easier to read).

```
D:\aa>ipconfig
Windows IP Configuration


Ethernet adapter Local Area Connection 2:

        Connection-specific DNS Suffix  . :
        IP Address. . . . . . . . . . . . : 148.64.133.73
```

```
        Subnet Mask . . . . . . . . . . . : 255.255.192.0
        Default Gateway . . . . . . . . . : 148.64.128.1
```

Listing 88-11: *Simplified configuration information from the Windows ipconfig utility*

```
D:\aa>ipconfig /all
Windows IP Configuration

   Host Name . . . . . . . . . . . . : ixl
   Primary Dns Suffix  . . . . . . . :
   Node Type . . . . . . . . . . . . : Hybrid
   IP Routing Enabled. . . . . . . . : No
   WINS Proxy Enabled. . . . . . . . : No

Ethernet adapter Local Area Connection 2:

   Connection-specific DNS Suffix  . :
   Description . . . . . . . . . . . : 3Com PCI Ethernet Adapter
   Physical Address. . . . . . . . . : 00-04-76-4E-75-3F
   Dhcp Enabled. . . . . . . . . . . : Yes
   Autoconfiguration Enabled . . . . : Yes
   IP Address. . . . . . . . . . . . : 148.64.133.73
   Subnet Mask . . . . . . . . . . . : 255.255.192.0
   Default Gateway . . . . . . . . . : 148.64.128.1
   DHCP Server . . . . . . . . . . . : 148.64.128.1
   DNS Servers . . . . . . . . . . . : 148.78.249.200
                                       148.78.249.201
   Lease Obtained. . . . . . . . . . : April 19, 2003 11:51:37 AM
   Lease Expires . . . . . . . . . . : April 19, 2003 12:21:37 PM
```

Listing 88-12: *Detailed configuration information from the Windows ipconfig utility*

The winipcfg Utility for Windows 95, 98, and Me

Windows 95, 98, and Me have a graphical tool called `winipcfg`, instead of the `ipconfig` command-line utility. This program allows you to examine the configuration parameters in much the same way as `ipconfig`, and also to release and renew DHCP leases, but it does not support the other options of `ipconfig` (such as displaying the host's DNS cache). An example of the main `winipcfg` screen is shown in Figure 88-2.

> **KEY CONCEPT** On UNIX systems, the `ifconfig` utility can be used to display or modify a large number of TCP/IP configuration settings. Windows systems provide either the command-line utility `ipconfig` or the graphical tool `winipcfg`. Both let an administrator see basic TCP/IP configuration information for a host and allow tasks to be performed such as renewing a DHCP lease, but they are otherwise quite limited compared with the UNIX `ifconfig` program.

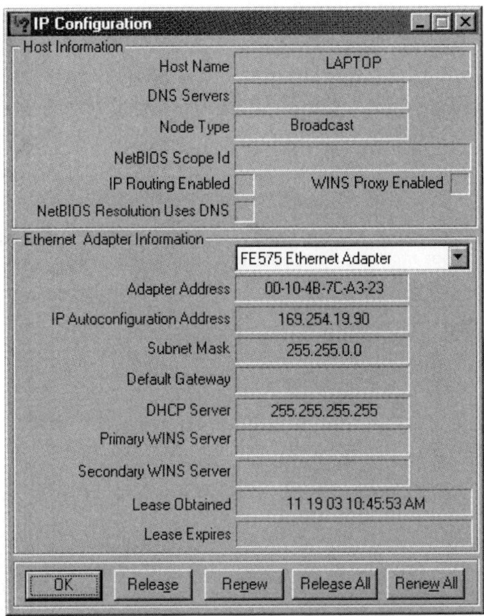

Figure 88-2: Windows 95/98/Me winipcfg utility *The* `winipcfg` *utility can be used in older, consumer-oriented versions of Windows to check the configuration of a host and release/renew DHCP leases.*

Miscellaneous TCP/IP Troubleshooting Protocols

As soon as you set up a network, it will very quickly develop problems that you will need to address. Recognizing that the complexity of TCP/IP internetworks would make diagnosing certain problems difficult, the suite's architects defined a number of miscellaneous utility protocols that can be helpful in testing and troubleshooting networks. Despite having been around for more than 20 years, these protocols are somewhat obscure and get little attention. However, even though they are no longer implemented on many systems, I feel they are worth a quick look.

These simple protocols are designed to be implemented as services that run on TCP/IP servers. Each listens for requests on a dedicated well-known port number and then responds with a particular type of information. These protocols can be used with both TCP and UDP, enabling each transport protocol to be tested. In the case of UDP, the server counts each UDP datagram sent to it as a request and sends a response to it. When used with TCP, a connection is first established by the client to the server. In some of the protocols, this connection is then used to send data continuously between the client and server; in others, the establishment of the connection is considered an implied request to the server, which will immediately send a response and then close the connection.

Table 88-15 provides a brief description of each of these troubleshooting protocols under both UDP and TCP. I have shown for each the port number that the service uses and also the RFC that defines it.

Table 88-15: Miscellaneous TCP/IP Troubleshooting Protocols

Protocol	Well-Known Port Number	Defining RFC	Description
Echo Protocol	7	862	Echoes received data back to its originator. When used on UDP, the payload of each message is simply packaged into a return UDP datagram and sent back. For TCP, each byte sent by the client is echoed back by the server until the connection is closed.
Discard Protocol	9	863	Throws away all data that is sent to it.
Character Generator Protocol	19	864	Generates random characters of data and sends them to a device. When used with UDP, each UDP message sent to the server causes it to send back a UDP message containing a random amount (0 to 512 bytes) of data. When used with TCP, the server just starts sending characters as soon as a client establishes a connection, and continues until the connection is terminated by the client.
Quote of the Day Protocol	17	865	Sends a short message (selected by the server's administrator) to a client device. For UDP, the message is sent for each incoming UDP message; for TCP, the message is sent by the server once when the connection is established, which is then closed.
Active Users	11	866	Sends a list of active users to a device. For UDP, the list is sent for each incoming UDP message; if it is longer than 512 bytes, it will be sent in multiple messages. For TCP, the list is sent automatically when the connection is made to the server, and then the connection is terminated.
Daytime Protocol	13	867	Returns the current time on the server in human-readable form, in response to receipt of a UDP message or an incoming TCP connection.
Time Protocol	37	868	Returns the current time in machine-readable form—specifically, the number of seconds since midnight, January 1, 1900 GMT. The time is sent for each UDP message received by the server or upon establishment of a TCP connection. Note that this protocol cannot be used for time synchronization of servers, because it does not compensate for variability in the time required for the messages to be carried over the internetwork.

INDEX

Numbers in *italics* refer to tables; numbers in **bold** refer to figures.

Numbers

100BASE-TX Fast Ethernet, 34
100VG-AnyLAN, 47
127.0.0.1, IPv4 loopback address, 266
30-Second Timer, RIP, 605
64-bit extended unique identifier. *See* EUI-64
6BONE experimental IPv6 network, 370
7-bit and 8-bit message encoding, MIME, 1258

A

AAAA (IPv6 Address) DNS resource record, 949
abbreviation, of URLs, 1156
absolute and relative domain names, DNS, 865
abstraction level, OSI Reference Model layers, 88
Accept, 1361
Accept-Charset, 1362
Accept-Encoding, 1362
Accept-Language, 1362
Accept-Ranges, 1364
access and retrieval
  email, 1285
  Usenet articles, 1403
access control commands, FTP, 1185
Access, MIB object characteristic, 1088
accredited registrars for DNS name registration, 877
Accredited Standards Committee X3, Information Technology, 50
ACFC (Address and Control Field Compression), 158, 186
ACK, 747, 753
acknowledgment ambiguity, TCP, 804
Acknowledgment messages, TFTP, 1213, *1213*
Acknowledgment Number, 784
active and passive opens, 751
active data connections, 1178
adaptive retransmission, 803
address allocation, 1000
Address and Control Field Compression (ACFC)
  PPP LCP option, 158
  use in PPP, 186
address books, 1230
address classes, 256
address designations, 214
address embedding, 392
address hexadecimal notation, 378
Address Mask Request and Address Mask Reply messages, ICMP4, 543, *544*
address ranges (scopes), 1009
address resolution, 203, 204
  at layers 2 and 3, 204
  direct mapping, 206, **207**
    ARCNet example, 207
    problems with large hardware address size, **208**
  dynamic, 209, **210**
    caching, 211
  email addressing and, 1226
  IP. *See* ARP
  IPv6, 224

address resolution, *continued*
MAC addresses and, 205
methods, 206
multicast
IEEE 802 addresses, 223
organizationally unique identifier (OUI), 223
Address Resolution Protocol. *See* ARP
Address Resolution Protocol utility (arp), 1471
Address resource record, DNS, 937, *937*, 946
address size
IP, 245
IPv6, 376
address space
IP, 246
IPv6, 376
allocation of, 381
address terminology, IP NAT, 430
address types, IPv6, 375
Address Unreachable, 549
addressing, 565
ARP, 214
BOOTP, 980
classful, 258, **259**
classless, 281
email. *See* email: addressing
hardware, 104, 244
IP. *See* IP: address
IPv6. *See* IPv6: address
MAC, 205
mailing list, 1231
Mobile IP, 483
multicast, 22
unicast, 22
Usenet, 1404
World Wide Web, 1326
adjacent layer communication (interfaces), OSI Reference Model, 91
Adj-RIBs-In, 656
Adj-RIBs-Out, 656
administration
DHCP servers, 1015
DNS name servers, 889
SNMP, 1075
administration and troubleshooting utilities and protocols, 1461
administrative contact, DNS domain contacts, 896
administratively scoped IP multicast addresses, 269
ADSL (Asymmetric Digital Subscriber Line), 41
Advanced Research Projects Agency. *See* ARPA
.AERO generic TLD, 872
Age, HTTP response header, 1364
agent
BOOTP relay/forwarding. *See* BOOTP: relay agent
DHCP relay. *See* DHCP: relaying
Mobile IP. *See* Mobile IP: agent
SNMP, 1073
agent-driven negotiation, HTTP, 1378
aggregation, route, CIDR, 359
AH (Authentication Header). *See* IPsec, AH
algorithms and metrics, in routing protocols, 594
algorithms, encryption/hashing, in IPsec, 453
aliases (CNAME resource records), DNS, 920
aliases and address books, email, 1230
all ones and zeros
IP addresses, 263
IP subnets, 285
allocation
DHCP leases, **1025**
DHCP address. *See* DHCP
IPv6 address space, 381
Allow, HTTP entity header, 1366
alpha, smoothing factor for TCP RTT calculation, 804
alt, Usenet newsgroup hierarchy, 1406
Alternate Checksum Request, 759, 773
Alternate Checksum, 773
American National Standards Institute (ANSI), 50
American Registry for Internet Numbers (ARIN), 56
analog information, 62
AND Boolean logical function, 74
clearing bits with, 76, *77*
truth table, *74*
anonymous FTP, 1177

ANSI (American National Standards Institute), 50
any state commands, IMAP, 1304, *1304*
anycast address. *See* IPv6: address
anycast routing, 421
API (application program interface), 109
APIPA (Automatic Private IP Addressing), DHCP. *See* DHCP
application and service parameters, *1049*
application categories, 1164
Application Layer
  OSI Reference Model. *See* OSI Reference Model
  TCP/IP model, 130
  TCP/IP protocol summary, 133
  TCP/IP protocols at, 821
application media type, MIME, 1251
application program interface (API). *See* API
applications
  direct and indirect methods, 1170
  general file transfer, 1164
  SNMP, 1073
  TCP, 691, 742
  TCP/IP, 707
  Telnet, 1440
  UDP, 692, 717
  using both TCP and UDP, 718
architecture
  DNS name, 858
  DNS name server, 888
  IPsec. *See* IPsec: architectures
  name, 831
  NFS, 957
  PPP, 145, **145**
  PPP Multilink Protocol (MP), 176
  routing protocol, 591
  SNMP Framework, 1076
  TCP/IP, 119
ARCNet, and direct mapping address resolution, 207
area border routers, OSPF, 631
area directors, IETF working groups, 53
areas, OSPF, 630
ARIN (American Registry for Internet Numbers), 56
arithmetic, 72
arp (Address Resolution Protocol utility), 1471
ARP (Address Resolution Protocol), 212, 214
  address designations, 214
  caching, 218
  gratuitous, 499
  messages
    format, 216, *217*, **218**
    Request and Reply, 214
  Mobile IP interaction, 498
  proxy ARP, 221, **222**
    Mobile IP and, 499, **500**
  role in IP datagram delivery, 354
  transaction process, **215**
ARPA (Advanced Research Projects Agency)
  ARPAnet, 122, 842, 1170
  ARPAnet host name lists, 842
  Network Control Protocol (NCP), 720, 1170
  security issues, 450
  TCP/IP history and, 122, 720
.ARPA generic TLD, 872
ARPAnet. *See* ARPA
article propagation, NNTP, **1415**
articles, Usenet. *See* Usenet
AS (autonomous system)
  BGP. *See* BGP
  routers, 593
  routing architecture, 592
ASCII control codes, 1445
ASCII data type, 1183
ASN.1, SNMP use of, 1116
Asymmetric Digital Subscriber Line (ADSL), 41
asymmetry, 41
Asynchronous Transfer Mode. *See* ATM
ATM (Asynchronous Transfer Mode)
  IP and, 17
  PPP over ATM (PPPoA), 146
  quality of service and, 44
attachments, 1243
audio media type, 1250
AUTH extension, 1281
Authenticate-Ack messages, 162
Authenticated state, 1301
  commands, 1307, *1308*
Authenticate-Nak, 162

Authenticate-Request, 162
authentication
DHCP, 1064
ESP. *See* IPsec
FTP, 1175
HTTP, 1389
HTTP proxy servers, 1388
IMAP, 1306
OSPF message, 639
POP-before-SMTP, 1278
PPP, 162
RIP-2, 618
RIPng, 621
Authentication Header, 461
Authentication phase, 149
Authentication Protocol, 158
authorities
DNS, 868
Internet registration, 55
IP address, 252
authority, 882
Authorization state, 1290
Authorization, 1362
autoconfiguration
DHCP, 1058
IPv6, 399
ND, 583
automatic allocation, DHCP, 1002
Automatic Private IP Addressing. *See* DHCP
autonomous system (AS) routing architecture, 592, **594**

B

backbone routers and topology, OSPF, 631
backbone, Usenet, 1413
BACP (PPP Bandwidth Allocation Control Protocol), 178–179
Bad Length, 534
bandwidth, 35
Bandwidth Allocation Control Protocol, 178
Bandwidth Allocation Protocol, 178
bandwidth reservation, 44
BAP (PPP Bandwidth Allocation Protocol), 178–179
base 2 numbers, 65
base 8 numbers, 67
base 10 numbers, 65
base 16 numbers, 67
base64, MIME encoding method, 1258, *1259*
base URLs, 1150
basic rate interface (BRI), 175
basic topology, OSPF, 628
Baudot, Jean-Maurice-Émile, 38
baud, 38
BBS (bulletin board system), 1458
Bell Laboratories, 1398
Bellman-Ford routing protocol algorithm, 594
Berkeley Remote (r) Commands, 1454
Berkeley Standard Distribution (BSD), UNIX
ephemeral port number ranges, 704
popularized RIP, 614
Berners-Lee, Tim, 1318
Best Current Practice, RFC category, 58
best-effort, description of IP, 237
BGP (Border Gateway Protocol), 647, 648
algorithm, 657
AS (autonomous system)
internal peer, 652
multihomed, 654
routing policies, 654
stub, 654
transit, 655
types, 654
border routers, 652
connection establishment, 662
decision process, 659
error reporting, 663
external BGP (EBGP), 652
functions and features, 650
hold timer, 672
hybrid routing protocol algorithm, 595
Internal BGP (IBGP), 652
limitations on efficient route selection, 661
Marker field, 665
message generation and transport, 663
messages
general format, 664, *664*, **665**

BGP, *continued*
messages, *continued*
Keepalive, 672, *673*, **673**
Notification, 673, 674, **674,** *675*
Open, 666, *666*, 667, **668**
Update, *671*, 667, 668, *669*, **670**
messaging, 662
neighbors and peers, 652
operation, 662, 663
path attributes, 659, *659*
route determination, 659
route information exchange, 662
route storage, 656
router roles, 652
routing information bases (RIBs), 656
routing policy issues, 655
speakers, 652
standards, *649*, *650*
topology, 651, **653**
traffic flow and types, 653
versions, 649, *649*
BGP-4. *See* BGP
bidirectional, IP NAT, 437–439
Big Eight newsgroup hierarchies, 1405
billing contact, 896
binary
addition, *72*
arithmetic, 72
conversion from decimal to, 70
digit (bit), 63
information, 62
group representations and terms, 63, *63*, **64**
transistors and, 62
notation, IP addresses, 245
numbers, decimal equivalent, 65, *66*
octal and hexadecimal digit conversion, *68*
representation of IPv6 addresses, **378**
representation of DNS resource records, 890
units, 38
bis, 1300
bit (binary digit), 63
bit mask, 76
bit masking
IP subnet masks, 277
using Boolean logical functions, 75
BITS (Bump in the Stack) IPsec architecture, 455
bits and bytes, 37
bits per second (bps), 38
bits, 63, 76
BITW (Bump in the Wire) IPsec architecture, 456
.BIZ generic TLD, 872
block mode, FTP, 1182
bogus authentication information, 1158
Boolean logic
expressions, 73, 75
functions, 73
AND and OR, 74
Exclusive-OR (XOR, EOR), 75
NOT, 73
true and false values, 73
BOOTP (Bootstrap Protocol), 977
addressing, 980
basis for DHCP, 999
bootstrapping and, 977, 983
broadcasts and port use, 981
Client IP Address (CIAddr) field, 984
client/server messaging, 980
clients, 980
forwarding agents, 991–994, **994**, 1056
history, 978
interoperability with DHCP, 1062
magic cookie, 989
messages
format, 985, *986*, **988**
HType values, *987*
messaging, 981
operation, 983, **985**
relay agent, 991
broadcast message use, 994
DHCP message relaying, 1056
function, 992
normal operation, 993, **994**
retransmission of lost messages, 982
server, 980
standards, 978
transport, 981
Vendor Information
extensions, 989
field format, *990*
fields, 990
Vendor-Specific Area, 988

BOOTP/DHCP relay agents, 991–994, 1056
Bootstrap Protocol. *See* BOOTP
bootstrapping
BOOTP and, 977
RARP and, 228
TFTP and, 1200
Border Gateway Protocol. *See* BGP
border routers
AS in, 593
BGP, 652
bottlenecks, 40
bps (bits per second), 38
branch, DNS name tree, 860
BRI (basic rate interface), 175
broadcast methods
name registration, 836
name resolution, 837
broadcast addresses
IPv6, 375
subnet, 314
browsers, 1321
buffers, 525
bulletin board system (BBS), 1458
Bump in the Stack (BITS), **455**
Bump in the Wire (BITW), **456**
Bush, Vannevar, 1318
business name conflicts, 879
byte, 64
versus octet, 64

C

cable modem, 41
cable segment, 29
Cache-Control directives, *1359*
caching, 902
ARP, 218
DNS, 903
dynamic address resolution, 210
HTTP. *See* HTTP: caching
name resolution, 839
negative, DNS, 904
NFS, 963
caching-only, DNS name servers, 895
Calculator program, Windows, 68
Callback-Request messages, 179
Callback-Response messages, 179
Call-Request messages, 179
Call-Response messages, 179
Call-Status-Indication messages, 179
Call-Status-Response messages, 179
campus area network (CAN), 27
Canonical Name resource record, 937, *938*, 946
care-of addresses. *See* Mobile IP: addresses
Carriage Control/FORTRAN, 1185
carriage return (CR), RFC 822 email message format, 1235
carriage return/line feed sequence. *See* CRLF
case
in DNS labels, 863
in DNS master files, 945
CBEMA (Computer and Business Equipment Manufacturers Association), 50
.CC country code TLD, 875
CCITT (Comité Consultatif International Téléphonique et Télégraphique), 50
OSI Reference Model and, 82
CCP (Compression Control Protocol). *See* PPP: CCP
ccTLDs, DNS country code (geopolitical) TLDs, 874
cell, message type, 18
central authority, DNS root domain, 868
centralized registration authorities, 55
CERN (Conseil Européen pour la Recherche Nucléaire), 1318
Challenge messages, PPP CHAP, 164
channels, IRC, 1459
CHAP (Challenge Handshake Authentication Protocol), PPP. *See* PPP: CHAP
character, information storage term, 64
checksum calculation, TCP, 774
checksum recalculations, IP NAT, 446
child, DNS name term, 862
chunked transfers, HTTP, 1375
CIAddr (Client IP Address) Field, BOOTP, 984
CIDR (Classless Inter-Domain Routing)
address blocks, *323*
addressing example, 324

CIDR, *continued*
difference between VLSM and, 296
hierarchical addressing, 319
hierarchical division of /15 CIDR address block, **325**
IANA and, 321
notation, 319, **320**
prefix length in, 319
circuit switching, **14**
circuit-switching and packet-switching networks, 13
Cisco Systems, 681
class determination algorithm, 258, **259**
classes
BGP path attribute, 658
DNS resource record, 893
ICMP message, 512
IP address, 256
SNMP PDU, 1103
classful addressing, 258, **259**
classless addressing, 281. *See also* CIDR
Classless Inter-Domain Routing (CIDR) notation, 281
clearing bits, 63, 76
using AND bit mask, 77, *77*
client and server roles, 23
client hardware, 126
client identifier, DHCP, 1017
client implementations, DHCP, 1056
client processes, 697
client software, 23, 126
client, BOOTP, 980
client/server
application port use, TCP/IP, 703
model of operation, TCP/IP, **126**, 697
name resolution method, 837
networking, 23, **25**
port number use, 705
structural models, 23
closing TCP send window, 808
CMIP (Common Management Information Protocol), 1070
CName (Canonical Name) DNS resource record, 892, 937
master file format, 946
coaxial cable segment, 29
Code-Reject messages
PPP CCP, 170
PPP ECP, 173
PPP LCP, 159
PPP NCPs, 160
collision domain, 29
co-located care-of address, Mobile IP, 485
colon hexadecimal notation, 379
.COM generic TLD, 872
Comité Consultatif International Téléphonique et Télégraphique (CCITT), 50
command extensions, NNTP, 1422
command tagging, IMAP, 1303
command-line, FTP interface, 1193
comments, in DNS master files, 945
common Internet scheme syntax for URLs, 1143
Common Management Information Protocol (CMIP), 1070
Communication with Destination Administratively Prohibited, 549
Communication with Destination Host Is Administratively Prohibited, 524
Communication with Destination Network Is Administratively Prohibited, 524
communication, OSI Reference Model
horizontal (corresponding layer), 93
vertical (adjacent layer), 91
community strings, SNMPv1, 1111
community-based SNMPv2 (SNMPv2c), 1078
composite media types, MIME, 1253
compressed SLIP (CSLIP), 143
compression
DNS message, 941
OSI Reference Model Presentation Layer function, 111
PPP field, 185
compression algorithms, 171, *171*
Computer and Business Equipment Manufacturers Association (CBEMA), 50
computing IP subnet host address shortcuts, 313
configuration parameter management
DHCP, 1016

Configure-Ack, Configure-Nak, Configure-Reject, Configure-Request messages
PPP CCP, 170
PPP ECP, 173
PPP LCP, 157, 158
PPP NCPs, 160
conflicts in DNS public registration, 878–879
congestion
collapse, 817
handling and avoidance, 817
connection identification using TCP/IP socket pairs, 706
Connection, HTTP general header, 1360
connectionless and connection-oriented protocols, 15
contacts, DNS domain, 896
content and transfer encodings, 1372
content negotiation, HTTP, 1378
Content-Description, MIME header, 1247–1248
Content-Encoding, HTTP entity header, 1366
Content-ID, MIME header, 1247
Content-Language, HTTP entity header, 1366
Content-Length
HTTP entity header, 1366
MIME header, 1248
Content-Location
HTTP entity Header, 1366
MIME header, 1248
Content-MD5, HTTP entity header, 1367
Content-Range, HTTP entity header, 1367
Content-Transfer-Encoding, MIME header, 1247, 1257
Content-Type
HTTP entity header, 1367
MIME header, 1246, 1248
Continue, HTTP preliminary reply, 1356
control connection, FTP, 1172
control messages, PPP. *See* PPP
conventional IP addressing, 258, **259**
conventions
ICMP message processing, 517
SMI textual, 1090
convergence, routing protocol, 607
cookie, magic, BOOTP, 989
cookies, HTTP, 1391
.COOP generic TLD, 873
Copied flag, and IP datagram fragmentation, 347
core protocols, IPsec, 453
core protocols, TCP/IP lower-layer, 135
core routers and core routing architecture, 592
corporate name conflicts, 878
counters, PPP LQR, 168
counting to infinity, RIP, 607, **608**
country code TLDs and authorities, DNS, 874
CRLF
logical end-of-line character, Telnet NVT, 1445
RFC 822 messages and, 1235
cross-posting, Usenet, 1407
cross-resolution, dynamic resolution, 211
CSLIP (Compressed SLIP), 143
custom subnet mask. *See* IP: subnetting: custom masks
cybersquatting, DNS public registration, 879

D

DARPA (Defense Advanced Research Projects Agency). *See* ARPA
data block numbering, TFTP, 1205
data connections, FTP, 1177
data definition, NFS, 959
data encapsulation, OSI Reference Model, 95, **96**
Data Encryption Standard (DES), 473
data framing, SLIP, 141
data handling, TCP, 728
Data Link Layer (Layer 2), OSI Reference Model, 103
Data messages, TFTP, 1212, *1212*
data representation, 61
data, message, 19

Database Description messages, OSPF, 638
  format of, 641
datagram
  IP. *See* IP: datagrams
  IPv6. *See* IPv6: datagrams
datagram placement and linking, 462
Date, HTTP general header, 1360
DDDS (Dynamic Delegation Discovery System), 1162
DDNS (Dynamic DNS), 907
de facto standards, 48
deceptive naming practices, 879
decimal numbers
  binary equivalent, *66*
  conversion, *69*, *70*, *71*
decimal units, 38
decision process, BGP, 659
decrypting data, PPP ECP, 174
dedicated circuits, 15
default gateway, IP, 251
default IP subnet masks, *282*
default MSS, TCP, 778
default router, 530
default routes, RIP, 604
Defense Advanced Research Projects Agency (DARPA). *See* ARPA
delayed delivery, TCP/IP email, 1222
DELETE, HTTP method, 1351
delimiting, URLs, 1155
delivery
  IP datagram, 352
  IPv6 datagram, 420
demultiplexing, **698**, 699
Department of Defense (DoD), United States, 371
deregistration of mobile nodes, Mobile IP, 491
deregulation of DNS registration, 877
DES (Data Encryption Standard), 473
descriptors, MIB object, 1091
Destination Host Unknown, 524
Destination Host Unreachable for Type of Service, 524
Destination Network Unknown, 524
Destination Network Unreachable for Type of Service, 524
Destination Options, IPv6 extension header, 413
Destination Unreachable messages
  ICMP4, 522, *522*
  ICMP6, 548, *549*
device
  renumbering, IPv6, 400
  roles, Mobile IP, 481
  types, SNMP, 1072
dhclient, UNIX DHCP client daemon, 1056
DHCP (Dynamic Host Configuration Protocol), 998, 1058, **1060**
  address assignment and allocation mechanisms, 1000
  address pool size selection, 1009
  APIPA, 1059, **1060**
    IP address block for, 267
    limitations, 1060
  authentication, 1064
  autoconfiguration, 1058
  automatic allocation, 1002
  BOOTP interoperability, 1062
  BOOTP relay agents for, 1057
  client and server responsibilities, 1014
  client finite state machine, 1017, *1018*, **1020**
  client identifier, 1017
  client/server roles, 1015
  clients, 1056
    BOOTP servers and, 1063
    dhclient UNIX daemon, 1056
    dhcpd UNIX daemon, 1056
    responsibilities, 1015
  configuration, 1013
  conflict detection, 1061
  development of, 980
  DHCPv6, 1065
  dynamic allocation, 1001
  extensions, 1050
  general operation, 1017
  history, 998
  IP Version 6. *See* DHCP; DHCPv6
  leases, 1003
    address ranges (scopes), 1009, **1010**
    allocation, 1021, **1025**
    early termination, 1031
    issues with Infinite leases, 1005
    length, 1003

DHCP, *continued*
leases, *continued*
life cycle phases, 1006, **1007**
multiple-server non-overlapping scopes, **1011**
reallocation, 1026, **1028**
release, 1031
renewal and rebinding, 1028, **1032**
renewal and rebinding timers, 1008
manual allocation, 1001
message
format, 1038, **1039**, *1039*
generation, 1036
transport, 1036
types, *1051*
options
See also DHCP/BOOTP options
categories, *1043*
format, **1042,** *1043*
overloading, 1044
parameter
configuration, 1033, **1034**
storage, 1017
rebinding timer (T2), 1008
relaying, 1057
renewal timer (T1), 1008
retransmission of lost messages, 1037
security, 1063
servers
BOOTP clients and, 1063
configuration parameters, 1014
conflict detection, 1061
implementations, 1054
Microsoft, 1061
number of, 1055
placement, setup, and maintenance, 1055
responsibilities, 1014
software features, 1054
standards, 998
transaction identifier (XID), 1036
winipcfg and, 1056
DHCP/BOOTP options, 1045
application and service parameters, *1049*
DHCP extensions, *1050*
IP layer parameters
per host, *1047*
per interface, *1047*
link layer parameters per interface, *1048*
RFC 1497 vendor extensions, *1045*
TCP parameters, 1048, *1048*
DHCP/BOOTP relay agents. *See* BOOTP: relay agents
dhcpd, DHCP UNIX client daemon, 1056
DHCPv6 (DHCP for IP Version 6), 1065
dial-up remote server, email access, 1311
Differentiated Services (DS), IP datagram TOS field, 335
Diffie-Hellman group, IKE, 473
dig utility, 1476
digital information, 62
direct and indirect
(routed) delivery of IP datagrams, **352**
network applications, 1170
direct mapping, address resolution. *See* address resolution: direct mapping
direct server email access, 1311
directives, DNS master file, 945
disconnected access model, 1287
discrete media, MIME, 1246, 1248
diskless workstations, 1200
dispute resolution, DNS, 878
disruption, TCP connection, 760
Distance Vector Multicast Routing Protocol (DVMRP), 361
Distance-Vector (Bellman-Ford) routing protocol algorithm, 594
distributed name database, DNS, 869
DNS (Domain Name System), 848, 941
A resource record, 937, *937*, 946
AAAA (IPv6 Address) resource record, 949
absolute domain names, 865
Address resource record, 937, *937*, 946
authority structure, 868
caching, 903, 915
Canonical Name resource record, 892, *938*, 946
changes to support IPv6, 948
client/server messaging, 928
CName resource record, 892, *938*, 946

DNS, *continued*
components, 853
country code designations, 874
leasing/sale of, 875
country code TLDs and authorities, 874
DDNS, 907
design goals, 851
development, 848
dispute resolution, name registration, 880
distributed name database, 869
DNS Update (Dynamic DNS), 907
domain contacts, 896
domain names, 863
domain-related terminology, 860
domains, 858
email
address notation, 941
communication and, 1266
name resolution, 924
extension mechanisms for, 929
fully qualified domain names (FQDNs), 865
functions, **853**
generic TLDs, 870, **872**, *872*
geopolitical (country code) TLDs, 874
IN-ADDR.ARPA reverse name resolution hierarchy, **922**
inverse querying, 921
IPv6 Address (AAAA) DNS resource record, 949
labels and domain name construction, 863, **864**
lookup utility, whois/nicname, 1477
Mail Exchange resource record, 892, *939*, 947
master files
directives, 945
format, 943
resource record examples, 946
sample, 948
syntax rules, 945
master name servers, 893
messages
compression, 941
format, 930, *930*, **931**
generation and transport, 928
header format, 932, *933*, **934**
question section format, 935, *935*, **935**
resource record field formats, 935, **937**
transport using UDP and TCP, 929
multiple address records, 904
MX resource record, 892, *939*, 947
name registration, 867
authorities, 877
coordination, 878
dispute resolution, 880
second-level domains, 876
name resolution, 912, **913**, 917
email, 924
example, 917, **919**
handling aliases, 920
impact of zones on, 882
IN-ADDR.ARPA hierarchy, **922**
local resolution, 915
recursive, 913, **914**
reverse, 920
techniques, 911
name resolvers
caching, 916
functions and operation, 910
stub, 911
user interface, 910
name servers, 887
architecture, **833**, 888
caching, 901
data storage, 890
efficiency issues, 894
enhancements, 905
load balancing, 904
multiple, 905
redundancy, 894
resource record, 892, *937*, 946
support functions, 889
types and roles, 893
names
absolute, 865
architecture, 832, 858
distributed database, 869
fully qualified domain names (FQDNs), 865
hierarchical tree structure, 858
name space, 854, 857, **859**, **862**
notation, **941**

DNS, *continued*
names, *continued*
partially qualified domain names (PQDNs), 866
terminology, 860–862
NAT and, 437, 444
notify, 906
NS resource record, 892, *937*, 946
operation, 888
organizational TLDs, 870, **872**, *872*
partially qualified domain names (PQDNs), 866
pointer resource record, 892, *938*, 947
PQDNs (partially qualified domain names), 866
primary name servers, 893
private name registration, 884
PTR resource record, 892, *938*, 947
relative domain names, 865
resolution. *See* DNS: name resolution
resolvers. *See* DNS: name resolvers
resource records, 892, *892*
address, 937, *937*, 946
canonical name, 892, *938*, 946
classes, 893
format, common, 936, *936*
IPv6 address, 949
Mail Exchange, 892, *939*, 947
master file (text) representation, 891
master file format, common, 944
name server, 892, *937*, 946
pointer, 892, *938*, 947
RData field formats, 936
representations, 890
setup for reverse resolution, 922
Start Of Authority, 892, *938*, 946
text, 892, *940*, 947
reverse name resolution, 920
root
authority, 868
domain, 860
name servers, 899
RR. *See* DNS: resource records
secondary name servers, 893
slave name servers, 893
SOA resource record, 892, *938*, 946
standards, 849, 850
Start Of Authority resource record, 892, *938*, 946
subdomains, 860
text resource record, 892, *940*, 947
top-level domains (TLDs), 860
tree-related terminology, 860, **861**
TXT resource record, 892, *940*, 947
Uniform Domain Name Dispute Resolution Policy (UDRP), 880
whois/nicname utility, 1477
zones, **883**, 895
domain contacts, 896
transfers, 898, 907
DoD (United States Department of Defense), 371
DoD (United States Department of Defense) Model, 87
domains. *See* DNS
don't fragment flag, IP, 347
dotted decimal notation
IP address, 245
subnet mask, 278
double word, unit, 64
downstream Usenet servers, 1413
Duke University, 1398
DVMRP (Distance Vector Multicast Routing Protocol), 361
dynamic address
mappings, IP NAT, 433
resolution, 209, **210**
dynamic allocation, DHCP, 1001
dynamic data length, HTTP, 1375
Dynamic Delegation Discovery System (DDDS), 1162
Dynamic DNS (DDNS), 907
dynamic router selection, ND, 581
dynamic routing protocols, 595

E

EBCDIC, FTP data type, 1183
EBGP (External BGP), 652
Echo (Request) and Echo Reply messages
ICMP4, 536, *536*, **537**
ICMP6, 558, *559*
ping utility, use of, 1464
ECP (Encryption Control Protocol), 173
editor, RFC, 57

EDNS0 (Extension Mechanisms for DNS), 929
.EDU generic TLD, 873
EGP (Exterior Gateway Protocol), 684
EHLO (extended hello), SMTP, 1269
EIA (Electronic Industries Alliance), 50
EIGRP (Enhanced Interior Gateway Routing Protocol), 682
Electronic Industries Alliance (EIA), 50
electronic mail. *See* email
email (electronic mail), 1215
  access
    direct server, 1311
    models, 1287
    Telnet, 1311
    World Wide Web, 1313
  access and retrieval protocols and methods, 1285
  address books, 1230
  addressing, 1226
    gatewaying, 1229
    historical, 1228
    multiple recipients, 1230
    notation, DNS, 941
    SMTP requirements, 1227
    standard DNS-based, 1226
    UUCP-style, 1229
  aliases, 1230
  communication, 1220
    early, using relaying, 1266
    model, 1222, **1223**
    modern, using DNS, 1266
    protocol roles, 1224
  decoupling of sender and receiver, 1222
  delayed delivery, 1222
  DNS resource records for, 924
  early days of, 1218
  history of TCP/IP-based, 1219
  messages
    difference between message and envelope, 1241
    formats and processing, 1233
    RFC 822, 1234
  name resolution, DNS, 924
  protocols, 1215
  system overview, 1219
  Unix-to-Unix Copy Protocol (UUCP) and, 1219
  URL scheme (mailto), 1147
embedding, IPv6/IPv4 addresses, 392
encapsulated message type, MIME, 1257
Encapsulating Security Payload. *See* IPsec: ESP
encoding
  HTTP, 1373
  MIME. *See* MIME: encoding
encryption
  HTTP, 1390
  PPP. *See* PPP: ECP
encryption/hashing algorithms, IPsec, 453
END character, SLIP, 141
end-to-end
  encoding, HTTP, 1373
  headers, HTTP, 1385
  transport, Transport Layer, 107
Enhanced Interior Gateway Routing Protocol (EIGRP), 682
enhanced status code replies, SMTP, 1284
entities
  HTTP, 1370
  MIME, 1246
  SNMP, 1073
entity headers, HTTP. *See* HTTP: entity headers
envelope, analogy to IP datagram encapsulation, 330
EOR, Exclusive-OR Boolean logical function, 75
ephemeral ports, 703
error messages
  TFTP, 1213, *1214*
  ICMPv4. *See* ICMPv4: error messages
  ICMPv6. *See* ICMPv6: error messages
error reporting, BGP, 663, 673
escape character (ESC)
  DNS Master Files, 945
  SLIP, 142
  Telnet protocol commands, 1447
ESP (IPsec Encapsulating Security Payload). *See* IPsec: ESP
ETag, HTTP response header, 1364
/etc/hosts UNIX configuration file, 843, 1463

Ethernet
100BASE-TX fast, 34
example link layer technology, 28
frames, 19
ETSI (European Telecommunications Standards Institute), 50
EUI-64 (64-bit extended unique identifier) format, IEEE, 388
modified, 388
European Telecommunications Standards Institute (ETSI), 50
Exclusive-OR Boolean logical function, 75
expect, HTTP request header, 1362
experimental
IP addresses, Class E, 257
IPv6 network, 6BONE, 370
RFCs, 58
expires, HTTP entity header, 1367
explicit URL delimiting, 1156
expressions, Boolean logic, 73
extended hello (EHLO), SMTP command, 1269
extension headers, IPv6, 407
extensions
DHCP, 1050, *1050*
DNS, for IPv6, and 949
FTP security and, 1176
Mobile IP Agent Advertisement messages, 488
NNTP command, 1422
SMTP, *1276*, 1281
Exterior Gateway Protocol (EGP), 684
exterior routing protocols, 593
external BGP (EBGP), 652
External Data Representation (XDR) Standard, NFS, 959
external peers, in autonomous system, 652
external performance limiters, networks, 40
extranet, 30

F

failure messages, PPP CHAP, 164
family-related terminology, DNS, 861
Fast Ethernet, 100BASE-TX, 34
open standards and, 47
FDDI (Fiber Distributed Data Interface), 340
Fiber Distributed Data Interface (FDDI), 340
fiber-optic communication, simplex operation, 42
FidoNet addressing, 1228
field compression, PPP, 185
file and message transfer applications, 1163
file concepts, 1164
file system model, NFS, 968
File Transfer Protocol. *See* FTP
File Transfer Protocol, Trivial. *See* TFTP
file, URL local file scheme syntax, 1149
FIN (finish) messages, TCP, 747
finite state machine. *See* FSM
flag, unit of information measure, 63
flat name
architecture, 832, **832**
space, 832, **832**
flow control, TCP, 793, 805
footer, message, 19
foreign agent care-of address, Mobile IP, 484, **484**
format control, FTP, 1184
format prefix, IPv6 addresses, 382
forwarding agents, BOOTP, 991
forwarding, 98
four-message exchange, DHCPv6, 1066
FQDNs (Fully Qualified Domain Names), DNS, 865
fragment extension header, IPv6, *411*
fragmentation
IP, **342**
IPv6, 418–419
PPP MP, 196–199
Fragmentation Needed and DF Set, 523
fragments, URL, 1145
frames
Ethernet, 19
PPP LCP, 156
Framework, Internet Standard Management. *See* SNMP Framework
framework, SNMP. *See* SNMP Framework
framing, SLIP, 141
from, HTTP request header, 1362

FSM (finite state machine), 746
DHCP client, 1017
IMAP, 1300, **1301**
POP3, 1290
TCP, 746
FTP (File Transfer Protocol), 1169–1171
active data connection, **1179**
anonymous, 1177
authentication, 1175
commands
access control, 1185, *1186*
protocol service, *1187*
transfer parameter, *1187*
compared to TFTP, 1201
compressed mode, 1182
connection
active data, **1179**
control, 1175
establishment and user authentication, **1176**
management, 1177
normal, 1178
passive data, 1178, **1180**
control connection establishment, 1175
data
communication, 1181
representation, 1182
data structures, 1185
data types, 1183
development, 1170
format control, 1184
IP NAT and, 447
login sequence, 1175
multiple-line text replies, 1192
normal data connections, 1178
operational model, 1172, **1173**
passive data connection, 1178, **1180**
PASV command, 1178
PORT command, 1178
process components and terminology, 1173
protocol service commands, *1187*
proxy FTP, 1174
replies, 1188
reply codes, 1188, **1190**, *1190*
security extensions, 1176
service commands, 1186
session, example, 1196
standardization, 1170
stream mode, 1181
Telnet NVT and, 1186
third-party file transfer, 1174
transfer parameter commands, *1187*
transmission modes, 1181
user
commands, 1193, *1194*
interfaces, 1193
ftp, URL File Transfer Protocol syntax, 1147
full newsgroup retrieval, NNTP, 1418
full-duplex communication, 42
fully qualified domain names (FQDNs), 865
fundamental network characteristics, 10

G

Garbage-Collection Timer, RIP, 606
gates, logic, 75
Gateway Information Protocol (GWINFO), 598
gatewaying, email, 1228
gateway, 353
default, IP, 251
protocols. *See* routing protocols
Gateway-to-Gateway Protocol (GGP), 592, 678
general headers, HTTP. *See* HTTP: general headers
generic TLDs, DNS, 870, **872**, *872*
geopolitical (country code) TLDs, DNS, 874
GET, HTTP method, 1349
GetResponse messages, SNMP. *See* SNMP Protocol: messages
GGP (Gateway-to-Gateway Protocol), 678
in TCP/IP core architecture, 592
giga, 38
Gigabit (1,000 Mbps) Ethernet, 40
global address, IP NAT, 430
global hierarchical domain architecture, DNS, **859**
global routing prefix, IPv6, 386
global unicast address format, IPv6, 383, *384*

Gopher Protocol, 1431
  client/server operation, 1432
  menus, 1433
  selector strings, 1432
  servers, 1432
  URL syntax, 1148
  World Wide Web and, 1434
.GOV generic TLD, 873
granularity, of IP address classes, 270, 316
gratuitous ARP, in Mobile IP, 499
GRE (Generic Routing Encapsulation), 496
group address, IP multicast, 268
group, multicast, 22
GWINFO (Gateway Information Protocol), 598

H

half-duplex
  operation, 42
  Telnet NVT, 1446
hardware
  addresses, 104, 244
    ARP, 214
  client and server, 126–127
hashing/encryption algorithms, IPsec, 453
HEAD, HTTP method, 1350
header
  caching, HTTP, 1385
  message, 19
HELLO (HELLO Protocol), 679
Hello messages, OSPF, 641
HELO command, SMTP, 1268
HEMP (High-level Entity Management Protocol), 1070
HEMS (High-level Entity Management System), 1070
hexadecimal
  IPv6 addresses, 378
  notation, 68
  numbers, 67
    arithmetic, 72, *72*
    conversion, 69, *69*, 70
  representation of IPv6 addresses, **378**
hierarchical
  name registration, 835
  routing and aggregation in IPv6, 421
  topology, OSPF. *See* OSPF: hierarchical topology
hierarchies, Usenet, 1405
High-Level Data Link Control (HDLC) protocol, 144, 182
historic RFCs, 58
HMAC-MD5, Mobile IP authentication, 503
hold timer, BGP, 672
home agent, Mobile IP, 482
hop-by-hop
  encoding, HTTP, 1373
  headers and caching, HTTP, 1385
  options, IPv6, 413
hops
  in RIP, 601
  in routing and address resolution, 205
  routing protocol metric, 594
horizontal communication, OSI Reference Model, 93
host configuration protocols, 975
host ID, IP, 247
host name
  history of, 842
  lists, ARPAnet, 842
  utility (hostname), 1462
Host Precedence Violation, 524
host redirection using ICMP Redirect message, **531**
host table name system, 843
  files, 842
  modern networks and, 846
  name registration and, 844
  name resolution and, 844
  weaknesses of, 845
Host Unreachable, 523
host Utility, 1475
Host, HTTP request header, 1362
host-host communication functions, ND, 583
hostname, TCP/IP host name utility, 1462
host-router discovery functions, ND, 582
HOSTS file, Windows, 843
Host-to-Host Transport Layer, 107
  protocols, 132

HTML (Hypertext Markup Language), 1322
  elements and tags, 1323, *1324*
  text formatting tags, 1326
HTTP (Hypertext Transfer Protocol), 1315
  agent-driven negotiation, 1378
  authentication methods, 1389
  cache
    benefits of, 1382
    control, 1384
    locations, 1383
    hop-by-hop headers and, 1385
    impact on communication, 1335
    intermediary, 1384
    Web client, 1383
    Web server, 1384
  chunked transfers, 1375
  client/server communication, 1333, **1334**
  connections, 1329
  content and transfer encodings, 1372
  content negotiation, 1378
  Continue (100) preliminary reply, 1356
  cookies, 1391
  data length issues, 1374
  end-to-end
    encoding, 1373
    headers, 1385
  entities, 1370
  entity headers, 1365
    Allow, 1366
    Content-Encoding, 1366
    Content-Language, 1366
    Content-Length, 1366
    Content-Location, 1366
    Content-MD5, 1367
    Content-Range, 1367
    Content-Type, 1367
    Expires, 1367
    Last-Modified, 1367
  features, 1381
  general headers, 1358
    Cache-Control, 1358, *1359*
    Connection, 1360
    Date, 1360
    Pragma, 1360
    Trailer, 1360
    Transfer-Encoding, 1361
    Upgrade, 1361
    Via, 1361
    Warning, 1359, *1360*
  headers, 1357
    entity. *See* HTTP: entity headers
    general. *See* HTTP: general headers
    request. *See* HTTP: request headers
    response. *See* HTTP: response headers
  hop-by-hop
    encoding, 1373
    headers and caching, 1385
  intermediaries, 1334, **1335**
  Internet media types, 1370
  media types and subtypes, 1370
  message trailers, 1375
  messages
    generic format, 1342
    Request messages
      format, 1343, **1344**
      headers, 1346
      request line, 1344
      request URI, 1345
    Response messages
      format, 1346, **1347**
      headers, 1348
      status line, 1347
  methods, 1349
    DELETE, 1351
    GET, 1349
    HEAD, 1350
    OPTIONS, 1350
    POST, 1350
    PUT, 1350
    TRACE, 1351
  MIME and, 1371
  operation, 1329
  persistent connections, 1337
  pipelining, 1337
  privacy, 1388, 1390
  proxying, 1386
    caching interaction, 1388
    comparing proxies and caches, 1387
    security and, 1386
  quality values, 1378

HTTP, *continued*
reason phrases, 1353, *1354*
request headers, 1361
Accept, 1361
Accept-Charset, 1362
Accept-Encoding, 1362
Accept-Language, 1362
Authorization, 1362
Expect, 1362
From, 1362
Host, 1362
If-Match, 1362
If-Modified-Since, 1362
If-None-Match, 1363
If-Range, 1363
If-Unmodified-Since, 1363
Max-Forwards, 1363
Proxy-Authorization, 1363
Range, 1363
Referer, 1363
TE, 1364
User-Agent, 1364
request/response chain, 1334, **1335**
resource paths and directory listings, 1328
response headers, 1364
Accept-Ranges, 1364
Age, 1364
ETag, 1364
Location, 1364
Proxy-Authenticate, 1365
Retry-After, 1365
Server, 1365
Vary, 1365
WWW-Authenticate, 1365
security and privacy, 1388
server-driven negotiation, 1378
state management, 1391
status codes, 1352, *1354*
transitory connections, 1336
uniform resource locators (URLs), 1326
URL syntax, 1327
versions, 1330
http, URL World Wide Web/Hypertext Transfer Protocol syntax, 1146
hybrid routing protocol algorithms, 595
hypermedia, 1319, 1336, 1370
hypertext, 1318

I

IAB (Internet Architecture Board), 53
IAC (Interpret As Command), Telnet, 1447
IANA (Internet Assigned Numbers Authority)
DNS root domain and, 869
OUI for multicast address resolution, 223
IANA, 55
IBGP (Internal BGP), 652
IBM (International Business Machines, Inc.), 67
ICANN (Internet Corporation for Assigned Names and Numbers), 55–56, 254
ICMP (Internet Control Message Protocol), 507–508
See also ICMPv4; ICMPv6
data encapsulation, 520
history, 508
messages
classes, 512
codes, 513
common format, 518, *518*, **519**
creation rules and RFC 1122, 516
processing conventions, 517
responses, limitations on, 516
summary, 513, *513*
types, 512
operation, 510, **511**
standards, 508
versions, 508
ICMPv4
See also ICMP; ICMPv6
error messages, 521
Destination Unreachable, 343, 522, *522*, **523**
Parameter Problem, 533, **533**, *534*
Redirect, 530, 531, **531**
Source Quench, 525, *526*, **526**
Time Exceeded, 349, 527, **528**, *529*, **529**
informational messages, 535
Address Mask Reply, 543, *544*, **544**
Address Mask Request, 543, **544**
Echo (Reply), *536*, **537**
Echo Request, 536, *536*, **537**

ICMPv4, *continued*
informational messages, *continued*
Information Reply, 536
Information Request, 536
Router Advertisement, 539
message format, 540, *541*, **541**
Router Solicitation, 539
message format, 542, *542*, **542**
router discovery, 581
Timestamp (Request), 537, *538*, **539**
Timestamp Reply, 537, *538*, **539**
Traceroute, 544, *545*, **546**
ICMPv6
error messages, 547
Destination Unreachable, 548, **548**, *549*
Packet Too Big, 550, *551*, **551**
Parameter Problem, 554, *555*, **555**
Redirect. *See* ICMPv6: informational messages
Time Exceeded, 552, *553*, **554**
informational messages, 557
Echo Reply, 558, *559*, **559**
Echo (Request), 558, *559*, **559**
Neighbor Advertisement, 563
message format, 563, *563*, **564**
Neighbor Solicitation, 563
message format, 564, *565*, **565**
options, 571
MTU, 574, *574*, **574**
Prefix Information, 572, *572*, **573**
Redirected Header, 573, *574*, **574**
Source Link-Layer Address, 571, *571*, **571**
Target Link-Layer Address, 572, *572*, **572**
Redirect, 566, *566*, **567**
Router Advertisement, 560
message format, 560, **560**, *561*
Router Renumbering, 568, **569**, *569*
Router Solicitation, 560
message format, 562, *562*, **562**
ICMPv6 Packet Too Big messages, 417
ICS (Internet Connection Sharing), 252
idempotence
HTTP methods and, 1351
SNMP message transmission and, 1115
IEEE (Institute of Electrical and Electronics Engineers), 50
IEEE 802
802.11 shared key authentication, 163
addresses and IP multicast address resolution, 223
networking architecture model, 87
Project, 51, 103
IEEE EUI-64, 388
IEN (Internet Engineering Note), 57
IEN 2, 123
IESG (Internet Engineering Steering Group), 53
IETF (Internet Engineering Task Force), 53
ifconfig utility, UNIX, 1484
If-Match, 1362
If-Modified-Since, 1362
If-None-Match, 1363
If-Range, 1363
If-Unmodified-Since, 1363
IGRP (Interior Gateway Routing Protocol), 681
IKE (IPsec Internet Key Exchange), 471
image
media type, MIME, 1250
FTP Data Type, 1183
IMAP (Internet Message Access Protocol), 1297–1299
any state commands, 1304, *1304*
authenticated state commands, 1307, *1308*
authentication methods, 1306
command groups, 1303
command tagging, 1303
FSM, 1300, **1301**
history, 1299
Not Authenticated state commands, 1306, *1306*
operation, 1300
preauthentication, 1302
response codes, 1305
result codes, 1305
selected state commands, 1309, *1310*
session establishment and greeting, 1302

IMAP, *continued*
session states, 1300
standards, 1299
IMAP4 (Internet Message Access Protocol version 4). *See* IMAP
IN-ADDR.ARPA hierarchy, DNS, 920, **922**
inbound NAT, 437, **438**, *439*
incremental zone tansfers, DNS, 907
indirect datagram delivery (routing), 353
indirect network applications, 1170
industry groups, networking, 51
infinite DHCP leases, 1005
.INFO generic TLD, 873
information representation and groups, binary, 63
Information Sciences Institute (ISI), 57
Information Technology Industry Council (ITIC), 50
information (analog or digital), 62
informational messages
ICMPv4. *See* ICMPv4: informational messages
ICMPv6. *See* ICMPv6: informational messages
information-oriented design, SNMP, 1084
information, binary, 62
Institute of Electrical and Electronics Engineers (IEEE), 50
.INT generic TLD, 873
integrated architecture, IPsec, 455
interactive and remote application protocols, 1437
interfaces, OSI Reference Model, 91
Interior Gateway Routing Protocol (IGRP), 681
interior
nodes, DNS tree, 860
routing protocols, 593
intermediaries, HTTP, 1334
intermediate devices, message routing, 98
internal BGP (IBGP), 652
internal routers, AS architecture, 593
international networking standards organizations, 49
International Organization for Standardization (ISO), 49
International Telecommunication Union—Telecommunication Standardization Sector (ITU-T), 50
Internet Activities Board, (IAB), 53
Internet Architecture Board (IAB), 53
Internet Assigned Numbers Authority. *See* IANA
Internet Connection Sharing (ICS), 252
Internet Control Message Protocol. *See* ICMP
Internet Corporation for Assigned Names and Numbers. *See* ICANN
Internet Engineering Note number 2 (IEN 2), 123
Internet Engineering Notes (IENs), 57
Internet Engineering Steering Group (IESG), 53
Internet Engineering Task Force (IETF), 53
Internet Key Exchange, IPsec. *See* IPsec: IKE
Internet Layer, TCP/IP, 129
Internet media types, 1370
Internet Message Access Protocol. *See* IMAP
Internet minimum MTU, IP, 343
Internet Network Information Center (InterNIC), 56
Internet Protocol Control Protocol (IPCP), 162
Internet Protocol Mobility Support. *See* Mobile IP
Internet Protocol Version 4. *See* IP
Internet Protocol Version 6. *See* IPv6
Internet Protocol. *See* IP
Internet registration authorities and registries, 55
Internet Relay Chat Protocol. *See* IRC
Internet Research Steering Group (IRSG), 53
Internet Research Task Force (IRTF), 53
Internet Security Association and Key Management Protocol (ISAKMP), 472
Internet Society (ISOC), 52

Internet Standard Management Framework. *See* SNMP Framework
Internet standardization process, 58
Internet standards, 57
Internet standards organizations, 52, **54**
Internet Stream Protocol, version 2, 240
internet, 28
internetwork, 28
internetwork datagram delivery, IP, **236**
InterNIC (Internet Network Information Center), 56, 880
Interpret As Command (IAC) command, Telnet, 1447
interrupt handling
  TCP, 1449
  Telnet, 1449
interrupt-driven communication, SNMP, 1102
interrupts, 791
intranet, 30
inverse querying, DNS, 921
inverting bits with XOR, 77, *77*
IP (Internet Protocol), 233, 236, 242, *256*
  address
    resolution and, 205
    all ones and all zeros, 263
    binary, hexadecimal, and dotted decimal representations, **246**
    block for DHCP APIPA, 267
    categories, 249
    classless, 281
    concepts, 241
    configuration, 244
    division, **248**
    dotted decimal notation, 245
    loopback, 266
    management of, 252
    multicast. *See* IP: multicast, addresses
    multihoming, 251, **253**
    notation, 245
    number of, 251
    patterns with special meanings, *264*
    private and public, 244
    reserved, private, and loopback, 267, *267*
    size, 245
    special meanings, *264*
    structure, 247
    subnet. *See* IP: subnetting
  address classes, 256, *256*
    bit assignments and network/host ID sizes, **261**
    bit patterns and address ranges, *260*
    class determination algorithm, 258, **259**
    determining class from first octet bit pattern, 260
    granularity of, 270, 316
    network and host capacities, 262, *262*
  address space, 246
  CIDR, 315–316
    addressing block sizes, 322
    addressing example, 324
    IP routing with, 359
    notation, 281
    rationale for, 257
  classes. *See* IP: address: classes
  classless addressing. *See* CIDR
  Classless Inter-Domain Routing. *See* CIDR
  datagram
    Copied flag, 347
    delivery, 352, **352**
    encapsulation, 330, **331**
    format, 332, *332*, **334**
    fragmentation-related header fields, 346
    options, 336, *337*, **337**, *338*
    size, 340
    Time to Live (TTL) field, 335
    Type of Service (TOS) field, 335, *336*
  feature protocols, 240
  fragmentation, **341**, **342**, 344
    impact on TCP MSS selection, 778
    multiple-stage, 342
    process, 344, **345**
  functions, 238
  history, 239
  internetwork datagram delivery, **236**
  maximum transmission unit, **341**
  mobile. *See* Mobile IP, 486

IP (Internet Protocol), *continued*
MTU, 341, **341**
MTU Path Discovery, 343
multicast, 360
multicast address, 268
resolution, 223
administratively scoped, 269
groups, 268
types and ranges, 268, *268*, **268**
well-known, 269, *269*
group management, 361
multicast routing, 361
NAT (Network Address Translation). *See* IP NAT
packets. *See* IP: datagram
reassembly, 347
routing
in a CIDR environment, 359
datagram delivery and, 352
next-hop, 355, **356**
router discovery and, 540
routers and, 239
in a subnet environment, 359
routes and routing tables, 357, **358**
security. *See* IPsec
standards, 239
subnetting, 273–274
address formulas, 309
addresses, 287
custom masks, 283, **285**
default masks, 281, *282*
design trade-off, **300**
determining host addresses, **312**
determining addresses, **307**, **308**
example, **277**, 297, **301**, **302**
ID determination, *279*, **279**, **280**
identifiers, 286
masks, 277–279
multi-level, 294
summary tables, 288
three-level hierarchy, 276
Variable Length Subnet Masking. *See* IP: VLSM
versions, 239
VLSM, 292
example, **295**
network split into conventional subnets, **293**
network split using VLSM, **294**
IP datagram expiration, example, **528**
IP encapsulation within IP, 496
IP layer parameters per host, 1046, *1047*
IP layer parameters per interface, 1047, *1047*
IP NAT (IP Network Address Translation), 426
address terminology, 430, **432**
advantages of, 428
bidirectional, 437, **438**, *439*
compatibility issues and special requirements, 429, 445
disadvantages of, 429
dynamic mappings, 433
FTP and, 447
inbound, 437, **438**, *439*
IPsec and, 447
mappings, 433
outbound, 434, *435*, **436**
overlapping, 442, *445*, **446**
overloaded, 439, **441**, *442*
PAT, 439, **441**, *442*
port-based, 439, **441**, *442*
static mappings, 433
traditional, 434, *435*, **436**
twice NAT, 442, *445*, **446**
two-way, 437, **438**, *439*
unidirectional, 434, *435*, **436**
IP Next Generation (IPng). *See* IPv6
IP Security. *See* IPsec
IP supernetting, 315
IP within IP encapsulation, 496
IP6.INT domain for IPv6 reverse resolution, 949
ipconfig
utility (Windows), 1486
role in DHCP client implementation, 1056
IPCP (PPP Internet Protocol Control Protocol), 162
IPng. *See* IPv6
IPsec (IP Security), 449
AH (Authentication Header), 461
datagram placement and linking, 462, **463**, 463
format, **464**, 465, *465*
architectures
Bump in the Stack (BITS), 455, **455**

IPsec (IP Security), *continued*
architectures, *continued*
Bump in the Wire (BITW), 456, **456**
integrated, 455
Authentication Header (AH), 461
components, 452
core protocols, 453
Encapsulating Security Payload. *See* IPsec: ESP
end-host implementation, 454
ESP (Encapsulating Security Payload), 450, 466
authentication data, 466
authentication field calculation and placement, 467
datagram placement and linking, **468**
fields, 466
format, **469**, 470, *470*, **471**
header, 466
operations, 467
trailer, 466–467
history, 450
IKE (Internet Key Exchange), 471
modes, 457
transport, **458**
tunnel, **459**
operation, 452
protocols and components, **453**
router implementation, 454
security constructs, 460
services and functions, 451
standards, *451*
support components, 453
transport mode, **458**
tunnel mode, **459**
IPv4. *See* IP
IPv6 (IP version 6), 363, 366
6BONE experimental network, 370
AAAA (IPv6 Address) resource record, DNS, 949
address resolution for, 224
address, 373
allocations, 381, *382*
anycast, 398
binary, decimal, and hexadecimal representations, **378**
broadcast, 375
colon hexadecimal notation, 379
global unicast address format, 383, *384*, **385**
global routing prefix, 386
historical routing prefix structure, *386*
routing prefix structure, *386*, **387**
hexadecimal notation, 378
interface identifiers, 388
IPv4-compatible, 392, **393**
IPv4-mapped, 392, **393**
IPv6/IPv4 embedding, 392
link-local, 391
loopback, 391
mixed notation, 380
model, 374
multicast. *See* IPv6: multicast: addresses
physical address mapping, 388
prefix length representation, 381
private/unregistered/nonroutable, 390
renumbering, 400
reserved, 390
site-local, 391
size, 376
solicited-node, 396, **397**
space, 376
special, 389
types, 375
unicast, 375
unspecified, 391
zero compression, 379
AH. *See* IPsec: AH
autoconfiguration, stateless, 399
changes and additions to, 368
datagrams, 402, *403*, **403**
delivery, 420
encapsulation, 401
Hop Limit field, 552
main header format, 404, *404*, **405**
Next Header field, 405
options, 412, 413, 414
sizing, 416
structure, 402
design goals, 367
development of RIPng for, 600
DHCP for. *See* DHCPv6
DNS changes for, 850, 948

IPv6 (IP version 6), *continued*
DNS extensions, 949
extension headers, 407
chaining using the Next Header field, 407, **408**
Fragment, 411, *411*, **411**
No Next Header, 409
Routing, 410, *410*, **410**
fragmentation, 418, **419**
global unicast address format, 383, *384*, **385**
maximum transmission unit (MTU), 416
MTU, 416
multicast
addresses, 394, **394**, *395*, 396
scopes, 395, **396**
ND (Neighbor Discovery protocol). *See* ND
Next Header values, *406*
router renumbering, 568
routing, 420
standards, 366
stateless autoconfiguration, 399
transition from IPv4, 370
IPX/SPX protocol suite, 109
IRC (Internet Relay Chat Protocol), 1458
client/server operation and, 1459
logical network, 1459
messaging and channels, 1459
modern Internet and, 1460
IRSG (Internet Research Steering Group), 53
IRTF (Internet Research Task Force), 53
ISAKMP (Internet Security Association and Key Management Protocol), 472
ISDN and PPP Multilink Protocol, 175
ISI (Information Sciences Institute), 57
island networks, host table name system and, 846
ISO (International Organization for Standardization), 49
OSI Reference Model and, 82
ISO Standard 3166-1, 875
ISOC (Internet Society), 52
isochronous transmissions, QoS, 44
iterative name resolution, DNS, 912, **913**
ITIC (Information Technology Industry Council), 50
ITU-T (International Telecommunication Union—Telecommunication Standardization Sector), 50

K

Karn's algorithm, 804
keepalive messages
BGP, 672–673
TCP, 761
kilo, 38
kludge, 429

L

labels, DNS, 863, **864**
lag, 36
LAN (Local Area Network), 26
Last-Modified, HTTP entity header, 1367
latency, 35
QoS and, 43
Layer 1 (Physical Layer), 102
Layer 2 (Data Link Layer), 103
Layer 3 (Network Layer), 105
Layer 4 (Transport Layer), 106
Layer 5 (Session Layer), 109
Layer 6 (Presentation Layer), 110
Layer 7 (Application Layer), 111
layer stack, OSI Reference Model, 88
layer terminology, OSI Reference Model, 89
layering, importance in TCP/IP, 123
layers, abstraction level, 88
layers. *See* OSI Reference Model
LCP (PPP Link Control Protocol). *See* PPP: LCP
leases, DHCP. *See* DHCP: leases
line feed (LF) character, RFC 822 messages, 1235
line-delimiting issues, FTP ASCII data type, 1184
link configuration, PPP LCP, **157**

link layer parameters per interface, DHCP/BOOTP options, *1048*
link state, OSPF. *See* OSPF
links, PPP. *See* PPP: LCP
link-state (shortest-path first), routing protocol algorithm, 595
listservs (list servers), email, 1231
load balancing, DNS, 904
local area networks (LANs), 26
local file URL scheme, 1149
local Internet registries, 57
local name mappings, 846
local resolution, DNS, 916
localhost, standard DNS domain name, 885
locality of reference, 211
  spatial, 915
  temporal, 915
Location, HTTP response header, 1364
Loc-RIB, BGP routing information base, 656
logic gates, 75
logical functions, Boolean, 73
loopback addresses
  IP, 266
  IPv6, 391
lower-layer core protocols, 135
LQR. *See* PPP: LQR

M

MAC address, 205
magic cookie, BOOTP, 989
Magic Number, PPP option, 158
Mail Box Protocol, 1219
Mail Exchange resource record, DNS, 892, 925, 939, *939*, 947
mail forwarding, 1275
Mail Transfer Protocol (MTP), 1264
mail, electronic. *See* email; SMTP
mailing list expansion, SMTP, 1275
mailing lists, 1231
mailto, URL electronic mail scheme syntax, 1147
Majordomo, 1231
MAN (Metropolitan Area Network), 27
managed nodes, SNMP, 1072
managed objects. *See* MIBs: objects
management framework. *See* SNMP Framework
management information bases. *See* MIBs
manager, SNMP, 1073
manual allocation, DHCP, 1001
manual host configuration, problems with, 974
masks
  bit, 76
  bit masking for IP subnet, 277
  IP custom subnet, 283
Massachusetts Institute of Technology (MIT), 265, 443, 923
master files, DNS. *See* DNS: master files
mathematics of computing, 61
Max Repetitions parameter, SNMPv2/v3, 1107
Max-Access MIB object characteristic, 1088
Max-Forwards, HTTP request header, 1363
maximum segment lifetime (MSL), TCP, 766
maximum segment size (MSS), TCP, 777
maximum transfer unit (MTU), 341
maximum transmission unit (MTU), IPv6, 416
MD5 (Message Digest 5), 453
media types, HTTP Internet, 1370
mega, 38
Memex, 1318
menus, Gopher, 1433
message
  addressing, 20, **21**
  formatting, 19, **19**
  headers, 19
  media type, MIME, *1257*
  nesting, 19
  routing, intermediate devices in, 98
  terminology, 17
  traceroute utility and, 1468
  transmission, 20, **21**
Message Digest 5 (MD5), 453
methods, HTTP. *See* HTTP: methods
metrics
  general routing protocol, 594
  OSPF, 629

metrics, *continued*
RIP, 600
metropolitan area networks (MANs), 27
MIBs (management information bases), 1084–1085
See also SMI; SNMP Protocol
modules, 1096
object, 1087
characteristics, 1087
descriptors, 1091
groups, 1094
identifiers, 1091
name hierarchy, 1092, **1092**
recursive definition of, 1094
SMI, 1086
data types, 1089
SNMP generic object groups, **1089**, *1095*
Microsoft
APIPA and, 1059
DHCP servers, 1061
networking, 858
Windows protocols, 12
.MIL generic TLD, 873
MIME (Multipurpose Internet Mail Extensions), 1242
attachments in, 1243
basic structures, 1246
capabilities, 1243
composite media types, 1253
Content-Transfer-Encoding header, 1257
Content-Type header, 1248
differences from HTTP constructs, 1371
discrete media types, 1246
encapsulated, 1257
encoding, 1257
7-bit and 8-bit message, 1258
base64, 1258, *1259*, **1260**
quoted-printable, 1258
entities, 1246
extension for non-ASCII mail message headers, 1261
headers
Content-Description, 1247
Content-Disposition, 1248
Content-ID, 1247
Content-Length, 1248
Content-Location, 1248
Content-Transfer-Encoding, 1247
Content-Type, 1246
MIME-Version, 1246
media types, 1248
application, 1251, *1252*
octet-stream subtype, 1252
audio, 1250, *1251*
encapsulated, 1257
image, 1250, *1250*
message, *1257*
model, 1251, *1251*
multipart, 1253, *1253*, **1256**
encoding, 1254
subtypes, 1253
text, 1250, *1250*
video, 1251, *1251*
motivation for, 1242
multipart, *1253*–**1256**
non-ASCII extension, 1261
standards, 1244, *1245*
Usenet and, 1411
Minimal Encapsulation within IP, Mobile IP, 496
Minnesota, University of, 1431
miscellaneous TCP/IP troubleshooting protocols, 1489, *1490*
MIT (Massachusetts Institute of Technology), 265, 443, 923
mixed notation, IPv6 addresses, 380
MLP (Multilink Protocol), PPP. *See* PPP: MP
mnemonics, OSI Reference Model, 116
Mobile IP (Internet Protocol Mobility Support), 475–476, 480, **481**
address, 483
co-located care-of, 485
foreign agent care-of, 484, **484**
agent
discovery, 486
registration, 492
ARP and, 498
proxying by home agent, **500**
data encapsulation, 495
device roles, 481
efficiency, 500
functions, 482
Generic Routing Encapsulation (GRE), 496

Mobile IP, *continued*
inefficiency, **502**
limitations of, 479
messages
Agent Advertisement, 488, **489**, *490*, **490**
Agent Solicitation, 487
Registration Reply, **495**
Registration Request, 493, *493*, **494**
Minimal Encapsulation within IP, 496
Mobility Agent Advertisement Extension, 488
operation, 480, **481**
registration, 492
reverse tunneling, 498
security and, 503
transmission triangle, 497
tunneling, 496, **497**
Mobility Agent Advertisement extension, Mobile IP, **489**, *489*
model media type, MIME, 1251
models, networking, 83
modems, 36
moderated mailing lists, 1231
moderated Usenet newsgroups, 1407
modified EUI-64 format, 388
modules, MIB, 1096
More Fragments, IP datagram field, 346
Mount Protocol, NFS, 968, *969*
MP (Multilink Protocol). *See* PPP: MP, 196
MRU (Maximum Receive Unit) PPP option, 158
MSL (maximum segment lifetime),TCP, 766
MSS (maximum segment size), TCP, 729, 777
MTP (Mail Transfer Protocol), 1264
MTU (maximum transmission unit)
IP, 341
IPv6, 416
MTU option, ICMPv6, 574, *574*
multicast
address resolution, 223
IP. *See* IP: multicast
IPv6. *See* IPv6: multicast
messages, 22
multihomed AS, BGP, 654
multihomed devices, IP internetwork, **253**
Multilink PPP architecture, **176**
Multilink Protocol, PPP. *See* PPP: MP
multipart media type, MIME, *1253*
multipart messages, MIME. *See* MIME: media types: multipart
multiplexing, **698**, 699
.MUSEUM generic TLD, 873
MX (Mail Exchange) resource record, DNS, 892, 925, 939, 947, 1227

N

"N" Notation, OSI, 89
Nagle, John, 815
Nagle's Algorithm, TCP, 815
name
architecture, 831
registration, 834
DNS. *See* DNS: name registration
methods, 835
resolution, 837
caching and, 839
DNS. *See* DNS: name resolution
host table, 844
load balancing and, 840
techniques, 836
servers, DNS. *See* DNS: name servers
spaces, 831
DNS, **862**
flat, **832**
systems, 823, 826
host table, 843
.NAME generic TLD, 873
Name Server resource record, DNS, 892, *937*, 946
names, DNS. *See* DNS names
NAT (Network Address Translation). *See* IP NAT
National Committee for Information Technology (NCITS), 50
national Internet registries, 57
NCITS (National Committee for Information Technology), 50
NCP (Network Control Protocol), ARPA, 720, 1170
NCPs (Network Control Protocols), PPP. *See* PPP: NCPs

ND (Neighbor Discovery Protocol), 575, 576, **578**
  duplicate address detection, 586
  functions compared to IPv4, 580
  host redirection, **587**
  host-host communication functions, 583
  host-router discovery functions, 582
  ICMPv6 messages used, 580
  neighbor unreachability detection, 585
  next-hop determination, 584
  operation, 578
  redirect function, 586
  standards, 577
  updating neighbors, 585
negative caching, 904
Neighbor Advertisement message, 563
Neighbor Discovery protocol. *See* ND
Neighbor Solicitation message, 563
Nelson, Ted, 1318
nesting, message, 19
.NET generic TLD, 873
NetBIOS, 109
NetBIOS/NetBEUI/NBF suite, 109
netiquette, 1400
netstat utility
  UNIX, 1480
  Windows, 1482
Network Address Translation. *See* IP NAT
network congestion avoidance, quality of service, 44
Network Control Protocol (NCP), ARPA, 720, 1170
Network Control Protocols (NCPs), PPP. *See* PPP: NCPs
network file and resource sharing, 953
Network File System. *See* NFS
Network Information Center (NIC), 869, 1477
Network Interface Layer, 128
  protocols, 137
Network Interface/Internet Layer protocols, TCP/IP, 132
Network Layer, OSI Reference Model, 105
network management. *See* SNMP Framework
network message formatting, **19**
Network News Transfer Protocol. *See* NNTP
network news. *See* Usenet
network segment, 28
Network Solutions, Inc. (NSI), 56
network standards and standards organizations, 45
network status utility (netstat), 1479
Network Time Protocol (NTP), 539
Network Unreachable, 523
Network Virtual Terminal (NVT), 1443, **1444**
networking, 6
  advantages, 7
  characteristics, 10
  client/server, 23, **25**
  costs, 8
  disadvantages, 8
  fundamentals, 3
  industry groups, 51
  layers, models, and architectures, 10
  Microsoft, 858
  nonperformance characteristics, 33
  peer-to-peer, 23
  performance, 32
  speed, 34
  standards, 48
    organizations, 49
  structural models, 23
networks, 28
newbies, 1400
news. *See* Usenet; NNTP
newsgroups, 1404
news, URL Network News/Usenet scheme syntax, 1148
Next Header
  field, IPv6, 405
  values, IPv6, *406*
NFS (Network File System), 953
  architecture and components, 957
  caching, 963
  client and server responsibilities, 963
  components, 957
  data definition, 959
  design goals, 955
  External Data Representation (XDR), 959
  file system model, 968

NFS (Network File System), *continued*
  Mount Protocol server procedures, *969*
  operation, 961
  remote procedure calls (RPCs), 961
  security in, 959
  server procedures and operations, 964
    Version 2 and Version 3, 964, *964*
    Version 4, 966, *966*
  standards, 956
  versions, 956
  XDR, 959
    data types, 960, *960*
nibble, binary information groups, 63
NIC (Network Information Center), 843, 869
nick, 1459
nicname (DNS Registry Database Lookup Utility), 1477
NMS (SNMP Network Management Station), 1073
NNTP (Network News Transfer Protocol), 1397, 1411
  article propagation, **1415**
  base commands, 1420, *1421*
  client-server communication, 1416
  command extensions, 1422
    LIST, *1423*
    newsreader, 1423, *1424*
    transport, 1423, *1423*
  command syntax, 1420
  interserver communication, 1413
  news access, 1418, **1419**
  news article propagation, 1413
  news posting and access, 1416
  newsgroup header retrieval, 1418
  propagation methods, 1414
  reply codes, 1426, *1428*
  SMTP, similarity to, 1412
  status responses, 1426
  streaming mode, 1416
  Telnet NVT and, 1420
No Next Header, IPv6 extension header, 409
No Operation, IPv4 option, 338
No Route to Destination, 549
nominal performance, 34
Non Repeaters Parameter, SNMPv2/v3 Table Traversal, 1107
noncontiguous subnet masks, 280
noncore routers, 592
non-overlapping scopes, DHCP leases, 1010, **1011**
nonperformance networking characteristics, 33
No-Operation, TCP option, 773
Not Authenticated state commands, IMAP, *1306*
NOT, Boolean logical function, *73*
Notification messages, BGP. *See* BGP: messages: Notification
Notify feature, DNS, 898
NS (Name Server) resource record, DNS, 892, 937, 946
nslookup Utility, 1473, *1474*
NTP (Network Time Protocol), 539
nttp, URL Network News Transfer Protocol scheme syntax, 1148
.NU country code TLD, 875
numbers
  base 8, 67
  base 16, 67
  base 10, 65
  base 2, 65
  binary, 65
  decimal, 65
  hexadecimal, 67
  octal, 65
NVT (Network Virtual Terminal), Telnet, 1443, **1444**
nybble, binary information group, 63

O

OACK (option acknowledgment) messages, TFTP, 1208
OAKLEY, IPsec IKE, 472
object-oriented programming, basis for HTTP methods, 1349
objects, MIB. *See* MIBs: objects
obscuration, URL, 1157
octal numbers, 66
  conversion, *68*
octet
  binary information grouping, 63
  versus byte, 64

octet-stream, MIME application media type subtype, 1252
offline access model, email, 1287
omission of URL syntax elements, 1144
One-Byte Padding Extension, Mobile IP Agent Advertisement message format, 488
online access model, email, 1287
opcodes, ARP, 216
Open message, BGP. *See* BGP: messages: Open
Open Shortest Path First. *See* OSPF
open standards, 47
Open Systems Interconnection Reference Model. *See* OSI Reference Model
option acknowledgment (OACK) messages, TFTP, 1208, *1214*
option
  negotiation, Telnet, 1452
  overloading, DHCP, 1044
OPTIONS, HTTP method, 1350
OR, Boolean logical function, 74, *74*
  setting groups of bits with, 76
organizational (generic) TLDs and authorities, DNS, 870
organizationally unique identifier (OUI), for IP multicast address resolution, 223
.ORG generic TLD, 873
OSI model. *See* OSI Reference Model
OSI protocol suite, 82
OSI Reference Model, 79, *117*
  analogy, 113, *114*
  Application Layer (Layer 7), 111
  compared to TCP/IP model, **129**
  concepts, 87
  data encapsulation, 95, **96**
  Data Link Layer (Layer 2), 103
    addresses, contrasting to IP addresses, 244
    MAC address, 104
    sublayers, 103
  entities, functions, facilities, and services, 90
  history of, 82
  importance of, 84
  interfaces, **92**
  layer, 80, 101
    abstraction level of, 88
    relationships and terminology, **91**
    stack, 88
    terminology, 89
  lower layers, 88
  mnemonics, 116, **116**
  "N" notation, 89
  Network Layer (Layer 3), 105
  network stacks, 90
  OSI protocol suite, 82
  other network architectures and protocol stacks, 86
  PDU and SDU encapsulation, **97**
  Physical Layer (Layer 1), 102
  Presentation Layer (Layer 6), 110
  protocol data units (PDUs) and service data units (SDUs), 95
  protocol stack, 90
  protocols, 93, **94**
  routing, 98, **99**
  Session Layer (Layer 5), 109
  Transport Layer (Layer 4), 106
  upper layers, 88
  WAN technologies and, 86
OSPF (Open Shortest Path First), 625–626
  areas, 630
  AS, **629**
  calculated OSPF routes, *637*
  common header format, **640**
  development, 626
  features, 627
  hierarchical topology, 630, **632**
    area border routers, 631
    backbone routers, 631
    router roles, 631
  link-state database (LSDB), 628, *629*
  messages, 638
    authentication, 639
    Database Description messages, 641, *642*, **642**
    header format, common, 639, *640*
    Hello messages, 641, *641*, **641**
    Link State Acknowledgment messages, 644, *644*, **644**
    Link State Advertisement messages, 644, *645*, **645**
    Link State Request messages, 643, *643*, **643**

OSPF, *continued*
messages, *continued*
Link State Update messages, 643, *643*, **644**
messaging, 638
multicast version, 361
operation, 637
route
calculation, *637*
determination using SPF trees, 633, **635**
SPF tree, **637**
topology, 628
OUI (organizationally unique identifier)
IP multicast address resolution, 223
outbound NAT, 434, *435*, **436**
overlapping/twice NAT, 442
overloaded IP NAT, 439, **441**, *442*

P

Packet Internet Groper, 1463
packet switching, 13, **14**
Packet Too Big messages, ICMPv6, 550, *551*
packets, 18
IP, 330
PPP LCP, 156
padding, in IPv6 options, 414
Palo Alto Research Center (PARC), Xerox, 598
PAP (Password Authentication Protocol), PPP. *See* PPP: PAP
parameter configuration, DHCP, **1034**
Parameter Problem messages
ICMPv4, 533, *534*
ICMPv6, 554, *555*
PARC (Xerox Palo Alto Research Center), 598
PARC Universal Protocol (PUP), 598
Partially Qualified Domain Names (PQDNs), DNS, 866
party-based security model, SNMPv2/SMNPv3, 1111
passive data connections, FTP, 1178
passive opens, TCP, 751
PASV command, FTP, 1178
path attributes, BGP, 657, *659*
payload
encapsulation, 97
message, 19
PDU and SDU encapsulation, OSI Reference Model, **97**
PDUs, SNMP, 1103
peer-to-peer networking, 23, **24**
performance measurement units, 37
performance, network, 31
persistent connections, HTTP, 1337
Physical Layer, OSI Reference Model, 102
ping utility, 1463–1464
use, 1464–1465
options and parameters, 1466
ping6 utility (ping for IPv6), 1463
pipelining, HTTP, 1337
Pointer Indicates the Error, 534
Pointer resource record, DNS, 892, 938, *938*, 947
Point-to-Point Protocol. *See* PPP
poisoned reverse, split horizon with, RIP, 612
poll-driven communication, SNMP, 1102
pool size selection, DHCP, 1009
POP (Post Office Protocol), 1288
See also POP3
POP3 (Post Office Protocol version 3), 1288
authentication process, 1291
commands, 1291
finite state machine, 1290, **1291**
mail exchange process and commands, 1293, *1294*, **1296**
operation, 1290
responses, 1290
session states, 1290, **1291**
update and session termination process and commands, 1295
user authentication process, **1292**
POP-before-SMTP authentication, 1278
PORT command, FTP, 1178
port mapper, RPC, 962
port numbers, IANA and management of, 707
Port Unreachable, 523, 549
port-based (overloaded) NAT, 439, **441**, *442*

ports, 698
application use of well-known and registered ports, 707
BOOTP use of, 981
client/server application port mechanics, 703, **705**
demultiplexing, 699
destination, 699
ephemeral, 703
multiplexing, 699
process multiplexing/demultiplexing, **700**
server, 701
source, 699
positive acknowledgment with retransmission (PAR), 732
positive caching, 904
Post Office Protocol. *See* POP; POP3
POST, HTTP method, 1350
Postel, Jonathan B. (Jon), 55, 123
PPP (Point-to-Point Protocol), 139, 144
advantages, 145
architecture, **145**
authentication protocols, 162
See also PPP: PAP; PPP: CHAP
BACP (Bandwidth Allocation Control Protocol), 178, 179
BAP (Bandwidth Allocation Protocol), 178
messages, 179
operation, 179
CCP (Compression Control Protocol), 169
compression and decompression, *171*
configuration, 171
messages, 170
operation, 170
CHAP (Challenge Handshake Authentication Protocol), 163, **164**
frame formats, 194, *194*, **195**
code values, 187
compression algorithms, 171
Compression Control Protocol. *See* PPP: CCP
control frames, *187*, 187, *188*, 190
option format, 188, *189*
data frames, **184**
development and standardization, 144
ECP (Encryption Control Protocol), 172
configuration, 173
encryption algorithms, 173, *174*
encryption and decryption, 174
messages, 173
operation, 173
Encryption Control Protocol. *See* PPP: ECP
feature protocols, 167
field compression, 185
frame format, 182, *182*, **183**
Protocol field ranges, 183, *184*
Protocol field values, 184
function and architecture, 145
functional groups, 147
Internet Protocol Control Protocol (IPCP), **161**, 162
LCP (Link Control Protocol), 155, **156**
frame formats, 190, *191*
link configuration, 157, **157**
link maintenance, 159
link termination, 159
messages, 156
Link Control Protocol. *See* PPP: LCP
link phases, 148
LQM (Link Quality Monitoring), 168
LQR (Link Quality Reporting), 168
MP (Multilink Protocol), 175
architecture, 176, **176**
fragment frame formats, 196, *197*, **197**, **198**
fragmentation process, 196, 198, **199**
ISDN and, 175
operation, 177
Multilink Protocol. *See* PPP: MP
NCPs (Network Control Protocols), 159
IPCP, **161**, 162
operation, 160
Network Control Protocols. *See* PPP: NCPs
operation, 147, **148**
options, 157

PPP, *continued*
PAP (Password Authentication Protocol), 162, **163**
frame formats, 192, *193*, **193**
phases, 148, **151**, *152*
PPP over ATM (PPPoA), 146
PPP over Ethernet (PPPoE), 146
SLIP versus, 140
standards, 151, *153*
PPPoA (PPP over ATM), 146
PPPoE (PPP over Ethernet), 146
PQDNs (Partially Qualified Domain Names), DNS, 866
Pragma, HTTP general header, 1360
preauthentication, IMAP, 1302
Precedence Cutoff in Effect, 524
prefix discovery, ND, 579
Prefix Information option, ICMPv6, 572, *572*
prefix length
CIDR, 319
representation, IPv6 addresses, 381
Prefix-Lengths extension, Mobile IP Agent Advertisement messages, 488, *490*, **490**
Presentation Layer (Layer 6), OSI Reference Model, 110
PRI (primary rate interface), ISDN, 175
primary DNS namer server, 893
privacy, in HTTP, 1390
private addresses
IP, 265
IPv6, 391
private name registration, DNS, 884
private/dynamic port numbers, TCP/UDP, 703
.PRO generic TLD, 873
probe segments, TCP, 811
procedures and operations, NFS, 964
processes
TCP/IP client and server, 697
multiplexing and demultiplexing, **698**
processing conventions and rules, ICMP, 515
propagation methods, NNTP, 1414
proprietary standards, 46
Protocol field
IP, use by TCP and UDP, 699
PPP, 183
protocol. *See also individual protocol names.*
administration and troubleshooting, 1461
Application Layer, 821
connection-oriented, 15
connectionless, 15
general file transfer, 1167
host configuration, 971
interactive, 1435
lower-layer core, 135
network file and resource sharing, 951
Network Interface Layer, 137
Network Interface/Internet Layer connection, 201
operations, SNMP, 1102
OSI Reference Model, 93
roles, email, 1224
routing, 589
stacks, 86
suites, 12
IPX/SPX, 109
OSI, 82
TCP/IP, 119
TCP/IP, 131
Transport Layer, 687
Protocol Unreachable, 11
proxies, HTTP. *See* HTTP: proxying
proxy ARP, 221
Proxy FTP (FTP Third-Party File Transfer), 1174
Proxy-Authenticate, HTTP response header, 1365
Proxy-Authorization HTTP request header, 1363
proxying, ARP, 221
proxying, HTTP. *See* HTTP: proxying
pseudo header
TCP, 774
UDP, 714
PTR (Pointer) resource record, DNS, 938, 947
public cache, 1384
PUP (PARC Universal Protocol), 598
push function, TCP, 790
PUT, HTTP method, 1350

Q

q (quality) values, HTTP, 1380
QoS (quality of service), 43
  ATM and, 44
  IP Datagram Type of Service (TOS) field and, 335
  latency and, 43
quadruple, TCP socket identifier, 750
quality of service. *See* QoS
Quality Protocol, PPP option, 158
quality values, HTTP, 1378
Question Section format, DNS, 935
quoted-printable encoding, MIME, 1258

R

r (Berkeley Remote) Commands, 1454
Range, HTTP request header, 1363
RARP (Reverse Address Resolution Protocol), 228, **229**
  bootstrapping and, 228
  limitations of, 231
  servers, 228
rate, signaling, 38
rated or nominal speed, 34
rcp (Remote Copy), 1457
RCV (receive) pointers, TCP, 781, 782
RData field formats, DNS, 936
read process, TFTP, 1205, **1206**
Read Request (RRQ) messages, TFTP, 1211
reallocation, DHCP leases, **1028**
reason phrases, HTTP, 1353
reassembly, IP message, 347
rebinding process, DHCP, 1028
Rebinding Timer (T2), DHCP, 1008
receive (RCV) Pointers, TCP, 781
receive categories, TCP, 780
receiver SWS avoidance, TCP, 815
Record Route, IP option, 338
recursive DNS name resolution, 913, **914**
Redirect function, ND, 586
Redirect messages
  ICMPv4, 530, *531*
  ICMPv6, 566, *566*
Redirected Header option, ICMPv6, 573, *574*
redundancy
  DNS name servers, 894
  DNS root name server, 899
reference model. *See* OSI Reference Model
reference, locality of, 211
Referer, HTTP request header, 1363
  misspelled as Referer in HTTP, 1363
Refresh field, DNS SOA resource record, 897
regional Internet registries (RIRs), 56, 254, 321
registered port numbers, 707
registration authorities, Internet, 55
Registration Reply messages, Mobile IP, 491, *495*, **495**
Registration Request messages, Mobile IP, 491, *493*, **494**
registration, DNS. *See* DNS: name registration
registration
  host table name, 844
  name, 834
  Mobile IP, 492
registries, national Internet, 57
relative domain names, DNS, 865
relative URLs. *See* URLs: relative
relaying
  BOOTP. *See* BOOTP relay agent
  DHCP, 1057
  email, 1266
reliability features, TCP, 793
remote (r) commands, Berkeley, 1454
remote copy (rcp), 1457
remote login (rlogin), 1455
Remote Network Monitoring (RMON), 1133, **1135**, *1135*
  alarms, events, and statistics, 1136
  MIB hierarchy and object groups, 1134
  standards, 1134
Remote Procedure Calls (RPCs), 109
remote server email access, 1311
remote shell (rsh), 1456
remote uptime (ruptime), 1457
remote who (rwho), 1457
renewal and rebinding, DHCP leases, **1032**
renewal process, DHCP, 1028

Renewal Timer (T1), DHCP, 1008
renumbering
  IPv6 device, 400
  IPv6 router, 568
replay attacks, 453, 503
Reply messages, ARP, 214
Reply Messages, Application of ICMPv6 Echo and Echo, 559
Request for Comment. *See* RFCs
request headers, HTTP, 1361
Request messages
  ARP, 214
  HTTP, 1343, **1344**
  RIP, 604
request/response chain, HTTP, 1334
requirements analysis
  for IP subnetting, 298
  for a network, 32
reregistration, Mobile IP, 491
Réseaux IP Européens Network Coordination Center (RIPE NCC) regional Internet registry, 57
reserved addresses
  IP, 265
  IPv6, 390
reserved port numbers, TCP/UDP, 702
reset function, TCP, 760
Reset-Ack and Reset-Request messages
  PPP CCP, 170
  PPP ECP, 173
resetting bits, 63
resolution
  address. *See* address resolution
  conflict, DNS, 880
  DNS. *See* DNS: name resolution
  URN, 1161
resolvers, DNS. *See* DNS: name resolvers
resource paths, HTTP, 1328
resource records, DNS. *See* DNS: resource records
response headers, HTTP, 1364
Response messages
  HTTP, 1346, **1347**
  PPP CHAP, 164
  RIP, 604
retransmissions
  BOOTP, 982
  DHCP, 1037
  TCP, 794
Retry field, DNS Start of Authority resource record, 897
Retry-After, HTTP response header, 1365
reverse address resolution, 227
Reverse Address Resolution Protocol (RARP), 228
reverse name resolution, DNS, 920
  IPv6, 949
reverse tunneling, Mobile IP, 498
RFC 1497 vendor extensions, DHCP/BOOTP options, *1045*
RFC 822 email message format, 1234
  development of, 1235
  header field, 1238
    groups, 1237, 1238, *1239*
    structure, 1237
  message, 1235
    structure, 1236
  processing and interpretation, 1241
RFC Editor, 57
RFCs (Requests for Comments), 57
  categories, 58
    Best Current Practice, 58
    Experimental, 58
    Historic, 58
    Informational, 58
    Internet Draft (ID), 58
    Internet Standard, 59
    Proposed Standard/Draft Standard/Standard, 58
  master list, 58
RFCs by number. *See* "RFCs by Number" *following this index*
RIBs (routing information bases), BGP, 656
RIP (Routing Information Protocol), 598, 604
  30-second timer, 605
  algorithm issues, 607
    counting to infinity, 607, **608**
    routing loops, 607
    slow convergence, 607
    small infinity, 609
  ASes (autonomous systems), **601**
  default routes, 604
  development of RIP-2 and RIPng, 600
  Garbage-Collection Timer, 606
  message types, 604

RIP, *continued*
metric, issues with, 610
problems, 606
RIP-1 (RIP version 1), 614
messaging, 615, *615*, **616**
version-specific features, 617
RIP-2 (RIP version 2), 617
messaging, 618, 619, *619*, **620**
version-specific features, 617
RIPng (RIP for IPv6), 620
messaging, 621, *622*, **622**
version-specific features, 620
route determination and information propagation, 601, **603**
routing information and route distance metric, 600
special features, 610
hold down, 613
split horizon, 611
split horizon with poisoned reverse, 612, **613**
standardization, 598
timeout timer, 605
triggered updates, 606, 612
update messaging, 605
version-specific features, 614
RIPE NCC (Réseaux IP Européens Network Coordination Center) regional Internet registry, 57
RIPng. *See* RIP: RIPng
RIPv6. *See* RIP: RIPng
RIRs (regional Internet registries), 56, 254, 321
rlogin (Berkeley remote login), 1455
RMON (Remote Network Monitoring), 1133, **1135**, *1135*
robots, mailing list, 1231
robustness principle, TCP, 726
roles
DHCP client/server, 1015
DNS name servers, 893
email communication, 1224
Mobile IP, 481
TCP/IP hardware and software, 127
root domain, DNS, 860
root name servers, DNS, 899
round-trip time (RTT) calculation, TCP, 804
routable protocols, vs. routing protocols, 358
route
aggregation, 359
determination
BGP, 659
OSPF, 633, **635**
RIP, 601
propagation, RIP, 601, **603**
Route Tracing Utility. *See* traceroute
routed, RIP daemon for UNIX, 598
Router Advertisement and Router Solicitation messages
ICMPv4, 539
ICMPv6, 560
router discovery
IP, 540
IPv6, 581
router loops, 335, 527, 552, **553**, 607
router renumbering, IPv6, 568, *569*
routers
core, 592
default, 530
IP routing and, 239
IPv6, 420
noncore, 592
OSI Reference Model Network Layer and, 106
OSPF, 631
used for proxy ARP, 221
routes and routing tables, IP, 357, **358**
routing
classless, benefits of, 317
IP, 355
IP classless, 281
IP multicast, 361
IPv6, 420
OSI Reference Model and, 98
software, 252
source, 338
routing entries, 357
Routing extension header, IPv6, 410, *410*
routing information bases (RIBs), 656
Routing Information Protocol. *See* RIP
routing
loops, 335, 527, 552, **553**, 607
policies, BGP, 654

routing, *continued*
prefix
IPv6 unicast addresses, 385
structure, IPv6 global unicast address format, *386*
protocols, 589
algorithms and metrics, 594
architectures and concepts, 591
exterior and interior, 593
static and dynamic, 595
tables, IP, 357
RPCs (Remote Procedure Calls), 109, 962
RR. *See* DNS: resource records
RRQ (Read Request) messages, TFTP, 1211
rsh (Berkeley Remote Shell), 1456
RTT (round-trip time) calculation, TCP, 804
ruptime (Berkeley remote uptime), 1457
rwho (Berkeley remote who), 1457

S

SACK (selective acknowledgment), TCP, 798
SAD (Security Association Database), IPsec, 460
safe and idempotent HTTP methods, 1351
SAs (Security Associations), IPsec, 460
scalability, TCP/IP, 124
schemes and scheme-specific syntaxes, URL, 1146
scopes (lease address ranges), DHCP, 1009, **1010**, 1010
scopes, IPv6 multicast, 395
SDLC (Synchronous Data Link Control) protocol, 144
SDOs (Standards Developing Organizations), 50
secondary DNS name server, 893
second-level DNS domains, 860
Secure Hash Algorithm 1 (SHA-1), 453
secure login (slogin), 1456
secure shell (ssh), 1457
Secure Sockets Layer (SSL), 111, 1390
security
DHCP, 1064
HTTP, 1388
IP. *See* IPsec
Mobile IP, 503
NFS, 959
SMTP, 1277
SNMP, 1075, 1110
security associations (SAs), IPsec, 460
security extensions, FTP, 1176
security methods, SNMPv2/v3, 1111
security parameter index (SPI), IPsec, 461
Security, IP option, 338
segment retransmission timers, TCP, 794
segment
coaxial cable, 29
network, 28
TCP. *See* TCP segments
Selected state, IMAP4, 1309, *1310*
selective acknowledgment (SACK), TCP, 798
Selective Acknowledgment Permitted, TCP option, 773
Selective Acknowledgment, TCP Option, 773
selector string, Gopher, 1432
selectors, IPsec, 461
send (SND) pointers, TCP, 781
send window and usable window, 737
sender and receiver in TCP/IP email, decoupling, 1222
sender SWS avoidance and Nagle's algorithm, 815
Sequence Number field
PPP MP, 197
TCP, 783
sequence number synchronization, TCP, 737, 758
Serial Line Internet Protocol. *See* SLIP
Server, HTTP response header, 1365
server-driven negotiation, HTTP, 1378
servers, 23
BOOTP, 980
conflict detection, DHCP, 1061
data transfer process (Server-DTP), FTP, 1174
DNS name. *See* DNS: name servers

servers, *continued*
hardware, 126
implementations, DHCP, 1054
procedures and operations, NFS, 964
processing, SMTP, 1241
RARP, 228
responsibilities, DHCP, 1014
roles, 23
software, 23, 126
software features, DHCP, 1054
structure, Usenet, 1413
support functions, DNS, 889
TCP port assignments, 742
UDP port assignments, 716
Web, 1321
service commands, FTP, 1186
services, TCP/IP, 125
Session Layer (Layer 5), OSI Reference Model, 109
SetRequest messages, SNMP, 1107
setting bits using OR bit mask, 76, *76*
SGML (Standard Generalized Markup Language), 1322
SGMP (Simple Gateway Monitoring Protocol), 1070, 1100
SHA-1 (Secure Hash Algorithm 1), 453
shared cache, 1384
shared key authentication, IEEE 802.11, 163
shortcuts for computing IP subnet host addresses, 313
shortest path first (link-state) routing protocol algorithm, 595
shrinking TCP window, problems with, 809, **810**
signaling rate, 38
Silly Window Syndrome (SWS), TCP, 812
Simple Gateway Monitoring Protocol (SGMP), 1070, 1100
Simple Mail Transfer Protocol. *See* SMTP
Simple Network Management Protocol. *See* SNMP Framework; SNMP Protocol
simple structure, MIME, 1246
simplex network operation, 41
simultaneous connection termination, TCP, 766
simultaneous open connection establishment, TCP, 755
site-local addresses, IPv6, 391
SIZE extension, SMTP, 1281
sizes of networks, 25
SKEME, IKE, 472
slash (CIDR) notation, 303, 319, **320**
sliding the TCP send window, 738, **739**
sliding window system, TCP. *See* TCP: sliding window system
SLIP (Serial Line Internet Protocol), 141
compressed (CSLIP), 143
data framing method and general operation, 141
escape character (ESC) in, 142
operation, **143**
PPP vs., 140
problems, 142
slogin (secure login), 1456
SMI (Structure of Management Information), 1083–1084
See also MIBs; SNMP Framework
data types, 1089, *1089*
defining MIB objects, 1086
textual conventions, 1090
smoothing factor, TCP RTT, 804
SMTP (Simple Mail Transfer Protocol), 1263–1264
commands, 1279, *1279*
communication and message transport methods, 1265
connection establishment, 1268
using SMTP extensions, 1269
connection termination, 1270
enhanced status code replies, 1284
extensions, 1276, *1276*
AUTH, 1281
mail transaction process, 1271, **1273**
reply codes, 1281, *1283*
security issues, 1277
SIZE extension, 1281
special features, 1275
address debugging, 1275
mail forwarding, 1275
mail gatewaying, 1275
mail relaying, 1275
mailing list expansion, 1275
turning, 1275

SMTP, *continued*
special requirements for email addresses, 1227
standards, 1264
Telnet NVT and, 1279
terminology, 1267
transaction session establishment and termination, **1269**
SND (send) pointers, TCP, 781–782
sneakernet, 7
SNMP (Simple Network Management Protocol), 1099
See also SNMP Framework; SNMP Protocol
SNMP Framework, 1070
See also SNMP Protocol
architecture, 1076
components, 1075
design goals, 1071
device types, 1072
early development of, 1070
entities, 1073
information-oriented design of, 1084
managed node entities, 1073
management information base (MIB), **1089**
generic object groups, *1095*
network management station entities, 1073
operational model, 1073, **1074**
SNMP agents, 1073
SNMP applications, 1073
SNMP management information base (MIB), 1073
SNMP manager, 1073
standards, 1079
SNMPsec, *1080*
SNMPv1, *1080*
SNMPv2c, *1081*
SNMPv2p, *1080*
SNMPv2u, *1081*
SNMPv3, *1082*
versions, 1076
SNMPsec, 1077
SNMPv1.5, 1078
SNMPv1, 1077
SNMPv2 (SNMPv2u), User-Based, 1078
SNMPv2* (SNMP "asterisk"), 1078
SNMPv2c (community-based SNMPv2), 1078
SNMPv2, 1078
SNMPv3, 1079
SNMP Protocol, 1099, 1100
See also SNMP Framework
communication methods, 1102
information notification process, 1109
information poll process, 1104, **1105**
messages
format, 1116, **1118**
generation, 1114
vs. PDUs, 1117
SNMPv1 message format, 1119, *1119*, **1119**
SNMPv1 PDU formats, 1120, **1121**, **1122**
SNMPv1 Trap-PDU format , *1121*
SNMPv2 common PDU format, *1126*, **1128**
SNMPv2 GetBulkRequest-PDU Format, *1129*
SNMPv2c message format, 1124, *1124*, **1124**
SNMPv2p message format, 1123, *1123*, **1123**
SNMPv2u message format, 1124, *1125*, **1125**
SNMPv3 message format, 1129, **1130**, *1130*
object modification process, 1107, **1108**
PDU
classes, 1103, *1103*
format, 1117
protocol operations, 1102
and transport mappings, 1101
security issues and methods, 1110
table traversal, 1106
transport mappings, 1114
variable binding format , *1118*
SOA (Start Of Authority) resource record, DNS, 938, 946
socket identifier quadruple, TCP, 750
sockets, 109, 706
software
client, 23, 126
roles, client/server, 127

software, *continued*
routing, 252
server, 23, 126
solicited-node multicast addresses, 396
sonar, 1463
Source Host Isolated, 524
Source Link-Layer Address option, ICMPv6, 571, *571*
source port and destination port numbers, TCP/UDP, 699
Source Quench messages, ICMPv4, 525, *526*
Source Route Failed, 524
source routing, 338
spam, 1157
spatial locality of reference, 915
SPD (Security Policy Database), IPsec, 460
speed
rated or nominal, 34
network, 34
SPF (shortest path first), 626
SPF trees, OSPF, 633, **637**
SPI (Security Parameter Index), IPsec, 461
split horizon with poisoned reverse, RIP, 611–**613**
ssh (secure shell), 1457
SSL (Secure Sockets Layer), 111, 1390
stack, OSI Reference Model layer, 88
standardization process, Internet, 58
standards
See also individual protocols
de facto, 48
networking, 48
open, 47
proprietary, 46
standards developing organizations (SDOs), 50
standards
organizations, Internet, **54**
track, RFC process, 58
Stanford University, 843, 1298
Start Of Authority resource record, DNS, 892, 938, *938*, 946
state management using cookies, HTTP, 1390
stateful autoconfiguration, 1065
stateless autoconfiguration, 399, 1065
static and dynamic
address mappings, IP NAT, 433
ARP cache entries, 219
routing protocols, 595
stream mode, FTP, 1181
streaming mode, NNTP, 1416
Strict Source Route, IP option, 338
Structure of Management Information. *See* SMI
structured name space, DNS, 832
stub AS, BGP, 654
stub resolver, DNS, 911
subdomains, DNS, 860
sublayers, 89
physical layer, 103
subnet, 28
subnetting. *See* IP: subnetting
subnetwork, 28
subprotocols, 87
Success message, PPP CHAP, 164
suites, protocol, 12
supernetting. *See* CIDR
support protocols, IP, 505
SWS (Silly Window Syndrome), TCP, 812
symbolic names for addressing, 826
symmetric operation of Telnet, 1440
SYN field and control messages, TCP, 753
Synchronous Data Link Control (SDLC) protocol, 144

T

T1 (Renewal Timer), DHCP, 1008
T2 (Rebinding Timer), DHCP, 1008
table name registration, 835
table traversal, SNMP, 1106
table-based name resolution, 837
tables, routing, 357
tags, HTML, 1323
TANSTAAFL, 8
Target Hardware Address, ARP, 214
Target Link-Layer Address option, ICMPv6, 572, *572*
Target Protocol Address, ARP, 214
TCB (Transmission Control Block), TCP, 751

TCP (Transmission Control Protocol), 720, 727
acknowledgment header flag (ACK), 747
acknowledgment mechanics, 780
adaptive retransmission, 803
aggressive retransmission, **800**
applications and server port assignments, 742
characteristics, 724
congestion collapse, 817
congestion
avoidance, 818
fast recovery, 819
fast retransmit, 819
handling, 816
slow start, 818
connections, 745
active and passive opens, 751
establishment, 752, *754*, **755**
parameter exchange, 759
sequence number synchronization, 757
SYN and ACK messages, 753
keepalive messages, 761
management, 760
preparation, 750
reset segments, 761
termination, 762, *764*, **765**
transmission control blocks (TCBs), 751
data handling and processing, 728
data stream processing and segment packaging, **730**
finite state machine (FSM), 746, *748*, **750**
functions, 722
history, 720
maximum segment lifetime (MSL), 766
maximum segment size. *See* TCP: MSS
messages. *See* TCP: segments
MSS (maximum segment size), 729, 777
default, 778
negotiation, 779
nondefault value specification, 779
selection, 778
MSS (maximum segment size) parameter, 759
operation, 721
options, *773*
ports and connection identification, 741
probe segments, 811
pseudo header for checksum calculations, 774, *775*, **775**
push function, 790
reliability and flow control features, 793
reset function, 760
retransmission timer calculations, 803
retransmissions and retransmission timers, 794
robustness principle, 726
RTT calculation, adaptive retransmission and, 803
segments, *771*
checksum calculation, 774, **776**
control bits, *772*
format, 770, **772**
packaging, 728
selective acknowledgment (SACK), 798, **802**
send window. *See* TCP: sliding window system
sequence number synchronization, 758, **759**
sequence numbers, 729
silly window syndrome, 812, **814**
avoidance algorithms, 815
sliding window system, 731
categories and send window terminology, **738**
closing send window, 808
mechanics, 780
receive categories and pointers, **783**
send (SND) and receive (RCV) pointers, 781
send window and usable window, 737
sliding the send window, 738
transmit and receive categories, 780, **782**
window management issues, 809
window size adjustment and flow control, 805, **807**
socket identifier quadruple, 750

TCP, *continued*
standards, 721
SWS. *See* TCP: sliding window system; TCP: silly window syndrome
three-way handshake. *See* TCP: connections: establishment
TIME-WAIT state, 765
transmission round-trip time (RTT), 803
UDP vs., 689
urgent function, 791
Telnet Interrupt Handling, 1449
usable window. *See* TCP: sliding window system
TCP parameters, DHCP/BOOTP options, 1048, *1048*
TCP/IP, 119, 122
See also specific protocols and technologies
architecture, 128
client processes, 697
client/server operation, **126**, 697
factors in success of, 123
history, 122
model, 128
vs. OSI Reference Model, **129**
ports. *See* ports
protocols, 131, *132*, **134**
role of host configuration protocols in, 975
server processes, 697
services, 125
sockets, 109
transactional roles, 127
TCP/UDP ports, 698, 702
TE, HTTP request header, 1364
Telecommunications Industry Association (TIA), 50
Telecommunications Standardization Sector of the International Telecommunication Union (ITU-T), 82
Telnet Protocol, 1438–1439
accessing other servers with, 1442
applications, 1440
commands, 1446, *1448*
communication and the Network Virtual Terminal (NVT), 1443, **1444**
ASCII control codes, 1445, *1445*
connections and client/server operation, 1441
history, 1438
interrupt handling, 1449
options, 1451, *1451*
negotiation, 1452
subnegotiation, 1453
sessions and client/server communication, 1441
symmetric operation of, 1440
URL scheme syntax (telnet), 1149
telnet, URL Telnet scheme syntax, 1149
temporal locality of reference, 915
Terminate-Ack and Terminate-Request messages
PPP CCP, 171
PPP ECP, 173
PPP LCP, 159
PPP NCPs, 160
text formatting tags, HTML, 1326
text media type, MIME, 1250
text representation, DNS master file, 891
Text resource record, DNS, 892, 939, *940*, 947
textual conventions, SMI, 1090
text, MIME text media type, 1250
TFTP (Trivial File Transfer Protocol), 1199–1200
bootstrapping and, 1200
connection
establishment, 1203
termination, 1202
data block numbering, 1205
FTP and, 1201
identification, 1203
initial message exchange, 1204
messages, 1211
Acknowledgment, 1213, *1213*, **1213**
Data, 1212, *1212*, **1213**
Error, 1213, **1213**, *1214*
Option Acknowledgment, 1214, *1214*, **1214**
Read Request and Write Request, 1211, *1212*, **1212**
messaging, 1204
operation, 1202, 1204

TFTP, *continued*
options, 1211, *1211*
negotiation, 1208
read process, 1205, **1206**
with option negotiation, **1210**
transfer identifier (TID), 1203
write process, 1206, **1207**
third-party
cookies, 1392
file transfer (Proxy FTP), 1174
threading, Usenet article, 1419
three-way handshake
PPP CHAP, 163
TCP, 753
throughput, 35
TIA (Telecommunications Industry Association), 50
TID (transfer identifier), TFTP, 1203
Time Exceeded messages
ICMPv4, 527, *529*
ICMPv6, 552, *553*
Time to Live (TTL)
field, IP Datagram, 335
interval, DNS, 902
Time-Remaining messages, PPP LCP, 159
Timestamp
IP option, 338
(Request) messages, ICMPv4, 537, *538*
Reply messages, ICMPv4, 537, *538*
TIME-WAIT state, TCP, 765
TLDs (top-level domains), DNS, 860
TLV encoding of BOOTP vendor information fields, 990
.TO country code TLD, 875
Token Ring, 28
top-level domains (TLDs), DNS, 860
TOS (Type of Service) field, IP, 335
Total Length field, use in IP fragmentation, 346
TRACE, HTTP method, 1351
Traceroute messages, ICMPv4, 544, *545*
traceroute utility, 1467
operation, 1468, **1469**
options and parameters, 1470
traceroute message and, 1468
traceroute, 1467
tracert, abbreviation, 1467
use, 1469
Traceroute, IP option, 338
Traditional NAT, 434, *435*, **436**
traffic
flow and types, BGP, 653
prioritization and shaping, quality of service, 44
trailer
calculation and placement, ESP, 467
footer, alias 19
Trailer, ESP, 466
Trailer, HTTP general header, 1360
trailers, HTTP, 1375
transaction identifier (XID), DHCP, 1036
transactional roles, TCP/IP, 127
transfer encodings, HTTP, 1372
transfer identifier (TID), TFTP, 1203
Transfer-Encoding, HTTP general Header, 1361
transistors and binary information, 62
transit
AS, BGP, 655
traffic, BGP, 654
transition from IPv4 to IPv6, 370
transitory connections, HTTP, 1336
Transmission Control Blocks (TCBs), TCP, 751
Transmission Control Program, original meaning of TCP, 122
Transmission Control Protocol. *See* TCP
transmission round-trip time (RTT), TCP, 803
transmission triangle, Mobile IP, 497
transport extensions, NNTP, 1423
Transport Layer (Layer 4), OSI Reference Model, 106
transport mappings, SNMP, 1114
transport mode, IPsec, 457, **458**
Trap and Trapv2 messages, SNMP, 1109
tree, DNS. *See* DNS: names
triggered updates, RIP, 606, 612
Trivial File Transfer Protocol. *See* TFTP
troubleshooting utilities and protocols, TCP/IP, 1461
miscellaneous, *1490*
true and false Boolean values, 73

Truscott, Tom, 1398
truth tables, Boolean logic, 73
TTL (Time to Live)
Field, IP, router loops and, 335
DNS, 903
tunnel mode, IPsec, 457, **459**
tunneling, Mobile IP, 496, **497**
turning, SMTP, 1275
.TV country code TLD, 875
Two-Way NAT, 437, **438**, *439*
TXT (text) resource record, DNS, 939, 947
Type of Service (TOS) field, IP datagram, 335, *336*

U

UDP (User Datagram Protocol), 711–712
applications and server port use, 717
messages, 714, **714**, *715*
operation, 713
pseudo header, 714, **715**
TCP vs., 689
UDRP (Uniform Domain Name Dispute Resolution Policy), DNS, 881
unary operator, NT, 73
UNC (University of North Carolina), 1399
unicast, 21, 22
address format, IPv6. *See* IPv6: global unicast address format
unidirectional IP NAT, 434, *435*, **436**
Uniform Domain Name Dispute Resolution Policy, DNS, 880
Uniform Resource Identifiers. *See* URIs; URLs; URNs
unintentional cookies, 1392
unit prefixes, 38
United States ASCII (US-ASCII) character set, 1444
United States Department of Defense (DoD), 371
units, 38
University of Minnesota, 1431
University of North Carolina (UNC), 1399
UNIX configuration file /etc/hosts, 843, 1463
Unix-to-Unix Copy Protocol (UUCP)
email and, 1219
Usenet and, 1398
unmoderated Usenet newsgroups, 1407
Unrecognized IPv6 Option Encountered, 556
Unrecognized Next Header Type Encountered, 556
unreliable protocol, **732**
unsafe characters in URLs, 1145
unspecified address, IPv6, 391
Update messages, BGP. *See* BGP: messages: Update
Upgrade, HTTP general Header, 1361
urgent function, TCP, 791
URIs (Uniform Resource Identifiers), 1140
See also URLs; URNs
categories (URLs and URNs), 1141
standards, 1142
URLs (Uniform Resource Locators)
See also URIs; URNs
abbreviation, 1156
common Internet scheme syntax, 1143
example, **1144**
explicit delimiting and redirectors, 1156
fragments, 1145
general syntax, 1142
length and complexity issues, 1154
obscuration and obfuscation, 1156
parameter strings, 1155
problems with, 1159
relative, *1152*
interpretation rules, 1151
syntax and base URLs, 1150
schemes and scheme-specific syntaxes, 1146
special encodings, 1145, *1145*
special syntax rules, 1149
unsafe characters, 1145
wrapping and delimiting, 1155
URNs (Uniform Resource Names), 1159–1160
See also URIs; URLs
namespaces, 1160
syntax, 1160
resolution and implementation difficulties, 1161

usable window, TCP, 737
US-ASCII (United States ASCII) character set, 1235, 1444
Usenet
See also NNTP
access, 1417
addressing, 1404
article propagation, 1414, 1416
Big Eight newsgroup hierarchies, *1405*
headers, *1409*, *1410*
history, 1398
message format, 1408
MIME messages and, 1411
model, 1401–**1403**
posting, 1417
newsgroup hierarchies, 1405–**1406**
newsgroups, 1404
operation, 1399
overview, 1398
reading, 1417
server sructure, 1413
threading, 1419
transport methods, 1400
user (registered) port numbers, 703
user commands, FTP, *1194*
User Datagram Protocol. *See* UDP
User-Agent, HTTP request header, 1364
user-based security model (USM), SNMPv2/SNMPv3, 1112
USM (User-Based Security Model), SNMPv2/SNMPv3, 1112
UUCP (Unix-to-Unix Copy Protocol)
email and, 1219
Usenet and, 1398
UUCP-style email addressing, 1229

V

VACM (View-Based Access Control Model), SNMPv2/v3, 1112
Variable Length Subnet Masking (VLSM), IP. *See* IP: VLSM
Vary, HTTP response header, 1365
vendor information
extensions, BOOTP, 989
fields, BOOTP, 990
vertical communication, OSI Reference Model layers, 91
Via, HTTP general header, 1361
video media type, MIME, 1251
View-Based Access Control Model (VACM), SNMPv2/v3, 1112
virtual private networking (VPN), 30, 496
VLSM, IP. *See* IP: VLSM
VPN (virtual private networking), 30, 496

W

WAN (Wide Area Network), 26
Warning, HTTP general header, 1359
Web. *See* World Wide Web
WECA (Wireless Ethernet Compatibility Alliance), 51
well-known
(privileged) TCP/UDP port numbers, 702
IP multicast addresses, 269, *269*
IPv6 multicast addresses, 396
white space, in DNS Master Files, 945
whois (DNS registry database lookup utility), 1477
Wide Area Network (WANs), 26
window, TCP. *See* TCP: sliding window system
Windows winipcfg utility, **1489**
Windows Calculator program, 68
Windows protocols, Microsoft, 12
Windows Sockets (Winsock), 706
winipcfg utility for Windows, 1488, **1489**
Winsock, 706
Wireless Ethernet Compatibility Alliance (WECA), 51
wireless
LANs (WLANs), 26
MANs (WMANs), 27
PANs (WPANs), 27
WANs (WWANs), 26
word, binary unit, 64
World Wide Web, 1318
See also HTTP
addressing through HTTP URLs, 1326
browsers, 1321
components, 1320
email access, 1313

World Wide Web, *continued*
history, 1318
major functional components, 1320
media and the Hypertext Markup Language (HTML), 1322
servers, 1321
WPANs (wireless PANs), 27
wrapper protocol, UDP, 714
Write Request (WRQ) messages, TFTP, 1211
WWANs (wireless WANs), 26
WWW-Authenticate, HTTP response header, 1365

X

X3 (Accredited Standards Committee X3, Information Technology), 50
Xanadu, 1318
XDR (External Data Representation), 959
data types, 960, *960*
Xerox Network System (XNS), 598
Xerox Palo Alto Research Center (PARC), 598
XID (transaction identifier), DHCP, 1036
XNS (Xerox Network System), 598
XOR (Exclusive OR)
Boolean logical function, 75
inverting bits with, 77
truth table, *75*

Z

zero compression, IPv6 Addresses, 379
zones of authority, DNS, **883**
zones, DNS. *See* DNS: zones

RFCs BY NUMBER

RFC 95, 1219
RFC 97, 1439
RFC 114, 1170
RFC 155, 1219
RFC 172, 1170
RFC 196, 1219
RFC 226, 842
RFC 265, 1170
RFC 354, 1170
RFC 542, 1170
RFC 606, 843
RFC 608, 843
RFC 675, 122, 720
RFC 733, 1235
RFC 760, 239
RFC 765, 1170
RFC 768, 712
RFC 772, 1219, 1264
RFC 780, 1264
RFC 783, 1201
RFC 788, 1264
RFC 791, 239
RFC 792, 508
RFC 793, 720
RFC 799, 843, 848
RFC 810, 843
RFC 812, 1477
RFC 813, 722
RFC 821, 1264
RFC 822. *See* RFC 822 email message format *in main index*
RFC 823, 678
RFC 826, 213
RFC 827, 684
RFC 854, 1439
RFC 855, 1450
RFC 865, 1046
RFC 879, 722, 778
RFC 881, 848
RFC 882, 849
RFC 883, 849
RFC 887, 1046
RFC 891, 679
RFC 894, 1048
RFC 896, 722, 816
RFC 903, 228
RFC 904, 684
RFC 918, 1288
RFC 937, 1289
RFC 943, 1477
RFC 950, 274, 285, 305, 509
RFC 951, 978
RFC 959, 1171
RFC 977, 1400, 1412
RFC 1001, 1049
RFC 1014, 959
RFC 1021, 1070
RFC 1022, 1070
RFC 1023, 1070
RFC 1024, 1070
RFC 1028, 1070, 1100
RFC 1032, 849
RFC 1033, 849
RFC 1034, 849
RFC 1035, 849
RFC 1036, 1408
RFC 1048, 979
RFC 1052, 1070
RFC 1055, 141
RFC 1058, 598
RFC 1064, 1299
RFC 1072, 801
RFC 1081, 1289
RFC 1084, 980
RFC 1094, 956
RFC 1105, 648, 649
RFC 1122, 722
  DHCP messaging and, 1037
  ICMP message creation rules and, 516
  ICMP standards and, 509
RFC 1131, 627
RFC 1134, 144
RFC 1146, 722
RFC 1155, 1080
RFC 1156, 1080
RFC 1157, 1080
RFC 1163, 649
RFC 1171, 144
RFC 1176, 1299
RFC 1179, 1046
RFC 1183, 850
RFC 1190, 240
RFC 1203, 1300
RFC 1213, 1080
RFC 1247, 627
RFC 1256, 509, 540
RFC 1267, 649
RFC 1271, 1134
RFC 1322, 658
RFC 1323, 722
RFC 1332, 153
RFC 1334, 153
RFC 1341, 1244
RFC 1342, 1244
RFC 1350, 1201
RFC 1351, 1080

RFC 1352, 1080
RFC 1353, 1080
RFC 1377, 153
RFC 1378, 153
RFC 1388, 600, 617
RFC 1393, 338, 509, 545
RFC 1395, 980
RFC 1425, 1265
RFC 1436, 1432
RFC 1441, 1080
RFC 1442, 1080
RFC 1443, 1080
RFC 1444, 1080
RFC 1445, 1081
RFC 1446, 1081
RFC 1447, 1081
RFC 1448, 1081
RFC 1449, 1081
RFC 1450, 1081
RFC 1451, 1081
RFC 1452, 1081
RFC 1459, 1458
RFC 1497, 980, 1043
RFC 1513, 1136
RFC 1521, 1244
RFC 1522, 1244
RFC 1531, 999
RFC 1532, 980
RFC 1533, 980
RFC 1534, 1063
RFC 1541, 999
RFC 1542, 980
RFC 1546, 398
RFC 1552, 153
RFC 1570, 153, 159
RFC 1579, 1180
RFC 1583, 627
RFC 1590, 1244
RFC 1597, 266
RFC 1618, 154
RFC 1630, 1142
RFC 1631, 427
RFC 1635, 1177
RFC 1651, 1265
RFC 1652, 1276
RFC 1654, 649
RFC 1661, 153
RFC 1662, 153, 182
RFC 1700, 707
RFC 1701, 496
RFC 1717, 175
RFC 1723, 600
RFC 1730, 1300
RFC 1731, 1300
RFC 1733, 1287
RFC 1734, 1293
RFC 1737, 1142, 1160
RFC 1738, 1142
RFC 1757, 1134
RFC 1771, 649
RFC 1782, 1202
RFC 1783, 1202
RFC 1784, 1202
RFC 1794, 850
RFC 1808, 1142
RFC 1812, 286, 509
RFC 1813, 956
RFC 1832, 959
RFC 1847, 1254
RFC 1869, 1265
RFC 1870, 1276
RFC 1885, 509
RFC 1886, 850, 949
RFC 1891, 1276
RFC 1893, 1276
RFC 1896, 1250
RFC 1901, 1081
RFC 1902, 1081
RFC 1903, 1081
RFC 1904, 1081
RFC 1905, 1081
RFC 1906, 1081
RFC 1907, 1081
RFC 1908, 1081
RFC 1909, 1081
RFC 1910, 1081
RFC 1918, 266
RFC 1939, 1289
RFC 1945, 1244, 1330
RFC 1952, 1374
RFC 1962, 153
RFC 1967, 171
RFC 1968, 153
RFC 1969, 174
RFC 1970, 577
RFC 1973, 154
RFC 1974, 171
RFC 1977, 171
RFC 1978, 171
RFC 1979, 171
RFC 1981, 417, 551
RFC 1989, 154
RFC 1990, 154, 175
RFC 1993, 171
RFC 1994, 153
RFC 1995, 850, 907
RFC 1996, 850, 906
RFC 2001, 817, 818
RFC 2002, 478
RFC 2003, 496
RFC 2004, 496
RFC 2012, 1097
RFC 2014, 53
RFC 2018, 722, 801
RFC 2026, 59
RFC 2043, 153
RFC 2045, 1245
RFC 2046, 1245
RFC 2047, 1245
RFC 2048, 1245
RFC 2049, 1245
RFC 2060, 1300
RFC 2068, 1331
RFC 2077, 1249, 1251
RFC 2080, 600, 620
RFC 2097, 153
RFC 2109, 1391
RFC 2118, 171
RFC 2125, 154, 178
RFC 2131, 1000
RFC 2132, 1043
RFC 2136, 850, 907, 908
RFC 2141, 1142, 1160
RFC 2178, 627
RFC 2181, 850
RFC 2183, 1244, 1248
RFC 2192, 1142
RFC 2224, 1142
RFC 2228, 1176
RFC 2290, 154
RFC 2302, 1250
RFC 2308, 850
RFC 2318, 1250
RFC 2328, 627
RFC 2364, 154
RFC 2368, 1142
RFC 2373, 367, 374

RFC 2374, 367, 374, 385
RFC 2384, 1142
RFC 2387, 1254
RFC 2396, 1142
RFC 2401, 451, 454
RFC 2402, 451
RFC 2403, 451
RFC 2404, 452
RFC 2406, 452
RFC 2408, 452
RFC 2409, 452, 471
RFC 2412, 452
RFC 2419, 174
RFC 2420, 174
RFC 2453, 600, 617
RFC 2460, 366, 374
RFC 2461, 367, 509, 577
RFC 2462, 399
RFC 2463, 367, 509, 516
RFC 2472, 153
RFC 2474, 335
RFC 2483, 1162
RFC 2516, 154
RFC 2554, 1276
RFC 2557, 1244, 1248
RFC 2576, 1082
RFC 2578, 1082
RFC 2579, 1082
RFC 2580, 1082
RFC 2581, 722
RFC 2615, 154
RFC 2616, 1331
RFC 2617, 1331
RFC 2671, 929
RFC 2694, 437
RFC 2717, 1142
RFC 2718, 1142
RFC 2774, 1332
RFC 2810, 1458
RFC 2819, 1134
RFC 2821, 1235
RFC 2822, 1235
RFC 2850, 53
RFC 2854, 1250
RFC 2870, 899
RFC 2874, 949
RFC 2894, 400, 509, 568
RFC 2920, 1276
RFC 2965, 1391
RFC 2980, 1400
RFC 2988, 722, 803
RFC 3003, 1251
RFC 3010, 956
RFC 3021, 322
RFC 3118, 1064
RFC 3160, 53
RFC 3189, 1251
RFC 3220, 478
RFC 3330, 1059
RFC 3344, 478
RFC 3363, 950
RFC 3364, 950
RFC 3401 to RFC 3405, 1162
RFC 3406, 1162
RFC 3410, 1082
RFC 3411, 1082
RFC 3412, 1082
RFC 3413, 1082
RFC 3414, 1082
RFC 3415, 1082
RFC 3416, 1082, 1101
RFC 3417, 1082, 1101
RFC 3418, 1082
RFC 3425, 921
RFC 3501, 1300
RFC 3513, 367, 374, 382
RFC 3530, 957
RFC 3587, 367, 374, 386
RFC 3927, 1059

UPDATES

Visit *https://www.nostarch.com/tcpip.htm* for updates, errata, and other information.

UPDATES

Visit **http://www.nostarch.com/tcpip.htm** for updates, errata, and other information.

COLOPHON

The TCP/IP Guide is set in New Baskerville, TheSansMono Condensed, Futura, and Dogma. The book was printed and bound at Sheridan Books, Inc. in Chelsea, Michigan. The paper is 45# Utopia Filmcote.